The Renaissance in England

THE RENAISSANCE IN ENGLAND

Non-dramatic
PROSE AND VERSE
of the Sixteenth Century

HYDER E. ROLLINS
HERSCHEL BAKER
HARVARD UNIVERSITY

D. C. HEATH AND COMPANY BOSTON

PREFACE

In this anthology we offer a generous sampling of texts to represent the non-dramatic literary activity of England in the sixteenth century. Major space has been given to the best writing of the period (with the exception of *The Faerie Queene,* for which adequate room could not be found), but we have also included various texts of more historical than literary importance to piece out the total picture and help to show the greater works in true perspective. Stanyhurst as well as Sidney casts light upon the critical controversies of the time; and Barclay and Googe aid the reader in assessing Spenser's achievement in *The Shepherd's Calendar.* For similar reasons we have printed from the original books a sizable quantity of prefatory material, which not only illuminates separate works but also, as a whole, tells much about conventions of authorship, publishing practices, the nature of the reading public, and other significant aspects of the literary scene. The ten headings under which the selections have been arranged, though somewhat arbitrary, do suggest the main lines along which sixteenth-century writers worked, and they will perhaps serve to guide the student confronted for the first time by the rich confusion of Renaissance literature.

We have taken uncommon care to insure reliable texts. With a few exceptions (duly noted in the introductions) we have based our readings upon a fresh examination of the earliest printed or manuscript sources. For each selection from a printed work the source is identified by the original titlepage and the corresponding entry-number in Pollard and Redgrave's *Short-Title Catalogue* (STC). Except for the selections from Spenser's poetry, which are reproduced in the original spelling as specimens of consciously archaic Elizabethan English, we have tried to steer a middle course between complete archaism and thoroughgoing (often misleading) modernization. A student who uses completely modernized texts not only misses much of the flavor of the old authors but will be helpless to decipher their meaning when he sees an actual Elizabethan text or a facsimile of one. We have therefore, as a general rule (but without attempting complete consistency), kept forms that occur in a main or subordinate entry (but not as variant spellings) in *A New English Dictionary on Historical Principles.* For example, we have retained the Tudors' *hit* and *hability* (for *it* and *ability*) and often their casual treatment of the vowels in words like *when:whan, then:than, not:nat, hunger:honger.* Where the original editions give sanction we usually print *agen* for *again,* *bankro(u)t* for *bankrupt,* *battail* for *battle,* *capitain* for *captain,* *herault* for *herald,* *norice* for *nurse,* *plage* for *plague,* *sodain* (or *suddain*) for *sudden,* *wordle* for *world,* and so on. The punctuation has been modernized throughout. Obvious misprints in the originals (for example, *of* for *or*) have been silently emended; occasional less certain emendations are enclosed in brackets, which are also used for editorial notes and explanations. Sometimes (as explained in separate introductions) pointed brackets (< >) have been used to supply missing lines from other manuscripts or later editions.

The annotation of texts in which numerous words requiring explanation reappear again and again presents a special difficulty. To avoid repetition and to keep the editorial apparatus at a spatial minimum we have substituted two full glossaries for footnotes. The first glossary defines or identifies all the English words and phrases the meaning or orthography of which may pose difficulties for the student; the second supplies explanations of all proper nouns and translations of foreign words and phrases. With the assistance of the glossaries and the introductory notes the student will have all the information he needs for a ready understanding of the texts.

H. E. R.
H. B.

CONTENTS

Part I. THE HISTORICAL SETTING

Part II. EARLY TUDOR LITERATURE

Part III. THE REFORMATION IN ENGLAND

Part VI. LATER ELIZABETHAN POETRY

Part VII. TRANSLATIONS

Part VIII. CRITICAL THEORY

Part IX. PROSE FICTION

Part X. MISCELLANEOUS PROSE

Part I THE HISTORICAL SETTING

MICHAEL DRAYTON

POLY-OLBION

When Michael Drayton chose the story of Brut to open his massive *Poly-Olbion* (see p. 423, below) he was following the precedent established by generations of Tudor historians and reworking a formula that had long proved its appeal to patriotic Englishmen. The twin legends of Brut, the mythological Trojan founder of Britain, and of King Arthur, his descendant who battled the Saxon invaders, had been contrived to fill in the dim beginnings of British history, and for obvious reasons they had been among the dearest fictions of the Tudors: they were stirring tales, and they provided a flattering if spurious historical impetus for British nationalism. Although they had long been accepted as true, by Drayton's time the facts were coming to light (as Selden's "Illustrations" to the first song make clear). We now know that Geoffrey of Monmouth, Bishop of St. Asaph (?1100–?1154), on some slender hints in Bede and Nennius and on a "most ancient book in the British tongue" allegedly given him by one Walter, Archdeacon of Oxford, fabricated the famous legends in his *Historia regum Britanniae*, a work so popular that it survives in more than two hundred manuscripts. Geoffrey's history was translated into Anglo-Norman by Geoffrey Gaimar (whose version is lost) and by Wace in his *Roman de Brut* (1155); then Wace's version was expanded into splendid Middle English by Layamon, a Worcestershire priest. His vigorous *Brut* (ca. 1205) more than doubles Wace's 15,000 lines and greatly develops the Arthurian materials, which thereafter were lovingly embellished in a wealth of metrical romances and prose chronicles. In the sixteenth

century such widely read historical writers as Grafton, Stow, and Holinshed (see pp. 20–21) dutifully repeated the well-worn fables as facts, and even the learned Leland professed belief. But by 1612, when the first part of *Poly-Olbion* appeared, the situation had changed. In spite of Drayton's throbbing patriotism and indefatigable energy, his recension of the Brut story could not, in the nature of things, be taken very seriously by a "critic age" that was learning to distinguish history from fable and was more interested in the growing menace of Stuart despotism than in the mythical exploits of Trojan warriors. Drayton's decision to open his *magnum opus,* and to begin British history, with such a legend indicates with sufficient clarity his conservative, not to say reactionary, aims and methods. As a historian he was an alien in the age that would produce Bacon's clinical dissection of Henry VII and Clarendon's realistic appraisal of contemporary events, and he perversely exulted in the fact (see his epistles on pp. 438-39, 441, below).

The part of Drayton's version here reprinted concerns the wanderings of Brutus (Brut), grandson of Ascanius and great-grandson of Aeneas, who, after many perils, landed at Totnes, founded Troynovant (New Troy, later London), and established a dynasty of mighty kings that included Bladud, Gorboduc, Ferrex and Porrex, Lud, Cymbeline, Vortigern, and Arthur. Our text is based upon *Poly-Olbion. Or A Chorographicall Description of Tracts, Rivers, Mountaines, Forests, and other Parts of this renowned Isle of Great Britaine . . . Digested in a Poem,* 1612 (STC 7226).

FROM POLY-OLBION (1612)

THE FIRST SONG

THE ARGUMENT

The sprightly muse her wing displays
And the French ilands first surveys,
Bears up with Neptune, and in glory
Transcends proud Cornwall's promontory;
There crowns Mount Michael, and discries
How all those riverets fall and rise;

Then takes in Tamer as she bounds
The Cornish and Devonian grounds.
And whilst the Devonshire nymphs relate
Their loves, their fortunes, and estate,
Dert undertaketh to revive
Our Brut, and sings his first arrive.
Then northward to the verge she bends,
And her first song at Axe she ends.

Of Albion's glorious ile the wonders whilst I write,
The sundry, varying soils, the pleasures infinite,
Where heat kills not the cold, nor cold expels the heat,
The calms too mildly small, nor winds too roughly great,
Nor night doth hinder day, nor day the night doth wrong,
The summer not too short, the winter not too long—
What help shall I invoke to aid my muse the while?

  Thou Genius of the place, this most renowned ile,
Which livedst long before the all-earth-drowning flood,
Whilst yet the world did swarm with her gigantic brood,   10
Go thou before me still thy circling shores about,
And in this wand'ring maze help to conduct me out;
Direct my course so right as with thy hand to show
Which way thy forests range, which way thy rivers flow;
Wise Genius, by thy help that so I may discry
How thy fair mountains stand and how thy valleys lie
From those clear, pearly cleeves which see the morning's pride
And check the surly imps of Neptune when they chide
Unto the big-swoll'n waves in the Iberian stream,
Where Titan still unyokes his fiery-hoofed team,   20
And oft his flaming locks in luscious nectar steeps
When from Olympus' top he plungeth in the deeps;
That from th' Armoric sands, on surging Neptune's leas,
Through the Hibernic gulf (those rough, Vergivian seas)
My verse with wings of skill may fly a lofty gait,
As Amphitrite clips this iland fortunate,
Till through the sleepy main to Thuly I have gone
And seen the frozen iles, the cold Ducalidon,
Amongst whose iron rocks grim Saturn yet remains,
Bound in those gloomy caves with adamantine chains.   30

  Ye sacred bards that to your harps' melodious strings
Sung th' ancient heroes' deeds (the monuments of kings)
And in your dreadful verse ingrav'd the prophecies,
The aged world's descents and genealogies,
If, as those Druids taught which kept the British rites
And dwelt in darksome groves, there counsailing with sprites
(But their opinions fail'd, by error led awry,
As since clear truth hath shew'd to their posterity),
When these our souls by death our bodies do forsake
They instantly again do other bodies take,   40
I could have wish'd your spirits redoubled in my breast
To give my verse applause to time's eternal rest. . . .

[Among the rivers of Cornwall and Devon the Dert (Dart) thus
declares her preeminence:]

        "There's not the proudest flood
That falls betwixt the Mount and Exmoor shall make good
Her royalty with mine, with me nor can compare.
I challenge any one to answer me that dare,
That was, before them all, predestinate to meet
My Britain-founding Brut when, with his puissant fleet,
At Totnes first he touch'd, which shall renown my stream
(Which now the envious world doth slander for a dream);   50
Whose fatal flight from Greece, his fortunate arrive

In happy Albion here whilst strongly I revive,
Dear Harburn, at thy hands this credit let me win,"
Quoth she, "that as thou hast my faithful handmaid been,
So now, my only brook, assist me with thy spring
Whilst of the godlike Brut the story thus I sing.
   "When long-renowned Troy lay spent in hostile fire
And aged Priam's pomp did with her flames expire,
Aeneas (taking thence Ascanius, his young son,
And his most reverent sire, the grave Anchises, won   60
From shoals of slaughtering Greeks) set out from Simois' shores
And through the Tyrrhene Sea, by strength of toiling oars,
Raught Italy at last, where King Latinus lent
Safe harbor for his ships with wrackful tempests rent.
When in the Latin court Lavinia young and fair
(Her father's only child and kingdom's only heir)
Upon the Trojan lord her liking strongly plac'd
And languish'd in the fires that her fair breast imbrac'd;
But Turnus at that time, the proud Rutulian king,
A suitor to the maid, Aeneas malicing,   70
By force of arms attempts his rival to extrude;
But, by the Teucrian power courageously subdu'd,
Bright Cytherea's son the Latin crown obtain'd,
And dying, in his stead his son Ascanius reign'd.
Next Silvius him succeeds, begetting Brut again.
Who in his mother's womb whilst yet he did remain
The oracles gave out that next-born Brut should be
His parents' only death, which soon they liv'd to see.
For in his painful birth his mother did depart,
And ere his fifteenth year, in hunting of a hart,   80
He with a luckless shaft his hapless father slew,
For which out of his throne their king the Latins threw.
   "Who, wand'ring in the world, to Greece at last doth get,
Where whilst he liv'd unknown and oft with want beset,
He of the race of Troy a remnant happ'd to find
There by the Grecians held; which (having still in mind
Their tedious ten years' war and famous heroes slain)
In slavery with them still those Trojans did detain
Which Pyrrhus thither brought (and did with hate pursue
To wreak Achilles' death at Troy, whom Paris slew),   90
There by Pandrasus kept in sad and servile awe.
Who, when they knew young Brut and that brave shape they saw,
They humbly him desire that he a mean would be
From those imperious Greeks his countrymen to free.
   "He, finding out a rare and sprightly youth to fit
His humor every way for courage, power, and wit,
Assaracus (who, though that by his sire he were
A prince amongst the Greeks, yet held the Trojans dear,
Descended of their stock upon the mother's side,
For which he by the Greeks his birthright was deni'd),   100
Impatient of his wrongs, with him brave Brut arose,
And of the Trojan youth courageous captains chose,
Rais'd earthquakes with their drums, the ruffling ensigns rear,
And, gathering young and old that rightly Trojan were,
Up to the mountains march through straits and forests strong,
Where, taking in the towns pretended to belong

Unto that Grecian lord, some forces there they put,
Within whose safer walls their wives and children shut;
Into the fields they drew for liberty to stand.
  "Which when Pandrasus heard he sent his strict command   110
To levy all the power he presently could make;
So to their strengths of war the Trojans them betake.
  "But whilst the Grecian guides (not knowing how or where
The Teucrians were entrench'd or what their forces were)
In foul, disord'red troups yet straggled as secure,
This looseness to their spoil the Trojans did allure,
Who fiercely them assail'd, where stanchless fury rap'd
The Grecians in so fast that scarcely one escap'd;
Yea, proud Pandrasus' flight himself could hardly free.
Who, when he saw his force thus frustrated to be   120
And by his present loss his passed error found
(As by a later war to cure a former wound),
Doth reinforce his power to make a second fight.
When they whose better wits had overmatch'd his might,
Loth what they got to lose, as politiquely cast
His armies to intrap in getting to them fast
Antigonus as friend and Anaclet, his phere
(Surpriz'd in the last fight), by gifts who hired were
Into the Grecian camp th' insuing night to go,
And fain they were stol'n forth to their allies to show   130
How they might have the spoil of all the Trojan pride,
And, gaining them belief, the credulous Grecians guide
Into th' ambushment near that secretly was laid.
So to the Trojans' hands the Grecians were betray'd,
Pandrasus' self surpriz'd, his crown who to redeem
(Which scarcely worth their wrong the Trojan race esteem)
Their slavery long sustain'd did willingly release,
And, for a lasting league of amity and peace,
Bright Innogen, his child, for wife to Brutus gave
And furnish'd them a fleet with all things they could crave   140
To set them out to sea. Who lanching, at the last
They on Lergecia light, an ile, and, ere they pass'd,
Unto a temple built to great Diana there
The noble Brutus went wise Trivia to enquire
To shew them where the stock of ancient Troy to place.
  "The goddess, that both knew and lov'd the Trojan race,
Reveal'd to him in dreams that furthest to the west
He should discry the ile of Albion, highly blest;
With giants lately stor'd, their numbers now decay'd,
By vanquishing the rest his hopes should there be stay'd,   150
Where, from the stock of Troy, those puissant kings should rise
Whose conquests from the west the world should scant suffice.
  "Thus answer'd, great with hope, to sea they put again
And, safely under sail, the hours do entertain
With sights of sundry shores which they from far discry.
And viewing with delight th' Azarian Mountains high,
One walking on the deck unto his friend would say
(As I have heard some tell), 'So goodly Ida lay.'
  "Thus talking mongst themselves they sunburn'd Africk keep
Upon the leeward still, and (sulking up the deep)   160

For Mauritania make, where, putting in, they find
A remnant yet reserv'd of th' ancient Dardan kind,
By brave Antenor brought from out the Greekish spoils
(O long-renowned Troy! Of thee and of thy toils
What country had not heard?), which to their general then
Great Corineus had, the strong'st of mortal men,
To whom (with joyful hearts) Diana's will they show.
   "Who eas'ly being won along with them to go,
They altogether put into the wat'ry plain.
Ofttimes with pirates, oft with monsters of the main   170
Distressed in their way, whom hope forbids to fear,
Those pillars first they pass which Jove's great son did rear,
And, cuffing those stern waves which like huge mountains roll
(Full joy in every part possessing every soul),
In Aquitaine at last the Ilion race arrive.
Whom strongly to repulse when as those recreants strive,
They (anchoring there at first but to refresh their fleet,
Yet saw those savage men so rudely them to greet)
Unshipp'd their warlike youth advancing to the shore.
The dwellers, which perceiv'd such danger at the door,   180
Their king, Groffarius, get to raise his powerful force,
Who, must'ring up an host of mingled foot and horse,
Upon the Trojans set, when suddainly began
A fierce and dangerous fight, where Corineus ran
With slaughter through the thick-set squadrons of the foes
And with his armed ax laid on such deadly blows
That heaps of liveless trunks each passage stopp'd up quite.
   "Groffarius, having lost the honor of the fight,
Repairs his ruin'd powers, not so to give them breath,
When they which must be freed by conquest or by death   190
And, conquering them before, hop'd now to do no less
(The like in courage still) stand for the like success.
Then stern and deadly war put on his horrid'st shape,
And wounds appear'd so wide as if the grave did gape
To swallow both at once, which strove as both should fall
When they with slaughter seem'd to be encircled all.
Where Turon (of the rest), Brut's sister's valiant son
(By whose approved deeds that day was chiefly won),
Six hundred slew outright through his peculiar strength;
By multitudes of men yet overpress'd at length.   200
His nobler uncle there, to his immortal name,
The city Turon built and well endow'd the same.
   "For Albion sailing then, th' arrived quickly here
(O never in this world men half so joyful were
With shouts heard up to heaven when they beheld the land),
And in this very place where Totnes now doth stand
First set their gods of Troy, kissing the blessed shore,
Then, foraging this ile long promis'd them before,
Amongst the ragged cleeves those monstrous giants sought,
Who (of their dreadful kind) t' appal the Trojans brought   210
Great Gogmagog, an oak that by the roots could tear—
So mighty were (that time) the men who lived there.
But for the use of arms he did not understand
(Except some rock or tree that, coming next to hand,

He raz'd out of the earth to execute his rage),
He challenge makes for strength and offereth there his gage,
Which Corin taketh up to answer by and by,
Upon this son of earth his utmost power to try.
  "All doubtful to which part the victory would go,
Upon that lofty place at Plymouth call'd the Hoe   220
Those mighty wrastlers met with many an ireful look
Who threat'ned as the one hold of the other took,
But, grapled, glowing fire shines in their sparkling eyes.
And whilst at length of arm one from the other lies,
Their lusty sinews swell like cables as they strive;
Their feet such trampling make as though they forc'd to drive
A thunder out of earth, which stagger'd with the weight.
Thus, either's utmost force urg'd to the greatest height,
Whilst one upon his hip the other seeks to lift
And th' adverse (by a turn) doth from his cunning shift,   230
Their short-fetch'd, troubled breath a hollow noise doth make
Like bellows of a forge. Then Corin up doth take
The giant twixt the grains and, voiding off his hold
(Before his combrous feet he well recover could),
Pitch'd headlong from the hill. As when a man doth throw
An axtree that with sleight deliver'd from the toe
Roots up the yielding earth, so that his violent fall
Strook Neptune with such strength, as should'red him withal,
That where the monstrous waves like mountains late did stand
They leap'd out of the place and left the bared sand   240
To gaze upon wide heaven; so great a blow it gave.
For which the conquering Brut on Corineus brave
This horn of land bestow'd and mark'd it with his name,
Of Corin Cornwall call'd to his immortal fame . . . ."

ILLUSTRATIONS

[The commentary or "illustrations" which the fabulously learned John Selden provided for Drayton make *Poly-Olbion* a rich mine of antiquarian lore. Selden's remarks on the legend of Brut are especially interesting because they show how that attractive fiction (so carefully sustained by Tudor historians) was destroyed under a genuinely critical scrutiny.]

I should the sooner have been of the author's opinion (in more then poetical form standing for Brut) if in any Greek or Latin story authentique, speaking of Aeneas and his planting in Latium, were mention made of any such like thing. To reckon the learned men which deny him, or at least permit him not in conjecture, were too long a catalogue; and, indeed, this critique age scarce any longer endures any nation their first supposed author's name: not Italus to the Italian, not Hispalus to the Spaniard, Bato to the Hollander, Brabo to the Brabantine, Francio to the French, Celtes to the Celt, Galathes to the Gaul, Scota to the Scot—no, nor scarce Romulus to his Rome—because of their unlikely and fictitious mixtures. Especially this of Brut . . . is most of all doubted. But, reserving my censure, I thus maintain the author. Although nor Greek nor Latin, nor our country stories of Bede and Malmesbury especially, nor that fragment yet remaining of Gildas speak of him; and that his name were not published until Geoffrey of Monmouth's edition of the British story, which grew and continues much suspected, in much rejected; yet observe that Taliessin, a great bard, more then 1,000 years since affirms it; Nennius (in some copies he is under name of Gildas), above 800 years past, and the gloss of Samuel Beaulan (or some other crept into his text) mention both the common report and descent from Aeneas, and withal (which I take to be Nennius his own) make him son to one Isicio or Hesichio (perhaps meaning Aschenaz, of whom more to the Fourth Song), continuing a pedigree to Adam, joining these words: "This genealogy I found by tradition of the ancients which were first inhabitants of Britain." In a manuscript epistle of Henry of Huntingdon to one Warin I read the Latin of this English: "You ask me, sir, why, omitting the succeeding reigns from Brut to Julius Caesar, I begin my story at Caesar. I answer you that neither by word nor writing could I find any certainty of those times, although with diligent search I oft inquired it. Yet this year, in my journey towards Rome, in the Abbey of Beccensam, even with amazement I found the story of Brut." And in his own printed book he affirms that what Bede had in this part omitted was supplied to him by other authors, of which Girald seems to have had use. The British story of Monmouth was a translation (but with much liberty and no exact faithfulness) of a Welsh book delivered to Geoffrey by one Walter, Archdeacon of Oxford, and hath been followed (the translator being a man of some credit and Bishop of St. Asaph's under King Stephen) by Ponticus Virunnius, an Italian, most of our country historians of middle times, and this age, speaking so certainly of him that they blazon his coat to you. . . . Arguments are there also drawn from

some affinity of the Greek tongue, and much of Trojan and Greek names, with the British. These things are the more enforc'd by Cambro-Britons through that universal desire, bewitching our Europe, to derive their blood from Trojans, which for them might as well be by supposition of their ancestors' marriages with the hither-deduced Roman colonies, who by original were certainly Trojan if their antiquities deceive not. . . . Briefly, seeing no national story (except such as Thucydides, Xenophon, Polybius, Caesar, Tacitus, Procopius, Cantacuzene, the late Guicciardin, Comines, Machiavel, and their like, which were employed in the state of their times) can justify themselves but by tradition, and that many of the Fathers and ecclesiastical historians (especially the Jewish rabbins, taking their highest learning of Cabala, but from antique and successive report) have inserted upon tradition many relations currant enough where Holy Writ crosses them not, you shall enough please Saturn and Mercury, presidents of antiquity and learning, if with the author you foster this belief. . . . But you blame me thus expatiating. Let me add for the author that our most judicious antiquary of the last age, John Leland, with reason and authority hath also for Brut argued strongly. . . .

WILLIAM WARNER

ALBION'S ENGLAND

In 1598 Francis Meres praised Spenser and Warner as "our chief heroical makers," a comment that suggests both Warner's high contemporary reputation and the Elizabethan habit of converting history and quasi-historical fable to the uses of literature. Through many editions since 1555 *A Mirror for Magistrates* (see pp. 269 ff.) had instructed and (it must be presumed) delighted a whole generation of readers and writers; and its great popularity established the precedent for the spate of ostensibly historical poems that appeared in the last years of Elizabeth's reign: Warner's *Albion's England,* Drayton's *Piers Gaveston, Cromwell, Mortimeriados,* and *Heroical Epistles,* Daniel's *Complaint of Rosamond* and *Civil Wars,* and many others. Odd as the fact may now seem, *Albion's England* was the most popular of all these works, enjoying continuous favor for some twenty-five years in many editions. The first four books (1586) of laborious fourteeners (supported by a highly euphuistic dedicatory epistle) begin with "arked Noah" and then rehearse the familiar legends of Brut, his antecedents, and his posterity;

but as the demand continued and was met with successive expansions, Warner's "historical map" became a loose collection of versified tales, at least one of which, that of Curan and Argentile in Book IV, Chapter XX, has real charm. Ultimately, the strange poem covered, after its fashion, everything between the Flood and the execution of Mary Queen of Scots. Whatever his demerits as a poet, Warner at least recognized a good thing when it came his way: two additional books were added to the second edition of 1589, two more to the third of 1592, four more in 1596 (reprinted in 1597), another (a summary of all British history) in 1602, and in 1606 the "continuance" attained sixteen books. In 1612 the whole work was printed with a "prose breviate of the true history of Aeneas and epitome." Our text is based upon *Albions England. Or Historicall Map of the same Island: prosecuted from the lives, Actes, and Labors of Saturne, Jupiter, Hercules, and Aeneas: Originalles of the Brutons and English-men, and Occasion of the Brutons their first aryvall in Albion, 1586* (STC 25079).

FROM ALBION'S ENGLAND OR HISTORICAL MAP OF THE SAME ISLAND (1586)

[Beginning at the beginning, Warner devotes the first two books (thirteen chapters) to the complicated genealogies of the Trojan heroes, a task which requires elaborate excursions into both sacred and profane history. The pedigree of Britain's founder, Brut, is thus summarized at the end of the second book:

> Aeneas dead, Ascanius reign'd; Ascanius dead, his brother
> Posthumus Sylvius did succeed; Lavinia was his mother,
> Her sire Latinus, Faunus his, and Picus him begot,
> And Saturn him. From mother thus Posthumus lacked not
> The noblest blood. On father's side his petigree was thus:
> Jove had Dardanus, and the same begot Erictheus;
> He, Tros; Tros, Assaracus; he, Capys; and the same,
> Anchisis; he Aeneas had; of him Posthumus came;
> And he was father unto Brut; and thus the Brutons bring
> Their petegree from Jupiter, of pagan gods the king;
> And add they may that Brut his sire of Venus' son did spring.
> Thrice five degrees from Noe was Brut, and four times six was he
> From Adam, and from Japhet's house doth fetch his petegree.]

THE THIRD BOOK OF ALBION'S ENGLAND

CHAPTER XIV

> Now of the conqueror this isle had Brutain unto name,
> And with his Trojans Brut began manurage of the same.
> For razed Troy to rear a Troy, fit place he searched then,
> And views the mounting northern parts. "These fit," quoth he, "for men
> That trust as much to flight as fight; our bulwarks are our breasts.
> The next arrivals here, perchance, will gladlier build their nests;
> A Trojan's corrage is to him a fortress of defense."
> And leaving so where Scots be now, he southward maketh thence,
> Whereas the earth more plenty gave and air more temp'rature,
> And nothing wanted that by wealth or pleasure might allure.   10
> And more, the Lady Flood of Floods, the River Thamis, it
> Did seem to Brut against the foe and with himself to fit,
> Upon whose fruitful banks, therefore, whose bounds are chiefly said
> The wantless counties Essex, Kent, with which the wealthy glade
> Of Hertfordshire for city's store affords no little aid,
> Did Brut build up his Troynovant, inclosing it with wall,
> Which Lud did after beautify and Lud's-Town did it call
> That now is London, evermore to rightful princes true.
> Yea, prince and people still to it as to their storehouse drew,
> For plenty and for popilous the like we nowhere view.   20
> Howbeit many neighbor towns as much ere now could say,
> But place for people, people place, and all for sin decay.
> When Brut should die thus to his sons he did the isle convey:
> To Camber Wales, to Albanact he Albany did leave,
> To Locrine Brutain, whom his queen of life did thus bereave.
>
> The furous Hun that, drowning there, to Humber left his name
> The king did vanquish and for spoil unto his navy came,
> Where Humber's daughter, paragon for beauty, such a dame

As Love himself could not but love, did Locrine inflame,
That Guendolene, the Cornish duke his daughter, Locrine's queen,   30
Grew in contempt; and, Coryn dead, his change of choice was seen.
To Cornwell goes the wrothful queen to seize her father's land,
From whence she brought, to work revenge, of warriors stout a band,
And bids her husband battle, and in battle is he slain;
And, for their son in nonage was, she to his use did reign.
The Lady Estrild, Locrine's love, and Sabrin wondrous fair,
Her husband's and his leman's imp, she, meaning not to spare,
Did bring unto the water that the wench's name doth bear.
There binding both and bobbing them then trembling at her ire,
She said: "If Scythia could have hild the wand'ring king, thy sire,   40
Then British waters had not been to him deserved bane;
But Estrild, snout-fair Estrild, she was spar'd, forsooth, to train
With whorish tricks a vicious king; but neither of you twain—
Thou stately drab nor this thy brat, a bastard as thyself—
Shall live in triumph of my wrong. First mother and her elf
Shall fish in flood for Humber's soul and bring him news to hell
That Locrine's wife on Locrine's whore revenged her so well."
    They lifting up their lily hands, from out their lovely eyes
Pour tears like pearls and wash those cheeks where naught save beauty lies;
And, seeking to excuse themselves and mercy to obtain,   50
With speeches good and prayers fair they speak and pray in vain.
Queen Guendolene so bids, and they into the flood are cast,
Whereas amongst the drenching waves the ladies breathe their last.
    As this his granddame, such appear'd Mempricius, Madan's son,
Whose brother Manlius trait'rously by him to death was done.
And since of noble Brut his line prodigious things I tell,
I, skipping to the tenth from him, will shew what befell.
    About a thirty years and five did Leir rule this land
When, doting on his daughters three, with them he fell in hand
To tell how much they loved him. The eldest did esteem   60
Her life inferior to her love; so did the second deem;
The youngest said her love was such as did a child behove,
And that how much himself was worth, so much she him did love.
The formost two did please him well, the youngest did not so;
Upon the Prince of Albany the first he did bestow,
The middle on the Cornish prince; their dowry was his throne
At his decease; Cordella's part was very small or none,
Yet, for her form and virtuous life, a noble Gallian king
Did her, undowed, for his queen into his country bring.
    Her sisters, sick of father's health, their husbands by consent   70
Did join in arms; from Leir so by force the scepter went;
Yet for they promise pentions large he rather was content.
In Albany the quondam king at eldest daughter's court
Was settled scarce when she repines and lessens still his port.
His second daughter then, he thought, would shew herself more kind,
To whom he going, for a while did frank allowance find.
Ere long abridging almost all, she keepeth him so low
That of two bads for better's choice he back again did go.
But Gonoril at his return not only did attempt
Her father's death, but openly did hold him in contempt.   80 ·
    His aged eyes pour out their tears when, holding up his hands,
He said: "O God, whoso thou art that my good hap withstands,
Prolong not life, defer not death, myself I overlive

When those that owe to me their lives to me my death would give.
Thou town, whose walls rose of my wealth, stand evermore to tell
Thy founder's fall and warn that none do fall as Leir fell.
Bid none affy in friends, for say his children wrought his wrack—
Yea, those that were to him most dear did loath and let him lack.
Cordella, well Cordella said she loved as a child,
But sweeter words we seek then sooth, and so are men beguil'd.   90
She only rests untried yet, but what may I expect
From her to whom I nothing gave when these do me reject?
Then die, nay try; the rule may fail and nature may assend;
Nor are they ever surest friends on whom we most do spend."
He ships himself to Gallia then, but maketh known before
Unto Cordella his estate, who rueth him so poor
And kept his there arrival close till she provided had
To furnish him in every want. Of him her king was glad,
And nobly intertained him; the queen, with tears among,
Her duty done, conferreth with her father of his wrong.   100
Such duty, bounty, kindness, and increasing love he found
In that his daughter and her lord that sorrows more abound
For his unkindly using her then for the others' crime.
And king-like thus in Agamp's court did Leir dwell till time
The noble king, his son-in-law, transports an army great
Of forcy Gauls, possessing him of dispossessed seat,
To whom Cordella did succeed, not reigning long in queate . . . .

SAMUEL DANIEL

THE CIVIL WARS

The Elizabethan vogue of versified history reached a kind of consummation in Daniel's eight books, in ottava rima, about Richard II and the first three Lancastrians. The first five books (called, misleadingly, *The First Four Books*) appeared as early as 1595, shortly after Daniel's great success with *Delia* and *The Complaint of Rosamond* (see p. 402). Book VI first appeared in *The Works of Samuel Daniel* in 1601, and eight years later the poem took its final form of eight books that ended with Edward IV's marriage to Elizabeth Woodville. Although the 1609 dedication to the dowager Countess of Pembroke asserts that a continuation to the reign of Henry VII may be expected, instead of going further with the already long poem Daniel turned to the composition of prose history, and *The History of England* duly appeared, in two parts, in 1612 and 1618.

In spite of Jonson's quip—"Daniel wrote Civil Wars and yet had not one battle in all his book"—he brought a new sophistication, both psychological and moral, to his version of a time-worn story. His subject is the same that interested Shakespeare in the major chronicle plays, and

his concern with moral causality is, if not Shakespearean, at any rate far beyond the reach of *A Mirror for Magistrates* and *Albion's England*. The credo of political conservatism so copiously explicated in *Musophilus* (see pp. 410–417) is given a pragmatic sanction in *The Civil Wars*, for it is a poem expressly written to demonstrate the evil consequences of disorder—"the deformities of civil dissension and the miserable events of rebellions, conspiracies, and bloody revengements which followed (as in a circle) upon that breach of the due course of succession by the usurpation of Henry IV." Although Daniel, like his model Lucan, is the patriot poet insisting on a moral reading of the lessons of the past, he is more; for he is incorrigibly interested in the personages, especially in the weak or pathetic personages like Richard II and his queen, who are at once the reasons for and the victims of their misfortunes. Our text is based upon *The First Fowre Bookes of the civile wars*, 1595 (STC 6244); for the epistle to the dowager Countess of Pembroke we have followed the edition of 1609 (STC 6245).

FROM THE CIVIL WARS (1595, 1609)

To the Right Noble Lady, the Lady Mary, Countess Dowager of Pembroke [1609]

This poem of our last civil wars of England (whereof the many editions shew what kind of intertainment it hath had with the world) I have now again sent forth with the addition of two books, the one continuing the course of the history, the other making up a part which (for haste) was left unfurnish'd in the former impressions. And, having nothing else to do with my life but to work whilst I have it, I held it my part to adorn, the best I could, this province Nature hath allotted to my charge, and which I desire to leave, after my death, in the best form I may, seeing I can erect no other pillars to sustain my memory but my lines, nor otherwise pay my debts and the reck'nings of my gratitude to their honor who have done me good and furthered this work.

And whereas this argument was long since undertaken (in a time which was not so well secur'd of the future as, God be blessed, now it is) with a purpose to shew the deformities of civil dissension and the miserable events of rebellions, conspiracies, and bloody revengements which followed (as in a circle) upon that breach of the due course of succession by the usurpation of Henry IV; and thereby to make the blessings of peace and the happiness of an established government (in a direct line) the better to appear; I trust I shall do a grateful work to my country to continue the same unto the glorious union of Henry VII, from whence is descended our present happiness.

In which work I have carefully followed that truth which is delivered in the history without adding to or substracting from the general receiv'd opinion of things as we find them in our common annals, holding it an impiety to violate that public testimony we have without more evident proof or to introduce fictions of our own imagination in things of this nature. . . .

I have only used that poetical licence of framing speeches to the persons of men according to their occasions, as C. Sallustius and T. Livius (though writers in prose, yet in that kind poets) have, with divers other ancient and modern writers, done before me. Wherein, though they have incroached upon others' rights and usurp'd a part that was not properly theirs, yet, seeing they hold so just a proportion with the nature of men and the course of affairs, they pass as the parts of the actor (not the writer) and are receiv'd with great approbation.

And although many of these images are drawn with the pencil of mine own conceiving, yet I know they are according to the portraiture of Nature, and carry a resemblance to the life of action and their complexions whom they represent. For I see ambition, faction, and affections speak ever one language, wear like colors (though in several fashions), feed and are fed with the same nutriments, and only vary but in time. . . .

For mine own part, I am not so far in love with this form of writing (nor have I sworn fealty only to rime) but that I may serve in any other state of invention with what weapon of utterance I will; and, so it may make good my mind, I care not. For I see judgment and discretion (with whatsoever is worthy) carry their own ornaments and are grac'd with their own beauties, be they appareled in what fashion they will. And because I find the common tongue of the world is prose, I purpose in that kind to write the history of England from the Conquest, being incouraged thereunto by many noble and worthy spirits. Although, madame, I must not neglect to prosecute the other part of this work, being thus revived by your goodness, to whom and to whose noble family I hold myself ever bound, and will labor to do you all the honor and service I can.

Samuel Daniel

FROM THE FIRST FOUR BOOKS (1595)

THE ARGUMENT OF THE FIRST BOOK

What times forego Richard the Second's reign,
The fatal causes of this civil war,
His uncles' pride, his greedy minions' gain,
Gloster's revolt and death delivered are;
Hereford, accus'd, exil'd, call'd back again,
Pretends t'amend what others' rule did mar;
The king from Ireland hastes, but did no good,
Whilst strange, prodigious signs foretoken blood.

I

I sing the civil wars, tumultuous broils,
And bloody factions of a mighty land,
Whose people hauty, proud with forain spoils,
Upon themselves turn back their conquering hand;
Whilst kin their kin, brother the brother foils,
Like ensigns all against like ensigns band,
Bows against bows, the crown against the crown,
Whilst all, pretending right, all right thrown down.

2

What fury, O what madness held you so,
Dear people, too too prodigal of blood,   10
To waste so much and war without a foe,
Whilst France to see your spoils at pleasure stood?
How much might you have purchas'd with less wo
T' have done you honor and your nephews good?
Yours might have been whatever lies between
The Perenei and Alps, Aquitaine and Rheine.

3

And yet, O God, we have no cause to plain,
Since hereby came the quiet calm we joy,
The bliss of thee, Eliza, happy gain
For all our loss, for that no other way   20
The heavens could find then [to] unite again
The fatal sev'red families that they
Might bring forth thee, that in thy peace might grow
That glory which no age could ever show.

4

O sacred goddess, I no muse but thee
Invoke in this great work I now entend;
Do thou inspire my thoughts, infuse in me
A power to bring the same to happy end;
Raise up a work for latter times to see,
That may thy glory and my pains commend;   30
Strengthen thy subject strange things to rehearse
And give peace to my life, life to my verse.

5

And thou, Charles Mountjoy, born the world's delight,
That hast receiv'd into thy quiet shore
Me, tempest-driven, fortune-tossed wight,
Tir'd with expecting and could hope no more,
And cheerest on my better years to write
A sadder subject then I took before,
Receive the work I consecrate to thee,
Born of that rest which thou dost give to me.   40

6

And Memory, preserv'ress of things done,
Come thou, unfold the wounds, the wrack, the waste;
Reveal to me how all the strife begun
Twixt Lancaster and York in ages past;
How causes, counsels, and events did run
So long as these unhappy times did last,
Unintermix'd with fictions, fantasies:
I versify the troth, not poetize.

7

And to the end we may with better ease
Judge the true progress, here begin to show   50
What were the times foregoing near to these,

That these we may with better profit know.
Tell how the world fell into this disease
And how so great distemperature did grow;
So shall we see by what degrees it came
How things grown full do soon grow out of frame . . . .

[There follows a rapid summary of the kings and the political disorders between William the Conqueror and Edward III. Edward himself is seen as inaugurating a new era of tranquillity and domestic amity.]

24

But now this great succeeder all repairs
And rebrings back that discontinued good;
He builds up strength and greatness for his heirs
Out of the virtues that adorn'd his blood;   60
He makes his subjects lords of more then theirs,
And sets their bounds far wider then they stood.
Could greatness have but kept what he had got,
It was enough he did and what he wrought.

25

And had his heir surviv'd him in due course,
What limits, England, had'st thou found, what bar?
What world could have resisted so great force?
O more then men, two thunderbolts of war,
Why did not time your joined worth divorce
T' have made your several glories greater far?   70
Too prodigal was Nature thus to do,
To spend in one age what should serve for two.

26

But now the scepter in this glorious state
Supported with strong pow'r and victory
Was left unto a child, ordain'd by fate
To stay the course of what might grow too high.
Here was a stop that greatness did abate
When pow'r upon so weak a base did lie;
For lest great fortune should presume too far
Such oppositions interposed are.   80

27

Never this iland better peopled stood,
Never more men of might and minds address'd,
Never more princes of the royal blood
(If not too many for the publique rest),
Nor ever was more treasure, wealth, and good
Then when this Richard first the crown possess'd,
Second of name, a name in two accurst,
And well we might have miss'd all but the first.

28

In this man's reign began this fatal strife,
The bloody argument whereof we treat,   90
That dearly cost so many a prince his life,

That spoil'd the weak and even consum'd the great,
That wherein all calamity was rife,
That Memory even grieves her to repeat.
And would that time would now this knowledge lose,
But that 'tis good to learn by others' woes.

29

Edward the Third, being dead, had left this child,
Son of his worthy son deceas'd of late,
The crown and scepter of this realm to wield,
Appointing the protectors of his state   100
Two of his sons to be his better shield,
Supposing uncles free from guile or hate
Would order all things for his better good
In the respect and honor of their blood.

30

Of these, John, Duke of Lancaster, was one
(Too great a subject grown for such a state,
The title of a king and what h' had done
In great exploits his mind did elevate
Above proportion kingdoms stand upon,
Which made him push at what his issue gate);   110
The other Edmond Langley, whose mild sprite
Affected quiet and a safe delight.

31

With these did interpose his proud unrest
Thomas of Woodstock, one most violent,
Impatient of command, of peace, of rest;
Whose brow would shew that which his heart had meant;
His open malice and repugnant breast
Procur'd much mischief by his discontent;
And these had all the charge of king and state
Till by himself he might it ordinate.   120

32

And in the first years of this government
Things pass'd as first: the wars in France proceed,
Though not with that same fortune and event,
Being now not followed with such careful heed;
Our people here at home, grown discontent
Through great exactions, insurrections breed;
Private respects hind'red the common weal,
And idle ease doth on the mighty steal.

33

Too many kings breed factions in the court,
The head too weak, the members grown too great;   130
O this is that which kingdoms doth transport;
This plague the heavens do for injustice threat
When children rule, who ever in this sort
Confound the state their ancestors did get;
For the ambitious, once inur'd to reign,
Can never brook a private state again.

34

And kingdoms ever suffer this distress,
For one or many guide the infant king,
Which one or many, tasting this excess
Of greatness and command, can never bring   140
Their thoughts again t' obey or to be less.
From hence these insolencies ever spring,
Contempt of others whom they seek to foil;
Then follow leagues, destruction, ruin, spoil.

35

Whether it were that they which had the charge
Suff'red the king to take a youthful vein
That they their private better might inlarge,
Or whether he himself would farther strain
(Thinking his years sufficient to discharge
The government), presum'd to take the reign,   150
We will not say; but now his ear he lends
To youthful counsel, and his lusts attends.

36

And courts were never barren yet of those
Which could with subtle train and apt advise
Work on the prince's weakness, and dispose
Of feeble frailty easiest to intice;
And such no doubt about this king arose,
Whose flattery (the dangerous nurse of vice)
Got hand upon his youth to pleasures bent,
Which, led by them, did others discontent.   160

37

For now his uncles grew much to mislike
These ill proceedings; were it that they saw
That others, favor'd, did aspiring seek
Their nephew from their counsels to withdraw,
Seeing his nature flexible and meek,
Because they only would keep all in awe;
Or that indeed they found the king and state
Abus'd by such as now in office sate.

38

Or rather else they all were in the fault,
Th' ambitious uncles, th' indiscreet young king,   170
The greedy counsel, and the minions naught,
And all togither did this tempest bring;
Besides the times, with all injustice fraught,
Concurr'd in this confus'd disordering,
That we may truly say this spoil'd the state:
Youthful counsel, private gain, partial hate.

39

And sure the king plainly discovereth
Apparant cause his uncles to suspect;
For John of Gaunt was said to seek his death
By secret means which came not to effect;   180

The Duke of Gloster likewise practiseth
In open world that all men might detect,
And leagues his nobles, and in greatest strength
Rises in arms against him too at length. . . .

[Owing to Richard's weakness of character, his minions'
avarice, his kinsmen's hostility, and an increasingly intimate alliance with France following the king's marriage
to the French princess, Isabella, the strains within the body
politic become almost intolerable. At last Richard seizes
the initiative. Urged on by the French ambassador, he
surprises and arrests Gloucester, Warwick, and Arundel
(the heads of the anti-French faction at his court). Gloucester is "strangled in secret" at Calais, Warwick is forced
to humble himself, and Arundel is "put to public death."]

57

Now storm his uncles, albeit in vain,
For that no remedy they could devise;
They might their sorrows inwardly complain,
But outwardly they needs must temporize.
The king was great, and they should nothing gain
T' attempt revenge or offer once to rise;   190
This league with France had made him now so strong
That they must needs as yet indure this wrong. . . .

59

For standing on himself he sees his might
Out of the compass of respective awe,
And now begins to violate all right
While no restraining fear at hand he saw.
Now he exacts of all, wastes in delight,
Riots in pleasure, and neglects the law;
He thinks his crown is licens'd to do ill,
That less should list that may do what it will.   200

60

Thus b'ing transported in this sensual course,
No friend to warn, no counsel to withstand,
He still proceedeth on from bad to worse,
Sooth'd in all actions that he took in hand
By such as all impiety did nurse,
Commending ever what he did command.
Unhappy kings that never may be taught
To know themselves or to discern their fault!

61

And whilst all silent grieve at what is done,
The Duke of Herford, then of courage bold   210
And worthily great John of Gaunt's first son,
Utters the passion which he could not hold,
In sad discourse upon this course begun,
Which he to Mowbray, Duke of Norfolk, told,
To th' end he, being great about the king,
Might do some good by better counseling.

62

The faithless duke, that presently takes hold
Of such advantage to insinuate,
Hastes to the king, perverting what was told;
And what came of good mind he makes it hate.   220
The king, that might not now be so controll'd
Or censur'd in his course, much frets thereat,
Sends for the duke, who doth such words deny
And craves the combat of his enemy.

63

Which straight was granted, and the day assign'd
When both in order of the field appear
To right each other as th' event should find;
And now both even at point of combat were
When lo, the king chang'd sodenly his mind,
Casts down his warder, and so stays them there   230
As better now advis'd what way to take
Which might for his assured safety make.

64

For now, considering (as it likely might)
The victory should hap on Herford's side,
A man most valiant and of noble sprite,
Belov'd of all, and ever worthy tri'd,
How much he might be grac'd in publique sight
By such an act as might advance his pride
And so become more popular by this,
Which he fears—too much he already is;   240

65

And therefore he resolves to banish both,
Though th' one in chiefest favor with him stood,
A man he dearly lov'd and might be loth
To leave him that had done him so much good;
Yet having cause to do as now he doth,
To mitigate the envy of his blood,
Thought best to loose a friend to rid a foe,
And such a one as now he doubted so.

66

And therefore to perpetual exile he
Mowbray condemns, Herford but for ten years,   250
Thinking (for that the wrong of this decree
Compar'd with greater rigor less appears)
It might of all the better liked be;
But yet such murmuring of the fact he hears
That he is fain four of the ten forgive,
And judg'd him six years in exile to live.

67

At whose departure hence out of the land,
O how the open multitude reveal
The wondrous love they bare him underhand,

Which now in this hot passion of their zeal   260
They plainly shew'd that all might understand
How dear he was unto the common weal;
They fear'd not to exclaim against the king
As one that sought all good men's ruining.

68

Unto the shore with tears, with sighs, with moan
They him conduct, cursing the bounds that stay
Their willing feet that would have further gone
Had not the fearful ocean stopp'd their way.
"Why, Neptune, hast thou made us stand alone,
Devided from the world," for this say they;   270
"Hemm'd in to be a spoil to tyranny,
Leaving affliction hence no way to fly?

69

"Are we lock'd up, poor souls, here t' abide
Within the watery prison of thy waves
As in a fold, where subject to the pride
And lust of rulers we remain as slaves?
Here in the reach of might, where none can hide
From th' eye of wrath, but only in their graves?
Happy confiners you of other lands
That shift your soil and oft scape tyrants' hands!   280

70

"Ah, must we leave him here that here were fit
We should retain the pillar of our state,
Whose virtues well deserve to govern it,
And not this wanton young effeminate?
Why should not he in regal honor sit,
That best knows how a realm to ordinate?
Yet one day, O we hope thou shalt bring back,
Dear Bullingbrooke, the justice that we lack. . . ."

76

But long the duke remain'd not in exile
Before that John of Gaunt, his father, dies,   290
Upon whose state the king seiz'd now this while,
Disposing of it as his enemy's.
This open wrong no longer could beguile
The world that saw these great indignities,
Which so exasperates the minds of all
That they resolv'd him home again to call.

77

For now they saw 'twas malice in the king,
Transported in his ill-conceived thought,
That made him so to prosecute the thing
Against all law and in a course so naught;   300
And this advantage to the duke did bring
Fitter occasions whereupon he wrought,
For to a man so strong and of such might
He gives him more that takes away his right.

78

The king, in this meantime, I know not how,
Was drawn into some actions forth the land
T' appease the Irish that revolted now;
And there, attending what he had in hand,
Neglects those parts from whence worse dangers grow,
As ignorant how his affairs did stand,   310
Whether the plot was wrought it should be so,
Or that his fate did draw him on to go. . . .

81

And now was all disorder in th' excess,
And whatsoever doth a change portend,
As idle luxury and wantonness,
Proteus-like varying pride, vain without end,
Wrong-worker riot, motive to oppress,
Endless exactions which the idle spend,
Consuming usury and credits crack'd
Call'd on this purging war that many lack'd. . . .   320

85

And all this makes for thee, O Bullingbrooke,
To work a way unto thy sovereignty;
This care the heavens, fate, and fortune took
To bring thee to thy scepter easily;
Upon thee falls that hap which him forsook,
Who, crown'd a king, a king yet must not die;
Thou wert ordain'd by providence to raise
A quarrel lasting longer then thy days. . . .

[As Richard's star falls, Bolingbroke's rises. Against the
king's ineffectual defense the invasion easily succeeds, and
Richard falls into his rival's hands. In Book II Daniel
treats the immediate consequences of this upheaval:

King Richard moans his wrong and wails his reign,
And here, betray'd, to London he is led,
Basely attir'd, attending Herford's train,
Where th' one is scorn'd, the other welcomed;
His wife, mistaking him, doth much complain,
And both togither greatly sorrowed;
In hope to save his life and ease his thrall
He yields up state, and rule, and crown, and all.

The following passage from the end of the second book
opens with the description of Richard's forced abdication.]

[BOOK II]

116

And forth h' is brought unto th' accomplishment,
Deck'd with the crown in princely robes that day,
Like as the dead in other lands are sent
Unto their graves in all their best array;
And even like good did him this ornament,

For what he brought he must not bear away,
But buries there his glory and his name,
Intomb'd forevermore in others' blame.

117

And there unto th' assembly of these states
His sorrow for their long indured wrong   10
Through his abus'd authority relates,
Excuses with confessions mix'd among,
And glad, he says, to finish all debates,
He was to leave the rule they sought for long,
Protesting if it might be for their good
He would as gladly sacrifice his blood.

118

There he his subjects all in general
Assoils and quites of oath and fealty,
Renounces interest, title, right, and all
That appertain'd to kingly dignity,   20
Subscribes thereto and doth to witness call
Both heaven and earth, and God and saints on high,
And all this did he but t' have leave to live,
The which was all he crav'd that they would give.

119

'Tis said with his own hands he gave the crown
To Lancaster, and wish'd to God he might
Have better joy thereof then he had known,
And that his pow'r might make it his by right,
And furthermore he crav'd of all his own
But life to live apart, a private wight;   30
The vanity of greatness he had tri'd,
And how unsurely stands the foot of pride.

120

This brought to pass, the lords return with speed
T' acquaint the Parlament with what is done;
Where they at large publish'd the king's own deed
And manner of his resignation,
When Canterbury urg'd them to proceed
Forthwith unto a new election,
And Henry make his claim both by discent
And resignation to the government.   40

121

Who there with full and general applause
Is straight proclaim'd as king and after crown'd,
The other clean rejected by the laws
As one the realm had most unworthy found.
And yet, O Lancaster, I would thy cause
Had had as lawful and as sure a ground
As had thy virtues and thy glorious worth,
For empire born, for government brought forth.

122

Then had not, O, that sad succeeding age
Her fields engrain'd with blood, her rivers dy'd   50
With purple streaming wounds of her own rage,
Nor seen her princes slain, her peers distroy'd;
Then had'st not thou, dear country, come to wage
War with thyself, nor those afflictions tri'd
Of all-consuming discord here so long,
Too mighty now, against thyself too strong.

123

So had the blood of thirteen battles fought
About this quarrel, fatal to our land,
Have been reserv'd with glory to have brought
Nations and kingdoms under our command;   60
So should all that thy son and thou had got
With glorious praise have still been in our hand,
And that great worthy, last of all thy name,
Had join'd the western empire to the same.

124

So should his great imperial daughter, now
Th' admired glory of the earth, hereby
Have had all this near-bord'ring world to bow
To her immortalized majesty;
Then proud Iberus' lord, not seeking how
T' attain a false-conceived monarchy,   70
Had kept his barrain bounds and not have stood
In vain attempts t' inrich the seas with blood,

125

Nor interpos'd his greedy, meddling hands
In other men's affairs t' advance his own,
Nor tyranniz'd over so many lands,
From late obscurity so mighty grown;
But we with our undaunted conquering bands
Had lent our ensigns unto lands unknown,
And now with more audacious force began
To march against th' earth's terror, Ottoman.   80

126

Where thou, O worthy Essex, whose dear blood
Reserv'd from these sad times to honor ours,
Should'st have conducted armies and now stood
Against the strength of all the eastern pow'rs;
There should thy valiant hand perform'd that good
Against the barbarism that all devours,
That all the states of the redeemed earth
Might thee admire and glorify thy birth.

127

Thence might thy valor have brought in despight
Eternal trophies to Eliza's name,   90

And laid down at her sacred feet the right
Of all thy deeds and glory of the same.
All that which by her pow'r and by thy might
Thou had'st attain'd to her immortal fame
Had made thee wond'red here, admir'd afar,
The Mercury of peace, the Mars of war.

128

And thou, my lord, the glory of my muse,
Pure-spirited Mountjoy, th' ornament of men,
Had'st had a large and mighty field to use
Thy holy gifts and learned counsels then;   100
Whole lands and provinces should not excuse
Thy trusty faith, nor yet sufficient been
For those great virtues to have ordered
And in a calm obedience governed.

129

Nor had I, then, at solitary brook
Sate framing bloody accents of these times,
Nor told of wounds that grieved eyes might look
Upon the horror of their fathers' crimes;
But rather a more glorious subject took

To register in everlasting rimes,   110
The sacred glories of Elizabeth,
T' have kept the wonder of her worth from death;

130

And likewise builded for your great designs,
O you two worthies, beauties of our state,
Immortal tombs of unconsuming lines
To keep your holy deeds inviolate;
You in whose actions yet the image shines
Of ancient honor ne'er worn out of date,
You that have virtue into fashion brought
In these neglected times respected nought.   120

131

But whither am I carried with the thought
Of what might have been, had not this been so?
O sacred Fury, how was I thus brought
To speak of glory that must tell of wo?
These acted mischiefs cannot be unwrought,
Though men be pleas'd to wish it were not so,
And therefore leave, sad muse, th' imagin'd good,
For we must now return again to blood.

THE CHRONICLERS

Although the sprawling Elizabethan annals which we compendiously call the chronicles rarely succeed either as literature or as history, they are not without interest for a student of the age. With a few exceptions—for example, Hall on Henry VIII or the venerable Camden on the glories of Elizabeth—they are partisan, plagiaristic, uncritical, and virtually innocent of form or style; but they served Shakespeare (and many others) well, and they throw a bright light on the sometimes fanatical patriotism which it was a consistent Tudor policy to encourage. In 1505 the first and wisest of the Tudors commissioned a learned Italian, Polydore Vergil, to begin the laborious *Anglica historia,* which at last appeared (with a dedication to Henry VIII) between 1534 and 1555. Although Vergil cannot be said to rise far above the low level set by the chronicles of John Hardyng (1378–?1465) and Robert Fabyan (d. 1513), he did reveal the ways in which a renewed interest in the national past could serve the needs of a new dynasty. Henry VIII must have realized this fact when, in 1533, he commissioned John Leland to assemble materials for a new history. After years of incessant toil and travel, Leland, ready with a preliminary report, presented his *Laborious Journey and Search* to his royal master as a new-year's gift in 1545; but, like many a scholar since, he could never shape his mountainous data into a book, and he died insane. But the data themselves,

published under the supervision (and with the expansions) of the learned John Bale in 1549, were admired and rifled by nearly all succeeding chroniclers, and so, happily, not all his fabulous erudition perished.

While Leland was tramping the almost inaccessible length and breadth of England, a very able writer, Edward Hall (or Halle), was putting together the chronicle published posthumously in 1548 as *The Union of the Two Noble and Illustrate Families of Lancaster and York.* A work obviously written to justify the Tudors' foreign and domestic policies, the *Union* has a difficult bibliographical history, even when we disregard the possibility of an alleged edition printed by Thomas Berthelet in 1542 (an edition which is almost surely mythical). Hall, a holder of various legal and municipal posts in the twenties and thirties, had sat in the important Reformation Parliament of 1529 and had ardently supported Henry VIII's ecclesiastical policy there and in subsequent Parliaments. Dying in 1547, he entrusted to the printer Richard Grafton the task of completing and publishing his manuscript, and Grafton executed his commission so promptly that by the spring of 1548 the *Union* was in the bookstalls. A puzzling job of editing and printing, it apparently combines a second printing of the first part (ending with the death of Edward IV) and a first printing of the second part (ending with the death of Henry VIII). Moreover, the style of much of the second part is patently superior to the style of the first; in particular those pages dealing with the momentous events from 1529 onward have an immediacy, a vivacity, and a mass of colorful detail that are in marked contrast to the conventionally stilted and rhetorical handling of the earlier sections. The disparity has led certain scholars to argue that the two sections are the work of two separate hands and even to suggest that the second section may be Grafton's, not Hall's. But there is nothing in the style of Grafton's known work to support such an ascription; and Grafton himself explained in his preface that Hall had completed the history to about 1533, and that he, as literary executor and printer, had put together Hall's rough notes on the last fourteen years of Henry's life, but "utterly without any addition of mine." Lacking more specific data, modern scholars have conjectured that the original core of Hall's chronicle was the 1529–1533 section, written as a sort of journal during Hall's participation in the events recorded and hence bearing the marks of immediate and warmly partisan observation; that perhaps after the publication (1534) of Polydore Vergil's *Anglica historia* (to which the *Union* is heavily indebted for the years from Henry IV to Henry VII) Hall conceived the idea of making his journal a part of a longer history; and that while he was preparing the earlier section he continued his record of contemporary events, which Grafton eventually put in order to carry the history to the death of Henry VIII. Whatever the precise details, there is no question that the *Union* comes to splendid life when Hall reaches the reign of his own monarch, whom he vastly admired as the apotheosis of patriotism and Protestantism. Although it may be fairly lamented that Hall often betrays an ignorance (or neglect) of the political and economic forces beneath the glittering surface of Henry's court—unlike Florence, Tudor England never produced a Machiavelli or a Guicciardini—he was wonderfully sensitive to that surface. The turgid rhetoric of the earlier sections (a legacy from his Latin source) yields to a vibrant prose; his imagination soars when he remembers the Field of the Cloth of Gold, and his pages on the color and the pageantry of his sovereign's court are a monument to the age he loved so well. It is no wonder that Shakespeare paid Hall the supreme compliment of quoting him directly. Our excerpts are from *The Union of the two noble and illustrate famelies of Lancastre & Yorke*, 1548 (STC 12721).

Richard Grafton himself had gained fame—and apparently fortune, of a sort—by publishing the first English translation of the Bible printed in England (see p. 131). He began his indefatigable career as a chronicler by printing (for the first time) Hardyng's *Chronicle;* there followed his editorial work on Hall's *Union,* and then, in 1562, Richard Tottel published his *Abridgment of the Chronicles of England,* a massive and lumbering exercise in wholesale borrowing which nevertheless went through five editions

between 1562 and 1572. In spite of sharp professional criticism—John Stow savagely attacked everything he did —Grafton exploited his popular success with a *Manual of the Chronicles of England* in 1565 and with *A Chronicle at large and meere History of the affayres of Englande* in 1569 (STC 12147), upon which our text is based.

Raphael Holinshed's *Chronicles of England, Scotland, and Ireland* (1577), a long paean by divers writers to the glory of the British Isles, is notable chiefly for its size and scope; but Shakespeare found it handy (as who would not?), and so its compiler has earned a niche in literary history. Securing employment as a translator with a publisher named Reginald Wolfe, a man who could obviously discern the tides of public taste, Holinshed was set to work by his master in compiling and editing a chronicle to end all chronicles, one that would begin with the Flood and end with Queen Elizabeth. As a special feature of the work Holinshed included both a "description" and a "history" of each of the three kingdoms comprising the British Isles. He himself "compiled" the English history, as the custom was, by copious pilferings from his predecessors, but he had the wisdom (or luck) to hire William Harrison to write the wonderful *Description of England* which tells us so much of what we know about Elizabeth's age and realm. Harrison is encyclopedic and therefore dull from time to time, but his penetrating survey of the social institutions, schools, architecture, geography, mineral deposits, flora and fauna —to name only a few of the topics in his four "books"— is for the most part a pure delight. To increase God's plenty Harrison expanded his *Description* for the second edition of the *Chronicles* in 1587. Holinshed enlisted Harrison's services in translating Hector Boece for the *Description of Scotland,* he himself patching together the history from Boece (?1465–1536) and Johannes Major (1469–1550). Richard Stanyhurst (who was to do such violence to Virgil [see p. 553]) and Edmund Campion, the Jesuit martyr, provided the *Description of Ireland,* the frisky history of Giraldus Cambrensis (in John Hooker's translation) supplying the chronicle for that country. Our excerpts from Holinshed and from Harrison are based upon the enlarged second edition, *The First and second volumes of Chronicles . . . First collected and published by Raphaell Holinshed, William Harrison, and others,* [1587] (STC 13569).

For decades before publishing his famous *Survey of London* (1598) John Stow had plied the trade of chronicler and antiquarian. He had edited Chaucer (1561), Matthew Paris (1571), and Thomas Walsingham (1574), made his fame and perpetuated his acid opinion of Richard Grafton through the many editions of his *Summary of English Chronicles* (1565 ff.) and *The Chronicles of England* (1580 ff.), and had seen the second (1587) edition of Holinshed through the press before addressing himself, at the end of his life, to the work by which his name lives. *A Survey* of London is a labor of both love and scholarship, a hymn to the most glorious of capitals and a systematic survey of its history, architecture, streets, and institutions. It constitutes our most intimate and reliable view of Shakespeare's London. Our text is based upon *A Survay of London,* 1598 (STC 23341).

Because William Camden's great *Annales rerum Anglicarum et Hibernicarum regnante Elizabetha* was written in Latin and not published until 1615 (the second part posthumously in 1627) it lies beyond the province of this anthology; none the less its merits deserve mention. One of the most learned and widely respected savants of his age, Camden had made his reputation with *Britannia* (1586), the result of a long journey through the British Isles and an exhaustive geographical, historical, and archeological survey which Philemon Holland (see p. 565) translated (1610) and Michael Drayton plundered for his *Poly-Olbion* (see p. 423). *The Remains of a Greater Work Concerning Britain* (1605) is another fascinating, if somewhat uncritical, gathering of antiquarian lore; but Camden's *magnum opus,* the *Annales,* is the most learned and artful of Tudor chronicles. If Grafton was a hack and Holinshed an able compiler, Camden was an artist-scholar. His magisterial command of the materials of English history, his judicial temper, and his unflagging patriotism made the *Annales* a monument to the dynasty, the queen, the religion, and the country that he loved. The fact that its merit was quickly recognized is attested by a string of translations in the earlier seventeenth century—a partial French version by Pierre de Bellegent (1624), an English translation (Books I–III) of the French by Abraham Darcy (1625), a translation of Book IV by Thomas Browne (1629, 1634), and a complete English version by Robert Norton which went through three editions between 1630 and 1635.

The first three selections below are arranged chronologically by subject matter, Hall's Henry VIII following Grafton's Henry IV and Holinshed's Henry V.

——————

RICHARD GRAFTON

Now after King Richard [II] was deposed, as you have heard, then Henry Plantagenet, born at Bolingbroke in the County of Lincoln, Duke of Lancaster and Hereford, Earl of Derby, Leicester, and Lincoln, son to John of Gaunt, Duke of Lancaster, took upon him the government of this realm, and was by sound of trumpet proclaimed king of England and of France and lord of Ireland, the twenty-ninth day of September in the year of our Lord 1399, by the name of King Henry the Fourth, and was crowned at Westminster the eleventh day of October then next following, which was the day of the translation of Edward the Confessor, with all triumph and solemnity.

And at the day of his coronation (as saith Hall) because he would not have it thought that he took upon him the crown without good title and right thereunto had, therefore he caused it to be proclaimed and published that he challenged the realm not only by conquest, but also for that he was by King Richard adopted as heir, and declared successor of him, and by resignation had accepted the crown and scepter, and also that he was next heir male of the blood royal to King Richard.

Shortly after his coronation, he created his eldest son, Henry, Prince of Wales, Duke of Cornwall. and Earl of Chester, being then of the age of twelve years, and caused him to be proclaimed heir apparent to the crown of this realm. And soon after he called his high court of Parliament, in the which was demanded by King Henry's friends what should be done with King Richard. And as the aforesaid Hall saith, whom I chiefly follow in this history for that he hath diligently travailed therein, the Bishop of Carlisle [Thomas Merke], which was a man well learned and of a good courage, stood up and said: "My lords, I require you to take heed what answer you make unto this question; for I think there is none of you worthy or meet to geve judgment on so noble a prince as King Richard is, whom we have taken and honored for our sovereign and liege lord by the space of twenty-two years, and I assure you there is not so rank a traitor, nor so arrant a thief, nor yet so cruel a murderer, apprehended or detained in prison for his offense, but he shall be brought before the justice to hear his judgment. And yet ye will proceed to the judgment of an anointed king, and hear neither his answer nor excuse. And I say that the Duke of Lancaster, whom you call king, hath more offended and more trespassed to King Richard and this realm then the king hath either done to him or to us. For it is manifest and well known that the duke was banished the realm by King Richard and his counsail, and by the judgment of his awn father (for the space of ten years) for what cause you all know, and yet without license of King Richard he is returned again into the realm, yea and that is worse, hath taken upon him the name, title, and preheminence of a king. And, therefore, I say that you have done manifest wrong to proceed in anything against King Richard without calling him openly to his answer and defense." As soon as the bishop had ended his tale, he was attached by the earl marshal, and committed to ward in the Abbey of Saint Albans.

And in the said Parliament it was concluded that King Richard should continue in a large prison, and should have all things honorably minist'red unto him, as well for his diet as also apparel. And that if any person or persons would presume to stir and rear war on the behalf of King Richard for his deliverance out of prison, that then King Richard himself should be the first that should die for that commotion. . . .

But now drew on the time the innocent must perish with the nocent and the unguilty with the guilty. For King Richard, being ignorant of this conspiracy [of the Earls of Rutland, Huntington, Salisbury, Kent, and Spencer, all of whom had been handily suppressed by Henry IV in 1400] and kept in miserable captivity, was by King Henry adjudged to die, for that he would deliver himself of all inward fear of his enemies; wherefore some write that he commanded him to be slain, and others say that he was agreeable thereunto, and some others affirm that he knew not of it until it was done. But howsoever it was, King Richard died of a violent death; and one writer saith that King Henry, sitting at his table and sore sighing, said, "Have I no faithful friend that will deliver me from him whose life will be my death, and whose death will be the preservation of my life?" This saying was noted of them that were present, and specially of one called Sir Piers of Exton. This knight incontinently departed the court with eight tall persons with him, and came to Pomfret, commanding that the esquire which was accustomed to sew and take the assay before King Richard, should no more use that manner of service, saying: "Let him eat well now, for he shall not long eat." King Richard sat down to dinner, and was served without courtesy or assay, he much marveling of the sodain mutation of the thing, demanded of the esquire why he did not his duty? "Sir," said he, "I am otherwise commanded by Sir Piers of Exton, which is newly come from King Henry." When he heard that word, he took the carving knife in his hand, and strake the esquire on the head, saying, "The devil take Henry of Lancaster and thee together." And with that word Sir Piers entered into the chamber well armed, with eight tall men in harness, every man having a bill in his hand. King Richard, perceiving them armed, knew well that they came to his confusion, and, putting the table from him, valiantly took the bill out of the first man's hand, and manfully defended himself, and slew four of them in a short space. Sir Piers, being somewhat dismayed with his resisting, leapt into the chair where King Richard was wont to sit, while the other four persons chased him about the chamber, which, being unarmed, defended himself against his enemies that were armed (which was a valiant act), but in conclusion he came by the chair where Sir Piers stood, who with a stroke of his pollax felled him to the ground, and soon after was rid out of his life in this world. When this knight perceived that he was dead, he lamented and said: "O Lord, what have we done? We have murdered him whom by the space of twenty-two years we obeyed and honored as our sovereign lord; now will all noble men abhor us and all good men hate us and point at us as the murderers of a noble prince." Thus have you heard the death and end of King Richard the Second as the best aucthors report of it. . . .

Now as the old proverb saith, after wind cometh rain, and after one evil commonly ensueth another. So during this time that King Henry was vexed and unquieted, both within the realm and without, Owen Glendower, a squire of Wales, perceiving the realm to be unquieted and the king not very well settled in his kingdom, purposed to take upon him the principality of Wales and the name and preheminence of the same; and, what with fair, flattering words and large promises, he inveigled and allured an undiscrete number of Welshmen, who took him for their prince and made to him an oath of allegiance and subjection. And being thus advanced and supported, he made sharp and cruel war. . . .

[The Scots having declared war on the English,] King Henry, forthwith gathering together a great puissance and army, entered into Scotland, brenning and spoiling towns, villages, and castles, sparing nothing but religious houses and churches, and brent a great part of the towns of Edinburgh and Leith. . . . [After Henry had withdrawn to England the whole border was soon aroused.] The Earl Douglas, being sore grieved with the loss of his nation and friends, and entending to requite the same if it were possible, did by the consent of the governor of Scotland gather together an army of twenty thousand tall men and mo. In the which army the Lord Mordack, Earl of Fife, son to the governor of Scotland, the Earl of Angus, and many other earls and barons of the nobility of Scotland. These valiant captains and courageous soldiers entered into Northumberland, with banners displayed like men that thought themselves hable to spoil the whole country of Northumberland. Now when they were ent'red into England, thinking no puissance hable to encounter with their force, sodainly there issued out of a valley beside a town called Homildon, the Lord Henry Percy, whom the Scots for his haut and valiant courage called Sir Henry Hotspur, and in his company the Lord George of Dunbar, Earl of March, before banished Scotland, as you have heard, with all the gentlemen of Northumberland and eight thousand men on horseback and on foot. The encounter was sharp, the fight was dangerous and doubtful, but in the end the victory chanced to the English nation. . . .

This year [1401] appeared a comet or blazing star of a great and huge quantity, which some expounded to signify great effusion of man's blood, and the same proved true, as after ye shall hear. For Henry, Earl of Northumberland, and Thomas, Earl of Worcester, his brother, and his son Lord Henry Percy, called Hotspur, which were to King Henry in the beginning of his reign both friends and aiders, perceiving now that the king had pacified all civil sedition, and repressed his enemies, and had brought his realm to a convenient quietness, they began now somewhat to envy his glory, and grudged at his wealth and felicity; and specially grieved because the king demanded of the earl and his son such Scottish prisoners as they had taken at the conflicts fought at Homildon and Nesbit, as you before have heard. For of all the captives which were then taken, there was delivered to the king's possession only Mordake, Earl of Fife, son to the Duke of Albany, governor of Scotland. For the king diverse and sundry times required them of the earl and his son, but the Percies, affirming them to be their awn proper prisoners and their peculiar preys, did utterly deny to deliver them, insomuch that the king openly said that if they would not deliver them, he would take them without deliverance. Wherewith they being sore discontent, by the counsail of Lord Thomas Percy, Earl of Worcester, whose study was ever to procure malice and to set all things in broil and uncertainty, feigning a cause to prove and tempt the king, came to him to Windsor, requiring him by ransom or otherwise to cause to be delivered out of prison Edmund Mortimer, Earl of March, their cousin-german, whom (as they reported) Owen Glendower kept in filthy prison, shackeled with irons, only for that he took the king's part and was to him faithful and true. . . .

When the king had well advised upon and considered this matter, he made answer and said that the Earl of March was not taken prisoner neither for his cause nor in his service, but willingly suffered himself to be taken, the which fraud the king caused to be openly published, and this answer pleased nothing the Earl of Worcester, but put him in a great choler and chafe, and departed in a great rage and fume, insomuch that Sir Henry Hotspur said afterwards openly: "Behold the heir of the realm is robbed of his right, and the robber with his awn will not redeem him." And now the Percies disposed and bent themselves in all that they might utterly to depose King Henry and to restore their cousin Edmund, Earl of March, unto the crown and diadem of the realm [Mortimer being the great-grandson of Edward III], whom they shortly after not only delivered out of the captivity of Owen Glendower, but also ent'red into a league and amity with the said Owen against King Henry and all his friends, to the great displeasure and long unquieting of King Henry and his partakers. . . .

The Lord Percy, with the Earl Douglas and other the earls of Scotland, with a great army departed out of the north parts, leaving his father sick (which promised upon his amendment and recovery without delay to follow) and came to Stafford, where his uncle, the Earl of Worcester, and he met, and there began to consult upon their great affairs; and there also they exhorted their soldiers to spare no travail for the liberty of their country, protesting openly that they made war only to restore the noble realm of England to his accustomed glory and freedom, which was governed by a tyrant and not by his lawful and right king. The captains sware, and the soldiers promised to fight, yea and to die for the liberty of their country.

When all things were prepared, they set forward toward Wales, looking every hour for new aid and succors. The king, hearing of the earls' approaching, thought it policy to encounter with them before that the Welshmen should join with their army, and therefore returned sodeinly to the town of Shrewsbury. He was scantly ent'red into the town but he was by his posts advertised that the earls, with banners displayed and battails ranged, were coming toward him, and were so hot and courageous that they with light horses began to skirmish with his host. The king, perceiving their doings, issued out and encamped himself without the east gate of the town. The earls nothing abashed, although their succors them deceived, embattailed themselves not far from the king's army. And the same night they sent the articles [listing their grievances and challenging Henry's claim to the throne]. . . .

When King Henry had read their articles and defiance, he answered the esquires that he was ready with dent of sword and fierce battail to prove their quarrel false and feigned, and not with writing and slanderous bills, and so in his righteous cause and just quarrel he doubted not but God would both aid and assist him against untrue persons and false forsworn traitors, with which answer the messengers departed.

The next day [July 21, 1403] in the morning early, which was the even of Mary Magdalene, the king perceived that the battail was nearer then he either thought or looked for; therefore, lest long tarrying might minish or hinder his strength, he did with all speed set his battails in good order; and likewise did his enemies, which both in puissance and courage was nothing to him inferior. Then sodainly the trumpets blew, and forthwith the battails joined. The Scots, which had the forward on the lords' side, entending to be revenged of their old displeasures done to them by the English nation, set fiercely on the king's forward, that they made them draw back and had almost put them out of their array. The Welshmen also, which sith the king's departure out of Wales had lurked and lien in woods and mountains, hearing of this battail toward, came to the aid of the earls, and refreshed the weary people with new succors. When a fearful messenger had declared to the king that his people were beaten down on every side, it was no need to bid him stir, for sodainly he approached with his fresh battail, and comforted, heartened, and encouraged his part so that they took their hearts to them and manfully fought with their enemies. The prince that day holp much his father, for although he were that day sore wounded in the face with an arrow, yet he never ceased either to fight where the battail was most strongest or to encourage them who seemed to him to faint. This sore and fierce battail continued three long hours with indifferent fortune on both parts; but at the last the king, crying victory, brake the array, and entered into the battail of his enemies, and fought fiercely, and entered so far into the battail that the Lord Douglas strake him down, and slew Sir Walter Blunt and three other appareled in the king's suit and clothing, saying: "I marvel to see so many kings to arise so sodainly again." But soon after the king was raised again, and that day he did many a noble feat of arms. For the Scots write, and Frenchmen also, though the Englishmen keep silence, that he himself slew with his awn hands that day thirty-six of his enemies, and the other of his part, encouraged by his doings, fought valiantly and slew the Lord Percy called Sir Henry Hotspur, the best captain on the part adverse; and when his death was known, they fled, and happy was he that was foremost. And in that flight the Earl Douglas, falling from the crag of a mountain, brake one of his stones, and so was taken, and for his valiantness was of the king freely

and frankly delivered. There was taken also Sir Thomas Percy, Earl of Worcester, and divers others. On the king's part were slain Sir Walter Blunt and sixteen hundreth other persons. But on the part of the rebels were slain the Earl of Stafford, the Lord Percy, and above five thousand other; and as for the Scots, few or none escaped alive.

After this great victory by the king obtained, he first rend'red his humble and hearty thanks to God Almighty, and caused the Earl of Worcester the next morrow after to be drawn, hanged, and quartered in the town of Shrewsbury, and his head to be sent to London and there set upon a pole upon London Bridge; and the same also were many mo captains executed in the said place. And this being done, the king, like a valiant conqueror, returned to London with great pomp, where he was by the magistrates of the city most solemply received and joyfully welcomed. But here a little to return, before his departure from Shrewsbury he, not forgetting his enterprise against Owen Glendower, sent into Wales with a great army Prince Henry, his eldest son, against the said Owen and his seditious complices, which, being dismayed and in a manner desperate of all comfort by the reason of the king's late victory, fled into desert places and solitary caves, where he received a final reward, meet and prepared by God's providence for such a rebel and seditious seducer. For being destitute of all comfort, and dreading to shew his face to any creature, lacking meat to sustain nature, for pure hunger and lack of food miserably ended his wretched life. Now after that the death of Owen was known to the prince, and that the prince with little labor and less loss had tamed and brideled the furious rage of the wild Welshmen, and had left governors to rule and govern the country, he returned to his father with great honor and no small praise. . . .

Now [in 1412] after that these great and fortunate chances had happened to King Henry, he, thinking that there could not a greater praise be geven to a king then for the execution of his office and the administration of justice, and entending to live in quietness, being now delivered of all civil division, with the which almost all Christendom was troubled, not only to the decay of Christ's religion and Christian creatures, but to the greater advancement of paynim princes, by the publishing and setting forth of that counterfeit and false prophet Mahomet. And that the king would shew himself mindful hereof, he called a great counsail of the three estates of his realm, in the which he deliberately consulted and concluded, as well for the politique governance of his realm, as also for the war to be made against the infidels, and specially for the recovery of the city of Jerusalem, in the which wars he entended to end his transitory life; and for that cause he prepared a great army, and gathered much treasure, entending to set forward in the same springtime. But see the chance, whatsoever man intendeth, God sodainly reverseth; what princes will, God will not; what we think stable, God maketh mutable, whereby Salomon's saying is found true: That the wisdom of men is but foolishness before God. When this prince was thus furnished with treasure sufficient, with valiant captains and hardy soldiers, with tall ships furnished with victuals, munitions, and all things necessary for such a journey royal, he was taken with a sore and sodain disease called an apoplexy, of the which he languished until his appointed hour. During which sickness, as some aucthors write, he caused the crown to be set on the pillow at his bed's head, and sodainly his pang so sore troubled him that he lay as though his breath and soul were departed from him, wherefore his chamberlains covered his face with a linen cloth.

The prince, his son, being thereof advertised, entered into the chamber and took away the crown and departed. The father, being sodainly revived out of his trance, quickly perceived the lack of his crown; and having knowledge that the prince, his son, had possessed it, caused him to repair to his presence, requiring of him to shew for what cause he had so misused himself. The prince with a good audacity answered: "Sir, to mine and all men's judgments you seemed dead in this world; wherefore I as your next and apparent heir took that as mine awn, and not as yours." "Well, fair son," said the king (with a great sigh), "what right I had to it, and how I enjoyed it, God knoweth." "Well," quod the prince, "if you die king, I will have the garland, and trust to keep it with the sword against all mine enemies as you have done." "Well," said the king, "I commit all to God, and remember you to do well." And with that turned himself in his bed, and shortly after departed unto God in a chamber of the Abbots of Westminster called Jerusalem, the twenty day of March, 1413, and in the year of his age forty-six, when he had reigned thirteen years, five moneths, and odd days, in much trouble and little pleasure, whose body with all funeral pomp was conveyed to Canterbury and there solemply buried, leaving behind him by the Lady Mary, daughter to Lord Humphrey, Earl of Hereford and Northampton, Henry, Prince of Wales, Thomas, Duke of Clarence, John, Duke of Bedford, Humphrey, Duke of Gloucester, Blanche, Duchess of Barre, and Philip, Queen of Denmark, for by his last wife, Queen Jane, he had no children.

The king was of a mean stature, well-proportioned and formally compact, quick and deliver, and of a stout courage. After that he had appeased all civil dissensions, he shewed himself so gently to all men that he gat him more love of the nobles in his later days then he had evil will of them in the beginning.

RAPHAEL HOLINSHED

FROM THE CHRONICLES OF ENGLAND (1587)

Henry, Prince of Wales, son and heir to King Henry the Fourth, born in Wales at Monmouth on the river of Wye, after his father was departed took upon him the regiment of this realm of England the twentieth of March, the morrow after proclaimed king by the name of Henry the Fift, in the year of the world 5375, after the birth of our Savior by our account 1413. . . .

Such great hope and good expectation was had of this man's fortunate success to follow that within three days after his father's decease diverse noblemen and honorable personages did to him homage and sware to him due obedience, which had not been seen done to any of his predecessors, kings of this realm, till they had been possessed of the crown. He was crowned the ninth of April, being Passion Sunday, which was a sore, ruggy, and tempestuous day with wind, snow, and sleet, that men greatly marveled thereat, making diverse interpretations what the same might signify. But this king even at first appointing with himself to shew that in his person princely honors should change public manners, he determined to put on him the shape of a new man. For whereas aforetime he had made himself a companion unto misruly mates of dissolute order and life, he now banished them all from his presence (but not unrewarded, or else unpreferred), inhibiting them upon a great pain not once to approach, lodge, or sojourn within ten miles of his court or presence; and in their places he chose men of gravity, wit, and high policy, by whose wise counsel he might at all times rule to his honor and dignity; calling to mind how once, to high offense of the king his father, he had with his fist stricken the chief justice [Sir William Gascoigne] for sending one of his minions (upon desert) to prison, when the justice stoutly commanded himself also streict to ward, and he (then prince) obeyed. The king after expelled him out of his privy council, banish'd him the court, and made the Duke of Clarence (his younger brother) president of council in his stead. . . .

But now that the king was once placed in the royal seat of the realm he, virtuously considering in his mind that all goodness cometh of God, determined to begin with something acceptable to His Divine Majesty, and therefore commanded the clergy sincerely and truly to preach the word of God and to live accordingly, that they might be the lanterns of light to the temporalty, as their profession required. The laymen he willed to serve God and obey their prince, prohibiting them above all things breach of matrimony, custom in swearing, and, namely, wilful perjury. Beside this, he elected the best-learned men in the laws of the realm to the offices of justice, and men of good living he preferred to high degrees and authority. Immediately after Easter he called a Parliament, in which diverse good statutes and wholesome ordinances for the preservation and advancement of the commonwealth were devised and established. On Trinity Sunday were the solemn exequies done at Canterbury for his father, the king himself being present thereat. . . .

Whilest in the Lent season [of 1414] the king lay at Killingworth, there came to him from Charles, dolphin of France, certain ambassadors that brought with them a barrel of Paris balls which from their maister they presented to him for a token that was taken in very ill part as sent in scorn to signify that it was more meet for the king to pass the time with such childish exercise than to attempt any worthy exploit. Wherefore the king wrote to him that yer ought long he would toss him some London balls that perchance should shake the walls of the best court in France. . . .

[The king needing money, his second Parliament obligingly debated a bill legalizing wholesale expropriation of those "temporal lands devoutly given and disordinately spent by religious and other spiritual persons."] This bill was much noted and more feared among the religious sort, whom surely it touched very near, and therefore to find remedy against it they determined to assay all ways to put by and overthrow this bill; wherein they thought best to try if they might move the king's mood with some sharp invention, that he should not regard the importunate petitions of the Commons. Whereupon, on a day in the Parliament Henry Chichele, Archbishop of Canterbury, made a pithy oration wherein he declared how not only the duchies of Normandy and Aquitaine, with the counties of Anjou and Maine, and the country of Gascoigne, were by undoubted title appertaining to the king as to the lawful and only heir of the same, but also the whole realm of France as heir to his great-grandfather King Edward the Third.

Herein did he much inveigh against the surmised and false feigned law Salic which the Frenchmen alledge ever against the kings of England in bar of their just title to the crown of France. The very words of that supposed law are these: *In terram Salicam mulieres ne succedant;* that is to say, into the Salic land let not women succeed. . . . [Although the Earl of Westmorland sought to check the archbishop's argument by urging a Scottish instead of a French war, his speech was all but lost in the Duke of Exeter's ringing denunciation of the French.] To be brief, the Duke of Excester used such earnest and pithy persuasions to induce the king and the whole assembly of the Parliament to credit his words that immediately after he had made an end all the company began to cry, "War, war! France, France!" Hereby the bill for dissolving of religious houses was clearly set aside, and nothing thought on but only the recovering of France, according as the archbishop had moved. And upon this point, after a few acts besides for the wealth of the realm established, the Parliament was prorogued unto Westminster. . . .

[Although the French, alarmed by England's aggressive gestures, sent ambassadors to urge restraint and conciliation, Henry was peremptory in pushing his demands: either full satisfaction of the English claims "or else fire and sword."] The Frenchmen, being not a little abashed at these demands, thought not to make any absolute answer in so weighty a cause till they had further breathed, and therefore prayed the English ambassadors to say to the king their maister that they, now having no opportunity to conclude in so high a matter, would shortly send ambassadors into England which should certify and declare to the king their whole mind, purpose, and intent. The English ambassadors returned with this answer, making relation of everything that was said or done. King Henry, after the return of his ambassadors, determined fully to make war in France, conceiving a good and perfect hope to have fortunate success, sith victory for the most part followeth where right leadeth, being advanced forward by justice and set forth by equity. . . .

[None the less, the French continued their futile negotiations, "offering to the king of England a great sum of money, with diverse countries, being in very deed but base and poor, as a dowry with the Lady Catherine in marriage, so that he would dissolve his army and dismiss his soldiers which he had gathered and put in a readiness." In reply the Archbishop of Canterbury insisted that unless the princess' dowry included Aquitaine, Anjou, "and all other seignories and dominions sometimes appertaining to the noble progenitors of the king of England," then war was inevitable: Henry "would with all diligence enter into France and destroy the people, waste the country, and subvert the towns with blood, sword, and fire, and never cease till he had recovered his ancient right and lawful patrimony. The king avowed the archbishop's saying, and in the word of a prince promised to perform it to the uttermost."]

The Archbishop of Bourges [chief of the French mission], much grieved that his ambassage was no more regarded, after certain brags blustered out with impatience, as more presuming upon his prelacy than respecting his duty of considerance to whom he spake and what became him to say, he prayed safe conduct to depart. Which the king gently granted, and added withal to this effect: "I little esteem your French brags, and less set by your power and strength. I know perfectly my right to my region which you usurp, and except you deny the apparant truth, so do yourselves also; if you neither do nor will know it, yet God and the world knoweth it. The power of your master you see, but my puissance ye have not yet tasted. If he have loving subjects, I am (I thank God) not unstored of the same, and I say this unto you, that before one year pass I trust to make the highest crown of your country to stoop and the proudest miter to learn his *humiliatedo*. In the meantime, tell this to the usurper your master, that within three moneths I will enter into France as into mine own true and lawful patrimony, appointing to acquire the same not with brag of words but with deeds of men and dint of sword, by the aid of God in whom is my whole trust and confidence. . . ."

When King Henry had fully furnished his navy with men, munition, and other provisions, perceiving that his captains misliked nothing so much as delay, determined his soldiers to go a-shipboard and away. But see the hap: the night before the day appointed for their departure he was credibly informed that Richard, Earl of Cambridge, brother to Edward, Duke of York, and Henry, Lord Scroop of Masham, lord treasurer, with Thomas Grey, a knight of Northumberland, being confederate togither, had conspired his death; wherefore he caused them to be apprehended. The said Lord Scroop was in such favor with the king that he admitted him sometime to be his bedfellow, in whose fidelity the king reposed such trust that when any private or public council was in hand this lord had much in the determination of it. . . . [This curious and unexpected conspiracy involved Richard, Earl of Cambridge, the second son of Edmund de Langley (and therefore a prince of the blood), who had married

Anne Mortimer, sister of the Earl of March; Lord Scroop, a presumably loyal follower of both Henry IV and Henry V, whose kinsman, the Archbishop of York, had been executed in 1405; and Thomas Grey of Heaton, a kinsman of the Percies. According to Cambridge's confession, they hoped to proclaim the Earl of March king of England as the rightful heir of Richard II; but when March was sounded out he immediately informed the king of the conspiracy. Grey, as a commoner, was beheaded at once. His two colleagues, as peers, claimed their privilege of trial before the House of Lords; they were tried, found guilty, and executed on August 5, 1415.]

These prisoners upon their examination confessed that, for a great sum of money which they had received of the French king, they intended verily either to have delivered the king alive into the hands of his enemies or else to have murthered him before he should arrive in the duchy of Normandy. When King Henry had heard all things opened which he desired to know, he caused all his nobility to come before his presence, before whom he caused to be brought the offenders also, and to them said: "Having thus conspired the death and destruction of me, which am the head of the realm and governor of the people, it may be no doubt but that you likewise have sworn the confusion of all that are here with me, and also the desolation of your own country. To what horror, O Lord, for any true English heart to consider, that such an execrable iniquity should ever so bewrap you as for pleasing of a forren enemy to imbrue your hands in your blood and to ruin your own native soil. Revenge herein touching my person though I seek not, yet for the safeguard of you, my dear friends, and for due preservation of all sorts I am by office to cause example to be shewed. Get ye hence, therefore, ye poor, miserable wretches, to the receiving of your just reward, wherein God's Majesty give you grace of his mercy and repentance of your heinous offenses." And so immediately they were had to execution. . . .

But now to proceed with King Henry's doings. After this, when the wind came about prosperous to his purpose, he caused the mariners to weigh up anchors and hoise up sails, and to set forward with a thousand ships on the vigil of Our Lady Day the Assumption [in August, 1415], and took land at Caux (commonly called Kidcaux), where the river of Seine runneth into the sea, without resistance. At his first coming on land he caused proclamation to be made that no person should be so hardy on pain of death either to take anything out of any church that belonged to the same or to hurt or do any violence either to priests, women, or any such as should be found without weapon or armor and not ready to make resistance; also that no man should renew any quarrel or strife whereby any fray might arise to the disquieting of the army.

The next day after his landing he marched toward the town of Harfleur, standing on the river of Seine between two hills. He besieged it on every side, raising bulwarks and a bastle in which the two Earls of Kent and Huntington were placed with Cornwall, Gray, Steward, and Porter. On that side towards the sea the king lodged with his field, and the Duke of Clarence on the further side towards Rone. . . . [Failing to secure relief from the dauphin, who told an emissary from Harfleur that "the king's power was not yet assembled in such number as was convenient to raise so great a siege," the hard-pressed citizens at last surrendered the town after a thirty-day siege.] The soldiers were ransomed and the town sacked, to the great gain of the Englishmen. . . . [Actually, Harfleur opened its gates on September 22 and so avoided the terrors of storming and sacking. None the less, Henry ruthlessly expelled all the inhabitants except those who did him homage as king of France. Their sorrowful departure made possible a heavy immigration from England within the next few months.]

The French king, hearing that the town of Harfleur was gotten and that the king of England was marching forward into the bowels of the realm of France, sent out proclamations and assembled people on every side, committing the whole charge of his army to his son the dolphin and Duke of Aquitaine, who incontinently caused the bridges to be broken and the passages to be kept. Also, they caused all the corn and vittles to be conveyed away or destroyed in all places where it was conjectured that the Englishmen would pass. The king of England, nothing dismayed herewith, kept his journey in spite of his enemies, constraining them within diverse towns and holds to furnish him with vittles. . . . [None the less, the English advance was difficult, and when they at last crossed the Somme King Henry] determined to make haste towards Calis, and not to seek for battle except he were thereto constrained, bicause that his army by sickness was sore diminished, insomuch that he had but only two thousand horsemen and thirteen thousand archers, billmen, and of all sorts of other footmen.

The Englishmen were brought into some distress in this journey by reason of their vittles in manner spent and no hope to get more; for the enemies had destroyed all the corn before they came. Rest could they none take, for their enemies with alarms did ever so infest them; daily it rained, and nightly it freezed; of fuel there was great scarcity, of fluxes plenty; money inough, but wares for their relief to bestow it on had they none. Yet in this great necessity the poor people of the country were not spoiled, nor anything taken of them without payment, nor any outrage or offense done by the Englishmen except one, which was that a soldier took a pyx out of a church, for which he was apprehended, and the king not once removed till the box was restored and the offender strangled. The people of the countries thereabout, hearing of such zeal in him to the maintenance of justice, minist'red to his army victuals and other necessaries, although by open proclamation so to do they were prohibited.

The French king, being at Rone and hearing that King Henry was passed the river of Somme, was much displeased therewith, and assembling his council to the number of five and thirty, asked their advice what was to be done. . . . At length, thirty of them agreed that the Englishmen should not depart unfought withal, and five were of a contrary opinion, but the greater number ruled the matter; and so Montjoy, king-at-arms, was sent to the king of England to defy him as the enemy of France and to tell him that he should shortly have battle. King Henry advisedly answered: "Mine intent is to do as it pleaseth God. I will not seek your maister at this time, but if he or his seek me I will meet with them, God willing. If any of your nation attempt once to stop me in my journey now towards Calis, at their jeopardy be it; and yet wish I not any of you so unadvised as to be the occasion that I dye your tawny ground with your red blood."

When he had thus answered the herald, he gave him a princely reward and license to depart. Upon whose return with this answer it was incontinently on the French side proclaimed that all men of war should resort to the constable to fight with the king of England. . . . [Pressing on resolutely in spite of French opposition, the English at last came upon the main body of the French army, which King Henry viewed from the top of a hill. Thereupon he] returned to his people and with cheerful countenance caused them to be put in order of battle, assigning to every captain such room and place as he thought convenient, and so kept them still in that order till night was come, and then determined to seek a place to incamp and lodge his army in for that night. There was not one amongst them that knew any certain place whither to go in that unknown country, but by chance they happened upon a beaten way, white in sight, by the which they were brought unto a little village, where they were refreshed with meat and drink somewhat more plenteously than they had been diverse days before.

Order was taken by commandement from the king after the army was first set in battle array that no noise or clamor should be made in the host, so that in marching forth to this village every man kept himself quiet; but at their coming into the village fires were made to give light on every side, as there likewise were in the French host, which was incamped not past two hundred and fifty paces distant from the English.

The chief leaders of the French host were these: the constable of France, the marshal, the admiral, the Lord Rambures, maister of the crossbows, and other of the French nobility, which came and pitched down their standards and banners in the county of Saint Paul, within the territory of Agincourt, having in their army, as some write, to the number of threescore thousand horsemen, besides footmen, wagoners, and other. They were lodged even in the way by the which the Englishmen must needs pass towards Calis, and all that night after their coming thither made great cheer and were very merry, pleasant, and full of game. The Englishmen also for their parts were of good comfort and nothing abashed of the matter, and yet they were both hungry, weary, sore travailed, and vexed with many cold diseases. Howbeit, reconciling themselves with God by housel and shrift, requiring assistance at his hands that is the only giver of victory, they determined rather to die than to yield or flee.

The day following was the five and twentieth of October in the year 1415, being then Friday and the feast of Crispin and Crispinian, a day fair and fortunate to the English but most sorrowful and unlucky to the French. In the morning the French captains made three battles. In the vaward were eight thousand helms of knights and esquires, four thousand archers, and fifteen hundred crossbows. . . . In the middleward were assigned as many persons, or more, as were in the foremost battle. . . . And in the rearward were all the other men of arms. . . . Thus the Frenchmen, being ordered under their standards and banners, made a great shew, for surely they were esteemed in number six times as many or more than was the whole company of the Englishmen with wagoners, pages, and all. They rested themselves, waiting for the bloody blast of the terrible trumpet, till the hour between nine and ten of the clock of the same day, during which season the constable made unto the captains and other men of war a pithy oration, exhorting and incouraging them to do valiantly, with many comfortable words and sensible reasons. King Henry, also like a leader and not as one led, like a sovereign and not an inferior, perceiving a plot of ground very strong and meet for his purpose, which on the back half was fenced with the village wherein he had lodged the night before and on both sides defended with hedges and bushes,

thought good there to imbattle his host, and so ordered his men in the same place as he saw occasion and as stood for his most advantage. First he sent privily two hundred archers into a low meadow which was near to the vauntguard of his enemies, but separated with a great ditch, commanding them there to keep themselves close till they had a token to them given to let drive at their adversaries. Beside this, he appointed a vaward, of the which he made captain Edward, Duke of York, who of an haulty courage had desired that office, and with him were the Lords Beaumont, Willoughby, and Fanhope, and this battle was all of archers. The middleward was governed by the king himself, with his brother, the Duke of Gloucester, and the Earls of Marshal, Oxenford, and Suffolk, in the which were all the strong billmen. The Duke of Excester, uncle to the king, led the rearward, which was mixed both with billmen and archers. The horsemen like wings went on every side of the battle.

Thus the king, having ordered his battles, feared not the puissance of his enemies, but yet, to provide that they should not with the multitude of horsemen break the order of his archers in whom the force of his army consisted, . . . he caused stakes bound with iron, sharp at both ends, of the length of five or six foot, to be pitched before the archers and of each side the footmen like an hedge, to the intent that if the barded horses ran rashly upon them they might shortly be gored and destroyed. . . . When he had thus ordered his battles, he left a small company to keep his camp and carriage, which remained still in the village, and then, calling his captains and soldiers about him, he made to them a right grave oration, moving them to play the men, whereby to obtain a glorious victory, as there was hope certain they should, the rather if they would but remember the just cause for which they fought and whom they should incounter, such faint-hearted people as their ancestors had so often overcome. To conclude, many words of courage he uttered to stir them to do manfully, assuring them that England should never be charged with his ransom nor any Frenchman triumph over him as a captive; for either by famous death or glorious victory would he, by God's grace, win honor and fame. It is said that as he heard one of the host utter his wish to another thus, "I would to God there were with us now so many good soldiers as are at this hour within England," the king answered: "I would not wish a man more here than I have. We are indeed in comparison to the enemies but a few, but if God of his clemency do favor us and our just cause—as I trust he will—we shall speed well inough. But let no man ascribe victory to our own strength and might, but only to God's assistance, to whom, I have no doubt, we shall worthily have cause to give thanks therefor. . . ."

Whilest the king was yet thus in speech, either army so maligned the other, being as then in open sight, that every man cried, "Forward! Forward!" The Dukes of Clarence, Gloucester, and York were of the same opinion, yet the king stayed a while lest any jeopardy were not foreseen or any hazard not prevented. The Frenchmen in the meanwhile, as though they had been sure of victory, made great triumph, for the captains had determined before how to divide the spoil, and the soldiers the night before had played the Englishmen at dice. The noblemen had devised a chariot wherein they might triumphantly convey the king captive to the city of Paris, crying to their soldiers, "Haste you to the spoil, glory, and honor!" little weening, God wot, how soon their brags should be blown away. . . .

But when both these armies, coming within danger either of other, set in full order of battle on both sides, they stood still at the first, beholding either other's demeanor, being not distant in sunder past three bow shoots. And when they had on both parts thus stayed a good while without doing anything—except that certain of the French horsemen, advancing forwards betwixt both the hosts, were by the English archers constrained to return back—advice was taken amongst the Englishmen what was best for them to do. Thereupon all things considered, it was determined that, sith the Frenchmen would not come forward, the king with his army imbattled (as ye have hard) should march towards them, and so leaving their truss and baggage in the village where they lodged the night before, only with their weapons, armor, and stakes prepared for the purpose, as ye have heard. These made somewhat forward, before whom there went an old knight, Sir Thomas Erpingham (a man of great experience in the war), with a warder in his hand, and when he cast up his warder all the army shouted; but that was a sign to the archers in the meadow, which therewith shot wholly altogither at the vaward of the Frenchmen, who, when they perceived the archers in the meadow and saw they could not come at them for a ditch that was betwixt them, with all haste set upon the foreward of King Henry; but yer they could join, the archers in the forefront and the archers on that side which stood in the meadow so wounded the footmen, galled the horses, and cumb'red the men of arms that the footmen durst not go forward, the horsemen ran togither upon plumps without order, some overthrew such as were next them, and the horses overthrew their masters; and so at the first joining the Frenchmen were foully discomforted and the Englishmen highly incouraged.

When the French vaward was thus brought to confusion, the English archers cast away their bows and took into their hands axes, malls, swords, bills, and other hand-weapons and with the same slew the Frenchmen until they came to the middleward. Then approached the king and so incouraged his people that shortly the second battle of the Frenchmen was overthrown and dispersed, not without great slaughter of men; howbeit, diverse were relieved by their varlets and conveyed out of the field. The Englishmen were so busied in fighting and taking of the prisoners at hand that they followed not in chase of their enemies, nor would once break out of their array of battle. Yet sundry of the Frenchmen strongly withstood the fierceness of the English when they came to handy strokes, so that the fight sometime was doubtful and perilous. Yet as part of the French horsemen set their course to have ent'red upon the king's battle, with the stakes overthrown, they were either taken or slain. Thus this battle continued three long hours.

The king that day shewed himself a valiant knight, albeit almost felled by the Duke of Alanson; yet with plain strength he slew two of the duke's company and felled the duke himself, whom, when he would have yielded, the king's guard—contrary to his mind—slew out of hand. In conclusion, the king, minding to make an end of that day's journey, caused his horsemen to fetch a compass about and to join with him against the rearward of the Frenchmen, in the which was the greatest number of people. When the Frenchmen perceived his intent, they were suddenly amazed and ran away like sheep, without order or array. Which when the king perceived, he incouraged his men and followed so quickly upon the enemies that they ran hither and thither, casting away their armor. Many on their knees desired to have their lives saved.

In the mean season, while the battle thus continued, and that the Englishmen had taken a great number of prisoners, certain Frenchmen on horseback, . . . hearing that the English tents and pavilions were a good way distant from the army without any sufficient guard to defend the same, either upon a covetous meaning to gain by the spoil or upon a desire to be revenged, ent'red upon the king's camp and there spoiled the hails, robbed the tents, brake up chests, and carried away caskets, and slew such servants as they found to make any resistance. For which treason and haskardy in thus leaving their camp at the very point of fight for winning of spoil where none to defend it, very many were after committed to prison and had lost their lives if the dolphin had longer lived. But when the outcry of the lackeys and boys, which ran away for fear of the Frenchmen thus spoiling the camp, came to the king's ears, he, doubting lest his enemies should gather together again and begin a new field, and mistrusting further that the prisoners would be an aid to his enemies or the very enemies to their takers indeed if they were suffered to live, contrary to his accustomed gentleness commanded by sound of trumpet that every man, upon pain of death, should incontinently slay his prisoner. When this dolorous decree and pitiful proclamation was pronounced, pity it was to see how some Frenchmen were suddenly sticked with daggers, some were brained with poleaxes, some slain with malls, other had their throats cut, and some their bellies paunched, so that in effect, having respect to the great number, few prisoners were saved. . . .

[King Henry let it be known that any other captives taken subsequently would be treated in like fashion, and the scattered, demoralized enemy made no further resistance.] The Frenchmen, fearing the sentence of so terrible a decree, without further delay parted out of the field. And so about four of the clock in the afternoon the king, when he saw no appearance of enemies, caused the retreat to be blown, and, gathering his army together, gave thanks to Almighty God for so happy a victory, causing his prelates and chaplains to sing this psalm, *In exitu Israel de Aegypto,* and commanding every man to kneel down on the ground at this verse, *Non nobis, Domine, non nobis, sed nomini tuo da gloriam.* Which done, he caused *Te Deum,* with certain anthems, to be sung, giving laud and praise to God without boasting of his own force or any human power. That night he and his people took rest and refreshed themselves with such victuals as they found in the French camp, but lodged in the same village where he lay the night before.

In the morning, Montjoy, king-at-arms, and four other French heralds came to the king to know the number of prisoners and to desire burial for the dead. Before he made them answer, to understand what they would say, he demanded of them why they made to him that request, considering that he knew not whether the victory was his or theirs. When Montjoy by true and just confession had cleared that doubt to the high praise of the king, he desired of Montjoy to understand the name of the castle near adjoining. When they told him that it was called Agincourt, he said, "Then shall this conflict be called the battle of Agincourt.". . .

When tidings of this great victory was blown into England, solemn processions and other praisings to Almighty God, with bonfires and joyful triumphs, were ordained in every town, city, and borough; and the mayor and citizens of London went the morrow after the day of Saint Simon and Jude [October 28] from the church of Saint Paul to the church of Saint Peter at Westminster in devout manner, rend'ring to God hearty thanks for such fortunate luck sent to the king and his army. The same Sunday that the king removed from the camp at Agincourt towards Calis divers Frenchmen came to the field to view again the dead bodies; and the peasants of the country spoiled the carcasses of all such apparel and other things as the Englishmen had left; who took nothing but gold and silver, jewels, rich apparel, and costly armor. But the plowmen and peasants left nothing behind, neither shirt nor clout, so that the bodies lay stark naked until Wednesday. On the which day diverse of the noblemen were conveyed into their countries, and the remnant were by Philip, Earl Charlois, sore lamenting the chance and moved with pity, at his costs and charge buried in a square plot of ground of fifteen hundred yards, in the which he caused to be made three pits wherein were buried by account five thousand and eight hundred persons, beside them that were carried away by their friends and servants, and others which, being wounded, died in hospitals and other places. . . .

[In spite of this famous victory Henry's French campaigns dragged on sporadically for six years longer. At last when negotiations looking toward a permanent peace were undertaken, the French princess Catherine became one of the most important pawns in the dynastic struggle. In May, 1419, the French and English courts met at Melun for preliminary discussions.] Likewise for the French part came Isabel, the French queen, bicause her husband was fallen into his old frantic disease, having in her company the Duke of Burgognie and the Earl of Saint Paul, and she had attending upon her the fair Lady Catherine, her daughter, with six and twenty ladies and damosels; and had also for her furniture a thousand men of war. The said Lady Catherine was brought by her mother only to the intent that the king of England, beholding her excellent beauty, should be so inflamed and rapt in her love that he to obtain her to his wife should the sooner agree to a gentle peace and loving concord. But though many words were spent in this treaty, and that they met at eight several times, yet no effect insued, nor any conclusion was taken by this friendly consultation. . . . By reason whereof no conclusion sorted to effect of all this communication save only that a certain spark of burning love was kindled in the king's heart by the sight of the Lady Catherine. . . . [The next year, however, were opened those negotiations leading to the peace of Troyes,] in which at length it was concluded that King Henry of England should come to Troyes and marry the Lady Catherine, and the king her father after his death should make him heir of his realm, crown, and dignity. It was also agreed that King Henry, during his father-in-law's life, should in his stead have the whole government of the realm of France as regent thereof, with many other covenants and articles. . . .

[After his marriage, Henry brought his bride to England for her coronation at Westminster on February 24, 1421. The feast following that ceremony was splendid.] Thus for the first course: brawn and mustard, eels in burneux, frument with balien, pike in herbage, lamprey powdered, trout, codling, plaice fried, martin fried, crabs, leach lumbard flourished, tarts; and a device called a pelican, sitting on her nest with her birds, and an image of Saint Katharine holding a book and disputing with doctors, holding this poesy in her right hand, written in fair and legible letters, "*Madame le Royne*," and the pelican answering:

> *C'e est la signe & du roy, pour tenir joy,*
> *Et a tout sa gent, elle mette sa entent.*

The second course was jelly colored with columbine flowers, white potage or cream of almonds, bream of the sea, conger, soles, cheven, barbill and roch, fresh salmon, halibut, gurnard, rochet broiled, smelts fried, crevis or lobster, leech damask, with the king's poesy flourished thereupon, "*Une sans plus*"; lamprey fresh baked, flampeyn flourished with a scutcheon royal, and therein three crowns of gold planted with *flour-de-luces,* and flower of camomile wrought of confections with a devise of a panther and an image of Saint Katharine with a wheel in one hand and a scroll with a poesy in the other, to wit,

> *La royne ma file, in cesta ile,*
> *Per bon resoun, aues renoun.*

The third course was dates in compost, cream mottle, carp deore, turbot, tench, perch with gojon, fresh sturgion with welks, porperous roasted, mennes fried, *crevisse de eau douce,* pranis, eels roasted with lamprey, a leech called the white leech flourished with hawthorn leaves and red haws, a marchpane garnished with diverse figures of angels, among which was set an image of Saint Katharine, holding this poesy,

> *Il est escrit, pur voir & eit,*
> *Per marriage pure, cest guerre ne dure.*

And lastly a devise of a tiger looking in a mirror, and a man sitting on horseback all armed, holding in his arms a tiger's whelp with this poesy, "*Per force sans resoun ie ay prise ceste best,*" and with his own hand making a countenance of throwing of mirrors at the great tiger, which held this poesy, "*Gile che mirrour ma feste distour.*" Thus with all honor was finished the solemn coronation. . . .

This year [1421] at Windsor on the day of Saint Nicholas in December [the sixth] the queen was delivered of a son named Henry, whose godfathers were John, Duke of Bedford, and Henry, Bishop of Winchester, and Jaquet or, as the Frenchmen called her, Jacqueline of Bavière, Countess of Holland, was his godmother. The king being certified hereof as he lay at siege before Meaux, gave God thanks, in that it had pleased his divine providence to send him a son which might succeed in his crown and scepter. But when he heard reported the place of his nativity, were it that he warned by some prophecy or had some foreknowledge or else judged himself of his son's fortune, he said unto the Lord Fitzhugh, his trusty chamberlain, these words: "My lord, I, Henry, born at Monmouth, shall small time reign and much get; and Henry born at Windsor shall long reign and all loose. But as God will, so be it."

[Henry's forebodings proved true. The next year, still pursuing his French will-o'-the-wisp, he "began to wax sick" at Senlis and was presently carried in a horse-litter to Bois de Vincennes, whither he summoned the Dukes of Bedford and Gloucester and the Earls of Salisbury and Warwick.] Now when he saw them pensife for his sickness and great danger of life wherein he presently lay, he with many grave, courteous, and pithy words recomforted them the best he could, and therewith exhorted them to be trusty and faithful unto his son and to see that he might be well and virtuously brought up. And as concerning the rule and governance of his realms, during the minority and young years of his said son, he willed them to join togither in friendly love and concord, keeping continual peace and amity with the Duke of Burgognie and never to make treaty with Charles that called himself dolphin of Vienne by the which any part either of the crown of France or of the duchies of Normandy and Guienne may be lessened or diminished; and further that the Duke of Orleance and the other princes should still remain prisoners till his son came to lawful age, lest, returning home again, they might kindle more fire in one day than might be quenched in three.

He further advised them that, if they thought it necessary, it should be good to have his brother Humphrey, Duke of Gloucester, to be protector of England during the nonage of his son, and his brother the Duke of Bedford, with the help of the Duke of Burgognie, to rule and to be regent of France, commanding him with fire and sword to persecute the dolphin till he had either brought him to reason and obeisance or else to drive and expel him out of the realm of France. And herewith he protested unto them that neither the ambitious desire to inlarge his dominions, neither to purchase vain renowm and worldly fame, nor any other consideration had moved him to take the wars in hand, but only that in prosecuting his just title he might in the end attain to a perfect peace and come to enjoy those pieces of his inheritance which to him of right belonged. . . .

The noblemen present promised to observe his precepts and to perform his desires, but their hearts were so pensife and replenished with sorrow that one could not for weeping behold another. Then he 10 said the Seven Psalms and received the sacrament, and in ⟨sa⟩ying the Psalms of the Passion ended his

days here in this world at Bois Saint Vincent the last of August, in the year a thousand four hundred twenty and two.

This Henry was a king of life without spot, a prince whom all men loved and of none disdained, a captain against whom fortune never frowned nor mischance once spurned; whose people him so severe a justicer both loved and obeyed, and so humane withal that he left no offense unpunished nor friendship unrewarded, a terror to rebels and suppresser of sedition, his virtues notable, his qualities most praiseworthy.

EDWARD HALL

FROM THE UNION OF THE TWO NOBLE AND ILLUSTRATE FAMILIES OF LANCASTER AND YORK (1548)

Richard Grafton to the Reader

I must crave of thee, most gentle reader, charitably to judge of me, the imprinter of this work, if ought herein shall be seen unto thee of purpose to be omitted, either not sufficiently delated and set furth or else something too plainly spoken, in the which might be noted affection, that thou wilt excuse me therein; for I profess that I have, as near as in me lay, neither altered nor added anything of myself in 10 the whole work otherwise then the aucthor writ the same. But this is to be noted, that the aucthor thereof, who though not to all men yet to many very well knowen, was a man in the later time of his life not so painful and studious as before he had been; wherefore he perfited and writ this history no farther then to the four and twenty year of King Henry the Eight; the rest he left noted in divers and many pamphlets and papers, which so diligently and truly as I could I gathered the same together and have in such wise 20 compiled them as may after the said years appear in this work, but utterly without any addition of mine. Therefore my request and desire, as aforesaid, is that thou wilt truly and charitably judge me, and so soon as my leisure will serve, for thine ease and ready finding of anything herein contained I purpose to gather an exact table of the whole work.

THE NAME OF THE HISTORIES CONTAINED IN THIS VOLUME

THE TRIUMPHANT REIGN OF KING HENRY THE EIGHTH

THE TWENTY-FIFTH YEAR [1533-34]

The king in the beginning of this twenty-fifth year kept the day of Sainct George at his manor of Greenwich with great solempnity, and the court was greatly replenished with lords, knights, and with ladies and gentlewomen to a great number with all solace and pleasure. You have hard, the last year, how the Parliament had enacted that no person should, after a day, appeal to Rome for any cause whatsoever it were, and that the queen, now called 20 the princess dowager, had appealed to the court of Rome before the act made, so that it was doubted whether that appeal were good or not. This question was well handeled in the Parliament House, but much better in the Convocation House; but in both houses it was alleged, yea and by books shewed, that in the counsails of Calcedon, Africk, Toletan, and divers other famous counsails in the primitive church, yea in the time of Sainct Augustine, it was affirmed, declared, and determined that a cause rising in one province should be determined in the same, and that neither the patriarch of Constantinople should meddle in causes moved in the jurisdiction of the patriarch of Antioch, nor no bishop should entermit within another's province or country; which things were so clerkly opened, so conningly set furth to all intents, that every man that had wit, and was determined to follow the truth, and not affectionate nor wilfully wedded to his own mind, might plainly see that all appeals made to Rome were clearly void and of none effect; which doctrines and counsails were shewed to the Lady Katerine, princess dowager, but she (as women love to lose no dignity) ever continued in her old song, trusting more to the pope's partiality then to the determination of Christ's verity. Whereupon the Archbishop of Canterbury, accompanied with the Bishops of London, Winchester, Bath, Lincoln, and divers other great clerks in a great number, rode to Dunstable (which is six mile from Ampthill, where the princess dowager lay) and there, by a doctor called Doctor Lee, she was ascited to appear before the said archbishop in cause of matrimony in the said town of Dunstable; and at the day of apparance she would not appear, but made defaut, and so she was called peremptory every day fifteen days together, and at the last, for lack of apparance and for contumacy, by th' assent of all the learned men there being present she was divorced from the king and their marriage declared to be void and of none effect; which sentence geven, the archbishop and all the other returned whether it pleased them.

After which divorce sued, many wise men said that the king was not well counsailed to marry the Lady Anne Boleyn before the divorce were adjudged, for by marrying before the first marriage was dissolved they said that the second marriage might be brought in question; and verily they said true, for so it was in the moneth of May three year following, as you shall hear after, when I come to the time. Of this divorce every man spake as his discretion and wisdom was, for wise men said that it was godly and honorably done for the discharge of the king's conscience and profitable for the surety of the realm, and that God loved this marriage, considering that the new queen was so soon with child. Other said that the bishop of Rome would curse all Englishmen and that th' emperor and he would invade the realm and destroy the people, and specially the Spaniards boasted much; but thanks be to God, their doings were much less then their words. But after every man had talked enough there was no more communing of the matter, but all was in peace. . . .

THE TWENTY-SEVENTH YEAR [1535-36]

In the beginning of this year the Duke of Norfolk and the Bishop of Ely went to Calais, and thether came the admiral of France. And the nineteenth day of June was three monks of the Charterhouse hanged, drawn, and quart'red at Tyburn and their quarters set up about London for denying the king to be supreme head of the church. Their names were Exmewe, Middlemore, and Nudigate. These men, when they were arraigned at Westminster, behaved themselves very stiffly and stubbornly, for, hearing their indictment read how traitorously they had spoken against the king's Majesty his crown and dignity, they neither blushed nor bashed at it, but very foolishly and hypocritically knowledged their treason; which maliciously they avouched, having no learning for their defense but rather, being asked divers questions, they used a malicious silence, thinking (as by their examinations afterward in the Tower of London it did appear, for so they said) that they thought those men (which was the Lord Cromwell and other that there sat upon them in judgment) to be heretiques and not of the church of God, and therefore not worthy to be either answered or spoken unto. And therefore as they deserved they received, as you have heard before.

Also the twenty-second day of the same moneth John Fisher, Bishop of Rochester, was beheaded and his head set upon London Bridge. This bishop was of very many men lamented, for he was reported to be a man of great learning and a man of very good life, but therein wonderfully deceived, for he maintained the pope to be supreme head of the church and very maliciously refused the king's title of supreme head. It was said that the pope, for that he held so manfully with him and stood so stiffly in his cause, did elect him a cardinal and sent the cardinal's hat as far as Calais; but the head it should have stand on was as high as London Bridge or ever the hat could come to Bishop Fisher, and then it was too late, and therefore he neither ware it nor enjoyed his office. This man, as I said, was accompted learned, yea and that very notably learned, and yet have you heard how he was deceived with Elizabeth Barton, that called herself the holy maid of Kent, and no doubt so was he in the defense of that usurped authority, the more pity. Wonderful it is that a man, being learned, should be so blind in the Scriptures of God that proveth the supreme aucthority of princes so manifestly. Also the sixth day of July was Sir Thomas More beheaded for the like treason before rehearsed, which, as you have heard, was for the denying of the king's Majesty's supremacy. This man was also coumpted learned, and as you have heard before he was lord chancellor of England, and in that time a great persecutor of such as detested the supremacy of the bishop of Rome, which he himself so highly favored that he stood to it till he was brought to the scaffold on the Tower Hill, where on a block his head was stricken from his shoulders and had no more harm. I cannot tell whether I should call him a foolish wise man or a wise foolish man, for undoubtedly he, beside his learning, had a great wit, but it was so mingled with taunting and mocking that it seemed to them that best knew him that he thought nothing to be well spoken except he had minist'red some mock in the communication; insomuch as at his coming to the Tower one of the officers demanded his upper garment for his fee, meaning his gown, and he answered he should have it, and took him his cap, saying it was the uppermost garment that he had. Likewise, even going to his death, at the Tower gate a poor woman called unto him and besought him to declare that he had certain evidences of hers in the time that he was in office (which, after he was apprehended, she could not come by) and that he would intreat she might have them again or else she was undone. He answered, "Good woman, have patience a little while, for the king is so good unto me that even within this half hour he will discharge me of all businesses and help thee himself." Also when he went up the stair on the scaffold he desired one of the shiriff's officers to geve him his hand to help him up, and said, "When I come down again let me shift for myself as well as I can." Also the hangman kneeled down to him, asking him forgeveness of his death (as the manner is), to whom he said, "I forgeve thee, but I promise thee that thou shalt never have honesty of the striking off my head, my neck is so short." Also even when he should lay down his head on the block he, having a great gray beard, striked out his beard and said to the hangman, "I pray you, let me lay my beard over the block lest ye should cut it." Thus with a mock he ended his life.

This year, in the time that the king went his progress (which was to Gloucester and so westward), the king of Scots was installed at Windsor by the Lord Erskine his procurator. And in October following Stephen Gardiner, Bishop of Winchester, was sent ambassador into France, where he remained three years after.

In November was a solempn procession through the city of London of all the priests and religious in and about the city for the recovering of the French king to his health. And the eighth day of January following died the princess dowager at Kimbalton and was buried at Peterborough. Queen Anne ware yellow for the mourning.

And in February following was Queen Anne brought abed of a child before her time, which was born dead.

This year in the moneth of September William Tyndale, otherwise called Hichins, was by the cruelty of the clergy of Louvain condempned and burned in a town beside Bruxelles in Braband called Vylford. This man translated the New Testament into English and first put it in print, and likewise he translated the five books of Moses, Joshua, Judicum, Ruth, the Books of the Kings, and the Books of Paralipomenon, Nehemias or the first of Esoras, the prophet Jonas, and no more of the Holy Scripture. He made also divers treatises which of many were well liked and highly praised and of many utterly dispised and abhorred, and especially of the most part of the bishops of this realm, who often by their great labors caused proclamations to be made against his books and gat them condempned and brent, as well the New Testament as other works of his doings. Such as best knew him reported him to be a very sober man, born upon the borders of Wales and brought up in the University of Oxford, and in life and conversation unreprovable; and at the last, being in Oxford, Luther then setting forth certain works against the bishop of Rome, Tyndale, occasioned by theim to search the Scriptures whether Luther said the truth or no, did thereby not only himself attain the knowledge of the usurped aucthority of the bishop of Rome and his superstitious and dampnable doctrines that he had taught and published through all Christendom, but also, lamenting the ignorant state that his native country of England was in, who altogether were wrapped in errors, thought it his duty (for that God had revealed the light of his Gospel to him) to bestow his talent to the honor of God and profit of his country, and thought no way so good to reduce the people from their error as first to make theim acquainted with God's Word, that they might know what God's will was that we should do, and what the bishop of Rome said that we must do; and therefore first, as is aforesaid, he translated into English the New Testament, a work no doubt very notable and to him very painful, for that he was forced to fly his own native country and to live in a strange land among people that as well varied from his manners as the persons to him were unknowen. Amongest whom, after great pains by him taken and many and divers treatises by him published, he was at Andwarp this year by one Phillips, an Englishman and then a scholar at Louvain, betrayed and taken, and, as many said, not without the help and procurement of some bishops of this realm; but true it is that after he had been in prison more then a year and almost forgotten, he was labored for by letters written by the Lord Cromwell, and then in all haste, because he would recant no part of his doings, was burned as you have heard before. But yet this report did the procurator general there (which we call here the lieutenant) make of him, that he was *homo doctus, pius, et bonus,* that is to say "learned, godly, and good."

The fourth day of February the king held his high court of Parliament at Westminster, in the which was many good and wholesome statutes and laws made and concluded. And in this time was geven unto the king by the consent of the great and fat abbots all religious houses that were of the value of three hundred mark and under, in hope that their great monasteries should have continued still; but even at that time one said in the Parliament House that these were as thorns, but the great abbots were putrefied old oaks and they must needs follow, "And so will other do in Christendom," quod Doctor Stokesley, Bishop of London, "or many years be passed."

THE TWENTY-EIGHTH YEAR [1536-37]

On May Day were a solempn justs kept at Greenwich, and sodainly from the justs the king departed, having not above six persons with him, and came in the evening from Greenwich to his place at Westminster. Of this sodain departing many men mused, but most chiefly the queen, who the next day was apprehended and brought from Greenwich to the Tower of London, where after she was arraigned of high treason and condempned. Also at the same time was likewise apprehended the Lord Rochford, brother to the said queen, and Henry Norris, Mark Smeton, William a Bruton, and Sir Francis Weston, all of the king's privy chamber. All these were likewise committed to the Tower, and after arraigned and condempned of high treason. And all the gentlemen were beheaded on the scaffold at the Tower Hill; but the queen was with a sword beheaded within the Tower. And these following were the words that she spake the day of her death, which was the nineteenth day of May, 1536: "Good Christen people, I am come hether to die, for according to the law and by the law I am judged to die, and therefore I will speak nothing against it. I am come hether to accuse no man, nor to speak anything of that whereof I am accused and condempned to die, but I pray God save the king and send him long to reign over you, for a gentler nor a more merciful prince was there never; and to me he was ever a good, a gentle, and sovereign lord. And if any person will meddle of my cause, I require them to judge the best. And thus I take my leave of the world and of you all, and I heartily desire you all to pray for me. O Lord, have mercy on me! To God I commend my soul!" And then she kneeled down, saying, "To Christ I commend my soul, Jesu receive my soul!" divers times till that her head was stricken off with the sword. And on the Ascension Day following the king ware white for mourning.

The week before Whitsuntide the king married Lady Jane, daughter to the right worshipful Sir John Seymour, knight, which at Whitsuntide was openly shewed as queen. . . .

WILLIAM HARRISON

FROM THE DESCRIPTION OF ENGLAND (1587)

THE SECOND BOOK

CHAPTER XI. Of Sundry Kinds of Punishments Appointed for Malefactors

In cases of felony, manslaughter, robbery, murther, rape, piracy, and such capital crimes as are not reputed for treason or hurt of the estate, our sentence pronounced upon the offender is to hang till he be dead. For of other punishments used in other countries we have no knowledge or use, and yet so few grievous crimes committed with us as elsewhere in the world. To use torment also or question by pain and torture in these common cases with us is greatly abhorred, sith we are found alway to be such as despise death and yet abhor to be tormented, choosing rather frankly to open our minds than to yield our bodies unto such servile halings and tearings as are used in other countries. And this is one cause wherefore our condemned persons do go so cheerfully to their deaths, for our nation is free, stout, hauty, prodigal of life and blood, as Sir Thomas Smith saith *lib*. II, *cap*. 25 *De republica,* and therefore cannot in any wise digest to be used as villans and slaves in suffering continually beating, servitude, and servile torments. No, our jailers are guilty of felony by an old law of the land if they torment any prisoner committed to their custody for the revealing of his complices.

The greatest and most grievous punishment used in England for such as offend against the state is drawing from the prison to the place of execution upon an hardle or sled, where they are hanged till they be half dead and then taken down and quartered alive, after that their members and bowels are cut from their bodies and thrown into a fire provided near hand and within their own sight, even for the same purpose. Sometimes, if the trespass be not the more heinous, they are suffered to hang till they be quite dead. And whensoever any of the nobility are convicted of high treason by their peers, that is to say equals (for an inquest of yeomen passeth not upon them, but only of the lords of the Parlement) this manner of their death is converted into the loss of their heads only, notwithstanding that the sentence do run after the former order. In trial of cases concerning treason, felony, or any other grievous crime not confessed the party accused doth yield, if he be a nobleman, to be tried by an inquest (as I have said) of his peers; if a gentleman, by gentlemen; and an inferior by God and by the country, to wit the yeomanry (for combat or battle is not greatly in use); and, being condemned of felony, manslaughter, etc., he is eftsoons hanged by the neck till he be dead, and then cut down and buried. But if he be convicted of wilful murther done either upon pretended malice or in any notable robbery, he is either hanged alive in chains near the place where the fact was committed, or else, upon compassion taken, first strangled with a rope, and so continueth till his bones consume to nothing. We have use neither of the wheel nor of the bar, as in other countries, but when wilful manslaughter is perpetrated, beside hanging, the offender hath his right hand commonly striken off before or near unto the place where the act was done, after which he is led forth to the place of execution and there put to death according to the law. . . .

If a woman poison her husband she is burned alive; if the servant kill his master he is to be executed for petty treason; he that poisoneth a man is to be boiled to death in water or lead, although the party die not of the practise; in cases of murther all the accessaries are to suffer pains of death accordingly. Perjury is punished by the pillory, burning in the forehead with the letter P, the rewalting of the trees growing upon the grounds of the offenders, and loss of all his movables. Many trespasses also are punished by the cutting off one or both ears from the head of the offender, as the utterance of seditious words against the magistrates, fray-makers, petty robbers, etc. Rogues are burned through the ears, carriers of sheep out of the land by the loss of their hands, such as kill by poison are either boiled or scalded to death in lead or seething water. Heretics are burned quick, harlots and their mates by carting, ducking, and doing of open penance in sheets in churches and marketsteads are often put to rebuke. Howbeit, as this is counted with some either as no punishment at all to speak of, or but smally regarded of the offenders, so I would wish adultery and fornication to have some sharper law. For what great smart is it to be turned out of an hot sheet into a cold, or after a little washing in the water to be let loose again unto their former trades? Howbeit, the dragging of some of them over the Thames between Lambeth and Westminster at the tail of a boat is a punishment that

most terrifieth them which are condemned thereto, but this is inflicted upon them by none other than the knight marshal, and that within the compass of his jurisdiction and limits only. . . .

Witches are hanged or sometimes burned, but thieves are hanged (as I said before) generally on the gibbet or gallows, saving in Halifax, where they are beheaded after a strange manner and whereof I find this report. There is and hath been of ancient time a law, or rather a custom, at Halifax that whosoever doth commit any felony and is taken with the same or confess the fact upon examination, if it be valued by four constables to amount to the sum of thirteen pence, half-penny, he is forthwith beheaded upon one of the next marketdays (which fall usually upon the Tuesdays, Thursdays, and Saturdays) or else upon the same day that he is so convicted, if market be then holden. The engine wherewith the execution is done is a square block of wood of the length of four foot and an half, which doth ride up and down in a slot, rabet, or regal between two pieces of timber that are framed and set upright, of five yards in height. In the neather end of the sliding block is an ax, keyed or fastened with an iron into the wood, which, being drawn up to the top of the frame, is there fast'ned by a wooden pin (with a notch made into the same after the manner of a Samson's post), unto the middest of which pin also there is a long rope fastened that cometh down among the people, so that when the offender hath made his confession and hath laid his neck over the neathermost block, every man there present doth either take hold of the rope or putteth forth his arm so near to the same as he can get, in token that he is willing to see true justice executed; and, pulling out the pin in this manner, the head block wherein the ax is fastened doth fall down with such a violence that if the neck of the transgressor were so big as that of a bull it should be cut in sunder at a stroke and roll from the body by an huge distance. . . .

Rogues and vagabonds are often stocked and whipped; scolds are ducked upon cucking-stools in the water. Such felons as stand mute and speak not at their arraignment are pressed to death by huge weights laid upon a boord that lieth over their breast and a sharp stone under their backs, and these commonly hold their peace, thereby to save their goods unto their wives and children, which if they were condemned should be confiscated to the prince. Thieves that are saved by their books and clergy for the first offense, if they have stolen nothing else but oxen, sheep, money, or such like which be no open robberies (as by the highway side or assailing of any man's house in the night without putting him in fear of his life or breaking up of his walls or doors) are burned in the left hand upon the brawn of the thomb with an hot iron, so that if they be apprehended again that mark bewrayeth them to have been arraigned of felony before, whereby they are sure at that time to have no mercy. I do not read that this custom of saving by the book is used anywhere else than in England, neither do I find (after much diligent inquiry) what Saxon prince ordained that law. Howbeit, this I generally gather thereof, that it was devised to train the inhabiters of this land to the love of learning, which before contemned letters and all good knowledge, as men only giving themselves to husbandry and the wars, the like whereof I read to have been amongst the Goths and Vandals, who for a time would not suffer even their princes to be learned for weakening of their courages. . . . Pirates and robbers by sea are condemned in the court of the admiralty and hanged on the shore at low-water mark, where they are left till three tides have overwashed them. Finally, such as having walls and banks near unto the sea and do suffer the same to decay (after convenient admonition) whereby the water entereth and drowneth up the country are by a certain ancient custom apprehended, condemned, and staked in the breach where they remain forever as parcel of the foundation of the new wall that is to be made upon them, as I have heard reported. . . .

CHAPTER XII. Of the Manner of Building and Furniture of Our Houses

The greatest part of our building in the cities and good towns of England consisteth only of timber, for as yet few of the houses of the communalty (except here and there in the west country towns) are made of stone, although they may (in my opinion) in diverse other places be builded so good cheap of the one as of the other. In old time the houses of the Britons were slightly set up with a few posts and many radels, with stable and all offices under one roof, the like whereof almost is to be seen in the fenny countries and northern parts unto this day, where, for lack of wood, they are inforced to continue this ancient manner of building. It is not in vain, therefore, in speaking of building to make a distinction between the plain and woody soils, for as in these our houses are commonly strong and well-timbered, so that in many places there are not above four, six, or nine inches between stud and stud, so in the open and champain countries they are inforced, for want of stuff, to use no studs at all, but only frankposts, raisins, beams, prickposts, groundsels, summers (or dormants), transoms, and such principals, with here and there a girding whereunto they fasten their splints or radels and then cast it all over with thick clay to keep out the wind, which otherwise would annoy them. Certes this rude kind of

building made the Spaniards in Queen Mary's days [following her marriage with Philip II] to wonder, but chiefly when they saw what large diet was used in many of these so homely cottages, insomuch that one of no small reputation amongst them said after this manner: "These English," quoth he, "have their houses made of sticks and dirt, but they fare commonly so well as the king." Whereby it appeareth that he liked better of our good fare in such coarse cabins than of their own thin diet in their prince-like habitations and palaces. . . .

The walls of our houses on the inner sides . . . be either hanged with tapistery, arras-work, or painted cloths, wherein either diverse histories or herbs, beasts, knots, and such like are stained, or else they are sealed with oak of our own or wainscot brought hither out of the east countries, whereby the rooms are not a little commended, made warm, and much more close than otherwise they would be. As for stoves, we have not hitherto used them greatly, yet do they now begin to be made in diverse houses of the gentry and wealthy citizens who build them not to work and feed in, as in Germany and elsewhere, but now and then to sweat in, as occasion and need shall require it. This also hath been common in England, contrary to the customs of all other nations, and yet to be seen (for example in most streets of London) that many of our greatest houses have outwardly been very simple and plain to sight, which inwardly have been able to receive a duke with his whole train and lodge them at their ease. Hereby, moreover, it is come to pass that the fronts of our streets have not been so uniform and orderly builded as those of forrein cities, where (to say truth) the utterside of their mansions and dwellings have oft more cost bestowed upon them than all the rest of the house, which are often very simple and uneasy within, as experience doth confirm. Of old time our country houses instead of glass did use much lattice, and that made either of wicker or fine rifts of oak in checkerwise. I read also that some of the better sort in and before the times of the Saxons (who notwithstanding used some glass also since the time of Benedic Biscop, the monk that brought the feat of glazing first into this land) did make panels of horn instead of glass and fix them in wooden calms. But as horn in windows is now quite laid down in every place, so our lattices are also grown into less use bicause glass is come to be so plentiful and within a very little so good cheap if not better then the other. . . .

The ancient manors and houses of our gentlemen are yet and for the most part of strong timber, in framing whereof our carpenters have been and are worthily preferred before those of like science among all other nations. Howbeit, such as be lately builded are commonly either of brick or hard stone or both; their rooms large and comely, and houses of office further distant from their lodgings. Those of the nobility are likewise wrought with brick and hard stone, as provision may best be made, but so magnificent and stately as the basest house of a baron doth often match in our days with some honors of princes in old time. So that if ever curious building did florish in England it is in these our years wherein our workmen excel and are in manner comparable in skill with old Vitruvius, Leo Baptista, and Serlo. Nevertheless, their estimation more than their greedy and servile covetousness, joined with a lingering humor, causeth them often to be rejected, and strangers preferred to greater bargains who are more reasonable in their takings and less wasters of time by a great deal than our own.

The furniture of our houses also exceedeth and is grown in manner even to passing delicacy, and herein I do not speak of the nobility and gentry only but likewise of the lowest sort in most places of our south country that have anything at all to take to. Certes, in noblemen's houses it is not rare to see abundance of arras, rich hangings of tapistry, silver vessel, and so much other plate as may furnish sundry cupboards to the sum, oftentimes, of a thousand or two thousand pounds at the least, whereby the value of this and the rest of their stuff doth grow to be almost inestimable. Likewise in the houses of knights, gentlemen, merchantmen, and some other wealthy citizens it is not geason to behold generally their great provision of tapistry, Turkey work, pewter, brass, fine linen, and thereto costly cupboards of plate worth five or six hundred or a thousand pounds to be deemed by estimation. But as herein all these sorts do far exceed their elders and predecessors, and in neatness and curiosity the merchant all other, so in time past the costly furniture stayed there, whereas now it is descended yet lower, even unto the inferior artificers and many farmers, who by virtue of their old and not of their new leases have for the most part learned also to garnish their cupboards with plate, their joined beds with tapistry and silk hangings, and their tables with carpets and fine napery, whereby the wealth of our country (God be praised therefor, and give us grace to imploy it well!) doth infinitely appear. Neither do I speak this in reproach of any man, God is my judge, but to shew that I do rejoice rather to see how God hath blessed us with his good gifts, and whilest I behold how that in a time wherein all things are grown to most excessive prices and what commodity soever is to be had is daily plucked from the communalty by such as look into every trade, we do yet find the means to obtain and atchieve such furniture as heretofore hath been unpossible. There are old men yet dwelling in the village where I remain which have noted three things to be marveilously alt'red in England within their sound remembrance and other three things too, too much increased. One is the multitude of chimneys lately erected, whereas in their young days there were not above two or three, if so many, in most uplandish towns of the realm (the religious houses and manor places of their lords always excepted, and peradventure some great personages), but each one made his fire against a reredos in the hall where he dined and dressed his meat.

The second is the great (although not general) amendment of lodging, for, said they, our fathers (yea and we ourselves also) have lien full oft upon straw pallets, on rough mats covered only with a sheet under coverlets made of dagswain or hopharlots (I use their own terms), and a good round log under their heads instead of a bolster or pillow. If it were so that our fathers or the goodman of the house had within seven years after his marriage purchased a matteres or flockbed, and thereto a sack of chaff to rest his head upon, he thought himself to be as well-lodged as the lord of the town, that peradventure lay seldom in a bed of down or whole feathers. . . .

The third thing they tell of is the exchange of vessel, as of treen platters into pewter and wooden spoons into silver or tin. For so common were all sorts of treen stuff in old time that a man should hardly find four pieces of pewter (of which one was peradventure a salt) in a good farmer's house, and yet, for all this frugality (if it may so be justly called), they were scarce able to live and pay their rents at their days without selling of a cow or an horse or more, although they paid but four pounds at the uttermost by the year. Such also was their poverty that if some one odd farmer or husbandman had been at the alehouse, a thing greatly used in those days, amongst six or seven of his neighbors and there in a bravery, to shew what store he had, did cast down his purse and therein a noble or six shillings in silver unto them (for few such men then cared for gold bicause it was not so ready payment, and they were oft inforced to give a penny for the exchange of an angel), it was very likely that all the rest could not lay down so much against it; whereas in my time, although peradventure four pounds of old rent be improved to forty, fifty, or an hundred pounds, yet will the farmer, as another palm or date tree, think his gains very small toward the end of his term if he have not six or seven years' rent lying by him, therewith to purchase a new lease, beside a fair garnish of pewter on his cupboard, with so much more in odd vessel going about the house, three or four featherbeds, so many coverlids and carpets of tapistry, a silver salt, a bowl for wine (if not an whole nest), and a dozen of spoons to furnish up the suit. . . .

JOHN STOW

FROM A SURVEY OF LONDON (1598)

As Rome, the chief city of the world, to glorify itself drew her original from the gods, goddesses, and demi-gods by the Trojan progeny, so this famous city of London, for greater glory and in emulation of Rome, deriveth itself from the very same original. For, as Jeffery of Monmouth, the Welch historian, reporteth, Brut descended from the demi-god Eneas, the son of Venus, daughter of Jupiter, about the year of the world 2855, the year before Christ's nativity 1108, builded a city near unto a river now called Thames, and named it Troynovant or Trenovant.

King Lud afterward not only repaired this city but also added fair buildings, tow'rs, and walls, and called it after his own name Caire-Lud or Lud's Town, and the strong gate which he builded in the west part of the city he likewise for his own honor named it Ludgate.

This Lud had issue two sons, Androgeus and Themantius, who being not of age to govern at the death of their father, their uncle Cassibilan took upon him the crown; about the eight year of whose reign Julius Caesar arrived in this land with a great power of Romains to conquer it, the manner of which conquest I will summarily set down out of his own *Commentaries*, which are of far better credit then the relations of Jeffery Monmouth. . . .

Of Towers and Castles

The city of London, saith Fitzstephen, hath in the east a very great and a most strong palatine tower whose turrets and walls do rise from a deep foundation, the morter thereof being tempered with the blood of beasts. In the west part are two most strong castles, etc. To begin, therefore, with the most famous Tower of London, situate in the east near unto the River of Thames, it hath been the common opinion, and some have written (but of none assured ground), that Julius Caesar, the first conquerer of the Britains, was the original author and founder as well thereof as also of many other towers, castles, and great buildings within this realm; but, as I have already before noted, Caesar remained not here so long, nor had he in his head any such matter, but only to dispatch a conquest of this barbarous country and to proceed to greater matters. Neither do the Romain writers make mention of any such buildings erected by him here. And therefore leaving this and proceeding to more grounded authority, I find in a fair register book of the acts of the bishops of Rochester, set down by Edmond of Hadenham, that

William the First (surnamed Conqueror) builded the Tower of London, to wit, the great white and square Tower there, about the year of Christ 1078, appointing Gundulph, then Bishop of Rochester, to be principal surveyer and overseer of that work, who was for that time lodged in the house of Edmere, a burgess of London. . . . This was the great square Tower which was then builded and hath been since at divers times inlarged with other buildings adjoining, as shall be shewed hereafter. This Tower was by tempest of wind sore shaken in the year 1090, the fourth of William Rufus, and was again by the said Rufus and Henry the First repaired. They also caused a castle to be builded under the said Tower, to weet, on the south side towards the Thames. . . .

In the year 1478 George, Duke of Clarence, was drowned in the Tower, and within five years after King Edward the Fifth with his brother were murdered in the Tower. In the year 1502 Queen Elizabeth, wife to Henry the Seventh, died of childbirth in the Tower. In the year 1512 the chapel in the high white Tower was burned. In the year 1536 Queen Anne Bullen was beheaded in the Tower. In the year 1541 Lady Katharine Howard, wife to King Henry the Eighth, was also beheaded there.

Thus much for these accidents; and now to conclude thereof in summary: this Tower is a citadel to defend or command the city, a royal palace for assemblies and treaties, a prison of estate for the most dangerous offenders, the only place of coinage for all England at this present, the armory for warlike provision, the treasury of the ornaments and jewels of the crown, and general conserver of the most ancient records of the king's courts of justice at Westminster. . . .

Sports and Pastimes of Old Time Used in This City

Let us now, saith Fitzstephen, come to the sports and pastimes, seeing it is fit that a city should not only be commodious and serious but also merry and sportful. . . . London, for the shews upon theaters and comical pastimes, hath holy plays, representations of miracles which holy confessors have wrought, or representations of torments wherein the constancy of martyrs appeared. Every year also, at Shrove Tuesday (that we may begin with children's sports, seeing we all have been children), the schoolboys do bring cocks of the game to their maister and all the forenoon they delight themselves in cockfighting; after dinner all the youths go into the fields to play at the ball. The schollers of every school have their ball (or bastion) in their hands; the ancient and wealthy men of the city come forth on horseback to see the sport of the young men and to take part of the pleasure in beholding their agility. Every Friday in Lent a fresh company of young men comes into the field on horseback, and the best horsemen conducteth the rest. Then march forth the citizens' sons and other young men with disarmed lances and shields, and there they practise feats of war. Many courtiers likewise, when the king lieth near, and attendants of noblemen do repair to these exercises, and while the hope of victory doth inflame their minds do shew good proof how serviceable they would be in martial affairs. In Easter holidays they fight battails on the water: a shield is hanged upon a pole fixed in the midst of the stream, a boat is prepared without oars to be carried by violence of the water, and in the forepart thereof standeth a young man ready to give charge upon the shield with his lance; if so be he breaketh his lance against the shield and doth not fall, he is thought to have performed a worthy deed. If so be without breaking his lance he runneth strongly against the shield, down he falleth into the water, for the boat is violently forced with the tide; but on each side of the shield ride two boats furnished with young men which recover him that falleth as soon as they may. Upon the bridge, wharfs, and houses by the river's side stand great numbers to see and laugh thereat. In the holy days all sommer the youths are exercised in leaping, dancing, shooting, wrastling, casting the stone, and practising their shields. The maidens trip it with their timbrels and dance as long as they can well see. In winter, every holy day before dinner the boars prepared for brawn are set to fight, or else bulls and bears are baited.

When the great fen or moor [later called Moorfields] (which watereth the walls of the city on the north side) is frozen, many young men play upon the ice; some, striding as wide as they may, do slide swiftly; others make themselves seats of ice as great as millstones; one sits down, many hand-in-hand do draw him, and one slipping on a sudden, all fall together; some tie bones to their feet and under their heels, and, shoving themselves by a little picked staff, do slide as swiftly as a bird flyeth in the air or an arrow out of a crossbow. Sometime two run together with poles and, hitting one the other, either one or both do fall, not without hurt; some break their arms, some their legs, but youth, desirous of glory, in this sort exerciseth itself against the time of war. Many of the citizens do delight themselves in hawks and hounds, for they have liberty of hunting in Middlesex, Hartfordshire, all Chiltron, and in Kent to the Water of Cray [that is, in the so-called "home counties" around London, including the Chiltern Hills (in Oxfordshire, Bucks, Hertfordshire, and Bedfordshire) and Kent as far south as Crayford, a town southeast of Greenwich]. Thus far Fitzstephen of sports.

These or the like exercises have been continued till our time, namely in stage plays, whereof ye may read in *anno* 1391 a play to be play'd by the parish clerks of London at the Skinners' well besides Smithfield; which play continued three days together, the king, queen, and nobles of the realm being present. And of another play'd in the year 1409 which lasted eight days and was of matter from the creation of the world, whereat was present most part of the nobility and gentry of England, etc. Of late time, in place of those stage plays hath been used comedies, tragedies, enterludes, and histories, both true and feigned. For the acting whereof certain public places, as the Theater, the Curtain, etc., have been erected. [Thus Stow traces the history of pre-Shakespearean English drama in a couple of sentences. The early "stage plays" he mentions were miracle plays, that is, medieval dramatic representations based on sacred history or on legends of the saints. Imported from France, the miracles reached their highest development in the early fourteenth century. Presented by the corporation of the towns, with responsibility for the various parts (e.g. the Creation, the Flood, the Resurrection, the Harrowing of Hell, etc.) assumed by the various guilds, the performances were both a municipal and a religious celebration. Four "cycles" of such miracles are extant.] Also cocks of the game are yet cherished by divers men for their pleasures, much money being laid on their heads when they fight in pits, whereon some be costly made for that purpose. The ball is used by noblemen and gentlemen in tennis courts, and by people of meaner sort in the open fields and streets. The youths of this city, time out of mind, have left off to practise the disarmed lance and shield on horseback in the fields, but I have seen some few upon the river of Thames rowed in boats, with staves flat at the fore-end, running one against another, and for the most part either one or both overthrown and well ducked. . . .

SIR THOMAS MORE

THE HISTORY OF KING RICHARD THE THIRD

Whether More actually composed the fragmentary life of Richard III or merely translated from the Latin of his old patron John Cardinal Morton, it is one of the few unquestioned triumphs of Tudor historiography. Completed (according to More's nephew William Rastell) in 1513, it was first printed, in a sadly mutilated version, in Grafton's continuation of Hardyng's *Chronicle* (1543); Hall drew on it heavily for his *Union . . . of Lancaster and York* (1548); and finally, in the 1557 edition of More's English *Works,* Rastell reprinted it from an allegedly authentic manuscript. Nine years later a Latin version was included in the collected edition of More's Latin works. It has been suggested on the evidence of the eyewitness vivacity, the strong Lancastrian bias, and the inferior quality of the Latin style that Morton must be the author of the original version; but between the Latin and the English there are significant differences, and few have questioned More's hand in the version here represented. Very probably More drew upon Morton's intimate knowledge of the later fifteenth century for some of his details; but, whatever the facts of its composition, the *History* draws with sharp, swift strokes an unforgettable portrait of the favorite villain of Tudor historiographers. The obvious fascination with and contempt for the hunchback king, the vigor of the writing, and the dramatic intensity of Richard's rise and fall make it an extraordinary performance, and we need not wonder that Shakespeare read it with delight and admiration. Our text is based upon *The History of king Richard the thirde (unfinished) writen by Master Thomas More* in *The workes of Sir Thomas More Knyght,* 1557 (STC 18076).

FROM THE HISTORY OF KING RICHARD THE THIRD (1557)

King Edward, of that name the fourth, after that he had lived fifty and three years, seven moneths, and six days, and thereof reigned two and twenty years, one moneth, and eight days, died at Westminster the ninth day of April, the year of our redemption a thousand, four hundred, four score, and three, leaving much fair issue, that is to wit: Edward the Prince, a thirteen year of age; Richard, Duke of York, two year younger; Elizabeth, whose fortune and grace was after to be queen, wife unto King Henry the Seventh and mother unto the Eighth; Cecily, not so fortunate as fair; Briget, which, representing the virtue of her whose name she bare, professed and observed a religious life in Dertford, an house of close nuns; Anne, that was after honorably married unto Thomas, than Lord Haward and after Earl of Surrey; and Katherine, which long time tossed in either fortune, sometime in wealth, oft in adversity, at the last, if this be the last (for yet she liveth), is by the benignity of her nephew, King Henry the Eight, in very prosperous estate and worthy her birth and virtue.

This noble prince deceased at his palice of Westminster, and, with great funeral honor and heaviness of his people from thence convey'd, was enterred at Windsor. A king of such governance and behavior in time of peace (for in war each part must needs be other's enemy) that there was never any prince of this land attaining the crown by battail so heartely beloved with the substance of the people; nor he himself so specially in any part of his life as at the time of his death. Which favor and affection yet after his decease, by the cruelty, mischief, and trouble of the tempestious world that followed, highly toward him more increased. . . . In which time of his latter days this realm was in quiet and prosperous estate: no fear of outward enemies, no war in hand, nor none toward but such as no man looked for; the people toward the prince not in a constrained fear but in a willing and loving obedience; among themself, the commons in good peace. The lords whom he knew at variance, himself in his death-bed appeased. . . . So deceased (as I have said) this noble king, in that time in which his life was most desired, whose love of his people and their entire affection toward him had been to his noble children (having in themself also as many gifts of nature, as many princely virtues, as much goodly towardness, as their age could receive) a mervailous forteress and sure armor, if division and dissension of their friends had not unarmed them and left them destitute, and the execrable desire of sovereignty provoked him to their destruction which, if either kind or kindness had holden place, must needs have been their chief defense. For Richard, the Duke of Gloucester, by nature their uncle, by office their protector, to their father beholden, to themself by oath and allegiance bounden, all the bands broken that binden man and man together, without any respect of God or the world, unnaturally contrived to bereave them not only their dignity but also their lives. But forasmuch as this duke's demeanor minist'reth in effect all the whole matter whereof this book shall entreat, it is therefore convenient somewhat to shew you ere we farther go what manner of man this was that could find in his heart so much mischief to conceive.

Richard, Duke of York, a noble man and a mighty, began not by war but by law to challenge the crown, putting his claim into the Parliament, where his cause was either for right or favor so far-forth avanced that, King Henry [VI] his blood (albeit he had a goodly prince) utterly rejected, the crown was by authority of Parliament entailed unto the Duke of York and his issue male in remainder, immediately after the death of King Henry. But the duke, not enduring so long to tarry, but entending under pretext of dissension and debate arising in the realm to prevent his time and to take upon him the rule in King Harry his life, was with many nobles of the realm at Wakefield slain, leaving three sons, Edward, George, and Richard. All three, as they were great states of birth, so were they great and stately of stomach, greedy and ambitious of authority, and impatient of parteners. Edward, revenging his father's death, deprived King Henry and attained the crown. George, Duke of Clarence, was a goodly, noble prince, and at all points fortunate, if either his own ambition had not set him against his brother or the envy of his enemies his brother against him. For were it by the queen and the lords of her blood, which highly maligned the king's kinred (as women commonly, not of malice but of nature, hate them whom their housebands love), or were it a proud appetite of the duke himself, entending to be king; at the leastwise, heinous treason was there laid to his charge and finally—were he fauty, were he faultless—attainted was he by Parliament and judged to the death, and thereupon hastely drowned in a butt of malmesey; whose death King Edward (albeit he commanded it) when he wist it was done pitiously bewailed and sorrowfully repented.

Richard, the third son, of whom we now entreat, was in wit and courage egal with either of them, in body and prowess far under them both: little of stature, ill-featured of limbs, crook-backed, his left shoulder much higher then his right, hard-favored of visage, and such as is in states called warly, in other men otherwise; he was malicious, wrathful, envious, and, from aforc his birth, ever froward. It is for trouth reported that the duchess, his mother, had so much ado in her travail that she could not be delivered of him uncut, and that he came into the world with the feet forward, as men be borne outward, and (as the fame runneth) also not untoothed—whither men of hatred report above the trouth, or

else that nature changed her course in his beginning which in the course of his life many things unnaturally committed. None evil captain was he in the war, as to which his disposition was more metely then for peace. Sundry victories had he, and sometimes overthrows, but never in default as for his own parson, either of hardiness or politic order. Free was he called of dispense and somewhat above his power liberal; with large gifts he get him unsteadfast friendship, for which he was fain to pill and spoil in other places and get him steadfast hatred. He was close and secret, a deep dissimuler, lowly of countenance, arrogant of heart, outwardly coumpinable where he inwardly hated, not letting to kiss whom he thought to kill; dispitious and cruel, not for evil will alway, but ofter for ambition, and either for the surety or encrease of his estate. Friend and foe was muchwhat indifferent; where his advantage grew he spared no man's death whose life withstood his purpose. He slew with his own hands King Henry the Sixt, being prisoner in the Tower, as men constantly say, and that without commandement or knowledge of the king, which would undoubtedly, if he had entended that thing, have appointed that butcherly office to some other then his own born brother. . . .

[Following the death of Edward IV, events moved very quickly. While the council and the queen-mother were jockeying for position, Richard, as brother of the late Edward IV and therefore uncle to the boy-king, Edward V, was appointed protector. But his position was not secure, for the new king was making his progress from Ludlow to London under the auspices of Earl Rivers (his maternal uncle) and of his half-brother, Sir Richard Grey, both of whom Richard had reason to distrust. With the aid of the Duke of Buckingham he took the initiative, joined the royal cavalcade, and sent Rivers and Grey under close guard to Pontefract. Sensing her danger, Elizabeth, the queen-mother, took sanctuary at Westminster. Then, even though the council confirmed his title as protector and though Edward V was safe in the Tower, Richard resolved to move against the queen's party and against Lord Hastings, its leading representative and lord chamberlain in the council.]

Whereupon soon after, that is to wit, on the Friday, the [thirteenth] day of [June], many lords assembled in the Tower, and there sat in counsail, devising the honorable solempnity of the king's coronation, of which the time appointed then so near approached that the pageants and suttelties were in making, day and night, at Westminster, and much victual killed therefor that afterward was cast away. These lords so sitting togither commoning of this matter, the protector came in among them, first about nine of the clock, saluting them curtesly, and excusing himself that he had been from them so long, saying merely that he had been asleep that day. And after a little talking with them he said unto the Bishop of Ely: "My lord, you have very good strawberries at your garden in Holborn; I require you let us have a mess of them." "Gladly, my lord," quoth he; "would God I had some better thing as ready to your pleasure as that." And therewith, in all the haste, he sent his servant for a mess of strawberries. The protector set the lords fast in commoning, and thereupon, praying them to spare him for a little while, departed thence.

And soon, after one hour, between ten and eleven, he returned into the chamber among them, all changed, with a wonderful sour, angry countenance, knitting the brows, frowning and frotting and knawing on his lips, and so sat him down in his place, all the lords much dismayed and sore merveiling of this manner of sodain change, and what thing should him ail. Then, when he had sitten still awhile, thus he began: "What were they worthy to have that compass and imagine the distruction of me, being so near of blood unto the king and protector of his rial person and his realm?" At this question all the lords sat sore astonied, musing much by whom this question should be meant, of which every man wist himself clear. Then the lord chamberlain, as he that for the love between them thought he might be boldest with him, answered and said that they were worthy to be punished as heighnous traitors, whatsoever they were. And all the other affirmed the same. "That is," quoth he, "yonder sorceress, my brother's wife, and other with her"—meaning the queen. At these words many of the other lords were greatly abashed that favored her. But the Lord Hastings was in his mind better content that it was moved by her then by any other whom he loved better; albeit his heart somewhat grudged that he was not afore made of counsel in this matter, as he was of the taking of her kinred [Rivers and Grey] and of their putting to death, which were by his assent before devised to be beheaded at Pontefract this self-same day, in which he was not ware that it was by other devised that himself should the same day be beheaded at London. Then said the protector: "Ye shall all see in what wise that sorceress and that other witch of her counsel, Shore's wife, with their affinity have by their sorcery and witchcraft wasted my body." And therewith he plucked up his doublet sleeve to his elbow upon his left arm, where he shewed a wearish, withered arm and small, as it was never other. And thereupon every man's mind sore misgave them, well perceiving that this matter was

but a quarrel. For well they wist that the queen was too wise to go about any such folly. And also if she would, yet would she of all folk least make Shore's wife of counsail, whom of all women she most hated, as that concubine whom the king, her husband, had most loved. And also no man was there present but well knew that his harm was ever such since his birth. Natheless, the lord chamberlain (which from the death of King Edward kept Shore's wife, on whom he somewhat doted in the king's life, saving, as it is said, he that while forbare her of reverence toward his king, or else of a certain kind of fidelity to his friend) answered and said: "Certainly, my lord, if they have so heinously done, they be worthy heinous punishment."

"What!" quod the protector. "Thou servest me, I ween, with 'ifs' and with 'ands'! I tell thee they have so done, and that I will make good on thy body, traitor!" And therewith, as in a great anger, he clapped his fist upon the bord a great rap. At which token given, one cried "treason" without the chamber. Therewith a door clapped, and in come there rushing men in harness, as many as the chamber might hold. And anon the protector said to the Lord Hastings: "I arrest thee, traitor!" "What, me, my lord?" quod he. "Yea, thee, traitor," quoth the protector. And another let fly at the Lord Standley, which shronk at the stroke and fell under the table, or else his head had been cleft to the teeth; for as shortly as he shrank, yet ran the blood about his ears. Then were they all quickly bestowed in diverse chambers, except the lord chamberlain, whom the protector bade speed and shrive him apace. "For by St. Paul," quoth he, "I will not to dinner till I see thy head off." It booted him not to ask why, but heavily he took a priest at adventure and made a short shrift, for a longer would not be suffered, the protector made so much haste to dinner; which he might not go to till this were done for saving of his oath. So was he brought forth into the green beside the chapel within the Tower, and his head laid down upon a long log of timber and there striken off, and afterward his body, with the head, ent'rred at Windsor, beside the body of King Edward, whose both souls our Lord pardon. . . .

Now flew the fame of this lord's death swiftly through the city, and so forth farder about like a wind in every man's ear. But the protector immediately after dinner, entending to set some color upon the matter, sent in all haste for many sembstantial men out of the city into the Tower; and at their coming, himself, with the Duke of Buckingham, stood harnessed in old, ill-faring briginders such as no man should ween that they would vouchsafe to have put upon their backs except that some sodain necessity had constrained them. And then the protector shewed them that the lord chamberlain and other of his conspiracy had contrived to have sodeinly destroy'd him and the duke there the same day in the counsel. And what they intended further was as yet not well known. Of which their treason he never had knowledge before ten of the clock the same forenoon. Which sodain fear drave them to put on for their defense such harness as came next to hand. And so had God holpen them that the mischief turned upon them that would have done it. And this he required them to report. Every man answered him fair, as though no man mistrusted the matter which, of trouth, no man believed. Yet for the further appeasing of the people's mind, he sent immediately after dinner in all the haste one herod of arms, with a proclamation to be made through the city in the king's name, containing that the Lord Hastings, with divers other of his traitorous purpose, had before conspired the same day to have slain the lord protector and the Duke of Buckingham, sitting in the counsel, and after to have taken upon them to rule the king and the realm at their pleasure, and thereby to pill and spoil whom they list, uncontrolled. . . .

Now was this proclamation made within two hours after that he was beheaded, and it was so curiously indited and so fair written in parchment, in so well a set hand, and therewith of itself so long a process, that every child might well perceive that it was prepared before. For all the time between his death and the proclaiming could scant have sufficed unto the bare writing alone, all had it been but in paper and scribbled forth in haste at adventure. So that upon the proclaiming thereof one that was schoolmaster of Paul's, of chance standing by and comparing the shortness of the time with the length of the matter, said unto them that stood about him: "Here is a gay, goodly cast, foul cast away for haste." And a merchant answered him that it was written by prophecy. Now then, by and by, as it were for anger, not for covetise, the protector sent into the house of Shore's wife (for her husband dwelled not with her) and spoiled her of all that ever she had, above the value of two or three thousand marks, and sent her body to prison. And when he had awhile laid unto her, for the manner sake, that she went about to bewitch him and that she was of counsel with the lord chamberlain to destroy him—in conclusion, when that no color could fasten upon these matters—then he laid heinously to her charge the thing that herself could not deny, that all the world wist was true, and that natheless every man laughed at to hear it then so sodainly so highly taken: that she was nought of her body. And for this cause

(as a goodly continent prince, clean and fautless of himself, sent out of heaven into this vicious world for the amendment of men's manners) he caused the Bishop of London to put her to open penance, going before the cross in procession upon a Sonday, with a taper in her hand. In which she went in countenance and pace demure so womanly, and albeit she were out of all array save her kirtle only, yet went she so fair and lovely, namely while the wondering of the people cast a comely rud in her cheeks (of which she before had most miss), that her great shame wan her much praise among those that were more amorous of her body then curious of her soul. And many good folk, also, that hated her living and glad were to see sin corrected, yet pitied they more her penance then rejoiced therein, when they consid'red that the protector procured it more of a corrupt intent then any virtuous affection.

This woman was born in London, worshipfully friended, honestly brought up, and very well married, saving somewhat too soon, her husband an honest citizen, young and goodly and of good substance. But forasmuch as they were coupled ere she were well ripe, she not very fervently loved for whom she never longed. Which was happely the thing that the more easily made her encline unto the king's appetite when he required her. Howbeit, the respect of his royalty, the hope of gay apparel, ease, pleasure, and other wanton wealth was hable soon to pierce a soft, tender heart. But when the king had abused her, anon her husband (as he was an honest man and one that could his good, not presuming to touch a king's concubine) left her up to him altogither. When the king died, the lord chamberlain took her. Which in the king's days, albeit he was sore enamored upon her, yet he forbare her, either for reverence or for a certain friendly faithfulness. Proper she was and fair, nothing in her body that you would have changed, but if you would have wished her somewhat higher. Thus say they that knew her in her youth. Albeit some that now see her (for yet she liveth) deem her never to have been well visaged. Whose judgment seemeth me somewhat like as though men should guess the beauty of one long before departed by her scalp taken out of the charnel house; for now is she old, lean, withered, and dried up, nothing left but rivel'd skin and hard bone. And yet, being even such, whoso well advise her visage might guess and devise which parts how filled would make it a fair face. Yet delighted not men so much in her beauty as in her pleasant behavior. For a proper wit had she, and could both read well and write, merry in company, ready and quick of answer, neither mute nor full of babble, sometime taunting without displeasure and not without disport. . . .

[Following the downfall of Hastings and Jane Shore, the protector moved more brazenly toward the throne. He arranged to have one Ralph Shaw, in a sermon at Paul's Cross, question the validity of Edward IV's marriage with Elizabeth Woodville and so impugn the legitimacy of their children, and even declare that of the three sons of the Duke of York—Edward IV, Clarence, and Gloucester—only Gloucester was born in wedlock, and only Gloucester could advance a proper claim to the throne. "While these words were in speaking, the protector, accompanied with the Duke of Buckingham, went thorow the people into the place where the doctors commonly stand, in the upper story, where he stood to harken the sermon. But the people were so far from crying 'King Richard!' that they stood as they had been turned into stones, for wonder of this shameful sermon. After which once ended, the preacher gate him home and never after durst look out for shame but keep him out of sight like an owl. And when he once asked one that had been his old friend what the people talked of him, all were it that his own conscience well shewed him that they talked no good, yet when the tother answered him that there was in every man's mouth spoken of him much shame, it so strake him to the heart that within few days after he withered and consumed away." But with the aid of Buckingham the protector succeeded in his audacious slander: on June 25 a servile Parliament confirmed Gloucester's title to the throne, and on July 6 he was crowned Richard III.]

Now fell there mischieves thick. And as the thing evil gotten is never well kept, through all the time of his reign never ceased there cruel death and slaughter till his own destruction ended it. But as he finished his time with the best death and the most righteous, that is to wit his own, so began he with the most piteous and wicked; I mean the lamentable murther of his innocent nephews, the young king and his tender brother [Edward V and the Duke of York]. Whose death and final infortune hath natheless so far comen in question that some remain yet in doubt whither they were in his days destroy'd or no. Not for that only that Perkin Warbeck, by many folk's malice and mo folk's folly, so long space abusing the world, was as well with princes as the poorer people reputed and taken for the younger of those two, but for that also all things were in late days so covertly demeaned, one thing pretended and another meant, that there was nothing so plain and openly proved but that yet, for the common custom of close and covert dealing, men had it ever inwardly suspect, as many well counterfaited jewels make the true mistrusted. . . . But . . . for this present matter I shall rehearse you the dolorous end of those babes, not after every way that I have heard, but after that way that I have so hard by such men and by such means as methinketh it were hard but it should be true.

King Richard, after his coronation, taking his way to Gloucester, to visit in his new honor the town of which he bare the name of his old, devised as he rode to fulfil that thing which he before had intended. And forasmuch as his mind gave him that, his nephews living, men would not reckon that he could have right to the realm, he thought therefore without delay to rid them, as though the killing of his kinsmen could amend his cause and make him a kindly king. Whereupon he sent one John Green, whom he specially trusted, unto Sir Robert Brackenbury, constable of the Tower, with a letter and credence also that the same Sir Robert should in any wise put the two children to death. This John Green did his errand unto Brackenbury, kneeling before our Lady in the Tower, who plainly answered that he would never put them to death, to die therefor; with which answer John Green, returning, recounted the same to King Richard at Warwick, yet in his way. Wherewith he took such displeasure and thought that the same night he said unto a secret page of his: "Ah, whom shall a man trust? Those that I have brought up myself, those that I had went would most surely serve me, even those fail me and at my commandement will do nothing for me."

"Sir," quod his page, "there lieth one on your paylet without that, I dare well say, to do your Grace pleasure, the thing were right hard that he would refuse," meaning this by Sir James Tyrell, which was a man of right goodly parsonage and for nature's gifts worthy to have served a much better prince, if he had well served God and by grace obtained as much trouth and good will as he had strength and wit. . . . [Tyrell readily agreed to the king's will and posted off for the Tower, where the two little princes lay with only one servant, Black Will or William Slaughter. Tyrell chose for his henchmen Miles Forest ("a fellow fleshed in murther beforetime") and John Dighton ("his own horse-keeper, a big, broad, square, strong knave").] Then, all the other being removed from them, this Miles Forest and John Dighton about midnight (the sely children lying in their beds) came into the chamber and sodainly lapped them up among the clothes, so bewrapped them and entangled them, keeping down by force the feather bed and pillows hard unto their mouths, that within a while, smored and stifled, their breath failing, they gave up to God their innocent souls into the joys of heaven, leaving to the tormentors their bodies dead in the bed. Which after that the wretches parceived, first by the struggling with the pains of death, and after long lying still, to be throughly dead, they laid their bodies naked out upon the bed, and fetched Sir James to see them. Which, upon the sight of them, caused those murtherers to bury them at the stair foot, metely deep in the ground, under a great heap of stones. Than rode Sir James in great haste to King Richard, and shewed him all the manner of the murther, who gave him great thanks and, as some say, there made him knight. But he allowed not, as I have heard, that burying in so vile a corner, saying that he would have them buried in a better place because they were a king's sons. . . . Which things on every part well pondered, God never gave this world a more notable example, neither in what unsurety standeth this worldly well, or what mischief worketh the proud enterprise of an high heart, or finally what wretched end ensu th such dispiteous cruelty. For first to begin with the ministers: Miles Forest at St. Martin's piecemeal rotted away; Dighton, indeed, yet walketh on alive, in good possibility to be hanged ere he die. But Sir James Tyrell died at Tower Hill, beheaded for treason. King Richard himself, as ye shall hereafter hear, slain in the field, hacked and hewed of his enemies' hands, harried on horseback dead, his hair

in despite torn and togged like a cur dog; and the mischief that he took within less then three years of the mischief that he did, and yet all the meantime spent in much pain and trouble outward, much fear, anguish, and sorrow within. For I have heard by credible report, of such as were secret with his chamberers, that after this abhominable deed done, he never had quiet in his mind, he never thought himself sure. Where he went abroad, his eyen whirled about, his body privily fenced, his hand ever on his dagger, his countenance and manner like one alway ready to strike again; he took ill rest a nights, lay long waking and musing, sore wearied with care and watch, rather slumb'red then slept, troubled with fearful dreams, sodainly sometime stert up, lep out of his bed, and run about the chamber, so was his restless heart continually tossed and tumbled with the tedious impression and stormy remembrance of his abominable deed. . . . [More's work breaks off with the defection of Buckingham to Richmond's party; thus he does not describe the civil disorders of 1484–85, Richmond's landing at Milford Haven, and the establishment of the Tudor line with the tyrant's death on Bosworth Field.]

WILLIAM ROPER

THE LIFE OF SIR THOMAS MORE

William Roper, a well-born and distinguished lawyer and public servant whose career spanned the reigns of four Tudor monarchs, holds a small but tidy place in English literature with only one work, a life of his famous father-in-law. Having entered More's household probably in 1518 at the age of twenty, he married Margaret More in 1521, the year in which he was admitted to the Society of Lincoln's Inn. Although his relations with More were not always tranquil—his brief flirtation with Lutheranism was a sore trial to them both—he and his wife the firm supports of More's last bitter years. When, a couple of decades after that great man's death on the scaffold, Roper recorded his memories of those "sixteen years and more" when he had been "in house conversant with him," he not only performed an act of filial devotion but also made a valuable analysis of the swirling legal and political currents that had swept More to his traitor's (or martyr's) death. As a result, his biography affords both a charming vignette of an unforgettable personality and a framework that gives the sketch uncommon depth and interest. Except for those with special interests, Roper's life of More is consequently far more

valuable than the later hagiographies of Harpsfield and other Elizabethan Catholics who lost sight of the man in adoring the martyr.

Roper's work survives in more than a dozen manuscript versions: six in the British Museum and others in the Cambridge University Library, in the Dyce and Forster Collection in the Library of the Victoria and Albert Museum, in the Bodleian Library, and elsewhere. Popular though it was, Elizabeth's mounting savagery against Roman Catholics delayed its publication until the early seventeenth century. In 1626 it was first printed by one T. P. (perhaps Thomas Plowden), but almost another century passed before the great antiquary Thomas Hearne published his edition in 1716. The Rev. John Lewis printed three further editions in 1729, 1731, and 1765; and in 1817 Samuel Weller Singer, who had performed a like office for Cavendish's life of Wolsey (see p. 53), published his version based on the recensions of T. P., Hearne, and Lewis. Our text is based upon the admirable edition of Elsie Vaughan Hitchcock (EETS, no. 197, 1935 [for 1934]), who established her version on a collation of thirteen manuscripts.

FROM THE LIFE OF SIR THOMAS MORE, KNIGHT (?1557)

Forasmuch as Sir Thomas More, knight, sometime lord chancellor of England, a man of singular virtue and of a clear, unspotted conscience, as witnesseth Erasmus, more pure and white then the whitest snow, and of such an angelical wit as England, he saith, never had the like before nor never shall again, univarsally as well in the laws of our own realm (a study, in effect, able to occupy the whole life of a man) as in all other sciences right well studied, was in his days accompted a man worthy perpetual famous memory; I, William Roper, though most unworthy, his son-in-law by marriage of his eldest daughter [Margaret], knowing at this day no one man living that of him and of his doings understood so much as myself, for that I was continually resident in his house by the space of sixteen years and more, thought it therefore my part to set forth such matters touching his life as I could at this present call to remembrance. Among which things, very many notable things (not meet to have been forgotten) through negligence and long continuance of time are slipped out of my mind. Yet to th' entent the same should not all utterly perish I have, at the desire of divers worshipful friends of mine (though very far from the grace and worthiness of them, neverthe-less as farforth as my mean wit, memory, and knowl-edge would serve me), declared so much thereof as in my poor judgment seemed worthy to be rememb'red.

This Sir Thomas More, after he had been brought up in the Latin tongue at St. Anthony's in London, was, by his father's procurement, [in 1490] received into the house of the right reverend, wise, and learned prelate, Cardinal Morton; where, though he was young of years, yet would he at Christmastide sod-denly sometimes step in among the players and, never studying for the matter, make a part of his own there presently among them, which made the lookers-on more sport then all the players beside. In whose wit and towardness the cardinal much delighting, would often say of him unto the nobles that divers times dined with him, "This child here waiting at the table, whosoever shall live to see it, will prove a mervailous man."

Whereupon [in 1492], for his better furtherance in learning, he placed him at Oxford, where, when he was both in the Greek and Latin tongue sufficiently instructed, he was then for the study of the law of the realm put to an inn of chancery called New Inn, where for his time he very well prospered; and from thence was admitted to Lincoln's Inn with very small allowance, continuing there his study until he was made and accompted a worthy utter barrister.

After this, to his great commendation, he read for a good space a public lecture of St. Augustine, De civitate Dei, in the church of St. Lawrence in the Old Jewry, whereunto there resorted Doctor Grocyn, an excellent cunning man, and all the chief learned of the city of London.

Then was he made reader of Furnival's Inn, so remaining by the space of three years and more.

After which time he gave himself to devotion and prayer in the Charterhouse of London, religiously living there, without vow, about four years [1499-1503], until he resorted to the house of one Master Colt, a gentleman of Essex that had oft invited him thither, having three daughters whose honest conver-sation and virtuous education provoked him there specially to set his affection. And albeit his mind most served him to the second daughter for that he thought her the fairest and best-favored, yet when he considered that it would be both great grief and some shame also to the eldest [i.e. Jane Colt] to see her younger sister in marriage preferred before her, he then, of a certain pity, framed his fancy towards her and soon after [in 1505] married her. Never the more discontinuing his study of the law at Lincoln's Inn, but applying still the same until he was called to the bench and had read there twice, which is as often as ordinarily any judge of the law doth read.

Before which time he had placed himself and his wife at Bucklersbury in London, where he had by her three daughters and one son, in virtue and learn-ing brought up from their youth, whom he would often exhort to take virtue and learning for their meat and play for their sauce.

Who, ere ever he had been reader in court, was in the latter time of King Henry the Seventh made a burgess of the Parliament, wherein there were by the king demanded, as I have heard reported, about three fifteens for the marriage of his eldest daughter [Margaret Tudor] that then should be the Scottish queen. At the last debating whereof he made such arguments and reasons thereagainst that the king's demands thereby were clean overthrown. So that one of the king's privy chamber, named Master Tyler, being present thereat, brought word to the king out of the Parliament House that a beardless boy had disappointed all his purpose. Whereupon the king, conceiving great indignation towards him, could not be satisfied until he had some way revenged it. And forasmuch as he, nothing having, nothing could loose, his Grace devised a causeless quarrel against his father, keeping him in the Tower until he had made him pay to him an hundreth pounds' fine. . . .

[Following the death of Henry VII, however, young More advanced rapidly, both as a lawyer and as a politician. In 1510 he was made an under-sheriff of London; in 1515 and 1517 he was on the Continent in the service of some English merchants; in 1517 he was made master of requests and, shortly afterwards, a knight. Inevitably he came to the attention of Henry VIII.]

And so from time to time was he by the prince advanced, continuing in his singular favor and trusty service twenty years and above, a good part whereof used the king upon holy days, when he had done his own devotions, to send for him into his travers and there sometime in matters of astronomy, geometry, devinity, and such other faculties, and sometimes of his worldly affairs, to sit and confer with him. And otherwhiles would he, in the night, have him up into his leads, there for to consider with him the diversities, courses, motions, and operations of the stars and planets. And because he was of a pleasant disposition it pleased the king and queen, after the counsel had supp'd, at the time of their supper, for their pleasure, commonly to call for him to be merry with them. Whom when he perceived so much in his talk to delight that he could not once in a moneth get leave to go home to his wife and children (whose company he most desired) and to be absent from the court two days together but that he should be thither sent for again, he, much misliking this restraint of his liberty, began thereupon somewhat to dissemble his nature, and so, by little and little, from his former accustomed mirth to disuse himself, that he was of them from thenceforth at such seasons no more so ordinarily sent for. . . .

[In Parliament, More's star continued to rise. He became under-secretary of the exchequer in 1521 and speaker of the House in 1523. In spite of angering Cardinal Wolsey by his independence, More remained high in the king's favor.]

And for the pleasure he took in his company would his Grace sodenly sometimes come home to his house at Chelsea to be merry with him. Whither, on a time, unlooked for, he came to dinner to him and after dinner, in a fair garden of his, walked with him by the space of an hour, holding his arm about his neck. As soon as his Grace was gone, I, rejoicing thereat, told Sir Thomas More how happy he was, whom the king had so familiarly entertained as I never had seen him to do to any other except Cardinal Wolsey, whom I saw his Grace once walk with, arm in arm. "I thank our Lord, son," quoth he, "I find his Grace my very good lord indeed, and I believe he doth as singularly favor me as any subject within this realm. Howbeit, Son Roper, I may tell thee I have no cause to be proud thereof, for if my head could win him a castle in France"—for than was there war between us—"it should not fail to go."

This Sir Thomas More, among all other his virtues, was of such meekness that if it had fortuned him with any learned men resorting to him from Oxford, Cambridge, or elsewhere, as there did divers, some for desire of his acquaintance, some for the famous report of his wisdom and learning, and some for suits of the universities, to have entered into argument, wherein few were comparable unto him, and so far to have discoursed with them therein that he might perceive they could not, without some inconvenience, hold out much further disputation against him; then, lest he should discomfort them, as he that sought not his own glory but rather would seem conquered then to discourage students in their studies, ever shewing himself more desirous to learn then to teach, would he by some witty devise courteously break off into some other matter and geve over. . . .

So on a time, walking with me along the Thames' side at Chelsea, in talking of other things he said unto me: "Now would to our Lord, Son Roper, upon condition that three things were well-established in Christendom, I were put in a sack and here presently cast into the Thames."

"What great things be those, sir," quoth I, "that should move you so to wish?"

"Wouldest thou know what they be, Son Roper?" quoth he.

"Yea, marry, with good will, sir, if it please you," quoth I.

"In faith, son, they be these," said he. "The first is that where the most part of Christen princes be at mortal war, they were all at an universal peace. The second, that where the Church of Christ is at this present sore afflicted with many errors and heresies, it were settled in a perfect uniformity of religion. The third, that where the king's matter of his marriage is now come in question, it were to the glory of God and quietness of all parts brought to a good conclusion." Whereby, as I could gather, he judged that otherwise it would be a disturbance to a great part of Christendom.

Thus did it by his doings throughout the whole course of his life appear that all his travail and pains, without respect of earthly commodities either to himself or any of his, were only upon the service of God, the prince, and the realm wholly bestowed and imployed, whom I heard in his later time to say that he never asked the king for himself the valew of one penny. . . .

[From the beginning More realized that the king's desire for a divorce might lead to serious trouble, and so far as was possible he sought not to be implicated in the increasing agitation.]

It fortuned, before the matter of the said matrimony brought in question, when I, in talk with Sir Thomas More, of a certain joy commended unto him the happy estate of this realm, that had so Chatholike a prince that no heretic durst shew his face, so virtuous and learned a clergy, so grave and sound a nobility, and so loving, obedient subjects all in one faith agreeing together, "Troth it is, indeed, Son Roper," quoth he, and in commending all degrees and estates of the same went far beyond me. "And yet, Son Roper, I pray God," said he, "that some of us, as high as we seem to sit upon the mountains, treading heretics under our feet like ants, live not the day that we gladly would wish to be at a league and composition with them to let them have their churches quietly to themselfs, so that they would be content to let us have ours quietly to ourselves." After that I had told him many considerations why he had no cause so to say, "Well," said he, "I pray God, Son Roper, some of us live not till that day," shewing me no reason why he should put any doubt therein. To whom I said: "By my troth, sir, it is very desperately spoken." That vile term, I cry God mercy, did I geve him who, by these words perceiving me in a fume, said merrily unto me: "Well, well, Son Roper, it shall not be so. It shall not be so." Whom, in sixteen years and more, being in house conversant with him, I could never perceive as much as once in a fume. . . .

[Following Wolsey's fall More was named chancellor (1529) and thereafter was drawn increasingly into the moves and countermoves about Henry's divorce. But in addition to his political activities More at this time (toward the end of the twenties) was much engaged with his controversial religious treatises.]

And as little leisure as he had to be occupied in the study of Holy Scripture and controversies upon religion and such other virtuous exercises, being in manner continually busied about th' affairs of the king and the realm, yet such watch and pain in setting forth of divers profitable works in defense of the true Christian religion against heresies secretly sown abroad in the realm, assuredly sustained he that the bishops, to whose pastoral cure the reformation thereof principally appertained, thinking themselfs by his travail, wherein, by their own confession, they were not able with him to make comparison, of their duties in that behalf discharged, and considering that for all his prince's favor he was no rich man, nor in yearly revenues advanced as his worthiness deserved; therefore, at a convocation among themselfs and other of the clergy, they agreed together and concluded upon a sum of four or five thousand pounds, at the least, to my remembrance, for his pains to recompense him. To the payment whereof every bishop, abbot, and the rest of the clergy were, after the rate of their abilities, liberal contributories, hoping this portion should be to his contentation.

Whereupon Tunstall, Bishop of Durham, Clerk,

Bishop of Bath, and (as far as I can call to mind) Veysey, Bishop of Exeter, repaired unto him, declaring how thankfully for his travails, to their discharge, in God's cause bestowed they reck'ned themselves bounden to consider him; and that, albeit they could not according to his deserts so worthily as they gladly would requite him therefor, but must reserve that only to the goodness of God, yet for a small part of recompense, in respect of his estate so unequal to his worthiness, in the name of their whole convocation they presented unto him that sum, which they desired him to take in good part.

Who, forsaking it, said that like as it was no small comfort unto him that so wise and learned men so well accepted his simple doings, for which he never intended to receive reward but at th' hands of God only, to whom alone was the thank thereof chiefly to be ascribed, so gave he most humble thanks to their Honors all for their so bountiful and friendly consideration. . . .

This lord chancellor, albeit he was to God and the world well known of notable virtue (though not so of every man considered), yet for the avoiding of singularity would he appear none otherwise then other men in his apparel and other behavior. And albeit outwardly he appeared honorable like one of his calling, yet inwardly he no such vanities esteeming, secretly next his body ware a shirt of hear; which my sister More, a young gentlewoman, in the sommer, as he sate at supper, singly in his doublet and hose, wearing thereupon a plain shirt without ruff or collar, chancing to spy, began to laugh at it. My wife, not ignorant of his manner, perceiving the same, privily told him of it. And he, being sorry that she saw it, presently amended it.

He used also sometimes to punish his body with whips, the cords knotted, which was known only to my wife, his eldest daughter, whom for her secrecy above all other he specially trusted, causing her, as need required, to wash the same shirt of hear.

Now shortly upon his entry into the high office of the chancellorship the king yet eftsoons again moved him to weigh and consider his great matter; who, falling down upon his knees, humbly besought his Highness to stand his gracious soveraign as he ever, since his entry into his Grace's service, had found him, saying there was nothing in the world had been so grievous unto his heart as to remember that he was not able, as he willingly would with the loss of one of his limbs, for that matter anything to find whereby he could, with his conscience, safely serve his Grace's contentation; as he that always bare in mind the most godly words that his Highness spake unto him at his first coming into his noble service, the most virtuous lesson that ever prince taught his servant, willing him first to look unto God and after God to him; as, in good faith, he said, he did, or else might his Grace well accompt him his most unworthy servant. To this the king awnswered that, if he could not therein with his conscience serve him, he was content t' accept his service otherwise; and, using the advice of other of his learned counsel, whose consciences could well inough agree therewith, would nevertheless continue his gracious favor towards him and never with that matter molest his conscience after. . . .

[Although More relinquished the Great Seal in May, 1532, the king apparently continued to hold him in high favor; nevertheless, his time of trouble was almost upon him.] In the time somewhat before his trouble he would talk with his wife and children of the joys of heaven and the pains of hell, of the lives of holy martyrs, of their grievous martyrdoms, of their marvelous patience, and of their passions and deaths that they suff'red rather then they would offend God; and what an happy and blessed thing it was, for the love of God, to suffer loss of goods, imprisonment, loss of lands and life also. He would further say unto them that, upon his faith, if he might perceive his wife and children would incourage him to die in a good cause, it should so comfort him that, for very joy thereof, it would make him merely run to death. He shewed unto them afore what trouble might after fall upon him. Wherewith and the like virtuous talk he had so long before his trouble incouraged them that, when he after fell into the trouble indeed, his trouble to them was a great deal the less. *Quia spicula previsa minus laedunt.* . . .

[His end was not far off. He refused to attend the marriage of Henry and Anne Boleyn or to swear to the new oath of supremacy.]

After this, as the Duke of Norfolk and Sir Thomas More chanced to fall in familiar talk together, the duke said unto him: "By the mass, Master More, it is perilous, striving with princes. And therefore I would wish you somewhat to incline to the king's pleasure. For by God body, Master More, *indignatio principis mors est.*"

"Is that all, my lord?" quoth he. "Then in good faith is there no more difference between your Grace and me but that I shall die today and you tomorrow." . . .

[Adamant against any suggestion of compromise, More was at last committed to the Tower on April 17, 1534.] Now when he had remained in the Tower a little more than a moneth, my wife, longing to see her father, by her earnest suit at length got leave to go to him. At whose coming, after the Seven Psalms and Letany said (which, whensoever she came to him, ere he fell in talk of any worldly matters he used accustomably to say with her), among other communication he said unto her: "I believe, Meg,

that they that have put me here ween they have done me a high displeasure. But I assure thee, on my faith, my own good daughter, if it had not been for my wife and you that be my children, whom I accompt the chief part of my charge, I would not have failed long ere this to have closed myself in as straight a room, and straighter too. But since I am come hither without mine own desert, I trust that God of his goodness will discharge me of my care, and with his gracious help supply my lack among you. I find no cause, I thank God, Meg, to reckon myself in worse case here then in my own house. For methinketh God maketh me a wanton and setteth me on his lap and dandleth me." Thus, by his gracious demeanor in tribulation, appeared it that all the troubles that ever chanced unto him, by his patient sufferance thereof, were to him no painful punishments, but of his patience profitable exercises. . . .

When Sir Thomas More had continued a good while in the Tower, my lady, his wife, obtained license to see him; who, at her first coming, like a simple, ignorant woman and somewhat worldly too, with this manner of salutation bluntly saluted him: "What the good year, Master More," quoth she. "I mervail that you, that have been always hitherto taken for so wise a man, will now so play the fool to lie here in this close, filthy prison and be content thus to be shut up amongst mice and rats, when you might be abroad at your liberty and with the favor and good will both of the king and his council, if you would but do as all the bishops and best-learned of this realm have done. And seeing you have at Chelsea a right fair house, your library, your books, your gallery, your garden, your orchard, and all other necessaries so handsome about you, where you might in the company of me, your wife, your children, and household, be merry, I muse what, a God's name, you mean here still thus fondly to tarry."

After he had a while quietly heard her, with a cheerful countenance he said unto her: "I pray thee, good Mistress Alice, tell me one thing." "What is that?" quoth she. "Is not this house," quoth he, "as nigh heaven as my own? . . ."

[After two examinations in the Tower More was indicted for high treason (July 1, 1535) and, although he defended his plea of not guilty with characteristic learning, sincerity, and wit, he was sentenced to death.]

When Sir Thomas More came from Westminster to the Tower-ward, again his daughter, my wife, desirous to see her father, whom she thought she should never see in this world after, and also to have his final blessing, gave attendance about the Tower Wharf where she knew he should pass by before he could enter into the Tower, there tarrying for his coming home. As soon as she saw him, after his blessing on her knees reverently received, she, hasting towards him and without consideration or care of herself pressing in among the middest of the throng and company of the guard that with halberds and bills went around about him, hastely ran to him and there openly, in the sight of them all, imbraced him, took him about the neck, and kissed him. Who, well liking her most natural and dear daughterly affection towards him, gave her his fatherly blessing and many godly words of comfort besides. From whom after she was departed, she, not satisfied with the former sight of him, and like one that had forgotten herself, being all ravished with the entire love of her dear father, having respect neither to herself nor to the press of the people and multitude that were there about him, sodainly torned back again, ran to him as before, took him about the neck, and divers times together most lovingly kissed him; and at last, with a full heavy heart, was fain to depart from him. The beholding whereof was to many of them that were present thereat so lamentable that it made them for very sorrow thereof to mourn and weep. . . .

And so upon the next morrow, being Tuesday, St. Thomas' Even and the utas of Saint Peter, in the year of our Lord 1535 . . . early in the morning came to him Sir Thomas Pope, his singular friend, on message from the king and his council, that he should before nine of the clock the same morning suffer death, and that therefore furthwith he should prepare himself thereunto.

"Master Pope," quoth he, "for your good tidings I most heartily thank you. I have been always much bounden to the king's Highness for the benefits and honors that he hath still, from time to time, most bountifully heaped upon me, and yet more bound am I to his Grace for putting me into this place where I have had convenient time and space to have remembrance of my end. And so help me God, most of all, Master Pope, am I bound to his Highness that it pleaseth him so shortly to rid me out of the miseries of this wretched world. And therefore will I not fail earnestly to pray for his Grace, both here and also in another world."

"The king's pleasure is further," quoth Master Pope, "that at your execution you shall not use many words."

"Master Pope," quoth he, "you do well to geve me warning of his Grace's pleasure, for otherwise I had purposed at that time somewhat to have spoken, but of no matter wherewith his Grace or any other should have had cause to be offended. Nevertheless, whatsoever I intended I am ready obediently to con-form myself to his Grace's commandments. And I beseek you, good Master Pope, to be a mean unto his Highness that my daughter Margaret may be at my burial."

"The king is content already," quoth Master Pope, "that your wife, children, and other your friends shall have liberty to be present thereat."

"O how much beholden then," said Sir Thomas More, "am I to his Grace, that unto my poor burial vouchsafeth to have so gracious consideration."

Wherewithal Master Pope, taking his leave of him, could not refrain from weeping. Which Sir Thomas More perceiving, comforted him in this wise: "Quiet yourself, good Master Pope, and be not discomforted; for I trust that we shall, once in heaven, see each other full merrily, where we shall be sure to live and love together in joyful bliss eternally. . . ."

And so was he by master lieutenant brought out of the Tower and from thence led towards the place of execution. Where, going up the scaffold, which was so weak that it was ready to fall, he said merrily to master lieutenant: "I pray you, master lieutenant, see me salf up, and for my coming down let me shift for myself."

Then desired he all the people thereabout to pray for him and to bear witness with him that he should now there suffer death in and for the faith of the Holy Chatholike Church. Which done, he kneeled down and, after his prayers said, turned to th' executioner, and with a cheerful countenance spake thus to him: "Pluck up thy spirits, man, and be not afraid to do thine office. My neck is very short; take heed, therefore, thou strike not awry, for saving of thine honesty."

So passed Sir Thomas More out of this world to God upon the very same day in which himself had most desired.

Soon after whose death came intelligence thereof to the Emperor Charles. Whereupon he sent for Sir Thomas Elyot, our English embassador, and said unto him: "My Lord Embassador, we understand that the king, your master, hath put his faithful servant and grave, wise counselor, Sir Thomas More, to death." Whereunto Sir Thomas Elyot awnswered that he understood nothing thereof. "Well," said the emperor, "it is too true. And this will we say, that if we had been master of such a servant, of whose doings ourself have had these many years no small experience, we would rather have lost the best city of our dominions then have lost such a worthy counselor." Which matter was by the same Sir Thomas Elyot to myself, to my wife, to Maister Clement and his wife, to Master John Heywood and his wife, and unto divers other his friends accordingly reported.

Finis. Deo gratias.

GEORGE CAVENDISH

THE LIFE AND DEATH OF THOMAS WOLSEY

George Cavendish's *Wolsey* would be noteworthy even if it had more serious rivals in Tudor biography. From his entrance into the great cardinal's service as a gentleman-usher about 1526 until his master's death in 1530, Cavendish had been a loyal retainer, who abandoned, as Wolsey himself said, his own country, family, and tranquillity to discharge his duties. It was not until about 1557, at the end of his uneventful later life in his native Suffolk, that he set in order his recollections of his former master. Though fascinated by his subject, Cavendish, a good Catholic and a good Englishman, saw Wolsey's life as a morality play, with Pride as the villain of the piece. He is not always accurate in details, and his bias is unmistakable; yet his artless but moving account of Wolsey's prodigious rise, long triumph, and precipitous fall has the inexorability of great tragedy. For obvious reasons Elizabeth's accession dashed all hopes of publication. The *Life* was known in manuscript—and quoted—by Stow and Speed, the chroniclers; and Shakespeare certainly used it for his *Henry VIII*. But the first printed edition (*The Negotiations of Thomas Wolsey*) was not made until 1641, and then in so mangled and perversely distorted a form as to be scarcely recognizable. Slightly less garbled versions appeared in 1667 and 1706, but not until 1810 did Christopher Wordsworth (brother of the poet) reconstruct a respectable text from two manuscripts in the Lambeth Palace Library for his *Ecclesiastical Biography*. Four years later Joseph Hunter finally established George Cavendish's authorship, and in 1815 Samuel W. Singer set up a supposedly trustworthy text in *Cavendish's Life of Cardinal Wolsey*. Our text is based upon a late sixteenth-century manuscript (Phillipps MS. No. 6390) now in the Houghton Library, Harvard University. Even though such a manuscript has no real authority, it may at least be presumed to be closer to Cavendish's own text than Singer's redaction (between which and our manuscript there are a great many discrepancies). Our emendations are enclosed in pointed brackets.

FROM THE LIFE AND DEATH OF THOMAS WOLSEY (?1557)

THE PROLOGUE

It seemeth no wisdom to credit every light tale blasted abroad by the blasphemous mouth of the rude comminalty. For we daily hear how with their blasphemous trump they spread abroad innumerable lies without either shame or honesty, which (*prima facie*) sheweth forth a visage of truth as though it were a perfect verity and matter indeed, wherein there is nothing more untrue. And among the wise sort so [10] it is esteemed, with whom those babblings be of small force or effect. . . .

I have heard and also seen set forth in divers printed books some untrue imaginations after the death of divers persons which in their lives were of great estimation, that were invented rather to bring their honest names into infamy and perpetual slander of the common multitude then otherwise.

The occasion therefore that maketh me to rehearse all these things is this: that forasmuch as I [20] intend, God willing, to write here some part of the proceedings of Cardinal Wolsey the archbishop his ascending unto honorous estate and sudden falling again from the same, whereof some part shall be of mine own knowledge and some part of credible persons' information.

Forsooth this cardinal was my lord and master whom in his life I served and so remained with him after his fall continually during the term of his trouble until he died, as well in the south as in the north parts, and noted all his demeanor and usage in all that time, as also in his wealthy triumph and glorious estate. And since his death I have heard divers sundry surmises and imagined tales made of his proceedings and dealings which I myself have perfectly known to be most untrue, unto the which I could have sufficiently answered according to the truth but, as meseemed then, it was much better for me to dissemble the matter and suffer the same to remain still as lies then to reply against their untruth, of whom I might, for my boldness, sooner have kindled a great flame of displeasure then to quench one spark of their untrue report. Therefore I committed the truth of the matter to the knowledge of God, who knoweth the truth of all things. For whatsoever any man hath conceived in him when he lived or since his death, thus much I dare be bold to say, without displeasure of any person or of affection, that in my judgment I never saw this realm in better obedience and quiet then in the time of his authority and rule, ne justice better minist'red with indifferency, as I could evidently prove if I should not be accused of too much affection, or else ⟨that⟩ I set forth more then truth. I will therefore leave to speak any more thereof and make here an end and proceed further to his original beginning and ascending with fortune's favor to high honors, dignities, promotions, and riches.

Truth it is that Cardinal Wolsey was an honest poor man's son of Ipswich in the county of Suffolk and there born, being but a child was very apt to be learned; wherefor by the means of his parents or of his good friends and masters he was conveyed to the University of Oxford, where he prospered shortly so in learning that (as he told me with his own mouth) he was made Batchelor of Art when he passed not fifteen years of age, insomuch that for the rareness of his age he was called most commonly thorough the university the boy-batchelor.

Thus prospering and increasing in learning, he was made fellow in Magdalen College and after elected or appointed schoolmaster of Magdalen School, at which time the Lord Marquess Dorset had three of his sons there to school, committing as well unto him their education as their instruction and learning. It pleased the said Lord Marquess, against a Christmas season, to send as well for the schoolmaster as for his children home to his house for their recreation in that pleasant and honorable feast. They being then there, my lord their father perceiving them to be right well employed in learning for their time, which contented him so well that he, hav⟨ing⟩ a benefice in his gift being at that present void, gave the same to the schoolmaster in reward for his diligence at his return after Christmas to the university. And having the presentation thereof, repaired to the ordinary for his institution and induction. And being furnished of his ordinary instruments at the ordinary's hands for his presentment, made speed without any further delay to the said benefice to take thereof possession. And being there for that intent, one Sir Ames Paulett, knight, dwelling in the said county thereabout, took an occasion of displeasure against him, upon what ground I know not; but, sir, by your leave he was so bold as to set the schoolmaster by the heels during his displeasure, which was neither forgiven nor forgotten. For when the schoolmaster mounted to the dignity to be chancellor of England, he was not oblivious of his old displeasure cruelly minist'red unto him by Master Paulett, but sent for him and after many sharp and heinous words injoined him to attend and not to depart out of London without licence obtained; so that he continued there within the Middle Temple the space of five or six years and lay in the gatehouse next the street, which he reedified very

sumptuously, garnishing the same all over the outside with the cardinal's arms, his hat, his cognizances and badges, with other devices in so glorious a sort that he thought thereby to have appeased his old displeasure. . . .

[Following the death of Dorset, young Wolsey lost his benefice and left the university; however, he soon secured a post with Sir John Nanphant, "a very grave and ancient knight who had a great room in Calais under King Henry the Seventh," in whose service he became so useful that he was presently appointed chaplain to the king himself. His obvious talent soon won for him an assignment to negotiate with the Emperor Maximilian in the Low Countries, a commission that he executed with uncommon speed and success. His reward came when the king appointed him dean of Lincoln, "which was at that time one of the worthiest promotions that he gave under the degree of a bishopric. And thus from thenceforward he grew more and more in estimation and aucthority, and after promoted to be almoner. Here may all men note the chances of Fortune, that followeth some whom she intendeth to promote, and to some her favor is clean contrary, although they travail never so much with all the painful diligence that they can devise or imagine, whereof, for my part, I have tasted by experience."]

When death, that favoreth no estate, king ne kaiser, had taken the wise and sage King Henry the Seventh out of this present life—on whose soul Jesu have mercy!—it was wonder to see what practises and compasses was then used about ⟨that⟩ young King Henry the Eighth, and the great provision that was made for the funeral of the one and costly devises for the coronation of the other, ⟨with⟩ the new Queen Catherine and mother after to the Queen's Highness that now is. . . . But I omit and leave all the circumstance of their solemn triumphs unto such as take upon them to write stories of princes and chronicles, for it is no part of my intendment.

After the finishing of all these solemnizations and costly triumphs, our natural, young, and lusty courageous prince and sovereign lord, King Henry the Eighth, ent'ring into the flour of lusty youth, took upon him the regal scepter and imperial diadem of this fertile and plentiful realm, which at that time florished in abundance and riches, whereof the king was inestimably furnished, called the golden world, such grace then reigned within this realm.

Now the almoner, of whom I have taken upon me to write, having a head full of subtile wit and perceiving a plain path to walk in towards his journey to promotion, handeled himself so politiquely that he found means to be one of the king's council and to grow in favor and estimation with the king, to whom the king gave an house at Bridewell, in Fleet Street, sometime Sir Richard Empson's house, where he kept house for his family, and so daily attended upon the king and in his special favor, having great suit made unto him, as counselors most commonly have. His sentences and witty persuasions among the counselors in the council chamber were always so pithy that they, as occasion moved them continually, for his filed tongue and excellent eloquence assigned him to be their expositor unto the king in all their proceedings. In whom the king conceived such a leaning and fancy, and especially in that he was most earnest and readiest in all the council to advance the king's will and pleasure, having no respect to the case. The king therefore perceiving him to be a meet instrument for the accomplishment of his devised pleasures, called him more near unto him, and esteemed him so highly that his only estimation and favor diminished the credit and trust that all other ancient counselors were in before. . . . Who was now in high favor but Master Almoner? And who ruled all under the king but Master Almoner? Thus preferred he still in favor till at last in came presents, gifts, and rewards so plentifully that I dare say that he lacked nothing that might either please his phantasy or enrich his coffers, Fortune smiled so favorably upon him. But to what end it brought him ye shall hereafter hear. Therefore let no man to whom Fortune extendeth her grace trust overmuch to her subtil favor and pleasant promises, under color whereof she carrieth venemous gall. For when she seeth her servant in most high aucthority, and he most assureth himself of her favor, then sodeinly turneth she her visage and pleasant countenance into frowning cheer and utterly forsaketh him; such assurance is in her inconstant favor and promise. . . .

[Thereafter, Wolsey's rise was spectacular: having, as his royal master thought, successfully conducted Henry's French expedition in 1513, in less than a year he was named to three bishoprics (Tournay, Lincoln, and York), and in 1515 he was made a cardinal by Leo X and lord chancellor by his king. Loaded with offices and powers, he lived in regal state.]

He had in his hall continually three boards kept severally with three principal officers, that is to say, a steward which was always a priest; a treasurer, a knight; a controller, an esquire; also a cofferer being a doctor, three marshals, three yeomen ushers in the hall, besides two grooms and almoners. Then he had in the hall-kitchen two clerks, a clerk controller, a surveyor of the dresser, a clerk of his spicery, which together kept a continual mess in the hall. Also in the hall-kitchen he had of master cooks two and of other cooks, laborers, and children of the kitchen

twelve plus four yeomen of the scullery and four other yeomen of his silver scullery, two yeomen of his pastery, with two other pasterers under the yeomen.

Then had he in his privy kitchen a master cook which went daily in velvet or in satin with a chain of gold, besides two other yeomen and six laborers in the same room; in the larder a yeoman and a groom, in the scalding house a yeoman and three grooms, in the scullery two persons, in the buttery two yeomen, two grooms, and two pages; in the ewery likewise so many; in the celler three yeomen and three pages; in the chandlery two yeomen, in the wafery two yeomen, in the wardrop of beds the master of the wardrop and ten persons, in the laundery a yeoman, a groom, thirteen pages; two yeomen purveyors and one groom purveyor; in the bakehouse a yeoman and two grooms, in the wood-yard a yeoman and a groom; in the barn one yeoman; in the garden a yeoman and two grooms. Porters at the gate two yeomen and two grooms, a yeoman of his barge, a master of his horse, a clerk of the stable, a yeoman of the same, the saddler, the farrier, a yeoman of the chariot, a sumpterman, a yeoman of his stirrup, a muleteer, sixteen grooms of the stable, every one of them keeping four geldings; in the almonry a yeoman and a groom.

Now will I declare unto you the officers of his chapel and singing-men of the same. First, he had there a dean, a great divine and a man of excellent learning, a sub-dean, a repeater of the quire, a gospeler, an episteler, of singing priests ten, a master of the children, the seculars of the chapel being singing men twelve, singing children ten, with one servant to wait upon [the said] children. In the vestry, a yeoman and two grooms; over and besides divers retainers that came thither at principal feasts. And for the furniture of this chapel it passeth my capacity to declare the number of the costly ornaments and rich jewels that were occupied in the same continually. For I have seen in procession about the hall forty-four very rich copes of one suit worn, besides the rich crosses and candlesticks, and other necessary ornaments to the furniture of the same. Now shall ye understand that he had two cross-bearers and two pillar-bearers; in the great chamber and in the privy chamber all these persons, first, the chief chamberlin, a vice-chamberlin, of gentlemen-ushers (besides one of his privy chamber) two. He also had twelve waiters and of gentlemen-waiters in his privy chamber he had six; and lords nine or ten who had each of them two men allowed to attend upon them, except the Earl of Darby, who had allowed five men. Then had he of gentlemen cupbearers, of carvers, of sewers, both of the privy chamber and of the great chamber, with gentlemen daily waiters there forty persons, of yeomen ushers he had six, of grooms in his chamber he had eight, of yeomen of his chamber he had daily forty-five. . . .

Now will I declare unto you his order in going to Westminster Hall daily in the term season. First, ere he came out of his privy chamber he heard most commonly every day two masses in his closet, and there said his daily service with his chaplain; and as I heard one of his chaplains say, which was a man of credence and excellent learning, the cardinal, what weighty matters soever he had in the day, never went to his bed with any part of his divine service unsaid, no not so much as one collect, wherein I doubt not but he deceived the opinions of divers persons. Then going again to his privy chamber he would demand if his servants of the said chamber were in a readiness, and furnished his chamber of presence and waiting chamber. He, being thereof advertised, came out of his privy chamber about eight of the clock appareled all in red like a cardinal; (that is to say) his upper garment was all either of fine scarlet or else fine crimson taffeta or else most commonly of fine crimson satin ingrained; his pillion of fine scarlet with a neck set in the inner side with black velvet, and a tippet of sables about his neck, holding in his hand an orange whereof the meat or substance within was taken out and filled again with the part of a sponge, wherein was vinegar and other confections against pestilent airs, the which he most commonly held to his nose when he came among the press, or else that he was pestered with many suitors. And before him was borne first the Great Seal of England and his cardinal's hat by a lord or some gentleman of worth, right solemnly. And as soon as he was ent'red into his chamber of presence where there were daily attending upon him as well noblemen of this realm as other worthy gentlemen as gentlemen of his own family, his two great crosses then were attending to be borne before him. Then cried the gentlemen ushers going before him bare-headed and said, "On before, my lords and masters, on before! Make way for my lord's Grace!" Thus went he down through the hall with a sergeant-of-arms before him, bearing a great mace of silver, and two gentlemen carrying two great pillars of silver, and when he came to the hall door his mule stood there, trapped all in crimson velvet with a saddle of the same with gilt stirrups. Then was there attending upon him, when he was mounted, his two cross-bearers, and his pillar-bearers in like case, upon great horses trapped all in fine scarlet. Then marched he forward with a train of gentlemen, having his foot-men four in number about him, bearing each of them a gilt pole-ax in their hands. And thus passed he forth until he came to Westminster Hall door. . . .

Thus in great honor, triumph, and glory he reigned a long season, ruling all things in this realm appertaining to the king by his wisdom and also other weighty matters of foreign regions with whom the king of this realm had any occasion to intermeddle. All ambassadors of foreign potentates were always dispatched by his wisdom, to whom they had continual access for their dispatch. His house was always resorted like a king's house with noblemen and gentlemen, going and coming in and out, feasting and banqueting these ambassadors divers times and all others right nobly.

And when it pleased the king's Majesty for his recreation to repair to the cardinal's house, as he did divers times in the year, there wanted no preparations of goodly furniture in <viands> of the finest sort that could be gotten for money or friendship. Such pleasures were then devised for the king's consolation or comfort that might be invented or imagined. Banquets were set forth with maskers and mummers in so gorgeous a sort and costly manner that it was a heaven to behold. There wanted no dames or damosels, meet or apt to dance with the maskers or to garnish the place for the time, with other goodly disports. Then was there all kind of music and harmony set forth with excellent fine voices both of men and children. I have seen the king come sodainly thither in a mask, with a dozen masquers, all in garments like shepherds, made of fine cloth of gold and fine crimson satin paned, and caps of the same with visards of good proportion of phisnomy; their hairs and beards either of fine gold wire or of silver, or else of black silk, having sixteen torch-bearers besides their drummers and other persons attending upon them with visards, clothed all in satin of the same color. . . .

Thus passed the cardinal his time from day to day, and year to year, in such great joy, wealth, triumph, and glory, having always on his side the king's especial favor, until Fortune, of whose favor no man is longer assured then she is disposed, began to wax something wroth with his prosperous estate, and for the better means to bring him low she procured Venus, the insatiate goddess, to be her instrument, who brought the king to be in love with a gentle-woman [Anne Boleyn], that, after she perceived and felt the king's good will towards her and how gladded he was to please her and to grant all her requests, she wrought the cardinal much displeasure, as hereafter shall be more at large declared. This gentle-woman was the daughter of Sir Thomas Bulleine, knight, at that time but only a batchelor knight, the which afterwards, for the love of his daughter, was promoted to high dignities. He bare at several times for the most part all the high offices of the king's household. . . . [The king] fantasied so his daughter that almost all things began to grow out of frame.

To tell you how the king's love began to take place and what followed thereof I will do as much as I know to declare the same to you. . . .

[Cavendish relates with copious details the events leading to Wolsey's downfall over Henry's divorce from Catherine of Aragon: the cardinal's negotiations with François I and with Clement VII, the arrival of Cardinal Campeggio and his supplanting Wolsey in the divorce proceedings, the increasing power of Thomas Cromwell and the increasing enmity of Anne Boleyn, the bill of indictment preferred against Wolsey (November, 1529), his arrest for high treason (November, 1530), and his last progress from York toward London. Accompanied by Sir William Kingston, constable of the Tower, and an armed guard, he thus makes his way from Nottingham to Leicester.]

And by the way <he> waxed so sick that he had almost fallen from his mule, so that it was night before we came to the abbey of Leicester, where at his coming in at the gates the abbot with all his convent met him with divers torches' light, whom they right honorably received and welcomed with great reverence. To whom my lord said, "Father Abbot, I am come hither to leave my bones among you"; riding so still till he came at the stairs of his chamber, where he alighted from his mule, and then Master Kingston took him by the arm and led him up the stairs; who told me afterwards that he never felt so heavy a burthen in all his life. And as soon as he was in his chamber he went incontinent to his bed, very sick. This was upon Saturday at night, and then continued he sicker and sicker.

And upon Monday in the morning, as I stood by his bedside about eight of the clock, the windows being close shut, having wax lights burning upon the cupboard, I beheld him (as meseemed) drawing fast towards death. He, perceiving my shadow upon the wall by his bedside, asked who was there. "Sir," quoth I, "I am here." "How do you?" quoth he to me. "Very well, sir," quoth I, "if I might see your Grace well." "What is it of the clock?" said he to me. "Sir," said I, "it is past eight in the morning." "Eight of the clock!" quoth he; "that cannot be," rehearsing divers times "eight of the clock, eight of the clock, nay, nay." Quoth he at the last: "It cannot be eight of the clock, for at eight of the clock you shall loose your master, for my time draweth near that I must depart this world." With that Doctor Palmes, a worshipful gentleman, being his chaplain and ghostly father, standing by, bade me secretly demand of him whether he would be shriven, and to be in a readiness towards God, whatsoever should

chance. At whose desire I asked him that question. "What have you to do to ask me any such question?" quoth he, and began to be very angry with me for my presumption, until that at the last Master Doctor took my part and talked with him in Latin, and so pacified him. . . .

My lord waxed very sick, most likely to die that night, and often swooned; as methought drew on fast unto his end, until it was four of the clock in the morning, at which time I spake unto him and asked him how he did. "Well," quoth he, "if I had any meat. I pray you give me some." "Sir, there is none ready," said I. "Iwis," quoth he, "ye be the more to blame, for you should have meat for me in a readiness to eat when my stomach serveth me; therefore I pray you get me some, for I intend this day to make me strong, to the intent that I may occupy myself in confession and make me ready to God." "Then, sir, I will call up the cooks to provide some meat for you, and will also, if it be your pleasure, call for Master Palmes that <ye> may commune with him till your meat be ready." "With a good will," quoth he. And therefore I went first and called up the cooks, bidding them to provide some meat for my lord; then went I to Master Palmes and told him what case my lord was in, willing him to rise and to resort to him with speed. And then I went to Master Kingston and gave him warning that, as I thought, my lord would not live, advising him that if <he> had anything to say to him that he should make haste, for he was in great danger. . . . After he had eaten of a collace made of a chicken a spoonful or two, at the last quoth he, "Whereof was this collace made?" "Forsooth," quoth I, "of a chicken." "Why," quoth he, "is it fasting day, being St. Andrew's Even?" "What though it be," quoth Doctor Palmes, "ye be excused by reason of your sickness." "Yea," quoth he, "though I will eat no more."

Then was he in confession, and Master Kingston came to him and bade him good-morrow, for it was about six of the clock, and asked him how he did. "Sir," said he, "I tarry but the pleasure of God, to render up my poor soul into his hands." "Not so," quoth Master Kingston, "with the grace of God ye shall live and do very well if ye will be of good cheer." "Nay in good sooth, Master Kingston, my disease is such that I cannot live; I have had some experience in phisick. Thus it is: I have a flux with a continual fever, the nature thereof <is>, if there be no alteration of the same within eight days, must ensue either excoriation of the entrails or phrenzy or else present death, and the best of three is death. . . . Well, well, Master Kingston, I see the matter maketh you much worse then you should against me, how it <is> framed I know not, but if I had served God as diligently as I have done the king He would not have given me over in my gray hairs. But this is the just reward that I must receive for my diligent pains and study that I have had to do him service, not regarding my service to God, but only to satisfy his pleasure. I pray you have me most heartily commended unto his royal Majesty and beseech him in my behalf to call to his remembrance all matters proceeding between him and me from the beginning of the world and the progress of the same; and most especially in his weighty matters"—meaning the matter between good Queen Catherine and him; "and then shall his Grace's conscience know whether I have offended him or no. He is a prince of a royal courage and hath a princely heart, and rather then he will miss or want any part of his will or pleasure he will endanger the loss of the one half of his realm. For I assure you I have often kneeled before him the space of sometime three hours to persuade him from his will and appetite, but I could never dissuade him therefrom. Therefore, Master Kingston, I warn you, if it be your chance hereafter to be one of his privy counsel, as for your wisdom you are very meet, be well assured and advised what you put in his head, for ye shall never put it out again.

"And say, furthermore, that I request of his Grace, in God's name, that he have a vigilant eye to depress this new sect of Lutherans, that it doth not increase through his negligence in such sort that he be at length compelled to put harness upon his back to subdue them, as the king of Bohemia did, who had good game to see his subjects and commons, being infected with Wycliffe's heresies, spoil the spiritual men of his realm, who at the last was constrained to call to the king and his nobles for succor against their frantique rage, of whom they could get no help nor refuge, but laughed and had

good game, not regarding their duty. . . . If these be not plain precedents and sufficient persuasions to admonish a prince to be circumspect against the semblable mischief, then will God strike and take from us our prudent rulers, and leave us in the hands of our enemies, and then shall ensue mischief, inconvenience upon inconvenience, all barrenness and scarcity for lack of good order in the commonweal to the utter ruin and desolation of this realm, from the which God of his tender mercy defend us.

"Master Kingston, farewell! I can no more say, but I wish, ere I die, all things to have good success. My time draweth on fast. I may not tarry with you. And forget not what I have said and charged you withal, for when I am dead ye shall peradventure remember my words better." And even with these words he began to draw his speech at length, and his tongue to fail, his eyes being perfectly set in his head, whose sight failed him. Then began we to put him in remembrance of Christ's passion, and caused the yeomen of the guard to stand by secretly to see him die and to be witnesses of his words at his departure, who heard his communication; and incontinent the clock strok eight, and then gave he up the ghost, and he departed this present life. And calling to remembrance how he said the day before, we should loose our master (as it is before rehearsed), one of us looking upon another, supposing that either he knew or prophesied of his departure, we sent for the abbot. . . . .

Here is the end and fall of pride and arrogancy of men, exalted by Fortune to dignities; for I assure you, in his time he was the haughtiest man in all his proceedings alive, having more respect to honors of his person then he had to his spiritual profession, wherein should be showed all meekness, humility, and charity, the discussing whereof I leave to divines. . . .

Part II EARLY TUDOR LITERATURE

STEPHEN HAWES

THE PASTIME OF PLEASURE

As a groom of the chamber in Henry VII's household, Hawes—who had been educated at Oxford—wrote and presented to the king about 1506 *The Pastime of Pleasure*. Both the date and the author's acknowledged indebtedness to Lydgate point to the traditional character of the work—an unconscionably long dream-allegory of some six thousand lines, arranged in forty-six chapters of seven-line stanzas riming *ababbcc*. The basic plot, built on the motif of the quest, is simple; but its florid developments and digressions make the poem a jungle of allegorical characters and episodes. Grand Amour, the hero, receives instruction at the Tower of Doctrine (whose seven daughters represent the seven sciences of the Trivium and the Quadrivium), the Castle of Chivalry, the Tower of Chastity, and the like. After many adventures, including a prodigious fight with a three-headed giant, he at last reaches the palace of La Belle Pucelle, whom he marries. At the end of his life (and of the poem) he dies under the watchful eyes of Contrition and Conscience. The poem was first published in 1509 by Wynkyn de Worde, who issued a second edition (with woodcuts) in 1517. In 1554 there appeared another edition from the press of John Wayland, and its success presumably called for two further editions by Richard Tottel and John Waley in 1555. Our text is based upon *The Pastime of Pleasure*, ed. William Edward Mead, EETS, no. 173, 1928 (for 1927).

FROM THE PASTIME OF PLEASURE (1517)

How Grand Amour Walked in a Meadow and Met with Fame Environed with Tongues of Fire

CAPITUM I

Whan Phoebus ent'red was in Gemine,
Shining above in his fair, golden spere,
And horned Dian than but one degree
In the Crab had ent'red fair and clear,
Whan that Aurora did well appear
In the depured air and cruddy firmament,
Forth than I walked without impediment

Into a meadow both gay and glorious
Which Flora depainted with many a color
Like a place of pleasure most solacious,
Encensing out the aromatic odor   10
Of Zepherus' breath, which that every flour,
Through his fume, doth alway engender.
So as I went among the flours tender

By sodain chance a fair path I found
On which I looked, and right oft I mused;
And than all about I beheld the ground
With the fair path which I saw so used.
My chance or fortune I nothing refused,
But in the path forth I went apace,   20
To know whither and unto what place

It would me bring by ony similitude.
So forth I went, were it right or wrong,
Till that I saw of rial pulcritude
Before my face an image fair and strong,
With two fair hands stretched out along
Unto two highways there in pertition,
And in the right hand was this description:

"This is the straight way of Contemplation
Unto the Joyful Tour perdurable.   30
Who that will walk unto that mansion
He must forsake all things variable,
With the vainglory so much deceivable.
And though the way be hard and dangerous,
The last end thereof shall be right precious."

And in the other hand right fair written was:
"This is the way of Worldly Dignity,
Of the actife life. Who will in it pass
Unto the tour of fair Dame Beauty,
Fame shall tell him of the way in certainty,   40
Unto La Belle Pucelle, the fair lady excellent,
Above all other in clear beauty splendent."

I beheld right well both the ways twain
And mused oft which was best to take:
The one was sharp; the other was more plain.
And unto myself I began to make
A sodain argument, for I might not slake
Of my great musing of this rial image
And of these two ways so much in usage.

61

For this goodly picture was in altitude   50
Nine foot and more of fair marble stone,
Right well favored and of great fortitude
Though it were made full many years agone.
Thus stood I musing myself all alone
By right long time, but at the last I went
The actife way with all my whole entent.

Thus all alone I began to travel
Forth on my way by long continuance,
But oftentimes I had great mervail
Of the bypaths so full of pleasance,   60
Which for to take I had great doubtance.
But evermore, as near as I might,
I took the way which went before me right.

And at the last, whan Phoebus in the west
Gan to avail with all his beams merry,
Whan clear Diana in the fair southest
Gan for to rise, lighting our emispery
With clouds clear, without the stormy pery,
Methought afer I had a vision
Of a picture of mervoilous fashion.   70

To which I went without lenger delay,
Beholding well the right fair purtraiture
Made of fine copper, shining fair and gay,
Full well truly, according to measure
And as I thought, nine foot of stature;
Yet in the breast, with letters fair and blue,
Was written a sentence old and true:

"This is the way and the situation
Unto the Tour of Famous Doctrine.
Who that will learn must be ruled by Reason,   80
And with all his diligence he must encline
Sloth to eschew, and for to determine
And set his heart to be intelligible.
To a willing heart is nought impossible."

Beside the image I adown me set,
After my labor myself to repose,
Till at the last, with a gasping net,
Sloth my heed caught with his whole purpose.
It vailed not the body for to dispose
Against the heed; whan it is applied   90
The heed must rule; it cannot be denied.

Thus as I sat in a deedly slomber
Of a great horn I heard a rial blast,
With which I awoke and had a great wonder
From whence it came. It made me sore aghast.
I looked about. The night was well-near past,
And fair, golden Phoebus, in the morrow gray,
With cloud red began to break the day.

I saw come riding, in a valley fer,
A goodly lady environed about   100
With tongues of fire as bright as ony ster
That fiery flambes ensensed alway out,
Which I beheld, and was in great doubt;
Her palfrey swift, renning as the wind,
With two white greyhounds that were not behind.

Whan that these greyhounds had me so espied,
With fawning cheer of great humility
In goodly haste they fast unto me hied.
I mused why and wherefore it should be,
But I welcomed them in every degree.   110
They leaped oft and were of me right fain;
I suff'red them and cherished them again.

Their collars were of gold and of tissue fine,
Wherein their names appeared by scripture
Of diamonds that clearly do shine.
The letters were graven fair and pure;
To read their names I did my besy cure;
The one was Governance, the other named Grace;
Than was I glad of all this sodain case.

And than the lady, with fiery flame   120
Of brenning tongues, was in my presence
Upon her palfrey, which had unto name
Pegase the swift, so fair in excellence,
Which sometime longed with his preminence
To King Persius, the son of Jubiter,
On whom he rode by the world so fer.

To me she said she mervailed much why
That her greyhound shewed me that favor.
What was my name, she axed me truly.
To whom I said it was La Grand Amour,   130
"Beseeching you to be to me succor
To the Tour of Doctrine, and also me tell
Your proper name and where you do dwell."

"My name," quod she, "in all the world is known,
Yclipped Fame in every region;
For I my horn in sondry wise have blown
After the death of many a champion
And with my tongues have made ay mention
Of their great acts, again to revive,
In flaming tongues for to abide on live...."   140

[After Fame describes to Grand Amour the beauty and
goodness of La Belle Pucelle he resolves to win her for
his own. Before such a consummation, however, he must
undergo not only physical but also moral and academic
probation, and so his quest is long and arduous. Thus,
when Fame directs him to the Tower of Doctrine to be
instructed in the seven sciences, he is first sent by Dame

Use of script is orthodox to explain cosmic origin.

Doctrine, its chatelaine, to Lady Grammar, and then in turn to Logic, Lady Rhetoric, Arithmetic, Dame Music (who introduces him to La Belle Pucelle), Dame Geometry, and Astronomy. Thus his conversation with Dame Astronomy:]

CAPITUM XXII

Than forth I went into a meadow green,
With Flora painted in many a sondry color
Like a gay goddess, of all flours the queen.
She encensed out her aromatic odor;
The breath of Zepherus encreased the flour;
Amiddes the meadow, fair resplendishant,
Was a pavilion right high and quadrant

Of green sarcenet bord'red with gold,
Wherein did hang a fair astrology
Which oft Astronomy did full well behold;   150
Unto whom than I came full shortly
And kneeled adown before her meekly,
Beseeching her of her great gentleness
Of her science to shew the perfitness.

"My science," said she, "it is right reasonable
And is the last of the sciences seven.
Unto man it is also right profitable,
Shewing the course above of the heaven
Right merveilous for ony man to neven.
Who knew astronomy at every manner season   160
Might set in order every thing by reason.

"Also, the other six sciences liberal
By astronomy principally were found;
And one were lost, they were vanished all,
Each upon other hath so sure a ground.
In all the world that is so wide and round
Is none so wise that can them multiply
Nor know them all right well and surely.

"The High Astronomer, that is God omnipotent,
That the first day devided all the light   170
From the derkness with his will prepotent,
And the second day with his excellent might
The waters above he did devide aright
From the earthly waters which are infernal.
The third day herbs and fruits in special

"In earth he planted for to have their life,
By divers virtues and sundry growing
So to continue and be vegetatife;
And the fourth day he set in working
The bodies above to have their moving,   180
In the twelve signs themself to domify,
Some rethrogard and some directly.

Static world
Pre-Copernican

"The fifth day he did fishes make
In the sea, the great stormy flood,
To and fro their courses for to take
And in the water for to have their food,
Like to the same cold alway their blood.
The sixth day beasts with souls sensative,
And man also with soul intellective.

"The seventh day he rested of his work,   190
Nothing constrained as of weariness,
As writeth many a right famous clerk,
But that he had accomplished, doubtless,
His purpensed purpose by infinite prowess,
As to us doth most plainly discure
The perfit ground of Holy Scripture.

Harmony of the spheres

"Thus God himself is chief astronomer,
That made all thing according to his will:
The sun, the moon, and every little ster
To a good intent and for no manner of ill.   200
Withouten vain he did all thing fulfill,
As astronomy doth make apparance
By reason he weighed all things in balance."

CAPITUM XXIII

"And forasmuch that he made Nature
First of all to have domination,
The power of her I shall anon discure,
How that she taketh her operation
And whereupon is her foundation.
I simple and rude, oppress'd with negligence,
Shall discrive the might of her preeminence.   210

Only God would be

"For though that angels be invisible,
Inpalpable, and also celestial,
Withouten substance as insensible,
Yet have they nature which is angelical;
For Nature naturing, naturate, made all
Heaven and earth and the bodies above
By course of nature for to work and move.

natura/naturans essens

"On man or beast, without ony miss,
She worketh directly after the aspect
Of the matter, be it more or less, iwis,   220
And doth thereof the whole fourm direct;
After the quality it doth take effect;
If there be more than may one suffice,
A by-member she will than more devise.

"As that in ure ye may it daily see
Upon one hand some hath thumbs twain,
And other also sometime arms three.
The superfluity is cause thereof certain
Which that Dame Nature doth constrain

So for to do, for she leseth nought   230
Of the matter, but hath it wholly wrought.

"And in like wise, where is not sufficient
Of the matter for the whole formation,
There lacketh a member by great impediment,
So that there can be no perfit fashion,
As may be judged by perfit reason;
After the quality of the matter lacking,
So lacketh they of Nature's fourming. . . ."

[Following such sober instruction in the seven sciences
Grand Amour proceeds to the Tower of Chivalry, where,
after a good deal of talk, he is knighted by King Melezyus.
Then, accompanied by Minerva, he sets forth on his
chivalric peregrination. Having sought assistance at the
Temple of Venus, he then has many adventures: a visit
to the dungeon of Dame Correction, an assault on a
triple-headed giant, an attack on a castle inhabited by
seven monsters (Dissimulation, Delay, Discomfort, et al.),
and so on. At last he reaches his lady's tower. The subsequent nuptials are duly grand:]

Of the Great Marriage between Grand Amour and La Belle Pucelle

CAPITUM XXXIX

Than Perseverance, in all goodly haste,
Unto the steward called Liberality   240
Gave warning for to make ready fast
Against this time of great solempnity
That on the morrow hallowed should be.
She warned the cook, called Temperance,
And after that the ewers' observance.

With pleasance the panter and Dame Curtesy,
The gentle butler with the ladies all,
Each in her office, was prepared shortly
Against this feast so much triumphal;
And La Belle Pucelle then in special   250
Was up betime in the morrow gray.
Right so was I whan I saw the day.

And right anon La Belle Pucelle me sent
Against my wedding of the satin fine,
White as the milk, a goodly garment
Brand'red with pearl that clearly did shine.
And so, the marriage for to determine,
Venus me brought to a rial chapel
Which of fine gold was wrought everydel.

And after that the gay and glorious   260
La Belle Pucelle to the chapel was led
In a white vesture fair and precious,
With a golden chaplet on her yallow head.

And Lex Ecclesie did me to her wed,
After which wedding there was a great fest.
Nothing we lacked, but had of the best.

What should I tarry by long continuance
Of the feast for? Of my joy and pleasure
Wisdom can judge withouten variance
That nought I lacked, as ye may be sure.   270
Paying the sweet due debt of nature,
Thus with my lady that was fair and clear
In joy I lived full right many a year.

O lusty youth and young, tender heart!
The true companion of my lady bright!
God let us never from other astert,
But all in joy to live both day and night.
Thus after sorrow joy arriveth aright;
After my pain I had sport and play.
Full little thought I that it should decay.   280

Till that Dame Nature, naturing, had made
All things to grow unto their fortitude,
And Nature, naturing, wax'd retrograde,
By strength my youth so for to exclude
As was ever her old consuetude.
First to augment and than to abate,
This is the custom of her high estate.

[When, after a long life, Grand Amour dies, Mercy and
Charity bury him and Remembrance writes his epitaph.
But when Dame Fame announces that she will cause his
name to be forever honored, Time suddenly appears:]

CAPITUM XLIV

And as Dame Fame was in laudation
Into the temple with mervailous likeness
Sodainly came Time in breviation,   290
Whose similitude I shall anon express:
Aged he was, with a beard doubtless;
Of swallows' feders his wings were long;
His body fed'red, he was high and strong.

In his left hand he had an horology
And in his right hand a fire brenning;
A swerd about him girt full surely,
His legs armed clearly shining,
And on his noddle, darkly flaming,
Was set Saturn pale as ony lead,   300
And Jupiter amiddes his forhed. . . .

"My name," quod he, "is in division:
As time was, time is, and the time future.
I mervail much of the presumption
Of the Dame Fame, so putting in ure

Thy great praise, saying it shall endure
For to be infinite, evermore in preace,
Seeing that I shall all thy honor cease.

"Shall not I, Time, distroy both sea and land,
The sun and moon? And the stars all,   310
By very reason thou shalt understand,
At last shall lese their course in general.
On time past it vaileth not to call.
Now by this horologe it doth well appear
That my last name doth evermore draw near. . . .

"I am the lodestar to Dame Eternity.
Whan man of earth hath his creation,
After the minute of his nativity
He taketh than his operation
Upon me, Time, at every season.   320
In the same hour the world was create
Originally I took mine estate. . . .

"Do not I, Time, cause Nature to augment?
Do not I, Time, cause Nature to decay?
Do not I, Time, cause man to be present?
Do not I, Time, take his life away?
Do not I, Time, cause death take his say?
Do not I, Time, pass his youth and age?
Do not I, Time, everything assuage?

"In time Troy, the city, was edified;   330
By time also was the distruction.
Nothing without time can be fortified;
No earthly joy nor tribulation
Without time is for to suffer passion.
The time of earth was our distruction,
And the time of earth was our redemption. . . .

"Of the day of dome than in the balance
Almighty God shall be just and egal
To every person withouten doubtance,

Each as they did deserve in general: 340
Some to have joy, some pain eternal.
Than I am past; I may no lenger be.
And after me is Dame Eternity."

[After a final exhortation by Dame Eternity the poet
brings his work to a close:]

The Excusation of the Auctor

CAPITUM XLVI

Unto all poets I do me excuse
If that I offend for lack of science.
This little book yet do ye not refuse,
Though it be devoid of famous eloquence.
Add or detray by your high sapience,
And pardon me of my high enterprise,
Which of late this fable did feign and devise.   350

Go, little book, I pray God thee save
From mismet'ring by wrong impression,
And who that ever list thee for to have
That he perceive well thine entention;
For to be grounded without presumption,
As for to eschew the sin of idleness,
To make such books I apply my besiness,

Beseeching God for to give me grace
Books to compile of moral virtue,
Of my maister Lydgate to follow the trace,   360
His noble fame for to laud and remeve
Which in his life thee, Sloth, did eschew,
Making great books to be in memory,
On whose soul I pray God have mercy.

Here endeth *The Pastime of Pleasure.* Inprinted at London
in Fleet Street at the Sign of the Sun by Wynkyn de
Worde the year of Our Lord MCCCCC and XVII,
third day of December.

JOHN SKELTON

"Beastly Skelton," as Pope called him, has had a long career of critical disesteem. The vulgarity and the savage personal abuse of his satires, the coarseness of his poems of low life, his intensely conservative (not to say reactionary) attitude toward some of the freshest currents of the English Renaissance, and the notorious metrical and structural license of his verse have conspired to make him *persona non grata* to many different kinds of readers. And yet he was the most considerable poet of early Tudor

England. By his own account a product of both universities (each named him laureate), a learned man as learning was accounted in his day, a beneficed clergyman, and a tutor of the future Henry VIII, he fully deserved Erasmus' flattering description as *unum Britannicarum literarum lumen ac decus.* He was uncommonly well read in four literatures, and his own Latin and English works, both original and translated, constitute an imposing corpus. In his *Garland of Laurel* (ca. 1520), a long dream-allegory reminiscent of Chaucer's *House of Fame* and the "Prologue" to the *Legend of Good Women,* he presents an impressive catalogue of his own writings: among other things, three morality plays (of which only *Magnificence* survives), an English grammar, a *Speculum principis* composed for his royal pupil, and a translation of Deguilleville's *Pèlerinage de la vie humaine.* In addition, William Caxton, in the preface to *Eneydos* (1490), applauds Skelton's translations of Cicero's *Epistolae familiares* and of Diodorus Siculus; and although nearly all these works are now lost, the bulk and variety of what remains are formidable.

To celebrate the exploits of his royal and noble patrons he composed, early in Henry VII's reign, such occasional pieces as elegies on Edward IV and Henry Percy, Earl of Northumberland, and later, after Henry VIII's accession, *Eulogium pro suorum temporum conditione,* "A Laud and Praise Made for Our Sovereign Lord the King," and "A Ballad of the Scottish King" (on James IV's defeat at Flodden Field in 1513). These and other similar pieces are mainly laudatory and conventional; but in *The Bowge of Court,* which was probably written before the turn of the sixteenth century, we have a striking example of Skelton's originality breaking through the formal limitations of the dream-allegory. Written in the traditional seven-line stanza which Chaucer had popularized, it is Skelton's wry, dramatically terse version of the seven deadly sins— but sins domesticated in court and disguised as royal favorites. The satire shows not only Skelton's superb eye for the significant detail, but also real comic energy and a kind of nameless terror at the fact of evil; and the tense conclusion (in which the poet jumps overboard to escape his sinister "friends") is unforgettable.

A scornful comment at the end of Alexander Barclay's *Ship of Fools* (?1509) fixes at least one limit for dating *Philip Sparrow.* Written apparently after Skelton, then about forty, had taken holy orders and had settled in his parish of Diss, in his native Norfolk, it is one of the earliest specimens of the famous Skeltonic meter—cascades of short, irregular lines that run through a bewildering variety of rimes. *Philip Sparrow* (which was perhaps suggested by Catullus' lovely dirge on a sparrow's death) is an elegy for a pet bird belonging to one Jane Scroop, a pupil of the Black Nuns (or Benedictines) at Carrow in Norfolk. Audaciously strung together on scraps from the office for the dead, the long, loose poem describes the sparrow's death in the jaws of a cat, the assembling of the winged mourners, and the tender grief of its mistress, who, though bountifully read, can scarcely bring herself to compose an epitaph. The "Addition," perhaps written in reply to Barclay's criticism, expands the portrait of Jane Scroop. A finer example of Skeltonic meter is the free-wheeling *Tunning of Elinour Rumming,* one of Skelton's funniest and most superbly vulgar poems and an overwhelming exposé of low life in early Tudor England.

A considerable stay at the court of Henry VIII is indicated by the series of four poems attacking Sir Christopher Garnesche (or Garneys), a gentleman-usher to the king. These, constituting a one-sided flyting (Garneys' work being lost), are coarse, vigorous examples of Skelton's court satire; they are also exercises in formal vilification, somewhat in the manner of the *Flyting* of Dunbar and Kennedy which inspired them. From about the time he finished the *Garland of Laurel* Skelton engaged in a bitter controversy with the powerful Cardinal Wolsey. Although he had earlier flattered Wolsey in "A Replication against Certain Young Scholers" (an attack on some projected theological and pedagogical reforms at Cambridge), in *Colin Clout* (ca. 1519) he assumes the role of a roaming rustic to comment savagely on the corruption of the English clergy—a luxury-loving, venal, and worldly crew who merely follow the example set by the primate. Of its two sequels, *Speak, Parrot* (which survives in so mutilated a state as to be nearly unintelligible) carries the attack on Wolsey to astonishing personal limits, and *Why Come Ye Not to Court?* (written about 1523) crushingly summarizes Skelton's charges against Henry's chancellor as a power-mad knave leading his country to ruin. It is not surprising that Wolsey's reaction was sufficient to keep the poems out of print and to drive Skelton into sanctuary at Westminster for a time. He died in 1529.

The bibliographical problems of Skelton's works are immense. Many of his separate pieces were published by such London printers as Wynkyn de Worde, Richard Pynson, and Richard Kele, but apparently almost all the original editions are lost, and those that have survived are undated. Some of the more scurrilous satires—like *Colin Clout* and *Why Come Ye Not to Court?*—were probably never printed in Skelton's lifetime. Dyce's excellent edition of the mid-nineteenth century shows the difficulties of collating the various contemporary texts, the many manuscripts, and the later Elizabethan versions. Thus, although we have a 1513 text for "A Ballad of the Scottish King," the earliest extant editions of *Philip Sparrow, Colin Clout,* and *Why Come Ye Not to Court?* must be dated about 1545; while parts of *Speak, Parrot* and the poems *Against Garnesche* were not printed until Dyce included them in his edition of 1843. Therefore we have based our texts upon the early Elizabethan collected edition of Skelton's main works, Thomas Marshe's *Pithy pleasaunt and profitable workes of maister Skelton,* 1568 (STC 22608). Certain additions for the sake of meaning or meter are supplied (in pointed brackets) from Dyce.

FROM PITHY, PLEASAUNT, AND PROFITABLE WORKS OF MAISTER SKELTON (1568)

SKELTON LAUREATE, UPON A
DEAD MAN'S HEAD THAT WAS
SENT TO HIM FROM AN HONOR-
ABLE GENTLEWOMAN FOR A
TOKEN, DEVISED THIS GHOSTLY
MEDITATION IN ENGLISH, COVE-
NABLE IN SENTENCE, COM-
MENDABLE, LAMENTABLE, LAC-
RIMABLE, PROFITABLE FOR THE
SOUL

Your ugly token
My mind hath broken
From worldly lust,
For I have discuss'd
We are but dust
And die we must.
  It is general
To be mortal:
I have well espi'd
No man may him hide   10
From Death hollow-eyed
With sinews widered,
With bones shidered,
With his worm-eaten maw,

And his ghastly jaw
Gasping aside,
Naked of hide,
Neither flesh nor fell.
  Then by my counsel
Look that ye spell   20
Well this gospel,
For whereso we dwell
Death will us quell
And with us mell.
  For all our pamper'd paunchis
There may no fraunchis
Nor worldly bliss
Redeem us from this:
Our days be dated
To be checkmated   30
With drawttis of Death,
Stopping our breath;
Our eyen sinking,
Our bodies stinking,
Our gums grinning,
Our souls brinning.
To whom, then, shall we sue
For to have rescue

But to sweet Jesu
On us then for to rue?   40
  O goodly Child
Of Mary mild,
Then be our shild,
That we be not exil'd
To the dyne dale
Of bottomless bale,
Nor to the lake
Of fiends black.
  But grant us grace
To see Thy face,   50
And to purchase
Thine heavenly place,
And thy palace
Full of solace
Above the sky
That is so high,
Eternally
To behold and see
The Trinity.
  Amen.

Mirres vous y.

ON THE DEATH OF THE NOBLE PRINCE
KING EDWARD THE FOURTH

Miseremini mei, ye that be my friends!
  This world hath formed me down to fall.
How may I endure when that everything ends?
  What creature is born to be eternal?
Now there is no more but pray for me all.
  Thus say I, Edward, that late was your king
And twenty-three years ruled this imperial,
  Some unto pleasure and some to no liking.
Mercy I ask of my misdoing;
  What availeth it, friends, to be my foe   10
Sith I cannot resist nor amend your complaining?
  Quia ecce, nunc in pulvere dormio.

I sleep now in mold, as it is natural
  As earth unto earth hath his reverture.
What ordained God to be terrestrial
  Without recourse to the earth of nature?
Who to live ever may be sure?
  What is it to trust on mutability,
Sith that in this world nothing may indure?
  For now am I gone, that late was in prosperity;   20
To presume thereupon it is but a vanity,

Not certain but as a cherry-fair full of wo.
Reigned not I of late in great felicity?
  Et ecce, nunc in pulvere dormio.

Where was in my life such one as I
  While Lady Fortune with me had continuance?
Granted not she me to have victory
  In England to reign and to contribute France?
She took me by the hand and led me a dance,
  And with her sug'red lips on me she smiled;   30
But what for her dissembled countenance
  I could not beware till I was beguiled.
Now from this world she hath me exil'd
  When I was lothest hence for to go,
And I am in age but, as who saith, a child.
  Et ecce, nunc in pulvere dormio.

I had inough, I held me not content,
  Without remembrance that I should die,
And moreover to incroach ready was I bent;
  I knew not how long I should it occupy.   40
I made the Tower strong, I wist not why;
  I knew not to whom I purchased Tetersall,
I amended Dover on the mountain high,
  And London I provoked to fortify the wall;

I made Nottingham a place royal,
   Windsor, Eltham, and many other mo,
Yet at the last I went from them all.
   Et ecce, nunc in pulvere dormio.

Where is now my conquest and victory?
   Where is my riches and my royal array?   50
Where be my coursers and my horses high?
   Where is my mirth, my solace, and play?
As vanity, to nought all is wand'red away.
   O Lady Bess, long for me may ye call,
For I am departed till domesday;
   But love ye that Lord that is sovereign of all.
Where be my castles and buildings royal?
   But Windsor alone, now I have no mo,
And of Eton the prayers perpetual.
   Et ecce, nunc in pulvere dormio.   60

Why should a man be proud or presume high?
   Sainct Bernard thereof nobly doth treat,
<Saith> a man is nothing but a sack of stercory,
   And shall return unto worm's meat.
Why, what came of Alexander the Great
   Or else of strong Sampson who can tell?
Were no worms ordained their flesh to frete?
   And of Salomon, that was of wit the well?
Absolon proffered his hear for to sell,
   Yet for all his beauty worms eat him also.   70
And I but late in honor did excel,
   Et ecce, nunc in pulvere dormio.

I have played my pageyond, now am I past.
   Ye wot well all I was of no great yeld.
Thus all thing concluded shall be at the last.
   When Death approacheth, then lost is the field.
Then sithen this world me no longer upheld,
   Nor nought would conserve me here in my place,
In manus tuas, Domine, my spirit up I yield,
   Humbly beseeching thee, God, of <thy> grace.   80
O ye curtess commons, your hearts unbrace,
   Benignly now to pray for me also,
For right well you know your king I was,
   Et ecce, nunc in pulvere dormio.

THE BOWGE OF COURT

THE PROLOGUE

In autumpn whan the sun *in Virgine*
By radiant heat enriped hath our corn,
Whan Luna, full of mutability,
As emperess the diadem hath worn
Of our pole arctic, smiling half in scorn
At our folly and our unsteadfastness,
The time whan Mars to war him did dress,

I, calling to mind the great auctority
Of poets old, which full craftily
Under as covert terms as could be   10
Can touch a truth and cloak <it> subtilly
With fresh utterance full sententiously,
Diverse in style, some spared not vice to write,
Some of mortality nobly did endite—

Whereby I rede their renome and their fame
May never die, but evermore endure—
I was sore moved to aforce the same,
But Ignorance full soon did me discure
And shewed that in this art I was not sure;
For to illumine, she said, I was too dull,   20
Advising me my pen away to pull

And not to write, for he so will attain
Exceedingly further than his cunning is;
His heed may be hard, but feeble is <his> brain,
Yet have I known such ere this.
But of reproach surely he may not miss
That climbeth higher than he may footing have;
What and he slide down, who shall him save?

Thus up and down my mind was drawn and cast
That I ne wist what to do was best,   30
So sore enwearied that I was at the last
Enforced to sleep and for to take some rest
And to lie down as soon as I me dress'd.
At Harwichport, slumb'ring as I lay
In mine host's house called Power's Key,

Methought I saw a ship goodly of sail
Come sailing forth into that haven broad,
Her tackling rich and of high apparail,
She cast an anchor, and there she lay at road;
Marchants her boarded to see what she had <load>;   40
Therein they found royal marchandise
Fraighted with pleasure of what ye could devise.

But than I thought I would not dwell behind;
Among all other I put myself in prece.
Than there could I none acquaintance find;
There was much noise; anon one cried, "Cease,"
Sharply commanding each man hold his peace.
"Maisters," he said, "the ship that ye here see,
The *Bowge of Court* it hight for certainty.

"The owner thereof is lady of estate   50
Whose name to tell is Dame Sans Peer;
Her marchandise is rich and fortunate,
But who will have it must pay therefore dear.
This royal chaffer that is shipped here
Is called favor, to stond in her good grace."
Than should ye see there, pressing in apace,

Of one and other that would this lady see,
Which sat behind a traves of silk fine,
Of gold of tessew the finest that might be,
In a trone which far clearer did shine   60
Than Phebus in his sphere celestine;
Whose beauty, honor, goodly port
I have too little cunning to report.

But of each thing there, as I took heed,
Among all other was written in her trone
In gold letters this word which I did read:
Gardez le fortune qui est mauvelz et bone!
And, as I stood reading this verse myself alone,
Her chief gentlewoman, Danger by her name,
Gave me a taunt and said I was to blame   70

To be so pert to prese so proudly up.
She said she trowed that I had eaten sauce;
She asked if ever I drank of sauce's cup.
And I than softly answered to that clause
That, so to say, I had given her no cause;
Than asked she me, "Sir, so God thee speed,
What is thy name?" And I said it was Drede.

"What moved thee," quod she, "hidder to come?"
"Forsooth," quod I, "to buy some of your ware."
And with that word on me she gave a glome   80
With brows bent, and gan on me to stare
Full dainously, and fro me she did fare,
Leaving me stonding as a mazed man,
To whom there came another gentlewoman.

Desire her name was, and so she me told,
Saying to me, "Brother, be of good cheer,
Abash you not, but hardely be bold;
Avance yourself to approach and come near.
What though our chaffer be never so dear,
Yet I avise you to speak, for ony drede.   90
Who spareth to speak, in faith, he spareth to speed."

"Maistress," quod I, "I have none acquaintance
That will for me be mediator and mean,
But this another, I have but small substance."
"Peace," quod Desire, "ye speak not worth a bean.
If ye have not, in faith, I will you lene
A precious jewel, no richer in this lond.
Bon Aventure have here now in your hond.

"Shift now therewith, let see, as ye can
In Bowge of Court chevisance to make,   100
For I dare say that there nis earthly man
But, and he can Bon Aventure take,
There can no favor nor friendship him forsake.
Bon Aventure may bring you in such case
That ye shall stond in favor and in grace.

"But of one thing I warn you ere I go:
She that steereth the ship, make her your friend."
"Maistress," quod I, "I pray you tell me why so,
And how I may that way and means find."
"Forsooth," quod she, "however blow the wind,   110
Fortune guideth and ruleth all our ship;
Whom she hateth shall over the shipboard skip;

"Whom she loveth, of all pleasure is rich,
Whiles she laugheth and hath lust for to play;
Whom she hateth she casteth in the dich,
For whan she frowneth she thinketh to make a fray.
She cherisheth him, and him she chaseth away."
"Alas," quod I, "how might I have her sure?"
"In faith," quod she, "by Bon Aventure."

Thus in a row of marchants a great rout   120
Sued to Fortune that she would be their friend;
They throng in fast and flocked her about,
And I with them prayed her to have in mind.
She promised to us all she would be kind;
Of Bowge of Court she asketh what we would have,
And we asked favor, and favor she us gave.

Thus endeth the prologue

DREDE

The sail is up, Fortune ruleth our helm,
We want no wind to pass now over all;
Favor we have tougher then any elm,
That will abide and never from us fall.   130
But under honey ofttime lieth bitter gall,
For, as methought, in our ship I did see
Full subtle persons, in number four and three.

The first was Favel, full of flattery,
With fables false that well could feign a tale;
The second was Suspect, which that daily
Misdempt each man, with face deadly and pale;
And Harvey Hafter, that well could pick a male,
With other four of their affinity,
Disdain, Riot, Dissimuler, Subtilty.   140

Fortune their friend, with whom oft she did dance,
They could not fail, they thought, they were so sure;
And oftentimes I would myself avance
With them to make solace and pleasure.
But my disport they could not well endure;
They said they hated for to deal with Drede.
Than Favel gan with fair speech me to feed.

FAVEL

"Nothing earthly that I wonder so sore
As of your cunning, that is so excellent.
Dainty to have with us such one in store,   150

So virtuously that hath his days spent.
Fortune to you gifts of grace hath lent.
Lo, what it is a man to have cunning!
All earthly treasour it is surmounting.

"Ye be an apt man as ony can be found
To dwell with us and serve my lady's grace;
Ye be to her, yea, worth a thousand pound.
I heard her speak of you within short space,
When there were diverse that sore did you menace,
And, though I say it, I was myself your friend,   160
For here be diverse to you that be unkind.

"But this one thing, ye may be sure of me;
For by that Lord that bought dear all mankind,
I cannot flatter, I must be plain to thee,
And ye need ought, man, shew to me your mind,
For ye have me whom faithful ye shall find.
Whiles I have ought, by God, thou shalt not lack,
And if need be, a bold word I dare crack.

"Nay, nay, be sure, whiles I am on your side,
Ye may not fall, trust me, ye may not fail.   170
Ye stand in favor, and Fortune is your guide;
And as she will, so shall our great ship sail.
These lewd cockwats shall nevermore prevail
Against you hardely; therefore be not afraid.
Farewell till soon—but no word that I said!"

DREDE

Than thanked I him for his great gentleness,
But, as methought, he ware on him a cloak
That lined was with doubtful doubleness;
Methought of words that he had full a poke;
His stomach stuffed ofttimes did reboke.   180
Suspicion, methought, met him at a braid,
And I drew near to herk what they two said.

"In faith," quod Suspect, "spake Drede no word of me?"
"Why, what than? Wilt thou let men to speak?
He saith he cannot well accord with thee."
"Twish," quod Suspect, "go play, him I ne reke."
"By Christ," quod Favel, "Drede is sullen freak.
What, let us hold him up, man, for a while!"
"Ye so," quod Suspect, "he may us both beguile."

And whan he came walking soberly,   190
With "whom" and "ha," and with a crooked look,
Methought his heed was full of jealousy,
His eyen rolling, his honds fast they quoke,
And to meward the straight way he took.
"Godspeed, brother," to me quod he than,
And thus to talk with me he began.

SUSPICION

"Ye remember the gentleman right now
That commaund with you, methought a ⟨pretty space⟩?
Beware of him, for, I make God avow,
He will beguile you and speak fair to your face.   200
Ye never dwelt in such another place,
For here is none that dare well other trust,
But I would tell you a thing and I durst.

"Spake he, a-faith, no word to you of me?
I wote and he did ye would me tell.
I have a favor to you, whereof it be
That I must shew you much of my counsel.
But I wonder what the devil of hell
He said of me whan he with you did talk.
By mine advise, use not with him to walk.   210

"The sovereign'st thing that any man may have
Is little to say, and much to hear and see;
For, but I trusted you, so God me save,
I would nothing so plain be;
To you only, methink, I durst shrive me,
For now am I plenarly disposed
To shew you things that may not be disclosed."

DREDE

Than I assured him my fidelity
His counsel secret never to discure,
If he could find in heart to trust me;   220
Else I prayed him, with all my besy cure,
To keep it himself, for than he might be sure
That no man earthly could him bewray,
Whiles of his mind it were lock'd with the key.

"By God," quod he, "this and thus it is!"
And of his mind he shewed me all and some.
"Farewell," quod he, "we will talk more of this."
So he departed there he would be come.
I dare not speak, I promised to be dumb,
But as I stood musing in my mind,   230
Harvey Hafter came leaping, light as lind.

Upon his breast he bare a versing-box,
His throat was clear, and lustily could feign.
Methought his gown was all furred with fox,
And ever he sang, "Sith I am nothing plain."
To keep him from picking it was a great pain.
He gazed on me with his goatish beard;
Whan I looked on him, my purse was half afeard.

HARVEY HAFTER

"Sir, God you save! Why look ye so sad?
What thing is that I may do for you?   240
A wonder thing that ye wax not mad,

For, and I study should as ye do now,
My wit would waste, I make God avow.
Tell me your mind. Methink ye make a verse;
I could it scan, and ye would <it> rehearse.

"But to the point shortly to proceed,
Where hath your dwelling been ere ye came here?
For, as I trow, I have seen you indeed
Ere this, whan that ye made me royal cheer.
Hold up the helm, look up, and let God steer!   250
I would be merry, what wind that ever blow!
'Heave and ho rumbelow, row the boat, Norman, row!'

" 'Princes of Yought' can ye sing by rote?
Or 'Shall I Sail with You' a fellowship assay?
For on the book I cannot sing a note.
Would to God it would please you some day
A ballad book before me for to lay
And learn me to sing re-mi-fa-sol!
And, when I fail, bob me on the noll. . . .

"For, as for me, I served here many a day,   260
And yet unneth I can have my living.
But I require you no word that I say,
For, and I know ony earthly thing
That is again you, ye shall have weeting.
And ye be welcome, sir, so God me save.
I hope hereafter a friend of you to have."

DREDE

With that, as he departed so fro me,
Anon there met with him, as methought,
A man, but wonderly beseen was he.
He looked haughty; he set each man at nought;   270
His gaudy garment with scorns was all wrought;
With indignation lined was his hood;
He frowned as he would swear by Cock's blood.

He bote the lip; he looked passing coy;
His face was belimmed as bees had him stung;
It was no time with him to jape nor toy;
Envy hath wasted his liver and his lung;
Hatred by the heart so had him wrung
That he looked pale as ashes to my sight.
Disdain, I ween, this comerous crab's hight.   280

To Harvey Hafter than he spake of me,
And I drew near to hark what they two said.
"Now," quod Disdain, "as I shall saved be,
I have great scorn and am right evil apayed."
Than quod Harvey, "Why art thou so dismay'd?"
"By Christ," quod he, "for it is shame to say:
To see Johan Dawes, that came but yesterday,

"How he is now taken in conceit.
This Doctor Dawcock, Drede, I ween, he hight!
By God's bones, but if we have some sleight   290
It is like he will stond in your light."
"By God," quod Harvey, "and it so happen might.
Let us therefore shortly, at a word,
Find some mean to cast him over the bord."

"By Him that me bought," than quod Disdain,
"I wonder sore he is in such conceit."
"Turd!" quod Hafter, "I will thee nothing sain:
There must for him be laid some pretty bait.
We twain, I trow, be not without disceit.
First pick a quarrel and fall out with him then,   300
And so outface him with a card of ten."

Forthwith he made on me a proud assawt,
With scornful look meved all in mood;
He went about to take me in a fawt:
He frown'd, he stared, he stamped where he stood.
I looked on him, I wend he had be wood.
He set the arm proudly under the side,
And in this wise he gan with me to chide.

DISDAIN

"Rememb'rest thou what thou said yesternight?
Wilt thou abide by the words again?   310
By God, I have of thee now great dispite!
I shall thee anger ones in every vein;
It is great scorn to see such an hain
As thou art, one that came but yesterday,
With us old servants such maisters to play. . . ."

DREDE

With that came Riot rushing all at ones,
A rusty galland, to-ragged and to-rent,
And on the bord he whirled a pair of bones,
"Quarter-trey-deuce," he clattered as he went;
"Now have at all, by Saint Thomas of Kent!"   320
And ever he threw and kyst I wote ne'er what;
His hair was grown thorow out his hat.

Than I behild how he disguised was:
His heed was heavy for watching overnight,
His eyen bleared, his face shone like a glass,
His gown so short that it ne cover might
His rump, he went so all for summer light;
His hose was garded with a list of green,
Yet at the knee they were broken, I ween. . . .

What should I tell more of his ribaudry?   330
I was ashamed so to hear him prate;
He had no pleasure but in harlotry.
"Ay," quod he, "in the Devil's date,

What art thou? I saw thee now but late."
"Forsooth," quod I, "in this court I dwell now."
"Welcome," quod Riot, "I make God avow."

RIOT

"And, sir, in faith, why com'st not us among
To make thee merry, as other fellows done?
Thou must swear and stare, man, all day long,
And wake all night, and sleep till it be noon.   340
Thou may'st not study or muse on the moon;
This world is nothing but eat, drink, and sleep,
And thus with us good company to keep. . . ."

DREDE

Gone is this knave, this ribaud foul and lewd.
He ran as fast as ever that he might.
Unthriftiness in him may well be shewed,
For whom Tyburn groaneth both day and night;
And as I stood and cast aside my sight,
Disdain I saw with Dissimulation
Standing in sad communication.   350

But there was pointing and nodding with the head,
And many words said in secret wise;
They wand'red ay, and stood still in no stead.
Methought alway Dissimuler did devise
Me passing sore; mine heart than gan agrise.
I dempt and dread their talking was not good.
Anon Dissimuler came where I stood.

Than in his hood I saw there faces twain:
That one was lean and like a pined ghost,
That other looked as he would me have slain;   360
And to meward as he gan for to coast,
Whan that he was even at me almost,
I saw a knife hid in his one sleeve,
Whereon was written this word, "Mischief."

And in his other sleeve methought I saw
A spoon of gold, full of honey sweet
To feed a fool and for to prey a daw;
And on that sleeve these words were wrete,
"A false abstract cometh from a false concrete."
His hood was side, his cope was roset gray.   370
These were the words that he to me did say.

DISSIMULATION

"How do ye, maister, ye look so soberly?
As I be saved at the dreadful day,
It is a perilous vice, this envy.
Alas, a cunning man ne dwell may
In no place well, but fools with <him> fray.
But as for that, cunning hath no foe
Save him that nought can—Scripture saith so.

"I know your virtue and your literature
By that little cunning that I have.   380
Ye be maligned sore, I you ensure,
But ye have craft yourself alway to save.
It is great scorn to see a misproud knave
With a clerk that cunning is to prate.
Let them go louse them, in the Devil's date!

"For albeit that this long not to me,
Yet on my back I bear such lewd dealing.
Right now I spake with one, I trow, I see—
But what?—a straw! I may not tell all thing
By God, I say there is great heart-brenning   390
Between the person ye wot of <and> you.
Alas, I could not deal so with an Yew.

"I would each man were as plain as I.
It is a world, I say, to hear of some.
I hate this feigning, fie upon it, fie!
A man cannot wote where to be come.
Iwis I could tell—but humlery, home!
I dare not speak, we be so laid await,
For all our court is full of desceit. . . ."

DREDE

Sodainly, as he departed me fro,   400
Came pressing in one in a wonder array.
Ere I was ware, behind me he said, "Bo!"
Than I, astonied of that sodain fray,
Stert all at ones, I liked nothing his play;
For if I had not quickly fled the touch,
He had pluck'd out the nobles of my pouch.

He was trussed in a garment strait;
I have not seen such another's page,
For he could well upon a casket wait,
His <hood> all pounced and garded like a cage.   410
Light lime-finger, he took none other wage.
"Harken," quod he, "lo, here mine hond in thine,
To us welcome thou art, by Sainct Quintine."

DISCEIT

"But by that Lord that is one, two, and three,
I have an errand to round in your ear.
He told me so, by God, ye may trust me.
Parde, remember whan ye were there,
There I winked on you—wot ye not where?
In A loco, I mean juxta B—
Wo is him that is blind and may not see!   420

"But to hear the subtilty and the craft
As I shall tell you, if ye will hark again,
And, whan I saw the whoresons would you haft,
To hold mine hond, by God, I had great pain

dream allegory (handwritten annotation)

For forthwith there I had him slain
But that I dread morder would come out.
Who dealeth with shrews hath need to look about."

Drede

And as he rounded thus in mine ear
Of false collusion confett'red by assent,
Methought I see lewd fellows here and there   430
Came for to slee me of mortal entent;
And, as they came, the shipboard fast I hent

And thought to leap, and even with that woke,
Caught pen and ink, and wrote this little book.

I would therewith no man were miscontent,
Beseeching you that shall it see or read,
In every point to be indifferent,
Sith all in substance of slumb'ring doth proceed.
I will not say it is matter indeed,
But yet ofttime such dreams be found true.   440
Now construe ye what is the residue.

PHILIP SPARROW

Pla ce bo,
Who is there, who?
Di le xi,
Dame Margery;
Fa, re, mi, mi,
Wherefore and why, why?
For the soul of Philip Sparrow,
That was late slain at Carrow
Among the Nuns Black.
For that sweet soul's sake,   10
And for all sparrows' souls
Set in our bead-rolls,
Pater noster qui,
With an *Ave Mari,*
And with the corner of a creed,
The more shall be your meed.

  Whan I remember again
How my Philip was slain,
Never half the pain
Was between you twain,   20
Pyramus and Thisbe,
As than befell to me.
I wept and I wailed,
The tears down hailed;
But nothing it availed
To call Philip again,
Whom Gib, our cat, hath slain.
  Gib, I say, our cat,
Worrowed her on that
Which I loved best.   30
It cannot be express'd
My sorrowful heaviness,
But all without redress;
For within that stound,
Half slumb'ring, in a sound
I fell down to the ground.
  Unneth I kest mine eyes
Toward the cloudy skies.
But when I did behold
My sparrow dead and cold,   40
No creature but that wold

Have rued upon me,
To behold and see
What heaviness did me pang;
Wherewith my hands I wrang,
That my senows cracked,
As though I had been racked,
So pained and so strained,
That no life well-nigh remained.
  I sighed and I sobbed,   50
For that I was robbed
Of my sparrow's life.
O maiden, widow, and wife,
Of what estate ye be,
Of high or low degree,
Great sorrow then ye might see,
And learn to weep at me!
Such paines did me frete,
That mine heart did beat,
My visage pale and dead,   60
Wan, and blue as lead;
The pangs of hateful death
Well-nigh stopped my breath.
Heu, heu, me,
That I am wo for thee!
Ad Dominum cum tribularer clamavi.
Of God nothing else crave I
But Philip's soul to keep
From the marees deep
Of Acheronte's well,   70
That is a flood of hell;
And from the great Pluto,
The prince of endless wo;
And from foul Alecto,
With visage black and blo;
And from Medusa, that mare,
That like a fiend doth stare;
And from Megera's edders,
For ruffling of Philip's feathers,
And from her fiery sparklings,   80
For burning of his wings;
And from the smokes sour
Of Proserpina's bower:

And from the dens dark,
Where Cerberus doth bark,
Whom Theseus did afray,
Whom Hercules did outray,
As famous poets say;
For that hell-hound,
That lieth in chains bound,   90
With ghastly heads three,
To Jupiter pray we
That Philip preserved may be!
Amen, say ye with me!
Do mi nus,
Help now, sweet Jesus!
Levavi oculos meos in montes:
Would God I had Zenophontes,
Or Socrates the wise,
To shew me their devise   100
Moderately to take
This sorrow that I make
For Philip Sparrow's sake!
So fervently I shake,
I feel my body quake;
So urgently I am brought
Into careful thought.
Like Andromaca, Hector's wife,
Was weary of her life,
When she had lost her joy,   110
Noble Hector of Troy;
In like manner also
Encreaseth my deadly wo,
For my sparrow is go.
It was so pretty a fool,
It would sit on a stool,
And learned after my school
For to keep his cut,
With "Philip, keep your cut!"
  It had a velvet cap,   120
And would sit upon my lap,
And seek after small worms,
And sometime white bread-crumbs;
And many times and oft
Between my breasts soft

It would lie and rest;
It was proper and prest.
   Sometime he would gasp
When he saw a wasp;
A fly or a gnat, 130
He would fly at that;
And pretely he would pant
When he saw an ant.
Lord, how he would pry
After the butterfly!
Lord, how he would hop
After the gressop!
And whan I said, "Phip, Phip!"
Then he would leap and skip,
And take me by the lip. 140
Alas, it will me slo,
That Philip is gone me fro!
   Si in i qui ta tes,
Alas, I was evil at ease!
De pro fun dis cla ma vi,
When I saw my sparrow die!
   Now, after my dome,
Dame Sulpicia at Rome,
Whose name regist'red was
Forever in tables of brass 150
Because she did pass
In poesy to endite
And eloquently to write,
Though she would pretend
My sparrow to commend,
I trow she could not amend
Reporting the virtues all
Of my sparrow royal.
   For it would come and go
And flee so to and fro; 160
And on me it would leap
Whan I was asleep,
And his feathers shake,
Wherewith he would make
Me often for to wake,
And for to take him in
Upon my naked skin.
God wot, we thought no sin:
What though he crept so low?
It was no hurt, I trow; 170
He did nothing, perdee,
But sit upon my knee.
Philip, though he were nice,
In him it was no vice.
Philip had leave to go
To pick my little toe;
Philip might be bold
And do what he wold;
Philip would seek and take
All the fleas blake 180

That he could there espy
With his wanton eye.
   O pe ra,
La, sol, fa, fa,
Confitebor tibi, Domine, <in> toto corde meo.
   Alas, I would ride and go
A thousand mile of ground
If any such might be found;
It were worth an hundreth pound
Of King Cresus' gold, 190
Or of Attalus the old,
The rich prince of Pargame,
Whoso list the story to see.
Cadmus, that his sister sought,
And he should be bought
For gold and fee,
He should over the sea
To weet if he could bring
Any of the <off>spring,
Or any of the blood. 200
But whoso understood
Of Medea's art,
I would I had a part
Of her crafty magic!
My sparrow than should be quick
With a charm or twain,
And play with me again.
But all this is in vain
Thus for to complain.
   I took my sampler ones, 210
Of purpose, for the nones,
To sew with stitches of silk
My sparrow white as milk,
That by representacion
Of his image and facion
To me it might import
Some pleasure and comfort
For my solace and sport;
But whan I was sewing his beak,
Methought my sparrow did speak, 220
And open his pretty bill,
Saying, "Maid, ye are in will
Again me for to kill,
Ye prick me in the head!"
With that my needle ware red,
Methought, of Philip's blood;
Mine hear right upstood,
And was in such a fray,
My speech was taken away.
I kest down that there was, 230
And said, "Alas, alas,
How cometh this to pass?"
My fingers, dead and cold,
Could not my sampler hold;

My needle and threde
I threw away for drede.
The best now that I may,
Is for his soul to pray:
A porta inferi,
Good Lord, have mercy 240
Upon my sparrow's soul,
Written in my bead-roll!
   Au di vi vo cem,
Japhet, Ham, and Sem,
Ma gni fi cat,
Shew me the right path
To the hills of Armony,
Wherefore the birds yet cry
Of your father's boat,
That was sometime afloat, 250
And now they lie and rote,
Let some poets write;
Deucalion's flood it hight;
But as verily as ye be
The natural sons three
Of Noe the patriarch,
That made that great ark,
Wherein he had apes and owls,
Beasts, birds, and fowls,
That if ye can find 260
Any of my sparrow's kind
(God send the soul good rest!)
I would yet have a nest
As pretty and as prest
As my sparrow was.
But my sparrow did pass
All sparrows of the wood
That were since Noe's flood;
Was never none so good.
King Philip of Macedony 270
Had no such Philip as I,
No, no, sir, hardely.
   That vengeance I ask and cry,
By way of exclamacion,
On all the whole nacion
Of cats wild and tame;
God send them sorrow and shame!
That cat specially
That slew so cruelly
My little pretty sparrow 280
That I brought up at Carrow.
   O cat of churlish kind,
The fiend was in thy mind
Whan thou my bird untwined!
I would thou haddest been blind!
The leopards savage,
The lions in their rage,
Might catch thee in their paws,
And gnaw thee in their jaws!

The serpents of Libany   290
Might sting thee venemously!
The dragons with their toungues
Might poison thy liver and lungs!
The manticors of the mountains
Might feed them on thy brains!
   Melanchates, that hound
That plucked Acteon to the ground,
Gave him his mortal wound,
Changed to a deer,
The story doth appear,   300
Was changed to an hart:
So thou, foul cat that thou art,
The selfsame hound
Might thee confound,
That his own lord bote,
Might bite asunder thy throat!
   Of Ind the greedy gripes
Might tear out all thy tripes!
Of Arcady the bears
Might pluck away thine ears!   310
The wild wolf Lycaon
Bite asunder thy backbone!
Of Ethna the brenning hill,
That day and night brenneth still,
Set in thy tail a blaze,
That all the world may gaze
And wonder upon thee,
From occion the great sea
Unto the Iles of Orchady,
From Tilbury Ferry   320
To the Plain of Salisbury!
So traitorously my bird to kill
That never ought thee evil will!
   Was never bird in cage
More gentle of corage
In doing his homage
Unto his soverain.
Alas, I say again,
Death hath departed us twain.
The false cat hath thee slain;   330
Farewell, Philip, adieu!
Our Lord thy soul rescue!
Farewell without restore,
Farewell for evermore!
   And it were a Jew,
It would make one rue,
To see my sorrow new.
These villanous false cats
Were made for mice and rats,
And not for birds small!   340
Alas, my face waxeth pale,
Telling this piteous tale,
How my bird so fair,
That was wont to repair,

And go in at my spair,
And creep in at my gore
Of my gown before,
Flickering with his wings!
Alas, my hert it stings,
Rememb'ring pretty things!   350
Alas, mine heart it sleeth,
My Philip's doleful death,
Whan I remember it,
How pretely it would sit,
Many times and oft,
Upon my finger aloft!
I played with him tittle-tattle,
And fed him with my spattle,
With his bill between my lips,
It was my pretty Phips!   360
Many a pretty kuss
Had I of his sweet muss;
And now the cause is thus,
That he is slain me fro,
To my great pain and wo.
   Of Fortune this the chance
Standeth on variance:
Ofttime after pleasance
Trouble and grievance.
No man can be sure   370
Alway to have pleasure;
As well perceive ye may
How my disport and play
From me was taken away
By Gib, our cat savage,
That in furious rage
Caught Philip by the head,
And slew him there stark dead.
       Kyrie, eleison,
       Christe, eleison,   380
       Kyrie, eleison!
For Philip Sparrow's soul,
Set in our bead-roll,
Let us now whisper
A Pater noster.
   Lauda, anima mea, Dominum!
To weep with me look that ye come,
All manner of birds in your kind;
See none be left behind.
To mourning look that ye fall   390
With dolorous songs funeral,
Some to sing, and some to say,
Some to weep, and some to pray,
Every bird in his lay.
The goldfinch, the wagtail;
The jangling jay to rail,
The flecked pie to chatter
Of this dolorous matter;
And robin redbreast,

He shall be the priest   400
The requiem mass to sing,
Softly warbeling,
With help of the reed-sparrow
And the chattering swallow,
This hearse for to hallow;
The lark with his long toe;
The spink and the martinet also;
The shoveler with his broad beck;
The dotterel, that foolish peck,
And also the mad coot,   410
With a bald face to toot;
The fieldfare and the snite;
The crow and the kite;
The raven, called Rolfe,
His plain-song to solfe;
The partrich, the quail;
The plover with us to wail;
The woodhack, that singeth "chur"
Hoarsely, as he had the murr;
The lusty chanting nightingale;   420
The popinjay to tell her tale,
That tooteth oft in a glass,
Shall read the Gospel at mass;
The mavis with her whistle
Shall read there the Pistle.
But with a large and a long
To keep just plain-song,
Our chanters shall be the cuckove,
The culver, the stockdove.
With puwyt the lapwing   430
The versicles shall sing.
The bitter with his bump,
The crane with his trump,
The swan of Menander,
The goose and the gander,
The duck and the drake,
Shall watch at this wake.
The peacock so proud,
Because his voice is loud,
And hath a glorious tail,   440
He shall sing the Grail.
The owl, that <is> so foul,
Must help us to howl.
The heron so gaunt,
And the cormorant,
With the pheasant,
And the gaggling gant,
And the churlish chough;
The rout and the kough;
The barnacle, the buzzard,   450
With the wild mallard;
The divendop to sleep;
The water-hen to weep;
The puffin and the teal

Money they shall deal
To poor folk at large,
That shall be their charge;
The seamew and the titmouse;
The woodcock with the long nose;
The threstil with her warbling;   460
The starling with her brabbling;
The rook, with the osprey
That putteth fishes to a fray;
And the dainty curlew,
With the turtle most true.

    At this *Placebo*
We may not well forgo
The count'ring of the co;
The stork also,
That maketh his nest   470
In chimneys to rest;
Within those walls
No broken galls
May there abide
Of cuckoldry side,
Or else philosophy
Maketh a great lie.

    The estridge, that will eat
An horshowe so great,
In the stead of meat,   480
Such fervent heat
His stomach doth freat;
He cannot well fly,
Nor sing tunably,
Yet at a brayd
He hath well assay'd
To solf above ela,
Fa, lorell, fa, fa;
Ne quando
Male cantando,   490
The best that we can,
To make him our bellman,
And let him ring the bells;
He can do nothing els.

    Chanticleer, our cock,
Must tell what is of the clock
By the astrology
That he hath naturally
Conceived and caught,
And was never taught   500
By Albumazer
The astronomer,
Nor by Ptolomy
Prince of astronomy,
Nor yet by Haly;
And yet he croweth daily
And nightly the tides
That no man abides,
With Partlot his hen,

Whom now and then   510
He plucketh by the head
Whan he doth her tread.

    The bird of Araby,
That potentially
May never die,
And yet there is none
But one alone;
A phoenix it is
This hearse that must bliss
With aromatic gums   520
That cost great sums,
The way of thurification
To make fumigation
Sweet of reflayre,
And redolent of ayre,
This corse for ⟨to⟩ sence
With great reverence,
As patriarch or pope
In a black cope.
Whiles he senceth ⟨the hearse⟩   530
He shall sing the verse,
Libera me,
In de, la, sol, re,
Softly bemole,
For my sparrow's soul.
Pliny sheweth all
In his story natural
What he doth find
Of the phoenix kind;
Of whose incineracion   540
There riseth a new creacion
Of the same facion
Without alteracion,
Saving that old age
Is turned into corage
Of fresh youth again:
This matter true and plain,
Plain matter indeed,
Whoso list to read.

    But for the eagle doth fly   550
Highest in the sky,
He shall be thy sedean,
The quere to demean,
As provost principal,
To teach them their ordinal.
Also the noble falcon,
With the gerfalcon,
The tarsel gentil,
They shall mourn soft and still
In their amisse of gray;   560
The saker with them shall say
Dirige for Philip's soul;
The goshawk shall have a roll
The querestrers to control;

The lanners and marlions   510
Shall stand in their mourning gowns;
The hobby and the musket
The censers and the cross shall fet;
The kestrel in all this wark
Shall be holy water clark.   570

    And now the dark cloudy night
Chaseth away Phoebus bright,
Taking his course toward the west,
God send my sparrow's soul good rest!
Requiem aeternam dona eis, Domine!
Fa, fa, fa, mi, re,
A por ta in fe ri,
Fa, fa, fa, mi, mi.
    Credo videre bona Domini,
I pray God, Philip to heaven may
    fly!   580
Domine, exaudi orationem meam!
To heaven he shall, from heaven he
    came!
    Do mi nus vo bis cum!
Of all good prayers God send him
    some!
    Oremus:
Deus, cui proprium est misereri et parcere,
On Philip's soul have pity!
For he was a pretty cock,
And came of a gentle stock,
And wrapt in a maiden's smock,   590
And cherished full daintily,
Till cruel fate made him to die:
Alas, for doleful destiny!
But whereto should I
Lenger mourn or cry?
To Jupiter I call,
Of heaven emperial,
That Philip may fly
Above the sterry sky,
To tread the pretty wren,   600
That is our Lady's hen:
Amen, amen, amen!

    Yet one thing is behind,
That now cometh to mind.
An epitaph I would have
For Philip's grave;
But for I am a maid,
Timerous, half afraid,
That never yet assay'd
Of Elicon's well,   610
Where the muses dwell—
Though I can read and spell,
Recount, report, and tell
Of the *Tales of Canterbury,*
Some sad stories, some merry. . . .

[Here Jane Scroop itemizes her extensive reading in elegiac poetry.]

For, as I tofore have said,
I am but a young maid,
And cannot in effect
My style as yet direct
With English words elect.   620
Our natural tongue is rude,
And hard to be enneude
With polished terms lusty;
Our language is so rusty,
So cankered and so full
Of frowards, and so dull,
That if I would apply
To write ordinately,
I wot not where to find
Terms to serve my mind.   630
    Gower's English is old,
And of no value is told;
His matter is worth gold,
And worthy to be enrol'd.
    In Chaucer I am sped,
His tales I have read.
His matter is delectable,
Solacious, and commendable;
His English well allowed,
So as it is enprowed,   640
For as it is employed
There is no English void,
At those days much commended;
And now men would have amended
His English, whereat they bark,
And mar all they wark:
Chaucer, that famous clark,
His terms were not dark,
But pleasant, easy and plain;
No word he wrote in vain.   650
    Also John Lydgate
Writeth after an higher rate;
It is diffuse to find
The sentence of his mind,
Yet writeth he in his kind,
No man that can amend
Those matters that he hath penn'd;
Yet some men find a faut,
And say he writeth too haut.
    Wherefore hold me excused   660
If I have not well perused
Mine English half abused;
Though it be refused,
In worth I shall it take,
And fewer words make.
    But, for my sparrow's sake,
Yet as a woman may,

My wit I shall assay
An epitaph to write
In Latin plain and light,   670
Whereof the elegy
Followeth by and by:
Flos volucrum formose, vale!
Philip, sub isto
Marmore iam recubas,
Qui mihi carus eras.
Semper erunt ni<t>ido
Radiantia sidera c<o>elo;
Impressusque meo
Pectore semper eris. . . .   680

THE TUNNING
OF ELINOUR RUMMING

Tell you I chill,
If that ye will
A while be still,
Of a comely gill
That dwelt on a hill:
But she is not grill,
For she is somewhat sage
And well worn in age.
For her visage
It would assuage   10
A man's courage.
    Her lothly lere
Is nothing clear,
But ugly of cheer,
Droopy and drowsy,
Scurvy and lousy;
Her face all bowsy,
Comely crinkled,
Wondersly wrinkled,
Like a roast pig's ear,   20
Bristled with hear.
    Her lewd lips twain,
They slaver, men sain,
Like a ropy rain,
A gummy glair.
She is ugly fair:
Her nose somedele hooked,
And camously crooked,
Never stopping,
But ever dropping;   30
Her skin loose and slack,
Grained like a sack;
With a crooked back.
    Her eyen gowndy
Are full unsowndy,
For they are bleared;
And she gray-heared,
Jawed like a jetty;
A man would have pity

To see how she is gummed,   40
Fingered and thumbed,
Gently jointed,
Greased and anointed
Up to the knuckles;
The bones <of> her <huckles>
<Like as they were with buckles>
Together made fast.
Her youth is far past.
Footed like a plane,
Legs like a crane;   50
And yet she will jet
Like a jolly fet,
In her furred flocket,
And gray russet rocket,
With simper-the-cocket.
Her huke of Lincoln green,
It had been hers, I ween,
More then forty year,
And so it doth appear;
And the green bare threeds   60
Look like sere weeds,
Withered like hay,
The wool worn away.
And yet I dare say
She thinketh herself gay
Upon the holy day
Whan she doth her array
And girdeth in her geets
Stitched and pranked with pleats;
Her kirtle Bristow-red,   70
With clothes upon her head
That they weigh a sow of lead,
Writhen in a wonder wise,
After the Sarasins' guise,
With a whim wham
Knit with a trim tram
Upon her brain pan;
Like an Egyptian
Capped about.
Whan she goeth out   80
Herself for to shew,
She driveth down the dew
With a pair of heels
As broad as two wheels;
She hobbles as a gose
With her blanket hose,
Her shone smeared with tallow,
Greased upon dirt
That baudeth her skirt.

PRIMUS PASSUS

And this comely dame,   90
I understand, her name
Is Elinour Rumming,

At home in her wonning;
And as men say
She dwelt in Sothray,
In a certain stead
Byside Lederhead.
She is a tonnish gib;
The devil and she be sib.

But to make up my tale, 100
She breweth noppy ale,
And maketh thereof port-sale
To travelers, to tinkers,
To sweaters, to swinkers,
And all good ale drinkers,
That will nothing spare
But drink till they stare
And bring themself bare,
With "Now away the mare,
And let us slay care," 110
As wise as an hare!

Come whoso will
To Elinour on the hill,
With "Fill the cup, fill,"
And sit thereby still,
Early and late.
Thither cometh Kate,
Cisly, and Sare,
With their legs bare,
And also their feet 120
Hardely full unsweet;
With their heels dagged,
Their kirtles all to-jagged,
Their smocks all to-ragged,
With titters and tatters,
Bring dishes and platters,
With all their might running
To Elinour Rumming,
To have of her tunning;
She leaneth them of the same, 130
And thus beginneth the game.

Some wenches come unbraced,
<Some huswives come unlaced,>
With their naked paps
That flips and flaps;
It wigs and it wags,
Like tawny saffron bags;
A sort of foul drabs
All scurvy with scabs.
Some be fly-bitten, 140
Some skewed as a kitten;
Some with a shoe-clout
Bind their heads about;
Some have no hear-lace,
Their locks about their face,
Their tresses untruss'd
All full of unlust;

Some look strawry,
Some cawry mawry;
Full untidy tegs, 150
Like rotten eggs.
Such a lewd sort
To Elinour resort
From tide to tide.
Abide, abide,
And to you shall be told
How her ale is sold
To Mawt and to Mold.

SECUNDUS PASSUS

Some have no money
That thither comey 160
For their ale to pay,
That is a shrewd array!
Elinour sweared, "Nay,
Ye shall not bear away
My ale for nought,
By Him that me bought."
With "Hey, dog, hey,
Have these dogs away!"
With "Get me a staff,
The swine eat my draff! 170
Strike the hogs with a club,
They have drunk up my swilling-
    tub!"
For, be there never so much prese,
These swine go to the high dese;
The sow with her pigs;
The boar his tail wrigs,
Against the high bench!
With "Fo, there is a stench!
Gather up, thou wench;
Seest thou not what is fall? 180
Take up drit and all,
And bear out of the hall:
God geve it ill preving
Cleanly as evil cheving!"
    But let us turn plain
There we left again.
For as ill a patch as that
The hens run in the mash-fat;
For they go to roost
Straight over the ale-joust, 190
And dung, whan it comes,
In the ale tuns.
Then Elinour taketh
The mash-bowl, and shaketh
The hens' dung away,
And skommeth it in a tray
Whereas the yeast is,
With her mangy fistis,
And sometime she blens

The dung of her hens 200
And the ale together;
And saith, "Gossip, come hither,
This ale shall be thicker,
And flower the more quicker;
For I may tell you,
I learned it of a Jew,
Whan I began to brew,
And I have found it true;
Drink now while it is new;
And ye may it brook, 210
It shall make you look
Younger then ye be
Years two or three,
For ye may prove it by me.
Behold," she said, "and see
How bright I am of ble!
Ich am not cast away,
That can my husband say,
Whan we kiss and play
In lust and in liking; 220
He calleth me his whiting,
His mulling and his miting,
His nobs and his cony,
His sweeting and his honey,
With 'Bass, my pretty bonny,
Thou art worth good and money!'
This make I my falyre fonny,
Till that he dream and dronny,
For, after all our sport,
Than will he rout and snort; 230
Then sweetly together we lie,
As two pigs in a sty."

    To cease me seemeth best,
And of this tale to rest,
And for to leave this letter,
Because it is no better,
And because it is no sweeter;
We will no farther rime,
Of it at this time;
But we will turn plain 240
Where we left again.

TERTIUS PASSUS

Instead of coin and money
Some bring her a cony,
And some a pot with honey,
Some a salt, and some a spoon,
Some their hose, some their shoon;
Some ran a good trot
With a skillet or a pot;
Some fill their pot full
Of good Lemster wool: 250
An huswife of trust
Whan she is a-thrust

Such a web can spin,
Her thrift is full thin.
    Some go straight thither,
Be it slaty or slider;
They hold the highway,
They care not what men say,
Be that as be may.
Some, loth to be espi'd,   260
Some start in at the back side,
Over the hedge and pale,
And all for the good ale.
Some ren till they swete,
Bring with them malt or wheat,
And Dame Elinour entreat
To birle them of the best.
Than cometh another guest;
She sweared by the rood of rest,
Her lips are so dry,   270
Without drink she must die;
"Therefore fill it by and by,
And have here a peck of rye."
    Anon cometh another,
As dry as the other,
And with her doth bring
Meal, salt, or other thing,
Her harvest girdle, her wedding ring,
To pay for her scot
As cometh to her lot.   280
Some bringeth her husband's hood,
Because the ale is good;
Another brought her his cap
To offer to the ale-tap,
With flax and with tow;
And some brought sour dough;
With "Hey," and with "Ho!
Sit we down a row,
And drink till we blow,
And pipe 'Tirly Tirlow'!"   290
    Some laid to pledge
Their hatchet and their wedge,
Their heckle and their reel,
Their rock, their spinning-wheel;
And some went so narrow,
They laid to pledge their wharrow,
Their ribskin and their spindle,
Their needle and their thimble.
Here was scant thrift
Whan they made such shift.   300
Their thrust was so great,
They asked never for meat,
But "Drink, still drink,
And let the cat wink,
Let us wash our gums
From the dry crumbs!"

QUARTUS PASSUS

Some for very need
Lay down a skein of threed,
And some a skein of yarn;
<Some brought from the barn>   310
Both beans and peas;
Small chaffer doth ease
Sometime, now and than.
Another there was that ran
With a good brass pan;
Her color was full wan;
She ran in all the haste
Unbraced and unlac'd;
Tawny, swart, and sallow
Like a cake of tallow.   320
I swear by all hallow,
It was a stale to take
The devil in a brake.
    And than came halting Joan,
And brought a gambone
Of bacon that was reasty;
But, Lord, as she was testy,
Angry as a waspy,
She began to yane and gaspy,
And bad Elinour go bet,   330
And fill in good met;
It was dear that was far fet.
    Another brought a spick
Of a bacon flick;
Her tongue was very quick,
But she spake somewhat thick.
Her fellow did stammer and stut,
But she was a foul slut,
For her mouth foamed
And her belly groaned: 340
Joan sain she had eaten a fiest.
"By Christ," said she, "thou liest,
I have as sweet a breath
As thou, with shamefull death!"
Then Elinour said, "Ye callets,
I shall break your palettes,
Without ye now cease!"
And so was made the drunken peace.
Than thider came drunken Ales,
And she was full of tales,   350
Of tidings in Wales,
And of Sainct James in Gales,
And of the Portingales,
With "Lo, gossip, iwis,
Thus and thus it is:
There hath been great war
Between Temple Bar
And the Cross in Cheap,
And there came an heap

Of millstones in a rout."   360
She speaketh thus in her snout,
Sneveling in her nose,
As though she had the pose.
"Lo, here is an old tippet,
And ye will geve me a sippet
Of your stale ale,
God send you good sale!"
And as she was drinking,
She fell in a winking
With a barleyhood,   370
She piss'd where she stood;
Than began she to weep,
And forthwith fell on sleep.
Elinour took her up,
And blessed her with a cup
Of new ale in corns;
Ales found herein no thorns,
But supped it up at ones,
She found therein no bones.

QUINTUS PASSUS

Now in cometh another rabble: 380
First one with a ladle,
Another with a cradle,
And with a side saddle;
And there began a fabble,
A clattering and a babble
Of foolis filly
That had a foal with Willy,
With "Jast you!" and "Gup, gilly!"
She could not lie stilly.
Then came in a jennet,   390
And sware, "By Sainct Bennet,
I drank not this sennet
A draught to my pay!
Elinour, I thee pray
Of thine ale let us assay,
And have here a pilch of gray:
I wear skins of cony
That causeth I look so donny."
Another than did hitch her,
And brought a pottle-pitcher,   400
A tonnel, and a bottle,
But she had lost the stopple;
She cut off her shoe sole,
And stopped therewith the hole.
    Among all the blommer,
Another brought a skommer,
A frying pan and a slice;
Elinour made the price
For good ale each whit.
    Than start in mad Kit   410
That had little wit;
She seemed somedeal sick,

And brought up a penny chick
To Dame Elinour,
For a draught of liquor.
Than Margery Milkduck
Her kirtle she did up tuck
An inch above her knee,
Her legs that ye might see;
But they were sturdy and stubbed, 420
Mighty pestles and clubbed,
As fair and as white
As the foot of a kite.
She was somewhat foul,
Crook-necked like an owl;
And yet she brought her fees,
A cantle of Essex cheese
Was well a foot thick,
Full of maggots quick;
It was huge and great,   430
And mighty strong meat
For the devil to eat;
It was tart and punyete.
Another sort of sluts,
Some brought walnuts,
Some apples, some pears,
Some brought their clipping shears,
Some brought this and that,
Some brought I wote ne'er what,
Some brought their husband's hat, 440
Some puddings and links,
Some tripes that stinks.
   But of all this throng
One came them among,
She seemed half a leech,
And began to preach
Of the Tuesday in the week
Whan the mare doth keke,
Of the virtue of an unset leek,
Of her husband's breek.   450
With the feaders of a quail
She could to ⟨Bordeaux⟩ sail;
And with good ale barm
She could make a charm
To help withal a stitch:
She seemed to be a witch.
Another brought two goslings
That were naughty froslings;
⟨She⟩ brought them in a wallet;
She was a comely callet.   460
The goslings were untied;
Elinour began to chide,
"They be wrethocks thou hast brought,
They are sheer shaking nought!"

SEXTUS PASSUS

Maud Ruggy thither skipped:

She was ugly hipped,
And ugly thick lipped.
Like an onion sided,
Like tan ledder hided.
She had her so guided   470
Between the cup and the wall
That she was therewithal
Into a palsy fall;
With that her head shaked,
And her hands quaked;
One's head would have ached
To see her naked!
She drank so of the dregs
The dropsy was in her legs;
Her face glist'ring like glass, 480
All foggy fat she was.
She had also the gout
In all her joints about;
Her breath was sour and stale,
And smelled all of ale:
Such a bedfellaw
Would make one cast his craw!
But yet for all that
She drank on the mash-fat.
There came an old ribibe;   490
She halted of a kibe,
And had broken her shin
At the threshold coming in,
And fell so wide open
That one might see her token,
The devil thereon be wroken!
What need all this be spoken?
She yelled like a calf.
"Rise up, on God's half,"
Said Elinour Rumming,   500
"I beshrew thee for thy coming!"
As she at her did pluck,
"Quake, quake," said the duck
In that lampatram's lap;
With "Fie, cover thy shap
With some flip flap!
God geve it ill hap,"
Said Elinour, "for shame!"
Like an honest dame.
Up she start, half lame,   510
And scantly could go
For pain and for wo.
   In came another dant,
With a goose and a gant;
She had a wide weasant,
She was nothing pleasant,
Necked like an oliphant;
It was a bullifant,
A greedy cormorant.
   Another brought her garlic heads;
Another brought her beads   521

Of jet or of coal,
To offer to the ale pole.
Some brought a wimble,
Some brought a thimble,
Some brought a silk lace,
Some brought a pincase,
Some her husband's gown,
Some a pillow of down,
Some of the napery;[1]   530
And all this shift they make
For the good ale sake.
"A straw!" said Bele, "stand utter,
For we have eggs and butter,
And of pigeons a pair."[1]
   Than stert forth a fisgig,
And she brought a boar pig;
The flesh thereof was rank,
And her breath strongly stank;
Yet, or she went, she drank,   540
And gate her great thank
Of Elinour for her ware
That she thither bare
To pay for her share.
Now truly, to my thinking,
This is a solempn drinking.

SEPTIMUS PASSUS

"Soft!" quod one hight Sybil,
"And let me with you bibble."
She sate down in the place,
With a sorry face   550
Whey-wormed about.
Garnished was her snout
With here and there a puscul
Like a scabbed muscul.
"This ale," said she, "is noppy;
Let us sip and soppy,
And not spill a droppy,
For so mote I hoppy,
It cooleth well my croppy.
Dame Elinour," said she,   560
"Have here is for me,
A clout of London pins!"
And with that she begins
The pot to her pluck,
And drank a "Good luck."
She swinged up a quart
At ones for her part;
Her paunch was so puffed,
And so with ale stuffed,
Had she not hied apace,   570
She had defoiled the place.
   Than began the sport
Among that drunken sort.

_____

[1]Line missing.

"Dame Elinour," said they,
"Lend here a cock of hay,
To make all thing clean—
Ye wot well what we mean!"
　　But, sir, among all
That sate in that hall
There was a prick-me-dainty　　580
Sate like a sainty,
And began to painty
As though she would fainty.
She made it as coy
As a lege de moy;
She was not half so wise
As she was peevish nice.
She said never a word,
But rose from the bord,

And called for our dame,　　590
Elinour by name.
We supposed, iwis,
That she rose to piss;
But the very ground
Was for to compound
With Elinour in the spence
To pay for her expense.
"I have no penny nor groat,
To pay," said she, "God wote,
For washing of my throat;　　600
But my beads of amber
Bear them to your chamber."
Then Elinour did them hide
Within her bed's side.
But some than sat right sad

That nothing had
There of their ⟨awn,⟩
Neither gelt nor pawn:
Such were there many
That had not a penny,　　610
But, whan they should walk,
Were fain with a chalk
To score on the balk,
Or score on the tale:
God geve it ill hail!
For my fingers itch;
I have written too mich
Of this mad mumming
Of Elinour Rumming.
Thus endeth the gest　　620
Of this worthy fest!

Quod Skelton, Laureat.

ALEXANDER BARCLAY

CERTAIN EGLOGUES

When, during the first decade of the sixteenth century, Barclay at various times set about composing his pastoral eclogues, he was turning a rich classical form to vernacular uses. Virgil had lent the form his immense prestige, for in imitating Theocritus' idylls in his *Bucolics,* he superimposed upon his model's charming reminiscences of Sicilian life an element of satire and instruction, and his precedent was too weighty to be ignored, partly because Renaissance writers knew more Latin than Greek, and partly because of Virgil's great popularity. It was, consequently, to Virgil that Petrarch and his imitators turned when they sought to revive the pastoral idyll. Petrarch's twelve Latin *Eglogae* (many of them severely critical of ecclesiastical abuses) and Boccaccio's sixteen were less influential than those of Baptista Spagnuoli (1448–1516), Shakespeare's "Old Mantuan," whose elegancies of phrase every Elizabethan schoolboy had by heart. Though a Carmelite who rose to be general of his order, Mantuan devoted four of his ten eclogues to anti-clerical satire, and he also broadened the range of his form by treating such topics as inordinate love, anti-feminism, the neglect of poets, and the evils of urban life—all themes copiously imitated throughout the sixteenth century.

It was Mantuan whom Barclay took as his model (and, in part, as his source) when he led the way in using the vernacular for a form hitherto reserved for the learned languages. His five eclogues appeared in various editions (of which only the last, affixed to John Cawood's printing of *The Ship of Fools* in 1570, is dated) and no doubt went through various revisions. Barclay himself tells us that the first three "contain the miseries of courtiers and courts of all princes in general, gathered out of a book named in Latin *Miseriae curialium*" which Aeneas Sylvius Piccolomini, later Pope Pius II (1405–64), composed to commemorate his unhappy stay at the imperial court of the Emperor Frederick III in Vienna; but Barclay's fourth is adapted from Mantuan's fifth, his fifth from Mantuan's sixth. The modern view that they were written through the first years of the sixteenth century and revised for publication about 1514 is supported by Barclay's autobiographical "Prologue" in Cawood's edition. Though often vigorous with their thumping couplets, and full of sharply observed details, Barclay's adaptations of his sources are fearfully long and generally of small intrinsic literary interest. Our excerpts from the Prologue and from the nearly 1,200 lines of the fourth eclogue are based upon *The Eclogues of Alexander Barclay from the Original Edition by John Cawood,* ed. Beatrice White, EETS, no. 175, 1928 (for 1927).

FROM CERTAIN EGLOGUES (1570)

THE PROLOGUE

The famous poets with the muses nine,
With wit inspired, fresh, pregnant, and divine,
Say, "Boldly indite in style substantial!"
Some in poems high and heroical,
Some them delight in heavy tragedies,
And some in wanton or merry comedies;
Some in satires against vices dare carp,
Some in sweet songs accordant with the harp;
And each of these all had laud and excellence
After their reason and style of eloquence.   10
Who in fair speech could briefly comprehend
Most fruitful matter, men did him most commend;
And who were fruitless and in speech superflue,
Men by their writing scantly set a qu.
Therefore wise poets, to sharp and prove their wit,
In homely jests wrote many a merry fit
Before they durst be of audacity
T' aventure things of weight and gravity.
In this said manner the famous Theocrite
First in Syracuse attempted for to write   20
Certain egloges or speeches pastoral,
Inducing shepherds, men homely and rural,
Which in plain language, according to their name,
Had sundry talking—sometime of mirth and game,
Sometime of things more like to gravity
And not exceeding their small capacity.
Most noble Virgil after him long while
Wrote also egloges after like manner style,
His wits proving in matters pastoral
Or he durst venture to style heroical.   30
And in like manner now lately in our days
Hath other poets attempted the same ways,
As the most famous Baptist Mantuan,
The best of that sort since poets first began;
And Francis Petrark also in Italy
In like manner style wrote plain and merrily. . . .
Now to my purpose: their works' worthy fame
Did in my young age my heart greatly inflame,
Dull slouth eschewing, myself to exercise
In such small matters or I durst enterprise   40
To higher matter, like as these children do
Which first use to creep and afterward to go. . . .
So where I in youth a certain work began
And not concluded, as oft doth many a man,
Yet thought I after to make the same perfit;
But long I missed that which I first did write.
But here a wonder: I, forty year save twain
Proceeded in age, found my first youth again.
To find youth in age is a problem diffuse,
But now hear the truth and then no longer muse: 50
As I late turned old books to and fro,
One little treatise I found among the mo;

Because that in youth I did compile the same,
Egloges of Youth I did call it by name,
And, seeing some men have in the same delight,
At their great instance I made the same perfit,
Adding and bating where I perceived need,
All them desiring which shall this treatise read
Not to be grieved with any plain sentence
Rudely conveyed for lack of eloquence.   60
It were not fitting a herd or man rural
To speak in terms gay and rhetorical.
So teacheth Horace in *Art of Poetry*
That writers namely their reason should apply,
Meet speech approp'ring to every personage
After his estate, behavor, wit, and age.
But if that any would now to me object
That this my labor shall be of small effect,
And to the reader not greatly profitable,
And by that manner as vain and reprovable   70
Because it maketh only relation
Of shepherds' manner and disputation,
If any such read my treatise to the end
He shall well perceive, if he thereto intend,
That it containeth both lauds of virtue
And man infourmeth misliving to eschew
With divers bourds and sentences moral
Closed in shadow of speeches pastoral,
As many poets (as I have said beforn)
Have used long time before that I was born. . . .   80
But to the reader now to return again,
First of this thing I will thou be certain:
That five egloges this whole treatise doth hold
To imitation of other poets old.
In which egloges shepherds thou may'st see
In homely language not passing their degree
Sometime disputing of courtly misery,
Sometime of Venus' disceatful tyranny,
Sometime commending love honest and laudable,
Sometime despising love false and deceivable,   90
Sometime despising and blaming avarice,
Sometime exciting virtue to exercise,
Sometime of war abhorring the outrage
And of the same time the manifold damage,
And other matters, as after shall appear
To their great pleasure which shall them read or hear.

THE FOURTH EGLOGE OF ALEXANDER BARCLAY, ENTITULED CODRUS AND MINALCAS, TREATING OF THE BEHAVIOR OF RICH MEN AGAINST POETS

THE ARGUMENT

Codrus, a shepherd lusty, gay, and stout,
Sat with his wethers at pasture round about,
And poor Minalcas, with ewes scarce fourteen,

Sat sadly musing in shadow on the green.
This lusty Codrus was cloaked for the rain
And double-decked with huddes one or twain;
He had a pautner with purses manifold,
And surely lined with silver and with gold;
Within his wallet were meats good and fine;
Both store and plenty had he of ale and wine. . . .   10
Sometime he danced and hobbled as a bear;
Sometime he pried how he became his gear.
He leapt; he song and ran to prove his might:
When purse is heavy ofttime the heart is light.
But though this Codrus had store inough of good,
He wanted wisdom, for nought he understood
Save worldly practise his treasor for to store;
However it came, small force had he therefore.
On the other side the poor Minalcas lay
With empty belly and simple, poor array,   20
Yet could he pipe and finger well a drone,
But sour is music when men for hunger groan.
Codrus had riches, Minalcas had cunning;
For God not geveth to one man everything.
At last this Codrus espied Minalcas,
And soon he knew what manner man he was,
For old acquaintance between them erst had been
Long time before they met upon the green,
And therefore Codrus down boldly by him sat
And in this manner began with him to chat.   30

Finis

Codrus first speaketh

All hail, Minalcas, now by my faith well met!
Lord Jesu mercy, what troubles did thee let
That this long season none could thee here espy?
With us was thou wont to sing full merrily
And to lie piping ofttime among the flours
What time thy beasts were feeding among ours.
In these old valleys we two were wont to bourd,
And in these shadows talk many a merry word,
And oft were we wont to wrastle for a fall,
But now thou droopest and hast forgotten all. . . .   10
In sloth thou slomb'rest as buried were thy song;
Thy pipe is broken, or somewhat else is wrong.

Minalcas

What time the cuckow's feathers mout and fall,
From sight she lurketh; her song is gone withal.
When back is bare and purse of coin is light
The wit is dulled and reason hath no might.
Adieu enditing when gone is liberty!
Enemy to muses is wretched poverty;
What time a knight is subject to a knave,
To just or tourney small pleasor shall he have.   20

Codrus

What, no man thee keepeth here in captivity,
And busy labor subdueth poverty,

And oft it is better, and much surer also,
As subject to obey then at free will to go.
As, for example, behold a wanton colt
In raging youth leapeth over hill and holt,
But while he skippeth at pleasure and at will
Ofttime doth he fall in danger for to spill.
Sometime on stubs his hofes sore he tears,
Or falls in the mud both over head and ears;   30
Sometime all the night abroad in hail or rain,
And oft among breres tangled by the mane;
And other perils he suff'reth infinite,
So mingled with sorrow is pleasor and delight.
But if this same colt be broken at the last,
His sitter ruleth and him refraineth fast;
The spur him pricketh, the bridle doth him hold
That he cannot prance at pleasor where he wold;
The rider him ruleth and saveth from danger.
By which example, Minalcas, it is clear   40
That free will is subject to inconvenience,
Where by subjection man voideth great offense,
For man of himself is very frail certain,
But oft a ruler his folly doth refrain;
But as for thyself, thou hast no cause, pardie;
To walk at pleasor is no captivity.

Minalcas

Seest thou not, Codrus, the fields round about
Compassed with floods that none may in nor out?
The muddy waters near choke me with the stink;
At every tempest they be as black as ink.   50
Poverty to me should be no discomfort
If other shepherds were all of the same sort,
But, Codrus, I claw oft where it doth not itch
To see ten beggers and half a dozen rich.
Truly methinketh this wrong pertition,
And namely sith all ought be after one. . . .

Codrus

May'st thou not sometime thy fold and sheep apply
And after, at leasor to live more quietly,
Dispose thy wits to make or to endite,
Renouncing cures for time while thou dost write?   60

Minalcas

Needs must a shepherd bestow his whole labor
In tending his flocks, scant may he spare one hour.
In going, coming, and often them to tend
Full lightly the day is brought unto an end.
Sometime the wolves with dogs must he chase,
Sometime his folds must he new compace,
And ofttime them change; and if he storms doubt,
Of his sheepcote daub the walls round about;
When they be broken, ofttimes them renew;
And hurtful pastures note well and them eschew;   70
Buy straw and litter and hay for winter cold;
Oft grease the scabs as well of young as old;

For dread of thieves oft watch up all the night;
Beside this, labor with all his mind and might,
For his poor household for to provide vitail
If by adventure his wool or lambs fail.
In doing all these no respite doth remain,
But well to indite requireth all the brain.
I tell thee, Codrus, a style of excellence
Must have all labor and all the diligence.   80
Both these two works be great, near importable
To my small power; my strength is much unable.
The one to intend, scant may I bide the pain;
Then it is harder for me to do both twain.
What time my wits be clear for to indite,
My daily charges will grant me no respite;
But if I follow, inditing at my will,
Each one disdaineth my charges to fulfill.
Though in these fields each other ought sustain,
Clean lost is that law; one may require in vain.   90
If coin command, then men count them as bound;
Else flee they labor, then is my charge on ground. . . .
It me repenteth, if I have any wit;
As for my science, I weary am of it.
And of my poor life I weary am, Codrus,
Sith my hard fortune for me disposeth thus,
That of the stars and planets each one
To poor Minalcas well fortunate is none. . . .

CODRUS

Men say that clerks which know astronomy
Know certain stars which long to destiny,   100
But all their saying is nothing veritable,
Yet hear the matter, though it be but a fable:
They say that Mercury doth poets favor;
Under Jupiter be princes of honor
And men of riches, of wealth or dignity,
And all such other as have aucthority.
Mercury geveth to poets laureate
Goodly conveyance, speech pleasant and ornate,
Inventife reason to sing or play on harp,
In goodly ditty or ballade for to carp.   110
This is thy lot—what seeketh thou riches?
No man hath all, this thing is true doubtless;
God all disposeth as he perceiveth best.
Take thou thy fortune and hold thee still in rest;
Take thou thy fortune and hold thyself content;
Let us have riches and rooms excellent.

MINALCAS

Thou hast of riches and goods haboundance,
And I have ditties and songs of pleasance;
To ask my cunning too covetous thou art.
Why is not thyself contented with thy part?   120
Why doest thou invade my part and portion?
Thou wantest, Codrus, wit and discretion.

CODRUS

Not so, Minalcas! Forsooth, thou art to blame
Of wrong invasion to geve to me the name.
I would no ditty nor ballade take thee fro,
No harp nor arms which long to Apollo;
But only, Minalcas, I sore desire and long
To geve mine ears to thy sweet-sounding song.
It feedeth hearing and is to one pleasant
To hear good reason and ballade consonant.   130

MINALCAS

If thou have pleasure to hear my melody,
I grant thee, Codrus, to joy my armony;
So have I pleasure and joy of thy riches,
So gifts doubled increaseth love doubtless.

CODRUS

He of my riches hath joy which loveth me,
And who me hateth, nothing content is he.
Envious wretches by malice commonly
Take others' fortune and pleasure heavily.

MINALCAS

In like wise may'st thou injoy of our science
And of our muses, though thou be fro presence;   140
And of our cunning thou joyest semblably
If nought provoke thee by malice and envy.
If I feed thy ears, feed thou my mouth again;
I loth were to spend my gifts all in vain.
Meat unto the mouth is food and sustenance,
And songs feed the ears with pleasance.
I have the muses; if thou wilt have of mine,
Then right requireth that I have part of thine.
This longeth to love, to nourish charity;
This feedeth pity, this doth to right agree;   150
This is the pleasure and will of God above,
Of him disposed for to ingender love. . . .

CODRUS

Lord God, Minalcas, why hast thou all this pain
Thuswise to forge so many words in vain?

MINALCAS

That vain thou countest which may hurt or inless
Thy loved treasure or minish thy riches.
If thou wilt harken or hear my muses sing,
Refresh my mind with confort and liking;
Rid me fro troubles and care of business;
Confort my courage which now is comfortless. . . .   160
I ask no palace nor lodging curious,
No bed of state, or raiment sumptuous,
For this I learned of the dean of Powel's.
I tell thee, Codrus, this man hath won some souls.
I ask no treasure nor store of worldly good,

But a quiet life, and only cloth and food,
With homely lodging to keep me warm and dry.
Induring my life, forsooth no more ask I.
If I were certain this living still to have,
Avoid of trouble, no more of God I crave. . . .   170

CODRUS

Then write of battails or acts of men bold,
Or mighty princes—they may thee well uphold.
These worthy rulers of fame and name royal
Of very reason ought to be liberal.
Some shalt thou find between this place and Kent
Which for thy labor shall thee right well content.

MINALCAS

Yea, some shall I find which be so prodigal
That in vain things spend and clean wasteth all,
But how should that man my poverty sustain
Which nought reserveth his honor to maintain?   180
For ancient blood nor ancient honor
In these our days be nought without treasure.
The coin avanceth, need doth the name deject;
And where is treasure old, honor hath effect.
But such as be rich and in promotion
Shall have my writing but in derision.
For in this season great men of excellence
Have to poems no greater reverence
Then to a brothel or else a brothel-house,
Mad ignorance is so contagious.   190

CODRUS

It is not seeming a poet thus to jest
In wrathful speech nor words dishonest.

MINALCAS

It is no jesting, be thou never so wroth,
In open language to say nothing but troth.
If peradventure thou would have troth kept still,
Provoke thou not me to anger at thy will.
When wrath is moved, then reason hath no might;
The tongue forgetteth discretion and right.

CODRUS

To move thy mind I truly were full loth;
To geve good counsel is far from being wroth.   200

MINALCAS

As touching counsel my mind is plentiful,
But need and troubles make all my reason dull.
If I had counsel and gold in like plenty,
I tell thee, Codrus, I had no need of thee.
How should a poet, poor, bare, and indigent,
Indite the acts of princes excellent
While scant is he worth a knife his pipe to mend,

To round the holes, to cleanse or pick the end?
Behold, my whittle almost hath lost the blade,
So long time past is sith the same was made.   210
The haft is bruised, the blade not worth a straw,
Rusty and toothed, not much unlike a saw. . . .
Beside this, Codrus, princes and men royal
In our inditings have pleasure faint and small.
So much power have they with men of might
As simple doves when eagles take their flight,
Or as great winds careth for leaves dry.
They live in pleasure and wealth continually;
In lust their liking is, and in idleness;
Few have their minds clean from all viciousness;   220
Pleasure is thing whereto they most intend;
That they most cherish they would have men concend.
If poets should their manners magnify,
They were supporters of blame and lechery;
Then should their writing be nothing commendable,
Containing jests and deeds detestable
Of stinking Venus or love inordinate,
Of ribaud words which fall not for a state,
Of right oppressed and beastly gluttony,
Of vice advanced, of slouth and injury,   230
And other deeds infame and worthy blame
Which were overlong here to recount or name.
These to commend, Codrus, do not agree
To any poet which loveth chastity. . . .

[As the argument winds its weary way along, Minalcas
at last agrees to compose for Codrus a "ballade extract of
sapience" in order to demonstrate the function of a good
poet. The following stanza is a sample:

As meadows painted with flours redolent
    The sight rejoice of such as them behold,
So man indued with virtue excellent
    Fragrantly shineth with beams manifold.
Virtue with wisdom exceedeth store of gold;
    If riches abound, set not on them thy trust.
When strength is sturdy, then man is pert and bold,
    But wit and wisdom soon lay him in the dust.

But after four stanzas Codrus rudely cuts him off with
"Of this have we inough." Nothing daunted, Minalcas
tries again to please him, this time with "The Description
of the Tower of Virtue and Honor," a tedious and prolix
excursion into moral allegory which, he says, the shepherd
Cornix had made as an elegy for Sir Edward Howard.]

CODRUS

Minalcas, I swear by holy Peter's cope,
If all thing fortune as I have trust and hope,
If happy wind blow I shall or it be long
Comfort thy sorrow and well reward thy song.
What! tarry, man, a while till better fortune come.
If my part be any, then shall thy part be some.   240

MINALCAS

If thou in purpose so to reward my hire,
God grant thee, Codrus, thy wishing and desire.

CODRUS

Forsooth, Minalcas, I wish thee so indeed,
And that shalt thou know if fortune with me speed.
Farewell, Minalcas, for this time; *Dieu te garde*.
Near is winter; the world is too hard.

MINALCAS

Go, wretched niggard, God send thee care and pain!
Our Lord let thee never come hither more again;
And as did Midas, God turn it all to gold
That ever thou touchest or shalt in hands hold,   250
For so much on gold is fixed thy liking
That thou despisest both virtue and cunning.

SIR THOMAS MORE

UTOPIA

In his correspondence More speaks of his *Utopia* as *Nusquama* ("nowhere"), a proper translation of the Greek title and a sufficient clue to understanding the book, for it is an imaginative projection of those social and moral ideals which, however dear to the humanists of the northern Renaissance, were not to be found in contemporary institutions. The second book was composed during More's first embassy to the Low Countries in 1515; the first, a year later after his return to England. In the opening dialogue, set in Antwerp, between Hythloday (the fictitious traveler), Peter Giles, and More himself, we are presented with a lively and sensitive analysis of those ills—economic, penal, sociological, and moral—besetting early Tudor England; in Hythloday's narrative of the second book these themes are, as it were, resolved in the picture of an ideal commonwealth. When More circulated his manuscript among such friends as Giles, Tunstall, and Erasmus, their response was so favorable that Erasmus himself arranged its publication at Louvain; and there, in December, 1516, it duly appeared as *Libellus vere aureus nec minus salutaris quam festivus de optimo reip. statu deque nova insula Utopia,* with appropriate congratulatory letters or poems by Giles, John Paludanus, Busleyden, and others. Immediately successful, it was reprinted in March, 1517, at Paris; and a year later from Froben's press at Basle appeared the handsomest of all the early editions, produced under Erasmus' own supervision and adorned with Hans Holbein's illustrations. There were also many contemporary translations: German in 1524, Italian in 1548, Dutch in 1553 and 1562, French in 1550 and 1559; and in 1551 there appeared Ralph Robinson's famous English version which has become a classic in its own right. It was republished in 1556, 1597, 1624, and 1639, and was without a rival until Gilbert Burnet, Bishop of Salisbury, in 1684 produced his more accurate but less interesting translation. Our text is based upon *A fruteful and pleasaunt worke of the beste state of a publyque weale, and of the newe yle called Utopia . . . translated . . . by Raphe Robynson, Citizein and Goldsmythe of London, 1551* (STC 18094).

FROM UTOPIA (1516; trans. 1551)

THE FIRST BOOK OF THE COMMUNICATION OF RAPHAEL HYTHLODAY, CONCERNING THE BEST STATE
OF A COMMONWEALTH

The most victorious and triumphant king of England, Henry, th' eight of that name, in all royal virtues prince most peerless, had of late in controversy with the right high and mighty king [Charles V] of Castell weighty matters and of great importance; for the debatement and final determination whereof, the king's Majesty sent me ambassador into Flanders, joined in commission with Cuthbert Tunstall, a man doubtless out of comparison, and whom the king's Majesty of late, to the great rejoicing of all men, did prefer to the office of maister of the rolls. But of this man's praises I will say nothing, not bycause I do fear that small credence shall be geven to the testimony that cometh out of a frind's mouth, but bicause his virtue and learning be greater, and of more excellency, than that I am able to praise them; and also in all places so famous and so perfectly well known that they need not nor ought not of me to be praised, unless I would seem to shew and set furth the brightness of the sun with a candle, as the proverb saith.

There met us at Bruges (for thus it was before

agreed) they whom their prince had for that matter appointed commissioners, excellent men all. The chief and the head of them was the margrave (as they call him) of Bruges, a right honorable man; but the wisest and the best-spoken of them was George Temsice, provost of Cassels, a man not only by learning but also by nature of singular eloquence, and in the laws profoundly learned; but in reasoning and debating of matters, what by his natural wit and what by daily exercise, surely he had few fellows. After that we had ones or twice met, and upon certain points or articles could not fully and throughly agree, they for a certain space took their leave of us, and departed to Bruxelle, there to know their prince's pleasure. I in the meantime (for so my business lay) went straight thence to Antwerp.

Whiles I was there abiding, oftentimes among other, but which to me was more welcome then any other, did visit me one Peter Giles, a citizen of Antwerp, a man there in his country of honest reputation, and also preferred to high promotions, worthy truly of the highest. For it is hard to say whether the young man be in learning or in honesty more excellent. For he is both of wonderful virtuous conditions, and also singularly well-learned, and towards all sorts of people exceeding gentle; but towards his frinds so kind-hearted, so loving, so faithful, so trusty, and of so earnest affection that it were very hard in any place to find a man that with him in all points of friendship may be compared. No man can be more lowly or courteous. No man useth less simulation or dissimulation; in no man is more prudent simplicity. Besides this, he is in his talk and communication so merry and pleasant, yea, and that without harm, that through his gentle intertainment and his sweet and delectable communication, in me was greatly abated and diminished the fervent desire that I had to see my native country, my wife, and my children, whom then I did much long and covet to see, bicause that at that time I had been more then four moniths from them.

Upon a certain day as I was hearing the divine service in Our Lady's Church, which is the fairest, the most gorgious and curious church of building in all the city and also most frequented of people, and, when the devine [service] was done, was ready to go home to my lodging, I chanced to espy this foresaid Peter talking with a certain stranger, a man well-striken in age, with a black, sunburned face, a long beard, and a cloak cast homely about his shoulders, whom by his favor and apparel forthwith I judged to be a mariner. But when this Peter saw me, he cometh to me and saluteth me. And as I was about to answer him, "See you this man?" saith he (and therewith he pointed to the man that I saw him talking with before); "I was minded," quod he, "to bring him straight home to you." "He should have been very welcome to me," said I, "for your sake." "Nay," quod he, "for his own sake, if you knew him; for there is no man this day living that can tell you of so many strange and unknown peoples and countries as this man can. And I know well that you be very desirous to hear of such news." "Than I conjectured not far amiss," quod I, "for even at the first sight I judged him to be a mariner."

"Nay," quod he, "there ye were greatly deceived. He hath sailed, indeed, not as the mariner Palinure, but as the expert and prudent prince Ulysses: yea, rather as the ancient and sage philosopher Plato. For this same Raphael Hythloday (for this is his name) is very well-learned in the Latin tongue, but profound and excellent in the Greek tongue, wherein he ever bestowed more study than in the Latin, because he had geven himself wholly to the study of philosophy. Whereof he knew that there is nothing extant in the Latin tongue that is to any purpose, saving a few of Seneca's and Cicero's doings. His patrimony that he was born unto he left to his brethern (for he is a Portugal born), and for the desire that he had to see and know the far countries of the world he joined himself in company with Amerike Vespuce, and in the three last voyages of those four that be now in print [*Quatuor Americi Vesputii navigationes,* 1507] and abroad in every man's hands, he continued still in his company, saving that in the last voyage he came not home again with him. For he made such means and shift, what by intreatance, and what by importune suit, that he got license of Maister Amerike (though it were sore against his will) to be one of the twenty-four which in the end of the last voyage were left in the country of Gulike. He was, therefore, left behind for his mind's sake, as one that took more thought and care for traveling then dying, having customably in his mouth these sayings: he that hath no grave is covered with the sky, and the way to heaven out of all places is of like length and distance. Which fantasy of his (if God had not been his better friend) he had surely bought full dear.

"But after the departing of Maister Vespuce, when he had traveled thorough and about many countries with five of his companions Gulikians, at the last by marvelous chance he arrived in Taprobane, from whence he went to Caliquit, where he chanced to find certain of his country ships, wherein he retorned again into his country, nothing less then looked for."

All this when Peter had told me, I thanked him for his gentle kindness, that he had vouchsafed to bring me to the speech of that man, whose communication he thought should be to me pleasant and acceptable. And therewith I turned me to Raphael. And when we had hailsed th' one th' other, and had spoken these commen words that be customably spoken at the first meeting and acquentance of strangers, we went thence to my house, and there in my garden upon a bench covered with green torves we sat down talking togethers.

There he told us how that, after the departing of Vespuce, he and his fellows that tarried behind in Gulike began by little and little, thorough fair and gentle speech, to win the love and favor of the people of that country, insomuch that within short space they did dwell amonges them not only harmless, but also occupied with them very familiarly. He told us also that they were in high reputation and favor with a certain great man (whose name and country is now quite out of my remembrance) which of his mere liberality did bear the costs and charges of him and his five companions, and besides that gave them a trusty guide to conduct them in their jorney (which by water was in boatis and by land in wagains) and to bring them to other princes with very frindly commendations. Thus after many days' journeys, he said, they found towns and cities and weal publiques, full of people, governed by good and wholesome laws.

"For under the line equinoctial and of both sides of the same, as far as the sun doth extend his course, lieth," quod he, "great and wide deserts and wildernesses, parched, burned, and dried up with continual and intolerable heat. All things be hideous, terrible, loathsome, and unpleasant to behold; all things out of fashion and comeliness, inhabited with wild beasts and serpents, or at the leastwise with people that be no less savage, wild, and noisome then the very beasts themselfes be. But a little farther beyond that, all things begin by little and little to wax pleasant: the air soft, temperate, and gentle; the ground covered with green grass; less wildness in the beasts. At the last shall ye come again to people, cities, and towns wherein is continual entercourse and occupying of marchandise and chaffar, not only among themselfes and with their borderers, but also with marchants of far countries, both by land and water.

"There I had occasion," said he, "to go to many countries of every side. For there was no ship ready to any voyage or jorney but I and my fellows were into it very gladly received." The ships that they found first were made plain, flat and broad in the bottom, troughwise. The sails were made of great rushes, or of wickers, and in some places of leather. Afterward they found ships with ridged keels and sails of canvas, yea, and shortly after, having all things like ours. The shipmen also very expert and conning, both in the sea and in the weather.

But he said that he found great favor and frindship among them for teaching them the feat and use of the lodestone, which to them before that time was unknown. And therefore they were wont to be very timerous and fearful upon the sea, nor to venter upon it but only in the sommer time. But now they have such a confidence in that stone that they fear not stormy winter, in so doing ferther from care then jeopardy, insomuch that it is greatly to be doubted lest that thing, thorough their own foolish hardiness, shall tourn them to evil and harm, which at the first was supposed should be to them good and commodious.

But what he told us that he saw in every country where he came, it were very long to declare; nother it is my purpose at this time to make rehearsal thereof. But peradventure in another place I will speak of it, chiefly such things as shall be profitable to be known, as in special be those decrees and ordinances that he marked to be well and wisely provided and enacted among such peoples as do live together in a civil policy and good order. For of such things did we busily enquire and demand of him, and he likewise very willingly told us of the same. But as for monsters, because they be no news, of them we were nothing inquisitive. For nothing is more easy to be found then be barking Scyllas, ravening Celenes, and Lestrygones, devourers of people, and such-like great and uncredible monsters. But to find citizens ruled by good and wholesome laws, that is an exceeding rare and hard thing.

But as he marked many fond and foolish laws in those new-found lands, so he rehearsed many acts and constitutions whereby these our cities, nations, countries, and kingdoms may take ensample to amend their faults, enormities, and errors. Whereof in another place (as I said) I will intreat. Now at this time I am determined to rehearse only that he told us of the manners, customs, laws, and ordinances of the Utopians. But first I will repeat our former communication, by th' occasion and, as I might say, the drift whereof he was brought into the mention of that weal publique.

For when Raphael had very prudently touched divers things that be amiss, some here and some there, yea, very many of both parts, and again had spoken of such wise and prudent laws and decrees as be established and used both here among us and also there among them, as a man so conning and expert in the laws and customs of every several country, as though into what place soever he came guestwise, there he had led all his life; then Peter, much merveling at the man: "Surely, Maister Raphael," quod he,

"I wonder greatly why you get you not into some king's court; for I am sure there is no prince living that would not be very glad of you, as a man not only able highly to delight him with your profound learning and this your knowledge of countries and peoples, but also are meet to instruct him with examples and help him with counsel. And thus doing, you shall bring yourself in a very good case, and also be in hability to help all your frinds and kinsfolk."

"As concerning my frinds and kinsfolk," quod he, "I pass not greatly for them. For I think I have sufficiently done my part towards them already. For these things that other men do not depart from until they be old and sick, yea, which they be then very loath to leave when they can no lenger keep, those very same things did I, being not only lusty and in good health but also in the flower of my youth, devide among my frinds and kinsfolks; which I think with this my liberality ought to hold them contented, and not to require nor to look that, besides this, I should for their sakes give myself in bondage to kings."

"Nay, God forbed," quod Peter, "it is not my mind that you should be in bondage to kings, but as a retainer to them at your pleasure; which surely, I think, is the nighest way that you can devise how to bestow your time fruitfully, not only for the private commodity of your friends and for the general profit of all sorts of people, but also for the avancement of yourself to a much wealthier state and condition then you be now in."

"To a wealthier condition," quod Raphael, "by that means that my mind standeth clean against? Now I live at liberty after my own mind and pleasure, which I think very few of these great states and peers of realms can say. Yea, and there be inow of them that seek for great men's frindships, and, therefore, think it no great hurt if they have not me, nor two or three such other as I am."

"Well, I perceive plainly, frind Raphael," quod I, "that you be desirous nother of riches nor of power. And truly I have in no less reverence and estimation a man that is of your mind then any of them all that be so high in power and aucthority. But you shall do as it becometh you, yea, and according to this wisdom, and this high and free courage of yours, if you can find in your heart so to appoint and dispose yourself that you may apply your wit and deligence to the profit of the weal publique, though it be somewhat to your own pain and hindrance. And this shall you never so well do, nor with so great profit perfourm, as if you be of some great prince's counsel, and put in his head (as I doubt not but you will) honest opinions and virtuous persuasions. For from the prince, as from a perpetual wellspring, cometh among the people the flood of all that is good or evil. But in you is so perfit learning that without any experience, and again so great experience that without any learning, you may well be any king's counselor."

"You be twice deceived, Maister More," quod he, "first in me, and again in the thing itself. For nother is in me that hability that you force upon me, and, if it were never so much, yet in disquieting mine own quietness I should nothing further the weal publique. For, first of all, the most part of all princes have more delight in warlike matters and feats of chevalry (the knowledge whereof I nother have nor desire) than in the good feats of peace; and employ much more study how by right or by wrong to enlarge their dominions than how well and peaceably to rule and govern that they have already. Moreover, they that be counselors to kings, every one of them either is of himself so wise indeed that he need not, or else he thinketh himself so wise that he will not, allow another man's counsel, saving that they do shamefully and flatteringly geve assent to the fond and foolish sayings of certain great men. Whose favors, bicause they be in high aucthority with their prince, by assentation and flattering they labor to optain. And verily it is naturally geven to all men to esteem their own inventions best. So both the raven and the ape think their own young ones fairest.

"Than if a man in such a company, where some disdain and have despite at other men's inventions, and some count their own best, if among such men, I say, a man should bring furth anything that he hath read done in times past or that he hath seen done in other places, there the hearers fare as though the whole existimation of their wisdom were in jeopardy to be overthrown, and that ever after they should be counted for very diserdes, unless they could in other men's inventions pick out matter to reprehend and find fawt at. If all other poor helps fail, then this is their extreme refuge: these things, say they, pleased our forefathers and auncetors; would God we could be so wise as they were. And as though they had wittily concluded the matter, and with this answer stopped every man's mouth, they sit down again. As who should say, it were a very dangerous matter if a man in any point should be found wiser then his forefathers were. And yet be we content to suffer the best and wittiest of their decrees to lie unexecuted; but if in anything a better order might have been taken than by them was, there we take fast hold and find many fawts. Many times have I chanced upon such proud, lewd, overthwart, and wayward judgments, yea, and ones in England."

"I pray you, sir," quod I, "have you been in our country?" "Yea, forsooth," quod he, "and there I tarried for the space of four or five moniths together, not long after the [Cornish] insurrection [of 1497] that the western Englishmen made against their king, which by their own miserable and pitiful slaughter was suppressed and ended. In the mean season I was much bound and beholden to the Right Reverend Father, John Morton, archbishop and cardinal of Canterbury, and at that time also lord chancellor of England—a man, Maister Peter (for Maister More knoweth already that I will say), not more honorable for his aucthority then for his prudence and virtue. He was of a mean stature, and though streken in age, yet bare he his body upright. In his face did shine such an amiable reverence as was pleasant to behold; gentle in communication, yet earnest and sage. He had great delight many times with rough speech to his suitors to prove, but without harm, what prompt wit and what bold sprite were in every man. In the which, as in a virtue much agreeing with his nature, so that therewith were not joined impudency, he took great delectation; and the same person, as apt and meet to have an administration in the weal publique, he did lovingly enbrace. In his speech he was fine, eloquent, and pithy. In the law he had profound knowledge, in wit he was incomparable, and in memory wonderful excellent. These qualities, which in him were by nature singular, he by learning and use had made perfit.

"The king put much trust in his counsel; the weal publique also in a manner leaned unto him when I was there. For even in the chief of his youth he was taken from school into the court, and there passed all his time in much trouble and business, and was continually troubled and tossed with divers misfortunes and adversities. And so by many and great dangers he learned the experience of the wordle which, so being learned, cannot easely be forgotten.

"It chanced on a certain day, when I sate at his table, there was also a certain layman cunning in the laws of your realm. Which, I cannot tell whereof taking occasion, began diligently and busily to praise that strait and rigorous justice which at that time was there executed upon felons, who, as he said, were for the most part twenty hanged together upon one gallows. And, seeing so few escaped punishment, he said he could not chewse but greatly wonder and marvel how and by what evil luck it should so come to pass that thieves, nevertheless, were in every place so rife and rank. 'Nay, sir,' quod I (for I durst boldly speak my mind before the cardinal), 'marvel nothing hereat; for this punishment of thieves passeth of the limits [of] justice, and is also very hurtful to the weal publique. For it is too extreme and cruel a punishment for theft, and

yet not sufficient to refrain men from theft. For simple theft is not so great an offense that it ought to be punished with death. Nother there is any punishment so horrible that it can keep them from stealing, which have no other craft whereby to get their living. Therefore, in this point, not you only, but also the most part of the wordle, be like evil schoolmasters which be readier to beat then to teach their scholers. For great and horrible punishments be appointed for thieves, whereas much rather provision should have been made that there were some means whereby they might get their living, so that no man should be driven to this extreme necessity, first to steal and then to die.' 'Yes,' quod he, 'this matter is well inough provided for already. There be handicrafts, there is husbandry, to get their living by, if they would not willingly be nought.' 'Nay,' quod I, 'you shall not scape so; for, first of all, I will speak nothing of them that come home out of war, maimed and lame, as not long ago out of Blackheath Field, and a little before that out of the wars in France. [On the death of Francis, Duke of Brittany, in 1488 Henry VII had sent a force to aid his daughter Anne against Charles VIII of France. Although the English besieged Boulogne (October, 1492), Henry and Charles resolved their difficulties at the peace of Etaples (November, 1492).] Such, I say, as put their lives in jeopardy for the weal publique's or the king's sake, and by the reason of weakness and lameness be not able to occupy their old crafts, and be too aged to learn new—of them I will speak nothing, because war, like the tide, ebbeth and floweth. But let us consider those things that chance daily before our eyes.

" 'First there is a great number of gentlemen which cannot be content to live idle themselfes, like dorres, of that which other have labored for; their tenants, I mean, whom they poll and shave to the quick by raising their rents (for this only point of frugality do they use, men else thorough their lavasse and prodigal spending able to bring themselfes to very beggery); these gentlemen, I say, do not only live in idleness themselfes, but also carry about with them at their tails a great flock or train of idle and loit'ring serving-men which never learned any craft whereby to get their livings. These men, as soon as their maister is dead, or be sick themselfes, be incontinent thrust out of doors. For gentlemen had rather keep idle persons then sick men, and many times the dead man's heir is not able to maintain so great a house and keep so many serving-men as his father did. Then in the mean season they that be thus destitute of service other starve for honger or manfully play the thieves. For what would you have them to do? When they have wand'red abroad so long until they have worn threadbare their apparel and also appaired their health, then gentlemen, because of their pale and sick faces and patched coats, will not take them into service. And husbandmen dare not set them awork, knowing well inough that he is nothing meet to do true and faithful service to a poor man with a spade and a mattock, for small wages and hard fare, which, being daintily and tenderly pampered up in idleness and pleasure, was wont with a sword and a buckeler by his side to jet through the street with a bragging look, and to think himself too good to be any man's mate.'

" 'Nay, by Saint Mary, sir,' quod the lawyer, 'not so, for this kind of men must we make most of. For in them, as men of stouter stomachs, bolder spirits, and manlier courages then handicraftsmen and plowmen be, doth consist the whole power, strength, and puissance of our host, when we must fight in battail.'

" 'Forsooth, sir, as well you might say,' quod I, 'that for war's sake you must cherish thieves. For surely you shall never lack thieves whiles you have them. No, nor thieves be not the most false and faint-hearted soldiers, nor soldiers be not the cowardliest thieves, so well these two crafts agree together. But this fawt, though it be much used among you, yet is it not peculiar to you only, but commen also almost to all nations. Yet France besides this is troubled and infected with a much sorer plague. The whole realm is filled and besieged with hired soldiers in peace time (if that be peace) which be brought in under the same color and pretense that hath persuaded you to keep these idle serving-men. For these wise fools and very archdolts thought the wealth of the whole country herein to consist, if there were ever in a readiness a strong and a sure garrison, specially of old, practised soldiers; for they put no trust at all in men unexercised. And therefore they must be fain to seek for war to th' end they may ever have practised soldiers and cunning mansleers, lest that (as it is prettily said of Sallust) their hands and their minds thorough idleness or lack of exercise should wax dull. . . . But yet this is not only the necessary cause of stealing. There is another, which, as I suppose, is proper and peculiar to you Englishmen alone.' 'What is that?' quod the cardinal. 'Forsooth,' quod I, 'your sheep, that were wont to be so meek and tame and so small eaters, now, as I hear say, be become so great devourers and so wild that they eat up and swallow down the very men themselfes. They consume, destroy, and devour whole fields, houses, and cities. For look in what parts of the realm doth grow the finest and therefore dearest wool, there noblemen and gentlemen, yea, and certain abbots (holy men, God wot!), not contenting themselfes with the yearly revenues and profits that were

wont to grow to their forefathers and predecessors of their lands, nor being content that they live in rest and pleasure, nothing profiting, yea, much noying the weal publique, leave no ground for tillage; they enclose all in pastures; they throw down houses; they pluck down towns, and leave nothing stonding but only the church to make of it a sheephouse. And as though you lost no small quantity of ground by forests, chases, launds, and parks, those good holy men turn all dwelling-places and all glebeland into desolation and wilderness.

" 'Therefore, that one covetous and unsatiable cormarant and very plage of his native country may compass about and inclose many thousand acres of ground together within one pale or hedge, the husbandmen be thrust out of their own, or else other by covin or fraud or by violent oppression they be put besides it, or by wrongs and injuries they be so wearied that they be compelled to sell all. By one means, therefore, or by other, other by hook or crook they must needs depart away, poor, silly, wretched souls, men, women, husbands, wives, fatherless children, widows, woful mothers with their young babes, and their whole household small in substance and much in nomber, as husbandry requireth many hands. Away they trudge, I say, out of their known and accustomed houses, finding no places to rest in. All their household stuff, which is very little worth, though it might well abide the sale, yet, being soddeinly thrust out, they be constrained to sell it for a thing of nought. And when they have, wandering about, soon spent that, what can they else do but steal, and then justly, God wot, be hanged, or else go about a-begging? And yet then also they be cast in prison as vagabonds, because they go about and work not, whom no man will set awork, though they never so willingly offer themselfes thereto. For one shepherd or herdman is inough to eat up that ground with cattle, to the occupying whereof about husbandry many hands were requisite.

" 'And this is also the cause that victuals be now in many places dearer. Yea, besides this the price of wool is so risen that poor folks, which were wont to work it and make cloth of it, be now able to buy none at all. And by this means very many be fain to forsake work, and to give themselfes to idleness. For after that so much ground was inclosed for pasture, an infinite multitude of sheep died of the rot, such vengeance God took of their inordinate and unsatiable covetousness, sending among the sheep that pestiferous morreyn which much more justly should have fallen on the sheepmasters' own heads. And though the number of sheep increase never so fast, yet the price falleth not one mite, because there be so few sellers. For they be almost all comen into a few rich men's hands, whom no need driveth to sell before they lust, and they lust not before they may sell as dear as they lust. Now the same cause bringeth in like dearth of the other kinds of cattle, yea, and that so much the more bycause that after farms plucked down and husbandry decayed, there is no man that passeth for the breeding of young store. For these rich men bring not up the young ones of great cattle as they do lambs. But first they buy them abroad very cheap, and afterward, when they be fatted in their pastures, they sell them again exceeding dear. And therefore, as I suppose, the whole incommodity hereof is not yet felt. For yet they make dearth only in those places where they sell. But when they shall fetch them away from thence where they be bred faster then they can be brought up, then shall there also be felt great dearth when store beginneth to fail, there where the ware is bought.

" 'Thus the unreasonable covetousness of a few hath turned that thing to the utter undoing of your iland, in the which thing the chief felicity of your realm did consist. For this great dearth of victuals causeth every man to keep as little houses and as small hospitality as he possible may, and to put away their servants. Whether, I pray you, but a-begging, or else (which these gentle bloods and stout stomachs will sooner set their minds unto) a-stealing?

" 'Now to amend the matters, to this wretched beggery and miserable poverty is joined great wantonness, importunate superfluity, and excessive riot. For not only gentlemen's servants, but also handicraftmen, yea, and almost the plowmen of the country, with all other sorts of people, use much strange and proud newfangleness in their apparel, and too much prodigal riot and sumptuous fare at their table. Now bawds, queans, whores, harlots, strumpets, brothel-houses, stews, and yet another stews, wine taverns, ale-houses and tippling-houses, with so many naughty, lewd, and unlawful games as dice, cards, tables, tennis, bowls, coits—do not all these send the haunters of them straight a-stealing when their money is gone?

" 'Cast out these pernicious abominations! Make a law that they which plucked down farms and towns of husbandry shall build them up again, or else yield and uprender the possession of them to such as will go to the cost of building them anew. Suffer not these rich men to buy up all, to ingross and forstall, and with their monopoly to keep the market alone as please them. Let not so many be brought up in idleness; let husbandry and tillage be restored again; let cloth-working be renewed, that there may be honest labors for this idle sort to pass their time in profitably, which hitherto other poverty hath caused to be thieves, or else now be other vagabonds or

idle serving-men, and shortly will be thieves. Doubtless, onless you find a remedy for these enormities, you shall in vain avaunce yourselfes of executing justice upon felons. For this justice is more beautiful then just or profitable. For by suffering your youth wantonly and viciously to be brought up and to be infected, even from their tender age, by little and little with vice, than, a God's name! to be punished when they commit the same faults after they be comen to man's state, which from their youth they were ever like to do! In this point, I pray you, what other thing do you, then make thieves and then punish them? . . .' "

[Having concluded his account of that long-past conversation at Cardinal Morton's table, Raphael Hythloday carries on with Giles and More a general discussion of economic and political theory. Finally he works around to a defense of the common ownership of all property as a device calculated to cure social ills.]

"Thus I do fully persuade meself that no equal and just distribution of things can be made, nor that perfect wealth shall ever be among men, onless this propriety be exiled and banished. But so long as it shall continue, so long shall remain among the most and best part of men the heavy and inevitable burden of poverty and wretchedness. Which, as I grant that it may be somewhat eased, so I utterly deny that it can wholly be taken away. For if there were a statute made that no man should possess above a certain measure of ground, and that no man should have in his stock above a prescript and appointed sum of money; if it were by certain laws decreed that nother the king should be of too great power, nother the people too proud and wealthy, and that offices should not be obtained by inordinate suit or by bribes and gifts, that they should nother be bought nor sold, nor that it should be needful for the officers to be at any cost or charge in their offices—for so occasion is geven to the officers by fraud and ravin to gather up their money again, and by reason of gifts and bribes the offices be geven to rich men, which should rather have been executed of wise men—by such laws, I say, like as sick bodies that be desperate and past cure be wont with continual good cherissing to be kept up, so these evils also might be lightened and mitigated. But that they may be perfectly cured and brought to a good and upright state, it is not to be hoped for whiles every man is maister of his own to himself. Yea, and whiles you go about to do your cure of one part, you shall make bigger the sore of another part, so the help of one causeth another's harm, forasmuch as nothing can be geven to any man onless it be taken from another."

"But I am of a contrary opinion," quod I, "for

methinketh that men shall never there live wealthily where all things be commen. For how can there be abundance of goods, or of anything, where every man withdraweth his hand from labor? Whom the regard of his own gains driveth not to work, and the hope that he hath in other men's travails maketh him slothful. Then, when they be pricked with poverty, and yet no man can by any law or right defend that for his own which he hath gotten with the labor of his own hands, shall not there of necessity be continual sedition and bloodshed? Specially the aucthority and reverend of magistrates being taken away, which, what place it may have with such men among whom is no difference, I cannot devise."

"I marvel not," quod he, "that you be of this opinion. For you conceive in your mind other none at all, or else a very false image and similitude of this thing. But if you had been with me in Utopia and had presently seen their fashions and laws, as I did, which lived there five years and more, and would never have comen thence but only to make that new land known here, then doubtless you would grant that you never saw people well ordered but only there."

"Surely," quod Maister Peter, "it shall be hard for you to make me believe that there is better order in that new land then is here in these countries that we know. For good wits be as well here as there, and I think our commonwealths be ancienter than theirs, wherein long use and experience hath found out many things commodious for man's life, besides that many things here among us have been found by chance, which no wit could ever have devised."

"As touching the ancientness," quod he, "of commonwealths, than you might better judge if you had read the histories and chronicles of that land, which if we may believe, cities were there before there were men here. Now what thing soever hitherto by wit hath been devised or found by chance, that might be as well there as here. But I think verily, though it were so that we did pass them in wit, yet in study and laborsome endeavor they far pass us. For, as their chronicles testify, before our arrival there they never hard anything of us, whom they call the ultra-equinoctials, saving that ones about

twelve hundred years ago a certain ship was lost by the ile of Utopia, which was driven thither by tempest. Certain Romains and Egyptians were cast on land, which after that never went thence.

"Mark now what profit they took of this one occasion through deligence and earnest travail. There was no craft nor science within the impery of Rome whereof any profit could rise but they other learned it of these strangers or, else of them taking occasion to search for it, found it out. So great profit was it to them that ever any went thither from hence. But if any like chance before this hath brought any man from thence hether, that is as quite out of remembrance, as this also perchance in time to come shall be forgotten that ever I was there. And like as they quickly, almost at the first meeting, made their own whatsoever is among us wealthily devised, so I suppose it would be long before we would receive anything that among them is better instituted then among us. And this, I suppose, is the chief cause why their commonwealths be wiselier governed and do florish in more wealth then ours, though we nother in wit nor in riches be their inferiors."

"Therefore, gentle Maister Raphael," quod I, "I pray you and beseech you describe unto us the iland. And study not to be short, but declare largely in order their grounds, their rivers, their cities, their people, their manners, their ordinances, their laws, and, to be short, all things that you shall think us desirous to know. And you shall think us desirous to know whatsoever we know not yet." "There is nothing," quod he, "that I will do gladlier. For all these things I have fresh in mind. But the matter requireth leisure." "Let us go in, therefore," quod I, "to dinner; afterward we will bestow the time at our pleasure." "Content," quod he, "be it." So we went in and dined.

When dinner was done, we came into the same place again and sate us down upon the same bench, commanding our servants that no man should trouble us. Then I and Maister Peter Giles desired Master Raphael to perform his promise. He, therefore, seeing us desirous and willing to harken to him, when he had sit still and paused a little while, musing and bethinking himself, thus he began to speak.

The end of the First Book

THE SECOND BOOK OF THE COMMUNICATION OF RAPHAEL HYTHLODAY, CONCERNING THE BEST STATE OF A COMMONWEALTH, CONTAINING THE DISCRIPTION OF UTOPIA, WITH A LARGE DECLARATION OF THE GODLY GOVERNMENT AND OF ALL THE GOOD LAWS AND ORDERS OF THE SAME ILAND

The iland of Utopia containeth in breadth in the middle part of it (for there it is broadest) two hundred miles. Which breadth continueth through the most part of the land, saving that by little and little it cometh in and waxeth narrower towards both the ends. Which, fetching about a circuit or compass of five hundred miles, do fashion the whole iland like to the new moon. Between these two corners the sea runneth in, dividing them asonder by the distance of eleven miles or thereabouts; and there surmounteth into a large and wide sea which, by reason that the land of every side compasseth it about and shilt'reth it from the winds, is not rough nor mounteth not with great waves, but almost floweth quietly, not much unlike a great standing pool; and maketh almost all the space within the belly of the land in manner of a haven, and to the great commodity of the inhabitants receiveth in ships towards every part of the land. The forefronts or frontiers of the two corners, what with fords and shelves and what with rocks, be very jeopardous and dangerous. In the middle distance between them both standeth up above the water a great rock, which therefore is nothing perilous bicause it is in sight. Upon the top of this rock is a fair and a strong tower builded, which they hold with a garrison of men. Other rocks there be that lie hid under the water, and therefore be dangerous. The channels be known only to themselfes. An therefore it seldom chanceth that any stranger, onless he be guided by a Utopian, can come into this haven; insomuch that they themselfes could scasely enter without jeopardy but that their way is directed and ruled by certain landmarks standing on the shore. By turning, translating, and removing this marks into other places they may destroy their enemies' navies, be they never so many. The outside of the land is also full of havens, but the landing is so surely defensed, what by nature and what by workmanship of man's hand, that a few defenders may drive back many armies.

Howbeit, as they say, and as the fashion of the place itself doth partly shew, it was not ever compassed about with the sea. But King Utopus, whose name as conqueror the iland beareth (for before that time it was called Abraxa), which also brought the rude and wild people to that excellent perfection in all good fashions, humanity, and civil gentleness wherein they now go beyond all the people of the world, even at his first arriving and entering upon the land, furthwith obtaining the victory, caused fifteen miles' space of uplandish ground (where the sea had no passage) to be cut and digged up, and so brought the sea round about the land. He set to this work not only the inhabitants of the iland (because they should not think it done in contumely and despite) but also all his own soldiers. Thus the work, being divided into so great a number of workmen, was with exceeding marvelous speed dispatched. Insomuch that the borderers, which at the first began to mock and to jest at this vain enterprise, then turned their laughter to marvel at the success and to fear.

There be in the iland fifty-four large and fair cities or shire-towns, agreeing all together in one tongue, in like manners, institutions, and laws. They be all set and situate alike, and in all points fashioned alike, as farfurth as the place or plot suffereth. Of these cities they that be nighest together be twenty-four miles asonder. Again there is none of them distant from the next above one day's jorney afoot.

There come yearly to Amaurote out of every city three old men, wise and well-experienced, there to entreat and debate of the common matters of the land. For this city (because it standeth just in the middes of the iland and is therefore most meet for the embassadors of all parts of the realm) is taken for the chief and head city. The precincts and bounds of the shires be so commodiously appointed out and set furth for the cities that never a one of them all hath of any side less then twenty miles of ground, and of some side also much more, as of that part where the cities be of farther distance asonder. None of the cities desire to enlarge the bounds and limits of their shires; for they count themselfes rather the good husbands then the owners of their lands.

They have in the country, in all parts of the shire, houses or ferms builded, well appointed and furnished with all sorts of instruments and tools belonging to husbandry. These houses be inhabited of the citizens, which come thither to dwell by course. No household or ferm in the country hath fewer then forty persons, men and women, besides two bonden men, which be all under the rule and order of the goodman and the goodwife of the house, being both very sage and discrete persons. And every thirty ferms or families have one head ruler which is called a phylarch, being as it were a head bailiff. Out of every one of these families or ferms cometh every year into the city twenty persons which have continued two years before in the country. In their place so many fresh be sent thither out of the city, which of them that have been there a year already, and be therefore expert and conning in husbandry, shall be instructed and taught, and they the next year shall teach other. This order is used for fear that other scarceness of victuals or some other like incommodity should chance through lack of knowledge if they should be altogether new and fresh and unexpert in husbandry. This manner and fashion of yearly changing and renewing the occupiers of husbandry, though it be solempn and customably used to th' intent that no man shall be constrained against his will to continue long in that hard and sharp kind of life, yet many of them have such a pleasure and delight in husbandry that they obtain a longer space of years. These husbandmen plow and till the ground, and breed up cattle, and make ready wood which they carry to the city, other by land or by water, as they may most conveniently. They bring up a great multitude of pullen, and that by a marvelous policy. For the hens do not sit upon the eggs, but by keeping them in a certain equal heat they bring life into them and hatch them. The chickens, as soon as they be come out of the shell, follow men and women instead of the hens.

They bring up very few horses, nor none but very fierce ones, and for none other use or purpose but only to exercise their youth in riding and feats of arms. For oxen be put to all the labor of plowing and drawing; which they grant to be not so good as horses [at a] sudden brunt and, as we say, at a dead lift, but yet they hold opinion that oxen will abide and suffer much more labor and pain then horses will. And they think that they be not in danger and subject unto so many diseases, and that they be kept and maintained with much less cost and charge, and, finally, that they be good for meat when they be past labor.

They sow corn only for bread. For their drink is other wine made of grapes or else of apples or pears, or else it is clean water, and many times meth made of honey or liqueress sod in water, for thereof they have great store. And though they know certainly (for they know it perfectly indeed) how much victuals the city with the whole country or shire round about it doth spend, yet they sow much more corn and breed up much more cattle then serveth for their own use. And the overplus they part among their borderers. Whatsoever necessary things be lacking in the country, all such stuff they fetch out of the city, where without any exchange they easely obtain it of the magistrates of the city. For every moneth many of them go into the city on the holy day. When their harvest day draweth near and is at hand, then the phylarchs, which be the head officers and bailiffs of husbandry, send word to the magistrates of the city what number of harvestmen is needful to be sent to them out of the city. The which company of harvestmen, being there ready at the day appointed, almost in one fair day dispatcheth all the harvest work. . . .

Of the Magistrates

Every thirty families or ferms chewse them yearly an officer which in their old language is called the syphogrant and by a newer name the phylarch. Every ten syphogrants, with all their three hundred families, be under an officer which was ones called the tranibore, now the chief phylarch.

Moreover, as concerning the election of the prince, all the syphogrants, which be in number two hundred, first be sworn to chewse him whom they think most meet and expedient. Then by a secret election they name prince one of those four whom the people before named unto them. For out of the four quarters of the city there be four chosen, out of every quarter one, to stand for the election, which be put up to the counsel. The prince's office continueth all his lifetime, onless he be deposed or put down for suspicion of tyranny. They chewse the tranibores yearly, but lightly they change them not. All the other offices be but for one year. The tranibores every third day, and sometimes, if need be, oftener, come into the councel-house with the prince. Their councel is concerning the commonwealth. If there be any controversies among the commoners, which be very few, they dispatch and end them by and by. They take ever two syphogrants to them in councel, and every day a new couple. And it is provided that no thing touching the commonwealth shall be confirmed and ratified onless it have been reasoned of and debated three days in the councel before it be decreed. It is death to have any consultation for the commonwealth out of the counsel, or the place of the common election. This statute, they say, was made to th' entent that the prince and tranibores might not easely conspire together to oppress the people by tyranny and to change the state of the weal publique. Therefore, matters of great weight and importance be brought to the election-house of the syphogrants, which open the matter to their families; and afterward, when they have consulted among themselfes, they shew their devise to the councel. Sometime the matter is brought before the councel of the whole iland.

Furthermore, this custom also the councel useth, to dispute or reason of no matter the same day that it is first proposed or put furth, but to defer it to the next sitting of the counsel. Bycause that no man when he hath rashly there spoken that cometh first to his tongue's end shall then afterward rather study for reasons wherewith to defend and confirm his first foolish sentence than for the commodity of the commonwealth, as one rather willing the harm or hinderance of the weal publique then any loss or diminution of his own existimation, and as one that would not for shame (which is a very foolish shame) be counted anything overseen in the matter at the first, who at the first ought to have spoken rather wisely then hastely or rashly. . . .

Of Their Living and Mutual Conversation Together

But now will I declare how the citizens use them-selfes one towards another, what familiar occupying and entertainment there is among the people, and what fashion they use in distributing everything. First, the city consisteth of families; the families most commonly be made of kindreds. For the women, when they be married at a lawful age, they go into their husbands' houses. But the male children, with all the whole male offspring, continue still in their own family, and be governed of the eldest and ancientest father, onless he dote for age; for then the next to him in age is put in his room.

But to th' intent the prescript number of the citizens should neither decrease nor above measure increase it is ordained that no family, which in every city be six thousand in the whole, besides them of the country, shall at ones have fewer children of the age of fourteen years or thereabout then ten or mo then sixteen; for of children under this age no number can be appointed. This measure or number is easely observed and kept by putting them that in fuller families be above the number into families of smaller increase. But if chance be that in the whole city the store encrease above the just number, therewith they fill up the lack of other cities. But if so be that the multitude throughout the whole iland pass and exceed the due number, then they chewse out of every city certain citizens, and build up a town under their own laws in the next land where the inhabitants have much waste and unoccupied ground, receiving also of the inhabitants to them if they will join and dwell with them. They, thus joining and dwelling together, do easely agree in one fashion of living, and that to the great wealth of both the peoples. For they so bring the matter about by their laws that the ground which before was neither good nor profitable for the one nor for the other is now sufficient and fruitful enough for them both. But if the inhabitants of that land will not dwell with them, to be ordered by their laws, then they drive them out of those bounds which they have limited and appointed out for themselves. And if they resist and rebel, then they make war against them. For they count this the most just cause of war, when any people holdeth a piece of ground void and vacant to no good nor profitable use, keeping other from

the use and possession of it, which notwithstanding by the law of nature ought thereof to be nourished and relieved. . . .

But now again to the conversation of the citizens among themselfes. The eldest, as I said, ruleth the family. The wifes be ministers to their husbands, the children to their parents, and, to be short, the younger to their elders. Every city is divided into four equal parts. In the middes of every quarter there is a market-place of all manner of things. Thether the works of every family be brought into certain houses. And every kind of thing is laid up several in barns or storehouses. From hence the father of every family or every householder fetcheth whatsoever he and his have need of, and carryeth it away with him without money, without exchange, without any gage or pledge. For why should anything be denied unto him, seeing there is abundance of all things and that it is not to be feared lest any man will ask more then he needeth? For why should it be thought that man would ask more then enough which is sure never to lack? Certainly, in all kinds of living creatures, other fear of lack doth cause covetousness and ravin, or in man only pride, which counteth it a glorious thing to pass and excel other in the superfluous and vain ostentation of things. The which kind of vice among the Utopians can have no place.

Next to the market-places that I spake of stond meat markets, whether be brought not only all sorts of herbs and the fruits of trees with bread, but also fish and all manner of four-footed beasts and wild fowl that be man's meat. But first the filthiness and ordure thereof is clean washed away in the running river without the city, in places appointed meet for the same purpose. From thence the beasts be brought in killed, and clean washed by the hands of their bondmen. For they permit not their free citizens to accustom theirselfes to the killing of beasts, through the use whereof they think that clemency, the gentlest affection of our nature, doth by little and little decay and perish. Nother they suffer anything that is filthy, lothsome, or uncleanly to be brought into the city, lest the air, by the stench thereof infected and corrupt, should cause pestilent diseases.

Moreover, every street hath certain great large halls set in equal distance one from another, every one known by a several name. In these halls dwell the syphogrants. And to every one of the same halls be appointed thirty families, of either side fifteen. The stewards of every hall at a certain hour come into the meat markets, where they receive meat according to the number of their halls.

But first and chiefly of all, respect is had to the sick that be cured in the hospitals. For in the circuit of the city, a little without the walls, they have four hospitals, so big, so wide, so ample, and so lardge that they may seem four little towns; which were devised of that bigness partly to th' intent the sick, be they never so many in number, should not lie too throng or strait, and therefore uneasely and incommodiously; and partly that they which were taken and holden with contagious diseases, such as be wont by infection to creep from one to another, might be laid apart far from the company of the residue. These hospitals be so well appointed, and with all things necessary to health so furnished, and moreover so diligent attendance through the continual presence of cunning physitians is geven, that though no man be sent thither against his will, yet notwithstanding there is no sick person in all the city that had not rather lie there then at home in his own house. When the steward of the sick hath received such meats as the physitians have prescribed, then the best is equally devided among the halls, according to the company of every one, saving that there is had a respect to the prince, the bishop, the tranibores, and to ambassadors and all strangers, if there be any, which be very few and seldom. But they also, when they be there, have certain houses appointed and prepared for them.

To these halls at the set hours of dinner and supper cometh all the whole syphogranty or ward, warned by the noise of a brazen trumpet, except such as be sick in the hospitals or else in their own houses. . . . In this hall all vile service, all slavery and drudgery, with all laborsome toil and business, is done by bondmen. But the women of every family by course have the office and charge of cookery, for seething and dressing the meat, and ordering all things thereto belonging. They sit at three tables or mo, according to the number of their company. The men sit upon the bench next the wall and the women against them on the other side of the table, that, if any sodein evil should chance to them, as many times happeneth to women with child, they may rise without trouble or disturbance of anybody, and go thence into the nursery.

The nourcies sit several alone with their young sucklings in a certain parlor appointed and deputed to the same purpose, never without fire and clean water nor yet without cradles, that when they will they may lay down the young infants and at their pleasure take them out of their swathing clothes and hold them to the fire and refresh them with play. Every mother is nource to her own child onless other death or sickness be the let. When that chanceth, the wives of the syphogrants quickly provide a nource. And that is not hard to be done. For they that can do it do proffer themselfes to no service so gladly as to that. Because that there this kind of pity is much praised, and the child that is nourished ever after taketh his nource for his own natural mother. Also among the nourcies sit all the children that be under the age of five years. All the other children of both kinds, as well boys as girls, that be under the age of marriage, do other serve at the tables or else, if they be too young thereto, yet they stand by with mervelous silence. That which is geven to them from the table they eat, and other several dinner-time they have none. The syphogrant and his wife sitteth in the middes of the high table, forasmuch as that is counted the honorablest place, and because from thence all the whole company is in their sight. For that table standeth overwhart the over end of the hall. To them be joined two of the ancientest and eldest. For at every table they sit four at a mess. But if there be a church standing in that syphogranty or ward, then the priest and his wife sitteth with the syphogrant, as chief in the company. On both sides of them sit young men, and next unto them again old men. And thus throughout all the house equal of age be set together, and yet be mix'd with unequal ages. This, they say, was ordained to the intent that the sage gravity and reverence of the elders should keep the youngers from wanton license of words and behavior, forasmuch as nothing can be so secretly spoken or done at the table but either they that sit on the one side or on the other must needs perceive it. The dishes be not set down in order from the first place, but all the old men (whose places be marked with some special token to be known) be first served of their meat, and then the residue equally. The old men devide their dainties as they think best to the younger that sit of both sides them. Thus the elders be not defrauded of their due honor, and nevertheless equal commodity cometh to every one.

They begin every dinner and supper of reading something that pertaineth to good manners and virtue. But it is short, because no man shall be grieved therewith. Hereof th' elders take occasion of honest communication, but nother sad nor unpleasant. Howbeit, they do not spend all the whole dinnertime themselfes with long and tedious talks, but they gladly hear also the young men, yea, and do purposely provoke them to talk, to th' entent that they may have a proof of every man's wit and towardness or disposition to virtue, which commonly in the liberty of feasting doth shew and utter itself. Their dinners be very short, but their suppers be somewhat longer, because that after dinner followeth labor, after supper sleep and natural rest, which they think to be of more strength and efficacy to wholesome and healthful digestion. No supper is passed without music, nor their bankets lack no conceits nor junkets. They burn sweet gums and speces for perfumes and pleasant smells, and sprinkle about sweet ointments and waters; yea, they leave nothing undone that maketh for the cheering of the company. For they be much enclined to this opinion: to think no kind of pleasure forbidden whereof cometh no harm.

Thus, therefore, and after this sort they live togethers in the city; but in the country they that dwell alone, far from any neighbors, do dine and sup at home in their own houses. For no family there lacketh any kind of victuals, as from whom cometh all that the citizens eat and live by.

Of Their Journeying or Traveling Abroad, with Divers Other Matters Cunningly Reasoned and Wittily Discussed

... They marvel also that gold, which of the own nature is a thing so unprofitable, is now among all people in so high estimation that man himself, by whom, yea, and for the use of whom it is so much set by, is in much less estimation then the gold itself. Insomuch that a lumpish, blockheaded churl, and which hath no more wit then an ass, yea, and as full of noughtiness and foolishness, shall have nevertheless many wise and good men in subjection and bondage only for this: bycause he hath a great heap of gold. Which if it should be taken from him by any fortune, or by some subtle wile of the law (which no less then fortune doth raise up the low and pluck down the high), and be geven to the most vile slave and abject drevel of all his household, then shortly after he shall go into the service of his servant, as an augmentation or an overplus beside his money. But they much more marvel at and detest the madness of them which to those rich men, in whose debt and danger they be not, do give almost divine honors for none other consideration but bicause they be rich; and yet knowing them to be such niggish pennyfathers that they be sure, as long as they live, not the worth of one farthing of that heap of gold shall come to them.

These and such-like opinions have they conceived partly by education, being brought up in that commonwealth whose laws and customs be far different from these kinds of folly, and partly by good literature and learning. For though there be not many in every city which be exempt and discharged of all other labors and appointed only to learning—that is to say, such in whom even from their very childhood they have perceived a singular towardness, a fine wit, and a mind apt to good learning—yet all in their childhood be instruct in learning. And the better part of the people, both men and women, throughout all their whole life, do bestow in learning those spare hours which we said they have vacant from bodily labors. They be taught learning in their own native tongue. For it is both copious in words and also pleasant to the ear, and for the utterance of a man's mind very perfect and sure. The most part of all that side of the wordle useth the same language, saving that among the Utopians it is finest and purest; and according to the diversity of the countries it is diversely altered.

Of all these philosophers whose names be here famous in this part of the wordle to us known, before our coming thether not as much as the fame of any of them was comen among them; and yet in music, logic, arithmetic, and geometry they have found out in a manner all that our ancient philosophers have taught. But as they in all things be almost equal to our old ancient clerks, so our new logicians in subtle inventions have far passed and gone beyond them. For they have not devised one of all those rules of restrictions, amplifications, and suppositions, very wittily invented in the small *Logicales,* which here our children in every place do learn. Furthermore, they were never yet able to find out the second intentions, insomuch that none of them all could ever see man himself in commen, as they call him, though he be (as you know) bigger then ever was any giant, yea, and pointed to of us even with our finger. But they be in the course of the stars and the movings of the heavenly spheres very expert and cunning. They have also wittily excogitated and devised instruments of divers fashions wherein is exactly comprehended and contained the movings and situations of the sun, the moon, and of all the other stars which appear in their horizon. But as for the amities and dissensions of the planets, and all that deceitful divination by the stars, they never as much as dreamed thereof. Rains, winds, and other courses of tempests they know before by certain tokens which they have learned by long use and observation. But of the causes of all these things, of the ebbing, flowing, and saltiness of the sea, and finally of the original beginning and nature of heaven and of the wordle, they hold partly the same opinions that our old philosophers hold, and partly, as our philosophers vary emong themselfes, so they also, whiles they bring new reasons of things, do disagree from all them, and yet emong themselfes in all points they do not accord.

In that part of philosophy which intreateth of manners and virtue their reasons and opinions agree with ours. They dispute of the good qualities of the soul, of the body, and of fortune; and whether the name of goodness may be applied to all these or only to the endowments and gifts of the soul. They reason of virtue and pleasure. But the chief and principal question is in what thing, be it one or mo, the felicity of man consisteth. But in this point they seem almost too much geven and enclined to the opinion of them which defend pleasure, wherein they determine other all or the chiefest part of man's felicity to rest. And (which is more to be marveled at) the defense of this so dainty and delicate an opinion they fetch even from their grave, sharp, bitter, and rigorous religion. For they never dispute of felicity or blessedness but they join to the reasons of philosophy certain principles taken out of religion, without the which to the investigation of true felicity they think reason of itself weak and unperfect. Those principles be these and such-like: that the soul is immortal and by the bountiful goodness of God ordained to felicity; that to our virtues and good deeds rewards be appointed after this life and to our evil deeds punishments. Though these be pertaining to religion, yet they think it meet that they should be believed and granted by proofs of reason. But if these principles were condempned and disannulled, then without any delay they pronounce no man to be so foolish which would not do all his diligence and endeavor to obtain pleasure by right or wrong, only avoiding this inconvenience, that the less pleasure should not be a let or hinderance to the bigger, or that he labored not for that pleasure which would bring after it displeasure, grief, and sorrow. For they judge it extreme madness to follow sharp and painful virtue, and not only to banish the pleasure of life, but also willingly to suffer grief without any hope of profit thereof. For what profit can there be if a man, when he hath passed over all his life unpleasantly, that is to say, wretchedly, shall have no reward after his death? But now, sir, they think not felicity to rest in all pleasure, but only in that pleasure that is good and honest, and that hereto, as to perfet blessedness, our nature is allured and drawn even of virtue, whereto only they that be of the contrary opinion do attribute felicity. For they define virtue to be a life ordered according to nature, and that we be hereunto ordained of God, and that he doth follow the course of nature which in desiring and refusing things is ruled by reason. Furthermore, that reason doth chiefly and principally kendle in men the love and veneration of the Divine Majesty of whose goodness it is that we be and that we be in possibility to attain felicity. And that, secondarily, it moveth and provoketh us to lead our life out of care in joy and mirth and to help all other, in respect of the society of nature, to obtain the same. For there was never man so earnest and painful a follower of virtue, and hater of pleasure, that would so injoin you labors, watchings, and fastings but he would also exhort you to ease and lighten to your power the lack and misery of others,

praising the same as a deed of humanity and pity. Then if it be a point of humanity for man to bring health and comfort to man, and specially (which is a virtue most peculiarly belonging to man) to mitigate and assuage the grief of others, and, by taking from them the sorrow and heaviness of life, to restore them to joy, that is to say pleasure, why may it not, then, be said that nature doth provoke every man to do the same to himself?

For a joyful life, that is to say, a pleasant life, is other evil—and if it be so, then thou shouldest not only help no man thereto but rather, as much as in thee lieth, help all men from it, as noisome and hurtful—or else, if thou not only mayst but also of duty art bound to procure it to others, why not chiefly to theeself, to whom thou art bound to shew as much favor as to other? For when nature biddeth thee to be good and gentle to other, she commandeth thee not to be cruel and ungentle to theeself. Therefore, even very nature, say they, prescribeth to us a joyful life, that is to say, pleasure, as the end of all our operations. And they define virtue to be life ordered according to the prescript of nature. But in that that nature doth allure and provoke men one to help another to live merrily (which surely she doth not without a good cause, for no man is so far above the lot of man's state or condition that nature doth cark and care for him only, which equally favoreth all that be comprehended under the communion of one shape, form, and fashion), verily she commandeth thee to use diligent circumspection that thou do not so seek for thine own commodities that thou procure others' incommodities.

Wherefore their opinion is that not only covenants and bargains made among private men ought to be well and faithfully fulfilled, observed, and kept, but also commen laws, which other a good prince hath justly published or else the people—nother oppressed with tyranny, nother deceived by fraud and guile—hath by their common consent constitute and ratified concerning the partition of the commodities of life, that is to say, the matter of pleasure. These laws not offended, it is wisdom that thou look to thine own wealth. And to do the same for the commonwealth is no less then thy duty if thou bearest any reverent love or any natural zeal and affection to thy native country. . . .

Pleasure they call every motion and state of the body or mind wherein man hath naturally delectation. Appetite they join to nature, and that not without a good cause. For like as not only the senses, but also right reason, coveteth whatsoever is naturally pleasant, so that it may be gotten without wrong or injury, not letting or debarring a greater pleasure nor causing painful labor, even so those things that men by vain imagination do feign against nature to be pleasant (as though it lay in their power to change the things as they do the names of things), as such pleasures they believe to be of so small help and furtherance to felicity that they count them great let and hinderance, because that in whom they have ones taken place, all his mind they possess with a false opinion of pleasure, so that there is no place left for true and natural delectations. For there be many things which of their own nature contain no pleasantness—yea, the most part of them much grief and sorrow—and yet, through the perverse and malicious flickering inticements of lewd and unhonest desires, be taken not only for special and sovereign pleasures, but also be counted among the chief causes of life. . . .

They make divers kinds of true pleasures. For some they attribute to the soul, and some to the body. To the soul they give intelligence, and that delectation that cometh of the contemplation of truth. Hereunto is joined the pleasant remembrance of the good life past.

The pleasure of the body they devide into two parts. The first is when delectation is sensibly felt and perceived, which many times chanceth by the renewing and refreshing of those parts which our natural heat drieth up; this cometh by meat and drink, and sometimes whiles those things be voided whereof is in the body overgreat abundance. This pleasure is felt when we do our natural easement, or when we be doing the act of generation, or when the itching of any part is eased with rubbing or scratching. Sometimes pleasure riseth, exhibiting to any member nothing that it desireth nor taking from it any pain that it feeleth, which for all that tickleth and moveth our senses with a certain secret efficacy but with a manifest motion, and turneth them to it, as is that which cometh of music.

The second part of bodily pleasure, they say, is that which consisteth and resteth in the quiet and upright state of the body. And that truly is every man's own proper health, entermingled and disturbed with no grief. For this, if it be not letted nor assaulted with no grief, is delectable of itself, though it be moved with no external or outward pleasure. For though it be not so plain and manifest to the sense as the greedy lust of eating and drinking, yet nevertheless many take it for the chiefest pleasure. All the Utopians grant it to be a right great pleasure, and, as you would say, the foundation and ground of all pleasures, as which even alone is able to make the state and condition of life delectable and pleasant; and, it being ones taken away, there is no place left for any pleasure. . . .

They imbrace chiefly the pleasures of the mind.

For them they count the chiefest and most principal of all. The chief part of them, they think, doth come of the exercise of virtue, and conscience of good life. Of these pleasures that the body minist'reth they give the preeminence to health. For the delight of eating and drinking, and whatsoever hath any like pleasantness, they determine to be pleasures much to be desired, but no other ways than for health's sake. . . .

Beauty, strength, nembleness, these, as peculiar and pleasant gifts of nature, they make much of. But those pleasures which be received by the ears, the eyes, and the nose, which nature willeth to be proper and peculiar to man—for no other kind of living beasts doth behold the fairness and the beauty of the wordle, or is moved with any respect of savors, but only for the diversity of meats, nother perceiveth the concordant and discordant distances of sounds and tunes—these pleasures, I say, they accept and allow as certain pleasant rejoicings of life. But in all things this cautel they use, that a less pleasure hinder not a bigger, and that the pleasure be no cause of displeasure, which they think to follow of necessity if the pleasure be unhonest. But yet to dispise the comeliness of beauty, to waste the bodily strength, to tourn nimbleness into sloughishness, to consume and make feeble the body with fasting, to do injury to health, and to reject the other pleasant motions of nature (onless a man neglect these his commodities whiles he doth with a fervent zeal procure the wealth of others, or the commen profit, for the which pleasure forborne he is in hope of a greater pleasure of God), else for a vain shadow of virtue, for the wealth and profet of no man, to punish himself or to the intent he may be able couragiously to suffer adversity which, perchance, shall never come to him—this to do they think it a point of extreme madness and a token of a man cruelly minded towards himself and unkind toward nature, as one so disdaining to be in her danger that he renounceth and refuseth all her benefits.

This is their sentence and opinion of virtue and pleasure. And they believe that by man's reason none can be found truer then this, onless any godlier be inspired into man from heaven. Wherein, whether they believe well or no, nother the time doth suffer us to discuss, nother it is now necessary. For we have taken upon us to shew and declare their lores and ordinances, and not to defend them. . . .

Of the Religions in Utopia

There be divers kinds of religion, not only in sondry parts of the iland but also in divers places of every city. Some worship for god the sun, some the moon, some some other of the planets. There be that give worship to a man that was ones of excellent virtue or of famous glory, not only as god, but also as the chiefest and highest god. But the most and the wisest part, rejecting all these, believe that there is a certain godly power unknown, everlasting, incomprehensible, inexplicable, far above the capacity and retch of man's wit, dispersed throughout all the world, not in bigness but in virtue and power. Him they call the father of all. To him alone they attribute the beginnings, the encreasings, the proceedings, the changes, and the ends of all things. Nother they give devine honors to any other then to him.

Yea, all the other also, though they be in divers opinions, yet in this point they agree all togethers with the wisest sort in believing that there is one chief and principal god, the maker and ruler of the whole world, whom they all commonly in their country language call Mythra. But in this they disagree, that among some he is counted one and among some another. For every one of them, whatsoever that is which he taketh for the chief god, thinketh it to be the very same nature to whose only devine might and majesty the sum and soverainty of all things, by the consent of all people, is attributed and geven. Howbeit, they all begin by little and little to forsake and fall from this variety of superstitions and to agree togethers in that religion which seemeth by reason to pass and excel the residue. And it is not to be doubted but all the other would long ago have been abolished, but that whatsoever unprosperous thing happened to any of them as he was minded to change his religion, the fearfulness of people did take it not as a thing coming by chance, but as sent from god out of heaven, as though the god whose honor he was forsaking would revenge that wicked purpose against him.

But after they hard us speak of the name of Christ, of his doctrine, laws, miracles, and of the no less wonderful constancy of so many martyrs, whose blood willingly shed brought a great number of nations throughout all parts of the world into their sect, you will not believe with how glad minds they agreed unto the same, whether it were by the secret inspiration of God, or else for that they thought it next unto that opinion which among them is counted the chiefest. Howbeit, I think this was no small help and furtherance in the matter, that they hard us say that Christ instituted among his all things commen, and that the same community doth yet remain amongest the rightest Christian companies. Verily, howsoever it came to pass, many of them consented togethers in our religion, and were washed in the holy water of baptism.

But because among us four (for no mo of us was left alive, two of our company being dead) there was no priest, which I am right sorry for, they being entered and instructed in all other points of our religion lack only those sacraments which here none but priests do minister. Howbeit, they understand and perceive them, and be very desirous of the same. Yea, they reason and dispute the matter earnestly among themselfes, whether, without the sending of a Christian bishop, one chosen out of their own people may receive the order of priesthood. And truly they were minded to chuse one, but at my departure from them they had chosen none. They also which do not agree to Christ's religion fear no man from it, nor speak against any man that hath received it. Saving that one of our company in my presence was sharply punished. He, as soon as he was baptized, began against our wills, with more earnest affection then wisdom, to reason of Christ's religion, and began to wax so hot in his matter that he did not only prefer our religion before all other but also did utterly despise an condempn all other, calling them prophane and the followers of them wicked and devilish and the children of everlasting dampnation. When he had thus long reasoned the matter, they laid hold on him, accused him, and condempned him into exile, not as a despiser of religion but as a seditious person and a raiser-up of dissension among the people. For this is one of the ancientest laws among them, that no man shall be blamed for reasoning in the maintenance of his own religion.

For King Utopus, even at the first beginning, hearing that the inhabitants of the land were before his coming thether at continual dissension and strife among themselfes for their religions, perceiving also that this common dissension, whiles every several sect took several parts in fighting for their country, was the only occasion of his conquest over them all, as soon as he had gotten the victory, first of all he made a decree that it should be lawful for every man to favor and follow what religion he would, and that he might do the best he could to bring other to his opinion, so that he did it peaceably, gently, quietly, and soberly, without hasty and contentious rebuking and inveihing against other. If he could not by fair and gentle speech induce them unto his opinion, yet he should use no kind of violence, and refrain from displeasant and seditious words. To him that would vehemently and fervently in this cause strive and contend was decreed banishment or bondage.

This law did King Utopus make not only for the maintenance of peace, which he saw through continual contention and mortal hatred utterly extinguished, but also because he thought this decree should make for the furtherance of religion. Whereof he durst define and determine nothing unadvisedly, as doubting whether God, desiring manifold and divers sorts of honor, would inspire sondry men with sondry kinds of religion. And this, surely, he thought a very unmeet and foolish thing and a point of arrogant presumption, to compel all other by violence and threatenings to agree to the same that thou believest to be true. Furthermore, though there be one religion which alone is true, and all other vain and superstitious, yet did he well foresee (so that the matter were handeled with reason and sober modesty) that the truth of the own power would at the last issue out and come to light. But if contention and debate in that behalf should continually be used, as the worst men be most obstinate and stubborn and in their evil opinion most constant, he perceived that then the best and holiest religion would be trodden under foot and destroyed by most vain superstitions, even as good corn is by thorns and weeds overgrown and choked. Therefore all this matter he left undiscussed, and gave to every man free liberty and choice to believe what he would, saving that he earnestly and straitly chardged them that no man should conceive so vile and base an opinion of the dignity of man's nature as to think that the souls do die and perish with the body, or that the world runneth at all aventures, governed by no divine providence. And therefore they believe that after this life vices be extremely punished and virtues bountifully rewarded. Him that is of a contrary opinion they count not in the number of men, as one that hath avaled the high nature of his soul to the vileness of brute beasts' bodies; much less in the number of their citizens, whose laws and ordinances, if it were not for fear, he would nothing at all esteem. For you may be sure that he will study other with craft previly to mock or else violently to break the commen laws of his country, in whom remaineth no further fear then of the laws nor no further hope then of the body. Wherefore he that is thus minded is deprived of all honors, excluded from all offices, and reject from all common administrations in the weal publique. And thus he is of all sort despised as of an unprofitable and of a base and vile nature. Howbeit, they put him to no punishment, because they be persuaded that it is in no man's power to believe what he list. No, nor they constrain him not with threat'nings to dissemble his mind and shew countenance contrary to his thought. For deceit, and falshed, and all manner of lies as next unto fraud they do mervelously detest and abhor. But they suffer him not to dispute in his opinion, and that only among the commen people. For else apart, among the priests and men of gravity, they do not only suffer but also exhort him to dispute and argue, hooping that at the last that madness will give place to reason.

There be also other, and of them no small number, which be not forbidden to speak their minds as grounding their opinion upon some reason, being in their living nother evil nor vicious. Their heresy is much contrary to the other. For they believe that the souls of brute beasts be immortal and everlasting, but nothing to be compared with ours in dignity, nother ordained and predestinate to like felicity. For all they believe certainly and surely that man's bless shall be so great that they do mourn and lament every man's sickness, but no man's death, onless it be one whom they see depart from his life carefully and against his will. For this they take for a very evil token, as though the soul, being in dispair and vexed in conscience, through some prevy and secret forefeeling of the punishment now at hand, were afear'd to depart. And they think he shall not be welcome to God which, when he is called, runneth not to Him gladly, but is drawn by force and sore against his will. They, therefore, that see this kind of death do abhor it, and them that so die they bury with sorrow and silence. And when they have prayed God to be merciful to the soul and mercifully to pardon the infirmities thereof, they cover the dead corse with earth.

Contrariwise, all that depart merely and full of good hoope, for them no man mourneth, but followeth the hearse with joyful singing, commending the souls to God with great affection. And at the last not with mourning sorrow, but with a great reverence, they bourn the bodies, and in the same place they set up a piller of stone with the dead man's titles therein graved. When they be come home they rehearse his virtuous manners and his good deeds. But no part of his life is so oft or gladly talked of as his merry death. They think that this remembrance of their virtue and goodness doth vehemently provoke and enforce the quick to virtue, and that nothing can be more pleasant and acceptable to the dead, whom they suppose to be present emong them when they talk of them, though to the dull and feeble eyesight of mortal men they be invisible. . . .

Thus when Raphael had made an end of his tale, though many things came to my mind which in the manners and laws of that people seemed to be instituted and founded of no good reason, not only in the fashion of their chevalry and in their sacrifices and religions and in other of their laws, but also, yea and chiefly, in that which is the principal foundation of all their ordinances, that is to say, in the community of their life and living without any occupying of money—by the which thing only all nobility, magnificence, worship, honor, and majesty, the true ornaments and honors, as the common opinion is, of a commonwealth utterly be overthrown and destroyed—yet bicause I knew that he was weary of talking, and was not sure whether he could abide that anything should be said against his mind, specially bicause I remember'd that he had reprehended this fault in other, which be afear'd lest they should seem not to be wise enough onless they could find some fault in other men's inventions; therefore I, praising both their institutions and his communication, took him by the hand and led him in to supper, saying that we would chuse another time to weigh

and examine the same matters, and to talk with him more at lardge therein. Which would to God it might ones come to pass. In the meantime, as I cannot agree and consent to all things that he said, being else without doubt a man singularly well-learned and also in all wordly matters exactly and profoundly experienced, so must I needs confess and grant that many things be in the Utopian weal publique which in our cities I may rather wish for then hoope after.

Thus endeth the afternoon's talk of Raphael Hythloday concerning the laws and institutions of the Iland of Utopia.

SIR THOMAS CHALONER (trans.)

ERASMUS' *PRAISE OF FOLLY*

At the urging of his old pupil, the fourth Baron Mountjoy—who hailed the accession of Henry VIII as the opening of a golden age for English letters—Erasmus crossed the Channel to England for the third time in the fall of 1509. Convalescing from an illness at More's house in Bucklersbury, London, he wrote, in about a week, his *Moriae encomium,* a trifle compared to his *Adagia* and his theological works but still the book by which he is best known. A parody of the classical oration by Folly, an attractive and very loquacious wench, it shows Erasmus in a new role of social commentator, sparing neither

king nor prince, pope nor friar, pedant nor sportsman his urbane but sharply edged indignation. More and his friends were delighted with it, as was Erasmus apparently, for in April, 1511, he himself took it to Paris to be secretly printed. Its instantaneous success resulted in no less than seven editions within a few months, and its subsequent popularity in translations (of which we reprint excerpts from the first in English) has made it one of the most widely read books ever written. Our text is based upon *The praise of Folie . . . by . . . Erasmus Roterodame. Englished by Sir Thomas Chaloner knight,* 1549 (STC 10500).

FROM THE PRAISE OF FOLLY . . . ENGLISHED BY SIR THOMAS CHALONER (1549)

To the Reader

A folly it may be thought in me to have spent time in Englishing of this book, entitled *The Praise of Folly,* whereas the name itself seemeth to set forth no wisdom or matter of gravity unless perhaps Erasmus, the autor thereof, delighted to mock men in calling it one thing and meaning another. To this I answer that Folly in all points is not (as I take it) so strange unto us but that her name may well be abidden as long as will we or nill we she will be sure to bear a stroke in most of our doings. Howsoever a certain sect of fault-finders condemn all things that fully square not with their own rules, yea twice blind in this, that amonges the commen errors and infirmities of mortal men they will bear nothing with their brethern—as who saith they were demigods, and not more than one or two ways linked in Folly's bands.

I have, therefore, bestowed an English livery upon this Latin book as well as I could, not so much to please all men as rather to shew how even this Folly toucheth all men. Wherein I would not be noted as a carper of any man particularly (for what more unsitting than in books or plays to touch men by name?), nor that herein I seek to have any kind of men noted for their trade of life otherwise than the abuse thereof deserveth, but only my meaning is such as Erasmus in this book shall express for us both. He of his modesty is content to set no great face upon it, nor would be noted to have spent great labor in making thereof, saving as in pastime to have essayed whether ought might be spoken in praise of Folly, whereas Wisdom, the virtue, can praise itself. And therefore he imagineth that Folly should be a goddess who, before all kinds of men assembled as to a sermon, should declare how many benefits they receive at her hands and how without her access nothing in this life is delectable, commodious, or tolerable unto us, no, not our own life. . . .

Seeing the vices of our days are such as cannot enough be spoken against, what know we if Erasmus in this book thought good between game and earnest to rebuke the same? And chiefly to persuade (if it might be) a certain contentation in every man to hold him agreed with such lot and state of living as ariseth to him. For which purpose was I also soonest moved to English it, to the end that mean men of baser wits and condition might have a manner comfort and satisfaction in theimselves, inasmuch as the high God who made us all of one earth hath natheless chosen some to rule and more to serve. Whereat so much lacketh that the inferiors should repine, as, rather, set in the meaner degree they should thank God the more, without aspiring to things above their reach, which should draw more trouble and perils than if they absteigned therefro and gave place to others who had greater gifts of God and were called by auctority of their prince or country to wield the same. . . .

This frankness of Folly's taunting I have presumed in some points to itch to the best, namely in two or three places which the learned reader, comparing with the Latin book, may easily perceive how either I have slipped over a line or two or eased the sour sense of the Latin with some mannerlier English word. Wherein I chose rather to be counted a scant true interpreter than otherwise to touch things which were better unsaid, as long as it hurted not the grace of the book though they were omitted. Likewise, in all my translation I have not pained myself to render word for word nor proverb for proverb, whereof many be Greek such as have no grace in our tongue; but rather, marking the sense, I applied it to the phrase of our English, and where the proverbs would take no English, I adventured to put English proverbs of like weight in their places; which may be thought by some cunning translators a deadly sin. But I stick not for all that in this foolish book to use mine own foolish cast. And if it be misliked I pass not greatly, though I lose the praise of my folly.

MORIAE ENCOMIUM

FOLLY speaketh:

Howsoever men commonly talk of me (as, pardy, I am not ignorant what lewd reports go on Folly, yea even amongs those that are veriest fools of all), yet that I am she, I only (I say), who through mine influence do glad both the gods and men, by this it may appear sufficiently, that as soon as I came forth to say my mind afore this your so notable assembly, by and by all your looks began to clear up, unbending the frowning of your brows, and laughing upon me with so merry a countenance as by my trouth meseemeth even that all ye (whom I see here present) do fare as if ye were well-whittled and thoroughly moisted with the nectar wine of the Homerical gods, not without a portion of the juice of that mervailous herb nepenthes, which hath force to put sadness and melancholy from the heart. Whereas before ye sat all heavy and glomming, as if ye had come lately from Trophonius' cave or Sainct Patrick's purgatory. But like as whan Phoebus displayeth his golden bright rays upon the earth, or whan, after a sharp stormy winter, the new primetide flourisheth with his calm sweet western winds, than, lo, a new likeness, a new hew, and a new youth (as it were) retourneth unto all things; even so, as soon as I appeared ye all began to look up lustily. So what thing these cunning rhetoricians, for all their long and fore-penned orations, can hardly bring about (I mean to drive care and pensiveness out of the hearers' minds), that have I with my only look and presence accomplished. And now ye shall wit to what entent at this time, in this so strange an apparel, I am come forth amonges you, upon condition ye will not think much to bestow on me your ears a while. I mean not those ears that ye carry with you to sermons, but those ye geve to players, to jesters, and to fools. . . .

All this life of mortal men, what is it else but a certain kind of stage play? Whereas men come forth disguised, one in one array, another in another, each playing his part till at last the maker of the play or book-bearer causeth theim to avoid the scaffold, and yet sometime maketh one man come in two or three times with sundry parts and apparail, as who before represented a king, being clothed all in purple, having no more but shifted himself a little should shew himself again like an wobegone miser. And all this is dooen under a certain veil or shadow which, taken away ones, the play can no more be played. Here now if one of these wisemen, come (I ween) from heaven, did sodeinly appear and say, "How even this great prince, whom all men honor as their god and sovereign, deserveth scarce to be called man, seeing, like the brute beasts, he is trained by affections and is none other than a servant of the basest sort, seeing willingly he obeyeth so many and so vile vices, his maisters." Or than again, would bid some other who mourned for his father's or friend's decease rather to laugh and be merry, because such dying to this world is the beginning of a better life, whereas this here is but a manner death, as it were. Furthermore, would call another glorying in his arms and ancestry both a villain and a bastard because he is so many discents disallied from virtue, which is the only root of true nobility. And in such like sort would rail upon all the rest. I pray you, what should he prevail thereby, but make men take him for frantic and distraught? For surely, as nothing can be more foolish than wisdom out of place, so is nothing more fond than prudence out of season. . . .

Now next unto the felicity of these maister doctors such do approach as people call religious men and monks, that is to say, solitary livers, but by both names evil applied, seeing the greatest part of them are most far from religion, and none so commenly shall you meet roving abroad, even in every ale-house. Whose trade and observance surely were most miserable and abject unless that I did many ways relieve them. For though this kind of men be commenly so abhorred as even to meet with theim at unwares or next a body's rising it is taken for a sign of evil luck all the day after, yet Lord! how they make theimselves to be more than cherubyns. For first they hold it a great holiness to meddle so little with books and learning as scarce they know how to read their own names. And whan they roar forth (like a meny of asses) in their monasteries a nomber of psalms not understanded, than they ween verily to feed saincts' ears with a mervailous melody. Moreover, some orders of them—namely friars—do take a pride in their beggery, in going from door to door to axe their bread with a great lowing voice, pest'ring men everywhere, both in inns, in wagons, and in passengers, not a little (I promise you) to the hindrance of other begsters. And thus, lo, the blind minions, what with their greasiness, doltishness, rudeness, and shameless hanging on men, do represent unto us (as theimselves say) the life of the apostles. But is it not a comeliness (trow ye) whan they do all things by certain presidents of their orders, much like

mathematical rules which in no wise without offense they may alter or swerve fro? As for example, how many windows they must make to their shoes, what color and nomber of knots goeth to their girdles, with what difference and whereof must their weeds be made, of what breadth their leather thongs, how many bushelfuls their cowls, how many inches long their knotted hear, and how many hours for sleeping? Now who is he that seeth not how unequal this equality of theirs is, namely in such a diverseness of bodies and dispositions? Yet under confidence of these trifles they not only set laymen as light as butterflies, but even amongs theimselves despise each other. So that for all the apostolic charity which they profess, ye shall not see them stick to fall together by the ears either for a girdle of a contrary fashion or a garment somewhat of a browner or lighter color. Yea, some of theim, being of a straighter rule, are so sore punishers of their flesh as outwardly they wear naught but sackcloth and inwardly no better than fine holland. Some others again dare as soon touch poison as money, never the more forbearing from wine nor contrectation of women. Finally, all their delight is to accord in no point as touching the rules of their religions. Nor they look not how to resemble Christ, but sooner how amongs theimselves to be dissemblable, esteeming further a great part of their felicity to consist in the names of their orders. For some of them rejoice to be called Grey Friars, some White, these Colletes, they Minors, other Observants, other Crossed, some Benedictines, some Bernardines, these Carmelites, those Augustines, these Guilhemites, those Jacobites, etc. As who saith it were too sclender a name for theim to be called bare Christians. . . .

SIR THOMAS ELYOT

Although he was one of the most accomplished classicists of the age, Elyot chose to write all his works in English. By precept and example thus showing the uses of the vernacular for literary purposes, he won a large contemporary reputation and an honored place in English literary history. *The Book Named the Governor* (1531), his first and biggest success, was written, as he tells Henry VIII in his dedication, "to describe in our vulgar tongue the form of a just public weal" and to prescribe the education "of them that hereafter may be deemed worthy to be governors of the public weal under your Highness." Thus it belongs to that large class of didactic manuals in which Renaissance humanists urged the rights and duties of an educated aristocracy. Elyot himself knew and used

such works as Patrizi's *De regno et regis institutione,* Erasmus' *Institutio principis Christiani,* Vives' *De tradendis disciplinis,* and Pontano's *De principe;* and the success of his book (which went through at least seven other editions by 1580) must have influenced Ascham's *Schoolmaster* (see pp. 813, 817–40) and Mulcaster's *Elementary* (see pp. 840–44). On the broad base of his introduction to Book I, which sets forth the advantages of a hierarchal society controlled by a necessarily small aristocracy, Elyot prescribes the curriculum and method for educating the governing class; Book II treats those virtues, nobility, mercy, liberality, and the like, which characterize a good ruler; and Book III (which, like all Elyot's other work, owes much to Plato) enlarges the discussion to embrace such moral absolutes as justice, fortitude, and temperance. The extraordinary range of Elyot's reading is everywhere apparent in the copious *exempla* and anecdotes that illustrate his principles. The whole, in spite of its large debts to other thinkers, must be accounted the most important and influential statement of Christian humanism of early Tudor England.

The remainder of Elyot's prolific production is represented by excerpts from *Of the Knowledge Which Maketh a Wise Man* (1533), an edifying but undeniably prosy dialogue between Plato and Aristippus on the correspondence of knowledge and virtue, and from *The Castle of Health* (?1534, 1539), a very lively and once popular essay on Galenic physiology. The dialogue attempts by quasi-Socratic but cumbersome methods to formulate the uses of rational self-control toward a virtuous life, and as such it is a fair specimen of the high moral seriousness of northern humanism. The fact that a medical treatise written in English by a layman attained an immediate success vexed a good many of Elyot's contemporaries, but he defended himself by pointing out that the physicians, angry at a medical book in English, should remember that the Greeks wrote in Greek, the Romans in Latin, and Avicenna in Arabic—their own proper and maternal tongues. Whatever its medical merits, Elyot's little treatise is a useful compendium of so-called faculty psychology, and its popularity long survived the early detractors.

Our texts are based upon *The boke named the Governour devised by Sr Thomas Elyot knight,* 1531 (STC 7635); *Of The Knowledeg* [sic] *whiche maketh a wise man,* 1533 (STC 7668); *The Castel of Helth, Corrected And in some places augmented by the fyrste authour therof, syr Thomas Elyot,* 1541 (STC 7644).

FROM THE BOOK NAMED THE GOVERNOR (1531)

THE FIRST BOOK

1. The signification of a public weal, and why it is called in Latin *respublica*

A public weal is in sundry wise defined by philosophers, but knowing by experience that the often repetition of anything of grave or sad importance will be tedious to the readers of this wark, who perchance for the more part have nat been trained in learning containing semblable matter, I have compiled one definition out of many, in as compendious fourm as my poor wit can devise: trusting that in those few words the true signification of a public weal shall evidently appear to them whom reason can satisfy.

A public weal is a body living, compact or made of sundry astates and degrees of men, which is disposed by the order of equity and governed by the rule and moderation of reason. In the Latin tongue hit is called *respublica,* of the which the word *res* hath divers significations, and doth nat only betoken that that is called a thing, which is distinct from a person, but also signifieth astate, condition, substance, and profit. In our old vulgar, profit is called weal. And it is called a wealthy country wherein is all thing that is profitable. And he is a wealthy man that is rich in money and substance. *Public* (as Varro saith) is dirivied of *people,* which in Latin is called *populus;* wherefore hit seemeth that men have been long abused in calling *rempublicam* a commune weal. And they which do suppose it so to be called for that that everything should be to all men in commune, without discrepance of any astate or condition, be thereto moved more by sensuality than by any good reason or inclination to humanity. And that shall soon appear unto them that will be satisfied either with autority or with natural order and example.

First, the proper and true signification of the words *public* and *commune,* which be borrowed of the Latin tongue for the insufficiency of our own language, shall sufficiently declare the blindness of them which have hitherto holden and maintained the said opinions. As I have said, *public* took his beginning of *people,* which in Latin is *populus,* in which word is contained all the inhabitants of a realm or city, of what astate or condition soever they be.

Plebs in English is called the communalty, which signifieth only the multitude, wherein be contained the base and vulgar inhabitants nat avanced to any honor or dignity, which is also used in our daily communication; for in the city of London and other cities they that be none aldermen or sheriffs be called communers. And in the country, at a sessions or other assembly, if no gentlemen be thereat, the saying is that there was none but the communalty, which proveth in mine opinion that *plebs* in Latin is in English *communalty;* and *plebeii* be *communers.* And consequently there may appear like diversity to be in English between a public weal and a commune weal, as should be in Latin between *res publica* and *res plebia.* And after that signification, if there should be a commune weal, either the communers only must be wealthy, and the gentle and noble men needy and miserable, or else, excluding gentility, all men must be of one degree and sort, and a new name provided. Forasmuch as *plebs* in Latin and *comminers* in English be words only made for the discrepance of degrees, whereof proceedeth order; which in things as well natural as supernatural hath ever had such a preeminence that thereby the incomprehensible majesty of God, as it were by a bright leam of a torch or candle, is declared to the blind inhabitants of this world. Moreover, take away order from all things, what should than remain? Certes nothing finally, except some man would imagine eftsoons *Chaos*, which of some is expound a confuse mixture. Also where there is any lack of order needs must be perpetual conflict, and in things subject to nature nothing of himself only may be norished; but whan he hath distroyed that wherewith he doth participate by the order of his creation, he himself of necessity must than perish, whereof ensueth universal dissolution.

But now to prove, by example of those things that be within the compass of man's knowledge, of what estimation order is, nat only among men but also with God, albeit his wisdom, bounty, and magnificence can be with no tongue or pen sufficiently expressed. Hath nat he set degrees and astates in all his glorious warks?

First in his heavenly ministers, whom, as the church affirmeth, he hath constituted to be in divers degrees called hierarchs. Also Christ saith by his evangelist that in the house of his father (which is God) be many mansions. But to treat of that which by natural understanding may be comprehended. Behold the four elements whereof the body of man is compact, how they be set in their places called spheres, higher or lower, according to the sovereignty of their natures, that is to say, the fire as the most pure element, having in it nothing that is corruptible, in his place is highest and above other elements. The air, which next to the fire is most pure in substance, is in the second sphere or place. The water, which is somewhat consolidate and approacheth to corruption, is next unto the earth. The earth, which is of substance gross and ponderous, is set of all elements most lowest.

Behold also the order that God hath put generally in all his creatures, beginning at the most inferior or base and ascending upward: he made nat only herbs to garnish the earth, but also trees of a more eminent stature than herbs, and yet in the one and the other be degrees of qualities; some pleasant to behold, some delicate or good in taste, other wholesome and medicinable, some commodious and necessary. Semblably in birds, beasts, and fishes, some be good for the sustenance of man, some bear things profitable to sundry uses, other be apt to occupation and labor;

in diverse is strength and fierceness only; in many is both strength and commodity; some other serve for pleasure; none of them hath all these qualities; few have the more part or many, specially beauty, strength, and profit. But where any is found that hath many of the said properties, he is more set by than all the other, and by that estimation the order of his place and degree evidently appeareth; so that every kind of trees, herbs, birds, beasts, and fishes, beside their diversity of fourms, have (as who saith) a peculiar disposition appropered unto them by God their creator. So that in everything is order, and without order may be nothing stable or permanent; and it may nat be called order except it do contain in it degrees, high and base, according to the merit or estimation of the thing that is ord'red.

Now to retourn to the astate of mankind, for whose use all the said creatures were ordained of God, and also excelleth them all by prerogatife of knowledge and wisdom, hit seemeth that in him should be no lass providence of God declared than in the inferior creatures, but rather with a more perfect order and disposition. And therefore hit appeareth that God giveth nat to every man like gifts of grace or of nature, but to some more, some less, as it liketh his divine majesty.

Ne they be nat in commune (as fantastical fools would have all things), nor one man hath nat all virtues and good qualities. Natwithstanding, forasmuch as understanding is the most excellent gift that man can receive in his creation, whereby he doth approach most nigh unto the similitude of God, which understanding is the principal part of the soul; it is therefore congruent and according that as one excelleth another in that influence, as thereby being next to the similitude of his Maker, so should the astate of his person be avanced in degree or place where understanding may profit: which is also distributed into sundry uses, faculties, and offices, necessary for the living and governance of mankind. And like as the angels which be most fervent in contemplation be highest exalted in glory (after the opinion of holy doctors), and also the fire which is the most pure of elements, and also doth clarify the other inferior elements, is deputed to the highest sphere or place, so in this world they which excel other in this influence of understanding, and do imploy it to the detaining of other within the bounds of reason, and shew them how to provide for their necessary living; such ought to be set in a more high place than the residue where they may see and also be seen, that by the beams of their excellent wit, shewed through the glass of auctority, other of inferior understanding may be directed to the way of virtue and commodious living.

And unto men of such virtue by very equity appertaineth honor, as their just reward and duty, which by other men's labors must also be maintained according to their merits. Forasmuch as the said persons, excelling in knowledge whereby other be governed, be ministers for the only profit and commodity of them which have nat equal understanding, where they which do exercise artificial science or corporal labor do nat travail for their superiors only, but also for their own necessity; so the husbandman feedeth himself and the cloth-maker, the cloth-maker apparaileth himself and the husband, they both succor other artificers, other artificers them, they and other artificers them that be governors. But they that be governors (as I before said) nothing do acquire by the said influence of knowledge for their own necessities, but do imploy all the powers of their wits and their diligence to the only preservation of other their inferiors; among which inferiors also behoveth to be a disposition and order according to reason, that is to say, that the slouthful or idle person do nat participate with him that is industrious and taketh pain, whereby the fruits of his labors should be diminished; wherein should be none equality, but thereof should proceed discourage, and, finally, dissolution for lack of provision. Wherefore it can none otherwise stand with reason, but that the astate of the person in pre-eminence of living should be esteemed with his understanding, labor, and policy, whereunto must be added an augmentation of honor and substance; which nat only impresseth a reverence, whereof proceedeth due obedience among subjects, but also inflameth men naturally inclined to idleness or sensual appetite to covet like fortune, and for that cause to dispose them to study or occupation.

Now to conclude my first assertion or argument, where all thing is commune, there lacketh order; and where order lacketh, there all thing is odious and uncomely. And that have we in daily experience; for the pans and pots garnisheth well the kitchen, and yet should they be to the chamber none ornament. Also the beds, testars, and pillows beseemeth nat the hall, no more than the carpets and kusshins becometh the stable. Semblably the potter and tinker, only perfect in their craft, shall little do in the ministration of justice. A plowman or carter shall make but a feeble answer to an ambassador. Also a weaver or fuller should be an unmeet capitain of an army, or in any other office of a governor.

Wherefore to conclude, it is only a public weal where, like as God hath disposed the said influence of understanding, is also appointed degrees and places according to the excellency thereof; and thereto also would be substance convenient and necessary for the ornament of the same, which also impresseth a reverence and due obedience to the vulgar people or communalty; and without that, it can be no more said that there is a public weal than it may be affirmed that a house without his proper and necessary ornaments is well and sufficiently furnished.

II. That one sovereign governor ought to be in a public weal. And what damage hath happened where a multitude hath had equal authority without any sovereign

Like as to a castle or fortress sufficeth one owner or sovereign, and where any mo be of like power and authority seldom cometh the wark to perfection, or being already made, where the one diligently over-seeth and the other neglecteth, in that contention all is subverted and cometh to ruin. In semblable wise doth a public weal that hath mo chief governors than one. Example we may take of the Greeks, among whom in divers cities were divers fourms of public weals governed by multitudes; wherein one was most tolerable where the governance and rule was alway permitted to them which excelled in virtue, and was in the Greek tongue called *aristocratia*, in Latin *optimorum potentia*, in English the rule of men of best disposition, which the Thebans of long time observed.

Another public weal was among the Atheniensis, where equality was of astate among the people, and only by their whole consent their city and dominions were governed; which mought well be called a monster with many heads, nor never it was certain nor stable; and oftentimes they banished or slew the best citezins, which by their virtue and wisdom had most profited to the public weal. This manner of governance was called in Greek *dimocratia*, in Latin *popularis potentia*, in English the rule of the comminalty. Of these two governances none of them may be sufficient. For in the first, which consisteth of good men, virtue is nat so constant in a multitude but that some, being ones in authority, be incensed with glory, some with ambition, other with covetise and desire of treasure or possessions whereby they fall into contention; and, finally, where any achieveth the superiority, the whole governance is reduced unto a few in number, which fearing the multitude and their mutability, to the intent to keep them in dread to rebel, ruleth by terror and cruelty, thinking thereby to keep themself in surety; natwithstanding, rancor coarcted and long detained in a narrow room at the last brasteth out with intolerable violence, and bringeth all to confusion. For the power that is practised to the hurt of many cannat continue. The popular astate, if it anything do vary from equality of substance or estimation, or that the multitude of people have overmuch liberty, of necessity one of these inconveniences must happen: either tyranny, where he that is too much in favor would be elevate and suffer none equality, or else into the rage of a communalty, which of all rules is most to be feared. For like as the communes, if they feel some severity, they do humbly serve and obey, so where they, imbracing a license, refuse to be bridled, they fling and plunge; and if they ones throw down their governor, they order everything without justice, only with vengeance and cruelty; and with incomparable difficulty and unneth by any wisdom be pacified and brought again into order. Wherefore undoubtedly the best and most sure governance is by one king or prince, which ruleth only for the weal of his people to him subject; and that manner of governance is best approved, and hath longest continued, and is most ancient. For who can deny but that all thing in heaven and earth is governed by one God, by one perpetual order, by one providence? One sun ruleth over the day, and one moon over the night; and to descend down to the earth, in a little beast which of all other is most to be marvailed at, I mean the bee, is left to man by nature, as hit seemeth, a perpetual figure of a just governance or rule: who hath among them one principal bee for their governor, who excelleth all other in greatness, yet hath he no prick or sting, but in him is more knowledge than in the residue. For if the day following shall be fair and dry, and that the bees may issue out of their stalls without peril of rain or vehement wind, in the morning early he calleth them, making a noise, as it were the sown of a horn or a trumpet; and with that all the residue prepare them to labor, and fleeth abroad, gathering nothing but that shall be sweet and profitable, although they sit oftentimes on herbs and other things that be venomous and stinking.

The capitain himself laboreth nat for his sustinance, but all the other for him; he only seeth that if any drane or other unprofitable bee ent'reth into the hive, and consumeth the honey gathered by other, that he be immediately expelled from that company. And whan there is another number of bees encreased, they semblably have also a capitain, which be nat suffered to continue with the other. Wherefore this new company gathered into a swarm, having their capitain among them, and environing him to preserve him from harm, they issue forth seeking a new habitation, which they find in some tree, except with some pleasant noise they be allured and conveyed unto another hive. I suppose who seriously beholdeth this example, and hath any commendable wit, shall thereof gather much matter to the fourming of a public weal. But bicause I may nat be long therein,

considering my purpose, I would that, if the reader hereof be learned, that he should repair to the *Georgics* of Virgil, or to Pliny, or Columella, where he shall find the example more ample and better declared. And if any desireth to have the governance of one person proved by histories, let him first resort to the Holy Scripture, where he shall find that Almighty God commanded Moses only to bring his elected people out of captivity, giving only to him that authority, without appointing to him any other assistance of equal power or dignity, except in the message to King Pharaoh, wherein Aaron, rather as a minister than a companion, went with Moses. But only Moses conducted the people through the Red Sea; he only governed them forty years in [the] desert. And bicause Dathan and Abiron disdained his rule, and coveted to be equal with him, the earth opened, and fire issued out, and swallowed them in, with all their whole family and confederates, to the number of 14,700. . . .

The Greeks, which were assembled to revenge the reproach of Menelaus that he took of the Trojans by the ravishing of Helen, his wife, did nat they by one assent elect Agamemnon to be their emperor or capitain, obeying him as their sovereign during the siege of Troy? Although that they had divers excellent princes nat only equal to him but also excelling him (as in prowess, Achilles and Ajax Telemonius; in wisdom, Nestor and Ulysses and his own brother Menelaus, to whom they mought have given equal authority with Agamemnon) but those wise princes considered that, without a general capitain, so many persons as were there of divers realms gathered togither should be by no means well governed; wherefore Homer calleth Agamemnon the shepherd of people. They rather were contented to be under one man's obedience than severally to use their authorities or to join in one power and dignity; whereby at the last should have sourded dissension among the people, they being separately enclined toward their natural sovereign lord, as it appeared in the particular contention that was between Achilles and Agamemnon for their concubines, where Achilles, renouncing the obedience that he with all other princes had before promised, at the battail first enterprised against the Trojans. For at that time no little murmur and sedition was meved in the host of the Greeks, which natwithstanding was wonderfully pacified, and the army unscattered by the majesty of Agamemnon, joining to him counsailors Nestor and the witty Ulysses. . . .

It is nat to be dispaired but that the king our sovereign lord now reigning, and this realm alway having one prince like unto his Highness, equal to the ancient princes in virtue and courage, it shall be reduced (God so disposing) unto a public weal excelling all other in preeminence of virtue and abundance of things necessary. But forasmuch as I do well perceive that to write of the office or duty of a sovereign governor or prince far exceedeth the compass of my learning, Holy Scripture affirming that the hearts of princes be in God's own hands and disposition, I will therefore keep my pen within the space that is discribed to me by the three noble maisters, reason, learning, and experience; and by their enseignment or teaching I will ordinately treat of the two parts of a public weal, whereof the one shall be named "Due Administration," the other "Necessary Occupation," which shall be divided into two volumes. In the first shall be comprehended the best fourm of education or bringing up of noble children from their nativity, in such manner as they may be found worthy and also able to be governors of a public weal. The second volume, which, God granting me quietness and liberty of mind, I will shortly after send forth, it shall contain all the reminant which I can either by learning or experience find apt to the perfection of a just public weal; in the which I shall so endeavor myself that all men, of what astate or condition soever they be, shall find therein occasion to be alway virtuously occupied and nat without pleasure, if they be nat of the schools of Aristippus or Apicius, of whom the one supposed felicity to be only in lechery, the other in delicate feeding and gluttony; from whose sharp talons and cruel teeth I beseech all gentle readers to defend these warks, which for their commodity is only compiled.

x. What order should be in learning, and which autors should be first read

Now let us retourn to the order of learning apt for a gentleman. Wherein I am of the opinion of Quintilian that I would have him learn Greek and Latin autors both at one time; or else to begin with Greek, forasmuch as that it is hardest to come by, by reason of the diversity of tongues, which be five in number; and all must be known, or else uneth any poet can be well understand. And if a child do begin therein at seven years of age, he may continually learn Greek autors three years, and in the meantime use the Latin tongue as a familiar language; which in a nobleman's son may well come to pass, having none other persons to serve him or keeping him company but such as can speak Latin elegantly. And what doubt is there but so may he as soon speak good Latin as he may do pure French, which now is brought into as many rules and figures and as long a grammer as is Latin or Greek? I will nat contend who, among them that do write grammers of Greek (which now

almost be innumerable), is the best; but that I refer to the discretion of a wise maister. Alway I would advise him nat to detain the child too long in that tedious labors, either in the Greek or Latin grammer. For a gentle wit is therewith soon fatigate.

Grammer being but an introduction to the understanding of autors, if it be made too long or exquisite to the learner, hit in a manner mortifieth his corage. And by that time he cometh to the most sweet and pleasant reading of old autors, the sparks of fervent desire of learning is extinct with the burden of grammer, like as a little fire is soon quenched with a great heap of small sticks, so that it can never come to the principal logs where it should long burn in a great pleasant fire.

Now to follow my purpose: after a few and quick rules of grammer, immediately, or interlacing hit therewith, would be read to the child Aesop's fables in Greek, in which argument children much do delight. And surely it is a much pleasant lesson and also profitable, as well for that it is elegant and brief (and natwithstanding it hath much variety in words, and therewith much helpeth to the understanding of Greek), as also in those fables is included much moral and politic wisdom. Wherefore, in the teaching of them, the maister diligently must gader togither those fables which may be most accommodate to the advancement of some virtue, whereto he perceiveth the child inclined, or to the rebuke of some vice, whereto he findeth his nature disposed. And therein the master ought to exercise his wit, as well to make the child plainly to understand the fable, as also declaring the signification thereof compendiously and to the purpose, foreseen alway, that as well this lesson as all other autors which the child shall learn, either Greek or Latin, verse or prose, be perfectly had without the book; whereby he shall nat only attain plenty of the tongues, called copy, but also encrease and nourish remembrance wonderfully.

The next lesson would be some quick and merry dialogues, elect out of Lucian, which be without ribawdry or too much scorning, for either of them is exactly to be eschewed, specially for a nobleman, the one annoying the soul, the other his estimation concerning his gravity. The comedies of Aristophanes may be in the place of Lucian, and by reason that they be in meter they be the sooner learned by heart. I dare make none other comparison between them for offending the friends of them both; but thus much dare I say, that it were better that a child should never read any part of Lucian than all Lucian.

I could rehearse divers other poets which for matter and eloquence be very necessary, but I fear me to be too long from noble Homer, from whom as from a fountain proceeded all eloquence and learning. For in his books be contained and most perfectly expressed, nat only the documents martial and discipline of arms, but also incomparable wisdoms and instructions for politic governance of people, with the worthy commendation and laud of noble princes; wherewith the readers shall be so all-inflamed that they most fervently shall desire and covet, by the imitation of their virtues, to acquire semblable glory. For the which occasion, Aristotle, most sharpest-witted and excellent-learned philosopher, as soon as he had received Alexander from King Philip his father, he before any other thing taught him the most noble warks of Homer; wherein Alexander found such sweetness and fruit that ever after he had Homer nat only with him in all his journeys, but also laid him under his pillow whan he went to rest, and oftentimes would purposely wake some hours of the night to take, as it were, his pastime with that most noble poet.

For by the reading of his wark called *Iliados,* where the assembly of the most noble Greeks again Troy is recited with their affairs, he gathered courage and strength again his enemies, wisdom and eloquence for consultations, and persuasions to his people and army. And by the other wark called *Odyssea,* which recounteth the sundry adventures of the wise Ulysses, he, by the example of Ulysses, apprehended many noble virtues, and also learned to escape the fraud and deceitful imaginations of sundry and subtil crafty wits. Also there shall he learn to ensearch and perceive the manners and conditions of them that be his familiars, sifting out (as I mought say) the best from the warst, whereby he may surely commit his affairs, and trust to every person after his virtues. Therefore I now conclude that there is no lesson for a young gentleman to be compared with Homer, if he be plainly and substantially expouned and declared by the maister.

Natwithstanding, forasmuch as the said warks be very long and do require therefore a great time to be all learned and canned, some Latin autor would be therewith mix'd, and specially Virgil; which, in his wark called *Aeneidos,* is most like to Homer, and almost the same Homer in Latin. Also, by the joining together of those autors, the one shall be the better understand by the other. And verily (as I before said) none one autor serveth to so divers wits as doth Virgil. For there is nat that affect or desire whereto any child's fantasy is disposed but in some of Virgil's warks may be founden matter thereto apt and propise.

For what thing can be more familiar than his *Bucolics?* Nor no wark so nigh approacheth to the commune dalliance and manners of children, and the praty controversies of the simple sheepherds, therein

contained, wonderfully rejoiceth the child that heareth hit well declared, as I know by mine own experience. In his *Georgics,* Lord, what pleasant variety there is: the divers grains, herbs, and flowers that be there described, that, reading therein, it seemeth to a man to be in a delectable gardein or paradise. What plowman knoweth so much of husbandry as there is expressed? Who, delighting in good horses, shall nat be thereto more enflamed, reading there of the breeding, cheesing, and keeping of them? In the declaration whereof Virgil leaveth far behind him all breeders, hackneymen, and scorsers. Is there any astronomer that more exactly setteth out the order and course of the celestial bodies; or that more truly doth devine in his pronostications of the times of the year, in their qualities, with the future astate of all things provided by husbandry, than Virgil doth recite in that wark? . . . Finally (as I have said) this noble Virgil, like to a good norise, giveth to a child, if he will take it, everything apt for his wit and capacity; wherefore he is in the order of learning to be preferred before any other autor Latin.

I would set next unto him two books of Ovid, the one called *Metamorphosios,* which is as much to say as changing of men into other figure or fourm; the other is intitled *De fastis,* where the ceremonies of the gentiles, and specially the Romans, be expressed; both right necessary for the understanding of other poets. But by cause there is little other learning in them, concerning either virtuous manners or policy, I suppose it were better that, as fables and ceremonies happen to come in a lesson, it were declared abundantly by the maister than that in the said two books a long time should be spent and almost lost, which mought be better employed on such autors that do minister both eloquence, civil policy, and exhortation to virtue. Wherefore in his place let us bring in Horace, in whom is contained much variety of learning and quickness of sentence.

This poet may be enterlaced with the lesson of *Odyssea* of Homer, wherein is declared the wonderful prudence and fortitude of Ulysses in his passage from Troy. And if the child were induced to make verses by the imitation of Virgil and Homer, it should minister to him much delectation and courage to study; ne the making of verses is nat discommended in a nobleman, sens the noble Augustus and almost all the old emperors made books in verses.

The two noble poets Silius and Lucan be very expedient to be learned; for the one setteth out the emulation in qualities and prowess of two noble and valiant capitains, one enemy to the other: that is to say, Silius writeth of Scipio the Roman and Hannibal duke of Cartaginensis; Lucan declareth a semblable matter, but much more lamentable, forasmuch as the wars were civil, and, as it were, in the bowels of the Romans, that is to say, under the standards of Julius Caesar and Pompey.

Hesiodus, in Greek, is more brief than Virgil, where he writeth of husbandry, and doth nat rise so high in philosophy, but is fuller of fables, and therefore is more illecebrous.

And here I conclude to speak any more of poets necessary for the childhood of a gentleman, forasmuch as these, I doubt nat, will suffice until he pass the age of thirteen years. In which time childhood declineth, and reason waxeth ripe, and deprehendeth things with a more constant judgment. Here I would should be rememb'red that I require nat that all these warks should be throughly rad of a child in this time, which were almost impossible. But I only desire that they have, in every of the said books, so much instruction that they may take thereby some profit. Than the child's courage, inflamed by the frequent reading of noble poets, daily more and more desireth to have experience in those things that they so vehemently do commend in them that they write of.

Leonidas, the noble king of Spartans, being ones demanded, of what estimation in poetry Tyrtaeus (as he supposed) was, it is written that he answering said that for steering the minds of young men he was excellent, forasmuch as they, being meved with his verses, do ren into the battail, regarding no peril, as men all inflamed in martial courage.

And whan a man is comen to mature years, and that reason in him is confirmed with serious learning and long experience, than shall he, in reading tragedies, execrate and abhor the intolerable life of tyrants, and shall contemn the folly and dotage expressed by poets lascivious.

Here will I leave to speak of the first part of a nobleman's study; and now will I write of the second part, which is more serious, and containeth in it sundry manners of learning.

XI. The most commodious and necessary studies succeeding ordinately the lesson of poets

After that fourteen years be passed of a child's age, his maister if he can, or some other studiously exercised in the art of an orator, shall first read to him somewhat of that part of logic that is called *topica,* either of Cicero, or else of that noble clerk of Almaine, which late floured, called [Rodolphus] Agricola, whose wark prepareth invention, telling the places from whence an argument for the proof of any matter may be taken with little study; and that lesson, with much and diligent learning, having

mix'd therewith none other exercise, will in the space of half a year be perfectly canned. Immediately after that, the art of rhetoric would be semblably taught, either in Greek out of Hermogenes, or of Quintilian in Latin, beginning at the third book, and instructing diligently the child in that part of rhetoric, principally, which concerneth persuasion, forasmuch as it is most apt for consultations. There can be no shorter instruction in rhetoric than the treatise that Tully wrate unto his son, which book is named the *Partition of Rhetoric.* And in good faith, to speak boldly that I think, for him that needeth nat, or doth nat desire, to be an exquisite orator, the little book made by the famous Erasmus (whom all gentle wits are bounden to thank and support), which he calleth *Copiam verborum et rerum,* that is to say, "plenty of words and matters," shall be sufficient.

Isocrates, concerning the lesson of orators, is everywhere wonderful profitable, having almost as many wise sentences as he hath words; and with that is so sweet and delectable to read that, after him, almost all other seem unsavory and tedious; and in persuading, as well a prince as a private person, to virtue, in two very little and compendious warks, whereof he made the one to King Nicocles, the other to his friend Demonicus, would be perfectly canned, and had in continual memory.

Demosthenes and Tully, by the consent of all learned men, have preeminence and sovereignty over all orators: the one reigning in wonderful eloquence in the public weal of the Romans, who had the empire and dominion of all the world; the other, of no lass estimation, in the city of Athens, which of long time was accounted the mother of sapience and the palaice of muses and all liberal sciences. Of which two orators may be attained nat only eloquence, excellent and perfect, but also precepts of wisdom and gentle manners, with most commodious examples of all noble virtues and policy. Wherefore the maister, in reading them, must well observe and express the parts and colors of rhetoric in them contained, according to the precepts of that art before learned.

The utility that a nobleman shall have by reading these orators is that whan he shall hap to reason in counsail, or shall speak in a great audience or to strange ambassadors of great princes, he shall nat be constrained to speak words sodain and disord'red, but shall bestow them aptly and in their places. Wherefore the most noble Emperor Octavius is highly commended, for that he never spake in the Senate, or to the people of Rome, but in an oration prepared and purposely made.

Also to prepare the child to understanding of histories, which, being replenished with the names of countries and towns unknown to the reader, do make the history tedious or else the lass pleasant, so if they be in any wise known, it encreaseth an inexplicable delectation. It shall be therefore, and also for refreshing the wit, a convenient lesson to behold the old *Tables* of Ptolemy, wherein all the world is painted, having first some introduction into the sphere, whereof now of late be made very good treatises, and more plain and easy to learn than was wont to be.

Albeit there is none so good learning as the demonstration of cosmography by material figures and instruments, having a good instructor. And surely this lesson is both pleasant and necessary. For what pleasure is it in one hour to behold those realms, cities, seas, rivers, and mountains that uneth in an old man's life cannat be journeyed and pursued; what incredible delight is taken in beholding the diversities of people, beasts, fowls, fishes, trees, fruits, and herbs; to know the sundry manners and conditions of people, and the variety of their natures, and that in a warm study or perler, without peril of the sea, or danger of long and painful journeys; I cannat tell what more pleasure should happen to a gentle wit than to behold in his own house everything that within all the world is contained. The commodity thereof knew the great King Alexander, as some writers do remember. For he caused the countries whereunto he purposed any enterprise diligently and cunningly to be discribed and painted, that, beholding the picture, he mought perceive which places were most dangerous, and where he and his host mought have most easy and covenable passage. . . .

Cosmography being substantially perceived, it is than time to induce a child to the reading of histories; but first, to set him in a fervent courage, the maister in the most pleasant and elegant wise expressing what incomparable delectation, utility, and commodity shall happen to emperors, kings, princes, and all other gentlemen by reading of histories: shewing to him that Demetrius Phalereus, a man of excellent wisdom and learning, and which in Athens had been long exercised in the public weal, exhorted Ptolemy [Lagi], king of Egypt, chiefly above all other studies to haunt and embrace histories and such other books, wherein were contained precepts made to kings and princes; saying that in them he should read those things which no man durst report unto his person. Also Cicero, father of the Latin eloquence, calleth an history the witness of times, maistress of life, the life of remembrance, of trouth the light, and messager of antiquity. . . .

By the time that the child do come to seventeen years of age, to the intent his courage be bridled

with reason, hit were needful to read unto him some warks of philosophy, specially that part that may enform him unto virtuous manners, which part of philosophy is called moral. Wherefore there would be rad to him, for an introduction, two the first books of the wark of Aristotle called *Ethicae*, wherein is contained the definitions and proper significations of every virtue; and that to be learned in Greek, for the translations that we yet have be but a rude and gross shadow of the eloquence and wisdom of Aristotle. Forthwith would follow the wark of Cicero called in Latin *De officiis*, whereunto yet is no proper English word to be given; but to provide for it some manner of exposition, it may be said in this fourm: "Of the duties and manners appertaining to men." But, above all other, the warks of Plato would be most studiously rad when the judgment of a man is come to perfection, and by the other studies is instructed in the fourm of speaking that philosophers used. Lord God, what incomparable sweetness of words and matter shall he find in the said warks of Plato and Cicero; wherein is joined gravity with dilectation, excellent wisdom with divine eloquence, absolute virtue with pleasure incredible, and every place is so infarced with profitable counsail joined with honesty that those three books be almost sufficient to make a perfect and excellent governor.

The proverbs of Salomon with the books of Ecclesiastes and Ecclesiasticus be very good lessons. All the historial parts of the Bible be right necessary for to be rad of a nobleman, after that he is mature in years. And the residue (with the New Testament) is to be reverently touched, as a celestial jewel or relic, having the chief interpreter of those books true and constant faith, and dreadfully to set hands thereon, rememb'ring that Oza, for putting his hand to the holy shrine that was called *Archa federis*, whan it was brought by King David from the city of Gaba, though it were wavering and in danger to fall, yet was he striken of God, and fell dead immediately. It would nat be forgotten that the little book of the most excellent doctor Erasmus Roterodame (which he wrate to Charles, now being emperor [Charles V] and than prince of Castile), which book is intitled *The Institution of a Christen Prince*, would be as familiar alway with gentlemen, at all times and in every age, as was Homer with the great King Alexander or Xenophon with Scipio; for as all men may judge that have rad that wark of Erasmus, that there was never book written in Latin that, in so little a portion, contained of sentence, eloquence, and virtuous exhortation a more compendious abundance. And here I make an end of the learning and study whereby noblemen may attain to be worthy to have autority in a public weal. Alway I shall exhort tutors and governors of noble children that they suffer them nat to use ingurgitations of meat or drink, ne to sleep much, that is to say, above eight hours at the most. For undoubtedly both repletion and superfluous sleep be capital enemies to study, as they be semblably to health of body and soul. Aulus Gellius saith that children, if they use of meat and sleep overmuch, be made therewith dull to learn, and we see that thereof slowness is taken, and the children's personages do wax uncomely and lass grown in stature. Galen will nat permit that pure wine, without alay of water, should in any wise be given to children, forasmuch as it humecteth the body, or maketh it moister and hotter than is convenient; also it filleth the head with fume, in them specially which be like as children of hot and moist temperature. These be well-nigh the words of the noble Galen.

XVI. Of sundry fourms of exercise necessary for every gentleman

Although I have hitherto advanced the commendation of learning, specially in gentlemen, yet it is to be considered that continual study without some manner of exercise shortly exhausteth the spirits vital and hindereth natural decoction and digestion, whereby man's body is the sooner corrupted and brought into divers sicknesses, and finally the life is thereby made shorter; where, contrariwise, by exercise, which is a vehement motion (as Galen, prince of phisitions, defineth), the health of man is preserved and his strength increased; forasmuch as the members by meving and mutual touching do wax more hard, and natural heat in all the body is thereby augmented. Moreover, it maketh the spirits of a man more strong and valiant, so that by the hardness of the members all labors be more tolerable; by natural heat the appetite is the more quick, the change of the substance received is the more ready, the nourishing of all parts of the body is the more sufficient and sure. By valiant motion of the spirits all things superfluous be expelled and the conduits of the body cleansed. Wherefore this part of physic is nat to be contemned or neglected in the education of children, and specially from the age of fourteen years upward, in which time strength with courage increaseth. Moreover, there be divers manners of exercises, whereof some only prepareth and helpeth digestion, some augmenteth also strength and hardness of body, other serveth for agility and nimbleness, some for celerity or speediness. There be also which ought to be used for necessity only. All these ought he that is a tutor to a nobleman to have in remembrance, and, as opportunity serveth, to put them in experience. And specially them which with

health do join commodity and (as I mought say) necessity: considering that be he never so noble or valiant, sometime he is subject to peril, or (to speak it more pleasantly) servant to fortune. Touching such exercises as many be used within the house or in the shadow (as is the old manner of speaking), as deambulations, laboring with poises made of lead or other metal, called in Latin *alteres*, lifting and throwing the heavy stone or bar, playing at tennis, and divers semblable exercises, I will for this time pass over; exhorting them which do understand Latin, and do desire to know the commodities of sundry exercises, to resort to the book of Galen of the governance of health, called in Latin *De sanitate tuenda*, where they shall be in that matter abundantly satisfied, and find in the reading much delectation; which book is translated into Latin wonderful eloquently by Doctor Linacre, late most worthy phisition to our most noble sovereign lord, King Henry the VIII. . . .

BOOK III

XXIII. What is the true signification of understanding

Forasmuch as in the beginning of the first book of this wark I endeavored myself to prove that, by the order of man's creation, preeminence in degree should be among men according as they do excel in the pure influence of understanding, which cannat be denied to be the principal part of the soul, some reader, perchance meved with disdain, will for that one assertion immediately reject this wark, saying that I am of a corrupt or foolish opinion; supposing that I do intend by the said words that no man should govern or be in authority but only he which surmounted all other in doctrine, which, in his hasty malice, he deemeth that I only do mean where I speak of understanding.

I suppose all men do know that man is made of body and soul, and that the soul in preeminence excelleth the body as much as the maister or owner excelleth the house, or the artificer excelleth his instruments, or the king his subjects. And therefore Sallust in *The Conspiracy of Catiline* saith: "We use specially the rule of the soul and service of the body; the one we participate with gods, the other with beasts." And Tully saith in *Tusculan Questions:* "Man's soul, being decerpt or taken of the portion of divinity called *mens,* may be compared with none other thing (if a man mought leefully speak it) but with God himself." Also the noble divine Chrysostomus saith that the body was made for the soul and nat the soul for the body. Now it is to be further known that the soul is of three parts: the one, wherein is the power or efficacy of growing, which is also in herbs and trees as well as in man, and that part is called vegetatife. Another part, wherein man doth participate with all other things living, which is called sensitife, by reason that thereof the senses do proceed, which be distributed into divers instrumental parts of the body; as sight into the eyen, hearing to the ears, smelling to the nose, tasting to the mouth, feeling to every part of the body wherein is blood, without the which undoughtedly may be no feeling. The third part of the soul is named the part intellectual or of understanding, which is of all the other most noble, as whereby man is most like unto God, and is preferred before all other creatures. For where other beasts by their senses do feel what thing do profit theim, and what doth annoy them, only man understandeth whereof the said contrary dispositions do come, and by what means they do either help or annoy; also he perceiveth the causes of the same thing, and knoweth how to resist, where and whan need doth require, and with reason and craft how to give remedy and also with labor and industry to provide that thing which is wholesome or profitable. This most pure part of the soul, and (as Aristotle saith) divine, impassible, and incorruptible, is named in Latin *intellectus,* whereunto I can find no proper English but "understanding." For intelligence, which cometh of *intelligentia,* is the perceiving of that which is first conceived by understanding, called *intellectus.* Also "intelligence" is now used for an elegant word where there is mutual treaties or appointments, either by letters or message, specially concerning wars, or like other great affairs between princes or noblemen. Wherefore I will use this word "understanding" for *intellectus,* until some other more proper English word may be founden and brought in custom. But to perceive more plainly what thing it is that I call understanding. It is the principal part of the soul which is occupied about the beginning or original causes of things that may fall into man's knowledge, and his office is, before that anything is attempted, to think, consider, and prepense, and, after often tossing it up and down in the mind, than to exercise that power, the property whereof is to espy, seek for, ensearch, and find out; which virtue is referred to wit, which is, as it were, the instrument of understanding.

Moreover, after the things be invented, conjected, perceived, and by long time and often considered, and that the mind disposeth herself to execution or actual operation, than the virtue named prudence first putteth herself forwards, and than appeareth her industry and labor; forasmuch as she teacheth, warneth, exhorteth, ordereth, and profiteth, like to a wise capitain that setteth his host in array. And therefore it is to be rememb'red that the office or duty of understanding precedeth the interprise of acts, and is in the beginning of things. I call that beginning, wherein, before any matter taken in hand, the mind and thought is occupied, and that a man searcheth, and doughteth whether it be to be enterprised and by what way and in what time it is to be executed. Who by this little introduction, knowing what understanding do signify, will nat suppose that he which therein doth excel is nat with honor to be advanced? Than it followeth nat by this argument that forasmuch as he that excelleth other in understanding should be preferred in honor, therefore no man should be preferred to honor but only they that excel other in learning. No man having natural reason, though he never rad logic, will judge this to be a good argument, considering that understanding, called in Latin *intellectus* and *mens,* is by itself sufficient, and is nat of any necessity annexed to doctrine, but doctrine proceedeth of understanding. But if doctrine be alway attending upon understanding, as the daughter upon the mother, undoughtedly than understanding must be the more perfect and of a more efficacy, being increased by the inventions and experiences of many other declared by doctrine, no one man without inspiration having knowledge of all thing. I call doctrine discipline intellectife or learning, which is either in writing or by report of things before known, which proceedeth from one man to another.

That which I have said is in this wise confirmed by Saloman, saying, "A man that is wise, by hearing shall become wiser, and he that hath understanding shall be a governor."

Seneca saith we instruct our children in liberal sciences, nat bycause those sciences may give any virtue, but bicause they prepare the mind and make it apt to receive virtue. Which, being considered, no man will deny but that they be necessary to every man that coveteth very nobility; which, as I have oftentimes said, is in the having and use of virtue. And verely in whom doctrine hath been so founden joined with virtue, there virtue hath seemed excellent and, as I mought say, triumphant. . . .

FROM OF THE KNOWLEDGE WHICH MAKETH A WISE MAN (1533)

THE SECOND DIALOGUE

PLATO
ARISTIPPUS

PLATO: . . . First remember that of all that which beareth the name of a thing there be two kinds. One hath no body and is ever steadfast and permanent; the other hath a body, but it is ever movable and uncertain. The first, bicause it may be understand only it is called intelligible. The second, bicause it may be felt by senses it is called sensible. The way to know the first is called raison, and the knowledge thereof is named understanding. The way to know the second is called sense or feeling; the knowledge thereof is named perceiving. Moreover, of that which is called intelligible there is the first and the second. In the first is that portion of divinity which is in man, whereby he is made to the image and similitude of God. In the other be numbers and figures. Of this beasts have no part, neither of the first nor yet of the second. Of the first I suppose thou wilt grant me; and as for the second, experience will prove it. For I dare say thou never hardest of beasts that could skill of nomb'ring.

ARISTIPPUS: I wot ne'er; I never called any yet to a reckoning.

PLATO: And though an ape or other like beast seem in taking of things to observe an order, as it were, in nomb'ring, yet if it be well considered it shall appear that it is by an imagination ingend'red of custom and not by nomb'ring. I have seen a man which was born blind, and used to be lad to three or four houses in the city which hath been a great distance asonder, at the last by custom hath known so well where they stood that without any man or dog leading, or any man telling him, he hath gone directly unto them. Whereat first I mervailed with many other, and whan I communed with him I have perceived that he never observed nomber, but that only custom had set the distance of the places in his imagination. Like may be spoken of figures. For that whereby beasts do discern one thing from another is not under-standing: that is to say, though they discern in quantity the more from the lass, yet they understand it not as round, quadrant, or triangle, or in other like figure; but the simulacre or image whereby they perceive the said diversity is only by custom formed and imprinted in the principal sense, which is the heart. And whan the thing self is removed out of sight, that impression that remaineth is called imagi-nation, who committeth it forthwith unto memory, which undoubted is not only in men but also in beasts; for they discern the time present and that which is passed, but the time to come they know not, and memory is only of the time passed. And there-fore the beasts that thou spakest of do perceive the diversity of things by imagination and memory, conceiving and retaining in the heart, which is the principal sense or fountain of senses, the image of the thing that is sensible. And thereby the dog per-ceiveth his master and fetcheth his glove which he hath been before taught for to do, and goeth to the places where he hath seen his maister been a little before. But that he knoweth not whether his maister be a man or a horse, Plato or Demosthenes, a philoso-pher or an orator, it is evident inough. For although my dog had abiden ten years continually with me and had heard me every day speak of Demosthenes and name him an orator and heard thee call me every day Plato and name me a philosopher, yet if thou wouldest deliver unto him anything and bid him carry it to the orator, he would straight bring it unto me and not to Demosthenes. Also, if I would cast a loaf unto my spaniel and bid him carry it to my horse, I suppose he would forthwith eat it himself and lie down whan he hath done, without seeking for my horse though he stood by him. Is it not so?

ARISTIPPUS: Yea, in good faith, methinketh thou sayest truly.

PLATO: And likewise may be raisoned of all other beasts, be they never so wily, if their acts be deeply considered?

ARISTIPPUS: It appeareth so.

PLATO: Than thy saying is not to be reproved, that a beast lacked knowledge of himself and of other?

ARISTIPPUS: No, as it seemeth.

PLATO: And that lack of knowledge is ignorance?

ARISTIPPUS: Yea, truly, and so said I also.

PLATO: And that ignorance made the diversity between man and beast?

ARISTIPPUS: Yea, and the same too.

PLATO: Than thou wilt conclude that man hath knowledge?

ARISTIPPUS: Yea, that I must needs; thou knowest well inough.

PLATO: And what callest thou that knowledge? Supposest thou it is where a man knoweth himself and other?

ARISTIPPUS: Yea, so I said, and thou hast also affirmed it.

PLATO: So I did indeed, but yet, good Aristippus, suffer me to demand of thee a few questions. We shall the sooner find out the knowledge that we seek for. Is it in figure and nomber that knowledge resteth?

ARISTIPPUS: Yea, so it appeareth.

PLATO: Nay, if thou remember thee, perdie, thou saidest thyself that thy horse knew not that thou were a man or that he was a horse.

ARISTIPPUS: So said I indeed.

PLATO: Thou considerest also that it was agreed by us both that the figure made not the man, but it was the soul with the body that caused the man to be so named; and that without the soul, notwithstanding the figure of man, yet were he no man but a brute beast.

ARISTIPPUS: It must needs be so; I cannot deny it.

PLATO: Than is there somewhat more that maketh the said knowledge besides the figure which is contained in the second part of that which we called intelligible?

ARISTIPPUS: So methinketh. But what hit is I cannot remember.

PLATO: It is no mervail. Thy wits be so involved in carnal affections that this clean and pure doctrine cannot enter into them without great difficulty; and whan they be ones in they cannot long abide, thy memory is so occupied about wanton and beastly fantasy. But yet will I ones again rehearse unto thee that which thou hast so shortly forgotten. Did not I say that in the first part of that which is named intelligible is that portion of divinity in man whereby he is made to the image and similitude of God?

ARISTIPPUS: Yes, I remember well that.

PLATO: And is that form printed in any other thing than in man's soul, which is immutable and of one proportion and figure? Although it lieth bounden in the body as it were in a prison, considering things diversely, as the substance and qualities of the body suff'reth him to take light, being deceived by the judgment of the senses or wits, esteeming things as they be sensible and visible, where that which the soul by himself doth consider is intelligible and also invisible.

ARISTIPPUS: I doubt me what I shall say. But supposest thou, Plato, that the image and similitude of God is not in the body of man as well as in the soul?

PLATO: Hast thou so soon forgotten that which I have so often rehearsed? That if the body of man were without a soul he were than but in the nomber of brute beasts, which have senses as well as he, and some more sharp and quicker. And no man that will affirm that God is will presume—as I trow—to say expressly that the image of God is in satyrs and other beasts and fishes which have form and shape like unto man. And to speak to thee merrily without reproach unto God's majesty, if that which is in every man's body were the image of God, certes than the image of God were not only divers but also horrible, monstruous, and in some part ridiculous—that is to say, to be laughed at. For every man hath not in visage and personage one proportion or figure. Some have a plain and equal visage, some look as they laughed, other as they wept, divers as they were ever angry, many have in the quantity of their bodies or members excess or lack. Wherefore to think that all these be like unto God—which as he is the creator of them all and may make and do what he listeth, so it agreeth with all raison that he incomparably excelleth them all in every perfection and consequently in beauty—it were of all other the greatest madness.

ARISTIPPUS: Thou answerest me raisonably, but now, I pray thee, declare to me as plainly how the image of God is in the soul as thou supposeth.

PLATO: Thou wilt not deny that God is without any body, invisible and immortal, whose form cannot be deprehended with the eyen of mortal men nor described by any sensible knowledge?

ARISTIPPUS: No, truly. . . .

PLATO: Also God is in power in all and every part of the world. And by his providence all thing is governed and moved. And he himself is of none other moved nor governed but is the first incomprehensible mover.

ARISTIPPUS: I can by no raison deny it except I would deny that God is and that I may not, sens that the order of all thing that is visible declareth that there must needs be one principal cause and beginning, which we call God. And also that order cannot be without providence and one perpetual governance.

PLATO: Yet thou sayest well, and as it beseemeth Socrates' scoler. But now, Aristippus, forasmuch as God is the first and principal cause, and as he is one in beginning so is he ever one in governance; and therefore having in him all sufficiency and power, wilt thou not grant me that he is of an absolute and full perfection?

ARISTIPPUS: Yes, that must I needs.

PLATO: And is not perfection in that it is perfect good also?

ARISTIPPUS: No man will deny it.

PLATO: Yea, peradventure the same perfection is goodness, sens goodness is alway complete, profitable, and without any lack. And goodness and evil the one is contrary and ever repugnant unto the other. How sayest thou? Is it not so?

ARISTIPPUS: Yea, that is true.

PLATO: Than is there ever variance between them?

ARISTIPPUS: So it appeareth.

PLATO: But in God can never be variance, which of his nature is ever one, and may never suffer division.

ARISTIPPUS: I grant thee.

PLATO: Than in God nor about God can be none evil; therefore all evil is far from God. But yet meseemeth we have spoken somewhat lass of God than we should do.

ARISTIPPUS: What meanest thou thereby?

PLATO: For sens we both have agreed that he is the first beginning and cause, we should have also concluded that all goodness proceeded of him and that he was the fountain and principal goodness.

ARISTIPPUS: I admit all to be true that thou sayest.

PLATO: Than thou grantest that evil is contrary to God?

ARISTIPPUS: Yea, verily.

PLATO: And all thing that is ill is contrary to that thing which is good?

ARISTIPPUS: Yea, surely. . . .

PLATO: That wherein things be like or unlike one to another, do we not call it an image or similitude?

ARISTIPPUS: Yes, undoubtedly.

PLATO: Hitherto we have well agreed. Now let see, Aristippus, sens thou hast confessed that the soul is invisible and immortal, how sayest thou? Shall it suffice that therein only he be like unto God and in all other thing unlike or contrary?

ARISTIPPUS: No, for than should he be in part like and in part unlike. And than were hit not well spoken to say that man was made to the image and similitude of God without joining thereto distinctly and particularly in what thing he was made to the said image and similitude. As if one would say that in thy son were thy proper image and similitude. If thou thyself diddest perceive that he were like to thee in favor, proportion of body, and conditions, thou wouldest hold thee pleased and say nothing. But if thou beheldest that in his personage he were like thee, but in some part of the visage, as in the nose, the eyen, or the mouth, he were unlike thee; also in liberality he followed thee, but in lechery he did degenerate from thee; shouldest thou not than be constrained to demand of him that spake wherein thy son is like to thee, or in what part of him thine image should appear to be most?

PLATO: Now on my faith, Aristippus, thou speakest very well and wisely. Lo, see how by our long communing thou art drawn from thy wanton affections and fantasies, whereby the sparks of wisdom that thou gatest of Socrates' lessons like as fire hid under askes and dead coals whan they be removed is found cind'ring in little imbers, so thine affections being withdrawn, wisdom doth begin to glitter and shew; which if it would abide kendling and not like unto imbers remove and flee away with every puff of wind, I doubt not but for the sharpness of thy wit of all Socrates' scolers thou shouldest be at the last one of the most wisest and excellent. . . . By that which we before have affirmed, that God is the first cause and principal goodness, it argueth that all thing which is not the self God is inferior unto him. Wherefore the image or similitude of God, although it be an imitation or following in likeness of that whereunto it is made and resembled, yet is it inferior to God, who by the virtue of his unity hath ever a preeminence and soverainty. Therefore we will stick no more thereupon. . . .

FROM THE CASTLE OF HEALTH (1541)

The elements be those original things, unmixt and uncompound, of whose temperance and mixture all other things having corporal substance be compact. Of them be four, that is to say earth, water, air, and fire. Earth is the most gross and ponderous element, and of her proper nature is cold and dry. Water is more subtle and light than earth, but in respect of air and fire it is gross and heavy, and of her proper nature is cold and moist. Air is more light and subtle than the other two, and, being not altered with any exterior cause, is properly hot and moist. Fire is absolutely light and clear, and is the clarifier of other elements if they be vitiate or out of their natural temperance, and is properly hot and dry. It is to be rememb'red that none of the said elements be commonly seen or felt of mortal men as they are in their original being, but they which by our senses be perceived be corrupted with mutual mixture and be rather earthy, wat'ry, airy, and fiery than absolutely earth, water, air, and fire.

Of the Complexion of Man

Complexion is a combination of two divers qualities of the four elements in one body, as hot and dry of the fire, hot and moist of the air, cold and moist of the water, cold and dry of the earth. But although all these complexions be assembled in every body of man and woman, yet the body taketh his denomination of those qualities which abound in him more than in the other, as hereafter insueth.

The body where heat and moisture have sovereignty is called sanguine, wherein the air hath preeminence, and it is perceived and known by these signs which do follow: carnosity or fleshliness, the veins and arteries large, hear plenty and red, the visage white and ruddy, sleep much, dreams of bloody things or things pleasant, pulse great and full, digestion perfect, angry shortly, siege, urine, and sweat abundant, falling shortly into bleeding, the urine red and thick.

Where cold with moisture prevaileth that body is called fleumatic, wherein water hath preeminence, and is perceived by these signs: fatness, quaving and soft, veins narrow, hear much and plain, color white, sleep superfluous, dreams of things wat'ry or of fish, slowness, dulness in learning, smallness of courage, pulse slow and little, digestion weak, spittle white, abundant, and thick, urine thick, white, and pale.

Choleric is hot and dry, in whom the fire hath preeminence, and is discerned by these signs following: leanness of body, costifeness, hear black or dark aburn curled, visage and skin red as fire or sallow, hot things noyful to him, little sleep, dreams of fire, fighting, or anger, wit sharp and quick, hardy and fighting, pulse swift and strong, urine high-colored and clear, voice sharp.

Melancholic is cold and dry, over whom the earth hath dominion, and is perceived by these signs: leanness with hardness of skin, hear plain and thin, color duskish or white with leanness, much watch, dreams fearful, stiff in opinions, digestion slow and ill, timerous and fearful, anger long and fretting, pulse little, seldom laughing, urine wat'ry and thin. . . .

Of Humors

In the body of man be four principal humors which continuing in the proportion that nature hath limited the body is free from all sickness. Contrariwise, by the increase or diminution of any of them in quantity or quality, over or under their natural assignment, inequal temperature cometh into the body, which sickness followeth more or lass according to the lapse or decay of the temperatures of the said humors, which be these following: blood, fleum, choler, melancholy.

Blood hath preeminence over all other humors in sustaining of all living creatures, for it hath more conformity with the original cause of living by reason of temperateness in heat and moisture, also nourisheth more the body and restoreth that which is decayed, being the very treasure of life, by loss whereof death immediately followeth. The distemperature of blood happ'neth by one of the other three humors by the inordinate or superfluous mixture of them.

Of Fleum

Fleum is of two sorts, natural and unnatural. Natural fleum is a humor cold and moist, white and sweet, or without taste, ingend'red by insufficient decoction in the second digestion of the wat'ry or raw parts of the matter decoct called *chilus*, by the last digestion made apt to be converted into blood. In this humor water hath dominion most principal.

Fleum unnatural is that which is mixt with other humors or is altered in his quality, and thereof is eight sondry kinds: wat'ry, which is found in spettle of great drinkers or of them which digest ill; slimy or raw; glassy, like to white glass, thick, viscous like birdlime and heavy; plast'ry, which is very gross and as it were chalky, such is found in the joints of them which have the gout; salt, which is mingled with choler; sour, mixt with melancholy, which cometh of corrupt digestion; harsh, thick and gross, which is seldom founden, which tasteth like green crabs or sloes; styptic or binding is not so gross nor cold as harsh, and hath the taste like to green red wine, or other like straining the tongue.

Choler doth participate with natural heat as long as it is in good temperance, and thereof is also two kinds, natural and unnatural.

Natural choler is the foam of blood, the color whereof is red and clear, or more like to an orange color, and is hot and dry, wherein the fire hath dominion, and is light and sharp, and is ingend'red of the most subtle part of matter decoct or boiled in the stomach, whose beginning is in the liver.

Unnatural choler is that which is mixt or corrupted with other humors, whereof be four kinds: citrine or yellow choler, which is the mixture of natural choler and watery fleum and therefore hath less heat than pure choler; yelky, like to yelks of eggs, which is of the mixture of fleum congealed and choler natural, and is yet lass hot than the other; green like to leeks, whose beginning is rather of the stomach than of the liver; green like to green canker of metal, and bourneth like venim and is of exceeding adustion of choler or fleum, and by these two kinds nature is mortified.

Melancholy or black choler is devided into two kinds: natural, which is the dregs of pure blood and is known by the blackness whan it issueth either downward or upward, and is verily cold and dry; unnatural, which proceedeth of the adustion of choleric mixture and is hotter and lighter, having in it violence to kill, with a dangerous disposition. . . .

The Dominion of Sundry Complexions

. . . None of the four complexions have sooly such dominion in one man or woman's body that no part of any other complexion is therewith mixt. For whan we call a man sanguine, choleric, fleumatic, or melancholy we do not mean that he hath blood only without any of the other humors, or choler without blood, or fleum without blood or melancholy, or melancholy without blood or choler. And therefore the man which is sanguine, the more that he draweth into age, whereby natural moisture decayeth, the more is he choleric, by reason that heat, surmounting moisture, needs must remain heat and dryth. Semblably the choleric man, the more that he waxeth into age the more natural heat in him is abated, and dryth surmounting natural moisture, he becometh melancholic. But some sanguine man hath in the proportion of temperatures a greater mixture with choler than another hath. Likewise the choleric or fleumatic man with the humor of sanguine or melancholy. And therefore late practisers of physic are wont to call men according to the mixture of their complexions which man receiveth in his generation; the humors whereof the same complexions do consist, being augmented superfluously in the body or members by any of the said things called not natural, every of them do semblably augment the complexion which is proper unto him and bringeth unequal temperature unto the body. And for these causes the sanguine or fleumatic man or woman, feeling any dyscrasy by choler happ'ned to them by the said things called not natural, they shall use the diet discribed hereafter to him which is naturally choleric. Semblably the choleric or melancholic man or woman, having any dyscrasy by fleum, to use the diet of him which is naturally fleumatic, alway rememb'ring that sanguine and fleumatic men have more respect unto dryth, choleric and melancholic unto moisture, and that alway, as the accidental complexion decayeth, to resort by little and little to the diet pertaining to his natural complexion. . . .

The Division of Melancholy and the Diet of Persons Melancholic

Melancholy is of two sorts. The one is called natural, which is only cold and dry; the other is called adust or burned. Natural melancholy is, as Galen saith, the residence or dregs of the blood, and therefore is colder and thicker than the blood. Melancholy adust is in four kinds. Either it is of natural melancholy adust, or of the more pure part of the blood adust, or of choler adust, or of salt fleum adust. But of all other that melancholy is warst which is ingend'red of choler. Finally, all adust melancholy annoyeth the wit and judgment of man, for whan that humor is hot it maketh men mad, and whan it is extinct it maketh men fools, forgetful and dull. The natural melancholy kept in his temperance profiteth much to true judgment of the wit, but yet if it be too thick it darkeneth the spirits, maketh one timorous, and the wit dull. If it be mixt with fleum it mortifieth the blood with too much cold. Wherefore it may not be so little that the blood and spirits in their ferventness be as it were unbridled, whereof do happen unstableness of wit and slipper remembrance; nor yet so much that by the weight thereof—for it is heavy, approaching nigh to the earth—that we seem to be alway in sleep and need a spur to prick us forward. Wherefore it is right expedient to keep that humor as thin as nature will suffer it, and not to have too much of it. But now to the diet pertaining to them whom this humor annoyeth. The knowledge that melancholy reigneth is oftentimes heaviness of mind, or fear without cause, sleepiness in the members, many cramps without repletion or emptiness, sodain fury, sodain incontinency of the tongue, much solicitude of light things, with paleness of the visage and fearful dreams of terrible visions, dreaming of darkness, deep pits, or death of friends or acquaintance, and of all thing that is black. The meats convenient are they which be temperate in heat, but specially they that be moist (meats soon digested, and they rather boiled than roasted, temperately mixt with spices), milk hot from the udder or late milked is very convenient for that complexion, sweet almonds blanched and almond milk, the yelks of rear eggs, and finally all things which ingender pure blood. . . . All these be ill for them: wine thick or troublous (specially red wine), meats hard, dry, very salt or sour, bourned meat, fried meat, much beef, hare's flesh, beans, rocket, coleworts, mustard, radish, garlic (except there be much wind in the body, for than is it very wholesome), onions, leeks, finally all things which heateth too much, keeleth too much, or drieth too much; also wrath, fear, compassion, sorrow, much study or care, much idleness or rest; all thing that is grievous to see, to smell, or to hear, but most specially darkness. . . .

JOHN HEYWOOD

Although the extant records of Heywood's life are meager, they are sufficient to establish him as the last minstrel or court jester. From 1515, when he was a boy chorister in Henry VIII's household, until he was forced into a recusant's exile after Elizabeth's accession (1558) his career was to entertain the royal family as a "singing man," "a player of the virginals," and a writer of dramatic pageants and interludes. The interludes—*The Pardoner* and the Friar, *The Play of the Weather, The Four P's,* and *Johan Johan the Husband, Tyb His Wife, and Sir Jhan the Priest*—contributed powerfully to the secularization of Tudor drama in the thirties and forties, but they lie beyond the scope of this anthology; nearly all Heywood's other major works—versified proverbs and epigrams and a long allegory called *The Spider and the Fly*—were printed in the forties and fifties, when old political and religious alignments were changing almost from month to month. Through them all, Heywood's loyalty to Mary Tudor and to the church they both revered remained steadfast; in spite of his professional role as jester, even buffoon, his was the voice of conservatism and tradition, and the merry quips which so delighted his royal patrons are often expressions of unyielding political and religious orthodoxy. The rough and insouciant vigor and the metrical naïveté of the epigrams stake Heywood to the very lowest slopes of Parnassus, but the same qualities give us a glimpse of Tudor literature just before it merged into the artful and self-conscious sophistication of Tottel's *Miscellany* (which, incidentally, contains one of Heywood's eulogies on Queen Mary). He published, in tedious dialogue form, a collection of proverbs in 1546 which was reprinted in 1549, 1556, and 1561; and the epigrams began appearing, in batches of a hundred, in 1556; finally, in 1562, the so-called *Woorkes* (STC 13285) brought together the epigrams (numbering six hundred) and the proverbs in a single book. The volume was so popular that it went through new editions in 1566, 1576, 1587, and 1598—long after English poets had attained a level far above Heywood's.

It is not to be wondered at that *The Spider and the Fly* has remained one of the least-read major poems of the sixteenth century. The critics and historians, from William Harrison on, who have troubled to flip its pages have generally dismissed Heywood's most ambitious work as an unreadable allegory of an unpopular cause. Yet, granting its immense prolixity and its technical insecurity, one should still recognize its very solid merits. As we learn from Heywood's "Conclusion," the work was begun "mo then twenty" years before (around 1536) and completed only after it had lain a fragment for nearly two decades. In view of its theme—the consequences of social and ecclesiastical disorder—the reason for Heywood's long delay is clear. Not until 1555 was England again reconciled with Rome for the first time in a generation, and not until that reconciliation had been effected could Heywood have ended his poem in the manner he desired. As the late Sir A. W. Ward has shown, a glance at some of the main events of Tudor history throws a flood of light on the author's intentions. Working on the obvious assumption that the flies represent the Roman Catholics, the spiders the Protestants, and the maid with the cleansing broom Queen Mary, we may infer that the narrative structure of the poem is based upon a sequence of civil and religious disorders beginning with the Pilgrimage of Grace of 1536 (a rising in the north against Henry's dissolution of the Catholic monasteries) and ending with the executions of Lady Jane Grey and the Duke of Northumberland and the failure of the younger Wyatt's rebellion (1553–54). Of course there are other points of satire, especially in the tedious opening chapters, that cannot be adjusted to the main allegorical line: for example, the parodies of scholastic disputation and legal chicanery in the early arguments between the spider and the fly and the recurrent anti-clericalism that Heywood shared with many good Roman Catholics (including Erasmus); but, as the narrative gathers momentum, the theme becomes clearer, and the great issue of a (Protestant) "murmuring mut'ring" seeking to overthrow the (Catholic) social order sanctioned by law, nature, custom, and conscience is deviously but artfully developed. Finally, the crushing of the spider under the maid's foot and the advent of a new dispensation in which she exerts her high authority under her master (Christ) and her "maistress" (the Holy Church) is accompanied by a paean to hierarchal order that brings us close to a dominant Tudor ideal. *The Spider and the Fly* was published by Thomas Powell in 1556; it did not reach a second edition until the late nineteenth century. Our text is based upon *The Spider and the Flie. A parable of the Spider and the Flie, made by John Heywood, 1556* (STC 13308).

FROM JOHN HEYWOOD'S WORKS (1562)

A DIALOGUE CONTAINING THE NUMBER OF THE EFFECTUAL PROVERBS IN THE ENGLISH TONGUE

THE PREFACE

Among other things profiting in our tongue
Those which much may profit both old and young,
Such as on their fruit will feed or take hold,
Are our common, plain, pithy proverbs old.
Some sense of some of which being bare and rude,
Yet to fine and fruitful effect they allude,
And their sentences include so large a reach
That almost in all things good lessons they teach.
This write I not to teach, but to touch, for why
Men know this as well or better then I,   10
But this and this rest I write for this:
Remember'ring and considering what the pith is
That by remembrance of these proverbs may grow,
In this tale, erst talked with a friend, I show
As many of them as we could fitly find,
Falling to purpose, that might fall in mind,
To th' entent that the reader readily may
Find them and mind them whan he will alway.

THE FIRST CHAPITER

Of mine acquaintance a certain young man,
Being a resorter to me now and than,   20
Resorted lately, showing himself to be
Desirous to talk at length alone with me.
And as we for this a meet place had won,
With this old proverb this young man begon:
"Whoso that knew what would be dear
Should need be a marchant but one year.
Though it," quoth he, "thing impossible be,
The full sequel of present things to foresee,
Yet doth this proverb provoke every man
Politicly (as man possible can)   30
In things to come after to cast eye before
To cast out or keep in things for forestore,
As the provision may seem most profitable
And the commodity most commendable.
Into this consideration I am wrought
By two things which Fortune to hands hath brought.
Two women I know, of which twain the tone
Is a maid of flow'ring age, a goodly one;
Th' other a widow who so many years bears
That all her whiteness li'th in her white hears.   40
This maid hath friends rich, but riches hath she none,
Nor none can her hands get to live upon.
This widow is very rich and her friends bare,
And both these for love to wed with me fond are.
And both would I wed, the better and the worse,
The tone for her person, the tother for her purse.
They woo not my substance, but myself they woo;
Goods have I none and small good can I do.
On this poor maid her rich friends, I clearly know,
So she wed where they will, great gifts will bestow,   50
But with them all I am so far from favor
That she shall sure have no groat if I have her.
And I shall have as little, all my friends swear,
Except I follow them to wed elsewhere.
The poor friends of this rich widow bear no sway,
But wed her and win wealth whan I will I may.
Now which of these twain is like to be dearest
In pain or pleasure to stick to me nearest?
The depth of all doubts with you to consither,
The sense of the said proverb send'th me hither.   60
The best bargain of both quickly to have scann'd,
For one of them think I to make out of hand."

THE FIRST HUNDRED OF EPIGRAMS

AN EPIGRAM ON THIS BOOK OF EPIGRAMS I

This book may seem, as it sorteth in suit,
A thin, trim trencher to serve folk at fruit;
But carver or reader can no way win
To eat fruit thereon or compt fruit therein.

OF THE SENSES 6

Speak not too much lest speech make thee speechless;
Go not too much for fear thou go behind;
Hear not too much lest hearing bring deafness;
Look not too much lest looking make thee blind;
Smell not too much lest smelling lose his kind;
Taste not too much lest taste mistaste thy chaps;
Touch not too much for fear of after-claps.

THE MAISTER AND THE MAN 23

A man and his man chanced late to be
Nigh where a crow stood crying in a tree.
"James," quoth the maister, "the crow hath spied thee."
"Nay, by God, he looketh on you, maister," quoth he.
"Taunts," quoth the maister, "rebound sometime, I see:
Where I thought to taunt thee thou dost taunt me."

THE COCK AND THE HEN 54

A cock and his hen perching in the night,
The cock at his hour crow'd loud as he might;
The hen, heavy of sleep, pray'd the cock that he
Would leave off his crowing, but it would not be.
The hen saw the cock stick to his tackling;
In her treble voice she fell so to cackling
That the cock pray'd her her cackling to cease
And he of his crowing would hold his peace.
"Nay, chorl," quoth she, "be sure that will I not,
And for thy learning henceforth mark this knot: 10
Whenever thou wouldest seem to overcrow me,
Than will I surely overcackle thee."

THREE HUNDRED EPIGRAMS UPON THREE HUNDRED PROVERBS

LOOKING AND LEAPING 5

Look ere thou leap; nay, thou canst in no wise brook
To look ere thou leap, for thou leapst ere thou look.

OF HOLDING OF A NOSE 34

Thou canst hold my nose to the grindstone.
So cannot I thine, for thou hast none.

ONE DRIVETH OUT ANOTHER 112

One nail driveth out another with strokes so stout
That the hammer-head which driveth them wear'th quite
out.

THE FIFTH HUNDRED OF EPIGRAMS

OF ONE HANGED 43

What faut had he done that was hang'd yesterday?
Of any faut done by him I can nought say.
Two or three twopenny trifles were laid to him,
But his fair, gay hang'd hose, man, did undo him.
Here is tit for tat, measure met very trim:
First he hang'd his hose, now his hose hath hang'd him

OF DIFFERENCE BETWEEN WISE MEN AND FOOLS 79

Between wise men and fools, among things many
This one differ'th: when both sorts get things any
Which to their pleasures are pleasantly allow'd,
Of those things won wise men are glad, fools be proud.

OF HEYWOOD 100

"Art thou Heywood with the mad, merry wit?"
"Yea forsooth, maister, that same is even hit."
"Are thou Heywood that applieth mirth more then
  thrift?"
"Yea, sir, I take merry mirth a golden gift."
"Art thou Heywood that hath made many mad plays?"
"Yea, many plays, few good works in all my days."
"Art thou Heywood that hath made men merry long?"
"Yea, and will, if I be made merry among."
"Art thou Heywood that would be made merry now?"
"Yea, sir, help me to it, now I beseech you."   10

A SIXT HUNDRED OF EPIGRAMS

OF REBELLION 1

Against God I daily offend by frailty,
But against my prince or native country

With as much as bodkin, when I rebel,
The next day after hang me up fair and well.
The next day after? Nay, the next day before
Wish thou thyself hang'd, in that case evermore.
Before, thou hang'st honestly unworthily;
After, thou hang'st worthily unhonestly.
But ho! at our first dish in our merry feast
Why talk we of hanging, our mirth to molest?   10
Be our cheese no better then our pottage is,
Better fast then feast at such feasts as is this.
But being true to God, queen, country, and crown,
We shall at all feasts not hang up but sit down.

OF A HUSBAND HANG'D 81

"Is thy husband hang'd?" "He was, but he is nat.
In spight of his foes I found friends to ease that:
For or my dear heart had hang'd fully hours twain
I gat his pardon and cut him down again."

OF TAKING THINGS WRONG 99

"Perceived and taken things right thou hast long,
But for one thing in thee long sens taken wrong
Thy credit is touch'd and thou thereby the worse."
"What thing sayst thou have I taken wrong?" "A purse."

FROM THE SPIDER AND THE FLY (1556)

*The introduction to the matter, showing how the fly chanced
to fall in the spider's copweb.* Capitum primum.

In season what time every growing thing
That ripeth by root hath lively taken heart—
Grass, leaf, and flow'r—in field so florishing
That wintered, withered stalks stand in covart,
Though weary withered hearts play than like part
Covertly couch'd in bed themselves to hide,
Yet hearts of lust the bed cannot abide,

But up they must, proof of that lust to make;
In which-like cheerful time it chanced me
From sleep one night so timely to awake   10
That how far night or how nigh day might be
It pass'd my reach of search sure sign to see;
But straight the search of nature wrought the crow
Of dawning of the day warning to show.

Upon which admonition I arose,
But by the time that I could get me out
The day appeareth and so broad breaketh lose,
Leading mine eye at large to look about
The fields so fresh that be ye out of doubt
For favor, sight, and hearing each bird's voice   20
No change could chance to choose the better choice.

Which I, rejoicingly, heard and beheld
Till such time as the sun was come in sight,
So that the dew, drawn by his pow'r, must yield
From th' earth to th' air from whence it fell that night;
And having herein had mine appetite
I made return temp'rately to remain
Out of whot sun to temp'rate house again.

Whereas, anon, a book I took in hand
Some thing to read to fode forth fantasy,   30
And, stepping to a window there to stand,
In at a lattice hole right sodenly,
Even at a fling, fast flew there in a fly
That sang as shrill and freshly in my mind
As any bird could do, bred of that kind.

About the parlor flew this fly full round,
And, as appear'd, he sought for food indeed,
But when in no wise ought would there be found,
Into the butt'ry hastily he yeed
And stale into the almery to feed,   40
Where he at pleasure triumph'd uncontroll'd,
Till he had there at will wrought what he would.

From whence anon couragiously he flang
Now here, now there; of wing he made no store,

But for a fly, O Lord, how he then sang
Two notes above his highest note before,
Wherein encreas'd his courage more and more.
He flew, he frisk'd, he toss'd, he turn'd about,
The fly of flies, no fly, I trow, so stout.

But as the firmament most clear and blue   50
The golden sunbeams bent to beautify,
The curtain drawn of cloudy, weeping hue
Withdraweth and changeth that crystal azure sky
From blue to black, so fareth it with the fly,
Amid whose joy at window to have pass'd
A copweb mask'th his wings and maketh him fast.

Thus chance hath, by exchange, the fly so trapp'd
That sodainly he lost his liberty.
The more he wrang, the faster was he wrapp'd,
And all to th' encrease of his jeoberdy.   60
Which paril when he did conceive and see,
Such was his rage in haste from thence to flit
As made him seem well nigh out of his wit.

He wafted his wings, he wagged his tail,
He shook his head, he frown'd, he stared wide,
He spurn'd, he kick'd, but when nought would avail
To rid him thence, but there he must abide;
As breath and breast would bear, loudly he cried,
And wofully as any one fly can
In following form this woful fly began.   70

[We need not follow in detail the leisurely and copious
narrative that follows. Through tens of chapters and
hundreds of lines the situation is slowly developed: the
fly's remorse, the spider's cupidity, the interminable
wrangling of the ant and butterfly who act as their advocates. A few of Heywood's chapter-headings will indicate
the course of their arguments:

"The spider chargeth the fly first with burglary,
which the fly answereth unto; than the spider
chargeth him with single felony, which the fly
reasoneth unto. *Capitum 11.*"

"The spider in a manner granteth that the fly came
into the copweb against the fly's own will, which the
spider so granteth, for such policy forthwith appearing as seemeth to weigh sore against the fly. *Capitum
12.*"

"They fall in comparison touching their evidence
written or unwritten. Whereunto the fly layeth
prescription of custom, which he before alleged,
supposing thereby that the spider ought both to
deliver him and make him amends. *Capitum 21.*"

"They agree to be tried by arbiterment, whether all
or how many holes in all windows belong to spiders
and how many to flies, the spider choosing for his
part the ant or pismere, the fly choosing for his side

the butterfly; whereupon they, th' one couple in one
part and th' other couple in another part, talk togither forthwith. *Capitum 28.*"

After interminable logic chopping and disputation the
litigants reach an impasse that can be resolved only with
force.]

*Upon the spider's and the fly's mutt'ring murmuring, sodenly
there come nigh about them a wonderful number of all manner
of flies in their warlike manner. Whereat with twink of an
eye, as it were, the head spider, with a great number of spiders,
hath builded a strong castle in that copweb with ordinance and
weapons and spiders ready in order of defense. Capitum 52.*

Herewith even sodenly, at twink of an eye,
Came such a flight of flies in scatt'red ray
As shadowed the sun from th' earth to the sky.
No kind of fly alive but was there that day.
Tag and rag, like lions raging now rage they.
Flesh flies, butterflies, land flies, water flies,
Bees, humblebees, wasps, hornets, gnats of all size.

The grand captain standing amidmong this rout
Was the fly that flang from thence in fury erst told.
Seld hath been seen such a sort, and all so stout,   80
Except here and there one temp'rate to behold;
Staves, bats, clubs, pitchforks most beggarly, most bold,
Wherewith the spiders that erst gave evidence
In the copweb took sentuary for defense.

Where whether this proud spider gave word before,
Who with that pert fly had before there prated,
Or that spiders of ordinary have store
Of all munition for wars ready rated
I wot not. But without more time delated,
Ordnance of all sorts round the copweb was laid,   90
And all spiders with all weapons press'd in aid.

Dags, handgoons, hakes, hagbussers, culverins, slings,
Potgoons, sakers, cannons double and demi,
Field pieces of all suits with all belonging things,
Bills, bows, partizans, pikes to push far or nigh
And to occupy all spiders plac'd aptly,
Each of them harness'd meet for his property,
The rest all in bright harness cap-a-pie.

The flies of all ordnance were not destitute
Nor furnished like as the spiders were: 100
Rusty rotten pieces their terror to bruit
They shot off and shot wide of marks everywhere.
Drums, fifes, flags, and wiflers none wanted there.
Banners display'd on both sides, all arms bearing,
In harold's books avow'd for both sides wearing.

The flies in number above the spiders far,
The spiders in order far better then they,

The flies will adventure to make or to mar,
The spiders (not sodenly) sob'rly weigh
To defend or offend the flies as they may.   110
The spiders in copweb will bide this jeoberty;
The flies in field will besiege them at liberty.

This huge heap of flies light about th' arbiters. Apprehending
th' ant, casting a halter about his neck, drawing him to their
tree of reformation (as they call it) to hang him straight; but at
his suit to be hard speak ere he die, one fly fleeth into the tree,
wherewith the captain commandeth silence. Capitum 53.

This innumerable flock of flies are now
March'd unto th' arbiters; and they there lighted,
They took th' ant prisoner with an unadvised vow,
To spight the spiders who had flies long spighted,
That he should straight be hang'd and then endited
Of felony against flies as an adherent
To spiders in their usurpation urgent.

"Hang him up," quoth one with wild words and wide wit,
"A false wretch he is, and well known everywhere,   121
And would be known nowhere; wherever he flit
He hath two names, one name here, another there,
In this place call'd ant, in that place call'd pismere.
And one suspected varlet two names to have
Is, in common judgment, judged a false knave."

Then stepp'd forth a sort of fell flies furiously
Who, having cast a halter about th' ant's neck,
To their tree of reformation standing by
They felly forc'd him with many a chorlish check.   130
A ladder to that tree was set at a beck,
Where he in haste hal'd up and the halter tied.
"Turn the thief off the ladder," thousands cried.

Small was the marvail though th' ant were much
  abash'd
To see this sore, soden, importable chance;
Who liveth in nature but he must be dash'd
Both out of corage and out of countenance,
That should straight be dash'd out of continuance?
When none, or few, being forewarn'd of death's hour
Can evenly bear feeling thought of that sharp show'r.   140

Right now in worship set high as a judge,
Even now standing in shame to be hang'd high,
It was to him a feeling grief of grudge
Unknown to all that have not feelingly
Felt of the same in their experiency;
His look and hue now and late so unlike
That to the heart a Jew that sight must strike.

In which agony, calling to him his wit,
One wise fly, at all former talk present,

Seeming with all flies present in good credit,   150
He pray'd to persuade all there to be content
To hear him speak ere he his life should relent.
"But reason," quoth that fly; and therewithal he,
To get th' ant that grace, gat him into that tree.

The fly there bent to speak, the captain grand
By mouth of an harold at trumpet sounded
In proclamation did silence straight command.
Whereat a few words here and there in ears rowned
To hear that fly speak their speech was all drowned,
Whereupon the captain bidding that fly say   160
These or these like few words, he said straightway.

The fly in the tree, to perswad the flies to hear the ant speak,
wadeth honestly, politicly to allure them to quiet hearing of
the ant before they put him to death. His which tale told, he
removeth to his place again. Capitum 54.

"Brothers and brotherly friends all, I doubt nat
Ye know me a fly and take me such a fly
As for ant or spider in any what
Will not be false to the flock, that naturally
I ought to be true unto to live or die
For this ant and all ants. What I shall say now
Shall approve me none of them, but one of you.

"Of whom each one another myself to say
And each one to other, I hope, likewise knit,   170
Let us all as one, ent'ring this one journey,
Enter the path as we may pass thorow it.
One deep enduction whereto, judged in my wit,
Is to flee rash deeds rashly done here. For such
Have undone all, in our like case, very much.

"One of which dangerous deeds, under correction,
We do in this deed, th' ant thus to death to draw
Without accusation or detection,
Whereby might appear any color of law
To kill him. This, lo, doth my conscience gnaw,   180
And yet more the number here in ire so stirr'd
That they would have him hang'd and not speak one word.

"Which deed if we do, where are our like monsters?
First to apprehend an ant undetected
By any color, that any word consters
To be either detected or suspected,
And not only straight unto death directed
But die not suff'red to speak; defame of us
That perpetual trump will blow in shame of us.

"Wherefore for us, and not for him, as I said,   190
I sue to you as he hath sued to me
To hear him speak, which speech of you heard and
  weigh'd,

As you shall be agreed, so shall I agree
To hang him or save him as we cause shall see."
This tale thus told, down the fly again flit'th,
And where he erst did sit, there he again sit'th.

[No sooner is the ant, after the most intricate maneuvering, reprieved and imprisoned than all the flies march in battle array on the cobweb castle, but they are repulsed in a furious fight and return to their own camp. Meanwhile the spider's wife and children beseech him on bended knees to make peace with the flies, and he takes lengthy counsel with his twelve chief advisers as to the policy they should follow. At long last both ants and flies decide that further war would be suicidal, and so they agree to compose the original litigation between the spider and the fly by discourse of reason, law, custom, and conscience. By these hallowed sanctions the fly is condemned to death, but just as he is about to meet his fate he is saved by a *dea ex machina*.]

As the spider is about to kill the fly the maid of the house cometh in and striketh down the copweb and the spider to the ground. Capitum 89.

The spider toward the fly furiously draws
And being stepp'd to the fly, staying in stop
As he would have pierc'd the fly's head with his paws,
The maid of the house to the window did chop,   200
Setting her broom hard to the copweb's top,
Where at one stroke with her broom striken round
The copweb and spider she strake to the ground.

The maid being at point to tread the spider to death, the spider prayeth her to hear him speak ere he die and then to adjudge him justly. The maid granting to use him (as he did use the fly) as may best stand with reason, law, custom, and conscience, she at his request for the time withdrawing her foot they fall to reasoning of the case. Capitum 90.

The maid by mine absence to be the more bold
To work her will, as she came in I went out,
And look'd in at the window her to behold.
She swept down the copweb; the fly flew about
The parlor round, never more lusty nor stout.
The spider on the ground under the maid's foot
To tread him to death, and was about to do 't.   210

But the spider, on knees, lift up his hands high,
Beseeching her of mild maidenly pity
To be content to hear him speak ere he die
And to declare first what he had done and then why
He did those deeds, and so to judge him justly,
And that she would, in meantime, her foot withdraw,
Sight whereof made his head ache and his stomock gnaw.

"To banish," quoth the maid, "all pershal pretense
I'll hear and judge thee as thou did'st the fly here,
As stand'th with reason, law, custom, and conscience, 220
So shalt thou have good, bad, high, low, far or near;
And since fear of my foot abateth thy cheer,
Lest thou might'st take harm of thine own conceit
That I withdraw." And so withdrew it straight.

[There follows the last of the many trial-scenes in the poem, but this one finds the spider in the unaccustomed role of defendant. Condemned to die by the law of custom, he bids his twelve counselors and his eldest son farewell, excogitates soberly on the necessity of civil order, and meets his death bravely under the maid's foot.]

The maid hath before her the twelve spiders and the twelve flies that had been before in place, and upon her show that all harms done by those generations is grown by misorder, she finally deviseth full redress in pointing them to grow to order. Capitum 95.

Upon this execution done, she hath now
Before her these twelve spiders and those twelve flies
That erst were there, they erst mentioned to you;
Unto which number she did there devise
Certain precepts geven in words weighty and wise,
Which to repeat as rightly as I can   230
I will. And in this wise her tale began.

"To train the time and tarry you," quoth she,
"In talk of your forefauts, folly it were.
The smart both doth and will still tell it ye;
But what thing brought that smart, each when and where,
That here to hear each one lay to his ear;
Which thing briefly to tell, brief end to forder,
Was only in you all this thing—misorder.

"As God orderly created creatures all,
So were they created to orderly entent   240
To use themselves, each creature in his call,
Of which created sort. The Creator meant
Spiders and flies twain to order to relent,
The lack whereof on your sides witnesseth well
To have wrought displeasure on all sides everydell.

"On all sides, I say, meaning these sides thereby:
Your sides, my side, my master and mistress' side.
First for your sides: the smart show'th feelingly;
On my side, such rebukes as I abide
Of them for you, seeming your fauts to hide;   250
And on their sides, their most displeasant sight
To see spiders and flies out of order quight. . . .

"That spiders and flies are the creatures of God
And all his creatures in their creation good
I know and aknowledge—or else gods forbod.

I hate neither the spiders' nor the flies' brood;
I love all, as behoveth maidenly mood.
All his creatures in an order we must love
That orderly use themselves, as doth behove.

"And such as be ill yet may we not hate   260
The persons but the ill in the persons seen.
This learn'd I of a preacher that preached late,
And of myself, I thank God, I have not been
So much given to hate—any person, I mean,
Be they spiders, be they flies, whatever they be—
But I can use all, as stand'th with charity . . . .

"This ancient order, in few words here geven,
Is all that I ax in you to be used;
In lack whereof in all sorrow you are dreven,
In use thereof in solace you inclused.   270
Misorder bringing you thus confused,
Let order by your leaving of misorder
Quietness on your sides and all sides forder.

"By order from misorder you to redeem,
From sorrows of all sorts to solace so sorted,
Is cause of my coming. Not by means extreme,
But by most mild means that may be imported
In order to set you and see you comforted
To keep order, wherein you obeying me,
We may live in love all, each in his degree.   280

"Each in his degree, I say: mark that point well.
Your lack of living, so ye see, marr'd you all,
Chiefly you spiders, usurping to excel
In governance out of your place natural;
Which for few years past brought and kept flies so thrall
That you well-nigh brought flies to grant to agree
You as head governors general be;

"In which usurpation ye offended
Nature, reason, my master, maistress, and me.
Governors Nature hath commonly bended   290
Over such kinds to govern as themselves be,
Beast over beasts, fowl over fowls, as we see
Man over men; and in fear and awe is than
Th' unreasonable beast to reasonable man.

"Nature ye offend in planted plain proof here
To take rule of other kinds then your kind is;
Reason ye offend in that ye here appear
To take upon you the use of mine office;
Me ye offend in the same, and unto this
My master and maistress ye offend, as thus   300
Head rule here is their gift by custom's discuss.

"But leave this and take that: mine order erst told,
Keep you your places and let me keep mine,

As Nature and custom willeth you of old,
While reason and custom do me clear encline
My master's and maistress' will to work in fine,
As I under them and you under me
May lovely live, I say, each in due degree. . . ."

[Having "thankfully" received this good advice of the maid, the spiders and the flies all "joyfully depart" to live thereafter in amity. The maid then sweeps the contested window "clean in every place as far as her broom and arm will stretch."]

The maid being gone, the auctor cometh in, and upon his beholding the window fair and clean swept without any comberous copwebs or excessive flocks of flies he departeth. Capitum 98.

Beholding the window, seeing every room
Clean and empty, save three flies amid that plat,   310
And in the top (without reach of the maid's broom)
Corners of copwebs unneth seen, and to that
All things in quiet case, so that I could nat
Of any matter be any furder winner,
I went from the window to the boord to dinner.
Finis

The Conclusion with an Exposition of the Auctor Touching One Piece of the Latter Part of This Parable

I have, good readers, this parable here penn'd,
After old beginning newly brought to end.
The thing years mo then twenty since it begun,
To the thing years mo then nineteen, nothing done.
The fruit was green; I durst not gather it than   320
For fear of rotting before riping began;
The loss (it on the fruiterer's hand lying)
Had in that mystery marr'd his occupying.
This work among my poor works thus hath it pass'd,
Begun with the first and ended with the last,
At end whereof, as at beginning, I pray
All readers that read it (in all that we may)
Each one reader to scan this parable so
As our most scanning diligently may go,
In speech of spiders' and flies' fauts here shown,   330
To considerate weighing of fauts of our own;
And them by grace t' amend for concord growing
As spiders and flies grow to herein showing. . . .
                                        Let us here
Play our parts in this part, all parts to appear
To this maid as spiders and flies to that maid.
Let our banners of obedience be display'd,
Of love the badge, of rejoicing the right root,
And of our own wealths the right and full boot.
Love we her and obey we her as we ought,   340
And also our suffraine lord Philip, to her brought
By God as God brought her to us. Which twain,
Conjoined one in matrimonial train,

Both one also in auctority regal;
These two thus made one, both one here we call,
Which two thus one rejoice we everychone,
And these two thus one obey we all as one
Effectually as those spiders and flies
Figuratively that one recongnies,
Beseeching God that brought them to keep them here 350
In long prosperous reign, and of his mercy mere

So to bliss us that on this blessed stock
He bring such imps as over their faithful flock,
As their progenitors do reign presently,
They after them may reign perpetually.
And for gift of these two thus one to us geven
To yield the Three and One thanks as we are drevin,
And also them conclude we this even thus:
Thank we God for them, and God and them for us.

Finis

Part III THE REFORMATION IN ENGLAND

Although the English had for centuries been turning parts of the Bible into their various dialects, there was no printed vernacular version until the middle of Henry VIII's reign. The Venerable Bede tells us that Caedmon had written Biblical paraphrases (in Old English) in the seventh century, and the eighth-century Bede himself made a now lost translation of part of St. John's Gospel; in addition there survive from the ninth and tenth centuries various fragmentary versions of the Psalms and the Gospels, and from about the end of the tenth century we have the interesting West Saxon translation of the Gospels and Aelfric's version of several books of the Old Testament.

Although the two centuries following the Norman Conquest, when the language was in a most uncertain state, are nearly barren of translation, in the fourteenth century portions of the Bible were translated in several versions, mainly in Midland and Northern dialects. The most notable Middle English version was that attributed to John Wyclif, the Lollard whose efforts to make the complete Bible available in the vernacular were viewed with the gravest alarm by the orthodox. To Wyclif (or to his followers and collaborators) we owe two distinct translations made during Chaucer's lifetime: the so-called Early Version, completed about the time of Wyclif's death in 1384, and the splendid Later Version that was completed about 1395–97. The muscular, idiomatic vernacular of the Later Version stands as a monument in the development of English prose. These two were the first complete translations, and the last until after Henry VIII had wrenched his national church from Rome in the fourth decade of the sixteenth century.

Indeed, a genuinely new translation was not possible until Renaissance scholarship had established a better text than the hopelessly imperfect Latin Vulgate upon which all early versions were based. After 1488 the Hebrew of the Old Testament was available in print, and in 1516 Erasmus achieved one of his major triumphs when he published the New Testament in Greek with his own Latin translation. The next year Luther sparked the German Reformation, and apparently by the early twenties William Tyndale, one of his most zealous English converts, conceived the notion of a new vernacular translation in accordance with his Protestant convictions. Meeting only discouragement and even hostility at home, in 1524 he went to Germany, the spiritual home of his faith, and there, at Cologne, he began to publish his version of the New Testament in 1525. Blocked by the Catholic officials of that city, he escaped to Worms, where he completed the Cologne edition and then printed a new one, copies of which were promptly smuggled into England. There they were welcomed by increasing numbers of English

Lutherans, and the fact that they were promptly confiscated by Wolsey's agents merely spurred Tyndale on to further efforts. In 1530, at Antwerp, he printed his version of the Pentateuch, and the next year that of Jonah. Meanwhile Richard Bayfield and other zealous English reformers sought to meet the large but surreptitious demand for Tyndale's Worms New Testament by smuggling at least three reprints into England and at last, in 1534, by issuing a somewhat altered English edition. In the same year, in Antwerp, Tyndale himself supervised a definitive new edition, with savagely controversial prologues to most of the various books and inflammatory marginal glosses. Before his execution in 1536 at Vilvorde, near Brussels, he contrived to get into print two further editions (1535, 1536), and with these his tireless efforts ended. Even though he never achieved his dream of translating the whole Bible, Tyndale has been credited with doing more toward shaping the King James Version of 1611 than any other man. Working directly from the Hebrew and the Greek—although he also consulted Erasmus' Latin and Luther's German versions—he sought to render the Scripture in faithful and idiomatic English. That he succeeded beyond most translators' wildest dreams was finally shown when his translation served as the basis for the King James Version nearly a century later. The text of our excerpt from Tyndale is based upon *The Newe Testament dylygently corrected and compared with the Greke*, 1534 (STC 2826).

After Tyndale's hazardous experiment on the eve of the English Reformation the floodgates were open. Even before that great man's death, Miles Coverdale, a former Augustinian friar who lived to become Bishop of Exeter (1551–53), compiled (and in part translated) his complete version, which was printed (probably at Zurich) in 1535. Its success prompted Edward Whitchurch and Richard Grafton (see p. 20) to publish, in 1537, another version which "Thomas Matthew" (John Rogers?) stitched together from Tyndale and Coverdale. Significantly, both it and the second (1537) edition of Coverdale were published with the king's "gracious license"—a wry commentary on ecclesiastical developments since Tyndale had been harried out of the land a little more than a decade earlier. Passing by the version which Richard Taverner edited (or pirated) from "Matthew" in 1539, we come next to the important Great Bible of the same year. As early as 1530 Henry VIII had named a committee to determine the feasibility of issuing an official vernacular translation; its report urged that the project be undertaken forthwith, but while the work languished, commercial printers like Whitchurch and Grafton were busy meeting the demand for Bibles in English. Against the king's caution (or lack of interest), however, the Convocation of Canterbury, Thomas Cromwell, and Thomas Cranmer, Archbishop of Canterbury, pushed the job forward as best they could. In 1538 Cromwell dispatched Coverdale and Grafton to Paris to see the great work through the press of Francis Regnault, but, when the French Catholics raised difficulties, the task was finished in London in April, 1539, as a huge black-letter folio, the frontispiece to which shows Henry VIII giving the "Word of God" to Cromwell and Cranmer for them to relay to his people. The second (1540) of the seven editions that followed within two years is sometimes called Cranmer's Bible from the long preface which he contributed. The text of our excerpts is based upon *The Byble in Englyshe, That is to Saye The Content of All the Holy Scrypture*, 1539 (STC 2068).

The last years of Henry's reign marked a return to his former restrictive policy, so that Tyndale's version was banned in 1543 and Coverdale's in 1546; thus the Great Bible was (legally, at least) for some years without serious competition. During the Marian persecution, after Cranmer had died at the stake, Coverdale and one William Whittingham, in exile in Geneva, began the preparation of a new Protestant Bible, and in 1557 a New Testament, with a preface by Calvin himself, was actually published. Both its Protestantism and its convenience—it was a handy quarto in clear Roman type with the text numbered by verses and sections—won it immediate popularity in England. In 1560, however, it was superseded by the famous Geneva Bible, the combined effort of Whittingham, Anthony Gilby, and Thomas Sampson. Also a quarto in clear Roman type, this version drew upon Tyndale's New Testament as well as upon the latest Greek and Hebrew scholarship, and its copious and vehemently Protestant marginalia endeared it to generations of English puritans. Its success may be gauged by its nearly one hundred fifty editions between 1560 and 1644 —all these in spite of the fact that its use was prohibited in Anglican churches. The text of our excerpts is based upon *The Bible and Holy Scriptures Conteyned in The Olde and Newe Testament. Translated According to the Ebrue and Greke . . . With moste profitable annotations upon all the hard places, and other things of great importance . . . , 1560* (STC 2093).

A Bible contrived for official use, and also as a check to the immense popularity of the Geneva version, was the so-called Bishops' Bible, which Archbishop Parker launched in the early sixties, and which, after the labors of at least eight of Elizabeth's prelates, was published as a sumptuous folio in 1568. For our excerpts we have followed the edition of 1572 (*The holie Bible*, STC 2107).

In order to meet the competition of both the new Anglican and Genevan versions a group of English Catholics who were refugees in the Low Countries arranged for the publication of their own New Testament at Rheims in 1582. Nearly three decades later the work was completed when the Old Testament was printed at Douai in 1609–10. Based on the Vulgate and conspicuous for its heavily Latinate diction and generally cumbersome style, the Rheims-Douai version is a literal and uninteresting translation, and it was not reprinted as a complete work until 1635. For the Old Testament our excerpts are based upon *The Second Tome of the Holie Bible Faithfully translated into English, out of the Authentical Latin . . . By the English College of Doway, 1610* (STC 2207); for the New Testament, on *The New Testament of Jesus Christ, Translated Faithfully into English, out of the authentical Latin . . . With Arguments of bookes and chapters, Annotations, and other necessarie helpes, for the better understanding of the text, and specially for the discoverie of the Corruptions of divers late translations, and for cleering the Controversies in religion, of these daies, 1582* (STC 2884).

The last and greatest of the Renaissance Bibles was the so-called King James Version. Initiated by James I in 1604 as a revision of the Bishops' Bible of 1568 (which was itself a revision of Henry VIII's Great Bible of 1539), and executed by some fifty-four clergymen and scholars, it was at last published and "appointed to be read in churches" in 1611. The translators, who represented both the Anglican and puritan wings of the church, and included such notables as Lancelot Andrewes, John Overall, William Bedwell, Sir Henry Savile, John Spenser, and Thomas Sanderson, were the academic and scholarly peers of the realm. About the results of their labors it is impossible to be too laudatory. In spite of certain mistranslations and anachronisms, their noble work has for centuries remained the greatest and most influential monument of English prose. Its phrases, its rhythms, and its sonorous beauty have informed the style of countless writers, and no one who claims English as his native tongue can fail to acknowledge its abiding influence. Our excerpts are based on *The Holy Bible, Conteyning the Old Testament, and the New. Newly Translated out of the Originall Tongues, 1611* (STC 2216).

FROM WILLIAM TYNDALE'S NEW TESTAMENT (1534)

THE GOSPEL OF SAINT MATTHEW

THE FIFTH CHAPTER

When he saw the people he went up into a mountain, and when he was set his disciples came to him, and he opened his mouth and taught them, saying: Blessed are the pover in sprete, for theirs is the kingdom of heaven. Blessed are they that mourn, for they shall be conforted. Blessed are the meek, for they shall inherit the earth. Blessed are they which hunger and thirst for rightewesnes, for they shall be filled. Blessed are the merciful, for they shall obtain mercy. Blessed are the pure in heart, for they shall see God. Blessed are the peacemakers, for they shall be called the children of God. Blessed are they which suffer persecution for rightewesnes' sake, for theirs is the kingdom of heaven. Blessed are ye when men revile you and persecute you and shall falsely say all manner of evil sayings against you for my sake. Rejoice and be glad, for great is your reward in heaven. For so persecuted they the prophets which were before your days.

Ye are the salt of the earth, but and if the salt have lost her saltness, what can be salted therewith? It is thenceforth good for nothing but to be cast out and to be troden underfeet of men. Ye are the light of the world. A city that is set on an hill cannot be hid; neither do men light a candle and put it under a bushel, but on a candlestick, and it lighteth all that are in the house. Let your light so shine before men that they may see your good works and glorify your Father which is in heaven.

Think not that I am come to destroy the law or the prophets: no, I am not come to destroy them but to fulfil them. For truly I say unto you, till heaven and earth perish, one jot or one tittle of the law shall not scape till all be fulfilled.

Whosoever breaketh one of these least commandments and teacheth men so, he shall be called the least in the kingdom of heaven. But whosoever observeth and teacheth, the same shall be called great in the kingdom of heaven.

For I say unto you, except your rightewesnes exceed the rightewesnes of the scribes and pharisees, ye cannot enter into the kingdom of heaven.

Ye have heard how it was said unto them of the old time: "Thou shalt not kill, for whosoever killeth shall be in danger of judgment." But I say unto you, whosoever is angry with his brother shall be in danger of judgment. Whosoever sayeth unto his brother "Racha" shall be in danger of a counsel. But whosoever sayeth "Thou fool!" shall be in danger of hell fire.

Therefore when thou off'rest thy gift at the altar and there rememb'rest that thy brother hath ought against thee, leave there thine off'ring before the altar and go thy way first and be reconciled to thy brother, and then come and offer thy gift.

Agree with thine adversary quickly whiles thou art in the way with him, lest that adversary deliver thee to the judge and the judge deliver thee to the minister and then thou be cast into preson. I say unto thee verily, thou shalt not come out thence till thou have paid the utmost farthing.

Ye have heard how it was said to them of old time: "Thou shalt not commit advoutry." But I say unto you that whosoever looketh on a wife lusting after her hath committed advoutry with her already in his heart.

Wherefore if thy right eye offend thee, pluck him out and cast him from thee. Better it is for thee that one of thy members perish then that thy whole body should be cast into hell. Also if thy right hond offend thee, cut him off and cast him from thee. Better it is that one of thy members perish then that all thy body should be cast into hell.

It is said, "Whosoever put away his wife, let him geve her a testimonial also of the devorcement." But I say unto you, whosoever put away his wife (except it be for fornication) causeth her to break matrimony. And whosoever marrieth her that is devorced breaketh wedlock.

Again ye have heard how it was said to them of old time, "Thou shalt not forswear thyself, but shalt perform thine oath to God." But I say unto you, swear not at all, neither by heaven, for it is God's seat, nor yet by the earth, for it is his footstool, neither by Jerusalem, for it is the city of that great king; neither shalt thou swear by thy heed, because thou canst not make one white heer or black. But your communication shall be "Yea, yea," "Nay, nay." For whatsoever is more then that cometh of evil.

Ye have heard how it is said, "An eye for an eye, a tooth for a tooth." But I say to you that ye resist not wrong. But whosoever geve thee a blow on thy right cheek, turn to him the other. And if any man will sue thee at the law and take away thy coote, let him have thy cloak also. And whosoever will compell thee to go a mile, go with him twain. Geve to him that axeth, and from him that would borrow turn not away.

Ye have heard how it is said, "Thou shalt love thine neighbor and hate thine enemy." But I say unto you, love your enemies. Bless them that curse you. Do good to them that hate you. Pray for them which do you wrong and persecute you, that ye may be the childern of your Father that is in heaven. For he maketh his sun to arise on the evil and on the good and sendeth his rain on the just and unjust. For if ye love them which love you, what reward shall ye have? Do not the publicans even so? And if ye be friendly to your brethren only, what singular thing do ye? Do not the publicans likewise? Ye shall therefore be perfect even as your Father which is in heaven is perfect.

FROM THE GREAT BIBLE (1539)

THE XXIII PSALM

Dominus regit me

A Psalm of David

The Lord is my shepherd; therefore can I lack nothing. He shall feed me in a green pasture and lead me forth beside the waters of comfort. He shall convert my soul and bring me forth in the paths of righteousness for his name's sake. Yea, though I walk thorow the valley of the shadow of death I will fear no evil, for thou art with me; thy rod and thy staff comfort me.

Thou shalt prepare a table before me against them that trouble me; thou hast anointed my head with oil, and my cup shall be full.

But thy loving kindness and mercy shall follow me all the days of my life, and I will dwell in the house of the Lord forever.

THE GOSPEL OF SAINT MATTHEW

THE FIFTH CHAPTER

In this chapter and in the two next following is contained the most excellent and loving sermon of Christ in the mount, which sermon is the very key that openeth the understanding into the law. In this fifth chapter, specially he preacheth of the eight beatitudes or blessings, of manslaughter, wrath and anger, of advoutry, of swearing, of suffering wrong, and of love even toward a man's enemies.

When he saw the people he went up into a mountain, and when he was set his disciples came to him; and after that he had opened his mouth, he taught them, saying, Blessed are the poor in sprete, for theirs is the kingdom of heaven. Blessed are they that mourn, for they shall receive comfort. Blessed are the meek, for they shall receive the inheritance of the earth. Blessed are they which hunger and thirst after rightwesnes, for they shall be satisfied. Blessed are the merciful, for they shall obtain mercy. Blessed are the pure in heart, for they shall see God. Blessed are the peacemakers, for they shall be called the children of God. Blessed are they which suffer persecution for rightwesnes' sake, for theirs is the kingdom of heaven. Blessed are ye when men revile you, and persecute you, and shall falsely say all manner of evil sayings against you for my sake. Rejoice and be glad, for great is your reward in heaven. For so persecuted they the prophets which were before you.

Ye are the salt of the earth, but if the salt have lost the saltness, what shall be seasoned therewith? It is thenceforth good for nothing but to be cast out and to be trodden down of men. Ye are the light of the world. A city that is set on an hill cannot be hid; neither do men light a candle and put it under a bushel, but on a candlestick, and it geveth light unto all that are in the house. Let your light so shine before men that they may see your good works and glorify your Father which is in heaven.

Think not that I am come to destroy the law or the prophets. No, I am not come to destroy, but to fulfil. For truly I say unto you, till heaven and earth pass, one jot or one tittle of the law shall not scape till all be fulfilled.

Whosoever therefore breaketh one of these least commandements, and teacheth men so, he shall be called the least in the kingdom of heaven. But whosoever doeth and teacheth, the same shall be called great in the kingdom of heaven.

For I say unto you, except your rightwesnes exceed the rightwesnes of the scribes and pharisees, ye cannot enter into the kingdom of heaven.

Ye have heard that it was said unto them of the old time, "Thou shalt not kill; whosoever killeth shall be in danger of judgment." But I say unto you that whosoever is angry with his brother (unadvisedly) shall be in danger of judgment. And whosoever say unto his brother "Racha" shall be in danger of a counsel. But whosoever sayeth "Thou fool!" shall be in danger of hell fire.

Therefore, if thou off'rest thy gift at the altar and there rememb'rest that thy brother hath ought against thee, leave there thine off'ring before the altar and go thy way first, and be reconciled to thy brother, and then come, and offer thy gift.

Agree with thine adversary quickly, whiles thou art in the way with him, lest at any time the adversary deliver thee to the judge, and the judge deliver thee to the minister, and then thou be cast into prison. Verily I say unto thee, thou shalt not come out thence till thou have paid the utmost farthing.

Ye have heard that it was said to them of old time, "Thou shall not commit advoutry." But I say unto you that whosoever looketh on another man's wife to lust after her hath committed advoutry with her already in his heart.

If thy right eye hinder thee, pluck him out and

cast him from thee. For better it is unto thee that one of thy members perish then that thy whole body should be cast into hell.

And if thy right hand hinder thee, cut him off, and cast him from thee. For better it is unto thee that one of thy members perish then that all thy body should be cast into hell.

It is said, "Whosoever putteth away his wife, let him geve her a letter of the devorcement." But I say unto you that whosoever doth put away his wife (except it be for fornication) causeth her to break matrimony. And whosoever marrieth her that is devorced committeth advoutry.

Again, ye have heard how it was said to them of old time, "Thou shalt not forswear thyself, but shalt perform unto the Lord those things that thou swearest." But I say unto you, swear not at all: neither by heaven, for it is God's seat, nor by the earth, for it is his footstool, neither by Jerusalem, for it is the city of the great king; neither shalt thou swear by thy head, because thou canst not make one hear white or black. But your communication shall be "Ye, ye," "Nay, nay." For whatsoever is added more then these, it cometh of evil.

Ye have heard that it is said, "An eye for an eye and a tooth for a tooth." But I say unto you that ye resist not evil. But whosoever geve thee a blow on the right cheek, turn to him the other also. And if any man will sue thee at the law and take away thy coat, let him have thy clook also. And whosoever will compel thee to go a mile, go with him twain. Geve to him that asketh thee, and from him that would borrow, turn not thou away.

Ye have heard that it is said, "Thou shalt love thine neighbor and hate thine enemy." But I say unto you, love your enemies; bless them that curse you; do good to them that hate you; pray for them which hurt you and persecute you, that ye may be the children of your Father which is in heaven. For he maketh his sun to arise on the evil and on the good, and sendeth rain on the just and unjust. For if ye love them which love you, what reward have ye? Do not the publicans also even the same? And if ye make much of your brethren only, what singular thing do ye? Do not also the publicans likewise? Ye shall therefore be perfect, even as your Father which is in heaven is perfect.

FROM THE GENEVA BIBLE (1560)

PSALM XXIII

A Psalm of David

Because the prophet had proved the great mercies of God at diverse times and in sundry manners he gathereth

a certain assurance, fully persuading himself that God will continue the very same goodness towards him forever.

1. The Lord is my shepherd; I shall not want.

2. He maketh me to rest in green pasture and leadeth me by the still waters.

3. He restoreth my soul and leadeth me in the paths of righteousness for his name's sake.

4. Yea, though I should walk through the valley of the shadow of death I will fear no evil, for thou art with me; thy rod and thy staff they comfort me.

5. Thou dost prepare a table before me in the sight of mine adversaries; thou dost anoint mine head with oil, and my cup runneth over.

6. Doutless kindness and mercy shall follow me all the days of my life, and I shall remain a long season in the house of the Lord.

SAINT MATTHEW

CHAPTER V

3 Christ teacheth who are blessed. 13 The salt of the earth and light of the world. 16 Good works. 17 Christ came to fulfil the law. 21 What is meant by killing. 23 Reconciliation. 27 Adultery. 29 Offences. 31 Divorcement. 33 Not to swear. 39 To suffer wrong. 43 To love our enemies. 48 Perfection.

1. And when he saw the multitude he went up into a mountain, and when he was set his disciples came to him.

2. And he opened his mouth and taught them, saying:

3. Blessed are the poor in spirit, for theirs is the kingdom of heaven.

4. Blessed are they that mourn, for they shall be comforted.

5. Blessed are the meek, for they shall inherit the earth.

6. Blessed are they which hunger and thirst for righteousness, for they shall be filled.

7. Blessed are the merciful, for they shall obtain mercy.

8. Blessed are the pure in heart, for they shall see God.

9. Blessed are the peacemakers, for they shall be called the children of God.

10. Blessed are they which suffer persecution for righteousness' sake, for theirs is the kingdom of heaven.

11. Blessed are ye when men revile you and persecute you, and say all manner of evil against you for my sake, falsely.

12. Rejoice and be glad, for great is your reward in heaven; for so persecuted they the prophets which were before you.

13. Ye are the salt of the earth, but if the salt have lost his savor, wherewith shall it be salted? It is thenceforth good for nothing but to be cast out and to be trodden underfoot of men.

14. Ye are the light of the world. A city that is set on an hill cannot be hid.

15. Neither do men light a candle and put it under a bushel, but on a candlestick, and it giveth light unto all that are in the house.

16. Let your light so shine before men that they may see your good works, and glorify your Father which is in heaven.

17. Think not that I am come to destroy the law or the prophets. I am not come to destroy them, but to fulfil them.

18. For truly I say unto you, till heaven and earth perish, one jot or one tittle of the law shall not scape till all things be fulfilled.

19. Whosoever therefore shall break one of these least commandments and teach men so, he shall be called the least in the kingdom of heaven; but whosoever shall observe and teach them, the same shall be called great in the kingdom of heaven.

20. For I say unto you, except your righteousness exceed the righteousness of the scribes and pharisees, ye shall not enter into the kingdom of heaven.

21. Ye have heard that it was said unto them of the old time, "Thou shalt not kill, for whosoever killeth shall be culpable of judgment."

22. But I say unto you, whosoever is angry with his brother unadvisedly shall be culpable of judgment. And whosoever saith unto his brother "Raca" shall be worthy to be punished by the counsel. And whosoever shall say "Fool!" shall be worthy to be punished with hell fire.

23. If then thou bring thy gift to the altar and there rememb'rest that thy brother hath ought against thee,

24. Leave there thine off'ring before the altar and go thy way; first be reconciled to thy brother, and then come and offer thy gift.

25. Agree with thine adversary quickly whiles thou art in the way with him, lest thine adversary deliver thee to the judge, and the judge deliver thee to the sergeant, and thou be cast into prison.

26. Verily I say unto thee, thou shalt not come out thence till thou hast paid the utmost farthing.

27. Ye have heard that it was said to them of old time, "Thou shalt not commit adultery."

28. But I say unto you that whosoever looketh on a woman to lust after her hath committed adultery with her already in his heart.

29. Wherefore if thy right eye cause thee to offend, pluck it out and cast it from thee; for better it is for thee that one of thy members perish then that thy whole body should be cast into hell.

30. Also if thy right hand make thee to offend, cut it off and cast it from thee; for better it is for thee that one of thy members perish then that thy whole body should be cast into hell.

31. It hath been said also, "Whosoever shall put away his wife, let him give her a testimonial of divorcement."

32. But I say unto you, whosoever shall put away his wife (except it be for fornication) causeth her to commit adultery; and whosoever shall marry her that is divorced committeth adultery.

33. Again, ye have heard that it was said to them of old time, "Thou shalt not forswear thyself, but shalt perform thine oaths to the Lord."

34. But I say unto you, swear not at all, neither by heaven, for it is the throne of God;

35. Nor yet by the earth, for it is his footstool; neither by Jerusalem, for it is the city of the great king.

36. Neither shalt thou swear by thine head, because thou canst not make one heer white or black.

37. But let your communication be "Yea, yea"; "Nay, nay." For whatsoever is more then these cometh of evil.

38. Ye have heard that it hath been said, "An eye for an eye, and a tooth for a tooth."

39. But I say unto you, resist not evil, but whosoever shall smite thee on thy right cheek, turn to him the other also.

40. And if any man will sue thee at the law and take away thy coat, let him have thy cloak also.

41. And whosoever will compel thee to go a mile, go with him twain.

42. Give to him that asketh, and from him that would borrow of thee turn not away.

43. Ye have heard that it hath been said, "Thou shalt love thy neighbor and hate thine enemy."

44. But I say unto you, love your enemies, bless them that curse you; do good to them that hate you, and pray for them which hurt you and persecute you,

45. That ye may be the children of your Father that is in heaven; for he maketh his sun to arise on the evil and the good, and sendeth rain on the just and unjust.

46. For if ye love them which love you, what reward shall you have? Do not the publicans even the same?

47. And if ye be friendly to your brethren only, what singular thing do ye? Do not even the publicans likewise?

48. Ye shall therefore be perfit as your Father which is in heaven is perfit.

FROM THE BISHOPS' BIBLE (1572)

Dominus regit me

PSALM XXIII

THE ARGUMENT

David, resembling God to a sheepherd and himself to a sheep, declareth that all commodities, plenty, quietness, and prosperity ensueth them that be fully persuaded of God's providence; for God feedeth, nourisheth, defendeth, and governeth those that put their whole trust in him, after a more ample sort then any sheepherd doth his sheep.

A Psalm of David

1. God is my sheepherd; therefore I can lack nothing. He will cause me to repose myself in pasture full of grass, and he will lead me unto calm waters.

2. He will convert my soul; he will bring me forth into the paths of righteousness for his name sake.

3. Yea, though I walk through the valley of the shadow of death I will fear no evil, for thou art with me; thy rod and thy staff be the things that do comfort me.

4. Thou wilt prepare a table before me in the presence of mine adversaries; thou hast anointed my head with oil, and my cup shall be brimful.

5. Truly, felicity and mercy shall follow me all the days of my life, and I will dwell in the house of God for a long time.

SAINT MATTHEW

THE FIFTH CHAPTER

In this chapter and in the two next following is contained the most excellent and loving sermon of Christ in the mount. Which sermon is the very key that openeth the understanding into the law. In this fifth chapter specially, 3 he preacheth of the eight beatitudes or blessings, 21 of manslaughter, 22 wrath and anger, 27 of adultry, 33 of swearing, 39 of suffering wrong, 44 and of love, even toward a man's enemy.

1. When he saw the multitude, he went up into a mountain; and when he was set, his disciples came to him.

2. And when he had opened his mouth, he taught them, saying:

3. Blessed are the poor in spirit, for theirs is the kingdom of heaven.

4. Blessed are they that mourn, for they shall be comforted.

5. Blessed are the meek, for they shall inherit the earth.

6. Blessed are they which do hunger and thirst after righteousness, for they shall be satisfied.

7. Blessed are the merciful, for they shall obtain mercy.

8. Blessed are the pure in heart, for they shall see God.

9. Blessed are the peacemakers, for they shall be called the children of God.

10. Blessed are they which have been persecuted for righteousness' sake, for theirs is the kingdom of heaven.

11. Blessed are ye when men shall revile you and persecute you and, lying, shall say all manner of evil saying against you for my sake.

12. Rejoice ye and be glad, for great is your reward in heaven. For so persecuted they the prophets which were before you.

13. Ye are the salt of the earth; but if the salt become unsavory, wherein shall it be salted? It is thenceforth good for nothing but to be cast out and to be trodden underfoot of men.

14. Ye are the light of the world. A city that is set on an hill cannot be hid.

15. Neither do men light a candle and put it under a bushel, but on a candlestick, and it geveth light unto all that are in the house.

16. Let your light so shine before men that they may see your good works and glorify your Father which is in heaven.

17. Think not that I am come to destroy the law or the prophets. I am not come to destroy, but to fulfil.

18. For truly I say unto you, till heaven and earth pass, one jot or one tittle of the law shall not scape till all be fulfilled.

19. Whosoever therefore shall break one of these least commandements, and shall teach men so, he shall be called the least in the kingdom of heaven; but whosoever shall do and teach so, the same shall be called great in the kingdom of heaven.

20. For I say unto you, except your righteousness shall exceed the righteousness of the scribes and pharisees ye shall in no case enter into the kingdom of heaven.

21. Ye have heard that it was said to them of old time, "Thou shalt not kill. Whosoever killeth shall be in danger of judgment."

22. But I say unto you that whosoever is angry with his brother unadvisedly shall be in danger of judgment, and whosoever shall say unto his brother "Racha" shall be in danger of a counsel; but whosoever shall say "Thou fool!" shall be in danger of hell fire.

23. Therefore if thou bring thy gift to the altar

and there rememb'rest that thy brother hath ought against thee,

24. Leave there thy gift before the altar and go thy way, first be reconciled to thy brother, and then come and offer thy gift.

25. Agree with thine adversary quickly whiles thou art in the way with him, lest at any time the adversary deliver thee to the judge, and the judge deliver thee to the minister, and then thou be cast into prison.

26. Verily I say unto thee, thou shalt by no means come out thence till thou hast paid the uttermost farthing.

27. Ye have heard that it was said unto them of old time, "Thou shalt not commit adultry."

28. But I say unto you that whosoever looketh on a woman to lust after her hath committed adultry with her already in his heart.

29. If thy right eye offend thee, pluck it out and cast it from thee, for it is profitable for thee that one of thy members should perish, and not that thy whole body should be cast into hell.

30. And if thy right hand offend thee, cut it off and cast it from thee, for it is profitable for thee that one of thy members should perish, and not that all thy body should be cast into hell.

31. It hath been said, "Whosoever will put away his wife, let him geve her a writing of divorcement."

32. But I say unto you that whosoever doth put away his wife, except it be for fornication, causeth her to commit adultry, and whosoever marrieth her that is divorced committeth adultry.

33. Again, ye have heard that it hath been said unto them of old time, "Thou shalt not forswear theeself, but shalt perform unto the Lord thine oaths."

34. But I say unto you, swear not at all, neither by heaven, for it is God's seat,

35. Nor by the earth, for it is his footstool, neither by Hierusalem, for it is the city of the great king.

36. Neither shalt thou swear by thy head, because thou canst not make one hear white or black.

37. But let your communication be "Yea, yea"; "Nay, nay." For whatsoever is more then these cometh of evil.

38. Ye have heard that it hath been said, "An eye for an eye and a tooth for a tooth."

39. But I say unto you that ye resist not evil, but whosoever will geve thee a blow on thy right cheek, turn to him the other also.

40. And if any man will sue thee at the law and take away thy coat, let him have thy cloak also.

41. And whosoever will compel thee to go a mile, go with him twain.

42. Geve to him that asketh thee; and from him that would borrow of thee, turn not thou away.

43. Ye have heard that it hath been said, "Thou shalt love thy neighbor and hate thine enemy."

44. But I say unto you, love your enemies, bless them that curse you, do good to them that hate you, pray for them which hurt you and persecute you;

45. That ye may be the children of your Father which is in heaven, for he maketh his sun to rise on the evil and on the good, and sendeth rain on the just and on the unjust.

46. For if ye love them which love you, what reward have ye? Do not the publicans even the same?

47. And if ye salute your brethren only, what singular thing do ye? Do not also the publicans likewise?

48. Ye shall therefore be perfect even as your Father which is in heaven is perfect.

FROM THE RHEIMS–DOUAI BIBLE
(1582, 1609–10)

PSALM XXII[1]

A form of thanksgeving for all spiritual benefits (described under the metaphor of temporal prosperity) even from a sinner's first conversion to final perseverance and eternal beatitude.

1. The Psalm of David:

2. Our Lord ruleth me, and nothing shall be wanting to me; in place of pasture there he hath placed me.

3. Upon the water of refection he hath brought me up; he hath converted my soul; he hath conducted me upon the paths of justice for his name.

4. For although I shall walk in the middes of the shadow of death I will not fear evils, because thou art with me; thy rod and thy staff they have comforted me.

5. Thou hast prepared in my sight a table against them that trouble me. Thou hast fatted my head with oil, and my chalice inebriating, how goodly is it!

6. And thy mercy shall follow me all the days of my life, and that I may dwell in the house of our Lord in longitude of days.

THE GOSPEL ACCORDING TO SAINT MATTHEW

CHAPTER V

First 3 he promiseth rewards, 13 and he layeth before the apostles their office. 17 Secondly, he protesteth unto us that we must keep the commandments, and that more exactly then the scribes and pharisees, whose justice was counted most perfit; but yet that it was unsufficient he sheweth in the precepts of 21 murder, 27 advoutry, 31 divorce, 33 swearing, 38 revenge, 42 usury, 43 enemies.

[1]This version follows the numbering of the Psalms in the Vulgate.

1 And seeing the multitudes, he went up into a mountain, and when he was set, his disciples came unto him, 2 and opening his mouth he taught them, saying:

3 Blessed are the poor in spirit, for theirs is the kingdom of heaven. 4 Blessed are the meek, for they shall possess the land. 5 Blessed are they that mourn, for they shall be comforted. 6 Blessed are they that hunger and thirst after justice, for they shall have their fill. 7 Blessed are the merciful, for they shall obtain mercy. 8 Blessed are the clean of heart, for they shall see God. 9 Blessed are the peacemakers, for they shall be called the children of God. 10 Blessed are they that suffer persecution for justice, for theirs is the kingdom of heaven. 11 Blessed are ye when they shall revile you and persecute you, and speak all that naught is against you untruly for my sake. 12 Be glad and rejoice, for your reward is very great in heaven. For so they persecuted the prophets that were before you.

13 You are the salt of the earth. 14 But if the salt leese his virtue, wherewith shall it be salted? It is good for nothing any more but to be cast forth and to be trodden of men. 15 You are the light of the world. A city cannot be hid, situated on a mountain. 16 Neither do men light a candle and put it under a bushel, but upon a candlestick, that it may shine to all that are in the house. 17 So let your light shine before men, that they may see your good works and glorify your Father which is in heaven.

18 Do not think that I am come to break the law or the prophets. I am not come to break, but to fulfil. 19 For assuredly I say unto you, till heaven and earth pass, one jot or one tittle shall not pass of the law till all be fulfilled. 20 He therefore that shall break one of these least commandments and shall so teach men shall be called the least in the kingdom of heaven. But he that shall do and teach, he shall be called great in the kingdom of heaven. 21 For I tell you that unless your justice abound more then that of the scribes and pharisees you shall not enter into the kingdom of heaven.

22 You have heard that it was said to them of old, "Thou shalt not kill, and whoso killeth shall be in danger of judgment." 23 But I say to you that whosoever is angry with his brother shall be in danger of judgment. And whosoever shall say to his brother "Raca" shall be in danger of a counsel. And whosoever shall say "Thou fool!" shall be guilty of the hell of fire. 24 If therefore thou offer thy gift at the altar and there thou remember that thy brother hath ought against thee, 25 leave there thy offering before the altar and go first to be reconciled to thy brother; and then coming thou shalt offer thy gift. 26 Be at agreement with thy adversary betimes whiles thou art in the way with him lest perhaps the adversary deliver thee to the judge, and the judge deliver thee to the officer and thou be cast into prison. 27 Amen, I say to thee, thou shalt not go out from thence till thou repay the last farthing.

28 You have heard that it was said to them of old, "Thou shalt not commit advoutry." 29 But I say to you that whosoever shall see a woman to lust after her hath already committed advoutry with her in his heart. 30 And if thy right eye scandalize thee, pluck it out and cast it from thee. For it is expedient for thee that one of thy limbs perish rather then thy whole body be cast into hell. 31 And if thy right hand scandalize thee, cut it off and cast it from thee; for it is expedient for thee that one of thy limbs perish rather then that thy whole body go into hell.

32 It was said also, "Whosoever shall dimiss his wife, let him give her a bill of divorcement." 33 But I say to you, whosoever shall dimiss his wife, excepting the cause of fornication, maketh her to commit advoutry. And he that shall marry her that is dimissed committeth advoutry.

34 Again, you have heard that it was said to them of old, "Thou shalt not commit perjury, but thou shalt perform thy oaths to our Lord." 35 But I say to you not to swear at all, neither by heaven, because it is the throne of God, neither by the earth, because it is the footstool of his feet, neither by Hierusalem, because it is the city of the great king. 36 Neither shalt thou swear by thy head, because thou canst not make one hear white or black. 37 Let your talk be "Yea, yea," "No, no," and that which is over and above these is of evil.

38 You have heard that it was said, "An eye for an eye and a tooth for a tooth." 39 But I say to you not to resist evil, but if one strike thee on thy right cheek, turn to him also the other; 40 and to him that will contend with thee in judgment and take away thy coat, let go thy cloak also unto him; 41 and whosoever will force thee one mile, go with him other twain. 42 He that asketh of thee, give to him; and to him that would borrow of thee, turn not away.

43 You have heard that it was said, "Thou shalt love thy neighbor and hate thine enemy." 44 But I say to you, love your enemies, do good to them that hate you, and pray for them that persecute and abuse you, 45 that you may be the children of your Father which is in heaven, who maketh his sun to rise upon good and bad, and raineth upon just and unjust. 46 For if you love them that love you, what reward shall you have? Do not also the publicans this? 47 And if you salute your brethren only, what do you more? Do not also the heathen this? 48 Be you perfect, therefore, as also your heavenly Father is perfect.

FROM THE KING JAMES VERSION (1611)

PSALM XXIII

David's Confidence in God's Grace
A Psalm of David

1. The Lord is my shepherd; I shall not want.

2. He maketh me to lie down in green pastures; he leadeth me beside the still waters.

3. He restoreth my soul; he leadeth me in the paths of righteousness for his name's sake.

4. Yea, though I walk through the valley of the shadow of death I will fear no evil, for thou art with me; thy rod and thy staff they comfort me.

5. Thou preparest a table before me in the presence of mine enemies; thou anointest my head with oil; my cup runneth over.

6. Surely goodness and mercy shall follow me all the days of my life, and I will dwell in the house of the Lord forever.

SAINT MATTHEW

CHAPTER V

Christ beginneth his sermon in the mount: 3 declaring who are blessed, 13 who are the salt of the earth, 14 the light of the world, the city on an hill, 15 the candle; 17 that he came to fulfil the law; 21 what it is to kill, 27 to commit adultery, 33 to swear; 38 exhorteth to suffer wrong, 44 to love even our enemies, 48 and to labor after perfectness.

1. And seeing the multitudes, he went up into a mountain, and when he was set, his disciples came unto him.

2. And he opened his mouth, and taught them, saying:

3. Blessed are the poor in spirit, for theirs is the kingdom of heaven.

4. Blessed are they that mourn, for they shall be comforted.

5. Blessed are the meek, for they shall inherit the earth.

6. Blessed are they which do hunger and thirst after righteousness, for they shall be filled.

7. Blessed are the merciful, for they shall obtain mercy.

8. Blessed are the pure in heart, for they shall see God.

9. Blessed are the peacemakers, for they shall be called the children of God.

10. Blessed are they which are persecuted for righteousness' sake, for theirs is the kingdom of heaven.

11. Blessed are ye when men shall revile you, and persecute you, and shall say all manner of evil against you falsely for my sake.

12. Rejoice, and be exceeding glad, for great is your reward in heaven. For so persecuted they the prophets which were before you.

13. Ye are the salt of the earth, but if the salt have lost his savor wherewith shall it be salted? It is thenceforth good for nothing but to be cast out and to be trodden underfoot of men.

14. Ye are the light of the world. A city that is set on an hill cannot be hid.

15. Neither do men light a candle and put it under a bushel, but on a candlestick, and it giveth light unto all that are in the house.

16. Let your light so shine before men that they may see your good works and glorify your Father which is in heaven.

17. Think not that I am come to destroy the law or the prophets. I am not come to destroy, but to fulfil.

18. For verily I say unto you, till heaven and earth pass, one jot or one tittle shall in no wise pass from the law till all be fulfilled.

19. Whosoever therefore shall break one of these least commandements, and shall teach men so, he shall be called the least in the kingdom of heaven; but whosoever shall do and teach them, the same shall be called great in the kingdom of heaven.

20. For I say unto you that except your righteousness shall exceed the righteousness of the scribes and pharisees ye shall in no case enter into the kingdom of heaven.

21. Ye have heard that it was said by them of old time, "Thou shalt not kill," and "Whosoever shall kill shall be in danger of the judgment."

22. But I say unto you that whosoever is angry with his brother without a cause shall be in danger of the judgment; and whosoever shall say to his brother "Racha" shall be in danger of the counsel; but whosoever shall say "Thou fool!" shall be in danger of hell fire.

23. Therefore if thou bring thy gift to the altar and there rememb'rest that thy brother hath ought against thee,

24. Leave there thy gift before the altar, and go thy way; first be reconciled to thy brother, and then come and offer thy gift.

25. Agree with thine adversary quickly, whiles thou art in the way with him, lest at any time the adversary deliver thee to the judge, and the judge deliver thee to the officer, and thou be cast into prison.

26. Verily I say unto thee, thou shalt by no means come out thence till thou hast paid the uttermost farthing.

27. Ye have heard that it was said by them of old time, "Thou shalt not commit adultery."

28. But I say unto you that whosoever looketh on a woman to lust after her hath committed adultery with her already in his heart.

29. And if thy right eye offend thee, pluck it out and cast it from thee. For it is profitable for thee that one of thy members should perish, and not that thy whole body should be cast into hell.

30. And if thy right hand offend thee, cut it off and cast it from thee. For it is profitable for thee that one of thy members should perish, and not that thy whole body should be cast into hell.

31. It hath been said, "Whosoever shall put away his wife, let him give her a writing of divorcement."

32. But I say unto you that whosoever shall put away his wife, saving for the cause of fornication, causeth her to commit adultery; and whosoever shall marry her that is divorced committeth adultery.

33. Again, ye have heard that it hath been said by them of old time, "Thou shalt not forswear thyself, but shalt perform unto the Lord thine oaths."

34. But I say unto you, swear not at all, neither by heaven, for it is God's throne;

35. Nor by the earth, for it is his footstool; neither by Hierusalem, for it is the city of the great king.

36. Neither shalt thou swear by thy head, because thou canst not make one hair white or black.

37. But let your communication be "Yea, yea";

"Nay, nay"; for whatsoever is more then these cometh of evil.

38. Ye have heard that it hath been said, "An eye for an eye, and a tooth for a tooth."

39. But I say unto you that ye resist not evil, but whosoever shall smite thee on thy right cheek, turn to him the other also.

40. And if any man will sue thee at the law and take away thy coat, let him have thy cloak also.

41. And whosoever shall compel thee to go a mile, go with him twain.

42. Give to him that asketh thee, and from him that would borrow of thee, turn not thou away.

43. Ye have heard that it hath been said, "Thou shalt love thy neighbor and hate thine enemy."

44. But I say unto you, love your enemies, bless them that curse you, do good to them that hate you, and pray for them which despitefully use you, and persecute you,

45. That ye may be the children of your Father which is in heaven, for he maketh his sun to rise on the evil and on the good, and sendeth rain on the just and on the unjust.

46. For if ye love them which love you, what reward have ye? Do not even the publicans the same?

47. And if ye salute your brethren only, what do you more then others? Do not even the publicans so?

48. Be ye therefore perfect even as your Father which is in heaven is perfect.

SIR THOMAS MORE

CONTROVERSIAL WORKS

When, toward the close of his own career and of Roman Catholic England, More turned to the composition of theological and controversial works in English, it was from both religious and patriotic motives; for, as he and many others who did not die in bed were to learn, politics and religion were reciprocal forces in Tudor England. First the growing peril of Lutheranism and then the widening breach with Rome over Henry VIII's divorce had by the late twenties led More to the painful conviction that both piety (unthinkable apart from orthodoxy) and the health of the body politic were in jeopardy. When his friend Cuthbert Tunstall, Bishop of London, asked More to answer Tyndale's heretical *Parable of the Wicked Mammon* (1528), he consented as a Christian duty, just as he had no doubt consented to assist in the writing of *Assertio septem sacramentorum,* the anti-Lutheran treatise that won for Henry and his successors the papal accolade *Defensor fidei.* Casting his reply to Tyndale in the classically

sanctioned form of the dialogue (the form of his *Utopia* and of his earlier Latin translations of Lucian), he constructed his defense of orthodoxy in four conversations between himself and an emissary from a friend who, exposed to and perplexed by heretical doctrine, wished to have More's views on certain disputed points. The conversations between More and his friend's "Messenger," held in the former's study at Chelsea, turn on those orthodox doctrines and practises (the veneration of saints, the authenticity of miracles, the infallibility of the Roman church, the persecution of heretics, the celibacy of the clergy) that were being fiercely attacked by the Lutheran reformers; in addition, from time to time in the give and take of the discussions More finds occasion to denounce Luther and Tyndale by name and to excoriate Tyndale's translation of the Bible. Everywhere the strength, agility, and learning (if not the liberality) of More's trained lawyer's mind is apparent. Alone of his controversial writings the *Dialogue* required a second edition (1530) in his lifetime. Our text is based upon *A Dialogue concernynge heresyes & matters of religion* in *The workes of Sir Thomas More Knyght . . . wrytten by him in the Englysh tonge, 1557* (STC 18076).

Of More's other controversial works—most of them written within a year of his resigning the chancellorship in 1532—the best known are *The Supplication of Souls* (1529), a defense of the doctrine of purgatory occasioned by Simon Fish's *Supplication for the Beggars; The Confutation of Tyndale's Answer* (2 parts, 1529 and 1546), a counter-statement to Tyndale's *Answer unto Sir Thomas More's Dialogue* (1530); a *Letter* (1533) against one of John Frith's several attacks on the doctrines of purgatory and transubstantiation; and the famous *Apology* (1533). This last poignant and intimate document, written from a sharp awareness of the waves of heresies beating against the true

faith, is more temperate and reasonable than some of the polemical works which do considerable violence to More's reputation as an apostle of sweetness and light. It was occasioned by the anonymous *Treatise Concerning the Division between the Spirituality and Temporality* (1532), whose author (probably Christopher Saint-German), professing to be a good Catholic desirous of composing the differences between clergy and laity, actually castigates priestcraft in a list of bitter accusations. More's answer, addressed ironically to the "Pacifier" who wrote the *Treatise,* is a defense both of professional churchmen and of More's role in championing their prerogatives as priests of the only true church. Thus his searching criticism of the "Book of Division," as he calls the *Treatise,* yields repeatedly to discussions of More's public and private life as a Catholic. Our text is based upon *The apologye of syr Thomas More knyght, 1533* (STC 18078).

An attempt to get to core of differences.

FROM A DIALOGUE CONCERNING HERESIES AND MATTERS OF RELIGION (1557)

BOOK I, CHAPTER 22

"And forbecause we speak of Scripture now, and that the Church in things needily requisite to salvation hath the right understanding of Holy Scripture, wherein I perceive ye be studious of the text alone, without great force of the old fathers' interpretations or any other science (of which ye reckon all seven, save grammar, almost to serve for nought), I have of you so good opinion that I trust all your study shall turn you to good. But surely I have seen to some folk so much harm to grow thereof that I never would advise any man else in the study of Scripture to take that way."

"Why so?" quod he.

"For I have known," quod I, "right good wits that hath set all other learning aside, partly for sloth refusing the labor and pain to be sustained in that learning, partly for pride by which they could not endure that redargution that should sometime fall to their part in dispicions. Which affections their inward secret favor toward themselves covered and cloaked under the pretext of simplicity and good Christian devotion borne to the love of Holy Scripture alone. But in little while after, the damnable spirit of pride that, unware to themself, lurked in their hearts hath begun to put out his horns and shew himself. For then have they longed under the praise of Holy Scripture to set out to shew their own study. Which because they would have seem the more to be set by, they have first fallen to the dispraise and derision of all other disciplines. And because in speaking or preach-

ing of such common things as all Christian men know they could not seem excellent, nor make it appear and seem that in their study they had done any great mast'ry to shew themself, therefore marvelously they set out paradoxes and strange opinions against the common faith of Christ's whole Church. And because they have therein the old holy doctors against them, they fall to the contempt and dispraise of them, either preferring their own fond glosses against the old conning and blessed fathers' interpretations, or else lean to some words of Holy Scripture that seem to say for them against many mo texts that plainly make against them, without receiving or ear-giving to any reason or authority of any man, quick or dead, or of the whole Church of Christ to the contrary. And thus once proudly persuaded a wrong way, they take the bridle in the teeth and run forth like an headstrong horse that all the world cannot pluck them back. But with sowing sedition, setting forth of errors and heresies, and spicing their preaching with rebuking of priesthood and prelacy for the people's pleasure they turn many a man to ruin and themself also. And then the Devil deceiveth them in their blind affections. They take for good zeal to the people their malicious envy and for a great virtue their ardent appetite to preach, wherein they have so great pride for the people's praise that preach, I ween, they would though God would [by] his own mouth command them the contrary."

"Why should ye ween so," quod he, "or whereby can ye be sure that ye do not now misconster their good mind? . . . Only God beholdeth the heart. And therefore, saith our Savior, judge not before the time."

"I judge not," quod I, "but upon open things and well-apparent. For I speak but of those whose erroneous opinions in their preaching and their obstinate pride in the defense of their worldly worship well declareth their minds. And some have I seen which, when they have for their perilous preaching been by their prelates prohibited to preach, have, that notwithstanding, proceeded on still; and for the maintenance of their disobedience have amended the matter with an heresy, boldly and stubbornly defending that sith they had conning to preach they were by God bounden to preach, and that no man nor no law that was made or could be made had any authority to forbid them. . . . For the fruit of strife among the hearers and persecution of the preacher cannot lightly grow among Christian men but by the preaching of some strange newelties, and bringing-up of some newfangle heresies to the infection of our old faith. One wist I that was for his pertinacy in that opinion, that he would and might and was bounden to preach—any prohibition notwithstanding—when he was after divers bold and open defense thereof at last before folk honorable and few reasoned withal, and not only the law shewed him to the contrary of his opinion (which law was made at a General Council) but also by plain authority of Holy Scripture proved that his opinion was erroneous, he so perceived himself satisfied that he meekly knowledged his error and offered to abjure it and to submit himself to penance. But on the morrow, when he came forth in open presence of the people and there saw many that had oft heard him preach, of his secret pride he fell in such an open passion of shame that those should hear him go back with his word, which had before had his sermons in great estimation, that, at the first sight of the people, revoked his revocation and said out aloud that he might well be heard, that his opinion was true, and that he was the day before deceived in that he had confessed it for false. And thus he held his own stubbornly, without reason, till the books were shewed him again and himself read them before all the people, so that he perceived the audience that stood about him to feel and understand his proud folly in the defense of his indefensible error. And thereupon at the last yielded himself again. Such secret pride had our ghostly enemy conveyed into the heart of him, which, I ensure you, seemed in all his other outward manner as meek a simple soul as a man should have seen in a summer's day. . . ."

"Would ye, then," quod he, "condemn that manner of study by which a man hath so great affection to the Scripture alone that he, for the delight thereof, feeleth little savor in anything else, but that we should lese time in philosophy, the mother of heresies, and let Scripture alone?"

"Nay," quod I; "that mind am I not of. There was never thing written in this world that can in any wise be comparable with any part of Holy Scripture. And yet I think other liberal science a gift of God also and not to be cast away, but worthy to wait and as handmaids to give attendance upon divinity. And in this point I think not thus alone. For ye shall find Saint Hierome, Saint Austin, Saint Basil, and many of the old holy doctors open and plain of the same opinion. And of divinity reckon I the best part to be contained in Holy Scripture. And this I say for him that shall have time thereto, and from youth entendeth to the churchward, and to make himself with God's help meet for the office of a preacher. Howbeit if any man either happen to begin so late that he shall peradventure have no time thereto, or else any man of youth to have that fervent appetite unto Scripture that he cannot find in his heart to read anything else—which affection whoso happeth to have given him is very fortunate if he with grace and meekness guide it well—then would I counsel him specially to study for the virtuous framing of his own affections and using great moderation and temperance in the preaching to other men, and in all thing to flee the desire of praise and show of conning, ever mistrusting his own inclinations, and live in dread and fear of the Devil's subtle sleight and inventions. . . .

"For the sure avoiding whereof, my poor advice were in the study thereof to have a special regard to the writings and comments of old holy fathers. And yet or he fall in hand with the one or the other—next grace and help of God to be gotten with abstinence and prayer and cleanness of living—afore all thing were it necessary to come well and surely enstructed in all such points and articles as the Church believeth. Which things once firmly had, and fastly for undoubted truths presupposed, then shall reason and they be two good rules to examine and expown all doubtful texts by, sith the reader shall be sure that no text is so to be understanden as it standeth against them both or against any point of the catholic faith of Christ's Church. And therefore if it seem to stand against any of them, either shall the light of natural reason, with the collation of other texts, help to find out the truth, or else (which is the surest way) he shall perceive the truth in the comments of the good holy doctors of old to whom God hath given the grace of understanding.

"Or finally, if all that he can either find in other men's works or invent by God's aid of his own study cannot suffice to satisfy, but that any text yet seem unto him contrary to any point of the Church's faith and belief, let him then, as Saint Augustine saith, make himself very sure that there is some fawt either in the translator or in the writer (or nowadays in the printer); or finally that for some one let or other he understandeth it not aright. And so let him reverently knowledge his ignorance, lean and cleave to the faith of the Church as to an undoubted truth, leaving that text to be better perceived whan it shall please our Lord with his light to reveal and disclose it. And in this wise shall he take a sure way by which he shall be sure of one of two things, that is, to wit, either to perceive and understand the Scripture right; or else, at the leastwise, never in such wise to take it wrong that ever may turn his soul to peril."

BOOK IV, CHAPTER 1

When we had after dinner a little paused, your friend and I drew ourself aside into the garden. And there, sitting down in an herber, he began to enter furth into the matter, saying that he had well perceived that not in his country only but also in the university where he had been there were that had none evil opinion of Luther, but thought that his books were by the clergy forboden of malice and evil will, to the end that folk should not surely see and perfitly perceive what he saith, or, at the least, what thing he meaneth by his words. . . . They think that the clergy will not have his books read because that in them laymen may read the priests' fauts, which was, they say, the very cause of that condemnation. For else, whether he had written well or evil, yet, they say, his books had been kept in men's hands and read. For there is, they think, therein, though some part were nought, many things yet well said, whereof there was no reason that men should lese the profit for the bad. And also reason, men think it were, that all were heard that can be said touching the truth to be known concerning the matters of our salvation, to the entent that, all heard and perceived, men may for their own surety the better chese and hold the right way.

"Forsooth," quod I, "if it were now doubtful and ambiguous whether the Church of Christ were in the right rule of doctrine or not, then were it very necessary to give them all good audience that could and would anything dispute on either party for it or against it, to the end that, if we were now in a wrong way, we might leave it and walk in some better. But now, on the other side, if it so be—as indeed it is— that Christ's Church hath the true doctrine already . . . what wisdom were it now therein to shew ourself so mistrustful and wavering that, for to search whether our faith were false or true, we should give hearing, not to an angel of heaven, but to a fond frere, to an apostate, to an open incestuous lecher, a plain limb of the Devil, and a manifest messenger of hell? . . .

For my part is it of necessity to tell how nought he is, because that the worse the man is, the more madness were it for wise men to give his false fables harkening against God's undoubted truth, by his Holy Spirit taught unto his Church, and by such multitude of miracles, by so much blood of holy martyrs, by the virtuous living of so many blessed confessors, by the purity and cleanness of so many chaste widows and undefiled virgins, by the wholesome doctrine of so many holy doctors, and, finally, by the whole consent and agreement of all Christian people this fifteen hundred year confirmed. And therefore not any respect unto his railing against the clergy is, as some would have it seem, the cause of his condemnation and suppression of his books. For the good men of the clergy be not so sore grieved with them that touch the faults of the bad, nor the bad themself be not so tender-eared, that for the only talking of their faults they would banish the books that were good in other things beside. For else could not the books of many old holy fathers have endured so long, wherein the vices of them that in the clergy be nought be very vehemently rebuked. But the very cause why his books be not suff'red to be read is because his heresies be so many and so abhominable, and the proves wherewith he pretendeth to make them probable be so far from reason and truth and so far against the right understanding of Holy Scripture, whereof, under color of great zeal and affection, he laboreth to destroy the credence and good use and, finally, so far stretcheth all thing against good manner and virtue, provoking the world to wrong opinions of God and boldness in sin and wretchedness, that there can no good but much harm grow by the reading. For if there were the substance good, and of error or oversight some cockle among the corn which might be sifted out and the remnant stand instead, men would have been content therewith as they be with such other. But now is his not besprent with a few spots, but with more than half venom [it hath] poisoned the whole wine, and that right rotten of itself. And this done of purpose and malice, not without an evil spirit, in such wise walking with his words that the contagion thereof were likely to infect a feeble soul, as the savor of a sickness sore infecteth an whole body. Nor the truth is not to be learned of every man's mouth. For as Christ was not content that the Devil should call him God's son, though it were true, so is he not content that a devil's limb, as Luther is or Tyndale, should teach his flock the truth, for infecting them with their false, devilish heresies besides. For likewise as the Holy Scripture of God, because of the good spirit that made it, is of his own nature apt to purge and amend the reader, though some that read it of their invincible malice turn it to their harm, so do such writings as Luther's is, in the making whereof the Devil is of counsel and giveth therewith a breath of his assistance—though the goodness of some men master the malice thereof, walking harmless with God's help, as the prophet saith, upon the serpent and the cockatrice, and treading upon the lion and the dragon—yet be such works of themself alway right unwholesome to meddle with, meet and apt to corrupt and infect the reader. For the proof whereof we need none other example than this that we be in hand withal, if we consider what good the reading of his books hath done in Saxony. And this find we more than too much proved here among us, that of ten that use to read his books ye shall scantly find twain but that they not only cast off prayer and fasting and all such godly virtues as Holy Scripture commendeth and the Church commandeth and virtuous people have ever had in great price, but also fall in plain contempt and hatred thereof. So that what fruit should grow of the reading ye may soon guess."

BOOK IV, CHAPTER 13

"The fear of these outrages and mischiefs to follow upon such sects and heresies, with the proof that men have had in some countries thereof, have been the cause that princes and people have been constrained to punish heresies by terrible death, whereas else more easy ways had been taken with them. And, therefore, here will I somewhat," said I to your friend, "answer the points which ye moved . . . when ye said that many men thought it an hard and an uncharitable way taken by the clergy to put men convict of heresy sometime to shame, sometime to death, and that Christ so far abhorred all such violence that he would not any of his flock should fight in any wise, neither in the defense of themself or any other, not so much as in the defense of Christ himself (for which he blamed Saint Peter), but that we should all live after him in sufferance and patience, so farforth that folk thought, as ye said, that we should not fight in defense of ourself against the Turks and infidels. These objections be soon answered.

"For neither doth the clergy therein any such thing as is laid and imputed unto them, nor the temporalty neither, albeit with good reason they might; yet had they never, indeed, fallen so sore to force and violence against heretics if the violent cruelty first used by the heretics themself against good Catholic folk [had not] driven good princes thereto for preservation, not of the faith only, but also of the peace among their people. . . . And yet were heresy well worthy to be as sore [punished] as any other fault, sith there is no fault that more offendeth God. Howbeit while they forbare violence there was little violence done to them. And surely though God be

able against all persecution to preserve and encrease his faith among the people, as he did in the beginning, for all the persecution of the paynims and the Jews, yet is it no reason to look that Christian princes should suffer the Catholic Christian people to be oppressed by Turks or by heretics worse than Turks."

"By my soul," quod your friend, "I would all the world were all agreed to take all violence and compulsion away upon all sides, Christian and heathen, and that no man were constrained to believe but as he could be by grace, wisdom, and good works enduced, and then he that would go to God, go on a God's name, and he that will go to the Devil, the Devil go with him."

"Forsooth," quod I, "and if it so were, yet would I little doubt but that the good seed being sown among the people should as well come up and be as strong to save itself as the cockle, and God should alway be stronger than the Devil. . . . Sith we should nothing so much regard as the honor of God and encreasing of the Christian faith and winning of men's souls to heaven, we should seem to dishonor God if we mistrusted that his faith preached among other indifferently without disturbance should not be able to prosper. And believing that it were, we should hinder the profit if we would refuse the condition, where there be many mo to be won to Christ on that side than to be lost from him on this side. But yet as for heretics rising among ourself and springing of ourself be in no wise to be suffered but to be oppressed and overwhelmed in the beginning. For by any covenant with them Christendom can nothing win. For as many as we suffer to fall to them we lese from Christ. And by all them we cannot win to Christ one the mo though we wan them all home again, for they were our own before. And yet, as I said, for all that in the beginning never were they by any temporal punishment of their bodies anything sharply handled till that they began to be violent themself.

"We read that in the time of Saint Austin, the great doctor of the Church, the heretics of Africa called the Donatists fell to force and violence, robbing, beating, tormenting, and killing such as they took of the true Christian flock, as the Lutherans have done in Almain. For avoiding whereof, that holy man, Saint Austin, which long had with great patience borne and suffered their malice, only writing and preaching in the reproof of their errors, and had not only done them no temporal harm but also had letted and resisted other that would have done it, did yet at the last for the peace of good people both suffer and exhort the Count Boniface and other to repress them with force and fear them with bodily punishment.

"Which manner of doing holy Saint Hierom and

other virtuous fathers have in other places allowed. And since that time hath (thereupon necessity perceived by great outrages committed against the peace and quiet of the people in sundry places of Christendom by heretics rising of a small beginning to an high and unruly multitude) many sore punishments been devised for them, and especially by fire, not only in Italy and Almain, but also in Spain, and in effect in every part of Christendom. Among which in England, as a good Catholic realm, it hath been long punished by death in the fire. And specially forasmuch as in the time of that noble prince of most famous memory, King Henry the Fifth, while the Lord Cobham maintained certain heresies, and that, by the means thereof, the number so grew and encreased that, within a while, though himself was fled into Wales, yet they assembled themself together in a field near unto London in such wise and such number that the king with his nobles were fain to put harness on their backs for the repression of them; whereupon they were distressed and many put to execution, and after that the Lord Cobham taken in Wales and burned in London. The king, his nobles, and his people thereupon, considering the great peril and jeopardy that the realm was like to have fallen in by those heresies, made at a Parliament very good and substantial provisions, beside all such as were made before, as well for the withstanding as the repressing and grievous punishment of any such as should be founden faulty thereof and by the clergy left unto the secular hands. For here ye shall understand that it is not the clergy that laboreth to have them punished by death. Well may it be that, as we be all men and not angels, some of them may have sometime either overfervent mind or undiscreet zeal or, percase, an angry and a cruel heart, by which they may offend God in the selfsame deed whereof they should else greatly merit. But surely the order of the spiritual law therein is both good, reasonable, piteous, and charitable, and nothing desiring the death of any man therein. For at the first fault he is abjured, forsweareth all heresies, doth such penance for his fault as the bishop assigneth him, and is, in such wise, graciously received again into the favor and suffrages of Christ's Church. But and if he be taken eftsoons with the same crime again, then is he put out of the Christian flock by excommunication. And because that, being such, his conversation were perilous among Christian men, the Church refuseth him, and thereof the clergy giveth knowledge to the temporalty, not exhorting the prince or any man else either to kill him or punish him, but only in the presence of the temporal officer the spiritualty not delivereth him but leaveth him to the secular hand and forsaketh him as one excommunicate and removed out of the Christian flock. And though the Church be not light and sudden in receiving him again, yet, at the time of his death, upon his request with tokens of repentance, he is absolved and received again."

FROM THE APOLOGY (1533)

CHAPTER XXXVI

But I suppose, in good faith, that this Pacifier hath, of some facility of his own good nature, been easy to believe some such as have told him lies, and hath been thereby persuaded to think that many other folk said and knew the thing that some few told him for very truth. And surely they that are of this new bretherhed be so bold and so shameless in lying that whoso shall hear them speak and knoweth not what sect they be of shall be very sore abused by them.

Myself have good experience of them. For the lies are neither few nor small that many of the blessed brethren have made and daily yet make by me.

Divers of them have said that of such as were in my house while I was chancellor I used to examine them with torments, causing them to be bounden to a tree in my garden and there pituously beaten.

And this tale had some of those good brethren so caused to be blown about that a right worshipful friend of mine did of late, within less than this fortnight, tell unto another near friend of mine that he had of late heard much speaking thereof.

What cannot these brethern say that can be so shameless to say thus? For of very truth, albeit that for a great robbery or an heighnous murder or sacrilege in a church (with carrying away the pyx with the Blessed Sacrament or villanously casting it out) I caused sometime such things to be done by some officers of the Marshalsea, or of some other prisons, with which ordering of them by their well-deserved pain, and without any great hurt that afterward should stick by them, I found out and repressed many such desperate wretches as else had not failed to have gone further abroad and to have done to many good folk a great deal mych more harm; yet though I so did in thieves, murderers, and robbers of churches (and notwithstanding also that heretics be yet mych worse then all they), yet, saving only their sure keeping, I never did else cause any such thing to be done to any of them all in all my life, except only twain. Of which the tone was a child and a servant of mine in mine own house whom his father had, ere ever he came with me, nouseled up in such matters and had set him to attend upon George Jaye or Gee (otherwise called Clerke, which is a priest and is now, for all that, wedded in Antwarp, into whose house there the two nuns were brought which John Byrt, otherwise called Adrian, stale out of their cloister to make them harlots). This George Jaye did teach this child his ungracious heresy against the Blessed Sacrament of the Altar, which heresy this child, afterward being in service with me, began to teach another child in my house which uttered his counsel. And upon that point perceived and known, I caused a servant of mine to stripe him like a child before mine household for amendment of himself and ensample of such other.

Another was one which, after that he had fallen into the frantic heresies, fell soon after into plain, open franzy beside. And albeit that he had therefore been put up in Bedelem and afterward, by beating and correction, gathered his remembrance to him and began to come again to himself, being thereupon set at liberty and walking about abroad, his old fancies began to fall again in his head. And I was fro divers good, holy places advertized that he used, in his wandering about, to come into the church and there make many mad toys and trifles to the trouble of good people in the divine service, and specially would he be most besy in the time of most silence while the priest was at the secrets of the mass about the levation. And if he spied any woman kneeling at a form, if her head hing anything low in her meditations, than would he steal behind her and, if he were not letted, would labor to lift up all her clothes and cast them quite over her head. Whereupon I, being advertized of these pageants, and being sent unto and required by very devout, religious folk to take some other order with him, caused him, as he came wandering by my door, to be taken by the constables and bounden to a tree in the street before the whole town; and there they striped him with rods therefore till he waxed weary and somewhat lenger. And it appeared well that his remembrance was good inough, save that it went about in grazing till it was beaten home. For he could than very well rehearse his fawts himself, and speak and treat very well, and promise to do afterward as well. And verily, God be thanked, I hear none harm of him now.

And of all that ever came in my hand for heresy, as help me God, saving, as I said, the sure keeping of them (and yet not so sure, neither, but that George Constantine could steal away), else had never any of them any stripe or stroke given them, so mych as a fillip on the forehead.

And some have said that whan Constantine was gotten away I was fallen for anger in a wonderful rage. But surely, though I would not have suff'red him go if it would have pleased him to have tarried still in the stocks, yet whan he was neither so feeble for lack of meat but that he was strong inough to break the stocks, nor waxen so lame of his legs with lying but that he was light inough to leap the walls, nor by any mishandling of his head so dulled or dazed in his brain but that he had wit inough (whan he was once out) wisely to walk his way, neither was I than so heavy for the loss but that I had youth inough left me to wear it out, nor so angry with any man of mine that I spake them any evil word for the matter, more then to my porter that he should see the stocks mended and locked fast, that the prisoner stale not in again. And as for Constantine himself, I could him in good faith good thank. For never will I, for my part, be so unreasonable as to be angry with any man that riseth if he can whan he findeth himself that he sitteth not at his ease.

But now tell the brethern many marvelous lies of mych cruel tormenting that heretics had in my house, so farforth that one Segar, a bookseller of Cambridge which was in mine house about four or five days, and never had either bodily harm done him or foul word spoken him while he was in mine house, hath reported since, as I hear say, to diverse that he was bounden to a tree in my garden, and thereto topituously beaten, and yet, beside that, bounden about the head with a cord and wrongen that he fell down dead in a swoon.

And this tale of his beating did Tyndale tell to an old acquaintance of his own and to a good lover of mine, with one piece farther yet: that while the man was in beating I spied a little purse of his hanging at his doublet, wherein the poor man had (as he said) five mark, and that caught I quickly to me, and pulled it from his doublet, and put it in my bosom, and that Segar never saw it after. And therein, I trow, he said true, for no more did I neither, nor before neither, nor, I trow, no more did Segar himself neither, in good faith.

But now, when I can come to goods by such goodly ways, it is no great marvel though I be so sodainly grown to so great substance of riches, as Tyndale told his acquaintance and my friend; to whom he said that he wist well that I was no less worth in money and plate and other movables then twenty thousand marks. And as mych as that have diverse of the good brethern affirmed here nearer home.

And surely this will I confess, that if I have heaped up so mych good together, then have I not gotten the tone-half by right. And yet by all the thieves, murderers, and heretics that ever came in my hands am I not, I thank God, the richer of one grote. And yet have they spent my twain. Howbeit, if either any of them, or of any kind of people else that any cause have had before me or otherwise any meddling with me, find himself so sore grieved with anything that I have taken of his, he had some time to speak thereof. And now, sith no man cometh forth to ask any restitution yet, but hold their peace and slack their time so long, I geve them all plain, peremptory warning now that they dreve it off no lenger. For if they tarry till yesterday, and then come and ask so great sums among them as shall amount to twenty thousand mark, I purpose to purchase such a protection for them that I will leave myself less then the fourth part, even of shrewdness, rather then ever I will pay them.

And now dare I say that if this Pacifier had, by experience, known the truth of that kind of people, he would not have geven so mych credence to their lamentable complainings as, it seemeth me by some of his "some say's," he doth.

Howbeit, what faith my words will have with him in these mine own causes I cannot very surely say, nor yet very greatly care. And yet stand I not in so mych doubt of myself but that I trust well that among many good and honest men, among which sort of folk I trust I may reckon him, mine own word would alone, even in mine own cause, be somewhat better believed then would the oaths of some twain of this new bretherhed in a matter of another man.

CHAPTER XLIX

And thus, good Cristen readers, I make an end of this matter—the book, I mean, of this division—wherein I have nothing touched nor entended but only that I would not the temporalty bare the spiritualty the worse mind or affection for any such suttle, invented ways that lay the fauts of the bad to the whole body (wherein be many good), and under a figure of "some say" say some things false themself; nor that men should causeless, upon such surmised and unproved cruelty, change the good laws byfore made against heretics, whereby, to the displeasure of God and provoking of his indignation, we were likely to have the faith decay, and more harm grow thereon then any man yet can tell.

The whole sum and effect, therefore, of my mind in this matter is that, as touching the spirituality, I bear a tender mind of truth toward (I say) the body, not toward those that are nought therein. And this mind is every man bound to bear, and, I trust, so doth this Pacifier too, and will of himself, I ween, do well inough if he use to the contrary none evil counsel.

As touching heretics, I hate that vice of theirs and not their persons, and very fain would I that the tone were destroyed and the tother saved. And that I have toward no man any other mind then this (how loudly soever these blessed new brethern, the professors and preachers of verity, belie me): if all the favor and pity that I have used among them to their amendment were known, it would, I warrant you, well and plain appear; whereof, if it were requisite, I could bring forth witnesses mo then men would ween.

And sure this one thing will I be bold to say, that I never found any yet but, had he been never so bad nor done never so mych harm before, yet, after that I found him once changed and in good mind to mend, I have been so glad thereof that I have used him fro thenceforth not as an evil man or an abject, nor as a stranger neither, but as a good man and my very friend.

Howbeit, because it were neither right nor honesty that any man should look for more thank then he deserveth, I will that all the world wit it, on the tother side, that whoso be so deeply grounded in malice (to the harm of his own soul and other men's too) and so set upon the sowing of seditious heresies that no good means that men may use unto him can pull that malicious folly out of his poisoned, proud, obstinate heart, I would rather be content that he were gone in time then overlong to tarry to the destruction of other.

Finally, as for the author of the *Book of Division,* because he professeth these heretic opinions for heresies (as they be), I trust in all his other things himself meaneth but well, but partly may be by some pitiful affection led. And some things he saith but upon report and some things affirmeth peradventure as of himself, because of the firm credence that he therein hath geven to some that were not so credible as he took them for. But, in conclusion, whatsoever he be, for anything that I perceive in his book he shall, I trust in conclusion, be founden no such manner of man as folk should, of reason, reckon to bear unto the weal of the prince and the realm any better mind then I. Howbeit, if his wit and his learning find a better way, then not only I (which am but a plain soul and can invent no newelties, but am content to stand to the old order and laws) but also then all they which, for this realm in special and for the whole Church of Christ in general, have made those provisions of old, I neither can nor will forbede any man to follow him.

But this will I be bold to counsel every man to whose part soever any such change shall pertain: first, that they have, as I doubt not but they will, a good Christen mind to the maintenance of Christ's Catholic faith, and that they therein stand by the old, without the contrary change of any point of our old bylief for anything brought up for new, not only by Luther, Tyndale, Frith, or Friar Barons but also if there would (as there never will) an angel (as Saint Paul saith) come out of heaven and preach a contrary new.

Secondly, forasmych as these new fathers of these new brethern, like as they make falsed truth and truth falsed, and faith heresies and heresies faith, so do call also the new old and the old new, not letting to call in their books that faith but new which themself confess in the same books to be more old than th' age of eight hundred year. I will advise you, therefore, good readers, for the true taking of the old faith and for the discerning thereof from all new, to stand to the common, well-known bylief of the common, known Catholic Church of all Christen people—such faith as, by yourself and your fathers and your grandfathers, you have known to be byleved and have, over that, heard by them that the contrary was in the times of their fathers and their grandfathers also taken evermore for heresy. And also ye that read but even in English books shall in many things perceive the same by stories five times as far afore that.

We must also, for the perceiving of the old faith from new, stand to the writings of old holy doctors and saints, by whose expositions we see what points are expressed in the Scripture and what points the Catholic Church of Crist hath, byside the Scripture, received and kept by the Spirit of God and tradition of his apostles.

And specially must we also stand, in this matter of faith, to the determinations of Crist's Catholic Church.

Now if any man will bear other in hand that this point or that point is not determined, or that the holy doctors of the Church write not in such wise but the contrary, than whosoever is not of such learning as to perceive by himself whither of those two say true that hold therein contrary parts, than, except the article be a plain, open, known thing of itself, not doubted of before, let him not be light of credence in the byleving either the tone disputer or the tother, though they would both preach high praises of their own conning, and say that (byside all their mych worldly business) they had spent many years about the study of Scripture, and boast that their books of divinity were worth never so mych money, or that by the Spirit they were inspired and with the celestial dew sodainly sprongen up divines (as lusty, fresh, and green as after any show'r of rain ever sprong any bed of leeks). Let no man, I say, be light in byleving them for all that, but let him, by my poor counsel, pray God inspire himself to byleve and follow the thing that may be His high pleasure; and let him thereupon appoint with himself to live well; and forthwith (to begin well) get himself a good ghostly father and shrive him of his sins and than, concerning the question, ask advice and counsel of those whom himself thinketh, bytween God and his new-cleansed conscience, for learning and virtue most likely, without any partial leaning, indifferently to tell him truth.

And thus far I say for the faith itself, because I hear some men mych speak and boast that they will labor for declarations of heresy, which (as meseemeth) is a thing that little needeth. For I never wist any man in my life put in trouble for any point of heresy but such points as were for heresy well and openly known among the common people. And Saint Paul saith that heresies be manifest and open, so that he thought, as it seemeth, that there needed none other declaration than the common, received faith of the Christen people to the contrary.

But now, as touching any new order concerning heresies, with the change of laws before devised for the repression of them, I have no more to say therein, but advise every good man endeavor himself to keep well the laws already made of old, except he see the cause of the making changed or some other great necessity, and that he see that point by more ordinary means proved than either by "some say" or "they say" or "many say," or else that he perceive well, at the least, that those folk which would labor to change them be better and wiser both than ever were those that made them. And thus finish I this matter concerning heresies, beseeching our Lord and Savior for his bitter passion that, as his holy sacraments thereof took their strength, so by the prayer of all those holy saints that have, both by their holy doctrine and ensample of living, some of them planted the faith and some of them in sundry times well watered the plants, so himself will, of his goodness, specially now vouchsafe, as the warm sun (the very, eternal, only begotten Son of his eternal Father), to spread his beams upon us, and aspire his breath into us, and in our hearts (as Saint Paul saith) geve his faith strength and encrease.

More seemed to claim somethig for himself
which he would not allow others.
kind of paradox.   Wanted heretics punished.

JOHN COLET and HUGH LATIMER

SERMONS

In our secular age we sometimes forget that between Chaucer and Milton a sizable majority of all books published in England were concerned in one way or another with religion. It could hardly have been otherwise in the age of the Reformation when—as Henry VIII's divorce, the recurrent problems of Tudor succession, and the conduct of foreign policy show—every public question was heavy with ecclesiastical and even theological implications. Although the mere quantity, to say nothing of the quality, of theological writing in the sixteenth century is appalling, a few oases stand out amid the sandy wastes: More's generally tedious and ill-tempered works of controversy are still cherished by some merely because More wrote them, and the wiry strength of the Martin Marprelate tracts reveals much about Elizabethan puritanism; but the great Tudor translations of the Bible, the Book of Common Prayer, and Hooker's *Of the Laws of Ecclesiastical Polity* have a timeless beauty. With a few notable exceptions, however, the English have never shown much talent for theological dialectics or systematic theology, and it is consequently sermons and moral treatises that most interestingly exhibit the quality of Tudor religion. Among the hundreds of unread and largely unreadable sermons that survive, those of a few men still stand out. John Fisher, who became Bishop of Rochester and died a martyr's death with More, was a great preaching prelate, and so was Hugh Latimer; Thomas Lever, a protégé of Bishop Ridley, lived to become one of the most influential non-conformists of Elizabeth's reign; and the "silver-tongued" Henry Smith retains some of the magic he had for his contemporaries. To represent, if inadequately, this mass of material we have chosen the work of two men—one a Roman Catholic dean and the other a Protestant martyr—who after the lapse of centuries still convey something of the intensity and the moral tremor of the early Reformation.

John Colet's great Convocation Sermon was delivered on February 6, 1512, when Archbishop Warham convened his clergy to consider ways of extirpating the newly revived Lollard heresy. Assigned to preach the preliminary sermon of the meeting, Colet chose to scourge not the Lollards but the bishops who sat before him. His sermon is the utterance of an intensely conservative man who, had he lived, would no doubt have followed More to the scaffold in defense of the old religion; none the less, it is laced with a moral strength that most of Henry VIII's worldly prelates knew little of. Colet anticipates the real force of the Protestant Reformation—that is, its individualism—in locating the center of the good life within the soul of the individual Christian. Denouncing the clergy's own sins of ignorance, simony, and sloth, he trumpets forth the ancient virtues of humility, honesty, and piety as he calls for the inward reformation of the church itself. Delivered and immediately published in Latin (*Oratio habita ad clerum in convocatione*), Colet's remarks so vexed some of the clergy that the Bishop of London preferred a formal charge of heresy against him. It is pleasant to record that Warham of Canterbury promptly dismissed the accusation. The English translation of the sermon, which was presumably made in Colet's lifetime, was printed by Thomas Berthelet about 1530. *A Right Fruitful Monition*, probably composed some six years before the Convocation Sermon, lucidly but earnestly expounds the uses of piety in daily life. Although it survives only in posthumous editions (1534, 1563, 1577 ff.), it was reprinted more than twenty times within the next two centuries. Our texts are based upon *The sermō of doctor Colete made to the Convocacion*, [?1530] (STC 5550); *A ryght frutefull monycion, cōcernyng the ordre of a good chrysten mannes lyfe . . . Made by the famouse doctour Colete, somtyme deane of Paules*, 1534 (STC 5547).

When Hugh Latimer, Bishop of Worcester, preached the muscular, earthy sermons of his old age at the court of Edward VI, much had changed since Colet reproved the bishops. For one thing, Colet had addressed his learned auditors in Latin, whereas Latimer, though a man of much learning, was a famed preacher in the vernacular; for another, Colet had gravely sought to purify the Roman Catholic clergy through moral therapy, whereas Latimer, a pillar of the Reformation, hammered his lay listeners with colloquialism, anecdote, invective, humor, abrupt change of pace—every weapon that he could marshal against the enervation of their spiritual lives. In their sinewy, colloquial vigor no less than their theme of faith revealed in works, Latimer's sermons are one of the earliest triumphs of English Protestantism. Delivered probably on January 18, 1548, the "Sermon of the Plow" went through three editions within the year. Its author, meanwhile, pursued the rugged reformist zeal that led him, in 1555, to a fiery death with Bishop Ridley (see pp. 176–178). Our text is based upon *A notable Sermō of yᵉ reverende father Maister Hughe Latemer, whiche he preached in yᵉ Shrouds at paules churche in Londō, on the xviii. daye of January. 1548* (STC 15291).

JOHN COLET

FROM THE SERMON OF DOCTOR COLET MADE TO THE CONVOCATION AT PAUL'S (?1530)

Printed — delivered 1512.

Ye are come together today, fathers and right wise men, to enter council, in the which what ye will do and what matters ye will handle yet we understand nat. But we wish that ones, rememb'ring your name and profession, ye would mind the reformation of the church's matter. For hit was never more need, and the state of the church did never desire more your endeavors. For the Spouse of Christ, the church whom ye would should be "without spot or wrinkle," is made foul and evil-favor'd, as saith Esaias, "The faithful city is made an harlot"; and as saith Hieremias, "She hath done lechery with many lovers, whereby she hath conceived many seeds of wickedness and daily bringeth forth very foul fruit."

Wherefore I came hither today, fathers, to warn you that in this your council with all your mind ye think upon the reformation of the church. But forsooth I came nat willingly, for I knew mine unworthiness. I saw, beside, how hard it was to please the precise judgment of so many men. For I judged it utterly unworthy and unmeet, yea, and almost too malapert, that I, a servant, should counsel my lords; that I, a son, should teach you, my fathers. Truly, it had been meeter for some one of the fathers; that is to say, you prelates might have done it with more grave auctority and greater wisdom. But the commandement was to be obeyed of the Most Reverent Father and Lord the Archbishop [Warham of Canterbury], president of this council, which laid upon me this burden, truly too heavy for me. We read that the prophet Samuel said, "Obedience is better than sacrifice." Wherefore, fathers and right worthy men, I pray you and beseech you that this day ye would sustain my weakness with your goodness and patience; farthermore, to help me at the beginning with your good prayers. . . .

To exhort you, reverent fathers, to the endeavor of reformation of the church's estate (bicause that nothing hath so disfigured the face of the church as hath the fashion of secular and worldly living in clerks and priests) I know nat where more conveniently to take beginning of my tale than of the Apostle Paul, in whose temple ye are gethered together. For he, writing unto the Romans, and under their name unto you, saith, "Be you nat conformed to this world, but be you reformed in the newness of your understanding, that ye may prove what is the good will of God, well-pleasing and perfect."

This did the apostle write to all Christen men, but most chiefly unto priests and bishops. Priests and bishops are the light of the world. For unto them said our Savior, "You are the light of the world." And he said also, "If the light that is in thee be darkness, how dark shall the darkness be?" That is to say, if priests and bishops, that should be as lights, run in the dark way of the world, how dark than shall the secular people be? Wherefore Saint Paul said chiefly unto priests and bishops, "Be you nat conformable to this world, but be ye reformed."

In the which words the apostle doth two things. First, he doth forbid that we be nat conformable to the world and be made carnal. Farthermore, he doth command that we be reformed in the spirit of God, whereby we are spiritual.

I entending to follow this order, I will speak first of conformation, than after of reformation. . . .

And first for to speak of pride of life: how much greediness and appetite of honor and dignity is nowadays in men of the church! How run they, yea, almost out of breath, from one benefice to another, from the less to the more, from the lower to the higher! Who seeth nat this? Who, seeing this, sorroweth nat? Moreover, these that are in the same dignities, the most part of them doth go with so stately a countenance and with so high looks that they seem nat to be put in the humble bishopric of Christ, but rather in the high lordship and power of the world, nat knowing nor advertizing what Christ, the maister of all meekness, said unto his disciples, whom he called to be bishops and priests. "The princes of people," saith he, "have lordship of them, and those that be in auctority have power; but do ye nat so; but he that is greater among you, let him be minister; he that is highest in dignity, be he the servant of all men. The Son of Man came nat to be minist'red unto, but to minister." By which words our Savior doth plainly teach that the mast'ry in the church is none other thing than a ministration, and the high dignity in a man of the church to be none other thing than a meek service.

The second secular evil is carnal concupiscence. Hath nat this vice so grown and waxen in the church as a flood of their lust, so that there is nothing looked for more diligently in this most besy time of the most part of priests than that that doth delight and please the senses? They give themself to feasts and banketing;

151

they spend themself in vain babbling; they give themself to sports and plays; they apply themself to hunting and hawking; they drown themself in the delights of this world. Procurers and finders of lusts they set by. Against the which kind of men Judas the apostle crieth out in his pistle, saying: "Wo unto them which have gone the way of Cain. They are foul and beastly, feasting in their meats, without fear feeding themself; floods of the wild sea, foaming, foaming out their confusions; unto whom the storm of darkness is reserved for everlasting."

Covetousness is the third secular evil, the which Saint John the apostle calleth concupiscence of the eyes. Saint Paul calleth hit idolatry. This abominable pestilence hath so ent'red in the mind almost of all priests, and so hath blinded the eyes of the mind, that we are blind to all things but only unto those which seem to bring unto us some gains. For what other thing seek we nowadays in the church than fat benefices and high promotions? Yea, and in the same promotions, of what other thing do we pass upon than of our tithes and rents, that we care nat how many, how chargeful, how great benefices we take so that they be of great valure? O covetousness! Saint Paul justly called thee the root of all evil. Of thee cometh this heaping of benefices upon benefices. Of thee, so great pensions assigned of many benefices resigned. Of thee, all the suing for tithes, for off'ring, for mortuaries, for delapidations—by the right and title of the church! For the which thing we strive no less than for our own life. O covetousness! Of thee cometh these chargeful visitations of bishops. Of thee cometh the corruptness of courts, and these daily new inventions wherewith the sely people are so sore vexed. Of thee cometh the besyty and wantonness of officials. O covetousness, mother of all iniquity, of thee cometh this fervent study of ordinaries to dilate their jurisdictions. Of thee cometh this wood and raging contention in ordinaries; of thee, insinuation of testaments; of thee cometh the undue sequestration of fruits; of thee cometh the superstitious observing of all those laws that sound to any lucre, setting aside and dispising those that concern the amendment of manners. What should I rehearse the rest? To be short, and to conclude at one word: all corruptness, all the decay of the church, all the offenses of the world come of the covetousness of priests; according to that of Saint Paul, that here I repeat again and beat into your ears, "Covetousness is the root of all evil."

The fourth secular evil that spotteth and maketh ill-favored the face of the church is the continual secular occupation wherein priests and bishops nowadays doth besy themself, the servants rather of men than of God, the warriors rather of this world than of Christ. . . . Without doubt, of this secularity, and that clerks and priests, leaving all spiritualness, do turmoil themself with earthly occupations, many evils do follow.

First, the dignity of priesthood is dishonored, the which is greater than other the kings' or emperors'; it is egall with the dignity of angels. But the brightness of this great dignity is sore shadowed whan priests are occupied in earthly things, whose conversation ought to be in heaven.

Secondarily, priesthood is dispised whan there is no difference betwixt such priests and lay people, but according to the prophecy of Ozee, "As the people be, so are the priests."

Thirdly, the beautiful order and holy dignity in the church is confused whan the highest in the church do meddle with vile and earthly things, and in their stead vile and abject persons do exercise high and heavenly things.

Fourthly, the lay people have great occasion of evils, and cause to fall, whan those men whose duty is to draw men from the affection of this world by their continual conversation in this world teach men to love this world, and of the love of the world cast them down heedling into hell. . . .

These be the four evils that I have spoken of, O fathers, O priests, by the which we are conformable to this world, by the which the face of the church is made evil-favored, by the which the state of it is distroyed truly much more than it was in the beginning by the persecution of tyrants or afterward by the invasion that followed of heretics. For in the persecution of tyrants the church, being vexed, was made stronger and brighter. In the invasion of heretics the church, being shaken, was made wiser and more cunning in Holy Writ. But sens this secularity was brought in, after that the secular manner of living crept in in the men of the church, the root of all spiritual life—that is to say, charity—was extinct. The which taken away, there can nother wise nor strong church be in God. . . .

Wherefore, you fathers, you priests, and all you of the clergy, at the last look up and awake from this your sleep in this forgetful world; and at the last, being well awaked, hear Paul crying unto you, "Be you nat conformable unto this world."

And this for the first part. Now let us come to the second.

THE SECOND PART, OF REFORMATION

"But be you reformed in the newness of your understanding."

The second thing that Saint Paul commandeth is that we be reformed into a new understanding, that we smell those things that be of God. Be we reformed unto those things that are contrary to those I spake of even now, that is to say, to meekness, to soberness, to charity, to spiritual occupation—that, as the said Paul writeth unto Titus, "Renying all wickedness and worldly desires, we live in this world soberly, truly, and virtuously."

This reformation and restoring of the church's estate must needs begin of you, our fathers, and so follow in us your priests and in all the clergy. You are our heeds, you are an example of living unto us. Unto you we look as unto marks of our direction. In you and in your life we desire to read, as in lively books, how and after what fashion we may live. Wherefore, if you will ponder and look upon our motes, first take away the blocks out of your eyes. Hit is an old proverb, "Phisition, heal thyself." You spiritual phisition, first taste you this medicine of purgation of manners, and than after offer us the same to taste.

The way whereby the church may be reformed into better fashion is nat for to make new laws. For there be laws many inow and out of number, as Salomon saith: "Nothing is new under the sun." For the evils that are now in the church were before in time past, and there is no faut but that fathers have provided very good remedies for hit. There are no trespasses but that there be laws against them in the body of the Canon Law. Therefore, hit is no need that new laws and constitutions be made, but that those that are made already be kept. Wherefore in this your assemble let those laws that are made be called before you and rehearsed—those laws, I say, that restrain vice and those that furder virtue.

First, let those laws be rehearsed that do warn you fathers that ye put nat oversoon your hands on every man, or admit unto holy orders. For there is the well of evils, that, the broad gate of holy orders opened, every man that offereth himself is all-where admitted without pulling back. Thereof springeth and cometh out the people that are in the church both of unlearned and evil priests. Hit is nat inough for a priest, after my judgment, to construe a collette, to put forth a question, or to answer to a sopheme; but much more a good, a pure, and a holy life, approved manners, meetly learning of Holy Scripture, some knowledge of the sacraments; chiefly and above all thing, the fear of God and love of the heavenly life.

Let the laws be rehearsed that command that benefices of the church be given to those that are worthy, and that promotions be made in the church by the right balance of virtue, nat by carnal affection, nat by the acception of persons; whereby hit happeneth nowadays that boys for old men, fools for wise men, evil for good, do reign and rule.

Let the laws be rehearsed that warreth against the spot of simony. The which corruption, the which infection, the which cruel and odible pestilence so creepeth now abroad as the canker evil in the minds of priests that many of them are nat afeard nowadays both by prayer and service, rewards and promesses, to get them great dignities.

Let the laws be rehearsed that command personal residence of curates in their churches. For of this many evils grow, bycause all things nowadays are done by vicaries and parish priests, yea, and those foolish also and unmeet, and oftentimes wicked, that seek none other thing in the people than foul lucre, whereof cometh occasion of evil heresies and ill Christendom in the people.

Let be rehearsed the laws and holy rules, given of fathers, of the life and honesty of clerks: that forbid that a clerk be no marchant, that he be no usurer, that he be no hunter, that he be no common player, that he bear no weapon; the laws that forbid clerks to haunt taverns, that forbid them to have suspect familiarity with women; the laws that command soberness and a measurableness in apparel and temperance in adorning of the body....

Above all things let the laws be rehearsed that pertain and concern you, my reverent fathers and lords-bishops, laws of your just and canonical election in the chapters of your churches, with the calling of the Holy Ghost. For bycause that is nat done nowadays, and bycause prelates are chosen oftentimes more by favor of men than by the grace of God, therefore truly have we nat a few times bishops full little spiritual men, rather worldly than heavenly, savoring more the spirit of this world than the spirit of Christ....

Let the laws be rehearsed of the good bestowing of the patrimony of Christ, the laws that command that the goods of the church be spent nat in costly building, nat in sumptuous apparel and pomps, nat in feasting and banketing, nat in excess and wantonness, nat in enriching of kinsfolk, nat in keeping of dogs, but in things profitable and necessary to the church. ...

At the last let be renewed those laws and constitutions of fathers of the celebration of councils, that command provincial councils to be oftener used for the reformation of the church. For there never happ'neth nothing more hurtful to the church of Christ than the lack both of council general and provincial....

Forsooth, if you keep the laws, and if you reform first your life to the rules of the Canon Laws, than shall ye give us light, in the which we may see what is to be done of our part—that is to say, the light of your good example. And we, seeing our fathers so keeping the laws, will gladly follow the steps of our fathers.

The clergy's and spiritual's part ones reformed in the church, than may we with a just order proceed to the reformation of the lay's part, the which truly will be very easy to do if we first be reformed. For the body followeth the soul, and such rulers as are in the city, like dwellers be in it. Wherefore, if priests that have the charge of souls be good, straight the people will be good. Our goodness shall teach them more clearly to be good than all other teachings and preachings. Our goodness shall compel them into the right way truly more effectuously than all your suspendings and cursings. . . .

These are they, reverent fathers and right famous men, that I thought to be said for the reformation of the church's estate. I trust ye will take them of your gentleness to the best. And if paraventure it be thought that I have pass'd my bounds in this sermon, or have said anything out of temper, forgive hit me; and ye shall forgive a man speaking of very zeal, a man sorrowing the decay of the church. And consider the thing hitself, nat regarding any foolishness. Consider the miserable fourm and state of the church and endeavor yourselfs with all your minds to reform it. Suffer nat, fathers, this your so great a gathering to depart in vain. Suffer nat this your congregation to slip for naught. Truly, ye are gethered oftentimes together, but, by your favor to speak the truth, yet I see nat what fruit cometh of your assembling, namely to the church.

Go ye now in the Spirit that ye have called on that, by the help of hit, ye may in this your council find out, decern, and ordain those things that may be profitable to the church, praise unto you, and honor unto God. Unto whom be all honor and glory forever more. Amen.

FROM A RIGHT FRUITFUL MONITION CONCERNING THE ORDER OF A GOOD CHRISTIAN MAN'S LIFE (1534)

Remember first of all, virtuous reader, that it is high wisdom and great perfection thyself to know and than thyself to dispise, as to know thou hast nothing that is good of thyself but of God. For the gifts of nature, and all other temporal gifts of this world which been lawfully and truly obtained, well-considered, been comen to thee by the infinite goodness and grace of God, and not of thyself. And most in especial it is necessary for thee to know how that God of his great grace hath made thee his image, having regard to thy memory, understanding, and free will; and to know how God is thy maker and thou his wretched creature; and to know how thou art redeemed of God by the passion of Christ Jesu; and to know how God is thy helper, thy refuge, and thy deliverer of all evil; and to consider and to know the goodly order which God of his infinite wisdom hath ordained thee to be ord'red by, as to have these temporal goods for the necessity of the body, the body and sensual appetites to be ord'red by thy soul, thy soul to be ord'red by reason and grace, by reason and grace to know thy duty to God and to thy neighbor. . . .

First and principally, honor God as thy maker, love him as thy redeemer, fear him as thy judge.

Secondarily, thy neighbor which is thy superior, obey. Have concord and peace with them which been even with thee in degree, and have mercy and pity on thine inferiors.

Thirdly, provide thee to have a clean heart and a good custody of thy tongue. Pray and take labor by grace to have wisdom and cunning to do thy duty to God and to thy neighbor. And in all thy words and deeds have ever in mind that God and his angels heareth and seeth everything, and that nothing is so privily done but it shall be made open. And in especial have in mind that thou shalt die shortly, and how Christ died for thee, the subtility and falseness of this temporal world, the joys of heaven, and the pains of hell. And every morning, among other thy meditations and prayers, pray unto thy Lord God that, the day following, thou (according to the degree the which of his infinite goodness and mercy hath called thee unto) mayst use this temporal, wretched world in thy thoughts, words, and deeds that, by them and the merit of Christ's passion, thou mayst eschew the pains of hell and come to the joy everlasting. . . .

If thou be religious, remember that the due execution of true religion is not in wearing of the habit, but with a clean mind in very deed to execute the rules and ordinances of religion. For so it is that to wear the habit and not to execute the rule and order of religion is rather to be deemed ypocrisy or apostasy than otherwise.

If thou be lay and unmarried, keep thee clean unto the time thou be married. And remember the sore and terrible punishment of Noe's flood, and of the terrible fire and brimstone and sore punishment of Sodom and Gomor, done to man for misusing of the flesh. And in especial call to remembrance the mervailous and horrible punishment of the abhominable great pox daily appearing to our sights, growing in and upon man's flesh, the which sore punishment, everything well-rememb'red, cannot be thought but principally for the inordinate misuse of the flesh.

And if thou entend to marry, or being married and hast a good wife, thank our Lord therefore, for she is of his sending. And remember that three things in especial been pleasant to the spirit of God: that is to say, concord between bretheren, love and charity between neighbors, and a man and his wife well agreeing. And if thou have an evil wife, take patience and thank God, for all is for the best, well-taken. Howbeit, thou art bounden to do and pray for her amendement, lest she go to the Devil from whom she came. And have in remembrance that the intent of marriage is not in the beastly appetite or pleasure ₁₀ in the thing, but the intent thereof is to eschew the sin of the flesh or else to have children. . . .

Keep a mannerly mean. Be not too strait. Forgive not too soon. Keep a convenient measure in all thy works.

Go not to meat as a beast, but, as a reasonable man, say thy grace. And than remember that mo been sick and die by superfluities of meats than otherwise. Wherefore eat with measure to live in health. At thy meal have none other but honest communication, and ₂₀ such as is according to thy conning.

Backbite no man. Be merry in honesty, for sorrow and care hath killed many, and no profit therein. In no wise swear without compulsion of the law. For whereas is great swearing, from thence is never the plage of God. . . .

Remember as a man loveth, so he is, for the lover is in the thing loved more properly than in himself. Wherefore, if a man love earthly things he may be called an earthly man. And if he love principally ₃₀

heavenly things or God, he may be called an heavenly or a godly man. And therefore love God and heavenly things, for undoubted that is best and most assured love. For they be, and ever shall, permanent, and all earthly things been soon vanished and ended, and so the love of theim is in vain.

Also it is wisdom to fear God, for as he sayeth himself, "Fear not him that may kill the body and cannot hurt the soul, but fear Him that can kill the body and also the soul and commit them to everlasting pain." Wherefore, every evening, ere thou go to bed, call to remembrance, as much as thou canst, thy thoughts, words, and deeds said and done that day; and if any have been to thine own profit and to the pleasure of God, heartily thank him, for by his grace it was done. And if ony have been contrary to his pleasure, ask heartily mercy and reconcile thyself shortly by repentance to eschew the everlasting and terrible pains of hell. For, as Saint Austin saith, there is not a greater madness than for a little temporal delectation, which is soon done, to lese the eternal joy and to be bound to everlasting pain. From the which the Almighty Father of heaven, by his infinite power and mercy, and [by the] bitter passion and infinite wisdom of Jesu Christ, and by the infinite goodness and charity of the Holy Ghost, keep us. Amen.

Deo gratias.

Use well temporal things.

Desire eternal things.

HUGH LATIMER

FROM A NOTABLE SERMON OF THE REVEREND FATHER, MAISTER HUGH LATIMER (1548) [SERMON OF THE PLOW]

Quaecumque scripta sunt ad nostram doctrinam scripta sunt.

"All things which are written, are written for our erudition and knowledge. All things that are written in God's book, in the Bible book, in the book of the Holy Scripture, are written to be our doctrine."

I told you in my first sermon, honorable audience, that I purposed to declare unto you two things: the one, what seed should be sown in God's field, in ₁₀ God's plowland, and the other, who should be the sowers. That is to say, what doctrine is to be taught in Christ's church and congregation, and what men should be the teachers and preachers of it. The first part I have told you in the three sermons past, in which I have assayed to set furth my plow, to prove what I could do. And now I shall tell you who be the

plowers: for God's word is a seed to be sown in God's field, that is, the faithful congregation, and the preacher is the sower. And it is in the Gospel, *Exivit qui seminat seminare semen suum:* "He that soweth, the husbandman, the plowman, went furth to sow his seed." So that a preacher is resembled to a plowman, as it is in another place, *Nemo admota aratro manu, et a tergo respiciens, aptus est regno Dei:* "No man that putteth his hand to the plow, and looketh back, is apt for the kingdom of God." That is to say, let no preacher be negligent in doing his office. Albeit this is one of the places that hath been racked, as I told you of racking Scriptures. And I have been one of them myself that hath racked it (I cry God mercy for it); and have been one of them that have believed and have expounded it against religious persons that would forsake their order which they had professed, and would go out of their cloister: whereas indeed it toucheth not monkery, nor maketh any thing at all for any such matter; but it is directly spoken of diligent preaching of the word of God.

For preaching of the Gospel is one of God's plowworks, and the preacher is one of God's plowmen. Ye may not be offended with my similitude, in that I compare preaching to the labor and work of plowing, and the preacher to a plowman: ye may not be offended with this my similitude; for I have been scland'red of some persons for such things. It hath been said of me, "O, Latimer! nay, as for him, I will never believe him while I live, nor never trust him; for he likened our Blessed Lady to a saffron-bag," where in deed I never used that similitude. But it was, as I have said unto you before now, according to that which Peter saw before in the spirit of prophecy, and said that there should come after men *per quos via veritatis maledictis afficeretur;* there should come fellows "by whom the way of truth should be ill spoken of, and scland'red." But in case I had used this similitude, it had not been to be reproved, but might have been without reproach. For I might have said thus: as the saffron-bag that hath been full of saffron, or hath had saffron in it, doth ever after savor and smell of the sweet saffron that it contained; so our Blessed Lady, which conceived and bare Christ in her womb, did ever after resemble the manners and virtues of that precious babe which she bare. And what had our Blessed Lady been the worse for this, or what dishonor was this to our Blessed Lady? But as preachers must be ware and circumspect, that they geve not any just occasion to be sclandered and ill spoken of by the hearers, so must not the auditors be offended without cause. For heaven is in the Gospel likened to a mustard-seed; it is compared also to a piece of leaven; as Christ saith that at the last day he will come like a thief. And what dishonor is this to God, or what derogation is this to heaven? Ye may not then, I say, be offended with my similitude, forbecause I liken preaching to a plowman's labor, and a prelate to a plowman. But now you will ask me whom I call a prelate. A prelate is that man, whatsoever he be, that hath a flock to be taught of him; whosoever hath any spiritual charge in the faithful congregation, and whosoever he be that hath cure of soul.

And well may the preacher and the plowman be likened together. First, for their labor of all seasons of the year; for there is no time of the year in which the plowman hath not some special work to do. As in my country in Leicestershire, the plowman hath a time to set furth, and to assay his plow, and other times for other necessary works to be done. And then they also may be likened together for the diversity of works and variety of offices that they have to do. For as the plowman first setteth furth his plow, and then tilleth his land, and breaketh it in furrows, and sometime ridgeth it up again, and at another time harroweth it and clotteth it, and sometime dungeth it and hedgeth it, diggeth it and weedeth it, purgeth and maketh it clean: so the prelate, the preacher, hath many divers offices to do. He hath first a busy work to bring his parishioners to a right faith, as Paul calleth it, and not to a swarving faith; but to a faith that enbraceth Christ, and trusteth to his merits; a lively faith, a justifying faith, a faith that maketh a man righteous, without respect of works, as ye have it very well declared and set furth in the homily. He hath then a busy work, I say, to bring his flock to a right faith, and then to confirm them in the same faith: now casting them down with the law, and with threatenings of God for sin; now ridging them up again with the Gospel, and with the promises of God's favor; now weeding them, by telling them their faults, and making them forsake sin; now clotting them, by breaking their stony hearts, and by making them supple-hearted, and making them to have hearts of flesh, that is, soft hearts, and apt for doctrine to enter in; now teaching to know God rightly, and to know their duty to God and to their neighbors; now exhorting them, when they know their duty, that they do it, and be diligent in it, so that they have a continual work to do. Great is their business, and therefore great should be their hire. They have great labors, and therefore they ought to have good livings, that they may commodiously feed their flock; for the preaching of the word of God unto the people is called meat. Scripture calleth it meat; not strawberries, that come but once a year, and tarry not long, but are soon gone. But it is meat; it is no dainties. The people must have meat that must be familiar and continual, and daily geven unto them to feed upon. Many make a strawberry of it, minist'ring it but once a year; but such do not the office of good prelates. For Christ saith, *Quis putas est servus prudens et fidelis? Qui dat cibum in tempore.* "Who, think you, is a wise and a faithful servant? He that geveth meat in due time." So that he must at all times convenient preach diligently: therefore saith He, "Who, trow you, is a faithful servant?" He speaketh it as though it were a rare thing to find such a one, and as though He should say, there be but a few of theim to find in the world. And how few of theim there be throughout this realm that geve meat to their flock as they should do, the Visitors can best tell. Too few, too few, the more is the pity, and never so few as now.

By this, then, it appeareth that a prelate, or any that hath cure of soul, must diligently and substantially work and labor. Therefore saith Paul to Timothy, *Qui episcopatum desiderat, hic bonum opus desiderat:* "He that desireth to have the office of a bishop, or a prelate, that man desireth a good work." Then if it be good work, it is work; ye can make but a work of it. It is God's work, God's plow, and that plow God would have still going. Such, then, as loiter and live idly are not good prelates or ministers. And of such as do not preach and teach, nor do not their duties, God saith by his prophet Hieremy, *Maledictus qui facit opus Dei fraudulenter:* ["Cursed be the man that doth the work of God fraudulently,"] "guilefully or deceitfully." Some books have it *negligenter,* "negligently or slackly." How many such prelates, how many such bishops, Lord, for thy mercy, are there now in England! And what shall we in this case do? Shall we company with them? O Lord, for thy mercy, shall we not company with them? O Lord, whither shall we flee from them? But "cursed be he that doth the work of God negligently or guilefully," a sore word for them that are negligent in discharging their office, or have done it fraudulently; for that is the thing that maketh the people ill.

But true it must be that Christ saith, *Multi sunt vocati, pauci vero electi:* "Many are called, but few are chosen." Here have I an occasion by the way somewhat to say unto you; yea, for the place that I alledged unto you before out of Hieremy, the forty-eighth chapter. And it was spoken of a spiritual work of God, a work that was commanded to be done; and it was of shedding blood, and of destroying the cities of Moab. For, saith he, "Cursed be he that keepeth back his sword from shedding of blood." As Saul, when he kept back the sword from shedding of blood at what time he was sent against Amalech, was refused of God for being disobedient to God's commandements, in that he spared Agag the king. So that that place of the prophet was spoken of them that went to the distruction of the cities of Moab, among the which there was one called Nebo, which was much reproved for idolatry, superstition, pride, avarice, cruelty, tyranny, and for hardness of heart; and for these sins was plagued of God and destroyed.

Now what shall we say of these rich citizens of London? What shall I say of them? Shall I call them proud men of London, malicious men of London, merciless men of London? No, no! I may not say so; they will be offended with me than. Yet must I speak. For is there not reigning in London as much pride, as much covetousness, as much cruelty, as much oppression, as much superstition, as was in Nebo? Yes, I think, and much more too. Therefore I say, repent, O London; repent, repent! Thou hearest thy faults told thee. Amend them! Amend them! I think if Nebo had had the preaching that

thou hast, they would have converted. And, you rulers and officers, be wise and circumspect, look to your charge, and see you do your duties; and rather be glad to amend your ill living then to be angry when you are warned or told of your fault. What ado was there made in London at a certain man because he said (and indeed at that time on a just cause), "Burgesses!" quod he, "nay, butterflies." Lord, what ado there was for that word! And yet would God they were no worse then butterflies! Butterflies do but their nature: the butterfly is not covetous, is not greedy, of other men's goods, is not full of envy and hatred, is not malicious, is not cruel, is not merciless. The butterfly glorieth not in her own deeds, nor preferreth the traditions of men before God's word; it committeth not idolatry, nor worshipeth false gods. But London cannot abide to be rebuked; such is the nature of man. If they be pricked, they will kick; if they be rubbed on the gall, they will wince; but yet they will not amend their faults, they will not be ill spoken of. But how shall I speak well of them? If you could be content to receive and follow the word of God, and favor good preachers, if you could bear to be told of your faults, if you could amend when you hear of them, if you would be glad to reform that is amiss; if I might see any such inclination in you, that leave to be merciless and begin to be charitable, I would then hope well of you, I would then speak well of you. But London was never so ill as it is now. In times past men were full of pity and compassion, but now there is no pity; for in London their brother shall die in the streets for cold; he shall lie sick at the door between stock and stock—I cannot tell what to call it—and perish there for hunger. Was there any more unmercifulness in Nebo? I think not. In times past, when any rich man died in London, they were wont to help the poor scholars of the universities with exhibition. When any man died, they would bequeath great sums of money toward the relief of the poor. When I was a scholer in Cambridge myself, I hard very good report of London, and knew many that had relief of the rich men of London; but now I can hear no such good report, and yet I enquire of it, and harken for it; but now charity is waxed cold: none helpeth the scholer, nor yet the poor. And in those days, what did they whan they helped the scholers? Marry, they maintained and gave theim livings that were very papists and professed the pope's doctrine; and now that the knowledge of God's word is brought to light, and many earnestly study and labor to set it forth, now almost no man helpeth to maintain them.

O London, London! Repent, repent! For I think God is more displeased with London then ever he was with the city of Nebo. Repent, therefore, repent,

London, and remember that the same God liveth now that punished Nebo, even the same God, and none other; and he will punish sin as well now as he did then; and he will punish the iniquity of London, as well as he did them of Nebo. Amend, therefore. And ye that be prelates, look well to your office; for right prelating is busy laboring, and not lording. Therefore, preach and teach, and let your plow be doing. Ye lords, I say, that live like loiterers, look well to your office; the plow is your office and charge. If you live idle and loiter, you do not your duty; you follow not your vocation. Let your plow, therefore, be going, and not cease, that the ground may bring forth fruit.

But now methinketh I hear one say unto me: "Wot you what you say? It is a work? It is a labor? How, then, hath it happened that we have had so many hundred years so many unpreaching prelates, lording loiterers, and idle ministers?" Ye would have me here to make answer, and to shew the cause thereof. Nay, this land is not for me to plow; it is too stony, too thorny, too hard for me to plow. They have so many things that make for them, so many things to lay for theimselves, that it is not for my weak team to plow them. They have to lay for themselves long customs, ceremonies, and authority, placing in Parliament, and many things more. And I fear me this land is not yet ripe to be plowed, for, as the saying is, it lacketh weathering. This gear lacketh weathering; at least way it is not for me to plow. For what shall I look for among thorns, but pricking and scratching? What among stones, but stumbling? What (I had almost said) among serpents, but stinging? But this much I dare say, that sence lording and loitering hath come up, preaching hath come down, contrary to the apostles' times. For they preached and lorded not, and now they lord and preach not. For they that be lords will ill go to plow: it is no meet office for theim; it is not seeming for their estate. Thus came up lording loiterers; thus crept in unpreaching prelates; and so have they long continued. For how many unlearned prelates have we now at this day! And no mervel, for if the plowmen that now be were made lords, they would clean geve over plowing; they would leave off their labor, and fall to lording outright, and let the plow stand. And then, both plows not walking, nothing should be in the commonweal but hunger. For ever sence the prelates were made lords and nobles, the plow standeth; there is no work done; the people sterve. They hawk, they hunt, they card, they dice; they pastime in their prelacies with gallant gentlemen, with their dancing minions, and with their fresh companions, so that plowing is set aside; and by the lording and loitering, preaching and plowing is clean gone. And thus if the plowmen of the country were as negligent in their office as prelates be, we should not long live for lack of sustenance. And as it is necessary for to have this plowing for the sustentation of the body, so must we have also the other for the satisfaction of the soul, or else we cannot live long ghostly. For as the body wasteth and consumeth away for lack of bodily meat, so doth the soul pine away for default of ghostly meat. But there be two kinds of inclosing, to let or hinder both these kinds of plowing; the one is an inclosing to let or hinder the bodily plowing, and the other to let or hinder the holy-day-plowing, the church-plowing.

The bodily plowing is taken in and enclosed thorow singular commodity. For what man will let go or diminish his private commodity for a communewealth? And who will sustain any damage for the respect of a publique commodity? The other plow, also, no man is diligent to set forward, nor no man will herken to it. But to hinder and let it, all men's ears are open; yea, and a great many of this kind of plowmen, which are very busy and would seem to be very good workmen. I fear me some be rather mock-gospelers then faithful plowmen. I know many myself that profess the Gospel, and live nothing thereafter. I know them, and have been conversant with some of theim. I know theim, and (I speak it with an heavy heart) there is as little charity and good living in them as in any other; according to that which Christ said in the Gospel to the great number of people that followed him, as though they had had an earnest zeal to his doctrine, whereas indeed they had it not: *Non quia vidistis signa, sed quia comedistis de panibus.* "Ye follow me," saith he, "not because ye have seen the signs and miracles that I have done; but because ye have eaten the bread, and refreshed your bodies, therefore you follow me." So that I think many one nowadays professeth the Gospel for the living sake, not for the love they bear to God's word. But they that will be true plowmen must work faithfully for God's sake, for the edifying of their brethren. And as diligently as the husbandman ploweth for the sustentation of the body, so diligently must the prelates and ministers labor for the feeding of the soul: both the plows must still be doing, as most necessary for man. And wherefore are magistrates ordained but that the tranquillity of the communeweal may be confirmed, limiting both plows?

But now for default of unpreaching prelates, methink I could guess what might be said for excusing of theim. They are so troubeled with lordly living, they be so placed in palaces, couched in courts, ruffeling in their rents, dancing in their dominions, burdened with ambassages, pampering of their paunches, like a monk that maketh his jubilee; munching in their mangers, and moiling in their gay manors and mansions, and so troubled with loitering in their lordships, that they cannot attend it. They are otherwise occupied, some in the king's matters, some are ambassadors, some of the Privy Council, some to furnish the court, some are lords of the Parliament, some are presidents, and some comptrollers of mints.

Well, well, is this their duty? Is this their office? Is this their calling? Should we have ministers of the church to be comptrollers of the mints? Is this a meet office for a priest that hath cure of souls? Is this his charge? I would here ask one question: I would fain know who comptrolleth the Devil at home at his parish, while he comptrolleth the mint. If the apostles might not leave the office of preaching to be deacons, shall one leave it for minting? I cannot tell you; but the saying is that since priests have been minters, money hath been worse then it was before. And they say that the evilness of money hath made all things dearer. And in this behalf I must speak to England. Hear, my country, England, as Paul said in his first Epistle to the Corinthians, sixth chapter; for Paul was no sitting bishop, but a walking and a preaching bishop. But when he went from them, he left there behind him the plow going still; for he wrote unto theim, and rebuked theim for going to law and pleading their causes before heathen judges. "Is there," saith he, "utterly among you no wise man to be an arbitrator in matters of judgment? What, not one of all that can judge between brother and brother; but one brother go to law with another, and that under heathen judges? *Constituite contemptos qui sunt in ecclesia,* etc.: Appoint them judges that are most abject and vile in the congregation." Which he speaketh in rebuking them, "for," saith he, "*ad erubescentiam vestram dico:* I speak it to your shame." So, England, I speak it to thy shame. Is there never a nobleman to be a lord president, but it must be a prelate? Is there never a wise man in the realm to be a comptroller of the mint? "I speak it to your shame. I speak it to your shame." If there be never a wise man, make a water-bearer, a tinker, a cobbler, a slave, a page comptroller of the mint; make a mean gentleman, a groom, a yeoman, make a poor beggar lord president.

Thus I speak, not that I would have it so, but "to your shame," if there be never a gentleman meet nor able to be lord president. For why are not the noblemen and young gentlemen of England so brought up in knowledge of God and in learning that they may be able to execute offices in the communeweal? The king hath a great many of wards, and I trow there is a Court of Wards. Why is there not a school for the wards, as well as there is a court for their lands? Why are they not set in schools where they may learn? Or why are they not sent to the universities, that they may be able to serve the king when they come to age? If the wards and young gentlemen were well brought up in learning and in the knowledge of God, they would not, when they come to age, so much geve theimselves to other vanities. And if the nobility be well trained in godly learning, the people would follow the same train. For truly, such as the noblemen be, such will the people be. And now the only cause why noblemen be not made lord presidents is because they have not been brought up in learning.

Therefore for the love of God appoint teachers and schoolmaisters, you that have charge of youth; and geve the teachers stipends worthy their pains, that they may bring theim up in grammar, in logic, in rhetoric, in philosophy, in the civil law, and in that which I cannot leave unspoken of, the word of God. Thanks be unto God, the nobility otherwise is very well brought up in learning and godliness, to the great joy and comfort of England, so that there is now good hope in the youth, that we shall another day have a florishing commonwealth, considering their godly education. Yea, and there be already noblemen inough, though not so many as I would wish, able to be lord presidents, and wise men inough for the mint. And as unmeet a thing it is for bishops to be lord presidents or priests to be minters as it was for the Corinthians to plead matters of variance before heathen judges. It is also a sclander to the noblemen, as though they lacked wisdom and learning to be able for such offices, or else were no men of conscience, or else were not meet to be trusted and able for such offices. And a prelate hath a charge and cure otherwise; and therefore he cannot discharge his duty and be a lord president too. For a presidentship requireth a whole man, and a bishop cannot be two men. A bishop hath his office, a flock to teach, to look unto; and therefore he cannot meddle with another office, which alone requireth a whole man. He should therefore geve it over to whom it is meet, and labor in his own business; as Paul writeth to the Thessalonians, "Let every man do his own business, and follow his calling." Let the priest preach, and the noblemen handle the temporal matters. Moses was a mervailous man, a good man: Moses was a wonderful fellow, and did his duty, being a married man. We lack such as Moses was. Well, I would all men would look to their duty, as God hath called them, and then we should have a florishing Christian communeweal.

And now I would ask a strange question: who is the most diligent bishop and prelate in all England,

Latimer

that passeth all the rest in doing his office? I can tell, for I know him who it is; I know him well. But now I think I see you listing and harkening that I should name him. There is one that passeth all the other, and is the most diligent prelate and preacher in all England. And will ye know who it is? I will tell you: it is the Devil. He is the most diligent preacher of all other; he is never out of his diocese; he is never from his cure; ye shall never find him unoccupied; he is ever in his parish; he keepeth residence at all times; ye shall never find him out of the way. Call for him when you will, he is ever at home; the diligentest preacher in all the realm; he is ever at his plow. No lording nor loitering can hinder him; he is ever applying his business. Ye shall never find him idle, I warrant you. And his office is to hinder religion, to maintain superstition, to set up idolatry, to teach all kind of popery. He is ready as can be wished for to set forth his plow; to devise as many ways as can be to deface and obscure God's glory. Where the Devil is resident, and hath his plow going, there away with books, and up with candles; away with Bibles, and up with beads; away with the light of the Gospel, and up with the light of candles, yea, at noondays. Where the Devil is resident, that he may prevail, up with all superstition and idolatry: censing, painting of images, candles, palms, ashes, holy water, and new service of men's inventing; as though man could invent a better way to honor God with then God himself hath appointed. Down with Christ's cross, up with purgatory pickpurse, up with him, the popish purgatory, I mean. Away with clothing the naked, the poor and impotent; up with decking of images, and gay garnishing of stocks and stones; up with man's

traditions and his laws, down with God's traditions and his most holy word. Down with the old honor due to God, and up with the new god's honor. Let all things be done in Latin. There must be nothing but Latin, not as much as *Memento, homo, quod cinis es, et in cinerem reverteris:* "Remember, man, that thou art ashes, and into ashes thou shalt return," which be the words that the minister speaketh to the ignorant people when he geveth them ashes upon Ash Wednesday. But it must be spoken in Latin: God's word may in no wise be translated into English. . . .

But in the meantime the prelates take their pleasures. They are lords, and no laborers, but the Devil is diligent at his plow. He is no unpreaching prelate: he is no lordly loiterer from his cure, but a busy plowman, so that among all the prelates, and among all the pack of them that have cure, the Devil shall go for my money, for he still applieth his business. Therefore, ye unpreaching prelates, learn of the Devil to be diligent in doing of your office; learn of the Devil, and if you will not learn of God, nor good men, for shame learn of the Devil. *Ad erubescentiam vestram dico:* "I speak it for your shame." If you will not learn of God, nor good man, to be diligent in your office, learn of the Devil. Howbeit there is now very good hope that the king's Majesty, being by the help of good governance of his most honorable counsailors he is trained and brought up in learning and knowledge of God's word, will shortly provide a remedy and set an order herein; which thing that it may be so, let us pray for him. Pray for him, good people, pray for him. Ye have great cause and need to pray for him.

THOMAS STERNHOLD and JOHN HOPKINS

METRICAL PSALMS

Versifying the Psalter was a favorite exercise of sixteenth-century poets and poetasters. In England the practise goes back at least to the early fourteenth century, from which period there survives a manuscript (sometimes attributed to Richard Rolle) of versified translations of the Psalms; but the age of the Reformation (with the great rise of congregational singing) saw an important development in this dubious literary form. In 1539 Miles Coverdale published his *Ghostly Psalms,* translated from Martin Luther; and the metrical versions in French (about 1540) of Clément Marot were used not only by his coreligionists at home but also in Protestant worship at Geneva. In the thirties and forties, after Henry VIII's

break with Rome, there appeared English paraphrases— some in verse, some in prose—by George Joye (1534), Sir John Croke (?1536), "Theodore Basille" or Thomas Becon (1542), and Sir Thomas Wyatt (1549). Even the poetical miscellanies of the Tudor period are liberally sprinkled with grave and generally disheartening versions of the Psalms—most of them so pedestrian that it is sometimes hard to choose between, say, Wyatt's and John Hall's (see p. 209); and at the end of the century the emphatically secular books of airs and madrigals by men like Byrd, Dowland, Morley, and Campion frequently contained a considerable number of versified Psalms for the use of the godly. But the unquestioned champions of the questionable art-form were Thomas Sternhold and John Hopkins, whose redactions in jogging ballad-meter set to easy, popular tunes were croaked or sung by tens of thousands who knew no other "poetry" at all.

In the early part of the reign of Edward VI (1547–53) Sternhold, a former groom of the robes to Henry VIII, dedicated to the young king his *Certain Psalms Chosen out of the Psalter of David and Drawn into English Meter,* a collection (printed by Edward Whitchurch) of nineteen Psalms without music; to these, in the second edition of 1549, following Sternhold's death in the same year, John Hopkins added seven Psalms in his own translation and eighteen more by Sternhold (*All Such Psalms of David as Thomas Sternhold . . . Did in His Lifetime Draw into English Meter*). As editions multiplied during the fifties so did the number of contributors: in addition to some forty Psalms versified by Sternhold and fifty-six by Hopkins there were others by William Whittingham, Thomas Norton (the translator of Calvin's *Institutes*), Thomas Kethe, Thomas Bastard, *et al.* The popularity of the work was immense. After Hopkins' edition of 1549 there was another in 1550,

three in 1551, two in 1553, one (printed with music at Geneva) in 1556, one in 1560, one in 1561, and finally all one hundred fifty Psalms were attached to the Book of Common Prayer in 1562. The continuing popularity of the work is indicated by the fact that in the British Museum there are more than six hundred editions between 1540 and 1828. For Sternhold and Hopkins' work our text is based upon the rare 1549 edition, *Al such Psalmes of David as Thomas Sternehold late grome of ye kinges Maiesties Robes, didde in his life time draw into English Metre* (STC 2420). To this we have added Robert Wisdom's notorious "Turk and Pope" from *The Whole Booke of Psalmes,* 1562 (STC 2430). This metrical prayer—it is not actually a Psalm—was registered at Stationers' Hall in 1565–66 as "a songe or psalme for the Delyveraunce of his people from the handes of the Turke and all heathen infidels to the tune of ye xix psalme." Translated from a hymn by Martin Luther, it probably met with more ridicule throughout the sixteenth and seventeenth centuries than any other single poem by an Elizabethan writer.

FROM ALL SUCH PSALMS OF DAVID AS THOMAS STERNHOLD . . . DID IN HIS LIFETIME DRAW INTO ENGLISH METER (1549)

To the Most Noble and Virtuous King
Our Sovereign Lord King Edward the Sixth . . .

Although, most noble sovereign, the grossness of my wit doth not suffice to search out the secret mysteries hidden in the Book of Psalms, which, by the opinion of many learned men, comprehendeth the effect of the whole Bible, yet, trusting to the goodness of God, which hath in his hand the key thereof, which shutteth and no man openeth, openeth and no man shutteth, albeit I cannot geve to your Majesty great loaves thereof or bring into the Lord's barn full handfuls; yet to th' intent I would not appear in the harvest utterly idle and barren, being warned with the example of the dry figtree, I am bold to present unto your Majesty a few crumbs which I have picked up from under the Lord's board. . . . Seeing . . . that your tender and godly zeal doth more delight in the holy songs of verity than in any feigned rimes of vanity, I am encouraged to travail further in the said Book of Psalms, trusting that, as your Grace taketh pleasure to hear them sung sometimes of me, so ye will also delight not only to see and read them yourself but also to command them to be sung to you of others. . . . The Lord of earthly kings geve your Grace daily increase of honor and

virtue, and fulfil all your godly requests in Him without whose gift we have or can obtain nothing. Amen.

Master Sternhold

THE PSALMS OF DAVID IN METER

Beatus vir. PSALM 1

How happy be the righteous men
This Psalm declareth plain,
And how the ways of wicked men
Be damnable and vain.

The man is blest that hath not gone
By wicked rede astray,
Ne sat in chair of pestilence,
Nor walk'd in sinners' way;

But in the law of God the Lord
Doth set his whole delight,
And in that law doth exercise
Himself both day and night.

And as the tree that planted is
Fast by the river side,

10

Even so shall he bring furth his fruit
In his due time and tide.

His leaf shall never fall away,
But florish still and stand;
Each thing shall prosper wonderous well
That he doth take in hand.

So shall not the ungodly do,
They shall be nothing so,
But as the dust which from the earth
The winds drive to and fro.   20

Therefore shall not the wicked men
In judgment stand upright,
Ne yet in counsel of the just,
But shall be void of might.

For why the way of godly men
Unto the Lord is known,
And eke the way of wicked men
Shall quite be overthrown.

Beati omnes. PSALM CXXVIII

God blesseth with his benefits
The man and eke the wife
That in his ways do rightly walk
And fear him all their life.

Blessed art thou that fearest God
And walkest in his way,
For of thy labor thou shalt eat;
Happy art thou, I say.

Like fruitful vines on the house sides,
So doth thy wife spring out;
Thy children stand like olive buds
Thy table round about.

Thus art thou blest that fearest God,
And he shall let thee see   10
The promised Jerusalem
And his felicity.

Thou shalt thy childer's children see
To thy great joy's increase
Full quietly in Israel
To pass their time in peace.

Finis
Here end the Psalms drawn into English meter by
Master Sternhold.

To the Reader

Thou hast here, gentle reader, unto the Psalms
that were drawn into English meter by Master

Sternhold seven mo adjoined. Not to the intent that
they should be fathered on the dead man and so,
through his estimation, to be the more highly esteemed; neither for that they are, in mine opinion, as
touching the meter in any part to be compared with
his most exquisite doings. But especially to fill up a
place which else should have been void, that the book
may rise to his just volume; and partly for that they
are fruitful, although they be not fine; and comfortable unto a Christian mind, although not so pleasant
in the mouth or ear. Wherefore, if thou, good
reader, shalt accept and take this my doing in good
part I have my hert's desire herein. Farewell.

J[ohn] H[opkins]

Lauda anima mea. PSALM CXLVI

A praise of God, in him alone
All folk should hope and trust,
And not in worldly men, of whom
The chief shall turn to dust.

My soul, praise thou the Lord always!
My God I will confess!
While breath and life prolong my days
My mouth no time shall cease.

Trust not in worldly princes, then,
Though they abound in wealth,
Nor in the sons of mortal men,
In whom there is no health.

For why their breath doth soon depart,
To earth anon they fall,   10
And than the counsels of their heart
Decay and perish all.

O happy is that man, I say,
Whom Jacob's God doth aid,
And he whose hope doth not decay,
But on the Lord is stay'd;

Which made the yearth and waters deep,
The heavens high withal,
Which doth his word and promise keep
In truth, and ever shall.   20

With right always doth he proceed,
For such as suffer wrong;
The poor and hungry he doth feed
And leuse the fetters strong.

The Lord doth ease the blind with sight,
The lame to lims restore;
The Lord, I say, doth love the right
And just man evermore.

He doth defend the fatherless,
The strangers sad in hert,   30
And quit the widow from distress,
And all ill ways subvert.

Thy Lord and God eternally,
O Sion, still shall reign,
In time of all posterity
Forever to remain.

[TURK AND POPE]
Robert Wisdom

Preserve us, Lord, by thy dear Word,
  from Turk and Pope defend us, Lord;
Which both would thrust out of his throne
  our Lord Jesus Christ, thy dear Son.

Lord Jesus Christ, shew forth thy might,
  that thou art Lord of Lords by right.
Thy poor afflicted flock defend,
  that they may praise thee without end.

God Holy Ghost, our comforter,
  be our patron, help, and succor;   10
Geve us one mind and perfect peace,
  all gifts of grace in us encrease.

Thou living God, in persons three,
  thy name be praised in unity;
In all our need so us defend
  that we may praise thee world without end.

THE BOOK OF COMMON PRAYER

The need for the uniform conduct of divine services in the vernacular became obvious almost as soon as Henry VIII, following his break with Rome, had created a national church. Through the centuries the far-flung Roman Catholic dioceses of western Europe had evolved a bewildering array of breviaries (books of daily public or canonical prayers), missals (books of ritual for the Mass), manuals (books of ritual for various other ceremonies), and pontificals (books of those offices performed by bishops); and in England alone the so-called Use (or ritual) of Sarum (or Salisbury), though very popular, was challenged by the quite different Uses of York and Hereford, Lincoln, Bangor, Exeter, Wells, and St. Paul's—to say nothing of the many variations or permutations that this or that bishop might choose to employ. Not only were these ancient rituals in Latin, and therefore incomprehensible to most of the faithful, but they were obviously not contrived to encourage the growth of the new and insecure national church; their "diversity in singing and saying" the divine offices made a deplorable lack of Anglican uniformity inevitable, and their perpetuation of so-called idolatrous Roman errors made their use by Tudor bishops extremely odd, to say the least.

Although the need for a unified and simplified ritual for the Anglican establishment was plain, the achievement of that unity and simplicity was very slow. As early as 1535 Rome itself had sought to remedy its own confusion by authorizing the widely used "Reformed Breviary" of the Spanish Cardinal Quignon; but Henry VIII, who, although he had audaciously broken with the pontiff, remained a good Catholic in matters of dogma and ritual, moved very timidly toward any real reformation of the doctrine and discipline of his new church. Not until

1542 did he authorize a revised edition of the Sarum breviary, and not until the year following did he order public reading of the vernacular Bible, the presence of which in all parish churches had been required by law in 1536. In 1544, at his monarch's command, Thomas Cranmer, then the primate, compiled an English litany, but this was as far as Henry cared to go in the direction of an English order of service, and further reforms had to await the accession of Edward VI. Promptly with the new reign, the tempo of reform became brisker. In 1547 a royal injunction required that the Epistle and the Gospel at high mass be read in English; for Easter of 1548 a new "Order of the Communion" was established by royal proclamation; and finally, in 1549, the first complete Book of Common Prayer was published and approved by Parliament (January 21) for compulsory use in all churches of the realm.

Owing to the loss of the records of Convocation in the great fire of 1666 the actual process of composition of this first prayer book of Edward remains a matter of some doubt. It is certain, however, that Cranmer took an active part in synthesizing and simplifying the various Roman rituals which were adapted for Anglican Uses; more important, the sonorous rhetoric to which generations of Englishmen have been baptized, confirmed, married, and buried must be largely attributed to his wonderful gift of prose style. Apparently an ecclesiastical commission was convened, first at Chertsey and then at Windsor, to study the problems of a thorough revision of Anglican ritual, for when Parliament accepted the prayer book in its Act of Uniformity (1549) it acknowledged that "the Archbishop of Canterbury and certain other learned men of this realm" had faithfully executed the royal mandate in drawing up "one convenient and meet order, rite, and fashion of common and open prayer and administration of the sacraments." Liturgical scholars have long agreed that the Use of Sarum provided the frame for Cranmer's work: morning and evening prayer (with the Psalter and the lesson) were adapted from the Sarum breviary; matins from the Sarum matins, lauds, and prime; evensong from the Sarum vespers and compline; the order of communion (with the collects, Epistles, and Gospels) derives from the Sarum missal; the sacramental offices from the Sarum manual; and services of consecration from the Sarum pontifical. But traces of other rituals are also discernible. Cardinal Quignon's recent breviary was used, and so was the so-called Mozarabic missal, as well as various Lutheran and other Continental service books. In short, Edward's first prayer book was a work of inspired eclecticism, but its incomparable style is all its own.

In 1550 this prayer book was altered to include the ordinal (prescribing the ritual for consecrating bishops and ordaining priests and deacons); and two years later it was thoroughly revised to mark the extreme limit of reformed doctrine and discipline in the history of the Anglican Church. After this second Edwardian prayer book had been in use for only eight months, Mary succeeded her half-brother and promptly abolished the slow reforms and revisions of the past twenty years. At Elizabeth's accession everything was again reversed with the restoration of Edward's second prayer book by the Act of Uniformity of April 28, 1559. Such alterations as Parliament required (for example, in extending the use of the rochet and surplice to all the clergy and in striking out the prayer for deliverance from the "tyranny" and the "detestable enormities" of the Bishop of Rome) tended to mitigate some of the harsher Protestantism of Edward's "Hot Gospelers." In 1561 the Elizabethan prayer book reached its final form with the addition of some prescribed holy days.

Our text is based upon *The booke of the common prayer and administracion of the Sacramentes, and other rites and ceremonies of the Churche: after the use of the Churche of England*, 1549 (STC 16267).

FROM THE BOOK OF THE COMMON PRAYER AND ADMINISTRATION OF THE SACRAMENTS (1549)

THE PREFACE

There was never anything by the wit of man so well devised or so surely established which in continuance of time hath not been corrupted, as (among other things) it may plainly appear by the common prayers in the church, commonly called divine service, the first original and ground whereof, if a man would search out by the ancient fathers, he shall find that the same was not ordained but of a good purpose and for a great advancement of godliness. For they so ord'red the matter that all the whole Bible (or the greatest part thereof) should be read over once in the year, intending thereby that the clergy, and specially such as were ministers of the congregation, should by often reading and meditation of God's word be stirred up to godliness themselfs, and be more able also to exhort other by wholesome doctrine, and to confute them that were adversaries to the trueth. And further that the people, by daily hearing of Holy Scripture read in the church, should continually profit more and more in the knowledge of God and be the more inflamed with the love of his true religion. But these many years passed this godly and decent order of the ancient fathers hath been so altered, broken, and neglected by planting in uncertain stories, legends, responds, verses, vain repetitions, commemorations, and synodals that commonly when any book of the Bible was begun, before three or four chapiters were read out, all the rest were unread. And in this sort the book of Esaie was begun in Advent and the book of Genesis in Septuagesima, but they were only begun and never read thorow. After a like sort were other books of Holy Scripture used. And moreover whereas St. Paul would have such language spoken to the people in the church as they might understand and have profit by hearing the same, the service in this Church of England these many years hath been read in Latin to the people, which they understood not, so that they have heard with their ears only, and their hearts, spirit, and mind have not been edified thereby. And furthermore, notwithstanding that the ancient fathers had devided the Psalms into seven portions, whereof every one was called a nocturn, now of late time a few of them have been daily said (and oft repeated) and the rest utterly omitted. Moreover, the number and hardness of the rules called the pie and the manifold changings of the service was the cause that to turn the book only was so hard and intricate a matter that many times there was more business to find out what should be read then to read it when it was found out.

These inconveniences therefore considered, here is set furth such an order whereby the same shall be redressed. And for a readiness in this matter here is drawn out a calendar for that purpose which is plain and easy to be understood, wherein (so much as may be) the reading of Holy Scripture is so set furth that all things shall be done in order without breaking one piece thereof from another. For this cause be cut off anthems, responds, invitatories, and such like things as did break the continual course of the reading of the Scripture. Yet because there is no remedy but that of necessity there must be some rules, therefore certain rules are here set furth which, as they be few in number, so they be plain and easy to be understanded. So that here you have an order for prayer (as touching the reading of Holy Scripture) much agreeable to the mind and purpose of the old fathers, and a great deal more profitable and commodious then that which of late was used. It is more profitable because here are left out many things, whereof some be untrue, some uncertain, some vain and superstitious; and is ordained nothing to be read but the very pure word of God, the Holy Scriptures, or that which is evidently grounded upon the same, and that in such a language and order as is most easy and plain for the understanding both of the readers and hearers. It is also more commodious both for the shortness thereof and for the plainness of the order, and for that the rules be few and easy. Furthermore, by this order the curates shall need none other books for their publique service but this book and the Bible, by the means whereof the people shall not be at so great charge for books as in time past they have been.

And where heretofore there hath been great diversity in saying and singing in churches within this realm, some following Salisbury use, some Hereford use, some the use of Bangor, some of York, and some of Lincoln, now from hencefurth all the whole realm shall have but one use. And if any would judge this way more painful because that all things must be read upon the book, whereas before, by the reason of so often repetition, they could say many things by heart, if those men will weigh their labor with the profit in knowledge which daily they shall obtain by reading upon the book, they will not refuse the pain in consideration of the great profit that shall ensue thereof. . . .

THE INTROITS, COLLECTS, EPISTLES, AND GOSPELS TO BE USED AT THE CELEBRATION OF THE LORD'S SUPPER AND HOLY COMMUNION THROUGH THE YEAR, WITH PROPER PSALMS AND LESSONS FOR DIVERS FEASTS AND DAYS

The First Sunday in Advent

Beatus vir. Psalm i

Blessed is that man that hath not walked in the counsail of the ungodly nor stand in the way of sinners, and hath not sit in the seat of the scornful;

But his delight is in the law of the Lord, and in His law will he exercise himself day and night.

And he shall be like a tree planted by the waterside, that will bring forth his fruit in due season.

His leaf also shall not wither, and look whatsoever he doth it shall prosper.

As for the ungodly, it is not so with them, but they are like the chaff which the wind scattereth away from the face of the yearth.

Therefore the ungodly shall not be hable to stand in the judgment, neither the sinners in the congregation of the righteous.

But the Lord knoweth the way of the righteous, and the way of the ungodly shall perish.

Glory be to the Father and to the Son and to the Holy Ghost.

As it was in the beginning, and is now, and ever shall be, world without end. Amen.

And so must every Introit be ended

Let us pray.

THE COLLECT

Almighty God, geve us grace that we may cast away the works of darkness and put upon us the armor of light now in the time of this mortal life (in the which thy Son Jesus Christ came to visit us in great humility), that in the last day when he shall come again in his glorious majesty to judge both the quick and the dead we may rise to the life immortal through him who liveth and reigneth with thee and the Holy Ghost now and ever. Amen.

THE EPISTLE. *Romans xiii*

Owe nothing to any man but this, that ye love one another. For he that loveth another fulfilleth the law. For these commandements—thou shalt not commit adultry, thou shalt not kill, thou shalt not steal, thou shalt bear no false witness, thou shalt not lust, and so forth (if there be any other commandement)—it is all comprehended in this saying, namely, "Love thy neighbor as thyself." Love hurteth not his neighbor; therefore is love the fulfilling of the law. This also: we know the season, how that it is time that we should now awake out of sleep, for now is our salvation nearer then when we believed. The night is passed, the day is come nigh; let us, therefore, cast away the deeds of darkness and let us put on the armor of light. Let us walk honestly, as it were in the daylight, not in eating and drinking, neither in chamboring and wantonness, neither in strife nor envying, but put ye on the Lord Jesus Christ. And make not provision for the flesh to fulfil the lusts of it.

The Gospel. *Matthew xxi*

And when they drew nigh to Jerusalem and were come to Bethphage, unto Mount Olivet, then sent Jesus two disciples, saying unto them, "Go into the town that lieth over against you, and anon ye shall find an ass bound and a colt with her; loose them and bring them unto me. And if any man say ought unto you, say ye, 'The Lord hath need of them,' and straightway he will let them go." All this was done that it might be fulfilled which was spoken by the prophet, saying, "Tell ye the daughter of Sion, 'Behold, thy king cometh unto thee, meek, sitting upon an ass and a colt, the foal of the ass used to the yoke.'" The disciples went and did as Jesus commanded them, and brought the ass and the colt, and put on them their clothes, and set him thereon. And many of the people spread their garments in the way. Other cut down branches from the trees and strawed them in the way. Moreover, the people that went before and they that came after cried, saying, "Hosanna to the son of David! Blessed is he that cometh in the name of the Lord! Hosanna in the highest!" And when he was come to Jerusalem all the city was moved, saying, "Who is this?" And the people said, "This is Jesus the prophet of Nazareth, a city of Galilee." And Jesus went into the temple of God and cast out all them that sold and bought in the temple, and overthrew the tables of money-changers and the seats of them that sold doves, and said unto them, "It is written, 'My house shall be called the house of prayer, but ye have made it a den of thieves.'"

THE ORDER FOR
THE BURIAL OF THE DEAD

The priest meeting the corps at the church stile shall say, or else the priests and clerks shall sing, and so go either into the church or towards the grave

I am the resurrection and the life, saith the Lord; he that believeth in me, yea though he were dead, yet shall he live. And whosoever liveth and believeth in me shall not die forever. *John xi.*

I know that my Redeemer liveth, and that I shall rise out of the yearth in the last day, and shall be covered again with my skin, and shall see God in my flesh; yea, and I myself shall behold him, not with other but with these same eyes. *Job xix.*

We brought nothing into this world, neither may we carry anything out of this world. The Lord geveth and the Lord taketh away. Even as it pleaseth the Lord, so cometh things to pass. Blessed be the name of the Lord. *I Timothy vi. Job i.*

When they come at the grave, whiles the corps is made ready to be laid into the earth, the priest shall say, or else the priest and clerks shall sing

Man that is born of a woman hath but a short time to live and is full of misery. He cometh up and is cut down like a flour; he flyeth as it were a shadow and never continueth in one stay. *Job ix.*

In the middest of life we be in death. Of whom may we seek for succor but of thee, O Lord, which for our sins justly art moved? Yet, O Lord God most holy, O Lord most mighty, O holy and most merciful savior, deliver us not into the bitter pains of eternal death! Thou knowest, Lord, the secrets of our hearts; shut not up thy merciful eyes to our prayers, but spare us, Lord most holy, O God most mighty, O holy and merciful savior, thou most worthy judge eternal. Suffer us not at our last hour for any pains of death to fall from thee.

Then the priest, casting earth upon the corps, shall say

I commend thy soul to God, the Father Almighty, and thy body to the ground, earth to earth, ashes to ashes, dust to dust, in sure and certain hope of resurrection to eternal life through our Lord Jesus Christ, who shall change our vile body that it may be like to his glorious body according to the mighty working whereby he is hable to subdue all things to himself.

Then shall be said or sung

I heard a voice from heaven saying unto me, "Write, 'Blessed are the dead which die in the Lord.' Even so sayeth the spirit, that they rest from their labors." *Apocalypse xiv.*

Let us pray.

We commend into thy hands of mercy, most merciful Father, the soul of this our brother departed, N[omen]. And his body we commit to the earth, beseeching thine infinite goodness to geve us grace to live in thy fear and love and to die in thy favor, that when the judgment shall come which thou hast committed to thy well-beloved Son, both this our brother and we may be found acceptable in thy sight and receive that blessing which thy well-beloved Son shall then pronounce to all that love and fear thee, saying, "Come, ye blessed children of my Father, receive the kingdom prepared for you before the beginning of the world." Grant this, merciful Father, for the honor of Jesu Christ our only savior, mediator, and advocate. Amen.

This prayer shall also be added

Almighty God, we geve thee hearty thanks for this thy servant, whom thou hast delivered from the miseries of this wretched world, from the body of death and all temptation, and, as we trust, hast brought his soul which he committed into thy holy hands into sure consolation and rest. Grant, we beseech thee, that at the day of judgment his soul and all the souls of thy elect departed out of this life may with us and we with them fully receive thy promises and be made perfit altogether thorow the glorious resurrection of thy son Jesus Christ our Lord.

These psalms with other suffrages following are to be said in the church either before or after the burial of the corps

Dilexi quoniam. Psalm cxvi

I am well pleased that the Lord hath heard the voice of my prayer.

That he hath enclined his ear unto me; therefore will I call upon him as long as I live.

The snares of death compassed me round about, and the pains of hell gat hold upon me. I shall find trouble and heaviness, and I shall call upon the name of the Lord. O Lord, I beseech thee deliver my soul.

Gracious is the Lord and righteous. Yea, our God is merciful.

The Lord preserveth the simple. I was in misery and he helped me.

Turn again, then, unto thy rest, O my soul, for the Lord hath rewarded thee.

And why? Thou hast delivered my soul from death, mine eyes from tears, and my feet from falling.

I will walk before the Lord in the land of the living.

I believed, and therefore will I speak; but I was sore troubled. I said in my haste, "All men are liars."

What reward shall I geve unto the Lord for all the benefits that he hath done unto me?

I will receive the cup of salvation and call upon the name of the Lord.

I will pay my vows now in the presence of all his people. Right dear in the sight of the Lord is the death of his saints.

Behold, O Lord, how that I am thy servant. I am thy servant and the son of thy handmaid. Thou hast broken my bonds in sunder.

I will offer to thee the sacrifice of thanksgeving and will call upon the name of the Lord.

I will pay my vows unto the Lord in the sight of all his people, in the courts of the Lord's house, even in the middest of thee, O Hierusalem.

Glory to the Father, etc.

As it was in the beginning, etc. . . .

[The burial service continues with Psalms cxlvi and cxxxix and with the "lesson" taken from the fifteenth chapter of I Corinthians.]

The lesson ended, then shall the priest say

Lord, have mercy upon us.

Christ, have mercy upon us.

Lord, have mercy upon us.

Our Father which art in heaven, etc.

And lead us not into temptation.

Answer: But deliver us from evil. Amen.

Priest: Enter not, O Lord, into judgment with thy servant.

Answer: For in thy sight no living creature shall be justified.

Priest: From the gates of hell.

Answer: Deliver their souls, O Lord.

Priest: I believe to see the goodness of the Lord.

Answer: In the land of the living.

Priest: O Lord, graciously hear my prayer.

Answer: And let my cry come unto thee.

Let us pray.

O Lord, with whom do live the spirits of them that be dead, and in whom the souls of them that be elected, after they be delivered from the burden of the flesh, be in joy and felicity, grant unto this thy servant that the sins which he committed in this world be not imputed unto him, but that he, escaping the gates of hell and pains of eternal darkness, may ever dwell in the region of light with Abraham, Isaac, and Jacob, in the place where is no weeping, sorrow, nor heaviness; and when that dreadful day of the general resurrection shall come, make him to rise also with the just and righteous, and receive this body again to glory, then made pure and incorruptible. Set him on the right hand of thy son Jesus Christ emong thy holy and elect, that then he may hear with them these most sweet and comfortable words: "Come to me, ye blessed of my Father, possess the kingdom which hath been prepared for you from the beginning of the world." Grant this, we beseech thee, O merciful Father, through Jesus Christ our mediator and redeemer. Amen.

CERTAIN NOTES FOR THE MORE PLAIN EXPLICATION AND DECENT MINISTRATION OF THINGS CONTAINED IN THIS BOOK

In the saying or singing of matins and evensong, baptizing and burying, the minister in parish churches and chapels annexed to the same shall use a surplice. And in all cathedral churches and colledges th' archdeacons, deans, provests, maisters, prebendaries, and fellows being graduates may use in the quiere beside their surplices such hoods as pertaineth to their several degrees which they have taken in any university within this realm. But in all other places every minister shall be at liberty to use any surplice or no. It is also seemly that graduates, when they do preach, should use such hoods as pertaineth to their several degrees.

And whensoever the bushop shall celebrate the Holy Communion in the church or execute any other publique ministration, he shall have upon him beside his rochette a surplice or alb and a cope or vestment, and also his pastoral staff in his hand, or else borne or holden by his chapeleyne.

As touching kneeling, crossing, holding-up of hands, knocking upon the breast, and other gestures, they may be used or left, as every man's devotion serveth without blame.

Also upon Christmas day, Easter day, the Ascension day, Whitsunday, and the Feast of the Trinity may be used any part of Holy Scripture hereafter to be certainly limited and appointed in the stead of the Letany.

If there be a sermon, or for other great cause, the curate by his discretion may leave out the Letany, *Gloria in excelsis,* the Creed, th' omely, and the exhortation to the communion.

JOHN JEWEL

AN APOLOGY

John Jewel was well prepared, both by training and by hard experience, for the work by which his fame was built and his name still lives. In turn a student and fellow of Corpus Christi College, Oxford, a protégé of Peter Martyr, a licensed preacher, an exile (at Frankfort and Strassburg) from the Marian terror, he promptly returned to England when he heard of Elizabeth's accession and was as promptly groomed by that young but sagacious sovereign to defend her ecclesiastical policy. As a preacher at St. Paul's Cross and as a commissioner for the visitation of western counties, he quickly made his (and his queen's) position clear: that the only feasible strategy for the tottery Anglican establishment was to follow a *via media* between the unreconstructed papists of the right and the extreme Calvinists, or "Hot Gospelers," of the left. Such was the strategy of reason and compromise to which Richard Hooker (one of Jewel's own admiring disciples at Oxford) was later to give consummate statement in *Of the Laws of Ecclesiastical Polity* (see pp. 179–187). Jewel's challenge to his Roman Catholic adversaries in a sermon at St. Paul's Cross on November 26, 1559—to cite any specific sanction for Roman doctrine or discipline from the Scripture, the fathers, the councils, or the practise of the church during the first six centuries after Christ—indicates

his policy of defending the Anglican establishment by discrediting the alleged exclusive divine franchise of the Roman church; and the pastoral and administrative labors following his consecration as Bishop of Salisbury (January, 1560) prepared him well for making a systematic defense of the Anglican position. At last, in 1562, his great work appeared as *Apologia pro Ecclesia Anglicana,* and it was at once recognized as the official Anglican answer to the counter-reformation launched at the Council of Trent (1545–63). As a description and learned defense of Anglican doctrine and discipline, a rebuttal to the Roman Catholic charge of Anglican heresy, a critical examination of the papacy's claims for supremacy *de fide,* and a manifesto for the continuing reformation of national churches, Jewel's *Apologia* laid down the lines which his church has, *mutatis mutandis,* followed ever since. Written in Latin to assure an adequate Continental reception, it went through fifteen editions (in Latin, Greek, and even Welsh) before 1622; and its English version by Ann, Lady Bacon (mother of Francis), which was made with the express approval of Matthew Parker, Elizabeth's great Archbishop of Canterbury, went through four. Our text is based upon *An Apologie, or aunswer in defence of the Church of England,* 1562 (STC 14590).

FROM AN APOLOGY OR ANSWER IN DEFENSE OF THE CHURCH OF ENGLAND CONCERNING THE STATE OF RELIGION USED IN THE SAME (1562)

It hath been always an old complaint, even from the times of the patriarchs and prophets, and confirmed by the writings and testimonies of all ages, that truth dwelleth as a stranger here upon earth, and soon findeth enemies and slanderers among such as

do not know her. The which thing, although peradventure it may seem incredible unto others such as have not diligently marked these things, specially bycause that the whole offspring of mankind, by very course of nature, without a teacher, even of his own inclination coveteth after truth, and Christ himself our Savior what time he was here conversant amongest men called himself the Truth, as by that name which most aptly did express all divine power, nevertheless we that are exercised in the Holy Scriptures and have read and seen what hath happened in manner to all godly men of all ages, even unto the prophets, unto the apostles, unto the holy martyrs, and unto Christ himself, with what reproaches, what revilings, what slanderous names they were vexed here in their lifetime for only truth's sake, we, I say, do see that it is a thing not only nothing new nor incredible but also very currant and common to all ages. Marry, on the other side it might seem much more merveilous and uncredible in case that the Devil, the very father of lies and enemy to all truth, should now sodainly change his natural disposition and hope to find some other way then by lying to oppress the truth; or that by other sleights then such as he hath always used he should now begin to establish his kingdom. For out of all records you shall scantly find any time (other whiles religion was newly growing and encreasing, or after it was staid and setteled, or when it began to spring again) wherein truth and innocency amongest men was not most unworthily and most shamefully entreated; for the Devil seeth whiles truth prevaileth he cannot prevail nor keep his own. . . .

Nowadays . . . [the Roman Catholics] cry everywhere that all we are heretics, that we are departed from the faith, and that we with our new persuasions and wicked doctrine have broken the consent of the Church; that we do raise, as it were out of hell, and restore to life again old heresies and such as long ago were condemned. We sow abroad new sects and furious fancies that never before were heard of; also that we now are devided into contrary factions and opinions and could never agree by any means among ourselves; that we are wicked men and make war after the manner of the giants (as the fable is) against God himself and do live altogither without care or reverence of God; that we do despise all good deeds and use no discipline of virtue, maintain no laws, no customs, no equity, no justice, no right; that we loose the bridle to all mischief and allure the people to all kind of license and lust; that we go about and seek how all the states of monarchies and kingdoms might be overthrown, and that all things might be brought unto the rash government of the people and to the rule of the unskilful multitude; that we have rebelliously withdrawn ourselves from the Catholic Church and shaken the whole world with a cursed schism and have troubled the common peace and the general quietness of the Church; and that like as in times past Dathan and Abiron severed themselves from Moses and Aaron, so we at this day depart from the pope of Rome without any sufficient and just cause; as for the authority of the ancient fathers and old councils, we do set at naught. All ancient ceremonies such as our grandfathers and great-grandfathers now many ages past, when better manners and better days did florish, were approved, we have rashly and arrogantly abolished, and have brought into the Church by our own private authority, without any commandement of any holy and sacred general council, new rites and ceremonies; and that we have done all these things not for any respect of religion, but only of a desire to maintain strife and contention. As for them, they have changed utterly nothing at all, but all things, even as they received them from the apostles and were approved by the most ancient fathers, so they have kept them from age to age unto this day.

But now, lest they should seem only to pick quarrels and to speak evil of us in corners only to the intent to bring us into hatred, the Romish bishops have provided themselves of certain men, eloquent inough and not unlearned, for to undertake this desperate cause and to set it forth with books and long orations to the intent that the matter, being cunningly handled after the best fashion, the simple and ignorant man might suppose there were somewhat in it; for truly they saw how their cause began to decline in all places, how their sleights were now espied and therefore less set by, and that their garrisons decayed every day; and therefore their cause to be such that it had great need of help. Now as touching those things which they do object against us, part of them are manifestly false and even by the judgment of the selfsame persons that do object them condemned for lies; part of them, although they be as false as the other, yet inasmuch as they carry a shew and a counterfeit of truth, in such the simple reader, if he take not heed specially, if unto the probability of the matter the painted and delicate speech of these fellows be cunningly applied, may easily be entrapped and carried out of the way; part of them, again, are such as we ought not to decline from them as crimes, but as things right well and advisedly done to acknowledge and to profess them; and even to tell you at a word how the matter goeth, these men do slander all our doings, even those things which themselves cannot deny to be well and orderly done, and as though it were not possible that anything should be other done or spoken well of us, so all our sayings and doings they most maliciously deprave. No doubt it had been their part to have gone more simply and more plainly to work if they had meant to deal truly, whereas now nother truly nor courteously nor Christianly, but covertly and craftily they assault us with lies, abusing the blindness of the people and the ignorance of princes to bring us into hatred and to oppress the truth. This is the power of darkness and property of men that for the furtherance of their cause have more confidence in the blockishness of the unskilful multitude and in darkness then in truth and light, and as St. Jerome saith, of such as with closed eyes do bark against the manifest truth. But we give thanks unto the Almighty God that our quarrel is such that even these men, would they never so fain, can say nothing in reproach thereof which might not be turned in reproof of the fathers, of the prophets, of the apostles, of Peter, of Paul, and of Christ himself. . . .

As for us, inasmuch as within these twenty years last past so many thousands of our brethren in the middest of their extreme torments have borne witness to the truth, and princes coveting to bridle the Gospel in moiling many ways have labored all in vain, and that the whole world in manner beginneth now to open their eyes to behold the light, we think that our cause is already sufficiently pleaded and defended, and that whereas the matter itself speaketh inough for itself there is no great need of words. For if the popes themselves would, or rather if they could, consider with themselves the whole matter, the beginnings and the manner of the encrease of our religion, how that their trash in manner every whit, whan no man touched it, without all help of man, fell down to the ground; again how our profession at the first, notwithstanding the continual resistence of emperors, of so many kings, of popes and bishops, of all men in manner hath encreased and by little and little spread over all the earth, and now also at the length is entered into the courts and palaces of kings; even these things only might be sufficient tokens whereby to understand that God himself doth fight in our defense and scorneth from heaven all their endeavors, and that so mighty is the power of truth that no force of man nor yet hell-gates can withstand it. For be ye sure, so many free cities, so many kings, so many princes as at this day have abandoned the See of Rome and adjoined themself to the Gospel of Christ are not become mad. . . .

To be short, this whole religion which Christian men do profess at this day, in the first beginnings thereof was called of heathen men a sect and an heresy; they with these voices always filled the ears of princes to the entent that they, being once brought upon an opinion conceived beforehand to hate us and to take whatsoever should be said on our behalf to be factious and heresy, might be carried from the matter itself and from hearing of the cause. But the greater and the horribler the fault is, so much ought it to be proved with greater and more evident arguments, specially in these days now that men have begun to give less credit unto these men's dreams and more diligently to examine their doctrine then afore

they were accustomed. For the people of God is otherwise instructed now then they were when all things that were set forth by the popes of Rome were taken for the Gospel, and all religion depended only upon their authority. The Holy Scriptures are now abroad, the writings of the apostles and prophets are abroad, out of the which both all truth and Catholic doctrine may be proved and all heresy confuted.

But whereas of all these authorities these men bring not a word against us, and nevertheless to be called heretics that have not declined nother from Christ, nor from the apostles, nor from the prophets, it is very injurious and too, too grievous. With this sword Christ repulsed the Devil when he was tempted of him; with these weapons all loftiness that avanceth itself against God must be overthrown and vanquished. For all Scripture, saith Paul, inspired of God is profitable to teach, to confute, to instruct, to reprove, that the man of God may be perfect and furnished unto all good works. Thus always the godly fathers fought against heretics with none other weapons but out of the Holy Scriptures. . . .

Wherefore if we be heretics, if these men be as they will be called Catholics, why do they not that thing which they see the fathers, true Catholic men indeed, always did? Why do they not convince us out of the Holy Scriptures? Why do they not call us to be tried by them? Why do they not make it appear that we have severed ourselves from Christ, from the prophets, from the apostles, from the holy fathers? Why stagger they? Why flee they? It is God's cause—why doubt they to commit it to God's word? But if we be heretics which refer all our controversies unto the Holy Scriptures and make our appeal unto the selfsame words which we know are sealed by God himself and do prefer them before all things that may be devised by man, what shall we say to these men, what manner of men or by what name were it convenient to call these that are afraid to stand to the trial of the sacred Scriptures, that is to say the judgment of God himself, and prefer before them their own dreams and most cold inventions, and for their own tradition's sake now many years have broken the ordinances of Christ and of the apostles? Sophocles the poet when he was accused, being an old man, to the judges of his sons for a dotard and a fool and as one that fondly consumed his goods and therefore seemed to have need of a tutor, for to purge himself of this slander came into the court and after he had read *Oedipus Coloneus,* a tragedy which even in the selfsame time that he was accused in he had written with great diligence and very elegantly, by and by he asked of the judges whether that verse seemed to be the verse of a doting man.

Even so we, bicause that unto these men we seem to be mad and are slandered of them as heretics, as who would say we had now nothing to do nother with Christ nor with the Church of God, have thought it should not be unconvenient nor unprofitable if we did plainly and freely declare unto the world that faith wherein we stand, and all our hope which we have in Jesus Christ, that all men may see what we do hold touching every part of Christian religion and may judge with themselves whether that faith which they shall see confirmed with the words of Christ, with the writings of the apostles, with the testimonies of the Catholic fathers, and with the examples of many ages be only a raging of mad men and a conspiracy of heretics.

We believe, therefore, that there is one divine nature and power which we do call God, and the same is distincted into three equal persons, the Father, the Son, and the Holy Ghost, all of one power, of one majesty, of one eternity, of one divinity, of one substance. . . .

We do believe that Jesus Christ, the only Son of the eternal Father, according as it was decreed long sithens before all beginnings, when the fulness of time was come, took flesh and the whole nature of man of that same blessed and pure Virgin to the entent to declare unto men the secret and hid will of his Father which was hidden from all ages and generations, and to the entent that in the body and nature of man he might accomplish the mystery of our redemption, nailing our sins and the same handwriting which was written against us unto the Cross.

We believe that for our sakes he died and was buried, descended into hell, the third day by divine power returned unto life and rose again; after forty days in the sight of his disciples he ascended into heaven for to fulfil all things, and the very same body wherein he was born, wherein he was conversant upon earth, wherein he was mocked, wherein he suffered most grievous torments and cruel kind of death, wherein he rose again, wherein he ascended unto the right hand of the Father, he hath placed in majesty and glory above all princely dignity and power and virtue and rule and all names that are named not only in this world but also in the world to come, and that now he sitteth there and shall sit until all things be perfectly finished. . . .

From that place we believe that Christ shall come again for to execute that same public and universal judgment as well over those which he shall find yet remaining alive in their bodies as those that be dead. . . .

We do believe that there is only one Church of God and that the same is not shut up as in time past among the Jews into any one corner or kingdom, but is catholic and universal and dispersed into all the world so that now there is no nation that may truly complain that they be excluded and can have no part with the Church and people of God. . . .

We say that Christ hath geven even unto ministers authority to bind, to loose, to open, and to shut. And that the office of loosing doth consist herein: when that other to such as are overthrown in their own consciences and are truly returned to a better mind, the minister by the preaching of the Gospel offereth the merits of Christ and absolution, and doth assure him of the remission of his sins and of the hope of eternal salvation; other when such as in any grievous and slanderous offense, and by some notable and public fault, have offended their brothren's consciences and thereby have in manner alienated themselves from the common society of the Church and from the body of Christ, after that they do return again to a better mind he doth reconcile, gather, and restore home again unto the fellowship and unity of the faithful; and the authority of binding and shutting, we say, he exerciseth as often as other unto the unbelievers and stubborn persons he shutteth up the gates of the kingdom of heaven and threateneth unto them the revenge of God and everlasting punishment, or when he excludeth out from the bosom of the Church such as are openly excommunicated, the sentence that is geven after this sort by the ministers of the Church God doth so confirm; that whatsoever by their ministery here in earth is loosed or bound, that same will he loose and bind and make good also in heaven. The key whereby they have power other to shut up or to open the kingdom of heaven, we say with St. Chrysostom that it is the knowledge of the Scriptures, and with Tertullian the interpretation of the law, and with Eusebius the word of God, and that the disciples of Christ received this authority not for to hear the secret confessions of the people or to occupy themselves about privy whisperings (which their sacrificing priests at this day, all of them, do in every corner and in such sort they do it as though the whole power and use of the keys did consist therein alone), but to the entent they should go, they should teach, they should openly preach the Gospel, that unto such as believed they might be a saver of life unto life, unto the unbelieving and unfaithful persons the saver of death unto death, to the entent that the minds of the godly, being ones astonied with the conscience of their life past and of their sins, after they should begin to behold the light of the Gospel and believe in Christ. . . .

Matrimony, we say, in all kinds and states of men, in patriarchs, in prophets, in apostles, in holy martyrs, in ministers of the church, in bishops, is holy and honorable. . . .

We do receive and embrace all the canonical Scriptures, both of the Old and of the New Testament, and we give thanks unto our God that he hath raised up that light before us that we might always have it before our eyes, lest that other by the deceit of men or guiles of the Devil we should be carried away after errors and fables. . . .

We do receive the sacraments of the Church, that is to say, certain holy tokens and ceremonies which Christ would have us to use, that in them he might set before our eyes the mysteries of our salvation and more strongly confirm that faith which we have in his blood and seal up his grace in our hearts. And these we do call, with Tertullian, Origen, Ambrose, Augustine, Hierome, Chrysostom, Basil, Dionyse, and other Catholic fathers, figures, signs, badges, patterns, counterpanes, forms, seals, tokens, similitudes, examples, images, remembrances, and memories. . . .

Of sacraments which are properly to be reckoned under that name we do acknowledge two: the sacrament of baptism and the sacrament of thanksgiving; for so many do we find delivered and consecrated by Christ and approved of the old fathers Ambrose and Augustine. . . .

We say that the bread and wine [in the sacrament of thanksgiving or the Lord's Supper] are holy and heavenly mysteries of the body and blood of Christ, and that in them Christ himself, the true bread of eternal life, is so presently delivered unto us that we do truly receive his body and blood through faith. Nevertheless we do not so speak it, as though we supposed that the natures of bread and wine were utterly changed and came to nothing, as many in these last ages have dreamed, though hetherto they could never well agree among themself of their dream. . . .

And in like wise say we that without faith the sacraments of Christ profit nothing, no, not the living, much less them that be dead. For as touching that they are wont to boast them of their purgatory, although we know it is not very newly invented, yet it is nothing but mere foolish and an old wife's tale. . . .

Touching the multitude of idle ceremonies, we know St. Augustine grievously complained of them in his time. Wherefore we have cut off a great number of them bicause we knew that men's consciences were grievously cumbered with them and the Church of God burthened.

Nevertheless we do retain and reverently exercise not only such as we know were commended unto us by the apostles, but also certain others, such as seemed unto us might be borne without any hurt in the church, bicause we would have all things done in the holy assembly, according as St. Paul commandeth, comely and in order. Again, all such as we perceived to be other very superstitious, or cold, or filthy, or foolish, or contrary to the Holy Scriptures, or that were unfit for men that had their right wits (of which sort of ceremonies there be at this day in the papacy an infinite number) without exception we have utterly refused bicause we would not have the right worship of God any longer defiled with such foolishness.

We pray, as it is meet, in that tongue which every man amongst us doth understand to th' intent that the people, as Paul doth admonish us, by the common prayer may receive a common profit according as all the good fathers and Catholic bishops, not only in the Old Testament but also in the New, both did pray themselfs and taught the people to pray also, lest that, as St. Augustine saith, like popingays and blackbirds we might seem to pronounce that thing which we know not what it meaneth. . . .

All pardoners, dataries, collectors, bawds, and others that think gain to be godliness, and serve not Jesus Christ but their own bellies, do grievously complain of us at this day, for in time past this kind of men had good days in the old world. But now whatsoever increase cometh unto Christ, that think they turneth them to loss. This is hit whereupon the pope himself complaineth at this day, that charity forsooth is waxen cold bycause his rents are less now then they were wont to be. Thus he bringeth us into hatered all that he may, and raileth upon us and condemneth us for heretics to the intent that they which understand not the matter should think there were no worse men upon earth. Yet we for all this nother are nor ought to be ashamed of the Gospel. For we regard more the glory of God then the estimation of men. We know that all these things which we do teach are true, neither can we either use violence against the knowledge of our own conscience nother yet present ourselfs as witnesses against God. For if we deny any part of the Gospel of Jesus Christ before men, he on the other side will deny us again before his Father. Now if there be any that will be offended and may not endure the doctrine of Christ, they be blind themself and leaders of such as are blind; nevertheless the truth must be preached and set forth by our open profession of the same, and patiently we must look for the judgment of God to come. In the meanwhile let these men take heed what they do; let them have some regard of their own salvation, and let them cease to hate and to persecute the Gospel of the Son of God lest at the length they find him to be the punisher and revenger of his own cause. God will not suffer himself to be mocked. Men do see already how the matter goeth. This flame, the more it is kept under, so much the more and more it breaketh out and flieth abroad. Their unfaithfulness shall not deface the faith of God, but if they dispose not themself to lay away this hardness of their hearts and to receive the Gospel the publicans and sinners shall go before them into the kingdom of God.

God, the Father of our Lord Jesus Christ, open all their eyes that they may see that same blessed hope whereunto they are called, that we may all together in one worship that same only and true God and that same Jesus Christ whom he sent down to us from heaven. To whom together with the Father and the Holy Ghost be given all honor and glory forever and ever. Amen.

JOHN FOXE

ACTS AND MONUMENTS

John Foxe's *Acts and Monuments* was one of the most popular and least artful literary by-products of the English Reformation. Like Ascham, Foxe was of the generation of Protestants who learned their Latin and their theology from such men as Tyndale, Cheke, Latimer, and Ridley, and then emerged onto the turbulent political scene of the mid-century. The result for most of them— and Foxe was no exception—was a life strenuously dedicated to perfecting the Reformation which Henry VIII had started and which his daughter Mary sought to destroy.

Foxe himself, who had resigned his fellowship at Magdalen College, Oxford, over a point of theology in 1545, began as an author with inflammatory Protestant tracts. Ordained by Bishop Ridley in 1550, his exile (1554–59) during Mary's bloody reign was inevitable for a man of his unyielding views. First at Strassburg and then at Basle he labored tirelessly at theological tracts, propaganda, and Protestant politics, writing pamphlets in both Latin and English, a once-famous apocalyptic drama in five acts (*Christus triumphans,* 1556), and the *Commentarii rerum in ecclesia gestarum* (1554), a Protestant martyrology that may be regarded as the first draft of the *Acts and Monuments.* The reign of terror in England provided almost daily work for a martyrologist of Foxe's energies, and Edmund Grindal urged him to write up the persecutions of notables like Bradford, Cranmer, and Philpot. Having done so, Foxe resolved to carry on with a systematic history (in Latin) of English martyrs down through Mary's reign. Completed in six books (and incorporating the earlier *Commentarii*), this work was published at Basle in 1559 (with a dedication to the Duke of Norfolk, a former pupil of Foxe) as *Rerum in ecclesia gestarum . . . commentarii.* Returning to England as soon as his great work was through the press, Foxe was ordained a priest by Grindal (now the Bishop of London) and presumably set to work at once on an English translation and expansion of the *Rerum in ecclesia gestarum . . . commentarii.* At last, on March 20, 1563, the printer John Day, a friend and perhaps a business associate of Foxe, published the *Acts and Monuments.*

Its instantaneous success won for its author not only such immediate rewards as a handsome purse from Magdalen, his old college, and a prebend's stall at Salisbury Cathedral (the gift of Bishop Jewel), but also a secure place in English ecclesiastical history. The second edition of 1570, in two volumes, was, at the command of Convocation, placed in every cathedral church, and, as the decades rolled by, Foxe's *Book of Martyrs,* as it was commonly called, found its way into many homes which boasted of only one other book, the Bible. There were new editions (in two volumes) in 1576 and 1583, an abridgment by Timothy Bright (author of the well-known *Treatise of Melancholy*) in 1589, a reissue of the second volume in 1597, and other complete editions in 1596, 1610, and 1632 (the last in three volumes). The edition of 1641 was prefaced by a life of Foxe, allegedly the work of his son Samuel, but of questionable authenticity. Later editions are legion, some of those in the nineteenth century being so grossly mutilated and expanded as to be hardly recognizable. As early as 1566 Foxe's veracity was questioned by Nicholas Harpsfield (the biographer of More) in his *Sex dialogi;* the celebrated (or notorious) Jesuit Robert Parsons denounced Foxe's work as a pack of lies in his *Treatise of Three Conversions* in 1603; and Archbishop Laud refused to license a new edition in 1638, an act of impiety for which he was duly charged at his examination in 1641 before being committed to the Tower. In spite of sporadic attacks, however, *The Book of Martyrs* quickly gained and long retained a unique position in the affections of pious Englishmen.

Although the work grew by massive exfoliations and expansions in later editions, the 1563 volume is sufficiently staggering. A tightly printed volume of nearly two thousand pages, it is introduced by prefatory matter consisting of a prayer "Ad Dominum Iesum Christum," a "Kalender" of martyrs in almanac form, an epistle to the queen, an epistle "Ad doctum lectorem," a scathing epistle "To the Persecutors of God's Truth, Commonly Called Papists," and "A Declaration Concerning the Utility and Profit of This History" translated from the *Rerum in ecclesia gestarum . . . commentarii* of 1559. The body of the work is appalling in its bulk and its titanic disorder. Foxe arranges his narratives after a rough and ready fashion into six books corresponding to the six principal periods in the history of Catholic persecutions since the Middle Ages, and he does preserve (or try to preserve) a chronological sequence in cataloguing the iniquities of the Roman church. Actually the book is a jungle of state papers (in both Latin and English), legal depositions, horrendous woodcuts of tortures and executions, grossly prejudiced history, propaganda, and (most important) Protestant martyrologies. It was the martyrologies, written with the zeal and the simplicity of a passionate man, that made the book famous. Foxe's accounts of such personages as Lord Cobham, Wyclif, and Hus are copious and often grotesquely prejudiced; but when he reaches his own century, and especially the persecutions of Bloody Mary, his tales of Protestant martyrs acquire a dramatic vigor that brings us very close indeed to the passion and the zeal of those turbulent years. Our text is based upon *Actes and Monuments of these latter and perillous dayes, touching matters of the Church, wherein ar comprehended and described the great persecutions & horrible troubles, that have bene wrought and practised by the Romishe Prelates, speciallye in this Realme of England and Scotlande, from the yeare of our Lorde a thousande, unto the tyme nowe present,* 1563 (STC 11222).

FROM ACTS AND MONUMENTS OF THESE LATTER AND PERILOUS DAYS TOUCHING MATTERS OF THE CHURCH (1563)

A Declaration Concerning the Utility and Profit of This History

. . . If we be wont gladly to occupy ourselves in other chronicles that do only entreat upon matters of policy, and do (as a man would say) rejoice to behold therein the divers haps of worldly affairs, the stratagems of capitains and men of war, the roar of foughten fields, the sacking of cities, the great hurly-burly of realms and people; and besides if we think 10 it very expedient for a commonwealth to keep antiquity in remembrance that is but prophane, to deck, trim, and set that out with the ornaments of wit and eloquence, how much more, then, is it meet for us to accept and embrace the lives and doings, not of rough warriors, but of most mild and constant martyrs, which may serve not so much to delight the ear as to garnish the life, to frame it with examples of great profit, and to enstruct the mind in all kind of Christian godliness. For first of all, they geve a lively 20 testimony that there is One above which ruleth all, contrary to the opinion of the godless and the whole nest of Epicures. Like as one said of Harpalus in times past, that his doings did truly testify that there was no God, because, in suffering of him a great space together, God seemed to neglect all care of reasonable creatures; so contrariwise, in these men we have an assured and plain witness of God, in whose life appeared a certain force of divine nature, and in their death a far greater signification whiles in such sharp- 30 ness of torments we beheld in them a strength so constant above man's reach, a readiness to answer, patience in prison, godliness in forgeving, cheerfulness in suffering, besides the manifold sense and feeling of the Holy Ghost, which they learned in many of their comforts, and we by them. Over and besides this, the mild deaths of the saints do much prevail for the attaining of a good conscience and the contempt of the world, and to come to the fear of God. They confirm the faith, encrease godliness, abate pride in prosperity, and in adversity do open an hope of heavenly comfort. For what is he that in the misery of the godly may not be put in mind of his own case, whether he be himself godly or godless. For if God geve adversity unto good men, what may either the better sort promise themselves or the evil not fear? And whereas for the most part we become more cunning by reading of prophane stories, by this, if we list, we are made the better in our livings, and besides are animated unto like conflicts, if by God's permission they shall happen hereafter, as men becoming wiser by their doctrine and more steadfast by their example. To be short, they declare to the world what true fortitude is, and a way to conquer which standeth not in the power of man but in hope of the resurrection to come, and is now, I trust, at hand. In consideration whereof methinks I have good cause to wish that like as other men, even so the heroical wits of kings and princes, which for the most part are delighted with heroical stories, would carry about with them such monuments of martyrs as this is, and lay them always in sight, not alonely to read, but to follow, and would paint them upon their walls, cups, rings, and gates. For undoubtedly these martyrs are much more worthy of this honor then six hundred Alexanders, Hectors, Scipios, and warring Julies. For though this world do judge preposterously of things, yet with God, the judge of all men, they are most reputed indeed, not that kill one another with a weapon (for by that reason we may attribute the renoum of fortitude unto bears, lions, wolves, leopards), but they which being constantly killed in God's cause do retain still an invincible spirit and stomach against the threats of tyrants and injuries of tormentors. These undoubtedly are the true conquerors of the world, at whose hand we learn true manhood, so many as fight under Christ and not under the world. . . .

Let us not shrink or make much ado if the case require martyrdom or loss of our lives; but, according to their example, let us yield up the same in the defense of the Lord's flock. Which thing, if men would do, much less contention and business would be in the world then there is. And thus much touching the utility and fruit to be taken of this history. After these things thus premised, now, the Lord Jesus prospering us with his grace, let us enter into the matter thereof, deducing the course of the said history from the time of the thousand year after Christ, that is from the beginning of these last five hundreth years, unto this present time as by the contents hereof may appear.

Acts and Monuments Touching Things Done and Practised by the Prelates of the Romish Church . . .

The Latter Enprisoning and Death of the Lord Cobham

. . . Upon the day appointed he was brought out of the Tower with his arms bound behind him, having a very cheerful countenance. Than was he laid upon an hardle, as though he had been a most hainous traitor to the crown, and so drawn forth into Saint Giles' Field whereas they had set up a new pair of gallows. As he was comen to the place of execution and was taken from the hardle he fell down devoutly upon his knees, desiring Almighty God to forgeve his enemies. Than stood he up and beheld the multitude, exhorting them in most godly manner to follow the laws of God written in the Scriptures, and in any wise to beware of such teachers as they see contrary to Christ in their conversation and living, with many other special counsels. Than was he hanged up there by the middle in chains of iron and so consumed alive in the fire, praising the name of God so long as his life lasted. In the end he commended his soul into the hands of God, and so departed hence most Christenly, his body resolved into ashes.

And this was done in the year of our Lord 1418, which was the sixt year of the reign of King Henry the Fift, the people there present shewing great dolor.

How the priests that time fared, blasphemed, and accursed, requiring the people not to pray for him but to judge him dampned in hell for that he departed not in the obedience of their pope, it were too long to write.

This terrible kind of death with gallows, chains, and fire appeareth not very precious in the eyes of men that be carnal, no more than did the death of Christ whan he was hanged up among thieves. The righteous seemeth to die, saith the wise man, in the sight of them which are unwise, and their end is taken for very destruction. Ungodly fools thinketh their lives very madness and their passage hence without all honor. But though they suffer pain before men, saith he, yet is their expectation full of immortality. They are accounted for the children of God and have their just portion among the saincts. As gold in the fornace doth God try his elect, and as a most pleasant brent offering receiveth he them to rest.

The more hard the passage be, the more glorious shall they appear in the latter resurrection. Not that the afflictions of this life are worthy of such a glory, but that it is God's heavenly pleasure so to reward them. Never are the judgments and ways of men like unto the judgments and ways of God, but contrary evermore unless they be taught of him. In the latter time, saith the Lord unto Daniel, shall many be chosen, proved, and purified by fire, yet shall the ungodly live wickedly still and have no understanding that is of faith. By an angel from heaven was John earnestly commanded to write that blessed are the dead which hence departeth in the Lord. Right dear, saith David, in the sight of God is the death of his true servants. Thus resteth this valiant Christen knight, Sir John Oldcastle, under the altar of God, which is Jesus Christ, among that godly company which in the kingdom of patience suff'red great tribulation with the death of their bodies for his faithful word and testimony, abiding there with them, he fulfilling of their whole number and the full restoration of his elects. The which be grant in effect at this time appointed, which is one God eternal. Amen.

Thus have you hard the whole matter concerning the martyrdom of the good Lord Cobham as we have gathered it partly out of the collectors of John Bale and others. Now if there be any that require the old monuments of the bishops themselves which had the doing in the matter for a further testimony to satisfy their minds, we have here annexed the epistle of Thomas Arundel, Archbishop of Canterbury, his persecutor therewithal, though it be not greatly necessary for the history sufficiently declared before, yet for th' antiquity thereof we thought it not to be omitted. . . .

[The Execution of More and Fisher]

The king, . . . calling his high court of Parliament, caused it to be provided by sufficient acts, the pope to be utterly abolished and he himself to be established and proclaimed supreme head of the Church of England, which thing the Bishop of Rochester and Sir Thomas More (whom ye have heard before were the autors of Frith's death), grudging against and in no wise willing to consent thereunto, but manifestly and openly resisting the same, they were accused and condempned of treason and beheaded at Tower Hill.

In like manner the same year was three Charterhouse monks hanged, drawn, and quartered at Tyburn for speaking divers traitorous words against the king's Majesty and obstinately persevered in the same even until their death. . . .

The Behavior of Doctor Ridley at His Supper the Night before His Suffering

The night before he suffered, his beard was washed and his legs; and as he sat at supper the same night at Maister Irishe's (who was his keeper) he bad his hosts and the rest at the bourd to his marriage. "For," saith he, "tomorrow I must be married." And so shewed himself to be as merry as ever he was at any time before. And wishing his sister at his marriage, he asked his brother (sitting at the table) whether she could find in her heart to be there or no, and she answered, "Yea, I dare say, with all her heart." At which word he said he was glad to hear of her so much therein. So at this talk Maistress Irishe wept.

But Maister Ridley comforted her and said, "O Maistress Irishe, you love me not now, I see well inough. For in that you weep it doth appear you will not be at my marriage, neither is content therewith. Indeed, you be not so much my friend as I thought you had been. But quiet yourself; though my breakfast shall be something sharp and painful, yet I am sure my supper shall be more pleasant and sweet." And when they rose from the table his brother offered him to watch all night with him. But he said, "No, no, that you shall not. For I mind, God willing, to go to bed and to sleep as quietly tonight as ever I did in my life." So his brother departed, exhorting him to be of good cheer and to take his cross quietly, for the reward was great, etc.

The Behavior of Doctor Ridley and Maister Latimer at the Time of Their Death

Upon the north side of the town, in the ditch over against Baily College, the place of execution was appointed; and for fear of any tumult that might arise to let the burning of them, my Lord Williams was commanded by the queen's letters and the house-holders of the city to be there assistant, sufficiently appointed. And when everything was in a readiness, they were brought to the stake by the mayor and bailiffs: Maister Ridley in a fair black gown, such as he was wont to wear when he was bishop, with a tippet of sables about his neck, nothing undressed; Maister Latimer in a poor Bristol frise frock all worn, with his buttoned cap and a kerchief on his head all ready to the fire, a new long shroud hanging over his hose down to his feet, which at the first sight stirred men's hearts to rue upon them, beholding on the one side the honor they sometime had, on the other the calamity whereunto they were then descended.

Maister Doctor Ridley, as he passed towards Bocardo, he looked up where Maister Cranmer did lie, and belike he would have seen him at the glass window, to have spoken unto him. But then Maister Cranmer was busy with Frier Soto and his fellows, disputing together, so that he could not see him through that occasion. Then Maister Ridley, looking back, espied Maister Latimer coming after. Unto whom he said, "O, be ye there?" "Yea," said Maister Latimer, "have after, as fast as I can follow." So he following a pretty way off, at length they came both to the stake one after the other, where first Doctor Ridley ent'ring the place, marvelous earnestly holding up both his hands, looked towards heaven, and so forth, and with a glimpse of his eye aside espying Maister Latimer, with a wonderful cheerful look ran unto him, and embraced and kissed him, and as they that stood near reported, comforted him, saying: "Be of good heart, brother, for God will either assuage the fury of the flame, or else strengthen us to abide it." With that went he to the stake, kneeled down by it, kissed it, most effectuously prayed, and behind him Maister Latimer kneeled, as earnestly calling upon God as he. After they arose, the one talked with the other a little while, till they which were appointed to see the execution, removed themselves out of the sun. What they said, I can learn of no man. Then Doctor Smith began his sermon to them upon this text of Sainct Paul in the thirteenth chapter of the first Epistle to the Corinthians: *Si corpus meum tradam igni, charitatem autem non habeo, nihil inde utilitatis capio,* which is thus much in English: "If I yield my body to the fire to be burnt, and have not charity, I shall gain nothing thereby." Wherein he alledged that the goodness of the cause nor the holiness of the person should not be judged by the order of the death, which he confirmed by the examples of Judas, and of a woman in Oxford that of late hanged herself, for that then they and such like (as he or two or three other recited) might be adjudged righteous, which desperately sund'red their lives from their bodies, as he feared that those men that stood before him would do. But he cried still to the people to beware of theim. For they were heretiques and died out of the Church. And on the other side, he declared their diversity in opinions, as Lutherans, Oecolampadians, Zwinlians, of which sect they were, and that was the worst. But the old Church of Christ and the Catholic Faith believed far otherwise. At which place they lifted up both hands and their eyes to heaven, as it were calling God to witness of the truth.

The which countenance they made in many other places of his sermon, whereas they thought he spake amiss: he ended with a very short exhortation to theim, to recant and come home again to the Church, and save their lives and souls, which else were condemned. His sermon was scant in all a quarter of an hour.

Doctor Ridley said unto Maister Latimer: "Will you begin to answer the sermon, or shall I?" Maister Latimer said: "Begin you first, I pray you." "I will," said Maister Ridley. Then the wicked sermon being ended, Doctor Ridley and Maister Latimer kneeled down upon their knees, towards my Lord Williams of Tame, the vice-chancellor of Oxford, and divers other commissioners appointed for that purpose, which sat upon a form thereby, unto whom Maister Ridley said: "I beseech you, my lord, even for Christ's sake, that I may speak but two or three words," and whilest my lord bent his head to the mayor and vice-chancellor, as it appeared, to know whether he might geve him leave to speak, the bailiffs and Doctor Marshall vice-chancellor ran hastily unto him, and with their hands stopped his mouth, and said: "Maister Ridley, if you will revoke your erroneous opinions and recant the same, you shall not only have liberty so to do, but also the benefit of a subject, that is, have your life."

"Not otherwise?" said Maister Ridley. "No," quod Doctor Marshall. "Therefore if you will not do so, then there is no remedy but you must suffer for your deserts." "Well," quod Maister Ridley, "so long as the breath is in my body, I will never deny my Lord God and his known truth. God's will be done in me." And with that he rose up, and said with a loud voice: "Well, then, I commit our cause to Almighty God, which shall indifferently judge all." To whose saying Maister Latimer added his old posy, "Well, there is nothing hid but it shall be opened." And he said he could answer Smith well inough, if he might be suffered. Incontinently they were commanded to make theim ready, which they with all meekness obeyed. Maister Ridley took his gown and his tippet, and gave it to his brother-in-law, Maister Shepside, who all his time of emprisonment, although he might not be suffered to come to him, lay there

at his own charges, to provide him necessaries, which from time to time he sent him by the sergeant that kept him. Some other of his apparail that was little worth he gave away; other the bailiffs took.

He gave away besides divers other small things to gentlemen standing by, and divers of theim pitifully weeping, as to Sir Henry Lee he gave a new groat, and to divers of my Lord Williams' gentlemen some napkins, some nutmegs, and raisins of ginger, his dial, and such other things as he had about him to everyone that stood next him. Some plucked the points of his hose; happy was he that might get any rag of him. Maister Latimer gave nothing, but very quietly suffered his keeper to pull off his hose and his other array, which to look unto was very simple. And being stripped into his shroud, seemed as comely a person to them that were there present as one should lightly see. And whereas in his clothes he appeared a withered and crooked sely old man, he now stood bolt upright, as comely a father as one might lightly behold.

Then Maister Ridley, standing as yet in his truss, said to his brother: "It were best for me to go in my truss still." "No," quod his brother, "it will put you to more pain; and the truss will do a poor man good." Whereunto Maister Ridley said, "Be it in the name of God," and so unlaced himself. Then being in his shirt, he stood upon the foresaid stone, and held up his hands, and said, "O heavenly Father, I geve unto thee most hearty thanks for that thou hast called me to be a professor of thee, even unto death. I beseech thee, Lord God, take mercy upon this realm of England, and deliver the same from all her enemies."

Then the smith took a chain of iron and brought the same about both Doctor Ridley and Maister Latimer's middles. And as he was knocking in a staple, Doctor Ridley took the chain in his hand, and shaked the same, for it did gird in his belly, and looking aside to the smith, said, "Good fellow, knock it in hard, for the flesh will have his course." Then his brother did bring him gunpowder in a bag, and would have tied the same about his neck. Maister Ridley asked what it was; his brother said, "Gunpowder." Then said he, "I take it to be sent of God; therefore I will receive it, as sent of him. And have you any," said he, "for my brother?"—meaning Maister Latimer. "Yea, sir, that I have," quod his brother. "Then geve it unto him," said he, "betime, lest you come too late." So his brother went and carried the same gunpowder unto Maister Latimer. The meantime Doctor Ridley spake unto my Lord Williams and said, "My lord, I must be a suitor unto your lordship in the behalf of diverse poor men, and especially in the cause of my poor sister. I have made a supplication to the queen's Majesty in their behalfs.

I beseech your lordship for Christ's sake to be a mean to her Grace for them. My brother here hath the supplication, and will resort to your lordship to certify you hereof. There is nothing in all the world that troubleth my conscience (I praise God), this only excepted. Whiles I was in the See of London, diverse poor men took leases of me, and agreed with me for the same. Now I hear say, the bishop that now occupieth the same room will not allow my grants unto theim made, but contrary unto all law and conscience hath taken from theim their livings, and will not suffer them to enjoy the same. I beseech you, my lord, be a mean for theim; you shall do a good deed, and God will reward you." Then brought they a faggot kindled with fire, and laid the same down at Doctor Ridley's feet; and when he saw the fire flaming up toward him, he cried with a wonderful loud voice, "*In manus tuas, Domine, commendo spiritum meum; Domine, recipe spiritum meum.*" And after repeated this latter part often in English: "Lord, Lord, receive my spirit." Maister Latimer, crying as vehemently on the other side, "O Father of heaven, receive my soul," who received the flame as it were embracing it. After, as he had stroked his face with his hands, and as it were bathed them a little in the fire, soon died, as it appeared with very little pain or none.

But Maister Ridley, by reason of the evil making of the fire unto him, because the wooden faggots were laid about the gorse and overhigh built, the fire burned first beneath, being kept down by the wood. Which when he felt, he desired theim for Christ's sake to let the fire come unto him. Which when his brother-in-law heard, but not well understood, entending to rid him of his pain (for the which cause he gave attendance), as one in such sorrow, not well advised what he did, heaped faggots upon him that he clean covered him, which made the fire more vehement beneath, that it burned clean all his nether parts before it once touched the upper, and that made him leap up and down under the faggots, and often desire theim to let the fire come unto him, saying, "I cannot burn," which indeed appeared well. For after his legs were consumed by reason of his struggling with the pain (whereof he had no release but only his contentation in God) he shewed that side towards us clean, shirt and all untouched with the flame; yet in all this torment he forgat not to call unto God still, having in his mouth, "Lord, have mercy upon me," intermeddling this cry, "Let the fire come unto me; I cannot burn." In which pangs he laboreth till one of the standersby with his bill pulled off the faggots above, and where he espied the fire flame up, he wrested himself unto that side. And when the flame touched the gunpowder he was seen stir no more, but

espied burning on the other side by Maister Latimer. Which some said happened by reason that the chain loosed; other said that he fell over the chain by reason of the poise of his body and the weakness of the nether limbs.

Some say that before he was like to fall from the stake he desired them to hold him to it with their bills. Howsoever it was, surely it moved hundreds to tears to behold the horrible sight. For I think there was none that had not clean exiled all humanity and mercy which would not have lamented to behold the fury of the fire to rage upon their bodies. Signs there were of sorrow on every side. Some took it grievously to see their deaths, whose lives they held full dear. Some pitied their persons, that thought their souls had no need thereof. His brother moved many men, seeing his miserable case, seeing, I say, him compelled to such infelicity that he thought then to do him best service when he hastened his end. Some cried out of fortune to see his endeavor, who most dearly loved him and sought his release, turn to his greater vexation and encrease of pain. But whoso considered their preferments in time past, the places of honor that they sometime occupied in this commonwealth, the favor they were in with their princes, and the opinion of learning they had in the university they studied, could not choose but sorrow with tears to see so great dignity, honor, and estimation, so necessary members sometime accompted, so many godly virtues, the study of so many years, such excellent learning, to be put into the fire, and consumed in one moment. Well, dead they are, and the reward of this world they have already.

THE SIXT TOME OR SECTION OF THE ECCLESIASTICAL HISTORY CONTAINING SUCH ACTS AND RECORDS AS HAPPENED IN THE MOST FLORISHING REIGN OF QUEEN ELIZABETH

Having thus, by the power of the Almighty, plainly and truly displayed the cruel practises and horrible persecutions of Queen Mary's reign, freely and boldly describing her tragical story where view is to be had of many things no less marveilous then miserable, no less dangerous then dolorous, no less uncharitable then unnatural; and now orderly coming to the florishing and long-wished-for reign of the most noble, virtuous, and renowned sister of the said Mary, this our dread and sovereign mistress and governess Queen Elizabeth, I thought my traveled pen not a little refreshed with ease and gladness, not so much for that having now overpassed the bitter and sorrowful matters of such terrible burning, imprisoning, murdering, famishing, racking, and tormenting, and spiteful handeling of the pitiful bodies of Christ's blessed saints, as also for that we are now ent'ring into the time and reign of such a worthy princess and queen, the remembrance and story whereof minist'reth not so much unto me matter to write upon as also delectation to labor and travail about the same. For what man reputing with himself the singular ornaments and noble graces given of God to this so princely a lady and puissant princess, the mildness of her nature, the clemency of her royal estate and majesty, the peaceableness of her reign, who, a virgin, so mildly ruleth men, governeth her subjects, keepeth all things in order, quieteth forain nations, recovereth towns, inlargeth her kingdom, nourisheth and concileth amity, uniteth hearts and love with forren enemies, helpeth neighbors, reformeth religion, quencheth persecution, redresseth the dross, frameth things out of joint, so feared with such love and so loved with such fear—what man considering this, I say, either can hold his pen, though he never wrote before, or being never so much wearied with writing will not shake off all tediousness, ent'ring into a matter so pleasant and delectable to entreat upon? . . .

RICHARD HOOKER

OF THE LAWS OF ECCLESIASTICAL POLITY

When in 1585 Hooker was named Master of the Temple by the Archbishop of Canterbury, he was quickly drawn into a defense of the Anglican establishment against the charges of Walter Travers, a zealous puritan who served as afternoon lecturer at the Temple, and who had been passed over in Hooker's favor. Their disagreements—pure Canterbury in the morning and Geneva in the afternoon, as Thomas Fuller later put it—focused the question that was to agitate English Protestants for another half-century and more: whether the Anglican Church (whose discipline and doctrine had been fixed by the Elizabethan Settlement of 1560–61) should surrender to the puritan demands for abolishing its prelatical organization in favor of the Genevan system prescribed in Calvin's *Institutes*. Although neither Elizabeth nor the early Stuarts showed the least intention of yielding to the puritans, to a man of Hooker's judicious and philosophical temper it was a moral compulsion to defend the Establishment on the basis of something other than *de facto* supremacy; and so, in 1591, he requested a country benefice where he might have the leisure to supply his church with a full-breathed defense on both philosophical and theological grounds.

Squarely meeting his antagonists' claim that every point of ecclesiastical discipline and ritual should have a specific Scriptural sanction, Hooker enlarges the area of discussion to include principles of reason, natural law, history, and tradition with which he countered the puritans' literalism. In his broad view, as nobly expounded in Book I of the *Laws,* God's creation is essentially rational, and therefore governed by a natural law which the Scriptures do not contradict but rather supplement and confirm. This natural law, embodying God's eternal reason, is the supreme authority in ecclesiastical as well as civil conduct, and therefore the Anglican Church, an institution established by law, must seek its sanctions in both law and Scripture.

First at Boscombe in Wiltshire, and then at Bishopsbourne near Canterbury, Hooker passed the rest of his life in developing his great thesis. The result is not only the classical statement of Anglican rationalism but also a monument of Elizabethan prose. By January 26, 1593, he was far enough along in his task to permit John Windet, a publisher, to begin the printing. Although Windet's small folio announces the full eight books, and lists the "things handled" therein, it actually contains only four books. The (very long) fifth book appeared in 1597 as a separate volume. No further editions were published before Hooker's death (on November 2, 1600), but in 1604 the first four books were reissued under John Spenser's supervision, and in 1611 there appeared a third edition of Books I–IV and a second of Book V. Although there were several new editions during the early seventeenth century, not until 1648 were the sixth and eighth books printed together as a work long expected, the editor apologizing for his failure to find a manuscript of Book VII. At last, in 1662, John Gauden's edition of Hooker's works provided the seventh book, and so the canon was finally complete. Inevitably, the authenticity of the three posthumously published books has been questioned. In his charming *Life* of Hooker published with the 1666 edition Izaak Walton charged Mrs. Hooker and her son-in-law Ezekiel Charke with destroying her husband's manuscripts, a charge lent credence by John Spenser's assertion (in his edition of 1604) that, although Hooker's papers survived only in "old, unperfect, and mangled draughts, dismembered into pieces" by malignant persons, it was intended that the world "shall see them as they are." When Spenser died (as president of Corpus Christi College, Oxford) in 1614, his collection of Hooker's papers passed to John King, Bishop of London, and then, after King's death, to Archbishop Abbot, who conveyed them to the Lambeth Palace library sometime before 1633. William Prynne, the notorious Presbyterian, gained control of the library after Archbishop Laud's downfall in 1640; and in 1644 the Long Parliament turned over Hooker's manuscripts to

Hugh Peters, another rabid puritan. Thereafter their history cannot be traced, but the careful work of modern scholars has fairly demonstrated (largely on the basis of internal evidence) that Books VI–VIII as we have them were probably worked up from Hooker's own rough notes. Our text is based upon *Of the Lawes of Ecclesiasticall Politie*, 1594 (STC 13712).

FROM OF THE LAWS OF ECCLESIASTICAL POLITY (1594)

BOOK I

I. He that goeth about to persuade a multitude that they are not so well governed as they ought to be shall never want attentive and favorable hearers; because they know the manifold defects whereunto every kind of regiment is subject, but the secret lets and difficulties, which in public proceedings are innumerable and inevitable, they have not ordinarily the judgment to consider. And because such as openly reprove supposed disorders of state are taken for principal friends to the common benefit of all, and for men that carry singular freedom of mind; under this fair and plausible color whatsoever they utter passeth for good and currant. That which wanteth in the weight of their speech is supplied by the aptness of men's minds to accept and believe it. Whereas on the other side, if we maintain things that are established, we have not only to strive with a number of heavy prejudices deeply rooted in the hearts of men, who think that herein we serve the time, and speak in favor of the present state because thereby we either hold or seek preferment; but also to bear such exceptions as minds so averted beforehand usually take against that which they are loth should be poured into them.

Albeit therefore much of that we are to speak in this present cause may seem to a number perhaps tedious, perhaps obscure, dark, and intricate (for many talk of the truth which never sounded the depth from whence it springeth; and therefore when they are led thereunto they are soon weary, as men drawn from those beaten paths wherewith they have been inured); yet this may not so far prevail as to cut off that which the matter itself requireth, howsoever the nice humor of some be therewith pleased or no. They unto whom we shall seem tedious are in no wise injuried by us, because it is in their own hands to spare that labor which they are not willing to indure. And if any complain of obscurity, they must consider that in these matters it cometh no otherwise to pass then

in sundry the works both of art and also of nature, where that which hath greatest force in the very things we see is notwithstanding itself oftentimes not seen. The stateliness of houses, the goodliness of trees, when we behold them delighteth the eye; but that foundation which beareth up the one, that root which minist'reth unto the other nourishment and life, is in the bosom of the earth concealed; and if there be at any time occasion to search into it, such labor is then more necessary then pleasant, both to them which undertake it and for the lookers-on. In like manner, the use and benefit of good laws all that live under them may enjoy with delight and comfort, albeit the grounds and first original causes from whence they have sprong be unknown, as to the greatest part of men they are. But when they who withdraw their obedience pretend that the laws which they should obey are corrupt and vicious, for better examination of their quality it behooveth the very foundation and root, the highest well-spring and fountain of them, to be discovered. Which because we are not oftentimes accustomed to do, when we do it the pains we take are more needful a great deal then acceptable, and the matters which we handle seem by reason of newness (till the mind grow better acquainted with them) dark, intricate, and unfamiliar. For as much help whereof as may be in this case, I have endeavored throughout the body of this whole discourse that every former part might give strength unto all that follow, and every later bring some light unto all before. So that if the judgments of men do but hold themselves in suspense as touching these first more general meditations till in order they have perused the rest that ensue, what may seem dark at the first will afterwards be found more plain, even as the later particular decisions will appear, I doubt not, more strong when the other have been read before.

The laws of the Church, whereby for so many ages together we have been guided in the exercise of Christian religion and the service of the true God, our rites, customs, and orders of ecclesiastical government are called in question; we are accused as men that will not have Christ Jesus to rule over them, but have wilfully cast his statutes behind their backs, hating to be reformed and made subject unto the scepter of his discipline. Behold, therefore, we offer the laws whereby we live unto the general trial and judgment of the whole world; heartily beseeching Almighty God, whom we desire to serve according to his own will, that both we and others (all kind of partial affection being clean laid aside) may have eyes to see and hearts to embrace the things that in his sight are most acceptable.

And because the point about which we strive is the quality of our laws, our first entrance hereinto cannot better be made then with consideration of the nature of law in general, and of that law which giveth life unto all the rest which are commendable, just, and good; namely, the law whereby the Eternal himself doth work. Proceeding from hence to the law, first of nature, then of Scripture, we shall have the easier access unto those things which come after to be debated, concerning the particular cause and question which we have in hand.

II. All things that are have some operation not violent or casual. Neither doth anything ever begin to exercise the same without some foreconceived end for which it worketh. And the end which it worketh for is not obtained unless the work be also fit to obtain it by. For unto every end every operation will not serve. That which doth assign unto each thing the kind, that which doth moderate the force and power, that which doth appoint the form and measure of working, the same we term a law. So that no certain end could ever be attained unless the actions whereby it is attained were regular; that is to say, made suitable, fit, and correspondent unto their end, by some canon, rule, or law. Which thing doth first take place in the works even of God himself.

All things therefore do work after a sort according to law; all other things according to a law whereof some superior, unto whom they are subject, is author; only the works and operations of God have him both for their worker and for the law whereby they are wrought. The being of God is a kind of law to his working; for that perfection which God is geveth perfection to that he doth. Those natural, necessary, and internal operations of God, the generation of the Son, the proceeding of the Spirit, are without the compass of my present intent; which is to touch only such operations as have their beginning and being by a voluntary purpose, wherewith God hath eternally decreed when and how they should be. Which eternal decree is that we term an eternal law.

Dangerous it were for the feeble brain of man to wade far into the doings of the Most High; whom although to know be life, and joy to make mention of his name, yet our soundest knowledge is to know that we know him not as indeed he is, neither can know him; and our safest eloquence concerning him is our silence, when we confess without confession that his glory is inexplicable, his greatness above our capacity and reach. He is above, and we upon earth; therefore it behoveth our words to be wary and few.

Our God is one, or rather very Oneness, and mere unity, having nothing but itself in itself, and not consisting (as all things do besides God) of many things. In which essential Unity of God a Trinity personal nevertheless subsisteth, after a manner far exceeding the possibility of man's conceipt. The works which outwardly are of God, they are in such sort of him being one that each Person hath in them somewhat peculiar and proper. For being three, and they all subsisting in the essence of one Deity (from the Father, by the Son, through the Spirit), all things are. That which the Son doth hear of the Father, and which the Spirit doth receive of the Father and the Son, the same we have at the hands of the Spirit as being the last and therefore the nearest unto us in order, although in power the same with the second and the first.

The wise and learned among the very heathens themselves have all acknowledged some first cause, whereupon originally the being of all things dependeth. Neither have they otherwise spoken of that cause then as an agent, which, knowing what and why it worketh, observeth in working a most exact order or law. Thus much is signified by that which Homer mentioneth, Διὸς δ' ἐτελείετο βουλή. Thus much acknowledged by Mercurius Trismegistus, Τὸν πάντα κόσμον ἐποίησεν ὁ δημιουργὸς οὐ χερσὶν ἀλλὰ λόγῳ. Thus much confess'd by Anaxagoras and Plato, terming the Maker of the world an *intellectual* Worker. Finally the Stoics, although imagining the first cause of all things to be fire, held nevertheless that the same fire having art did ὁδῷ βαδίζειν ἐπὶ γενέσει κόσμου. They all confess therefore in the working of that first cause that counsel is used, reason followed, a way observed; that is to say, constant order and law is kept; whereof itself must needs be author unto itself. Otherwise it should have some worthier and higher to direct it, and so could not itself be the first. Being the first, it can have no other then itself to be the author of that law which it willingly worketh by.

God therefore is a law both to himself and to all other things besides. To himself he is a law in all those things whereof our Savior speaketh, saying, "My Father worketh as yet, so I." God worketh nothing without cause. All those things which are done by him have some end for which they are done; and the end for which they are done is a reason of his will to do them. His will had not inclined to create woman, but that he saw it could not be well if she were not created. *Non est bonum:* "It is not good man should be alone; therefore let us make an helper for him." That and nothing else is done by God, which to leave undone were not so good.

If therefore it be demanded why, God having power and hability infinite, th' effects notwithstanding of that power are all so limited as we see they are, the reason hereof is the end which he hath proposed, and the law whereby his wisdom hath stinted th' effects of his power in such sort that it doth not work infinitely, but correspondently unto that end for which it worketh, even all things χρηστῶς, in most decent and comely sort, all things in measure, number, and weight.

The general end of God's external working is the exercise of his most glorious and most abundant virtue. Which abundance doth shew itself in variety, and for that cause this variety is oftentimes in Scripture express'd by the name of riches. "The Lord hath made all things for his own sake." Not that anything is made to be beneficial unto him, but all things for him to shew beneficence and grace in them.

The particular drift of every act proceeding externally from God we are not able to discern, and therefore cannot always give the proper and certain reason of his works. Howbeit undoubtedly a proper and certain reason there is of every finite work of God, inasmuch as there is a law imposed upon it; which if there were not, it should be infinite, even as the worker himself is.

They err therefore who think that of the will of God to do this or that there is no reason besides his will. Many times no reason known to us; but that there is no reason thereof I judge it most unreasonable to imagine, inasmuch as he worketh all things κατὰ τὴν βουλὴν τοῦ θελήματος αὐτοῦ, not only according to his own will, but "the counsel of his own will." And whatsoever is done with counsel or wise resolution hath of necessity some reason why it should be done, albeit that reason be to us in some things so secret that it forceth the wit of man to stand, as the blessed apostle himself doth, amazed thereat: "O the depth of the riches both of the wisdom and knowledge of God! How unsearchable are his judgments, etc." That law eternal which God himself hath made to himself, and thereby worketh all things whereof he is the cause and author; that law in the admirable frame whereof shineth with most perfect beauty the countenance of that wisdom which hath testified concerning herself, "The Lord possessed me in the beginning of his way; even before his works of old I was set up, etc."; that law which hath been the

pattern to make, and is the card to guide the world by; that law which hath been of God and with God everlastingly; that law, the author and observer whereof is one only God to be blessed forever; how should either men or angels be able perfectly to behold? The book of this law we are neither able nor worthy to open and look into. That little thereof which we darkly apprehend we admire, the rest with religious ignorance we humbly and meekly adore.

Seeing therefore that according to this law He worketh "of whom, through whom, and for whom, are all things"; although there seem unto us confusion and disorder in th' affairs of this present world, *Tamen quoniam bonus mundum rector temperat, recte fieri cuncta ne dubites:* "Let no man doubt but that everything is well done, because the world is ruled by so good a guide" as transgresseth not his own law, then which nothing can be more absolute, perfect, and just.

The law whereby he worketh is eternal, and therefore can have no shew or color of mutability; for which cause, a part of that law being opened in the promises which God hath made (because his promises are nothing else but declarations what God will do for the good of men), touching those promises the apostle hath witnessed that God may as possibly deny himself and not be God as fail to perform them. And concerning the counsel of God, he termeth it likewise a thing unchangeable; the counsel of God and that law of God whereof now we speak being one. Nor is the freedom of the will of God any whit abated, let, or hindered by means of this; because the imposition of this law upon himself is his own free and voluntary act. This law therefore we may name eternal, being that order which God before all ages hath set down with himself, for himself to do all things by.

III. I am not ignorant that by "law eternal" the learned for the most part do understand the order, not which God hath eternally purposed himself in all his works to observe, but rather that which with himself he hath set down as expedient to be kept by all his creatures, according to the several condition wherewith he hath indued them. They who thus are accustomed to speak apply the name of law unto that only rule of working which superior authority imposeth; whereas we, somewhat more enlarging the sense thereof, term any kind of rule or canon whereby actions are framed a law. Now that law which, as it is laid up in the bosom of God, they call eternal, receiveth according unto the different kinds of things which are subject unto it different and sundry kinds of names. That part of it which ordereth natural agents we call usually nature's law; that which angels do clearly behold and without any swarving observe is a law celestial and heavenly; the law of reason, that which bindeth creatures reasonable in this world, and with which by reason they may most plainly perceive themselves bound; that which bindeth them, and is not known but by special revelation from God, divine law; human law, that which out of the law either of reason or of God men probably gathering to be expedient, they make it a law. All things, therefore, which are as they ought to be are conformed unto this second law eternal; and even those things which to this eternal law are not conformable are notwithstanding in some sort ordered by the first eternal law. For what good or evil is there under the sun, what action correspondent or repugnant unto the law which God hath imposed upon his creatures, but in or upon it God doth work according to the law which himself hath eternally purposed to keep; that is to say, the first law eternal? So that a two-fold law eternal being thus made, it is not hard to conceive how they both take place in all things.

Wherefore to come to the law of nature: albeit thereby we sometimes mean that manner of working which God hath set for each created thing to keep; yet forasmuch as those things are termed most properly natural agents which keep the law of their kind unwittingly, as the heavens and elements of the world, which can do no otherwise then they do; and forasmuch as we give unto intellectual natures the name of voluntary agents, that so we may distinguish them from the other; expedient it will be that we sever the law of nature observed by the one from that which the other is tied unto. Touching the former, their strict keeping of one tenure, statute, and law is spoken of by all, but hath in it more then men have as yet attained to know, or perhaps ever shall attain, seeing the travail of wading herein is geven of God to the sons of men, that perceiving how much the least thing in the world hath in it more then the wisest are able to reach unto, they may by this means learn humility. Moses, in describing the work of creation, attributeth speech unto God: "God said, Let there be light; let there be a firmament; let the waters under the heaven be gathered together into one place; let the earth bring forth; let there be lights in the firmament of heaven." Was this only the intent of Moses, to signify the infinite greatness of God's power by the easiness of his accomplishing such effects without travail, pain, or labor? Surely it seemeth that Moses had herein besides this a further purpose, namely, first to teach that God did not work as a necessary but a voluntary agent, intending beforehand and decreeing with himself that which did outwardly proceed from him; secondly, to shew

that God did then institute a law natural to be observed by creatures, and therefore, according to the manner of laws, the institution thereof is described as being established by solemn injunction. His commanding those things to be which are, and to be in such sort as they are, to keep that tenure and course which they do, importeth the establishment of nature's law. This world's first creation, and the preservation since of things created, what is it but only so farforth a manifestation by execution what the eternal law of God is concerning things natural? And as it cometh to pass in a kingdom rightly ordered that after a law is once published it presently takes effect far and wide, all states framing themselves thereunto; even so let us think it fareth in the natural course of the world. Since the time that God did first proclaim the edicts of his law upon it, heaven and earth have heark'ned unto his voice, and their labor hath been to do his will. He "made a law for the rain." He gave his "decree unto the sea, that the waters should not pass his commandement." Now if nature should intermit her course and leave altogether, though it were but for a while, the observation of her own laws; if those principal and mother elements of the world, whereof all things in this lower world are made, should loose the qualities which now they have; if the frame of that heavenly arch erected over our heads should loosen and dissolve itself; if celestial spheres should forget their wonted motions, and by irregular volubility turn themselves any way as it might happen; if the prince of the lights of heaven, which now as a giant doth run his unwearied course, should, as it were through a languishing faintness, begin to stand and to rest himself; if the moon should wander from her beaten way, the times and seasons of the year blend themselves by disordered and confused mixture, the winds breathe out their last gasp, the clouds yield no rain, the earth be defeated of heavenly influence, the fruits of the earth pine away as children at the withered breasts of their mother no longer able to yield them relief;— what would become of man himself, whom these things now do all serve? See we not plainly that obedience of creatures unto the law of nature is the stay of the whole world?

Notwithstanding, with nature it cometh sometimes to pass as with art. Let Phidias have rude and obstinate stuff to carve, though his art do that it should, his work will lack that beauty which otherwise in fitter matter it might have had. He that striketh an instrument with skill may cause notwithstanding a very unpleasant sound, if the string whereon he striketh chance to be uncapable of harmony. In the matter whereof things natural consist, that of Theophrastus taketh place, Πολὺ τὸ οὐχ ὑπακοῦον οὐδὲ δεχόμενον τὸ εὖ: "Much of it is oftentimes such as will by no means yield to receive that impression which were best and most perfect." Which defect in the matter of things natural they who gave themselves unto the contemplation of nature amongst the heathen observed often; but the true original cause thereof, divine malediction, laid for the sin of man upon these creatures which God had made for the use of man, this being an article of that saving truth which God hath revealed unto his Church, was above the reach of their merely natural capacity and understanding. But howsoever these swarvings are now and then incident into the course of nature, nevertheless so constantly the laws of nature are by natural agents observed that no man denieth but those things which nature worketh are wrought, either always or for the most part, after one and the same manner.

If here it be demanded what that is which keepeth nature in obedience to her own law, we must have recourse to that higher law whereof we have already spoken, and because all other laws do thereon depend, from thence we must borrow so much as shall need for brief resolution in this point. Although we are not of opinion, therefore, as some are, that nature in working hath before her certain exemplary draughts or patterns, which subsisting in the bosom of the Highest, and being thence discovered, she fixeth her eye upon them as travelers by sea upon the pole-star of the world, and that according thereunto she guideth her hand to work by imitation; although we rather embrace the oracle of Hippocrates, that "each thing both in small and in great fulfilleth the task which destiny hath set down," and concerning the manner of executing and fulfilling the same, "what they do they know not, yet is it in show and appearance as though they did know what they do; and the truth is they do not discern the things which they look on"; nevertheless, forasmuch as the works of nature are no less exact then if she did both behold and study how to express some absolute shape or mirror always present before her; yea, such her dexterity and skill appeareth that no intellectual creature in the world were able by capacity to do that which nature doth without capacity and knowledge; it cannot be but nature hath some director of infinite knowledge to guide her in all her ways. Who the guide of nature, but only the God of nature? "In him we live, move, and are." Those things which nature is said to do are by divine art performed, using nature as an instrument; nor is there any such art or knowledge divine in nature herself working, but in the Guide of nature's work.

Whereas therefore things natural which are not in the number of voluntary agents (for of such only we now speak, and of no other) do so necessarily observe their certain laws that as long as they keep those forms which give them their being they cannot possibly be apt or inclinable to do otherwise then they do; seeing the kinds of their operations are both constantly and exactly framed according to the several ends for which they serve, they themselves in the meanwhile, though doing that which is fit, yet knowing neither what they do, nor why, it followeth that all which they do in this sort proceedeth originally from some such agent as knoweth, appointeth, holdeth up, and even actually frameth the same.

The manner of this divine efficiency being far above us, we are no more able to conceive by our reason then creatures unreasonable by their sense are able to apprehend after what manner we dispose and order the course of our affairs. Only thus much is discerned, that the natural generation and process of all things receiveth order of proceeding from the settled stability of divine understanding. This appointeth unto them their kinds of working; the disposition whereof in the purity of God's own knowledge and will is rightly termed by the name of Providence. The same being referred unto the things themselves here disposed by it was wont by the ancient to be called natural destiny. That law the performance whereof we behold in things natural is as it were an authentical or an original draught written in the bosom of God himself; whose Spirit, being to execute the same, useth every particular nature, every mere natural agent, only as an instrument created at the beginning, and ever since the beginning used to work his own will and pleasure withal. Nature therefore is nothing else but God's instrument, in the course whereof Dionysius, perceiving some suddain disturbance, is said to have cried out, *Aut Deus naturae patitur, aut mundi machina dissolvitur:* "Either God doth suffer impediment, and is by a greater then himself hindered; or if that be impossible, then hath he determined to make a present dissolution of the world, the execution of that law beginning now to stand still, without which the world cannot stand."

This workman, whose servitor nature is, being in truth but only one, the heathens imagining to be mo gave him in the sky the name of Jupiter, in the air the name of Juno, in the water the name of Neptune, in the earth the name of Vesta and sometimes of Ceres, the name of Apollo in the sun, in the moon the name of Diana, the name of Aeolus and divers others in the winds; and to conclude, even so many guides of nature they dreamed of as they saw there were kinds of things natural in the world. These they honored, as having power to work or cease accordingly as men deserved of them. But unto us there is one only Guide of all agents natural, and he both the Creator and the Worker of all in all, alone to be blessed, adored, and honored by all forever.

That which hitherto hath been spoken concerneth natural agents considered in themselves. But we must further remember also (which thing to touch in a word shall suffice) that as in this respect they have their law, which law directeth them in the means whereby they tend to their own perfection; so likewise another law there is, which toucheth them as they are sociable parts united into one body, a law which bindeth them each to serve unto other's good, and all to prefer the good of the whole before whatsoever their own particular; as we plainly see they do, when things natural in that regard forget their ordinary natural wont, that which is heavy mounting sometime upwards of its own accord, and forsaking the center of the earth which to itself is most natural, even as if it did hear itself commanded to let go the good it privately wisheth, and to relieve the present distress of nature in common. . . .

V. God alone excepted (who actually and everlastingly is whatsoever he may be, and which cannot hereafter be that which now he is not), all other things besides are somewhat in possibility, which as yet they are not in act. And for this cause there is in all things an appetite or desire, whereby they incline to something which they may be; and when they are it, they shall be perfecter then now they are. All which perfections are contained under the general name of goodness. And because there is not in the world anything whereby another may not some way be made the perfecter, therefore all things that are are good. Again, sith there can be no goodness desired which proceedeth not from God himself, as from the supreme cause of all things, and every effect doth after a sort contain, at leastwise resemble, the cause from which it proceedeth, all things in the world are said in some sort to seek the highest, and to covet more or less the participation of God himself. Yet this doth nowhere so much appear as it doth in man; because there are so many kinds of perfections which man seeketh.

The first degree of goodness is that general perfection which all things do seek, in desiring the continuance of their being. All things therefore coveting as much as may be to be like unto God in being ever, that which cannot hereunto attain personally doth seek to continue itself another way, that is by offspring and propagation. The next degree of goodness is that which each thing coveteth by affecting resemblance with God, in the constancy and excellency of those operations which belong unto their kind. The immutability of God they strive unto by working either always or for the most part after one and the same manner; his absolute exactness they imitate by tending unto that which is most exquisite in every particular. Hence have arisen a number of axioms in philosophy showing how the works of nature do always aim at that which cannot be bettered.

These two kinds of goodness rehearsed are so nearly united to the things themselves which desire them that we scarcely perceive the appetite to stir in reaching forth her hand towards them. But the desire of those perfections which grow externally is more apparent, especially of such as are not expressly desired unless they be first known, or such as are not for any other cause then for knowledge itself desired. Concerning perfections in this kind, that by proceeding in the knowledge of truth and by growing in the exercise of virtue, man amongst the creatures of this inferior world aspireth to the greatest conformity with God, this is not only known unto us whom he himself hath so instructed, but even they do acknowledge who amongst men are not judged the nearest unto him. With Plato what one thing more usual then to excite men unto the love of wisdom by showing how much wise men are thereby exalted above men; how knowledge doth raise them up into heaven; how it maketh them, though not gods, yet as gods, high, admirable, and divine? . . .

VI. In the matter of knowledge there is between the angels of God and the children of men this difference: angels already have full and complete knowledge in the highest degree that can be imparted unto them; men, if we view them in their spring, are at the first without understanding or knowledge at all. Nevertheless from this utter vacuity they grow by degrees till they come at length to be even as the angels themselves are. That which agreeth to the one now, the other shall attain unto in the end; they are not so far disjoined and severed but that they come at length to meet. The soul of man being therefore at the first as a book wherein nothing is and yet all things may be imprinted, we are to search by what steps and degrees it riseth unto perfection of knowledge.

Unto that which hath been already set down concerning natural agents this we must add, that albeit therein we have comprised as well creatures living as void of life, if they be in degree of nature beneath men, nevertheless a difference we must observe between those natural agents that work altogether unwittingly and those which have, though weak, yet some understanding what they do, as fishes, fowls, and beasts have. Beasts are in sensible capacity as ripe even as men themselves, perhaps more ripe. For as stones, though in dignity of nature inferior unto plants, yet exceed them in firmness of strength or durability of being, and plants, though beneath the excellency of creatures indued with sense, yet exceed them in the faculty of vegetation and of fertility, so beasts, though otherwise behind men, may notwithstanding in actions of sense and phancy go beyond them, because the endeavors of nature, when it hath an higher perfection to seek, are in lower the more remiss, not esteeming thereof so much as those things do which hath no better proposed unto them.

The soul of man therefore, being capable of a more divine perfection, hath (besides the faculties of growing unto sensible knowledge which is common unto us with beasts) a further hability whereof in them there is no show at all, the ability of reaching higher then unto sensible things. Till we grow to some ripeness of years the soul of man doth only store itself with conceipts of things of inferior and more open quality, which afterwards do serve as instruments unto that which is greater; in the meanwhile above the reach of meaner creatures it ascendeth not. When once it comprehendeth anything above this, as the differences of time, affirmations, negations, and contradictions in speech, we then count it to have some use of natural reason. Whereunto if afterwards there might be added the right helps of true art and learning (which helps, I must plainly confess, this age of the world, carrying the name of a learned age, doth neither much know nor greatly regard), there would undoubtedly be almost as great difference in maturity of judgment between men therewith inured and that which now men are as between men that are now and innocents. Which speech if any condemn as being overhyperbolical, let them consider but this one thing: no art is at the first finding out so perfect as industry may after make it. Yet the very first man that to any purpose knew the way we speak of and followed it hath alone thereby performed more very near in all parts of natural knowledge then sithence in any one part thereof the whole world besides hath done. . . .

Education and instruction are the means, the one by use, the other by precept, to make our natural faculty of reason both the better and the sooner able to judge rightly between truth and error, good and evil. But at what time a man may be said to have attained so farforth the use of reason as sufficeth to make him capable of those laws whereby he is then bound to guide his actions, this is a great deal more easy for common sense to discern then for any man by skill and learning to determine; even as it is not in philosophers, who best know the nature both of fire and of gold, to teach what degree of the one will serve to purify the other so well as the artisan, who doth this by fire, discerneth by sense when the fire hath that degree of heat which sufficeth for his purpose.

VII. By reason man attaineth unto the knowledge of things that are and are not sensible. It resteth, therefore, that we search how man attaineth unto the knowledge of such things unsensible as are to be known that they may be done. . . .

Man in perfection of nature being made according to the likeness of his Maker resembleth him also in the manner of working, so that whatsoever we work as men, the same we do wittingly work and freely; neither are we according to the manner of natural agents any way so tied but that it is in our power to leave the things we do undone. The good which either is gotten by doing or which consisteth in the very doing itself causeth not action unless, apprehending it as good, we so like and desire it; that we do unto any such end, the same we choose and prefer before the leaving of it undone. Choice there is not unless the thing which we take be so in our power that we might have refused and left it. If fire consume the stubble it chooseth not so to do, because the nature thereof is such that it can do no other. To choose is to will one thing before another. And to will is to bend our souls to the having or doing of that which they see to be good. Goodness is seen with the eye of the understanding. And the light of that eye is reason. So that two principal fountains there are of humain action, knowledge and will, which will, in things tending towards any end, is termed choice. Concerning knowledge, "Behold," saith Moses, "I have set before you this day good and evil, life and death." Concerning will, he addeth immediately, "Choose life." That is to say, the things that tend unto life, them choose. . . .

Where understanding therefore needeth, in those things reason is the director of man's will by discovering in action what is good. For the laws of well-doing are the dictates of right reason. Children which are not as yet come unto those years whereat they may have, again, innocents which are excluded by natural defect from ever having, thirdly, madmen which for the present cannot possibly have the use of right reason to guide themselves have for their guide the reason that guideth other men, which are tutors over them to seek and to procure their good for them. In the rest there is that light of reason whereby good may be known from evil and which, discovering the same rightly, is termed right.

The will, notwithstanding, doth not incline to have or do that which reason teacheth to be good unless the same do also teach it to be possible. For albeit the appetite, being more general, may wish anything which seemeth good, be it never so impossible, yet for such things the reasonable will of man doth never seek. Let reason teach impossibility in anything, and the will of man doth let it go; a thing impossible it doth not affect, the impossibility thereof being manifest.

There is in the will of man naturally that freedom

whereby it is apt to take or refuse any particular object whatsoever being presented unto it. Whereupon it followeth that there is no particular object so good but it may have the show of some difficulty or unpleasant quality annexed to it, in respect whereof the will may shrink and decline it; contrariwise (for so things are blended) there is no particular evil which hath not some appearance of goodness whereby to insinuate itself. For evil as evil cannot be desired; if that be desired which is evil, the cause is the goodness which is or seemeth to be joined with it. Goodness doth not move by being, but by being apparent; and therefore many things are neglected which are most precious only because the value of them lieth hid. . . . Reason, therefore, may rightly discern the thing which is good, and yet the will of man not incline itself thereunto, as oft the prejudice of sensible experience doth oversway.

Nor let any man think that this doth make anything for the just excuse of iniquity. For there was never sin committed wherein a less good was not preferred before a greater, and that wilfully; which cannot be done without the singular disgrace of nature and the utter disturbance of that divine order whereby the preeminence of chiefest acceptation is by the best things worthily challenged. . . .

XVI. Thus far, therefore, we have endeavored in part to open of what nature and force laws are, according unto their several kinds: the law which God with himself hath eternally set down to follow in his own works, the law which he hath made for his creatures to keep, the law of natural and necessary agents, the law which angels in heaven obey, the law whereunto by the light of reason men find themselves bound in that they are men, the law which they make by composition for multitudes and politique societies of men to be guided by, the law which belongeth unto each nation, the law that concerneth the fellowship of all, and lastly the law which God himself hath supernaturally revealed. It might, peradventure, have been more popular and more plausible to vulgar ears if this first discourse had been spent in extolling the force of laws, in shewing the great necessity of them when they are good, and in aggravating their offense by whom publique laws are injuriously traduced. But forasmuch as with such kind of matter the passions of men are rather stirred one way or other then their knowledge any way set forward unto the trial of that whereof there is doubt made, I have therefore turned aside from that beaten path and chosen, though a less easy, yet a more profitable way in regard of the end we propose. . . .

It is both commonly said, and truly, that the best men otherwise are not always the best in regard of society. The reason whereof is for that the law of men's actions is one if they be respected only as men, and another when they are considered as parts of a politique body. Many men there are then whom nothing is more commendable when they are singled; and yet in society with others none less fit to answer the duties which are looked for at their hands. Yea, I am persuaded that of them with whom in this cause we strive there are whose betters amongst men would be hardly found if they did not live amongst men, but in some wilderness by themselves. The cause of which their disposition, so unframable unto societies wherein they live, is for that they discern not aright what place and force these several kinds of laws ought to have in all their actions. Is there question either concerning the regiment of the Church in general or about conformity between one church and another, or of ceremonies, offices, powers, jurisdictions in our own church? Of all these things they judge by that rule which they frame to themselves with some show of probability, and what seemeth in that sort convenient, the same they think themselves bound to practise; the same by all means they labor mightily to uphold; whatsoever any law of man to the contrary hath determined they weigh it not. Thus, by following the law of private reason where the law of publique should take place, they breed disturbance. . . .

And as here [in the matter of dietary restrictions] men's private phancies must give place to the higher judgment of that church which is in authority a mother over them, so the very actions of whole churches have, in regard of commerce and fellowship with other churches, been subject to laws concerning food, the contrary unto which laws had else been thought more convenient for them to observe, as by that order of abstinence from strangled and blood may appear an order grounded upon that fellowship which the churches of the Gentiles had with the Jews.

Thus we see how even one and the selfsame thing is under divers considerations conveyed through many laws, and that to measure by any one kind of law all the actions of men were to confound the admirable order wherein God hath disposed all laws, each as in nature, so in degree, distinct from other.

Wherefore that here we may briefly end: of law there can be no less acknowledged then that her seat is the bosom of God, her voice the harmony of the world; all things in heaven and earth do her homage, the very least as feeling her care and the greatest as not exempted from her power; both angels and men and creatures of what condition soever, though each in different sort and manner, yet all with uniform consent admiring her as the mother of their peace and joy.

Part IV POETICAL MISCELLANIES, BALLADS, AND SONG BOOKS

THE COURT OF VENUS and A BOOK OF BALLETS

Although the practise of collecting, in commonplace-books, poems and songs that struck one's fancy must have been fairly common in the early Tudor court, the printing and commercial distribution of such collections (or miscellanies) did not begin until the last years of Henry VIII. Skelton and Barclay and Heywood were, so to speak, professionals who wrote mainly in longer forms; but the Tudor court was prolific in minor "courtly makers"—men of birth and breeding who, as Renaissance gentlemen, fancied that they could polish off a graceful ·lyric or a translation as deftly as they could make love or wage war. Towards the close of the century Puttenham's *Art of English Poesy* (1589) records that "in the latter end" of Henry's reign there "sprung up a new company of courtly makers, of whom Sir Thomas Wyatt th' Elder and Henry, Earl of Surrey, were the two chieftains"; and it was these men and their imitators whose poems, handed around in manuscript, furnished copy for enterprising printers and thus inaugurated the great succession of poetical miscellanies which contain some of the finest writing of the age.

The earliest extant miscellany is a thing of shreds and patches that survives in three black-letter fragments. One, in the Bodleian Library (Douce G.3), contains fifteen leaves which were perhaps printed in the late thirties. Another, in the Stark Collection of the University of Texas, contains two leaves (discovered in 1928 as end-papers in a copy of the 1551 edition of Ralph Robinson's translation of More's *Utopia*) with the running title, *A Boke of Balettes;* it was printed perhaps in the late forties. The third, in the Folger Shakespeare Library, contains eight leaves with a titlepage, *The Court of Venus,* but with no imprint or date. Furthermore, there was entered in the Stationers' Register sometime between July, 1557, and July, 1558, another edition of *The Court of Venus* which has presumably not survived. Thus we know of four editions (and have fragments of three) of the earliest Tudor miscellany. Although the chronological and other relations of the four can only be conjectured, it seems likely that the first (the Bodleian fragment) was put together about 1536 from a manuscript of Wyatt's poems and from *The Pilgrim's Tale,* a pseudo-Chaucerian and coarsely anti-clerical allegory by one Robert Shyngleton, and duly appeared as *The Court of Venus.* The satire of *The Pilgrim's Tale* must have made the little book offensive to the clergy, and so we may surmise that it was suppressed. Perhaps a decade later certain of the lyrics were reprinted as *A Boke of Balettes* (of which only the Stark fragment remains). Apparently the lost edition mentioned in the Stationers' Register next appeared, and finally, in the early sixties, this lost edition was reprinted under the original title of *The Court of Venus* (the Folger fragment represents this reprint). Whatever the exact details of their publication, these various fragments obviously possess great historical importance; moreover, they preserve the earliest printed versions of some charming lyrics, including a few pieces by Wyatt that reappeared later in Tottel's *Miscellany.* We have based our text upon photostats of the three extant fragments, silently correcting the typographical errors in which they abound; readings in pointed brackets in the last two poems are supplied by the better versions in Tottel's *Miscellany.*

FROM THE COURT OF VENUS (ca. 1536)

[DRIVEN BY DESIRE TO SET AFFECTION]

Driven by desire to set affection
A great way, alas, above my degree,
Chosen I am, I think, by election
To covet that thing that will not be.

I serve in love not like to speed;
I look, alas, a little too high;
Against my will I do indeed
Covet that thing that will not be.

My fancy, alas, doth me so bind
That I can see no remedy   10

But still to follow my foolish mind
And covet that thing that will not be.

I hoped well whan I began,
And sens the prove is contrary
Why should I any longer than
Covet that thing that will not be?

But rather to leave now at the last
Then still to follow fancy,
Content with the pain that is past
And not covet that thing that will not be.   20

[Anonymous]

191

FROM A BOOK OF BALLETS (ca. 1545)

[LOVE WHOM YE LIST AND SPARE NOT]

Love whom ye list and spare not;
Therewith I am content.
Hate whom ye list and spare not,
For even I am indifferent.

Do what ye list and dread not,
After your own fantasy.
Think what you list and fear not,
For all is one to me.

For as for me I am not
Wavering as the wind,
But even as one that recketh not
Which way ye turn your mind.

For in your love I doubt not,
But as one that recketh not,
Whether you hate or hate not
Is least charge of my thought.

Wherefore I pray you forget not
But that I am well content
To love whom ye list and spare not,
For I am indifferent.

[Anonymous]

[SHALL SHE NEVER OUT OF MY MIND]

Shall she never out of my mind?
Nor shall I never out of this pain?
Alas, her love doth me so blind,
Except her help I am now slain.

I never told her of my mind,
What pain I suffer for her sake.
Alas, what means might I now find
That no displeasure with me she take?

If I speak fair she saith I flatter,
And if I do not I shall not speed;
If I to her do write a letter,
Then will she say she cannot read.

Shall I despair yet for all this?
Nay, nay, my heart will not do so.
I would ones my sweetheart kiss,
A thousand times to bind more wo.

I am abashed when I should speak.
Alas, I cannot my mind express.
It maketh my heart in pieces break
To see her loving gentleness.

[Anonymous]

FROM THE COURT OF VENUS (ca. 1562)

THE PROLOGUE

In the moneth of May when the new tender green
Hath smoothly covered the ground that was bare,
Powd'red with flours so well-beseen,
I would have brought my heart out of care.
And as I walked in the wood so fair,
Thick of grass among the flours sweet
And many a wholesome herb fair under the feet,

I heard one hunt; methought it did blow
In a great horn of stiff sown
At the root of the heart, as far as I could know.
Toward the cry I had me fast bown,
And at the last, forweary, I sat me down,
Thinking a while to take my resting.
The hounds were gone out of my hearing.

And for that I knew myself to be alone
And sodeinly my grief I began to complain;
Methought I had good place myself to moan
And ease my heart of mine own pain,
Beseeching Venus to lose me out of chain.
I was so fast and sure stung through the heart
With the fiery chain that I could not start.

And as I was making my complaint
Of my true service to my lady dear,
And how nothing I was repentant
Save to her presence I was not taken near,
Genius came and asked me, "What cheer?"
Who is with Venus put in such trust
That like to die for love, confess them he must.

Venus knew I had a woful heart,
And where we thus contend she knoweth her relief.
To me, therefore, she sent her own clark
To slack my sorrows and help me of my grief
That was so far in danger and mischief.
For whether I would, she knew I durst not speak,
Which caused my heart in sunder to break.

I laid my head, betwixt my life and death,
Upon his knee, and what he said I heard,
And by that time I scarcely drew my breath

But hard his tale or I answered.
It hath been pity him to have disturbed.   40
Oftentimes he bad that I should leave my wo,
And said of my disease there were five hundreth mo.

He bad, therefore, that I with pen and ink
Ready with writing should make my complaint:
"There shall be a redress sooner then ye think";
And bad no more that my hear should raint.
And of our bills, he said, he would none want
Of them he thought to have good comfort
And would present himself in Venus' court.

"For she entendeth, and that is in all haste,   50
To surmount the parliament as fast as can be done.
And Jupiter himself within this day past
Hath commanded Marcury for to be gone
Upon his message—some call him Stillbon—
With his commission also, for to compel
Minos to come, the judge of dreful hell,

"To the Mount of Cethro, where Venus doth
    dwell.
The preparement made is so far exceeding
That of such triumph no stories doth tell;   60
That is above all other so far transcending.
And for the while she had me by copying
Of these complaints which doth follow;
And after that I should know the matter thorow."

The whole fashion of everything
He would me send; therefore we must be gone,
Of matters determined as well as of the meeting.
But I besought him, or ever I were alone,
That of Venus' court he would interpret the fashion
Something to make, but he would not consent   70
Till it were concluded by the parliament. . . .

And therefore I must, my reader, intreat,
Desiring you heartily to be content.
For though I have not, I will not forget
To describe the court. I will be diligent,
And at the end of this complaint set it;
But I as nothing of mine induction
Will once report of Genius' instruction.

And here followeth, wherein you may read,
To the court of Venus a great number;   80
Their hearts, they say, be as heavy as lead.
Their sorrowful wo I am sure you will tender,
For if that I were maden uncumber
And had such might as she hath moan,
Out of their pain they should be letten gone.

[Anonymous]

[MY LUTE, AWAKE][1]

My lute, awake! Perform the last
Labor that thou and I shall waste,
And end that I have new begun.
For when this song is gone and past,
My lute, be still, for I have done.

As to be heard where ear is none,
As lead to grave in a marble stone,
My song may pierce heart as soon.
Should we then sing, weep, or moan?
No more, my lute, for I have done.   10

The rock doth not so cruelly
Repulse the waves continually
As she my suit and affection,
So that I am past all remedy,
Whereby my lute and I have done.

Proud of the spleen that thou hast shot,
Of simple heart, through loves got
Unkind, although thou hast them won,
Think not he hath his own forgot
Although my lute and I have done.   20

Vengeance may fall on such disdain
That maketh but game of earnest pain.
Trow not alone under the sun
Ungently to cause to lovers plain
Although my lute and I have done.

And then may chance thee to repent
The time that thou hast lost and spent
To cause thy lover to sigh and sown.
Then shalt thou know beauty but lent,
And wish and want as I have done.   30

My lute, be still! This is the last
Labor that thou and I shall waste,
And end that I have begun.
Or when this song is sung and past,
My lute, be still, for I have done.

[Sir Thomas Wyatt]

[DISDAIN ME NOT WITHOUT DESERT]

Disdain me not without desert,
Nor leave me not so sodeynly,
Sence well ye wot that in my heart
I mean nothing but honesty.
    Disdain me not.

---

[1] We print this poem unemended (except for the correction of a
few obvious misprints) and for comparison supply Tottel's
version in full on p. 200.

Refuse me not without cause why,
Nor think me not to be unjust,
Since that, by lot of fantasy,
The careful knot needs knit I must.
    Refuse me not.   10

Mistrust me not, though some there be
That fain would spot <my> steadfastness.
Believe them not, seeing that ye see
The proof is not as they express.
    Mistrust me not.

Forsake me not till I deserve,
Nor hate me not till <I offend,
Destroy me not till that> I swarve,
For sith you know what I entend,
    Forsake me not.   20

Disdain me not, being your own;
Refuse me not that am so true;
Mistrust me not till all be known;
Forsake me never for no new.
    Disdain me not.

                      [Sir Thomas Wyatt]

[MARVEL NO MORE]

Mervail no more, although
The songs I sing do moan,
For other life then woe
I never proved none.
And in my heart also

Is graven with letters deep
<A thousand sighs and mo,
A flood> of tears to weep.

How may a man in smart
Find matter to rejoice?   10
How may a woful heart
Set forth a pleasant voice?
<Play whoso can that part;>
In me must needs appear
How fortune overthwart
<Doth cause my mourning cheer>.

Perdie there is no man
If he never saw sight
That parfectly tell can
The nature of the light.   20
<Alas!> How should I, than,
That never tasted but sour,
But do as I began,
Continually to lower?

Such chance perchance may chance
To cause me change my tune.
And when such chance doth chance
Then shall I thank fortune.
And if such chance do chance
Perchance or it be long   30
For such a pleasant chance
To sing some pleasant song.

                      [Sir Thomas Wyatt]

TOTTEL'S MISCELLANY

Whatever the gaps in our knowledge of *The Court of Venus* (see p. 191), we know a good deal about the first great Tudor poetical miscellany, the volume published by Richard Tottel on June 5, 1557, as *Songs and Sonnets Written by the Right Honorable Lord Henry Haward Late Earl of Surrey and Other* and today cherished by lovers of poetry as Tottel's *Miscellany*. This collection, one of the largest and most successful of the century, contains two hundred seventy-one pieces attributed as follows: to Surrey forty poems, to Wyatt ninety-seven, to Nicholas Grimald forty, and to "Uncertain Authors" ninety-four. The fact that Grimald is represented so copiously among his courtly betters has led to the suggestion—now disproved—that he was engaged by Tottel to be the editor or compiler of the book. In the completely reset second edition (July 1, 1557) thirty of Grimald's forty poems are omitted.

Following the two editions of 1557 there were others in 1559 (two), 1565, 1567, 1574, 1585, and 1587—an astonishing record of nine editions within thirty years. First and last, Tottel's *Miscellany* gives us the texts of three hundred ten poems, including not only the great work of Wyatt and the facile work of Surrey, but also pieces by Lord Vaux, John Heywood, Chaucer, Sir Francis Bryan, Sir John Cheke, John Harington, Thomas Norton (who also translated Calvin's *Institutes* and wrote part of *Gorboduc*), Sir Anthony St. Leger, Thomas Churchyard, John Hall, and others. Moreover, it demonstrates a remarkable metrical range: the sonnet is liberally represented (with about thirty examples by Wyatt, about fifteen by Surrey, three by Grimald, and others by the "Uncertain Authors"), and so are ottava rima, terza rima, poulter's measure, heroic couplets, septenaries, rime royal, hexameters, blank verse, dizains, and douzains. There is a comparable richness of poetical forms: epigrams, satires, at least one pastoral, elegies, and a great variety of amorous lyrics. The book marks a surging response to the literary forms and styles of the Continental Renaissance; and, in spite of its archaic diction, its heavy (and sometimes inept) imitations of Petrarch and others, and its frequent technical insecurity, Tottel's *Miscellany* is one of the great books of the century. As much as any other it inaugurated the high period of the English Renaissance, and it was

unquestionably the most influential literary achievement of Elizabeth's early reign. Our texts are based upon the first edition of 1557 (STC 13860). To our excerpts from Wyatt's share of the volume we have appended five poems by him from manuscripts in the British Museum: "Help Me to Seek" from Egerton MS. 2711, and "Forget Not Yet," "And Wilt Thou Leave Me Thus," "Blame Not My Lute," and "Since You Will Needs" from Additional MS. 17492.

FROM SONGS AND SONNETS, WRITTEN BY THE RIGHT HONORABLE LORD HENRY HOWARD, LATE EARL OF SURREY, AND OTHER (1557) [TOTTEL'S *MISCELLANY*]

The Printer to the Reader

That to have well written in verse, yea and in small parcels, deserveth great praise, the works of divers Latins, Italians, and other do prove sufficiently. That our tongue is able in that kind to do as praiseworthily as the rest, the honorable style of the noble Earl of Surrey and the weightiness of the deep-witted Sir Thomas Wyatt the Elder's verse, with several graces in sundry good English writers, do show abundantly. It resteth now, gentle reader, that thou think it not 10 evil done to publish, to the honor of the English tongue and for profit of the studious of English

eloquence, those works which the ungentle hoarders-up of such treasure have heretofore envied thee. And for this point, good reader, thine own profit and pleasure, in these presently and in mo hereafter, shall answer for my defense. If, parhaps, some mislike the stateliness of style removed from the rude skill of common ears, I ask help of the learned to defend their learned friends, the authors of this work. And I exhort the unlearned by reading to learn to be more skilful and to purge that swinelike grossness that maketh the sweet marjoram not to smell to their delight.

HENRY HOWARD, EARL OF SURREY

In Poulter's measure

DESCRIPTION OF SPRING, WHEREIN EACH THING RENEWS SAVE ONLY THE LOVER

The soote season that bud and bloom furth brings
With green hath clad the hill and eke the vale;
The nightingale with feathers new she sings;
The turtle to her make hath told her tale.
Summer is come, for every spray now springs,
The hart hath hung his old head on the pale,
The buck in brake his winter coat he flings,
The fishes float with new repaired scale,
The adder all her slough away she slings,
The swift swallow pursueth the flies small,   10
The busy bee her honey now she mings.
Winter is worn that was the flowers' bale.
And thus I see among these pleasant things
Each care decays, and yet my sorrow springs.

COMPLAINT OF A LOVER THAT DEFIED LOVE AND WAS BY LOVE AFTER THE MORE TORMENTED

When summer took in hand the winter to assail,
With force of might and virtue great his stormy blasts
    to quail,
And when he clothed fair the earth about with green
    And every tree new garmented, that pleasure was to
    seen,
Mine heart gan new revive, and changed blood did stir
    Me to withdraw my winter wo that kept within the
    door.
"Abroad," quod my desire, "assay to set thy foot
    Where thou shalt find the savor sweet, for sprong is
    every root;
And to thy health, if thou were sick in any case,

Nothing more good than in the spring the air to feel a
    space.   10
There shalt thou hear and see all kinds of birds ywrought
    Well tune their voice with warble small, as nature hath
      them tought."
Thus pricked me my lust the sluggish house to leave,
    And for my health I thought it best such counsail to
      receive.
So on a morrow furth, unwist of any wight,
    I went to prove how well it would my heavy burden
      light.
And when I felt the air so pleasant round about,
    Lord! to myself how glad I was that I had gotten out.
There might I see how Ver had every blossom hent,
    And eke the new betrothed birds ycoupled how they
      went.   20
And in their songs, methought, they thanked Nature much
    That by her license all that year to love their hap was
      such
Right as they could devise to chose them feres throughout.
    With much rejoicing to their lord thus flew they all
      about;
Which when I gan resolve and in my head conceive
    What pleasant life, what heaps of joy these little birds
      receive,
And saw in what estate I, weary man, was brought
    By want of that they had at will and I reject at nought,
Lord! how I gan in wrath unwisely me demean:
    I cursed Love and him defied; I thought to turn the
      stream.   30
But whan I well beheld he had me under awe
    I asked mercy for my fault that so transgress'd his law.
"Thou blinded god," quod I, "forgeve me this offense;
    Unwillingly I went about to malice thy pretense."
Wherewith he gave a beck, and thus, methought, he
      swore:
    "Thy sorrow ought suffice to purge thy fault if it were
      more."
The virtue of which sound mine heart did so revive
    That I, methought, was made as whole as any man alive.
But here ye may perceive mine error all and some,
    For that I thought that so it was, yet was it still un-
      done;   40
And all that was no more but mine empressed mind
    That fain would have some good relief of Cupid well
      assign'd.
I turned home forthwith, and might perceive it well
    That he agrieved was right sore with me for my rebel.
My harms have ever since increased more and more,
    And I remain, without his help, undone for evermore.
A mirror let me be unto ye lovers all:
    Strive not with love, for if ye do it will ye thus befall.

COMPLAINT OF A LOVER REBUKED

Love that liveth and reigneth in my thought,
That built his seat within my captive breast,

Clad in the arms wherein with me he fought,
Oft in my face he doth his banner rest.
She that me taught to love and suffer pain,
My doubtful hope and eke my hot desire
With shamefast cloak to shadow and refrain,
Her smiling grace converteth straight to ire.
And coward Love then to the heart apace
Taketh his flight, whereas he lurks, and plains   10
His purpose lost, and dare not shew his face.
For my lord's guilt thus faultless bide I pains.
Yet from my lord shall not my foot remove.
Sweet is his death that takes his end by love.

DESCRIPTION AND PRAISE OF HIS LOVE GERALDINE

From Tuscan came my lady's worthy race;
Fair Florence was sometime her ancient seat.
The western ile, whose pleasant shore doth face
Wild Camber's cliffs, did geve her lively heat.
Fostered she was with milk of Irish breast;
Her sire an earl, her dame of princes' blood.
From tender years in Britain she doth rest
With king's child, where she tasteth costly food.
Hunsdon did first present her to mine eyen.
Bright is her hue, and Geraldine she hight.   10
Hampton me taught to wish her first for mine,
And Windsor, alas! doth chase me from her sight.
Her beauty of kind, her virtues from above,
Happy is he that can obtain her love.

THE FRAILTY AND HURTFULNESS OF BEAUTY

Brittle beauty that nature made so frail,
Whereof the gift is small and short the season,
Flow'ring today, tomorrow apt to fail,
Tickle treasure abhorred of reason,
Dangerous to deal with, vain, of none avail,
Costly in keeping, pass'd not worth two peas,
Slipper in sliding as is an eel's tail,
Hard to attain, once gotten not geason,
Jewel of jeopardy that peril doth assail,
False and untrue, enticed oft to treason,   10
En'my to youth—that most may I bewail.
Ah! bitter-sweet infecting as the poison,
Thou farest as fruit that with the frost is taken:
Today ready ripe, tomorrow all to-shaken.

HOW EACH THING SAVE THE LOVER IN SPRING REVIVETH TO PLEASURE

When Windsor walls sustained my wearied arm,
My hand my chin to ease my restless head,
The pleasant plot revested green with warm,
The blossom'd boughs with lusty Ver yspread,
The flow'red meads, the wedded birds so late,
Mine eyes discover. And to my mind resort
The jolly woes, the hateless short debate,
The rakehell life that longs to love's disport.

Wherewith, alas! the heavy charge of care
Heap'd in my breast breaks forth against my will   10
In smoky sighs that overcast the air.
My vapor'd eyes such dreary tears distill,
The tender spring which quicken where they fall,
And I half-bent to throw me down withal.

PRISONED IN WINDSOR, HE RECOUNTETH HIS PLEASURE THERE PASSED

So cruel prison how could betide, alas,
As proud Windsor? Where I in lust and joy
With a king's son my childish years did pass
In greater feast than Priam's sons of Troy;
Where each sweet place returns a taste full sour:
The large green courts where we were wont to hove
With eyes cast up into the maidens' tower,
And easy sighs, such as folk draw in love;
The stately seats, the ladies bright of hue,
The dances short, long tales of great delight;   10
With words and looks that tigers could but rue,
Where each of us did plead the other's right;
The palm-play where, despoiled for the game,
With dazed eyes oft we by gleams of love
Have miss'd the ball and got sight of our dame,
To bait her eyes, which kept the leads above;
The gravel ground, with sleeves tied on the helm,
On foaming horse, with swords and friendly hearts,
With cheer, as though one should another whelm,
Where we have fought, and chased oft with darts;   20
With silver drops the mead yet spread for ruth,
In active games of nimbleness and strength,
Where we did strain, trained with swarms of youth,
Our tender lims that yet shot up in length;
The secret groves which oft we made resound
Of pleasant plaint and of our ladies' praise,
Recording oft what grace each one had found,
What hope of speed, what dread of long delays;
The wild forest, the clothed holts with green,
With reins avaled, and swift ybreathed horse,   30
With cry of hounds and merry blasts between,
Where we did chase the fearful hart of force;
The wide vales eke that harbor'd us each night,
Wherewith, alas, reviveth in my breast
The sweet accord; such sleeps as yet delight,
The pleasant dreams, the quiet bed of rest;
The secret thoughts imparted with such trust,
The wanton talk, the divers change of play,
The friendship sworn, each promise kept so just,
Wherewith we pass'd the winter night away.   40
And with this thought the blood forsakes the face,
The tears berain my cheeks of deadly hue,
The which as soon as sobbing sighs, alas,

Upsupped have, thus I my plaint renew:
"O place of bliss, renewer of my woes,
Geve me accompt—where is my noble fere,
Whom in thy walls thou dost each night enclose,
To other lief, but unto me most dear?"
Echo, alas, that doth my sorrow rue,
Returns thereto a hollow sound of plaint.   50
Thus I alone, where all my freedom grew,
In prison pine with bondage and restraint;
And with remembrance of the greater grief
To banish the less, I find my chief relief.

[OF THE DEATH OF SIR THOMAS WYATT THE ELDER]

W[yatt] resteth here, that quick could never rest;
Whose heavenly gifts encreased by disdain,
And virtue sank the deeper in his breast,
Such profit he by envy could obtain.
  A head where wisdom mysteries did frame,
Whose hammers beat still in that lively brain
As on a stith, where that some work of fame
Was daily wrought to turn to Britain's gain.
  A visage stern and mild, where both did grow
Vice to contemn, in virtue to rejoice;   10
Amid great storms whom grace assured so
To live upright and smile at fortune's choice.
  A hand that taught what might be said in rime,
That reft Chaucer the glory of his wit,
A mark the which (unparfited, for time)
Some may approach, but never none shall hit.
  A tongue that served in foreign realms his king;
Whose courteous talk to virtue did enflame
Each noble heart; a worthy guide to bring
Our English youth by travail unto fame.   20
  An eye whose judgment none affect could blind,
Friends to allure and foes to reconcile;
Whose piercing look did represent a mind
With virtue fraught, reposed, void of guile.
  A heart where dread was never so impress'd
To hide the thought that might the trouth avance;
In neither fortune loft nor yet repress'd,
To swell in wealth or yield unto mischance.
  A valiant corps where force and beauty met,
Happy—alas, too happy, but for foes!   30
Lived, and ran the race that nature set,
Of manhood's shape where she the mold did lose.
  But to the heavens that simple soul is fled,
Which left with such as covet Christ to know
Witness of faith that never shall be dead;
Sent for our health, but not received so.
Thus for our guilt this jewel have we lost:
The earth, his bones; the heavens possess his ghost.

SIR THOMAS WYATT

THE LOVER FOR SHAMEFASTNESS HIDETH HIS DESIRE WITHIN HIS FAITHFUL HEART

The long love that in my thought I harber,
And in my heart doth keep his residence,
Into my face preaseth with bold pretense
And there campeth, displaying his banner.
She that me learns to love and to suffer,
And wills that my trust and lust's negligence
Be reined by reason, shame, and reverence,
With his hardiness takes displeasure.
Wherewith love to the heart's forest he fleeth,
Leaving his enterprise with pain and cry,   10
And there him hideth and not appeareth.
What may I do, when my maister feareth,
But in the field with him to live and die?
For good is the life ending faithfully.

THE ABUSED LOVER SEETH HIS FOLLY AND ENTENDETH TO TRUST NO MORE

Was never file yet half so well yfiled
To file a file for any smith's intent
As I was made a filing instrument
To frame other while that I was beguiled.
But reason, lo! hath at my folly smiled
And pardoned me, since that I me repent
Of my lost years and of my time misspent.
For youth led me, and falsehood me misguided.
Yet this trust I have of great apparence:
Since that deceit is ay returnable,   10
Of very force it is agreeable
That therewithal be done the recompense.
Then guile beguiled plained should be never,
And the reward is little trust forever.

THE LOVER DESCRIBETH HIS BEING STRIKEN WITH SIGHT OF HIS LOVE

The lively sparks that issue from those eyes,
Against the which there vaileth no defense,
Have pierc'd my heart and done it none offense,
With quaking pleasure, more then once or twice.
Was never man could anything devise
Sunbeams to turn with so great vehemence
To daze man's sight as by their bright presence
Dazed am I; much like unto the guise
Of one striken with dint of lightening,
Blind with the stroke, and erring here and there.   10
So call I for help, I not when nor where,
The pain of my fall patiently bearing.
For straight after the blaze (as is no wonder)
Of deadly [nay] hear I the fearful thunder.

THE LOVER, HAVING DREAMED ENJOYING OF HIS LOVE, COMPLAINETH THAT THE DREAM IS NOT EITHER LONGER OR TRUER

Unstable dream, according to the place,
Be steadfast ones or else at least be true.
By tasted sweetness make me not to rue
The soden loss of thy false feigned grace.
By good respect in such a dangerous case
Thou broughtest not her into these tossing seas,
But madest my sprite to live, my care t' encrease,
My body in tempest her delight t' imbrace.
The body dead, the sprite had his desire.
Painless was th' one, the other in delight.   10
Why, then, alas! did it not keep it right,
But thus return to leap into the fire?
And where it was at wish, could not remain?
Such mocks of dreams do turn to deadly pain.

DESCRIPTION OF THE CONTRARIOUS PASSIONS IN A LOVER

I find no peace, and all my war is done.
I fear and hope, I burn and freeze like ice.
I fly aloft, yet can I not arise;
And nought I have, and all the world I season.
That locks nor loseth holdeth me in prison
And holds me not, yet can I scape nowise;
Nor lets me live nor die at my devise,
And yet of death it geveth me occasion.
Without eye I see, without tongue I plain.
I wish to perish, yet I ask for health;   10
I love another, and thus I hate myself.
I feed me in sorrow and laugh in all my pain.
Lo! thus displeaseth me both death and life,
And my delight is causer of this strife.

THE LOVER COMPARETH HIS STATE TO A SHIP IN PERILOUS STORM TOSSED ON THE SEA

Petrarchan

My galley charged with forgetfulness
Through sharp seas in winter nights doth pass
Tween rock and rock; and eke my foe, alas,
That is my lord, steereth with cruelness.
And every [oar] a thought in readiness,
As though that death were light in such a case;
An endless wind doth tear the sail apace
Of forced sighs and trusty fearfulness.
A rain of tears, a cloud of dark disdain,
Have done the wearied cords great hinderance,   10
Wreathed with error and with ignorance.
The stars be hid that led me to this pain.
Drown'd is reason that should be my comfort,
And I remain, dispearing of the port.

THE LOVER SHEWETH HOW HE IS FORSAKEN
OF SUCH AS HE SOMETIME ENJOYED

They flee from me that sometime did me seek,
With naked foot stalking within my chamber.
Once have I seen them gentle, tame, and meek
That now are wild, and do not once remember
That sometime they have put themselves in danger
To take bread at my hand. And now they range,
Busily seeking in continual change.

Thanked be fortune it hath been otherwise
Twenty times better, but once especial:
In thin array, after a pleasant guise,   10
When her loose gown did from her shoulders fall
And she me caught in her arms long and small,
And therewithal so sweetly did me kiss
And softly said, "Dear heart, how like you this?"

It was no dream, for I lay broad awaking.
But all is turn'd now through my gentleness
Into a bitter fashion of forsaking,
And I have leave to go of her goodness,
And she also to use newfangleness.
But since that I unkindly so am served,   20
How like you this? What hath she now deserved?

TO A LADY TO ANSWER DIRECTLY WITH
YEA OR NAY

Madame, withouten many words,
Once I am sure you will or no;
And if you will, then leave your boords
And use your wit, and shew it so,
For with a beck you shall me call.
And if of one that burns alway
Ye have pity or ruth at all,
Answer him fair with yea or nay.
If it be yea, I shall be fain;
If it be nay, friends as before.   10
You shall another man obtain,
And I mine own, and yours no more.

A RENOUNCING OF HARDLY ESCAPED LOVE

Farewell the heart of cruelty,
Though that with pain my liberty
Dear have I bought and wofully
Finish'd my fearful tragedy.
Of force I must forsake such pleasure.
A good cause just, since I endure
Thereby my wo, which, be ye sure,
Shall therewith go me to recure.

I fare as one escap'd that fleeth,
Glad he is gone, and yet still feareth   10
Spied to be caught, and so dreadeth
That he for nought his pain leseth.
In joyful pain rejoice, my heart,
Thus to sustain of each a part.

Let not this song from thee astart.
Welcome among my pleasant smart.

THE LOVER TO HIS BED, WITH DESCRIBING
OF HIS UNQUIET STATE

The restful place, renewer of my smart;
The labor's salve, encreasing my sorrow;
The body's ease and troubler of my heart;
Quieter of mind, mine unquiet foe;
Forgetter of pain, rememb'rer of my wo;
The place of sleep wherein I do but wake;
Besprent with tears, my bed, I thee forsake!

The frosty snows may not redress my heat,
Nor heat of sun abate my fervent cold.
I know nothing to ease my pains so great.   10
Each cure causeth encrease by twentyfold,
Renewing cares upon my sorrows old;
Such overthwart effects in me they make,
Besprent with tears, my bed for to forsake.

But all for nought! I find no better ease
In bed or out. This most causeth my pain:
Where I do seek how best that I may please,
My lost labor, alas! is all in vain.
My heart once set, I cannot it refrain.
No place from me my grief away can take,   20
Wherefore with tears, my bed, I thee forsake!

OF HIS LOVE THAT PRICKED HER FINGER
WITH A NEEDLE

She sat and sewed that hath done me the wrong
Whereof I plain, and have done many a day;
And, whilst she heard my plaint in piteous song,
She wish'd my heart the sampler that it lay.
The blind maister whom I have served so long,
Grudging to hear that he did hear her say,
Made her own weapon do her finger bleed
To feel if pricking were so good indeed.

COMPLAINT FOR TRUE LOVE UNREQUITED

What vaileth troth, or by it to take pain?
To strive by steadfastness for to attain
How to be just and flee from doubleness?
Since all alike, where ruleth craftiness,
Rewarded is both crafty-false and plain.
Soonest he speeds that most can lie and feign.
True-meaning heart is had in high disdain.
Against deceit and cloaked doubleness
What vaileth troth or parfit steadfastness?
Deceiv'd is he, by false and crafty train,   10
That means no guile and faithful doth remain
Within the trap, without help or redress.
But for to love, lo! such a stern maistress
Where cruelty dwells, alas! it were in vain.

THE LOVER COMPARETH HIS HEART TO THE OVERCHARGED GUN

The furious gun, in his most raging ire,
When that the bowl is rammed in too sore,
And that the flame cannot part from the fire,
Cracks in sunder, and in the air do roar
The shevered pieces. So doth my desire,
Whose flame encreaseth ay from more to more;
Which to let out I dare not look nor speak;
So inward force my heart doth all to-break.

THE LOVER REJOICETH THE ENJOYING OF HIS LOVE

Once, as methought, fortune me kiss'd
And bade me ask what I thought best,
And I should have it as me list,
Therewith to set my heart in rest.

I asked but my lady's heart
To have for evermore mine own;
Then at an end were all my smart,
Then should I need no more to moan.

Yet for all that a stormy blast
Had overturn'd this goodly day,   10
And fortune seemed at the last
That to her promise she said nay.

But like as one out of dispair
To sodain hope revived I.
Now fortune sheweth herself so fair
That I content me wondersly.

My most desire my hand may reach;
My will is alway at my hand;
Me need not long for to beseech
Her that hath power me to command.   20

What earthly thing more can I crave?
What would I wish more at my will?
Nothing on earth more would I have
Save that I have to have it still.

For fortune hath kept her promess
In granting me my most desire.
Of my sovereign I have redress,
And I content me with my hire.

THE LOVER COMPLAINETH THE UNKINDNESS OF HIS LOVE[1]

My lute, awake! Perform the last
Labor that thou and I shall waste,
And end that I have now begun;
And when this song is sung and past,
My lute, be still, for I have done.

As to be heard where ear is none,
As lead to grave in marble stone,

My song may pierce her heart as soon.
Should we then sigh, or sing, or moan?
No, no, my lute, for I have done.   10

The rocks do not so cruelly
Repulse the waves continually
As she my suit and affection,
So that I am past remedy,
Whereby my lute and I have done.

Proud of the spoil that thou hast got
Of simple hearts through Love's shot,
By whom, unkind, thou hast them won,
Think not he hath his bow forgot,
Although my lute and I have done.   20

Vengeance shall fall on thy disdain,
That makest but game on earnest pain.
Think not alone under the sun
Unquit to cause thy lovers plain,
Although my lute and I have done.

May chance thee lie wither'd and old
In winter nights that are so cold,
Plaining in vain unto the moon.
Thy wishes then dare not be told;
Care then who list, for I have done.   30

And then may chance thee to repent
The time that thou hast lost and spent
To cause thy lovers sigh and swown;
Then shalt thou know beauty but lent,
And wish and want as I have done.

Now cease, my lute! This is the last
Labor that thou and I shall waste,
And ended is that we begun.
Now is this song both sung and past.
My lute, be still, for I have done.   40

THE LOVER'S LIFE COMPARED TO THE ALPS

Petrarchan

Like unto these unmeasurable mountains
So is my painful life, the burden of ire;
For high be they, and high is my desire;
And I of tears, and they be full of fountains.
Under craggy rocks they have barren plains;
Hard thoughts in me my woful mind doth tire.
Small fruit and many leaves their tops do attire;
With small effect great trust in me remains.
The boistous winds oft their high boughs do blast;
Hot sighs in me continually be shed.   10
Wild beasts in them, fierce love in me is fed.
Unmovable am I, and they steadfast.
Of singing birds they have the tune and note,
And I always plaints passing through my throat.

A RENOUNCING OF LOVE

Farewell, love, and all thy laws forever!
Thy baited hooks shall tangle me no more;
Senec and Plato call me from thy lore

To parfit wealth, my wit for to endeavor.
In blind error when I did parsever,
Thy sharp repulse, that pricketh ay so sore,
Taught me in trifles that I set no store,
But scape forth thence, since liberty is lever.
Therefore, farewell! Go trouble younger hearts,
And in me claim no more auctority.   10
With idle youth go use thy proparty,
And thereon spend thy many brittle darts,
For, hitherto though I have lost my time,
Me list no lenger rotten boughs to clime.

DESCRIPTION OF A GUN

Vulcan begat me; Minerva me taught;
Nature, my mother; Craft nourish'd me year by year.
Three bodies are my food; my strength is in naught.
Anger, wrath, waste, and noise are my children dear.
Guess, friend, what I am and how I am wrought—
Monster of sea, or of land, or of elsewhere.
Know me and use me, and I may thee defend;
And if I be thine en'my, I may thy life end.

THE COURTIER'S LIFE

In court to serve, decked with fresh array,
Of sug'red meats feeling the sweet repast,
The life in bankets and sundry kinds of play
Among the press of lordly looks to waste—
Hath with it join'd ofttimes such bitter taste
That whoso joys such kind of life to hold,
In prison joys, fett'red with chains of gold.

OF HIS RETURN FROM SPAIN

Tagus, farewell, that westward with thy streams
Turns up the grains of gold already tried,
For I with spur and sail go seek the Thames,
Gainward the sun that sheweth her wealthy pride,
And to the town that Brutus sought by dreams,
Like bended moon that leans her lusty side.
My king, my country, I seek for whom I live.
O mighty Jove! the winds for this me geve.

OF THE MEAN AND SURE ESTATE
Written to John Poins

My mother's maids when they do sew and spin,
They sing a song made of the fieldish mouse;
That forbecause her livelod was but thin,
Would needs go see her townish sister's house.
She thought herself endured too grievous pain;
The stormy blasts her cave so sore did sowse
That when the furrows swimmed with the rain,
She must lie cold and wet, in sorry plight.
And worse then that, bare meat there did remain
To comfort her when she her house had dight: 10
Sometime a barley corn, sometime a bean,

For which she labored hard both day and night
In harvest time, while she might go and glean.
And when her store was stroyed with the flood,
Then wellaway, for she undone was clean.
Then was she fain to take instead of food
Sleep, if she might, her hunger to beguile.
"My sister," quod she, "hath a living good,
And hence from me she dwelleth not a mile.
In cold and storm she lieth warm and dry   20
In bed of down, the dirt doth not defile
Her tender foot, she labors not as I;
Richly she feeds, and at the rich man's cost,
And for her meat she needs not crave nor cry.
By sea, by land, of delicates the most
Her cater seeks, and spareth for no peril;
She feeds on boil meat, bake meat, and on roast,
And hath therefore no whit of charge nor travail.
And when she list, the liquor of the grape
Doth glad her heart, till that her belly swell."   30
And at this journey makes she but a jape;
So forth she goes, trusting of all this wealth
With her sister her part so for to shape
That if she might there keep herself in health,
To live a lady while her life doth last.
And to the door now is she come by stealth,
And with her foot anon she scrapes full fast.
Th' other for fear durst not well scarce appear,
Of every noise so was the wretch aghast.
At last she asked softly who was there.   40
And in her language as well as she could,
"Peep," quod the other, "sister, I am here."
"Peace," quod the town mouse, "why speakest thou so
     loud?"
And by the hand she took her fair and well,
"Welcome," quod she, "my sister, by the rood."
She feasted her that joy it was to tell
The fare they had, they drank the wine so clear;
And as to purpose, now and then it fell
She cheered her with "How, sister, what cheer?"
Amid this joy befell a sorry chance,   50
That, wellaway, the stranger bought full dear
The fare she had. For as she look'd askance,
Under a stool she spied two steaming eyes
In a round head, with sharp ears; in France
Was never mouse so fear'd, for the unwise
Had not yseen such a beast before;
Yet had nature taught her, after her guise,
To know her foe and dread him evermore.
The town mouse fled, she knew whither to go;
The other had no shift, but wonders sore,   60
Fear'd of her life; at home she wish'd her tho,
And to the door, alas, as she did skip,
The heaven it would, lo, and eke her chance was so,
At the threshold her seely foot did trip,
And ere she might recover it again.

The traitor cat had caught her by the hip,
And made her there against her will remain,
That had forgot her poor surety and rest
For seeming wealth, wherein she thought to reign.
Alas, my Poins, how men do seek the best   70
And find the worst, by error as they stray.
And no marvel, when sight is so oppress'd,
And blinds the guide; anon out of the way
Goeth guide and all in seeking quiet life.
O wretched minds, there is no gold that may
Grant that you seek, no war, no peace, no strife.
No, no, although thy head were hoop'd with gold,
Sergeant with mace, with hawbart, sword, nor knife,
Cannot repulse the care that follow should.
Each kind of life hath with him his disease.   80
Live in delight, even as thy lust would,
And thou shalt find when lust doth most thee please,
It irketh straight, and by itself doth fade.
A small thing is it that may thy mind appease;
None of you all there is that is so mad
To seek for grapes on brambles or on briers;
Nor none I trow that hath his wit so bad
To set his hay for conies over rivers,
Nor ye set not a dragnet for an hare;
And yet the thing that most is your desire   90
You do misseek with more travail and care.
Make plain thine heart, that it be not knotted
With hope or dread, and see thy will be bare
From all affects, whom vice hath ever spotted.
Thyself content with that is thee assign'd,
And use it well that is to thee allotted.
Then seek no more out of thyself to find
The thing that thou hast sought so long before,
For thou shalt feel it sticking in thy mind;
Mad, if ye list to continue your sore,   100
Let present pass, and gape on time to come,
And deep yourself in travail more and more.
Henceforth, my Poins, this shall be all and some;
These wretched fools shall have nought else of me;
But to the great God and to his dome,
None other pain pray I for them to be,
But when the rage doth lead them from the right,
That looking backward, virtue they may see
Even as she is, so goodly fair and bright.
And whilst they clasp their lusts in arms across, 110
Grant them, good Lord, as thou mayst of thy might,
To fret inward for losing such a loss.

OF THE COURTIER'S LIFE

Written to John Poins

Mine own John Poins, since ye delight to know
The causes why that homeward I me draw,
And flee the prease of courts, whereso they go,
Rather then to live thrall under the awe

Of lordly looks, wrapped within my cloak,
To will and lust learning to set a law;
It is not because I scorn or mock
The power of them, whom fortune here hath lent
Charge over us, of right to strike the stroke.
But true it is that I have always meant   10
Less to esteem them then the common sort,
Of outward things that judge in their entent
Without regard what inward doth resort.
I grant sometime of glory that the fire
Doth touch my heart. Me list not to report
Blame by honor, and honor to desire.
But how may I this honor now attain
That cannot dye the color black a liar?
My Poins, I cannot frame my tune to feign,
To cloak the truth, for praise without desert,   20
Of them that list all [vice] for to retain.
I cannot honor them that set their part
With Venus and Bacchus all their life long;
Nor hold my peace of them, although I smart.
I cannot crouch nor kneel to such a wrong,
To worship them like God on earth alone,
That are as wolves these seely lambs among.
I cannot with my words complain and moan
And suffer nought, nor smart without complaint,
Nor turn the word that from my mouth is gone;   30
I cannot speak and look like as a saint,
Use wiles for wit, and make disceit a pleasure;
Call craft counsail, for lucre still to paint;
I cannot wrest the law to fill the coffer,
With innocent blood to feed myself fat,
And do most hurt where that most help I offer.
I am not he that can allow the state
Of high Caesar, and damn Cato to die;
That with his death did scape out of the gate
From Caesar's hands, if Livy doth not lie,   40
And would not live where liberty was lost,
So did his heart the common wealth apply.
I am not he, such eloquence to boast,
To make the crow in singing as the swan,
Nor call the lion of coward beasts the most,
That cannot take a mouse as the cat can;
And he that dieth for hunger of the gold,
Call him Alexander, and say that Pan
Passeth Apollo in music manifold;
Praise Sir Thopas for a noble tale,   50
And scorn the story that the Knight told;
Praise him for counsel that is drunk of ale;
Grin when he laughs that beareth all the sway,
Frown when he frowns, and groan when he is pale;
On others' lust to hang both night and day.
None of these points would ever frame in me;
My wit is nought, I cannot learn the way.
And much the less of things that greater be,
That asken help of colors to devise

To join the mean with each extremity; 60
With nearest virtue ay to cloak the vice.
And as to purpose likewise it shall fall,
To press the virtue that it may not rise;
As drunkenness good fellowship to call;
The friendly foe, with his fair double face,
Say he is gentle and curties therewithal;
Affirm that favel hath a goodly grace
In eloquence; and cruelty to name
Zeal of justice, and change in time and place;
And he that suff'reth offense without blame, 70
Call him pitiful, and him true and plain
That raileth rechless unto each man's shame;
Say he is rude that cannot lie and feign;
The lecher a lover, and tyranny
To be the right of a prince's reign.
I cannot, I; no, no, it will not be.
This is the cause that I could never yet
Hang on their sleeves, that weigh, as thou mayst see,
A chip of chance more then a pound of wit.
This maketh me at home to hunt and hawk, 80
And in foul weather at my book to sit,
In frost and snow then with my bow to stalk.
No man doth mark whereso I ride or go.
In lusty leas at liberty I walk,
And of these news I feel nor weal nor wo,
Save that a clog doth hang yet at my heel.
No force for that, for it is ord'red so
That I may leap both hedge and dike full well;
I am not now in France to judge the wine,
With sav'ry sauce those delicates to feel, 90
Nor yet in Spain where one must him incline,
Rather then to be, outwardly to seem.
I meddle not with wits that be so fine,
Nor Flanders cheer lets not my sight to deem
Of black and white, nor takes my wits away
With beastliness; such do those beasts esteem.
Nor I am not where truth is geven in prey
For money, poison, and treason; of some
A common practise, used night and day.
But I am here in Kent and Christendom, 100
Among the muses, where I read and rime;
Where if thou list, mine own John Poins, to come,
Thou shalt be judge how I do spend my time.

OF HIS LOVE CALLED ANNA

What word is that that changeth not
Though it be turned and made in twain?
It is mine Anna, God it wot,
The only causer of my pain,
My love that meedeth with disdain.
Yet is it loved, what will you more?
It is my salve and eke my sore.

HE RULETH NOT THOUGH HE REIGN OVER REALMS THAT IS SUBJECT TO HIS OWN LUSTS

If thou wilt mighty be, flee from the rage
Of cruel will, and see thou keep thee free
From the foul yoke of sensual bondage;
For though thy empire stretch to Indian Sea,
And for thy fear trembleth the fardest Thulee,
If thy desire have over thee the power,
Subject, then, art thou and no governor.
If to be noble and high thy mind be meved,
Consider well thy ground and thy beginning.
For He that hath each star in heaven fixed, 10
And geves the moon her horns and her eclipsing,
Alike hath made thee noble in his working,
So that wretched no way thou may bee
Except foul lust and vice do conquer thee.
All were it so thou had a flood of gold,
Unto thy thirst yet should it not suffice.
And though with Indian stones a thousandfold
More precious then can thyself devise
Ycharged were thy back, thy covetise
And busy biting yet should never let 20
Thy wretched life ne do thy death profet.

Poems from Manuscripts

[HELP ME TO SEEK]

Help me to seek, for I lost it there,
And if that ye have found it, ye that be here,
And seek to convey it secretly,
Handle it soft and treat it tenderly,
Or else it will plain, and then appair.

But rather restore it mannerly,
Since that I do ask it thus honestly,
For to lese it, it sitteth me too near.
 Help me to seek!

Alas, and is there no remedy? 10
But have I thus lost it wilfully?
Iwis it was a thing all too dear
To be bestowed, and wist not where:
It was mine heart. I pray you heartily
 Help me to seek!

[FORGET NOT YET]

Forget not yet the tried entent
Of such a truth as I have meant,
My great travail, so gladly spent,
 Forget not yet.

Forget not yet when first began
The weary life ye know, since whan

The suit, the service none tell can,
  Forget not yet.

Forget not yet the great assays,
The cruel wrong, the scornful ways;   10
The painful patience in denays,
  Forget not yet.

Forget not yet, forget not this,
How long ago hath been, and is,
The mind that never meant amiss,
  Forget not yet.

Forget not, then, thine own approved,
The which so long hath thee so loved,
Whose steadfast faith yet never moved,
  Forget not this.   20

[AND WILT THOU LEAVE ME THUS]

  And wilt thou leave me thus?
Say nay, say nay! for shame,
To save thee from the blame
Of all my grief and grame.
And wilt thou leave me thus?
Say nay, say nay!

  And wilt thou leave me thus,
That hath loved thee so long
In wealth and wo among?
And is thy heart so strong   10
As for to leave me thus?
Say nay, say nay!

  And wilt thou leave me thus,
That hath given thee my heart,
Never for to depart
Nother for pain nor smart?
And wilt thou leave me thus?
Say nay, say nay!

  And wilt thou leave me thus,
And have no more pity   20
Of him that loveth thee?
Helas, thy cruelty!
And wilt thou leave me thus?
Say nay, say nay!

[BLAME NOT MY LUTE]

Blame not my lute, for he must sound
Of this and that as liketh me;
For lack of wit the lute is bound
To give such tunes as pleaseth me.
Though my songs be somewhat strange,
And speaks such words as touch thy change,
  Blame not my lute.

My lute, alas, doth not offend,
Though that perforce he must agree
To sound such tunes as I entend   10
To sing to them that heareth me;
Then though my songs be somewhat plain
And toucheth some that use to feign,
  Blame not my lute.

My lute and strings may not deny,
But as I strike they must obey;
Break not them, than, so wrongfully,
But wreak thyself some wiser way;
And though the songs which I endight
[Do] quit thy change with rightful spite,   20
  Blame not my lute.

Spight asketh spight, and changing change,
And falsed faith must needs be known;
The faut so great, the case so strange,
Of right it must abroad be blown.
Then since that by thine own desart
My songs do tell how true thou art,
  Blame not my lute.

Blame but theeself that hast misdone
And well desarved to have blame;   30
Change thou thy way so evil begun
And then my lute shall sound that same;
But if till then my fingers play,
By thy desart, their wonted way,
  Blame not my lute.

Farewell, unknown, for though thou brake
My strings in spight, with great disdain,
Yet have I found out for thy sake
Strings for to string my lute again.
And if perchance this foolish rime   40
Do make thee blush at any time,
  Blame not my lute.

[SINCE YOU WILL NEEDS]

Since you will needs that I shall sing,
Take it in worth, sich as I have,
Plenty of plaint, moan, and mourning
In deep dispair and deadly pain,
Bootless for boot, crying to crave,
  To crave in vain.

Such hammers work within my head
That sound nought else unto my ears
But fast at board, and wake abed;
Such tune the temper to my song   10
To wail my wrong, that I want tears
  To wail my wrong.

Death and dispair afore my face,
My days decays, my grief doth grow;
The cause thereof is in this place,
Whom cruelty doth still constrain
For to rejoice, though it be wo
  To hear me plain.

A broken lute, untuned strings
With such a song may well bear part,   20
That neither pleaseth him that sings

Nor theim that hear, but her alone
That with her heart would strain my heart,
  To hear it groan.

If it grieve you to hear this same
That you do feel but in my voice,
Consider, then, what pleasant game
I do sustain in every part
To cause me sing or to rejoice
  Within my heart.   30

NICHOLAS GRIMALD

CONCERNING VIRGIL'S AENEIDS

By heaven's high gift, in case revived were
Lysip, Apelles, and Homer the great—
The most renowm'd, and each of them sans peer
In graving, painting, and the poet's feat—
Yet could they not, for all their vein divine,
In marble, table, paper more or less,
With cheezel, pencil, or with pointel fine
So grave, so paint, or so by style express
(Though they beheld of every age and land
The fairest books in every tongue contrived   10
To frame a fourm and to direct their hand)
Of noble prince the lively shape descrived
As, in the famous work that Aeneids hight,
The namecouth Virgil hath set forth in sight.

MAN'S LIFE AFTER POSIDONIUS OR CRATES

What path list you to tread? What trade will you assay?
The courts of plea by brawl and bate drive gentle peace
  away.
In house, for wife and child, there is but cark and care;
With travail and with toil inough in fields we use to fare.
Upon the seas lieth dread; the rich in forain land
Do fear the loss; and there the poor like misers poorly
  stand.
Strife with a wife; without, your thrift full hard to see.
Young brats a trouble; none at all, a maim it seems to be.
Youth fond; age hath no heart and pincheth all too nigh.
Choose, then, the liefer of these two: no life, or soon to
  die.   10

THE GARDEN

The issue of great Jove, draw near, you muses nine!
Help us to praise the blissful plot of garden ground so fine.
The garden gives good food and aid for leech's cure;
The garden, full of great delight, his master doth allure.
Sweet sallet herbs be here, and herbs of every kind;
The ruddy grapes, the seemly fruits, be here at hand to
  find.

Here pleasance wanteth not to make a man full fain;
Here marvelous the mixture is of solace and of gain.
To water sundry seeds, the furrow by the way
A running river, trilling down with liquor, can convey. 10
Behold, with lively hue fair flow'rs that shine so bright;
With riches, like the orient gems, they paint the mold in
  sight.
Bees, humming with soft sound (their murmur is so
  small),
Of blooms and blossoms suck the tops; on dewed leaves
  they fall.
The creeping vine holds down her own bewedded elms,
And, wandering out with branches thick, reeds folded
  overwhelms.
Trees spread their coverts wide with shadows fresh and
  gay;
Full well their branched bows defend the fervent sun
  away.
Birds chatter, and some chirp, and some sweet tunes do
  yield;
All mirthful, with their songs so blithe, they make both
  air and field.   20
The garden it allures, it feeds, it glads the sprite;
From heavy hearts all doleful dumps the garden chaseth
  quite.
Strength it restores to lims, draws and fulfils the sight;
With cheer revives the senses all and maketh labor light.
O, what delights to us the garden ground doth bring!
Seed, leaf, flow'r, fruit, herb, bee, and tree, and more then
  I may sing!

A FUNERAL SONG UPON THE DECEASE
OF ANNES, HIS MOTHER

Yea, and a good cause why thus should I plain;
For what is he can quietly sustain
So great a grief with mouth as still as stone?
My love, my life, of joy my jewel is gone.
This hearty zeal if any wight disprove
As woman's work, whom feeble mind doth move,

He neither knows the mighty nature's laws
Nor touching elders' deeds hath seen old saws.
Martius, to vanquish Rome, was set on fire,
But vanquish'd fell, at mother's boon, his ire.   10
Into Hesperian land Sertorius fled,
Of parent, ay, chief care had in his head.
Dear weight on shoulders Sicil brethren bore
While Etna's giant spouted flames full sore.
Not more of Tyndar's imps hath Sparta spoke
Than Arge of charged necks with parents' yoke.
Nor only them thus did foretime entreat:
Then was the nurse also in honor great.
Caiet the Phrygian from amid fireflame
Rescued, who gave to Latin stronds the name.   20
Acca, in double sense Lupa ycleped,
To Roman calendars a feast hath heaped.
His Capra Jove among the sters hath pight;
In welkin clear yet, lo! she shineth bright.
Hyades as gratefully Lyai did place,
Whom, in primetide, supports the Bull's fair face.
And should not I express my inward wo
When you, most loving dam, so soon hence go?
I, in your fruitful womb conceived, borne was
While wandering moon ten months did overpass.   30
Me, brought to light, your tender arms sustain'd,
And with my lips your milky paps I strain'd.
You me embraced, in bosom soft you me
Cherished as I your only child had be.
Of issue fair with numbers were you blest,
Yet I the best beloved of all the rest.
Good luck certain forereading mothers have,
And you of me a special judgment gave.
Then, when firm pace I fixed on the ground,
When tongue gan cease to break the lisping sound,   40
You me straightway did to the muses send,
Ne suffered long a loitering life to spend.
What gain the wool, what gain the web had braught,
It was his meed that me there daily taught.
When with Minerve I had acquaintance won,
And Phoebus seem'd to love me as his son,
Brownshold I bad, at parents' hest, farewell,
And gladly there in schools I gan to dwell
Where Granta gives the ladies nine such place
That they rejoice to see their blissful case.   50
With joys at heart in this Pernasse I bode
While through his signs five times great Titan glode;
And twice as long by that fair ford whereas
Swan-feeder Thames no furder course can pass.
O, what desire had you, therewhile, of me?
Mid doubtful dreads, what joys were wont to be?
Now linen clothes, wrought with those fingers fine,
Now other things of yours did you make mine.
Till your last threads gan Clotho to untwine
And of your days the date extreme assign.   60

Hearing the chance, your neighbors made much moan;
A dearworth dame, they thought their comfort gone.
Kinswomen wept; your charge, the maidens, wept;
Your daughters wept whom you so well had kept.
But my good sire gave, with soft words, relief,
And cloaks with outward cheer his inward grief,
Lest, by his care, your sickness should augment
And on his case your thoughtful heart be bent.
You, not forgetting yet a mother's mood,
When at the door dart-thirling death there stood,   70
Did say, "Adieu, dear spouse, my race is run.
Whereso he be, I have left you a son."
And "Nicholas" you nam'd and nam'd again,
With other speech, aspiring heavenly reign,
When into air your sprite, departed, fled
And left the corps a-cold in lukewarm bed.
Ah, could you thus, dear Mother, leave us all?
Now should you live that yet, before your fall,
My songs you might have sung, have heard my voice,
And in commodities of your own rejoice.   80
My sisters yet unwedded who shall guide?
With whose good lessons shall they be applied?
Have, Mother, monuments of our sore smart:
No costly tomb, arear'd with curious art,
Nor Mausolean mass hung in the air,
Nor lofty steeples that will once appair,
But wailful verse and doleful song accept.
By verse the names of ancient peers be kept;
By verse lives Hercules; by verse, Achil;
Hector, Ene, by verse, be famous still.   90
Such former years, such death hath chanced thee;
Clos'd with good end good life is wont to be.
But now, my sacred parent, fare you well!
God shall cause us again togither dwell
What time this universal globe shall hear
Of the last trump the ringing voice—great fear
To some, to such as you a heavenly cheer.
Till then, repos'd, rest you in gentle sleep
While He, whom to you are bequeath'd, you keep.

MARCUS TULLIUS CICERO'S DEATH

Therefore, when restless rage of wind and wave
He saw, "By fates, alas! call'd for," quod he,
"Is hapless Cicero. Sail on! Shape course
To the next shore, and bring me to my death!
Perdie these thanks, rescued from civil sword,
Wilt thou, my country, pay? I see mine end.
So pow'rs divine, so bid the gods above,
In city saved that Consul Marcus shend."
Speaking no more, but drawing from deep heart
Great groans, even at the name of Rome rehears'd,   10
His eyes and cheeks with show'rs of tears he wash'd.
And though a rout in daily dangers worn,

With forced face the shipmen held their tears
And, striving long the sea's rough floods to pass,
In angry winds and stormy stours made way,
And at the last safe anchor'd in the road.
Came heavy Cicero a-land; with pain
His fainted lims the aged sire doth draw,
And round about their master stood his band,
Nor greatly with their own hard hap dismay'd   20
Nor plighted faith prone in sharp time to break;
Some swords prepare; some their dear lord assist.
In litter laid, they lead him uncouth ways,
If so deceive Antonius' cruel gleaves
They might, and threats of following routs escape.
Thus lo, that Tully went, that Tullius
Of royal robe and sacred senate prince.
When he afar the men approach espieth
And of his fone the ensigns doth aknow,
And, with drawn sword, Popillius threat'ning death   30
(Whose life and whole estate, in hazard once,
He had preserv'd when Rome, as yet to free,
Heard him, and at his thund'ring voice amaz'd).
Herennius eke, more eager than the rest,
Present enflam'd with fury, him pursues.
What might he do? Should he use in defense
Disarmed hands? Or pardon ask, for meed?
Should he with words attempt to turn the wrath
Of th' armed knight whose safeguard he had wrought?
No! Age forbids and, fix'd within deep breast,   40
His country's love and falling Rome's image.

"The charet turn," saith he; "let loose the reins. . . .
Slay me. Yet all th' offspring to come shall know,
And this decease shall bring eternal life.
Yea, and unless I fail, and all in vain,
Rome, I sometime thy augur chosen was,
Not evermore shall friendly fortune thee
Favor, Antonius. Once the day shall come
When her dear wights, by cruel spight thus slain,
Victorious Rome shall at thy hands require.   50
Me likes, therewhile, go see the hoped heaven."
Speech had he left, and therewith he, good man,
His throat prepar'd and held his head unmoved.
His hasting to those fates the very knights
Be loth to see, and rage rebated when
They his bare neck beheld and his hoar hairs.
Scant could they hold the tears that forth gan burst,
And almost fell from bloody hands the swords.
Only the stern Herennius, with grim look,
"Dastards, why stand you still?" he saith, and straight 60
Swaps off the head with his presumptuous iron.
Ne with that slaughter yet is he not fill'd;
Foul shame on shame to heap is his delight.
Wherefore the hands also doth he off smite
Which durst Antonius' life so lively paint.
Him, yielding strained ghost, from welkin high
With lothly cheer Lord Phoebus gan behold,
And in black cloud, they say, long hid his head.
The Latin muses, and the Grays, they wept,
And, for his fall, eternally shall weep. . . .   70

UNCERTAIN AUTHORS

COMPARISON OF LIFE AND DEATH

   The life is long that lothsomely doth last;
The doleful days draw slowly to their date;
The present pangs and painful plages forepast
Yield grief ay green to stablish this estate;
So that I feel, in this great storm and strife,
The death is sweet that endeth such a life.
   Yet by the stroke of this strange overthrow,
At which conflict in thraldom I was thrust,
The Lord be praised, I am well taught to know
From whence man came and eke whereto he must,   10
And by the way upon how feeble force
His term doth stand till death doth end his course.
   The pleasant years that seem so swift that run,
The merry days to end so fast that fleet,
The joyful nights of which day daweth so soon,
The happy hours which mo do miss then meet,

Do all consume as snow against the sun;
And death makes end of all that life begun.
   Since death shall dure till all the world be waste,
What meaneth man to dread death then so sore?   20
As man might make that life should alway last,
Without regard the Lord hath led before
The dance of death which all must run on row,
Though how, or when, the Lord alone doth know.
   If man would mind what burdens life doth bring,
What grievous crimes to God he doth commit,
What plages, what pangs, what perils thereby spring,
With no sure hour in all his days to sit,
He would sure think, as with great cause I do,
The day of death were better of the two.   30
   Death is a port whereby we pass to joy;
Life is a lake that drowneth all in pain.
Death is so dear it ceaseth all annoy;

Life is so lewd that all it yields is vain.
And as by life to bondage man is braught,
Even so likewise by death was freedom wraught.
  Wherefore with Paul let all men wish and pray
To be dissolv'd of this foul fleshy mass,
Or at the least be armed against the day,
That they be found good soldiers, prest to pass   40
From life to death, from death to life again—
To such a life as ever shall remain.

A PRAISE OF PETRARCH AND OF LAURA, HIS LADY

O Petrarch, head and prince of poets all,
Whose lively gift of flowing eloquence
Well may we seek but find not how or whence
So rare a gift with thee did rise and fall,
Peace to thy bones, and glory immortal
Be to thy name and to her excellence
Whose beauty lighted in thy time and sense
So to be set forth as none other shall!
Why hath not our pens rimes so perfit wrought?
Ne why our time forth bringeth beauty such   10
To try our wits as gold is by the touch
If to the style the matter aided ought?
But there was never Laura more then one,
And her had Petrarch for his paragon.

A COMPARISON OF HIS LOVE WITH THE FAITHFUL AND PAINFUL LOVE OF TROILUS TO CRESSID

  I read how Troilus served in Troy
A lady long and many a day,
And how he bode so great annoy
For her, as all the stories say,
That half the pain had never man
Which had this woful Troyan than.
  His youth, his sport, his pleasant cheer,
His courtly state and company
In him so strangely alt'red were
With such a face of contrary   10
That every joy became a wo.
This poison new had turned him so.
  And what men thought might most him ease
And most that for his comfort stode,
The same did most his mind displease
And set him most in furious mode;
For all his pleasure ever lay
To think on her that was away.
  His chamber was his common walk
Wherein he kept him secretly;   20
He made his bed the place of talk,
To hear his great extremity.
In nothing else had he delight
But even to be a martyr right.

  And now to call her by her name
And straight therewith to sigh and throb.
And when his fancies might not frame,
Then into tears and so to sob.
All in extremes and thus he lies,
Making two fountains of his eyes.   30
  As agues have sharp shifts of fits
Of cold and heat successively,
So had his head like change of wits.
His patience wrought so diversly—
Now up, now down, now here, now there,
Like one that was he wist not where.
  And thus, though he were Priam's son
And comen of the king's high blood,
This care he had ere he her won;
Till she that was his maistress good,   40
And loth to see her servant so,
Became phisicion to his wo,
  And took him to her hands and grace,
And said she would her mind apply
To help him in his woful case
If she might be his remedy.
And thus, they say, to ease his smart
She made him owner of her heart.
  And truth it is, except they lie,
From that day forth her study went   50
To shew to love him faithfully
And his whole mind full to content.
So happy a man at last was he,
And eke so worthy a woman she.
  Lo! lady, then, judge you by this
Mine ease and how my case doth fall,
For sure between my life and his
No difference there is at all.
His care was great; so was his pain;
And mine is not the least of twain.   60
  For what he felt in service true
For her whom that he loved so,
The same I feel as large for you
To whom I do my service owe.
There was that time in him no pain
But now the same in me doth reign.
  Which if you can compare and weigh,
And how I stand in every plight,
Then this for you I dare well say:
Your heart must needs remorse of right   70
To grant me grace and so to do
As Cressid then did Troilus to.
  For well I wot you are as good
And even as fair as ever was she,
And comen of as worthy blood,
And have in you as large pity
To tender me your own true man
As she did him her servant than.
  Which gift I pray God for my sake

Full soon and shortly you me send;   80
So shall you make my sorrows slake,
So shall you bring my wo to end,
And set me in as happy case
As Troilus with his lady was.

THE PROMISE OF A CONSTANT LOVER

As laurel leaves that cease not to be green
From parching sun nor yet from winter's thret,

As hardened oak that fear'th no sword so keen,
As flint for tool in twain that will not fret,
As fast as rock or pillar surely set,
So fast am I to you and ay have been;
Assuredly whom I cannot forget
For joy, for pain, for torment, nor for teen,
For loss, for gain, for frowning, nor for thret;
But ever one, yea both in calm or blast,   10
Your faithful friend, and will be to my last.

JOHN HALL

THE COURT OF VIRTUE

Although its contents are contemptible as literature, *The Court of Virtue* is a quaint reminder of certain puritanical Elizabethans' reaction to secular and amatory verse. Hall, who mingled poetry and medicine, evidently intended his book as a sharp challenge to the vogue signalized by the success of *The Court of Venus* and Tottel's *Miscellany*. It is a collection of the author's various works written at various times, all of them dedicated to the proposition that the uses of literature are moral and didactic. A long "Prologue" in the form of a dream-allegory shows the troubled poet wandering in the country; presently he falls asleep and dreams of three fair ladies who proffer him advice. Madame Hope tries to console him, but Lady Virtue (or Arete) tartly denounces the depraved condition of man and the lamentable reading habits of the public.

> Such as in carnal love rejoice,
> Trim songs of love they will compile;
> And sinfully with tune and voice
> They sing their songs in pleasant style
> To Venus, that same strumpet vile,
> And make of her a goddess dear
> In lechery that had no peer.

> A book also of songs they have,
> And *Venus' Court* they do it name;
> No filthy mind a song can crave
> But therein he may find the same,
> And in such songs is all their game,
> Whereof right divers books be made
> To nourish that most filthy trade.

In view of this calamity Lady Virtue charges the poet to provide an antidote by showing the compatibility of godly doctrine and lyric poetry; she commands him

> To make a book of songs holy,
> Godly, and wise, blaming folly.

After Love, the third lady, encourages the poet to exercise charity, he addresses himself to his task.

The result is not very lyrical, but it is incorrigibly godly. In his one-man miscellany Hall includes songs built around specific Scriptural citations and dramatized through speakers like Jeremiah and Christ (for instance, "The Praise of Godly Love or Charity out of I. Corinthians xiii and John iv"); he versifies the Apostles' Creed, the Pater Noster, and the Ten Commandments; he writes metrical paraphrases of the Psalms; he composes a long dream-allegory on the evils of witchcraft; he even inserts a ballad, "The Description . . . of a Monstrous Child Born in the Town of Maidstone in the County of Kent in the Year of Our Salvation 1561 the 29 Day of September." But most interestingly for our purposes, he "moralizes" some of the lyrics of Sir Thomas Wyatt, and thus shows how the most worldly and amorous poetry can, by a few skilful changes, be converted to the uses of piety. Our excerpts include "A Song of the Lute in the Praise of God and Dispraise of Idolatry," derived from "My Lute, Awake," and "A Ditty of the Pen Inveighing against Usury and False Dealing," from "My Pen, Take Blame." Many of Hall's "songs" are accompanied by musical notation; others (for example, "A Song of the Lute") merely indicate the tune through the title of a popular refrain.

Although Hall's book survives in several mutilated copies, we do not possess the original titlepage. An entry in the Stationers' Register sometime between July, 1564, and July, 1565, gives the title as *The Couurte of vertu contaynynge many holy or spretuall songes Sonettes psalmes ballettes shorte sentences as well of holy scriptures as others &c.;* our text is based upon the fragmentary copies in the British Museum and the Huntington Library (STC 12632).

from THE COURT OF VIRTUE (1565)

AN EXAMPLE OF THE PRAISE OF GOD FOR HIS OMNIPOTENCY, OUT OF THE CXIII PSALM

King David, knowing well
How virtue did excel
All other worldly thing,
Did chiefly in God's fear
All wickedness forbear
That may God's anger bring.

For God is of such pow'r
That nothing at no hour
Can him withstand or bide,
For he may work his will   10
All mortal men until
At every time and tide.

Therefore we are all bound
That dwel in this world round
To praise the living Lord,
And in that Lord of Might
To set our whole delight
And in his Holy Word.

Wherefore this noble king
Studied above all thing   20
His duty to walk in;
To sing God's laud and praise
He maketh no delays,
But thus he doth begin.

Laudate pueri dominum

Ye servants, praise the Lord
And with hearty accord
See that ye do the same.
Look that ye render store
Of praises evermore
Unto his blessed name.   30

His name that we should praise
He is worthy always,
Even from the rising-time
Of the sun fair and bright
Until it be in sight
That down he doth incline.

The Lord is high of might;
There is no kind of wight
That can with him compare;
His glories certainly   40
Above the heavens high
Remain and ever are.

Who is like unto him
Or will presume to clim
Where he so high doth dwel¹?
Yet is this Lord so meek
To behold and take keep
Of earth and heaven well;

Who doth the simple take
Out of the miry lake   50
To set them up again;
He takes out of the dust
All that in him do trust
To rid them from their pain,

So that he may them set
Among the princes great
By his great pow'r and might,
The princes all among
Which govern do the throng
Of people day and night.   60

He doth redeem also
The woman from her wo
That barren long hath been;
A mother full of bliss
Of children now she is;
Her household may be seen.

A SONG OF THE LUTE IN THE PRAISE OF GOD AND DISPRAISE OF IDOLATRY

Sing this as "My Pen Obey, etc."

My lute, awake and praise the Lord,
My heart and hands thereto accord,
Agreeing as we have begun
To sing out of God's Holy Word,
And so proceed till we have done.

Praise we the Lord in this our song
And sing it Christen men among,
That in a godly race do run,
The which, although it be not long,
Shall be right good or it be done.   10

This pleasant song shall not sung be
To the goddess of lechery,
Nor to nothing under the sun
But praising of the Almighty,
My lute and I till we have done.

This teacheth us David the king,
With harp and lute geve God praising,

All men that in this world do won.
To God, therefore, geve praise and sing,
As my lute and I have begun.   20

This Lord first made all things of nought,
And when against his law we wrought,
From heaven he sent down his Son,
Which with his Gospel us all taught,
After the which we have not done.

Although in man were nothing good,
Him to redeem, Christ shed his blood.
With thorns the Jews our Lord did crown;
He suff'red death upon the rood;
Lo, thus our saving health was done.   30

On this, therefore, we fix our faith,
That Jesus Christ, as Scripture saith,
Is only our salvation.
Upon this rock who so him stay'th,
Thus saith the Lord, it is well done.

But one thing sore my heart doth grieve,
That hypocrites made us believe
In idols both of wood and stone.
From Christ our rock they did us drive;
Wo be to them what have they done.   40

Which canker still within their hearts
Doth yet remain and few converts,
For at God's Word they fret and frown;
Therefore, my lute, it is our parts
Them to rebuke as we have done.

God sent his Word unto this end,
That we our sinful lives should mend,
And yet repenteth few or none.
My lute, therefore, let us intend
To say the truth till we have done.   50

If in our song we should recite
How each estate doth not upright
(Which will be their confusion),
Which know the truth and do not right,
My lute, when should our song be done?

But to be short, my heart's intent
Is to praise God omnipotent,
Who of our health the thread hath spun
And hath his Word to us now sent
To mend our lives till we have done.   60

Man's soul to save, Christ died therefore,
Who of us men doth ask no more

But this lesson to learn and con,
With love to keep his holy lore
In which all perfect works are done.

Lord, grant us to thy Word to cleave
That no man other do deceive,
And in that zeal that I begun,
Lauding our Lord God, here I leave.
Be still, my lute; my song is done.   70

A DITTY OF THE PEN INVEIGHING AGAINST USURY AND FALSE DEALING

My pen, obey my will a while
Till I see good to end this style,
For if all men would sin abhor,
Such songs we need not to compile,
Nor my pen should write so no more.

If all men of their word were true
Promise to keep and pay their due,
What need had pens to work therefore?
But sith no wight will truth ensue,
Pens were as good to write no more.   10

Pens are abus'd, and that daily,
About all craft and usury;
We may well say alas therefore,
And yet, lest we make them angry,
It seems as good to write no more.

Yet let us shew the Lord's intent
How that for gains nought should be lent;
All falsehood God will plage right sore;
And yet, my pen, lest we be shent,
It seems as good to write no more.   20

For all in vain we speak Scripture
To such as will in sin endure,
For they amend never the more,
But hate all godly counsail pure
That warneth them to sin no more.

Yet if all men with such pretense
Should cease to shew their conscience,
They should transgress God's holy lore,
Yet sith none will it reverence,
It seems as good to write no more.   30

The Scripture thus doth specify
In David's Psalms, "Blessed is he
That lendeth freely rich and poor
Without all gain of usury."
Yet do they use it still the more.

Though some for writing will us blame,
These crafty men (whom we not name)
These false-got goods they must restore
To those of whom they got the same,
Or else be damn'd forever more.   40

For though some men have done ere this
In usury that did amiss
And have been warn'd of it before,
That do repent yet few there is,
But rather use it more and more.

But sure in hell their bed is made,
And all that use of craft the trade
Are like the same to rue right sore.
In craft and guile yet sith they wade,
It were as good to write no more.   50

God grant as in this song is meant
We may amend all and repent,
Rooting out vice to the hard core
To serve the Lord omnipotent
In love and truth forever more.

THE PARADISE OF DAINTY DEVICES

In a sense the successor to Tottel's anthology was *The Paradise of Dainty Devices*, the most popular and frequently reprinted of all Elizabethan miscellanies. Between 1576 and 1606 it went through at least ten editions (1576, 1577[?], 1578, 1580, 1585, 1590[?], 1596 [two], 1600, 1606). As Henry Disle, its publisher, tells us, it was the compilation of Richard Edwards, a man "both of worship and credit, for his private use," and the book (which was published posthumously) clearly reflects its compiler's taste for ditties that are "both pithy and pleasant, as well for the invention as meter, and will yield a far greater delight, being as they are so aptly made to be set to any song in five parts or sung to instrument." Since Edwards died in 1566, his collection was no doubt inspired by the success of Tottel's *Miscellany*, whether or not he intended that it should fall into the hands of Disle and be set forth in print.

The first edition contains ninety-nine pieces, but in its various reprintings the *Paradise* reached a total of one hundred twenty-seven poems by some thirty authors, who included Edwards himself, Thomas Churchyard, Sir Richard Grenville, Jasper Heywood, William Hunnis, Francis Kinwelmarsh, someone called "My Luck Is Loss" (who has been identified, on inconclusive evidence, with George Gascoigne), Edward de Vere, Earl of Oxford, Barnabe Rich, Lord Vaux, George Whetstone, and others, like the tantalizing "Master Bewe," who cannot now be identified. Although there are some conventional amatory poems in the early editions of the *Paradise*, the tone of the collection is set by the opening piece, a translation of St. Bernard's verses on "the unstable felicity of this wayfaring world"; and in later editions the deletions and additions were all dictated by piety and gravity. Our excerpts are all from the first edition except for Churchyard's "He Persuadeth His Friend from the Fond Affects of Love" (of which the first three stanzas are in 1576, the rest in 1578), Hunnis' "No Pains Comparable to His Attempt" (1578), and Rich's "An Epitaph upon the Death of Sir William Drury" (1580). Our text is based upon the editions of 1576, 1578, and 1580 (STC 7516, 7517, 7519).

FROM THE PARADISE OF DAINTY DEVICES (1576)

IN HIS EXTREME SICKNESS

What grieves my bones and makes my body faint?
What pricks my flesh and tears my head in twain?
Why do I wake when rest should me attaint?
When others laugh, why do I live in pain?
I toss, I turn, I change from side to side,
And stretch me oft, in sorrow's links beti'd.

I toss as one betoss'd in waves of care;
I turn to flee the woes of lothsome life;
I change to spy if death this corps might spare;
I stretch to heaven to rid me of this strife.   10
Thus do I stretch and change and toss and turn,
While I, in hope of heaven, my life do burn.

Then hold thee still, let be thy heaviness,
Abolish care, forget thy pining woe;
For by this means soon shalt thou find redress;
When oft betoss'd, hence thou to heaven must go.
Then toss and turn and tumble frank and free.
O happy thrice when thou in heaven shalt be!

Lord Vaux

FOR CHRISTMAS DAY

Rejoice, rejoice, with heart and voice;
In Christes[1] birth this day rejoice.

From Virgin's womb this day [to us] did spring
The precious seed that only saved man.
This day let man rejoice and sweetly sing,
Since on this day salvation first began.
This day did Christ man's soul from death remove,
With glorious saints to dwell in heaven above.

This day to man came pledge of perfect peace,
This day to man came love and unity,   10
This day man's grief began for to surcease,
This day did man receive a remedy
For each offense and every deadly sin,
With guilty heart, that erst he wand'red in.

In Christes flock let love be surely plac'd,
From Christes flock let concord hate expel,
Of Christes flock let love be so embrac'd
As we in Christ and Christ in us may dwell.
Christ is the aucthor of all unity,
From whence proceedeth all felicity.   20

O sing unto this glittering, glorious king!
O praise his name, let every living thing!
Let heart and voice like bells of silver ring
The comfort that this day [to us] did bring.
Let lute, let shalm, with sound of sweet delight,
The joy of Christes birth this day recite.

F[rancis] K[inwelmarsh]

EASTER DAY

All mortal men, this day rejoice
In Christ that you redeemed hath,
By death, with death. Sing we with voice
To him that hath appeased God's wrath,
Due unto man for sinful path
Wherein, before, he went astray.
Geve thanks to Him with perfect faith
That for mankind hath made this glorious day.

This day he rose from tomb again,
Wherein his precious corse was laid;   10
Whom cruelly the Jews had slain,
With bloody wounds full ill array'd.
O man, be now no more dismay'd
If thou henceforth from sin do stay;
Of death thou needest not be afraid:
Christ conquered death for this, his glorious day.

His death prevailed had no whit,
As Paul the apostle well doth write,
Except he had uprisen yet
From death to life by Godlike might   20
With most triumphant, glittering light.
This day his glory shined, I say,[2]
And made us bright as sun this glorious day.

O man, arise with Christ therefore,
Since he from sin hath made thee free.
Beware thou fall in sin no more,
But rise as Christ did rise for thee.
So mayst thou him in glory see
When he at day of doom shall say,
"Come thou, my child, and dwell with me."   30
God grant us all to see that glorious day!

Jasper Heywood

WANTING HIS DESIRE, HE COMPLAINETH

The sailing ships with joy at length do touch the long-desired port,
The hewing ax the oak doth waste, the batt'ring cannon breaks the fort;
Hard haggard hawks stoop to the lure, wild colts in time the bridle tames;
There is nothing so out of ure but to his kind long time it frames.
Yet this I find in time: no time can win my suit;
Though oft the tree I clime, I cannot catch the fruit.

And yet the pleasant branches oft in yielding wise to me do bow;
When I would touch they spring aloft, soon are they gone, I wot not how.

---

[1] For the sake of the meter we preserve here (and occasionally elsewhere) the archaic genitive ending.

[2] Line missing.

Thus I pursue the fleeting flood, like Tantalus in hell below.
Would God my case she understood which can full soon relieve my wo,   10
Which if to her were known the fruit were surely mine:
She would not let me groan and browze upon the rine.

But if my ship with tackle [torn], with rented sails must needs retire,
And stream and wind had plainly sworn by force to hinder my desire,
Like one that strikes upon the rocks, my weary wrack I should bewail,
And learn to know false Fortune's mocks, who smiles on me to small avail.
Yet sith she only can my rented ship restore,
To help her wracked man but once I seek no more.

Master Edwards

HIS GOOD NAME BEING BLEMISHED, HE BEWAILETH

[Framed in the front of forlorn hope] past all recovery,
I stayless stand to abide the shock of shame and infamy.
My life, through ling'ring long, is lodg'd in lair of lothsome ways,
My death delay'd to keep from life the harm of hapless days.
My sprites, my heart, my wit and force in deep distress are drown'd;
The only loss of my good name is of these griefs the ground.

And since my mind, my wit, my head, my voice, and tongue are weak
To utter, move, devise, conceive, sound forth, declare, and speak
Such piercing plaints as answer might, or would, my woful case,
Help crave I must, and crave I will, with tears upon my face,   10
Of all that may in heaven or hell, in earth or air, be found
To wail with me this loss of mine, as of these griefs the ground.

Help gods, help saints, help sprites and powers that in the heaven do dwell!
Help ye that are to wail ay wont, ye howling hounds of hell!
Help man, help beasts, help birds and worms that on the earth doth toil!
Help fish, help fowl that flocks and feeds upon the salt sea soil!
Help echo that in air doth flee, shrill voices to resound,
To wail this loss of my good name, as of these griefs the ground.

E. O. [Edward de Vere, Earl of Oxford]

OF FORTUNE'S POWER

Polycrates, whose passing hap caus'd him to lose his fate,
A golden ring cast in the seas to change his constant state,
And in a fish yet at his bourd the same he after found;
Thus Fortune, lo, to whom she takes, for bounty doth abound.

The misers unto might she mounts, a common case we see,
And mighty in great misery she sets in low degree;
Whom she today doth rear on high, upon her whirling wheel,
Tomorrow next she dingeth down and casteth at her heel.

No measure hath she in her gifts, she doth reward each sort:
The wise, that counsel have, no more then fools that maketh sport;   10
She useth never partial hands for to offend or please.
"Geve me good Fortune," all men says, "and throw me in the seas."

It is no fault or worthiness that makes men fall or rise;
I rather be born fortunate then to be very wise.

The blindest [runs] right soon, that by good Fortune guided is;
To whom that pleasant Fortune pipes can never dance amiss.

Master Edwards

AMANTIUM IRAE AMORIS REDINTEGRATIO EST

In going to my naked bed, as one that would have slept,
I heard a wife sing to her child that long before had wept;
She sighed sore and sang full [sweet] to bring the babe to rest
That would not rest but cried still, in sucking at her breast.
She was full weary of her watch, and grieved with her child;
She rocked it and rated it until on her it smil'd.
Then did she say, "Now have I found the proverb true to prove:
The falling out of faithful friends is the renewing of love."

Then took I paper, pen, and ink, this proverb for to write,
In register for to remain of such a worthy wight.   10
As she proceeded thus in song unto her little brat,
Much matter uttered she of weight in place whereas she sat,
And proved plain there was no beast nor creature bearing life
Could well be known to live in love without discord and strife.
Then kissed she her little babe and sware by God above
The falling out of faithful friends is the renewing of love.

She said that neither king ne prince ne lord could live aright
Until their puissance they did prove, their manhood and their might.
When manhood shall be matched so that fear can take no place
Then weary works makes warriors each other to embrace,   20
And leave their force that failed them, which did consume the rout,
That might before have lived their time [and days] and nature out.
Then did she sing as one that thought no man could her reprove,
"The falling out of faithful friends is the renewing of love."

She said she saw no fish ne fowl nor beast within her haunt
That met a stranger in their kind but could geve it a taunt.
Since flesh might not indure, but rest must wrath succeed,
And force the fight to fall to play in pasture where they feed,
So noble nature can well end the works she hath begun,
And bridle well that will not cease, her tragedy in some.   30
Thus in her song she oft rehears'd, as did her well behove,
"The falling out of faithful friends is the renewing of love.

"I mervail much, pardy," quoth she, "for to behold the rout,
To see man, woman, boy, and beast to toss the world about:
Some kneel, some crouch, some beck, some check, and some can smoothly smile,
And some embrace others in arms, and there think many a wile.
Some stand aloof at cap and knee, some humble and some stout,
Yet are they never friends indeed until they once fall out."
Thus ended she her song, and said before she did remove,
"The falling out of faithful friends is the renewing of love."   40

Master Edwards

FORTITUDE. A YOUNG MAN OF EGYPT AND VALERIAN

Each one deserves great praise to have, but yet not like, I think,
Both he that can sustain the yoke of pains and doth not shrink,
And he whom Cupid's covert craft can nothing move at all
Into the hard and tangled knots of Venus' snares to fall

Bestir you, then, whoso delights in virtue's race to run
The flying boy with bow ybent by strength to overcome,
As one did once when he was young and in his tender days,
Whose stout and noble deed of his hath got immortal praise.
The wicked Romains did pursue the seely Christians than,
What time Valerian emperor was, a wicked, cruel man,   10
Who spared not with bloody draughts to quench his own desire,
Dispatching all that stuck to Christ with hot, consuming fire.
At length a man of tender years was brought before his sight,
Such one as Nature seemed to make a witness of her might;
For every part so well was set that nothing was depraved,
So that the cruel king himself would gladly have him saved.
So loth he was to see a work, so rare of Nature's power,
So finely built, so sodainly destroyed within an hour;
Then means he sought to overcome, or win him at the lest,
To slip from Christ whom he before had earnestly profess'd.   20
A bed prepar'd, so finely deck'd, such divers pleasant smells,
That well it might appear a place where pleasure only dwells;
By him he laid a naked wench, a Venus' darling sure,
With sug'red speech and lovely toys that might his mind allure.
Such wanton lures as these, he thought, might eas'ly him entice,
Which things, he knew, with lusty youth had always been in price.
Such ways, I think, the gods themselves could have invented none,
For flattering Venus overcomes the senses everychone;
And he himself was even at point to Venus to consent
Had not his stout and manly mind resisted his entent.   30
When he perceived his flesh to yield to pleasure's wanton toys,
And was by sleight almost provoked to taste of Venus' joys,
More cruel to himself then those that glad would him undo,
With bloody tooth his tender tongue bote quite and clean in two.
Thus was the pain so passing great of this his bloody bit
That all the fire and carnal lust was quenched every whit.
Do ill, and all thy pleasures, then, full soon will pass away;
But yet the shame of those thy deeds will nevermore decay.
Do well, and though thy pains be great, yet soon each one will cease;
But yet the praise of those thy deeds will evermore increase.   40

[Richard Edwards]

[BEWARE OF SIRENS]

When sage Ulysses sailed by
The perilous seas where Sirens sing,
Himself unto the mast did tie,
Lest their alluring tunes might bring
His mind on maze and make him stay,
And he with his become their prey.

Ulysses, O thou valiant wight,
It seemed Dame Circes loved thee well
What time she told to thee aright
The seas wherein the Sirens dwell,   10
By mean where[of] against thy sail
Their subtil songs could not prevail.

Were thou amongs us here again
And heard our Sirens' melody,
Not Circes' skill nor yet thy brain
Could keep thee from their treachery,
Such Sirens have we nowadays
That tempt us by a thousand ways.

They sing, they dance, they sport, they play,
They humbly fall upon their knees,   20
They sigh, they sob, they prate, they pray.
With such dissembling shifts as these
They calculate, they chant, they charm
To conquer us that mean no harm.

Good ladies all, let's join in one
And banish clean this Siren kind.
What need we yield to hear their moan,
Since their deceipt we daily find?
Let not your hearts to them apply;
Defy them all, for so will I.   30

And if where Circes now doth dwell
You [wish your] wit advise to learn,
Lo, I am [he] that best can tell
Their Sirens' songs and them discern,
For why experience yieldeth skill
To me that scap'd that Siren's ill.

Master Bewe

A LOVER REJECTED COMPLAINETH

The trickling tears that falls along my cheeks,
The secret sighs that shows my inward grief,
The present pains perforce that love ay seeks
Bids me renew my cares without relief,
In woful song in dole display
My pensive heart for to bewray.

Bewray thy grief, thou woful heart, with speed;
Resign thy voice to her that caus'd thy wo;
With irksome cries bewail thy late-done deed,
For she thou lovest is sure thy mortal foe,   10
And help for thee there is none sure,
But still in pain thou must endure.

The striken deer hath help to heal his wound,
The haggard hawk with toil is made full tame,
The strongest tower the cannon lays on ground,
The wisest wit that ever had the fame
Was thrall to love by Cupid's sleights.
Then weigh my case with equal weights.

She is my joy, she is my care and wo,
She is my pain, she is my ease therefore,   20
She is my death, she is my life also,
She is my salve, she is my wounded sore.
In fine, she hath the hand and knife
That may both save and end my life.

And shall I live on yearth to be her thrall?
And shall I sue and serve her all in vain?
And [shall I] kiss the steps that she lets fall,
And shall I pray the gods to keep the pain
From her that is so cruel still?
No, no, on her work all your will!   30

And let her feel the power of all your might,
And let her [lose] her most desire with speed,
And let her pine away both day and night,
And let her moan and none lament her need,
And let all those that shall her see
Despise her state and pity me.

E. O. [Edward de Vere, Earl of Oxford]

OF A CONTENTED MIND

When all is done and said, in the end thus shall you find,
He most of all doth bathe in bliss that hath a quiet mind,
And, clear from worldly cares, to deem can be content
The sweetest time in all his life in thinking to be spent.

The body subject is to fickle Fortune's power,
And to a million of mishaps is casual every hour;
And death in time doth change it to a clod of clay,
Whenas the mind, which is devine, runs never to decay.

Companion none is like unto the mind alone,
For many have been harm'd by speech, through thinking few or none;   10
Few oftentimes restraineth words, but makes not thoughts to cease,
And he speaks best that hath the skill when for to hold his peace.

Our wealth leaves us at death, our kinsmen at the grave,
But virtues of the mind unto the heavens with us we have.
Wherefore for virtue's sake I can be well content
The sweetest time of all my life to deem in thinking spent.

Lord Vaux

HE PERSUADETH HIS FRIEND FROM THE FOND AFFECTS OF LOVE

Why art thou bound and mayst go free? Shall reason yield to raging will?
Is thraldom like to liberty? Wilt thou exchange thy good for ill?
Then shalt thou learn a childish play, and of each part to taste and prove;
The lookers-on shall judge and say, "Lo, this is he that lives by love."

Thy wits with thoughts shall stand at stay, thy head shall have but heavy rest;
Thy eyes shall watch for wanton prey, thy tongue shall shew thy heart's request;
Thy ears shall hear a thousand [nays], thy hand shall put thy pen to pain;
And in the end thou shalt dispraise thy life so spent for such small gain.

If love and list might ever cope, or youth might run in reason's race,
Or if strong suit might win sure hope, I would less blame a lover's case;   10
For love is hot with great desire, and sweet delight makes youth so fond
That little sparks will prove great fire, and bring free hearts to endless bond.

First count the care and then the cost, and mark what fraud in faith is found,
Then after come and make thy boast, and shew some cause why thou art bound.
For when the wine doth run full low you shall be fain to drink the lees,
And eat the flesh, full well I know, that hath been blown with many flies.

We see where great devotion is, the people kneel and kiss the cross,
And though we find small fault of this, yet some will gild a bridle's boss.
A fool his bable will not change, not for the scepter of a king;
A lover's life is nothing strange, for youth delights none other thing.   20

Thomas Churchyard

NO PAINS COMPARABLE TO HIS ATTEMPT

Like as the doleful dove delights alone to be,
And doth refuse the bloomed branch, chusing the leafless tree,
Whereon, wailing his chance, with bitter tears besprent,
Doth with his bill his tender breast oft pierce and all to-rent,
Whose grievous groanings tho, whose grips of pining pain,
Whose ghastly looks, whose bloody streams outflowing from each vein,
Whose falling from the tree, whose panting on the ground
Examples be of mine estate, tho there appear no wound.

W[illiam] Hunnis

AN EPITAPH UPON THE DEATH OF SIR
WILLIAM DRURY, KNIGHT, LORD JUSTICE
AND GOVERNOR OF IRELAND, DECEASED
AT WATERFORD THE THIRD OF OCTOBER,
AN. DO. 1579

Give pardon, then, to him that takes in hand,
Though never taught with poet's pen to write,
Will yet presume to let you understand
No strange event, although a seldom sight   10
Which late I saw, a doleful tale to tell,
And followeth thus; then mark how it befell.

In place where wants Apollo with his lute,
There peevish Pan may prease to pipe a dance;
Where men of skill and learned clarks are mute,
There fools may prate and hit the truth perchance.
Why spare I, then, to speak, when all are mum,
And virtue left forgot in time to come?

I saw Report in mourning weed array'd,
Whose blubbered eyes bewray'd some secret grief,
Besprent with tears, with sighs and sobs he said,
"You martial wights, abandon all relief;
Come wail with me whose loss is not alone
When you yourselves have greatest cause to moan.

"For Drury, he, the choice of all your train,
Your greatest guide and lamp of clearest light,   20
The only man Bellona did retain
Her champion chief, and made Sir Mars his knight,
Even he is now bereaved of his breath;
'Tis you, 'tis you may most lament his death."

Then might I see a warlike crew appear,
Came marching on with weapons trail'd on ground;
Their outward show bewray'd their inward cheer,
Their drums and trumps did yield a doleful sound;
They marched thus in sad and solemn sort,
As men amaz'd to hear this late Report.   30

And in the midst of this their heavy muse
I might perceive in sight a worthy dame,
Who by her speech and tenure of her news
I knew her well and saw 'twas Lady Fame
With trump in hand, and thus methought she said:
"You worthy wights, your Drury is not dead.

"He liveth, he, amongst the blessed rout
Whose noble acts hath purchas'd endless fame;
Whilst world doth last no time shall wear him out,
Nor death for all his spight abridge his name.   40
But Drury still forever shall remain;
His fame shall live in Flanders, France, and Spain.

"The Germans eke, Italians, and the rest
Can well discourse of Drury's deeds at large,
With whom he serv'd, a champion ready prest,
At all assaults the foremost to give charge;
In many a fray himself he did advance
'Tween Charles of Rome and Henry, king of France.

"In vain to vaunt the credit he attain'd
In native soil where he was known so well,   50
And bruit hath blown what glory he hath gain'd
In Scottish land, where they themselves can tell
In Edinburgh he wan their Maiden Tower
By first assault, perforce the Scottish power.

"But Ireland, thou, thou thrice accursed soil!
Thy luck is loss, thy fortune still withstood.
What mischief more to work thy greater spoil
Then loss of him that meant thee greatest good?
Yet canst thou say, 'Sir Drury's noble name
In Ireland still shall bide in lasting fame.'   60

"Wherefore, you worthy wights, leave off to wail!
Your Drury lives, his fame for ay shall last,
His virtues bide though wretched life do fail."
And taking then her trump she blew a blast
Which sounded more his praise then I can write,
Or with my tongue express in order right.

Then might I hear the soldiers give a shout,
The sound whereof redounded in the sky.
Great joy was made amongst the armed rout;
With strained throats then all at once they cry,   70
"He lives, he lives, our Drury is not dead.
His virtues rare by Fame shall still be spread."

In order, then, themselves they did retire,
Their weapons vanc'd, with ensigns brave display'd.
What would you more? Report is made a liar,
Sir Drury lives, sufficeth what is said.
What though his corps entombed be in clay,
His virtues shine that never shall decay.

Vivit post funaera virtus.

Barnabe Rich

A GORGEOUS GALLERY OF GALLANT INVENTIONS

A Gorgeous Gallery of Gallant Inventions, the least attractive and least successful of all the Elizabethan poetical miscellanies, must have been inspired by *The Paradise of Dainty Devices* (1576). Sponsored by the same Richard Jones who in 1566 had published *Very Pleasant Sonnets and Stories in Meter* (known to us as *A Handful of Pleasant Delights,* 1584), *A Gorgeous Gallery* was entered in the Stationers' Register on June 5, 1577, as *A Handful of Hidden Secrets* and then as *Delicate Dainties,* and described as a work "collected together by R. Williams." But both Williams and the foregoing titles in the Register were abandoned, for when the book appeared in the next year it was as *A Gorgeous Gallery,* and the editor was named on the titlepage as Thomas Proctor, a printer and ballad-writer who may have succeeded Owen Roydon after Roydon had succeeded the mysterious Williams. Proctor, a man of gravely moral views but of little poetical talent, contributed (and initialed) eleven pieces and Roydon at least two; some of the other contributors—whose work was probably used without permission—may be conjecturally identified as Lord Vaux the Elder, Thomas Churchyard, Thomas Howell, Clement Robinson (who edited *A Handful of Pleasant Delights*), and Jasper Heywood. *A Gorgeous Gallery* is frankly a miscellany, made up, as the titlepage admits, of pieces "first framed and fashioned in sundry forms by divers worthy workmen of late days, and now joined together and builded up." Proctor, as editor, drew heavily on the now lost *Pleasant Sonnets* and to a lesser extent on Tottel's *Miscellany* and *The Paradise of Dainty Devices;* he also reprinted a fair number of broadside ballads. In spite of such varied sources the pieces in *A Gorgeous Gallery* are uncommonly uniform and monotonous in tone and subject; the tone is lugubrious and the subject is the vanity of earthly pleasures; but

they do exhibit an extraordinary range of metrical variation (poulter's measure, septenary couplets, octosyllabic anapestic couplets, hexameter couplets, irregular heroic verse, iambic trimeter, rime royal, ottava rima). Whatever its interest for the literary historian, *A Gorgeous Gallery* did not please the Elizabethans, and apparently the collection never went beyond its first edition (STC 20402), on which our text is based.

FROM A GORGEOUS GALLERY OF GALLANT INVENTIONS (1578)

A[nthony] M[unday] unto All Young Gentlemen in Commendation of this Gallery and Workmen Thereof

See, gallants, see this gallery of delights,
With buildings brave, imboss'd of variant hue,
With dainties deck'd, devis'd by worthy wights,
Which, as time serv'd, unto perfection grew.
By study's toil with phrases fine they fraught
This peerless piece, fill'd full of pretty pith,
And trimm'd it, with what skill and learning taught,
In hope to please your longing minds therewith.
Which workmanship, by worthy workmen wrought,
Perus'd lest in oblivion it should lie,   10
A willing mind each part together sought
And term'd the whole *A Gorgious Gallery;*
Wherein you may, to recreate the mind,
Such fine inventions find for your delight,
That, for desart, their doings will you bind
To yield them praise, so well a work to wright.
                              A[nthony] M[unday]

THE LOVER IN DISTRESS EXCLAIMETH AGAINST FORTUNE

How can the cripple get, in running race, the game?
Or he in fight defend himself whose arms are broken lame?
How can th' imprisoned man, whose legs be wrapp'd in chains,
Think this his life a pleasant time who knoweth nothing but pains?
So how can I rejoice that have no pleasant thing
That may revive my doleful sprits or cause me for to sing?
My legs be lame to go, mine arms cannot embrace,
My heart is sore, mine eyes be blind, for lack of Fortune's grace.
All this is Fortune's fault that keeps these senses so;
She may advance them if she list, and rid them of this wo.   10

It is her cruel will always on me to lower,
To keep from me her pleasant gifts, to make me know her power.
Alas, alas, fie, Fortune, fie! Why art thou so unkind
To me that fain would be thy son, and ever in thy mind?
Now do I thee beseech with pleasures me to freight,
To temper this my woful life, or else to kill me straight.
                                        [Anonymous]

A PROPER DITTY

To the Tune of "Lusty Gallant"

The glittering shows of Flora's dames
Delights not so my careful mind,
Ne gathering of the fragrant flames
That oft in Flora's nymphs I find,
Ne all the notes of birds so shrill
Melodiously in woods that sing,
Whose solemn quires the skies doth fill
With note on note that heavenly ring;

The frisking fish in streams that spring
And sport them on the river's side,   10
The hound, the hawk, and everything
Wherein my joys did once abide
Doth nothing else but breed my wo,
Sith that I want which I desire,
And death is eke become my foe,
Denying that I most require.

But if that Fortune's friendly grace
Would grant mine eyes to take the view
Of her whose port and amorous face
My senses all doth so subdue,   20
That, ranging to and fro to gain
The prey that most delighteth me,
At last I find that breeds me pain;
She flies so fast it will not be.

Then in myself with lingering thoughts
A sodain strife begins to grow;
I then do wish such birds at noughts
That from their lovers flyeth so.
At last I see the fowler's gin
Prepared for this bird and me;   30
Then wish'd I, lo! his head therein,
So that my bird and I were free.

[Anonymous]

THE LOVER COMPLAINETH OF HIS LADY'S UNCONSTANCY

To the Tune of "I Loathe That I Did Love"

You graves of grisly ghosts,
Your charge from coffins send;
From roaring rout in Pluto's coasts
You furies up ascend.

You trampling steeds of hell,
Come tear a woful wight
Whose hapless hap no tongue can tell,
Ne pen can well endight.

I hate this loathsome life.
O Atropos, draw nigh,   10
Untwist the thread of mortal strife,
Send death, and let me die.

For Beauty's tainted troop
Hath made my cares assay,
And Fickleness with her did cope
To fordge my whole decay.

My faith, alas, I gave
To wight of Cressid's kind,
For steadfast love I love did crave,
As curtesy doth bind.   20

She likewise troth doth plight
To be a constant love,
And prove herself even mauger spight
A faithful turtle-dove.

But lo! a woman's mind
Cloak'd whole with deep deceit,
And driven with every gale of wind
To bite at fresher bait!

For when bewitch'd she had
My mind, that erst was free,   30
And that her comely beauty bad
My wounded heart agree.

And fix'd on Fancy's lore
(As world can witness bear)
No other saint I did adore,
Or idol anywhere.

Ne will, no wo, or smart
Could mind from purpose fet,
But that I had a Jason's heart,
The golden fleece to get.   40

Ne for my part, I swear
By all the gods above,
I never thought on other fere
Or sought for other love.

In her the like consent
I saw full oft appear,
If eyes be judge of that it meant,
Or ears have power to hear.

Yet words be turn'd to wind.
A new-found guest hath got   50
The fort which once, to undermine
And win, I planted shot.

Her friend that meant her well
Out of conceit is quite,
While other bears away the bell
By hitting of the white.

In this our wavering age
So light are women's minds
As aspen leaf that still doth rage
Though Aeole calm his winds.   60

No place hath due desart;
No place hath constancy;
In every mood their minds back start,
As daily we may see.

What paps did give them food,
That weave such webs of wo?
What beast is of so cruel mood,
That counts his friend for foe?

Yet women do reward
With cares the loving wight;   70
They constancy no whit regard;
In change is their delight.

You gallant youths, therefore,
In time beware by me!
Take heed of women's subtile lore,
Let me example be.

[Anonymous]

THE LOVER IN THE PRAISE OF HIS BELOVED
AND COMPARISON OF HER BEAUTY

Not she for whom proud Troy did fall and burn,
The Greeks eke slain that bloody race did run;
Nor she for spight that did Actaeon turn
Into an hart her beauty coy did shun;
Nor she whose blood upon Achilles' tomb
[Was sprent], whose face would tame a tiger's heart;
Nor she that wan by wise of Paris' dome
Th' apple of gold for beauty to her part;
Nor she whose eyes did pierce true Troylus' breast,
And made him yield that knew in love no law,   10
Might be compared to the fairest and the best
Whom Nature made to keep the rest in awe.
For Beauty's sake sent down from Jove above,
Thrice happy is he that can attain her love.

[Anonymous]

THE LOVER DECEIVED BY HIS LADY'S
UNCONSTANCY WRITETH UNTO HER
AS FOLLOWETH

The heat is past that did me fret,
The fire is out that nature wrought,
The plants of youth that I did set
Are dry and dead within my thought.
The frost hath slain the kindly sap
That kept the heart in lively state;
The sodain storm and thunder-clap
Hath turned love to mortal hate.

The mist is gone that blear'd mine eyes;
The low'ring clouds I see appear;   10
Though that the blind eat many flies,
I would you knew my sight is clear.
Your sweet, deceiving, flatt'ring face
Did make me think that you were white;
I muse how you had such a grace
To seem a hawk and be a kite.

Where precious ware is to be sold,
They shall it have that giveth most;
All things, we see, are won with gold;
Few things is had where is no cost.   20
And so it fareth now by me,
Because I preace to give no gifts:
She takes my suit unthankfully
And drives me off with many drifts.

Is this the end of all my suit,
For my good will to have a scorn?
Is this of all my pains the fruit,
To have the chaff instead of corn?
Let them that list possess such dross,
For I deserve a better gain;   30

Yet had I rather leave with loss
Then serve and sue—and all in vain.

[Thomas Churchyard]

A LOVER APPROVING HIS LADY UNKIND
IS FORCED UNWILLING TO UTTER HIS MIND

Willow, willow, willow, sing all of green willow,
Sing all of green willow shall be my garland.

My love, what misliking in me do you find
(Sing all of green willow),
That on such a soddain you alter your mind?
(Sing willow, willow, willow.)
What cause doth compel you so fickle to be
(Willow, willow, willow, willow)
In heart which you plighted most loyal to me?
(Willow, willow, willow, willow.)   10

I faithfully fixed my faith to remain
(Sing all of green willow),
In hope I, as constant, should find you again.
(Sing willow, willow, willow.)
But perjur'd as Jason, you faithless I find,
Which makes me, unwilling, to utter my mind.
Willow, willow, willow, sing all of green willow,
Sing all of green willow shall be my garland.

Your beauty brave-decked, with shows gallant-gay
(Sing all of green willow),   20
Allured my fancy, I could not say nay.
(Sing willow, willow, willow.)
Your phrases fine-filed did force me agree
(Willow, willow, willow, willow)
In hope as you promis'd you loyal would be.
(Willow, willow, willow, willow.)

But now you be frisking, you list not abide
(Sing all of green willow),
Your vow most unconstant and faithless is tried.
(Sing willow, willow, willow.)   30
Your words are uncertain, not trusty you stand,
Which makes me to wear the willow garland.
Willow, willow, willow, sing all of green willow,
Sing all of green willow shall be my garland.

Hath light of love lull'd you so soft in her lap?
(Sing all of green willow.)
Hath fancy provok'd you? Did love you intrap?
(Sing willow, willow, willow.)
That now you be flurting and will not abide
(Willow, willow, willow, willow)   40
To me which most trusty in time should have tried?
(Willow, willow, willow, willow.)

Is modest demeanure thus turn'd to untrust?
  (Sing all of green willow.)
Are faith and troth fixed approved unjust?
  (Sing willow, willow, willow.)
Are you she which constant forever would stand,
And yet will you give me the willow garland?
  Willow, willow, willow, sing all of green willow,
  Sing all of green willow shall be my garland.　　50

What motion hath mov'd you to mask in delight?
  (Sing all of green willow.)
What toy have you taken? Why seem you to spight
  (Sing willow, willow, willow)
Your love which was ready for ay to indure
  (Willow, willow, willow, willow),
According to promise most constant and sure?
  (Willow, willow, willow, willow.)

What gallant you conquer'd, what youth mov'd your
    mind
  (Sing all of green willow)　　60
To leave your old lover and be so unkind
  (Sing willow, willow, willow)
To him which you plighted both faith, troth, and hand
Forever—yet gives me the willow garland?
  Willow, willow, willow, sing all of green willow,
  Sing all of green willow shall be my garland.

Hath wealth you allured, the which I do want?
  (Sing all of green willow.)
Hath pleasant devises compell'd you recant?
  (Sing willow, willow, willow.)　　70
Hath feature forc'd you your words to deny?
  (Willow, willow, willow, willow.)
Or is it your fashion to cog and to lie?
  (Willow, willow, willow, willow.)

What, are your sweet smiles quite turn'd into low'rs?
  (Sing all of green willow.)
Or is it your order to change them by hours?
  (Sing willow, willow, willow.)
What, have you sufficient, think you, in your hand
To pay for the making of my willow garland?　　80
  Willow, willow, willow, sing all of green willow,
  Sing all of green willow shall be my garland.

Farewell then, most fickle, untrue, and unjust!
  (Sing all of green willow.)
Thy deeds are ill dealings, in thee is no trust!
  (Willow, willow, willow, willow.)
Thy vows are uncertain, thy words are but wind.
  (Willow, willow, willow, willow.)
God grant thy new lover more trusty thee find.
  (Willow, willow, willow, willow.)　　90

Be warned then, gallants, by proof I unfold
  (Sing willow, willow, willow):
Maids' love is uncertain, soon hot and soon cold.
  (Sing willow, willow, willow.)
They turn as the reed, not trusty they stand,
Which makes me to wear the willow garland.
  Willow, willow, willow, sing all of green willow,
  Sing all of green willow shall be my garland.

                      [Anonymous]

A MIRROR OF MORTALITY

Shall clammy clay shroud such a gallant gloze,
Must beauty brave be shrin'd in dankish earth,
Shall crawling worms devour such lively shows
When valiant corps shall yield the latter breath?
  Shall pleasure vade, must puffing pride decay,
  Shall flesh consume, must thought resign to clay?
Shall haughty heart have hire to his desart,
Must deep desire die, drench'd in direful dread?
Shall deeds lewd-done in fine reap bitter smart,
Must each [man] vade when life shall leave us dead?　　10
  Shall lands remain, must wealth be left behind?
  Is sense depriv'd when flesh in earth is shrin'd?
Seek, then, to shun the snares of vain delight,
Which moves the mind in youth from virtue's lore;
Leave off the vaunt of pride and manly might,
Sith all must yield when death the flesh shall gore.
  And weigh these words: as soon for to be sold,
  To market comes the young sheep as the old;
No trust in time, our days uncertain be;
Like as the flower, bedeck'd with splendant hue,　　20
Whose gallant show soon dri'd with heat we see
Of scorching beams, though late it bravely grew.
  We must all yield; the best shall not deny.
  Unsure is death, yet certain we shall die.
Although a while we vaunt in youthful years,
In young delights we seem to live at rest,
We subject be to grief, each horror fears
The valianst hearts when death doth daunt the breast.
  Then use thy talent here unto thee lent,
  That thou mayst well account how it is spent.　　30
                    T[homas] P[roctor]

RESPICE FINEM

Lo, here the state of every mortal wight.
See here the fine of all their gallant joys.
Behold their pomp, their beauty and delight,
Whereof they vaunt as safe from all annoys.
To earth the stout, the proud, the rich shall yield;
The weak, the meek, the poor shall shrouded lie
In dampish mold; the stout with spear and shield
Cannot defend himself when he shall die.
The proudest wight, for all his lively shows,
Shall leave his pomp, cut off by dreadful death.　　10

The rich, whose hutch with golden ruddocks flows,
At length shall rest, uncoin'd in dampish earth.
By Nature's law we all are born to die,
But where or when the best uncertain be.
No time prefix'd, no goods our life shall buy
Of dreadful death, no friends shall set us free.
We subject be a thousand ways to death:
Small sickness moves the valiant heart to fear;

A little push bereaves your breathing breath
Of brave delights, whereto you subject are.   20
Your world is vain, no trust in earth you find;
Your valiant prime is but a brittle glass;
Your pleasures vade, your thoughts a puff of wind,
Your ancient years are but a withered grass.
          Mors omnibus communis.

                              T[homas] P[roctor]

A HANDFUL OF PLEASANT DELIGHTS

Although *A Handful of Pleasant Delights* survives only in an imperfect British Museum copy dated 1584 (and in two undated fragments, representing two earlier editions, of one leaf and four leaves respectively), that copy is a reissue, with some changes and additions and with a misleading titlepage, of a now lost *Very Pleasant Sonnets and Stories in Meter,* a collection of broadside ballads published in 1566. Chronologically, therefore, it may be regarded as the first of the many imitations of Tottel's *Miscellany,* even though its contents, which are all ballads, are a far cry from the would-be urbanities and sophistications of the earlier collection. The titlepage of the *Handful* promises the reader a book of ballads "newly devised to the newest tunes that are now in use to be sung, every sonnet orderly pointed to his proper tune," but actually it is a compilation (by one Clement Robinson) of ballads that were not new even in 1566, and the "newest tunes" were even older. Thus the *Handful* is the first "garland"

(or collection of broadside ballads), and it established a precedent that Thomas Deloney and others were to follow with much success later in the century. Although the thin little book was apparently not reprinted after 1584, its compiler's astute gauging of popular taste may be inferred from echoes, quotations, and allusions sprinkled through the more literary works of many Elizabethans, particularly of Shakespeare. In her madness Ophelia (*Hamlet,* IV.v.174 ff.) remembers that rosemary is for remembrance; and "Greensleeves" (one of the most popular ballads of the period) is twice mentioned in *The Merry Wives of Windsor* (II.i.64; V.v.22). But since most of the broadsides in the *Handful* had already established their popularity before Robinson brought them together, we cannot wonder that his little anthology went through at least three editions. Our text is based upon the edition of 1584 (STC 21105).

FROM A HANDFUL OF PLEASANT DELIGHTS (1584)

The Printer to the Reader

You that in music do delight
    your minds for to solace,
This little book of sonnets may
    well like you in that case.
Peruse it well ere you pass by;
    here may you wish and have
Such pleasant songs to each new tune
    as lightly you can crave.
Or if fine histories you would read,
    you need not far to seek;   10

Within this book such may you have
    as ladies may well like.
Here may you have such pretty things
    as women much desire;
Here may you have of sundry sorts
    such songs as you require.
Wherefore, my friend, if you regard
    such songs to read or hear,
Doubt not to buy this pretty book—
    the price is not so dear.   20

A NOSEGAY ALWAYS SWEET FOR LOVERS TO SEND FOR TOKENS OF LOVE AT NEW YEAR'S TIDE OR FOR FAIRINGS, AS THEY IN THEIR MINDS SHALL BE DISPOSED TO WRITE

A nosegay, lacking flowers fresh,
  to you now I do send;
Desiring you to look thereon,
  when that you may intend.
For flowers fresh begin to fade,
  and Boreas in the field,
Even with his hard congealed frost,
  no better flowers doth yield.

But if that winter could have sprung
  a sweeter flower than this,   10
I would have sent it presently
  to you withouten miss.
Accept this, then, as time doth serve,
  be thankful for the same,
Despise it not, but keep it well,
  and mark each flower his name.

Lavender is for lovers true
  which evermore be fain,
Desiring always for to have
  some pleasure for their pain;   20
And when that they obtained have
  the love that they require,
Then have they all their perfect joy,
  and quenched is the fire.

Rosemary is for remembrance
  between us day and night;
Wishing that I might always have
  you present in my sight.
And when I cannot have,
  as I have said before,   30
Then Cupid with his deadly dart
  doth wound my heart full sore.

Sage is for sustenance
  that should man's life sustain,
For I do still lie languishing,
  continually in pain,
And shall do still until I die,
  except thou favor show.
My pain and all my grievous smart
  full well you do it know.   40

Fennel is for flatterers,
  an evil thing it is sure;
But I have always meant truly,
  with constant heart most pure,
And will continue in the same

as long as life doth last,
Still hoping for a joyful day
  when all our pains be past.

Violet is for faithfulness,
  which in me shall abide;   50
Hoping likewise that from your heart
  you will not let it slide,
And will continue in the same
  as you have now begun,
And then forever to abide,
  then you my heart have won.

Thyme is to try me,
  as each be tried must,
Letting you know while life doth last
  I will not be unjust;   60
And if I should I would to God
  to hell my soul should bear,
And eke also that Belzebub
  with teeth he should me tear.

Roses is to rule me
  with reason as you will,
For to be still obedient
  your mind for to fulfil;
And thereto will not disagree
  in nothing that you say,   70
But will content your mind truly
  in all things that I may.

Jeliflowers is for gentleness,
  which in me shall remain,
Hoping that no sedition shall
  depart our hearts in twain.
As soon the sun shall loose his course,
  the moon against her kind
Shall have no light, if that I do
  once put you from my mind.   80

Carnations is for graciousness,
  mark that now by the way.
Have no regard to flatterers,
  nor pass not what they say;
For they will come with lying tales
  your ears for to fulfil.
In any case do you consent
  nothing unto their will.

Marigolds is for marriage,
  that would our minds suffice,   90
Lest that suspicion of us twain
  by any means should rise.
As for my part, I do not care,
  myself I will still use

That all the women in the world
    for you I will refuse.

Pennyrial is to print your love
    so deep within my heart,
That when you look this nosegay on,
    my pain you may impart;   100
And when that you have read the same,
    consider well my wo,
Think ye then how to recompense
    even him that loves you so.

Cowslops is for counsel,
    for secrets us between,
That none but you and I alone
    should know the thing we mean.
And if you will thus wisely do,
    as I think to be best,   110
Then have you surely won the field,
    and set my heart at rest.

I pray you keep this nosegay well,
    and set by it some store.
And thus farewell! The gods thee guide
    both now and evermore!
Not as the common sort do use,
    to set it in your breast,
That when the smell is gone away,
    on ground he takes his rest.   120

                    [Anonymous]

A NEW COURTLY SONNET OF THE LADY GREENSLEEVES

To the New Tune of "Greensleeves"

Greensleeves was all my joy,
    Greensleeves was my delight,
Greensleeves was my heart of gold,
    And who but Lady Greensleeves?

Alas, my love, ye do me wrong
    to cast me off discurteously,
And I have loved you so long,
    delighting in your company.
Greensleeves was all my joy,
    Greensleeves was my delight,   10
Greensleeves was my heart of gold,
    And who but Lady Greensleeves?

I have been ready at your hand
    to grant whatever you would crave;
I have both waged life and land
    your love and good will for to have.
        Greensleeves was all my joy, etc.

I bought thee kerchers to thy head
    that were wrought fine and gallantly;
I kept thee both at boord and bed,
    which cost my purse well favoredly.   20
        Greensleeves was all my joy, etc.

I bought thee petticoats of the best,
    the cloth so fine as fine might be;
I gave thee jewels for thy chest,
    and all this cost I spent on thee.
        Greensleeves was all my joy, etc.

Thy smock of silk, both fair and white,
    with gold embrodered gorgeously;
Thy petticoat of sendal right;
    and thus I bought thee gladly.   30
        Greensleeves was all my joy, etc.

Thy girdle of gold so red,
    with pearls bedecked sumptuously,
The like no other lasses had,
    and yet thou wouldst not love me.
        Greensleeves was all my joy, etc.

Thy purse and eke thy gay gilt knives,
    thy pincase gallant to the eye,
No better wore the burgess-wives,   40
    and yet thou wouldst not love me.
        Greensleeves was all my joy, etc.

Thy crimson stockings all of silk,
    with gold all wrought above the knee,
Thy pumps as white as was the milk,
    and yet thou wouldst not love me.
        Greensleeves was all my joy, etc.

Thy gown was of the grossy green,
    thy sleeves of satin hanging by,
Which made thee be our harvest queen,   50
    and yet thou wouldst not love me.
        Greensleeves was all my joy, etc.

Thy garters fringed with the gold,
    and silver aglets hanging by,
Which made thee blithe for to behold,
    and yet thou wouldst not love me.
        Greensleeves was all my joy, etc.

My gayest gelding I thee gave
    to ride wherever liked thee;
No lady ever was so brave,   60
    and yet thou wouldst not love me.
        Greensleeves was all my joy, etc.

My men were clothed all in green,
  and they did ever wait on thee;
All this was gallant to be seen,
  and yet thou wouldst not love me.
      Greensleeves was all my joy, etc.

They set thee up, they took thee down,
  they served thee with humility,
Thy foot might not once touch the ground,   70
  and yet thou wouldst not love me.
      Greensleeves was all my joy, etc.

For every morning when thou rose,
  I sent thee dainties orderly
To cheer thy stomach from all woes,
  and yet thou wouldst not love me.
      Greensleeves was all my joy, etc.

Thou couldst desire no earthly thing
  but still thou hadst it readily;
Thy music still to play and sing,   80
  and yet thou wouldst not love me.
      Greensleeves was all my joy, etc.

And who did pay for all this gear
  that thou didst spend when pleased thee?
Even I that am rejected here,
  and thou disdain'st to love me.
      Greensleeves was all my joy, etc.

Well, I will pray to God on high
  that thou my constancy may'st see,
And that yet once before I die   90
  thou wilt vouchsafe to love me.
      Greensleeves was all my joy, etc.

Greensleeves, now farewell, adieu!
  God I pray to prosper thee,
For I am still thy lover true;
  come once again and love me.
      Greensleeves was all my joy, etc.

                    [Anonymous]

A PROPER SONNET INTITULED:
I SMILE TO SEE HOW YOU DEVISE

To Any Pleasant Tune

I smile to see how you devise
New masking nets my eyes to blear;

Yourself you cannot so disguise,
But as you are you must appear.

Your privy winks at boord I see,
And how you set your roving mind;
Yourself you cannot hide from me;
Although I wink, I am not blind.

The secret sighs and feigned cheer
That oft doth pain thy careful breast,   10
To me right plainly doth appear;
I see in whom thy heart doth rest.

And though thou makest a feigned vow
That love no more thy heart should nip,
Yet think I know as well as thou
The fickle helm doth guide the ship.

The salamander in the fire
By course of kind doth bathe his lims;
The floating fish taketh his desire
In running streams whereas he swims.   20

So thou in change dost take delight;
Full well I know thy slippery kind.
In vain thou seem'st to dim my sight,
Thy rolling eyes bewrayeth thy mind.

I see him smile that doth possess
Thy love which once I honored most.
If he be wise, he may well guess
Thy love, soon won, will soon be lost.

And sith thou canst no man intice
That he should still love thee alone,   30
Thy beauty now hath lost her price;
I see thy savory scent is gone.

Therefore, leave off thy wonted play,
But, as thou art, thou wilt appear,
Unless thou canst devise a way
To dark the sun that shines so clear.

And keep thy friend that thou hast won,
In truth to him thy love supply,
Lest he at length, as I have done,
Take off thy bells and let thee fly.   40
                    [Anonymous]

BRETON'S BOWER OF DELIGHTS

Breton's Bower of Delights was, like *A Handful of Pleasant Delights* and *A Gorgeous Gallery*, the venture of Richard Jones, an enterprising but none too scrupulous publisher, who, though he seems to have specialized in broadside ballads, numbered works by Whetstone, Lodge, Nashe, and Marlowe among the some ninety books that came from his press. On May 3, 1591, Jones entered the *Bower* in the Stationers' Register, and when the book appeared he explained in his preface "To the Gentlemen Readers" that it had been put together "in the author's absence." Actually the *Bower* is not, as the titlepage seems to suggest, entirely Nicholas Breton's work, but Jones used his name prominently in order to attract buyers. Breton was annoyed, for in his preface to *The Pilgrimage to Paradise* (1592) he complained that the *Bower* "was done altogether without my consent or knowledge, and many things of other men's mingled with few of mine." Jones ignored the protest, and two years later used Breton's name again for *The Arbor of Amorous Devices*, with as little propriety as before (as he himself admits in his preface); moreover, in 1597 he again issued under Breton's name both the *Bower* and the *Arbor*, the former in a considerably shortened edition.

The original fifty-six poems of the *Bower* make up a very pretty, though carelessly printed, collection. Jones himself attributes one to the Earl of Oxford and includes two others that were probably written by that poetical nobleman; three have been ascribed to Raleigh; one is a condensation of a lyric by Surrey in Tottel's *Miscellany*; and another is perhaps by Sidney. Breton himself acknowledged the first and longest poem, an elegy on Sidney entitled "Amoris Lachrimae," but it has been conjectured that some twenty-six of the fifty-six are his work. The *Bower* is metrically interesting, containing six sonnets (and ten lyrics loosely called sonnets after the Elizabethan usage), four alleged pastorals, a couple of broadside ballads, seven poems in poulter's measure, and twenty-three in the six-line iambic pentameter stanza of Shakespeare's *Venus and Adonis*. We may infer that the *Bower* was reasonably popular, not only because it gained a second edition within six years, but also because *The Phoenix Nest* (1593) printed three poems and part of a fourth (probably from the authors' manuscripts) that had already appeared in it and because *England's Helicon* (1600) lifted four poems from its pages. Our text is based upon *Brittons Bowre of Delights*, 1591 (STC 3633).

FROM BRETON'S BOWER OF DELIGHTS (1591)

To the Gentlemen Readers

Gentlemen, I present you here, in the author's absence, with sundry fine devices and rare conceits, in English verse, by the names of epitaphs, poems, pastorals, and sonnets, some of worthiness and some of wantonness, yet all (in my poor censure) witty, pleasant, and commendable. If any like you (as I hope they will), partly for the well-penning of them but specially for the subject and worthiness of the persons they do concern, though haply you esteem the rest 10 of less regard, I then have my desire and count my labor and charges well bestowed. I am only the printer of them, chiefly to pleasure you and partly to profit myself if they prove to your good liking; if otherwise, my hope is frustrate, my labor lost, and all my cost is cast away. Pardon me, good gentlemen, of my presumption, and protect me, I pray you, against those cavilers and findfaults that never like of anything that they see printed, though it be never so well compiled. And where you happen to find any fault, impute it to be committed by the printer's negligence then otherwise by any ignorance in the author. . . . So shall your poor printer have just cause hereafter to be more careful and acknowledge himself most bounden at all times to do you service to the utmost of his power.

Yours,
R[ichard] J[ones], Printer

[GO, MUSE, UNTO THE BOWER]

Go, muse, unto the bower whereas my mistress dwells
And tell her of her servant's love, but tell her nothing els.
And speak but in her ear, that none may hear but she,
That if she not the sooner help there is no help for me.
Not that I fear to speak, but it is strange to hear
That she will never look on him that holds her love so
  dear.

Perhaps she knows it not, or if she do she will not,
Yet let her kindness have a care that, though she hurt, she
    kill not;
And though it be too strange, yet let her this believe me:
That dead men live, yet I am dead, yet live if she relieve
    me;   10
For yet are not so cold the coals of kind desire
But in the ashes lives a spark to kindle love a fire,
Which fire his fuel hath but from those fairest eyes
Where faith doth burn and fancy flame and favor never
    dies.

                [Nicholas Breton]

[LIKE TO AN HERMIT POOR]

Like to an hermit poor in place obscure
I mean to spend my days in endless doubt,
To wail such woes as time cannot recure,
Where none but Love shall ever find me out.
My food shall be of care and sorrow made,
My drink nought else but tears fall'n from mine eyes,
And for my light in such obscured shade
The flames shall serve that from my heart arise.
A gown of grief my body shall attire,
And broken hope the staff of all my stay;   10
Of late repentance link'd with long desire
The couch is made whereon my bones to lay.
    And at my gate Dispair shall linger still
    To let in Death when Love and Fortune will.

             [?Sir Walter Raleigh]

A SONNET

Those eyes that hold the hand of every heart,
That hand that holds the heart of every eye,
That wit that goes beyond all nature's art,
The sense too deep for wisdom to discry;
    That eye, that hand, that wit, that heavenly sense
    Doth shew my only mistress' excellence.

O eyes that pierce into the purest heart,
O hands that hold the highest thoughts in thrall,
O wit that weighs the depth of all desart,
O sense that shews the secret sweet of all,   10
    The heaven of heavens with heavenly powers preserve
      thee!
    Love but thyself and give me leave to serve thee.

To serve, to live, to look upon those eyes,
To look, to live, to kiss that heavenly hand,
To sound that wit that doth amaze the [wise],
To know that sense no sense can understand,
    To understand that all the world may know
    Such wit, such sense, eyes, hands, there are no mo.

               [Nicholas Breton]

RARE NEWS

News from the heavens! All wars are at an end,
Twixt higher powers a happy peace concluded;
Fortune and Faith are sworn each other's friend,
And Love's desire shall never be deluded.

Time hath set down the compass of his course,
Nature her work and Excellence her art,
Care his content and Cruelty his curse,
Labor his desire and Honor his desart.

Words shall be deeds, and men shall be divine,
Women all saints or angels in degrees;   10
Clouds shall away, the sun shall ever shine,
Heavens shall have power to hinder none of these.
    These are the articles of the conclusion,
    Which, when they fall, then look for a confusion.

               [Nicholas Breton]

HIS COMPLAINT AGAINST LOVE
AND FORTUNE

If heaven and earth were both not fully bent
To plague a wretch with an infernal pain,
To rob the heart of all his high content
And leave a wound that should not heal again;
If cruel Fortune did not seek to kill
The careful spirit of my kind affect,
And Care did not so crucify me still
That Love had left no hope of his effect;
If she whom most my heart hath ever loved
Were not unkind in care of my distress,   10
And she by whom my grief might be removed
Did not hold back the mean of my redress;
If all these thoughts and many thousands mo—
Too long to tell, too deadly to endure—
Did not consume my heart in sorrow so
That Care hath left no hope of any cure;
Then might I yet, amid my greatest grief,
Persuade my patience with some heavenly power,
That when I most despair of my relief
My hopeless heart might find some happy hour.   20
But since that Fortune so doth frown upon me
That Care hath thus of comfort all bereft me,
Think it not strange to see me, wo-begone me,
Where no good hope of no good hap is left me.
And since I see all kindness so unkind,
And friendship grown to such contrary thought,
And such a thought the torment of the mind
That Care and Sorrow hath consumed to nought,
I will resolve (though patience be perforce)
To sit me down and thus in secret cry: 30
"Dead is my heart! O earth, receive my corse!
Heaven be my life, for in the world I die!"

               [Nicholas Breton]

OF THE BIRTH AND BRINGING-UP OF DESIRE

"When wert thou born, Desire?" "In pomp and prime
    of May."
"By whom, sweet boy, wert thou begot?" "By good
    conceit, men say."
"Tell me, who was thy nurse?" "Fresh youth in sug'red
    joy."
"What was thy meat and daily food?" "Sore sighs with
    great annoy."
"What had you then to drink?" "Unfeigned lovers' tears."
"What cradle were you rocked in?" "In hope, devoid of
    fears."
"What brought you then asleep?" "Sweet speech that
    liked men best."
"And where is now your dwelling-place?" "In gentle
    hearts I rest."
"Doth company displease?" "It doth in many one."
"Where would Desire then choose to be?" "He likes to
    muse alone."   10
"What feedeth most your sight?" "To gaze on favor still."
"Who find you most to be your foe?" "Disdain of my
    good will."
"Will ever age or death bring you into decay?"
"No, no, Desire both lives and dies ten thousand times a
    day."

             [Edward de Vere,] Earl of Ox[ford]

A PASTORAL

Sweet birds, that sit and sing amid the shady valleys,
And see how sweetly Phyllis walks amid her garden alleys,
Go round about her bower and sing as ye are bidden.
To her is only known his faith that from the world is
    hidden.
And she among you all that hath the sweetest voice
Go chirp of him that never told, yet never chang'd, his
    choice,
And not forget his faith, that liv'd forever lov'd,
Yet never made his fancy known, nor ever favor mov'd.
And ever let your ground of all your grace be this:
To you, to you, to you the due of love and honor is; 10
On you, on you, on you our music all attendeth;
For as on you our muse begun, in you all music endeth.

                 [Nicholas Breton]

A SHEPHERD'S DREAM

A silly shepherd lately sate
    among a flock of sheep,
Where, musing long on this and that,
    at last he fell asleep.

And in the slumber as he lay
    he gave a piteous groan;
He thought his sheep were run away,
    and he was left alone.

He whop'd, he whistled, and he call'd,
    but not a sheep came near him,   10
Which made the shepherd sore appall'd
    to see that none would hear him.

But, as the swain amazed stood
    in this most solemn vein,
Came Phyllida out of the wood,
    and stood before the swain.

Whom when the shepherd did behold
    he straight began to weep,
And at the heart he grew acold
    to think upon his sheep.   20

For well he knew where came the queen
    the shepherd durst not stay,
And where that he durst not be seen
    the sheep must needs away.

To ask her if she saw his flock
    might happen patience move,
And have an answer with a mock
    that such demanders prove.

Yet forbecause he saw her come
    alone out of the wood,   30
He thought he would not stand as dumb
    when speech might do him good.

And, therefore, falling on his knees
    to ask but for his sheep,
He did awake and so did leese
    the honor of his sleep.

                 [Nicholas Breton]

THE PHOENIX NEST

The Phoenix Nest, one of the most distinguished repositories of Elizabethan poetry, appeared when Tottel's *Miscellany* was in its ninth and *The Paradise of Dainty Devices* in its sixth edition, and it marks a real advance over such stalwart predecessors. Produced under the supervision of R. S., a gentleman of the Inner Temple, it differs from other Elizabethan miscellanies in being a literary rather than a commercial venture, and thus in achieving a high level of taste and elegance unmatched by all its rivals except the beautiful *England's Helicon* of 1600. According to the titlepage the work of "noble men, worthy knights, gallant gentlemen, Masters of Arts, and brave scholars," *The Phoenix Nest* makes a virtue of gentility, for it was written by and addressed to cultured men; and, although Elizabethan propriety hardly sanctioned a gentleman's acknowledged authorship, the initials with which the poems are signed suggest a roster of splendid contributors. "G. P., Master of Arts" is probably George Peele; E. O. is almost certainly Edward de Vere, seventeenth Earl of Oxford; "N. B., Gentleman" must be Nicholas Breton; T. L. is unquestionably Thomas Lodge, most of whose sixteen contributions appeared also in his *Phyllis* (1593); and T. W. may (or may not) be Thomas Watson, the author of The Ἑκατομπαθία (1582). But R. S., the compiler, defies certain identification. Richard Stanyhurst is a wildly improbable candidate, as anyone who has ever looked at his translation of Virgil must realize; and no stronger case can be made for Robert Southwell, the Jesuit martyr. Though Thomas Warton's early suggestion of Richard Stapleton has found general favor, probably no positive attribution can ever be made.

Whoever R. S. was, he produced an uncommonly fine text; *The Phoenix Nest* is remarkable, among other things, for being one of the most carefully printed books of the century. Its contents, too, are important. Three elegies on Sidney by Matthew Roydon, Raleigh, and, so many scholars believe, Fulke Greville sufficiently explain the title (for in his admirers' verses Sidney came again to life); the pieces immediately following are almost medieval in tone and subject (Peele's "Praise of Chastity," a tedious prose dialogue between Constancy and Inconstancy, and dream-poems by Breton and perhaps Greene); but the second half of the collection, described as "excellent ditties of divers kinds and rare invention," represents the best type of late Elizabethan lyric poetry in a wide variety of forms and meters, and especially in the sonnet, which was having so great a vogue. In this section the contributors (like those in Tottel's *Miscellany* a generation earlier and in *A Poetical Rhapsody* a decade later) lie in heavy debt to such Continental writers as Petrarch, Desportes, and Ronsard.

In view of its special, aristocratic appeal it is not surprising that *The Phoenix Nest* enjoyed more literary than popular success. It provided the text for the last three Astrophel poems at the end of Spenser's *Colin Clout,* and it was liberally rifled by the editors of *England's Helicon* and *A Poetical Rhapsody,* but presumably the stream of contemporary sonnet sequences (*Chloris* and *Phyllis* and others) captured the public's fancy. If *The Phoenix Nest* gained a second edition, no trace of it remains. Our text is based upon the edition of 1593 (STC 21516).

FROM THE PHOENIX NEST (1593)

AN EPITAPH UPON THE RIGHT HONORABLE SIR PHILIP SIDNEY, KNIGHT, LORD GOVERNOR OF FLUSHING

To praise thy life or wail thy worthy death
And want thy wit—thy wit high, pure, divine—
Is far beyond the pow'r of mortal line,
Nor anyone hath worth that draweth breath.

Yet rich in zeal, though poor in learning's lore,
And friendly care obscur'd in secret breast,
And love that envy in thy life suppress'd,
Thy dear life done, and death hath doubled more.

And I, that in thy time and living state
Did only praise thy virtues in my thought,   10
As one that seld the rising sun hath sought,
With words and tears now wail thy timeless fate.

Drawn was thy race aright from princely line,
Nor less than such (by gifts that Nature gave,
The common mother that all creatures have)
Doth virtue shew, and princely linage shine.

A king gave thee thy name, a kingly mind
That God thee gave, who found it now too dear
For this base world, and hath resum'd it near
To sit in skies and sort with pow'rs divine.   20

Kent thy birth days and Oxford held thy youth;
The heavens made haste, and stay'd nor years nor time;
The fruits of age grew ripe in thy first prime;
Thy will, thy words; thy words, the seals of truth.

Great gifts and wisdom rare imploy'd thee thence
To treat from kings with those more great than kings—
Such hope men had to lay the highest things
On thy wise youth, to be transported hence.

Whence to sharp wars sweet honor did thee call,
Thy country's love, religion, and thy friends—   30
Of worthy men the marks, the lives, and ends—
And her defense, for whom we labor all.

There didst thou vanquish shame and tedious age,
Grief, sorrow, sickness, and base fortune's might;
Thy rising day saw never woful night,
But pass'd with praise from off this worldly stage.

Back to the camp by thee that day was brought
First thine own death, and after thy long fame,
Tears to the soldiers, the proud Castilians' shame,
Virtue express'd, and honor truly taught.   40

What hath he lost that such great grace hath won?
Young years for endless years, and hope unsure
Of fortune's gifts for wealth that still shall dure.
O happy race with so great praises run!

England doth hold thy lims that bred the same,
Flanders thy valure where it last was tried,
The camp thy sorrow where thy body died,
Thy friends thy want, the world thy virtue's fame,

Nations thy wit, our minds lay up thy love,
Letters thy learning, thy loss years long to come.   50
In worthy hearts sorrow hath made thy tomb;
Thy soul and spright enrich the heavens above.

Thy liberal heart imbalm'd in grateful tears,
Young sighs, sweet sighs, sage sighs bewail thy fall;
Envy her sting, and Spite hath left her gall;
Malice herself a mourning garment wears.

That day their Hannibal died, our Scipio fell—
Scipio, Cicero, and Petrarch of our time,
Whose virtues, wounded by my worthless rime,
Let angels speak, and heavens thy praises tell.   60

[?Sir Walter Raleigh]

ANOTHER OF THE SAME, EXCELLENTLY WRITTEN BY A MOST WORTHY GENTLEMAN

Silence augmenteth grief; writing encreaseth rage;
Stall'd are my thoughts which lov'd and lost the wonder of our age.
Yet quick'ned now with fire, though dead with frost ere now,
Enrag'd I write, I know not what—dead, quick, I know not how.

Hard-hearted minds relent, and Rigor's tears abound,
And Envy strangely rues his end in whom no fault she found;
Knowledge her light hath lost; Valor hath slain her knight.
Sidney is dead, dead is my friend, dead is the world's delight!

Place, pensive, wails his fall whose presence was her pride;
Time crieth out, "My ebb is come; his life was my springtide!"   10
Fame mourns in that she lost the ground of her reports;
Each living wight laments his lack, and all in sundry sorts.

He was—wo worth that word!—to each well-thinking mind
A spotless friend, a matchless man whose virtue ever shin'd,
Declaring in his thoughts, his life, and that he writ
Highest conceits, longest foresights, and deepest works of wit.

He, only like himself, was second unto none,
Whose death (though life) we rue, and wrong, and all in vain do moan.
Their loss, not him, wail they that fill the world with cries;
Death slew not him, but he made death his ladder to the skies.   20

Now sink of sorrow I who live (the more the wrong),
Who wishing death, whom death denies, whose thread is all too long,
Who tied to wretched life, who looks for no relief,
Must spend my ever-dying days in never-ending grief.

Heart's ease and only I like [parallels] run on,
Whose equal length keep equal breadth and never meet in one;
Yet, for not wronging him, my thoughts, my sorrow's cell,
Shall not run out, though leak they will for liking him so well.

Farewell to you, my hopes, my wonted, waking dreams.
Farewell, sometimes enjoyed joy, eclipsed are thy beams.   30
Farewell, self-pleasing thoughts, which quietness brings forth,
And farewell, friendship's sacred league, uniting minds of worth;

And farewell, merry heart, the gift of guiltless minds,
And all sports which for live's restore variety assigns.
Let all that sweet is, void! In me no mirth may dwell:
Philip, the cause of all this wo, my live's content, farewell!

Now rime, the son of rage, which art no kin to skill,
And endless grief, which deads my life, yet knows not how to kill,
Go seek that hapless tomb, which if ye hap to find,
Salute the stones that keep the lims that held so good a mind.   40
                              [?Fulke Greville, Lord Brooke]

THE PREAMBLE TO N[ICHOLAS] B[RETON] HIS GARDEN-PLOT

Sweet fellow, whom I sware such sure, affected love
As neither weal, nor wo, nor want can from my mind remove,
To thee, my fellow sweet, this woful tale I tell
To let thee see the dark distress wherein my mind doth dwell.

On loathed bed I lay, my lustless lims to rest,
Where still I tumble to and fro to seek which side were best.
At last I catch a place, where long I cannot lie,
But strange conceits from quiet sleeps do keep awake mine eye.

The time of year, meseems, doth bid me, sloven, rise,
And not from shew of sweet delight to shut my sleepy eyes;   10
But sorrow, by and by, doth bid me, slave, lie still
And slug amongst the wretched souls whom care doth seek to kill.

For sorrow is my spring which brings forth bitter tears,
The fruits of friendship all forlorn, as feeble fancy fears.
                              [Nicholas Breton]

A STRANGE DESCRIPTION OF A RARE GARDEN-PLOT, WRITTEN BY N[ICHOLAS] B[RETON] GENT.

My garden-ground of grief, where self-will's seeds are sown,
Whereof comes up the weeds of wo that joys have overgrown,
With patience paled round to keep in secret spight,
And quickset round about with care to keep out all delight,

Four quarters squared out I find in sundry sort,
Whereof, according to their kinds, I mean to make report.
The first, the knot of Love, drawn even by true desire,
Like as it were two hearts in one, and yet both would be nigher.

The herb is call'd isop, the juice of such a taste
As with the sour makes sweet conceits to fly away too fast.   10
The borders round about are set with privy sweet,
Where never bird but nightingale presum'd to set her feet.

From this I stepp'd aside unto the knot of Care,
Which so was cross'd with strange conceits as tongue cannot declare.
The herb was called thyme which set out all that knot,
And like a maze methought it was when in the crooks I got.

The borders round about are savory unsweet,
An herb not much in my conceit, for such a knot unmeet.
From this to Friendship's knot I stepp'd and took the view
How it was drawn and then, again, in order how it grew.   20

The course was not unlike a kind of hand in hand,
But many fingers were away that there should seem to stand.
The herb that set the knot was pennyrial round,
And, as meseem'd, it grew full close and near unto the ground,

And parched here and there, so that it seemed not
Full as it should have been indeed, a perfect Friendship knot.
Hereat I paus'd a while and took a little view
Of an odd quarter drawn in beds where herbs and flowers grew.

The flow'rs were buttons fine for batchelors to bear,
And by those flow'rs there grew an herb was called maidenhear.   30

Amid this garden-ground a condit strange I found,
Which water fetch'd from Sorrow's spring to water all the ground,
To this, my heavy house, the dungeon of Distress,
Where fainting heart lies panting still, despairing of redress.

Whence from my window, lo! this sad prospect I have:
A piece of ground whereon to gaze would bring one to his grave.
Lo! thus the welcome spring, that others lends delight,
Doth make me die to think I lie thus drowned in despight,

That up I cannot rise and come abroad to thee,
My fellow sweet, with whom God knows how oft I wish to be.   40
And thus, in haste, adieu; my heart is grown so sore,
And care so crooks my fingers' ends, that I can write no more.
                                        [Nicholas Breton]

[OF CEASELESS THOUGHTS MY MIND HATH FRAM'D HIS WINGS]

Of ceaseless thoughts my mind hath fram'd his wings,
Wherewith he soars and climes above conceit;
And, midst his flight, for endless joy he sings
To spy those double lamps whose sweet receit
   Must be the heaven whereas my soul shall rest,
   Though by their shine my body be depress'd.

Her eyes shroud pity, piety, and pure;
Her face shields roses, lilies, and delight;
Her hand hath pow'r to conquer and allure;
Her heart holds honor, love, remorse, and right;   10
   Her mind is fraught with wisdom, faith, and love.
   All what is hers is borrowed from above.

Then mount, my mind, and fear no future fall;
Exceed conceit, for she exceeds conceit.
Burn, lovely lamps, to whom my looks are thrall;
My soul shall glory in so sweet receit.
   Tho in your flames my corse to cinders wend,
   Yet am I proud to gain a phoenix' end.
               T[homas] L[odge]

[MY FRAIL AND EARTHLY BARK, BY REASON'S GUIDE]

My frail and earthly bark, by Reason's guide
(Which holds the helm whilst Will doth [wield] the sail),
By my desires (the winds of bad betide),
Hath sail'd these worldly seas with small avail.
Vain objects serve for dreadful rocks to quail
   My brittle boat, from haven of life that flies
   To haunt the sea of mundane miseries.

My soul, that draws impressions from above,
And views my course, and sees the winds aspire,
Bids Reason watch to scape the shoals of Love;   10
But lawless Will, enflam'd with endless ire,
Doth steer in poop whilst Reason doth retire;
   The storms increase; my bark Love's billows fill.
   Thus are they wrack'd that guide their course by Will.
               T[homas] L[odge]

[FOR PITY, PRETTY EYES, SURCEASE]

For pity, pretty eyes, surcease
To give me war, and grant me peace!
Triumphant eyes, why bear you arms
Against a heart that thinks no harms,
A heart already quite appall'd,
A heart that yields and is enthrall'd?
Kill rebels proudly that resist,
Not those that in true faith persist
And, conquered, serve your deity.

Will you, alas, command me die?   10
Then die I yours, and death my cross,
But unto you pertains the loss.
               T[homas] [Lodge]

[MY BONNY LASS, THINE EYE]

My bonny lass, thine eye,
     So sly,
Hath made me sorrow so;
Thy crimson cheeks, my dear,
     So clear,
Have so much wrought my wo;

Thy pleasing smiles and grace,
     Thy face,
Have ravish'd so my sprights
That life is grown to nought   10
     Through thought
Of Love, which me affrights.

For Fancy's flames of fire
     Aspire
Unto such furious pow'r
As, but the tears I shed
     Make dead,
The brands would me devour.

I should consume to nought
     Through thought   20
Of thy fair shining eye,
Thy cheeks, thy pleasing smiles,
     The wiles
That forc'd my heart to die,

Thy grace, thy face, the part
     Where art
Stands gazing still to see
The wondrous gifts and pow'r
     Each hour
That hath bewitched me.   30
               T[homas] L[odge]

[THOSE EYES WHICH SET MY FANCY ON AFIRE]

Those eyes which set my fancy on afire,
Those crisped hairs which hold my heart in chains,
Those dainty hands which conquer'd my desire,
That wit which of my thoughts doth hold the reins!

Those eyes for clearness do the stars surpass,
Those hairs obscure the brightness of the sun,
Those hands more white than ever ivory was,
That wit even to the skies hath glory won!

O eyes that pierce our hearts without remorse,
O hairs of right that wears a royal crown,   10
O hands that conquer more than Caesar's force,
O wit that turns huge kingdoms upside down!

Then, Love, be judge what heart may thee withstand—
Such eyes, such hair, such wit, and such a hand!
                                        [Anonymous]

[HER FACE, HER TONGUE, HER WIT]

Her face,	Her tongue,	Her wit,
So fair,	So sweet,	So sharp,
First bent,	Then drew,	Then hit,
Mine eye,	Mine ear,	My heart.

Mine eye,	Mine ear,	My heart,
To like,	To learn,	To love,
Her face,	Her tongue,	Her wit,
Doth lead,	Doth teach,	Doth move.

O face,	O tongue,	O wit,
With frowns,	With check,	With smart, 10
Wrong not,	Vex not,	Wound not,
Mine eye,	Mine ear,	My heart.

Mine eye,	Mine ear,	My heart,
To learn,	To know,	To fear,
Her face,	Her tongue,	Her wit,
Doth lead,	Doth teach,	Doth swear.

                                        [Anonymous]

A NOTABLE DESCRIPTION OF THE WORLD

Of thick and thin, light, heavy, dark, and clear;	*Mixtures*
White, black, and blue, red, green, and purple dye;	*Colors*
Gold, silver, brass, lead, iron, tin, and copper;	*Metals*
Moist air, hot fire, cold water, earth full dry;	*Elements*
Blood, choler, flegm, and melancholy by;	*Complexions*
A mixed mass, a chaos all confus'd—	*Chaos*
Such was the world till God division us'd.	

In framing heav'n and earth, God did divide
The first day's light and darkth to night and day.   1
The second, he a firmament appli'd.   2
Third, fruitful earth appear'd; seas took their way. 3
Fourth, sun and moon with stars in skies he fix'd.   4
Fift, fish and fowl the sea and land possess'd.   5
And God made man like to himself the sixt.   6

The seventh day, when all things he had bless'd,   7
He hallowed that, and therein took his rest.
                                W. S. [?William Smith]

A DESCRIPTION OF LOVE

Now what is love, I pray thee tell.
It is that fountain and that well
Where pleasure and repentance dwell;
It is, perhaps, that saucing bell
    That tolls all into heaven or hell;
    And this is love, as I hear tell.

Yet what is love, I pray thee say.
It is a work on holiday;
It is December match'd with May;
When lusty bloods, in fresh array,   10
    Hear, ten months after, of the play.
    And this is love, as I hear say.

Yet what is love, I pray thee sain.
It is a sunshine mix'd with rain;
It is a toothache, or like pain;
It is a game where none doth gain.
    The lass saith no, and would full fain.
    And this is love, as I hear sain.

Yet what is love, I pray thee say.
It is a yea, it is a nay,   20
A pretty kind of sporting fray;
It is a thing will soon away.
    Then take the vantage while you may.
    And this is love, as I hear say.

Yet what is love, I pray thee show.
A thing that creeps—it cannot go;
A prize that passeth to and fro,
A thing for one, a thing for mo;
    And he that proves must find it so.
    And this is love, sweet friend, I trow. 30
                                        [Anonymous]

[O NIGHT, O JEALOUS NIGHT, REPUGNANT TO MY PLEASURES]

O night, O jealous night, repugnant to my pleasures,
O night so long desir'd, yet cross to my content!
There's none but only thou that can perform my pleasures,
Yet none but only thou that hindereth my intent.

Thy beams, thy spiteful beams, thy lamps that burn too
    brightly,
Discover all my trains, and naked lay my drifts,
That night by night I hope, yet fail my purpose nightly,
Thy envious, glaring gleam defeateth so my shifts.

Sweet night, withhold thy beams, withhold them till
    tomorrow,
Whose joys in lack so long a hell of torments breeds.   10

Sweet night, sweet, gentle night, do not prolong my
    sorrow.
Desire is guide to me, and Love no loadstar needs.

Let sailors gaze on stars and moon so freshly shining,
Let them that miss the way be guided by the light.
I know my lady's bow'r; there needs no more divining;
Affection sees in dark, and Love hath eyes by night.

Dame Cynthia, couch awhile; hold in thy horns for
    shining,

And glad not low'ring night with thy too glorious rays;
But be she dim and dark, tempestuous and repining,
That in her spite my sport may work thy endless praise. 20

And when my will is wrought, then, Cynthia, shine, good
    lady,
All other nights and days in honor of that night,
That happy, heavenly night, that night so dark and shady,
Wherein my love had eyes that lighted my delight.

[Anonymous]

ENGLAND'S HELICON

Although its dazzling gallery of contributors—Barn-field, Breton, Browne, Drayton, Greene, Fulke Greville, Lodge, Marlowe, Peele, Raleigh, Shakespeare, Sidney, Spenser, and Surrey among others—makes *England's Helicon* (1600) the loveliest of Elizabethan miscellanies, it is by no means an irreplaceable book, some hundred twenty-seven of its one hundred fifty poems surviving elsewhere. It is, then, a real anthology, and, like many present-day anthologies, it was built on a definite plan—to contain nothing but pastoral poetry. Such a limitation incurred grave risks, for, its distinguished contributors notwithstanding, its compiler printed a good deal that was trivial and tedious.

Just who that compiler was has long been a matter of speculation. A commendatory sonnet by A. B. addressed to John Bodenham (whose arms are on the verso of the titlepage) and praising his work on "Wit's Common-wealth" (i.e. *Politeuphuia*), "Wit's Theater," "The Muses' Garden" (i. e. *Belvedere*), and "thy Helicon" has led many to believe Bodenham the compiler of these four anthologies (see p. 650). But as has been recently shown (from evidence too technical to rehearse here), Bodenham must be regarded as "the originator and patron, but not the editor, of the four books mentioned in A. B.'s sonnet. He did all, or most, of the preliminary work on *Politeuphuia* and *Belvedere,* he outlined the two as well as *Wit's Theater* and *England's Helicon,* but all four he entrusted to the editorial skill of a second person, who then dedicated each book to him, and who was in all likelihood rewarded with a substantial gift of money." It is at least a plausible guess that the actual editor of *England's Helicon* was the L. N. who signed the preface "To the Reader, If In-different," and that the signature is the transposed initials of Nicholas Ling, the publisher of *Politeuphuia* and *Wit's Theater* and a man known to have been on intimate terms with Bodenham.

At any rate, the moving spirit behind the collection was obviously a person of some cultivation and of rather rarefied literary tastes; otherwise it is unlikely that he should have conceived the notion of a pastoral anthology. Given the broad Elizabethan conception of pastoral poetry, however, virtually any poem mentioning a shepherd or nymph or swain was grist to his mill, and so he could (and did) draw upon Spenser's *Shepherd's Calendar,* Bartholomew Yong's translation of Monte-mayor's influential *Diana,* pastoral novels like Sidney's *Arcadia,* Greene's *Menaphon,* and Lodge's *Rosalynde,* plays like Peele's *Arraignment of Paris,* song books like Dowland's and Morley's, and earlier miscellanies like Tottel's, *Breton's Bower of Delights,* and *The Phoenix Nest.* With a freedom of conscience that modern editors may envy but cannot imitate, he treated his texts to suit his purpose, changing words, substituting pastoral for non-pastoral names, inventing titles, and adding lines. Consequently the texts of *England's Helicon* are usually unreliable, and, except when they are not found else-where, they must invariably yield to the readings of their sources. We include them only to provide a sampling from so famous a miscellany. Of our excerpts, only Drayton's "The Shepherd's Anthem" and Browne's "Thyrsis' Praise of His Mistress" made their first printed appearance in *England's Helicon,* the former in the first edition, the latter in the second (1614). For the others the editor of *England's Helicon* used the following sources:

Sidney's "Astrophel's Love Is Dead" and "In Wonted Walks" were reprinted from *Certain Sonnets Written by Sir Philip Sidney* affixed to the 1598 edition of the *Arcadia;* "Dorus His Comparisons,' "Astrophel to Stella, His Third Song," and "An Excellent Sonnet of a Nymph" from the text of the 1598 *Arcadia.*

Breton's "Phyllida and Corydon" from *The Honorable Entertainment Given to the Queen's Majesty. . . at Elvetham in Hampshire* (1591).

Shakespeare's "The Passionate Shepherd's Song" from *The Passionate Pilgrim* (1599), which in turn reprinted it from *Love's Labor's Lost* (IV.iii 101–20).

Lodge's "The Solitary Shepherd's Song" from *A Margarite of America* (1596).

Yong's "The Nymph Diana's Song" from his translation of Montemayor's *Diana* (1598).

Marlowe's famous "The Passionate Shepherd to His Love" and its counterpart, "The Nymph's Reply" (perhaps by Raleigh), from *The Passionate Pilgrim*.

Peele's "Colin, the Enamored Shepherd" from *The Arraignment of Paris* (1584).

The continued popularity of *England's Helicon* has made it one of the most successful books of the Elizabethan period. Following its second edition in 1614—with the

original one hundred fifty poems rearranged and nine new ones added—it retained an astonishing popularity during the next two centuries (when most other Elizabethan miscellanies were quite forgotten); it was edited and widely admired in the nineteenth century; and it has been one of the most fertile sources for modern anthologies of Elizabethan poetry. Our text is based upon the first edition of 1600 (STC 3191), except for Browne's "Thyrsis' Praise of His Mistress," which appeared first in the second edition of 1614 (STC 3192).

FROM ENGLAND'S HELICON (1600)

To the Reader, If Indifferent

Many honored names have heretofore (in their particular interest) patronized some part of these inventions; many here be that only these collections have brought to light, and not inferior (in the best opinions) to any before published. The travail that hath been taken in gathering them from so many hands hath wearied some hours; which, severed, might in part have perished; digested into this mean volume, may, in the opinion of some, not be alto- 10 gether unworthy the labor. If any man hath been defrauded of anything by him composed, by another man's title put to the same, he hath this benefit by this collection: freely to challenge his own in publique where else he might be robb'd of his proper due. No one thing being here placed by the collector of the same under any man's name, either at large or in letters, but as it was delivered by some especial copy coming to his hands. No one man that shall take offense that his name is published to any invention 20 of his but he shall, within the reading of a leaf or two, meet with another in reputation every way equal with himself, whose name hath been before printed to his poem, which now taken away were more then theft; which may satisfy him that would fain seem curious or be intreated for his fame.

Now if any stationer shall find fault that his copies are robb'd by anything in this collection, let me ask him this question: why more in this then in any divine or human author? From whence a man writing 30 of that argument shall gather any saying, sentence, simile, or example, his name put to it who is the author of the same. This is the simplest of many reasons that I could urdge, though perhaps the nearest his capacity, but that I would be loth to trouble myself to satisfy him. Further, if any man whatsoever, in prizing of his own birth or fortune, shall

take in scorn that a far meaner man in the eye of the world shall be placed by him, I tell him plainly, whatsoever so excepting that, that man's wit is set by his, not that man by him. In which degree the names of poets (all fear and duty ascribed to her great and sacred name!) have been placed with the names of the greatest princes of the world by the most autentique and worthiest judgments without disparagement to their sovereign titles; which if any man, taking exception thereat in ignorance, know not, I 10 hold him unworthy to be placed by the meanest that is but graced with the title of a poet. Thus, gentle reader, I wish thee all happiness.

L. N. [?Nicholas Ling]

ASTROPHEL'S LOVE IS DEAD

Ring out your bells, let mourning shews be spread,
    For love is dead.
  All love is dead, infected
  With plague of deep disdain,
  Worth as nought worth rejected,
  And faith fair scorn doth gain.
    From so ungrateful fancy,
    From such a female frenzy,
    From them that use men thus,
      Good Lord, deliver us!   10

Weep, neighbors, weep. Do you not hear it said
    That love is dead?
  His death-bed peacocks' folly,
  His winding-sheet is shame;
  His will false, seeming holy,
  His sole exec'tor blame.
    From so ungrateful fancy,
    From such a female frenzy,
    From them that use men thus,
      Good Lord, deliver us!   20

Let dirge be sung and trentals richly read,
    For love is dead.
    And wrong his tomb ordaineth
    My mistress' marble heart,
    Which epitaph containeth,
    "Her eyes were once his dart."
      From so ungrateful fancy,
      From such a female frenzy,
      From them that use men thus,
        Good Lord, deliver us!   30

Alas, I lie. Rage hath this error bred.
    Love is not dead.
    Love is not dead, but sleepeth
    In her unmatched mind,
    Where she his counsel keepeth
    Till due desert she find.
      Therefore from so vile fancy,
      To call such wit a frenzy,
      Who love can temper thus,
        Good Lord, deliver us!   40

                Sir Philip Sidney

PHYLLIDA AND CORYDON

In the merry moneth of May
In a morn by break of day
Forth I walked by the woodside
Whenas May was in his pride.
There I spied all alone
Phyllida and Corydon.
Much ado there was, God wot:
He would love and she would not.
She said never man was true;
He said, "None was false to you."   10
He said he had lov'd her long;
She said love should have no wrong.
Corydon would kiss her then;
She said maids must kiss no men
Till they did for good and all.
Then she made the shepherd call
All the heavens to witness truth:
Never lov'd a truer youth.
Thus with many a pretty oath,
Yea and nay, and faith and troth,   20
Such as silly shepherds use
When they will not love abuse,
Love, which had been long deluded,
Was with kisses sweet concluded.
And Phyllida with garlands gay
Was made the Lady of the May.

                N[icholas] Breton

THE PASSIONATE SHEPHERD'S SONG

On a day (alack the day)
Love, whose moneth was ever May,

Spied a blossom passing fair
Playing in the wanton air.
Through the velvet leaves the wind
All unseen gan passage find,
That the shepherd, sick to death,
Wish'd himself the heaven's breath.
"Air," quoth he, "thy cheeks may blow;
Air, would I might triumph so.   10
But alas, my hand hath sworn
Ne'er to pluck thee from thy thorn.
Vow, alack, for youth unmeet,
Youth so apt to pluck a sweet—
Thou for whom Jove would swear
Juno but an Ethiop were
And deny himself for Jove,
Turning mortal for my love."

             W[illiam] Shakespeare

THE SOLITARY SHEPHERD'S SONG

O shady vales, O fair enriched meads,
O sacred woods, sweet fields, and rising mountains,
O painted flowers, green herbs where Flora treads,
Refresh'd by wanton winds and wat'ry fountains!

O all you winged queristers of wood
That, perch'd aloft, your former pains report,
And straight again recount, with pleasant mood,
Your present joys in sweet and seemly sort!

O all you creatures whosoever thrive
On mother earth, in seas, by air, by fire!   10
More blest are you then I here under sun.
Love dies in me, whenas he doth revive
In you. I perish under beauty's ire,
Where, after storms, winds, frosts, your life is won.

                Thomas Lodge

DORUS HIS COMPARISONS

My sheep are thoughts which I both guide and serve;
Their pasture is fair hills of fruitless love.
On barren sweets they feed, and, feeding, sterve;
I wail their lot but will not other prove.
My sheep-hook is wanhope, which all upholds;
My weeds, desires, cut out in endless folds.
  What wool my sheep shall bear, while thus they live,
  In you it is; you must the judgment give.

                Sir Philip Sidney

THE NYMPH DIANA'S SONG

When that I, poor soul, was born
I was born unfortunate.
Presently the Fates had sworn
To foretell my hapless state.

Titan his fair beams did hide;
Phoebe 'clips'd her silver light.
In my birth my mother died,
Young and fair in heavy plight.

And the nurse that gave me suck
Hapless was in all her life;   10
And I never had good luck,
Being maid or married wife.

I lov'd well and was belov'd,
And forgetting was forgot;
This a hapless marriage mov'd,
Grieving that it kills me not.

With the earth would I were wed
Then in such a grave of woes
Daily to be buried,
Which no end nor number knows.   20

Young my father married me,
Forc'd by my obedience.
Syrenus, thy faith and thee
I forgot without offense.

Which contempt I pay so far
Never like was paid so much.
Jealousies do make me war
But without a cause of such.

I do go with jealous eyes
To my folds and to my sheep,   30
And with jealousy I rise
When the day begins to peep.

At his table I do eat,
In his bed with him I lie;
But I take no rest nor meat
Without cruel jealousy.

If I ask him what he ails
And whereof he jealous is,
In his answer then he fails;
Nothing can he say to this.   40

In his face there is no cheer,
But he ever hangs the head;
In each corner he doth peer,
And his speech is sad and dead.

> Ill the poor soul lives, ywis,
> That so hardly married is.

Bartholomew Yong

ASTROPHEL TO STELLA, HIS THIRD SONG

If Orpheus' voice had force to breathe such musique's love
Through pores of senseless trees as it could make them
        move,
If stones good measure danc'd, the Theban walls to build
To cadence of the tunes which Amphion's lyre did yield,
    More cause a like effect at leastwise bringeth.
    O stones, O trees, learn hearing! Stella singeth.

If love might sweet'n so a boy of shepherd's brood
To make a lizard dull to taste love's dainty food,
If eagle fierce could so in Grecian maid delight
As his light was her eyes, her death his endless night,   10
    Earth gave that love; heav'n, I trow, love defineth.
    O beasts, O birds, look! Love, lo! Stella shineth.

The birds, [beasts,] stones, and trees feel this, and, feeling,
        love;
And if the trees nor stones stir not the same to prove,
Nor beasts nor birds do come unto this blessed gaze,
Know that small love is quick and great love doth amaze.
    They are amaz'd, but you with reason armed,
    O eyes, O ears of men, how are you charmed?

Sir Philip Sidney

THE SHEPHERD'S ANTHEM

Near to a bank with roses set about,
Where pretty turtles joining bill to bill,
And gentle springs steal softly murmuring out,
Washing the foot of pleasure's sacred hill,
    There little Love, sore wounded, lies,
        his bow and arrows broken,
    Bedew'd with tears from Venus' eyes—
        O that it should be spoken.

Bear him my heart, slain with her scornful eye,
Where sticks the arrow that poor heart did kill,   10
With whose sharp pile yet will him, ere he die,
About my heart to write his latest will.
    And bid him send it back to me
        at instant of his dying,
    That cruel, cruel she may see
        my faith and her denying.

His hearse shall be a mournful cypress shade,
And for a chantry Philomel's sweet lay,
Where prayer shall continually be made
By pilgrim lovers passing by that way.   20
    With nymphs and shepherds yearly moan,
        his timeless death beweeping,
    And telling that my heart alone
        hath his last will in keeping.

Michael Drayton

[IN WONTED WALKS, SINCE WONTED FANCIES CHANGE]

In wonted walks, since wonted fancies change,
Some cause there is which of strange cause doth rise;
For in each thing whereto my mind doth range
Part of my pain meseems engraved lies.

The rocks, which were of constant mind the mark,
In climbing steep now hard refusal show;
The shading woods seem now my sun to dark,
And stately hills disdain to look so low.

The restful caves now restless visions give.
In dales I see each way a hard ascent.   10
Like late-mown meads, late cut from joy I live.
Alas, sweet brooks do in my tears augment.
  Rocks, woods, hills, caves, dales, meads, brooks
      answer me:
  "Infected minds infect each thing they see."
                              Sir Philip Sidney

THE PASSIONATE SHEPHERD TO HIS LOVE

Come live with me and be my love,
And we will all the pleasures prove
That valleys, groves, hills, and fields,
Woods or steepy mountain yields.

And we will sit upon the rocks,
Seeing the shepherds feed their flocks
By shallow rivers, to whose falls
Melodious birds sings madrigals.

And I will make thee beds of roses
And a thousand fragrant poesies,   10
A cap of flowers and a kirtle
Imbroid'red all with leaves of myrtle;

A gown made of the finest wool
Which from our pretty lambs we pull,
Fair-lined slippers for the cold,
With buckles of the purest gold;

A belt of straw and ivy buds
With coral clasps and amber studs.
And if these pleasures may thee move,
Come live with me and be my love.   20

The shepherds' swains shall dance and sing
For thy delight each May-morning.
If these delights thy mind may move,
Then live with me and be my love.
                              Christopher Marlowe

THE NYMPH'S REPLY TO THE SHEPHERD

If all the world and love were young,
And truth in every shepherd's tongue,
These pretty pleasures might me move
To live with thee and be thy love.

Time drives the flocks from field to fold
When rivers rage and rocks grow cold
And Philomel becometh dumb;
The rest complains of cares to come.

The flowers do fade, and wanton fields
To wayward winter reckoning yields.   10
A honey tongue, a heart of gall
Is fancy's spring but sorrow's fall.

Thy gowns, thy shoes, thy beds of roses,
Thy cap, thy kirtle, and thy poesies
Soon break, soon wither, soon forgotten—
In folly ripe, in reason rotten.

Thy belt of straw and ivy buds,
Thy coral clasps and amber studs,
All these in me no means can move
To come to thee and be thy love.   20

But could youth last and love still breed,
Had joys no date nor age no need,
Then these delights my mind might move
To live with thee and be thy love.
                              [?Sir Walter Raleigh]

AN EXCELLENT SONNET OF A NYMPH

Virtue, beauty, and speech did strike, wound, charm
My heart, eyes, ears with wonder, love, delight;
First, second, last did bind, enforce, and arm
His works, shows, suits with wit, grace, and vow's might.

Thus honor, liking, trust much, far, and deep
Held, pierc'd, possess'd my judgment, sense, and will;
Till wrongs, contempt, deceit did grow, steal, creep
Bands, favor, faith to break, defile, and kill.

Then grief, unkindness, proof took, kindled, taught
Well-grounded, noble, due spite, rage, disdain.   10
But ah, alas, in vain my mind, sight, thought
Doth him, his face, his words leave, shun, refrain.
  For nothing, time, nor place can loose, quench, ease
  Mine own embraced, sought knot, fire, disease.
                              Sir Philip Sidney

COLIN, THE ENAMORED SHEPHERD, SINGETH THIS PASSION OF LOVE

O gentle love, ungentle for thy deed,
  thou makest my heart,
   a bloody mark,
  With piercing shot to bleed.

Shoot soft, sweet love, for fear thou shoot amiss,
  for fear too keen
   thy arrows been
  And hit the heart where my beloved is.

Too fair that fortune were, nor never I
  shall be so blest   10
   among the rest
  That love shall seize on her by sympathy.

Then since with love my prayers bear no boot
  this doth remain
   to ease my pain:
  I take the wound and die at Venus' foot.

          George Peele

THYRSIS' PRAISE OF HIS MISTRESS

On a hill that grac'd the plain
Thyrsis sate, a comely swain.
  Comelier swain ne'er grac'd a hill.
Whilst his flock that wand'red nigh
Cropp'd the green grass busily
  Thus he tun'd his oaten quill:

"Ver hath made the pleasant field
Many sev'ral odors yield,
  Odors aromatical.

From fair Astra's cherry lip   10
Sweeter smells forever skip;
  They in pleasing passen all.

"Leavy groves now mainly ring
With each sweet bird's sonneting,
  Notes that make the echoes long.
But when Astra tunes her voice
All the mirthful birds rejoice
  And are list'ning to her song.

"Fairly spreads the damask rose
Whose rare mixture doth disclose 20
  Beauties pencils cannot feign;
Yet if Astra pass the bush
Roses have been seen to blush.
  She doth all their beauties stain.

"Phoebus shining bright in sky
Gilds the floods, heats mountains high,
  With his beams' all-quick'ning fire.
Astra's eyes—most sparkling ones—
Strikes a heat in hearts of stones
  And enflames them with desire. 30

"Fields are blest with flow'ry wreath;
Air is blest when she doth breathe;
  Birds make happy ev'ry grove;
She each bird when she doth sing;
Phoebus' heat to earth doth bring;
  She makes marble fall in love.

"Those, blessings of the earth we swains do call.
Astra can bless those blessings, earth and all."

         W[illiam] Browne

A POETICAL RHAPSODY

A Poetical Rhapsody, the last and one of the most valuable of the Elizabethan miscellanies, presents an uncommon number of bibliographical problems. Entered on May 28, 1602, in the Stationers' Register as "a book called *Pastorals and Eglogues, Odes and Madrigals,*" it was published under its present title early in the following summer; other editions and expansions followed in 1608, 1611, and 1621. The one hundred seventy-six poems of the first edition were reprinted in the second and third, and all but three of them in the fourth; furthermore, the second edition added sixty-four new poems, the third eight, and the fourth two. Thus, first and last, *A Poetical Rhapsody* preserves the text of two hundred fifty poems. Representing such writers as Sidney, Raleigh, Campion,

Sir John Davies, Spenser, Watson, the Davisons, and many others, it is a big and an important collection.

If we may accept the word of Francis Davison, its projector and first editor, the original design was more modest; for Davison intended the book to be an anthology of his, his brother Walter's, and a dear anonymous friend's work. He asks the reader to remember "that those [poems] under the name of Anomos were written . . . when poetry was far from that perfection to which it hath now attained; that my brother is by profession a soldier, and was not eighteen years old when he writ these toys; that mine own were made, most of them, six or seven years since at idle times as I journeyed up and down during my travels." In the first edition Anomos is credited with sixty-nine poems, Walter Davison with nineteen, and Francis Davison with forty-two; for the rest the editor emphatically denies any responsibility "as being done by the printer [John Bailey], either to grace the forefront with Sir Philip Sidney's and others' names, or to make the book grow to a competent volume."

In spite of the "never yet published" on the titlepage, Bailey included a fair number of poems that had been in print for years. Of the first section (nos. 1–11) two are assigned to Sidney, two to Anomos, one to the Countess of Pembroke, one to Walter Davison, two to Francis Davison, one to A. W., one to Ignoto, and one is unsigned. The fact that Francis Davison himself, in a manuscript catalogue of A. W.'s poems (MS. Harleian 280), ascribed eighty-one poems to A. W. has led to many futile speculations about that mysterious contributor's identity; it is a fair guess, however, that the initials stand

merely for "anonymous writer." The second section of the miscellany is assigned to the Davison brothers, forty to Francis and eighteen to Walter. Of the remaining poems, sixty-seven are by Anomos, and the rest are scattered among Sir John Davies, Thomas Campion, Henry Constable, Sir Walter Raleigh, Sir Henry Wotton, Spenser, *et al.* It is indeed "a competent volume," its varied content comprising pastorals, translations (of Anacreon, Martial, Horace, Ovid), imitations of many Italian and French forms (of which Francis Davison had acquired a thorough knowledge on his travels), madrigals, and airs. Although Davison himself probably retired from the project after the second edition, he had done his work well, and *A Poetical Rhapsody* remained popular throughout the earlier seventeenth century. Our text is based upon the edition of 1602 (STC 6373).

FROM A POETICAL RHAPSODY (1602)

To the Reader

Being induced by some private reasons and by the instant intreaty of special friends to suffer some of my worthless poems to be published, I desired to make some written by my dear friend Anomos and my dearer brother to bear them company. Both without their consent, the latter being in the Low Country wars and the former utterly ignorant thereof. My friend's name I concealed; mine own and my brother's I willed the printer to suppress as well as I had concealed the other; which he having put in without my privity, we must both now undergo a sharper censure perhaps then our nameless works should have done, and I especially. For if their poems be liked, the praise is due to their invention; if disliked, the blame both by them and all men will be derived upon me for publishing that which they meant to suppress. . . .

For these poems in particular, I could alledge these excuses: that those under the name of Anomos were written (as appeareth by divers things to Sir Philip Sidney living and of him dead) almost twenty years since, when poetry was far from that perfection to which it hath now attained; that my brother is by profession a soldier, and was not eighteen years old when he writ these toys; that mine own were made, most of them, six or seven years since at idle times as I journeyed up and down during my travels. But to leave their works to justify themselves, or the authors to justify their works, and to speak of mine

own, thy mislikes I contemn; thy praises (which I neither deserve nor expect) I esteem not, as hoping (God willing) ere long to regain thy good opinion if lost, or more deservedly to continue it if already obtained, by some graver work. Farewell.

Francis Davison

A DIALOGUE BETWEEN TWO SHEPHERDS, THENOT AND PIERS, IN PRAISE OF ASTREA

MADE BY THE EXCELLENT LADY, THE LADY MARY, COUNTESS OF PEMBROKE, AT THE QUEEN'S MAJESTY'S BEING AT HER HOUSE AT [WILTON], ANNO 15[99]

THENOT.   I sing divine Astrea's praise.
       O muses, help my wits to raise
         And heave my verses higher.

PIERS.   Thou need'st the truth but plainly tell,
       Which much I doubt thou canst not well,
         Thou art so oft a liar.

THENOT.   If in my song no more I show
       Than heav'n and earth and sea do know,
         Then truly I have spoken.

PIERS.   Sufficeth not no more to name,   10
       But, being no less, the like, the same;
         Else laws of truth be broken.

THENOT.   Then say she is so good, so fair,
       With all the earth she may compare,
         Not Momus self denying.

PIERS   Compare may think where likeness holds;
             Nought like to her the earth enfolds.
                  I look'd to find you lying.

THENOT.   Astrea sees with wisdom's sight,
             Astrea works by virtue's might,   20
                  And jointly both do stay her.
PIERS.   Nay, take from them her hand, her mind,
             The one is lame, the other blind.
                  Shall still your lying stain her?

THENOT.   Soon as Astrea shews her face
             Straight every ill avoids the place,
                  And every good aboundeth.
PIERS.   Nay, long before her face doth show,
             The last doth come, the first doth go.
                  How loud this lie resoundeth!   30

THENOT.   Astrea is our chiefest joy,
             Our chiefest guard against annoy,
                  Our chiefest wealth, our treasure.
PIERS.   Where chiefest are, [there] others be,
             To us none else but only she.
                  When wilt thou speak in measure?

THENOT.   Astrea may be justly said
             A field in flow'ry robe array'd,
                  In season freshly springing.
PIERS.   That spring indures but shortest time;   40
             This never leaves Astrea's clime.
                  Thou liest, instead of singing.

THENOT.   As heavenly light that guides the day,
             Right so doth [shine] each lovely ray
                  That from Astrea flieth.
PIERS.   Nay, darkness oft that light enclouds;
             Astrea's beams no darkness shrouds.
                  How loudly Thenot lieth!

THENOT.   Astrea rightly term I may
             A manly palm, a maiden bay,   50
                  Her verdure never dying.
PIERS.   Palm oft is crooked, bay is low;
             She, still upright, still high doth grow.
                  Good Thenot, leave thy lying.

THENOT.   Then, Piers, of friendship tell me why,
             My meaning true, my words should lie
                  And strive in vain to raise her.
PIERS.   Words from conceit do only rise;
             Above conceit her honor flies.
                  But silence nought can praise her.   60

                        Mary, Countess of Pembroke

SONNET I. DEDICATION OF THESE RIMES TO HIS FIRST LOVE

If my harsh, humble style and rimes ill-dressed
     Arrive not to your worth and beauty glorious,
     My muse's shoulders are with weight oppressed,
     And heavenly beams are o'er my sight victorious.
If these dim colors have your worth expressed,
     Laid by love's hand and not by art laborious,
     Your sun-like rays have my wit's harvest blessed,
     Enabling me to make your praise notorious.
But if, alas (alas, the heavens defend it),
     My lines your eyes, my love your heart, displeasing,   10
     Breed hate in you and kill my hope of easing,
     Say with yourself, "How can the wretch amend it?
I wondrous fair, he wondrous dearly loving,
How can his thoughts but make his pen be moving?"

                                    Francis Davison

SONNET III. UPON HIS ABSENCE FROM HER

The fairest eyes (O eyes in blackness fair!)
     That ever shin'd, and the most heav'nly face,
     The daintiest smiling, the most conquering grace
     And sweetest breath that e'er perfum'd the air;
The cherriest lips, whose kiss might well repair
     A dead man's state, that speech which did displace
     All mean desires and all affections base,
     Clogging swift Hope and winging dead Dispair;
That snow-white breast and all those faultless features
     Which made her seem a personage divine   10
     And far excelling fairest human creatures
     Hath absence banish'd from my cursed eyen.
But in my heart, as in a mirror clear,
All these perfections to my thoughts appear.

                                    Francis Davison

MADRIGAL V. ALLUSION TO THE CONFUSION OF BABEL

     The wretched life I live
In my weak senses such confusion maketh
     That, like th' accursed rabble
     That built the tow'r of Babel,
          My wit mistaketh
And unto nothing a right name doth give.

I term her my dear love that deadly hates me;
My chiefest good, her that's my chiefest evil;
Her saint and goddess who's a witch, a devil;
Her my sole hope that with despair amates me.   10
     My balm I call her that with poison fills me,
     And her I term my life that daily kills me.

                                    Francis Davison

ODE V. HIS FAREWELL TO HIS UNKIND AND UNCONSTANT MISTRESS

Sweet, if you like and love me still,
And yield me love for my good will,
And do not from your promise start
When your fair hand gave me your heart;
   If dear to you I be
   As you are dear to me,
Then yours I am and will be ever;
Nor time nor place my love shall sever,
But faithful still I will persever
   Like constant marble stone,   10
   Loving but you alone.

But if you favor mo than me
(Who love thee still, and none but thee),
If others do the harvest gain
That's due to me for all my pain;
   If that you love to range
   And oft to chop and change,
Then get you some newfangled mate.
My doting love shall turn to hate,
Esteeming you (though too too late)   20
   Not worth a pebble-stone,
   Loving not me alone.

               Francis Davison

ODE VIII. THAT ALL OTHER CREATURES HAVE THEIR ABIDING IN HEAVEN, HELL, EARTH, AIR, WATER, OR FIRE; BUT HE IN ALL OF THEM

In heav'n the blessed angels have their being;
In hell the fiends appointed to damnation.
To men and beasts earth yields firm habitation;
The wing'd musicians in the air are fleeing.
   With fins the people gliding
   Of water have th' enjoying.
   In fire (all else destroying)
The salamander finds a strange abiding.
But I, poor wretch, since I did first aspire
To love your beauty, beauties all excelling,   10
   Have my strange, diverse dwelling
In heaven, hell, earth, water, air, and fire.

Mine ear, while you do sing, in heav'n remaineth;
My mind in hell through hope and fear's contention.
Earth holds my drossy wit and dull invention.
Th' ill food of airy sighs my life sustaineth.
   To streams of tears still flowing
   My weeping eyes are turned.
   My constant heart is burned
In quenchless fire within my bosom glowing.   20
O fool, no more, no more so high aspire!

In heaven is no beauty more excelling,
   In hell no such pride dwelling,
Nor heart so hard in earth, air, water, fire.

               Francis Davison

TO SAMUEL DANIEL, PRINCE OF ENGLISH POETS

Upon His Three Several Sorts of Poesy:
Lyrical, in His Sonnets,
Tragical, in *Rosamond* and *Cleopatra*,
Heroical, in His *Civil Wars*

Olympias' matchless son, whenas he knew
   How many crowns his father's sword had gain'd,
With smoking sighs and deep-fetch'd sobs did rue
And his brave cheeks with scalding tears bedew
   Because that kingdoms now so few remain'd
   By his victorious arm to be obtain'd.

So, learned Daniel, whenas thou didst see
   That Spenser erst so far had spread his fame
That he was monarch deem'd of poesy,
Thou didst (I guess) ev'n burn with jealousy   10
   Lest laurel were not left enough to frame
   A nest sufficient for thine endless name.

But as that pearl of Greece soon after pass'd
   In wondrous conquests his renowned sire
And others all whose names by Fame are plac'd
In highest seat, so hath thy muse surpass'd
   Spenser and all that do with hot desire
   To the thunder-scorning laurel crown aspire.

And as his empire's linked force was known,
   When each of those that did his kingdoms share   20
The mighti'st kings in might did match alone,
So of thy skill the greatness thus is shown
   That each of those great poets deemed are
   Who may in no one kind with thee compare.

One shar'd out Greece, another Asia held,
   And fertile Egypt to a third did fall,
But only Alexander all did wield.
So in soft, pleasing lyrics some are skill'd,
   In tragic some, some in heroical,
   But thou alone art matchless in them all.   30

       Non equidem invideo, miror magis.
               Francis Davison

THREE EPITAPHS UPON THE DEATH OF A RARE CHILD OF SIX YEARS OLD

i

Wit's perfection, Beauty's wonder,
Nature's pride, the Graces' treasure,

Virtue's hope, his friends' sole pleasure,
This small marble stone lies under,
   Which is often moist with tears
   For such loss in such young years.

ii

Lovely boy, thou art not dead,
But from earth to heaven fled;
For base earth was far unfit
For thy beauty, grace, and wit.

iii

Thou alive on earth, sweet boy,
Hadst an angel's wit and face;
And now dead thou dost enjoy
In high heaven an angel's place.

Francis Davison

SONNET I. HE DEMANDS PARDON FOR LOOKING, LOVING, AND WRITING

Let not, sweet saint, let not these lines offend you,
   Nor yet the message that these lines impart—
   The message my unfeigned love doth send you,
   Love which yourself hath planted in my heart.
For, being charm'd by the bewitching art
   Of those inveigling graces which attend you,
   Love's holy fire makes me breathe out in part
   The never-dying flames my breast doth lend you.
Then if my lines offend, let Love be blamed;
   And if my love displease, accuse mine eyes;   10
   If mine eyes sin, their sin's cause only lies
   On your bright eyes which have my heart inflamed.
Since eyes, love, lines err then by your direction,
Excuse mine eyes, my lines, and my affection.

Walter Davison

SONNET VII. OF HIS LADY'S WEEPING

What need I say how it doth wound my breast
   By fate to be thus banish'd from thine eyes,
   Since your own tears with me do sympathize,
   Pleading with slow departure there to rest?
For when with floods of tears they were oppress'd,
   Over those ivory banks they did not rise
   Till others, envying their felicities,
   Did press them forth that they might there be bless'd.
Some of which tears, press'd forth by violence,
   Your lips with greedy kissing straight did drink;   10
   And other some, unwilling to part thence,
   Inamor'd on your cheeks in them did sink.
And some which from your face were forc'd away
In sign of love did on your garments stay.

Walter Davison

ODE IV. UPON VISITING HIS LADY BY MOONLIGHT

The night, say all, was made for rest,
And so say I, but not for all.
To them the darkest nights are best,
Which give them leave asleep to fall;
   But I, that seek my rest by light,
   Hate sleep and praise the clearest night.

Bright was the moon, as bright as day,
And Venus glist'red in the west,
Whose light did lead the ready way
That brought me to my wished rest.   10
   Then each of them encreas'd their light
   While I injoy'd her heavenly sight.

Say, gentle dames, what mov'd your mind
To shine so bright above your wont.
Would Phoebe fair Endymion find?
Would Venus see Adonis hunt?
   No, no, you feared by her sight
   To loose the praise of beauty bright.

At last for shame you shrunk away
And thought to reave the world of light;   20
Then shone my dame with brighter ray
Then that which comes from Phoebus' sight.
   None other light but hers I praise,
   Whose nights are clearer then the days.

Anomos

HOPELESS DESIRE SOON WITHERS AND DIES

Though naked trees seem dead to sight
When winter wind doth keenly blow,
Yet if the root maintain her right
The spring their hidden life will show.
   But if the root be dead and dry
   No marvel though the branches die.

While Hope did live within my breast
No winter storm could kill Desire;
But now Disdain hath Hope oppress'd,
Dead is the root, dead is the spire.   10
   Hope was the root, the spire was Love,
   No sap beneath, no life above.

And as we see the rootless stock
Retain some sap and spring a while,
Yet quickly prove a lifeless block
Because the root doth life beguile,
   So lives Desire which Hope hath left,
   As twilight shines when sun is reft.

Anomos

AN ALTAR AND SACRIFICE TO DISDAIN FOR FREEING HIM FROM LOVE

My muse, by thee restor'd to life,
To thee, Disdain, this altar rears,
Whereon she offers causeless strife,
Self-spending sighs, and bootless tears,
    Long suits in vain,
    Hate for good will,
    Still-dying pain,
    Yet living still,
    Self-loving Pride,
    Looks coyly strange,   10
    Will, Reason's guide,
    Desire of change,
    And last of all
    Blind Fancy's fire,
    False Beauty's thrall
    That binds Desire;—
All these I offer to Disdain,
By whom I live from Fancy free,
With vow that if I love again
My life the sacrifice shall be.   20
Vicinus et domitum pedibus calcamus amorem.

                        Anomos

SAPPHICS UPON THE PASSION OF CHRIST

Hatred eternal, furious revenging,
Merciless raging, bloody persecuting,
Slanderous speeches, odious revilings,
    Causeless abhorring;
Impious scoffings by the very abjects,
Dangerous threat'ning by the priests anointed,
Death full of torment in a shameful order
    Christ did abide here.
He that in glory was above the angels
Changed his glory for an earthly carcass,   10
Yielded his glory to a sinful outcast,
    Glory refusing.
Me that in bondage many sins retained
He for his goodness, for his only goodness,
Brought from hell-torments to the joys of heaven
    Not to be numb'red.
Dead in offenses, by his aid revived,
Quick'ned in spirit by the grace he yieldeth,
Sound then his praises to the world's amazement,
    Thankfully singing.   20

                        Anomos

BROADSIDE BALLADS

Although their literary status may be dubious, the broadside ballads of Tudor and early Stuart England constitute a fascinating record of public passions, prejudices, and topics of interest. In the days when there were no newspapers, and when books were beyond the means and intellectual capacities of many people, the broadside ballad served the purposes of journalism, propaganda, and occasionally even poetry for a large, if uncultivated, public. Generically the broadside ballad was a song set to a popular tune, printed on a single sheet ornamented with crude woodcuts, and hawked by professional singers whose artistic and moral qualifications were (like Autolycus') liable to the most serious doubts. More sophisticated writers commonly ridiculed these singers, their wares, and the hack poets who ground out the doggerel verses; and indeed all three, judged by almost any standards of music, typography, and literature, were usually appalling. Yet such poets as Surrey ("The Lover Comforteth Himself"), Lord Vaux ("The Aged Lover Renounceth Love"), Gascoigne ("Gascoigne's Arraignment"), Marlowe ("The Passionate Shepherd to His Love"), and Raleigh ("The Nymph's Reply to the Shepherd") were represented on broadsides, and some of the most famous lyrics of the age were croaked by nameless ballad-singers. On the other hand, many poems originally printed as broadside ballads found their way into respectable miscellanies like Tottel's, *The Paradise of Dainty Devices,* and *A Gorgeous Gallery of Gallant Inventions;* and one notable collection—*A Handful of Pleasant Delights*—contains nothing but such pieces.

Almost anything could (and did) furnish a subject for the ballad-writers: the sack of Antwerp, the report of a prodigious fish, the death of Bishop Jewel, the hot hatred of the pope and all his works, the assassination of Henri IV, the savage executions of heretics and criminals, a ditty of love, a change of dynasties, the age-old injunctions of piety and Protestant zeal. Some few of the ballad-writers—John Skelton, Thomas Churchyard, William Elderton, Thomas Deloney, Martin Parker— became notorious if not famous; and their work, beginning about the time that Henry VIII broke with Rome and temporarily ending with the Parliamentary ban on ballad-printing and ballad-singing in 1649, remains one of the most interesting literary bypaths of the Renaissance.

The following selections from this huge mass of material, supplemented by the pieces from *A Handful of Pleasant Delights* (see pp. 224–27), provide a fair sampling of the main types of broadside ballads. The epitaph of Bishop Jewel (no. 11 in Herbert L. Collmann's edition, for the Roxburghe Club, of *Ballads & Broadsides Chiefly of the Elizabethan Period*) may have been among the lost entries (1571–76) of the Stationers' Register; its author was probably the same Nicholas Bourman in whose name three other broadsides are licensed between 1570–71 and 1602; since it is without any indication of tune it may be regarded as a verse broadside rather than a ballad proper. Of the two pieces by the famous and long-lived Thomas Churchyard, "Davy Dicar's Dream" (Collmann, no. 19), perhaps written before the middle of the century, was printed by the Richard Lant who published more than thirty titles between 1542 and 1563, most of them broadsides (see H. R. Plomer, *Hand-Lists of English Printers 1501–56*). The elegy on Queen Elizabeth (Collmann, no. 32) survives as a unique broadside in the British Museum. Since Churchyard died in 1604, it must be one of the last products of his fifty-year career. William Elderton's edifying account of the "monsterous child" of Stony Stratford (Collmann, no. 40) was entered in the Stationers' Register in 1564–65. The savage exultation about John Felton's martyrdom (Collmann, no. 70) refers to that unfortunate man's nailing the papal bull of Elizabeth's excommunication to the gates of the Bishop of London's palace on May 15, 1570. Its author may have been the Stephen Peele mentioned as a bookseller in the records of the Stationers' Company between 1570 and

1593; and its tune, "Row Well, Ye Mariners," taken from a very popular song to which several other extant ballads were set, is preserved in William Chappell's *Popular Music of the Olden Time*, I, 112–13. Our last selection, "Francis' New Jig," is important as the only surviving printed Elizabethan dramatic jig, that is, a miniature farce set in ballad-measure and sung to popular tunes, which was performed in song and dance as a kind of skit at the end of a play. Licensed in the Stationers' Register on October 14, 1595, and now preserved in the great collection of broadsides which Samuel Pepys bequeathed to Magdalene College, Cambridge, its attribution to George Attowell (or Atwell), an Elizabethan actor, probably means no more than that he danced one of the roles. Of the four tunes it employs, "As I Went to Walsingham" and "Go from My Window" are preserved in Chappell, I, 121, 140–41; "Bugle Bow" and "The Jewish Dance" have not survived. Our texts are based upon the original ballads: for the epitaph on Jewel, the elegy on Elizabeth, the ballad of the monstrous birth, the ballad on John Felton, and the jig the appropriate STC numbers are 3414, 5256, 7565, 19549, and 903 respectively; "Davy Dicar's Dream," which is preserved in the Society of Antiquaries, London, is listed by Robert Lemon, *Catalogue of a Collection of Printed Broadsides* (London, 1866), p. 7.

AN EPITAPH UPON THE DEATH OF THE RIGHT REVERENT FATHER IN GOD J. JEWEL, DOCTOR OF DIVINITY AND BISHOP OF SARISBURY, WHO DECEASED THE TWENTY-SECOND OF SEPTEMBER, 1571

If publique weal or country's claim might languish and bewail
    The late decease of such devines as chiefly did prevail
And clean extirp such shadowed works as Antichristians' ire
    Or Arius' flock, most Tityrus-like, began for to conspire
To overwhelm the verity; then may we Christians say
    We do sustain a double loss of Jewel at this day;
Whose name doth not import so much the value or the price
    As is his miss accompted of by fathers sage and wise.
No pearl or precious substance may so much bewailed be
    As country soil hath cause to moan, dear Jewel, now for thee.   10
Who hath detected prudently, and publish'd very plain,
    Such errors as unworthy are in Christians to remain.
As warrior-like thou, Jewel, hast laid batt'ry to thy foes,
    As Harding, with like popish sects, that papists captain chose
For to defend their heresies; by thee his fond delusion,
    Apparantly as proved is, was brought unto confusion.
Thy zealous mind, thy sacred spright, by west, by north, by south
    Hath driven off raging papists' sect, a snaffle in the mouth.
Whereon so long time they have fed that Christes Ghospel clear
    Unto the lay and common sort most brightly doth appear.   20

So that deservedly of right, by golden trump of fame,
  Thou dost deserve the title of a Jewel unto name.
For why by thee most worthily thy virtues stood in stead;
  By thee, likewise, the flock of Christ most preciously were fed;
By thee the path of heavenly health, by thee true faith, was shown;
  By thee the fruits of charity in deeds and words were known;
By thee the inward man was clad and nourish'd very well.
  In any soil scarce is there found such jewels for to dwell.
Thy deeds agreed with steadfast words, fast founded on the rock,
  To Christian state a father dear and patron to the flock,   30
Which bears the title of the church, or sheepfold of the Lord,
  Approved by testimonial acts as Scriptures do record.
If thus much then th' accompt was made, what creature can denay
  But England she too soon hath lost a Jewel at this day,
Whom neither benefit of wealth could cause to wander fro
  The compass of the heavenly card, his duty to bestow
Among his brethren dear in Christ; then as we have begun
  Let us suppose that we have lost this Jewel all too soon.
Desiring God that as he is, no doubt, with Him on high,
  We may become true jewels all until the time we die.   40
So shall the heavenly verity most brightly florish still,
  And spread her branches fair abroad all over Sion Hill;
Whereby the popish train may fall that erst hath been so high,
  And clean diminish'd from the earth as withered plants that die.
Grant this, O God, for evermore, and pierce thy pastors' hearts
  That valiantly, as Jewel did, they play true pastors' parts;
And leave behind such worthy works to glorify God's name
  As he hath done, and so confound the popish sect with shame,
That by such mean no papist may the perfect Scripture wrest
  As Harding hath done heretofore, whom Jewel hath suppress'd.   50
And thus farewell, dear Jewel, now, sith God's good pleasure is
  To have thee hence from us among to his eternal bliss.
With tears I end this simple verse, proceeding of good will,
  Let learned sort take pen in hand and frame their filed quill
To spread this Jewel's fame abroad, though corps be clad in clay.
  His worthy works and virtues rare Dame Fame shall sure display.
                        N[icholas] Bour[man]

Imprinted at London in the upper end of Fleetlane by
Richard Jones, and are to be sold at his shop joining
to the southwest door of Sainct Paul's Church. 1571.
October 2.

DAVY DICAR'S DREAM

When faith in friends bear fruit and foolish fancies fade,
  And crafty catchers come to nought and hate great love hath made,
When fraud flieth far from town and lewterers leave the field,
  And rude shall run a rightful race and all men be well [will'd],
When gropers after gain shall carp for common wealth,
  And wily workers shall disdain to fig and live by stealth,
When wisdom walks aloft and folly sits full low,
  And virtue vanquish pamp'red vice and grace begins to grow,
When justice joins to truth and law looks not to meed,
  And bribes help not to build fair bow'rs, nor gifts great gluttons feed,   10

When hunger hides his head and plenty please the poor,
 And niggards to the needy men shall never shut their door,
When double dark deceit is out of credit worn,
 And fawning speech is falshed found and craft is laugh'd to scorn,
When pride which picks the purse gapes not for garments gay,
 No javels wear no velvet weeds nor wand'ring wits bear sway,
When riches wrongs no right, nor power poor put back,
 Nor covetous creeps not into court, nor learned livings lack,
When slipper sleights are seen and far-fatchers be found,
 And private profit and self-love shall both be put in pound, 20
When debt no sergeant dreads and courtiers credit keep,
 And might mells not with merchandise, nor lords shall sell no sheep,
When lucre lasts not long and hurd great heaps doth hate,
 And every wight is well content to walk in his estate,
When truth doth tread the streets and liars lurk in den,
 And rex doth reign and rule the roast and weeds out wicked men,
Then baleful barns be blithe that here in England won,
 Your strife shall stint, I undertake, your dreadful days are done!
   Finis   Quod T[homas] Churchyard

    Imprinted at London in Aldersgate Street
       by Richard Lant

SORROWFUL VERSES MADE ON [THE] DEATH
OF OUR MOST SOVEREIGN LADY QUEEN
ELIZABETH MY GRACIOUS MISTRESS

England may mourn, as many kingdoms may,
 A loss of late that gold nor pearl redeems,
A gale of wind that made kings hoise up sails
 When blust'ring blasts brought barks in great extremes.
Her realm she rul'd and bridled as God would
 With reason's rein, that holds back Bayard's bit,
To purchase peace paid massy sums of gold,
 Did what she might to win a world with wit.
Wisdom rules stars, climbs up to heaven's gate,
 Makes peace and wars, and stays a tottering state. 10
Her insight saw all outward flaws of wind,
 Her judgment crept into our cunning age;
No practise could surpass her princely mind;
 Her calmy words could swelling sea assuage;
Religion burn'd like lamp in her bare breast,
 And for her faith she still set up her rest.
She gave great things to thousands, world well knows,
 As at well-head and fountain water flows.
Caesar's sharp spirit her speeches utt'red oft;
 Cyrus' great power and wealth she wanted not. 20
She pluck'd down pride to set meek hearts aloft;
 Her matchless deeds great fame and glory got,
Opened her bags to such as suffered wrong,
 Much money lent but felt the loss too long,
Escap'd bad men that sought to shed her blood,
 Forgave great faults to win world's love and zeal.
But when most safe in health we thought she stood,

Her ghost pass'd hence from crown and commonweal
To God's high throne like torch and candle blaze,
Lost earthly light and left us in a maze. 30

    Finis
    T[homas] Churchyard, Esquire

This Phoenix dead, from her warm cinders straight
In form of man another Phoenix rose,
Who clapp'd his wings and flew up such a height
So near the sun that he God's glory shows.

THE TRUE FORM
AND SHAPE OF A MONSTEROUS CHILD
WHICH WAS BORN IN STONY STRATFORD
IN NORTHAMPTONSHIRE THE YEAR OF
OUR LORD MCCCCCLXV

This child was born on Friday, being the twenty-sixth
day of January, betwixt six and seven of the clock in the
morning, and lived two hours, and was christened by
the midwife, and are both women children, having two
bodies joining together. With four arms and four legs
perfect, and from the navel upwards one face, two eyes,
one nose, and one mouth, and three ears, one being upon
the backside of the head a little above the nape of the neck,
having hear growing upon the head. Which child was
born out of wedlock. The father's name is Richard
Sotherne, who is now fled; and the mother is yet living
in the same town. And this child was brought up to London where it was seen of divers worshipful men and

women of the city, and also of the country. To witness
that it is a truth and no fable, but a warning of God to
move all people to amendment of life:

You that do see this child disfigured here,
　　Two babes in one, disguised to behold,
Think with yourselves, when such things do appear,
　　All is not well, as wise heads may be bold.
But God that can in secrets shew the sign
Can bring much more to pass by pow'r devine.

And we that live to see this wonder, how
　　The gaze is geven to make this mervail great,
Let one by one that this beholdeth now
　　Be warned, as the wonder gives conceit,　　10
To live to mend the wonderous shape we see,
Contrary much in all that ought to be.

For as we find this figure seemeth strange
　　Because it shows proportion not in ure,
So bear in mind how time can chop and change,
　　Disguising works in wills that be unsure.
From mean to more, from more to much excess,
Where Nature wills desire should be less.
　　　　　　　　Finis　　　　W[illiam] Elderton

Imprinted at London in Fleet Street beneath the
Conduit at the sign of St. John Evangelist by
Thomas Colwell

A LETTER TO ROME, TO DECLARE TO THE POPE
JOHN FELTON, HIS FRIEND, IS HANG'D IN A ROPE,
AND FARTHER, ARIGHT HIS GRACE TO ENFORM,
HE DIED A PAPIST AND SEEM'D NOT TO TURN

To the Tune of "Row Well, Ye Mariners"

Who keeps Saint Angel gates?
Where lieth our holy father, say?
　　I muse that no man waits,
Nor comes to meet me on the way.
　　Sir Pope, I say? If you be near
Bow down to me your list'ning ear;
　　Come forth, bestir you then apace,
For I have news to show your Grace.
　　Stay not, come on,
That I from hence were shortly gone.　　10
　　Hark well, hear me,
What tidings I have brought to thee.

The bull so lately sent
To England by your holy Grace,
　　John Felton may repent
For setting up the same in place.
　　For he upon a goodly zeal
He bare unto your commonweal

Hath ventured life to pleasure you,
And now is hang'd, I tell you true.　　20
　　Wherefore, Sir Pope,
In England have you lost your hope.
　　Curse on, spare not,
Your knights are like to go to pot.

But further to declare,
He died your obedient child
　　And never seem'd to spare
For to exalt your doctrine wild,
　　And told the people every one
He died your obedient son,　　30
　　And as he might he did set forth
Your dignity that's nothing worth.
　　Your trash, your toys
He took to be his only joys;
　　Therefore hath won
Of you the crown of martyrdom.

Let him be shrined then
According to his merits due,
　　As you have others done
That prove unto their prince untrue;　　40
　　For these, Sir Pope, you love of life
That with their princes fall at strife,
　　Defending of your supreme pow'r,
Yet some have paid full dear therefore,
　　As now lately
Your friend John Felton seem'd to try.
　　Therefore I pray
That you a mass for him will say.

Ring all the bells in Rome
To do his sinful soul some good,　　50
　　Let that be done right soon
Because that he hath shed his blood.
　　His quarters stand not all together,
But ye may hap to ring them thether
　　In place where you would have them be,
Then might you do as pleaseth ye.
　　For why they hang
Unshrined each one upon a stang;
　　Thus stands the case:
On London gates they have a place.　　60

His head upon a pole
Stands wavering in the wherling wind,
　　But where should be his soul
To you belongeth for to find.
　　I wish you purgatory look
And search each corner with your hook
　　Lest it might chance, or you be ware,
The devils to catch him in a snare.
　　If ye him see,

From purgatory set him free.   70
  Let not, trudge than,
Fetch Felton out and if ye can.

I wish you now, Sir Pope,
To look unto your faithful friends
  That in your bulls have hope
To have your pardon for their sins.
  For here, I tell you, every lad
Doth scoff and scorn your bulls too bad,
  And think they shall the better fare
For hating of your cursed ware.   80
  Now do I end.
I came to show you as a friend
  Whether bless or curse
You send to me, I am not the worse.
Finis   Steven Peele

Imprinted by Alexander Lacy for Henry Kirkham,
dwelling at the sign of the Black Boy at the middle north
door of Paul's Church

FRANCIS' NEW JIG BETWEEN FRANCIS, A GENTLEMAN, AND RICHARD, A FARMER

To the Tune of "Walsingham"

1

Bess. As I went to Walsingham
  to the shrine with speed,
Met I with a jolly palmer
  in a pilgrim's weed. [*Enter* Francis]
Now God you save, you jolly palmer!
  Francis. Welcome, lady gay,
Oft have I sued to thee for love.
  Bess. Oft have I said you nay.

Francis. My love is fixed. Bess. And so is mine,
  but not on you,   10
For to my husband whilst I live
  I will ever be true.
Francis. I'll give thee gold and rich array.
  Bess. Which I shall buy too dear.
Francis. Nought shalt thou want, then say not nay.
  Bess. Naught would you make me, I fear.

3

What though you be a gentleman,
  and have lands great store?
I will be chaste, do what you can,
  though I live ne'er so poor.   20
Francis. Thy beauty rare hath wounded me,
  and pierc'd my heart.
Bess. Your foolish love doth trouble me.
  Pray you, sir, depart.

4

Francis. Then tell me, sweet, wilt thou consent
  unto my desire?
Bess. And if I should, then tell me, sir,
  what is it you require?
Francis. For to injoy thee as my love.
  Bess. Sir, you have a wife;   30
Therefore let your suit have an end.
  Francis. First will I lose my life.

5

All that I have thou shalt command.
  Bess. Then my love you have.
Francis. Your meaning I well understand.
  Bess. I yield to what you crave.
Francis. But tell me, sweet, when shall I enjoy
  my heart's delight?
Bess. I prethee, sweet heart, be not coy,
  even soon at night.   40

6

My husband is rid ten miles from home,
  money to receive;
In the evening see you come.
  Francis. Till then I take my leave. [*Exit*]
Bess. Thus have I rid my hands full well
  of my amorous love,
And my sweet husband will I tell,
  how he doth me move.

Enter Richard, *Bess's husband*
To the Tune of "The Jewish Dance"

7

Richard. Hey doun a doun,
  hey doun, a doun, a doun,   50
There is never a lusty farmer
  in all our town
That hath more cause
  to lead a merry life
Then I that am married
  to an honest, faithful wife.
Bess. I thank you, gentle husband;
  you praise me to my face.
Richard. I cry thee mercy, Bessie,
  I knew thee not in place.   60

8

Bess. Believe me, gentle husband,
  if you knew as much as I,
The words that you have spoken
  you quickly would deny.
For since you went from home
  a suitor I have had
Who is so far in love with me

that he is almost mad.
He'll give me gold and silver store,
   and money for to spend,   70
And I have promis'd him, therefore,
   to be his loving friend.

9

RICHARD. Believe me, gentle wife,
   but this makes me to frown;
There is no gentleman nor knight,
   nor lord of high renown,
That shall enjoy thy love, girl,
   though he were ne'er so good.
Before he wrong my Bessie so
   I'll spend on him my blood.   80
And therefore tell me who it is
   that doth desire thy love.
BESS. Our neighbor, Master Francis,
   that often did me move.

10

To who I gave consent,
   his mind for to fulfil,
And promis'd him this night
   that he should have his will.
Nay, do not frown, good Dickie,
   but hear me speak my mind,   90
For thou shalt see, I'll warrant thee,
   I'll use him in his kind.
For unto thee I will be true
   so long as I do live;
I'll never change thee for a new,
   nor once my mind so give.

11

Go you to Mistriss Francis
   and this to her declare,
And will her with all speed
   To my house to repair,   100
Where she and I'll devise
   some pretty knavish wile,
For I have laid the plot,
   her husband to beguile.
Make haste, I pray, and tarry not,
   for long he will not stay.
RICHARD. Fear not, I'll tell her such a tale
   shall make her come away. [Exit]

12

BESS. Now, Bess, bethink thee
   what thou hast to do.   110
Thy lover will come presently,
   and hardly will he woo.
I will teach my gentleman
   a trick that he may know

I am too crafty and too wise
   to be o'erreached so.
But here he comes now—not a word,
   but fall to work again. [She sews. Enter FRANCIS]
FRANCIS. How now, sweetheart, at work so hard?
   BESS. Ay, sir, I must take pains.   120

13

FRANCIS. But say, my lovely sweeting,
   thy promise wilt thou keep?
Shall I enjoy thy love
   this night with me to sleep?
BESS. My husband rid from home;
   here safely may you stay.
FRANCIS. And I have made my wife believe
   I rid another way.
BESS. Go in, good sir, whate'er betide,
   this night and lodge with me.   130
FRANCIS. The happiest night that ever I had,
   thy friend still will I be. [Exit FRANCIS. BESS retires]

THE SECOND PART OF ATTOWELL'S NEW JIG

To the Tune of "Bugle Bow"
Enter MISTRESS FRANCIS *with* RICHARD

14

WIFE. I thank you, neighbor Richard,
   for bringing me this news.
RICHARD. Nay, thank my wife that loves me so,
   and will not you abuse.
WIFE. But see whereas she stands
   and waiteth our return.
RICHARD. You must go cool your husband's heat
   that so in love doth burn.   140
BESS. Now, Dickie, welcome home,
   and, mistress, welcome hither;
Grieve not although you find
   your husband and I together.
For you shall have your right,
   nor will I wrong you so;
Then change apparel with me straight
   and unto him do go.
WIFE. For this your kind good will
   a thousand thanks I give,   150
And make account I will requite
   this kindness if I live.

15

BESS. I hope it shall not need,
   Dick will not serve me so;
I know he loves me not so ill
   a-ranging for to go.
RICHARD. No, faith, my lovely Bess,
   first will I lose my life

Before I'll break my wedlock bonds
    or seek to wrong my wife. [*Exit* WIFE]   160
Now thinks good Master Francis
    he hath thee in his bed,
And makes account he is grafting
    of horns upon my head.
But softly stand aside,
    now shall we know his mind,
And how he would have used thee
    if thou hadst been so kind.

Enter MASTER FRANCIS *with his own wife*
having a mask before her face, supposing
her to be Bess
To the Tune of "Go from My Window"

16

FRANCIS. Farewell, my joy and heart's delight,
    till next we meet again.   170
Thy kindness to requite for lodging me all night,
    here's ten pound for thy pain;
And more to shew my love to thee,
    wear this ring for my sake.
WIFE. Without your gold or fee you shall have more of
    me.
    FRANCIS. No doubt of that I make.
WIFE. Then let your love continue still.
    FRANCIS. It shall till life doth end.
WIFE. Your wife I greatly fear. FRANCIS. For her thou
    need'st not care,
    so I remain thy friend.   180
WIFE. But you'll suspect me without cause
    that I am false to you,
And then you'll cast me off and make me but a scoff,
    since that I prove untrue.

17

FRANCIS. Then never trust man for my sake
    if I prove so unkind.
WIFE. So often have you sworn, sir, since that you were
    born,
    and soon have chang'd your mind.
FRANCIS. Nor wife nor life, nor goods nor lands,
    shall make me leave my love,   190
Nor any worldly treasure make me forgo my pleasure,
    nor once my mind remove.

18

WIFE. But soft a while, who is yonder? Do you see
    my husband? Out, alas.
FRANCIS. And yonder is my wife. Now shall we have a life!
    How cometh this to pass?
RICHARD. Come hither, gentle Bess. I charge thee do
    confess
    what makes Master Francis here.

WIFE. Good husband, pardon me. I'll tell the troth to thee.
    RICHARD. Then speak and do not fear.   200

19

FRANCIS. Nay, neighbor Richard, hark to me.
    I'll tell the troth to you.
BESS. Nay, tell it unto me, good sir, that I may see
    what you have here to do.
But you can make no scuse to color this abuse,
    this wrong is too too great.
RICHARD. Good sir, I take great scorn you should proffer
    me the horn.
    WIFE. Now must I cool this heat. [WIFE *unmasks*]

20

Nay, neighbor Richard, be content,
    thou hast no wrong at all;   210
Thy wife hath done thee right, and pleasur'd me this night.
    FRANCIS. This frets me to the gall.
Good wife, forgive me this offense;
    I do repent mine ill.
WIFE. I thank you with mine heart for playing this kind
    part,
    though sore against your will.

21

Nay, gentle husband, frown not so,
    for you have made amends;
I think it is good gain to have ten pound for my pain,
    then let us both be friends.   220
FRANCIS. Ashamed I am and know not what to say;
    good wife, forgive this crime.
Alas, I do repent. WIFE. Tut, I could be content
    to be served so many a time.

22

FRANCIS. Good neighbor Richard, be content;
    I'll woo thy wife no more.
I have enough of this. WIFE. Then all forgiven is.
    I thank thee, Dick, therefore,
And to thy wife I'll give this gold;
    I hope you'll not say no,   230
Since I have had the pleasure, let her enjoy the treasure.
    FRANCIS. Good wife, let it be so.

23

BESS. I thank you, gentle mistress. RICHARD. Faith, and
    so do I.
Sir, learn your own wife to know,
And shoot not in the dark for fear you miss the mark.
    BESS. He hath paid for this, I trow.
All women learn of me. FRANCIS. All men by me take heed
    how you a woman trust.
WIFE. Nay, women, trust no men. FRANCIS. And if they
    do, how then?
    WIFE. There's few of them prove just.   240

24

Farewell, neighbor Richard. Farewell, honest Bess.
  I hope we are all friends.

And if you stay at home, and use not thus to roam,
  here all our quarrel ends.

Finis   George Attowell
At London Printed for I.W.

SONG BOOKS

Although from *The Court of Venus* (?1536) through Davison's *Poetical Rhapsody* (1602 ff.) there had been a rich succession of poetical miscellanies, the song books, with both lyrics and their musical settings, reached their highest development around the turn of the sixteenth century. As early as 1530 Wynkyn de Worde had published *XX Songs*, but Thomas Whythorne's *Songs of Three, Four, and Five Voices* (1571) was the only work of its kind thereafter for nearly sixty years. In 1588, however, Nicholas Yonge, one of the singing-men at St. Paul's Cathedral, put together, out of imported books from Italy, *Musica Transalpina,* thus starting a vogue for madrigals that lasted for a generation or more. The vogue was powerfully stimulated by the song books of William Byrd, a great composer in the larger choral forms, who helped to domesticate the madrigal among English amateurs. His three volumes of secular and religious songs (1588, 1589, 1611) were expressly fashioned for non-professional singing (an "exercise . . . delightful to nature, and good to preserve the health of man" because it "doth strengthen all parts of the breast, and doth open the pipes"). Byrd generally used metrical versions of the Psalms for his songs of piety, but he set his songs of mirth from Sidney, the seventeenth Earl of Oxford, and many other contemporaries, adorning (and sometimes concealing) the texts in a rich texture of polyphonic writing for three, four, five, or six voices. Such books were published in small quartos, each part containing the music for one voice.

An older English tradition—sporadically indicated in the poetical miscellanies and in the broadside ballads—was that of the simple "air" or monophonic setting, which was melodically and rhythmically easier than the madrigal. This was the form that John Dowland's four books of airs for lute accompaniment (1597, 1600, 1603, 1612) helped to popularize, and to which Thomas Campion brought his superb gifts as both a poet and a melodist.

Both the madrigal and the air enjoyed great popularity. Although the preface to Rosseter's *Book of Airs* (1601)

comments tartly on the madrigal as "long, intricate, bated with fugue, chain'd with syncopation," the Italian importation was obviously welcomed by a wide audience. From Thomas Watson's *First Set of Italian Madrigals Englished* (1590), Thomas Morley's *Madrigals to Four Voices* (1594) and *First Book of Ballets to Five Voices* (1595), Yonge's second volume of *Musica Transalpina* (1597), John Wilbye's *First Set of English Madrigals* (1598), and many others, we may infer a growing demand for these lovely polyphonic forms. One of the most attractive books of this group is Thomas Morley's *Triumphs of Oriana* (1601), a collection of madrigals in honor of Queen Elizabeth, to which John Milton's father contributed "Fair Oriana in the Morn."

Our texts are based upon William Byrd, *Psalmes, Sonets, & songs of sadnes and pietie, made into Musicke of fiue parts,* 1588 (STC 4253); William Byrd, *Songs of sundrie natures, some of gravitie, and others of myrth, fit for all companies and voyces,* 1589 (STC 4256); Nicholas Yonge, *Musica Transalpina. Madrigales translated of foure, five and sixe parts,* 1588 (STC 26094); John Dowland, *The First Booke of Songes or Ayres of fowre partes with Tableture for the Lute,* 1597 (STC 7091); John Dowland, *The Second Booke of Songs or Ayres, of 2. 4. and 5. parts,* 1600 (STC 7095); John Dowland, *The Third and Last Book of Songs or Aires,* 1603 (STC 7096); Thomas Morley, *Madrigales The Triumphes of Oriana, to 5. and 6. voices: composed by divers severall aucthors,* 1601 (STC 18130); [Thomas Campion], *A Book of Ayres, Set foorth to be song to the Lute, Orpherian, and Base Violl, by Philip Rosseter,* 1601 (STC 21332). (Mr. Percival Vivian, Campion's most authoritative editor, is inclined [*Campion's Works,* 1909, pp. lii–liii] to attribute both the lyrics and settings of Part I to Campion, perhaps some of the lyrics and all of the settings of Part II to Rosseter. Although the whole was published under Rosseter's name, he himself, in his dedication to Sir Thomas Monson, seems to suggest such an attribution.)

WILLIAM BYRD

FROM PSALMS, SONNETS, AND SONGS OF SADNESS AND PIETY (1588)

Reasons Briefly Set Down by th' Auctor to Persuade Everyone to Learn to Sing

1. First, it is a knowledge easely taught and quickly learned where there is a good master and an apt scoler.

2. The exercise of singing is delightful to nature, and good to preserve the health of man.

3. It doth strengthen all parts of the breast, and doth open the pipes.

4. It is a singuler good remedy for a stutting and 10 stammering in the speech.

5. It is the best means to procure a perfect pronunciation and to make a good orator.

6. It is the only way to know where nature hath bestowed the benefit of a good voice, which gift is so rare as there is not one among a thousand that hath it, and in many that excellent gift is lost because they want art to express nature.

7. There is not any music of instruments whatsoever comparable to that which is made of the voices 20 of men where the voices are good and the same well-sorted and ordered.

8. The better the voice is, the meeter it is to honor and serve God therewith, and the voice of man is chiefly to be imployed to that end.

Omnis spiritus laudet Dominum.

Since singing is so good a thing,
I wish all men would learn to sing.   30

The Epistle to the Reader

Benign reader, here is offered unto thy courteous acceptation music of sundry sorts and to content divers humors. If thou be disposed to pray, here are psalms; if to be merry, here are sonnets; if to lament for thy sins, here are songs of sadness and piety. If thou delight in music of great compass, here are divers songs which, being originally made for in- 40 struments to express the harmony and one voice to pronounce the ditty, are now framed in all parts for voices to sing the same. If thou desire songs of small compass and fit for the reach of most voices, here are most in number of that sort. Whatsoever pains I have taken herein I shall think to be well imployed if the same be well accepted, music thereby the better loved and the more exercised.

In the expressing of these songs, either by voices or instruments, if there happen to be any jar or dis- 50 sonance, blame not the printer, who, I do assure thee, through his great pains and diligence, doth here deliver to thee a perfect and true copy. If in the composition of these songs there be any fault by me committed, I desire the skilful either with courtesy to let the same be concealed or in friendly sort to be thereof admonished, and at the next impression he shall find the error reformed, rememb'ring always that it is more easy to find a fault then to amend it.

If thou find anything here worthy of liking and commendation, give praise unto God, from whom, as from a most pure and plentiful fountain, all good gifts of science do flow, whose name be glorified forever.

The most assured friend to all
that love or learn music,
William Byrd

Sonnets and Pastorals

[WHO LIKES TO LOVE, LET HIM TAKE HEED]

Who likes to love, let him take heed,
    And wot you why?
Among the gods it is decreed
    That Love shall die,
And every wight that takes his part
Shall forfait each a mourning heart.

The cause is this, as I have heard,
    A sort of dames
Whose beauty he did not regard
    Nor secret flames   10
Complain'd before the gods above
That gold corrupts the god of love.

The gods did storm to hear this news,
    And there they swore
That sith he did such dames abuse
    He should no more
Be god of love, but that he should
Both die and forfait all his gold.

His bow and shafts they took away
    Before their eyes,   20
And gave these dames a longer day
    For to devise
Who should them keep, and they be bound
That love for gold should not be found.

These ladies, striving long, at last
  They did agree
To give them to a maiden chaste
  Whom I did see,
Who with the same did pierce my breast.
Her beauty's rare, and so I rest.   30

[WHAT PLEASURE HAVE GREAT PRINCES]

What pleasure have great princes
More dainty to their choice
Then herdmen wild? Who careless
In quiet life rejoice,
And fortune's fate not fearing,
Sing sweet in summer morning.

Their dealings plain and rightful
Are void of all disceit;
They never know how spightful
It is to kneel and wait   10
On favorite presumptious,
Whose pride is vain and sumptious.

All day their flocks each tendeth;
At night they take their rest,
More quiet than who sendeth
His ship into the East,
Where gold and pearl are plenty,
But getting, very dainty.

For lawyers and their pleading
They 'steem it not a straw;   20
They think that honest meaning
Is of itself a law,
Whence conscience judgeth plainly
They spend no money vainly.

O happy who thus liveth,
Not caring much for gold,
With clothing which sufficeth
To keep him from the cold;
Though poor and plain his diet,
Yet merry it is, and quiet.   30

Songs of Sadness and Piety

[ALL AS A SEA, THE WORLD NO OTHER IS]

All as a sea, the world no other is;
Ourselves are ships still tossed to and fro,
And lo, each man, his love to that or this,
Is like a storm that drives the ship to go,
That thus our life in doubt of shipwrack stands,
Our wills the rocks, our want of skill the sands.

Our passions be the pirates still that spoil
And overboard casts out our reason's fraight;
The mariners, that day and night do toil,
Be our conceits that do on pleasure wait;   10
Pleasure, maister, doth tyrannize the ship
And giveth virtue secretly the nip.

The compass is a mind to compass all,
Both pleasure, profit, place, and fame for naught;
That winds that blow men overweening call,
The merchandise is wit full dearly bought;
Trial the anker cast upon experience,
For labor, life, and all ado the recompense.

[WHY DO I USE MY PAPER, INK, AND PEN]

Why do I use my paper, ink, and pen,
And call my wits to counsel what to say?
Such memories were made for mortal men;
I speak of saints whose names cannot decay.
An angel's trump were fitter for to sound
Their glorious death, if such on earth were found.

That store of such were once on earth pursu'd
The histories of ancient times record,
Whose constancy great tyrants' rage subdu'd
Through patient death, professing Christ their Lord,   10
As his apostles perfect witness bear
With many more that blessed martyrs were.

Whose patience rare and most couragious mind
With fame renoum'd perpetual shall endure,
By whose examples we may rightly find
Of holy life and death a pattern pure.
That we therefore their virtues may embrace
Pray we to Christ to guide us with his grace!

FROM SONGS OF SUNDRY NATURES (1589)

To the Curteous Reader

    Finding that my last impression of music, most gentle reader, through thy curtesy and favor hath had good passage and utterance, and that since the publishing thereof the exercise and love of that art to have exceedingly encreased, I have been encouraged thereby to take further pains therein and to make thee pertaker thereof because I would shew myself grateful to thee for thy love and desirous to delight thee with variety, whereof, in my opinion, no science

is more plentifully adorned then music. For which purpose I do now publish for thee songs of three, four, five, and six parts to serve for all companies and voices, whereof some are easy and plain to sing, other more hard and difficult, but all such as any young practicioner in singing with a little foresight may easely perform. If I find thy curtesy to extend as well to these my present travels as it hath done to my former endeavors, I will make myself endebted to thee during my life, of whatsoever is in me to   10
yield thy delight in music any satisfaction.

> The most affectionate friend
> to all that love or learn music,
> William Byrd

[IS LOVE A BOY]

THE FIRST PART

Is Love a boy? What means he then to strike?
Or is he blind? Why will he be a guide?
Is he a man? Why doth he hurt his like?
    Is he a god? Why doth he men deride?

No one of these, but one compact of all:
A wilful boy, a man still dealing blows,
Of purpose blind to lead men to their thrall,
    A god that rules unruly, God he knows.

THE SECOND PART

Boy, pity me that am a child again;
    Blind be no more my guide to make me stray;   10

Man, use thy might to force away my pain;
    God, do me good and lead me to my way.
And if thou be'st a pow'r to me unknown,
Pow'r of my life, let here thy grace be shown.

[O LORD MY GOD, LET FLESH AND BLOOD]

O Lord, my God, let flesh and blood
    Thy servant not subdue,
Nor let the world deceive me with
    His glory most untrue.

Let not, O Lord, O mighty God,
    Let not thy mortal foe,
Let not the fiend with all his craft,
    Thy servant overthrow.

But to resist give fortitude,
    Give patience to endure,   10
Give constancy that always Thine
    I may persever sure.

[WHEN FIRST BY FORCE OF FATAL DESTINY]

When first by force of fatal destiny
    From Carthage town the Trojan knight did sail,
Queen Dido fair with woful, weeping eye
    His strange depart did grievously bewail.
And when no sighs nor tears could ease her smart,
With sword full sharp she pierc'd her tender heart.

NICHOLAS YONGE

FROM MUSICA TRANSALPINA (1588)

To the Right Honorable Gilbert, Lord Talbot . . .
Nicholas Yonge Wisheth Increase of Honor
with All Happiness

Right honorable, since I first began to keep house in this city it hath been no small comfort unto me that a great number of gentlemen and merchants of good accompt, as well of this realm as of forrein nations, have taken in good part such entertainment of pleasure as my poor ability was able to afford   10
them, both by the exercise of music daily used in my house and by furnishing them with books of that kind yearly sent me out of Italy and other places. . . .

And albeit there be some English songs lately set forth by a great maister of music [i.e. William Byrd],

which for skill and sweetness may content the most curious, yet because they are not many in number, men (delighted with variety) have wished more of the same sort. For whose cause chiefly I endeavored to get into my hands all such English songs as were praiseworthy, and amongst others I had the hap to find in the hands of some of my good friends certain Italian madrigals, translated, most of them five years ago, by a gentleman for his private delight (as not long before certain Napolitans had been Englished by a very honorable personage, and now a councilor of estate, whereof I have seen some, but never possessed any). And finding the same to be singulerly well-liked not only of those for whose cause I gathered them but of many skilful gentlemen and other great musicians who affirmed the accent of the words to be well maintained, the descant not hind'red though some few notes alt'red, and in every place the due decorum kept, I was so bold (being well acquainted with the gentleman) as to entreat the rest, who willingly gave me such as he had (for of some he kept no copies) and also some other more lately done at the request of his particular friends.

Now when the same were seen to arise to a just number sufficient to furnish a great set of books, divers of my friends aforesaid required with great instance to have them printed, whereunto I was as willing as the rest, but could never obtain the gentleman's consent, though I sought it by many great means. For his answer was ever that those trifles (being but an idle man's exercise, of an idle subject, written only for private recreation) would blush to be seen otherwise then by twilight, much more to be brought into the common view of all men. . . . Wherefore I kept them, or the most of them, for a long time by me, not presuming to put my sickle in another man's corn, till such time as I heard that the same, being dispersed into many men's hands, were by some persons altogither unknown to the owner like to be published in print. Which made me adventure to set this work in hand (he being neither privy nor present, nor so near this place as by any reasonable means I could give him notice), wherein though he may take a just offense that I have laid open his labors without his license, yet since they were in hazard to come abroad by strangers, lame and unperfect by means of false copies, I hope that this which I have done to avoid a greater ill shall deserve a more favorable excuse. . . . From London, the first of October, 1588.

Your lordship's most humble at commandement,

N[icholas] Yonge

[AS IN THE NIGHT WE SEE THE SPARKS REVIVED]

As in the night we see the sparks revived,
    And quite extinct so soon as day appeareth,
So when I am of my sweet sun deprived,
    New fears approach, and joy my heart forbeareth.
But not so soon she is again arrived
    As fear retireth and present hope me cheereth.

O sacred light, O turn again to bless me,
And drive away this fear that doth oppress me.

[SUSANNA FAIR, SOMETIME OF LOVE REQUESTED]

Susanna fair, sometime of love requested
    By two old men whom her sweet looks allur'd,
Was in her heart full sad and sore molested,
    Seeing the force her chastity endur'd.
To them she said, "If I, by craft procur'd,
    Do yield to you my body to abuse it,
I kill my soul, and if I do refuse it
    You will me judge to death reproachfully.
But better it is in innocence to chuse it
Then by my fault t' offend my God on high."

[LADY, IF YOU SO SPIGHT ME]

Lady, if you so spight me,
Wherefore do you so oft kiss and delight me?
Sure, that my heart, oppress'd and overjoyed,
May break and be destroyed!
If you seek so to spill me,
Come kiss me, sweet, and kill me.
So shall your heart be eased,
And I shall rest content and die well pleased.

[THE FAIR YOUNG VIRGIN IS LIKE THE ROSE UNTAINTED]

The fair young virgin is like the rose untainted
    In garden fair, while tender stalk doth bear it,
Sole and untouch'd, with no resort acquainted;
    No shepherd nor his flock doth once come near it;
Th' air full of sweetness, the morning fresh depainted,
    The earth, the water with all their favors cheer it;
Dainty young gallants and ladies most desired
    Delight to have therewith their heads and breasts attired.

THE SECOND PART

But not so soon: from green stock where it growed
    The same is pluck'd and from the branch removed,
As lost is all from heaven and earth that flowed,
    Both favor, grace, and beauty best beloved.
The virgin fair that hath the flower bestowed
    (Which more then life to guard it her behoved)
Loseth her praise and is no more desired
    Of those that late unto her love aspired.

JOHN DOWLAND

FROM THE FIRST BOOK OF SONGS OR AIRS (1597)

To the Courteous Reader

. . . About sixteen years past I traveled the chiefest parts of France, a nation furnish'd with great variety of music; but lately, being of a more confirmed judgment, I bent my course towards the famous provinces of Germany, where I found both excellent masters and most honorable patrons of music, namely, those two miracles of this age for virtue and magnificence, Henry Julio, Duke of Brunswick, and learned Maritius, Lantzgrave of Hessen, of whose 10 princely virtues and favors towards me I can never speak sufficiently. . . .

Thus having spent some moneths in Germany to my great admiration of that worthy country, I pass'd over the Alps into Italy, where I found the cities furnish'd with all good arts, but especially music. What favor and estimation I had in Venice, Padua, Genoa, Ferrara, Florence, and divers other places I willingly suppress lest I should any way seem partial in mine own indeavors. . . 20

There have been divers lute lessons of mine lately printed without my knowledge, false and unperfect, but I purpose shortly myself to set forth the choicest of all my lessons in print and also an introduction for fingering, with other *Books of Songs* whereof this is the first. And as this finds favor with you, so shall I be affected to labor in the rest. Farewell.

John Dowland

[CAN SHE EXCUSE MY WRONGS WITH VIRTUE'S CLOAK]

Can she excuse my wrongs with virtue's cloak?
Shall I call her good when she proves unkind?
Are those clear fires which vanish into smoke?
Must I praise the leaves where no fruit I find?

No, no! Where shadows do for bodies stand
Thou may'st be abus'd if thy sight be dim.
Cold love is like to words written on sand
Or to bubbles which on the water swim.

Wilt thou be thus abused still,
Seeing that she will right thee never?   10
If thou canst not o'ercome her will
Thy love will be thus fruitless ever.

Was I so base that I might not aspire
Unto those high joys which she holds from me?
As they are high, so high is my desire;
If she this deny, what can granted be?

If she will yield to that which reason is,
It is Reason's will that Love should be just.
Dear, make me happy still by granting this
Or cut off delays if that die I must.   20

Better a thousand times to die
Then for to live thus still tormented.
Dear, but remember it was I
Who for thy sake did die contented.

[GO, CRYSTAL TEARS]

Go, crystal tears, like to the morning showers,
And sweetly weep into thy lady's breast,
And as the dews revive the drooping flowers,
So let your drops of pity be address'd
    To quicken up the thoughts of my desert,
    Which sleeps too sound, whilst I from her depart.

Haste, hapless sighs, and let your burning breath
Dissolve the ice of her indurate heart,
Whose frozen rigor, like forgetful death,
Feels never any touch of my desart.   10
    Yet sighs and tears to her I sacrifice,
    Both from a spotless heart and patient eyes.

[COME AWAY, COME, SWEET LOVE]

Come away, come, sweet love,
    The golden morning breaks.
All the earth, all the air
    Of love and pleasure speaks.
Teach thine arms then to embrace
    And sweet rosy lips to kiss,
And mix our souls in mutual bliss.
    Eyes were made for beauty's grace,
Viewing, ruing love's long pains,
    Procur'd by beauty's rude disdain.   10

Come away, come, sweet love,
    The golden morning wastes,
While the sun from his sphere
    His fiery arrows casts,
Making all the shadows fly,
    Playing, staying in the grove
To entertain the stealth of love.
    Thither, sweet love, let us hie,
Flying, dying in desire,
    Wing'd with sweet hopes and heav'nly fire.   20

Come away, come, sweet love,
  Do not in vain adorn
Beauty's grace that should rise
  Like to the naked morn.
Lilies on the river's side
  And fair Cyprian flowers new blown
Desire no beauties but their own;
  Ornament is nurse of Pride,
Pleasure measure, Love's delight.
  Haste then, sweet love, our wished flight!   30

[HIS GOLDEN LOCKS TIME HATH TO SILVER TURN'D]
[From George Peele's *Polyhymnia*, 1590]

His golden locks Time hath to silver turn'd,
O Time too swift, O swiftness never ceasing!
His youth gainst Time and Age hath ever spurn'd,
But spurn'd in vain: youth waneth by encreasing.
  Beauty, strength, youth are flowers but fading seen:
  Duty, faith, love are roots, and ever green.

His helmet now shall make a hive for bees,
And lover's sonnets turn to holy psalms.
A man-at-arms must now serve on his knees
And feed on prayers, which are Age's alms.   10
  But though from court to cottage he depart,
  His saint is sure of his unspotted heart.

And when he saddest sits in homely cell,
He'll teach his swains this carol for a song:
"Blest be the hearts that wish my sovereign well!
Curst be the soul that thinks her any wrong!"
  Goddess, allow this aged man his right
  To be your beadsman now that was your knight.

[COME, HEAVY SLEEP]

Come, heavy Sleep, the image of true death,
  And close up these my weary, weeping eyes
Whose spring of tears doth stop my vital breath
  And tears my heart with sorrow's sigh-swoll'n cries.
  Come and possess my tired thoughts, worn soul
  That living dies till thou on me bestoul.

Come, shadow of my end and shape of rest,
  Allied to death, child to this black-fac'd night,
Come thou and charm these rebels in my breast,
  Whose waking fancies doth my mind affright.   10
  O come, sweet Sleep, come or I die forever!
  Come ere my last sleep comes, or come never!

FROM THE SECOND BOOK OF SONGS OR AIRS (1600)

[PRAISE BLINDNESS, EYES]

Praise blindness, eyes, for seeing is deceit;
Be dumb, vain tongue, words are but flattering winds:
Break, heart, and bleed, for there is no receit
To purge inconstancy from most men's minds.
  And so I wak'd amaz'd and could not move;
  I know my dream was true, and yet I love.

And if thine ears, false haralds to thy heart,
Convey into thy head hopes to obtain,
Then tell thy hearing thou art deaf by art;
Now love is art, that wonted to be plain.   10
  And so I wak'd amaz'd and could not move;
  I know my dream was true, and yet I love.

Now none is bald except they see his brains,
Affection is not known till one be dead,
Reward for love are labors for his pains,
Love's quiver's made of gold, his shafts of lead.
  And so I wak'd amaz'd and could not move;
  I know my dream was true, and yet I love.

[NOW CEASE, MY WAND'RING EYES]

Now cease, my wand'ring eyes,
  Strange beauties to admire:
In change least comfort lies,
  Long joys yield long desire.
  One faith, one love
Makes our frail pleasures eternal, and in sweetness prove.
  New hopes, new joys
Are still with sorrow declining unto deep annoys.

One man hath but one soul
  Which art cannot devide;   10
If all one soul must love,
  Two loves must be deni'd.
  One soul, one love,
By faith and merit united cannot remove.
  Distracted spirits
Are ever changing and hapless in their delights.

Nature two eyes hath given
  All beauty to impart
As well in earth as heaven,
  But she hath given one heart,   20
  That though we see
Ten thousand beauties, yet in us one should be:
  One steadfast love
Because our hearts stand fix'd although our eyes
  do move.

FROM THE THIRD AND LAST BOOK OF SONGS OR AIRS (1603)

[ME, ME, AND NONE BUT ME]

Me, me, and none but me dart home, O gentle Death!
  And quickly, for I draw too long this idle breath.
O how I long till I may fly to heaven above,
  Unto my faithful and beloved turtle dove!

Like to the silver swan, before my death I sing,
  And, yet alive, my fatal knell I help to ring,
Still I desire from earth and earthly joys to fly:
  He never happy liv'd that cannot love to die.

[FLOW NOT SO FAST, YE FOUNTAINS]

Flow not so fast, ye fountains.
  What needeth all this haste?
Swell not above your mountains,
  Nor spend your time in waste.
Gentle springs, freshly your salt tears
Must still fall, dropping from their spheres.

Weep they apace, whom Reason
  Or ling'ring Time can ease;
My sorrow can no season
  Nor ought besides appease,   10
Gentle springs, freshly your salt tears
Must still fall, dropping from their spheres.

Time can abate the terror
  Of every common pain,
But common grief is error,
  True grief will still remain.
Gentle springs, freshly your salt tears
Must still fall, dropping from their spheres.

[WEEP YOU NO MORE, SAD FOUNTAINS]

Weep you no more, sad fountains.
  What need you flow so fast?
Look how the snowy mountains
  Heaven's sun doth gently waste.
But my sun's heav'nly eyes
  View not your weeping,

That now lies sleeping
Softly, now softly lies sleeping.

Sleep is a reconciling,
  A rest that peace begets;   10
Doth not the sun rise smiling
  When fair at e'en he sets?
Rest you, then, rest, sad eyes,
Melt not in weeping
  While she lies sleeping
Softly, now softly lies sleeping.

[WHAT POOR ASTRONOMERS ARE THEY]

What poor astronomers are they
  Take women's eyes for stars!
And set their thoughts in battle ray
  To fight such idle wars,
When in the end they shall approve
  'Tis but a jest drawn out of love.

And love itself is but a jest
  Devis'd by idle heads
To catch young fancies in the nest
  And lay [them] in fools' beds,   10
That being hatch'd in beauty's eyes
  They may be fledge ere they be wise.

But yet it is a sport to see
  How wit will run on wheels
While wit cannot persuaded be
  With that which reason feels:
That women's eyes and stars are odd,
  And love is but a feigned god.

But such as will run mad with will
  I cannot clear their sight,   20
But leave them to their study still
  To look where is no light.
Till time too late we make them try,
  They study false astronomy.

THOMAS CAMPION

FROM A BOOK OF AIRS (1601)

To the Reader

What epigrams are in poetry, the same are airs in music, then in their chief perfection when they are short and well-seasoned. But to clog a light song with a long praeludium is to corrupt the nature of it. Many rests in music were invented either for neces-sity of the fugue or granted as an harmonical license in songs of many parts; but in airs I find no use they have unless it be to make a vulgar and trivial modula-tion seem to the ignorant strange and to the judicial tedious. A naked air without guide, or prop, or color but his own is easily censured of every ear, and requires so much the more invention to make it please. And as Martial speaks in defense of his short epigrams, so may I say in th' apology of airs that where there is a full volume there can be no imputation of shortness. The lyric poets among the Greeks and Latins were first inventers of airs, tying themselves strictly to the number and value of their syllables, of which sort you shall find here only one song in sapphic verse; the rest are after the fashion of the time, ear-pleasing rimes without art. The subject of 10 them is for the most part amorous, and why not amorous songs as well as amorous attires? Or why not new airs as well as new fashions? For the note and tableture, if they satisfy the most, we have our desire; let expert masters please themselves with better. And if any light error hath escaped us, the skilful may easily correct it; the unskilful will hardly perceive it. But there are some who, to appear the more deep and singular in their judgment, will admit no music but that which is long, intricate, bated 20 with fugue, chain'd with syncopation, and where the nature of every word is precisely express'd in the note. . . . But such childish observing of words is altogether ridiculous, and we ought to maintain as well in notes as in action a manly carriage, gracing no word but that which is eminent and emphatical. . . .

[MY SWEETEST LESBIA]

My sweetest Lesbia, let us live and love,
And though the sager sort our deeds reprove,
Let us not weigh them. Heav'n's great lamps do dive
Into their west, and straight again revive,
But soon as once set is our little light,
Then must we sleep one ever-during night.

If all would lead their lives in love like me,
Then bloody swords and armor should not be;
No drum nor trumpet peaceful sleeps should move,
Unless alarm came from the camp of love. 10
But fools do live, and waste their little light,
And seek with pain their ever-during night.

When timely death my life and fortune ends,
Let not my hearse be vex'd with mourning friends,
But let all lovers, rich in triumph, come
And with sweet pastimes grace my happy tomb;
And Lesbia, close up thou my little light,
And crown with love my ever-during night.

[I CARE NOT FOR THESE LADIES]

I care not for these ladies
That must be woo'd and pray'd;
Give me kind Amaryllis,
The wanton country maid.

Nature art disdaineth;
Her beauty is her own.
  Her when we court and kiss,
  She cries, "Forsooth, let go!"
  But when we come where comfort is,
  She never will say, "No!" 10

If I love Amaryllis
She gives me fruit and flowers,
But if we love these ladies
We must give golden showers.
Give them gold that sell love;
Give me the nutbrown lass
  Who, when we court and kiss,
  She cries, "Forsooth, let go!"
  But when we come where comfort is,
  She never will say, "No!" 20

These ladies must have pillows
And beds by strangers wrought;
Give me a bower of willows,
Of moss and leaves unbought,
And fresh Amaryllis
With milk and honey fed,
  Who, when we court and kiss,
  She cries, "Forsooth, let go!"
  But when we come where comfort is,
  She never will say, "No!" 30

[WHEN TO HER LUTE CORINNA SINGS]

When to her lute Corinna sings,
Her voice revives the leaden strings,
And doth in highest notes appear
As any challeng'd echo clear;
But when she doth of mourning speak,
Ev'n with her sighs the strings do break.

And as her lute doth live or die,
Led by her passion, so must I:
For when of pleasure she doth sing,
My thoughts enjoy a sodain spring, 10
But if she doth of sorrow speak,
Ev'n from my heart the strings do break.

[THE CYPRESS CURTAIN OF THE NIGHT IS SPREAD]

The cypress curtain of the night is spread,
And over all a silent dew is cast.
The weaker cares by sleep are conquered,
But I alone, with hideous grief aghast,
In spite of Morpheus' charms, a watch do keep
Over mine eyes to banish careless sleep.

Yet oft my trembling eyes through faintness close,
And then the map of hell before me stands,

Which ghosts do see, and I am one of those
Ordain'd to pine in Sorrow's endless bands,   10
Since from my wretched soul all hopes are reft
And now no cause of life to me is left.

Grief, ceaze my soul, for that will still endure
When my cras'd body is consum'd and gone;
Bear it to thy black den, there keep it sure
Where thou ten thousand souls dost tire upon.
But all do not afford such food to thee
As this poor one, the worser part of me.

[FOLLOW YOUR SAINT]

Follow your saint, follow with accents sweet;
Haste you, sad notes, fall at her flying feet.
There, wrapp'd in cloud of sorrow, pity move,
And tell the ravisher of my soul I perish for her love.
But if she scorns my never-ceasing pain,
Then burst with sighing in her sight and ne'er return again.

All that I sung still to her praise did tend,
Still she was first, still she my songs did end.
Yet she my love and music both doth fly,
The music that her echo is and beauty's sympathy.   10
Then let my notes pursue her scornful flight:
It shall suffice that they were breath'd and died for her
     delight.

[THOU ART NOT FAIR]

Thou art not fair for all thy red and white,
    For all those rosy ornaments in thee;
Thou art not sweet, though made of mere delight,
    Nor fair nor sweet, unless thou pity me.
I will not soothe thy fancies; thou shalt prove
That beauty is no beauty without love.

Yet love not me, nor seek thou to allure
    My thoughts with beauty, were it more devine;
Thy smiles and kisses I cannot endure,
    I'll not be wrapp'd up in those arms of thine.   10
Now shew it, if thou be a woman right,—
Embrace, and kiss, and love me in despight.

[WHEN THE GOD OF MERRY LOVE]

When the god of merry love
As yet in his cradle lay,
Thus his wither'd nurse did say,
"Thou a wanton boy wilt prove
To deceive the powers above,
For by thy continual smiling
I see thy power of beguiling."

Therewith she the babe did kiss,
When a sodain fire out came

From those burning lips of his   10
That did her with love enflame,
But none would regard the same,
So that to her day of dying
The old wretch liv'd ever-crying.

[HARK, ALL YOU LADIES THAT DO SLEEP]

Hark, all you ladies that do sleep!
    The fairy queen Proserpina
Bids you awake and pity them that weep.
    You may do in the dark
    What the day doth forbid;
    Fear not the dogs that bark,
    Night will have all hid.

But if you let your lovers moan,
    The fairy queen Proserpina
Will send abroad her fairies ev'ry one,   10
    That shall pinch black and blue
    Your white hands and fair arms
    That did not kindly rue
    Your paramours' harms.

In myrtle arbors on the downs
    The fairy queen Proserpina,
This night by moonshine leading merry rounds,
    Holds a watch with sweet love,
    Down the dale, up the hill;
    No plaints or groans may move   20
    Their holy vigil.

All you that will hold watch with love,
    The fairy queen Proserpina
Will make you fairer then Dione's dove;
    Roses red, lilies white,
    And the clear damask hue,
    Shall on your cheeks alight;
    Love will adorn you.

All you that love, or lov'd before,
    The fairy queen Proserpina   30
Bids you encrease that loving humor more;
    They that yet have not fed
    On delight amorous,
    She vows that they shall lead
    Apes in Avernus.

[WHEN THOU MUST HOME]

When thou must home to shades of underground,
    And there arriv'd, a new admired guest,
The beauteous spirits do engirt thee round,
    White Iope, blithe Helen, and the rest,
To hear the stories of thy finish'd love
From that smooth tongue whose music hell can move,

Then wilt thou speak of banqueting delights,
  Of masks and revels which sweet youth did make,
Of tourneys and great challenges of knights,
  And all these triumphs for thy beauty's sake;   10
When thou hast told these honors done to thee,
Then tell, O tell, how thou didst murther me.

[COME, LET US SOUND WITH MELODY THE PRAISES]

Come, let us sound with melody the praises
Of the kings' King, th' omnipotent Creator,
Author of number, that hath all the world in
        Harmony framed.

Heav'n is his throne perpetually shining,
His devine power and glory; thence he thunders,
One in all, and all still in one abiding,
        Both Father and Son.

O sacred Sprite, invisible, eternal,
Ev'rywhere yet unlimited, that all things   10
Canst in one moment penetrate, revive me,
        O Holy Spirit.

Rescue, O rescue me from earthly darkness,
Banish hence all these elemental objects,
Guide my soul that thirsts to the lively fountain
        Of thy devineness.

Cleanse my soul, O God, thy bespotted image,
Altered with sin so that heav'nly pureness
Cannot acknowledge me but in thy mercies,
        O Father of Grace.   20

But when once thy beams do remove my darkness,
O then I'll shine forth as an angel of light
And record, with more than an earthly voice, thy
        Infinite honors.

THOMAS MORLEY

FROM THE TRIUMPHS OF ORIANA (1601)

[LIGHTLY SHE WHIPPED O'ER THE DALES]

Lightly she whipped o'er the dales,
  Making the woods proud with her presence;
Gently she trod the flow'rs, and they as gently kiss'd her
        tender feet.
The birds in their best language bade her welcome,
  Being proud that Oriana heard their song;
The clove-foot satyrs, singing, made music to the fauns
        a-dancing,
And both together with an emphasis sang Oriana's praises
Whilst the ajoining woods with melody did entertain
        their sweet harmony.
Then sang the shepherds and nymphs of Diana,
        "Long live fair Oriana!"   10
                        John Mundy

[FAIR ORIANA, BEAUTY'S QUEEN]

Fair Oriana, Beauty's queen,
Tripped along the verdant green;
The fauns and satyrs, running out,
Skipped and danced round about.
Flora forsook her painted bow'rs
And made a coronet of flow'rs.
Then sang the nymphs of chaste Diana,
        "Long live fair Oriana!"
                        John Hilton

[FAIR ORIANA IN THE MORN]

Fair Oriana in the morn
  Before the day was born;
With velvet steps on ground,
  Which made nor print nor sound,
Would see her nymphs abed,
  What lives those ladies led.
The roses, blushing, said,
  "O stay, thou shepherd's maid,"
And on a sodain all
  They rose and heard her call.   10
Then sang those shepherds and nymphs of Diana,
        "Long live fair Oriana!"
                        John Milton

[HARD BY A CRYSTAL FOUNTAIN]

Hard by a crystal fountain
  Oriana, the bright, lay down a-sleeping;
The birds they finely chirped, the winds were stilled;
  Sweetly with these accenting, the air was filled;
This is that fair whose head a crown deserveth,
  Which heaven for her reserveth.
Leave, shepherds, your lambs' keeping upon the barren
        mountain,
And, nymphs, attend on her and leave your bow'rs!
  For she the shepherd's life maintains and yours.
    Then sang the shepherds and nymphs of Diana,   10
        "Long live fair Oriana!"
                        Thomas Morley

Part V EARLY ELIZABETHAN POETRY

A MIRROR FOR MAGISTRATES

Odd as the fact may now seem, *A Mirror for Magistrates* was one of the spectacular popular successes of the Elizabethan period. Satisfying two basic desires of the age—to hear a story and to be edified—this compilation of instructive "tragedies" went through eight editions in about thirty years (?1555, 1559, 1563, 1571, 1574, 1575, 1578, 1587), not only earning for itself immense prestige among both readers and writers but also producing, toward the end of the century, notable imitations by such worthies as Daniel and Drayton, and even exerting a profound influence on the rise of the chronicle play in the eighties and nineties. Few other English books have had so pervasive an influence. Yet its beginnings were inauspicious, for the first (?1555) edition was suppressed by the lord chancellor himself as (presumably) a threat to the precarious *status quo* of Mary's reign. In the Dyce Collection at the Victoria and Albert Museum there is a unique titlepage of an undated edition of Lydgate's *Fall of Princes*, published by John Wayland, which promises the reader in addition to Lydgate's work accounts of "the fall of such as since that time [i.e. Lydgate's] were notable in England, diligently collected out of the chronicles." On the verso of this titlepage, in "The Printer to the Reader," Wayland announces that *The Fall of Princes* will be followed by a "continuation . . . concerning the chief princes of this iland, penned by the best clerks in such kind of matters that be this day living, not unworthy to be matched with Maister Lydgate." Other copies of Wayland's edition have, inserted at the end of the volume, a second titlepage which reads, "A memorial of such princes as since the time of King Richard the Second have been unfortunate in the realm of England." These two variant titlepages, plus one leaf (in the British Museum) containing a prose-link and eighteen stanzas of the tragedy of Owen Glendower, are presumably all that remains of the first edition of the *Mirror*. That this edition was suppressed is made clear by William Baldwin, editor of the 1559 edition, in his outspoken preface. "The work was begun," Baldwin ruefully remarks, "and part of it printed four year ago [i.e. in 1555], but hind'red by the lord chancellor that then was; nevertheless, through the means of my Lord Stafford, lately perused and licensed."

In his address to the reader, Baldwin tells us more of his part in the undertaking: that when the printer (Thomas Marsh), in response to a popular demand, resolved to issue the *Mirror* he solicited Baldwin's aid; that Baldwin's acceptance was made contingent on his having "the help of such as in wit were apt, in learning allowed, and in judgment and estimation able to wield and furnish so weighty an enterprise"; that seven such eligible collaborators met with him and laid out the work, each of them taking "for his part to be sundry personages and in their behalfs to bewail unto me [as interlocutor] their grievous chances, heavy destinies, and woful misfortunes." This cooperative plan was followed, the seven contributors working more or less independently on their separate assignments, and Baldwin himself, as editor, providing prose-links and commentaries for the tragedies narrated in the first person; and so the *Mirror* was duly published.

Attributions of authorship for the nineteen tragedies in the second edition must remain largely conjectural. Subsequent editions credit Baldwin with three tragedies (Richard, Earl of Cambridge, Richard, Duke of York, and George, Duke of Clarence), Sir Thomas Chaloner (the translator of Erasmus) with one (Richard II), Thomas Phaer (the translator of Virgil) with one (Owen Glendower); and internal evidence (such as the prefaces and the prose-links) suggests that George Ferrers wrote the tragedies of Tresilian and Thomas of Woodstock, as well as others that were "stayed" for some reason (Edmund, Duke of Somerset, Eleanor Cobham, and Humphrey, Duke of Gloucester).

The third (1563) edition of the *Mirror* represents a notable expansion, for to the contents of the second it adds a new preface by Baldwin, eight new tragedies, and the customary prose-links. Among the eight new pieces are two of the purple passages of Tudor literature—Churchyard's Jane Shore and Sackville's Henry, Duke of Buckingham, with its splendid "Induction." Though it contains no new work, the fourth (1571) edition drastically rearranges the contents of its predecessor. In the same year as the fifth edition (1574) there appeared also a new *Mirror* (called, oddly enough, "The First Part") by John Higgins, and subsequent editions of the so-called "original" *Mirror* as well as of its imitations, whose dating and description constitute a bibliographical headache, made further changes and additions to the original canon. Not until 1610, when Richard Niccols virtually rewrote and recast the entire work, did *A Mirror for Magistrates* complete its extraordinary career with the Elizabethan and Jacobean reading public.

Our texts are based upon *A Myrroure For Magistrates. Wherein may be seen by example of other, with howe grevous plages vices are punished,* 1559 (STC 1247); *A Myrrour for Magistrates. Wherein maye be seen by example of other, with howe grevous plages vices are punished,* 1563 (STC 1248).

from A MIRROR FOR MAGISTRATES (1559)

LOVE AND LIVE

To the nobility and all other in office, God grant wisdom and all things needful for the preservation of their estates. Amen.

Plato among many other of his notable sentences concerning the government of a commonweal hath this: "Well is that realm governed in which the ambitious desire not to bear office." Whereby you may perceive, right honorable, what offices are where they be duly executed: not gainful spoils for the greedy to hunt for, but painful toils for the heedy to be charged with. You may perceive also by this sentence that there is nothing more necessary in a commonweal than that officers be diligent and trusty in their charges. And sure in whatsoever realm such provision is made that officers be forced to do their duties, there is it as hard a matter to get an officer as it is in other places to shift off and put by those that, with flattery, bribes, and other shifts, sue and preace for offices. For the ambitious—that is to say prollers for power or gain—seek not for offices to help other, for which cause offices are ordained, but with the undoing of other to prank up themselves. And therefore bar them once of this bait, and force them to do their duties, and they will geve more to be rid fro their charges than they did at the first to buy them; for they seek only their commodity and ease. And therefore, where the ambitious seek no office, there no doubt offices are duly minist'red; and where offices are duly minist'red, it cannot be chosen but the people are good, whereof must needs follow a good commonweal. For if the officers be good, the people cannot be ill. Thus the goodness or badness of any realm lieth in the goodness or badness of the rulers. And therefore not without great cause do the holy apostles so earnestly charge us to pray for the magistrates; for indeed the wealth and quiet of every commonweal, the disorder also and miseries of the same, come specially through them. I need not go either to the Romans or Greeks for proof hereof, neither yet to the Jews or other nations, whose commonweals have alway florished while their officers were good, and decayed and ran to ruin whan naughty men had the regiment. Our own country stories (if we read and mark them) will shew us examples inow; would God we had not seen mo than inow. I purpose not to stand here upon the particulars, because they be in part set furth in the tragedies. Yet by the way this I note (wishing all other to do the like), namely, that as good governors have never lacked their deserved renowm, so have not the bad escaped infamy, besides such plages as are horrible to hear of.

For God (the ordainer of offices), although he suffer them for punishment of the people to be often occupied of such as are rather spoilers and Judases than toilers or justices (whom the Scripture therefore calleth hypocrites), yet suff'reth he them not to scape unpunished because they dishonor him. For it is God's own office, yea his chief office, which they bear and abuse. For as justice is the chief virtue, so is the ministration thereof the chiefest office; and therefore hath God established it with the chiefest name, honoring and calling kings and all officers under them by his own name, gods. Ye be all gods, as many as have in your charge any ministration of justice. What a foul shame were it for any now to take upon them the name and office of God and in their doings to shew themselves divils! God cannot, of justice, but plage such shameless presumption and hypocrisy, and that with shameful death, diseases, or infamy. How he hath plaged evil rulers from time to time in other nations, you may see gathered in Bochas' book intituled *The Fall of Princes* [i.e. *De casibus virorum*], translated into English by Lydgate. How he hath dealt with some of our countrymen your ancestors, for sundry vices not yet left, this book named *A Mirror for Magistrates* can shew: which therefore I humbly offer unto your Honors, beseeching you to accept it favorably. For here as in a looking-glass you shall see (if any vice be in you) how the like hath been punished in other heretofore, whereby, admonished, I trust it will be a good occasion to move you to the sooner amendment. This is the chiefest end why it is set furth, which God grant it may attain.

The work was begun and part of it printed four year ago, but hind'red by the lord chancellor [Stephen Gardiner] that then was; nevertheless, through the means of my Lord [Henry] Stafford, lately perused and licensed. Whan I first took it in hand, I had the help of many granted, and off'red of some, but of few performed, scarce of any; so that where I entended to have continued it to Queen Mary's time, I have been fain to end it much sooner. Yet so, that it may stand for a pattern till the rest be ready; which with God's grace (if I may have any help) shall be shortly. In the meanwhile, my lords and gods (for so I may call you), I most humbly beseech you favorably to accept this rude mirror and diligently to read and consider it. And although you shall find in it that some have for their virtue been envied and murdered, yet cease not you to be virtuous, but do your offices to the uttermost. Punish sin boldly both in yourselves and other; so shall God (whose lieutenants you are) either so maintain you that no malice shall prevail, or, if it do, it shall be for your good and to your eternal glory both here and in heaven, which I beseech God you may covet and attain. Amen.

Yours most humble,
William Baldwin

A Brief Memorial of Sundry Unfortunate Englishmen. William Baldwin to the Reader

Whan the printer had purposed with himself to print Lydgate's book of *The Fall of Princes,* and had made privy thereto many both honorable and worshipful, he was counsailed by divers of theim to procure to have the story continued from whereas Bochas left unto this present time, chiefly of such as Fortune had dallied with here in this iland; which might be as a mirror for all men as well noble as others, to shew the slippery deceits of the wavering lady and the due reward of all kind of vices. Which advice liked him so well that he required me to take pains therein; but because it was a matter passing my wit and skill, and more thankless than gainful to meddle in, I refused utterly to undertake it except I might have the help of such as in wit were apt, in learning allowed, and in judgment and estimation able to wield and furnish so weighty an enterprise, thinking even so to shift my hands. But he, earnest and diligent in his affairs, procured Atlas to set under his shoulder; for, shortly after, divers learned men whose many gifts need few praises consented to take upon theim part of the travail. And whan certain of theim to the number of seven were through a general assent at an appointed time and place gathered together to devise thereupon, I resorted unto them, bearing with me the book of Bochas, translated by Dan Lydgate, for the better observation of his order; which, although we liked well, yet would it not comelily serve, seeing that both Bochas and Lydgate were dead; neither were there any alive that meddled with like argument, to whom the unfortunate might make their moan.

To make, therefore, a state meet for the matter, they all agreed that I should usurp Bochas' room, and the wretched princes complain unto me; and took upon themselves every man for his part to be

sundry personages, and in their behalfs to bewail unto me their grievous chances, heavy destinies, and woful misfortunes.

This done, we opened such books of chronicles as we had there present, and Maister Ferrers, after he had found where Bochas left, which was about the end of King Edward the Third's reign, to begin the matter, said thus:

"I mervail what Bochas meaneth to forget among his miserable princes such as were of our nation, whose number is as great as their adventures wonderful; for to let pass all, both Britons, Danes, and Saxons, and to come to the last Conquest, what a sort are they, and some even in his own time! As for example, King Richard the First, slain with a quarl in his chief prosperity, also King John his brother, as some say, poisoned. Are not their histories rueful and of rare example? But, as it should appear, he, being an Italian, minded most the Roman and Italic story, or else perhaps he wanted our country chronicles. It were therefore a goodly and a notable matter to search and discourse our whole story from the first beginning of the inhabiting of the ile. But seeing the printer's mind is to have us follow where Lydgate left, we will leave that great labor to other that may intend it, and (as blind Bayard is always boldest) I will begin at the time of Richard the Second, a time as unfortunate as the ruler therein. And forasmuch, friend Baldwin, as it shall be your charge to note and pen orderly the whole process, I will, so far as my memory and judgment serveth, somewhat further you in the truth of the story. And therefore omitting the ruffle made by Jack Straw and his meinie and the murder of many notable men which thereby happened—for Jack, as ye know, was but a poor prince—I will begin with a notable example which within a while after ensued. And although he be no great prince, yet sithens he had a princely office, I will take upon me the miserable person of Sir Robert Tresilian, chief justice of England, and of other which suff'red with him, thereby to warn all of his authority and profession to take heed of wrong judgments, misconstruing of laws, or wresting the same to serve the princes' turns, which rightfully brought theim to a miserable end, which they may justly lament in manner ensuing." [Then follows the first tragedy, "The Fall of Robert Tresilian."]

FROM A MIRROR FOR MAGISTRATES (1563)

THOMAS SACKVILLE, EARL OF DORSET

THE INDUCTION

The wrathful winter, proaching on apace,
With blust'ring blasts had all ybared the treen,
And old Saturnus, with his frosty face,
With chilling cold had pierc'd the tender green;
The mantles rent wherein enwrapped been
The gladsome groves that now lay overthrown,
The tapets torn, and every bloom down blown.

The soil, that erst so seemly was to seen,
Was all despoiled of her beauty's hue;
And soote fresh flowers, wherewith the summer's queen
Had clad the earth, now Boreas' blasts down blew;   11
And small fowls flocking, in their song did rue
The winter's wrath, wherewith each thing defac'd
In woful wise bewail'd the summer past.

Hawthorn had lost his motley livery,
The naked twigs were shivering all for cold,
And dropping down the tears abundantly;
Each thing, methought, with weeping eye me told
The cruel season, bidding me withhold
Myself within; for I was gotten out   20
Into the fields, whereas I walk'd about.

When lo, the night with misty mantles spread
Gan dark the day and dim the azure skies;
And Venus in her message Hermes sped
To bloody Mars, to will him not to rise,
While she herself approach'd in speedy wise;
And Virgo, hiding her disdainful breast,
With Thetis now had laid her down to rest.

Whiles Scorpio, dreading Sagittarius' dart,
Whose bow, prest bent in sight, the string had slipp'd, 30
Down slid into the ocean-flood apart;
The Bear, that in the Irish seas had dipp'd
His griesly feet, with speed from thence he whipp'd;
For Thetis, hasting from the Virgin's bed,
Pursued the Bear, that ere she came was fled.

And Phaeton now, near reaching to his race
With glistering beams, gold streaming where they bent,
Was prest to enter in his resting place;
Erythius, that in the cart first went,
Had even now attain'd his journey's stent;   40
And, fast declining, hid away his head,
While Titan couched him in his purple bed.

And pale Cynthea, with her borrowed lignt,
Beginning to supply her brother's place,
Was past the noonstead six degrees in sight,
When sparkling stars amid the heaven's face
With twinkling light shone on the earth apace.
That, while they brought about the nightes chare,
The dark had dimmed the day ere I was ware.

And sorrowing I to see the summer flowers,   50
The lively green, the lusty leas forlorn,
The sturdy trees so shattered with the showers,
The fields so fade that florish'd so beforn,
It taught me well all earthly things be born
To die the death, for nought long time may last;
The summer's beauty yields to winter's blast.

Then looking upward to the heaven's leams,
With nightes stars thick powd'red everywhere,
Which erst so glistened with the golden streams
That cheerful Phoebus spread down from his sphere,   60
Beholding dark oppressing day so near;
The sodain sight reduced to my mind
The sundry changes that in earth we find;

That musing on this worldly wealth in thought,
Which comes and goes more faster than we see
The flickering flame that with the fire is wrought,
My busy mind presented unto me
Such fall of peers as in this realm had be,
That oft I wish'd some would their woes descrive,
To warn the rest whom Fortune left alive.   70

And strait forth stalking with redoubled pace,
For that I saw the night drew on so fast,
In black all clad there fell before my face
A piteous wight, whom wo had all forwaste;
Furth from her eyen the crystal tears outbrast,
And sighing sore, her hands she wrung and fold,
Tare all her hear, that ruth was to behold.

Her body small, forwithered and forspent,
As is the stalk that summer's drought oppress'd;
Her wealked face with woful tears besprent,   80
Her color pale, and, as it seemed her best,
In wo and plaint reposed was her rest;
And as the stone that drops of water wears,
So dented were her cheeks with fall of tears.

Her eyes swollen with flowing streams afloat;
Wherewith, her looks thrown up full piteously,
Her forceless hands together oft she smote,
With doleful shrieks that echoed in the sky;
Whose plaint such sighs did strait accompany
That, in my doom, was never man did see   90
A wight but half so wobegone as she.

I stood aghast, beholding all her plight,
Tween dread and dolor, so distrain'd in heart
That, while my hears upstarted with the sight,
The tears outstream'd for sorrow of her smart;
But when I saw no end that could apart
The deadly dewle which she so sore did make,
With doleful voice then thus to her I spake:

"Unwrap thy woes, whatever wight thou be,
And stint betime to spill thyself with plaint;   100
Tell what thou art, and whence, for well I see
Thou canst not dure, with sorrow thus attaint."
And with that word of sorrow, all forfaint
She looked up, and prostrate as she lay,
With piteous sound, lo, thus she gan to say:

"Alas, I, wretch whom thus thou seest distrained
With wasting woes that never shall aslake,
Sorrow I am, in endless torments pained
Among the Furies in the infernal lake,
Where Pluto, god of hell, so griesly black,   110
Doth hold his throne, and Letheus' deadly taste
Doth reave remembrance of each thing forepast.

"Whence come I am, the dreary destiny
And luckless lot for to bemoan of those
Whom Fortune, in this maze of misery,
Of wretched chance, most woful mirrors chose;
That when thou seest how lightly they did lose
Their pomp, their power, and that they thought most
    sure,
Thou mayest soon deem no earthly joy may dure."

Whose rueful voice no sooner had outbrayed   120
Those woful words wherewith she sorrowed so,
But out, alas, she shright and never stayed,
Fell down, and all to-dash'd herself for wo;
The cold pale dread my lims gan overgo,
And I so sorrowed at her sorrows eft
That, what with grief and fear, my wits were reft.

I stretch'd myself and strait my heart revives,
That dread and dolor erst did so appale;
Like him that with the fervent fever strives,
When sickness seeks his castle health to scale,   130
With gathered spirits so forc'd I fear to avale;
And rearing her with anguish all fordone,
My spirits return'd and then I thus begun:

"O Sorrow, alas, sith Sorrow is thy name,
And that to thee this drear doth well pertain,
In vain it were to seek to cease the same;
But as a man himself with sorrow slain,
So I, alas, do comfort thee in pain,
That here in sorrow art forsunk so deep
That at thy sight I can but sigh and weep."   140

I had no sooner spoken of a sike,
But that the storm so rumbled in her breast
As Eolus could never roar the like;
And showers down rained from her eyen so fast
That all bedrent the place, till at the last
Well eased they the dolor of her mind,
As rage of rain doth swage the stormy wind.

For furth she paced in her fearful tale:
"Come, come," quod she, "and see what I shall shew;
Come hear the plaining and the bitter bale   150
Of worthy men by Fortune overthrow;
Come thou and see them ruing all in row;
They were but shades that erst in mind thou roll'd;
Come, come with me, thine eyes shall them behold."

What could these words but make me more aghast,
To hear her tell whereon I mus'd whilere?
So was I mazed therewith, till at the last,
Musing upon her words, and what they were,
All sodainly well-lessoned was my fear;
For to my mind returned how she tell'd   160
Both what she was and where her won she held.

Whereby I knew that she a goddess was,
And therewithal resorted to my mind
My thought, that late presented me the glass
Of brittle state, of cares that here we find,
Of thousand woes to silly men assign'd;
And how she now bid me come and behold,
To see with eye that erst in thought I roll'd.

Flat down I fell, and with all reverence
Adored her, perceiving now that she,   170
A goddess sent by godly providence,
In earthly shape thus showed herself to me,
To wail and rue this world's uncertainty;
And while I honor'd thus her godhead's might,
With plaining voice these words to me she shright:

"I shall thee guide first to the griesly lake
And thence unto the blissful place of rest
Where thou shalt see and hear the plaint they make
That whilom here bare swinge among the best;
This shalt thou see, but great is the unrest   180
That thou must bide before thou canst attain
Unto the dreadful place where these remain."

And with these words, as I upraised stood,
And gan to follow her that straight furth paced,
Ere I was ware, into a desert wood
We now were come, where, hand in hand imbraced,
She led the way and through the thick so traced
As, but I had been guided by her might,
It was no way for any mortal wight.

But lo, while thus amid the desert dark   190
We passed on with steps and pace unmeet,
A rumbling roar, confus'd with howl and bark
Of dogs, shook all the ground under our feet,
And stroke the din within our ears so deep
As, half distraught, unto the ground I fell,
Besought return, and not to visit hell.

But she, forthwith, uplifting me apace,
Removed my dread, and with a steadfast mind
Bade me come on; for here was now the place,
The place where we our travel end should find;   200
Wherewith I arose, and to the place assign'd
Astoin'd I stalk, when strait we approached near
The dreadful place that you will dread to hear.

An hideous hole all vast, withouten shape,
Of endless depth, o'erwhelm'd with ragged stone,
With ugly mouth and grisly jaws doth gape,
And to our sight confounds itself in one;
Here ent'red we, and yeding forth, anon
An horrible loathly lake we might discern,
As black as pitch, that cleped is Avern.   210

A deadly gulf where nought but rubbish grows,
With foul black swelth in thick'ned lumps that lies,
Which up in the air such stinking vapors throws
That over there may fly no fowl but dies,
Chok'd with the pestilent savors that arise;
Hither we come, whence forth we still did pace,
In dreadful fear amid the dreadful place.

And first, within the portch and jaws of hell,
Sate deep Remorse of Conscience, all besprent
With tears, and to herself oft would she tell   220
Her wretchedness, and cursing never stent
To sob and sigh, but ever thus lament
With thoughtful care as she that, all in vain,
Would wear and waste continually in pain.

Her eyes unsteadfast, rolling here and there,
Whirl'd on each place, as place that vengeance brought,
So was her mind continually in fear,
Tossed and tormented with the tedious thought
Of those detested crimes which she had wrought;
With dreadful cheer and looks thrown to the sky, 230
Wishing for death, and yet she could not die.

Next saw we Dread, all trembling how he shook,
With foot uncertain proffered here and there,
Benumb'd of speech, and with a ghastly look,
Search'd every place, all pale and dead for fear,
His cap borne up with staring of his hear,
Stoin'd and amaz'd at his own shade for dreed,
And fearing greater dangers than was need.

And next, within the entry of this lake,
Sate fell Revenge, gnashing her teeth for ire,   240
Devising means how she may vengeance take,
Never in rest till she have her desire;
But frets within so farforth with the fire
Of wreaking flames, that now determines she
To die by death, or veng'd by death to be.

When fell Revenge, with bloody foul pretense,
Had showed herself as next in order set,
With trembling lims we softly parted thence,
Till in our eyes another sight we met,
When fro my heart a sigh forthwith I fet,   250
Ruing, alas, upon the woful plight
Of Misery, that next appeared in sight.

His face was lean and somedeal pined away,
And eke his hands consumed to the bone,
But what his body was I cannot say,
For on his carcass raiment had he none
Save clouts and patches, pieced one by one;
With staff in hand and scrip on shoulders cast,
His chief defence against the winter's blast.

His food, for most, was wild fruits of the tree, 260
Unless sometime some crums fell to his share,
Which in his wallet long, God wot, kept he,
As on the which full daint'ly would he fare;
His drink, the running stream; his cup, the bare
Of his palm closed; his bed, the hard cold ground;
To this poor life was Misery ybound.

Whose wretched state when we had well beheld,
With tender ruth on him and on his feres,
In thoughtful cares furth then our pace we held;
And by and by another shape appears,   270
Of greedy Care, still brushing up the breres,
His knuckles knobb'd, his flesh deep dented in,
With tawed hands and hard ytanned skin.

The morrow gray no sooner had begun
To spread his light, even peeping in our eyes,
When he is up and to his work yrun;
But let the night's black misty mantles rise,
And with foul dark never so much disguise
The fair bright day, yet ceaseth he no while,
But hath his candles to prolong his toil.   280

By him lay heavy Sleep, the cousin of Death,
Flat on the ground and still as any stone,
A very corps, save yielding forth a breath;
Small keep took he whom Fortune frowned on
Or whom she lifted up into the trone
Of high renown; but as a living death,
So, dead alive, of life he drew the breath.

The body's rest, the quiet of the heart,
The travail's ease, the still night's fere was he,
And of our life in earth the better part;   290
Reaver of sight, and yet in whom we see
Things oft that tide, and oft that never be;
Without respect, esteeming equally
King Croesus' pomp and Irus' poverty.

And next in order sad Old Age we found,
His beard all hoar, his eyes hollow and blind,
With drooping cheer still poring on the ground,
As on the place where nature him assign'd
To rest, when that the sisters had untwin'd
His vital thread and ended with their knife   300
The fleeting course of fast declining life.

There heard we him with broken and hollow plaint
Rue with himself his end approaching fast,
And all for nought his wretched mind torment
With sweet remembrance of his pleasures past,
And fresh delights of lusty youth forwaste;
Recounting which, how would he sob and shriek,
And to be young again of Jove beseek!

But, and the cruel fates so fixed be
That time forepast cannot return again,   310
This one request of Jove yet prayed he,
That in such withered plight and wretched pain
As eld, accompanied with his loathsome train,
Had brought on him, all were it wo and grief,
He might a while yet linger forth his life,

And not so soon descend into the pit
Where Death, when he the mortal corps hath slain,
With retchless hand in grave doth cover it,
Thereafter never to enjoy again
The gladsome light, but in the ground ylain,   320
In depth of darkness waste and wear to nought,
As he had never into the world been brought.

But who had seen him sobbing, how he stood
Unto himself and how he would bemoan
His youth forepast, as though it wrought him good
To talk of youth, all were his youth foregone,
He would have mused and mervail'd much, whereon
This wretched Age should life desire so fain,
And knows full well life doth but length his pain.

Crookback'd he was, tooth-shaken, and blear-eyed,   330
Went on three feet, and sometime crept on four,
With old lame bones that rattled by his side,
His scalp all pill'd and he with eld forlore;
His withered fist still knocking at Death's door,
Fumbling and driveling as he draws his breath;
For brief, the shape and messenger of Death.

And fast by him pale Malady was plac'd,
Sore sick in bed, her color all forgone,
Bereft of stomach, savor, and of taste,
Ne could she brook no meat but broths alone;   340
Her breath corrupt, her keepers every one
Abhorring her, her sickness past recure,
Detesting physic and all physic's cure.

But O, the doleful sight that then we see!
We turn'd our look and on the other side
A griesly shape of Famine mought we see,
With greedy looks and gaping mouth that cried
And roar'd for meat, as she should there have died;
Her body thin and bare as any bone,
Whereto was left nought but the case alone.   350

And that, alas, was knawn on everywhere,
All full of holes that I ne mought refrain
From tears to see how she her arms could tear,
And with her teeth gnash on the bones in vain,
When all for nought she fain would so sustain
Her starven corps, that rather seem'd a shade
Then any substance of a creature made.

Great was her force, whom stone wall could not stay,
Her tearing nails snatching at all she saw;
With gaping jaws that by no means ymay   360
Be satisfied from hunger of her maw,
But eats herself as she that hath no law;
Gnawing, alas, her carcass all in vain,
Where you may count each sinow, bone, and vein.

On her while we thus firmly fix'd our eyes,
That bled for ruth of such a dreary sight,
Lo, sodainly she shright in so huge wise
As made hell gates to shiver with the might;
Wherewith a dart we saw, how it did light
Right on her breast, and therewithal, pale Death   370
Enthrilling it, to reave her of her breath.

And by and by a dum dead corps we saw,
Heavy and cold, the shape of Death aright,
That daunts all earthly creatures to his law;
Against whose force in vain it is to fight;
Ne peers, ne princes, nor no mortal wight,
No towns, ne realms, cities, ne strongest tower,
But all, perforce, must yield unto his power.

His dart, anon, out of the corps he took,
And in his hand, a dreadful sight to see,   380
With great triumph eftsoons the same he shook,
That most of all my fears affrayed me;
His body dight with nought but bones, perdy,
The naked shape of man there saw I plain,
All save the flesh, the sinow, and the vein.

Lastly, stood War, in glittering arms yclad,
With visage grim, stern looks, and blackly hued;
In his right hand a naked sword he had,
That to the hilts was all with blood embrued;
And in his left, that kings and kingdoms rued,   390
Famine and fire he held, and therewithal
He razed towns and threw down towers and all.

Cities he sack'd and realms that whilom flow'red
In honor, glory, and rule above the best,
He overwhelm'd and all their fame devour'd,
Consumed, destroyed, wasted, and never ceas'd
Till he their wealth, their name, and all oppress'd;
His face forhewed with wounds, and by his side
There hung his targe, with gashes deep and wide.

In mids of which, depainted there, we found   400
Deadly Debate, all full of snaky hear,
That with a bloody fillet was ybound,
Outbreathing nought but discord everywhere,
And round about were portray'd, here and there,
The hugy hosts, Darius and his power,
His kings, princes, his peers, and all his flower.

Whom great Macedo vanquish'd there in sight
With deep slaughter, despoiling all his pride,
Pierc'd through his realms and daunted all his might;
Duke Hannibal beheld I there beside,   410
In Canna's field victor how he did ride,
And woful Romains that in vain withstood,
And Consul Paulus covered all in blood.

Yet saw I more: the fight at Thrasimene,
And Trebey field, and eke when Hannibal
And worthy Scipio last in arms were seen
Before Carthago gate, to try for all
The world's empire, to whom it should befall;
There saw I Pompey and Caesar clad in arms,
Their hosts allied and all their civil harms,   420

With conquerors' hands, forbath'd in their own blood,
And Caesar weeping over Pompey's head;
Yet saw I Sylla and Marius where they stood,
Their great cruelty and the deep bloodshed
Of friends; Cyrus I saw and his host dead,
And how the queen with great despite hath flung
His head in blood of them she overcome.

Xerxes, the Persian king, yet saw I there
With his huge host that drank the rivers dry,
Dismounted hills, and made the vales uprear,   430
His host and all yet saw I slain, perdy;
Thebes I saw, all raz'd how it did lie
In heaps of stones, and Tyrus put to spoil,
With walls and towers flat evened with the soil.

But Troy, alas, methought above them all,
It made mine eyes in very tears consume,
When I beheld the woful word befall,
That by the wrathful will of gods was come;
And Jove's unmoved sentence and foredoom
On Priam king, and on his town so bent,   440
I could not lin, but I must there lament.

And that the more, sith destiny was so stern
As, force perforce, there might no force avail,
But she must fall, and by her fall we learn
That cities, towers, wealth, world, and all shall quail;
No manhood, might, nor nothing mought prevail
All were there prest full many a prince and peer,
And many a knight that sold his death full dear.

Not worthy Hector, worthiest of them all,
Her hope, her joy, his force is now for nought;   450
O Troy, Troy, there is no boot but bale,
The hugy horse within thy walls is brought;
Thy turrets fall, thy knights, that whilom fought
In arms amid the field, are slain in bed,
Thy gods defil'd and all thy honor dead.

The flames upspring and cruelly they creep
From wall to roof till all to cinders waste;
Some fire the houses where the wretches sleep,
Some rush in here, some run in there as fast;
In everywhere or sword or fire they taste;   460
The walls are torn, the towers whirl'd to the ground;
There is no mischief but may there be found.

Cassandra yet there saw I how they haled
From Pallas' house, with spercled tress undone,
Her wrists fast bound and with Greeks' rout empaled;
And Priam eke, in vain how did he run
To arms, whom Pyrrhus with despite hath done
To cruel death, and bathed him in the bain
Of his son's blood, before the altar slain.

But how can I descrive the doleful sight   470
That in the shield so livelike fair did shine?
Sith in this world I think was never wight
Could have set furth the half, not half so fine;
I can no more but tell how there is seen
Fair Ilium fall in burning red gledes down,
And from the soil great Troy, Neptunus' town.

Herefrom when scarce I could mine eyes withdraw,
That fill'd with tears as doth the springing well,
We passed on so farfurth till we saw
Rude Acheron, a loathsome lake to tell,   480
That boils and bubs up swelth as black as hell;
Where grisly Charon, at their fixed tide,
Still ferries ghosts unto the farder side.

The aged god no sooner Sorrow spied,
But hasting strait unto the bank apace,
With hollow call unto the rout he cried
To swarve apart and geve the goddess place;
Strait it was done, when to the shore we pace,
Where, hand in hand as we then linked fast,
Within the boat we are together plac'd.   490

And furth we launch full fraughted to the brink,
Whan with the unwonted weight, the rusty keel
Began to crack as if the same should sink;
We hoise up mast and sail, that in a while
We fet the shore, where scarcely we had while
For to arrive, but that we heard anon
A three-sound bark confounded all in one.

We had not long furth pass'd but that we saw
Black Cerberus, the hideous hound of hell,
With bristles rear'd and with a three-mouthed jaw   500
Fordinning the air with his horrible yell,
Out of the deep dark cave where he did dwell;
The goddess strait he knew, and by and by
He peas'd and couched while that we passed by.

Thence come we to the horror and the hell,
The large great kingdoms and the dreadful reign
Of Pluto in his trone where he did dwell,
The wide waste places and the hugy plain,
The wailings, shrieks, and sundry sorts of pain,
The sighs, the sobs, the deep and deadly groan,   510
Earth, air, and all, resounding plaint and moan.

Here pewled the babes, and here the maids unwed
With folded hands their sorry chance bewailed,
Here wept the guiltless slain, and lovers dead,
That slew themselves when nothing else availed;

A thousand sorts of sorrows here, that wailed
With sighs and tears, sobs, shrieks, and all yfere,
That O, alas, it was a hell to hear.

We stayed us strait, and with a rueful fear
Beheld this heavy sight, while from mine eyes   520
The vapored tears down stilled here and there,
And Sorrow eke, in far more woful wise,
Took on with plaint, upheaving to the skies
Her wretched hands, that with her cry the rout
Gan all in heaps to swarm us round about.

"Lo here," quoth Sorrow, "princes of renown,
That whilom sat on top of Fortune's wheel,
Now laid full low, like wretches whirled down,
Even with one frown, that stayed but with a smile;
And now behold the thing that thou, erewhile,   530
Saw only in thought, and what thou now shalt hear,
Recompt the same to kesar, king, and peer."

Then first came Henry, Duke of Buckingham,
His cloak of black all pill'd and quite forworn,
Wringing his hands, and Fortune oft doth blame,
Which of a duke hath made him now her scorn;
With ghastly looks, as one in manner lorn,
Oft spread his arms, stretch'd hands he joins as fast
With rueful cheer and vapored eyes upcast.

His cloak he rent, his manly breast he beat,   540
His hear all torn, about the place it lay;
My heart so molt to see his grief so great,
As feelingly methought it dropp'd away;
His eyes they whirled about withouten stay,
With stormy sighs the place did so complain,
As if his heart at each had burst in twain.

Thrice he began to tell his doleful tale,
And thrice the sighs did swallow up his voice,
At each of which he shrieked so withal,
As though the heavens rived with the noise;   550
Till at the last, recovering his voice,
Supping the tears that all his breast berain'd,
On cruel Fortune, weeping, thus he plain'd.

THOMAS CHURCHYARD

HOW SHORE'S WIFE, EDWARD THE FOURTH'S CONCUBINE, WAS BY KING RICHARD DESPOILED OF ALL HER GOODS AND FORCED TO DO OPEN PENANCE

Among the rest by Fortune overthrown
I am not least, that most may wail her fate.
My fame and bruit abroad the world is blown;
Who can forget a thing thus done so late?

My great mischance, my fall, and heavy state
Is such a mark whereat each tongue doth shoot,
That my good name is pluck'd up by the root.

This wand'ring world bewitched me with wiles
And won my wits with wanton sug'red joys.
In Fortune's frekes who trusts her when she smiles   10
Shall find her false and full of fickle toys;
Her triumphs all but fill our ears with noise,
Her flattering gifts are pleasures mix'd with pain;
Yea, all her words are thunders threat'ning rain.

The fond desire that we in glory set
Doth thirl our hearts to hope in slipper hap,
A blast of pomp is all the fruit we get,
And under that lies hid a sodain clap.
In seeking rest unwares we fall in trap,
In groping flowers with nettles stung we are,   20
In laboring long we reap the crop of care.

O dark deceit with painted face for show,
O poisoned bait that makes us eager still,
O feigned friend deceiving people so,
O world, of thee we cannot speak too ill,
Yet fools we are that bend so to thy skill!
The plage and scourge that thousands daily feel
Should warn the wise to shun thy whirling wheel.

But who can stop the stream that runs full swift,
Or quench the fire that is crept in the straw?   30
The thirsty drinks, there is no other shift,
Perforce is such that need obeys no law.
Thus bound we are in worldly yokes to draw,
And cannot stay, nor turn again in time,
Nor learn of those that sought too high to clime.

Myself for proof, lo, here I now appear
In woman's weed with weeping, watered eyes,
That bought her youth and her delights full dear;
Whose loud reproach doth sound unto the skies
And bids my corse out of the grave to rise,   40
As one that may no longer hide her face,
But needs must come and shew her piteous case.

The sheet of shame wherein I shrouded was
Did move me oft to plain before this day,
And in mine ears did ring the trump of brass,
Which is defame that doth each vice bewray.
Yea, though full dead and low in earth I lay,
I heard the voice of me what people said,
But then to speak, alas, I was affrayed.

And now a time for me I see prepar'd,   50
I hear the lives and falls of many wights;
My tale, therefore, the better may be heard,
For at the torch the little candle lights.
Where pageants be, small things fill out the sights.
Wherefore geve ear, good Baldwin, do thy best,
My tragedy to place among the rest.

Because that truth shall witness well with thee,
I will rehearse in order as it fell
My life, my death, my doleful destiny,
My wealth, my wo, my doing every deal,   60
My bitter bliss, wherein I long did dwell.
A whole discourse of me, Shore's wife by name,
Now shalt thou hear as thou hadst seen the same.

Of noble blood I cannot boast my birth,
For I was made out of the meanest mold,
Mine heritage but seven foot of earth,
Fortune ne gave to me the gifts of gold.
But I could brag of nature, if I would,
Who fill'd my face with favor fresh and fair,
Whose beauty shone like Phoebus in the air.   70

My shape, some said, was seemly to each sight,
My countenance did shew a sober grace,
Mine eyes in looks were never proved light,
My tongue in words were chaste in every case,
Mine ears were deaf, and would no lovers place,
Save that, alas! a prince did blot my brow.
Lo, there the strong did make the weak to bow.

The majesty that kings to people bear,
The stately port, the awful cheer they show,
Doth make the mean to shrink and couch for fear,   80
Like as the hound that doth his maister know.
What then, since I was made unto the bow?
There is no cloak can serve to hide my fault,
For I agreed the fort he should assault.

The eagle's force subdues each bird that flies.
What metal may resist the flaming fire?
Doth not the sun dazzle the clearest eyes,
And melt the ice, and make the frost retire?
Who can withstand a puissant king's desire?
The stiffest stones are pierced through with tools.   90
The wisest are with princes made but fools.

If kind had wrought my form in common frames,
And set me forth in colors black and brown,
Or beauty had been parched in Phoebus' flames,
Or shamefast ways had pluck'd my feathers down,
Then had I kept my name and good renown;
For nature's gifts was cause of all my grief.
A pleasant prey enticeth many a thief.

Thus wo to thee that wrought my peacock's pride
By clothing me with nature's tapistry,   100
Wo worth the hue wherein my face was dyed,
Which made me think I pleased every eye.
Like as the sters make men behold the sky,
So beauty's show doth make the wise full fond,
And brings free hearts full oft to endless bond.

But clear from blame my friends cannot be found;
Before my time my youth they did abuse:
In marriage a prentice was I bound,
When that mere love I knew not how to use.
But, wellaway, that cannot me excuse,   110
The harm is mine, though they devised my care,
And I must smart and sit in sland'rous snare.

Yet geve me leave to plead my case at large.
If that the horse do run beyond his race,
Or anything that keepers have in charge
Do break their course, where rulers may take place,
Or meat be set before the hungry's face,
Who is in fault? The offender, yea or no,
Or they that are the cause of all this wo?

Note well what strife this forced marriage makes,   120
What loathed lives do come where love doth lack,
What scratting briers do grow upon such brakes,
What commonweals by it are brought to wrack,
What heavy load is put on patience' back,
What strange delights this branch of vice doth breed,
And mark what grain springs out of such a seed.

Compel the hawk to sit that is unmann'd,
Or make the hound untaught to draw the deer,
Or bring the free against his will in band,
Or move the sad a pleasant tale to hear,   130
Your time is lost and you are never the near.
So love ne learns of force the knot to knit;
She serves but those that feel sweet fancy's fit.

The less defame redounds to my dispraise,
I was entic'd by trains, and trapp'd by trust;
Though in my power remained yeas or nays,
Unto my friends yet needs consent I must
In everything, yea lawful or unjust.
They brake the boughs and shak'd the tree by sleight,
And bent the wand that might have grown full streight.

What help is this? The pale thus broken down,   141
The deer must needs in danger run astray.
At me therefore why should the world so frown?
My weakness made my youth a prince's prey.
Though wisdom should the course of nature stay,
Yet try my case who list, and they shall prove
The ripest wits are soonest thralls to love.

What need I more to clear myself too much?
A king me wan, and had me at his call:
His royal state, his princely grace was such,   150
The hope of will (that women seek for all),
The ease and wealth, the gifts which were not small,
Besieged me so strongly round about,
My power was weak, I could not hold him out.

Duke Hannibal in all his conquest great,
Or Caesar yet, whose triumphs did exceed,
Of all their spoils, which made them toil and sweat,
Were not so glad to have so rich a meed
As was this prince when I to him agreed,
And yielded me a prisoner willingly,   160
As one that knew no way away to flee.

The nightingale for all his merry voice,
Nor yet the lark that still delights to sing,
Did never make the hearers so rejoice
As I with words have made this worthy king.
I never jarr'd, in tune was every string,
I tempered so my tongue to please his ear
That what I said was current everywhere.

I join'd my talk, my gestures, and my grace
In witty frames that long might last and stand,   170
So that I brought the king in such a case
That to his death I was his chiefest hand.
I governed him that ruled all this land:
I bare the sword, though he did wear the crown;
I strake the stroke that threw the mighty down.

If justice said that judgment was but death,
With my sweet words I could the king persuade,
And make him pause and take therein a breath,
Till I with suit the fautor's peace had made.
I knew what way to use him in his trade,   180
I had the art to make the lion meek,
There was no point wherein I was to seek.

If I did frown, who then did look awry?
If I did smile, who would not laugh outright?
If I but spake, who durst my words deny?
If I pursued, who would forsake the flight?
I mean my power was known to every wight.
On such a height good hap had built my bower,
As though my sweet should never have turn'd to sour.

My husband then, as one that knew his good,   190
Refused to keep a prince's concubine,
Foreseeing the end and mischief as it stood,
Against the king did never much repine;
He saw the grape whereof he drank the wine.
Though inward thought his heart did still torment,
Yet outwardly he seem'd he was content.

To purchase praise and win the people's zeal,
Yea, rather bent of kind to do some good,
I ever did uphold the common weal,
I had delight to save the guiltless blood.   200
Each suitor's cause when that I understood,
I did prefer as it had been mine own,
And help'd them up that might have been o'erthrown.

My power was prest to right the poor man's wrong,
My hands were free to geve where need required,
To watch for grace I never thought it long,
To do men good I need not be desired.
Nor yet with gifts my heart was never hired.
But when the ball was at my foot to guide,
I played to those that Fortune did abide.   210

My want was wealth, my wo was ease at will,
My robes were rich and braver then the sun;
My fortune then was far above my skill,
My state was great, my glass did ever run;
My fatal thread so happily was spun
That then I sat in earthly pleasures clad,
And for the time a goddess' place I had.

But I had not so soon this life possess'd
But my good hap began to slip aside.
And Fortune then did me so sore molest   220
That unto plaints was turned all my pride.
It booted not to row against the tide:
Mine oars were weak, my heart and strength did fail,
The wind was rough, I durst not bear a sail.

What steps of strife belong to high estate?
The climbing up is doubtful to indure,
The seat itself doth purchase privy hate,
And honor's fame is fickle and unsure.
And all she brings is flours that be unpure,
Which fall as fast as they do sprout and spring,   230
And cannot last, they are so vain a thing.

We count no care to catch that we do wish,
But what we win is long to us unknown.
Till present pain be served in our dish,
We scarce perceive whereon our grief hath grown.
What grain proves well that is so rashly sown?
If that a mean did measure all our deeds,
Instead of corn we should not gather weeds.

The settl'd mind is free from Fortune's power.
They need not fear who look not up aloft,   240
But they that clime are careful every hour,
For when they fall they light not very soft.
Examples hath the wisest warned oft
That where the trees the smallest branches bear,
The storms do blow and have most rigor there.

Where is it strong but near the ground and root?
Where is it weak but on the highest sprays?
Where may a man so surely set his foot
But on those boughs that groweth low always?
The little twigs are but unsteadfast stays;   250
If they break not, they bend with every blast:
Who trusts to them shall never stand full fast

The wind is great upon the highest hills,
The quiet life is in the dale below,
Who treads on ice shall slide against their wills,
They want no care that curious arts would know,
Who lives at ease and can content him so
Is perfect wise, and sets us all to school;
Who hates this lore may well be called a fool.

What greater grief may come to any life   260
Than after sweet to taste the bitter sour?
Or after peace to fall at war and strife?
Or after mirth to have a cause to lower?
Under such props false Fortune builds her bower;
On sodain change her flitting frames be set,
Where is no way for to escape her net.

The hasty smart that Fortune sends in spite
Is hard to brook, where gladness we imbrace.
She threatens not, but sodainly doth smite;
Where joy is most, there doth she sorrow place.   270
But sure I think this is too strange a case
For us to feel such grief amid our game,
And know not why until we taste the same.

As erst I said, my bliss was turn'd to bale;
I had good cause to weep and wring my hands,
And show sad cheer with countenance full pale,
For I was brought in sorrow's woful bands.
A pirrie came and set my ship on sands.
What should I hide or color care and noy?
King Edward died in whom was all my joy.   280

And when the earth received had his corse,
And that in tomb this worthy prince was laid,
The world on me began to shew his force,
Of troubles then my part I long assayed;
For they of whom I never was afraid
Undid me most, and wrought me such despite
That they bereft from me my pleasure quite.

As long as life remain'd in Edward's breast,
Who was but I? Who had such friends at call?
His body was no sooner put in chest   290
But well was him that could procure my fall.
His brother was mine enemy most of all,
Protector then, whose vice did still abound
From ill to worse till death did him confound.

He falsely feigned that I of counsail was
To poison him, which thing I never meant;
But he could set thereon a face of brass
To bring to pass his lewd and false entent.
To such mischief this tyrant's heart was bent,
To God ne man he never stood in awe,   300
For in his wrath he made his will a law.

Lord Hastings' blood for vengeance on him cries,
And many mo that were too long to name;
But most of all, and in most woful wise,
I had good cause this wretched man to blame.
Before the world I suff'red open shame:
Where people were as thick as is the sand
I penance took with taper in my hand.

Each eye did stare and look me in the face;
As I pass'd by the rumors on me ran,   310
But Patience then had lent me such a grace
My quiet looks were praised of every man.
The shamefast blood brought me such color than
That thousands said, which saw my sober cheer,
"It is great ruth to see this woman here."

But what prevail'd the people's pity there?
This raging wolf would spare no guiltless blood.
O wicked womb that such ill fruit did bear,
O cursed earth that yieldeth forth such mud!
The hell consume all things that did thee good,   320
The heavens shut their gates against thy sprite,
The world tread down thy glory under feet!

I ask of God a vengeance on thy bones!
Thy stinking corps corrupts the air I know;
Thy shameful death no earthly wight bemoans,
For in thy life thy works were hated so
That every man did wish thy overthrow.
Wherefore I may, though percial now I am,
Curse every cause whereof thy body came.

Wo worth the man that fathered such a child,   330
Wo worth the hour wherein thou wast begate,
Wo worth the breasts that have the world beguil'd
To norish thee that all the world did hate!
Wo worth the gods that gave thee such a fate
To live so long, that death deserved so oft!
Wo worth the chance that set thee up aloft!

Ye princes all, and rulers everychone,
In punishment beware of hatred's ire.
Before ye scourge, take heed, look well thereon.
In wrath's ill will if malice kindle fire,   340
Your hearts will burn in such a hot desire
That in those flames the smoke shall dim your sight,
Ye shall forget to join your justice right.

You should not judge till things be well deserned.
Your charge is still to maintain upright laws.
In conscience' rules ye should be throughly learned;
Where clemency bids wrath and rashness pause,
And further saith, "Strike not without a cause,
And when ye smite do it for justice' sake,"
Then in good part each man your scourge will take.   35

If that such zeal had moved this tyrant's mind
To make my plague a warning for the rest,
I had small cause such fault in him to find;
Such punishment is used for the best;
But by ill will and power I was oppress'd.
He spoiled my goods, and left me bare and poor,
And caused me to beg from door to door.

What fall was this, to come from prince's fare
To watch for crums among the blind and lame?
When alms was dealt I had a hungry share,   360
Bycause I knew not how to ask, for shame,
Till force and need had brought me in such frame
That starve I must, or learn to beg an alms,
With book in hand, and say St. David's Psalms.

Where I was wont the golden chains to wear,
A pair of beads about my neck was wound,
A linen cloth was lapp'd about my hear,
A ragged gown that trailed on the ground,
A dish that clapp'd and gave a heavy sound,
A staying staff and wallet therewithal,   370
I bare about as witness of my fall.

I had no house wherein to hide my head,
The open street my lodging was perforce,
Full oft I went all hungry to my bed,
My flesh consumed, I looked like a corse.
Yet in that plight who had on me remorse?
O God, thou knowest my friends forsook me than,
Not one holp me that succored many a man.

They frown'd on me that fawn'd on me before,
And fled from me that followed me full fast;   380
They hated me, by whom I set much store,
They knew full well my fortune did not last.
In every place I was condemn'd and cast.
To plead my cause at bar it was no boot,
For every man did tread me under foot.

Thus long I lived all weary of my life,
Till death approach'd and rid me from that wo.
Example take by me, both maid and wife,
Beware, take heed, fall not to folly so,
A mirror make of my great overthrow;   390
Defy this world and all his wanton ways;
Beware by me that spent so ill her days.

This was so well liked that all together exhorted
me instantly to procure Maister Churchyard to undertake and to pen as many mo of the remainder a
might by any means be attainted at his hands.
And when I had promised I would do my diligence
therein, they asked me if I had any mo tragedies yet
unread, for the evening was now at hand and there

were enow already read to make a handsome volume. "Indeed," quod I, "I purpose here to end the second part of this volume, for here endeth the cruel reign of King Richard the Third. And in another volume hereafter to discourse the residue from the beginning of King Henry the Seventh to the end of this king and queen's reign (if God so long will grant us life); and I beseech you all that you will diligently perform such stories as you have undertaken and procure your friends such as be learned to help us with the rest; for there is in this part matter enough to set all the poets in England in

work, and I would wish that every fine, apt wit would at the least undertake one. For so would it be a notable volume. For my part, I entend to be so impudent and importunate a suitor to so many as I knew or may hereafter be acquainted with that no excuse shall serve to shake me off; and I desire you all to be as earnest. And to occupy the time while we be now together I will read unto you Edmund, the Duke of Somerset, which must be placed in the first part, and than the Blacksmith, which must serve for third volume, to th' end I may know your judgment therein." "Do so, we pray you," quoth they.

THOMAS TUSSER

As his contemporaries did not fail to note, although Thomas Tusser apparently knew everything about agricultural and domestic economy, he found it impossible to remain solvent. Like Mr. Micawber, he spent his life waiting for something to turn up. First a singing-boy at St. Paul's under John Redford, he then passed on to Eton (where he acquired a lasting resentment of Nicholas Udall's floggings) and thence (1543) to King's College and Trinity Hall, Cambridge. Forced by ill health to leave the university without a degree, he entered the service of William Lord Paget as a musician, and it was to the powerful Pagets that he thereafter looked for such meager patronage as came his way. By 1553 he was farming in Suffolk, an experience that led, in 1557, to Richard Tottel's publishing *A Hundreth Good Points of Husbandry*. An ailing wife forced his removal from Suffolk to Ipswich, and with her successor he moved to Norfolk, then to Norwich (where he apparently served as a singing-man in the cathedral), then to Essex, then to London (where a son was christened in 1572/73), then to Cambridge (where he was a servant in his old college). At last he died in a London debtors' prison in 1580. The grim facts of Tusser's luckless life (some of which he versifies in the 1573 edition of *Five Hundreth Points of Good Husbandry*) are curiously discordant with his encyclopedic knowledge of rural and domestic economy. In the *Hundreth Good Points* (1557), then in a reprint expanded with *A Hundreth*

Good Points of Huswifery (1570, 1571), and finally in *Five Hundreth Points of Good Husbandry United to As Many of Good Huswifery* (three issues in 1573 and others, variously expanded, in 1574, 1577, 1580, 1585, 1586, 1590, 1593, 1597, 1599, as well as six more editions between 1604 and 1638) Tusser became a perennial best-seller. And no wonder, for generations of common readers learned from his galloping anapests thousands of approved maxims of planting, reaping, storing, housekeeping, domestic finance, meteorology, rural superstitions, morality, and Protestant piety. Arranging his lore in the form of an almanac, Tusser edified while he entertained. He possessed not only a minute knowledge of the farmer's day-to-day problems but also an extraordinary metrical facility and versatility. Most of the *Five Hundreth Points* is in rushing couplets of anapestic tetrameter, but the many prefatory and autobiographical digressions employ complicated stanzaic forms, Skeltonics, iambic tetrameters in sonnet-like stanzas, amphibrachs, and acrostics. However prosy Tusser's material—and it is usually of the earth earthy—he had a superb ear, and his nuggets of agricultural morality exhibit some of the most interesting metrics of Tudor literature. Our texts are based upon *A hundreth good pointes of husbandrie*, [1557] (STC 24372); *Five hundred pointes of good Husbandrie, as well for the Champion, or open countrie, as also for the woodland, or Severall, mixed in everie Month with Huswiferie*, 1580 (STC 24380).

FROM A HUNDRETH GOOD POINTS OF HUSBANDRY (1557)

A hundreth good points of good husbandry
Maintaineth good household, with huswifry.
Housekeeping and husbandry, if it be good,
Must love one another as cousins in blood.
The wife, too, must husband as well as the man,
Or farewell thy husbandry, do what thou can.

SEPTEMBER

Thresh seed and go fan, for the plow may not lie;
September doth bid to be sowing of rye.
The redges well-harrow'd, or ever thou strike,
Is one point of husbandry rye land do like.

Geve winter corn leave for to have full his lust;
Sow wheat as thou mayst, but sow rye in the dust.
Be careful for seed, for such seed as thou sow,
As true as thou livest, look justly to mow.

The seed being sown, water-forow thy ground
That rain, when it cometh, may run away round.   10
The ditches kept scoured, the hedge clad with thorn,
Doth well to drain water and saveth thy corn.

Then furth with thy slings and thine arrows and bows,
Till ridges be green keep the corn from the crows.
A good boy abroad, by the day-star appear,
Shall scare goodman crow that he dare not come near.

At Michelmas, mast would be looked upon,
And lay to get some, or the mast-time be gone.
It saveth thy corn well; it fatteth thy swine;
In frost it doth help them where else they should pine. 20

MARCH

In March sow thy barley, thy lond not too cold,
The drier the better, a hundreth times told.
That tilth harrow'd finely, set seed-time an end,
And praise and pray God a good harvest to send.

Sow wheat in a mean, sow thy rye not too thin;
Let peason and beans, here and there, take therein.
Sow barley and oats good and thick, do not spare;
Give land leave her seed or her weed for to bear.

For barley and peas, harrow after thou sow;
For rye harrow first, seldom after, I trow.   10
Let wheat have a clod for to cover the head
That after a frost it may out and go spread.

A DIGRESSION FROM HUSBANDRY TO A POINT OR TWO OF HUSWIFERY

Now here I think needful a pause for to make
To treat of some pains a good huswife must take.

For huswifes must husband as well as the man,
Or farewell thy husbandry, do what thou can.

In March and in April, from morning to night,
In sowing and setting good huswives delight
To have in their garden or some other plot,
To trim up their house and to furnish their pot.

Have millons at Michelmas, parsneps in Lent,
In June butt'red beans saveth fish to be spent.   10
With those and good pottage, inough having than,
Thou winnest the heart of thy laboring man.

JULY

Then muster thy folk, play the captain thyself,
Providing them weapon and such kind of pelf.
Get bottles and bags, keep the field in the heat;
The fear is not much, but the danger is great.

With toiling and raking and setting on cocks
The grass that was green is now hay for an ox.
That done, leave the tithe, load thy cart and away,
The battle is fought, thou hast gotten the day.

Then down with thy headlonds, thy corn round about;
Leave never a dallop unmown or had out.   10
Though grass be but thin about barley and peas,
Yet picked up clean, it shall do thee good ease.

Thry-fallow betime, for destroying of weed,
Lest thistle and dock fall a-blooming and seed.
Such season may hap it shall stand thee upon
To till it again or the sommer be gone.

And better thou wart so to do for thy haste
Then hardness for slought make thy land to lie waste.
A ready good forehorse is dainty to find;
Be hind'red at first, and come alway behind.   20

Thy houses and barns would be looked upon,
And all thing amended or harvest come on.
Things thus set in order, at quiet and rest,
Thy harvest goeth forward and prospereth best.

Saint James willeth husbands get reapers at hand,
The corn being ripe, do but shed as it stand.
Be saving and thankful for that God hath sent;
He sendeth it thee for the selfsame entent.

Reap well, scatter not, gather clean that is shorn;
Bind fast, shock apace, pay the tenth of thy corn.   30
Load fast, carry home, lose no time being fair;
Golf just in the barn, it is out of despair.

This done, set the poor over all for to glean,
And after thy cattle to eat it up clean.
Then spare it for pasture till rowen be past;
To lengthen thy dairy no better thou hast.

Then welcome thy harvest folk, servants and all;
With mirth and good cheer let them furnish thine hall.

The harvest-lord nightly must geve thee a song;
Fill him then the black bowl, or else he hath wrong.   40

Thy harvest thus ended in mirth and in joy,
Please everyone gently, man, woman, and boy.
Thus doing with alway such help as they can,
Thou winnest the name of a right husbandman.

FROM FIVE HUNDRED POINTS OF GOOD HUSBANDRY (1580)

THE LADDER TO THRIFT

To take thy calling thankfully
    and shun the path to beggery,
To grudge in youth no drudgery,
    to come by knowledge perfectly,
To count no travel slavery
    that brings in penny saverly,
To follow profit earnestly
    but meddle not with pilfery,
To get by honest practisie,
    and keep thy gettings covertly,   10
To lash not out too lashingly
    for fear of pinching penury,
To get good plot to occupy,
    and store and use it husbandly,
To shew to landlord curtesy
    and keep thy covenants orderly,
To hold that thine is lawfully
    for stoutness or for flattery,
To wed good wife for company
    and live in wedlock honestly,   20
To furnish house with householdry
    and make provision skilfully, . . .
To bear thy crosses patiently,
    for worldly things are slippery,
To lay to keep from misery
    age, coming on so creepingly,
To pray to God continually
    for aid against thine enemy,
To spend thy Sabbath holily
    and help the needy poverty,   30
To live in conscience quietly
    and keep thyself from malady,
To ease thy sickness speedily
    ere help be past recovery,
To seek to God for remedy,
    for witches prove unluckily.

    These be the steps unfeignedly
    To climb to thrift by husbandry.

    These steps both reach and teach thee shall
    To come by thrift to shift withal.   40

A DESCRIPTION OF THE PROPERTIES
OF WINDS ALL THE TIMES OF THE YEAR

North winds send hail, south winds bring rain,
East winds we bewail, west winds blow amain;
Northeast is too cold, southeast not too warm,
Northwest is too bold, southwest doth no harm.

The north is a noyer to grass of all suits,
The east a destroyer to herb and all fruits;
The south with his showers refresheth the corn,
The west to all flowers may not be forborne.

The west, as a father, all goodness doth bring;
The east, a forbearer no manner of thing;   10
The south, as unkind, draweth sickness too near;
The north, as a friend, maketh all again clear.

With temperate wind we be blessed of God;
With tempest, we find, we are beat with his rod;
All power we know to remain in his hand
However wind blow, by sea or by land.

    Though winds do rage as winds were wood,
    And cause spring tides to raise great flood,
    And lofty ships leave anker in mud,
    Bereafing many of life and of blood,   20
    Yet true it is, as cow chaws cud
    And trees at spring do yield forth bud,
    Except wind stands as never it stood,
    It is an ill wind turns none to good.

THE AUTHOR'S LIFE

Now, gentle friend, if thou be kind,
Disdain thou not, although the lot
Will now with me no better be
    than doth appear;
Nor let it grieve that thus I live,
But rather guess, for quietness,
As others do, so do I too
    content me here.

By leave and love of God above
I mind to shew, in verses few,   10

How through the breers my youthful years
   have run their race;
And further say why thus I stay
And mind to live, as bee in hive,
Full bent to spend my life to an end
   in this same place.

It came to pass that born I was
Of linage good, of gentle blood,
In Essex lair, in village fair,
   that Rivenhall hight,   20
Which village lied by Banktree side;
There spend did I mine infancy,
There then my name in honest fame
   remain'd in sight.

I yet but young, no speech of tongue
Nor tears withal that often fall
From mother's eyes when child outcries
   to part her fro,
Could pity make good father take,
But out I must to song be thrust;   30
Say what I would, do what I could,
   his mind was so.

O painful time, for every crime,
What toesed ears, like baited bears!
What bobbed lips, what jerks, what nips,
   what hellish toys!
What robes, how bare! What colledge fare!
What bread, how stale! What penny ale!
Then Wallingford, how wart thou abhorr'd
   of silly boys!   40

Thence for my voice I must—no choice—
Away of force like posting horse,
For sundry men had plagards then
   such child to take;
The better breast, the lesser rest,
To serve the queere, now there, now here;
For time so spent I may repent
   and sorrow make.

But mark the chance, myself to vance
By friendship's lot to Paul's I got,   50
So found I grace a certain space
   still to remain;
With Redford there, the like nowhere

For cunning such, and virtue much,
By whom some part of music art
   so did I gain.

From Paul's I went, to Eton sent,
To learn streightways the Latin phrase,
Where fifty-three stripes given to me
   at once I had;   60
For fault but small, or none at all,
It came to pass thus beat I was.
See, Udall, see, the mercy of thee
   to me, poor lad!

From London hence to Cambridge thence,
With thanks to thee, O Trinity,
That to thy hall, so passing all,
   I got at last;
Where joy I felt, there trim I dwelt,
There heaven from hell I shifted well,   70
With learned men, a number then,
   the time I pass'd.

Long sickness had, then was I glad
To leave my book, to prove and look
In court what gain, by taking pain,
   mought well be found;
Lord Paget than, that noble man,
Whose soul, I trust, is with the just,
That same was he enriched me
   with many a pound.   80

When this betide, good parents died,
One after one, till both were gone,
Whose petigree, who list may see
   in harold's book;
Whose souls in bliss be long ere this,
For hope we must, as God is just,
So here that crave shall mercy have
   that mercy look.

By court I spi'd, and ten years tri'd
That cards and dice, with Venus' vice,   90
And peevish pride, from virtue wide,
   with some so wraught
That Tyburn play made them away,
Or begger's state as evil to hate;
By suchlike evils I saw such devils
   to come to naught. . . .

BARNABE GOOGE

Barnabe Googe, a well-educated kinsman and retainer of Sir William Cecil, Lord Burghley, made his first quasi-literary flight with a translation of Marcellus Palingenius' (Angelo Manzolli's) *Zodiac of Life* (*Zodiacus vitae*, 1543), publishing the first three books in 1560, the first six in 1561, and all twelve in 1565; but while this ambitious work was in progress he seems to have been forced into a different kind of authorship. Going abroad in 1561, he left with a friend the manuscript of his eclogues, apparently an early work which he had modestly consigned to "continual darkness." But when on his return (perhaps at the end of 1562) he learned that it had already been sent to press, he reluctantly assented to its publication, mainly, if one may believe him, to protect the investment of the "poor printer." In 1563, then, the thin volume duly appeared as a miscellaneous group of eight eclogues in clumsy fourteeners, two genuine sonnets (which the printer broke up into twenty-eight lines each), epitaphs on such notables as Thomas Phaer, Richard Edwards, and Nicholas Grimald, and some travel-poems resulting from his trip abroad. The eight eclogues are not without interest: bridging the long gap between Barclay's and Spenser's use of the form, they show to what stern moral (and even Calvinistic) uses the pastoral eclogue could be forced, and the two of them (the fifth and sixth) derived from Montemayor's *Diana* inaugurate the long and powerful influence of Spanish romance in English literature. None the less, Googe's first impulse to let his juvenilia lie in darkness was probably sound. At any rate he never again attempted original composition, and the 1563 volume remains a grim little testimonial to the continuing influence of Tottel's *Miscellany*. Our text is based upon *Eglogs Epytaphes, and Sonettes. Newly written by Barnabe Googe,* 1563 (STC 12048).

FROM EGLOGUES, EPITAPHS, AND SONNETS (1563)

To the Right Worshipful Master William Lovelace, Esquire, Reader of Gray's Inn, Barnabe Googe Wisheth Health

How loth I have been, being of long time earnestly required, to suffer these trifles of mine to come to light, it is not unknown to a great number of my familiar acquaintance, who both daily and hourly moved me thereunto, and little of long time prevailed therein. For I both considered and weighed with myself the grossness of my style which, thus 10 committed to the gazing shew of every eye, should forthwith disclose the manifest folly of the writer; and also I feared and mistrusted the disdainful minds of a number both scornful and carping correctors, whose heads are ever busied in taunting judgments, lest they should otherwise interpret my doings than indeed I meant them. These two so great mischiefs utterly dissuaded me from the following of my friends' persuasions and willed me rather to condemn them to continual darkness, whereby no in- 20 convenience could happen, than to endanger myself in giving them to light, to the disdainful doom of any offended mind. Notwithstanding, all the diligence that I could use in the suppression thereof could not suffice; for I myself being at that time out of the realm, little fearing any such thing to happen, a very friend of mine, bearing, as it seemed, better will to my doings than respecting the hazard of my name, committed them, altogether unpolished, to the hands of the printer. In whose hands, during his absence from the city till his return of late, they remained. At which time he declared the matter wholly unto me, shewing me that, being so far past, and paper provided for the impression thereof, it could not without great hinderance of the poor printer be now revoked. His sodain tale made me, at the first, utterly amazed, and doubting a great while what was best to be done. At the length, agreeing both with necessity and his counsel, I said with Martial, *Jam sed poteras tutior esse domi.* And, calling to mind to whom I might chiefly commit the fruits of my smiling muse, sodainly was cast before my eyes the perfect view of your friendly mind, gentle Maister Lovelace, unto whom, for the numb'red heaps of sundry friendships accounting myself as bound, I have thought best to give them, not doubting but that they shall be as well taken as I do presently mean them.

Desiring you therein, as all such as shall read them, especially to bear with the unpleasant form of my too hastily finished "Dream," the greater part whereof with little advice I lately ended bycause the beginning of it, as a senseless head separated from the body, was given with the rest to be printed. And thus, desiring but for recompense the friendly receiving of my slender gift, I end, wishing unto you, good Maister Lovelace, in this life the happy enjoying of prosperous years and hereafter the blessed estate of never-ceasing joy.

Yours assuredly,
Barnabe Googe

EGLOGA SECUNDA

DAMETAS

My beasts, go feed upon the plain
   and let your herdman lie.
Thou seest her mind, and fear'st thou now,
   Dametas, for to die?
Why stayest thou thus? Why dost thou stay?
   Thy life too long doth last.
Account this flood thy fatal grave,
   sith time of hope is past.
What mean'st thou thus to linger on?
   Thy life would fain depart.   10
Alas, the wound doth fester still
   of cursed Cupid's dart.
No salve but this can help thy sore;
   no thing can move her mind.
She hath decreed that thou shalt die;
   no help there is to find.
Now sith there is no other help,
   nor ought but this to try,
Thou seest her mind; why fear'st thou than,
   Dametas, for to die?   20
Long hast thou served, and served true,
   but all, alas, in vain;
For she thy service nought esteems,
   but deals thee grief for gain.
For thy good will a gay reward,
   disdain for love, she gives;
Thou lovest her while thy life doth last;
   she hates thee while she lives.
Thou flam'st whenas thou seest her face
   with heat of high desire;   30
She flames again, but how? Alas,
   with deep, disdainful ire!
The greatest pleasure is to thee
   to see her void of pain;
The greatest grief to her again
   to see thy health remain.
Thou covet'st ever her to find;
   she seeks from thee to fly.
Thou seest her mind, why fear'st thou than,
   Dametas, for to die?   40
Dost thou account it best to keep
   thy life in sorrows still?

Or think'st thou best it now to live
   contrary to her will?
Think'st thou thy life for to retain
   when she is not content?
Canst thou addict thyself to live,
   and she to murder bent?
Dost thou entend again to sue
   for mercy at her hands?   50
As soon thou may'st go plow the rocks
   and reap upon the sands.
Draw near, O mighty herd of beasts,
   sith no man else is by;
Your herdman long that hath you kept,
   Dametas, now must die.
Resolve your brutish eyes to tears,
   and all together cry;
Bewail the woful end of love;
   Dametas now must die.   60
My pleasant songs now shall you hear
   no more on mountains high;
I leave you all, I must be gone;
   Dametas now must die.
To Tityrus I you resine,
   in pasture good to lie,
For Tityrus shall keep you though
   Dametas now must die.
O cursed cause that hath me slain,
   my troth, alas, to try!   70
O shepherds all, be witnesses:
   Dametas here doth die!

EGLOGA QUINTA

MOPSUS
AGON

[MOPSUS.] Some doleful thing there is at hand,
     thy countenance doth declare.
     Thy face, good Agon, void of blood,
      thine eyes, amazed, stare.
     I see thy tears how they do still
      disclose thy secret mind.
     Hath Fortune frowned late on thee?
      Hath Cupid been unkind?

AGON.   A piteous thing to be bewail'd,
     a desperate act of love,   10
     O Destinies, such cruel broils
      how have you power to move?
     Here lived a lady fair of late
      that Claudia men did call,
     Of goodly form, yea, such a one
      as far surmounted all.
     The stately dames that in this court
      to show themselves do lie:
     There was not one in all the crew
      that could come Claudia nigh.   20

A worthy knight did love her long
  and for her sake did feel
The pangs of love that happen still
  by frowning Fortune's wheel.
He had a page Valerius named
  whom so much he did trust
That all the secrets of his heart
  to him declare he must,
And made him all the only means
  to sue for his redress   30
And to entreat for grace to her
  that caused his distress.
She, whanas first she saw his page,
  was straight with him in love,
That nothing could Valerius' face
  from Claudia's mind remove.
By him was Faustus often hard;
  by him his suits took place;
By him he often did aspire
  to see his lady's face.   40
This passed well till, at the length,
  Valerius sore did sue,
With many tears beseeching her
  his maister's grief to rue;
And told her that if she would not
  release his maister's pain,
He never would attempt her more,
  nor see her once again.
She then, with mazed count'nance there
  and tears that gushing fell,   50
Astonied answer'd thus: "Lo, now,
  alas, I see too well
How long I have deceived been
  by thee, Valerius, here.
I never yet believed before
  nor till this time did fear
That thou didst for thy maister sue,
  but only for my sake.
And for my sight, I ever thought,
  thou didst thy travail take.   60
But now I see the contrary.
  Thou nothing car'st for me
Since first thou knew'st the fiery flames
  that I have felt by thee.
O Lord, how ill thou dost requite
  that I for thee have done!
I curse the time that friendship first
  to show I have begun.
O Lord, I thee beseech, let me
  in time revenged be,   70
And let him know that he hath sinn'd
  in this misusing me.
I cannot think but Fortune once
  shall thee reward for all,
And vengeance due for thy deserts
  in time shall on thee fall.

And tell thy maister Faustus now,
  if he would have me live,
That nevermore he sue to me,
  This answer last I give.   80
And thou, O traitor vile
  and en'my to my life,
Absent thyself from out my sight;
  procure no greater strife.
Since that these tears had never force
  to move thy stony heart,
Let never these my wearied eyes
  see thee no more. Depart!"
This said, in haste she hieth in,
  and there doth vengeance call,   90
And strake herself with cruel knife,
  and bloody down doth fall.
This doleful chance whan Faustus heard,
  lamenting loud, he cries,
And tears his hear, and doth accuse
  the unjust and cruel skies.
And in this raging mood away
  he stealeth out alone,
And gone he is, no man knows where;
  each man doth for him moan.   100
Valerius, whan he doth perceive
  his maister to be gone,
He weeps and wails in piteous plight,
  and forth he runs anon.
No man knows where he is become.
  Some say the woods he took,
Intending there to end his life,
  on no man more to look.
The court laments, the princess eke
  herself doth weep for wo.   110
Lo, Faustus fled and Claudia dead,
  Valerius vanished so.

AN EPITAPH OF THE DEATH OF NICHOLAS GRIMALD

Behold this fleeting world, how all things fade,
How everything doth pass and wear away.
Each state of life, by common course and trade,
Abides no time, but hath a passing day.
For look: as Life, that pleasant dame, hath brought
The pleasant years and days of lustiness,
So Death, our foe, consumeth all to nought,
Envying these, with dart doth us oppress.
And that which is the greatest grief of all,
The greedy gripe doth no estate respect,   10
But where he comes he makes them down to fall,
Ne stays he at the high, sharp-witted sect.
For if that wit or worthy eloquence
Or learning deep could move him to forbear,
O Grimald, then thou had'st not yet gone hence,
But here haddest seen full many an aged year.
Ne had the muses lost so fine a flour.

Nor had Minerva wept to leave thee so.
If Wisdom might have fled the fatal hour,
Thou had'st not yet been suff'red for to go.   20
A thousand doltish geese we might have spar'd,
A thousand witless heads Death might have found,
And taken them for whom no man had car'd
And laid them low in deep, oblivious ground.
But Fortune favors fools, as old men say,
And lets them live and takes the wise away.

Sonnets

TO DOCTOR BALE

Good, aged Bale, that, with thy hoary hears,
Dost yet persist to turn the painful book,
O happy man, that hast obtain'd such years
And leav'st not yet on papers pale to look,
Give over now to beat thy wearied brain,
And rest thy pen that long hath labored sore.
For aged men unfit, sure, is such pain,
And thee beseems to labor now no more.
But thou, I think, Don Plato's part will play,
With book in hand to have thy dying day.   10

OF EDWARDS OF THE CHAPEL

Devine Camenes, that with your sacred food
Have fed and foster'd up from tender years
A happy man that in your favor stood,
Edwards, in court that cannot find his feres,
Your names be blest that, in this present age,
So fine a head by art have framed out,
Whom some hereafter, help'd by poet's rage,
Perchance may match but none shall pass, no doubt.
O Plautus, if thou wert alive again,
That comedies so finely didst endite,   10
Or Terence, thou that, with thy pleasant brain,
The hearers' minds on stage didst much delight,
What would you say, sirs, if you should behold,
As I have done, the doings of this man?
No word at all, to swear I durst be bold,
But burn with tears that which with mirth began;
I mean your books, by which you gat your name,

To be forgot you would commit to flame.
Alas, I would, Edwards, more tell thy praise,
But at thy name my muse amazed stays.   20

GOING TOWARDS SPAIN

Farewell, thou fertile soil
    that Brutus first out found
When he, poor soul, was driven clean
    from out his country ground;
That northward lay'st thy lusty sides
    amid the raging seas,
Whose wealthy land doth foster up
    thy people all in ease,
While others scrape and cark abroad,
    their simple food to get,   10
And sely souls take all for good
    that cometh to the net
Which they, with painful pains, do pitch
    in barren, burning realms,
While we have all without restraint
    among thy wealthy streams.
O blest of God, thou pleasant ile,
    where Wealth herself doth dwell,
Wherein my tender years I pass'd,
    I bid thee now farewell.   20
For Fancy drives me forth abroad
    and bids me take delight
In leaving thee and ranging far
    to see some stranger sight.
And faith, I was not framed here
    to live at home with ease,
But, passing forth for knowledge' sake,
    to cut the foaming seas.

COMING HOMEWARD OUT OF SPAIN

O raging seas and mighty Neptune's reign,
In monstrous hills that throwest thyself so high,
That with thy floods dost beat the shores of Spain
And break the clives that dare thy force envy,
Cease now thy rage and lay thine ire aside,
And Thou that hast the governance of all,
O mighty God, grant weather, wind, and tide
Till in my country coast our anker fall.

THOMAS HOWELL

Thomas Howell, a shadowy but graceful anachronism, was one of the last of the courtly makers who wrote merely to please their titled friends and patrons. We hear of him first in the early sixties as a retainer of Lady Anne Talbot, and apparently his whole adult life was spent in the great households of the Earl of Shrewsbury and then of Mary, Countess of Pembroke. Almost all his verse

(which stays timidly in the tradition of Tottel's *Miscellany*) was written about or for the Talbot and Sidney families. Indeed, his *Devices* (1581), a sort of collected edition of his earlier *Arbor of Amity* and *Pleasant Sonnets* (both apparently published in 1568) together with some later poems, is dedicated to the Countess of Pembroke, and one of its lyrics ("Written in a Most Excellent Book") contains the earliest known reference to her brother's *Arcadia*, a manuscript of which Howell must have read at Wilton. Although he was emphatically a minor figure, Howell's verses are among the most accomplished and urbane of the barren sixties and seventies. Our text is based upon *The Arbor of Amitie, wherin is comprised pleasant Poems and pretie Poesies, set foorth by Thomas Howell Gentleman,* 1568 (STC 13874).

FROM THE ARBOR OF AMITY (1568)

WHEN HE THOUGHT HIMSELF CONTEMNED

O heart, why dost thou sigh, and wilt not break?
O doleful chance, thou hast a cause thereto;
For thy reward in love and kindness eke
Is recompens'd by hate and deadly wo.

Have I so plight my heart and mind to thee?
Have I been bent so whole unto thy hand,
And others now obtain the fruit from me?
Thou art unkind, forsooth, such foe to stand.

O doleful heart, thus plung'd in pinching pain,
Lament no more, but break, thy truth to try;   10
For where thy comfort was and joy did reign,
Now hate returns no news, O heart, now die!

Lo, thus the breeding birds their nests do build,
But others take the gains and fruits of them;
The crooked clown so ear'th the toiling field,
But oft the crop remains to other men.

Well, time may come wherein my fruitless part,
So ill bestow'd, some others may bewail,
And wish they had receiv'd my yielding heart
Whose loving root took ground to small avail.   20

THE ROSE

Whenas the mildest month
   Of jolly June doth spring,
And gardens green with happy hue
   Their famous fruits do bring;
When eke the lustiest time
   Reviveth youthly blood,
Then springs the finest featur'd flower
   In border fair that stood;
Which moveth me to say,
   In time of pleasant year,   10
Of all the pleasant flowers in June
   The red rose hath no peer.

JACK SHOWS HIS QUALITIES AND GREAT
GOOD WILL TO JONE

Mine own zweet Jone, let me not moan,
   no more I thee require,
But as I crave, so let me have
   the thing I do desire.
And ich shall still even at thy will
   be ready at thy hand,
To fling, to spring, and run at ring
   whilst ich am able stand.
With cap and knee ich will serve thee,
   what should ich more declare?   10
Thy mind to please and body ease
   is only all my care.
Though ich am not zo seemly, chwot,
   as been the courtnoles gay,
Yet chave a flail that will not fail
   to thrash both night and day.
And vor manhood cham zure cham good,
   vor all our town can zay
How stout ich stood with Robart Whood
   when Baldoone volk vetcht May;   20
And eke ich pass both more and lass
   in dancing Downtoone's round:
To trip, to skip, and handle a whip
   cham zure my peer's not vound.
To clout a shoe, ich may tell you,
   veow cunnigare there be;
And eke to theatch, whare can ye veatch
   another like to me?
In husbandry ich am truly
   ycounted to excel;   30
Yea, and ich can, if need be than,
   wait at the table well.
For once ich went up into Kent
   with the head man of our town,
Where ich did wait at every bait,
   chee vore thee cham no clown.
Why, for my manor, ich bear the banner
   before my Lord of May;
No country man there is that can
   teach me, though I do zay.   40
And furthermore thou knowest gay store
   of good will fall to me;
Vor vather zed, when he is dead
   that all mine own shall be:
Both calf and cow and our great zow
   that vifteen pigs did varrow

Even at one time, shall then be mine,
  and eke our new wheelbarrow.
Beside all this, ich shall not miss
  of red ones to have store,   50
That zaw no zun, nor yet the moon,

of years cham zure a score.
And all, my Jone, shalt thou alone
  at thy commandment have,
If thou wilt let me friscoles vet
  in place where ich do crave.

GEORGE TURBERVILE

As another writer, of good intentions but little talent, whose Bible was Tottel's *Miscellany*, George Turbervile is the Rosencrantz to Googe's Guildenstern. Like Googe, he wrote little original poetry (although Anthony Wood mentions a now lost volume of poems about his trip to Russia in 1568–69), and the little that he wrote is not very interesting. *Epitaphs, Epigrams, Songs, and Sonnets,* his one surviving original book—which, with conventional modesty but alarming accuracy, he called "the unripe seeds of my barren brain"—appeared in 1567 as "newly corrected with additions," but no earlier copy is known. Another edition (either the second or the third) was published in 1570. For the most part a loosely connected group of amatory poems, dedicated to Anne, Countess of Warwick, about "Tymetes" and "Pyndara," the volume also contains a good many epigrams adapted from those in Janus Carnarius' Latin collection of 1529. Although Turbervile made a significant advance in smoothing and regularizing the rough meter and

wrenched accent of his immediate predecessors, the kindest thing to say about his poetry is that it shows how pervasive the influence of Tottel's *Miscellany* was in the sixties and seventies. Perhaps more interesting than his own verse are his translations. His faithful rendering of Ovid's *Heroides* (*The Heroical Epistles,* 1567) not only employs poulter's measure and fourteeners, but also experiments with blank verse; its popularity justified new editions in 1569, 1570, 1580, and 1600. His translation of Mantuan's eclogues is notable for spreading the wide popularity of "old Mantuan" and for seeking at least to approximate the style to the subject: "I have . . . used the common country phrase according to the person of the speakers in every eglogue as though indeed the man himself should tell his tale." Our texts are based upon *The Eglogs of the Poet B. Mantuan Carmelitan,* 1567 (STC 22990); *Epitaphes, Epigrams, Songs, and Sonets, with a Discourse of the Friendly affections of Tymetes to Pyndara his Ladie. Newly corrected with additions,* 1570 (STC 24327).

─────────❧─────────

FROM THE EGLOGS OF THE POET B. MANTUAN CARMELITAN TURNED INTO ENGLISH VERSE AND SET FORTH WITH THE ARGUMENT TO EVERY EGLOGE (1567)

To the Reader

Having translated this poet, gentle reader, although basely and with barren pen, [I] thought it not good nor friendly to withhold it from thee, knowing of old thy wonted curtesy in perusing books and discretion in judging them without affection. I shall think my pains passing well imployed if thou shew thy accustomed favor to this book which I have now forced to a new and forrain language from that it was. Though I have altered the tongue, I trust I have 10 not changed the author's meaning or sense in anything, but played the part of a true interpreter, observing that which we term decorum in each respect as far as the poet and our mother tongue would give me leave. For as the conference betwixt shephierds is familiar stuff and homely, so have I shap'd my style and temp'red it with such common and ordinary

phrase of speech as countrymen do use in their affairs, alway minding the saying of Horace, whose sentence I have thus Englished:

To set a manly head upon a horse's neck,
And all the lims with divers plumes of divers hue to deck,
Or paint a woman's face aloft to open show
And make the picture end in fish with scaly skin below,
I think, my friends, would cause you laugh and smile to see
How ill these ill-compacted things and members would
    agree.

For, indeed, he that shall translate a shephierd's tale and use the talk and style of an heroical personage, expressing the siely man's meaning with lofty, thundering words, in my simple judgment joins (as Horace saith) a horse's neck and a man's head togither. For as the one were monstrous to see, so were the other too fond and foolish to read. Wherefore I have, I say, used the common country phrase according to the person of the speakers in every egloge as though indeed the man himself should tell his tale. And the sooner to let thee understand the matter contained in every treatise I have (I hope to thy good liking) foreset the argument. If there be anything herein that thou shalt happen to mislike, neither blame the learned poet nor control the clownish shephierd, good reader, but me that presum'd rashly to offer so unworthy matter to thy survey. But if thou fancy or like well with ought contained herein, commend Mantuan, extol the shephierd; sufficeth me to avoid scot-free from slanderous snare. If I gain thy good will I have the guerdon of my travail. Thus presuming upon thy patience in perusing this book, thy uncorrupt judgment in condemning and allowing the same, I end my preface, craving thee to lend quiet ear to Fortunatus and the rest of his companions.

10

George Turbervile

THE SECOND EGLOGE ENTITULED FORTUNATUS

THE ARGUMENT

The pranks that Padus play'd
    in breaking down his bounds,
And how he had dismay'd
    men, sheep, and pasture grounds,
His Faustus' tale to quite
    here Fortunatus gan,
And after to recite
    the fond affects of man.
Of mad Amyntas' love
    and passing rage to tell
For other men's behove
    this zealous shepherd fell.

THE SPEAKERS' NAMES
FAUSTUS
FORTUNATUS

FAUSTUS: How happ'd, my friend, you come so late?
    A week is past and gone.
    What bred thy stay? Annoys thy sheep
    the soil they feed upon?

FORTUNATUS: O Faustus, Pade, the flood that fleets
    and runs alongst our grounds,
    Was woxen egal with the banks;
    it had so pass'd his bounds
    That we, not forcing on our flocks,
    for private profit's sake
    And common safety were constrain'd
    both day and night to make

10

    A bay to beat the waters back
    and cause them to recoil,
    For fear lest Padus would have drown'd
    and overflown our soil.

FAUSTUS: Yea, Padus sundry times, when he
    doth swell above his banks
    (As Tityrus can witness well),
    plays many spiteful pranks.   20

FORTUNATUS: Even as thou sayst, perhaps he doth
    when, out of mean and time,
    He boils by force of summer blaze
    and bove the bank doth clime.
    But now the year requires the same,
    for from the frosty hills
    The winter snow descendeth down.
    The mount with water fills
    The slacked floods and doth discharge
    himself; the flood as fast   30
    Conveys his burden and the waves
    to gultching seas doth cast.
    They play the part that men are wont,
    for when the heavy pack
    Doth pinch our lims we cast it on
    our needy neighbor's back.
    But now the channel hath revok'd
    his spouting spring again.

FAUSTUS: O Fortunatus (wonder 'tis
    and monstrous thing to sain),   40
    Though Padus do decrease, our lake
    with greater surge doth swell.
    The city swims aloft the stream,
    a strangy tale to tell.
    The vaults and cellars ditches are;
    in whirries men resort
    Unto the barrels; drawers have
    a joyly glee and sport
    To go by water with their jacks
    and fetch the wine away   50
    By bottles full that erst full dry
    in secret cellar lay.
    On townish men (though happy they
    appear to open sight)
    Yet many times unhappy haps
    and cruel chances light.

FORTUNATUS: From every pleasure doth arise
    displeasure in the end,
    And ay from every blessed hap
    both baleful luck depend.   60

FAUSTUS: Thus much of Padus hath been told;
    now let's recite our love,

Since friendly Venus thereunto
  in each respect doth move.
The weather is full warm, we see;
  the soil is green to view;
The fowls about the field do sing;
  now everything doth mew
And shifts his rusty winter robe.

FORTUNATUS: Thou hast in shepherd's verse   70
Declar'd thy love, but I will gin
  another's to rehearse
(A shepherd whom thou know'st full well)
  to make it plain in sight
What force there rests in Venus' flame
  and shew her stately might.
Amyntas—poor, God wot, and born
  unlucky under sign—
Six calves of egal age possess'd
  and had as many kine.   80
Whom as he drave to pasture with
  a bull that father was
To all the hierd, it was his chance
  by Coytus to pass,
A place where Mincius with his clear
  and silver channel flows
And swiftly all the grassy soil
  and meadows overgoes.
A castle new with battled walls
  there faceth on the flood,   90
High raised up, that Coyte hight
  and on the marish stood.
Here, resting him by river's side
  where grew a goodly vine
That with his boughs did shade the banks
  and waters passing fine,
He stay'd to catch the gliding fish
  with baited hook and line.
'Twas harvest time, the scorching beams
  of scalding Phoebus' rays   100
Had sing'd the soil; the nightingale
  had laid aside her lays.
The ground was with'red in such wise
  as neither flock could feed
Thereon by day nor dew was left
  for grasshoppers at need
By night to moist their cricking chaps.
  Here, whilst he spent the tide
About the river and this fond
  and vain devise appli'd,   110
The bull, first vexed with the wasp
  and next with curs (they say),
And last by filching soldiers mean
  was quite convey'd away,
Not to be found in field. Which when
  the boy had understood,

He gat him to a mountain by
  and cried out agood
For bull unhaply lost of late,
  and all the country sought   120
With greedy, gazing eye. But when
  he saw it booted nought
And that his pain could not prevail,
  his bended bow he took
And painted quiver full of shafts
  and for his beast gan look
Through woods where was no haunted path,
  through every flock and fold,
Through pastures eke to see where he
  his bullock might behold.   130
About Benacus' banks he went,
  and mounts with olive tree
Beset, and places where both fig
  and vine was green to see.
At length a haughty hill he hent
  where did a chapel stand
Of sulphur, and from thence he cast
  his eyes about the land
And overview'd Benacus' bounds
  and all the country round   140
To see where in that coast there were
  his bullock to be found.
It was Sainct Peter's day by course
  and custom of the year;
The youth of every village by
  at afternoon was there,
And underneath a greenish elm
  that shadowed all the soil
At sound of pleasant country pipe
  they danc'd and kept a coil.   150

FAUSTUS: The country cloins cannot be tam'd
  by any kind of art;
Unquiet, they delight in sweat;
  when priest hath done his part
And morning prayers ended are,
  the holy day (when all
Should cease from toil), impatient they
  of rest and hunger fall
To filling of their greedy maws
  and tossing of the cup,   160
And hie to dance as soon as minstrel gins to pipe it up.
They tread it tricksy under tree:
  one skips as he were mad,
Another jumps as 'twere an ox
  unto the altar lad.
The sacred soil (that sin it were
  to turn with toiling share
And cut with crooked culter) they
  cannot endure to spare,   170

But frisk thereon like frantic fools.
    Unwieldy wights, God wot,
With leaden legs and heavy heels
    about the churchyard trot,
And all the day do cry and laugh
    and lay their lips to pot.

FORTUNATUS: Thou dolt, why dost thou chat of this?
    Thyself a rustic born,
The manners of the country cloins
    and rustic rout dost scorn.   180
Thou dost thyself condemn withal;
    thou art thy proper foe.

FAUSTUS: Tush! Of Amyntas let us chat;
    let all these matters go.
I spake it but in sport, my friend,
    I trust you take it so.
He stay'd and, leaning gainst his staff
    ymade of acer tree,
Did stint from travail till the heat
    might somewhat swaged be.   190
O most unhappy, hapless youth!
    in shade a greater flash
Will seize thy corps. Shut up thine eyes,
    lest whilst Diana wash
Her lovely lims in silver stream
    thou naked her espy,
Or lend a list'ning ear unto
    the sirens when they cry.
Thy luck with Narciss' heavy love
    may well compared be,   200
For whilst in well he sought to slake
    his thirst, the more was he
(Unlucky lad) with drought attach'd;
    so whilst thou dost devise
This outward heat to flee, an in-
    ward flame doth thee surprise.
How much had better been, I pray,
    and happier for thee
(Unless the fatal gods would had
    thy dest'ny so to be)   210
To thy remainder flock in field
    to have returned back,
And kept thy kye and let alone
    the bull that was a lack,
And taken in good part the loss
    of that one beast alone,
Than thus, in seeking nought to find,
    thyself to have forgone.

FAUSTUS: O friend, who is not wise become
    when things are at the worst?   220
'Tis naught to give advise in fine
    that should been had at first.

FORTUNATUS: The counsel that comes after all
    things are dispatch'd at last
Is like a show'r of rain that falls
    when sowing-time is past.
Among the rest of all the rout
    a passing proper lass,
A white-hair'd trull of twenty years
    or near about, there was: 230
In stature passing all the rest,
    a gallant girl for hue,
To be compar'd with townish nymphs,
    so fair she was to view.
Her forehead cloth with gold was purl'd
    a little here and there;
With copper clasp about her neck
    a kerchief did she wear
That reached to her breast and paps;
    the wench about her waist   240
A gallant, gaudy riband had
    that girt her body fast.
In petticoat of country stuff
    mockado like she goes;
'Twas plaited brave, the length was such
    it hung nigh to her toes.
As soon as her the youth had spi'd
    he perish'd by and by.
By sight he sucked in the flame
    and [beam] of wanton eye;   250
He swallow'd up the blinding fire
    and in his belly plac'd
The coals that neither waves could quench
    nor rainy imber waste,
No, not inchantments, witches' words,
    it clung so close and fast.
Forgetful he of former flock
    and damage done with waves,
Was all inraged with this flash;
    at night he nought but raves.   260
The season that for quiet sleep
    by Nature pointed was
In bitter plaints and cruel cries
    this burning boy did pass.
I sundry times, for pity's sake,
    his growing flame to stay
And stop the frantic fury, would
    to him full often say:
"O lamentable lad, what god
    hath forc'd thee thus to fare?   270
But sure it was no work of gods
    that bred this bitter care.
Nay, rather 'twas the cruel'st imp
    and spiteful'st fiend of hell
Of those with Lucifer that from
    the skies to dungeon fell,
That nine days' space were tumbling down.

I pray thee make me show
And call to mind wherever yet
   thou any man didst know   280
By foolish love advanc'd to wealth,
   or any office borne,
Or rais'd by means thereof his house,
   or stuff'd his barns with corn.
Didst ever any know that hath
   thereby enlarg'd his bounds,
Increas'd his flock, or for his hierd
   ygotten fruitful grounds?
Among so many countries tell
   me if thou heardst of one.   290
At any time, through all the earth,
   I think was never none.
There are that to their bloody boords
   our crushed bodies bear,
And butcher-like, with greedy teeth,
   our rented corses tear.
There are, I say, whom spiteful fiends
   unto such practise drive,
Yet is there no such kind of men
   so cruel here alive.   300
No country is so barbarous,
   is none so savage sect,
As doth not hate the woman's love
   and fancies fond reject.
Thence brawls are bred, thence chidings
     come,
   thence broiling war and strife,
Yea, often eke with shedding blood
   the cruel loss of life.
By means thereof are cities sack'd
   and bulwarks beat to ground;   310
Moreover, laws and sacred books,
   in iron chains ybound,
Forbid and give us charge to flee
   in any case this love.
With words expressly Cupid they
   and all his toys disprove."
Amyntas had no sooner heard
   the name of laws rehears'd
But answered (for in city he
   a boy was fost'red erst):   320
"Thou goest about to far surmount,
   by giving this advice,
The Catos both and to be thought
   both circumspect and wise.
This error and this madness bears
   each-where a cruel sway.
Man flatt'reth with himself and would
   be counted crafty, ay,
A creature able to foresee;
   yet many a snare and gin   330
And ditch that he himself hath delv'd

the miser falleth in.
He first was free, but to his neck
   himself did frame the yoke;
In servile chain himself he bound
   and bands of freedom broke.
So weighty are those laws (myself
   have seen the books ere this)
As neither predecessors nor
   ourselves can keep iwiss,   340
Nor aftercomers shall observe
   the meaning of the same.
Behold the foolish wit of man
   that thinks such feat to frame,
As to the heavens to aspire
   and hopes at length to get
Among the glist'ring stars aloft
   a stately room and seat.
Perhaps when life is lost he shall
   into a fowl convart,   350
And then his feath'red soul with wings
   to welkin shall depart."
"And then," quod I, "what brawl is this?
   Since God did so devise
The laws, 'twere foul offense for man
   His statutes to despise."

FAUSTUS: These are debates of great affairs
   and weighty things indeed.

FORTUNATUS: Wott'st thou what kind of man I was?
   Though ragged be my weed   360
And I a rustic now to see,
   then, both in force and mind
And looks, I was a roisting lad.
   Thou shouldst not lightly find
A shepherd to be match'd with me.

FAUSTUS: And yet, if bolt upright
Thou stalk with count'nance cast aloft,
   thou wilt appear in sight
A second Marius to be.
   Let barber shave thy face   370
With razor, and in countenance thou
   wilt match with Carbo's grace.

FORTUNATUS: Amyntas would like answer make
   when I his folly blam'd.
But to proceed: "When God had man
   in perfect figure fram'd,
He did repine thereat and thought
   the pleasures he allow'd
Too passing were, and did restrain
   our lust with law, and bow'd   380
Our rebel minds with new decrees,
   as horsemen use to tie

Their jades with brakes about the jaws
   for fear they go awry.
Herein love makes me shew my mind
   and fancy freely tell:
Whoso debars his wife to go
   in common doth not well,
But envious may accompted be.
   But yet this spiteful hate   390
The cloak of honest custom doth
   in some respect abate;
For whilst each man unto himself
   (not forcing common good)
Reserv'd his private joys and to
   his marriage bargain stood,
A common custom is incroach'd
   that honesty is hight.
God saith to make such peevish laws
   'twas mad and foolish spight.   400
A hateful thing is love, God wot,
   and pleasure spiteful eke."
Then I, no longer daring to

   the youth athwart to speak,
Shook off the raging, wanton boy
   that seem'd bereft of sense,
And on my former voyage I
   eftsoon departed thence.

FAUSTUS: Seest how this vile affection fond
   our inward eyes of mind   410
Shuts up in such despiteous sort
   and makes us men so blind
As headlong we to errors run
   and to deceiptful snare,
Till time we be in wilful trap
   and nipp'd with cutting care?

FORTUNATUS: O dost thou see, friend Faustus, how
   the pitchy clouds upon
Mount Baldus to a cluster go
   and join themselves in one?   420
It hails! For fear our cattle be
   dispersed, let's be gone.

FROM EPITAPHS, EPIGRAMS, SONGS, AND SONNETS (1570)

To the Reader

Here have I, gentle reader, according to promise in my translation, given thee a few sonnets, the unripe seeds of my barren brain, to pleasure and recreate thy weary mind and troubled head withal, trusting that thou wilt not loth the bestowing thy time at vacant hours in perusing the same. Weighing that for thy solace alone (the bounden duty which I owed the noble countess [of Warwick] reserved) I under- 10 took this slender toil, and not for any pleasure I did myself in penning thereof. As I deem thou canst not, so do I hope thou wilt not mislike it at all. But if there be anything herein that may offend thee, re- fuse it; read and peruse the rest with patience; let not the misliking of one member procure thee rashly to condemn the whole. I stand to thy judgment; I ex- pect thy equity. Read the good and reject the evil; yea, rather condemn it to perpetual silence. For so would I wish thee to deal with unworthy books. But assuredly there is nothing in this whole slender 20 volume that was meant amiss of me, the writer, how- soever the letter go in thy judgment that art the reader. Whatsoever I have penned, I write not to this purpose, that any youthly head should follow or pursue such frail affections or taste of amorous bait; but by mere fiction of these fantasies, I would warn (if I might) all tender age to flee that fond and filthy affection of poisoned and unlawful love. Let this be a glass and mirror for them to gaze upon; the sooner may I, I trust, prevail in my persuasion, for that my- 30

self am of their years and disposition. And as I am not the first that in this sort hath written and imploy'd his time, so shall I not be the last that, without desart perhaps, shall be misdeemed for attempting the same. But let those curious knights cast an eye to home and look well about whether they themselves are blameless, or as well worthy reproach as others. This done and my intent considered, hoping of thy curtesy, I end, always ready to pleasure thee by my pains, wishing unto thee, that art the patient reader, as to myself, the writer and thy very friend.

George Turbervile

THE LOVER EXTOLLETH THE SINGULAR BEAUTY OF HIS LADY

Let Myron muse at Nature's passing might
And quite resign his pievish painter's right,
For sure he cannot frame her featur'd shape
That for her face excels the Greekish rape.

Let Zeuxis' grapes not make him proud at all,
Though fowls for them did skirr against a wall;
For if he should assay my love to paint,
His art would fail, his cunning fist would faint.

Let Praxitel presume with pencil rude
Base things to blaze, the people to delude;   10
Her featur'd lims to draw let him not dare
That with the fair Diana may compare.

Though Venus' form Apelles made so well
As Greece did judge the painter to excel,
Yet let not that enbold the Greek to grave
Her shape that beauty's praise deserves to have.

For Nature, when she made her, did entend
To paint a piece that no man might amend,
A pattern for the rest that after should
Be made by hand or cast in cunning mould.   20

VERSE IN PRAISE OF LORD HENRY HOWARD, EARL OF SURREY

What should I speak in praise of Surrey's skill
Unless I had a thousand tongues at will?
No one is able to depaint at full
The flowing fountain of his sacred skull;
Whose pen approv'd what wit he had in mue,
Where such a skill in making sonnets grew,
Each word in place with such a sleight is couch'd,
Each thing whereof he treats so firmly touch'd,
As Pallas seem'd within his noble breast
To have sojourn'd and been a daily guest.   10
Our mother tongue by him hath got such light
As ruder speech thereby is banish'd quite;
Reprove him not for fancies that he wrought,
For fame thereby, and nothing else, he sought.
What though his verse with pleasant toys are fright?
Yet was his Honor's life a lamp of light.
A mirror he the simple sort to train,
That ever beat his brain for Britain's gain.
By him the nobles had their virtues blaz'd
When spiteful death their Honors' lives had raz'd. 20
Each that in life had well deserved aught
By Surrey's means an endless fame hath caught.
To quite his boon and ay well-meaning mind
Whereby he did his sequel seem to bind,
Though want of skill to silence me procures,
I write of him whose fame for ay endures,
A worthy wight, a noble for his race,
A learned lord that had an earl's place.

THE LOVER TO THE THAMES OF LONDON TO FAVOR HIS LADY PASSING THEREON

Thou stately stream that, with the swelling tide,
Gainst London walls incessantly dost beat,
Thou Thames, I say, where barge and boat doth ride
And snow-white swans do fish for needful meat,
   Whenso my love of force or pleasure shall
Flit on thy flood as custom is to do,
Seek not with dread her courage to appal,
But calm thy tide and smoothly let it go
As she may joy, arriv'd to siker shore,
To pass the pleasant stream she did before.   10
   To welter up and surge in wrathful wise
(As did the flood where Helle drenched was)

Would but procure defame of thee to rise;
Wherefore let all such ruthless rigor pass,
So wish I that thou mayst with bending side
Have power for ay in wonted gulf to glide.

THE LOVER EXHORTETH HIS LADY TO TAKE TIME WHILE TIME IS

Though brave your beauty be
   and feature passing fair,
Such as Apelles to depaint
   might utterly dispair,
Yet drowsy, drooping age,
   incroaching on apace,
With pensive plow will raze your hue
   and beauty's beams deface.
Wherefore in tender years
   how crooked age doth haste   10
Revoke to mind, so shall you not
   your mind consume in waste.
Whilst that you may, and youth
   in you is fresh and green,
Delight yourself, for years to flit
   as fickle flouds are seen;
For water slipped by
   may not be call'd again,
And to revoke forepassed hours
   were labor lost in vain.   20
Take time whilst time applies;
   with nimble foot it goes,
Nor to compare with passed prime
   thy after-age suppose.
The holts that now are hoar,
   both bud and bloom I saw;
I ware a garland of the brier
   that puts me now in awe.
The time will be when thou
   that dost thy friends defy   30
A cold and crooked beldame shalt
   in lothsome cabin lie.
Nor with such nightly brawls
   thy postern gate shall sound,
Nor roses straw'd afront thy door
   in dawning shall be found.
How soon are corpses, Lord,
   with filthy furrows fill'd!
How quickly beauty, brave of late,
   and seemly shape is spill'd!   40
Even thou, that from thy youth
   to have been so, wilt swear,
With turn of hand, in all thy head
   shalt have gray-powd'red hear.
The snakes with shifted skins
   their lothsome age do way;
The buck doth hang his head on pale
   to live a longer day.

Your good without recure
doth pass; receive the flow'r,   50
Which, if you pluck not from the stalk,
will fall within this hour.

THAT DEATH IS NOT SO MUCH TO BE FEARED AS DAILY DISEASES ARE

What? Is 't not folly for to dread
and stand of death in fear,
That mother is of quiet rest,
and griefs away doth wear,
That brings release to want of wealth
and poor, oppressed wights?
He comes but once to mortal men,
but once for all he smites.
Was never none that twice hath felt
of cruel death the knife.   10
But other griefs and pining pains
do linger on the life,
And oftentimes on selfsame corse
with furious fits molest,
When death, by one dispatch'd of life,
doth bring the soul to rest.

TO HIS FRIEND RIDING TO LONDONWARD

As Troylus did rejoice
when Cressid yielded grace
And deigned him, from service true,

so near her heart to place,
So have I joy'd, my dear,
for friendship which I found,
And love requited with the like,
which cur'd my careful wound.
As he full shrilly shright
and dool'd his woful chance,   10
On Greekish steed from Trojan town
when Cressid gan to prance
And leave the liked soil
where did sojourn her joy,
I mean the worthy Troylus,
and loving'st youth in Troy;
Even so I wail at thy
departure, would thou wist,
And out I cry, a wretched wight
that thought himself yblist.   20
O London, lothsome lodge,
why dost thou now procure
My love to leave this pleasant soil
that hath my heart in cure?
Since needs it must be so,
gainsend her home in haste;
Let her retire with harmless health
that sickless hence is past.
Yield me a good account
of her that is my joy,   30
And send her to her Troylus
that longs for her in Troy.

GEORGE GASCOIGNE

In 1573, when Gascoigne was serving as a soldier in the Low Countries (perhaps to escape an investigation by the Privy Council at the urging of his many creditors), there appeared a collection of prose and verse called *A Hundreth Sundry Flowers Bound Up in One Small Posy,* the titlepage of which, pushing the metaphor hard, explains that the contents had been "gathered partly by translation in the fine outlandish gardens of Euripides, Ovid, Petrarch, Ariosto, and others; and partly by invention out of our own fruitful orchards in England." In a studiously mystifying epistle the printer (Richard Smith) disclaims responsibility for the collection, and professes ignorance of the compiler's identity, thus discharging himself of any "misliking as the graver sort of gray-heared judges might perhaps conceive in the publication of these pleasant pamphlets." The book itself, once regarded as a miscellany but definitely shown by Professor Prouty to be Gascoigne's work, falls into three parts: two plays, *Jocasta* and *Supposes,* translated from Euripides and Ariosto; an interesting if salacious novel, *A Discourse of*

the Adventures Passed by Master F. J., that, unlike the *novelle* of Painter and his imitators, employs an English setting for an extraordinary novel of character rather than of sensational incident; a hundred poems (hence the title of the volume) of which twenty-one are ascribed to Gascoigne and the rest to ostensibly unknown authors, and a rambling set of semi-autobiographical stanzas called "The Delectable History of Dan Bartholmew of Bath." The titlepage and the printer's epistle tell us nothing about the author except that a certain G. T. had lent a manuscript of pieces in prose and verse to H. W., who in turn had requested his friend A. B. to have the work printed.

Perhaps this hocus-pocus had the desired effect of concealing Gascoigne's identity against the outcry raised by some allegedly personal allusions—but not for long, since Gascoigne tacitly acknowledged authorship of the *Flowers* two years later. In 1575 he published *The Posies of George Gascoigne Corrected, Perfected, and Augmented,* perhaps the most interesting literary work between Tottel's *Miscellany* and *The Shepherd's Calendar.* In an epistle "To the Reverend Divines" Gascoigne laments the offensive nature of parts of the *Flowers* and asserts the piety of his intentions; he then recasts the 1573 volume so as to bring out its moral utility. Some of the earlier poems are omitted, and the rest (as is explained in an epistle "To All Young Gentlemen") are rearranged under the weird rubrics of Flowers (works, "to be smelled unto," of "rare invention"), Herbs ("more profitable than pleasant"), and Weeds (pieces of questionable merit, but "none so vile or stinking but that it hath in it some virtue if it be rightly handled"). In addition, the *Posies* contains commendatory poems by no less than nineteen contemporaries, a considerably bowdlerized version of *Master F. J.* (now passed off as a translation from a fictitious Italian named Bartello and refurbished with Italian characters and place-names), a long autobiographical poem based upon Gascoigne's recent soldiering ("Dulce bellum inexpertis"), and

Certain Notes of Instruction, a brisk little *catalogue raisonné* of metrical forms that is the earliest critical treatise on prosody in the language (see pp. 596–99).

The Steel Glass, an interesting example of type-satire in blank verse addressed to Lord Grey of Wilton (who was later to be Spenser's patron), was first published, a year before Gascoigne's death, with *The Complaint of Philomene,* a lugubrious retelling of the classic myth that is possibly an allegory of the author's own mishaps. Certainly the personal element in *The Steel Glass* is obvious to all who run and read.

Our texts are based upon *A Hundreth sundrie Flowres bounde up in one small Poesie,* 1573 (STC 11635); *The Posies of George Gascoigne Esquire. Corrected, perfected, and augmented,* 1575 (STC 11636); and *The Steele Glas. A Satyre . . . togither with the Complainte of Phylomene,* 1576 (STC 11645).

FROM THE POSIES (1575)

To the Reverend Divines unto Whom These *Posies* Shall Happen to Be Presented. . .

Right reverend, I have thought it my part, before I wade further in publishing of these *Posies,* to lay open before your grave judgments as well the cause which presently moveth me to present them as also the depth and secrets of some conceits which, being passed in clouds and figurative speeches, might percase both be offensive to your gravity and perilous to my credit.

It is very near two years past since (I being in Holland in service with the virtuous Prince of Orange) the most part of these *Posies* were imprinted; and now at my return I find that some of them have not only been offensive for sundry wanton speeches and lascivious phrases, but further I hear that the same have been doubtfully construed, and, therefore, scandalous. . . .

It is most true—and I call heaven and earth to witness—that I never received of the printer, or of any other, one groat or penny for the first copies of these *Posies.* True it is that I was not unwilling the same should be imprinted, and that not of a vainglorious desire to be thought a pleasant poet, neither yet of a light mind to be counted a cunning lover. For though in youth I was often overhardy to put my name in balance of doubtful judgments, yet now I am become so bashful that I could rather be content to leese the praise of my follies than to hazard the misconceit of the grave and gray-headed judges. But to confess a truth unto you, right reverend (with

whom I may not dissemble in cases which so generally do touch all men), I was the rather contented to see them imprinted for these sundry considerations.

First, for that I have seen diverse authors (both learned and well learned) which, after they have both reformed their lives and converted their studies, have not yet disdained to read the poems which they let pass their pens in youth. For it seemeth unto me that in all ages poetry hath been not only permitted, but also it hath been thought a right good and excellent quality.

Next unto this, I have always been of opinion that it is not unpossible either in poems or in prose to write both compendiously and perfectly in our English tongue. And therefore, although I challenge not unto myself the name of an English poet, yet may the reader find out in my writings that I have more faulted in keeping the old English words (*quamvis iam obsoleta*) than in borrowing of other languages such epithets and adjectives as smell of the inkhorn.

Thirdly, as I seek advancement by virtue, so was I desirous that there might remain in public record some pledge or token of those gifts wherewith it hath pleased the Almighty to endue me, to the end that thereby the virtuous might be incouraged to employ my pen in some exercise which might tend both to my preferment and to the profit of my country. . . .

Fourthly, because I had written sundry things which could not chuse but content the learned and godly reader, therefore I hoped the same should serve as undoubted proof that I had laid aside vanities and delighted to exercise my pen in moral discourses; at least the one passing, cheek by cheek, with the other must of necessity persuade both the learned and the light-minded that I could as well sow good grain as grains or draff. And I thought not meet, being intermingled as they were, to cast away a whole bushel of good seed for two or three grains of darnel or cockle.

Lastly, I persuaded myself that as in the better sort of the same I should purchase good liking with the honorable aged, so even in the worst sort I might yet serve as a mirror for unbridled youth to avoid those perils which I had passed. For little may he do which hath escaped the rock or the sands if he cannot waft with his hand to them that come after him.

These considerations, right reverend, did first move me to consent that these poems should pass in print. . . .

And for full proof of mine earnest zeal in God's service I require of you, reverend, most instantly that, if hereby my skill seem sufficient to wade in matters of greater importance, you will then vouchsafe to employ me accordingly. Surely you shall find me no less ready to undertake a whole year's travail in any work which you shall think me able to overcome than I have been willing heretofore to spend three hours in penning of an amorous sonnet. Even so being desirous that all men generally, and you especially, should conceive of me as I mean, I have thus far troubled your learned eyes with this plain epistle, written for my purgation, in matters which else might both have offended you and given great battery to the ramparts of my poor credit. The God of peace vouchsafe to govern and product you, and me, and all his in quiet of conscience and strength of spirit. Amen. From my poor house at Walthamstow in the Forest this last day of January, 1574 [i.e. 1575].

To All Young Gentlemen, and Generally to the Youth of England. . .

. . . To speak English, it is your using, my lusty gallants, or misusing of these *Posies* that may make me praised or dispraised for publishing of the same. For if you, where you may learn to avoid the subtile sands of wanton desire, will run upon the rocks of unlawful lust, then great is your folly, and greater will grow my rebuke. If you, where you might gather wholesome herbs to cure your sundry infirmities, will spend the whole day in gathering of sweet-smelling posies, much will be the time that you shall misspend, and much more the harm that you shall heap upon my head. Or if you will rather beblister your hands with a nettle than comfort your senses by smelling to the pleasant marjoram, then wanton is your pastime, and small will be your profit.

I have here presented you with three sundry sorts of posies: *Flowers, Herbs,* and *Weeds.* In which division I have not meant that only the *Flowers* are to be smelled unto, nor that only the *Weeds* are to be rejected. I term some *Flowers* bycause, being indeed invented upon a very light occasion, they have yet in them, in my judgment, some rare invention and method before not commonly used. And therefore, being more pleasant than profitable, I have named them *Flowers.*

The second, being indeed moral discourses and reformed inventions, and therefore more profitable than pleasant, I have named *Herbs.*

The third, being *Weeds,* might seem to some judgments neither pleasant nor yet profitable, and therefore meet to be cast away. But as many weeds are right medicinable, so may you find in this none so vile or stinking but that it hath in it some virtue if it be rightly handled. Marry, you must take heed how you use them. For if you delight to put hemlock in your fellow's pottage you may chance both to poison him and bring yourself in peril. But if you take example by the harms of others who have eaten it before you, then may you chance to become so wary that you will look advisedly on all the perceley that you gather, lest amongst the same one branch of hemlock might annoy you. . . .

The scope of mine intent, and the mark whereat I shoot, is double. I mean grounded upon two sundry causes: the one that, being indebted unto the world (at the least five thousand days very vainly spent) I may yield him yet some part of mine account in these poems. Wherein as he may find great diversity both in style and sense, so may the good be incouraged to set me on work at last, though it were noon before I sought service. The other reason is that, bicause I have, to mine own great detriment, misspent my golden time, I may serve as ensample to the youthful gentlemen of England, that they run not upon the rocks which have brought me to shipwrack. Beware, therefore, lusty gallants, how you smell to these *Posies.* And learn you to use the talent which I have highly abused. Make me your mirror. And if hereafter you see me recover mine estate, or reedify the decayed walls of my youth, then begin you sooner to build some foundation which may beautify your palace. If you see me sink in distresses (notwithstanding that you judge me quick of capacity), then learn you to maintain yourselves swimming in prosperity, and eschew betimes the whirlpool of misgovernment. . . .

From my poor house at Walthamstow in the Forest, the second of January, 1575.

Flowers

THE ANATOMY OF A LOVER

To make a lover known by plain anatomy,
You lovers all that list, beware! Lo, here behold you me,
Who, though mine only looks your pity well might move,
Yet every part shall play his part to paint the pangs of love—
If first my feeble head have so much matter left,
If fancy's raging force have not his feeble skill bereft.
These locks that hang unkempt, these hollow, dazzled eyes,
These chattering teeth, this trembling tongue well-tewed with careful cries,
These wan and wrinkled cheeks, well-wash'd with waves of wo,
May stand for pattern of a ghost whereso this carcass go.   10
These shoulders they sustain the yoke of heavy care,
And on my bruised, broken back the burden must I bear.
These arms quite brawn-fall'n are with beating on my breast.
This right hand weary is to write; this left hand craveth rest.
These sides enclose the forge where sorrow plays the smith,
And hot desire hath kindled fire to work this metal with.
The anvil is my heart; my thoughts they strike the stroke;
My lights and lungs like bellows blow, and sighs ascend for smoke.
My secret parts are so with secret sorrow soaken
As, for the secret shame thereof, deserves not to be spoken.   20
My thighs, my knees, my legs, and last of all my feet
To serve a lover's turn are so unable and unmeet
That scarce they sustain up this restless body well,
Unless it be to see the bower wherein my love doth dwell;
And there by sight eftsoon to feed my gazing eye,
And so content my hungry corps till dolors do me die.
Yet for a just reward of love so dearly bought
I pray you say, "Lo, this was he whom love had worn to nought."
                              Ever or Never

———————————

THE ARRAIGNMENT OF A LOVER

At Beauty's bar as I did stand,
When false Suspect accused me,
"George," quod the judge, "hold up thy hand;
Thou art arraign'd of flattery.
Tell, therefore, how thou wilt be tried.
Whose judgment here wilt thou abide?"

"My lord," quod I, "this lady here,
Whom I esteem above the rest,
Doth know my guilt if any were;
Wherefore her doom shall please me best.   10
Let her be judge and juror both
To try me guiltless by mine oath."

Quod Beauty, "No, it fitteth not,
A prince herself to judge the cause.
Will is our justice, well you wot,
Appointed to discuss our laws.

If you will guiltless seem to go,
God and your country quit you so."

Then Craft, the cryer, call'd a quest,
Of whom was Falsehood foremost fere;   20
A pack of pickthanks were the rest
Which came false witness for to bear.
The jury such, the judge unjust,
Sentence was said I should be truss'd.

Jealous, the jailor, bound me fast
To hear the verdict of the bill.
"George," quod the judge, "now thou art cast,
Thou must go hence to Heavy Hill
And there be hang'd, all but the head.
God rest thy soul when thou art dead!"   30

Down fell I then upon my knee
All flat before Dame Beauty's face,

And cried, "Good lady, pardon me
Which here appeal unto your grace!
You know if I have been untrue
It was in too much praising you.

"And though this judge do make such haste
To shed with shame my guiltless blood,
Yet let your pity first be plac'd
To save the man that meant you good.   40
So shall you shew yourself a queen,
And I may be your servant seen."

Quod Beauty, "Well, bicause I guess
What thou dost mean henceforth to be—
Although thy faults deserve no less
Than justice here hath judged thee—
Wilt thou be bound to stint all strife
And be true prisoner all thy life?"

"Yea, madame," quod I, "that I shall.
Lo, Faith and Truth my sureties!"   50
"Why, then," quod she, "come when I call;
I ask no better warrantise."
Thus am I Beauty's bounden thrall
At her command when she doth call.
                        Ever or Never

A STRANGE PASSION OF A LOVER

Amid my bale I bathe in bliss,
I swim in heaven, I sink in hell;
I find amends for every miss,
And yet my moan no tongue can tell.
I live and love (what would you more?)
As never lover liv'd before.

I laugh sometimes with little lust;
So jest I oft and feel no joy;
Mine ease is builded all on trust,
And yit mistrust breeds mine annoy.   10
I live and lack, I lack and have,
I have and miss the thing I crave.

These things seem strange, yet are they true.
Believe me, sweet. my state is such,
One pleasure which I would eschew
Both slakes my grief and breeds my grutch.
So doth one pain which I would shun
Renew my joys where grief begun.

Then like the lark that pass'd the night
In heavy sleep with cares oppress'd,   20
Yit when she spies the pleasant light,
She sends sweet notes from out her breast;

So sing I now because I think
How joys approach when sorrows shrink.

And as fair Philomene, again,
Can watch and sing when other sleep,
And taketh pleasure in her pain,
To wray the wo that makes her weep;
So sing I now for to bewray
The loathsome life I lead alway.   30

The which to thee, dear wench, I write,
That know'st my mirth but not my moan.
I pray God grant thee deep delight
To live in joys when I am gone.
I cannot live—it will not be:
I die to think to part from thee.
                        Ferendo natura

THE LULLABY OF A LOVER

Sing lullaby, as women do,
Wherewith they bring their babes to rest,
And lullaby can I sing too
As womanly as can the best.
With lullaby they still the child,
And if I be not much beguil'd,
Full many wanton babes have I
Which must be still'd with lullaby.

First, lullaby my youthful years,
It is now time to go to bed,   10
For crooked age and hoary hears
Have won the haven within my head;
With lullaby, then, youth be still,
With lullaby, content thy will,
Since courage quails and comes behind,
Go sleep, and so beguile thy mind.

Next, lullaby my gazing eyes,
Which wonted were to glance apace,
For every glass may now suffice
To shew the furrows in my face;   20
With lullaby, then, wink awhile,
With lullaby, your looks beguile,
Let no fair face nor beauty bright
Entice you eft with vain delight.

And lullaby, my wanton will,
Let reason's rule now reign thy thought,
Since all too late I find by skill
How dear I have thy fancies bought;
With lullaby, now take thine ease,
With lullaby, thy doubts appease;   30
For trust to this, if thou be still,
My body shall obey thy will.

Eke, lullaby my loving boy,
My little Robin, take thy rest;
Since age is cold and nothing coy,
Keep close thy coin, for so is best;
With lullaby, be thou content,
With lullaby, thy lusts relent;
Let others pay which have mo pence,
Thou art too poor for such expense.   40

Thus lullaby, my youth, mine eyes,
My will, my ware, and all that was!
I can no mo delays devise,
But welcome pain, let pleasure pass;
With lullaby, now take your leave,
With lullaby, your dreams deceive,
And when you rise with waking eye,
Remember, then, this lullaby.

Ever or Never

GASCOIGNE'S GOODNIGHT

When thou hast spent the ling'ring day in pleasure and delight,
Or after toil and weary way dost seek to rest at night,
Unto thy pains or pleasures past add this one labor yet,
Ere sleep close up thine eye too fast: do not thy God forget.
But search within thy secret thoughts what deeds did thee befall,
And, if thou find amiss in ought, to God for mercy call.
Yea, though thou find nothing amiss which thou canst call to mind,
Yet evermore remember this, there is the more behind;
And think, how well soever it be that thou hast spent the day,
It came of God, and not of thee, so to direct thy way.   10
Thus if thou try thy daily deeds, and pleasure in this pain,
Thy life shall cleanse thy corn from weeds, and thine shall be the gain.
But if thy sinful, sluggish eye will venter for to wink
Before thy wading will may try how far thy soul may sink,
Beware and wake! for else thy bed, which soft and smooth is made,
May heap more harm upon thy head than blows of en'my's blade.
Thus if this pain procure thine ease, in bed as thou dost lie,
Perhaps it shall not God displease to sing thus soberly:
"I see that sleep is lent me here to ease my weary bones,
As Death at last shall eke appear to ease my grievous groans.   20
My daily sports, my paunch full fed, have caus'd my drowsy eye,
As careless life in quiet led might cause my soul to die.
The stretching arms, the yawning breath, which I to bedward use,
Are patterns of the pangs of Death when life will me refuse;
And of my bed each sundry part in shadows doth resemble
The sundry shapes of Death, whose dart shall make my flesh to tremble.
My bed itself is like the grave, my sheets the winding-sheet,
My clothes the mold which I must have to cover me most meet.
The hungry fleas, which frisk so fresh, to worms I can compare,
Which greedily shall gnaw my flesh and leave the bones full bare.   30
The waking cock that early crows to wear the night away
Puts in my mind the trump that blows before the latter day.
And as I rise up lustily when sluggish sleep is past,
So hope I to rise joyfully to judgment at the last.
Thus will I wake, thus will I sleep, thus will I hope to rise,
Thus will I neither wail nor weep, but sing in godly wise.
My bones shall in this bed remain, my soul in God shall trust,
By whom I hope to rise again from death and earthly dust."

Haud ictus sapio

THE FRUITS OF WAR, WRITTEN UPON THIS
THEME, *DULCE BELLUM INEXPERTIS,* AND IT
WAS WRITTEN BY PIECEMEAL AT SUNDRY
TIMES AS THE AUCTHOR HAD VACANT
LEISURES FROM SERVICE, BEING BEGUN AT
DELF IN HOLLAND. . . .

To write of war and wot not what it is,
Nor ever yet could march where war was made,
May well be thought a work begun amiss,
A rash attempt, in worthless verse to wade,
To tell the trial, knowing not the trade;
Yet such a vein even now doth feed my muse
That in this theme I must some labor use.

And herewithal I cannot but confess
How unexpert I am in feats of war,
For more than writing doth the same express;   10
I may not boast of any cruel jar,
Nor vaunt to see full valiant facts from far.
I have nor been in Turkey, Denmark, Greece,
Ne yet in Colch to win a golden fleece.

But natheless I somewhat read in writ
Of high exploits by martial men ydone,
And thereupon I have presumed yet
To take in hand this poem now begun,
Wherein I mean to tell what race they run
Who follow drums before they know the dub,   20
And brag of Mars before they feel his club. . . .

The poets old in their fond fables feign
That mighty Mars is god of war and strife;
These astronomers think where Mars doth reign
That all debate and discord must be rife;
Some think Bellona goddess of that life,
So that some one and some another judge
To be the cause of every grievous grudge. . . .

Well, then, let see what saith the common voice;
These old-said saws of war what can they say?   30
Who list to harken to their whisp'ring noise
May hear them talk and tattle day by day
That princes' pride is cause of war alway.
Plenty brings pride, pride plea, plea pine, pine peace,
Peace plenty, and so, say they, they never cease.

And though it have been thought as true as steel
Which people prate and preach above the rest,
Yet could I never any reason feel
To think *Vox populi vox Dei est.*
As for my skill I compt him but a beast   40
Which trusteth truth to dwell in common speech,
Where every lourden will become a leech. . . .

And, for my part, my fancy for to wright,
I say that war is even the scourge of God,
Tormenting such as dwell in princely plight
Yet not regard the reaching of his rod,
Whose deeds and duties oftentimes are odd,
Who range at randon, jesting at the just,
As though they reign'd to do even what they lust.

Whom neither plague can pull into remorse,   50
Nor dearth can draw to mend that is amiss;
Within whose hearts no pity findeth force,
Nor right can rule to judge what reason is;
Whom sickness salveth not, nor bale brings bliss;
Yet can high Jove, by waste of bloody war,
Send schoolmaisters to teach them what they are. . . .

But if war be, as I have said before,
God's scourge which doth both prince and people tame,
Then warn the wiser sort by learned lore
To flee from that which bringeth naught but blame,   60
And let men compt it grief, and not a game,
To feel the burden of God's mighty hand
When he concludes in judgment for to stand.

O prince, be pleas'd with thine own diadem;
Confine thy countries with their common bounds;
Enlarge no land, ne stretch thou not thy stream;
Pen up thy pleasure in Repentance' pounds
Lest thine own sword be cause of all thy wounds;
Claim nought by war where title is not good.
It is God's scourge. Then, prince, beware thy blood!   70

O dukes, O earls, O barons, knights, and squires,
Keep you content with that which is your own;
Let bravery never bring you in his briers;
Seek not to mow where you no seed have sown;
Let not your neighbor's house be overthrown
To make your garden straight, round, even, and
     square,
For that is war, God's scourge. Then, lords, beware!

O bishops, deacons, prelates, priests, and all,
Strive not for tithes, for glebeland, nor for fees,
For polling Peter pence, for popish pall,   80
For proud pluralities, nor new degrees;
And though you think it lubberlike to leese,
Yet should you lend that one-half of your coat.
Then, priests, leave war, and learn to sing that note.

O lawless lawyers, stop your too-long nose
Wherewith you smell your needy neighbors' lack;
Which can pretend a title to suppose,
And in your rules uplandish louts can rack

Till you have brought their wealth unto the wrack.
This is plain war, although you term it strife,   90
Which God will scourge. Then, lawyers, leave this life.

O merchants, make more conscience in an oath;
Sell not your silks by danger nor deceit;
Break not your banks with coin and credit both;
Heap not your hoards by wiliness of weight;
Set not to sale your subtilties by sleight;
Breed no debate by bargaining for days,
For God will scourge such guiles ten thousand ways.

O country clowns, your closes see you keep
With hedge and ditch, and mark your mead with
        mears;   100
Let not Dame Flattery in your bosom creep
To tell a fitten in your landlord's ears,
And say the ground is his, as plain appears,
Where you but set the bounders forth too far.
Ply you the plow, and be no cause of war.

O common people, claim nothing but right,
And cease to seek that you have never lost;
Strive not for trifles; make not all your might
To put your neighbor's purse to needless cost.
When your own gilt is spent, then farewell frost.   110
The lawyer gains, and leads a lordly life,
Whiles you leese all and beg to stint your strife.

Knew kings and princes what a pain it were
To win mo realms than any wit can wield,
To pine in hope, to fret as fast for fear,
To see their subjects murd'red in the field,
To loose at last, and then themselves to yield,
To break sound sleep with cark and inward care,
They would love peace and bid war well to fare. . . .

Herbs

HE WROTE TO THE SAME FRIEND FROM EXCESTER THIS SONNET FOLLOWING

A hundreth suns—in course but not in kind—
Can witness well that I possess no joy.
The fear of death which fretteth in my mind
Consumes my heart with dread of dark annoy.
And for each sun a thousand broken sleeps
Devide my dreams with fresh recourse of cares.
The youngest sister sharp her shear she keeps
To cut my thread, and thus my life it wears.
Yet let such days, such thousand restless nights,
Spit forth their spite, let Fates eke show their force!   10
Death's daunting dart, whereso his buffet lights,
Shall shape no change within my friendly corse.
But dead or live, in heaven, in earth, in hell
I will be thine whereso my carcass dwell.
                Si fortunatus infoelix

HE WROTE UNTO A SCOTTISH DAME WHOM HE CHOSE FOR HIS MISTRESS IN THE FRENCH COURT AS FOLLOWETH

Lady, receive, receive in gracious wise
This ragged verse, these rude, ill-scribbled lines,
Too base an object for your heavenly eyes.
For he that writes, his freedom, lo! resigns
Into your hands, and freely yields as thrall
His sturdy neck, erst subject to no yoke,
But bending now, and headlong prest to fall
Before your feet—such force hath beauty's stroke.
Since, then, mine eyes, which scorn'd our English dames,
In forrain courts have chosen you for fair,   10
Let be this verse true token of my flames,
And do not drench your own in deep despair.
Only I crave, as I nill change for new,
That you vouchsafe to think your servant true.
                Si fortunatus infoelix

Weeds

IN PRAISE OF A GENTLEWOMAN WHO, THOUGH SHE WERE NOT VERY FAIR, YET WAS SHE AS HARD-FAVORED AS MIGHT BE

If men may credit give to true-reported fames,
Who doubts but stately Rome had store of lusty, loving dames?
Whose ears have been so deaf as never yet heard tell
How far the fresh Pompeia for beauty did excel?
And golden Marcus, he that sway'd the Romain sword,
Bare witness of Boemia by credit of his word.
What need I mo rehearse, since all the world did know
How high the floods of beauty's blaze within those walls did flow?
And yet in all that choice a worthy Romain knight,

Antonius, who conquered proud Egypt by his might,   10
Not all to please his eye but most to ease his mind
Chose Cleopatra for his love, and left the rest behind.
A wondrous thing to read: in all his victory
He snapp'd but her for his own share, to please his fantasy.
She was not fair, God wot! The country breeds none bright;
Well may we judge her skin the foil, because her teeth were white.
Percase her lovely looks some praises did deserve,
But brown, I dare be bold, she was, for so the soil did serve.
And could Antonius forsake the fair in Rome?
To love his nutbrown lady best, was this an equal doom?   20
I dare well say dames there did bear him deadly grudge;
His sentence had been shortly said if Faustine had been judge.
For this I dare avow—without vaunt be it spoke—
So brave a knight as Antony held all their necks in yoke.
I leave not Lucrece out, believe in her who list;
I think she would have lik'd his lure and stooped to his fist.
What mov'd the chieftain then to link his liking thus?
I would some Romain dame were here the question to discuss.
But [I that] read her life do find therein by fame
How clear her curtesy did shine in honor of her name.   30
Her bounty did excel, her truth had never peer,
Her lovely looks, her pleasant speech, her lusty, loving cheer,
And all the worthy gifts that ever yet were found
Within this good Egyptian queen did seem for to abound.
Wherefore he worthy was to win the golden fleece
Which scorn'd the blazing stars in Rome to conquer such a piece.
And she to quite his love, in spite of dreadful death,
Enshrin'd with snakes within his tomb did yield her parting breath.

ALLEGORIA

If fortune favor'd him, then may that man rejoice
And think himself a happy man by hap of happy choice,   40
Who loves and is belov'd of one as good, as true,
As kind as Cleopatra was, and yet more bright of hue.
Her eyes as gray as glass, her teeth as white as milk,
A ruddy lip, a dimpled chin, a skin as smooth as silk.
A wight (what could you more?) that may content man's mind,
And hath supplies for ev'ry want that any man can find;
And may himself assure, when hence his life shall pass,
She will be stung to death with snakes, as Cleopatra was.
                    Si fortunatus infoelix

FROM THE STEEL GLASS. A SATIRE (1576)

. . . For whiles I mark this weak and wretched world
Wherein I see how every kind of man
Can flatter still, and yet deceives himself,
I seem to muse from whence such error springs,
Such gross conceits, such mists of dark mistake,
Such surquedry, such weening overwell
(And yet, indeed, such dealings too too bad);
And as I stretch my weary wits to weigh

The cause thereof, and whence it should proceed,
My batt'red brains (which now be shrewdly bruis'd   10
With cannon shot of much misgovernment)
Can spy no cause but only one conceit
Which makes me think the world goeth still awry.

I see and sigh (bycause it makes me sad)
That peevish pride doth all the world possess;

And every wight will have a looking-glass
To see himself, yet so he seeth him not.
Yea, shall I say, a glass of common glass,
Which glist'reth bright and shews a seemly shew,
Is not enough: the days are past and gone   20
That beryl glass, with foils of lovely brown,
Might serve to shew a seemly favor'd face.
That age is dead, and vanish'd long ago,
Which thought that steel both trusty was and true,
And needed not a foil of contraries,
But shew'd all things even as they were indeed.
Instead whereof, our curious years can find
The crystal glass, which glimseth brave and bright,
And shews the thing much better than it is,
Beguil'd with foils of sundry subtile sights,   30
So that they seem, and covet not to be.

This is the cause (believe me now, my lord)
That realms do rue from high prosperity,
That kings decline from princely government,
That lords do lack their ancestors' good will,
That knights consume their patrimony still,
That gentlemen do make the merchant rise,
That plowmen beg, and craftsmen cannot thrive,
That clergy quails and hath small reverence,
That laymen live by moving mischief still,   40
That courtiers thrive at latter Lammas Day,
That officers can scarce enrich their heirs,
That soldiers sterve, or preach at Tyburn cross,
That lawyers buy, and purchase deadly hate,
That merchants clime, and fall again as fast,
That roisters brag above their betters' room,
That sycophants are counted jolly guests,
That Lais leads a lady's life aloft,
And Lucrece lurks with sober, bashful grace.

This is the cause (or else my muse mistakes)   50
That things are thought which never yet were wrought,
And castles built above in lofty skies
Which never yet had good foundation.
And that the same may seem no feigned dream,
But words of worth, and worthy to be weighed,
I have presum'd my lord for to present
With this poor glass, which is of trusty steel,
And came to me by will and testament
Of one that was a glass-maker indeed.

Lucilius this worthy man was nam'd,   60
Who at his death bequeath'd the crystal glass
To such as love to seem but not to be;
And unto those that love to see themselves,
How foul or fair soever that they are,
He gan bequeath a glass of trusty steel,
Wherein they may be bold always to look,
Because it shews all things in their degree.

And since myself (now pride of youth is past)
Do love to be, and let all seeming pass;
Since I desire to see myself indeed—   70
Not what I would, but what I am, or should—
Therefore I like this trusty glass of steel. . . .

I see a world of worthy government:
A commonwealth with policy so rul'd
As neither laws are sold nor justice bought,
Nor riches sought unless it be by right;
No cruelty nor tyranny can reign,
No right revenge doth raise rebellion,
No spoils are ta'en although the sword prevail,
No riot spends the coin of common wealth,   80
No rulers hoard the country's treasure up,
No man grows rich by subtilty nor sleight,
All people dread the magistrate's decree,
And all men fear the scourge of mighty Jove.
Lo! This, my lord, may well deserve the name
Of such a land as milk and honey flows,
And this I see within my glass of steel
Set forth even so by Solon, worthy wight,
Who taught King Croesus what it is to seem
And what to be, by proof of happy end.   90
The like Lycurgus, Lacedemon king,
Did set to shew by view of this my glass
And left the same, a mirror to behold,
To every prince of his posterity.

But now, aye me, the glazing crystal glass
Doth make us think that realms and towns are rich
Where favor sways the sentence of the law,
Where all is fish that cometh to the net,
Where mighty power doth overrule the right,
Where injuries do foster secret grudge,   100
Where bloody sword makes every booty prize,
Where banqueting is compted comely cost,
Where officers grow rich by princes' pence,
Where purchase comes by covin and deceit,
And no man dreads but he that cannot shift,
Nor none serve God but only tongue-tied men.
Again I see within my glass of steel
But four estates to serve each country soil:
The king, the knight, the peasant, and the priest.
The king should care for all the subjects still,   110
The knight should fight for to defend the same,
The peasant he should labor for their ease,
And priests should pray for them and for themselves.

But, out alas, such mists do blear our eyes,
And crystal gloss doth glister so therewith,
That kings conceive their care is wonderous great
Whenas they beat their busy, restless brains
To maintain pomp and high, triumphant sights,
To feed their fill of dainty delicates,

To glad their hearts with sight of pleasant sports,   120
To fill their ears with sound of instruments,
To break with bit the hot, couragious horse,
To deck their halls with sumpteous cloth of gold,
To clothe themselves with silks of strange devise,
To search the rocks for pearls and precious stones,
To delve the ground for mines of glistering gold—
And never care to maintain peace and rest,
To yield relief where needy lack appears,
To stop one ear until the poor man speak,
To seem to sleep when justice still doth wake,   130
To guard their lands from sodain sword and fire,
To fear the cries of guiltless suckling babes
Whose ghosts may call for vengeance on their blood
And stir the wrath of mighty thund'ring Jove.

I speak not this by any English king,
Nor by our queen whose high foresight provides
That dire debate is fled to forain realms
Whiles we enjoy the golden fleece of peace. . . .

O crystal glass, thou settest things to shew
Which are, God knoweth! of little worth indeed.   140
All eyes behold, with eager, deep desire,
The falcon fly, the greyhound run his course,
The baited bull and bear at stately stake,
These enterludes, these new Italian sports,
And every gawd that glads the mind of man;
But few regard their needy neighbors' lack,
And few behold, by contemplation,
The joys of heaven ne yet the pains of hell.
Few look to law, but all men gaze on lust.

A sweet consent of music's sacred sound   150
Doth raise our minds, as rapt, all up on high;
But sweeter sounds of concord, peace, and love
Are out of tune, and jar in every stop.

To toss and turn the sturdy, trampling steed,
To bridle him and make him meet to serve,
Deserves, no doubt, great commendation;
But such as have their stables full yfraught
With pamp'red jades ought therewithal to weigh
What great excess upon them may be spent,
How many poor (which need nor brake nor bit)   160
Might therewithal in godly wise be fed,
And kings ought not so many horse to have.

The sumpteous house declares the prince's state,
But vain excess bewrays a prince's faults.

Our bumbast hose, our treble-double ruffs,
Our suits of silk, our comely guarded capes,
Our knit silk stocks, and Spanish leather shoes
(Yea, velvet serves ofttimes to trample in),

Our plumes, our spangs, and all our quaint array
Are pricking spurs provoking filthy pride,   170
And snares, unseen, which lead a man to hell. . . .

O blind desire! O high aspiring hearts!
The country squire doth covet to be knight,
The knight a lord, the lord an earl or a duke,
The duke a king, the king would monarch be,
And none content with that which is his own.
Yet none of these can see in crystal glass
(Which glistereth bright and blears their gazing eyes)
How every life bears with him his disease.
But in my glass, which is of trusty steel,   180
I can perceive how kingdoms breed but care,
How lordship lives with lots of less delight
(Though cap and knee do seem a reverence,
And court-like life is thought another heaven)
Than common people find in every coast.

The gentleman which might in country keep
A plenteous boord and feed the fatherless
With pig and goose, with mutton, beef, and veal
(Yea, now and then a capon and a chick)
Will break up house and dwell in market towns,   190
A loit'ring life, and like an Epicure.

But who, meanwhile, defends the common wealth?
Who rules the flock when shepherds so are fled?
Who stays the staff which should uphold the state?
Forsooth, good sir, the lawyer leapeth in—
Nay, rather leaps both over hedge and ditch,
And rules the roast—but few men rule by right.

O knights, O squires, O gentle bloods yborn,
You were not born all only for yourselves!
Your country claims some part of all your pains.   200
There should you live, and therein should you toil
To hold up right and banish cruel wrong,
To help the poor, to bridle back the rich,
To punish vice, and virtue to advance,
To see God serv'd and Belzebub suppress'd.
You should not trust leftenants in your room
And let them sway the scepter of your charge
Whiles you, meanwhile, know scarcely what is done,
Nor yet can yield accompt if you were call'd. . . .

But holla! Here I see a wondrous sight!   210
I see a swarm of saints within my glass.
Behold! Behold! I see a swarm indeed
Of holy saints which walk in comely wise,
Not deck'd in robes nor garnished with gold,
But some unshod, yea, some full thinly cloth'd;
And yet they seem so heavenly for to see
As if their eyes were all of diamonds,
Their face of rubies, sapphires, and jacincts,

Their comely beards and hear of silver wires;
And, to be short, they seem angelical.   220
What should they be, my lord, what should they be?

O gracious God, I see now what they be.
These be my priests which pray for ev'ry state;
These be my priests divorced from the world
And wedded yet to heaven and holiness;
Which are not proud, nor covet to be rich,
Which go not gay, nor feed on dainty food,
Which envy not, nor know what malice means,
Which loath all lust, disdaining drunkenness,
Which cannot feign, which hate hypocrisy,   230
Which never saw Sir Simony's deceits,
Which preach of peace, which carp contentions,
Which loiter not, but labor all the year,
Which thunder threats of God's most grievous wrath,
And yet do teach that mercy is in store.

Lo! these, my lord, be my good praying priests,
Descended from Melchizedek by line,
Cousins to Paul, to Peter, James, and John.
These be my priests, the seas'ning of the earth,
Which will not leese their sav'riness, I trow.   240

Not one of these, for twenty hundreth groats,
Will teach the text that bids him take a wife
And yet be cumb'red with a concubine.

Not one of these will read the holy writ
Which doth forbid all greedy usury
And yet receive a shilling for a pound.

Not one of these will preach of patience
And yet be found as angry as a wasp.

Not one of these can be content to sit
In taverns, inns, or alehouses all day,   250
But spends his time devoutly at his book.

Not one of these will rail at rulers' wrongs
And yet be blotted with extortion.

Not one of these will paint out worldly pride,
And he himself as gallant as he dare.

Not one of these rebuketh avarice
And yet procureth proud pluralities.

Not one of these reproveth vanity
Whiles he himself, with hawk upon his fist
And hounds at heel, doth quite forget his text.   260

Not one of these corrects contentions
For trifling things, and yet will sue for tithes.

Not one of these, not one of these, my lord,
Will be asham'd to do even as he teacheth.

My priests have learnt to pray unto the Lord,
And yet they trust not in their lip-labor.

My priests can fast, and use all abstinence
From vice and sin, and yet refuse no meats.

My priests can give in charitable wise
And love also to do good alms-deeds,   270
Although they trust not in their own deserts.

My priests can place all penance in the heart
Without regard of outward ceremonies.

My priests can keep their temples undefiled
And yet defy all superstition.

Lo now, my lord, what think you by my priests,
Although they were the last that shewed themselves?
I said at first their office was to pray;
And since the time is such, even nowadays,
As hath great need of prayers truly pray'd,   280
Come forth, my priests, and I will bid your beads.
I will presume, although I be no priest,
To bid you pray as Paul and Peter pray'd.

Then pray, my priests, yea, pray to God himself
That he vouchsafe, even for his Christes sake,
To give his word free passage here on earth,
And that his church, which now is militant,
May soon be seen triumphant over all;
And that he deign to end this wicked world
Which walloweth still in sinks of filthy sin.   290

Eke pray, my priests, for princes and for kings,
Emperors, monarchs, dukes, and all estates
Which sway the sword of royal government
(Of whom our queen, which lives without compare,
Must be the chief, in bidding of my beads,
Else I deserve to lese both beads and bones);
That God give light unto their noble minds,
To maintain truth, and therewith still to weigh
That here they reign not only for themselves,
And that they be but slaves to common wealth,   300
Since all their toils and all their broken sleeps
Shall scant suffice to hold it still upright.

Tell some in Spain how close they keep their closets,
How seld the wind doth blow upon their cheeks,
Whileas, meanwhile, their sunburnt suitors sterve
And pine before their process be preferr'd.
Then pray, my priests, that God will give his grace
To such a prince, his fault in time to mend.

Tell some in France how much they love to dance,
While suitors dance attendance at the door.   310
Yet pray, my priests, for prayers princes mend.

Tell some in Portugal how cold they be
In setting forth of right religion;
Which more esteem the present pleasures here
Then stablishing of God his holy word.
And pray, my priests, lest God such princes spit
And vomit them out of his angry mouth.

Tell some Italian princes how they wink
At stinking stews, and say they are, forsooth,
A remedy to quench foul, filthy lust;   320
Whenas indeed they be the sinks of sin.
And pray, my priests, that God will not impute
Such wilful facts unto such princes' charge,
When he himself commandeth every man
To do none ill that good may grow thereby.

And pray likewise for all that rulers be
By kings' commands, as their leftenants here,
All magistrates, all councilors, and all
That sit in office or authority.
Pray, pray, my priests, that neither love nor meed   330
Do sway their minds from furdering of right,
That they be not too saintish nor too sour,
But bear the bridle evenly between both;
That still they stop one ear, to hear him speak
Which is accused, absent as he is;
That evermore they mark what mood doth move
The mouth which makes the information;
That faults forepast (so that they be not huge
Nor do exceed the bonds of loyalty)
Do never quench their charitable mind   340
Whenas they see repentance hold the reins
Of heady youth, which wont to run astray;
That malice make no mansion in their minds,
Nor envy fret to see how virtue climes.
The greater birth the greater glory, sure,
If deeds maintain their ancestors' degree.

Eke pray, my priests, for them and for yourselves,
For bishops, prelates, archdeans, deans, and priests,
And all that preach, or otherwise profess
God's holy word, and take the cure of souls.   350
Pray, pray, that you, and every one of you,
May walk upright in your vocation;
And that you shine like lamps of perfect life,
To lend a light and lantern to our feet.

Say therewithal that some (I see them, I,
Whereas they fling in Flanders all afar,
For why my glass will shew them as they be)

Do neither care for God nor yet for devil,
So liberty may launch about at large.

And some, again (I see them well enough,   360
And note their names, in liegeland where they lurk),
Under pretense of holy humble hearts,
Would pluck adown all princely diadem.
Pray, pray, my priests for these; they touch you near.

Shrink not to say that some do, Romain-like,
Esteem their pall and habit overmuch.
And therefore pray, my priests, lest pride prevail.

Pray that the souls of sundry damned ghosts
Do not come in, and bring good evidence
Before the God which judgeth all men's thoughts   370
Of some whose wealth made them neglect their charge,
Till secret sins, untouch'd, infect their flocks
And bred a scab which brought the sheep to bane.

Some other ran before the greedy wolf,
And left the fold unfended from the fox,
Which durst nor bark nor bawl for both their ears.
Then pray, my priests, that such no more do so.

Pray for the nources of our noble realm,
I mean the worthy Universities
(And Cantabridge shall have the dignity,   380
Whereof I was unworthy member once),
That they bring up their babes in decent wise:
That Philosophy smell no secret smoke
Which Magic makes, in wicked mysteries;
That Logic leap not over every stile
Before he come a furlong near the hedge,
With curious quids to maintain argument;
That Sophistry do not deceive itself;
That Cosmography keep his compass well;
And such as be historiographers   390
Trust not too much in every tattling tongue,
Nor blinded be by partiality;
That Physic thrive not overfast by murder;
That numb'ring men, in all their evens and odds,
Do not forget that only Unity
Unmeasurable, infinite, and one;
That Geometry measure not so long
Till all their measures out of measure be;
That Music with his heavenly harmony
Do not allure a heavenly mind from heaven,   400
Nor set men's thoughts in worldly melody
Till heavenly hierarchies be quite forgot;
That Rhetoric learn not to overreach;
That Poetry presume not for to preach,
And bite men's faults with satire's corrosives,
Yet pamper up her own with pultesses,
Or that she dote not upon Erato,

Which should invoke the good Calliope;
That Astrology look not overhigh
And light, meanwhile, in every puddled pit; 410
That Grammer grudge not at our English tongue
Bycause it stands by *monosyllaba*
And cannot be declin'd, as others are.
Pray thus, my priests, for Universities.
And if I have forgotten any art
Which hath been taught or exercised there,
Pray you to God the good be not abus'd
With glorious shew of overloading skill.

Now these be past, my priests, yet shall you pray
For common people, each in his degree, 420
That God vouchsafe to grant them all his grace.
Where should I now begin to bid my beads?
Or who shall first be put in common place?
My wits be weary and my eyes are dim,
I cannot see who best deserves the room;
Stand forth, good Pierce, thou plowman, by thy name—
Yet so, the sailor saith I do him wrong.
That one contends his pains are without peer;
That other saith that none be like to his;
Indeed they labor both exceedingly. 430
But since I see no shipman that can live
Without the plow, and yet I many see
Which live by land that never saw the seas,
Therefore I say, stand forth, Pierce Plowman, first;
Thou win'st the room by very worthiness.

Behold him, priests, and though he stink of sweat
Disdain him not. For, shall I tell you what?
Such clime to heaven before the shaven crowns.
But how? Forsooth, with true humility.
Not that they hoard their grain when it is cheap, 440
Nor that they kill the calf to have the milk,
Nor that they set debate between their lords
By earing up the balks that part their bounds;
Nor forbecause they can both crouch and creep
(The guileful'st men that ever God yet made)
Whenas they mean most mischief and deceit;
Nor that they can cry out on landlords loud,
And say they rack their rents an ace too high,
When they themselves do sell their landlord's lamb
For greater price then ewe was wont be worth. 450
(I see you, Pierce; my glass was lately scour'd.)
But for they feed with fruits of their great pains
Both king and knight, and priests in cloister pent,
Therefore I say that sooner some of them
Shall scale the walls which lead us up to heaven
Than corn-fed beasts whose belly is their god,
Although they preach of more perfection.

And yet, my priests, pray you to God for Pierce,
As Pierce can pinch it out for him and you.

And if you have a paternoster spare, 460
Then shall you pray for sailors (God them send
More mind of him whenas they come to land,
For toward shipwrack many men can pray),
That they once learn to speak without a lie,
And mean good faith without blaspheming oaths;
That they forget to steal from every freight,
And for to forge false cockets, free to pass;
That manners make them give their betters place,
And use good words, though deeds be nothing gay.

But here methinks my priests begin to frown 470
And say that thus they shall be overcharg'd
To pray for all which seem to do amiss;
And one I hear, more saucy than the rest,
Which asketh me, "When shall our prayers end?"

I tell thee, priest: when shoemakers make shoes
That are well sewed, with never a stitch amiss,
And use no craft in utt'ring of the same;
When tailors steal no stuff from gentlemen;
When tanners are with corriers well agreed,
And both so dress their hides that we go dry; 480
When cutlers leave to sell old rusty blades,
And hide no cracks with soder nor deceit;
When tinkers make no more holes than they found,
When thatchers think their wages worth their work,
When colliers put no dust into their sacks,
When maltmen make us drink no furmenty,
When Davie Diker digs, and dallies not,
When smiths shoe horses as they would be shod,
When millers toll not with a golden thumb,
When bakers make not barm bear price of wheat, 490
When brewers put no baggage in their beer,
When butchers blow not over all their flesh,
When horse-corsers beguile no friends with jades,
When weavers' weight is found in huswives' web.
(But why dwell I so long among these louts?)

When mercers make more bones to swear and lie,
When vintners mix no water with their wine,
When printers pass none errors in their books,
When hatters use to buy none old cast robes,
When goldsmiths get no gains by sod'red crowns, 500
When upholsters sell feathers without dust,
When pewterers infect no tin with lead,
When drapers draw no gains by giving day,
When parchmenteers put in no ferret silk,
When surgeons heal all wounds without delay.
(Tush! these are toys, but yet my glass sheweth all.)

When purveyors provide not for themselves,
When takers take no bribes nor use no brags,
When customers conceal no covin us'd,

When searchers see all corners in a ship   510
(And spy no pence by any sight they see),
When shrives do serve all process as they ought,
When bailiffs strain none other thing but strays,
When auditors their counters cannot change,
When proud surveyors take no parting pence,
When silver sticks not on the tellers' fingers,
And when receivers pay as they receive,
When all these folk have quite forgotten fraud.

(Again. .ny priests, a little, by your leave.)
When sycophants can find no place in court   520
But are espied for echoes, as they are;
When roisters ruffle not above their rule,
Nor color craft by swearing precious coals;
When fencers' fees are like to apes' rewards,

A piece of bread and therewithal a bob;
When Lais lives not like a lady's peer,
Nor useth art in dyeing of her hear;—
When all these things are ord'red as they ought,
And see themselves within my glass of steel,
Even then, my priests, may you make holiday   530
And pray no more but ordinary prayers.

And yet therein I pray you, my good priests,
Pray still for me and for my glass of steel
That it nor I do any mind offend
Bycause we shew all colors in their kind.
And pray for me, that since my hap is such
To see men so, I may perceive myself.
O, worthy words to end my worthless verse—
Pray for me, priests, I pray you pray for me.
                    Tam Marti quam Mercurio

GEORGE WHETSTONE

George Whetstone (or Whetstones)—perhaps the least interesting of all the uninteresting writers (such as Googe, Turbervile, and Howell) in the lean years between Tottel's *Miscellany* and *The Shepherd's Calendar*—apparently became an author, as a last resort, in order to eat. Having tried wenching, gambling, and soldiering, he finally tried writing; and his first book, *The Rock of Regard,* is a collection (almost a one-man miscellany) of some sixty-eight pieces, in prose and verse, that he arranged on the model of his friend Gascoigne's *Posies* (1575). To point their moral and didactic uses Gascoigne had grouped his poems under the rubrics of "Flowers," "Herbs," and "Weeds"; Whetstone—who could speak from considerable experience on the dangers of sin—arranged his under such far-fetched headings as "The Castle of Delight" and "The Orchard of Repentance," each of the four sections carrying a separate dedication. Although fearfully uninspired, many of his pieces are narratives adapted from Italian sources, and thus they serve to remind us of the continuing vogue of Italianate *novelle,* a vogue contributed to by Painter, Pettie, Riche, and many others, and one which Whetstone himself exploited in such later works as *An Heptameron of Civil Discourses* (1582). Our text is based upon *The Rocke of Regard divided into foure parts,* 1576 (STC 25348).

FROM THE ROCK OF REGARD (1576)

To All the Young Gentlemen of England to Whose Perusing This Book Shall Happen, George Whetstones Wisheth Both Health and Good Hap

Worthy gentlemen, I have presented unto your friendly acceptance a work so worthless (in respect of the homely handling thereof) as will, I fear, neither content you in reading nor any ways commend my pains in writing; and yet I am right well assured (curious contentment set apart) it importeth neces- 10 sary matter of direction for unstayed youth, who, having the reins at liberty, are so hot in expense as that they be many times surfited with incumberancies, yea, tired outright with prodigality, before they be brought into any perfect order of spending. For whose behalf and forewarning I have collected together a number of my unlearned devises (invented for the most of experience) and more boldly then well-advised have guarded them with the title of *The Rock of Regard,* not for that it containeth only needful matter but for that you, having noted the discommodities of the unnecessary, might read the necessary considerations with more regard. . . .

[Whetstone explains the headings of the various sections thus: "The Castle of Delight," the first part of the collection, seeks to "join commodity with the reader's pleasure"; "The Garden of Unthriftiness" contains "a number of vain, wanton, and worthless sonnets" that will serve "to make the rest of the book more profitable" and to pluck away "the visard of 10 self-conceit" from hot desires; "The Arbor of Virtue" is included chiefly "for the delight of virtuous ladies and gentlewomen"; "The Orchard of Repentance" is "planted with experience, the fruits therein growing (think I) be wholesome, although to curious appetites not greatly toothsome."]

Now, worthy gentlemen, have you heard my honest intent as touching the imprinting of this my book; mine was the pain in framing the plots wherein these fruits and flowers grow; yours is the pleasure 20 and profit of both. Marry, if you misuse my well-meaning so far that you (where sea-room serveth you to avoid the sands of wanton love) will wilfully run upon the rocks of unlawful lust, the folly is yours and no fault in me; or if you (where you may gather friendly fruits of admonition that will cure your wounds of prodigality and preserve you from the infection of cousening cutthroats) will continually be smelling unto unthrifty flowers, you not only vainly spend your time but work a discredit 30 unto my painful labors. Wherefore, I earnestly require you that you use the first increase of my barren brain so rightly as I may be incouraged hereafter to beat my head about some matter of more worth rather then by the misuse of them to be discouraged from attempting any honest labor. And thus wishing good success in your virtuous enterprises, I commit you to the pleasure of the Highest. From my lodging in Holborn, the 15 of October, 1576.

40

The Castle of Delight

THE ARGUMENT FOR *Cressid's Complaint*

The inconstancy of Cressid is so ready in every man's mouth as it is a needless labor to blaze at full her abuse towards young Troilus, her frowning on Sir Diomede, her wanton lures and love; nevertheless her company scorned of thousands sometimes sought, her beggery after bravery, her lothsome leprosy after lively beauty, her wretched age after wanton youth, and her perpetual 50 infamy after violent death are worthy notes (for others' heed) to be rememb'red. And forasmuch as Cressid's heirs in every corner live, yea more cunning then Cressid herself in wanton exercises, toys, and inticements, to forewarn all men of such filths, to persuade the infected

to fall from their follies, and to raise a fear in dames untainted to offend, I have reported the subtile sleights, the lewd life, and evil fortunes of a courtisane in Cressid's name, whom you may suppose in tattered weeds, half hunger-starved, miserably array'd, with scabs, leprosy, and maingy to complain as followeth.

CRESSID'S COMPLAINT

You ramping girls which rage with wanton lust,
Behold in me the bitter blooms of change:
Forworn with wo, who wallows in the dust
And leper-like is double-mail'd with mainge.
For my desart this fortune is not strange;
Disdain my life, but listen to my moan;
Without good heed the hap may be your own.

Though now I am anointed with annoy,
My hide bepatch'd with scabs of sundry hue,
I sometime was the star of stately Troy, 10
With beauty blist, my veins as azures blue,
No fault in me but that I was untrue.
In Priam's court who did not Cressid like?
In lieu of love who gave she not the gleak?

Where I was lov'd I seemed always strange;
Where little weigh'd I won with gleams of grace;
My gadding mind had such delight in change
As seldom twice the best I did imbrace,
And once beguil'd with beauty of my face,
With ebbs of grief did fall his floods of joy; 20
He su'd and serv'd, but Cressid then was coy.

I did intice King Priam's sons to love
And did repine the poorest should go free;
My thralls for grace a thousand ways did prove,
On whom I smil'd a happy man was he;
The wisest wits were thus bewitch'd by me.
But as the hawk in mew at random lives,
Yet diet keeps her gorge as seldom grieves,

So I that liv'd with store of food at large,
When hunger pinch'd on lusty youths I prey'd; 30
If boistrous lads my gorge did overcharge,
For tiring meat the dainty boys were weigh'd.
Thus with a mean my prime of pride was stay'd;
Then was I fair, my train with oil was trick'd,
My feathers fresh were daily prun'd and pick'd.

No toy, no gaud, ne strange devise I see,
Though not the first, the same I second had;
Glad was the youth that fast'ned ought on me;
Of brave array in change I still was clad.
My cost to see, the courtly dames were mad; 40
They did repine the peers should Cressid love
When rascals scarce to them did liking move.

Such fancies strange were figur'd in my face
As few there were but my good will did move;
I train'd them on with outward shew of grace:
My garter one, another had my glove,
My colors all did wear in sine of love,
But where in heart I lov'd and liked best,
He ever wore the spoil of all the rest.

Sir Diomede got both brooch and belt of cost,   50
The which in right to Troilus belongs—
An eyesore sure to him that lov'd me most,
Who might repine, but not revenge, his wrongs,
Least notes of hope were turn'd to desperate songs.
The rest did love as courtiers do in show,
But he, good soul, did pine away with wo.

Yet cruel I did smile to see his smart
Who sometime warm'd his woes with slender hap,
Which freez'd again with frownings overthwart;
And when with joy he prattled in my lap,   60
With peevish speech I would his pleasures snap.
For wronging whom the Trojans did me paint
In heart a fiend, in face and form a saint. . . .

But I so long on carren crows did prey
My poisoned blood in color waxed pale:
In Nature's aid mine age had wrought decay.
Now listen, ramps, for here begins my tale;

Before my bliss, but now I blaze my bale;
For physic's art my surfets cannot cure;
Bound so, perforce, the worst I must indure.   70

In seeking sport, my hair did shed in jest,
A sorry joy to ceaseless sorrow plight,
French fevers now in me can take no rest
From bones to flesh, from flesh in open sight
With grinckcome's grease behold a monstrous wight:
My lovers old with "fawth!" their brows doth bend.
Of Cressid's lust, lo here the lothsome end.

Glad is she now a brownbread crust to gnaw,
Who dainty once on finest cates did frown,
To couch upon soft seams a pad of straw,   80
Where half mislik'd were stately beds of down.
By need enforc'd, she begs on every clown
On whom but late the best would gifts bestow;
But squeamish then, "God dyld ye," she said no. . . .

Take heed in time lest had I wist you rue,
And thus perforce I hold my tired tongue.
Methinks I hear the bell to sound adieu;
My withered corps with deadly cold is clung.
A happier turn if I had died young.
My shrouding sheet then had not been of shame,   90
Who dying now doth live in filthy fame.
                    Sive bonum sive malum fama est.

Part VI LATER ELIZABETHAN POETRY

THOMAS WATSON

Thomas Watson was one of the most learned and least interesting poets of the late sixteenth century. Educated probably at St. Mary's Hall, Oxford (he left without a degree), and deeply read in classical literature, he came to London, dabbled in the law, and quickly became something of a legend for his knowledge of foreign literatures, ancient and modern. Visiting Paris in 1581, he deeply impressed one Stephen Broelmann, a scholar of Cologne, who urged him to print some of his Latin works that were already circulating in manuscript. As a result, in 1581 he published a Latin version of Sophocles' *Antigone*, together with a set of allegorical verses called "Pompae" and four "Themata" illustrating different forms of classical prosody. Watson's chief contribution to English literature came the following year. On March 31, 1582, his "Passions" were licensed, and were published shortly thereafter as The ῾Εκατομπαθία *or Passionate Century of Love*, a set of one hundred eighteen-line "sonnets" treating both the author's "sufferance" in love and his "long farewell" to love, as well as some half-dozen Latin poems of various sorts. An elaborate volume containing a euphuistic epistle by Lyly as well as commendatory verses by Thomas Acheley, Matthew Roydon, George Peele, and others, it marks an important stage in the Elizabethans' literary relations with the Continent, even if it cannot be regarded as a work of original genius. The "passions"— the majority of them prefaced by prose notes concerning theme and sources—are translated or adapted from an imposing list of foreign authors: Petrarch, Serafino de' Ciminelli Aquilano, Poliziano, Baptista Mantuanus, Strozza, and Ronsard among the moderns, Sophocles, Theocritus, Virgil, Horace, Tibullus, and Ovid among the ancients.

Although Watson's work was widely admired, it really exerted no great influence on the development of the English sonnet. When the vogue of the sonnet did develop some ten years later, it was under the stimulus of Sidney's *Astrophel and Stella* (see p. 323), and neither for his form nor for the intensity of his amorous emotion could Sidney (who also wrote in the early eighties) have owed much to Watson's passionless but accomplished exercises in translation. In his other major work also, Watson's influence on native literature was at best oblique and peripheral. His paraphrase (1585) in Latin hexameters of Tasso's *Aminta* acquired such popularity in Abraham Fraunce's English version (1587) that it went through four editions within four years. But not until the fourth edition (1591), called *The Countess of Pembroke's Ivy-Church*, did Fraunce make a tardy and equivocal acknowledgment of his debt to Watson. Our text is based upon *The ῾Εκατομπαθία or Passionate Centurie of Love, Divided into two parts: whereof, the first expresseth the Authors sufferance in Love: the latter, his long farewell to Love and all his tyrannie*, 1582 (STC 25118).

FROM THE ΕΚΑΤΟΜΠΑΘΙΑ OR PASSIONATE CENTURY OF LOVE (1582)

John Lyly to the Author, His Friend

My good friend, I have read your new passions, and they have renewed mine old pleasures, the which brought to me no less delight then they have done to yourself commendations. And certes, had not one of mine eyes about serious affairs been watchful, both by being too too busy had been wanton: such is the nature of persuading pleasure that it melteth the marrow before it scorch the skin, and burneth before it warmeth. Not unlike unto the oil of jet, which rotteth the bone and never rankleth the flesh, or the scarab flies, which enter into the root and never touch the rind.

And whereas you desire to have my opinion, you may imagine that my stomach is rather cloyed then queasy, and therefore mine appetite of less force then mine affection, fearing rather a surfet of sweetness then desiring a satisfying. The repeating of love wrought in me a remembrance of liking, but, searching the very veins of my heart, I could find nothing but a broad scar where I left a deep wound, and loose strings where I tied hard knots, and a table of steel where I framed a plot of wax.

Whereby I noted that young swans are grey, and the old white; young trees tender, and the old tough; young men amorous, and growing in years either wiser or warier. The coral in the water is a soft weed, on the land a hard stone; a sword frieth in the fire like a black eel, but laid in earth like white snow; the heart in love is altogether passionate, but free from desire altogether careless.

But it is not my intent to inveigh against love, which women account but a bare word and that men reverence as the best god. Only this I would add without offense to gentlewomen: that were not men more superstitious in their praises then women are constant in their passions, love would either shortly be worn out of use, or men out of love, or women out of lightness. I can condemn none but by conjecture, nor commend any but by lying, yet suspicion is as free as thought, and, as far as I see, as necessary as credulity.

Touching your mistress, I must needs think well, seeing you have written so well; but as false glasses shew the fairest faces, so fine gloses amend the baddest fancies. Apelles painted the phoenix by hearsay, not by sight; and Lysippus engraved Vulcan with a straight leg, whom nature framed with a poult-foot, which proveth men to be of greater affection then judgment. But in that so aptly you have varied upon women, I will not vary from you; for confess I must (and if I should not, yet mought I be compelled) that to love were the sweetest thing in the earth if women were the faithfullest, and that women would be more constant if men were more wise.

And seeing you have used me so friendly as to make me acquainted with your passions, I will shortly make you privy to mine, which I would be loth the printer should see, for that my fancies being never so crooked, he would put them in straight lines unfit for my humor, necessary for his art, who setteth down *blinde* in as many letters as *seeing*. Farewell.

To the Author

If graver heads shall count it overlight
To treat of love, say thou to them, "A stain
Is incident unto the finest dye."
And yet no stain at all it is for thee
These lays of love, as mirth to melancholy,
To follow fast thy sad *Antigone*,
Which may bear out a broader work then this,
Compil'd with judgment, order, and with art,
And shroud thee under shadow of his wings
Whose gentle heart and head with learning freight   10
Shall yield thee gracious favor and defense.

G[eorge] Peele

2

In this passion the author describeth in how pitious a case the heart of a lover is, being (as he feigneth here) seperated from his own body and removed into a darksome and solitary wilderness of woes. The conveyance of his invention is plain and pleasant enough of itself, and therefore needeth the less annotation before it.

My heart is set him down, twixt hope and fears,
Upon the stony bank of high desire

To view his own made flood of blubbering tears,
Whose waves are bitter salt and hot as fire.
   There blows no blast of wind, but ghostly groans,
   Nor waves make other noise then pitious moans;
As life were spent, he waiteth Charon's boat
And thinks he dwells on side of Stygian lake.
But black despair sometimes with open throat
Or spightful jealousy doth cause him quake: 10
   With howling shrikes on him they call and cry
   That he as yet shall neither live nor die.
Thus void of help, he sits in heavy case
And wanteth voice to make his just complaint.
No flow'r but hiacynth in all the place,
No sun comes there, nor any heav'nly saint,
   But only she which in himself remains
   And joys her ease though he abound in pains.

18

This sonnet is perfectly pathetical, and consisteth in two principal points, whereof the first containeth an accusation of love for his hurtful effects and usual tyranny; the second part is a sudden recantation or excuse of the author's evil words by casting the same upon the neck of his beloved, as being the only cause of his late frenzy and blasphemous rage so lavishly poured forth in foul speeches.

Love is a sour delight, a sug'red grief,
A living death, an ever-dying life,
A breach of reason's law, a secret thief,
A sea of tears, an everlasting strife,
   A bait for fools, a scourge of noble wits,
   A deadly wound, a shot which ever hits.
Love is a blinded god, an angry boy,
A labyrinth of doubts, an idle lust,
A slave to beauty's will, a witless toy,
A ravening bird, a tyrant most unjust,   10
   A burning heat, a cold, a flatt'ring foe,
   A private hell, a very world of wo.
Yet, mighty Love, regard not what I say
Which lie in trance, bereft of all my wits,
But blame the light that leads me thus astray
And makes my tongue blaspheme by frantic fits.
   Yet hurt her not, lest I sustain the smart
   Which am content to lodge her in my heart.

34

The author in this sonnet very highly commendeth the most rare excellencies of his mistress, avouching her to have no equal. And he imitateth the second sonnet *nelle rime di* Messer Agnolo Fiorenzuola, the Florentine, whose beginning is all one with that here; and this it is:

> *Deh le mie belle donne et amorose,*
> *Ditemi il ver per vostra cortesia,*
> *Non è chiara tra voi la donna mia,*
> *Come è'l Sol chiar tra tutte l'altre cose?*

Ye stately dames, whose beauties far excel,
Of courtesy confess, at my request,
Doth not my love amongst you bear the bell
As Phoebus' golden rays obscures the rest
    Of planet stars, and dimmeth ev'ry light
    That shines in heav'n or earth by day or night?
Take wistly heed in viewing her sweet face
Where Nature hath express'd what ere she could,
Either for beauty's blaze or comely grace;
Since when, to prize her work, she brake the mold,   10
    So that who seeks to find her equal out
    Intends a thing will ne'er be brought about.
Therefore, sweet ladies all, voutchsafe with me
To follow her desert and my desire
By praising her unto the ninth degree;
For honor by due right is virtue's hire,
    And Envy's mouth must say, when all is done,
    No bird but one is sacred to the sun.

39

The second part of this passion is borrowed from out the
fift sonnet in Petrarch, part I. . . .

When first these eyes beheld with great delight
The phoenix of this world, or second sun,
Her beams or plumes bewitched all my sight,
And Love encreas'd the hurt that was begun,
    Since when my grief is grown so much the more
    Because I find no way to cure the sore.
I have attempted oft to make complaint
And with some doleful words to tell my grief,
But through my fearful heart my voice doth faint
And makes me mute where I should crave relief.   10
    Another while I think to write my pain,
    But straight my hand lays down the pen again.
Sometimes my mind with heaps of doubtful cares
Conjoin'd with fawning hopes is sore oppress'd,
And sometime suddein joy at unawares
Doth move too much, and so doth hurt my breast.
    What man doth live in more extremes then these,
    Where death doth seem a life and pains do please?

53

The two first parts of this sonnet are an imitation of certain
Greek verses of Theocritus, which verses, as they are
translated by many good poets of later days, so most
aptly and plainly by C. Urcinus Velius in his *Epigrams.* . . .

Where tender Love had laid him down to sleep,
A little bee so stung his finger's end

That burning ache enforced him to weep
And call for Phoebus' son to stand his friend,
    To whom he cried, "I muse so small a thing
    Can prick thus deep with such a little sting."
"Why so, sweet boy?" quoth Venus, sitting by.
"Thyself is young, thy arrows are but small,
And yet thy shot makes hardest hearts to cry."
To Phoebus' son she turned therewithal   10
    And pray'd him shew his skill to cure the sore
    Whose like her boy had never felt before.
Then he with herbs recured soon the wound,
Which being done, he threw the herbs away,
Whose force, through touching Love in selfsame ground,
By hapless hap did breed my heart's decay.
    For there they fell where long my heart had li'n
    To wait for Love and what he should assign.

91

MY LOVE IS PAST

In the latter part of this sonnet the author imitateth those
verses of Horace [*Ad Pyrrham*, ode V]:

> *Me tabula sacer*
> *Votiva paries indicat uvida*
> *Suspendisse potenti*
> *Vestimenta maris Deo.*

Whom also that renowned Florentine, Messer Agnolo
Fi[o]renzuola, did imitate long ago, both in like manner
and matter, as followeth:

> *O miseri coloro,*
> *Che non provar di donna fede mai.* . . .

Ye captive souls of blindfold Cyprian's boat,
Mark with advise in what estate ye stand:
Your boatman never whistles merry note,
And Folly, keeping stern, still puts from land
    And makes a sport to toss you to and fro
    Twixt sighing winds and surging waves of wo.
On Beauty's rock she runs you at her will,
And holds you in suspense twixt hope and fear,
Where, dying oft, yet are you living still,
But such a life as death much better were.   10
    Be therefore circumspect and follow me
    When chance or change of manners sets you free.
Beware how you return to seas again;
Hang up your votive tables in the quire
Of Cupid's church in witness of the pain
You suffer now by forced fond desire;
    Then hang your through-wet garments on the wall
    And sing with me that love is mix'd with gall.

As Miss Latham, Raleigh's latest editor, ruefully points out, his poems pose formidable textual problems. For many reasons one of the most admired figures of the age, his poetry was widely read and praised (for example, by Harvey, Puttenham, Meres, Spenser), yet he himself printed none of it, nor did he leave any authoritative manuscript collection. The problems have been compounded ever since Thomas Warton, in his *History of English Poetry* (1774–81), blandly announced that the commonly used Ignoto ("anonymous" or "unknown") was Raleigh's "constant signature"—an error which led nineteenth-century editors to distend grossly the Raleigh canon. The handful of pieces that competent modern scholars assign to Raleigh have, then, various and dubious sources: commendatory pieces in Gascoigne's *Steel Glass* (1576) and in Spenser's *Faerie Queene* (1590), quoted verses in Puttenham's *Art of English Poesy* (1589), anonymous contributions to *The Phoenix Nest* (1593), *England's Helicon* (1600), and *A Poetical Rhapsody* (1602) that have been ascribed to Raleigh on plausible grounds, and a few pieces in commonplace-books that have been preserved at Hatfield House or in the Rawlinson and Harley manuscripts in the Bodleian Library and the British Museum. Of the poems which we reprint, "Nature, That Wash'd Her Hands in Milk" is ascribed to Raleigh in Harley MS. 6917 and in other manuscripts of the early seventeenth century; "My Body in the Walls Captived" is in a Hatfield House MS. (Cecil Papers 144); "The Ocean to Cynthia," the ambitious poem which Raleigh read to Spenser at Kilcolman in 1589,[1] survives as a fragment (the eleventh book and part of the twelfth) in the author's own hand among the Hatfield MSS. (Cecil Papers 144); "As You Came from the Holy Land," ascribed to "Sir W. R." in Rawlinson Poet. 85, although included in a late (1678) edition of Thomas Deloney's *Garland of Good Will*, cannot have been from Deloney's pen; for details about an early Huntington Library MS. see *The Pepys Ballads* (ed. Hyder Edward Rollins), VIII, 9; "Sir Walter Raleigh to His Son" is from British Museum MS. Additional 23,229. Our texts are based mainly upon *The Poems of Sir Walter Ralegh*, ed. Agnes M. C. Latham, 1951.

[NATURE, THAT WASH'D HER HANDS IN MILK]

Nature, that wash'd her hands in milk
　And had forgot to dry them,
Instead of earth took snow and silk
　At Love's request to try them,
If she a mistress could compose
To please Love's fancy out of those.

Her eyes, he would, should be of light,
　A violet breath, and lips of jelly,
Her hair not black nor overbright,
　And of the softest down her belly. 　10
As for her inside, he'ld have it
Only of wantonness and wit.

At Love's entreaty, such a one
　Nature made, but with her beauty
She hath framed a heart of stone,
　So as Love, by ill destiny,
Must die for her whom Nature gave him
Because her darling would not save him.

But Time, which Nature doth despise
　And rudely gives her love the lie, 　20
Makes Hope a fool and Sorrow wise,

His hands doth neither wash nor dry,
But, being made of steel and rust,
Turns snow and silk and milk to dust.

The light, the belly, lips, and breath
　He dims, discolors, and destroys;
With those he feeds, but fills not, death,
　Which sometimes were the food of joys.
Yea, Time doth dull each lively wit,
And dries all wantonness with it. 　30

O cruel Time, which takes in trust
　Our youth, our joys, and all we have,
And pays us but with age and dust;
　Who, in the dark and silent grave
When we have wand'red all our ways,
Shuts up the story of our days.

[MY BODY IN THE WALLS CAPTIVED]

My body in the walls captived
Feels not the wounds of spiteful envy,
But my thrall'd mind, of liberty deprived,
Fast-fettered in her ancient memory,

---

[1]See *Colin Clout's Come Home Again*, lines 56 ff. (p. 359, below).

Doth nought behold but Sorrow's dying face.
Such prison erst was so delightful
As it desir'd no other dwelling-place,
But Time's effects and destinies despiteful
Have changed both my keeper and my fare.
Love's fire and Beauty's light I then had store, 10
But now, close-kept as captives wonted are,
That food, that heat, that light I find no more.
　　Dispair bolts up my doors, and I alone
　　Speak to dead walls—but those hear not my moan.

THE OCEAN TO CYNTHIA

Sufficeth it to you, my joys interred,
In simple words that I my woes complain:
You that then died when first my fancy erred,
Joys under dust that never live again.

If to the living were my muse addressed,
Or did my mind her own spirit still inhold,
Were not my living passion so repressed,
As to the dead the dead did these unfold,

Some sweeter words, some more becoming verse,
Should witness my mishap in higher kind; 10
But my love's wounds, my fancy in the hearse,
The idea but resting of a wasted mind,

The blossoms fallen, the sap gone from the tree,
The broken monuments of my great desires—
From these so lost, what may th' affections be,
What heat in cinders of extinguish'd fires?

Lost in the mud of those high-flowing streams
Which through more fairer fields their courses bend,
Slain with self-thoughts, amaz'd in fearful dreams,
Woes without date, discomforts without end, 20

From fruitful trees I gather with'red leaves
And glean the broken ears with miser's hands,
Who sometime did injoy the weighty sheaves;
I seek fair flours amid the brinish sand. . . .

O hopeful love, my object and invention,
O true desire, the spur of my consait,
O worthiest spirit, my mind's impulsion,
O eyes transpersant, my affections' bait!

O princely form, my fancy's adamant,
Divine conceit, my pains' acceptance, 30
O all in one, O heaven on yearth transparant,
The seat of joys and Love's abundance!

Out of that mass of miracles my muse
Gathered those flours to her pure senses pleasing,

Out of her eyes (the store of joys) did chuse
Equal delights, my sorrows' counterpoising.

Her regal looks my rigorous sithes suppressed;
Small drops of joys sweet'ned great worlds of woes;
One gladsome day a thousand cares redressed.
Whom Love defends what fortune overthrows? 40

When she did well, what did there else amiss?
When she did ill, what empires could have pleased,
No other power effecting wo or bliss?
She gave, she took, she wounded, she appeased.

The honor of her love love still devising,
Wounding my mind with contrary consait,
Transferr'd itself, sometime to her aspiring,
Sometime the trumpet of her thoughts' retrait.

To seek new worlds for gold, for praise, for glory,
To try desire, to try love severed far, 50
When I was gone she sent her memory,
More strong then were ten thousand ships of war,

To call me back, to leave great honor's thought,
To leave my friends, my fortune, my attempt,
To leave the purpose I so long had sought,
And hold both cares and comforts in contempt. . . .

But stay, my thoughts; make end, geve Fortune way.
Harsh is the voice of wo and sorrow's sound;
Complaints cure not, and tears do but allay
Griefs for a time, which after more abound. 60

To seek for moisture in th' Arabian sand
Is but a loss of labor and of rest.
The links which time did break of hearty bands[1]

Words cannot knit, or wailings make anew.
Seek not the sun in clouds when it is set.
On highest mountains where those cedars grew,
Against whose banks the troubled ocean bet,

And were the marks to find thy hoped port,
Into a soil far off themselves remove.
On Sestos' shore, Leander's late resort, 70
Hero hath left no lamp to guide her love.

Thou lookest for light in vain, and storms arise.
She sleeps thy death that erst thy danger sithed;
Strive then no more; bow down thy weary eyes—
Eyes which to all these woes thy heart have guided.

──────────

[1]Stanza imperfect in MS.

She is gone. She is lost. She is found. She is ever fair.
Sorrow draws weakly where Love draws not too.
Wo's cries sound nothing but only in Love's ear.
Do then by dying what life cannot do.

Unfold thy flocks and leave them to the fields   80
To feed on hills or dales, where likes them best,
Of what the summer or the springtime yields;
For Love and Time hath geven thee leave to rest.

Thy heart which was their fold—now in decay
By often storms and winter's many blasts—
All torn and rent becomes misfortune's prey.
False hope my shepherd's staff, now age hath brast

My pipe, which Love's own hand gave my desire
To sing her praises and my wo upon,
Dispair hath often threat'ned to the fire   90
As vain to keep, now all the rest are gone.

Thus home I draw, as death's long night draws on.
Yet every foot old thoughts turn back mine eyes;
Constraint me guides as old age draws a stone
Against the hill, which overweighty lies

For feeble arms or wasted strenght to move;
My steps are backward, gazing on my loss.
My mind's affection, and my soul's sole love,
Not mix'd with Fancy's chase or Fortune's dross,

To God I leave it who first gave it me,   100
And I her gave, and she return'd again.
As it was hers, so let His mercies be
Of my last comforts the essential mean.
    But be it so or not, th' effects are pass'd.
    Her love hath end. My wo must ever last.

[AS YOU CAME FROM THE HOLY LAND]

"As you came from the holy land
    Of Walsingham,
Met you not with my true love
    By the way as you came?"

"How shall I know your true love,
    That have met many one
As I went to the holy land,
    That have come, that have gone?"

"She is neither white nor brown,
    But as the heavens fair.
There is none hath a form so divine   10
    In the earth or the air."

"Such an one did I meet, good sir,
    Such an angelic face,

Who, like a queen, like a nymph, did appear
    By her gait, by her grace."

"She hath left me here all alone,
    All alone as unknown,
Who sometimes did me lead with herself,
    And me lov'd as her own."   20

"What's the cause that she leaves you alone
    And a new way doth take,
Who loved you once as her own
    And her joy did you make?"

"I have lov'd her all my youth,
    But now old, as you see,
Love likes not the falling fruit
    From the withered tree."

"Know that Love is a careless child,
    And forgets promise pass'd;   30
He is blind; he is deaf when he list,
    And in faith never fast.

"His desire is a dureless content
    And a trustless joy;
He is won with a world of despair
    And is lost with a toy."

"Of womenkind such indeed is the love,
    Or the word 'love' abused,
Under which many childish desires
    And conceits are excus'd.   40

"But love is a durable fire
    In the mind ever burning:
Never sick, never old, never dead,
    From itself never turning."

SIR WALTER RALEIGH TO HIS SON

Three things there be that prosper up apace
And flourish whilst they grow asunder far;
But on a day they meet all in one place,
And when they meet they one another mar.
And they be these: the wood, the weed, the wag.
The wood is that which makes the gallow-tree;
The weed is that which strings the hangman's bag;
The wag, my pretty knave, betokeneth thee.
Mark well, dear boy, whilst these assemble not,
Green springs the tree, hemp grows, the wag is wild;   10
But when they meet it makes the timber rot,
It frets the halter, and it chokes the child.
    Then bless thee, and beware, and let us pray
    We part not with thee at this meeting-day.

SIR PHILIP SIDNEY

Sir Philip Sidney, a paragon to his contemporaries and an inspiration to posterity, was very influential in three important areas of Elizabethan literature. As his *Arcadia* (see pp. 737–51) domesticated the pastoral romance in England and his *Defense of Poesy* (see pp. 599 f., 605–24) is the most substantial critical treatise of the age, so his *Astrophel and Stella* initiated the vogue of sonnet sequences that is one of the most conspicuous developments of later Elizabethan literary history. Written in the late seventies and early eighties (just before and just after Sidney's projected marriage to Penelope Devereux, Lord Essex' eldest daughter, was blasted by her match with Lord Rich), it probably took its final form about 1582, when Sidney, temporarily in the queen's disfavor for opposing her matrimonial overtures to the Duke of Anjou, was living in retirement at Wilton with his sister, the Countess of Pembroke. Sidney ostentatiously disclaims literary affectation and protests his anguished sincerity (as in Sonnets 1, 3, 15), and indeed he does invest the stereotyped theme of frustrated passion with a new poignancy of love for his lady and of contempt for his successful rival (as in Sonnets 24 and 37); but conventional Petrarchan elements are everywhere apparent, and the real distinction of *Astrophel and Stella* lies in its metrical skill, its music, and its philosophical gravity. It splendidly illustrates the blending of English puritanism with the most advanced belletristic influences of the late Renaissance.

In its final form comprising one hundred eight sonnets and eleven songs (or "other sonnets of variable verse"), *Astrophel and Stella* has a tumultuous bibliographical history. Although Sidney, as a characteristically aristocratic gesture, never published any of his works himself, the great success of the first (unauthorized) edition of the *Arcadia* in 1590 must have prompted the printer Thomas Newman to issue the already "famous device" of *Astrophel and Stella* in 1591 with an epistle to his friend Francis Flower, a breezy epistle by Thomas Nashe (who, as Newman hints, perhaps served as editor), and an appendix of "sundry other rare sonnets of divers noblemen and gentlemen" (among them Samuel Daniel, part of whose *Delia* was thus printed without his permission [see p. 402]). Although Newman, with a flourish of altruism, declared his purpose to be the correction of the "corruption" "spread abroad" by many "ill writers" in manuscript versions, and although Nashe extravagantly boasted that "Apollo hath resigned his ivory harp unto Astrophel," thus initiating a new era of English poetry, there were those who were vexed at the entrepreneurs' presumption. As we learn from the records of the Stationers Company, before the year was out a group of Sidney's friends sought to suppress the edition, but none the less Matthew Lownes, another printer of more enterprise than integrity, issued his own unauthorized edition late in 1591, about the same time that Newman himself published a second edition without the offensive epistles and with many textual changes. Like Sidney's other works, *Astrophel and Stella* at last acquired a canonical text in the handsome folio which Lady Pembroke authorized in 1598. This edition vastly increased the number of textual changes, first printed the famous Sonnet 37 (which attacks Lord Rich by name), added two songs (nos. 8 and 9), rearranged the order of the contents, and appended a group of "certain sonnets of Sir Philip Sidney never before printed" (among them the two celebrated sonnets of recantation, "Thou Blind Man's Mark" and "Leave Me, O Love," as well as the lovely "Ring Out Your Bells" that was given a place of honor in *England's Helicon* two years later [see pp. 238 f.]). Our texts of Newman's and Nashe's epistles are based upon the first unauthorized quarto of 1591, *Syr P. S. His Astrophel and Stella* (STC 22536); for the poetry itself we have used the authorized folio of 1598 (STC 22541).

<hr>

FROM ASTROPHEL AND STELLA (1591, 1598)

To the Worshipful and His Very Good Friend Master Francis Flower Esquire, Increase of All Content

It was my fortune, right worshipful, not many days since to light upon the famous device of *Astrophel and Stella,* which, carrying the general commendation of all men of judgment and being reported to be one of the rarest things that ever any Englishman set abroad, I have thought good to publish it under your name, both for I know the excellency of your Worship's conceit above all other to be such as is only fit to discern of all matters of wit, as also for the credit and countenance your patronage may give to such a work. Accept of it, I beseech you, as the first fruits of my affection, which desires to approve itself in all duty unto you; and though the argument perhaps may seem too light for your grave view, yet, considering the worthiness of the author, I hope you will entertain it accordingly. For my part, I have been very careful in the printing of it, and whereas, being spread abroad in written copies, it had gathered much corruption by ill writers, I have used their help and advice in correcting and restoring it to his first dignity, that I know were of skill and experience in those matters. And the rather was I moved to set it forth because I thought it pity anything proceeding from so rare a man should be obscured, or that his fame should not still be nourish'd in his works, whom the works with one united grief bewailed. Thus craving pardon for my bold attempt, and desiring the continuance of your Worship's favor unto me, I end.

Yours always to be commanded,
Thomas Newman

Somewhat to Read for Them That List

Tempus adest plausus aurea pompa venit: so ends the scene of idiots, and enter Astrophel in pomp. Gentlemen that have seen a thousand lines of folly drawn forth *ex uno puncto impudentiae* and two famous mountains to go to the conception of one mouse, that have had your ears deaf'ned with the echo of Fame's brazen tow'rs when only they have been touch'd with a leaden pen, that have seen Pan sitting in his bower of delights and a number of Midasses to admire his miserable hornpipes, let not your surfeted sight (new come from such puppet play) think scorn to turn aside into this theater of pleasure, for here you shall find a paper stage strew'd with pearl, an artificial heav'n to overshadow the fair frame, and crystal walls to encounter your curious eyes whiles the tragicomedy of love is performed by starlight. The chief actor here is Melpomene, whose dusky robes dipp'd in the ink of tears as yet seem to drop when I view them near. The argument cruel chastity, the prologue hope, the epilogue dispair, *videte quaeso et linguis animisque favete.* And here, peradventure, my witless youth may be tax'd with a margent note of presumption for offering to put up any motion of applause in the behalf of so excellent a poet, the least syllable of whose name sounded in the ears of judgment is able to give the meanest line he writes a dowry of immortality; yet those that observe how jewels oftentimes come to their hands that know not their value, and that the cockscombs of our days, like Esop's cock, had rather have a barley kernel wrapp'd up in a ballet then they will dig for the

wealth of wit in any ground that they know not, I hope will also hold me excused, though I open the gate to his glory and invite idle ears to the admiration of his melancholy. . . .

Put out your rush candles, you poets and rimers, and bequeath your crazed quarterzains to the chandlers, for lo, here he cometh that hath broken your legs. Apollo hath resigned his ivory harp unto Astrophel, and he, like Mercury, must lull you asleep with his music. Sleep Argus, sleep Ignorance, sleep Impudence! For Mercury hath Io, and only *io paean* belongeth to Astrophel. Dear Astrophel, that in the ashes of thy love livest again like the phoenix, O might thy body (as thy name) live again likewise here amongst us; but the earth, the mother of mortality, hath snatch'd thee too soon into her chilled cold arms and will not let thee by any means be drawn from her deadly imbrace; and thy divine soul, carried on an angel's wings to heaven, is installed in Hermes' place, sole prolocutor to the gods. Therefore mayest thou never return from the Elysian fields like Orpheus; therefore must we ever mourn for our Orpheus.

Fain would a second spring of passion here spend itself on his sweet remembrance, but religion, that rebuketh prophane lamentation, drinks in the rivers of those dispairful tears which languorous ruth hath outwelled and bids me look back to the house of honor where from one and the selfsame root of renown I shall find many goodly branches derived, and such as with the spreading increase of their virtues may somewhat overshadow the grief of his loss. Amongst the which, fair sister of Phoebus and eloquent secretary to the muses, most rare Countess of Pembroke, thou art not to be omitted, whom arts do adore as a second Minerva and our poets extol as the patroness of their invention; for in thee the Lesbian Sappho with her lyric harp is disgraced, and the laurel garland which thy brother so bravely advanc'd on his lance is still kept green in the temple of Pallas. Thou only sacrificest thy soul to contemplation, thou only entertainest empty-handed Homer, and keepest the springs of Castalia from being dried up. Learning, wisdom, beauty, and all other ornaments of nobility whatsoever seek to approve themselves in thy sight and get a further seal of felicity from the smiles of thy favor. . . .

Gentlemen, I fear I have too much presumed on your idle leisure and been too bold to stand talking all this while in another man's door, but now I will leave you to survey the pleasures of Paphos and offer your smiles on the altars of Venus.

Yours in all desire to please,
Thomas Nashe

ASTROPHEL AND STELLA

1

Loving in truth, and fain in verse my love to show,
  That she, dear she, might take some pleasure of my pain,
  Pleasure might cause her read, reading might make her
    know,
  Knowledge might pity win, and pity grace obtain—
I sought fit words to paint the blackest face of wo,
  Studying inventions fine, her wits to entertain,
  Oft turning others' leaves to see if thence would flow
  Some fresh and fruitful showers upon my sunburn'd
    brain.
But words came halting forth, wanting Invention's stay;
  Invention, Nature's child, fled step-dame Study's
    blows,   10
  And others' feet still seem'd but strangers in my way.
Thus, great with child to speak, and helpless in my throes,
  Biting my trewand pen, beating myself for spite,
  "Fool," said my muse to me, "look in thy heart and
    write."

2

Not at the first sight, nor with a dribbed shot,
  Love gave the wound which, while I breathe, will
    bleed;
  But known worth did in mine of time proceed,
  Till by degrees it had full conquest got.
I saw and liked; I liked but loved not;
  I loved, but straight did not what Love decreed;
  At length to Love's decrees I, forc'd, agreed,
  Yet with repining at so partial lot.
Now even that footstep of lost liberty
  Is gone, and now, like slave-born Muscovite,   10
  I call it praise to suffer tyranny;
And now employ the remnant of my wit
  To make meself believe that all is well,
  While, with a feeling skill, I paint my hell.

3

Let dainty wits cry on the sisters nine,
  That, bravely mask'd, their fancies may be told;
  Or Pindar's apes flaunt they in phrases fine,
  Enam'ling with pied flowers their thoughts of gold;
Or else let them in statelier glory shine,
  Ennobling new-found tropes with problems old;
  Or with strange similes enrich each line,
  Of herbs or beasts which Ind or Afric hold.
For me, in sooth, no muse but one I know;
  Phrases and problems from my reach do grow,   10
  And strange things cost too dear for my poor sprites.
How then? even thus: in Stella's face I read
  What love and beauty be, then all my deed
  But copying is what in her Nature writes.

6

Some lovers speak, when they their muses entertain,
  Of hopes begot by fear, of wot not what desires,
  Of force of heav'nly beams infusing hellish pain,
  Of living deaths, dear wounds, fair storms, and freezing
    fires;
Someone his song in Jove and Jove's strange tales attires,
  Bord'red with bulls and swans, powd'red with golden
    rain;
  Another, humbler wit to shepherd's pipe retires,
  Yet hiding royal blood full oft in rural vein;
To some a sweetest plaint a sweetest style affords,
  While tears pour out his ink, and sighs breathe out his
    words,   10
  His paper pale dispair, and pain his pen doth move.
I can speak what I feel, and feel as much as they,
  But think that all the map of my state I display
  When trembling voice brings forth that I do Stella love.

7

When Nature made her chief work, Stella's eyes,
  In color black why wrapp'd she beams so bright?
  Would she in beamy black, like painter wise,
  Frame daintiest luster mix'd of shades and light?
Or did she else that sober hue devise
  In object best to knit and strength our sight,
  Lest, if no veil these brave gleams did disguise,
  They, sunlike, should more dazzle then delight?
Or would she her miraculous power show,
  That, whereas black seems beauty's contrary,   10
  She even in black doth make all beauties flow?
Both so, and thus: she, minding Love should be
  Placed ever there, gave him this mourning weed
  To honor all their deaths who for her bleed.

15

You that do search for every purling spring
  Which from the ribs of old Parnassus flows,
  And every flour, not sweet perhaps, which grows
  Near thereabouts into your poesy wring;
Ye that do dictionaries' method bring
  Into your rimes, running in rattling rows;
  You that poor Petrarch's long-deceased woes
  With new-born sighs and denizen'd wit do sing;
You take wrong ways; those farfet helps be such
  As do bewray a want of inward touch,   10
  And sure at length stol'n goods do come to light.
But if, both for your love and skill, your name
  You seek to nurse at fullest breasts of Fame,
  Stella behold, and then begin to endite.

20

Fly, fly, my friends, I have my death-wound, fly;
  See there that boy, that murth'ring boy, I say,
  Who, like a thief, hid in dark bush doth lie
  Till bloody bullet get him wrongful prey.
So tyran he no fitter place could spy,
  Nor so fair level in so secret stay,
  As that sweet black which veils the heav'nly eye;
  There himself with his shot he close doth lay.
Poor passenger, pass now thereby I did,
  And stay'd, pleas'd with the prospect of the place,   10
  While that black hue from me the bad guest hid;
But straight I saw motions of lightning grace,
  And then descried the glist'ring of his dart;
  But ere I could fly thence, it pierc'd my heart.

21

Your words, my friend (right healthful caustics), blame
  My young mind marr'd, whom Love doth windlass so
  That mine own writings, like bad servants, show
  My wits quick in vain thoughts, in virtue lame;
That Plato I read for nought but if he tame
  Such coltish years; that to my birth I owe
  Nobler desires, lest else that friendly foe,
  Great expectation, wear a train of shame.
For since mad March great promise made of me,
  If now the May of my years much decline,   10
  What can be hoped my harvest time will be?
Sure, you say well, "Your wisdom's golden mine
  Dig deep with learning's spade." Now tell me this,
  Hath this world ought so fair as Stella is?

24

Rich fools there be whose base and filthy heart
  Lies hatching still the goods wherein they flow,
  And damning their own selves to Tantal's smart,
  Wealth breeding want, more [rich] more wretched
     grow.
Yet to those fools heav'n such wit doth impart,
  As what their hands do hold their heads do know;
  And knowing, love; and loving, lay apart
  As sacred things, far from all danger's show.
But that rich fool who by blind Fortune's lot
  The richest gem of love and life enjoys   10
  And can with foul abuse such beauties blot,
Let him, depriv'd of sweet but unfelt joys,
  Exil'd for ay from those high treasures which
  He knows not, grow in only folly rich.

28

You that with allegory's curious frame
  Of others' children changelings use to make,
  With me those pains, for God's sake, do not take;
  I list not dig so deep for brazen fame.

When I say Stella, I do mean the same
  Princess of beauty for whose only sake
  The reins of love I love, though never slake,
  And joy therein, though nations count it shame
I beg no subject to use eloquence,
  Nor in hid ways do guide philosophy;   10
  Look at my hands for no such quintessence,
But know that I in pure simplicity
  Breathe out the flames which burn within my heart,
  Love only reading unto me this art.

30

Whether the Turkish new moon minded be
  To fill his horns this year on Christian coast;
  How Poles' right king means without leave of host
  To warm with ill-made fire cold Moscovy;
If French can yet three parts in one agree;
  What now the Dutch in their full diets boast;
  How Holland hearts, now so good towns be lost,
  Trust in the shade of pleasing Orange tree;
How Ulster likes of that same golden bit
  Wherewith my father once made it half tame;   10
  If in the Scotch court be no welt'ring yet:
These questions busy wits to me do frame.
  I, cumb'red with good manners, answer do,
  But know not how, for still I think of you.

31

With how sad steps, O moon, thou climb'st the skies!
  How silently, and with how wan a face!
  What! may it be that even in heav'nly place
  That busy archer his sharp arrows tries?
Sure, if that long-with-love-acquainted eyes
  Can judge of love, thou feel'st a lover's case;
  I read it in thy looks—thy languish'd grace
  To me, that feel the like, thy state descries.
Then, ev'n of fellowship, O moon, tell me,
  Is constant love deem'd there but want of wit?   10
  Are beauties there as proud as here they be?
Do they above love to be lov'd, and yet
  Those lovers scorn whom that love doth possess?
  Do they call virtue there ungratefulness?

34

Come, let me write. And to what end? To ease
  A burth'ned heart. How can words ease, which are
  The glasses of thy daily vexing care?
  Oft cruel fights well pictured forth do please.
Art not asham'd to publish thy disease?
  Nay, that may breed my fame, it is so rare.
  But will not wise men think thy words fond ware?
  Then be they close, and so none shall displease.
What idler thing then speak and not be hard?
  What harder thing then smart and not to speak?   10
  Peace, foolish wit! with wit my wit is marr'd.

Thus write I, while I doubt to write, and wreak
　My harms on ink's poor loss. Perhaps some find
　Stella's great pow'rs, that so confuse my mind.

35

What may words say, or what may words not say,
　Where truth itself must speak like flattery?
　Within what bounds can one his liking stay,
　Where nature doth with infinite agree?
What Nestor's counsel can my flames allay,
　Since Reason's self doth blow the coal in me?
　And ah, what hope that hope should once see day,
　Where Cupid is sworn page to chastity?
Honor is honor'd, that thou dost possess
　Him as thy slave, and now long-needy Fame   10
　Doth even grow rich, naming my Stella's name.
Wit learns in thee perfection to express.
　Not thou by praise, but praise in thee is rais'd;
　It is a praise to praise, when thou art prais'd.

37

My mouth doth water, and my breast doth swell,
　My tongue doth itch, my thoughts in labor be;
　Listen then, lordings, with good ear to me,
　For of my life I must a riddle tell.
Toward Aurora's court a nymph doth dwell,
　Rich in all beauties which man's eye can see;
　Beauties so far from reach of words that we
　Abase her praise saying she doth excel;
Rich in the treasure of deserv'd renown,
　Rich in the riches of a royal heart,   10
　Rich in those gifts which give th' eternal crown;
Who, though most rich in these and every part
　Which make the patents of true worldly bliss,
　Hath no misfortune but that Rich she is.

39

Come sleep! O sleep, the certain knot of peace,
　The baiting-place of wit, the balm of wo,
　The poor man's wealth, the prisoner's release,
　Th' indifferent judge between the high and low;
With shield of proof shield me from out the prease
　Of those fierce darts dispair at me doth throw;
　O make in me those civil wars to cease;
　I will good tribute pay, if thou do so.
Take thou of me smooth pillows, sweetest bed,
　A chamber deaf to noise and blind to light,   10
　A rosy garland and a weary head;
And if these things, as being thine by right,
　Move not thy heavy grace, thou shalt in me,
　Livelier then elsewhere, Stella's image see.

41

Having this day my horse, my hand, my lance
　Guided so well that I obtain'd the prize,

Both by the judgment of the English eyes
　And of some sent from that sweet enemy, France;
Horsemen my skill in horsemanship advance,
　Townfolks my strength; a daintier judge applies
　His praise to sleight which from good use doth rise;
　Some lucky wits impute it but to chance;
Others, because of both sides I do take
　My blood from them who did excel in this,   10
　Think nature me a man of arms did make.
How far they shot awry! The true cause is,
　Stella look'd on, and from her heav'nly face
　Sent forth the beams which made so fair my race.

53

In martial sports I had my cunning tried,
　And yet to break more staves did me address,
　While with the people's shouts, I must confess,
　Youth, luck, and praise even fill'd my veins with pride;
When Cupid, having me, his slave, descried
　In Mars's livery prancing in the press:
　"What now, Sir Fool!" said he—I would no less—
　"Look here, I say!" I look'd, and Stella spied,
Who, hard by, made a window send forth light.
　My heart then quak'd, then dazzled were mine eyes,   10
　One hand forgat to rule, th' other to fight,
Nor trumpets' sound I heard nor friendly cries.
　My foe came on, and beat the air for me,
　Till that her blush taught me my shame to see.

FIRST SONG

Doubt you to whom my muse these notes entendeth,
Which now my breast, o'ercharg'd, to music lendeth?
To you, to you, all song of praise is due;
Only in you my song begins and endeth.

Who hath the eyes which marry state with pleasure?
Who keeps the key of nature's chiefest treasure?
To you, to you, all song of praise is due;
Only for you the heav'n forgate all measure.

Who hath the lips where wit in fairness reigneth?
Who womankind at once both decks and staineth?   10
To you, to you, all song of praise is due;
Only by you Cupid his crown maintaineth.

Who hath the feet whose step of sweetness planteth?
Who else, for whom fame worthy trumpets wanteth?
To you, to you, all song of praise is due;
Only to you her scepter Venus granteth.

Who hath the breast whose milk doth passions nourish?
Whose grace is such that when it chides doth cherish?
To you, to you, all song of praise is due;
Only through you the tree of life doth flourish.   20

Who hath the hand which without stroke subdueth?
Who long-dead beauty with increase reneweth?
To you, to you, all song of praise is due;
Only at you all envy hopeless rueth.

Who hath the hair which, loosest, fastest tieth?
Who makes a man live then glad when he dieth?
To you, to you, all song of praise is due;
Only of you the flatterer never lieth.

Who hath the voice which soul from senses sunders?
Whose force but yours the bolts of beauty thunders?   30
To you, to you, all song of praise is due;
Only with you not miracles are wonders.

Doubt you to whom my muse these notes intendeth,
Which now my breast, o'ercharg'd, to music lendeth?
To you, to you, all song of praise is due;
Only in you my song begins and endeth.

71

Who will in fairest book of Nature know
    How virtue may best lodg'd in beauty be,
    Let him but learn of Love to read in thee,
Stella, those fair lines which true goodness show.
There shall he find all vices' overthrow,
    Not by rude force, but sweetest soveraignty
    Of reason, from whose light those nightbirds fly,
That inward sun in thine eyes shineth so.
And, not content to be Perfection's heir,
    Thyself dost strive all minds that way to move,   10
    Who mark in thee what is in thee most fair.
So while thy beauty draws the heart to love,
    As fast thy virtue bends that love to good.
    But, ah, Desire still cries, "Give me some food."

74

I never drank of Aganippe well,
    Nor ever did in shade of Tempe sit,
    And muses scorn with vulgar brains to dwell;
Poor layman I, for sacred rites unfit.
Some do I hear of poets' fury tell,
    But, God wot, wot not what they mean by it;
    And this I swear by blackest brook of hell,
I am no pickpurse of another's wit.
How falls it then that with so smooth an ease
    My thoughts I speak, and what I speak doth flow   10
    In verse, and that my verse best wits doth please?
Guess we the cause. What, is it thus? Fie, no.
    Or so? Much less. How then? Sure thus it is,
    My lips are sweet, inspired with Stella's kiss.

76

She comes, and streight therewith her shining twins do
        move
    Their rays to me, who in her tedious absence lay

Benighted in cold wo; but now appears my day,
    The only light of joy, the only warmth of love.
She comes with light and warmth, which, like Aurora,
        prove
    Of gentle force, so that mine eyes dare gladly play
    With such a rosy morn, whose beams, most freshly
        gay,
    Scorch not, but only do dark chilling sprites remove.
But lo, while I do speak, it groweth noon with me,
    Her flamy glist'ring lights increase with time and
        place,   10
    My heart cries, "Ah, it burns!" Mine eyes now dazzled
        be.
No wind, no shade can cool. What help then in my case,
    But with short breath, long looks, staid feet, and
        walking head,
    Pray that my sun go down with meeker beams to bed?

FOURTH SONG

Only joy, now here you are,
Fit to hear and ease my care,
Let my whispering voice obtain
Sweet reward for sharpest pain;
Take me to thee, and thee to me.
No, no, no, no, my dear, let be.

Night hath clos'd all in her cloak,
Twinkling stars love-thoughts provoke,
Danger hence good care doth keep,
Jealousy itself doth sleep;   10
Take me to thee, and thee to me.
No, no, no, no, my dear, let be.

Better place no wit can find
Cupid's yoke to loose or bind;
These sweet flowers on fine bed, too,
Us in their best language woo;
Take me to thee, and thee to me.
No, no, no, no, my dear, let be.

This small light the moon bestows
Serves thy beams but to disclose;   20
So, to raise my hap more high,
Fear not else, none can us spy;
Take me to thee, and thee to me.
No, no, no, no, my dear, let be.

That you heard was but a mouse,
Dumb sleep holdeth all the house.
Yet asleep, methinks they say,
"Young folks, take time while you may."
Take me to thee, and thee to me.
No, no, no, no, my dear, let be.   30

Niggard Time threats, if we miss
This large offer of our bliss,
Long stay ere he grant the same.
Sweet, then, while each thing doth frame,
Take me to thee, and thee to me.
No, no, no, no, my dear, let be.

Your fair mother is a-bed,
Candles out and curtains spread;
She thinks you do letters write.
Write, but first let me indite: 40
Take me to thee, and thee to me.
No, no, no, no, my dear, let be.

Sweet, alas, why strive you thus?
Concord better fitteth us;
Leave to Mars the force of hands,
Your power in your beauty stands.
Take thee to me, and me to thee.
No, no, no, no, my dear, let be.

Wo to me, and do you swear
Me to hate but I forbear?   50
Cursed be my dest'nies all
That brought me so high to fall.
Soon with my death I will please thee.
No, no, no, no, my dear, let be.

100

O tears, no tears, but rain from Beauty's skies,
   Making those lilies and those roses grow
   Which ay most fair, now more then most fair show,
   While graceful Pity Beauty beautifies.
O honey'd sighs which from that breast do rise
   Whose pants do make unspilling cream to flow,
   Wing'd with whose breath so pleasing zephires blow
   As can refresh the hell where my soul fries.
O plaints conserv'd in such a sugar'd phrase
   That Eloquence itself envies your praise,   10
   While sobb'd-out words a perfect music give.
Such tears, sighs, plaints, no sorrow is, but joy;
   Or if such heavenly signs must prove annoy,
   All mirth farewell, let me in sorrow live.

ELEVENTH SONG

Who is it that this dark night
Underneath my window plaineth?
   It is one who from thy sight
Being, ah, exil'd, disdaineth
   Every other vulgar light.

Why, alas, and are you he?
Be not yet those fancies changed?
   Dear, when you find change in me,
Though from me you be estranged,
   Let my change to ruin be.   10

Well, in absence this will die;
Leave to see, and leave to wonder.
   Absence sure will help, if I
Can learn how myself to sunder
   From what in my heart doth lie.

But time will these thoughts remove;
Time doth work what no man knoweth.
   Time doth as the subject prove;
With time still the affection groweth
   In the faithful turtledove.   20

What if you new beauties see,
Will not they stir new affection?
   I will think they pictures be
(Image-like, of saints' perfection),
   Poorly counterfeting thee.

But your reason's purest light
Bids you leave such minds to nourish.
   Dear, do reason no such spite;
Never doth thy beauty florish
   More then in my reason's sight.   30

But the wrongs love bears will make
Love at length leave undertaking.
   No, the more fools it do shake,
In a ground of so firm making
   Deeper still they drive the stake.

Peace, I think that some give ear.
Come no more, lest I get anger.
   Bliss, I will my bliss forbear,
Fearing, sweet, you to endanger;
   But my soul shall harbor there.   40

Well, begone, begone, I say,
Lest that Argus' eyes perceive you.
   O unjust[est] fortune's sway,
Which can make me thus to leave you,
   And from louts to run away!

Certain Sonnets
TRANSLATED OUT OF
HORACE WHICH BEGINS *RECTIUS VIVES*

You better sure shall live not evermore
   Trying high seas, nor while seas' rage you flee,
   Pressing too much upon ill-harbor'd shore.

The golden mean who loves lives safely free
   From filth of foreworn house, and quiet lives
   Releas'd from court where envy needs must be.

The winds most oft the hugest pine tree grieves;
   The stately towers come down with greater fall;
   The highest hills the bolt of thunder cleaves.

Evil haps do fill with hope, good haps appal   10
    With fear of change, the courage well prepar'd;
    Foul winters, as they come, away they shall.

Though present times and past with evils be snar'd,
    They shall not last; with cithern silent muse
    Apollo wakes, and bow hath sometime spar'd.

In hard estate with stout shew valor use.
    The same man still in whom wise doom prevails,
    In too full wind draw in thy swelling sails.

A FAREWELL

Oft have I mus'd, but now at length I find
    Why those that die, men say they do depart—
    "Depart," a word so gentle, to my mind,
    Weakly did seem to paint death's ugly dart.

But now the stars with their strange course do bind
    Me one to leave with whom I leave my heart.
    I hear a cry of spirits faint and blind,
    That parting thus my chiefest part I part.

Part of my life, the loathed part to me,
    Lives to impart my weary clay some breath;   10
    But that good part wherein all comforts be
    Now dead doth shew departure is a death.
        Yea, worse than death: death parts both wo and joy;
        From joy I part still living in annoy.

[THOU BLIND MAN'S MARK,
THOU FOOL'S SELF-CHOSEN SNARE]

Thou blind man's mark, thou fool's self-chosen snare,
Fond fancy's scum, and dregs of scatt'red thought,
Band of all evils, cradle of causeless care,
Thou web of will whose end is never wrought,

Desire, Desire, I have too dearly bought
With prize of mangled mind thy worthless ware!
Too long, too long asleep thou hast me brought
Who should my mind to higher things prepare.

But yet in vain thou hast my ruin sought;
In vain thou madest me to vain things aspire;   10
In vain thou kindlest all thy smoky fire.

For Virtue hath this better lesson taught:
Within myself to seek my only hire,
Desiring nought but how to kill desire.

[LEAVE ME, O LOVE,
WHICH REACHEST BUT TO DUST]

Leave me, O Love, which reachest but to dust,
And thou, my mind, aspire to higher things.
Grow rich in that which never taketh rust.
Whatever fades but fading pleasure brings.

Draw in thy beams and humble all thy might
To that sweet yoke where lasting freedoms be,
Which breaks the clouds and opens forth the light
That doth both shine and give us sight to see.

O take fast hold; let that light be thy guide
In this small course which birth draws out to death,   10
And think how evil becometh him to slide
Who seeketh heav'n and comes of heav'nly breath.
    Then farewell, world! Thy uttermost I see!
    Eternal Love, maintain thy life in me.

EDMUND SPENSER

Like Shakespeare and Milton, his mighty opposites in English Renaissance literature, Spenser turned to poetry at an early age. For nearly a decade before the publication of *The Shepherd's Calendar* in 1579 he had been learning his craft. About the time he left Richard Mulcaster's stern but thorough teaching at the Merchant Taylors' School he contributed to John van der Noot's *Theater Wherein Be Represented the Miseries That Follow the Voluptuous Worldlings* (1569) some translations from Petrarch and Du Bellay; and at Pembroke Hall, Cambridge, he read widely in three foreign languages as well as his own, became intimate with Gabriel Harvey and Edward Kirke (the one a fellow and the other a sizar of his college), and presumably determined upon a career in literature. After proceeding M. A. in 1576, Spenser seems to have spent some time in the north of England (where he may have met and wooed the "Rosalind" of *The Shepherd's Calendar*), joined the Earl of Leicester's brilliant household in London around 1579, and began the bookish but revealing correspondence with Harvey (1579-80; see pp. 624-27) which tells us so much about Spenser's own literary aspirations and about the literary activity of the so-called Areopagus of Leicester's circle. At the urging of Sidney, Dyer, and Harvey the young poet was attracted—happily not for long—by the idea of classical meters in English. But, as we learn from the letters to Harvey and from E. K.'s glosses to *The Shepherd's Calendar*, he was also buzzing with other plans. From a long list of now lost works whose titles have survived—something called *The Dying Pelican*, a prose tract on *The English Poet*, nine

English comedies, *Dreams, Legends, Pageants,* and *Epithalamion Thamesis* among others—we may infer that in these heady years he was writing incessantly. A letter of October 5, 1579, announces to Harvey that *The Faerie Queene* is already in progress, and perhaps some of these apprentice works eventually came to rest within its capacious spread; moreover, it is possible, and even probable, that two of the *Hymns in Honor of Love and Beauty* and *Prosopopoia* were also products of this period, and were exhumed and revised for publication in the nineties after *The Faerie Queene* had established Spenser's fame. In the late seventies, however, the major work in hand was *The Shepherd's Calendar,* and its publication in 1579 marks not only Spenser's emergence as a poet of the first rank but also the advent of the high Elizabethan Renaissance after the lean years of Googe, Turbervile, and Gascoigne.

Though issued modestly as the work of "Immerito," *The Shepherd's Calendar* was carefully ushered into the world with a dedication to Sidney and a flattering prefatory letter addressed to Harvey by E. K. (?Edward Kirke), who also contributed an elaborate set of glosses. Following the plan of the *Kalendrier des Bergers,* a French almanac or cyclopedia of devotion and popular science, Spenser contrives an eclogue for each of the twelve months; moreover, as thoroughly conversant with the pastoral tradition embracing Theocritus, Virgil, Baptista Mantuanus, Jacopo Sannazaro, Clément Marot (*Eglogue au roi, Complaincte de ma Dame Loyse de Savoye*), Montemayor, Alexander Barclay, and Barnabe Googe, Spenser draws freely on many predecessors. Affecting (to the displeasure of Sidney and later of Jonson) a studiously archaic diction and employing a rich variety of meters and stanzas (ranging from ballad measure to so intricate a form as the sestina), he imitates or adapts Bion ("March"), Theocritus ("August"), Mantuan ("July," "September," "October"), and Marot ("November," "December"). Also in the tradition of the Renaissance pastoral he varies the amorous eclogues built around Colin's hopeless love for Rosalind ("January," "March," "June," "December") with a set of eclogues on religion ("February," "May," "July," "September"), as well as others that praise Queen Elizabeth ("April"), lament the death of "Dido" ("November"), illustrate the conventional singing-match ("August"), and deplore the neglect of poets ("October"). Colin Clout, the lovelorn shepherd whose name Spenser got from Skelton, must be taken to represent the poet himself, but other characters also clearly have some biographical significance: Hobbinol is Harvey, Algrind is Archbishop Grindal, Roffy (or Roffyn) is Bishop John Young (the Master of Pembroke during Spenser's years at Cambridge), Eliza is Queen Elizabeth, Lobbin is perhaps the Earl of Leicester, and Tityrus is variously Virgil or Chaucer. Rosalind may have been Machabeus Chyld, whom Spenser seems to have married in 1579, and about whose later life nothing is known.

The success of *The Shepherd's Calendar,* which had reached five editions before Spenser's death in 1599 (1579, 1581, 1586, 1591, 1597), at once raised the young poet to the first rank of contemporary writers. Sidney praised him in the noble *Defense* (?1581), and Webbe trumpeted his advent in his *Discourse* (1586). Meanwhile, however, Spenser, while following his political career in Ireland, was pushing steadily forward with the composition of *The Faerie Queene.* The publication of its first three books at Raleigh's instigation in 1590 had brought Spenser back to England in 1589; and, although his stay of some two years did not result in the preferment he had hoped for and deserved, it did bring him into contact with many writers, confirmed his reputation, and led to the publication of *Daphnaida* (1591), an elegy for Douglas Howard, daughter of Henry, Lord Howard, and wife of Sir Arthur Gorges. Spenser's impressions of court life and of the contemporary literary scene are beautifully ordered in *Colin Clout's Come Home Again,* a charming pastoral that, though perhaps written shortly after his return to Ireland, was not published until 1595. Although the allusions to Raleigh (the Shepherd of the Ocean), Queen Elizabeth (Cynthia), and Sidney (Astrophel) are as obvious as that to young Samuel Daniel (who alone, except for William Alabaster, is not given a pseudonym), the identification of the other pastoral names has been the source of much conjecture, some of it well-informed, some ridiculous. The suggestions for identifying Harpalus have included Googe, Churchyard, Turbervile, and Sackville; for Corydon, Abraham Fraunce and Sir Edward Dyer; for Alcyon, Gorges (whose wife's death provided the subject for *Daphnaida*); for Palin, Sir Thomas Chaloner, Peele, and Giles Fletcher the Elder; for Alcon, Thomas Watson, Lodge, and even James VI of Scotland; for Palemon, Gascoigne, Churchyard, and Arthur Golding; for Amyntas, Ferdinando Stanley, fifth Earl of Derby, and Thomas Watson; for Aetion, Drayton and Shakespeare. Whatever the facts behind such artful evasions, we may be sure that in the rhapsodic praise of ideal love we are very close to Spenser's most intimate convictions. In its softly cadenced pentameter quatrains and its firm lyrical structure *Colin Clout's Come Home Again* is one of Spenser's most shapely and successful poems. The volume is pieced out with Spenser's *Astrophel* and others' elegies on Sidney.

To exploit the popularity of the "new poet," William Ponsonby, his publisher, hurried through the press a volume of *Complaints* (1591) consisting mainly of juvenilia refurbished for the occasion. These included *The Ruins of Time, The Tears of the Muses* (both on conventional themes of mutability and the neglect of art), *Virgil's Gnat* (an ottava rima adaptation of the Latin *Culex* long mistakenly attributed to Virgil), *Muiopotmos* (a lovely *jeu d'esprit* about a butterfly caught in a spider's web that allegorizes perhaps Sidney's career or perhaps the enmity of Leicester and Burghley), and two revised contributions to Van der Noot's *Theater* of 1569 (*The Visions of Bellay* and *The Visions of Petrarch*). To represent this volume we have chosen excerpts from *Prosopopoia, or Mother Hubberd's Tale*, a piece which Spenser himself deprecates as "long sithens composed in the raw conceipt of my youth." Perhaps originally two separate poems, a satirical beast-fable and an allegory of usurped royalty, in its rather unwieldy printed form the work obviously echoes events of Spenser's brief stay in Leicester's household. The portrait of the good courtier (in the first part) may represent young Spenser's idealized view of Sidney; the sleeping lion (of the second part) is perhaps Elizabeth, and the fox who appropriates her royal prerogatives is sometimes equated with Burghley, whose threat to the crown (with his proposed match between the queen and the Duke d'Alençon) was checked by Leicester (Mercury).

In 1594 Spenser sent to Ponsonby for publication his sonnet sequence called *Amoretti* and the richly woven *Epithalamion*, both works of high autobiographical value which were printed together in 1595. In their blend of conventional and personal elements, the eighty-nine sonnets, a record of his courtship of Elizabeth Boyle, testify not only to the sonnet-vogue of the nineties but also to the intensity of Spenser's devotion to the woman who became his wife. As for the *Epithalamion*, it is one of the permanent splendors of English literature. A nuptial hymn written for Spenser's bride, its twenty-three stanzas and envoy lead us through the wedding day from dawn to midnight, and its flawless symmetry is only enhanced by the variety of its diction, imagery, pageantry, and soaring lyricism.

In 1596, again in London to see Books IV-VI of *The Faerie Queene* through the press, Spenser was commissioned by the Earl of Worcester to write the *Prothalamion* for the marriages of his daughters, Lady Elizabeth and Lady Katherine Somerset. This beautiful wedding song was published separately. In the same year appeared *Four Hymns*, of which the first two hymns were written, as Spenser explains in his dedication, in the "greener times" of his youth, the last two contrived "by way of retraction to reform them." Drawing on Christian myth, Calvinistic theology, and a big body of Platonic and Neo-Platonic lore from Ficino (*Commentarium in Convivium*), Giordano Bruno (*De gl' heroici furori*), Castiglione (*Il Cortegiano*), Benivieni (*Canzone dello amore celeste et divino*), and others, the *Hymns*, in graceful rime royal, achieve a characteristically rich fusion of some of the main elements in Spenser's syncretistic philosophy.

Our texts are based upon *The Shepheardes Calender. Conteyning twelue Æglogues proportionable to the twelue monethes*, 1579 (STC 23089); *Complaints. Containing sundrie small Poemes of the Worlds Vanitie*, 1591 (STC 23078); *Colin Clouts Come home againe*, 1595 (STC 23077); *Amoretti and Epithalamion. Written not long since by Edmunde Spenser*, 1595 (STC 23076); *Fowre Hymnes, Made by Edm. Spenser*, 1596 (STC 23086); *Prothalamion Or A Spousall Verse made by Edm. Spenser*, 1596 (STC 23088).

FROM THE SHEPHEARDES CALENDER CONTEYNING TWELVE ÆGLOGVES PROPORTIONABLE TO THE TWELVE MONETHES (1579)

ENTITLED TO THE NOBLE AND VERTVOUS GENTLEMAN MOST WORTHY OF ALL TITLES BOTH OF LEARNING AND CHEVALRIE, M. PHILIP SIDNEY

TO HIS BOOKE

Goe little booke: thy selfe present,
As child whose parent is vnkent,
To him that is the president
Of noblesse and of cheualree,
And if that Enuie barke at thee,
As sure it will, for succoure flee
  Vnder the shadow of his wing,
And asked, who thee forth did bring,
A shepheards swaine saye did thee sing,

All as his straying flocke he fedde: 10
And when his honor has thee redde,
Craue pardon for my hardyhedde.
  But if that any aske thy name,
Say thou wert base begot with blame:
Forthy thereof thou takest shame.
And when thou art past ieopardee,
Come tell me what was sayd of mee:
And I will send more after thee.

                             Immeritô

To the Most Excellent and Learned Both Orator and Poete, Mayster Gabriell Haruey, His Verie Special and
Singular Good Frend E. K. Commendeth the Good Lyking of This His Labour, and the Patronage
of the New Poete

Vncouthe, vnkiste, Sayde the olde famous Poete
Chaucer: whom for his excellencie and wonderfull
skil in making, his scholler Lidgate, a worthy scholler
of so excellent a maister, calleth the Loadestarre of
our Language: and whom our Colin clout in his
Æglogue calleth Tityrus the God of shepheards, comparing hym to the worthines of the Roman Tityrus,
Virgile. Which prouerbe, myne owne good friend
Maister Haruey, as in that good old Poete it serued
well Pandares purpose, for the bolstering of his   10
baudy brocage, so very well taketh place in this our
new Poete, who for that he is vncouthe (as said
Chaucer) is vnkist, and vnknown to most men, is
regarded but of few. But I dout not, so soone as his
name shall come into the knowledg of men, and his
worthines be sounded in the tromp of fame, but that
he shall be not onely kiste, but also beloued of all,
embraced of the most, and wondred at of the best.
No lesse, I thinke, deserueth his wittinesse in deuising,
his pithinesse in vttering, his complaints of loue so   20
louely, his discourses of pleasure so pleasantly, his
pastorall rudenesse, his morall wisenesse, his dewe
obseruing of Decorum euerye where, in personages,
in seasons, in matter, in speach, and generally in al
seemely simplycitie of handeling his matter, and
framing his words: the which of many thinges which
in him be straunge, I know will seeme the straungest,
the words them selues being so auncient, the knitting
of them so short and intricate, and the whole Periode
and compasse of speache so delightsome for the   30
roundnesse, and so graue for the straungenesse. And
firste of the wordes to speake, I graunt they be something hard, and of most men vnused, yet both
English, and also vsed of most excellent Authors and
most famous Poetes. In whom whenas this our Poet
hath bene much traueiled and throughly redd, how
could it be (as that worthy Oratour sayde) but that
walking in the sonne although for other cause he
walked, yet needes he mought be sunburnt; and
hauing the sound of those auncient Poetes still ring-   40
ing in his eares, he mought needes in singing hit out
some of theyr tunes. But whether he vseth them by
such casualtye and custome, or of set purpose and
choyse, as thinking them fittest for such rusticall
rudenesse of shepheards, eyther for that theyr rough
sounde would make his rymes more ragged and
rustical, or els because such olde and obsolete wordes
are most vsed of country folke, sure I think, and
think I think not amisse, that they bring great grace
and, as one would say, auctoritie to the verse. For   50

albe amongst many other faultes it specially be ob-
iected of Valla against Liuie, and of other against
Saluste, that with ouer much studie they affect
antiquitie, as coueting thereby credence and honor of
elder yeeres, yet I am of opinion, and eke the best
learned are of the lyke, that those auncient solemne
wordes are a great ornament both in the one and in
the other; the one labouring to set forth in hys worke
an eternall image of antiquitie, and the other carefully discoursing matters of grauitie and importaunce.
For if my memory fayle not, Tullie, in that booke
wherein he endeuoureth to set forth the paterne of a
perfect Oratour, sayth that ofttimes an auncient
worde maketh the style seeme graue, and as it were
reuerend: no otherwise then we honour and reuerence
gray heares for a certein religious regard which we
haue of old age. Yet nether euery where must old
words be stuffed in, nor the commen Dialecte and
maner of speaking so corrupted therby, that as in old
buildings it seme disorderly and ruinous. But all as in
most exquisite pictures they vse to blaze and portraict not onely the daintie lineaments of beautye,
but also rounde about it to shadow the rude thickets
and craggy clifts, that by the basenesse of such parts,
more excellency may accrew to the principall; for
oftimes we fynde ourselues, I knowe not how,
singularly delighted with the shewe of such naturall
rudenesse, and take great pleasure in that disorderly
order. Euen so doe those rough and harsh termes
enlumine and make more clearly to appeare the
brightnesse of braue and glorious words. So oftentimes a dischorde in Musick maketh a comely con-
cordaunce: so great delight tooke the worthy Poete
Alceus to behold a blemish in the ioynt of a wel
haped body. But if any will rashly blame such his
purpose in choyse of old and vnwonted words, him
may I more iustly blame and condemne, or of witlesse headinesse in iudging, or of heedelesse hardinesse in condemning; for not marking the compasse
of hys bent, he wil iudge of the length of his cast. For
in my opinion it is one special prayse, of many
whych are dew to this Poete, that he hath laboured
to restore, as to theyr rightfull heritage, such good
and naturall English words as haue ben long time out
of vse and almost cleane disherited. Which is the
onely cause that our Mother tonge, which truely of
it self is both ful enough for prose and stately enough
for verse, hath long time ben counted most bare and
barrein of both. Which default when as some en-
deuoured to salue and recure, they patched vp the

holes with peces and rags of other languages, borrowing here of the french, there of the Italian, euery
where of the Latine, not weighing how il those
tongues accorde with themselues, but much worse
with ours. So now they haue made our English
tongue a gallimaufray or hodgepodge of al other
speches. Other some not so wel seene in the English
tonge as perhaps in other languages, if they happen
to here an olde word, albeit very naturall and significant, crye out streight way that we speak no English, but gibbrish, or rather such as in old time
Euanders mother spake. Whose first shame is, that
they are not ashamed, in their own mother tonge
straungers to be counted and alienes. The second
shame no lesse then the first, that what so they
vnderstand not, they streight way deeme to be sencelesse, and not at al to be vnderstode. Much like to
the Mole in Æsopes fable, that, being blynd her selfe,
would in no wise be perswaded that any beast could
see. The last more shameful then both, that of their
owne country and natural speach, which together
with their Nources milk they sucked, they haue so
base regard and bastard iudgement, that they will not
onely themselues not labor to garnish and beautifie
it, but also repine that of other it should be embellished. Like to the dogge in the maunger, that him
selfe can eate no hay, and yet barketh at the hungry
bullock, that so faine would feede: whose currish
kind, though it cannot be kept from barking, yet I
conne them thanke that they refrain from byting.

Now for the knitting of sentences, whych they call
the ioynts and members therof, and for al the compasse of the speach, it is round without roughnesse,
and learned wythout hardnes, such indeede as may
be perceiued of the leaste, vnderstoode of the moste,
but iudged onely of the learned. For what in most
English wryters vseth to be loose, and as it were
vngyrt, in this Authour is well grounded, finely
framed, and strongly trussed vp together. In regard
wherof, I scorne and spue out the rakehellye route
of our ragged rymers (for so themselues vse to hunt
the letter) which without learning boste, without
iudgement iangle, without reason rage and fome, as
if some instinct of Poeticall spirite had newly rauished
them aboue the meanenesse of commen capacitie.
And being in the middest of all theyr brauery,
sodenly eyther for want of matter, or of ryme, or
hauing forgotten theyr former conceipt, they seeme
to be so pained and traueiled in theyr remembrance,
as it were a woman in childebirth or as that same
Pythia, when the traunce came vpon her: *Os rabidum
fera corda domans* &c.

Nethelesse let them a Gods name feede on theyr
owne folly, so they seeke not to darken the beames of
others glory. As for Colin, vnder whose person the
Author selfe is shadowed, how furre he is from such
vaunted titles and glorious showes, both him selfe
sheweth, where he sayth:

> Of Muses Hobbin. I conne no skill.   And,
>
> Enough is me to paint out my vnrest, &c.[1]

And also appeareth by the basenesse of the name,
wherein, it semeth, he chose rather to vnfold great
matter of argument couertly then, professing it, not
suffice thereto accordingly. Which moued him
rather in Æglogues then other wise to write, doubting perhaps his habilitie, which he little needed, or
mynding to furnish our tongue with this kinde,
wherein it faulteth, or following the example of the
best and most auncient Poetes, which deuised this
kind of wryting, being both so base for the matter,
and homely for the manner, at the first to trye theyr
habilities: and, as young birdes, that be newly crept
out of the nest, by little first to proue theyr tender
wyngs, before they make a greater flyght. So flew
Theocritus, as you may perceiue he was all ready full
fledged. So flew Virgile, as not yet well feeling his
winges. So flew Mantuane, as being not full somd.
So Petrarque. So Boccace. So Marot, Sanazarus, and
also diuers other excellent both Italian and French
Poetes, whose foting this Author euery where followeth, yet so as few, but they be wel sented, can trace
him out. So finally flyeth this our new Poete, as a
bird whose principals be scarce growen out, but yet
as that in time shall be hable to keepe wing with the
best.

Now as touching the generall dryft and purpose
of his Æglogues, I mind not to say much, him selfe
labouring to conceale it. Onely this appeareth, that

---

[1] A reference to "June" (lines 65–80), in which Colin Clout modestly tells Hobbinol:

> Of muses, Hobbinol, I conne no skill,
> For they bene daughters of the hyghest Ioue,
> And holden scorne of homely shepheards quill.
> For sith I heard that Pan with Phœbus stroue,
> Which him to much rebuke and Daunger droue,
> I neuer lyst presume to Parnasse hyll;
> But pyping lowe in shade of lowly groue,
> I play to please my selfe, all be it ill.
>
> Nought weigh I who my song doth prayse or blame,
> Ne striue to winne renowne, or passe the rest.
> With shepheard sittes not followe flying fame,
> But feede his flocke in fields, where falls hem best.
> I wote my rymes bene rough, and rudely drest;
> The fytter they my carefull case to frame.
> Enough is me to paint out my vnrest,
> And poore my piteous plaints out in the same.

He continues with praise of "the God of shepheards, Tityrus"
(i.e. Chaucer), "who taught me homely, as I can, to make."

his vnstayed yougth had long wandred in the common Labyrinth of Loue, in which time to mitigate and allay the heate of his passion, or els to warne (as he sayth) the young shepheards, scilicet his equalls and companions of his vnfortunate folly, he compiled these xij. Æglogues, which for that they be proportioned to the state of the xij. monethes, he termeth the *Shepheards Calendar,* applying an olde name to a new worke. Hereunto haue I added a certain Glosse or scholion for thexposition of old wordes and harder phrases: which maner of glosing and commenting, well I wote, wil seeme straunge and rare in our tongue: yet for somuch as I knew many excellent and proper deuises both in wordes and matter would passe in the speedy course of reading, either as vnknowen, or as not marked, and that in this kind, as in other, we might be equal to the learned of other nations, I thought good to take the paines vpon me, the rather for that by meanes of some familiar acquaintaunce I was made priuie to his counsell and secret meaning in them, as also in sundry other works of his. Which albeit I know he nothing so much hateth as to promulgate, yet thus much haue I aduentured vpon his frendship, him selfe being for long time furre estraunged, hoping that this will the rather occasion him to put forth diuers other excellent works of his, which slepe in silence, as his Dreames, his Legendes, his Court of Cupide, and sondry others; whose commendations to set out were verye vayne; the thinges though worthy of many, yet being knowen to few. These my present paynes if to any they be pleasurable or profitable, be you iudge, mine own good Maister Haruey, to whom I haue both in respect of your worthinesse generally, and otherwyse vpon some particular and special considerations, voued this my labour, and the maydenhead of this our commen frends Poetrie, himselfe

hauing already in the beginning dedicated it to the Noble and worthy Gentleman, the right worshipfull Maister Philip Sidney, a special fauourer and maintainer of all kind of learning. Whose cause I pray you, sir, yf Enuie shall stur vp any wrongful accusasion, defend with your mighty Rhetorick and other your rare gifts of learning, as you can, and shield with your good wil, as you ought, against the malice and outrage of so many enemies, as I know wilbe set on fire with the sparks of his kindled glory. And thus recommending the Author vnto you, as vnto his most special good frend, and my selfe vnto you both, as one making singuler account of two so very good and so choise frends, I bid you both most hartely farwel, and commit you and your most commendable studies to the tuicion of the greatest.

> Your owne assuredly to
> be commaunded E. K.

Post script

Now I trust, Maister Haruey, that vpon sight of your speciall frends and fellow Poets doings, or els for enuie of so many vnworthy Quidams, which catch at the garlond which to you alone is dewe, you will be perswaded to pluck out of the hateful darknesse those so many excellent English poemes of yours which lye hid, and bring them forth to eternall light. Trust me, you doe both them great wrong, in depriuing them of the desired sonne, and also yourselfe, in smoothering your deserued prayses, and all men generally, in withholding from them so diuine pleasures, which they might conceiue of your gallant English verses, as they haue already doen of your Latine Poemes, which in my opinion both for inuention and Elocution are very delicate and superexcellent. And thus againe, I take my leaue of my good Mayster Haruey. From my lodging at London thys 10. of Aprill. 1579.

THE GENERALL ARGVMENT OF THE WHOLE BOOKE

Little, I hope, needeth me at large to discourse the first Originall of Æglogues, hauing alreadie touched the same. But for the word Æglogues I know is vnknowen to most, and also mistaken of some the best learned (as they think), I wyll say somewhat thereof, being not at all impertinent to my present purpose.

They were first of the Greekes the inuentours of them called Æglogai, as it were αἴγον or αἰγονόμων λόγοι, that is Goteheards tales. For although in Virgile and others the speakers be more shepheards then Goteheards, yet Theocritus in whom is more

ground of authoritie then in Virgile, this specially from that deriuing, as from the first head and welspring the whole Inuention of his Æglogues, maketh Goteheards the persons and authors of his tales. This being, who seeth not the grossenesse of such as by colour of learning would make vs beleeue that they are more rightly termed Eclogai, as they would say, extraordinary discourses of vnnecessarie matter, which definition albe in substaunce and meaning it agree with the nature of the thing, yet no whit answereth with the ἀνάλυσις and interpretation of the word. For they be not termed Eclogues, but

Æglogues. Which sentence this authour very well obseruing, vpon good iudgement, though indeede few Goteheards haue to doe herein, nethelesse doubteth not to cal them by the vsed and best knowen name. Other curious discourses hereof I reserue to greater occasion. These xij. Æclogues euery where answering to the seasons of the twelue monthes may be well deuided into three formes or ranckes. For eyther they be Plaintiue, as the first, the sixt, the eleuenth, and the twelfth; or recreatiue, such as al those be which conceiue matter of loue, or commendation of special personages; or Moral, which for the most part be mixed with some Satyrical bitternesse, namely the second of reuerence dewe to old age, the fift of coloured deceipt, the seuenth and ninth of dissolute shepheards and pastours, the tenth of contempt of Poetrie and pleasaunt wits. And to this diuision may euery thing herein be reasonably applyed, a few onely except, whose speciall purpose and meaning I am not priuie to. And thus much generally of these xij. Æclogues. Now will we speake particularly of all, and first of the first, which he calleth by the first monethes name Ianuarie: wherein to some he may seeme fowly to haue faulted, in that he erroniously beginneth with that moneth which beginneth not the yeare. For it is wel known, and stoutely mainteyned with stronge reasons of the learned, that the yeare beginneth in March. For then the sonne reneweth his finished course, and the seasonable spring refresheth the earth, and the plesaunce thereof, being buried in the sadnesse of the dead winter now worne away, reliueth. This opinion maynteine the olde Astrologers and Philosophers, namely the reuerend Andalo, and Macrobius in his holydayes of Saturne, which accoumpt also was generally obserued both of Grecians and Romans. But sauing the leaue of such learned heads, we mayntaine a custome of coumpting the seasons from the moneth Ianuary, vpon a more speciall cause then the heathen Philosophers euer coulde conceiue, that is, for the incarnation of our mighty Sauiour and eternall Redeemer the Lord Christ, who as then renewing the state of the decayed world, and returning the compasse of expired yeres to theyr former date and first commencement, left to vs his heires a memoriall of his birth in the ende of the last yeere and beginning of the next. Which reckoning, beside that eternall monument of our saluation, leaneth also vppon good proofe of special iudgement. For albeit that in elder times, when as yet the coumpt of the yere was not

perfected, as afterwarde it was by Iulius Caesar, they began to tel the monethes from Marches beginning, and according to the same God (as is sayd in Scripture) comaunded the people of the Iewes to count the moneth Abib, that which we call March, for the first moneth, in remembraunce that in that moneth he brought them out of the land of Ægipt, yet according to tradition of latter times it hath bene otherwise obserued, both in gouernment of the church and rule of Mightiest Realmes. For from Iulius Cæsar, who first obserued the leape yeere which he called *Bissextilem Annum,* and brought in to a more certain course the odde wandring dayes which of the Greekes were called ὑπερβαίνοντες, of the Romanes *intercalares* (for in such matter of learning I am forced to vse the termes of the learned), the monethes haue bene nombred xij, which in the first ordinaunce of Romulus were but tenne, counting but CCCiiij dayes in euery yeare, and beginning with March. But Numa Pompilius, who was the father of al the Romain ceremonies and religion, seeing that reckoning to agree neither with the course of the sonne, nor of the Moone, thereunto added two monethes, Ianuary and February: wherin it seemeth, that wise king minded vpon good reason to begin the yeare at Ianuarie, of him therefore so called *tanquam Ianua anni,* the gate and entraunce of the yere, or of the name of the god Ianus, to which god for that the old Paynims attributed the byrth and beginning of all creatures new comming into the worlde, it seemeth that he therfore to him assigned the beginning and first entraunce of the yeare. Which account for the most part hath hetherto continued. Notwithstanding that the Ægiptians beginne theyr yeare at September, for that according to the opinion of the best Rabbins, and very purpose of the scripture selfe, God made the worlde in that Moneth, that is called of them *Tisri.* And therefore he commaunded them to keepe the feast of Pauilions in the end of the yeare, in the xv. day of the seuenth moneth, which before that time was the first.

But our Authour, respecting nether the subtiltie of thone parte, nor the antiquitie of thother, thinketh it fittest according to the simplicitie of commen vnderstanding, to begin with Ianuarie, wening it perhaps no decorum that Shepheard should be seene in matter of so deepe insight, or canuase a case of so doubtful iudgment. So therefore beginneth he, and so continueth he throughout.

IANVARYE
Ægloga prima

ARGVMENT

In this fyrst Æglogue Colin cloute, a shepheardes boy,
complaineth him of his vnfortunate loue, being but newly
(as semeth) enamoured of a countrie lasse called Rosalinde:
with which strong affection being very sore traueled, he
compareth his carefull case to the sadde season of the yeare,
to the frostie ground, to the frosen trees, and to his owne
winterbeaten flocke. And lastlye, fynding himselfe robbed
of all former pleasaunce and delights, hee breaketh his
Pipe in peeces, and casteth him selfe to the ground.

COLIN CLOVTE

A Shepeheards boye (no better doe him call)
When Winters wastful spight was almost spent,
All in a sunneshine day, as did befall,
Led forth his flock, that had bene long ypent.
So faynt they woxe, and feeble in the folde,
That now vnnethes their feete could them vphold.

All as the Sheepe, such was the shepeheards looke,
For pale and wanne he was (alas the while),
May seeme he lovd, or els some care he tooke:
Well couth he tune his pipe, and frame his stile.   10
Tho to a hill his faynting flocke he ledde,
And thus him playnd, the while his shepe there fedde.

"Ye Gods of loue, that pitie louers payne
(If any gods the paine of louers pitie),
Looke from aboue, where you in ioyes remaine,
And bowe your eares vnto my dolefull dittie.
And Pan, thou shepheards God, that once didst loue,
Pitie the paines that thou thy selfe didst proue.

"Thou barrein ground, whome winters wrath hath wasted,
Art made a myrrhour, to behold my plight: 20
Whilome thy fresh spring flowrd, and after hasted
Thy sommer prowde with Daffadillies dight.
And now is come thy wynters stormy state,
Thy mantle mard, wherein thou maskedst late.

"Such rage as winters reigneth in my heart,
My life bloud friesing with vnkindly cold:
Such stormy stoures do breede my balefull smart,
As if my yeare were wast and woxen old.
And yet, alas, but now my spring begonne,
And yet, alas, yt is already donne.   30

"You naked trees, whose shady leaues are lost,
Wherein the byrds were wont to build their bowre:
And now are clothd with mosse and hoary frost,
Instede of bloosmes, wherwith your buds did flowre:
I see your teares, that from your boughes doe raine,
Whose drops in drery ysicles remaine.

"All so my lustfull leafe is drye and sere,
My timely buds with wayling all are wasted:
The blossome which my braunch of youth did beare
With breathed sighes is blowne away and blasted;   40
And from mine eyes the drizling teares descend,
As on your boughes the ysicles depend.

"Thou feeble flocke, whose fleece is rough and rent,
Whose knees are weake through fast and euill fare,
Mayst witnesse well by thy ill gouernement,
Thy maysters mind is ouercome with care.
Thou weake, I wanne: thou leane, I quite forlorne:
With mourning pyne I, you with pyning mourne.

"A thousand sithes I curse that carefull hower,
Wherein I longd the neighbour towne to see: 50
And eke tenne thousand sithes I blesse the stoure,
Wherein I sawe so fayre a sight as shee.
Yet all for naught: such sight hath bred my bane.
Ah God, that loue should breede both ioy and payne.

"It is not Hobbinol, wherefore I plaine,
Albee my loue he seeke with dayly suit:
His clownish gifts and curtsies I disdaine,
His kiddes, his cracknelles, and his early fruit.
Ah foolish Hobbinol, thy gyfts bene vayne:
Colin them giues to Rosalind againe.   60

"I loue thilke lasse (alas why doe I loue?),
And am forlorne (alas why am I lorne?).
Shee deignes not my good will, but doth reproue,
And of my rurall musick holdeth scorne.
Shepheards deuise she hatcth as the snake,
And laughes the songes that Colin Clout doth make.

"Wherefore, my pype, albee rude Pan thou please,
Yet for thou pleasest not where most I would:
And thou, vnlucky Muse, that wontst to ease
My musing mynd, yet canst not, when thou should: 70
Both pype and Muse shall sore the while abye."
So broke his oaten pype, and downe dyd lye.

By that, the welked Phœbus gan availe
His weary waine, and nowe the frosty Night
Her mantle black through heauen gan ouerhaile.
Which seene, the pensife boy halfe in despight
Arose, and homeward droue his sonned sheepe,
Whose hanging heads did seeme his carefull case to weepe.

Colins Embleme
Anchôra speme.

GLOSSE

Colin Cloute) is a name not greatly vsed, and yet haue I
sene a Poesie of Maister Skeltons vnder that title. But
indeede the word Colin is Frenche, and vsed of the

French Poete Marot (if he be worthy of the name of a Poete) in a certein Æglogue. Vnder which name this Poete secretly shadoweth himself, as sometime did Virgil vnder the name of Tityrus, thinking it much fitter, then such Latine names, for the great vnlikelyhoode of the language.

vnnethes) scarcely.

couthe) commeth of the verbe Conne, that is, to know or to haue skill. As well interpreteth the same the worthy Sir Thomas Smitth in his booke of gouerment: wherof I haue a perfect copie in wryting, lent me by his kinseman, and my verye singular good freend, Maister Gabriel Haruey: as also of some other his most graue and excellent wrytings.

Sythe) time. Neighbour towne) the next towne: expressing the Latine *Vicina.*

Stoure) a fitt.   Sere) withered.

His clownish gyfts) imitateth Virgils verse,

> *Rusticus es Corydon, nec munera curat Alexis.*

Hobbinol) is a fained country name, whereby, it being so commune and vsuall, seemeth to be hidden the person of some his very speciall and most familiar freend, whom he entirely and extraordinarily beloued, as peraduenture shall be more largely declared hereafter. In thys place seemeth to be some sauour of disorderly loue, which the learned call *pæderastice:* but it is gathered beside his meaning. For who that hath red Plato his dialogue called *Alcybiades,* Xenophon, and Maximus Tyrius, of Socrates opinions, may easily perceiue that such loue is muche to be alowed and liked of, specially so meant as Socrates vsed it: who sayth, that in deede he loued Alcybiades extremely, yet not Alcybiades person, but hys soule, which is Alcybiades owne selfe. And so is *pæderastice* much to be præferred before *gynerastice,* that is the loue whiche enflameth men with lust toward woman kind. But yet let no man thinke that herein I stand with Lucian or hys deuelish disciple Vnico Aretino, in defence of execrable and horrible sinnes of forbidden and vnlawful fleshlinesse. Whose abominable errour is fully confuted of Perionius, and others.

I loue) a prety Epanorthosis in these two verses, and withall a Paronomasia or playing with the word, where he sayth, I loue thilke lasse (alas &c.

Rosalinde) is also a feigned name, which being wel ordered, wil bewray the very name of hys loue and mistresse, whom by that name he coloureth. So as Ouide shadoweth hys loue vnder the name of Corynna, which of some is supposed to be Iulia, themperor Augustus his daughter, and wyfe to Agryppa. So doth Aruntius Stella euery where call his Lady Asteris and Ianthis, albe it is wel knowen that her right name was Violantilla: as witnesseth Statius in his *Epithalamium.* And so the famous Paragone of Italy, Madonna Cœlia,

in her letters enuelopeth her selfe vnder the name of Zima: and Petrona vnder the name of Bellochia. And this generally hath bene a common custome of counterfeicting the names of secret Personages.

Auail) bring downe.

Ouerhaile) drawe ouer.

Embleme

His Embleme or Poesye is here vnder added in Italian, *Anchóra speme:* the meaning wherof is, that notwithstande his extreme passion and lucklesse loue, yet leaning on hope, he is some what recomforted.

APRILL
Ægloga quarta

ARGVMENT

This Æglogue is purposely intended to the honor and prayse of our most gracious souereigne, Queene Elizabeth. The speakers herein be Hobbinoll and Thenott, two shepheardes: the which Hobbinoll, being before mentioned greatly to haue loued Colin, is here set forth more largely, complayning him of that boyes great misaduenture in Loue, whereby his mynd was alienate and with drawen not onely from him, who moste loued him, but also from all former delightes and studies, aswell in pleasaunt pyping, as conning ryming and singing, and other his laudable exercises. Whereby he taketh occasion, for proofe of his more excellencie and skill in poetrie, to recorde a songe which the sayd Colin sometime made in honor of her Maiestie, whom abruptely he termeth Elysa.

| THENOT | HOBBINOLL |

Tell me, good Hobbinoll, what garres thee greete?
What! hath some Wolfe thy tender Lambes ytorne?
Or is thy Bagpype broke, that soundes so sweete?
Or art thou of thy loued lasse forlorne?

Or bene thine eyes attempred to the yeare,
Quenching the gasping furrowes thirst with rayne?
Like April shoure, so stremes the trickling teares
Adowne thy cheeke, to quenche thy thristye payne.

HOBBINOLL

Nor thys, nor that, so muche doeth make me mourne,
But for the ladde whome long I lovd so deare   10
Nowe loues a lasse that all his loue doth scorne:
He plongd in payne, his tressed locks dooth teare.

Shepheards delights he dooth them all forsweare,
Hys pleasaunt Pipe, whych made vs meriment,
He wylfully hath broke, and doth forbeare
His wonted songs, wherein he all outwent.

THENOT

What is he for a Ladde you so lament?
Ys loue such pinching payne to them that proue?
And hath he skill to make so excellent,
Yet hath so little skill to brydle loue? 20

HOBBINOLL

Colin thou kenst, the Southerne Shepheardes boye:
Him Loue hath wounded with a deadly darte.
Whilome on him was all my care and ioye,
Forcing with gyfts to winne his wanton heart.

But now from me hys madding mynd is starte,
And woes the Widdowe daughter of the glenne:
So nowe fayre Rosalind hath bredde hys smart,
So now his frend is chaunged for a frenne.

THENOT

But if hys ditties bene so trimly dight,
I pray thee, Hobbinoll, recorde some one: 30
The whiles our flockes doe graze about in sight,
And we close shrowded in thys shade alone.

HOBBINOL

Contented I: then will I singe his laye
Of fayre Eliza, Queene of shepheardes all:
Which once he made, as by a spring he laye,
And tuned it vnto the Waters fall.

"Ye dayntye Nymphs, that in this blessed Brooke
    doe bathe your brest,
Forsake your watry bowres, and hether looke,
    at my request: 40
And eke you Virgins that on Parnasse dwell,
Whence floweth Helicon, the learned well,
    Helpe me to blaze
    Her worthy praise
Which in her sexe doth all excell.

"Of fayre Elisa be your siluer song,
    that blessed wight:
The flowre of Virgins, may shee florish long,
    In princely plight.
For shee is Syrinx daughter without spotte, 50
Which Pan the shepheards God of her begot:
    So sprong her grace
    Of heauenly race,
No mortall blemishe may her blotte.

"See, where she sits vpon the grassie greene
    (O seemely sight!),
Yclad in Scarlot like a mayden Queene,
    And Ermines white.
Vpon her head a Cremosin coronet,
With Damaske roses and Daffadillies set: 60

Bayleaues betweene
And Primroses greene
Embellish the sweete Violet.

"Tell me, haue ye seene her angelick face,
    Like Phœbe fayre?
Her heauenly haueour, her princely grace,
    can you well compare?
The Redde rose medled with the White yfere,
In either cheeke depeincten liuely chere.
    Her modest eye, 70
    Her Maiestie,
Where haue you seene the like, but there?

"I sawe Phœbus thrust out his golden hedde,
    vpon her to gaze:
But when he sawe how broade her beames did spredde,
    it did him amaze.
He blusht to see another Sunne belowe,
Ne durst againe his fyrye face out showe:
    Let him, if he dare,
    His brightnesse compare 80
With hers, to haue the ouerthrowe.

"Shewe thy selfe, Cynthia, with thy siluer rayes,
    and be not abasht:
When shee the beames of her beauty displayes,
    O how art thou dasht?
But I will not match her with Latonaes seede;
Such follie great sorow to Niobe did breede:
    Now she is a stone,
    And makes dayly mone,
Warning all other to take heede. 90

"Pan may be proud that euer he begot
    such a Bellibone,
And Syrinx reioyse that euer was her lot
    to beare such an one.
Soone as my younglings cryen for the dam,
To her will I offer a milkwhite Lamb:
    Shee is my goddesse plaine,
    And I her shepherds swayne,
Albee forswonck and forswatt I am.

"I see Calliope speede her to the place 100
    where my Goddesse shines:
And after her the other Muses trace,
    with their Violines.
Bene they not Bay braunches which they doe beare,
All for Elisa in her hand to weare?
    So sweetely they play,
    And sing all the way,
That it a heauen is to heare.

"Lo how finely the graces can it foote
   to the Instrument: 110
They dauncen deffly, and singen soote,
   in their meriment.
Wants not a fourth Grace, to make the daunce euen?
Let that rowme to my Lady be yeuen:
   She shalbe a Grace,
   To fyll the fourth place,
And reigne with the rest in heauen.

"And whither rennes this beuie of Ladies bright,
   raunged in a rowe?
They bene all Ladyes of the lake behight,   120
   that vnto her goe.
Chloris, that is the chiefest Nymph of al,
Of Oliue braunches beares a Coronall:
   Oliues bene for peace,
   When wars doe surcease:
Such for a Princesse bene principall.

"Ye shepheards daughters, that dwell on the greene,
   hye you there apace:
Let none come there but that Virgins bene,
   to adorne her grace.   130
And when you come whereas shee is in place,
See that your rudenesse doe not you disgrace:
   Binde your fillets faste,
   And gird in your waste,
For more finesse, with a tawdrie lace.

"Bring hether the Pincke and purple Cullambine,
   with Gelliflowres:
Bring Coronations, and Sops in wine,
   worne of Paramoures.
Strowe me the ground with Daffadowndillies,   140
And Cowslips, and Kingcups, and loued Lillies:
   The pretie Pawnce,
   And the Cheuisaunce,
Shall match with the fayre flowre Delice.

"Now ryse vp Elisa, decked as thou art,
   in royall aray:
And now ye daintie Damsells may depart
   echeone her way,
I feare I haue troubled your troupes to longe:
Let dame Eliza thanke you for her song.   150
   And if you come hether
   When Damsines I gether,
I will part them all you among."

THENOT

And was thilk same song of Colins owne making?
Ah foolish boy that is with loue yblent!
Great pittie is, he be in such taking,
For naught caren, that bene so lewdly bent.

HOBBINOL

Sicker I hold him for a greater fon,
That loues the thing he cannot purchase.
But let vs homeward, for night draweth on,   160
And twincling starres the daylight hence chase.

Thenots Embleme
O quam te memorem virgo?
Hobbinols Embleme
O dea certe.

GLOSSE

Gars thee greete) causeth thee weepe and complain.

Forlorne) left and forsaken.

Attempred to the yeare) agreeable to the season of the yeare, that is Aprill, which moneth is most bent to shoures and seasonable rayne: to quench, that is, to delaye the drought, caused through drynesse of March wyndes.

The Ladde) Colin Clout.   The Lasse) Rosalinda.

Tressed locks) wrethed and curled.

Is he for a ladde) A straunge manner of speaking, scilicet what maner of Ladde is he?

To make) to rime and versifye. For in this word making, our olde Englishe Poetes were wont to comprehend all the skil of Poetrye, according to the Greeke woorde ποιεῖν, to make, whence commeth the name of Poetes.

Colin thou kenst) knowest. Seemeth hereby that Colin perteyneth to some Southern noble man, and perhaps in Surrye or Kent, the rather bicause he so often nameth the Kentish downes, and before, "As lythe as lasse of Kent."

The Widowes) He calleth Rosalind the Widowes daughter of the glenne, that is, of a country Hamlet or borough, which I thinke is rather sayde to coloure and concele the person, then simply spoken. For it is well knowen, euen in spighte of Colin and Hobbinoll, that shee is a Gentle woman of no meane house, nor endewed with anye vulgare and common gifts both of nature and manners: but suche, indeede, as neede nether Colin be ashamed to haue her made knowne by his verses, nor Hobbinol be greued that so she should be commended to immortalitie for her rare and singular Vertues. Specially deseruing it no lesse then eyther Myrto, the most excellent Poete Theocritus his dearling, or Lauretta, the diuine Petrarches Goddesse, or Himera, the worthye Poete Stesichorus hys Idole: Vpon whom he is sayd so much to haue doted that, in regard of her excellencie, he scorned and wrote against the beauty of Helena. For which his præsumptuous and vnheedie hardinesse, he is sayde by vengeaunce of the Gods, thereat being offended, to haue lost both his eyes.

Frenne) a straunger. The word, I thinke, was first poetically put, and afterwarde vsed in commen custome of speach for forenne.

Dight) adorned. Laye) a songe. As Roundelayes and Virelayes. In all this songe is not to be respected, what the worthinesse of her Maiestie deserueth, nor what to the highnes of a Prince is agreeable, but what is moste comely for the meanesse of a shepheards witte, or to conceiue, or to vtter. And therefore he calleth her Elysa, as through rudenesse tripping in her name: and a shepheards daughter, it being very vnfit that a shepheards boy brought vp in the shepefold should know, or euer seme to haue heard of a Queenes roialty.

Ye daintie) is, as it were, an *Exordium ad preparandos animos.*

Virgins) the nine Muses, daughters of Apollo and Memorie, whose abode the Poets faine to be on Parnassus, a hill in Grece, for that in that countrye specially florished the honor of all excellent studies.

Helicon) is both the name of a fountaine at the foote of Parnassus, and also of a mounteine in Bæotia, out of which floweth the famous Spring Castalius, dedicate also to the Muses: of which spring it is sayd that, when Pegasus the winged horse of Perseus (whereby is meant fame and flying renowme) strooke the grownde with his hoofe, sodenly thereout sprange a wel of moste cleare and pleasaunte water, which fro thence forth was consecrate to the Muses and Ladies of learning.

Your siluer song) seemeth to imitate the lyke in Hesiodus ἀργυρέον μέλος.

Syrinx) is the name of a Nymphe of Arcadie, whom when Pan being in loue pursued, she flying from him, of the Gods was turned into a reede. So that Pan catching at the Reedes in stede of the Damosell, and puffing hard (for he was almost out of wind), with hys breath made the Reedes to pype: which he seeing, tooke of them, and in remembraunce of his lost loue, made him a pype thereof. But here by Pan and Syrinx is not to bee thoughte that the shephearde simplye meante those Poetical Gods: but rather supposing (as seemeth) her graces progenie to be diuine and immortall, so as the Paynims were wont to iudge of all Kinges and Princes, according to Homeres saying,

Θυμὸς δὴ μέγας ἐστὶ διοτρεφέως βασιλήως,
τιμὴ δ' ἐκ διός ἐστι, φιλεῖ δε ὁ μητίετα Ζεύς,

could deuise no parents in his iudgement so worthy for her, as Pan the shepeheards God and his best beloued Syrinx. So that by Pan is here meant the most famous and victorious King, her highnesse Father, late of worthy memorye K. Henry the eyght. And by that name, oftymes (as hereafter appeareth) be noted kings and mighty Potentates: And in some place Christ himselfe, who is the verye Pan and god of Shepheardes.

Cremosin coronet) he deuiseth her crowne to be of the finest and most delicate flowers, instede of perles and precious stones, wherewith Princes Diademes vse to bee adorned and embost.

Embellish) beautifye and set out.

Phebe) the Moone, whom the Poets faine to be sister vnto Phæbus, that is the Sunne.

Medled) mingled.

Yfere) together. By the mingling of the Redde rose and the White is meant the vniting of the two principall houses of Lancaster and of Yorke: by whose longe discord and deadly debate this realm many yeares was sore traueiled, and almost cleane decayed. Til the famous Henry the seuenth, of the line of Lancaster, taking to wife the most vertuous Princesse Elisabeth, daughter to the fourth Edward of the house of Yorke, begat the most royal Henry the eyght aforesayde, in whom was the firste vnion of the Whyte Rose and the Redde.

Calliope) one of the nine Muses; to whome they assigne the honor of all Poetical Inuention, and the firste glorye of the Heroicall verse. Other say that shee is the Goddesse of Rhetorick: but by Virgile it is manifeste, that they mystake the thyng. For there in hys Epigrams, that arte semeth to be attributed to Polymnia, saying,

Signat cuncta manu, loquiturque Polymnia gestu;

which seemeth specially to be meant of Action and elocution, both special partes of Rhetorick: besyde that her name, which (as some construe it) importeth great remembraunce, conteineth another part. But I holde rather with them which call her Polymnia or Polyhymnia of her good singing.

Bay branches) be the signe of honor and victory, and therfore of myghty Conquerors worn in theyr triumphes, and eke of famous Poets, as saith Petrarch in hys Sonets,

Arbor vittoriosa triomphale,
Honor d' Imperadori & di Poëti, &c.

The Graces) be three sisters, the daughters of Iupiter (whose names are Aglaia, Thalia, Euphrosyne, and Homer onely addeth a fourth, scilicet Pasithea), otherwise called Charites, that is thanks. Whom the Poetes feyned to be the Goddesses of all bountie and comelines, which therefore (as sayth Theodontius) they make three, to wete, that men first ought to be gracious and bountiful to other freely, then to receiue benefits at other mens hands curteously, and thirdly to requite them thankfully: which are three sundry Actions in liberalitye. And Boccace saith, that they be painted naked (as they were indeede on the tombe of C. Iulius Cæsar), the one hauing her backe toward vs, and her face fromwarde, as proceeding from vs; the other two toward vs, noting double thanke to be due to vs for the benefit we haue done.

Deaffly) Finelye and nimbly.   Soote) Sweete.

Meriment) Mirth.

Beuie) A beauie of Ladyes is spoken figuratiuely for a

company or troupe. The terme is taken of Larkes. For they say a Beuie of Larkes, euen as a Couey of Partridge, or an eye of Pheasaunts.

Ladyes of the lake) be Nymphes. For it was an olde opinion amongste the Auncient Heathen, that of euery spring and fountaine was a goddesse the Soueraigne. Whiche opinion stucke in the myndes of men not manye yeares sithence, by meanes of certain fine fablers and lowd lyers, such as were the Authors of King Arthure the great and such like, who tell many an vnlawfull leasing of the Ladyes of the Lake, that is, the Nymphes. For the word Nymphe in Greeke signifieth Well water, or otherwise a Spouse or Bryde.

Behight) called or named.

Cloris) the name of a Nymph, and signifieth greenesse, of whome is sayd, that Zephyrus, the Westerne wind, being in loue with her, and coueting her to wyfe, gaue her for a dowrie the chiefedome and soueraigntye of al flowres and greene herbes growing on earth.

Oliues bene) The Oliue was wont to be the ensigne of   20 Peace and quietnesse, eyther for that it cannot be planted and pruned, and so carefully looked to, as it ought, but in time of peace: or els for that the Oliue tree, they say, will not growe neare the Firre tree, which is dedicate to Mars the God of battaile, and vsed most for speares and other instruments of warre. Whereupon is finely feigned, that when Neptune and Minerua stroue for the naming of the citie of Athens, Neptune, striking the ground with his mace, caused a horse to come forth, that importeth warre, but at Mineruaes stroke sprong   30 out an Oliue, to note that it should be a nurse of learning and such peaceable studies.

Binde your) Spoken rudely, and according to shepheardes simplicitye.

Bring) all these be names of flowers. Sops in wine a flowre in colour much like to a Coronation, but differing in smel and quantitye. Flowre delice, that which they vse to misterme Flowre de luce, being in Latine called Flos delitiarum.

A Bellibone) or a Bonibell. Homely spoken for a fayre   40 mayde or Bonilasse.

Forswonck and forswatt) ouerlaboured and sunneburnt.

I saw Phæbus) the sunne. A sensible Narration and present view of the thing mentioned, which they call παρουσία.

Cynthia) the Moone, so called of Cynthus, a hyll where she was honoured.

Latonaes seede) Was Apollo and Diana. Whom when as Niobe the wife of Amphion scorned, in respect of the noble fruict of her wombe, namely her seuen sonnes and so many daughters, Latona, being therewith dis-   50 pleased, commaunded her sonne Phœbus to slea al the sonnes, and Diana all the daughters: whereat the vnfortunate Niobe, being sore dismayed, and lamenting out of measure, was feigned of the Poetes to be turned into a stone vpon the sepulchre of her children. For

which cause the shepheard sayth he will not compare her to them, for feare of like mysfortune.

Now rise) is the conclusion. For hauing so decked her with prayses and comparisons, he returneth all the thanck of hys laboure to the excellencie of her Maiestie.

When Damsins) A base reward of a clownish giuer.

Yblent) Y is a poeticall addition. Blent, blinded.

Embleme

This Poesye is taken out of Virgile, and there of him vsed   10 in the person of Æneas to his mother Venus, appearing to him in likenesse of one of Dianaes damosells: being there most diuinely set forth. To which similitude of diuinitie Hobbinoll comparing the excelency of Elisa, and being through the worthynes of Colins song, as it were, ouercome with the hugenesse of his imagination, brusteth out in great admiration (*O quam te memorem virgo?*), being otherwise vnhable, then by soddein silence, to expresse the worthinesse of his conceipt. Whom Thenot answereth with another part of the like verse, as confirming by his graunt and approuaunce, that Elisa is no whit inferiour to the Maiestie of her of whome that Poete so boldly pronounced *O dea certe*.

IVLYE
Ægloga septima
ARGVMENT

This Æglogue is made in the honour and commendation of good shepeheardes, and to the shame and disprayse of proude and ambitious Pastours. Such as Morrell is here imagined to bee.

THOMALIN   MORRELL

Is not thilke same a goteheard prowde,
   that sittes on yonder bancke,
Whose straying heard them selfe doth shrowde
   emong the bushes rancke?

MORRELL

What ho, thou iollye shepheards swayne,
   come vp the hyll to me:
Better is, then the lowly playne,
   als for thy flocke, and thee.

THOMALIN

Ah God shield, man, that I should clime,
   and learne to looke alofte,   10
This reede is ryfe, that oftentime
   great clymbers fall vnsoft.
In humble dales is footing fast,
   the trode is not so tickle:
And though one fall through heedlesse hast,
   yet is his misse not mickle.

And now the Sonne hath reared vp
  his fyriefooted teme,
Making his way betweene the Cuppe,
  and golden Diademe: 20
The rampant Lyon hunts he fast,
  with Dogge of noysome breath,
Whose balefull barking bringes in hast
  pyne, plagues, and dreery death.
Agaynst his cruell scortching heate
  where hast thou couerture?
The wastefull hylls vnto his threate
  is a playne ouerture.
But if thee lust to holden chat
  with seely shepherds swayne,   30
Come downe, and learne the little what
  that Thomalin can sayne.

MORRELL

Syker, thous but a laesie loord,
  and rekes much of thy swinck,
That with fond termes and weetlesse words
  to blere myne eyes doest thinke.
In euill houre thou hentest in hond
  thus holy hylles to blame,
For sacred vnto saints they stond,
  and of them han theyr name.   40
S. Michels mount who does not know,
  that wardes the Westerne coste?
And of S. Brigets bowre, I trow,
  all Kent can rightly boaste:
And they that con of Muses skill,
  sayne most what, that they dwell
(As goteheards wont) vpon a hill,
  beside a learned well.
And wonned not the great God Pan
  vpon mount Oliuet,   50
Feeding the blessed flocke of Dan,
  which dyd himselfe beget?

THOMALIN

O blessed sheepe, O shepheard great,
  that bought his flocke so deare,
And them did saue with bloudy sweat
  from Wolues, that would them teare.

MORREL

Besyde, as holy fathers sayne,
  there is a hyllye place,
Where Titan ryseth from the mayne,
  to renne hys dayly race.   60
Vpon whose toppe the starres bene stayed,
  and all the skie doth leane;
There is the caue where Phebe layed
  the shepheard long to dreame.
Whilome there vsed shepheards all

to feede theyr flocks at will,
Till by his foly one did fall,
  that all the rest did spill.
And sithens shepheardes bene foresayd
  from places of delight: 70
Forthy I weene thou be affrayd
  to clime this hilles height.
Of Synah can I tell thee more,
  and of our Ladyes bowre:
But little needes to strow my store;
  suffice this hill of our.
Here han the holy Faunes resourse,
  and Syluanes haunten rathe.
Here has the salt Medway his sourse,
  wherein the Nymphes doe bathe,   80
The salt Medway, that trickling stremis
  adowne the dales of Kent,
Till with his elder brother Themis
  his brackish waues be meynt.
Here growes Melampode euery where,
  and Teribinth good for Gotes:
The one, my madding kiddes to smere;
  the next, to heale theyr throtes.
Hereto, the hills bene nigher heuen,
  and thence the passage ethe.   90
As well can proue the piercing leuin,
  that seeldome falls bynethe.

THOMALIN

Syker thou speakes lyke a lewde lorrell,
  of Heauen to demen so:
How be I am but rude and borrell,
  yet nearer wayes I knowe.
To Kerke the narre, from God more farre,
  has bene an old sayd sawe.
And he that striues to touch the starres
  oft stombles at a strawe.   100
Alsoone may shepheard clymbe to skye,
  that leades in lowly dales,
As Goteherd prowd that sitting hye,
  vpon the Mountaine sayles.
My seely sheepe like well belowe,
  they need not Melampode:
For they bene hale enough, I trowe,
  and liken theyr abode.
But if they with thy Gotes should yede,
  they soone myght be corrupted: 110
Or like not of the frowie fede,
  or with the weedes be glutted.
The hylls where dwelled holy saints
  I reuerence and adore:
Not for themselfe, but for the sayncts,
  Which han be dead of yore.
And nowe they bene to heauen forewent,
  theyr good is with them goe:

Theyr sample onely to vs lent,
  that als we mought doe soe.   120
Shepheards they weren of the best,
  and liued in lowlye leas:
And sith theyr soules bene now at rest,
  why done we them disease?
Such one he was (as I haue heard
  old Algrind often sayne)
That whilome was the first shepheard,
  and liued with little gayne:
As meeke he was, as meeke mought be,
  simple, as simple sheepe,   130
Humble, and like in eche degree
  the flocke which he did keepe.
Often he vsed of hys keepe
  a sacrifice to bring,
Nowe with a Kidde, now with a sheepe
  the Altars hallowing.
So lowted he vnto hys Lord,
  such fauour couth he fynd,
That sithens neuer was abhord
  the simple shepheards kynd.   140
And such I weene the brethren were
  that came from Canaan:
The brethren twelue, that kept yfere
  the flockes of mighty Pan.
But nothing such thilk shephearde was
  whom Ida hyll dyd beare,
That left hys flocke, to fetch a lasse,
  whose loue he bought to deare:
For he was proude, that ill was payd
  (no such mought shepheards bee),   150
And with lewde lust was ouerlayd:
  tway things doen ill agree:
But shepheard mought be meeke and mylde,
  well eyed, as Argus was,
With fleshly follyes vndefyled,
  and stoute as steede of brasse.
Sike one (sayd Algrin) Moses was,
  that sawe hys makers face,
His face more cleare then Christall glasse,
  and spake to him in place.   160
This had a brother (his name I knewe),
  the first of all his cote,
A shepheard trewe, yet not so true
  as he that earst I hote.
Whilome all these were lowe, and lief,
  and loued their flocks to feed;
They neuer strouen to be chiefe,
  and simple was theyr weede.
But now (thanked be God therefore)
  the world is well amend,   170
Their weedes bene not so nighly wore,
  such simplesse mought them shend:
They bene yclad in purple and pall,

so hath theyr god them blist;
They reigne and rulen ouer all,
  and lord it as they list:
Ygyrt with belts of glitterand gold
  (mought they good sheepeheards bene),
Theyr Pan theyr sheepe to them has sold,
  I saye as some haue seene.   180
For Palinode (if thou him ken)
  yode late on Pilgrimage
To Rome (if such be Rome), and then
  he sawe thilke misusage.
For shepheards (sayd he) there doen leade
  as Lordes done other where;
Theyr sheepe han crustes, and they the bread,
  the chippes, and they the chere;
They han the fleece, and eke the flesh
  (O seely sheepe the while);   190
The corne is theyrs, let other thresh,
  their hands they may not file.
They han great stores and thriftye stockes,
  great freendes and feeble foes:
What neede hem caren for their flocks?
  theyr boyes can looke to those.
These wisards weltre in welths waues,
  pampred in pleasures deepe,
They han fatte kernes, and leany knaues,
  their fasting flockes to keepe.   200
Sike mister men bene all misgone,
  they heapen hylles of wrath:
Sike syrlye shepheards han we none,
  they keepen all the path.

MORRELL

Here is a great deale of good matter
  lost for lacke of telling;
Now sicker I see, thou doest but clatter:
  harme may come of melling.
Thou medlest more then shall haue thanke,
  to wyten shepheards welth: 210
When folke bene fat, and riches rancke,
  it is a signe of helth.
But say me, what is Algrin he,
  that is so oft bynempt?

THOMALIN

He is a shepheard great in gree,
  but hath bene long ypent.
One daye he sat vpon a hyll
  (as now thou wouldest me:
But I am taught by Algrins ill,
  to loue the lowe degree).   220
For sitting so with bared scalpe,
  an Eagle sored hye,
That weening hys whyte head was chalke,
  a shell fish downe let flye.

She weend the shell fishe to haue broake,
  But therewith bruzd his brayne,
So now, astonied with the stroke,
  he lyes in lingring payne.

MORRELL

Ah good Algrin, his hap was ill,
  but shall be better in time.   230
Now farwell, shepheard, sith thys hyll
  thou hast such doubt to climbe.

Thomalins Embleme
In medio virtus.

Morrells Embleme
In summo fœlicitas.

GLOSSE

A Goteheard) By Gotes in scrypture be represented the
  wicked and reprobate, whose pastour also must needes   20
  be such.

Banck) is the seate of honor.

Straying heard) which wander out of the waye of truth.

Als) for also.

Clymbe) spoken of Ambition.

Great clymbers) according to Seneca his verse, *Decidunt
  celsa grauiore lapsu.*

Mickle) much.

The sonne) A reason, why he refuseth to dwell on
  Mountaines, because there is no shelter against the   30
  scortching sunne. According to the time of the yeare,
  whiche is the whotest moneth of all.

The Cupp and Diademe) Be two signes in the Firmament, through which the sonne maketh his course in
  the moneth of Iuly.

Lion) Thys is Poetically spoken, as if the Sunne did hunt
  a Lion with one Dogge. The meaning whereof is, that
  in Iuly the sonne is in Leo. At which tyme the Dogge
  starre, which is called Syrius or Canicula, reigneth,
  with immoderate heate causing Pestilence, drougth,   40
  and many diseases.

Ouerture) an open place. The word is borrowed of the
  French, and vsed in good writers.

To holden chatt) to talke and prate.

A loorde) was wont among the old Britons to signifie a
  Lorde. And therefore the Danes, that long time vsurped
  theyr Tyrannie here in Brytanie, were called for more
  dread then dignitie, Lurdanes, scilicet Lord Danes. At
  which time it is sayd, that the insolencie and pryde of
  that nation was so outragious in thys Realme, that if it 50
  fortuned a Briton to be going ouer a bridge, and sawe
  the Dane set foote vpon the same, he muste retorne
  back, till the Dane were cleane ouer, or els abyde the
  pryce of his displeasure, which was no lesse then
  present death. But being afterwarde expelled that name

of Lurdane became so odious vnto the people, whom
  they had long oppressed, that euen at this daye they
  vse for more reproche to call the Quartane ague the
  Feuer Lurdane.

Recks much of thy swinck) counts much of thy paynes.

Weetelesse) not vnderstoode.

S. Michels mount) is a promontorie in the West part of
  England.

A hill) Parnassus afforesayd.   Pan) Christ.

Dan) One trybe is put for the whole nation *per Synecdo-* 10
  chen.

Where Titan) the Sonne. Which story is to be redde in
  Diodorus Syculus of the hyl Ida; from whence he
  sayth, all night time is to bee seene a mightye fire, as
  if the skye burned, which toward morning beginneth
  to gather into a rownd forme, and thereof ryseth the
  sonne, whome the Poetes call Titan.

The Shepheard) is Endymion, whom the Poets fayne to
  haue bene so beloued of Phœbe, scilicet the Moone,   20
  that he was by her kept a sleepe in a caue by the space
  of xxx. yeares, for to enioye his companye.

There) that is, in Paradise, where, through errour of
  shepheards vnderstanding, he sayth, that all shepheards
  did vse to feede theyr flocks, till one (that is, Adam),
  by hys follye and disobedience, made all the rest of hys
  ofspring be debarred and shutte out from thence.

Synah) a hill in Arabia, where God appeared.

Our Ladyes bowre) a place of pleasure so called.

Faunes or Syluanes) be of Poetes feigned to be Gods of 30
  the Woode.

Medway) the name of a Ryuer in Kent, which, running
  by Rochester, meeteth with Thames; whom he calleth
  his elder brother, both because he is greater, and also
  falleth sooner into the Sea.

Meynt) mingled.

Melampode and Terebinth) be hearbes good to cure
  diseased Gotes. Of thone speaketh Mantuane, and of
  thother Theocritus.

τερμίνθου τράγων ἔσχατον ἀκρεμόνα.   40

Nigher heauen) Note the shepheards simplenesse, which
  supposeth that from the hylls is nearer waye to heauen.

Leuin) Lightning; which he taketh for an argument to
  proue the nighnes to heauen, because the lightning
  doth comenly light on hygh mountaynes, according to
  the saying of the Poete, *Feriuntque summos fulmina
  montes.*

Lorrell) A losell.   A borell) a playne fellowe.

Narre) nearer.   Hale) for hole.   50

Yede) goe.   Frowye) mustye or mossie.

Of yore) long agoe.   Forewente) gone afore.

The firste shepheard) was Abell the righteous, who (as
  scripture sayth) bent hys mind to keeping of sheepe, as
  did hys brother Cain to tilling the grownde.

His keepe) hys charge, scilicet his flocke.

Lowted) did honour and reuerence.

The brethren) the twelue sonnes of Iacob, whych were shepemaisters, and lyued onelye thereupon.

Whom Ida) Paris, which, being the sonne of Priamus, king of Troy, for his mother Hecubas dreame, which being with child of hym, dreamed shee broughte forth a firebrand, that set all the towre of Ilium on fire, was cast forth on the hyll Ida; where being fostered of 10 shepheards, he eke in time became a shepheard, and lastly came to knowledge of his parentage.

A lasse) Helena, the wyfe of Menelaus, king of Lacedemonia, was by Venus, for the golden Aple to her geuen, then promised to Paris, who thereupon with a sorte of lustye Troyanes stole her out of Lacedemonia, and kept her in Troye. Which was the cause of the tenne yeares warre in Troye, and the moste famous citye of all Asia most lamentably sacked and defaced.

Argus) was of the Poets deuised to be full of eyes, and therefore to hym was committed the keeping of the 20 transformed Cow Io: So called because that in the print of a Cowes foote there is figured an I in the middest of an O.

His name) he meaneth Aaron: whose name for more Decorum the shephearde sayth he hath forgot, lest his remembraunce and skill in antiquities of holy writ should seeme to exceede the meanenesse of the Person.

Not so true) for Aaron in the absence of Moses started aside, and committed Idolatry.

In purple) Spoken of the Popes and Cardinalles, which 30 vse such tyrannical colours and pompous paynting.

Belts) Girdles.

Glitterand) Glittering. A Participle vsed sometime in Chaucer, but altogether in I. Goore.

Theyr Pan) that is, the Pope, whom they count theyr God and greatest shepheard.

Palinode) A shephearde, of whose report he seemeth to speake all thys.

Wisards) greate learned heads.

Welter) wallowe. 40

Kerne) a Churle or Farmer.

Sike mister men) such kinde of men.

Surly) stately and prowde.

Melling) medling.

Bett) better.   Bynempte) named.

Gree) for degree.

Algrin) the name of a shepheard afforesayde, whose myshap he alludeth to the chaunce that happened to the Poet Æschylus, that was brayned with a shellfishe.

Embleme

By thys poesye Thomalin confirmeth that which in hys 50 former speach by sondrye reasons he had proued. For being both hymselfe sequestred from all ambition and also abhorring it in others of hys cote, he taketh oc-

casion to prayse the meane and lowly state, as that wherein is safetie without feare, and quiet without danger, according to the saying of olde Philosophers, that vertue dwelleth in the middest, being enuironed with two contrary vices: whereto Morrell replieth with continuaunce of the same Philosophers opinion, that albeit all bountye dwelleth in mediocritie, yet perfect felicitye dwelleth in supremacie. For they say, and most true it is, that happinesse is placed in the highest degree, so as if any thing be higher or better, then that streight way ceaseth to be perfect happines. Much like to that which once I heard alleaged in defence of humilitye out of a great doctour, *Suorum Christus humillimus:* which saying a gentle man in the company taking at the rebownd, beate backe again with lyke saying of another Doctoure, as he sayde, *Suorum deus altissimus.*

OCTOBER
Ægloga decima

ARGVMENT

In Cuddie is set out the perfecte paterne of a Poete, whiche, finding no maintenaunce of his state and studies, complayneth of the contempte of Poetrie, and the causes thereof: Specially hauing bene in all ages, and euen amongst the most barbarous, always of singular accounpt and honor, and being indede so worthy and commendable an arte: or rather no arte, but a diuine gift and heauenly instinct not to bee gotten by laboure and learning, but adorned with both: and poured into the witte by a certaine ἐνθουσιασμός and celestiall inspiration, as the Author hereof els where at large discourseth in his booke called the English Poete, which booke being lately come to my hands, I mynde also by Gods grace vpon further aduisement to publish.

PIERCE   CVDDIE

Cuddie, for shame hold vp thy heauye head,
And let vs cast with what delight to chace,
And weary thys long lingring Phœbus race.
Whilome thou wont the shepheards laddes to leade
In rymes, in ridles, and in bydding base:
Now they in thee, and thou in sleepe art dead.

CVDDYE

Piers, I haue pyped erst so long with payne,
That all mine Oten reedes bene rent and wore:
And my poore Muse hath spent her spared store,
Yet little good hath got, and much lesse gayne.   10
Such pleasaunce makes the Grashopper so poore,
And ligge so layd, when Winter doth her straine:

The dapper ditties that I wont deuise,
To feede youthes fancie and the flocking fry,

Delighten much: what I the bett forthy?
They han the pleasure, I a sclender prise.
I beate the bush, the byrds to them doe flye:
What good thereof to Cuddie can arise?

PIERS

Cuddie, the prayse is better then the price,
The glory eke much greater then the gayne: 20
O what an honor is it to restraine
The lust of lawlesse youth with good aduice:
Or pricke them forth with pleasaunce of thy vaine,
Whereto thou list their trayned willes entice.

Soone as thou gynst to sette thy notes in frame,
O how the rurall routes to thee doe cleaue:
Seemeth thou dost their soule of sence bereaue,
All as the shepheard that did fetch his dame
From Plutoes balefull bowre withouten leaue:
His musicks might the hellish hound did tame.   30

CVDDIE

So praysen babes the Peacoks spotted traine,
And wondren at bright Argus blazing eye:
But who rewards him ere the more forthy?
Or feedes him once the fuller by a graine?
Sike prayse is smoke that sheddeth in the skye,
Sike words bene wynd, and wasten soone in vayne.

PIERS

Abandon then the base and viler clowne,
Lyft vp thy selfe out of the lowly dust,
And sing of bloody Mars, of wars, of giusts,
Turne thee to those that weld the awful crowne.   40
To doubted Knights, whose woundlesse armour rusts,
And helmes vnbruzed wexen dayly browne.

There may thy Muse display her fluttryng wing,
And stretch herselfe at large from East to West:
Whither thou list in fayre Elisa rest,
Or if thee please in bigger notes to sing,
Aduaunce the worthy whome shee loueth best,
That first the white beare to the stake did bring.

And when the stubborne stroke of stronger stounds
Has somewhat slackt the tenor of thy string: 50
Of loue and lustihead tho mayst thou sing,
And carrol lowde, and leade the Myllers rownde,
All were Elisa one of thilke same ring.
So mought our Cuddies name to Heauen sownde.

CVDDYE

Indeede the Romish Tityrus, I heare,
Through his Mecœnas left his Oaten reede,
Whereon he earst had taught his flocks to feede,
And laboured lands to yield the timely eare,

And eft did sing of warres and deadly drede,
So as the Heauens did quake his verse to here.   60

But ah Mecœnas is yclad in claye,
And great Augustus long ygoe is dead:
And all the worthies liggen wrapt in leade,
That matter made for Poets on to play:
For, euer, who in derring doe were dreade,
The loftie verse of hem was loued aye.

But after vertue gan for age to stoupe,
And mighty manhode brought a bedde of ease,
The vaunting Poets found nought worth a pease,
To put in preace emong the learned troupe.   70
Tho gan the streames of flowing wittes to cease,
And sonnebright honour pend in shamefull coupe.

And if that any buddes of Poesie,
Yet of the old stocke gan to shoote agayne,
Or it mens follies mote be forst to fayne,
And rolle with rest in rymes of rybaudrye,
Or, as it sprong, it wither must agayne:
Tom Piper makes vs better melodie.

PIERS

O pierlesse Poesye, where is then thy place?
If nor in Princes pallace thou doe sitt   80
(And yet is Princes pallace the most fitt)
Ne brest of baser birth doth thee embrace.
Then make thee winges of thine aspyring wit,
And, whence thou camst, flye backe to heauen apace.

CVDDIE

Ah, Percy, it is all to weake and wanne,
So high to sore, and make so large a flight:
Her peeced pyneons bene not so in plight,
For Colin fittes such famous flight to scanne:
He, were he not with loue so ill bedight,
Would mount as high, and sing as soote as Swanne.   90

PIERS

Ah fon, for loue does teach him climbe so hie,
And lyftes him vp out of the loathsome myre:
Such immortall mirrhor, as he doth admire,
Would rayse ones mynd aboue the starry skie.
And cause a caytiue corage to aspire,
For lofty loue doth loath a lowly eye.

CVDDIE

All otherwise the state of Poet stands,
For lordly loue is such a Tyranne fell
That, where he rules, all power he doth expell.
The vaunted verse a vacant head demaundes,   100
Ne wont with crabbed care the Muses dwell.
Vnwisely weaues, that takes two webbes in hand.

Who euer casts to compasse weightye prise,
And thinks to throwe out thondring words of threate,
Let powre in lauish cups and thriftie bitts of meate,
For Bacchus fruite is frend to Phœbus wise.
And when with Wine the braine begins to sweate,
The nombers flowe as fast as spring doth ryse.

Thou kenst not, Percie, howe the ryme should rage.
O if my temples were distaind with wine,   110
And girt in girlonds of wild Yuie twine,
How I could reare the Muse on stately stage,
And teache her tread aloft in buskin fine,
With queint Bellona in her equipage.

But ah my corage cooles ere it be warme,
Forthy, content vs in thys humble shade:
Where no such troublous tydes han vs assayde,
Here we our slender pipes may safely charme.

PIERS   20

And when my Gates shall han their bellies layd,
Cuddie shall haue a Kidde to store his farme.   120

Cuddies Embleme
Agitante calescimus illo &c.

GLOSSE

This Æglogue is made in imitation of Theocritus his
xvi. Idilion, wherein hee reproued the Tyranne Hiero   30
of Syracuse for his nigardise towarde Poetes, in whome
is the power to make men immortal for theyr good
dedes, or shameful for their naughty lyfe. And the lyke
also is in Mantuane. The style hereof, as also that in
Theocritus, is more loftye then the rest, and applyed
to the heighte of Poeticall witte.

Cuddie) I doubte whether by Cuddie be specified the
authour selfe, or some other. For in the eyght Æglogue
the same person was brought in, singing a Cantion of
Colins making, as he sayth. So that some doubt that   40
the persons be different.

Whilome) sometime.   Oaten reedes) *Auena.*
Ligge so layde) lye so faynt and vnlustye.
Dapper) pretye.
Frye) is a bold Metaphore, forced from the spawning
fishes. For the multitude of young fish be called the
frye.
To restraine) This place seemeth to conspyre with Plato,
who in his first booke *de Legibus* sayth, that the first
inuention of Poetry was of very vertuous intent. For   50
at what time an infinite number of youth vsually came
to theyr great solemne feastes called Panegyrica, which
they vsed euery fiue yeere to hold, some learned man
being more hable then the rest for speciall gyftes of
wytte and Musicke, would take vpon him to sing fine
verses to the people, in prayse eyther of vertue or of

victory or of immortality or such like. At whose
wonderful gyft al men being astonied and as it were
rauished with delight, thinking (as it was indeed) that
he was inspired from aboue, called him *vatem:* which
kinde of men afterwarde framing their verses to lighter
musick (as of musick be many kinds, some sadder, some
lighter, some martiall, some heroical: and so diuersely
eke affect the mynds of men) found out lighter matter
of Poesie also, some playing wyth loue, some scorning
at mens fashions, some powred out in pleasures, and so
were called Poetes or makers.

Sence bereaue) what the secrete working of Musick is
in the myndes of men, aswell appeareth, hereby, that
some of the auncient Philosophers, and those the moste
wise, as Plato and Pythagoras, held for opinion, that the
mynd was made of a certaine harmonie and musicall
nombers, for the great compassion and likenes of affection in thone and in the other, as also by that memorable
history of Alexander: to whom when as Timotheus,
the great Musitian, playd the Phrygian melodie, it is
said, that he was distraught with such vnwonted fury,
that streight way rysing from the table in great rage,
he caused himselfe to be armed, as ready to goe to warre
(for that musick is very war like). And immediatly
whenas the Musitian chaunged his stroke into the
Lydian and Ionique harmony, he was so furr from
warring, that he sat as styl as if he had bene in matters
of counsell. Such might is in musick. Wherefore Plato
and Aristotle forbid the Arabian Melodie from children
and youth. For that being altogither on the fyft and vii
tone, it is of great force to molifie and quench the
kindly courage which vseth to burne in yong brests.
So that it is not incredible which the Poete here sayth,
that Music can bereaue the soule of sence.

The shepheard that) Orpheus: of whom is sayd, that by
his excellent skil in Musick and Poetry, he recouered
his wife Eurydice from hell.

Argus eyes) of Argus is before said, that Iuno to him committed hir husband Iupiter his Paragon Io, bicause he
had an hundred eyes: but afterwarde Mercury wyth
hys Musick lulling Argus aslepe, slew him and brought
Io away, whose eyes it is sayd that Iuno for his eternall
memory placed in her byrd the Peacocks tayle. For
those coloured spots indeede resemble eyes.

Woundlesse armour) vnwounded in warre, doe rust
through long peace.

Display) A poeticall metaphore: whereof the meaning
is that, if the Poet list showe his skill in matter of more
dignitie then is the homely Æglogue, good occasion is
him offered of higher veyne and more Heroicall argument, in the person of our most gratious soueraign,
whom (as before) he calleth Elisa. Or if mater of
knighthoode and cheualrie please him better, that there
be many Noble and valiaunt men, that are both worthy
of his payne in theyr deserued prayses, and also fauour-
ers of hys skil and faculty.

The worthy) he meaneth (as I guesse) the most honorable and renowmed the Erle of Leycester, whom by his cognisance (although the same be also proper to other) rather then by his name he bewrayeth, being not likely that the names of noble princes be known to country clowne.

Slack) that is when thou chaungest thy verse from stately discourse to matter of more pleasaunce and delight.

The Millers) a kind of daunce.

Ring) company of dauncers.

The Romish Tityrus) wel knowen to be Virgile, who by Mecænas means was brought into the fauour of the Emperor Augustus, and by him moued to write in loftier kinde then he erst had doen.

Whereon) in these three verses are the three seuerall workes of Virgile intended. For in teaching his flocks to feede is meant his *Æglogues*. In labouring of lands is hys *Bucoliques*. In singing of wars and deadly dreade is his diuine *Æneis* figured.

In derring doe) In manhoode and cheualrie.

For euer) He sheweth the cause why Poetes were wont be had in such honor of noble men; that is, that by them their worthines and valor shold through theyr famous Posies be commended to al posterities. Wherfore it is sayd, that Achilles had neuer bene so famous, as he is, but for Homeres immortal verses. Which is the only aduantage which he had of Hector. And also that Alexander the great comming to his tombe in Sigeus, with naturall teares blessed him, that euer was his hap to be honoured with so excellent a Poets work: as so renowmed and ennobled onely by hys meanes. Which being declared in a most eloquent Oration of Tullies, is of Petrarch no lesse worthely sette forth in a sonet,

> Giunto Alexandro a la famosa tomba
> Del fero Achille sospírando disse
> O fortunato che si chiara tromba. Trouasti &c.

And that such account hath bene alwayes made of Poetes, aswell sheweth this that the worthy Scipio in all his warres against Carthage and Numantia had euermore in his company, and that in a most familiar sort, the good olde Poet Ennius: as also that Alexander destroying Thebes, when he was enformed that the famous Lyrick Poet Pindarus was borne in that citie, not onely commaunded streightly that no man should vpon payne of death do any violence to that house by fire or otherwise: but also specially spared most, and some highly rewarded, that were of hys kinne. So fauoured he the only name of a Poete. Whych prayse otherwise was in the same man no lesse famous, that when he came to ransacking of king Darius coffers, whom he lately had ouerthrowen, he founde in a little coffer of siluer the two bookes of Homers works, as layd vp there for speciall iewells and richesse, which he,

taking thence, put one of them dayly in his bosome, and thother euery night layde vnder his pillowe. Such honor haue Poetes alwayes found in the sight of princes and noble men. Which this author here very well shewth, as els where more notably.

But after) he sheweth the cause of contempt of Poetry to be idlenesse and basenesse of mynd.

Pent) shut vp in slouth, as in a coope or cage.

Tom piper) An Ironicall Sarcasmus, spoken in derision of these rude wits whych make more account of a ryming rybaud then of skill grounded vpon learning and iudgment.

Ne brest) the meaner sort of men.

Her peeced pineons) vnperfect skil. Spoken wyth humble modestie.

As soote as Swanne) The comparison seemeth to be strange: for the swanne hath euer wonne small commendation for her swete singing: but it is sayd of the learned that the swan a little before hir death singeth most pleasantly, as prophecying by a secrete instinct her neere destinie. As wel sayth the Poete elswhere in one of his sonetts,

> The siluer swanne doth sing before her dying day
> As shee that feeles the deepe delight that is in death &c.

Immortall myrrhour) Beauty, which is an excellent obiect of Poeticall spirites, as appeareth by the worthy Petrarchs saying,

> Fiorir faceua il mio debile ingegno
> A la sua ombra, et crescer ne gli affanni.

A caytiue corage) a base and abiect minde.

For lofty loue) I think this playing with the letter to be rather a fault then a figure, aswel in our English tongue as it hath bene alwayes in the Latine, called *Cacozelon*.

A vacant) imitateth Mantuanes saying, *vacuum curis diuina cerebrum Poscit*.

Lauish cups) Resembleth that comen verse, *Fœcundi calices quem non fecere disertum*.

O if my) He seemeth here to be rauished with a Poetical furie. For (if one rightly mark) the numbers rise so ful, and the verse groweth so big, that it seemeth he hath forgot the meanenesse of shepheards state and stile.

Wild yuie) for it is dedicated to Bacchus, and therefore it is sayd that the Mænades (that is Bacchus franticke priestes) vsed in theyr sacrifice to carry Thyrsos, which were pointed staues or Iauelins, wrapped about with yuie.

In buskin) it was the maner of Poetes and plaiers in tragedies to were buskins, as also in Comedies to vse stockes and light shoes. So that the buskin in Poetry is vsed for tragical matter, as is said in Virgile, *Sola sophocleo tua carmina digna cothurno*. And the like in Horace, *Magnum loqui, nitique cothurno*.

Queint) strange Bellona, the goddesse of battaile, that is

Pallas, which may therefore wel be called queint for that (as Lucian saith) when Iupiter hir father was in traueile of her, he caused his sonne Vulcane with his axe to hew his head. Out of which leaped forth lustely a valiant damsell armed at all poyntes, whom seeing Vulcane so faire and comely, lightly leaping to her, proferred her some cortesie, which the Lady disdeigning, shaked her speare at him, and threatned his saucinesse. Therefore such straungenesse is well applyed to her.   10
Æquipage) order.   Tydes) seasons.

Charme) temper and order. For charmes were wont to be made by verses as Ouid sayth,

Aut si carminibus.

Embleme

Hereby is meant, as also in the whole course of this Æglogue, that Poetry is a diuine instinct and vnnatural rage passing the reache of comen reason. Whom Piers answereth Epiphonematicos as admiring the excellencye of the skyll whereof in Cuddie hee hadde alreadye hadde a taste.

FROM COMPLAINTS (1591)

PROSOPOPOIA: OR MOTHER HVBBERDS TALE

It was the month in which the righteous Maide
That, for disdaine of sinfull worlds vpbraide,
Fled back to heauen, whence she was first conceiued,
Into her siluer bowre the Sunne receiued;
And the hot Syrian Dog on him awayting,
After the chased Lyons cruell bayting,
Corrupted had th'ayre with his noysome breath,
And powr'd on th'earth plague, pestilence, and death.
Emongst the rest a wicked maladie
Raign'd emongst men, that manie did to die,   10
Depriu'd of sense and ordinarie reason;
That it to Leaches seemed strange and geason.
My fortune was, mongst manie others moe,
To be partaker of their common woe;
And my weake bodie, set on fire with griefe,
Was rob'd of rest and naturall reliefe.
In this ill plight, there came to visite mee
Some friends, who, sorie my sad case to see,
Began to comfort me in chearfull wise,
And meanes of gladsome solace to deuise.   20
But seeing kindly sleep refuse to doe
His office, and my feeble eyes forgoe,
They sought my troubled sense how to deceaue
With talke, that might vnquiet fancies reaue;
And sitting all in seates about me round,
With pleasant tales (fit for that idle stound)
They cast in course to waste the wearie howres:
Some tolde of Ladies, and their Paramoures;
Some of braue Knights, and their renowned Squires;
Some of the Faeries and their strange attires;   30
And some of Giaunts hard to be beleeued,
That the delight thereof me much releeued.
Amongst the rest a good old woman was,
Hight Mother Hubberd, who did farre surpas
The rest in honest mirth, that seem'd her well:
She, when her turne was come her tale to tell,
Tolde of a strange aduenture, that betided

Betwixt the Foxe and th'Ape by him misguided;
The which, for that my sense it greatly pleased,
All were my spirite heauie and diseased,   40
Ile write in termes as she the same did say,
So well as I her words remember may.
No Muses aide me needes heretoo to call;
Base is the style, and matter meane withall.
¶ Whilome (said she) before the world was ciuill,
The Foxe and th'Ape, disliking of their euill
And hard estate, determined to seeke
Their fortunes farre abroad, lyeke with his lyeke:
For both were craftie and vnhappie witted;
Two fellowes might no where be better fitted.   50
The Foxe, that first this cause of griefe did finde,
Gan first thus plaine his case with words vnkinde:
"Neighbour Ape, and my Goship eke beside
(Both two sure bands in friendship to be tide),
To whom may I more trustely complaine
The euill plight that doth me sore constraine,
And hope thereof to finde due remedie?
Heare then my paine and inward agonie.
Thus manie yeares I now haue spent and worne,
In meane regard, and basest fortunes scorne,   60
Dooing my Countrey seruice as I might,
No lesse I dare saie than the prowdest wight;
And still I hoped to be vp aduaunced,
For my good parts; but still it hath mischaunced.
Now therefore that no lenger hope I see,
But froward fortune still to follow mee,
And losels lifted high, where I did looke,
I meane to turne the next leafe of the booke.
Yet ere that anie way I doo betake,
I meane my Gossip priuie first to make."   70
"Ah my deare Gossip" (answer'd then the Ape),
"Deeply doo your sad words my wits awhape,
Both for because your griefe doth great appeare,
And eke because my selfe am touched neare:
For I likewise haue wasted much good time,
Still wayting to preferment vp to clime,

Whilest others always haue before me stept,
And from my beard the fat away haue swept;
That now vnto despaire I gin to growe,
And meane for better winde about to throwe.   80
Therefore to me, my trustie friend, aread
Thy councell: two is better than one head."
"Certes" (said he) "I meane me to disguize
In some straunge habit, after vncouth wize,
Or like a Pilgrime, or a Lymiter,
Or like a Gipsen, or a Iuggeler,
And so to wander to the worlds ende,
To seeke my fortune, where I may it mend;
For worse than that I haue I cannot meete.
Wide is the world, I wote, and euerie streete   90
Is full of fortunes and aduentures straunge,
Continuallie subiect vnto chaunge.
Say, my faire brother, now if this deuice
Doth like you, or may you to like entice."
"Surely" (said th'Ape) "it likes me wondrous well;
And would ye not poore fellowship expell,
My selfe would offer you t'accompanie
In this aduentures chauncefull ieopardie.
For to wexe olde at home in idlenesse
Is disaduentrous, and quite fortunelesse: 100
Abroad, where change is, good may gotten bee."
The Foxe was glad, and quickly did agree:
So both resolu'd, the morrow next ensuing,
So soone as day appeard to peoples vewing,
On their intended iourney to proceede;
And ouer night, whatso theretoo did neede,
Each did prepare, in readines to bee.
The morrow next, so soone as one might see
Light out of heauens windowes forth to looke,
Both their habiliments vnto them tooke,   110
And put themselues (a Gods name) on their way.
Whenas the Ape beginning well to wey
This hard aduenture, thus began t'aduise:
"Now read, Sir Reynold, as ye be right wise,
What course ye weene is best for vs to take,
That for our selues we may a liuing make.
Whether shall we professe some trade or skill?
Or shall we varie our deuice at will,
Euen as new occasion appeares?
Or shall we tie our selues for certaine yeares   120
To anie seruice, or to anie place?
For it behoues ere that into the race
We enter, to resolue first herevpon."
"Now surely, brother" (said the Foxe anon)
"Ye haue this matter motioned in season:
For euerie thing that is begun with reason
Will come by readie meanes vnto his end;
But things miscounselled must needs miswend.
Thus therefore I aduize vpon the case:
That not to anie certaine trade or place,   130
Nor anie man we should our selues applie:

For why should he that is at libertie
Make himselfe bond? sith then we are free borne,
Let vs all seruile base subiection scorne;
And as we bee sonnes of the world so wide,
Let vs our fathers heritage diuide,
And chalenge to our selues our portions dew
Of all the patrimonie which a few
Now hold in hugger mugger in their hand,
And all the rest doo rob of good and land.   140
For now a few haue all and all haue nought,
Yet all be brethren ylike dearly bought:
There is no right in this partition,
Ne was it so by institution
Ordained first, ne by the law of Nature,
But that she gaue like blessing to each creture
As well of worldly liuelode as of life,
That there might be no difference nor strife,
Nor ought cald mine or thine: thrice happie then
Was the condition of mortall men.   150
That was the golden age of Saturne old,
But this might better be the world of gold:
For without golde now nothing wilbe got.
Therefore (if please you) this shalbe our plot:
We will not be of anie occupation;
Let such vile vassalls borne to base vocation
Drudge in the world, and for their liuing droyle,
Which haue no wit to liue withouten toyle.
But we will walke about the world at pleasure
Like two free men, and make our ease a treasure.   160
Free men some beggers call, but they be free,
And they which call them so more beggers bee:
For they doo swinke and sweate to feed the other,
Who liue like Lords of that which they doo gather,
And yet doo neuer thanke them for the same,
But as their due by Nature doo it clame.
Such will we fashion both our selues to bee,
Lords of the world, and so will wander free
Where so vs listeth, vncontrol'd of anie:
Hard is our hap, if we (emongst so manie)   170
Light not on some that may our state amend;
Sildome but some good commeth ere the end."
Well seemd the Ape to like this ordinaunce:
Yet, well considering of the circumstaunce,
As pausing in great doubt awhile he staid,
And afterwards with graue aduizement said:
"I cannot, my lief brother, like but well
The purpose of the complot which ye tell:
For well I wot (compar'd to all the rest
Of each degree) that Beggers life is best: 180
And they that thinke themselues the best of all
Oft-times to begging are content to fall.
But this I wot withall that we shall ronne
Into great daunger like to bee vndonne,
Thus wildly to wander in the worlds eye,
Without pasport or good warrantie,

For feare least we like rogues should be reputed,
And for eare marked beasts abroad be bruted.
Therefore I read that we our counsells call,
How to preuent this mischiefe ere it fall,   190
And how we may with most securitie,
Beg amongst those that beggers doo defie."
"Right well, deere Gossip, ye aduized haue"
(Said then the Foxe), "but I this doubt will saue:
For ere we farther passe, I will deuise
A pasport for vs both in fittest wize,
And by the names of Souldiers vs protect;
That now is thought a ciuile begging sect.
Be you the Souldier, for you likest are
For manly semblance, and small skill in warre: 200
I will but wayte on you, and as occasion
Falls out, my selfe fit for the same will fashion."
The Pasport ended, both they forward went,
The Ape clad Souldierlike, fit for th'intent,
In a blew iacket with a crosse of redd
And manie slits, as if that he had shedd
Much blood throgh many wounds therein receaued,
Which had the vse of his right arme bereaued;
Vpon his head an old Scotch cap he wore,
With a plume feather all to peeces tore: 210
His breeches were made after the new cut,
Al Portugese, loose like an emptie gut;
And his hose broken high aboue the heeling,
And his shooes beaten out with traueling.
But neither sword nor dagger he did beare,
Seemes that no foes reuengement he did feare;
In stead of them a handsome bat he held,
On which he leaned, as one farre in elde.
Shame light on him, that through so false illusion,
Doth turne the name of Souldiers to abusion,   220
And that, which is the noblest mysterie,
Brings to reproach and common infamie.
Long they thus trauailed, yet neuer met
Aduenture, which might them a working set:
Yet manie waies they sought, and manie tryed;
Yet for their purposes none fit espyed.
At last they chaunst to meete vpon the way
A simple husbandman in garments gray;
Yet though his vesture were but meane and bace,
A good yeoman he was of honest place,   230
And more for thrift did care than for gay clothing:
Gay without good is good hearts greatest loathing.
The Foxe, him spying, bad the Ape him dight
To play his part, for loe! he was in sight,
That (if he er'd not) should them entertaine,
And yeeld them timely profite for their paine.
Eftsoones the Ape himselfe gan vp to reare,
And on his shoulders high his bat to beare,
As if good seruice he were fit to doo;
But little thrift for him he did fit too: 240
And stoutly forward he his steps did straine,

That like a handsome swaine it him became.
When as they nigh approached, that good man
Seeing them wander loosly, first began
T'enquire of custome, what and whence they were?
To whom the Ape, "I am a Souldiere,
That late in warres haue spent my deerest blood,
And in long seruice lost both limbs and good,
And now constrain'd that trade to ouergiue,
I driuen am to seeke some meanes to liue: 250
Which might it you in pitie please t'afford,
I would be readie both in deed and word,
To doo you faithfull seruice all my dayes.
This yron world" (that same he weeping sayes)
"Brings downe the stowtest hearts to lowest state:
For miserie doth brauest mindes abate,
And make them seeke for that they wont to scorne,
Of fortune and of hope at once forlorne."
The honest man, that heard him thus complaine,
Was grieu'd, as he had felt part of his paine;   260
And well disposd' him some reliefe to showe,
Askt if in husbandrie he ought did knowe,
To plough, to plant, to reap, to rake, to sowe,
To hedge, to ditch, to thrash, to thetch, to mowe;
Or to what labour els he was prepar'd?
For husbands life is labourous and hard.
Whenas the Ape him hard so much to talke
Of labour, that did from his liking balke,
He would haue slipt the coller handsomly,
And to him said: "good Sir, full glad am I,   270
To take what paines may anie liuing wight:
But my late maymed limbs lack wonted might
To doo their kindly seruices, as needeth:
Scarce this right hand the mouth with diet feedeth,
So that it may no painfull worke endure,
Ne to strong labour can it selfe enure.
But if that anie other place you haue,
Which askes small paines, but thriftines to saue,
Or care to ouerlooke, or trust to gather,
Ye may me trust as your owne ghostly father."   280
With that the husbandman gan him auize
That it for him were fittest exercise
Cattell to keep, or grounds to ouersee;
And asked him, if he could willing bee
To keep his sheep, or to attend his swyne,
Or watch his mares, or take his charge of kyne?
"Gladly" (said he) "what euer such like paine
Ye put on me, I will the same sustaine:
But gladliest I of your fleecie sheepe
(Might it you please) would take on me the keep.   290
For ere that vnto armes I me betooke,
Vnto my fathers sheepe I vsde to looke,
That yet the skill thereof I haue not loste:
Thereto right well this Curdog by my coste"
(Meaning the Foxe) "will serue, my sheepe to gather,
And driue to follow after their Belwether. . . ."

[Rascals that they are, the ape and the fox kill and eat all the new-born sheep, "and when lambes fail'd, the old sheepes liues they reft." Having thus destroyed the flock, they flee to avoid a reckoning with the farmer.]

And now the Foxe had gotten him a gowne,
And th'Ape a cassocke sidelong hanging downe;
For they their occupation meant to change,
And now in other state abroad to range:
For since their souldiers pas no better spedd,
They forg'd another, as for Clerkes booke-redd.
Who passing foorth, as their aduentures fell,
Through manie haps, which needs not here to tell,   360
At length chaunst with a formall Priest to meete,
Whom they in ciuill manner first did greete,
And after askt an almes for Gods deare loue.
The man straight way his choler vp did moue,
And with reproachfull tearmes gan them reuile,
For following that trade so base and vile;
And askt what license, or what Pas they had?
"Ah" (said the Ape, as sighing wondrous sad)
"Its an hard case, when men of good deseruing
Must either driuen be perforce to steruing,   370
Or asked for their pas by euerie squib,
That list at will them to reuile or snib:
And yet (God wote) small oddes I often see
Twixt them that aske, and them that asked bee.
Natheles because you shall not vs misdeeme,
But that we are as honest as we seeme,
Yee shall our pasport at your pleasure see,
And then ye will (I hope) well mooued bee."
Which when the Priest beheld, he vew'd it nere,
As if therein some text he studying were,   380
But little els (God wote) could thereof skill:
For read he could not euidence nor will,
Ne tell a written word, ne write a letter,
Ne make one title worse, ne make one better:
Of such deep learning little had he neede,
Ne yet of Latine, ne of Greeke, that breede
Doubts mongst Diuines, and difference of texts,
From whence arise diuersitie of sects,
And hatefull heresies, of God abhor'd.
But this good Sir did follow the plaine word,   390
Ne medled with their controuersies vaine.
All his care was, his seruice well to saine,
And to read Homelies vpon holidayes:
When that was done, he might attend his playes;
An easie life, and fit high God to please.
He hauing ouerlookt their pas at ease,
Gan at the length them to rebuke againe,
That no good trade of life did entertaine,
But lost their time in wandring loose abroad,
Seeing the world, in which they bootles boad,   400
Had wayes enough for all therein to liue;
Such grace did God vnto his creatures giue.

Said then the Foxe: "Who hath the world not tride,
From the right way full eath may wander wide.
We are but Nouices, new come abroad,
We haue not yet the tract of anie troad,
Nor on vs taken anie state of life,
But readie are of anie to make preife.
Therefore might please you, which the world haue proued,
Vs to aduise, which forth but lately moued,   410
Of some good course, that we might vndertake;
Ye shall for euer vs your bondmen make."
The Priest gan wexe halfe proud to be so praide,
And thereby willing to affoord them aide;
"It seemes" (said he) "right well that ye be Clerks,
Both by your wittie words, and by your werks.
Is not that name enough to make a liuing
To him that hath a whit of Natures giuing?
How, manie honest men see ye arize
Daylie thereby, and grow to goodly prize?   420
To Deanes, to Archdeacons, to Commissaries,
To Lords, to Principalls, to Prebendaries;
All iolly Prelates, worthie rule to beare,
Who euer them enuie: yet spite bites neare.
Why should ye doubt, then, but that ye likewise
Might vnto some of those in time arise?
In the meane time to liue in good estate,
Louing that loue, and hating those that hate;
Being some honest Curate, or some Vicker
Content with little in condition sicker."   430
"Ah but" (said th'Ape) "the charge is wondrous great,
To feed mens soules, and hath an heauie threat."
"To feede mens soules" (quoth he) "is not in man:
For they must feed themselves, doo what we can.
We are but charg'd to lay the meate before:
Eate they that list, we need to doo no more.
But God it is that feedes them with his grace,
The bread of life powr'd downe from heauenly place.
Therefore said he, that with the budding rod
Did rule the Iewes, *All shalbe taught of God.*   440
That same hath Iesus Christ now to him raught,
By whom the flock is rightly fed and taught:
He is the Shepheard, and the Priest is hee;
We but his shepheard swaines ordain'd to bee.
Therefore herewith doo not your selfe dismay;
Ne is the paines so great, but beare ye may;
For not so great as it was wont of yore,
It's now a dayes, ne halfe so streight and sore:
They whilome vsed duly euerie day
Their seruice and their holie things to say,   450
At morne and euen, besides their Anthemes sweete,
Their penie Masses, and their Complynes meete,
Their Dirges, their Trentals, and their shrifts,
Their memories, their singings, and their gifts.
Now all these needlesse works are laid away:
Now once a weeke vpon the Sabbath day,

It is enough to doo our small deuotion,
And then to follow any merrie motion.
Ne are we tyde to fast, but when we list,
Ne to weare garments base of wollen twist,   460
But with the finest silkes vs to aray,
That before God we may appeare more gay,
Resembling Aarons glorie in his place:
For farre vnfit it is, that person bace
Should with vile cloaths approach Gods maiestie,
Whom no vncleannes may approachen nie:
Or that all men, which anie master serue,
Good garments for their seruice should deserue,
But he that serues the Lord of hoasts most high,
And that in highest place, t'approach him nigh,   470
And all the peoples prayers to present
Before his throne, as on ambassage sent
Both too and fro, should not deserue to weare
A garment better than of wooll or heare.
Beside we may haue lying by our sides
Our louely Lasses, or bright shining Brides:
We be not tyde to wilfull chastitie,
But haue the Gospell of free libertie."
By that he ended had his ghostly sermon,
The Foxe was well induc'd to be a Parson;   480
And of the Priest eftsoones gan to enquire,
How to a Benefice he might aspire. . . .

[The worldly clergyman advises the two aspirants to attach themselves to a powerful nobleman as the quickest road to preferment. But when they do get a place—the fox disguised as a priest and the ape as his clerk—they so scandalously abuse their office that they are again compelled to flee. Traveling forth once more, they meet a richly bedecked mule who urges them to try their luck at court, and to brazen out their incompetence with "a good bold face, And with big words, and with a stately pace." Again disguised—the ape as a gentleman and the fox as his groom—they follow the mule's advice and do attain a measure of success. A truly good courtier, however, would not stoop to their flattery and deceit.]

Yet the braue Courtier, in whose beauteous thought
Regard of honour harbours more than ought,
Doth loath such base condition, to backbite
Anies good name for enuie or despite: 720
He stands on tearmes of honourable minde,
Ne will be carried with the common winde
Of Courts inconstant mutabilitie,
Ne after euerie tattling fable flie;
But heares, and sees the follies of the rest,
And thereof gathers for himselfe the best:
He will not creepe, nor crouche with fained face,
But walkes vpright with comely stedfast pace,
And vnto all doth yeeld due curtesie;
But not with kissed hand belowe the knee,   730
As that same Apish crue is wont to doo:
For he disdaines himselfe t'embase theretoo.

He hates fowle leasings, and vile flatterie,
Two filthie blots in noble Gentrie;
And lothefull idlenes he doth detest,
The canker worme of euerie gentle brest;
The which to banish with faire exercise
Of knightly feates, he daylie doth deuise:
Now menaging the mouthes of stubborne steedes,
Now practising the proofe of warlike deedes,   740
Now his bright armes assaying, now his speare,
Now the nigh aymed ring away to beare;
At other times he casts to sew the chace
Of swift wilde beasts, or runne on foote a race
T'enlarge his breath (large breath in armes most needfull),
Or els by wrestling to wex strong and heedfull,
Or his stiffe armes to stretch with Eughen bowe,
And manly legs, still passing too and fro,
Without a gowned beast him fast beside;
A vaine ensample of the Persian pride,   750
Who after he had wonne th' Assyrian foe,
Did euer after scorne on foote to goe.
Thus when this Courtly Gentleman with toyle
Himselfe hath wearied, he doth recoyle
Vnto his rest, and there with sweete delight
Of Musicks skill reuiues his toyled spright,
Or els with Loues and Ladies gentle sports,
The ioy of youth, himselfe he recomforts:
Or lastly, when the bodie list to pause,
His minde vnto the Muses he withdrawes;   760
Sweete Ladie Muses, Ladies of delight,
Delights of life, and ornaments of light:
With whom he close confers with wise discourse,
Of Natures workes, of heauens continuall course,
Of forreine lands, of people different,
Of kingdomes change, of diuers gouernment,
Of dreadfull battailes of renowmed Knights;
With which he kindleth his ambitious sprights
To like desire and praise of noble fame,
The onely vpshot whereto he doth ayme.   770
For all his minde on honour fixed is,
To which he leuels all his purposis,
And in his Princes seruice spends his dayes,
Not so much for to gaine, or for to raise
Himselfe to high degree, as for his grace,
And in his liking to winne worthie place,
Through due deserts and comely carriage,
In whatso please employ his personage,
That may be matter meete to gaine him praise;
For he is fit to vse in all assayes,   780
Whether for Armes and warlike amenaunce,
Or else for wise and ciuill gouernaunce.
For he is practiz'd well in policie,
And thereto doth his Courting most applie:
To learne the enterdeale of Princes strange,
To marke th'intent of Counsells, and the change
Of states, and eke of priuate men somewhile,

Supplanted by fine falshood and faire guile;
Of all the which he gathereth what is fit
T'enrich the storehouse of his powerfull wit,   790
Which through wise speaches and graue conference
He daylie eekes, and brings to excellence.
Such is the rightfull Courtier in his kinde:
But vnto such the Ape lent not his minde;
Such were for him no fit companions,
Such would descrie his lewd conditions:
But the yong lustie gallants he did chose
To follow, meete to whom he might disclose
His witlesse pleasance and ill pleasing vaine.
A thousand wayes he them could entertaine,   800
With all the thriftles games that may be found;
With mumming and with masking all around,
With dice, with cards, with balliards farre vnfit,
With shuttelcocks, misseeming manlie wit,
With courtizans, and costly riotize,
Whereof still somewhat to his share did rize:
Ne, them to pleasure, would he sometimes scorne
A Pandares coate (so basely was he borne);
Thereto he could fine louing verses frame,
And play the Poet oft. But ah, for shame,   810
Let not sweete Poets praise, whose onely pride
Is vertue to aduaunce, and vice deride,
Be with the worke of losels wit defamed,
Ne let such verses Poetrie be named.
Yet he the name on him would rashly take,
Maugre the sacred Muses, and it make
A seruant to the vile affection
Of such as he depended most vpon,
And with the sugrie sweete thereof allure
Chast Ladies eares to fantasies impure.   820
To such delights the noble wits he led
Which him relieu'd, and their vaine humours fed
With fruitles follies and vnsound delights.
But if perhaps into their noble sprights
Desire of honor or braue thought of armes
Did euer creepe, then with his wicked charmes
And strong conceipts he would it driue away,
Ne suffer it to house there halfe a day.
And whenso loue of letters did inspire
Their gentle wits, and kindly wise desire,   830
That chieflie doth each noble minde adorne,
Then he would scoffe at learning, and eke scorne
The Sectaries thereof, as people base
And simple men, which neuer came in place
Of worlds affaires, but in darke corners mewd,
Muttred of matters, as their bookes them shewd,
Ne other knowledge euer did attaine,
But with their gownes their grauitie maintaine.
From them he would his impudent lewde speach
Against Gods holie Ministers oft reach,   840
And mocke Diuines and their profession:
What else then did he by progression,

But mocke high God himselfe, whom they professe?
But what car'd he for God, or godlinesse?
All his care was himselfe how to aduaunce,
And to vphold his courtly countenaunce
By all the cunning meanes he could deuise;
Were it by honest wayes, or otherwise,
He made small choyce: yet sure his honestie
Got him small gaines, but shameless flatterie,   850
And filthie brocage, and vnseemly shifts,
And borowe base, and some good Ladies gifts:
But the best helpe, which chiefly him sustain'd,
Was his man Raynolds purchase which he gain'd.
For he was school'd by kinde in all the skill
Of close conueyance, and each practise ill
Of coosinage and cleanly knauerie,
Which oft maintain'd his masters brauerie.
Besides he vsde another slipprie slight,
In taking on himselfe, in common sight,   860
False personages, fit for euerie sted,
With which he thousands cleanly coosined:
Now like a Merchant, Merchants to deceaue,
With whom his credite he did often leaue
In gage, for his gay Masters hopelesse dett:
Now like a Lawyer, when he land would lett,
Or sell fee-simples in his Masters name,
Which he had neuer, nor ought like the same:
Then would he be a Broker, and draw in
Both wares and money, by exchange to win: 870
Then would he seeme a Farmer, that would sell
Bargaines of woods, which he did lately fell,
Or corne, or cattle, or such other ware,
Thereby to coosin men not well aware;
Of all the which there came a secret fee
To th'Ape, that he his countenaunce might bee.
Besides all this, he vsd' oft to beguile
Poore suters, that in Court did haunt some while:
For he would learne their busines secretly,
And then informe his Master hastely,   880
That he by meanes might cast them to preuent,
And beg the sute the which the other ment.
Or otherwise false Reynold would abuse
The simple Suter, and wish him to chuse
His Master, being one of great regard
In Court, to compas anie sute not hard,
In case his paines were recompenst with reason:
So would he worke the silly man by treason
To buy his Masters friuolous good will,
That had not power to doo him good or ill.   890
So pitifull a thing is Suters state.
Most miserable man, whom wicked fate
Hath brought to Court, to sue for had ywist,
That few haue found, and manie one hath mist.
Full little knowest thou that hast not tride,
What hell it is, in suing long to bide:
To loose good dayes, that might be better spent:

To waste long nights in pensiue discontent;
To speed to day, to be put back to morrow;
To feed on hope, to pine with feare and sorrow;   900
To haue thy Princes grace, yet want her Peeres;
To haue thy asking, yet waite manie yeeres;
To fret thy soule with crosses and with cares;
To eate thy heart through comfortlesse dispaires;
To fawne, to crowche, to waite, to ride, to ronne,
To spend, to giue, to want, to be vndonne.
Vnhappie wight, borne to desastrous end,
That doth his life in so long tendance spend.
Who euer leaues sweete home, where meane estate
In safe assurance, without strife or hate,   910
Findes all things needfull for contentment meeke,
And will to Court for shadowes vaine to seeke,
Or hope to gaine, himselfe will a daw trie:
That curse God send vnto mine enemie. . . .

[At length the fox's "craftie feates" become so gross that
he is exposed and banished, whereupon the ape, "wanting
his huckster man," is so discredited that he is forced to
take flight. Joining forces again, they resume their wanderings, and at last come upon the sleeping lion, king of the
beasts, "His Crowne and Scepter lying him beside." After
the ape has audaciously appropriated the regalia the fox
assents to his masquerading as king on condition "that ye
ruled bee In all affaires, and counselled by mee." For a
time their ruse succeeds: the other animals fall prostrate
before the royal diadem on the ape's brow, and the two
adventurers prepare to exploit their good fortune.]

The Ape, thus seized of the Regall throne,
Eftsones by counsell of the Foxe alone
Gan to prouide for all things in assurance,
That so his rule might lenger haue endurance.
First to his Gate he pointed a strong gard,
That none might enter but with issue hard:
Then for the safegard of his personage,
He did appoint a warlike equipage
Of forreine beasts, not in the forest bred,
But part by land and part by water fed;   1120
For tyrannie is with strange ayde supported.
Then vnto him all monstrous beasts resorted
Bred of two kindes, as Griffons, Minotaures,
Crocodiles, Dragons, Beauers, and Centaures:
With those himselfe he strengthned mightelie,
That feare he neede no force of enemie.
Then gan he rule and tyrannize at will,
Like as the Foxe did guide his graceles skill,
And all wylde beasts made vassals of his pleasures,
And with their spoyles enlarg'd his priuate treasures. 1130
No care of iustice, nor no rule of reason,
No temperance, nor no regard of season
Did thenceforth euer enter in his minde,
But crueltie, the signe of currish kinde,
And sdeignfull pride, and wilfull arrogaunce;
Such followes those whom fortune doth aduaunce.

But the false Foxe most kindly plaid his part:
For whatsoeuer mother wit or arte
Could worke, he put in proofe: no practise slie,
No counterpoint of cunning policie,   1140
No reach, no breach, that might him profit bring,
But he the same did to his purpose wring.
Nought suffered he the Ape to giue or graunt,
But through his hand must passe the Fiaunt.
All offices, all leases by him lept,
And of them all whatso he likte he kept.
Iustice he solde iniustice for to buy,
And for to purchase for his progeny.
Ill might it prosper, that ill gotten was,
But so he got it, little did he pas.   1150
He fed his cubs with fat of all the soyle,
And with the sweete of others sweating toyle;
He crammed them with crumbs of Benefices;
And fild their mouthes with meeds of malefices;
He cloathed them with all colours saue white,
And loded them with lordships and with might,
So much as they were able well to beare,
That with the weight their backs nigh broken were.
He chaffred Chayres in which Churchmen were set,
And breach of lawes to priuie ferme did let;   1160
No statute so established might bee,
Nor ordinaunce so needfull, but that hee
Would violate, though not with violence,
Yet vnder colour of the confidence
The which the Ape repos'd in him alone,
And reckned him the kingdomes corner stone.
And euer, when he ought would bring to pas,
His long experience the platforme was:
And when he ought not pleasing would put by,
The cloke was care of thrift, and husbandry,   1170
For to encrease the common treasures store;
But his owne treasure he encreased more
And lifted vp his loftie towres thereby,
That they began to threat the neighbour sky;
The whiles the Princes pallaces fell fast
To ruine (for what thing can euer last?),
And whilest the other Peeres for pouertie
Were forst their auncient houses to let lie,
And their olde Castles to the ground to fall,
Which their forefathers, famous ouer all,   1180
Had founded for the Kingdomes ornament,
And for their memories long moniment.
But he no count made of Nobilitie,
Nor the wilde beasts whom armes did glorifie,
The Realmes chiefe strength and girlond of the crowne;
All these through fained crimes he thrust adowne,
Or made them dwell in darknes of disgrace:
For none but whom he list might come in place.
Of men of armes he had but small regard,
But kept them lowe, and streigned verie hard.   1190
For men of learning little he esteemed;

His wisedome he aboue their learning deemed.
As for the rascall Commons least he cared;
For not so common was his bountie shared.
"Let God" (said he) "if please, care for the manie,
I for my selfe must care before els anie."
So did he good to none, to manie ill,
So did he all the kingdome rob and pill,
Yet none durs speake, ne none durst of him plaine;
So great he was in grace, and rich through gaine. . . . 1200
[Again the rogues overplay their hand, however, and at
last their tyranny and fraud become so obvious that Jove,
beholding "the troubled kingdome of wilde beasts" from
his "turret hye," almost strikes the spurious king with a
thunderbolt. On second thought, however, he resolves
"with scornfull shame Him to auenge, and blot his brutish
name."

Forthwith he Mercurie vnto him cal'd,
And bad him flie with neuer resting speed
Vnto the forrest, where wilde beasts doo breed,
And there enquiring priuily, to learn
What did of late chaunce to the Lyon stearne,   1250
That he rul'd not the Empire, as he ought;
And whence were all those plaints vnto him brought
Of wrongs and spoyles by saluage beasts committed;
Which done, he bad the Lyon be remitted
Into his seate, and those same treachours vile
Be punished for their presumptuous guile.
The Sonne of Maia soone as he receiu'd
That word, streight with his azure wings he cleau'd
The liquid clowdes and lucid firmament;
Ne staid, till that he came with steep descent   1260
Vnto the place, where his prescript did showe.
There stouping like an arrowe from a bowe,
He soft arriued on the grassie plaine,
And fairly paced forth with easie paine,
Till that vnto the Pallace nigh he came.
Then gan he to himselfe new shape to frame,
And that faire face, and that Ambrosiall hew,
Which wonts to decke the Gods immortall crew,
And beautefie the shinie firmament,
He doft, vnfit for that rude rabblement.   1270
So standing by the gates in strange disguize,
He gan enquire of some in secret wize,
Both of the King, and of his gouernment,
And of the Foxe, and his false blandishment:
And euermore he heard each one complaine
Of foule abuses both in realme and raine.
Which yet to proue more true, he meant to see,
And an ey-witnes of each thing to bee.
Tho on his head his dreadfull hat he dight,
Which maketh him inuisible in sight,   1280
And mocketh th'eyes of all the lookers on,
Making them thinke it but a vision.
Through power of that, he runnes through enemies
    swerds;

Through power of that, he passeth through the herds
Of rauenous wilde beasts, and doth beguile
Their greedie mouthes of the expected spoyle;
Through power of that, his cunning theeueries
He wonts to worke, that none the same espies;
And through the power of that, he putteth on
What shape he list in apparition.   1290
That on his head he wore, and in his hand
He tooke Caduceus, his snakie wand,
With which the damned ghosts he gouerneth,
And furies rules, and Tartare tempereth.
With that he causeth sleep to seize the eyes,
And feare the harts of all his enemyes;
And when him list, an vniuersall night
Throughout the world he makes on euerie wight,
As when his Syre with Alcumena lay.
Thus dight, into the Court he tooke his way,   1300
Both through the gard, which neuer did describe,
And through the watchmen, who him neuer spide:
Thenceforth he past into each secrete part,
Whereas he saw, that sorely grieu'd his hart,
Each place abounding with fowle iniuries,
And fild with treasure rackt with robberies:
Each place defilde with blood of guiltles beasts,
Which had been slaine, to serue the Apes beheasts;
Gluttonie, malice, pride, and couetize,
And lawlesnes raigning with riotize;   **1310**
Besides the infinite extortions,
Done through the Foxes great oppressions,
That the complaints thereof could not be tolde.
Which when he did with lothfull eyes beholde,
He would no more endure, but came his way,
And cast to seeke the Lion, where he may,
That he might worke the auengement for this shame
On those two caytiues, which had bred him blame.
And seeking all the forrest busily,
At last he found where sleeping he did ly: 1320
The wicked weed, which there the Foxe did lay,
From vnderneath his head he tooke away,
And then him waking, forced vp to rize.
The Lion looking vp gan him auize,
As one late in a traunce, what had of long
Become of him: for fantasie is strong.
"Arise" (said Mercurie) "thou sluggish beast,
That here liest senseles, like the corpse deceast,
The whilste thy kingdome from thy head is rent,
And thy throne royall with dishonour blent: 1330
Arise, and doo thy selfe redeeme from shame,
And be aueng'd on those that breed thy blame."
Thereat enraged, soone he gan vpstart,
Grinding his teeth, and grating his great hart,
And rouzing vp himselfe, for his rough hide
He gan to reach; but no where it espide.
Therewith he gan full terribly to rore,
And chafte at that indignitie right sore.

But when his Crowne and scepter both he wanted,
Lord how he fum'd, and sweld, and rag'd, and panted;
And threatned death, and thousand deadly dolours 1341
To them that had purloyn'd his Princely honours.
With that in hast, disrobed as he was,
He toward his owne Pallace forth did pas;
And all the way he roared as he went,
That all the forrest with astonishment
Thereof did tremble, and the beasts therein
Fled fast away from that so dreadfull dinn.
At last he came vnto his mansion,
Where all the gates he found fast lockt anon,   1350
And manie warders round about them stood.
With that he roar'd alowd, as he were wood,
That all the Pallace quaked at the stound,
As if it quite were riuen from the ground,
And all within were dead and hartles left;
And th'Ape himselfe, as one whose wits were reft,
Fled here and there, and euerie corner sought,
To hide himselfe from his owne feared thought.
But the false Foxe, when he the Lion heard,
Fled closely forth, streightway of death afeard,   1360
And to the Lion came, full lowly creeping,
With fained face, and watrie eyne halfe weeping,
T'excuse his former treason and abusion,

And turning all vnto the Apes confusion:
Nath'les the royall Beast forbore beleeuing,
But bad him stay at ease till further preeuing.
Then when he saw no entrance to him graunted,
Roaring yet lowder that all harts it daunted,
Vpon those gates with force he fiercely flewe,
And rending them in pieces, felly slewe   1370
Those warders strange, and all that els he met.
But th'Ape still flying, he no where might get:
From rowme to rowme, from beame to beame he fled
All breathles, and for feare now almost ded:
Yet him at last the Lyon spide, and caught,
And forth with shame vnto his iudgement brought.
Then all the beasts he causd' assembled bee,
To heare their doome, and sad ensample see:
The Foxe, first Author of that treacherie,
He did vncase, and then away let flie.   1380
But th'Apes long taile (which then he had) he quight
Cut off, and both eares pared of their hight;
Since which, all Apes but halfe their eares haue left,
And of their tailes are vtterlie bereft.

So Mother Hubberd her discourse did end:
Which pardon me, if I amisse haue pend;
For weake was my remembrance it to hold,
And bad her tongue that it so bluntly tolde.

FROM COLIN CLOVTS COME HOME AGAINE (1595)

To the Right Worthy and Noble Knight
Sir Walter Raleigh, Captaine of Her Maiesties
Guard, Lord Wardein of the Stanneries,
and Lieutenant of the Countie of
Cornwall

Sir, that you may see that I am not alwaies ydle as
yee thinke, though not greatly well occupied, nor
altogither vndutifull, though not precisely officious,
I make you present of this simple pastorall, vnworthie
of your higher conceit for the meanesse of the stile,   10
but agreeing with the truth in circumstance and
matter. The which I humbly beseech you to accept
in part of paiment of the infinite debt in which I
acknowledge my selfe bounden vnto you, for your
singular fauours and sundrie good turnes shewed to
me at my late being in England, and with your good
countenance protect against the malice of euill
mouthes, which are alwaies wide open to carpe at
and misconstrue my simple meaning. I pray continually for your happinesse. From my house of   20
Kilcolman the 27. of December. 1591.

Yours euer humbly,
Ed[mund] Sp[enser]

The shepheards boy (best knowen by that name)
That after Tityrus first sung his lay,
Laies of sweet loue, without rebuke or blame,
Sate (as his custome was) vpon a day,
Charming his oaten pipe vnto his peres,
The shepheard swaines that did about him play:
Who all the while with greedie listfull eares
Did stand astonisht at his curious skill,
Like hartlesse deare, dismayd with thunders sound.
At last when as he piped had his fill,   10
He rested him: and sitting then around,
One of those groomes (a iolly groome was he,
As euer piped on an oaten reed,
And lou'd this shepheard dearest in degree,
Hight Hobbinol) gan thus to him areed:
    "Colin my liefe, my life, how great a losse
Had all the shepheards nation by thy lacke!
And I poore swaine of many greatest crosse:
That, sith thy Muse first since thy turning backe
Was heard to sound as she was wont on hye,   20
Hast made vs all so blessed and so blythe.
Whilest thou wast hence, all dead in dole did lie:
The woods were heard to waile full many a sythe,
And all their birds with silence to complaine:

The fields with faded flowers did seem to mourne,
And all their flocks from feeding to refraine:
The running waters wept for thy returne,
And all their fish with languour did lament:
But now both woods and fields, and floods reviue,
Sith thou art come, their cause of meriment,   30
That vs, late dead, hast made againe aliue.
But were it not too painfull to repeat
The passed fortunes, which to thee befell
In thy late voyage, we thee would entreat,
Now at thy leisure them to vs to tell."

   To whom the shepheard gently answered thus:
"Hobbin, thou temptest me to that I couet:
For of good passed newly to discus,
By dubble vsurie doth twise renew it.
And since I saw that Angels blessed eie,   40
Her worlds bright sun, her heauens fairest light,
My mind, full of my thoughts satietie,
Doth feed on sweet contentment of that sight:
Since that same day in nought I take delight,
Ne feeling haue in any earthly pleasure,
But in remembrance of that glorious bright,
My lifes sole blisse, my hearts eternall threasure.
Wake then, my pipe, my sleepie Muse awake,
Till I haue told her praises lasting long:
Hobbin desires, thou maist it not forsake,   50
Harke then, ye iolly shepheards, to my song."

   With that they all gan throng about him neare,
With hungrie eares to heare his harmonie:
The whiles their flocks, deuoyd of dangers feare,
Did round about them feed at libertie.

   "One day" (quoth he) "I sat (as was my trade)
Vnder the foote of Mole, that mountaine hore,
Keeping my sheepe amongst the cooly shade
Of the greene alders by the Mullaes shore.
There a straunge shepheard chaunst to find me out,   60
Whether allured with my pipes delight,
Whose pleasing sound yshrilled far about,
Or thither led by chaunce, I know not right:
Whom when I asked from what place he came,
And how he hight, himselfe he did ycleepe,
The shepheard of the Ocean by name,
And said he came far from the main-sea deepe.
He, sitting me beside in that same shade,
Prouoked me to plaie some pleasant fit,
And when he heard the musicke which I made,   70
He found himselfe full greatly pleasd at it:
Yet aemuling my pipe, he tooke in hond
My pipe before that aemuled of many,
And plaid theron (for well that skill he cond);
Himselfe as skilfull in that art as any.
He pip'd, I sung; and when he sung, I piped,
By chaunge of turnes, each making other mery,
Neither enuying other, nor enuied,
So piped we, vntill we both were weary. . . .

His song was all a lamentable lay,
Of great vnkindnesse, and of vsage hard,
Of Cynthia, the Ladie of the sea,
Which from her presence faultlesse him debard.
And euer and anon with singults rife
He cryed out, to make his vndersong,
'Ah my loues queene, and goddesse of my life,   170
Who shall me pittie, when thou doest me wrong?'. . . .

   "When thus our pipes we both had wearied well"
(Quoth he), "and each an end of singing made,
He gan to cast great lyking to my lore,   180
And great dislyking to my lucklesse lot,
That banisht had my selfe, like wight forlore,
Into that waste, where I was quite forgot.
The which to leaue, thenceforth he counseld mee,
Vnmeet for man in whom was ought regardfull,
And wend with him, his Cynthia to see,
Whose grace was great, and bounty most rewardfull.
Besides her peerlesse skill in making well
And all the ornaments of wondrous wit,
Such as all womankynd did far excell,   190
Such as the world admyr'd and praised it:
So what with hope of good, and hate of ill,
He me perswaded forth with him to fare;
Nought tooke I with me, but mine oaten quill:
Small needments else need shepheard to prepare.
So to the sea we came; the sea? that is
A world of waters heaped vp on hie,
Rolling like mountaines in wide wildernesse,
Horrible, hideous, roaring with hoarse crie. . . ."

[As Colin tells the listening shepherds, the tempestuous
voyage to Cynthia's court was made frightful by the
"ghastly dreadfull" surges of the deep. But his fears were
assuaged by his companion's report of the peace and splendor of her realm. Even the unruly sea is her "Regiment": the waves obey her commands, and "Triton,
blowing loud his wreathed horne," is her shepherd of
the deep. As the voyage ends, the sight of the great queen's
land fills Colin with elation.]

   "Both heauen and heauenly graces do much more"
(Quoth he) "abound in that same land then this.
For there all happie peace and plenteous store   310
Conspire in one to make contented blisse:
No wayling there nor wretchednesse is heard,
No bloodie issues nor no leprosies,
No griesly famine, nor no raging sweard,
No nightly bodrags, nor no hue and cries;
The shepheards there abroad may safely lie,
On hills and downes, withouten dread or daunger:
No rauenous wolues the good mans hope destroy,
Nor outlawes fell affray the forest raunger.
There learned arts do florish in great honor,   320
And Poets wits are had in peerlesse price:
Religion hath lay powre to rest vpon her,
Aduancing vertue and suppressing vice.

For end, all good, all grace there freely growes,
Had people grace it gratefully to vse:
For God his gifts there plenteously bestowes,
But gracelesse men them greatly do abuse."

    "But say on further," then said Corylas,
"The rest of thine aduentures, that betyded."

    "Foorth on our voyage we by land did passe"   330
(Quoth he), "as that same shepheard still vs guyded,
Vntill that we to Cynthiaes presence came:
Whose glorie, greater then my simple thought,
I found much greater then the former fame;
Such greatnes I cannot compare to ought:
But if I her like ought on earth might read,
I would her lyken to a crowne of lillies,
Vpon a virgin brydes adorned head,
With Roses dight and Goolds and Daffadillies;
Or like the circlet of a Turtle true,   340
In which all colours of the rainbow bee;
Or like faire Phebes garlond shining new,
In which all pure perfection one may see.
But vaine it is to thinke, by paragone
Of earthly things, to iudge of things diuine:
Her power, her mercy, and her wisedome, none
Can deeme, but who the Godhead can define.
Why then do I, base shepheard bold and blind,
Presume the things so sacred to prophane?
More fit it is t'adore with humble mind   350
The image of the heauens in shape humane."

    With that Alexis broke his tale asunder,
Saying, "By wondring at thy Cynthiaes praise,
Colin, thy selfe thou mak'st vs more to wonder,
And, her vpraising, doest thy selfe vpraise.
But let vs heare what grace she shewed thee,
And how that shepheard strange thy cause aduanced?"

    "The shepheard of the Ocean" (quoth he)
"Vnto that Goddesse grace me first enhanced,
And to mine oaten pipe enclin'd her eare,   360
That she thenceforth therein gan take delight,
And it desir'd at timely houres to heare,
All were my notes but rude and roughly dight.
For not by measure of her owne great mynd
And wondrous worth she mott my simple song,
But ioyd that country shepheard ought could fynd
Worth harkening to, emongst the learned throng."

    "Why?" (said Alexis then) "what needeth shee
That is so great a shepheardesse her selfe,
And hath so many shepheards in her fee,   370
To heare thee sing, a simple silly Elfe?
Or be the shepheards which do serue her laesie,
That they list not their mery pipes applie?
Or be their pipes vntunable and craesie,
That they cannot her honour worthylie?"

    "Ah nay" (said Colin) "neither so, nor so:
For better shepheards be not vnder skie,
Nor better hable, when they list to blow

Their pipes aloud, her name to glorifie.
There is good Harpalus, now woxen aged   380
In faithfull seruice of faire Cynthia:
And there is Corydon, though meanly waged,
Yet hablest wit of most I know this day.
And there is sad Alcyon, bent to mourne,
Though fit to frame an euerlasting dittie,
Whose gentle spright for Daphnes death doth tourn
Sweet layes of loue to endlesse plaints of pittie.
Ah! pensiue boy, pursue that braue conceipt,
In thy sweet *Eglantine of Meriflure,*
Lift vp thy notes vnto their wonted height,   390
That may thy Muse and mates to mirth allure.
There eke is Palin, worthie of great praise,
Albe he enuie at my rustick quill:
And there is pleasing Alcon, could he raise
His tunes from laies to matter of more skill.
And there is old Palemon free from spight,
Whose carefull pipe may make the hearer rew:
Yet he himselfe may rewed be more right,
That sung so long vntill quite hoarse he grew.
And there is Alabaster throughly taught,   400
In all this skill, though knowen yet to few,
Yet were he knowne to Cynthia as he ought,
His *Eliseïs* would be redde anew.
Who liues that can match that heroick song,
Which he hath of that mightie Princesse made?
O dreaded Dread, do not thy selfe that wrong,
To let thy fame lie so in hidden shade:
But call it forth, O call him forth to thee,
To end thy glorie which he hath begun:
That when he finisht hath as it should be,   410
No brauer Poeme can be vnder Sun.
Nor Po nor Tyburs swans so much renowned,
Nor all the brood of Greece so highly praised,
Can match that Muse when it with bayes is crowned,
And to the pitch of her perfection raised.
And there is a new shepheard late vp sprong,
The which doth all afore him far surpasse:
Appearing well in that well tuned song
Which late he sung vnto a scornfull lasse.
Yet doth his trembling Muse but lowly flie,   420
As daring not too rashly mount on hight,
And doth her tender plumes as yet but trie
In loues soft laies and looser thoughts delight.
Then rouze thy feathers quickly, Daniell,
And to what course thou please thy selfe aduance:
But most, me seemes, thy accent will excell
In Tragick plaints and passionate mischance.
And there that shepheard of the Ocean is,
That spends his wit in loues consuming smart:
Full sweetly tempred is that Muse of his   430
That can empierce a Princes mightie hart.
There also is—ah! no, he is not now,
But since I said he is, he quite is gone,

Amyntas quite is gone and lies full low,
Hauing his Amaryllis left to mone.
Helpe, O ye shepheards, helpe ye all in this,
Helpe Amaryllis this her losse to mourne:
Her losse is yours, your losse Amyntas is,
Amyntas, floure of shepheards pride forlorne:
He whilest he liued was the noblest swaine   440
That euer piped in an oaten quill:
Both did he other which could pipe maintaine,
And eke could pipe himselfe with passing skill.
And there, though last not least, is Aetion,
A gentler shepheard may no where be found:
Whose Muse, full of high thoughts inuention,
Doth like himselfe Heroically sound.
All these and many others mo remaine,
Now after Astrofell is dead and gone:
But while as Astrofell did liue and raine,   450
Amongst all these was none his Paragone.
All these do florish in their sundry kynd,
And do their Cynthia immortall make:
Yet found I lyking in her royall mynd,
Not for my skill, but for that shepheards sake. . . ."

[When one of his auditors, Lucida, "a louely lasse," asks
Colin to describe the "Nymphs" that adorn Cynthia's
court, he catalogues the virtue and the beauty of "Vrania,
sister vnto Astrofell" (Mary, Countess of Pembroke),
Theana (Anne Russell, wife of Ambrose Dudley, Earl of
Warwick), Marian (Margaret, Countess of Cumberland),
Amaryllis, Charillis, and Phyllis (Alice, Anne, and Eliza-
beth Spenser), and many others.]

So hauing said, Aglaura him bespake:
"Colin, well worthie were those goodly fauours
Bestowd on thee, that so of them doest make,
And them requitest with thy thankfull labours.
But of great Cynthiaes goodnesse and high grace
Finish the storie which thou hast begunne."

"More eath" (quoth he) "it is in such a case   590
How to begin, then know how to haue donne.
For euerie gift and euerie goodly meed,
Which she on me bestowd, demaunds a day;
And euerie day in which she did a deed
Demaunds a yeare it duly to display.
Her words were like a streame of honny fleeting,
The which doth softly trickle from the hiue:
Hable to melt the hearers heart vnweeting,
And eke to make the dead againe aliue.
Her deeds were like great clusters of ripe grapes,   600
Which load the braunches of the fruitfull vine:
Offring to fall into each mouth that gapes,
And fill the same with store of timely wine.
Her lookes were like beames of the morning Sun,
Forth looking through the windowes of the East:
When first the fleecie cattell haue begun
Vpon the perled grasse to make their feast.
Her thoughts are like the fume of Franckincence,

Which from a golden Censer forth doth rise:
And throwing forth sweet odours mounts fro thence   610
In rolling globes vp to the vauted skies.
There she beholds with high aspiring thought
The cradle of her owne creation:
Emongst the seats of Angels heauenly wrought,
Much like an Angell in all forme and fashion."

"Colin" (said Cuddy then) "thou hast forgot
Thy selfe, me seemes, too much, to mount so hie:
Such loftie flight base shepheard seemeth not,
From flocks and fields to Angels and to skie."

"True" (answered he) "but her great excellence   620
Lifts me aboue the measure of my might:
That being fild with furious insolence,
I feele my selfe like one yrapt in spright.
For when I thinke of her, as oft I ought,
Then want I words to speake it fitly forth:
And when I speake of her what I haue thought,
I cannot thinke according to her worth.
Yet will I thinke of her, yet will I speake,
So long as life my limbs doth hold together,
And when as death these vitall bands shall breake,   630
Her name recorded I will leaue for euer.
Her name in euery tree I will endosse,
That, as the trees do grow, her name may grow:
And in the ground each where will it engrosse,
And fill with stones, that all men may it know.
The speaking woods and murmuring waters fall
Her name Ile teach in knowen termes to frame:
And eke my lambs, when for their dams they call,
Ile teach to call for Cynthia by name.
And long while after I am dead and rotten,   640
Amongst the shepheards daughters dancing rownd
My layes made of her shall not be forgotten,
But sung by them with flowry gyrlonds crownd.
And ye, who so ye be, that shall surviue,
When as ye heare her memory renewed,
Be witnesse of her bountie here aliue,
Which she to Colin her poore shepheard shewed."

Much was the whole assembly of those heards
Moov'd at his speech, so feelingly he spake:
And stood awhile astonisht at his words,   650
Till Thestylis at last their silence brake,
Saying, "Why, Colin, since thou foundst such grace
With Cynthia and all her noble crew,
Why didst thou euer leaue that happie place,
In which such wealth might vnto thee accrew,
And back returnedst to this barrein soyle,
Where cold and care and penury do dwell,
Here to keep sheepe, with hunger and with toyle?
Most wretched he, that is and cannot tell."

"Happie indeed" (said Colin) "I him hold   660
That may that blessed presence still enioy,
Of fortune and of enuy vncomptrold,
Which still are wont most happie states t'annoy:

But I, by that which little while I prooued,
Some part of those enormities did see,
The which in Court continually hooued,
And followd those which happie seemd to bee.
Therefore I, silly man, whose former dayes
Had in rude fields bene altogether spent,
Durst not aduenture such vnknowen wayes,   670
Nor trust the guile of fortunes blandishment,
But rather chose back to my sheep to tourne,
Whose vtmost hardnesse I before had tryde,
Then, hauing learnd repentance late, to mourne
Emongst those wretches which I there descryde."
     "Shepheard" (said Thestylis) "it seemes of spight
Thou speakest thus gainst their felicitie,
Which thou enuiest, rather then of right
That ought in them blameworthie thou doest spie."
     "Cause haue I none" (quoth he) "of cancred will   680
To quite them ill that me demeand so well:
But selfe-regard of priuate good or ill
Moues me of each, so as I found, to tell,
And eke to warne yong shepheards wandring wit,
Which, through report of that liues painted blisse,
Abandon quiet home to seeke for it,
And leaue their lambes to losse, misled amisse.
For, sooth to say, it is no sort of life
For shepheard fit to lead in that same place,
Where each one seeks with malice and with strife   690
To thrust downe other into foule disgrace
Himselfe to raise: and he doth soonest rise
That best can handle his deceitfull wit,
In subtil shifts and finest sleights deuise,
Either by slaundring his well deemed name,
Through leasings lewd and fained forgerie:
Or else by breeding him some blot of blame,
By creeping close into his secrecie;
To which him needs a guilefull hollow hart,
Masked with faire dissembling curtesie,   700
A filed toung furnisht with tearmes of art,
No art of schoole, but Courtiers schoolery.
For arts of schoole haue there small countenance,
Counted but toyes to busie ydle braines,
And there professours find small maintenance,
But to be instruments of others gaines.
Ne is there place for any gentle wit,
Vnlesse to please, it selfe it can applie:
But shouldred is, or out of doore quite shit,
As base, or blunt, vnmeet for melodie.   710
For each mans worth is measured by his weed,
As harts by hornes, or asses by their eares:
Yet asses been not all whose eares exceed,
Nor yet all harts that hornes the highest beares.
For highest lookes haue not the highest mynd,
Nor haughtie words most full of highest thoughts:
But are like bladders blowen vp with wynd,
That being prickt do vanish into noughts.

Euen such is all their vaunted vanitie,
Nought else but smoke, that fumeth soone away;   720
Such is their glorie that in simple eie
Seeme greatest when their garments are most gay.
So they themselues for praise of fooles do sell,
And all their wealth for painting on a wall;
With price whereof they buy a golden bell,
And purchace highest rowmes in bowre and hall:
Whiles single Truth and simple honestie
Do wander vp and downe despys'd of all;
Their plaine attire such glorious gallantry
Disdaines so much, that none them in doth call. 730
          "Love most aboundeth there.
For all the walls and windows there are writ
All full of loue, and loue, and loue my deare,
And all their talke and studie is of it.
Ne any there doth braue or valiant seeme,
Vnlesse that some gay Mistresse badge he beares: 780
Ne any one himselfe doth ought esteeme,
Vnlesse he swim in loue vp to the eares.
But they of loue and of his sacred lere
(As it should be) all otherwise deuise
Then we poore shepheards are accustomd here,
And him do sue and serue all otherwise.
For with lewd speeches and licentious deeds
His mightie mysteries they do prophane,
And vse his ydle name to other needs,
But as a complement for courting vaine.   790
So him they do not serue as they professe,
But make him serue to them for sordid vses,
Ah! my dread Lord, that doest liege hearts possesse,
Auenge thy selfe on them for their abuses.
But we poore shepheards, whether rightly so,
Or through our rudenesse into errour led,
Do make religion how we rashly go
To serue that God that is so greatly dred;
For him the greatest of the Gods we deeme,
Borne without Syre or couples, of one kynd,   800
For Venus selfe doth soly couples seeme,
Both male and female, through commixture ioynd,
So pure and spotlesse Cupid forth she brought,
And in the gardens of Adonis nurst:
Where growing, he his owne perfection wrought,
And shortly was of all the Gods the first.
Then got he bow and shafts of gold and lead,
In which so fell and puissant he grew,
That Ioue himselfe his powre began to dread,
And taking vp to heauen, him godded new.   810
From thence he shoots his arrowes euery where
Into the world, at randon as he will,
On vs fraile men, his wretched vassals here,
Like as himselfe vs pleaseth saue or spill.
So we him worship, so we him adore
With humble hearts to heauen vplifted hie,
That to true loues he may vs euermore

Preferre, and of their grace vs dignifie:
Ne is there shepheard, ne yet shepheards swaine,
What euer feeds in forest or in field,   820
That dare with euil deed or leasing vaine
Blaspheme his powre, or termes vnworthie yield."

  "Shepheard, it seemes that some celestiall rage
Of loue" (quoth Cuddy) "is breath'd into thy brest,
That powreth forth these oracles so sage,
Of that high powre, wherewith thou art possest.
But neuer wist I till this present day,
Albe of loue I alwayes humbly deemed,
That he was such an one as thou doest say,
And so religiously to be esteemed.   830
Well may it seeme by this thy deep insight,
That of that God the Priest thou shouldest bee:
So well thou wot'st the mysterie of his might,
As if his godhead thou didst present see."

  "Of loues perfection perfectly to speake,
Or of his nature rightly to define,
Indeed" (said Colin), "passeth reasons reach,
And needs his priest t'expresse his powre diuine.
For long before the world he was ybore
And bred aboue in Venus bosome deare: 840
For by his powre the world was made of yore,
And all that therein wondrous doth appeare.
For how should else things so far from attone
And so great enemies as of them bee,
Be euer drawne together into one,
And taught in such accordance to agree?
Through him the cold began to couet heat,
And water fire; the light to mount on hie,
And th'heauie downe to peize; the hungry t'eat,
And voydnesse to seeke full satietie.   850
So, being former foes, they wexed friends,
And gan by litle learne to loue each other:
So, being knit, they brought forth other kynds
Out of the fruitfull wombe of their great mother.
Then first gan heauen out of darknesse dread
For to appeare, and brought forth chearfull day;
Next gan the earth to shew her naked head,
Out of deep waters which her drownd alway.
And shortly after, euerie liuing wight
Crept forth like wormes out of her slimie nature,   860
Soone as on them the Suns life giuing light
Had powred kindly heat and formall feature.
Thenceforth they gan each one his like to loue,
And like himselfe desire for to beget:
The Lyon chose his mate, the Turtle Doue
Her deare, the Dolphin his owne Dolphinet:
But man, that had the sparke of reasons might
More then the rest to rule his passion,
Chose for his loue the fairest in his sight,
Like as himselfe was fairest by creation.   870
For beautie is the bayt which with delight
Doth man allure, for to enlarge his kynd,

Beautie, the burning lamp of heauens light,
Darting her beames into each feeble mynd:
Against whose powre nor God nor man can fynd
Defence, ne ward the daunger of the wound,
But, being hurt, seeke to be medicynd
Of her that first did stir that mortall stownd.
Then do they cry and call to loue apace,
With praiers lowd importuning the skie,   880
Whence he them heares, and when he list shew grace,
Does graunt them grace that otherwise would die.
So loue is Lord of all the world by right,
And rules the creatures by his powrfull saw:
All being made the vassalls of his might,
Through secret sence which therto doth them draw.
Thus ought all louers of their lord to deeme,
And with chaste heart to honor him alway:
But who so else doth otherwise esteeme
Are outlawes, and his lore do disobay.   890
For their desire is base, and doth not merit
The name of loue, but of disloyall lust:
Ne mongst true louers they shall place inherit,
But as Exuls out of his court be thrust."

  So hauing said, Melissa spake at will:
"Colin, thou now full deeply hast divynd
Of loue and beautie, and with wondrous skill
Hast Cupid selfe depainted in his kynd.
To thee are all true louers greatly bound,
That doest their cause so mightily defend: 900
But most, all wemen are thy debtors found,
That doest their bountie still so much commend."

  "That ill" (said Hobbinol) "they him requite;
For hauing loued euer one most deare,
He is repayd with scorne and foule despite,
That yrkes each gentle heart which it doth heare."

  "Indeed" (said Lucid) "I haue often heard
Faire Rosalind of diuers fowly blamed:
For being to that swaine too cruell hard,
That her bright glorie else hath much defamed.   910
But who can tell what cause had that faire Mayd
To vse him so that vsed her so well?
Or who with blame can iustly her vpbrayd
For louing not? for who can loue compell?
And sooth to say, it is foolhardie thing,
Rashly to wyten creatures so diuine,
For demigods they be and first did spring
From heauen, though graft in frailnesse feminine.
And well I wote that oft I heard it spoken,
How one that fairest Helene did reuile,   920
Through iudgement of the Gods, to been ywroken,
Lost both his eyes and so remaynd long while,
Till he recanted had his wicked rimes,
And made amends to her with treble praise:
Beware therefore, ye groomes, I read betimes,
How rashly blame of Rosalind ye raise."

  "Ah! shepheards" (then said Colin) "ye ne weet

How great a guilt vpon your heads ye draw:
To make so bold a doome with words vnmeet,
Of thing celestiall which ye neuer saw.   930
For she is not like as the other crew
Of shepheards daughters which emongst you bee,
But of diuine regard and heauenly hew,
Excelling all that euer ye did see.
Not then to her that scorned thing so base,
But to my selfe the blame that lookt so hie:
So hie her thoughts as she her selfe haue place,
And loath each lowly thing with loftie eie.
Yet so much grace let her vouchsafe to grant
To simple swaine, sith her I may not loue,   940
Yet that I may her honour paravant,

And praise her worth, though far my wit aboue.
Such grace shall be some guerdon for the griefe
And long affliction which I haue endured:
Such grace sometimes shall giue me some reliefe,
And ease of paine which cannot be recured.
And ye, my fellow shepheards, which do see
And heare the languours of my too long dying,
Vnto the world for euer witnesse bee
That hers I die, nought to the world denying   950
This simple trophe of her great conquest."
    So, hauing ended, he from ground did rise,
And after him vprose eke all the rest:
All loth to part, but that the glooming skies
Warnd them to draw their bleating flocks to rest.

FROM AMORETTI AND EPITHALAMION (1595)

AMORETTI

I

Happy ye leaues, when as those lilly hands,
Which hold my life in their dead doing might,
Shall handle you and hold in loues soft bands,
Lyke captiues trembling at the victors sight.
And happy lines, on which with starry light,
Those lamping eyes will deigne sometimes to look,
And reade the sorrowes of my dying spright,
Written with teares in harts close bleeding book.
And happy rymes, bath'd in the sacred brooke
Of Helicon whence she deriued is,   10
When ye behold that Angels blessed looke,
My soules long lacked foode, my heauens blis.
Leaues, lines, and rymes, seeke her to please alone,
Whom if ye please, I care for other none.

5

Rudely thou wrongest my deare harts desire,
In finding fault with her too portly pride:
The thing which I doo most in her admire
Is of the world vnworthy most enuide.
For in those lofty lookes is close implide
Scorn of base things, and sdeigne of foule dishonor
Thretning rash eies which gaze on her so wide,
That loosely they ne dare to looke vpon her.
Such pride is praise, such portlinesse is honor,
That boldned innocence beares in hir eies;
And her faire countenance, like a goodly banner,
Spreds in defiaunce of all enemies.
Was neuer in this world ought worthy tride,
Without some spark of such self-pleasing pride.

13

In that proud port which her so goodly graceth,
Whiles her faire face she reares vp to the skie,

And to the ground her eie lids low embaseth,
Most goodly temperature ye may descry:
Myld humblesse mixt with awfull maiesty.
For looking on the earth whence she was borne,
Her minde remembreth her mortalitie:
What so is fayrest shall to earth returne.
But that same lofty countenance seemes to scorne
Base thing, and thinke how she to heauen may clime,   10
Treading downe earth as lothsome and forlorne,
That hinders heauenly thoughts with drossy slime.
Yet lowly still vouchsafe to looke on me,
Such lowlinesse shall make you lofty be.

15

Ye tradefull Merchants, that with weary toyle
Do seeke most pretious things to make your gain,
And both the Indias of their treasures spoile,
What needeth you to seeke so farre in vaine?
For loe my loue doth in her selfe containe
All this worlds riches that may farre be found:
If Saphyres, loe her eies be Saphyres plaine;
If Rubies, loe hir lips be Rubies sound;
If Pearles, hir teeth be pearles both pure and round;
If Yuorie, her forhead yuory weene;   10
If Gold, her locks are finest gold on ground;
If siluer, her faire hands are siluer sheene.
But that which fairest is but few behold,
Her mind adornd with vertues manifold.

19

The merry Cuckow, messenger of Spring,
His trompet shrill hath thrise already sounded,
That warnes al louers wayt vpon their king,
Who now is comming forth with girland crouned.
With noyse whereof the quyre of Byrds resounded
Their anthemes sweet devized of loues prayse,
That all the woods theyr ecchoes back rebounded,

As if they knew the meaning of their layes.
But mongst them all which did Loues honor rayse,
No word was heard of her that most it ought,   10
But she his precept proudly disobayes,
And doth his ydle message set at nought.
Therefore, O loue, vnlesse she turne to thee
Ere Cuckow end, let her a rebell be.

23

Penelope, for her Vlisses sake,
Deuiz'd a Web her wooers to deceaue,
In which the worke that she all day did make,
The same at night she did againe vnreaue.
Such subtile craft my Damzell doth conceaue,
Th'importune suit of my desire to shonne:
For all that I in many dayes doo weaue
In one short hour I find by her vndonne.
So when I thinke to end that I begonne,
I must begin and neuer bring to end: 10
For with one looke she spils that long I sponne,
And with one word my whole yeares work doth rend.
Such labour like the Spyders web I fynd,
Whose fruitlesse worke is broken with least wynd.

28

The laurell leafe which you this day doe weare
Giues me great hope of your relenting mynd:
For since it is the badg which I doe beare,
Ye, bearing it, doe seeme to me inclind.
The powre thereof, which ofte in me I find,
Let it lykewise your gentle brest inspire
With sweet infusion, and put you in mind
Of that proud mayd whom now those leaues attyre:
Proud Daphne scorning Phæbus louely fyre,
On the Thessalian shore from him did flie.   10
For which the gods in theyr reuengefull yre
Did her transforme into a laurell tree.
Then fly no more, fayre loue, from Phebus chace,
But in your brest his leafe and loue embrace.

33

Great wrong I doe, I can it not deny,
To that most sacred Empresse, my dear dred,
Not finishing her Queene of faëry,
That mote enlarge her liuing prayses dead.
But Lodwick, this of grace to me aread:
Doe ye not thinck th'accomplishment of it
Sufficient worke for one mans simple head,
All were it as the rest but rudely writ?
How then should I, without another wit,
Thinck euer to endure so tædious toyle,   10
Sins that this one is tost with troublous fit
Of a proud loue, that doth my spirite spoyle?
Ceasse then, till she vouchsafe to grawnt me rest,
Or lend you me another liuing brest.

34

Like as a ship that through the Ocean wyde
By conduct of some star doth make her way,
Whenas a storme hath dimd her trusty guyde,
Out of her course doth wander far astray;
So I, whose star, that wont with her bright ray
Me to direct, with cloudes is ouercast,
Doe wander now in darknesse and dismay,
Through hidden perils round about me plast.
Yet hope I well that when this storme is past
My Helice, the lodestar of my lyfe,   10
Will shine again, and looke on me at last,
With louely light to cleare my cloudy grief.
Till then I wander, carefull, comfortlesse,
In secret sorow and sad pensiuenesse.

44

When those renoumed noble Peres of Greece,
Thrugh stubborn pride amongst themselues did iar,
Forgetfull of the famous golden fleece,
Then Orpheus with his harp theyr strife did bar.
But this continuall cruell ciuill warre,
The which my selfe against my selfe doe make,
Whilest my weak powres of passions warreid arre,
No skill can stint nor reason can aslake.
But when in hand my tunelesse harp I take,
Then doe I more augment my foes despight,   10
And griefe renew, and passions doe awake
To battaile, fresh against my selfe to fight.
Mongst whome the more I seeke to settle peace,
The more I fynd their malice to increace.

54

Of this worlds Theatre in which we stay,
My loue lyke the Spectator ydly sits,
Beholding me, that all the pageants play,
Disguysing diuersly my troubled wits.
Sometimes I ioy when glad occasion fits,
And mask in myrth lyke to a Comedy:
Soone after when my ioy to sorrow flits,
I waile and make my woes a Tragedy.
Yet she, beholding me with constant eye,
Delights not in my merth nor rues my smart: 10
But when I laugh she mocks, and when I cry
She laughes, and hardens euermore her hart.
What then can moue her? if nor merth nor mone,
She is no woman, but a sencelesse stone.

62

The weary yeare his race now hauing run,
The new begins his compast course anew:
With shew of morning mylde he hath begun,
Betokening peace and plenty to ensew.
So let vs, which this chaunge of weather vew,
Chaunge eeke our mynds and former liues amend,

The old yeares sinnes forepast let vs eschew,
And fly the faults with which we did offend.
Then shall the new yeares ioy forth freshly send
Into the glooming world his gladsome ray;   10
And all these stormes which now his beauty blend,
Shall turne to caulmes and tymely cleare away.
So likewise, loue, cheare you your heauy spright,
And chaunge old yeares annoy to new delight.

68

Most glorious Lord of lyfe, that on this day
Didst make thy triumph ouer death and sin,
And hauing harrowd hell, didst bring away
Captiuity thence captiue vs to win:
This ioyous day, deare Lord, with ioy begin,
And grant that we for whom thou diddest dye,
Being with thy deare blood clene washt from sin,
May liue for euer in felicity:
And that thy loue we weighing worthily,
May likewise loue thee for the same againe;   10
And for thy sake that all lyke deare didst buy,
With loue may one another entertayne.
So let vs loue, deare loue, lyke as we ought:
Loue is the lesson which the Lord vs taught.

70

Fresh spring, the herald of loues mighty king,
In whose cote armour richly are displayd
All sorts of flowers the which on earth do spring
In goodly colours gloriously arrayd,
Goe to my loue, where she is carelesse layd,
Yet in her winters bowre not well awake;
Tell her the ioyous time wil not be staid
Vnlesse she doe him by the forelock take.
Bid her therefore her selfe soone ready make,
To wayt on loue amongst his louely crew,   10
Where euery one that misseth then her make
Shall be by him amearst with penance dew.
Make hast therefore, sweet loue, whilest it is prime,
For none can call againe the passed time.

75

One day I wrote her name vpon the strand,
But came the waues and washed it away:
Agayne I wrote it with a second hand,
But came the tyde, and made my paynes his pray.
Vayne man, sayd she, that doest in vaine assay
A mortall thing so to immortalize,
For I my selue shall lyke to this decay,
And eek my name bee wyped out lykewize.
Not so (quod I); let baser things deuize
To dy in dust, but you shall liue by fame: 10
My verse your vertues rare shall eternize,
And in the heuens wryte your glorious name;
Where whenas death shall all the world subdew,
Our loue shall liue, and later life renew.

77

Was it a dreame, or did I see it playne?
A goodly table of pure yuory,
All spred with iuncats, fit to entertayne
The greatest Prince with pompous roialty:
Mongst which there in a siluer dish did ly
Twoo golden apples of vnualewd price,
Far passing those which Hercules came by,
Or those which Atalanta did entice;
Exceeding sweet, yet voyd of sinfull vice,
That many sought yet none could euer taste,   10
Sweet fruit of pleasure brought from paradice
By loue himselfe, and in his garden plaste.
Her brest that table was so richly spredd,
My thoughts the guests, which would thereon haue fedd.

79

Men call you fayre, and you doe credit it,
For that your selfe ye dayly such doe see:
But the trew fayre, that is the gentle wit
And vertuous mind, is much more praysd of me.
For all the rest, how euer fayre it be,
Shall turne to nought and loose that glorious hew:
But onely that is permanent and free
From frayle corruption, that doth flesh ensew.
That is true beautie: that doth argue you
To be diuine and borne of heauenly seed,   10
Deriu'd from that fayre Spirit from whom al true
And perfect beauty did at first proceed.
He onely fayre, and what he fayre hath made,
All other fayre lyke flowres vntymely fade.

80

After so long a race as I haue run
Through Faery land, which those six books compile,
Giue leaue to rest me, being halfe fordonne,
And gather to my selfe new breath awhile.
Then as a steed refreshed after toyle,
Out of my prison I will breake anew:
And stoutly will that second worke assoyle,
With strong endeuour and attention dew.
Till then giue leaue to me in pleasant mew
To sport my muse and sing my loues sweet praise: 10
The contemplation of whose heauenly hew
My spirit to an higher pitch will rayse.
But let her prayses yet be low and meane,
Fit for the handmayd of the Faery Queene.

82

Ioy of my life, full oft for louing you
I blesse my lot, that was so lucky placed:
But then the more your owne mishap I rew,
That are so much by so meane loue embased.
For had the equall heuens so much you graced
In this as in the rest, ye mote inuent
Some heuenly wit, whose verse could haue enchased

Your glorious name in golden moniment.
But since ye deignd so goodly to relent
To me your thrall, in whom is little worth,   10
That little that I am shall all be spent
In setting your immortall prayses forth;
Whose lofty argument vplifting me
Shall lift you vp vnto an high degree.

EPITHALAMION

Ye learned sisters which haue oftentimes
Beene to me ayding, others to adorne,
Whom ye thought worthy of your gracefull rymes,
That euen the greatest did not greatly scorne
To heare theyr names sung in your simple layes,
But ioyed in theyr prayse;
And when ye list your owne mishaps to mourne,
Which death, or loue, or fortunes wreck did rayse,
Your string could soone to sadder tenor turne,
And teach the woods and waters to lament   10
Your dolefull dreriment.
Now lay those sorrowfull complaints aside,
And hauing all your heads with girland crownd,
Helpe me mine owne loues prayses to resound,
Ne let the same of any be enuide:
So Orpheus did for his owne bride,
So I vnto my selfe alone will sing,
The woods shall to me answer, and my Eccho ring.

Early before the worlds light giuing lampe
His golden beame vpon the hils doth spred,   20
Hauing disperst the nights vnchearefull dampe,
Doe ye awake, and with fresh lustyhed,
Go to the bowre of my beloued loue,
My truest turtle doue,
Bid her awake; for Hymen is awake,
And long since ready forth his maske to moue,
With his bright Tead that flames with many a flake,
And many a bachelor to waite on him,
In theyr fresh garments trim.
Bid her awake, therefore, and soone her dight,   30
For lo the wished day is come at last,
That shall for al the paynes and sorrowes past
Pay to her vsury of long delight:
And whylest she doth her dight,
Doe ye to her of ioy and solace sing,
That all the woods may answer, and your eccho ring.

Bring with you all the Nymphes that you can heare,
Both of the riuers and the forrests greene:
And of the sea that neighbours to her neare,
Al with gay girlands goodly wel beseene.   40
And let them also with them bring in hand
Another gay girland,
For my fayre loue, of lillyes and of roses,

Bound trueloue wize with a blew silke riband.
And let them make great store of bridale poses,
And let them eeke bring store of other flowers
To deck the bridale bowers.
And let the ground whereas her foot shall tread,
For feare the stones her tender foot should wrong,
Be strewed with fragrant flowers all along,   50
And diapred lyke the discolored mead.
Which done, doe at her chamber dore awayt,
For she will waken strayt,
The whiles doe ye this song vnto her sing,
The woods shall to you answer, and your Eccho ring.

Ye Nymphes of Mulla, which with carefull heed
The siluer scaly trouts doe tend full well,
And greedy pikes which vse therein to feed
(Those trouts and pikes all others doo excell),
And ye likewise which keepe the rushy lake,   60
Where none doo fishes take,
Bynd vp the locks the which hang scatterd light,
And in his waters which your mirror make,
Behold your faces as the christall bright,
That when you come whereas my loue doth lie,
No blemish she may spie.
And eke ye lightfoot mayds which keepe the deere
That on the hoary mountayne vse to towre,
And the wylde wolues which seeke them to deuoure,
With your steele darts doo chace from comming neer, 70
Be also present heere,
To helpe to decke her and to help to sing,
That all the woods may answer, and your eccho ring.

Wake now, my loue, awake; for it is time,
The Rosy Morne long since left Tithones bed,
All ready to her siluer coche to clyme,
And Phœbus gins to shew his glorious hed.
Hark how the cheerefull birds do chaunt theyr laies
And carroll of loues praise.
The merry Larke hir mattins sings aloft,   80
The thrush replyes, the Mauis descant playes,
The Ouzell shrills, the Ruddock warbles soft,
So goodly all agree with sweet consent,
To this dayes merriment.
Ah my deere loue, why doe ye sleepe thus long,
When meeter were that ye should now awake,
T'awayt the comming of your ioyous make,
And hearken to the birds louelearned song
The deawy leaues among?
For they of ioy and pleasance to you sing,   90
That all the woods them answer, and theyr eccho ring.

My loue is now awake out of her dreame,
And her fayre eyes, like stars that dimmed were
With darksome cloud, now shew theyr goodly beams
More bright then Hesperus his head doth rere.

Come now, ye damzels, daughters of delight,
Helpe quickly her to dight,
But first come ye fayre houres which were begot,
In Ioues sweet paradice, of Day and Night,
Which doe the seasons of the yeare allot,   100
And al that euer in this world is fayre
Doe make and still repayre.
And ye three handmayds of the Cyprian Queene,
The which doe still adorne her beauties pride,
Helpe to addorne my beautifullest bride:
And as ye her array, still throw betweene
Some graces to be seene,
And as ye vse to Venus, to her sing,
The whiles the woods shal answer, and your eccho ring.

Now is my loue all ready forth to come,   110
Let all the virgins therefore well awayt,
And ye fresh boyes that tend vpon her groome,
Prepare your selues; for he is comming strayt.
Set all your things in seemely good aray,
Fit for so ioyfull day,
The ioyfulst day that euer sunne did see.
Faire Sun, shew forth thy fauourable ray,
And let thy lifull heat not feruent be
For feare of burning her sunshyny face,
Her beauty to disgrace.   120
O fayrest Phœbus, father of the Muse,
If euer I did honour thee aright,
Or sing the thing that mote thy mind delight,
Doe not thy seruants simple boone refuse,
But let this day, let this one day, be myne,
Let all the rest be thine.
Then I thy souerayne prayses loud wil sing,
That all the woods shal answer, and theyr eccho ring.

Harke how the Minstrels gin to shrill aloud
Their merry Musick that resounds from far,   130
The pipe, the tabor, and the trembling Croud,
That well agree withouten breach or iar.
But most of all the Damzels doe delite,
When they their tymbrels smyte,
And thereunto doe daunce and carrol sweet,
That all the sences they doe rauish quite,
The whyles the boyes run vp and downe the street,
Crying aloud with strong confused noyce,
As if it were one voyce.
"Hymen io Hymen, Hymen," they do shout,   140
That euen to the heauens theyr shouting shrill
Doth reach, and all the firmament doth fill,
To which the people standing all about,
As in approuance doe thereto applaud
And loud aduaunce her laud,
And euermore they "Hymen Hymen" sing,
That al the woods them answer, and theyr eccho ring.

Loe where she comes along with portly pace,
Lyke Phœbe from her chamber of the East,
Arysing forth to run her mighty race,   150
Clad all in white, that seemes a virgin best.
So well it her beseemes that ye would weene
Some angell she had beene.
Her long loose yellow locks lyke golden wyre,
Sprinckled with perle, and perling flowres a-tweene,
Doe lyke a golden mantle her attyre,
And being crowned with a girland greene,
Seeme lyke some mayden Queene.
Her modest eyes abashed to behold
So many gazers as on her do stare,   160
Vpon the lowly ground affixed are.
Ne dare lift vp her countenance too bold,
But blush to heare her prayses sung so loud,
So farre from being proud.
Nathlesse doe ye still loud her prayses sing,
That all the woods may answer, and your eccho ring.

Tell me, ye merchants daughters, did ye see
So fayre a creature in your towne before,
So sweet, so louely, and so mild as she,
Adornd with beautyes grace and vertues store?   170
Her goodly eyes lyke Saphyres shining bright,
Her forehead yuory white,
Her cheekes lyke apples which the sun hath rudded,
Her lips lyke cherryes charming men to byte,
Her brest like to a bowle of creame vncrudded,
Her paps lyke lyllies budded,
Her snowie necke lyke to a marble towre,
And all her body like a pallace fayre,
Ascending vppe with many a stately stayre,
To honors seat and chastities sweet bowre.   180
Why stand ye still, ye virgins, in amaze,
Vpon her so to gaze,
Whiles ye forget your former lay to sing,
To which the woods did answer, and your eccho ring?

But if ye saw that which no eyes can see,
The inward beauty of her liuely spright,
Garnisht with heauenly guifts of high degree,
Much more then would ye wonder at that sight,
And stand astonisht lyke to those which red
Medusaes mazeful hed.   190
There dwels sweet loue and constant chastity,
Vnspotted fayth and comely womanhood,
Regard of honour and mild modesty,
There vertue raynes as Queene in royal throne,
And giueth lawes alone,
The which the base affections doe obay,
And yeeld theyr seruices vnto her will,
Ne thought of thing vncomely euer may
Thereto approch to tempt her mind to ill.
Had ye once seene these her celestial threasures,   200

And vnreuealed pleasures,
Then would ye wonder and her prayses sing,
That al the woods should answer, and your echo ring.

Open the temple gates vnto my loue,
Open them wide that she may enter in,
And all the postes adorne as doth behoue,
And all the pillours deck with girlands trim,
For to recyue this Saynt with honour dew,
That commeth in to you.
With trembling steps and humble reuerence,   210
She commeth in, before th'almighties vew:
Of her ye virgins learne obedience,
When so ye come into those holy places,
To humble your proud faces.
Bring her vp to th'high altar, that she may
The sacred ceremonies there partake,
The which do endlesse matrimony make,
And let the roring Organs loudly play
The praises of the Lord in liuely notes,
The whiles with hollow throates   220
The Choristers the ioyous Antheme sing,
That al the woods may answere, and their eccho ring.

Behold whiles she before the altar stands,
Hearing the holy priest that to her speakes
And blesseth her with his two happy hands,
How the red roses flush vp in her cheekes,
And the pure snow with goodly vermill stayne,
Like crimsin dyde in grayne,
That euen th'Angels which continually
About the sacred Altare doe remaine,   230
Forget their seruice and about her fly,
Ofte peeping in her face that seemes more fayre,
The more they on it stare.
But her sad eyes, still fastened on the ground,
Are gouerned with goodly modesty,
That suffers not one looke to glaunce awry,
Which may let in a little thought vnsownd.
Why blush ye, loue, to giue to me your hand,
The pledge of all our band?
Sing, ye sweet Angels, Alleluya sing,   240
That all the woods may answere, and your eccho ring.

Now al is done; bring home the bride againe,
Bring home the triumph of our victory,
Bring home with you the glory of her gaine,
With ioyance bring her and with iollity.
Neuer had man more ioyfull day then this,
Whom heauen would heape with blis.
Make feast therefore now all this liue long day,
This day for euer to me holy is,
Poure out the wine without restraint or stay,   250
Poure not by cups, but by the belly full,
Poure out to all that wull,

And sprinkle all the postes and wals with wine,
That they may sweat, and drunken be withall.
Crowne ye God Bacchus with a coronall,
And Hymen also crowne with wreathes of vine,
And let the Graces daunce vnto the rest,
For they can doo it best:
The whiles the maydens doe theyr carroll sing,
To which the woods shal answer, and theyr eccho ring.

Ring ye the bels, ye yong men of the towne,   261
And leaue your wonted labors for this day:
This day is holy; doe ye write it downe,
That ye for euer it remember may.
This day the sunne is in his chiefest hight,
With Barnaby the bright,
From whence declining daily by degrees,
He somewhat loseth of his heat and light,
When once the Crab behind his back he sees.
But for this time it ill ordained was,   270
To chose the longest day in all the yeare,
And shortest night, when longest fitter weare:
Yet neuer day so long, but late would passe.
Ring ye the bels, to make it weare away,
And bonefiers make all day,
And daunce about them, and about them sing:
That all the woods may answer, and your eccho ring.

Ah when will this long weary day haue end,
And lende me leaue to come vnto my loue?
How slowly do the houres theyr numbers spend!   280
How slowly does sad Time his feathers moue!
Hast thee, O fayrest Planet, to thy home
Within the Westerne fome:
Thy tyred steedes long since haue need of rest.
Long though it be, at last I see it gloome,
And the bright euening star with golden creast
Appeare out of the East.
Fayre childe of beauty, glorious lampe of loue,
That all the host of heauen in rankes doost lead,
And guydest louers through the nightes dread,   290
How chearefully thou lookest from aboue,
And seemst to laugh atweene thy twinkling light,
As ioying in the sight
Of these glad many which for ioy doe sing,
That all the woods them answer, and their echo ring.

Now ceasse, ye damsels, your delights forepast;
Enough is it that all the day was youres
Now day is doen, and night is nighing fast:
Now bring the Bryde into the brydall boures.
Now night is come, now soone her disaray,   300
And in her bed her lay;
Lay her in lillies and in violets,
And silken courteins ouer her display,
And odourd sheetes, and Arras couerlets.

Behold how goodly my faire loue does ly
In proud humility;
Like vnto Maia, when as Ioue her tooke,
In Tempe, lying on the flowry gras,
Twixt sleepe and wake, after she weary was
With bathing in the Acidalian brooke.   310
Now it is night, ye damsels may be gon,
And leaue my loue alone,
And leaue likewise your former lay to sing:
The woods no more shal answere, nor your echo ring.

Now welcome night, thou night so long expected,
That long daies labour doest at last defray,
And all my cares, which cruell loue collected,
Hast sumd in one, and cancelled for aye:
Spread thy broad wing ouer my loue and me,
That no man may vs see,   320
And in thy sable mantle vs enwrap,
From feare of perrill and foule horror free.
Let no false treason seeke vs to entrap,
Nor any dread disquiet once annoy
The safety of our ioy:
But let the night be calme and quietsome,
Without tempestuous storms or sad afray:
Lyke as when Ioue with fayre Alcmena lay,
When he begot the great Tirynthian groome:
Or lyke as when he with thy selfe did lie,   330
And begot Maiesty.
And let the mayds and yongmen cease to sing:
Ne let the woods them answer, nor theyr eccho ring.

Let no lamenting cryes, nor dolefull teares,
Be heard all night within nor yet without.
Ne let false whispers, breeding hidden feares,
Breake gentle sleepe with misconceiued dout.
Let no deluding dreames, nor dreadful sights
Make sudden sad affrights;
Ne let housefyres, nor lightnings helpelesse harmes,   340
Ne let the Pouke, nor other euill sprights,
Ne let mischiuous witches with theyr charmes,
Ne let hob Goblins, names whose sence we see not,
Fray vs with things that be not,
Let not the shriech Oule, nor the Storke be heard:
Nor the night Rauen that still deadly yels,
Nor damned ghosts cald vp with mighty spels,
Nor griesly vultures make vs once affeard:
Ne let th'unpleasant Quyre of Frogs still croking
Make vs to wish theyr choking.   350
Let none of these theyr drery accents sing;
Ne let the woods them answer, nor theyr eccho ring.

But let stil Silence trew night watches keepe,
That sacred peace may in assurance rayne,
And tymely sleep, when it is tyme to sleepe,
May poure his limbs forth on your pleasant playne,

The whiles an hundred little winged loues,
Like diuers fethered doues,
Shall fly and flutter round about your bed,
And in the secret darke, that none reproues,   360
Their prety stealthes shal worke, and snares shal spread
To filch away sweet snatches of delight,
Conceald through couert night.
Ye sonnes of Venus, play your sports at will:
For greedy pleasure, carelesse of your toyes,
Thinks more vpon her paradise of ioyes,
Then what ye do, albe it good or ill.
All night therefore attend your merry play,
For it will soone be day:
Now none doth hinder you, that say or sing,   370
Ne will the woods now answer, nor your Eccho ring.

Who is the same which at my window peepes?
Or whose is that faire face that shines so bright?
Is it not Cinthia, she that neuer sleepes,
But walkes about high heauen al the night?
O fayrest goddesse, do thou not enuy
My loue with me to spy:
For thou likewise didst loue, though now vnthought,
And for a fleece of woll, which priuily
The Latmian shephard once vnto thee brought,   380
His pleasures with thee wrought.
Therefore to vs be fauorable now;
And sith of wemens labours thou hast charge,
And generation goodly dost enlarge,
Encline thy will t'effect our wishfull vow,
And the chast wombe informe with timely seed,
That may our comfort breed:
Till which we cease our hopefull hap to sing,
Ne let the woods vs answere, nor our Eccho ring.

And thou great Iuno, which with awful might   390
The lawes of wedlock still dost patronize,
And the religion of the faith first plight
With sacred rites hast taught to solemnize:
And eeke for comfort often called art
Of women in their smart,
Eternally bind thou this louely band,
And all thy blessings vnto vs impart.
And thou glad Genius, in whose gentle hand
The bridale bowre and geniall bed remaine,
Without blemish or staine,   400
And the sweet pleasures of theyr loues delight
With secret ayde doest succour and supply,
Till they bring forth the fruitfull progeny,
Send vs the timely fruit of this same night.
And thou fayre Hebe, and thou Hymen free,
Grant that it may so be.
Til which we cease your further prayse to sing,
Ne any woods shal answer, nor your Eccho ring.

And ye high heauens, the temple of the gods,
In which a thousand torches flaming bright   410
Doe burne, that to vs wretched earthly clods
In dreadful darknesse lend desired light;
And all ye powers which in the same remayne,
More then we men can fayne,
Poure out your blessing on vs plentiously,
And happy influence vpon vs raine,
That we may raise a large posterity,
Which from the earth, which they may long possesse,
With lasting happinesse,
Vp to your haughty pallaces may mount,   420
And for the guerdon of theyr glorious merit
May heauenly tabernacles there inherit,
Of blessed Saints for to increase the count.
So let vs rest, sweet loue, in hope of this,
And cease till then our tymely ioyes to sing,
The woods no more vs answer, nor our eccho ring.

Song made in lieu of many ornaments
With which my loue should duly haue bene dect,
Which cutting off through hasty accidents,
Ye would not stay your dew time to expect,   430
But promist both to recompens,
Be vnto her a goodly ornament,
And for short time an endlesse moniment.

PROTHALAMION (1596)

Calme was the day, and through the trembling ayre
Sweete breathing Zephyrus did softly play,
A gentle spirit, that lightly did delay
Hot Titans beames, which then did glyster fayre:
When I whom sullein care,
Through discontent of my long fruitlesse stay
In Princes Court, and expectation vayne
Of idle hopes, which still doe fly away,
Like empty shaddowes, did aflict my brayne,
Walkt forth to ease my payne   10
Along the shoare of siluer streaming Themmes;
Whose rutty Bancke, the which his Riuer hemmes,
Was paynted all with variable flowers,
And all the meades adornd with daintie gemmes,
Fit to decke maydens bowres,
And crowne their Paramours,
Against the Brydale day, which is not long:
   Sweete Themmes, runne softly till I end my Song.

There, in a Meadow, by the Riuers side,
A Flocke of Nymphes I chaunced to espy,   20
All louely Daughters of the Flood thereby,
With goodly greenish locks all loose vntyde,
As each had bene a Bryde,
And each one had a little wicker basket,
Made of fine twigs entrayled curiously,

In which they gathered flowers to fill their flasket:
And with fine Fingers cropt full feateously
The tender stalkes on hye.
Of euery sort which in that Meadow grew
They gathered some; the Violet pallid blew,   30
The little Dazie that at euening closes,
The virgin Lillie, and the Primrose trew,
With store of vermeil Roses,
To decke their Bridegromes posies,
Against the Brydale day, which was not long:
   Sweete Themmes, runne softly till I end my Song.

With that, I saw two Swannes of goodly hewe
Come softly swimming downe along the Lee;
Two fairer Birds I yet did neuer see:
The snow which doth the top of Pindus strew   40
Did neuer whiter shew,
Nor Joue himselfe, when he a Swan would be
For loue of Leda, whiter did appeare:
Yet Leda was they say as white as he,
Yet not so white as these, nor nothing neare;
So purely white they were
That euen the gentle streame, the which them bare,
Seem'd foule to them, and bad his billowes spare
To wet their silken feathers, least they might
Soyle their fayre plumes with water not so fayre   50
And marre their beauties bright,
That shone as heauens light,
Against their Brydale day, which was not long:
   Sweete Themmes, runne softly till I end my Song.

Eftsoones the Nymphes, which now had Flowers their
      fill,
Ran all in haste to see that siluer brood,
As they came floating on the Christal Flood.
Whom when they sawe, they stood amazed still,
Their wondring eyes to fill,
Them seem'd they neuer saw a sight so fayre,   60
Of Fowles so louely, that they sure did deeme
Them heauenly borne, or to be that same payre
Which through the Skie draw Venus siluer Teeme;
For sure they did not seeme
To be begot of any earthly Seede,
But rather Angels or of Angels breede:
Yet were they bred of Somers-heat, they say,
In sweetest Season, when each Flower and weede
The earth did fresh aray;
So fresh they seem'd as day,   70
Euen as their Brydale day, which was not long:
   Sweete Themmes, runne softly till I end my Song.

Then forth they all out of their baskets drew
Great store of Flowers, the honour of the field,
That to the sense did fragrant odours yeild,
All which vpon those goodly Birds they threw,
And all the Waues did strew,

That like old Peneus Waters they did seeme,
When downe along by pleasant Tempes shore,
Scattred with Flowres, through Thessaly they streeme, 80
That they appeare through Lillies plenteous store,
Like a Brydes Chamber flore.
Two of those Nymphes, meane while, two Garlands
  bound
Of freshest Flowres which in that Mead they found,
The which presenting all in trim Array,
Their snowie Foreheads therewithall they crownd,
Whil'st one did sing this Lay,
Prepar'd against that Day,
Against their Brydale day, which was not long:
 Sweete Themmes, runne softly till I end my Song. 90

"Ye gentle Birdes, the worlds faire ornament,
And heauens glorie, whom this happie hower
Doth leade vnto your louers blisfull bower,
Ioy may you haue and gentle hearts content
Of your loues couplement:
And let faire Venus, that is Queene of loue,
With her heart-quelling Sonne vpon you smile,
Whose smile, they say, hath vertue to remoue
All Loues dislike, and friendships faultie guile
For euer to assoile.   100
Let endlesse Peace your steadfast hearts accord,
And blessed Plentie wait vpon your bord,
And let your bed with pleasures chast abound,
That fruitfull issue may to you afford,
Which may your foes confound,
And make your ioyes redound,
Vpon your Brydale day, which is not long:
 Sweete Themmes, run softlie till I end my Song."

So ended she; and all the rest around
To her redoubled that her vndersong,   110
Which said their bridale daye should not be long.
And gentle Eccho from the neighbour ground
Their accents did resound.
So forth those ioyous Birdes did passe along,
Adowne the Lee, that to them murmurde low,
As he would speake, but that he lackt a tong,
Yeat did by signes his glad affection show,
Making his streame run slow.
And all the foule which in his flood did dwell
Gan flock about these twaine, that did excell   120
The rest so far as Cynthia doth shend
The lesser starres. So they, enranged well,
Did on those two attend,
And their best seruice lend,
Against their wedding day, which was not long:
 Sweete Themmes, run softly till I end my song.

At length they all to mery London came,
To mery London, my most kyndly Nurse,

That to me gaue this Lifes first natiue sourse;
Though from another place I take my name,   130
An house of auncient fame.
There when they came, whereas those bricky towres,
The which on Themmes brode aged backe doe ryde,
Where now the studious Lawyers haue their bowers,
There whylome wont the Templer Knights to byde,
Till they decayd through pride:
Next whereunto there standes a stately place,
Where oft I gayned gifts and goodly grace
Of that great Lord which therein wont to dwell,
Whose want too well now feeles my freendles case: 140
But Ah! here fits not well
Olde woes but ioyes to tell
Against the bridale daye, which is not long:
 Sweete Themmes, runne softly till I end my Song.

Yet therein now doth lodge a noble Peer,
Great Englands glory and the Worlds wide wonder,
Whose dreadfull name late through all Spaine did thunder,
And Hercules two pillors standing neere
Did make to quake and feare:
Faire branch of Honor, flower of Cheualrie,   150
That fillest England with thy triumphs fame,
Ioy haue thou of thy noble victorie,
And endlesse happinesse of thine owne name
That promiseth the same:
That through thy prowesse and victorious armes
Thy country may be freed from forraine harmes;
And great Elisaes glorious name may ring
Through al the world, fil'd with thy wide Alarmes,
Which some braue muse may sing
To ages following,   160
Vpon the Brydale day, which is not long:
 Sweete Themmes, runne softly till I end my Song.

From those high Towers this noble Lord issuing,
Like Radiant Hesper when his golden hayre
In th'Ocean billowes he hath Bathed fayre,
Descended to the Riuers open vewing,
With a great traine ensuing.
Aboue the rest were goodly to bee seene
Two gentle Knights of louely face and feature,
Beseeming well the bower of anie Queene,   170
With gifts of wit and ornaments of nature
Fit for so goodly stature:
That like the twins of Ioue they seem'd in sight,
Which decke the Bauldricke of the Heauens bright.
They two, forth pacing to the Riuers side,
Receiued those two faire Brides, their Loues delight,
Which at th'appointed tyde,
Each one did make his Bryde,
Against their Brydale day, which is not long:
 Sweete Themmes, runne softly till I end my Song. 180

FROM FOWRE HYMNES (1596)

To the Right Honorable and Most Vertuous Ladies,
the Ladie Margaret Countesse of Cumberland,
and the Ladie Marie Countesse of Warwicke

Hauing in the greener times of my youth composed these former two Hymnes in the praise of
Loue and beautie, and finding that the same too
much pleased those of like age and disposition, which
being too vehemently caried with that kind of affection, do rather sucke out poyson to their strong
passion, then hony to their honest delight, I was   10
moued by the one of you two most excellent Ladies,
to call in the same. But being vnable so to doe, by
reason that many copies thereof were formerly
scattered abroad, I resolued at least to amend and by
way of retractation to reforme them, making in stead
of those two Hymnes of earthly or naturall love and
beautie, two others of heauenly and celestiall. The
which I doe dedicate ioyntly vnto you two honorable sisters, as to the most excellent and rare ornaments of all true loue and beautie, both in the one   20
and the other kinde, humbly beseeching you to
vouchsafe the patronage of them, and to accept this
my humble seruice, in lieu of the great graces and
honourable fauours which ye dayly shew vnto me,
vntill such time as I may by better meanes yeeld you
some more notable testimonie of my thankfull mind
and dutifull deuotion.

And euen so I pray for your happinesse.
Greenwich this first of September.
1596.   30
Your Honors most bounden euer
in all humble seruice.
Ed[mund] Sp[enser]

AN HYMNE IN HONOVR OF LOVE

Loue, that long since hast to thy mighty powre
Perforce subdude my poore captiued hart,
And raging now therein with restlesse stowre,
Doest tyrannize in euerie weaker part;
Faine would I seeke to ease my bitter smart
By any seruice I might do to thee,
Or ought that else might to thee pleasing bee.

And now t'asswage the force of this new flame,
And make thee more propitious in my need,
I meane to sing the praises of thy name,   10
And thy victorious conquests to areed;
By which thou madest many harts to bleed
Of mighty Victors, with wyde wounds embrewed,
And by thy cruell darts to thee subdewed.

Onely I feare my wits, enfeebled late
Through the sharpe sorrowes which thou hast me bred,

Should faint, and words should faile me to relate
The wondrous triumphs of thy great godhed.
But if thou wouldst vouchsafe to ouerspred
Me with the shadow of thy gentle wing,   20
I should enabled be thy actes to sing.

Come then, O come, thou mightie God of loue,
Out of thy siluer bowres and secret blisse,
Where thou doest sit in Venus lap aboue,
Bathing thy wings in her ambrosiall kisse,
That sweeter farre then any Nectar is;
Come softly, and my feeble breast inspire
With gentle furie, kindled of thy fire.

And ye, sweet Muses, which haue often proued
The piercing points of his auengefull darts;   30
And ye, faire Nimphs, which oftentimes haue loued
The cruell worker of your kindly smarts,
Prepare your selues, and open wide your harts,
For to receiue the triumph of your glorie,
That made you merie oft, when ye were sorie.

And ye, faire blossomes of youths wanton breed,
Which in the conquests of your beautie bost,
Wherewith your louers feeble eyes you feed,
But sterue their harts, that needeth nourture most,
Prepare your selues to march amongst his host,   40
And all the way this sacred hymne do sing,
Made in the honor of your Soueraigne king.

Great god of might, that reignest in the mynd,
And all the bodie to thy hest doest frame,
Victor of gods, subduer of mankynd,
That doest the Lions and fell Tigers tame,
Making their cruell rage thy scornefull game,
And in their roring taking great delight,
Who can expresse the glorie of thy might?

Or who aliue can perfectly declare   50
The wondrous cradle of thine infancie?
When thy great mother Venus first thee bare,
Begot of Plentie and of Penurie,
Though elder then thine owne natiuitie;
And yet a chyld, renewing still thy yeares,
And yet the eldest of the heauenly Peares.

For ere this worlds still mouing mightie masse
Out of great Chaos vgly prison crept,
In which his goodly face long hidden was
From heauens view, and in deepe darknesse kept,   60
Loue, that had now long time securely slept
In Venus lap, vnarmed then and naked,
Gan reare his head, by Clotho being waked.

And taking to him wings of his owne heate,
Kindled at first from heauens life-giuing fyre,
He gan to moue out of his idle seate,
Weakely at first, but after with desyre
Lifted aloft, he gan to mount vp hyre,
And, like fresh Eagle, make his hardie flight
Through all that great wide wast, yet wanting light. 70

Yet wanting light to guide his wandring way,
His owne faire mother, for all creatures sake,
Did lend him light from her owne goodly ray:
Then through the world his way he gan to take,
The world that was not till he did it make,
Whose sundrie parts he from them selues did seuer,
The which before had lyen confused euer.

The earth, the ayre, the water, and the fyre,
Then gan to raunge them selues in huge array,
And with contrary forces to conspyre   80
Each against other, by all meanes they may,
Threatning their owne confusion and decay:
Ayre hated earth, and water hated fyre,
Till Loue relented their rebellious yre.

He then them tooke and, tempering goodly well
Their contrary dislikes with loued meanes,
Did place them all in order, and compell
To keepe them selues within their sundrie raines,
Together linkt with Adamantine chaines;
Yet so, as that in euery liuing wight   90
They mixe themselues, and shew their kindly might.

So euer since they firmely haue remained,
And duly well obserued his beheast;
Through which now all these things that are contained
Within this goodly cope, both most and least,
Their being haue, and dayly are increast,
Through secret sparks of his infused fyre,
Which in the barraine cold he doth inspyre.

Thereby they all do liue, and moued are
To multiply the likenesse of their kynd,   100
Whilest they seeke onely, without further care,
To quench the flame which they in burning fynd:
But man, that breathes a more immortall mynd,
Not for lusts sake, but for eternitie,
Seekes to enlarge his lasting progenie.

For hauing yet in his deducted spright
Some sparks remaining of that heauenly fyre,
He is enlumind with that goodly light,
Vnto like goodly semblant to aspyre:
Therefore in choice of loue, he doth desyre   110
That seemes on earth most heauenly, to embrace,
That same is Beautie, borne of heauenly race.

For sure of all that in this mortall frame
Contained is, nought more diuine doth seeme,
Or that resembleth more th'immortall flame
Of heauenly light, then Beauties glorious beame.
What wonder, then, if with such rage extreme
Fraile men, whose eyes seek heauenly things to see,
At sight thereof so much enrauisht bee?

Which well perceiuing, that imperious boy   120
Doth therwith tip his sharp empoisned darts;
Which glancing through the eyes with countenance coy,
Rest not till they haue pierst the trembling harts,
And kindled flame in all their inner parts,
Which suckes the blood, and drinketh vp the lyfe
Of carefull wretches with consuming griefe.

Thenceforth they playne, and make ful piteous mone
Vnto the author of their balefull bane;
The daies they waste, the nights they grieue and grone,
Their liues they loath, and heauens light disdaine;   130
No light but that whose lampe doth yet remaine
Fresh burning in the image of their eye,
They deigne to see, and seeing it still dye.

The whylst thou, tyrant Loue, doest laugh and scorne
At their complaints, making their paine thy play;
Whylest they lye languishing like thrals forlorne,
The whyles thou doest triumph in their decay,
And otherwhyles, their dying to delay,
Thou doest emmarble the proud hart of her,
Whose loue before their life they doe prefer.   140

So hast thou often done (ay me the more!)
To me thy vassall, whose yet bleeding hart
With thousand wounds thou mangled hast so sore
That whole remaines scarse any little part;
Yet to augment the anguish of my smart,
Thou hast enfrosen her disdainefull brest,
That no one drop of pitie there doth rest.

Why then do I this honor vnto thee,
Thus to ennoble thy victorious name,
Since thou doest shew no fauour vnto mee,   150
Ne once moue ruth in that rebellious Dame,
Somewhat to slacke the rigour of my flame?
Certes small glory doest thou winne hereby,
To let her liue thus free, and me to dy.

But if thou be indeede, as men thee call,
The worlds great Parent, the most kind preseruer
Of liuing wights, the soueraine Lord of all,
How falles it, then, that with thy furious feruour,
Thou doest afflict as well the not deseruer,
As him that doeth thy louely heasts despize,   160
And on thy subjects most doest tyrannize?

*3ohnes ib all
beauty*

Yet herein eke thy glory seemeth more,
By so hard handling those which best thee serue,
That ere thou doest them vnto grace restore,
Thou mayest well trie if they will euer swerue,
And mayest them make it better to deserue;
And hauing got it, may it more esteeme.
For things hard gotten men more dearely deeme.

So hard those heauenly beauties be enfyred,
As things diuine least passions doe impresse,   170
The more of stedfast mynds to be admyred,
The more they stayed be on stedfastnesse:
But baseborne mynds such lamps regard the lesse,
Which at first blowing take not hastie fyre;
Such fancies feele no loue, but loose desyre.

For loue is Lord of truth and loialtie,
Lifting himselfe out of the lowly dust
On golden plumes vp to the purest skie,
Aboue the reach of loathly sinfull lust,
Whose base affect, through cowardly distrust   180
Of his weake wings, dare not to heauen fly,
But like a moldwarpe in the earth doth ly.

His dunghill thoughts, which do themselues enure
To dirtie drosse, no higher dare aspyre,
Ne can his feeble earthly eyes endure
The flaming light of that celestiall fyre,
Which kindleth loue in generous desyre,
And makes him mount aboue the natiue might
Of heauie earth, vp to the heauens hight.

Such is the powre of that sweet passion,   190
That it all sordid basenesse doth expell,
And the refyned mynd doth newly fashion
Vnto a fairer forme, which now doth dwell
In his high thought, that would it selfe excell;
Which he beholding still with constant sight,
Admires the mirrour of so heauenly light.

Whose image printing in his deepest wit,
He thereon feeds his hungrie fantasy,
Still full, yet neuer satisfyde with it,
Like Tantale, that in store doth sterued ly: 200
So doth he pine in most satiety,
For nought may quench his infinite desyre,
Once kindled through that first conceiued fyre.

Thereon his mynd affixed wholly is,
Ne thinks on ought, but how it to attaine;
His care, his ioy, his hope is all on this,
That seemes in it all blisses to containe,
In sight whereof, all other blisse seemes vaine.
Thrise happie man, might he the same possesse;
He faines himselfe, and doth his fortune blesse.   210

And though he do not win his wish to end,
Yet thus farre happie he him selfe doth weene,
That heauens such happie grace did to him lend,
As thing on earth so heauenly to haue seene,
His harts enshrined saint, his heauens queene,
Fairer then fairest, in his fayning eye,
Whose sole aspect he counts felicitye.

Then forth he casts in his vnquiet thought,
What he may do, her fauour to obtaine;
What braue exploit, what perill hardly wrought,   220
What puissant conquest, what aduenturous paine,
May please her best, and grace vnto him gaine:
He dreads no danger, nor misfortune feares,
His faith, his fortune, in his breast he beares.

Thou art his god, thou art his mightie guyde,
Thou, being blind, letst him not see his feares,
But cariest him to that which he hath eyde,
Through seas, through flames, through thousand swords
    and speares:
Ne ought so strong that may his force withstand,
With which thou armest his resistlesse hand.   230

Witnesse Leander in the Euxine waues,
And stout Æneas in the Troiane fyre,
Achilles preassing through the Phrygian glaiues,
And Orpheus daring to prouoke the yre
Of damned fiends, to get his loue retyre:
For both through heauen and hell thou makest way,
To win them worship which to thee obay.

And if by all these perils and these paynes,
He may but purchase lyking in her eye,
What heauens of ioy then to himselfe he faynes,   240
Eftsoones he wypes quite out of memory
What euer ill before he did aby:
Had it bene death, yet would he die againe,
To liue thus happie as her grace to gaine.

Yet when he hath found fauour to his will,
He nathemore can so contented rest,
But forceth further on, and striueth still
T'approch more neare, till in her inmost brest
He may embosomd bee, and loued best;
And yet not best, but to be lou'd alone: 250
For loue can not endure a Paragone.

The feare whereof, O how doth it torment
His troubled mynd with more then hellish paine!
And to his fayning fansie represent
Sights neuer seene, and thousand shadowes vaine,
To breake his sleepe and waste his ydle braine;
Thou that hast neuer lou'd canst not beleeue
Least part of th'euils which poore louers greeue.

The gnawing enuie, the hart-fretting feare,
The vaine surmizes, the distrustfull showes,   260
The false reports that flying tales doe beare,
The doubts, the daungers, the delayes, the woes,
The fayned friends, the vnassured foes,
With thousands more then any tongue can tell,
Doe make a louers life a wretches hell.

Yet is there one more cursed then they all,
That cancker worme, that monster Gelosie,
Which eates the hart, and feedes vpon the gall,
Turning all loues delight to miserie,
Through feare of loosing his felicitie.   270
Ah Gods, that euer ye that monster placed
In gentle loue, that all his ioyes defaced.

By these, O Loue, thou doest thy entrance make
Vnto thy heauen, and doest the more endeère
Thy pleasures vnto those which them partake,
As after stormes, when clouds begin to cleare,
The Sunne more bright and glorious doth appeare;
So thou thy folke, through paines of Purgatorie,
Dost beare vnto thy blisse, and heauens glorie.

There thou them placest in a Paradize   280
Of all delight and ioyous happie rest,
Where they doe feede on Nectar heauenly wize,
With Hercules and Hebe, and the rest
Of Venus dearlings, through her bountie blest,
And lie like Gods in yuorie beds arayd,
With rose and lillies ouer them displayd.

There with thy daughter Pleasure they doe play
Their hurtlesse sports, without rebuke or blame,
And in her snowy bosome boldly lay
Their quiet heads, deuoyd of guilty shame,   290
After full ioyance of their gentle game,
Then her they crowne their Goddesse and their Queene,
And decke with floures thy altars well beseene.

Ay me, deare Lord, that euer I might hope,
For all the paines and woes that I endure,
To come at length vnto the wished scope
Of my desire, or might my selfe assure,
That happie port for euer to recure.
Then would I thinke these paines no paines at all,
And all my woes to be but penance small.   300

Then would I sing of thine immortall praise
An heauenly Hymne, such as the Angels sing,
And thy triumphant name then would I raise
Boue all the gods, thee onely honoring,
My guide, my God, my victor, and my king;
Till then, dread Lord, vouchsafe to take of me
This simple song, thus fram'd in praise of thee.

AN HYMNE OF HEAVENLY LOVE

Loue, lift me vp vpon thy golden wings
From this base world vnto thy heauens hight,
Where I may see those admirable things,
Which there thou workest by thy soueraine might,
Farre aboue feeble reach of earthly sight,
That I thereof an heauenly Hymne may sing
Vnto the god of Loue, high heauens king.

Many lewd layes (ah woe is me the more!)
In praise of that mad fit which fooles call loue,
I haue in th'heat of youth made heretofore,   10
That in light wits did loose affection moue.
But all those follies now I do reproue,
And turned haue the tenor of my string,
The heauenly prayses of true loue to sing.

And ye that wont with greedy vaine desire
To reade my fault, and wondring at my flame,
To warme your selues at my wide sparckling fire,
Sith now that heat is quenched, quench my blame,
And in her ashes shrowd my dying shame:
For who my passed follies now pursewes,   20
Beginnes his owne, and my old fault renewes.

Before this worlds great frame, in which al things
Are now containd, found any being place,
Ere flitting Time could wag his eyas wings
About that mightie bound, which doth embrace
The rolling Spheres, and parts their houres by space,
That high eternall powre, which now doth moue
In all these things, mou'd in it selfe by loue.

It lou'd it selfe, because it selfe was faire;
(For faire is lou'd); and of it selfe begot   30
Like to it selfe his eldest sonne and heire,
Eternall, pure, and voide of sinfull blot,
The firstling of his ioy, in whom no iot
Of loues dislike or pride was to be found,
Whom he therefore with equall honour crownd.

With him he raignd, before all time prescribed,
In endlesse glorie and immortall might,
Together with that third from them deriued,
Most wise, most holy, most almightie Spright,
Whose kingdomes throne no thought of earthly wight   40
Can comprehend, much lesse my trembling verse
With equall words can hope it to reherse.

Yet O most blessed Spirit, pure lampe of light,
Eternall spring of grace and wisedome trew,
Vouchsafe to shed into my barren spright
Some little drop of thy celestiall dew,
That may my rymes with sweet infuse embrew,

And giue me words equall vnto my thought,
To tell the maruciles by thy mercie wrought.

Yet being pregnant still with powrefull grace,   50
And full of fruitfull loue, that loues to get
Things like himselfe, and to enlarge his race,
His second brood though not in powre so great,
Yet full of beautie, next he did beget
An infinite increase of Angels bright,
All glistring glorious in their Makers light.

To them the heauens illimitable hight
(Not this round heauen, which we from hence behold,
Adornd with thousand lamps of burning light,
And with ten thousand gemmes of shyning gold)   60
He gaue as their inheritance to hold,
That they might serue him in eternall blis,
And be partakers of those ioyes of his.

There they in their trinall triplicities
About him wait, and on his will depend,
Either with nimble wings to cut the skies,
When he them on his messages doth send,
Or on his owne dread presence to attend,
Where they behold the glorie of his light,
And caroll Hymnes of loue both day and night.   70

Both day and night is vnto them all one,
For he his beames doth still to them extend,
That darknesse there appeareth neuer none,
Ne hath their day, ne hath their blisse an end,
But there their termelesse time in pleasure spend,
Ne euer should their happinesse decay,
Had not they dar'd their Lord to disobay.

But pride, impatient of long resting peace,
Did puffe them vp with greedy bold ambition,
That they gan cast their state how to increase   80
Aboue the fortune of their first condition,
And sit in Gods owne seat without commission:
The brightest Angell, euen the Child of light,
Drew millions more against their God to fight.

Th'Almighty, seeing their so bold assay,
Kindled the flame of his consuming yre,
And with his onely breath them blew away
From heauens hight, to which they did aspyre,
To deepest hell, and lake of damned fyre;
Where they in darknesse and dread horror dwell,   90
Hating the happie light from which they fell.

So that next off-spring of the Makers loue,
Next to himselfe in glorious degree,
Degendering to hate, fell from aboue
Through pride (for pride and loue may ill agree);

And now of sinne to all ensample bee.
How then can sinfull flesh it selfe assure,
Sith purest Angels fell to be impure?

But that eternall fount of loue and grace,
Still flowing forth his goodnesse vnto all,   100
Now seeing left a waste and emptie place
In his wyde Pallace, through those Angels fall,
Cast to supply the same, and to enstall
A new vnknowen Colony therein,
Whose root from earths base groundworke shold begin.

Therefore of clay, base, vile, and next to nought,
Yet form'd by wondrous skill, and by his might,
According to an heauenly patterne wrought,
Which he had fashiond in his wise foresight,
He man did make, and breathd a liuing spright   110
Into his face most beautifull and fayre,
Endewd with wisedomes riches, heauenly, rare.

Such he him made, that he resemble might
Himselfe, as mortall thing immortall could;
Him to be Lord of euery liuing wight,
He made by loue out of his owne like mould,
In whom he might his mightie selfe behould:
For loue doth loue the thing belou'd to see,
That like it selfe in louely shape may bee.

But man forgetfull of his makers grace,   120
No lesse then Angels, whom he did ensew,
Fell from the hope of promist heauenly place
Into the mouth of death, to sinners dew,
And all his off-spring into thraldome threw:
Where they for euer should in bonds remaine,
Of neuer dead, yet euer dying, paine.

Till that great Lord of Loue, which him at first
Made of meere loue, and after liked well,
Seeing him lie like creature long accurst
In that deepe horror of despeyred hell,   130
Him wretch in doole would let no lenger dwell,
But cast out of that bondage to redeeme,
And pay the price, all were his debt extreeme.

Out of the bosome of eternall blisse,
In which he reigned with his glorious syre,
He downe descended, like a most demisse
And abiect thrall, in fleshes fraile attyre,
That he for him might pay sinnes deadly hyre,
And him restore vnto that happie state
In which he stood before his haplesse fate.   140

In flesh at first the guilt committed was,
Therefore in flesh it must be satisfyde:
Nor spirit, nor Angell, though they man surpas,

Could make amends to God for mans misguyde,
But onely man himselfe, who selfe did slyde.
So, taking flesh of sacred virgins wombe,
For mans deare sake he did a man become.

And that most blessed bodie, which was borne
Without all blemish or reprochfull blame,
He freely gaue to be both rent and torne   150
Of cruell hands, who with despightfull shame
Reuyling him, that them most vile became,
At length him nayled on a gallow tree,
And slew the iust by most vniust decree.

O huge and most vnspeakeable impression
Of loues deepe wound, that pierst the piteous hart
Of that deare Lord with so entyre affection,
And sharply launching euery inner part,
Dolours of death into his soule did dart;
Doing him die, that neuer it deserued,   160
To free his foes, that from his heast had swerued.

What hart can feele least touch of so sore launch,
Or thought can think the depth of so deare wound,
Whose bleeding sourse their streames yet neuer staunch,
But stil do flow, and freshly still redound,
To heale the sores of sinfull soules vnsound,
And clense the guilt of that infected cryme,
Which was enrooted in all fleshly slyme?

O blessed well of loue, O floure of grace,
O glorious Morning starre, O lampe of light,   170
Most liuely image of thy fathers face,
Eternall King of glorie, Lord of might,
Meeke lambe of God before all worlds behight,
How can we thee requite for all this good?
Or what can prize that thy most precious blood?

Yet nought thou ask'st in lieu of all this loue,
But loue of vs for guerdon of thy paine.
Ay me! what can vs lesse then that behoue?
Had he required life of vs againe,
Had it beene wrong to aske his owne with gaine?   180
He gaue vs life, he it restored lost;
Then life were least, that vs so litle cost.

But he our life hath left vnto vs free,
Free that was thrall, and blessed that was band;
Ne ought demaunds, but that we louing bee.
As he himselfe hath lou'd vs afore hand,
And bound therto with an eternall band,
Him first to loue, that vs so dearely bought,
And next, our brethren to his image wrought.

Him first to loue, great right and reason is,   190
Who first to vs our life and being gaue;
And after, when we fared had amisse,

Vs wretches from the second death did saue;
And last the food of life, which now we haue,
Euen himselfe in his deare sacrament,
To feede our hungry soules vnto vs lent.

Then next to loue our brethren, that were made
Of that selfe mould, and that selfe makers hand,
That we, and to the same againe shall fade,
Where they shall haue like heritage of land,   200
How euer here on higher steps we stand;
Which also were with selfe same price redeemed
That we, how euer of vs light esteemed.

And were they not, yet since that louing Lord
Commaunded vs to loue them for his sake,
Euen for his sake, and for his sacred word,
Which in his last bequest he to vs spake,
We should them loue, and with their needs partake;
Knowing that whatsoere to them we giue,
We giue to him, by whom we all doe liue.   210

Such mercy he by his most holy reede
Vnto vs taught, and, to approue it trew,
Ensampled it by his most righteous deede,
Shewing vs mercie, miserable crew,
That we the like should to the wretches shew,
And loue our brethren; thereby to approue
How much himselfe that loued vs, we loue.

Then rouze thy selfe, O earth, out of thy soyle,
In which thou wallowest like to filthy swyne,
And doest thy mynd in durty pleasures moyle,   220
Vnmindfull of that dearest Lord of thyne;
Lift vp to him thy heauie clouded eyne,
That thou his soueraine bountie mayst behold,
And read through loue his mercies manifold.

Beginne from first, where he encradled was
In simple cratch, wrapt in a wad of hay,
Betweene the toylefull Oxe and humble Asse,
And in what rags, and in how base aray,
The glory of our heauenly riches lay,
When him the silly Shepheards came to see,   230
Whom greatest Princes sought on lowest knee.

From thence reade on the storie of his life,
His humble carriage, his vnfaulty wayes,
His cancred foes, his fights, his toyle, his strife,
His paines, his pouertie, his sharpe assayes,
Through which he past his miserable dayes,
Offending none, and doing good to all,
Yet being malist both of great and small.

And looke at last how of most wretched wights
He taken was, betrayd, and false accused,   240
How with most scornefull taunts, and fell despights,

He was reuyld, disgrast, and foule abused,
How scourgd, how crownd, how buffeted, how brused;
And lastly how twixt robbers crucifyde,
With bitter wounds through hands, through feet and syde.

Then let thy flinty hart that feeles no paine,
Empierced be with pittifull remorse,
And let thy bowels bleede in euery vaine,
At sight of his most sacred heauenly corse,
So torne and mangled with malicious forse,   250
And let thy soule, whose sins his sorrows wrought,
Melt into teares, and grone in grieued thought.

With sence whereof whilest so thy softened spirit
Is inly toucht, and humbled with meeke zeale,
Through meditation of his endlesse merit,   *death of*
Lift vp thy mind to th'author of thy weale,   *Christ mor—*
And to his soueraine mercie doe appeale;   *than Resurr*
Learne him to loue, that loued thee so deare,
And in thy brest his blessed image beare.

With all thy hart, with all thy soule and mind,   260
Thou must him loue, and his beheasts embrace;
All other loues, with which the world doth blind
Weake fancies, and stirre vp affections base,
Thou must renounce, and vtterly displace,

And giue thy selfe vnto him full and free,
That full and freely gaue himselfe to thee.

Then shalt thou feele thy spirit so possest,
And rauisht with deuouring great desire
Of his deare selfe, that shall thy feeble brest
Inflame with loue, and set thee all on fire   270
With burning zeale, through euery part entire,
That in no earthly thing thou shalt delight,
But in his sweet and amiable sight.

Thenceforth all worlds desire will in thee dye,   *goes*
And all earthes glorie on which men do gaze   *beyond*
Seeme durt and drosse in thy pure sighted eye,   *Castiglione*
Compar'd to that celestiall beauties blaze,
Whose glorious beames all fleshly sense doth daze
With admiration of their passing light,
Blinding the eyes and lumining the spright.   280

Then shall thy rauisht soule inspired bee
With heauenly thoughts, farre aboue humane skil,
And thy bright radiant eyes shall plainely see
Th'Idee of his pure glorie, present still
Before thy face, that all thy spirits shall fill
With sweete enragement of celestiall loue,
Kindled through sight of those faire things aboue.

Uses the imagery more than dogma

ROBERT GREENE

As we may infer from the popularity of poetical miscellanies, broadside ballads, books of songs and airs, and the hundreds of musical interpolations in Tudor drama, the sixteenth century was preeminently an age of song. It is, then, not surprising that even in prose fiction writers should often inject lyrics which, though scarcely compatible with modern presuppositions about the "realistic" novel were wonderfully suited to the Arcadian and pastoral romances of the Elizabethan age. As an extremely prolific and popular writer of such romances (see pp. 751–62), Robert Greene turned out scores of fragile and melodious songs. Although he published only one volume of non-dramatic poetry (an elegy on Sir Christopher Hatton called *A Maiden's Dream*, 1591), his poetical production scattered through his novels and tales is large, varied, and generally excellent. For thus inter-mingling prose and poetry Greene had no precedents in the Italianate *novelle* of Elizabeth's early reign or in the two novels of Lyly, but the Arcadian romance from Sannazaro on (see p. 737) had made the practice com-mon, and of course Sidney had used his *Arcadia* as a sort

of laboratory of metrical experiments. After Sidney, in fact, it became almost *de rigueur* for Elizabethan novelists—even Deloney in his tales of merchants and apprentices—to string out their plots on beads of inter-polated lyrics. In *Rosalynde* (see pp. 763–88) Thomas Lodge was to reach a lyrical eminence that Greene rarely attained, but no man who could write so lovely a thing as Sephestia's lullaby in *Menaphon* (see p. 754) can be ignored. The following selection from Greene's large production fairly represents his range and his merits. Our texts are based upon *Arbasto, The Anatomie of Fortune*, 1584 (STC 12218); *Morando The Tritameron of Love: The first and second part*, 1587 (STC 12277); *Perimedes The Blacke-Smith, A golden methode, how to use the minde in pleasant and profitable exercise*, 1588 (STC 12295); *Ciceronis Amor. Tullies Love*, 1589 (STC 12224); *Greenes farewell to Folly. Sent to Courtiers and Schollers as a president to warne them from the vaine delights that drawes youth on to repentance*, 1591 (STC 12241); *Philomela. The Lady Fitzwaters Night-ingale*, 1592 (STC 12296).

FROM ARBASTO, THE ANATOMY OF FORTUNE (1584)

[IN TIME WE SEE THAT SILVER DROPS]

In time we see that silver drops
   The craggy stones make soft;
The slowest snail in time, we see,
   Doth creep and climb aloft.

With feeble puffs the tallest pine
   In tract of time doth fall;
The hardest heart in time doth yield
   To Venus' luring call.

Where chilling frost alate did nip,
   There flasheth now a fire;   10
Where deep disdain bred noisome hate,
   There kindleth now desire.

Time causeth hope to have his hap;
   What care in time not eas'd?
In time I loath'd that now I love,
   In both content and pleas'd.

FROM MORANDO, THE TRITAMERON OF LOVE (1587)

[THE FICKLE SEAT WHEREON PROUD FORTUNE SITS]

The fickle seat whereon proud Fortune sits,
   The restless globe whereon the Fury stands,
Bewrays her fond and far inconstant fits;
   The fruitful horn she handleth in her hands
Bids all beware to fear her flattering smiles,
   That giveth most when most she meaneth guiles.
The wheel that turning never taketh rest,
   The top whereof fond worldlings count their bliss,
Within a minute makes a black exchange,
   And then the vild and lowest better is;   10
Which emblem tells us the inconstant state
   Of such as trust to Fortune or to Fate.

FROM PERIMEDES THE BLACKSMITH (1588)

[OBSCURE AND DARK IS ALL THE GLOOMY AIR]

Obscure and dark is all the gloomy air;
   The curtain of the night is overspread;
The silent mistress of the lowest sphere
   Puts on her sable-colored veil and lower.

Nor star nor milk-white circle of the sky
   Appears where Discontent doth hold her lodge;
She sits shrin'd in a cannapy of clouds,
   Whose massy darkness mazeth every sense.

Wan is her looks, her cheeks of azure hue,
   Her hairs as Gorgons' foul retorting snakes,   10
Envy the glass wherein the hag doth gaze,
   Restless the clock that chimes her fast asleep,

Disquiet thoughts the minutes of her watch.
   Forth from her cave the fiend full oft doth fly;
To kings she goes and troubles them with crowns,
   Setting those high-aspiring brands on fire

That flame from earth unto the seat of Jove;
   To such as Midas, men that dote on wealth
And rent the bowels of the middle earth
   For coin; who gape, as did fair Danae,   20

For showers of gold, their discontent in black;
   Throws forth the viols of her restless cares
To such as sit at Paphos for relief
   And offer Venus many solemn vows;

To such as Hymen in his saffron robe
   Hath knit a Gordian knot of passions.
To these, to all, parting the glomy air,
   Black Discontent doth make her bad repair.

[IN CYPRES SAT FAIR VENUS BY A FOUNT]

In Cypres sat fair Venus by a fount,
   Wanton Adonis toying on her knee;
She kiss'd the wag, her darling of accompt;
   The boy gan blush, which, when his lover see,
     She smil'd and told him love might challenge debt,
     And he was young and might be wanton yet.

The boy wax'd bold, fired by fond desire,
   That woo he could and court her with conceit.
Reason spied this and sought to quench the fire
   With cold disdain, but wily Adon straight   10
     Cheer'd up the flame and said, "Good sir, what let?
     I am but young and may be wanton yet."

Reason replied that beauty was a bane
   To such as feed their fancy with fond love,
That when sweet youth with lust is overta'en
   It rues in age. This could not Adon move,
     For Venus taught him still this rest to set:
     That he was young and might be wanton yet.

Where Venus strikes with beauty to the quick
   It little vails sage Reason to reply;   20
Few are the cares for such as are love-sick
   But love. Then though I wanton it awry
     And play the wag, from Adon this I get:
     I am but young and may be wanton yet.

[FAIR IS MY LOVE FOR APRIL IN HER FACE]

Fair is my love for April in her face,
 Her lovely breasts September claims his part,
And lordly July in her eyes takes place,
 But cold December dwelleth in her heart.
  Blest be the months that sets my thoughts on fire,
  Accurst that month that hind'reth my desire.

Like Phoebus' fire so sparkles both her eyes;
 As air perfum'd with amber is her breath;
Like swelling waves her lovely teats do rise;
 As earth her heart, cold, dateth me to death.   10
  Aye me, poor man, that on the earth do live
  When unkind earth death and dispair doth give!

In pomp sits Mercy seated in her face,
 Love twixt her breasts his trophies doth imprint;
Her eyes shines favor, courtesy, and grace,
 But touch her heart, ah, that is fram'd of flint,
  That fore my harvest in the grass bears grain,
  The rocks will wear, wash'd with a winter's rain.

FROM CICERONIS AMOR: TULLY'S LOVE (1589)

[WHEN GODS HAD FRAM'D THE SWEET OF WOMEN'S FACE]

When gods had fram'd the sweet of women's face,
 And lock'd men's looks within their golden hair,
That Phoebus blush'd to see their matchless grace,
 And heavenly gods on earth did make repair,
  To quip fair Venus' overweening pride
  Love's happy thoughts to jealousy were tied;

Then grew a wrinkle on fair Venus' brow,
 The amber sweet of love was turn'd to gall;
Gloomy was heaven; bright Phoebus did avow
 He could be coy and would not love at all,   10
  Swearing no greater mischief could be wrought
  Then love united to a jealous thought.

FROM GREENE'S FAREWELL TO FOLLY (1591)

[SWEET ARE THE THOUGHTS THAT SAVOR OF CONTENT]

Sweet are the thoughts that savor of content;
 the quiet mind is richer then a crown;
Sweet are the nights in careless slumber spent;
 the poor estate scorns Fortune's angry frown.
Such sweet content, such minds, such sleep, such bliss
 beggars injoy when princes oft do miss.

The homely house that harbors quiet rest,
 the cottage that affords no pride nor care,
The mean that grees with country music best,
 the sweet consort of mirth and music's fare,   10
Obscured life sets down a type of bliss.
 A mind content both crown and kingdom is.

FROM PHILOMELA. THE LADY FITZWATER'S NIGHTINGALE (1592)

PHILOMELA'S ODE THAT SHE SUNG IN HER ARBOR

Sitting by a river side
 Where a silent stream did glide,
Muse I did of many things
 That the mind in quiet brings.
I gan think how some men deem
 Gold their god, and some esteem
Honor is the chief content
 That to man in life is lent.
And some others do contend
 Quiet none like to a friend.   10
Others hold there is no wealth
 Compared to a perfit health.
Some man's mind in quiet stands
 When he is lord of many lands.
But I did sigh, and said all this
 Was but a shade of perfit bliss,
And in my thoughts I did approve
 Nought so sweet as is true love.
Love twixt lovers passeth these
 When mouth kisseth and heart grees,   20
With folded arms and lippes meeting,
 Each soul another sweetly greeting.
For by the breath the soul fleeteth,
 And soul with soul in kissing meeteth.
If love be so sweet a thing
 That such happy bliss doth bring,
Happy is love's sug'red thrall,
 But unhappy maidens all
Who esteem your virgin's blisses
 Sweeter than a wive's sweet kisses.   30
No such quiet to the mind
 As true love with kisses kind.
But if a kiss prove unchaste,
 Then is true love quite disgrac'd;
Though love be sweet, learn this of me:
 No love sweet but honesty.

THOMAS LODGE

Following the publication of *An Alarum against Usurers* (1584; see pp. 844–48) Thomas Lodge, presumably disheartened by the hazards of authorship, sought adventure in foreign parts. Like Gascoigne, Rich, Whetstone, and other writers of those lean years, he seems to have tried soldiering for a while, and then, in 1588, he signed on for a voyage to the islands of Terceira and the Canaries with one Captain Clark. But he had not abandoned literature: *Rosalynde,* his greatest success, was "hatched in storms" and "feathered in the surges of many perilous seas," and shortly after his return he published an elaborate volume of poetry. His decision to issue *Scylla's Metamorphosis* was perhaps prompted, as he hints in the dedication, by an unauthorized edition of his "unperfit poems." Although so far as is known he had printed nothing for five years, it is a fair inference that his works were sufficiently popular in manuscript to become the loot of unscrupulous printers. Possibly *Scylla's Metamorphosis* and the irregular "sonnets" accompanying it were products of his college days in the mid-seventies that had been exhumed and revised for publication in the late eighties; at any rate they are a young man's work, full of a lush, bookish Hellenism that reminds one of the early Keats. The first erotic narrative poem of the period, *Scylla's Metamorphosis* is important as a predecessor of (and perhaps an inspiration for) a swarm of quasi-Ovidian imitations in the nineties: Marlowe's *Hero and Leander* (see pp. 388–96), Shakespeare's *Venus and Adonis* (which employs the quatrain-couplet stanza of Lodge's piece), Drayton's *Endymion and Phoebe* (see pp. 428–31), Marston's *Metamorphosis of Pygmalion's Image,* and others. Our text

is based upon *Scillaes Metamorphosis: Enterlaced with the unfortunate love of Glaucus. Whereunto is annexed the delectable discourse of the discontented Satyre: with sundrie other most absolute Poems and Sonnets,* 1589 (STC 16674).

Lodge went to sea again in 1591, by which time his literary work was sufficiently admired to win praise from Spenser in *Colin Clout's Come Home Again* (where Lodge seems to be addressed as Alcon). Two years later, in 1593, Lodge was apparently encouraged to publish *Phyllis,* a volume containing some forty sonnets, assorted lyrics, and a long narrative poem in the tradition of *A Mirror for Magistrates;* in the same year this work was followed by a historical romance, *The Life and Death of William Longbeard.* The fact that Lodge was copiously represented in *The Phoenix Nest* (1593; see p. 231) attests to his rising reputation, and in his next volume of poetry, *A Fig for Momus* (1595), he seems to be writing with the ease of an established man of letters. It is a varied work, containing not only some interesting imitations of Roman satire which anticipate the later work of Hall and Marston (see pp. 455–63) but also a pastoral dialogue "To Rowland" and verse epistles to Daniel and Drayton. These epistles, as Lodge comments, "are in that kind wherein no Englishman of our time hath publiquely written." Epistle 5, revealing a warm friendship between Drayton and Lodge, closes with a sympathetic account of the curious mathematical digression on the "learned nines and threes" in *Endymion and Phoebe* (see p. 431). Our text is based upon *A fig for Momus: Containing Pleasant varietie, included in Satyres, Eclogues, and Epistles, by T. L. of Lincolnes Inne Gent,* 1595 (STC 16658).

FROM SCYLLA'S METAMORPHOSIS (1589)

THE MOST PITHY AND PLEASANT HISTORY OF GLAUCUS AND SCYLLA

Walking alone, all only full of grief,
Within a thicket near to Isis' flood,
Weeping my wants and wailing scant relief,
Wringing mine arms as one with sorrow wood,
  The piteous streams, relenting at my moan,
  Withdrew their tides and stay'd to hear me groan.

From forth the channel, with a sorrowing cry,
The sea-god Glaucus, with his hallowed hears

Wet in the tears of his sad mother's dye,
With piteous looks, before my face appears;   10
  For whom the nymphs a mossy coat did frame
  Embroadered with his Scylla's heavenly name;

And, as I sat under a willow tree,
The lovely honor of fair Thetis' bower,
Repos'd his head upon my faintful knee;
And when my tears had ceas'd their stormy shower
  He dried my cheeks and then bespake him so
  As when he wail'd I straight forgot my wo.

"Infortunate, why wand'reth thy content
From forth his scope as wearied of itself?   20
Thy books have school'd thee from this fond repent,
And thou canst talk by proof of wavering pelf:
    Unto the world such is inconstancy
    As sap to tree, as apple to the eye.

"Mark how the morn in roseate color shines
And straight with clouds the sunny tract is clad;
Then see how pomp through wax and wane declines
From high to low, from better to the bad.
    Take moist from sea, take color from his kind,
    Before the world devoid of change thou find. . . ."   30

Here gan he pause and shake his heavy head,
And fold his arms and then unfold them straight;
Fain would he speak, but tongue was charm'd by dread,
Whilst I, that saw what woes did him aweight,
    Comparing his mishaps and moan with mine,
    Gan smile for joy and dry his drooping ey'n.

But lo, a wonder! From the channel's glide
A sweet, melodious noise of music rose
That made the stream to dance a pleasant tide;
The weeds and sallows near the bank that grows   40
    Gan sing as when the calmest winds accord
    To greet with balmy breath the fleeting ford.

Upon the silver bosom of the stream
First gan fair Themis shake her amber locks,
Whom all the nymphs that wait on Neptune's realm
Attended from the hollow of the rocks.
    In brief, while these rare paragons assemble,
    The wat'ry world to touch their teats do tremble.

Footing it featly on the grassy ground
These damsels, circling with their brightsome fairs   50
The love-sick god and I, about us wound
Like stars that Ariadne's crown repairs.
    Who once hath seen or pride of morn or day
    Would deem all pomp within their cheeks did play. . . .

But pensive Glaucus, passionate with painings,
Amidst their revel thus began his ruth:
"Nymphs, fly these groves, late-blasted with my
        plainings,
For cruel Scylla nill regard my truth.
    And leave us two, consorted in our groanings,
    To register with tears our bitter moanings. . . .   60

"But, tender nymphs, to you belongs no teen;
Then favor me in flying from this bower
Whereas but care and thought of crosses been;
Leave me that loose myself through fancy's power,
    Through fancy's power which, had I leave to loose it,
    No fancy then should see me for to choose it. . . .

"Go you in peace to Neptune's wat'ry sound;
No more may Glaucus play him with so pretty.
But shun resort where solace nill be found
And plain my Scylla's pride and want of pity.   70
    Alas, sweet nymphs, my godhead's all in vain,
    For why this breast includes immortal pain.

"Scylla hath eyes, but too sweet eyes hath Scylla;
Scylla hath hands, fair hands but coy in touching;
Scylla in wit surpasseth grave Sibylla;
Scylla hath words, but words well-stor'd with grutching;
    Scylla a saint in look, no saint in scorning.
    Look, saint-like Scylla, lest I die with mourning! . . ."

[Swooning away with unrequited love, Glaucus is
tenderly revived by the solicitous nymphs, and at their
request he finally consents to tell his mournful story. In
his youthful folly Glaucus was both irresistible and indifferent to the nymphs who flocked about him—indifferent,
that is, until he happened to see Scylla.]

"Her hair not truss'd, but scatter'd on her brow,
Surpassing Hybla's honey for the view   80
Or soft'ned golden wires. I know not how
Love, with a radiant beauty, did pursue
    My too judicial eyes in darting fire
    That kindled straight in me my fond desire.

"Within these snares first was my heart intrapped,
Till through those golden shrouds mine eyes did see
An ivory-shadowed front wherein was wrapped
Those pretty bow'rs where graces couched be,
    Next which her cheeks appear'd like crimson silk,
    Or ruddy rose bespread on whitest milk.   90

"Twixt which the nose in lovely tenor bends
(Too trait'rous pretty for a lover's view),
Next which her lips like violets commends
By true proportion that which doth insue;
    Which, when they smile, present unto the eyes
    The ocean's pride and ivory paradise. . . .

"The lovely breast where all this beauty rested
Shrouded within a world of deep disdain,
For where I thought my fancy should be feasted
With kind affect, alas, unto my pain,   100
    When first I woo'd, the wanton straight was flying,
    And gave repulse before we talk'd of trying.

"How oft have I (too often have I done so)
In silent night, when every eye was sleeping,
Drawn near her cave in hope her love were won so,
Forcing the neighboring waters through my weeping
    To wake the winds, who did afflict her dwelling
    Whilst I with tears my passion was a-telling.

"When midst the Caspian Seas the wanton play'd,
I drew whole wreaths of coral from the rocks   110
And in her lap my heavenly presents laid;
But she, unkind, rewarded me with mocks.
   Such are the fruits that spring from ladies' coying,
   Who smile at tears and are intrapp'd with toying. . . .

"Wretched Love, let me die! End my love by my death.
Dead, alas, still I live, fly my life, fade my love.
Out alas, Love abides, still I joy vital breath.
Death is love, love is death, wo is me that do prove.
   Pain and wo, care and grief, every day about me hovers.
   Then, but death, what can quell all the plages of
      hapless lovers? . . ."   120

[Scorned by Scylla, Glaucus wandered forlorn until he came, far in the west, to a "sweet and fruitful field" where Isis, "the lady of that lovely stream," and her attendant nymphs made him welcome. Here he stayed, giving such comfort as he could to hapless mortals who, like himself, were victims of love.]

The woful Glaucus thus with woes attainted,
The pensive nymphs agriev'd to see his plight,
The floods and fields with his laments acquainted,
Myself amaz'd to see this heavy sight,
   On sodain Thetis with her train approached
   And gravely thus her amorous son reproached:

"My son," said she, "immortal have I made thee.
Amidst my wat'ry realms who may compare
Or match thy might? Why, then, should care invade thee
That art so young, so lovely, fresh, and fair?   130
   Alas, fond god, it merits great reproving
   In states of worth to dote on foolish loving.

"Come, wend with me, and midst thy father's bow'r
Let us disport and frolic for a while
In spite of Love, although he pout and low'r.
Good exercise will idle lusts beguile;
   Let wanton Scylla coy her where she will,
   Live thou, my son, by reason's level still."

Thus said the goddess, and although her words
Gave signs of counsail, pomp, and majesty.   140
Yet natheless her piteous eye affords
Some pretty witness to the standers-by
   That in her thoughts, for all her outward show,
   She mourn'd to see her son amated so. . . .

[Seeing that nothing will revive him but Scylla's love, Thetis prays to Venus to be of aid to Glaucus. The obliging goddess at once appears, in great splendor, and commands her son Cupid to set matters straight. He does so by shooting another arrow into the very wound that he had made before, and Glaucus immediately arose, "reviv'd, reliev'd, and free from fancy's cup."]

No more of love, no more of hate he spoke;
No more he forc'd the sighs from out his breast;
His sodain joy his pleasing smiles provoke,
And all aloft he shakes his bushy crest,
   Greeting the gods and goddesses beside,
   And every nymph upon that happy tide.   150

Cupid and he together, hand in hand,
Approach the place of this renowned train.
"Ladies," said he, "releas'd from amorous band,
Receive my prisoner to your grace again."
   Glaucus gave thanks when Thetis, glad with bliss,
   Embrac'd his neck and his kind cheeks did kiss. . . .

[Just at this moment of general rejoicing Scylla happens to come floating by and meets with a very mixed reception: Venus admires her beauty, Glaucus smiles to see his "lovely foe," Thetis almost tears her heart asunder with rage, and the nymphs cast envious looks upon her obvious charms. Approaching Cupid, Thetis makes a startling request:]

"O, if there dwell within thy breast, my boy,
Or grace or pity or remorse," said she,
"Now bend thy bow, abate yon wanton's joy,
And let these nymphs thy rightful justice see."   160
   The god, soon won, gan shoot and cleft her heart
   With such a shaft as caus'd her endless smart.

The tender nymph, attainted unawares,
Fares like the Lybian lioness that flies
The hunter's lance that wounds her in his snares;
Now gins she love, and straight on Glaucus cries,
   Whilst on the shore the goddesses rejoice
   And all the nymphs afflict the air with noise.

To shore she flits, and swift as Afric wind
Her footing glides upon the yielding grass,   170
And, wounded by affect, recure to find
She sodainly with sighs approach'd the place
   Where Glaucus sat, and, weary with her harms,
   Gan clasp the sea-god in her amorous arms.

"Glaucus, my love," quoth she, "look on thy lover.
Smile, gentle Glaucus, on the nymph that likes thee."
But stark as stone sat he and list not prove her.
(Ah, silly nymph, the selfsame god that strikes thee
   With fancy's dart, and hath thy freedom slain,
   Wounds Glaucus with the arrow of disdain.)   180

O kiss no more, kind nymph. He likes no kindness;
Love sleeps in him to flame within thy breast;
Clear'd are his eyes where thine are clad with blindness;
Freed be his thoughts where thine must taste unrest.
   Yet nill she leave, for never love will leave her,
   But fruitless hopes and fatal haps deceive her.

Lord, how her lips do dwell upon his cheeks,
And how she looks for babies in his eyes,
And how she sighs and swears she loves and leeks,
And how she vows, and he her vows envies.   190
 Trust me, the envious nymphs, in looking on,
 Were forc'd with tears for to assist her moan. . . .

To make long tale were tedious to the woful,
Woful that read what woful she approved;
In brief, her heart with deep dispair was so full
As, since she might not win her sweet beloved,
 With hideous cries like wind borne back she fled
 Unto the sea and toward Sicillia sped. . . .

[Eager to learn what she will do in her desperation, all
the others—the nymphs, Venus, Thetis "in pomp upon a
'Triton's back," and Glaucus and the poet riding together
on a dolphin—set out in hot pursuit. When they find her,
returned to her native Sicily, her sorrow is wonderful to
behold. Fury, Rage, Dispair, Wanhope, and Wo—a
grisly crew dispatched by Ate—lay violent hands on the
bereft Scylla.]

These five at once the sorrowing nymph assail,
And captive lead her bound into the rocks   200
Where, howling still, she strives for to prevail.
With no avail yet strives she, for her locks
 Are chang'd with wonder into hideous sands,
 And hard as flint become her snow-white hands.

The waters howl with fatal tunes about her,
The air doth scowl whenas she turns within them,
The winds and waves with puffs and billows scout her;
Waves storm, air scowls, both wind and waves begin them
 To make the place this mournful nymph doth weep in
 A hapless haunt whereas no nymph may keep in.   210

The seaman, wand'ring by that famous isle,
Shuns all with fear dispairing Scylla's bow'r;
Nymphs, sea-gods, sirens, when they list to smile,
Forsake the haunt of Scylla in that stour.
 "Ah, nymphs," thought I, "if every coy one felt
 The like mishaps their flinty hearts would melt."

Thetis rejoic'd to see her foe depress'd;
Glaucus was glad since Scylla was enthrall'd;
The nymphs gan smile to boast their Glaucus' rest;
Venus and Cupid, in their thrones enstall'd,   220
 At Thetis' beck to Neptune's bow'r repair,
 Whereas they feast amidst his palace fair.

Of pure, immortal nectar is their drink,
And sweet ambrosia dainties do repast them;
The Tritons sing, Palemon smiles to think
Upon the chance, and all the nymphs do haste them
 To trick up mossy garlands where they won
 For lovely Venus and her conquering son.

From forth the fountains of his mother's store
Glaucus let fly a dainty crystal bain   230
That wash'd the nymphs with labor tir'd before;
Cupid he trips among this lovely train.
 Alonely I apart did write this story
 With many a sigh and heart full sad and sorry.

Glaucus, when all the goddesses took rest,
Mounted upon a dolphin full of glee,
Convey'd me friendly from this honored feast
And, by the way, such sonnets sung to me
 That all the dolphins neighboring of his glide
 Danc'd with delight his reverend course beside.   240

At last he left me where at first he found me,
Willing me let the world and ladies know
Of Scylla's pride; and then by oath he bound me
To write no more of that whence shame doth grow,
 Or tie my pen to penny-knaves' delight,
 But live with fame and so for fame to write.

L'Envoy

Ladies, he left me, trust me I missay not;
But so he left me as he will'd me tell you
That nymphs must yield when faithful lovers stray not,
Lest through contempt, almighty Love compel you   250
 With Scylla in the rocks to make your biding—
 A cursed plague for women's proud backsliding.

FROM A FIG FOR MOMUS (1595)

To the Gentlemen Readers Whatsoever

Gentlemen, I know you wonder that, having so long time kept silence, I salute the world with so peremptory a title; but, if thou consider the reasons before you enter into mislike, you shall be satisfied and I excused.

I entitle my book *A Fig for Momus* not in contempt of the learned, for I honor them; not in disdain of the well-minded, because they cherish science; but in despight of the detractor who, having no learning to judge, wanteth no liberty to reprove.

Who worthily deserving the name of Momus shall rather at my hands have a fig to choke him then he and his lewd tongue shall have a frump to check me. Sheep are soonest worried by cur dogs because they are mild, but he that nips him soundly, that bites him cowardly, purchaseth his own peace and escapes much peril. . . . Where detraction is given to challenge, it is good striking first, for whelps that are whipp'd for brawling are quickly quiet.

This cause, gentlemen, hath drawn me to use this title, and under this title I have thought good to include satires, eclogues, and epistles; first, by reason that I study to delight with variety; next, because I would write in that form wherein no man might challenge me with servile imitation (wherewith heretofore I have been unjustly taxed). My satires, to speak truth, are by-pleasures, rather placed here to prepare and try the ear then to feed it, because if they pass well the whole centon of them, already in my hands, shall sodainly be published.

In them, under the names of certain Romains, where I reprehend vice I purposely wrong no man, but observe the laws of that kind of poem. If any repine thereat, I am sure he is guilty, because he bewrayeth himself. For my eclogues, I commend them to men of approved judgment; whose margents though I fill not with quotations, yet their matter and handling will show my diligence. For my epistles, they are in that kind wherein no Englishman of our time hath publiquely written, which, if they please, may draw on more; if displease, have their priviledge by authority. Briefly, I have so written as I have read, so read as I can judge. In which respect, if any man doubt, let him ask and I will resolve him; if any man reprove, let him look to it, I will nip him. For as I am ready to satisfy the reasonable, so I have a gird in store for a railer. Finally, gentlemen, as Prometheus, after he had formed his image of earth, presented it to the sun, and Ops, when she had brought forth Jupiter (for fear lest he should be devoured by Time, figured in Saturn), gave him in keeping to the Cureti, so I present this frail image of my wit to take life and light from the sun of your approved judgments; and desirous to commend this infant of my wit to immortality and defend it from the assaults of time and envy, commit and submit it to your protection, the true Cureti of all cunning; who, accepting these fragments in good worth, shall shortly receive from me matters both worthy regard and reading. *Vale*, 6 Maii 1595.

Yours as you use him,

T[homas] L[odge]

TO MASTER E[VERARD] DIG[BY]

SATIRE 1

Digby, whence comes it that the world begins
To wink at follies and to soothe up sins?
Can other reason be alledg'd then this:
The world soothes sin because it sinful is?
The man that lives by bribes and usury
Winks, like a fox, at lothsome lechery;

Craft gives Ambition leave to lay his plot
And cross his friend because he sounds him not.
All men are willing with the world to halt,
But no man takes delight to know his fault.   10
He is a gallant fit to serve my lord,
Which claws and soothes him up at every word,
That cries, when his lame poesy he hears,
"'Tis rare, my lord! 'Twill pass the nicest ears."
This makes Anphidius welcome to good cheer
And spend his master forty pounds a year
And keep his plaice-mouth'd wife in welts and guards;
For flattery can never want rewards.
And therefore Humphrey holds this paradox:
'Tis better be a fool then be a fox,   20
For folly is rewarded and respected
Where subtility is hated and rejected.
Self-will doth frown when honest Zeal reproves;
To hear good counsel Error never loves.
Tell pursy Rollus, lusking in his bed,
That humors by excessive ease are bred,
That sloth corrupts and chokes the vital sprights,
And kills the memory and hurts the lights.
He will not stick, after a cup of sack,
To flout his counselor behind his back.   30
For with a world of mischiefs and offense
Unbridled Will rebels against the sense,
And thinketh it no little prejudice
To be reproved, though by good advice.
For wicked men repine their sins to hear,
And Folly flings if Counsail touch him near.
Tell Sextus' wife (whose shoes are underlaid)
Her gait is girlish and her foot is splay'd;
She'll rail with open mouth, as Martial doth;
But if you praise her, though you speak not sooth,   40
You shall be welcome both to bed and board,
And use herself, her husband, and his sword.
Tell blear-ey'd Linus that his sight is clear,
He'll pawn himself to buy thee bread and beer;
But touch me Quintus with his stinking breath,
The dastard will defy thee to the death.
Thus, though men's great deformities be known,
They grieve to hear and take them for their own.
Find me a niggard that doth want the shift
To call his cursed avarice good thrift;   50
A rakehell, sworn to prodigality,
That dares not term it liberality;
A letcher, that hath lost both flesh and fame,
That holds not letchery a pleasant game.
And why? Because they cloak their shame by this
And will not see the horror what it is.
And cunning Sin, being clad in Virtue's shape,
Flies much reproof and many scorns doth scape.
Last day I chanc'd, in crossing of the street,
With Diffilus the innkeeper to meet.   60
He wore a silken nightcap on his head

And look'd as if he had been lately dead.
I ask'd him how he far'd. "Not well," quoth he,
"An ague this two months hath troubled me."
I let him pass and laugh'd to hear his scuse,
For I knew well he had the pox by Luce,
And wore his nightcap-ribbind at the ears
Because of late he sweat away his hears.
But had a stranger chanc'd to spy him than,
He might have deem'd him for a civil man.   70
Thus with the world the world dissembles still,
And to their own confusions follow will,
Holding it true felicity to fly
Not from the sin but from the seeing eye.
Then in this world who winks at each estate
Hath found the means to make him fortunate:
To color hate with kindness, to defraud
In private those in publique we applaud,
To keep this rule, "Kaw me and I kaw thee,"
To play the saints whereas we divels be,   80
Whate'er men do let them not reprehend,
For cunning knaves will cunning knaves defend.
Truth is pursu'd by hate; then is he wise
That to the world his worldly wit applies.
What, is he wise? I, as Amphestus strong,
That burnt his face because his beard was long.

TO MASTER MICHAEL DRAYTON

EPISTLE 5

Michael, as much good hap unto thy state
As orators have figures to dilate!
As many crowns as alchemists have shifts!
Briefly, so many goods as thou hast gifts!
I hear some upstart rimer set agog
By writing poems on the Lician frog,
Or Tithon's grasshopper grows envious
And will be famous with Archilochus.
Alas for them that by scurrility
Would purchase fame and immortality.   10
But know this, friend, true excellence depends
On numbers aim'd to good and happy ends.
What else hath wanton poetry enjoy'd
But this: "Alas, thy wit was ill imploy'd"?
What reason mov'd the golden Augustine
To name our poetry vain error's wine?
Or Hierome, deeply sighted in these evils,
To term it nothing but the food of devils?
Nought but the misimployment of our gifts,
Ordain'd for arts but spent in shameless shifts.   20
Look as the sunbeam in a burning glass
Doth kindle fire wherever it doth pass,
But, freely spread upon th' ingend'ring earth,
Eggs on the spring and kills the cause of dearth;
So poetry, restrain'd in error's bounds,
With poisoned words and sinful sweetness wounds;

But clothing virtue and adorning it,
Wit shines in virtue, virtue shines in wit.
True science, suited in well-couched rimes,
Is nourished for fame in after-times.   30
Thou, then, sweet friend, grieve not though Folly thrive;
Fame got by it dies ere it is alive.
Be thou a prentice to a blessed muse,
Which grace with thy good words will still infuse.
O let that holy flame, that heavenly light,
That led old Abraham's race in darksome night,
O let that star which, shining, never ceas'd
To guide the sages of balm-breathing east
Conduct thy muse unto that lofty pitch
Which may thy style with praises more enritch.   40
They wash a Moor, they strive to dry the seas
And plane proud Atlas, that intend to please
By filthy words, by railing and detraction
Proper to Momus and his hateful faction.
For when they think they have deserved most,
Alas, faith, wisdom, all this toil is lost.
But all this while I have forgot my text;
I must remember now what follows next.
I have perus'd thy learned nines and threes
And scann'd them in their natures and degrees,   50
And to thy choice apology apply
This sodain tribute of my memory.
And first for three, which Bartas wisely names
The first of odds, which, multiplied, frames
The sacred number nine. Three doth include
The name beloved by Beatitude;
Three doth express the link and union
That knitteth one to two and two in one;
Three doth include his infinite in three
And is the step to immortality;   60
Three hath his center of the second one,
His true beginning and his end alone.
The true Pythagorists, as I have read,
Do term the triangle Minerva's head,
And in their purifying bathing us'd,
By threes, to sprinkle water once infus'd.
These threes so famous are the steps to nine,
Sacred unto the muses most divine;
This number in proportions musical
Is dissonant, and astrologians call   70
The same *sinister* for some secret work
Or hidden fate that in the same doth lurk.
Hesiodus in his *Theogony*
Under Styx' nine-fold stream doth signify
The discords and complexions of man's body.
Pierias, Michael, if thou list to see,
Will tell thee more; this shall suffice for me.
Here must I needs abruptly make an end,
Call'd to discourse with old Aminta's friend.
When he is gone and I get time to write,   80
Thou shalt have more. Till then, sweet friend, goodnight.

CHRISTOPHER MARLOWE

HERO AND LEANDER

Although John Wolf had licensed *Hero and Leander* (with Marlowe's translation of Lucan; see p. 558) on September 28, 1593, a few months after the author's violent death, he apparently made no effort to publish it, and consequently Edward Blount's edition of 1598 is the first we have. But the copyright for *Hero and Leander* that Blount had secured from Wolf he in turn transferred, on March 2, 1598, to Paul Linley, who shortly thereafter published at least one complete version of the work, including Chapman's continuation. Linley himself died in 1600, and on June 26 of that year the Stationers' Register recorded the transfer of copyright of twenty-four titles from his estate to the printer John Flasket, among them "Hero and Leander with the 1 booke of Lucan by Marlowe." Flasket duly published the poem later in the same year (and again in 1606), but his titlepage makes no mention of Chapman's continuation (which he included in his edition) and does advertise the partial translation of Lucan (which he omitted). Although we shall probably never learn all the details of these puzzling transactions, it is safe to assume that Blount's edition of 1598 (containing only Marlowe's fragment of some 800 lines) is the *editio princeps*. The immense popularity of the poem is attested not only by the many subsequent editions—as Tucker Brooke computes them, three in 1598 and others in 1600, 1606, 1609, 1613, 1616, 1617, 1622, 1629, and 1637—but also by a great many references to it in the literature of the period. Apparently about the time of Blount's edition, Chapman had busied himself (possibly at Marlowe's own wish, as lines 183–198 of the third sestiad seem to suggest) with a characteristically opaque continuation of four sestiads (as he called them); and on April 14, 1598, a poetaster named Henry Petowe secured a license for his own feeble continuation of Marlowe's poem.

Commonly assumed to be one of its author's last works, *Hero and Leander* is a dazzling witness to the vogue of Ovidian and erotic narrative that also produced such works as Lodge's *Scylla's Metamorphosis* (1589), Shakespeare's *Venus and Adonis* (1593), Drayton's *Endymion and Phoebe* (1595), and Marston's *Metamorphosis of Pygmalion's Image* (1598). Although Marlowe could have read the story of Hero and Leander in Ovid's *Heroides* (which Turbervile had translated in 1567), he must have been acquainted with the widely popular Greek version of Musaeus, an Alexandrian who lived at the beginning of the sixth century after Christ. Musaeus' poem had been published about 1484, and subsequently was translated into Latin, Italian (by Tasso), and French (by Marot). Whether Marlowe was familiar with these versions is not known, but at any rate his poem is *sui generis,* a product of his own boundless imagination and of his own mastery of the heroic couplet. Our text is based upon *Hero and Leander,* 1598 (STC 17413), but we follow all modern editions in transposing lines 279–90, 291–300 of the Second Sestiad.

HERO AND LEANDER (1598)

To the Right Worshipful Sir Thomas Walsingham, Knight

Sir, we think not ourselves discharged of the duty we owe to our friend when we have brought the breathless body to the earth, for albeit the eye there taketh his ever farewell of that beloved object, yet the impression of the man that hath been dear unto us, living an after life in our memory, there putteth us in mind of farther obsequies due unto the deceased. And namely of the performance of whatsoever we 10 may judge shall make to his living credit and to the effecting of his determinations prevented by the stroke of death. By these meditations (as by an intellectual will) I suppose myself executor to the unhappily deceased author of this poem, upon whom, knowing that in his lifetime you bestowed many kind favors, entertaining the parts of reckoning and worth which you found in him with good countenance and liberal affection, I cannot but see so far into the will of him dead that whatsoever issue of his brain should chance to come abroad that the first breath it should take might be the gentle air of your liking; for since his self had been accustomed thereunto, it would prove more agreeable and thriving to his right children than any other foster countenance whatsoever. At this time, seeing that this unfinished tragedy happens under my hands to be imprinted, of a double duty, the one to yourself, the other to the deceased, I present the same to your most favorable allowance, off'ring my utmost self now and ever to be ready. At your Worship's disposing,

Edward Blunt

[First Sestiad]

On Hellespont, guilty of true love's blood,
In view and opposite two cities stood,
Sea-borderers, disjoin'd by Neptune's might;
The one Abydos, the other Sestos hight.
At Sestos Hero dwelt; Hero the fair,
Whom young Apollo courted for her hair,
And off'red as a dower his burning throne,
Where she should sit for men to gaze upon.
The outside of her garments were of lawn,
The lining purple silk, with gilt stars drawn;   10
Her wide sleeves green, and bordered with a grove
Where Venus in her naked glory strove
To please the careless and disdainful eyes
Of proud Adonis that before her lies.
Her kirtle blue, whereon was many a stain,
Made with the blood of wretched lovers slain.
Upon her head she ware a myrtle wreath,
From whence her veil reach'd to the ground beneath.
Her veil was artificial flowers and leaves,
Whose workmanship both man and beast deceives;   20
Many would praise the sweet smell as she pass'd,
When 'twas the odor which her breath forth cast;
And there for honey bees have sought in vain,
And, beat from thence, have lighted there again.
About her neck hung chains of pebble-stone,
Which, light'ned by her neck, like diamonds shone.
She ware no gloves, for neither sun nor wind
Would burn or parch her hands, but to her mind
Or warm or cool them, for they took delight
To play upon those hands, they were so white.   30
Buskins of shells all silvered used she,
And branch'd with blushing coral to the knee,
Where sparrows perch'd, of hollow pearl and gold,
Such as the world would wonder to behold;
Those with sweet water oft her handmaid fills,
Which, as she went, would cherup through the bills.
Some say, for her the fairest Cupid pin'd,
And, looking in her face, was strooken blind.
But this is true: so like was one the other,
As he imagin'd Hero was his mother;   40
And oftentimes into her bosom flew,
About her naked neck his bare arms threw,
And laid his childish head upon her breast,
And, with still panting rock'd, there took his rest.
So lovely fair was Hero, Venus' nun,
As Nature wept, thinking she was undone,
Because she took more from her than she left
And of such wondrous beauty her bereft;
Therefore, in sign her treasure suff'red wrack,
Since Hero's time hath half the world been black.   50
Amorous Leander, beautiful and young
(Whose tragedy divine Musaeus sung),
Dwelt at Abydos; since him dwelt there none
For whom succeeding times make greater moan.

His dangling tresses that were never shorn,
Had they been cut and unto Colchos borne,
Would have allur'd the vent'rous youth of Greece
To hazard more than for the Golden Fleece.
Fair Cynthia wish'd his arms might be her sphere;
Grief makes her pale, because she moves not there.   60
His body was as straight as Circe's wand;
Jove might have sipp'd out nectar from his hand.
Even as delicious meat is to the taste,
So was his neck in touching, and surpass'd
The white of Pelops' shoulder. I could tell ye
How smooth his breast was, and how white his belly,
And whose immortal fingars did imprint
That heavenly path, with many a curious dint,
That runs along his back; but my rude pen
Can hardly blazon forth the loves of men,   70
Much less of powerful gods; let it suffice
That my slack muse sings of Leander's eyes,
Those orient cheeks and lips, exceeding his
That leapt into the water for a kiss
Of his own shadow, and, despising many,
Died ere he could enjoy the love of any.
Had wild Hippolytus Leander seen,
Enamored of his beauty had he been;
His presence made the rudest paisant melt
That in the vast uplandish country dwelt;   80
The barbarous Thracian soldier, mov'd with nought,
Was mov'd with him, and for his favor sought.
Some swore he was a maid in man's attire,
For in his looks were all that men desire:
A pleasant smiling cheek, a speaking eye,
A brow for love to banquet royally;
And such as knew he was a man, would say,
"Leander, thou art made for amorous play;
Why art thou not in love, and lov'd of all?
Though thou be fair, yet be not thine own thrall."   90
    The men of wealthy Sestos every year,
For his sake whom their goddess held so dear,
Rose-cheek'd Adonis, kept a solemn feast.
Thither resorted many a wand'ring guest
To meet their loves; such as had none at all
Came lovers home from this great festival;
For every street, like to a firmament,
Glistered with breathing stars, who, where they went,
Frighted the melancholy earth, which deem'd
Eternal heaven to burn, for so it seem'd   100
As if another Phaeton had got
The guidance of the sun's rich chariot.
But, far above the loveliest, Hero shin'd,
And stole away th' inchanted gazer's mind;
For like sea nymphs' inveigling harmony,
So was her beauty to the standers-by.
Nor that night-wand'ring pale and wat'ry star
(When yawning dragons draw her thirling car
From Latmus Mount up to the glomy sky,

Where, crown'd with blazing light and majesty,   110
She proudly sits) more overrules the flood
Than she the hearts of those that near her stood.
Even as when gawdy nymphs pursue the chase,
Wretched Ixion's shaggy-footed race,
Incens'd with savage heat, gallop amain
From steep pine-bearing mountains to the plain,
So ran the people forth to gaze upon her,
And all that view'd her were enamor'd on her.
And as in fury of a dreadful fight,
Their fellows being slain or put to flight,   120
Poor soldiers stand with fear of death dead-strooken,
So at her presence all, surpris'd and tooken,
Await the sentence of her scornful eyes;
He whom she favors lives, the other dies.
There might you see one sigh, another rage,
And some, their violent passions to asswage,
Compile sharp satires; but alas, too late,
For faithful love will never turn to hate.
And many, seeing great princes were denied,
Pin'd as they went, and, thinking on her, died.   130
On this feast day, O cursed day and hour!
Went Hero thorow Sestos, from her tower
To Venus' temple, where unhappily,
As after chanc'd, they did each other spy.
So fair a church as this had Venus none;
The walls were of discolored jasper stone,
Wherein was Proteus carved, and o'erhead
A lively vine of green sea-agget spread,
Where, by one hand, light-headed Bacchus hoong,
And, with the other, wine from grapes outwroong.   140
Of crystal shining fair the pavement was;
The town of Sestos call'd it Venus' glass;
There might you see the gods in sundry shapes,
Committing heady riots, incest, rapes;
For know that underneath this radiant floor
Was Danae's statue in a brazen tower;
Jove slyly stealing from his sister's bed
To dally with Idalian Ganymed,
And for his love Europa bellowing loud,
And tumbling with the rainbow in a cloud;   150
Blood-quaffing Mars heaving the iron net
Which limping Vulcan and his Cyclops set;
Love kindling fire to burn such towns as Troy;
Silvanus weeping for the lovely boy
That now is turn'd into a cypress tree,
Under whose shade the wood-gods love to be.
And in the midst a silver altar stood;
There Hero sacrificing turtles' blood,
Veil'd to the ground, veiling her eyelids close,
And modestly they opened as she rose;   160
Thence flew Love's arrow with the golden head,
And thus Leander was enamored.
Stone still he stood, and evermore he gazed,
Till with the fire that from his count'nance blazed,

Relenting Hero's gentle heart was strook;
Such force and virtue hath an amorous look.
     It lies not in our power to love or hate,
For will in us is overrul'd by fate.
When two are stripp'd, long ere the course begin,
We wish that one should lose, the other win;   170
And one especially do we affect
Of two gold ingots, like in each respect.
The reason no man knows, let it suffice,
What we behold is censur'd by our eyes.
Where both deliberate, the love is slight;
Who ever lov'd, that lov'd not at first sight?
     He kneel'd, but unto her devoutly pray'd;
Chaste Hero to herself thus softly said:
"Were I the saint he worships, I would hear him";
And as she spake those words, came somewhat near him.
He started up; she blush'd as one asham'd;   181
Wherewith Leander much more was inflam'd.
He touch'd her hand; in touching it she trembled;
Love deeply grounded hardly is dissembled.
These lovers parled by the touch of hands;
True love is mute, and oft amazed stands.
Thus while dumb signs their yielding hearts entangled,
The air with sparks of living fire was spangled,
And night, deep drench'd in misty Acheron,
Heav'd up her head, and half the world upon   190
Breath'd darkness forth (dark night is Cupid's day).
And now begins Leander to display
Love's holy fire with words, with sighs, and tears,
Which like sweet music ent'red Hero's ears;
And yet at every word she turn'd aside,
And always cut him off as he repli'd.
At last, like to a bold sharp sophister,
With cheerful hope thus he accosted her:
     "Fair creature, let me speak without offense;
I would my rude words had the influence   200
To lead thy thoughts as thy fair looks do mine!
Then shouldst thou be his prisoner who is thine.
Be not unkind and fair; misshapen stuff
Are of behavior boisterous and ruff.
O shun me not, but hear me ere you go,
God knows I cannot force love, as you do.
My words shall be as spotless as my youth,
Full of simplicity and naked truth.
This sacrifice, whose sweet perfume descending
From Venus' altar to your footsteps bending,   210
Doth testify that you exceed her far,
To whom you offer, and whose nun you are.
Why should you worship her? her you surpass
As much as sparkling diamonds flaring glass.
A diamond set in lead his worth retains;
A heavenly nymph, belov'd of human swains,
Receives no blemish, but ofttimes more grace;
Which makes me hope, although I am but base,
Base in respect of thee, divine and pure,

Dutiful service may thy love procure,   220
And I in duty will excel all other,
As thou in beauty dost exceed Love's mother.
Nor heaven, nor thou, were made to gaze upon;
As heaven preserves all things, so save thou one.
A stately builded ship, well rigg'd and tall,
The ocean maketh more majestical;
Why vowest thou then to live in Sestos here,
Who on Love's seas more glorious wouldst appear?
Like untun'd golden strings all women are,
Which, long time lie untouch'd, will harshly jar.   230
Vessels of brass, oft handled, brightly shine;
What difference betwixt the richest mine
And basest mold but use? for both, not us'd,
Are of like worth. Then treasure is abus'd
When misers keep it; being put to loan,
In time it will return us two for one.
Rich robes themselves and others do adorn;
Neither themselves nor others, if not worn.
Who builds a palace, and rams up the gate,
Shall see it ruinous and desolate.   240
Ah, simple Hero, learn thyself to cherish!
Lone women, like to empty houses, perish.
Less sins the poor rich man that starves himself
In heaping up a mass of drossy pelf,
Than such as you; his golden earth remains,
Which, after his discease, some other gains;
But this fair gem, sweet in the loss alone,
When you fleet hence, can be bequeath'd to none.
Or if it could, down from th' enamel'd sky
All heaven would come to claim this legacy,   250
And with intestine broils the world destroy,
And quite confound nature's sweet harmony.
Well therefore by the gods decreed it is
We human creatures should enjoy that bliss.
One is no number; maids are nothing, then,
Without the sweet society of men.
Wilt thou live single still? one shalt thou be
Though never-singling Hymen couple thee.
Wild savages, that drink of running springs,
Think water far excels all earthly things,   260
But they that daily taste neat wine, despise it;
Virginity, albeit some highly prize it,
Compar'd with marriage, had you tried them both,
Differs as much as wine and water doth.
Base boullion for the stamp's sake we allow;
Even so for men's impression do we you,
By which alone, our reverend fathers say,
Women receive perfection every way.
This idol which you term virginity
Is neither essence subject to the eye,   270
No, nor to any one exterior sense,
Nor hath it any place of residence,
Nor is 't of earth or mold celestial,
Or capable of any form at all.

Of that which hath no being do not boast;
Things that are not at all are never lost.
Men foolishly do call it virtuous;
What virtue is it that is born with us?
Much less can honor be ascrib'd thereto;
Honor is purchas'd by the deeds we do.   280
Believe me, Hero, honor is not won
Until some honorable deed be done.
Seek you, for chastity, immortal fame,
And know that some have wrong'd Diana's name?
Whose name is it, if she be false or not,
So she be fair, but some vile tongues will blot?
But you are fair, aye me, so wondrous fair,
So young, so gentle, and so debonair,
As Greece will think, if thus you live alone,
Some one or other keeps you as his own.   290
Then, Hero, hate me not, nor from me fly
To follow swiftly blasting infamy.
Perhaps thy sacred priesthood makes thee loath;
Tell me, to whom mad'st thou that heedless oath?"
    "To Venus," answered she, and as she spake,
Forth from those two tralucent cesterns brake
A stream of liquid pearl, which down her face
Made milk-white paths, whereon the gods might trace
To Jove's high court. He thus repli'd: "The rites
In which love's beauteous empress most delights   300
Are banquets, Doric music, midnight revel,
Plays, masks, and all that stern age counteth evil.
Thee as a holy idiot doth she scorn,
For thou, in vowing chastity, hast sworn
To rob her name and honor, and thereby
Commit'st a sin far worse than perjury,
Even sacrilege against her deity,
Through regular and formal purity.
To expiate which sin, kiss and shake hands;
Such sacrifice as this Venus demands."   310
    Thereat she smil'd, and did deny him so
As, put thereby, yet might he hope for mo.
Which makes him quickly reenforce his speech,
And her in humble manner thus beseech:
    "Though neither gods nor men may thee deserve,
Yet for her sake whom you have vow'd to serve,
Abandon fruitless, cold virginity,
The gentle queen of love's sole enemy.
Then shall you most resemble Venus' nun,
When Venus' sweet rites are perform'd and done.   320
Flint-breasted Pallas joys in single life,
But Pallas and your mistress are at strife.
Love, Hero, then, and be not tyrannous,
But heal the heart that thou hast wounded thus;
Nor stain thy youthful years with avarice;
Fair fools delight to be accounted nice.
The richest corn dies if it be not reap'd;
Beauty alone is lost, too warily kept."
    These arguments he us'd, and many more,

Wherewith she yielded, that was won before.   330
Hero's looks yielded, but her words made war;
Women are won when they begin to jar.
Thus having swallow'd Cupid's golden hook,
The more she striv'd, the deeper was she strook;
Yet, evilly feigning anger, strove she still,
And would be thought to grant against her will.
So having paus'd awhile, at last she said:
"Who taught thee rhetoric to deceive a maid?
Aye me! such words as these should I abhor,
And yet I like them for the orator."   340
    With that Leander stoop'd to have embrac'd her,
But from his spreading arms away she cast her,
And thus bespake him: "Gentle youth, forbear
To touch the sacred garments which I wear.
Upon a rock, and underneath a hill,
Far from the town, where all is whist and still,
Save that the sea playing on yellow sand
Sends forth a rattling murmur to the land,
Whose sound allures the golden Morpheus
In silence of the night to visit us,   350
My turret stands; and there, God knows, I play
With Venus' swans and sparrows all the day.
A dwarfish beldame bears me company,
That hops about the chamber where I lie,
And spends the night, that might be better spent,
In vain discourse and apish merriment.
Come thither." As she spake this, her toong tripp'd,
For unawares "Come thither" from her slipp'd;
And sodainly her former color chang'd,
And here and there her eyes, through anger, rang'd.   360
And like a planet moving several ways   *Conceits*
At one self instant, she, poor soul, assays,
Loving, not to love at all, and every part
Strove to resist the motions of her heart;
And hands so pure, so innocent, nay such
As might have made heaven stoop to have a touch,
Did she uphold to Venus, and again
Vow'd spotless chastity, but all in vain.
Cupid beats down her prayers with his wings;
Her vows above the empty air he flings;   370
All deep enrag'd, his sinowy bow he bent,
And shot a shaft that burning from him went;
Wherewith she, strooken, look'd so dolefully,
As made Love sigh to see his tyranny.
And as she wept, her tears to pearl he turn'd,
And wound them on his arm, and for her mourn'd.
Then towards the palace of the Destinies,
Laden with languishment and grief, he flies,
And to those stern nymphs humbly made request,
Both might enjoy each other and be blest.   380
But with a ghastly dreadful countenance,
Threat'ning a thousand deaths at every glance,
They answered Love, nor would vouchsafe so much
As one poor word, their hate to him was such.

Harken awhile, and I will tell you why:
Heaven's winged herald, Jove-born Mercury,
The selfsame day that he asleep had laid
Inchanted Argus, spied a country maid,
Whose careless hair, instead of pearl t' adorn it,
Glist'red with dew, as one that seem'd to scorn it;   390
Her breath as fragrant as the morning rose,
Her mind pure, and her toong untaught to glose;
Yet proud she was, for lofty pride that dwells
In tow'red courts is oft in sheapherds' cells,
And too too well the fair vermilion knew
And silver tincture of her cheeks that drew
The love of every swain. On her this god
Enamored was, and with his snaky rod
Did charm her nimble feet, and made her stay,
The while upon a hillock down he lay,   440
And sweetly on his pipe began to play,
And with smooth speech her fancy to assay;
Till in his twining arms he lock'd her fast,
And then he woo'd with kisses, and at last,
As sheapherds do, her on the ground he laid,
And, tumbling in the grass, he often stray'd
Beyond the bounds of shame, in being bold
To eye those parts which no eye should behold.
And like an insolent commanding lover,
Boasting his parentage, would needs discover   410
The way to new Elysium; but she,
Whose only dower was her chastity,
Having striv'n in vain, was now about to cry,
And crave the help of sheapherds that were nigh.
Herewith he stay'd his fury, and began
To give her leave to rise; away she ran;
After went Mercury, who us'd such cunning,
As she, to hear his tale, left off her running;
Maids are not won by brutish force and might,
But speeches full of pleasure and delight;   420
And, knowing Hermes courted her, was glad
That she such loveliness and beauty had
As could provoke his liking, yet was mute,
And neither would deny nor grant his suit.
Still vow'd he love, she wanting no excuse
To feed him with delays, as women use,
Or thirsting after immortality—
All women are ambitious naturally—
Impos'd upon her lover such a task
As he ought not perform, nor yet she ask.   430
A draught of flowing nectar she requested,
Wherewith the king of gods and men is feasted.
He, ready to accomplish what she will'd,
Stole some from Hebe (Hebe Jove's cup fill'd)
And gave it to his simple rustic love;
Which being known (as what is hid from Jove?)
He inly storm'd, and wax'd more furious
Than for the fire filch'd by Prometheus,
And thrusts him down from heaven; he wand'ring here

In mournful terms, with sad and heavy cheer, 440
Complain'd to Cupid. Cupid, for his sake,
To be reveng'd on Jove did undertake;
And those on whom heaven, earth, and hell relies,
I mean the adamantine Destinies,
He wounds with love, and forc'd them equally
To dote upon deceitful Mercury.
They off'red him the deadly fatal knife
That shears the slender threads of human life;
At his fair feathered feet the engines laid
Which th' earth from ougly Chaos' den upweigh'd; 450
These he regarded not, but did intreat
That Jove, usurper of his father's seat,
Might presently be banish'd into hell,
And aged Saturn in Olympus dwell.
They granted what he crav'd, and once again
Saturn and Ops began their golden reign.
Murder, rape, war, lust, and treachery
Were with Jove clos'd in Stygian empery.
But long this blessed time continued not;
As soon as he his wished purpose got, 460
He, reckless of his promise, did despise
The love of th' everlasting Destinies.
They, seeing it, both Love and him abhorr'd,
And Jupiter unto his place restor'd.
And but that Learning, in despight of Fate,
Will mount aloft, and enter heaven gate,
And to the seat of Jove itself advance,
Hermes had slept in hell with Ignorance;
Yet as a punishment they added this,
That he and Poverty should always kiss. 470
And to this day is every scholler poor;
Gross gold from them runs headlong to the boor.
Likewise, the angry sisters thus deluded,
To venge themselves on Hermes, have concluded
That Midas' brood shall sit in Honor's chair,
To which the muses' sons are only heir;
And fruitful wits that inaspiring are
Shall, discontent, run into regions far;
And few great lords in virtuous deeds shall joy,
But be surpris'd with every garish toy; 480
And still inrich the lofty servile clown,
Who with incroaching guile keeps learning down.
Then muse not Cupid's suit no better sped,
Seeing in their loves the Fates were injured.

[Second Sestiad]

By this, sad Hero, with love unacquainted,
Viewing Leander's face, fell down and fainted.
He kiss'd her and breath'd life into her lips,
Wherewith, as one displeas'd, away she trips.
Yet as she went, full often look'd behind,
And many poor excuses did she find
To linger by the way, and once she stay'd
And would have turn'd again, but was afraid,

In off'ring parley, to be counted light.
So on she goes, and in her idle flight 10
Her painted fan of curled plumes let fall,
Thinking to train Leander therewithal.
He, being a novice, knew not what she meant,
But stay'd, and after her a letter sent,
Which joyful Hero answer'd in such sort
As he had hope to scale the beauteous fort
Wherein the liberal graces lock'd their wealth,
And therefore to her tower he got by stealth.
Wide open stood the door, he need not climb;
And she herself, before the pointed time, 20
Had spread the boord, with roses strowed the room,
And oft look'd out, and mus'd he did not come.
At last he came; O who can tell the greeting
These greedy lovers had at their first meeting?
He ask'd, she gave, and nothing was denied;
Both to each other quickly were affied.
Look how their hands, so were their hearts united,
And what he did she willingly requited.
Sweet are the kisses, the imbracements sweet,
When like desires and affections meet; 30
For from the earth to heaven is Cupid rais'd,
Where fancy is in equal balance pais'd.
Yet she this rashness sodainly repented,
And turn'd aside, and to herself lamented,
As if her name and honor had been wrong'd
By being possess'd of him for whom she long'd;
Aye and she wish'd, albeit not from her heart,
That he would leave her turret and depart.
The mirthful god of amorous pleasure smil'd
To see how he this captive nymph beguil'd; 40
For hitherto he did but fan the fire,
And kept it down that it might mount the higher.
Now wax'd she jealous lest his love abated,
Fearing her own thoughts made her to be hated.
Therefore unto him hastily she goes,
And, like light Salmacis, her body throws
Upon his bosom, where with yielding eyes
She offers up herself a sacrifice,
To slake his anger, if he were displeas'd.
O what god would not therewith be appeas'd? 50
Like Aesop's cock, this jewel he enjoyed,
And as a brother with his sister toyed,
Supposing nothing else was to be done,
Now he her favor and good will had won.
But know you not that creatures wanting sense
By nature have a mutual appetence,
And wanting organs to advance a step,
Mov'd by love's force, unto each other lep?
Much more in subjects having intellect,
Some hidden influence breeds like effect. 60
Albeit Leander, rude in love and raw,
Long dallying with Hero, nothing saw
That might delight him more, yet he suspected

Some amorous rites or other were neglected.
Therefore unto his body hers he clung;
She, fearing on the rushes to be flung,
Striv'd with redoubled strength; the more she strived,
The more a gentle pleasing heat revived,
Which taught him all that elder lovers know;
And now the same gan so to scorch and glow,   70
As in plain terms, yet cunningly, he crav'd it;
Love always makes those eloquent that have it.
She, with a kind of granting, put him by it,
And ever as he thought himself most nigh it,
Like to the tree of Tantalus she fled,
And, seeming lavish, sav'd her maidenhead.
Ne'er king more sought to keep his diadem,
Than Hero this inestimable gem.
Above our life we love a steadfast friend,
Yet when a token of great worth we send,   80
We often kiss it, often look thereon,
And stay the messenger that would be gone;
No marvel then though Hero would not yield
So soon to part from that she dearly held;
Jewels being lost are found again, this never;
'Tis lost but once, and once lost, lost forever.
    Now had the morn espi'd her lover's steeds,
Whereat she starts, puts on her purple weeds,
And, red for anger that he stay'd so long,
All headlong throws herself the clouds among.   90
And now Leander, fearing to be miss'd,
Imbrac'd her sodainly, took leave, and kiss'd.
Long was he taking leave, and loath to go,
And kiss'd again, as lovers use to do.
Sad Hero wroong him by the hand and wept,
Saying, "Let your vows and promises be kept."
Then, standing at the door, she turn'd about,
As loath to see Leander going out.
And now the sun that through th' orizon peeps,
As pitying these lovers, downward creeps,   100
So that in silence of the cloudy night,
Though it was morning, did he take his flight.
But what the secret trusty night conceal'd,
Leander's amorous habit soon reveal'd;
With Cupid's myrtle was his bonnet crown'd,
About his arms the purple riband wound
Wherewith she wreath'd her largely spreading hear;
Nor could the youth abstain, but he must wear
The sacred ring wherewith she was endow'd
When first religious chastity she vow'd;   110
Which made his love through Sestos to be known,
And thence unto Abydos sooner blown
Than he could sail; for incorporeal Fame,
Whose weight consists in nothing but her name,
Is swifter than the wind, whose tardy plumes
Are reeking water and dull earthly fumes.
Home, when he came, he seem'd not to be there,
But like exiled heir thrust from his sphere,
Set in a forren place; and straight from thence,

Alcides like, by mighty violence   120
He would have chas'd away the swelling main
That him from her unjustly did detain.
Like as the sun in a diameter
Fires and inflames objects removed far,
And heateth kindly, shining lat'rally,
So beauty sweetly quickens when 'tis nigh,
But being separated and removed,
Burns where it cherish'd, murders where it loved.
Therefore even as an index to a book,
So to his mind was young Leander's look.   130
O none but gods have power their love to hide;
Affection by the count'nance is descri'd.
The light of hidden fire itself discovers,
And love that is conceal'd betrays poor lovers.
His secret flame apparantly was seen;
Leander's father knew where he had been,
And for the same mildly rebuk'd his son,
Thinking to quench the sparkles new begun.
But love, resisted once, grows passionate,
And nothing more than counsail lovers hate;   140
For as a hot, proud horse highly disdains
To have his head controll'd, but breaks the reins,
Spits forth the ringled bit, and with his hooves
Checks the submissive ground, so he that loves,
The more he is restrain'd, the worse he fares.
What is it now but mad Leander dares?
"O Hero, Hero!" thus he cried full oft,
And then he got him to a rock aloft,
Where having spi'd her tower, long star'd he on 't,
And pray'd the narrow toiling Hellespont   150
To part in twain, that he might come and go;
But still the rising billows answered "No."
With that he stripp'd him to the iv'ry skin,
And crying, "Love, I come!" leap'd lively in.
Whereat the sapphire-visag'd god grew proud,
And made his cap'ring Triton sound aloud,
Imagining that Ganymede, displeas'd,
Had left the heavens; therefore on him he seiz'd.
Leander striv'd; the waves about him wound,
And pull'd him to the bottom, where the ground   160
Was strew'd with pearl, and in low coral groves
Sweet singing meremaids sported with their loves
On heaps of heavy gold, and took great pleasure
To spurn in careless sort the shipwrack treasure.
For here the stately azure palace stood
Where kingly Neptune and his train abode.
The lusty god imbrac'd him, call'd him "love,"
And swore he never should return to Jove.
But when he knew it was not Ganymede,
For under water he was almost dead,   170
He heav'd him up, and, looking on his face,
Beat down the bold waves with his triple mace,
Which mounted up, intending to have kiss'd him,
And fell in drops like tears because they miss'd him.
Leander, being up, began to swim,

And, looking back, saw Neptune follow him;
Whereat aghast, the poor soul gan to cry,
"O, let me visit Hero ere I die!"
The god put Helle's bracelet on his arm,
And swore the sea should never do him harm.   180
He clapp'd his plump cheeks, with his tresses play'd,
And, smiling wantonly, his love bewray'd.
He watch'd his arms, and, as they open'd wide,
At every stroke betwixt them would he slide,
And steal a kiss, and then run out and dance,
And as he turn'd cast many a lustful glance,
And throw him gawdy toys to please his eye,
And dive into the water, and there pry
Upon his breast, his thighs, and every lim,
And up again, and close beside him swim,   190
And talk of love. Leander made reply:
"You are deceiv'd, I am no woman, I."
Thereat smil'd Neptune, and then told a tale
How that a sheapherd, sitting in a vale,
Play'd with a boy so lovely, fair, and kind,
As for his love both earth and heaven pin'd;
That of the cooling river durst not drink
Lest water nymphs should pull him from the brink;
And when he sported in the fragrant lawns,
Goat-footed satyrs and up-staring fauns   200
Would steal him thence. Ere half this tale was done,
"Aye me," Leander cri'd, "th' enamored sun,
That now should shine on Thetis' glassy bower,
Descends upon my radiant Hero's tower.
O that these tardy arms of mine were wings!"
And as he spake, upon the waves he springs.
Neptune was angry that he gave no ear,
And in his heart revenging malice bare;
He flung at him his mace, but as it went
He call'd it in, for love made him repent.   210
The mace returning back, his own hand hit,
As meaning to be veng'd for darting it.
When this fresh bleeding wound Leander view'd,
His color went and came, as if he ru'd
The grief which Neptune felt. In gentle breasts
Relenting thoughts, remorse, and pity rests;
And who have hard hearts and obdurate minds
But vicious, harebrain'd, and illit'rate hinds?
The god, seeing him with pity to be moved,
Thereon concluded that he was beloved.   220
(Love is too full of faith, too credulous,
With folly and false hope deluding us.)
Wherefore, Leander's fancy to surprise,
To the rich ocean for gifts he flies.
'Tis wisdom to give much; a gift prevails
When deep persuading oratory fails.
  By this, Leander, being near the land,
Cast down his weary feet and felt the sand.
Breathless albeit he were, he rested not
Till to the solitary tower he got,   230
And knock'd and call'd, at which celestial noise

The longing heart of Hero much more joys
Then nymphs or sheapherds when the timbrel rings,
Or crooked dolphin when the sailor sings.
She stay'd not for her robes, but straight arose,
And, drunk with gladness, to the door she goes;
Where seeing a naked man, she scriech'd for fear
(Such sights as this to tender maids are rare),
And ran into the dark herself to hide.
Rich jewels in the dark are soonest spi'd;   240
Unto her was he led, or rather drawn,
By those white lims which sparkled through the lawn.
The nearer that he came, the more she fled,
And, seeking refuge, slipp'd into her bed.
Whereon Leander sitting thus began,
Through numming cold all feeble, faint, and wan:
  "If not for love, yet, love, for pity sake,
Me in thy bed and maiden bosom take;
At least vouchsafe these arms some little room,
Who, hoping to imbrace thee, cherely swom;   250
This head was beat with many a churlish billow,
And therefore let it rest upon thy pillow."
Herewith, affrighted, Hero shrunk away,
And in her lukewarm place Leander lay,
Whose lively heat, like fire from heaven fet,
Would animate gross clay, and higher set
The drooping thoughts of base declining souls
Then drery Mars carousing nectar bowls.
His hands he cast upon her like a snare;
She, overcome with shame and sallow fear,   260
Like chaste Diana when Actaeon spied her,
Being sodainly betray'd, div'd down to hide her;
And as her silver body downward went,
With both her hands she made the bed a tent,
And in her own mind thought herself secure,
O'ercast with dim and darksome coverture.
And now she lets him whisper in her ear,
Flatter, intreat, promise, protest, and swear;
Yet ever as he greedily assay'd
To touch those dainties, she the harpy play'd,   270
And every lim did, as a soldier stout,
Defend the fort and keep the foeman out.
For though the rising iv'ry mount he scal'd,
Which is with azure circling lines empal'd,
Much like a globe (a globe may I term this,
By which love sails to regions full of bliss),
Yet there with Sisyphus he toil'd in vain,
Till gentle parley did the truce obtain.
Wherein Leander on her quivering breast,
Breathless spoke something, and sigh'd out the rest; 280
Which so prevail'd, as he with small ado
Inclos'd her in his arms and kiss'd her too.
And every kiss to her was as a charm,
And to Leander as a fresh alarm,
So that the truce was broke, and she, alas,
Poor silly maiden, at his mercy was.
Love is not full of pity, as men say,

But deaf and cruel where he means to prey.
Even as a bird, which in our hands we wring,
Forth plungeth and oft flutters with her wing,   290
She trembling strove; this strife of hers, like that
Which made the world, another world begat
Of unknown joy. Treason was in her thought,
And cunningly to yield herself she sought.
Seeming not won, yet won she was at length;
In such wars women use but half their strength.
Leander now, like Theban Hercules,
Ent'red the orchard of th' Esperides,
Whose fruit none rightly can describe but he
That pulls or shakes it from the golden tree.   300
And now she wish'd this night were never done,
And sigh'd to think upon th' approaching sun;
For much it griev'd her that the bright daylight
Should know the pleasure of this blessed night,
And them like Mars and Erycine display,
Both in each other's arms chain'd as they lay.
Again she knew not how to frame her look,
Or speak to him who in a moment took
That which so long, so charily she kept;
And fain by stealth away she would have crept,   310
And to some corner secretly have gone,

Leaving Leander in the bed alone.
But as her naked feet were whipping out,
He on the suddain cling'd her so about
That meremaid-like unto the floor she slid,
One half appear'd, the other half was hid.
Thus near the bed she blushing stood upright,
And from her countenance behold ye might
A kind of twilight break, which through the air,
As from an orient cloud, glims here and there;   320
And round about the chamber this false morn
Brought forth the day before the day was born.
So Hero's ruddy cheek Hero betray'd,
And her all naked to his sight display'd;
Whence his admiring eyes more pleasure took
Than Dis on heaps of gold fixing his look.
By this, Apollo's golden harp began
To sound forth music to the ocean;
Which watchful Hesperus no sooner heard,
But he the day-bright-bearing car prepar'd,   330
And ran before, as harbenger of light,
And with his flaring beams mock'd ougly Night
Till she, o'ercome with anguish, shame, and rage,
Dang'd down to hell her loathsome carriage.

Desunt nonnulla.

RICHARD BARNFIELD

Richard Barnfield, whose talent was graceful but thin and short-lived, has ridden into a kind of minor fame on Shakespeare's coat-tails. Three of his lyrics—"To His Friend Maister R. L. in Praise of Musique and Poetry," "An Ode" ("As it fell upon a day / In the merry month of May"), and "The Unknown Shepherd's Complaint" —were included in *The Passionate Pilgrim* (1599), a volume which the unscrupulous printer William Jaggard published as Shakespeare's. The first two lyrics had appeared earlier in Barnfield's "Poems in Divers Humors" appended to *The Encomium of Lady Pecunia* (1598), and the second turned up again in *England's Helicon* (1600). At any rate, by the late nineties Barnfield had almost shot his literary bolt. A graduate of Brasenose College, Oxford (B.A., 1592), on coming down to London he formed friendships with the learned Thomas Watson, the less learned Francis Meres, Drayton, perhaps Shakespeare, and others who wrote or were interested in writing. In 1594 he published anonymously *The Affectionate Shepherd*, a set of three long pastoral variations on Virgil's second eclogue accompanied by a lugubrious "Complaint of Chastity" and some curious hexameters called "Helen's Rape, or a Light Lanthorn for Light Ladies." Apart from facile and melodious versifying, the most conspicuous feature of the pastorals is their lightly veiled advocacy of homosexuality, and the same unsavory theme also informs Barnfield's next volume, *Cynthia, with Certain Sonnets and the Legend of Cassandra* (1595). Its eponymous paean to Elizabeth (its subject-matter cribbed from Peele's *Arraignment of Paris* and its stanza from *The Faerie Queene*) is a rich brocade of adulation of the queen, but the twenty sonnets, most of them addressed to a young man for whom the poet languishes in vain, are cloying and offensive. Three years later Barnfield published *The Encomium of Lady Pecunia*. Its title-poem, a jingling, flippant hymn to the power of money, is bracketed with two long, quasi-satirical pieces ("The Complaint of Poetry for the Death of Liberality" and "The Combat between Conscience and Covetousness in the Mind of Man") as well as with the "Poems in Divers Humors" already noted. In 1605 Barnfield issued a second edition of *The Encomium* (with additions on Elizabeth's death and James's accession); thereafter he apparently retired from literary production to enjoy the considerable Staffordshire estate which he had inherited. Our texts are based upon *Cynthia. With Certaine Sonnets, and the Legend of Cassandra*, 1595 (STC 1483); *Poems: In divers humors*, 1598 (STC 1488); *Lady Pecunia, or The praise of Money . . . Newly corrected and inlarged, by Richard Barnfield, Graduate in Oxford*, 1605 (STC 1486).

FROM CYNTHIA, WITH CERTAIN SONNETS (1595)

To the Curteous Gentlemen Readers

Gentlemen, the last term [that is, November, 1594] there came forth a little toy of mine intituled *The Affectionate Shepherd,* in the which his country content found such friendly favor that it hath incouraged me to publish my second fruits, *The Affectionate Shepherd* being the first, howsoever undeservedly, I protest, I have been thought of some to have been the author of two books heretofore. I need not to name them, because they are too well- 10 known already; nor will I deny them because they are dislik'd but because they are not mine. This protestation, I hope, will satisfy th' indifferent; as for them that are maliciously envious, as I cannot so I care not to please. Some there were that did interpret *The Affectionate Shepherd* otherwise then, in truth, I meant, touching the subject thereof, to wit the love of a shepherd to a boy—a fault the which I will not excuse, because I never made. Only this I will unshadow my conceit, being nothing else but an 20 imitation of Virgil in the second eglogue of Alexis. . . . Thus, hoping you will bear with my rude conceit of Cynthia—if for no other cause yet for that it is the first imitation of the verse of that excellent poet, Maister Spenser, in his *Faerie Queene*—I leave you to the reading of that which I so much desire may breed your delight.

Richard Barnfield

CYNTHIA

Now was the welkin all inveloped
  With dusky mantle of the sable night,
  And Cynthia, lifting up her drooping head,
  Blush'd at the beauty of her borrowed light,
  When Sleep now summon'd every mortal wight.
  Then lo, methought, I saw or seem'd to see
  An heavenly creature like an angel bright
  That in great haste came pacing towards me;
Was never mortal eye beheld so fair a she.

"Thou lazy man," quoth she, "what mak'st thou here, 10
  Lull'd in the lap of honor's enemy?
  I here command thee now for to appear
  By virtue of Jove's mickle majesty
  In yonder wood"—which with her finger she
  Out-pointing had no sooner turn'd her face,
  And leaving me to muse what she should be,
  Yvanished into some other place,
But straight, methought, I saw a rout of heavenly race.

Down in a dale, hard by a forest side,
  Under the shadow of a lofty pine,   20

Not far from whence a trickling stream did glide,
  Did Nature by her secret art combine
  A pleasant arbor of a spreading vine;
  Wherein Art strove with Nature to compare,
  That made it rather seem a thing divine,
  Being scituate all in the open air;
A fairer ne'er was seen, if any seen so fair.

There might one see, and yet not see indeed,
  Fresh Flora flourishing in chiefest prime,
  Arrayed all in gay and gorgeous weed,   30
  The primrose and sweet-smelling eglantine,
  As fitted best, beguiling so the time;
  And ever as she went she strew'd the place,
  Red roses mix'd with daffadillies fine,
  For gods and goddesses that in like case
In this same order sat with ill-beseeming grace.

First, in a royal chair of massy gold,
  Barr'd all about with plates of burning steel,
  Sat Jupiter, most glorious to behold,
  And in his hand was placed Fortune's wheel,   40
  The which he often turn'd, and oft did reel.
  And next to him, in grief and jealousy,
  If sight may censure what the heart doth feel,
  In sad lament was placed Mercury,
That, dying, seem'd to weep, and weeping seem'd to
    die. . . .

[Beside Jupiter and Mercury, the distinguished gathering includes the three Furies, "King Priam's son that Alexander hight," and three goddesses—Hera, Venus, and Pallas Minerva. In a tearful complaint Hera tells how Paris, named to award the title "Pulcherrima" to one of them, gave the prize to Venus, and she petitions Jupiter for a redress of her grievance. The chief of the gods gravely reviews the case, and concludes that the prize really belongs to none of them, but to that peerless queen who is the epitome of "wisdom, beauty, wealth."]

"In western world, amids the ocean main,
  In complete virtue shining like the sun,
  In great renown a maiden queen doth reign,
  Whose royal race, in ruin first begun,
  Till heaven's bright lamps dissolve shall ne'er be
    done;   50
  In whose fair eyes Love link'd with virtues been,
  In everlasting peace and union;
  Which sweet consort in her full well beseem
Of bounty and of beauty fairest faery queen.

"And to conclude, the gifts in her yfound
  Are all so noble, royal, and so rare,

That more and more in her they do abound;
In her, most peerless prince without compare,
Endowing still her mind with virtuous care,
That through the world so wide the flying fame   60
And name that Envy's self cannot impair
Is blown of this fair queen, this gorgeous dame,
Fame borrowing all men's mouths to royalize the same."

And with this sentence Jupiter did end:
    "This is the prick," quoth he, "this is the praise
To whom this as a present I will send,
That shameth Cynthia in her silver rays,
If so you three this deed do not displease.
Then one and all and every one of them
To her that is the honor of her days,   70
A second Judith in Jerusalem,
To her we send this pearl, this jewel, and this gem."

Then call'd he up the winged Mercury,
    The mighty messenger of gods enroll'd,
And bad him hither hastily to hie,
Whom, tended by her nymphs, he should behold,
Like pearls ycouched all in shining gold;
    And even with that from pleasant slumb'ring sleep,
Desiring much these wonders to unfold,
I, wak'ning when Aurora gan to peep,   80
Depriv'd so soon of my sweet dream, gan almost weep.

THE CONCLUSION

Thus, sacred virgin, muse of chastity,
    This difference is betwixt the moon and thee:
She shines by night, but thou by day dost shine;
She monthly changeth, thou dost ne'er decline;
And as the sun to her doth lend his light,
So he by thee is only made so bright;
Yet neither sun nor moon thou canst be named,
Because thy light hath both their beauties shamed.
    Then since an heavenly name doth thee befall,
    Thou Virgo art, if any sign at all.   90

CERTAIN SONNETS

SONNET 3

The Stoics think (and they come near the truth)
That virtue is the chiefest good of all;

The Academics on Idea call;
The Epicures in pleasure spend their youth;
The Peripatetics judge felicity
To be the chiefest good above all other.
One man thinks this, and that conceives another,
So that in one thing very few agree.
Let Stoics have their virtue if they will,
And all the rest their chief-supposed good;   10
Let cruel Martialists delight in blood,
And misers joy their bags with gold to fill.
    My chiefest good, my chief felicity,
    Is to be gazing on my love's fair eye.

SONNET 8

Sometimes I wish that I his pillow were
So might I steal a kiss and yet not seen,
So might I gaze upon his sleeping eyen,
Although I did it with a panting fear.
But when I well consider how vain my wish is,
"Ah, foolish bees," think I, "that do not suck
His lips for honey, but poor flowers do pluck
Which have no sweet in them, when his sole kisses
Are able to revive a dying soul—
Kiss him, but sting him not, for if you do   10
His angry voice your flying will pursue.
But when they hear his tongue, what can control
Their back-return? For then they plain may see
How honeycombs from his lips dropping be."

SONNET 20

But now my muse, toil'd with continual care,
Begins to faint and slack her former pace,
Expecting favor from that heavenly grace
That may, in time, her feeble strength repair.
Till when, sweet youth, the essence of my soul—
Thou that dost sit and sing at my heart's grief,
Thou that dost send thy shepherd no relief—
Behold these lines, the sons of Tears and Dole.
Ah, had great Colin, chief of shepherds all,
Or gentle Rowland, my professed friend,   10
Had they thy beauty, or my penance penn'd,
Greater had been thy fame and less my fall.
    But since that every one cannot be witty,
    Pardon I crave of them, and of thee pity.

FROM POEMS IN DIVERS HUMORS (1598)

To The Learned and Accomplish'd Gentleman Maister Nicholas Blackleech of Gray's Inn

To you, that know the touch of true conceit
(Whose many gifts I need not to repeat),

I write these lines, fruits of unriper years,
Wherein my muse no harder censure fears,
Hoping in gentle worth you will them take
Not for the gift but for the giver's sake.

TO HIS FRIEND MAISTER R[ICHARD?] L[INCHE?] IN PRAISE OF MUSIQUE AND POETRY

If musique and sweet poetry agree,
As they must needs (the sister and the brother),
Then must the love be great twixt thee and me,
Because thou lov'st the one, and I the other.
Dowland to thee is dear, whose heavenly touch
Upon the lute doth ravish human sense;
Spenser to me, whose deep conceit is such
As, passing all conceit, needs no defense.
Thou lov'st to hear the sweet melodious sound
That Phoebus' lute (the queen of musique) makes;   10
And I in deep delight am chiefly drown'd
Whenas himself to singing he betakes.
One god is god of both (as poets feign),
One knight loves both, and both in thee remain.

A REMEMBRANCE OF SOME ENGLISH POETS

Live, Spenser, ever in thy *Faerie Queene,*
Whose like for deep conceit was never seen;
Crown'd mayst thou be unto thy more renown
As king of poets with a laurel crown.

And Daniel, praised for thy sweet-chaste verse,
Whose fame is grav'd on Rosamond's black hearse,
Still mayst thou live and still be honored
For that rare work, *The White Rose and the Red.*

And Drayton, whose well-written tragedies
And sweet *Epistles* soar thy fame to skies,   10
Thy learned name is equal with the rest,
Whose stately numbers are so well-address'd.

And Shakespeare, thou whose honey-flowing vein,
Pleasing the world, thy praises doth obtain,
Whose *Venus* and whose *Lucrece,* sweet and chaste,
Thy name in fame's immortal book have plac'd,
    Live ever you, at least in fame live ever:
    Well may the body die, but fame dies never.

AN ODE

As it fell upon a day
In the merry month of May,
Sitting in a pleasant shade
Which a grove of myrtles made,
Beasts did leap and birds did sing,
Trees did grow and plants did spring;
Everything did banish moan,
Save the nightingale alone.
She, poor bird, as all forlorn,
Lean'd her breast up-till a thorn   10
And there sung the doleful'st ditty,
That to hear it was great pity.
"Fie, fie, fie," now would she cry,

"Teru, teru," by and by;
That to hear her so complain,
Scarce I could from tears refrain;
For her griefs so lively shown
Made me think upon mine own.
Ah, thought I, thou mourn'st in vain;
None takes pity on thy pain;   20
Senseless trees, they cannot hear thee;
Ruthless bears, they will not cheer thee.
King Pandion, he is dead,
All thy friends are lapp'd in lead.
All thy fellow birds do sing,
Careless of thy sorrowing.
Whilst as fickle fortune smil'd,
Thou and I were both beguil'd.
Every one that flatters thee
Is no friend in misery: 30
Words are easy, like the wind,
Faithful friends are hard to find;
Every man will be thy friend
Whilst thou hast wherewith to spend,
But if store of crowns be scant,
No man will supply thy want.
If that one be prodigal,
Bountiful they will him call;
And with such-like flattering
Pity but he were a king.   40
If he be addict to vice,
Quickly him they will entice;
If to women he be bent,
They have at commandement;
But if fortune once do frown,
Then farewell his great renown;
They that fawn'd on him before
Use his company no more.
He that is thy friend indeed
He will help thee in thy need: 50
If thou sorrow, he will weep;
If thou wake, he cannot sleep;
Thus of every grief, in heart,
He with thee doth bear a part.
These are certain signs to know
Faithful friend from flatt'ring foe.

AN EPITAPH
UPON THE DEATH OF SIR PHILIP SIDNEY, KNIGHT, LORD-GOVERNOR OF VLISSING

That England lost, that Learning lov'd, that every
    mouth commended,
That Fame did praise, that prince did raise, that country
    so defended,
Here lies the man, like to the swan, who, knowing she
    shall die,
Doth tune her voice unto the spheres and scorns
    mortality.

Two worthy earls his uncles were, a lady was his
    mother,
A knight his father, and himself a noble countess'
    brother.
Belov'd, bewail'd, alive, now dead, of all, with tears
    forever,

Here lies Sir Philip Sidney's corps, whom cruel Death
    did sever;
He liv'd for her, he died for her; for whom he died, he
    lived.
O grant, O God, that we of her may never be
    deprived!   10

FROM LADY PECUNIA OR THE PRAISE OF MONEY (1605)

To the Gentlemen Readers

Gentlemen, being incouraged through your gentle
acceptance of my *Cynthia,* I have once more vent'red
on your curtesies, hoping to find you (as I have done
heretofore) friendly. Being determined to write of
something, and yet not resolved of anything, I considered with myself, if one should write of love, they
will say, "Everyone writes of love." If of virtue,
"Why, who regards virtue?" To be short, I could
think of nothing but either it was common or not   10
at all in request. At length I bethought myself of a
subject both new (as having never been written upon
before) and pleasing, as I thought, because man's
nature commonly loves to hear that praised with
whose presence he is most pleased.

Erasmus, the glory of Netherland and the refiner
of the Latin tongue, wrote a whole book in the
praise of folly. Then if so excellent a scholler writ in
praise of vanity, why may not I write in praise of
that which is profitable? There are not two countries   20
where gold is esteemed less than in India and more
then in England; the reason is because the Indians are
barbarous and our nation civil. . . .

[1]

I sing not of Angelica the fair,
For whom the Paladin of France fell mad,
Nor of sweet Rosamond, old Clifford's heir,
Whose death did make the second Henry sad;
    But of the fairest fair Pecunia,
    The famous queen of rich America.

2

Goddess of gold, great empress of the earth,
O thou that canst do all things under heaven,
That dost convert the saddest mind to mirth,
Of whom the elder age was quite bereaven,   10
    Of thee I'll sing, and in thy praise I'll write:
    You golden angels, help me to indite. . . .

5

When Saturn liv'd and wore the kingly crown,
And Jove was yet unborn, but not unbred,

This lady's fame was then of no renown,
For gold was then no more esteem'd then lead;
    Then truth and honesty were only us'd;
    Silver and gold were utterly refus'd.

6

But when the world grew wiser in conceit
And saw how men in manners did decline,   20
How charity began to lose her heat,
And one did at another's good repine,
    Then did the aged first of all respect her,
    And vow'd from thenceforth never to reject her.

7

Thus with the world her beauty did increase,
And many suitors had she to obtain her;
Some sought her in the wars and some in peace,
But few of youthful age could ever gain her;
    Or if they did, she soon was gone again,
    And could with them but little time remain.   30

8

For why against the nature of her sex,
That commonly despise the feeble old,
She loves old men, but young men she rejects,
Because to her their love is quickly cold;
    Old men, like husbands jealous of their wives,
    Lock her up fast and keep her as their lives.

9

The young man, careless to maintain his life,
Neglects her love as though he did abhor her,
Like one that hardly doth obtain a wife,
And when he hath her once he cares not for her;   40
    She, seeing that the young man doth despise her,
    Leaves the frank heart and flies unto the miser. . . .

16

But now unto her praise I will proceed,
Which is as ample as the world is wide.
What great contentment doth her presence breed
In him that can his wealth with wisdom guide!
    She is the sovereign queen of all delights;
    For her the lawyer pleads, the soldier fights.

17

For her the merchant ventures on the seas,
For her the scholler studies at his book,   50
For her the usurer (with greater ease)
For silly fishes lays a silver hook,
　For her the townsman leaves the country village,
　For her the plowman gives himself to tillage;

18

For her the gentleman doth raise his rents,
For her the servingman attends his maister,
For her the curious head new toys invents,
For her to sores the surgeon lays his plaister;
　In fine, for her each man in his vocation
　Applies himself in every sev'ral nation. . . .   60

34

The time was once when fair Pecunia here
Did basely go attired all in leather,
But in Eliza's reign it did appear
Most richly clad in gold or silver either;
　Nor reason is it that her golden reign
　With baser coin eclipsed should remain.

35

And as the coin she did repurify
From baser substance to the purest metals,
Religion so did she refine beside
From papistry to truth, which daily settles   70
　Within the peoples' hearts, though some there be
　That cleave unto their wonted papistry.

36

No flock of sheep but some are still infected,
No piece of lawn so pure but hath some fret;
All buildings are not strong that are erected;
All plants prove not that in good ground are set;
　Some tares are sown amongst the choicest seed;
　No garden can be clean'd of every weed.

37

But now more angels then on earth yet wear
Her golden impress have to heaven attended   80
Her virgin soul; now, now she sojourns there,
Tasting more joys then may be comprehended.
　Life she hath chang'd for life (O countless gain),
　An earthly rule for an eternal reign;

38

Such a successor leaving in her stead,
So peerless worthy and so royal wise,
In him her virtues live, though she be dead.
Bounty and zeal in him both sovereignize;
　To him alone Pecunia doth obey,
　He ruling her that doth all others sway. . . .   90

45

Stand forth, who can, and tell and truly say
When England, Scotland, Ireland, and France
He ever saw Pecunia to display
Before these days, O wondrous happy chance!
　Nor doth Pecunia only please the eye,
　But charms the ear with heavenly harmony. . . .

48

Had I the sweet, inchanting tongue of Tully,
That charm'd the hearers like the sirens' song,
Yet could I not discribe the praises fully
Which to Pecunia justly doth belong;   100
　Let it suffice her beauty doth excel,
　Whose praise no pen can paint, no tongue can tell. . . .

50

Whether ye list to look into the city,
Where money tempts the poor beholder's eye,
Or to the country towns, devoid of pity,
Where to the poor each place doth alms deny,
　All things for money now are bought and sold,
　That either heart can think or eye behold.

51

Nay more, for money, as report doth tell,
Thou mayst obtain a pardon for thy sins;   110
The pope of Rome for money will it sell,
Whereby thy soul no small salvation wins.
　But how can he, of pride the chief beginner,
　Forgive thy sins, that is himself a sinner?

52

Then sith the pope is subject unto sin,
No marvel tho divine Pecunia tempt him
With her fair beauty, whose good will to win
Each one contends; and shall we then exempt him?
　Did never mortal man yet look upon her
　But straightway he became enamour'd on her. . . . 120

56

Then how can I sufficiently commend
Her beauty's worth which makes the world to wonder?
Or end her praise whose praises have no end,
Whose absence brings the stoutest stomach under?
　Let it suffice Pecunia hath no peer,
　No wight, no beauty held more fair, more dear.

THE AUTHOR'S PRAYER TO PECUNIA

Great lady, sith I have compil'd thy praise
According to my skill and not thy merit,
And sought thy fame above the stars to raise,
Had I sweet Ovid's vein or Virgil's spirit,   130
　I crave no more but this for my good will,
　That in my want thou wilt supply me still.

Samuel Daniel enters literary history through the back door, as it were. When Thomas Newman, a printer of questionable integrity, in 1591 published an unauthorized edition of Sidney's *Astrophel and Stella* (see p. 323) he included as padding "sundry other rare sonnets," among which were twenty-eight by Daniel. To be sure, Daniel had six years earlier issued a somewhat florid translation of Paulus Jovius' (or Giovio's) treatise on *imprese* and heraldic devices; but Newman's thrusting him out into the world as a poet was sufficiently vexing for him to revise and publish in the following year twenty-three of the sonnets that had been "bewray'd to the world uncorrected," plus twenty-seven new ones. These constituted the famous *Delia*, one of the first fruits of the sonneteering rage which afflicted many Elizabethans after Sidney's cycle had appeared. A more traditional inclusion in the same volume was *The Complaint of Rosamond*, a graceful testimony to the continuing popularity of the complaint literature inaugurated by *A Mirror for Magistrates*. Already beginning his maddening habit of revising with each reprinting, Daniel issued in 1592 a second edition which increased the number of sonnets to fifty-four, and in 1594 a third edition which furnished many new readings, omitted certain sonnets and inserted others, added twenty-three stanzas to *Rosamond*, replaced the original prose dedication to Lady Pembroke with a sonnet, and introduced to the world *Cleopatra*, a Senecan closet drama designed as a companion-piece to Lady Pembroke's *Antony* of 1592. In 1595 Daniel launched the first instalment of his *Civil Wars* (see pp. 12–19), but for four years thereafter he published nothing new, although *Delia* continued its stately progress through a fifth edition in 1595. At last, in 1599, he dedicated to Charles Blount, Lord Mountjoy (the lover of Sidney's "Stella," Lady Rich), his *Poetical Essays*, a collection that shows how his successive works grew by accretion. It reprints (with the inevitable new readings) *Rosamond*, *Cleopatra*, and the *Civil Wars*, and adds to them a *Letter from Octavia to Marcus Antonius* (in the style of *Rosamond*) and the celebrated *Musophilus*. This latter grave and lovely poem, a dialogue between a crass worldling and a lover of art,

learning, and tradition, remains one of the most moving statements of Renaissance humanism. Its dedication to Fulke Greville is one more token of Daniel's long intimacy with the Sidney circle.

Daniel greeted the accession of James I in 1603 with a *Panegyric Congratulatory* which was printed together with a group of "Poetical Epistles" addressed to six of his titled friends, three men and three women; to the second edition of this volume, in the same year, he added the notable *Defense of Rime*, his rejoinder to Campion's *Observations in the Art of English Poesy* (see pp. 653–62). Thereafter the successively collected and expanded editions of Daniel's works constitute a bibliographical labyrinth. In 1601 Simon Waterson, his printer ever since the 1592 *Delia*, commemorated Daniel's continuing popularity with a folio ("newly augmented," of course) of *The Works*; a year later the unsold copies were apparently reissued with a new titlepage. As the years passed, and as Daniel's production and reputation increased, other such collections followed: *Certain Small Poems Lately Printed* (including the tragedy of *Philotas*) in 1605, *Certain Small Works Heretofore Divulged . . . Now Again Corrected and Augmented* in 1607 (of which a second issue with a different title appeared in the same year), another issue ("corrected and augmented") of the 1607 title in 1611, and finally a posthumous *Whole Works* which his brother and literary executor published in 1623.

The extracts below are reprinted from the following texts: *Delia* from the second edition, *Delia. Containing certaine Sonnets: with the complaynt of Rosamond*, 1592 (STC 6253); *The Complaint of Rosamond* from the third edition, *Delia and Rosamond augmented*, 1594 (STC 6254); *Musophilus* from *The Poeticall Essayes of Sam. Danyel. Newly corrected and augmented*, 1599 (STC 6261); *Ulysses and the Siren* from *Certaine Small Poems Lately Printed*, 1605 (STC 6239); the remaining pieces from *A Panegyrike Congratulatorie Delivered to the Kings Most Excellent Maiestie . . . Also Certaine Epistles, With a Defence of Ryme, Heretofore Written, and Now Published by the Author,* [1603] (STC 6259).

FROM DELIA. CONTAINING CERTAIN SONNETS: WITH THE COMPLAINT OF ROSAMOND (1592)

To the Right Honorable the Lady Mary,
Countess of Pembroke

Right honorable, although I rather desired to keep in the private passions of my youth from the multi-

tude as things utter'd to myself and consecrated to silence, yet, seeing I was betray'd by the indiscretion of a greedy printer and had some of my secrets bewray'd to the world uncorrected, doubting the like of the rest, I am forced to publish that which I never meant. But this wrong was not only done to me, but to him whose unmatchable lines have indured the like misfortune, Ignorance sparing not to commit sacriledge upon so holy reliques. Yet Astrophel, flying with the wings of his own fame a higher pitch then the gross-sighted can discern, hath regist'red his own name in the annals of eternity and cannot be disgraced, howsoever disguised. And for myself, seeing I am thrust out into the world and that my unbold'ned muse is forced to appear so rawly in publique, I desire only to be graced by the countenance of your protection, whom the fortune of our time hath made the happy and judicial patroness of the muses (a glory hereditary to your house) to preserve them from those hidious beasts, Oblivion and Barbarism. Whereby you do not only possess the honor of the present but also do bind posterity to an ever-grateful memory of your virtues, wherein you must survive yourself. And if my lines hereafter better labored shall purchase grace in the world, they must remain the monuments of your honorable favor and record the zealous duty of me, who am vowed to your Honor in all observancy forever.

Samuel Daniel

SONNETS TO DELIA

SONNET I

Unto the boundless ocean of thy beauty
Runs this poor river, charg'd with streams of zeal,
Returning thee the tribute of my duty
Which here my love, my youth, my plaints reveal.
Here I unclasp the book of my charg'd soul
Where I have cast th' accounts of all my care;
Here have I summ'd my sighs; here I enrol
How they were spent for thee, look what they are.
Look on the dear expenses of my youth
And see how just I reckon with thine eyes;   10
Examine well thy beauty with my truth
And cross my cares ere greater sums arise.
  Read it, sweet maid, though it be done but slightly.
  Who can shew all his love doth love but lightly.

SONNET 6

Fair is my love, and cruel as sh' is fair.
Her brow shades frowns although her eyes are sunny;
Her smiles are lightning though her pride dispair;
And her disdains are gall, her favors honey.
A modest maid, deck'd with a blush of honor,
Whose feet do tread green paths of youth and love,
The wonder of all eyes that look upon her,
Sacred on earth, design'd a saint above.
Chastity and Beauty, which were deadly foes,

Live reconciled friends within her brow;   10
And had she pity to conjoin with those,
Then who had heard the plaints I utter now?
  O had she not been fair and thus unkind,
  My muse had slept, and none had known my mind.

SONNET 7

O had she not been fair and thus unkind,
Then had no finger pointed at my lightness;
The world had never known what I do find,
And clouds obscure had shaded still her brightness.
Then had no censor's eye these lines survey'd,
Nor graver brows have judg'd my muse so vain;
No sun my blush and error had bewray'd,
Nor yet the world had heard of such disdain.
Then had I walk'd with bold, erected face;
No downcast look had signified my miss.   10
But my degraded hopes with such disgrace
Did force me groan out griefs and utter this.
  For, being full, should not I then have spoken,
  My sense, oppress'd, had fail'd, and heart had broken.

SONNET 25

Reign in my thoughts, fair hand, sweet eye, rare voice!
Possess me whole, my heart's triumvirate!
Yet heavy heart to make so hard a choice
Of such as spoil thy poor, afflicted state!
For whilst they strive which shall be lord of all,
All my poor life by them is trodden down;
They all erect their trophies on my fall
And yield me nought that gives them their renown.
When back I look, I sigh my freedom pass'd
And wail the state wherein I present stand,   10
And see my fortune ever like to last,
Finding me rein'd with such a heavy hand.
  What can I do but yield? And yield I do,
  And serve all three, and yet they spoil me too.

SONNET 31

The star of my mishap impos'd this paining,
To spend the April of my years in wailing
That never found my fortune but in waning,
With still fresh cares my present woes assailing.
Yet her I blame not, though she might have bless'd me,
But my desire's wings, so high aspiring,
Now melted with the sun that hath possess'd me,
Down do I fall from off my high desiring,
And in my fall do cry for mercy speedy.
No pitying eye looks back upon my mourning,   10
No help I find when now most favor need I;
Th' ocean of my tears must drown me burning,
  And this my death shall christen her anew
  And give the cruel fair her title dew.

SONNET 34

I once may see when years shall wreck my wrong,
When golden hairs shall change to silver wire,
And those bright rays that kindle all this fire
Shall fail in force, their working not so strong;
Then Beauty, now the burthen of my song,
Whose glorious blaze the world doth so admire,
Must yield up all to tyrant Time's desire;
Then fade those flowers which deck'd her pride so long.
When, if she grieve to gaze her in her glass
Which then presents her winter-with'red hew,   10
Go you, my verse, go tell her what she was,
For what she was she best shall find in you.
    Your fiery heat lets not her glory pass,
    But, phoenix-like, shall make her live anew.

SONNET 38

When winter snows upon thy golden hears,
And frost of age hath nipp'd thy flowers near,
When dark shall seem thy day that never clears,
And all lies with'red that was held so dear,
Then take this picture, which I here present thee,
Limmed with a pencil not all unworthy;
Here see the gifts that God and Nature lent thee,
Here read thyself and what I suff'red for thee.
This may remain thy lasting monument
Which happily posterity may cherish;   10
These colors with thy fading are not spent,
These may remain when thou and I shall perish.
    If they remain, then thou shalt live thereby;
    They will remain, and so thou canst not die.

SONNET 42

Fair and lovely maid, look from the shore,
See thy Leander striving in these waves;
Poor soul, quite spent, whose force can do no more.
Now send forth hopes, for now calm pity saves,
And waft him to thee with those lovely eyes,
A happy convoy to a holy land;
Now shew thy pow'r, and where thy virtue lies;
To save thine own, stretch out the fairest hand.
Stretch out the fairest hand, a pledge of peace,
That hand that darts so right and never misses;   10
I'll not revenge old wrongs, my wrath shall cease,
For that which gave me wounds I'll give it kisses.
    Once let the ocean of my cares find shore,
    That thou be pleas'd and I may sigh no more.

SONNET 48

Drawn with th' attractive virtue of her eyes,
My touch'd heart turns it to that happy cost,
My joyful north, where all my fortune lies,
The level of my hopes desired most,
There where my Delia, fairer then the sun,
Deck'd with her youth, whereon the world now smileth,
Joys in that honor which her beauty won,
Th' eternal volume which her fame compileth.
Florish, fair Albion, glory of the north,
Neptune's darling held between his arms,   10
Devided from the world as better worth,
Kept for himself, defended from all harms.
    Still let disarmed peace deck her and thee,
    And muse-foe Mars abroad far fost'red be!

SONNET 49

Care-charmer Sleep, son of the sable Night,
Brother to Death, in silent darkness born,
Relieve my languish and restore the light;
With dark, forgetting of my cares, return,
And let the day be time enough to morn
The shipwrack of my ill-advent'red youth;
Let waking eyes suffice to wail their scorn
Without the torment of the Night's untruth.
Cease dreams, th' imagery of our day desires,
To model forth the passions of the morrow;   10
Never let rising sun approve you liars
To add more griefs to aggravate my sorrow.
    Still let me sleep, imbracing clouds in vain,
    And never wake to feel the day's disdain.

SONNET 50

Let others sing of knights and paladines
In aged accents and untimely words,
Paint shadows in imaginary lines,
Which well the reach of their high wits records;
But I must sing of thee, and those fair eyes
Autentique shall my verse in time to come,
When yet th' unborn shall say, "Lo where she lies
Whose beauty made him speak that else was domb."
These are the arks, the trophies I erect,
That fortify thy name against old age,   10
And these thy sacred virtues must protect
Against the dark and Time's consuming rage.
    Though th' error of my youth they shall discover,
    Suffice they shew I liv'd and was thy lover.

from DELIA AND ROSAMOND AUGMENTED (1594)

THE COMPLAINT OF ROSAMOND

"Out from the horror of infernal deeps
My poor, afflicted ghost comes here to plain it,
Attended with my shame that never sleeps,
The spot wherewith my kind and youth did stain it;
My body found a grave where to contain it,
    A sheet could hide my face, but not my sin,
    For fame finds never tomb t' inclose it in.

"And which is worse, my soul is now denied
Her transport to the sweet Elysian rest,
The joyful bliss for ghosts repurified,   10
Th' ever-springing gardens of the blest;
Charon denies me waftage with the rest,
    And says my soul can never pass the river,
    Till lovers' sighs on earth shall it deliver.

"So shall I never pass, for how should I
Procure this sacrifice amongst the living?
Time hath long since worn out the memory
Both of my life and live's unjust depriving;
Sorrow for me is dead for ay reviving.
    Rosamond hath little left her but her name,   20
    And that disgrac'd, for time hath wrong'd the same.

"No muse suggests the pity of my case;
Each pen doth overpass my just complaint,
Whilst others are preferr'd, though far more base;
Shore's wife is grac'd, and passes for a saint;
Her legend justifies her foul attaint.
    Her well-told tale did such compassion find
    That she is pass'd, and I am left behind.

"Which seen with grief, my miserable ghost
(Whilom invested in so fair a veil,   30
Which whilst it liv'd was honored of the most,
And being dead, gives matter to bewail)
Comes to solicit thee, since others fail,
    To take this task and in thy woful song
    To form my case and register my wrong.

"Although I know thy just, lamenting muse,
Toil'd in th' affliction of thine own distress,
In others' cares hath little time to use,
And therefore mayst esteem of mine the less;
Yet as thy hopes attend happy redress,   40
    Thy joys depending on a woman's grace,
    So move thy mind a woful woman's case.

"Delia may hap to deign to read our story,
And offer up her sigh among the rest,
Whose merit would suffice for both our glory,
Whereby thou might'st be grac'd and I be bless'd;

That indulgence would profit me the best.
    Such power she hath by whom thy youth is led.
    To joy the living and to bless the dead.

"So I, through beauty made the woful'st wight,   50
By beauty might have comfort after death;
That dying fairest, by the fairest might
Find life above on earth, and rest beneath.
She that can bless us with one happy breath,
    Give comfort to thy muse to do her best,
    That thereby thou mayst joy and I might rest."

Thus said, forthwith mov'd with a tender care
And pity, which myself could never find,
What she desir'd my muse deign'd to declare,
And therefore will'd her boldly tell her mind;   60
And I more willing took this charge assign'd
    Because her griefs were worthy to be known,
    And telling hers, might hap forget mine own.

"Then write," quoth she, "the ruin of my youth,
Report the downfall of my slipp'ry state;
Of all my life reveal the simple truth,
To teach to others what I learnt too late.
Exemplify my frailty, tell how fate
    Keeps in eternal dark our fortunes hidden,
    And ere they come, to know them 'tis forbidden.   70

"For whilst the sunshine of my fortune lasted,
I joy'd the happiest warmth, the sweetest heat
That ever yet imperious beauty tasted;
I had what glory ever flesh could get,
But this fair morning had a shameful set.
    Disgrace dark'd honor, sin did cloud my brow,
    As note the sequel, and I'll tell thee how.

"The blood I stain'd was good and of the best,
My birth had honor and my beauty fame;
Nature and fortune join'd to make me bless'd,   80
Had I had grace t' have known to use the same.
My education shew'd from whence I came,
    And all concurr'd to make me happy first,
    That so great hap might make me more accurs'd.

"Happy liv'd I whilst parents' eye did guide
The indiscretion of my feeble ways,
And country home kept me from being ey'd,
Where best unknown I spent my sweetest days;
Till that my friends mine honor sought to raise
    To higher place, which greater credit yields,   90
    Deeming such beauty was unfit for fields.

"From country then to court I was preferr'd,
From calm to storms, from shore into the deeps;

There where I perish'd, where my youth first err'd;
There where I lost the flow'r which honor keeps;
There where the worser thrives, the better weeps.
  Ah me, poor wench, on this unhappy shelf
  I grounded me and cast away myself.

"For thither com'd (when years had arm'd my youth
With rarest proof of beauty ever seen,   100
When my reviving eye had learnt the truth
That it had pow'r to make the winter green,
And flow'r affections whereas none had been),
  Soon could I teach my brow to tyrannize,
  And make the world do homage to mine eyes.

"For age I saw, though years with cold conceit
Congeal'd their thoughts against a warm desire,
Yet sigh their want, and look at such a bait;
I saw how youth was wax before the fire;
I saw by stealth, I fram'd my look a liar,   110
  Yet well perceiv'd how fortune made me then
  The envy of my sex, and wonder unto men.

"Look how a comet at the first appearing
Draws all men's eyes with wonder to behold it;
Or as the saddest tale at suddain hearing
Makes silent list'ning unto him that told it;
So did my speech when rubies did unfold it,
  So did the blazing of my blush appear
  T' amaze the world, that holds such sights so dear.

"Ah, beauty, siren, fair enchanting good!   120
Sweet silent rhetorique of persuading eyes!
Dumb eloquence, whose power doth move the blood
More then the words or wisdom of the wise!
Still harmony, whose diapason lies
  Within a brow, the key which passions move
  To ravish sense and play a world in love!

"What might I then not do whose power was such?
What cannot women do that know their pow'r?
What woman knows it not (I fear too much)
How bliss or bale lies in their laugh or low'r,   130
Whilst they enjoy their happy blooming flow'r,
  Whilst nature decks her with her proper fair,
  Which cheers the world, joys each sight, sweetens th'
    air.

"Such one was I, my beauty was mine own,
No borrowed blush which bankrot beauties seek;
That new-found shame, a sin to us unknown,
Th' adulterate beauty of a falsed cheek,
Vild stain to honor and to women eke,
  Seeing that time our fading must detect,
  Thus with defect to cover our defect   140

"Impiety of times, chastity's abator,
Falsehood, wherein thyself thyself deniest,
Treason to counterfeit the seal of nature,
The stamp of heaven, impressed by the highest,
Disgrace unto the world, to whom thou liest,
  Idol unto thyself, shame to the wise,
  And all that honor thee idolatrize.

"Far was that sin from us whose age was pure,
When simple beauty was accounted best,
The time when women had no other lure   150
But modesty, pure cheeks, a virtuous breast;
This was the pomp wherewith my youth was bless d;
  These were the weapons which mine honor won
  In all the conflicts which my eyes begun;

"Which were not small—I wrought on no mean object;
A crown was at my feet, scepters obey'd me;
Whom fortune made my king, love made my subject;
Who did command the land most humbly pray'd me;
Henry the Second, that so highly weigh'd me,
  Found well, by proof, the privilege of beauty,   160
  That it had pow'r to countermand all duty.

"For after all his victories in France,
Triumphing in the honor of his deeds,
Unmatch'd by sword, was vanquish'd by a glance,
And hotter wars within his bosom breeds,
Wars whom whole legions of desires feeds,
  Against all which my chastity opposes
  The field of honor virtue never loses. . . .

"And safe mine honor stood, till that in truth
One of my sex, of place and nature bad,   170
Was set in ambush to intrap my youth,
One in the habit of like frailty clad,
One who the liv'ry of like weakness had,
  A seeming matron, yet a sinful monster,
  As by her words the chaster sort may conster.

"She set upon me with the smoothest speech
That court and age could cunningly devise;
Th' one autentique made her fit to teach,
The other learn'd her how to subtilize.
Both were enough to circumvent the wise,   180
  A document that well may teach the sage
  That there's no trust in youth, nor hope in age. . . .

"So well the golden balls cast down before me
Could entertain my course, hinder my way;
Whereat my retchless youth, stooping to store me,
Lost me the goal, the glory, and the day.
Pleasure had set my well-school'd thoughts to play,
  And bade me use the virtue of mine eyes,
  For sweetly it fits the fair to wantonize.

"Thus wrought to sin, soon was I train'd from court 190
T' a solitary grange, there to attend
The time the king should thither make resort,
Where he love's long-desired work should end.
Thither he daily messages doth send,
　　With costly jewels, orators of love,
　　Which (ah, too well men know) do women move.

"The day before the night of my defeature
He greets me with a casket richly wrought,
So rare that art did seem to strive with nature
T' express the cunning workman's curious thought; 200
The mystery whereof I prying sought,
　　And found engraven on the lid above
　　Amymone, how she with Neptune strove;

"Amymone, old Danaus' fairest daughter,
As she was fetching water all alone
At Lerna, whereas Neptune came and caught her,
From whom she striv'd and struggled to be gone,
Beating the air with cries and piteous moan;
　　But all in vain, with him sh' is forc'd to go.
　　'Tis shame that men should use poor maidens so. 210

"There might I see described how she lay,
At those proud feet not satisfied with prayer;
Wailing her heavy hap, cursing the day,
In act so piteous to express dispair.
And by how much more griev'd, so much more fair;
　　Her tears upon her cheeks, poor careful girl,
　　Did seem, against the sun, crystal and pearl;

"Whose pure clear streams, which lo, so fair appears,
Wrought hotter flames; O miracle of love
That kindles fire in water, heat in tears,　　　　220
And makes neglected beauty mightier prove,
Teaching afflicted eyes affects to move;
　　To shew that nothing ill becomes the fair
　　But cruelty, which yields unto no prayer.

"This having view'd, and therewith something moved,
Figured I find within the other squares
Transformed Io, Jove's dearly loved,
In her affliction how she strangely fares,
Strangely distress'd (O beauty, born to cares),
　　Turn'd to a heifer, kept with jealous eyes,　　230
　　Always in danger of her hateful spies.

"These presidents presented to my view,
Wherein the presage of my fall was shown,
Might have forewarn'd me well what would ensue,
And others' harms have made me shun mine own;
But fate is not prevented, though foreknown,
　　For that must hap, decreed by heavenly powers
　　Who work our fall yet make the fault still ours.

"Witness the world, wherein is nothing rifer
Then miseries unkenn'd before they come.　　240
Who can the characters of chance discipher,
Written in clouds of our concealed dome?
Which though perhaps have been reveal'd to some,
　　Yet that so doubtful (as success did prove them)
　　That men must know they have the heavens above
　　　　them.

"I saw the sin wherein my foot was ent'ring,
I saw how that dishonor did attend it,
I saw the shame whereon my flesh was vent'ring,
Yet had I not the power for to defend it.
So weak is sense, when error hath condemn'd it;　　250
　　We see what's good, and thereto we consent,
　　But yet we choose the worst, and soon repent. . . ."

[In the interests of secrecy and safety Henry installs his
mistress in "a stately pallace" set in a labyrinth of "intricate, innumerable wayes," through which "he himselfe came guided by a threed." Here Rosamond lives
"inclos'd from all the world a sunder."]

"What greater torment ever could have been
Then to inforce the fair to live retir'd?
For what is beauty if it be not seen?
Or what is 't to be seen if not admir'd,
And though admir'd, unless in love desir'd?
　　Never were cheeks of roses, locks of amber,
　　Ordain'd to live imprison'd in a chamber.

"Nature created beauty for the view,　　　　260
Like as the fire for heat, the sun for light;
The fair do hold this privilege as due
By ancient charter, to live most in sight,
And she that is debarr'd it hath not right.
　　In vain our friends in this use their dehorting,
　　For beauty will be where is most resorting.

"Witness the fairest streets that Thames doth visit,
The wondrous concourse of the glittering fair;
For what rare woman deck'd with beauty is it
That thether covets not to make repair?　　270
The solitary country may not stay her;
　　Here is the center of all beauties best,
　　Excepting Delia, left t' adorn the west.

"Here doth the curious with judicial eyes
Contemplate beauty gloriously attired;
And herein all our chiefest glory lies,
To live where we are prais'd and most desired.
O, how we joy to see ourselves admired,
　　Whilst niggardly our favors we discover;
　　We love to be belov'd, yet scorn the lover.　　280

"Yet would to God my foot had never mov'd
From country safety, from the fields of rest,
To know the danger to be highly lov'd,
And live in pomp to brave among the best;
Happy for me, better had I been bless'd,
  If I unluckily had never stray'd,
  But liv'd at home a happy country maid,

"Whose unaffected innocency thinks
No guileful fraud, as doth the courtly liver;
She's deck'd with truth; the river where she drinks   290
Doth serve her for her glass, her counsel-giver;
She loves sincerely, and is loved ever;
  Her days are peace, and so she ends her breath——
  True life, that knows not what's to die till death.

"So should I never have been regist'red
In the black book of the unfortunate,
Nor had my name enroll'd with maids misled,
Which bought their pleasures at so high a rate;
Nor had I taught, through my unhappy fate,
  This lesson, which myself learnt with expense,   300
  How most it hurts that most delights the sense.

"Shame follows sin, disgrace is duly given,
Impiety will out, never so closely done;
No walls can hide us from the eye of heaven,
For shame must end what wickedness begun;
Forth breaks reproach when we least think thereon,
  And this is ever proper unto courts,
  That nothing can be done but fame reports.

"Fame doth explore what lies most secret hidden,
Ent'ring the closet of the palace dweller,   310
Abroad revealing what is most forbidden,
Of truth and falsehood both an equal teller;
'Tis not a guard can serve for to expel her.
  The sword of justice cannot cut her wings,
  Nor stop her mouth from utt'ring secret things.

"And this our stealth she could not long conceal
From her whom such a forfeit most concerned,
The wronged queen, who could so closely deal
That she the whole of all our practice learned,
And watch'd a time when least it was discerned,   320
  In absence of the king, to wreak her wrong
  With such revenge as she desired long.

"The laberinth she ent'red by that thread
That serv'd a conduct to my absent lord,
Left there by chance, reserv'd for such a deed,
Where she surpris'd me whom she so abhorr'd.
Enrag'd with madness, scarce she speaks a word,
  But flies with eager fury to my face,
  Off'ring me most unwomanly disgrace.

"Look how a tigress that hath lost her whelp   330
Runs fiercely raging through the woods astray,
And seeing herself depriv'd of hope or help,
Furiously assaults what's in her way,
To satisfy her wrath, not for a prey;
  So fell she on me in outragious wise,
  As could disdain and jealousy devise.

"And after all her vile reproaches us'd,
She forc'd me take the poison she had brought
To end the life that had her so abus'd,
And free her fears and ease her jealous thought.   340
No cruelty her wrath would leave unwrought,
  No spightful act that to revenge is common,
  For no beast fiercer then a jealous woman.

"'Here take,' saith she, 'thou impudent, unclean,
Base, graceless strumpet, take this next your heart;
Your love-sick heart, that overcharg'd hath been
With pleasure's surfeit, must be purg'd with art.
This potion hath a power that will convart
  To nought those humors that oppress you so;
  And, girl, I'll see you take it ere I go.   350

"'What, stand you now amaz'd, retire you back?
Tremble you, minion? Come, dispatch with speed;
There is no help, your champion now you lack,
And all these tears you shed will nothing steed;
Those dainty fingers needs must do the deed.
  Take it, or I will drench you else by force,
  And trifle not, lest that I use you worse.'

"Having this bloody doom from hellish breath,
My woful eyes on every side I cast,
Rigor about me, in my hand my death,   360
Presenting me the horror of my last,
All hope of pity and of comfort past.
  No means, no pow'r, no forces to contend,
  My trembling hands must give myself my end.

"Those hands that beauty's ministers had been,
They must give death, that me adorn'd of late;
That mouth that newly gave consent to sin
Must now receive destruction in threat;
That body which my lust did violate
  Must sacrifice itself t' appease the wrong: 370
  So short is pleasure, glory lasts not long.

"And she no sooner saw I had it taken
But forth she rushes, proud with victory,
And leaves m' alone, of all the world forsaken,
Except of death, which she had left with me;
Death and myself alone together be,
  To whom she did her full revenge refer;
  Ah, poor weak conquest both for him and her

"Then straight my conscience summons up my sin
T' appear before me in a hideous face;   380
Now doth the terror of my soul begin,
When ev'ry corner of that hateful place
Dictates mine error and reveals disgrace;
    Whilst I remain oppress'd in every part,
    Death in my body, horror at my heart.

"Down on my bed my loathsome self I cast,
The bed that likewise gives in evidence
Against my soul, and tells I was unchaste,
Tells I was wanton, tells I followed sense;
And therefore cast by guilt of mine offence,   390
    Must here the right of heaven needs satisfy,
    And where I wanton lay must wretched die.

"Here I began to wail my hard mishap,
My suddain, strange, unlook'd-for misery;
Accusing them that did my youth intrap,
To give me such a fall of infamy.
And, 'Poor distressed Rosamond,' said I,
    'Is this thy glory got, to die forlorn
    In deserts where no ear can hear thee mourn?

" 'Nor any eye of pity to behold   400
The woful end of thy sad tragedy?
But that thy wrongs unseen, thy tale untold,
Must here in secret silence buried lie,
And with thee thine excuse together die.
    Thy sin reveal'd, but thy repentance hid,
    Thy shame alive, but dead what thy death did.'. . .

"This, and much more, I would have utter'd then,
A testament to be recorded still,
Sign'd with my blood, subscrib'd with Conscience' pen,
To warn the fair and beautiful from ill.   410
And O I wish, by th' example of my will,
    I had not left this sin unto the fair,
    But died intestate to have had no heir.

"But now the poison spread through all my veins
Gan dispossess my living senses quite,
And nought-respecting death, the last of pains,
Plac'd his pale colors, th' ensign of his might,
Upon his new-got spoil before his right;
    Thence chas'd my soul, setting my day ere noon,
    When I least thought my joys could end so soon. 420

"And as convey'd t' untimely funerals,
My scarce-cold corse not suff'red longer stay,
Behold, the king, by chance returning, falls
T' incounter with the same upon the way,
As he repair'd to see his dearest joy;
    Not thinking such a meeting could have been,
    To see his love and, seeing, been unseen.

"Judge those whom chance deprives of sweetest treasure,
What 'tis to lose a thing we hold so dear,
The best delight wherein our soul takes pleasure,   430
The sweet of life that penetrates so near.
What passions feels that heart, inforc'd to bear
    The deep impression of so strange a sight,
    Tongue, pen, nor art can never shew aright.

"Amaz'd he stands, nor voice nor body steers,
Words had no passage, tears no issue found,
For sorrow shut up words, wrath kept in tears;
Confus'd affects each other do confound;
Oppress'd with grief his passions had no bound.
    Striving to tell his woes, words would not come, 440
    For light cares speak when mighty griefs are dumb.

"At length extremity breaks out a way,
Through which th' imprisoned voice with tears attended
Wails out a sound that sorrows do bewray,
With arms across and eyes to heaven bended,
Vaporing out sighs that to the skies ascended—
    Sighs, the poor ease calamity affords,
    Which serve for speech when sorrow wanteth words.

" 'O heavens,' quoth he, 'why do mine eyes behold
The hateful rays of this unhappy sun?   450
Why have I light to see my sins controll'd,
With blood of mine own shame thus vildly done?
How can my sight endure to look thereon?
    Why doth not black eternal darkness hide
    That from mine eyes my heart cannot abide?

" 'What saw my life wherein my soul might joy?
What had my days, whom troubles still afflicted,
But only this to counterpoise annoy?
This joy, this hope, which death hath interdicted;
This sweet whose loss hath all distress inflicted;   460
    This that did season all my sour of life,
    Vex'd still at home with broils, abroad in strife.

" 'Vex'd still at home with broils, abroad in strife,
Dissension in my blood, jars in my bed,
Distrust at boord, suspecting still my life,
Spending the night in horror, days in dread:
Such life hath tyrants, and this life I led.
    These miseries go mask'd in glittering shows,
    Which wise men see, the vulgar little knows.'

"Thus as these passions do him overwhelm,   470
He draws him near my body to behold it;
And as the vine married unto the elm
With strict imbraces, so doth he infold it;
And as he in his careful arms doth hold it,
    Viewing the face that even death commends,
    On senseless lips millions of kisses spends.

" 'Pitiful mouth,' saith he, 'that living gavest
The sweetest comfort that my soul could wish,
O, be it lawful now that dead thou havest
This sorrowing farewell of a dying kiss;   480
And you, fair eyes, containers of my bliss,
  Motives of love, born to be matched never,
  Entomb'd in your sweet circles sleep forever.

" 'Ah, how methinks I see death dallying seeks
To entertain itself in love's sweet place;
Decayed roses of discolored cheeks
Do yet retain dear notes of former grace,
And ugly death sits fair within her face;
  Sweet remnants resting of vermillion red,
  That death itself doubts whether she be dead.   490

" 'Wonder of beauty, O receive these plaints,
These obsequies, the last that I shall make thee;
For lo, my soul that now already faints,
That lov'd thee living, dead will not forsake thee,
Hastens her speedy course to overtake thee.
  I'll meet my death, and free myself thereby,
  For, ah, what can he do that cannot die?

" 'Yet ere I die, thus much my soul doth vow,
Revenge shall sweeten death with ease of mind,
And I will cause posterity shall know   500
How fair thou wert above all womenkind,
And after-ages monuments shall find
  Shewing thy beauty's title, not thy name,
  Rose of the world, that sweet'ned so the same.'

"This said, though more desirous yet to say,
For sorrow is unwilling to give over,
He doth repress what grief would else bewray,
Lest he too much his passions should discover;
And yet respect scarce bridles such a lover,
  So far transported that he knew not whither,   510
  For love and majesty dwell ill together.

"Then were my funerals not long deferred,
But done with all the rites pomp could devise,
At Godstow, where my body was interred,
And richly tomb'd in honorable wise,
Where yet as now scarce any note descries
  Unto these times the memory of me,
  Marble and brass so little lasting be. . . .

"But here an end, I may no longer stay thee,
I must return t' attend at Stygian flood;   520
Yet, ere I go, this one word more I pray thee:
Tell Delia now her sigh may do me good,
And will her note the frailty of our blood;
  And if I pass unto those happy banks,
  Then she must have her praise, thy pen her thanks."

So vanish'd she, and left me to return
To prosecute the tenor of my woes,
Eternal matter for my muse to mourn;
But, ah, the world hath heard too much of those;
My youth such errors must no more disclose.   530
  I'll hide the rest, and grieve for what hath been;
  Who made me known must make me live unseen.

FROM POETICAL ESSAYS (1599)

MUSOPHILUS

To the Right Worthy and Judicious Favorer of Virtue, Maister Fulke Greville

I do not here, upon this hum'rous stage,
Bring my transformed verse apparailed
With others' passions or with others' rage,
With loves, with wounds, with factions furnished;
But here present thee, only modeled
In this poor frame, the form of mine own heart;
Here, to revive myself, my muse is led
With motions of her own t' act her own part,
Striving to make her now contemned art
As fair t' herself as possibly she can,   10
Lest, seeming of no force, of no desart,
She might repent the course that she began,
  And, with these times of dissolution, fall
  From goodness, virtue, glory, fame, and all.

PHILOCOSMUS

Fond man, Musophilus, that thus dost spend
In an ungainful art thy dearest days,
Tiring thy wits, and toiling to no end
But to attain that idle smoke of praise,
Now when this busy world cannot attend
Th' untimely music of neglected lays;
  Other delights then these, other desires,
  This wiser profit-seeking age requires.

MUSOPHILUS

Friend Philocosmus, I confess indeed
  I love this sacred art thou sett'st so light,   10
  And though it never stand my life in steed,
  It is inough it gives myself delight;
  The whiles my unafflicted mind doth feed
  On no unholy thoughts for benefit.
Be it that my unseasonable song
  Come out of time; that fault is in the time,

And I must not do, Virtue so much wrong
  As love her ought the worse for others' crime.
  And yet I find some blessed spirits among
  That cherish me, and like and grace my rime.   20
Again, that I do more in soul esteem
  Then all the gain of dust the world doth crave;
  And if I may attain but to redeem
  My name from dissolution and the grave,
  I shall have done enough, and better deem
  T' have liv'd to be, then to have died to have.
Short-breath'd mortality would yet extend
  That span of life so farforth as it may
  And rob her fate; seek to beguile her end
  Of some few ling'ring days of after-stay,   30
  That all this little All might not descend
  Into the dark, a universal prey.
  And give our labors yet this poor delight,
  That when our days do end, they are not done;
  And though we die, we shall not perish quite,
  But live two lives, where other have but one.

Philocosmus

Silly desires of self-abusing man,
  Striving to gain th' inheritance of air,
  That having done the uttermost he can
  Leaves yet, perhaps, but beggery to his heir.   40
  All that great purchase of the breath he wan
  Feeds not his race, or makes his house more fair.
And what art thou the better, thus to leave
  A multitude of words to small effect,
  Which other times may scorn, and so deceive
  Thy promis'd name of what thou dost expect?
  Besides, some viperous cretick may bereave
  Th' opinion of thy worth, for some defect,
And get more reputation of his wit
  By but controlling of some word or sense   50
  Then thou shalt honor for contriving it,
  With all thy travail, care, and diligence;
  Being learning now enough to contradict
  And censure others with bold insolence.
Besides, so many so confusedly sing,
  Whose divers discords have the music marr'd,
  And in contempt that mystery doth bring,
  That he must sing aloud that will be heard.
  And the receiv'd opinion of the thing,
  For some unhallow'd strings that vildly jarr'd,   60
Hath so unseason'd now the ears of men
  That who doth touch the tenor of that vein
  Is held but vain; and his unreck'ned pen
  The title but of levity doth gain;
  A poor, light gain to recompense their toil
  That thought to get eternity the while.
And therefore, leave the left and outworn course
  Of unregarded ways, and labor how
  To fit the times with what is most in force;

Be new with men's affections that are new;   70
  Strive not to run an idle counter-course
  Out from the scent of humors men allow.
For not discreetly to compose our parts
  Unto the frame of men (which we must be)
  Is to put off ourselves, and make our arts
  Rebels to nature and society;
  Whereby we come to bury our desarts
  In th' obscure grave of singularity.

Musophilus

Do not profane the work of doing well,
  Seduced man, that canst not look so high   80
  From out that mist of earth, as thou canst tell
  The ways of right, which virtue doth descry;
  That overlooks the base, contemptible,
  And low-laid follies of mortality.
Nor mete out truth and right-deserving praise
  By that wrong measure of confusion,
  The vulgar foot, that never takes his ways
  By reason, but by imitation,
  Rolling on with the rest, and never weighs
  The course which he should go, but what is gone.   90
Well were it with mankind, if what the most
  Did like were best; but ignorance will live
  By others' square, as by example lost;
  And man to man must th' hand of error give
  That none can fall alone, at their own cost;
  And all because men judge not, but believe.
For what poor bounds have they whom but th' earth
    bounds?
  What is their end whereto their care attains,
  When the thing got relieves not, but confounds,
  Having but travail to succeed their pains?   100
  What joy hath he of living that propounds
  Affliction but his end and grief his gains?
Gath'ring, incroaching, wresting, joining to,
  Destroying, building, decking, furnishing,
  Repairing, alt'ring, and so much ado
  To his soul's toil and body's travailing.
  And all this doth he, little knowing who
  Fortune ordains to have th' inheriting.
And his fair house rais'd high in Envy's eye,
  Whose pillars rear'd, perhaps, on blood and wrong,   110
  The spoils and pillage of iniquity,
  Who can assure it to continue long?
  If Rage spar'd not the walls of piety,
  Shall the profanest piles of sin keep strong?
How many proud aspiring palaces
  Have we known made the prey of wrath and pride,
  Level'd with th' earth, left to forgetfulness,
  Whilest titlers their pretended rights decide,
  Or civil tumults, or an orderless
  Order, pretending change of some strong side!   120
Then where is that proud title of thy name,

Written in ice of melting vanity?
Where is thine heir left to possess the same?
Perhaps not so well as in beggery.
Something may rise to be beyond the shame
Of vile and unregarded poverty.
Which, I confess, although I often strive
To clothe in the best habit of my skill,
In all the fairest colors I can give,
Yet for all that, methinks she looks but ill.   130
I cannot brook that face which, dead-alive,
Shews a quick body but a buried will.
Yet oft we see the bars of this restraint
Holds goodness in, which loose wealth would let fly;
And fruitless riches barrener then want
Brings forth small worth from idle liberty;
Which when disorders shall again make scant,
It must refetch her state from poverty.
But yet in all this interchange of all,
Virtue, we see, with her fair grace, stands fast.   140
For what high races hath there come to fall,
With low disgrace, quite vanished and past,
Since Chaucer liv'd; who yet lives and yet shall,
Though (which I grieve to say) but in his last.
Yet what a time hath he wrested from Time
And won upon the mighty waste of days,
Unto th' immortal honor of our clime,
That by his means came first adorn'd with bays;
Unto the sacred relics of whose rime
We yet are bound in zeal to offer praise.   150
And could our lines, begotten in this age,
Obtain but such a blessed hand of years,
And scape the fury of that threat'ning rage
Which in confused clouds ghastly appears,
Who would not strain his travails to ingage
When such true glory should succeed his cares?
But whereas he came planted in the spring
And had the sun before him of respect,
We, set in th' autumn, in the withering
And sullen season of a cold defect,   160
Must taste those sour distastes the times do bring
Upon the fulness of a cloy'd neglect;
Although the stronger constitutions shall
Wear out th' infection of distemp'red days,
And come with glory to outlive this fall,
Recov'ring of another spring of praise,
Clear'd from th' oppressing humors wherewithal
The idle multitude surcharge their lays.
Whenas, perhaps, the words thou scornest now
May live, the speaking picture of the mind,   170
The extract of the soul, that labored how
To leave the image of herself behind,
Wherein posterity, that love to know,
The just proportion of our spirits may find;
For these lines are the veins, the arteries,
And undecaying life-strings of those hearts

That still shall pant, and still shall exercise
The motion spirit and nature both imparts;
And shall with those alive so sympathize
As, nourish'd with their powers, injoy their parts.   180
O blessed Letters, that combine in one
All ages past, and make one live with all,
By you we do confer with who are gone,
And the dead-living unto counsel call;
By you th' unborn shall have communion
Of what we feel, and what doth us befall.
Soul of the world, Knowledge, without thee
What hath the earth that truly glorious is?
Why should our pride make such a stir to be,
To be forgot? What good is like to this,   190
To do worthy the writing, and to write
Worthy the reading and the world's delight?
And let th' unnatural and wayward race,
Born of one womb with us but to our shame,
That never read t' observe but to disgrace,
Raise all the tempest of their pow'r to blame.
That puff of folly never can deface
The work a happy genius took to frame.
Yet why should civil Learning seek to wound
And mangle her own members with despight?   200
Prodigious wits! that study to confound
The life of wit, to seem to know aright;
As if themselves had fortunately found
Some stand from off the earth beyond our sight,
Whence, overlooking all as from above,
Their grace is not to work but to reprove.
But how came they plac'd in so high degree,
Above the reach and compass of the rest?
Who hath admitted them only to be
Free denizens of skill to judge the best,   210
From whom the world as yet could never see
The warrant of their wit soundly express'd?
T' acquaint our times with that perfection
Of high conceit which only they possess,
That we might have things exquisitely done,
Measur'd with all their strict observances,
Such would, I know, scorn a translation,
Or bring but others' labors to the press;
Yet oft these monster-breeding mountains will
Bring forth small mice of great expected skill.   220
Presumption, ever fullest of defects,
Fails, in the doing, to perform her part;
And I have known proud words and poor effects
Of such indeed as do condemn this art.
But let them rest; it ever hath been known
They others' virtues scorn that doubt their own.
And for the divers disagreeing cords
Of interjangling ignorance, that fill
The dainty ears and leave no room for words,
The worthier minds neglect, or pardon, will.   230
Knowing the best he hath, he frankly fords,

And scorns to be a niggard of his skill;
And that the rather, since this short-liv'd race,
   Being fatally the sons but of one day,
   That now with all their pow'r ply it apace
   To hold out with the greatest might they may
   Against Confusion, that hath all in chase
   To make of all a universal prey.
For now great Nature hath laid down at last
   That mighty birth wherewith so long she went   240
   And overwent the times of ages past,
   Here to lie in, upon our soft content;
   Where fruitful she hath multiplied so fast
   That all she hath on these times seem'd t' have spent.
All that which might have many ages grac'd
   Is born in one, to make one cloy'd with all;
   Where plenty hath impress'd a deep distaste
   Of best and worst and all in general;
   That Goodness seems Goodness to have defac'd,
   And Virtue hath to Virtue given the fall.   250
For Emulation, that proud nurse of Wit,
   Scorning to stay below or come behind,
   Labors upon that narrow top to sit
   Of sole perfection in the highest kind.
   Envy and Wonder looking after it
   Thrust likewise on, the selfsame bliss to find;
And so long striving till they can no more,
   Do stuff the place, or others' hopes shut out;
   Who, doubting to overtake those gone before,
   Give up their care and cast no more about;   260
   And so in scorn leave all as fore-possess'd,
   And will be none where they may not be best.
Even like some empty creek that long hath lain
   Left or neglected of the river by,
   Whose searching sides, pleas'd with a wand'ring vein,
   Finding some little way that close did lie,
   Steal in at first, then other streams again
   Second the first, then more, then all supply,
Till all the mighty main hath borne at last
   The glory of his chiefest pow'r that way,   270
   Plying this new-found pleasant room so fast
   Till all be full, and all be at a stay,
   And then about and back again doth cast,
   Leaving that full to fall another way:
So fares this humorous world, that evermore,
   Rapt with the current of a present course,
   Runs into that which lay contemn'd before,
   Then, glutted, leaves the same and falls t' a worse;
   Now Zeal holds all, no life but to adore,
   Then cold in spirit, and faith is of no force.   280
Straight all that holy was unhallowed lies,
   The scattered carcasses of ruin'd vows;
   Then Truth is false, and now hath Blindness eyes,
   Then Zeal trusts all, now scarcely what it knows;
   That evermore, to foolish or to wise,
   It fatal is to be seduc'd with shows.

Sacred Religion, mother of Form and Fear,
   How gorgeously sometimes dost thou sit deck'd!
   What pompous vestures do we make thee wear!
   What stately piles we prodigal erect!   290
   How sweet perfum'd thou art, how shining clear!
   How solemnly observ'd, with what respect!
Another time, all plain and quite threadbare,
   Thou must have all within and nought without,
   Sit poorly without light, disrob'd, no care
   Of outward grace to amuse the poor devout;
   Pow'rless, unfollowed, scarcely men can spare
   The necessary rites to set thee out.
Either Truth, Goodness, Virtue are not still
   The selfsame which they are, and always one,   300
   But alter to the project of our will,
   Or we our actions make them wait upon,
   Putting them in the livery of our skill,
   And cast them off again when we have done.
You mighty lords that with respected grace
   Do at the stern of fair example stand,
   And all the body of this populace
   Guide with the only turning of your hand,
   Keep a right course, bear up from all disgrace,
   Observe the point of glory to our land;   310
Hold up disgraced Knowledge from the ground,
   Keep Virtue in request, give Worth her due,
   Let not Neglect with barbarous means confound
   So fair a good to bring in night anew.
   Be not, O be not accessary found
   Unto her death that must give life to you.
Where will you have your virtuous name safe laid?
   In gorgeous tombs, in sacred cells secure?
   Do you not see those prostrate heaps betray'd
   Your fathers' bones, and could not keep them sure?   320
   And will you trust deceitful stones fair laid,
   And think they will be to your honor truer?
No, no, unsparing Time will proudly send
   A warrant unto Wrath, that with one frown
   Will all these mock'ries of Vainglory rend,
   And make them, as before, ungrac'd, unknown;
   Poor idle honors that can ill defend
   Your memories, that cannot keep their own.
And whereto serve that wondrous trophy now
   That on the goodly plain near Wilton stands?   330
   That huge dumb heap that cannot tell us how,
   Nor what, nor whence it is, nor with whose hands,
   Nor for whose glory, it was set to shew
   How much our pride mocks that of other lands?
Whereon whenas the gazing passenger
   Hath greedy look'd with admiration,
   And fain would know his birth, and what he were,
   How there erected and how long agone,
   Enquires and asks his fellow traveler
   What he hath heard and his opinion,   340
And he knows nothing; then he turns again

And looks, and sighs, and then admires afresh,
  And in himself with sorrow doth complain
  The misery of dark forgetfulness;
  Angry with Time that nothing should remain
  Our greatest wonder's wonder to express.
Then Ignorance, with fabulous discourse,
  Robbing fair Art and Cunning of their right,
  Tells how those stones were by the Divel's force
  From Africk brought to Ireland in a night,   350
  And thence to Britanny by magic course,
  From giant's hand redeem'd by Merlin's sleight,
And then near Ambri plac'd, in memory
  Of all those noble Britons murth'red there
  By Hengist and his Saxon treachery,
  Coming to parle in peace at unaware.
  With this old legend then Credulity
  Holds her content, and closes up her care.
But is Antiquity so great a liar?
  Or do her younger sons her age abuse,   360
  Seeing after-comers still so apt t' admire
  The grave authority that she doth use,
  That Reverence and Respect dares not require
  Proof of her deeds, or once her words refuse?
Yet wrong they did us to presume so far
  Upon our easy credit and delight;
  For, once found false, they straight became to mar
  Our faith and their own reputation quite,
  That now her truths hardly believed are;
  And, though sh' avouch the right, she scarce hath
    right.   370
And as for thee, thou huge and mighty frame
  That stands corrupted so with Time's despight,
  And giv'st false evidence against their fame
  That set thee there to testify their right,
  And art become a traitor to their name
  That trusted thee with all the best they might,
Thou shalt stand still belied and slandered,
  The only gazing-stock of ignorance;
  And by thy guile the wise, admonished,
  Shall never more desire such heaps t' advance,   380
  Nor trust their living glory with the dead
  That cannot speak, but leave their fame to chance.
Considering in how small a room do lie,
  And yet lie safe, as fresh as if alive,
  All those great worthies of antiquity,
  Which long fore-liv'd thee, and shall long survive,
  Who stronger tombs found for eternity
  Then could the pow'rs of all the earth contrive;
Where they remain these trifles to obraid,
  Out of the reach of spoil and way of rage;   390
  Though Time with all his power of years hath laid
  Long battery, back'd with undermining Age,
  Yet they make head, only with their own aid,
  And war with his all-conquering forces wage;
Pleading the heavens' prescription to be free
And t' have a grant t' indure as long as he.

PHILOCOSMUS

Behold how every man, drawn with delight
  Of what he doth, flatters him in his way;
  Striving to make his course seem only right,
  Doth his own rest and his own thoughts betray;   400
  Imagination bringing bravely dight
  Her pleasing images in best array,
With flattering glasses that must shew him fair
  And others foul, his skill and his wit best,
  Others seduc'd, deceiv'd, and wrong in their,
  His knowledge right, all ignorant the rest;
  Not seeing how these minions in the air
  Present a face of things falsely express'd,
  And that the glimmering of these errors shown
  Are but a light to let him see his own.   410
Alas, poor Fame, in what a narrow room,
  As an incaged parrot, art thou pent
  Here amongst us, where even as good be dumb
  As speak and to be heard with no attent!
  How can you promise of the time to come
  Whenas the present are so negligent?
Is this the walk of all your wide renown,
  This little point, this scarce discerned ile,
  Thrust from the world, with whom our speech
    unknown
  Made never any traffic of our style?   420
  And is this all, where all this care is shown,
  T' inchant your fame to last so long a while?
  And for that happier tongues have won so much,
  Think you to make your barbarous language such?
Poor narrow limits for so mighty pains
  That cannot promise any forrain vent!
  And yet, if here, to all, your wondrous veins
  Were generally known, it might content.
  But lo, how many reads not, or disdains
  The labors of the chief and excellent!   430
How many thousands never heard the name
  Of Sidney, or of Spenser, or their books?
  And yet brave fellows, and presume of fame,
  And seem to bear down all the world with looks.
  What then shall they expect of meaner frame,
  On whose indeavors few or none scarce looks?
Do you not see these pamphlets, libels, rimes,
  These strange confused tumults of the mind,
  Are grown to be the sickness of these times,
  The great disease inflicted on mankind?   440
  Your virtues, by your follies made your crimes,
  Have issue with your indiscretion join'd.
Schools, arts, professions, all in so great store,
  Pass the proportion of the present state;
  Where, being as great a number as before
  And fewer rooms them to accommodate,
  It cannot be but they must throng the more
  And kick and thrust and shoulder with debate. . . .
This sweet inchanting Knowledge turns you clean
  Out from the fields of natural delight,   450

And makes you hide, unwilling to be seen
In th' open concourse of a public sight.
This skill, wherewith you have so cunning been,
Unsinews all your pow'rs, unmans you quite.
Public society and commerce of men
Require another grace, another port. . . .
A manly style, fitted to manly ears,
Best grees with wit. Not that which goes so gay
And commonly the gaudy liv'ry wears
Of nice corruptions, which the times do sway,   460
And waits on th' humor of his pulse that bears
His passions set to such a pleasing kay;
Such dainties serve only for stomachs weak;
For men do foulest when they finest speak.
Yet do I not dislike that in some wise
Be sung the great heroical deserts
Of brave renowned spirits, whose exercise
Of worthy deeds may call up others' hearts,
And serve a model for posterities,
To fashion them fit for like glorious parts;   470
But so that all our spirits may tend hereto
To make it not our grace to say, but do.

MUSOPHILUS

Much thou hast said, and willingly I hear,
As one that am not so possess'd with love
Of what I do, but that I rather bear
An ear to learn then a tongue to disprove.
I know men must, as carried in their sphere,
According to their proper motions, move,
And that course likes them best which they are on;
Yet truth hath certain bounds, but falsehood none.   480
I do confess our limits are but small
Compar'd with all the whole vast earth beside;
All which, again, rated to that great All,
Is likewise as a point scarcely descried;
So that in these respects we may this call
A point but of a point, where we abide.
But if we shall descend from that high stand
Of overlooking contemplation,
And cast our thoughts but to and not beyond
This spatious circuit which we tread upon,   490
We then may estimate our mighty land
A world within a world, standing alone;
Where if our fame confin'd cannot get out,
What, shall we then imagine it is penn'd
That hath so great a world to walk about,
Whose bounds with her reports have both one end?
Why shall we not rather esteem her stout,
That farther then her own scorn to extend?
Where being so large a room, both to do well
And eke to hear th' applause of things well done,   500
That farther if men shall our virtues tell,
We have more mouths, but not more merit, won;
It doth not greater make that which is laudable;
The flame is bigger blown, the fire all one.

And for the few that only lend their ear,
That few is all the world, which with a few
Doth ever live and move and work and stir;
This is the heart doth feel and only know.
The rest of all, that only bodies bear,
Roll up and down, and fill up but the row,   510
And serves as others' members, not their own,
The instruments of those that do direct.
Then what disgrace is this, not to be known
To those know not to give themselves respect?
And though they swell with pomp of folly blown,
They live ungrac'd and die but in neglect.
And for my part, if only one allow
The care my laboring spirits take in this,
He is to me a theater large inow
And his applause only sufficient is;   520
All my respect is bent but to his brow,
That is my all; and all I am is his.
And if some worthy spirits be pleased too,
It shall more comfort breed, but not more will.
But what if none? It cannot yet undo
The love I bear unto this holy skill.
This is the thing that I was born to do,
This is my scene, this part must I fulfil. . . .
And see how soon this rolling world can take
Advantage for her dissolution,   530
Fain to get loose from this withholding stake
Of civil science and discretion.
How glad it would run wild, that it might make
One formless form of one confusion!
Like tyrant Ottoman's blindfolded state,
Which must know nothing more but to obey;
For this seeks greedy Ignorance t' abate
Our number, order, living, form, and sway;
For this it practises to dissipate
Th' unshelt'red troops, till all be made away.   540
For, since our fathers' sins pull'd first to ground
The pale of their disservered dignity,
And overthrew that holy reverent bound
That parted learning and the laity,
And laid all flat in common, to confound
The honor and respect of piety,
It did so much invile the estimate
Of th' opened and invulgar'd mysteries,
Which now reduc'd unto the basest rate
Must wait upon the Norman subtleties,   550
Who, being mounted up into their state,
Do best with wrangling rudeness sympathize.
And yet, though now set quite behind the train
Of vulgar sway, and light of pow'r weigh'd light,
Yet would this giddy innovation fain
Down with it lower, to abase it quite;
And those poor remnants that do yet remain
The spoiled marks of their devided right
They wholly would deface, to leave no face
Of reverent distinction and degree,   560

As if they weigh'd no difference in this case
Betwixt Religion's age and infancy;
Where th' one must creep, th' other stand with grace,
Lest turn'd to a child it overturned be.
Though to pull back th' on-running state of things
(Gathering corruption, as it gathers days)
Unto the form of their first orderings
Is the best means that dissolution stays,
And to go forward, backward, right, men brings
T' observe the line from whence they took their
    ways,   570
Yet being once gone wide, and the right way
Not level to the time's condition,
To alter course may bring men more astray,
And leaving what was known, to light on none;
Since every change the reverence doth decay
Of that which alway should continue one.
For this is that close-kept Palladium
Which, once remov'd, brings ruin evermore.
This stirr'd makes men, fore-settled, to become
Curious to know what was believ'd before;   580
Whilst Faith disputes, that used to be dumb,
And more men strive to talk then to adore.
For never headstrong Reformation will
Rest, till to th' extreme opposite it run,
And overrun the mean, distrusted still
As being too near of kin to that men shun;
For good, and bad, and all must be one ill
When once there is another truth begun.
So hard it is an even hand to bear
In tampering with such maladies as these,   590
Lest that our forward passions launce too near,
And make the cure prove worse then the disease.
For with the worst we will not spare the best,
Because it grows with that which doth displease;
And faults are easier look'd in then redress'd;
Men running with such eager violence,
At the first view of errors fresh in quest,
As they, to rid an inconvenience,
Stick not to raise a mischief in the steed,
Which after mocks their weak improvidence.   600
And, therefore, O make not your own sides bleed
To prick at others, you that would amend
By pulling down, and think you can proceed
By going back unto the farther end;
Let stand that little covert left behind,
Whereon your succors and respects depend. . . .
I grant that some unlettered practique may
(Leaving beyond the Alps faith and respect
To God and man) with impious cunning sway
The courses fore-begun with like effect,   610
And without stop maintain the turning on,
And have his errors deem'd without defect.
But when some pow'rful opposition
Shall, with a sound incount'ring shock, disjoint

The fore-contrived frame, and thereupon
Th' experience of the present disappoint,
And other stirring spirits, and other hearts
Built huge for action, meeting in a point,
Shall drive the world to summon all their arts,
And all too little for so real might,   620
When no advantages of weaker parts
Shall bear out shallow counsels from the light,
And this sense-opening action (which doth hate
Unmanly craft) shall look to have her right,
Who then holds up the glory of the State,
Which lettered arms and armed letters won?
Who shall be fittest to negotiate,
Contemn'd Justinian or else Littleton?
When it shall not be held wisdom to be
Privately made, and publiquely undone;   630
But sound designs that judgment shall decree
Out of a true discern of the clear ways
That lie direct, with safe-going equity,
Imbroiling not their own and others' days;
Extending forth their providence, beyond
The circuit of their own particular;
That even the ignorant may understand
How that Deceipt is but a caviler,
And true unto itself can never stand,
But still must with her own conclusions war.   640
Can Truth and Honesty, wherein consists
The right repose on earth, the surest ground
Of Trust, come weaker arm'd into the lists
Then Fraud or Vice, that doth itself confound?
Or shall Presumption, that doth what it lists,
Not what it ought, carry her courses sound?
Then, what safe place out of confusion
Hath plain-proceeding Honesty to dwell?
What suit of grace hath Virtue to put on,
If Vice shall wear as good and do as well?   650
If Wrong, if Craft, if Indiscretion
Act as fair parts, with ends as laudable?
Which all this mighty volume of events,
The world, the universal map of deeds,
Strongly controls, and proves from all dissents
That the directest courses best succeeds,
When Craft, wrapp'd still in many cumberments,
With all her cunning thrives not, though it speeds.
For should not grave and learn'd Experience,
That looks with th' eyes of all the world beside,   660
And with all ages holds intelligence,
Go safer then Deceipt without a guide,
Which in the bypaths of her diffidence
Crossing the ways of Right, still runs more wide?
Who will not grant? And therefore this observe,
No state stands sure but on the grounds of right,
Of virtue, knowledge, judgment to preserve,
And all the pow'rs of learning's requisite;
Though other shifts a present turn may serve,

Yet in the trial they will weigh too light.   670
And do not thou contemn this swelling tide
    And stream of words, that now doth rise so high
    Above the usual banks, and spreads so wide
    Over the borders of antiquity;
    Which, I confess, comes ever amplifi'd
    With th' abounding humors that do multiply;
And is with that same hand of happiness
    Inlarg'd, as vices are out of their bands;
    Yet so, as if let out but to redress,
    And calm, and sway th' affections it commands,   680
    Which as it stirs, it doth again repress
    And brings in th' outgone malice that withstands.
Pow'r above pow'rs, O heavenly Eloquence,
    That with the strong rein of commanding words
    Dost manage, guide, and master th' eminence
    Of men's affections, more then all their swords:
    Shall we not offer to thy excellence
    The richest treasure that our wit affords?
Thou that canst do much more with one poor pen
    Then all the pow'rs of princes can effect,   690
    And draw, divert, dispose, and fashion men
    Better then force or rigor can direct:
    Should we this ornament of glory then,
    As th' unmaterial fruits of shades, neglect?
Or should we careless come behind the rest
    In pow'r of words, that go before in worth,
    Whenas our accents equal to the best
    Is able greater wonders to bring forth;
    When all that ever hotter spirits express'd
    Comes bettered by the patience of the North?   700
And who, in time, knows whither we may vent
    The treasure of our tongue, to what strange shores
    This gain of our best glory shall be sent,
    T' inrich unknowing nations with our stores?
    What worlds in th' yet unformed Occident
    May come refin'd with th' accents that are ours?
Or who can tell for what great work in hand
    The greatness of our style is now ordain'd?
    What pow'rs it shall bring in, what spirits command,
    What thoughts let out, what humors keep restrain'd,
    What mischief it may pow'rfully withstand,   711
    And what fair ends may thereby be attain'd?
And as for Poesy, mother of this force,

That breeds, brings forth, and nourishes this might,
    Teaching it in a loose, yet measured course,
    With comely motions how to go upright,
    And fost'ring it with bountiful discourse
    Adorns it thus in fashions of delight,
What should I say? since it is well approv'd
    The speech of heaven, with whom they have
        commerce   720
    That only seem out of themselves remov'd
    And do with more then human skills converse.
    Those numbers wherewith heaven and earth are mov'd
    Shew, weakness speaks in prose, but pow'r in verse.
Wherein thou likewise seemest to allow
    That th' acts of worthy men should be preserv'd,
    As in the holiest tombs we can bestow
    Upon their glory that have well deserv'd;
    Wherein thou dost no other virtue show
    Then what most barbarous countries have observ'd,
    When all the happiest nations hitherto   731
    Did with no lesser glory speak then do.
Now to what else thy malice shall object,
    For schools, and arts, and their necessity,
    When from my lord, whose judgment must direct
    And form and fashion my ability,
    I shall have got more strength, thou shalt expect,
    Out of my better leisure, my reply.
And if herein the curious sort shall deem
    My will was carried far beyond my force,   740
    And that it is a thing doth ill beseem
    The function of a poem to discourse,
    Thy learned judgment which I most esteem,
    Worthy Fulke Greville, must defend this course;
By whose mild grace and gentle hand at first
    My infant muse was brought in open sight
    From out the darkness wherein it was nurs'd
    And made to be partaker of the light,
    Which peradventure never else had durst
    T' appear in place, but had been smothered quite;   750
And now, herein incourag'd by thy praise,
    Is made so bold and vent'rous to attempt
    Beyond example and to try those ways
    That malice from our forces thinks exempt,
    To see if we our wronged lines could raise
    Above the reach of lightness and contempt.

FROM A PANEGYRIC CONGRATULATORY . . . ALSO CERTAIN EPISTLES (1603)

TO THE LADY MARGARET, COUNTESS OF CUMBERLAND

He that of such a height hath built his mind,
And rear'd the dwelling of his thoughts so strong
As neither fear nor hope can shake the frame
Of his resolved pow'rs, nor all the wind

Of vanity or malice pierce to wrong
His settled peace, or to disturb the same,
What a fair seat hath he, from whence he may
The boundless wastes and wilds of man survey.

And with how free an eye doth he look down
Upon these lower regions of turmoil,   10

Where all these storms of passions mainly beat
On flesh and blood; where honor, power, renown
Are only gay afflictions, golden toil;
Where greatness stands upon as feeble feet
As frailty doth, and only great doth seem
To little minds, who do it so esteem.

He looks upon the mightiest monarchs' wars
But only as on stately robberies,
Where evermore the fortune that prevails
Must be the right, the ill-succeeding mars   20
The fairest and the best-fac'd enterprise;
Great pirate, Pompey, lesser pirates quails.
Justice, he sees, as if seduced, still
Conspires with pow'r, whose cause must not be ill.

He sees the face of right t' appear as manifold
As are the passions of uncertain man,
Who puts it in all colors, all attires,
To serve his ends and make his courses hold;
He sees that let deceit work what it can,
Plot and contrive base ways to high desires,   30
That the all-guiding Providence doth yet
All disappoint, and mocks this smoke of wit.

Nor is he mov'd with all the thunder-cracks
Of tyrants' threats, or with the surly brow
Of power, that proudly sits on others' crimes,
Charg'd with more crying sins then those he checks;
The storms of sad confusion that may grow
Up in the present, for the coming times,
Appal not him, that hath no side at all
But of himself, and knows the worst can fall.   40

Although his heart, so near allied to earth,
Cannot but pity the perplexed state
Of troublous and distress'd mortality,
That thus make way unto the ugly birth
Of their own sorrows, and do still beget
Affliction upon imbecility;
Yet seeing thus the course of things must run,
He looks thereon, not strange, but as foredone.

And whilst distraught ambition compasses
And is incompass'd, whilst as craft deceives   50
And is deceiv'd, whilst man doth ransack man,
And builds on blood, and rises by distress,
And th' inheritance of desolation leaves
To great-expecting hopes, he looks thereon
As from the shore of peace with unwet eye,
And bears no venture in impiety.

Thus, madame, fares the man that hath prepar'd
A rest for his desires, and sees all things
Beneath him, and hath learnt this book of man,

Full of the notes of frailty, and compar'd   60
The best of glory with her sufferings,
By whom I see you labor all you can
To plant your heart, and set your thought as near
His glorious mansion as your pow'rs can bear;

Which, madame, are so soundly fashioned
By that clear judgment that hath carried you
Beyond the feeble limits of your kind,
As they can stand against the strongest head
Passion can make, inur'd to any hew
The world can cast, that cannot cast that mind   70
Out of her form of goodness, that doth see
Both what the best and worst of earth can be.

Which makes that, whatsoever here befalls,
You in the region of yourself remain,
Where no vain breath of th' impudent molests;
That hath secur'd within the brazen walls
Of a clear conscience that without all stain
Rises in peace, in innocency rests,
Whilst all what malice from without procures
Shews her own ugly heart, but hurts not yours.   80

And whereas none rejoice more in revenge
Then women use to do, yet you well know
That wrong is better check'd by being contemn'd
Then being pursu'd, leaving to him t' avenge
To whom it appertains; wherein you show
How worthily your clearness hath condemn'd
Base malediction, living in the dark,
That at the rays of goodness still doth bark.

Knowing the heart of man is set to be
The center of this world, about the which   90
These revolutions of disturbances
Still roll, where all th' aspects of misery
Predominate, whose strong effects are such
As he must bear, being pow'rless to redress;
And that unless above himself he can
Erect himself, how poor a thing is man!

And how turmoil'd they are that level lie
With earth, and cannot lift themselves from thence;
That never are at peace with their desires,
But work beyond their years, and even deny   100
Dotage her rest, and hardly will dispense
With death; that when ability expires,
Desire lives still, so much delight they have
To carry toil and travail to the grave.

Whose ends you see, and what can be the best
They reach unto, when they have cast the sum
And reck'nings of their glory, and you know
This floating life hath but this port of rest—

A heart prepar'd, that fears no ill to come,
And that man's greatness rests but in his show,   110
The best of all whose days consumed are
Either in war or peace conceiving war.

This concord, madame, of a well-tun'd mind
Hath been so set by that all-working hand
Of heaven, that though the world hath done his worst
To put it out by discords most unkind,
Yet doth it still in perfect union stand
With God and man, nor ever will be forc'd
From that most sweet accord, but still agree,
Equal in fortune's inequality.   120

And this note, madame, of your worthiness
Remains recorded in so many hearts,
As time nor malice cannot wrong your right
In th' inheritance of fame you must possess;
You that have built you by your great desarts,
Out of small means, a far more exquisite
And glorious dwelling for your honored name
Then all the gold that leaden minds can frame.

TO THE LADY LUCY, COUNTESS OF BEDFORD

Though virtue be the same when low she stands
    In th' humble shadows of obscurity,
    As when she either sweats in martial bands
Or sits in court clad with authority,
    Yet, madame, doth the strictness of her room
    Greatly detract from her ability;
For, as in-wall'd within a living tomb
    Her hands and arms of action labor not,
    Her thoughts, as if abortive from the womb,
Come never born, though happily begot.   10
But where she hath, mounted in open sight,
    An eminent and spacious dwelling got
    Where she may stir at will and use her might,
There is she more herself and more her own;
    There in the fair attire of honor dight
    She sits at ease and makes her glory known;
Applause attends her hands, her deeds have grace;
    Her worth, new-born, is straight as if full grown.
    With such a goodly and respected face
Doth virtue look, that's set to look from high,   20
    And such a fair advantage by her place
    Hath state and greatness to do worthily.
And therefore well did your high fortunes meet
    With her, that gracing you, comes grac'd thereby;
    And well was let into a house so sweet,
So good, so fair, so fair, so good a guest,
    Who now remains as blessed in her seat,
    As you are with her residency bless'd.
And this fair course of knowledge whereunto
    Your studies, learned lady, are address'd   30

Is th' only certain way that you can go
Unto true glory, to true happiness;
    All passages on earth besides are so
    Incumb'red with such vain disturbances
As still we loose our rest in seeking it,
    Being but deluded with apparances;
    And no key had you else that was so fit
T' unlock that prison of your sex as this,
    To let you out of weakness, and admit
    Your powers into the freedom of that bliss   40
That sets you there where you may oversee
    This rolling world, and view it as it is,
    And apprehend how th' outsides do agree
With th' inward, being of the things we deem
    And hold in our ill-cast accounts to be
    Of highest value and of best esteem;
Since all the good we have rests in the mind,
    By whose proportions only we redeem
    Our thoughts from out confusion, and do find
The measure of ourselves and of our pow'rs;   50
    And that all happiness remains confin'd
    Within the kingdom of this breast of ours,
Without whose bounds all that we look on lies
    In others' jurisdictions, others' pow'rs,
    Out of the circuit of our liberties.
All glory, honor, fame, applause, renown,
    Are not belonging to our royalties,
    But t' others' wills, wherein th' are only grown;
And that unless we find us all within,
    We never can without us be our own,   60
    Nor call it right our life that we live in,
But a possession held for others' use,
    That seem to have most int'rest therein;
    Which we do so dissever, part, traduce,
Let out to custom, fashion, and to shew,
    As we enjoy but only the abuse
    And have no other deed at all to shew.
How oft are we constrained to appear
    With other countenance then that we owe,
    And be ourselves far off, when we are near!   70
How oft are we forc'd on a cloudy heart
    To set a shining face and make it clear,
    Seeming content to put ourselves apart
To bear a part of others' weaknesses!
    As if we only were compos'd by art,
    Not nature, and did all our deeds address
T' opinion, not t' a conscience what is right;
    As fram'd b' example, not advisedness,
    Into those forms that intertain our sight.
And though books, madame, cannot make this mind   80
    Which we must bring apt to be set aright,
    Yet do they rectify it in that kind,
And touch it so as that it turns that way
    Where judgment lies; and though we cannot find
    The certain place of truth, yet do they stay

And intertain us near about the same,
  And give the soul the best delight that may
  Encheer it most, and most our spirits inflame
To thoughts of glory, and to worthy ends;
  And therefore in a course that best became   90
  The clearness of your heart, and best commends
Your worthy pow'rs, you run the rightest way
  That is on earth, that can true glory give,
  By which, when all consumes, your fame shall live.

A PASTORAL

O happy golden age,
  Not for that rivers ran
With streams of milk, and honey dropp'd from trees,
  Not that the earth did gauge
  Unto the husbandman
Her voluntary fruits, free without fees,
  Not for no cold did freeze
  Nor any cloud beguile
Th' eternal-flow'ring spring,
  Wherein liv'd everything   10
And whereon th' heavens perpetually did smile,
  Not for no ship had brought
From forrain shores or wars or wares ill sought,
  But only for that name,
  That idle name of wind,
That idol of deceit, that empty sound
  Call'd Honor, which became
  The tyran of the mind
And so torments our nature without ground,
  Was not yet vainly found,   20
  Nor yet sad griefs imparts
Amidst the sweet delights
  Of joyful, amorous wights,
Nor were his hard laws known to freeborn hearts,
  But golden laws like these
  Which Nature wrote, "That's lawful which doth
    please."
Then amongst flow'rs and springs
  Making delightful sport

Sate lovers without conflict, without shame,
  And nymphs and shepherds sing,   30
  Mixing in wanton sort
Whisp'rings with songs, then kisses with the same,
  Which from affection came.
  The naked virgin then
Her roses fresh reveals
  Which now her vail conceals,
  The tender apples in her bosom seen;
And oft in rivers clear
  The lovers with their loves consorting were.
Honor, thou first didst close   40
  The spring of all delight;
Denying water to the amorous thirst,
  Thou taught'st fair eyes to lose
  The glory of their light,
Restrain'd from men and on themselves revers'd.
  Thou in a lawn didst first
  These golden hairs incase,
Late spread unto the wind;
  Thou mad'st loose grace unkind,
Gav'st bridle to their words, art to their pace.   50
  O Honor, it is thou
That mak'st that stealth which love doth free allow.
It is thy work that brings
  Our griefs and torments thus.
But thou, fierce lord of Nature and of love,
  The qualifier of kings,
  What dost thou here with us
That are below thy power, shut from above?
  Go, and from us remove;
  Trouble the mighty's sleep;   60
Let us, neglected, base,
  Live still without thy grace
And th' use of th' ancient, happy ages keep.
  Let's love! This life of ours
  Can make no truce with time that all devours.

    Let's love! The sun doth set and rise again,
    But whenas our short light
    Comes once to set, it makes eternal night.

FROM CERTAIN SMALL POEMS LATELY PRINTED (1605)

ULYSSES AND THE SIREN

SIREN   Come, worthy Greek, Ulysses, come,
Possess these shores with me!
The winds and seas are troublesome,
And here we may be free.
    Here may we sit and view their toil
That travail in the deep,
And joy the day in mirth the while,
And spend the night in sleep.

ULYSSES   Fair nymph, if fame or honor were
To be attain'd with ease,   10
Then would I come and rest with thee
And leave such toils as these.
    But here it dwells, and here must I
With danger seek it forth;
To spend the time luxuriously
Becomes not men of worth.

SIREN   Ulysses, O be not deceiv'd
With that unreal name.
This honor is a thing conceiv'd,
And rests on others' fame;   20
    Begotten only to molest
Our peace and to beguile
(The best thing of our life) our rest,
And give us up to toil.

ULYSSES   Delicious nymph, suppose there were
Nor honor nor report,
Yet manliness would scorn to wear
The time in idle sport.
    For toil doth give a better touch
To make us feel our joy,   30
And ease finds tediousness as much
As labor yields annoy.

SIREN   Then pleasure likewise seems the shore
Whereto tends all your toil,
Which you forgo to make it more,
And perish oft the while.
    Who may disport them diversly
Find never tedious day,
And ease may have variety
As well as action may.   40

ULYSSES   But natures of the noblest frame
These toils and dangers please,
And they take comfort in the same
As much as you in ease;

And with the thought of actions past
Are recreated still,
When pleasure leaves a touch at last
To shew that it was ill.

SIREN   That doth opinion only cause;
That's out of custom bred,   50
Which makes us many other laws
Then ever Nature did.
    No widows wail for our delights;
Our sports are without blood;
The world, we see, by warlike wights
Receives more hurt then good.

ULYSSES   But yet the state of things require
These motions of unrest,
And these great spirits of high desire
Seem born to turn them best,   60
    To purge the mischiefs that increase
And all good order mar;
For oft we see a wicked peace
To be well chang'd for war.

SIREN   Well, well, Ulysses, then I see
I shall not have thee here,
And therefore I will come to thee
And take my fortunes there.
    I must be won that cannot win,
Yet lost were I not won,   70
For beauty hath created been
T' undo or be undone.

MICHAEL DRAYTON

The Harmony of the Church, Drayton's first published work, was entered in the Stationers' Register on February 1, 1591, and published in the same year. It is a useful reminder that great writers should not be judged by their maiden efforts. A set of nineteen Biblical paraphrases in the tradition of Sternhold and Hopkins (see pp. 160 f.), it is introduced by a grim little epistle that, forswearing the false allures of secular poetry, promises verity instead of vanity, truths instead of "tales." In spite of his high moral purpose, however, Drayton here writes badly: the verse-forms are ludicrously old-fashioned (the fourteeners and poulter's measure rarely giving way to more flexible stanzaic structures), the alliteration is forced and heavy, and the tight-lipped severity is hardly ever relieved by any grace of diction or real intensity of religious emotion. There is a possibility that the book was quickly withdrawn; at any rate, the second and last issue (called *A Heavenly Harmony of Spiritual Songs*) did not appear until

nineteen years later. Our text is based upon *The Harmonie of the Church. Containing, The Spirituall Songes and holy Hymnes. . . . Now (newlie) reduced into sundrie kinds of English Meeter: meete to be read or sung, for the solace and comfort of the godly,* 1591 (STC 7199).

Fortunately for his reputation and for the history of English literature, Drayton sought a new style and a new subject for his second work. Entered in the Stationers' Register on April 23, 1593, and published in the same year, *Idea, the Shepherd's Garland* derives not from mid-Tudor hymnology but from Spenser and the new poetry of the eighties. After *The Shepherd's Calendar* (see pp. 331, 333–50) and Sidney's *Arcadia* (see pp. 737–51) the vogue of the pastoral had reached its zenith, and by the time Drayton himself attempted the eclogue it was a form rich in convention and possibilities. Drayton exploits them fully in a wide variety of set styles that include the singing-match, the dirge, the ballad, the beast-fable, the debate, the love-complaint. Throughout, his heaviest debt is, not unnaturally, to *The Shepherd's Calendar;* but he does not use Spenser's archaic diction or his calendar-structure, and he is little interested in contemporary affairs, ecclesiastical or political. Except for a dirge on Sidney (Eclogue IV) and panegyrics on Elizabeth and Lady Pembroke (Eclogues III and VI), the theme of the nine eclogues is Rowland's hopeless love for Idea. In 1606 a thoroughly revised, rearranged, and improved version (enlarged by one eclogue) appeared as *Eglogues* in *Poems Lyric and Pastoral.* Like all Drayton's other successive revisions—notably those of his sonnets—it shows the steady growth of his taste and talent. Among the significant additions to the 1606 version are the interpolated songs, of which a ballad, in Chaucer's *Sir Thopas* meter, about Dowsabel and her shepherd boy is one of his happiest inspirations. Our text is based upon *Idea. The Shepheards Garland, Fashioned in nine Eglogs. Rowlands Sacrifice to the nine Muses,* 1593 (STC 7202).

Like *The Shepherd's Garland, Idea's Mirror* (entered in the Stationers' Register on May 30, 1594) is another effort to exploit a literary vogue. Mindful of the thundering success of Sidney's *Astrophel and Stella* (see p. 323), to say nothing of the sonnets of Watson, Daniel, Constable, Barnes, Lodge, and Giles Fletcher (see p. 496), a young poet could hardly have refrained from sonneteering in the mid-nineties. Although Drayton, following Sidney's example, claims originality for his "passions," it is clear that the sonnets in *Idea's Mirror* are vastly indebted not only to his immediate English predecessors (especially Daniel) but also to Ronsard and Desportes. Most of the fifty-one sonnets are in the English form of three quatrains and a couplet, but Drayton frequently seeks variety in Alexandrines and in changing the customary *abab* rime to *abba.* Whether written to Anne Goodere (the youngest daughter of his patron) or to a Platonic idea of perfect womanhood, in their first version the sonnets generally stay within the limits of metaphor and theme made common by earlier writers: the shipwreck of hopeless love, the lover's despair, the lady's unapproachable virtue, the expectation of immortality through poetry, and the like. On no other work did Drayton lavish such care in revision. From 1594 to his death in 1631 he supervised eleven new editions, many of them (for example, in 1599, 1600, 1602, 1605, 1619) the result of drastic correcting, rearranging, and rewriting, until the number of sonnets was more than doubled and the style altered almost beyond recognition. To remember that the famous "Since there's no help, come, let us kiss and part" —one of the authentic masterpieces in the form—appeared first in the recension made for the 1619 *Poems* is to realize how far Drayton had come from the stale conceits, the prissy affectation, and the stereotyped emotion of the original *Idea's Mirror.* Our texts are based upon *Ideas Mirrour. Amours in Quartorzains,* 1594 (STC 7203); *Poems*

by Michael Drayton Esquyer. Collected into one Volume, With sondry Peeces inserted never before Imprinted, 1619 (STC 7222).

Endymion and Phoebe (licensed on April 12, 1595) is Drayton's distinguished contribution to the vogue of the mythological and amatory poem that, inaugurated by Lodge's *Scylla's Metamorphosis* (see pp. 382–385), had already produced Marlowe's *Hero and Leander* (see pp. 388–396) and Shakespeare's *Venus and Adonis* (1593). The chief inspiration of these and similar works was Ovid; but Drayton, though preserving the customarily rich embellishments of style and diction in his lush couplets, erects them on a ground-base of austere Platonism. For this motif, as well as for the planetary and cosmological inlays, Mrs. Tillotson found striking analogues in Saluste du Bartas' *Semaines;* but in both style and theme the dominant contemporary influence is Spenser. Although the allegory cannot be pushed too far, it is fairly clear that Endymion, the mortal who regards the nymph Phoebe as a rival of the moon-goddess, to some degree represents Drayton, and that Phoebe is the same Idea (Anne Goodere?) who inspired so much of his other work. The epilogue to Colin (Spenser), Museus (Daniel) and Goldey (Lodge) seems to promise a continuation of the work, but actually Drayton never even reissued *Endymion and Phoebe,* and when he did finally return to it ten years later he recast the whole work as a thorny satire (*The Man in the Moon*) for the 1606 *Poems.* Our text is based upon *Endimion and Phoebe. Ideas Latmus,* 1595 (STC 7192).

Drayton had already attempted historical poetry when —no doubt inspired by Daniel's *Complaint of Rosamond* (see p. 402)—he reverted to the *Mirror for Magistrates* tradition (see p. 269) to write the "legends" of *Piers Gaveston* (1594), *Matilda* (1594), and *Robert, Duke of Normandy* (1596); but, as he hints in the preface to *Matilda,* he had at least begun thinking about a larger work as early as 1594. Perhaps stimulated by Marlowe's *Edward II,* he had read widely in fourteenth-century history for his *Piers Gaveston,* and he surely knew Daniel's *Civil Wars* (see pp. 12–19). Entered in the Stationers' Register on April 15, 1596, and shortly thereafter published with a dedication to Lucy, Countess of Bedford, *Mortimeriados* was the most ambitious work he had yet written. Taking as his subject the internecine strife (1321–30) between Edward II and the barons that led to Mortimer's capture by Edward III, Drayton lengthily explores, in rime royal, the political and moral implications of the battles, intrigues, and derring-do of those troubled years. There are epic suggestions in the invocations, the classical parallels, and the ostensibly heroic treatment of warfare, but the poem lacks unity because it lacks a hero. As a result it seems rather a series of set pieces (for example, the bloody fields of Burton and Boroughbridge, Edward II's deposition, Mortimer's escape) than a poem whose theme generates its energy.

When, some years later, he revised (or rather rewrote) *Mortimeriados,* it was with his characteristic thoroughness: in *The Barons' Wars* (1603), as he called the new work, he substituted the ottava rima of Daniel's *Civil Wars* for rime royal (thus changing thousands of rimes), added several hundred lines, eliminated much of the Spenserian decoration, and tried to strengthen and unify the theme of calamity following civil disorder. *The Barons' Wars* was again revised for the 1619 *Poems.* Our text is based upon *Mortimeriados. The Lamentable civell warres of Edward the second and the Barons,* 1596 (STC 7207).

Throughout the late nineties Drayton continued to be indefatigable. *England's Heroical Epistles* (1597 ff.), in the tradition of Ovid's *Heroides,* is a spirited exchange of letters, in wonderfully fluent couplets, by twelve pairs of notable lovers like Henry II and Rosamond, Queen Isabel and Mortimer, Queen Catherine and Owen Tudor, Edward IV and Jane Shore, Surrey and Geraldine, Guild- ford Dudley and Lady Jane Grey. Though they are all on the theme of unhappy love, these epistles attain a flexibility and richness of characterization, a dramatic immediacy, and a psychological penetration that make them one of Drayton's most splendid achievements. Beginning with five pairs of epistles in the first (1597) edition, he reissued and enlarged the collection in 1598 and 1599, and before he died it went through other editions (either as a single volume or in combination with his other works) in 1600, 1602, 1603, 1605, 1610, 1613, and 1630; moreover, there is another issue of uncertain date. Our excerpt, Surrey's epistle to Geraldine, first appeared in the second (1598) edition (STC 7194), which forms the basis of our text.

Before the old queen died Drayton was already at work on his gigantic *Poly-Olbion,* one of the most ambitious projects in English literary history. Seeking a big subject for a big poem, he chose to sing the glories of England with a characteristically Elizabethan ardor and extrava- gance. Like Spenser earlier and young Milton and Dryden later, he was enchanted with his theme; and although he worked against fearsome odds for some twenty years, he failed to complete the "herculean labor" that he had begun as a relatively young man. Unlike Spenser and Milton and Dryden he did not try to convert English history to the uses of a "heroic poem" (that is, an epic); instead he set himself a task perhaps even more difficult: to treat poetically and systematically the flora, fauna, topography, mythology, history, and quasi-history of his native land. Fragmentary though it is, *Poly-Olbion* is unique in our language. In the course of thirty "songs" composed of many thousands of hexameter couplets Drayton relentlessly plods, county by county, from the Channel Islands to the borders of Scotland and from Brut's arrival at Totnes to the personages and events of his own time. Given the difficulties of travel in Drayton's day it is improbable that (like Leland for his *Itinerary* or Camden for his *Britannia*) he actually visited all the regions he discusses; but he was a bookish man, and he drew copiously on the chroniclers, on Camden, and on such county histories as Richard Carew's *Survey of Cornwall* (1602)—and he missed very little. In spite of Drayton's obstinate ardor, the handsome maps, and the learned commentary contributed by John Selden, *Poly-Olbion* ("land of many blessings") must be accounted a splendid failure. The first eighteen songs were published in 1612, the last twelve in 1622, and both instalments were ac- companied by ill-natured epistles denouncing and derid- ing the lack of patrons, the scurrility of printers, and the debased reading habits of the public. The fact is that for all its sporadic charms—and the section from the thirteenth song on Drayton's native Warwickshire is a fair specimen (see also pp. 3–9)—*Poly-Olbion* is an unconscionably long and often prosy poem. Our texts are based upon *Poly- Olbion. Or A Chorographicall Description of Tracts, Rivers, Mountaines, Forests, and other Parts of this renowned Isle of Great Britaine . . . Digested in a Poem,* 1612 (STC 7226); *The Second Part, or a Continuance of Poly-Olbion from the Eighteenth Song,* 1622 (STC 7229).

When the accession of James I failed to bring the royal preferment which Drayton thought he deserved, he turned briefly to a kind of sour satire (*The Owl* in 1604 and *The Man in the Moon* in the 1606 *Poems*) that belongs to his Jacobean rather than his Elizabethan phase. In 1606, however, in the *Poems Lyric and Pastoral* (a revised and collected edition of nearly all his previous works), there appeared the celebrated odes so dear to generations of English patriots and to all anthologists. Some Elizabethans had used the term *ode* to describe any particularly com- plicated poem, others as a loose synonym for *song,* but, as Drayton himself points out, none had even approached the great classical models. He admiringly mentions Pindar (whom Jonson was to imitate so superbly) and Anacreon, but his own preference is for Horace, whose "mixed" odes he takes as a model. "New they are, and the work of playing hours," he says of his efforts; "but what other commendation is theirs and whether inherent in the sub- ject must be thine to judge." Frequently their jagged, almost Skeltonic, lines and their telescoped syntax make for obscurity, but throughout they reveal a masterly variety of structure; and in the famous patriotic pieces, "To the Virginian Voyage" and "Agincourt," all difficul- ties are triumphantly overcome. In subsequent revisions Drayton greatly improves without actually rewriting the earlier versions. Our text is based upon *Poems by Michael Drayton Esquyer. Collected into one Volume. With sondry Peeces inserted never before Imprinted,* 1619 (STC 7222).

FROM THE HARMONY OF THE CHURCH (1591)

To the Curteous Reader

Gentle reader, my meaning is not with the variety of verse to feed any vain humor, neither to trouble thee with devises of mine own invention, as carrying an overweening of mine own wit; but here I present thee with these psalms or songs of praise so exactly translated as the prose would permit or sense would any way suffer me, which (if thou shalt be the same in heart thou art in name, I mean a Christian) I doubt not but thou wilt take as great delight in these as in any poetical fiction. I speak not of Mars, the god of wars, nor of Venus, the goddess of love, but of the Lord of Hosts that made heaven and earth; not of toys in Mount Ida, but of triumphs in Mount Sion; not of vanity, but of verity; not of tales, but of truths.

Thus submitting myself unto thy clemency and my labors unto thy indifferency, I wish thee as myself.

Thine as his own,   20
M[ichael] D[rayton]

THE MOST EXCELLENT SONG WHICH WAS SALOMON'S . . .

THE THIRD CHAPTER

By night within my bed I roamed here and there,
But all in vain: I could not find my love and friendly fere.
Then straightways up I rose and searching every street
Throughout the city far and near, but him I could not meet.
The watchmen found me tho, to whom I then can say,
"Have ye not seen mine own true love of late come this a-way?"
Then, passing them, I found my love I long had sought,
And to my mother's chamber then my darling have I brought.
I charge you by the roes and hinds this vow to me you make,
Ye Jewish daughters, not to call my love till she do wake.   10
Who's that which doth from wilderness in mighty smoke appear
Like the perfumes of odors sweet which merchants hold so dear?
About the bed of Salomon, behold, there is a band
Of threescore valiant Israelites which all in armor stand,
All expert men of war with sword still ready prest

Lest foes in nighttime should approach when men suspect them least.
King Salomon hath made of Lyban tree so sure
A palace brave, whose pillars strong are all of silver pure.
The pavement beaten gold, the hangings purple grain,
The daughters of Jerusalem with joy to entertain.   20
Ye Sion daughters, see where Salomon is set
In royal throne, and on his head the princely coronet
Wherewith his mother first adorn'd him, as they say,
When he in marriage linked was, even on his wedding day.

THE SONG OF JONAH IN THE WHALE'S BELLY

IN THE SECOND CHAPTER OF JONAH

In grief and anguish of my heart my voice I did extend
Unto the Lord, and he thereto a willing ear did lend;
Even from the deep and darkest pit and the infernal lake
To me he hath bow'd down his ear for his great mercy's sake.
For thou into the middest of surging seas so deep
Hast cast me forth, whose bottom is so low and wondrous steep,
Whose mighty wallowing waves, which from the floods do flow,
Have with their power up swallowed me and overwhelm'd me tho.
Then said I, "Lo, I am exil'd from presence of thy face,
Yet will I once again behold thy house and dwelling-place.   10
The waters have encompass'd me, the floods inclos'd me round,
The weeds have sore encomb'red me which in the seas abound.
Unto the valleys down I went, beneath the hills which stand,
The earth hath there environ'd me with force of all the land.
Yet hast thou still preserved me from all these dangers here
And brought my life out of the pit, O Lord my God so dear."
My soul consuming thus with care, I prayed unto the Lord,
And he from out his holy place heard me with one accord.
Who to vain lying vanities doth wholly him betake
Doth err also; God's mercy he doth utterly forsake.   20
But I will offer unto him the sacrifice of praise,
And pay my vows, ascribing thanks unto the Lord always.

from IDEA. THE SHEPHERD'S GARLAND FASHIONED IN NINE EGLOGS (1593)

THE NINTH EGLOG

When coal-black night with sable veil
    eclips'd the gladsome light,
Rowland in darksome shade alone
    bemoans his woful plight.

What time the weatherbeaten flocks
    forsook the fields to shroud them in the fold,
The groves dispoil'd of their fair summer locks,
    the leaveless branches nipp'd with frosty cold,
The drooping trees, their gayness all agone,
In mossy mantles do express their moan.

When Phoebus from his leman's lovely bower
    throughout the sphere had jerk'd his angry jades,
His car, now pass'd the heavens' high, welked tower,
    gan drag adown the occidental slades;   10
In silent shade of desart all alone
Thus to the night Rowland bewrays his moan:

"O blessed stars which lend the darkness light,
    the glorious painting of that circled throne,
You eyes of heaven, you lanthorns of the night,
    to you, bright stars, to you I make my moan:
Or end my days or ease me of my grief;
The earth is frail and yields me no relief.

"And thou, fair Phoebe, clearer to my sight
    then Titan is when brightest he hath shone,   20
Why should'st thou now shut up thy blessed light
    and sdeign to look on thy Endymion?
Perhaps the heavens me thus despight have done
Because I durst compare thee with their sun.

"If dreary sighs, the tempests of my breast,
    or streams of tears from floods of weeping eyes,
If downcast looks with darksome clouds oppress'd,
    or words which with sad accents fall and rise,
If these nor her nor you to pity move,
There's neither help in you nor hope in love.   30

"O fair'st that lives, yet most unkindest maid,
    O whilom thou the joy of all my flock,
Why have thine eyes these eyes of mine betray'd
    unto thy heart more hard then flinty rock,
And lastly thus depriv'd me of their sight
From whom my love derives both life and light?

"Those dapper ditties penn'd unto her praise
    and those sweet strains of tuneful pastoral
She scorneth as the lourdayn's clownish lays
    and recketh as the rustic madrigal.   40
Her lips prophane Idea's sacred name
And sdeign to read the annals of her fame.

"Those gorgeous garlands and those goodly flowers
    wherewith I crown'd her tresses in the prime
She most abhors, and shuns those pleasant bowers
    made to disport her in the summertime;
She hates the sports and pastimes I invent
And, as the toad, flies all my merriment.

"With holy verses heryed I her glove
    and dew'd her cheeks with fountains of my tears,   50
And carol'd her full many a lay of love,
    twisting sweet roses in her golden hairs.
Her wand'ring sheep full safely have I kept
And watch'd her flock full oft when she hath slept.

"Oenon never upon Ida hill
    so oft hath call'd on Alexander's name
As hath poor Rowland with an angel's quill
    erected trophies of Idea's fame;
Yet that false shepherd, Oenon, fled from thee;
I follow her that ever flies from me.   60

"There's not a grove that wonders not my wo;
    there's not a river weeps not at my tale;
I hear the echoes, wand'ring to and fro,
    resound my grief in every hill and dale;
The beasts in field with many a woful groan,
The birds in air help to express my moan.

"Where been those lines, the heralds of my heart,
    my plaints, my tears, my vows, my sighs, my prayers?
O what availeth faith, or what my arts?
    O love, O hope, quite turn'd into despairs!   70
She stops her ears as adder to the charms
And lets me lie and languish in my harms.

"All is agone, such is my endless grief,
    and my mishaps amended naught with moan;
I see the heavens will yield me no relief;
    what helpeth care when cure is past and gone?
And tears, I see, do me avail no good,
But as great show'rs increase the rising flood."

With folded arms, thus hanging down his head,
    he gave a groan as though his heart had broke,   80
Then, looking pale and wan as he were dead,
    he fetch'd a sigh but never a word he spoke.
For now his heart wax'd cold as any stone,
Was never man alive so wobegone.

With that, fair Cynthia stoops her glittering veil
    and dives adown into the ocean flood;
The eastern brow which erst was wan and pale
    now in the dawning blusheth red as blood;
The whistling lark, ymounted on her wings,
To the gray morrow her good morrow sings.   90

When this poor shepherd, Rowland of the Rock,
  whose fainting legs his body scarce upheld,
Each shepheard now returning to his flock,

alone poor Rowland fled the pleasant field,
And in his cote got to a vechy bed;
Was never man alive so hard bested.

FROM IDEA'S MIRROR. AMOURS IN QUARTORZAINS (1594)

To the Dear Child of the Muses and His Ever Kind Mecaenas, Master Anthony Cooke, Esquire

Vouchsafe to grace these rude, unpolish'd rimes,
Which long, dear friend, have slept in sable night
And, come abroad now in these glorious times,
Can hardly brook the pureness of the light.
But sith you see their destiny is such
That in the world their fortune they must try,
Perhaps they better shall abide the tuch,
Wearing your name their gracious livery.
Yet these mine own; I wrong not other men,   10
Nor traffique further then this happy clime,
Nor filch from Portes' nor from Petrarch's pen—
A fault too common in this latter time.
    Divine Sir Philip, I avouch thy writ:
    I am no pickpurse of another's wit.

                    Yours devoted,
                        M[ichael] Drayton

AMOUR 1

Read here, sweet maid, the story of my wo,
The dreary abstracts of my endless cares,
With my live's sorrow enterlined so,
Smok'd with my sighs and blotted with my tears;
The sad memorials of my miseries
Penn'd in the grief of mine afflicted ghost,
My live's complaint in doleful elegies,
With so pure love as time could never boast.
Receive the incense which I offer here,
By my strong faith ascending to thy fame,   10
My zeal, my hopes, my vows, my praise, my prayer,
My soul's oblations to thy sacred name;
    Which name my muse to highest heaven shall raise
    By chaste desire, true love, and virtue's praise.

AMOUR 7

Stay, stay, sweet Time! Behold, or ere thou pass
From world to world, thou long hast sought to see
That wonder now wherein all wonders be,
Where heaven beholds her in a mortal glass.
Nay, look thee, Time, in this celestial glass,
And thy youth past in this fair mirror see;
Behold world's Beauty in her infancy,
What she was then and thou or ere she was.
Now pass on, Time, to after-worlds tell this:
Tell truly, Time, what in thy time hath been,   10

That they may tell more worlds what Time hath seen,
And heaven may joy to think on past worlds' bliss.
    Here make a period, Time, and say for me,
    "She was, the like that never was nor never more
        shall be."

AMOUR 21

Letters and lines, we see, are soon defaced;
Mettles do waste and fret with cankers' rust;
The diamond shall once consume to dust,
And freshest colors with foul stains disgraced.
Paper and ink can paint but naked words;
To write with blood of force offends the sight,
And if with tears I find them all too light,
And sighs and signs a silly hope affords,
O sweetest shadow, how thou serv'st my turn,
Which still shalt be as long as there is sun,   10
Nor, whilst the world is, never shall be done
Whilst moon shall shine by night or any fire shall burn,
    That everything whence shadow doth proceed
    May in his shadow my love's story read.

AMOUR 44

My heart the anvil where my thoughts do beat,
My words the hammers fashioning my desires,
My breast the forge including all the heat,
Love is the fuel which maintains the fire.
My sighs the bellows which the flame increaseth,
Filling mine ears with noise and nightly groaning;
Toiling with pain, my labor never ceaseth,
In grievous passions my woes still bemoaning.
Mine eyes with tears against the fire striving,
With scorching gleed my heart to cinders turneth,   10
But with those drops the coals again reviving,
Still more and more unto my torment burneth.
    With Sisyphus thus do I roll the stone
    And turn the wheel with damned Ixion.

AMOUR 45

Black, pitchy Night, companion of my wo,
The inn of care, the nurse of dreary sorrow,
Why length'nest thou thy darkest hours so,
Still to prolong my long-time-look'd-for morrow?
Thou sable shadow, image of dispair,
Portrait of hell, the air's black mourning weed,
Recorder of revenge, remembrancer of care,
The shadow and the veil of every sinful deed;
Death like to thee, so live thou still in death,

The grave of joy, prison of day's delight,   10
Let heavens withdraw their sweet, ambrosian breath,
Nor moon nor stars lend thee their shining light.
  For thou alone renew'st that old desire
  Which still torments me in day's burning fire.

[The following sonnets are printed from the last major
revision of *Idea*, in the 1619 *Poems*.]

IDEA. IN SIXTY-THREE SONNETS

TO THE READER OF THESE SONNETS

Into these loves who but for passion looks,
At this first sight here let him lay them by
And seek elsewhere, in turning other books
Which better may his labor satisfy.
No far-fetch'd sigh shall ever wound my breast;
Love from mine eye a tear shall never wring,
Nor in "ah-me's" my whining sonnets dress'd.
A libertine, fantasticly I sing.
My verse is the true image of my mind,
Ever in motion, still desiring change;   10
And as thus to variety inclin'd,
So in all humors sportively I range.
  My muse is rightly of the English strain
  That cannot long one fashion intertain.

6

How many paltry, foolish, painted things
That now in coaches trouble ev'ry street
Shall be forgotten, whom no poet sings,
Ere they be well wrapp'd in their winding-sheet!
Where I to thee eternity shall give
When nothing else remaineth of these days,
And queens hereafter shall be glad to live
Upon the alms of thy superfluous praise.
Virgins and matrons, reading these my rimes,
Shall be so much delighted with thy story   10
That they shall grieve they liv'd not in these times
To have seen thee, their sex's only glory.
  So shalt thou fly above the vulgar throng
  Still to survive in my immortal song.

8

There's nothing grieves me but that age should haste
That in my days I may not see thee old,
That where those two clear sparkling eyes are plac'd
Only two loopholes then I might behold;
That lovely, arched, ivory, polish'd brow
Defac'd with wrinkles that I might but see;
Thy dainty hair, so curl'd and crisped now,
Like grizzled moss upon some aged tree;
Thy cheek, now flush with roses, sunk and lean;
Thy lips with age as any wafer thin;   10
Thy pearly teeth out of thy head so clean
That when thou feed'st, thy nose shall touch thy chin.

These lines that now [thou] scorn'st, which should
    delight thee,
  Then would I make thee read but to despight thee.

20

An evil spirit, your beauty haunts me still,
Wherewith, alas, I have been long possess'd,
Which ceaseth not to tempt me to each ill
Nor gives me once but one poor minute's rest.
In me it speaks whether I sleep or wake,
And when by means to drive it out I try,
With greater torments then it me doth take
And tortures me in most extremity.
Before my face it lays down my despairs
And hastes me on unto a sudden death,   10
Now tempting me to drown myself in tears,
And then in sighing to give up my breath.
  Thus am I still provok'd to every evil
  By this good-wicked spirit, sweet angel-devil.

50

As in some countries, far remote from hence,
The wretched creature destined to die,
Having the judgment due to his offense,
By surgeons begg'd their art on him to try,
Which on the living work without remorse,
First make incision on each mast'ring vein,
Then stanch the bleeding, then transpierce the corse,
And with their balms recure the wounds again,
Then poison, and with physic him restore,
Not that they fear the hopeless man to kill,   10
But their experience to increase the more:
Ev'n so my mistress works upon my ill,
  By curing me and killing me each hour
  Only to shew her beauty's sov'reign pow'r.

61

Since there's no help, come, let us kiss and part.
Nay, I have done, you get no more of me,
And I am glad, yea glad with all my heart
That thus so cleanly I myself can free;
Shake hands forever, cancel all our vows,
And when we meet at any time again
Be it not seen in either of our brows
That we one jot of former love retain.
Now at the last gasp of Love's latest breath,
When, his pulse failing, Passion speechless lies,   10
When Faith is kneeling by his bed of death
And Innocence is closing up his eyes,
  Now if thou would'st, when all have given him over,
  From death to life thou might'st him yet recover.

63

Truce, gentle love, a parley now I crave!
Methinks 'tis long since first these wars begun,

Nor thou, nor I, the better yet can have;
Bad is the match where neither party won.
I offer free conditions of fair peace:
My heart for hostage that it shall remain,
Discharge our forces, here let malice cease,
So for my pledge thou give me pledge again.

Or if no thing but death will serve thy turn,
Still thirsting for subversion of my state,   10
Do what thou canst—raze, massacre, and burn;
Let the world see the utmost of thy hate.
  I send defiance, since, if overthrown,
  Thou vanquishing, the conquest is mine own.

FROM ENDYMION AND PHOEBE (1595)

In Ionia whence sprang old poets' fame,
From whom that sea did first derive her name,
The blessed bed whereon the muses lay,
Beauty of Greece, the pride of Asia,
Whence Archelaus, whom times historify,
First unto Athens brought philosophy,
In this fair region, on a goodly plain,
Stretching her bounds unto the bord'ring main,
The mountain Latmos overlooks the sea,
Smiling to see the ocean billows play—   10
Latmos, where young Endymion us'd to keep
His fairest flock of silver-fleeced sheep.
To whom Silvanus often would resort
At barley-break to see the satyrs sport,
And when rude Pan his tab'ret list to sound
To see the fair nymphs foot it in a round
Under the trees which on this mountain grew.
As yet the like Arabia never knew,
For all the pleasures Nature could devise,
Within this plot she did imparadise;   20
And great Diana, of her special grace,
With vestal rites had hallowed all the place.
Upon this mount there stood a stately grove
Whose reaching arms to clip the welkin strove,
Of tufted cedars and the branching pine,
Whose bushy tops themselves do so intwine
As seem'd, when Nature first this work begun,
She then conspir'd against the piercing sun,
Under whose covert (thus divinely made)
Phoebus' green laurel florish'd in the shade.   30
Fair Venus' myrtle, Mars his warlike fir,
Minerva's olive, and the weeping myrrh,
The patient palm which thrives in spite of hate,
The poplar to Alcides consecrate,
Which Nature in such order had disposed
And therewithal these goodly walks inclosed
As serv'd for hangings and rich tapestry
To beautify this stately gallery;
Imbraud'ring these in curious trails along
The clust'red grapes, the golden citrons hung.   40
More glorious then the precious fruit were these
Kept by the dragon in Hesperides,
Or gorgious arras in rich colors wrought
With silk from Africk or from Indie brought.
Out of this soil sweet, bubbling fountains crept

As though for joy the senseless stones had wept,
With straying channels dancing sundry ways,
With often turns like to a curious maze,
Which, breaking forth, the tender grass bedewed,
Whose silver sand with orient pearl was strewed,   50
Shadowed with roses and sweet eglantine
Dipping their sprays into this crystalline
From which the birds the purple berries pruned
And to their loves their small recorders tuned.
The nightingale, woods' herald of the spring,
The whistling woosel, mavis caroling,
Tuning their trebles to the waters' fall,
Which made the musique more angelical,
Whilst gentle Zephyr, murmuring among,
Kept time and bare the burthen to the song.   60
About whose brims, refresh'd with dainty showers,
Grew amaranthus and sweet gilliflowers,
The marigold, Phoebus' beloved friend,
The moly, which from sorcery doth defend,
Violet, carnation, balm, and cassia,
Idea's primrose, coronet of May.
Above this grove a gentle, fair ascent
Which by degrees of milk-white marble went;
Upon the top, a paradise was found
With which Nature this miracle had crown'd,   70
Empal'd with rocks of rarest precious stone
Which, like the flames of Aetna, brightly shone,
And serv'd as lanthorns furnished with light
To guide the wand'ring passengers by night,
For which, fair Phoebe, sliding from her sphere,
Used ofttimes to come and sport her there,
And from the azure, starry-painted sky
Embalm'd the banks with precious lunary,
That now her Menalus she quite forsook
And unto Latmos wholly her betook,   80
And in this place her pleasure us'd to take,
And all was for her sweet Endymion's sake—
Endymion, the lovely shepherds' boy,
Endymion, great Phoebe's only joy,
Endymion, in whose pure-shining eyes
The naked fairies danc'd the hay-de-guise.
The shag-hair'd satyrs' mountain-climbing race
Have been made tame by gazing in his face;
For this boy's love the water-nymphs have wept,
Stealing ofttimes to kiss him whilst he slept,   90

And tasting once the nectar of his breath,
Surfet with sweet and languish unto death;
And Jove, ofttimes bent to lascivious sport
And coming where Endymion did resort,
Hath courted him, inflamed with desire,
Thinking some nymph was cloth'd in boy's attire;
And oftentimes the simple rural swains,
Beholding him in crossing o'er the plains,
Imagined Apollo from above
Put on this shape to win some maiden's love.   100
This shepherd Phoebe ever did behold,
Whose love already had her thoughts controll'd;
From Latmos' top (her stately throne) she rose,
And to Endymion down beneath she goes. . . .

   Thus came she where her love Endymion lay,
Who with sweet carols sang the night away,
And, as it is the shepherds' usual trade,
Oft on his pipe a roundelay he play'd.
As meek he was as any lamb might be,
Nor never liv'd a fairer youth then he.   110
His dainty hand the snow itself did stain
Or her to whom Jove show'r'd in golden rain,
From whose sweet palm the liquid pearl did swell
Pure as the drops of Aganippa's well,
Clear as the liquor which fair Hebe spilt;
His sheephook silver, damask'd all with gilt,
The staff itself of snowy ivory
Studded with curral, tipp'd with ebony;
His tresses of the raven's shining black,
Straggling in curls along his manly back;   120
The balls which Nature in his eyes had set,
Like diamonds inclosing globes of jet,
Which sparkled from their milky lids outright
Like fair Orion's heaven-adorning light. . . .
"Sweet boy," quod she, "take what thy heart can wish!
When thou dost angle, would I were a fish;
When thou art sporting by the silver brooks,
Put in thy hand—thou need'st no other hooks.
Hard-hearted boy, Endymion, look on me!
Nothing on earth I hold too dear for thee.   130
I am a nymph and not of humain blood,
Begot by Pan on Isis' sacred flood;
When I was born, upon that very day
Phoebus was seen the reveler to play;
In Jove's high house the gods assembled all,
And Juno held her sumptuous festival;
Oceanus that hour was dancing spied,
And Tithon seen to frolic with his bride;
The halcyons that season sweetly sang,
And all the shores with shouting sea-nymphs rang;   140
And on that day, my birth to memorize,
The shepherds hold a solemn sacrifice. . . .
I'll lay thee on the swan's soft, downy plume,
And all the wind shall gently breath perfume;
I'll plat thy locks with many a curious pleat

And chafe thy temples with a sacred heat;
The muses still shall keep thee company
And lull thee with inchanting harmony.
If not all these, yet let my virtues move thee;
A chaster nymph, Endymion, cannot love thee."   150
   But he imagin'd she some nymph had been
Because she was appareled in green,
Or happily some of fair Flora's train
Which oft did use to sport upon the plain.
He tells her he was Phoebe's servant sworn,
And oft in hunting had her quiver borne,
And that to her virginity he vowed
Which in no hand by Venus was allowed.
Then unto her a catalogue recites
Of Phoebe's statutes and her hallowed rites,   160
And of the grievous penalty inflicted
On such as her chaste laws had interdicted.
Now he requests that she would stand aside,
Because the fish her shadow had espied;
Then he intreats her that she would be gone
And at this time to let him be alone. . . .

[Repulsed in all her advances, Phoebe at length returns
to Latmos, leaving Endymion to bewail his apparently
hopeless love.]

   Now fast by Latmos, near unto a grove
Which by the mount was shadowed from above,
Upon a bank Endymion sat by night,
To whom fair Phoebe lent her friendly light,   170
And sith his flocks were laid them down to rest,
Thus gives his sorrows passage from his breast:
"Sweet leaves," quod he, "which with the air do tremble,
O how your motions do my thoughts resemble!
With that mild breath, by which [you] only move,
Whisper my words in silence to my love;
Convey my sighs, sweet civet-breathing air,
In doleful accents to my heavenly fair;
You murmuring springs, like doleful instruments,
Upon your gravel sound my sad laments,   180
And in your silent bubbling, as you go,
Consort yourselves like music to my wo."
And lifting now his sad and heavy eyes
Up towards the beauty of the burnish'd skies,
"Bright lamps," quod he, "the glorious welkin bears,
Which clip about the planets' wand'ring spheres
And in your circled maze do ever roll,
Dancing about the never-moving pole,
Sweet nymph, which in fair Elice dost shine,
Whom thy surpassing beauty made divine,   190
Now in the artic constellation
Smile, sweet Callisto, on Endymion. . . .
And you great wand'ring lights, if from your spheres
You have regard unto a sheepherd's tears,
Or, as men say, if over earthly things
You only rule as potentates and kings,

Unto my love's event, sweet stars, direct
Your kindest revolution and aspect,
And bend your clear eyes from your thrones above
Upon Endymion pining thus in love. . . ."   200

[The next day, descending from Latmos, Phoebe finds
Endymion asleep, and so wasted with melancholy that
his "vital spirits" and his "parts organical" have been
exhausted. With soft caresses she breathes into his soul
"the fiery nature of a heavenly muse" and gently awakens
him. He reacts so violently with amorous passion that,
mistaking the "queen of chastity" for a mere nymph, he
urges her to ease his torments. But Phoebe, jealous of
her honor, repeats the familiar warnings of "men's subtleties and natural deceits," at which he makes a mighty
vow of constancy.]

She, hearing this, thought time that she reveal'd
That kind affection which she long conceal'd,
Determineth to make her true love known
Which she had borne unto Endymion.
"I am no huntress, nor no nymph," quoth she,
"As thou perhaps imagin'st me to be.
I am great Phoebe, Latmos' sacred queen,
Who from the skies have hether pass'd unseen,
And by thy chaste love hether was I led,
Where full three years thy fair flock have I fed   210
Upon these mountains and these fertile plains
And crown'd thee king of all the sheepherds' swains;
Nor wanton nor lascivious is my love,
Nor never lust my chaste thoughts once could move,
But sith thou thus hast offer'd at my shrine
And of the gods hast held me most divine,
Mine altars thou with sacrifice hast stor'd,
And in my temples hast my name ador'd,
And, of all other, most hast honor'd me,
Great Phoebe's glory thou alone shalt see."   220
    This spake, she putteth on her brave attire,
As being burnish'd in her brother's fire,
Purer then that celestial, shining flame
Wherein great Jove unto his leman came,
Which quickly had his pale cheeks overspread
And tincted with a lovely, blushing red;
Which, whilst her brother Titan for a space
Withdrew himself to give his sister place.
She now is dark'ned to all creatures' eyes,
Whilst in the shadow of the earth she lies,   230
For that the earth, of nature cold and dry,
A very chaos of obscurity
Whose globe exceeds her compass by degrees
Fixed upon her superficies,
When in his shadow she doth hap to fall
Doth cause her darkness to be general.
    Thus whilst he laid his head upon her lap
She in a fiery mantle doth him wrap
And carries him up from this lumpish mold

Into the skies, whereas he might behold   240
The earth in perfect roundness of a ball
Exceeding globes most artificial,
Which in a fixed point Nature disposed
And with the sundry elements inclosed,
Which as the center permanent doth stay
Whenas the skies in their diurnal sway
Strongly maintain the ever-turning course,
Forced alone by their first mover source,
Where he beholds the airy regions
Whereas the clouds and strange impressions   250
Maintain'd by coldness often do appear
And by the highest region of the air
Unto the clearest element of fire
Which to her silver footstool doth aspire;
Then doth she mount him up into her sphere,
Imparting heavenly secrets to him there,
Where, light'ned by her shining beams, he sees
The powerful planets all in their degrees,
Their sundry revolutions in the skies,
And by their working how they sympathize,   260
All in their circles severally prefix'd
And in due distance each with other mix'd;
The mansions which they hold in their estate,
Of which by nature they participate,
And how those signs their several places take
Within the compass of the zodiac. . . .
And now to him her greatest power she lent
To lift him to the starry firmament. . . .
And having imp'd the wings of his desire
And kindled him with this celestial fire,   270
She sets him down and, vanishing his sight,
Leaves him inwrapped in this true delight.
Now wheresoever he his fair flock fed,
The muses still Endymion followed;
His sheep as white as swans or driven snow,
Which beautified the soil with such a show
As where he folded in the darkest night
There never needed any other light;
If that he hung'red and desired meat,
The bees would bring him honey for to eat,   280
Yet from his lips would not depart away
Till they were loaden with ambrosia;
And if he thirsted, often there was seen
A bubbling fountain spring out of the green,
With crystal liquor fill'd unto the brim,
Which did present her liquid store to him;
If he would hunt, the fair nymphs at his will
With bows and quivers would attend him still,
And whatsoever he desir'd to have,
That he obtain'd if he the same would crave.   290
    And now at length the joyful time drew on
She meant to honor her Endymion
And glorify him on that stately mount

Whereof the goddess made so great account.
She sends Jove's winged herald to the woods,
The neighbor fountains, and the bord'ring floods,
Charging the nymphs which did inhabit there
Upon a day appointed to appear
And to attend her sacred majesty
In all their pomp and great solemnity. . . .   300

[Phoebe makes the most elaborate preparations: assembling the satyrs, the oreads, the hamadryads, the
dryads ("on dappled stags"), she appropriately bedecks
Endymion for the rite.]

Upon a chariot was Endymion laid,
In snowy tissue gorgiously array'd,
Of precious ivory covered o'er with lawn,
Which by four stately unicorns was drawn.
Of ropes of orient pearl their traces were,
Pure as the path which doth in heaven appear,
With rarest flowers inchas'd and overspread,
Which serv'd as curtains to this glorious bed,
Whose seat of crystal in the sunbeams shone
Like thunder-breathing Jove's celestial throne;   310
Upon his head a coronet install'd
Of one intire and mighty emerald,
With richest bracelets on his lily wrists
Of heliotropium link'd with golden twists,
A bevy of fair swans which, flying over,
With their large wings him from the sun do cover
And, easily wafting as he went along,
Do lull him still with their inchanting song,
Whilst all the nymphs on solemn instruments
Sound dainty music to their sweet laments.   320

[Phoebe herself appears in radiant glory, attended by
"twenty and eight great gorgious lamps," protected by
Astraea, and followed by the nine muses "crowned with
triumphant laurel boughs." After a long digression on the
sacred number nine—with explanations of the corresponding heavenly hierarchies, of famous constellations,
of musical harmonies, and even of the Christian Trinity—
Drayton returns to his narrative.]

  But to my tale I must return again:
Phoebe to Latmos thus convey'd her swain
Under a bushy laurel's pleasing shade,
Amongst whose boughs the birds sweet music made,
Whose fragrant, branch-imbosted canopy
Was never pierc'd with Phoebus' burning eye;
Yet never could this paradise want light,
Elumin'd still with Phoebe's glorious sight.
She laid Endymion on a grassy bed,

With sommer's arras richly overspread,   330
Where from her sacred mansion next above
She might descend and sport her with her love,
Which thirty years the sheepherd safely kept,
Who in her bosom soft and soundly slept;
Yet as a dream he thought the time not long,
Remaining ever beautiful and young,
And what in vision there to him befell
My weary muse some other time shall tell.

  Dear Colin, let my muse excused be
Which rudely thus presumes to sing by thee,   340
Although her strains be harsh, untun'd, and ill,
Nor can attain to thy divinest skill.
  And thou, the sweet Museus of these times,
Pardon my rugged and unfiled rimes,
Whose scarce invention is too mean and base
When Delia's glorious muse doth come in place.
  And thou, my Goldey, which in sommer days
Hast feasted us with merry roundelays,
And when my muse scarce able was to fly
Didst imp her wings with thy sweet poesy.   350
  And you, the heirs of ever-living fame,
The worthy titles of a poet's name,
Whose skill and rarest excellence is such
As spiteful Envy never yet durst touch,
To your protection I this poem send
Which from proud Momus may my lines defend.
  And if, sweet maid, thou deign'st to read this story
Wherein thine eyes may view thy virtue's glory,
Thou purest spark of Vesta's kindled fire,
Sweet nymph of Ancor, crown of my desire,   360
The plot which for their pleasure heaven devis'd
Where all the muses be imparadis'd,
Where thou dost live, there let all graces be,
Which want their grace if only wanting thee;
Let stormy winter never touch the clime,
But let it florish as in April's prime;
Let sullen night that soil ne'er overcloud,
But in thy presence let the earth be proud.
If ever Nature of her work might boast,
Of thy perfection she may glory most,   370
To whom fair Phoebe hath her bow resign'd,
Whose excellence doth live in thee refin'd,
And that thy praise Time never should impair
Hath made my heart thy never-moving sphere.
Then if my muse give life unto thy fame,
Thy virtues be the causers of the same,
And from thy tomb some oracle shall rise
To whom all pens shall yearly sacrifice.

from MORTIMERIADOS. THE LAMENTABLE CIVIL WARS OF EDWARD THE SECOND AND THE BARONS (1596)

To the Excellent and Most Accomplish'd Lady, Lucy, Countess of Bedford

Rarest of ladies, all of all I have,
Anchor of my poor, tempest-beaten state,
Which givest life to that life Nature gave
And to thyself dost only consecrate,
   My hope's true goddess, guider of my fate,
Vouchsafe to grace what here to light is brought,
Begot by thy sweet hand, born of my thought.

And though I sing of this tumultuous rage,
Still painting passions in these tragedies,
Thy milder looks this fury can assuage,   10
Such is the virtue of thy sacred eyes
   Which do contain a thousand purities,
And like themselves can make their object such
As doth th' elixar all things it doth touch. . . .

The Haringtons, whose house thy birth hath blest,
Adding such honor to their family,
And famous Bedfords' greatness still increas'd,
Raising the height of their nobility,
   That earldom's title more to dignify,
That virtue, lively pictur'd forth in thee,   20
May truly be discern'd what she should be.

And laurel-crowned Sidney, Nature's pride,
Whom heaven to earth but only shew'd this good,
Betwixt the world and thee did then devide
His fame and virtues, which both equal stood;
   The world his fame, to thee of her own blood
He gave his virtues, that in his own kind
His never-matched worth might be enshrin'd. . . .

And in despight of tyrannizing times
This hope, great lady, yet to thee is left: 30
Thy name shall live in steel-outduring rimes,
Still scorning age's sacraligious theft;
   What fame doth keep can never be bereft,
Nor can thy past-priz'd honor ever die
If lines can give thee immortality.

Leaving unto succeeding times to see
How much thy sacred gifts I did adore,
What power thy virtues ever had in me,
And what thou wert compar'd with those before,
   Which shall in age thy youth again restore,   40
And still shall add more vigor to thy fame
Then earthly honors or a countess' name;

Proclaiming unto ages yet to come
Whilst Bedford liv'd what living Bedford was,
Enclosing thee in this immortal tomb,
More durable then letter-graven brass,
   To shew what thy great power could bring to pass,
And other hopes I utterly refuse,
And thou my hope, my lady, and my muse.

MORTIMERIADOS

The low'ring heaven had mask'd her in a cloud,
Dropping sad tears upon the sullen earth,
Bemoaning in her melancholy shroud
The angry stars which reign'd at Edward's birth,
   With whose beginning ended all our mirth:
Edward the Second, but the first of shame,
Scourge of the crown, eclipse of England's fame. . . .

The rageful fire which burn'd Carnarvon's breast,
Blown with revenge of Gaveston's disgrace,
Awakes the barons from their nightly rest   10
And maketh way to give the Spencers place,
   Whose friendship Edward only doth embrace,
By whose allurements he is fondly led
To leave his queen and fly his lawful bed.

This planet stirr'd up that tempestious blast
By which our fortune's anchorage was torn,
The storm wherewith our spring was first defac'd,
Whereby all hope unto the ground was borne;
   Hence came the grief, the tears, the cause to mourn;
This bred the blemish which her beauty stain'd,   20
Whose ugly scars to aftertimes remain'd.

In all this heat his greatness first began,
The serious subject of my sadder vein,
Great Mortimer, the wonder of a man
Whose fortunes here my muse must entertain,
   And from the grave his griefs must yet complain
To shew our vice nor virtues never die,
Though underground a thousand years we lie.

This gust first threw him on that blessed coast
Which never age discovered before;   30
This lucky chance drew all King Edward lost,
This shipwrack cast the prize upon his shore,
   And this all-drowning deluge gave him more;
From hence the sun of his good fortune shone,
The fatal step to Edward's fatal throne. . . .

And whilst this poor wife-widowed queen alone
In this dispairing passion pines away,
Beyond all hope, to all but heaven unknown
A little spark which yet in secret lay
   Breaks forth in flame and turns her night to day,   40
The woful winter of her sorrows cheering
Even as the world at the fair sun's appearing. . . .

Pale Jealousy, child of insatiate Love,
Of heart-sick thoughts with Melancholy bred,
A hell-tormenting fear no faith can move,
By discontent with deadly poison fed,
　　With heedless youth and error vainly led,
A mortal plague, a virtue-drowning flood,
A hellish fire not quenched but with blood.

The hate-swoll'n lords with fury set on fire,　　50
Whom Edward's wrongs to vengeance do provoke,
With Lancaster and Herford now conspire
No more to bear the Spencers' servile yoke;
　　The bonds of their allegiance they have broke,
Resolv'd with blood their liberty to buy,
To live with honor or with fame to die.

Amid this faction Mortimer doth enter,
The ghastly prologue to this tragic act,
His youth and courage boldly bids him venter
And tells him still how strongly he was back'd.　　60
　　Sinon persuades how Ilion might be sack'd,
The people still applauding in his ears
The fame and credit of the Mortimers. . . .

[THE DEATH OF EDWARD]

He on a lean, ill-favored beast is set,
Death upon Famine moralizing right;
His cheeks with tears, his head with rain bewet,
Night's very picture, wand'ring still by night.
　　When he would sleep, like dreams they him affright,
His food torment, his drink a poisoned bane,
No other comfort but in deadly pain.　　70

And yet, because they fear to have him known,
They shave away his princely tressed hair,
And now become not worth a hair of 's own,
Body and fortune now be equal bare.
　　Thus void of wealth, O were he void of care,
But O, our joys are shadows and deceive us,
But cares, even to our deaths, do never leave us.

A silly molehill is his kingly chair,
With puddle water must he now be dress'd,
And his perfume the lothsome fenny air,　　80
An iron skull a bason fitting best,
　　A bloody workman suiting with the rest,
His lothed eyes within this filthy glass
Truly behold how much deform'd he was.

The drops which from his eyes' abundance fall,
A pool of tears still rising by this rain,
Even fighting with the water and withal
A circled compass makes it to retain,
　　Billow'd with sighs like to a little main,
Water with tears contending whether should　　90
Make water warm or make the warm tears cold.

Vile traitors, hold off your unhallowed hands!
The cruel'st beast the lion's presence fears,
And can you keep your sovereign then in bands?
How can your eyes behold th' anointed's tears?
　　Are not your hearts even pierced through your ears?
The mind is free, whate'er afflict the man,
A king's a king, do Fortune what she can. . . .

To Berkeley thus they lead this wretched king,
The place of horror which they had forethought.　　100
O heavens, why suffer you so vile a thing,
And can behold this murther to be wrought,
　　But that your ways are all with judgment frought?
Now ent'rest thou, poor Edward, to thy hell;
Thus take thy leave and bid the world farewell.

O Berkeley, thou which hast been famous long,
Still let thy walls shriek out a deadly sound
And still complain thee of thy grievous wrong;
Preserve the figure of King Edward's wound
　　And keep their wretched footsteps on the ground,　　110
That yet some power again may give them breath,
And thou again mayst curse them both to death.

The croaking raven's hideous voice he hears
Which through the castle sounds with deadly yells,
Imprinting strange, imaginary fears,
The heavy echoes like to passing bells,
　　Chiming far off his doleful burying knells;
The jarging casements which the fierce wind drives
Puts him in mind of fetters, chains, and gyves.

By silent night the ugly, shrieking owls　　120
Like dreadful spirits with terror do torment him;
The envious dog, angry with darkness, howls
Like messengers from damned ghosts were sent him,
　　Or with hell's noisome terror to present him
Under his roof the buzzing night-crow sings,
Clapping his window with her fatal wings.

Death still prefigur'd in his fearful dreams
Of raging fiends and goblins that he meets,
Of falling down from steep rocks into streams,
Of tombs, of graves, of pits, of winding sheets,　　130
　　Of strange temptations and seducing sprits;
And with his cry awak'd, calling for aid,
His hollow voice doth make himself afraid.

Oft in his sleep he sees the queen to fly him,
Stern Mortimer pursue him with his sword,
His son in sight, yet dares he not come nigh him,
To whom he calls, who answereth not a word;
　　And like a monster wond'red and abhorr'd,
Widows and orphans following him with cries,
Stabbing his heart, and scratching out his eyes.　　140

Next comes the vision of his bloody reign,
Masking along with Lancaster's stern ghost,
Of eight and twenty barons hang'd and slain,
Attended with the rueful, mangled host,
  At Burton and at Borough battle lost,
Threat'ning with frowns and trembling every lim,
With thousand thousand curses cursing him. . . .

Thus, on his careful cabin falling down,
Enter the actors of his tragedy,
Opening the doors which made a hollow soun   150
As they had howl'd against their cruelty,
  Or of his pain as they would prophesy,
To whom, as one which died before his death,
He yet complains whilst pain might lend him breath.

"O be not authors of so vile an act
To bring my blood on your posterity,
That babes even yet unborn do curse the fact;
I am a king, though king of misery,
  I am your king, though wanting majesty,
But he who is the cause of all this teen   160
Is cruel March, the champion of the queen.

"He hath my crown, he hath my son, my wife,
And in my throne triumpheth in my fall.
Is 't not inough but he will have my life?
But more, I fear that yet this is not all:
  I think my soul to judgment he will call,
And in my death his rage yet shall not die,
But persecute me so immortally.

"And for you deadly hate me, let me live
For that advantage angry heaven hath left;   170
Fortune hath taken all that she did give,
Yet that revenge should not be quite bereft,
  She leaves behind this remnant of her theft:
That Misery should find that only I
Am far more wretched then is Misery."

Betwixt two beds these devils straight enclos'd him,
Thus done, uncovering of his secret part,
When for his death they fitly had dispos'd him,
With burning iron thrust him to the heart.
  O pain beyond all pain how much thou art!   180
Which words, as words, may verbally confess
But never pen precisely could express! . . .

FROM ENGLAND'S HEROICAL EPISTLES (1598)

HENRY HOWARD, EARL OF SURREY, TO GERALDINE

THE ARGUMENT

  Henry Howard, that true noble Earl of Surrey and
excellent poet, falling in love with Geraldine, descended
of the noble family of the Fitzgeralds of Ireland, a fair
and modest lady and one of the honorable maids to
Queen Katherine Dowager, eternizeth her praises in
many excellent poems, of rare and sundry inventions,
and after some few years, being determined to see that
famous Italy, the source and Helicon of all excellent arts,
first visiteth that renowned Florence, from whence the
Geralds challenge their descent, from the ancient family
of the Geraldi. There in honor of his mistress he advanceth
her picture, and challengeth to maintain her beauty by
deeds of arms against all that durst appear in the lists,
where after the proof of his brave and incomparable
valor, whose arm crowned her beauty with eternal
memory, he writeth this epistle to his dearest mistress.

From learned Florence, long time rich in fame,
From whence thy race, thy noble grandsires, came
To famous England, that kind nurse of mine,
Thy Surrey sends to heavenly Geraldine;
Yet let not Thuscan think I do her wrong,
That I from thence write in my native tongue,

That in these harsh-tun'd cadences I sing,
Sitting so near the muses' sacred spring;
But rather think herself adorn'd thereby,
That England reads the praise of Italy.   10
Though to the Thuscans I the smoothness grant,
Our dialect no majesty doth want
To set thy praises in as high a key
As France, or Spain, or Germany, or they.
  That day I quit the foreland of fair Kent,
And that my ship her course for Flanders bent,
Yet think I with how many a heavy look
My leave of England and of thee I took,
And did intreat the tide, if it might be,
But to convey me one sigh back to thee.   20
Up to the deck a billow lightly skips,
Taking my sigh, and down again it slips;
Into the gulf itself it headlong throws,
And as a post to England-ward it goes.
As I sit wond'ring how the rough seas stirr'd,
I might far off perceive a little bird,
Which, as she fain from shore to shore would fly,
Hath lost herself in the broad vasty sky,
Her feeble wing beginning to deceive her,
The seas of life still gaping to bereave her;   30
Unto the ship she makes, which she discovers,
And there, poor fool, a while for refuge hovers.
And when at length her flagging pineon fails,

Panting she hangs upon the rattling sails,
And being forc'd to loose her hold with pain,
Yet beaten off, she straight lights on again,
And toss'd with flaws, with storms, with wind, with
    weather,
Yet still departing thence, still turneth thither;
Now with the poop, now with the prow doth bear,
Now on this side, now that, now here, now there.   40
Methinks these storms should be my sad depart;
The silly helpless bird is my poor heart,
The ship to which for succor it repairs,
That is yourself, regardless of my cares.
Of every surge doth fall, or wave doth rise,
To some one thing I sit and moralize.
    When for thy love I left the Belgic shore,
Divine Erasmus and our famous More,
Whose happy presence gave me such delight
As made a minute of a winter's night,   50
With whom a while I stay'd at Rotterdame,
Now so renowned by Erasmus' name;
Yet every hour did seem a world of time
Till I had seen that soul-reviving clime,
And thought the foggy Netherlands unfit,
A wat'ry soil to clog a fiery wit.
And as that wealthy Germany I pass'd,
Coming unto the emperor's court at last,
Great learn'd Agrippa, so profound in art,
Who the infernal secrets doth impart,   60
When of thy health I did desire to know,
Me in a glass my Geraldine did shew,
Sick in thy bed and, for thou couldst not sleep,
By a watch taper set thy light to keep.
I do remember thou didst read that ode
Sent back whilst I in Thanet made abode,
Whereas thou cam'st unto the word of love,
Even in thine eyes I saw how passion strove.
That snowy lawn which covered thy bed
Methought look'd white, to see thy cheek look red;   70
Thy rosy cheek, oft changing in my sight,
Yet still was red, to see the lawn so white;
The little taper which should give thee light
Methought wax'd dim, to see thy eye so bright;
Thine eye again supplies the taper's turn,
And with his beams doth make the taper burn;
The shrugging air about thy temples hurls
And wraps thy breath in little clouded curls,
And as it doth ascend, it straight doth cease it,
And as it sinks, it presently doth raise it.   80
Canst thou by sickness banish beauty so?
Which if put from thee knows not where to go,
To make her shift and for her succor seek
To every rivel'd face, each bankrupt cheek.
If health preserv'd, thou beauty still dost cherish,
If that neglected, beauty soon doth perish.
Care draws on care, wo comforts wo again,

Sorrow breeds sorrow, one grief brings forth twain;
If live or die, as thou dost so do I,
If live, I live, and if thou die, I die: 90
One heart, one love, one joy, one grief, one troth,
One good, one ill, one life, one death to both.
    If Howard's blood thou hold'st as but too vile,
Or not esteem'st of Norfolk's princely style,
If Scotland's coat no mark of fame can lend,
That lion plac'd in our bright silver bend
(Which as a trophy beautifies our shield
Since Scottish blood discolored Flodden Field,
When the proud Cheviot our brave ensign bare
As a rich jewel in her icy hair,   100
And did fair Bramston's neighboring valleys choke
With clouds of cannon's fire-disgorging smoke),
Or Surrey's earldom insufficient be
And not a dower so well contenting thee,
Yet am I one of great Apollo's heirs,
The sacred muses challenge me for theirs.
By princes my immortal lines are sung,
My flowing verses grac'd with every tongue;
The little children, when they learn to go,
By painful mothers daded to and fro,   110
Are taught my sug'red numbers to rehearse,
And have their sweet lips season'd with my verse.
    When heaven would strive to do the best she can,
And put an angel's spirit into a man,
Then all her power she in that work doth spend
When she a poet to the world doth send;
The difference rests betwixt the gods and us,
Allow'd by them is but distinguish'd thus:
They give men breath, men by their power are born;
That life they give, the poet doth adorn;   120
And from the world when they dissolve man's breath,
They in the world do give man life in death.
    When time shall turn those amber curls to gray,
My verse again shall gild and make them gay,
And trick them up in knotted curls anew,
And in the autumn give a summer's hue.
That sacred power that in my ink remains
Shall put fresh blood into thy wither'd veins,
And on thy red decay'd, thy whiteness dead,
Shall set a white more white, a red more red.   130
When thy dim sight thy glass cannot discry,
Thy crazed mirrhor cannot see thine eye,
My verse to tell what eye, what mirrhor, was,
Glass to thine eye, an eye unto thy glass,
Where both thy mirrhor and thine eye shall see
What once thou saw'st in that, that saw in thee,
And to them both shall tell the simple truth,
What that in pureness was, what thou in youth.
    If Florence once should lose her old renown,
As famous Athens, now a fisher town,   140
My lines for thee a Florence shall erect
Which great Apollo ever shall protect,

And with the numbers from my pen that falls
Bring marble mines to build again those walls.
Nor beauteous Stanhope, whom all tongues report
To be the glory of the English court,
Shall by our nation be so much admir'd,
If ever Surrey truly were inspir'd.
And famous Wyatt, who in numbers sings
To that inchanting Thracian harper's strings,   150
To whom Phoebus, the poets' god, did drink
A bowl of nectar fill'd unto the brink,
And sweet-tongu'd Bryan, whom the muses kept
And in his cradle rock'd him whilst he slept,
In sacred verses so divinely penn'd,
Upon thy praises ever shall attend.
  What time I came unto this famous town
And made the cause of my arrival known,
Great Medices a list for triumphs built;
Within the which, upon a tree of gilt,   160
With thousand sundry rare devices set,
I did erect thy lovely counterfet
To answer those Italian dames' desire,
Which daily came thy beauty to admire;
By which my lion, in his gaping jaws,
Holdeth my lance, and in his dreadful paws
Reacheth my gauntlet unto him that dare
A beauty with my Geraldine's compare.
Which when each manly valiant arm assays,
After so many brave triumphant days   170
The glorious prize upon my lance I bare,
By herald's voice proclaim'd to be thy share.
The shivered staves, here for thy beauty broke,
With fierce encounters pass'd at every shock,
When stormy courses answered cuff for cuff,
Denting proud beavers with the counter-buff,
Upon an altar burnt with holy flame,
And sacrific'd as ensence to thy fame;
Where, as the phoenix from her spiced fume
Renews herself in that she doth consume,   180
So from these sacred ashes live we both,
Even as that one Arabian wonder doth.
  When to my chamber I myself retire,
Burnt with the sparks that kindled all this fire,
Thinking of England, which my hope contains,
The happy ile where Geraldine remains,
Of Hunsdon, where those sweet celestial eyne
At first did pierce this tender breast of mine,
Of Hampton Court and Windsor, where abound
All pleasures that in paradise were found.   190
Near that fair castle is a little grove,
With hanging rocks all covered from above,
Which on the bank of lovely Thames doth stand,
Clipp'd by the water from the other land,
Whose bushy top doth bid the sun forbear
And checks those proud beams that would enter there;
Whose leaves still muttering as the air doth breathe,

With the sweet bubbling of the stream beneath,
Doth rock the senses, whilst the small birds sing,
Lulled asleep with gentle murmuring;   200
Where light-foot fairies sport at prison-base
(No doubt there is some power frequents the place),
There the soft poplar and smooth beech do bear
Our names together carved everywhere,
And Gordian knots do curiously entwine
The names of Henry and of Geraldine.
O, let this grove in that time yet to come
Be call'd the lovers' blest Elysium;
Whither my love was wonted to resort,
In summer's heat in those sweet shades to sport;   210
A thousand sundry names I have it given,
And call'd it beauty-hider, cover-heaven,
The roof where beauty her rich court doth keep,
Under whose compass all the stars do sleep.
There is one tree which now I call to mind,
Doth bear these verses carved in his rind:
When Geraldine shall sit in thy fair shade,
Fan her sweet tresses with perfumed air,
Let thy large boughs a canopy be made
To keep the sun from gazing on my fair;   220
And when thy spreading branched arms be sunk,
And thou no sap nor pith shalt more retain,
Ev'n from the dust of thy unwieldy trunk
I will renew thee, phoenix-like, again,
And from thy dry decayed root will bring
A new-born stem, another Aeson's spring.
  I find no cause, nor judge I reason why
My country should give place to Lombardy;
As goodly flowers on Thamisis do grow
As beautify the banks of wanton Po;   230
As many nymphs as haunt rich Arnus' strand,
By silver Sabrine tripping hand in hand;
Our shade's as sweet, though not to us so dear,
Because the sun hath greater power here;
This distant place but gives me greater wo;
Far off, my sighs the farther have to go.
Ah absence! why thus shouldst thou seem so long?
Or wherefore shouldst thou offer time such wrong,
Summer so soon should steal on winter's cold,
Or winter's blasts so soon make summer old?   240
Love did us both with one self arrow strike,
Our wounds both one, our cure should be the like,
Except thou hast found out some mean by art,
Some powerful med'cine to withdraw the dart;
But mine is fix'd, and absent's physic proved,
It sticks too fast, it cannot be removed.
  Adieu, adieu, from Florence when I go
By my next letters Geraldine shall know,
Which if good fortune shall my course direct,
From Venice by some messenger expect;   250
Till when, I leave thee to thy heart's desire:
By him that lives thy virtues to admire.

NOTES OF THE CHRONICLE HISTORY
From learned Florence, long time rich in fame.

Florence, a city of Thuscan, standing upon the River Arnus, celebrated by Dante, Petrarch, and other the most noble wits of Italy, was the original of the family out of which this Geraldine did spring, as Ireland the place of her birth, which is intimated by these verses of the Earl of Surrey's:

> From Thuscan came my lady's worthy race,
> Fair Florence was sometime her ancient seat,
> The western ile, whose pleasant shore doth face
> Wild Camber's cliffs, did give her lively heat.

Great learn'd Agrippa, so profound in art.

Cornelius Agrippa, a man in his time so famous for magic (which the books published by him concerning that argument do partly prove) as in this place needs no further remembrance. Howbeit, as those abstruse and gloomy arts are but illusions, so in the honor of so rare a gentleman as this earl (and therewithal so noble a poet, a quality by which his other titles receive their greatest luster) invention may make somewhat more bold with Agrippa above the barren truth.

That lion set in our bright silver bend.

The blazon of the Howards' honorable armor was *Gules between six crossless fitches a bend argent,* to which afterwards was added by atchievement, *In the canton point of the bend an escutcheon or, within the Scottish tressure a demi-lion rampant gules,* etc., as Master Camden, now Clarenceaulx, from authority noteth. Never shall time nor bitter envy be able to obscure the brightness of so great a victory as that for which this addition was obtained. The historian of Scotland George Buchanan reporteth that the Earl of Surrey gave for his badge a silver lion (which from antiquity belonged to the name) tearing in pieces *a lion prostrate gules,* and withal that this which he terms insolency was punished in him and his posterity, as if it were fatal to the conqueror to do his sovereign such loyal service as a thousand such severe censurers were never able to perform.

Since Scottish blood discolored Flodden Field.

The battle was fought at Bramstone near to Flodden Hill, being a part of the Cheviot, a mountain that exceedeth all the mountains in the north of England for bigness, in which the wilful perjury of James the Fifth was punished from heaven by the Earl of Surrey, being left by King Henry the Eight (then in France before Turwin) for the defence of his realm.

Nor beauteous Stanhope, whom all tongues report
To be the glory. etc.

Of the beauty of that lady, he himself testifies in an elegy which he writ of her refusing to dance with him, which he seemeth to allegorize under a lion and a wolf. As of himself he saith:

> A lion saw I late, as white as any snow.

And of her:

> I might perceive a wolf as white as whale's bone,
> A fairer beast, of fresher hue, beheld I never none,
> But that her looks were coy, and froward was her grace.

And famous Wyatt, who in numbers sings.

Sir Thomas Wyatt the elder, a most excellent poet, as his poems extant do witness, besides certain encomions written by the Earl of Surrey upon some of David's Psalms by him translated:

> What holy grave, what worthy sepulcher,
> To Wyatt's Psalms shall Christians purchase then?

And afterward upon his death the said earl writeth thus:

> What virtues rare were temp'red in thy breast?
> Honor that England such a jewel bred,
> And kiss the ground whereas thy corps did rest.

At Hunsdon where those sweet celestial eyne.

It is manifest by a sonnet written by this noble earl that the first time he beheld his lady was at Hunsdon:

> Hunsdon did first present her to mine eyne.

Which sonnet, being altogether a description of his love, I do alledge in divers places of this gloss as proofs of what I write.

Of Hampton Court and Windsor, where abound
All pleasures, etc.

That he injoyed the presence of his fair and virtuous mistress in those two places, by reason of Queen Katherine's usual abode there (on whom this Lady Geraldine was attending), I prove by these verses of his:

> Hampton me taught to wish her first for mine,
> Windsor alas doth chase me from her sight.

And in another sonnet following:

> When Windsor walls sustain'd my wearied arm,
> My hand my chin, to ease my restless head.

And that his delight might draw him to compare Windsor to Paradise an elegy may prove, where he rememb'reth his past pleasures in that place:

> With a king's son my childish years I pass'd,
> In greater feast then Priam's son of Troy.

And again in the same elegy:

> Those large green courts, where we were wont
>   to rove,
> With eyes cast up unto the maidens' tower,
> With easy sighs, such as men draw in love.

And again in the same:

> The stately seats, the ladies bright of hue,
> The dances short, long tales of sweet delight.

And for the pleasantness of the place, these verses of his may testify in the same elegy before recited:

> The secret groves which we have made resound.
> With silver drops the meads yet spread for ruth.

> *As goodly flowers by Thamisis do grow, etc.*   10

I had thought in this place not to have spoken of Thames, being so oft rememb'red by me before in sundry other places on this occasion; but thinking of that excellent epigram, which as I judge either to be done by the said earl or Sir Francis Bryan for the worthiness thereof I will here insert, which as it seems to me was compiled at the author's being in Spain:

> Tagus, farewell, which westward with thy streams
> Turn'st up the grains of gold already try'd,
> For I with spur and sail go seek the Thames,
> Against the sun that shews her wealthy pride
> And to the town that Brutus sought by dreams,
> Like bended moon that leans her lusty side;
> To seek my country now, for whom I live,
> O mighty Jove, for this the winds me give.

> *Finis*

FROM POLY-OLBION (1612, 1622)

To the General Reader [1612]

In publishing this essay of my poem there is this great disadvantage against me: that it cometh out at this time when verses are wholly deduc'd to chambers, and nothing esteem'd in this lunatique age but what is kept in cabinets and must only pass by transcription. In such a season, when the idle, humorous world must hear of nothing that either savors of antiquity or may awake it to seek after more then dull and slothful ignorance may easily reach unto, these, I say, make much against me, and especially in a poem from any example, either of ancient or modern that have proved in this kind, whose unusual tract may perhaps seem difficult to the female sex, yea, and I fear, to some that think themselves not meanly learned, being not rightly inspired by the muses. Such I mean as had rather read the fantasies of forrain inventions then to see the rarities and history of their own country delivered by a true native muse. Then, whosoever thou be, possess'd with such stupidity and dulness that, rather then thou wilt take pains to search into ancient and noble things, choosest to remain in the thick fogs and mists of ignorance, as near the common laystall of a city, refusing to walk forth into the Tempe and fields of the muses, where, through most delightful groves, the angelique harmony of birds shall steal thee to the top of an easy hill; where, in artificial caves cut out of the most natural rock, thou shalt see the ancient people of this ile delivered thee in their lively images; from whose height thou mayst behold both the old and later times, as in thy prospect, lying far under thee, then conveying thee down by a soul-pleasing descent through delicate, embroidered meadows, often veined with gentle gliding brooks in which thou mayst fully view the dainty nymphs in their simple, naked beauties bathing them in crystalline streams, which shall lead thee to most pleasant downs where harmless shepherds are, some exercising their pipes, some singing roundelays to their gazing flocks. If, as I say, thou hadst rather (because it asks thy labor) remain where thou wert then strain thyself to walk forth with the muses, the fault proceeds from thy idleness, not from any want in my industry. And to any that shall demand wherefore, having promised this poem of the general iland so many years, I now publish only this part of it, I plainly answer that many times I had determined with myself to have left it off, and have neglected my papers sometimes two years together, finding the times since his Majesty's happy coming-in to fall so heavily upon my distressed fortunes after my zealous soul had labored so long in that which, with the general happiness of the kingdom, seem'd not then impossible somewhat also to have advanced me. But I instantly saw all my long-nourish'd hopes even buried alive before my face, so uncertain, in this world, be the ends of our clearest endeavors. And whatever is herein that tastes of a free spirit, I thankfully confess it to proceed from the continual bounty of my truly noble friend Sir Walter Aston, which hath given me the best of those hours whose leisure hath effected this which I now publish. Sundry other songs I have also, though yet not so perfect that I dare commit them to publique censure; and the rest I determine to go forward with, God enabling me, may I find means to assist my endeavor. Now, reader, for the further understanding of my poem thou hast three especial helps: first, the argument to direct thee still where thou art and through what shires the muse makes her journey and what she chiefly handles in the song thereto belonging; next, the map, lively delineating to thee every mountain, forest, river, and valley, expressing in their sundry postures their loves, delights, and natural situations; then hast thou the illustration of this learned gentleman [John Selden], my friend, to explain every hard matter of history that, lying far from the way of common reading, may, without question, seem difficult unto thee. Thus wishing thee thy heart's desire and committing my poem to thy charitable censure, I take my leave.

Thine as thou art mine,

Michael Drayton

The Thirteenth Song

THE ARGUMENT

This song our shire of Warwick sounds,
Revives old Arden's ancient bounds.
Through many shapes the muse here roves;
Now, sporting in those shady groves,
The tunes of birds oft stays to hear;
Then, finding herds of lusty deer,
She huntress-like the hart pursues;
And like a hermit walks, to chuse
The simples everywhere that grow;
Comes Ancor's glory next to show,
Tells Guy of Warwick's famous deeds;
To th' vale of Red Horse then proceeds,
To play her part the rest among;
There shutteth up her thirteenth song.

Upon the Midlands now th' industrious muse doth fall,
That shire which we the heart of England well may call,
As she herself extends (the midst which is decreed)
Betwixt St. Michael's Mount and Berwick-bord'ring Tweed,
Brave Warwick, that abroad so long advanc'd her bear,
By her illustrious earls renowned everywhere,
Above her neighboring shires which always bore her head.
  My native country then, which so brave spirits hath bred,
If there be virtue yet remaining in thy earth,
Or any good of thine thou breath'dst into my birth,   10
Accept it as thine own whilst now I sing of thee,
Of all thy later brood th' unworthiest though I be.
  Muse, first of Arden tell, whose footsteps yet are found
In her rough woodlands more then any other ground
That mighty Arden held even in her height of pride,
Her one hand touching Trent, the other Severn's side.
  The very sound of these the wood nymphs doth awake,
When thus of her own self the ancient forest spake:
  "My many goodly sites when first I came to show,
Here opened I the way to mine own overthrow;   20
For when the world found out the fitness of my soil,
The gripple wretch began immediately to spoil
My tall and goodly woods, and did my grounds inclose,
By which in little time my bounds I came to lose.
  "When Britain first her fields with villages had fill'd,
Her people wexing still and wanting where to build,
They oft dislodg'd the hart and set their houses where
He in the broom and brakes had long time made his leir.
Of all the forests here within this mighty ile,
If those old Britains then me sovereign did instyle,   30
I needs must be the great'st, for greatness 'tis alone
That gives our kind the place, else were there many a one
For pleasantness of shade that far doth me excel.
But of our forests' kind the quality to tell,
We equally partake with woodland as with plain,
Alike with hill and dale, and every day maintain

The sundry kinds of beasts upon our copious wastes
That men for profit breed, as well as those of chase."
    Here Arden of herself ceas'd any more to show,
And with her sylvan joys the muse along doth go.   40
    When Phoebus lifts his head out of the winter's wave,
No sooner doth the earth her flowery bosom brave,
At such time as the year brings on the pleasant spring,
But hunt's-up to the morn the feath'red sylvans sing,
And in the lower grove, as in the rising knoll,
Upon the highest spray of every mounting pole,
Those quiristers are perch'd with many a speckled breast.
Then from her burnish'd gate the goodly glitt'ring east
Gilds every lofty top, which late the humorous night
Bespangled had with pearl to please the morning's sight;   50
On which the mirthful quires with their clear open throats
Unto the joyful morn so strain their warbling notes
That hills and valleys ring, and even the echoing air
Seems all compos'd of sounds, about them everywhere.
The throstle, with shrill sharps, as purposely he song
T' awake the lustless sun, or chiding that so long
He was in coming forth that should the thickets thrill;
The woosell near at hand, that hath a golden bill,
As Nature him had mark'd of purpose t' let us see
That from all other birds his tunes should different be;   60
For with their vocal sounds they sing to pleasant May.
Upon his dulcet pipe the merle doth only play;
When in the lower brake the nightingale hard by
In such lamenting strains the joyful hours doth ply
As though the other birds she to her tunes would draw;
And but that Nature, by her all-constraining law,
Each bird to her own kind this season doth invite,
They else, alone to hear that charmer of the night
(The more to use their ears), their voices sure would spare,
That moduleth her tunes so admirably rare,   70
As man to set in parts at first had learn'd of her.
    To Philomel the next, the linnet we prefer,
And by that warbling bird the wood-lark place we then,
The red sparrow, the nope, the redbreast, and the wren,
The yellowpate, which though she hurt the blooming tree,
Yet scarce hath any bird a finer pipe then she;
And of these chanting fowls the goldfinch not behind
That hath so many sorts descending from her kind.
The tydie for her notes as delicate as they,
The laughing hecco, then the counterfetting jay,   80
The softer with the shrill (some hid among the leaves,
Some in the taller trees, some in the lower greaves),
Thus sing away the morn, until the mounting sun
Through thick exhaled fogs his golden head hath run,
And through the twisted tops of our close covert creeps
To kiss the gentle shade, this while that sweetly sleeps.
    And near to these our thicks, the wild and frightful herds,
Not hearing other noise but this of chattering birds,
Feed fairly on the launds; both sorts of seasoned deer,
Here walk the stately red, the freckled fallow there,   90
The bucks and lusty stags amongst the rascals strew'd,
As sometime gallant spirits amongst the multitude. . . .

To Any That Will Read It [1622]

When I first undertook this poem or (as some very skilful in this kind have pleased to term it) this herculean labor, I was by some virtuous friends persuaded that I should receive much comfort and incouragement therein, and for these reasons: first, that it was a new, clear way, never before gone by any; then, that it contained all the delicacies, delights, and rarities of this renowned isle interwoven with the histories of the Britans, Saxons, Normans, and the later English; and, further, that there is scarcely any of the nobility or gentry of this land but that he is some way or other by his blood interested therein. But it hath fallen out otherwise; for instead of that comfort which my noble friends, from the freedom of their spirits, proposed as my due I have met with barbarous ignorance and base detraction; such a cloud hath the Devil drawn over the world's judgment, whose opinion is in few years fallen so far below all ballatry, that the lethargy is incurable. Nay, some of the stationers that had the selling of the first part of this poem, because it went not so fast away in the sale as some of their beastly and abominable trash (a shame both to our language and nation), have either despightfully left out or at least carelessly neglected the epistles to the readers and so have cousoned the buyers with unperfected books; which these that have undertaken the second part have been forced to amend in the first for the small number that are yet remaining in their hands. And some of our outlandish, unnatural English (I know not how otherwise to express them) stick not to say that there is nothing in this island worthy studying for and take a great pride to be ignorant in anything thereof. For these, since they delight in their folly, I wish it may be hereditary from them to their posterity, that their children may be begg'd for fools to the fift generation, until it may be beyond the memory of man to know that there was ever any other of their families. Neither can this deter me from going on with Scotland, if means and time do not hinder me, to perform as much as I have promised in my first song:

Till to the sleepy main to Thuly I have gone
And seen the frozen isles, the cold Deucalidon,
Amongst whose iron rocks grim Saturn yet remains
Bound in those gloomy caves with adamantine chains.

And as for those cattle whereof I spake before, *odi profanum vulgus et arceo,* of which I account them, be they never so great; and so I leave them. To my friends and the lovers of my labors I wish all happiness.

Michael Drayton

FROM POEMS . . . WITH SUNDRY PIECES (1619)

To the Reader

Odes I have called these my few poems which how happy soever they prove, yet criticism itself cannot say that the name is wrongfully usurped; for (not to begin with definitions against the rule of oratory, nor *ab ovo* against the prescript rule of poetry in a poetical argument, but somewhat only to season thy palate with a slight description) an ode is known to have been properly a song moduled to the ancient harp, and neither too short-breathed, as hasting to the end, nor composed of the longest verses, as unfit for the sudden turns and lofty tricks with which Apollo used to manage it. They are, as the learned say, divers: some transcendently lofty and far more high then the epic (commonly called the heroique poem), witness those of the inimitable Pindarus consecrated to the glory and renown of such as returned in triumph from Olympus, Elis, Isthmus, or the like; others, among the Greeks, are amorous, soft, and made for chambers, as other for theaters, as were Anacreon's, the very delicacies of the Grecian Erato, which muse seemed to have been the minion of that Teian old man which composed them; of a mixed kind were Horace's, and may truly therefore be called his mixed. Whatsoever else are mine, little partaking of the high dialect of the first—

Though we be all to seek
Of Pindar, that great Greek—

nor altogether of Anacreon, the arguments being amorous, moral, or what else the muse pleaseth. To write much in this kind neither know I how it will relish nor, in so doing, can I but injuriously presuppose ignorance or slouth in thee, or draw censure upon myself for sinning against the decorum of a preface by reading a lecture where it is inough to sum the points. New they are, and the work of playing hours, but what other commendation is theirs and whether inherent in the subject must be thine to judge. But to act the go-between of my poems and thy applause is neither my modesty nor confidence, that oft'ner then once have acknowledged thee kind and do not doubt hereafter to do somewhat in which I shall not fear thee just; and would at this time also gladly let thee understand what I think above the rest of the last ode of this number or, if thou wilt, ballad in my book; for both the great master of Italian rimes, Petrarch, and our Chaucer, and other of the upper house of the muses have thought their canzons honored in the title of a ballad, which, for that I labor to meet truly therein with the old English garb, I hope as able to justify as the learned Colin Clout his roundelay. Thus requesting thee in thy better judgment to correct such faults as have escaped in the printing, I bid thee farewell.

M[ichael] Drayton

TO THE VIRGINIAN VOYAGE

You brave heroique minds,
Worthy your country's name,
   That honor still pursue,
   Go and subdue,
Whilst loit'ring hinds
Lurk here at home with shame.

Britans, you stay too long;
Quickly aboord bestow you,
   And with a merry gale
   Swell your stretch'd sail,   10
With vows as strong
As the winds that blow you.

Your course securely steer,
West and by south forth keep,
   Rocks, lee shores, nor shoals,
   When Aeolus scowls,
You need not fear,
So absolute the deep.

And cheerfully at sea
Success you still intice,   20
   To get the pearl and gold,
   And ours to hold
Virginia,
Earth's only paradise,

Where nature hath in store
Fowl, venison, and fish,
   And the fruitful'st soil
   Without your toil
Three harvests more,
All greater then your wish.   30

And the ambitious vine
Crowns with his purple mass
   The cedar reaching high
   To kiss the sky,
The cypress, pine,
And useful sassafras.

To whose the golden age
Still nature's laws doth give,

No other cares that tend,
   But them to defend   40
From winter's age
That long there doth not live.

Whenas the luscious smell
Of that delicious land
   Above the seas that flows
   The clear wind throws,
Your hearts to swell
Approaching the dear strand,

In kenning of the shore,
Thanks to God first given,   50
   O you, the happi'st men,
   Be frolic then,
Let cannons roar,
Frighting the wide heaven.

And in regions far
Such heroes bring ye forth
   As those from whom we came,
   And plant our name
Under that star
Not known unto our north.   60

And as there plenty grows
Of laurel everywhere,
   Apollo's sacred tree,
   You it may see
A poet's brows
To crown that may sing there.

Thy voyages attend,
Industrious Hakluyt,
   Whose reading shall inflame
   Men to seek fame,   70
And much commend
To after-times thy wit.

AN ODE WRITTEN IN THE PEAK

This while we are abroad
   Shall we not touch our lyre?
Shall we not sing an ode?
   Shall that holy fire
In us that strongly glow'd
   In this cold air expire?

Long since the summer laid
   Her lusty brav'ry down;
The autumn half is weigh'd,
   And Boreas gins to frown   10
Since now I did behold
   Great Brut's first builded town.

Though in the utmost Peak
  A while we do remain,
Amongst the mountains bleak
  Expos'd to sleet and rain,
No sport our hours shall break
  To exercise our vein.

What though bright Phoebus' beams
  Refresh the southern ground,   20
And though the princely Thames
  With beautious nymphs abound,
And by old Camber's streams
  Be many wonders found?

Yet many rivers clear
  Here glide in silver swaths,
And what of all most dear,
  Buckston's delicious baths,
Strong ale and noble cheer
  T' assuage breem winter's scaths.   30

Those grim and horrid caves
  Whose looks affright the day
Wherein nice Nature saves
  What she would not bewray,
Our better leisure craves
  And doth invite our lay.

In places far or near,
  Or famous or obscure,
Where wholesome is the air
  Or where the most impure,   40
All times and everywhere
  The muse is still in ure.

HIS DEFENSE AGAINST THE IDLE CRITIC

The rime nor mars nor makes
Nor addeth it nor takes
  From that which we propose;
Things imaginary
Do so strangely vary
  That quickly we them lose.

And what's quickly begot
As soon again is not;
  This do I truly know.
Yea, and what's borne with pain,   10
That sense doth long'st retain,
  Gone with a greater flow.

Yet this critic so stern,
But whom none must discern
  Nor perfectly have seeing,
Strangely lays about him
As nothing without him
  Were worthy of being.

That I myself betray
To that most publique way   20
  Where the world's old bawd,
Custom, that doth humor
And by idle rumor
  Her dotages applaud.

That whilst she still prefers
Those that be wholly hers,
  Madness and ignorance,
I creep behind the time
From spertling with their crime
  And glad too with my chance.   30

O wretched world the while,
When the evil most vile
  Beareth the fairest face,
And inconstant lightness
With a scornful slightness
  The best things doth disgrace;

Whilst this strange knowing beast,
Man, of himself the least,
  His envy declaring,
Makes virtue to descend,   40
Her title to defend
  Against him much preparing;

Yet these me not delude,
Nor from my place extrude
  By their resolved hate,
Their vileness that do know
Which to myself I show
  To keep above my fate.

TO HIS COY LOVE, A CANZONET

I pray thee leave, love me no more,
  Call home the heart you gave me.
I but in vain that saint adore
  That can but will not save me.
These poor half kisses kill me quite;
  Was ever man thus served,
Amidst an ocean of delight
  For pleasure to be sterved?

Shew me no more those snowy breasts
  With azure riverets branched,   10
Where whilst mine eye with plenty feasts
  Yet is my thirst not stanched.
O Tantalus, thy pains ne'er tell;
  By me thou art prevented;
'Tis nothing to be plagu'd in hell,
  But thus in heaven tormented.

Clip me no more in those dear arms,
  Nor thy life's comfort call me;

O, these are but too pow'rful charms
  And do but more inthrall me.   20
But see how patient I am grown
  In all this coil about thee:
Come, nice thing, let thy heart alone,
  I cannot live without thee.

TO THE CAMBRO-BRITANS AND
THEIR HARP, HIS BALLAD OF AGINCOURT

Fair stood the wind for France,
When we our sails advance,
Nor now to prove our chance
  Longer will tarry;
But putting to the main,
At Kaux, the mouth of Seine,
With all his martial train,
  Landed King Harry.

And taking many a fort,
Furnish'd in warlike sort,   10
Marcheth tow'rds Agincourt
  In happy hour;
Skirmishing day by day
With those that stopp'd his way,
Where the French gen'ral lay
  With all his power.

Which in his hight of pride,
King Henry to deride,
His ransom to provide
  To the king sending;   20
Which he neglects the while
As from a nation vile,
Yet with an angry smile
  Their fall portending.

And turning to his men,
Quoth our brave Henry then:
"Though they to one be ten,
  Be not amazed.
Yet have we well begun,
Battles so bravely won   30
Have ever to the sun
  By fame been raised.

"And for myself," quoth he,
"This my full rest shall be;
England, ne'er mourn for me,
  Nor more esteem me;
Victor I will remain
Or on this earth lie slain,
Never shall she sustain
  Loss to redeem me.   40

"Poiters and Cressy tell,
When most their pride did swell,
Under our swords they fell;
  No less our skill is
Then when our grandsire great,
Claiming the regal seat,
By many a warlike feat
  Lopp'd the French lilies."

The Duke of York so dread
The eager vaward led;   50
With the main Henry sped
  Amongst his henchmen.
Excester had the rear,
A braver man not there,
O Lord, how hot they were
  On the false Frenchmen!

They now to fight are gone,
Armor on armor shone,
Drum now to drum did groan,
  To hear was wonder,   60
That with cries they make
The very earth did shake,
Trumpet to trumpet spake,
  Thunder to thunder.

Well it thine age became,
O noble Erpingham,
Which didst the signal aim
  To our hid forces;
When from a meadow by,
Like a storm suddenly,   70
The English archery
  Stuck the French horses,

With Spanish ewgh so strong,
Arrows a cloth-yard long,
That like to serpents stung,
  Piercing the weather;
None from his fellow starts,
But playing manly parts,
And like true English hearts,
  Stuck close together.   80

When down their bows they threw,
And forth their bilboes drew,
And on the French they flew,
  Not one was tardy;
Arms were from shoulders sent,
Scalps to the teeth were rent,
Down the French peasants went;
  Our men were hardy.

This while our noble king,
His broadsword brandishing,   90
Down the French host did ding,
  As to o'erwhelm it;
And many a deep wound lent,
His arms with blood besprent,
And many a cruel dent
  Bruised his helmet.

Gloster, that duke so good,
Next of the royal blood,
For famous England stood
  With his brave brother;   100
Clarence, in steel so bright,
Though but a maiden knight,
Yet in that furious fight
  Scarce such another.

Warwick in blood did wade,
Oxford the foe invade,
And cruel slaughter made
  Still as they ran up;
Suffolk his ax did ply,
Beaumont and Willoughby   110
Bare them right doughtily,
  Ferrers and Fanhope.

Upon Saint Crispin's day
Fought was this noble fray,
Which fame did not delay
  To England to carry;
O, when shall English men
With such acts fill a pen,
Or England breed again
  Such a King Harry?   120

GEORGE CHAPMAN

Chapman's poetry is generally graceless and obscure, but he himself, in various angry epistles, defended it on both moral and esthetic grounds. With an almost Miltonic sense of poetic calling, and with a superb contempt for the amenities of conventional verse, he sought to make poetry a vehicle for the various Christian, Stoic, and Neo-Platonic doctrines with which his mind was fired— truths that demanded of both himself and his reader the most strenuous exertions. "From flints must the gorgonean fount be smitten," he explains to Matthew Roydon, and those who read "but to curtoll a tedious hour" stupidly think that the Muse "should prostitutely shew them her secrets, when she will scarcely be look'd upon by others but with invocation, fasting, watching—yea, not without having drops of their souls like an heavenly familiar." On such Olympian convictions Chapman erects an esthetic of stylized obscurity. He does concede that "obscurity in affection of words and indigested concets is pedantical and childish; but where it shroudeth itself in the heart of his subject, utter'd with fitness of figure and expressive epethits, with that darkness will I still labor to be shadowed." And yet, as he confesses in dedicating *Achilles' Shield* to the mathematician Thomas Harriot in 1598, he was unable to reach the heights he sought:

> Rich mine of knowledge, O that my strange muse
> Without this body's nourishment could use
> Her zealous faculties only t' aspire
> Instructive light from your whole sphere of fire!
> But wo is me, what zeal or power soever
> My free soul hath, my body will be never
> Able t' attend. Never shall I enjoy
> Th' end of my hapless birth, never employ
> That smother'd fervor that in lothed embers

> Lies swept from light, and no clear hour remembers.
> O had your perfect eye organs to pierce
> Into that chaos whence this stifled verse
> By violence breaks, where glowworm-like doth shine
> In nights of sorrow this hid soul of mine,
> And how her genuine forms struggle for birth
> Under the claws of this foul panther earth;
> Then under all those forms you should discern
> My love to you in my desire to learn.

Chapman's view of the poet's exalted function and his unfortunate identification of obscurity with profundity need to be kept in mind by readers of his first published poem, Σκιὰ νυκτός, *The Shadow of Night*. Some theorists have cited it to establish Chapman's alleged connection with a so-called School of Night, a literary and quasi-philosophical group (including Raleigh, Marlowe, and Harriot) whose affectations Shakespeare is said to have ridiculed in *Love's Labor's Lost*. Be that as it may, the poem somberly celebrates the darkness and obscurity whose ennobling merits the world cannot comprehend. Of its two "Hymns," the first (*Hymnus in Noctem*) sets forth in rapturous but somewhat muddy terms Chapman's theory of poetic inspiration and of poetry; the second (*Hymnus in Cynthiam*) contains such a circumstantial account of Sir Francis Vere's Netherlands campaign that some critics have supposed it reflects Chapman's otherwise unrecorded experiences as a soldier. Entered in the Stationers' Register in December, 1593, and published in 1594, the work, for reasons sufficiently plain, never attained a second edition.

Apparently its failure was instructive, for although Chapman, smarting from a sense of injured merit, continued to expound his esthetics of obscurity, he turned to a very different style for his next work. No doubt inspired by the vogue of Ovidian narrative verse, and more immediately by the reading, in manuscript, of Marlowe's *Hero and Leander,* he abandoned his murky philosophizing for the erotic narrative of *Ovid's Banquet of Sense.* To be sure, the eroticism is grounded upon a strongly Neo-Platonic doctrine of love perhaps suggested by Marsilio Ficino, but the theme—that man must exploit all his capacity for sensual gratification in order to attain the highest stages of spiritual love—permits a good deal of lush amatory description in the mode of Marlowe, Shakespeare, and Lodge. Prefaced by commendatory sonnets from Richard Stapleton, Thomas Williams, and

Sir J[ohn] D[avies], *Ovid's Banquet of Sense* is followed by a set of ten sonnets called "A Coronet for His Mistress Philosophy," an unfortunate translation of Gilles Durant's *Le zodiac amoureux,* and "The Amorous Contention of Phyllis and Flora," a pleasing little pastoral that is probably the work of Richard Stapleton. First published in 1595, the volume finally reached a second (and posthumous) edition in 1639.

Our texts are based on Σκιὰ νυκτὸς [*sic*]. *The Shadow of Night: Containing Two Poeticall Hymnes,* 1594 (STC 4990); *Ovids Banquet of Sence. A Coronet for his Mistresse Philosophie, and his amorous Zodiacke,* 1595 (STC 4985).

FROM ΣΚΙΑ ΝΥΚΤΟΣ, THE SHADOW OF NIGHT, CONTAINING TWO POETICAL HYMNS (1594)

To My Dear and Most Worthy Friend Master Mathew Roydon

It is an exceeding rapture of delight in the deep search of knowledge (none knoweth better then thyself, sweet Mathew) that maketh men manfully indure th' extremes incident to that herculean labor; from flints must the gorgonean fount be smitten. Men must be shod by Mercury, girt with Saturn's adamantine sword, take the shield from Pallas, the helm from Pluto, and have the eyes of Graea (as   10 Hesiodus arms Perseus against Medusa) before they can cut off the viperous head of benumming ignorance, or subdue their monstrous affections to most beautiful judgment.

How, then, may a man stay his marvailing to see passion-driven men, reading but to curtoll a tedious hour and altogether hidebound with affection to great men's fancies, take upon them as killing censures as if they were Judgment's butchers or as if the life of truth lay tottering in their verdits.   20

Now what a supererogation in wit this is to think Skill so mightily pierc'd with their loves that she should prostitutely shew them her secrets, when she will scarcely be look'd upon by others but with invocation, fasting, watching—yea, not without having drops of their souls like an heavenly familiar. Why, then, should our *intonsi Catones,* with their profit-ravish'd gravity, esteem her true favors such questionless vanities as, with what part soever thereof they seem to be something delighted, they queimishly   30 commend it for a pretty toy? Good Lord, how serious and eternal are their idolatrous plats for

riches! No marvail, sure, they here do so much good with them. And heaven, no doubt, will grovel on the earth (as they do) to imbrace them. But I stay this spleen when I remember, my good Mathew, how joyfully oftentimes you reported unto me that most ingenious Darby [Ferdinando Stanley], deep-searching Northumberland [Sir Henry Percy, 1564–1632], and skill-imbracing heir of Hunsdon [George Carey] had most profitably entertained learning in themselves, to the vital warmth of freezing science and to the admirable luster of their true nobility, whose high-deserving virtues may cause me hereafter strike that fire out of darkness which the brightest day shall envy for beauty. I should write more, but my hasting out of town taketh me from the paper. So, preferring thy allowance in this poor and strange trifle to the passport of a whole city of others, I rest as resolute as Seneca, satisfying myself if but a few, if one, or if none like it.

> By the true admirer of thy virtues
> and perfectly vowed friend,
> G[eorge] Chapman

HYMNUS IN NOCTEM

Great goddess, to whose throne in Cynthian fires
This earthly altar endless fumes exspires,
Therefore, in fumes of sighs and fires of grief,
To fearful chances thou send'st bold relief;
Happy, thrice happy, type and nurse of death
Who, breathless, feeds on nothing but our breath,
In whom must Virtue and her issue live
Or die forever, now let humor give

Seas to mine eyes that I may quickly weep
The shipwrack of the world. Or let soft sleep,   10
Binding my senses, lose my working soul
That, in her highest pitch, she may control
The court of skill, compact of mystery,
Wanting but franchisement and memory
To reach all secrets. Then in blissful trance
Raise her, dear Night, to that perseverance
That in my torture she all earths may sing
And force to tremble in her trumpeting
Heaven's crystal temples. In her pow'rs implant
Skill of my griefs, and she can nothing want.   20

   Then, like fierce bolts well-ramm'd with heat and cold
In Jove's artillery, my words unfold
To break the labyrinth of every ear
And make each frighted soul come forth and hear.
Let them break hearts as well as yielding airs
That all men's bosoms (pierc'd with no affairs
But gain of riches) may be lanced wide
And with the threats of virtue terrified.

   Sorrow's dear sovereign and the queen of rest,
That, when unlightsome, vast, and indigest   30
The formless matter of this world did lie,
Fill'dst every place with thy divinity,
Why did thy absolute and endless sway
License heaven's torch, the scepter of the day,
Distinguish'd intercession to thy throne
That, long before, all matchless rul'd alone?
Why let'st thou order orderless disperse
The fighting parents of this universe?
When earth, the air, and sea in fire remain'd,
When fire, the sea, and earth the air contain'd,   40
When air, the earth, and fire the sea enclos'd,
When sea, fire, air in earth were indispos'd,
Nothing, as now, remain'd so out of kind.
All things in gross were finer then refin'd;
Substance was sound within and had no being.
Now form gives being, all our essence seeming.
Chaos had soul without a body then;
Now bodies live without the souls of men,
Lumps being digested, monsters in our pride. . . .

   A stepdame, Night of Mind, about us clings   50
Who broods beneath her hell-obscuring wings
Worlds of confusion where, the soul defam'd,
The body had been better never fram'd.
Beneath thy soft and peaceful covert then,
Most sacred mother both of gods and men,
Treasures unknown and more unpriz'd did dwell;
But in the blind-born shadow of this hell
This horrid stepdame, Blindness of the Mind,
Nought worth the sight, no sight, but worse then blind,
A gorgon that, with brass and snaky brows,   60
Most harlot-like her naked secrets shows.
For in th' expansure and distinct attire
Of light and darkness, of the sea and fire,

Of air and earth and all, all these create,
First set and rul'd in most harmonious state,
Disjunction shows in all things now amiss
By that first order what confusion is.
Religious curb, that manag'd men in bounds
Of publique welfare, lothing private grounds,
Now cast away by Self-Love's paramours,   70
All are transform'd to Calydonian boars
That kill our bleeding vines, disploy our fields,
Rend groves in pieces, all things nature yields
Supplanting, tumbling up in hills of dearth
The fruitful disposition of the earth.
Ruin creates men all to slaughter bent,
Like envy, fed with others' famishment. . . .

   If, then, we frame man's figure by his mind,
And that at first his fashion was assign'd
Erection in such God-like excellence   80
For his soul's sake and her intelligence,
She so degenerate and grown depress'd,
Content to share affections with a beast,
The shape wherewith he should be now indu'd
Must bear no sign of man's similitude.
Therefore Promethean poets, with the coals
Of their most genial, more then human, souls,
In living verse created men like these
With shapes of centaurs, harpies, Lapithes,
That they, in prime of erudition,   90
When almost savage vulgar men were grown,
Seeing themselves in those Pierian founts,
Might mend their minds, asham'd of such accounts.
So when ye hear the sweetest muse's son
With heavenly rapture of his music won
Rocks, forests, floods, and winds to leave their course
In his attendance, it bewrays the force
His wisdom had to draw men grown so rude
To civil love of art and fortitude.
And not for teaching others insolence   100
Had he his date-exceeding excellence
With sovereign poets, but for use applied,
And in his proper acts exemplified,
And that in calming the infernal kind,
To wit, the perturbations of his mind,
And bringing his Eurydice from hell
(Which Justice signifies) is proved well.
But if in right's observance any man
Look back, with boldness less then Orphean,
Soon falls he to the hell from whence he rose.   110
The fiction, then, would temp'rature dispose
In all the tender motives of the mind
To make man worthy his hell-danting kind.
The golden chain of Homer's high device
Ambition is, or cursed Avarice,
Which, all gods haling, being tied to Jove,
Him from his settled height could never move,
Intending this: that though that pow'rful chain,

Of most herculean vigor to constrain
Men from true virtue or their pristine states,   120
Attempt a man that manless changes hates,
And is ennobled with a deathless love
Of things eternal, dignified above,
Nothing shall stir him from adorning still
This shape with virtue and his pow'r with will. . . .
  So to the chaos of our first descent
(All days of honor and of virtue spent)
We basely make retrait, and are no less
Then huge, impolish'd heaps of filthiness.
Men's faces glitter, and their hearts are black.   130
But thou, great mistress of heaven's gloomy rack,
Art black in face and glitter'st in thy heart.
There is thy glory, riches, force, and art.
Opposed earth beats black and blue thy face
And often doth thy heart itself deface
For spite that, to thy virtue-famed train,
All the choice worthies that did ever reign
In eldest age were still preferr'd by Jove,
Esteeming that due honor to his love.
There shine they, not to seamen guides alone   140
But sacred presidents to every one.
There fix'd forever where the day is driven
Almost four hundred times a year from heaven.
In hell, then, let her sit and never rise
Till morns leave blushing at her cruelties.
  Meanwhile, accept, as followers of thy train
(Our better parts aspiring to thy reign)
Virtues obscur'd and banished the day,
With all the glories of this spongy sway
Prison'd in flesh, and that poor flesh in bands   150
Of stone and steel, chief flow'rs of virtue's garlands.
  O then most tender fortress of our woes
That, bleeding, lie in virtue's overthrows,
Hating the whoredom of this painted light,
Raise thy chaste daughters, ministers of right,
The dreadful and the just Eumenides;
And let them wreak the wrongs of our disease,
Drowning the world in blood, and stain the skies
With their spilt souls, made drunk with tyrannies. . . .
  Kneel, then, with me! Fall worm-like on the ground,

And, from th' infectious dunghill of this round,   161
From men's brass wits and golden foolery,
Weep, weep your souls into felicity.
Come to this house of mourning, serve the Night,
To whom pale Day (with whoredom soaked quite)
Is but a drudge, selling her beauty's use
To rapes, adult'ries, and to all abuse. . . .
  All you possess'd with indepressed spirits,
Indu'd with nimble and aspiring wits,
Come consecrate with me to sacred Night   170
Your whole endeavors, and detest the light.
Sweet Peace's richest crown is made of stars,
Most certain guides of honor'd marinars;
No pen can anything eternal write
That is not steep'd in humor of the Night.
  Hence, beasts and birds, to caves and bushes then,
And welcome Night, ye noblest heirs of men.
Hence, Phoebus, to thy glassy strumpet's bed,
And never more let Themis' daughters spread
Thy golden harness on thy rosy horse,   180
But in close thickets run thy oblique course.
  See now ascends the glorious bride of brides,
Nuptials and triumphs glitt'ring by her sides.
Juno and Hymen do her train adorn,
Ten thousand torches round about them borne.
Dumb Silence, mounted on the Cyprian star,
With becks rebukes the winds before his car
Where she advanc'd; beats down with cloudy mace
The feeble light to black Saturnius' palace.
Behind her, with a brace of silver hinds,   190
In ivory chariot swifter then the winds
Is great Hyperion's horned daughter drawn
Enchantress-like, deck'd in disparent lawn,
Circled with charms and incantations
That ride huge spirits and outragious passions.
Music and mood she loves, but Love she hates
(As curious ladies do their publique cates).
This train, with meteors, comets, lightenings,
The dreadful presence of our empress sings,
Which grant forever, O eternal Night,   200
Till virtue flourish in the light of light.
                              Explicit Hymnus

FROM OVID'S BANQUET OF SENSE (1595)

To the Truly Learned and My Worthy Friend
Master Mathew Roydon

  Such is the wilful poverty of judgments, sweet
M[athew], wand'ring, like passportless men, in contempt of the divine discipline of poesy, that a man
may well fear to frequent their walks. The prophane
multitude I hate, and only consecrate my strange
poems to these searching spirits whom learning hath
made noble and nobility sacred, endeavoring that
material oration which you call *schema,* varying in
some rare fiction from popular custom even for the
pure sakes of ornament and utility. . . .

But that poesy should be as pervial as oratory, and plainness her special ornament, were the plain way to barbarism, and to make the ass run proud of his ears, to take away strength from lions and give camels horns.

That *enargia,* or clearness of representation, requir'd in absolute poems is not the perspicuous delivery of a low invention, but high and hearty invention express'd in most significant and unaffected phrase. It serves not a skilful painter's turn to draw [10] the figure of a face only to make known who it represents, but he must limn, give luster, shadow, and height'ning; which, though ignorants will esteem spic'd and too curious, yet such as have the judicial perspective will see it hath motion, spirit, and life.

There is no confection made to last but it is admitted more cost and skill then presently to be used simples; and, in my opinion, that which, being with a little endeavor searched, adds a kind of majesty to poesy is better then that which every cobbler may [20] sing to his patch.

Obscurity in affection of words and indigested concets is pedantical and childish; but where it shroudeth itself in the heart of his subject, utter'd with fitness of figure and expressive epethits, with that darkness will I still labor to be shadowed. Rich minerals are digg'd out of the bowels of the earth, not found in the superficies and dust of it; charms made of unlearned characters are not consecrate by the muses, which are divine artists, but by Evippe's [30] daughters, that challeng'd them with mere nature, whose breasts, I doubt not, had been well worthy commendation if their comparison had not turn'd them into pies.

Thus, not affecting glory for mine own slight labors, but desirous other should be more worthily glorious, nor professing sacred poesy in any degree, I thought good to submit to your apt judgment, acquainted long since with the true habit of poesy; and now, since your laboring wits endeavor heaven- [40] high thoughts of nature, you have actual means to sound the philosophical conceits that my new pen so seriously courteth. I know that empty and dark spirits will complain of palpable night; but those that before-hand have a radiant and light-bearing intellect will say they can pass through Corinna's garden without the help of a lantern.

Your own most worthily and sincerely affected,

George Chapman [50]

THE ARGUMENT

Ovid, newly enamored of Julia, daughter to Octavius Augustus Caesar, after by him called Corinna, secretly convey'd himself into a garden of the emperor's court, in an arbor whereof Corinna was bathing, playing upon her lute, and singing; which Ovid, overhearing, was exceedingly pleas'd with the sweetness of her voice, and to himself uttered the comfort he conceived in his sense of hearing.

Then the odors she us'd in her bath breathing a rich savor, he expresseth the joy he felt in his sense of smelling.

Thus growing more deeply enamored, in great contentation with himself, he venters to see her in the pride of her nakedness, which doing by stealth, he discovered the comfort he conceived in seeing, and the glory of her beauty.

Not yet satisfied, he useth all his art to make known his being there without her offense; or, being necessarily offended, to appease her, which done, he entreats a kiss to serve for satisfaction of his taste, which he obtains.

Then proceeds he to entreaty for the fift sense and there is interrupted.

Narratio

The earth from heavenly light conceived heat
Which mixed all her moist parts with her dry,
When with right beams the sun her bosom beat
And with fit food her plants did nutrify;
　They (which to earth as to their mother cling
In forked roots), now sprinkled plenteously
　With her warm breath, did hasten to the spring,
Gather their proper forces, and extrude
All power but that with which they stood indu'd,

Then did Cyrrhus fill his eyes with fire, [10]
Whose ardor curl'd the foreheads of the trees,
And made his green love burn in his desire
When youth and ease (collectors of Love's fees)
　Entic'd Corinna to a silver spring
Enchasing a round bower, which with it sees
　(As with a diamant doth an amel'd ring),
Into which eye most pitifully stood
Niobe, shedding tears that were her blood. . . .

In a loose robe of tinsel forth she came,
Nothing but it betwixt her nakedness [20]
And envious light. The downward-burning flame
Of her rich hair did threaten new access
　Of vent'rous Phaeton to scorch the fields.
And thus to bathing came our poet's goddess,
　Her handmaids bearing all things pleasure yields
To such a service: odors most delighted
And purest linen which her looks had whited.

Then cast she off her robe and stood upright,
As lightning breaks out of a laboring cloud,
Or as the morning heaven casts off the night, [30]
Or as that heaven cast off itself and show'd

Heaven's upper light, to which the brightest day
Is but a black and melancholy shroud,
  Or as when Venus striv'd for sovereign sway
Of charmful beauty in young Troy's desire;
So stood Corinna vanishing her tire. . . .

And now she us'd the fount where Niobe,
Tomb'd in herself, pour'd her lost soul in tears
Upon the bosom of this Romain Phoebe,
Who, bath'd and odor'd, her bright lims she rears   40
  And, drying her on that disparent ground,
Her lute she takes t' enamor heavenly ears
  And try if with her voice's vital sound
She could warm life through those cold statues spread
And cheer the dame that wept when she was dead. . . .

While this was singing, Ovid, young in love
With her perfections, never proving yet
How merciful a mistress she would prove,
Boldly embrac'd the power he could not let
  And, like a fiery exhalation,   50
Follow'd the sun he wish'd might never set,
  Trusting herein his constellation
Rul'd by love's beams which Julia's eyes erected,
Whose beauty was the star his life directed.

And, having drench'd his ankles in those seas,
He needs would swim, and car'd not if he drown'd.
Love's feet are in his eyes, for if he please
The depth of Beauty's gulfy flood to sound
  He goes upon his eyes, and up to them
At the first step he is. No shader ground   60
  Could Ovid find, but in Love's holy stream
Was past his eyes, and now did wet his ears,
For his high sovereign's silver voice he hears.

Whereat his wit assumed fiery wings,
Soaring above the temper of his soul;
And he the purifying rapture sings
Of his ears' sense, takes full the Thespian bowl
  And it carouseth to his mistress' health,
Whose sprightful verdure did dull flesh control;
  And his conceit he crowneth with the wealth   70
Of all the muses in his pleased senses
When with the ears' delight he thus commences:

"Now, muses, come, repair your broken wings
(Pluck'd and prophan'd by rustic Ignorance)
With feathers of these notes my mistress sings;
And let quick Verse her drooping head advance
  From dungeons of contempt to smite the stars.
In Julia's tunes, led forth by furious trance,
  A thousand muses come to bid you wars,
Dive to your spring, and hide you from the stroke.   80
All poets' furies will her tunes invoke.

"Never was any sense so set on fire
With an immortal ardor as mine ears.
Her fingers to the strings doth speech inspire
And number'd laughter, that the descant bears
  To her sweet voice, whose species through my sense
My spirits to their highest function rears;
  To which, impress'd with ceaseless confluence,
It useth them as proper to her pow'r,
Marries my soul, and makes itself her dow'r. . . .   90

"O that as man is call'd a little world,
The world might shrink into a little man
To hear the notes about this garden hurl'd,
That skill, dispers'd in tunes so Orphean,
  Might not be lost in smiting stocks and trees
That have no ears, but, grown as it began,
  Spread their renowns as far as Phoebus sees
Through earth's dull veins, that she, like heaven, might
    move
In ceaseless music and be fill'd with love.

"In precious incense of her holy breath   100
My love doth offer hecatombs of notes
To all the gods, who now despise the death
Of oxen, heifers, wethers, swine, and goats.
  A sonnet in her breathing sacrifiz'd
Delights them more then all beasts' bellowing throats,
  As much with heaven as with my hearing priz'd.
And as gilt atoms in the sun appear,
So greet these sounds the grissells of mine ear,

"Whose pores do open wide to their regreet,
And my implanted air that air embraceth   110
Which they impress. I feel their nimble feet
Tread my ears' labyrinth; their sport amazeth,
  They keep such measure, play themselves, and dance.
And now my soul in Cupid's furnace blazeth,
  Wrought into fury with their dalliance.
And as the fire the parched stubble burns,
So fades my flesh, and into spirit turns. . . ."

Now in his glowing ears her tunes did sleep,
And as a silver bell, with violent blow
Of steel or iron, when his sounds most deep   120
Do from his sides and air's soft bosom flow,
  A great while after murmurs at the stroke,
Letting the hearer's ears his hardness know,
  So chid the air to be no longer broke,
And left the accents panting in his ear
Which in this banquet his first service were. . . .

[Having had all his other senses ravished, Ovid at last
requests Corinna to gratify his sense of touch.]

"Then, sacred madam, since my other senses
Have in your graces tasted such content,

Let wealth not to be spent fear no expenses,
But give thy bounty true eternizement, 130
   Making my senses' groundwork, which is Feeling,
Effect the other, endless excellent,
   Their substance with flint-soft'ning softness steeling.
Then let me feel, for know, sweet Beauty's queen,
Dames may be felt as well as heard or seen.

"For if we be allow'd to serve the ear
With pleasing tunes, and to delight the eye
With gracious shows, the taste with dainty cheer,
The smell with odors, is 't immodesty
   To serve the senses' emperor, sweet Feeling, 140
With those delights that fit his empery?
   Shall subjects free themselves and bind their king?
Minds taint no more with body's touch or tire
Then bodies nourish with the mind's desire. . . ."

Herewith, even glad his arguments to hear,
Worthily willing to have lawful grounds
To make the wondrous power of heaven appear
In nothing more then her perfections found,
   Close to her navel she her mantle wrests,
Slacking it upwards, and the folds unwound, 150
   Showing Latona's twins, her plenteous breasts,
The Sun and Cynthia, in their triumph-robes
Of lady-skin, more rich then both their globes. . . .

[When, at Corinna's request, Ovid touches her "with fear and reverence" he attains the summit of sensual pleasure, a pleasure that he rationalizes thus:]

"O Nature, how dost thou defame in this
Our human honors, yoking men with beasts
And noblest minds with slaves? Thus Beauty's bliss,
Love, and all virtues that quick spirit feasts
   Surfet on flesh; and thou that banquets minds,
Most bounteous mistress, of thy dull-tongu'd guests
   Reap'st not due thanks. Thus rude frailty binds 160
What thou giv'st wings; thus joys I feel in thee
Hang on my lips and will not uttered be.

"Sweet, touch the engine that Love's bow doth bend,
The sense wherewith he feels him deified,
The object whereto all his actions tend,
In all his blindness his most pleasing guide.
   For thy sake will I write the *Art of Love*,
Since thou dost blow his fire and feed his pride,
   Since in thy sphere his health and life doth move.
For thee I hate who hate society, 170
And such as self-love makes his slavery. . . .

"To me, dear sovereign, thou art patroness,
And I, with that thy graces have infused,
Will make all fat and foggy brains confess
Riches may from a poor verse be deduced,
   And that gold's love shall leave them groveling here
When thy perfections shall to heaven be mused,
   Deck'd in bright verse, where angels shall appear
The praise of virtue, love, and beauty singing,
Honor to noblesse, shame to avarice bringing." 180

Here Ovid, interrupted with the view
Of other dames who then the garden painted,
Shrouded himself and did as death eschew
All note by which his love's fame might be tainted.
   And as when mighty Macedon had won
The monarchy of earth, yet when he fainted,
   Griev'd that no greater action could be done
And that there were no more worlds to subdue,
So Love's defects Love's conqueror did rue.

But as, when expert painters have display'd 190
To quickest life a monarch's royal hand
Holding a scepter, there is yet bewray'd
But half his fingers, when we understand
   The rest not to be seen, and never blame
The painter's art, in nicest censures scann'd,
   So in the compass of this curious frame
Ovid well knew there was much more intended,
With whose omission none must be offended.
            Intentio animi actio.
            Explicit Convivium

A CORONET FOR HIS MISTRESS PHILOSOPHY

[SONNET 10]

Muses that Fame's loose feathers beautify,
   And such as scorn to tread the theater
   As ignorant, the seed of memory
   Have most inspir'd and shown their glories there;
To noblest wits and men of highest doom,
   That for the kingly laurel bent affair,
   The theaters of Athens and of Rome
   Have been the crowns and not the base empair.
Far, then, be this foul, cloudy-brow'd contempt
   From like-plum'd birds, and let your sacred rimes 10
   From Honor's court their servile feet exempt
   That live by soothing moods and serving times.
And let my love adorn with modest eyes
Muses that sing Love's sensual emperies.

ROBERT SOUTHWELL

Like George Herbert a little later, Robert Southwell sought to use the techniques of secular verse for religious purposes. A Jesuit martyr whose piety was almost incandescent, Southwell won quick posthumous fame with *St. Peter's Complaint* (1595), a long narrative and meditative poem about Christ's passion and Peter's remorse for his unstable faith; not only is it written in the stanza of Shakespeare's *Venus and Adonis* (1593), but its style exhibits a persistent and sometimes grotesque effort to render spiritual and moral values in extravagantly sensuous conceits. Southwell must have known Italian poetry from his residence at the English College in Rome, and he reveals a baroque tendency to merge the timeless and the temporal, seeking an immediate sensuous apprehension of what he regarded as eternal truths. Thus he is able to project his martyr's piety in lyrics where the convolutions of conceits, paradoxes, and wit-writing seem the results of artifice rather than holiness. Although virtually all his shorter pieces are on such themes as

contemptus mundi and the beauty of death, in form and texture they often recall the amatory poems of an obsolescent Petrarchan tradition. All Southwell's English poetry was published posthumously, *St. Peter's Complaint* shortly after he had won his long-sought and barbarous martyrdom at Tyburn (1595) and *Moeoniae* (a loose collection of poems on religious and miraculous subjects) in at least two editions during the same year. *St. Peter's Complaint* was so popular that it was reprinted (with various additions) thirteen times by 1638. An edition in 1602 first contained "The Burning Babe," a poem which Ben Jonson admired immensely and which has remained a favorite of anthologists. Our texts are based upon *Moeoniae. Or, Certaine excellent Poems and spirituall Hymnes,* 1595 (STC 22954); *Saint Peters complaynt. With other Poems,* 1595 (STC 22956); *St Peters Complain[t]e Mary Magdal. teares Wth other workes of the author R:S:,* 1636 (STC 22968).

FROM MOEONIAE, OR CERTAIN EXCELLENT POEMS AND SPIRITUAL HYMNS (1595)

THE VIRGIN MARY'S CONCEPTION

Our second Eve puts on her mortal shroud,
Earth breeds a heaven for God's new dwelling-place,
Now riseth up Elias' little cloud
That, growing, shall distill the show'r of grace.
Her being now begins who, ere she end,
Shall bring our good that shall our ill amend;
Both grace and nature did their force unite
To make this babe the sum of all their best:
Our most her least, our million but her mite.
She was at easiest rate worth all the rest;   10
What grace to men or angels God did part
Was all united in this infant's heart.
Four only wights bred without fault are nam'd,
And all the rest conceived were in sin:
Without both man and wife was Adam fram'd,
Of man but not of wife did Eve begin,
Wife without touch of man Christ's mother was,
Of man and wife this babe was born in grace.

CHRIST'S BLOODY SWEAT

Fat soil, full spring, sweet olive, grape of bliss
That yields, that streams, that powers, that dost distill,
Untill'd, undrawn, unstamp'd, untouch'd of press,
Dear fruit, clear brooks, fair oil, sweet wine at will.
Thus Christ unforc'd prevents in sheeding blood

The whips, the thorns, the nail, the spear, and rood.
He pelican's, he phoenix' fate doth prove,
Whom flames consume when streams enforce to die.
How burneth blood, how bleedeth burning love?
Can one in flame and stream both bathe and fry?   10
How would he join a phoenix' fiery pains
In fainting pelican's still bleeding veins?

UPON THE IMAGE OF DEATH

Before my face the picture hangs
   That daily should put me in mind
Of those cold names and bitter pangs
   That shortly I am like to find;
But yet, alas, full little I
   Do think hereon that I must die.

I often look upon a face
   Most ugly, grisly, bare, and thin;
I often view the hollow place
   Where eyes and nose have sometimes bin;   10
I see the bones across that lie,
   Yet little think that I must die.

I read the label underneath,
   That telleth me whereto I must;
I see the sentence eke that saith,

"Remember, man, that thou art dust!"
But yet, alas, but seldom I
 Do think indeed that I must die.

Continually at my bed's head
 A hearse doth hang, which doth me tell   20
That I yer morning may be dead,
 Though now I feel myself full well;
But now, alas, for all this, I
 Have little mind that I must die.

The gown which I do use to wear,
 The knife wherewith I cut my meat,
And eke that old and ancient chair
 Which is my only usual seat—
All those do tell me I must die,
 And yet my life amend not I.   30

My ancestors are turn'd to clay,
 And many of my mates are gone;
My youngers daily drop away,
 And can I think to scape alone?
No, no, I know that I must die,
 And yet my life amend not I.

Not Salomon for all his wits,
 Nor Sampson, though he were so strong,
No king nor ever person yet
 Could scape but death laid him along;   40
Wherefore I know that I must die,
 And yet my life amend not I.

Though all the East did quake to hear
 Of Alexander's dreadful name,
And all the West did likewise fear
 To hear of Julius Caesar's fame,

Yet both by death in dust now lie;
 Who then can scape but he must die?

If none can scape Death's dreadful dart,
 If rich and poor his beck obey,   50
If strong, if wise, if all do smart,
 Then I to scape shall have no way.
O grant me grace, O God, that I
 My life may mend, sith I must die.

SEEK FLOWERS OF HEAVEN

Soar up, my soul, unto thy rest,
 cast off this loathsome load;
Long is the date of thy exile,
 too long the strict abode;
Graze not on worldly withered weed,
 it fitteth not thy taste;
The flowers of everlasting spring
 do grow for thy repaste.
Their leaves are stain'd in beauty's dye
 and blazed with their beams,   10
Their stalks inamel'd with delight
 and limm'd with glorious gleams;
Life-giving juice of living love
 their sug'red veins doth fill,
And wat'red with everlasting showers
 they nectared drops distill.
These flowers do spring from fertile soil,
 though from unmanur'd field;
Most glittering gold in lieu of glebe
 these fragrant flowers do yield,   20
Whose sovereign scent, surpassing sense,
 so ravisheth the mind
That worldly weeds needs must he loath
 that can these flowers find.

FROM SAINT PETER'S COMPLAINT. WITH OTHER POEMS (1595)

LOVE'S SERVILE LOT

Love mistress is of many minds,
 Yet few know whom they serve;
They reckon least how little love
 Their service doth deserve.

The will she robbeth from the wit,
 The sense from reason's lore;
She is delightful in the rine,
 Corrupted in the core.

She shroudeth vice in virtue's veil,
 Pretending good in ill,   10
She offereth joy, affordeth grief,
 A kiss where she doth kill.

A honey-shower rains from her lips,
 Sweet lights shine in her face;
She hath the blush of virgin mild,
 The mind of viper's race.

She makes thee seek yet fear to find,
 To find but not enjoy;
In many frowns some gliding smiles
 She yields—to more annoy.   20

She woos thee to come near her fire,
 Yet doth she draw it from thee;
Far off she makes thy heart to fry
 And yet to freeze within thee.

She letteth fall some luring baits
    For fools to gather up;
To sweet, to sour, to every taste,
    She tempereth her cup.

Soft souls she binds in tender twist,
    Small flies in spinner's web;   30
She sets afloat some luring streams
    But makes them soon to ebb.

Her wat'ry eyes have burning force,
    Her floods and flames conspire;
Tears kindle sparks, sobs fuel are,
    And sighs do blow her fire.

May never was the month of love,
    For May is full of flowers,
But rather April, wet by kind,
    For love is full of showers.   40

Like tyrant cruel wounds she gives,
    Like surgeon salve she lends,
But salve and sore have equal force,
    For death is both their ends.

With soothing words inthralled souls
    She chains in servile bands;
Her eye in silence hath a speech
    Which eye best understands.

Her little sweet hath many sours;
    Short hap, immortal harms;   50
Her loving looks are murd'ring darts,
    Her songs, bewitching charms.

Like winter rose and summer ice
    Her joys are still untimely;
Before her, hope; behind, remorse;
    Fair first, in fine unseemly.

Moods, passions, fancies, jealous fits
    Attend upon her train;

She yieldeth rest without repose,
    A heav'n in hellish pain.   60

Her house is sloth, her door deceit,
    And slippery hope her stairs;
Unbashful boldness bids her guests
    And every vice repairs.

Her diet is of such delight
    As please till they be past,
But then the poison kills the heart
    That did entice the taste.

Her sleep in sin doth end in wrath,
    Remorse rings her awake;   70
Death calls her up, shame drives her out,
    Dispairs her upshot make.

Plow not the seas, sow not the sands,
    Leave off your idle pain;
Seek other mistress for your minds,
    Love's service is in vain.

I DIE ALIVE

O life, what lets thee from a quick decease?
O death, what draws thee from a present prey?
My feast is done, my soul would be at ease,
    My grace is said—O death, come take away.

I live, but such a life as ever dies;
I die, but such a death as never ends;
My death to end my dying life denies,
    And life my living death no whit amends.

Thus still I die, yet still I do revive,
My living death by dying life is fed;   10
Grace more then nature keeps my heart alive,
    Whose idle hopes and vain desires are dead.

Not where I breathe but where I love I live,
Not where I love but where I am I die;
The life I wish must future glory give;
    The deaths I feel in present dangers lie.

FROM ST. PETER'S COMPLAINT . . . WITH OTHER WORKS OF THE AUTHOR (1636)

NEW PRINCE NEW POMP

Behold a silly, tender babe
    In freezing winter night
In homely manger trembling lies—
    Alas, a piteous sight.
The inns are full; no man will yield
    This little pilgrim bed,
But forc'd he is with silly beasts
    In crib to shroud his head.

Despise him not for lying there,
    First what he is enquire;   10
An orient pearl is often found
    In depth of dirty mire.
Weigh not his crib, his wooden dish,
    Nor beasts that by him feed;
Weigh not his mother's poor attire
    Nor Joseph's simple weed.
This stable is a prince's court.
    The crib his chair of state;

The beasts are parcel of his pomp,
  The wooden dish his plate.   20
The persons in that poor attire
  His royal liveries wear;
The prince himself is come from heaven,
  This pomp is prized there.
With joy approach, O Christian wight!
  Do homage to thy king,
And highly praise his humble pomp
  Which he from heaven doth bring.

THE BURNING BABE

As I in hoary winter's night
  stood shivering in the snow,
Surpris'd I was with sudden heat
  which made my heart to glow;
And lifting up a fearful eye
  to view what fire was near,
A pretty babe all burning bright
  did in the air appear;
Who, scorched with excessive heat,
  such floods of tears did shed   10

As though his floods should quench his flames,
  which with his tears were bred.
"Alas," quoth he, "but newly born
  in fiery heats I fry,
Yet none approach to warm their hearts
  or feel my fire but I;
My faultless breast the fornace is,
  the fuel wounding thorns;
Love is the fire and sighs the smoke,
  the ashes shames and scorns;   20
The fuel Justice layeth on,
  and Mercy blows the coals;
The metal in this fornace wrought
  are men's defiled souls,
For which as now on fire I am
  to work them to their good,
So will I melt into a bath
  to wash them in my blood."
With this he vanish'd out of sight
  and swiftly shrunk away,   30
And straight I called unto mind
  that it was Christmas day.

JOSEPH HALL

The work of Skelton, Wyatt, Lodge, and Donne—which Joseph Hall surely knew—somewhat undercuts his famous boast of being the first English satirist. Yet when he published the first part of *Virgidemiae* in 1597, a year after he had proceeded M.A. at Emmanuel College, Cambridge, he leapt into literary fame. And with good reason, for by producing the first Juvenalian satire in the language he had opened a path that many were to tread. The essential qualities of Juvenal's satire (and of Hall's imitation) are its stylized obscurity and its moral vigor. The jagged transitions, cryptic and often disguised allusions to actual persons, and high rhetorical polish are its hallmarks just as surely as its rigidly moral function of castigating folly through ridicule. *Virgidemiae* means "a harvest of switches," and Hall obviously regarded satire as an agency of moral indictment and therapy. None the less, the first instalment of his work (the three books of so-called "toothless satires") reaches no great heights of moral indignation. Book I contains a good deal of interesting literary comment, if not criticism, on such contemporaries as the Petrarchan sonneteers, Spenser, and Marlowe; and the second and third books ironically survey such frauds as astrologers, whining lovers, and parsimonious patrons. The "biting satires" of the second instalment (1598) more nearly approach Juvenal both in their fiendish obscurity and in their attacks on persons rather than types: Lollio is a grubby miser whose son wastes his money and is ashamed to acknowledge his father; Gallio is so effeminate and refined that he is a monster of self-indulgence; Virginius is a finicky bachelor who waits too long to marry.

Hall's work was successful enough to spawn a host of imitators, among them Marston, Guilpin, and the author of *Microcynicon;* but on June 1, 1599, John Whitgift and Richard Bancroft, the Archbishop of Canterbury and the Bishop of London respectively, dismayed by the spate of scurrilous literature, condemned and ordered burned by the common hangman a long list of such offensive books, both satirical and erotic. The list included Hall's *Virgidemiae,* Marston's *Metamorphosis of Pygmalion's Image,* Guilpin's *Skialetheia,* Thomas Cutwode's *Caltha Poetarum,* Marlowe's *Elegies* and Davies' *Epigrams* (which were printed together), *Microcynicon, The XV Joys of Marriage,* and all the items in the Nashe-Harvey controversy (see pp. 859–60); in addition, the authorities decreed "that no satires or epigrams be printed hereafter" and "that no English histories be printed except they be allowed by some of her Majesty's privy council." For some reason Hall's and Cutwode's books were at the last minute reprieved, but the others were publicly destroyed on June 4, 1599.

Shortly after this holocaust Hall took holy orders, and as a loyal and articulate Anglican divine he lived long enough to lock horns with young John Milton on the eve of the Great Rebellion. Our text is based upon *Virgidemiarum, Six Bookes. . . . Corrected and amended,* 1598 (STC 12716).

FROM VIRGIDEMIARUM, SIX BOOKS (1598)

Liber I

PROLOGUE

I first adventure, with foolhardy might,
To tread the steps of perilous despight;
I first adventure; follow me who list,
And be the second English satirist.
Envy waits on my back, Truth on my side;
Envy will be my page and Truth my guide.
Envy the margent holds and Truth the line;
Truth doth approve, but Envy doth repine.
For in this smoothing age who durst indite
Hath made his pen an hired parasite   10
To claw the back of him that beastly lives
And prank base men in proud superlatives.
Whence damned Vice is shrouded quite from shame
And crown'd with Virtue's meed, immortal name;
Infamy, dispossess'd of native due,
Ordain'd of old on looser life to sue;
The world's eye bleared with those shameless lies,
Mask'd in the shew of meal-mouth'd poesies.
Go, daring muse, on with thy thankless task,
And do the ugly face of Vice unmask;   20
And if thou canst not thine high flight remit
So as it mought a lowly satire fit,
Let lowly satires rise aloft to thee.
Truth be thy speed and Truth thy patron be.

SATIRE VII

Great is the folly of a feeble brain
O'errul'd with love and tyrannous disdain,
For love, however in the basest breast
It breeds high thoughts that feed the fancy best,
Yet is he blind, and leads poor fools awry
While they hang, gazing, on their mistress' eye.
The love-sick poet, whose importune prayer
Repulsed is with resolute dispair,
Hopeth to conquer his disdainful dame
With publique plaints of his conceived flame;   10
Then pours he forth in patched sonnetings
His love, his lust, and lothsome flatterings,
As tho the staring world hang'd on his sleeve
When once he smiles to laugh and when he sighs to grieve.
Careth the world thou love, thou live, or die?
Careth the world how fair thy fair one be?
Fond wittold, that wouldst load thy witless head
With timely horns before thy bridal bed!
Then can he term his dirty, ill-fac'd bride
Lady and queen and virgin deifi'd;   20
Be she all sooty-black or berry-brown,
She's white as morrow's milk or flakes new-blown;

And tho she be some dunghill drudge at home,
Yet can he her resign some refuse room
Amids the well-known stars. Or, if not there,
Sure will he saint her in his calender.

Liber II

SATIRE VI

A gentle squire would gladly intertain
Into his house some trencher-chaplain,
Some willing man that might instruct his sons
And that would stand to good conditions.
First, that he lie upon the truckle-bed
Whiles his young maister lieth o'er his head;
Secondly, that he do, on no default,
Ever presume to sit above the salt;
Third, that he never change his trencher twice;
Fourth, that he use all comely courtesies,   10
Sit bare at meals and one-half rise and wait;
Last, that he never his young master beat
But he must ask his mother to define
How many jerks she would his breech should line.
All these observ'd, he could contented be
To give five marks and winter livery.

Liber III

SATIRE II

Great Osmond knows not how he shall be known
When once great Osmond shall be dead and gone,
Unless he rear up some rich monument
Ten furlongs nearer to the firmament.
Some stately tomb he builds, Egyptian-wise,
Rex regum written on the pyramis,
Whereas great Arthur lies in ruder oak
That never felt none but the feller's stroke.
Small honor can be got with gawdy grave,
Nor it thy rotting name from death can save.   10
The fairer tomb, the fouler is thy name,
The greater pomp procuring greater shame.
Thy monument make thou thy living deeds;
No other tomb then that true virtue needs.
What? Had he nought whereby he might be known
But costly pilements of some curious stone?
The matter Nature's and the workman's frame
His purse's cost—where, then, is Osmond's name?
Deserv'dst thou ill? Well were thy name and thee
Wert thou inditched in great secrecy   20
Whereas no passenger might curse thy dust,
Nor dogs sepulchral sate their gnawing lust.
Thine ill desarts cannot be grav'd with thee
So long as on thy grave they engraved be.

Liber IV

SATIRE VI

Quid placet ergo?

I wot not how the world's degenerate
That men or know or like not their estate.
Out from the Gades up to the eastern morn
Not one but holds his native state forlorn.
When comely striplings wish it were their chance
For Caenis' distaff to exchange their lance,
And wear curl'd periwigs, and chalk their face,
And still are poring on their pocket-glass;
Tir'd with pinn'd ruffs and fans and partlet strips
And busks, and verdingales about their hips,   10
And tread on corked stilts a prisoner's pace,
And make their napkin for their spitting-place,
And gripe their waist within a narrow span.
Fond Caenis that wouldst wish to be a man,
Whose mannish huswives like their refuse state
And make a drudge of their uxorious mate,
Who, like a cotquean, freezeth at the rock
Whiles his breech'd dame doth man the foreign stock.
Is 't not a shame to see each homely groom
Sit perched in an idle chariot room   20
That were not meet some panel to bestride
Surcingled to a galled hackney's hide?
Each muckworm will be rich with lawless gain,
Although he smother up mows of seven years' grain
And hang himself when corn grows cheap again;
Altho he buy whole harvests in the spring
And foist in false strikes to the measuring;
Although his shop be muffled from the light,
Like a day-dungeon or Cimmerian night.
Not full nor fasting can the carl take rest   30
Whiles his George-nobles rusten in his chest.
He sleeps but once and dreams of burglary,
And wakes and casts about his frighted eye,
And gropes for thieves in every darker shade,
And if a mouse but stir he calls for aid.
The sturdy plowman doth the soldier see
All scarfed with pi'd colors to the knee,
Whom Indian pillage hath made fortunate;
And now he gins to loth his former state;
Now doth he inly scorn his Kendal-green,   40
And his patch'd cockers now despised been.
Nor list he now go whistling to the car,
But sells his team and settleth to the war.
O war, to them that never tried thee sweet!
When his dead mate falls groveling at his feet,
And angry bullets whistlen at his ear,
And his dim eyes see nought but death and drere,
O happy plowman, were thy weal well known,
O happy all estates except his own!
Some dronken rimer thinks his time well spent   50

If he can live to see his name in print,
Who, when he is once fleshed to the press
And sees his handsel have such fair success,
Sung to the wheel and sung unto the pail,
He sends forth thraves of ballads to the sale,
Nor then can rest, but volumes up bodg'd rimes
To have his name talk'd of in future times.
The brainsick youth that feeds his tickled ear
With sweet-sauc'd lies of some false traveler
Which hath the Spanish *Decades* read a while,   60
Or whetstone leasings of old Mandeville,
Now with discourses breaks his midnight sleep
Of his adventures through the Indian deep,
Of all their massy heaps of golden mines,
Or of the antique tombs of Palestine,
Or of Damascus' magic wall of glass,
Of Salomon his sweating piles of brass,
Of the bird ruc that bears an elephant,
Of mermaids that the southern seas do haunt,
Of headless men, of savage cannibals   70
The fashions of their lives and governals.
What monstrous cities there erected be,
Cairo or the City of the Trinity.
Now are they dunghill cocks that have not seen
The bordering Alps or else the neighbor Rhene;
And now he plies the newsful grasshopper
Of voyages and ventures to enquire.
His land mortgag'd, he, sea-beat in the way,
Wishes for home a thousand sithes a day;
And now he deems his homebred fare as leefe   80
As his parch'd bisket or his barrel'd beef.
Mongst all these sturs of discontented strife
O let me lead an academic life:
To know much and to think we nothing know,
Nothing to have, yet think we have enough;
In skill to want, and, wanting, seek for more;
In weal nor want nor wish for greater store.
Envy, ye monarchs with your proud excess,
At our low sail and our high happiness.

A Postscript to the Reader

It is not for everyone to relish a true and natural
satire, being of itself, besides the native and inbred
bitterness and tartness of the perticulars, both hard
of concept and harsh of style, and therefore cannot
but be unpleasing both to the unskilful and over-
musical ear; the one being affected with only a shallow and easy matter, the other with a smooth and
currant disposition. So that I well foresee in the timely
publication of these my concealed satires I am set
upon the rack of many merciless and peremptory
censures, which sith the calmest and most plausible
writer is almost fatally subject unto in the curiosity
of these nicer times, how may I hope to be exempted

upon the occasion of so busy and stirring a subject? One thinks it misbeseeming the author because a poem, another unlawful in itself because a satire, a third harmless to others for the sharpness, a fourth un-satire-like for the mildness. The learned, too perspicuous, being named with Juvenal, Persius, and the other ancient satires; the unlearned, savorless because too obscure, and obscure because not under their reach. What a monster must he be that would please all! . . .

For my satires themselves, I see two obvious cavils to be answered. One concerning the matter, then which, I confess, none can be more open to danger, to envy, sith faults loth nothing more then the light, and men love nothing more then their faults; and therefore, what through the nature of the faults and fault of the persons, it is impossible so violent an appeachment should be quietly brooked. But why should vices be unblamed for fear of blame? And if thou mayst spit upon a toad unvenomed, why mayst thou not speak of a vice without danger? Especially so warily as I have indeavored, who, in the unpartial mention of so many vices, may safely profess to be altogether guiltless in myself to the intention of any guilty person who might be blemished by the likelihood of my conceived application, thereupon choosing rather to mar mine own verse then another's name. Which notwithstanding, if the injurious reader shall wrest to his own spight and disparaging of others, it is a short answer: Art thou guilty? Complain not, thou art not wronged. Art thou guiltless? Complain not, thou art not touched. The other concerning the manner, wherein perhaps too much stooping to the low reach of the vulgar I shall be thought not to have any whit kindly raught my ancient Roman predecessors, whom, in the want of more late and familiar presidents, I am constrained thus far off to imitate, which thing I can be so willing

to grant that I am further ready to warrant my action therein to any indifferent censure. First, therefore, I dare boldly avouch that the English is not altogether so natural to a satire as the Latin, which I do not impute to the nature of the language itself, being so far from disabling it anyway that, methinks, I durst equal it to the proudest in every respect, but to that which is common to it with all other common languages—Italian, French, Germain, etc.—in their poesies: the fettering together the series of the verses with the bonds of like cadence or desinence of rime, which, if it be usually abrupt and not dependent in sense upon so near affinity of words, I know not what a lothsome kind of harshness and discordance it breedeth to any judicial ear. Which if any more confident adversary shall gainsay, I wish no better trial then the translation of one of Persius his satires into English, the difficulty and dissonance whereof shall make good my assertion, besides the plain experience thereof in the satires of Ariosto, save which and one base French satire I could never attain the view of any for my direction. . . . Let my second ground be the well-known daintiness of the time, such that men rather choose carelessly to lease the sweet of the kernel then to urge their teeth with breaking of the shell wherein it is wrapped. . . . Thirdly, the end of this pains was a satire, but the end of my satire a further good, which whether I attain or no I know not, but let me be plain with hope of profit rather then purposely obscure only for a bare name's sake.

Notwithstanding in the expectation of this quarrel, I think my first satire doth somewhat resemble the sour and crabbed face of Juvenal's, which I, indeavoring in that, did determinately omit in the rest for these forenamed causes, that so I might have somewhat to stop the mouth of every accuser. The rest to each man's censure, which let be as favorable as so thankless a work can deserve or desire.

JOHN MARSTON

Fresh from Brasenose College, Oxford, and from a conventional flirtation with the law, John Marston erupted into literature as flamboyantly as possible. His *Metamorphosis of Pygmalion's Image and Certain Satires*, a pornographic imitation of the Ovidian narratives of Lodge, Marlowe, Shakespeare, Drayton, and others, was published anonymously in 1598 with a dedication signed W. K. On September 8 of the same year *The Scourge of Villany* was licensed and shortly thereafter published. It at once established its author as the *enfant terrible* of con-

temporary letters. With his two instalments of *Virgidemiae* (1597–98) Joseph Hall, launching the vogue of knotty, obscure satire in the style of Juvenal, had not only claimed the title of the first English satirist but had perhaps ridiculed Marston as "Labeo" (VI.i.185–6). Marston promptly excoriated Hall in a satire called "Reactio," and in the preface to the second (1599) edition of the *Scourge* defended his "plainness gainst the verjuice face of the crabbed'st satirist that ever stuttered." This preface, signed W. Kinsayder (which perhaps means "cutter of dogs' tails"), is as ostentatiously ill-tempered as the ten satires it introduces. The work of a bookish and peevish young man commenting darkly (and often obscenely) on life in London, it is dedicated "To his most esteemed and best-beloved self," "presented" to "Detraction," and allegedly motivated by a savage indignation at the sins and crimes of urban life. Yet Marston is repeatedly more lascivious than his subjects; and although there is some valuable commentary on his fellow writers (especially in Satire VI), it is hard to tell how much of his work derives from a genuine misanthropy and disenchantment, how much from the theatrical posturing of a modish malcontent. Both his tedious little quarrel with Hall (which seems to have been whipped up mainly by Marston) and the audacious railing at his other contemporaries were abruptly silenced by an ecclesiastical ban on such works in June, 1599. Our text is based upon *The Scourge of Villanie. Corrected, with the addition of newe Satyres,* 1599 (STC 17486).

FROM THE SCOURGE OF VILLANY (1599)

To Detraction I Present My Poesy

Foul canker of fair, virtuous action,
Vile blaster of the freshest blooms on earth,
Envy's abhorred child, Detraction,
I here expose to thy all-tainting breath
The issue of my brain. Snarl, rail, bark, bite!
Know that my spirit scorns Detraction's spite.

Know that the Genius which attendeth on
And guides my powers intellectual
Holds in all vile repute Detraction—
My soul an essence metaphysical   10
That, in the basest sort, scorns critics' rage
Because he knows his sacred parentage.

My spirit is not puff'd up with fat fume
Of slimy ale nor Bacchus' heating grape.
My mind disdains the dungy, muddy scum
Of abject thoughts and envy's raging hate.
True judgment slight regards opinion;
A sprightly wit disdains Detraction.

A partial praise shall never elevate
My settled censure of mine own esteem.   20
A cankered verdit of malignant hate
Shall ne'er provoke me worse myself to deem.
Spite of despite and rancor's villany
I am myself. So is my poesy.

To Those That Seem Judicial Perusers

Know I hate to affect too much obscurity and harshness, because they profit no sense. To note vices so that no man can understand them is as fond as the French execution in picture. Yet there are some (too many) that think nothing good that is so curteous as to come within their reach, terming all satires bastard which are not palpable dark and so rough writ that the hearing of them read would set a man's teeth on edge. For whose unseason'd palate I wrote the first satire in some places too obscure, in all places misliking me. Yet when, by some scurvy chance, it shall come into the late perfumed fist of judicial Torquatus (that, like some rotten stick in a troubled water, hath got a great deal of barmy froth to stick to his sides) I know he will vouchsafe it some of his new-minted epithets (as *real, intrinsicate, delphic*) when, in my conscience, he understands not the least part of it. But from thence proceeds his judgment. Persius is crabby because ancient, and his jerks (being particularly given to private customs of his time) dusky. Juvenal (upon the like occasion) seems to our judgment gloomy. Yet both of them go a good, seemly pace, not stumbling, shuffling. Chaucer is hard even to our understandings. Who knows not the reason? How much more those old satires which express themselves in terms that breathed not long even in their days! But had we then lived, the understanding of them had been nothing hard. I will not deny there is a seemly decorum to be observed, and a peculiar kind of speech for a satire's lips, which I can willinglier conceive then dare to prescribe; yet let me have the substance rough, not the shadow. I cannot—nay, I will not—delude your sight with mists; yet I dare defend my plainness gainst the verjuice face of the crabbed'st satirist that ever stuttered. He that thinks worse of my rimes then myself, I scorn him, for he cannot; he that thinks better is a fool. So favor me, good opinion, as I am far from being a Suffenus. If thou perusest me with an unpartial eye, read on; if otherwise, know I neither value thee nor thy censure.

                                                    W. Kinsayder

PROEMIUM IN LIBRUM PRIMUM

I bear the scourge of just Rhamnusia,
Lashing the lewdness of Britannia.
Let others sing, as their good genius moves,
Of deep designs or else of clipping loves;
Fair fall them all that, with wit's industry,
Do clothe good subjects in true poesy.
But as for me, my vexed, thoughtful soul
Takes pleasure in displeasing sharp control.

    Thou nursing mother of fair Wisdom's lore,
Ingenuous Melancholy, I implore   10
Thy grave assistance! Take thy gloomy seat!
Inthrone thee in my blood, let me intreat.
Stay his quick, jocund skips and force him run
A sad-pac'd course until my whips be done.
Daphne, unclip thine arms from my sad brow!
Black cypress crown me whilst I up do plow
The hidden entrails of rank villany,
Tearing the veil from damn'd impiety.

    Quake, guzzle dogs, that live on putrid slime!
Scud from the lashes of my yerking rime.   20

SATIRE II
Difficile est satyram non scribere

I cannot hold, I cannot, I, indure
To view a big-womb'd, foggy cloud immure
The radiant tresses of the quick'ning sun.
Let custards quake. My rage must freely run.
Preach not the Stoic's patience to me!
I hate no man, but men's impiety.
My soul is vex'd. What power will'th desist
Or dares to stop a sharp-fang'd satirist?
Who'll cool my rage? Who'll stay my itching fist,
But I will plague and torture whom I list?   10
If that the three-fold walls of Babylon
Should hedge my tongue, yet I should rail upon
This fusty world that now dare put in ure
To make Jehovah but a coverture
To shade rank filth. Loose conscience is free
From all conscience. What else hath liberty?
As 't please the Thracian Boreas to blow,
So turns our airy conscience to and fro.

    What icy Saturnist, what northern pate,
But such gross lewdness would exasperate?   20
I think the blind doth see the flame-god rise
From sister's couch each morning to the skies,
Glowing with lust. Walk but in dusky night
With Lynceus' eyes, and to thy piercing sight
Disguised gods will show in peasants' shape,
Prest to commit some execrable rape.
Here Jove's lust-pander, Maia's juggling son,
In clown's disguise doth after milkmaids run;
And fore he'll loose his brutish lechery
The trulls shall taste sweet nectar's surquedry.   30
There Juno's brat forsakes Nereis' bed

And, like a swaggerer, lust-fired,
Attended only with his smock-sworn page,
Pert Gallus, slyly slips along to wage
Tilting incounters with some spurious seed
Of marrow pies and yawning oysters' breed.
        O damn'd! . . .

    O what dry brain melts not sharp mustard rime
To purge the snottery of our slimy time?
Hence, idle *cave!* Vengeance pricks me on   40
When mart is made of fair religion.
Reform'd, bald Trebus swore in Romish quiere
He sold God's essence for a poor denier.
The Egyptians adored onions,
To garlic yielding all devotions:
O happy garlic, but thrice happy you
Whose scenting gods in your large gardens grew.
Democritus, rise from thy putrid slime;
Sport at the madness of that hotter clime.
Deride their frenzy that, for policy,   50
Adore wheat dough as real deity.
Almighty men that can their Maker make,
And force his sacred body to forsake
The cherubines to be gnawn actually,
Deviding *individuum,* really,
Making a score of gods with one poor word—
Aye, so I thought, in that you could afford
So cheap a pennyworth. O ample field
In which a satire may just weapon wield!
But I am vex'd when swarms of Julians   60
Are still manur'd by lewd precisians
Who, scorning church rites, take the symbol up
As slovenly as careless courtiers slup
Their mutton gruel. Fie, who can withhold,
But must of force make his mild muse a scold
When that he, grieved, sees, with red, vex'd eyes,
That Athens' ancient, large immunities
Are eyesores to the Fates? Poor cells forlorn!
Is 't not enough you are made an abject scorn
To jeering apes, but must the shadow, too,   70
Of ancient substance be thus wrung from you?
O split my heart lest it do break with rage
To see th' immodest looseness of our age.
Immodest looseness? Fie, too gentle word
When every sign can brothelry afford,
When lust doth sparkle from our females' eyes,
And modesty is rousted in the skies. . . .

SATIRE IV
Cras

. . . Vice, from privation of that sacred grace
Which God withdraws but puts not vice in place.
Who says the sun is cause of ugly night?
Yet when he veils our eyes from his fair sight
The gloomy curtain of the night is spread.

Ye curious sots, vainly by Nature led,
Where is your vice or virtuous habit now?
For *Sustine pro nunc* doth bend his brow,
And old, crabb'd Scotus on th' *Organon*
Pay'th me with snaphaunce, quick distinction: 10
"Habits that intellectual termed be
Are got, or else infus'd, from Deity."
Dull Sorbonist, fly contradiction!
Fie, thou oppugn'st the definition.
If one should say, "Of things term'd rational
Some reason have, others mere sensual,"
Would not some freshman, reading Porphyry,
Hiss and deride such blockish foolery?
"Then vice nor virtue have from habit place:
The one from want, the other sacred grace;   20
Infus'd, displac'd, not in our will or force,
But as it please Jehovah have remorse."
"I will," cries Zeno. O presumption!
"I can"—thou mayst, dogged opinion
Of thwarting Cynics. Today vicious,
List to their precepts, next day virtuous.
Peace, Seneca, thou belchest blasphemy:
"To live from God, but to live happily"
(I hear thee boast) "from thy philosophy
And from thyself." O ravening lunacy!   30
Cynics, ye wound yourselves; for destiny,
Inevitable fate, necessity,
You hold, doth sway the acts spiritual
As well as parts of that we mortal call.
Where's then "I will"? Where's that strong deity
You do ascribe to your philosophy?
Confounded Nature's brats, can will and fate
Have both their seat and office in your pate?
O hidden depth of that dread secrecy
Which I do trembling touch in poetry!   40
Today, today implore obsequiously!
Trust not tomorrow's will, lest utterly
Ye be attach'd with sad confusion
In your grace-tempting, lewd presumption.
   But I forget. Why sweat I out my brain
In deep designs to gay boys lewd and vain?
These notes were better sung mong better sort.
But to my pamphlet few save fools resort.
                    Libri primi finis

SATIRE VII
A Cynic Satire

"A man, a man, a kingdom for a man!"
"Why, how now, currish, mad Athenian?
Thou Cynic dog, seest not streets do swarm
With troops of men?" "No, no, for Circe's charm
Hath turn'd them all to swine. I never shall
Think those same Samian saws authentical,
But rather I dare swear the souls of swine
Do live in men; for that same radiant shine,

That luster wherewith Nature's nature [foiled]
Our intellectual part, that gloss, is soiled   10
With staining spots of vile impiety
And muddy dirt of sensuality.
These are no men, but apparitions,
Ignes fatui, glowworms, fictions,
Meteors, rats of Nilus, fantasies,
Colosses, pictures, shades, resemblances.

            "Ho, Linceus!
Seest thou yon gallant in the sumptuous clothes,
How brisk, how spruce, how gorgiously he shows?
Note his French herring-bones, but note no more   20
Unless thou spy his fair appendant whore
That lackeys him. Mark nothing but his clothes,
His new-stamp'd complement, his cannou oaths.
Mark those, for naught but such lewd viciousness
Ere graced him save Sodom beastliness.
Is this a man? Nay, an incarnate devil
That struts in vice and glorieth in evil.
   "A man, a man!" "Peace, Cynic. Yon is one,
A complete soul of all perfection."
"What, mean'st thou him that walks all open-breasted,   30
Drawn through the ear with ribands, plumy crested?
He that doth snort in fat-fed luxury
And gapes for some grinding monopoly?
He that in effeminate invention,
In beastly source of all pollution,
In riot, lust, and fleshly-seeming sweetness
Sleeps sound secure under the shade of greatness?
Mean'st thou that senseless, sensual Epicure?
That sink of filth, that guzzle most impure?
What, he? Linceus, on my word thus presume: 40
He's nought but clothes and scenting sweet perfume.
His very soul, assure thee, Linceus,
Is not so big as is an atomus.
Nay, he is sprightless; sense or soul hath none
Since last Medusa turn'd him to a stone. . . .

   "Now rail no more at my sharp Cynic sound,
Thou brutish world that, in all vileness drown'd,
Hast lost thy soul; for naught but shades I see;
Resemblances of men inhabit thee.
   "Yon tissue-slop, yon holy-crossed pane   50
Is but a water spaniel that will fawn
And kiss the water whilst it pleasures him,
But, being once arrived at the brim,
He shakes it off.
   "Yon in the cap'ring cloak, a mimic ape
That only strives to seem another's shape.
   "Yon Aesop's ass, yon sad civility,
Is but an ox that, with base drudgery,
Ears up the land whilst some gilt ass doth chaw
The golden wheat, he well-apay'd with straw.   60
   "Yon's but a muckhill overspread with snow,
Which with that veil doth even as fairly show

As the green meads whose native, outward fair
Breathes sweet perfumes into the neighbor air.
   "Yon effeminate, sanguine Ganymede
Is but a beaver, hunted for the bed."
   "Peace, Cynic! See what yonder doth approach?"
"A cart? A tumbrel?" "No, a badged coach."
"What's in 't? Some man?" "No, nor yet womankind,
But a celestial angel, fair refin'd."   70
"The Devil as soon." "Her mask so hinders me
I cannot see her beauty's deity."
"Now that is off, she is so vizarded,
So steep'd in lemon's juice, so surphuled,
I cannot see her face. Under one hood
Two faces, but I never understood
Or saw one face under two hoods till now.
'Tis the right semblance of old Janus' brow.
   "Her mask, her vizard, her loose-hanging gown
For her loose-lying body, her bright, spangled crown, 80
Her long slit sleeve, stiff busk, puff verdingall
Is all that makes her thus angelical.
Alas, her soul struts round about her neck;
Her seat of sense is her rebato set;
Her intellectual is a feigned niceness,
Nothing but clothes and simpering preciseness.
   "Out on these puppets, painted images,
Haberdashers' shops, torchlight maskeries,
Perfuming pans, Dutch ancients, glowworms bright
That soil our souls and damp our reason's light!   90
Away, away! Hence, coachman, go inshrine
Thy new-glaz'd puppet in Port Esquiline.
Blush, Martia, fear not or look pale. All's one;
Margara keeps thy set complexion.
Sure I ne'er think those axioms to be true
That souls of men from that great Soul ensue
And of his essence do participate
As 't were by pipes, when so degenerate,
So adverse, is our nature's motion
To his immaculate condition—   100
That such foul filth from such fair purity,
Such sensual acts from such a Deity,
Can ne'er proceed. But if that dream were so,
Then sure the slime that from our souls do flow
Have stopp'd those pipes by which it was convey'd,
And now no human creatures once disray'd
Of that fair gem.
Beasts' sense, plants' growth, like being as a stone.
But out, alas, our cognizance is gone."
                                          Finis libri secundi

SATIRE VIII
Inamorato Curio

Curio, ay me! Thy mistress' monkey's dead!
Alas, alas, her pleasure's buried.
Go, woman's slave, perform his exequies,

Condole his death in mournful elegies.
Tut, rather paeans sing, hermaphrodite,
For that sad death gives life to thy delight.
   Sweet-fac'd Corinna, deign the riband tie
Of thy cork shoe or else thy slave will die.
Some puling sonnet tolls his passing bell;
Some sighing elegy must ring his knell.   10
Unless bright sunshine of thy grace revive
His wambling stomach, certes he will dive
Into the whirlpool of devouring death
And to some mermaid sacrifice his breath.
Then O, O then, to thy eternal shame
And to the honor of sweet Curio's name
This epitaph upon the marble stone
Must fair be grav'd of that true-loving one:

             Here lieth he, he lieth here,
                 that bounc'd and pity cried.   20
             The door not op'd, fell sick, alas,
                 alas, fell sick and died.

What Myrmidon or hard Dolopian,
What savage-minded, rude Cyclopian
But such a sweet, pathetique Paphian
Would force to laughter? . . .
   Publius hates vainly to idolatrize
And laughs that papists honor images,
And yet—O madness!—these mine eyes did see
Him melt in moving plaints, obsequiously   30
Imploring favor, twining his kind arms,
Using inchantments, exorcisms, charms,
The oil of sonnets, wanton blandishment,
The force of tears, and seeming languishment
Unto the picture of a painted lass.
I saw him court his mistress' looking-glass,
Worship a busk-point (which in secrecy,
I fear, was conscious of strange villany).
I saw him crouch, devote his livelihood,
Swear, protest, vow peasant servitude   40
Unto a painted puppet. To her eyes
I heard him swear his sighs to sacrifice.
But if he get her itch-allaying pin,
O sacred relique, straight he must begin
To rave outright—then thus: "Celestial bliss,
Can heaven grant so rich a grace as this?
Touch it not, by the Lord, sir, 'tis divine.
It once beheld her radiant eyes bright shine;
Her hair imbrac'd it, O thrice-happy prick
That there was thron'd and in her hair didst stick!"   50
Kiss, bless, adore it, Publius. Never lin.
Some sacred virtue lurketh in the pin.
   O frantic, fond, pathetique passion!
Is 't possible such sensual action
Should clip the wings of contemplation?
O, can it be the spirit's function,

The soul, not subject to dimension,
Should be made slave to reprehension
Of crafty nature's paint? Fie, can our soul
Be underling to such a vile control? . . .   60
    What should I say? Lust hath confounded all.
The bright gloss of our intellectual
Is foully soil'd. The wanton wallowing
In fond delights and amorous dallying
Hath dusk'd the fairest splendor of our soul;
Nothing now left but carcass, loathsome, foul.
For sure if that some sprite remained still
Could it be subject to lewd Lais' will?
    Reason, by prudence in her function,
Had wont to tutor all our action,   70
Aiding with precepts of philosophy
Our feebled nature's imbecility.
But now affection, will, concupiscence
Have got o'er reason chief preheminence.
'Tis so, else how should such vile baseness taint
As force it be made slave to nature's paint?
Methinks the spirit's Pegase, Fantasy,
Should hoise the soul from such base slavery;
But now I see, and can right plainly show,
From whence such abject thoughts and actions grow.   80
    Our adverse body, being earthly, cold,
Heavy, dull, mortal, would not long infold
A stranger inmate that was backward still
To all his dungy, brutish, sensual will;
Now hereupon our intellectual,
Compact of fire all celestial,
Invisible, immortal, and divine,
Grew straight to scorn his landlord's muddy slime;
And therefore now is closely slunk away
(Leaving his smoky house of mortal clay),   90
Adorn'd with all his beauty's lineaments
And brightest gems of shining ornaments,
His parts divine, sacred, spiritual
Attending on him, leaving the sensual
Base hangers-on lusking at home in slime,
Such as wont to stop Port Esqueline.
Now doth the body, led with senseless will
(The which in Reason's absence ruleth still),
Rave, talk idly, as 't were some deity
Adoring female painted puppetry,   100
Playing at put-pin, doting on some glass
Which, breath'd but on, his falsed gloss doth pass;
Toying with babies and with fond pastime,
Some children's sport, deflow'ring of chaste time,
Imploying all his wits in vain expense,
Abusing all his organons of sense.
    Return, return, sacred Synderesis,
Inspire our trunks; let not such mud as this
Pollute us still. Awake our lethargy.
Raise us from out our brainsick foolery.   110

TO EVERLASTING OBLIVION

Thou mighty gulf, insatiate cormorant,
Deride me not, though I seem petulant
To fall into thy chops. Let others pray
Forever their fair poems flourish may.
But as for me, hungry Oblivion,
Devour me quick. Accept my orison,
My earnest prayers which do importune thee,
With gloomy shade of thy still empery
To veil both me and my rude poesy.
Far worthier lines in silence of thy state   10
Do sleep securely, free from love or hate,
From which this, living, ne'er can be exempt,
But whilst it breathes will hate and fury tempt.
Then close his eyes with thy all-dimming hand
Which not right glorious actions can withstand.
Peace, hateful tongues! I now in silence pace
Unless some hound do wake me from my place.
    I with this sharp yet well-meant poesy
    Will sleep secure, right free from injury
    Of cank'red hate or rankest villany.   20

To Him That Hath Perused Me

Gentle or ungentle hand that holdest me, let not thine eye be cast upon privateness, for I protest I glance not on it. If thou hast perused me, what lesser favor canst thou grant then not to abuse me with unjust application? Yet I fear me I shall be much, much injuried by two sorts of readers: the one being ignorant, not knowing the nature of a satire (which is under feigned, private names to note general vices), will needs wrest each feigned name to a private, unfeigned person; the other, too subtile, bearing a private malice to some greater personage then he dare in his own person seem to malingn, will strive, by a forced application of my general reproofs, to broach his private hatred—then the which I know not a greater injury can be offered to a satirist. I durst presume—knew they how guiltless and how free I were from prying into privateness—they would blush to think how much they wrong themselves in seeking to injure me. Let this protestation satisfy our curious searchers. So may I obtain my best hopes, as I am free from endeavoring to blast any private man's good name. If any one (forced with his own guilt) will turn it home and say, " 'Tis I," I cannot hinder him. Neither do I injure him. For other faults of poesy I crave no pardon, in that I scorn all penance the bitterest censurer can impose upon me. Thus, wishing each man to leave enquiring who I am and learn to know himself, I take a solemn congee of this fusty world.

Theriomastix

EVERARD GUILPIN

Like Marston's *Scourge of Villany*, *Skialetheia* was one of the many imitations of Joseph Hall's *Virgidemiae* (1597-98) which poured from the presses in the late nineties. Hall, seeking to revive Juvenalian satire, had popularized a crabbed, wilful obscurity which Marston reduced nearly to absurdity, and which Guilpin and other poetasters did their best to emulate. Although *Skialetheia*, which was licensed September 15, 1598, was published anonymously, seven extracts from it are ascribed to "Edw. Guilpin" in *England's Parnassus* (1600), and the little autobiography in Epigram 22 serves to identify its author with an Everard Guilpin who was at Emmanuel College, Cambridge, in the late eighties and a member of Gray's Inn in 1591. Whatever the facts of Guilpin's career (and they are very obscure), his one little book of seventy epigrams, a "Satyre Preludium," and six satires permits us to infer a good deal about him. He was a close observer of the London scene, a habitué of the theater (as the satirical portrait of Essex as "great Foelix," a parody of a famous passage in Shakespeare's *Richard II*, shows), and a wittily obscene *bon vivant* whose work fairly represents the kind of audacious personal satire abruptly silenced by ecclesiastical decree in June, 1599. Our text is based upon *Skialetheia. Or, A shadowe of Truth, in certaine Epigrams and Satyres*, 1598 (STC 12504).

FROM SKIALETHEIA, OR A SHADOW OF TRUTH IN CERTAIN EPIGRAMS AND SATIRES (1598)

PROEMIUM 1

As in the greatest of societies
The first beginners, like good-natur'd souls,
Bear with their neighbors' poor infirmities,
But after, when ambition controls
Their calm proceedings, they imperiously
(As great things still o'erwhelm themselves with weight)
Envy their countrymen's prosperity
And in contempt of poorer fates delight;
So England's wits, now mounted the full height,
Having confounded monstrous barbarisms,   10
Puff'd up by conquest, with self-wounding spight
Engrave themselves in civil war's abysms,
   Seeking by all means to destroy each other,
   The unhappy children of so dear a mother.

OF TITUS 3

Titus oft vaunts his gentry everywhere,
Blazoning his coat, deriving 's pedegree.
What needest thou daily, Titus, jade mine ear?
I will believe thy house's ancestry:
   If that be ancient which we do forget,
   Thy gentry is so. None can remember it.

TO DELONEY 8

Like to the fatal, ominous raven which tolls
The sick man's dirge within his hollow beak,
So every paper-clothed post in Poules
To thee, Deloney, mourningly doth speak
And tells thee of thy hempen tragedy.
The wracks of hungry Tyburn naught to thine,
Such massacre's made of thy balladry,
And thou in grief for wo thereof mayst pine.
   At every street's end Fuscus' rimes are read,
   And thine in silence must be buried.   10

TO CLODIUS 22

I prethee, Clodius, tell me what's the reason
Thou dost expect I should salute thee first.
I have sized in Cambridge, and my friends a season
Some exhibition for me there disburs'd.
Since that, I have been in Goad his weekly roll
And been acquaint with Monsieur Littleton;
I have walk'd in Poules, and duly din'd at noon,
And sometimes visited the dancing school.
   Then how art thou my better, that I should
   Speak always first, as I incroach fain would?   10
   But in a whore-house thou canst swagger too,
   Clodius, good day—'tis more then I can do.

TO THE READER 47

Excuse me, reader, though I now and than
In some light lines do shew myself a man,
Nor be so sour, some wanton words to blame:
They are the language of an epigram.

OF PANSA 52

Fine, spruce young Pansa's grown a malcontent,
A mighty malcontent though young and spruce.
As heresy he shuns all merriment,
And, turn'd good husband, puts forth sighs to use;
Like hate-man Timon in his cell he sits

Misted with darkness like a smoky room,
And if he be so mad to walk the streets,
To his sight's life his hat becomes a tomb.
What is the cause of this melancholy?
His father's dead? No, such news revives him.   10
Wants he a whore? Nor that. Loves he? That's folly.
Mount his high thoughts? O no. Then what grieves him?
Last night which did our Inns of Court men call
In silken suits like gaudy butterflies
To paint the torchlight summer of the hall
And shew good legs, spite of slops smothering thighs,
    He, passing from his chamber through the court,
    Did spoil a pair of new white pumps with dirt.

DE IGNOTO 56

There's an odd fellow (I'll not tell his name
Because from my lines he shall get no fame),
Reading mine epigrams, bathes every limb
In angry sweat, swearing that I mean him.
Content thyself. I write of better men;
Thou art no worthy subject for my pen.

SATIRA PRIMA

Shall I still miche in silence and give aim
To other wits which make court to bright fame?
A schoolboy still, shall I lend ear to other
And mine own private muse's music smother,
Especially in this sin-leapered age
Where every player-vice comes on the stage
Mask'd in a virtuous robe, and fools do sit
More honored then the Prester John of wit?
Where virtue, like a common gossop, shields
Vice with her name and her defects o'er-gilds?   10
No, no, my muse, be valiant to control,
Play the scold bravely, fear no cucking-stool,
Begall thy spirit; like shrill trumpets' clangor
Vent forth th' impatience and alarm thine anger;
Gainst sin's invasions rend the foggy cloud
Whose all-black womb far blacker vice doth shroud;
    Tell giant greatness a more great did frame
Th' imaginary colosse of the same,
    And then expostulate why Titus should
Make shew of Etna's heat, yet be as cold   20
As snow-drown'd Athos in his frozen zeal,
Both to religion and his commonweal.
    Or why should Caelius injure thrift so much
As to entitle his extortion such?
    Or desperate Drus cloak the confusion
Of heady rage with resolution?
    Pale, trembling Matho dyes his milk-stain'd liver
In color of a discreet counsel-giver
And cool advisement, yet the world doth know
He's a rank coward—but who dares tell him so?   30
    The world's so bad that virtue's over-aw'd

And forc'd, poor soul, to become vice's bawd. . . .
    O world, O time, that ever men should be
So blind besotted with hypocrisy
Poison to call an wholesome antidote,
And made carouse the same, although they know 't.
    How now, my muse, this is right woman's fashion
To fall from brawling to a blubbering passion.
Have done, have done, and to a nimbler key
Set thy wind instrument, and sprightly play!   40
This leaden-heeled passion is too dull
To keep pace with this satyr-footed gull,
This mad-cap world, this whirligigging age.
Thou must have words compact of fire and rage,
Terms of quick camphire and saltpeter phrases
As in a mine to blow up the world's graces
And blast her antic, apish complements,
Her juggling tricks and mists which mock the sense,
Make Catiline or Alcibiades
To seem a Cato or a Socrates.   50
    This vizar-fac'd, pole-head dissimulation,
This parasite, this guide to reprobation,
This squint-ey'd slave which looks two ways at once,
This fork'd dilemma, oil of passions,
Hath so bewray'd the world with his foul mire
That naked truth may be suspect a liar.
    For when great Foelix, passing through the street,
Vaileth his cap to each one he doth meet,
And when no broom-man that will pray for him
Shall have less truage then his bonnet's brim,   60
Who would not think him perfect curtesy,
Or the honeysuckle of humility?
The Devil he is as soon—he is the Devil
Brightly accoust'red to bemist his evil.
Like a swartrutter's hose his puff thoughts swell
With yeasty ambition. Signior Machiavel
Taught him this mumming trick, with curtesy
T' entrench himself in popularity
And for a writhen face and body's move
Be barricado'd in the people's love.   70
    Yonder comes Clodius, give him the salute,
An oily slave. He, angling for repute,
Will gently entertain thee and prevent
Thy worse conceit with many a complement;
But turn thy back, and then he turns the word;
The foul-mouth'd knave will call thee Goodman Tord.
    Nothing but cosenage doth the world possess
And stuffs the large arms of his emptiness.
    Make suit to Fabius for his favor, he
Will straight protest of his love's treasury;   80
Believ'st thou him, then wear a motley coat,
He'll be the first man which shall cut thy throat.
    Come to the court and Balthazar affords
Fountains of holy and rosewater words;
Hast thou need of him and would'st find him kind?
Nay then, go by—the gentleman is blind.

Thus all our actions in a sympathy
Do dance an antic with hypocrisy,
And motley-fac'd Dissimulation
Is crept into our every fashion,   90
Whose very titles too are dissembled.
The now all-buttock'd and no-bellied
Doublet and hose which I do revel in
Was my great-grandsire's when he did begin
To woo my grandame, when he first bespake her
And witness to the jointure he did make her;
Witness some ancient, painted history
Of Assuerus, Haman, Mardoche,
For though some gulls me to believe are loth,
I know they'll credit print and painted cloth;   100
Yet, like th' old ballad of the Lord of Lorn
Whose last line in King Harry's days was born,
It still retains the title of as new
And proper a fashion as you ever knew. . . .

Methinks I see the piebald whoreson tremble
To hear of Aretine; he doth dissemble,
There is no trust to be had to his quaking.
To him once more, and rouse him from his shaking
Fever of feigned fear, hold whip and cord,
Muse, play the beadle, a lash at every word.   110
No, no, let be, he's a true cosener still,
And like the crampfish darts even through my quill
His sly, insinuating, poisonous juice,
And doth the same into my spirit infuse.
Methinks already I applaud myself
For nettle-stinging thus this fairy elf,
And though my conscience says I merit not
Such dear reward, dissembling yet (God wot),
I hunt for praise and do the same expect.
Hence, crafty enchanter! Welcome, base Neglect!   120
Scoffs make me know myself; I must not err:
Better a wretch then a dissembler.

JOHN WEEVER

The literary merit of John Weever's *Epigrams* is so negligible that nothing but the names of the illustrious contemporaries whom he addresses could have kept his thin little volume from oblivion. Weever, a Lancashire man who was an undergraduate at Queen's College, Cambridge, from 1594 to about 1598, was merely writing tritely in the vogue signalized by the work of Hall, Marston, Guilpin, and others; and his only distinction is to have mentioned so many writers—among them Spenser, Marston, Jonson, Daniel, Drayton, Warner, and Shakespeare—whom posterity has found interesting. Introduced by a dedication to Sir Richard Houghton and a set of explanatory and commendatory verses by Weever and certain of his friends, the *Epigrams* is arranged under seven "weeks," each of which contains some twenty epigrams and (except the first) a separate dedication to various persons whom Weever knew or wished to know. Internal evidence (such as an allusion to Marston's *Scourge of Villany* and the death of Spenser) suggests that the collection was probably put together just before its publication in 1599, in which year it was published by Thomas Bushell as *Epigrammes in the oldest cut, and newest fashion. A twise seven houres (in so many weekes) studie No longer (like the fashion) not unlike to continue* (STC 25224), upon which our text is based.

FROM EPIGRAMS IN THE OLDEST CUT AND NEWEST FASHION (1599)

To the Generous Readers

Epigrams are much like unto almanacs, serving especially for the year for the which they are made; then these, right judging readers, being for one year penn'd and in another printed, are past date before they come from the press, that you may put them up in your pockets (like your old almanacs) as not befitting this triumphant year of jubilee. Yet I beseech you shew me some curtesy in hope to have the next calculated more carefully. If you look for some reasons because I keep no order in the placing of my epistles and epigrams, let this suffice: I write epigrams, and there is an old saying,

Non locus hominem, sed homo locum, etc.

> The placing gives no grace
> Unto the man, but man unto the place.

Some faults you shall find in the printing and more in the penning, all which I refer to your own correction, and myself to your mild censures.

John Weever

The First Week
EPIGRAM I. *DE SE*

Nor do I fear the satire's venim'd bite,
Nor choploge's teeth, ne railer's vile reproach,
Nor malcontented Envy's pois'ned spight,
Jove's thunderbolt, nor Momus' long, sharp broach;
Nor that I have in high Parnassus slept,
Or pledg'd Apollo cups of Massic wine,
Or by the fount of Helicon have kept
That none dare carp these epigrams of mine;
   But that I think I shall be carp'd of none,
   For who'll wrest water from a flinty stone?   10

EPIGRAM 2. *AD LECTOREM*

Of all my epigrams, reader, read not one,
Ne yet read two, but rather read just none.
Then read them all, or let them all alone.

EPIGRAM 23. *AD MICHAELEM DRAYTON*

The peers of heav'n kept a parliament,
And for Wit's mirror Philip Sidney sent
(To keep another when they do intend,
Twenty to one for Drayton they will send),
   Yet bade him leave his learning, so it fled
   And vow'd to live with thee since he was dead.

The Fourth Week
EPIGRAM 22. *AD GULIELMUM SHAKESPEARE*

Honey-tong'd Shakespeare, when I saw thine issue
I swore Apollo got them and none other;
Their rosy-tainted features, cloth'd in tissue,
Some heaven-born goddess said to be their mother.
Rose-cheeck'd Adonis with his amber tresses,
Fair, fire-hot Venus charming him to love her,
Chaste Lucretia virgin-like her dresses,
Proud, lust-stung Tarquin seeking still to prove her,
Romea, Richard, more whose names I know not—
Their sug'red tongues and power-attractive beauty   10
Say they are saints, although that saints they shew not,
For thousands vows to them subjective duty.
They burn in love; thy children, Shakespeare, het them.
Go, woo thy muse, more nymphist brood beget them.

EPIGRAM 23. *IN ED. ALLEN*

Rome had her Roscius and her theater,
Her Terence, Plautus, Ennius, and Meander.
The first to Allen Phoebus did transfer;
The next, Thames' swans receiv'd fore he could land her.
Of both, more worthy we, by Phoebus' doom,
Then t' Allen Roscius yield, to London Rome.

The Sixt Week
EPIGRAM 10. *AD SAMUELEM DANIEL*

Daniel, thou in tragic note excels,
As *Rosamond* and *Cleopatra* tells.
Why dost thou not in a drawn, bloody line
Offer up tears at Ferdinando's shrine?
   But those that, ere he died, bewitch'd him then,
   Belike bewitcheth now each poet's pen.

EPIGRAM 11. *AD JO. MARSTON ET BEN. JONSON*

Marston, thy muse enharbors Horace' vein;
Then some Augustus give thee Horace' merit.
And thine, embuskin'd Jonson, doth retain
So rich a style and wondrous gallant spirit
That if to praise your muses I desired
My muse would muse. Such wits must be admired.

EPIGRAM 13. *AD GULIELMUM WARNER*

Live, prince of poets! Thy affections guide
Where Wit attires herself in Virtue's suit;
Whilst England's fame thy flowing verse doth pride,
This be thy praise: thy *Albion*'s absolute.

EPIGRAM 23. *IN OBITUM ED. SPENSER POETAE PRESTANISS.*

Colin's gone home, the glory of his clime,
The muses' mirror, and the shepherds' saint.
Spenser is ruin'd, of our latter time
The fairest ruin, faery's foulest want.
Then his *Time-Ruins* did our ruin show
Which by his ruin we untimely know.
Spenser, therefore thy *Ruins* were call'd in,
Too soon to sorrow lest we should begin.

SIR JOHN DAVIES

Sir John Davies' poetry, like that of many other Elizabethans, was the work of a man for whom literature was an avocation. A prominent lawyer who had been educated at Winchester, Oxford, and the Middle Temple, he was one of the most popular of those learned amateurs who, from Chaucer's time to Fulke Greville's, accounted for a large part of the literary production of England. The audacious Martialian *Epigrams* which was printed (supposedly at "Middleburgh in Holland") together with Marlowe's *Elegies* (see p. 557-58) must have been tossed off when Davies was a bencher of the Temple and a gay blade around town; the confiscation and public burning of the book in 1599 at the instigation of the ecclesiastical authorities could have seemed only an act of simple justice to many sober-sided Elizabethans. But Davies' more important works would have pleased almost any reader, so fluent, so impeccably moral, and so conventional they were.

In June, 1594, when he was still a member of the Middle Temple, *Orchestra, or a Poem of Dancing* was entered in the Stationers' Register; possibly, therefore, the earliest extant edition, which is dated 1596, is not the first. A long poem of some one hundred thirty seven-line stanzas, it learnedly and at times whimsically explores the social, musical, astronomical, and cosmological implications of order and measured movement. The Richard Martin to whom it is dedicated in a graceful sonnet was the same colleague whom Davies viciously assaulted at the barristers' table of the Temple in 1597, thus incurring the grave penalty of disbarment (1597/98). His enforced leisure of the next three years—he was reinstated in 1601 —presumably gave him time for the slow maturing of his *magnum opus,* the famous *Nosce Teipsum* ("Know Thyself"), which was published with a dedication to the queen in 1599. This poem, one of the most meditative and ambitious of the late sixteenth century, is a very long and often very prosy compendium of Elizabethan philosophy, psychology, physiology, and theology. In two parts labeled respectively "Of Human Knowledge" and "Of the Soul of Man and the Immortality Thereof,"

its swift and facile quatrains rarely lift either Davies or his reader to new heights; none the less it is the work of an intelligent and well-read man, who asks the right questions, even if he is incapable of formulating any original answers. Its popularity was sufficient to warrant further editions in 1602, 1608, and 1619; in 1622 Davies himself included it (with *Orchestra* and *Hymns of Astraea* [1599], a panegyric to Elizabeth in acrostics, but, significantly, without the *Epigrams*) in a collected edition of his work.

After Davies' readmission to the Middle Temple he quickly became immersed in the duties of an important political career. In 1603 James I named him solicitor-general of Ireland, partly, so gossip had it, because he so much admired *Nosce Teipsum.* Inevitably the brilliant young poet of the Middle Temple, who could both shock with his licentious and edify with his didactic poems, became a grave man of large affairs. He died unexpectedly in 1626 just after Charles I had appointed him chief-justice.

Our texts are based upon *Epigrammes and Elegies. By J. D. and C. M.,* [?1590] (STC 6350); *Orchestra Or A Poeme of Dauncing. Iudicially prooving the true observation of time and measure, in the Authenticall and laudable use of Dauncing,* 1596 (STC 6360); *Nosce teipsum. This Oracle expounded in two Elegies. 1. Of Humane knowledge. 2. Of the Soule of Man, and the immortalitie thereof,* 1599 (STC 6355).

FROM EPIGRAMS AND ELEGIES BY J. D[AVIES] AND C. M[ARLOWE] (?1590)

AD MUSAM 1

Fly, merry muse, unto that merry town
Where thou mayst plays, revels, and triumphs see,
The house of fame and theater of renown
Where all good wits and spirits love to be.

Fall in between their hands that praise and love thee,
And be to them a laughter and a jest;
But as for them which, scorning, shall reprove thee,
Disdain their wits and think thine own the best.

But if thou find any so gross and dull
That think I do to private taxing lean,   10
Bid him go hang, for he is but a gull,
And knows not what an epigram doth mean:
    Which taxeth under a particular name
    A general vice that merits public blame.

IN RUFUM 3

Rufus the courtier, at the theater
Leaving the best and most conspicuous place,
Doth either to the stage himself transfer
Or through a grate doth shew his doubtful face;

For that the clamorous fry of Inns of Court
Fills up the private rooms of greater price,
And such a place where all may have resort
He, in his singularity, doth despise.

Yet doth not his particular humor shun
The common stews and brothels of the town,   10
Though all the world in troops do thither run,
Clean and unclean, the gentle and the clown.
    Then why should Rufus in his pride abhor
    A common seat, that loves a common whore?

IN TITUM 6

Titus, the brave and valorous young gallant,
Three years together in this town hath been,
Yet my lord chancellor's tomb he hath not seen,
Nor the new water-work, nor the Elephant.
   I cannot tell the cause without a smile:
   He hath been in the Counter all this while.

IN SEVERUM 13

The Puritan Severus oft doth read
This text that doth pronounce vain speech a sin,
That thing defiles a man that doth proceed
From out the mouth, not that which enters in;
Hence is it that we seldom hear him swear,
And thereof like a Pharisee he vaunts,
But he devours more capons in a year
Then would suffice a hundreth Protestants;
And sooth, those sectaries are gluttons all,
As well the threadbare cobbler as the knight;   10
For those poor slaves which have not wherewithal
Feed on the rich till they devour them quite;
And so, like Pharaoh's kine, they eat up clean
Those that be fat, yet still themselves be lean.

IN GERONTEM 20

Geron, whose moldy memory corrects
Old Holinshed, our famous chronicler,
With moral rules and policy collects
Out of all actions done this four-score year;
   Accounts the times of every odd event
   Not from Christ's birth nor from the prince's reign
   But from some other famous accident
   Which in men's general notice doth remain—
The siege of Bulloigne and the plaguy sweat,
The going to Saint Quintine's and New Haven,   10
The Rising in the North, the frost so great
That cartwheel-prints on Thames's face were seen,
   The fall of money and burning of Paul's steeple,
   The blazing star and Spaniards' overthrow—
   By these events, notorious to the people,
   He measures times and things forepast doth shew.
But most of all he chiefly reckons by
A private chance, the death of his curst wife;
This is to him the dearest memory
And th' happiest accident of all his life.   20

IN CIPRIUM 22

The fine youth Ciprius is more tierse and neat
Then the new garden of the old Temple is,
And still the newest fashion he doth get

And, with the time, doth change from that to this.
He wears a hat now of the flat crown block,
The treble ruffs, long cloak, and doublet French;
He takes tobacco and doth wear a lock,
And wastes more time in dressing then a wench.
   Yet this new fangled youth, made for these times,
   Doth above all praise old Gascoigne's rimes.   10

IN HAYWODUM 29

Heywood, which did in epigrams excel,
Is now put down since my light muse arose,
As buckets are put down into a well
Or as a schoolboy putteth down his hose.

OF TABACCO 36

Homer of moly and nepenthe sings:
Moly, the gods' most sovereign herb divine,
Nepenthe, heaven's drink which gladness brings,
Heart's grief expels, and doth the wits refine.
   But this our age another world hath found
   From whence an herb of heavenly power is brought;
   Moly is not so sovereign for a wound,
   Nor hath nepenthe so great wonders brought.
It is tabacco, whose sweet substantial fume
The hellish torment of the teeth doth ease,   10
By drawing down and drying up the rheum,
The mother and the nurse of each disease.
   It is tabacco which doth cold expel,
   And clears the obstructions of the arteries,
   And surfeits threat'ning death digesteth well,
   Decocting all the stomach's crudities.
It is tabacco which hath power to clarify
The cloudy mists before dim eyes appearing;
It is tabacco which hath power to rarefy
The thick, gross humor which doth stop the hearing,   20
   The wasting hectic and the quartan fever
   Which doth of physic make a mockery;
   The gout it cures, and helps ill breaths forever,
   Whether the cause in tooth or stomach be.
And though ill breaths were by it but confounded,
Yet that medicine it doth far excel
Which by Sir Thomas More hath been propounded,
For this is thought a gentlemanlike smell.
   O that I were one of these mountebanks
   Which praise their oils and powders which they sell,   30
   My customers would give me coin with thanks,
   I for this ware so smooth a tale would tell.
Yet would I use none of those terms before;
I would but say that it the pox will cure.
This were enough, without discoursing more,
All our brave gallants in the town t' allure.

FROM ORCHESTRA OR A POEM OF DANCING (1596)

Where lives the man that never yet did hear
Of chaste Penelope, Ulysses' queen?
Who kept her faith unspotted twenty year
Till he return'd that far away had been,
And many men and many towns had seen;
    Ten year at siege of Troy he ling'ring lay,
    And ten year in the midland sea did stray.

Homer, to whom the muses did carouse
A great, deep cup with heavenly nectar fill'd,
The greatest, deepest cup in Jove's great house   10
(For Jove himself had so expressly will'd),
He drank of all, ne let one drop be spill'd;
    Since when, his brain that had before been dry
    Became the wellspring of all poetry—

Homer doth tell in his aboundant verse
The long, laborious travails of the man,
And of his lady, too, he doth rehearse,
How she illudes with all the art she can
Th' ungrateful love which other lords began;
    For of her lord false Fame long since had sworn   20
    That Neptune's monsters had his carcass torn.

All this he tells, but one thing he forgot,
One thing most worthy his eternal song;
But he was old and blind and saw it not,
Or else he thought he should Ulysses wrong
To mingle it his tragic acts among.
    Yet was there not in all the world of things
    A sweeter burden for his muse's wings.

The courtly love Antinous did make,
Antinous, that fresh and jolly knight,   30
Which of the gallants that did undertake
To win the widow had most wealth and might,
Wit to persuade, and beauty to delight—
    The courtly love he made unto the queen
    Homer forgot as if it had not been.

Sing then, Terpsichore, my light muse, sing
His gentle art and cunning curtesy.
You, lady, can remember everything,
For you are daughter of Queen Memory.
But sing a plain and easy melody,   40
    For the soft mean that warbleth but the ground
    To my rude ear doth yield the sweetest sound.

One only night's discourse I can report.
When the great torch-bearer of heaven was gone
Down in a mask unto the ocean's court
To revel it with Tethys, all alone

Antinous, disguised and unknown,
    Like to the spring in gaudy ornament
    Unto the castle of the princess went.

The sovereign castle of the rocky ile   50
Wherein Penelope the princess lay
Shone with a thousand lamps which did exile
The dim, dark shades and turn'd the night to day.
Not Jove's blue tent, what time the sunny ray
    Behind the bulwark of the earth retires,
    Is seen to sparkle with more twinkling fires.

That night the queen came forth from far within
And in the presence of her court was seen,
For the sweet singer Phemius did begin
To praise the worthies that at Troy had been.   60
Somewhat of her Ulysses she did ween
    In his grave hymn the heav'nly man would sing,
    Or of his wars, or of his wandering. . . .

[When Antinous asks Penelope to dance with him she
professes ignorance of "this new rage," whereupon he
seeks to persuade her that dancing is the oldest and most
significant of arts.]

"Dancing, bright lady, then began to be
When the first seeds whereof the world did spring,
The fire, air, earth, and water, did agree,
By Love's persuasion, Nature's mighty king,
To leave their first disord'red combating,
    And in a dance such measure to observe
    As all the world their motion should preserve.   70

"Since when they still are carried in a round
And, changing, come one in another's place,
Yet do they neither mingle nor confound,
But everyone doth keep the bounded space
Wherein the dance doth bid it turn or trace.
    This wondrous miracle did Love devise,
    For dancing is Love's proper exercise.

"Like this he fram'd the gods' eternal bower,
And of a shapeless and confused mass
By his through-piercing and digesting power   80
The turning vault of heaven framed was,
Whose starry wheels he hath so made to pass
    As that their movings do a music frame,
    And they themselves still dance unto the same.

"Or if this all, which round about we see
(As idle Morpheus some sick brains hath taught),
Of undivided motes compacted be,
How was this goodly architecture wrought?
Or by what means were they together brought?

They err that say they did concur by chance.   90
  Love made them meet in a well-ordered dance. . . ."

This said, the queen with her sweet lips divine
Gently began to move the subtile air,
Which, gladly yielding, did itself incline
To take a shape between those rubies fair,
And, being formed, softly did repair
  With twenty doublings in the empty way
  Unto Antinous' ears, and thus did say:

"What eye doth see the heav'n but doth admire
When it the movings of the heav'ns doth see?   100
Myself, if I to heav'n may once aspire,
If that be dancing will a dancer be.
But as for this, your frantic jollity,
  How it began, or whence you did it learn,
  I never could with reason's eye discern."

Antinous answered: "Jewel of the earth,
Worthy you are that heav'nly dance to lead,
But, for you think our dancing base of birth
And newly born but of a brainsick head,
I will forthwith his antique gentry read,   110
  And for I love him will his herault be,
  And blaze his arms, and draw his petigree.

"When Love had shap'd this world, this great fair wight
That all wights else in his wide womb contains,
And had instructed it to dance aright
A thousand measures with a thousand strains,
Which it should practise with delightful pains
  Until that fatal instant should revolve
  When all to nothing should again resolve,

"The comely order and proportion fair   120
On every side did please his wand'ring eye
Till, glancing through the thin, transparent air,
A rude, disordered rout he did espy
Of men and women that most spitefully
  Did one another throng and crowd so sore
  That his kind eye in pity wept therefore.

"And swifter then the lightning down he came,
Another shapeless chaos to digest;
He will begin another world to frame
(For Love, till all be well, will never rest);   130
Then with such words as cannot be express'd
  He cuts the troops, that all asunder fling,
  And ere they wist he casts them in a ring.

"Then did he rarefy the element
And in the center of the ring appear;
The beams that from his forehead shining went
Begot an horror and religious fear

In all the souls that round about him were,
  Which in their ears attentiveness procures
  While he, with such like sounds, their minds allures. 140

" 'How doth Confusion's mother, headlong Chance,
Put Reason's noble squadron to the rout?
Or how should you, that have the governance
Of Nature's children, heaven and earth throughout,
Prescribe them rules and live yourselves without?
  Why should your fellowship a trouble be,
  Since man's chief pleasure is society?

" 'If sense hath not yet taught you, learn of me
A comely moderation and discreet,
That your assemblies may well-ordered be;   150
When my uniting power shall make you meet,
With heav'nly tunes it shall be tempered sweet,
  And be the model of the world's great frame,
  And you, earth's children, dancing shall it name.

" 'Behold the world, how it is whirled round,
And for it is so whirl'd, is named so;
In whose large volume many rules are found
Of this new art, which it doth fairly show;
For your quick eyes in wand'ring to and fro,
  From east to west, on no one thing can glance,   160
  But, if you mark it well, it seems to dance. . . .

" 'Under that spangled sky five wand'ring flames,
Besides the king of day and queen of night,
Are wheel'd around, all in their sundry frames,
And all in sundry measures do delight,
Yet altogether keep no measure right.
  For by itself each doth itself advance,
  And by itself each doth a galliard dance.

" 'Venus, the mother of that bastard Love
Which doth usurp the world's great marshal's name, 170
Just with the sun her dainty feet doth move
And unto him doth all her gestures frame.
Now after, now afore, the flattering dame
  With divers cunning passages doth err,
  Still him respecting that respects not her.

" 'For that brave sun, the father of the day,
Doth love this earth, the mother of the night,
And, like a reveler in rich array,
Doth dance his galliard in his leman's sight.
Both back and forth and sideways passing light,   180
  His gallant grace doth so the gods amaze
  That all stand still and at his beauty gaze. . . .

" 'Who doth not see the measures of the moon
Which thirteen times she danceth every year,
And ends her pavine thirteen times as soon

As doth her brother, of whose golden hair
She borroweth part and proudly doth it wear?
　　Then doth she coyly turn her face aside,
　　That half her cheek is scarce sometimes discri'd. . . .

" 'If, then, fire, air, wand'ring and fixed lights   190
In every province of th' imperial sky
Yield perfect forms of dancing to your sights,
In vain I teach the ear that which the eye
With certain view already doth descry.
　　But for your eyes perceive not all they see
　　In this I will your senses' master be.

" 'For, lo, the sea that fleets about the land
And like a girdle clips her solid waist,
Music and measure both doth understand;
For his great crystal eye is always cast   200
Up to the moon, and on her fixed fast,
　　And as she danceth in her pallid sphere
　　So danceth he about the center here. . . .

" 'Only the earth doth stand forever still;
Her rocks remove not, nor her mountains meet
(Although some wits, enrich'd with learning's skill,
Say heav'n stands firm and that the earth doth fleet
And swiftly turneth underneath their feet);
　　Yet though the earth is ever steadfast seen,
　　On her broad breast hath dancing ever been,   210

" 'For those blue veins that through her body spread,
Those sapphire streams which from great hills do spring
(The earth's great dugs, for every wight is fed
With sweet, fresh moisture from them issuing),
Observe a dance in their wild wandering;
　　And still their dance begets a murmur sweet,
　　And still the murmur with the dance doth meet. . . .

" 'Hark how the birds do sing! And mark then how,
Jump with the modulation of their lays,
They lightly leap and skip from bough to bough;   220
Yet do the cranes deserve a greater praise,
Which keep such measure in their airy ways,
　　As when they all in order ranked are
　　They make a perfect form triangular. . . .

" 'But why relate I every singular?
Since all the world's great fortunes and affairs
Forward and backward rapt and whirled are
According to the music of the spheres,
And Chance herself her nimble feet upbears
　　On a round, slippery wheel that rolleth ay,   230
　　And turns all states with her impetuous sway.

" 'Learn then to dance, you that are princes born
And lawful lords of earthly creatures all!

Imitate them, and thereof take no scorn,
For this new art to them is natural.
And imitate the stars celestial,
　　For when pale Death your vital twist shall sever,
　　Your better parts must dance with them forever.'

"Thus Love persuades, and all the crowd of men
That stands around doth make a murmuring,   240
As when the wind, loos'd from his hollow den,
Among the trees a gentle bass doth sing,
Or as a brook through peebles wandering;
　　But in their looks they uttered this plain speech:
　　That they would learn to dance if Love would teach.

"Then, first of all, he doth demonstrate plain
The motions seven that are in nature found:
Upward and downward, forth and back again,
To this side and to that, and turning round
(Whereof a thousand brawls he doth compound),   250
　　Which he doth teach unto the multitude,
　　And ever with a turn they must conclude. . . .

"Thus Love taught men, and men thus learn'd of Love
Sweet music's sound with feet to counterfait,
Which was long time before high-thundering Jove
Was lifted up to heav'n's imperial seat.
For though by birth he were the prince of Crete,
　　Nor Crete nor heav'n should the young prince have
　　　　seen
　　If dancers with their timbrels had not been.

"Since when all ceremonious mysteries,   260
All sacred orgies and religious rites,
All pomps and triumphs and solemnities,
All funerals, nuptials, and like public sights,
All parliaments of peace and warlike fights,
　　All learned arts and every great affair
　　A lively shape of dancing seems to bear. . . .

"Lo, this is Dancing's true nobility:
Dancing, the child of Music and of Love,
Dancing itself both love and harmony,
Where all agree and all in order move,   270
Dancing, the art that all arts do approve,
　　The fair character of the world's consent,
　　The heav'ns' true figure and th' earth's ornament."

The queen, whose dainty ears had borne too long
The tedious praise of that she did despise,
Adding once more the music of the tongue
To the sweet speech of her alluring eyes,
Began to answer in such winning wise
　　As that forthwith Antinous' tongue was tied,
　　His eyes fast fix'd, his ears were open wide.   280

"Forsooth," quoth she, "great glory you have won
To your trim minion Dancing all this while
By blazing him Love's first begotten son,
Of every ill the hateful father vile
That doth the world with sorceries beguile,
   Cunningly mad, religiously prophane,
   Wit's monster, reason's canker, sense's bane.

"Love taught the mother that unkind desire
To wash her hands in her own infant's blood;
Love taught the daughter to betray her sire   290
Into most base unworthy servitude;
Love taught the brother to prepare such food
   To feast his brothers that the all-seeing sun,
   Wrapp'd in a cloud, that wicked sight did shun.

"And even this selfsame Love hath dancing taught,
An art that sheweth th' idea of his mind,
With vainness, frenzy, and misorder fraught;
Sometimes with blood and cruelties unkind,
For in a dance Tereus' mad wife did find
   Fit time and place, by murthering her son,   300
   T' avenge the wrong his traitorous sire had done.

"What mean the mermaids when they dance and sing
But certain death unto the mariner?
What tidings do the dancing dolphins bring
But that some dangerous storm approacheth near?
Then sith both Love and Dancing liveries bear
   Of such ill hap, unhappy may they prove
   That, sitting free, will either dance or love!"

Yet once again Antinous did reply:
"Great queen, condemn not Love, the innocent,   310
For this mischievous lust which traitorously
Usurps his name and steals his ornament.
For that true Love which dancing did invent
   Is he that tun'd the world's whole harmony
   And link'd all men in sweet society.

"He first extracted from th' earth-mingled mind
That heav'nly fire, or quintessence divine,
Which doth such sympathy in beauty find
As is between the elm and fruitful vine,
And so to beauty ever doth encline.   320
   Live's life it is, and cordial to the heart,
   And of our better part the better part. . . .

"Love in the twinkling of your eyelids danceth,
Love danceth in your pulses and your veins,
Love, when you sew, your needle's point advanceth,
And makes it dance a thousand curious strains
Of winding rounds, whereof the form remains
   To shew that your fair hands can dance the hay
   Which your fine feet would learn as well as they.

"And when your ivory fingers touch the strings   330
Of any silver-sounding instrument
Love makes them dance to those sweet murmurings
With busy skill and cunning excellent.
O that your feet those tunes would represent
   With artificial motions to and fro,
   That Love this art in every part might show!

"Yet your fair soul, which came from heav'n above
To rule this house, another heav'n below,
With divers powers in harmony doth move;
And all the virtues that from her do flow   340
In a round measure hand in hand do go.
   Could I now see, as I conceive, this dance,
   Wonder and Love would cast me in a trance. . . .

"But if these eyes of yours (loadstars of Love
Shewing the world's great dance to your mind's eye)
Cannot with all their demonstrations move
Kind apprehension in your fantasy
Of dancing's virtue and nobility,
   How can my barbarous tongue win you thereto
   Which heav'n and earth's fair speech could never do?

"O Love, my king, if all my wit and power   351
Have done you all the service that they can,
O be you present in this present hour
And help your servant and your true liegeman
End that persuasion which I erst began.
   For who in praise of dancing can persuade
   With such sweet force as Love, which dancing made?"

Love heard his prayer, and swifter then the wind,
Like to a page in habit, face, and speech,
He came and stood Antinous behind,   360
And many secrets to his thoughts did teach.
At last a crystal mirror he did reach
   Unto his hands, that he with one rash view
   All forms therein by Love's revealing knew,

And, humbly honoring, gave it to the queen
With this fair speech: "See, fairest queen," quoth he,
"The fairest sight that ever shall be seen
And th' only wonder of posterity,
The richest work in Nature's treasury,
   Which she disdains to shew on this world's stage   370
   And thinks it far too good for our rude age.

"But in another world, divided far,
In the great, fortunate, triangled ile
Thrice twelve degrees remov'd from the North Star,
She will this glorious workmanship compile
Which she hath been conceiving all this while
   Since the world's birth; and will bring forth at last
   When six and twenty hundreth years are past."

Penelope the queen, when she had view'd
The strange, eye-dazzling, admirable sight,   380
Fain would have prais'd the state and pulchritude,
But she was stroken dumb with wonder quite,
Yet her sweet mind retain'd her thinking might;
   Her ravish'd mind in heav'nly thoughts did dwell,
   But what she thought no mortal tongue can tell.

You, lady muse, whom Jove the Counselor
Begot of Memory, Wisdom's treasures,
To your divining tongue is given a power
Of uttering secrets large and limitless.
You can Penelope's strange thoughts express   390
   Which she conceiv'd, and then would fain have
      told,
   When she the wondrous crystal did behold.

Her winged thoughts bore up her mind so high
As that she ween'd she saw the glorious throne
Where the bright moon doth sit in majesty;
A thousand sparkling stars about her shone,
But she herself did sparkle more alone
   Then all those thousand beauties would have done
   If they had been confounded all in one.

And yet she thought those stars mov'd in such measure
To do their sovereign honor and delight,   401
As sooth'd her mind with sweet, enchanting pleasure,
Although the various change amaz'd her sight
And her weak judgment did entangle quite.
   Beside, their moving made them shine more clear,
   As diamonds mov'd more sparkling do appear.

This was the picture of her wondrous thought,
But who can wonder that her thought was so
Sith Vulcan, king of fire, that mirror wrought

(Which things to come, present, and past doth know)
And there did represent in lively show   411
   Our glorious English court's divine image
   As it should be in this, our golden age.

Away, Terpsichore, light muse, away!
And come, Uranie, prophetess divine!
Come, muse of heav'n, my burning thirst allay!
Even now for want of sacred drink I tine.
In heav'nly moisture dip this pen of mine
   And let my mouth with nectar overflow,
   For I must more then mortal glory show.   420

O that I had Homer's aboundant vein!
I would hereof another *Ilias* make,
Or else the man of Mantua's charmed brain,
In whose large throat great Jove the thunder spake.
O that I could old Geoffery's muse awake,
   Or borrow Colin's fair heroic style,
   Or smooth my rimes with Delia's servant's file! . . .

Yet Astrophel might one for all suffice,
Whose supple muse cameleon-like doth change
Into all forms of excellent devise.   430
So might the swallow, whose swift muse doth range
Through rare ideas and inventions strange,
   And ever doth enjoy her joyful spring,
   And sweeter then the nightingale doth sing.

O that I might that singing swallow hear
To whom I owe my service and my love!
His sug'red tunes would so enchant mine ear
And in my mind such sacred fury move
As I should knock at heav'n's great gate above
   With my proud rimes, while of this heav'nly state   440
   I do aspire the shadow to relate.

FROM NOSCE TEIPSUM. THIS ORACLE EXPOUNDED IN TWO ELEGIES (1599)

To My Most Gracious Dread Sovereign

To that clear majesty which, in the north,
Doth like another sun in glory rise,
Which standeth fix'd yet spreads her heavenly worth,
Loadstone to hearts and loadstar to all eyes,

Like heav'n in all, like th' earth in this alone,
That though great states by her support do stand,
Yet she herself supported is of none
But by the finger of th' Almighty's hand. . . ,

I offer up some sparkles of that fire
Whereby we reason, live, and move, and be.   10
These sparks by nature evermore aspire,
Which makes them to so high an highness flee.

Fair soul, since to the fairest body knit
You give such lively life, such quick'ning power,
Such sweet, celestial influence to it
As keeps it still in youth's immortal flower

(As where the sun is present all the year
And never doth retire his golden ray
Needs must the spring be everlasting there
And every season like the month of May),   20

O many, many years may you remain
A happy angel to this happy land!
Long, long may you on earth our empress reign
Ere you in heaven a glorious angel stand.

Stay long, sweet spirit, ere thou to heaven depart,
Which mak'st each place a heaven wherein thou art.

Her Majesty's least and unworthiest subject,
John Davies

OF HUMAN KNOWLEDGE

Why did my parents send me to the schools
That I with knowledge might enrich my mind,
Since the desire to know first made men fools
And did corrupt the root of all mankind?

For when God's hand had written in the hearts
Of the first parents all the rules of good,
So that their skill enfus'd did pass all arts
That ever were, before or since the flood,

And when their reason's eye was sharp and clear
And (as an eagle can behold the sun)   10
Could have approach'd th' eternal light as near
As the intellectual angels could have done;

Even then to them the spirit of lies suggests
That they were blind because they saw not ill,
And breathes into their incorrupted breasts
A curious wish which did corrupt their will.

For that same ill they straight desir'd to know;
Which ill (being nought but a defect of good)
And all God's works the Divel could not show
While man, their lord, in his perfection stood.   20

So that themselves were first to do the ill
Ere they thereof the knowledge could attain,
Like him that knew not poison's power to kill
Until, by tasting it, himself was slain.

Even so, by tasting of that fruit forbid,
Where they sought knowledge they did error find;
Ill they desir'd to know, and ill they did,
And to give passion eyes made reason blind. . . .

What can we know or what can we discern
When error chokes the windows of the mind?   30
The diverse forms of things how can we learn
That have been ever from our birthday blind?

When reason's lamp, which, like the sun in sky,
Throughout man's little world her beams did spread,
Is now become a sparkle, which doth lie
Under the ashes, half extinct and dead,

How can we hope that through the eye and ear
This dying sparkle in this cloudy place

Can recollect these beams of knowledge clear
Which were enfus'd in the first minds by grace? . . .   40

We seek to know the moving of each sphere
And the strange cause of th' ebbs and floods of Nile,
But of that clock within our breasts we bear
The subtile motions we forget the while.

We that acquaint ourselves with every zone,
And pass both tropics, and behold the poles,
When we come home are to ourselves unknown,
And unacquainted still with our own souls.

We study speech, but others we persuade;
We leechcraft learn, but others cure with it;   50
We interpret laws which other men have made,
But read not those which in our hearts are writ. . . .

If ought can teach us ought, Affliction's looks
(Making us look into ourselves so near)
Teach us to know ourselves beyond all books
Or all the learned schools that ever were.

This mistress lately pluck'd me by the ear,
And many a golden lesson hath me taught,
Hath made my senses quick and reason clear,
Reform'd my will, and rectifi'd my thought.   60

So do the winds and thunders cleanse the air,
So working [lees] settle and purge the wine,
So lopp'd and pruned trees do florish fair,
So doth the fire the drossy gold refine.

Neither Minerva, nor the learned muse,
Nor rules of art, nor precepts of the wise
Could in my brain those beams of skill enfuse
As but the glance of this dame's angry eyes.

She within lists my ranging mind hath brought,
That now beyond myself I list not go.   70
Myself am center of my circling thought;
Only myself I study, learn, and know.

I know my body's of so frail a kind
As force without, fevers within, can kill;
I know the heavenly nature of my mind,
But 'tis corrupted both in wit and will.

I know my soul hath power to know all things,
Yet is she blind and ignorant in all;
I know I am one of Nature's little kings,
Yet to the least and vilest things am thrall.   80

I know my life's a pain and but a span;
I know my sense is mock'd with everything;
And, to conclude, I know myself a man,
Which is a proud and yet a wretched thing.

OF THE SOUL OF MAN AND THE
IMMORTALITY THEREOF

The lights of heaven (which are the world's fair eyes)
Look down into the world, the world to see,
And, as they turn or wander in the skies,
Survey all things that on this center be.

And yet the lights which in my tow'r do shine,
Mine eyes, which view all objects nigh and far,
Look not into this little world of mine,
Nor see my face wherein they fixed are.

Since Nature fails us in no needful thing,
Why want I means mine inward self to see?   10
Which sight the knowledge of myself might bring,
Which to true wisdom is the first degree.

That pow'r which gave me eyes the world to view,
To view myself enfus'd an inward light
Whereby my soul, as by a mirror true,
Of her own form may take a perfect sight.

But as the sharpest eye discerneth nought
Except the sunbeams in the air do shine,
So the best sense with her reflecting thought
Sees not herself without some light divine.   20

O light which mak'st the light which makes the day,
Which set'st the eye without and mind within,
Lighten my spirit with one clear heavenly ray
Which now to view itself doth first begin.

For her true form how can my spark discern,
Which, dim by nature, art did never clear;
When the great wits, of whom all skill we learn,
Are ignorant both what she is and where?

One thinks the soul is air, another fire,
Another blood defus'd about the heart,   30
Another saith the elements conspire
And to her essence each doth give a part.

Musicians think our souls are harmonies;
Physicians hold that they complexions be;
Epicures make them swarms of atomies
Which do by change into our bodies flee.

Some think one general soul fills every brain
As the bright sun sheds light in every star,
And others think the name of soul is vain
And that we only well-mix'd bodies are.   40

In judgment of her substance thus they vary,
And thus they vary in judgment of her seat;
For some her chair up to the brain do carry,
Some thrust it down into the stomach's heat.

Some place it in the root of life, the heart,
Some in the liver, fountain of the veins;
Some say she is all in all, and all in part;
Some say she is not contain'd, but all contains.

Thus these great clerks their little wisdom show
While with their doctrines they at hazard play,   50
Tossing their light opinions to and fro
To mock the lewd, as learn'd in this as they.

For no craz'd brain could ever yet propound,
Touching the soul, so vain and fond a thought
But some among these maisters have been found
Which in their schools the self-same thing have taught.

God only wise, to punish pride of wit,
Among men's wits hath this confusion wrought,
As the proud tow'r whose points the clouds did hit
By tongues' confusion was to ruin brought.   60

But Thou which didst man's soul of nothing make,
And when to nothing it was fallen agen,
To make it new the form of man didst take,
And God with God becam'st a man with men;

Thou that hast fashioned twice this soul of ours
So that she is by double title thine,
Thou only knowest her nature and her powers;
Her subtile form thou only canst define. . . .

Thou, like the sun, dost with indifferent ray
Into the palace and the cottage shine,   70
And shew'st the soul both to the clark and lay
By the clear lamp of thy oracle divine.

This lamp through all the regions of my brain,
Where my soul sits, doth spread such beams of grace
As now, methinks, I do distinguish plain
Each subtile line of her immortal face.

The soul a substance and a spirit is
Which God himself doth in the body make,
Which makes the man, for every man from this
The nature of a man and name doth take.   80

And though this spirit be to the body knit
As an apt mean her powers to exercise,
Which are life, motion, sense, and will, and wit,
Yet she survives although the body dies.

She is a substance and a real thing
Which hath itself an actual working might,
Which neither from the senses' power doth spring
Nor from the body's humors temp'red right.

She is a vine which doth no propping need
To make her spread herself or spring upright;   90

She is a star whose beams do not proceed
From any sun, but from a native light.

For when she sorts things present with things past
And thereby things to come doth oft foresee,
When she doth doubt at first and choose at last,
These acts her own without the body be. . . .

When in th' effects she doth the causes know,
And, seeing the stream, thinks where the spring doth
   rise,
And, seeing the branch, conceives the root below,
These things she views without the body's eyes. . . . 100

When she defines, argues, divides, compounds,
Considers virtue, vice, and general things,
And, marrying diverse principles and grounds,
Out of their match a true conclusion brings;

These actions in her closet all alone,
Retir'd within herself, she doth fulfill;
Use of her body's organs she hath none
When she doth use the powers of wit and will.

Yet in the body's prison so she lies
As through the body's windows she must look   110
Her diverse powers of sense to exercise
By gathering notes out of the world's great book.

Nor can herself discourse or judge of ought
But what the sense collects and home doth bring,
And yet the power of her discoursing thought
From these collections is a diverse thing. . . .

So, though this cunning mistress and this queen
Doth as her instruments the senses use
To know all things that are felt, heard, or seen,
Yet she herself doth only judge and choose.   120

Even as our great wise empress that now reigns
By sovereign title over sundry lands
Borrows in mean affairs her subjects' pains,
Sees by their eyes, and writeth by their hands;

But things of weight and consequence indeed
Herself doth in her chamber them debate,
Where all her counselors she doth exceed
As far in judgment as she doth in state. . . .

Her harmonies are sweet and full of skill
When on the body's instrument she plays,   130
But the proportions of the wit and will,
Those sweet accords, are even the angels' lays.

These tunes of reason are Amphion's lyre
Wherewith he did the Theban city found·

These are the notes wherewith the heavenly quire
The praise of Him which spreads the heaven doth sound.

Then herself, being Nature, shines in this,
That she performs her noblest works alone.
The work the touchstone of the nature is,
And by their operations things are known.   140

Are they not senseless then that think the soul
Nought but a fine perfection of the sense,
Or of the forms which fancy doth enroll
A quick resulting and a consequence?

What is it then that doth the sense accuse
Both of false judgments and fond appetites?
Which makes us do what sense doth most refuse?
Which oft in torment of the sense delights?

Sense thinks the planets' spheres not much asunder.
What tells us, then, their distance is so far?   150
Sense thinks the lightning borne before the thunder.
What tells us, then, they both together are?

When men seem crows far off upon a tow'r,
Sense saith th' are crows. What makes us think them
   men?
When we in agues think all sweet things sour,
What makes us know our tongues' false judgments
   then? . . .

Then is the soul a nature which contains
The pow'r of sense within a greater pow'r,
Which doth employ and use the senses' pains,
But sits and rules within her private bow'r. . . .   160

Since then the soul works by herself alone,
Springs not from sense nor humors well agreeing,
Her nature is peculiar and her own;
She is a substance and a perfect being.

But though this substance be the root of sense,
Sense knows her not, which doth but bodies know;
She is a spirit and a heavenly influence
Which from the fountain of God's spirit doth flow. . . .

Were she a body how could she remain
Within this body, which is less then she?   170
Or how could she the world's great shape contain
And in our narrow breasts contained be?

All bodies are confin'd within some place,
But she all place within herself confines;
All bodies have their measure and their space,
But who can draw the soul's dimensive lines?

No body can at once two forms admit
Except the one the other do deface,
But in the soul ten thousand forms do sit,
And none intrudes into her neighbor's place. . . .   180

From their gross matter she abstracts the forms
And draws a kind of quintessence from things,
Which to her proper nature she transforms
To bear them light on her celestial wings.

This doth she when from things particular
She doth abstract the universal kinds,
Which bodiless and immaterial are
And can be lodg'd but only in our minds.

And thus from diverse accidents and acts,
Which do within her observation fall,   190
She goddesses and pow'rs divine abstracts,
As Nature, Fortune, and the virtues all. . . .

Since body and soul have such diversities
Well might we muse how first their match began,
But that we learn that He that spread the skies
And fix'd the earth first form'd the soul in man.

This true Prometheus first made man of earth
And shed in him a beam of heavenly fire;
Now in their mothers' wombs before their birth
Doth in all sons of men their souls inspire. . . .   200

God doubtless makes her and doth make her good,
And graffs her in the body, there to spring,
Which, though it be corrupted, flesh and blood
Can no way to the soul corruption bring.

And yet this soul, made good by God at first
And not corrupted by the body's ill,
Even in the womb is sinful and accurst
Ere she can judge by wit or choose by will.

Yet is not God the author of her sin,
Though author of her being and being there,   210
And if we dare to judge our judge herein,
He can condemn us and himself can clear.

First God from infinite eternity
Decreed what hath been, is, or shall be done,
And was resolv'd that every man should be,
And, in his turn, his race of life should run;

And so did purpose all the souls to make
That ever have been made or ever shall,
And that their being they should only take
In human bodies or not be at all.   220

Was it then fit that such a weak event
(Weakness itself, the sin and fall of man)
His counsel's execution should prevent,
Decreed and fix'd before the world began?

Or that one penal law by Adam broke
Should make God break his own eternal law,
The settled order of the world revoke,
And change all forms of things which he foresaw?

Could Eve's weak hand, extended to the tree,
In sunder rent that adamantine chain   230
Whose golden links effects and causes be,
And which to God's own chair doth fix'd remain?

O could we see how cause from cause doth spring,
How mutually they link'd and folded are,
And hear how oft one disagreeing string
The harmony doth rather make then mar!

And view at once how death by sin is brought,
And how from death a better life doth rise,
How this God's justice and his mercy taught,
We this decree would praise as right and wise. . . .   240

Then let us praise that power which makes us be
Men as we are, and rest contented so,
And, knowing man's fall was curiosity,
Admire God's counsels which we cannot know.

And let us know that God the maker is
Of all the souls in all the men that be,
Yet their corruption is no fault of his,
But the first man's that broke God's first decree.

This substance and this spirit of God's own making
Is in the body plac'd and planted here   250
That, both of God and of the world partaking,
Of all that is, man might the image bear.

God first made angels bodiless pure minds;
Then other things which mindless bodies be;
Last he made man th' horizon twixt both kinds,
In whom we do the world's abridgment see. . . .

But how shall we this union well express?
Nought ties the soul, her subtilty is such;
She moves the body which she doth possess,
Yet no part toucheth but by virtue's touch.   260

Then dwells she not therein as in a tent,
Nor as a pilot in his ship doth sit,
Nor as a spider in her web is pent,
Nor as the wax retains the print in it. . . ,

But as the fair and cheerful morning light
Doth here and there her silver beams impart
And in an instant doth herself unite
To the transparent air in all and part;

Still resting whole when blows the air divide,
Abiding pure when th' air is most corrupted,   270
Throughout the air her beams dispersing wide,
And when the air is toss'd not interrupted;

So doth the piercing soul the body fill,
Being all in all and all in part diffus'd,
Indivisible, uncorruptible still,
Not forc'd, encount'red, troubled, or confus'd.

And as the sun above the light doth bring,
Though we behold it in the air below,
So from th' eternal light the soul doth spring,
Though in the body she her powers do show. . . .   280

Her quick'ning power in every living part
Doth as a nurse or as a mother serve,
And doth employ her economic art
And busy care her household to preserve.

Here she attracts and there she doth retain;
There she decocts and doth the food prepare;
There she distributes it to every vein;
There she expels what she may fitly spare. . . .

And though the soul may not this power extend
Out of the body, but still use it there,   290
She hath a power which she abroad doth send,
Which views and searcheth all things everywhere.

This power is sense, which from abroad doth bring
The color, taste, and touch, and scent, and sound,
The quantity and shape of everything
Within th' earth's center or heaven's circle found.

This power, in parts made fit, fit objects takes,
Yet not the things but forms of things receives,
As when a seal in wax impression makes
The print therein, but not itself it leaves.   300

And though things sensible be numberless,
But only five the senses' organs be,
And in those five all things their forms express
Which we can touch, taste, feel, or hear, or see. . . .

First the two eyes, which have the seeing power,
Stand as one watchman, spy, or sentinel,
Being plac'd aloft within the head's high tower;
And though both see, yet both but one thing tell. . . .

Now let us hear how she the ears employs.
Their office is the troubled air to take,   310
Which in their mazes forms a sound or noise
Whereof herself doth true distinction make.

These wickets of the soul are plac'd on high
Because all sounds do lightly mount aloft,
And that they may not pierce too violently,
They are delayed with turns and windings oft. . . .

The body's life with meats and air is fed;
Therefore the soul doth use the tasting power
In veins which, through the tongue and palate spread,
Distinguish every relish, sweet and sour. . . .   320

Next in the nosthrils she doth use the smell;
As God the breath of life in them did give,
So makes he now his power in them to dwell
To judge all airs whereby we breathe and live. . . .

Lastly the feeling power, which is life's root,
Through every living part itself doth shed
By sinews which extend from head to foot
And like a net all o'er the body spread. . . .

These are the outward instruments of sense;
These are the guards which everything must pass   330
Ere it approach the mind's intelligence
Or touch the phantasy, wit's looking-glass.

And yet these porters, which all things admit,
Themselves perceive not, nor discern the things;
One common power doth in the forehead sit
Which all their proper forms together brings.

For all those nerves, which spirits of sense do bear
And to those outward organs spreading go,
United are as in a center there,
And there this power those sundry forms doth know.   340

Those outward organs present things receive;
This inward sense doth absent things retain,
Yet straight transmits all forms she doth perceive
Unto a higher region of the brain,

Where phantasy, near handmaid to the mind,
Sits and beholds and doth discern them all;
Compounds in one things diverse in their kind,
Compares the black and white, the great and small. . . .

Yet always all may not afore her be;
Successively she this and that intends;   350
Therefore such forms as she doth cease to see
To memory's large volume she commends. . . .

Here senses' apprehension end doth take,
As when a stone is into water cast
One circle doth another circle make
Till the last circle touch the bank at last.

But though the apprehensive power do pause,
The motive virtue then begins to move,
Which in the heart below doth passions cause—
Joy, grief, and fear, and hope, and hate, and love.   360

These passions have a free commanding might,
And diverse actions in our life do breed;
For all acts done without true reason's light
Do from the passion of the sense proceed.

But sith the brain doth lodge these powers of sense,
How makes it in the heart those passions spring?
The mutual love, the kind intelligence
Twixt heart and brain, this sympathy doth bring.

From the kind heat which in the heart doth reign
The spirits of life do their beginning take;   370
These spirits of life, ascending to the brain,
When they come there the spirits of sense do make.

These spirits of sense in phantasy's high court
Judge of the forms of objects ill or well;
And so they send a good or ill report
Down to the heart where all affections dwell.

If the report be good, it causeth love,
And longing hope, and well-assured joy;
If it be ill, then doth it hatred move,
And trembling fear, and vexing grief's annoy.   380

Yet were these natural affections good
(For they which want them blocks or divels be),
If reason in her first perfection stood
That she might nature's passions rectify.

Besides, another motive power doth rise
Out of the heart, from whose pure blood do spring
The vital spirits, which, borne in arteries,
Continual motion to all parts do bring.

This makes the pulses beat and lungs respire;
This holds the sinews like a bridle's reins,   390
And makes the body to advance, retire,
To turn or stop, as she them slacks or strains.

Thus the soul tunes the body's instrument;
These harmonies she makes with life and sense;
The organs fit are by the body lent,
But th' actions flow from the soul's influence.

But now I have a will yet want a wit
To express the workings of the wit and will,
Which, though their root be to the body knit,
Use not the body when they use their skill.   400

These powers the nature of the soul declare,
For to man's soul these only proper be,
For on the earth no other wights there are
Which have these heavenly powers, but only we.

The wit, the pupil of the soul's clear eye
And in man's world th' only shining star,
Looks in the mirror of the phantasy
Where all the gatherings of the senses are.

From thence this power the shapes of things abstracts,
And them within her passive part receives,   410
Which are enlight'ned by that part which acts
And so the forms of single things perceives.

But after, by discoursing to and fro,
Anticipating and comparing things,
She doth all universal natures know,
And all effects into their causes brings.

When she rates things and moves from ground to ground
The name of reason she obtains by this;
But when by reasons she the truth hath found
And standeth fix'd, she understanding is.   420

When her assent she lightly doth encline
To either part, she is opinion light;
But when she doth by principles define
A certain truth, she hath true judgment's sight.

And as from senses reason's work doth spring,
So many reasons understanding gain,
And many understandings knowledge bring,
And by much knowledge wisdom we obtain.

So, many stairs we must ascend upright
Ere we attain to wisdom's high degree;   430
So doth this earth eclipse our reason's light
Which else, in instants, would like angels' be. . . .

Will puts in practise what the wit deviseth;
Will ever acts, and wit contemplates still,
And as from wit the power of wisdom riseth,
All other virtues daughters are of will.

Will is the prince and wit the counselor
Which doth for common good in counsel sit;
And when wit is resolv'd, will lends her power
To execute what is advis'd by wit.   440

Wit is the mind's chief judge which doth comptrol
Of fancy's court the judgments false and vain;
Will holds the royal scepter in the soul,
And on the passions of the heart doth reign.

Will is as free as any emperor;
Nought can restrain her gentle liberty;
No tyrant nor no torment hath the pow'r
To make us will when we unwilling be. . . .

The quick'ning power would be, and so would rest;
The sense would not be only, but be well;   450
But wit's ambition longeth to be best,
For it desires in endless bliss to dwell.

And these three powers three sorts of men do make:
For some, like plants, their veins do only fill;
And some, like beasts, their senses' pleasure take;
And some, like angels, do contemplate still. . . .

Yet these three pow'rs are not three souls, but one;
As one and two are both contain'd in three,
Three being one number by itself alone,
A shadow of the blessed Trinity.   460

O what is man, great Maker of mankind,
That thou to him so great respect dost bear?
That thou adorn'st him with so bright a mind,
Mak'st him a king, and even an angel's peer?

O what a lively life, what heavenly pow'r,
What spreading virtue, what a sparkling fire,
How great, how plentiful, how rich a dow'r
Dost thou within this dying flesh inspire!

Thou leav'st thy print in other works of thine,
But thy whole image thou in man hast writ.   470
There cannot be a creature more divine
Except, like thee, it should be infinite.

But it exceeds man's thought to think how high
God hath rais'd man since God a man became;
The angels do admire this mystery
And are astonish'd when they view the same.

Nor hath He given these blessings for a day,
Nor made them on the body's life depend;
The soul, though made in time, survives for ay,
And, though it hath beginning, sees no end.   480

Her only end is never-ending bliss,
Which is th' eternal face of God to see,

Who last of ends and first of causes is,
And to do this she must eternal be. . . .

[Through the following section of the poem—some one
hundred forty quatrains—Davies argues at tedious length
for the immortality of the soul.]

O ignorant, poor man, what dost thou bear
Lock'd up within the casket of thy breast?
What jewels and what riches hast thou there?
What heavenly treasure in so weak a chest?

Look in thy soul and thou shalt beauties find
Like those which drown'd Narcissus in the flood;   490
Honor and pleasure both are in thy mind,
And all that in the world is counted good.

Think of her worth, and think that God did mean
This worthy mind should worthy things embrace;
Blot not her beauties with thy thoughts unclean,
Nor her dishonor with thy passions base.

Kill not her quick'ning power with surfetings,
Mar not her sense with sensuality,
Cast not her serious wit on idle things,
Make not her free will slave to vanity.   500

And when thou think'st of her eternity,
Think not that death against her nature is;
Think it a birth, and, when thou goest to die,
Sing like a swan, as if thou went'st to bliss.

And if thou, like a child, didst fear before,
Being in the dark where thou didst nothing see,
Now I have brought the torchlight, fear no more;
Now, when thou diest, thou canst not hudwink'd be.

And thou, my soul, which turn'st thy curious eye
To view the beams of thine own form divine,   510
Know that thou canst know nothing perfectly
While thou art clouded with this flesh of mine.

Take heed of overweening, and compare
Thy peacock's feet with thy gay peacock's train.
Study the best and highest things that are,
But of thyself an humble thought retain.

Cast down thyself, and only strive to raise
The glory of thy Maker's sacred name;
Use all thy powers that blessed power to praise,
Which gives thee power to be and use the same.   520

JOHN DONNE

Owing perhaps to his remarkable mutation from wild Jack Donne to Dr. Donne, dean of St. Paul's, one of the most interesting of late Elizabethan poets left most of his verse in manuscript. Between his conversion from Rome to Canterbury in the late nineties and his taking holy orders (1615) Donne had presumably authorized the publication of some serious elegiac pieces (the two "Anniversaries" for Elizabeth Drury and a threnody for Prince Henry), but almost all the rest of his poetry, including even the "Holy Sonnets" of his latter years, remained unprinted. It was not until 1633, two years after his death, that the ill-printed and chaotically arranged *Poems by J. D. with Elegies on the Author's Death* was published by John Marriot. Two years later the volume was reissued with considerable alterations, including new groupings of "Songs and Sonnets," "Epigrams," "Elegies," "Epithalamions or Marriage Songs," "Satires," and the like. None the less, the 1635 edition is textually more corrupt than its predecessor, for it began the evil practice of including poems which modern scholars know to be uncanonical. Although Donne's son in 1637 had secured from the Archbishop of Canterbury a decree prohibiting further unauthorized publication of his father's work, Marriot issued new editions in 1639 and 1649; at last, however, in 1650, the younger Donne enforced his filial and legal rights by supervising an edition (oddly enough, also published by Marriot) to which were added "divers copies under his [John Donne's] own hand never before in print" and a flowery dedication (by Donne *fils*) to William, Lord Craven, Baron of Hamsted Marshall. Actually, young Donne's efforts amounted to nothing: the text and the canon of the 1650 edition are as carelessly handled as those of its predecessors, and the new "divers copies," miscellaneous pieces in Latin and English of questionable authenticity, add nothing to John Donne's reputation. This edition of 1650 was reprinted in 1654, and the last edition presumably from manuscript sources finally appeared in 1669, seven years after the younger Donne's death.

Long before this string of unsatisfactory editions appeared, Donne's poetry was widely circulated in manuscript recensions, and those that have survived have obvious value in determining both the text and the canon. Thus a small quarto manuscript (no. 216) in the library of Queen's College, Oxford, provides excellent texts for five satires, "The Storm," and "The Calm"; the so-called Westmoreland Manuscript (dating from about 1625), formerly in the possession of Sir Edmund Gosse, contains the satires, thirteen elegies, an epithalamion, the "Holy Sonnets," a group of "Paradoxes" in prose, and some epigrams; and there are many other such collections which, though without even the qualified authority of the 1633 *Poems,* are none the less useful in solving the many textual cruxes that such difficult and widely disseminated poetry as Donne's presents.

In order to stay within the chronological limits of this anthology we have confined our excerpts to Donne's early work—those "best pieces," as Jonson told Drummond, written "ere he was twenty-five years old" (that is, Jonson thought, by 1598). Although Donne's poetry is notoriously hard to date, it is the consensus of all authorities (including Sir Herbert Grierson, who has made the subject his own) that the "Songs and Sonnets"—whether cynical and often obscene pieces like "The Indifferent," passionate love songs (probably written for Anne More, who became his wife) like "The Canonization," or complicated essays in metaphysics like "The Extasy"—belong to his earliest work. The satires, too, must be dated before Elizabeth's death—between 1593 and 1595 in Sir Herbert Grierson's opinion; and "The Storm" and "The Calm" can be precisely ascribed to 1597, the year of the ill-starred "Islands Expedition" organized to seek out and destroy the second Armada which Philip II was preparing to send against England in retaliation for the Cadiz expedition of 1596. Our texts are based upon *Poems, By J. D. With Elegies on the Authors Death,* 1633 (STC 7045).

FROM POEMS (1633)

The Printer to the Understanders

For this time I must speak only to you; at another, readers may perchance serve my turn; and I think this a way very free from exception, in hope that very few will have a mind to confess themselves ignorant.

If you look for an epistle as you have before ordinary publications, I am sorry that I must deceive you; but you will not lay it to my charge when you shall consider that this is not ordinary, for if I should say it were the best in this kind that ever this kingdom hath yet seen, he that would doubt of it must go out of the kingdom to enform himself, for the best judgments within it take it for granted.

You may imagine (if it please you) that I could endear it unto you by saying that importunity drew it on, that had it not been presented here it would have come to us from beyond the seas (which perhaps is true enough), that my charge and pains in procuring of it hath been such and such. I could add hereto a promise of more correctness or enlargement in the next edition if you shall in the meantime content you with this. But these things are so common as that I should profane this piece by applying them to it. . . . I shall satisfy myself with the conscience of well-doing in making so much good common.

Howsoever it may appear to you, it shall suffice me to enform you that it hath the best warrant that can be: publique authority and private friends. . . . Farewell. . . .

EPIGRAMS

HERO AND LEANDER

Both robb'd of air, we both lie in one ground,
Both whom one fire had burn'd, one water drown'd.

PYRAMUS AND THISBE

Two, by themselves, each other, love, and fear
Slain, cruel friends by parting have join'd here.

FALL OF A WALL

Under an undermin'd and shot-bruis'd wall
A too-bold captain perish'd by the fall,
Whose brave misfortune happiest men envi'd
That had a town for tomb, his bones to hide.

AN OBSCURE WRITER

Philo, with twelve years' study, hath been griev'd
To'be[1] understood. When will he be believ'd?

THE STORM
To Mr. Christopher Brooke

Thou which art I ('tis nothing to be so),
Thou which art still thyself, by these shalt know
Part of our passage; and a hand or eye
By Hilliard drawn is worth an history
By a worse painter made; and (without pride)
When by thy judgment they are dignifi'd
My lines are such. 'Tis the preheminence
Of friendship only to'impute excellence.
England, to whom we'owe what we be and have,
Sad that her sons did seek a forrain grave   10

---

[1] We retain from the 1633 text this use of the apostrophe to indicate, presumably, that two syllables are to be read in the time normally occupied by one.

(For Fate's or Fortune's drifts none can soothsay;
Honor and misery have one face and way),
From out her pregnant intrails sigh'd a wind
Which at th' air's middle marble room did find
Such strong resistance that itself it threw
Downward again; and so, when it did view
How in the port our fleet dear time did leese,
Withering like prisoners which lie but for fees,
Mildly it kiss'd our sails, and, fresh and sweet
As to a stomach sterv'd, whose insides meet,   20
Meat comes, it came; and swole our sails, when we
So joy'd, as Sara'her swelling joy'd to see.
But 'twas but so kind as our countrymen
Which bring friends one day's way and leave them then.
Then like two mighty kings which, dwelling far
Asunder, meet against a third to war,
The south and west winds join'd, and, as they blew,
Waves like a rolling trench before them threw.
Sooner then you read this line did the gale,
Like shot not fear'd till felt, our sails assail;   30
And what at first was call'd a gust, the same
Hath now a storm's, anon a tempest's, name.
Jonas, I pity thee and curse those men
Who, when the storm rag'd most, did wake thee then.
Sleep is pain's easiest salve, and doth fulfil
All offices of death except to kill.
But when I wak'd I saw that I saw not;
I, and the sun, which should teach me,'had forgot
East, west, day, night; and I could only say
If'the world had lasted, now it had been day.   40
Thousands our noises were, yet we 'mongst all
Could none by his right name, but thunder, call.
Lightning was all our light, and it rain'd more
Then if the sun had drunk the sea before.
Some coffin'd in their cabins lie,'equally
Griev'd that they are not dead and yet must die;
And as sin-burd'ned souls from graves will creep
At the last day, some forth their cabins peep
And tremblingly'ask what news, and do hear so,
Like jealous husbands, what they would not know.   50
Some, sitting on the hatches, would seem there
With hideous gazing to fear away fear.
Then note they the ship's sicknesses, the mast
Shak'd with this ague, and the hold and waist
With a salt dropsy clogg'd, and all our tacklings
Snapping like too-high-stretched treble strings.
And from our totter'd sails rags drop down so
As from one hang'd in chains a year ago.
Even our ordinance, plac'd for our defense,
Strive to break loose and scape away from thence.   60
Pumping hath tir'd our men, and what's the gain?
Seas into seas thrown we suck in again;
Hearing hath deaf'd our sailors, and if they
Knew how to hear, there's none knows what to say.
Compar'd to these storms death is but a qualm,

Hell somewhat lightsome, and the 'Bermuda calm.
Darkness, Light's elder brother, his birthright
Claims o'er this world and to heaven hath chas'd light.
All things are one, and that one none can be,
Since all forms uniform deformity   70
Doth cover, so that we, except God say
Another *Fiat,* shall have no more day.
So violent yet long these furies be
That though thine absence sterve me, 'I wish not thee.

THE CALM

Our storm is past, and that storm's tyrannous rage
A stupid calm, but nothing it, doth swage.
The fable is inverted, and far more
A block afflicts now then a stork before.
Storms chafe, and soon wear out themselves or us;
In calms, heaven laughs to see us languish thus.
As steady 'as I can wish that my thoughts were,
Smooth as thy mistress' glass, or what shines there,
The sea is now; and as the iles which we
Seek when we can move, our ships rooted be.   10
As water did in storms, now pitch runs out,
As lead when a fir'd church becomes one spout;
And all our beauty, and our trim, decays
Like courts removing or like ended plays.
The fighting place now seamen's rags supply,
And all the tackling is a frippery.
No use of lanthorns; and in one place lay
Feathers and dust, today and yesterday.
Earth's hollownesses, which the world's lungs are,
Have no more wind then the upper vault of air.   20
We can nor lost friends nor sought foes recover,
But meteor-like, save that we move not, hover.
Only the calenture together draws
Dear friends, which meet dead in great fishes' jaws;
And on the hatches, as on altars, lies
Each one, his own priest and own sacrifice;
Who live, that miracle do multiply
Where walkers in hot ovens do not die.
If in despite of these we swim, that hath
No more refreshing then our brimstone bath;   30
But from the sea into the ship we turn,
Like parboil'd wretches on the coals to burn.
Like Bajazet encag'd, the shepherds' scoff,
Or like slack-sinew'd Sampson, his hair off,
Languish our ships. Now as a myriad
Of ants durst th' emperor's loved snake invade,
The crawling galleys, sea-gaols, finny chips,
Might brave our pinnaces, now bed-rid ships.
Whether a rotten state, and hope of gain,
Or to disuse me from the queasy pain   40
Of being belov'd, and loving, or the thirst
Of honor or fair death outpush'd me first,
I lose my end; for here as well as I
A desperate may live, and a coward die.

Stag, dog, and all which from or towards flies,
Is paid with life or prey or, doing, dies.
Fate grudges us all, and doth subtly lay
A scourge, 'gainst which we all forget to pray;
He that at sea prays for more wind, as well
Under the poles may beg cold, heat in hell.   50
What are we then? How little more, alas,
Is man now then before he was! He was
Nothing; for us, we are for nothing fit;
Chance or ourselves still disproportion it.
We have no power, no will, no sense—I lie!
I should not then thus feel this misery.

[*Songs and Sonnets*]

A NOCTURNAL UPON SAINT LUCY'S DAY,
BEING THE SHORTEST DAY

'Tis the year's midnight, and it is the day's,
Lucy's, who scarce seven hours herself unmasks;
    The sun is spent, and now his flasks
    Send forth light squibs, no constant rays;
        The world's whole sap is sunk;
The general balm th' hydroptique earth hath drunk,
Whither, as to the bed's feet, life is shrunk,
Dead and enterr'd; yet all these seem to laugh,
Compar'd with me, who am their epitaph.

Study me then, you who shall lovers be   10
At the next world, that is, at the next spring;
    For I am every dead thing,
    In whom Love wrought new alchimy.
        For his art did express
A quintessence even from nothingness,
From dull privations, and lean emptiness;
He ruin'd me, and I am re-begot
Of absence, darkness, death—things which are not.

All others from all things draw all that's good,
Life, soul, form, spirit, whence they being have; 20
    I, by Love's limbeck, am the grave
    Of all that's nothing. Oft a flood
        Have we two wept, and so
Drown'd the whole world, us two; oft did we grow
To be two chaoses, when we did show
Care to ought else; and often absences
Withdrew our souls, and made us carcasses.

But I am by her death, which word wrongs her,
Of the first nothing the elixir grown;
    Were I a man, that I were one   30
    I needs must know; I should prefer,
        If I were any beast,
Some ends, some means; yea plants, yea stones detest
And love; all, all some properties invest;
If I an ordinary nothing were,
As shadow, a light and body must be here.

But I am none; nor will my sun renew.
You lovers, for whose sake the lesser sun
   At this time to the Goat is run
    To fetch new lust, and give it you,   40
      Enjoy your summer all;
Since she enjoys her long night's festival,
Let me prepare towards her, and let me call
This hour her vigil and her eve, since this
Both the year's and the day's deep midnight is.

A VALEDICTION FORBIDDING MOURNING

As virtuous men pass mildly away,
   And whisper to their souls to go,
Whilst some of their sad friends do say,
   "The breath goes now," and some say, "No";

So let us melt, and make no noise,
   No tear-floods nor sigh-tempests move;
'Twere prophanation of our joys
   To tell the laity our love.

Moving of th' earth brings harms and fears,
   Men reckon what it did and meant;   10
But trepidation of the spheres,
   Though greater far, is innocent.

Dull sublunary lovers' love,
   Whose soul is sense, cannot admit
Absence, because it doth remove
   Those things which elemented it.

But we by a love so much refin'd
   That ourselves know not what it is,
Interassured of the mind,
   Care less eyes, lips, hands to miss.   20

Our two souls, therefore, which are one,
   Though I must go, endure not yet
A breach, but an expansion,
   Like gold to airy thinness beat.

If they be two, they are two so
   As stiff twin compasses are two;
Thy soul, the fix'd foot, makes no show
   To move, but doth if the'other do.

And though it in the center sit,
   Yet when the other far doth roam,   30
It leans, and harkens after it,
   And grows erect as that comes home.

Such wilt thou be to me who must,
   Like th' other foot, obliquely run;
Thy firmness makes my circle just,
   And makes me end where I begun.

SONG

Go and catch a falling star,
   Get with child a mandrake root,
Tell me where all past years are,
   Or who cleft the Devil's foot,
Teach me to hear mermaids singing,
   Or to keep off envy's stinging,
      And find
      What wind
Serves to advance an honest mind.

If thou beest born to strange sights,   10
   Things invisible to see,
Ride ten thousand days and nights,
   Till age snow white hairs on thee;
Thou, when thou retorn'st, wilt tell me
All strange wonders that befell thee,
      And swear
      Nowhere
Lives a woman true and fair.

If thou find'st one, let me know;
   Such a pilgrimage were sweet;   20
Yet do not, I would not go,
   Though at next door we might meet;
Though she were true when you met her,
And last till you write your letter,
      Yet she
      Will be
False, ere I come, to two or three.

WOMAN'S CONSTANCY

Now thou hast lov'd me one whole day,
Tomorrow when thou leav'st, what wilt thou say?
Wilt thou then antedate some new-made vow?
      Or say that now
We are not just those persons which we were?
Or, that oaths made in reverential fear
Of Love and his wrath any may forswear?
Or, as true deaths true marriages untie,
So lovers' contracts, images of those,
Bind but till sleep, death's image, them unloose?   10
      Or, your own end to justify,
For having purpos'd change and falsehood, you
Can have no way but falsehood to be true?
Vain lunatique, against these scapes I could
      Dispute and conquer, if I would;
      Which I abstain to do,
For by tomorrow I may think so too.

THE SUN RISING

   Busy old fool, unruly sun,
     Why dost thou thus
   Through windows and through curtains call on us?
   Must to thy motions lovers' seasons run?

Saucy, pedantique wretch, go chide
Late schoolboys and sour prentices;
Go tell court-huntsmen that the king will ride;
Call country ants to harvest offices.
Love, all alike, no season knows, nor clime,
Nor hours, days, moneths, which are the rags of time.   10

Thy beams so reverend and strong
Why shouldst thou think?
I could eclipse and cloud them with a wink
But that I would not lose her sight so long.
If her eyes have not blinded thine,
Look, and tomorrow late tell me
Whether both the'Indias of spice and mine
Be where thou left'st them or lie here with me.
Ask for those kings whom thou saw'st yesterday,
And thou shalt hear, all here in one bed lay.   20

She'is all states, and all princes I;
Nothing else is.
Princes do but play us; compar'd to this
All honor's mimique, all wealth alchimy.
Thou, sun, art half as happy'as we
In that the world's contracted thus;
Thine age asks ease, and since thy duties be
To warm the world, that's done in warming us.
Shine here to us, and thou art everywhere;
This bed thy center is, these walls thy sphere.   30

THE INDIFFERENT

I can love both fair and brown,
Her whom abundance melts, and her whom want
betrays,
Her who loves loneness best, and her who masks and
plays,
Her whom the country form'd, and whom the town,
Her who believes, and her who tries,
Her who still weeps with spungy eyes,
And her who is dry cork and never cries;
I can love her and her and you and you,
I can love any, so she be not true.

Will no other vice content you?   10
Will it not serve your turn to do as did your mothers?
Or have you all old vices spent, and now would find out
others?
Or doth a fear that men are true torment you?
O, we are not, be not you so,
Let me, and do you, twenty know.
Rob me, but bind me not, and let me go.
Must I, who came to travail thorow you,
Grow your fix'd subject because you are true?

Venus heard me sigh this song,
And by love's sweetest part, variety, she swore,   20

She heard not this till now, and that it should be so no
more.
She went, examin'd, and return'd ere long,
And said, "Alas, some two or three
Poor heretiques in love there be,
Which think to stablish dangerous constancy.
But I have told them, 'Since you will be true,
You shall be true to them who'are false to you.' "

THE CANONIZATION

For Godsake hold your tongue and let me love,
Or chide my palsy or my gout,
My five gray hairs or ruin'd fortune flout,
With wealth your state, your mind with arts improve,
Take you a course, get you a place,
Observe his Honor or his Grace,
Or the king's real or his stamped face
Contemplate. What you will, approve,
So you will let me love.

Alas, alas, who's injur'd by my love?   10
What merchant's ships have my sighs drown'd?
Who says my tears have overflow'd his ground?
When did my colds a forward spring remove?
When did the heats which my veins fill
Add one more to the plaguy bill?
Soldiers find wars, and lawyers find out still
Litigious men which quarrels move,
Though she and I do love.

Call us what you will, we are made such by love.
Call her one, me another fly,   20
We'are tapers too, and at our own cost die,
And we in us find the'eagle and the dove.
The phoenix' riddle hath more wit
By us; we two, being one, are it.
So to one neutral thing both sexes fit;
We die and rise the same, and prove
Mysterious by this love.

We can die by it if not live by love,
And if unfit for tombs and hearse
Our legend be, it will be fit for verse.   30
And if no piece of chronicle we prove,
We'll build in sonnets pretty rooms.
As well a well-wrought urn becomes
The greatest ashes as half-acre tombs.
And by these hymns all shall approve
Us canoniz'd for love;

And thus invoke us: "You whom reverend love
Made one another's hermitage,
You to whom love was peace that now is rage;
Who did the whole world's soul contract and drove   40
Into the glasses of your eyes

(So made such mirrors and such spies
That they did all to you epitomize)
    Countries, towns, courts: beg from above
    A pattern of your love!"

SONG

Sweetest love, I do not go
    For weariness of thee,
Nor in hope the world can show
    A fitter love for me;
    But since that I
Must die at last, 'tis best
To use myself in jest
    Thus by feign'd deaths to die.

Yesternight the sun went hence,
    And yet is here today;   10
He hath no desire nor sense,
    Nor half so short a way;
    Then fear not me,
But believe that I shall make
Speedier journeys, since I take
    More wings and spurs then he.

O, how feeble is man's power,
    That if good fortune fall,
Cannot add another hour,
    Nor a lost hour recall!   20
    But come bad chance,
And we join to it our strength,
And we teach it art and length,
    Itself o'er us to'advance.

When thou sigh'st, thou sigh'st not wind,
    But sigh'st my soul away;
When thou weep'st, unkindly kind,
    My life's blood doth decay.
    It cannot be
That thou lov'st me, as thou say'st,   30
If in thine my life thou waste;
    Thou art the best of me.

Let not thy divining heart
    Forethink me any ill;
Destiny may take thy part,
    And may thy fears fulfil;
    But think that we
Are but turn'd aside to sleep;
They who one another keep
    Alive, ne'er parted be.   40

THE ANNIVERSARY

All kings, and all their favorites,
    All glory of honors, beauties, wits,
The sun itself, which makes times as they pass,

Is elder by a year now, then it was
When thou and I first one another saw;
All other things to their destruction draw,
    Only our love hath no decay;
This no tomorrow hath, nor yesterday;
Running, it never runs from us away,
But truly keeps his first, last, everlasting day.   10

Two graves must hide thine and my corse;
    If one might, death were no divorce.
Alas, as well as other princes, we,
Who prince enough in one another be,
Must leave at last in death these eyes and ears,
Oft fed with true oaths and with sweet salt tears;
    But souls where nothing dwells but love,
All other thoughts being inmates, then shall prove
This, or a love increased there above,
When bodies to their graves, souls from their graves,
    remove.   20

And then we shall be throughly blest,
    But we no more then all the rest;
Here upon earth we'are kings, and none but we
Can be such kings, nor of such subjects be.
Who is so safe as we, where none can do
Treason to us, except one of us two?
    True and false fears let us refrain;
Let us love nobly, and live, and add again
Years and years unto years, till we attain
To write threescore; this is the second of our reign.   30

TWICK'NAM GARDEN

Blasted with sighs, and surrounded with tears,
    Hither I come to seek the spring,
    And at mine eyes, and at mine ears,
Receive such balms as else cure everything;
    But O, self traitor, I do bring
The spider love, which transubstantiates all,
    And can convert manna to gall;
And that this place may thoroughly be thought
    True paradise, I have the serpent brought.

'Twere wholesomer for me that winter did   10
    Benight the glory of this place,
    And that a grave frost did forbid
These trees to laugh and mock me to my face;
    But that I may not this disgrace
Indure, nor yet leave loving, Love, let me
    Some senseless piece of this place be;
Make me a mandrake, so I may groan here,
    Or a stone fountain weeping out my year.

Hither with crystal vials, lovers, come
    And take my tears, which are love's wine,   20
    And try your mistress' tears at home,

For all are false that taste not just like mine;
    Alas, hearts do not in eyes shine,
Nor can you more judge woman's thoughts by tears
    Then by her shadow what she wears.
O perverse sex, where none is true but she
    Who's therefore true because her truth kills me.

A VALEDICTION OF WEEPING

    Let me pour forth
My tears before thy face whilst I stay here,
For thy face coins them, and thy stamp they bear,
And by this mintage they are something worth,
      For thus they be
      Pregnant of thee;
Fruits of much grief they are, emblems of more—
When a tear falls, that thou fall'st which it bore,
So thou and I are nothing then, when on a divers shore.

    On a round ball   10
A workman that hath copies by can lay
An Europe, Afrique, and an Asia,
And quickly make that which was nothing, all;
      So doth each tear
      Which thee doth wear,
A globe, yea world, by that impression grow,
Till thy tears mix'd with mine do overflow
This world; by waters sent from thee, my heaven
    dissolved so.

    O more then moon,
Draw not up seas to drown me in thy sphere;   20
Weep me not dead in thine arms, but forbear
To teach the sea what it may do too soon;
      Let not the wind
      Example find,
To do me more harm then it purposeth;
Since thou and I sigh one another's breath,
Whoe'er sighs most is cruelest, and hastes the other's
    death.

THE FLEA

Mark but this flea, and mark in this,
How little that which thou deny'st me is;
It suck'd me first, and now sucks thee,
And in this flea our two bloods mingled be;
Thou know'st that this cannot be said
A sin, nor shame, nor loss of maidenhead;
    Yet this enjoys before it woo,
    And pamper'd swells with one blood made of two,
    And this, alas, is more then we would do.

O stay, three lives in one flea spare,   10
Where we almost, yea, more then married are.
This flea is you and I, and this
Our marriage bed and marriage temple is;

Though parents grudge, and you, w' are met
And cloister'd in these living walls of jet.
    Though use make you apt to kill me,
    Let not to that self-murder added be,
    And sacrilege, three sins in killing three.

Cruel and sodain, hast thou since
Purpled thy nail in blood of innocence?   20
Wherein could this flea guilty be,
Except in that drop which it suck'd from thee?
Yet thou triumph'st and say'st that thou
Find'st not thyself nor me the weaker now;
    'Tis true, then learn how false fears be:
    Just so much honor, when thou yield'st to me,
    Will waste as this flea's death took life from thee.

THE EXTASY

Where, like a pillow on a bed,
    A pregnant bank swell'd up to rest
The violet's reclining head,
    Sat we two, one another's best.
Our hands were firmly cimented
    With a fast balm, which thence did spring;
Our eye-beams twisted, and did thread
    Our eyes upon one double string;
So to'entergraft our hands, as yet
    Was all the means to make us one,   10
And pictures in our eyes to get
    Was all our propagation.
As 'twixt two equal armies fate
    Suspends uncertain victory,
Our souls, which to advance their state
    Were gone out, hung 'twixt her and me.
And whilst our souls negotiate there,
    We like sepulchral statues lay;
All day, the same our postures were,
    And we said nothing, all the day.   20
If any, so by love refin'd
    That he soul's language understood,
And by good love were grown all mind,
    Within convenient distance stood,
He, though he knew not which soul spake,
    Because both meant, both spake the same,
Might thence a new concoction take
    And part far purer then he came.
This extasy doth unperplex,
    We said, and tell us what we love: 30
We see by this it was not sex,
    We see we saw not what did move;
But as all several souls contain
    Mixture of things, they know not what,
Love these mix'd souls doth mix again
    And makes both one, each this and that.
A single violet transplant,
    The strength, the color, and the size,

All which before was poor and scant,
  Redoubles still and multiples.   40
When love with one another so
  Interinanimates two souls,
That abler soul, which thence doth flow,
  Defects of loneliness controls.
We then, who are this new soul, know
  Of what we are compos'd and made,
For th' atomies of which we grow
  Are souls, whom no change can invade.
But O, alas, so long, so far,
  Our bodies why do we forbear?   50
They are ours, though they are not we; we are
  The intelligences, they the sphere.
We owe them thanks, because they thus
  Did us to us at first convey,
Yielded their forces, sense, to us,
  Nor are dross to us, but allay.
On man heaven's influence works not so,
  But that it first imprints the air;
So soul into the soul may flow,
  Though it to body first repair.   60
As our blood labors to beget
  Spirits, as like souls as it can,
Because such fingers need to knit
  That subtile knot which makes us man,
So must pure lovers' souls descend
  T' affections, and to faculties,
Which sense may reach and apprehend,
  Else a great prince in prison lies.
To'our bodies turn we then, that so
  Weak men on love reveal'd may look;   70
Love's mysteries in souls do grow,
  But yet the body is his book.
And if some lover, such as we,
  Have heard this dialogue of one,
Let him still mark us, he shall see
  Small change when we'are to bodies gone.

THE RELIQUE

When my grave is broke up again
Some second ghest to entertain
(For graves have learn'd that womanhead,
  To be to more then one a bed),
    And he that digs it spies
A bracelet of bright hair about the bone,
    Will he not let'us alone,
And think that there a loving couple lies,
Who thought that this device might be some way
To make their souls, at the last busy day,   10
Meet at this grave and make a little stay?

  If this fall in a time or land
    Where misdevotion doth command,
  Then he that digs us up will bring

Us to the bishop and the king,
    To make us reliques; then
Thou shalt be a Mary Magdalen, and I
    A something else thereby;
All women shall adore us, and some men;
And since at such time miracles are sought,   20
I would have that age by this paper taught
What miracles we harmless lovers wrought.

  First, we lov'd well and faithfully,
    Yet knew not what we lov'd, nor why;
  Difference of sex no more we knew
    Then our guardian angels do;
      Coming and going, we
Perchance might kiss, but not between those meals;
    Our hands ne'er touched the seals
Which nature, injur'd by late law, sets free;   30
These miracles we did, but now alas,
All measure and all language I should pass,
Should I tell what a miracle she was.

Satires

SATIRE III

Kind pity chokes my spleen; brave scorn forbids
Those tears to issue which swell my eyelids;
I must not laugh, nor weep sins and be wise;
Can railing then cure these worn maladies?
Is not our mistress, fair religion,
As worthy of all our souls' devotion
As virtue was to the first blinded age?
Are not heaven's joys as valiant to asswage
Lusts as earth's honor was to them? Alas,
As we do them in means, shall they surpass   10
Us in the end? and shall thy father's spirit
Meet blind philosophers in heaven, whose merit
Of strict life may be imputed faith, and hear
Thee, whom he taught so easy ways and near
To follow, damn'd? O, if thou dar'st, fear this;
This fear great courage and high valor is.
Dar'st thou aid mutinous Dutch, and dar'st thou lay
Thee in ships, wooden sepulchers, a prey
To leaders' rage, to storms, to shot, to dearth?
Dar'st thou dive seas and dungeons of the earth?   20
Hast thou couragious fire to thaw the ice
Of frozen North discoveries? and thrice
Colder then salamanders, like divine
Children in th' oven, fires of Spain and the line,
Whose countries limbecks to our bodies be,
Canst thou for gain bear? and must every he
Which cries not "Goddess!" to thy mistress draw
Or eat thy poisonous words? Courage of straw!
O desperate coward, wilt thou seem bold and
To thy foes and His, who made thee to stand   30
Sentinel in his world's garrison, thus yield,

And for forbidden wars leave th' appointed field?
Know thy foes: the foul Devil, whom thou
Strivest to please, for hate, not love, would allow
Thee fain his whole realm to be quit; and as
The world's all parts wither away and pass,
So the world's self, thy other lov'd foe, is
In her decrepit wane, and thou, loving this,
Dost love a withered and worn strumpet; last,
Flesh, itself's death, and joys which flesh can taste   40
Thou lovest, and thy fair goodly soul, which doth
Give this flesh power to taste joy, thou dost loathe.
Seek true religion. O, where? Mirreus,
Thinking her unhous'd here and fled from us,
Seeks her at Rome; there, because he doth know
That she was there a thousand years ago;
He loves her rags so, as we here obey
The statecloth where the prince sat yesterday.
Crantz to such brave loves will not be inthrail'd,
But loves her only who at Geneva is call'd   50
Religion, plain, simple, sullen, young,
Contemptuous, yet unhansome; as, among
Lecherous humors, there is one that judges
No wenches wholesome but coarse country drudges.
Graius stays still at home here, and because
Some preachers, vile ambitious bawds, and laws,
Still new like fashions, bid him think that she
Which dwells with us is only perfect, he
Imbraceth her whom his godfathers will
Tender to him, being tender; as wards still   60
Take such wives as their guardians offer, or
Pay valews. Careless Phrygius doth abhor
All, because all cannot be good; as one,
Knowing some women whores, dares marry none.
Gracchus loves all as one, and thinks that so
As women do in divers countries go
In divers habits, yet are still one kind,
So doth, so is, religion; and this blind-
Ness too much light breeds; but unmoved, thou
Of force must one, and forc'd but one allow,   70
And the right; ask thy father which is she,

Let him ask his; though truth and falsehood be
Near twins, yet truth a little elder is;
Be busy to seek her; believe me this,
He's not of none, nor worst, that seeks the best.
To adore, or scorn an image, or protest,
May all be bad. Doubt wisely; in strange way
To stand inquiring right is not to stray;
To sleep, or run wrong, is. On a huge hill,
Cragged and steep, Truth stands, and he that will   80
Reach her, about must and about must go,
And what the hill's suddenness resists, win so.
Yet strive so that before age, death's twilight,
Thy soul rest, for none can work in that night.
To will implies delay, therefore now do
Hard deeds, the body's pains; hard knowledge to
The mind's indeavors reach, and mysteries
Are like the sun, dazzling, yet plain to all eyes.
Keep the truth which thou hast found; men do not stand
In so ill case that God hath with his hand   90
Signed kings blank charters to kill whom they hate;
Nor are they vicars, but hangmen, to fate.
Fool and wretch, wilt thou let thy soul be tied
To man's laws, by which she shall not be tried
At the last day? Will it then boot thee
To say a Philip or a Gregory,
A Harry or a Martin, taught thee this?
Is not this excuse for mere contraries
Equally strong? Cannot both sides say so?
That thou mayest rightly obey power, her bounds
    know;   100
Those past, her nature and name is chang'd; to be
Then humble to her is idolatry.
As streams are, power is; those blest flowers that dwell
At the rough stream's calm head, thrive and do well,
But having left their roots, and themselves given
To the stream's tyrannous rage, alas, are driven
Through mills and rocks and woods, and at last, almost
Consum'd in going, in the sea are lost.
So perish souls, which more chuse men's unjust
Power from God claim'd, then God himself to trust. 110

BEN JONSON

Although a complete edition of Jonson's non-dramatic poetry has remained the task of modern scholars, the three collections which appeared in his lifetime and shortly after his death presumably contain most of the pieces that he himself valued most highly. *Epigrams* (which was licensed on May 15, 1612) and *The Forest* were included in the folio *Works* of 1616, *Underwoods* in the second volume of the second folio in 1640. The *Epigrams,* which Jonson himself hailed as "the ripest of my studies," is a remarkable hodge-podge of beauty, wit, and brutality. Its one hundred thirty-three pieces polish and also distend the genre that ever since the Greek Anthology had enjoyed a wide reputation and that had been especially popular with the Elizabethans, both in the vernacular and in Latin imitations of Martial. However the epigram is defined—and perhaps it may safely be described as a short poem making a pithy (and ostensibly witty) comment, often of a critical or satirical nature—the name itself had been attached to hundreds of pieces in the sixteenth century. Sir Thomas More in Latin and Wyatt in English wrote epigrams that were widely admired and imitated, and John Heywood (who often merely refurbished proverbs [see p. 121]) was so prolific in the form as to earn the sobriquet "Epigramist"; but many poets of Elizabeth's early reign—Gascoigne, Googe, Turbervile, Timothy Kendall—as well as later writers like Harington, John Weever, Sir John Davies, Donne, Lodge, Everard Guilpin—created or translated epigrams with infectious enthusiasm. Moreover, the rise of euphuism, with its labored but pointed turns of antithetical wit, helped to popularize the technique of the epigram in prose, and that technique was readily assimilated into the *Essays* of Bacon and the character-books of the early seventeenth

century. Although Jonson had, then, copious precedent for his efforts in this form, he also used it for new purposes. As a classical scholar he knew and admired the Martialian epigrams, both those that wittily and lightly sketch a person or a thing and those that cap a longer "narration" with a pointed judgment at the end of some sharply observed particulars. Jonson's *Epigrams* contains many specimens of both types. In addition to its satirical poems, however, the collection includes some lovely chiseled epitaphs reminiscent of the Greek Anthology, a grotesque mock-epic ("On the Famous Voyage"), coarse jests in rime, and stately poems of commendation. The fifteen poems in *The Forest,* an even more miscellaneous group, include not only some of his most famous songs but also a fragmentary Pindaric ode and several inimitably grave and formal epistles to persons of honor. Our texts are based upon *Epigrammes. 1. Booke* and *The Forrest* in *The Workes,* volume I, 1616 (STC 14751).

FROM EPIGRAMS (1616)

To the Great Example of Honor and Virtue, the Most Noble William, Earl of Pembroke, Lord Chamberlain, etc.

My lord, while you cannot change your merit I dare not change your title. It was that made it, and not I. Under which name I here offer to your lordship the ripest of my studies, my *Epigrams,* which, though they carry danger in the sound, do not therefore seek your shelter. For when I made them, I had nothing in my conscience to expressing of which I did need a cipher. But if I be fall'n into those times wherein, for the likeness of vice and facts, everyone thinks another's ill deeds objected to him, and that in their ignorant and guilty mouths the common voice is (for their security), "Beware the poet," confessing therein so much love to their diseases as they would rather make a party for them then be either rid or told of them; I must expect at your lordship's hand the protection of truth and liberty while you are constant to your own goodness. In thanks whereof, I return you the honor of leading forth so many good and great names (as my verses mention on the better part) to their remembrance with posterity. Amongst whom, if I have praised unfortunately any one that doth not deserve, or if all answer not in all numbers the pictures I have made

of them, I hope it will be forgiven me that they are no ill pieces, though they be not like the persons. But I foresee a nearer fate to my book then this: that the vices therein will be own'd before the virtues (though there I have avoided all particulars as I have done names) and that some will be so ready to discredit me as they will have the impudence to belie themselves. For if I meant them not, it is so. Nor can I hope otherwise. For why should they remit anything of their riot, their pride, their self-love, and other inherent graces to consider truth or virtue, but, with the trade of the world, lend their long ears against men they love not and hold their dear mountebank or jester in far better condition then all the study or studiers of humanity? For such, I would rather know them by their vizards still then they should publish their faces, at their peril, in my theater, where Cato, if he liv'd, might enter without scandal.

Your lordship's most faithful honorer,

Ben Jonson

To The Reader

Pray thee, take care, that tak'st my book in hand,
To read it well; that is, to understand.

TO MY BOOK

It will be look'd for, Book, when some but see
Thy title *Epigrams,* and nam'd of me,
Thou should'st be bold, licentious, full of gall,
Wormwood, and sulphur, sharp, and tooth'd withal;
Become a petulant thing, hurl ink and wit
As madmen stones, not caring whom they hit.
Deceive their malice who could wish it so,
And, by thy wiser temper, let men know
Thou art not covetous of least self-fame
Made from the hazard of another's shame,   10
Much less with lewd, prophane, and beastly phrase
To catch the world's loose laughter or vain gaze.
He that departs with his own honesty
For vulgar praise doth it too dearly buy.

TO WILLIAM CAMDEN

Camden, most reverend head, to whom I owe
All that I am in arts, all that I know
(How nothing's that!), to whom my country owes
The great renown and name wherewith she goes,
Then thee the age sees not that thing more grave,
More high, more holy, that she more would crave.
What name, what skill, what faith hast thou in things!
What sight in searching the most antique springs!
What weight and what authority in thy speech!
Man scarce can make that doubt but thou canst teach. 10
Pardon free truth, and let thy modesty,
Which conquers all, be once overcome by thee.
Many of thine this better could then I,
But for their powers accept my piety.

ON REFORMED GAMESTER

Lord, how is Gamester chang'd! His hair close cut,
His neck fenc'd round with ruff, his eyes half shut!
His clothes two fashions off, and poor! His sword
Forbid his side, and nothing but the Word
Quick in his lips! Who hath this wonder wrought?
The late ta'en bastinado. So I thought.
What several ways men to their calling have!
The body's stripes, I see, the soul may save.

ON MY FIRST DAUGHTER

Here lies, to each her parents' ruth,
Mary, the daughter of their youth.
Yet all heaven's gifts being heaven's due,
It makes the father less to rue.
At six moneths' end she parted hence
With safety of her innocence,
Whose soul heaven's Queen (whose name she bears),
In comfort of her mother's tears,
Hath plac'd amongst her virgin train;
Where while that, sever'd, doth remain,   10
This grave partakes the fleshly birth;
Which cover lightly, gentle earth.

ON MARGARET RATCLIFFE

M arble, weep, for thou dost cover
A dead beauty underneath thee,
R ich as Nature could bequeath thee.
G rant, then, no rude hand remove her.
A ll the gazers on the skies
R ead not in fair heaven's story
E xpresser truth or truer glory
T hen they might in her bright eyes.
R are as wonder was her wit,
A nd like nectar ever-flowing,   10
T ill Time, strong by her bestowing,
C onquer'd hath both life and it,
L ife whose grief was out of fashion
I n these times. Few so have ru'd
F ate in a brother. To conclude,
F or wit, feature, and true passion,
E arth, thou hast not such another.

ON MY FIRST SON

Farewell, thou child of my right hand and joy!
My sin was too much hope of thee, lov'd boy.
Seven years thou wert lent to me, and I thee pay,
Exacted by thy fate, on the just day.
O, could I loose all father now! For why
Will man lament the state he should envy?
To have so soon scap'd world's and flesh's rage,
And, if no other misery, yet age?
Rest in soft peace, and, ask'd, say here doth lie
Ben Jonson his best piece of poetry,   10
For whose sake, henceforth, all his vows be such
As what he loves may never like too much.

TO CENSORIOUS COURTLING

Courtling, I rather thou should'st utterly
Dispraise my work then praise it frostily.
When I am read, thou feign'st a weak applause,
As if thou wert my friend, but lack'dst a cause.
This but thy judgment fools; the other way
Would both thy folly and thy spite betray.

OF LIFE AND DEATH

The ports of death are sins, of life, good deeds,
Through which our merit leads us to our meeds.
How wilful blind is he, then, that would stray
And hath it in his powers to make his way!
This world Death's region is, the other, Life's;
And here it should be one of our first strifes
So to front death as men might judge us past it.
For good men but see death; the wicked taste it.

TO EDWARD ALLEN

If Rome so great, and in her wisest age,
Fear'd not to boast the glories of her stage,
As skilful Roscius and grave Aesop, men

Yet crown'd with honors as with riches then,
Who had no less a trumpet of their name
Then Cicero, whose every breath was fame—
How can so great example die in me
That, Allen, I should pause to publish thee?
Who both their graces in thyself hast more
Outstripp'd then they did all that went before,   10
And present worth in all dost so contract
As others speak but only thou dost act.
Wear this renown. 'Tis just that who did give
So many poets life by one should live.

TO LUCY, COUNTESS OF BEDFORD,
WITH MR. DONNE'S SATIRES

Lucy, you brightness of our sphere, who are
Life of the muses' day, their morning star!
If works (not th' authors) their own grace should look,
Whose poems would not wish to be your book?
But these, desir'd by you, the maker's ends
Crown with their own. Rare poems ask rare friends.
Yet satires, since the most of mankind be
Their unavoided subject, fewest see;
For none ere took that pleasure in sin's sense
But, when they heard it tax'd, took more offense.   10
They, then, that, living where the matter is bred,
Dare for these poems yet both ask and read
And like them too, must needfully, though few,
Be of the best—and mongst those best are you,
Lucy, you brightness of our sphere, who are
The muses' evening, as their morning, star.

TO JOHN DONNE

Who shall doubt, Donne, where I a poet be
When I dare send my *Epigrams* to thee?
That so alone canst judge, so alone dost make,
And in thy censures evenly dost take
As free simplicity to disavow
As thou hast best authority t' allow.
Read all I send, and if I find but one
Mark'd by thy hand, and with the better stone,
My title's seal'd. Those that for claps do write,
Let pui'nees', porters', players' praise delight,   10

And, till they burst, their backs like asses load.
A man should seek great glory, and not broad.

EPITAPH ON S[ALOMON] P[AVY], A CHILD
OF QUEEN ELIZABETH'S CHAPEL

Weep with me, all you that read
    This little story,
And know for whom a tear you shed
    Death's self is sorry.
'Twas a child that so did thrive
    In grace and feature
As heaven and nature seem'd to strive
    Which own'd the creature.
Years he numb'red scarce thirteen
    When Fates turn'd cruel,   10
Yet three fill'd zodiacs had he been
    The stage's jewel,
And did act, what now we moan,
    Old men so duly
As, sooth, the Parcae thought him one,
    He play'd so truly.
So, by error, to his fate
    They all consented;
But, viewing him since (alas, too late),
    They have repented   20
And have sought (to give new birth)
    In baths to steep him;
But, being so much too good for earth,
    Heaven vows to keep him.

EPITAPH ON ELIZABETH, LADY H.

Would'st thou hear what man can say
    In a little? Reader, stay.
Underneath this stone doth lie
    As much beauty as could die,
Which in life did harbor give
    To more virtue then doth live.
If at all she had a fault,
    Leave it buried in this vault.
One name was Elizabeth,
    Th' other, let it sleep with death: 10
Fitter where it died to tell
    Then that it liv'd at all. Farewell.

FROM THE FOREST (1616)

TO PENSHURST

Thou art not, Penshurst, built to envious show
    Of touch or marble, nor canst boast a row
Of polish'd pillars or a roof of gold;
    Thou hast no lanthern whereof tales are told,
Or stair, or courts, but stand'st an ancient pile,
    And, these grudg'd at, art reverenc'd the while.

Thou joy'st in better marks of soil, of air,
    Of wood, of water; therein thou art fair.
Thou hast thy walks for health as well as sport,
    Thy mount to which the dryads do resort,   10
Where Pan and Bacchus their high feasts have made
    Beneath the broad beech and the chestnut shade,
That taller tree which of a nut was set

At his great birth where all the muses met.
There in the writhed bark are cut the names
   Of many a sylvan taken with his flames,
And thence the ruddy satyrs oft provoke
   The lighter fauns to reach thy lady's oak.
Thy copps, too, nam'd of Gamage, thou hast there
   That never fails to serve thee season'd deer   20
When thou would'st feast or exercise thy friends.
   The lower land, that to the river bends,
Thy sheep, thy bullocks, kine, and calves do feed,
   The middle grounds thy mares and horses breed.
Each bank doth yield thee conies, and the tops,
   Fertile of wood, Ashore and Sidney's copps,
To crown thy open table, doth provide
   The purpled pheasant with the speckled side.
The painted partrich lies in every field
   And, for thy mess, is willing to be kill'd.   30
And if the high-swoll'n Medway fail thy dish,
   Thou hast thy ponds that pay thee tribute fish,
Fat, aged carps that run into thy net;
   And pikes, now weary their own kind to eat,
As loth the second draught or cast to stay,
   Officiously at first themselves betray;
Bright eels that emulate them and leap on land
   Before the fisher, or into his hand.
Then hath thy orchard fruit, thy garden flowers
   Fresh as the air and new as are the hours.   40
The early cherry, with the later plum,
   Fig, grape, and quince, each in his time doth come;
The blushing apricot and woolly peach
   Hang on thy walls, that every child may reach.
And though thy walls be of the country stone,
   They are rear'd with no man's ruin, no man's groan;
There's none that dwell about them wish them down,
   But all come in, the farmer and the clown,
And no one empty-handed, to salute
   Thy lord and lady, though they have no suit.   50
Some bring a capon, some a rural cake,
   Some nuts, some apples; some that think they make
The better cheeses bring hem, or else send
   By their ripe daughters whom they would commend
This way to husbands, and whose baskets bear
   An emblem of themselves in plum or pear.
But what can this (more then express their love)
   Add to thy free provisions, far above
The need of such? Whose liberal board doth flow
   With all that hospitality doth know!   60
Where comes no guest but is allow'd to eat
   Without his fear, and of thy lord's own meat,
Where the same beer and bread and self-same wine
   That is his lordship's shall be also mine.
And I not fain to sit (as some, this day,
   At great men's tables) and yet dine away.
Here no man tells my cups, nor, standing by,
   A waiter doth my gluttony envy,

But gives me what I call and lets me eat;
   He knows, below, he shall find plenty of meat;   70
Thy tables hoard not up for the next day,
   Nor, when I take my lodging, need I pray
For fire or lights or livory: all is there,
   As if thou, then, wert mine, or I reign'd here.
There's nothing I can wish for which I stay.
   That found King James when, hunting late this way
With his brave son, the prince, they saw thy fires
   Shine bright on every hearth, as the desires
Of thy penates had been set on flame
   To entertain them; or the country came   80
With all their zeal to warm their welcome here.
   What—great I will not say, but—sodain cheer
Did'st thou, then, make hem! And what praise was
     heap'd
   On thy good lady then, who therein reap'd
The just reward of her high huswifery
   To have her linen, plate, and all things nigh
When she was far, and not a room but dress'd
   As if it had expected such a guest!
These, Penshurst, are thy praise, and yet not all.
   Thy lady's noble, fruitful, chaste withal;   90
His children thy great lord may call his own,
   A fortune, in this age, but rarely known.
They are, and have been, taught religion; thence
   Their gentler spirits have suck'd innocence.
Each morn and even they are taught to pray
   With the whole household, and may, every day,
Read in their virtuous parents' noble parts
   The mysteries of manners, arms, and arts.
Now, Penshurst, they that will proportion thee
   With other edifices, when they see   100
Those proud, ambitious heaps and nothing else,
   May say, "Their lords have built, but thy lord dwells."

TO CELIA

Come, my Celia, let us prove,
   While we may, the sports of love.
Time will not be ours forever;
   He at length our good will sever.
Spend not, then, his gifts in vain;
   Suns that set may rise again,
But if once we lose this light
   'Tis, with us, perpetual night.
Why should we defer our joys?
   Fame and rumor are but toys.   10
Cannot we delude the eyes
   Of a few poor household spies?
Or his easier ears beguile,
   So removed by our wile?
'Tis no sin love's fruit to steal,
   But the sweet theft to reveal,
To be taken, to be seen,
   These have crimes accounted been.

SONG. THAT WOMEN ARE BUT MEN'S SHADOWS

Follow a shadow, it still flies you;
  Seem to fly it, it will pursue.
So court a mistress, she denies you;
  Let her alone, she will court you.
Say, are not women truly, then,
  Styl'd but the shadows of us men?
At morn and even shades are longest;
  At noon they are or short or none.
So men at weakest, they are strongest,
  But grant us perfect, they're not known.   10
Say, are not women truly, then,
  Styl'd but the shadows of us men?

SONG. TO CELIA

Drink to me only with thine eyes,
  And I will pledge with mine;
Or leave a kiss but in the cup,
  And I'll not look for wine.
The thirst that from the soul doth rise
  Doth ask a drink divine,
But might I of Jove's nectar sup,
  I would not change for thine.

I sent thee late a rosy wreath,
  Not so much honoring thee   10
As giving it a hope that there
  It could not withered be.
But thou thereon did'st only breathe
  And sent'st it back to me,

Since when it grows and smells, I swear,
  Not of itself, but thee.

TO HEAVEN

Good and great God, can I not think of thee
  But it must straight my melancholy be?
Is it interpreted in me disease
  That, laden with my sins, I seek for ease?
O, be thou witness, that the reins dost know
  And hearts of all, if I be sad for show;
And judge me after if I dare pretend
  To ought but grace, or aim at other end.
As thou art all, so be thou all to me,
  First, midst, and last, converted one and three,   10
My faith, my hope, my love; and in this state
  My judge, my witness, and my advocate.
Where have I been this while exil'd from thee?
  And whither rapt, now thou but stoop'st to me?
Dwell, dwell here still! O Being everywhere,
  How can I doubt to find thee ever here?
I know my state, both full of shame and scorn,
  Conceiv'd in sin, and unto labor born,
Standing with fear, and must with horror fall,
  And destin'd unto judgment after all.   20
I feel my griefs, too, and there scarce is ground
  Upon my flesh t' inflict another wound.
Yet dare I not complain or wish for death
  With holy Paul, lest it be thought the breath
Of discontent, or that these prayers be
  For weariness of life, not love of thee.

SONNET SEQUENCES

The rage for sonnet sequences, commonly deprecated as the most unfortunate development of late Elizabethan literature, was mercifully short-lived. And yet we should remember that the greatest writers of the age produced many distinguished sonnets to follow the fashion. The inanities of Percy, Barnes, and Tofte are hard to tolerate, but the beauties of Sidney, Daniel, and Spenser—to say nothing of the glories of Shakespeare—serve to remind us that great writers can master and exploit the same convention that stifles lesser men.

When Wyatt and Surrey domesticated the sonnet in the English language they imported a form that had enjoyed immense popularity on the Continent for more than two centuries. Dante had lent his great prestige to the form by casting twenty-five of the thirty-one lyrics of the *Vita nuova* as regular sonnets; but it was Petrarch, the most imitated writer of the Italian Renaissance, who securely established not only the form but also the themes of the Continental sonnet. In his *Rime* there are two sets

of sonnets (one addressed to Laura in life, the other to Laura in death) comprising three hundred seventeen quatorzains interspersed with ballades, sestinas, madrigals, and odes. Petrarch's theme, like Dante's, was Platonic love, and he made the stock figures of the unapproachable lady and the despairing lover indispensable for generations of young men with amatory or literary aspirations. Of the many Italian writers who limped or galloped after Petrarch the most important were Serafino de' Ciminelli Aquilano, Pietro Bembo, Luigi Alemanni, and the two great epic poets Ariosto and Tasso. In the early sixteenth century Mellin de St. Gelais and Clément Marot established the sonnet in France, and Joachim du Bellay, in his influential *Défense et illustration de la langue française* (written in 1549 to publicize the literary program of the Pléiade), singled out the Petrarchan sonnet as especially appropriate for French writers to imitate. Not only did Du Bellay follow his own advice, but his colleague Pierre de Ronsard published nearly a thousand sonnets, and in the later sixteenth century Philippe Desportes was almost as prolific and popular. If, as Sir Sidney Lee has estimated, more than 300,000 sonnets were written in sixteenth-century Europe, then the Elizabethans' exercises in that form must be regarded as a small part of a large whole—but a part that none the less includes Shakespeare's *Sonnets*.

After the publication of Tottel's *Miscellany* (1557) the true sonnet enjoyed no great popularity, even though ungifted writers like Googe occasionally employed the form (see p. 286); it more frequently gave its name to almost any "little song" or short lyric. Young Spenser seems to have contributed some sonnets (derived from Petrarch through Marot and Du Bellay) to Van der Noot's *Theater* in 1569 (see p. 330), and a few years later Gascoigne included some thirty sonnets in his *Hundreth Sundry Flowers* (1573) and even defined the form as a poem of fourteen pentameter lines in *Certain Notes of Instruction* (1575; see p. 598). Although the hundred "sonnets" in Thomas Watson's Ἑκατομπαθία (1582; see pp. 317–19) contain eighteen lines each, the "passionate century of love" (as he called his work) does constitute a sort of sequence, and so it anticipates the development of the sonnet cycles in the nineties. However, by the time Watson published his frigid translations and adaptations (obligingly listing their sources), Sir Philip Sidney had no doubt written most of *Astrophel and Stella,* the work which, when surreptitiously published in 1591 with a part of Daniel's *Delia,* brilliantly launched the sonnet vogue which the following selections represent. About the same time that Sidney was recording his courtship of Penelope Devereux (see p. 323), his friend, schoolmate, and biographer Fulke Greville must have written the sonnets to "Caelica," a collection pieced out with later work and finally published posthumously in 1633 (the same year, incidentally, as Donne's *Poems* containing the early "Songs and Sonnets").

The floodgates, then, were opened with the appearance of *Astrophel and Stella* in 1591. The next year Daniel issued an authorized edition of *Delia,* a work revised and "augmented" in 1594, when Drayton printed his *Idea's Mirror,* and followed quickly by Spenser's great *Amoretti* (1595). By this time all manner of poets and poetasters were scribbling and plagiarizing "amours in quatorzains." Henry Constable's *Diana,* which first appeared in 1592, was in 1594 "augmented with divers quatorzains of honorable and learned personages" to eight "decades." In 1593 Thomas Lodge published his *Phyllis* and Barnabe Barnes his *Parthenophil and Parthenophe,* followed in 1595 by his *Divine Century of Spiritual Sonnets.* In *Licia* (1593) Giles Fletcher had urbanely confessed that his lady could be somebody or nobody, perhaps "learning's image, or some heavenly wonder which the precisest may not mislike," and his caveat against searching for autobiographical passion (which Sidney, somewhat disingenuously, had claimed) may be applied to most of the sonnet sequences

that flooded the bookstalls in the mid-nineties. The forty "canzons" in the anonymous *Zepheria* (1594), like William Percy's twenty pieces in *Sonnets to the Fairest Coelia* of the same year, gain distinction of a dubious sort from their legal jargon reminiscent of the Inns of Court. Shortly thereafter, Bartholomew Griffin's sixty-two sonnets in *Fidessa More Chaste Than Kind* (1596) plagiarized with disarming impartiality from Daniel, Drayton, Watson, and several approved Continental writers.

With William Smith's *Chloris* (1596), Robert Tofte's *Laura* (1597) properly brings up the rear of the sonneteers whom Lee lumped together as *poetae minimi.* Most of Tofte's one hundred twenty metrically irregular poems in three "parts" were, as he says in his dedication, conceived in Italy, and his unfortunately large collection may be accounted one of the last flickers of Petrarch's influence in English poetry. Most of these writers—and others not represented in this anthology—were men of very slender taste and talent. Their unblushing plagiarism, their affectation, and their prosodic incompetence lead one to think that surely nothing worth saying about unhappy love had been left unsaid. But then, a decade after the vogue had died, there appeared the *Sonnets* of Shakespeare.

The *Sonnets* may well be called the most puzzling single book of lyric poems ever published in our language. Although no other work has stimulated more scholarship, interpretation, and foolish conjecture, what we actually know of its history may be quickly set forth: in *Palladis Tamia* (1598) Francis Meres alluded to Shakespeare's "sugared sonnets" in circulation among his "private friends"; the next year two of the sonnets (nos. 138 and 144) were included in *The Passionate Pilgrim. By W. Shakespeare,* a piratical anthology published by William Jaggard; ten years later (May 20, 1609) Thomas Thorpe, a not quite reputable publisher, registered at Stationers' Hall a book entitled *Shake-speares Sonnets: Never before Imprinted;* and shortly thereafter a quarto containing Thorpe's dedication to "Mr. W. H.," one hundred fifty-four sonnets, and an obscure poem called "A Lover's Complaint" was offered for sale by two booksellers (John Wright and William Aspley), each of them under his own imprint. Perhaps because the edition was suppressed or perhaps because the vogue of sonnet sequences had waned, there was no second printing until one hundred forty-six of the sonnets (rearranged as seventy-two titled "poems") were included in John Benson's edition of *Poems: Written by Wil. Shakespeare, Gent.* in 1640, twenty-four years after the author's death.

On the basis of these facts and on the alleged autobiographical evidence of the sonnets themselves, scholars, zealots, and amateur detectives have erected a dizzying mass of scholarship and guesswork. In spite of the mountainous labors of certain irrepressible—and sometimes ridiculous—interpreters, the informed consensus is that

Thorpe's edition was unauthorized, and that therefore Shakespeare cannot be held accountable for the dedication or the puzzling arrangement of the sonnets; that most of the sonnets were composed in the mid-nineties, and that the majority of nos. 1–126 were addressed to a handsome and aristocratic young man who may have been but probably was not the "Mr. W. H." of Thorpe's dedication; that a second series (nos. 127–152) concerns the poet's tangled relations with a mistress "black as hell"; and that the last two (obviously inferior) sonnets are either spurious or at any rate thematically unrelated to the earlier poems. Within this broad area of agreement, however, there is ample room for disagreement and contradictory conjecture. Does the "begetter" thanked in Thorpe's dedication refer to the inspirer of the poems or to the procurer who provided Thorpe with the manuscript (there being absolutely no evidence that Shakespeare himself was involved in the transaction)? Does "Mr. W. H." refer to William Herbert, third Earl of Pembroke, to Henry Wriothesley, third Earl of Southampton, to an unknown William Hughes, to Sir William Hervey? Is the subject of nos. 1–126 one young man or several young men? Did the "dark woman" of nos. 127–152 contribute to an adulterous triangle with

the poet and his friend? Do the sonnets (nos. 78–83, 85, 86) about a "rival poet" refer to Spenser, to Marlowe, to Barnabe Barnes, to Chapman, to Jonson, to Drayton—or to several or none of them? These and many similar questions will no doubt continue to agitate the scholarship or curiosity of all readers, but the sonnets, inscrutable as the Sphinx, remain the most precious lyrics of the Elizabethan or any other age of English literature.

Our texts are based upon *Certaine Learned and Elegant Workes of the Right Honorable Fulke Lord Brooke, Written in his Youth, and familiar Exercise with Sir Philip Sidney*, 1633 (STC 12361); *Licia, or Poemes of Love, In Honour of the admirable and singular vertues of his Lady, to the imitation of the best Latin Poets, and others*, [1593] (STC 11055); *Diana. Or, The excellent conceitful Sonnets of H. C. Augmented with divers Quatorzains of honorable and lerned personages. Devided into viij. Decads*, [1594] (STC 5638); *Sonnets to the Fairest Coelia*, 1594 (STC 19618); *Zepheria*, 1594 (STC 26124); *Fidessa, more chaste then kinde*, 1596 (STC 12367); *Laura. The Toyes of a Traveller. Or The Feast of Fancie. Divided into three Parts*, 1597 (STC 24097); *Shake-speares sonnets. Never before imprinted*, 1609 (STC 22353).

FULKE GREVILLE

FROM CERTAIN LEARNED AND ELEGANT WORKS (1633)

CAELICA
SONNET 4

You little stars that live in skies
And glory in Apollo's glory,
In whose aspects conjoined lies
The heaven's will and nature's story,
Joy to be likened to those eyes,
Which eyes make all eyes glad or sorry;
  For when you force thoughts from above,
  These overrule your force by love.

And thou, O Love, which in these eyes
Hast married reason with affection,   10
And made them saints of beauty's skies,
Where joys are shadows of perfection,
Lend me thy wings that I may rise
Up, not by worth, but thy election;
  For I have vow'd in strangest fashion,
  To love, and never seek compassion.

SONNET 7

The world, that all contains, is ever moving;
The stars within their spheres forever turned;
Nature, the queen of change, to change is loving,
And form to matter new is still adjourned.

Fortune, our fancy-god, to vary liketh;
Place is not bound to things within it placed;
The present time upon time passed striketh;
With Phoebus' wand'ring course the earth is graced.

The air still moves, and by its moving cleareth;
The fire up ascends and planets feedeth;   10
The water passeth on and all lets weareth;
The earth stands still, yet change of changes breedeth.

Her plants, which summer ripes, in winter fade;
Each creature in unconstant mother lieth;
Man made of earth, and for whom earth is made,

Still dying lives and living ever dieth;
  Only, like fate, sweet Myra never varies,
  Yet in her eyes the doom of all change carries.

SONNET 16

Fie, foolish earth, think you the heaven wants glory
Because your shadows do yourself benight?
All's dark unto the blind, let them be sorry;
The heavens in themselves are ever bright.

Fie, fond desire, think you that love wants glory
Because your shadows do yourself benight?
The hopes and fears of lust may make men sorry,
But love still in herself finds her delight.

Then earth, stand fast, the sky that you benight
Will turn again and so restore your glory;   10
Desire, be steady, hope is your delight,
An orb wherein no creature can be sorry,
  Love being plac'd above these middle regions
  Where every passion wars itself with legions.

SONNET 52

Away with these self-loving lads
Whom Cupid's arrow never glads!
Away, poor souls, that sigh and weep
In love of those that lie asleep!
  For Cupid is a meadow god
  And forceth none to kiss the rod.

Sweet Cupid's shafts, like destiny,
Doth causeless good or ill decree;
Desert is born out of his bow,
Reward upon his wing doth go.   10
  What fools are they that have not known
  That Love likes no laws but his own!

My songs they be of Cynthia's praise,
I wear her rings on holidays;
In every tree I write her name,
And every day I read the same.
  Where Honor Cupid's rival is,
  There miracles are seen of his.

If Cynthia crave her ring of me,
I blot her name out of the tree;   20
If doubt do darken things held dear,
Then well fare nothing once a year.
  For many run, but one must win;
  Fools, only, hedge the cuckoo in.

The worth that worthiness should move
Is love, that is the bow of Love;

And love as well the foster can
As can the mighty nobleman.
  Sweet saint, 'tis true you worthy be,
  Yet without love nought worth to me.   30

SONNET 82

Under a throne I saw a virgin sit,
The red and white rose quarter'd in her face;
Star of the north! and for true guards to it,
Princes, church, states, all pointing out her grace;
The homage done her was not born of wit;
Wisdom admir'd, zeal took ambitious place,
State in her eyes taught order how to sit
And fix confusion's unobserving race.
  Fortune can here claim nothing truly great
  But that this princely creature is her seat.   10

SONNET 110

Sion lies waste, and thy Jerusalem,
O Lord, is fall'n to utter desolation;
Against thy prophets and thy holy men
The sin hath wrought a fatal combination;
  Prophan'd thy name, thy worship overthrown,
  And made thee, living Lord, a God unknown.

Thy powerful laws, thy wonders of creation,
Thy Word incarnate, glorious heaven, dark hell,
Lie shadowed under man's degeneration;
Thy Christ still crucifi'd for doing well;   10
  Impiety, O Lord, sits on thy throne,
  Which makes thee, living light, a God unknown.

Man's superstition hath thy truths entomb'd,
His atheism again her pomps defaceth;
That sensual unsatiable vast womb
Of thy seen church thy unseen church disgraceth.
  There lives no truth with them that seem thine own,
  Which makes thee, living Lord, a God unknown.

Yet unto thee, Lord, mirror of transgression,
We who for earthly idols have forsaken   20
Thy heavenly image, sinless, pure impression,
And so in nets of vanity lie taken,
  All desolate implore that to thine own,
  Lord, thou no longer live a God unknown.

Yet, Lord, let Israel's plagues not be eternal,
Nor sin forever cloud thy sacred mountains,
Nor with false flames, spiritual but infernal,
Dry up thy mercy's ever-springing fountains.
  Rather, sweet Jesus, fill up time and come
  To yield the sin her everlasting doom.   30

GILES FLETCHER

FROM LICIA (1593)

To the Reader

I had thought, curteous and gentle reader, not to have troubled thy patience with these lines, but that in the neglect thereof I should either scorn thee as careless of thine opinion (a thing savoring of a proud humor) or dispair to obtain thy favor, which I am loth to conceive of thy good nature. . . .

For this kind of poetry wherein I wrote, I did it only to try my humor. And for the matter of love, it may be I am so devoted to some one into whose hands these may light by chance that she may say, which thou now sayest, that surely he is in love; which if she do, then have I the full recompense of my labor, and the poems have dealt sufficiently for the discharge of their own duty.

This age is learnedly wise and faultless in this kind of making their wits known, thinking so basely of our bare English, wherein thousands have travailed with such ill luck, that they deem themselves barbarous and the iland barren unless they have borrowed from Italy, Spain, and France their best and choicest conceits. For my own part, I am of this mind, that our nation is so exquisite (neither would I overweeningly seem to flatter our homespun stuff or diminish the credit of our brave travailers) that neither Italy, Spain, nor France can go beyond us for exact invention. For if anything be odious amongst us it is the exile of our old manners and some baseborn phrases stuff'd up with such new terms as a man may sooner feel us to flatter by our incrouching eloquence than suspect it from the ear.

And for the matter of love, where every man takes upon him to court exactly, I could justly grace (if it be a grace to be excellent in that kind) the Inns of Court and some gentlemen-like students in both universities whose learning and bringing-up, together with their fine natures, makes so sweet a harmony as, without partiality, the most injurious will prefer them before all others; and therefore they only are fittest to write of love.

For others, for the most part, are men of mean reach, whose imbased minds prey upon every bad dish—men unfit to know what love means, deluded fondly with their own conceit, misdeeming so divine a fancy, taking it to be the contentment of themselves, the shame of others, the wrong of virtue, and the refiner of the tongue, boasting of some few favors. These and such like errors—errors hateful to an upright mind—commonly by learnless heads are reputed for love's kingdom. But vain men, naturally led, deluded themselves, deceive others. . . .

If thou muse what my Licia is, take her to be some Diana, at the least chaste; or some Minerva; no Venus, fairer far. It may be she is learning's image, or some heavenly wonder which the preciest may not mislike. . . . It may be, I mean that kind courtesy which I found at the patroness of these poems; it may be some colledge. It may be my conceit, and portend nothing. Whatsoever it be, if thou like it, take it; and thank the worthy Lady Mollineux, for whose sake thou hast it—worthy indeed, and so not only reputed by me in private affection of thankfulness, but so equally to be esteemed by all that know her.

For if I had not received of her and good Sir Richard, of kind and wise Master Lee, of courteous Master Houghton, all matchless, matched in one kindred, those unrequitable favors, I had not thus idly toyed.

If thou mislike it, yet she, or they, or both, or divine Licia, shall patronize it; or if none, I will, and can, do it myself. Yet I wish thy favor. Do but say thou art content, and I rest thine. If not, farewell till we both meet. September 8, 1593.

1

Sad, all alone, not long I musing sat,
But that my thoughts compelled me to aspire;
A laurel garland in my hand I gat,
So the Muses I approach'd the nigher.
My suit was this, a poet to become,
To drink with them, and from the heavens be fed.
Phoebus denied, and sware there was no room,
Such to be poets as fond fancy led.
With that I mourn'd and sat me down to weep;
Venus she smil'd, and smiling to me said,   10
"Come drink with me, and sit thee still, and sleep."
This voice I heard; and Venus I obey'd.
    That poison, sweet, hath done me all this wrong,
    For now of love must needs be all my song.

9

Love was laid down, all weary, fast asleep,
Whereas my love his armor took away.
The boy awak'd, and straight began to weep,

But stood amaz'd, and knew not what to say.
"Weep not, my boy," said Venus to her son,
"Thy weapons none can wield but thou alone.
Licia the Fair this harm to thee hath done;
I saw her here, and presently was gone.
She will restore them, for she hath no need
To take thy weapons, where thy valor lies.   10
For men to wound, the Fates have her decreed
With favor, hands, with beauty, and with eyes."
    No, Venus, no, she scorns them, credit me,
    But robb'd thy son, that none might care for thee.

23

My love was mask'd and armed with a fan
To see the sun so careless of his light,
Which stood and gaz'd, and, gazing, waxed wan
To see a star himself that was more bright.
Some did surmise she hid her from the sun,
Of whom, in pride, she scorn'd for to be kiss'd,
Or fear'd the harm by him to others done—
But these the reason of this wonder miss'd;
Nor durst the sun, if that her face were bare,
In greatest pride presume to take a kiss,   10
But she, more kind, did shew she had more care
Then with her eyes eclipse him of his bliss.
    Unmask you, sweet, and spare not. Dim the sun.
    Your light's inough, although that his were done.

25

Seven are the lights that wander in the skies,
And at these seven I wonder in my love;
To see the moon, how pale she doth arise,
Standing amaz'd as though she durst not move;
So is my sweet much paler than the snow,
Constant her looks, those looks that cannot change.
Mercury the next, a god sweet-tongu'd we know,
But her sweet voice doth wonders speak more strange.
The rising sun doth boast him of his pride,
And yet my love is far more fair than he.   10
The warlike Mars can wieldless weapons guide,
But yet that god is far more weak than she.
The lovely Venus seemeth to be fair,
But at her best, my love is far more bright.
Saturn for age with groans doth dim the air,
Whereas my love with smiles doth give it light.
    Gaze at her brows, where heaven ingrafted is;
    Then sigh, and swear there is no heaven but this.

28

In time the strong and stately turrets fall,
In time the rose and silver lilies die,
In time the monarchs captive are and thrall,
In time the sea and rivers are made dry;
The hardest flint in time doth melt asunder;
Still-living fame in time doth fade away;

The mountains proud we see in time come under;
And earth, for age, we see in time decay.
The sun in time forgets for to retire
From out the east where he was wont to rise;   10
The basest thoughts we see in time aspire,
And greedy minds in time do wealth despise.
    Thus all, sweet fair, in time must have an end,
    Except thy beauty, virtues, and thy friend.

47

Like Memnon's rock, touch'd with the rising sun,
Which yields a sound and echoes forth a voice;
But when it's drown'd in western seas is done,
And drowsy-like leaves off to make a noise;
So I, my love, inlight'ned with your shine,
A poet's skill within my soul I shroud—
Not rude, like that which finer wits decline,
But such as muses to the best allow'd.
But when your figure and your shape is gone,
I speechless am, like as I was before;   10
Or if I write, my verse is fill'd with moan,
And blurr'd with tears by falling in such store;
    Then muse not, Licia, if my muse be slack,
    For when I wrote I did thy beauty lack.

52

O sug'red talk, wherewith my thoughts do live;
O brows, Love's trophy and my senses' shrine;
O charming smiles, that death or life can give;
O heavenly kisses from a mouth devine;
O wreaths, too strong, and trammels made of hair;
O pearls inclosed in an ebon pale;
O rose and lilies in a field most fair
Where modest white doth make the red seem pale.
O voice whose accents live within my heart,
O heavenly hand that more then Atlas holds,   10
O sighs perfum'd that can release my smart,
O happy they whom in her arms she folds.
    Now if you ask where dwelleth all this bliss,
    Seek out my love, and she will shew you this.

AN ELEGY

Down in a bed, and on a bed of down,
Love, she, and I to sleep together lay.
She, like a wanton, kiss'd me with a frown,
"Sleep, sleep," she said, but meant to steal away.
I could not choose but kiss, but wake, but smile
To see how she thought us two to beguile.

She feign'd a sleep; I wak'd her with a kiss;
A kiss to me she gave to make me sleep.
"If I did wrong, sweet love, my fault was this,
In that I did not you thus waking keep.   10
Then kiss me, sweet, that so I sleep may take;
Or let me kiss to keep you still awake."

The night drew on, and needs she must be gone.
She waked Love and bid him learn to wait;
She sigh'd, she said, to leave me there alone,
And bid Love stay, but practise no deceit.
Love wept for grief, and sighing made great moan,
And could not sleep, nor stay, if she were gone.

"Then stay, sweet love!" A kiss with that I gave.
She could not stay, but gave my kiss again; 20
A kiss was all that I could get or crave,
And with a kiss she bound me to remain.
"Ah, Licia," still I in my dreams did cry;
"Come, Licia, come, or else my heart will die."

HENRY CONSTABLE

FROM DIANA (1594)

The First Decade

9

My lady's presence makes the roses red
Because to see her lips they blush for shame.
The lily's leaves, for envy, pale became,
And her white hands in them this envy bred.
The marigold the leaves abroad doth spread
Because the sun's and her power is the same.
The violet of purple color came,
Dy'd in the blood she made my heart to shed.
In brief, all flowers from her their virtue take;
From her sweet breath their sweet smells do proceed; 10
The living heat which her eyebeams doth make
Warmeth the ground and quickeneth the seed.
The rain wherewith she watereth the flowers
Falls from mine eyes, which she dissolves in showers.

The Third Decade

1

Uncivil sickness, hast thou no regard,
But dost presume my dearest to molest,
And without leave dar'st enter in that breast
Whereto sweet Love approach yet never dar'd?
Spare thou her health which my life hath not spar'd!
Too bitter such revenge of my unrest!
Although with wrongs my thought she hath oppress'd,
My wrongs seek not revenge—they crave reward.
Cease, sickness! Cease in her then to remain,
And come, and welcome, harbor thou in me 10
Whom Love long since hath taught to suffer pain.
So she which hath so oft my pain increas'd—
O God, that I might so revenged be!—
By my poor pain might have her pain releas'd.

The Fifth Decade

8

Dear to my soul, then leave me not forsaken!
Fly not, my heart within thy bosom sleepeth.
Even from myself and sense I have betaken
Me unto thee for whom my spirit weepeth,

And on the shore of that salt teary sea,
Couch'd in a bed of unseen seeming pleasure,
Where in imaginary thoughts thy fair self lay;
But being wak'd, robbed of my live's best treasure,
I call the heavens, air, earth, and seas to hear
My love, my truth, and black disdain'd estate; 10
Beating the rocks with bellowings of dispair,
Which still with plaints my words reverberate;
Sighing, "Alas, what shall become of me?"
Whilst Echo cries, "What shall become of me?"

9

Whilst Echo cries, "What shall become of me?"
And desolate, my desolations pity,
Thou in thy beauty's carrack sit'st to see
My tragic downfall and my funeral ditty.
No timbrel, but my heart thou play'st upon,
Whose strings are stretch'd unto the highest key;
The diapason, love; love is the unison;
In love my life and labors waste away.
Only regardless to the world thou leav'st me,
Whilst slain hopes, turning from the feast of sorrow 10
Unto dispair, their king which ne'er deceives me,
Captives my heart, whose black night hates the morrow;
And he in ruth of my distressed cry
Plants me a weeping star within mine eye.

The Sixth Decade

2

To live in hell, and heaven to behold;
To welcome life and die a living death;
To sweat with heat and yet be freezing cold;
To grasp at stars and lie the earth beneath;
To tread a maze that never shall have end;
To burn in sighs and starve in daily tears;
To climb a hill and never to descend;
Giants to kill, and quake at childish fears;
To pine for food and watch th' Hesperian tree;
To thirst for drink, and nectar still to draw; 10
To live accurs'd, whom men hold blest to be,
And weep those wrongs which never creature saw:
If this be love, if love in these be founded,
My heart is love, for these in it are grounded.

WILLIAM PERCY

FROM SONNETS TO THE FAIREST COELIA (1594)

To the Reader

Courteous Reader,

    Whereas I was fully determined to have concealed
my sonnets as things privy to myself, yet, of courtesy
having lent them to some, they were secretly committed to the press and almost finished before it came
to my knowledge. Wherefore making, as they say,
virtue of necessity, I did deem it most convenient to
prepose mine epistle only to beseech you to account
of them as of toys and amorous devices; and ere long   10
I will impart unto the world another poem which
shall be both more fruitful and ponderous.

    In the meanwhile I commit these as a pledge to
your indifferent censures.

    London, 1594.

                      W[illiam] Percy

1

Judg'd by my goddess' doom to endless pain,
Lo, here I ope my sorrow's passion,
That ev'ry silly eye may view most plain
A sentence given on no occasion.
If that by chance they fall (most fortunate)
Within those cruel hands that did enact it,
Say but "Alas, he was too passionate,
My doom is pass'd, nor can be now unactit."
So mayst thou see I was a spotless lover,
And grieve withal that e'er thou dealt so sore;   10
Unto remorse who goes about to move her,
Pursues the winged winds and tills the shore.
    Lovely is her semblance, hard is her heart,
    Wavering is her mind, sure is her dart.

7

If it be sin so dearly for to love thee,
Come, bind my hands—I am thy prisoner.
Yet if a spark of pity may but move thee,
First sit upon the cause, commissioner.
The same, well heard, may wrest incontinent
Two floods from forth those rocks of adamant,
Which, streaming down with force impatient,
May melt the breast of my fierce Rhadamant.
Dearest cruel, the cause, I see, dislikes thee,
On us thy brows thou bends so direfully.   10
Enjoin me penance whatsoever likes thee;
Whate'er it be I'll take it thankfully.
    Yet since for love it is I am thy bondman,
    Good Coelia, use me like a gentleman.

15

ECHO

What is the fair to whom so long I plead? *Lead.*
What is her face so angel-like? *Angel-like.*
Then unto saints in mind sh' is not unlike. *Unlike.*
What may be hop'd of one so evil-nat'red? *Hatred.*
O then my woes how shall I ope best? *Hope best.*
Then she is flexible. *She is flexible.*
Fie, no, it is impossible. *Possible.*
About her straight then only our best! *You're best.*
How must I first her loves to me approve? *Prove.*
How if she say I may not kiss her? *Kiss her.*   10
For all her bobs I must then bear, or miss her? *Yes, sir.*
Then will she yield at length to love? *To love.*
    Ev'n so? *Ev'n so.* By Narcisse, is it true? *True.*
    Of thine honesty? *Aye.* Adieu. *Adieu.*

19

It shall be said I died for Coelia;
Then quick, thou griesly man of Erebus,
Transport me hence unto Proserpina,
To be adjudg'd as wilful amorous;
To be hung up within the liquid air,
For all the sighs which I in vain have wasted;
To be through Lethe's waters cleansed fair,
For those dark clouds which have my looks o'ercasted;
To be condemn'd to everlasting fire,
Because at Cupid's fire I wilful brent me;   10
And to be clad for deadly dumps in mire.
Among so many plagues which shall torment me
    One solace I shall find, when I am over—
    It will be known I died a constant lover.

20

Receive these writs, my sweet and dearest friend,
The lively patterns of my liveless body,
Where thou shalt find in hebon pictures penn'd
How I was meek, but thou extremely bloody.
I'll walk forlorn along the willow shades
Alone, complaining of a ruthless dame;
Where'er I pass, the rocks, the hills, the glades
In piteous yells shall sound her cruel name.
There I will wail the lot which Fortune sent me
And make my moans unto the savage ears;   10
The remnant of the days which Nature lent me,
I'll spend them all, conceal'd, in ceaseless tears.
    Since unkind fates permit me not t' enjoy her,
    No more, burst eyes! I mean for to annoy her.

ANONYMOUS

FROM ZEPHERIA (1594)

Alli veri figlioli delle Muse

Ye modern laureates, famous'd for your writ,
Who for your pregnance may in Delos dwell,
On your sweet lines eternity doth sit,
Their brows ennobling with applause and laurel.
Triumph and honor ay invest your writ!
   Ye fet your pens from wing of singing swan,
When (sweetly warbling to herself) she floats
Adown Meander streams, and like to organ
Imparts into her quills melodious notes.
   Ye from the father of delicious phrases   10
Borrow such hymns as make your mistress live
When time is dead; nay, Hermes tunes the praises
Which ye in sonnets to your mistress give.
   Report throughout our western isle doth ring
The sweet-tun'd accents of your Delian sonnetry,
Which to Apollo's violin ye sing—
O then, your high strains drown his melody.
   From forth dead sleep of everlasting dark,
Fame, with her trump's shrill summon, hath awak'd
The Romain Naso and the Tuscan Petrarch,   20
Your spirit-ravishing lines to wonder at.
   O, theme befitting high-mus'd Astrophil,
He to your silvery songs lent sweetest touch,
Your songs, the immortal spirit of your quill!
O pardon, for my artless pen too much
Doth dim your glories through his infant skill.
   Though may I not with you the spoils devide
(Ye sacred offspring of Mnemosyne)
Of endless praise, which have your pens atchiev'd
(Your pens the trumps to immortality),   30
Yet be it leful that like maims I bide,
Like brunts and scars in your love's warfare,
And here, though in my homespun verse, of them declare.

CANZON 8

Illuminating lamps, ye orbs [crystallite],
Transparent mirrolds, globes devining beauty,
How have I joy'd to wanton in your light,
Though was I slain by your artillery.
Ye blithesome stars, like Leda's lovely twins
When clear they twinkle in the firmament,
Promise *esperance* to the seamen's wand'rings,
So have your shine made ripe mine heart's content.
Or as the light which Sestian Hero show'd
Arm-finn'd Leander to direct in waves   10
When through the raging Hellespont he row'd,
Steering to Love's port; so by thine eyes' clear rays
   Blest were my ways! But since no light was found,
   Thy poor Leander in the deep is drown'd.

CANZON 13

Proud in thy love, how many have I cited
Impartial thee to view, whose eyes have lavish'd.
Sweet beauteous objects oft have men delighted;
But thou above delight their sense hast ravish'd.
They, amorous artists, thee pronounc'd love's queen,
And unto thy supremacy did swear
(Venus, at Paphos keep, no more be seen!)
Now Cupid after thee his shafts shall bear.
How have I spent my spirit of invention
In penning amorous stanzas to thy beauty,   10
But heavenly graces may not brook dimension;
No more may thine, for infinite they be.
   But now in harsh tune I of amours sing,
   My pipe for them grows hoarse, but [shrill] to
     plaining.

CANZON 23

Thy coral-colored lips, how should I portray
Unto the unmatchable pattern of their sweet?
A draught of blessedness I stole away
From them when last I kiss'd. I taste it yet;
So did that sug'ry touch my lips ensucket.
On them, Minerva's honey birds do hive
Mellifluous words, when so thou please to frame
Thy speech to entertainment. Thence I derive
My heart's sole paradise and my lips' sweet game.
Ye are the coral gates of temple's clarion,   10
Whereout the Pythius preach'd divinity.
Unto thy voice bequeath'd the good Arion
His silvery lyre. Such paean melody
   Thy voice the organ-pipe of angels' quire
   Trebles. Yet, one kiss, and I'll raise them higher.

CANZON 26

When we, in kind embracements, had agreed
To keep a royal banquet on our lips,
How soon have we another feast decreed,
And how, at parting, have we mourn'd by fits!
Eftsoons, in absence have we wail'd much more
Till those void hours of intermission
Were spent, that we might revel as before.
How have we bribed time for expedition!
And when remitted to our former love-plays.
How have we, overweening in delight,   10
Accus'd the Father-Sexton of the days
That then with eagle's wings he took his flight.
   But now, old man, fly on as swift as thought,
   Sith eyes from love, and hope from heart, is wrought.

BARTHOLOMEW GRIFFIN

FROM FIDESSA MORE CHASTE THAN KIND (1596)

To the Gentlemen of the Inns of Court

Curteous Gentlemen:

It may please you, intertain with patience this poor pamphlet, unworthy, I confess, so worthy patronage. If I presume, I crave pardon; if offend, it is the first fruit of any my writings; if dislike, I can be but sorry. Sweet gentlemen, censure mildly, as protectors of a poor stranger. Judge the best, as incouragers of a young beginner. So shall I make true report of your undeserved favors, and you shall be yourselves ever curteous.

In this hope, if promise may go for currant, I willingly make the same unto you of a pastoral, yet unfinished, that my purpose was to have added for variety sake to this little volume of sonnets. The next term you may expect it. In the meantime, I wholly rely on your gentle acceptance.

Yours ever,

B[artholomew] Griffin

3

Venus and young Adonis sitting by her,
Under a myrtle shade, began to woo him;
She told the youngling how god Mars did try her,
And as he fell to her, so fell she to him.
"Even thus," quoth she, "the wanton god embrac'd
　　me"—
And then she clasp'd Adonis in her arms.
"Even thus," quoth she, "the warlike god unlaced me"—
As if the boy should use like loving charms.
But he, a wayward boy, refus'd her offer
And ran away, the beauteous queen neglecting,　　10
Shewing both folly to abuse her proffer
And all his sex of cowardice detecting.
　　O that I had my mistress at that bay,
　　To kiss and clip me till I ran away!

5

Arraign'd, poor captive at the bar I stand,
The bar of beauty, bar to all my joys;
And up I hold my ever-trembling hand,
Wishing or life or death to end annoys.
And when the judge doth question of the guilt
And bids me speak, then sorrow shuts up words.
Yea, though he say, "Speak boldly what thou wilt,"
Yet my confus'd affects no speech affords.
For why, alas, my passions have no bound,
For fear of death that penetrates so near;　　10
And still one grief another doth confound,
Yet doth at length a way to speech appear.

Then, for I speak too late, the judge doth give
His sentence that in prison I shall live.

15

Care-charmer sleep, sweet ease in restless misery,
The captive's liberty and his freedom's song,
Balm of the bruised heart, man's chief felicity,
Brother of quiet death, when life is too, too long!
A comedy it is, and now an history—
What is not sleep unto the feeble mind!
It easeth him that toils and him that's sorry,
It makes the deaf to hear, to see the blind.
Ungentle sleep, thou helpest all but me,
For when I sleep my soul is vexed most.　　10
It is Fidessa that doth master thee;
If she approach, alas, thy power is lost.
　　But here she is. See, how he runs amain!
　　I fear at night he will not come again.

23

Fly to her heart, hover about her heart,
With dainty kisses mollify her heart,
Pierce with thy arrows her obdurate heart,
With sweet allurements ever move her heart,
At midday and at midnight touch her heart,
Be lurking closely, nestle about her heart,
With power (thou art a god) command her heart,
Kindle thy coals of love about her heart,
Yea, even into thyself transform her heart.
Ah, she must love! Be sure thou have her heart,　　10
And I must die if thou have not her heart,
Thy bed, if thou rest well, must be her heart,
He hath the best part sure that hath the heart.
What have I not, if I have but her heart!

24

Striving is past. Ah, I must sink and drown,
And that in sight of long-descried shore.
I cannot send for aid unto the town;
All help is vain, and I must die therefore.
Then, poor distressed caitiff, be resolved
To leave this earthly dwelling fraught with care.
Cease will thy woes, thy corps in earth involved;
Thou diest for her that will no help prepare.
O see, my case herself doth now behold.
The casement open is. She seems to speak.　　10
But she is gone. O then I dare be bold
And needs must say, "She caus'd my heart to break."
　　I die before I drown, O heavy case!
　　It was because I saw my mistress' face.

47

I see, I hear, I feel, I know, I rue
My fate, my fame, my pain, my loss, my fall.
Mishap, reproach, disdain, a crown, her hue,
Cruel, still-flying, false, fair, funeral,
To cross, to shame, bewitch, deceive, and kill
My first proceedings in their flow'ring bloom.
My worthless pen fast chained to my will,
My erring life through an uncertain doom,
My thoughts that yet in lowliness do mount,
My heart the subject of her tyranny.   10
What now remains but her severe account
Of murther's crying guilt—foul butchery!
   She was unhappy in her cradle breath
   That given was to be another's death.

54

If great Apollo offered as a dower
His burning throne to beauty's excellence;
If Jove himself came in a golden shower
Down to the earth, to fetch fair Io thence;
If Venus in the curled locks were tied
Of proud Adonis not of gentle kind;
If Tellus for a shepherd's favor died,
The favor cruel love to her assign'd;
If heaven's winged herald, Hermes, had
His heart inchanted with a country maid;   10
If poor Pygmalion were for beauty mad;
If gods and men have all for beauty stray'd:
   I am not then asham'd to be included
   Mongst those that love, and be with love deluded.

ROBERT TOFTE

FROM LAURA (1597)

To the Gentle and Gentlemen Readers Whatsoever

Gentlemen: As the fencer first maketh a flourish with his weapon before he cometh to strokes in playing his prize, so I thought good, *pro forma* only, to use these few lines unto you before you come to the pith of the matter.

What the gentleman was that wrote these verses I know not; and what she is for whom they are devised I cannot guess; but thus much I can say: that as they came into the hands of a friend of mine by mere fortune, so happ'ned I upon them by as great a chance.

Only in this I must confess we are both to blame, that whereas he, having promised to keep private the original, and I, the copy secret, we have both consented to send it abroad as common, presuming chiefly upon your accustomed curtesies. Assuring ourselves, if we may have your protections, we shall think ourselves as safe as Ulysses did when he was shadowed under the shield of Pallas against furious Ajax; so we, by your countenances, shall be sufficiently furnished to encounter against any foulmouthed jacks whatsoever.

To censure of this work is for better wits than mine own, and it is for poets, not for printers, to give judgment of this matter. Yet if I may be bold to report what I have heard other gentlemen affirm, many have written worse, some better, few so well, the work being so full of choice and change as, it is thought, it will rather delight every way than dislike any way.

Thus, curteous gentlemen, building upon my wonted foundation of your friendly acceptance, I rest your debtors, and will study, in what I can, daily to make you amends.

         Yours always,
           [Valentine Simmes]

The First Part

7

Down from the neck unto that dainty breast
(Which Nature made a mirror of delight,
And where a world of beauties sweet do rest)
Doth hang a costly chain of pearl most bright;
   And of proportion are so just and round
   That such in India rich cannot be found.
Besides, their orient brightness is alike,
So that mine eyes are dazzled with the same,
And, not much us'd to see so fair a sight
(A sight which doth the sun in glory stain),   10
   Can well discern, though them they both do see,
   If breast be pearl or pearl in bosom be.

20

What time with brow the loveliest gins to scowl,
Shewing disdain and fury in her face,
Methinks I see the clouds wex dark and foul,
And gloomy night begins to run his race.
But then again, when she to show begins
Her smiling cheer adorn'd with favor rare,
Straightways the sun in chariot bright forth springs;
Clear are the skies, the gladsome day most fair.
   Thus in one face I see, against my will,
   The rising of the sun and falling still.   10

29

As burnish'd gold, such are my sovereign's hears,
A brace of stars devine her blackish eyes;
Like to the fairest black the raven bears,
Or fairer, if you fairer can devise;
  So likewise fair's the beauty of her breasts,
  Where pleasure lurks, where joy still dallying rests.
This Venus' bower you rightly may compare
To whitest snow that e'er from heaven fell,
Or to the mines of alabaster fair.
Wo's me! 'Tis sweet to sleep in Cupid's cell,   10
  Whilst he the heart makes surfet with delight
  Through golden hair, black eyes, and breast most white.

The Second Part

9

When I did part from thee the other night,
Methought a foul black dog, with ugly shape,
Did follow me, and did me sore affright,
And all the way did greedy on me gape.
  Nor I this cur, how he at me did howl,
  Can well as yet forget, with chaps most foul.
Then, thinking of his color, hateful black,
Methought some ill my thought did fear to come,
And said within me, "Turn again, turn back.
If forward thou dost go thou art undone."   10
  Then pardon, lady, if I back again
  Am come this night with you for to remain.

23

Two winds, one calm, another fierce to see,
Th' one of the spring, of winter th' other right,
I plainly, lady, do discern in thee.
The first, which makes me joy, breathes from thy sight
  Such dainty flowers, in diverse colored show,
  As makes to blush Dame Iris' rainy bow.
The second, which makes me to pine away,
Blows from thine inward breast a deadly blast,
Where doth eternal hardness always stay,
Which I do see eternal ay to last.   10
  So as calm Zephyrus in face thou art,
  But rough as boistrous Boreas in thine heart.

The Third Part

7

When she was born she came with smiling eye
Laughing into the world, a sign of glee;
When I was born, to her quite contrary,

Wailing I came into the world to see.
  Then mark this wonder strange: what nature gave,
  From first to th' last this fashion kept we have.
She in my sad laments doth take great joy;
I through her laughing die, and languish must
Unless that love, to save me from this noy,
Do unto me, unworthy, shew so just   10
  As for to change her laughter into pain,
  And my complaints into her joy again.

8

In love his kingdom great, two fools there be:
My lady's one, myself the other am.
The fond behavior of both which to see,
Whoso but nicely marks will say the same.
  Foolish our thoughts are; foolish our desire;
  Foolish our hearts in fancy's flame to fry;
Foolish to burn in love's hot scorching fire,—
But what! Fools are we none. My tongue doth lie.
  For who most foolish is and fond, in love,
  More wiser far than others oft doth prove.   10

34

Strange is this thing! My horse I cannot make
With spur, with speech, nor yet with rod in hand
Force him to go, although great pains I take.
Do what I can, he still as tir'd doth stand.
  No doubt he feels an heavy weight of me,
  Which is the cause he standeth still as stone;
Nor is he ware that now he carrieth three—
He thinks, poor jade, I am on's back alone.
  But three we are: with mine own self, I prove,
  Laura is in my heart, in soul is Love.   10

A Friend's Just Excuse about the Book and Author in His Absence

Without the author's knowledge, as is before said
by the printer, this poem is made thus publiquely
known, which with my best indeavor the gentleman
himself, suspecting what is now proved to be true,
at my coming up earnestly intreated me to prevent.
But I came at the last sheet's printing, and find more
than thirty sonnets not his intermix'd with his.
Help'd it cannot be but by the well-judging reader,
who will with less pain distinguish between them
than I, on this sodain, possibly can. To him, then, I
refer that labor. . . .

With the author bear, I pray ye, whom I must
intreat to bear with me.

R. B.

WILLIAM SHAKESPEARE

FROM SONNETS (1609)

To the only begetter of
these insuing sonnets
Mr. W. H. all happiness
and that eternity
promised
by
our ever-living poet
wisheth
the well-wishing
adventurer in
setting
forth.
                    T[homas] T[horpe]

2

When forty winters shall besiege thy brow
And dig deep trenches in thy beauty's field,
Thy youth's proud livery, so gaz'd on now,
Will be a totter'd weed of small worth held.
Then being ask'd where all thy beauty lies,
Where all the treasure of thy lusty days,
To say within thine own deep-sunken eyes
Were an all-eating shame and thriftless praise.
How much more praise deserv'd thy beauty's use
If thou couldst answer, "This fair child of mine   10
Shall sum my count and make my old excuse,"
Proving his beauty by succession thine!
   This were to be new made when thou art old
   And see thy blood warm when thou feel'st it cold.

7

Lo, in the orient when the gracious light
Lifts up his burning head, each under eye
Doth homage to his new-appearing sight,
Serving with looks his sacred majesty;
And having climb'd the steep-up heavenly hill,
Resembling strong youth in his middle age,
Yet mortal looks adore his beauty still,
Attending on his golden pilgrimage;
But when from highmost pitch, with weary car,
Like feeble age he reeleth from the day,   10
The eyes, fore duteous, now converted are
From his low tract and look another way.
   So thou, thyself outgoing in thy noon,
   Unlook'd on diest unless thou get a son.

12

When I do count the clock that tells the time
And see the brave day sunk in hidious night,

When I behold the violet past prime
And sable curls all silver'd o'er with white,
When lofty trees I see barren of leaves,
Which erst from heat did canopy the herd,
And summer's green all girded up in sheaves
Borne on the bier with white and bristly beard;
Then of thy beauty do I question make
That thou among the wastes of time must go,   10
Since sweets and beauties do themselves forsake
And die as fast as they see others grow;
   And nothing gainst Time's scythe can make defense
   Save breed, to brave him when he takes thee hence.

15

When I consider everything that grows
Holds in perfection but a little moment,
That this huge stage presenteth nought but shows
Whereon the stars in secret influence comment;
When I perceive that men as plants increase,
Cheered and check'd even by the selfsame sky,
Vaunt in their youthful sap, at height decrease,
And wear their brave state out of memory;
Then the conceit of this inconstant stay
Sets you most rich in youth before my sight,   10
Where wasteful Time debateth with Decay
To change your day of youth to sullied night;
   And, all in war with Time for love of you,
   As he takes from you, I ingraft you new.

18

Shall I compare thee to a summer's day?
Thou art more lovely and more temperate.
Rough winds do shake the darling buds of May,
And summer's lease hath all too short a date.
Sometime too hot the eye of heaven shines,
And often is his gold complexion dimm'd;
And every fair from fair sometime declines,
By chance, or nature's changing course, untrimm'd;
But thy eternal summer shall not fade
Nor lose possession of that fair thou ow'st,   10
Nor shall Death brag thou wand'rest in his shade
When in eternal lines to time thou grow'st.
   So long as men can breathe or eyes can see,
   So long lives this, and this gives life to thee.

19

Devouring Time, blunt thou the lion's paws,
And make the earth devour her own sweet brood;
Pluck the keen teeth from the fierce tiger's jaws,
And burn the long-liv'd phoenix in her blood;

Make glad and sorry seasons as thou fleets,
And do whate'er thou wilt, swift-footed Time,
To the wide world and all her fading sweets;
But I forbid thee one most heinous crime:
O, carve not with thy hours my love's fair brow,
Nor draw no lines there with thine antique pen!   10
Him in thy course untainted do allow
For beauty's pattern to succeeding men.
    Yet do thy worst, old Time! Despite thy wrong,
    My love shall in my verse ever live young.

25

Let those who are in favor with their stars
Of public honor and proud titles boast,
Whilst I, whom fortune of such triumph bars,
Unlook'd for joy in that I honor most.
Great princes' favorites their fair leaves spread
But as the marigold at the sun's eye;
And in themselves their pride lies buried,
For at a frown they in their glory die.
The painful warrior famosed for fight,
After a thousand victories once foil'd,   10
Is from the book of honor rased quite,
And all the rest forgot for which he toil'd.
    Then happy I, that love and am beloved
    Where I may not remove nor be removed.

29

When, in disgrace with Fortune and men's eyes,
I all alone beweep my outcast state,
And trouble deaf heaven with my bootless cries,
And look upon myself and curse my fate,
Wishing me like to one more rich in hope,
Featur'd like him, like him with friends possess'd,
Desiring this man's art, and that man's scope,
With what I most enjoy contented least;
Yet in these thoughts myself almost despising,
Haply I think on thee, and then my state,   10
Like to the lark at break of day arising
From sullen earth, sings hymns at heaven's gate;
    For thy sweet love rememb'red such wealth brings
    That then I scorn to change my state with kings.

30

When to the sessions of sweet silent thought
I summon up remembrance of things past,
I sigh the lack of many a thing I sought,
And with old woes new wail my dear time's waste.
Then can I drown an eye (unus'd to flow)
For precious friends hid in death's dateless night,
And weep afresh love's long since cancel'd woe,
And moan th' expense of many a vanish'd sight.
Then can I grieve at grievances foregone,
And heavily from woe to woe tell o'er   10
The sad account of fore-bemoaned moan,

Which I new pay as if not paid before.
    But if the while I think on thee, dear friend,
    All losses are restor'd and sorrows end.

33

Full many a glorious morning have I seen
Flatter the mountain tops with sovereign eye,
Kissing with golden face the meadows green,
Gilding pale streams with heavenly alcumy;
Anon permit the basest clouds to ride
With ugly rack on his celestial face,
And from the forlorn world his visage hide,
Stealing unseen to west with this disgrace.
Even so my sun one early morn did shine
With all-triumphant splendor on my brow;   10
But, out alack! he was but one hour mine,
The region cloud hath mask'd him from me now.
    Yet him for this my love no whit disdaineth;
    Suns of the world may stain when heaven's sun staineth.

50

How heavy do I journey on the way
When what I seek (my weary travel's end)
Doth teach that ease and that repose to say,
"Thus far the miles are measur'd from thy friend!"
The beast that bears me, tired with my woe,
Plods dully on, to bear that weight in me,
As if by some instinct the wretch did know
His rider lov'd not speed, being made from thee.
The bloody spur cannot provoke him on
That sometimes anger thrusts into his hide;   10
Which heavily he answers with a groan,
More sharp to me than spurring to his side;
    For that same groan doth put this in my mind—
    My grief lies onward and my joy behind.

54

O, how much more doth beauty beauteous seem
By that sweet ornament which truth doth give!
The rose looks fair, but fairer we it deem
For that sweet odor which doth in it live.
The canker blooms have full as deep a dye
As the perfumed tincture of the roses,
Hang on such thorns, and play as wantonly
When summer's breath their masked buds discloses;
But, for their virtue only is their show,
They live unwoo'd and unrespected fade,   10
Die to themselves. Sweet roses do not so:
Of their sweet deaths are sweetest odors made.
    And so of you, beauteous and lovely youth,
    When that shall vade, by verse distills your truth.

55

Not marble nor the gilded monuments
Of princes shall outlive this pow'rful rime;

But you shall shine more bright in these contents
Than unswept stone, besmear'd with sluttish time.
When wasteful war shall statues overturn,
And broils root out the work of masonry,
Nor Mars his sword nor war's quick fire shall burn
The living record of your memory.
Gainst death and all-oblivious enmity
Shall you pace forth; your praise shall still find room   10
Even in the eyes of all posterity
That wear this world out to the ending doom.
   So, till the Judgment that yourself arise,
    You live in this, and dwell in lovers' eyes.

60

Like as the waves make towards the pebbled shore,
So do our minutes hasten to their end;
Each changing place with that which goes before,
In sequent toil all forwards do contend.
Nativity, once in the main of light,
Crawls to maturity, wherewith being crown'd,
Crooked eclipses gainst his glory fight,
And Time that gave doth now his gift confound.
Time doth transfix the flourish set on youth
And delves the parallels in beauty's brow,   10
Feeds on the rarities of nature's truth,
And nothing stands but for his scythe to mow;
   And yet to times in hope my verse shall stand,
    Praising thy worth, despite his cruel hand.

64

When I have seen by Time's fell hand defaced
The rich proud cost of outworn buried age;
When sometime lofty towers I see down-rased
And brass eternal slave to mortal rage;
When I have seen the hungry ocean gain
Advantage on the kingdom of the shore,
And the firm soil win of the wat'ry main,
Increasing store with loss and loss with store;
When I have seen such interchange of state,
Or state itself confounded to decay,   10
Ruin hath taught me thus to ruminate,
That Time will come and take my love away.
   This thought is as a death, which cannot choose
    But weep to have that which it fears to lose.

68

Thus is his cheek the map of days outworn,
When beauty liv'd and died as flowers do now,
Before these bastard signs of fair were born
Or durst inhabit on a living brow;
Before the golden tresses of the dead,
The right of sepulchers, were shorn away
To live a second life on second head;
Ere beauty's dead fleece made another gay.

In him those holy antique hours are seen,
Without all ornament, itself and true,   10
Making no summer of another's green,
Robbing no old to dress his beauty new;
   And him as for a map doth Nature store,
    To show false Art what beauty was of yore.

71

No longer mourn for me when I am dead
Than you shall hear the surly sullen bell
Give warning to the world that I am fled
From this vile world, with vildest worms to dwell.
Nay, if you read this line, remember not
The hand that writ it; for I love you so
That I in your sweet thoughts would be forgot
If thinking on me then should make you woe.
O, if, I say, you look upon this verse
When I, perhaps, compounded am with clay,   10
Do not so much as my poor name rehearse,
But let your love even with my life decay,
   Lest the wise world should look into your moan
    And mock you with me after I am gone.

73

That time of year thou mayst in me behold
When yellow leaves, or none, or few, do hang
Upon those boughs which shake against the cold,
Bare ruin'd quires where late the sweet birds sang.
In me thou seest the twilight of such day
As after sunset fadeth in the west,
Which by and by black night doth take away,
Death's second self, that seals up all in rest.
In me thou seest the glowing of such fire
That on the ashes of his youth doth lie,   10
As the deathbed whereon it must expire,
Consum'd with that which it was nourish'd by.
   This thou perceiv'st, which makes thy love more strong,
    To love that well which thou must leave ere long.

76

Why is my verse so barren of new pride?
So far from variation or quick change?
Why, with the time, do I not glance aside
To new-found methods and to compounds strange?
Why write I still all one, ever the same,
And keep invention in a noted weed,
That every word doth almost tell my name,
Showing their birth, and where they did proceed?
O, know, sweet love, I always write of you,
And you and love are still my argument: 10
So all my best is dressing old words new,
Spending again what is already spent;
   For as the sun is daily new and old,
    So is my love still telling what is told.

97 - 98   - ssg - playors wer
at of the Provinces -

86

Was it the proud full sail of his great verse,
Bound for the prize of all-too-precious you,
That did my ripe thoughts in my brain inhearse,
Making their tomb the womb wherein they grew?
Was it his spirit, by spirits taught to write
Above a mortal pitch, that struck me dead?
No, neither he, nor his compeers by night
Giving him aid, my verse astonished.
He, nor that affable familiar ghost
Which nightly gulls him with intelligence,   10
As victors, of my silence cannot boast—
I was not sick of any fear from thence;
    But when your countenance fill'd up his line,
    Then lacked I matter; that enfeebled mine.

87

Farewell! thou art too dear for my possessing,
And like enough thou know'st thy estimate.
The charter of thy worth gives thee releasing;
My bonds in thee are all determinate.
For how do I hold thee but by thy granting,
And for that riches where is my deserving?
The cause of this fair gift in me is wanting,
And so my patent back again is swerving.
Thyself thou gav'st, thy own worth then not knowing,
Or me, to whom thou gav'st it, else mistaking;   10
So thy great gift, upon misprision growing,
Comes home again, on better judgment making.
    Thus have I had thee as a dream doth flatter—
    In sleep a king, but waking no such matter.

90

Then hate me when thou wilt! if ever, now!
Now, while the world is bent my deeds to cross,
Join with the spite of fortune, make me bow,
And do not drop in for an after-loss.
Ah, do not, when my heart hath scap'd this sorrow,
Come in the rearward of a conquer'd woe;
Give not a windy night a rainy morrow,
To linger out a purpos'd overthrow.
If thou wilt leave me, do not leave me last,
When other, petty griefs have done their spite,   10
But in the onset come. So shall I taste
At first the very worst of fortune's might;
    And other strains of woe, which now seem woe,
    Compar'd with loss of thee will not seem so.

97

How like a winter hath my absence been
From thee, the pleasure of the fleeting year!
What freezings have I felt, what dark days seen!
What old December's bareness everywhere!
And yet this time remov'd was summer's time,
The teeming autumn, big with rich increase,

Bearing the wanton burthen of the prime,
Like widowed wombs after their lords' decease;
Yet this abundant issue seem'd to me
But hope of orphans and unfathered fruit;   10
For summer and his pleasures wait on thee,
And, thou away, the very birds are mute;
    Or, if they sing, 'tis with so dull a cheer
    That leaves look pale, dreading the winter's near.

these go together

98

From you have I been absent in the spring,
When proud-pied April, dress'd in all his trim,
Hath put a spirit of youth in everything,
That heavy Saturn laugh'd and leapt with him,
Yet nor the lays of birds, nor the sweet smell
Of different flowers in odor and in hue,
Could make me any summer's story tell,
Or from their proud lap pluck them where they grew;
Nor did I wonder at the lily's white,
Nor praise the deep vermilion in the rose: 10
They were but sweet, but figures of delight,
Drawn after you, you pattern of all those.
    Yet seem'd it winter still, and, you away,
    As with your shadow I with these did play.

104

To me, fair friend, you never can be old,
For as you were when first your eye I eyed,
Such seems your beauty still. Three winters cold
Have from the forests shook three summers' pride,
Three beauteous springs to yellow autumn turn'd
In process of the seasons have I seen,
Three April perfumes in three hot Junes burn'd,
Since first I saw you fresh, which yet are green.
Ah, yet doth beauty, like a dial hand,
Steal from his figure, and no pace perceived!   10
So your sweet hue, which methinks still doth stand,
Hath motion, and mine eye may be deceived;
    For fear of which, hear this, thou age unbred:
    Ere you were born was beauty's summer dead.

106

When in the chronicle of wasted time
I see descriptions of the fairest wights,
And beauty making beautiful old rime
In praise of ladies dead and lovely knights,
Then, in the blazon of sweet beauty's best,
Of hand, of foot, of lip, of eye, of brow,
I see their antique pen would have express'd
Even such a beauty as you master now.
So all their praises are but prophecies
Of this our time, all you prefiguring;   10
And, for they look'd but with divining eyes,
They had not skill enough your worth to sing;
    For we, which now behold these present days,
    Have eyes to wonder, but lack tongues to praise.

107

Not mine own fears, nor the prophetic soul
Of the wide world, dreaming on things to come,
Can yet the lease of my true love control,
Supposed as forfeit to a confin'd doom.
The mortal moon hath her eclipse endur'd,
And the sad augurs mock their own presage;
Incertainties now crown themselves assur'd,
And peace proclaims olives of endless age.
Now with the drops of this most balmy time
My love looks fresh, and Death to me subscribes,   10
Since, spite of him, I'll live in this poor rime,
While he insults o'er dull and speechless tribes;
    And thou in this shalt find thy monument
    When tyrants' crests and tombs of brass are spent.

110

Alas, 'tis true I have gone here and there
And made myself a motley to the view,
Gor'd mine own thoughts, sold cheap what is most dear,
Made old offenses of affections new.
Most true it is that I have look'd on truth
Askance and strangely; but, by all above,
These blenches gave my heart another youth,
And worse essays prov'd thee my best of love.
Now all is done, have what shall have no end!
Mine appetite I never more will grind   10
On newer proof, to try an older friend,
A god in love, to whom I am confin'd.
    Then give me welcome, next my heaven the best,
    Even to thy pure and most most loving breast.

116

Let me not to the marriage of true minds
Admit impediments. Love is not love
Which alters when it alteration finds
Or bends with the remover to remove.
O, no! it is an ever-fixed mark
That looks on tempests and is never shaken;
It is the star to every wand'ring bark,
Whose worth's unknown, although his height be taken.
Love's not Time's fool, though rosy lips and cheeks
Within his bending sickle's compass come.   10
Love alters not with his brief hours and weeks,
But bears it out even to the edge of doom.
    If this be error, and upon me proved,
    I never writ, nor no man ever loved.

119

What potions have I drunk of siren tears,
Distill'd from limbecks foul as hell within,
Applying fears to hopes and hopes to fears,
Still losing when I saw myself to win!
What wretched errors hath my heart committed
Whilst it hath thought itself so blessed never!

How have mine eyes out of their spheres been fitted
In the distraction of this madding fever!
O benefit of ill! Now I find true
That better is by evil still made better;   10
And ruin'd love, when it is built anew,
Grows fairer than at first, more strong, far greater.
    So I return rebuk'd to my content,
    And gain by ills thrice more than I have spent.

126

O thou, my lovely boy, who in thy power
Dost hold Time's fickle glass, his sickle, hour;
Who hast by waning grown, and therein show'st
Thy lovers withering as thy sweet self grow'st;
If Nature (sovereign mistress over wrack),
As thou goest onwards, still will pluck thee back,
She keeps thee to this purpose, that her skill
May Time disgrace and wretched minutes kill.
Yet fear her, O thou minion of her pleasure!
She may detain, but not still keep, her treasure;   10
Her audit, though delay'd, answer'd must be,
And her quietus is to render thee.

127

In the old age black was not counted fair,
Or, if it were, it bore not beauty's name;
But now is black beauty's successive heir,
And beauty slander'd with a bastard shame;
For since each hand hath put on nature's power,
Fairing the foul with art's false borrow'd face,
Sweet beauty hath no name, no holy bower,
But is profan'd, if not lives in disgrace.
Therefore my mistress' brows are raven black,
Her eyes so suited, and they mourners seem   10
At such who, not born fair, no beauty lack,
Sland'ring creation with a false esteem.
    Yet so they mourn, becoming of their woe,
    That every tongue says beauty should look so.

128

How oft, when thou, my music, music play'st
Upon that blessed wood whose motion sounds
With thy sweet fingers when thou gently sway'st
The wiry concord that mine ear confounds,
Do I envy those jacks that nimble leap
To kiss the tender inward of thy hand,
Whilst my poor lips, which should that harvest reap,
At the wood's boldness by thee blushing stand!
To be so tickled they would change their state
And situation with those dancing chips   10
O'er whom thy fingers walk with gentle gait,
Making dead wood more blest than living lips.
    Since saucy jacks so happy are in this,
    Give them thy fingers, me thy lips to kiss.

129

Th' expense of spirit in a waste of shame
Is lust in action; and, till action, lust
Is perjur'd, murd'rous, bloody, full of blame,
Savage, extreme, rude, cruel, not to trust;
Enjoy'd no sooner but despised straight;
Past reason hunted, and no sooner had,
Past reason hated, as a swallowed bait
On purpose laid to make the taker mad;
Mad in pursuit, and in possession so;
Had, having, and in quest to have, extreme;   10
A bliss in proof—and prov'd, a very woe;
Before, a joy propos'd; behind, a dream.
  All this the world well knows; yet none knows well
  To shun the heaven that leads men to this hell.

130

My mistress' eyes are nothing like the sun;
Coral is far more red than her lips' red;
If snow be white, why then her breasts are dun;
If hairs be wires, black wires grow on her head.
I have seen roses damask'd, red and white,
But no such roses see I in her cheeks;
And in some perfumes is there more delight
Than in the breath that from my mistress reeks.
I love to hear her speak; yet well I know
That music hath a far more pleasing sound.   10
I grant I never saw a goddess go:
My mistress, when she walks, treads on the ground;
  And yet, by heaven, I think my love as rare
  As any she belied with false compare.

133

Beshrew that heart that makes my heart to groan
For that deep wound it gives my friend and me!
Is 't not enough to torture me alone
But slave to slavery my sweet'st friend must be?
Me from myself thy cruel eye hath taken,
And my next self thou harder hast engrossed.
Of him, myself, and thee I am forsaken—
A torment thrice threefold thus to be crossed.
Prison my heart in thy steel bosom's ward;
But then my friend's heart let my poor heart bail;   10
Whoe'er keeps me, let my heart be his guard:
Thou canst not then use rigor in my jail.
  And yet thou wilt; for I, being pent in thee,
  Perforce am thine, and all that is in me.

139

O, call not me to justify the wrong
That thy unkindness lays upon my heart!
Wound me not with thine eye but with thy tongue;
Use power with power, and slay me not by art!

Tell me thou lov'st elsewhere; but in my sight,
Dear heart, forbear to glance thine eye aside.
What need'st thou wound with cunning when thy might
Is more than my o'erpress'd defense can bide?
Let me excuse thee:—Ah, my love well knows
Her pretty looks have been mine enemies;   10
And therefore from my face she turns my foes,
That they elsewhere might dart their injuries.
  Yet do not so; but since I am near slain,
  Kill me outright with looks and rid my pain.

144

Two loves I have, of comfort and despair,
Which like two spirits do suggest me still.
The better angel is a man right fair,
The worser spirit a woman color'd ill.
To win me soon to hell, my female evil
Tempteth my better angel from my side,
And would corrupt my saint to be a devil,
Wooing his purity with her foul pride.
And whether that my angel be turn'd fiend
Suspect I may, yet not directly tell;   10
But being both from me, both to each friend,
I guess one angel in another's hell.
  Yet this shall I ne'er know, but live in doubt,
  Till my bad angel fire my good one out.

146

Poor soul, the center of my sinful earth,
. . . these rebel pow'rs that thee array,[1]
Why dost thou pine within and suffer dearth,
Painting thy outward walls so costly gay?
Why so large cost, having so short a lease,
Dost thou upon thy fading mansion spend?
Shall worms, inheritors of this excess,
Eat up thy charge? Is this thy body's end?
Then, soul, live thou upon thy servant's loss,
And let that pine to aggravate thy store;   10
Buy terms divine in selling hours of dross;
Within be fed, without be rich no more.
  So shalt thou feed on Death, that feeds on men,
  And Death once dead, there's no more dying then.

147

My love is as a fever, longing still
For that which longer nurseth the disease;
Feeding on that which doth preserve the ill,
Th' uncertain sickly appetite to please.
My reason, the physician to my love,
Angry that his prescriptions are not kept,
Hath left me, and I desperate now approve
Desire is death, which physic did except.

---

[1] By an obvious error the 1609 text repeats the last three words of
line 1 at the beginning of line 2.

Past cure I am, now reason is past care,
And frantic-mad with evermore unrest;   10
My thoughts and my discourse as madmen's are,
At randon from the truth vainly express'd;
  For I have sworn thee fair, and thought thee bright,
  Who art as black as hell, as dark as night.

152

In loving thee thou know'st I am forsworn,
But thou art twice forsworn, to me love swearing;
In act thy bed-vow broke, and new faith torn
In vowing new hate after new love bearing.
But why of two oaths' breach do I accuse thee
When I break twenty? I am perjur'd most;
For all my vows are oaths but to misuse thee,
And all my honest faith in thee is lost;
For I have sworn deep oaths of thy deep kindness,
Oaths of thy love, thy truth, thy constancy;   10
And, to enlighten thee, gave eyes to blindness,

Or made them swear against the thing they see;
  For I have sworn thee fair—more perjur'd I,
  To swear against the truth so foul a lie!

154

The little Love-god, lying once asleep,
Laid by his side his heart-inflaming brand,
Whilst many nymphs that vow'd chaste life to keep
Came tripping by; but in her maiden hand
The fairest votary took up that fire
Which many legions of true-hearts had warm'd;
And so the general of hot desire
Was, sleeping, by a virgin hand disarm'd.
This brand she quenched in a cool well by,
Which from Love's fire took heat perpetual,   10
Growing a bath and healthful remedy
For men diseas'd; but I, my mistress' thrall,
  Came there for cure, and this by that I prove—
  Love's fire heats water, water cools not love.

Part VII TRANSLATIONS

HENRY HOWARD, EARL OF SURREY (trans.)

VIRGIL'S *AENEID*

Although Surrey holds his modern reputation through his contributions to Tottel's *Miscellany* (1557), his immediate admirers were perhaps more impressed by his incomplete translation of Virgil. The burly Scots version which Gawin Douglas had made about 1512 included all the *Aeneid* as well as the so-called thirteenth book of Mapheus Vegius; but, for obvious linguistic and political reasons, readers south of the Tweed could never rejoice in it as they rejoiced in Surrey's scrappy work. Indeed, whatever its intrinsic merit, the latter is significant for two reasons: it is the first English effort to render a poem which the Renaissance admired above all others, and it is the first specimen of blank verse in our language.

Surrey's translation survives in three versions which seem to be bibliographically unrelated: in Tottel's well-known edition of Books II and IV (1557), in William Awen's (or Owen's) of Book IV (1554), and in a manuscript version discovered in 1903 in a commonplace-book in the Hargrave collection (MS. Hargrave 205) in the British Museum. Although Tottel's *Certain Books of Virgil's Aeneis*, published on June 21, 1557, just sixteen days after the famous *Miscellany*, was long regarded as the *editio princeps*, scholars since the eighteenth century have been vaguely aware of a perhaps earlier and unrelated edition. Not until 1858, however, did the unique copy of an undated *Fourth Book of Virgil* which John Day printed

for Awen, or Owen, turn up for sale by Sotheby's, and not until 1922 was it acquired by Mr. Carl H. Pforzheimer and so made available for scholarly inspection. Owen's edition is now generally regarded as the first. The dedication to Surrey's son, the fourth Duke of Norfolk (who came into his title in August, 1554), establishes a *terminus a quo*, and Day's imprisonment in October of the same year for printing heretical books a *terminus ad quem;* therefore the book probably appeared in the early fall of 1554. Nicholas Grimald had, in the late forties, experimented with blank verse in a couple of translated poems that were later included in Tottel's *Miscellany* (see "Marcus Tullius Cicero's Death," pp. 206-7), but Surrey's translation of Virgil into unrimed decasyllables may be plausibly assigned to 1538 or 1540, and therefore in point of both composition and publication the *Fourth Book* may claim priority. Since Owen boasts in his dedication that his text was "taken of one written with the author's own hand" and compared with two other copies "written out by other men," it is a fair inference that Surrey's translation had circulated in manuscript long before it came to the attention of Owen or Tottel. Our text is based upon *The fourth boke of Virgill . . . translated into English, and drawne into a straunge metre by Henrye late Earle of Surrey,* 1554. The volume is not listed in the *Short Title Catalogue.*

FROM THE FOURTH BOOK OF VIRGIL, INTREATING OF THE LOVE BETWEEN AENEAS AND DIDO, TRANSLATED INTO ENGLISH AND DRAWN INTO A STRANGE METER (1554)

To the Most Puissant Prince Thomas, Duke of Norfolk, William Awen, His Most Humble Orator, Wisheth Perpetual Health and Felicity

When it chanced a copy of this part of Virgil, translated by your Grace's father, right honorable lord, by the means of a friend of mine to come to my hands, I not only held the same as no small treasure because I had heard it, like as others the monuments of that noble wit of his (which was in this kind no doubt incomparable), of all men to be commended; but also my desire was great at one time or other, if by a means convenient I might, to publish the same; and that the rather because I could understand of no man that had a copy thereof but he

was more willing the same should be kept as a private treasure in the hands of a few then published to the common profit and delectation of many. But forasmuch as my copy, although it were taken of one written with the author's own hand, was not yet so certain that it might be thought of itself sufficient to be published, partly for that the writer had not time sufficient to the due examination thereof after it was written, and also because the reading of the author's copy itself, by reason of speedy writing thereof, was somewhat doubtful; for these causes, getting two other copies also, written out by other men, I caused mine to be conferred with them both and of theim that to be received as most worthy to be allowed which was both to the Latin most agreeable and also best standing with the dignity of that kind of miter.

And this my doing, I trust, no honest man shall be able to reprove, but rather it shall be an occasion to such as favor the moniments of so noble a wit if they have a better copy to publish the same. As for the unthankful, I pass not how much they repine at my deed, so that I may understand your Grace to take in good part my good will herein. Which, if you do (as I nothing doubt of your Grace's goodness), it shall no little encourage me hereafter to bring other his works to light as they shall come to my hands.

Thus beseeching our Lord God to continue your Grace in wealth and increase of virtue, I wish you heartily well to fare.

Your Grace's most humble orator,
William Owen

The Fourth Book of Virgil

But now the wounded queen, with heavy care,
Throughout the veins she nourisheth the play,
Surprised with blind flame; and to her mind
Gan eke resort the prowess of the man
And honor of his race, whiles in her breast
Imprinted stack his words and picture's form;
Ne to her lims care granteth quiet rest.
The next morrow with Phoebus' lamp the earth
Alight'ned clear, and eke the dawning day
The shadows dark gan from the pole remove,   10
When all unsound her sister of like mind
Thus spake she to: "O sister Anne, what dreams
Be these that me, tormented, thus affray?
What new guest is this that to our realm is come?
What one of cheer? How stout of heart in arms?
Truly I think (ne vain is my belief)
Of goddish race some offspring should he be.
Cowardry notes hearts swarved out of kind.
He driven—Lord!—with how hard destiny,
What battails eke atchieved did he tell?   20
But that my mind is fix'd unmovably
Never with wight in wedlock ay to join,
Sith my first love me left by death dissevered,
If genial brands and bed me lothed not,
To this one fault perchance yet might I yield.
Ay me! For I grant, sith wretched Sychaeus' death,
My spouse and house with brothers' feud defiled,
The only man he hath my senses bent
And pricked forth my mind that gan to slide;
Now feelingly I taste the steps of mine old flame.   30
But first I wish the earth me swallow down
With thunder, or the mighty Lord me send
To the pale ghosts of hell and darkness deep,
Or I thee stain, shamefastness, or thy law.
He that with me first coupled took away
My love with him; still enjoy he [it] in grave!"

Thus did she say, and with supprised tears
Bained her breast. . . .

[Having been loved and deserted by Aeneas, Dido prepares a massive funeral pyre for her intended suicide.]

But trembling Dido, all eagerly now bent
Upon her stern determination,   40
Her blood-shot eyes roiling within her head,
Her quivering cheeks flecked with deadly stain,
Both pale and wan to think on death to come,
Into the inward wards of her palace
She rusheth in, and clam up as bestraught
The burial stack, and drew the Trojan sweard,
Her gift sometime, but meant to no such use.
Where, when she saw his weed and well-known bed,
Weeping a while, in study gan she stay,
Fell on the bed, and these last words she said: 50
"Sweet spoils, whiles God and destiny did permit,
Receive this spirit and rid me of these cares.
I lived and ran the course fortune did grant,
And under earth my great ghost now shall wend.
A goodly town I built, and saw my walls;
Happy, alas too happy, if these coasts
The Trojan ships had never touched ay."
This said, she laid her mouth close to the bed.
"Why, then," quoth she, "unwroken shall we die?
But let us die, for thus and in this sort   60
It liketh us to seek the shadows dark.
And from the seas the cruel Trojan eyes
Shall well decern this flame, and take with him
Eke these unlucky tokens of my death."
As she had said, her damsel might perceive
Her with these words fall pierced on the sword,
The boiling blood with gore and hands embrued.
The clamor rang unto the palace top;
The bruit ran throughout all th' astoined town
With wailing great and women's lamenting.   70
The roofs gan roar, the air resound with plaint
As though Carthage or ancient town of Tyre
With prease of ent'red enemies swarmed full,
Or when the rage of furious flame doth take
The temples' tops and mansions eke of men.
Her sister Anne, spriteless for dread to hear
This fearful stir, with nails gan tear her face.
She smote her breast and rushed through the rout,
And dying thus she clepes her by her name:
"Sister, for this did you with craft me bourd?   80
The stake, the flame, the auters breed they this?
What shall I first complain, forsaken wight?
Lothest thou in death thy sister's fellowship?
Thou should have called me to like destiny;
One wo, one sword, one hour mought end us both.
This funeral stake built I with these hands,
[And] with this voice cleped our native gods
As cruel for to absent me from thy death.
Distroyed thou hast, sister, both thee and me,

Thy people eke, and princes born at Tyre.   90
Geve here, I shall with water wash her wounds
And suck with mouth her breath, if ought be left."
　　This said, unto the high degrees she mounted,
Embracing fast her sister, now half dead,
With wailful plaint, whom in her lap she laid,
The black, swart [gore] wiping dry with her clothes.
But Dido strave for to lift up again
Her heavy eyen, and hath no power thereto.
Deep under her breast the fixed wound doth gape.
Thrice leaning on her elbow gan she raise   100
Herself upward, and thrice she overthrew
Upon the bed, ranging with wand'ring eyes
The skies for light, and wept when she it found.
　　Almighty Juno, having ruth by this
Of her long pains and eke her ling'ring death,
From heaven she sent the goddess Iris down

The thralling spirit and jointed lims to loose.
For that neither by lot of destiny
Nor yet by natural death she perished,
But wretchedly before her fatal day,   110
And kindled with a sodain rage of flame,
Proserpine had not yet from her head bereft
The golden hear, nor judged her to hell.
The dewy Iris thus with golden wings,
A thousand hues shewing against the sun,
Amid the skies then did she fly adown
On Dido's head, whereas she gan alight.
"This hear," quoth she, "to Pluto consecrate,
Commanded I bereave, and eke thy spirit unloose
From this body." And when she had thus said,   120
With her right hand she cut the hear in twain.
And therewithal the natural heat gan quench,
And into wind the life forthwith resolve.

THOMAS PHAER (trans.)

VIRGIL'S *AENEID*

Phaer, who had begun his career as a lawyer and then had turned to medicine, drifted into literary history toward the end of his life with a contribution (the tragedy of Owen Glendower) to the first (?1555) edition of *A Mirror for Magistrates*. About the same time, in the spring of 1555, he translated the first book of the *Aeneid* in the jogging fourteener of ballad meter. His progress was so easy that each book required, on the average, about twenty days. On December 7, 1557, he completed the seventh book, and in the following year he published, with a dedication to Queen Mary, the entire seven, hoping, as he explained in a prose epilogue, to engage the interest of "the nobility, gentlemen, and ladies that study not Latin." The reception accorded his work was apparently favorable enough to spur him on, so that he had completed two more books by April, 1560, when he injured his hand. Although he himself was dead by the following August, the nine books that he had translated (together "with so much of [the] tenth book as since his death could be found in unperfit papers at his house in Kilgerran Forest in Pembrokeshire") were published in 1562 by William Wightman, "receptor of Wales." In 1584 Thomas Twyne finally brought out the first complete translation of the *Aeneid* in English by adding to Phaer's nine books his own version of the last three and, for good measure, the popular "thirteenth book" of Mapheus Vegius. Our text is based upon *The seven first bookes of the Eneidos of Virgill, converted in Englishe meter by Thomas Phaer Esquier, sollicitour to the king and quenes maiesties, attending their honorable counsaile in the Marchies of Wales,* 1558 (STC 24799).

─────────

FROM THE SEVEN FIRST BOOKS OF THE ENEIDOS OF VIRGIL (1558)

To Our Supreme Sovereign and Lady,
　　Queen Mary. . .

My translation of seven the first books of Virgil's *Eneidos,* a man of all writers most famous and excellent, I do of duty present and dedicate to your gracious Highness, being the most famous and excellent princess, with the travail of your poorest servant, to you, my most sovereign good lady and only redoubted maistress. To the end that, like as my diligence employed in your service in the Marchies may otherwise appear to your Grace by your honorable counsail there, so your Highness hereby may receive the accompts of my pastime in all my vacations, in which vacations I made the said work, since I have been preferred to your service by your right noble and faithful counsailor William, Lord Marquis of Winchester, my first bringer-up and patron. If this my beginning may please your Majesty and, by

the same, your nobility and others that shall vouchsave to read it, I entend, God willing, to set forth the
rest as soon as I can (if leisure will permit me). And
in the mean season, and evermore during my life, I
shall pray Almighty God for your preeminent estate
to encrease in all virtue, honor, prosperity, and quiet.

Your Grace's most humble servitor and subject,

Thomas Phaer

The First Book of the Eneidos of Virgil

I that my slender oaten pipe in verse was wont to sound
Of woods, and, next to that, I taught for husbandmen the ground,
How fruit unto their greedy lust they might constrain to bring,
A work of thanks, lo, now of Mars and dreadful wars I sing,
Of arms and of the man of Troy that first by fatal flight
Did thence arrive to Lavine land, that now Italia hight,
But shaken sore with many a storm, by seas and lands ytoss'd,
And all for Juno's endless wrath, that wrought to have had him lost,
And sorrows great in wars he bode ere he the walls could frame
Of mighty Rome and bring the gods to avance the Romain name.   10
Now, muse, direct my song to tell for what offense and why;
What ailed so this queen of gods to drive thus cruelly
This noble prince, of virtue mild, from place to place to toil,
Soch pains to take. May heavenly minds so sore in rancor boil?

    There was a town of ancient time, Carthago of old it hight,
Against Italia and Tiber's mouth lay loof at seas aright;
Both rich in wealth and sharp in war the people it held of Tyre;
This town above all towns to reise was Juno's most desire;
Forsook her seat at Samos Ile and here her arms she set,
Her char, and here she minds to make (if all gods do not let)   20
An empire all the world to rule. But hard she had beforn
From Troy should rise a stock by whom their tow'rs should all be torn,
That far and wide should bear the rule, so fierce in war to feel
That Liby land destroy they should, so Fortune turns the wheel;
For fear of that, and calling eft the old war to her mind
That she at Troy had done before for Greeks, her friends so kind,
Ne from her heart the causes old of wrath and sore disdain
Was slaked yet, but in her breast high spite did still remain,
How Paris Venus' beauty praised and hers esteemed at naught;
She abhors the stock of Ganymede, whom Jove to heaven had raught;   30
Thus flamed in her mode she kest through all the seas to throw
The sely, poor remain of Troy that Greeks had layed so low;
And them that wild Achilles' wrath had spared alive at last,
From Italy she thought to keep till destinies should be past.
And many a year they wand'red wide in seas and sundry pine.
So huge a work of weight it was to build of Rome the ligne.

    Scant from the sight of Sicil Ile, their sails in merry array
Went under wind, and through the seas and salt foam made their way;
When Juno her bethought again of her immortal wound
Onto herself, "And shall I thus be conquer'd and confound?   40
And shall I leave it thus?" quoth she. "Shall yet this Troyan king,
For all my work, to Italy this people safely bring?
I trow the Destiny wills it so, but did not Pallas burn
A fleet of Greeks and in the seas them did all overturn,
For one man's sin and for the faut of Ajax made to fall?
She threw the fires of mighty Jove from skies upon them all
And drown'd their ships; and he himself, with whirlwind set afire,
All smoking, on the rocks she kest his carcas to expire.

But I, that queen of gods am call'd and sister of Jove in throne
And eke his wife, how long I war with this poor stock alone   50
So many a year! And who shall now Dame Juno's godhead know,
Or shortly upon mine altars who due honors will bestow?"
    Thus rolling in her burning breast, she straight to Eolia hied,
Into the country of cloudy skies where blust'ring winds abide.
King Eolus the wrastling winds in caves he locks full low;
In prison strong the storms he keeps, forbidden abroad to blow;
They, for disdain, with murmur great at every mouth do rage,
But he aloft with mace in hand their force doth all assuage.
If he so did not, lands and seas and skies they would so sweep,
Within a while, that all were gone. Therefore in dungeons deep   60
Almighty Jove did close them up, and hills hath overset,
And made a king that should know when to loose them, when to let.
Whom to entreat this Juno came, and thus to him she spake:
"King Eolus, for onto thee the great god hath betake
And given thee leave to lift the floods and calm to make them still,
On Tyrrhene sea there sails a fleet that bears me no good will;
To Italy they mind to pass, a new Troy there to build.
Let out thy winds, and all their ships do drown with waters wild;
Disperse them all to sundry shores or whelm them down with deep.
Of precious ladies seven and seven about me do I keep,   70
Whereof the fairest of them all, that call'd is Deiopey,
Shall be thine own for evermore, my mind if thou obey;
And of a goodly son," quoth she, "she shall thee make a sire."
    To that said Eolus: "O queen, what needs all this desire?
Command me, dame, I must obey; my duty it is of right.
By you this kingdom first I gat and grace of Jove on hight;
You make me sit among the gods at bankets (this ye know);
You gave me might these stormy winds to strain or make to blow."
He turn'd his sword when this was said, and through the hill he push'd,
And at that gap with throngs atones the winds forth out they rush'd.   80
The whirlwinds to the lands went out, and than to seas they flew
Both east and west, and from the sands the waves aloft they threw.
The stormy south again the clives the waters drives so high
That cables all began to crack and men for dreed to cry.
Anon was take from Troyans' eyes both sight and light of sun,
And on the sea the grim, dark night to close all in begun.
The thunders roar'd, and lightnings lept full oft on every side;
There was no man but present death before his face espied. . . .

Thus farforth [through the seventh book], good readers, as well for defense of my country language (which I have heard discommended of many, and esteemed of some to be more than barbarous) as also for honest recreation of you, the nobility, gentlemen, and ladies that study not Latin, I have taken some travail to express this most excellent writer, as far as my simple ability extended. And if God send me life and leisure I purpose to set forth the rest, unless it may like some other that is better armed with learn- [10] ing to prevent my labors; whereof, I assure you, I would be right glad, contenting myself sufficiently with this: that by me first this gate is set open. If now the young writers will vouchsafe to enter, they may find in this language both large and aboundant camps of variety, wherein they may gather innumerable sorts of most beautiful flours, figures, and phrases, not only to supply the imperfection of me but also to garnish all kinds of their own verses with a more clean and compendious order of meter than hereto-fore commonly hath been accustomed. And if any further help I may do to that purpose, I shall more gladly bestow my travail hereafter if I may know that these my beginnings be of you gently taken and embraced. Trusting that you, my right worshipful maisters, and students of universities, and such as be teachers of childern, and readers of this auctor in Latin, will not be too much offended though every verse answer not to your expectation. For, besides the diversity between a construction and a translation, you know there be many mystical secrets in this writer which, uttered in English, would shew little pleasure and in mine opinion are better to be untouched than to deminish the grace of the rest with tediousness or darkness. I have, therefore, followed the counsel of Horace, teaching the duty of a good interpretor: *Qui quae desperat nitescere posse, relinquit.* By which occasion, somewhat I have in places omitted, somewhat have alt'red, and some thing I have expounded, and all to the ease of inferior readers; for you that are learned need not to be instructed. I mean not to prejudice any that can do finer; only I desire you to bear with my travail, and among other to pardon my first book, wherein I found this new kind of fingering somewhat strange unto me, and, to say truth, I had never any quiet from troubles to confer or peruse that book, or any of the rest, as I most desired. You may therefore accept them as things roughly begun rather than polished; and where you understand a faut, I desire you with silence patiently pass it, and upon knowledge given to me I shall, in

10 the next setting-forth, endeavor to reform it. And if any with this will not be contented, than let him take it in hand and do it anew himself; and I nothing mistrust but he shall find it an easier thing to control a piece or two than amend the whole of this enterpretation. Thus I commit you to God, gentle readers. . . .

SIR THOMAS HOBY (trans.)

CASTIGLIONE'S *COURTIER*

Since to an extraordinary degree Baldassare Castiglione built his career around the values enshrined in his great book, both *Il Cortegiano* and its author are fine and characteristic products of the high Italian Renaissance. Conceived, in a sense, as a memorial to the glittering ceremonial of a culture that was passing away, *The Courtier* is a repository of highly civilized ethical, social, and political values that young Thomas Hoby's translation made available, on the threshold of Elizabeth's reign, to a nation that was just entering the noontide splendor of its own belated Renaissance. Sketched "in a few days" in 1508, shortly after the death of Castiglione's master, Guidobaldo Malatesta, Duke of Urbino, the book sought to commemorate "the savor of the virtues" that the great Malatesta family had made possible in their ducal court. But as Castiglione explains in his "Epistle," the pressure of his new commitments and his desire to perfect his style long delayed publication. Internal evidence and allusions to contemporary events (such as the lament for the death of Cesare Gonzaga, who died in 1512) suggest that Book IV was probably completed at Rome about 1516; but in 1518 Castiglione was still tinkering with his manuscript after he had submitted it to Cardinal Bembo and Bishop Jacopo Sadoleto for their opinions, and even after he had arrived in Spain in 1524 he was, as he wrote to Lady Vittoria Colonna, vexed that the wide and unauthorized circulation of the manuscript was compelling him to rush his work to the printer before he had completed polishing it. Finally, some twenty years after its inception, *Il Cortegiano* was published at Venice in 1528, shortly before Castiglione's death at Toledo in the following year.

Its success, both in Italy and elsewhere, was immediate. In 1534 Juan Boscán issued his Spanish version; Abbé Jacques Colin, almoner to François I, made a French translation which Etienne Dolet presumably saw through the press about 1538; and by the early fifties Hoby was at work on his English translation which was finally published in 1561. Following a stay of three years, mainly in Italy, on the Continent (1547–50), Hoby returned to the court of Edward VI after he had already begun (at Paris, as his diary records) translating the third book of *Il Cortegiano* at the request of the wife of his patron the Marquess of Northampton. The task was completed, apparently at Padua, in 1556, after Hoby had found it prudent to leave England following Mary's accession; and it was perhaps then that Sir John Cheke (who was also at Padua in order to avoid the Marian persecutions) agreed to write his commendatory letter on the translator's art, a letter dated from London in the following year. Publication had to wait, however, until Mary had been succeeded by Elizabeth and Hoby had settled down to the life of a landed gentleman at Bisham, Berkshire. In 1560 his diary records a thirteen-weeks' visit to London, no doubt for the purpose of seeing his manuscript through the press; and sometime between March 8 and April 14, 1561, the printer William Seres entered in the Stationers' Register *The Courtier. Done into English by T. Hoby.* There were other editions in 1577 and 1603, and in 1587 an elaborate edition with the Italian, French, and English versions in parallel columns was published by John Wolfe. Our text is based upon *The Courtyer of Count Baldessar Castilio divided into foure bookes . . . done into Englyshe by Thomas Hoby,* 1561 (STC 4778).

FROM THE COURTIER OF COUNT BALDESSAR CASTILIO (1561)

Thomas Sackville in Commendation of the Work to the Reader

These royal kings that rear up to the sky
Their palaice tops, and deck them all with gold,
With rare and curious works they feed the eye,
And show what riches here great princes hold.
A rarer work and richer far in worth
Castilio's hand presenteth here to thee.
No proud ne golden court doth he set furth,
But what in court a courtier ought to be.
The prince he raiseth huge and mighty walls;
Castilio frames a wight of noble fame.
The king with gorgeous tissue clads his halls;
The count with golden virtue decks the same,
Whose passing skill, lo, Hoby's pen displays
To Britain folk, a work of worthy praise.

To the Right Honorable the Lord Henry Hastings, Son and Heir Apparent to the Noble Earl of Huntington

Themistocles, the noble Athenian, in his banishment entertained most honorably with the king of Persia, willed upon a time to tell his cause by a spokesman, compared it to a piece of tapestry that, being spread abroad, discloseth the beauty of the workmanship but, folded together, hideth it; and therefore demanded respite to learn the Persian tongue to tell his own cause. Right so, honorable lord, this *Courtier* hath long stray'd about this realm, and the fruit of him either little or unperfectly received to the commune benefit; for either men skilful in his tongue have delighted in him for their own private commodity, or else he hath eftsoons spoken in piecemeal by an interpreter to such as desired to know his mind and to practise his principles, the which how unperfect a thing it is, Themistocles and experience teach. But now, though late indeed yet for all that at length, beside his three principal languages in the which he hath a long time haunted all the courts of Christendom, he is become an Englishman (which many a long time have wished, but few attempted and none atchieved) and well willing to dwell in the court of England and in plight to tell his own cause. In whose commendation I shall not need to use any long process of words, for he can so well speak for himself, and answer to the opinion men have a long time conceived of him, that whatsoever I should write therein were but labor in waste, and rather a diminishing then a setting-forth of his worthiness; and a great deal better it were to pass it over with silence then to use briefness. Only for the little acquaintance I have with him, and for

the general profit is in him, my desire is he should now at his first arrival, a new man in this kind of trade, be well entertained and much honored. And forsomuch as none but a young gentleman, and trained up all his lifetime in court and of worthy qualities, is meet to receive and entertain so worthy a courtier, that like may fellowship and get estimation with his like, I do dedicate him unto your good lordship, that through your means and under your patronage he may be commune to a great meany. . . .

Generally ought this to be in estimation with all degrees of men, for to princes and great men it is a rule to rule themselves that rule others; and one of the books that a noble philosopher exhorted a certain king to provide him, and diligently to search, for in them he should find written such matters that friends durst not utter unto kings. To men grown in years, a pathway to the beholding and musing of the mind, and to whatsoever else is meet for that age; to young gentlemen, an encouraging to garnish their mind with moral virtues and their body with comely exercises, and both the one and the other with honest qualities to attain unto their noble end; to ladies and gentlewomen, a mirror to deck and trim themselves with virtuous conditions, comely behaviors, and honest entertainment toward all men; and to them all in general, a storehouse of most necessary implements for the conversation, use, and training-up of man's life with courtly demeanors. . . .

As I . . . have to my small skill bestowed some labor about this piece of work, even so could I wish, with all my heart, profound, learned men in the Greek and Latin should make the like proof, and every man store the tongue according to his knowledge and delight above other men in some piece of learning, that we alone of the world may not be still counted barbarous in our tongue, as in time out of mind we have been in our manners. And so shall we perchance in time become as famous in England as the learned men of other nations have been and presently are; and though the hardness of this present matter be such, and mine unskilfulness to undertake this enterprise so great, that I might with good cause have despaired to bring to an end it that many excellent wits have attempted, yet could I not choose but yield to the continual requests and often persuasions of many young gentlemen which have (may chance) an opinion that to be in me that is not indeed; and unto whom in any reasonable matter I were skilful in, neither I could nor ought of duty to want in fulfilling their desire. Notwithstanding, a great while I forbare and lingered the time to see if any of a more perfect understanding in the tongue, and better practised in the matter of the book (of whom we want not a number in this realm) would take the matter in hand, to do his country so great a benefit; and this imagination prevailed in me a long space after my duty done in translating the third book (that entreateth of a gentlewoman of the court), persuaded thereto, in that I was enformed it was as then in some forwardness by another whose wit and style was greatly to be allowed, but since prevented by death he could not finish it. But of late, being instantly craved upon afresh, I whetted my style and settled myself to take in hand the other three books (that entreat of the perfection of a gentleman of the court) to fulfil their petition in what I am able, having time and leisure thereto, the which I have done— though not in effect, yet in apparance—and that in a

great deal shorter time then the hardness of the matter required. . . .

Wherefore receive you this as a token of my good will, and so receive it that the fruit, whatever it be, may be acknowledged at your hands; and you pass the expectation of men in this as in all other things, which, no doubt, is very great of you; and I, to acknowledge this benefit, where my hability stretcheth to nothing else, shall at the least evermore wish unto your lordship long life, that you may go forward as you do in these beginnings, which promise a lucky end to the honor of yourself, comfort of your friends, and forwardness of the commune weal of your country. 1556.

Your lordship's most bounden

Thomas Hoby

The First Book of the Courtier of Count Baldessar Castilio, unto Maister Alphonsus Ariosto

I have a long time doubted with myself, most loving Master Alphonsus, which of the two were harder for me: either to deny you the thing that you have with such instance many times required of me, or to take it in hand; bicause on the one side methought it a very hard matter to deny anything, especially the request being honest, to the person whom I love dearly, and of whom I perceive myself dearly beloved. Again, on the other side, to undertake an enterprise which I do not know myself able to bring to an end, I judged it uncomely for him that weigheth due reproofs so much as they ought to be weighed. At length, after much debating, I have determined to prove in this behalf what aid that affection and great desire to please can bring unto my diligence, which in other things is wont to encrease the labor of men.

You, then, require me to write what is, to my thinking, the trade and manner of courtiers, which is most fitting for a gentleman that liveth in the court of princes, by the which he may have the knowledge how to serve them perfectly in every reasonable matter, and obtain thereby favor of them and praise of other men. Finally, of what sort he ought to be that deserveth to be called so perfect a courtier that there be no want in him.

Wherefore I, considering this kind of request, say that in case it should not appear to myself a greater blame to have you esteem me to be of small friendship then all other men of little wisdom, I would have rid my hands of this labor for fear lest I should be counted rash of all such as know what a hard matter it is, among such diversity of manners that

are used in the courts of Christendom, to pick out the perfectest trade and way, and, as it were, the flour of this courtiership. Because use maketh us many times to delight in and to set little by the self-same things; whereby sometime it proceedeth that manners, garments, customs, and fashions which at some time have been in price become not regarded; and contrariwise, the not regarded become of price. Therefore it is manifestly to be descerned that use hath greater force then reason to bring up new inventions emong us and to abolish the old, of the which whoso goeth about to judge the perfection is oftentimes deceived.

For which consideration, perceiving this and many other lets in the matter propounded for me to write upon, I am constrained to make a piece of an excuse, and to open plainly that this error (if it may be termed an error) is commune to us both, that if any blame happen to me about it, it may be also part'ned with you. For it ought to be reck'ned a no less offense in you to lay upon me a burden that passeth my strength then in me to take it upon me.

Let us, therefore, at length settle ourselves to begin that is our purpose and drift, and, if be it possible, let us fashion such a courtier as the prince that shall be worthy to have him in his service, although his state be but small, may notwithstanding be called a mighty lord.

We will not in these books follow any certain order or rule of appointed precepts, the which for the most part is wont to be observed in the teaching of anything whatsoever it be. But after the manner of men of old time, renewing a grateful memory, we will repeat certain reasonings that were debated in times past between men very excellent for that purpose. And although I was not there present—but at the time when they were debated it was my chance to be in England—yet soon after my return I heard them of a person that faithfully reported them unto me. And I will endeavor myself, forsomuch as my memory will serve me, to call them particularly to remembrance that you may see what men worthy great commendation, and unto whose judgment a man may in every point geve an undoubted credit, have judged and believed in this matter. Neither shall we swarve from the purpose to arrive in good order at the end, unto the which all our communication is directed, if we disclose the cause of the reasonings that hereafter follow.

As every man knoweth, the little city of Urbin is situated upon the side of the Apennine (in a manner) in the middes of Italy, towards the Gulf of Venice. The which for all it is placed emong hills, and those not so pleasant as perhaps some other that we behold in many places, yet in this point the element hath been favorable unto it, that all about the country is very plentiful and full of fruits; so that beside the wholesomeness of air, it is very aboundant and stored with all things necessary for the life of man. But among the greatest felicities that men can reckon it to have, I count this the chief, that now a long time it hath always been governed with very good princes; although in the commune calamities of the wars of Italy it remained also a season without any at all.

But without searching further of this we may make a good proof with the famous memory of Duke Frederick, who in his days was the light of Italy. Neither do we want true and very large testimonies yet remaining of his wisdom, courtesy, justice, liberality, of his invincible courage and policy of war. And of this do so many victories make proof, chiefly his conquering of places impregnable, his sodein readiness in setting forward to geve battail, his putting to flight sundry times with a small number very great and puissant armies, and never sustained loss in any conflict. So that we may, not without cause, compare him to many famous men of old time.

This man, among his other deeds praiseworthy, in the hard and sharp situation of Urbin built a palaice, to the opinion of many men the fairest that was to be found in all Italy, and so fornished it with every necessary implement belonging thereto that it appeared not a palaice but a city in fourm of a palaice, and that not only with ordinary matters (as silver plate, hangings for chambers of very rich cloth of gold, of silk, and other like) but also for sightliness; and to deck it out withal placed there a wonderous number of ancient images of marble and metal, very excellent peinctings, and instruments of music of all sorts; and nothing would he have there but what was most rare and excellent.

To this, with very great charges he gathered together a great number of most excellent and rare books in Greek, Latin, and Hebrew, the which all he garnished with gold and silver, esteeming this to be the chiefest ornament of his great palaice.

This duke, then, following the course of nature when he was sixty-five years of age, as he had lived, so did he end his life with glory. And left duke after him a child of ten years, having no more male, and without mother, who hight Guidobaldo. This child, as of the state, so did it appear also that he was heir of all his father's virtues; and sodenly with a marvelous towardness began to promise so much of himself as a man would not have thought possible to be hoped of a man mortal. So that the opinion of men was that of all Duke Frederick's notable deeds there was none greater then that he begat such a son. But Fortune, envying this so great virtue, with all her might gainstood this so glorious a beginning, in such wise that before Duke Guidobaldo was twenty years of age he fell sick of the gout, the which, encreasing upon him with most bitter pains, in a short time so numbed him of all his members that he could neither stand on foot nor move himself. And in this manner was one of the best-favored and towardliest personages in the world deformed and marred in his green age. And beside, not satisfied with this, Fortune was so contrary to him in all his purposes that very sildom he brought to pass anything to his mind. And for all he had in him most wise counsail, and an invincible courage, yet it seemed that whatsoever he took in hand, both in feats of arms and in every other thing, small or great, it came always to ill success. And of this make proof his many and divers calamities, which he always bore out with such stoutness of courage that virtue never yielded to Fortune. But with a bold stomach, despising her storms, lived with great dignity and estimation among all men— in sickness as one that was sound, and in adversity as one that was most fortunate. So that, for all he was thus diseased in his body, he served in time of war with most honorable entertainment under the most famous kings of Naples, Alphonsus and Ferdinand the younger; afterward with Pope Alexander VI, with the lords of Venice and Florence. And when Julius II was created pope, he was then made general captain of the church; at which time, proceeding in his accustomed usage, he set his delight above all things to have his house furnished with most noble and valiant gentlemen, with whom he lived very familiarly, enjoying their conversation, wherein the pleasure which he gave unto other men was no less then that he received of other, because he was very well seen in both tongues, and together with a loving behavior and pleasantness he had also accompanied the knowledge of infinite things. And beside this, the greatness of his courage so quickened him that, where he was not in case with his person to practise the feats of chivalry, as he had done long before, yet did he take very great delight to behold them in other men, and with his words sometime correcting and otherwise praising every man according to his deserts, he declared evidently how great a judgment he had in those matters.

And upon this at tilt, at tourney, in riding, in playing at all sorts of weapon, also in inventing devices, in pastimes, in music, finally in all exercises meet for noble gentlemen, every man strived to show himself such a one as might deserve to be judged worthy of so noble an assembly. Therefore were all the hours of the day devided into honorable and pleasant exercises, as well of the body as of the mind. But because the duke used continually, by reason of his infirmity, soon after supper to go to his rest, every man ordinarily at that hour drew where the duchess was, the Lady Elizabeth Gonzaga. Where also continually was the Lady Emilia Pia, who for that she was endowed with so lively a wit and judgment as you know, seemed the maistress and ringleader of all the company, and that every man at her received understanding and courage. There was then to be heard pleasant communication and merry conceits, and in every man's countenance a man might perceive peincted a loving jocundness. So that this house truly might well be called the very mansion-place of mirth and joy. And I believe it was never so tasted in other place, what manner a thing the sweet conversation is that is occasioned of an amiable and loving company, as it was once there.

For leaving apart what honor it was to all us to serve such a lord as he whom I declared unto you right now, every man conceived in his mind an high contentation every time we came into the duchess' sight. And it appeared that this was a chain that kept all linked together in love, in such wise that there was never agreement of will or hearty love greater between brethren then there was between us all. The like was between the women, with whom we had such free and honest conversation that every man might commune, sit, dally, and laugh with whom he had lusted. But such was the respect which we bore to the duchess' will that the selfsame liberty was a very great bridle. Neither was there any that thought it not the greatest pleasure he could have in the world to please her and the greatest grief to offend her. For this respect were there most honest

conditions coupled with wonderous great liberty and devises of pastimes and laughing matters temp'red in her sight, beside most witty jests, with so comely and grave a majesty that the very sober mood and greatness that did knit together all the acts, words, and gestures of the duchess in jesting and laughing made them also that had never seen her in their life before to count her a very great lady. And all that came in her presence, having this respect fixed in their breast, it seemed she had made them to her beck. So that every man enforced himself to follow this trade, taking, as it were, a rule and ensample of fair conditions at the presence of so great and so virtuous a lady. Whose most excellent qualities I entend not now to express, for it is neither my purpose and again they are well inough known to the world, and much better then I am able either with tongue or with pen to indite. And such as would perhaps have lien hid a space, Fortune, as she that wond'reth at so rare virtues, hath thought good with many adversities and temptations of miseries to disclose them, to make trial thereby that in the tender breast of a woman, in company with singular beauty, there can dwell wisdom, and stoutness of courage, and all other virtues that in grave men themselves are most seldom.

But leaving this apart, I say that the manner of all the gentlemen in the house was immediately after supper to assemble together where the duchess was. Where, among other recreations, music and dancing, which they used continually, sometime they propounded feat questions, otherwhile they invented certain witty sports and pastimes, at the device sometime of one, sometime of another, in the which, under sundry coverts, oftentimes the standers-by opened subtilly their imaginations unto whom they thought best. At other times there arose other disputations of divers matters, or else jestings with prompt inventions. Many times they fell into purposes, as we nowadays term them, where in this kind of talk and debating of matters there was wonderous great pleasure on all sides; because, as I have said, the house was replenished with most noble wits. . . . So that thither ran continually poets, musicians, and all kind of men of skill, and the excellentest in every faculty that were in all Italy.

After Pope Julius II had with his own presence, by the aid of the Frenchmen, brought Bolonia to the obedience of the Apostolic See again, in the year 1506, in his return toward Rome he took Urbin in his way, where he was received as honorably as was possible, and with as sumptuous and costly preparation as could have been in any other city of Italy, whatsoever it be. So that, beside the pope, all the cardinals and other courtiers thought themselves throughly satisfied. And some there were that, provoked with the sweetness of this company, after the pope and the court was departed continued many days together in Urbin. At which time they did not only proceed in their accustomed trade of disporting and ordinary recreations, but also every man set to his helping hand to augment them somewhat, and especially in pastimes, which they had up almost every night. And the order thereof was such that, as soon as they were assembled where the duchess was, every man sat him down at his will, or as it fell to his lot, in a circle together, and in sitting were devided a man and a woman, as long as there were women, for always, lightly, the number of men was far the greater. Then were they governed as the duchess thought best, which many times gave this charge unto the Lady Emilia. . . .

[Following the pope's departure it is agreed that the company shall divert itself by discussions of set topics, the topic finally chosen being the character of the perfect courtier. Count Lewis of Canossa agrees to begin by enumerating some of his necessary attributes.]

"I will have this our courtier, therefore, to be a gentleman born and of a good house. For it is a great deal less dispraise for him that is not born a gentleman to fail in the acts of virtue then for a gentleman. If he swarve from the steps of his ancestors he staineth the name of his family, and doth not only not get but loseth that is already gotten. For nobleness of birth is, as it were, a clear lamp that sheweth forth and bringeth into light works both good and bad, and enflameth and provoketh unto virtue as well with the fear of slander as also with the hope of praise. And whereas this brightness of nobleness doth not discover the works of the unnoble, they have a want of provocation and of fear of slander, and they reckon not themselves bound to wade any further then their auncetors did before theim; whereas the noble of birth count it a shame not to arrive at the least at the bounds of their predecessors set forth unto them. Therefore it chanceth always in a manner, both in arms and in all other virtuous acts, that the most famous men are gentlemen. Because nature in everything hath deeply sowed that privy seed which geveth a certain force and property of her beginning unto whatsoever springeth of it, and maketh it like unto herself. . . .

"The courtier, therefore, beside nobleness of birth I will have him to be fortunate in this behalf, and by nature to have not only a wit and a comely shape of person and countenance, but also a certain grace, and, as they say, a hue that shall make him at the first sight acceptable and loving unto whoso beholdeth him. And let this be an ornament to frame and accompany all his acts, and to assure men in his

look such a one to be worthy the company and favor of every great man."

Here, without any longer tarrying, the Lord Gaspar Pallavicin said: "That our pastime may have the form and manner agreed upon, and lest it should appear that we little esteem the aucthority geven us to contrary you, I say, in mine advise, that this nobleness of birth is not so necessary for the courtier. And if I wist that any of you thought it a strange or a new matter I would alledge unto you sundry, who for all they were born of most noble blood yet have they been heaped full of vices; and contrariwise many unnoble that have made famous their posterity. And if it be true that you said before, that the privy force of the first seed is in everything, we should all be in one manner condition, for that we had all one self beginning, and one should not be more noble then another. But beside the diversities and degrees in us of high and low, I believe there be many other matters, wherein I judge Fortune to be the chief; because we see her bear a stroke in all worldly things, and, as it were, take a pastime to exalt many times whom pleaseth her without any desert at all, and bury in the bottomless depth the most worthy to be exalted. . . ."

Then answered Count Lewis: "I deny not but in men of base degree may reign the very same virtues that are in gentlemen. But to avoid rehearsal of that we have already said, with many other reasons that might be alledged in commendation of nobleness, the which is evermore honored of all men because it standeth with reason that good should spring of good; forsomuch as our entent is to fashion a courtier without any manner default or lack in him, and heaped with all praise, methink it a necessary matter to make him a gentleman, as well for many other respects as also for the common opinion, which by and by doth lean to nobleness. . . .

"But to come to some particularity, I judge the principal and true profession of a courtier ought to be in feats of arms, the which above all I will have him to practise lively, and to be known among other for his hardiness, for his achieving of enterprises, and for his fidelity toward him whom he serveth. And he shall purchase himself a name with these good conditions in doing the deeds in every time and place, for it is not for him to faint at any time in this behalf without a wonderous reproach. And even as in women honesty once stained doth never return again to the former astate, so the fame of a gentleman that carrieth weapon, if it once take a foil in any little point through dastardliness or any other reproach, doth evermore continue shameful in the world and full of ignorance. . . . He, therefore, that we seek for, where the enemies are shall shew himself most fierce, bitter, and evermore with the first. In every place beside, lowly, sober, and circumspect, fleeing above all thing bragging and unshameful praising himself; for therewith a man always purchaseth himself the hatred and ill will of the hearers."

"And I," answered the Lord Gaspar, "have known few men excellent in anything, whatsoever it be, but they praise themselves. And methink it may well be borne in them, for he that is of skill, whan he seeth that he is not known for his works of the ignorant, hath a disdeign that his cunning should lie buried, and needs must he open it one way lest he should be defrauded of the estimation that belongeth to it, which is the true reward of virtuous travails. . . ."

[Presently Master Bernard Bibiena introduces another consideration.] "As for the grace and beauty of phisnamy, I think not the contrary but they are in me, and therefore do so many women burn for the love of me, as you know. But for the comeliness of person, I stand somewhat in doubt, and especially by reason of my legs here, for methink indeed they are not so well made as I could wish they were; the body and the rest is meetly well. Therefore declare somewhat more particularly this comeliness of person, what it should be, that I may be out of this doubt and set my heart at rest."

Whan they had a while laughed at this the count said: "Certes, the grace of the phisnamy may well be said to be in you without any lie. And no other example do I alledge but this, to declare what manner thing it should be; for undoubtedly we see your countenance is most acceptable and pleasant to behold unto every man, although the proportion and draughts of it be not very delicate, but it is manly and hath a good grace withal. And this quality have many and sundry shapes of visages.

"And such a countenance as this is will I have our courtier to have, and not so soft and womanish as many procure to have, that do not only curl the hear and pick the brows, but also pamper themselves in every point like the most wanton and dishonest women in the world; and a man would think them in going, in standing, and in all their gestures so tender and faint that their members were ready to flee one from another; and their words they pronounce so drawningly that a man would ween they were at that instant yielding up the ghost; and the higher in degree the men are they talk withal, the more they use such fashions. These men, seeing nature (as they seem to have a desire to appear and to be) hath not made them women, ought not to be esteemed in place of good women, but like common harlots to be banished, not only out of princes' courts but also out of the company of gentlemen.

"To come, therefore, to the quality of the person,

I say he is well if he be neither of the least nor of the greatest size. For both the one and the other hath with it a certain spiteful wonder, and such men are marveled at almost as much as men marvel to behold monstrous things. Yet if there must needs be a default in one of the two extremities, it shall be less hurtful to be somewhat of the least then to exceed the common stature in height. For men so shut up of body, beside that many times they are of a dull wit, they are also unapt for all exercises of nimbleness, which I much desire to have in the courtier. And therefore will I have him to be of a good shape and well-proportioned in his lims, and to shew strength, lightness, and quickness, and to have understanding in all exercises of the body that belong to a man of war. And herein I think the chief point is to handle well all kind of weapon, both for footman and horseman, and to know the vantages in it. And especially to be skilful on those weapons that are used ordinarily emong gentlemen. . . .

"And because it is the peculiar praise of us Italians to ride well, to manege with reason especially rough horses, to run at the ring and at tilt, he shall be in this among the best Italians. At tournament in keeping a passage, in fighting at barriers, he shall be good emong the best Frenchmen. At *joco di canne,* running at bull, casting of spears and darts he shall be among the Spaniards excellent. But principally let him accompany all his motion with a certain good judgment and grace, if he will deserve that general favor which is so much set by. . . ."

[And so the conversation winds on, touching urbanely such of the ideal courtier's other attributes as social graces and unaffected demeanor. Presently the talk turns to his use of language, and to the advantages of pure (if archaic) Tuscan over other dialects. To clarify a rather desultory discussion the duchess finally asks Count Lewis to state explicitly what a courtier needs "to speak and to write well, be it Tuscan or whatever else."]

The count answered . . . : "This our tongue which we name the vulgar tongue is tender and new, for all it hath been now used a long while. For in that Italy hath been not only vexed and spoiled but also inhabited a long time with barbarous people, by the great resort of those nations the Latin tongue was corrupted and destroyed, and of that corruption have sprung other tongues. The which like the rivers that depart from the top of the Apennine and run abroad toward the two seas, so are they also divided; and some dyed with the Latin speech have spread abroad sundry ways, some into one part and some into another, and one dyed with barbarousness hath remained in Italy. This, then, hath a long time been among us out of order and diverse, because there was none that would bestow diligence about it, nor write in it, ne yet seek to geve it brightness or any grace; yet hath it been afterward brought into better frame in Tuscan then in the other parts of Italy.

"And by this it appeareth that the flow'r of it hath remained there ever since those first times, because that nation hath kept proper and sweet accents in the pronunciation and an order of grammer, where it was meet, more then the other. And hath had three noble writers [i.e. Dante, Petrarch, and Boccaccio] which wittily, both in the words and terms that custom did allow in their time, have expressed their conceits; and that hath happened (in my mind) with a better grace to Petrarca, in matters of love, then to any of the other.

"Where there arose afterward from time to time, not only in Tuscan but in all Italy, among gentlemen brought up in court, in arms, and in letters some study to speak and to write more finely then they did in that first rude age, whan the turmoil of the miseries that arose through barbarous nations was not as yet quieted; many words have been left out as well in Florence itself and in all Tuscan as in the residue of Italy, and other brought in in their stead and made in this behalf the alteration that happeneth in all worldly things, the which also hath evermore chanced in other tongues. . . . Therefore would I, for my part, always shun the use of those ancient words, except it were in certain clauses, and in them very seldom. And, in my judgment, he that useth them otherwise committeth a no less error then whoso would, to follow them of old time, feed upon mast where he hath now aboundance of corn found out.

"And because you say the ancient words only with the brightness of antiquity deck out so highly every matter, how base soever it be, that it may make it worthy great commendation, I say unto you that not of these ancient words only but of those that be good indeed I make so small accompt that I suppose without the juice of fair sentences they ought of reason to be little set by. For to divide the sentences from the words is the deviding of the soul from the body, the which cannot be done, neither in the one nor in the other, without destruction ensue upon it. That, therefore, which is the principal matter and necessary for a courtier to speak and write well, I believe, is knowledge. For he that hath not knowledge and the thing in his mind that deserveth to be understood can neither speak nor write it.

"Then must he couch in a good order that he hath to speak or to write, and afterward express it well with words, the which, if I be not deceived, ought to be apt chosen, clear, and well applied, and (above all) in use also among the people; for very such make the greatness and gorgeousness of an oration, so he

that speaketh have a good judgment and heedfulness withal, and the understanding to pick such as be of most proper signification for that he entendeth to speak and commend, and, temp'ring them like wex after his own mind, applieth them in such part and in such order that at the first show they may set furth and do men to understand the dignity and brightness of them, as tables of peincting placed in their good and natural light. . . ."

[The conversation ripples on to the affectations of women, to literature, to music and painting, until presently there is heard "a great scraping of feet in the floor, with a cherm of loud speaking; and upon that every man turning himself about saw at the chamber door appear a light of torches, and by and by after ent'red in the lord general" (i.e. Francesco della Rovere, the adopted heir of Duke Frederick and nephew of Pope Julius II) "with a great and noble train who was then returned from accompanying the pope a piece of the way." The arrival of the newcomers disrupting the conversation, it is agreed to "bestow the small time that remaineth about some other pastime without ambition."]

The which being agreed upon of all hands, the duchess willed the Lady Margaret and the Lady Constance Fregosa to shew them a dance. Wherefore Barletta immediately, a very pleasant musician and an excellent dancer who continually kept all the court in mirth and joy, began to play upon his instruments; and they, hand in hand, shewed them a dance or two with a very good grace and great pleasure to the lookers-on. That done, because it is far in night, the duchess arose upon her feet, and so every man, taking his leave reverently of her, departed to his rest.

THE FOURTH BOOK

[The fourth and final book is concerned with more serious matters than the earlier books: the moral obligation that ties a courtier to his prince, the nature of virtue and the necessity of temperance, monarchy and democracy, the attributes of a good ruler, and the nature of love and beauty. On this last topic Master Peter Bembo undertakes to speak.]

Then the Lord Gaspar: "I remember," quoth he, "that these lords yesternight reasoning of the courtier's qualities did allow him to be a lover; and in making rehearsal of as much as hitherto hath been spoken, a man may pick out a conclusion that the courtier which with his worthiness and credit must incline his prince to virtue must in manner of necessity be aged, for knowledge cometh very sildom times before years, and specially in matters that be learned with experience. I cannot see, whan he is well drawn in years, how it will stand well with him to be a lover, considering, as it hath been said the other night, love frameth not with old men, and the tricks that in young men be gallantness, courtesy, and preciseness so acceptable to women, in them are mere follies and fondness to be laughed at, and purchase him that useth them hatred of women and mocks of others. Therefore, in case this your Aristotle, an old courtier, were a lover and practised the feats that young lovers do, as some that we have seen in our days, I fear me he would forget to teach his prince; and paraventure boys would mock him behind his back, and women would have none other delight in him but to make him a jesting-stock."

Then said the Lord Octavian: "Since all the other qualities appointed to the courtier are meet for him, although he be old, methink we should not then bar him from this happiness to love."

"Nay rather," quoth the Lord Gaspar, "to take this love from him is a perfection over and above, and a making him to live happily out of misery and wretchedness."

Master Peter Bembo said: "Remember you not, my Lord Gaspar, that the Lord Octavian declared the other night in his device of pastimes, although he be not skilful in love, to know yet that there be some lovers which reckon the disdeigns, the angers, the debates and torments which they receive of their ladies, sweet? Whereupon he required to be taught the cause of this sweetness. Therefore, in case our courtier, though he be old, were kendled with those loves that be sweet without any bitter smack, he should feel no misery nor wretchedness at all. And being wise, as we set case he is, he should not be deceived in thinking to be meet for him whatsoever were meet for young men, but in loving should perhaps love after a sort that might not only not bring him in sclander, but to much praise and great happiness, without any lothsomeness at all, the which very sildom or in manner never happeneth to young men; and so should he neither lay aside the teaching of his prince, nor yet commit anything that should deserve the mocking of boys."

Then spake the duchess: "I am glad, Master Peter, that you have not been much troubled in our reasonings this night, for now we may be the bolder to give you in charge to speak, and to teach the courtier this so happy a love, which bringeth with it neither sclander nor any inconvenience; for perhaps it shall be one of the necessariest and profitablest qualities that hitherto hath been given him; therefore speak of good fellowship as much as you know therein."

Master Peter laughed and said: "I would be loth,

madam, where I say it is leful for old men to love, it should be an occasion for these ladies to think me old; therefore hardly give ye this enterprise to another."

The duchess answered: "You ought not to refuse to be counted old in knowledge, though ye be young in years. Therefore say on, and excuse yourself no more. . . ."

And here, after they had laughed a while, Master Peter proceeded: "I say, therefore, that according as it is defined of the wise men of old time, love is nothing else but a certain coveting to enjoy beauty; and forsomuch as coveting longeth for nothing but for things known, it is requisite that knowledge go evermore before coveting, which of his own nature willeth the good, but of himself is blind and knoweth it not. Therefore hath nature so ordained that to every virtue of knowledge there is annexed a virtue of longing. And bicause in our soul there be three manner ways to know, namely, by sense, reason, and understanding: of sense there ariseth appetite or longing, which is commune to us with brute beasts; of reason ariseth election or choice, which is proper to man; of understanding, by the which man may be partner with angels, ariseth will. Even as therefore the sense knoweth not but sensible matters and that which may be felt, so the appetite or coveting only desireth the same; and even as the understanding is bent but to behold things that may be understood, so is that will only fed with spiritual goods. Man of nature indowed with reason, placed, as it were, in the middle between these two extremities, may, through his choice inclining to sense or reaching to understanding, come nigh to the coveting, sometime of the one, sometime of the other part. In these sorts, therefore, may beauty be coveted, the general name whereof may be applied to all things, either natural or artificial, that are framed in good proportion and due temper, as their nature beareth. But speaking of the beauty that we mean, which is only it that appeareth in bodies, and especially in the face of man, and moveth this fervent coveting which we call love, we will term it an influence of the heavenly bountifulness, the which for all it stretcheth over all things that be created (like the light of the sun), yet whan it findeth out a face well proportioned, and framed with a certain lively agreement of several colors, and set furth with lights and shadows, and with an orderly distance and limits of lines, thereinto it distilleth itself and appeareth most well-favored, and decketh out and light'neth the subject where it shineth with a marvelous grace and glist'ring, like the sunbeams that strike against beautiful plate of fine gold wrought and set with precious jewels, so that it draweth unto it men's eyes with pleasure, and piercing through them imprinteth himself in the soul, and with an unwonted sweetness all to-stirreth her and delighteth, and setting her on fire maketh her to covet him. Whan the soul then is taken with coveting to enjoy this beauty as a good thing, in case she suffer herself to be guided with the judgment of sense, she falleth into most deep errors, and judgeth the body in which beauty is descerned to be the principal cause thereof; whereupon to enjoy it she reckoneth it necessary to join as inwardly as she can with that body, which is false; and therefore whoso thinketh in possessing the body to injoy beauty, he is far deceived, and is moved to it, not with true knowledge by the choice of reason, but with false opinion by the longing of sense. Whereupon the pleasure that followeth it is also false and of necessity full of errors. . . ."

Here Bembo paused a while, as though he would breathe him, and whan all things were whist Master Morello, of Ortona, said: "And in case there were some old man more fresh and lusty and of a better complexion then many young men, why would you not have it leful for him to love with the love that young men love?"

The duchess laughed, and said: "If the love of young men be so unlucky, why would you, Master Morello, that old men should also love with this unluckiness? But in case you were old, as these men say you be, you would not thus procure the hurt of old men."

Master Morello answered: "The hurt of old men, meseemeth, Master Peter Bembo procureth, who will have them to love after a sort that I for my part understand not; and, methink, the possessing of this beauty which he praiseth so much, without the body, is a dream."

"Do you believe, Master Morello," quoth then Count Lewis, "that beauty is always so good a thing as Master Peter Bembo speaketh of?"

"Not I, in good sooth," answered Master Morello. "But I remember rather that I have seen many beautiful women of a most ill inclination, cruel and spiteful, and it seemeth that, in a manner, it happeneth always so, for beauty maketh them proud, and pride, cruel."

Count Lewis said, smiling: "To you perhaps they seem cruel, bicause they content you not with it that you would have. But cause Master Peter Bembo to teach you in what sort old men ought to covet beauty, and what to seek at their ladies' hands, and what to content themselves withal; and in not passing out of these bounds ye shall see that they shall be neither proud nor cruel, and will satisfy you with what you shall require."

Master Morello seemed then somewhat out of patience, and said: "I will not know the thing that toucheth me not. But cause you to be taught how the young men ought to covet this beauty that are not so fresh and lusty as old men be."

Here Sir Frederick, to pacify Master Morello and to break their talk, would not suffer Count Lewis to make answer, but interrupting him said: "Perhaps Master Morello is not altogether out of the way in saying that beauty is not always good, for the beauty of women is many times cause of infinite evils in the world—hatred, war, mortality, and destruction, whereof the rasing of Troy can be a good witness; and beautiful women for the most part be either proud and cruel, as is said, or unchaste; but Master Morello would find no fault with that. There be also many wicked men that have the comeliness of a beautiful countenance, and it seemeth that Nature hath so shaped them bicause they may be the readier to deceive, and that this amiable look were like a bait that covereth the hook."

Then Master Peter Bembo: "Believe not," quoth he, "but beauty is always good."

Here Count Lewis, bicause he would return again to his former purpose, interrupted him and said: "Since Master Morello passeth not to understand that which is so necessary for him, teach it me, and show me how old men may come by this happiness of love, for I will not care to be counted old, so it may profit me."

Master Peter Bembo laughed, and said: "First will I take that error out of these gentlemen's mind, and afterward will I satisfy you also." So beginning afresh: "My lords," quoth he, "I would not that with speaking ill of beauty, which is a holy thing, any of us as prophane and wicked should purchase him the wrath of God. Therefore, to give Master Morello and Sir Frederick warning, that they lose not their sight, as Stesichorus did—a pain most meet for whoso dispraiseth beauty—I say that beauty cometh of God and is like a circle, the goodness whereof is the center. And therefore, as there can be no circle without a center, no more can beauty be without goodness. Whereupon doth very sildom an ill soul dwell in a beautiful body. And therefore is the outward beauty a true sign of the inward goodness, and in bodies this comeliness is imprinted, more and less as it were, for a mark of the soul, whereby she is outwardly known; as in trees, in which the beauty of the buds giveth a testimony of the goodness of the fruit. And the very same happeneth in bodies, as it is seen that palmastrers by the visage know many times the conditions and otherwhile the thoughts of men. And, which is more, in beasts also a man may descern by the face the quality of the courage, which in the body declareth itself as much as it can. Judge you how plainly in the face of a lion, a horse, and an eagle, a man shall descern anger, fierceness, and stoutness; in lambs and doves, simpleness and very innocency; the crafty subtilty in foxes and wolves; and the like, in a manner, in all other living creatures. The foul, therefore, for the most part be also evil, and the beautiful good. Therefore it may be said that beauty is a face pleasant, merry, comely, and to be desired for goodness; and foulness a face dark, uglesome, unpleasant, and to be shunned for ill. And in case you will consider all things, ye shall find that whatsoever is good and profitable hath also evermore the comeliness of beauty. Behold the state of this great engine of the world, which God created for the health and preservation of everything that was made: the heaven round beset with so many heavenly lights; and in the middle the earth invironed with the elements and upheld with the very weight of itself; the sun that, compassing about, giveth light to the whole, and in winter season draweth to the lowermost sign, afterward by little and little climeth again to the other part; the moon, that of him taketh her light, according as she draweth nigh or goeth farther from him; and the other five sters that diversly keep the very same course. These things emong themselves have such force by the knitting together of an order so necessarily framed that, with altering them any one jot, they should all be lewsed and the world would decay. They have also such beauty and comeliness that all the wits men have cannot imagine a more beautiful matter.

"Think now of the shape of man, which may be called a little world, in whom every percel of his body is seen to be necessarily framed by art and not by hap, and then the form altogether most beautiful, so that it were a hard matter to judge whether the members (as the eyes, the nose, the mouth, the ears, the arms, the breast, and in like manner the other parts) give either more profit to the countenance and the rest of the body or comeliness. The like may be said of all other living creatures. Behold the feathers of fowls, the leaves and boughs of trees, which be given them of nature to keep them in their being, and yet have they withal a very great sightliness. Leave nature, and come to art. What thing is so necessary in sailing vessels as the forepart, the sides, the mainyards, the mast, the sails, the stern, oars, anchors, and tacklings? All these things notwithstanding are so well-favored in the eye that unto whoso beholdeth them they seem to have been found out as well for pleasure as for profit. Pillars and great beams uphold high buildings and palaices, and yet are they no less pleasureful unto the eyes of the beholders then profitable to the buildings. When men began first to build, in the middle of temples and

houses they reared the ridge of the roof, not to make the works to have a better show, but bicause the water might the more commodiously avoid on both sides; yet unto profit there was furthwith adjoined a fair sightliness, so that if, under the sky where falleth neither hail nor rain, a man should build a temple without a reared ridge, it is to be thought that it could have neither a sightly show nor any beauty. Beside other things, therefore, it giveth a great praise to the world in saying that it is beautiful. It is praised in saying the beautiful heaven, beautiful earth, beautiful sea, beautiful rivers, beautiful woods, trees, gardeins, beautiful cities, beautiful churches, houses, armies. In conclusion, this comely and holy beauty is a wonderous setting-out of everything. And it may be said that good and beautiful be after a sort one self thing, especially in the bodies of men; of the beauty whereof the nighest cause, I suppose, is the beauty of the soul; the which, as a partner of the right and heavenly beauty, maketh sightly and beautiful whatever she toucheth, and most of all if the body, where she dwelleth, be not of so vile a matter that she cannot imprint in it her property. Therefore beauty is the true monument and spoil of the victory of the soul, whan she with heavenly influence beareth rule over material and gross nature, and with her light overcometh the darkness of the body. It is not, then, to be spoken that beauty maketh women proud or cruel, although it seem so to Master Morello. Neither yet ought beautiful women to bear the blame of that hatred, mortality, and destruction which the unbridled appetites of men are the cause of. I will not now deny that it is possible also to find in the world beautiful women unchaste; yet not bicause beauty inclineth them to unchaste living, for it rather plucketh them from it, and leadeth them into the way of virtuous conditions, through the affinity that beauty hath with goodness; but otherwhile ill bringing-up, the continual provocations of lovers, tokens, poverty, hope, deceits, fear, and a thousand other matters, overcome the steadfastness, yea, of beautiful and good women; and for these and like causes may also beautiful men become wicked."

Then said the Lord Cesar: "In case the Lord Gaspar's saying be true of yesternight, there is no doubt but the fair women be more chaste then the foul."

"And what was my saying?" quoth the Lord Gaspar.

The Lord Cesar answered: "If I do well bear in mind, your saying was that the women that are sued to always refuse to satisfy him that sueth to them, but those that are not sued to sue to others. There is no doubt but the beautiful women have always more suitors, and be more instantly laid at in love, then the foul. Therefore the beautiful always deny, and consequently be more chaste then the foul, which, not being sued to, sue unto others."

Master Peter Bembo laughed, and said: "This argument cannot be answered to." Afterward he proceeded: "It chanceth also, oftentimes, that as the other senses, so the sight is deceived and judgeth a face beautiful which indeed is not beautiful. And bicause in the eyes and in the whole countenance of some women a man beholdeth otherwhile a certain lavish wantonness peincted, with dishonest flickerings, many, whom that manner delighteth bicause it promiseth them an easiness to come by the thing that they covet, call it beauty; but indeed it is a cloaked unshamefastness, unworthy of so honorable and holy a name."

Master Peter Bembo held his peace, and those lords still were earnest upon him to speak somewhat more of this love and of the way to enjoy beauty aright, and at the last: "Methink," quoth he, "I have showed plainly inough that old men may love more happily then young, which was my drift; therefore it belongeth not to me to enter any farther."

Count Lewis answered: "You have better declared the unluckiness of young men then the happiness of old men, whom you have not as yet taught what way they must follow in this love of theirs; only you have said that they must suffer themselves to be guided by reason, and the opinion of many is that it is unpossible for love to stand with reason."

Bembo notwithstanding sought to make an end of reasoning, but the duchess desired him to say on, and he began thus afresh: "Too unlucky were the nature of man, if our soul, in the which this so fervent coveting may lightly arise, should be driven to nourish it with that only which is commune to her with beasts, and could not turn it to the other noble part, which is proper to her. Therefore, since it is so your pleasure, I will not refuse to reason upon this noble matter. And bicause I know myself unworthy to talk of the most holy mysteries of Love, I beseech him to lead my thought and my tongue so that I may show this excellent courtier how to love contrary to the wonted manner of the commune ignorant sort. And even as from my childhood I have dedicated all my whole life unto him, so also now that my words may be answerable to the same intent, and to the praise of him, I say, therefore, that since the nature of man in youthful age is so much inclined to sense, it may be granted the courtier, while he is young, to love sensually; but in case afterward also, in his riper years, he chance to be set on fire with this coveting of love, he ought to be good and circumspect, and heedful that he beguile not himself to be led wilfully into the wretchedness that in young men

deserveth more to be pitied then blamed, and contrariwise in old men, more to be blamed then pitied. Therefore whan an amiable countenance of a beautiful woman cometh in his sight, that is accompanied with noble conditions and honest behaviors, so that, as one practised in love, he wotteth well that his hue hath an agreement with hers, as soon as he is aware that his eyes snatch that image and carry it to the heart, and that the soul beginneth to behold it with pleasure, and feeleth within herself the influence that stirreth her and by little and little setteth her in heat, and that those lively spirits that twinkle out through the eyes put continually fresh nourishment to the fire, he ought in this beginning to seek a speedy remedy and to raise up reason, and with her to fence the fortress of his heart, and to shut in such wise the passages against sense and appetites that they may enter neither with force nor subtil practise. Thus, if the flame be quenched, the jeopardy is also quenched. But in case it continue or encrease, then must the courtier determine, when he perceiveth he is taken, to shun throughly all filthiness of commune love, and so enter into the holy way of love with the guide of reason, and first consider that the body where that beauty shineth is not the fountain from whence beauty springeth, but rather bicause beauty is bodiless and, as we have said, an heavenly shining beam, she loseth much of her honor whan she is coopled with that vile subject and full of corruption, bicause the less she is partner thereof, the more perfect she is, and, clean sund'red from it, is most perfect. And as a man heareth not with his mouth, nor smelleth with his ears, no more can he also in any manner wise enjoy beauty, nor satisfy the desire that she stirreth up in our minds, with feeling, but with the sense unto whom beauty is the very butt to level at, namely, the virtue of seeing. Let him lay aside, therefore, the blind judgment of the sense, and enjoy with his eyes the brightness, the comeliness, the loving sparkles, laughters, gestures, and all the other pleasant fournitours of beauty, especially with hearing the sweetness of her voice, the tunableness of her words, the melody of her singing and playing on instruments (in case the woman beloved be a musician), and so shall he with most dainty food feed the soul through the means of these two senses which have little bodily substance in them and be the ministers of reason, without ent'ring farther toward the body with coveting unto any longing otherwise then honest. Afterward let him obey, please, and honor with all reverence his woman, and reckon her more dear to him then his own life, and prefar all her commodities and pleasures before his own, and love no less in her the beauty of the mind then of the body. Therefore let him have a care not to suffer her to rep into any error, but with lessons and good exhortations seek always to frame her to modesty, to temperance, to true honesty, and so to work that there may never take place in her other then pure thoughts and far wide from all filthiness of vices. And thus in sowing of virtue in the gardein of that mind, he shall also gather the fruits of most beautiful conditions, and savor them with a marvelous good relish. And this shall be the right engend'ring and imprinting of beauty in beauty, the which some hold opinion to be the end of love. In this manner shall our courtier be most acceptable to his lady, and she will always show herself toward him tractable, lowly, and sweet in language, and as willing to please him as to be beloved of him; and the wills of them both shall be most honest and agreeable, and they consequently shall be most happy."

Here Master Morello: "The engend'ring," quoth he, "of beauty in beauty aright were the engend'ring of a beautiful child in a beautiful woman; and I would think it a more manifest token a great deal that she loved her lover if she pleased him with this then with the sweetness of language that you speak of."

Master Peter Bembo laughed, and said: "You must not, Master Morello, pass your bounds. I may tell you it is not a small token that a woman loveth whan she giveth unto her lover her beauty, which is so precious a matter; and by the ways that be a passage to the soul (that is to say, the sight and the hearing) sendeth the looks of her eyes, the image of her countenance, and the voice of her words, that pierce into the lover's heart and give a witness of her love."

Master Morello said: "Looks and words may be, and oftentimes are, false witnesses. Therefore whoso hath not a better pledge of love, in my judgment he is in an ill assurance. And surely I looked still that you would have made this woman of yours somewhat more courteous and free toward the courtier then my Lord Julian hath made his; but meseemeth ye be both of the property of those judges that, to appear wise, give sentence against their own."

Bembo said: "I am well pleased to have this woman much more courteous toward my courtier not young then Lord Julian's is to the young; and that with good reason, bicause mine coveteth but honest matters, and therefore may the woman grant him them all without blame. But my Lord Julian's woman, that is not so assured of the modesty of the young man, ought to grant him the honest matters only, and deny him the dishonest. Therefore more happy is mine, that hath granted him whatsoever he requireth, then the other, that hath part granted and

part denied. And bicause you may moreover the better understand that reasonable love is more happy then sensual, I say unto you that selfsame things in sensual ought to be denied otherwhile, and in reasonable granted; bicause in the one they be honest, and in the other dishonest. Therefore the woman, to please her good lover, beside the granting him merry countenances, familiar and secret talk, jesting, dallying hand-in-hand, may also lawfully and without blame come to kissing, which in sensual love, according to Lord Julian's rules, is not leful. For since a kiss is a knitting together both of body and soul, it is to be feared lest the sensual lover will be more inclined to the part of the body then of the soul; but the reasonable lover wotteth well that although the mouth be a percel of the body, yet is it an issue for the words that be the enterpreters of the soul, and for the inward breath, which is also called the soul; and therefore hath a delight to join his mouth with the woman's beloved with a kiss—not to stir him to any unhonest desire, but bicause he feeleth that that bond is the opening of an entry to the souls, which, drawn with a coveting the one of the other, pour themselves by turn the one into the other's body, and be so mingled together that each of them hath two souls, and one alone so framed of them both ruleth, in a manner, two bodies. Whereupon a kiss may be said to be rather a coopling together of the soul then of the body, bicause it hath such force in her that it draweth her unto it, and, as it were, seperateth her from the body. For this do all chaste lovers covet a kiss as a coopling of souls together. And therefore Plato, the divine lover, saith that in kissing his soul came as far as his lips to depart out of the body. And bicause the separating of the soul from the matters of the sense, and the through coopling her with matters of understanding, may be betokened by a kiss, Salomon saith in his heavenly book of ballats, 'O that he would kiss me with a kiss of his mouth,' to express the desire he had that his soul might be ravished through heavenly love to the beholding of heavenly beauty in such manner that, coopling herself inwardly with it, she might forsake the body."

They stood all herkening heedfully to Bembo's reasoning, and after he had stay'd awhile and saw that none spake, he said: "Since you have made me to begin to show our not young courtier this happy love, I will lead him yet somewhat farther forwards, bicause to stand still at this stay were somewhat perilous for him, considering, as we have oftentimes said, the soul is most inclined to the senses, and for all reason with discourse chooseth well, and knoweth that beauty not to spring of the body, and therefore setteth a bridle to the unhonest desires, yet to behold it always in that body doth oftentimes corrupt the right judgment. And where no other inconvenience insueth upon it, one's absence from the wight beloved carrieth a great passion with it; bicause the influence of that beauty whan it is present giveth a wonderous delight to the lover, and, setting his heart on fire, quickeneth and melteth certain virtues in a trance and congealed in the soul, the which, nourished with the heat of love, flow about and go bubbling nigh the heart, and thrust out through the eyes those spirits which be most fine vapors made of the purest and clearest part of the blood, which receive the image of beauty and deck it with a thousand sundry fournitures. Whereupon the soul taketh a delight, and with a certain wonder is aghast, and yet enjoyeth she it, and, as it were, astonied together with the pleasure, feeleth the fear and reverence that men accustomably have toward holy matters, and thinketh herself to be in paradise. The lover, therefore, that considereth only the beauty in the body, loseth this treasure and happiness as soon as the woman beloved with her departure leaveth the eyes without their brightness, and consequently the soul as a widow without her joy. For since beauty is far off, that influence of love setteth not the heart on fire, as it did in presence. Whereupon the pores be dried up and withered, and yet doth the remembrance of beauty somewhat stir those virtues of the soul in such wise that they seek to scatter abroad the spirits, and they, finding the ways closed up, have no issue, and still they seek to get out, and so with those shootings inclosed prick the soul and torment her bitterly, as young children whan in their tender gums they begin to breed teeth. And hence come the tears, sighs, vexations, and torments of lovers; bicause the soul is always in affliction and travail and, in a manner, wexeth wood, until the beloved beauty cometh before her once again, and then is she immediately pacified and taketh breath, and, throughly bent to it, is nourished with most dainty food, and by her will would never depart from so sweet a sight. To avoid, therefore, the torment of this absence, and to enjoy beauty without passion, the courtier by the help of reason must full and wholly call back again the coveting of the body to beauty alone, and, in what he can, behold it in itself simple and pure, and frame it within his imagination sund'red from all matter, and so make it friendly and loving to his soul, and there enjoy it, and have it with him day and night, in every time and place, without mistrust ever to lose it; keeping always fast in mind that the body is a most diverse thing from beauty, and not only not encreaseth but diminisheth the perfection of it. In this wise shall our not young courtier be out of all

bitterness and wretchedness that young men feel, in a manner continually, as jealousies, suspicions, disdeigns, angers, desperations, and certain rages full of madness, whereby many times they be led into so great error that some do not only beat the women whom they love, but rid themselves out of their life. He shall do no wrong to the husband, father, brethren, or kinsfolk of the woman beloved. He shall not bring her in sclander. He shall not be in case with much ado otherwhile to refrain his eyes and tongue from discovering his desires to others. He shall not take thought at departure or in absence, bicause he shall evermore carry his precious treasure about with him shut fast within his heart. And beside, through the virtue of imagination, he shall fashion within himself that beauty much more fair then it is indeed. But emong these commodities the lover shall find another yet far greater, in case he will take this love for a stair, as it were, to clime up to another far higher then it. The which he shall bring to pass, if he will go and consider with himself what a streict bond it is to be always in the trouble to behold the beauty of one body alone. And therefore, to come out of this so narrow a room, he shall gather in his thought by little and little so many ornaments that meddling all beauties together he shall make an universal concept, and bring the multitude of them to the unity of one alone, that is generally spread over all the nature of man. And thus shall he behold no more the particular beauty of one woman, but an universal that decketh out all bodies. Whereupon, being made dim with this greater light, he shall not pass upon the lesser, and, burning in a more excellent flame, he shall little esteem it that he set great store by at the first. This stair of love, though it be very noble and such as few arrive at it, yet is it not in this sort to be called perfect, forsomuch as where the imagination is of force to make conveyance and hath no knowledge but through those beginnings that the senses help her withal, she is not clean purged from gross darkness; and therefore, though she do consider that universal beauty in sunder and in itself alone, yet doth she not well and clearly descern it, nor without some doubtfulness, by reason of the agreement that the fancies have with the body. Wherefore such as come to this love are like young birds almost flush, which for all they flitter a little their tender wings, yet dare they not stray far from the nest, nor commit theimselves to the wind and open weather. Whan our courtier, therefore, shall be come to this point, although he may be called a good and happy lover, in respect of them that be drowned in the misery of sensual love, yet will I not have him to set his heart at rest, but boldly proceed farther, following the highway after his guide, that leadeth him to the point of true happiness. And thus, instead of going out of his wit with thought, as he must do that will consider the bodily beauty, he may come into his wit to behold the beauty that is seen with the eyes of the mind, which then begin to be sharp and thorough-seeing whan the eyes of the body lose the flour of their sightliness.

"Therefore the soul, rid of vices, purged with the studies of true philosophy, occupied in spiritual, and exercised in matters of understanding, turning her to the beholding of her own substance, as it were raised out of a most deep sleep, openeth the eyes that all men have and few occupy, and seeth in herself a shining beam of that light which is the true image of the angel-like beauty partened with her, whereof she also part'neth with the body a feeble shadow; therefore, wexed blind about earthly matters, is made most quick of sight about heavenly. And otherwhile whan the stirring virtues of the body are withdrawn alone through earnest beholding, either fast bound through sleep, whan she is not hind'red by them, she feeleth a certain prevy smell of the right angel-like beauty, and, ravished with the shining of that light, beginneth to be inflamed, and so greedily followeth after that in a manner she wexeth drunken and beside herself, for coveting to coople herself with it, having found, to her wening, the footsteps of God, in the beholding of whom, as in her happy end, she seeketh to settle herself. And therefore, burning in this most happy flame, she ariseth to the noblest part of her, which is the understanding, and there, no more shadowed with the dark night of earthly matters, seeth the heavenly beauty; but yet doth she not for all that enjoy it altogether perfectly, bicause she beholdeth it only in her perticular understanding, which cannot conceive the passing great universal beauty; whereupon, not throughly satisfied with this benefit, love giveth unto the soul a greater happiness. For like as through the perticular beauty of one body he guideth her to the universal beauty of all bodies, even so in the last degree of perfection through perticular understanding he guideth her to the universal understanding. Thus the soul kindled in the most holy fire of true heavenly love fleeth to coople herself with the nature of angels, and not only clean forsaketh sense, but hath no more need of the discourse of reason, for, being changed into an angel, she understandeth all things that may be understood; and without any veil or cloud she seeth the main sea of the pure heavenly beauty, and receiveth it into her, and enjoyeth that sovereign happiness that cannot be comprehended of the senses. Since, therefore, the beauties which we daily see with these our dim eyes in bodies subject to corruption, that nevertheless be nothing else but dreams and most thin shadows of beauty, seem unto us so well-favored and comely that oftentimes they kendle in us a most burning fire, and with such delight that we reckon no happiness may be compared to it that we feel otherwhile through the only look which the beloved countenance of a woman casteth at us; what happy wonder, what blessed abashment, may we reckon that to be that taketh the souls which come to have a sight of the heavenly beauty? What sweet flame, what soote incense, may a man believe that to be which ariseth of the fountain of the sovereign and right beauty? Which is the origin of all other beauty, which never encreaseth nor diminisheth, always beautiful, and of itself, as well on the one part as on the other, most simple, only like itself, and partner of none other, but in such wise beautiful that all other beautiful things be beautiful because they be partners of the beauty of it.

"This is the beauty unseperable from the high bounty which with her voice calleth and draweth to her all things; and not only to the indowed with understanding giveth understanding, to the reasonable reason, to the sensual sense and appetite to live, but also partaketh with plants and stones, as a print of herself, stirring, and the natural provocation of their properties. So much, therefore, is this love greater and happier then others as the cause that stirreth it is more excellent. And therefore, as commune fire trieth gold and maketh it fine, so this most holy fire in souls destroyeth and consumeth whatsoever there is mortal in them, and relieveth and maketh beautiful the heavenly part, which at the first by reason of the sense was dead and buried in them. This is the great fire in the which, the poets write, that Hercules was burned on the top of the montaigne Oeta, and, through that consuming with fire, after his death was holy and immortal. This is the fiery bush of Moses; the divided tongues of fire; the inflamed chariot of Helias; which doobleth grace and happiness in their souls that be worthy to see it, whan they forsake this earthly baseness and flee up into heaven. Let us, therefore, bend all our force and thoughts of soul to this most holy light, that showeth us the way which leadeth to heaven; and after it, putting off the affections we were clad withal at our coming down, let us clime up the stairs which at the lowermost step have the shadow of sensual beauty, to the high mansion-place where the heavenly, amiable, and right beauty dwelleth, which lieth hid in the innermost secrets of God, lest unhallowed eyes should come to the sight of it; and there shall we find a most happy end for our desires, true rest for our travails, certain remedy for miseries, a most healthful medicine for sickness, a most sure haven in the troublesome storms of the tempestuous sea of this life.

"What tongue mortal is there then, O most holy love, that can sufficiently praise thy worthiness? Thou most beautiful, most good, most wise, art derived of the unity of heavenly beauty, goodness, and wisdom, and therein dost thou abide, and unto it through it, as in a circle, turnest about. Thou the most sweet bond of the world, a mean betwext heavenly and earthly things, with a bountiful temper bendest the high virtues to the government of the lower, and turning back the minds of mortal men to their beginning, cooplest them with it. Thou with agreement bringest the elements in one, stirrest nature to bring furth and that which ariseth and is born for the succession of the life. Thou bringest severed matters into one, to the unperfect givest perfection, to the unlike likeness, to enimity amity, to the earth fruits, to the sea calmness, to the heaven lively light. Thou art the father of true pleasures, of grace, peace, lowliness, and good will, enemy to rude wildness and sluggishness—to be short, the beginning and end of all goodness. And forsomuch as thou delightest to dwell in the flour of beautiful bodies and beautiful souls, I suppose that thy abiding-place is now here emong us, and from above otherwhile showest thyself a little to the eyes and minds of them that be worthy to see thee. Therefore vouchsafe, Lord, to harken to our prayers, pour thyself into our hearts, and with the brightness of thy most holy fire lighten our darkness, and, like a trusty guide in this blind maze, show us the right way; reform the falsehood of the senses, and after long wand'ring in vanity give us the right and sound joy. Make us to smell those spiritual savors that relieve the virtues of the understanding, and to hear the heavenly harmony so tunable that no discord of passion take place any more in us. Make us drunken with the bottomless fountain of contentation that always doth delight and never giveth fill, and that giveth a smack of the right bliss unto whoso drinketh of the renning and clear water thereof. Purge with the shining beams of thy light our eyes from misty ignorance, that they may no more set by mortal beauty, and well perceive that the things which at the first they thought themselves to see be not indeed, and those that they saw not to be in effect. Accept our souls that be off'red unto thee for a sacrifice. Burn them in the lively flame that wasteth all gross filthiness, that after they be clean sund'red from the body they may be copled with an everlasting and most sweet bond to the heavenly beauty. And we, severed from ourselves, may be changed like right lovers into the beloved, and, after we be drawn from the earth, admitted to the feast of the angels, where, fed with im-

mortal ambrosia and nectar, in the end we may die a most happy and lively death, as in times past died the fathers of old time, whose souls with most fervent zeal of beholding thou diddest hale from the body and coopledst them with God."

When Bembo had hitherto spoken with such vehemency that a man would have thought him, as it were, ravished and beside himself, he stood still without once moving, holding his eyes toward heaven as astonied, whan the Lady Emilia, which together with the rest gave most diligent ear to this talk, took him by the plait of his garment and plucking him a little, said: "Take heed, Master Peter, that these thoughts make not your soul also to forsake the body."

"Madam," answered Master Peter, "it should not be the first miracle that love hath wrought in me."

Then the duchess and all the rest began afresh to be instant upon Master Bembo that he would proceed once more in his talk, and every one thought he felt in his mind, as it were, a certain sparkle of that godly love that pricked him, and they all coveted to hear farther; but Master Bembo: "My lords," quoth he, "I have spoken what the holy fury of love hath, unsought for, indited to me; now that, it seemeth, he inspireth me no more, I wot not what to say. And I think verily that love will not have his secrets discovered any farther, nor that the courtier should pass the degree that his pleasure is I should show him, and therefore it is not perhaps leful to speak any more in this matter."

"Surely," quoth the duchess, "if the not young courtier be such a one that he can follow this way which you have showed him, of right he ought to be satisfied with so great a happiness, and not to envy the younger."

Then the Lord Cesar Gonzaga: "The way," quoth he, "that leadeth to this happiness is so steep, in my mind, that I believe it will be much ado to get to it."

The Lord Gaspar said: "I believe it be hard to get up for men, but unpossible for women."

The Lady Emilia laughed, and said: "If ye fall so often to offend us, I promise you you shall be no more forgiven."

The Lord Gaspar answered: "It is no offense to you in saying that women's souls be not so purged from passions as men's be, nor accustomed in beholdings, as Master Peter hath said is necessary for them to be that will taste of the heavenly love. Therefore it is not read that ever woman hath had this grace; but many men have had it, as Plato, Socrates, Plotinus, and many other, and a number of our holy fathers, as Saint Francis, in whom a fervent spirit of love imprinted the most holy seal of the five wounds. And nothing but the virtue of love could hale up

Saint Paul the apostle to the sight of those secrets which is not lawful for man to speak of; nor show Saint Stephan the heavens open."

Here answered the Lord Julian: "In this point men shall nothing pass women, for Socrates himself doth confess that all the mysteries of love which he knew were oped unto him by a woman, which was Diotima. And the angel that with the fire of love imprinted the five wounds in Saint Francis hath also made some women worthy of the same print in our age. You must remember, moreover, that Saint Mary Magdalen had many faults forgeven her, bicause she loved much; and perhaps with no less grace then Saint Paul was she many times through angelic love haled up to the third heaven. And many other, as I showed you yesterday more at large, that for love of the name of Christ have not passed upon life, nor feared torments, nor any other kind of death how terrible and cruel ever it were. And they were not, as Master Peter will have his courtier to be, aged, but soft and tender maidens, and in the age when he saith that sensual love ought to be borne withal in men."

The Lord Gaspar began to prepare himself to speak, but the duchess: "Of this," quoth she, "let Master Peter be judge, and the matter shall stand to his verdit, whether women be not as meet for heavenly love as men. But bicause the plead between you may happen be too long, it shall not be amiss to defer it until tomorrow."

"Nay, tonight," quoth the Lord Cesar Gonzaga.

"And how can it be tonight?" quoth the duchess.

The Lord Cesar answered: "Bicause it is day already," and showed her the light that began to enter in at the clifts of the windows. Then every man arose upon his feet with much wonder, because they had not thought that the reasonings had lasted lenger then the accustomed wont, saving only that they were begun much later, and with their pleasantness had deceived so the lords' minds that they wist not of the going away of the hours. And not one of them felt any heaviness of sleep in his eyes, the which often happeneth whan a man is up after his accustomed hour to go to bed. Whan the windows then were opened on the side of the palaice that hath his prospect toward the high top of Mount Catri, they saw already risen in the east a fair morning like unto the color of roses, and all stars voided, saving only the sweet governess of the heaven, Venus, which keepeth the bounds of the night and the day, from which appeared to blow a sweet blast that, filling the air with a biting cold, began to quicken the tunable notes of the pretty birds emong the hushing woods of the hills at hand. Whereupon they all, taking their leave with reverence of the duchess, departed toward their lodgings without torch, the light of the day sufficing.

And as they were now passing out at the great chamber door, the lord general turned him to the duchess and said: "Madam, to take up the variance between the Lord Gaspar and the Lord Julian, we will assemble this night with the judge sooner then we did yesterday."

The Lady Emilia answered: "Upon condition that in case my Lord Gaspar will accuse women, and geve them, as his wont is, some false report, he will also put us in surety to stand to trial, for I reckon him a wavering starter."

A LETTER OF SIR J[OHN] CHEKE'S TO HIS LOVING FRIEND MAISTER THOMAS HOBY

For your opinion of my good will unto you as you writ, you cannot be deceived; for submitting your doings to my judgment, I thank you; for taking this pain of your translation, you worthily deserve great thanks of all sorts. I have taken some pain at your request chiefly in your preface, not in the reading of it (for that was pleasant unto me both for the roundness of your sayings and well-speakings of the same) but in changing certain words which might very well be let alone, but that I am very curious, in my friends' matters, not to determine but to debate what is best. Wherein I seek not the bestness haply by truth, but by mine own phancy and shew of goodness.

I am of this opinion, that our own tongue should be written clean and pure, unmix'd and unmangeled with borrowing of other tongues, wherein if we take not heed by time, ever borrowing and never paying, she shall be fain to keep her house as bankrupt. For then doth our tongue naturally and praisably utter her meaning when she borroweth no counterfeitness of other tongues to attire herself withal, but useth plainly her own, with such shift as nature, craft, experience, and following of other excellent doth lead her unto; and if she want at any time (as being unperfight she must), yet let her borrow with such bashfulness that it may appear that if either the mold of our own tongue could serve us to fashion a word of our own, or if the old denisoned words could content and ease this need, we would not boldly venture of unknown words. This I say not for reproof of you, who have scarcely and necessarily used where occasion serveth a strange word so as it seemeth to grow out of the matter and not to be sought for, but for mine own defense, who might be counted overstraight a deemer of things if I gave not this accompt to you, my friend and wise, of my marring this your handiwork. But I am called away; I pray you pardon my shortness; the rest of my sayings should be but praise and exhortation in this your doings, which at more leisure I should do better. From my house in Woodstreet, the 16 of July, 1557.

Yours assured,
John Cheke

ARTHUR GOLDING (trans.)

OVID'S *METAMORPHOSES*

There is a certain irony in the fact that Arthur Golding, a landed, well-connected puritan of the sternest piety, should be remembered mainly for his translation of the licentious Ovid. As a man of property and solid learning, a half-uncle of Edward de Vere, seventeenth Earl of Oxford, and a friend of such notables as Burghley, Sidney, Sir Walter Mildmay, Sir Christopher Hatton, and Archbishop Grindal, he moved in high circles and boasted himself a "gentleman." Most of his many translations were of authors befitting a person of his gravity, his reputation, and his flinty Calvinist principles. He published English versions of Caesar's *Commentaries* (1565), Beza's *Book of Christian Questions and Answers* (1572), Seneca's *Concerning Benefiting* (1578), Jacques Hurault's *Politic, Moral, and Martial Discourses* (1595), as well as a whole swarm of Calvin's treatises—among others, his *Little Book Concerning Offenses* (1567), his commentaries on the Psalms (1571), and his sermons on Galatians (1574), Job (1574), Ephesians (1577), and Deuteronomy (1583). Moreover, Golding was commissioned by Sidney, departing on his fatal expedition to the Low Countries, to finish the partial translation of Philippe de Mornay's *Work Concerning the Trueness of the Christian Religion* which the young courtier and his sister had been working on with characteristic piety. The volume duly appeared in 1587, a year after Sidney's untimely death. Of all the nearly two dozen translations attributed to Golding, however, the one on which his contemporary fame and his posthumous reputation securely rest is that of Ovid's *Metamorphoses*. The *First Four Books* was published, with a long verse-epistle to the Earl of Leicester, in 1565, and all fifteen books followed two years later. The epistle is interesting not only as an elaborate critical and exegetical account of the *Metamorphoses* but as a laborious defense—by a puritan who conventionally denounced stage plays on the Sabbath—of erotic pagan poetry in terms of its moral allegory. In its plodding fourteener couplets Golding's Ovid is often flat, sometimes energetic, and occasionally even poetic; but the prevailing impression is one of competent mediocrity. If he rises to no great height, neither does he fall into bathos, and at least until George Sandys' translation (1626) Golding and Ovid were virtually synonymous to generations of English readers, including, of course, Shakespeare. Our text is based upon *The .XV. Bookes of P. Ouidius Naso, entytuled Metamorphosis, translated oute of Latin into English meeter, by Arthur Golding Gentleman, A worke very pleasaunt and delectable*, 1567 (STC 18956).

FROM THE FIFTEEN BOOKS OF P. OVIDIUS NASO ENTITULED METAMORPHOSIS (1567)

To the Right Honorable and His Singular Good Lord, Robert, Earl of Leicester . . .
Arthur Golding, Gentleman, Wisheth Continuance of Health, with Prosperous Estate and Felicity

At length my chariot wheel about the mark hath found the way,
And at their weary race's end my breathless horses stay.
The work is brought to end by which the author did account
(And rightly) with eternal fame above the stars to mount.

For whatsoever hath been writ of ancient time in Greek
By sundry men dispersedly, and in the Latin eke,
Of this same <u>dark philosophy</u> of turned shapes, the same
Hath Ovid into one whole mass in this book brought in frame.
Four kind of things in this his work the poet doth contain:
That nothing under heaven doth ay in steadfast state remain;   10
And next that nothing perisheth, <u>but that each substance takes</u>
<u>Another shape than that it had.</u> Of theis two points he makes
The proof by shewing through his work the wonderful exchange
Of gods, men, beasts, and elements to sundry shapes right strange,
Beginning with creation of the world and man of slime,
And so proceeding with the turns that happened till his time.
Then sheweth he the soul of man from dying to be free
By samples of the noblemen who for their virtues be
Accounted and canonized for gods by heathen men,
And by the pains of Limbo lake and blissful state agen   20
Of spirits in th' Elysian Fields. And though that of theis three
He make discourse dispersedly, yit specially they be
Discussed in the latter book in that oration where
He bringeth in Pythagoras dissuading men from fear
Of death and preaching abstinence from flesh of living things.
But as for that opinion which Pythagoras there brings
Of souls removing out of beasts to men, and out of men
To birds and beasts both wild and tame, both to and fro agen,
It is not to be understand of that same soul whereby
We are endu'd with reason and discretion from on high,   30
But of that soul or life the which brute beasts as well as we
Enjoy. Three sorts of life or soul (for so they termed be)
Are found in things. The first gives pow'r to thrive, encrease, and grow,
And this in senseless herbs and trees and shrubs itself doth show.
The second giveth pow'r to move and use of senses five,
And this remains in brutish beasts and keepeth them alive.
Both theis are mortal, as the which received of the air
By force of Phoebus after death do thither eft repair.
The third gives understanding, wit, and reason; and the same
Is it alonely which with us of soul doth bear the name.   40
And as the second doth contain the first, even so the third
Containeth both the other twain. And neither beast nor bird
Nor fish nor herb nor tree nor shrub nor any earthly wight—
Save only man—can of the same partake the heavenly might.
I grant that when our breath doth from our bodies go away
It doth eftsoons return to air, and of that air there may
Both bird and beast participate, and we of theirs likewise.
For while we live—the thing itself appeareth to our eyes—
Both they and we draw all one breath. But for to deem or say
Our noble soul (which is divine and permanent for ay)   50
Is common to us with the beasts, I think it nothing less
Than for to be a point of him that wisdom doth profess.
Of this I am right well assur'd: there is no Christen wight
That can by fondness be so far seduced from the right.
And finally he doth proceed in shewing that not all
That bear the name of men (how strong, fierce, stout, bold, hardy, tall,
How wise, fair, rich, or highly born, how much renown'd by fame
Soe'er they be, although on earth of gods they bear the name)
Are for to be accounted men; but such as under awe

Of reason's rule continually do live in virtue's law;   60
And that the rest do differ nought from beasts, but rather be
Much worse than beasts bicause they do abase their own degree.
To natural philosophy the formest three pertain,
The fourth to moral, and in all are pithy, apt, and plain
Instructions which import the praise of virtues and the shame
Of vices, with the due rewards of either of the same. . . .

[After summarizing the fifteen books of the *Metamorphoses* Golding
seeks to establish a fundamental harmony between Ovid's pagan poetry
and the Bible. Ending a long and knotty comparison between Ovid
(and his sources) and Genesis, he concludes:]

If any man will say theis things may better learned be
Out of divine philosophy or Scripture, I agree
That nothing may in worthiness with Holy Writ compare.
Howbeit, so farforth as things no whit impeachment are   70
To virtue and to godliness, but furtherers of the same,
I trust we may them savely use without desert of blame.
And yet there are (and those not of the rude and vulgar sort,
But such as have of godliness and learning good report)
That think the poets took their first occasion of theis things
From Holy Writ as from the well from whence all wisdom springs.
What man is he but would suppose the author of this book
The first foundation of his work from Moses' writings took?
Not only in effect he doth with Genesis agree,
But also in the order of creation, save that he   80
Makes no distinction of the days. For what is else at all
That shapeless, rude, and pest'red heap which Chaos he doth call
Than even that universal mass of things which God did make
In one whole lump before that each their proper place did take,
Of which the Bible saith that in the first beginning God
Made heaven and earth. . . ?
Consid'ring, then, of things before rehears'd the whole effect,
I trust there is already shew'd sufficient to detect
That poets took the ground of all their chiefest fables out
Of Scripture, which they, shadowing with their gloses, went about   90
To turn the truth to toys and lies. And of the selfsame rate
Are also theis: their Phlegeton, their Styx, their blissful state
Of spirits in th' Elysian Fields. Of which the former twain
Seem counterfetted of the place where damned souls remain,
Which we call hell. The third doth seem to fetch his pedegree
From paradise, which Scripture shews a place of bliss to be.
If poets, then, with leesings and with fables shadowed so
The certain truth, what letteth us to pluck those visers fro
Their doings and to bring again the darkened truth to light,
That all men may behold thereof the clearness shining bright?   100
The readers therefore earnestly admonish'd are to be
To seek a further meaning than the letter gives to see.
The travail ta'en in that behalf, although it have some pain,
Yit makes it double recompence with pleasure and with gain:
With pleasure for variety and strangeness of the things,
With gain for good instruction which the understanding brings.
And if they, happening for to meet with any wanton word
Or matter lewd, according as the person doth avoord
In whom the evil is describ'd, do feel their minds thereby
Provok'd to vice and wantoness (as nature commonly   110

Is prone to evil), let them thus imagine in their mind:
"Behold, by scent of reason and by perfect sight I find
A panther here whose painted coat with yellow spots like gold
And pleasant smell allure mine eyes and senses to behold.
But well I know his face is grim and fierce, which he doth hide
To this intent, that while I thus stand gazing on his hide
He may devour me unbewares." Ne let them more offend
At vices in this present work in lively colors penn'd
Than if that in a crystal glass foul images they found,
Resembling folks' foul visages that stand about it round.   120
For sure theis fables are not put in writing to th' entent
To further or allure to vice, but rather this is meant,
That men, beholding what they be when vice doth reign instead
Of virtue, should not let their lewd affections have the head.
For as there is no creature more divine than man as long
As reason hath the sovereignty and standeth firm and strong,
So is there none more beastly, vile, and devilish than is he
If reason, giving over, by affection mated be.
The use of this same book, therefore, is this: that every man,
Endeavoring for to know himself as nearly as he can,   130
As though he in a chariot sate well-ordered, should direct
His mind by reason in the way of virtue, and correct
His fierce affections with the bit of temp'rance, lest perchance
They, taking bridle in the teeth like wilful jades, do prance
Away and headlong carry him to every filthy pit
Of vice, and drinking of the same defile his soul with it;
Or else do headlong harry him upon the rocks of sin
And, overthrowing forcibly the chariot he sits in,
Do tear him worse than ever was Hippolytus, the son
Of Theseus, when he went about his father's wrath to shun.   140
This worthy work, in which of good examples are so many,
This orchard of Alcinous in which there wants not any
Herb, tree, or fruit that may man's use for health or pleasure serve,
This plenteous horn of Acheloy which justly doth deserve
To bear the name of treasury of knowledge I present
To your good lordship once again not as a member rent
Or parted from the res'due of the body any more,
But fully now accomplished, desiring you therefore
To let your noble courtesy and favor countervail
My faults where art or eloquence on my behalf doth fail,   150
For sure the mark whereat I shoot is neither wreaths of bay
Nor name of poet, no, nor meed, but chiefly that it may
Be liked well of you and all the wise and learned sort,
And next that every wight that shall have pleasure for to sport
Him in this gardein may as well bear wholesome fruit away
As only on the pleasant flow'rs his rechless senses stay.
But why seem I theis doubts to cast, as if that he who took
With favor and with gentleness a parcel of the book
Would not likewise accept the whole? Or even as if that they
Who do excel in wisdom and in learning would not weigh   160
A wise and learned work aright? Or else as if that I
Ought ay to have a special care how all men do apply
My doings to their own behoof? As of the former twain
I have great hope and confidence, so would I also fain
The other should according to good meaning find success.

If otherwise, the fault is theirs, not mine, they must confess.
And therefore briefly to conclude, I turn again to thee,
O noble Earl of Leicester, whose life God grant may be
As long in honor, health, and wealth as ancient Nestor's was,
Or rather as Tithonus's, that all such students as   170
Do travail to enrich our tong with knowledge heretofore
Not common to our vulgar speech may daily more and more
Proceed through thy good furtherance and favor in the same
To all men's profit and delight and thy eternal fame,
And that—which is a greater thing—our native country may
Long time enjoy thy counsel and thy travail to her stay.

> At Barwick the twentieth of April, 1567.

> Your good lordship's most humbly to command,
> Arthur Golding

The Fourth Book

. . . Within the town (of whose huge walls so monstrous high and thick
The fame is given Semiramis for making them of brick)
Dwelt hard together two young folk in houses join'd so near
That under all one roof well nigh both twain conveyed were.
The name of him was Pyramus, and Thisbe call'd was she.
So fair a man in all the East was none alive as he,
Nor ne'er a woman, maid, nor wife in beauty like to her.
This neighbrod bred acquaintance first, this neighbrod first did stir
The secret sparks, this neighbrod first an entrance in did show
For love to come to that to which it afterward did grow.   10
And if that right had taken place they had been man and wife,
But still their parents went about to let which (for their life)
They could not let. For both their hearts with equal flame did burn.
No man was privy to their thoughts. And for to serve their turn
Instead of talk they used signs; the closelier they suppress'd
The fire of love the fiercer still it raged in their breast.
The wall that parted house from house had riven therein a crany
Which shronk at making of the wall; this fault not mark'd of any
Of many hundred years before (what doth not love espy?)
These lovers first of all found out and made a way whereby   20
To talk togither secretly, and through the same did go
Their loving whisp'rings very light and safely to and fro.
Now as at one side Pyramus and Thisbe on the tother
Stood often drawing one of them the pleasant breath from other,
"O thou envious wall," they said, "why let'st thou lovers thus?
What matter were it if that thou permitted both of us
In arms each other to embrace? Or if thou think that this
Were overmuch, yet mightest thou at least make room to kiss.
And yet thou shalt not find us churls. We think ourselves in debt
For this same piece of courtesy, in vouching safe to let   30
Our sayings to our friendly ears thus freely come and go."
Thus having where they stood in vain complained of their wo,
When night drew near they bad adieu and each gave kisses sweet
Unto the parget on their side, the which did never meet.
Next morning with her cheerful light had driven the stars aside,
And Phebus with his burning beams the dewy grass had dry'd,
These lovers at their wonted place by foreappointment met,
Where, after much complaint and moan, they covenanted to get

Away from such as watched them and in the evening late
To steal out of their fathers' house and eke the city gate,   40
And to th' entent that in the fields they stray'd not up and down
They did agree at Ninus' tomb to meet without the town,
And tarry underneath a tree that by the same did grow
Which was a fair high mulberry with fruit as white as snow,
Hard by a cool and trickling spring. This bargain pleas'd them both,
And so daylight (which to their thought away but slowly go'th)
Did in the ocean fall to rest, and night from thence doth rise.
As soon as darkness once was come, straight Thisbe did devise
A shift to wind her out of doors, that none that were within
Perceived her, and muffling her with cloths about her chin   50
That no man might discern her face, to Ninus' tomb she came
Unto the tree, and sat her down there underneath the same.
Love made her bold. But see the chance: there comes besmear'd with blood
About the chaps a lioness all foaming from the wood,
From slaughter lately made of kine to stanch her bloody thirst
With water of the foresaid spring. Whom Thisbe, spying first
Afar by moonlight, thereupon with fearful steps gan fly,
And in a dark and irksome cave did hide herself thereby.
And as she fled away for haste she let her mantle fall,
The which for fear she left behind, not looking back at all.   60
Now when the cruel lioness her thirst had stanched well,
In going to the wood she found the slender weed that fell
From Thisbe, which with bloody teeth in pieces she did tear.
The night was somewhat further spent ere Pyramus came there,
Who, seeing in the subtle sand the print of lion's paw,
Wax'd pale for fear. But when also the bloody cloak he saw
All rent and torn, "One night," he said, "shall lovers two confound,
Of which long life deserved she of all that live on ground.
My soul deserves of this mischance the peril for to bear.
I, wretch, have been the death of thee which to this place of fear   70
Did cause thee in the night to come and came not here before.
My wicked limbs and wretched guts with cruel teeth therefore
Devour ye, O ye lions all that in this rock do dwell!
But cowards use to wish for death." The slender weed that fell
From Thisbe up he takes, and straight doth bear it to the tree
Which was appointed erst the place of meeting for to be.
And when he had bewept and kiss'd the garment which he knew,
"Receive thou my blood too," quoth he, and therewithal he drew
His sword, the which among his guts he thrust, and by and by
Did draw it from the bleeding wound beginning for to die,   80
And cast himself upon his back. The blood did spin on high,
As when a conduit pipe is crack'd, the water bursting out
Doth shoot itself a great way off and pierce the air about.
The leaves that were upon the tree besprinkled with his blood
Were dyed black. The root also bestained as it stood,
A deep dark purple color straight upon the berries cast.
Anon, scarce ridded of her fear with which she was aghast,
For doubt of disappointing him comes Thisbe forth in haste,
And for her lover looks about, rejoicing for to tell
How hardly she had scap'd that night the danger that befell.   90
And as she knew right well the place and fashion of the tree
(As which she saw so late before), even so when she did see
The color of the berries turn'd she was uncertain whither

It were the tree at which they both agreed to meet togither.
While in this doubtful stound she stood she cast her eye aside
And there bewelt'red in his blood her lover she espy'd
Lie sprawling with his dying limbs. At which she started back
And looked pale as any box. A shudd'ring through her strack
Even like the sea which sodenly with whissing noise doth move
When with a little blast of wind it is but touch'd above.   100
But when, approaching nearer him, she knew it was her love
She beat her breast, she shricked out, she tare her golden hears,
And taking him between her arms did wash his wounds with tears.
She meynt her weeping with his blood, and kissing all his face
(Which now became as cold as ice) she cry'd in woful case,
"Alas, what chance, my Pyramus, hath parted thee and me?
Make answer, O my Pyramus, it is thy Thisb, even she
Whom thou dost love most heartily that speaketh unto thee.
Give ear and raise thy heavy head!" He, hearing Thisbe's name,
Lift up his dying eyes and, having seen her, clos'd the same.   110
But when she knew her mantle there and saw his scabberd lie
Without the sword, "Unhappy man, thy love hath made thee die!
Thy love," she said, "hath made thee slay thyself. This hand of mine
Is strong inough to do the like. My love no less than thine
Shall give me force to work my wound. I will pursue thee dead,
And, wretched woman as I am, it shall of me be said
That like as of thy death I was the only cause and blame
So am I thy companion eke and partner in the same,
For death, which only could, alas, asunder part us twain,
Shall never so dissever us but we will meet again.   120
And you, the parents of us both, most wretched folk alive,
Let this request that I shall make in both our names bylive
Entreat you to permit that we whom chaste and steadfast love
And whom even death hath join'd in one may, as it doth behove,
In one grave be together laid. And thou, unhappy tree,
Which shroudest now the corse of one and shalt anon through me
Shroud two, of this same slaughter hold the sicker signs for ay.
Black be the color of thy fruit and mourning-like alway,
Such as the murder of us twain may evermore bewray."
This said, she took the sword yet warm with slaughter of her love,   130
And setting it beneath her breast did to her heart it shove.
Her prayer with the gods and with their parents took effect,
For when the fruit is throughly ripe the berry is bespeck'd
With color tending to a black. And that which after fire
Remained rested in one tomb as Thisbe did desire. . . .

SIR THOMAS NORTH (trans.)

PLUTARCH'S *LIVES*

The *Parallel Lives,* since the Renaissance one of the most popular and influential of all the literary legacies of antiquity, appears to have been written during Plutarch's later years in his native Chaeronea, a Boeotian village, after his return from Rome, where his lectures on rhetoric and philosophy had earned for him consular rank from the Emperor Trajan. Although the work was perhaps begun as merely a gallery of biographical sketches, the notion of coupling a Grecian with a Roman celebrity in "parallel lives" is described (and the title itself used) in the dedication (to Sosius Senecio) of "Theseus" and "Romulus." None the less, it is by no means certain that Plutarch himself consistently carried out the parallelism, even though in all modern editions most of the lives (for example, "Lycurgus" and "Numa," "Solon" and "Publicola") are arranged so as to compare and contrast the careers of eminent legislators, statesmen, warriors, and the like. Of the fifty lives generally accepted as authentic only four (those of Artaxerxes, Aratus of Sicyon, Galba, and Otho) are single biographies.

No man was ever more fortunate in his translators than Plutarch, for the popularity of the *Parallel Lives* is largely attributable to a couple of happy accidents—the wonderful French version (1559) of Jacques Amyot and then the translation (1579) of the French into the vigorous and supple English of Sir Thomas North. The fact that North occasionally corrects or amplifies Amyot's version permits the inference that he had the Greek (or perhaps a Latin translation) before him, but Amyot was his principal source, and his great work is actually a translation of a translation. Thanks to its incomparable prose, it is also one of the noblest products of the Tudor age. North's translation became a revered textbook of political wisdom, a storehouse of classical lore, and, most important, the indispensable source for three of Shakespeare's ripest plays (*Antony and Cleopatra, Coriolanus,* and *Julius Caesar*) as well as a contributing source for two others (*A*

Midsummer-Night's Dream and *Timon of Athens*). Rarely has one great writer so closely followed another, and it is North's highest praise that the greatest of all writers was indebted to him not only for facts but also for words, phrases, and even whole passages.

The first edition (which Thomas Vautrollier put forth in two issues) in 1579 was not followed by another until 1595. In 1602, however, there appeared a collection of fifteen new biographies (*The Lives of Epaminondas, of Philip of Macedon* . . .) allegedly translated by North from Aemilius Probus (that is, Cornelius Nepos); and this work in the following year became the second part of a two-part edition of the *Lives* printed three times by Richard Field. Another two-part edition followed in 1610 and 1612, and still another in 1631. According to Anthony Wood, the learned John Selden had a hand in the editions of 1631 and 1657, and the last complete edition (before our day) appeared in 1676. Thereafter, although Englishmen continued to read Plutarch's *Lives,* they usually followed the translation superintended by Dryden (1683–86) or that of John and William Langhorne (1770).

Our text is based upon *The Lives of the Noble Grecians and Romanes . . . Translated out of Greeke into French by Iames Amyot . . . and out of French into Englishe, by Thomas North,* 1579 (STC 20065).

FROM THE LIVES OF THE NOBLE GRECIANS AND ROMANS COMPARED TOGETHER BY . . . PLUTARCH OF CHAERONEA, TRANSLATED OUT OF GREEK INTO FRENCH BY JAMES AMYOT . . . AND OUT OF FRENCH INTO ENGLISH BY THOMAS NORTH (1579)

To the Most High and Mighty Princess Elizabeth, by the Grace of God of England, France, and Ireland Queen, Defender of the Faith, etc.

Under hope of your Highness' gratious and accustomed favor, I have presumed to present here unto your Majesty Plutarch's *Lives* translated as a book fit to be protected by your Highness and meet to be set forth in English. For who is fitter to give countenance to so many great states than such an high and mighty princess? Who is fitter to revive the dead memory of their fame than she that beareth the lively image of their virtues? Who is fitter to authorize a work of so great learning and wisdom than she whom all do honor as the muse of the world? Therefore I humbly beseech your Majesty to suffer the simpleness of my translation to be covered under the

ampleness of your Highness' protection. For, most gracious Sovereign, though this book be no book for your Majesty's self, who are meeter to be the chief story than a student therein, and can better understand it in Greek than any man can make it English, yet I hope the common sort of your subjects shall not only profit themselves hereby but also be animated to the better service of your Majesty. For among all the profane books that are in reputacion at this day there is none—your Highness best knows—that teacheth so much honor, love, obedience, reverence, zeal, and devotion to princes as these *Lives* of Plutarch do. How many examples shall your subjects read here of several persons and whole armies, of noble and base, of young and old, that both by sea and land, at home and abroad have strained their wits, not regarded their states, ventured their persons, cast away their lives not only for the honor and safety but also for the pleasure of their princes?

Then well may the readers think if they have done this for heathen kings, what should we do for Christian princes? If they have done this for glory, what should we do for religion? If they have done this without hope of heaven, what should we do that look for immortality? And so, adding the encouragement of these exsamples to the forwardness of their own dispositions, what service is there in war, what honor in peace, which they will not be ready to do for their worthy queen?

And therefore that your Highness may give grace to the book and the book may do his service to your Majesty, I have translated it out of French, and do here most humbly present the same unto your Highness, beseeching your Majesty with all humility not to reject the good meaning but to pardon the errors of your most humble and obedient subject and servant, who prayeth God long to multiply all graces and blessings upon your Majesty. Written the sixteen day of January, 1579.

Your Majesty's most humble
and obedient servant,
Thomas North

To the Reader

The profit of stories and the praise of the author are sufficiently declared by Amyot in his epistle to the reader, so that I shall not need to make many words thereof. And, indeed, if you will supply the defects of this translation with your own diligence and good understanding, you shall not need to trust him; you may prove yourselves that there is no prophane study better then Plutarch. All other learning is private, fitter for universities then cities, fuller of contemplation than experience, more commendable in the students themselves than profitable unto others. Whereas stories are fit for every place, reach to all persons, serve for all times, teach the living, revive the dead, so far excelling all other books as it is better to see learning in noble men's lives than to read it in philosophers' writings. Now for the author I will not deny but love may deceive me, for I must needs love him with whom I have taken so much pain; but I believe I might be bold to affirm that he hath written the profitablest story of all authors. For all other were fain to take their matter as the fortune of the countries whereof they wrote fell out, but this man, being excellent in wit, learning, and experience, hath chosen the special acts of the best persons of the famosest nations of the world. But I will leave the judgment to yourselves. My only purpose is to desire you to excuse the faults of my translation with your own gentleness and with the opinion of my diligence

and good entent. And so I wish you all the profit of the book. Fare ye well. The four and twenty day of January, 1579.

Thomas North

[North's "To the Reader" is followed by his translation of Amyot's long defense of Plutarch's *Lives* as a document of moral instruction and delight: "it may be reasonably avowed that men are more beholding to such good wits as by their grave and wise writing have deserved the name of historiographers then they are to any other kind of writers, bicause an history is an orderly register of notable things said, done, or happened in time past to maintain the continual remembrance of them and to serve for the instruction of them to come."]

THE LIFE OF JULIUS CAESAR

... The time of the great armies and conquests he made afterwards [following his first consulship], and of the war in the which he subdued all the Gauls, ent'ring into another course of life far contrary unto the first, made him to be known for as valiant a soldier and as excellent a captain to lead men as those that afore him had been counted the wisest and most valiantest generals that ever were, and that by their valiant deeds had atchieved great honor. For whosoever would compare the house of the Fabians, of the Scipios, of the Metellians, yea, those also of his own time or long before him, as Sylla, Marius, the two Lucullians, and Pompey self,

Whose fame ascendeth up unto the heavens,

it will appear that Caesar's prowess and deeds of arms did excel them all together. The one in the hard countries where he made wars, another in enlarging the realms and countries which he joined unto the Empire of Rome, another in the multitude and power of his enemies whom he overcame, another in the rudeness and austere nature of men with whom he had to do, whose manners afterwards he soft'ned and made civil, another in curtesy and clemency which he used unto them whom he had conquered, another in great bounty and liberality bestowed upon them that served under him in those wars; and, in fine, he excelled them all in the number of battles he had fought and in the multitude of his enemies he had slain in battle. For in less then ten years' war [58–49 B.C.] in Gaul he took by force and assault above eight hundred towns; he conquered three hundred several nations; and, having before him in battle thirty hundred thousand soldiers, at sundry times he slew ten hundred thousand of them and took as many more prisoners. Furthermore, he was so entirely beloved of his soldiers that to do him service (where otherwise they were no more then other men in any private quarrel), if Caesar's honor were touched, they were invincible and would so desperately venter themselves, and with such fury, that no man was able to abide them. . . . Furthermore, they did not wonder so much at his valiantness in putting himself at every instant in such manifest danger and in taking so extreme pains as he did, knowing that it was his greedy desire of honor that set him afire and pricked him forward to do it; but that he always continued all labor and hardness, more then his body could bear, that filled them all with admiration. For concerning the constitucion of his body he was lean, white, and soft-skinned, and often subject to headache and otherwhile to the falling sickness, the which took him the first time, as it is reported, in Corduba, a city of Spain; but yet therefore yielded not to the disease of his body to make it a cloak to cherish him withal, but contrarily took the pains of war as a medicine to cure his sick body, fighting always with his disease, traveling continually, living soberly, and commonly lying abroad in the field. For the most nights he slept in his coach or litter, and thereby bestowed his rest to make him always able to do something, and in the daytime he would travel up and down the country to see towns, castles, and strong places. He had always a secretary with him in his coach who did still write as he went by the way, and a soldier behind him that carried his sword. He made such speed the first time he came from Rome, when he had his office, that in eight days he came to the River of Rhone. He was so excellent a rider of horse from his youth that, holding his hands behind him, he would gallop his horse upon the spur. In his wars in Gaul he did further exercise himself to indite letters as he rode by the way, and did occupy two secretaries at once with as much as they could write. . . .

Now when he had burnt all the country of his enemies and confirmed the league with the confederates of the Romans, he returned back again into Gaul after he had tarried eighteen days at the most in Germany, on th' other side of the Rhine. The jorney he made also into England [55 and 54 B.C.] was a noble enterprise and very commendable. For he was the first that sailed the west ocean with an army by sea, and that passed through the Sea Atlanticum with his army to make war in that so great and famous iland (which many ancient writers would not believe that it was so indeed, and did make them vary about it, saying that it was but a fable and a lie), and was the first that enlarged the Roman Empire beyond the earth inhabitable. For twice he passed over the narrow sea against the firm land of Gaul and, fighting many battles there, did hurt his

enemies more then enrich his own men, bicause of men hardly brought up and poor there was nothing to be gotten. Whereupon his war had not such success as he looked for, and therefore, taking pledges only of the king and imposing a yearly tribute apon him to be paid unto the people of Rome, he returned again into Gaul. . . .

[His Gallic victories consolidated, Caesar returned to Rome where, through political machinations and bribery, he gained a wide popular following. Pompey's prudent flight merely stirred him to fresh endeavors that came to a climax with his great triumph at Pharsalia (48 B.C.). With his enemies dispersed he passed over the sea to Alexandria.]

And for the war he made in Alexandria, some say he needed not have done it, but that he willingly did it for the love of Cleopatra, wherein he wan little honor and besides did put his person in great danger. Others do lay the fault upon the king of Egypt's ministers, but specially on Pothinus the eunuch, who, bearing the greatest sway of all the king's servants, after he had caused Pompey to be slain and driven Cleopatra from the court, secretly laid wait all the ways he could, how he might likewise kill Caesar. Wherefore Caesar, hearing an inkling of it, began thenceforth to spend all the night long in feasting and banketing, that his person might be in the better safety. But besides all this, Pothinus the eunuch spake many things openly not to be borne, only to shame Caesar and to stir up the people to envy him. For he made his soldiers have the worst and oldest wheat that could be gotten; then if they did complain of it, he told them they must be contented, seeing they eat at another man's cost. And he would serve them also at the table in treen and earthen dishes, saying that Caesar had away all their gold and silver, for a debt that the king's father (that then reigned) did owe unto him, which was a thousand seven hundred and fifty myriads, whereof Caesar had before forgiven seven hundred and fifty thousand unto his children. Howbeit, then he asked a million to pay his soldiers withal. Thereto Pothinus answered him, that at that time he should do better to follow his other causes of greater importance, and afterwards that he should at more leisure recover his debt, with the king's good will and favor. Caesar replied unto him and said that he would not ask counsel of the Egyptians for his affairs, but would be paid, and thereupon secretly sent for Cleopatra, which was in the country, to come unto him. She, only taking Apollodorus Sicilian of all her friends, took a little boat and went away with him in it in the night and came and landed hard by the foot of the castle. Then, having no other mean to come into the court without being known, she laid herself down upon a mattress or flockbed, which

Apollodorus her friend tied and bound up together like a bundle with a great leather thong, and so took her up on his back and brought her thus hamper'd in this fardel unto Caesar, in at the castle gate. This was the first occasion (as it is reported) that made Caesar to love her, but afterwards, when he saw her sweet conversation and pleasant entertainment, he fell then in further liking with her, and did reconcile her again unto her brother the king, with condition that they two jointly should reign together. Apon this new reconciliation, a great feast being prepared, a slave of Caesar's that was his barber, the fearfulest wretch that lived, still busily prying and listening abroad in every corner, being mistrustful by nature, found that Pothinus and Achillas did lie in wait to kill his maister Caesar. This being proved unto Caesar, he did set such sure watch about the hall where the feast was made that, in fine, he slew the eunuch Pothinus himself. Achillas, on th' other side, saved himself, and fled unto the king's camp where he raised a marvelous dangerous and difficult war for Caesar, bicause he having then but a few men about him as he had, he was to fight against a great and strong city. The first danger he fell into was for the lack of water he had, for that his enemies had stopped the mouth of the pipes the which conveyed the water unto the castle. The second danger he had was that, seeing his enemies came to take his ships from him, he was driven to repulse that danger with fire, the which burnt the arsenal where the ships lay and that notable library of Alexandria withal. The third danger was in the battle by sea, that was fought by the tower of Phar, where, meaning to help his men that fought by sea, he lept from the pier into a boat. Then the Egyptians made toward him with their oars on every side, but he, leaping into the sea, with great hazard saved himself by swimming. It is said that, then holding divers books in his hand, he did never let them go, but kept them always upon his head above water and swam with the other hand, notwithstanding that they shot marvelously at him, and was driven sometime to duck into the water. Howbeit, the boat was drowned presently. In fine, the king coming to his men that made war with Caesar, he went against him and gave him battle and wan it with great slaughter and effusion of blood. But for the king, no man could ever tell what became of him after. Thereupon Caesar made Cleopatra, his sister, queen of Egypt, who, being great with child by him, was shortly brought to bed of a son whom the Alexandrians named Caesarion.

From thence he went into Syria, and so, going into Asia, there it was told him that Domitius was overthrown in battle by Pharnaces, the son of King Mithridates, and was fled out of the realm of Ponte with a few men with him, and that this King Pharnaces, greedily following his victory, was not contented with the winning of Bithynia and Cappadocia but further would needs attempt to win Armenia the Less, procuring all those kings, princes, and governors of the provinces thereabouts to rebel against the Romans. Thereupon Caesar went thither straight with three legions and fought a great battle with King Pharnaces by the city of Zela, where he slew his army and drave him out of all the realm of Ponte [47 B.C.]. And bicause he would advertize one of his friends of the sodainness of this victory he only wrote three words unto Anitius at Rome: *Veni, vidi, vici*, to wit, "I came, I saw, I overcame." These three words, ending all with like sound and letters in the Latin, have a certain short grace, more pleasant to the ear then can be well expressed in any other tongue.

After this he returned again into Italy and came to Rome, ending his year for the which he was made dictator the second time, which office before was never granted for one whole year but unto him. Then he was chosen consul for the year following. . . .

[Caesar waged his last victorious campaigns against Cato and Scipio and then against the sons of Pompey. With their defeat in 46 and 45 his dominion was absolute.]

The Romans, inclining to Caesar's prosperity and taking the bit in the mouth, supposing that to be ruled by one man alone it would be a good mean for them to take breath a little after so many troubles and miseries as they had abidden in these civil wars, they chose him perpetual dictator. This was a plain tyranny, for to this absolute power of dictator they added this: never to be afraid to be deposed. Cicero propounded before the senate that they should geve him such honors as were meet for a man; howbeit others afterwards added to honors beyond all reason. For men striving who should most honor him, they made him hateful and troublesome to themselves that most favored him by reason of the unmeasurable greatness and honors which they gave him. . . . But his enemies, notwithstanding, that envied his greatness, did not stick to find fault withal. As Cicero the orator, when one said, "Tomorrow the star Lyra will rise," "Yea," said he, "at the commandement of Caesar," as if men were compelled so to say and think by Caesar's edict. But the chiefest cause that made him mortally hated was the covetous desire he had to be called king, which first gave the people just cause and next his secret enemies honest color to bear him ill will. . . . When they had decreed divers honors for him in the senate, the consuls and praetors, accompanied with the whole assembly of the senate, went unto him in the market-place, where he was set by the pulpit for orations to tell him what honors they had decreed for him in his absence. But he, sitting still in his majesty, disdaining to rise up unto them when they came in, as if they had been private men, answered them that his honors had more need to be cut off then enlarged. This did not only offend the senate but the common people also, to see that he should so lightly esteem of the magistrates of the commonwealth, insomuch as every man that might lawfully go his way departed thence very sorrowfully. Thereupon also Caesar, rising, departed home to his house, and tearing open his doublet collar, making his neck bare, he cried out aloud to his friends that his throat was ready to offer to any man that would come and cut it. Notwithstanding, it is reported that afterwards, to excuse this folly, he imputed it to his disease, saying that their wits are not perfit which have his disease of the falling evil, when, standing of their feet, they speak to the common people, but are soon troubled with a trembling of their body and a sodain dimness and giddiness. But that was not true. . . .

[At the feast of Lupercalia Caesar presided over the celebrations in great state.] Caesar sate to behold that sport apon the pulpit for orations in a chair of gold, appareled in triumphing manner. Antonius, who was consul at that time, was one of them that ran this holy course [in the traditional Lupercalian races]. So when he came into the market-place the people made a lane for him to run at liberty, and he came to Caesar and presented him a diadem wreathed about with laurel. Whereupon there rose a certain cry of rejoicing, not very great, done only by a few appointed for the purpose. But when Caesar refused the diadem, then all the people together made an outcry of joy. Then Antonius offering it him again, there was a second shout of joy, but yet of a few. But when Caesar refused it again the second time, then all the whole people shouted. Caesar, having made this proof, found that the people did not like of it, and thereupon rose out of his chair and commanded the crown to be carried unto Jupiter in the Capitol. After that there were set up images of Caesar in the city with diadems upon their heads, like kings. Those the two tribunes, Flavius and Marullus, went and pulled down, and furthermore, meeting with them that first saluted Caesar as king, they committed them to prison. The people followed them rejoicing at it and called them Brutes bicause of Brutus, who had in old time driven the kings out of Rome, and that brought the kingdom of one person unto the government of the senate and people. Caesar was so offended withal that he deprived Marullus and Flavius of their tribuneships and, accusing them, he spake also against the people and called them Bruti

and Cumani, to wit, "beasts and fools." Hereupon the people went straight unto Marcus Brutus, who from his father came of the first Brutus and by his mother of the house of the Servilians, a noble house as any was in Rome, and was also nephew and son-in-law of Marcus Cato. Notwithstanding, the great honors and favor Caesar shewed unto him kept him back, that of himself alone he did not conspire nor consent to depose him of his kingdom. For Caesar did not only save his life after the battle of Pharsalia when Pompey fled, and did at his request also save many moe of his friends besides, but furthermore he put a marvelous confidence in him. For he had already preferred him to the praetorship for that year, and furthermore was appointed to be consul the fourth year after that, having through Caesar's friendship obtained it before Cassius, who likewise made suit for the same; and Caesar also, as it is reported, said in this contention, "Indeed, Cassius hath alleged best reason, but yet shall he not be chosen before Brutus." Some, one day accusing Brutus while he practised this conspiracy, Caesar would not hear of it, but clapping his hand on his body told them, "Brutus will look for this skin," meaning thereby that Brutus for his virtue deserved to rule after him, but yet that for ambition's sake he would not shew himself unthankful nor dishonorable. Now they that desired change and wished Brutus only their prince and governor above all other, they durst not come to him themselves to tell him what they would have him to do, but in the night did cast sundry papers into the praetor's seat where he gave audience, and the most of them to this effect: "Thou sleepest, Brutus, and art not Brutus indeed." Cassius, finding Brutus' ambition sturred up the more by these seditious bills, did prick him forward and egg him on the more for a private quarrel he had conceived against Caesar, the circumstance whereof we have set down more at large in Brutus' life.

Caesar also had Cassius in great jealousy and suspected him much. Whereupon he said on a time to his friends, "What will Cassius do, think ye? I like not his pale looks." Another time when Caesar's friends complained unto him of Antonius and Dolabella, that they pretended some mischief towards him, he answered them again, "As for those fat men and smooth-combed heads," quoth he, "I never reckon of them, but these pale-visaged and carrion-lean people, I fear them most" (meaning Brutus and Cassius). Certainly destiny may easier be foreseen then avoided, considering the strange and wonderful signs that were said to be seen before Caesar's death. For, touching the fires in the element and spirits running up and down in the night, and also these solitary birds to be seen at noondays sitting in the great market-place—are not all these signs perhaps worth the noting in such a wonderful chance as happened? But Strabo the philosopher writeth that divers men were seen going up and down in fire, and, furthermore, that there was a slave of the soldiers that did cast a marvelous burning flame out of his hand, insomuch as they that saw it thought he had been burnt, but when the fire was out, it was found he had no hurt. Caesar self, also doing sacrifice unto the gods, found that one of the beasts which was sacrificed had no heart, and that was a strange thing in nature, how a beast could live without a heart. Furthermore, there was a certain soothsayer that had geven Caesar warning long time afore to take heed of the day of the Ides of March (which is the fifteenth of the moneth), for on that day he should be in great danger. That day being come, Caesar going unto the senate house, and speaking merrily to the soothsayer, told him, "The Ides of March be come." "So be they," softly answered the soothsayer, "but yet are they not past." And the very day before, Caesar, supping with Marcus Lepidus, sealed certain letters as he was wont to do at the bord. So talk falling out amongst them, reasoning what death was best, he, preventing their opinions, cried out aloud, "Death unlooked for." Then going to bed the same night as his manner was and lying with his wife Calpurnia, all the windows and doors of his chamber flying open, the noise awoke him and made him afraid when he saw such light, but more when he heard his wife Calpurnia, being fast asleep, weep and sigh and put forth many fumbling lamentable speeches. For she dreamed that Caesar was slain and that she had him in her arms. Others also do deny that she had any such dream, as amongst other Titus Livius writeth that it was in this sort: The senate having set upon the top of Caesar's house, for an ornament and setting-forth of the same, a certain pinnacle, Calpurnia dreamed that she saw it broken down and that she thought she lamented and wept for it. Insomuch that Caesar rising in the morning, she prayed him if it were possible not to go out of the doors that day, but to adjorn the session of the senate until another day. And if that he made no reckoning of her dream, yet that he would search further of the soothsayers by their sacrifices, to know what should happen him that day. Thereby it seemed that Caesar likewise did fear and suspect somewhat, bicause his wife Calpurnia until that time was never geven to any fear or supersticion, and then for that he saw her so troubled in mind with this dream she had. But much more afterwards when the soothsayers, having sacrificed many beasts one after another, told him that none did like them. Then he determined to send Antonius to adjorn the session of

the senate. But in the meantime came Decius Brutus, surnamed Albinus, in whom Caesar put such confidence that in his last will and testament he had appointed him to be his next heir, and yet was of the conspiracy with Cassius and Brutus; he, fearing that if Caesar did adjorn the session that day the conspiracy would out, laughed the soothsayers to scorn, and reproved Caesar, saying that he gave the senate occasion to mislike with him and that they might think he mocked them, considering that by his commandement they were assembled and that they were ready, willingly, to grant him all things, and to proclaim him king of all the provinces of the Empire of Rome out of Italy, and that he should wear his diadem in all other places, both by sea and land. And, furthermore, that if any man should tell them from him they should depart for that present time and return again when Calpurnia should have better dreams, what would his enemies and ill-willers say, and how could they like of his friends' words? And who could persuade them otherwise but that they would think his dominion a slavery unto them and tyrannical in himself? "And yet if it be so," said he, "that you utterly mislike of this day, it is better that you go yourself in person, and, saluting the senate, to dismiss them till another time." Therewithal he took Caesar by the hand, and brought him out of his house. Caesar was not gone far from his house but a bondman, a stranger, did what he could to speak with him, and when he saw he was put back by the great prease and multitude of people that followed him, he went straight unto his house, and put himself into Calpurnia's hands to be kept till Caesar came back again, telling her that he had great matters to impart unto him. . . .

For these things, they may seem to come by chance, but the place where the murther was prepared, and where the senate were assembled, and where also there stood up an image of Pompey dedicated by himself amongst other ornaments which he gave unto the theater—all these were manifest proofs that it was the ordinance of some god that made this treason to be executed, specially in that very place. It is also reported that Cassius (though otherwise he did favor the doctrine of Epicurus), beholding the image of Pompey, before they ent'red into the action of their traiterous enterprise, he did softly call upon it to aid him. But the instant danger of the present time taking away his former reason did sodainly put him into a furious passion and made him like a man half besides himself. Now Antonius, that was a faithful friend to Caesar and a valiant man besides of his hands, him Decius Brutus Albinus entertained out of the senate house, having begun a long tale of set purpose. So Caesar coming into the house, all the senate stood up on their feet to do him honor. Then part of Brutus' company and confederates stood round about Caesar's chair, and part of them also came towards him as though they made suit with Metellus Cimber to call home his brother again from banishment, and thus prosecuting still their suit, they followed Caesar till he was set in his chair. Who, denying their petitions and being offended with them one after another bicause the more they were denied the more they pressed upon him and were the earnester with him, Metellus, at length taking his gown with both his hands, pulled it over his neck, which was the sign geven the confederates to set apon him. Then Casca behind him strake him in the neck with his sword, howbeit the wound was not great nor mortal bicause it seemed the fear of such a devilish attempt did amaze him and take his strength from him, that he killed him not at the first blow. But Caesar, turning straight unto him, caught hold of his sword and held it hard, and they both cried out, Caesar in Latin, "O vile traitor Casca, what dost thou?" and Casca in Greek to his brother, "Brother, help me!" At the beginning of this stur they that were present, not knowing of the conspiracy, were so amazed with the horrible sight they saw that they had no power to fly, neither to help him, not so much as once to make any outcry. They on th' other side that had conspired his death compassed him in on every side with their swords drawn in their hands, that Caesar turned him nowhere but he was striken at by some, and still had naked swords in his face, and was hacked and mangeled among them as a wild beast taken of hunters. For it was agreed among them that every man should geve him a wound, bicause all their parts should be in this murther; and then Brutus himself gave him one wound about his privities. Men report also that Caesar did still defend himself against the rest, running every way with his body, but when he saw Brutus with his sword drawn in his hand, then he pulled his gown over his head and made no more resistance, and was driven either casually or purposedly by the counsel of the conspirators against the base whereupon Pompey's image stood, which ran all of a goar-blood till he was slain. . . .

Caesar died at six and fifty years of age, and Pompey also lived not passing four years more then he. So he reaped no other fruit of all his reign and dominion (which he had so vehemently desired all his life and pursued with such extreme danger) but a vain name only and a superficial glory that procured him the envy and hatred of his country. But his great prosperity and good fortune that favored him all his lifetime did continue afterwards in the revenge of his death, pursuing the murtherers both by sea and land till they had not left a man more to be executed of all them that were actors or counselers in the conspiracy of his death. Furthermore, of all the chances that happen unto men upon the earth, that which came to Cassius above all other is most to be wond'red at. For he, being overcome in the battle at the jorney of Philippes, slew himself with the same sword with the which he strake Caesar. Again, of signs in the element, the great comet which seven nights together was seen very bright after Caesar's death, the eight night after was never seen more. Also the brightness of the sun was darkened, the which all that year through rose very pale and shined not out, whereby it gave but small heat; therefore the air, being very cloudy and dark by the weakness of the heat that could not come forth, did cause the earth to bring forth but raw and unripe fruit which rotted before it could ripe. But above all, the ghost that appeared unto Brutus shewed plainly that the gods were offended with the murther of Caesar. The vision was thus: Brutus, being ready to pass over his army from the city of Abydos to the other coast lying directly against it, slept every night (as his manner was) in his tent, and being yet awake, thinking of his affairs—for by report he was as careful a captain and lived with as little sleep as ever man did—he thought he heard a noise at his tent door, and, looking towards the light of the lamp that waxed very dim, he saw a horrible vision of a man of a wonderful greatness and dreadful look which at the first made him marvelously afraid. But when he saw that it did him no hurt, but stood by his bedside and said nothing, at length he asked him what he was. The image answered him: "I am thy ill angel, Brutus, and thou shalt see me by the city of Philippes." Then Brutus replied again and said, "Well, I shall see thee then." Therewithal the spirit presently vanished from him. After that time Brutus, being in battle near unto the city of Philippes, against Antonius and Octavius Caesar, at the first battle he wan the victory and, overthrowing all them that withstood him, he drave them into young Caesar's camp, which he took. The second battle being at hand, this spirit appeared again unto him, but spake never a word. Thereupon Brutus, knowing he should die, did put himself to all hazard in battle, but yet fighting could not be slain. So, seeing his men put to flight and overthrown, he ran unto a little rock not far off and there, setting his sword's point to his breast, fell upon it and slew himself, but yet, as it is reported, with the help of his friend that dispatched him.

RICHARD STANYHURST (trans.)

· VIRGIL'S *AENEID*

Richard Stanyhurst's translation of the first four books of the *Aeneid* is surely one of the most grotesque works of the Elizabethan or any other period. His earlier commentary on Porphyry (*Harmonia seu catena dialectica in Porphyrianas institutiones*, 1570), published when he was only twenty-three, sufficiently established his competence in ancient tongues, and the account of his native Ireland contributed to Holinshed's *Chronicles* (1577) revealed him to be a close observer and a writer of spirited, if very odd, English prose. To learn Latin is one thing, however, and to possess literary taste is another; and, if we may judge by his Virgil, no amount of scholarship and no theory of metrics and orthography, however labored, could teach Stanyhurst to tell a hawk from a handsaw in matters of poetry. The result of his fatal deficiency became a jest for such contemporaries as Nashe and Puttenham, and a monitory monument to posterity.

In his dedicatory epistle Stanyhurst justifies the undertaking with characteristic vigor—and he was nothing if not vigorous. Following Ascham's injunction ("in his golden pamphlet intituled *The Schoolmaster*") to beautify the English language with "heroical verses," he resolved to translate Virgil's epic, a work of "peerless style and matchless stuff." That Thomas Phaer had anticipated him with such "pick'd and lofty words" increased rather than lessened his own labors, not only because he was forced "to weed out" from his own verses "such choice words as were forestall'd" by Phaer, but also because he was "moved to shun Master Phaer his enterpretation and cling more near to the meaning of mine author in slicing the husk and cracking the shell to bestow the kernel upon the witty and enquisitive reader." In spite of these formidable difficulties, Stanyhurst boasts that he "huddled up" in ten days the fourth book that had taken Phaer fifteen. His theory of translation, as he explains it in a preface "To the Learned Reader," proceeds upon the assumption (recently urged by Gabriel Harvey and the members of the so-called Areopagus in Leicester House) that quantitative verse in Latin should be rendered by quantitative verse in English. None the less, against the "pricisianists" who would make English too "stiffly tied" to classical precepts Stanyhurst insists that "nature will not permit us to fashion our words in all points correspondent to the Latinists." Consequently, although he renders Virgil in allegedly quantitative hexameters (and with a peculiar orthography that we have not wholly reproduced), he does so with considerable freedom, for Virgil, like Ovid, is so "tickle in some places" that he requires a "construction" rather than a line-for-line "translation."

Stanyhurst's Virgil was published at Leyden in 1582 together with versifications of the first four Psalms in classical quantitative meter and a group of original poems and epitaphs in Latin and English. Although the Leyden volume was reissued, slightly revised, in London in 1583 (and again, two years after Stanyhurst's death, in 1620), it quickly became more ridiculed than read, and for the rest of his life the translator, an ardent Catholic convert who wisely shunned the fate of more indiscreet, or more zealous, English Catholics by staying on the Continent, devoted himself mainly to the composition of saints' lives in Latin. Our text is based upon *The First Foure Bookes of Virgil his Aeneis,* 1582 (STC 24806).

FROM THE FIRST FOUR BOOKS OF VIRGIL HIS AENEIS (1582)

To the Right Honorable, My Very Loving Brother, the Lord Baron of Dunsany

What deep and rare points of hidden secrets Virgil hath seal'd up in his twelve books of *Aeneis* may easely appear to such reaching wits as bend their endewors to the unfolding thereof, not only by gnibbling upon the outward rine of a supposed history but also by groaping the pith that is shrin'd up within the bark and body of so exquisite and singular a discourse. For whereas the chief praise of a writer consisteth in the enterlacing of pleasure with profit, our author hath so wisely allayed the one with the other as the shallow reader may be delighted with a smooth tale and the diving searcher may be advantaged by sowning a precious treatise. . . .

Having, therefore, my good lord, taken upon me to execute some part of Maister Ascham his will, who, in his golden pamphlet intituled *The Schoolmaster,* doth wish the university students to apply their wits in beautifying our English language with heroical verses, I held no Latinist so fit to geve the onset on as Virgil, who, for his peerless style and matchless stuff, doth bear the prick and price among all the Roman poets. Howbeit I have here half a guess that two sorts of carpers will seem to spurn at this mine enterprise, the one utterly ignorant, the other meanly letter'd. The ignorant will imagine that the passage was nothing craggy inasmuch as Master Phaer hath broken the ice before me; the meaner clarks will suppose my travail in these heroical verses to carry no great difficulty in that it lay in my choice to make what word I would short or long, having no English writer before me in this kind of poetry with whose squire I should level my syllables. To shape, therefore, an answer to the first, I say they are altogether in a wrong box, considering that such words as fit Master Phaer may be very unapt for me, which they would confess if their skill were so much as spare in these verses. Furthermore, I stand so nicely on my pantofles that way as, if I could, yet I would not ren on the score with Master Phaer, or any other, by borrowing his terms in so copious and fluent a language as our English tongue is. And in good sooth, although the gentleman hath translated Virgil into English rythme with such surpassing excellency as a very few (in my conceit) for pick'd and lofty words can burd him, none, I am well assured, overgo him; yet he hath rather doubled, then defalk'd aught of, my pains by reason that in conferring his translation with mine I was forced to weed out from my verses such choice words as were forestall'd by him, unless they were so feeling as others could not countervail their signification; in which case it were no reason to sequester my pen from their acquaintance, considering that, as Master Phaer was not the first founder, so he may not be accompted the only owner of such terms. . . .

Now to come to theim that guess my travail to be easy by reason of the liberty I had in English words —for as I cannot devine upon such books that happly ruck in students' mews, so, I trust, I offer no man injury if I assume to myself the maidenhead of all works that hath been before this time in print, to my knowledge, divulged in this kind of verse—I will not greatly wrangle with theim therein; yet this much they are to consider, that as the first applying of a word may ease me in the first place, so, perhaps, when I am occasioned to use the selfsame word elsewhere, I may be as much hindered as at the beginning I was furth'red. For example, in the first verse of Virgil I make *season* long; in another place it would stead me percase more if I made it short, and yet I am now tied to use it as long. So that the advantage that way is not very great. But as for the general facility, this much I dare warrant young beginners: that when they shall have some firm footing in this kind of poetry, which by a little painful exercise may be purchas'd, they shall find as easy a vein in the English as in the Latin verses, yea, and much more easy than in the English rythmes. Touching mine own trial, this much I will discover: the three first books I translated by starts, as my leisure and pleasure would serve me; in the fourth book I did task myself and pursued the matter somewhat hotly. Master Phaer took to the making of that book fifteen days. I huddled up mine in ten. Wherein I covet no praise, but rather do crave pardon. . . .

Good God! What a fry of such wooden rhythmers doth swarm in stationers' shops, who, never enstructed in any grammar school, not attaining to the parings of the Latin or Greek tongue, yet like blind bayards rush on forward, fost'ring their vain conceits with such overweening, silly follies as they reck not to be condemned of the learned for ignorant, so they be commended of the ignorant for learned. The readiest way, therefore, to flap these drones from the sweet-scenting hives of poetry is for the learned to apply theimselves wholly—if they be delighted with that vein—to the true making of verses in such wise as the Greeks and Latins, the fathers of knowledge, have done; and to leave to these doltish coistrels their rude rythming and balductum ballads. To the sturring, therefore, of the riper and the encouraging of the younger gentlemen of our universities I have taken some pains that way, which I thought good to betake to your lordship his patronage, being of itself otherwise so tender as happily it might scant endure the tip of a frumping phillip. And thus omitting all other ceremonial complementos between your lordship and me, I commit you and your proceedings to the guarding and guiding of the Almighty.

From Leiden in Holland the last of June, 1582.

Your lordship his loving brother,

Richard Stanyhurst

To the Learned Reader

In the observation of quantities of syllables, some happly will be so stiffly tied to the ordinances of the Latins as what shall seem to swarve from their maxims they will not stick to score up for errors. In which resolution such curious pricisianists do attribute greater prerogative to the Latin tongue than reason will afford, and less liberty to our language than nature may permit. For inasmuch as the Latins have not been authors of these verses, but traced in the steps of the Greeks, why should we with the strings of the Latin rules cramp our tongue more than the Latins do fetter their speech, as it were, with the chains of the Greek precepts? Also, that nature will not permit us to fashion our words in all points correspondent to the Latinists may easely appear in such terms as we borrow of theim. For example, the first of *breviter* is short; the first of *briefly* with us must be long. Likewise, *sonans* is short, yet *sowning* in English must be long—and much more if it were *sounding*, as the ignorant generally but falsely do write. Nay, that whereat I wonder more, the learned trip their pens at this stone, insomuch as Master Phaer in the very first verse of Virgil mistaketh the word; yet *sound* and *sown* differ as much in English as *solidus* and *sonus* in Latin. . . . *Mother* I make long, yet *grandmother* must be short. *Buckler* is long, yet *swashbuckler* is short. And albeit that word be long by position, yet doubtless the natural dialect of English will not allow of that rule in middle syllables, but it must be of force with us excepted where the natural pronunciation will so have it. For otherwise we should banish a number of good and necessary words from our verses, as Master Gabriel Harvey (if I mistake not the gentleman his name) hath very well observed in one of his *Familiar Letters,* where he layeth down divers words straying from the Latin precepts, as *majesty, royalty, honesty,* etc. And soothly, to my seeming, if the conjunction *and* were made common in English it were not amiss, although it be long by position; for the Romans are greatly advantaged by their words *et, que, quoque, atque,* which, were they disjointed from the Latin poetry, many good verses would be ravel'd and dismemb'red that now carry a good grace among theim, having their joints knit with these copulative sinews. . . .

The final end of a verse is to please the ear, which must needs be the umpire of the word, and according to that weight our syllables must be poised. Wherefore, sith the poets theimselves advouch, *tu nihil invita facies, dicesve Minerva,* that nothing may be done or spoken against nature, and that art is also bound to shape itself by all imitation to nature, we must request these grammatical precisians that, as every country hath his peculiar law, so they permit every language to use his particular lore. For my part, I purpose not to beat on every childish tittle that concerneth *prosodia,* neither do I undertake to chalk out any lines or rules to others, but to lay down to the reader his view the course I took in this my travail. Such words as proceed from the Latin, and be not alt'red by our English, in theim I observe the quantity of the Latin, as *honest, honor.* A few I excepted, as the first of *apeared, aventure, aproached* I make short, although they are long in Latin, as *appareo, advenio, appropinquo.* For which and percase a few such words I must crave pardon of the curteous reader. For otherwise it were like enough that some grammatical pullet, hatch'd in Dis pater his satchel,

would stand clocking against me as though he had found an horse-nest in laying that down for a fault that perhaps I do know better then he. . . .

Touching the termination of syllables, I made a *prosodia* to myself, squaring somewhat from the Latin in this wise:

a finita communia.

b, d, t brevia; yet these words that end like diphthongs are common, as *mouth, south,* etc.

c common. *e* common. If it be short I write it usually with a single *e,* as *the, me;* if long, with two, as *thee, mee,* although I would not wish the quantity of syllables to depend so much upon the gaze of the eye as the censure of the ear.

f brevia.

g brevia, sometime long by position where *d* may be enterserted, as *passage* is short, but if you make it long, *passadge* with *d* would be written, albeit, as I said right now, the ear, not orthography, must decide the quantity as near as is possible.

i common.

k common.

l brevia, praeter Hebraea, ut Michael, Gabriel.

n brevia, yet words ending in diphthongwise would be common, as *plain, fain, swain.*

o common, *praeter ô longum.*

p brevia.

r brevia, except words ending like diphthongs that may be common, as *your, our, hour, four, succor,* etc.

as and *es* common.

is brevia.

os common.

us brevia.

v common.

As for *m,* it is either long by position or else clipp'd if the next word begin with a vocal, as *fame, name;* for albeit *e* be the last letter, that must not salve *m* from accurtation, because in the ear *m* is the last letter and *e* doth nought else but lengthen and mollify the pronunciation. As for *i, y, w,* inasmuch as they are mongrels (sometime consonants, sometime vocals), where they further, I do not reject theim; where they hinder, I do not greatly weigh theim. As the middle of *following* I make short, notwithstanding the *w,* and likewise the first of *power.* But where a consonant immediately followeth the *w,* I make it always long, as *fowling.*

This much I thought good to acquaint the gentle reader withal, rather to discover with what private precepts I have embayed my verses then to publish a directory to the learned, who, in their travails, may frankly use their own discretion without my direction.

The Second Book of Virgil His Aeneis

With tentive list'ning each wight was settled in hark'ning.
Thus Father Aeneas chronicled from lofty bed haughty:
"You me bid, O princess, to scarify a festered old sore,
How that the Trojans were press'd by Greecian army,
Whose fatal misery my sight hath witnessed heavy,
In which sharp bick'ring myself, as party, remained.
What rutter of Dolopans were so cruel-hearted in
     hark'ning?
What curst Myrmidons, what karn of cank'red Ulysses,
That, void of all weeping, could ear so mortal an hazard?
And now with moisture the night from welkin is
     hast'ning,   10
And stars to slumber do stur men's natural humors.
Howbeit, princely regent, if that thy affection earnest
Thy mind enflameth to learn our fatal aventures,
The toils of Trojans, and last infortunate affray,
Though my queasy stomach that bloody recital abhorreth,
And tears with trilling shall bain my phisnomy deeply,
Yet thine hot affected desire shall gain the rehearsal.
The Greekish captains, with wars and destiny mated,
Fetching from Pallas some wise, celestial engine,
Fram'd a steed of timber, steaming like mountain in
     hudgeness.   20
A vow for passadge they feign'd, and bruit so reported.
In this odd, hudge ambry they ramm'd a number of hardy,
Tough knights, thick-farcing the ribs with clustered
     armor.
In sight is Tenedos of Troy, the famosed island,
Whilst Priamus flourish'd a seat with riches abounding,
But now for shipping a rough and dangerous harbor.
There lurk'd these minions in sort most secret abiding.
All we then had deemed to Greece that the army retired;
Therefore the Trojans their long-borne sadness abandon.
The gates unclosed, they scud with a lively vagary,   30
The tents of the enemies marking, and desolate haven.
Here fought the Dolopans, there stoutly encount'red
     Achilles,
Here rode the navy, there battails bloody were off'red.
Some do look on dismal present of lofty Minerva;
Also they gaze wond'ring at the horse his mervelous
     hudgeness.
And first exhorteth the Trojans seely Tymetes
To bring the monument into the city, then after
For to place in stately castle the monsterous idol
(Whether he meant treasons, or so stood destiny Trojan).
But Capys and others, diving more deeply to bottom,   40
Warely suspecting in gifts the treachery Greekish,
Did wish the wooden monster were drowned, or
     harbor'd
In scorching firebrands, or ribs to spatter asunder.
The wavering commons in kim-kam sects are haled.
First, then, among others, with no small company
     guarded,
Laocoon, storming from princely castle, is hast'ning

And afar off bellowing, 'What fond, phantastical,
     harebrain
Madness hath enchanted your wits, you townsmen
     unhappy?
Ween you, blind hoddypecks, the Greekish navy
     returned?
Or that their presents want craft? Is subtil Ulysses   50
So soon forgotten? My life for an halfpenny, Trojans,
Either here are crouching some troups of Greekish
     asembly
Or to crush our bulwarks this work is forged, all houses
For to pry surmounting the town. Some practise or other
Here lurks of cunning. Trust not this treacherous ensign.
And, for a full reck'ning, I like not barrel or herring;
The Greeks bestowing their presents Greekish I fear me.'
Thus said, he stout rested. With his chap'd staff speedily
     running
Strong the steed he chargeth, the plank ribs manfully
     riving.
Then the jade, hit, shivered, the vauts half shrilly
     rebounded   60
With clush-clash buzzing, with drumming, clattered
     humming.
Had gods or fortune no such coarse destiny knedded,
Or that all our senses were not so bluntly benummed,
Their sleight and stratagems had been discovered eas'ly,
Now Troy with Priamus' castle most stately remaining.
     "But lo! The mean season, with shouting, clamorous
     hallow
Of Troy-town the shepherds a younker manacled haling
Present to Priamus. This guest full slyly did offer
Himself for captive, thereby to compass his hesting,
And Trojan city to his Greekish countrymen open.   70
A brass-bold merchant in causes dangerous hardy,
In doubtful matters thus stands he flatly resolved
Or to cog or certain for knavery to purchase a Tyburn.
The Trojan striplings, crowding, do cluster about him;
Some view the captive, some frumping quillities utter.
     "Now listen, lordings, to Greekish coosinage harken,
And of one odd, subtil stratagem, most treacherous
     handling,
Conster all.
For when this princox in midst of throng stood unarmed
Heedily the Trojans marking with phisnomy staring,   80
'O,' quod he, 'what region shall shroud me, villainous
     outcast?
Whereto shall I take me, forlorn, unfortunate, hopelost?
From Greekish country do I stand quite banished. Also
The wrath hot of Trojans my blood now fiercely
     requireth.'
     "Thus with a sob sighing, our minds with mercy
     relenting,
Greedily we covet to learn his kindred, his errand,
His state, eke his meaning, his mind, his fortune, his
     hazard.

Then the squire—embold'ned, dreadless—thus coined an
 answer:
'King, my faith I plight here to relate the verity soothly.
I may not, I will not, deny my Greecian offspring. 90
Though Sinon a caitiff by fortune scurvy be framed,
A liar him never may she make, nor cogger unhonest.
If that, king puissant, ye have heard erst happily reported
The name of the famous Palamedes, greatly renowmed,
The Greeks this captain with villainous injury murd'red.
Him they, lying, charged with treasons falsely, for
  hind'ring,
Forsooth, their warfares; him dead now dolefully mourn
 they.
To serve this worthy, to him nearly in kinred allied,
My father unwealthy me sent, then a pretty page, hither.
Whilst he stood in kingdom cocksure, whilst counsel
 availed, 100
Then we were of reck'ning; our feats were duly regarded.
But when my cousin was snapp'd by wicked Ulysses—
A story far-publish'd, no glozing fable I twattle—
With cholerique fretting I dump'd and rankled in anguish.
My tongue not charming, with fuming, fustian anger,
Plainly without cloaking, I vow'd to be kindly revenged,
Ever if I backward to native country returned.
And thus with menacing lip-threats I purchased hatred.
Hence grew my cross-bars; hence always after Ulysses
With new-forg'd treasons me, his foe, to terrify
 covets. 110
Oft he gave out rumors, he fabled sundry reports,
Me to trap in matters of state with forgery knavish.
His malice he fost'red till that priest Calchas he gained.
But lo! to what purpose do I chat such janglery trim-
 trams?
What needs this ling'ring? Sith Greeks ye hold equal in
 hatred,
Sith this eke heard serveth, speed furth your bloody
 revengement.
So ye may full pleasure the Greeks, and profit Ulysses.'
The less he furth prattled, the more we longed in harking
To learn all the reasons, no Greekish villainy doubting.
The rest, chill shivering, he with heart delivered
 hollow. . . . 120

But mark what follow'd, what chance and luck cruel
 happ'ned
Jump with this cogging, our minds and senses apalling.
As priest Laocoon, by lot to Neptune apointed,
A bull for sacrifice full-siz'd did slaughter at altars,
Then, lo ye, from Tenedos through standing deep flood
 apeased
—I shiver in telling—two serpents monsterous ugly
Plash'd the water sulking, to the shore most hastily
 swinging;
Whose breasts upsteaming and manes blood-speckled
 inhanced
High the sea surmounted; the rest in smooth flood is
 hidden.
Their tails, with crumpled knot twisting, swashly they
 wriggled. 130
The water is roused; they do frisk with flounce to the
 shoreward,
The land with staring eyes, bloody and firy, beholding.
Their fangs in lapping they stroke with brandished hot
 tongues.
All we flee from sacrifice with sight so grisled afrighted.
They charge Laocoon, but first they raght to the sucklings,
His two young children with circle poisoned hooking.
Theim they do chew, renting their members tender
 asunder.
In vain Laocoon, the assault like a stickler apeasing,
Is too soon embayed with wrapping girdle ycompass'd,
His middle embracing with wig-wag circuled hooping,
His neck eke chaining with tails, him in quantity topping,
He with his hands labored their knots to squeeze, but all
  hopeless 142
He strives. His temples with black, swart poison are oincted.
He freams and, scrawling to the sky, brays terrible
 hoiseth;
Much like as a fat bull belloweth that, settled on altar,
Half-kill'd, escapeth the missing butcherous hatchet.
But these bloody dragons to sacred temple aproached,
Under feet lurking and shield of mighty Minerva.
A fear then general men's mated senses atached.
We judge Laocoon to be justly and worthily punished 150
For that he rash charged with lance the mystical idol. . . ."

CHRISTOPHER MARLOWE (trans.)

OVID'S *ELEGIES* and LUCAN'S *PHARSALIA*

There can be no doubt that the volume containing
Marlowe's translation of Ovid's *Elegies* and Sir John
Davies' *Epigrams* (see p. 467–68) was a surreptitious but
popular publishing venture. The six early editions that
survive (all ostensibly printed at "Middleburgh in Hol-

land") are undated (although two are probably from the
mid-seventeenth century); but we do know, from the
Stationers' Register, that Archbishop Whitgift's decree
against scurrilous satires and epigrams resulted in the
public burning, on June 4, 1599, of the unlicensed volume

—a fact that at least establishes a *terminus ad quem* for dating the first edition. A *terminus a quo* is, unfortunately, not so easy to establish. In a late edition entitled *All Ovid's Elegies* the presence of Ben Jonson's accomplished version of I.xv sufficiently demonstrates the immaturity of Marlowe's translations; and indeed their general stiffness and ineptness, as well as the frequently licentious subject matter, have led Marlowe's most authoritative editor to regard the *Elegies* as "almost certainly" the work of his college days in Cambridge. In *The Unfortunate Traveler* (1594) Nashe quotes Marlowe's version of II.iii.3–4, in *The Merchant of Venice* (V.i.109) Shakespeare imitates Marlowe's rendering of I.xiii.43 ("The moon sleeps with Endymion every day"), and Davies' twenty-ninth epigram is twice alluded to in Thomas Bastard's *Chrestoleros* (1598); but these passages could mean no more than that their authors saw the work of Marlowe and Davies in manuscript, and cannot be taken as proof of publication in the early nineties. The two excerpts which we reprint are dreary testimonials to the fact that even greater writers do not always write well. Our text is based upon *All Ovids Elegies: 3. Bookes. By C. M. Epigrams by J. D.,* [?1640] (STC 18933).

The printer John Wolf entered in the Stationers' Register on the same day (September 28, 1593) both "Lucan's first book of the famous civil war betwixt Pompey and Caesar Englished by Christopher Marlowe" and "a book intituled Hero and Leander, being an amorous poem devised by Christopher Marlowe"; but the earliest extant copy of the *Lucan* was presumably published by Thomas Thorpe in 1600, and Thorpe's chatty epistle to Edward Blount (who, in 1598, had published the earliest extant edition of *Hero and Leander*) speaks of the latter's "old right" in the book. But also in 1598 Paul Linley had published an edition of *Hero and Leander*, and in 1600 John Flasket issued another edition with the title-page *Hero and Leander, Begun by Christopher Marlowe. Whereunto Is Added the First Book of Lucan Translated Line for Line by the Same Author*—a puzzling title since the volume contains the complete *Hero and Leander* (including Chapman's long continuation) but not a trace of the *Lucan*. As Tucker Brooke suggested, it is probable that Wolf had transferred his right in both poems to Blount, who in turn relinquished his interest to Linley in 1598, after which Flasket secured the rights for his edition of 1600. But how Thorpe entered the picture is by no means clear. His part in the publication of Shakespeare's *Sonnets* (1609) at least permits the inference that he was not the most scrupulous man in the world, but perhaps Flasket transferred the right in the *Lucan* to him when Chapman's continuation of *Hero and Leander* made it necessary to omit the *Lucan* from the 1600 edition with the misleading titlepage. Although certainly a more respectable performance than the *Elegies*, Marlowe's *Lucan* is full of errors and incoherencies that are only partially compensated for by the occasionally majestic movement of the blank verse. At any rate, it is of great interest in showing how a master of blank verse learned to control that medium. Our text is based upon *Lucans First Booke Translated Line for Line, By. Chr. Marlow,* 1600 (STC 16883 [B]).

FROM ALL OVID'S ELEGIES: THREE BOOKS (?1640)

Liber primus

ELEGIA 15

Ad invidos, quod fama poetarum sit perennis

Envy, why carpest thou my time is spent so ill
And term'st my works fruits of an idle quill?
Or that, unlike the line from whence I come,
War's rusty honors are refus'd, being young?
Nor that I study not the brawling laws,
Nor set my voice to sale in every cause?
Thy scope is mortal, mine eternal fame,
That all the world may ever chant my name.
Homer shall live while Tenedos stands and Ide,
Or into sea swift Simois doth slide.   10
Ascraeus lives whiles grapes with new wine swell,
Or men with crooked sickles corn down fell,

The world shall of Callimachus ever speak:
His art excell'd although his wit was weak.
Forever lasts high Sophocles' proud vein;
With sun and moon Aratus shall remain;
While bondmen cheat, fathers hoard, bawds [be] whorish,
And strumpets flatter, shall Menander flourish.
Rude Ennius and Plautus full of wit
Are both in Fame's eternal legend writ.   20
What age of Varro's name shall not be told,
And Jason's Argos and the fleece of gold?
Lofty Lucretius shall live that hour
That Nature shall dissolve this earthly bower.
Aeneas' war and Tityrus shall be read
While Rome of all the conquered world is head.
Till Cupid's bow and fiery shafts be broken

Thy verses, sweet Tibullus, shall be spoken,
And Gallus shall be known from east to west;
So shall Lycoris whom he loved best.   30
Therefore, when flint and iron wear away,
Verse is immortal, and shall ne'er decay.
To verse let kings give place, and kingly shows,
And banks o'er which gold-bearing Tagus flows.
Let base, conceited wits admire vild things,
Fair Phoebus lead me to the muses' springs.
About my head [be] quivering myrtle wound,
And in sad lovers' heads let me be found.
The living, not the dead, can Envy bite,
For after death all men receive their right.   40
Then, though Death takes my bones in funeral fire,
I'll live, and as he pulls me down mount higher.

THE SAME BY B[EN] J[ONSON]

Envy, why twit'st thou me my time's spent ill,
And call'st my verse fruits of an idle quill?
Or that, unlike the line from whence I sprung,
War's dusty honors I pursue not young?
Or that I study not the tedious laws
And prostitute my voice in every cause?
Thy scope is mortal, mine eternal fame,
Which through the world shall ever chant my name.
Homer will live while Tenedos stands and Ide,
Or to the sea fleet Simois doth slide;   10
And so shall Hesiod too while vines do bear
Or crooked sickles crop the ripened ear;
Callimachus, though in invention low,
Shall still be sung, since he in art doth flow.
No loss shall come to Sophocles' proud vein;
With sun and moon Aratus shall remain.
Whilst slaves be false, fathers hard, and bawds be
    whorish,
Whilst harlots flatter, shall Menander flourish.
Ennius, though rude, and Accius' high-rear'd strain
A fresh applause in every age shall gain.   20
Of Varro's name what ear shall not be told?
Or Jason's Argo and the fleece of gold?
Then shall Lucretius' lofty numbers die
When earth and seas in fire and flames shall fry.
Tityrus, Tillage, Aeney, shall be read
Whilst Rome of all the conquer'd world is head.
Till Cupid's fires be out and his bow broken
Thy verses, neat Tibullus, shall be spoken.

Our Gallus shall be known from east to west;
So shall Lycoris, whom he now loves best.   30
The suffering plowshare or the flint may wear,
But heavenly poesy no death can fear.
Kings shall give place to it, and kingly shows,
The banks o'er which gold-bearing Tagus flows.
Kneel hinds to trash, me let bright Phoebus swell
With cups full flowing from the muses' well.
The frost-dead myrtle shall impale my head,
And of sad lovers I'll be often read.
Envy the living, not the dead, doth bite,
For after death all men receive their right.   40
Then when this body falls in funeral fire
My name shall live, and my best part aspire.

Liber secundus

ELEGIA 12

Exultat, quod amica potitus sit

About my temples go triumphant bays:
Conquer'd Corinna in my bosom lays—
She whom her husband, guard, and gate, as foes,
Lest art should win her, firmly did enclose.
That victory doth chiefly triumph merit
Which without bloodshed doth the prey inherit.
No little ditched towns, no lowly walls,
But to my share a captive damsel falls.
When Troy by ten years' battail tumbled down,
With the Atrides many gain'd renown;   10
But I no partner of my glory brook,
Nor can another say his help I took.
I, guide and soldier, won the field and wear her;
I was both horseman, footman, standard-bearer.
Nor in my act hath fortune mingled chance.
O care-got triumph, hitherwards advance!
Nor is my war's cause new: but for a queen
Europe and Asia in firm peace had been.
The Lapithes and the Centaurs for a woman
To cruel arms their drunken selves did summon.   20
A woman forc'd the Trojans new to enter
Wars, just Latinus, in thy kingdom's center.
A woman against late-built Rome did send
The Sabine fathers who sharp wars intend.
I saw how bulls for a white heifer strive;
She, looking on them, did more courage give.
And me with many, but yet without murther,
Cupid commands to move his ensigns further.

FROM LUCAN'S FIRST BOOK TRANSLATED LINE FOR LINE (1600)

To His Kind and True Friend, Edward Blunt

Blount: I purpose to be blunt with you and out of my dulness to encounter you with a dedication in the memory of that pure, elemental wit, Christopher Marlowe, whose ghost or genius is to be seen walk the Churchyard in (at the least) three or four sheets. Methinks you should presently look wild now, and grow humorously frantique upon the taste of it. Well, lest you should, let me tell you: this spirit was sometime a familiar of your own, *Lucan's First Book Translated,* which, in regard of your old right in it, I have rais'd in the circle of your patronage. But stay now, Edward, if I mistake not, you are to accommodate yourself with some few instructions touching the property of a patron that you are not yet possess'd of, and to study them for your better grace as our gallants do fashions. First, you must be proud and think you have merit inough in you, though you are ne'er so empty; then, when I bring you the book, take physic and keep state, assign me a time by your man to come again, and, afore the day, be sure to have chang'd your lodging; in the meantime sleep little and sweat with the invention of some pitiful dry jest or two which you may happen to utter, with some little (or not at all) marking of your friends when you have found a place for them to come in at; or if by chance something has dropp'd from you worth the taking-up, weary all that come to you with the often repetition of it; censure scornfully inough, and somewhat like a travailer; commend nothing, lest you discredit your (that which you would seem to have) judgment. These things, if you can mold yourself to them, Ned, I make no question but they will not become you. One special virtue in our patrons of these days I have promis'd myself you shall fit excellently, which is to give nothing. Yes, thy love I will challenge as my peculiar object both in this and (I hope) many more succeeding offices. Farewell! I affect not the world should measure my thoughts to thee by a scale of this nature. Leave to think good of me when I fall from thee.

Thine in all rites of perfect friendship,
Thomas Thorpe

THE FIRST BOOK OF LUCAN
TRANSLATED INTO ENGLISH

Wars worse then civil on Thessalian plains
And outrage strangling law and people strong
We sing, whose conquering swords their own breasts
    launch'd,
Armies allied, the kingdoms' league uprooted,

Th' affrighted world's force bent on publique spoil,
Trumpets and drums like deadly threat'ning other,
Eagles alike display'd, darts answering darts.
    Romans, what madness, what huge lust of war
Hath made barbarians drunk with Latin blood?
Now Babylon, proud through our spoil, should stoop 10
While slaught'red Crassus' ghost walks unreveng'd.
Will ye wadge war for which you shall not triumph?
    Ay me, O what a world of land and sea
Might they have won whom civil broils have slain!
As far as Titan springs where night dims heaven—
Ay to the torrid zone where midday burns—
And where stiff winter, whom no spring resolves,
Fetters the Euxine Sea with chains of ice,
Scythia and wild Armenia had been yok'd,
And they of Nilus' mouth (if there live any).   20
    Rome, if thou take delight in impious war,
First conquer all the earth, then turn thy force
Against thyself; as yet thou wants not foes,
That now the walls of houses half-rear'd totter,
That rampiers fallen down, huge heaps of stone
Lie in our towns, that houses are abandon'd,
And few live that behold their ancient seats.
Italy many years hath lien untill'd
And chok'd with thorns; that greedy earth wants hinds.
Fierce Pyrrhus, neither thou nor Hannibal   30
Art cause; no foreign foe could so afflict us;
These plagues arise from wreak of civil power.
    But if for Nero, then unborn, the fates
Would find no other means (and gods not slightly
Purchase immortal thrones, nor Jove joy'd heaven
Until the cruel giants' war was done),
We plain not heavens, but gladly bear these evils
For Nero's sake. Pharsalia, groan with slaughter,
And Carthage souls be glutted with our bloods;
At Munda let the dreadful battails join;   40
Add, Caesar, to these ills Perusian famine,
The Mutin toils, the fleet at Leuca sunk,
And cruel field near burning Aetna fought.
    Yet Rome is much bound to these civil arms
Which made thee emperor, thee (seeing thou, being old,
Must shine a star) shall heaven (whom thou lovest)
Receive with shouts, where thou wilt reign as king,
Or mount the sun's flame-bearing chariot
And with bright, restless fire compass the earth,
Undaunted though her former guide be chang'd.   50
Nature and every power shall give thee place,
What god it please thee be or where to sway,
But neither chuse the north t' erect thy seat
Nor yet the adverse reeking southern pole,
Whence thou should'st view thy Rome with squinting
    beams.
If any one part of vast heaven thou swayest,

The burdened axes with thy force will bend.
The midst is best; that place is pure and bright;
There, Caesar, may'st thou shine and no cloud dim thee;
Then men from war shall bide in league and ease;   60
Peace through the world from Janus' phane shall fly
And bolt the brazen gates with bars of iron.
Thou, Caesar, at this instant art my god.
Thee if I invocate, I shall not need
To crave Apollo's aid or Bacchus' help;
Thy power inspires the muse that sings this war.
   The causes first I purpose to unfold
Of these garboils, whence springs a long discourse,
And what made madding people shake off peace.
   The fates are envious; high seats quickly perish;   70
Under great burdens falls are ever grievous;
Rome was so great it could not bear itself;
So when this world's compounded union breaks,
Time ends and to old Chaos all things turn,
Confused stars shall meet, celestial fire
Fleet on the floods, the earth shoulder the sea,
Affording it no shore, and Phoebe's wain
Chase Phoebus and inrag'd affect his place,
And strive to shine by day and, full of strife,
Dissolve the engines of the broken world.   80
All great things crush themselves; such end the gods

Allot the height of honor; men so strong
By land and sea no foreign force could ruin:
O Rome, thyself art cause of all these evils;
Thyself thus shivered out to three men's shares;
Dire league of partners in a kingdom last not.
   O faintly join'd friends, with ambition blind,
Why join you force to share the world betwixt you?
While th' earth the sea, and air the earth sustains,
While Titan strives against the world's swift course   90
Or Cynthia (Night's queen) waits upon the day,
Shall never faith be found in fellow kings.
Dominion cannot suffer partnership;
This needs no foreign proof nor farfet story.
Rome's infant walls were steep'd in brothers' blood,
Nor then was land or sea to breed such hate;
A town with one poor church set them at odds.
   Caesar's and Pompey's jarring love soon ended;
'Twas peace against their wills; betwixt them both
Stepp'd Crassus in. Even as the slender isthmus   100
Betwixt the Aegean and the Ionian sea
Keeps each from other, but, being worn away,
They both burst out and each incounter other;
So whenas Crassus' wretched death, who stay'd them,
Had fill'd Assyrian Carra's walls with blood,
His loss made way for Roman outrages. . . .

SIR JOHN HARINGTON (trans.)

ARIOSTO'S *ORLANDO FURIOSO*

Ariosto's *Orlando Furioso*—which takes its place with Boiardo's *Orlando Innamorato* (1494) and Tasso's *Gerusalemme Liberata* (1581) in the triad of Renaissance Italian epics—was begun (as a sequel to Boiardo's fragment) about 1503. The first forty cantos were published in 1516 and the last six in 1532, a year before the author's death. Harington's spirited translation in the meter of the original was begun (with the story of Giocondo from Canto XXVIII) to amuse the ladies of Elizabeth's court; but the queen, vexed with Harington for corrupting her ladies' morals with so indelicate an episode, ordered him to translate the whole as a penance before entering her presence again. In 1591 the penance was accomplished, and in the same year it was published in a stately folio, with the translator's witty "Apology of Poetry" (see pp. 647-50) by way of preface.

The fertility of Ariosto's imagination, the intricate but delicately controlled convolutions of his plot, make *Orlando Furioso* one of the marvels of European literature. Generically related to the Charlemagne legends, the poem is built around Orlando's (i.e. Roland's) madness at the faithlessness of Angelica. When, in Paris, Rinaldo falls in love with her, the king puts her in the custody of Namo (Duke Namus of Bavaria). Fleeing to the island of Ebuda, she is found and freed from a sea-monster by Rogero, after which she herself liberates Orlando from the enchanted castle of Atlantes. When she subsequently elopes with Medoro, a wounded Moor, to Cathay, the jilted Orlando goes mad with jealousy, his wits being taken from him for three months and deposited in the moon. His friend Astolpho, however, restores him by flying to the moon in Elijah's chariot and retrieving the urn containing Orlando's wits from St. John himself. The long poem ends with the siege of Paris by the Moors under Agrimant and a great Christian victory when Rogero (the true hero of the poem and a Christianized Moor) meets Rodomont, the Moorish champion, in single combat and destroys him.

There were later editions of Harington's translation in 1607 and 1634. Our text is based upon *Orlando Furioso in English Heroical Verse, by John Harington Esquire*, 1591 (STC 746).

FROM ORLANDO FURIOSO IN ENGLISH HEROICAL VERSE (1591)

THE FIRST BOOK OR CANTO OF ORLANDO FURIOSO

THE ARGUMENT

Charles hath the foil, Angelica flies thence;
Renaldo's horse holp him his love to find;
Ferraw with him doth fight in her defense;
She flies again, they stay not long behind.
Argalia's ghost reproves Ferraw's offense;
The Spaniard to new vow himself doth bind;
His mistress' presence Sacrapant enjoyeth;
Bradamant and Renaldo him annoyeth.

1

Of dames, of knights, of arms, of love's delight,
Of curtesies, of high attempts I speak:
Then when the Moors transported all their might
On Afric seas, the force of France to break,
Drawn by the youthful heat and raging spite
Of Agramant, their king, that vow'd to wreak
The death of King Trayano (lately slain)
Upon the Roman emperor Charlemain.

2

I will no less Orlando's acts declare
(A tale in prose ne verse yet sung or said),   10
Who fell bestraught with love, a hap most rare
To one that erst was counted wise and staid.
If my sweet saint, that causeth my like care,
My slender muse afford some gracious aid,
I make no doubt but I shall have the skill
As much as I have promis'd to fulfill.

3

Vouchsafe, O prince of most renowmed race,
The ornament and hope of this our time,
T' accept this gift presented to your Grace
By me, your servant, rudely here in rime;   20
And though I pay paper and ink in place
Of deeper debt, yet take it for no crime;
It may suffice a poor and humble debtor
To say and if he could it should be better.

4

Here shall you find among the worthy peers
Whose praises I prepare to tell in verse
Rogero; him from whom of ancient years
Your princely stems derived I rehearse;
Whose noble mind by princely acts appears,
Whose worthy fame even to the sky doth perse,   30
So you vouchsafe my lowly style and base
Among your high conceits a little place.

5

Orlando, who long time had loved dear
Angelica the fair, and for her sake
About the world in nations far and near
Did high attempts perform and undertake,
Return'd with her into the west that year
That Charles his power against the Turks did make,
And with the force of Germany and France
Near Pyren Alps his standard did advance,   40

6

To make the kings of Afric and of Spain
Repent their rash attempts and foolish vaunts.
One having brought from Afric in his train
All able men to carry sword or lance,
The tother mov'd the Spaniards now again
To overthrow the goodly realm of France;
And hither, as I said, Orlando went,
But of his coming straight he did repent.

7

For here—behold how human judgments arr
And how the wiser sort are oft mistaken—   50
His lady, whom he guarded had so far
Nor had in fights nor dangers great forsaken,
Without the dint of sword or open war
Amid his friends away from him was taken.
For Charles the Great, a valiant prince and wise,
Did it to quench a broil that did arise.

8

Between Orlando and Renaldo late
There fell about Angelica a brall,
And each of them began the other hate,
This lady's love had made them both so thrall;   60
But Charles, who much mislikes that such debate
Between such friends should rise on cause so small,
To Namus of Bavier in keeping gave her,
And suff'red neither of them both to have her;

9

But promis'd he would presently bestow
The damsel fair on him that in that fight
The plainest proof should of his prowess show
And danger most the pagans with his might;
But, ay the while, the Christens take the blow:
Their soldiers slain, their captains put to flight,   70
The duke himself a pris'ner there was taken,
His tent was quite abandon'd and forsaken.

10

Where when the damsel fair a while had stay'd
That for the victor pointed was a prey,
She took her horse, ne farther time delay'd,
But secretly convey'd herself away;
For she foresaw and was full sore afraid
That this to Charles would prove a dismal day;
And riding through a wood she happ'd to meet
A knight that came against her on his feet,   80

11

His curats on, his helmet not undone,
His sword and target ready to the same,
And through the wood so swiftly he did run
As they that go half naked for a game.
But never did a shepherd's daughter shun
More speedily a snake that on her came
Then fair Angelica did take her flight
Whenas she once had knowledge of the knight.

12

This valiant knight was Lord of Clarimount,
Duke Ammon's son, as you shall understand,   90
Who, having lost his horse of good account,
That by mishap was slipp'd out of his hand,
He follow'd him in hope again to mount
Until this lady's sight did make him stand,
Whose face and shape proportion'd were so well
They seem the house where Love itself did dwell.

13

But she that shuns Renaldo all she may
Upon her horse's neck doth lay the rein;
Through thick and thin she galloppeth away,
Ne makes the choice of beaten way or plain,   100
But gives her palfrey leave to chuse the way,
And being mov'd with fear and with disdain
Now up, now down she never leaves to ride
Till she arrived by a river side.

14

Fast by the stream Ferraw she sees anone
Who, 'noy'd in part with dust and part with sweat,
Out of the battle hither came alone
With drink his thirst, with air to 'suage his heat;
And minding back again to have been gone
He was detain'd with an unlook'd-for let: 110
Into the stream by hap his helmet fell,
And how to get it out he cannot tell.

15

And hearing now the noise and mournful cry
Of one with piteous voice demanding aid,
Seeing the damsel eke approaching nigh
That nought but help against Renaldo pray'd,

What wight it was he guessed by and by
Though looking pale, like one that had been fray'd;
And, though she had not late been in his sight,
He thought it was Angelica the bright.   120

16

And being both a stout and curteous knight
And love a little kindling in his breast,
He promis'd straight to aid her all he might
And to perform whatever she request;
And though he want a helmet, yet to fight
With bold Renaldo he will do his best,
And both the one the other straight defied,
Oft having either other's value tried.

17

Between them two a combat fierce began
With strokes that might have pierc'd the hardest rock,
While they thus fight on foot, and man to man,   131
And give and take so hard and heavy knocks,
Away the damsel posteth all she can;
Their pain and travail she requites with mocks;
So hard she rode while they were at their fight
That she was clean escaped out of sight. . . .

[Angelica having fled, the two knights very sensibly agree
to stop fighting each other and to look for her instead.
Presently coming upon the brook where he had lost his
helmet, Ferraw tries to dredge it up again.]

25

Hard by the bank a tall young poplar grew
Which he cut down, thereof a pole to make
With which each place in feeling and in view
To find his skull he up and down doth rake;   140
But lo, a hap unlook'd for doth ensue
While he such needless, fruitless pain doth take:
He saw a knight arise out of the brook
Breast-high, with visage grim and angry look.

26

The knight was arm'd at all points save the head,
And in his hand he held the helmet plain—
That very helmet that such care had bred
In him that late had fought it with such pain.
And looking grimly on Ferraw he said:
"A faithless wretch, in promise false and vain,   150
It grieves thee now this helmet so to miss,
That should of right be rend'red long ere this.

27

"Remember, cruel pagan, when you killed
Me, brother to Angelica the bright?
You said you would, as I then dying willed,
Mine armor drown when finish'd were the fight.
Now if that Fortune have the thing fulfilled

Which thou thyself should'st have perform'd in right,
Grieve not thyself, or, if thou wilt be grieved,
Grieve that thy promise cannot be believed.   160

28

"But if to want an helmet thou repine,
Get one wherewith thine honor thou may'st save;
Such hath Orlando, County Paladine,
Renaldo such, or one perchance more brave
That was from Almont ta'en, this from Mambrine.
Win one of these that thou with praise may'st have,
And as for this, surcease to seek it more,
But leave it as thou promis'd me before."

29

Ferraw was much amaz'd to see the sprite
That made this strange appearance unexpected;   170
His voice was gone, his hair did stand upright,
His senses all were so to fear subjected.
His heart did swell with anger and despite
To hear his breach of promise thus objected,
And that Argalia (so the knight was named)
With just reproof could make him thus ashamed.

30

And wanting time the matter to excuse
And being guilty of no little blame,
He rested mute, and in a senseless muse,
So sore his heart was tainted with the shame.   180
And by Lanfusa's life he vow'd to use
No helmet till such time he gat the same
Which from the stout Almont Orlando wan
Whenas they two encount'red man to man. . . .

[Meanwhile Angelica, after a hectic flight from her two warriors, at last finds a shady retreat near a river. There she overhears the amorous plaints of Sacrapant, a knight exhausted with frustrated love for a lady who had fled to the protection of Charlemagne and Orlando. Indeed, the lady was none other than Angelica herself, and when she recognizes her old lover she resolves to exploit his passion once again.]

50

But being now with danger compass'd round
She thought it best to take him for her guide,
For one that were in water almost drown'd
Were very stout if for no help he cried.
If she let pass the fortune now she found,
She thinks to want the like another tide;   190
And furthermore for certain this she knew,
That Sacrapant had been her lover true.

51

Ne meant she tho to quench the raging fires
That ay consum'd his faithful, loving heart,

Ne yet with that a lover most desires
T' assuage the pain in all or yet in part;
She means he first shall pull her from the briers,
And feed him then with words and women's art
To make him first of all to serve her turn,
That done, to wonted coyness to return.   200

52

Unto the river side she doth descend,
And toward him most goddess-like she came
And said, "Peace be to thee, my dearest friend!"
With modest look, and call'd him by his name;
Further she said, "The gods and you defend
My chastity, mine honor, and my fame;
And never grant by their divine permission
That I give cause of any such suspicion."

53

With how great joy a mother's mind is fill'd
To see a son for whom she long had mourned,   210
Whom she hard late in battle to be kill'd
And saw the troops without him home returned,
Such joy had Sacrapant when he behild
His lady dear; his tears to smiles are turned
To see her beauty rare, her comely favor,
Her princely presence, and her stately havor. . . .

[With a certain justice Sacrapant decides to "gather now the fresh and fragrant rose" which he has sought so long, but just as he is about to lay violent hands on Angelica a strange warrior suddenly appears to challenge him. After a fearful encounter, the strange knight overthrows Sacrapant's horse and leaves his antagonist bruised and breathless. Angelica tries to comfort him after the stranger has departed.]

68

Thus while she gives him comfort all she may,
Behold there came a messenger in post,
Blowing his horn and riding down the way
Where he before his horse and honor lost.   220
And coming nearer he of them doth pray
To tell if they had seen pass by that cost
A champion arm'd at all points like a knight,
The shield, the horse, and armor all of white.

69

"I have both seen the knight and felt his force,"
Said Sacrapant, "for here, before you came,
He cast me down and also kill'd my horse,
Ne know I—that doth grieve me most—his name."
"Sir," quoth the post, "the name I will not force
To tell, sith you desire to know the same;   230
First, know that you were conquer'd in this fight
By vallew of a damsel fair and bright,

70

"Of passing strength but of more passing hew,
And Bradamant this damsel fair is named.
She was the wight whose meeting you may rew
And all your life hereafter be ashamed."
This said, he turn'd his horse and bad adew,
But Sacrapant, with high disdain enflamed,
Was first so wroth and then so sham'd thereto
He knew not what to say nor what to do. . . .   240

[As Sacrapant and Angelica, both on one horse, make
their way off, they come across Bayard, Orlando's famous
steed, wandering in the woods. Angelica appropriates him
for her own mount.]

77

And being newly settled in her seat
She saw a man on foot all armed run;
Straight in her mind she gan to chafe and fret
Because she knew it was Duke Ammon's son.
Most earnestly he sued her love to get,
More earnestly she seeks his love to shun;
Once she lov'd him, he hated her as much;
And now he loves, she hates, his hap was such.

78

The cause of this first from two fountains grew,
Like in the taste but in effects unlike,   250
Plac'd in Ardenna, each in other's view;
Who tastes the one, love's dart his heart doth strike;
Contrary of the other doth ensue:
Who drink thereof, their lovers shall mislike.

Renaldo drank of one, and love much pained him;
The other drank this damsel that disdained him.

79

This liquor thus with secret venim mingled
Makes her to stand so stiffly in the nay,
On whom Renaldo's heart was wholly kindled,
Though scarce to look on him she can away,   260
But from his sight desiring to be singled,
With soft, low voice the pagan she doth pray
That he approach no nearer to this knight,
But fly away with all the speed he might.

80

"Why then," quoth he, "make you so small esteem
Of me, as though that I to him should yield?
So weak and faint my forces do you deem
That safe from him yourself I cannot shield?
Then you forget Albracca, it should seem,
And that same night when I, amid the field,   270
Alone, unarmed, did defend you then
Against King Agrican and all his men."

81

"No, sir," said she— ne knows she what to say—
Because Renaldo now approach'd so nigh
And threat'ned sore the pagan in the way
When under him his horse he did espy
And saw the damsel taken as a prey,
In whose defense he means to live and die.
But what fell out between these warriors fearce
Within the second book I do rehearse.   280

PHILEMON HOLLAND (trans.)

PLUTARCH'S *MORALS*

Plutarch's diversified and voluminous writings exclusive of the *Parallel Lives*, compendiously called the *Opera moralia*, consist of about sixty essays, many of them very long and some of dubious authenticity. Whether all are genuine or not, they are a storehouse of classical humanism and literary history; and even though they present no systematic philosophical view other than an urbane regard for education and rational common sense, some of them—for example, the famous "On the Education of Children" (which Elyot had translated about 1535), "How a Young Man Ought to Hear Poetry," "On Virtue and Vice," "Precepts about Health" (Erasmus' Latin version of which had been Englished about 1530), "On Isis and Osiris," "On the Cessation of Oracles," "On Exile," and "Precepts on Governing"—had been admired by generations of Renaissance humanists for both their content and their style. Holland's version of the complete collection, one of the first of his incredible exertions in the translator's weary art, constitutes a bulky folio based partly on Plutarch's Greek and partly on Jacques Amyot's French (1559). Licensed to William Ponsonby on April 18, 1600, it was actually published by Arnold Hatfield in 1603 with a fulsome (and unrewarded) dedication to James I. Our text is based upon *The Philosophie, commonlie called, the Morals Written by the learned Philosopher Plutarch of Chaeronea. Translated out of Greeke into English, and conferred with the Latine translations and the French, by Philemon Holland of Coventrie, Doctor in Physicke*, 1603 (STC 20063).

FROM THE PHILOSOPHY COMMONLY CALLED THE MORALS WRITTEN BY THE LEARNED PHILOSOPHER PLUTARCH (1603)

To the Most High and Mighty Prince James, by the Grace of God King of England, Scotland, France, and Ireland, Defender of the Faith, etc.

In this general joy of affectionate and loyal subjects, testified by their frequent confluence from all parts, longing for nothing so much as the full fruition of that beautiful star which lately, upon the shutting-in of the evening with us after our long summer's day, immediately by his radiant beams maintained still a twilight from the north and within some few hours appeared bright shining above our horizon, suffering neither the dark night and confused chaos of anarchy to overspread and subvert nor the turbulent tempests and bloody broils of factious sidings to trouble and pervert our state, I also, for my part, could not stay behind, but in testimony of semblable love and allegiance shew myself and withal most humbly present unto your Highness this *Philosophy of Plutarch;* which, being first naturally bred in Greece, then transplanted in Italy, France, and other regions of the continent, after sundry nativities, if I may so speak, reserved (not without some divine providence) unto these days, is now in this our iland newly come to light, ready both to congratulate your Majesty's first entry upon the inheritance of these kingdoms and desirous also to enjoy the benefit of that happy horoscope and fortunate ascendent under which it was born, even the favorable aspect of your gracious countenance, by virtue whereof it may not only be marked to long life, feeble otherwise of itself, but also yield pleasure with profit to the English nation.

Vouchsafe therefore, my dear lord and dread sovereign, to accept that now at my hands whole and entire which in part Trajanus, the best Romain emperor that ever was, received sometime from the first author and stockfather himself; protect the same in English habit whom in French attire Amyot dedicated to the late most Christian king [Charles IX], and deign unto her no less favor and grace than her younger sister, to wit, the *History or Parallel Lives,* hath already obtained, which, being transported out of France into England by that worthy knight Sir Thomas North, our countryman, was patronized by our late sovereign lady of famous memory, Elizabet. . . . These regards, albeit they were sufficient motives in themselves to induce me for to attempt none other patronage than the name of my liege lord so gracious, nor to submit my labors to the censure of any person before a king so judicious, yet was I more animated to enterprise the same by the former experience that I had of a prince's benignity in that behalf what time [i.e. 1600] as I consecrated my English translation of the Roman history written by Titus Livius unto the immortal memory of the said noble and renowmed queen. Now, seeing that with her realms and dominions the best parts and gifts that were in her be likewise hereditarily descended upon your royal person, and the same multiplied in greater measure proportionable to the dignity of sex, the addition of scepters and diadems and the weighty charge of so puissant and populous an empire, it were in me a gross absurdity, if not mere impiety, to make any doubt of that excellent virtue of all others whereby princes come nearest unto the nature of God, whose majesty here upon earth they represent. . . .

Your Majesty's most humble and obedient subject,

Philemon Holland

THAT VIRTUE MAY BE TAUGHT AND LEARNED

THE SUMMARY

Plutarch, refuting here the error of those who are of opinion that by good and diligent instruction a man cannot become the better, recommendeth sufficiently the study of virtue. And to prove this assertion of his he sheweth that the apprentissage of that which is of small consequence in this world witnesseth enough that a man ought to be trained from day to day to the knowledge of things that are beseeming and worthy his person. Afterwards he declareth that as much travel should be employed to make him comprehend such things as be far distant from the capacity and excellency of his spirit, in which discourse he taxeth covertly those vain and giddy heads who (as they say) run after their own shadow, whereas they should stay and rest upon that which is firm and permanent.

We dispute of virtue and put in question whether prudence, justice, loyalty, and honesty may be taught or no. And do we admire then the works of orators, sailors and shipmasters, architects, husbandmen, and an infinite number of other such which be extant? Whereas of good men we have nothing but their bare and simple names, as if they were hippocentaurs, giants, or cyclops, and mervail we that of virtuous actions which be entire, perfect, and unblamable none can be found, ne yet any manners so composed according to duty but that they be tainted with some passions and vicious perturbations? Yea, and if it happen that Nature of herself bring forth some good and honest actions, the same straightways are darkened, corrupted, and in a manner marred by certain strange mixtures of contrary matters that creep into them, like as when among good corn there grow up weeds and wild bushes that choke the same, or when some kind and gentle fruit is clean altered by savage nourishment. Men learn to sing, to dance, to read and write, to till the ground, and to ride horses; they learn likewise to shew themselves, to do on their apparel decently; they are taught to wait at cup and trencher, to give drink at the table, to season and dress meat; and none of all this can they skill to perform and do handsomely if they be not trained thereto; and yet shall that for which these and such-like qualities they learn, to wit, good life and honest conversation, be reckoned a mere casual thing, coming by chance and fortune, and which can neither be taught nor learned? O good sirs, what a thing is this! In saying that virtue cannot be taught, we deny withal that it is or hath any being. For if it be true that the learning of it is the generation and breeding thereof, certes he that hindereth the one disannulleth the other, and in denying that it may be taught we grant that no such thing there is at all. And yet, as Plato saith, for the neck of a lute not made in proportion to the rest of the body there was never known one brother go to war with another, nor a friend to quarrel with his friend, ne yet two neighbor cities to fall out and maintain deadly feud to the interchangeable working and suff'ring of those miseries and calamities which follow open war. Neither can any man come forth and say that by occasion of an accent (as, for example, whether the word *telchines* should be pronounced with the accent over the second syllable or no) there arose sedition and dissension in any city, or debate in a house between man and wife about the warp and woof of any web; howbeit never man yet would take in hand to wear a piece of cloth, nor handle a book, nor play upon the lute or harp unless he had learned before; for albeit he were not like to sustain any great loss and no tall damage thereby, yet he would fear to be mocked and laughed to scorn for his labor, in which case, as Heraclitus saith, it were better for a man to conceal his own ignorance; and may such an one think, then, that he could order a house well, rule a wife, and behave himself as it becometh in marriage, bear magistracy or govern a commonweal as he ought, being never bound and brought up to it? Diogenes, espying upon a time a boy eating greedily and unmannerly, gave his master or tutor a good cuff on the ear, and good reason he had so to do as imputing the fault rather to him who had not taught than to the boy who had not learned better manners. And is it so indeed? Ought they of necessity who would be mannerly at the table both

in putting hand to a dish of meat and taking the cup with a good grace, or, as Aristophanes saith,

> At board not feeding greedily
> Nor laughing much, undecently,
> Nor crossing feet full wantonly,

to be taught even from their infancy? And is it possible that the same should know how to behave themselves in wedlock, how to manage the affairs of state, how to converse among men, how to bear office without touch and blame unless they have learned first how to carry themselves one toward another? Aristippus answered upon a time, when one said unto him, "And are you, sir, everywhere?" "I should," quoth he, laughing merrily, "cast away the fare for ferriage which I pay unto the mariner if I were everywhere." And why might not a man say likewise if children be not the better for their teaching the salary is lost which men bestow upon their masters and teachers? But we see that they, taking them into their governance presently from their nources, like as they did form their lims and joints featly with their hands, do prepare and frame their manners accordingly, and set them in the right way to virtue. And to this purpose answered very wisely a Laconian schoolmaster to one who demanded of him what good he did to the child of whom he had the charge. "Marry," quoth he, "I make him to take joy and pleasure in those things that be honest." And to say a truth, these teachers and governors instruct children to hold up their heads straight as they go in the street and not to bear it forward; also not to dip into sauce but with one finger, not to take bread or fish but with twain, to rub or scratch after this or that manner, and thus and thus to truss and hold up their clothes. What shall we say, then, to him who would make us believe that the art of physic professeth to scour the morphew or heal a whitflaw, but not to cure a pleurisy, fever, or the phrenzy? And what differeth he from them who hold that there be schools and rules to teach petties and little children how to be mannerly and demean themselves in small matters, but as for great, important, and absolute things it must be nothing else but use and custom, or else mere chance and fortune that doth effect them? For like as he were ridiculous and worthy to be laughed at who should say that no man ought to lay hand upon the oar for to row but he that hath been prentise to it, but sit at the stern and guide the helm he may who was never taught it; even so he who maintaineth that in some inferior arts there is required apprentissage, but for the attaining of virtue none at all, deserveth likewise to be mocked. And verily he should do contrary unto the Scythians, for they, as Herodotus writeth, use to put out the eyes of their slaves only to the end that, being blind, they might turn round about with their milk and so stir and shake it. But he forsooth putteth the eye of reason into these base and inferior arts which are no better than servants waiting upon others, but plucketh it from virtue. Iphicrates answered contrariwise, being demanded of Callias, the son of Chabrias, by way of contempt and derision in this wise: "What are you, sir? An archer? A targeteer? A man-at-arms? Or a light-armed soldier?" "I am none," quoth he, "of all these, but rather one of those who commandeth them all." Well, ridiculous then is he, and very absurd, who would say there were an art to be taught of drawing a bow and shooting, of fighting close at hand being armed at all pieces, of discharging bullets with a sling, or of sitting and riding an horse; but forsooth to lead and conduct an army there was none at all. As who would say that

feat were a thing not learned but coming by chance, I know not how. And yet I must needs say more sottish and foolish were he who should hold and affirm that prudence only could not be taught, without which no other arts and sciences be worth ought or avail any whit. That this is true and that she is alone the guide which leadeth and guideth all other sciences, arts, and virtues, giving them every one their due place and honor, and making them profitable to mankind, a man may know by this if there were nothing else: that there would be no grace at a feast, though the meat were never so well-dressed and served up by skilful cooks, though there were proper escuirs or shewers to set the dishes upon the boord, carvers, tasters, skinkers, and other servitors and waiters enough, unless there be some good order observed among the said ministers to place and dispose everything as it ought.

JOHN FLORIO (trans.)

MONTAIGNE'S *ESSAYS*

Montaigne's *Essais,* one of the great and original works of European literature, has a tangled bibliographical history. When the first edition was published in 1580 it was in two books; the second edition of 1582 contains a few expansions and additions; the third, 1587, virtually reprints the second; and the last edition (1588) published in Montaigne's lifetime (called the fifth on the titlepage, although no copy of a fourth is known) contains not only a new third book but also many important textual changes and additions. In 1595, three years after Montaigne's death, there appeared the first posthumous edition, which, because of its many new readings in all three books, was long regarded as authoritative (and so was used by Florio for his translation). The discovery, at a convent near Bordeaux in the late eighteenth century, of a copy of the 1588 edition that Montaigne had apparently used in preparing a new recension for the press raised many problems. For one thing, a contemporary hand has altered the "fifth edition" of the titlepage to "sixth"; for another, almost every page shows copious interlineations and marginal corrections, erasures, and rewritings. It is now known that most of these changes actually found their way into the 1595 text; but since that text contains a good many readings not in the Bordeaux copy, as well as readings altered from the Bordeaux copy, the basis of the 1595 text remains a puzzle. Since Mlle Marie de Jars de Gournay, Montaigne's *fille d'alliance,* who in 1635

published her own edition of the *Essais,* was perhaps responsible for the 1595 readings, scholars have come to regard the Bordeaux copy as the most authentic text. As such it was used for the superb "Edition Municipale" published by the city of Bordeaux.

These problems meant nothing to John Florio, who quite properly translated from the 1595 text as the latest and ostensibly the most authoritative. Before tackling the formidable job of rendering the *Essais* in English he had for some twenty years been a familiar figure in the London literary scene as author, translator, teacher of languages, and lexicographer. In 1598 he published, with dedications to the Earls of Rutland and Southampton and the Countess of Rutland, his notable *World of Words,* an Italian-English lexicon that long enjoyed great popularity. In the following year his translation of Montaigne was licensed to Edward Blount, and in 1603 it appeared in a sumptuous small folio containing a bombastic preface, commendatory verses by "Il Candido" (Dr. Matthew Gwinne?) and Samuel Daniel, and a dedication for each of the three books—the first addressed to Lucy, Countess of Bedford, and Lady Harington, the second to Elizabeth, Countess of Rutland, and Lady Rich (Sidney's "Stella"), and the third to Lady Grey and Lady Nevill. A second edition, dedicated to Queen Anne, appeared in 1613, and a third in 1632. Our text follows *The Essayes or Morall, Politike and Millitarie Discourses,* 1603 (STC 18041).

from MICHEL EYQUEM MONTAIGNE'S *ESSAYS* (1603)

To the Curteous Reader

Shall I apologize translation? Why, but some hold (as for their freehold) that such conversion is the subversion of universities. God hold with them, and withhold them from impeach or empair. It were an ill turn, the turning of books should be the over-turning of libraries. Yea, but my old fellow Nolano told me, and taught publicly, that from translation all science had its offspring. Likely, since even philosophy, grammar, rhetoric, logic, arithmetic, geometry, astronomy, music, and all the mathe-matics yet hold their name of the Greeks; and the Greeks drew their baptizing water from the conduit-pipes of the Egyptians, and they from the well-springs of the Hebrews or Chaldees. And can the well-springs be so sweet and deep, and will the well-drawn water be so sour and smell? And were their countries so ennobled, advantaged, and embellished by such deriving; and doth it drive our noblest colonies upon the rocks of ruin? And did they well? And proved they well? And must we prove ill that do so? Why, but learning would not be made com-mon. Yea, but learning cannot be too common, and the commoner the better. . . . If nothing can be now said but hath been said before . . . , what is that that hath been? That that shall be (as he said that was wisest). What do the best, then, but glean after others' harvest, borrow their colors, inherit their possessions? What do they but translate, perhaps usurp, at least collect? If with acknowledgment, it is well; if by stealth, it is too bad; in this our conscience is our accuser, posterity our judge; in that our study is our advocate, and you readers our jury. . . . Sup-pose Homer took nothing out of any, for we hear of none good before him, and there must be a first; yet Homer by Virgil is often so translated as Scaliger conceives there is the armor of Hercules most puissant put on the back of Bacchus most delicate; and Petrarch, if well tracked, would be found in their footsteps, whose very garbage less poets are noted to have gathered. . . . Why, then, belike I have done by Montaigne as Terence by Menander, made of good French no good English. If I have done no worse, and it be no worse taken, it is well. As he, if no poet, yet am I no thief, since I say of whom I had it, rather to imitate his and his authors' negligence then any backbiters' obscure diligence. His horse I set before you, perhaps without his trappings, and his meat without sauce. . . . He, most writing of himself, and the worst rather then the best, dis-claimeth all memory, authorities, or borrowing of the ancient or modern; whereas in course of his dis-course he seems acquainted not only with all, but no

other but authors. . . . Why, but essays are but men's school-themes pieced together; you might as well say, several texts. All is in the choice and handling. Yea marry, but Montaigne, had he wit, it was but a French wit, ferdillant, legier, and extravagant. Now say you English wits by the staidest censure of as learned a wit as is among you. The counsel of that judicious, worthy counselor, honorable Sir Edward Wotton, would not have embarked me to this dis-covery had not his wisdom known it worth my pains and your perusing. And should or would any dog-tooth'd critic or adder-tongu'd satirist scoff or find fault that in the course of his discourses, or web of his essays, or entitling of his chapters he holdeth a disjointed, broken, and gadding style; and that many times they answer not his titles, and have no co-herence together; to such I will say little, for they deserve but little; but if they list, else let them chuse, I send them to the ninth chapter of the third book, folio 596, where himself preventeth their carping, and, foreseeing their criticism, answereth them for me at full. . . . But some errors are mine, and mine by more then translation. Are they in grammer or ortography? As easy for you to right as me to be wrong. Or in construction, as misattributing *him, her,* or *it* to things alive or dead or neuter? You may soon know my meaning and eftsoons use your mending. Or are they in some uncouth terms, as *entrain, conscientious, endear, tarnish, comport, efface, facilitate, amusing, debauching, regret, effort, emotion,* and such like? If you like them not, take others most commonly set by them to expound them, since there they were set to make such likely French words familiar with our English, which well may bear them. . . . This printer's wanting a diligent corrector, my many employments, and the distance between me and my friends I should confer with may ex-tenuate, if not excuse, even more errors. In sum, if any think he could do better, let him try; then will he better think of what is done. Seven or eight of great wit and worth have assayed, but found these essays no attempt for French apprentices or Little-tonians. If thus done it may please you, as I wish it may and I hope it shall, I with you shall be pleased; though not, yet still I am the same resolute

John Florio.

The Author to the Reader

Reader, lo, here a well-meaning book. It doth at the first entrance forewarn thee that in contriving the same I have proposed unto myself no other then a familiar and private end; I have had no respect or consideration at all either to thy service or to my glory; my forces are not capable of any such desseign. I have vowed the same to the particular commodity of my kinsfolks and friends, to the end that loosing me (which they are likely to do ere long) they may therein find some lineaments of my conditions and humors, and by that means reserve more whole and more lively foster the knowledge and acquaintance they have had of me. Had my intention been to forestall and purchase the world's opinion and favor I would surely have adorned myself more quaintly, or kept a more grace and solemn march. I desire therein to be delineated in mine own genuine, simple, and ordinary fashion, without contention, art, or study; for it is myself I pourtray. My imperfections shall therein be read to the life, and my natural form discerned so farforth as public reverence hath permitted me. For if my fortune had been to have lived among those nations which yet are said to live under the sweet liberty of Nature's first and uncorrupted laws, I assure thee I would most willingly have pourtrayed myself fully and naked. Thus, gentle reader, myself am the groundwork of my book. It is, then, no reason thou shouldest employ thy time about so frivolous and vain a subject. Therefore farewell. From Montaigne, the first of March, 1580.

BOOK I, CHAPTER 18: That We Should Not Judge of Our Happiness until after Our Death

Scilicet ultima semper
Expectanda dies homini est, dicique beatus
Ante obitum nemo, supremaque funera debet.
[Ovid, *Metamorphoses* iii.135]

We must expect of man the latest day,
Nor, ere he die, he's happy, can we say.

The very children are acquainted with the story of Croesus to this purpose: who, being taken by Cyrus and by him condemned to die, upon the point of his execution cried out aloud: "O Solon, Solon!" Which words of his being reported to Cyrus, who inquiring what he meant by them, told him he now at his own cost verified the advertisement Solon had beforetimes given him, which was that no man, what cheerful and blandishing countenance soever Fortune shewed them, may rightly deem himself happy till such time as he have passed the last day of his life, by reason of the uncertainty and vicissitude of human things, which, by a very light motive and slight occasion, are often changed from one to another clean contrary state and degree. And therefore Agesilaus answered one that counted the king of Persia happy because, being very young, he had gotten the garland of so mighty and great a dominion. "Yea, but," said he, "Priam at the same age was not unhappy." Of the kings of Macedon that succeeded Alexander the Great some were afterward seen to become joiners and scriveners at Rome; and of tyrants of Sicily, schoolmaisters at Corinth. One that had conquered half the world, and been emperor over so many armies, became an humble and miserable suitor to the rascally officers of a king of Egypt. At so high a rate did that great Pompey purchase the irksome prolonging of his life but for five or six months. And in our fathers' days Lodowick Sforce, tenth duke of Milan, under whom the state of Italy had so long been turmoiled and shaken, was seen to die a wretched prisoner at Loches in France, but not till he had lived and lingered ten years in thraldom, which was the worst of his bargain. O inhumane and barbarous cruelty! So various and inconstant is the hand of Fortune in disposing of empires and kingdoms. And a thousand such like examples. For it seemeth that as the sea-billows and surging waves rage and storm against the surly pride and stubborn height of our buildings, so is there above certain spirits that envy the rising prosperities and greatness here below.

Usque adeo res humanas vis abdita quaedam
Obterit, et pulchros fasces saevasque secures
Proculcare, ac ludibrio sibi habere videtur.
Lucretius lib. v.1233

A hidden pow'r so men's states hath outworn,
Fair swords, fierce scepters, signs of honors borne
It seems to trample and deride in scorn.

And it seemeth Fortune doth sometimes narrowly watch the last day of our life, thereby to shew her power and in one moment to overthrow what for many years together she had been erecting, and makes us cry after Laberius, *Nimirum hac die una plus vixi, mihi quam vivendum fuit.* Thus it is: "I have lived longer by this one day then I should." So may that good advice of Solon be taken with reason. But forsomuch as he is a philosopher with whom the favors or disfavors of Fortune and good or ill luck have no place and are not regarded by them, and puissances and greatnesses and accidents of quality are well-nigh indifferent, I deem it very likely he had a further reach, and meant that the same good fortune of our life (which dependeth of the tranquillity and contentment of a well-borne mind and of the resolution and assurance of a well-ordered soul) should never be ascribed unto man until he have been seen play the last act of his comedy, and without doubt the hardest. In all the rest there may be some mask; either these sophistical discourses of philosophy are not in us but by countenance, or accidents that never touch us to the quick give us always leisure to keep our countenance settled. But when that last part of death and of ourselves comes to be acted, then no dissembling will avail; then is it high time to speak plain English and put off all vizards; then whatsoever the pot containeth must be shewn, be it good or bad, foul or clean, wine or water.

> *Nam verae voces tum demum pectore ab imo*
> *Ejiciuntur, et eripitur persona, manet res.*
> Lucretius lib. iii.57

> For then are sent true speeches from the heart;
> We are ourselves; we leave to play a part.

Lo here, why at this last cast all our live's other actions must be tried and touched. It is the maister-day, the day that judgeth all others; it is the day, saith an ancient writer, that must judge of all my fore-passed years. To death do I refer the essay of my studies' fruit. There shall we see whether my discourse proceed from my heart or from my mouth. I have seen diverse by their death, either in good or evil, give reputation to all their forepassed life. Scipio, father-in-law to Pompey, in well dying re-

paired the ill opinion which until that hour men had ever held of him. Epaminondas, being demanded which of the three he esteemed most, either Chabrias or Iphicrates or himself, "It is necessary," said he, "that we be seen to die, before your question may well be resolved." Verily we should steal much from him if he should be weighed without the honor and greatness of his end. God hath willed it as he pleased it; but in my time three of the most execrable persons that ever I knew in all abhomination of life, and the most infamous, have been seen to die very orderly and quietly, and in every circumstance composed even unto perfection. There are some brave and fortunate deaths. I have seen her [i.e. Atropos, one of the Three Fates] cut the twine of some man's life with a progress of wonderful advancement, and with so worthy an end, even in the flow'r of his growth and spring of his youth, that in mine opinion his ambitious and haughty couragious designs thought nothing so high as might interrupt them; who, without going to the place where he pretended, arrived there more gloriously and worthily than either his desire or hope aimed at. And by his fall forewent the power and name whither by his course he aspired. When I judge of other men's lives I ever respect how they have behaved themselves in their end; and my chiefest study is I may well demean myself at my last gasp, that is to say, quietly and constantly.

BOOK II, CHAPTER 12: An Apology of Raymond Sebond

... My house hath long since ever stood open to men of understanding, and is very well known to many of them; for my father, who commanded the same fifty years and upward, set on fire by that new kind of earnestness wherewith King Francis the First embraced letters and raised them unto credit, did with great diligence and much cost endeavor to purchase the acquaintance of learned men, receiving and entertaining them as holy persons, and who had some particular inspiration of divine wisdom; collecting their sentences and discourses as if they had been oracles, and with so much more reverence and religious regard by how much less authority he had to judge of them, for he had no knowledge of letters, no more than his predecessors before him. As for me, I love them indeed, but yet I worship them not. Amongst others, Peter Bunel (a man, in his time, by reason of his learning, of high esteem), having sojourned a few days at Montaigne with my father and others of his coat, being ready to depart thence, presented him with a book entituled *Theologia*

naturalis, sive liber creaturarum magistri Raimondi de Sebonda. And forsomuch as the Italian and Spanish tongues were very familiar unto him and that the book was written in a kind of Latinized Spanish, whereof diverse words had Latin terminations, he hoped that with little aid he might reap no small profit by it, and commended the same very much unto him as a book most profitable and fitting the days in which he gave it him. It was even at what time the newfangles of Luther began to creep in favor and in many places to shake the foundation of our ancient belief. Wherein he seemed to be well advised as he who by discourse of reason foresaw that this budding disease would easily turn to an execrable atheism; for the vulgar many, wanting the faculty to judge of things by themselves, suffering itself to be carried away by fortune and led on by outward apparances, if once it be possessed with the boldness to despise and malapertness to impugn the opinions which tofore it held in awful reverence (as are those wherein consisteth their salvation), and that some articles of their religion be made doubtful and questionable, they will soon and easily admit an equal uncertainty in all other parts of their belief, as they that had no other grounded aucthority or foundation but such as are now shaken and weakened, and immediately reject (as a tyrannical yoke) all impressions they had in former times received by the aucthority of laws or reverence of ancient custom. . . .

My father, a few days before his death lighting by chance upon this book which before he had neglected, amongst other writings commanded me to translate the same into French. It is easy to translate such aucthors, where nothing but the matter is to be represented, but hard and dangerous to undertake such as have added much to the grace and elegancy of the language, namely to reduce them into a weaker and poorer tongue. It was a strange task and new occupation for me, but by fortune being then at leisure, and unable to gainsay the commandement of the best father that ever was, I came ere long (as well as I could) to an end of it; wherein he took singular delight and commanded the same to be printed, which accordingly was after his decease performed. I found the conceits of the author to be excellent, the contexture of his work well followed, and his project full of piety. Now forasmuch as diverse amuse themselves to read it, and especially ladies (to whom we owe most service), it hath often been my hap to help them, when they were reading it, to discharge the book of two principal objections which are brought against the same. His drift is bold and his scope advent'rous, for he undertaketh by human and natural reasons to establish and verify all the articles of Christian religion against atheists. Wherein (to say truth) I find him so resolute and so happy as I deem it a thing impossible to do better in that argument and think that none equaleth him. Which book seeming to me both overrich and exquisite, being written by an aucthor whose name is so little known and of whom all we know is that he was a Spaniard who, about two hundred years since, professed physic in Toulouse, I demanded once of Adrianus Turnebus (a man who knew all things) what such a book might be, who answered that he deemed the same to be some quintessence extracted from out Saint Thomas Aquinas; for, in good truth, only such a spirit, fraught with so infinite erudition and so full of admirable subtilty, was capable of such and so rare imaginations. So it is that whosoever be the author or deviser of it (the title whereof ought not, without further reason, to be taken from Sebond) he was a very sufficient-worthy man, and endowed with sundry other excellent qualities.

The first thing he is reproved for in his book is that Christians wrong themselves much in that they ground their belief upon human reasons, which is conceived but by faith and by a particular inspiration of God. Which objection seemeth to contain some zeal of piety, by reason whereof we ought with so much more mildness and regard endeavor to satisfy them that propose it. It were a charge more befitting a man conversant, and suitable to one acquainted, with the Holy Scriptures than me, who am altogether ignorant in them. Nevertheless, I think that, even as to a matter so divine and high and so much exceeding all human understanding as is this verity wherewith it hath pleased the goodness of God to enlighten us, it is most requisite that he afford and lend us his help, and that, with an extraordinary and privileged favor, that so we may the better conceive and entertain the same. For I suppose that means merely human can no way be capable of it, which, if they were, so many rare and excellent minds, and so plenteously stored with natural faculties, as have been in times past would never, by their discourse, have miss'd the attaining of this knowledge. It is faith only which lively and assuredly embraceth the high mysteries of our religion. And no man can doubt but that it is a most excellent and commendable enterprise properly to accommodate and fit to the service of our faith the natural helps and human implements which God hath bestowed upon us. And no question is to be made but that it is the most honorable employment we can put them unto, and that there is no occupation or intent more worthy a good Christian than by all means, studies, and imaginations carefully to endeavor how to embellish, amplify, and extend the truth of his belief and religion. It is not enough for us to serve God in spirit and soul; we owe him besides, and we yield unto him, a corporal worshiping; we apply our lims, our motions, and all external things to honor him. The like ought to be done, and we should accompany our faith with all the reason we possess, yet always with this proviso, that we think it doth not depend of us, and that all our strength and arguments can never attain to so supernatural and divine a knowledge. . . .

[Taking as his point of departure this studiously commonplace summary of natural theology, Montaigne ironically sets about to defend Sebond from his detractors. Actually he marshals against the most cherished principles of rational theology a massive attack, bringing into play all his great reserves of wit, learning, and irony. In this, the longest and most elaborate of the *Essays,* he examines man's alleged superiority to animals, man's philosophical achieve ments, man's knowledge of God, man's knowledge of himself—in fact, all the central tenets of Renaissance optimism—only to conclude that *homo sapiens,* in spite of his pride, is an impotent and ridiculous creature. Thus, near the opening of the "Apology," he sketches in his aims and methods.]

Some say his [i.e. Sebond's] arguments are weak, and simple to verify what he would. . . . Such fellows must somewhat more roughly be handled, for they are more dangerous and more malicious then the first [i.e. those who object to Sebond's system of natural theology]. Man doth willingly apply other men's sayings to the advantage of the opinions he hath forejudged in himself. To an atheist all writings make for atheism. He with his own venom infecteth the innocent matter. These have some preoccupation of judgment that makes their taste wallowish and tasteless to conceive the reasons of Sebond. As for the rest, they think to have fair play offered them if they have free liberty to combat our religion with mere worldly weapons, which they durst not charge did they behold her in her majesty, full of aucthority and commandement. The means I use to suppress this frenzy, and which seemeth the fittest for my purpose, is to bruze, to crush, and trample this pride and fierceness of man under foot and violently to pull out of their hands the silly weapons of their reason; to make them stoop and bite and snarl at the ground under the aucthority and reverence of God's majesty. Only to her belongeth science and wisdom; it is she alone can judge of herself, and from her we steal whatsoever we repute, value, and count ourselves to be. . . .

They must be taught that to convince the weakness of their reason we need not go far to cull out rare examples; and that it is so defective and blind as there is no facility so clear that is clear enough unto her; that easy and uneasy is all one to her; that all subjects equally, and Nature in general, disavoweth her jurisdiction and interposition. What preacheth truth unto us when it biddeth us fly and shun worldly philosophy, when it so often telleth us that all our wisdom is but folly before God, that of all vanities man is the greatest, that man (who presumeth of his knowledge) doth not yet know what knowledge is, and that man, who is nothing if he but think to be something, seduceth and deceiveth himself? These sentences of the Holy Ghost do so lively and manifestly express what I would maintain as I should need no other proof against such as with all submission and obeisance would yield to his authority. But these will needs be whipp'd to their own cost, and cannot abide their reason to be combated but by itself.

Let us now but consider man alone, without other help, armed but with his own weapons, and unprovided of the grace and knowledge of God—which is all his honor, all his strength, and all the ground of his being. Let us see what holdfast or freehold he hath in this gorgeous and goodly equipage. Let him with the utmost power of his discourse make me understand upon what foundation he hath built those great advantages and odds he supposeth to have over other creatures. Who hath persuaded him that this admirable moving of heaven's vaults, that the eternal light of these lamps so fiercely rolling over his head, that the horror-moving and continual motion of this infinite vast ocean were established and continue so many ages for his commodity and service? Is it possible to imagine anything so ridiculous as this miserable and wretched creature, which is not so much as maister of himself, exposed and subject to the offenses of all things, and yet dareth call himself maister and emperor of this universe? In whose power it is not to know the least part of it, much less to command the same. And the priviledge, which he so fondly challengeth, to be the only absolute creature in this huge world's frame perfectly able to know the absolute beauty and several parts thereof, and that he is only of power to yield the great Architect thereof due thanks for it, and to keep account both of the receipts and layings-out of the world. Who hath sealed him this patent? Let him shew us his letters of priviledge for so noble and so great a charge. . . .

Presumption is our natural and original infirmity. Of all creatures, man is the most miserable and frail, and therewithal the proudest and disdainfullest. Who perceiveth and seeth himself placed here amidst the filth and mire of the world, fast tied and nailed to the worst, most senseless, and drooping part of the world, in the vilest corner of the house and farthest from heaven's cope, with those creatures that are the worst of the three conditions—and yet dareth imaginarily place himself above the circle of the moon and reduce heaven under his feet. It is through the vanity of the same imagination that he dare equal himself to God, that he ascribeth divine conditions unto himself, that he selecteth and separateth himself from out the rank of other creatures, to which his fellow-brethren and compeers he cuts out and shareth their parts and allotteth them what portions of means or forces he thinks good. How knoweth he, by the virtue of his understanding, the inward and secret motions of beasts? By what comparison from them to us doth he conclude the brutishness he ascribeth unto them? When I am playing with my cat, who knows whether she have more sport in dallying with me then I have in gaming with her? We entertain one another with mutual apish tricks; if I have my hour to begin or to refuse, so hath she hers. . . .

Suppose beasts had all the virtue, the knowledge, the wisdom, and sufficiency of the Stoics, they should still be beasts; nor might they ever be compared unto a miserable, wretched, and senseless man. For when all is done, whatsoever is not as we are is not of any worth. And God, to be esteemed of us, must (as we will shew anon) draw somewhat near it. Whereby it appeareth that it is not long of a true discourse but of a foolish hardiness and self-presuming obstinacy we prefer ourselves before other creatures, and sequester ourselves from their condition and society.

But to return to our purpose, we have for our part inconstancy, irresolution, uncertainty, sorrow, superstition, carefulness for future things (yea, after our life), ambition, covetousness, jealousy, envy, inordinate, mad, and untamed appetites, war, falsehood, disloyalty, detraction, and curiosity. Surely we have strangely overpaid this worthy discourse whereof we so much glory, and this readiness to judge or capacity to know, if we have purchased the same with the price of so infinite passions to which we are uncessantly enthralled. . . .

[Having thus devastatingly compared man to beasts, Montaigne turns his attention to human reason.] I have, in my days, seen a hundred artificers and as many laborers more wise and more happy then some rectors in the university, and whom I would rather resemble. Methinks learning hath a place amongest things necessary for man's life (as glory, nobleness, dignity, or at most as riches and such other qualities which, indeed, stead the same), but afar off, and more in conceit than by nature. We have not much more need of offices, of rules, and laws how to live in our commonwealth than the cranes and ants have in theirs. Which notwithstanding, we see how orderly, and without instruction, they maintain themselves. If man were wise, he would value everything according to its worth, and as it is either more profitable or more necessary for life. He that shall number us by our actions and proceedings shall doubtless find many more excellent ones amongest the ignorant then among the wiser sort; I mean in all kind of virtues. My opinion is that ancient Rome brought forth many men of much more valor and sufficiency, both for peace and war, then this late, learned Rome, which with all her wisdom hath overthrown her erst-flourishing estate. . . .

So long as man shall be persuaded to have means or power of himself, so long will he deny and never acknowledge what he oweth unto his Maister; he shall always, as the common saying is, make shift with his own. He must be stripped into his shirt. Let us consider some notable example of the effect of philosophy. Posidonius, having long time been grieved with a painful ling'ring disease, which with the smarting pain made him to wring his hands and gnash his teeth, thought to scorn grief with exclaiming and crying out against it: "Do what thou list, yet will I never say that thou art peril or pain." He feeleth the same passions that my lackey doth, but he boasteth himself that at least he containeth his tongue under the laws of his sect. . . .

Be it supposed that learning and knowledge should work those effects they speak of, that is, to blunt and abate the sharpness of those accidents or mischances that follow and attend us. Doth she any more than what ignorance effecteth much more evidently and simply? The philosopher Pyrrho, being at sea and by reason of a violent storm in great danger to be cast away, presented nothing unto those that were with him in the ship to imitate but the security of an hog which was aboard, who, nothing at all dismay'd, seemed to behold and outstare the tempest. Philosophy, after all her precepts, gives us over to the examples of a wrestler or of a muleteer, in whom we ordinarily perceive much less feeling of death, of pain, of grief, and other inconveniences, and more undaunted constancy then ever learning or knowledge could store a man withal, unless he were born and of himself, through some natural habitude, prepared unto it. . . . Beasts do manifestly declare unto us how many infirmities our minds' agitation brings us. That which is told us of those that inhabit Bresill, who die only through age, which some impute to the clearness and calmness of their air, I rather ascribe to the calmness and clearness of their minds, void and free from all passions, cares, toiling, and unpleasant labors, as a people that pass their life in a wonderful kind of simplicity and ignorance, without letters or laws, and without kings or any religion. . . .

[After a destructive analysis of the Aristotelian, Epicurean, and Stoic philosophies Montaigne comes to Pyrrhonism or skepticism. Of all man's intellectual constructs it appeals to him the most, precisely because it is the least pretentious.] That ignorance which is known, judged, and condemned is not an absolute ignorance; for, to be so, she must altogether be ignorant of herself. So that the profession of the Pyrrhonians is ever to waver, to doubt, and to enquire; never to be assured of anything nor to take any warrant of himself. Of the three actions or faculties of the soul, that is to say the imaginative, the concupiscible, and the consenting, they allow and conceive the two former; the last they hold and defend to be ambiguous, without inclination or approbation either of one or other side. . . . How many arts are there which profess to consist more in conjecture than in the science, that distinguish not between truth and falsehood but only follow seeming? There is both truth and false, say they, and there are means in us to seek it out, but not to stay it when we touch it. It is better for us to suffer the order of the world to manage us without further inquisition. A mind warranted from prejudice hath a marvelous preferment to tranquillity. Men that censure and control their judges do never duly submit themselves unto them. How much more docile and tractable are simple and uncurious minds found both towards the laws of religion and politic decrees then these overvigilant and nice wits, teachers of divine and human causes? There is nothing in man's invention wherein is so much likelihood, possibility, and profit. This representeth man bare and naked, acknowledging his natural weakness, apt to receive from above some strange power, disfurnished of all human knowledge, and so much the more fit to harbor divine understanding, disannulling his judgment that so he may give more place unto faith; neither misbelieving nor establishing any doctrine or opinion repugnant unto common laws and observances, humble, obedient, disciplinable, and studious; a sworn enemy to heresy, and by consequence exempting himself from all vain and irreligious opinions invented and brought up by false sects. . . .

[Finally, after a long and very discursive analysis of philosophy, rational theology, and psychology, Montaigne brings his essay in skepticism to a close with a discussion of epistemology. He systematically undercuts the validity of both reason and sensation as the bases of cognition, and is therefore left with the solipsist proposition that man can know nothing with certainty.]

Our fantasy doth not apply itself to strange things, but is rather conceived by the interposition of senses; and senses cannot comprehend a strange subject, nay, not so much as their own passions; and so nor the fantasy nor the apparance is the subject's, but rather the passion's only, and sufferance of the sense, which passion and subject are divers things. Therefore, who judgeth by apparances judgeth by a thing different from the subject. And to say that the senses' passions

refer the quality of strange subjects by resemblance unto the soul, how can the soul and the understanding rest assured of that resemblance, having of itself no commerce with forraign subjects? Even as he that knows not Socrates, seeing his picture, cannot say that it resembleth him. . . . May it be that some choice apparances rule and direct the others? This choice must be verified by another choice, the second by a third, and so shall we never make an end. In few, there is no constant existence, neither of our being nor of the objects. And we and our judgment and all mortal things else do uncessantly roll, turn, and pass away. Thus can nothing be certainly established, nor of the one nor of the other, both the judging and the judged being in continual alteration and motion. We have no communication with being, for every human nature is ever in the middle between being born and dying, giving nothing of itself but an obscure apparance and shadow, and an uncertain and weak opinion. And if, perhaps, you fix your thought to take its being, it would be even as if one should go about to prison the water; for how much the more he shall close and press that which, by its own nature, is ever gliding, so much the more he shall loose what he would hold and fasten. Thus, seeing all things are subject to pass from one change to another, reason, which therein seeketh a real subsistence, finds herself deceived as unable to apprehend anything subsistent and permanent, forsomuch as each thing either cometh to a being and is not yet altogether, or beginneth to die before it be born. . . .

"O, what a vile and abject thing is man . . . unless he raise himself above humanity!" Observe here a notable speech and a profitable desire, but likewise absurd. For to make the handful greater than the hand, and the embraced greater then the arm, and to hope to straddle more than our legs' length, is impossible and monstrous; nor that man should mount over and above himself or humanity, for he cannot see but with his own eyes, nor take hold but with his own arms. He shall raise himself up if it please God extraordinarily to lend him His helping hand. He may elevate himself by forsaking and renouncing his own means, and suff'ring himself to be elevated and raised by mere heavenly means. It is for our Christian faith, not for his Stoic virtue, to pretend or aspire to this divine metamorphosis or miraculous transmutation.

Book II, Chapter 28: All Things Have Their Season

Those who compare Cato the Censor to Cato the Younger (that killed himself) compare two notable natures, and in form near one unto another. The first exploited his sundry ways and excelleth in military exploits and utility of his public vacations. But the younger's virtue (besides that it were blasphemy, in vigor to compare any unto him) was much more sincere and unspotted. For who will discharge the Censor of envy and ambition, that durst countercheck the honor of Scipio, in goodness and all other parts of excellency far greater and better then him or any other man living in his age? Amongst other things reported of him this is one: that in his eldest years he gave himself with so earnest a longing to learn the Greek tongue as if it had been to quench a long-burning thirst; a thing in mine opinion not very honorable in him. It is properly that which we call doting or to become a child again. All things have their season, yea, the good and all. And I may say my Pater noster out of season. As T. Quintius Flaminius was accused, forasmuch as being general of an army, even in the hour of the conflict he was seen to withdraw himself apart, amusing himself to pray God although he gained the battle.

> *Imponit finem sapiens et rebus honestis.*
>> Juvenal, *Satires* vi.444

> A wise man will use moderation
> Even in things of commendation.

Eudemonidas, seeing Xenocrates, very old, laboriously apply himself in his school lectures, said, "When will this man know something, since he is yet learning?" And Philopoemen, to those who highly extolled King Ptolemy [V̄?] because he daily hard'ned his body to the exercise of arms: "It is not," said he, "a matter commendable in a king of his age in them to exercise himself; he should now really and substantially imploy them." Wise men say that young men should make their preparations and old men enjoy them. And the greatest vice they note in us is that our desires do uncessantly grow younger and younger. We are ever beginning anew to live. Our studies and our desires should sometimes have a feeling of age. We have a foot in the grave, and our appetites and pursuits are but new-born.

> *Tu secanda marmora*
> *Locas sub ipsum funus, et supulchri*
> *Immemor, struis domos.*
>> Horace, *Car.* ii, *Od.* xviii.17

> You, when you should be going to your grave,
> Put marble out to work, build houses brave,
> Unmindful of the burial you must have.

The longest of my desseigns doth not extend to a whole year; now I only apply myself to make an end; I shake off all my new hopes and enterprises; I bid my last farewell to all the places I leave, and daily dispossess myself of what I have. *Olim jam nec perit quicquam mihi, nec acquiritur. Plus superest viatici quam viae.* "It is a good while since I neither loose nor get anything; I have more to bear my charges then way to go."

> *Vixi, et quem dederat cursum fortuna peregi.*
>> Virgil, *Aeneid* iv.653

> I have liv'd, and the race have pass'd
> Wherein my fortune had me plac'd.

To conclude, it is all the ease I find in my age, and that it suppresseth many cares and desires in me wherewith life is much disquieted. The care of the world's course, the care of riches, of greatness, of knowledge, of health, and of myself. This man learneth to speak when he should rather learn to hold his peace forever. A man may always continue his study, but not schooling. O fond-foolish for an old man to be ever an abcedarian.

> *Diversos diversa juvant, non omnibus annis*
> *Omnia conveniunt.*
>> Catullus, *Eleg.* [*recte* Maximianus
>> (Pseudo-Gallus)] i.104

> Diverse delights to diverse, nor to all
> Do all things at all years convenient fall.

If we must needs study, let us study something sortable to our condition, that we may answer, as he did who, being demanded what his studies would stead him in his decrepity, answered that he might the better and with more ease leave this world. Such a study was young Cato's in forefeeling his approaching end, who light upon Plato's discourse of the soul's immortality [i.e. the *Phaedo*]. Not, as it may be supposed, that long before he had not stored himself with all sorts of munition for such a dislodging. Of assurance, of constancy, and instruction he had more then Plato hath in all his writings. His science and his courage were in this respect above all philosophy. He undertook this occupation not for the service of his death, but as one who did not so much as interrupt his sleep in a deliberation of such consequence, who ever without choice or change continued his wonted studies and all other accustomed actions of his life. The same night wherein the praetorship was refused him he passed over in play. That wherein he must die he spent in reading. The loss of life or office was all one to him.

GEORGE CHAPMAN (trans.)

HOMER'S *ILIAD* and *ODYSSEY*

Unlike Virgil, Homer (and the Greeks in general) had been neglected by Tudor translators. In 1580 Thomas Purfoote had registered for publication a wretched thing called *The Strange, Wonderful, and Bloody Battle between Frogs and Mice* (a translation by William Fowldes in "heroical verse" finally published in 1603), but the only serious effort to render Homer in English before Chapman did the work that, as he boasted, he was born to do, was Arthur Hall's version (1581) of *Ten Books of Homer's Iliads* from the French of Hagues Salel (1555)—an ungainly and inaccurate copy of a copy in fourteeners. Chapman apparently turned to his great task sometime in the mid-nineties, and in 1598 he published the first fruits of his labors as *Seven Books of the Iliads of Homer, Prince of Poets. Translated According to the Greek in Judgment of His Best Commentaries.* Consisting of Books I–II and VII–XI in septenary couplets, it was dedicated to the Earl of Essex with a preface advancing a characteristically exalted view of the moral uses of poetry. *Achilles' Shield*, published later in the same year, a translation in the decasyllabic couplets which Chapman was to use later in his version of the *Odyssey*, contains Books XII–XVIII, a vehement attack (in the dedication to Essex) on the critical views of Scaliger, and a defense of the preface to the *Seven Books* in an epistle to the "Understander." At an uncertain date (perhaps 1610) the work was carried on with *Homer, Prince of Poets, Translated According to the Greek in Twelve Books of His Iliads*, a volume containing the 1598 translation of Books I–II and VII–XI plus III–VI

and XII, a grave and eloquent verse epistle to Prince Henry, a sonnet to Queen Anne, fifteen complimentary poems and sonnets to various personages of honor, and a poem "To the Reader." The complete *Iliad* was at last entered in the Stationers' Register on April 18, 1611, and shortly after (probably in the same year) there was published in folio *The Iliads of Homer, Prince of Poets. Never Before in Any Language Truly Translated. With a Comment on Some of the Chief Places.* Books I–II (down to the catalogue of ships) had been newly translated for this edition, and Books XIII–XXIV, as Chapman admits in his preface, had been tossed off in less than fifteen weeks. The angry preface defends the translator from the malicious charge of using other versions to conceal his ignorance of Greek. The translation of the *Odyssey* did not require so long a time. "Twenty-four books of Homer's Odysseys" was entered in the Stationers' Register on November 2, 1614, and presumably in the same year the first twelve books were published as *Homer's Odysses* with a dedication to Robert Carr, Earl of Somerset. Finally, in 1616, there appeared in a single handsome folio *The Whole Works of Homer*, a title that was eventually justified (?1624) when Chapman published his version of the allegedly Homeric *Batrachomyomachia*, hymns, and epigrams. Our text is based upon *The Whole Works of Homer; Prince of Poetts In his Iliads, and Odysses. Translated according to the Greeke, By Geo: Chapman*, 1616 (STC 13624).

FROM THE WHOLE WORKS OF HOMER, PRINCE OF POETS, IN HIS ILIADS AND ODYSSES, TRANSLATED ACCORDING TO THE GREEK (1616)

To the High-Born Prince of Men, Henry, Thrice Royal Inheritor to the United Kingdoms of Great Britain, etc.

Since perfect happiness, by princes sought,
Is not with birth born nor exchequers bought,
Nor follows in great trains, nor is possess'd
With any outward state, but makes him blest
That governs inward and beholdeth there
All his affections stand about him bare,
That by his power can send to Tow'r and death
All trait'rous passions, marshaling beneath

His justice his mere will, and in his mind   10
Holds such a scepter as can keep confin'd
His whole life's actions in the royal bounds
Of virtue and religion, and their grounds
Takes in to sow his honors, his delights,
And complete empire, you should learn these rights,
Great prince of men, by princely presidents;
Which here, in all kinds, my true zeal presents
To furnish your youth's groundwork and first state,
And let you see one godlike man create
All sorts of worthiest men; to be contriv'd

In your worth only, giving him, reviv'd,   20
For whose life Alexander would have given
One of his kingdoms, who, as sent from heaven
And thinking well that so divine a creature
Would never more enrich the race of nature,
Kept as his crown his works, and thought them still
His angels, in all power to rule his will;
And would affirm that Homer's poesy
Did more advance his Asian victory
Then all his armies. O, 'tis wondrous much
(Though nothing priz'd) that the right virtuous touch 30
Of a well-written soul to virtue moves!
Nor have we souls to purpose if their loves
Of fitting objects be not so inflam'd.
How much, then, were this kingdom's main soul maim'd
To want this great inflamer of all powers
That move in human souls! All realms but yours
Are honor'd with him and hold blest that state
That have his works to read and contemplate,
In which humanity to her height is rais'd,
Which all the world (yet none enough) hath prais'd. . . .

    And lastly, great prince, mark and pardon me,   41
As in a flourishing and ripe fruit tree
Nature hath made the bark to save the bole,
The bole the sap, the sap to deck the whole
With leaves and branches, they to bear and shield
The useful fruit, the fruit itself to yield
Guard to the kernel, and for that all those
(Since out of that again the whole tree grows),
So in our tree of man, whose nervy root
Springs in his top, from thence even to his foot,   50
There runs a mutual aid through all his parts,
All join'd in one to serve his queen of arts,
In which doth Poesy, like the kernel, lie
Obscur'd, though her Promethean faculty
Can create men and make even death to live,
For which she should live honor'd; kings should give
Comfort and help to her that she might still
Hold up their spirits in virtue, make the will
That governs in them to the power conform'd,
The power to justice, that the scandals storm'd   60
Against the poor dame clear'd by your fair Grace,
Your Grace may shine the clearer, her low place
Not shewing her the highest leaves obscure.
Who raise her raise themselves, and he sits sure
Whom her wing'd hand advanceth, since on it
Eternity doth (crowning virtue) sit.
All whose poor seed, like violets in their beds,
Now grow with bosom-hung and hidden heads,
For whom I must speak (though their fate convinces
Me worst of poets) to you, best of princes.   70

    By the most humble and faithful implorer for
    all the graces to your Highness eternized by
    your divine Homer,
                                    George Chapman

The Preface to the Reader

Of all books extant in all kinds Homer is the first and best. No one before his (Josephus affirms) nor before him (saith Velleius Paterculus) was there any whom he imitated, nor after him any that could imitate him. And that poesy may be no cause of detraction from all the eminence we give him Spondanus (preferring it to all arts and sciences) unanswerably argues and proves. For to the glory of God and the singing of his glories, no man dares deny, man was chiefly made. And what art performs this chief end of man with so much excitation and expression as poesy? Moses, David, Salomon, Job, Esay, Jeremy, etc. chiefly using that to the end above said. And since the excellence of it cannot be obtained by the labor and art of man (as all easily confess it), it must needs be acknowledged a divine infusion. To prove which in a word this distich, in my estimation, serves something nearly:

    Great poesy, blind Homer, makes all see
    Thee capable of all arts, none of thee.

For out of him, according to our most grave and judicial Plutarch, are all arts deduced, confirmed, or illustrated. It is not, therefore, the world's vilifying of it that can make it vile, for so we might argue and blaspheme the most incomparably sacred. It is not of the world indeed, but, like truth, hides itself from it. Nor is there any such reality of wisdom's truth in all human excellence as in poets' fictions. That most vulgar and foolish receipt of poetical license being of all knowing men to be exploded, excepting it (as if poets had a tale-telling priviledge above others), no artist being so strictly and inextricably confined to all the laws of learning, wisdom, and truth as a poet. For were not his fictions composed of the sinews and souls of all those, how could they differ far from and be combined with eternity? To all sciences, therefore, I must still (with our learned and ingenious Spondanus) prefer it as having a perpetual commerce with the Divine Majesty, embracing and illustrating all his most holy precepts, and enjoying continual discourse with his thrice perfect and most comfortable Spirit. And as the contemplative life is most worthily and divinely preferred by Plato to the active, as much as the head to the foot, the eye to the head, reason to sense, the soul to the body, the end itself to all things directed to the end, quiet to motion, and eternity to time, so much prefer I divine poesy to all worldly wisdom. To the only shadow of whose worth yet I entitle not the bold rimes of every apish and impudent braggart (though he dares assume anything); such I turn over to the weaving of cobwebs, and shall but chatter on molehills, far under the hill of the muses, when their fortunat'st self-love and ambition hath advanced them highest. Poesy is the flower of the sun and disdains to open to the eye of a candle. So kings hide their treasures and counsels from the vulgar. *Ne evilescant,* saith our Spondanus. We have example sacred enough that true poesy's humility, poverty, and contempt are badges of divinity, not vanity. Bray, then, and bark against it, ye wolf-fac'd worldlings. . . . I, for my part, shall ever esteem it much more manly and sacred, in this harmless and pious study, to sit till I sink into my grave then shine in your vainglorious bubbles and impieties, all your poor policies, wisdoms, and their trappings at no more valuing then a musty nut. And much less I weigh the frontless detractions of some stupid ignorants, that no more knowing me then their own beastly ends, and I ever (to my knowledge) bless'd from their sight, whisper behind me, vilifying of my translation; out of the French affirming them, when both in French and all other languages but his own our with-all-skill-enriched poet is so poor and unpleasing that no man can discern from whence flowed his so generally given eminence and admiration. And therefore, by any reasonable creature's conference of my slight comment and conversion, it will easily appear how I shun them, and whether the original be my rule or not. In which he shall easily see I understand the understandings of all other interpreters and commenters in places of his most depth, importance, and rapture; in whose exposition and illustration, if I abhor from the sense that others wrest and rack out of him, let my best detractor examine how the Greek word warrants me. For my other fresh fry, let them fry in their foolish galls, nothing so much weighed as the barking of puppies or foisting hounds, too vile to think of our sacred Homer or set their prophane feet within their lives' lengths of his thresholds. If I fail in something, let my full performance in other some restore me, haste spurring me on with other necessities. For as at my conclusion I protest, so here at my entrance, less then fifteen weeks was the time in which all the last twelve books were entirely new translated, no conference had with anyone living in all the novelties I presume I have found. . . .

The First Book of Homer's Iliads

Achilles' baneful wrath resound, O goddess that impos'd
Infinite sorrows on the Greeks and many brave souls los'd
From breasts heroique, sent them far to that invisible cave
That no light comforts, and their lims to dogs and vultures gave.
To all which Jove's will gave effect, from whom first strife begun
Betwixt Atrides, king of men, and Thetis' godlike son.
 What god gave Eris their command and op'd that fighting vein?
Jove's and Latona's son, who, fir'd against the king of men
For contumely shown his priest, infectious sickness sent
To plague the army, and to death by troops the soldiers went.   10
Occasion'd thus, Chryses the priest came to the fleet to buy,
For presents of unvalued price, his daughter's liberty,
The golden scepter and the crown of Phoebus in his hands
Proposing, and made suit to all, but most to the commands
Of both th' Atrides, who most rul'd. "Great Atreus' sons," said he,
"And all ye well-greav'd Greeks, the gods, whose habitations be
In heavenly houses, grace your powers with Priam's razed town
And grant ye happy conduct home; to win which wish'd renown
Of Jove by honoring his son, far-shooting Phoebus, deign
For these fit presents to dissolve the ransomable chain   20
Of my lov'd daughter's servitude." The Greeks entirely gave
Glad acclamations for sign that their desires would have
The grave priest reverenc'd, and his gifts of so much price embrac'd.
The general, yet, bore no such mind, but viciously disgrac'd
With violent terms the priest, and said: "Dotard, avoid our fleet,
Where ling'ring be not found by me, nor thy returning feet
Let ever visit us again, lest nor thy godhead's crown
Nor scepter save thee. Her thou seek'st I still will hold mine own
Till age deflour her. In our court at Argos, far transferr'd

From her lov'd country, she shall ply her web and see prepar'd   30
With all fit ornaments my bed. Incense me then no more,
But, if thou wilt be safe, be gone!" This said, the sea-beat shore,
Obeying his high will, the priest trod off with haste and fear,
And walking silent till he left far off his enemies' ear,
Phoebus, fair-hair'd Latona's son, he stirr'd up with a vow
To this stern purpose: "Hear, thou god that bear'st the silver bow,
That Chrysa guard'st, rulest Tenedos with strong hand, and the round
Of Cilla most divine dost walk! O Smintheus, if crown'd
With thankful offerings thy rich phane I ever saw, or fir'd
Fat thighs of oxen and of goats to thee, this grace desir'd   40
Vouchsafe to me: pains for my tears let these rude Greeks repay,
Forc'd with thy arrows." Thus he pray'd, and Phoebus heard him pray,
And, vex'd at heart, down from the tops of steep heaven stoop'd; his bow
And quiver cover'd round his hands did on his shoulders throw;
And of the angry deity the arrows, as he mov'd,
Rattl'd about him. Like the night he rang'd the host and rov'd
(Apart the fleet set) terribly; with his hard-loosing hand
His silver bow twang'd, and his shafts did first the mules command
And swift hounds; then the Greeks themselves his deadly arrows shot.
The fires of death went never out, nine days his shafts flew hot   50
About the army, and the tenth Achilles call'd a court
Of all the Greeks. Heaven's white-arm'd queen (who everywhere cut short
Beholding her lov'd Greeks by death) suggested it, and he,
All met in one, arose and said: "Atrides, now I see
We must be wandering again; flight must be still our stay
(If flight can save us now); at once sickness and battle lay
Such strong hand on us. Let us ask some prophet, priest, or prove
Some dream-interpreter (for dreams are often sent from Jove)
Why Phoebus is so much incens'd. If unperformed vows
He blames in us or hecatombs, and if these knees he bows   60
To death may yield his graves no more, but offering all supply
Of savors burn'd from lambs and goats, avert his fervent eye
And turn him temperate." Thus he sate, and then stood up to them
Calchas, sirnamed Thestorides, of augurs the supreme;
He knew things present, past, to come, and rul'd the equipage
Of th' Argive fleet to Ilion for his prophetique rage
Given by Apollo, who, well seen in th' ill they felt, propos'd
This to Achilles: "Jove's belov'd, would thy charge see disclos'd
The secret of Apollo's wrath? Then covenant and take oath
To my discovery, that with words and pow'rful actions both   70
Thy strength will guard the truth in me, because I well conceive
That he whose empire governs all, whom all the Grecians give
Confirm'd obedience, will be mov'd; and then you know the state
Of him that moves him when a king hath once mark'd for his hate
A man inferior. Though that day his wrath seems to digest
Th' offense he takes, yet evermore he rakes up in his breast
Brands of quick anger, till revenge hath quench'd to his desire
The fire reserved. Tell me, then, if whatsoever ire
Suggests in hurt of me to him, thy valor will prevent."
    Achilles answer'd: "All thou know'st, speak, and be confident;   80
For by Apollo, Jove's belov'd (to whom performing vows,
O Calchas, for the state of Greece, thy spirit prophetique shows
Skills that direct us), not a man of all these Grecians here
(I living and enjoying the light shot through this flow'ry sphere)

Shall touch thee with offensive hands, though Agamemnon be
The man in question, that doth boast the mightiest empery
Of all our army." Then took heart the prophet unreprov'd
And said: "They are not unpaid vows nor hecatombs that mov'd
The god against us; his offense is for his priest empair'd
By Agamemnon, that refus'd the present he preferr'd   90
And kept his daughter. This is cause why heaven's far-darter darts
These plagues amongst us, and this still will empty in our hearts
His deathful quiver uncontain'd till to her loved sire
The black-ey'd damsel be resign'd, no redemptory hire
Took for her freedom, not a gift, but all the ransom quit
And she convey'd, with sacrifice, till her enfranchis'd feet
Tread Chrysa under. Then the god, so pleas'd, perhaps we may
Move to remission. . . ."

THE SIXTH BOOK OF HOMER'S ILIADS
[Hector and Andromache]

            "I myself will now go home and see
My household, my dear wife, and son, that little hope of me.
For, sister, 'tis without my skill if I shall evermore
Return and see them, or to earth her right in me restore.
The gods may stoop me by the Greeks." This said, he went to see
The virtuous princess, his true wife, white-arm'd Andromache.
She, with her infant son and maid, was climb'd the tow'r about
The sight of him that sought for her, weeping and crying out.
Hector, not finding her at home, was going forth, retir'd,
Stood in the gate, her woman call'd, and curiously enquir'd   10
Where she was gone, bad tell him true if she were gone to see
His sisters or his brothers' wives, or whether she should be
At temple with the other dames t' implore Minerva's ruth.
    Her woman answer'd, since he ask'd and urg'd so much the truth,
The truth was she was neither gone to see his brothers' wives,
His sisters, nor t' implore the ruth of Pallas on their lives;
But, she advertiz'd of the bane Troy suffer'd, and how vast
Conquest had made herself for Greece, like one distraught made haste
To ample Ilion with her son and nurse, and all the way
Mourn'd and dissolv'd in tears for him. Then Hector made no stay,   20
But trod her path, and through the streets (magnificently built)
All the great city pass'd, and came where (seeing how blood was spilt)
Andromache might see him come; who made as he would pass
The ports without saluting her, not knowing where she was.
She, with his sight, made breathless haste to meet him, she, whose grace
Brought him withal so great a dow'r, she that of all the race
Of King Aetion only liv'd, Aetion, whose house stood
Beneath the mountain Placius, environ'd with the wood
Of Theban Hippoplace, being court to the Cilician land.
She ran to Hector and with her, tender of heart and hand,   30
Her son, borne in his nurse's arms, when like a heavenly sign
Compact of many golden stars the princely child did shine,
Whom Hector call'd Scamandrius but whom the town did name
Astyanax because his sire did only prop the same.
Hector, though grief bereft his speech, yet smil'd upon his joy;
Andromache cried out, mix'd hands, and to the strength of Troy
Thus wept forth her affection: "O noblest in desire,
Thy mind, inflam'd with others' good, will set thyself on fire,

Nor pitiest thou thy son nor wife, who must thy widow be
If now thou issue. All the field will only run on thee;   40
Better my shoulders underwent the earth then thy decease,
For then would earth bear joys no more, then comes the black increase
Of griefs (like Greeks on Ilion). Alas, what one survives
To be my refuge? One black day bereft seven brothers' lives
By stern Achilles; by his hand my father breath'd his last;
His high-wall'd, rich Cilician Thebes sack'd by him and laid waste;
The royal body yet he left unspoil'd; religion charm'd
That act of spoil; and, all in fire, he burn'd him complete arm'd,
Built over him a royal tomb, and to the monument
He left of him, th' Oreades (that are the high descent   50
Of aegis-bearing Jupiter) another of their own
Did add to it, and set it round with elms, by which is shown,
In theirs, the barrenness of death; yet might it serve beside
To shelter the sad monument from all the ruffinous pride
Of storms and tempests, us'd to hurt things of that noble kind.
The short life yet my mother liv'd he sav'd, and serv'd his mind
With all the riches of the realm, which not enough esteem'd,
He kept her prisoner whom small time but much more wealth redeem'd.
And she in sylvan Hippoplace Cilicia rul'd again,
But soon was overrul'd by death; Diana's chaste disdain   60
Gave her a lance and took her life. Yet, all these gone from me,
Thou amply render'st all; thy life makes still my father be,
My mother, brothers; and besides thou art my husband too,
Most lov'd, most worthy. Pity then, dear love, and do not go;
For thou gone, all these go again. Pity our common joy,
Lest of a father's patronage, the bulwark of all Troy,
Thou leav'st him a poor widow's charge. Stay, stay then, in this tow'r
And call up to the wild fig tree all thy retired pow'r,
For there the wall is easiest scal'd and fittest for surprise,
And there th' Ajaces, Idomen, th' Atrides, Diomed thrice   70
Have both survey'd and made attempt, I know not if induc'd
By some wise augur or the fact was naturally infus'd
Into their wits or courages." To this great Hector said:
"Be well assur'd, wife, all these things in my kind cares are weigh'd;
But what a shame and fear it is to think how Troy would scorn
(Both in her husbands and her wives, whom long-train'd gowns adorn)
That I should cowardly fly off! The spirit I first did breath
Did never teach me that, much less since the contempt of death
Was settl'd in me and my mind knew what a worthy was,
Whose office is to lead in fight and give no danger pass   80
Without improvement. In this fire must Hector's trial shine;
Here must his country, father, friends be in him made divine.
And such a stormy day shall come, in mind and soul I know,
When sacred Troy shall shed her tow'rs for tears of overthrow,
When Priam, all his birth and pow'r, shall in those tears be drown'd.
But neither Troy's posterity so much my soul doth wound,
Priam, nor Hecuba herself, nor all my brothers' woes
(Who, though so many and so good, must all be food for foes)
As thy sad state, when some rude Greek shall lead thee weeping hence,
These free days clouded and a night of captive violence   90
Loading thy temples, out of which thine eyes must never see,
But spin the Greek wives webs of task, and their fetch-water be
To Argos from Messeides or clear Hyperia's spring;
Which, howsoever thou abhorr'st, Fate's such a shrewish thing

She will be mistress, whose curst hands, when they shall crush out cries
From thy oppressions, being beheld by other enemies,
Thus they will nourish thy extremes: 'This dame was Hector's wife,
A man that at the wars of Troy did breath the worthiest life
Of all their army.' This again will rub thy fruitful wounds
To miss the man that to thy bands could give such narrow bounds.   100
But that day shall not wound mine eyes; the solid heap of night
Shall interpose and stop mine ears against thy plaints and plight."
    This said, he reach'd to take his son, who, of his arms afraid,
And then the horsehair plume, with which he was so overlaid,
Nodded so horribly, he cling'd back to his nurse and cried.
Laughter affected his great sire, who doft and laid aside
His fearful helm, that on the earth cast round about it light.
Then took and kiss'd his loving son, and, balancing his weight
In dancing him, these loving vows to living Jove he us'd,
And all the other bench of gods: "O you that have infus'd   110
Soul to this infant, now set down this blessing on his star:
Let his renown be clear as mine, equal his strength in war,
And make his reign so strong in Troy that years to come may yield
His facts his fame, when, rich in spoils, he leaves the conquer'd field
Sown with his slaughters. These high deeds exceed his father's worth,
And let this echo'd praise supply the comforts to come forth
Of his kind mother with my life." This said, th' heroic sire
Gave him his mother, whose fair eyes fresh streams of love's salt fire
Billow'd on her soft cheeks to hear the last of Hector's speech
In which his vows compris'd the sum of all he did beseech   120
In her wish'd comfort. So she took into her odorous breast
Her husband's gift, who, mov'd to see her heart so much oppress'd,
He dried her tears, and thus desir'd: "Afflict me not, dear wife,
With these vain griefs. He doth not live that can disjoin my life
And this firm bosom but my Fate—and Fate whose wings can flee?
Noble, ignoble, Fate controls; once born, the best must die.
Go home and set thy huswif'ry on these extremes of thought,
And drive war from them with thy maids; keep them from doing nought.
These will be nothing; leave the cares of war to men and me,
In whom, of all the Ilion race, they take their high'st degree."   130
    On went his helm, his princess home, half cold with kindly fears
When every fear turn'd back her looks, and every look shed tears. . . .

THE TWELFTH BOOK OF HOMER'S ODYSSES

Our ship now pass'd the streights of th' ocean flood;
She plow'd the broad sea's billows, and made good
The ile Aeaea, where the palace stands
Of th' early riser with the rosy hands,
Active Aurora, where she loves to dance
And where the sun doth his prime beams advance.
    When here arriv'd, we drew her up to land
And trod ourselves the resaluted sand,
Found on the shore fit resting for the night,
Slept, and expected the celestial light.   10
    Soon as the white-and-red-mix'd-finger'd dame
Had gilt the mountains with her saffron flame
I sent my men to Circes' house before
To fetch deceas'd Elpenor to the shore.

Straight swell'd the high banks with fell'd heaps of
    trees,
And, full of tears, we did due exequies
To our dead friend, whose corse consum'd with fire
And honor'd arms, whose sepulcher entire
And over that a column rais'd, his oar,
Curiously carv'd to his desire before,   20
Upon the top of all his tomb we fix'd;
Of all rites fit his funeral pile was mix'd.
    Nor was our safe ascent from hell conceal'd
From Circes' knowledge, nor so soon reveal'd
But she was with us with her bread and food
And ruddy wine, brought by her sacred brood
Of woods and fountains. In the midst she stood
And thus saluted us: "Unhappy men,

That have, inform'd with all your senses, been
In Pluto's dismal mansion, you shall die   30
Twice now, where others, that Mortality
In her fair arms holds, shall but once decease.
But eat and drink out all conceit of these,
And this day dedicate to food and wine,
The following night to sleep. When next shall shine
The cheerful morning, you shall prove the seas.
Your way and every act ye must address
My knowledge of their order shall design,
Lest with your own bad counsels ye encline
Events as bad against ye, and sustain   40
By sea and shore the woful ends that reign
In wilful actions." Thus did she advise,
And, for the time, our fortunes were so wise
To follow wise directions. All that day
We sate and feasted. When his lower way
The sun had enter'd and the even the high,
My friends slept on their gables; she and I,
Led by her fair hand to a place apart,
By her well-sorted, did to sleep convert
Our timed pow'rs. When all things Fate let fall   50
In our affair she ask'd, I told her all.
To which she answer'd: "These things thus took end,
And now to those that I inform, attend;
Which you rememb'ring, God himself shall be
The blessed author of your memory.

"First, to the Sirens ye shall come, that taint
The minds of all men whom they can acquaint
With their attractions. Whosoever shall,
For want of knowledge mov'd, but hear the call
Of any Siren, he will so despise   60
Both wife and children, for their sorceries,
That never home turns his affections' stream;
Nor they take joy in him, nor he in them.
The Sirens will so soften with their song
(Shrill, and in sensual appetite so strong)
His loose affections that he gives them head.
And then observe: They sit amidst a mead,
And round about it runs a hedge or wall
Of dead men's bones, their wither'd skins and all
Hung all along upon it, and these men   70
Were such as they had fawn'd into their fen,
And then their skins hung on their hedge of bones.
Sail by them, therefore; thy companions
Beforehand causing to stop every ear
With sweet, soft wax so close that none may hear
A note of all their charmings. Yet may you,
If you affect it, open ear allow
To try their motion, but presume not so
To trust your judgment when your senses go
So loose about you, but give straight command   80
To all your men to bind you foot and hand
Sure to the mast, that you may safe approve
How strong in instigation to their love

Their rapting tunes are. If so much they move
That, spite of all your reason, your will stands
To be enfranchis'd both of feet and hands,
Charge all your men before to slight your charge
And rest so far from fearing to enlarge
That much more sure they bind you. When your friends
Have outsail'd these, the danger that transcends   90
Rests not in any counsail to prevent
Unless your own mind finds the tract and bent
Of that way that avoids it. I can say
That in your course there lies a twofold way,
The right of which, your own taught present wit
And grace divine must prompt. In general yet
Let this inform you: near these Sirens' shore
Move two steep rocks, at whose feet lie and roar
The black seas' cruel billows; the blest gods
Call them the Rovers. Their abhorr'd abods   100
No bird can pass, no, not the doves, whose fear
Sire Jove so loves that they are said to bear
Ambrosia to him, can their ravine scape,
But one of them falls ever to the rape
Of those sly rocks. Yet Jove another still
Adds to the rest, that so may ever fill
The sacred number. Never ship could shun
The nimble peril wing'd there, but did run
With all her bulk and bodies of her men   110
To utter ruin. . . ."

TO THE RUINS OF TROY AND GREECE

Troy rac'd, Greece wrack'd, who mourns? Ye both may
    boast,
Else th' *Iliads* and *Odysses* had been lost.

AD DEUM

The only true God, betwixt whom and me
I only bound my comforts, and agree
With all my actions, only truly knows
And can judge truly me with all that goes
To all my faculties. In whose free grace
And inspiration I only place
All means to know (with my means, study, pray'r,
In and from his word taken) stair by stair
In all continual contentation rising
To knowledge of his truth, and practising   10
His will in it with my sole Savior's aid,
Guide, and enlight'ning. Nothing done nor said
Nor thought that good is but acknowledg'd by
His inclination, skill, and faculty.
By which, to find the way out to his love
Past all the worlds, the sphere is where doth move
My studies, pray'rs, and pow'rs. No pleasure taken
But sign'd by him, for which, my blood forsaken,
My soul I cleave to, and what (in his blood
That hath redeem'd, cleans'd, taught her) fits her good. 20
    Deo opt. max. gloria

Part VIII CRITICAL THEORY

SIR THOMAS ELYOT

FROM THE BOOK NAMED THE GOVERNOR (1531)[1]

BOOK I

XIII . . . . Decay of Learning among Gentlemen

. . . But sens we be now occupied in the defense
of poets, it shall nat be incongruent to our matter to
shew what profit may be taken by the diligent reading of ancient poets, contrary to the false opinion
that now reigneth, of them that suppose that in the
warks of poets is contained nothing but bawdry
(such is their foul word of reproach) and unprofitable   10
leasings.

But first I will interpret some verses of Horace
wherein he expresseth the office of poets, and after
will I resort to a more plain demonstration of some
wisdoms and counsails contained in some verses of
poets. Horace, in his second book of *Epistles,* saith in
this wise or much like:

> The poet fashioneth by some pleasant mean
> The speech of children tender and unsure;
> Pulling their ears from words unclean,
> Giving to them precepts that are pure,   20
> Rebuking envy and wrath if it dure;
> Things well done he can by example commend.
> The needy and sick he doth also his cure
> To recomfort, if aught he can amend.

But they which be ignorant in poets will perchance
object, as is their manner, again these verses, saying
that in Terence and other that were writers of
comedies, also Ovid, Catullus, Martialis, and all that
rout of lascivious poets that wrate epistles and ditties   30
of love, some called in Latin *elegiae* and some *epigrammata,* is nothing contained but incitation to
lechery.

First, comedies, which they suppose to be a
doctrinal of ribaudry, they be undoubtedly a picture
or, as it were, a mirror, of man's life wherein evil is
nat taught but discovered; to the intent that men
beholding the promptness of youth unto vice, the
snares of harlots and bawds laid for young minds, the
disceipt of servants, the chances of fortune contrary   40
to men's expectation, they being thereof warned
may prepare themself to resist or prevent occasion.
Semblably rememb'ring the wisdoms, advertisements, counsails, dissuasion from vice, and other
profitable sentences, most eloquently and familiarly
shewed in those comedies, undoubtedly there shall
be no little fruit out of them gathered. And if the
vices in them expressed should be cause that minds

of the readers should be corrupted, than by the same
argument nat only enterludes in English but also
sermons, wherein some vice is declared, should be to
the beholders and hearers like occasion to encrease
sinners.

And that by comedies good counsail is minist'red,
it appeareth by the sentence of Parmeno, in the
second comedy of Terence [*Eunuchus*]:

> In this thing I triumph in mine own conceipt,
> That I have founden for all young men the way
> How they of harlots shall know the deceipt,
> Their wits, their manners, that thereby they may
> Them perpetually hate; forsomuch as they
> Out of their own houses be fresh and delicate,
> Feeding curiously; at home all the day
> Living beggarly in most wretched astate.

There be many mo words spoken which I purposely omit to translate, natwithstanding the substance of the whole sentence is herein comprised. But
now to come to other poets, what may be better   50
said than is written by Plautus in his first comedy
[*Amphitruo*]?

> Verily, virtue doth all things excel.
> For if liberty, health, living, and substance,
> Our country, our parents, and children do well,
> It happ'neth by virtue; she doth all advance.
> Virtue hath all thing under governance,
> And in whom of virtue is founden great plenty,
> Anything that is good may never be dainty.

Also Ovidius, that seemeth to be most of all poets
lascivious, in his most wanton books hath right commendable and noble sentences; as for proof thereof
I will recite some that I have taken at adventure.

> Time is in medicine if it shall profit;
> Wine given out of time may be annoyance.
> A man shall irritate vice if he prohibit
> Whan time is nat meet unto his utterance.
> Therefore, if thou yet by counsail art recuperable,
> Flee thou from idleness and alway be stable.

Martialis, which, for his dissolute writing, is most
seldom rad of men of much gravity, hath natwithstanding many commendable sentences and right
wise counsails, as among divers I will rehearse one
which is first come to my remembrance.

> If thou wilt eschew bitter adventure
> And avoid the gnawing of a pensiful heart,
> Set in no one person all wholly thy pleasure;
> The lass joy shalt thou have, but the lass shalt   50
>   thou smart.

[1] For a note on this text see pp. 105-6.

I could recite a great number of semblable good sentences out of these and other wanton poets, who in the Latin do express them incomparably with more grace and delectation to the reader than our English tongue may yet comprehend.

Wherefore, sens good and wise matter may be picked out of these poets, it were no reason, for some light matter that is in their verses, to abandon therefore all their warks, no more than it were to forbear or prohibit a man to come into a fair gardein lest the redolent savors of sweet herbs and flours shall meve him to wanton courage, or lest in gad'ring good and wholesome herbs he may happen to be stung with a nettle. No wise man ent'reth into a gardein but he soon espieth good herbs from nettles, and treadeth the nettles under his feet while he gad'reth good herbs. Whereby he taketh no damage, or if he be stungen he maketh light of it and shortly forgetteth it. Semblably if he do read wanton matter mix'd with wisdom he putteth the warst under foot and sorteth out the best, or, if his courage be stirred or provoked, he remem'breth the little pleasure and great detriment that should ensue of it, and withdrawing his mind to some other study or exercise shortly forgetteth it.

And therefore among the Jews, though it were prohibited to children until they came to ripe years to read the books of Genesis, of the Judges, *Cantica canticorum,* and some part of the book of Ezekiel the prophet, for that in them was contained some matter which mought happen to incense the young mind wherein were sparks of carnal concupiscence, yet after certain years of men's ages it was leeful for every man to read and diligently study those warks. So, although I do nat approve the lesson of wanton poets to be taught unto all children, yet think I convenient and necessary that whan the mind is become constant and courage is assuaged, or that children of their natural disposition be shamefast and continent, none ancient poet would be excluded from the lesson of such one as desireth to come to the perfection of wisdom. . . .

THOMAS WILSON

THE ART OF RHETORIQUE

Like his other principal works—*The Rule of Reason* (1551) and a translation of seven orations of Demosthenes (1570)—Wilson's *Art of Rhetorique* (1553) represents a significant effort on the part of a post-Reformation savant to domesticate the fruits of classical learning in the vernacular. Wilson, who had gone from Eton to King's College, Cambridge, was, like Ascham and Haddon and others who appear so prominently in *The Schoolmaster,* a product of an extraordinary flowering of classical studies in the thirties and forties. Cheke, whom Wilson revered, was named provost of King's during his residence, and he taught a whole generation of brilliant students both the virtues of sound training and a scholarly *noblesse oblige* in transmitting the moral and esthetic uses of that training in lucid, unpretentious English. Ascham's book is the finest theoretical statement of this broad program, and Wilson's logical and rhetorical treatises are its practical exemplification. It follows that neither *The Rule of Reason* nor *The Art of Rhetorique* can be called original. The one is frigidly Aristotelian (though published nearly a decade after Ramus' *Dialectica* had revolutionized the study of logic), and the other is an urbane restatement, fleshed out with *exempla* and anecdotes, of the rhetorical principles which had been common knowledge ever since the Renaissance rediscovered Cicero and Quintilian. Although his was not the earliest rhetorical treatise in English—it had been preceded, for example, by Leonard Cox's in 1524 and Richard Sherry's in 1550, both of them, however, nothing more than schoolbooks—Wilson gave a significant impetus to the continuing interest in classical rhetoric, and the many editions of his book (1553, 1560, 1562, 1563, 1567, 1580, 1584, 1585) carried on its popularity until it was superseded by such favorites as Talaeus' *Rhetorica* (on which Abraham Fraunce built his *Arcadian Rhetoric* of 1588), Charles Butler's *Rhetoricae libri duo* (1598), John Brinsley's *Ludus literarius or the Grammar School* (1612), and Thomas Farnaby's *Index rhetoricus* (1625).

For both his plan and his terminology Wilson goes straight to Quintilian. Book I is given over to basic definitions and to an exposition of the canonical requirements of a properly trained orator (namely, invention, disposition, elocution, memory, and utterance), with the exposition itself frequently relieved by *exempla* both translated (like Erasmus' epistle on the advantages of marriage) and original. Book II is mainly a discussion of disposition, or of the ways in which a rhetorician may develop the parts of an oration (for example, the entrance, the narration, the confirmation, and the conclusion). Book III, which leans heavily on Cicero, is devoted to elocution, memory, and utterance, the first topic allowing for a large treatment of the classical figures or tropes, with copious examples.

Our text is based upon the editions of 1553 and 1560:

"The Prologue to the Reader" (in which Wilson's intransigent Protestantism is vividly set forth) and the bracketed words in the pedantic epistle which illustrates the evils of inkhorn terms are from the second (1560) edition, where they make their first appearance (STC 25800); for the remainder we follow *The Arte of Rhetorique, for the use of all suche as are studious of Eloquence, sette forth in English, by Thomas Wilson*, 1553 (STC 25799).

FROM THE ART OF RHETORIQUE, FOR THE USE OF ALL SUCH AS ARE STUDIOUS OF ELOQUENCE (1553)

A Prologue to the Reader [1560]

. . . Two years past, at my being in Italy, I was charged in Rome town, to my great danger and utter undoing (if God's goodness had not been the greater), to have written this book of *Rhetorique,* and the *Logic* also, for the which I was coumpted an heretic, notwithstanding the absolution granted to all the realm by Pope Julie the Third for all former offenses or practises devised against the Holy Mother Church, as they call it. A strange matter, that things done in England seven years before, and the same universally forgiven, should afterwards be laid to a man's charge in Rome. But what cannot malice do? Or what will not the wilful devise, to satisfy their minds, for undoing of others? God be my judge, I had then as little fear (although death was present and the torment at hand, whereof I felt some smart) as ever I had in all my life before. For when I saw those that did seek my death to be so maliciously set to make such poor shifts for my readier dispatch and to burden me with those back reckonings, I took such courage, and was so bold, that the judges then did much mervail at my stoutness, and, thinking to bring down my great heart, told me plainly that I was in farther peril then whereof I was aware, and sought thereupon to take advantage of my words and to bring me in danger by all means possible. And after long debating with me, they willed me at any hand to submit myself to the Holy Father and the devout College of Cardinals. For otherwise there was no remedy. With that, being fully purposed not to yield to any submission, as one that little trusted their colorable deceit, I was as ware as I could be not to utter anything for mine own harm, for fear I should come in their danger. For then either should I have died or else have denied, both openly and shamefully, the known truth of Christ and his Gospel. In the end, by God's grace, I was wonderfully delivered through plain force of the worthy Romains (an enterprise heretofore in that sort never attempted), being then without hope of life and much less of liberty. And now that I am come home, this book is shewed me, and I desired to look upon it to amend it where I thought meet. "Amend it?" quoth I. "Nay, let the book first amend itself, and make me amends. . . ." But I think some will read it, before whom I do wash my hands if any harm should come to them hereafter, and let theim not say but that they are warned. I never hard a man yet troubled for ignorance in religion. And yet methinks it is as great an heresy not to know God as to err in the knowledge of God. But some, perhaps, may say unto me: "Sir, you are much to be blamed that are so fearful, and do cast such perils beforehand to discourage men from well-doing." I answer: "My mind is not to discourage any man, but only to shew how I have been tried for this book's sake, *tanquam per ignem.* For, indeed, the prison was on fire when I came out of it, and whereas I feared fire most (as who is he that doth not fear it?) I was delivered by fire and sword together. And yet now thus fearful am I, that having been thus swinged and restrained of liberty, I would first rather hasard my life presently hereafter to die upon a turk then to abide again, without hope of liberty, such painful imprisonment forever. So that I have now got courage with suffering damage, and made myself, as you see, very willing from henceforth to die, being then brought only but in fear of death. They that love sorrow upon sorrow, God send it theim. I, for my part, had rather be without sense of grief then forever to live in grief. And I think the troubles before death being long suffered and without hope continued are worse a great deal then present death itself can be, especially to him that maketh little accoumpt of this life and is well armed with a constant mind to Godward." Thus I have talked of myself more then I needed, some will say, and yet not more (may I well say) then I have needed indeed. For I was without all help and without all hope, not only of liberty, but also of life, and therefore what thing needed I not? Or with what words sufficiently could I set forth my need? God be praised, and thanks be given to him only, that not only hath delivered me out of the lion's mouth but also hath brought England, my dear country, out of great thraldom and foreign bondage.

And God save the Queen's Majesty, the realm, and

the scattered flock of Christ; and grant, O merciful God, an universal quietness of mind, perfit agreement in doctrine, and amendment of our lives, that we may be all one sheepfold and have one pastor, Jesus, to whom, with the Father and the Holy Ghost, be honor and glory, world without end. Amen. This seventh of December, *anno Domini* 1560.

Eloquence First Given by God, After Lost by Man, and Last Repaired by God Again

Man, in whom is poured the breath of life, was made at his first being an ever-living creature unto the likeness of God, endued with reason, and appointed lord over all other things living. But after the fall of our first father, sin so crept in that our knowledge was much darkened, and by corruption of this our flesh man's reason and entendment were both overwhelmed. At what time God, being sore grieved with the folly of one man, pitied of his mere goodness the whole state and posterity of mankind. And therefore (whereas through the wicked suggestion of our ghostly enemy the joyful fruition of God's glory was altogether lost) it pleased our heavenly Father to repair mankind of his free mercy and to grant an ever-living enheritance unto all such as would by constant faith seek earnestly thereafter. Long it was ere that man knew himself, being destitute of God's grace, so that all things waxed savage, the earth untilled, society neglected, God's will not known, man against man, one against another, and all against order. Some lived by spoil; some, like brute beasts, grazed upon the ground; some went naked; some roamed like woodoses; none did anything by reason, but most did what they could by manhood. None almost considered the ever-living God, but all lived most communely after their own lust. By death they thought that all things ended; by life they looked for none other living. None rememb'red the true observation of wedlock; none tendered the education of their children; laws were not regarded; true dealing was not once used. For virtue, vice bare place; for right and equity, might used aucthority. And, therefore, whereas man through reason might have used order, man through folly fell into error. And thus for lack of skill, and for want of grace, evil so prevailed that the Devil was most esteemed, and God either almost unknown emong them all or else nothing feared emong so many. Therefore, even now when man was thus past all hope of amendment, God, still tendering his own workmanship, stirred up his faithful and elect to persuade with reason all men to society. And gave his appointed ministers knowledge both to see the natures of men and also granted them the gift of utterance, that they might with ease win folk at their will and frame theim by reason to all good order.

And, therefore, whereas men lived brutishly in open fields, having neither house to shroud them in nor attire to clothe their backs, nor yet any regard to seek their best avail, these appointed of God called theim together by utterance of speech and persuaded with them what was good, what was bad, and what was gainful for mankind. And although at first the rude could hardly learn, and either for strangeness of the thing would not gladly receive the offer or else for lack of knowledge could not perceive the goodness, yet, being somewhat drawn and delighted with the pleasantness of reason and the sweetness of utterance, after a certain space they became, through nurture and good advisement, of wild, sober; of cruel, gentle; of fools, wise; and of beasts, men. Such force hath the tongue, and such is the power of eloquence and reason, that most men are forced even to yield in that which most standeth against their will. And therefore the poets do feign that Hercules, being a man of great wisdom, had all men linked together by the ears in a chain to draw them and lead them even as he lusted. For his wit was so great, his tongue so eloquent, and his experience such that no one man was able to withstand his reason, but every one was rather driven to do that which he would and to will that which he did, agreeing to his advise both in word and work in all that ever they were able.

Neither can I see that men could have been brought by any other means to live together in fellowship of life, to maintain cities, to deal truly, and willingly to obey one another if men at the first had not by art and eloquence persuaded that which they full oft found out by reason. For what man, I pray you, being better able to maintain himself by valiant courage then by living in base subjection, would not rather look to rule like a lord then to live like an underling if by reason he were not persuaded that it behoveth every man to live in his own vocation and not to seek any higher room then whereunto he was at the first appointed? Who would dig and delve from morn till evening? Who would travail and toil with the sweat of his brows? Yea, who would for his king's pleasure adventure and hasard his life if wit had not so won men that they thought nothing more needful in this world, nor anything whereunto they were more bounden, then here to live in their duty and to train their whole life according to their calling? Therefore, whereas men are in many things weak by nature and subject to much infirmity, I think in this one point they pass all other creatures living, that they have the gift of speech and reason.

And among all other I think him most worthy fame, and emongest men to be taken for half a god, that therein doth chiefly and above all other excel men, wherein men do excel beasts. For he that is emong the reasonable of all most reasonable, and emong the witty of all most witty, and emong the eloquent of all most eloquent, him think I emong all men not only to be taken for a singular man but rather to be counted for half a god. For in seeking the excellency hereof, the sooner he draweth to perfection, the nigher he cometh to God, who is the chief wisdom and therefore called God because he is most wise, or rather wisdom itself.

Now then, seeing that God geveth his heavenly grace unto all such as call unto him with stretched hands and humble heart, never wanting to those that want not to themselves, I purpose by his grace and especial assistance to set forth precepts of eloquence, and to shew what observation the wise have used in handeling of their matters, that the unlearned, by seeing the practise of other, may have some knowledge themselves, and learn by their neighbors' devise what is necessary for themselves in their own case.

THE ART OF RHETORIQUE

What is rhetorique

Rhetorique is an art to set furth by utterance of words matter at large; or, as Cicero doth say, it is a learned, or rather an artificial, declaration of the mind in the handeling of any cause called in contention that may through reason largely be discussed.

The matter whereupon an orator must speak

An orator must be able to speak fully of all those questions which by law and man's ordinance are enacted and appointed for the use and profit of man, such as are thought apt for the tongue to set forward. Now astronomy is rather learned by demonstration then taught by any great utterance. Arithmetique smally needeth the use of eloquence, seeing it may be had wholly by numb'ring only. Geometry rather asketh a good square then a clean, flowing tongue to set out the art. Therefore an orator's profession is to speak only of all such matters as may largely be expounded for man's behove, and may with much grace be set out for all men to hear theim. . . .

The end of rhetorique

Three things are required of an orator: to teach, to delight, and to persuade.

First, therefore, an orator must labor to tell his tale that the hearers may well know what he meaneth and understand him wholly, the which he shall with ease do if he utter his mind in plain words such as are usually received, and tell it orderly without going about the bush. That if he do not this, he shall never do the other. For what man can be delighted, or yet be persuaded, with the only hearing of those things which he knoweth not what they mean? The tongue is ordained to express the mind that one might understand another's meaning. Now what availeth to speak when none can tell what the speaker meaneth? Therefore, Phavorinus, the philosopher, as Gellius telleth the tale, did hit a young man over the thumbs very handsomely for using overold and overstrange words. "Sirrah," quoth he, "when our old, great ancestors and grandsires were alive they spake plainly in their mothers' tongue, and used old language such as was spoken then at the building of Rome. But you talk me such Latin as though you spake with them even now, that were two or three thousand years ago, and only because you would have no man to understand what you say. Now were it not better for thee a thousandfold, thou foolish fellow, in seeking to have thy desire to hold thy peace and speak nothing at all? For then, by that means, few should know what were thy meaning. But thou sayest the old antiquity doth like thee best because it is good, sober, and modest. Ah, live, man, as they did before thee, and speak thy mind now as men do at this day! And remember that which Caesar saith: 'Beware, as long as thou livest, of strange words as thou wouldest take heed and eschew great rocks in the sea.' "

The next part that he hath to play is to cheer his guests and to make them take pleasure with hearing of things wittily devised and pleasantly set furth. Therefore every orator should earnestly labor to file his tongue that his words may slide with ease and that in his deliverance he may have such grace as the sound of a lute or any such instrument doth geve. Then his sentences must be well-framed and his words aptly used throughout the whole discourse of his oration.

Thirdly, such quickness of wit must be shewed, and such pleasant saws so well applied, that the ears may find much delight, whereof I will speak largely when I shall entreat of moving laughter. And, assuredly, nothing is more needful then to quicken these heavy-loaden wits of ours, and much to cherish these our lumpish and unwieldy natures, for except men find delight they will not long abide. Delight theim and win them; weary theim, and you lose theim forever. And that is the reason that men commonly tarry the end of a merry play, and cannot abide the half-hearing of a sour, checking sermon. Therefore even these ancient preachers must now and then play the fools in the pulpit to serve the tickle ears of their fleeting audience, or else they are like sometimes to preach to the bare walls; for though the spirit be apt and our will prone, yet our flesh is so heavy, and humors so overwhelm us, that we cannot without refreshing long abide to hear any one thing. Thus we see that to delight is needful, without the which weightier matters will not be heard at all; and therefore him cun I thank that both can and will ever mingle sweet emong the sour, be he preacher, lawyer—yea, or cook either, hardly when he dresseth a good dish of meat. Now I need not tell that scurrility, or ale-house jesting, would be thought odious, or gross mirth would be deemed madness, considering that even the mean-witted do know that already; and as for other that have no wit, they will never learn it; therefore God speed them. Now when these two are done, he must persuade and move the affections of his hearers in such wise that they shall be forced to yield unto his saying, whereof (because the matter is large, and may more aptly be declared when I shall speak of amplification) I will surcease to speak anything thereof at this time.

By what means eloquence is attained

First needful it is that he which desireth to excel in this gift of oratory and longeth to prove an eloquent man must naturally have a wit and an aptness thereunto; then must he to his book, and learn to be well-stored with knowledge that he may be able to minister matter for all causes necessary. The which when he hath got plentifully, he must use much exercise, both in writing and also in speaking. For though he have a wit and learning together, yet shall they both little avail without much practise. What maketh the lawyer to have such utterance? Practise. What maketh the preacher to speak so roundly? Practise. Yea, what maketh women go so fast away with their words? Marry, practise, I warrant you. . . .

Now, before we use either to write or speak eloquently we must dedicate our minds wholly to follow the most wise and learned men, and seek to fashion as well their speech and gesturing as their wit or enditing. The which when we earnestly mind to do we cannot but in time appear somewhat like theim. For if they that walk much in the sun and think not of it are yet, for the most part, sunburnt, it cannot be but that they which wittingly and willingly travail to counterfect other must needs take some color of theim and be like unto theim in some one thing or other; according to the proverb, by companying with the wise a man shall learn wisdom.

To what purpose this art is set furth

To this purpose and for this use is the art compiled together by the learned and wise men: that those which are ignorant might judge of the learned, and labor (when time should require) to follow their works accordingly. Again, the art helpeth well to dispose and order matters of our awn invention, the which we may follow as well in speaking as in writing; for though many by nature, without art, have proved worthy men, yet is art a surer guide then nature, considering we see as lively by the art what we do as though we read a thing in writing, whereas nature's doings are not so open to all men. Again, those that have good wits by nature shall better encrease theim by art, and the blunt also shall be whetted through art, that want nature to help them forward.

Five things to be considered in an orator

Anyone that will largely handle any matter must fasten his mind first of all upon these five especial points that follow, and learn theim every one:

    i. Invention of matter
    ii. Disposition of the same
    iii. Elocution
    iv. Memory
    v. Utterance

The finding-out of apt matter, called otherwise invention, is a searching-out of things true or things likely, the which may reasonably set furth a matter and make it appear probable. The places of logique geve good occasion to find out plentiful matter. And therefore they that will prove any cause and seek only to teach thereby the truth must search out the places of logique, and no doubt they shall find much plenty. But what availeth much treasure and apt matter if man cannot apply it to his purpose? Therefore, in the second place is mentioned the setteling or ordering of things invented for this purpose, called in Latin *dispositio,* the which is nothing else but an apt bestowing and orderly placing of things, declaring where every argument shall be set and in what manner every reason shall be applied for confirmation of the purpose.

But yet what helpeth it, though we can find good reasons and know how to place theim, if we have not apt words and picked sentences to commend the whole matter? Therefore this point must needs follow to beautify the cause, the which, being called elocution, is an applying of apt words and sentences to the matter found out to confirm the cause. When all these are had together it availeth little if man have no memory to contain theim. The memory, therefore, must be cherished, the which is a fast holding both of matter and words couched together to confirm any cause.

Be it now that one have all these four, yet if he want the fift all the other do little profit. For though a man can find out good matter and good words, though he can handsomely set them together and carry them very well away in his mind, yet it is to no purpose if he have no utterance when he should speak his mind and shew men what he hath to say. Utterance, therefore, is a framing of the voice, countenance, and gesture after a comely manner.

Thus we see that every one of these must go together to make a perfect orator, and that the lack of one is an hinderance of the whole, and that as well all may be wanting as one if we look to have an absolute orator.

There are seven parts in every oration

   i. The enterance or beginning
   ii. The narration
   iii. The proposition
   iv. The division or several parting of things
   v. The confirmation
   vi. The confutation
   vii. The conclusion

The enterance or beginning is the former part of the oration, whereby the will of the standers-by or of the judge is sought for and required to hear the matter.

The narration is a plain and manifest pointing of the matter and an evident setting-furth of all things that belong unto the same, with a brief rehearsal grounded upon some reason.

The proposition is a pithy sentence, comprehending in a small room the sum of the whole matter.

The division is an opening of things, wherein we agree and rest upon and wherein we stick and stand in traverse, shewing what we have to say in our awn behalf.

The confirmation is a declaration of our awn reasons, with assured and constant proofs.

The confutation is a dissolving or wiping away of all such reasons as make against us.

The conclusion is a clarkly gathering of the matter spoken before, and a lapping-up of it altogether. . . .

The Third Book

Of apt chusing and framing of words and sentences together, called elocution

And now we are come to that part of rhetorique, the which above all other is most beautiful, whereby not only words are aptly used but also sentences are in right order framed. For whereas invention helpeth to find matter, and disposition serveth to place arguments, elocution getteth words to set furth invention, and with such beauty commendeth the matter that reason seemeth to be clad in purple, walking afore both bare and naked. . . . If we think it comeliness and honesty to set furth the body with handsome apparel, and think theim worthy to have money that both can and will use it accordingly, I cannot otherwise see but that this part deserveth praise which

standeth wholly in setting furth matter by apt words and sentences together, and beautifieth the tongue with great change of colors and variety of figures.

Four parts belonging to elocution

   i. Plainness
   ii. Aptness
   iii. Composition
   iv. Exornation

Emong all other lessons this should first be learned, that we never affect any strange inkhorn terms, but so speak as is commonly received, neither seeking to be overfine nor yet living overcareless, using our speech as most men do and ord'ring our wits as the fewest have done. Some seek so far for outlandish English that they forget altogether their mothers' language. And I dare swear this, if some of their mothers were alive they were not able to tell what they say; and yet these fine English clerks will say they speak in their mother tongue, if a man should charge them for counterfeiting the king's English. Some far-journeyed gentlemen at their return home, like as they love to go in forrein apparel, so they will powder their talk with oversea language. He that cometh lately out of France will talk French English and never blush at the matter. Another chops in with Angleso-Italiano. . . . I know them that think rhetorique to stand wholly upon dark words, and he that can catch an inkhorn term by the tail, him they compt to be a fine Englishman and a good rhetorician. And the rather to set out this folly, I will add here such a letter as William Sommer himself could not make a better for that purpose. Some will think, and swear too, that there was never any such thing written. Well, I will not force any man to believe it, but I will say thus much, and abide by it too, the like have been made heretofore and praised above the moon.

[A letter devised by a Lincolnshire man for a void benefice to a gentleman that then waited upon the lord chancellor for the time being]

Pondering, expending, and revoluting with myself your ingent affability and ingenious capacity for mundane affairs, I cannot but celebrate and extol your magnifical dexterity above all other. For how could you have adepted such illustrate prerogative and dominical superiority if the fecundity of your ingeny had not been so fertile and wonderful pregnant? Now, therefore, being accersited to such splendent renowm and dignity splendidious, I doubt not but you will adjuvate such poor adnichilate orphans as whilom ware condisciples with you and of antique familiarity in Lincolnshire. Emong whom I, being a scholastical panion, obtestate your sublimity to extol mine infirmity. There is a sacerdotal dignity in my native country contiguate to me, where I now contemplate, which your worshipful benignity could soon impetrate for me if it would like you to extend your scedules and collaud me in them to the right honorable lord chancellor, or rather archigrammatian of England. You know my literature, you know the pastoral promotion; I obtestate your clemency to invigilate thus much for me, according to my confidence and as you know my condign merits for such a compendious living. But now I relinquish to fatigate your intelligence with any more frivolous verbosity, and therefore He that rules the climates be evermore your beautreux, your fortress, and your bulwark. Amen.

[Dated at my dome, or rather mansion-place, in Lincolnshire, the penult of the month sextile. *Anno millimo, quillimo, trillimo.*

Per me Iohannes Octo]

What wise man, reading this letter, will not take him for a very calf that made it in good earnest, and thought by his ink-pot terms to get a good personage? Doth wit rest in strange words, or else standeth it in wholesome matter and apt declaring of a man's mind? Do we not speak because we would have other to understand us, or is not the tongue geven for this end, that one might know what another meaneth? And what unlearned man can tell what half this letter signifieth? Therefore, either we must make a difference of English, and say some is learned English and other some is rude English, or the one is court talk, the other is country speech; or else we must of necessity banish all such affected rhetorique, and use altogether one manner of language. When I was in Cambridge, and student in the King's College, there came a man out of the town with a pint of wine in a pottle pot to welcome the provost of that house [i.e. John Cheke], that lately came from the court. And because he would bestow his present like a clerk, dwelling emong the schoolers, he made humbly his three curtsies and said in this manner: "Cha good even, my good lord, and well might your lordship vare. Understanding that your lordship was come and knowing that you are a worshipful Pilate and keeps abominable house, I thought it my duty to come incantivanty and bring you a pottle a wine, the which I beseech your lordship take in good worth." Here the simple man, being desirous to amend his mother's tongue, shewed himself not to be the wisest man that ever spake with tongue. . . .

Now whereas words be received, as well Greek as Latin, to set furth our meaning in th' English tongue, either for lack of store or else because we would enrich the language, it is well done to use them; and no man therein can be charged for any affectation when all other are agreed to follow the same way. There is no man agrieved when he heareth "letters patents," and yet "patents" is Latin and signifieth "open to all men." The "communion" is a fellowship or a coming together, rather Latin then English; the king's "prerogative" declareth his power royal above all other; and yet I know no man grieved for these terms being used in their place, nor yet any one suspected for affectation when such general words are spoken. The folly is espied when either we will use such words as few men do use, or use theim out of place, when another might serve much better. Therefore, to avoid such folly we may learn of that most excellent orator Tully, who in his third book, where he speaketh of a perfect orator, declareth under the name of Crassus that for the choice of words four things should chiefly be observed. First, that such words as we use should be proper unto the tongue wherein we speak; again, that they be plain for all men to perceive; thirdly, that they be apt and meet, most properly to set out the matter; fourthly, that words translated from one signification to another (called of the Grecians *tropes*) be used to beautify the sentence, as precious stones are set in a ring to commend the gold. . . .

What a figure is

A figure is a certain kind either of sentence, oration, or word used after some new or strange wise, much unlike to that which men communely use to speak.

The division of figures

There are three kinds of figures; the one is when the nature of words is changed from one signification to another, called a *trope* of the Grecians; the other serveth for words when they are not changed by nature, but only altered by speaking, called of the Grecians a *scheme;* the third is when by diversity of invention a sentence is many ways spoken, and also matters are amplified by heaping examples, by dilating arguments, by comparing of things together, by similitudes, by contraries, and by divers other like, called by Tully "exornation of sentences" or colors of rhetorique.

By all which figures every oration may be much beautified, and without the same not one can attain to be counted an orator, though his learning otherwise be never so great.

Of the first use of *tropes*

When learned and wise men gan first to enlarge their tongue and sought with great utterance of speech to commend causes, they found full oft much want of words to set out their meaning. And therefore, rememb'ring things of like nature unto those whereof they spake, they used such words to express their mind as were most like unto other. As for example, if I should speak against some notable Pharisee I might use translation of words in this wise: "Yonder man is of a crooked judgment, his wits are cloudy, he liveth in deep darkness, dusked altogether with blind ignorance, and drowned in the raging sea of bottomless superstition." Thus is the ignorant set out by calling him crooked, cloudy, dark, blind, and drown'd in superstition. All which words are not proper unto ignorance, but borrowed of other things that are of like nature unto ignorance. . . .

And not only do men use translation of words (called *tropes*) for need sake when they cannot find other, but also when they may have most apt words at hand, yet will they of a purpose use translated words. And the reason is this. Men count it a point of wit to pass over such words as are at hand, and to use such as are far-fetch'd and translated; or else it is because the hearer is led by cogitation upon rehearsal of a metaphor, and thinketh more by remembrance of a word translated then is there expressly spoken; or else because the whole matter seemeth by a similitude to be opened; or, last of all, bicause every translation is commenly and for the most part referred to the senses of the body, and especially to the sense of seeing, which is the sharpest and quickest above all other. . . .

The division of *tropes*

Tropes are either of a word or of a long-continued speech or sentence.

Tropes of a word are these

A metaphor or translation of words
A word-making [*onomatopoeia*, "when we make words of our own mind, such as be derived from the nature of things"]
Intellection [*synecdoche*, "when we gather or judge the whole by the part, or part by the whole"]
Abusion [*catachresis*, "when for a certain proper word we use that which is most nigh unto it, as in calling some water a fish pond, though there be no fish in it at all"]
Transmutation of a word [*metonymy*, "when a word hath a proper signification of the own, and, being referred to another thing, hath another meaning. . . . As thus: 'Put upon you the Lord Jesus Christ';

that is to say, be in living such a one as he was. 'The pope is banished England'; that is to say, all his superstition and hypocrisy either is or should be gone to the Devil, by the king's express will and commandement"]
Transumption ["when by degrees we go to that which is to be shewed"]
Change of a name [*antonomasia*, "when for the proper name some name of an office or other calling is used"]
Circumlocution [*periphrasis*, "a large description, either to set forth a thing more gorgeously, or else to hide it if the ears cannot bear the open speaking"]

Tropes of a long-continued speech or sentence are these

An allegory, or inversion of words ["a metaphor used throughout a whole sentence or oration"]
Mounting ["when we do set furth things exceedingly and above all men's expectation, meaning only that they are very great"]
Resembling of things
Similitude ["a likeness when two things, or mo then two, are so compared and resembled together that they both in some one property seem like"]
Example. . . .

The division of *schemes*

Strange using of any word or sentence contrary to our daily wont is either when we add or take away a syllable or a word to encrease a sentence by change of speech, contrary to the commune manner of speaking.

Figures of a word

Those be called figures of a word when we change a word and speak it contrary to our vulgar and daily speech. Of the which sort there are six in number:

i. Addition at the first [*prosthesis*: "He did all to berattle him. Wherein appeareth that a syllable is added to this word 'rattle' "]
ii. Abstraction from the first [*apheresis*: "As I roamed all alone, I gan to think of matters great. In which sentence 'gan' is used for 'began' "]
iii. Interlacing in the middest [*epenthesis*: " 'Relligion' for 'religion' "]
iv. Cutting from the middest [*syncope*: " 'Idolatry' for 'idololatry' "]
v. Adding at the end [*proparalepsis*: " 'Hasten your business' for 'haste your business' "]
vi. Cutting from the end [*apocope*: "A fair 'may' for 'maid' "]

GEORGE GASCOIGNE

FROM CERTAIN NOTES OF INSTRUCTION CONCERNING THE MAKING OF VERSE OR RIME IN ENGLISH, WRITTEN AT THE REQUEST OF MASTER EDOUARDO DONATI (1575)[1]

Signor Edouardo, since promise is debt, and you, by the law of friendship, do burden me with a promise that I should lend you instructions towards the making of English verse or rime, I will assay to discharge the same, though not so perfectly as I would, yet as readily as I may; and therewithal I pray you consider that *quot homines, tot sententiae,* especially in poetry, wherein, nevertheless, I dare not challenge any degree, and yet will I at your request adventure to set down my simple skill in such simple manner as I have used, referring the same hereafter to the correction of the laureate. And you shall have it in these few points following.

The first and most necessary point that ever I found meet to be considered in making of a delectable poem is this, to ground it upon some fine invention. For it is not inough to roll in pleasant words, nor yet to thunder in *rym, ram, ruff* by letter (quoth my master Chaucer), nor yet to abound in apt vocables or epithets unless the invention have in it also *aliquid salis.* By this *aliquid salis* I mean some good and fine devise shewing the quick capacity of a writer; and where I say some good and fine invention I mean that I would have it both fine and good. For many inventions are so superfine that they are *vix* good. And again, many inventions are good and yet not finely handled. And for a general forewarning, what theme soever you do take in hand, if you do handle it but *tanquam in oratione perpetua* and never study for some depth of device in the invention and some figures also in the handling thereof, it will appear to the skilful reader but a tale of a tub. To deliver unto you general examples it were almost unpossible, sithence the occasions of inventions are, as it were, infinite; nevertheless, take in worth mine opinion and perceive my furder meaning in these few points. If I should undertake to write in praise of a gentlewoman I would neither praise her crystal eye nor her cherry lip, etc. For these things are *trita et obvia.* But I would either find some supernatural cause whereby my pen might walk in the superlative degree, or else I would undertake to answer for any imperfection that she hath and thereupon raise the praise of her commendation. Likewise, if I should disclose my pretense in love, I would either make a strange discourse of some intolerable passion, or find occasion to plead by the example of some history, or

discover my disquiet in shadows *per allegoriam,* or use the covertest mean that I could to avoid the uncomely customs of common writers. Thus much I adventure to deliver unto you, my friend, upon the rule of invention, which of all other rules is most to be marked and hardest to be prescribed in certain and infallible rules; nevertheless, to conclude therein, I would have you stand most upon the excellency of your invention and stick not to study deeply for some fine device. For that being found, pleasant words will follow well inough and fast inough.

2. Your invention being once devised, take heed that neither pleasure of rime nor variety of device do carry you from it, for as to use obscure and dark phrases in a pleasant sonnet is nothing delectable, so to entermingle merry jests in a serious matter is an indecorum.

3. I will next advise you that you hold the just measure wherewith you begin your verse. I will not deny but this may seem a preposterous order, but bycause I covet rather to satisfy you particularly than to undertake a general tradition I will not so much stand upon the manner as the matter of my precepts. I say, then, remember to hold the same measure wherewith you begin, whether it be in a verse of six syllables, eight, ten, twelve, etc.; and though this precept might seem ridiculous unto you, since every young scholler can conceive that he ought to continue in the same measure wherewith he beginneth, yet do I see and read many men's poems nowadays which, beginning with the measure of twelve in the first line and fourteen in the second (which is the common kind of verse), they will yet, by that time they have passed over a few verses, fall into fourteen and fourteen, *et sic de similibus,* the which is either forgetfulness or carelessness.

4. And in your verses remember to place every word in his natural emphasis or sound; that is to say, in such wise and with such length or shortness, elevation or depression of syllables, as it is commonly pronounced or used. To express the same we have three manner of accents, *gravis, levis, et circumflexa,* the which I would English thus, the long accent, the short accent, and that which is indifferent; the grave accent is marked by this caract /, the light accent is noted thus \, and the circumflex or indifferent is thus signified ~. The grave accent is drawn out or elevate, and maketh that syllable long whereupon it is placed; the light accent is depressed or snatched up, and

1 For a note on this text see pp. 298-99.

maketh that syllable short upon the which it lighteth; the circumflex accent is indifferent, sometimes short, sometimes long, sometimes depressed and sometimes elevate. For example of th' emphasis or natural sound of words, this word *treasure* hath the grave accent upon the first syllable, whereas if it should be written in this sort, *treasúre*, now were the second syllable long, and that were clean contrary to the common use wherewith it is pronounced. For furder explanation hereof note you that commonly now- 10 adays in English rimes (for I dare not call them English verses) we use none other order but a foot of two syllables, whereof the first is depressed or made short and the second is elevate or made long, and that sound or scanning continueth throughout the verse. . . .

Also our father Chaucer hath used the same liberty in feet and measures that the Latinists do use, and whosoever do peruse and well consider his works he shall find that, although his lines are not always 20 of one selfsame number of syllables, yet, being read by one that hath understanding, the longest verse and that which hath most syllables in it will fall to the ear correspondent unto that which hath fewest syllables in it; and likewise that which hath in it fewest syllables shall be found yet to consist of words that have such natural sound as may seem equal in length to a verse which hath many mo syllables of lighter accents. And surely I can lament that we are fallen into such a plain and simple manner of writing 30 that there is none other foot used but one, whereby our poems may justly be called rhythms and cannot by any right challenge the name of a verse. But since it is so, let us take the ford as we find it, and let me set down unto you such rules or precepts that even in this plain foot of two syllables you wrest no word from his natural and usual sound. I do not mean hereby that you may use none other words but of two syllables, for therein you may use discretion according to occasion of matter; but my meaning is 40 that all the words in your verse be so placed as the first syllable may sound short or be depressed, the second long or elevate, the third short, the fourth long, the fifth short, etc. . . .

5. Here, by the way, I think it not amiss to fore-warn you that you thrust as few words of many syllables into your verse as may be, and hereunto I might alledge many reasons. First, the most ancient English words are of one syllable, so that the more monosyllables that you use the truer Englishman you 50 shall seem and the less you shall smell of the inkhorn. Also, words of many syllables do cloy a verse and make it unpleasant, whereas words of one syllable will more easily fall to be short or long as occasion requireth, or will be adapted to become circumflex or of an indifferent sound.

6. I would exhort you also to beware of rime without reason. My meaning is hereby that your rime lead you not from your first invention, for many writers, when they have laid the platform of their invention, are yet drawn sometimes by rime to forget it or at least to alter it, as when they cannot readily find out a word which may rime to the first and yet continue their determinate invention, they do then either botch it up with a word that will rime —how small reason soever it carry with it—or else they alter their first word and so percase decline or trouble their former invention. But do you always hold your first determined invention, and do rather search the bottom of your brains for apt words than change good reason for rumbling rime.

7. To help you a little with rime (which is also a plain young scholler's lesson), work thus: when you have set down your first verse, take the last word thereof and compt over all the words of the selfsame sound by order of the alphabet. As, for example, the last word of your first line is *care;* to rime therewith you have *bare, clare, dare, fare, gare, hare,* and *share, mare, snare, rare, stare,* and *ware,* etc. Of all these take that which best may serve your purpose, carry-ing reason with rime; and if none of them will serve so, then alter the last word of your former verse, but yet do not willingly alter the meaning of your invention.

8. You may use the same figures or tropes in verse which are used in prose, and in my judgment they serve more aptly and have greater grace in verse than they have in prose; but yet therein remember this old adage, *ne quid nimis,* as many writers which do not know the use of any other figure than that which is expressed in repetition of sundry words beginning all with one letter, the which (being modestly used) lendeth good grace to a verse; but they do so hunt a letter to death that they make it *crambe,* and *crambe bis positum mors est.* Therefore, *ne quid nimis.*

9. Also, as much as may be, eschew strange words or *obsoleta et inusitata* unless the theme do give just occasion. Marry, in some places a strange word doth draw attentive reading, but yet I would have you therein to use discretion.

10. And as much as you may, frame your style to perspicuity and to be sensible, for the haughty, obscure verse doth not much delight, and the verse that is too easy is like a tale of a roasted horse; but let your poem be such as may both delight and draw attentive reading and therewithal may deliver such matter as be worth the marking.

11. You shall do very well to use your verse after th' English phrase and not after the manner of other languages. The Latinists do commonly set the ad-jective after the substantive, as, for example, *femina pulchra, aedes altae,* etc.; but if we should say in

English "a woman fair," "a house high," etc., it would have but small grace, for we say "a good man" and not "a man good," etc. And yet I will not altogether forbid it you, for in some places it may be borne, but not so hardly as some use it which write thus:

> Now let us go to temple ours.
> I will go visit mother mine, etc.

Surely, I smile at the simplicity of such devisers which might as well have said it in plain English phrase, and yet have better pleased all ears than they satisfy their own fancies by such superfinesse. Therefore, even as I have advised you to place all words in their natural or most common and usual pronunciation, so would I wish you to frame all sentences in their mother phrase and proper *idioma;* and yet sometimes, as I have said before, the contrary may be borne, but that is rather where rime enforceth, or *per licentiam poeticam,* than it is otherwise lawful or commendable.

12. This poetical license is a shrewd fellow and covereth many faults in a verse. It maketh words longer, shorter, of mo syllables, of fewer, newer, older, truer, falser; and, to conclude, it turkeneth all things at pleasure, for example, *ydone* for *done, adown* for *down, o'ercome* for *overcome, ta'en* for *taken, power* for *pow'r, heaven* for *heav'n, thews* for *good parts* or *good qualities,* and a number of other which were but tedious and needless to rehearse, since your own judgment and reading will soon make you espy such advantages.

13. There are also certain pauses or rests in a verse which may be called ceasures, whereof I would be loth to stand long, since it is at discretion of the writer and they have been first devised, as should seem, by the musicians; but yet thus much I will adventure to write, that, in mine opinion, in a verse of eight syllables the pause will stand best in the middest; in a verse of ten it will best be placed at the end of the first four syllables; in a verse of twelve, in the midst; in verses of twelve in the first and fourteen in the second we place the pause commonly in the midst of the first and at the end of the first eight syllables in the second. In rhythm royal it is at the writer's discretion and forceth not where the pause be until the end of the line.

14. And here, bycause I have named rhythm royal, I will tell you also mine opinion as well of that as of the names which other rimes have commonly borne heretofore. Rhythm royal is a verse of ten syllables, and seven such verses make a staff, whereof the first and third lines do answer across in like terminations and rime, the second, fourth, and fifth do likewise answer each other in terminations, and the two last do combine and shut up the sentence. This hath been called rhythm royal, and surely it is a royal kind of verse, serving best for grave discourses. There is also another kind called ballade, and thereof are sundry sorts; for a man may write ballade in a staff of six lines, every line containing eight or six syllables, whereof the first and third, second and fourth do rime across, and the fifth and sixth do rime together in conclusion. You may write also your ballade of ten syllables, riming as before is declared; but these two were wont to be most commonly used in ballade, which proper name was, I think, derived of this word in Italian *ballare,* which signifieth "to dance." And indeed those kinds of rimes serve best for dances or light matters. Then have you also a rondlet, the which doth always end with one selfsame foot or repetition and was thereof, in my judgment, called a rondlet. This may consist of such measure as best liketh the writer. Then have you sonnets: some think that all poems being short may be called sonnets, as indeed it is a diminutive word derived of *sonare,* but yet I can best allow to call those sonnets which are of fourteen lines, every line containing ten syllables. The first twelve do rime in staves of four lines by cross-meter, and the last two riming togither do conclude the whole. There are dizains and sixains, which are of ten lines and of six lines, commonly used by the French, which some English writers do also term by the name of "sonnets." Then is there an old kind of rhythm called "verlays," derived, as I have read, of this word *verd,* which betokeneth "green," and "lay," which betokeneth "a song," as if you would say "green songs"; but I must tell you, by the way, that I never read any verse which I saw by aucthority called "verlay" but one, and that was a long discourse in verses of ten syllables, whereof the four first did rime across and the fifth did answer to the first and third, breaking off there and so going on to another termination. Of this I could shew example of imitation in mine own verses written to the right honorable the Lord Grey of Wilton upon my journey into Holland, etc. There are also certain poems devised of ten syllables, whereof the first answereth in termination with the fourth, and the second and third answer each other; these are more used by other nations than by us, neither can I tell readily what name to give them. And the commonest sort of verse which we use nowadays (viz., the long verse of twelve and fourteen syllables) I know not certainly how to name it unless I should say that it doth consist of poulter's measure, which giveth twelve for one dozen and fourteen for another. But let this suffice—if it be not too much—for the sundry sorts of verses which we use nowadays.

15. In all these sorts of verses, whensoever you undertake to write, avoid prolixity and tediousness, and ever, as near as you can, do finish the sentence and meaning at the end of every staff where you write staves and at the end of every two lines where you write by couples or poulter's measure; for I see many writers which draw their sentences in length and make an end at latter Lammas; for commonly, before they end, the reader hath forgotten where he begun. But do you, if you will follow my advise, eschew prolixity and knit up your sentences as compendiously as you may, since brevity, so that it be not drowned in obscurity, is most commendable.

16. I had forgotten a notable kind of rime called riding rime, and that is such as our maister and father Chaucer used in his *Canterbury Tales* and in divers other delectable and light enterprises; but though it come to my remembrance somewhat out of order, it shall not yet come altogether out of time, for I will now tell you a conceipt which I had before forgotten to write. (You may see, by the way, that I hold a preposterous order in my traditions, but, as I said before, I write moved by good will and not to shew my skill.) Then to return to my matter: as this riding rime serveth most aptly to write a merry tale, so rhythm royal is fittest for a grave discourse. Ballades are best of matters of love, and rondlets most apt for the beating or handling of an adage or common proverb; sonnets serve as well in matters of love as of discourse; dizains and sixains for short fantasies; verlays for an effectual proposition (although by the name you might otherwise judge of verlays); and the long verse of twelve and fourteen syllables, although it be nowadays used in all themes, yet in my judgment it would serve best for psalms and hymns.

I would stand longer in these traditions were it not that I doubt mine own ignorance; but, as I said before, I know that I write to my friend, and, affying myself thereupon, I make an end.

GOSSON—LODGE—SIDNEY

Stephen Gosson acquired such fame as he now has in a hard way—by annoying a great man. He came down from Oxford in the same year (1576/77) in which James Burbage built the first public theater in London, and for a time, at least, tried to make his way in the world by writing plays. Although none of them has survived, they must have been sufficiently bad; for, turning from aspiring playwright to disgruntled playwright to detractor of all playwrights, he attacked the popular drama (and, by implication, all imaginative literature) with a vehemence that allied him at once with the puritan obscurantists— men of unyielding piety who thought (with some cause) that playhouses were sinks of iniquity, that popular amusements were sinful, and that poetry was a sinister form of untruth. About 1577 John Northbrooke's *Spiritus est vicarius Christi in terra: A Treatise Wherein Dicing, Dancing, Vain Plays or Interludes with Other Idle Pastimes . . . Are Reproved*—a dialogue between a wise old man and a foolish young one—had initiated the puritan onslaught; but Gosson's *School of Abuse* (1579)—and his novel-like *Ephemerides of Phialo* of the same year, also a yeasty specimen of euphuistic prose—seems to have attracted much more attention. Audaciously dedicated without permission to Sir Philip Sidney, it was answered not only by that eminent man but also by young Thomas Lodge in a noisy, intemperate rebuttal—apparently suppressed as soon as it appeared—that has survived without titlepage or date. Whatever Lodge's zeal against Gosson and the author (probably Anthony Munday) of *A Second and Third Blast of Retrait from Plays and Theaters* (1580),

he cannot be said to have contributed anything of importance to critical theory; and when Gosson answered him with *Plays Confuted in Five Actions* (1582) it was simply to labor the argument *ad hominem* that both contestants mistook for the discourse of reason. Philip Stubbes's grave *Anatomy of Abuses* (1583), certainly a more judicious work than either Gosson's or Lodge's, subordinated the attack on the stage to a larger discussion, in dialogue form, of the moral health of Ailgna (that is, Anglia or England)—a discussion that restates the common puritan strictures on Sabbath-breaking and other sinful pastimes, but with a barrage of circumstantial detail that gives the work considerable value.

The whole tedious altercation continued to sputter for years through the donnish controversy between William Gager and John Rainolds of Oxford, Harington's saucy preface to his translation of *Orlando Furioso,* Nashe's defense of plays in *Pierce Penniless,* and countless puritan tracts and sermons; but it acquired a new dimension only in Sidney's *Defense of Poesy,* a luminous *apologia* for imaginative literature that time has not tarnished. Written in the early eighties as a refutation of Gosson's foolish little book, Sidney's essay was not published until 1595, and then in two versions—one, by William Ponsonby, as *The Defense of Poesy,* and another, by Henry Olney, as *An Apology for Poetry;* but since Ponsonby's version contains passages not found in Olney's, and since it was chosen by the Countess of Pembroke for the authorized edition (1598) of her brother's work, there can be no doubt that its text is preferable. Much of what Sidney has to say is commonplace enough, but he says it with a grace, urbanity, and ironical humor new to English prose. Building his *Defense* on the lines of a classical oration, he defends poetry on the score of its antiquity and its prestige, and he conventionally describes its neoclassical "kinds" (or genres); but his real intent is to evaluate and justify the kind of truth available in poetry, and his central section is a splendid analysis of the creative imagination which raises the poet far above the mere historian, the philosopher, and the mathematician. Only toward the end of his treatise does Sidney answer the attacks on drama that had been the stock in trade of Gosson

and his fellows, and it is then that his aristocratic, neoclassical bent most strongly appears. A valuable coda on the state of English literature brings this most distinguished treatise to a close.

Our texts are based upon *The S[c]hoole of Abuse, Conteining a plesaunt invective against Poets, Pipers, Plaiers, Jesters, and such like Caterpillers of a Commonwelth*, 1579 (STC 12097); *Reply to Stephen Gosson Touching Plays* (the original titlepage is lost, and so the title is conjectural), [1579] (STC 16663); *The Defence of Poesie. By Sir Phillip Sidney, Knight*, 1595 (STC 22535).

STEPHEN GOSSON

FROM THE SCHOOL OF ABUSE (1579)

To the Right Noble Gentleman, Master Philip Sidney, Esquire, Stephen Gosson Wisheth Health of Body, Wealth of Mind, Reward of Virtue, Advancement of Honor, and Good Success in Godly Affairs

Caligula, lying in France with a great army of fighting men, brought all his force on a sudden to the seaside as though he intended to cut over and invade England; when he came to the shore, his soldiers were presently set in array, himself shipped in a small bark, weighed anchors, and lanched out. [10] He had not played long in the sea, wafting to and fro at his pleasure, but he returned again, stroke sail, gave alarm to his soldiers in token of battail, and charged every man to gather cockles. I know not, right worshipful, whether myself be as frantic as Caligula in my proceedings, because that, after I have set out the flag of defiance to some abuses, I may seem well inough to strike up the drum and bring all my power to a vain skirmish. The title of my book doth promise much; the volume, you see, [20] is very little; and sithence I cannot bear out my folly by authority, like an emperor, I will crave pardon for my phrenzy by submission, as your Worship's to command. The school which I build is narrow, and, at the first blush, appeareth but a dog-hole; yet small clouds carry water, slender threads sew sure stitches, little hears have their shadow, blunt stones whet knives, from hard rocks flow soft springs, the whole world is drawn in a map, Homer's *Iliads* in a nutshell, a king's picture in a penny, little chests may [30] hold great treasure, a few cyphers contain the substance of a rich merchant, the shortest pamphlet may shroud matter, the hardest head may geve light, and the harshest pen may set down somewhat worth the reading. . . .

If your Worship vouchsafe to enter the school door and walk an hour or twain within for your pleasure, you shall see what I teach, which present my school, my cunning, and myself to your worthy patronage. Beseeching you, though I bid you to dinner, not to look for a feast fit for the curious taste of a perfect courtier, but to imitate Philip of Macedon, who, being invited to a farmer's house when he came from hunting, brought a greater train then the poor man looked for. When they were set, the good Philip, perceiving his host sorrowful for want of meat to satisfy so many, exhorted his friends to keep their stomachs for the second course; whereupon every man fed modestly on that which stood before him and left meat inough at the taking-up of the table. And I trust if your Worship feed sparingly on this (to comfort your poor host) in hope of a better course hereafter, though the dishes be few that I set before you, they shall for this time suffice yourself and a great many mo.

Your Worship's to command,

Stephen Gosson

To the Reader

Gentlemen and others, you may well think that I sell you my corn and eat chaff, barter my wine and drink water, sith I take upon me to deter you from plays when mine own works are daily to be seen upon stages as sufficient witnesses of mine own folly and severe judges against myself. But if you saw how many tears of sorrow my eyes shed when I behold them, or how many drops of blood my heart sweats when I remember them, you would not so much blame me for misspending my time, when I knew not what I did, as commend me at the last for recovering my steps with graver counsel. After-wits are ever best; burnt children dread the fire. I have seen that which you behold, and I shun that which you frequent. And that I might the easier pull your minds from such studies, draw your feet from such places, I have sent you a school of those abuses which I have gathered by observation.

Theodorus the atheist complained that his schollers were wont, how plain soever he spake, to misconster him; how right soever he wrote, to wrest him. And I look for some such auditors in my school as of rancor will hit me howsoever I ward, or of stomach assail me howsoever I be guarded, making black of white, chalk of cheese, the full moon of a mess of cruds. These are such as with curst curs bark at every man but their own friends; these snatch up bones in open streets and bite them with madness in secret corners; these, with sharp winds, pierce subtiler in narrow lanes then large fields. And sith there is neither authority in me to bridle their tongues nor reason in them to rule their own talk, I am contented to suffer their taunts, requesting you which are gentlemen of curtesy to bear with me and, because you are learned, amend the faults friendly which escape the press. The ignorant, I know, will swallow them down and digest them with ease. Farewell!

Yours,
Stephen Gosson

THE SCHOOL OF ABUSE

. . . As I cannot but commend his wisdom which, in banqueting, feeds most upon that that doth nourish best, so must I dispraise his method in writing which, following the course of amarous poets, dwelleth longest in those points that profit least, and, like a wanton whelp, leaveth the game to run riot. The scarab flies over many a sweet flower and lights in a cowshard; it is the custom of the fly to leave the sound places of the horse and suck at the botch; the nature of coloquintida to draw the worst humors to itself; the manner of swine to forsake the fair fields and wallow in the mire; and the whole practise of poets, either with fables to shew their abuses or with plain terms to unfold their mischief, discover their shame, discredit themselves, and disperse their poison through all the world. Virgil sweats in describing his gnat; Ovid bestirreth him to paint out his flea; the one shews his art in the lust of Dido, the other his cunning in the incest of Myrrha and that trumpet of bawdry, *The Craft of Love.*

I must confess that poets are the whetstones of wit, notwithstanding that wit is dearly bought; where honey and gall are mix'd it will be hard to sever the one from the other. The deceitful phisition geveth sweet syrops to make his poison go down the smoother; the juggler casteth a mist to work the closer; the siren's song is the sailor's wrack; the fowler's whistle the bird's death; the wholesome bait the fish's bane. The harpies have virgins' faces and vultures' talents; hyena speaks like a friend and devours like a foe; the calmest seas hide dangerous rocks; the wolf jets in wethers' fells. Many good sentences are spoken by Davus to shadow his knavery and written by poets as ornaments to beautify their works and set their trumpery to sale without suspect. . . .

Because I have been matriculated myself in the school where so many abuses florish I will imitate the dogs of Egypt which, coming to the banks of Nilus to quench their thirst, sip and away, drink running, lest they be snapp'd short for a prey to crocodiles. I should tell tales out of the school and be ferruled for my fault or hissed at for a blab if I laid all the orders open before your eyes. You are no sooner ent'red but liberty looseth the reins and geves you head, placing you with poetry in the lowest form; when his skill is shown to make his scholer as good as ever twang'd, he prefers you to piping, from piping to playing, from play to pleasure, from pleasure to sloth, from sloth to sleep, from sleep to sin, from sin to death, from death to the Devil, if you take your learning apace and pass through every form without revolting. Look not to have me discourse these at large. The crocodile watcheth to take me tardy. Whichsoever of them I touch is a bile. Trip and go, for I dare not tarry. . . .

Consider with thyself, gentle reader, the old discipline of England. Mark what we were before, and what we are now. Leave Rome a while and cast thine eye back to thy predecessors, and tell me how wonderfully we have been changed since we were schooled with these abuses. Dion saith that Englishmen could suffer watching and labor, hunger and thirst, and bear off all storms with head and shoulders; they used slender weapons, went naked, and were good soldiers; they fed upon roots and barks of trees; they would stand up to the chin many days in marshes without victuals; and they had a kind of sustenance in time of need, of which if they had taken but the quantity of a bean or the weight of a pease, they did neither gape after meat nor long for the cup a great while after. The men in valure not yielding to Scythia, the women in courage passing the Amazons. The exercise of both was shooting and darting, running and wrestling, and trying such maisteries as either consisted in swiftness of feet, agility of body, strength of arms, or martial discipline.

But the exercise that is now among us is banqueting, playing, piping, and dancing, and all such delights as may win us to pleasure or rock us asleep. . . .

In our assemblies at plays in London you shall see such heaving and shoving, such itching and should'ring to sit by women, such care for their garments that they be not trod on, such eyes to their laps that no chips light in them, such pillows to their backs that they take no hurt, such masking in their ears (I know not what), such geving them pippins to pass the time, such playing at foot-saunt without cards, such ticking, such toying, such smiling, such winking, and such manning them home when the sports are ended that it is a right comedy to mark their behavior, to watch their conceits, as the cat for the mouse, and as good as a course at the game itself to dog them a little, or follow aloof by the print of their fee , and so discover by slot where the deer taketh soil. If this were as well noted as ill seen, or as openly punished as secretly practised, I have no doubt but the cause would be feared to dry up the effect, and these pretty rabbets very cunningly ferreted from their borrows. For they that lack customers all the week, either because their haunt is unknown or the constables and officers of their parish watch them so narrowly that they dare not queatch, to celebrate the Sabboth flock to theaters and there keep a general market of bawdry. Not that any filthiness, indeed, is committed within the compass of that ground (as was once done in Rome), but that every wanton and his paramour, every man and his mistress, every John and his Joan, every knave and his quean, are there first acquainted and cheapen the marchandise in that place which they pay for elsewhere as they can agree. . . .

God hath now blessed England with a queen in virtue excellent, in power mighty, in glory renowmed, in government politic, in possession rich, breaking her foes with the bent of her brow, ruling her subjects with shaking her hand, removing debate by diligent foresight, filling her chests with the fruits of peace, minist'ring justice by order of law, reforming abuses with great regard, and bearing her sword so even that neither the poor are trod under foot nor the rich suff'red to look too high; nor Rome, nor France, nor tyrant, nor Turk dare for their lives to enter the list. But we, unworthy servants of so mild a mistress, degenerate children of so good a mother, unthankful subjects of so loving a prince, wound her sweet heart with abusing her lenity and stir Jupiter to anger to send us a stork that shall devour us. How often hath her Majesty, with the grave advice of her whole council, set down the limits of apparel to every degree, and how soon again hath the pride of our hearts overflown the channel? How many times hath access to theaters been restrained, and how boldly again have we reent'red? Overlashing in apparel is so common a fault that the very hirelings of some of our players (which stand at reversion of six shillings by the week) jet under gentlemen's noses in suits of silk, exercising themselves to prating on the stage, and common scoffing when they come abroad, where they look askance over the shoulder at every man of whom the Sunday before they begged an alms. . . .

Man is enriched with reason and knowledge; with knowledge to serve his Maker and govern himself, with reason to distinguish good and ill, and choose the best, neither referring the one to the glory of God nor using the other to his own profit. Fire and air mount upwards, earth and water sink down, and every insensible body else never rests till it bring itself to his own home. But we, which have both sense, reason, wit, and understanding, are ever overlashing, passing our bounds, going beyond our limits, never keeping ourselves within compass nor once looking after the place from whence we came and whither we must in spight of our hearts. . . .

Let us but shut up our ears to poets, pipers, and players, pull our feet back from resort to theaters, and turn away our eyes from beholding of vanity, the greatest storm of abuse will be overblown and a fair path trodden to amendment of life. Were not we so foolish to taste every drug and buy every trifle, players would shut in their shops and carry their trash to some other country. . . .

Therefore I will content myself to shew you no more abuses in my school then myself have seen, nor so many by hundreds as I have heard of. Lions fold up their nails when they are in their dens for wearing them in the earth, and need not; eagles draw in their tallants as they set in their nests for blunting them there among dross; and I will cast anchor in these abuses, rest my bark in this simple road, for grating my wits upon needless shelves. And because I accuse other for treading awry, which, since I was born, never went right; because I find so many faults abroad, which have at home more spots on my body then the leopard, more stains on my coat then the wicked Nessus, more holes in my life then the open sieve, more sins in my soul then hears on my head, if I have been tedious in my lecture, or yourselves be weary of your lesson, harken no longer for the clock; shut up the school, and get you home.

THOMAS LODGE

... There came to my hands lately a little—would God a witty—pamphlet bearing a fair face as though it were the *School of Abuse;* but, being by me advisedly weighed, I find it the oftscome of imperfections, the writer fuller of words then judgment, the matter certainly as ridiculous as serious. Assuredly his mother-wit wrought this wonder, the child to dispraise his father, the dog to bite his maister for his dainty morsel; but I see, with Seneca, that the wrong is to be suffered, since he dispraiseth who by custom hath left to speak well. But I mean to be short and teach the maister what he knoweth not, partly that he may see his own folly and partly that I may discharge my promise. Both bind me; therefore I would wish the good schoolmaister to overlook his abuses again with me; so shall he see an ocean of enormities which begin in his first principle in the dispraise of poetry.

And first let me familiarly consider with this find-fault what the learned have always esteemed of poetry. Seneca, though a Stoic, would have a poetical son; and amongst the ancientest Homer was no less accompted then *humanus deus.* What made Alexander, I pray you, esteem of him so much? Why allotted he for his works so curious a closet? Was there no fitter underprop for his pillow then a simple pamphlet? In all Darius' coffers was there no jewel so costly? Forsooth, methinks, these two—the one the father of philosophers, the other the chieftain of chivalry—were both deceived if all were as a Gosson would wish them. If poets paint naught but paltery toys in verse, their studies tended to foolishness, and in all their indeavors they did naught else but *agendo nihil agere.* ...

But I see you would seem to be that which you are not, and, as the proverb saith, *nodum in scirpo quaerere.* Poets, you say, use colors to cover their inconveniences and witty sentences to burnish their bawdery; and you, divinity to cover your knavery. But tell me truth, Gosson, speakest thou as thou thinkest? What colors findest thou in a poet not to be admitted? Are his speeches unperfect? Savor they of inscience? I think if thou hast any shame, thou canst not but like and approve them. Are their gods displeasant unto thee? Doth Saturn in his majesty move thee? Doth Juno with her riches displease thee? Doth Minerva with her weapon discomfort thee? Doth Apollo with his harping harm thee? ... For wot thou that in the person of Saturn our decaying years are signified; in the picture of angry Juno our affections are dissiphered; in the person of Minerva is our understanding signified, both in respect of war as policy. When they feign that Pallas was begotten of the brain of Jupiter their meaning is none other but that all wisdom, as the learned say, is from above and cometh from the Father of Lights; in the portraiture of Apollo all knowledge is denotated. So that, what so they wrote, it was to this purpose: in the way of pleasure to draw men to wisdom; for, seeing the world in those days was unperfect, it was necessary that they, like good phisitions, should so frame their potions that they might be appliable to the queasy stomachs of their wearish patients. But our students by your means have made shipwrack of their labors; our schoolmaisters have so offended that by your judgment they shall *subire poenam capitis* for teaching poetry; the university is little beholding to you—all their practises in teaching are frivolous. Wit hath wrought that in you that years and study never settled in the heads of our sagest doctors. No mervel though you dispraise poetry when you know not what it means.

Erasmus will make that the pathway to knowledge which you dispraise, and no mean fathers vouchsafe in their serious questions of devinity to insert poetical censures. I think, if we shall well overlook the philosophers, we shall find their judgments not half perfect. Poets, you say, fail in their fables, philosophers in the very secrets of nature. Though Plato could wish [*The Republic,* bk. X] the expulsion of poets from his well-publiques (which he might do with reason), yet the wisest had not all that same opinion; it had been better for him to have search'd more narrowly what the soul was, for his definition was very frivolous, when he would make it naught else but *substantiam intellectu predictam.* If you say that poets did labor about nothing, tell me, I beseech you, what wonders wrought those your dunce doctors in their reasons *de ente, et non ente,* in their definition of no force and less wit? How sweat they, poor souls, in making more things then could be? That I may use your own phrase, did not they spend one candle by seeking another? Democritus, Epicurus, with their scholler Metrodorus, how labored they in finding out more worlds then one? Your Plato in midst of his preciseness wrought that absurdity that never may be read in poets: to make a yearthly creature to bear the person of the Creator, and a corruptible substance an incomprehensible God! For, determining of the principal causes of all things, a made them naught else but an Idea, which, if it be conferred with the truth, his sentence will savor of inscience. ...

Men hope that scollers should have wit, brought up in the university; but your sweet self, with the cattle of Euboea, since you left your college, have lost your learning. You dispraise Maximius Tyrius' policy, and that thing that he wrote to manifest learned poets' meaning you attribute to folly. O holy-headed man! Why may not Juno resemble the air? Why not Alexander valor? Why not Ulysses policy? Will you have all for your own tooth? Must men write that you may know their meaning, as though your wit were to wrest all things? Alas, simple Irus, beg at knowledge' gate awhile; thou hast not won the mastery of learning. Wean thyself to wisdom and use thy talent in zeal, not for envy. Abuse not thy knowledge in dispraising that which is peerless. I should blush from a player to become an envious preacher—if thou had'st zeal to preach. If for Sion's sake thou couldst not hold thy tongue, thy true-dealing were praiseworthy, thy revolting would counsel me to reverence thee. Pity were it that poetry should be displaced; full little could we want Buchanan's works, and Boethius' comforts may not be banished. What made Erasmus labor in Euripides' tragedies? Did he indeavor by painting them out of Greek into Latin to manifest sin unto us or to confirm us in goodness? Labor, I pray thee, in pamphlets more praiseworthy. Thou hast not saved a senator, therefore not worthy a laurel wreath; thou hast not, in disproving poetry, reproved an abuse, and therefore not worthy commendation. . . .

It is a pretty sentence—yet not so pretty as pithy—*poeta nascitur, orator fit;* as who should say poetry cometh from above, from a heavenly seat of a glorious God unto an excellent creature, man; an orator is but made by exercise. For if we examine well what befell Ennius among the Romans and Hesiodus among his countrymen the Grecians, how they came by their knowledge, whence they received their heavenly fury, the first will tell us that, sleeping on the Mount of Parnassus, he dreamed that he received the soul of Homer into him, after the which he became a poet; the next will assure you that it cometh not by labor, neither that night-watchings bringeth it, but that we must have it thence whence he fetched it, which was, he saith, from a well of the muses which Cabelimus calleth Porum, a draught whereof drew him to his perfection; so of a shepherd he became an eloquent poet. Well, then, you see that it cometh not by exercise of playmaking, neither insertion of gauds, but from nature and from above; and I hope that Aristotle hath sufficiently taught you that *natura nihil fecit frustra.* . . .

I must arm myself now, for here is the greatest bob I can gather out of your book—forsooth Ovid's abuses, in describing whereof you labor very vehemently, terming him lecher, and in his person dispraise all poems. But shall one man's folly destroy a universal commodity? What gift, what perfit knowledge, hath there been among the professors of which there hath not been a bad one? The angels have sinned in heaven, Adam and Eve in earthly paradise, among the holy apostles ungracious Judas. I reason not that all poets are holy, but I affirm that poetry is a heavenly gift, a perfit gift, then which I know not greater pleasure. . . . I abhor those poets that savor of ribaldry; I will, with the zealous, admit the expulsion of such enormities; poetry is dispraised, not for the folly that is in it, but for the abuse which many ill writers color by it. Believe me, the magistrates may take advice—as I know wisely can—to root out those odd rimes which runs in every rascal's mouth, savoring of ribaldry—those foolish ballets that are admitted make poets' good and godly practises to be refused. I like not of a wicked Nero that will expel Lucan, yet admit I of a zealous governor that will seek to take away the abuse of poetry. I like not of an angry Augustus which will banish Ovid for envy. I love a wise senator which in wisdom will correct him and with advise burn his follies. Unhappy were we if, like poor Scaurus, we should find Tiberius that will put us to death for a tragedy-making; but most blessed were we if we might find a judge that severely would amend the abuses of tragedies. . . .

If it be not tedious to Gosson to harken to the learned, the reader shall perceive the antiquity of playmaking, the inventors of comedies, and therewithal the use and commodity of them. So that in the end I hope my labor shall be liked and the learned will sooner conceive his folly. For tragedies and comedies, Donate the grammarian saith they were invented by learned fathers of the old time to no other purpose but to yield praise unto God for a happy harvest or plentiful year. . . . You see, then, that the first matter of tragedies was to give thanks and praises to God and a grateful prayer of the countrymen for a happy harvest, and this, I hope, was not discommendable. I know you will judge it farthest from abuse. But to wade farther, this form of invention being found out, as the days wherein it was used did decay and the world grew to more perfection, so the wit of the younger sort became more riper; for they, leaving this form, invented another, in the which they altered the nature but not the name; for, for sonnets in praise of the gods, they did set forth the sour fortune of many exiles, the miserable fall of hapless princes, the ruinous decay of many countries; yet, not content with this, they presented the lives of satyrs so that they might wisely, under the abuse of that name, discover the follies of many their foolish fellow-citizens. And those monsters were then as our parasites are nowadays, such as with pleasure reprehended abuse. . . .

But let me apply those days to ours, their actors to our players, their autors to ours. Surely we want not a Roscius, neither are there great scarcity of Terence's profession, but yet our men dare not nowadays presume so much as the old poets might, and therefore they apply their writing to the people's vein, whereas if in the beginning they had ruled we should nowadays have found small spectacles of folly. But of truth I must confess, with Aristotle, that men are greatly delighted with imitation, and that it were good to bring those things on stage that were altogether tending to virtue. All this I admit and heartily wish, but you say unless the thing be taken away the vice will continue. Nay, I say if the style were changed the practise would profit. . . . If our poets will now become severe, and for prophane things write of virtue, you, I hope, should see a reformed state in those things, which, I fear me, if they were not, the idle-headed commons would work more mischief. I wish as zealously as the best that all

abuse of playing were abolished, but for the thing, the antiquity causeth me to allow it, so it be used as it should be. I cannot allow the prophaning of the Sabaoth. I praise your reprehension in that; you did well in discommending the abuse, and surely I wish that that folly were disclaimed; it is not to be admitted; it makes those sin which perhaps, if it were not, would have been present at a good sermon. It is in the magistrate to take away that order and appoint it otherwise. But sure it were pity to abolish that which hath so great virtue in it because it is abused. . . .

And because I think myself to have sufficiently answered that I supposed, I conclude with this: God preserve our peaceable princess and confound her enemies; God enlarge her wisdom, that like Saba she may seek after a Salomon; God confound the imaginations of her enemies and perfit his graces in her, that the days of her rule may be continued in the bonds of peace, that the house of the chosen Israelites may be maintained in happiness. Lastly, I friendly bid Gosson farewell, wishing him to temper his pen with more discretion.

SIR PHILIP SIDNEY

THE DEFENSE OF POESY (1595)

When the right virtuous E[dward] W[otton] and I were at the Emperor's [Maximilian II's] court togither, we gave ourselves to learn horsemanship of John Pietro Pugliano, one that with great commendation had the place of an esquire in his stable. And he, according to the fertileness of the Italian wit, did not only afford us the demonstration of his practise, but sought to enrich our minds with the contemplations therein which he thought most precious. But with none I remember mine ears were at any time more loaden then when (either ang'red with slow payment or moved with our learner-like admiration) he exercised his speech in the praise of his faculty. He said soldiers were the noblest estate of mankind, and horsemen the noblest of soldiers. He said they were the maisters of war and ornaments of peace; speedy goers and strong abiders; triumphers both in camps and courts. Nay, to so unbelieved a point he proceeded, as that no earthly thing bred such wonder to a prince as to be a good horseman. Skill of government was but a *pedanteria* in comparison. Then would he add certain praises by telling what a peerless beast the horse was, the only serviceable courtier without flattery, the beast of most beauty, faithfulness, courage, and such more that, if I had not been a

piece of a logician before I came to him, I think he would have persuaded me to have wished myself a horse. But thus much at least with his no few words he drave into me, that self-love is better then any gilding to make that seem gorgious wherein ourselves be parties.

Wherein, if Pugliano's strong affection and weak arguments will not satisfy you, I will give you a nearer example of myself, who (I know not by what mischance), in these my not old years and idlest times having slipp'd into the title of a poet, am provoked to say something unto you in the defense of that my unelected vocation, which if I handle with more good will then good reasons, bear with me, since the scholler is to be pardoned that followeth the steps of his maister. And yet I must say that, as I have more just cause to make a pitiful defense of poor poetry, which from almost the highest estimation of learning is fall'n to be the laughing-stock of children, so have I need to bring some more available proofs, since the former is by no man barr'd of his deserved credit, the silly latter hath had even the names of philosophers used to the defacing of it, with great danger of civil war among the muses.

And first, truly, to all them that professing learning inveigh against poetry may justly be objected, that they go very near to ungratefulness, to seek to deface that which, in the noblest nations and languages that are known, hath been the first light-giver to ignorance, and first nurse, whose milk little and little enabled them to feed afterwards of tougher knowledges. And will you play the hedgehog that, being received into the den, drave out his host, or rather the vipers that with their birth kill their parents? Let learned Greece in any of his manifold sciences be able to shew me one book before Musaeus, Homer, and Hesiod, all three nothing else but poets. Nay, let any history be brought that can say any writers were there before them, if they were not men of the same skill, as Orpheus, Linus, and some other are named, who, having been the first of that country that made pens deliverers of their knowledge to the posterity, may justly challenge to be called their fathers in learning, for not only in time they had this priority (although in itself antiquity be venerable) but went before them, as causes to draw with their charming sweetness the wild untamed wits to an admiration of knowledge, so as Amphion was said to move stones with his poetry to build Thebes, and Orpheus to be list'ned to by beasts—indeed stony and beastly people. So among the Romans were Livius Andronicus and Ennius. So in the Italian language the first that made it aspire to be a treasure-house of science were the poets Dante, Boccace, and Petrarch. So in our English were Gower and Chaucer, after whom, encouraged and delighted with their excellent foregoing, others have followed, to beautify our mother tongue, as well in the same kind as other arts.

This did so notably shew itself, that the philosophers of Greece durst not a long time appear to the world but under the mask of poets. So Thales, Empedocles, and Parmenides sang their natural philosophy in verses; so did Pythagoras and Phocylides their moral counsels; so did Tyrtaeus in war matters, and Solon in matters of policy: or rather, they, being poets, did exercise their delightful vein in those points of highest knowledge, which before them lay hidden to the world. For that wise Solon was directly a poet it is manifest, having written in verse the notable fable of the Atlantic Iland, which was continued by Plato. And truly, even Plato, whosoever well considereth shall find that in the body of his work, though the inside and strength were philosophy, the skin as it were and beauty depended most of poetry: for all stands upon dialogues, wherein he feigns many honest burgesses of Athens speak of such matters that, if they had been set on the rack, they would never have confessed them, besides his poetical describing the circumstances of their meetings, as the well ordering of a banquet, the delicacy of a walk, with enterlacing mere tales, as Gyges' Ring, and others, which who knows not to be flowers of poetry did never walk into Apollo's garden.

And even historiographers (although their lips sound of things done, and verity be written in their foreheads) have been glad to borrow both fashion and perchance weight of the poets. So Herodotus entituled his history by the name of the nine muses; and both he and all the rest that followed him either stale or usurped of poetry their passionate describing of passions, the many particularities of battles, which no man could affirm, or, if that be denied me, long orations put in the mouths of great kings and captains, which it is certain they never pronounced. So that, truly, neither philosopher nor historiographer could at the first have entered into the gates of popular judgments if they had not taken a great passport of poetry, which in all nations at this day where learning flourisheth not is plain to be seen, in all which they have some feeling of poetry.

In Turkey, besides their law-giving divines, they have no other writers but poets. In our neighbor country Ireland, where truly learning goes very bare, yet are their poets held in a devout reverence. Even among the most barbarous and simple Indians where no writing is, yet have they their poets, who make and sing songs, which they call *areytos*, both of their ancestors' deeds and praises of their gods—a sufficient probability that, if ever learning come among them, it must be by having their hard dull wits softened and sharpened with the sweet delights of poetry. For until they find a pleasure in the exercise of the mind, great promises of much knowledge will little persuade them that know not the fruits of knowledge. In Wales, the true remnant of the ancient Britons, as there are good authorities to shew the long time they had poets, which they called bards, so thorow all the conquests of Romans, Saxons, Danes, and Normans, some of whom did seek to ruin all memory of learning from among them, yet do their poets, even to this day, last; so as it is not more notable in the soon beginning then in long continuing. But since the authors of most of our sciences were the Romans, and before them the Greeks, let us a little stand upon their authorities, but even so far as to see what names they have given unto this now scorned skill.

Among the Romans a poet was called *vates*, which is as much as a diviner, foreseer, or prophet, as by his conjoined words *vaticinium* and *vaticinari* is manifest; so heavenly a title did that excellent people bestow upon this heart-ravishing knowledge. And so far were they carried into the admiration thereof, that they thought in the chanceable hitting upon any such verses great foretokens of their following fortunes were placed. Whereupon grew the word of *sortes Virgilianae,* when, by suddain opening Virgil's book, they lighted upon some verse of his, as it is reported by many, whereof the histories of the emperors' lives are full, as of Albinus, the governor of our iland, who in his childhood met with this verse, *Arma amens capio nec sat rationis in armis;* and in his age performed it: although it were a very vain and godless superstition, as also it was to think spirits were commanded by such verses—whereupon this word "charms," derived of *carmina,* cometh—so yet serveth it to shew the great reverence those wits were held in. And altogither not without ground, since both the oracles of Delphos and Sibylla's prophecies were wholly delivered in verses. For that same exquisite observing of number and measure in the words, and that high-flying liberty of conceit proper to the poet, did seem to have some divine force in it.

And may not I presume a little farther, to shew the reasonableness of this word *vates,* and say that the holy David's Psalms are a divine poem? If I do, I shall not do it without the testimony of great learned men, both ancient and modern. But even the name of "Psalms" will speak for me, which, being interpreted, is nothing but songs; then that it is fully written in meter, as all learned Hebricians agree, although the rules be not yet fully found; lastly and principally, his handling his prophecy, which is merely poetical. For what else is the awaking his musical instruments, the often and free changing of persons, his notable *prosopopeias,* when he maketh you, as it were, see God coming in his majesty, his telling of the beasts' joyfulness, and hills' leaping, but a heavenly poesy, wherein almost he sheweth himself a passionate lover of that unspeakable and everlasting beauty to be seen by the eyes of the mind, only cleared by faith? But truly now having named him, I fear I seem to prophane that holy name, applying it to poetry, which is among us thrown down to so ridiculous an estimation. But they that with quiet judgments will look a little deeper into it shall find the end and working of it such, as, being rightly applied, deserveth not to be scourged out of the Church of God.

But now let us see how the Greeks have named it, and how they deemed of it. The Greeks named him ποιητήν, which name hath, as the most excellent, gone through other languages. It cometh of this word ποιεῖν, which is "to make": wherein, I know not whether by luck or wisdom, we Englishmen have met with the Greeks in calling him "a maker": which name, how high and incomparable a title it is, I had rather were known by marking the scope of other sciences then by any partial allegation.

There is no art delivered unto mankind that hath not the works of Nature for his principal object, without which they could not consist, and on which they so depend as they become actors and players, as it were, of what Nature will have set forth. So doth the astronomer look upon the stars, and, by that he seeth, set down what order Nature hath taken therein. So doth the geometrician and arithmetician in their diverse sorts of quantities. So doth the musicians in times tell you which by nature agree, which not. The natural philosopher thereon hath his name, and the moral philosopher standeth upon the natural virtues, vices, or passions of man; and "follow Nature" (saith he) "therein, and thou shalt not err." The lawyer saith what men have determined; the historian what men have done. The grammarian speaketh only of the rules of speech; and the rhetorician and logician, considering what in Nature will soonest prove and persuade, thereon give artificial rules, which still are compassed within the circle of a question according to the proposed matter. The physician weigheth the nature of man's body, and the nature of things helpful or hurtful unto it. And the metaphysic, though it be in the second and abstract notions, and therefore be counted supernatural, yet doth he indeed build upon the depth of Nature. Only the poet, disdaining to be tied to any such subjection, lifted up with the vigor of his own invention, doth grow in effect into another nature, in making things either better then Nature bringeth forth, or, quite anew, forms such as never were in Nature, as the Heroes, Demigods, Cyclops, Chimeras, Furies, and such like: so as he goeth hand in hand with Nature, not enclosed within the narrow warrant of her gifts, but freely ranging within the zodiac of his own wit.

Nature never set forth the earth in so rich tapistry as diverse poets have done—neither with so pleasant rivers, fruitful trees, sweet-smelling flowers, nor whatsoever else may make the too much loved earth more lovely. Her world is brazen, the poets only deliver a golden. But let those things alone, and go to man—for whom as the other things are, so it seemeth in him her uttermost [cunning] is imployed—and know whether she have brought forth so true a lover as Theagenes, so constant a friend as Pylades, so valiant a man as Orlando, so right a prince as Xenophon's Cyrus, so excellent a man every way as Virgil's Aeneas. Neither let this be jestingly conceived, because the works of the one be essential, the other in imitation or fiction; for every understanding knoweth the skill of each artificer standeth in that idea or foreconceit of the work, and not in the work itself. And that the poet hath that idea is manifest, by delivering them forth in such excellency as he had imagined them. Which delivering forth also is not wholly imaginative, as we are wont to say by them that build castles in the air: but so far substantially it worketh, not only to make a Cyrus, which had been but a particular excellency, as Nature might have done, but to bestow a Cyrus upon the world, to make many Cyruses, if they will learn aright why and how that maker made him.

Neither let it be deemed too saucy a comparison to balance the highest point of man's wit with the efficacy of Nature; but rather give right honor to the heavenly Maker of that maker, who, having made man to his own likeness, set him beyond and over all the works of that second nature: which in nothing he sheweth so much as in poetry, when with the force of a divine breath he bringeth things forth surpassing her doings, with no small arguments to the incredulous of that first accursed fall of Adam, since our erected wit maketh us know what perfection is, and yet our infected will keepeth us from reaching unto it. But these arguments will by few be understood, and by fewer granted. Thus much (I hope) will be given me, that the Greeks with some probability of reason gave him the name above all names of learning. Now let us go to a more ordinary opening of him, that the truth may be the more palpable: and so I hope, though we get not so unmatched a praise as the etymology of his names will grant, yet his very description, which no man will deny, shall not justly be barred from a principal commendation.

Poesy therefore is an art of imitation, for so Aristotle termeth it in the word μίμησις, that is to say, a representing, counterfeiting, or figuring-forth —to speak metaphorically, a speaking picture; with this end, to teach and delight. Of this have been three general kinds.

The chief, both in antiquity and excellency, were they that did imitate the unconceivable excellencies of God. Such were David in his Psalms; Salomon in his Song of Songs, in his Ecclesiastes, and Proverbs; Moses and Debora in their Hymns; and the writer of Job; which, beside other, the learned Emanuel Tremellius and F[ranciscus] Junius do entitle the poetical part of the Scripture. Against these none will speak that hath the Holy Ghost in due holy reverence. In this kind, though in a full wrong divinity, were Orpheus, Amphion, Homer in his Hymns, and many other, both Greek and Romans, and this poesy must be used by whosoever will follow St. Paul's counsail in singing psalms when they are merry, and I know is used with the fruit of comfort by some, when, in sorrowful pangs of their death-bringing sins, they find the consolation of the never-leaving goodness.

The second kind is of them that deal with matters philosophical: either moral, as Tyrtaeus, Phocylides, [and] Cato; or natural, as Lucretius and Virgil's *Georgics;* or astronomical, as Manilius and Pontanus; or historical, as Lucan; which who mislike, the fault is in their judgment quite out of taste, and not in the sweet food of sweetly uttered knowledge.

But bicause this second sort is wrapped within the fold of the proposed subject, and takes not the free course of his own invention, whether they properly be poets or no let grammarians dispute; and go to the third, indeed right poets, of whom chiefly this question ariseth; betwixt whom and these second is such a kind of difference as betwixt the meaner sort of painters, who counterfeit only such faces as are set before them, and the more excellent, who, having no law but wit, bestow that in colors upon you which is fittest for the eye to see, as the constant though lamenting look of Lucretia, when she punished in herself another's fault, wherein he painteth not Lucretia, whom he never saw, but painteth the outward beauty of such a virtue. For these third be they which most properly do imitate to teach and delight, and to imitate borrow nothing of what is, hath been, or shall be, but range, only reined with learned discretion, into the divine consideration of what may be, and should be. These be they that, as the first and most noble sort may justly be termed *vates,* so these are waited on in the excellentest languages and best understandings with the foredescribed name of poets; for these indeed do merely make to imitate, and imitate both to delight and teach, and delight to move men to take that goodness in hand which without delight they would fly as from a stranger, and teach to make them know that goodness whereunto they are moved: which being the noblest scope to which ever any learning was directed, yet want there not idle tongues to bark at them.

These be subdivided into sundry more special denominations. The most notable be the heroic, lyric, tragic, comic, satiric, iambic, elegiac, pastoral, and certain others, some of these being termed according to the matter they deal with, some by the sort of verse they liked best to write in; for indeed the greatest part of poets have appareled their poetical inventions in that numbrous kind of writing which is called verse—indeed but appareled, verse being but an ornament and no cause to poetry, since there have been many most excellent poets that never versified, and now swarm many versifiers that need never answer to the name of poets. For Xenophon, who did imitate so excellently as to give us *effigiem iusti imperii,* "the portraiture of a just empire," under the name of Cyrus (as Cicero saith of him), made therein

(Poetry should imitate the ideal)

Renaissance view

an absolute heroical poem. So did Heliodorus in his sug'red invention of that picture of love in Theagenes and Chariclea; and yet both these wrote in prose: which I speak to shew that it is not riming and versing that maketh a poet—no more then a long gown maketh an advocate, who though he pleaded in armor should be an advocate and no soldier. But it is that feigning notable images of virtues, vices, or what else, with that delightful teaching, which must be the right describing note to know a poet by, although indeed the Senate of Poets hath chosen verse as their fittest raiment, meaning, as in matter they passed all in all, so in manner to go beyond them—not speaking (table-talk fashion or like men in a dream) words as they chanceably fall from the mouth, but peasing each syllable of each word by just proportion according to the dignity of the subject.

Now therefore it shall not be amiss first to weigh this latter sort of poetry by his works, and then by his parts, and, if in neither of these anatomies he be condemnable, I hope we shall obtain a more favorable sentence. This purifying of wit, this enriching of memory, enabling of judgment, and enlarging of conceit, which commonly we call learning, under what name soever it come forth, or to what immediate end soever it be directed, the final end is to lead and draw us to as high a perfection as our degenerate souls, made worse by their clay lodgings, can be capable of. This, according to the inclination of man, bred many-formed impressions. For some that thought this felicity principally to be gotten by knowledge and no knowledge to be so high or heavenly as acquaintance with the stars, gave themselves to astronomy; others, persuading themselves to be demigods if they knew the causes of things, became natural and supernatural philosophers; some an admirable delight drew to music; and some the certainty of demonstration to the mathematics. But all, one and other, having this scope—to know, and by knowledge to lift up the mind from the dungeon of the body to the enjoying his own divine essence. But when by the balance of experience it was found that the astronomer looking to the stars might fall in a ditch, that the inquiring philosopher might be blind in himself, and the mathematician might draw forth a straight line with a crooked heart, then, lo, did proof, the overruler of opinions, make manifest that all these are but serving sciences, which, as they have a private end in themselves, so yet are they all directed to the highest end of the mistress Knowledge, by the Greeks called ἀρχιτεκτονική, which stands (as I think) in the knowledge of a man's self, in the ethic and politique consideration, with the end of well doing and not of well knowing only—even

as the saddler's next end is to make a good saddle, but his further end to serve a nobler faculty, which is horsemanship; so the horseman's to soldiery, and the soldier not only to have the skill, but to perform the practise of a soldier. So that, the ending end of all earthly learning being virtuous action, those skills that most serve to bring forth that have a most just title to be princes over the rest. Wherein, if we can shew, the poet is worthy to have it before any other competitors. Among whom principally to challenge it step forth the moral philosophers, whom, methinks, I see coming towards me with a sullain gravity, as though they could not abide vice by daylight, rudely clothed for to witness outwardly their contempt of outward things, with books in their hands against glory, whereto they set their names, sophistically speaking against subtility, and angry with any man in whom they see the foul fault of anger. These men, casting largess as they go of definitions, divisions, and distinctions, with a scornful interrogative do soberly ask whether it be possible to find any path so ready to lead a man to virtue as that which teacheth what virtue is—and teacheth it not only by delivering forth his very being, his causes, and effects, but also by making known his enemy, vice (which must be destroyed), and his cumbersome servant, passion (which must be mast'red); by shewing the generalities that contains it, and the specialities that are derived from it; lastly, by plain setting down how it extends itself out of the limits of a man's own little world to the government of families and maintaining of public societies.

Phil—

The historian scarcely gives leisure to the moralist to say so much, but that he, loaden with old mouse-eaten records, authorizing himself (for the most part) upon other histories, whose greatest authorities are built upon the notable foundation of hearsay; having much ado to accord differing writers and to pick truth out of partiality; better acquainted with a thousand years ago then with the present age, and yet better knowing how this world goes then how his own wit runs; curious for antiquities and inquisitive of novelties; a wonder to young folks and a tyrant in table talk, denieth, in a great chafe, that any man for teaching of virtue, and virtue's actions, is comparable to him. "I am *testis temporum, lux veritatis, vita memoriae, magistra vitae, nuncia vetustatis,* etc. The philosopher" (saith he) "teacheth a disputative virtue, but I do an active. His virtue is excellent in the dangerless Academy of Plato, but mine sheweth forth her honorable face in the battails of Marathon, Pharsalia, Poitiers, and Agincourt. He teacheth virtue by certain abstract considerations, but I only bid you follow the footing of them that have gone before you. Old-aged experience goeth beyond the fine-

comparative argument covered

witted philosopher, but I give the experience of many ages. Lastly, if he make the song-book, I put the learner's hand to the lute; and if he be the guide, I am the light."

Then would he allege you innumerable examples, confirming story by stories, how much the wisest senators and princes have been directed by the credit of history, as Brutus, Alphonsus of Aragon, and who not, if need be? At length the long line of their disputation makes a point in this, that the one giveth the precept, and the other the example.

Now, whom shall we find (since the question standeth for the highest form in the school of learning) to be moderator? Truly, as meseemeth, the poet; and if not a moderator, even the man that ought to carry the title from them both, and much more from all other serving sciences. Therefore compare we the poet with the historian and with the moral philosopher; and, if he go beyond them both, no other humain skill can match him. For as for the divine, with all reverence it is ever to be excepted, not only for having his scope as far beyond any of these as eternity exceedeth a moment, but even for passing each of these in themselves. And for the lawyer, though Jus be the daughter of Justice, the chief of virtues, yet because he seeks to make men good rather *formidine poenae* then *virtutis amore,* or, to say righter, doth not endeavor to make men good, but that their evil hurt not others, having no care, so he be a good citizen, how bad a man he be: therefore, as our wickedness maketh him necessary, and necessity maketh him honorable, so is he not in the deepest truth to stand in rank with these who all endeavor to take naughtiness away, and plant goodness even in the secretest cabinet of our souls. And these four are all that any way deal in the consideration of men's manners, which being the supreme knowledge, they that best breed it deserve the best commendation.

The philosopher, therefore, and the historian are they which would win the goal, the one by precept, the other by example. But both, not having both, do both halt. For the philosopher, setting down with thorny arguments the bare rule, is so hard of utterance, and so misty to be conceived, that one that hath no other guide but him shall wade in him till he be old before he shall find sufficient cause to be honest. For his knowledge standeth so upon the abstract and general, that happy is that man who may understand him, and more happy that can apply what he doth understand. On the other side, the historian, wanting the precept, is so tied, not to what should be but to what is, to the particular truth of things and not to the general reason of things, that his example draweth no necessary consequence, and therefore a less fruitful doctrine.

Now doth the peerless poet perform both: for whatsoever the philosopher saith should be done, he gives a perfect picture of it by someone by whom he presupposeth it was done; so as he coupleth the general notion with the particular example. A perfect picture, I say, for he yieldeth to the powers of the mind an image of that whereof the philosopher bestoweth but a wordish description, which doth neither strike, pierce, nor possess the sight of the soul so much as that other doth.

For as in outward things, to a man that had never seen an elephant or a rhinoceros, who should tell him most exquisitely all their shape, color, bigness, and particular marks, or of a gorgious palace an architecture who declaring the full beauties might well make the hearer able to repeat, as it were by rote, all he had heard, yet should never satisfy his inward conceit with being witness to itself of a true lively knowledge: but the same man, as soon as he might see those beasts well painted, or that house well in model, should straightways grow, without need of any description, to a judicial comprehending of them: so no doubt the philosopher with his learned definition—be it of virtue or vices, matters of public policy or private government—replenisheth the memory with many infallible grounds of wisdom, which, notwithstanding, lie dark before the imaginative and judging pow'r, if they be not illuminated or figured forth by the speaking picture of poesy.

Tully taketh much pains, and many times not without poetical helps, to make us know the force love of our country hath in us. Let us but hear old Anchises speaking in the middest of Troy's flames, or see Ulysses in the fulness of all Calypso's delights bewail his absence from barrain and beggarly Ithaca. Anger, the Stoics said, was a short madness: let but Sophocles bring you Ajax on a stage, killing or whipping sheep and oxen, thinking them the army of Greeks, with their chieftains Agamemnon and Menelaus, and tell me if you have not a more familiar insight into anger then finding in the Schoolmen his genus and difference. See whether wisdom and temperance in Ulysses and Diomedes, valure in Achilles, friendship in Nisus and Euryalus, even to an ignorant man carry not an apparant shining, and, contrarily, the remorse of conscience in Oedipus, the soon-repenting pride in Agamemnon, the self-devouring cruelty in his father Atreus, the violence of ambition in the two Theban brothers, the sour-sweetness of revenge in Medea, and, to fall lower, the Terentian Gnatho and our Chaucer's Pandar so express'd that we now use their names to signify their trades; and finally, all virtues, vices, and passions so in their own natural states laid to the view, that we seem not to hear of them, but clearly to see through them. But even in the most excellent determination of goodness, what philosopher's counsail can so readily direct a prince, as the feigned Cyrus in Xenophon; or a virtuous man in all fortunes, as Aeneas in Virgil; or a whole commonwealth, as the way of Sir Thomas More's *Utopia?* I say the way, because where Sir Thomas More erred, it was the fault of the man and not of the poet, for that way of patterning a commonwealth was most absolute, though he perchance hath not so absolutely performed it. For the question is, whether the feigned image of poetry or the regular instruction of philosophy hath the more force in teaching: wherein if the philosophers have more rightly shewed themselves philosophers then the poets have attained to the high top of their profession, as in truth, *Mediocribus esse poetis, Non Dii, non homines, non concessere columnae;* it is, I say again, not the fault of the art, but that by few men that art can be accomplished.

Certainly, even our Savior Christ could as well have given the moral commonplaces of uncharitableness and humbleness as the divine narration of Dives and Lazarus; or of disobedience and mercy, as that heavenly discourse of the lost child and the gracious father; but that his through-searching wisdom knew the estate of Dives burning in hell and of Lazarus in Abraham's bosom would more constantly (as it were) inhabit both the memory and judgment. Truly, for myself, meseems I see before mine eyes the lost child's disdainful prodigality, turned to envy a swine's dinner: which by the learned divines are thought not historical acts, but instructing parables. For conclusion, I say the philosopher teacheth, but he teacheth obscurely, so as the learned only can understand him; that is to say, he teacheth them that are already taught. But the poet is the food for the tend'rest stomachs, the poet is indeed the right popular philosopher, whereof Aesop's tales give good proof: whose pretty allegories, stealing under the formal tales of beasts, makes many, more beastly then beasts, begin to hear the sound of virtue from those dumb speakers.

But now may it be alledged that, if this imagining of matters be so fit for the imagination, then must the historian needs surpass, who brings you images of true matters, such as indeed were done, and not such as fantastically or falsely may be suggested to have been done. Truly, Aristotle himself, in his discourse of poesy, plainly determineth this question, saying that poetry is φιλοσοφώτερον and σπουδαιότερον, that is to say, it is more philosophical and more [serious] then history. His reason is because poesy dealeth with καθόλου, that is to say, with the universal consideration, and the history with καθ' ἕκαστον, the particular. "Now," saith he, "the universal

weighs what is fit to be said or done, either in likelihood or necessity (which the poesy considereth in his imposed names), and the particular only marketh whether Alcibiades did, or suffered, this or that." Thus far Aristotle: which reason of his (as all his) is most full of reason. For indeed, if the question were whether it were better to have a particular act truly or falsely set down, there is no doubt which is to be chosen, no more then whether you had rather have Vespasian's picture right as he was, or at the painter's pleasure nothing resembling. But if the question be, for your own use and learning, whether it be better to have it set down as it should be, or as it was, then certainly is more doctrinable the feigned Cyrus in Xenophon then the true Cyrus in Justin, and the feigned Aeneas in Virgil then the right Aeneas in Dares Phrygius: as to a lady that desired to fashion her countenance to the best grace, a painter should more benefit her to portrait a most sweet face, writing Canidia upon it, then to paint Canidia as she was, who, Horace sweareth, was full ill-favored.

If the poet do his part aright, he will shew you in Tantalus, Atreus, and such like, nothing that is not to be shunned; in Cyrus, Aeneas, Ulysses, each thing to be followed; where the historian, bound to tell things as things were, cannot be liberal (without he will be poetical) of a perfect pattern, but, as in Alexander or Scipio himself, shew doings, some to be liked, some to be misliked. And then how will you discern what to follow but by your own discretion, which you had without reading Q[uintus] Curtius? And whereas a man may say, though in universal consideration of doctrine the poet prevaileth, yet that the history, in his saying such a thing was done, doth warrant a man more in that he shall follow; the answer is manifest: that if he stand upon that *was*—as if he should argue, because it rained yesterday, therefore it should rain today—then indeed it hath some advantage to a gross conceit; but if he know an example only enforms a conjectured likelihood, and so go by reason, the poet doth so far exceed him, as he is to frame his example to that which is most reasonable, be it in warlike, politic, or private matters; where the historian in his bare *was* hath many times that which we call fortune to overrule the best wisdom. Many times he must tell events whereof he can yield no cause: or, if he do, it must be poetically.

For that a feigned example hath as much force to teach as a true example (for as for to move, it is clear, since the feigned may be tuned to the highest key of passion), let us take one example wherein an historian and a poet did concur. Herodotus and Justin doth both testify that Zopyrus, King Darius' faithful servant, seeing his maister long resisted by the rebellious Babylonians, feigned himself in extreme disgrace of his king; for verifying of which, he caused his own nose and ears to be cut off, and so flying to the Babylonians, was received, and for his known valure so far credited that he did find means to deliver them over to Darius. Much like matter doth Livy record of Tarquinius and his son. Xenophon excellently feigneth such another stratagem performed by Abradates in Cyrus' behalf. Now would I fain know, if occasion be presented unto you to serve your prince by such an honest dissimulation, why you do not as well learn it of Xenophon's fiction as of the other's verity—and truly so much the better, as you shall save your nose by the bargain; for Abradates did not counterfeit so far. So then the best of the historian is subject to the poet; for whatsoever action, or faction, whatsoever counsail, policy, or war stratagem the historian is bound to recite, that may the poet (if he list) with his imitation make his own, beautifying it both for further teaching and more delighting as it please him, having all, from Dante his heaven to his hell, under the authority of his pen. Which if I be asked what poets have done so, as I might well name some, so yet say I, and say again, I speak of the art and not of the artificer.

Now, to that which commonly is attributed to the praise of history, in respect of the notable learning is got by marking the success, as though therein a man should see virtue exalted and vice punished—truly that commendation is peculiar to poetry and far off from history. For indeed poetry ever sets Virtue so out in her best colors, making Fortune her well-waiting handmaid, that one must needs be enamored of her. Well may you see Ulysses in a storm and in other hard plights; but they are but exercises of patience and magnanimity, to make them shine the more in the near-following prosperity. And of the contrary part, if evil men come to the stage, they ever go out (as the tragedy writer answered to one that misliked the shew of such persons) so manicled as they little animate folks to follow them. But the history, being captived to the truth of a foolish world, is many times a terror from well-doing, and an encouragement to unbridled wickedness.

For see we not valiant Miltiades rot in his fetters; the just Phocion and the accomplished Socrates put to death like traitors; the cruel Severus live prosperously; the excellent Severus miserably murthered; Sylla and Marius dying in their beds; Pompey and Cicero slain then when they would have thought exile a happiness? See we not virtuous Cato driven to kill himself, and rebel Caesar so advanced that his name yet, after 1,600 years, lasteth in the highest honor? And mark but even Caesar's own words of the forenamed Sylla (who in that only did honestly, to put down his dishonest tyranny), *literas nescivit,* as if want of learning caused him to do well. He meant it not by poetry, which, not content with earthly plagues, deviseth new punishments in hell for tyrants, nor yet by philosophy, which teacheth *occidendos esse;* but no doubt by skill in history, for that indeed can afford you Cypselus, Periander, Phalaris, Dionysius, and I know not how many more of the same kennel, that speed well inough in their abhominable injustice of usurpation. I conclude, therefore, that he excelleth history, not only in furnishing the mind with knowledge, but in setting it forward to that which deserves to be called and accounted good: which setting forward, and moving to well-doing, indeed setteth the laurel crown upon the poets as victorious, not only of the historian, but over the philosopher, howsoever in teaching it may be questionable.

For suppose it be granted (that which I suppose with great reason may be denied) that the philosopher, in respect of his methodical proceeding, teach more perfectly then the poet, yet do I think that no man is so much φιλοφιλόσοφος as to compare the philosopher, in moving, with the poet.

And that moving is of a higher degree then teaching, it may by this appear, that it is well-nigh both the cause and effect of teaching. For who will be taught, if he be not moved with desire to be taught, and what so much good doth that teaching bring forth (I speak still of moral doctrine) as that it moveth one to do that which it doth teach? For, as Aristotle saith, it is not γνῶσις but πρᾶξις must be the fruit. And how πρᾶξις can be, without being moved to practise, it is no hard matter to consider.

The philosopher sheweth you the way, he enformeth you of the particularities, as well of the tediousness of the way, as of the pleasant lodging you shall have when your journey is ended, as of the many by-turnings that may divert you from your way. But this is to no man but to him that will read him, and read him with attentive studious painfulness; which constant desire whosoever hath in him, hath already pass'd half the hardness of the way, and therefore is beholding to the philosopher but for the other half. Nay, truly, learned men have learnedly thought that where once reason hath so much overmastered passion as that the mind hath a free desire to do well, the inward light each mind hath in itself is as good as a philosopher's book; since in nature we know it is well to do well, and what is well and what is evil, although not in the words of art which philosophers bestow upon us. For out of natural conceit the philosophers drew it. But to be moved to do that which we know, or to be moved with desire to know, *hoc opus, hic labor est.*

Now therein of all sciences (I speak still of humane, and according to the humane conceit) is our poet the monarch. For he doth not only shew the way, but giveth so sweet a prospect into the way as will entice any man to enter into it. Nay, he doth, as if your journey should lie through a fair vineyard, at the very first give you a cluster of grapes, that, full of that taste, you may long to pass further. He beginneth not with obscure definitions, which must blur the margent with interpretations, and load the memory with doubtfulness; but he cometh to you with words set in delightful proportion, either accompanied with, or prepared for, the well-enchanting skill of music; and with a tale forsooth he cometh unto you, with a tale which holdeth children from play and old men from the chimney corner. And, pretending no more, doth intend the winning of the mind from wickedness to virtue: even as the child is often brought to take most wholesome things by hiding them in such other as have a pleasant taste: which, if one should begin to tell them the nature of the aloes or rhabarbarum they should receive, would sooner take their physic at their ears then at their mouth. So is it in men (most of which are childish in the best things, till they be cradled in their graves): glad they will be to hear the tales of Hercules, Achilles, Cyrus, Aeneas; and, hearing them, must needs hear the right description of wisdom, valure, and justice; which, if they had been barely, that is to say philosophically, set out, they would swear they be brought to school again.

That imitation whereof poetry is, hath the most conveniency to Nature of all other, insomuch that, as Aristotle saith, those things which in themselves are horrible, as cruel battails, unnatural monsters, are made in poetical imitation delightful. Truly, I have known men that even with reading *Amadis de Gaule* (which God knoweth wanteth much of a perfect poesy) have found their hearts moved to the exercise of courtesy, liberality, and especially courage. Who readeth Aeneas carrying old Anchises on his back that wisheth not it were his fortune to perform so excellent an act? Whom doth not those words of Turnus move, the tale of Turnus having planted his image in the imagination?—*Fugientem haec terra videbit? Usque adeone mori miserum est?* Where the philosophers, as they think scorn to delight, so must they be content little to move, saving wrangling whether virtue be the chief or the only good, whether the contemplative or the active life do excel: which Plato and Boethius well knew, and therefore made Mistress Philosophy very often borrow the masking raiment of poesy. For even those hard-hearted evil men who think virtue a school name, and know no other good but *indulgere genio,* and therefore despise

the austere admonitions of the philosopher, and feel not the inward reason they stand upon, yet will be content to be delighted—which is all the good-fellow poet seemeth to promise—and so steal to see the form of goodness, which seen they cannot but love ere themselves be aware, as if they took a medicine of cherries.

Infinite proofs of the strange effects of this poetical invention might be alleged; only two shall serve, which are so often rememb'red as I think all men know them; the one of Menenius Agrippa, who, when the whole people of Rome had resolutely divided themselves from the Senate, with apparant shew of utter ruin, though he were (for that time) an excellent orator, came not among them upon trust either of figurative speeches or cunning insinuations, and much less with farfet maxims of philosophy, which (especially if they were Platonic) they must have learned geometry before they could well have conceived; but forsooth he behaveth himself like a homely and familiar poet. He telleth them a tale, that there was a time when all the parts of the body made a mutinous conspiracy against the belly, which they thought devoured the fruits of each other's labor: they concluded they would let so unprofitable a spender starve. In the end, to be short (for the tale is notorious, and as notorious that it was a tale), with punishing the belly they plagued themselves. This applied by him wrought such effect in the people, as I never read that only words brought forth but then so suddain and so good an alteration; for upon reasonable conditions a perfect reconcilement ensued. The other is of Nathan the prophet, who, when the holy David had so far forsaken God as to confirm adultery with murther, when he was to do the tend'rest office of a friend, in laying his own shame before his eyes, sent by God to call again so chosen a servant, how doth he it but by telling of a man whose beloved lamb was ungratefully taken from his bosom?—the application most divinely true, but the discourse itself feigned. Which made David (I speak of the second and instrumental cause) as in a glass see his own filthiness, as that heavenly psalm of mercy well testifieth.

By these, therefore, examples and reasons, I think it may be manifest that the poet, with that same hand of delight, doth draw the mind more effectually then any other art doth: and so a conclusion not unfitly ensues, that, as virtue is the most excellent resting-place for all worldly learning to make his end of, so poetry, being the most familiar to teach it, and most princely to move towards it, in the most excellent work is the most excellent workman. But I am content not only to decipher him by his works (although works in commendation and dispraise must ever hold a high authority), but more narrowly will examine his parts: so that, as in a man, though all togither may carry a presence full of majesty and beauty, perchance in some one defectuous piece we may find blemish. Now in his parts, kinds, or species (as you list to term them), it is to be noted that some poesies have coupled togither two or three kinds, as the tragical and comical, whereupon is risen the tragicomical. Some, in the [like] manner, have mingled prose and verse, as Sannazaro and Boethius. Some have mingled matters heroical and pastoral. But that cometh all to one in this question, for, if severed they be good, the conjunction cannot be hurtful. Therefore, perchance forgetting some, and leaving some as needless to be rememb'red, it shall not be amiss in a word to cite the special kinds, to see what faults may be found in the right use of them.

Is it then the pastoral poem which is misliked? For perchance where the hedge is lowest they will soonest leap over. Is the poor pipe disdained, which sometimes out of Melibeus' mouth can shew the misery of people under hard lords and ravening soldiers, and again, by Tityrus, what blessedness is derived to them that lie lowest from the goodness of them that sit highest; sometimes, under the pretty tales of wolves and sheep, can enclude the whole considerations of wrongdoing and patience; sometimes shew that contentions for trifles can get but a trifling victory; where perchance a man may see that even Alexander and Darius, when they strave who should be cock of this world's dunghill, the benefit they got was that the after-livers may say, *Haec memini et victum frustra contendere Thirsim: Ex illo Coridon, Coridon est tempore nobis?* Or is it the lamenting elegiac, which in a kind heart would move rather pity then blame, who bewaileth with the great philosopher Heraclitus the weakness of mankind and the wretchedness of the world; who surely is to be praised, either for compassionate accompanying just causes of lamentations, or for rightly painting out how weak be the passions of wofulness? Is it the bitter but wholesome iambic, who rubs the galled mind, in making shame the trumpet of villany with bold and open crying out against naughtiness? Or the satiric, who *omne vafer vitium ridenti tangit amico;* who sportingly never leaveth till he make a man laugh at folly, and, at length ashamed, to laugh at himself, which he cannot avoid without avoiding the folly; who, while *circum praecordia ludit,* giveth us to feel how many headaches a passionate life bringeth us to; how, when all is done, *est Ulubris, animus si nos non deficit aequus?* No, perchance it is the comic, whom naughty playmakers and stage-keepers have justly made odious. To the arguments of abuse I will after answer. Only thus much now is to be said, that the comedy is an imitation of the common errors of our life, which he representeth in the most ridiculous and scornful sort that may be, so as it is impossible that any beholder can be content to be such a one.

Now, as in geometry the oblique must be known as well as the right, and in arithmetic the odd as well as the even, so in the actions of our life who seeth not the filthiness of evil wanteth a great foil to perceive the beauty of virtue. This doth the comedy handle so in our private and domestical matters, as with hearing it we get as it were an experience what is to be looked for of a niggardly Demea, of a crafty Davus, of a flattering Gnatho, of a vainglorious Thraso; and not only to know what effects are to be expected, but to know who be such, by the signifying badge given them by the comedient. And little reason hath any man to say that men learn the evil by seeing it so set out; since, as I said before, there is no man living but, by the force truth hath in nature, no sooner seeth these men play their parts, but wisheth them in *pistrinum;* although perchance the sack of his own faults lie so behind his back that he seeth not himself to dance the same measure; whereto yet nothing can more open his eyes then to see his own actions contemptibly set forth. So that the right use of comedy will (I think) by nobody be blamed, and much less of the high and excellent tragedy, that openeth the greatest wounds, and sheweth forth the ulcers that are covered with tissue; that maketh kings fear to be tyrants, and tyrants manifest their tyrannical humors; that, with stirring the affects of admiration and commiseration, teacheth the uncertainty of this world and upon how weak foundations gilden roofs are builded; that maketh us know, *Qui sceptra saevus duro imperio regit, Timet timentes, metus in authorem redit.* But how much it can move, Plutarch yieldeth a notable testimony of the abhominable tyrant Alexander Pheraeus, from whose eyes a tragedy, well made and represented, drew abundance of tears, who, without all pity, had murthered infinite numbers, and some of his own blood, so as he that was not ashamed to make matters for tragedies, yet could not resist the sweet violence of a tragedy. And if it wrought no further good in him, it was that he, in despight of himself, withdrew himself from harkening to that which might mollify his hardened heart.

But it is not the tragedy they do mislike; for it were too absurd to cast out so excellent a representation of whatsoever is most worthy to be learned. Is it the lyric that most displeaseth, who with his tuned lyre and well-accorded voice giveth praise, the reward of virtue, to virtuous acts, who giveth moral precepts and natural problems, who sometime raiseth up his voice to the height of the heavens, in singing

If poetry has defects it is the fault of the poet + not of poetry.

Marvelous summary

SIR PHILIP SIDNEY 615

the lauds of the immortal God? Certainly, I must confess mine own barbarousness; I never heard the old song of Percy and Douglas that I found not my heart moved more then with a trumpet; and yet is it sung but by some blind crowder, with no rougher voice then rude style; which, being so evil appareled in the dust and cobwebs of that uncivil age, what would it work trimmed in the gorgious eloquence of Pindar? In Hungary I have seen it the manner at all feasts, and other such-like meetings, to have songs of their ancestors' valure; which that right soldierlike nation think one of the chiefest kindlers of brave courage. The incomparable Lacedemonians did not only carry that kind of music ever with them to the field, but even at home, as such songs were made, so were they all content to be singers of them, when the lusty men were to tell what they did, the old men what they had done, and the young what they would do. And where a man may say that Pindar many times praiseth highly victories of small moment, rather matters of sport then virtue, as it may be answered, it was the fault of the poet, and not of the poetry; so indeed the chief fault was in the time and custom of the Greeks, who set those toys at so high a price that Philip of Macedon reckoned a horse race won at Olympus among his three fearful felicities. But as the unimitable Pindar often did, so is that kind most capable and most fit to awake the thoughts from the sleep of idleness to embrace honorable enterprises.

There rests the heroical, whose very name (I think) should daunt all backbiters; for by what conceit can a tongue be directed to speak evil of that which draweth with him no less champions then Achilles, Cyrus, Aeneas, Turnus, Tydeus, Rinaldo? who doth not only teach and move to a truth, but teacheth and moveth to the most high and excellent truth; who maketh magnanimity and justice shine through all misty fearfulness and foggy desires; who, if the saying of Plato and Tully be true, that who could see Virtue would be wonderfully ravished with the love of her beauty—this man setteth her out to make her more lovely in her holiday apparel to the eye of any that will deign not to disdain until they understand. But if anything be already said in the defense of sweet poetry, all concurreth to the maintaining the heroical, which is not only a kind, but the best and most accomplished kind of poetry. For as the image of each action stirreth and instructeth the mind, so the lofty image of such worthies most enflameth the mind with desire to be worthy, and enforms with counsail how to be worthy. Only let Aeneas be worn in the tablet of your memory, how he governeth himself in the ruin of his country, in the preserving his old father, and carrying away his religious cere-

monies, in obeying God's commandment to leave Dido, though not only all passionate kindness, but even the humane consideration of virtuous gratefulness, would have craved other of him; how in storms, how in sports, how in war, how in peace, how a fugitive, how victorious, how besieged, how besieging, how to strangers, how to allies, how to enemies, how to his own, lastly, how in his inward self, and how in his outward government, and, I think, in a mind most prejudiced with a prejudicating humor, he will be found in excellency fruitful, yea, as Horace saith, *melius Chrysippo et Crantore*. But truly I imagine it falleth out with these poet-whippers as with some good women who often are sick but in faith they cannot tell where. So the name of Poetry is odious to them, but neither his cause nor effects, neither the sum that contains him nor the particularities descending from him, give any fast handle to their carping dispraise.

Since, then, poetry is of all humane learnings the most ancient and of most fatherly antiquity, as from whence other learnings have taken their beginnings; since it is so universal that no learned nation doth despise it, nor barbarous nation is without it; since both Roman and Greek gave such divine names unto it, the one of "prophesying," the other of "making," and that indeed that name of "making" is fit for him, considering that, where all other arts retain themselves within their subject and receive, as it were, their being from it, the poet only only bringeth his own stuff, and doth not learn a conceit out of a matter, but maketh matter for a conceit; since neither his description nor end containing any evil, the thing described cannot be evil; since his effects be so good as to teach goodness and delight the learners of it; since therein (namely in moral doctrine, the chief of all knowledges) he doth not only far pass the historian but for instructing is well-nigh comparable to the philosopher, for moving leaveth him behind him; since the Holy Scripture (wherein there is no uncleanness) hath whole parts in it poetical, and that even our Savior Christ vouchsafed to use the flowers of it; since all his kinds are not only in their united forms but in their severed dissections fully commendable; I think (and think I think rightly) the laurel crown appointed for triumphant captains doth worthily (of all other learnings) honor the poet's triumph. But bicause we have ears as well as tongues, and that the lightest reasons that may be will seem to weigh greatly, if nothing be put in the counterbalance, let us hear, and, as well as we can, ponder, what objections be made against this art, which may be worthy either of yielding or answering.

First, truly, I note not only in these μισομούσοι, poet-haters, but in all that kind of people who seek a praise by dispraising others, that they do prodigally spend a great many wand'ring words in quips and scoffs, carping and taunting at each thing, which, by stirring the spleen, may stay the brain from a through beholding the worthiness of the subject. Those kind of objections, as they are full of a very idle easiness, since there is nothing of so sacred a majesty but that an itching tongue may rub itself upon it, so deserve they no other answer but, instead of laughing at the jest, to laugh at the jester. We know a playing wit can praise the discretion of an ass, the comfortableness of being in debt, and the jolly commodities of being sick of the plague. So of the contrary side, if we will turn Ovid's verse, *Ut lateat virtus proximitate mali*, that "good lie hid in nearness of the evil," Agrippa will be as merry in shewing the vanity of science as Erasmus was in commending of folly. Neither shall any man or matter escape some touch of these smiling railers. But for Erasmus and Agrippa, they had another foundation then the superficial part would promise. Marry, these other pleasant faultfinders, who will correct the verb before they understand the noun, and confute others' knowledge before they confirm their own, I would have them only remember that scoffing cometh not of wisdom; so as the best title in true English they get with their merriments is to be called good fools, for so have our grave forefathers ever termed that humorous kind of jesters.

But that which giveth greatest scope to their scorning humor is riming and versing. It is already said (and, as I think, truly said) it is not riming and versing that maketh poesy. One may be a poet without versing, and a versifier without poetry. But yet presuppose it were inseparable (as indeed it seemeth Scaliger judgeth), truly it were an inseparable commendation. For if *oratio* next to *ratio*, speech next to reason, be the greatest gift bestowed upon mortality, that cannot be praiseless which doth most polish that blessing of speech; which considereth each word, not only (as a man may say) by his forcible quality, but by his best-measured quantity, carrying even in themselves a harmony (without, perchance, number, measure, order, proportion be in our time grown odious). But lay aside the just praise it hath, by being the only fit speech for music (music, I say, the most divine striker of the senses), thus much is undoubtedly true, that if reading be foolish without rememb'ring, memory being the only treasure of knowledge, those words which are fittest for memory are likewise most convenient for knowledge.

Now, that verse far exceedeth prose in the knitting up of the memory, the reason is manifest—the words (besides their delight, which hath a great affinity to memory) being so set as one word cannot be lost but

the whole work fails; which, accusing itself, calleth the remembrance back to itself, and so most strongly confirmeth it. Besides, one word so, as it were, begetting another, as, be it in rime or measured verse, by the former a man shall have a near guess to the follower. Lastly, even they that have taught the art of memory have shewed nothing so apt for it as a certain room divided into many places well and throughly known. Now, that hath the verse in effect perfectly, every word having his natural seat, which seat must needs make the word remenb'red. But what needs more in a thing so known to all men? Who is it that ever was scholler that doth not carry away some verses of Virgil, Horace, or Cato, which in his youth he learned, and even to his old age serve him for hourly lessons? As *Percontatorem fugito nam garrulus idem est; Dum tibi quisque placet credula turba sumus.* But the fitness it hath for memory is notably proved by all delivery of arts: wherein for the most part, from grammar to logic, mathematics, physic, and the rest, the rules chiefly necessary to be borne away are compiled in verses. So that, verse being in itself sweet and orderly, and being best for memory, the only handle of knowledge, it must be in jest that any man can speak against it.

Now then go we to the most important imputations laid to the poor poets. For aught I can yet learn, they are these. First, that there being many other more fruitful knowledges, a man might better spend his time in them then in this. Secondly, that it is the mother of lies. Thirdly, that it is the nurse of abuse, infecting us with many pestilent desires, with a siren's sweetness drawing the mind to the serpent's tail of sinful fancies—and herein, especially, comedies give the largest field to ear (as Chaucer saith)—how both in other nations and in ours, before poets did soften us, we were full of courage, given to martial exercises, the pillars of manlike liberty, and not lulled asleep in shady idleness with poets' pastimes. And lastly, and chiefly, they cry out with open mouth, as if they had overshot Robin Hood, that Plato banished them out of his commonwealth. Truly, this is much, if there be much truth in it. First, to the first, that a man might better spend his time is a reason indeed, but it doth (as they say) but *petere principium;* for if it be, as I affirm, that no learning is so good as that which teacheth and moveth to virtue, and that none can both teach and move thereto so much as poetry, then is the conclusion manifest that ink and paper cannot be to a more profitable purpose imployed. And certainly, though a man should grant their first assumption, it should follow (methinks) very unwillingly that good is not good because better is better. But I still and utterly deny that there is sprung out of earth a more fruitful knowledge. To the second, therefore, that they should be the principal liars, I answer paradoxically, but, truly, I think truly, that of all writers under the sun the poet is the least liar, and, though he would, as a poet can scarcely be a liar. The astronomer, with his cousin the geometrician, can hardly escape, when they take upon them to measure the height of the stars. How often, think you, do the physicians lie, when they aver things good for sicknesses, which afterwards send Charon a great number of souls drown'd in a potion before they come to his ferry? And no less of the rest which take upon them to affirm. Now, for the poet, he nothing affirmeth, and therefore never lieth. For, as I take it, to lie is to affirm that to be true which is false; so as the other artists, and especially the historian, affirming many things, can, in the cloudy knowledge of mankind, hardly escape from many lies. But the poet (as I said before) never affirmeth. The poet never maketh any circles about your imagination to conjure you to believe for true what he writeth. He citeth not authorities of other histories, but even for his entry calleth the sweet muses to inspire unto him a good invention; in troth, not laboring to tell you what is, or is not, but what should or should not be. And therefore, though he recount things not true, yet because he telleth them not for true, he lieth not—without we will say that Nathan lied in his speech, before alleged, to David; which as a wicked man durst scarce say, so think I none so simple would say that Aesop lied in the tales of his beasts; for who thinketh that Aesop wrote it for actually true were well worthy to have his name chronicled among the beasts he writeth of. What child is there that, coming to a play and seeing *Thebes* written in great letters upon an old door, doth believe that it is Thebes? If then a man can arrive to the child's age, to know that the poet's persons and doings are but pictures what should be, and not stories what have been, they will never give the lie to things not affirmatively but allegorically and figuratively written. And therefore, as in history, looking for truth, they may go away full fraught with falsehood, so in poesy, looking but for fiction, they shall use the narration but as an imaginative groundplat of a profitable invention.

But hereto is replied that the poets give names to men they write of, which argueth a conceit of an actual truth, and so, not being true, proveth a falsehood. And doth the lawyer lie then, when under the names of "John of the Stile" and "John of the Nokes" he putteth his case? But that is easily answered. Their naming of men is but to make their picture the more lively, and not to build any history; painting men, they cannot leave men nameless. We see we cannot play at chests but that we must give names to our chessmen; and yet, methinks, he were a very partial champion of truth that would say we lied for giving a piece of wood the reverend title of a bishop. The poet nameth Cyrus and Aeneas no other way then to shew what men of their fames, fortunes, and estates should do.

Their third is, how much it abuseth men's wit, training it to wanton sinfulness and lustful love; for indeed that is the principal, if not the only, abuse I can hear alledged. They say the comedies rather teach then reprehend amorous conceits. They say the lyric is larded with passionate sonnets, the elegiac weeps the want of his mistress, and that even to the heroical Cupid hath ambitiously climbed. Alas, Love, I would thou couldest as well defend thyself as thou canst offend others. I would those on whom thou dost attend could either put thee away, or yield good reason why they keep thee. But grant love of beauty to be a beastly fault (although it be very hard, since only man, and no beast, hath that gift to discern beauty); grant that lovely name of Love to deserve all hateful reproaches (although even some of my maisters the philosophers spent a good deal of their lamp-oil in setting forth the excellency of it); grant, I say, what they will have granted, that not only love, but lust, but vanity, but (if they list) scurrility, possess many leaves of the poets' books: yet think I, when this is granted, they will find their sentence may with good manners put the last words foremost, and not say that poetry abuseth man's wit, but that man's wit abuseth poetry.

For I will not deny but that man's wit may make poesy, which should be εἰκαστική, which some learned have defined, "figuring forth good things," to be φανταστική, which doth, contrariwise, infect the fancy with unworthy objects, as the painter should give to the eye either some excellent perspective, or some fine picture fit for building or fortification or containing in it some notable example, as Abraham sacrificing his son Isaac, Judith killing Holofernes, David fighting with Golias, may leave those, and please an ill-pleased eye with wanton shews of better-hidden matters. But what, shall the abuse of a thing make the right use odious? Nay truly, though I yield that poesy may not only be abused, but that being abused, by the reason of his sweet charming force, it can do more hurt then any other army of words, yet shall it be so far from concluding that the abuse should give reproach to the abused, that contrariwise it is good reason that whatsoever, being abused, doth most harm, being rightly used (and upon the right use each thing receives his title), doth most good.

Do we not see skill of physic (the best ramper to our often-assaulted bodies), being abused, teach poison, the most violent destroyer? Doth not knowledge of law, whose end is to even and right all things, being abused, grow the crooked fosterer of horrible injuries? Doth not (to go to the highest) God's word abused breed heresy, and his name abused become blasphemy? Truly, a needle cannot do much hurt, and as truly (with leave of ladies be it spoken) it cannot do much good. With a sword thou mayst kill thy father, and with a sword thou mayst defend thy prince and country. So that, as in their calling poets fathers of lies they said nothing, so in this their argument of abuse they prove the commendation.

They alledge herewith, that before poets began to be in price our nation had set their hearts' delight upon action, and not imagination, rather doing things worthy to be written, then writing things fit to be done. What that before-time was, I think scarcely Sphinx can tell, since no memory is so ancient that hath the precedence of poetry. And certain it is that, in our plainest homeliness, yet never was the Albion nation without poetry. Marry, this argument, though it be leveled against poetry, yet is it indeed a chain-shot against all learning, or bookishness, as they commonly term it. Of such mind were certain Goths, of whom it is written that, having in the spoil of a famous city taken a fair library, one hangman, belike fit to execute the fruits of their wits, who had murthered a great number of bodies, would have set fire in it. "No," said another very gravely, "take heed what you do, for while they are busy about those toys, we shall with more leisure conquer their countries."

This indeed is the ordinary doctrine of ignorance, and many words sometimes I have heard spent in it, but bicause this reason is generally against all learning, as well as poetry, or rather, all learning but poetry; because it were too large a digression to handle it, or at least too superfluous (since it is manifest that all government of action is to be gotten by knowledge, and knowledge best by gathering many knowledges, which is reading), I only, with Horace, to him that is of that opinion, *iubeo stultum esse libenter;* for as for poetry itself, it is the freest from this objection. For poetry is the companion of camps.

I dare undertake, Orlando Furioso or honest King Arthur will never displease a soldier; but the quiddity of *ens* and *prima materia* will hardly agree with a corslet. And therefore, as I said in the beginning, even Turks and Tartars are delighted with poets. Homer, a Greek, flourished before Greek flourished. And if to a slight conjecture a conjecture may be apposed, truly it may seem that, as by him their learned men took almost their first light of knowledge, so their active men received their first motions of courage. Only Alexander's example may serve, who by Plutarch is accounted of such virtue that Fortune was not his guide but his footstool; whose acts speak for him, though Plutarch did not—indeed the phoenix of warlike princes. This Alexander left his schoolmaister, living Aristotle, behind him, but took dead Homer with him. He put the philosopher Callisthenes to death for his seeming philosophical, indeed mutinous, stubbornness, but the chief thing he was ever heard to wish for was that Homer had been alive. He well found he received more bravery of mind by the pattern of Achilles then by hearing the definition of fortitude: and therefore, if Cato misliked Fulvius for carrying Ennius with him to the field, it may be answered that, if Cato misliked it, the noble Fulvius liked it, or else he had not done it: for it was not the excellent Cato Uticensis (whose authority I would much more have reverenced), but it was the former, in truth a bitter punisher of faults, but else a man that had never sacrificed to the Graces. He misliked and cried out against all Greek learning, and yet, being fourscore years old, began to learn it, belike fearing that Pluto understood not Latin. Indeed, the Roman laws allowed no person to be carried to the wars but he that was in the soldiers' roll, and therefore, though Cato misliked his unmust'red person, he misliked not his work. And if he had, Scipio Nasica, judged by common consent the best Roman, loved him. Both the other Scipio brothers, who had by their virtues no less surnames then of Asia and Afric, so loved him that they caused his body to be buried in their sepulture. So as Cato's authority being but against his person, and that answered with so far greater then himself, is herein of no validity.

But now indeed my burthen is great, that Plato his name is laid upon me, whom, I must confess, of all philosophers I have ever esteemed most worthy of reverence, and with good reason, since of all philosophers he is the most poetical. Yet if he will defile the fountain out of which his flowing streams have proceeded, let us boldly examine with what reasons he did it. First, truly, a man might maliciously object that Plato, being a philosopher, was a natural enemy of poets. For indeed, after the philosophers had picked out of the sweet mysteries of poetry the right discerning true points of knowledge, they forthwith, putting it in method, and making a school art of that which the poets did only teach by a divine delightfulness, beginning to spurn at their guides, like ungrateful prentices were not content to set up shop for themselves but sought by all means to discredit their maisters; which by the force of delight being barred them, the less they could overthrow them, the more they hated them. For, indeed, they found for Homer seven cities strave who should have him for their citizen; where many cities banished philosophers as not fit members to live among them. For only repeating certain of Euripides' verses, many Athenians had their lives saved of the Syracusians, where the Athenians themselves thought many philosophers unworthy to live. Certain poets, as Simonides and Pindarus, had so prevailed with Hiero the First that of a tyrant they made him a just king; where Plato could do so little with Dionysius that he himself of a philosopher was made a slave. But who should do thus, I confess, should requite the objections made against poets with like cavilations against philosophers; as likewise one should do that should bid one read *Phaedrus* or *Symposium* in Plato, or the discourse of love in Plutarch, and see whether any poet do authorize abhominable filthiness, as they do. Again, a man might ask out of what commonwealth Plato doth banish them. In sooth, thence where he himself alloweth community of women. So as belike this banishment grew not for effeminate wantonness, since little should poetical sonnets be hurtful when a man might have what woman he listed. But I honor philosophical instructions, and bless the wits which bred them: so as they be not abused, which is likewise stretched to poetry.

St. Paul himself sets a watchword upon philosophy —indeed upon the abuse. So doth Plato upon the abuse, not upon poetry. Plato found fault that the poets of his time filled the world with wrong opinions of the gods, making light tales of that unspotted essence, and therefore would not have the youth depraved with such opinions. Herein may much be said; let this suffice: the poets did not induce such opinions, but did imitate those opinions already induced. For all the Greek stories can well testify that the very religion of that time stood upon many and many-fashioned gods, not taught so by the poets, but followed according to their nature of imitation. Who list may read in Plutarch the discourses of Isis and Osiris, of the cause why oracles ceased, of the divine providence, and see whether the theology of that nation stood not upon such dreams which the poets indeed superstitiously observed, and truly (since they had not the light of Christ) did much better in it then the philosophers, who, shaking off superstition, brought in atheism. Plato therefore (whose authority I had much rather justly consture then unjustly resist) meant not in general of poets, in those words of which Julius Scaliger saith, *Qua authoritate barbari quidam atque hispidi abuti velint ad poetas e republica exigendos;* but only meant to drive out those wrong opinions of the Deity (whereof now, without further law, Christianity hath taken away all the hurtful belief), perchance (as he thought) nourished by the then esteemed poets. And a man need go no further then to Plato himself to know his meaning: who, in his dialogue called *Ion,* giveth high and rightly divine commendation unto poetry. So as Plato, banishing the abuse, not the thing, not banishing it, but giving due honor to it, shall be our patron and not our adversary. For indeed I had much rather (since truly I may do it) shew their mistaking of Plato (under whose lion's skin they would make an ass-like braying against poesy) then go about to overthrow his authority; whom, the wiser a man is, the more just cause he shall find to have in admiration; especially since he attributeth unto poesy more then myself do, namely, to be a very inspiring of a divine force, far above man's wit, as in the fore-named dialogue is apparant.

Of the other side, who would shew the honors have been by the best sort of judgments granted them, a whole sea of examples would present themselves: Alexanders, Caesars, Scipios, all favorers of poets; Laelius, called the Roman Socrates, himself a poet, so as part of *Heautontimorumenon* in Terence was supposed to be made by him; and even the Greek Socrates, whom Apollo confirmed to be the only wise man, is said to have spent part of his old time in putting Aesop's fables into verses. And therefore, full evil should it become his scholler Plato to put such words in his maister's mouth against poets. But what needs more? Aristotle writes the Art of Poesy, and why, if it should not be written? Plutarch teacheth the use to be gathered of them, and how, if they should not be read? And who reads Plutarch's either history or philosophy shall find he trimmeth both their garments with guards of poesy. But I list not to defend poesy with the help of his underling historiography. Let it suffice to have shewed it is a fit soil for praise to dwell upon; and what dispraise may set upon it is either easily overcome or transformed into just commendation. So that, since the excellencies of it may be so easily and so justly confirmed, and the low-creeping objections so soon trodden down; it not being an art of lies, but of true doctrine; not of effeminateness, but of notable stirring of courage; not of abusing man's wit, but of strengthening man's wit; not banished, but honored by Plato; let us rather plant more laurels for to ingarland the poets' heads (which honor of being laureate, as besides them only triumphant captains wear, is a sufficient authority to shew the price they ought to be held in) then suffer the ill-savored breath of such wrong-speakers once to blow upon the clear springs of poesy.

But since I have run so long a career in this matter, methinks, before I give my pen a full stop, it shall be but a little more lost time to enquire why England (the mother of excellent minds) should be grown so hard a stepmother to poets, who certainly in wit ought to pass all others, since all only proceeds from their wit, being indeed makers of themselves, not takers of others. How can I but exclaim, *Musa, mihi causas memora, quo numine laeso!* Sweet poesy, that hath anciently had kings, emperors, senators, great captains, such as, besides a thousand others, David, Adrian, Sophocles, Germanicus, not only to favor poets, but to be poets; and of our nearer times can present for her patrons a Robert, king of Sicil, the great King Francis of France, King James [I] of Scotland; such cardinals as Bembus and Bibiena; such famous preachers and teachers as Beza and Melancthon; so learned philosophers as Fracastorius and Scaliger; so great orators as Pontanus and Muretus; so piercing wits as George Buchanan; so grave counsailors as, besides many, but before all, that Hospital of France, then whom (I think) that realm never brought forth a more accomplished judgment, more firmly builded upon virtue—I say these, with numbers of others, not only to read others' poesies, but to poetize for others' reading—that poesy, thus embraced in all other places, should only find in our time a hard welcome in England, I think the very earth laments it, and therefore decks our soil with fewer laurels then it was accustomed. For heretofore poets have in England also flourished, and, which is to be noted, even in those times when the trumpet of Mars did sound loudest. And now that an over-faint quietness should seem to strow the house for poets, they are almost in as good reputation as the mountebanks at Venice. Truly even that, as of the one side it giveth great praise to poesy, which like Venus (but to better purpose) had rather be troubled in the net with Mars then enjoy the homely quiet of Vulcan; so serveth it for a piece of a reason why they are less grateful to idle England, which now can scarce endure the pain of a pen. Upon this necessarily followeth that base men with servile wits undertake it, who think it inough if they can be rewarded of the printer. And so as Epaminondas is said, with the honor of his virtue, to have made an office, by his exercising it, which before was contemptible, to become highly respected, so these men, no more but setting their names to it, by their own disgracefulness disgrace the most graceful poesy. For now, as if all the muses were got with child to bring forth bastard poets, without any commission they do post over the banks of Helicon till they make the readers more weary then post-horses, while, in the meantime, they, *queis meliore luto finxit praecordia Titan,* are better content to suppress the outflowings of their wit, then, by publishing them, to be accounted knights of the same order. But I that, before ever I

durst aspire unto the dignity, am admitted into the company of the paper-blurrers, do find the very true cause of our wanting estimation is want of desert, taking upon us to be poets in despite of Pallas. Now wherein we want desert were a thankworthy labor to express: but if I knew, I should have mended myself. But as I never desired the title, so have I neglected the means to come by it. Only, overmastered by some thoughts, I yielded an inky tribute unto them. Marry, they that delight in poesy itself should seek to know what they do, and how they do, and, especially, look themselves in an unflattering glass of reason, if they be inclinable unto it. For poesy must not be drawn by the ears; it must be gently led, or rather it must lead; which was partly the cause that made the ancient learned affirm it was a divine gift, and no humane skill; since all other knowledges lie ready for any that have strength of wit; a poet no industry can make, if his own genius be not carried into it; and therefore is an old proverb, *Orator fit, poeta nascitur.* Yet confess I always that as the fertilest ground must be manured, so must the highest-flying wit have a Daedalus to guide him. That Daedalus, they say, both in this and in other, hath three wings to bear itself up into the air of due commendation: that is, Art, Imitation, and Exercise. But these, neither artificial rules nor imitative patterns, we much cumber ourselves withal. Exercise indeed we do, but that very fore-backwardly; for where we should exercise to know, we exercise as having known, and so is our brain delivered of much matter which never was begotten by knowledge. For there being two principal parts—matter to be expressed by words and words to express the matter—in neither we use Art or Imitation rightly. Our matter is *quodlibet* indeed, though wrongly performing Ovid's verse, *Quicquid conabar dicere, versus erat:* never marshaling it into any assured rank, that almost the readers cannot tell where to find themselves.

Chaucer, undoubtedly, did excellently in his *Troilus and Cressid;* of whom, truly, I know not whether to mervail more either that he in that misty time could see so clearly or that we in this clear age go so stumblingly after him. Yet had he great wants, fit to be forgiven in so reverent an antiquity. I account the *Mirror of Magistrates* meetly furnished of beautiful parts, and in the Earl of Surrey's lyrics many things tasting of a noble birth and worthy of a noble mind. The *Shepherd's Calendar* hath much poetry in his egloges, indeed worthy the reading, if I be not deceived. That same framing of his style to an old rustic language I dare not allow, since neither Theocritus in Greek, Virgil in Latin, nor Sannazaro in Italian did affect it. Besides these, I do not remember to have seen but few (to speak boldly) printed that have poetical sinews in them; for proof whereof, let but most of the verses be put in prose, and then ask the meaning, and it will be found that one verse did but beget another, without ordering at the first what should be at the last, which becomes a confused mass of words, with a tingling sound of rime, barely accompanied with reason.

Our tragedies and comedies (not without cause cried out against), observing rules neither of honest civility nor skilful poetry, excepting *Gorboduc* (again, I say, of those that I have seen), which notwithstanding as it is full of stately speeches and well-sounding phrases, climbing to the height of Seneca his style, and as full of notable morality, which it doth most delightfully teach, and so obtain the very end of poesy, yet in truth it is very defective in the circumstances, which grieves me, because it might not remain as an exact model of all tragedies. For it is faulty both in place and time, the two necessary companions of all corporal actions. For where the stage should alway represent but one place, and the uttermost time presupposed in it should be, both by Aristotle's precept and common reason, but one day, there is both many days and many places inartificially imagined. But if it be so in *Gorboduc,* how much more in all the rest, where you shall have Asia of the one side, and Afric of the other, and so many other under-kingdoms that the player, when he comes in, must ever begin with telling where he is, or else the tale will not be conceived? Now you shall have three ladies walk to gather flowers, and then we must believe the stage to be a garden. By and by we hear news of shipwrack in the same place; then we are to blame if we accept it not for a rock. Upon the back of that comes out a hideous monster, with fire and smoke, and then the miserable beholders are bound to take it for a cave. While in the meantime two armies fly in, represented with four swords and bucklers, and then what hard heart will not receive it for a pitched field? Now, of time they are much more liberal, for ordinary it is that two young princes fall in love. After many traverses, she is got with child, delivered of a fair boy; he is lost, groweth a man, falleth in love, and is ready to get another child; and all this in two hours' space—which, how absurd it is in sense, even sense may imagine, and art hath taught, and all ancient examples justified, and, at this day, the ordinary players in Italy will not err in. Yet will some bring in an example of *Eunuch* in Terence that containeth matter of two days, yet far short of twenty years. True it is, and so was it to be played in two days, and so fitted to the time it set forth. And though Plautus have in one place done amiss, let us hit it with him, and not miss with him. But they will say, "How then shall we set forth a story which contains both many places and many times?" And do they not know that a tragedy is tied to the laws of poesy and not of history; not bound to follow the story, but having liberty either to feign a quite new matter or to frame the history to the most tragical conveniency? Again, many things may be told which cannot be shewed, if they know the difference betwixt reporting and representing. As, for example, I may speak (though I am here) of Peru, and in speech digress from that to the description of Calicut; but in action I cannot represent it without Pacolet's horse. And so was the manner the ancients took, by some Nuntius to recount things done in former time or other place. Lastly, if they will represent an history, they must not (as Horace saith) begin *ab ovo,* but they must come to the principal point of that one action which they will represent. By example this will be best expressed. I have a story of young Polydorus, delivered for safety's sake, with great riches, by his father Priamus to Polymnestor, king of Thrace, in the Troyan war time. He, after some years, hearing the overthrow of Priamus, for to make the treasure his own, murthereth the child. The body of the child is taken up by Hecuba. She, the same day, findeth a sleight to be revenged most cruelly of the tyrant. Where now would one of our tragedy writers begin but with the delivery of the child? Then should he sail over into Thrace, and so spend I know not how many years, and travel numbers of places. But where doth Euripides? Even with the finding of the body, the rest leaving to be told by the spirit of Polydorus. This needs no further to be enlarged; the dullest wit may conceive it.

But besides these gross absurdities, how all their plays be neither right tragedies nor right comedies, mingling kings and clowns, not because the matter so carrieth it, but thrust in the clown by head and shoulders, to play a part in majestical matters, with neither decency nor discretion, so as neither the admiration and commiseration, nor the right sportfulness, is by their mongrel tragicomedy obtained. I know Apuleius did somewhat so, but that is a thing recounted with space of time, not represented in one moment: and I know the ancients have one or two examples of tragicomedies, as Plautus hath *Amphitrio.* But, if we mark them well, we shall find that they never, or very daintily, match hornpipes and funerals. So falleth it out that, having indeed no right comedy, in that comical part of our tragedy we have nothing but scurrility, unworthy of any chaste ears, or some extreme shew of doltishness, indeed fit to lift up a loud laughter and nothing else; where the whole tract of a comedy should be full of delight, as the tragedy should be still maintained in a well-raised admiration. But our comedients think there is no delight without laughter, which is very wrong, for though laughter may come with delight, yet cometh it not of delight, as though delight should be the cause of laughter; but well may one thing breed both togither. Nay, rather in themselves they have, as it were, a kind of contrariety; for delight we scarcely do but in things that have a conveniency to ourselves or to the general nature; laughter almost ever cometh of things most disproportioned to ourselves and nature. Delight hath a joy in it, either permanent or present. Laughter hath only a scornful tickling.

For example, we are ravished with delight to see a fair woman, and yet are far from being moved to laughter. We laugh at deformed creatures, wherein certainly we cannot delight. We delight in good chances, we laugh at mischances; we delight to hear the happiness of our friends and country, at which he were worthy to be laughed at that would laugh. We shall, contrarily, laugh sometimes to find a matter quite mistaken and go down the hill against the bias, in the mouth of some such men as for the respect of them one shall be heartily sorry he cannot chuse but laugh; and so is rather pained then delighted with laughter. Yet deny I not but that they may go well togither. For as in Alexander's picture well set out we delight without laughter, and in twenty mad antiques we laugh without delight, so in Hercules, painted with his great beard and furious countenance, in a woman's attire, spinning at Omphale's commandement, it breeds both delight and laughter. For the representing of so strange a power in love procures delight, and the scornfulness of the action stirreth laughter. But I speak to this purpose, that all the end of the comical part be not upon such scornful matters as stir laughter only, but mix with it that delightful teaching which is the end of poesy. And the great fault even in that point of laughter, and forbidden plainly by Aristotle, is that they stir laughter in sinful things, which are rather execrable then ridiculous; or in miserable, which are rather to be pitied then scorned. For what is it to make folks gape at a wretched begger and a beggerly clown; or, against law of hospitality, to jest at strangers because they speak not English so well as we do? What do we learn? Since it is certain *Nil habet infelix paupertas durius in se, Quam quod ridiculos homines facit.* But rather a busy loving courtier, and a heartless threat'ning Thraso, a self-wise-seeming schoolmaister, a wry-transformed traveler—these if we saw walk in stage names, which we play naturally, therein were delightful laughter, and teaching delightfulness, as in the other the tragedies of Buchanan do justly bring forth a divine admiration. But I have lavished out too many words of this play-matter. I do it because,

as they are excelling parts of poesy, so is there none so much used in England, and none can be more pitifully abused; which, like an unmannerly daughter shewing a bad education, causeth her mother Poesy's honesty to be called in question.

Other sort of poetry almost have we none but that lyrical kind of songs and sonnets; which, Lord, if he gave us so good minds, how well it might be employed, and with how heavenly fruits, both private and public, in singing the praises of the immortal beauty, the immortal goodness of that God who giveth us hands to write and wits to conceive; of which we might well want words, but never matter; of which we could turn our eyes to nothing but we should ever have new-budding occasions. But truly many of such writings as come under the banner of unresistable love, if I were a mistress, would never persuade me they were in love; so coldly they apply fiery speeches, as men that had rather read lovers' writings, and so caught up certain swelling phrases (which hang togither like a man that once told me the wind was at northwest, and by south, because he would be sure to name winds inough), then that in truth they feel those passions, which easily (as I think) may be bewrayed by that same forcibleness or *energia* (as the Greeks call it) of the writer. But let this be a sufficient though short note, that we miss the right use of the material point of poesy.

Now, for the outside of it, which is words, or (as I may term it) diction, it is even well worse. So is it that honey-flowing matron Eloquence appareled, or rather disguised, in a courtisan-like painted affectation: one time with so farfet words that many seem monsters, but must seem strangers, to any poor Englishman; another time, with coursing of a letter, as if they were bound to follow the method of a dictionary; another time, with figures and flowers extremely winter-starved. But I would this fault were only peculiar to versifiers, and had not as large possession among prose-printers, and (which is to be mervailed) among many schollers, and (which is to be pitied) among some preachers. Truly I could wish, if at least I might be so bold to wish in a thing beyond the reach of my capacity, the diligent imitators of Tully and Demosthenes (most worthy to be imitated) did not so much keep Nizolian paper-books of their figures and phrases, as by attentive translation (as it were) devour them whole, and make them wholly theirs. For now they cast sugar and spice upon every dish that is served to the table, like those Indians not content to wear earrings at the fit and natural place of the ears, but they will thrust jewels through their nose and lips, because they will be sure to be fine. Tully, when he was to drive out Catiline, as it were with a thunderbolt of eloquence,

use of language

often useth the figure of repetition, as *Vivit. Vivit? Immo in senatum venit,* etc. Indeed, enflamed with a well-grounded rage, he would have his words (as it were) double out of his mouth, and so do that artificially which we see men do in choler naturally. And we, having noted the grace of those words, hale them in sometimes to a familiar epistle, when it were too much choler to be choleric. How well store of *similiter cadenses* doth sound with the gravity of the pulpit I would but invoke Demosthenes' soul to tell, who with a rare daintiness useth them. Truly they have made me think of the sophister that with too much subtility would prove two eggs three, and though he might be counted a sophister had none for his labor. So these men, bringing in such a kind of eloquence, well may they obtain an opinion of a seeming fineness, but persuade few, which should be the end of their fineness.

Now for similitudes in certain printed discourses, I think all herbarists, all stories of beasts, fowls, and fishes are rifled up, that they may come in multitudes to wait upon any of our conceits; which certainly is as absurd a surfet to the ears as is possible; for the force of a similitude not being to prove anything to a contrary disputer, but only to explain to a willing hearer, when that is done, the rest is a most tedious prattling, rather overswaying the memory from the purpose whereto they were applied then any whit enforming the judgment already either satisfied, or by similitudes not to be satisfied. For my part, I do not doubt, when Antonius and Crassus, the great forefathers of Cicero in eloquence, the one (as Cicero testified of them) pretended not to know art, the other not to set by it, because with a plain sensibleness they might win credit of popular ears; which credit is the nearest step to persuasion; which persuasion is the chief mark of oratory—I do not doubt (I say) but that they used these knacks very sparingly; which who doth generally use, any man may see doth dance to his own music; and so to be noted by the audience more careful to speak curiously then truly.

Undoubtedly (at least to my opinion undoubtedly) I have found in divers small-learned courtiers a more sound style then in some professors of learning, of which I can guess no other cause but that the courtier, following that which by practise he findeth fittest to nature, therein (though he know it not) doth according to art, though not by art; where the other, using art to shew art, and not hide art (as in these cases he should do), flieth from nature, and indeed abuseth art.

Use in connection with M

But what! Methinks I deserve to be pounded for straying from poetry to oratory, but both have such an affinity in the wordish consideration that I think

this digression will make my meaning receive the fuller understanding—which is not to take upon me to teach poets how they should do but only, finding myself sick among the rest, to shew some one or two spots of the common infection grown among the most part of writers; that, acknowledging ourselves somewhat awry, we may bend to the right use both of matter and manner, whereto our language giveth us great occasion, being indeed capable of any excellent exercising of it. I know some will say it is a mingled language. And why not so much the better, taking the best of both the other? Another will say it wanteth grammer. Nay truly, it hath that praise, that it wants not grammer; for grammer it might have, but it needs it not; being so easy in itself, and so void of those cumbersome differences of cases, genders, moods, and tenses, which I think was a piece of the Tower of Babylon's curse, that a man should be put to school to learn his mother tongue. But for the uttering sweetly and properly the conceit of the mind, which is the end of speech, that hath it equally with any other tongue in the world; and is perticularly happy in compositions of two or three words togither, near the Greek, far beyond the Latin, which is one of the greatest beauties can be in a language.

Now, of versifying there are two sorts, the one ancient, the other modern: the ancient marked the quantity of each syllable, and according to that framed his verse; the modern observing only number (with some regard of the accent), the chief life of it standeth in that like sounding of the words which we call rime. Whether of these be the most excellent would bear many speeches. The ancient, no doubt, more fit for music, both words and time observing quantity, and more fit lively to express divers passions, by the low or lofty sound of the well-weighed syllable. The latter likewise, with his rime, striketh a certain music to the ear; and, in fine, since it doth delight, though by another way, it obtains the same purpose, there being in either sweetness, and wanting in neither majesty. Truly the English, before any vulgar language I know, is fit for both sorts: for, for the ancient, the Italian is so full of vowels that it must ever be cumb'red with elisions; the Dutch so, of the other side, with consonants, that they cannot yield the sweet sliding fit for a verse; the French, in his whole language, hath not one word that hath his accent in the last syllable saving two, called *antepenultima,* and little more hath the Spanish, and, therefore, very gracelessly may they use dactyls. The English is subject to none of these defects.

Now, for rime, though we do not observe quantity, yet we observe the accent very precisely; which other languages either cannot do, or will not do so absolutely. That cesura, or breathing place in the midst of the verse, neither Italian nor Spanish have, the French and we never almost fail of. Lastly, even the very rime itself the Italian cannot put in the last syllable, by the French named the "masculine rime," but still in the next to the last, which the French call the "female," or the next before that, which the Italian [term] *sdrucciola*. The example of the former is *buono: suono*, of the *sdrucciola, femina: semina*. The French, of the other side, hath both the male, as *bon: son*, and the female, as *plaise: taise*, but the *sdrucciola* he hath not: where the English hath all three, as *due: true, father: rather, motion: potion*, with much more which might be said, but that already I find the triflings of this discourse is much too much enlarged.

So that since the ever-praiseworthy poesy is full of virtue-breeding delightfulness, and void of no gift that ought to be in the noble name of learning; since the blames laid against it are either false or feeble; since the cause why it is not esteemed in England is the fault of poet-apes, not poets; since, lastly, our tongue is most fit to honor poesy, and to be honored by poesy; I conjure you all that have had the evil luck to read this ink-wasting toy of mine, even in the name of the nine muses, no more to scorn the sacred mysteries of poesy, no more to laugh at the name of "poets," as though they were next inheritors to fools, no more to jest at the reverent title of a "rimer"; but to believe, with Aristotle, that they were the ancient treasurers of the Grecians' divinity; to believe, with Bembus, that they were first bringers-in of all civility; to believe, with Scaliger, that no philosopher's precepts can sooner make you an honest man then the reading of Virgil; to believe, with Clauserus, the translator of Cornutus, that it pleased

the heavenly Deity, by Hesiod and Homer, under the veil of fables, to give us all knowledge, logic, rhetoric, philosophy, natural and moral, and *quid non;* to believe, with me, that there are many mysteries contained in poetry, which of purpose were written darkly lest by prophane wits it should be abused; to believe, with Landin, that they are so beloved of the gods that whatsoever they write proceeds of a divine fury; lastly, to believe them-selves, when they tell you they will make you im-mortal by their verses.

Thus doing, your name shall florish in the printers' shops; thus doing, you shall be of kin to many a poetical preface; thus doing, you shall be most fair, most rich, most wise, most all; you shall dwell upon superlatives. Thus doing, though you be *libertino patre natus,* you shall sodeinly grow *Herculea proles, Si quid mea carmina possunt.* Thus doing, your soul shall be placed with Dante's Beatrix or Virgil's Anchises. But if (fie of such a but) you be born so near the dull-making cataract of Nilus that you can-not hear the planet-like music of poetry, if you have so earth-creeping a mind that it cannot lift itself up to look to the sky of poetry, or rather, by a certain rustical disdain, will become such a mome as to be a Momus of poetry; then, though I will not wish unto you the ass's ears of Midas, nor to be driven by a poet's verses (as Bubonax was) to hang himself, nor to be rimed to death, as is said to be done in Ireland; yet thus much curse I must send you, in the behalf of all poets, that while you live, you live in love, and never get favor for lacking skill of a sonnet, and, when you die, your memory die from the earth for want of an epitaph.

THE SPENSER-HARVEY CORRESPONDENCE

The correspondence consisting of two letters by Ed-mund Spenser and three by Gabriel Harvey that was published in 1580, just after *The Shepherd's Calendar* had appeared, is important not only because it affords us a glimpse of a great poet on the threshold of his greatest work but also because it tells us a good deal about the stage of literary cultivation in England at the time when Elizabethan literature was entering its golden period. While an undergraduate, Spenser had known and ad-mired Harvey as a fellow of Pembroke Hall, Cambridge; and when, in 1576, after proceeding M.A. and leaving the university, he was recommended by Harvey to the powerful Earl of Leicester and joined the cultivated circle at Leicester House—a circle including Sidney, Dyer,

Thomas Drant, and others—the former "poor scholler" of Pembroke Hall must have been dazzled by his good fortune. Full of enthusiasm for the social elegance and the literary aspirations of the Areopagus (as he called his new friends), his letters to Harvey, though sometimes ludicrously mannered and fastidious, tell a great deal about the growth of a poet's mind. Harvey's replies—heavily jocose, patronizing, and instructive (as to the merits of English verse in classical meter, for example)—give a wonderful sketch of an Elizabethan pedant. Both correspondents later wished it thought that the publica-tion of the letters was unauthorized: "it was the sinister hap of those infortunate letters," wrote Harvey in 1592, "to fall into the left hands of malicious enemies or undiscreet friends who adventured to imprint in earnest that was scribbled in jest"; but it is likely that the writers themselves arranged for the printing. The letters were entered in the Stationers' Register on June 30, 1580, and appeared in the same year in a quarto volume divided into two sections with separate titlepages—*Three Proper, and wittie, familiar Letters* and *Two Other, very commendable Letters* (STC 23095)—upon which our excerpts from Spenser's first letter and Harvey's reply are based.

FROM THREE PROPER AND WITTY FAMILIAR LETTERS and TWO OTHER VERY COMMENDABLE LETTERS (1580)

Nota envy of Harvey

To the Worshipful His Very Singular Good Friend, Maister G[abriel] H[arvey], Fellow of Trinity Hall in Cambridge

Good Master G[abriel], I perceive by your most curteous and friendly letters your good will to be no less indeed than I always esteemed. In recompense whereof, think, I beseech you, that I will spare neither speech nor writing nor aught else whensoever and wheresoever occasion shall be off'red me; yea, I will not stay till it be off'red, but will seek it in all that [10] possibly I may. And that you may perceive how much your counsel in all things prevaileth with me and how altogither I am ruled and overruled thereby, I am now determined to alter mine own former purpose and to subscribe to your advizement, being notwithstanding resolved still to abide your farther resolution. My principal doubts are these. First, I was minded for a while to have intermitted the uttering of my writings lest, by overmuch cloying their noble ears, I should gather a contempt of my- [20] self or else seem rather for gain and commodity to do it for some sweetness that I have already tasted. Then also meseemeth the work too base for his excellent lordship, being made in honor of a private personage unknown, which of some ill-willers might be upbraided not to be so worthy as you know she is, or the matter not so weighty that it should be off'red to so weighty a personage, or the like. The self former title still liketh me well inough, and your fine addition no less. If these and the like doubts may [30] be of importance in your seeming to frustrate any part of your advice, I beseech you without the least self-love of your own purpose counsel me for the best; and the rather do it faithfully and carefully for that in all things I attribute so much to your judgment that I am evermore content to adnihilate mine own determinations in respect thereof. And, indeed, for yourself too it sitteth with you now to call your wits and senses togither (which are always at call) when occasion is so fairly offered of estimation and [40] preferment. For whiles the iron is hot it is good striking, and minds of nobles vary as their estates. *Verum ne quid durius.*

I pray you bethink you well hereof, good Maister G[abriel], and forthwith write me those two or three special points and caveats for the nonce *de quibus in superioribus illis mellitissimis, longissimisque litteris tuis.* Your desire to hear of my late being with her Majesty must die in itself. As for the two worthy gentlemen, Master Sidney and Master Dyer, they have me, I thank them, in some use of familiarity; of whom and to whom, what speech passeth for your credit and estimation I leave yourself to conceive, having always so well conceived of my unfeigned affection and zeal towards you. And now they have proclaimed in their ἀρείῳ πάγῳ a general surceasing and silence of bald rimers—and also of the very best too; instead whereof they have, by authority of their whole senate, prescribed certain laws and rules of quantities of English syllables for English verse, having had thereof already great practise, and drawn me to their faction. New books I hear of none, but only of one that, writing a certain book called *The School of Abuse* and dedicating it to Maister Sidney, was for his labor scorned, if at least it be in the goodness of that nature to scorn. Such folly it is not to regard aforehand the inclination and quality of him to whom we dedicate our books. Such might I happily incur entituling my *Slumber* and the other pamphlets unto his Honor. I meant them rather to Maister Dyer. But I am of late more in love with my English versifying than with riming, which I should have done long since if I would then have followed your [30] counsel. *Sed te solum iam tum suspicabar cum Aschamo sapere; nunc aulam video egregios alere poetas Anglicos.* Maister E. K. heartily desireth to be commended unto your Worship, of whom what accompt he maketh yourself shall hereafter perceive by his painful and dutiful verses of yourself.

Thus much was written at Westminster yesternight, but, coming this morning, being the sixteenth of October, to Mistress Kirk's to have it delivered to the carrier, I received your letter sent me the last [40] week; whereby I perceive you otherwhiles continue your old exercise of versifying in English, which glory I had now thought should have been only ours here at London and the court.

Trust me, your verses I like passingly well and

florid generality

envy your hidden pains in this kind, or rather malign and grudge at yourself that would not once impart so much to me. But once or twice you make a breach in Maister Drant's rules: *quod tamen condonabimus tanto poetae, tuaeque ipsius maximae in his rebus autoritati*. You shall see, when we meet in London (which, when it shall be, certify us), how fast I have followed after you in that course. Beware lest in time I overtake you. *Veruntamen te solum sequar (ut saepenumero sum professus), nunquam sane assequar, dum vivam*. And now requite I you with the like, not with the very best but with the very shortest, namely with a few iambics. I dare warrant they be precisely perfect for the feet (as you can easily judge), and vary not one inch from the rule. I will impart yours to Maister Sidney and Maister Dyer at my next going to the court. I pray you, keep mine close to yourself or your very entire friends Maister [Thomas] Preston, Maister [John] Still, and the rest.

Iambicum trimetrum

Unhappy verse, the witness of my unhappy state,
  Make thyself flutt'ring wings of thy fast-flying
  Thought and fly forth unto my love, wheresoever she
  be,
Whether lying restless in heavy bed, or else
  Sitting so cheerless at the cheerful boord, or else
  Playing alone, careless, on her heavenly virginals.
If in bed, tell her that my eyes can take no rest;
  If at boord, tell her that my mouth can eat no meat;
  If at her virginals, tell her I can hear no mirth.
Asked why, say waking love suffereth no sleep;
  Say that raging love doth appal the weak stomach;
  Say that lamenting love marreth the musical.
Tell her that her pleasures were wont to lull me asleep;
  Tell her that her beauty was wont to feed mine eyes;
  Tell her that her sweet tongue was wont to make me
  mirth.
Now do I nightly waste, wanting my kindly rest;
  Now do I daily starve, wanting my lively food;
  Now do I always die, wanting thy timely mirth.
And if I waste, who will bewail my heavy chance?
  And if I starve, who will record my cursed end?
  And if I die, who will say, "This was *Immerito*"?

I thought once again here to have made an end with a hearty *vale* of the best fashion, but lo (an ill-favored mischance), my last farewell, whereof I made great accompt, and much marveled you should make no mention thereof, I am now told (in the Divel's name) was thorough one man's negligence quite forgotten, but should now undoubtedly have been sent whether I had come or no. Seeing it can now be no otherwise, I pray you take all togither with all their faults; and now I hope you will vouchsafe me an answer of the largest size, or else, I tell you true, you shall be very deep in my debt, notwithstanding this other sweet but short letter and fine but few verses. But I would rather I might yet see your own good self and receive a reciprocal farewell from your own sweet mouth. . . .

[There follows a Latin poem of more than a hundred lines addressed "*Ad ornatissimum virum . . . G. H.*," which opens:

  Sic malus egregium, sic non inimicus amicum,
  Sicque novus veterem jubet ipse poeta poetam
  Salvere. . . .]

I was minded also to have sent you some English verses, or rimes, for a farewell, but by my troth I have no spare time in the world to think on such toys that, you know, will demand a freer head than mine is presently. I beseech you, by all your curtesies and graces, let me be answered ere I go, which will be (I hope, I fear, I think) the next week if I can be dispatched of my lord [the Earl of Leicester]. I go thither as sent by him and maintained mostwhat of him, and there am to employ my time, my body, my mind to his Honor's service. Thus, with many superhearty commendations and recommendations to yourself and all my friends with you, I end my last farewell, not thinking any more to write unto you before I go and withal committing to your faithful credence the eternal memory of our everlasting friendship, the inviolable memory of our unspotted friendship, the sacred memory of our vowed friendship. Which I beseech you continue with usual writings as you may, and of all things let me hear some news from you. As gentle Master Sidney, I thank his good Worship, hath required of me and so promised to do again. *Qui monet, ut facias, quod iam facis*—you know the rest. You may always send them most safely to me by Mistress Kirk and by none other. So once again, and yet once more, farewell most heartily, mine own good Master H[arvey], and love me as I love you, and think upon poor *Immerito* as he thinketh upon you.

  Leicester House, this fifth of October, 1579.
  Per mare, per terras,
  Vivus mortuusque,
  Tuus Immerito

To My Very Friend, M[aster] *Immerito*

Liberalissimo Signor Immerito, in good sooth my poor storehouse will presently afford me nothing either to recompense or countervail your gentle mastership's long, large, lavish, luxurious, laxative letters withal—now, a God's name, when did I ever in my life hunt the letter before? But belike there's no remedy, I must needs be even with you once in my days—but only, forsooth, a few millions of recommendations and a running copy of the verses enclosed. Which verses (*extra iocum*) are so well done in Latin by two doctors and so well translated into English by one odd gentleman and generally so well allowed of all that chanced to have the perusing of them that, trust me, G[abriel] H[arvey] was at the first hardly intreated to shame himself and, truly, now blusheth to see the first letters of his name stand so near their names, as of necessity they must. . . . I am at this instant very busily and hotly employed in certain great and serious affairs whereof (notwithstanding for all your vowed and long-experimented secrecy) you are not like to hear a word more at the most till I myself see a world more at the least. And therefore for this once, I beseech you (notwithstanding your great expectation of I know not what volumes for an answer), content your good self with these presents—pardon me, I came lately out of a scrivener's shop—and in lieu of many gentle farewells and goodly Godbewyes at your departure, give me once again leave to play the counsailor a while, if it be but to justify your liberal mastership's *nostri Cato maxime saecli*. And I conjure you, by the contents of the verses and rimes enclosed and by all the good and bad spirits that attend upon the authors themselves, immediately upon the contemplation thereof to abandon all other fooleries and honor virtue, the only immortal and surviving accident amongst so many mortal and ever-perishing substances. . . . But a word or two to your large, lavish, laxative letters, and then, for this time, adieu. Of my credit, your doubts are not so redoubted as yourself oversuspiciously imagine, as I purpose shortly to advize you more at large. Your hot iron is so hot that it striketh me to the heart; I dare not come near to strike it. The tide tarrieth no man, but many a good man is fain to tarry the tide. And I know some, which could be content to be their own carvers, that are glad to thank other for their courtesy. But beggars, they say, must be no choosers.

Your new-founded ἄρειον πάγον I honor more than you will or can suppose, and make greater accompt of the two worthy gentlemen than of two hundreth *Dionisii Areopagitae* or the very notablest senators that ever Athens did afford of that number. Your English *trimetra* I like better than perhaps you will easily believe, and am to requite them with better, or worse, at more convenient leisure. Marry, you must pardon me, I find not your warrant so sufficiently good and substantial in law that it can persuade me they are all so precisely perfect for the feet as yourself overpartially ween and overconfidently avouch, especially the third, which hath a foot more than a louse (a wonderous deformity in a

right and pure senary), and the sixt, which is also in the same predicament, unless happily one of the feet be sawed off with a pair of syncopes. And then should the orthography have testified so much, and instead of *hēavēnly̆ vīrgĭnāls* you should have written *hēav'nly̆ virg'nāls*, and *virg'nāls* again in the ninth, and should have made a curtol of *Immĕrĭtō* in the last, being all notwithstanding usual and tolerable enough in a mix'd and licentious iambic; and of two evils better, no doubt, the first than the last, a third superfluous syllable than a dull spondee. Then, methinketh, you have in my fancy somewhat too many spondees beside, and whereas trochee sometime presumeth in the first place (as namely, in the second verse, *make thy*, which *thy*, by your maistership's own authority, must needs be short), I shall be fain to supply the office of the art memorative and put you in mind of a pretty fable in Abstemio, the Italian, implying thus much, or rather thus little, in effect.

A certain lame man, being invited to a solempn nuptial feast, made no more ado but sate me him roundly down foremost at the highest end of the table. The master of the feast, suddainly spying his presumption and handsomely removing him from thence, placed me this halting gentleman below at the nether end of the bourd, alleging for his defense the common verse, *Sedes nulla datur praeterquam sexta trochaeo*, and pleasantly alluding to this foot which, standing upon two syllables (the one long, the other short), much like, of a like, his guest's feet, is always thrust down to the last place in a true hexameter and quite thrust out of doors in a pure and just senary. . . . Your Latin farewell is a goodly, brave, yonkerly piece of work, and Goddilge ye, I am always marvelously beholding unto you for your bountiful titles. I hope by that time I have been resident a year or two in Italy I shall be better qualified in this kind and more able to requite your lavish and magnificent liberality that way. . . . And as for your speedy and hasty travel, methinks I dare still wager all the books and writings in my study, which you know I esteem of greater value than all the gold and silver in my purse or chest, that you will not (and yet I must take heed how I make my bargain with so subtile and intricate a sophister), that you shall not, I say, be gone oversea, for all your saying, neither the next nor the next week. And then, peradventure, I may personally perform your request and bestow the sweetest farewell upon your sweet-mouthed maship that so unsweet a tongue and so sour a pair of lips can afford. . . .

Trinity Hall, still in my gallery, 23 October 1579. In haste.

Yours, as you know,

G[abriel] H[arvey]

WILLIAM WEBBE

A DISCOURSE OF ENGLISH POETRY

William Webbe, a shadowy figure in Elizabethan literature, wrote nothing of importance except the graceful *Discourse of English Poetry* (1586). Educated at St. John's College, Cambridge (B.A., 1572/73), where he must have known such contemporaries as Harvey and Spenser, he seems to have acquired considerable reading and fair taste, and it was while serving as tutor to the sons of Edward Sulyard, of Flemyngs in Essex, that he put together, at odd hours, the treatise by which his name lives. The work of a well-informed and intelligent (but by no means highly talented) lover of literature, it is a potpourri of many elements: it respectfully follows Sidney's noble *Defense* in justifying works of the imagination, it surveys (after a fashion) the history of English literature, it keeps alive Harvey's foolish campaign for the use of classical meters (and even turns most of the April eclogue of *The Shepherd's Calendar* into sapphics, as well as two Virgilian eclogues into hexameters), but most importantly it announces the advent of a great "new poet." In Webbe's enthusiastic praise of *The Shepherd's Calendar*—whose author, significantly, he does not name—we have a valuable statement of Spenser's impact on his contemporaries. Entered in the Stationers' Register on September 4, 1586, Webbe's essay was published, with a dedication to Edward Sulyard, in the same year. Our text is based upon *A Discourse of English Poetrie*, 1586 (STC 25172).

FROM A DISCOURSE OF ENGLISH POETRY (1586)

A Preface to the Noble Poets of England

Among the innumerable sorts of English books and infinite fardles of printed pamphlets wherewith this country is pestered, all shops stuffed, and every study furnished, the greatest part, I think, in any one kind are such as are either mere poetical or which tend in some respect (as either in matter or form) to poetry. Of such books, therefore, sith I have been one that have had a desire to read not the fewest, and because it is an argument which men of great learning have [10] no leisure to handle (or, at the least, having to do with more serious matters, do least regard), if I write something concerning what I think of our English poets, or adventure to set down my simple judgment of English poetry, I trust the learned poets will give me leave and vouchsafe my book passage as being for the rudeness thereof no prejudice to their noble studies, but even (as my intent is) an *instar cotis* to stir up some other of meet ability to bestow travail in this matter; whereby I think we [20] may not only get the means, which we yet want, to discern between good writers and bad, but perhaps also challenge from the rude multitude of rustical rimers, who will be called poets, the right practise and orderly course of true poetry.

It is to be wond'red at of all, and is lamented of many, that whereas all kind of good learning have aspired to royal dignity and stately grace in our English tongue, being not only founded, defended, maintained, and enlarged, but also purged from faults, weeded of errors, and polished from barbar- [30] ousness by men of great authority and judgment, only poetry hath found fewest friends to amend it, those that can reserving their skill to themselves, those that cannot running headlong upon it, thinking to garnish it with their devises but more corrupting it with fantastical errors. What should be the cause that our English speech in some of the wisest men's judgments hath never attained to any sufficient ripeness, nay, not full avoided the reproach of barbarousness in poetry? The rudeness of the country, or baseness of wits, or the coarse dialect of the speech? Experience utterly disproveth it to be any of these. What then? Surely the cank'red enmity of curious custom, which, as it never was great friend to any good learning, so in this hath it grounded in the most such a negligent persuasion of an impossibility in matching the best that the finest wits and most divine heads have contented themselves with a base kind of fingering, rather debasing their faculties in setting forth their skill in the coarsest manner then, for breaking custom, they would labor to adorn their country and advance their style with the highest and most learned'st top of true poetry. The rudeness or unaptness of our country to be either none or no hinderance, if reformation were made accordingly, the exquisite excellency in all kinds of good learning now flourishing among us, inferior to none other nation, may sufficiently declare.

That there be as sharp and quick wits in England [30] as ever were among the peerless Grecians or renowmed Romains, it were a note of no wit at all in me to deny. And is our speech so coarse or our phrase so harsh that poetry cannot therein find a vein whereby it may appear like itself? Why should we think so basely of this rather then of her sister—I mean rhetorical elocution? Which, as they were by birth twins, by kind the same, by original of one descent, so, no doubt, as eloquence hath found such favorers in the English tongue as she frequenteth not any more gladly, so would poetry, if there were the like welcome and entertainment given her by our English poets, without question aspire to wonderful perfection and appear far more gorgeous and delectable among us. Thus much I am bold to say in behalf of poetry, not that I mean to call in question the reverend and learned works of poetry written in our tongue by men of rare judgment and most excellent poets, but even, as it were, by way of supplication to the famous and learned laureate masters of England, that they would but consult one half-hour with their heavenly muse what credit they might win to their native speech, what enormities they might wipe out of English poetry, what a fit vein they might frequent wherein to shew forth their worthy faculties, if English poetry were truly reformed and some perfect platform or *prosodia* of versifying were by them ratified and set down, either in imitation of Greeks and Latins or, where it would scant abide the touch of their rules, the like observations selected and established by the natural affectation of the speech. Thus much I say, not to persuade you that are the favorers of English poetry, but to move it to you, being not the first that have thought upon this matter but one that by consent of others have taken upon me to lay it once again in your ways, if perhaps you may stumble upon it and chance to look so low from your divine cogitations when your muse mounteth to the stars and ransacketh the spheres of heaven; whereby, perhaps, you may take compassion of noble poetry, pitifully mangled and defaced by rude smatterers and barbarous imitators of your worthy studies. If the motion be worthy your regard, it is enough to move it; if not, my words would simply prevail in persuading you; and therefore I rest upon this only request, that of your courtesies you will grant passage, under your favorable corrections, for this my simple censure of English poetry, wherein, if you please to run it over, you shall know briefly mine opinion of the most part of our accustomed poets and particularly, in his place, the little somewhat which I have sifted out of my weak brain concerning this reformed versifying.

W[illiam] W[ebbe]

. . . I know no memorable work written by any poet in our English speech until twenty years past, where, although learning was not generally decay'd at any time, especially since the conquest of King William, Duke of Normandy (as it may appear by many famous works and learned books—though not of this kind—written by bishops and others), yet surely that poetry was in small price among them it is very manifest and no great marvail; for even that light of Greek and Latin poets which they had they much contemned, as appeareth by their rude versifying, which of long time was used (a barbarous use it was), wherein they converted the natural property of the sweet Latin verse to be a bald kind of riming, thinking nothing to be learnedly written in verse which fell not out in rime, that is, in words whereof the middle word of each verse should sound alike with the last, or of two verses the end of both should fall in the like letters. . . .

This brutish poetry, though it had not the beginning in this country, yet so hath it been affected here that the infection thereof would never—nor, I think, ever will—be rooted up again. I mean this tinkerly verse which we call rime. Master Ascham saith that it first began to be followed and maintained among the Huns and Gothians and other barbarous nations who, with the decay of all good learning, brought it into Italy; from thence it came into France, and so to Germany; at last conveyed into England by men, indeed, of great wisdom and learning but not considerate nor circumspect in that behalf. But of this I must intreat more hereafter.

Henry, the first king of that name in England, is wonderfully extolled in all ancient records of memory for his singular good learning in all kind of noble studies, insomuch as he was named by his surname Beauclerk. . . . What knowledge he attained in the skill of poetry I am not able to say. I report his name for proof that learning in this country was not little esteemed of at that rude time, and that like it is, among other studies, a king would not neglect the faculty of poetry. The first of our English poets that I have heard of was John Gower, about the time of King Richard the Second, as it should seem by certain conjectures both a knight and questionless a singular well-learned man, whose works I could wish they were all whole and perfect among us, for no doubt they contained very much deep knowledge and delight (which may be gathered by his friend Chaucer, who speaketh of him oftentimes in divers places of his works). Chaucer, who for that excellent fame which he obtained in his poetry was always accounted the God of English poets (such a title for honor's sake hath been given him), was next after, if not equal in time to, Gower, and hath left many works both for delight and profitable knowledge far exceeding any other that as yet ever since his time directed their studies that way. Though the manner of his style may seem blunt and coarse to many fine English ears at these days, yet, in truth, if it be equally pondered and with good judgment advised and confirmed with the time wherein he wrote, a man shall perceive thereby even a true picture or perfect shape of a right poet. He by his delightsome vein so gulled the ears of men with his devises that, although corruption bare such sway in most matters that learning and truth might scant be admitted to shew itself, yet without controlment might he gird at the vices and abuses of all states, and gall with very sharp and eager inventions, which he did so learnedly and pleasantly that none therefore would call him into question. For such was his bold spirit that what enormities he saw in any he would not spare to pay them home, either in plain words or else in some pretty and pleasant covert that the simplest might espy him.

Near in time unto him was Lydgate, a poet surely for good proportion of his verse and meetly currant style, as the time afforded, comparable with Chaucer, yet more occupied in superstitious and odd matters then was requisite in so good a wit; which, though he handled them commendably, yet, the matters themselves being not so commendable, his estimation hath been the less. The next of our ancient poets that I can tell of I suppose to Pierce Plowman, who in his doings is somewhat harsh and obscure but indeed a very pithy writer, and—to his commendation I speak it—was the first that I have seen that observed the quantity of our verse without the curiosity of rime.

Since these, I know none other till the time of Skelton, who writ in the time of King Henry the Eight, who, as indeed he obtained the laurel garland, so may I with good right yield him the title of a poet. He was doubtless a pleasant, conceited fellow and of a very sharp wit, exceeding bold, and would nip to the very quick where he once set hold. Next him, I think, I may place Master George Gascoigne, as painful a soldier in the affairs of his prince and country as he was a witty poet in his writing, whose commendations, because I found in one of better judgment then myself, I will set down his words and suppress mine own. Of him thus writeth E. K. upon the ninth [really the eleventh] eglogue of the new poet [Spenser]: "Master George Gascoigne, a witty gentleman and the very chief of our late rimers, who, and if some parts of learning wanted not (albeit is well known he altogether wanted not learning), no doubt would have attained to the excellency of those famous poets. For gifts of wit and natural promptness appear in him aboundantly."

I might next speak of the divers works of the old Earl of Surrey, of the Lord Vaux, of Norton of Bristow, [Richard] Edwards, Tusser, Churchyard, William Hunnis, Heywood, Sand, Hill, S. Y., M. D., and many others; but to speak of their several gifts and aboundant skill shewed forth by them in many pretty and learned works would make my discourse much more tedious.

I may not omit the deserved commendations of many honorable and noble lords and gentlemen in her Majesty's court which in the rare devises of poetry have been, and yet are, most excellent skilful, among whom the right honorable Earl of Oxford may challenge to himself the title of the most excellent among the rest. I can no longer forget those learned gentlemen which took such profitable pains in translating the Latin poets into our English tongue, whose deserts in that behalf are more then I can utter. Among these I ever esteemed, and while I live in my conceit I shall account, Master D[octor] Phaer without doubt the best, who, as indeed he had the best piece of poetry whereon to set a most gallant verse, so performed he it accordingly and in such sort as, in my conscience, I think would scarcely be done again —if it were to do again. Notwithstanding, I speak it but as mine own fancy, not prejudicial to those that list to think otherwise. His work whereof I speak is the Englishing of *Aeneidos* of Virgil, so farforth as it pleased God to spare him life, which was to the half part of the tenth book, the rest being since with no less commendations finished by that worthy scholler and famous phisition, Master Thomas Twyne.

Equally with him may I well adjoin Master Arthur Golding for his labor in Englishing Ovid's *Metamorphosis,* for which gentleman surely our country hath for many respects greatly to give God thanks as for him which hath taken infinite pains without ceasing, travaileth as yet indefatigably, and is addicted without society by his continual labor to profit this nation and speech in all kind of good learning. The next very well deserveth Master Barnabe Googe to be placed as a painful furtherer of learning his help to poetry, besides his own devises, as the translating of Palingenius' *Zodiac.* Abraham Fleming, as in many pretty poesies of his own, so in translating hath done to his commendations. To whom I would here adjoin one of his name whom I know to have excelled as well in all kind of learning as in poetry most especially, and would appear so if the dainty morsels and fine poetical inventions of his were as common abroad as I know they be among some of his friends. I will crave leave of the laudable authors of Seneca in English, of the other parts of Ovid, of Horace, of Mantuan, and divers other, because I would hasten to end this rehearsal, perhaps offensive to some whom, either by forgetfulness or want of knowledge, I must needs overpass. . . .

This place have I purposely reserved for one who,

if not only yet in my judgment principally, deserveth the title of the rightest English poet that ever I read, that is, the author of *The Shepherd's Calendar,* intituled to the worthy gentleman Master Philip Sidney. Whether it was Master Sp[enser] or what rare scholler in Pembroke Hall soever, because himself and his friends (for what respect I know not) would not reveal it, I force not greatly to set down. Sorry I am that I cannot find none other with whom I might couple him in this catalogue in his rare gift of poetry; although one there is, though now long since seriously occupied in graver studies (Master Gabriel Harvey), yet as he was once his most special friend and fellow poet, so because he hath taken such pains not only in his Latin poetry (for which he enjoyed great commendations of the best both in judgment and dignity in this realm), but also to reform our English verse and to beautify the same with brave devises, of which I think the chief lie hid in hateful obscurity; therefore will I adventure to set them together as two of the rarest wits and learned'st masters of poetry in England. Whose worthy and notable skill in this faculty I would wish, if their high dignities and serious businesses would permit, they would still grant to be a furtherance to that reformed kind of poetry which Master Harvey did once begin to ratify; and surely, in mine opinion, if he had chosen some graver matter and handled but with half that skill which I know he could have done, and not poured it forth at a venture as a thing between jest and earnest, it had taken greater effect then it did.

As for the other gentleman, if it would please him or his friends to let those excellent poems whereof I know he hath plenty come abroad, as his *Dreams,* his *Legends,* his *Court of Cupid,* his *English Poet,* with other, he should not only stay the rude pens of myself and others, but also satisfy the thirsty desires of many which desire nothing more then to see more of his rare inventions. If I join to Master Harvey his two brethren, I am assured, though they be both busied with great and weighty callings (the one [Richard] a godly and learned divine, the other [John] a famous and skilful phisition), yet if they listed to set to their helping hands to poetry they would as much beautify and adorn it as any others.

If I let pass the uncountable rabble of riming ballet-makers and compilers of senseless sonnets, who be most busy to stuff every stall full of gross devises and unlearned pamphlets, I trust I shall with the best sort be held excused. For though many such can frame an ale-house song of five- or six-score verses, hobbling upon some tune of a *Northern Jig,* or *Robin Hood,* or *La Lubber,* etc., and perhaps observe just number of syllables (eight in one line, six in another, and therewithal an -*a* to make a jerk in the end), yet if these might be accounted poets (as it is said some

of them make means to be promoted to the laurel), surely we shall shortly have whole swarms of poets; and every one that can frame a book in rime, though for want of matter it be but in commendations of copper noses or bottle ale, will catch at the garland due to poets; whose potical (poetical I should say) heads I would wish at their worshipful Commencements might instead of laurel be gorgiously garnished with fair green barley in token of their good affection to our English malt. . . .

Now . . . will I with like brevity make trial what I can say concerning our English poetry, first in the matter thereof, then in the form, that is, the manner of our verse. . . .

English poetry, therefore, being considered according to common custom and ancient use, is where any work is learnedly compiled in measurable speech and framed in words containing number or proportion of just syllables, delighting the readers or hearers as well by the apt and decent framing of words in equal resemblance of quantity (commonly called verse) as by the skilful handling of the matter whereof it is intreated. . . .

The matters whereof verses were first made were either exhortations to virtue, dehortations from vices, or the praises of some laudable thing. From thence, they began to use them in exercises of imitating some virtuous and wise man at their feasts, whereas some one should be appointed to represent another man's person of high estimation, and he sang fine ditties and witty sentences tunably to their music notes. Of this sprang the first kind of comedies, when they began to bring into these exercises more persons then one, whose speeches were devised dialogue-wise in answering one another. And of such like exercises or, as some will needs have it, long before the other, began the first tragedies. . . . There grew at last to be a greater diversity between tragedy-writers and comedy-writers, the one expressing only sorrowful and lamentable histories, bringing in the persons of gods and goddesses, kings and queens, and great states, whose parts were chiefly to express most miserable calamities and dreadful chances which increased worse and worse till they came to the most woful plight that might be devised. The comedies, on the other side, were directed to a contrary end, which, beginning doubtfully, drew to some trouble or turmoil and by some lucky chance always ended to the joy and appeasement of all parties. This distinction grew, as some hold opinion, by imitation of the works of Homer, for out of his *Iliads* the tragedy-writers found dreadful events whereon to frame their matters, and the other out of his *Odyssea* took arguments of delight and pleasant ending after dangerous and troublesome doubts.

So that, though there be many sorts of poetical

writings, and poetry is not debarred from any matter which may be expressed by pen or speech, yet for the better understanding and briefer method of this discourse I may comprehend the same in three sorts, which are comical, tragical, historical. Under the first may be contained all such epigrams, elegies, and delectable ditties which poets have devised respecting only the delight thereof; in the second, all doleful complaints, lamentable chances, and whatsoever is poetically expressed in sorrow and heaviness; in the third we may comprise the rest of all such matters which as indifferent between the other two do commonly occupy the pens of poets: such are the poetical compiling of chronicles, the friendly greetings between friends, and very many sorts besides, which for the better distinction may be referred to one of these three kinds of poetry. . . .

Now will I speak somewhat of that princely part of poetry wherein are displayed the noble acts and valiant exploits of puissant captains, expert soldiers, wise men, with the famous reports of ancient times, such as are the heroical works of Homer in Greek and the heavenly verse of Virgil's *Aeneidos* in Latin; which works, comprehending, as it were, the sum and ground of all poetry, are verily and incomparably the best of all other. To these, though we have no English work answerable in respect of the glorious ornaments of gallant handling, yet our ancient chroniclers and reporters of our country affairs come most near them; and, no doubt, if such regard of our English speech and curious handling of our verse had been long since thought upon and from time to time been polished and bettered by men of learning, judgment, and authority, it would ere this have matched them in all respects. A manifest example thereof may be the great good grace and sweet vein which eloquence hath attained in our speech because it hath had the help of such rare and singular wits as from time to time might still add some amendment to the same. Among whom, I think, there is none that will gainsay but Master John Lyly hath deserved most high commendations, as he which hath stepp'd one step further therein then any, either before or since he first began the witty discourse of his *Euphues*. Whose works, surely, in respect of his singular eloquence and brave composition of apt words and sentences, let the learned examine and make trial thereof thorough all the parts of rhetoric, in fit phrases, in pithy sentences, in gallant tropes, in flowing speech, in plain sense, and surely, in my judgment, I think he will yield him that verdict which Quintilian giveth of both the best orators, Demosthenes and Tully, that from the one nothing may be taken away, to the other nothing may be added. But a more nearer example to prove my former assertion

true—I mean the meetness of our speech to receive the best form of poetry—may be taken by conference of that famous translation of Master D[octor] Phaer with the copy itself, whosoever please with courteous judgment but a little to compare and mark them both together and weigh with himself whether the English tongue might by little and little be brought to the very majesty of a right heroical verse. . . .

But concerning the matter of our English writers let this suffice. Now shall ye hear my simple skill in what I am able to say concerning the form and matter of our English verse. . . .

The falling-out of verses together in one like sound is commonly called in English rime, taken from the Greek word ῥυθμός, which surely, in my judgment, is very abusively applied to such a sense; and by this the unworthiness of the thing may well appear, in that wanting a proper name whereby to be called, it borroweth a word far exceeding the dignity of it and not appropriate to so rude and base a thing. For rime is properly the just proportion of a clause or sentence, whether it be in prose or meter, aptly comprised together, whereof there is both a natural and an artificial composition in any manner or kind of speech, either French, Italian, Spanish, or English, and is proper not only to poets, but also to readers, orators, pleaders, or any which are to pronounce or speak anything in public audience. . . .

There be three special notes necessary to be observed in the framing of our accustomed English rime. The first is that one meter or verse be answerable to another in equal number of feet or syllables, or proportionable to the tune whereby it is to be read or measured. The second, to place the words in such sort as none of them be wrested contrary to the natural inclination or affectation of the same, or more truly the true quantity thereof. The third, to make them fall together mutually in rime, that is, in words of like sound, but so as the words be not disordered for the rime's sake, nor the sense hindered. . . .

But now to proceed to the reformed kind of English verse which many have before this attempted to put in practise and to establish for an accustomed right among English poets, you shall hear in like manner my simple judgment concerning the same.

I am fully and certainly persuaded that if the true kind of versifying in imitation of Greeks and Latins had been practised in the English tongue and put in ure from time to time by our poets, who might have continually been mending and polishing the same, every one according to their several gifts, it would, long ere this, have aspired to as full perfection as in any other tongue whatsoever. For why may I not think so of our English, seeing that among the Romains a long time, yea even till the days of Tully, they esteemed not the Latin poetry almost worth anything in respect of the Greek, as appeareth in the oration *Pro Archia poeta;* yet afterwards it increased in credit more and more, and that in short space, so that in Virgil's time wherein were they not comparable with the Greeks? So likewise now it seemeth not currant for an English verse to run upon true quantity and those feet which the Latins use because it is strange; and the other barbarous custom, being within compass of every base wit, hath worn it out of credit or estimation. But if our writers, being of learning and judgment, would rather infringe this curious custom then omit the occasion of inlarging the credit of their native speech and their own praises, by practising that commendable kind of writing in true verse, then, no doubt, as in other parts of learning so in poetry should not stoop to the best of them all in all manner of ornament and comeliness. But some object that our words are nothing resemblant in nature to theirs and therefore not possible to be framed with any good grace after their use; but cannot we, then, as well as the Latins did, alter the canon of the rule according to the quality of our word; and where our words and theirs will agree, there to jump with them; where they will not agree, there to establish a rule of our own to be directed by? Likewise, for the tenor of the verse, might we not (as Horace did in the Latin) alter their proportions to what sorts we listed, and to what we saw would best become the nature of the thing handled or the quality of the words? Surely it is to be thought that

if any one of sound judgment and learning should put forth some famous work containing divers forms of true verses, fitting the measures according to the matter, it would of itself be a sufficient authority, without any prescription of rules, to the most part of poets for them to follow and by custom to ratify. . . .

Epilogus

This small travail, courteous reader, I desire thee take in good worth which I have compiled, not as an exquisite censure concerning this matter, but (as thou mayst well perceive, and in truth to that only end) that it might be an occasion to have the same throughly and with greater discretion taken in hand and labored by some other of greater ability, of whom I know there be many among the famous poets in London who, both for learning and leisure, may handle this argument far more pithily then myself. Which if any of them will vouchsafe to do, I trust we shall have English poetry at a higher price in short space; and the rabble of bald rimes shall be turned to famous works, comparable, I suppose, with the best works of poetry in other tongues. In the meantime, if my poor skill can set the same anything forward I will not cease to practise the same towards the framing of some apt English *prosodia,* still hoping and heartily wishing to enjoy first the benefit of some other's judgment whose authority may bear greater credit and whose learning can better perform it.

ABRAHAM FRAUNCE

THE ARCADIAN RHETORIC

Fraunce's *Arcadian Rhetoric* (1588) is interesting not only as an adaptation (almost a translation) of a famous Continental treatise on rhetoric but also as an anthology, embracing several ancient and modern literatures, of passages chosen to illustrate the terms and principles under discussion. After his education at St. John's College, Cambridge (B.A., 1580), and an intimate association with the brilliant social and literary circle around Sir Philip Sidney and his sister Lady Pembroke, Fraunce in 1588 published two works—*The Lawyer's Logic* and *The Arcadian Rhetoric*—which are significant commentaries on the popularity of Ramean thought in England. The more than fifty books of Petrus Ramus (or Pierre de la Ramée, 1515–72) had made him both a champion and a *bête noire* of the French Renaissance: a champion of anti-scholastic reformers in theology and pedagogy and a *bête*

noire to the orthodox traditionalists. From the publication of his anti-Aristotelian logic (*Dialectica,* 1543) until his barbarous death as a Protestant martyr on St. Bartholomew's Day (1572), Ramus had labored tirelessly to simplify and methodize the logic, rhetoric, and pedagogy of the liberal arts. In England, and especially at Cambridge, his work had exerted a profound influence on Protestant intellectuals, and the two books published by Fraunce in 1588 fairly represent the kind of impact that Ramus had in the late sixteenth century. The expository parts of *The Arcadian Rhetoric* are heavily indebted to the *Rhetorica* of Audemarus Talaeus (Omer Talon), a favorite disciple of Ramus who had published his *praelectiones* on the master's *Dialectica* in 1552, and whose own *Rhetorica* had in turn been graced with Ramus' *praelectiones* in 1567. As Miss Ethel Seaton has recently shown, Fraunce constructed his rhetorical treatise largely on the scheme of this 1567 edition, often merely translating whole sentences and even paragraphs. It is in his illustrations that he shows his learning and his originality; for, instead of limiting himself to Talaeus' examples of rhetorical tropes and figures from classical prose orators, Fraunce ranges learnedly and tastefully through a half-dozen literatures—including, significantly, English. From the Greek he cites Homer, from the Latin Virgil, Horace, Ovid, Catullus, Martial, Boethius, and Joseph of Exeter, from the Italian Petrarch and Tasso (but, oddly enough, not Ariosto), from the French Du Bartas, Etienne Tabourot's popular anthology called *Les Bigarrures*, and Rémy Belleau, from the Spanish Juan Boscán (translator of Castiglione) and Garcilasso (Garci Lasso de la Vega). But the most important and interesting of his illustrations

are those from English writers: there are more than a hundred excerpts from Sidney (whose works had not yet been published), only three from Spenser (perhaps because Spenser is so copiously represented in Webbe's *Discourse of English Poetry*, 1586, and in Fraunce's own *Lawyer's Logic*), one from *Piers Plowman*, and three from Richard Willey (or Willes), author of the *Poemata* (1573) and editor of Richard Eden's translation of Petrus Martyr's *Decades* (*The History of Travel*, 1577). Thus Fraunce's little book is both a handy manual of rhetoric and a tastefully arranged anthology. Entered in the Stationers' Register on June 11, 1588, it was probably published in the same year. Our text is based upon *The Arcadian Rhetorike: Or The Praecepts of Rhetorike made plaine by examples, Greeke, Latin, English, Italian, French, Spanish*, 1588 (STC 11338).

FROM THE ARCADIAN RHETORIC (1588)

THE FIRST CHAPTER OF THE FIRST BOOK

What Rhetoric Is

Rhetoric is an art of speaking. It hath two parts, elocution and pronunciation. Elocution is the first part of rhetoric, concerning the ordering and trimming of speech. It hath also two parts, congruity and bravery. Congruity is that which causeth the speech to be pure and coherent; and it is performed either by etymology, which concerneth the affections of several words, or *syntaxis,* which doth orderly conjoin them together. Here should all grammatical rules (as they call them) be placed. I omit them for this time, as being scarce resolved in this conceipt. Bravery of speech consisteth in tropes, or turnings, and in figures, or fashionings. A trope or turning is when a word is turned from his natural signification to some other so conveniently as that it seem rather willingly led than driven by force to that other signification. This was first invented of necessity for want of words, but afterwards continued and frequented by reason of the delight and pleasant grace thereof. Sometimes these tropes be excessive, signifying in word more than can be true in deed; and then are they termed hyperboles. The excellency of tropes is, then, most apparant when either many be fitly included in one word or one so continued in many as that with what thing it begin, with the same it also end; and then it is called an allegory or inversion. And so much of the general proprieties of tropes; now to the divers kinds thereof.

CAP. 2. Of the *Metonymia* of the Cause

There be two kinds of tropes. The first containeth *metonymia,* the change of name, and *ironia,* a scoffing or jesting speech; the second comprehendeth a metaphor and synecdoche. *Metonymia* is a trope which useth the name of one thing for the name of another that agreeth with it, as when the cause is turned to signify the thing caused, the thing caused to signify the cause, the subject to express the adjunct, or the adjunct the subject. The *metonymia* of the cause is double, of the efficient or material cause; of the efficient as when the autor and inventor is put for the things by him invented and found. . . .

Sir Philip Sidney in the second act of *Arcadia* [*Works,* ed. Feuillerat, IV, 120], speaking of the furious multitude: "Bacchus, they say, was begotten of thunder. I think that ever since made him so full of stir and debate; Bacchus indeed it was which sounded the first trumpet of this rude alarum."

Second act [*Works,* IV, 142]:
Therefore, alas, you use vile Vulcan's spite,
Which nothing spares, to melt that virgin's wax
Which, while it is, it is all Asia's light.

Third act [*Works,* I, 220]:
More white than Neptune's foamy face
When struggling rocks he would embrace.

Fourth act [*Works,* IV, 284], Philanax speaking of Pyrocles and Philoclea: "The violence the gentleman spake of is now turned to marriage; he alledged Mars, but she speaks of Venus." . . .

The *metonymia* of the material cause is when the matter is put for the thing thereof made. . . .

> Virgil, *Aeneid* I [line 35]:
> *Spumas salis aere ruebant.*

> *Georgics* II [line 506]:
> *Ut gemma bibat, et sarrhano dormiat ostro.* . . .

> Sir Philip Sidney, act IV [*Works*, IV, 136]:
> Who evermore will love Apollo's quill? . . .

CAP. 3. Of the *Metonymia* of the Thing Caused

The *metonymia* of the thing caused is when we attribute that to the efficient which is made by the efficient. And hereof come most of poets' and orators' epithets. . . .

> Sir P[hilip] Sid[ney], second act [*Works*, IV, 141]:
> Nay, even cold death, inflam'd with hot desire,
> Her to enjoy where joy itself is thrall,
> Will spoil the earth of her most rich attire. . . .

CAP. 6. Of *Ironia*

Ironia is a trope that by naming one contrary intendeth another. The special grace whereof is in jesting and merry conceipted speeches. This trope continued maketh a most sweet allegory, and it is perceived by the contrariety of the matter itself, or by the manner of utterance 'quite differing from the sense of the words; for then it is apparant that we speak but jestingly, and not as we think. . . .

> [Sir Philip Sidney, *Arcadia*, act] III [*Works*, IV, 183], of Mopsa: "So that the pretty pig, laying her sweet burden about his neck, 'My Dorus,' said she, 'tell me these wonders.'"

> In the same book [*Works*, IV, 199] Philoclea saith: "'O kind mother of mine,' said she, 'did you bestow the light upon me for this? Or did you bear me to be the author of my burial? A trim purchase you have made of your own shame—robbed your daughter to ruin yourself.'"

> In [act] IV [*Works*, IV, 302–3], Timantus of Philanax: "O notable affection, for the love of the father to kill the wife and disenherit the children! O single-minded modesty, to aspire to no less than to the princely diadem!"

CAP. 7. Of a Metaphor

Thus much of the first kind of trope in *metonymia* and *ironia*. Now followeth the second, containing a metaphor and synecdoche. A metaphor is when the like is signified by the like; so then a metaphor is nothing but a similitude contracted into one word. There is no trope more florishing than a metaphor, especially if it be applied to the senses, and among the senses chiefly to the eye, which is the quickest of all the senses. . . .

> Sir Philip Sid[ney], 23d son[net]:
> Alas, the race
> Of all my thoughts hath neither stop nor start,
> But only Stella's eyes and Stella's heart.

> Of Pyrocles, [act] I Ar[cadia] [*Works*, IV, 13]: "For besides his eyes sometimes even great with tears."

> In the same place [*Works*, IV, 13]: "And might perceive in him store of thoughts rather stirred than digested." . . .

CAP. 8. Of Synecdoche of the Part

Synecdoche is when the name of the whole is given to the part, or the name of the part to the whole. Synecdoche of the part is when by a part we mean the whole, and it is either of the member or of the special. Of the member, when by one integral member the whole is signified. . . .

> Sir P[hilip] Sidney, [act] II [*Works*, IV, 108], of Basilius: "Basilius having comb'd and trick'd himself more curiously than any times forty winters before."

CAP. 12. Of Figures *schemes*

Now of figures. A figure is a certain decking of speech whereby the usual and simple fashion thereof is altered and changed to that which is more elegant and conceipted. For as a trope is of single words, so a figure of coopled and conjoined; and as of words some be proper, some turned, so of speeches, some be simple and natural, some finely fashioned and figured artificially. A figure is either in the word or in the sentence. A figure of the word is that whereby the words do sweetly and fitly sound among themselves. In these figures especially consisteth the conceipted pleasance and delicacy of speech.

CAP. 13. Of Verse and Rime

The figure of words consisteth either in the just dimension and measuring of sounds or words, or else in the pleasant repetition of the same. This dimension or measuring is either belonging to poets or used of orators. Poetical dimension is that which is bound to the continual observation of prescript spaces. Poetical dimension maketh either rime or verse. Rime containeth a certain number of syllables ending alike.

> Sir P[hilip] Sid[ney] [*Works*, IV, 187]:
> My heart, my hand, my hand hath given my heart;
> The giver given from gifts shall never part.

CAP. 14.

Verse or meter is a poetical dimension comprehending certain feet settled in certain places. A foot is a dimension of certain syllables with a strict observation of distinct time or quantity. A foot is either of two syllables or three, and both of them either simple or compound. The simple one of two syllables is *spondaeus*, consisting of two long syllables (as ἔστω, *musas, learning, tutta, chacun, obras*); or *pyrrichius*, containing two short syllables (as λόγος, *deus, pretty, ove, amis, mia*). The compound one of two syllables is either *iambus*, of one short and one long (as νεῶν, *deos, revenge, tuoi, seras, aguas*); or *choreus*, of one long and one short (as ἄλλα, *arma, noble, notte, vaincre, porne*). . . . [And so on through the other metrical forms. To illustrate the various meters, both simple and compound, Fraunce quotes largely from Sidney's experiments in quantitative verse. Thus the following sapphics from *Arcadia* (*Works*, [I, 76):]

> If mine eyes can speak to do hearty arrant,
> Or mine eyes' language she do hap to judge of,
> So that eyes' message be of her received,
>   Hope, we do live yet.
>
> But if eyes fail then, when I most do need them,
> Or if eyes' language be not unto her known,
> So that eyes' message do return rejected,
>   Hope, we do both die.
>
> Yet dying and dead do we sing her honor,
> So become our tombs monuments of her praise,
> So become our losses the triumph of her gain,
>   Hers be the glory, etc.

THE SECOND BOOK

I CAP. Of Utterance or Pronunciation

Of elocution, which was the first part of rhetoric, we have spoken already; it now remaineth to talk of utterance or pronunciation, the second part. Utterance is a fit delivering of the speech already beautified. It hath two parts, voice and gesture, the one pertaining to the ear, the other belonging to the eye. A good voice is to be wished; but although it be but mean, we must have care to keep and better it, that whatsoever we utter it may be pronounced with a voice fit for the thing delivered. The voice must be neither too low nor too high, but mean; for

as the one disgraceth all contention and earnest speech, so the other bewrayeth a brawling disposition. Nothing is either better for his voice that speaketh, or more pleasant to the ears of them that hear, than often changing; nothing more hurtful to the one, or harsh to the other, than continual straining without intermission. To brawl in the beginning with a shriking voice is rude and unmannerly. It is best to begin with a submiss voice, and so ascend by degrees as occasion serveth. The consideration of voice is to be had either in severed words or in the whole sentence. In the particular applying of the voice to several words we make tropes that be most excellent plainly appear. For without this change of voice neither any *ironia* nor lively metaphor can well be discerned.

By that kind of voice which belongeth to whole sentences, all kinds of figures and passionate ornaments of speech are made manifest. In figures of words which altogether consist in sweet repetitions and dimensions is chiefly conversant that pleasant and delicate tuning of the voice which resembleth the consent and harmony of some well-ord'red song. In other figures of affections the voice is more manly, yet diversly, according to the variety of passions that are to be expressed. . . .

CAP. 3. Of Action of Gesture of the Whole Body

Hetherto of voice; now of gesture and action, which is both more excellent and more universal than voice, as belonging not only to those that use the same speech but generally to all people, yea, to beasts and senseless creatures, as the very pictures which, being dumb, yet speak by gesture and action. The gesture must follow the change and variety of the voice, answering thereunto in every respect, yet not parasitically, as stage-players use, but gravely and decently as becometh men of greater calling. Let the body, therefore, with a manlike and grave motion of his sides rather follow the sentence than express every particular word. Stand upright and straight, as nature hath appointed; much wavering and overcurious and nice motion is very ridiculous. . . .

THOMAS NASHE

"PREFACE" TO GREENE'S *MENAPHON* (1589)[1]

To the Gentlemen Students of Both Universities

Curteous and wise, whose judgments (not entangled with envy) enlarge the deserts of the learned

by your liberal censures, vouchsafe to welcome your scholler-like shepherd with such university entertainment as either the nature of your bounty or the custom of your common civility may afford. To you he appeals that knew him *ab extrema pueritia*, whose

---

[1] For a note on this text see p. 751.

placet he accounts the *plaudite* of his pains, thinking his day-labor was not altogether lavish'd *sine linea* if there be anything of all in it that doth *olere Atticum* in your estimate. I am not ignorant how eloquent our gowned age is grown of late, so that every mechanical mate abhors the English he was born to and plucks with a solemn periphrasis his *ut vales* from the inkhorn; which I impute not so much to the perfection of arts as to the servile imitation of vainglorious tragedians who contend not so seriously to excel in action as to embowel the clouds in a speech of comparison, thinking themselves more than initiated in poets' immortality if they but once get Boreas by the beard and the heavenly Bull by the dewlap. But herein I cannot so fully bequeath them to folly as their idiot art-masters that intrude themselves to our ears as the alcumists of eloquence, who, mounted on the stage of arrogance, think to outbrave better pens with the swelling bumbast of a bragging blank verse. Indeed, it may be the ingrafted overflow of some kill-cow conceit that overcloyeth their imagination with a more than drunken resolution, being not extemporal in the invention of any other means to vent their manhood, commits the disgestion of their choleric incumbrances to the spacious volubility of a drumming decasyllabon. Mongst this kind of men that repose eternity in the mouth of a player I can but ingross some deep-read grammarians, who, having no more learning in their skull than will serve to take up a commodity, nor art in their brain than was nourished in a servingman's idleness, will take upon them to be the ironical censors of all when God and poetry doth know they are the simplest of all. To leave these to the mercy of their mother tongue, that feed on nought but the crumbs that fall from the translator's trencher, I come, sweet friend, to thy Arcadian *Menaphon,* whose attire, though not so stately, yet comely, doth entitle thee above all other to that *temperatum dicendi genus* which Tully in his *Orator* [XXVIII, 98] termeth true eloquence. Let other men, as they please, praise the mountain that in seven years brings forth a mouse, or the Italianate pen of a packet of pilfries affordeth the press a pamphlet or two in an age, and then in disguised array vaunts Ovid's and Plutarch's plumes as their own; but give me the man whose extemporal vein in any humor will excel our greatest art-master's deliberate thoughts, whose invention, quicker than his eye, will challenge the proudest rethorician to the contention of like perfection with like expedition. What is he amongst students so simple that cannot bring forth (*tandem aliquando*) some or other thing singular, sleeping betwixt every sentence? Was it not Maro's twelve years' toil that so famed his twelve *Aeneidos?* Or Peter Ramus' sixteen years' pains that

so praised his petty *Logic?* How is it, then, our drooping wits should so wonder at an exquisite line that was his master's day-labor? . . .

I will not deny but in scholler-like matters of controversy a quicker style may pass as commendable and that a quip to an ass is as good as a goad to an ox; but when an irregular idiot that was up to the ears in divinity before ever he met with *probabile* in the university shall leave *pro and contra* before he can scarcely pronounce it, and come to correct commonweals that never heard of the name of magistrate before he came to Cambridge, it is no mervail if every ale-house vaunt the table of the world turned upside down, since the child beats his father and the ass whips his master. But lest I might seem with these night crows *nimis curiosus in aliena republica* I'll turn back to my first text of studies of delight, and talk a little in friendship with a few of our trivial translators. It is a common practise nowadays amongst a sort of shifting companions, that run through every art and thrive by none, to leave the trade of noverint, whereto they were born, and busy themselves with the indeavors of art that could scarcely latinize their neck-verse if they should have need; yet English Seneca read by candlelight yields many good sentences (as "Blood is a beggar" and so forth), and if you intreat him fair in a frosty morning he will afford you whole *Hamlets*—I should say handfuls of tragical speeches. But O grief! *Tempus edax rerum!* What's that will last always? The sea exhaled by drops will in continuance be dry; and Seneca, let blood line by line and page by page, at length must needs die to our stage; which makes his famish'd followers to imitate the kid in Aesop, who, enamored with the fox's newfangles, forsook all hopes of life to leap into a new occupation; and these men, renouncing all possibilities of credit or estimation, to intermeddle with Italian translations, wherein how poorly they have plodded—as those that are neither provenzal men nor are able to distinguish of articles— let all indifferent gentlemen that have travailed in that tongue discern by their two-penny pamphlets. And no mervail though their home-born mediocrity be such in this matter, for what can be hoped of those that thrust Elysium into hell and have not learned, so long as they have lived in the spheres, the just measure of the horizon without an hexameter? Sufficeth them to bodge up a blank verse with *if*'s and *and*'s and otherwhile for recreation after their candle-stuff (having starched their beards most curiously) to make a peripatetical path into the inner parts of the city and spend two or three hours in turning over French dowdy, where they attract more infection in one minute than they can do eloquence all days of their life by conversing with any authors of like argument. But lest in this declamatory vein I should condemn all and commend none, I will propound to your learned imitation those men of import that have labored with credit in this laudable kind of translation. In the forefront of whom I cannot but place that aged father Erasmus that invested most of our Greek writers in the robes of the ancient Romains, in whose traces Philip Melancthon, Sadolet, Plantin, and many other reverent Germains insisting, have reedified the ruins of our decayed libraries and merveilously inriched the Latin tongue with the expense of their toil. Not long after, their emulation being transported into England, every private scholler—William Turner and who not—began to vaunt their smattering of Latin in English impressions. But amongst others in that age, Sir Thomas Elyot's elegance did sever itself from all equals, although Sir Thomas More with his comical wit at that instant was not altogether idle; yet was not knowledge fully confirmed in her monarchy amongst us till that most famous and fortunate nurse of all learning, St. John's in Cambridge, that at that time was as an university within itself, shining so far above all other houses, halls, and hospitals whatsoever that no colledge in the town was able to compare with the tithe of her students, having (as I have heard grave men of credit report) more candles' light in it every winter morning before four of the clock than the four-of-clock bell gave strokes—till she, I say, as a pitying mother, put to her helping hand and sent from her fruitful womb sufficient schollers both to support her own weal as also to supply all other inferior foundations' defects, and namely that royal erection of Trinity College, which the university orator [Roger Ascham], in an epistle to the Duke of Somerset, aptly termed *colonia diducta* from the suburbs of St. John's. In which extraordinary conception, *uno partu in rempublicam prodiere,* the exchequer of eloquence, Sir John Cheke, a man of men, supernaturally traded in all tongues, Sir John Mason, Doctor Watson, Redman, Ascham, Grindal, Lever, Pilkington, all which have, either by their private readings or publique works, repurged the errors of arts expell'd from their purity and set before our eyes a more perfect method of study. . . .

Whoever my private opinion condemneth as faulty, Master Gascoigne is not to be abridged of his deserved esteem, who first beat the path to that perfection which our best poets have aspired to since his departure, whereto he did ascend by comparing the Italian with the English, as Tully did *Graeca cum Latinis.* Neither was Master Turbervile the worst of his time, although in translating he attributed too much to the necessity of rime. And in this page of praise I cannot omit aged Arthur Golding for his industrious toil in Englishing Ovid's *Metamorphosis,* besides many other exquisite editions of divinity turned by him out of the French tongue into our own. Master Phaer, likewise, is not to be forgot in regard of his famous Virgil, whose heavenly verse had it not been blemish'd by his haughty thoughts, England might have long insulted in his wit and *corrigat qui potest* have been subscribed to his works. But Fortune, the mistress of change, with a pitying compassion respecting Master Stanyhurst's praise, would that Phaer should fall that he might rise, whose heroical poetry, infired (I should say inspired) with an hexameter fury, recalled to life whatever hissed barbarism hath been buried this hundred year and revived by his ragged quill such carterly variety as no Hodge Plowman in a country but would have held as the extremity of clownery, a pattern whereof I will propound to your judgments, as near as I can, being part of one of his descriptions of a tempest, which is thus:

> Then did he make heaven's vault to rebound with rounce robble hobble
> Of ruff-raff roaring, with thwick-thwack thurlery bouncing.

Which strange language of the firmament, never subject before to our common phrase, makes us, that are not used to terminate heaven's movings in the accents of any voice, esteem of their triobolar interpreter as of some thrasonical huff-snuff, for so terrible was his style to all mild ears as would have affrighted our peaceable poets from intermeddling hereafter with that quarreling kind of verse, had not sweet Master Fraunce, by his excellent translation of Master Thomas Watson's sug'red *Amyntas,* animated their dulled spirits to such high-witted endeavors. . . .

"Tut," says our English Italians, "the finest wits our climate sends forth are but dry-brain'd dolts in comparison of other countries." Whom if you interrupt with *redde rationem,* they will tell you of Petrarch, Tasso, Celiano, with an infinite number of others, to whom if I should oppose Chaucer, Lydgate, Gower, with such like that lived under the tyranny of ignorance, I do think their best lovers would be much discontented with the collation of contraries if I should write over all their heads, "Hail, fellow, well met!" One thing I am sure of, that each of these three have vaunted their meters with as much admiration in English as ever the proudest Ariosto did his verse in Italian. What should I come to our court, where the otherwhile vacations of our graver nobility are prodigal of more pompous wit and choice of words than ever tragic Tasso could attain to? But as for pastoral poems I will not make the comparison, lest our countrymen's credit should be discountenanc'd by the contention, who, although they cannot fare with such inferior facility, yet I know would carry the bucklers full easily from all forrein bravers if their *subjectum circa quod* should savor of anything haughty. And, should the challenge of deep conceit be intruded by any forreiner to bring our English wits to the touchstone of art, I would prefer divine Master Spenser, the miracle of wit, to bandy line for line for my life in the honor of England gainst Spain, France, Italy, and all the world. Neither is he the only swallow of our summer (although Apollo, if his *tripos* were up again, would pronounce him his Socrates), but, he being forborne, there are extant about London many most able men to revive poetry, through it were executed ten thousand tin es, as in Plato's, so in puritans' commonwealth; as, for example, Matthew Roydon, Thomas Atchelow, and George Peele, the first of whom, as he hath shewed himself singular in the immortal "Epitaph" of his beloved Astrophel, besides many other most absolute comic inventions (made more publique by every man's praise than they can be by my speech), so the second hath more than once or twice manifested his deep-witted schollership in places of credit; and for the last, though not the least of them all, I dare commend him to all that know him as the chief supporter of pleasance now living, the Atlas of poetry and *primus verborum artifex,* whose first encrease, *The Arraignment of Paris,* might plead to your opinions his pregnant dexterity of wit and manifold variety of invention, wherein, *me judice,* he goeth a step beyond all that write. Sundry other sweet gentlemen I know that have vaunted their pens in private devices and trick'd up a company of taffeta fools with their feathers, whose beauty if our poets

had not pick'd with the supply of their periwigs, they might have antick'd it until this time up and down the country with the king of fairies and din'd every day at the pease-porredge ordinary with Delphrigus. . . .

As poetry hath been honored in those her forenamed professors, so it hath not been any whit disparaged by William Warner's absolute *Albion's [England].* And here authority hath made a full point, in whose reverence insisting I cease to expose to your sport the picture of those pamphleteers and poets that make a patrimony of "In speech" and more then a younger brother's inheritance of their ABC. Read favorably to incourage me in the firstlings of my folly, and persuade yourselves I will persecute those idiots and their heirs unto the third generation that have made art bankrout of her ornaments and sent poetry a-begging up and down the country. It may be my *Anatomy of Absurdities* may acquaint you ere long with my skill in surgery, wherein the diseases of art, more merrily discovered, may make our maimed poets put together their blanks unto the building of an hospital.

If you chance to meet it in Paul's, shaped in a new suit of similitudes as if, like the eloquent apprentice of Plutarch, it were propped at seven years' end in double apparel, think his master hath fulfilled covenants and only canceled the indentures of duty. If I please, I will think my ignorance indebted unto you that applaud it; if not, what rests but that I be excluded from your courtesy, like Apocrypha from your Bibles?

However, yours ever,
Thomas Nashe

GEORGE PUTTENHAM

THE ART OF ENGLISH POESY

Although the most ambitious (and next to Sidney's the best) of Elizabethan critical treatises was published (1589) anonymously, it has, thanks to the careful scholarship of Misses Willcock and Walker, at last been plausibly established as the work of George (not his brother Richard) Puttenham. Its printer Richard Field, in a dedication to Lord Burghley, professed ignorance of its author, but he was probably lying, for there is good reason to believe that the work was revised with substantial alterations while it was going through the press. George Puttenham, an elderly man when the *Art* appeared, was a nephew of Sir Thomas Elyot who had gone from Cambridge to the Inns of Court (in the fifties

a center of literary activity), traveled widely on the Continent, and enjoyed sufficient intimacy with Elizabeth's court to write for the queen in 1579 a series of poems called *Partheniades.* As both a rhetoric and a poetics his treatise is closer in tone and purpose to such humanistic monuments as his uncle's *Book Named the Governor* and Ascham's *Schoolmaster* than to the apologetic literature of Lodge, Sidney, Webbe, Harington, Nashe, and others. Indeed, it was probably drafted in the late sixties (before the puritan attack gathered strength) and revised for publication in the mid-eighties. A carefully planned work that reveals an intimate knowledge of both foreign and mid-Tudor literature, it proceeds from a general account (Book I) of poetry and its various kinds (tragedy, comedy, epic, pastoral, and the like) to a review (Book II) of the metrical forms in use by English poets of the mid-century to a searching analysis (Book III) of the ingredients (language, style, and rhetorical devices) from which poetry is constructed. As the word "art" suggests, Puttenham's main interest is in the technique of a craft, and he never gets far from the actual structure of poetry itself. Certain inconsistencies of style and doctrine may perhaps be attributed to a hurried revision. Entered in the Stationers' Register on November 9, 1588, on April 7, 1589, the printer's rights were "put over" to Richard Field, who published the book (in at least three issues) in the same year. The work at once acquired the prestige that it has enjoyed ever since. Sir John Harington in the preface to his *Orlando Furioso* (1591) and the eminent Camden in his *Remains* (1605) recognized its authority, Ben Jonson owned a copy (now in the British Museum), Francis Meres plundered it freely for his *Palladis Tamia* (1598), and various writers of the early seventeenth century mentioned it or its unknown author with admiration. Our text is based upon *The Arte of English Poesie. Contrived into three Bookes: The first of Poets and Poesie, the second of Proportion, the third of Ornament*, 1589 (STC 20519).

FROM THE ART OF ENGLISH POESY (1589)

Book I: Of Poets and Poesy

Chap. i. What a Poet and Poesy Is, and Who May Be Worthily Said the Most Excellent Poet of Our Time

A poet is as much to say as a maker. And our English name well conforms with the Greek word, for of ποιεῖν, "to make," they call a maker *poeta*. Such as, by way of resemblance and reverently, we may say of God, who without any travail to his divine imagination made all the world of nought nor also by any pattern or mold (as the Platonics with their Idees do phantastically suppose). Even so the very poet makes and contrives out of his own brain both the verse and matter of his poem, and not by any foreign copy or example as doth the translator, who therefore may well be said a versifier but not a poet. The premises considered, it giveth to the name and profession no small dignity and preheminence above all other artificers, scientific or mechanical. And nevertheless, without any repugnancy at all, a poet may in some sort be said a follower or imitator, because he can express the true and lively of everything is set before him and which he taketh in hand to describe; and so in that respect is both a maker and a counterfaitor, and poesy an art not only of making but also of imitation. And this science in his perfection cannot grow but by some divine instinct (the Platonics call it *furor*), or by excellency of nature and complexion, or by great subtilty of the spirits and wit, or by much experience and observation of the world and course of kind, or peradventure by all or most part of them. Otherwise how was it possible that Homer, being but a poor private man and, as some say, in his later age blind, should so exactly set forth and describe, as if he had been a most excellent captain or general, the order and array of battles, the conduct of whole armies, the sieges and assaults of cities and towns? Or, as some great prince's majordomo and perfect surveyor in court, the order, sumptuousness, and magnificence of royal bankets, feasts, weddings, and interviews? Or, as a politician very prudent and much inured with the private and publique affairs, so gravely examine the laws and ordinances civil, or so profoundly discourse in matters of estate and forms of all politique regiment? Finally, how could he so naturally paint out the speeches, countenance, and manners of princely persons and private, to wit, the wrath of Achilles, the magnanimity of Agamemnon, the prudence of Menelaus, the prowess of Hector, the majesty of King Priamus, the gravity of Nestor, the policies and eloquence of Ulysses, the calamities of the distressed queens, and valiance of all the captains and adventurous knights in those lamentable wars of Troy? It is therefore of poets thus to be conceived that, if they be able to devise and make all these things of themselves without any subject of verity, that they be—by manner of speech—as creating gods. If they do it by instinct divine or natural, then surely much favored from above; if by their experience, then no doubt very wise men; if by any president or pattern laid before them, then truly the most excellent imitators and counterfaitors of all others. But you, madame,[1] my most honored and gracious, if I should seem to offer you this my devise for a discipline and not a delight, I might well be reputed of all others the most arrogant and injurious, yourself being already, of any that I know in our time, the most excellent poet. Forsooth by your princely purse, favors, and countenance, making in manner what ye list—the poor man rich, the lewd well-learned, the coward

---

[1] Presumably Queen Elizabeth.

couragious, and vile both noble and valiant. Then for imitation no less, your person as a most cunning counterfaitor lively representing Venus in countenance, in life Diana, Pallas for government, and Juno in all honor and regal magnificence.

CHAP. II. That There May Be an Art of Our English Poesy As Well As There Is of the Latin and Greek

Then as there was no art in the world till by experience found out, so if poesy be now an art, and of all antiquity hath been among the Greeks and Latins, and yet were none until by studious persons fashioned and reduced into a method of rules and precepts, then no doubt may there be the like with us. And if th' art of poesy be but a skill appertaining to utterance, why may not the same be with us as well as with them, our language being no less copious, pithy, and significative then theirs, our conceipts the same, and our wits no less apt to devise and imitate then theirs were? If, again, art be but a certain order of rules prescribed by reason and gathered by experience, why should not poesy be a vulgar art with us as well as with the Greeks and Latins, our language admitting no fewer rules and nice diversities then theirs? But peradventure mo, by a peculiar which our speech hath, in many things differing from theirs, and yet in the general points of that art allowed to go in common with them; so as if one point perchance, which is their feet whereupon their measures stand and indeed is all the beauty of their poesy—and which feet we have not, nor as yet never went about to frame, the nature of our language and words not permitting it—we have instead thereof twenty other curious points in that skill more then they ever had, by reason of our rime and tunable concords or symphony, which they never observed. Poesy, therefore, may be an art in our vulgar, and that very methodical and commendable.

CHAP. III. How Poets Were the First Priests, the First Prophets, the First Legislators and Politicians in the World

The profession and use of poesy is most ancient from the beginning and not, as many erroneously suppose, after but before any civil society was among men. For it is written that poesy was th' original cause and occasion of their first assemblies, when before the people remained in the woods and mountains, vagarant and dispersed like the wild beasts, lawless and naked or very ill-clad, and of all good and necessary provision for harbor or sustenance utterly unfurnished, so as they little diff'red for their manner of life from the very brute beasts of the field. Whereupon it is feigned that Amphion and Orpheus, two poets of the first ages, one of them, to wit Amphion, builded up cities and reared walls with the stones that came in heaps to the sound of his harp, figuring thereby the mollifying of hard and stony hearts by his sweet and eloquent persuasion. And Orpheus assembled the wild beasts to come in herds to harken to his music and by that means made them tame, implying thereby how, by his discreet and wholesome lessons uttered in harmony and with melodious instruments, he brought the rude and savage people to a more civil and orderly life, nothing, as it seemeth, more prevailing or fit to redress and edify the cruel and sturdy courage of man then it. And as these two poets, and Linus before them and Musaeus also and Hesiodus in Greece and Arcadia, so by all likelihood had mo poets done in other places and in other ages before them, though there be no remembrance left of them by reason of the records by some accident of time perished and failing. Poets, therefore, are of great antiquity. Then forasmuch as they were the first that entended to the observation of Nature and her works—and specially of the celestial courses, by reason of the continual motion of the heavens searching after the first mover and from thence by degrees coming to know and consider of the substances separate and abstract which we call the divine intelligences or good angels (demones)—they were the first that instituted sacrifices of placation, with invocations and worship to them as to gods, and invented and stablished all the rest of the observances and ceremonies of religion and so were the first priests and ministers of the holy mysteries. And because, for the better execution of that high charge and function, it behoved them to live chaste and in all holiness of life and in continual study and contemplation, they came by instinct divine and by deep meditation and much abstinence (the same assubtiling and refining their spirits) to be made apt to receive visions, both waking and sleeping, which made them utter prophecies and foretell things to come. So also were they the first prophets or seers, videntes, for so the Scripture termeth them in Latin after the Hebrew word; and all the oracles and answers of the gods were given in meter or verse and published to the people by their direction. And for that they were aged and grave men, and of much wisdom and experience in th' affairs of the world, they were the first lawmakers to the people and the first politicians, devising all expedient means for th' establishment of common wealth to hold and contain the people in order and duty by force and virtue of good and wholesome laws made for the preservation of the publique peace and tranquillity, the same peradventure not purposely intended but greatly furthered by the awe of their gods and such scruple of conscience as the terrors of their late-invented religion had led them into.

CHAP. IX. How Poesy Should Not Be Imployed upon Vain Conceits or Vicious or Infamous

Wherefore, the nobility and dignity of the art considered as well by universality as antiquity and the natural excellence of itself, poesy ought not to be abased and imployed upon any unworthy matter and subject, nor used to vain purposes; which nevertheless is daily seen, and that is to utter conceits infamous and vicious, or ridiculous and foolish, or of no good example and doctrine. Albeit in merry matters—not unhonest—being used for man's solace and recreation it may be well allowed; for, as I said before, poesy is a pleasant manner of utterance, varying from the ordinary of purpose to refresh the mind by the ear's delight. Poesy also is not only laudable because I said it was a metrical speech used by the first men, but because it is a metrical speech correcte l and reformed by discreet judgments, and with no less cunning and curiosity then the Greek and Latin poesy, and by art beautified and adorned and brought far from the primitive rudeness of the first inventors; otherwise it might be said to me that Adam and Eve's aperns were the gayest garments because they were the first, and the shepherd's tent or pavilion the best housing because it was the most ancient and most universal; which I would not have so taken, for it is not my meaning but that art and cunning concurring with nature, antiquity, and universality in things indifferent and not evil do make them more laudable. And right so our vulgar riming poesy, being by good wits brought to that perfection we see, is worthily to be preferred before any other manner of utterance in prose for such use and to such purpose as it is ordained and shall hereafter be set down more particularly.

CHAP. X. The Subject or Matter of Poesy

Having sufficiently said of the dignity of poets and poesy, now it is time to speak of the matter or subject of poesy, which to mine intent is whatsoever witty and delicate conceit of man meet or worthy to be put in written verse for any necessary use of the present time or good instruction of the posterity. But the chief and principal is the laud, honor, and glory of the immortal gods (I speak now in phrase of the Gentiles); secondly, the worthy gests of noble princes, the memorial and registry of all great fortunes, the praise of virtue and reproof of vice, the instruction of moral doctrines, the revealing of sciences natural and other profitable arts, the redress of boist'rous and sturdy courages by persuasion, the consolation and repose of temperate minds; finally,

the common solace of mankind in all his travails and cares of this transitory life; and in this last sort, being used for recreation only, may allowably bear matter not always of the gravest or of any great commodity or profit, but rather in some sort vain, dissolute, or wanton, so it be not very scandalous and of evil example. But as our intent is to make this art vulgar for all Englishmen's use, and therefore are of necessity to set down the principal rules therein to be observed, so in mine opinion it is no less expedient to touch briefly all the chief points of this ancient poesy of the Greeks and Latins so farforth as it conformeth with ours. So as it may be known what we hold of them as borrowed and what as of our own peculiar. Wherefore, now that we have said what is the matter of poesy, we will declare the manner and forms of poems used by the ancients.

CHAP. XI. Of Poems and Their Sundry Forms and How Thereby the Ancient Poets Received Surnames

As the matter of poesy is divers, so was the form of their poems and manner of writing, for all of them wrote not in one sort, even as all of them wrote not upon one matter. Neither was every poet alike cunning in all as in some one kind of poesy, nor uttered with like felicity. But wherein anyone most excelled, thereof he took a surname, as to be called a poet heroic, lyric, elegiac, epigrammatist, or otherwise. Such therefore as gave themselves to write long histories of the noble gests of kings and great princes, entermeddling the dealings of the gods, half-gods, or heroes of the Gentiles and the great and weighty consequences of peace and war, they called poets heroic, whereof Homer was chief and most ancient among the Greeks, Virgil among the Latins. Others who more delighted to write songs or ballads of pleasure to be sung with the voice and to the harp, lute, or citheron, and such other musical instruments, they were called melodious poets (*melici*) or by a more common name lyric poets, of which sort was Pindarus, Anacreon, and Callimachus with others among the Greeks, Horace and Catullus among the Latins. There were another sort who sought the favor of fair ladies and coveted to bemoan their estates at large and the perplexities of love in a certain piteous verse called elegy, and thence were called elegiac; such among the Latins were Ovid, Tibullus, and Propertius. There were also poets that wrote only for the stage—I mean plays and interludes—to recreate the people with matters of disport, and to that intent did set forth in shews pageants, accompanied with speech, the common behaviors and manner of life of private persons and such as were the meaner sort of men; and they were called comical poets, of whom among the Greeks Menander and Aristophanes were most excellent, with the Latins Terence and Plautus. Besides those poets comic there were other who served also the stage but meddled not with so base matters, for they set forth the doleful falls of infortunate and afflicted princes, and were called poets tragical; such were Euripides and Sophocles with the Greeks, Seneca among the Latins. There were yet others who mounted nothing so high as any of them both, but, in base and humble style by manner of dialogue, uttered the private and familiar talk of the meanest sort of men, as shepherds, heywards, and such like; such was among the Greeks Theocritus, and Virgil among the Latins; their poems were named eglogues or shepherdly talk. There was yet another kind of poet who intended to tax the common abuses and vice of the people in rough and bitter speeches, and their invectives were called satires and themselves satiricques; such were Lucilius, Juvenal, and Persius among the Latins, and with us he that wrote the book called *Piers Plowman*. Others of a more fine and pleasant head were given wholly to taunting and scoffing at undecent things, and in short poems uttered pretty merry conceits, and these men were called epigrammatists. There were others that for the people's good instruction and trial of their own wits used in places of great assembly to say by rote numbers of short and sententious meters, very pithy and of good edification, and thereupon were called poets mimists, as who would say imitable and meet to be followed for their wise and grave lessons. . . . Thus have you how the names of the poets were given them by the forms of their poems and manner of writing.

CHAP. XXXI. Who in Any Age Have Been the Most Commended Writers in Our English Poesy, and the Author's Censure Given upon Them

It appeareth by sundry records of books both printed and written that many of our countrymen have painfully travailed in this part, of whose works some appear to be but bare translations, other some matters of their own invention and very commendable, whereof some recital shall be made in this place to th' intent chiefly that their names should not be defrauded of such honor as seemeth due to them for having by their thankful studies so much beautified our English tongue as at this day it will be found our nation is in nothing inferior to the French or Italian for copy of language, subtilty of device, good method and proportion in any form of poem, but that they may compare with the most and perchance pass a great many of them. And I will not reach above the time of King Edward the Third and Richard the Second for any that wrote in English meter, because

before their times, by reason of the late Norman conquest which had brought into this realm much alteration both of our language and laws and therewithal a certain martial barbarousness whereby the study of all good learning was so much decay'd as long time after no man or very few entended to write in any laudable science, so as beyond that time there is little or nothing worth commendation to be found written in this art. And those of the first age were Chaucer and Gower, both of them, as I suppose, knights. After whom followed John Lydgate, the monk of Bury, and that nameless who wrote the satire called *Piers Plowman;* next him followed Hardyng the chronicler; then, in King Henry th' Eight's times, Skelton (I wot not for what great worthiness) surnamed the poet laureate. In the latter end of the same king's reign sprong up a new company of courtly makers of whom Sir Thomas Wyatt th' elder and Henry, Earl of Surrey, were the two chieftains, who, having traveled into Italy and there tasted the sweet and stately measures and style of the Italian poesy, as novices newly crept out of the schools of Dante, Ariosto, and Petrarch, they greatly polished our rude and homely manner of vulgar poesy from that it had been before, and for that cause may justly be said the first reformers of our English meter and style. In the same time or not long after was the Lord Nicholas Vaux, a man of much facility in vulgar makings. Afterward, in King Edward the Sixth's time, came to be in reputation for the same faculty Thomas Sternhold, who first translated into English certain psalms of David, and John Heywood, the epigrammatist, who for the mirth and quickness of his conceits more then for any good learning was in him came to be well benefited by the king. But the principal man in this profession at the same time was Maister Edward [or rather George] Ferrers, a man of no less mirth and felicity that way but of much more skill and magnificence in his meter, and therefore wrate for the most part to the stage in tragedy and sometimes in comedy or enterlude, wherein he gave the king so much good recreation as he had thereby many good rewards. In Queen Mary's time florished above any other Doctor Phaer, one that was well learned and excellently well translated into English verse heroical certain books of Virgil's *Aeneidos*. Since him followed Maister Arthur Golding, who with no less commendation turned into English meter the *Metamorphosis* of Ovid, and that other doctor [Thomas Twyne] who made the supplement to those books of Virgil's *Aeneidos* which Maister Phaer left undone. And in her Majesty's time that now is are sprong up another crew of courtly makers, noblemen and gentlemen of her Majesty's own servants, who have written excellently well, as it would appear if their doings could be found out and made public with the rest; of which number is first that noble gentleman Edward, Earl of Oxford, Thomas, Lord of Buckhurst, when he was young, Henry, Lord Paget, Sir Philip Sidney, Sir Walter Raleigh, Maister Edward Dyer, Maister Fulke Greville, Gascon, Britton, Turbervile, and a great many other learned gentlemen whose names I do not omit for envy but to avoid tediousness, and who have deserved no little commendation. But of them all particularly this is mine opinion, that Chaucer with Gower, Lydgate, and Hardyng for their antiquity ought to have the first place, and Chaucer as the most renowmed of them all, for the much learning appeareth to be in him above any of the rest. And though many of his books be but bare translations out of the Latin and French, yet are they well handled, as his books of *Troilus and Cresseid* and *The Romaunt of the Rose,* whereof he translated but one-half—the device was John de Mehune's, a French poet. *The Canterbury Tales* were Chaucer's own invention, as I suppose, and where he sheweth more the natural of his pleasant wit then in any other of his works; his similitudes, comparisons, and all other descriptions are such as cannot be amended. His meter heroical of *Troilus and Cresseid* is very grave and stately, keeping the staff of seven and the verse of ten; his other verses of *The Canterbury Tales* be but riding rime, nevertheless very well becoming the matter of that pleasant pilgrimage, in which every man's part is play'd with much decency. Gower, saving for his good and grave moralities, had nothing in him highly to be commended, for his verse was homely and without good measure, his words strained much deal out of the French writers, his rime wrested, and in his inventions small subtilty. The applications of his moralities are the best in him, and yet those many times very grossly bestowed; neither doth the substance of his works sufficiently answer the subtilty of his titles. Lydgate, a translator only and no deviser of that which he wrate, but one that wrate in good verse. Hardyng, a poet epic or historical, handled himself well according to the time and manner of his subject. He that wrote the satire of *Piers Plowman* seemed to have been a malcontent of that time, and therefore bent himself wholly to tax the disorders of that age and specially the pride of the Roman clergy, of whose fall he seemeth to be a very true prophet. His verse is but loose meter and his terms hard and obscure, so as in them is little pleasure to be taken. Skelton, a sharp satirist but with more railing and scoffery then became a poet laureate; such among the Greeks were called *pantomimi,* with us buffoons, altogether applying their wits to scurrilities and other ridiculous matters. Henry, Earl of Surrey, and Sir

Thomas Wyatt, between whom I find very little difference, I repute them (as before) for the two chief lanterns of light to all others that have since employed their pens upon English poesy. Their conceits were lofty, their styles stately, their conveyance cleanly, their terms proper, their meter sweet and well proportioned, in all imitating very naturally and studiously their maister, Francis Petrarca. The Lord Vaux his commendation lieth chiefly in the facility of his meter and the aptness of his descriptions such as he taketh upon him to make, namely in sundry of his songs, wherein he sheweth the counterfait action very lively and pleasantly. Of the later sort I think thus. That for tragedy the Lord of Buckhurst and Maister Edward [i.e. George] Ferrys, for such doings as I have seen of theirs, do deserve the highest price; th' Earl of Oxford and Maister Edwards of her Majesty's chapel for comedy and enterlude. For eglogue and pastoral poesy, Sir Philip Sidney and Maister Chaloner and that other gentleman [i.e. Spenser] who wrate the late *Shepherd's Calendar.* For ditty and amorous ode I find Sir Walter Raleigh's vein most lofty, insolent, and passionate. Maister Edward Dyer for elegy most sweet, solempn, and of high conceit. Gascon for a good meter and for a plentiful vein. Phaer and Golding for a learned and well-corrected verse, specially in translation clear and very faithfully answering their authors' intent. Others have also written with much facility, but more commendably perchance if they had not written so much nor so popularly. But last in recital and first in degree is the queen our sovereign lady, whose learned, delicate, noble muse easily surmounteth all the rest that have written before her time or since for sense, sweetness, and subtilty, be it in ode, elegy, epigram, or any other kind of poem heroic or lyric wherein it shall please her Majesty to employ her pen, even by as much odds as her own excellent estate and degree exceedeth all the rest of her most humble vassals.

BOOK II: OF PROPORTION POETICAL

CHAP. IX. How the Good Maker Will Not Wrench His Word to Help His Rime Either by Falsifying His Accent or by Untrue Orthography

Now there cannot be in a maker a fouler fault then to falsify his accent to serve his cadence or by untrue orthography to wrench his words to help his rime, for it is a sign that such a maker is not copious in his own language or (as they are wont to say) not half his craft's maister. As for example, if one should rime to this word *restore* he may not match him with *door* or *poor,* for neither of both are of like terminant, either by good orthography or in natural sound; therefore such rime is strained; so is it to this word ram to say *came*, or to *bean, den*, for they sound not nor be written alike; and many other like cadences which were superfluous to recite and are usual with rude rimers who observe not precisely the rules of prosody. Nevertheless, in all such cases (if necessity constrained) it is somewhat more tolerable to help the rime by false orthography then to leave an unpleasant dissonance to the ear by keeping true orthography and loosing the rime, as for example it is better to rime *dore* with *restore* then in his truer orthography, which is *door,* and to this word *desire* to say *fier* than *fire,* though it be otherwise better written *fi e.* For since the chief grace of our vulgar poesy consisteth in the symphony, as hath been already said, our maker must not be too licentious in his concords, but see that they go even, just, and melodious in the ear and right so in the numerosity or currantness of the whole body of his verse and in every other of his proportions. For a licentious maker is in truth but a bungler and not a poet. Such men were, in effect, the most part of all your old rimers, and specially Gower, who, to make up his rime, would for the most part write his terminant syllable with false orthography and many times not stick to put in a plain French word for an English; and so, by your leave, do many of our common rimers at this day, as he [Timothy Kendall] that by all likelihood having no word at hand to rime to this word *joy* he made his other verse end in *roy,* saying very impudently thus:

O mighty lord of love, Dame Venus' only joy,
Who art the highest god of any heavenly roy.

Which word was never yet received in our language for an English word. Such extreme licentiousness is utterly to be banished from our school, and better it might have been borne with in old riming writers, bycause they lived in a barbarous age and were grave, moral men but very homely poets, such also as made most of their works by translation out of the Latin and French tongue and few or none of their own engine, as may easely be known to them that list to look upon the poems of both languages.

Finally, as ye may rime with words of all sorts, be they of many syllables or few, so nevertheless is there a choice by which to make your cadence (before rememb'red) most commendable; for some words of exceeding great length, which have been fetched from the Latin inkhorn or borrowed of strangers, the use of them in rime is nothing pleasant, saving perchance to the common people, who rejoice much to be at plays and enterludes and, besides their natural ignorance, have at all such times their ears so attentive to the matter and their eyes upon the shews of the stage that they take little heed to the cunning of the rime, and therefore be as well satisfied with that which is gross as with any other finer and more delicate.

BOOK III: OF ORNAMENT

CHAP. IV. Of Language

Speech is not natural to man saving for his only hability to speak, and that he is by kind apt to utter all his conceits with sounds and voices diversified many manner of ways: by means of the many and fit instruments he hath by nature to that purpose, as a broad and voluble tongue, thin and movable lips, teeth even and not shagged, thick-ranged, a round, vaulted palate, and a long throat, besides an excellent capacity of wit that maketh him more disciplinable and imitative then any other creature. Then as to the form and action of his speech it cometh to him by art and teaching and by use or exercise. But after a speech is fully fashioned to the common understanding and accepted by consent of a whole country and nation, it is called a language and receiveth none allowed alteration but by extraordinary occasions, by little and little, as it were insensibly, bringing in of many corruptions that creep along with the time.... Then when I say language I mean the speech wherein the poet or maker writeth, be it Greek or Latin or, as our case is, the vulgar English; and when it is peculiar unto a country it is called the mother speech of that people. The Greeks term it *idioma;* so is ours at this day the Norman-English. Before the conquest of the Normans it was the Angle-Saxon, and before that the British, which, as some will, is at this day the Welsh or, as others affirm, the Cornish. I for my part think neither of both, as they be now spoken and pronounced. This part in our maker or poet must be heedily looked unto that it be natural, pure, and the most usual of all his country; and for the same purpose rather that which is spoken in the king's court or in the good towns and cities within the land then in the marches and frontiers, or in port towns where strangers haunt for traffic sake, or yet in universities where schollers use much peevish affectation of words out of the primitive languages, or finally in any uplandish village or corner of a realm where is no resort but of poor rustical or uncivil people. Neither shall he follow the speech of a craftsman or carter or other of the inferior sort, though he be inhabitant or bred in the best town and city in this realm, for such persons do abuse good speeches by strange accents or ill-shapen sounds and false ortography. But he shall follow generally the better-brought-up sort, such as the Greeks call *charientes*— men civil and graciously behavored and bred. Our maker, therefore, at these days shall not follow *Piers Plowman* nor Gower nor Lydgate nor yet Chaucer, for their language is now out of use with us; neither shall he take the terms of northern men such as they use in daily talk (whether they be noblemen or gentlemen or of their best clarks, all is a matter); nor in effect any speech used beyond the River of Trent, though no man can deny but that theirs is the purer English-Saxon at this day, yet it is not so courtly nor so currant as our southern English is; no more is the far western man's speech. Ye shall, therefore, take the usual speech of the court and that of London and the shires lying about London within sixty miles and not much above. I say not this but that in every shire of England there be gentlemen and others that speak—but specially write—as good southern as we of Middlesex or Surrey do, but not the common people of every shire, to whom the gentlemen and also their learned clarks do for the most part condescend. But herein we are already ruled by th' English dictionaries and other books written by learned men, and therefore it needeth none other direction in that behalf. Albeit peradventure some small admonition be not impertinent, for we find in our English writers many words and speeches amendable, and ye shall see in some many inkhorn terms so ill-affected brought in by men of learning, as preachers and schoolmasters, and many strange terms of other languages by secretaries and merchants and travelers, and many dark words and not usual nor well-sounding though they be daily spoken in court. Wherefore great heed must be taken by our maker in this point that his choice be good. And peradventure the writer hereof be in that behalf no less faulty then any other, using many strange and unaccustomed words and borrowed from other languages, and in that respect himself no meet magistrate to reform the same errors in any other person; but, since he is not unwilling to acknowledge his own fault and can the better tell how to amend it, he may seem a more excusable corrector of other men's. He entendeth, therefore, for an indifferent way and universal benefit to tax himself first and before any others.

These be words used by th' author in this present treatise: *scientific*, but with some reason, for it answereth the word *mechanical*, which no other word could have done so properly, for when he spake of all artificers which rest either in science or in handicraft it followed necessarily that *scientifique* should be coupled with *mechanical*, or else neither of both to have been allowed but in their places—a man of science liberal and a handicraftsman, which had not been so cleanly a speech as the other. *Major-domo*: in truth this word is borrowed of the Spaniard and Italian, and therefore new and not usual but to them that are acquainted with the affairs of court, and so for his jolly magnificence—as this case is—may be accepted among courtiers, for whom this is specially

written. A man might have said instead of *major-domo* the French word *maître d'hôtel*, but ill-favoredly, or the right English word *lord steward*. But methinks for my own opinion this word *major-domo*, though he be borrowed, is more acceptable than any of the rest; other men may judge otherwise. *Politien*: this word also is received from the Frenchmen, but at this day usual in court and with all good secretaries, and cannot find an English word to match him, for to have said *a man politique* had not been so well bicause in truth that had been no more than to have said a civil person. *Politien* is rather a surveyor of civility than civil, and a publique minister or counselor in the state. Ye have also this word *conduct*, a French word but well allowed of us and long since usual; it sounds somewhat more than this word *leading*, for it is applied only to the leading of a captain and not as a little boy should lead a blind man; therefore more proper to the case when he said *conduct* of whole armies. Ye find also this word *idiom* taken from the Greeks, yet serving aptly when a man wanteth to express so much unless it be in two words, which surplusage to avoid we are allowed to draw in other words single and as much significative. This word *significative* is borrowed of the Latin and French, but to us brought in first by some nobleman's secretary, as I think, yet doth so well serve the turn as it could not now be spared. And many more like usurped Latin and French words, as *method, methodical, placation, function, assubtiling, refining, compendious, prolix, figurative, inveigle* (a term borrowed of our common lawyers), *impression* (also a new term, but well expressing the matter and more than our English word). These words *numerous, numerosity, metrical, harmonical*, but they cannot be refused, specially in this place for description of the art. Also ye find these words *penetrate, penetrable, indignity*, which I cannot see how we may spare them, whatsoever fault we find with inkhorn terms, for our speech wanteth words to such sense so well to be used; yet instead of *indignity* ye have *unworthiness*, and for *penetrate* we may say *pierce* (and that a French term also) or *broach* or *enter into with violence*, but not so well-sounding as *penetrate*. Item, *savage* for *wild, obscure* for *dark*. Item, these words *declination, delineation, dimension* are scholastical terms indeed, and yet very proper. But peradventure—and I could bring a reason for it—many other like words borrowed out of the Latin and French were not so well to be allowed by us, as these words *audacious* (for *bold*), *facundity* (for *eloquence*), *egregious* (for *great or notable*), *implete* (for *replenished*), *attemptate* (for *attempt*), *compatible* (for *agreeable in nature*), and many more. . . .

SIR JOHN HARINGTON

FROM A PREFACE OR RATHER A BRIEF APOLOGY OF POETRY AND OF THE AUTHOR AND TRANSLATOR PREFIXED TO *ORLANDO FURIOSO* (1591)[1]

The learned Plutarch, in his laconical apothegms, tells of a sophister that made a long and tedious oration in praise of Hercules, and expecting at the end thereof for some great thanks and applause of the hearers, a certain Lacedemonian demanded him who had dispraised Hercules. Methinks the like may be now said to me, taking upon me the defense of poesy; for surely if learning in general were of that account among us as it ought to be among all men, and is among wise men, then should this my apology of poesy (the very first nurse and ancient grandmother of all learning) be as vain and superfluous as was that sophister's, because it might then be answered—and truly answered—that no man disgraced it. But sith we live in such a time in which nothing can escape the envious tooth and backbiting tongue of an impure mouth and wherein every blind corner hath a squint-eyed Zoilus that can look aright upon no man's doings (yea, sure there be some that will not stick to call Hercules himself a dastard because, forsooth, he fought with a club and not at the rapier and dagger), therefore I think no man of judgment will judge this my labor needless in seeking to remove away those slanders that either the malice of those that love it not, or the folly of those that understand it not, hath devised against it. For indeed, as the old saying is, *scientia non habet inimicum praeter ignorantem:* knowledge hath no foe but the ignorant. But now, because I make account, I have to deal with three sundry kinds of reprovers: one, of those that condemn all poetry, which, how strong head soever they have, I count but a very weak faction; another, of those that allow poetry but not this particular poem, of which kind sure there cannot be many; a third, of those that can bear with the art, and like of the work, but will find fault with my not well handling of it, which they may not only probably but, I doubt, too truly do, being a thing as commonly done as said, that where the hedge is lowest there doth every man go over. Therefore against these three I must arm me with the best defensive weapons I can, and if I happen to give a blow now and then in mine own defense, and, as good fencers use, to ward and strike at once, I must crave pardon of course, seeing our law allows that is done *se defendendo* and the law of nature teacheth *vim vi repellere.*

First, therefore, of poetry itself. For those few that generally disallow, it might be sufficient to alledge those many that generally approve it, of which I could bring in such an army, not of soldiers, but of famous kings and captains, as not only the sight but the very sound of them were able to vanquish and dismay the small forces of our adversaries. For who would once dare to oppose himself against so many Alexanders, Caesars, Scipios (to omit infinite other princes both of former and later ages, and of forrain and nearer countries) that, with favor, with study, with practise, with example, with honors, with gifts, with preferments, with great and magnificent cost, have encoraged and advanced poets and poetry? . . . My meaning is, plainly and *bona fide* confessing all the abuses that can truly be objected against some kind of poets, to shew you what good use there is of poetry. Neither do I suppose it to be greatly behooveful for this purpose to trouble you with the curious definitions of a poet and poesy, and with the subtle distinctions of their sundry kinds; nor to dispute how high and supernatural the name of a maker is, so christ'ned in English by that unknown godfather [i.e. Puttenham] that this last year save one, viz. 1589, set forth a book called *The Art of English Poetry;* and least of all do I purpose to bestow any long time to argue whether Plato, Xenophon, and Erasmus, writing fictions and dialogues in prose, may justly be called poets; or whether Lucan, writing a story in verse, be an historiographer; or whether Master Phaer, translating Virgil, Master Golding, translating Ovid's *Metamorphosis,* and myself, in this work that you see, be any more then versifiers, as the same *Ignoto* termeth all translators. For as for al, or the most part, of such questions, I will refer you to Sir Philip Sidney's *Apology,* who doth handle them right learnedly, or to the forenamed treatise, where they are discoursed more largely. . . .

But to come to the purpose and to speak after the phrase of the common sort that term all that is written in verse poetry, and, rather in scorn then in praise, bestow the name of a poet on every base rimer and ballad-maker, this I say of it—and I think I say truly—that there are many good lessons to be learned out of it, many good examples to be found in it, many good uses to be had of it, and that therefore it is not nor ought not to be despised by the wiser sort, but so to be studied and imployed as was intended by the first writers and devisers thereof, which is to soften and polish the hard and rough dispositions of men and make them capable of virtue and good discipline.

[1] For a note on this text see p. 567.

I cannot deny but to us that are Christians, in respect of the high end of all, which is the health of our souls, not only poetry but all other studies of philosophy are in a manner vain and superfluous. Yea, as the wise man saith, whatsoever is under the sun is vanity of vanities, and nothing but vanity. But sith we live with men and not with saints, and because few men can embrace this strict and stoical divinity; or rather, indeed, for that the Holy Scriptures, in which those high mysteries of our salvation are contained, are a deep and profound study and not subject to every weak capacity—no, nor to the highest wits and judgments except they be first illuminate by God's Spirit or instructed by his teachers and preachers—therefore we do first read some other authors, making them, as it were, a looking-glass to the eyes of our mind; and then, after we have gathered more strength, we enter into profounder studies of higher mysteries, having first, as it were, enabled our eyes by long beholding the sun in a bason of water at last to look upon the sun itself. So we read how that great Moses, whose learning and sanctity is so renowned over all nations, was first instructed in the learning of the Egyptians before he came to that high contemplation of God and familiarity (as I may so term it) with God. So the notable prophet Daniel was brought up in the learning of the Chaldeans, and made that the first step of his higher vocation to be a prophet. If, then, we may by the example of two such special servants of God spend some of our young years in studies of humanity, what better and more meet study is there for a young man then poetry? Specially heroical poesy, that with her sweet stateliness doth erect the mind and lift it up to the consideration of the highest matters, and allureth them that of themselves would otherwise loth them to take and swallow and digest the wholesome precepts of philosophy, and many times even of the true divinity. . . .

But briefly to answer to the chief objections: Cornelius Agrippa, a man of learning and authority not to be despised, maketh a bitter invective against poets and poesy, and the sum of his reproof of it is this (which is all that can with any probability be said against it): that it is a nurse of lies, a pleaser of fools, a breeder of dangerous errors, and an inticer to wantonness. I might here warn those that will urge this man's authority to the disgrace of poetry to take heed (of what calling soever they be) lest with the same weapon that they think to give poetry a blow they give themselves a maim. For Agrippa taketh his pleasure of greater matters then poetry; I marvel how he durst do it, save that I see he hath done it; he hath spared neither miters nor scepters. The courts of princes where virtue is rewarded, justice maintained,

oppressions relieved, he calls them a colledge of giants, of tyrants, of oppressors, warriors; the most noble sort of noble men he termeth cursed, bloody, wicked, and sacrilegious persons. . . . But for the rejecting of his writings, I refer it to others that have pow'r to do it and to condemn him for a general libeler; but for that he writeth against poetry, I mean to speak a word or two in refuting thereof.

And first for lying. I might, if I list, excuse it by the rule of *poetica licentia* and claim a priviledge given to poets, whose art is but an imitation (as Aristotle calleth it) and therefore are allowed to feign what they list. . . . But what if they lie least of all other men? What if they lie not at all? Then, I think, that great slander is very unjustly raised upon them. For in my opinion they are said properly to lie that affirm that to be true that is false; and how other arts can free themselves from this blame, let them look that profess them. But poets, never affirming any for true, but presenting them to us as fables and imitations, cannot lie though they would; and because this objection of lies is the chief, and that upon which the rest be grounded, I will stand the longer upon the clearing thereof.

The ancient poets have indeed wrapped, as it were, in their writings divers and sundry meanings which they call the senses or mysteries thereof. First of all for the literal sense (as it were, the utmost bark or rine) they set down in manner of an history the acts and notable exploits of some person's worthy memory; then in the same fiction, as a second rine and somewhat more fine—as it were, nearer to the pith and marrow—they place the moral sense profitable for the active life of man, approving virtuous actions and condemning the contrary. Many times, also, under the selfsame words they comprehend some true understanding of natural philosophy, or sometimes of politic government, and now and then of divinity; and these same senses that comprehend so excellent knowledge we call the allegory, which Plutarch defineth to be when one thing is told and by that another is understood. Now let any man judge if it be a matter of mean art or wit to contain in one historical narration, either true or feigned, so many, so diverse, and so deep conceits. But for making the matter more plain, I will alledge an example thereof.

Perseus, son of Jupiter, is feigned by the poets to have slain Gorgon, and, after that conquest atchieved, to have flown up to heaven. The historical sense is this: Perseus, the son of Jupiter, by the participation of Jupiter's virtues that were in him, or rather coming of the stock of one of the kings of Crete (or Athens, so called), slew Gorgon, a tyrant in that country (Gorgon in Greek signifieth "earth"), and was for his virtuous parts exalted by men up unto heaven. Morally, it signifieth this much: Perseus, a wise man, son of Jupiter, endued with virtue from above, slayeth sin and vice, a thing base and earthly signified by Gorgon, and so mounteth up to the sky of virtue. It signifies in one kind of allegory thus much: the mind of man, being gotten by God and so the child of God, killing and vanquishing the earthliness of this Gorgonical nature, ascendeth up to the understanding of heavenly things, of high things, of eternal things, in which contemplation consisteth the perfection of man. This is the natural allegory, because man [is] one of the chief works of nature. It hath also a more high and heavenly allegory: that the heavenly nature, daughter of Jupiter, procuring with her continual motion corruption and mortality in the inferior bodies, severed itself at last from these earthly bodies and flew up on high and there remaineth forever. It hath also another theological allegory: that the angelical nature, daughter of the most high God, the Creator of all things, killing and overcoming all bodily substance, signified by Gorgon, ascended into heaven. The like infinite allegories I could pike out of other poetical fictions, save that I would avoid tediousness. It sufficeth me, therefore, to note this: that the men of greatest learning and highest wit in the ancient times did of purpose conceal these deep mysteries of learning, and, as it were, cover them with the veil of fables and verse for sundry causes. One cause was that they might not be rashly abused by prophane wits, in whom science is corrupted like good wine in a bad vessel; another cause why they wrote in verse was conservation of the memory of their precepts, as we see yet the general rules almost of every art, not so much as husbandry, but they are oft'ner recited and better rememb'red in verse then in prose; another, and a principal cause of all, is to be able with one kind of meat and one dish (as I may so call it) to feed divers tastes. . . .

But because I have named the two parts of poetry, namely invention or fiction and verse, let us see how well we can authorize the use of both these. . . . The prophet Nathan, reproving King David for his great sin of adultery and murther, doth he not come to him with a pretty parable of a poor man and his lamb that lay in his bosom and eat of his bread; and the rich man, that had whole flocks of his own, would needs take it from him? In which, as it is evident it was but a parable, so it were unreverent and almost blasphemous to say it was a lie. But to go higher, did not our Savior himself speak in parables? As that divine parable of the sower, that comfortable parable of the prodigal son, that dreadful parable of Dives and Lazarus, though I know of this last many of the fathers hold that it is a story indeed and no parable.

But in the rest it is manifest that he was all holiness, all wisdom, all truth, used parables, and even such as discreet poets use, where a good and honest and wholesome allegory is hidden in a pleasant and pretty fiction; and therefore for that part of poetry of imitation, I think nobody will make any question but it is not only allowable, but godly and commendable, if the poet's ill-handling of it do not mar and pervert the good use of it.

The other part of poetry, which is verse—as it were the clothing or ornament of it—hath many good uses. Of the help of memory I spake somewhat before; for the words being couched together in due order, measure, and number, one doth, as it were, bring on another, as myself have often proved, and so, I think, do many beside; though for my own part I can rather boast of the marring a good memory then of having one, yet I have ever found that verse is easier to learn and far better to preserve in memory then is prose. Another special grace in verse is the forcible manner of phrase in which, if it be well made, it far excelleth loose speech or prose. A third is the pleasure and sweetness to the ear which makes the discourse pleasant unto us oftentime when the matter itself is harsh and unacceptable. . . . But now for the authority of verse, if it be not sufficient to say for them that the greatest philosophers and gravest senators that ever were have used them both in their speeches and in their writings, that precepts of all arts have been delivered in them, that verse is as ancient a writing as prose, and indeed more ancient in respect that the oldest works extant be verse, as Orpheus, Linus, Hesiodus, and others beyond memory of man or mention almost of history—if none of these will serve for the credit of it, yet let this serve: that some part of the Scripture was written in verse, as the Psalms of David, and certain other songs of Deborah, of Salomon, and others, which the learnedest divines do affirm to be verse and find that they are in meter, though the rule of the Hebrew verse they agree not on. Sufficeth it me only to prove that by the authority of Sacred Scriptures both parts of poesy, invention or imitation and verse, are allowable, and consequently that great objection of lying is quite taken away and refuted.

Now the second objection is pleasing of fools. I have already showed how it displeaseth not wise men. Now if it have this virtue too, to please the fools and ignorant, I would think this an article of praise, not of rebuke; wherefore I confess that it pleaseth fools, and so pleaseth them that, if they mark it and observe it well, it will in time make them wise; for in verse is both goodness and sweetness, rhubarb and sugar candy, the pleasant and the profitable. . . .

Now for the breeding of errors, which is the third

objection. I see not why it should breed any when none is bound to believe that they write, nor they look not to have their fictions believed in the literal sense; and therefore he that well examines whence errors spring shall find the writers of prose and not of verse the authors and maintainers of them; and this point I count so manifest as it needs no proof.

The last reproof is lightness and wantonness. This is indeed an objection of some importance sith, as Sir Philip Sidney confesseth, Cupido is crept even into the heroical poems and consequently makes that also subject to this reproof. I promised in the beginning not partially to praise poesy, but plainly and honestly to confess that that might truly be objected against it, and, if anything may be, sure it is this lasciviousness; yet this I will say, that of all kind of poesy the heroical is least infected therewith. The other kinds I will rather excuse then defend, though of all the kinds of poesy it may be said, where any scurrility and lewdness is found, there poetry doth not abuse us, but writers have abused poetry.

And briefly to examine all the kinds. First, the tragical is merely free from it, as representing only the cruel and lawless proceedings of princes, moving nothing but pity or detestation. The comical, whatsoever foolish playmakers make it offend in this kind, yet, being rightly used, it represents them so as to make the vice scorned and not embraced. The satiric is merely free from it, as being wholly occupied in mannerly and covertly reproving of all vices. The elegy is still mourning. As for the pastoral, with the sonnet or epigram, though many times they savor of wantonness and love and toying, and, now and then breaking the rules of poetry, go into plain scurrility, yet even the worst of them may be not ill-applied and are, I must confess, too delightful. . . .

But to end this part of my apology, as I count and conclude heroical poesy allowable and to be read and studied without all exception, so I may as boldly say that tragedies well handled be a most worthy kind of poesy, that comedies may make men see and shame at their own faults, that the rest may be so written and so read as much pleasure and some profit may be gathered out of them. And for mine own part, as Scaliger writeth of Virgil, so I believe that the reading of a good heroical poem may make a man both wiser and honester. . . . And thus much be said for poesy.

FRANCIS MERES

PALLADIS TAMIA

Thanks to its famous catalogue of contemporary writers, including Shakespeare, *Palladis Tamia* has long attracted far more attention than it deserves, for as a contribution to critical theory it is a picayune performance, euphuistic in style and derivative in content. The work of a conventionally and superficially educated graduate of Pembroke College, Cambridge, it is the second volume in a series of commonplace-books on moral philosophy, religion, and literature. Projected and probably subsidized by John Bodenham, the series includes, besides *Palladis Tamia*, Nicholas Ling's *Polit-euphuia, Wit's Commonwealth* (1597), Robert Allott's *Wit's Theater of the Little World* (1599), John Bodenham and Anthony Munday's *Belvedere* (1600, 1610), and William Wrednot's *Palladis Palatium* (?1600, 1604).

Meres's contribution, which was entered in the Stationers' Register on September 7, 1598, and published in the same year, is ostensibly a gathering of apothegms and critical judgments on religion, practical conduct, literature, music, and painting, but it has been cherished by posterity for its section entitled "A Comparative Discourse of Our English Poets with the Greek, Latin, and Italian Poets." Here Meres purposes to survey the whole gallery of English poets from Chaucer on and to compare or contrast each with his counterpart in classical or Italian literature. In dealing with over a hundred English authors and ranging through immense tracts of foreign literatures to find their opposite numbers Meres, to say the least, gives the impression of wide and various learning. Actually, however, as Professor Don Cameron Allen has shown, he was a superficial plagiarist who lifted names, sentences, and whole passages from quotation books, epithet books, and encyclopedias that were standard works of reference for every Elizabethan undergraduate. One such omnium-gatherum that had been thumbed by generations of students was the massive *Polyanthea* (1507 ff.) of Dominicus Nannus Mirabellius, a work that through many editions and additions reached a length of fifteen hundred pages by the early seventeenth century. Anyone who remembered the alphabet and could read schoolboy Latin might find in the *Polyanthea* approved quotations listed under such rubrics as *Abnegatio, Absolutio, Abstemii,* and so on, with each main heading generally subdivided as to definition and etymology, Biblical *sententiae*, Biblical *exempla*, patristic *sententiae*, patristic *exempla*, philosophical and poetical *sententiae*, and the like. Other works of the same sort were Erasmus' *Adagia*, Ravisius Textor's famous *Epitheta* (a huge collection of familiar classical quotations arranged by subject), and his *Officina*, a compendium which savants like Ascham derogated but in which men of less learning could find copious information conveniently arranged under such headings as *De diis, De mundo, De homine* (containing more than a hundred sub-sections), and *De artibus liberalibus*. With these arsenals of learning at his elbow, Meres's task was fairly easy, and he performed it in the easiest way, as Professor Allen's long lists of cribbings prove. He not only rifled the encyclopedias ("As Sotades Maronites, the iambic poet, gave himself wholly to write impure and lascivious things" for Textor's "Sotades Maronites poeta fuit iambographus, impurissimus et plenus lasciviae"), but he also borrowed from contemporary English romances and transferred, with only negligible changes, whole passages from the critical treatises of Ascham, Sidney, Webbe, and Puttenham. Our text is based upon *Palladis Tamia. Wits Treasury Being the Second part of Wits Common wealth. By Francis Meres Maister of Artes of both Universities*, 1598 (STC 17834).

FROM PALLADIS TAMIA (1598)

POETS

. . . As Cato, when he was a scholler, would not believe his maister except he rendered a reason of that he taught him, so we are not to believe poets in all that they write or say except they yield a reason. [*Plutarchus.*]

As in the same pasture the bee seizeth on the flower, the goat grazeth on the shrub, the swine on the root, and the oxen, kine, and horses on the grass, so in poets one seeketh for history, another for ornament of speech, another for proof, and another for precepts of good life. *Idem*. . . .

As in the portraiture of murder or incest we praise the art of him that drew it but we detest the thing itself, so in lascivious poets let us imitate their elocution but execrate their wantonness. *Idem*. . . .

As we are delighted in the picture of a viper or a spider artificially enclosed within a precious jewel, so poets do delight us in the learned and cunning depainting of vices. . . .

As God giveth life unto man, so a poet giveth ornament unto it.

As the Greek and Latin poets have won immortal credit to their native speech, being encouraged and graced by liberal patrons and bountiful benefactors, so our famous and learned laureate masters of England would entitle our English to far greater admired excellency if either the Emperor Augustus or Octavia, his sister, or noble Mecaenas were alive to reward and countenance them; or if our witty comedians and stately tragedians (the glorious and goodly representers of all fine wit, glorified phrase, and quaint action) be still supported and upheld, by which means for lack of patrons—O ingrateful and damned age!—our poets are solely or chiefly maintained, countenanced, and patronized. . . .

As the holy prophets and sanctified apostles could never have foretold nor spoken of such supernatural matters unless they had been inspired of God, so Cicero in his *Tusculan Questions* is of the mind that a poet cannot express verses aboundantly, sufficiently, and fully, neither his eloquence can flow pleasantly or his words sound well and plenteously, without celestial instinction. . . .

And our famous English poet Spenser, who in his *Shepherd's Calendar* lamenting the decay of poetry at these days, saith most sweetly to the same:

Then make thee wings of thine aspiring wit,
And, whence thou camest, fly back to heaven
apace, etc. . . .

A COMPARATIVE DISCOURSE OF OUR ENGLISH POETS WITH THE GREEK, LATIN, AND ITALIAN POETS

As Greece had three poets of great antiquity, Orpheus, Linus, and Musaeus, and Italy other three ancient poets, Livius Andronicus, Ennius, and Plautus, so hath England three ancient poets, Chaucer, Gower, and Lydgate. . . .

As Homer was the first that adorned the Greek tongue with true quantity, so *Piers Plowman* was the first that observed the true quantity of our verse without the curiosity of rime.

Ovid writ a chronicle from the beginning of the world to his own time, that is, to the reign of Augustus the emperor; so hath Hardyng the chronicler, after his manner of old harsh riming, from Adam to his time, that is, to the reign of King Edward the Fourth.

As Sotades Maronites, the iambic poet, gave himself wholly to write impure and lascivious things, so Skelton—I know not for what great worthiness surnamed the poet laureate—applied his wit to scurrilities and ridiculous matters; such among the Greeks were called *pantomimi*, with us, buffoons.

As Consalvo Periz, that excellent learned man and secretary to King Philip of Spain, in translating the *Ulysses* of Homer out of Greek into Spanish, hath, by good judgment, avoided the fault of riming although not fully hit perfect and true versifying, so hath Henry Howard, that true and noble Earl of Surrey, in translating the fourth book of Virgil's *Aeneas,* whom Michael Drayton in his *England's Heroical Epistles* hath eternized for an "Epistle to His Fair Geraldine." . . .

As the Greek tongue is made famous and eloquent by Homer, Hesiod, Euripides, Aeschylus, Sophocles, Pindarus, Phocylides, and Aristophanes; and the Latin tongue by Virgil, Ovid, Horace, Silius Italicus, Lucanus Lucretius, Ausonius, and Claudianus; so the English tongue is mightily enriched and gorgeously invested in rare ornaments and resplendent abiliments by Sir Philip Sidney, Spenser, Daniel, Drayton, Warner, Shakespeare, Marlowe, and Chapman.

As Xenophon, who did imitate so excellently as to give us *effigiem justi imperii* (the portraiture of a just empire) under the name of Cyrus, as Cicero saith of him, made therein an absolute heroical poem; and as Heliodorus writ in prose his sug'red invention of that picture of love in Theagenes and Chariclea, and yet both excellent admired poets; so Sir Philip Sidney writ his immortal poem, *The Countess of Pembroke's Arcadia,* in prose, and yet our rarest poet.

As Sextus Propertius said, *Nescio quid magis nascitur Iliade,* so I say of Spenser's *Faerie Queene,* "I know not what more excellent or exquisite poem may be written."

As Achilles had the advantage of Hector because it was his fortune to be extolled and renowned by the heavenly verse of Homer, so Spenser's Elisa, the Faerie Queene, hath the advantage of all the queens in the world to be eternized by so divine a poet.

As Theocritus is famoused for his *Idyllia* in Greek and Virgil for his *Eclogues* in Latin, so Spenser, their imitator in his *Shepherd's Calendar,* is renowned for the like argument and honored for fine poetical invention and most exquisite wit.

As Parthenius Nicaeus excellently sung the praises of his Arete, so Daniel hath divinely sonneted the matchless beauty of his Delia.

As everyone mourneth when he heareth of the lamentable plangors of Thracian Orpheus for his dearest Eurydice, so everyone passionateth when he readeth the afflicted death of Daniel's distressed Rosamond.

As Lucan hath mournfully depainted the civil wars of Pompey and Caesar, so hath Daniel the civil wars of York and Lancaster, and Drayton the civil wars of Edward the Second and the barons. . . .

As Joannes Honterus, in Latin verse, writ three books of cosmography with geographical tables, so Michael Drayton is now in penning, in English verse, a poem called *Poly-Olbion,* geographical and hydrographical, of all the forests, woods, mountains, fountains, rivers, lakes, floods, baths, and springs that be in England.

As Aulus Persius Flaccus is reported among all writers to be of an honest life and upright conversation, so Michael Drayton, *quem toties honoris et amoris causa nomino,* among schollers, soldiers, poets, and all sorts of people is held for a man of virtuous disposition, honest conversation, and well-governed carriage; which is almost miraculous among good wits in these declining and corrupt times when there is nothing but roguery in villanous man and when cheating and craftiness is counted the cleanest wit and soundest wisdom.

As Decius Ausonius Gallus, *in libris fastorum,* penned the occurrences of the world from the first creation of it to his time, that is, to the reign of the Emperor Gratian, so Warner, in his absolute *Albion's England,* hath most admirably penned the history of his own country from Noah to his time, that is, to the reign of Queen Elizabeth. I have heard him term'd, of the best wits of both our universities, our English Homer.

As Euripides is the most sententious among the Greek poets, so is Warner among our English poets.

As the soul of Euphorbus was thought to live in Pythagoras, so the sweet witty soul of Ovid lives in mellifluous and honey-tongued Shakespeare; witness his *Venus and Adonis,* his *Lucrece,* his sug'red sonnets among his private friends, etc.

As Plautus and Seneca are accounted the best for comedy and tragedy among the Latins, so Shakespeare among the English is the most excellent in both kinds for the stage. For comedy, witness his *Gentlemen of Verona,* his *Errors,* his *Love Labor's Lost,* his *Love Labor's Won,* his *Midsummer's-Night Dream,* and his *Merchant of Venice;* for tragedy, his *Richard the Second, Richard the Third, Henry the Fourth, King John, Titus Andronicus,* and his *Romeo and Juliet.*

As Epius Stolo said that the muses would speak with Plautus' tongue if they would speak Latin, so I say that the muses would speak with Shakespeare's fine-filed phrase if they would speak English.

As Musaeus, who wrote the love of Hero and Leander, had two excellent schollers, Thamyras and Hercules, so hath he in England two excellent poets, imitators of him in the same argument and subject, Christopher Marlowe and George Chapman. . . .

As Italy had Dante, Boccace, Petrarch, Tasso, Celiano, and Ariosto, so England had Matthew Roydon, Thomas Atchelow, Thomas Watson, Thomas Kyd, Robert Greene, and George Peele.

As there are eight famous and chief languages, Hebrew, Greek, Latin, Syriac, Arabic, Italian, Spanish, and French, so there are eight notable several kinds of poets, heroic, lyric, tragic, comic, satiric, iambic, elegiac, and pastoral.

As Homer and Virgil among the Greeks and Latins are the chief heroic poets, so Spenser and Warner be our chief heroical makers.

As Pindarus, Anacreon, and Callimachus among the Greeks, and Horace and Catullus among the Latins, are the best lyric poets, so in this faculty the best among our poets are Spenser (who excelleth in all kinds), Daniel, Drayton, Shakespeare, Breton.

As these tragic poets flourished in Greece: Aeschylus, Euripides, Sophocles, Alexander Aetolus, Achaeus Erithriaeus, Astydamas Atheniensis, Apollodorus Tarsensis, Nicomachus Phrygius, Thespis Atticus, and Tirion Apolloniates; and these among the Latins: Accius, Marcus Attilius, Pomponius Secundus, and Seneca; so these are our best for tragedy: the Lord Buckhurst, Doctor Legge of Cambridge, Doctor Edes of Oxford, Maister Edward Ferris, the author of the *Mirror for Magistrates,* Marlowe, Peele, Watson, Kyd, Shakespeare, Drayton, Chapman, Dekker, and Benjamin Jonson. . . .

As Horace, Lucilius, Juvenal, Persius, and Lucullus are the best for satire among the Latins, so with us, in the same faculty, these are chief: Piers Plowman, Lodge, Hall of Emmanuel College in Cambridge,

the author [John Marston] of *Pygmalion's Image and Certain Satires,* the author [Everard Guilpin] of *Skialetheia.* . . .

As Achilles tortured the dead body of Hector, and as Antonius and his wife Fulvia tormented the liveless corpse of Cicero, so Gabriel Harvey hath shewed the same inhumanity to Greene, that lies full low in his grave.

As Eupolis of Athens used great liberty in taxing the vices of men, so doth Thomas Nashe, witness the brood of the Harveys! . . .

As Anacreon died by the pot, so George Peele by the pox.

As Archesilaus Pyrtanaeus perished by wine at a drunken feast, as Hermippus testified in Diogenes [Laertius], so Robert Greene died of a surfet taken at pickled herrings and Rhenish wine, as witnesseth Thomas Nashe, who was at the fatal banquet.

As Jodelle, a French tragical poet, being an Epicure and an atheist, made a pitiful end, so our tragical poet Marlowe for his Epicurism and atheism had a tragical death. You may read of this Marlowe more at large in *The Theater of God's Judgments,* in the twenty-fifth chapter entreating of "Epicures and Atheists."

As the poet Lycophron was shot to death by a certain rival of his, so Christopher Marlowe was stabb'd to death by a bawdy servingman, a rival of his in his lewd love.

THOMAS CAMPION and SAMUEL DANIEL

Under the hallowed doctrine of imitation—which held, among other things, that since the ancients were peerless in imitating nature, moderns could do no better than to imitate the ancients—English humanists ever since Ascham had waged a long war on vernacular prosody. Ascham, who took his classics very seriously, bitterly denounced the rude, beggarly riming of English poets; Gabriel Harvey (and others of the so-called Areopagus in Leicester's circle) worked hard to show young Spenser the dangers of rime; Stanyhurst perpetrated a major calamity in trying to render part of Virgil in English hexameters; and though Sidney preserved a discreet neutrality in the controversy (see p. 623), he made several interesting experiments in classical meters for his *Arcadia.* In varying degrees they all endorsed Campion's position: "Old customs, if they be better, why should they not be recall'd, as the yet florishing custom of numerous [that is, quantitative] poesy used among the Romans and the Grecians?" The purists' ignorance of Middle English led them (and, much later, Dryden) to dismiss Chaucer's prosody as barbaric; and they regarded as upstart challenges to their revered elegiacs, sapphics, and hexameters the Continental forms (sonnet, *canzone,* ottava rima, terza rima, and others) that had been imported in Tottel's *Miscellany* and described in Gascoigne's *Certain Notes of Instruction* (see pp. 596–99). Such importations, sneers Campion, the products of "lack-learning times" in "barbarized Italy," make up "that vulgar and easy kind of poesy which is now in use throughout most parts of Christendom." When one remembers the steady campaign to wrench English accents to the demands of quantitative meters, Campion's *Observations* and Daniel's *Defense,* coming at the very end of the Elizabethan age, appear as documents of great importance—the one because it so ably summarized an anachronistic position, the other because it so effectively argued that position out of court. It is ironical that Campion, with one of the best ears of the age, should have marshaled his learning against the very technique that he had mastered; but at any rate he exhibits more taste than Ascham and Harvey and Stanyhurst in dismissing all English efforts to imitate classical dactylic verse as "pitiful" and "against the nature of our language." And although he is, consequently, left with only iambic and trochaic lines, he is able to endorse no less than eight meters as sanctioned by classical precept and confirmed by modern practise. Daniel's gracefully devastating reply to this pedantry is superb, not only as a refutation of Campion's eight meters but also as a *coup de grâce* to a moribund tradition and as a manifesto of literary independence. To his "adversary's" proposition that "our measures go wrong, all riming is gross, vulgar, barbarous," Daniel replies by showing that the eight types could all be accommodated within the practise of English metrics; more importantly, he justifies rime (and, by implication, all original vernacular literature) by the high sanction of both custom and nature—"custom that is before all law, nature that is above all art." With deep sincerity, and out of an obvious love for his language and its literature, he insists upon the emancipation of English writers from authoritarian precept. "Here I stand forth only to make good the place we have thus taken up and to defend the sacred monuments erected therein, which contain the honor of the dead, the fame of the living, the glory of peace, and the best power of our speech, and wherein so many honorable spirits have sacrificed to memory their dearest passions, shewing by what divine influence they have been moved and under what stars they lived." Campion's work, entered in the Stationers' Register on October 21, 1591, was published eleven years later as *Observations in the Art of English Poesie* (STC 4543); Daniel's prompt answer was inserted in the second issue of *A Panegyrike Congratulatorie,* [1603] (STC 6259). Our texts are based upon the first editions.

THOMAS CAMPION

FROM OBSERVATIONS IN THE ART OF ENGLISH POESY (1602)

The First Chapter, Intreating of Numbers in General

There is no writing too brief that, without obscurity, comprehends the intent of the writer. These my late observations in English poesy I have thus briefly gathered that they might prove the less troublesome in perusing and the more apt to be retain'd in memory. And I will first generally handle the nature of numbers. Number is *discreta quantitas,* so that when we speak simply of number we intend only the dissever'd quantity; but when we speak of a poem written in number we consider not only the distinct number of the syllables, but also their value which is contained in the length or shortness of their sound. As in music we do not say a strain of so many notes, but so many sem'briefs (though sometimes there are no more notes then sem'briefs), so in a verse the numeration of the syllables is not so much to be observed as their weight and due proportion. In joining of words to harmony there is nothing more offensive to the ear then to place a long syllable with a short note, or a short syllable with a long note, though in the last the vowel often bears it out. The world is made by symmetry and proportion and is in that respect compared to music, and music to poetry; for Terence saith, speaking of poets, *artem qui tractant musicam,* confounding music and poesy together. What music can there be where there is no proportion observed? Learning first flourished in Greece; from thence it was derived unto the Romains, both diligent observers of the number and quantity of syllables, not in their verses only but likewise in their prose. Learning, after the declining of the Romain empire and the pollution of their language through the conquest of the barbarians, lay most pitifully deformed till the time of Erasmus, Reuchlin, Sir Thomas More, and other learned men of that age who brought the Latin tongue again to light, redeeming it with much labor out of the hands of the illiterate monks and friars (as a scoffing book, entituled *Epistolae obscurorum virorum,* may sufficiently testify). In those lack-learning times and in barbarized Italy began that vulgar and easy kind of poesy which is now in use throughout most parts of Christendom, which we abusively call rime and meter, of *rithmus* and *metrum,* of which I will now discourse.

The Second Chapter, Declaring the Unaptness of Rime in Poesy

I am not ignorant that whosoever shall by way of reprehension examine the imperfections of rime must encounter with many glorious enemies (and those very expert and ready at their weapon) that can, if need be, extempore (as they say) rime a man to death. Besides, there is grown a kind of prescription in the use of rime to forestall the right of true numbers, as also the consent of many nations, against all which it may seem a thing almost impossible and vain to contend. All this and more cannot yet deter me from a lawful defense of perfection or make me any whit the sooner adhere to that which is lame and unbeseeming. For custom, I allege that ill uses are to be abolish'd, and that things naturally imperfect cannot be perfected by use. Old customs, if they be better, why should they not be recall'd, as the yet florishing custom of numerous poesy used among the Romans and Grecians? But the unaptness of our tongues and the difficulty of imitation disheartens us; again, the facility and popularity of rime creates as many poets as a hot summer flies.

But let me now examine the nature of that which we call rime. By rime is understood that which ends in the like sound, so that verses in such manner composed yield but a continual repetition of that rhetorical figure which we term *similiter desinentia;* and that, being bι t *figura verbi,* ought (as Tully and all other rhetoricians have judicially observ'd) sparingly to be us'd lest it should offend the ear with tedious affectation. Such was that absurd following of the letter amongst our English so much of late affected, but now hiss'd out of Paul's Churchyard; which foolish, figurative repetition crept also into the Latin tongue, as it is manifest in the book of *p*'s call'd *Praelia porco-rum* and another pamphlet all of *f*'s which I have seen imprinted; but I will leave these follies to their own ruin and return to the matter intended. The ear is a rational sense and a chief judge of proportion, but in our kind of riming what proportion is there kept where there remains such a confus'd inequality of syllables? Iambic and trochaic feet, which are oppos'd by nature, are by all rimers confounded; nay, oftentimes they place instead of an iambic the foot Pyr-rhicius (consisting of two short syllables), curtaling their verse, which they supply in reading with a ridiculous and unapt drawing of their speech. As for example:

Was it my destiny, or dismal chance?

In this verse the two last syllables of the word *destiny,* being both short and standing for a whole foot in the verse, cause the line to fall out shorter then it ought by nature. The like impure errors have in time of rudeness been used in the Latin tongue, as the *Carmina proverbialia* can witness, and many other such reverend bables. But the noble Grecians and Romains, whose skilful monuments outlive barbarism, tied themselves to the strict observation of poetical numbers, so abandoning the childish titillation of riming that it was imputed a great error to Ovid for setting forth this one riming verse: *Quot caelum stellas/ tot habet tua Roma puellas.*

. . . There is yet another fault in rime altogether intolerable, which is that it inforceth a man oftentimes to abjure his matter and extend a short conceit beyond all bounds of art. For in quatorzains, methinks, the poet handles his subject as tyrannically as

Procrustes, the thief, his prisoners, whom, when he had taken, he used to cast upon a bed, which if they were too short to fill he would stretch them longer, if too long he would cut them shorter. Bring before me now any the most self-lov'd rimer and let me see if without blushing he be able to read his lame, halting rimes. Is there not a curse of nature laid upon such rude poesy when the writer is himself asham'd of it, and the hearers in contempt call it riming and ballating? What devine in his sermon, or grave counselor in his oration, will allege the testimony of a rime? But the devinity of the Romains and Grecians was all written in verse; and Aristotle, Galen, and the books of all the excellent philosophers are full of the testimonies of the old poets. By them was laid the foundation of all human wisdom, and from them the knowledge of all antiquity is derived. . . .

The Third Chapter, of our English Numbers in General

There are but three feet which generally distinguish the Greek and Latin verses: the dactyl, consisting of one long syllable and two short, as *vīvĕrĕ;* the trochee, of one long and one short, as *vītă;* and the iambic, of one short and one long, as *ămōr.* The spondee of two long, the tribrach of three short, the anapestic of two short and a long are but as servants to the first. Divers other feet, I know, are by the grammarians cited, but to little purpose. The heroical verse that is distinguish'd by the dactyl hath been oftentimes attempted in our English tongue, but with passing pitiful success; and no wonder, seeing it is an attempt altogether against the nature of our language. For both the concourse of our monosyllables make our verses unapt to slide; and also, if we examine our polysyllables, we shall find few of them, by reason of their heaviness, willing to serve in place of a dactyl. . . . If we therefore reject the dactyl as unfit for our use (which of necessity we are enforc'd to do) there remain only the iambic foot, of which the iambic verse is fram'd, and the trochee, from which the trochaic numbers have their original. Let us now, then, examine the property of these two feet and try if they consent with the nature of our English syllables. And first for the iambics: they fall out so naturally in our tongue that, if we examine our own writers, we shall find they unawares hit oftentimes upon the true iambic numbers but always aim at them as far as their ear, without the guidance of art, can attain unto, as it shall hereafter more evidently appear. The trochaic foot, which is but an iambic turn'd over and over, must of force in like manner accord in proportion with our British syllables and so produce an English trochaical verse. Then, having these two principal kinds of verses, we may easily out of them derive other forms as the Latins and Greeks before us have done, whereof I will make plain demonstration, beginning at the iambic verse.

The Fourth Chapter, of the Iambic Verse

I have observed, and so may anyone that is either practis'd in singing or hath a natural ear able to time a song, that the Latin verses of six feet, as the heroic and iambic, or of five feet, as the trochaic, are in nature all of the same length of sound with our English verses of five feet; for either of them, being tim'd with the hand, *quinque perficiunt tempora,* they fill up the quantity, as it were, of five sem'briefs, as, for example, if any man will prove to time these verses with his hand:

A pure iambic: *Suis et ipsa Roma viribus ruit.*

A licentiate iambic: *Ducunt volentes fata, nolentes trahunt.*

An heroic verse: *Tityre, tu patulae recubans sub tegmine fagi.*

A trochaic verse: *Nox est perpetua una dormienda.*

English iambics pure:
The more secure, the more the stroke we feel
Of unprevented harms; so gloomy storms
Appear the sterner if the day be clear.

Th' English iambic licentiate:
Hark how these winds do murmur at thy flight.

The English trochee:
Still where envy leaves, remorse doth enter.

The cause why these verses differing in feet yield the same length of sound is by reason of some rests which either the necessity of the numbers or the heaviness of the syllables do beget. For we find in music that oftentimes the strains of a song cannot be reduc'd to true number without some rests prefix'd in the beginning and middle, as also at the close if need requires. Besides, our English monosyllables enforce many breathings which no doubt greatly lengthen a verse, so that it is no wonder if for these reasons our English verses of five feet hold pace with the Latins of six. The pure iambic in English needs small demonstration, because it consists simply of iambic feet; but our iambic licentiate offers itself to a farther consideration, for in the third and fift place we must of force hold the iambic foot; in the first,

second, and fourth place we may use a spondee or iambic and sometime a tribrach or dactyl, but rarely an anapestic foot, and that in the second or fourth place. . . .

The Ninth Chapter, of the Anacreontic Verse

. . . Thus have I briefly described eight several kinds of English numbers, simple or compound. The first was our iambic pure and licentiate. The second, that which I call our dimeter, being derived either from the end of our iambic or from the beginning of our trochaic. The third which I delivered was our English trochaic verse. The fourth our English elegiac. The fift, sixt, and seventh were our English sapphic and two other lyrical numbers, the one beginning with that verse which I call our dimeter, the other ending with the same. The eight and last was a kind of Anacreontic verse, handled in this chapter. These numbers which, by my long observation, I have found agreeable with the nature of our syllables I have set forth for the benefit of our language, which I presume the learned will not only imitate but also polish and amplify with their own inventions. Some ears accustomed altogether to the fatness of rime may perhaps except against the cadences of these numbers; but let any man judicially examine them, and he shall find they close of themselves so perfectly that the help of rime were not only in them superfluous but also absurd. Moreover, that they agree with the nature of our English it is manifest, because they entertain so willingly our own British names, which the writers in English heroics could never aspire unto; and even our rimers themselves have rather delighted in borrowed names then in their own, though much more apt and necessary. . . I will briefly recite and dispose in order all such feet as are necessary for composition of the verses before described. They are six in number, three whereof consist of two syllables, and as many of three.

Feet of two syllables:

iambic		revēnge
trochaic	as	bēautў
spondee		cōnstānt

Feet of three syllables:

tribrach		mĭsĕrў
anapestic	as	mĭsĕries
dactyl		dēstĭnў

SAMUEL DANIEL

FROM A DEFENSE OF RIME (1603)

To All the Worthy Lovers and Learned Professors of Rime within His Majesty's Dominions, S[amuel] D[aniel]

Worthy gentlemen, about a year since, upon the great reproach given to the professors of rime and the use thereof, I wrote a private letter as a defense of mine own undertakings in that kind to a learned gentleman, a great friend of mine then in court. Which I did rather to confirm myself in mine own courses, and to hold him from being won from us, then with any desire to publish the same to the world.

But now, seeing the times to promise a more regard to the present condition of our writings in respect of our sovereign's happy inclination this way, whereby we are rather to expect an incoragement to go on with what we do then that any innovation should check us with a shew of what it would do in another kind (and yet do nothing but deprave), I have now given a greater body to the same argument and here present it to your view under the patronage of a noble earl, who in blood and nature is interessed to take our part in this cause with others, who cannot, I know, but hold dear the monuments that have been left unto the world in this manner of composition, and who, I trust, will take in good part this my *Defense,* if not as it is my particular yet in respect of the cause I undertake, which I here invoke you all to protect.

Sa[muel] D[aniel]

To William Herbert, Earl of Pembroke

The general custom and use of rime in this kingdom, noble lord, having been so long (as if from a grant of nature) held unquestionable, made me to imagine that it lay altogither out of the way of contradiction, and was become so natural as we should never have had a thought to cast it off into reproach or be made to think that it ill became our language. But now I see, when there is opposition made to all things in the world by words, we must now at length likewise fall to contend for words themselves and make a question whether they be right or not. For we are told how that our measures go wrong, all riming is gross, vulgar, barbarous; which, if it be so, we have lost much labor to no purpose; and, for mine own particular, I cannot but blame the fortune of the times and mine own genius that cast me upon so wrong a course, drawn with the current of custom and an unexamined example. Having been first incourag'd or fram'd thereunto by your most worthy and honorable mother, receiving the first notion for the formal ordering of those compositions at Wilton (which I must ever acknowledge to have been my best school, and thereof always am to hold a feeling and grateful memory), afterward drawn farther on by the well-liking and approbation of my worthy lord, the fosterer of me and my muse, I adventured to bestow all my whole powers therein, perceiving it agreed so well both with the complexion of the times and mine own constitution as I found not wherein I might better imploy me. But yet now, upon the great discovery of these new measures, threat'ning to overthrow the whole state of rime in this kingdom, I must either stand out to defend or else be forced to forsake myself and give over all. And though irresolution and a self-distrust be the most apparent faults of my nature—and that the least check of reprehension, if it savor of reason, will as easily shake my resolution as any man's living—yet in this case I know not how I am grown more resolved and, before I sink, willing to examine what those powers of judgment are that must bear me down and beat me off from the station of my profession, which by the law of nature I am set to defend; and the rather for that this detractor (whose commendable rimes, albeit now himself an enemy to rime, have given heretofore to the world the best notice of his worth) is a man of fair parts and good reputation; and therefore the reproach forcibly cast from such a hand may throw down mor: at once then the labors of many shall in long time build up again, specially upon the slippery foundation of opinion and the world's inconstancy, which knows not well what it would have. . . . And he who is thus become our unkind adversary must pardon us if we be as jealous of our fame and reputation as he is desirous of credit by his new-old art, and must consider that we cannot, in a thing that concerns us so near, but have a feeling of the wrong done, wherein every rimer in this universal iland, as well as myself, stands interessed. . . .

We could well have allowed of his numbers had he not disgraced our rime, which both custom and nature doth most powerfully defend—custom that is before all law, nature that is above all art. Every language hath her proper number or measure fitted to use and delight, which custom, intertaining by the allowance of the ear, doth indenize and make natural. All verse is but a frame of words confin'd within certain measure, differing from the ordinary speech and introduced, the better to express men's conceipts, both for delight and memory. Which frame of words consisting of *rithmus* or *metrum,* number or measure, are disposed into divers fashions according to the humor of the composer and the set of the time. And these *rhythmi,* as Aristotle saith, are familiar amongst all nations and *e naturali et sponte fusa compositione;* and they fall as naturally already in our language as ever art can make them, being such as the ear of itself doth marshal in their proper rooms; and they of themselves will not willingly be put out of their rank, and that in such a verse as best comports with the nature of our language. And for our rime (which is an excellency added to this work of measure, and a harmony far happier than any proportion antiquity could ever shew us) doth add more grace and hath more of delight than ever bare numbers, howsoever they can be forced to run in our slow language, can possibly yield. Which, whether it be deriv'd of *rhythmus* or of *romance,* which were songs the bards and Druids about rimes used, and thereof were called *Remensi,* as some Italians hold; or howsoever, it is likewise number and harmony of words, consisting of an agreeing sound in the last syllables of several verses, giving both to the ear an echo of a delightful report and to the memory a deeper impression of what is delivered therein. For as Greek and Latin verse consists of the number and quantity of syllables, so doth the English verse of measure and accent. And though it doth not strictly observe long and short syllables, yet it most religiously respects the accent; and as the short and the long make number, so the acute and grave accent yield harmony. And harmony is likewise number, so that the English verse, then, hath number, measure, and harmony in the best proportion of music. . . .

Methinks it is a strange imperfection that men should thus overrun the estimation of good things with so violent a censure, as though it must please none else because it likes not them. . . .

"Ill customs are to be left." I grant it, but I see not how that can be taken for an ill custom which nature hath thus ratified, all nations received, time so long confirmed, the effects such as it performs those offices of motion for which it is imployed; delighting the ear, stirring the heart, and satisfying the judgment in such sort as I doubt whether ever single numbers will do in our climate if they shew no more work of wonder then yet we see. And if ever they prove to become anything, it must be by the approbation of many ages that must give them their strength for any operation, or before the world will feel where the pulse, life, and energy lies; which now we are sure where to have in our rimes, whose known frame hath those due stays for the mind, those incounters of touch, as makes the motion certain though the variety be infinite.

Nor will the general sort for whom we write (the wise being above books) taste these labored measures but as an orderly prose when we have all done. For this kind acquaintance and continual familiarity ever had betwixt our ear and this cadence is grown to so intimate a friendship as it will now hardly ever be brought to miss it. For be the verse never so good, never so full, it seems not to satisfy nor breed that delight as when it is met and combined with alike-sounding accents; which seems as the jointure without which it hangs loose and cannot subsist, but runs wildly on like a tedious fancy without a close. Suffer, then, the world to injoy that which it knows and what it likes. . . .

For seeing it is matter that satisfies the judicial, appear it in what habit it will, all these pretended proportions of words, howsoever placed, can be but words, and peradventure serve but to embroil our understanding; whilst seeking to please our ear we inthrall our judgment; to delight an exterior sense we smooth up a weak, confused sense, affecting sound to be unsound—and all to seem *servum pecus,* only to imitate the Greeks and Latins, whose felicity in this kind might be something to themselves, to whom their own *idioma* was natural, but to us it can yield no other commodity then a sound. We admire them not for their smooth-gliding words nor their measures, but for their inventions; which treasure, if it were to be found in Welsh and Irish, we should hold those languages in the same estimation; and they may thank their sword that made their tongues so famous and universal as they are. For to say truth, their verse is many times but a confused deliverer of their excellent conceits, whose scattered limbs we are fain to look out and join together to discern the image of what they represent unto us. And even the Latins, who profess not to be so licentious as the Greeks, shew us many times examples but of strange cruelty in torturing and dismemb'ring of words in the middest or disjoining such as naturally should be married and march together, by setting them as far asunder as they can possibly stand. . . .

I have wished there were not that multiplicity of rimes as is used by many in sonnets, which yet we see in some so happily to succeed, and hath been so far from hindering their inventions as it hath begot conceit beyond expectation and comparable to the best inventions of the world; for sure in an eminent spirit, whom nature hath fitted for that mystery, rime is no impediment to his conceit but rather gives him wings to mount and carries him, not out of his course, but, as it were, beyond his power to a far happier flight. All excellencies being sold us at the hard price of labor, it follows where we bestow most thereof we buy the best success; and rime, being far more laborious then loose measures (whatsoever is objected), must needs, meeting with wit and industry, breed greater and worthier effects in our language. So that if our labors have wrought out a manumission from bondage, and that we go at liberty notwithstanding these ties, we are no longer the slaves of rime, but we make it a most excellent instrument to serve us. . . .

Methinks we should not so soon yield our consents captive to the authority of antiquity unless we saw more reason; all our understandings are not to be built by the square of Greece and Italy. We are the children of Nature as well as they; we are not so placed out of the way of judgment but that the same sun of discretion shineth upon us; we have our portion of the same virtues as well as of the same vices. *Et Catilinam quocunque in populo videas, quocunque sub axe.* Time and the turn of things bring about these faculties according to the present estimation; and *res temporibus, non tempora rebus, servire oportet.* So that we must never rebel against use*, quem penes arbitrium est et vis et norma loquendi.* It is not the observing of trochaicques nor their iambicques that will make our writings ought the wiser. All their poesy, all their philosophy, is nothing unless we bring the discerning light of conceit with us to apply it to use. It is not books but only that great book of the world and the all-overspreading grace of heaven that makes men truly judicial. Nor can it be but a touch of arrogant ignorance to hold this or that nation barbarous, these or those times gross, considering how this manifold creature man, wheresoever he stand in the world, hath always some disposition of worth, intertains the order of society, affects that which is most in use, and is eminent in some one thing or other that fits his humor and the times. The Grecians held all other nations barbarous but themselves, yet Pyrrhus, when he saw the well-ordered marching of the Romans, which made them see their presumptuous error, could say it was no barbarous manner of proceeding. The Goths, Vandals, and Longobards, whose coming down like an inundation overwhelmed, as they say, all the glory of learning in Europe, have yet left us still their laws and customs as the originals of most of the provincial constitutions of Christendom, which, well considered with their other courses of government, may serve to clear them from this imputation of ignorance. And though the vanquished never yet spake well of the conqueror, yet even thorow the unsound coverings of malediction appear those monuments of truth as argue well their worth and proves them not without judgment, though without Greek and Latin.

Will not experience confute us if we should say the state of China, which never heard of anapestiques, crochees, and tribracques, were gross, barbarous, and uncivil? And is it not a most apparant ignorance, both of the succession of learning in Europe and the general course of things, to say "that all lay pitifully deformed in those lack-learning times from the declining of the Roman empire till the light of the Latin tongue was revived by Reuchlin, Erasmus, and More" when for three hundred years before them, about the coming-down of Tamburlaine into Europe, Franciscus Petrarca (who then, no doubt, likewise found whom to imitate) shewed all the best notions of learning in that degree of excellency both in Latin, prose and verse, and in the vulgar Italian as all the wits of posterity have not yet much overmatched him in all kinds to this day? His great volumes written in moral philosophy shew his infinite reading and most happy power of disposition: his twelve *Eglogues,* his *Africa* (containing nine books of the last Punic war) with his three books of *Epistles* in Latin verse shew all the transformations of wit and invention that a spirit naturally born to the inheritance of poetry and judicial knowledge could express; all which, notwithstanding, wrought him not that glory and fame with his own nation as did his poems in Italian, which they esteem above all whatsoever wit could have invented in any other form then wherein it is, which questionless they will not change with the best measures Greeks or Latins can shew them, howsoever our adversary imagines. . . . Hereupon [after the revival of Greek studies and the spread of printing] came that mighty confluence of learning in these parts which, returning as it were *per postliminium* and here meeting then with the new-invented stamp of printing, spread itself indeed in a more universal sort then the world ever heretofore had it; when Pomponius Laetus, Aeneas Sylvius, Angelus Politianus, Hermolaus Barbarus, Johannes Picus de Mirandula (the miracle and phoenix of the world) adorned Italy and wakened up other nations likewise with this desire of glory long before it brought forth Reuchlin, Erasmus, and More— worthy men, I confess, and the last a great ornament to this land, and a rimer. . . .

We must not look upon the immense course of times past as men overlook spacious and wide countries from off high mountains, and are never the near to judge of the true nature of the soil or the particular site and face of those territories they see. Nor must we think, viewing the superficial figure of a region in a map, that we know straight the fashion and place as it is. Or reading an history (which is but a map of men, and doth no otherwise acquaint us with the true substance of circumstances than a superficial card doth the seaman with a coast never seen, which always proves other to the eye than the imagination forecast it), that presently we know all the world and can distinctly judge of times, men, and manners just as they were; when the best measure of man is to be taken by his own foot, bearing ever the nearest proportion to himself, and is never so far different and unequal in his powers that he hath all in perfection at one time and nothing at another. The distribution of gifts are universal, and all seasons hath them in some sort. We must not think but that there were Scipios, Caesars, Catos, and Pompeys born elsewhere then at Rome; the rest of the world hath ever had them in the same degree of nature, though not of state. . . .

Let us go no further but look upon the wonderful architecture of this state of England, and see whether they were deformed times that could give it such a form: where there is no one the least pillar of majesty but was set with most profound judgment and borne up with the just conveniency of prince and people; no court of justice but laid by the rule and square of nature, and the best of the best commonwealths that ever were in the world; so strong and substantial as it hath stood against all the storms of factions, both of belief and ambition, which so powerfully beat upon it, and all the tempestuous alterations of humorous times whatsoever, being continually in all ages furnish'd with spirits fit to maintain the majesty of her own greatness and to match in an equal concurrency all other kingdoms round about her with whom it had to incounter.

But this innovation, like a viper, must ever make way into the world's opinion thorow the bowels of her own breeding, and is always borne with reproach in her mouth; the disgracing others is the best grace it can put on to win reputation of wit; and yet is it never so wise as it would seem, nor doth the world ever get so much by it as it imagineth, which, being so often deceived and seeing it never performs so much as it promises, methinks men should never give more credit unto it. For let us change never so often, we cannot change man; our imperfections must still run on with us. . . . But shall we not tend to perfection? Yes, and that ever best by going on in the course we are in, where we have advantage, being so far onward of him that is but now setting forth. For we shall never proceed if we be ever beginning, nor arrive at any certain port, sailing with all winds that blow—*non convalescit planta quae saepius transfertur*—and therefore let us hold on in the course we have undertaken and not still be wand'ring. Perfection is not the portion of man, and, if it were, why may we not as well get to it this way as another, and suspect these great undertakers lest they have conspired with envy to betray our proceedings and put us by the honor of our attempts with casting us back upon another course, of purpose to overthrow

the whole action of glory when we lay the fairest for it and were so near our hopes? I thank God that I am none of these great schollers if thus their high knowledges do but give them more eyes to look out into uncertainty and confusion, accounting myself rather beholding to my ignorance that hath set me in so low an under-room of conceipt with other men and hath given me as much distrust as it hath done hope, daring not adventure to go alone but plodding on the plain tract I find beaten by custom and the time, contenting me with what I see in use. . . .

Were it not far better to hold us fast to our old custom than to stand thus distracted with uncertain laws wherein right shall have as many faces as it pleases passion to make it, that wheresoever men's affections stand, it shall still look that way? What trifles doth our unconstant curiosity call up to contend for? What colors are there laid upon indifferent things to make them seem other then they are, as if it were but only to intertain contestation amongst men who, standing according to the prospective of their own humor, seem to see the selfsame things to appear otherwise to them then either they do to other or are indeed in themselves, being but all one in nature? For what ado have we here? What strange precepts of art about the framing of an iambique verse in our language? Which, when all is done, reaches not by a foot, but falleth out to be the plain ancient verse consisting of ten syllables or five feet, which hath ever been used amongst us, time out of mind, and, for all this cunning and counterfeit name, can or will [not] be any other in nature then it hath been ever heretofore. And this new dimeter is but the half of this verse divided in two, and no other then the cesura or breathing-place in the middest thereof, and therefore it had been as good to have put two lines in one but only to make them seem diverse. Nay, it had been much better for the true English reading and pronouncing thereof, without violating the accent, which now our adversary hath herein most unkindly done; for, being as we are to sound it according to our English march, we must make a rest and raise the last syllable, which falls out very unnatural in *desolate, funeral, Elizabeth, prodigal,* and in all the rest, saving the monosyllables. Then follows the English trochaic, which is said to be a simple verse, and so indeed it is, being without rime, having here no other grace then that in sound it runs like the known measure of our former ancient verse ending (as we term it according to the French) in a feminine foot, saving that it is shorter by one syllable at the beginning, which is not much missed by reason it falls full at the last. Next comes the elegiac, being the fourth kind, and that likewise is no other then our old accustomed measure of five feet; if there be any difference it must be made in the reading, and therein we must stand bound to stay where often we would not and sometimes either break the accent or the due course of the word. And now for the other four kinds of numbers, which are to be employed for odes, they are either of the same measure or such as have ever been familiarly used amongst us.

So that of all these eight several kinds of new-promised numbers, you see what we have: only what was our own before, and the same but appareled in forrain titles, which, had they come in their kind and natural attire of rime, we should never have suspected that they had affected to be other or sought to degenerate into strange manners, which now we see was the cause why they were turn'd out of their proper habit and brought in as aliens, only to induce men to admire them as far-comers. But see the power of nature! It is not all the artificial coverings of wit that can hide their native and original condition, which breaks out thorow the strongest bands of affectation and will be itself, do singularity what it can. And as for those imagined quantities of syllables, which have been ever held free and indifferent in our language, who can inforce us to take knowledge of them, being *in nullius verba jurati* and owing fealty to no forrain invention? Especially in such a case where there is no necessity in nature, or that it imports either the matter or form, whether it be so or otherwise. But every versifier that well observes his work finds in our language, without all these unnecessary precepts, what numbers best fit the nature of her idiom, and the proper places destined to such accents as she will not let into any other rooms then into those for which they were born. . . .

But now for whom hath our adversary taken all this pains? For the learned, or for the ignorant, or for himself to shew his own skill? If for the learned, it was to no purpose, for every grammarian in this land hath learned his *prosodia* and already knows all this art of numbers; if for the ignorant, it was vain, for if they become versifiers we are like to have lean numbers instead of fat rime. And if Tully would have his orator skill'd in all the knowledges appertaining to God and man, what should they have who would be a degree above orators? Why, then, it was to shew his own skill, and what himself had observed; so he might well have done without doing wrong to the fame of the living and wrong to England in seeking to lay reproach upon her native ornaments and to turn the fair stream and full course of her accents into the shallow current of a less uncertainty, clean out of the way of her known delight. And I had thought it could never have proceeded from the pen of a scholler (who sees no profession free from the impure mouth of the scorner) to say the reproach

of others' idle tongues is the curse of nature upon us, when it is rather her curse upon him that knows not how to use his tongue. What? Doth he think himself is now gotten so far out of the way of contempt that his numbers are gone beyond the reach of obloquy and that, how frivolous or idle soever they shall run, they shall be protected from disgrace—as though that light rimes and light numbers did not weigh all alike in the grave opinion of the wise? . . .

Here I stand forth only to make good the place we have thus taken up and to defend the sacred monuments erected therein, which contain the honor of the dead, the fame of the living, the glory of peace, and the best power of our speech, and wherein so many honorable spirits have sacrificed to memory their dearest passions, shewing by what divine influence they have been moved and under what stars they lived.

But yet notwithstanding all this which I have here delivered in the defense of rime I am not so far in love with mine own mystery, or will seem so froward, as to be against the reformation and the better settling these measures of ours. Wherein there be many things I could wish were more certain and better ordered, though myself dare not take upon me to be a teacher therein, having so much need to learn of others. And I must confess that to mine own ear those continual cadences of couplets used in long and continued poems are very tiresome and unpleasing by reason that still, methinks, they run on with a sound of one nature and a kind of certainty which stuffs the delight rather then intertains it. But yet, notwithstanding, I must not out of mine own daintiness condemn this kind of writing which peradventure to another may seem most delightful; and many worthy compositions we see to have passed with commendation in that kind. Besides, methinks, sometimes to beguile the ear with a running out and passing over the rime, as no bound to stay us in the line where the violence of the matter will break thorow, is rather graceful then otherwise. Wherein I find my Homer-Lucan, as if he gloried to seem to have no bounds, albeit he were confined within his measures, to be, in my conceipt, most happy. For so thereby they who care not for verse or rime may pass it over without taking notice thereof and please themselves with a well-measured prose. And I must confess my adversary hath wrought this much upon me, that I think a tragedy would indeed best comport with a blank verse and dispense with rime, saving in the chorus or where a sentence shall require a couplet. And to avoid this overglutting the ear with that always certain and full incounter of rime I have assay'd in some of my *Epistles* to alter the usual place of meeting and to set it further off by one verse, to try how I could disuse my own ear and to ease it of this continual burthen which indeed seems to surcharge it a little too much; but as yet I cannot come to please myself therein, this alternate or cross rime holding still the best place in my affection.

Besides, to me this change of number in a poem of one nature fits not so well, as to mix uncertainly feminine rimes with masculine, which, ever since I was warned of that deformity by my kind friend and countryman Maister Hugh Samford, I have always [10] so avoided it as there are not above two couplets in that kind in all my poem of the *Civil Wars;* and I would willingly, if I could, have altered it in all the rest, holding feminine rimes to be fittest for ditties, and either to be set certain or else by themselves. But in these things, I say, I dare not take upon me to teach that they ought to be so, in respect myself holds them to be so, or that I think it right, for indeed there is no right in these things that are continually in a wand'ring motion, carried with the violence of [20] our uncertain likings, being but only the time that gives them their power. For if this right or truth should be no other thing then that we make it, we shall shape it into a thousand figures, seeing this excellent painter, man, can so well lay the colors which himself grinds in his own affections as that he will make them serve for any shadow and any counterfeit. But the greatest hinderer to our proceedings and the reformation of our errors is this self-love whereunto we versifiers are ever noted to be especially subject— [30] a disease of all other the most dangerous and incurable, being once seated in the spirits, for which there is no cure but only by a spiritual remedy.

Multos puto ad sapientiam potuisse pervenire, nisi putassent se pervenisse. And this opinion of our sufficiency makes so great a crack in our judgment as it will hardly ever hold anything of worth. *Caecus amor sui;* and though it would seem to see all without it, yet certainly it discerns but little within. For there is not the simplest writer that will ever tell himself he doth ill, but, as if he were the parasite only to sooth his own doings, persuades him that his lines cannot but please others which so much delight himself. . . .

Next to this deformity stands our affectation wherein we always bewray ourselves to be both unkind and unnatural to our own native language in disguising or forging strange or unusual words as if it were to make our verse seem another kind of speech out of the course of our usual practise, displacing our words or investing new only upon a singularity, when our own accustomed phrase, set in the due place, would express us more familiarly and to better delight than all this idle affectation of antiquity or novelty can ever do. And I cannot but wonder at the strange presumption of some men that dare so audaciously adventure to introduce any whatsoever forrain words, be they never so strange, and of themselves, as it were, without a parliament, without any consent or allowance, establish them as free denizens in our language. But this is but a character of that perpetual revolution which we see to be in all things that never remain the same, and we must herein be content to submit ourselves to the law of time, which in few years will make all that for which we now contend *nothing.*

BEN JONSON

TIMBER

Although an artist and a profoundly learned man with a poised critical faculty, Jonson left virtually no criticism outside an occasional short preface (for example, to *Volpone*) or note (like the remarks on tragedy in *Sejanus*). We know that he wrote a preface (in dialogue, with Donne as one of the speakers) to his version of Horace's *Ars poetica;* but it perished in the fire that he immortalized in "An Execration upon Vulcan." The major source of his critical opinions, therefore, is a disorderly collection of reading-notes and commentaries—almost surely the gleanings of his commonplace-book—which was printed in the posthumous 1640 folio of his works. Entitled (probably by Jonson himself) *Timber or Discoveries Made upon Men and Matter as They Have Flowed out of His Daily Readings,* this hodge-podge has generally been regarded

as Jonson's own arrangement of his notes on his fabulously wide reading over many years. There are many different things in the collection: terse paraphrases and even translations from his beloved Latin classics, epigrams and apothegms on subjects of general interest, autobiographical fragments, tight little critical essays on those contemporaries (like Shakespeare and Bacon) whom he had known and admired, and trenchant (if usually derivative) neo-classical pronouncements on literary theory. It is the greatest pity that Jonson left no fullbreathed critical treatise like Sidney's or Daniel's; and yet the *Discoveries,* scrappy as it is, does provide an intimate glimpse of a great man of letters in an informal aspect. Our text is based upon *The Workes of Benjamin Jonson,* 1640 (STC 14753).

FROM TIMBER OR DISCOVERIES MADE UPON MEN AND MATTER (1640)

Opinion is a light, vain, crude, and imperfect thing settled in the imagination but never arriving at the understanding, there to obtain the tincture of reason. We labor with it more then truth. There is much more holds us then presseth us. An ill fact is one thing; an ill fortune is another. Yet both oftentimes sway us alike by the error of our thinking. . . .

What a deal of cold business doth a man misspend the better part of life in! In scattering complements, tend'ring visits, gathering and venting news, following feasts and plays, making a little winter-love in a dark corner. . . .

In being able to counsel others, a man must be furnish'd with an universal store in himself to the knowledge of all nature. That is the matter and seed-plot; there are the seats of all argument and invention. But especially you must be cunning in the nature of man. There is the variety of things, which are as the elements and letters, which his art and wisdom must rank and order to the present occasion. For we see not all letters in single words, nor all places in particular discourses. That cause seldom happens wherein a man will use all arguments.

The two chief things that give a man reputation in counsel are the opinion of his honesty and the opinion of his wisdom. The authority of those two will persuade when the same counsels utter'd by other persons less qualified are of no efficacy or working. . . .

I cannot think Nature is so spent and decay'd that she can bring forth nothing worth her former years. She is always the same, like herself; and when she collects her strength is abler still. Men are decay'd, and studies; she is not.

I know nothing can conduce more to letters then to examine the writings of the ancients, and not to rest in their sole authority or take all upon trust from them, provided the plagues of judging and pronouncing against them be away (such as are envy, bitterness, precipitation, impudence, and scurrile scoffing). For to all the observation of the ancients we have our own experience, which if we will use and apply, we have better means to pronounce. It is true they open'd the gates and made the way that went before us, but as guides, not commanders: *non domini nostri, sed duces fuere.* Truth lies open to all; it is no man's several. *Patet omnibus veritas; nondum est occupata. Multum ex illa etiam futuris relicta est.* . . .

Nothing is of more credit or request now then a petulant paper or scoffing verses, and it is but convenient to the times and manners we live with, to have then the worst writings and studies flourish when the best begin to be despis'd. Ill arts begin where good end.

The time was when men would learn and study good things, not envy those that had them. Then men were had in price for learning; now letters only make men vile. He is upbraidingly call'd a poet, as if it were a most contemptible nickname. But the professors, indeed, have made the learning cheap. Railing and tinkling rimers, whose writings the vulgar more greedily read as being taken with the scurrility and petulancy of such wits. He shall not have a reader now unless he jeer and lie. It is the food of men's natures, the diet of the times. Gallants cannot sleep else. The writer must lie, and the gentle reader rests happy to hear the worthiest works misinterpreted, the clearest actions obscured, the innocent'st life traduc'd. And in such a license of lying, a field so fruitful of slanders, how can there be matter wanting to his laughter? Hence comes the epidemical infection. For how can they escape the contagion of the writings whom the virulency of the calumnies hath not stav'd off from reading?

Nothing doth more invite a greedy reader then an unlook'd-for subject. And what more unlook'd for then to see a person of an unblam'd life made ridiculous or odious by the artifice of lying? But it is the disease of the age, and no wonder if the world, growing old, begin to be infirm. Old age itself is a disease. It is long since the sick world began to doat and talk idly. Would she had but doated still, but her dotage is now broke forth into a madness, and become a mere phrenzy. . . .

Expectation of the vulgar is more drawn and held with newness then goodness. We see it in fencers, in players, in poets, in preachers, in all where fame promiseth anything; so it be new, though never so naught and depraved, they run to it and are taken. Which shews that the only decay or hurt of the best men's reputation with the people is their wits have outliv'd the people's palates. They have been too much or too long a feast. . . .

Eloquence is a great and diverse thing. Nor did she yet ever favor any man so much as to become wholly his. He is happy that can arrive to any degree of her grace. Yet there are who prove themselves masters of her, and absolute lords; but I believe they may mistake their evidence. For it is one thing to be eloquent in the schools or in the hall, another at the bar or in the pulpit. There is a difference between mooting and pleading, between fencing and fighting. To make arguments in my study and confute them is easy, where I answer myself, not an adversary. So I can see whole volumes dispatch'd by the umbratical doctors on all sides. But draw these forth into the just lists; let them appear *sub dio,* and they are chang'd with the place. Like bodies bred i' the shade they cannot suffer the sun or a show'r, nor bear the open air; they scarce can find themselves, that they were wont to domineer so among their auditors; but indeed I would no more chuse a rhetorician for reigning in a school then I would a pilot for rowing in a pond. . . .

Memory, of all the powers of the mind, is the most delicate and frail. It is the first of our faculties that age invades. Seneca, the father, the rhetorician, confesseth of himself he had a miraculous one, not only to receive but to hold. I myself could, in my youth, have repeated all that ever I had made, and so continued till I was past forty. Since, it is much decay'd in me. Yet I can repeat whole books that I have read, and poems of some selected friends which I have lik'd to charge my memory with. It was wont to be faithful to me, but shaken with age now and sloth (which weakens the strongest abilities), it may perform somewhat but cannot promise much. By exercise it is to be made better and serviceable. Whatsoever I pawn'd with it while I was young and a boy, it offers me readily and without stops; but what I trust to it now, or have done of later years, it lays up more negligently and oftentimes loses, so that I receive mine own (though frequently call'd for) as if it were new and borrow'd. Nor do I always find presently from it what I do seek, but while I am doing another thing, that I labor'd for will come. And what I sought with trouble will offer itself when I am quiet. Now in some men I have found it as happy as nature who, whatsoever they read or pen, they can say without book presently, as if they did then write in their mind. And it is more a wonder in such as have a swift style, for their memories are commonly slowest; such as torture their writings, and go into council for every word, must needs fix somewhat, and make it their own at last, though but through their own vexation. . . .

Man is read in his face, God in his creatures; but not as the philosopher, the creature of glory, reads him, but as the divine, the servant of humility. Yet even he must take care not to be too curious. For to utter truth of God (but as he thinks only) may be dangerous, who is best known by our not knowing. Some things of him, so much as he hath revealed or commanded, it is not only lawful but necessary for us to know, for therein our ignorance was the first cause of our wickedness.

Truth is man's proper good, and the only immortal thing was given to our mortality to use. No good Christian or ethnic, if he be honest, can miss it; no statesman or patriot should. For without truth all the actions of mankind are craft, malice, or what you will, rather then wisdom. Homer says he hates him worse then hell-mouth that utters one thing with his tongue and keeps another in his breast. Which high expression was grounded on divine reason. For a lying mouth is a stinking pit, and murthers with the contagion it venteth. Beside, nothing is lasting that is feign'd; it will have another face then it had ere long. . . .

Nothing in our age, I have observ'd, is more preposterous then the running judgments upon poetry and poets, when we shall hear those things commended and cry'd up for the best writings which a man would scarce vouchsafe to wrap any wholesome drug in; he would never light his tobacco with them. And those men almost nam'd for miracles who yet are so vile that if a man should go about to examine and correct them he must make all they have done but one blot. . . . But a man cannot imagine that thing so foolish or rude but will find and enjoy an admirer, at least a reader or spectator. The puppets are seen now in despight of the players; [John] Heath's *Epigrams* and the Sculler's [John Taylor's] poems have their applause. There are never wanting that dare prefer the worst preachers, the worst pleaders, the worst poets; not that the better have left to write or speak better, but that they that hear them judge worse: *non illi peius dicunt, sed hi corruptius judicant.* Nay, if it were put to the question of the water-rimer's works against Spenser's I doubt not but they would find more suffrages, because the most favor common vices out of a prerogative the vulgar have to lose their judgments and like that which is naught.

Poetry in this latter age hath prov'd but a mean mistress to such as have wholly addicted themselves to her or given their names up to her family. They who have but saluted her on the by, and now and then tend'red their visits, she hath done much for and advanced in the way of their own professions (both the Law and the Gospel) beyond all they could have hoped or done for themselves without her favor. Wherein she doth emulate the judicious but preposterous bounty of the time's grandees, who accumulate all they can upon the parasite or freshman in their friendship, but think an old client or honest servant bound by his place to write and starve. . . .

I remember the players have often mentioned it as an honor to Shakespeare that in his writing (whatsoever he penn'd) he never blotted out line. My answer hath been, would he had blotted a thousand. Which they thought a malevolent speech. I had not told posterity this but for their ignorance, who choose that circumstance to commend their friend by wherein he most faulted; and to justify mine own candor, for I lov'd the man, and do honor his memory, on this side idolatry, as much as any. He was, indeed, honest, and of an open and free nature;

had an excellent phantasy, brave notions, and gentle expressions, wherein he flow'd with that facility that sometime it was necessary he should be stopp'd. *Sufflaminandus erat,* as Augustus said of Haterius. His wit was in his own power; would the rule of it had been so too. Many times he fell into those things could not escape laughter, as when he said in the person of Caesar, one speaking to him, "Caesar, thou dost me wrong," he replied: "Caesar did never wrong but with just cause," and such like, which were ridiculous. But he redeemed his vices with his virtues. There was ever more in him to be praised then to be pardoned. . . .

Some that turn over all books and are equally searching in all papers, that write out of what they presently find or meet without choice; by which means it happens that what they have discredited and impugned in one work, they have before or after extolled the same in another. Such are all the essayists, even their master, Montaigne. These in all they write confess still what books they have read last, and therein their own folly so much that they bring it to the stake raw and undigested; not that the place did need it neither, but that they thought themselves furnished, and would vent it. . . .

Knowledge is the action of the soul, and is perfect without the senses as having the seeds of all science and virtue in itself, but not without the service of the senses. By those organs the soul works; she is a perpetual agent, prompt and subtile, but often flexible and erring, intangling herself like a silkworm. But her reason is a weapon with two edges, and cuts through. In her indagations ofttimes new scents put her by, and she takes in errors into her by the same conduits she doth truths. . . .

Some controverters in divinity are like swaggerers in a tavern that catch that which stands next them, the candlestick or pots, turn everything into a weapon; ofttimes they fight blindfold, and both beat the air. The one milks a he-goat, the other holds under a sieve. Their arguments are as fluxive as liquor spill'd upon a table, which with your finger you may drain as you will. Such controversies or disputations (carried with more labor then profit) are odious, where most times the truth is lost in the midst or left untouch'd. And the fruit of their fight is that they spit one upon another and are both defil'd. These fencers in religion I like not. . . .

For a man to write well there are required three necessaries: to read the best authors, observe the best speakers, and much exercise of his own style. In style, to consider what ought to be written and after what manner, he must first think and excogitate his matter, then choose his words, and examine the weight of either. Then take care in placing and rank-ing both matter and words that the composition be comely, and to do this with diligence and often. No matter how slow the style be at first, so it be labor'd and accurate; seek the best, and be not glad of the forward conceipts or first words that offer themselves to us, but judge of what we invent and order what we approve. Repeat often what we have formerly written, which, beside that it helps the consequence and makes the juncture better, it quickens the heat of imagination (that often cools in the time of setting down) and gives it new strength, as if it grew lustier by the going back. As we see in the contention of leaping, they jump farthest that fetch their race largest; or as in throwing a dart or javelin we force back our arms to make our loose the stronger. Yet if we have a fair gale of wind I forbid not the steering-out of our sail, so the favor of the gale deceive us not. For all that we invent doth please us in the conception or birth, else we would never set it down. But the safest is to return to our judgment and handle over again those things, the easiness of which might make them justly suspected. So did the best writers in their beginnings; they impos'd upon themselves care and industry. They did nothing rashly. They obtain'd first to write well, and then custom made it easy and a habit. . . .

A master should temper his own powers and descend to the other's infirmity. If you pour a glut of water upon a bottle it receives little of it, but with a funnel, and by degrees, you shall fill many of them and spill little of your own; to their capacity they will all receive and be full. And as it is fit to read the best authors to youth first, so let them be of the openest and clearest, as Livy before Sallust, Sidney before Donne; and beware of letting them taste Gower or Chaucer at first, lest, falling too much in love with antiquity and not apprehending the weight, they grow rough and barren in language only. When their judgments are firm and out of danger, let them read both the old and the new, but no less take heed that their new flowers and sweetness do not as much corrupt as the others' dryness and squalor, if they choose not carefully. Spenser, in affecting the ancients, writ no language, yet I would have him read for his matter, but as Virgil read Ennius. The reading of Homer and Virgil is counsel'd by Quintilian as the best way of informing youth and confirming man. For besides that the mind is rais'd with the height and sublimity of such a verse, it takes spirit from the greatness of the matter, and is tincted with the best things. Tragic and lyric poetry is good too, and comic with the best, if the manners of the reader be once in safety. In the Greek poets, as also in Plautus, we shall see the economy and disposition of poems better observed then in Terence and the later, who thought the sole grace and virtue of their fable the sticking-in of sentences, as ours do the forcing-in of jests. . . .

It was well noted by the late Lord St. Alban that the study of words is the first distemper of learning, vain matter the second. And a third distemper is deceit, or the likeness of truth—imposture held up by credulity. All these are the cobwebs of learning, and to let them grow in us is either sluttish or foolish. Nothing is more ridiculous then to make an author a dictator as the schools have done Aristotle. The damage is infinite knowledge receives by it. For to many things a man should owe but a temporary belief and a suspension of his own judgment, not an absolute resignation of himself or a perpetual captivity. Let Aristotle and others have their dues, but if we can make farther discoveries of truth and fitness then they, why are we envied? Let us beware, while we strive to add we do not diminish or deface; we may improve but not augment. By discrediting falsehood truth grows in request. We must not go about like

men anguish'd and perplex'd for vicious affectation of praise, but calmly study the separation of opinions, find the errors have intervened, awake antiquity, call former times into question, but make no parties with the present nor follow any fierce undertakers, mingle no matter of doubtful credit with the simplicity of truth, but gently stir the mold about the root of the question and avoid all digladiations, facility of credit, or superstitious simplicity; seek the consonancy and concatenation of truth; stoop only to point of necessity and what leads to convenience. Then make exact animadversion where style hath degenerated, where flourish'd and thriv'd in choiceness of phrase, round and clean composition of sentence, sweet falling of the clause, varying an illustration by tropes and figures, weight of matter, worth of subject, soundness of argument, life of invention, and depth of judgment. This is *monte potiri,* to get the hill. For no perfect discovery can be made upon a flat or a level. . . .

Part IX PROSE FICTION

If, as Bernard Shaw once said, drama begins with two primitive desires, to hear a story and to have a dance, then the origins of the novel may surely be sought in the aboriginal and apparently universal fondness for tales and anecdotes. Be that as it may, there can be no doubt of the intimate relationship between Tudor jestbooks and the fiction of writers like Nashe and Deloney. However the jestbook may be defined—and Ernst Schulz's definition as a collection of comic prose tales or anecdotes contrived for the reader's entertainment is conveniently inclusive—its history in the sixteenth century is extremely complex. The hugely popular *Facetiae* of Poggio Bracciolini (1380–1459), a learned secretary to the papal curia who delighted in dressing out vernacular tales in Ciceronian Latin, was partially translated and printed by William Caxton in 1484 as *Fables of Poge the Florentine;* but there were no doubt hundreds of such tales, in many forms and languages, that never reached the dignity of print. The earliest extant Tudor jestbook is *A Hundred Merry Tales* (1525/26), a big collection of *fabliau*-like jests which Shakespeare knew and which we can still read with amusement. Its subjects are the misadventures of married women no better than they should be, clerical rascality and venality, gulls preyed upon by knaves, and similarly broad topics—all of which were plagiarized, adapted, and added to by the scores of jestbooks which poured

from the presses of Tudor publishers. As Schulz and F. P. Wilson agree, it is possible to catalogue the spate of these ephemeral pamphlets under three main rubrics: collections of detached jests like the *Fables of Poge, A Hundred Merry Tales,* and Robert Armin's *Nest of Ninnies* (1608); jest-biographies of a quasi-legendary wag like *The Merry Jests and Witty Shifts of Scoggin* (1565/66), *Merry Tales . . . by Maister Skelton* (1566/67), and *Dobson's Dry Bobs* (1607); and collections of rather complicated *novella*-like jests like *Tarlton's News out of Purgatory* (1590) and *Westward for Smelts* (1619/20). Within these broad classifications there is much diversity. *Merry Tales and Quick Answers* (1535), though generically related to *A Hundred Merry Tales,* reflects the influence of Poggio and Erasmus in capping each jest with an illustrative Latin quotation that reminds one of the medieval *exemplum;* and the collections built around Scoggin and Skelton, reminiscent of the German accretions about Till Eulenspiegel, at least suggest, if they did not actually influence, the development of such picaresque novels as Nashe's *Unfortunate Traveler* (see p. 788). To represent this sprawling body of almost sub-literary material we have chosen some of the jests that, oddly enough, came to be associated with John Skelton. Our text is based upon *Merie Tales Newly Imprinted & made by Maister Skelton Poet Laureat,* 1567 (STC 22618).

FROM MERRY TALES NEWLY IMPRINTED AND MADE BY MAISTER SKELTON (1567)

HOW SKELTON CAME LATE HOME TO OXFORD FROM ABINGTON. TALE I

Skelton was an Englishman born as Scoggin was, and he was educated and brought up in Oxford. And there was he made a poet lauriat. And on a time he had been at Abington to make merry, where that he had eat salt meats, and he did come late home to Oxford, and he did lie in an inn named the Tabor (which is now the Angel), and he did drink and went to bed. About midnight he was so thirsty or dry that 10 he was constrained to call to the tapster for drink, and the tapster hard him not. Then he cried to his ost and his ostess, and to the ostler for drink, and no man would hear him. "Alack," said Skelton, "I shall perish for lack of drink. What remedy?" At the last he did cry out and said, "Fire! Fire! Fire!"

Then Skelton hard every man bustled himself upward, and some of them were naked, and some were half asleep and amazed. And Skelton did cry, "Fire! Fire!" still, that every man knew not whether 20 to resort. Skelton did go to bed, and the ost and ostess

and the tapster, with the ostler, did wend to Skelton's chamber, with candles lighted in their hands, saying, "Where, where, where is the fire?" "Here, here, here," said Skelton, and pointed his finger to his mouth, saying, "Fetch me some drink to quench the fire and the heat and the dryness in my mouth." And so they did. Wherefore it is good for every man to help his own self in time of need with some policy or craft, so be it there be no deceit nor falshed used.

HOW SKELTON TOLD THE MAN THAT CHRIST WAS VERY BUSY IN THE WOODS WITH THEM THAT MADE FAGGOTS. TALE III

When Skelton did come to London there were many men at the table at dinner. Amongst all other there was one said to Skelton: "Be you of Oxford or of Cambridge a scholer?" Skelton said, "I am of Oxford." "Sir," said the man, "I will put you a question. You do know well that after Christ did rise from death to life it was forty days after ere he did ascend into heaven, and he was but certain times with his disciples, and when that he did appear to them he did never tarry long amongest them, but sodainly vanished from theim. I would fain know," saith the man to Skelton, "where Christ was all these forty days." "Where he was," saith Skelton, "God knoweth. He was very busy in the woods among his laborers that did make faggots to burn heretics, and such as thou art, the which dost ask such diffuse questions. But now I will tell thee more: when he was not with his mother and his disciples he was in paradise to comfort the holy patriarchs' and prophets' souls, the which before he had set out of hell. And at the day of his ascension he took them all up with him into heaven."

How the Friar Asked Leave of Skelton to Preach at Diss, Which Skelton Would Not Grant. Tale VIII

There was a friar the which did come to Skelton to have license to preach at Diss. "What would you preach there?" said Skelton. "Do not you think that I am sufficient to preach there in mine own cure?" "Sir," said the freer, "I am the limiter of Norwich, and once a year one of our place doth use to preach with you to take the devotion of the people, and if I may have your good will, so be it, or else I will come and preach against your will by the authority of the Bishop of Rome; for I have his bulls to preach in every place, and therefore I will be there on Sunday next coming." "Come not there, freer, I do counsel thee," said Skelton. The Sunday next following, Skelton laid watch for the coming of the freer, and as soon as Skelton had knowledge of the freer he went into the pulpit to preach. At last the freer did come into the church with the Bishop of Rome's bulls in his hand. Skelton then said to all his parish: "See, see, see," and pointed to the frier. All the parish gazed on the freer. Then said Skelton: "Maisters, here is as wonderful a thing as ever was seen. You all do know that it is a thing daily seen: a bull doth beget a calf, but here, contrary to all nature, a calf hath gotten a bull. For this frier, being a calf, hath gotten a bull of the Bishop of Rome." The friar, being ashamed, would never after that time presume to preach at Diss.

How the Vintener's Wife Put Water into Skelton's Wine. Tale XV

Skelton did love well a cup of good wine. And on a day he did make merry in a tavern in London, and the morrow after he sent to the same place again for a quart of the same wine he drunk of before, the which was clean changed and brewed again. Skelton perceiving this, he went to the tavern and did sit down in a chair and did sigh very sore and made great lamentation. The wife of the house, perceiving this, said to Master Skelton: "How is it with you, Master Skelton?" He answered and said, "I did never so evil." And then he did reach another great sigh, saying, "I am afraid that I shall never be saved nor come to heaven." "Why," said the wife, "should you dispair so much, in God's mercy?" "Nay," said he, "it is past all remedy." Then said the wife, "I do pray you break your mind unto me." "O," said Skelton, "I would gladly shew you the cause of my dolor if that I wist that you would keep my counsel." "Sir," said she, "I have been made of counsel of greater matters then you can shew me." "Nay, nay," said Skelton, "my matter passeth all other matters, for I think I shall sink to hell for my great offenses. For I sent this day to you for wine to say mass withal, and we have a strong law that every priest is bound to put into his chalice when he doth sing or say mass some wine and water, the which doth signify the water and blood that did run out of Christ's side when Longeous, the blind knight, did thrust a spear to Christ's heart; and this day I did put no water into my wine when that I did put wine into my chalice." Then said the vintiner's wife: "Be merry, Maister Skelton, and keep my counsel, for by my faith I did put into the vessel of wine that I did send you of today ten gallands of water. And therefore take no thought, Master Skelton, for I warrant you." Then said Skelton, "Dame, I do beshrew thee for thy labor, for I thought so much before, for through such uses and brewing of wine many men be deceived and be hurt by drinking of such evil wine. For all wines must be strong and fair and well-colored. It must have a redolent savor. It must be cold and sprinkeling in the piece or in the glass."

Thus endeth the merry tales of Maister Skelton, very pleasant for the recreation of the mind.

PAINTER, FENTON, PETTIE, and RICH

THE *NOVELLE* IN ENGLISH

The domestication, early in Elizabeth's reign, of Continental (and especially Italian) prose narratives was an event of great importance; for the translations, or free adaptations, of William Painter and then of his imitators Sir Geoffrey Fenton and George Pettie introduced a large body of foreign literature to a popular audience, provided a ground for stylistic experimentation, and supplied an arsenal of plots and characters to Shakespeare and many other dramatists. In Painter, for example, Shakespeare might have found ideas for *Lucrece, Coriolanus, Timon of Athens, All's Well,* and *Romeo and Juliet;* Webster, for *Appius and Virginia* and *The Duchess of Malfi;* Fletcher and Marston, for *The Maid of the Mill* and for *The Dutch Courtesan* and *Sophonisba.* However vehemently patriots and savants like Ascham might denounce the enervating effects of importing a glibly immoral literature in translation, the Elizabethan reading public cordially welcomed the sensationalism and the amorous complexities of the Italian *novelle;* and the success of the new form marked a significant stage in emancipating Tudor literature from dogma and didacticism.

Painter, the pioneer of the movement, began his excursions into foreign literature when, still in his teens, he translated from the Latin of Nicholas à Moffa an account of the death of the Sultan Solyman (for which he found a place in the second edition of *The Palace of Pleasure*); and in 1562, after he had been appointed clerk of her Majesty's ordnance in the Tower, the printer William Jones secured a license for *The City of Civility,* which, though now lost or never published, was perhaps an early version of *The Palace of Pleasure.* That famous book was begun, as Painter explains, as an attempt to render such stories from Livy as the translator "deemed most worthy the provulgation in our native tongue," but as he ventured onward he broadened his scope to include narratives from other sources, and when the first volume was published in 1566 it contained sixty "novels" adapted from both classical and modern writers. A second volume of thirty-four further tales appeared a year later; in 1569 the first volume was reissued; and in 1575 there appeared a complete edition "beautified, corrected, and augmented" with seven new tales. *The Palace of Pleasure* was by far the biggest book of prose tales in Tudor literature. Vigorously and simply written, with a sharp emphasis on plot and boldness of characterization, the one hundred one "novels" of the 1575 edition offered God's plenty in opening up the riches of foreign literature to Englishmen. "The lives, gests, conquests, and high enterprises of great princes," "the terrible combats of corageous personages," "the chaste hearts of constant ladies," "the ugly shapes of insolency and pride, the deform figures of incontinence

and rape, the cruel aspects of spoil, breach of order, treason, ill luck, and overthrow of states and other persons," "merry talk, sporting practises, deceitful devises, and nipping taunts"—these, as Painter copiously explains, are his subjects. As Professor Bush has shown, the "first authors and elucubrators" whom Painter rifled form an imposing gallery. Although Painter apparently never translated directly from the Greek, he drew largely on classical sources: in his book there are two tales from Herodotus, three from Claudius Aelianus, one from Plutarch's *Moralia,* twelve from Aulus Gellius, eight from Livy, three from Quintus Curtius, and one from Xenophon. For the rest, he tapped the fertile, sensuous tradition of the Italian *novella.* Boccaccio's *Decamerone* supplied sixteen tales, Matteo Bandello's *Novelle* (through the French of Belleforest or Boaistuau de Launay) twenty-six; and Giraldi Cinthio's *Hecatommithi,* Masuccio Salernitano's *Novellino,* Giovanni Francesco Straparola's *Tredici piacevoli notti,* Giovanni Fiorentino's *Pecorone,* Queen Margaret of Navarre's *Heptameron,* and others made up the remainder. As for our excerpts, "The Rape of Lucrece" was worked up from Book I of Livy's *Annales,* "Candaules and Gyges" from Herodotus (I.vii), and "Giletta of Narbona" (a source for Shakespeare's *All's Well*) from Boccaccio's *Decamerone* (III.ix). Our text is based upon *The Palace of Pleasure Beautified; Corrected and Augmented,* 1575 (STC 19123).

Compared to Painter's flowing bowl, the *Certain Tragical Discourses* (1567) of Fenton is a thin trickle indeed. The book, no doubt inspired by the success of Painter's, is a collection of thirteen tales, all adapted with precious stylistic elaboration from the French translation of Bandello's *Novelle,* Boaistuau and Belleforest's *Histoires tragiques* (1559). A young man of good birth and education, much impressed with the refinements of Continental literature, Fenton evidently resolved to achieve similar refinement in his own language, but like many other young writers intent upon elegance he succeeded in becoming only affected. As he wordily explains in dedicating his translation of a translation to Lady Mary Sidney, it was his purpose to demonstrate the advantages of both literary elegance and female chastity in presenting to his uncultivated countrymen a group of tales concerned with good ladies in distress. But his "discourses," for all their alleged didactic intent and painful sophistication of style, reveal an effeminacy of writing and a sticky lusciousness of content that are sadly remote from the blunt, robust vulgarity of Painter. None the less, the success of Fenton's collection warranted a second edition in 1579. Our text is based upon *Certaine Tragicall Discourses,* 1567 (STC 10791)

671

Fenton's unfortunate stylistic developments were carried on to something closely anticipating euphuism in George Pettie's *Petite Palace of Pettie His Pleasure* (1576), a collection of twelve "novels," of which all but one ("St. Alexius") are founded upon well-known classical stories. Addressing his collection to "gentle gentlewomen," Pettie coyly deprecates any similarity to the rough and ready Painter (whose title the publisher had shamelessly cribbed), and just as coyly admits to cultivating "new fashions in words and phrases." In spite, or perhaps because, of his style Pettie's overwritten and sentimental little book became popular at once. His use of antithesis, alliteration, simile, and a whole bag of rhetorical tricks strongly suggests a direct model for Lyly's *Euphues* of two years later; and that the Elizabethan public liked his artifice is attested by two further (undated) editions of the *Petite Palace* within four or five years. Indeed, long after Painter's work was apparently forgotten, Pettie's was twice again reprinted—in 1605 and 1613. Our text is based upon *A petite Pallace of Pettie his pleasure: Contayning many pretie Hystories,* 1576 (STC 19819).

The vogue of Italian *novelle* remained strong through the seventies and early eighties, and both in prose and lumbering verse, tales of intrigue and violence continued to find publishers and readers. George Whetstone's *Rock of Regard* (1576) presents, among other things, a versified rendition of the tale of the Countess of Celant which Painter had borrowed from Bandello, as well as a prose version of the tale of Rinaldo and Giletta; Henry Wotton's *Courtly Controversy of Cupid's Cautels* (1578) apes the plan of the *Decamerone* in presenting five tales told by three gentlemen and two ladies of Poitou; Robert Smythe's *Strange, Lamentable, and Tragical Histories Translated out of French* (1577), Whetstone's *Heptameron of Civil Discourses* (1582), and William Warner's *Pan His Syrinx* (1584, 1597) are all in the genre that Painter had made popular. *Rich His Farewell to Military Profession* (1581), from which we reprint a tale Shakespeare borrowed in *Twelfth Night,* is a representative and pleasant specimen of these later collections. In 1585 Rich, a self-educated soldier who had somehow acquired a knowledge of French and Italian, explained ruefully that he had spent thirty years in the profession of arms; but like Gascoigne, Churchyard, Turbervile, and Whetstone he had also drifted into authorship, and before he died (in 1617) he had, if we may believe him, produced some thirty-five or forty books, mainly of prose fiction and autobiographical narrative. Of these he is best remembered for *The Strange and Wonderful Adventures of Don Simonides* (1581, 1584), a two-part romance that stylistically owes a good deal to *Euphues,* and for the *Farewell,* a collection of eight tales that Rich had put together because, as he explained, "it is less painful to follow a fiddle in a gentlewoman's chamber then to march after a drum in the field." Securely buttressed fore and aft with a dedicatory epistle "To the Right Courteous Gentlewomen Both of England and Ireland," a rambling essay in autobiography addressed "To the Noble Soldiers Both of England and Ireland," an epistle "To the Readers in General," and a gossipy "Conclusion" in the form of an epilogue, the *Farewell* contains five tales (nos. 1, 2, 5, 7, 8) "forged only for delight, neither credible to be believed nor hurtful to be perused," and three "Italian histories written likewise for pleasure by Maister L. B."—an attribution that has puzzled a good many scholars, since the initials fit no Italian writer whom Rich could have known. However, it is at least probable, as Edmond Malone scribbled in his copy of the 1606 edition (now in the Bodleian), that L. B. was Lodowick Bryskett. We know that Bryskett had beguiled the time in Ireland with translating Cinthio's *Tre dialoghi della vita civile* (dialogues inserted between Decades V and VI of *Gli Hecatommithi*) and had published them in 1606 as *A Discourse of Civil Life;* and since Bryskett and Rich were in Ireland at the same time, both under the patronage of Sir Francis Walsingham and Sir Robert Cecil, it would be a plausible guess that Rich had read Bryskett's translations in manuscript. Our text is based upon *Riche his Farewell to Militarie profession: conteinyng verie pleasaunt discourses fit for a peaceable tyme,* 1581 (STC 20996).

WILLIAM PAINTER

FROM THE PALACE OF PLEASURE (1575)

To the Right Honorable, My Very Good Lord, Ambrose, Earl of Warwick, Baron of Lisle, of the Most Noble Order of the Garter Knight . . .

. . . Incensed with the generosity and natural instinct of your noble mind, I purposed many times to imploy indeavor by some small beginnings to give **your Honor to understand** outwardly what the inward desire is willing to do, if ability thereunto were correspondent. And as opportunity served (respiring, as it were, from the weighty affairs of that office [i.e. lieutenant of the Order of the Garter] wherein it hath pleased our most drad Sovereign Lady worthily to place you the chief and general) I perused such volumes of noble authors as wherewith my poor armary is furnished, and amonges other chanced upon that excellent historiographer Titus Livius. In whom is contained a large camp of noble facts and exploits atchieved by valiant personages of the Romain state. By whom also is rememb'red the beginning and continuation of their famous commonwealth. And viewing in him great plenty of strange histories, I thought good to select such as were the best and principal, wherein travailing not far I occurred upon some which I deemed most worthy the provulgation in our native tongue, reducing them into such compendious form as I trust shall not appear unpleasant. Which when I had finished, seeing them but a handful in respect of the multitude, I fully determined to proceed in the rest. But when I considered mine own weakness and the majesty of the author, the cank'red infirmity of a cowardly mind stayed my conceived purpose, and yet not so stayed as utterly to suppress mine attempt. Wherefore advancing again the ensign of courage, I thought good (leaving where I left in that author till I knew better how they would be liked) to adventure into divers other, out of whom I decerped and chose (*raptim*) sondry proper and commendable histories, which I may boldly so term because the authors be commendable and well approved. And thereunto have joined many other, gathered out of Boccaccio, Bandello, Ser Giovanni Fiorentino, Straparole, and other Italian and French authors. All which I have recueled and bound together in this volume, under the title of *The Palace of Pleasure,* presuming to consecrate the same and the rest of my benevolent mind to your Honor. . . . In these histories (which by another term I call novels) be described the lives, gests, conquests, and high enterprises of great princes, wherein also be not forgotten the cruel acts and tyranny of some. In these be set forth the great valiance of noble gentlemen, the terrible combats of corageous personages, the virtuous minds of noble dames, the chaste hearts of constant ladies, the wonderful patience of puissant princes, the mild sufferance of well-disposed gentlewomen, and, in divers, the quiet bearing of adverse fortune. In these histories be depainted in lively colors the ugly shapes of insolency and pride, the deform figures of incontinence and rape, the cruel aspects of spoil, breach of order, treason, ill luck, and overthrow of states and other persons. Wherein also be intermixed pleasant discourses, merry talk, sporting practises, deceitful devises, and nipping taunts to exhilarate your Honor's mind. And although by the first face and view some of these may seem to intreat of unlawful love and the foul practises of the same, yet, being throughly read and well considered, both old and young may learn how to avoid the ruin, overthrow, inconvenience, and displeasure that lascivious

desire and wanton will doth bring to their suitors and pursuers. All which may render good examples, the best to be followed and the worst to be avoided, for which intent and purpose be all things good and bad recited in histories, chronicles, and monuments by the first authors and elucubrators of the same. . . .

Near the Tower of London, the first of January, 1566.

By your lordship's most bounden
William Painter

To the Reader

. . . To give thee full advertisement of the whole collection of these novels, understand that six of them have I selected out of Titus Livius, two out of Herodotus, certain out of Aelianus, Xenophon, Aulus Gellius, Plutarch, and other like approved authors. Other novels have I adjoined, chosen out of divers Italian and French writers. Wherein I confess myself not to be so well trained, peradventure, as the fine heads of such travailers would desire, and yet I trust sufficiently to express the sense of every of the same. Certain have I culled out of the *Decamerone* of Giovan Boccaccio, wherein be contained one hundred novels, amonges which there be some (in my judgment) that be worthy to be condempned to perpetual prison, but of them such have I redeemed to the liberty of our vulgar as may be best liked and better suffered. Although the sixt part of the same hundreth may full well be permitted. And as I myself have already done many other of the same work, yet for this present I have thought good to publish only ten in number; the rest I have referred to them that be able with better style to express the author's eloquence, or until I adjoin to this another tome, if none other in the meantime do prevent me, which with all my heart I wish and desire; because the works of Boccaccio for his style, order of writing, gravity, and sententious discourse is worthy of intire provulgation. Out of Bandello I have selected seven, chosing rather to follow Launay and Belleforest, the French translators, than the barren soil of his own vein, who, being a Lombard, doth frankly confess himself to be no fine Florentine or trim Thoscane, as eloquent and gentle Boccaccio was. Divers other also be extracted out of other Italian and French authors. All which, I trust, be both profitable and pleasant, and will be liked of the indifferent reader. . . .

THE RAPE OF LUCRECE

Sextus Tarquinius ravished Lucrece, and she, bewailing the loss of her chastity, killed herself.

THE SECOND NOVEL

Great preparation was made by the Romains against a people called Rutuli, who had a city named

Ardea, excelling in wealth and riches, which was the cause that the Romain king, being exhausted and quite void of money by reason of his sumptuous buildings, made wars upon that country. In the time of the siege of that city the young Romain gentlemen banqueted one another, amongs whom there was one called Collatinus Tarquinius, the son of Egerius. And by chance they ent'red in communication of their wives, every one praising his several spouse. At length the talk began to grow hot, whereupon Collatinus said that words were vain. For within few hours it might be tried how much his wife Lucretia did excel the rest. "Wherefore," quoth he, "if there be any livelihood in you, let us take our horse to prove which of our wives doth surmount." Whereupon they rode to Rome in post. At their coming they found the king's daughters sporting themselves with sondry pastimes. From thence they went to the house of Collatinus, where they found Lucrece not as the other before named spending time in idleness, but late in the night occupied and busy amonges her maids in the middes of her house, spinning of wool. The victory and praise whereof was given to Lucretia, who, when she saw her husband, gently and lovingly intertained him and curteously bade the Tarquinians welcome. Immediately Sextus Tarquinius, the son of Tarquinius Superbus (that time the Romain king), was incensed with a libidinous desire to construpate and deflow'r Lucrece. When the young gentlemen had bestowed that night pleasantly with their wives they retourned to the camp. Not long after, Sextus Tarquinius with one man retourned to Collatia unknown to Collatinus, and ignorant to Lucrece and the rest of her household for what purpose he came; who, being well intertained, after supper was conveighed to his chamber. Tarquinius, burning with the love of Lucrece, after he perceived the household to be at rest and all things in quiet, with his naked sword in his hand went to Lucrece being asleep, and keeping her down with his left hand, said: "Hold thy peace, Lucrece; I am Sextus Tarquinius; my sword is in my hand; if thou cry I will kill thee." The gentlewoman, sore afrayed, being newly awaked out of her sleep and seeing imminent death, could not tell what to do. Then Tarquinius confessed his love and began to intreat her, and therewithal used sundry minacing words, by all means attempting to make her quiet; when he saw her obstinate, and that she would not yield to his request, notwithstanding his cruel threats, he added shameful and villanous speech, saying that he would kill her, and when she was slain he would also kill his slave and place him by her, that it might be reported how she was slain, being taken in adultery. She vanquished with his terrible and infamous threat, his fleshly and licentious enter-

prise overcame the purity of her chaste and honest heart; which done, he departed. Then Lucrece sent a post to Rome to her father and another to Ardea to her husband, requiring them that they would make speed to come unto her with certain of their trusty friends, for that a cruel fact was chanced. Then Sp. Lucretius with P[ublius] Valerius (the son of Volesius) and Collatinus with L[ucius] Junius Brutus made haste to Lucrece, where they found her sitting very pensive and sad in her chamber. So soon as she saw them she began pitiously to weep. Then her husband asked her whether all things were well, unto whom she said these words:

"No, dear husband, for what can be well or safe unto a woman when she hath lost her chastity? Alas, Collatine, the steps of another man be now fixed in thy bed. But it is my body only that is violated; my mind, God knoweth, is guiltless, whereof my death shall be witness. But if you be men, give me your hands and trouth that the adulterer may not escape unrevenged. It is Sextus Tarquinius, who, being an enemy instead of a friend, the other night came unto me armed with his sword in his hand and by violence carried away from me (the gods know) a woful joy." Then every one of them gave her their faith and comforted the pensife and languishing lady, imputing the offence to the author and doer of the same, affirming that her body was polluted and not her mind, and where consent was not, there the crime was absent. Whereunto she added: "I pray you consider with yourselves what punishment is due for the malefactor. As for my part, though I clear myself of the offence, my body shall feel the punishment, for no unchaste or ill woman shall hereafter impute no dishonest act to Lucrece." Then she drew out a knife which she had hidden secretly under her kirtle and stabbed herself to the heart. Which done, she fell down groveling upon her wound and died. Whereupon her father and husband made great lamentation, and as they were bewailing the death of Lucrece, Brutus plucked the knife out of the wound, which gushed out with aboundance of blood, and holding it up said: "I swear by the chaste blood of this body here dead, and I take you, the immortal gods, to witness, that I will drive and extirpate out of this city both L[ucius] Tarquinius Superbus and his wicked wife with all the race of his children and progeny, so that none of them, ne yet any others, shall reign any longer in Rome." Then he delivered the knife to Collatinus, Lucretius, and Valerius, who marveled at the strangeness of his words, and from whence he should conceive that determination. They all swore that oath and followed Brutus, as their captain, in his conceived purpose. The body of Lucrece was brought into the market-place, where the people wond'red at the vileness of that fact, every man complaining upon the mischief of that facinorous rape committed by Tarquinius. Whereupon Brutus persuaded the Romains that they should cease from tears and other childish lamentations, and to take weapons in their hands to shew themselves like men.

Then the lustiest and most desperate persons within the city made themselves prest and ready to attempt any enterprise; and after a garrison was placed and bestowed at Collatia, diligent watch and ward was kept at the gates of the city to the intent the king should have no advertisement of that stir. The rest of the soldiers followed Brutus to Rome.

When he was come thither the armed multitude did beat a marvelous fear throughout the whole city; but yet, because they saw the chiefest parsonages go before, they thought that the same enterprise was taken in vain. Wherefore the people out of all places of the city ran into the market-place, where Brutus complained of the abhominable rape of Lucrece committed by Sextus Tarquinius; and thereunto he added the pride and insolent behavior of the king, the misery and drudgery of the people, and how they which in time past were victors and conquerors were made of men of war artificers and laborers. He rememb'rd also the infamous murder of Servius Tullius, their late king. These and such-like he called to the people's remembrance, whereby they abrogated and deposed Tarquinius, banishing him, his wife, and children. Then he levied an army of chosen and piked men and marched to the camp at Ardea, committing the government of the city to Lucretius, who before was by the king appointed lieutenant. Tullia in the time of this hurly-burly fled from her house, all the people cursing and crying vengeance upon her. News brought into the camp of these events, the king with great fear retourned to Rome to repress those tumults; and Brutus, hearing of his approach, marched another way, because he would not meet him. When Tarquinius was come to Rome the gates were shut against him, and he himself commanded to avoid into exile. The camp received Brutus with great joy and triumph for that he had delivered the city of such a tyrant. Then Tarquinius with his children fled to Caere, a city of the Hetrurians. And as Sextus Tarquinius was going he was slain by those that premeditated revengement of old murder and injuries by him done to their predecessors. This L[ucius] Tarquinius Superbus reigned twenty-five years. The reign of the kings from the first foundation of the city continued two hundred forty-four years, after which government two consuls were appointed for the order and administration of the city. And for that year L[ucius] Junius Brutus and L[ucius] Tarquinius Collatinus.

CANDAULES AND GYGES

Candaules, king of Lydia, shewing the secrets of his wive's beauty to Gyges, one of his guard, was by counsail of his wife slain by the said Gyges and deprived of his kingdom.

THE SIXT NOVEL

Of all follies wherewith vain men be affected, the folly of immoderate love is most to be detested. For that husband which is beautified with a comely and honest wife, whose rare excellency doth surpass other as well in lineaments, proportion, and feature of body as with inward qualities of mind, if he cannot retain in the secrecy and silence of his breast that excelling gift and benefit, is worthy to be inaugured with a laurel crown of folly. Beauty, each man knoweth, is one of nature's ornaments, by her wisdom ordained not to enter in triumph, as victors use upon gain of victory, with bravery to ostentate their glory by sound of shalm and drum, but thankfully for the same to proclaim the due praise to the Author of nature. For there is nothing more frail and fading then the luring looks of Dame Beauty's eyes, altogether like the flaring marigold flour which in the most fervent heat of the sommer's day doth appear most glorious, and upon retire of the night's shadow appeareth as though it had never been the same. And therefore he that conceiveth rejoice in her uncertain state is like to him that in his slomb'ring dream doth imagine he hath found a peerless jewel of price inestimable, beset with glist'ring diamond; and perfectly awaked knoweth he hath none such. If God hath indued a man with a wife that is beautiful and honest, he is furnished with double pleasure, such as rather thanks to Him then vain ostentation is to be rememb'red; otherwise he doateth either in jealousy or openeth proud vaunts thereof to such as he thinketh to be his most assured friends. What joy the sequel thereof doth bring let the history insuing report.

Candaules, king of Lydia, had a marvelous beautiful gentlewoman to his queen and wife whom he loved very dearly, and for that great love which he bare her thought her the fairest creature of the world. Being in this loving concept, he extolled the praise of his wife to one of his guard called Gyges, the son of Dascylus (whom he loved above all the rest of his household, and used his counsail in all his weighty causes). Within a while after, he said unto Gyges these words: "It seemeth unto me, Gyges, that thou dost not greatly believe the words which I speak unto thee of the beauty of my wife, but because eyes be better witnesses of things then ears thou shalt see her naked." With these words Gyges, being amazed, cried out, saying, "What words be these, sir king! Methink you are not well advised to require me to view and behold the lady, my maistress, in that sort. For a woman seen naked doth with her clothes put off also her chastity. In old time honest things were devised for man's instruction, emonges which was used this one thing: that every man ought to behold the things that were his own. But, sir, I do believe assuredly that she is the fairest woman in the world; wherefore desire me not to things that be unlawful." In this sort Gyges replied, and yet feared lest some danger might happen unto him. Whom Candaules encouraged, saying: "Be of good cheer, and be not afraid that either I or my wife go about to deceive thee, or that thou shalt incur any danger. For I will take upon me so to use the matter as she by no means shall know that thou hast seen her. I will place thee behind the portal of our chamber. When I go to bed, my wife commonly doth follow. And she being in the chamber, a chair is set ready upon which she layeth her clothes as she putteth them off. Which done, she sheweth herself a good time naked; and when she riseth from her chair to go to bed, her back being toward thee, thou mayest easily conveigh thyself out again. But in any wise take heed she do not see thee as thou goest out. Whereunto I pray thee to have a special regard." Gyges, seeing that by no means he could avoid the vain request of the king, was ready at the time appointed. Candaules, about the hour of bedtime, went into the chamber and conveighed Gyges into the same, and after the king the queen followeth, whom Gyges beheld at her going in and at the putting-off of her clothes. When her back was towards him (as he was going out) she perceived him. The queen, understanding by her husband the circumstance of the fact, neither for shame did cry out ne yet made countenance as though she had seen Gyges; but in her mind purposed to revenge her husband's folly. For emonges the Lydians (as for the most part with all other nations) it is coumpted a great shame to see a naked [wo]man. The gentlewoman counterfaited her grief and kept silence. In the morning, when she was ready, by such of her servants whom she best trusted she sent for Gyges, who thought that she had known nothing of that which chanced. Being come before her presence, she said unto him: "Gyges, I offer unto thee now two conditions; take whether thou wilt. For either thou must kill Candaules and take me to thy wife and the kingdom also, or else thou must die thyself that thou mayest understand how in all things not meet to be known it is not necessary to obey Candaules. For either he must needs die which gave thee that counsail, or thyself which diddest see me naked, and thereby committed a thing unlawful." Which words for a while did

wonderfully amaze Gyges; then he besought the queen that she would pardon him from that unlawful choice. When he saw that he could not persuade her, he required her to shew him by what means he might attempt that enterprise. "Marry," quoth she, "even in that place where thou sawest me naked; when he is asleep thou shalt commit that fact." After they had devised the treason, night approached. And Gyges with stout courage bent himself thereunto, for he saw no remedy but that he must kill or else be killed. Wherefore with a dagger, which the queen delivered him, he killed Candaules when he was asleep, and so got from him both his wife and kingdom. A goodly example to declare that the secrets of marriage ought not to be disclosed, but with reverence to be covered, lest God do plague such offences with death or other shame to manifest to the world how dearly he esteemeth that honorable state.

GILETTA OF NARBONA

Giletta, a phisition's daughter of Narbonne, healed the French king of a fistula, for reward whereof she demanded Beltramo, Count of Rossiglione, to husband. The count, being married against his will, for despite fled to Florence and loved another. Giletta, his wife, by policy found means to lie with her husband in place of his lover, and was begotten with child of two sons; which known to her husband, he received her again and afterwards he lived in great honor and felicity.

THE THIRTY-EIGHTH NOVEL

In France there was a gentleman called Isnardo, the Count of Rossiglione, who, because he was sickly and diseased, kept always in his house a phisition named Maister Gerardo of Narbona. This count had one only son called Beltramo, a very young child, amiable and fair. With whom there was nourished and brought up many other children of his age, amonges whom one of the daughters of the said phisition, named Giletta, who fervently fell in love with Beltramo more then was meet for a maiden of her age. This Beltramo, when his father was dead, and left under the royal custody of the king, was sent to Paris, for whose departure the maiden was very pensife. A little while after, her father being likewise dead, she was desirous to go to Paris only to see the young count if for that purpose she could get any good occasion. But being diligently looked unto by her kinsfolk (because she was rich and fatherless) she could see no convenient way for her intended journey; and being now marriageable, the love she bare to the count was never out of her remembrance, and refused many husbands with whom her kinsfolk would have matched her, without making them privy to the cause of her refusal. Now it chanced that she burned more in love with Beltramo then ever she did before because she heard tell that he was grown to the state of a goodly young gentleman. She heard by report that the French king had a swelling upon his breast which, by reason of ill cure, was grown to be a fistula, which did put him in marvelous pain and grief, and that there was no phisition to be found (although many were proved) that could heal it, but rather did impair the grief and made it worse and worse. Wherefore the king, like one in despair, would take no more counsel or help. Whereof the young maiden was wonderful glad, thinking to have by this means not only a lawful occasion to go to Paris but, if the disease were such as she supposed, easely to bring to pass that she might have the Count Beltramo to her husband. Whereupon with such knowledge as she had learned at her father's hands beforetime, she made a powder of certain herbs which she thought meet for that disease and rode to Paris. And the first thing she went about when she came thither was to see the Count Beltramo. And then she repaired to the king, praying his Grace to vouchsafe to shew her his grief. The king, perceiving her to be a fair young maiden and a comely, would not hide it, but opened the same unto her. So soon as she saw it she put him in comfort that she was able to heal him, saying: "Sir, if it may please your Grace, I trust in God without any great pain unto your Highness within eight days to make you whole of this disease." The king, hearing her say so, began to mock her, saying: "How is it possible for thee, being a young woman, to do that which the best-renowmed phisitions in the world cannot?" He thanked her for her good will and made her a direct answer that he was determined no more to follow the counsail of any phisition. Whereunto the maiden answered: "Sir, you despise my knowledge because I am young and a woman, but I assure you that I do not minister physic by profession, but by the aid and help of God, and with the cunning of Maister Gerardo of Narbona, who was my father and a phisition of great fame so long as he lived." The king, hearing those words, said to himself: "This woman peradventure is sent unto me of God, and therefore why should I disdain to prove her cunning, forsomuch as she promiseth to heal me within a little space, without any offence or grief unto me?" And being determined to prove her he said: "Damosel, if thou dost not heal me, but make me to break my determination, what wilt thou shall follow thereof?" "Sir," said the maiden, "let me be kept in what guard and keeping you list; and if I do not heal you within these eight days let me be burnt; but if I do heal your Grace, what recompense shall I

have then?" To whom the king answered: "Because thou art a maiden and unmarried, if thou heal me according to thy promise I will bestow thee upon some gentleman that shall be of right good worship and estimation." To whom she answered: "Sir, I am very well content that you bestow me in marriage, but I beseech your Grace let me have such a husband as I myself shall demand, without presumption to any of your children or other of your blood." Which request the king incontinently granted. . . .

[The agreement made, Giletta proceeded to cure the king and exact her reward, which was, of course, Beltramo for a husband. The count, however, bitterly resented being allied to a woman not "of a stock convenable to his nobility." When the king insisted on keeping his word, Beltramo went through the ceremony with bad grace, and immediately fled to Tuscany, where he was honorably received as a soldier. Giletta meanwhile returned to Rossiglione, assumed her place as the count's lady, and quickly tidied up those public affairs which "were spoiled and out of order," thus winning the esteem of her subjects.]

This notable gentlewoman, having restored all the country again to their ancient liberties, sent word to the count, her husband, by two knights, to signify unto him that if it were for her sake that he had abandoned his country, upon retourn of answer, she to do him pleasure would depart from thence. To whom he chorlishly replied: "Let her do what she list; for I do purpose to dwell with her when she shall have this ring"—meaning a ring which he wore—"upon her finger and a son in her arms begotten by me." He greatly loved that ring and kept it very carefully, and never took it from his finger for a certain virtue that he knew it had. The knights, hearing the hard condition of two things impossible and seeing that by them he could not be removed from his determination, retourned again to the lady, telling her his answer; who, very sorrowful, after she had a good while bethought her, purposed to find means to attain the two things that thereby she might recover her husband. And having advised herself what to do, she assembled the noblest and chiefest of her country, declaring unto them in lamentable wise what she had already done to win the love of the count, shewing them also what followed thereof. And in the end said unto theim that she was loth the count for her sake should dwell in perpetual exile; therefore she determined to spend the rest of her time in pilgrimages and devotion for preservation of her soul, praying theim to take the charge and government of the country, and that they would let the count understand that she had forsaken his house and was removed far from thence, with purpose never to return to Rossiglione again. Many tears were shed by the people as she was speaking those words, and divers supplications were made unto him to alter his opinion, but all in vain. Wherefore, commending them all unto God, she took her way with her maid and one of her kinsmen in the habit of a pilgrim, well furnished with silver and precious jewels, telling no man whither she went, and never rested till she came to Florence; where, arriving by fortune at a poor widow's house, she contented herself with the state of a poor pilgrim, desirous to hear news of her lord, whom by fortune she saw the next day passing by the house (where she lay) on horseback with his company. . . .

[Giletta learns that her husband is in love with the daughter of an impoverished gentlewoman of the neighborhood; she goes to the widow, explains her situation, and offers to the mother enough "ready money" to marry her daughter honorably in return for her assistance.]

The countess' offer was very well liked of the lady, because she was poor, yet, having a noble heart, she said unto her: "Madame, tell me wherein I may do you service, and if it be a thing honest, I will gladly perform it, and the same being brought to pass, do as it shall please you." Then said the countess: "I think it requisite that by someone whom you trust you give knowledge to the count, my husband, that your daughter is and shall be at his commandment; and to the intent she may be well assured that he loveth her indeed above any other, she must pray him to send her a ring that he weareth upon his finger, which ring, as she knoweth, he loveth very dearly; and when he sendeth the ring, you shall give it unto me and afterwards send him word that your daughter is ready to accomplish his pleasure, and then you shall cause him secretly to come hither, and place me by him instead of your daughter. Peradventure God will give me the grace that I may be with child, and so, having this ring on my finger and the child in mine arms begotten by him, I may recover him, and by your means continue with him as a wife ought to do with her husband." This thing seemed difficult unto the gentlewoman, fearing that there would follow reproach unto her daughter. Notwithstanding, considering what an honest part it were to be a mean that the good lady might recover her husband and that she might do it for a good purpose, having affiance in her honest affection, not only promised the countess to bring this to pass, but in few days, with great subtilty following the order wherein she was instructed, she had gotten the ring, although it was with the count's ill will, and took order that the countess instead of her daughter did lie with him. And at the first meeting so effectuously desired by the count, God so disposed the matter that the countess was begotten with child of two goodly sons, and her delivery chanced at the due time. Whereupon the gentlewoman not only contented the countess at that time with the company of her husband but at many other times so secretly as it was never known, the count not thinking that he had lien with his wife but with her whom he loved. To whom at his uprising in the morning he used many curteous and amiable words, and gave divers fair and precious jewels which the countess kept most carefully; and when she perceived herself with child she determined no more to trouble the gentlewoman, but said unto her: "Madame, thanks be to God and you, I have the thing that I desire, and even so it is time to recompense your desert, that afterwards I may depart." The gentlewoman said unto her that if she had done any pleasure agreeable to her mind she was right glad thereof, which she did not for hope of reward, but because it appertained to her by well-doing so to do. Whereunto the countess said: "Your saying pleaseth me well, and for my part I do not purpose to give unto you the thing you shall demand in reward but for consideration of your well-doing, which duty forceth me to do." The gentlewoman then, constrained with necessity, demanded of her with great bashfulness an hundred pounds to marry her daughter. The countess, perceiving the shamefastness of the gentlewoman and her curteous demand, gave her five hundred pounds and so many fair and costly jewels as almost amounted to like valor. For which the gentlewoman, more then contented, gave most hearty thanks to the countess, who departed from the gentlewoman and retourned to her lodging. The gentlewoman, to take occasion from the count of any farther repair or sending to her house, took her daughter with her and went into the country to her friends. The Count Beltramo, within few days after being revoked home to his own house by his subjects (hearing that the countess was departed from thence), retourned. The countess, knowing that her husband was gone from Florence and retourned home, was very glad, continuing in Florence till the time of her childbed, being brought abed of two sons which were very like unto their father, and caused them carefully to be noursed and brought up; and when she saw time she took her journey (unknown to any) and arrived at Montpellier, and resting herself there for certain days, hearing news of the count and where he was, and that upon the day of All Saints he purposed to make a great feast and assembly of ladies and knights, in her pilgrim's weed she repaired thither. And knowing that they were all assembled at the palace of the count, ready to sit down at the table, she passed through the people without change of apparel, with her two sons in her arms; and when she was come up into the hall, even to the place where the count sat, falling down prostrate at his feet, weeping, saying unto him: "My lord, I am thy poor, infortunate wife, who to th' intent thou mightest retourn and dwell in thine own house have been a great while begging about the world. Therefore I now beseech thee, for the honor of God, that thou wilt observe the conditions which the two knights that I sent unto thee did command me to do; for behold, here in mine arms not only one son begotten by thee, but twain, and likewise thy ring. It is now time then, if thou keep promise, that I should be received as thy wife." The count, hearing this, was greatly astonned, and knew the ring and the children also, they were so like him. "But tell me," quod he, "how is this come to pass?" The countess, to the great admiration of the count and of all those that were in presence, rehearsed unto them in order all that which had been done, and the whole discourse thereof. For which cause the count, knowing the things she had spoken to be true, and perceiving her constant mind and good wit, and the two fair young boys, to keep his promise made and to please his subjects and the ladies that made suit unto him to accept her from that time forth as his lawful wife and to honor her, abjected his obstinate rigor, causing her to rise up, and imbraced and kissed her, acknowledging her again for his lawful wife. And after he had appareled her according to her estate, to the great pleasure and contentation of those that were there and of all his other friends, not only that day but many others he kept great cheer, and from that time forth he loved and honored her as his dear spouse and wife.

SIR GEOFFREY FENTON

FROM CERTAIN TRAGICAL DISCOURSES WRITTEN OUT OF FRENCH AND LATIN (1567)

To the Right Honorable and Virtuous Lady, the Lady Mary Sidney, Geoffrey Fenton Wisheth a Happy Encrease of Honor and Years in This Life

. . . There is required in all estates both a faith and fear in God, and also an outward policy in wordly things, whereof, according to the philosophers, the one is to be learned by perusing the Scripture and the other cannot be gotten but by the assistance of histories, who are the only and true tables whereon are drawn in perfect colors the virtues and vices of every condition of man, both their florishing time (whilest they embraced the first) and miserable fall (when they grew in delight with the wickedness of the last). If a man be a magistrate, or bear authority in public affairs, what labor is better bestowed then in searching the acts of such as have supplied equal dignity and place, to accommodate himself to their virtues? And to the private person antiquity gives choice of admonitions for obedience to his superiors, with charge to apply and employ all his care for the commodity of his country. If he be a citizen, he shall there find what belongeth to his proper office, either in the service of his public weal or in his peculiar affairs at home. And to a woman, what store of examples are there to instruct her in her duty, either for the married to keep her faith to her husband, with Lucretia, or the unmarried to defend her virginity, with Virginia. Finally, that excellent treasore and full library of all knowledge yields us freely presidents for all cases that may happen, both for imitation of the good, detesting the wicked, avoiding a present mischief, and preventing any evil afore it fall. Wherein also, as in every art there be certain special principles and rules for the direction of such as search out their disposition, so histories do swarm with examples of all kind of virtues, wherein both the dignity of virtue and foulness of vice appeareth much more lively then in any moral teaching, seeing therein is figured, under certain forms and shapes of men and their doings past, all and every such diversity and change which philosophy doth teach by way of precepts. . . . Wherein, seeing in this world the nature of man in all ages, although the singular persons be changed, remaineth still one, so also the good fortunes, felicities, calamities, and miseries which happen, both in public government and to every private state, turn always to one effect and are like those of times past; so that, by the benefit of stories presenting afore our eyes a true calendar of things of ancient date, by the commendation of virtuous and valiant persons and acts we be drawn by desire to tread the steps of their renowm. And on th' other side, considering the sinister fortune and horrible cases which have happened to certain miserable souls, we behold both th' extreme points whereunto the frail condition of man is subject by infirmity, and also are thereby taught by the view of other men's harms to eschew the like inconveniences in ourselves. Wherein, right honorable, like as I have rather touched slightly then used terms of commendation at large, according to the worthiness of so precious a jewel as the knowledge of histories—for that nowadays every man's mouth is open to commend the fruit distilling from so florishing a vine—so, for my part, being more forward then hable to discharge my zeal in that behalf, have bestowed some of my void hours, whilest I was in the other sides the sea, in forcing certain *Tragical Discourses* out of their French terms into our English phrase, presuming to commend unto your ladyship the fruits and effect of my travail; following therein the order of such as have spent time in the like study, who are wont to declare their good will by bestowing their labors. Wherewith, being unhappily denied other friendship of fortune to make good my desire in giving an unfeigned show of the duty and service I owe you and the house whereof you took your beginning, am here, upon terms of humility, for preferment of this rude and simple dedication of these forrein reapports to your Honor. . . . And albeit at the first sight these discourses may import certain vanities or fond practises in love, yet I doubt not to be absolved of such intent by the judgment of the indifferent sort, seeing I have rather noted diversity of examples in sundry young men and women, approving sufficiently the inconvenience happening by the pursuit of licentious desire, then affected in any sort such uncertain follies. For here may be seen such patterns of chastity, and maids so assured and constant in virtue, that they have not doubted rather to reappose a felicity in the extreme pangs of death then to fall by any violent force into the danger of the fleshly enemy to their honor. In like sort appeareth here an experience of wonderful virtues in men; who, albeit had power to use and command the thing they chiefly desired, yet, bridling with main hand the humor of their inordinate lust, vanquished all motions of sensuality, and became maisters of theimselves by abstaining from that whereunto they felt provocation by nature. . . . Which shall suffice for this time, good madam, for the commendation of that which is sufficiently perfect of itself, and so generally honored of all degrees that it need not th' assistance of any peculiar praise; humbly craving, for my part, a priviledge of favor at your hands, so farfurth as it may be lawful for me to lay these first fruits of my travel upon the altar already garnished with other oblations of your everlasting glory as a remembrance of an humble sacrifice which I make of my little labor and continual service vowed to your ladyship, so long as God and nature will allow my abode in this miserable vale.

At my chamber at Paris, 22 *Junii*, 1567.

Your ladyship's to command,
Geoffrey Fenton

George Turbervile in Praise of the Translator of This Book

If handycraftmen have great praise for working well,
By toiling trade, the trifling wares which they for money sell,
Then why should Fenton fear to purchase praise of men
To whom he frankly gives the gift of this, his pleasant pen?
If he his busy brow have beat for our avail,
And for our pleasure taken pains, why should his guerdon fail?
No greedy golden fee, no gem or jewel brave,
But, of the reader, good report this writer longs to have.
No man of meanest wit, no beast of slender brain,
That thinks that such a volume great is wrought with slender pain.
The thing itself declares what toil he undertook
Ere Fenton's curious file could frame this passing pleasant book.
The French to English phrase, his mother language, he,
The dark to light, the shade to sun, hath brought, as you may see.
The learned stories erst and sug'red tales that lay
Remov'd from simple common sense this writer doth display.
And what, before he took his painful quill to write,
Did lurk unknown, is plainly now to be discerned in sight.
Now men of meanest skill, what Bandel wrought, may view,
And tell the tale in English well that erst they never knew,
Discourse of sundry strange and tragical affairs,
Of loving ladies' hapless haps, their deaths, and deadly cares;
And divers things beside, whereby to flee the dart
Of vile, deceitful Cupid's bow that wounds the lover's heart.
Since this by Fenton's mean and travail thou dost gain,
Good reader, yield him earned praise and thanks for taken pain.
Then I that made this verse shall think as well of thee
As Fenton's work doth well deserve accompted of to be.

[DISCOURSE IX]
THE IMPUDENT LOVE OF THE LADY OF CHABRY WITH HER PROCURER TOLONIO, TOGETHER WITH THE DETESTABLE MORDERS COMMITTED BETWEEN THEIM

THE ARGUMENT

There was never mischief of former time nor vice in present use wherein men are, or have been, more drowned or drawn by a beastly desire then in th' execrable and deadly sin of whoredom. By the which, besides that the spiritual fornication is figured in some sort, yet is it forbidden unto us expressly by th' inviolable laws, not written in the tables where th' ancients were wont to grave directions and orders to politique states of the Romains, Athenians, Egyptians, or Spartans, but recorded in th' everlasting Book within the which the very finger of God hath sealed his infallible statutes. Whereof as he would that his children and faithful heirs of his kingdom were made partakers with desire and indeavor of imitation, so we are all warned by the same defence that, besides the wrong and harm we do to our own bodies, we offend heinously against the health of our souls, specially in corrupting the wife of our neighbor with th' abuse of that part of her which is necessary to be guarded with as great care and watch as we read was used sometime in the superstitious ceremonies of the vestals of Rome in keeping a continual fire in their temple. . . . Behold here, you ladies, a familiar profe in the black picture or portraiture of this bloody gentlewoman who, forgetting the virtue of her youth worthily renowmed of all men, could not be satisfied with th' abuse of her age and hoary hears, touching th' incestious prostitution of her body, without the number of unnatural morders wherewith you may see her tyrannous hands dyed, and th' innocent souls of her husband and two sons kneeling afore the troan of justice for vengeance of her wickedness.

If we may credit the reapports of France and Italy, we need not doubt of the singularities of Provincia which the chronicles of both countries do advouch to owe nothing to any one corner in Christendom, either for the glorious site and situation of the place, fertility and plenty of everything which pleasure or necessity can wish, rich and stately cities builded with a form of majesty more then the common sort of towns and peopled besides with every sort of civility and curtesy inhabitants. In the middest whereof is a little village called Lagrassa, planted, as it seems, in a pleasant vale, yielding a chiefest beauty and furniture of glory to the whole plat or circuit of Provincia; for it is assisted on every part with the champain, furnished with all sorts of delight both by wood and water, with a glistering glee of the green meadows, who yield such a continual fertility that, if it were not the devouring jaws of their greedy cattle, a man would think they were specially favored with a springtime at all seasons in the year. In diverse parts of this herbage, florishing with blossoms of every enticing flower, shall you see, as it were, certain close arbors and open alleys, beautified with the small sprays of limon trees, orinhges, and granades, off'ring to be thankful (with their several fruits) to strangers passing that way, with every other graft of pleasant view or taste, dispersed with such order,

both in round, quadrant, and triangle form, that only Nature herself is to be thought the chief work-woman in that mystical conveigh. . . .

In this provincial paradise, then, and not far from the said town, is a castle whereof was lord and owner a noble gentleman of the country, who, in the entry of his florishing time, married a young gentlewoman of equal honor and height of estate to himself; who, for her part, had a grace to govern the hot time of her youth with such modesty that her honest conveigh and integrity of life seemed to deserve no less then the virtue of Lucrecia, according to t' historians, or chaste abstinence of Penelope; by the fictions of the poets. But whether the secret hypocrasy of her infected mind could no longer conceal or refrain to event the fruits of such villany, or whether age had abated the former force of her husband, draining his sinews and veins of their ancient moisture, with conversion of his sap of strenght into withered humors of debility, or participating, paradventure, with the desire and disposition of such as delight in the taste of inordinate pleasure with often change of diot, having already passed the uttermost of fifty years, of a chaste and virtuous young lady became an old strumpet without honesty or shame; and whose delicate youth gave more arguments and effect of staid life then her old age hable to mortify or keep under the [privations] proper only to the folly of unbridled youth, to whom alone is due the title of fond affection, with acts of small discretion. And as the French adage advoucheth that of a young saint proceeds an old Sathan, and a timely hermit makes a tyrannous devil, so this diabolical lady, supplying the years of her youth with loyalty towards her husband, necessary prayer and invocation to God, with due respect to the order and guide of her house, was seen to make a conversion of these virtues into a desire and effect of no less detestation then the offense of Cain or other morderer; for that, without respect to the number of her children or view of hoary hairs with other arguments of age, she began to practise policies in love, wishing in her husband a continuance of that which nature cannot give twice to any man, and that whereof she seemed not half so desirous in the very heat of the flame which kindleth the sensual appetite, making us sometime exceed the order of reason in performing the sommonce of sensuality. Wherein feeling a want in her husband to satisfy her filthy thirst, and weary already with his cold comffort in bed, ent'red into devise to furnish her lack that way. Whereby, as it chanced, she wrought the web of destruction to herself, with continual infamy to her house forever. Which be the ordinary fruits of this beastly pleasure, breeding the tempest under a masque or counterfait veil of calm seas, and then to drench the passingers when they are most persuaded of assurance. And who will not confess, by this authority both familiar and true, but love is an undoubted rage and fury, seeing he forceth and giveth fire to that which ought to quench and conquer the flame kindled first by his suggestion?

This gentleman of the Castle of Chabry had for one of his next neighbors a doctor of the law called Messieur Tolonio, whom (for the credit of his learning) he used as a chief companion; by which means, also, he had the favor of familiar conference with his wife without suspicion, not refusing divers times in the absence of the knight to enter the bedchamber and consult with her upon her pillow. . . . [Such familiarity leads to disaster, for after Tolonio, with her encouragement, has seduced the Lady of Chabris he quickly falls in with her proposal that they get rid of her old husband. They agree "to procure some speedy mean of delivery or release from this loathsome torment."]

Here, besides a consummation and effect of detestable whoredom, wherein the one with impudency obtaineth a gloot of her insatiable lust and the other unhappily yields to th' unbridled will of a devilish woman, yet is the foundation laid between the two wretches to encrease their offence with an act of greater sin; for, besides the vice of contamination of another man's bed, the wicked doctor agreed to a mortal conspiracy and treason against him who was neither doubtful of his honesty nor suspicious of his faith, and whose liberality deserved a return of more credit then to weave the web of his distruction, for that his chiefest mean of sustentation grew by the fees and other assistance of the gentleman. . . . Let every man behold here an experience of the malice of those that, under the veil of good learning, bolstered with a dissembled show of a certain vain knowledge and skill to discern the good from the evil, and try the difference of the just from the unjust, do study altogether the perversion of justice, to seduce all good order and honesty, and abuse (under color of honest faith) the simplicity of the good sort. Whereof how many examples of iniquity do we see nowadays in diverse our professors of learning, whose vanity procureth so many divorcements between the man and wife, and yet they affirm, for the most part, that such acts are not tolerable, neither by th' ordinance of God, institution of men, nor any authority in the civilian school. Besides, how many are to be seen who, puffed up with a little smattering skill in either of the laws, which rather sets abroach the humor of their vanity then confirms them in good order or integrity of judgment or living, do trade only in corrupting the good and sound parts of evervone.

inducing some to sedition, other to theft, perjury, and false witness-bearing, others to habandon their country and parents, with the society and fellowship of all their friends. . . . Wherein I am moved to such a plainness touching the vanity of diverse our learned men nowadays by the sinister success and diversity of rare matters happening amongst us, and for that we see the most parts of Christendom rather tormented by such as abuse the virtue of true knowledge with desire to incense contrariety of sects then invaded with th' incursions of the blasphemous infidels and enemies of our religion.

And truly the domestical servant, in credit or trust with his maister, and evil-given or -affected towards his lord, is more to be feared then a whole army of enemies standing in battail array in the field. Whereof the Lord of Chabry may be a familiar experience by the means of this pernicious advocate; who abusing the lady, and she committing like wrong on the behalf of her husband, determined both (for the better conveigh of their abhominable life) the death of the poor gentleman. Whereunto they added th' execution with more then an ordinary speed, for this villanous lawyer practised immediately with a knave of his own disposition; who, receiving some two or three hundreth crowns with promise of further reward, consented to perform the meaning of his bloody request, attending so diligently th' assistance of convenient time and place that one morning he dogged the knight; who, walking in the fatal path of his misfortune to a warren of conies, a good distance from his castle, was soddeinly invaded by the hired enemy to his life, with one other of equal intent; who had no sooner performed their cursed charge on the unhappy gentleman but they retired in such secret manner to the place where the morder was first conspired that they were unseen of everyone, and their doings known to no man. By which means they were neither taken, and much less doubted, for any such offence; neither would any have ent'red into suspicion either against the lady or her procurer Tolonio, considering both their former credit with th' innocent now dead, and also their present sleight in coloring their late detestable traison. For the dead knight was no sooner discovered by certain passengers that way by chance but the counterfait image his wife (feigning a necligent care and desperation of herself) falleth without respect upon the disfigured and bleeding body of her husband, renting her hair and garments, watering his dead face with a whole river of feigned tears, and, as one thorowly instructed afore in the office of th' ypocrite, forgat no sort of feminine cries; sometime wringing her hands with a dolorous regard to his dead body, kissing every part of his senseless ghost, and preferring sometime a soddain scilence, forced (as it were) by her passion of secret sorrow, retired at last to a broken voice, with open exclamation against the doleful chance in this sort:

"Ah, infortunate gentleman! to whose virtuous life thy destinies have done manifest wrong in taking thee away amid the solace of thy old years, with abridgment of the rest and reappose exspected in age, and that by a train of mortal and bloody treason. . . . That I would to God I might participate with his fortune in embracing in the grave the ghost of him whose remembrance and love will never lose harbor in th' intrals of my heart till my body lie shrined within the sheet that shroods his dismemb'red corps! O cruell morderer! Whosoever thou art, what desolation am I brought unto by thy wickedness! How many floods of tears will never cease hencefurth to gush and distil upon the tomb of him whom thou hast traitorously slain! What torches, what incense, what sacrifice shall not cease to fry and burn upon the altar that covereth his guiltless bones!" . . . Wherewith the doctor, having filled all the country with hue and cry to apprehend the traitors whom he lodged within his house, was at her elbow or she wist; and, joying not a little in her artificial skill in playing that part of the tragedy whereof himself performed the first act, began to persuade her to consolation and (not without th' assistance of some suborned tears) willed her not to sorrow for that which could not be recovered. . . .

But now, the funerals performed to the dead Lord of Chabry, the lady, albeit she dismissed by little and little the greatness of her dolor, yet she ceased not her diligence in the search of the morderer, nor forgat to promise large hire to such as could bring her the ministers of the fact. There was public information and secret inquiry, with every point and circumstance so sifted to the quick that there lack'd nothing but the confession of him that was dead, which was impossible to be had, or the testimony of the bloody parties, which were the commissioners appointed to enquire of the morder; whose hands smelled of the blood of the dead innocent. Whereupon the matter was hush'd for a time. In which Tolonio was not idle to ransick every secret corner in the house, not forgetting (I think) to visit the treasor he chiefly affected, and for a simple pleasure of the which he had been so prodigal of his conscience; who, yet not satisfied with the sacrifice of innocent life, stirred up desire of greater sin. For this tyrannous widow had four sons, whereof as two of theim were continually in the house, so the eldest, jalous (not without cause) of the familiarity between his mother and her doctor—whose haunt he judged to exceed the compass of his commission and limits

of honor—could not so conceal nor disgest the conceit of that which persuaded a stain of infamy in the forhead or forefront of his house, but that he thought to belong to his duty to impart unto her the cause of his suspicion, with persuasion (in humble sort) to be indiff'rently careful to keep her former glory of virtuous life, and curious to defend the remainder of her years from worthy crime or spot of foul imputation. . . .

[The eldest son, therefore, roundly denounces his mother for her "incestuous life" with Tolonio, and threatens her with public disgrace and her lover with death: "If hereafter you become as careless of the honor of your children as heretofore you have been void of regard to your own reputation, the world shall punish the abuse of your old years with open exclamation against your lascivious order of life, devesting you of all titles of high degree; and these hands only shall send Maister Doctor to visit his process in th' infernal senate and preach in other pulpit then the highest theater within the castle of Chabry." She fears her son, but defends herself with fulsome hypocrisy: "Alas, what is he that dare undertake the defense of this desolate widow if mine own children seek to set abroach my dishonor. . . ? You grieve with the familiarity between Tolonio and me, but chiefly because we use conference now and then in my chamber. Do not you know it is he by whose counsel are guided the whole affairs of the house; or do you see his liberty enlarged since the death of your father, in whose time he practised in sort as he doth now, and yet was he never jealous of his access hether at any hour?" But even as she allays his suspicions she is plotting her son's murder.]

For th' execution whereof her wickedness devised this speedy and necessary mean. There was within the castle a high gallery, boarded underfoot with certain planks fast'ned to rotten planchers; whereas the young gentleman used his daily recreation in walking, by reason of the delightful air and pleasant prospect upon diverse fields and gardens, so the tigress his mother reserved that place as a most chief and mortal minister in the death of her son. For she and her pernicious procurer one evening knocked out of either end of diverse of the planks the nails that kept theim close to the plancher, in such sort that the next that happened to make his walk there should have no leisure to discover the traison, and much less live to bring reapport of the hardness of the rocks growing in the ditches under the said gallery. Which chanced unhappily to the son of this she-wolf; who, no more happy in a mother then his father fortunate in a wife, renewed the next day his accustomed walks in the vault, where he had not spent three or four turns but his destiny brought him to tread upon the fatal boards; who, having no hold nor stay to rest upon, disjoined theimselves with the weight of th' infortunate gentleman, who, falling soddainly upon the rocks with his head forward, was bruised to pieces, being dead indeed almost so soon as he felt th' apprehension of death. . . .

[No sooner do the two murderers thus secure their safety, as they think, than the second son makes it clear that he, too, has his suspicions. His mother, "not liking to have any tutor to note or control her villany, and hard'ned withal in th' execution of flesh and life, judged it no offence to embrue her hands with the blood of this innocent, and paint every post and postern of her castle with the brains of her posterity." Therefore she and Tolonio succeed in having the second son murdered, while hunting, by the same villains who had killed his father. And now, in spite of the fact that "her servants kept eye and watch upon her with suspicion of her vicious dealing," the widow and Tolonio resolve to marry. This decision necessitates the murder of Tolonio's wife, for he, "not ignorant of the large revenue and great sums of money of the Lady of Chabry, with store of other wealth about the castle, accompted it a commodity to exchange the life of his wife for the filthy use of so great riches; meaning, notwithstanding, to enjoy the spoils of so plentiful a prey and after to send her packing and make her pass by the path of so many morders committed both by the one and th' other." Tolonio murders his wife with his own hands, strangling "her in bed with a napking of thin holland wound fast about her neck," and explaining to the servants "that it was the soddain fall of a cold rheum, with superfluity of flegm, that had forced this mortal suffocation in his wife."]

Which was easely believed of his men, and had so stayed without further inquiry of the case if God had not awaked with the noise of the cry the aged man her father, who the same night supped with his daughter, and left her in as good estate as she was ever afore. In whom the consent of the destinies of Tolonio and the justice of the Highest seemed of indifferent operation in the view of his tragedy; for that, notwithstanding his tears and sorrow, he gave diligent regard to the face and throat of his daughter; whereof the one was swelled and pooffed up with black blood and in the other appeared a circle or print of the thing that wrought th' effect of her death. Whereupon followed a secret judgment in himself that she was distressed by mortal violence, and the defluxion which smothered and stopped the conduits of her breath were the hands of her husband, or some other by his appointment. Wherein, notwithstanding, he was so constant in dissimuling his opinion for the present that he forbare, as then, to give any show of

his grudge, attending a more fit time and opportunity for the revenge of so great a villainy, and that to the terror and example of all ages, touching such heinous abuses to their honest wives. Whereupon, willing his son-in-law to consider of the obsequies according to the merit of both their houses, he said he would go procure the company of diverse their friends in the city for the more pomp and better furniture of the funeral. . . . [Instead, the old father hastens to the "judge criminal of the place," to whom he makes a most circumstantial accusation of his wicked son-in-law. During the examination that follows, the old man's grief moves the judge "to such remorse on the behalf of the morder that, what with the scilence and other drooping arguments of guilty conscience in Tolonio (who albeit was an orator of sufficient eloquence in the senate, yet he made no one simple offer of confutation to the old man's complaint) and resolution of physicians who gave sentence against him, with judgment that her life was forced to leave her by the main strength of man, he caused the sergeants to apprehend him, sending him furthwith to embrace the bottom of a dungeon in place of his pretended marriage with the widow of Chabry." Tolonio's wife is buried with much pomp, he himself confesses to her murder and is remanded "to the court of parliament of Aix," and the Lady of Chabris prudently gathers together her jewels and flees to the castle of Pogetto in Savoy. And none too soon, for at his trial in Aix Tolonio "advouched eftsoons the points of his former confession, with the discovery of his incesteous trade with the Lady of Chabry, the abhominable morders, th' occasions of the same, and the names of theim that assisted the bloody execution. Whereupon the sentence of that court dismissed him to Lagrassa to be pinched with th' extremity of every torture and rack appointed to torment offenders." In prison, awaiting execution, his remorse is horrible.]

"Respect not, O Lord, the number of my faults, for that they exceed computation, nor deal not with me according to the greatness of the least of theim, for that (without th' assistance of thy special goodness) hell is the reward and merit of my wicked life. Which I wish may work a warning to all degrees of equal disposition to myself that, although they feed for a time of a flattering pleasure or favor of this world, yet seeing their iniquities in th' end are discovered by themselves, whereby they are sure to receive (with me) the hire of their evil by an infamous death, I wish them stand in awe of th' infallible judgment, and pray with the prophet to participate in the general satisfaction which the death of His Son hath made for all flesh, fallen for want of grace in the first man, whose faults have been already purified by the blood of that most innocent Lamb into whose hands I commend my penitent sprite." In th' end of which prayer he was drawn out of the prison and led to the theater of public execution, where he received the reward of his bad life by a worthy death, to the special contentment of his father-in-law and general joy of all the ladies and gentlewomen of the country except the miserable widow of Chabry, who, being adjorned and not appearing, accordingly was condemned and executed by figure, according to the custom in France in that behalf. Whereof she was made to understand by some secret spy, who also warned her of the diligent inquisition and means that were made to find her, to th' end justice might pass upon her. Whereupon, doubting either assurance or savety at Pogetto, went to Jeynes with one man only called Jacques Pallyero, who, somewhat jealous of the coming away of his mistress, or rather fearing in the end to be partaker of the punishment of her wicked life, made no conscience one day, as she was in her devotions in the church, to rob her of every part and parcel of her money and jewels, with other necessaries, saving such as she ware about her; which was such a corsay of secret and fretting grief for the time that she was at point to admit th' offer of dispair. Albeit, being already ent'red into repentance and judging that misfortune of little or no value in respect of th' infinite abuses of her former time, gave God thanks for his visitation, and ent'ring into devise for means to

support the residue of her years, addressed her to an ancient widow; to whom as she accompts her present necessity proceeding of the villainy of her man—without any mention (I am sure) of her detestable trade past, or cause of her present being there—so she found such favor in this matron that, in respect of her show of honest behavior and gravity, arguing her discent from nobility, she committed unto her the government and bringing-up of her daughters. In which trade she ended very poorly, albeit with more honor then she deserved, her unhappy days.

Here you see the misery of this wretch, who erst hath commanded over a household of servants and gentlewomen at her beck, is now brought to live under the awe of one inferior to her house and calling; and who, passing her youth with all pomp and delicate nouriture and now drawing to th' end of her years, is forced to an experience of continual exile, subject to the will and pleasure of another, and press'd (as she did indeed) to die out of her country without the company or comfort of any her friends to close her eyes, or couch her bones in other shrine or sepulcher, then by th' appointment of strangers. Wherein, certainly, appeareth rightly the infallible judgment of God, who, forsaken of such as yield honor to their proper desires, suff'reth theim also to fall in such sort that in the end they are constrained to confess their faults, with detestation of their sin, when they feel his just vengeance poured upon theim. . . .

GEORGE PETTIE

FROM A PETITE PALACE OF PETTIE HIS PLEASURE CONTAINING MANY PRETTY HISTORIES BY HIM SET FORTH IN COMELY COLORS AND MOST DELIGHTFULLY DISCOURSED (1576)

To the Gentle Gentlewomen Readers

Gentle readers, whom by my will I would have only gentlewomen and therefore to you I direct my words, may it please you to understand that the great desire I have to procure your delight hath caused me somewhat to transgress the bounds of faithful friendship; for having with great earnestness obtained of my very friend Master George Pettie the copy of certain histories by himself, upon his own and certain of his friends' private occasions, drawn into discourses, I saw such witty and pithy pleasantness contained in them that I thought I could not any way do greater pleasure or better service to your noble sex then to publish them in print, to your common profit and pleasure. And though I am sure hereby to incur his displeasure, for that he willed me

in any wise to keep them secret, yet if it please you thankfully to accept my good will I force the less of his ill will. For to speak my fancy without feigning, I care not to displease twenty men to please one woman; for the friendship amongst men is to be counted but cold kindness in respect of the fervent affection between men and women; and our nature is rather to dote of women then to love men. And yet it lieth in your powers so to think of his doings, and to yield him such courteous consideration for the same, that he shall have more cause to thank me then think ill of my faithless dealing towards him. Which if your courtesies shall perform, you shall increase my duty towards you and his good will towards me; you shall make me shew my will and him his skill another time to pleasure you; you shall bind both of us to remain ready at your commandments. For mine own part, I can challenge no part of praise or thanks for this work, for that I have taken no pains therein neither by adding argument, note, or anything, but even have set them forth as they were sent me; only I have christened them with the name of a *Palace of Pleasure.* I dare not compare this work with the former *Palaces of Pleasure* because comparisons are odious and because they contain histories translated out of grave authors and learned writers, and this containeth discourses devised by a green, youthful capacity and reported in a manner extempore, as I myself for divers of them am able to testify. I dare not commend them because I am partial; I dare dedicate them to you, gentlewomen, because you are curteous. And that you may the better understand the drift of these devices I have caused the letter also which my friend sent me with this work to be set down to your sight. Thus commending mine own faithless enterprise and my friend's fruitful labor and learning to your courteous protection, I wish you all beauty with bounty and comeliness with curtesy. From my lodging in Fleet Street.

Yours readily to command,
R. B.

The Letter of G. P. to R. B. Concerning This Work

Forced by your earnest importunity and furthered by mine own idle opportunity, I have set down in writing, and according to your request sent unto you, certain of those tragical trifles which you have heard me in sundry companies at sundry times report, and so near as I could I have written them word for word as I then told them; but if any of them seem better unto you now then they did then, you must attribute it to my lisping lips, which perchance did somewhat disgrace the grace of them; and if any seem worse now then than, you must impute it to this, that perchance there was then some Pallas in place which furthered my invention. . . . If you like not of some words and phrases used contrary to their common custom, you must think that, seeing we allow of new fashions in cutting of beards, in long-waisted doublets, in little short hose, in great caps, in low hats, and almost in all things, it is as much reason we should allow of new fashions in phrases and words. But these faults, or whatsoever else, I care not to excuse unto you, who are the only cause I committed them, by your earnest desire to have me set down these trifles in writing. And as my words hitherto have tended to this end, that you should take these trifles well, so now I am to exhort you that you will use them well; that with the spider you suck not out poison out of them, that by some light example you be not the sooner incited to lightness. For believe me—I speak it friendly, therefore take it friendly—I think it more needful to send you a bridle then a spur that way. . . .

From my lodging in Holborn this twelfth of July.

G. P.

ADMETUS AND ALCEST

Admetus, son to Atys, king of Lybia, falling in love with Alcest, daughter to Lycabas, king of Assur, who recompensed him with semblable affection, are restrained each from other by their parents, but being secretly married, wander in wildernesses like poor pilgrims. Atys shortly after dieth, whereof Admetus, being advertised, returneth with his wife and is established in the kingdom. The Destinies grant him a double date of life if he can find one to die for him, which Alcest herself performeth; for whose death Admetus most wofully lamenting, she was eftsoons by Proserpina restored to her life and lover again.

It is a saying no less common then commonly proved true that marriages are guided by destiny; and, amongst all the contracts which concern the life of man, I think they only be not in our own power or pleasure. Which may plainly appear by this, that when the choice of such marriages doth chance unto us as we ourselves can wish, when they may by their parents and friends countenance us, by their dowry and portion profit us, by their person and beauty pleasure us, by their virtue and perfection every way place us in paradise, yet it is often seen that we set little by them, neither make any account of such profitable proffers, but by a contrary course of the heavens and Destinies are carried, as it were against our wills, some other way and caused to settle in affection there where heaven and earth seem to withstand our desire, where friends frown on us, where wealth wants, where there is neither felicity in pursuing, neither felicity in possessing; which the history which you shall hear shall more plainly set forth unto you.

There reigned in the land of Lybia one Atys, who had to his neighbor, more near then was necessary, one Lycabas, king of Assur; which princes, rather coveting their neighbors' dominions then contenting themselves with their own, incroached each one upon other's right and continued continual war one against the other. But at length Atys, whether he were wearied and wasted with war, or whether he had occasion to bend his force some other way, or whether he were disposed to enter into league and amity with his neighbors, I know not; but he sent his one son Admetus to Lycabas to parley of a peace. Now Lycabas, either thinking he had him at some advantage, either not minding to put up injuries before received, would accept no conditions of peace, but by Admetus sent his father flat defiance. So that the war continued between them in as great rage as it had done the former time of their reign. But yet hate caused not such hot skirmishes between the parents but that love forced as fierce assaults between the children. For it was so that Lycabas had a daughter named Alcest, who, what time Admetus was in her father's court to intreat of peace, chanced out at her chamber window to have a sight of him, and he at the same time happened to incounter a view of her. And as small drops of rain ingender great floods, and as of little seeds grow great trees, so of this little look and sight grew such great love and delight that death itself could not dissolve it. For as women be of delicate and fine metal and therefore soon subject to love, so Alcest after this first sight was so overgone in good will towards Admetus that she fixed her only felicity in framing in her fancy the form of his face, and printing in her heart the perfection of his person. And as nothing breedeth bane to the body sooner then trouble of mind, so she persevered so long in such pensive passions and careful cogitations that her body was brought so low for lack of the use of sleep and meat that she was fain to keep her bed; and by reason that she covertly concealed her grief, it burned so furiously within her that it had almost clean consumed her away. Her father, seeing her in this heavy case, assembled all the learned phisitions he could learn of in the country, who, having seen her, were all altogether ignorant of her disease, and were at their wits' end what medicine to apply to her malady. Some thought it a consumption, some a burning fever, some a melancholy humor, some one thing, some another. And her father examining her how it held her and what disease she thought it to be, she answered that it was a sickness which it pleased God to send her, and that it was not in the help of physic to heal her, but her health was only to be had at God's hands. Now Admetus, on the other side, having the proffer of many princes made him in the way of marriage, made very careless account thereof, and seemed in his mind to be very angry with those offers; and as the sight of meat is very loathsome to him whose stomach is ill or hath already eaten his fill, so that little sight which he had of Alcest had fed his fancy so full that to see, or so much as think, of any other woman was most grievous unto him. And notwithstanding the griping pain of love caused some grafts of grief to begin to grow in his heart, yet, by reason that he had the conducting of the army royal under his father, he was so busily occupied that he had no great leisure to lodge any loving thoughts within his breast. But see how the Destinies dealt to drive this bargain thorow! There arose a quarrel between the two armies touching certain points wherein the law of arms was thought to be broken, to decide which controversy Admetus was sent post to Lycabas, who, sitting by his daughter's bedside, had word brought him that Admetus was come to the court to impart matters of importance unto him. Now at this instant there chanced one of the phisitions to hold Alcest by the arm and to feel her pulses, and where before they beat very feebly as if she had been ready to yield to the sommance of death, she no sooner heard that message brought up to her father but that her pulses began to beat with great force and liveliness; which the phisition, perceiving, persuaded himself he had found the cause of her calamity; but for more assured proof he whistered the king in the ear, desiring him that Admetus might be sent for thither, and there to make relation of his message unto him; which the king caused to be done accordingly. Admetus was no sooner admitted into the chamber but her pulses began to beat again with wonderful swiftness, and so continued all the while he was in the chamber. Who, seeing his love in such danger of her life, though he understood not the cause thereof, yet he cast such a careful countenance towards her that she easely perceived he did participate in pain with her; which made her cast such glances of good will towards him that he easely understood it was for his sake she sustained such sorrow and sickness. But the fear of her father, who was his mortal foe, and the urgent necessity of his affairs forced him to depart without manifesting unto her the manifold good will he bare her. And though his departure were little better then death to the damsel, yet for that she knew her love to be incount'red with like affection, whereof before she stood in doubt, she began to drive away the dark clouds of dispair and to suffer the bright light of hope to shine upon her. . . .

[When the king learns from the physician the true nature of Alcest's illness he is "mervailously disquieted," but neither by "sharp threat'nings" nor by "gentle persuasions" is he able to check her passion for Admetus. Indeed, Alcest writes her lover, begging forgiveness for refusing to stand "upon the nice terms of my maiden's estate" lest they both "pine away in pain for lack of being privy to each other's mind and purpose," offering herself as his "lawful and loving spouse," and promising to steal away secretly "to what place you will have me." Admetus, receiving this letter just after a stormy interview with his father (who angrily refuses to countenance the love affair), answers her with flowing rhetoric: "If Croesus came and offered me all his wealth, if Alexander yielded me his empire, if Juno came from heaven with her kingdoms, Pallas with her wisdom, or Venus with her Helen, assure thyself, sweet mistress, that neither any one of them, neither all of them together, should be so gratefully or gladly received of me as the proffer which your letters have made me. . . . If it please you so much to dishonor yourself and to do me so much honor as meet me the tenth of this moneth at the chapel of Diana, standing, as you know, six leagues from your father's court, I will there, God willing, meet you, and a priest with me to marry us; which done, we will shift ourselves into pilgrims' apparel, and so disguised indure together such fortune as the fates shall assign us." The lovers meet and marry according to plan, and then, in their pilgrims' weeds, go "hand in hand, and heart in heart, wailfully and wilfully, wand'ring out of their own native country to avoid their parents' punishment and displeasure."]

O lamentable lots of love, which drave two princes from their pleasant palaices, from their flourishing friends, from their train of servants, from their sumptuous fare, from their gorgeous garments, from variety of delights, from secure quietness, yea, from heavenly happiness, to wild wilderness, to desert dens, to careful caves, to hard cheer with haws and hips, to pilgrims' pelts, to peril of spoiling, to danger of devouring, to misery of mind, to affliction of body, yea, to hellish heaviness! O pitiless parents, to prefer their own hate before their children's love, their own displeasures before their children's pleasure; to forget that themselves were once young and subject to love, to measure the fiery flames of youth by the dead coals of age, to govern their children by their own lust which now is, not which was in times past, to seek to alter their natural affection from their children upon so light a cause, shewing themselves rebels to nature, to indeavor to undo the Destinies and disappoint the appointment of the gods, shewing themselves traitors to the gods. But the one of them, the father of Admetus, reaped the just reward of his rigor. For Atys, after the departure of his son, took the matter very heavily, abandoned all pleasures, avoided all company, and spent most part of his time in discoursing with himself in this sorrowful sort:

"If nature, by the devine providence of God, did not move us to the maintenance of mankind, surely the charge of children is such a heavy burthen that it would fear men from ent'ring into the holy state of matrimony. For to omit the inconveniences of their infancy, which are infinite, when they draw once to man's estate, what time they should be a stay to our staggering state, good God, what troubles do they torment us with! What cares do they consume us with! What annoys do they afflict our old years withal! They say we are renewed and revived, as it were, in our offspring, but we may say we die daily in thinking of the desperate deeds of our children. And as the spider feeleth if her web be prick'd but with the point of a pin, so if our children be touched but with the least trouble that is, we feel the force of it to pierce us to the heart. . . . My son—ah, why do I call him son?—hath not only wish'd my death, but wrought it. He knew he was my only delight; he knew I could not live, he being out of my sight; he knew his desperate disobedience would drive me to a desperate death. And could he so much dote of a light damsel to force so little of his loving father? Alas, a wife is to be preferred before father and friend. But had he none to fix his fancy on but the daughter of my most furious foe? Alas, love hath no respect of persons. Yet was not my good will and consent to be craved therein? Alas, he saw no possibility to obtain it. But now, alas, I would grant my good will; but now, alas, it is too late. His fear of my fury is too great ever to be found; his fault is too great ever to look me in the face more, and my sorrow is too great ever to be saluted." And thereupon got him to bed, and in five days' space his natural moisture with secret sorrow was so soaken away that he could no longer continue his careful life, but yielded willingly to desired death. So it pleased God to provide for the poor pilgrims, who, having pass'd many a fearful forest and dangerous desert, were now come to the seashore, minding to take ship and travel into unknown coasts, where they might not by any means be known. And being on shipboard, they heard the maister of the ship make report that Atys, king of the Lybians, was dead. Whereupon Admetus desired to be set on shore again, and, dissembling the cause thereof, pretended some other matter and got to the next town, where with the money and jewels he had about him he furnished himself and his lady with the best apparel could be provided in the town, and with such a train of men as he could there take up; which done, he made the greatest expedition he could unto his own country, where he was royally received as prince, and shortly after joyfully crowned king. And being quietly settled in the regal seat, he presently dispatched ambassadors to Lycabas, his father's foe and his father-in-law, whose ambassade contained these two points: the one to intreat a peace for his people, the other to crave a pardon for his wife; who willingly granted both the one and the other, whereby he now lived in great quiet and tranquillity. A mervailous mutability of fortune which in the space of a moneth could bring him from happy joy to heavy annoy, and then from annoy again to greater joy then his former joy! For as the sun, having been long time overwhelmed with dark clouds, when it hath banished them from about it seems to shine more brightly then at any time before, so the state and condition of this prince, having been covered with the clouds of care, now it was cleared of them seemed more pleasant and happy then at any time before. And, verily, as sharp sauce gives a good taste to sweet meat, so trouble and adversity makes quiet and prosperity far more pleasant. For he knoweth not the pleasure of plenty who hath not felt the pain of penury; he takes no delight in meat who is never hungry; he careth not for ease who was never troubled with any disease.

But notwithstanding the happy life of this prince, albeit he abounded in as great riches as he required, albeit he had as many kingdoms as he coveted, albeit he had such a wife as he wished for, yea, and injoyed all things which either God could give him, fortune further him to, or nature bestow upon him; yet to shew that there is no sun shineth so bright but that clouds may overcast it, no ground so good but that it bringeth forth weeds as well as flowers, no king so surely guarded but that the gamesome goddess Fortune will at least check him if not mate him, no state so plentiful in pleasure but that it is mixed with pain, he had some weeds of wo which began to grow up amongst his flowers of felicity, and some chips of sorry chance did light in the heap of his happiness. Yea, Fortune presented herself once again upon the stage, and meant to have one fling more at him. For this prince, possessing such a pleasant life, took great delight in good housekeeping, and gave such good entertainment to strangers that his fame was far spread into forrain countries; yea, the rumor thereof reached to the skies, insomuch that Apollo, as the poets report, having occasion to discend from heaven to the earth, went to see the entertainment of Admetus; who was so royally received by him that the god thought good with some great kindness to requite his great curtesy. And as Philemon and Baucis for their hearty housekeeping were preserved by the gods from drowning when all the country and people besides were overflown, so the god Apollo meant to preserve his life when all his country and people then living should lie full low in their graves. And of the Destinies of death obtained thus much for him, that if when the time and term of his natural life drew to an end, if any could be found who would willingly die and loose their own life for him, he should begin the course of his life again, and continue on earth another age.

Now when the time of his natural life drew to an end, there was diligent inquiry made who would be content to abridge their own days to prolong their prince's life. And first the question was put to his friends, who were nearest to themselves; then to his kinsfolk, whose love was as much of custom as of kindness; then to his subjects, whose affection was as much for fear as for favor; then to his servants, who thought their life as sweet as their maister did his; then to his children, who thought it reason that, as their father did first enter into this life, so he should first depart out of this life; so that there could none be found so frank of their life to set this prince free from the force of death. Now Alcest, seeing the death of her dear husband draw near, and knowing her own life without his life and love would be but loathsome unto her, of her own accord off'red herself to be sacrificed for her husband's sake and to hasten her own death to prolong his life. O loyal, loving wife! O wight good inough for God himself! And yet had she a husband good inough for herself; for he loved her so intirely that though by loosing her he might have gained life long time, yet would he not by any means consent to her death, saying without her life his life would be more grievous unto him then a thousand deaths. But she persuaded with him against herself all that she could, saying, "I would not, O peerless prince, you should take the matter so kindly at my hands, as though for your sake only I off'red up my life; for it is indeed the commodity of your country and mine own, being under your dominion, which driveth me hereto, knowing myself unable to govern them, you being gone. And considering the daily war, the spoilful wastes, the bloody blasts, the troublesome strife which your realm is subject to, I thought you had not loved me so little as to leave me behind you to bear on my weak back such a heavy burthen as I think Atlas himself could scarce sustain. Again, considering that death is but a fleeting from one life into another, and that from a most miserable life to a most happy life, yea, from bale to bliss, from care to quiet, from purgatory to paradise, I thought you had not envied me so much as to think me unworthy of it. Do you not know that Cleobis and Biton had death bestowed on them as the best gift which God could devise to give them, and do you think it can do me harm, especially seeing I may thereby do you good?" "Alas, sweet wife," saith Admetus, "this your piety is unprofitable which is subject to so many perils. But if death be so good, good wife, let me injoy it, who am injoined to it, and to whom only it will be good, for death is only good to me [to] whom it is given, not to you who are not appointed to it. For it is not lawful for anyone to leave this life without special permission of the gods. And as in our court it is lawful for none to have access unto us unless by us he be sent for, so neither is it lawful for anyone to appear before the heavenly throne unless by the gods he be summoned. Neither will death be so easy to you as to me, whose nature is apt to yield unto it. For you see fruit which is not ripe will scarce with strength be torn from the tree, whereas that which is ripe falleth easely of its own accord. Therefore, good wife, give me leave to die to whom it will be only good and easy to die." "Why, sweet husband," saith she, "the god Apollo allowed any that would to die for you; otherwise to what purpose was that which he obtained of the Destinies for you? And for the uneasiness of death, nothing can be uneasy or hard unto a willing heart. But bicause your pleasure is so, I am content to continue my careful life, and with sorrow to survive you." And so left her husband, and went privily to the altar, and off'red up herself to death to prolong her husband's life. Which when the king knew, he would presently have spoiled himself, but his hands had not the power to do it, for that by the decree of the Destinies he must now of force live another age on earth. Which when he saw, he filled the court with such pitiful wailing, such bitter weeping, such hellish howling, that it pierced the heavens, and moved the gods to take remorse on his misery. And Proserpine, the goddess of hell, especially pitying the parting of this loving couple, for that she herself knew the pain of parting from friends, being by Dis stolen from her mother Ceres, put life into his wife again, and with speed sent her unto him. Who, being certified hereof in his sleep, early in the morning waited for her coming. Seeing her come afar off, he had much ado to keep his soul in his body from flying to meet her. Being come, he received her as joyfully as she came willingly, and so they lived long time together in most contented happiness.

This seemeth strange unto you, gentlewomen, that a woman should die and then live again; but the meaning of it is this, that you should die to yourselves and live to your husbands; that you should

count their life your life, their death your distruction; that you should not care to disease yourselves to please them; that you should in all things frame yourselves to their fancies; that if you see them disposed to mirth, you should indeavor to be pleasant; if they be solemn, you should be sad; if they hard, you having; if they delight in hawks, that you should love spaniels; if they hunting, you hounds; if they good company, you good housekeeping; if they be hasty, that you should be patient; if they be jealous, that you should lay aside all light looks; if they frown, that you fear; if they smile, that you laugh; if they kiss, that you clepe, or at least give them two for one; and so that in all things you should conform yourselves to their contentation. So shall there be one will in two minds, one heart in two bodies, and two bodies in one flesh. Methinks I hear my wish wish me such a wife as I have spoken of; verily, good wish, you wish your wealth great wealth, and God make me worthy of you, wish, and your wish; and if I might have my wish I am persuaded you should have your wish. But if I be so good a husband as Admetus was; if I forgo father, friends, and living; if I be content to change joy for annoy, court for care, pleasure for pilgrimage, for my wive's sake; if I had rather die myself then she should; if, she being dead, with mournful cries I move the gods to raise her to life again—I shall think myself worthy of so good a wife as Alcest was. I shall [hope] to have a wife who with Cleopatra will sting herself to death with serpents at the death of her Antonius; who with Hylonomo will slay herself at the death of her Cyllar; who with Singer will vanish away into air for the loss of her Picus; and who with Alcest will be content to lose her life to preserve her Admetus!

BARNABE RICH

FROM RICH HIS FAREWELL TO MILITARY PROFESSION (1581)

To the Right Courteous Gentlewomen Both of England and Ireland Barnabe Riche Wisheth All Things They Should Have Appertaining to Their Honor, Estimation, and All Other Their Honest Delights

Gentlewomen, I am sure there are many, but especially of such as best know me, that will not a little wonder to see such alteration in me that, having spent my younger days in the wars emongest men and vowed myself only unto Mars, should now in my riper years desire to live in peace emongest women and to consecrate myself wholly unto Venus. But

yet the wiser sort can very well consider that the older we wax the riper our wit, and the longer we live the better we can conceive of things appertaining to our own profits. Though harebrained youth overhaled me for a time, that I knew not bale from bliss, yet wisdom now hath warned me that I well know cheese from chalk. I see now it is less painful to follow a fiddle in a gentlewoman's chamber then to march after a drum in the field. And more sound sleeping under a silken canapy close by a friend then under a bush in the open field within a mile of our foe. And nothing so dangerous to be wounded with the luring look of our beloved mistress as with the cruel shot of our hateful enemy, the one possess'd with a pitiful heart to help where she hath hurt, the other with a deadly hate to kill where they might save. . . .

But now, gentlewomen, as I have vowed myself to be at your dispositions, so I know not how to frame myself to your contentations when I consider with how many commendable qualities he ought to be endued that should be welcomed into your blessed companies. I find in myself no one manner of exercise that might give me the least hope to win your good likings. . . .

And here, gentlewomen, the better to manifest the farther regard of my duty I have presented you with a few rough-heawen histories, yet I dare undertake so warely polished that there is nothing let slip that might breed offense to your modest minds.

I have made bold to publish theim under your savecundites, and I trust it shall nothing at all offend you. My last request is that at your pleasures you will peruse theim and with your favors you will defend them, which if I may perceive not to be misliked of emongest you, my encouragement will be such that I trust within a very short space you shall see me grow from a young puny to a sufficient scholer. And thus, gentlewomen, wishing to you all what yourselves do best like of, I humbly take my leave.

Yours in the way of honesty,
Barnabe Riche

To the Noble Souldiours Both of England and Ireland Barnabe Riche Wisheth As to Himself

There is an old proverb, noble souldiours, and thus it followeth: it is better to be happy then wise; but what it is to be happy, how should I discipher, who never in my life could yet attain to any hap at all that was good, and yet I have had souldiour's luck and speed as well as the rest of my profession. And with wisdom I will not meddle (I never came where it grew), but this I dare boldly affirm—and the experience of the present time doth make daily proof—that wit stands by in a threadbare coat where folly sometime sits in a velvet gown, and how often is it seen that vice shall be advanced where virtue is little or naught at all regarded, small desert shall highly be preferred where well-doing shall go unrewarded, and flattery shall be welcomed for a guest of great accompt where plain Tom Tell-Troth shall be thrust out of doors by the shoulders; and to speak a plain truth indeed, do ye not see pipers, parasites, fiddlers, dancers, players, jesters, and such others better esteemed and made of, and greater benevolence used toward them, then to any others that indeavors themselves to the most commendable qualities? . . .

[Rich continues with a long and gossipy account of his misadventures in the military profession, developing the thesis that without money it is impossible for an old soldier to enter a reputable civilian calling.]

And here I cannot but speak of the bounty of that noble gentleman, Sir Christofer Hatton, my very good maister and upholder; who, having builded a house in Northamptonshire called by the name of Holdenby, which house for the bravery of the buildings, for the stateliness of the chambers, for the rich furniture of the lodgings, for the conveighance of the offices, and for all other necessaries appertenent to a palace of pleasure is thought by those that have judgment to be incomparable and to have no fellow in England that is out of her Majesty's hands; and although this house is not yet fully finished and is but a new erection, yet it differeth far from the works that are used nowadays in many places. I mean where the houses are built with a great number of chimneys, and yet the smoke comes forth but at one only tunnel. This house is not built on that manner, for as it hath sundry chimneys, so they cast forth several smokes; and such worthy port and daily hospitality kept that although the owner himself useth not to come there once in two years, yet I dare undertake there is daily provision to be found convenient to entertain any nobleman with his whole train that should hap to call in of a sodain. And how many gentlemen and strangers that comes but to see the house are there daily welcomed, feasted, and well lodged? From whence should he come, be he rich, be he poor, that should not there be entertained if it please him to call in? To be short, Holdenby giveth daily relief to such as be in want for the space of six or seven miles' compass.

Peradventure those that be envious will think this tale nothing appertinent to the matter that I was in hand withal, but I trust my offense is the less, considering I have spoken but a truth, and do wish that every other man were able to say as much for his maister, and so an end.

And now where I left off I was telling what pride, what covetousness, what whoredom, what glotony, what blasphemy, what riot, what excess, what dronkenness, what swearing, what bribery, what extortion, what usury, what oppression, what deceipt, what forgery, what vice in general is daily entertained and practised in England. . . . [In spite of which indictment Rich closes his epistle with an ornate eulogy of Queen Elizabeth and of the happy realm in her care.]

And thus, noble souldiours and gentlemen all, I have held you with a long sermon, neither can I tell how my preaching will be allowed of. I crave no more but wish you all better fortune then I know the present time will afford you, and so will rest at your disposition.

Barnabe Riche

To the Readers in General

I assure thee, gentle reader, when I first took in hand to write these discourses I meant nothing less then to put theim in print, but writ theim at the request of some of my dearest friends, sometimes for their disport to serve their private use. And now, again by great importunity, I am forced to send them all to the printer. The histories altogether are eight in number, whereof the first, the second, the fift, the seventh, and eight are tales that are but forged only for delight, neither credible to be believed nor hurtful to be perused. The third, the fourth, and the sixt are Italian histories written likewise for pleasure by Maister L. B. [?Lodowick Bryskett]. And here, gentil reader, I must instantly intreat thee that if thou findest any words or terms seeming more undecent then peradventure thou wilt like of, think that I have set them down as more appropriate to express the matter they intreat of then either for want of judgment or good manners. Trusting that as I have written them in jest so thou wilt read them but to make thyself merry, I wish they might as well please thee in the reading as they displease me in putting them forth. I bid thee heartely farewell.

Barnabe Riche

OF APOLONIUS AND SILLA

THE ARGUMENT OF THE SECOND HISTORY

Apolonius Duke, having spent a year's service in the wars against the Turk, returning homeward with his company by sea, was driven by force of weather to the Ile of Cyprus, where he was well received by Pontus, governor of the same ile, with whom Silla, daughter to Pontus, fell so strangely in love that after Apolonius was departed to Constantinople Silla with one man followed, and, coming to Constantinople, she served Apolonius in the habit of a man, and, after many pretty accidents falling out, she was known to Apolonius, who in requital of her love married her.

There is no child that is born into this wretched world but before it doeth suck the mother's milk it taketh first a soope of the cup of error, which maketh us when we come to riper years not only to enter into actions of injury but many times to stray from that is right and reason; but in all other things wherein we shew ourselves to be most dronken with this poisoned cup it is in our actions of love, for the lover is so estranged from that is right and wandereth so wide from the bounds of reason that he is not able to deem white from black, good from bad, virtue from vice, but only led by the appetite of his own affections and grounding them on the foolishness of his own fancies will so settle his liking on such a one as either by desert or unworthiness will merit rather to be loathed then loved. . . .

During the time that the famous city of Constantinople remained in the hands of the Christians, emongst many other noblemen that kept their abiding in that florishing city there was one whose name was Apolonius, a worthy duke who, being but a very young man and even then new come to his possessions, which were very great, levied a mighty band of men at his own proper charges, with whom he served against the Turk during the space of one whole year, in which time, although it were very short, this young duke so behaved himself as well by prowess and valiance shewed with his own hands as otherwise by his wisdom and liberality used towards his souldiors that all the world was filled with the fame of this noble duke. When he had thus spent one year's service, he caused his trompet to sound a retrait and, gathering his company together and imbarking themselves, he set sail, holding his course towards Constantinople; but being upon the sea, by the extremity of a tempest which sodainly fell, his fleet was desevered some one way and some another, but he himself recovered the Ile of Cyprus, where he was worthily received by Pontus, duke and governor of the same ile, with whom he lodged while his ships were new repairing.

This Pontus, that was lord and governor of this famous ile, was an ancient duke and had two children, a son and a daughter; his son was named Silvio, of whom hereafter we shall have further occasion to speak, but at this instant he was in the parts of Africa serving in the wars.

The daughter her name was Silla, whose beauty was so peerless that she had the sovereignty emongest all other dames as well for her beauty as for the nobleness of her birth. This Silla, having heard of the worthiness of Apolonius, this young duke, who, besides his beauty and good graces, had a certain natural allurement that, being now in his company in her father's court, she was so strangely attached with the love of Apolonius that there was nothing might content her but his presence and sweet sight, and although she saw no manner of hope to attain to that she most desired, knowing Apolonius to be but a geast and ready to take the benefit of the next wind and to depart into a strange country, whereby she was bereaved of all possibility ever to see him again and therefore strived with herself to leave her fondness—but all in vain, it would not be, but like the fowl which is once limed, the more she striveth, the faster she tieth herself. So Silla was now constrained perforce her will to yield to love, wherefore from time to time she used so great familiarity with him as her honor might well permit, and fed him with such amorous baits as the modesty of a maid could reasonably afford; which when she perceived did take but small effect, feeling herself so much outraged with the extremity of her passion by the only countenance that she bestowed upon Apolonius, it might have been well perceived that the very eyes pleaded unto him for pity and remorse. But Apolonius, coming but lately from out the field, from the chasing of his enemies, and his fury not yet throughly desolved nor purged from his stomach, gave no regard to those amorous enticements which by reason of his youth he had not been acquainted withal. But his mind ran more to hear his pilots bring news of a merry wind to serve his turn to Constantinople, which in the end came very prosperously; and, giving Duke Pontus hearty thanks for his great entertainment, taking his leave of himself and the Lady Silla his daughter, departed with his company, and with a happy gaale arrived at his desired port. Gentlewomen, according to my promise I will here, for brevity's sake, omit to make repetition of the long and dolorous discourse recorded by Silla for this sodain departure of her Apolonius, knowing you to be as tenderly hearted as Silla herself, whereby you may the better conjecture the fury of her fever.

But Silla, the further that she saw herself bereaved of all hope ever any more to see her beloved Apolonius, so much the more contagious were her passions and made the greater speed to execute that she had premeditated in her mind, which was this: emongest many servants that did attend upon her there was one whose name was Pedro, who had a long time waited upon her in her chamber, whereby she was well assured of his fidelity and trust. To that Pedro, therefore, she bewrayed first the fervency of her love borne to Apolonius, conjuring him in the name of the goddess of love herself, and binding him by the duty that a servant ought to have that tendereth his mistress' safety and good liking, and desiring him with tears trickling down her cheeks that he would give his consent to aid and assist her in that she had determined, which was for that she was fully resolved to go to Constantinople where she might again take the view of her beloved Apolonius; that he, according to the trust she had reposed in him, would not refuse to give his consent secretly to convey her from out her father's court according as she should give him direction, and also to make himself pertaker of her journey and to wait upon her till she had seen the end of her determination. . . .

[With some misgivings assenting to her proposal, Pedro secures passage to Constantinople for himself and his "sister," and in due time they steal away from Pontus' court. But on the voyage their captain soon "was better pleased in beholding of her face then in taking the height either of the sun or star, and thinking her, by the homeliness of her apparel, to be but some simple maiden, calling her into his cabin, he began to break with her after the sea-fashion, desiring her to use his own cabin for her better ease, and during the time that she remained at the sea she should not want a bed, and then, wispering softly in her ear, he said that for want of a bedfellow he himself would supply that room." Silla very properly rejects his offer, at which the enraged and lustful captain swears to have his pleasure with her that very night. But as the distraught maiden prays to God for help in preserving her chastity, a mighty storm blows up and drives the ship on the shore. Although Pedro and most of the crew are drowned, "by the only providence of God" Silla rides safely ashore on the captain's sea-chest. The chest provides both money and man's clothing, and so Silla, taking her brother Silvio's name and disguising herself as a man, indomitably pushes on toward Constantinople.]

In this manner she traveled to Constantinople, where she inquired out the palace of the Duke Apolonius, and, thinking herself now to be both fit and able to play the servingman, she presented herself to the duke, craving his service; the duke, very willing to give succor unto strangers, perceiving him to be a proper smogue young man, gave him entertainment. Silla thought herself now more then satisfied for all the casualties that had happened unto her in her journey that she might at her pleasure take but the view of the Duke Apolonius, and above the rest of his servants was very diligent and attendant upon him, the which the duke perceiving began likewise to grow into good liking with the diligence of his man, and therefore made him one of his chamber. Who but Silvio then was most neat about him in helping of him to make him ready in a morning, in the setting of his ruffs, in the keeping of his chamber? Silvio pleased his maister so well that above all the rest of his servants about him he had the greatest credit, and the duke put him most in trust.

At this very instant there was remaining in the city a noble dame, a widow whose houseband was but lately deceased, one of the noblest men that were in the parts of Grecia, who left his lady and wife large possessions and great livings. This lady's name was called Julina, who, besides the aboundance of her wealth and the greatness of her revenues, had likewise the sovereignty of all the dames of Constantinople for her beauty. To this Lady Julina Apolonius became an earnest suitor, and according to the manner of wooers, besides fair words, sorrowful sighs, and piteous countenances, there must be sending of loving letters, chains, bracelets, brooches, rings, tablets, gems, jewels, and presents I know not what. So my duke, who in the time that he remained in the Ile of Cyprus had no skill at all in the art of love, although it were more then half proffered unto him, was now become a scholler in love's school and had already learned his first lesson, that is, to speak pitifully, to look ruthfully, to promise largely, to serve diligently, and to please carefully. Now he was learning his second lesson, that is, to reward liberally, to give bountifully, to present willingly, and to write lovingly. Thus Apolonius was so busied in his new study that I warrant you there was no man that could challenge him for playing the truant, he followed his profession with so good a will. And who must be the messenger to carry the tokens and love letters to the Lady Julina but Silvio, his man? In him the duke reposed his only confidence to go between him and his lady.

Now, gentilwomen, do you think there could have been a greater torment devised wherewith to afflict the heart of Silla then herself to be made the instrument to work her own mishap and to play the atturney in a cause that made so much against herself? But Silla, altogether desirous to please her maister, cared nothing at all to offend herself, followed his business with so good a will as if it had been in her own preferment.

Julina, now having many times taken the gaze of this young youth Silvio, perceiving him to be of such excellent perfect grace, was so intangeled with the often sight of this sweet temptation that she fell into as great a liking with the man as the maister was with herself. And on a time Silvio, being sent from his maister with a message to the Lady Julina, as he began very earnestly to solicet in his maister's behalf, Julina, interrupting him in his tale, said: "Silvio, it is enough that you have said for your maister; from henceforth either speak for yourself or say nothing at all." Silla, abashed to hear these words, began in her mind to accuse the blindness of love, that Julina, neglecting the good will of so noble a duke, would prefer her love unto such a one as Nature itself had denayed to recompense her liking. . . .

[Meanwhile the true Silvio returns to Cyprus and learns of the departure of Pedro and Silla. Thinking the servant has abducted his sister, he sets out to find them and gain revenge, and after many wanderings comes to Constantinople. There, "walking in an evening for his own recreation on a pleasant greenyard without the walls of the city," he meets Julina. Owing to his extraordinary similarity to Silla, Julina

addresses him in the affectionate terms she has come to use with Apolonius' man, and, after an equivocal conversation, the pleased but puzzled Silvio agrees to a supper rendezvous the following night. Both await their meeting with amorous impatience.]

Silvio hastening himself to the palace of Julina, where by her he was friendly welcomed, and a sumpteous supper being made ready, furnished with sondry sorts of delicate dishes, they sat them down, passing the suppertime with amarous looks, loving countenances, and secret glances conveighed from the one to the other, which did better satisfy them then the feeding of their dainty dishes.

Suppertime being thus spent, Julina did think it very unfitly if she should tourn Silvio to go seek his lodging in an evening, desired him therefore that he would take a bed in her house for that night, and, bringing him up into a fair chamber that was very richly furnished, she found such means that, when all the rest of her household servants were abed and quiet, she came herself to bear Silvio company, where, concluding upon conditions that were in question between them, they passed the night with such joy and contentation as might in that convenient time be wished for, but only that Julina, feeding too much of some one dish above the rest, received a surfet, whereof she could not be cured in forty weeks after—a natural inclination in all women which are subject to longing and want the reason to use a moderation in their diet. But the morning approaching, Julina took her leave and conveighed herself into her own chamber, and when it was fair daylight Silvio, making himself ready, departed likewise about his affairs in the town, debating with himself how things had happened, being well assured that Julina had mistaken him, and therefore for fear of further evils determined to come no more there, but took his journey towards other places in the parts of Grecia to see if he could learn any tidings of his sister Silla. . . .

[Julina, deciding to rid herself of Apolonius' unwelcome attentions once for all, tells him that she loves another; Apolonius manfully withdraws, but when he learns, through his servants' gossip, that Julina has showered her affections on Silvio, he immediately "caused him [i.e. the disguised Silla] to be thrust into a dongeon, where he was kept prisoner in a very pitiful plight." When Julina (who, "assuring herself to be with child, fearing to become quite bankrout of her honor, did think it more then time to seek out a father") comes to request Silvio's release, a painful scene follows. Apolonius charges Silvio with "forgeries and perjured protestations, not only hateful unto me . . . but most habominable . . . in the presence and sight of God." Silvio protests innocence and fidelity to Apolonius and calls upon the "sacred gods" to "consume me straight with flashing flames of fire" if he has made any commitments to Julina, but her only answer is to call him the father of her unborn child and her "spouse and loyal housband" in the sight of God. At last she calls on death to release her and collapses in a flood of tears.]

The duke, who stood by all this while and heard this whole discourse, was wonderfully moved with compassion towards Julina, knowing that from her infancy she had ever so honorably used herself that there was no man able to detect her of any misdemeanor otherwise then beseemed a lady of her estate; wherefore, being fully resolved that Silvio his man had committed this villany against her, in a great fury drawing his rapier he said unto Silvio:

"How canst thou, arrant thief, shew thyself so cruel and careless to such as do thee honor? Hast thou so little regard of such a noble lady as humbleth herself to such a villain as thou art, who without any respect either of her renowm or noble estate canst be content to seek the wrack and utter ruin of her honor? But frame thyself to make such satisfaction as she requireth, although I know, unworthy wretch, that thou art not able to make her the least part of amends, or I swear by God that thou shalt not escape the death which I will minister to thee with my own hands, and therefore advise thee well what thou doest."

Silvio, having heard this sharp sentence, fell down on his knees before the duke, craving for mercy, desiring that he might be suffered to speak with the Lady Julina apart, promising to satisfy her according to her own contentation.

"Well," quoth the duke, "I take thy word, and therewithal I advise thee that thou perform thy promise, or otherwise, I protest before God, I will make thee such an example to the world that all traitors shall tremble for fear how they do seek the dishonoring of ladies."

But now Julina had conceived so great grief against Silvio that there was much ado to persuade her to talk with him, but rememb'ring her own case, desirous to hear what excuse he could make, in the end she agreed, and, being brought into a place severally by themselves, Silvio began with a piteous voice to say as followeth:

"I know not, madame, of whom I might make complaint, whether of you or of myself, or rather of Fortune, which hath conducted and brought us both into so great adversity. I see that you receive great wrong, and I am condemned against all right, you in peril to abide the bruit of spightful tongues and I in danger to loose the thing that I most desire; and although I could alledge many reasons to prove my sayings true, yet I refer myself to the experience and bounty of your mind." And herewithal loosing his garments down to his stomach and shewed Julina his breasts and pretty teats, surmounting far the whiteness of snow itself, saying, "Lo, madame, behold here the party whom you have challenged to be the father of your child! See, I am a woman, the daughter of a noble duke, who only for the love of him whom you so lightly have shaken off have forsaken my father, abandoned my country, and in manner as you see am become a servingman, satisfying myself but with the only sight of my Apolonius. And now, madame, if my passion were not vehement and my torments without comparison, I would wish that my feigned griefs might be laughed to scorn and my desembled pains to be rewarded with flouts. But my love being pure, my travail continual, and my griefs endless, I trust, madame, you will not only excuse me of crime but also pity my distress, the which I protest I would still have kept secret if my fortune would so have permitted."

Julina did now think herself to be in a worse case then ever she was before, for now she knew not whom to challenge to be the father of her child; wherefore when she had told the duke the very certainty of the discourse which Silvio had made unto her, she departed to her own house with such grief and sorrow that she purposed never to come out of her own doors again alive to be a wonder and mocking-stock to the world.

But the duke, more amazed to hear this strange discourse of Silvio, came unto him, whom when he had viewed with better consideration perceived indeed that it was Silla, the daughter of Duke Pontus, and imbracing her in his arms he said:

"O the branch of all virtue and the flow'r of curtesy itself, pardon me, I beseech you, of all such discourtesies as I have ignorantly committed towards you, desiring you that without farther memory of ancient griefs you will accept of me who is more joyful and better contented with your presence then if the whole world were at my commandment. Where hath there ever been found such liberality in a lover, which, having been trained up and nourished emongest the delicacies and banquets of the court, accompanied with trains of many fair and noble ladies, living in pleasure and in the middest of delights, would so prodigally adventure yourself, neither fearing mishaps nor misliking to take such pains as I know you have not been accustomed unto. O liberality never heard of before! O faith that can never be sufficiently rewarded! O true love most pure and unfeigned!" Herewithal, sending for the most artificial workmen, he provided for her sondry suits of sumpteous apparel and the marriage day appointed, which was celebrated with great triumph through the whole city of Constantinople, everyone praising the nobleness of the duke; but so many as did behold the excellent beauty of Silla gave her the praise above all the rest of the ladies in the troop.

The matter seemed so wonderful and strange that the bruit was spread throughout all the parts of Grecia, insomuch that it came to the hearing of Silvio, who, as you have heard, remained in those parts to enquire of his sister. He, being the gladdest 10 man in the world, hasted to Constantinople, where, coming to his sister, he was joyfully received and most lovingly welcomed and entertained of the duke, his brother-in-law. After he had remained there two or three days the duke revealed unto Silvio the whole discourse how it happened between his sister and the Lady Julina, and how his sister was challenged for getting a woman with child. Silvio, blushing with these words, was striken with great remorse to make Julina amends, understanding her to be a noble lady, 20 and was left defamed to the world through his default; he therefore bewrayed the whole circumstance to the duke, whereof the duke, being very joyful, immediately repaired with Silvio to the house of Julina, whom they found in her chamber in great lamentation and mourning. To whom the duke said, "Take courage, madam, for behold here a gentilman that will not stick both to father your child and to take you for his wife—no inferior person, but the son and heir of a noble duke, worthy of your estate and 30 dignity."

Julina, seeing Silvio in place, did know very well that he was the father of her child and was so ravished with joy that she knew not whether she were awake or in some dream. Silvio, imbracing her in his arms, craving forgiveness of all that pass'd, concluded with her the marriage day, which was presently accomplished with great joy and contentation to all parties. And thus Silvio having attained a noble wife and Silla his sister her desired houseband, they passed the 40 residue of their days with such delight as those that have accomplished the perfection of their felicities.

The Conclusion [to the book]

Gentle reader, now thou hast perused these histories to the end I doubt not but thou wilt deem of them as they worthely deserve and think such vanities more fitter to be presented on a stage (as some of them have been) then to be published in print (as, till now, they have never been), but to excuse myself of the folly that here might be imputed unto me, that myself being the first that have put them to the 10 print should likewise be the first that should condemn them as vain; for mine own excuse herein I answer that in the writing of them I have used the same manner that many of our young gentlemen useth nowadays in the wearing of their apparel, which is rather to follow a fashion that is new (be it never so foolish) then to be tied to a more decent custom that is clean out of use: sometime wearing their hair freeseled so long that makes them look like a water spaniel, sometimes so short like a new-shorn sheep, 20 their beards sometimes cut round like a Philip's dollar, sometimes square like the King's Head in Fish Street, sometimes so near the skin that a man might judge by his face the gentleman had had very pill'd luck; their caps and hats sometimes so big as will hold more wit then three of them have in their heads, sometimes so little that it will hold no wit at all; their ruffs sometimes so huge as shall hang about their necks like a cart-wheel, sometimes a little falling band that makes theim look like one of the queen's 30 silk women. . . .

Now I am sure if any of theim were asked why he used such variety in his apparel he would answer, because he would follow the fashion. Let this, then, suffice likewise for mine excuse, that myself seeing trifles of no accompt to be now best in season, and such vanities more desired then matters of better purpose, and the greatest part of our writers still busied with the like, so I have put forth this book because I would follow the fashion. . . .

THOMAS UNDERDOWN

AN ETHIOPIAN HISTORY

Thomas Underdown's *Ethiopian History* (?1569) introduced to English readers the fertile tradition of the so-called Greek romance—a loose term for the lush prose-fictions of the early Christian era whose plot-formulas reappear in many guises, both dramatic and non-dramatic, in the later sixteenth century. The standard plot of the

Greek romances—Heliodorus' *Aethiopica*, Achilles Tatius' *Leucippe and Cleitophon*, and Longus' *Daphnis and Chloe* were the best-known—concerns a pair (or pairs) of high-born lovers who, involved in a perplexed dynastic situation, resort to flight (or exile) and disguise in order to achieve, after many travels and hazards, the eventual triumph of true love and political justice. A résumé of Heliodorus' tortuous plot will perhaps indicate the pattern and the stylized complexity of the romances that were so popular in Shakespeare's day, both in translations like Underdown's and in adaptations like the *Arcadia* of Sir Philip Sidney:

At the moment of conception Persina, the wife of King Hydaspes of Ethiopia, had looked upon a marble statue and, as she feared, had thus affected the color of her unborn child. When her daughter is born white, she, trying to evade a charge of adultery, gives the baby over to Sisimithres, a gymnosophist, who takes her to Egypt and there entrusts her to Charicles, a Pythian priest. Charicles takes the child back with him to Delphi, where she becomes a priestess of Apollo under the name of Chariclea. Meeting and falling in love with Theagenes, a Thessalian warrior visiting the shrine to do sacrifice, she flees with him from Delphi; and after many changes and chances by land and sea they at last fall into her father's hands. Just as Chariclea is about to die in a sacrificial fire, her identity is revealed, and so all ends well, with the lovers married and restored to their patrimony.

Underdown, who apparently had small Latin and less Greek, made his translation from the Latin version (1551) of Stanislaus Warschewiczki. Entered in the Stationers'

Register in 1568–69, it was presumably published in 1569, and so great was its popularity that it went through successively revised editions in 1577, 1587, 1605 (reissued in 1606), and 1622; a new version by William L'isle appeared in 1631 and again in 1638.

Like Heliodorus, we begin our excerpts *in medias res.* In Book I Theagenes and Cariclea,[1] having already fled from the temple at Delphi, have been captured by Thyamis, "captain of the thieves of Egypt." In his house they meet Cnemon, a Greek, who, after Thyamis himself has been abducted by Mitranes, goes in search of his friend. In Book II Cnemon meets Calasiris, Thyamis' father, "who telleth him a notable tale of his own ill hap and annexeth thereto the beginning of the story of the whole book, how Caricles came by Cariclea, and how Theagenes was sent out of Thessalia to perform the funeral of Pyrrhus, Achilles his son." Book III carries on this story-within-a-story of Calasiris. It contains, as Underdown summarizes the action, "the manner of the funerals and how Theagenes fell in love with Cariclea and she with him, and the moan that Caricles made for her to Calasiris." We ourselves begin with Calasiris' account to Cnemon of Cariclea's origin as he had heard it from Caricles. Our text is based upon *An Aethiopian Historie written in Greeke by Heliodorus: very wittie and pleasaunt, Englished by Thomas Underdoune,* [?1569] (STC 13041).

FROM AN ETHIOPIAN HISTORY (?1569)

To The Right Honorable Edward Deviere, Lord Boulbeck, Earl of Oxenford, Lord Great Chamberlain of England, Thomas Underdowne Wisheth Long and Blessed Life with Encrease of Honor

As they somewhat be more precise than I, right honorable Earl, which would have noble men, and such as bear sway and rule in the weal public, to be in all manner of sciences great artists and altogether bookish, so do I far dissent from them that would contrarily have them utterly unlettered and flat idiots. For the bookish man busily attending his own study cannot carefully yenough tender the state; for such is the property of knowledge that it breedeth a contempt of all other things in respect of itself. As for the ignorant, it is most evident and plain that he can have no manner of governance or skill of regiment in his head. The Greeks in all manner of knowledge and learning did far surmount the Romans, but the Romans in administ'ring their state, in warlike facts, and in common sense were much their superiors; for the Greeks were wedded to their learning alone; the Romans, content with a mediocrity, applied themselves to greater things. I do not

deny but that in many matters—I mean matters of learning—a nobleman ought to have a sight; but to be too much addicted that way, I think, is not good. Now of all knowledge fit for a noble gentleman I suppose the knowledge of histories is most seeming. For furthering whereof, I have Englished a passing fine and witty history written in Greek by Heliodorus, and for right good cause consecrated the same to your honorable lordship. For such virtues be in your Honor, so hauty courage joined with great skill, such sufficiency in learning, so good nature and common sense that in your Honor is, I think, expressed the right pattern of a noble gentleman, which in my head I have conceived. It nothing did dismay me, or for that I was not known to your Honor, neither may it seem any rash attempt for that cause. For such is the force of virtue that she maketh us to love not only our own countrymen by sight unknown but also strangers which by land and sea be severed from us. Therefore I beseech your Honor favorably to accept this my small travail in

---

[1]Here and later we use Underdown's spellings *Cariclea* and *Caricles.*

translating Heliodorus, whom, if I have so well translated as he is worthy, I am persuaded that your Honor will like very well of. Sure I am that of other translators he hath been dedicated to mighty kings and princes. Therefore accept my good will, honorable Earl, and if opportunity shall serve hereafter, there shall greater things appear under your Honor's name. Almighty God geve you increase of honor, and keep and defend you for ever and ever.

Your Honor's most humble to command,
Thomas Underdowne

THE ETHIOPIAN HISTORY

The Second Book

" 'After I [i.e. Caricles, whose words Calasiris is quoting to Cnemon] had traveled over many countries, at length I came into your Egypt and into the city Catadupi, to see the sluces of Nilus. And thus, my friend, I have told you the manner of my travel into those places. But I desire that you should know the principal cause why I tell you this tale. As I walked about in the city, as my leisure served, and did buy such things as are very scarce in Greece (for now, by continuance of time having well digested my sorrows, I hasted to return into my country), there came a sober man to me, and such a one as by countenance appeared to be wise, that had lately passed his youthful years, of color black, and saluted me and said that he would talk with me about a certain matter (not speaking Greek very well). And when he saw that I was willing to go with him he brought me into a certain temple, and by and by said: "I saw you buy certain herbs and roots that grow in India and Ethiopia. If you will buy such things of me, in good faith and without guile I will shew you them with all my heart." "That I will," quod I; "shew me them, I pray you." With that he took a little bag from under his arm and shewed me certain precious stones of wonderful price. For there were margarites among them as big as a little nut, perfit round, and smaradges and hiachinths. They were in color as the green grass and shined very bright. These were like the sea bank that lieth under a hard rock which maketh all that is underneath to be like purple color. At few words, their mingled and divers shining color delighted and pleased the eyes wonderfully, which as soon as I saw, "You must seek other chapmen," quod I, "good sir, for I and all my riches are scant able to buy one of the stones that I see." "Why," said he, "if you be not able to buy them, yet are you able to take them if they be geven you." "I am able," said I, "to receive them indeed, but I know not what you mean so to mock me." "I mock you not," quod he, "but mean good faith, and I swear by the god of this church that I

will geve you all these things if you will take them, beside another gift which far excelleth them all." I laughed when I heard this. He asked me why I laughed. "Because," quod I, "it is a thing to be laughed at, seeing you promise me things of so great price and yet assure me to geve me more." "Trust me," said he. "But swear that you will use this gift well and as I shall teach you." I marvailed what he meant, and stayed a while; yet in hope of those greater rewards I took an oath. After I had sworn as he willed me, he brought me to his lodging and shewed me a maid of excellent beauty which he said was but seven year old. Methought she was almost marriageable, such grace doth excellent beauty geve to the tallness of stature. I stood in a maze, as well for that I knew not what he meant as also for the unsatiable desire I had to look upon her. Then spake he thus to me: "Sir, the mother of this maid which you see, for a certain cause that you shall know hereafter, laid her forth wrapped in such apparel as is commonly used for such purposes, committing her to a doubtfulness of fortune. And I, by chance finding her, took her up, for it is not lawful to despise and neglect a soul in danger after it hath once entered into an human body. For this is one of the wise men's precepts that are with us, to be whose scholer myself was once judged worthy. Besides that, even in the infant's eyes there appeared some wonderful thing: she beheld me with such a steady and amiable countenance as I looked upon her. With her was also found this bag of precious stones which I shewed you of late, and a silken cloth wrought with letters in her mother tongue, wherein was her whole estate contained, her mother, as I ghess, procuring the same. Which after I had read I knew whence and what she was, and so I carried her into the country far from the city, and delivered her to certain shepherds to be brought up, with charge that they should tell no man. As for those things that were found with her, I detained with myself, lest for them the maid should be brought into any danger. And thus at the first this matter was concealed. But after, in process of time, the maid growing on and becoming more fair then other women were (for beauty, in mine opinion, cannot be concealed, though it were under the ground, but would thence also appear), fearing lest her estate should be known and so she killed and I brought in trouble therefore, I sued that I might be sent in ambassadge to the deputy of Egypt, and obtained; wherefore I come and bring her with me, desirous to set her business in good order. And now must I utter to him the cause of mine ambassadge, for he hath appointed this day for the hearing of me. As touching the maid, I commend her to you, and the gods who have hitherto conserved her, upon such conditions as you are bound by oath to perform. That is, that you will use her as a free woman and marry her to a free man, as you receive her at my hand or rather of her mother, who hath so left her. . . . As for other secrecies belonging to the maid, I will tell you them tomorrow in more ample wise if you will meet with me about Isis' temple." I did as he requested, and carried the maid muffled to mine own house, and used her very honorably that day, comforting her with many fair means, and gave God great thanks for her, from that time hitherto accompting and meaning her my daughter. The next day I went to Isis' temple as I had appointed with the stranger, and after I had walked there a great while alone and saw him not, I went to the deputy's house and inquired whether any man saw the legate of Ethiopia. The one told me that he was gone, or rather driven homeward, the last day before sunset, for that the deputy threat'ned to kill him if presently he departed not. I asked him the cause. "For that," quoth he, "by his ambassadge he willed him not to meddle with the mines out of which the smaragdes were digged as those that appertained to Ethiopia." I came home again much grieved, like one that had had some great mishap, because I could not know anything as touching the maid, neither whence she was or who were her parents.' " "Marvail not thereat," said Cnemon [interrupting] him, "for I myself take it heavily that I cannot know it now; yet perhaps I shall know it hereafter." "You shall indeed," said Calasiris. "But now will I tell you what Caricles said more. 'After I came into my house,' quoth he, 'the maid came forth to meet me but said nothing bicause she could not yet speak Greek; yet she took me by the hand and made me good cheer with her countenance. I marveiled that even as good greyhounds do fawn upon everyone though they have but little acquaintance with them, so she quickly perceived my good will toward her, and did imbrace me as if I had been her father. I determined, therefore, not to tarry any longer in Catadupi lest some spite of the gods should deprive me of my other daughter too, and so, coming by boat down along Nilus to the sea, I got a ship and sailed home, and now is this my daughter with me—this daughter, I say, surnamed also by my name, for whose sake I lead scant a quiet life. And beside other things, wherein she is better then I could wish, she learned the Greek tongue in so short space, and came to perfit age with such speed, as if she had been a peerless branch; and so far passed all other in excellent beauty that all men's eyes, as well strangers' as Greeks', were set on her.' " . . .

[Although Caricles is eager to marry his ward to his nephew, she herself has become "Diana's servant" and dedicated her life to chastity. But then Theagenes, a Thessalian warrior, appears with his soldiers at the temple where Caricles is priest of Pyrrhus, having arrived to do sacrifice to the son of the great Achilles whom they claim as ancestor. When Theagenes comes before Caricles his beauty and his grace are at once evident.] "Therewith entered in a young man of Achilles' courage indeed, who in countenance and stomach appeared no less, with a straight neck, high foreheaded, with his hear in comely sort rebending down, his nose and nosthrils wide inough to take breath (which is a token of courage and strength), his eyes not very gray, but gray and black, which made him look somewhat fiercely and yet very amiably, not much unlike the sea which is new calmed after a boisterous tempest. After he had saluted us, as the manner was, and we him again, 'It is time,' said he, 'to do sacrifice to the god, that we may finish the noble man's rights and the pomp thereto belonging by times.' 'Let it be so,' said Caricles, and as he rose he told me [Calasiris] softly, 'You shall see Cariclea today if you have not seen her before, for she must be at the pomp and funerals of Neoptolemus by custom.' I had seen the maid before, Cnemon, and done sacrifice with her, and she would enquire of me of our holy customs and ordinances. Yet I said nothing to him, waiting to see what would come hereof, and so we went to the temple both together. For all things that belonged to the sacrifices were made ready by the Thessalians. As soon as we came to the altar and the young man began to do the sacrifice, having leave first of the priest, Pythia said thus:

> Ye men of Delphi, sing of her,
> and goddes offspring praise,
> Who now in grace begins to grow,
> but fame shall end her days;
> Who leaving these my temples here,
> and passing surging streams,
> Shall come at length to country scortch
> with Phoebus' blazing beams;
> Where they, as recompenses due,
> that virtues rare do gain,
> In time to come, ere it be long,
> white miters shall obtain.

After the god had said thus, those that stood by cast many doubts, but knew not what that answer should mean. Every man had his several exposition, and as he desired, so he conjectured, yet could none attain to the true meaning thereof, for oracles and dreams are for the most part understood when they be come to pass. And although the men of Delphos were in amaze for that was said, yet they hasted to go to this gorgeous solemnity, not caring to make any diligent enquiry of the answer which was geven."

Here endeth the second book.

[In the tenth and last book the plot is resolved and the characters are appropriately disposed of. As Underdown summarizes the action, it relates "how Hydaspes was received into his own country, and the manner of the sacrifices which he did; then the acknowledging of Cariclea to be his daughter, and the entertaining of the strange embassadors, with certain active feats of Theagenes. After this is Theagenes assured to Cariclea by Hydaspes, and they are made priests, he the sun's and she the moon's, and do sacrifice. Then go they to Meroe, where the secreter things appertaining to the marriage are finished." We pick up the action just as Hydaspes, who is preparing to sacrifice Cariclea and Theagenes, begins to learn their identities through a letter from Oroondates.]

The Tenth Book

. . . "To Hydaspes, the gentle and fortunate king of the Ethiopians, Oroondates, the great king's deputy, sendeth greeting.

"Forasmuch as when you overcame me in battail, but more in lofty courage of mind, you gave me a whole deputyship of your own courtesy, I shall think it no marveil if you perform a small request now. There was a certain maid who, in carriage from Memphis, happened to fall into your hands by chance of war, and it was told me of such as were with her and escaped out of your danger, that you commanded her to be carried captive into Ethiopia. This wench I desire you to send me, both for her own sake, but most for her father's, for whom I would see her safe kept. He hath traveled far for her, and in this travel he was taken prisoner in this time of war by my soldiers, which lay in garrison in Eliphantina; whom I spied when I took the view of those that escaped out of the battail, and he desired that he might be sent to your clemency. You have him such a man emong the rest of the ambassadors as may with his manners alone declare that he is a gentleman and worthy only with his behavior to obtain his desire at your hand. Send him back again to me, O king, marry, who is not called only but hath been ere now a father too." When he had read this he asked which of these is this that seeketh for his daughter. They shewed him a certain old man, to whom he said: "Stranger, I will do anything at Oroondates' request, but I commanded ten only to be brought hither, and forasmuch as one of them is known not to be thine, look upon all the rest. If thou canst find her, take her with thee." The old man fell down and kissed his feet, and after he had looked upon them all, as they were brought before him, and found her not whom he sought, he was very sad, and said, "None of these, O king, is she." "You know," quod Hydaspes, "there is no want of good will in me. If you find her not that you seek for, blame Fortune. For I geve you

leave to look that neither here is any other beside these, nor in the tents." When the old man had bent his brows and wept, he lift up his face and looked round about him, and suddainly ran forth as though he had been mad. And when he came to the altar he did wind his cloak round like a rope (for he had a cloak on then by chance), and cast it about Theagenes' neck, and cried that all men might hear: "I have found thee, mine enemy. I have gotten thee, thou mischievous and accursed fellow." And although the officers would have stayed him and plucked him from him, he hanged so fast upon him that he obtained leave to bring him before Hydaspes and the counsel. And there he spake thus: "This man, O king, is he who like a thief hath taken my daughter from me; this is he who hath made my house desolate and without any child. He hath taken my heart even from the altars of Apollo. And now he sitteth at the altars of the gods like a good and devout man." All that were there were moved with that which he did —marry, they understood not his words, but they marvailed at his work. And when Hydaspes bad him tell plainly what he meant, the old man (that was Caricles) concealed the truth of Cariclea, fearing lest if she were dead by the way that he should have much ado with her true parents. But he told that briefly that was little hurtful in this sort: "I had a daughter, O king; if you had seen how wise and fair withal she had been you would have thought that I had good cause to say as I do. She led her life in virginity, and was one of Diana's priests, which is honored at Delphi. That maid this jolly Thessalian hath stolen out of Apollo's church as he came, being captain of a holy ambassage, to Delphi, my native city, there to celebrate a certain feast. Wherefore it may well be deemed that he hath offended also against you, for that he hath displeased your god Apollo (which is all one with the sun) and defiled his temple. Furthermore, a false priest of Memphis was his companion in performance of this his shameful and heinous fact. After I had been in Thessalia and required to have this fellow, and they were all content to deliver him to me as a common plague of their country, wheresoever he were found, I went to Memphis, which I deemed to be a place whither Calasiris would go for divers causes. When I came thither I found him dead, as well he had deserved, and was told by his son Thyamis of all that belonged to my daughter: how that she was sent to Siene to Oroondates, where not finding Oroondates (for I came thither too), at Eliphantina I was taken prisoner and stayed, from whence I came at this present in humble sort to seek my daughter, and you shall do me, unhappy man, a good turn and a deed well beseeming a king if you will accept the deputy's request made in my behalf." And then he held his peace, and wept bitterly to confirm that he said. Hydaspes turned to Theagenes. "And what say you to this?" quod he. Theagenes answered: "All that he hath laid against me in this accusation is true. I am the thief, the unjust man, and the robber. As touching him, yet have I done you a good turn." Therefore said Hydaspes: "Restore that which is not your own, that because ye are vowed to the gods ye may be a clean and glorious sacrifice and not seem to be punished for your offense." "Nay," quod Theagenes, "not he that did the wrong, but he that hath the commodity of it ought by justice to make restitution. Seeing, therefore, you have her, restore her, for it is Cariclea whom he also will confess to be your daughter." No man could rule himself any longer, but they were disord'red in every place. Sisimithres, who had withheld himself a good while, for all that he knew the whole matter that was in handling, till it were bolted out, which by little and little came to light, then he came to them and imbraced Caricles and said: "Your adoptive daughter, which I once delivered you, is well found and known to be their daughter whom you know yourself well yenough." Cariclea also ran out of the tabernacle like a mad woman, without regard what became of her kind and age, and fell at Caricles' feet and said: "O father, no less dear to me then those that begat me, take what revenge you will of me without any regard to the excuse which some man might allege that it was the gods' will and their doing." Persina on the other side kissed Hydaspes and said: "Husband, judge that all this is so, and be sure that this young Greek is your daughter's husband." The people in another place rejoiced and almost danced for joy, and with one consent were all glad of that which was done. Marry, all they understood not, but gathered the most part of Cariclea. Perhaps also they were stirred to understand the troth by inspiration of the gods, whose will it was that this should fall out wonderfully, as in a comedy. Surely they made very contrary things agree, and joined sorrow and mirth, tears and laughter together, and turned fearful and terrible things into a joyful banquet in the end; many that wept began to laugh, and such as were sorrowful to rejoice, when they found that they sought not for and lost that they hoped to find; and to be short the cruel slaughters which were looked for every moment were turned into holy sacrifice. Then said Hydaspes to Sisimithres: "Right wise man, what must we do? To refuse the sacrifice of the gods is a wicked act, but to offer them which they have provided for us is the duty of devout men. We must, therefore, bethink us what is best to do." Whereto Sisimithres answered, not in Greek but in the Ethiopian tongue, that all might understand him, thus: "Through too much pleasure, O king, the wisest men are oftentimes blinded. You might have perceived at the first that the gods liked not the sacrifice was ordained, who have now every way declared that happy Cariclea is your daughter, even at the very altars, and have brought him that brought her up out of the middest of Greece, as it had been of purpose. They have feared and troubled the horses and bullocks, too, that stood before the altars, whereby they declared that the greater sacrifices which have been used emong our ancestors should now cease and be used no more; and beside declared this young Greek to be the maid's husband, which may be the end and conclusion of this comedy. Let us, therefore, suffer these divine miracles to sink in our minds, and be helpers of their will, and do more acceptable sacrifices to them, and leave murthering of men and women forever hereafter." After Sisimithres had said thus so loud that all might hear him, Hydaspes, who understood also the tongue wherein he spoke, took up Theagenes and Cariclea, and said: "Seeing that these things been thus appointed by the will and pleasure of the gods, I think—how seemeth it to you that be here also?— that it is not good to strive against them. Wherefore, before them who have preordained this and you also which seem with your consent to follow their fates and destinies, I wish that these two may increase and grow in wedlock, and geve them leave to rejoice either other, that they may engender and have children. And if you shall think it good, let this decree be confirmed with sacrifice, and let us fall to worshiping of the gods." The army consented thereto, and with clapping their hands gave a sign that they were contented with the match. Hydaspes then came to the altars and, ready to begin sacrifice, said thus: "O Sun our lord, and Lady Moon, forasmuch as Theagenes and Cariclea are declared to be man and wife by your good wills, I am sure you will accept of their offerings and suffer them to do sacrifice to you." This said, he took off his own miter and Persina's, which were the notes of their priesthood, and set one upon Theagenes' head, which was his own, and the other upon Cariclea's, that was Persina's. When this was done, Caricles rememb'red himself of the oracle's answer at Delphi, and saw that fulfilled indeed which was promised before of the gods. Which was that after they fled from Delphi, they

> Should come at length to country scorch
>   with burning Phoebus' beams,
> Where they, as recompenses due,
>   that virtues rare do gain,
> In time to come, ere it be long,
>   white miters shall obtain.

Thus after they had on these white miters and were made priests by the voice and opinion of Hydaspes, and had done sacrifice very well, they rode in chariots drawn with horses, Hydaspes and Theagenes in one, Sisimithres and Cariclea in another, and Persina with Cariclea in the third; but theirs was drawn with two white oxen to Meroe with great joy and melody of instruments of music, to accomplish the secreter affairs of wedlock in the city for more solemnity's sake.

Thus endeth the Ethiopian History of Theagenes and Cariclea, the author whereof is Heliodorus of Emesos, a city in Phoenicia, son of Theodosius, which fetcheth his petigree from the same.

GEORGE GASCOIGNE

FROM A DISCOURSE OF THE ADVENTURES PASSED BY MASTER F. J. (1573)[1]

. . . F. J. chanced once in the north parts of this realm to fall in company of a very fair gentlewoman whose name was Mistress Elinor, unto whom, bearing a hot affection, he first adventured to write this letter following.

G. T.

Mistress, I pray you understand that being altogether a stranger in these parties, my good hap hath been to behold you to my no small contentation; and my evil hap accompanies the same, with such imperfection of my deserts as that I find always a ready repulse in mine own forwardness. So that, considering the natural climate of the country, I must say that I have found fire in frost. And yet, comparing the inequality of my deserts with the least part of your worthiness, I feel a continual frost in my most fervent fire. Such is, then, th' extremity of my passions, the which I could never have been content to commit unto this telltale paper were it not that I am destitute of all other help. Accept, therefore, I beseek you, the earnest good will of a more trusty than worthy servant, who, being thereby encouraged, may supply the defects of his ability with ready trial of dutiful loyalty. And let this poor paper, besprent with salt tears and blown over with scalding sighs, be saved of you as a safeguard for your sampler or a bottom to wind your sewing silk, that when your last needleful is wrought you may return to reading thereof and consider the care of him who is

More yours than his own,
F. J.

This letter by her received, as I have hard him say, her answer was this: she took occasion one day, at his request, to dance with him, the which doing, she bashfully began to declare unto him that she had read over the writing which he delivered unto her, with like protestation that as at delivery thereof she understood not for what cause he thrust the same into her bosom, so now she could not perceive thereby any part of his meaning; nevertheless at last seemed to take upon her the matter, and though she disabled herself, yet gave him thanks as etc. Whereupon he brake the brawl and, walking abroad, devised immediately these few verses following.

G. T.

Fair Bersabe the bright, once bathing in a well,
With dew bedimm'd King David's eyes that ruled
   Israel;
And Salomon himself, the source of sapience,
Against the force of such assaults could make but small
   defense.
To it the stoutest yield and strongest feel like wo;
Bold Hercules and Sampson both did prove it to be so.
What wonder seemeth, then, when stars stand thick in
   skies
If such a blazing star have power to dim my dazzled eyes?

L'envoi

To you these few suffice; your wits be quick and good.
You can conject by change of hue what humors feed my
   blood.

F. J.

I have heard the aucthor say that these were the first verses that ever he wrote upon like occasion. The which, considering the matter precedent, may in my judgment be well allowed; and to judge his doings by the effects he declared unto me that before he could put the same in legible writing it pleased the said Mistress Elinor of her curtesy thus to deal with him. Walking in a garden among divers other gentlemen and gentlewomen, with a little frowning smile in passing by him, she delivered unto him a paper with these words: "For that I understand not," quoth she, "th' intent of your letters, I pray you take them here again and bestow them at your pleasure." The which done and said, she passed by without change either of pace or countenance. F. J., somewhat troubled with her angry look, did sodenly leave the company, and, walking into a park near

---

1 For a note on this text see pp. 298–99.

adjoining, in great rage began to wreak his malice on this poor paper, and the same did rend and tear in pieces. When sodenly at a glance he perceived it was not of his own handwriting, and, therewithal abashed, upon better regard he perceived in one piece thereof written in Romain these letters: SHE. Wherefore placing all the pieces thereof as orderly as he could, he found therein written these few lines hereafter following.

G. T.   10

Your soden departure from our pastime yesterday did enforce me for lack of chosen company to return unto my work, wherein I did so long continue till at the last the bare bottom did draw unto my remembrance your strange request. And although I found therein no just cause to credit your colored words, yet have I thought good hereby to requite you with like curtesy, so that at least you shall not condemn me for ungrateful. But as to the matter therein contained, if I could persuade myself that there were in me any coals to kindle such sparks of   20 fire I might yet peradventure be drawn to believe that your mind were frozen with like fear. But as no smoke ariseth where no coal is kindled, so without cause of affection the passion is easy to be cured. This is all that I understand of your dark letters. And as much as I mean to answer.

SHE.

My friend F. J. hath told me divers times that immediately upon receit hereof he grew in jealousy   30 that the same was not her own devise. And therein I have no less allowed his judgment then commended his invention of the verses and letters before rehearsed. For as by the style this letter of hers bewrayeth that it was not penned by a woman's capacity, so the sequel of her doings may discipher that she had mo ready clerks then trusty servants in store. Well, yet as the perfect hound, when he hath chased the hurt deer amid the whole herd, will never give over till he have singled it again, even so   40 F. J., though somewhat abashed with this doubtful shew, yet still constant in his former intention, ceased not by all possible means to bring this deer yet once again to the bows, whereby she might be the more surely striken, and so in the end enforced to yield. Wherefore he thought not best to commit the said verses willingly into her custody, but privily lost them in her chamber, written in counterfeit. And after on the next day thought better to reply, either upon her or upon her secretary, in this wise as here   50 followeth.

G. T.

The much that you have answered is very much, and much more than I am able to reply unto; nevertheless in mine own defense thus much I allege: that if my sodein departure pleased not you, I cannot myself therewith be pleased as one that seeketh not to please many and more desirous to please you then any. The cause of mine affection I suppose you behold daily. For, self-love avoided, every wight may judge of themselves as much as reason persuadeth; the which if it be in your good nature suppressed with bashfulness, then mighty Jove grant you may once behold my wan cheeks washed in wo, that therein my salt tears may be a mirror to represent your own shadow, and that like unto Narcissus you may be constrained to kiss the cold waves wherein your counterfait is so lively portrayed. For if aboundance of other matters failed to draw my gazing eyes in contemplation of so rare excellency, yet might these your letters both frame in me an admiration of such divine *esprit* and a confusion to my dull understanding, which so rashly presumed to wander in this endless laberinth. Such I esteem you, and thereby am become such, and even

HE.   F. J.

This letter finished and fair written over, his chance was to meet her alone in a gallery of the same house, where (as I have heard him declare) his manhood in this kind of combat was first tried; and therein I can compare him to a valiant prince who, distressed with power of enemies, had committed the safeguard of his person to treaty of ambassade, and sodenly (surprised with a *camnassado* in his own trenches) was enforced to yield as prisoner. Even so my friend F. J., lately overcome by the beautiful beams of this Dame Elinor, and having now committed his most secret intent to these late rehearsed letters, was at unwares encount'red with his friendly foe and constrained either to prepare some new defense or else, like a recreant, to yield himself as already vanquished. Wherefore, as in a trance, he lifted up his dazzled eyes, and so continued in a certain kind of admiration, not unlike the astronomer who, having after a whole night's travail in the gray morning found his desired star, hath fixed his hungry eyes to behold the comet long looked for; whereat this gracious dame, as one that could discern the sun before her chamber windows were wide open, did deign to embolden the feinting knight with these or like words.

"I perceive now," quod she, "how mishap doth follow me, that, having chosen this walk for a simple solace, I am here disquieted by the man that meaneth my distruction." And therewithal, as half angry,   50 began to turn her back, whenas my friend F. J., now awaked, gan thus salute her.

"Mistress," quod he, "and I perceive now that good hap haunts me, for being by lack of opportunity constrained to commit my welfare unto these blabbing leaves of bewraying paper"—shewing that in his hand—"I am here recomforted with happy view of my desired joy." And therewithal reverently kissing his hand, did softly distrain her slender arm and so stayed her departure. The first blow thus proffered and defended, they walked and talked, traversing divers ways, wherein I doubt not but that my friend F. J. could quit himself reasonably well. And though it stood not with duty of a friend that I should therein require to know his secrets, yet of himself he declared thus much: that after long talk she was contented to accept his proffer'd service, but yet still disabling herself and seeming to marvel what cause had moved him to subject his liberty so wilfully, or at least in a prison (as she termed it) so unworthy. Whereunto I need not rehearse his answer, but suppose now that thus they departed, saving I had forgotten this: she required of him the last-rehearsed letter, saying that his first was lost, and now she lacked a new bottom for her silk, the which I warrant you he granted. And so proffering to take an humble *congé* by *bezo las manos,* she graciously gave him the *zuccado des labros,* and so for then departed. . . .

[As a result of this colloquy, and of another poetical exercise which F. J. contrived for her to find, Elinor discovers herself to be in love; but since she refuses to acknowledge the fact she begins to sicken, and especially to suffer from nosebleed. Through the good offices of Mistress Frances, another gentlewoman in the house, F. J. is brought to her with what he promises to be a sovereign cure. Coming to her "chamber," he finds her "set in a chair, leaning on the one side over a silver bason."]

After his due reverence, he laid his hand on her temples and, privily rounding her in her ear, desired her to command a hazel stick and a knife, the which being brought he delivered unto her, saying on this wise: "Mistress, I will speak certain words in secret to myself, and do require no more but when you hear me say openly this word *amen* that you with this knife will make a nick upon this hazel stick; and when you have made five nicks command me also to cease." The dame, partly of good will to the knight and partly to be stenched of her bleeding, commanded her maid and required the other gentles somewhat to stand aside; which done, he began his oraisons, wherein he had not long muttered before he pronounced *amen,* wherewith the lady made a nick on the stick with her knife. The said Ferdinando continued to another *amen,* when the lady, having made another nick, felt her bleeding began to steinch; and so by the third *amen* throughly steinched. Ferdinando, then changing his prayers into private talk, said softly unto her: "Mistress, I am glad that I am hereby enabled to do you some service, and as the staunching of your own blood may some way recomfort you, so if the shedding of my blood may any way content

you I beseech you command it, for it shall be evermore readily employed in your service." And therewithal with a loud voice pronounced *amen,* wherewith the good lady, making a nick, did secretly answer thus: "Good servant," quod she, "I must needs think myself right happy to have gained your service and good will, and be you sure that, although there be in me no such desert as may draw you into this depth of affection, yet such as I am I shall be always glad to shew myself thankful unto you; and now, if you think yourself assured that I shall bleed no more, do then pronounce your fifth *amen.*" The which pronounced, she made also her fifth nick and held up her head, calling the company unto her and declaring unto them that her bleeding was throughly steinched. <Well, it were long to tell what sundry opinions were pronounced upon this act, and I do dwell overlong in the discourses of this F. J., especially having taken in hand only to copy out his verses; but for the circumstance doth better declare the effect, I will return to my former tale.>[1] And Ferdinando, tarrying a while in the chamber, found opportunity to lose his sequence near to his desired mistress, and, after *congé* taken, departed. After whose departure the lady arose out of her chair, and her maid, going about to remove the same, espied and took up the writing, the which her mistress perceiving, gan sodenly conjecture that the same had in it some like matter to the verses once before left in like manner, and made semblant to mistrust that the same should be some words of conjuration; and, taking it from her maid, did peruse it and immediately said to the company that she would not forgo the same for a great treasure. . . . But to be plain, I think that, F. J. excepted, she was glad to be rid of all company until she had with sufficient leisure turned over and retossed every card in this sequence. And not long after, being now tickled thorough all the veins with an unknown humor, adventured of herself to commit unto a like ambassador the disciphering of that which hitherto she had kept more secret, and thereupon wrote with her own hand and head in this wise.

G. T.

Good servant, I am out of all doubt much beholding unto you, and I have great comfort by your means in the steinching of my blood, and I take great comfort to read your letters, and I have found in my chamber divers songs which I think to be of your making, and I promise you they are excellently made, and I assure you that I will be ready to do for you any pleasure that I can during my life; wherefore I pray you come to my chamber once in a day till I come abroad again, and I will be glad

---

[1] The sentence here enclosed in pointed brackets does not occur in all copies of the 1573 edition.

of your company, and forbecause that you have promised to be my HE I will take upon me this name, your SHE.

This letter I have seen of her own handwriting, and as therein the reader may find great difference of style from her former letter, so may you now understand the cause. She had in the same house a friend, a servant, a secretary—what should I name him? Such one as she esteemed in time past more than was cause in time present, and to make my tale good, I will (by report of my very good friend F. J.) describe him unto you. He was in height the proportion of two pigmies, in breadth the thickness of two bacon hogs, of presumption a giant, of power a gnat, apishly witted, knavishly manner'd, and crabbedly favor'd. What was there in him, then, to draw a fair lady's liking? Marry sir, even all in all, a well-lined purse wherewith he could at every call provide such pretty conceits as pleased her peevish fantasy, and by that means he had throughly (long before) insinuated himself with this amorous dame. This manling, this minion, this slave, this secretary was now by occasion ridden to London, forsooth; and though his absence were unto her a disfurnishing of eloquence, it was yet unto F. J. an opportunity of good advantage, for when he perceived the change of her style, and thereby grew in some suspicion that the same proceeded by absence of her chief chancelor, he thought good now to smite while the iron was hot, and to lend his mistress such a pen in her secretary's absence as he should never be able at his return to amend the well-writing thereof; wherefore, according to her command, he repaired once every day to her chamber at the least, whereas he guided himself so well, and could devise such store of sundry pleasures and pastimes, that he grew in favor not only with his desired but also with the rest of the gentlewomen. . . .

[Although F. J. continues to ingratiate himself with Elinor through his witty small talk and his poetry, her jealousy grows with her interest. For at supper, after F. J. has charmed the whole company with his conversation, Elinor, in her "night attire," comes from her chamber; she insists that F. J. dance with Frances ("unto F. J. a kinswoman, a virgin of rare chastity, singular capacity, notable modesty, and excellent beauty"), but she is torn by jealousy in watching them weave through their paces. She flings herself angrily away to her chamber, causes her maid "to clap to the door," and the next day fails to keep a rendezvous with her "servant." Meanwhile, Frances determines to save F. J. from Elinor, who, as she tells him, is a born coquette: although a married woman, she has deserted two former lovers and will no doubt desert him too, so infatuated is she with her knavish secretary (to whom she "had

of long time been yielded"). However, when at dinner Elinor coyly invites F. J. to visit her again in her chamber he eagerly assents.]

Supper-time came and passed over, and not long after came the handmaid of the Lady Elinor into the great chamber, desiring F. J. to repair unto their mistress, the which he willingly accomplished; and being now ent'red into her chamber, he might perceive his mistress in her night's attire, preparing herself towards bed, to whom F. J. said: "Why, how now, mistress? I had thought this night to have seen you dance (at least or at last) amongst us." "By my troth, good servant," quod she, "I adventured so soon unto the great chamber yesternight that I find myself somewhat sickly disposed, and therefore do strain curtesy (as you see) to go the sooner to my bed this night; but before I sleep," quod she, "I am to charge you with a matter of weight." And taking him apart from the rest declared that (as that present night) she would talk with him more at large in the gallery near ajoining to her chamber. Hereupon F. J., discreetly dissimuling his joy, took his leave and returned into the great chamber, where he had not long continued before the lord of the castle commanded a torch to light him unto his lodging, whereas he prepared himself and went to bed, commanding his servant also to go to his rest. And when he thought as well his servant as the rest of the household to be safe, he arose again and, taking his nightgown, did under the same convey his naked sword, and so walked to the gallery, where he found his good mistress walking in her nightgown and attending his coming. The moon was now at the full, the skies clear, and the weather temperate, by reason whereof he might the more plainly and with the greater contentation behold his long-desired joys; and, spreading his arms abroad to embrace his loving mistress, he said: "O my dear lady! When shall I be able with any desert to countervail the least part of this your bountiful goodness?" The dame (whether it were of fear indeed or that the wiliness of womanhood had taught her to cover her conceits with some fine dissimulation) stert back from the knight, and, shriching (but softly), said unto him: "Alas, servant, what have I deserved that you come against me with naked sword as against an open enemy?" F. J., perceiving her entent, excused himself, declaring that he brought the same for their defense, and not to offend her in any wise. The lady being therewith somewhat appeased, they began with more comfortable gesture to expel the dread of the said late affright, and sithens to become bolder of behavior, more familiar in speech, and most kind in accomplishing of common comfort. But why hold I so long discourse in discribing the joys which (for lack of like experience) I cannot set out to the full? Were it not that I know to whom I write, I would the more beware what I write. F. J. was a man, and neither of us are senseless, and therefore I should slander him (over and besides a greater obloquy to the whole genealogy of Aeneas) if I should imagine that of tender heart he would forbear to express her more tender limbs against the hard floor. Sufficed that of her curteous nature she was content to accept bords for a bed of down, mats for cameric sheets, and the nightgown of F. J. for a counterpoint to cover them; and thus, with calm content instead of quiet sleep, they beguiled the night until the proudest ster began to abandon the firmament, when F. J. and his mistress were constrained also to abandon their delights, and with ten thousand sweet kisses and strait embracings did frame themselves to play "Loath to depart." Well, remedy was there none, but Dame Elinor must return unto her chamber, and F. J. must also convey himself (as closely as might be) into his chamber, the which was hard to do, the day being so far sprung, and he having a large base-court to pass over before he could recover his stairfoot door. And though he were not much perceived, yet the Lady Frances, being no less desirous to see an issue of these enterprises then F. J. was willing to cover them in secrecy, did watch; and even at the ent'ring of his chamber door perceived the point of his naked sword glist'ring under the skirt of his nightgown; whereat she smiled and said to herself, "This gear goeth well about." Well, F. J. having now recovered his chamber, he went to bed, and there let him sleep, as his mistress did on that other side. Although the Lady Frances, being throughly tickled now in all the veins, could not enjoy such quiet rest, but arising, took another gentlewoman of the house with her and walked into the park to take the fresh air of the morning. They had not long walked there but they retorned, and though F. J. had not yet slept sufficiently for one which had so far travailed in the night past, yet they went into his chamber to raise him, and coming to his bed's side found him fast on sleep. "Alas," quod that other gentlewoman, "it were pity to awake him." "Even so it were," quod Dame Frances, "but we will take away somewhat of his whereby he may perceive that we were here." And looking about the chamber his naked sword presented itself to the hands of Dame Frances, who took it with her, and, softly shutting his chamber door again, went down the stairs and recovered her own lodging in good order and unperceived of anybody, saving only that other gentlewoman which accompanied her. . . .

[Although the next day, owing to the loss of his sword and to certain innuendoes of Frances, F. J.

has reason to think that his affair with Elinor will become public, Elinor contrives to steal the sword herself and return it to her lover. Thereafter they meet more freely and frequently, "their affairs being no less politicly governed then happily atchieved." And so they pass their time "in exceeding contentation and more than speakable pleasures, in which time F. J. did compile very many verses according to sundrie occasions proff'red." Not even the return of Elinor's husband (of whom we have heard virtually nothing before) interferes with their "pleasures."]

The husband of the Lady Elinor, being all this while absent from her, gan now retorn and kept cut at home, with whom F. J. found means so to ensignuate himself that familiarity took deep root between them, and seldom but by stealth you could find the one out of the other's company. On a time the knight, riding on hunting, desired F. J. to accompany him, the which he could not refuse to do, but like a lusty younker, ready at all assays, appareled himself in green, and about his neck a bugle, pricking and gallowping amongst the foremost according to the manner of that country. And it chanced that the married knight thus gallowping lost his horn, which some devines might have interpreted to be but moulting, and that by God's grace he might have a new come up again shortly instead of that. Well, he came to F. J., requiring him to lend him his bugle. "For," said the knight, "I hard you not blow this day, and I would fain encourage the hounds if I had a horn." Quod F. J.: "Although I have not been over-lavish of my coming hitherto, I would you should not doubt but that I can tell how to use a horn well enough; and yet I may little do if I may not lend you a horn." And therewithal took his bugle from his neck and lent it to the knight, who, making in unto the hounds, gan assay to rechate; but the horn was too hard for him to wind, whereat F. J. took pleasure, and said to himself: "Blow till you break that; I made thee one within these few days that thou wilt never crack whiles thou livest." And hereupon (before the fall of the buck) devised this sonnet following, which at his home-coming he presented unto his mistress.

G. T.

As some men say there is a kind of seed
Will grow to horns if it be sowed thick,
Wherewith I thought to try if I could breed
A brood of buds well-sharped on the prick.
And by good proof of learned skill I found,
As on some special soil all seeds best frame,
So jealous brains do breed the battle ground
That best of all might serve to bear the same.
Then sought I forth to find such supple soil,

And call'd to mind thy husband had a brain,
So that percase, by travail and by toil,
His fruitful front might turn my seed to gain.
And as I groped in that ground to sow it,
Start up a horn, thy husband could not blow it.

                                              F. J.

This sonnet treateth of a strange seed, but it tasteth most of rye, which is more common amongst men nowadays. Well, let it pass amongst the rest, and he that liketh it not, turn over the leaf to another. I doubt not but in this register he may find some to content him, unless he be too curious; and here I will surcease to rehearse any more of his verses until I have expressed how that his joys, being now exalted to the highest degree, began to bend towards declination. For now the unhappy secretary, whom I have before rememb'red, was returned from London, on whom F. J. had no sooner cast his eyes but immediately he fell into a great passion of mind which might be compared unto a fever. . . . Well, such was the grief unto him that he became sickly and kept his chamber. The ladies, having received the news thereof, gan all at once lament his misfortune and of common consent agreed to visit him. They marched thither in good equipage, I warrant you, and found F. J. lying upon his bed languishing, whom they all saluted generally and sought to recomfort; but especially his mistress, having in her hand a branch of willow wherewith she defended her from the whot air, gan thus say unto him: "Servant," quod she, "for that I suppose your malady to proceed of none other cause but only slouthfulness, I have brought this pretty rod to beat you a little, nothing doubting but when you feel the smart of a twig or twain you will, like a tractable young scholler, pluck up your quick'ned spirits and cast this drowsiness apart." F. J. with a great sigh answered: "Alas, good mistress," quod he, "if any like chastisement might quicken me, how much more might the presence of all you lovely dames recomfort my dulled mind, whom to behold were sufficient to revive an eye now dazzled with the dread of death, and that not only for the heavenly aspects which you represent but also much the more for your exceeding curtesy, in that you have deigned to visit me, so unworthy a servant. But, good mistress," quod he, "as it were shame for me to confess that ever my heart could yield for fear, so I assure you that my mind cannot be content to induce infirmity by sluggish conceit. But in truth, mistress, I am sick," quod he. And therewithal the trembling of his heart had sent up such a throbbing into his throat as that his voice, now deprived of breath, commanded the tongue to be still. When Dame Elinor for com-

passion distilled into tears and drew towards the window, leaving the other gentlewomen about his bed, who, being no less sorry for his grief, yit for that they were none of them so touched in their secret thoughts, they had bolder sprites and freer speech to recomfort him. Amongest the rest the Lady Frances (who indeed loved him deeply and could best conjecture the cause of his conceipts) said unto him: "Good Trust," quod she, "if any help of physic may cure your malady I would not have you hurt yourself with these doubts which you seem to retain. If choice of diet may help, behold us here your cooks, ready to minister all things needful; if company may drive away your annoy, we mean not to leave you solitary; if grief of mind be cause of your infirmity, we all here will offer our devoir to turn it into joy; if mishap have given you cause to fear or dread anything, remember hope, which never faileth to recomfort an afflicted mind. And, good Trust," quod she, distreining his hand right heartily, "let this simple proof of our poor good wills be so accepted of you as that it may work thereby the effect of our desires." F. J., as one in a trance, had marked very little of her curteous talk, and yet gave her thanks and so held his peace; whereat the ladies being all amazed, there became a silence in the chamber on all sides. Dame Elinor, fearing thereby that she might the more easely be espied and having now dried up her tears, returned to F. J., recomforting him by all possible means of common curtesy, promising that since in her sickness he had not only staunched her bleeding but also by his gentle company and sundry devices of honest pastime had driven away the pensiveness of her mind, she thought herself bound with like willingness to do her best in anything that might restore his health. . . . After their departure he gan cast in his mind the exceeding curtesy used towards him by them all, but above all other the bounty of his mistress; and therewithal took a sound and firm opinion that it was not possible for her to counterfeit so deeply (as indeed I believe that she then did not), whereby he sodenly felt his heart greatly eased, and began in himself thus to reason: "Was ever man of so wretched a heart? I am the most bounden to love," quod he, "of all them that ever professed his service. I enjoy one the fairest that ever was found, and I find her the kindest that ever was heard of; yit in mine own wicked heart I could villainously conceive that of her which, being compared with the rest of her virtues, is not possible to harbor in so noble a mind. Hereby I have brought myself without cause into this feebleness, and good reason that for so high an offence I should be punished with great infirmity. What shall I then do? Yield to the same? No, but according to my late protestation I will recomfort this languishing mind of mine to the end I may live but only to do penance for this so notable a crime so rashly committed." And thus saying he start from his bed and gan to walk towards the window; but the venimous serpent which (as before I rehearsed) had stung him could not be content that these medicines applied by the mouth of his gentle mistress should so soon restore him to guerison. And although indeed they were such mithridate to F. J. as that they had now expelled the rancor of the poison, yit that ougly, hellish monster had left behind her in the most secret of his bosom (even between the mind and the man) one of her familiars named Suspect, which gan work in the weak sprites of F. J. effects of no less peril than before he had conceived. His head swelling with these troublesome toys and his heart swimming in the tempests of tossing fantasy, he felt his legs so feeble that he was constrained to lie down on his bed again; and, repeating in his own remembrance every word that his mistress had spoken unto him, he gan to dread that she had brought the willow braunce to beat him with in token that he was of her forsaken; for so lovers do most commonly expound the willow garland, and this to think did cut his heart in twain. . . .

[After supper, the whole bevy of "dames" returned to visit the sick man and to beguile the time with expounding riddles and allegories of love. But Elinor had more on her mind than urbane conversation, for in taking her departure she whispered to him that she would return later that night.]

About ten or eleven of the clock came his mistress in her nightgown, who, knowing all privy ways in that house very perfectly, had conveyed herself into F. J. chamber unseen and unperceived, and, being now come unto his bed's side, kneeled down and, laying her arm over him, said these or like words: "My good servant, if thou knewest what perplexities I suffer in beholding of thine infirmities it might then suffice either utterly to drive away thy malady or much more to augment thy griefs; for I know thou lovest me, and I think also that thou hast had sufficient proof of mine unfeigned good will, in remembrance whereof I fall into sundry passions. . . ." [Elinor's account of their affair brings to F. J. such remorse for his ill-founded jealousy that he swoons in her arms, at which Elinor promptly provides amatory resuscitation.] For my friend F. J. hath to me emported that, returning to life, the first thing which he felt was that his good mistress lay pressing his breast with the whole weight of her body and biting his lips with her friendly teeth. . . . F. J., now awaked, could no less do than of his curteous nature receive his mistress into his bed; who, as one that knew that way better than how to help his swooning, gan gently

strip off her clothes, and, lovingly embracing him, gan demand of him in this sort: "Alas, good servant," quod she, "what kind of malady is this that so extremely doth torment thee?" F. J. with fainting speech answered: "Mistress, as for my malady, it hath been easely cured by your bountiful medicines applied. But I must confess that in receiving that guerison at your hands I have been constrained to fall into an ecstasy through the galding remembrance of mine own unworthiness. Nevertheless, good mistress, since I perceive such fidelity remaining between us as that few words will persuade such trust as lovers ought to embrace, let these few words suffice to crave your pardon. . . ." Dame Elinor, who had rather have found her servant perfectly revived than thus with strange conceipts encomb'red, and musing much at his dark speech, became importunate to know the certainty of his thoughts. And F. J., as one not maister of himself, gan at the last plainly confess how he had mistrusted the change of her vowed affections. Yea, and (that more was) he plainly expressed with whom, of whom, by whom, and to whom she bent her better liking.

Now, here I would demand of you and such other as are expert: is there any greater impediment to the fruition of a lover's delights than to be mistrusted? Or rather, is it not the ready way to race all love and former good will out of remembrance to tell a guilty mind that you do mistrust it? It should seem yes by Dame Elinor, who began now to take the matter whotly; and of such vehemency were her fancies that she now fell into flat defiance with F. J., who, although he sought by many fair words to temper her choleric passions and by yielding himself to get the conquest of another, yet could he by no means determine the quarrel. The soft pillows being present at all these whot words put forth themselves as mediators for a truce between these enemies, and desired that, if they would needs fight, it might be in their presence but only one push of the pike, and so from thenceforth to become friends again forever. But the dame denied flatly, alledging that she found no cause at all to use such curtesy unto such a recreant, adding further many words of great reproach, the which did so enrage F. J. as that, having now forgotten all former curtesies, he drew upon his new professed enemy and bare her up with such a violence against the bolster that before she could prepare the ward he thrust her through both hands, and etc.; whereby the dame, swooning for fear, was constrained (for a time) to abandon her body to the enemy's curtesy. At last, when she came to herself, she rose sodeinly and determined to save herself by flight, leaving F. J. with many dispiteful words, and swearing that he should never (eftsoons) take her at the like advantage, the which oath she kept better than her former professed good will; and having now recovered her chamber (because she found her hurt to be nothing dangerous) I doubt not but she slept quietly the rest of the night. As F. J., also persuading himself that he should with convenient leisure recover her from this hagger conceipt, took some better rest towards the morning than he had done in many nights forepast.

So let them both sleep whiles I turn my pen unto the before-named secretary, who, being (as I said) come lately from London, had made many proffers to renew his accustomed consultations; but the sorrow which his mistress had conceived in F. J. his sickness, togither with her continual repair to him during the same, had been such lets unto his attempts as it was long time before he could obtain audience. At the last these new accidents fell so favorably for the furtherance of his cause that he came to his mistress' presence and there pleaded for himself. Now, if I should at large write his allegations, togither with her subtile answers, I should but cumber your ears with unpleasant rehearsal of feminine frailty. To be short, the late disdainful mood which she had conceived against F. J., togither with a scrupule which lay in her conscience touching the eleventh article of her belief, moved her presently with better will to consult with this secretary as well upon a speedy revenge of her late-received wrongs as also upon the reformation of her religion. And in very deed it fell out that the secretary, having been of long time absent, and thereby his quills and pens not worn so near as they were wont to be, did now prick such fair large notes that his mistress liked better to sing faburden under him than to descant any longer upon F. J. plain-song; and thus they continued in good accord until it fortuned that Dame Frances came into her chamber upon such sodein as she had like to have marred all the music. Well, they conveyed their clifs as closely as they could, but yit not altogether without some suspicion given to the said Dame Frances, who, although she could have been content to take any pain in F. J. behalf, yit otherwise she would never have bestowed the watching about so worthless a prize. . . .

[Hereafter, the affair between F. J. and Elinor languishes to a softly cadenced close. As F. J. recovers his health and resumes the social intercourse of the great hall, he is made to understand that things between him and his lady are not as they once were. Elinor herself is conspicuously indifferent to his advances; and Frances, eager to see the termination of an affair so little to the credit of the man she vainly loves, tells him a thinly disguised allegory of the debasing effects of such an intrigue as his and Elinor's,

At last F. J. is made to realize that the episode has ended.]

F. J. smell'd how the world went about, and therefore did one day in the gray morning adventure to pass through the gallery towards his mistress' chamber, hoping to have found the door open; but he found the contrary, and there, attending in good devotion, heard the parting of his mistress and her secretary, with many kind words; whereby it appeared that the one was very loth to depart from the other. F. J. was enforced to bear this burden, and after he had attended there as long as the light would give him leave, he departed also to his chamber and, apparelling himself, could not be quiet until he had spoken with his mistress, whom he burdened flatly with this despiteful treachery; and she as fast denied it until, at last being still urged with such evident tokens as he alleged, she gave him this bone to gnaw upon. "And if I did so," quod she, "what than?" Whereunto F. J. made none answer, but departed with this farewell: "My loss is mine own, and your gain is none of yours; and sooner can I recover my loss than you enjoy the gain which you gape after." And whan he was in place solitary he compiled these following for a final end of the matter.

G. T.

"And if I did, what then?
Are you agriev'd therefore?
The sea hath fish for every man,
And what would you have more?"

Thus did my mistress once
Amaze my mind with doubt,
And popp'd a question for the nonce
To beat my brains about.

Whereto I thus replied:
"Each fisherman can wish
That all the sea at every tide
Were his alone to fish.

"And so did I, in vain,
But since it may not be,
Let such fish there as find the gain,
And leave the loss for me.

"And with such luck and loss
I will content myself
Till tides of turning time may toss
Such fishers on the shelf.

"And when they stick on sands,
That every man may see,
Then will I laugh and clap my hands
As they do now at me."

F. J.

It is time now to make an end of this thriftless history, wherein, although I could wade much further as to declare his departure, what thanks he gave to his Hope, etc., yet I will cease, as one that had rather leave it unperfect than make it too plain. I have pass'd it over with "quod he" and "quod she," after my homely manner of writing, using sundry names for one person, as "the dame," "the lady," "mistress," etc., "the lord of the castle," "the master of the house," and "the host"; nevertheless for that I have seen good aucthors term every gentlewoman a lady and every gentleman *domine* I have thought it no greater fault then petty treason thus to entermingle them, nothing doubting but you will easely understand my meaning, and that is as much as I desire. Now henceforwards I will trouble you no more with such a barbarous style in prose. . . .

G. T.

JOHN LYLY

EUPHUES

Unlike most young writers, Lyly won fame with his first literary effort. As a hanger-on to the powerful Lord Burghley and his son-in-law the Earl of Oxford after he had proceeded M.A. at Oxford (1575), he finished *Euphues: The Anatomy of Wit* in the summer of 1578; by early winter he had found a publisher, for on December 2 Gabriel Cawood entered it in the Stationers' Register; by Christmas, as Lyly himself said, it was lying "bound on the stationer's stall"; and within a few months he was famous as the author of a new kind of romance—a kind destined for a fertile but relatively short history. Developing with tedious if ingenious intensity the stylistic devices of precariously balanced sentence structure and rhetorical figuration, Lyly used the tricks of antithesis, alliteration, repetition, *exempla, sententiae,* and *similia* with fiendish ingenuity. They were tricks long familiar in classical rhetoric, and already domesticated in the vernacular by such writers as North (in his translation of *The Dial of Princes,* 1557), Pettie (in *A Petite Palace of Pettie His Pleasure,* 1576), and John Grange (in *The Golden Aphroditis,* 1577), as well as by John Rainolds, fellow (1566–86) of Corpus Christi College, in his Latin lectures at Oxford. Although Lyly was first famous and then notorious for his style, his real contribution to prose fiction lay in the uses to which he put this style: he applied his technical skill to a prose comedy of manners based on the social modes and affectations of contemporary life, and his delighted readers welcomed *Euphues* as a heady change from the unfashionable (and anachronistic) conventions of chivalric romance. Lyly's clever blend of stylistic elegance, amorous narrative, didacticism, and satire made *Euphues* a dazzling popular success; moreover, when Euphues' *education sentimentale* is considered in its larger implications, it takes its proper place in the rich and various tradition of Renaissance ethical writing that includes the greater work of Castiglione, Elyot, Ascham, Sidney, and even of Spenser. The reception of *Euphues* was so cordial that a new edition (with many revisions and even additions, including a mollifying address to the "gentlemen scholars" of Oxford) was ready by the summer of 1579; and a sequel, *Euphues and His England* (ambiguously announced at the end of its predecessor) was launched almost immediately, entered by Cawood in the Stationers' Register on July 24, 1579, and published (perhaps in the spring) the next year. Even though Lyly's *preciosité* had itself become an object of ridicule by the nineties, the popularity of his novels continued long into the seventeenth century. The original *Euphues* went through thirteen editions by 1613, the sequel through twelve by 1609, and the two novels were printed together four times between 1617 and 1638. Our text is based upon *Euphues. The Anatomy of Wyt. Very pleasant for all Gentlemen to reade, and most necessary to remember . . . By John Lylly Master of Arte,* 1578 (STC 17053); *Euphues and his England. Containing his voyage and adventures, myxed with sundry pretie discourses of honest Love, the discription of the countrey, the Court, and the manners of that Isle . . . By Iohn Lyly, Maister of Arte,* 1580 (STC 17068).

FROM EUPHUES: THE ANATOMY OF WIT (1578)

To the Gentlemen Readers

I was driven into a quandary, gentlemen, whether I might send this my pamphlet to the printer or to he pedler. I thought it too bad for the press and too good for the pack. But seeing my folly in writing to be as great as others', I was willing my fortune should be as ill as any man's. We commonly see the book that at Christmas lieth bound on the stationer's stall, at Easter to be broken in the haberdasher's shop, which sith it is the order of proceeding, I am content this winter to have my doings read for a toy, that in sommer they may be ready for trash. It is not strange, whenas the greatest wonder lasteth but nine days, that a new work should not endure but three moneths. Gentlemen use books as gentlewomen handle their flow'rs, who in the morning stick them in their heads, and at night straw them at their heels. Cherries be fulsome when they be through ripe, bicause they be plenty, and books be stale when they be printed, in that they be common. In my mind printers and tailors are bound chiefly to pray for gentlemen: the one hath so many fantasies to print, the other such divers fashions to make, that the pressing-iron of the one is never out of the fire, nor the printing press of the other any time lieth still. But a fashion is but a day's wearing, and a book but an hour's reading, which seeing it is so, I am of a shoemaker's mind, who careth not so the shoe hold the plucking-on, [nor] I, so my labors last the running-over. He that cometh in print bicause he would be known is like the fool that cometh into the market bicause he would be seen. I am not he that seeketh praise for his labor, but pardon for his offense; neither do I set this forth for any devotion in print, but for duty which I owe to my patron. If one write never so well, he cannot please all, and write he never so ill, he shall please some. Fine heads will pick a quarrel with me if all be not curious, and flatterers a thank if anything be currant. But this is my mind, let him that findeth fault amend it, and him that liketh it use it. Envy braggeth but draweth no blood; the malicious have more mind to quip then might to cut. I submit myself to the judgment of the wise, and I little esteem the censure of fools. The one will be satisfied with reason, the other are to be answered with silence. I know gentlemen will find no fault without cause, and bear with those that deserve blame; as for others I care not for their jests, for I never meant to make them my judges. Farewell.

There dwelt in Athens a young gentleman of great patrimony, and of so comely a personage that it was doubted whether he were more bound to Nature for the liniaments of his person or to Fortune for the encrease of his possessions. But Nature, impatient of comparisons, and as it were disdaining a companion or co-partner in her working, added to this comeliness of his body such a sharp capacity of mind that not only she proved Fortune counterfait, but was half of that opinion that she herself was only currant. This young gallant, of more wit then wealth, and yet of more wealth then wisdom, seeing himself inferior to none in pleasant conceipts, thought himself superior to all in honest conditions, insomuch

that he deemed himself so apt to all things that he gave himself almost to nothing but practising of those things commonly which are incident to these sharp wits, fine phrases, smooth quipping, merry taunting, using jesting without mean, and abusing mirth without measure. As therefore the sweetest rose hath his prickle, the finest velvet his brack, the fairest flour his bran, so the sharpest wit hath his wanton will, and the holiest head his wicked way. And true it is that some men write and most men believe that in all perfect shapes a blemish bringeth rather a liking every way to the eyes then a loathing any way to the mind. Venus had her mole in her cheek which made her more amiable; Helen her scar on her chin which Paris called *cos amoris,* the whetstone of love, Aristippus his wart, Lycurgus his wen. So likewise in the disposition of the mind, either virtue is overshadowed with some vice, or vice overcast with some virtue. Alexander valiant in war, yet given to wine. Tully eloquent in his gloses, yet vainglorious. Solomon wise, yet too too wanton. David holy but yet an homicide. None more witty then Euphues, yet at the first none more wicked. The freshest colors soonest fade, the teenest razor soonest turneth his edge, the finest cloth is soonest eaten with moths, and the cambric sooner stained then the coarse canvas; which appeared well in this Euphues, whose wit being like wax apt to receive any impression, and having the bridle in his own hands either to use the rein or the spur, disdaining counsail, leaving his country, loathing his old acquaintance, thought either by wit to obtain some conquest or by shame to abide some conflict, and leaving the rule of reason, rashly ran unto destruction.

It hath been an old-said saw, and not of less truth then antiquity, that wit is the better if it be the dearer bought; as in the sequel of this history shall most manifestly appear. It happened this young imp to arrive at Naples, a place of more pleasure then profit, and yet of more profit then piety, the very walls and windows whereof shewed it rather to be the tabernacle of Venus then the temple of Vesta.

There was all things necessary and in readiness that might either allure the mind to lust or entice the heart to folly, a court more meet for an atheist then for one of Athens, for Ovid then for Aristotle, for a graceless lover then for a godly liver; more fitter for Paris then Hector and meeter for Flora then Diana.

Here my youth (whether for weariness he could not or for wantonness would not go any further) determined to make his abode; whereby it is evidently seen that the fleetest fish swalloweth the delicatest bait, that the highest soaring hawk traineth to the lure, and that the wittest sconce is invegled with the soddeyn view of alluring vanities.

Here he wanted no companions, which courted

him continually with sundry kinds of devices, whereby they might either soak his purse to reap commodity or soothe his person to win credit, for he had guests and companions of all sorts.

There frequented to his lodging and mansion-house as well the spider to suck poison of his fine wit as the bee to gather honey, as well the drone as the dove, the fox as the lamb, as well Damocles to betray him as Damon to be true to him. Yet he behaved himself so warily that he could single out his game wisely, insomuch that an old gentleman in Naples, seeing his pregnant wit, his eloquent tongue somewhat taunting, yet with delight, his mirth without measure, yet not without wit, his sayings vainglorious, yet pithy, began to bewail his nurture and to muse at his nature, being incensed against the one as most pernicious, and enflamed with the other as most precious; for he well knew that so rare a wit would in time either breed an intolerable trouble or bring an incomperable treasure to the common-weal; at the one he greatly pitied, at the other he rejoiced.

Having therefore gotten opportunity to communicate with him his mind, with wat'ry eyes, as one lamenting his wantonness, and smiling face, as one loving his wittiness, encount'red him on this manner:

"Young gentleman, although my acquaintance be small to intreat you, and my authority less to command you, yet my good will in giving you good counsail should induce you to believe me, and my hoary hairs, ambassadors of experience, enforce you to follow me; for by how much the more I am a stranger to you, by so much the more you are beholding to me; having therefore opportunity to utter my mind, I mean to be importunate with you to follow my meaning. As thy birth doth shew the express and lively image of gentle blood, so thy bringing-up seemeth to me to be a great blot to the linage of so noble a brute, so that I am enforced to think that either thou diddest want one to give thee good instructions, or that thy parents made thee a wanton with too much cockering; either they were too foolish in using no discipline, or thou too froward in rejecting their doctrine; either they willing to have thee idle, or thou wilful to be ill employed. Did they not remember that which no man ought to forget, that the tender youth of a child is like the tempering of new wax, apt to receive any form? He that will carry a bull with Milo must use to carry him a calf also; he that coveteth to have a straight tree must not bow him being a twig. The potter fashioneth his clay when it is soft, and the sparrow is taught to come when he is young. As therefore the iron being hot receiveth any form with the stroke of the hammer, and keepeth it, being cold, forever, so the tender wit of a child, if with diligence it be instructed in youth, will with industry use those qualities in his age.

"They might also have taken example of the wise husbandmen, who in their fattest and most fertile ground sow hemp before wheat, a grain that drieth up the superfluous moisture and maketh the soil more apt for corn. Or of good gardeners, who in their curious knots mix hyssop with thyme as aiders the one to the growth of the other, the one being dry, the other moist; or of cunning painters, who for the whitest work cast the blackest ground, to make the picture more amiable. If therefore thy father had been as wise an husbandman as he was a fortunate husband, or thy mother as good a huswife as she was a happy wife, if they had been both as good gard'ners to keep their knot as they were grafters to bring forth such fruit, or as cunning painters as they were happy parents, no doubt they had sowed hemp before wheat, that is, discipline before affection, they had set hyssop with thyme, that is, manners with wit, the one to aid the other; and to make thy dexterity more, they had cast a black ground for their white work, that is, they had mixed threats with fair looks.

"But things past are past calling again; it is too late to shut the stable door when the steed is stolen. The Troyans repented too late when their town was spoiled. Yet the remembrance of thy former follies might breed in thee a remorse of conscience, and be a remedy against further concupiscence. But now to thy present time: the Lacedemonians were wont to shew their children dronken men and other wicked men, that by seeing their filth they might shun the like fault and avoid such vices when they were at the like state. The Persians to make their youth abhor gluttony would paint an epicure sleeping with meat in his mouth and most horribly overladen with wine, that by the view of such monsterous sights they might eschew the means of the like excess.

"The Parthians, to cause their youth to loathe the alluring trains of women's wiles and deceiptful enticements, had most curiously carved in their houses a young man blind, besides whom was adjoined a woman so exquisite that in some men's judgment Pygmalion's image was not half so excellent, having one hand in his pocket, as noting their theft, and holding a knife in the other hand to cut his throat. If the sight of such ugly shapes caused a loathing of the like sins, then, my good Euphues, consider their plight and beware of thine own peril. Thou art here in Naples a young sojourner, I an old senior; thou a stranger, I a citizen; thou secure, doubting no mishap, I sorrowful, dreading thy misfortune. Here mayst thou see that which I sigh to see, dronken sots wallowing in every house, in every chamber, yea, in every channel; here mayst thou behold that which I cannot without blushing behold nor without blubbering utter, those whose bellies be their gods, who offer their goods as sacrifice to their guts; who sleep with meat in their mouths, with sin in their hearts, and with shame in their houses.

"Here, yea, here, Euphues, mayst thou see not the carved visard of a lewd woman, but the incarnate visage of a lascivious wanton, not the shadow of love, but the substance of lust. My heart melteth in drops of blood to see a harlot with the one hand rob so many coffers and with the other to rip so many corses.

"Thou art here amiddest the pikes between Scylla and Charybdis, ready if thou shun Syrtes to sink into Symphlagades. Let the Lacedemonian, the Persian, the Parthian, yea, the Neapolitan, cause thee rather to detest such villany, at the sight and view of their vanity.

"Is it not far better to abhor sins by the remembrance of others' faults then by repentance of thine own follies? Is not he accompted most wise whom other men's harms do make most wary? But thou wilt haply say, that although there be many things in Naples to be justly condemned, yet there are some things of necessity to be commended, and as thy will doth lean unto the one, so thy wit would also embrace the other.

"Alas, Euphues, by how much the more I love the high climbing of thy capacity, by so much the more I fear thy fall. The fine crystal is sooner crazed then the hard marble, the greenest beech burneth faster then the driest oak, the fairest silk is soonest soiled, and the sweetest wine turneth to the sharpest vineger, the pestilence doth most rifest infect the clearest complection, and the caterpiller cleaveth unto the ripest fruit, the most delicate wit is allured with small enticement unto vice, and most subject to yield unto vanity; if therefore thou do but harken to the sirens, thou wilt be enamored; if thou haunt their houses and places, thou shalt be enchanted.

"One drop of poison infecteth the whole tun of wine, one leaf of colliquintida marreth and spoileth the whole pot of porredge, one iron mole defaceth the whole piece of lawn. Descend into thine own conscience, and consider with thyself the great difference between staring and stark blind, wit and wisdom, love and lust. Be merry but with modesty, be sober but not too sullen, be valiant but not too venterous. Let thy attire be comely but not costly, thy diet wholesome but not excessive; use pastime as the word importeth, to pass the time in honest recreation. Mistrust no man without cause, neither

be thou credulous without proof; be not light to follow every man's opinion, nor obstinate to stand in thine own conceipt. Serve God, love God, fear God, and God will so bless thee as either heart can wish or thy friends desire. And so I end my counsail, beseeching thee to begin to follow it."

This old gentleman having finished his discourse, Euphues began to shape him an answer in this sort:

"Father and friend (your age sheweth the one, your honesty the other), I am neither so suspicious to mistrust your good will, nor so sottish to mislike your good counsail; as I am therefore to thank you for the first, so it stands me upon to think better on the latter. I mean not to cavil with you as one loving sophistry, neither to control you as one having superiority; the one would bring my talk into the suspicion of fraud, the other convince me of folly. Whereas you argue I know not upon what probabilities, but sure I am upon no proof, that my bringing-up should be a blemish to my birth, I answer, and swear too, that you were not therein a little overshot; either you gave too much credit to the report of others, or too much liberty to your own judgment; you convince my parents of peevishness, in making me a wanton, and me of lewdness, in rejecting correction. But so many men, so many minds; that may seem in your eye odious which in another's eye may be gracious. Aristippus, a philosopher, yet who more courtly? Diogenes, a philosopher, yet who more carterly? Who more popular then Plato, retaining always good company? Who more envious then Timon, denouncing all humain society? Who so severe as the Stoics, which like stocks were moved with no melody? Who so secure as the Epicures, which wallowed in all kind of licentiousness? Though all men be made of one metal, yet they be not cast all in one mold; there is framed of the selfsame clay as well the tile to keep out water as the pot to contain liquor, the sun doth harden the dirt and melt the wax, fire maketh the gold to shine and the straw to smother, perfumes doth refresh the dove and kill the betil, and the nature of the man disposeth that consent of the manners. Now whereas you seem to love my nature and loathe my nurture, you bewray your own weakness in thinking that nature may any ways be altered by education, and as you have ensamples to confirm your pretense, so I have most evident and infallible arguments to serve for my purpose. It is natural for the vine to spread; the more you seek by art to alter it, the more in the end you shall augment it. It is proper for the palm tree to mount; the heavier you load it the higher it sprouteth. Though iron be made soft with fire it returneth to his hardness; though the falcon be reclaimed to the fist she retireth to her haggardness; the whelp of a mastiff will never be taught to retrieve the partridge; education can have no shew where the excellency of nature doth bear sway. The silly mouse will by no manner of means be tamed; the subtil fox may well be beaten, but never broken from stealing his prey; if you pound spices they smell the sweeter; season the wood never so well, the wine will taste of the cask; plant and translate the crab tree where and whensoever it please you and it will never bear sweet apple.

"Infinite and innumerable were the examples I could alledge and declare to confirm the force of Nature, and confute these your vain and false forgeries, were not the repetition of them needless, having shewed sufficient, or bootless, seeing those alledged will not persuade you. And can you be so unnatural, whom Dame Nature hath nourished and brought up so many years, to repine as it were against Nature?

"The similitude you rehearse of the wax argueth your waxing and melting brain, and your example of the hot and hard iron sheweth in you but cold and weak disposition. Do you not know that which all men do affirm and know, that black will take no other color? that the stone abeston being once made hot will never be made cold? that fire cannot be forced downward? that Nature will have course after kind? that everything will dispose itself according to Nature? Can the Ethiop change or alter his skin? or the leopard his hue? Is it possible to gather grapes of thorns, or figs of thistles? or to cause anything to strive against Nature?

"But why go I about to praise Nature, the which as yet was never any imp so wicked and barbarous, any Turk so vile and brutish, any beast so dull and senseless, that could or would or durst dispraise or contemn? Doth not Cicero conclude and allow that if we follow and obey Nature, we shall never err? Doth not Aristotle alledge and confirm that Nature frameth or maketh nothing in any point rude, vain, and unperfect?

"Nature was had in such estimation and admiration among the heathen people that she was reputed for the only goddess in heaven. If Nature, then, have largely and bountifully endewed me with her gifts, why deem you me so untoward and graceless? If she have dealt hardely with me, why extol you so much my birth? If Nature bear no sway, why use you this adulation? If Nature work the effect, what booteth any education? If Nature be of strength or force, what availeth discipline or nurture? If of none, what helpeth Nature? But let these sayings pass, as known evidently and granted to be true, which none can or may deny unless he be false, or that he be an enemy to humanity.

"As touching my residence and abiding here in Naples, my youthly and lusty affections, my sports and pleasures, my pastimes, my common dalliance, my delights, my resort and company, and companions which daily use to visit me; although to you they breed more sorrow and care then solace and comfort, bicause of your crabbed age, yet to me they bring more comfort and joy then care and grief, more bliss then bale, more happiness then heaviness, bicause of my youthful gentleness. Either you would have all men old as you are, or else you have quite forgotten that you yourself were young, or ever knew young days; either in your youth you were a very vicious and ungodly man, or now, being aged, very superstitious and devout above measure.

"Put you no difference between the young flourishing bay tree and the old withered beech? no kind of distinction between the waxing and the waning of the moon? and between the rising and the setting of the sun? Do you measure the hot assaults of youth by the cold skirmishes of age? whose years are subject to more infirmities then our youth, we merry, you melancholy, we zealous in affection, you jealous in all your doings, you testy without cause, we hasty for no quarrel. You careful, we careless, we bold, you fearful, we in all points contrary unto you, and ye in all points unlike unto us.

"Seeing therefore we be repugnant each to the other in nature, would you have us alike in qualities? Would you have one potion minist'red to the burning fever and to the cold palsy? one plaister to an old issue and a fresh wound? one salve for all sores? one sauce for all meats? No, no, Eubulus, but I will yield to more then either I am bound to grant, either thou able to prove: suppose that which I never will believe, that Naples is a cank'red storehouse of all strife, a common stews for all strumpets, the sink of shame and the very nurse of all sin. Shall it therefore follow of necessity that all that are wooed of love should be wedded to lust? Will you conclude as it were *ex consequenti* that whosoever arriveth here shall be enticed to folly, and being enticed, of force shall be entangled? No, no, it is the disposition of the thought that altereth the nature of the thing. The sun shineth upon the dunghill and is not corrupted; the diamond lieth in the fire and is not consumed; the crystal toucheth the toad and is not poisoned; the bird trochilus liveth by the mouth of the crocodile and is not spoiled; a perfect wit is never bewitched with lewdness, neither enticed with lasciviousness.

"Is it not common that the holm tree springeth amidst the beach? that the ivy spreadeth upon the hard stones? that the soft feather-bed breaketh the hard blade? If experience have not taught you this, you have lived long and learned little, or if your moist brain have forgot it, you have learned much and profited nothing. But it may be that you measure my affections by your own fancies, and knowing yourself either too simple to raise the siege of policy, or too weak to resist the assault by prowess, you deem me of as little wit as yourself, or of less force, either of small capacity, or of no courage. In my judgment, Eubulus, you shall as soon catch a hare with a taber as you shall persuade youth, with your aged and overworn eloquence, to such severity of life, which as yet there was never Stoic so strict, nor Jesuit so superstitious, neither votary so devout, but would rather allow it in words then follow it in works, rather talk of it then try it. Neither were you such a saint in your youth, that abandoning all pleasures, all pastimes, and delights, you would chuse rather to sacrifice the first fruits of your life to vain holiness then to youthly affections. But as to the stomach quatted with dainties all delicates seem queasy, and as he that surfeteth with wine useth afterward to allay with water; so these old huddles, having over-charged their gorges with fancy, accompt all honest recreation mere folly, and having taken a surfet of delight seem now to savor it with despight. Seeing therefore it is labor lost for me to persuade you, and wind vainly wasted for you to exhort me, here I found you, and here I leave you, having neither bought nor sold with you, but changed ware for ware; if you have taken little pleasure in my reply, sure I am that by your counsail I have reaped less profit. They that use to steal honey burn hemlock to smoke the bees from their hives, and it may be that to get some advantage of me you have used these smoky arguments, thinking thereby to smother me with the conceipt of strong imagination. But as the camelion though he have most guts draweth least breath, or as the elder tree though he be fullest of pith is farthest from strength, so though your reasons seem inwardly to yourself somewhat substantial, and your persuasions pithy in your own conceipt, yet being well weighed without, they be shadows without substance, and weak without force. The bird taurus hath a great voice but a small body, the thunder a great clap yet but a little stone, the empty vessel giveth a greater sound then the full barrel. I mean not to apply it, but look into yourself and you shall certainly find it; and thus I leave you seeking it, but were it not that my company stay my coming I would surely help you to look it, but I am called hence by my acquaintance."

Euphues having thus ended his talk departed, leaving this old gentleman in a great quandary; who, perceiving that he was more enclined to wantonness then to wisdom, with a deep sigh, the tears trickling down his cheeks, said: "Seeing thou wilt not buy counsel at the first hand good cheap, thou shalt buy repentance at the second hand, at such an unreasonable rate that thou wilt curse thy hard pennyworth, and ban thy hard heart." And im-mediately he went to his own house, heavily be-wailing the young man's unhappiness.

Here ye may behold, gentlemen, how lewdly wit standeth in his own light, how he deemeth no penny good silver but his own, preferring the blossom before the fruit, the bud before the flower, the green blade before the ripe ear of corn, his own wit before all men's wisdoms. Neither is that geason, seeing for the most part it is proper to all those of sharp capacity to esteem of themselves as most proper; if one be hard in conceiving, they pronounce him a dolt; if given to study, they proclaim him a dunce; if merry, a jester; if sad, a saint; if full of words, a sot; if without speech, a cipher. If one argue with them boldly, then is he impudent; if coldly, an innocent; if there be reasoning of divinity, they cry, *Quae supra nos nihil ad nos;* if of humanity, *Sententias loquitur carnifex.* Hereof cometh such great familiarity between the ripest wits, when they shall see the dis-position the one of the other, the *sympathia* of affections and as it were but a pair of shears to go between their natures, one flattereth another in his own folly, and layeth cushions under the elbow of his fellow when he seeth him take a nap with fancy, and as their wit wresteth them to vice, so it forgeth them some feat excuse to cloak their vanity.

Too much study doth intoxicate their brains, for (say they) although iron the more it is used the brighter it is, yet silver with much wearing doth waste to nothing; though the cammock the more it is bowed the better it serveth, yet the bow the more it is bent and occupied the weaker it waxeth; though the camomile the more it is trodden and pressed down the more it spreadeth, yet the violet the oft'ner it is handled and touched the sooner it withereth and decayeth. Besides this, a fine wit, a sharp sense, a quick understanding is able to attain to more in a moment or a very little space then a dull and blockish head in a month; the scythe cutteth far better and smoother then the saw; the wax yieldeth better and sooner to the seal then the steel to the stamp or hammer; the smooth and plain beech is easier to be carved and occupied then the knotty box. For neither is there anything but that hath his contraries. Such is the nature of these novices that think to have learning without labor and treasure without travail, either not understanding or else not rememb'ring that the finest edge is made with the blunt whetstone and the fairest jewel fashioned with the hard hammer. I go not about, gentlemen, to inveigh against wit, for then I were witless; but frankly to confess mine own little wit, I have ever thought so superstitiously of wit that I fear I have committed idolatry against wisdom, and if Nature had dealt so beneficially with me to have given me any wit, I should have been readier in the defense of it to have made an apology then any way to turn to apostasy. But this I note, that for the most part they stand so on their pantuffles that they be secure of perils, obstinate in their own opinions, impatient of labor, apt to conceive wrong, credulous to believe the worst, ready to shake off their old acquaintance without cause and to condempn them without color. All which humors are by so much the more easier to be purged, by how much the less they have fest'red the sinews. But return we again to Euphues.

Euphues having sojourned by the space of two moneths in Naples, whether he were moved by the courtesy of a young gentleman named Philautus or inforced by destiny, whether his pregnant wit or his pleasant conceits wrought the greater liking in the mind of Euphues, I know not for certainty; but Euphues shewed such entire love towards him that he seemed to make small accompt of any others, determining to enter into such an inviolable league of friendship with him as neither time by piecemeal should empair, neither fancy utterly dissolve, nor any suspicion infringe. "I have read," saith he, "and well I believe it, that a friend is in prosperity a pleasure, a solace in adversity, in grief a comfort, in joy a merry companion, at all times another I, in all places the express image of mine own person; insomuch that I cannot tell whether the immortal gods have bestowed any gift upon mortal men either more noble or more necessary then friendship. Is there anything in the world to be reputed (I will not say compared) to friendship? Can any treasure in this transitory pilgrimage be of more valew then a friend? In whose bosom thou mayst sleep secure without fear, whom thou mayst make partner of all thy secrets without suspicion of fraud, and pertaker of all thy misfortune without mistrust of fleeting, who will accompt thy bale his bane, thy mishap his misery, the pricking of thy finger the piercing of his heart. But whether am I carried? Have I not also learned that one should eat a bushel of salt with him whom he meaneth to make his friend? that trial maketh trust? that there is falsehood in fellowship? And what then? Doth not the sympathy of manners make the conjunction of minds? Is it not a byword, "Like will to like"? Not so common as commendable it is, to see young gentlemen choose them such friends with whom they may seem being absent to be present, being asunder to be conversant, being dead to be alive. I will therefore have Philautus for my phere, and by so much the more I make myself sure to have Philautus, by how much the more I view in him the lively image of Euphues."

Although there be none so ignorant that doth not know, neither any so impudent that will not confess, friendship to be the jewel of humain joy; yet whosoever shall see this amity grounded upon a little affection will soon conjecture that it shall be dissolved upon a light occasion; as in the sequel of Euphues and Philautus you shall see, whose hot love waxed soon cold. For as the best wine doth make the sharpest vinaigar, so the deepest love turneth to the deadliest hate. Who deserved the most blame, in mine opinion it is doubtful, and so difficult that I dare not presume to give verdit. For love being the cause for which so many mischiefs have been attempted, I am not yet persuaded whether of them was most to be blamed, but certainly neither of them was blameless. I appeal to your judgment, gentlemen, not that I think any of you of the like disposition able to decide the question, but, being of deeper discretion then I am, are more fit to debate the quarrel. Though the discourse of their friendship and falling-out be somewhat long, yet, being somewhat strange, I hope the delightfulness of the one will attenuate the tediousness of the other.

Euphues had continual access to the place of Philautus and no little familiarity with him, and, finding him at convenient leisure, in these short terms unfolded his mind unto him:

"Gentleman and friend, the trial I have had of thy manners cutteth off divers terms which to another I would have used in the like matter. And sithens a long discourse argueth folly, and delicate words incur the suspicion of flattery, I am determined to use neither of them, knowing either of them to breed offense. Weighing with myself the force of friendship by the effects, I studied ever since my first coming to Naples to enter league with such a one as might direct my steps being a stranger, and resemble my manners being a scholar, the which two qualities as I find in you able to satisfy my desire, so I hope I shall find a heart in you willing to accomplish my request. Which if I may obtain, assure yourself that Damon to his Pythias, Pylades to his Orestes, Titus to his Gysippus, Theseus to his Pyrothus, Scipio to his Laelius, was never found more faithful then Euphues will be to his Philautus."

Philautus, by how much the less he looked for this discourse, by so much the more he liked it, for he saw all qualities both of body and mind in Euphues, unto whom he replied as followeth:

"Friend Euphues (for so your talk warranteth me to term you), I dare neither use a long process, neither loving speech, lest unwittingly I should cause you to convince me of those things which you have already condemned. And verily I am bold to presume upon your curtesy, since you yourself have used so little curiosity, persuading myself that my short answer will work as great an effect in you as your few words did in me. And seeing we resemble (as you say) each other in qualities, it cannot be that the one should differ from the other in curtesy; seeing the sincere affection of the mind cannot be expressed by the mouth, and that no art can unfold the entire love of the heart, I am earnestly to beseech you not to measure the firmness of my faith by the fewness of my words, but rather think that the overflowing waves of good will leave no passage for many words. Trial shall prove trust; here is my hand, my heart, my lands, and my life at thy commandment. Thou mayst well perceive that I did believe thee, that so soon I did love thee, and I hope thou wilt the rather love me, in that I did believe thee."

After many embracings and protestations one to another, they walked to dinner, where they wanted neither meat, neither music, neither any other pastime, and, having banqueted, to digest their sweet confections they danced all that afternoon; they used not only one boord but one bed, one book (if so be it they thought not one too many). Their friendship augmented every day, insomuch that the one could not refrain the company of the other one minute; all things went in common between them, which all men accompted commendable. Philautus being a town-born child, both for his own continuance and the great countenance which his father had while he lived, crept into credit with Don Ferardo, one of the chief governors of the city, who although he had a courtly crew of gentlewomen sojourning in his palace, yet his daughter, heir to his whole revenues, stained the beauty of them all, whose modest bashfulness caused the other to look wan for envy, whose lily cheeks dyed with a vermillion red made the rest to blush at her beauty. For as the finest ruby staineth the color of the rest that be in place, or as the sun dimmeth the moon that she cannot be discerned, so this gallant girl more fair then fortunate, and yet more fortunate then faithful, eclipsed the beauty of them all and changed their colors. Unto her had Philautus access, who wan her by right of love, and should have worn her by right of law, had not Euphues by strange destiny broken the bonds of marriage and forbidden the banes of matrimony.

It happened that Don Ferardo had occasion to go to Venice about certain his own affairs, leaving his daughter the only steward of his household, who spared not to feast Philautus, her friend, with all kinds of delights and delicates, reserving only her honesty as the chief stay of her honor. Her father being gone, she sent for her friend to supper, who came not as he was accustomed, solitarily alone, but accompanied with his friend Euphues. The gentlewoman, whether it were for niceness or for niggardness of curtesy, gave him such a cold welcome that he repented that he was come.

Euphues, though he knew himself worthy every way to have a good countenance, yet could he not perceive her willing any way to lend him a friendly look. At the last, supper being ready to come in, Philautus said unto her: "Gentlewoman, I was the bolder to bring my shadow with me"—meaning Euphues—"knowing that he should be the better welcome for my sake." Unto whom the gentlewoman replied: "Sir, as I never when I saw you thought that you came without your shadow, so now I cannot a little mervail to see you so overshot in bringing a new shadow with you." Euphues, though he perceived her coy nip, seemed not to care for it, but taking her by the hand said:

"Fair lady, seeing the shade doth often shild your beauty from the parching sun, I hope you will the better esteem of the shadow, and by so much the less it ought to be offensive, by how much the less it is able to offend you, and by so much the more you ought to like it, by how much the more you use to lie in it."

"Well, gentleman," answered Lucilla, "in arguing of the shadow, we forgo the substance. Pleaseth it you therefore to sit down to supper?" And so they all sate down; but Euphues fed of one dish which ever stood before him, the beauty of Lucilla.

Here Euphues at the first sight was so kindled with desire that almost he was like to burn to coals. Supper being ended, the order was in Naples that the gentlewomen would desire to hear some discourse either concerning love or learning. And although Philautus was requested, yet he posted it over to Euphues, whom he knew most fit for that purpose. Euphues, being thus tied to the stake by their importunate intreaty, began as followeth:

"He that worst may is always enforced to hold the candle; the weakest must still to the wall; where none will, the Devil himself must bear the cross. But were it not, gentlewomen, that your list stands for law, I would borrow so much leave as to resign mine office to one of you, whose experience in love hath made you learned, and whose learning hath made you so lovely; for me to entreat of the one, being a novice, or to discourse of the other, being a trewant, I may well make you weary but never the wiser, and give you occasion rather to laugh at my rashness then to like my reasons. Yet I care the less to excuse my boldness to you, who were the cause of my blindness. And since I am at mine own choice either to talk of love or of learning, I had rather for this time be deemed an unthrift in rejecting profit, then a Stoic in renouncing pleasure.

"It hath been a question often disputed but never determined, whether the qualities of the mind, or the composition of the man, cause women most to like, or whether beauty or wit move men most to love. Certes, by how much the more the mind is to be preferred before the body, by so much the more the graces of the one are to be preferred before the gifts of the other, which if it be so, that the contemplation of the inward quality ought to be respected more then the view of the outward beauty, then doubtless women either do or should love those best whose virtue is best, not measuring the deformed man with the reformed mind. The foul toad hath a fair stone in his head, the fine gold is found in the filthy earth, the sweet kernel lieth in the hard shell. Virtue is harbored in the heart of him that most men esteem misshapen. Contrariwise, if we respect more the outward shape then the inward habit, good God, into how many mischiefs do we fall, into what blindness are we led? Do we not commonly see that in painted pots is hidden the deadliest poison? that in the greenest grass is the greatest serpent? in the clearest water the ugliest toad? Doth not experience teach us that in the most curious sepulcher are enclosed rotten bones? that the cypress tree beareth a fair leaf but no fruit? that the estridge carrieth fair feathers but rank flesh? How frantic are those lovers which are carried away with the gay glistering of the fine face, the beauty whereof is parched with the sommer's blaze and chipped with the winter's blast, which is of so short continuance that it fadeth before one perceive it florish, of so small profit that it poisoneth those that possess it, of so little value with the wise that they accompt it a delicate bait with a deadly hook, a sweet panther with a devouring paunch, a sour poison in a silver pot. Here I cold enter into discourse of such fine dames as being in love with their own looks make such coarse accompt of their passionate lovers; for commonly if they be adorned with beauty, they be so straight-laced, and made so high in the instep, that they disdain them most that most desire them. It is a world to see the doting of their lovers and their dealing with them, the revealing of whose subtle trains would cause me to shed tears and you, gentlewomen, to shut your modest ears. Pardon me, gentlewomen, if I unfold every wile, and shew every wrinkle of women's disposition. Two things do they cause their servants to vow unto them, secrecy and sovereignty, the one to conceal their enticing sleights, by the other to assure themselves of their only service. Again—but ho there! If I shold have waded any further and

sounded the depth of their deceipt, I should either have procured your displeasure or incurred the suspicion of fraud, either armed you to practise the like subtlety or accused myself of perjury. But I mean not to offend your chaste minds with the rehearsal of their unchaste manners, whose ears I perceive to glow and hearts to be grieved at that which I have already uttered, not that amongst you there be any such, but that in your sex there should be any such. Let not gentlewomen therefore make too much of their painted sheath, let them not be so curious in their own conceit or so currish to their loyal lovers. When the black crow's foot shall appear in their eye or the black ox tread on their foot, when their beauty shall be like the blasted rose, their wealth wasted, their bodies worn, their faces wrinkled, their fingers crooked, who will like of them in their age who loved none in their youth? If you will be cherished when you be old, be curteous while you be young; if you look for comfort in your hoary hairs, be not coy when you have your golden locks; if you would be embraced in the waning of your bravery, be not squeamish in the waxing of your beauty; if you desire to be kept like the roses when they have lost their color, smell sweet as the rose doth in the bud; if you would be tasted for old wine, be in the mouth a pleasant grape; so shall you be cherished for your curtesy, comforted for your honesty, embraced for your amity, so shall you be preserved with the sweet rose and dronk with the pleasant wine. Thus far I am bold, gentlewomen, to counsel those that be coy that they weave not the web of their own wo nor spin the threed of their own thraldom by their own overthwartness. And seeing we are even in the bowels of love, it shall not be amiss to examine whether man or woman be soonest allured, whether be most constant the male or the female. And in this point I mean not to be mine own carver, lest I should seem either to pick a thank with men or a quarrel with women. If, therefore, it might stand with your pleasure, Mistress Lucilla, to give your censure, I would take the contrary, for sure I am though your judgment be sound yet affection will shadow it."

Lucilla, seeing his pretense, thought to take advantage of his large proffer, unto whom she said: "Gentleman, in mine opinion women are to be won with every wind, in whose sex there is neither force to withstand the assaults of love, neither constancy to remain faithful. And bicause your discourse hath hetherto bred delight, I am loth to hinder you in the sequel of your devices."

Euphues, perceiving himself to be taken napping, answered as followeth: "Mistress Lucilla, if you speak as you think, these gentlewomen present have little cause to thank you; if you cause me to commend women, my tale will be accompted a mere trifle and your words the plain truth. Yet knowing promise to be debt, I will pay it with performance. And I would the gentlemen here present were as ready to credit my proof as the gentlewomen are willing to hear their own praises, or I as able to overcome as Mistress Lucilla would be content to be overthrown. Howsoever the matter shall fall out, I am of the surer side, for if my reasons be weak, then is our sex strong, if forcible, then your judgment feeble; if I find truth on my side, I hope I shall for my wages win the good will of women; if I want proof, then, gentlewomen, of necessity you must yield to men. But to the matter.

"Touching the yielding to love, albeit their hearts seem tender, yet they harden them like the stone of Sicilia, the which the more it is beaten the harder it is. For being framed as it were of the perfection of men, they be free from all such cogitations as may any way provoke them to uncleanness, insomuch as they abhor the light love of youth which is grounded upon lust and dissolved upon every light occasion. When they see the folly of men turn to fury, their delight to doting, their affection to frenzy; when they see them as it were pine in pleasure and to wax pale through their own peevishness, their suits, their service, their letters, their labors, their loves, their lives seem to them so odious that they harden their hearts against such concupiscence, to the end they might convert them from rashness to reason, from such lewd disposition to honest discretion. Hereof it cometh that men accuse women of cruelty; bicause they themselves want civility, they accompt them full of wiles in not yielding to their wickedness, faithless for resisting their filthiness. But I had almost forgot myself; you shall pardon me, Mistress Lucilla, for this time, if thus abruptly I finish my discourse; it is neither for want of good will or lack of proof, but that I feel in myself such alteration that I can scarcely utter one word. Ah, Euphues! Euphues!"

The gentlewomen were stroock into such a quandary with this sodain change that they all changed color. But Euphues, taking Philautus by the hand and giving the gentlewomen thanks for their patience and his repast, bade them all farewell and went immediately to his chamber. But Lucilla, who now began to fry in the flames of love, all the company being departed to their lodgings, enter'd into these terms and contrarieties:

"Ah, wretched wench, Lucilla, how art thou perplexed! What a doubtful fight dost thou feel betwixt faith and fancy, hope and fear, conscience and concupiscence! O my Euphues, little dost thou know the sodain sorrow that I sustain for thy sweet sake.

Whose wit hath bewitched me, whose rare qualities have deprived me of mine old quality, whose courteous behavior without curiosity, whose comely feature without fault, whose filed speech without fraud hath wrapped me in this misfortune. And canst thou, Lucilla, be so light of love in forsaking Philautus to fly to Euphues? Canst thou prefer a stranger before thy countryman? a starter before thy companion? Why, Euphues doth perhaps desire my love, but Philautus hath deserved it. Why, Euphues' feature is worthy as good as I, but Philautus his faith is worthy a better. I, but the latter love is most fervent. I, but the first ought to be most faithful. I, but Euphues hath greater perfection. I, but Philautus hath deeper affection.

"Ah, fond wench, dost thou think Euphues will deem thee constant to him, when thou hast been unconstant to his friend? Weenest thou that he will have no mistrust of thy faithfulness when he hath had trial of thy fickleness? Will he have no doubt of thine honor when thou thyself callest thine honesty in question? Yes, yes, Lucilla, well doth he know that the glass once crased will with the least clap be cracked, that the cloth which staineth with milk will soon lose his color with vineger, that the eagle's wing will waste the feather as well of the phoenix as of the pheasant, that she that hath been faithless to one will never be faithful to any. But can Euphues convince me of fleeting, seeing for his sake I break my fidelity? Can he condemn me of disloyalty when he is the only cause of my disliking? May he justly condemn me of treachery who hath this testimony as trial of my good will? Doth not he remember that the broken bone once set together is stronger then ever it was? that the greatest blot is taken off with the pommice? that though the spider poison the fly, she cannot infect the bee? that although I have been light to Philautus, yet I may be lovely to Euphues? It is not my desire, but his deserts, that moveth my mind to this choice, neither the want of the like good will in Philautus, but the lack of the like good qualities, that removeth my fancy from the one to the other.

"For as the bee that gathereth honey out of the weed, when she espieth the fair flower flieth to the sweetest; or as the kind spaniel, though he hunt after birds, yet forsakes them to retrieve the partridge; or as we commonly feed on beef hungerly at the first, yet, seeing the quail more dainty, change our diet: so I, although I loved Philautus for his good properties, yet, seeing Euphues to excel him, I ought by nature to like him better. By so much the more therefore my change is to be excused, by how much the more my choice is excellent; and by so much the less I am to be condemned, by how much the more Euphues is to be commended. Is not the diamond of more valew then the ruby bicause he is of more virtue? Is not the emerald preferred before the sapphire for his wonderful property? Is not Euphues more praiseworthy then Philautus, being more witty? But fye, Lucilla, why dost thou flatter thyself in thine own folly? Canst thou feign Euphues thy friend, whom by thine own words thou hast made thy foe? Diddest not thou accuse women of inconstancy? Diddest not thou accompt them easy to be won? Diddest not thou condemn them of weakness? What sounder argument can he have against thee then thine own answer? what better proof then thine own speech? what greater trial then thine own talk? If thou hast belied women, he will judge thee unkind; if thou have revealed the troth, he must needs think thee unconstant; if he perceive thee to be won with a nut, he will imagine that thou wilt be lost with an apple; if he find thee wanton before thou be wooed, he will guess thou wilt be wavering when thou art wedded.

"But suppose that Euphues love thee, that Philautus leave thee, will thy father, thinkest thou, give thee liberty to live after thine own lust? Will he esteem him worthy to enherit his possessions whom he accompteth unworthy to enjoy thy person? Is it like that he will match thee in marriage with a stranger, with a Grecian, with a mean man? I, but what knoweth my father whether he be wealthy, whether his revenues be able to countervail my father's lands, whether his birth be noble, yea or no? Can any one make doubt of his gentle blood that seeth his gentle conditions? Can his honor be called into question whose honesty is so great? Is he to be thought thriftless who in all qualities of the mind is peerless? No, no, the tree is known by his fruit, the gold by his touch, the son by the sire. And as the soft wax receiveth whatsoever print be in the seal and sheweth no other impression, so the tender babe, being sealed with his father's gifts, representeth his image most lively. But were I once certain of Euphues' good will, I would not so superstitiously accompt of my father's ill will. Albeit I can no way quench the coals of desire with forgetfulness, yet will I rake them up in the ashes of modesty; seeing I dare not discover my love for maidenly shamefastness, I will dissemble it till time I have opportunity. And I hope so to behave myself as Euphues shall think me his own, and Philautus persuade himself I am none but his. But I would to God Euphues would repair hether, that the sight of him might mitigate some part of my martyrdom."

She, having thus discoursed with herself her own miseries, cast herself on the bed; and there let her lie, and return we to Euphues, who was so caught in the gin of folly that he neither could comfort himself nor durst ask counsel of his friend, suspecting that which indeed was true, that Philautus was corrival with him and cookemate with Lucilla. Amiddest, therefore, these his extremities between hope and fear, he uttered these or the like speeches:

"What is he, Euphues, that, knowing thy wit and seeing thy folly, but will rather punish thy lewdness then pity thy heaviness? Was there ever any so fickle so soon to be allured? any ever so faithless to deceive his friend? ever any so foolish to bathe himself in his own misfortune? Too true it is that as the sea crab swimmeth always against the stream, so wit always striveth against wisdom; and as the bee is oftentimes hurt with her own honey, so is wit not seldom plagued with his own conceit.

"O ye gods, have ye ordained for every malady a medicine, for every sore a salve, for every pain a plaister, leaving only love remediless? Did ye deem no man so mad to be entangled with desire, or thought ye them worthy to be tormented that were so misled? Have ye dealt more favorable with brute beasts then with reasonable creatures?

"The filthy sow when she is sick eateth the sea crab and is immediately recured; the torteyse having tasted the viper sucketh origanum and is quickly revived; the bear ready to pine licketh up the ants and is recovered; the dog having surfeted, to procure his vomit eateth grass, and findeth remedy; the hart being pierced with the dart runneth out of hand to the herb dictanum and is healed. And can men by no herb, by no art, by no way procure a remedy for the impatient disease of love? Ah, well I perceive that love is not unlike the fig tree, whose fruit is sweet, whose root is more bitter then the claw of a bitter, or like the apple in Persia, whose blossom savoreth like honey, whose bud is more sour then gall.

"But O impiety! O broad blasphemy against the heavens! Wilt thou be so impudent, Euphues, to accuse the gods of iniquity? No, fond fool, no. Neither is it forbidden us by the gods to love, by whose divine providence we are permitted to live, neither do we want remedies to recure our maladies, but reason to use the means. But why go I about to hinder the course of love with the discourse of law? Hast thou not read, Euphues, that he that loppeth the vine causeth it to spread fairer? that he that stoppeth the stream forceth it to swell higher? that he that casteth water on the fire in the smith's forge maketh it to flame fiercer? Even so he that seeketh by counsail to moderate his overlashing affections encreaseth his own misfortune. Ah, my Lucilla, wold thou wert either less fair or I more fortunate, either I wiser or thou milder, either would I were out of this mad mood, either I would we were both of one mind. But how should she be persuaded of my loyalty, that yet had never one simple proof of my love? Will she not rather imagine me to be intangled with her beauty then with her virtue? that my fancy being so lewdly chained at the first will be as lightly changed at the last? that there is nothing which is permanent that is violent? Yes, yes, she must needs conjecture so, although it be nothing so, for by how much the more my affection cometh on the suddain, by so much the less will she think it certain. The rattling thunderbolt hath but his clap, the lightening but his flash, and as they both come in a moment, so do they both end in a minute.

"I, but, Euphues, hath she not heard also that the dry touchwood is kindled with lime? that the greatest mushromp groweth in one night? that the fire quickly burneth the flax? that love easily ent'reth into the sharp wit without resistance, and is harbored there without repentance?

"If therefore the gods have endewed her with as much bounty as beauty; if she have no less wit then she hath comeliness; certes she will neither conceive sinisterly of my sodain suit, neither be coy to receive me into her service, neither suspect me of lightness in yielding so lightly, neither reject me disdainfully for loving so hastely. Shall I not, then, hazard my life to obtain my love? and deceive Philautus to receive Lucilla? Yes, Euphues, where love beareth sway, friendship can have no shew. As Philautus brought me for his shadow the last supper, so will I use him for my shadow till I have gained his saint. And canst thou, wretch, be false to him that is faithful to thee? Shall his curtesy be cause of thy cruelty? Wilt thou violate the league of faith to enherit the land of folly? Shall affection be of more force then friendship, love then law, lust then loyalty? Knowest thou not that he that looseth his honesty hath nothing else to loose?

"Tush, the case is light where reason taketh place; to love and to live well is not granted to Jupiter. Whoso is blinded with the caul of beauty decerneth no color of honesty. Did not Gyges cut Candaules a coat by his own measure? Did not Paris, though he were a welcome guest to Menelaus, serve his host a slippery prank? If Philautus had loved Lucilla, he would never have suffered Euphues to have seen her. Is it not the prey that enticeth the thief to rifle? Is it not the pleasant bait that causeth the fleetest fish to bite? Is it not a byword amongst us that gold maketh an honest man an ill man? Did Philautus accompt Euphues too simple to decipher beauty, or superstitious not to desire it? Did he deem him a saint in rejecting fancy, or a sot in not discerning?

"Thought he him a Stoic that he would not be moved, or a stock that he could not?

"Well, well, seeing the wound that bleedeth inward is most dangerous, that the fire kept close burneth most furious, that the oven dammed up baketh soonest, that sores having no vent fester inwardly, it is high time to unfold my secret love to my secret friend. Let Philautus behave himself never so craftily, he shall know that it must be a wily mouse that shall breed in the cat's ear, and bicause I resemble him in wit I mean a little to dissemble with him in wiles. But O, my Lucilla, if thy heart be made of that stone which may be mollified only with blood, would I had sipped of that river in Caria which tourneth those that drink of it to stones. If thine ears be anointed with the oil of Syria that bereaveth hearing, would mine eyes had been rubbed with the sirrop of the cedar tree, which taketh away sight."

Euphues having thus talked with himself, Philautus entered the chamber, and finding him so worn and wasted with continual mourning, neither joying in his meat nor rejoicing in his friend, with wat'ry eyes uttered this speech:

"Friend and fellow, as I am not ignorant of thy present weakness, so I am not privy of the cause, and although I suspect many things, yet can I assure myself of no one thing. Therefore, my good Euphues, for these doubts and domps of mine, either remove the cause or reveal it. Thou hast hetherto found me a cheerful companion in thy mirth, and now shalt thou find me as careful with thee in thy moan. If altogether thou mayst not be cured, yet mayst thou be comforted. If there be anything that either by my friends may be procured, or by my life attained, that may either heal thee in part or help thee in all, I protest to thee by the name of a friend that it shall rather be gotten with the loss of my body then lost by getting a kingdom. Thou hast tried me, therefore trust me; thou hast trusted me in many things, therefore try me in this one thing. I never yet failed, and now I will not faint. Be bold to speak and blush not; thy sore is not so angry but I can salve it, thy wound not so deep but I can search it, thy grief not so great but I can ease it. If it be ripe it shall be lanced, if it be broken it shall be tainted, be it never so desperate it shall be cured. Rise, therefore, Euphues, and take heart at grass, younger thou shalt never be; pluck up thy stomach, if love itself have stong thee it shall not stifle thee. Though thou be enamored of some lady thou shalt not be enchanted. They that begin to pine of a consumption, without delay preserve themselves with cullisses, he that feeleth his stomach enflamed with heat cooleth it eftsoons with conserves; delays breed dangers, nothing so perilous as procrastination." Euphues hearing this comfort and friendly counsail dissembled his sorrowing heart, with a smiling face answering him forthwith as followeth:

"True it is, Philautus, that he which toucheth the nettle tenderly is soonest stoung, that the fly which playeth with the fire is singed in the flame, that he that dallieth with women is drawn to his wo. And as the adamant draweth the heavy iron, the harp the fleet dolphin, so beauty allureth the chaste mind to love and the wisest wit to lust; the example whereof I would it were no less profitable then the experience to me is like to be perilous. The vine watered with wine is soon withered, the blossom in the fattest ground is quickly blasted, the goat the fatter she is the less fertile she is; yea, man the more witty he is the less happy he is. So it is, Philautus (for why should I conceal it from thee, of whom I am to take counsail?), that since my last and first being with thee at the house of Ferardo, I have felt such a furious battail in mine own body, as if it be not speedily repressed by policy it will carry my mind (the grand captain in this fight) into endless captivity. Ah, Livia, Livia, thy courtly grace without coyness, thy blazing beauty without blemish, thy curteous demeanor without curiosity, thy sweet speech savored with wit, thy comely mirth tempered with modesty, thy chaste looks yet lovely, thy sharp taunts yet pleasant have given me such a check that sure I am at the next view of thy virtues I shall take the mate. And taking it not of a pawn, but of a prince, the loss is to be accompted the less. And though they be commonly in a great choler that receive the mate, yet would I willingly take every minute ten mates to enjoy Livia for my loving mate. Doubtless if ever she herself have been scorched with the flames of desire, she will be ready to quench the coals with curtesy in another; if ever she have been attached of love, she will rescue him that is drenched in desire; if ever she have been taken with the fever of fancy, she will help his ague who by a quotidian fit is converted into phrenzy. Neither can there be under so delicate a hew lodged deceit, neither in so beautiful a mold a malicious mind. True it is that the disposition of the mind followeth the composition of the body; how then can she be in mind any way imperfect, who in body is perfect every way? I know my success will be good, but I know not how to have access to my goddess; neither do I want courage to discover my love to my friend, but some color to cloak my coming to the house of Ferardo, for if they be in Naples as jealous as they be in the other parts of Italy, then it behoveth me to walk circumspectly and to forge some cause for mine often coming. If, therefore, Philautus, thou canst set but this feather to mine arrow, thou shalt see me shoot so near that thou wilt accompt me for a cunning archer. And verily if I had not loved thee well I wold have swallowed mine own sorrow in silence, knowing that in love

nothing is so dangerous as to perticipate the means thereof to another, and that two may keep counsel if one be away. I am therefore enforced perforce to challenge that courtesy at thy hands which erst thou diddest promise with thy heart, the performance whereof shall bind me to Philautus and prove thee faithful to Euphues."

Philautus, thinking all to be gold that glistered and all to be gospel that Euphues uttered, answered his forged glose with this friendly close:

"In that thou hast made me privy to thy pourpose, I will not conceal my practise; in that thou cravest my aid, assure thyself I will be the finger next the thumb, insomuch as thou shalt never repent thee of the one or the other. Concerning Livia, though she be fair, yet is she not so amiable as my Lucilla, whose servant I have been the term of three years; but lest comparisons should seem odious, chiefly where both the parties be without comparison, I will omit that, and seeing that we had both rather be talking with them then tattling of them, we will immediately go to them. And truly, Euphues, I am not a little glad that I shall have thee not only a comfort in my life but also a companion in my love. As thou hast been wise in thy choice, so I hope thou shalt be fortunate in thy chance. Livia is a wench of more wit then beauty, Lucilla of more beauty then wit, both of more honesty then honor, and yet both of such honor as in all Naples there is not one in birth to be compared with any of them both. How much, therefore, have we to rejoice in our choice! Touching our access, be thou secure, I will flap Ferardo in the mouth with some conceit, and fill his old head so full of new fables that thou shalt rather be earnestly entreated to repair to his house then evil entreated to leave it. As old men are very suspicious to mistrust everything, so are they very credulous to believe anything; the blind man doth eat many a fly."

"Yea, but," said Euphues, "take heed, my Philautus, that thou thyself swallow not a gudgen." Which word Philautus did not mark until he had almost digested it. "But," said [Philautus], "let us go devoutly to the shrine of our saints, there to offer our devotion." To the which Euphues consented willingly, smiling to himself to see how he had brought Philautus into a fool's paradise.

Here you may see, gentlemen, the falsehood in fellowship, the fraud in friendship, the painted sheath with the leaden dagger, the fair words that make fools fain; but I will not trouble you with superfluous addition unto whom I fear me I have been tedious with the bare discourse of this rude history.

Philautus and Euphues repaired to the house of Ferardo, where they found Mistress Lucilla and Livia accompanied with other gentlewomen, neither being idle nor well employed, but playing at cards. But when Lucilla beheld Euphues she could scarcely contain herself from embracing him, had not womanly shamefastness, and Philautus his presence, stayed her wisdom.

Euphues on the other side was fallen into such a trance that he had not the power either to succor himself or salute the gentlewomen. At the last Lucilla began as one that best might be bold, on this manner:

"Gentlemen, although your long absence gave me occasion to think that you disliked your late entertainment, yet your coming at the last hath cut off my former suspicion. And by so much the more you are welcome, by how much the more you were wished for. But you, gentleman"—taking Euphues by the hand—"were the rather wished for, for that your discourse being left unperfect caused us all to long (as women are wont for things that like them) to have an end thereof."

Unto whom Philautus replied as followeth: "Mistress Lucilla, though your courtesy made us nothing to doubt of our welcome, yet modesty caused us to pinch courtesy who should first come; as for my friend, I think he was never wished for here so earnestly of any as of himself, whether it might be to renew his talk or to recant his sayings, I cannot tell."

But whilest he was yet speaking Ferardo entered, whom they all dutifully welcomed home, who rounding Philautus in the ear desired him to accompany him immediately without farther pausing, protesting it should be as well for his preferment as for his own profit. Philautus consenting, Ferardo said to his daughter:

"Lucilla, the urgent affairs I have in hand will scarce suffer me to tarry with you one hour; yet my retourn I hope will be so short that my absence shall not breed thy sorrow. In the mean season I commit all things into thy custody, wishing thee to use thy accustomable courtesy. And seeing I must take Philautus with me, I will be so bold to crave you, gentleman, his friend, to supply his room, desiring you to take this hasty warning for a hearty welcome and so to spend this time of mine absence in honest mirth. And thus I leave you."

Philautus knew well the cause of this sodain departure, which was to redeem certain lands that were morgaged in his father's time to the use of Ferardo, who on that condition had beforetime promised him his daughter in marriage. But retourn we to Euphues.

Euphues was surprised with such incredible joy at this strange event that he had almost sounded, for seeing his co-rival to be departed, and Ferardo to give him so friendly entertainment, doubted not

in time to get the good will of Lucilla. Whom finding in place convenient without company, with a bold courage and comely gesture he began to assay her in this sort:

"Gentlewoman, my acquaintance being so little, I am afraid my credit will be less, for that they commonly are soonest believed that are best beloved, and they liked best whom we have known longest; nevertheless the noble mind suspecteth no guile without cause, neither condemneth any wight without proof; having therefore notice of your heroical heart, I am the better persuaded of my good hap. So it is, Lucilla, that coming to Naples but to fetch fire, as the byword is, not to make my place of abode, I have found such flames that I can neither quench them with the water of free will, neither cool them with wisdom. For as the hop, the pole being never so high, groweth to the end, or as the dry beech, kindled at the root, never leaveth until it come to the top, or as one drop of poison disperseth itself into every vein, so affection, having caught hold of my heart and the sparkles of love kindled my liver, will sodeinly, though secretly, flame up into my head, and spread itself into every sinew. It is your beauty (pardon my abrupt boldness), lady, that hath taken every part of me prisoner, and brought me to this deep distress; but seeing women when one praiseth them for their deserts deem that he flattereth them to obtain his desire, I am here present to yield myself to such trial as your courtesy in this behalf shall require. Yet will you commonly object this to such as serve you and sterve to win your good will, that hot love is soon cold, that the bavin though it bourn bright is but a blaze, that scalding water if it stand a while tourneth almost to ice, that pepper though it be hot in the mouth is cold in the maw, that the faith of men though it fry in their words, it freezeth in their works. Which things, Lucilla, albeit they be sufficient to reprove the lightness of some one, yet can it not convince everyone of lewdness, neither ought the constancy of all to be brought in question through the subtilty of a few. For although the worm entereth almost into every wood, yet he eateth not the cedar tree; though the stone cylindrus at every thunder clap roll from the hill, yet the pure sleekstone mounteth at the noise; though the rust fret the hardest steel, yet doth it not eat into the emerald; though polypus change his hew, yet the salamander keepeth his color; though Proteus transform himself into every shape, yet Pygmalion retaineth his old form; though Aeneas were too fickle to Dido, yet Troylus was too faithful to Cressida; though others seem counterfait in their deeds, yet, Lucilla, persuade yourself that Euphues will be always currant in his dealings. But as the true gold is tried by the touch, the pure flint by the stroke of the iron, so the loyal heart of the faithful lover is known by the trial of his lady; of the which trial, Lucilla, if you shall accompt Euphues worthy, assure yourself, he will be as ready to offer himself a sacrifice for your sweet sake as yourself shall be willing to employ him in your service. Neither doth he desire to be trusted any way until he shall be tried every way, neither doth he crave credit at the first, but a good countenance till time his desire shall be made manifest by his deserts. Thus not blinded by light affection, but dazzled with your rare perfection, and boldened by your exceeding courtesy, I have unfolded mine entire love, desiring you having so good leisure to give so friendly an answer as I may receive comfort and you commendation."

Lucilla, although she were contented to hear this desired discourse, yet did she seem to be somewhat displeased. And truly, I know not whether it be peculiar to that sex to dissemble with those whom they most desire, or whether by craft they have learned outwardly to loath that which inwardly they most love; yet wisely did she cast this in her head, that if she should yield at the first assault he would think her a light huswife, if she should reject him scornfully, a very haggard; minding therefore that he should neither take hold of her promise, neither unkindness of her preciseness, she fed him indifferently with hope and despair, reason and affection, life and death. Yet in the end arguing wittily upon certain questions, they fell to such agreement as poor Philautus would not have agreed unto if he had been present, yet always keeping the body undefiled. And thus she replied:

"Gentleman, as you may suspect me of idleness in giving ear to your talk, so may you convince me of lightness in answering such toys; certes as you have made mine ears glow at the rehearsal of your love, so have you galled my heart with the remembrance of your folly. Though you came to Naples as a stranger, yet were you welcome to my father's house as a friend. And can you then so much transgress the bounds of honor (I will not say of honesty) as to solicit a suit more sharp to me then death? I have hetherto, God be thanked, lived without suspicion of lewdness, and shall I now incur the danger of sensual liberty? What hope can you have to obtain my love, seeing yet I could never afford you a good look? Do you therefore think me easely enticed to the bent of your bow, bicause I was easely entreated to listen to your late discourse? Or seeing me (as finely you glose) to excel all other in beauty, did you deem that I would exceed all other in beastliness? But yet I am not angry, Euphues, but in an agony, for who is she that will fret or fume with one that loveth her, if

this love to delude me be not dissembled? It is that which causeth me most to fear, not that my beauty is unknown to myself, but that commonly we poor wenches are deluded through light belief, and ye men are naturally enclined craftely to lead your life. When the fox preacheth the geese perish. The crocodile shroudeth greatest treason under most pitiful tears; in a kissing mouth there lieth a galling mind. You have made so large proffer of your service, and so fair promises of fidelity, that were I not overchary of mine honesty, you would inveigle me to shake hands with chastity. But certes I will either lead a virgin's life in earth (though I lead apes in hell) or else follow thee rather then thy gifts; yet am I neither so precise to refuse thy proffer, neither so peevish to disdain thy good will. So excellent always are the gifts which are made acceptable by the virtue of the giver. I did at the first entrance discern thy love but yet dissemble it. Thy wanton glances, thy scalding sighs, thy loving signs caused me to blush for shame, and to look wan for fear, lest they should be perceived of any. These subtil shifts, these painted practises (if I were to be won) would soon wean me from the teat of Vesta to the toys of Venus. Besides this, thy comely grace, thy rare qualities, thy exquisite perfection were able to move a mind half mortified to transgress the bonds of maidenly modesty. But God shield, Lucilla, that thou shouldest be so careless of thine honor as to commit the state thereof to a stranger. Learn thou by me, Euphues, to dispise things that be amiable, to forgo delightful practises; believe me, it is piety to abstain from pleasure.

"Thou art not the first that hath solicited this suit, but the first that goeth about to seduce me, neither discernest thou more then other, but darest more then any, neither hast thou more art to discover thy meaning, but more heart to open thy mind. But thou preferrest me before thy lands, thy livings, thy life; thou offerest thyself a sacrifice for my security, thou profferest me the whole and only sovereignty of thy service. Truly, I were very cruel and hardhearted if I should not love thee; hardhearted albeit I am not, but truly love thee I cannot, whom I doubt to be my lover.

"Moreover, I have not been used to the court of Cupid, wherein there be more sleights then there be hares in Athon, then bees in Hybla, then stars in heaven. Besides this, the common people here in Naples are not only both very suspicious of other men's matters and manners, but also very jealous over other men's children and maidens; either therefore dissemble thy fancy, or desist from thy folly.

"But why shouldest thou desist from the one, seeing thou canst cunningly dissemble the other?

My father is now gone to Venice, and as I am uncertain of his retourn, so am I not privy to the cause of his travel. But yet is he so from hence that he seeth me in his absence. Knowest thou not, Euphues, that kings have long arms and rulers large reaches? Neither let this comfort thee, that at his departure he deputed thee in Philautus' place. Although my face cause him to mistrust my loyalty, yet my faith enforceth him to give me this liberty; though he be suspicious of my fair hew, yet is he secure of my firm honesty. But alas, Euphues, what truth can there be found in a traveler? What stay in a stranger? whose words and bodies both watch but for a wind, whose feet are ever fleeting, whose faith plighted on the shore is tourned to perjury when they hoist sail. Who more traiterous to Phyllis then Demophoon? Yet he a traveler. Who more perjured to Dido then Aeneas? And he a stranger. Both these queens, both they caitiffs. Who more false to Ariadne then Theseus? Yet he a sailer. Who more fickle to Medea then Jason? Yet he a starter. Both these daughters to great princes, both they unfaithful of promises. Is it then likely that Euphues will be faithful to Lucilla, being in Naples but a sojourner? I have not yet forgotten the invective (I can no otherwise term it) which thou madest against beauty, saying it was a deceiptful bait with a deadly hook and a sweet poison in a painted pot. Canst thou then be so unwise to swallow the bait which will breed thy bane? to swill the drink that will expire thy date? to desire the wight that will work thy death? But it may be that with the scorpion thou canst feed on the earth, or with the quail and roebuck be fat with poison, or with beauty live in all bravery. I fear me thou hast the stone continens about thee, which is named of the contrary, that though thou pretend faith in thy words, thou devisest fraud in thy heart; that though thou seem to prefer love, thou art inflamed with lust. And what for that? Though thou have eaten the seeds of rockat, which breed incontinency, yet have I chewed the leaf cress, which maintaineth modesty. Though thou bear in thy bosom the herb araxa, most noisome to virginity, yet have I the stone that groweth in the Mount Tmolus, the upholder of chastity. You may, gentleman, accompt me for a cold prophet, thus hastely to divine of your disposition; pardon me, Euphues, if in love I cast beyond the moon, which bringeth us women to endless moan. Although I myself were never burnt, whereby I should dread the fire, yet the scorching of others in the flames of fancy warneth me to beware. Though I as yet never tried any faithless, whereby I should be fearful, yet have I read of many that have been perjured, which causeth me to be careful. Though I am able to convince none by proof, yet am I enforced to suspect one upon

probabilities. Alas, we silly souls which have neither wit to decipher the wiles of men, nor wisdom to dissemble our affection, neither craft to train in young lovers, neither courage to withstand their encounters, neither discretion to discern their doubling, neither hard hearts to reject their complaints—we, I say, are soon enticed, being by nature simple and easily entangled, being apt to receive the impression of love. But alas, it is both common and lamentable to behold simplicity intrapped by subtility, and those that have most might to be infected with most malice. The spider weaveth a fine web to hang the fly, the wolf weareth a fair face to devour the lamb, the merlin striketh at the partridge, the eagle often snappeth at the fly, men are always laying baits for women, which are the weaker vessels; but as yet I could never hear man by such snares to intrap man. For true it is that men themselves have by use observed that it must be a hard winter when one wolf eateth another. I have read that the bull being tied to the fig tree loseth his strength, that the whole herd of deer stand at the gaze if they smell a sweet apple, that the dolphin by the sound of music is brought to the shore. And then no mervail it is that if the fierce bull be tamed with the fig tree, if that women being as weak as sheep be overcome with a fig, if the wild deer be caught with an apple, that the tame damsel is won with a blossom, if the fleet dolphin be allured with harmony, that women be entangled with the melody of men's speech, fair promises, and solemn protestations. But folly it were for me to mark their mischiefs, sith I am neither able, neither they willing, to amend their manners; it becometh me rather to shew what our sex should do then to open what yours doth. And seeing I cannot by reason restrain your importunate suit, I will by rigor done on myself cause you to refrain the means. I would to God Ferardo were in this point like to Lysander, which would not suffer his daughters to wear gorgeous apparel, saying it would rather make them common then comely. I would it were in Naples a law, which was a custom in Egypt, that women should always go barefoot, to the intent they might keep themselves always at home, that they should be ever like to that snail which hath ever his house on his head. I mean so to mortify myself that instead of silks I will wear sackcloth, for owches and bracelets, leer and caddis, for the lute, use the distaff, for the pen, the needle, for lovers' sonnets, David's Psalms. But yet I am not so senseless altogether to reject your service; which if I were certainly assured to proceed of a simple mind, it shold not receive so simple a reward. And what greater trial can I have of thy simplicity and truth then thine own request which desireth a trial? I, but in the coldest flint there is hot fire, the bee that hath honey in her mouth hath a sting in her tail, the tree that beareth the sweetest fruit hath a sour sap, yea, the words of men, though they seem smooth as oil, yet their hearts are as crooked as the stalk of ivy. I would not, Euphues, that thou shouldest condemn me of rigor, in that I seek to assuage thy folly by reason, but take this by the way, that although as yet I am disposed to like of none, yet whensoever I shall love any, I will not forget thee; in the mean season accompt me thy friend, for thy foe I will never be."

Euphues was brought into a great quandary and, as it were, a cold shivering to hear this new kind of kindness, such sweet meat, such sour sauce, such fair words, such faint promises, such hot love, such cold desire, such certain hope, such sodain change, and stood like one that had looked on Medusa's head, and so had been tourned into a stone.

Lucilla, seeing him in this pitiful plight and fearing he would take stand if the lure were not cast out, took him by the hand and wringing him softly, with a smiling countenance began thus to comfort him:

"Methinks, Euphues, changing so your color upon the sodain, you will soon change your copy. Is your mind on your meat? A penny for your thought."

"Mistress," quod he, "if you would buy all my thoughts at that price, I should never be weary of thinking, but seeing it is too dear, read it, and take it for nothing."

"It seems to me," said she, "that you are in some brown study what colors you might best wear for your lady."

"Indeed, Lucilla, you level shrewdly at my thought, by the aim of your own imagination, for you have given unto me a true love's knot wrought of changeable silk, and you deem me that I am devising how I might have my colors changeable also, that they might agree. But let this with such toys and devices pass. If it please you to command me any service, I am here ready to attend your leisure."

"No service, Euphues, but that you keep silence until I have uttered my mind, and secrecy when I have unfolded my meaning."

"If I should offend in the one I were too bold, if in the other, too beastly."

"Well then, Euphues," said she, "so it is that for the hope that I conceive of thy loyalty and the happy success that is like to ensue of this our love, I am content to yield thee the place in my heart which thou desirest and deservest above all other; which consent in me if it may any ways breed thy contentation, sure I am that it will every way work my comfort. But as either thou tenderest mine honor or thine own safety, use such secrecy in this matter that my father have

no inkling hereof before I have framed his mind fit for our purpose. And though women have small force to overcome men by reason, yet have they good fortune to undermine them by policy. The soft drops of rain pierce the hard marble, many strokes overthrow the tallest oak, a silly woman in time may make such a breach into a man's heart as her tears may enter without resistance; then doubt not but I will so undermine mine old father, as quickly I will enjoy my new friend. Tush, Philautus was liked for fashion sake, but never loved for fancy sake, and this I vow by the faith of a virgin and by the love I bear thee (for greater bands to confirm my vow I have not), that my father shall sooner martyr me in the fire then marry me to Philautus. No, no, Euphues, thou only hast won me by love, and shalt only wear me by law; I force not Philautus his fury, so I may have Euphues his friendship; neither will I prefer his possessions before thy person, neither esteem better of his lands then of thy love. Ferardo shall sooner disherit me of my patrimony then dishonor me in breaking my promise. It is not his great manors, but thy good manners, that shall make my marriage. In token of which my sincere affection, I give thee my hand in pawn and my heart forever to be thy Lucilla."

Unto whom Euphues answered in this manner:

"If my tongue were able to utter the joys that my heart hath conceived, I fear me, though I be well beloved, yet I should hardly be believed. Ah, my Lucilla, how much am I bound to thee, which preferrest mine unworthiness before thy father's wrath, my happiness before thine own misfortune, my love before thine own life! How might I excel thee in curtesy whom no mortal creature can exceed in constancy? I find it now for a settled truth, which erst I accompted for a vain talk, that the purple dye will never stain, that the pure civet will never loose his savor, that the green laurel will never change his color, that beauty can never be blotted with discourtesy. As touching secrecy in this behalf, assure thyself that I will not so much as tell it to myself. Command Euphues to run, to ride, to undertake any exploit, be it never so dangerous, to hazard himself in any enterprise, be it never so desperate."

As they were thus pleasantly conferring the one with the other, Livia (whom Euphues made his stale) entered into the parlor, unto whom Lucilla spake in these terms: "Dost thou not laugh, Livia, to see my ghostly father keep me here so long at shrift?" "Truly," answered Livia, "methinks that you smile at some pleasant shift; either he is slow in enquiring of your faults, or you slack in answering of his questions." And thus being supper time they all sat down, Lucilla well pleased, no man better content then Euphues, who after his repast having no opportunity to confer with his lover had small lust to continue with the gentlewomen any longer; seeing therefore he could frame no means to work his delight, he coined an excuse to hasten his departure, promising the next morning to trouble them again as a guest more bold then welcome, although indeed he thought himself to be the better welcome in saying that he would come.

But as Ferardo went in post, so he retourned in haste, having concluded with Philautus that the marriage should immediately be consummated, which wrought such a content in Philautus that he was almost in an ecstasy through the extremity of his passions; such is the fulness and force of pleasure, that there is nothing so dangerous as the fruition. Yet knowing that delays bring dangers, although he nothing doubted of Lucilla, whom he loved, yet feared he the fickleness of old men, which is always to be mistrusted. He urged therefore Ferardo to break with his daughter, who being willing to have the match made was content incontinently to procure the means; finding therefore his daughter at leisure, and having knowledge of her former love, spake to her as followeth:

"Dear daughter, as thou hast long time lived a maiden, so now thou must learn to be a mother, and as I have been careful to bring thee up a virgin, so am I now desirous to make thee a wife. Neither ought I in this matter to use any persuasions, for that maidens commonly nowadays are no sooner born but they begin to bride it; neither to offer any great portions, for that thou knowest thou shalt inherit all my possessions. Mine only care hath been hetherto to match thee with such an one as should be of good wealth able to maintain thee, of great worship able to compare with thee in birth, of honest conditions to deserve thy love, and an Italian born to enjoy my lands. At the last I have found one answerable to my desire, a gentleman of great revenues, of a noble progeny, of honest behavior, of comely personage, born and brought up in Naples, Philautus, thy friend as I gess, thy husband, Lucilla, if thou like it; neither canst thou dislike him who wanteth nothing that should cause thy liking, neither hath anything that should breed thy loathing. And surely I rejoice the more that thou shalt be linked to him in marriage, whom thou hast loved, as I hear, being a maiden; neither can there any jars kindle between them where the minds be so united, neither any jealousy arise where love hath so long been settled. Therefore, Lucilla, to the end the desire of either of you may now be accomplished, to the delight of you both, I am here come to finish the contract by giving hands, which you have already begun between yourselves

by joining of hearts, that as God doth witness the one in your consciences, so the world may testify the other by your conversations; and therefore, Lucilla, make such answer to my request as may like me and satisfy thy friend."

Lucilla, abashed with this sodein speech of her father, yet boldened by the love of her friend, with a comely bashfulness answered him in this manner:

"Reverend sir, the sweetness that I have found in the undefiled estate of virginity causeth me to loath the sour sauce which is mixed with matrimony, and the quiet life which I have tried being a maiden maketh me to shun the cares that are always incident to a mother; neither am I so wedded to the world that I should be moved with great possessions, neither so bewitched with wantonness that I should be enticed with any man's proportion, neither if I were so disposed would I be so proud to desire one of noble progeny, or so precise to choose one only in mine own country, for that commonly these things happen always to the contrary. Do we not see the noble to match with the base, the rich with the poor, the Italian oftentimes with the Portingale? As love knoweth no laws, so it regardeth no conditions; as the lover maketh no pause where he liketh, so he maketh no conscience of these idle ceremonies. In that Philautus is the man that threateneth such kindness at my hands and such courtesy at yours, that he should accompt me his wife before he woo me, certainly he is like for me to make his reckoning twice bicause he reckoneth without his hostess. And in this Philautus would either shew himself of great wisdom to persuade, or me of great lightness to be allured. Although the loadstone draw iron, yet it cannot move gold; though the jet gather up the light straw, yet can it not take up the pure steel; although Philautus think himself of virtue sufficient to win his lover, yet shall he not obtain Lucilla. I cannot but smile to hear that a marriage should be solemnized where never was any mention of assuring, and that the wooing should be a day after the wedding. Certes, if when I looked merrily on Philautus he deemed it in the way of marriage, or if seeing me disposed to jest he took me in good earnest, then sure he might gather some presumption of my love, but no promise. But methinks it is good reason that I should be at mine own bridal, and not given in the church before I know the bridegroom. Therefore, dear father, in mine opinion as there can be no bargain where both be not agreed, neither any indentures sealed where the one will not consent, so can there be no contract where both be not content, no banes asked lawfully where one of the parties forbiddeth them, no marriage made where no match was meant. But I will hereafter frame myself to be coy, seeing I am claimed for a wife bicause I have been courteous, and give myself to melancholy, seeing I am accompted won in that I have been merry. And if every gentleman be made of the metal that Philautus is, then I fear I shall be challenged of as many as I have used to company with, and be a common wife to all those that have commonly resorted hether.

"My duty therefore ever reserved, I here on my knees forswear Philautus for my husband, although I accept him for my friend, and seeing I shall hardly be induced ever to match with any, I beseech you, if by your fatherly love I shall be compelled, that I may match with such a one as both I may love and you may like."

Ferardo, being a grave and wise gentleman, although he were throughly angry, yet he dissembled his fury, to the end he might by craft discover her fancy, and whispering Philautus in the ear (who stood as though he had a flea in his ear) desired him to keep silence until he had undermined her by subtilty, which Philautus having granted, Ferardo began to sift his daughter with this device:

"Lucilla, thy color sheweth thee to be in a great choler, and thy hot words bewray thy heavy wrath; but be patient, seeing all my talk was only to try thee. I am neither so unnatural to wrest thee against thine own will, neither so malicious to wed thee to any against thine own liking; for well I know what jars, what jealousy, what strife, what storms ensue, where the match is made rather by the compulsion of the parents then by consent of the parties; neither do I like thee the less, in that thou likest Philautus so little, neither can Philautus love thee the worse, in that thou lovest thyself so well, wishing rather to stand to thy chance then to the choice of any other. But this grieveth me most, that thou art almost vowed to the vain order of the vestal virgins, despising, or at the least not desiring, the sacred bands of Juno her bed. If thy mother had been of that mind when she was a maiden, thou haddest not now been born to be of this mind to be a virgin. Weigh with thyself what slender profit they bring to the commonwealth, what slight pleasure to themselves, what great grief to their parents, which joy most in their offspring and desire most to enjoy the noble and blessed name of a grandfather.

"Thou knowest that the tallest ash is cut down for fuel bycause it beareth no good fruit, that the cow that gives no milk is brought to the slaughter, that the drone that gathereth no honey is contemned, that the woman that maketh herself barren by not marrying is accompted among the Grecian ladies worse then a carrion, as Homer reporteth. Therefore, Lucilla, if thou have any care to be a comfort to my hoary hairs or a commodity to thy commonweal,

frame thyself to that honorable estate of matrimony, which was sanctified in paradise, allowed of the patriarchs, hallowed of the old prophets, and commended of all persons. If thou like any, be not ashamed to tell it me, which only am to exhort thee, yea, and as much as in me lieth to command thee, to love one. If he be base thy blood will make him noble, if beggerly thy goods shall make him wealthy, if a stranger thy freedom may enfranchise him; if he be young he is the more fitter to be thy phere, if he be old the liker to thine aged father. For I had rather thou shouldest lead a life to thine own liking in earth then to thy great torments lead apes in hell. Be bold therefore to make me partner of thy desire, which will be partaker of thy disease, yea, and a furtherer of thy delights, as far as either my friends, or my lands, or my life will stretch."

Lucilla, perceiving the drift of the old fox her father, weighed with herself what was best to be done; at the last not weighing her father's ill will, but encouraged by love, shaped him an answer which pleased Ferardo but a little, and pinched Philautus on the parson's side, on this manner:

"Dear father Ferardo, although I see the bait you lay to catch me, yet I am content to swallow the hook, neither are you more desirous to take me napping then I willing to confess my meaning. So it is that love hath as well inveigled me as others which make it as strange as I. Neither do I love him so meanly that I should be ashamed of his name, neither is his personage so mean that I should love him shamefully. It is Euphues, that lately arrived here at Naples, that hath battered the bulwark of my breast and shall shortly enter as conqueror into my bosom. What his wealth is I neither know it nor weigh it, what his wit is all Naples doth know it, and wonder at it, neither have I been curious to enquire of his progenitors, for that I know so noble a mind could take no original but from a noble man, for as no bird can look against the sun but those that be bred of the eagle, neither any hawk soar so high as the brood of the hobby, so no wight can have such excellent qualities except he descend of a noble race, neither be of so high capacity unless he issue of a high progeny. And I hope Philautus will not be my foe, seeing I have chosen his dear friend, neither you, father, be displeased in that Philautus is displaced. You need not muse that I should so sodeinly be intangled; love gives no reason of choice, neither will it suffer any repulse. Myrrha was enamored of her natural father, Biblis of her brother, Phaedra of her son-in-law; if nature can no way resist the fury of affection, how should it be stayed by wisdom?"

Ferardo interrupting her in the middle of her discourse, although he were moved with inward grudge, yet he wisely repressed his anger, knowing that sharp words would but sharpen her froward will, and thus answered her briefly:

"Lucilla, as I am not presently to grant my good will, so mean I not to reprehend thy choice, yet wisdom willeth me to pause until I have called what may happen to my remembrance, and warneth thee to be circumspect, lest thy rash conceit bring a sharp repentance. As for you, Philautus, I would not have you dispair, seeing a woman doth oftentimes change her desire."

Unto whom Philautus in few words made answer: "Certainly, Ferardo, I take the less grief in that I see her so greedy after Euphues, and by so much the more I am content to leave my suit, by how much the more she seemeth to disdain my service; but as for hope, bicause I would not by any means taste one dram thereof, I will abjure all places of her abode and loath her company, whose countenance I have so much loved; as for Euphues——" and there staying his speech, he flang out of the doors, and repairing to his lodging uttered these words:

"Ah, most dissembling wretch, Euphues, O counterfait companion, couldest thou under the shew of a steadfast friend cloak the malice of a mortal foe? under the color of simplicity shroud the image of deceit? Is thy Livia tourned to my Lucilla, thy love to my lover, thy devotion to my saint? Is this the curtesy of Athens, the caviling of scholars, the craft of Grecians? Couldest thou not remember, Philautus, that Greece is never without some wily Ulysses, never void of some Synon, never to seek of some deceitful shifter? Is it not commonly said of Grecians that craft cometh to them by kind, that they learn to deceive in their cradle? Why then did his pretended curtesy bewitch thee with such credulity? Shall my good will be the cause of his ill will? Bicause I was content to be his friend, thought he me meet to be made his fool? I see now that as the fish scolopidus in the flood Araris at the waxing of the moon is as white as the driven snow and at the waning as black as the burnt coal, so Euphues, which at the first encreasing of our familiarity was very zealous, is now at the last cast become most faithless. But why rather exclaim I not against Lucilla, whose wanton looks caused Euphues to violate his plighted faith? Ah, wretched wench, canst thou be so light of love as to change with every wind? so unconstant as to prefer a new lover before thine old friend? Ah, well I wot that a new broom sweepeth clean, and a new garment maketh thee leave off the old though it be fitter, and new wine causeth thee to forsake the old though it be better, much like to the men in the Island Scyrum, which pull up the old tree when they see the young begin to spring, and not unlike unto

the widow of Lesbos which changed all her old gold for new glass. Have I served thee three years faithfully, and am I served so unkindly? Shall the fruit of my desire be tourned to disdain? But unless Euphues had inveigled thee thou haddest yet been constant. Yea, but if Euphues had not seen thee willing to be won, he would never have wooed thee. But had not Euphues enticed thee with fair words, thou wouldest never have loved him. But haddest thou not given him fair looks he would never have liked thee. I, but Euphues gave the onset. I, but Lucilla gave the occasion. I, but Euphues first brake his mind. I, but Lucilla first bewrayed her meaning. Tush, why go I about to excuse any of them, seeing I have just cause to accuse them both? Neither ought I to dispute which of them hath proffered me the greatest villany, sith that either of them hath committed perjury. Yet although they have found me dull in perceiving their falsehood, they shall not find me slack in revenging their folly. As for Lucilla, seeing I mean altogether to forget her, I mean also to forgive her, lest in seeking means to be revenged mine old desire be renewed."

Philautus having thus discoursed with himself began to write to Euphues as followeth:

"Although hetherto, Euphues, I have shrined thee in my heart for a trusty friend, I will shun thee hereafter as a trothless foe, and although I cannot see in thee less wit then I was wont, yet do I find less honesty. I perceive at the last (although being deceived it be too late) that musk, although it be sweet in the smell, is sour in the smack, that the leaf of the cedar tree, though it be fair to be seen, yet the syrup depriveth sight, that friendship, though it be plighted by shaking the hand, yet it is shaken off by fraud of the heart. But thou hast not much to boast of, for as thou hast won a fickle lady, so hast thou lost a faithful friend. How canst thou be secure of her constancy when thou hast had such trial of her lightness? How canst thou assure thyself that she will be faithful to thee, which hath been faithless to me? Ah, Euphues, let not my credulity be an occasion hereafter for thee to practise the like cruelty. Remember this, that yet there hath never been any faithless to his friend that hath not also been fruitless to his God. But I weigh this treachery the less, in that it cometh from a Grecian, in whom is no troth. Though I be too weak to wrastle for a revenge, yet God who permitteth no guile to be guiltless will shortly requite this injury; though Philautus have no policy to undermine thee, yet thine own practises will be sufficient to overthrow thee.

"Couldest thou, Euphues, for the love of a fruitless pleasure violate the league of faithful friendship? Diddest thou weigh more the enticing looks of a lewd wench then the entire love of a loyal friend? If thou diddest determine with thyself at the first to be false, why diddest thou swear to be true? If to be true, why art thou false? If thou wast minded both falsely and forgedly to deceive me, why diddest thou flatter and dissemble with me at the first? If to love me, why doest thou flinch at the last? If the sacred bands of amity did delight thee, why diddest thou break them? If dislike thee, why diddest thou praise them? Dost thou not know that a perfect friend should be like the glazeworm, which shineth most bright in the dark? or like the pure frankencense, which smelleth most sweet when it is in the fire? or at the least not unlike to the damask rose, which is sweeter in the still then on the stalk? But thou, Euphues, dost rather resemble the swallow which in the summer creepeth under the eaves of every house, and in the winter leaveth nothing but dirt behind her, or the humble bee which having sucked honey out of the fair flower doth leave it and loath it, or the spider which in the finest web doth hang the fairest fly. Dost thou think, Euphues, that thy craft in betraying me shall any whit cool my courage in revenging thy villany? Or that a gentleman of Naples will put up such an injury at the hands of a scholler? And if I do, it is not for want of strength to maintain my just quarrel, but of will which thinketh scorn to get so vain a conquest. I know that Menelaus for his ten years' war endured ten years' wo, that after all his strife he wan but a strumpet, that for all his travels he reduced (I cannot say reclaimed) but a straggeler; which was as much in my judgment as to strive for a broken glass which is good for nothing. I wish thee rather Menelaus' care then myself his conquest, that thou, being deluded by Lucilla, mayst rather know what it is to be deceived then I, having conquered thee, should prove what it were to bring back a dissembler. Seeing therefore there can no greater revenge light upon thee then that as thou hast reaped where another hath sown, so another may thresh that which thou hast reaped, I will pray that thou mayst be measured unto with the like measure that thou hast meten unto others; that as thou hast thought it no conscience to betray me, so others may deem it no dishonesty to deceive thee; that as Lucilla made it a light matter to forswear her old friend, Philautus, so she may make it a mock to forsake her new phere, Euphues. Which if it come to pass, as it is like by my compass, then shalt thou see the troubles and feel the torments which thou hast already thrown into the hearts and eyes of others. Thus hoping shortly to see thee as hopeless as myself is hapless, I wish my wish were as effectually ended as it is heartely looked for. And so I leave thee.

Thine once,

Philautus"

Philautus, dispatching a messenger with this letter speedely to Euphues, went into the fields to walk, there either to digest his choler or chew upon his melancholy. But Euphues having read the contents was well content, setting his talk at naught and answering his taunts in these gibing terms:

"I remember, Philautus, how valiantly Ajax boasted in the feats of arms, yet Ulysses bare away the armor; and it may be that though thou crake of thine own courage, thou mayst easely lose the conquest. Dost thou think Euphues such a dastard that he is not able to withstand thy courage, or such a dullard that he cannot descry thy craft? Alas, good soul! It fareth with thee as with the hen, which when the puttock hath caught her chicken beginneth to cackle; and thou having lost thy lover beginnest to prattle. Tush, Philautus, I am in this point of Euripides his mind, who thinks it lawful for the desire of a kingdom to transgress the bounds of honesty, and for the love of a lady to violate and break the bands of amity.

"The friendship between man and man as it is common so is it of course; between man and woman as it is seldom so is it sincere; the one proceedeth of the similitude of manners, the other of the sincerity of the heart. If thou haddest learned the first point of hawking thou wouldst have learned to have held fast, or the first note of descant thou wouldest have kept thy sol fa to thyself.

"But thou canst blame me no more of folly in leaving thee to love Lucilla then thou mayst reprove him of foolishness that having a sparrow in his hand letteth her go to catch the pheasant, or him of unskilfulness that seeing the heron leaveth to level his shoot at the stock-dove, or that woman of coyness that having a dead rose in her bosom throweth it away to gather the fresh violet. Love knoweth no laws. Did not Jupiter transform himself into the shape of Amphitrio to imbrace Alcmena? into the form of a swan to enjoy Leda? into a bull to beguile Io? into a shower of gold to win Danae? Did not Neptune change himself into a heifer, a ram, a flood, a dolphin, only for the love of those he lusted after? Did not Apollo convert himself into a shepherd, into a bird, into a lion, for the desire he had to heal his disease? If the gods thought no scorn to become beasts to obtain their best beloved, shall Euphues be so nice in changing his copy to gain his lady? No, no; he that cannot dissemble in love is not worthy to live. I am of this mind, that both might and malice, deceit and treachery, all perjury, any impiety may lawfully be committed in love, which is lawless. In that thou arguest Lucilla of lightness, thy will hangs in the light of thy wit. Dost thou not know that the weak stomach if it be cloyed with one diet doth soon surfet? that the clown's garlic cannot ease the courtier's disease so well as the pure treacle? that farfet and dear

bought is good for ladies? that Euphues being a more dainty morsel then Philautus ought better to be accepted? Tush, Philautus, set thy heart at rest, for thy hap willeth thee to give over all hope both of my friendship and her love; as for revenge, thou art not so able to lend a blow as I to ward it, neither more venterous to challenge the combat then I valiant to answer the quarrel. As Lucilla was caught by fraud, so shall she be kept by force, and as thou wast too simple to espy my craft, so I think thou wilt be too weak to withstand my courage; but if thy revenge stand only upon thy wish, thou shalt never live to see my wo, or to have thy will; and so farewell.
                                        Euphues"

This letter being dispatched, Euphues sent it, and Philautus read it, who disdaining those proud terms, disdained also to answer them, being ready to ride with Ferardo.

Euphues having for a space absented himself from the house of Ferardo, bicause he was at home, longed sore to see Lucilla, which now opportunity offered unto him, Ferardo being gone again to Venice with Philautus; but in his absence one Curio, a gentleman of Naples of little wealth and less wit, haunted Lucilla her company, and so enchanted her that Euphues was also cast off with Philautus; which thing being unknown to Euphues caused him the sooner to make his repair to the presence of his lady, whom he finding in her muses began pleasantly to salute in this manner:

"Mistress Lucilla, although my long absence might breed your just anger (for that lovers desire nothing so much as often meeting), yet I hope my presence will dissolve your choler (for that lovers are soon pleased when of their wishes they be fully possessed). My absence is the rather to be excused in that your father hath been always at home, whose frowns seemed to threaten my ill fortune, and my presence at this present the better to be accepted in that I have made such speedy repair to your presence."

Unto whom Lucilla answered with this glyeke:
"Truly, Euphues, you have miss'd the cushion, for I was neither angry with your long absence, neither am I well pleased at your presence; the one gave me rather a good hope hereafter never to see you, the other giveth me a greater occasion to abhor you."

Euphues being nipped on the head, with a pale countenance, as though his soul had forsaken his body, replied as followeth:

"If this sodayn change, Lucilla, proceed of any desert of mine, I am here not only to answer the fact, but also to make amends for my fault; if of any new motion or mind to forsake your new friend, I am rather to lament your inconstancy then revenge it; but I hope that such hot love cannot be so soon cold,

neither such sure faith be rewarded with so sodeyn forgetfulness."

Lucilla, not ashamed to confess her folly, answered him with this frump:

"Sir, whether your deserts or my desire have wrought this change it will boot you little to know, neither do I crave amends, neither fear revenge; as for fervent love, you know there is no fire so hot but it is quenched with water, neither affection so strong but is weakened with reason. Let this suffice thee, that thou know I care not for thee."

"Indeed," said Euphues, "to know the cause of your alteration would boot me little, seeing the effect taketh such force. I have heard that women either love entirely or hate deadly, and seeing you have put me out of doubt of the one, I must needs persuade myself of the other. This change will cause Philautus to laugh me to scorn, and double thy lightness in turning so often. Such was the hope that I conceived of thy constancy that I spared not in all places to blaze thy loyalty; but now my rash conceit will prove me a liar and thee a light huswife."

"Nay," said Lucilla, "now shalt not thou laugh Philautus to scorn, seeing you have both drunk of one cup; in misery, Euphues, it is a great comfort to have a companion. I doubt not but that you will both conspire against me to work some mischief, although I nothing fear your malice; whosoever accompteth you a liar for praising me may also deem you a letcher for being enamored of me, and whosoever judgeth me light in forsaking of you may think thee as lewd in loving of me, for thou that thoughtest it lawful to deceive thy friend must take no scorn to be deceived of thy foe."

"Then I perceive, Lucilla," said he, "that I was made thy stale, and Philautus thy laughing-stock; whose friendship (I must confess indeed) I have refused to obtain thy favor; and sithens another hath won that we both have lost, I am content for my part, neither ought I to be grieved, seeing thou art fickle."

"Certes, Euphues," said Lucilla, "you spend your wind in waste, for your welcome is but small and your cheer is like to be less; fancy giveth no reason of his change, neither will be controlled for any choice; this is therefore to warn you that from henceforth you neither solicit this suit neither offer any way your service. I have chosen one (I must needs confess) neither to be compared to Philautus in wealth, nor to thee in wit, neither in birth to the worst of you both. I think God gave it me for a just plague for renouncing Philautus and choosing thee, and sithens I am an ensample to all women of lightness, I am like also to be a mirror to them all of unhappiness, which ill luck I must take by so much the more patiently, by how much the more I acknowledge myself to have deserved it worthely."

"Well, Lucilla," answered Euphues, "this case breedeth my sorrow the more, in that it is so sodein, and by so much the more I lament it, by how much the less I looked for it. In that my welcome is so cold and my cheer so simple, it nothing toucheth me, seeing your fury is so hot, and my misfortune so great, that I am neither willing to receive it nor you to bestow it. If tract of time or want of trial had caused this metamorphosis my grief had been more tolerable, and your fleeting more excusable, but coming in a moment undeserved, unlooked for, unthought of, it encreaseth my sorrow and thy shame."

"Euphues," quoth she, "you make a long harvest for a little corn, and angle for the fish that is already caught. Curio, yea, Curio is he that hath my love at his pleasure, and shall also have my life at his commandement, and although you deem him unworthy to enjoy that which erst you accompted no wight worthy to embrace, yet seeing I esteem him more worth then any, he is to be reputed as chief. The wolf chooseth him for her make that hath or doth endure most travail for her sake. Venus was content to take the blacksmith with his polt-foot. Cornelia here in Naples disdained not to love a rude miller. As for changing, did not Helen the pearl of Greece, thy countrywoman, first take Menelaus, then Theseus, and last of all Paris? If brute beasts give us ensamples that those are most to be liked of whom we are best beloved, or if the princess of beauty, Venus, and her heirs, Helen and Cornelia, shew that our affection standeth on our free will, then am I rather to be excused then accused. Therefore, good Euphues, be as merry as you may be, for time may so tourn that once again you may be."

"Nay, Lucilla," said he, "my harvest shall cease, seeing others have reaped my corn; as for angling for the fish that is already caught, that were but mere folly. But in my mind if you be a fish you are either an eel, which as soon as one hath hold of her tail will slip out of his hand, or else a minnow, which will be nibbling at every bait but never biting. But what fish soever you be, you have made both me and Philautus to swallow a gudgen. If Curio be the person, I would neither wish thee a greater plague nor him a deadlier poison. I for my part think him worthy of thee, and thou unworthy of him, for although he be in body deformed, in mind foolish, an innocent born, a begger by misfortune, yet doth he deserve a better then thyself, whose corrupt manners have stain'd thy heavenly hew, whose light behavior hath dimmed the lights of thy beauty, whose unconstant mind hath betrayed the innocency of so many a gentleman. And in that you bring in the example of a beast to confirm your folly, you shew therein your beastly disposition, which is ready to follow such beastliness. But Venus played false! And for what? Seeing her lightness serveth for an example, I would wish thou mightest try her punishment for a reward, that being openly taken in an iron net all the world might judge whether thou be fish or flesh; and certes in my mind no angle will hold thee, it must be a net. Cornelia loved a miller, and thou a miser; can her folly excuse thy fault? Helen of Greece, my countrywoman born but thine by profession, changed and rechanged at her pleasure, I grant. Shall the lewdness of others animate thee in thy lightness? Why then dost thou not haunt the stews bicause Lais frequented them? Why doest thou not love a bull, seeing Pasiphae loved one? Why art thou not enamored of thy father, knowing that Myrrha was so incensed? These are set down that we, viewing their incontinency, should fly the like impudency, not follow the like excess, neither can they excuse thee of any inconstancy. Merry I will be as I may, but if I may hereafter as thou meanest, I will not; and therefore farewell, Lucilla, the most inconstant that ever was nursed in Naples; farewell, Naples, the most cursed town in all Italy; and women all, farewell!"

Euphues having thus given her his last farewell yet being solitary began afresh to recount his sorrow on this manner:

"Ah, Euphues, into what a quandary art thou brought! In what sodein misfortune art thou wrapped! It is like to fare with thee as with the eagle, which dieth neither for age nor with sickness, but with famine, for although thy stomach hunger yet thy heart will not suffer thee to eat. And why shouldest thou torment thyself for one in whom is neither faith nor fervency? O the counterfait love of women! O inconstant sex! I have lost Philautus, I have lost Lucilla, I have lost that which I shall hardly find again, a faithful friend. Ah, foolish Euphues, why diddest thou leave Athens, the nourse of wisdom, to inhabit Naples, the nourisher of wantonness? Had it not been better for thee to have eaten salt with the philosophers in Greece then sugar with the courtiers of Italy? But behold the course of youth, which always inclineth to pleasure; I forsook mine old companions to search for new friends, I rejected the grave and fatherly counsail of Eubulus, to follow the brainsick humor of mine own will. I addicted myself wholly to the service of women to spend my life in the laps of ladies, my lands in maintenance of bravery, my wit in the vanities of idle sonnets. I had thought that women had been as we men, that is true, faithful, zealous, constant, but I perceive they be rather wo unto men by their falsehood, gelousy, inconstancy. I was half persuaded that they were made of the perfection of men, and would be comforters, but now I see they have tasted of the infection of the serpent, and will be corasives. The phisition saith it is dangerous to minister physic unto the patient that hath a cold stomach and a hot liver, lest in giving warmth to the one he inflame the other; so verely it is hard to deal with a woman whose words seem fervent, whose heart is congealed into hard ice, lest trusting their outward talk he be-trayed with their inward treachery. I will to Athens, there to toss my books, no more in Naples to live with fair looks. I will so frame myself as all youth hereafter shall rather rejoice to see mine amendement then be animated to follow my former life. Phi-losophy, physic, divinity shall be my study. O the hidden secrets of nature, the express image of moral virtues, the equal balance of justice, the medicines to heal all diseases, how they begin to delight me! The axiomaes of Aristotle, the maxims of Justinian, the aphorisms of Galen, have sodainly made such a breach into my mind that I seem only to desire them which did only erst detest them. If wit be employed in the honest study of learning, what thing so pretious as wit? If in the idle trade of love, what thing more pestilent then wit? The proof of late hath been verefied in me, whom nature hath endued with a little wit, which I have abused with an obstinate will; most true it is that the thing the better it is the greater is the abuse, and that there is nothing but through the malice of man may be abused.

"Doth not the fire (an element so necessary that without it man cannot live) as well burn the house as burn in the house, if it be abused? Doth not treacle as well poison as help if it be taken out of time? Doth not wine if it be immoderately taken kill the stomach, enflame the liver, murther the droncken? Doth not physic destroy if it be not well temp'red? Doth not law accuse if it be not rightly interpreted? Doth not divinity condemn if it be not faithfully construed? Is not poison taken out of the honeysuckle by the spider, venim out of the rose by the canker, dung out of the maple tree by the scorpion? Even so the greatest wickedness is drawn out of the greatest wit, if it be abused by will, or entangled with the world, or inveigled with women.

"But seeing I see mine own impiety, I will en-deavor myself to amend all that is past and to be a mirror of godliness hereafter. The rose though a little it be eaten with the canker, yet being distilled yieldeth sweet water, the iron though fretted with the rust, yet being burnt in the fire shineth brighter, and wit although it hath been eaten with the canker of his own conceit and fretted with the rust of vain love, yet, being purified in the still of wisdom and tried in the fire of zeal, will shine bright and smell sweet in the nosethrills of all young novices.

"As therefore I gave a farewell to Lucilla, a farewell to Naples, a farewell to women, so now do I give a farewell to the world, meaning rather to macerate myself with melancholy then pine in folly, rather choosing to die in my study amiddest my books then to court it in Italy, in the company of ladies."

It happened immediately Ferardo to retourn home, who hearing this strange event was not a little amazed, and was now more ready to exhort Lucilla from the love of Curio then before to the liking of Philautus. Therefore in all haste, with wat'ry eyes and a woful heart, began on this manner to reason with his daughter:

"Lucilla (daughter I am ashamed to call thee, seeing thou hast neither care of thy father's tender affection nor of thine own credit), what sprite hath enchanted thy spirit that every minute thou alterest thy mind? I had thought that my hoary hairs should have found comfort by thy golden locks and my rotten age great ease by thy ripe years. But, alas, I see in thee neither wit to order thy doings, neither will to frame thyself to discretion, neither the nature of a child, neither the nurture of a maiden, neither (I cannot without tears speak it) any regard of thine honor, neither any care of thine honesty.

"I am now enforced to remember thy mother's death, who I think was a prophetess in her life, for oftentimes she would say that thou haddest more beauty then was convenient for one that should be honest and more cockering then was meet for one that should be a matron.

"Would I had never lived to be so old or thou to be so obstinate; either would I had died in my youth in the court or thou in thy cradle. I would to God that either I had never been born or thou never bred. Is this the comfort that the parent reapeth for all his care? Is obstinacy paid for obedience, stubbernness rend'red for duty, malicious desperateness for filial fear? I perceive now that the wise painter saw more then the foolish parent can, who painted love going downward, saying it might well descend, but ascend it could never. Danaus, whom they report to be the father of fifty children, had among them all but one that disobeyed him in a thing most dishonest, but I that am father to one more then I would be, although one be all, have that one most disobedient to me in a request lawful and reasonable. If Danaus seeing but one of his daughters without awe became himself without mercy, what shall Ferardo do in this case who hath one and all most unnatural to him in a most just cause? Shall Curio enjoy the fruit of my travails, possess the benefit of my labors, enherit the patrimony of mine ancestors, who hath neither wis-dom to increase them nor wit to keep them? Wilt thou, Lucilla, bestow thyself on such an one as hath neither comeliness in his body, nor knowledge in his mind, nor credit in his country? O I would thou haddest either been ever faithful to Philautus, or never faithless to Euphues, or would thou wouldest be more fickle to Curio! As thy beauty hath made thee [the] blaze of Italy, so will thy lightness make thee the byword of the world. O Lucilla, Lucilla, would thou wert less fair or more fortunate, either of less honor or greater honesty, either better minded or soon buried! Shall thine old father live to see thee match with a young fool? Shall my kind heart be rewarded with such unkind hate? Ah, Lucilla, thou knowest not the care of a father nor the duty of a child, and as far art thou from piety as I from cruelty.

"Nature will not permit me to disherit my daughter, and yet it will suffer thee to dishonor thy father. Affection causeth me to wish thy life, and shall it entice thee to procure my death? It is mine only comfort to see thee florish in thy youth, and is it thine to see me fade in mine age? To conclude, I desire to live to see thee prosper, and thou to see me perish. But why cast I the effect of this unnaturalness in thy teeth, seeing I myself was the cause? I made thee a wanton, and thou hast made me a fool; I brought thee up like a cockney, and thou hast handled me like a cockscomb (I speak it to mine own shame). I made more of thee then became a father, and thou less of me then beseemed a child. And shall my loving care be cause of thy wicked cruelty? Yea, yea, I am not the first that hath been too careful, nor the last that shall be handled so unkindly; it is common to see fathers too fond and children too froward. Well, Lucilla, the tears which thou seest trickle down my cheeks and the drops of blood (which thou canst not see) that fall from my heart enforce me to make an end of my talk; and if thou have any duty of a child, or care of a friend, or courtesy of a stranger, or feeling of a Christian, or humanity of a reasonable creature, then release thy father of grief, and acquite thyself of ungratefulness; otherwise thou shalt but hasten my death and encrease thine own defame, which if thou do the gain is mine and the loss thine, and both infinite."

Lucilla, either so bewitched that she could not relent, or so wicked that she would not yield to her father's request, answered him on this manner:

"Dear father, as you would have me to shew the duty of a child, so ought you to shew the care of a parent, and as the one standeth in obedience, so the other is grounded upon reason. You would have me as I owe duty to you to leave Curio, and I desire you as you owe me any love that you suffer me to enjoy him. If you accuse me of unnaturalness in that I yield not to your request, I am also to condemn you of unkindness in that you grant not my petition. You object I know not what to Curio, but it is the eye of the maister that fatteth the horse and the love of the woman that maketh the man. To give reason for

fancy were to weigh the fire and measure the wind. If, therefore, my delight be the cause of your death, I think my sorrow would be an occasion of your solace. And if you be angry bicause I am pleased, certes I deem you would be content if I were deceased; which if it be so that my pleasure breed your pain, and mine annoy your joy, I may well say that you are an unkind father and I an unfortunate child. But, good father, either content yourself with my choice, or let me stand to the main chance, otherwise the grief will be mine and the fault yours, and both untolerable."

Ferardo, seeing his daughter to have neither regard of her own honor nor his request, conceived such an inward grief that in short space he died, leaving Lucilla the only heir of his lands and Curio to possess them; but what end came of her, seeing it is nothing incident to the history of Euphues, it were superfluous to insert it, and so incredible that all women would rather wonder at it then believe it, which event being so strange, I had rather leave them in a muse what it should be then in a maze in telling what it was.

Philautus having intelligence of Euphues his success and the falsehood of Lucilla, although he began to rejoice at the misery of his fellow, yet, seeing her fickleness, could not but lament her folly and pity his friend's misfortune; thinking that the lightness of Lucilla enticed Euphues to so great liking.

Euphues and Philautus having conference between themselves, casting discourtesy in the teeth each of the other, but chiefly noting disloyalty in the demeanor of Lucilla, after much talk renewed their old friendship, both abandoning Lucilla as most abhominable. Philautus was earnest to have Euphues tarry in Naples, and Euphues desirous to have Philautus to Athens, but the one was so addicted to the court, the other so wedded to the university, that each refused the offer of the other; yet this they agreed between themselves, that, though their bodies were by distance of place severed, yet the conjunction of their minds should neither be seperated by the length of time nor alienated by change of soil. "I for my part," said Euphues, "to confirm this league give thee my hand and my heart." And so likewise did Philautus, and so shaking hands they bid each other farewell. [Although the parting of the two friends thus closes the formal narrative, the novel has an elaborate coda consisting of various epistles and dialogues calculated to show the effects of Euphues' education: "A Cooling Card for Philautus and All Fond Lovers," an epistle "To the Grave Matrons and Honest Maidens of Italy," a long dialogue on education (adapted from Plutarch) between Euphues and Ephoebus, a letter from Euphues "To the Gentlemen Schollers in Athens," a dialogue on religion between

Euphues and Atheos (i.e. an atheist), and a set of "Certain Letters" between Euphues, Philautus, Eubulus, Livia, and others. The quality of Euphues' revulsion from his youthful follies is suggested in his last stern letter to Philautus when he comments on Lucilla's frightful end: living a life of "practised sin," she was "stricken sodainly, being troubled with no sickness," and so she died "in great beggery in the streets." From such a death following such a life, Euphues warns his friend, he should learn to improve his ways. "If thou mean to keep me as a friend, shake off those vain toys and dalliances with women. . . . If thou mean not to amend thy manners, I desire thee to write no more to me, for I will neither answer thee nor read them."]

FROM EUPHUES AND HIS ENGLAND (1580)

To the Ladies and Gentlewomen of England, John Lyly Wisheth What They Would

Arachne having woven in cloth of arras a rainbow of sundry silks, it was objected unto her by a lady more captious then cunning, that in her work there wanted some colors; for that in a rainbow there should be all. Unto whom she replied, "If the colors lack thou lookest for, thou must imagine that they are on the other side of the cloth. For in the sky we can discern but one side of the rainbow, and what colors are in the other, see we cannot, guess we may."

In the like manner, ladies and gentlewomen, am I to shape an answer in the behalf of Euphues, who framing divers questions and quirks of love, if, by some more curious then needeth, it shall be told him that some sleights are wanting, I must say they are noted on the backside of the book. When Venus is painted, we cannot see her back but her face; so that all other things that are to be recounted in love, Euphues thinketh them to hang at Venus' back in a budget, which bicause he cannot see, he will not set down.

These discourses I have not clapp'd in a cluster, thinking with myself that ladies had rather be sprinkled with sweet water then washed; so that I have sowed them here and there like strawberries, not in heaps like hops; knowing that you take more delight to gather flowers one by one in a garden then to snatch them by handfuls from a garland.

It resteth, ladies, that you take the pains to read it, but at such times as you spend in playing with your little dogs; and yet will I not pinch you of that pastime, for I am content that your dogs lie in your laps, so Euphues may be in your hands, that when you shall be weary in reading of the one you may be ready to sport with the other; or handle him as you do your junkets, that when you can eat no more, you tie some in your napkin for children; for if you be filled with the first part, put the second in your pocket for your waiting maids. Euphues had rather lie shut in a lady's casket then open in a scholler's study.

Yet after dinner you may overlook him to keep you from sleep, or, if you be heavy, to bring you asleep, for to work upon a full stomach is against physic, and therefore better it were to hold Euphues in your hands, though you let him fall when you be willing to wink, then to sew in a clout, and prick your fingers when you begin to nod.

Whatsoever he hath written, it is not to flatter, for he never reaped any reward by your sex but repentance; neither can it be to mock you, for he never knew anything by your sex but righteousness.

But I fear no anger for saying well, when there is none but thinketh she deserveth better.

She that hath no glass to dress her head will use a bowl of water; she that wanteth a sleekstone to smooth her linen will take a pebble; the country dame girdeth herself as straight in the waist with a coarse caddis as the madame of the court with a silk riband; so that seeing everyone so willing to be pranked, I could not think anyone unwilling to be praised.

One hand washeth another, but they both wash the face; one foot goeth by another, but they both carry the body; Euphues and Philautus praise one another, but they both extol women. Therefore in my mind you are more beholding to gentlemen that make the colors then to the painters that draw your counterfaits; for that Apelles' cunning is nothing if he paint with water, and the beauty of women not much if they go unpraised.

If you think this love dreamed, not done, yet methinketh you may as well like that love which is penned and not practised as that flower that is wrought with the needle and groweth not by nature. The one you wear in your heads, for the fair sight, though it have no favor; the other you may read for to pass the time, though it bring small pastime. You chuse cloth that will wear whitest, not that will last longest, colors that look freshest, not that endure soundest, and I would you would read books that have more shew of pleasure then ground of profit; then should Euphues be as often in your hands, being but a toy, as lawn on your heads, being but trash; the one will be scarce liked after once reading, and the other is worn out after the first washing.

There is nothing lighter then a feather, yet is it set aloft in a woman's hat; nothing slighter then hair, yet is it most frizzled in a lady's head; so that I am in good hope, though there be nothing of less account then Euphues, yet he shall be marked with ladies' eyes, and liked sometimes in their ears. For this I have diligently observed, that there shall be nothing found that may offend the chaste mind with unseemly terms or uncleanly talk.

Then, ladies, I commit myself to your curtesies, craving this only, that, having read, you conceal your censure, writing your judgments as you do the posies in your rings, which are always next to the finger, not to be seen of him that holdeth you by the hands, and yet known to you that wear them on your hands. If you be wrong (which cannot be done without wrong), it were better to cut the shoe then burn the last.

If a tailor make your gown too little, you cover his fault with a broad stomacher; if too great, with a number of plights; if too short, with a fair guard; if too long, with a false gathering. My trust is you will deal in the like manner with Euphues, that if he have not fed your humor, yet you will excuse him more then the tailor; for could Euphues take the measure of a woman's mind, as the tailor doth of her body, he would go as near to fit them for a fancy as the other doth for a fashion.

He that weighs wind must have a steady hand to hold the balance, and he that searcheth a woman's thoughts must have his own stayed. But lest I make my epistle, as you do your newfound bracelets, endless, I will frame it like a bullet, which is no sooner in the mold but it is made; committing your ladyships to the Almighty, who grant you all you would have and should have, so your wishes stand with his will. And so humbly I bid you farewell.

Your ladyships' to command,

John Lyly

To the Gentlemen Readers

Gentlemen, Euphues is come at the length, though too late, for whose absence I hope three bad excuses shall stand in stead of one good reason.

First, in his travel you must think he loitered, tarrying many a month in Italy viewing the ladies in a painter's shop, when he should have been on the seas in a merchant's ship, not unlike unto an idle huswife who is catching of flies when she should sweep down copwebs.

Secondly, being a great start from Athens to England, he thought to stay for the advantage of a leap year, and had not this year leap'd with him, I think he had not yet leap'd hether.

Thirdly, being arrived, he was as long in viewing of London as he was in coming to it, not far differing from gentlewomen, who are longer a-dressing their heads then their whole bodies.

But now he is come, gentlemen, my request is only to bid him welcome, for divers there are, not that they mislike the matter but that they hate the man, that will not stick to tear Euphues bicause they do envy Lyly; wherein they resemble angry dogs, which bite the stone, not him that throweth it, or the choleric horse-rider, who, being cast from a young colt and not daring to kill the horse, went into the stable to cut the saddle.

These be they that thought Euphues to be drowned and yet were never troubled with drying of his clothes; but they gessed as they wished, and I would it had happened as they desired.

They that loath the fountain's head will never drink of the little brooks; they that seek to poison the fish will never eat the spawn; they that like not me will not allow anything that is mine.

But as the serpent porphirius, though he be full of poison, yet having no teeth hurteth none but himself, so the envious, though they swell with malice till they burst, yet having no teeth to bite I have no cause to fear.

Only my suit is to you, gentlemen, that if anything be amiss, you pardon it; if well, you defend it; and howsoever it be, you accept it.

Faults escaped in the printing, correct with your pens; omitted by my negligence, overslip with patience; committed by ignorance, remit with favor.

If in every part it seem not alike, you know that it is not for him that fashioneth the shoe to make the grain of the leather.

The old hermit will have his talk savor of his cell; the old courtier, his love taste of Saturn; yet the last lover may happely come somewhat near Jupiter.

Lovers when they come into a garden, some gather nettles, some roses, one thyme, another sage, and every one that, for his lady's favor, that she favoreth; insomuch as there is no weed almost but it is worn. If you, gentlemen, do the like in reading, I shall be sure all my discourses shall be regarded, some for the smell, some for the smart, all for a kind of loving smack; let everyone follow his fancy, and say that is best which he liketh best. And so I commit every man's delight to his own choice, and myself to all your courtesies.

Yours to use,

John Lyly

SIR PHILIP SIDNEY

ARCADIA

Sir Philip Sidney's *Arcadia,* one of the most popular and influential works of the late sixteenth century, is the great exemplar in English of a genre represented on the Continent by Sannazaro's Italian *Arcadia* (1504) and Montemayor's Spanish *Diana Enamorada* (?1559). These rambling works, blending the plot-formulas of Greek and chivalric romance with the conventions of the pastoral eclogue, are episodic prose narratives, of high-born characters in a pastoral setting, interspersed with songs and bucolic eclogues. There can be no doubt that Sidney knew and used the Greek romances (see pp. 696 f.), the pastoral novels of Sannazaro and Montemayor, and Spanish chivalric romances about Amadis and Palmerin when, to beguile the time at Wilton in the early eighties, he began work on his *Arcadia.* In a studiously casual dedication to his sister, the Countess of Pembroke, he characteristically belittled his labors as the idle fancy of idle hours, and perhaps he did undertake them merely for the delectation of the countess and her literary coterie. None the less, he took his work seriously enough to re-cast and greatly expand much of the bulky manuscript, and as a result his novel survives in two widely different forms. The so-called "Old *Arcadia,*" which many Elizabethans knew in manuscript but which was not printed until Professor Albert Feuillerat's edition of 1926, is a charming but conventional pastoral romance in five "books" separated by long eclogues in both regular and quantitative verse. Employing all the tricks of mystery, suspense, complicated digressions, and abrupt reversals, Sidney builds his plot around the amorous adventures of two shipwrecked and disguised princes, Musidorus of Thessaly and Pyrocles of Macedon. Cast ashore in Arcadia, they fall in love with Pamela and Philoclea, daughters of King Basilius, who, in compliance with a mysterious and enigmatic oracle, has established himself in a deep forest. In order to woo the maidens the princes disguise themselves as rustics; and the already complicated situation becomes more intense when Musidorus and Pamela flee to the seacoast and Pyrocles (posing as the shepherdess Zelmane) is courted by both Basilius and his lustful queen Gynecia (who has penetrated Pyrocles' disguise). Sporadic comic relief is provided by the clown Dametas and his foolish wife and daughter. When Basilius drinks the love-potion prepared by Gynecia for Pyrocles, he falls into a swoon that is mistaken for death; then General Philanax and his troops seek to restore order by capturing and haling back the eloping Musidorus and Pamela, exposing the false Zelmane, and charging both princes with murder, rape, and treason. Their situation looks hopeless when King Evarchus of Macedon (Pyrocles' father) condemns them to death at the end of a

great trial scene, but in the nick of time Basilius comes to his senses, exonerates the two royal adventurers, explains the mysterious oracle, and tidily unravels the plot by pairing off the lovers.

Tailored for the elegant and aristocratic audience whose tastes Sidney knew so well, this tale must be accounted a spirited and successful adaptation of the Continental romance. The invention is fertile, the action brisk and varied, the style vigorous, and the characters drawn with a psychological and moral subtlety that more than compensates for the recurrent melodrama. But Sidney was sufficiently dissatisfied with his work to begin at once a thoroughgoing revision that was broken off (at his untimely death in 1586) with an uncompleted sentence in an uncompleted chapter in the middle of the third book. In 1590 this fragmentary revision (the "New *Arcadia*") was more or less surreptitiously published by William Ponsonby; three years later Ponsonby's quarto text was pieced out to five books and rearranged with new episodes and eclogues from "several loose sheets" in the possession of Lady Pembroke; finally, in 1598, that great lady (who gloried in her function as her brother's literary executor) allowed the publication of a presumably authoritative edition "with sundry new additions" in a handsome folio that also contained the previously printed *Defense of Poesy* and *Astrophel and Stella,* as well as a gathering of unpublished *Certain Sonnets.* All these post-humous editions—the quarto of 1590 and the folios of 1593 and 1598—are obviously defective: the quarto because it is only a three-book fragment, and the folios because they merely tack onto the fragmentary "New *Arcadia*" the concluding books of the "Old *Arcadia.*" Incomplete as it is, the "New *Arcadia*" is of extraordinary interest in showing how a skilful artist tried to transform a romance into a prose epic. By heightening the style, recasting the chronologically simple narrative on the model of the Virgilian epic, artfully enriching the plot with interpolated episodes, and enlarging the thematic implications, Sidney was obviously trying to create out of the original *Arcadia* "an heroic poem in prose." Garbled and incongruous as the parts of the successive Elizabethan versions were, the book enjoyed immense prestige. There were two issues of the 1590 quarto, the "augmented and ended" folio of 1593, the authorized folio of 1598, a pirated Edinburgh edition of 1599, two folio issues in 1605, and other editions or issues in 1613 (2), 1621 (at Dublin), 1622, 1623, 1627-28, 1629 (2), 1633, and ("now the ninth time published") 1638. Our text is based upon *The Countesse of Pembrokes Arcadia,* 1590 (STC 22539).

FROM THE COUNTESS OF PEMBROKE'S ARCADIA (1590)

To My Dear Lady and Sister, the Countess of Pembroke

Here now have you, most dear and most worthy to be most dear lady, this idle work of mine; which, I fear, like the spider's web will be thought fitter to be swept away then worn to any other purpose. For my part, in very truth, as the cruel fathers among the Greeks were wont to do to the babes they would not foster, I could well find in my heart to cast out in some desert of forgetfulness this child which I am 10 loth to father. But you desired me to do it, and your desire, to my heart, is an absolute commandment. Now it is done only for you, only to you; if you keep it to yourself, or to such friends who will weigh errors in the balance of good will, I hope, for the father's sake, it will be pardoned, perchance made much of, though in itself it have deformities. For indeed, for severer eyes it is not, being but a trifle, and that triflingly handled. Your dear self can best witness the manner, being done in loose sheets of 20 paper, most of it in your presence, the rest by sheets sent unto you as fast as they were done. In sum, a young head, not so well stayed as I would it were (and shall be when God will), having many, many fancies begotten in it, if it had not been in some way delivered would have grown a monster, and more sorry might I be that they came in then that they gat out. But his chief safety shall be the not walking abroad; and his chief protection the bearing the livery of your name, which, if much, much good will 30 do not deceive me, is worthy to be a sanctuary for a greater offender. This say I because I know the virtue so, and this say I because it may be ever so; or, to say better, because it will be ever so. Read it, then, at your idle times, and the follies your good judgment will find in it blame not, but laugh at. And so, looking for no better stuff then, as in an haberdasher's shop, glasses or feathers, you will continue to love the writer, who doth exceedingly love you; and most, most heartily prays you may 40 long live to be a principal ornament to the family of the Sidneys.

Your loving brother,
Philip Sidney

The division and summing of the chapters was not of Sir Philip Sidney's doing, but adventured by the overseer of the print for the more ease of the readers. He therefore submits himself to their judgment, and if his labor answer not the worthiness of the book 50 desireth pardon for it. As also if any defect be found in the eclogues, which, although they were of Sir Philip Sidney's writing, yet were they not perused by him, but left till the work had been finished, that then choice should have been made, which should have been taken and in what manner brought in. At this time they have been chosen and disposed as the overseer thought best.

THE FIRST BOOK

CHAPTER I

The shepherdish complaints of the absented lovers Strephon and Claius. The second shipwrack of Pyrocles and Musidorus. Their strange saving, enterview, and parting.

It was in the time that the earth begins to put on her new apparel against the approach of her lover, and that the sun running a most even course becomes an indifferent arbiter between the night and the day, when the hopeless shepherd Strephon was come to the sands which lie against the Island of Cithera; where viewing the place with a heavy kind of delight, and sometimes casting his eyes to the ile-ward, he called his friendly rival, the pastor Claius, unto him, and setting first down in his darkened countenance a doleful copy of what he would speak:

"O my Claius," said he, "hether we are now come to pay the rent for which we are so called unto by overbusy Remembrance, Remembrance, restless Remembrance, which claims not only this duty of us, but for it will have us forget ourselves. I pray you, when we were amid our flock, and that of other shepherds some were running after their sheep strayed beyond their bounds, some delighting their eyes with seeing them nibble upon the short and sweet grass, some medicining their sick ewes, some setting a bell for an ensign of a sheepish squadron, some with more leisure inventing new games of exercising their bodies and sporting their wits—did Remembrance grant us any holiday, either for pastime or devotion, nay, either for necessary food or natural rest? but that still it forced our thoughts to work upon this place, where we last (alas that the word 'last' should so long last) did gaze our eyes upon her ever-flourishing beauty; did it not still cry within us, 'Ah, you base-minded wretches, are your thoughts so deeply bemired in the trade of ordinary worldlings, as for respect of gain some paltry wool may yield you, to let so much time pass without knowing perfectly her estate, especially in so troublesome a season, to leave that shore unsaluted from whence you may see to the island where she dwelleth, to leave those steps unkissed wherein Urania printed the farewell of all beauty?' Well, then, Remembrance commanded, we obeyed, and here we find that as our remembrance came ever clothed unto us in the form of this place, so this place gives new heat to the fever of our languishing remembrance. Yonder, my Claius, Urania lighted; the very horse (methought) bewailed to be so disburd'ned; and as for thee, poor Claius, when thou went'st to help her down, I saw reverence and desire so devide thee that thou didst at one instant both blush and quake, and instead of bearing her wert ready to fall down thyself. There she sat, vouchsafing my cloak (then most gorgeous) under her; at yonder rising of the ground she turned herself, looking back toward her wonted abode, and because of her parting bearing much sorrow in her eyes, the lightsomeness whereof had yet so natural a cheerfulness as it made even sorrow seem to smile; at that turning she spake unto us all, opening the cherry of her lips, and Lord, how greedily mine ears did feed upon the sweet words she uttered! And here she laid her hand over thine eyes, when she saw the tears springing in them, as if she would conceal them from other, and yet herself feel some of thy sorrow. But wo is me, yonder, yonder did she put her foot into the boat, at that instant, as it were, deviding her heavenly beauty between the earth and the sea. But when she was imbarked, did you not mark how the winds whistled and the seas danc'd for joy, how the sails did swell with pride, and all because they had Urania? O Urania, blessed be thou, Urania, the sweetest fairness and fairest sweetness!"

With that word his voice brake so with sobbing that he could say no further; and Claius thus answered: "Alas, my Strephon," said he, "what needs this score to recken up only our losses? What doubt is there but that the light of this place doth call our thoughts to appear at the court of affection, held by that racking steward, Remembrance? As well may sheep forget to fear when they spy wolves as we can miss such fancies when we see any place made happy by her treading. Who can choose that saw her but think where she stayed, where she walk'd, where she turned, where she spoke? But what is all this? Truly, no more but as this place served us to think of those things, so those things serve as places to call to memory more excellent matters. No, no, let us think with consideration, and consider with acknowledging, and acknowledge with admiration, and admire with love, and love with joy in the midst of all woes; let us in such sort think, I say, that our poor eyes were so inriched as to behold, and our

low hearts so exalted as to love, a maid who is such that, as the greatest thing the world can shew is her beauty, so the least thing that may be praised in her is her beauty. Certainly as her eyelids are more pleasant to behold then two white kids climbing up a fair tree and browsing on his tend'rest branches, and yet are nothing compared to the day-shining stars contained in them; and as her breath is more sweet then a gentle southwest wind which comes creeping over flow'ry fields and shadowed waters in the extreme heat of summer, and yet is nothing compared to the honey-flowing speech that breath doth carry; no more all that our eyes can see of her (though when they have seen her what else they shall ever see is but dry stubble after clover's grass) is to be matched with the flock of unspeakable virtues laid up delightfully in that best-builded fold. But indeed, as we can better consider the sun's beauty by marking how he gilds these waters and mountains then by looking upon his own face, too glorious for our weak eyes; so it may be our conceits (not able to bear her sun-staining excellency) will better weigh it by her works upon some meaner subject employed. And alas, who can better witness that then we, whose experience is grounded upon feeling? Hath not the only love of her made us (being silly ignorant shepherds) raise up our thoughts above the ordinary level of the world, so as great clerks do not disdain our conference? Hath not the desire to seem worthy in her eyes made us, when others were sleeping, to sit viewing the course of heavens; when others were running at base, to run over learned writings; when other mark their sheep, we to mark ourselves? Hath not she thrown reason upon our desires, and, as it were, given eyes unto Cupid? Hath in any, but in her, love-fellowship maintained friendship between rivals, and beauty taught the beholders chastity?"

He was going on with his praises, but Strephon bad him stay and look. And so they both perceived a thing which floated, drawing nearer and nearer to the bank; but rather by the favorable working of the sea then by any self-industry. They doubted a while what it should be, till it was cast up even hard before them; at which time they fully saw that it was a man. Whereupon running for pity sake unto him, they found his hands (as it should appear, constanter friends to his life then his memory) fast gripping upon the edge of a square small coffer, which lay all under his breast; else in himself no shew of life, so as the board seemed to be but a bier to carry him a-land to his sepulcher. So drew they up a young man of so goodly shape and well-pleasing favor that one would think death had in him a lovely countenance;

and that, though he were naked, nakedness was to him an apparel. That sight increased their compassion, and their compassion called up their care; so that, lifting his feet above his head, making a great deal of salt water to come out of his mouth, they laid him upon some of their garments and fell to rub and chafe him, till they brought him to recover both breath, the servant, and warmth, the companion of living.

At length, opening his eyes, he gave a great groan, a doleful note but a pleasant ditty, for by that they found not only life but strength of life in him. They therefore continued on their charitable office, until, his spirits being well returned, he, without so much as thanking them for their pains, gate up, and looking round about to the uttermost limits of his sight, and crying upon the name of Pyrocles, nor seeing nor hearing cause of comfort: "What," said he, "and shall Musidorus live after Pyrocles?" Therewithal he offered wilfully to cast destruction and himself again into the sea; a strange sight to the shepherds, to whom it seemed that before being in apparance dead had yet saved his life, and now coming to his life should be a cause to procure his death; but they ran unto him, and pulling him back (then too feeble for them) by force stickled that unnatural fray. "I pray you," said he, "honest men, what such right have you in me as not to suffer me to do with myself what I list? And what policy have you to bestow a benefit where it is counted an injury?"

They hearing him speak in Greek, which was their natural language, became the more tender-hearted towards him; and considering, by his calling and looking, that the loss of some dear friend was great cause of his sorrow, told him they were poor men that were bound by course of humanity to prevent so great a mischief, and that they wish'd him, if opinion of somebody's perishing bred such desperate anguish in him, that he should be comforted by his own proof, who had lately escaped as apparant danger as any might be.

"No, no," said he, "it is not for me to attend so high a blissfulness; but since you take care of me, I pray you find means that some bark may be provided that will go out of the haven, that if it be possible we may find the body, far, far too precious a food for fishes. And for the hire," said he, "I have within this casket of value sufficient to content them."

Claius presently went to a fisherman, and having agreed with him, and provided some apparel for the naked stranger, he imbarked, and the shepherds with him; and were no sooner gone beyond the mouth of the haven but that some way into the sea they might discern, as it were, a stain of the water's color, and by times some sparks and smoke mounting thereout.

But the young man no sooner saw it, but that, beating his breast, he cried that there was the beginning of his ruin, intreating them to bend their course as near unto it as they could; telling how that smoke was but a small relique of a great fire, which had driven both him and his friend rather to commit themselves to the cold mercy of the sea then to abide the hot cruelty of the fire; and that therefore, though they both had abandoned the ship, that he was (if anywhere) in that course to be met withal. They steered therefore as near thetherward as they could; but when they came so near as their eyes were full masters of the object, they saw a sight full of piteous strangeness: a ship, or rather the carcass of the ship, or rather some few bones of the carcass, hulling there, part broken, part burned, part drowned; death having used more then one dart to that destruction. About it floated great store of very rich things, and many chests which might promise no less. And amidst the precious things were a number of dead bodies, which likewise did not only testify both elements' violence, but that the chief violence was grown of human inhumanity; for their bodies were full of grisly wounds, and their blood had, as it were, filled the wrinkles of the sea's visage; which it seemed the sea would not wash away, that it might witness it is not always his fault when we condemn his cruelty. In sum, a defeat where the conquered kept both field and spoil; a shipwreck without storm or ill footing; and a waste of fire in the midst of water.

But a little way off they saw the mast, whose proud height now lay along, like a widow having lost her make of whom she held her honor; but upon the mast they saw a young man (at least if he were a man) bearing shew of about eighteen years of age, who sate as on horseback, having nothing upon him but his shirt, which being wrought with blew silk and gold had a kind of resemblance to the sea; on which the sun (then near his western home) did shoot some of his beams. His hair (which the young men of Greece used to wear very long) was stirred up and down with the wind, which seemed to have a sport to play with it, as the sea had to kiss his feet; himself full of admirable beauty, set forth by the strangeness both of his seat and gesture; for, holding his head up full of unmoved majesty, he held a sword aloft with his fair arm, which often he waved about his crown as though he would threaten the world in that extremity. But the fishermen, when they came so near him that it was time to throw out a rope, by which hold they might draw him, their simplicity bred such amazement, and their amazement such a superstition, that, assuredly thinking it was some god begotten between Neptune and Venus that had made all this terrible slaughter, as they went under sail by him held up their hands and made their prayers. Which when Musidorus saw, though he were almost as much ravished with joy as they with astonishment, he lept to the mariner and took the rope out of his hand, and—saying, "Dost thou live and art well?" who answered, "Thou canst tell best, since most of my well-being stands in thee"—threw it out; but already the ship was passed beyond Pyrocles; and therefore Musidorus could do no more but persuade the mariners to cast about again, assuring them that he was but a man, although of most divine excellencies, and promising great rewards for their pain.

And now they were already come upon the stays, when one of the sailors descried a galley which came with sails and oars directly in the chase of them, and straight perceived it was a well-known pirate, who hunted not only for goods, but for bodies of men, which he imployed either to be his galley slaves or to sell at the best market. Which when the maister understood, he commanded forthwith to set on all the canvas they could and fly homeward, leaving in that sort poor Pyrocles, so near to be rescued. But what did not Musidorus say? What did he not offer to persuade them to venture the fight? But fear, standing at the gates of their ears, put back all persuasions; so that he had nothing to accompany Pyrocles but his eyes, nor to succor him but his wishes. Therefore praying for him, and casting a long look that way, he saw the galley leave the pursuit of them and turn to take up the spoils of the other wrack; and, lastly, he might well see them lift up the young man; and, "Alas!" said he to himself, "dear Pyrocles, shall that body of thine be enchained? Shall those victorious hands of thine be commanded to base offices? Shall virtue become a slave to those that be slaves to viciousness? Alas, better had it been thou hadst ended nobly thy noble days. What death is so evil as unworthy servitude?" But that opinion soon ceased when he saw the galley setting upon another ship, which held long and strong fight with her; for then he began afresh to fear the life of his friend, and to wish well to the pirates, whom before he hated, lest in their ruin he might perish. But the fishermen made such speed into the haven that they absented his eyes from beholding the issue; where being ent'red, he could procure neither them nor any other as then to put themselves into the sea; so that, being as full of sorrow for being unable to do anything as void of counsel how to do anything, besides that sickness grew something upon him, the honest shepherds Strephon and Claius (who, being themselves true friends, did the more perfectly judge the justness of his sorrow) advise him that he should mitigate somewhat of his wo, since he had gotten an amendment in fortune, being come

from assured persuasion of his death to have no cause to dispair of his life, as one that had lamented the death of his sheep should after know they were but strayed, would receive pleasure, though readily he knew not where to find them.

CHAPTER II

The pastors' comforts to the wracked Musidorus. His passage into Arcadia. The descriptions of Laconia, Arcadia, Kalander's person, house, and entertainment to Musidorus, now called Palladius. His sickness, recovery, and perfections.

"Now, sir," said they, "thus for ourselves it is. We are in profession but shepherds, and in this country of Laconia little better then strangers, and therefore neither in skill nor hability of power greatly to stead you. But what we can present unto you is this: Arcadia, of which country we are, is but a little way hence, and even upon the next confines. There dwelleth a gentleman, by name Kalander, who vouchsafeth much favor unto us; a man who for his hospitality is so much haunted that no newsstir but comes to his ears; for his upright dealing so beloved of his neighbors that he hath many ever ready to do him their uttermost service, and, by the great good will our prince bears him, may soon obtain the use of his name and credit, which hath a principal sway, not only in his own Arcadia, but in all these countries of Peloponnesus; and, which is worth all, all these things give him not so much power as his nature gives him will to benefit, so that it seems no music is so sweet to his ear as deserved thanks. To him we will bring you, and there you may recover again your health, without which you cannot be able to make any diligent search for your friend, and, therefore, but in that respect you must labor for it. Besides, we are sure the comfort of curtesy and ease of wise counsel shall not be wanting."

Musidorus (who, besides he was merely unacquainted in the country, had his wits astonished with sorrow) gave easy consent to that from which he saw no reason to disagree; and therefore, defraying the mariners with a ring bestowed upon them, they took their journey together through Laconia, Claius and Strephon by course carrying his chest for him, Musidorus only bearing in his countenance evident marks of a sorrowful mind supported with a weak body; which they perceiving, and knowing that the violence of sorrow is not at the first to be striven withal (being, like a mighty beast, sooner tamed with following than overthrown by withstanding), they gave way unto it for that day and the next, never troubling him either with asking questions or finding fault with his melancholy, but rather fitting to his dolor dolorous discourses of their own and other folk's misfortunes. Which speeches, though they had not a lively entrance to his senses shut up in sorrow, yet, like one half asleep, he took hold of much of the matters spoken unto him, so as a man may say, ere sorrow was aware, they made his thoughts bear away something else beside his own sorrow, which wrought so in him that at length he grew content to mark their speeches, then to marvel at such wit in shepherds, after to like their company, and lastly to vouchsafe conference; so that the third day after, in the time that the morning did strow roses and violets in the heavenly floor against the coming of the sun, the nightingales, striving one with the other which could in most dainty variety recount their wrong-caused sorrow, made them put off their sleep; and, rising from under a tree, which that night had been their pavilion, they went on their journey, which by and by welcomed Musidorus' eyes, wearied with the wasted soil of Laconia, with delightful prospects. There were hills which garnished their proud heights with stately trees; humble valleys whose base estate seemed comforted with refreshing of silver rivers; meadows enamel'd with all sorts of eye-pleasing flowers; thickets which, being lined with most pleasant shade, were witnessed so to by the cheerful desposition of many well-tuned birds; each pasture stored with sheep feeding with sober security, while the pretty lambs, with bleating oratory, craved the dams' comfort; here a shepherd's boy piping, as though he should never be old; there a young shepherdess knitting, and withal singing, and it seemed that her voice comforted her hands to work, and her hands kept time to her voice's music. As for the houses of the country (for many houses came under their eye), they were all scattered, no two being one by th' other, and yet not so far off as that it barred mutual succor: a shew, as it were, of an accompanable solitariness and of a civil wildness.

"I pray you," said Musidorus, then first unsealing his long-silent lips, "what countries be these we pass through, which are so divers in shew, the one wanting no store, th' other having no store but of want?"

"The country," answered Claius, "where you were cast ashore, and now are pass'd through, is Laconia, not so poor by the barrenness of the soil (though in itself not passing fertile) as by a civil war, which, being these two years within the bowels of that estate, between the gentlemen and the peasants (by them named Helots), hath in this sort, as it were, disfigured the face of nature and made it so unhospital as now you have found it; the towns neither of the one side nor the other willingly opening their gates

to strangers, nor strangers willingly ent'ring, for fear of being mistaken. But this country, where now you set your foot, is Arcadia; and even hard by is the house of Kalander, whether we lead you; this country being thus decked with peace and (the child of peace) good husbandry. These houses you see so scattered are of men, as we two are, that live upon the commodity of their sheep, and therefore, in the division of the Arcadian estate, are termed shepherds; a happy people, wanting little, because they desire not much."

"What cause, then," said Musidorus, "made you venter to leave this sweet life and put yourself in yonder unpleasant and dangerous realm?"

"Guarded with poverty," answered Strephon, "and guided with love."

"But now," said Claius, "since it hath pleased you to ask anything of us, whose baseness is such as the very knowledge is darkness, geve us leave to know something of you and of the young man you so much lament, that at least we may be the better instructed to enform Kalander, and he the better know how to proportion his entertainment."

Musidorus, according to the agreement between Pyrocles and him to alter their names, answered that he called himself Palladius and his friend Daiphantus. "But, till I have him again," said he, "I am indeed nothing, and therefore my story is of nothing. His entertainment, since so good a man he is, cannot be so low as I account my estate; and, in sum, the sum of all his curtesy may be to help me by some means to seek my friend."

They perceived he was not willing to open himself further, and therefore, without further questioning, brought him to the house; about which they might see (with fit consideration both of the air, the prospect, and the nature of the ground) all such necessary additions to a great house as might well shew Kalander knew that provision is the foundation of hospitality, and thrift the fewel of magnificence.

The house itself was built of fair and strong stone, not affecting so much any extraordinary kind of fineness as an honorable representing of a firm stateliness; the lights, doors, and stairs rather directed to the use of the guest then to the eye of the artificer, and yet as the one chiefly heeded, so the other not neglected; each place handsome without curiosity, and homely without lothsomeness; not so dainty as not to be trod on, nor yet slubber'd up with goodfellowship; all more lasting then beautiful, but that the consideration of the exceeding lastingness made the eye believe it was exceeding beautiful; the servants, not so many in number as cleanly in apparel and serviceable in behavior, testifying even in their countenances that their maister took as well care to be served as of them that did serve. One of them was forthwith ready to welcome the shepherds, as men who, though they were poor, their maister greatly favored; and understanding by them that the young man with them was to be much accounted of, for that they had seen tokens of more then common greatness, howsoever now eclipsed with fortune, he ran to his master, who came presently forth, and pleasantly welcoming the shepherds, but especially applying him to Musidorus, Strephon privately told him all what he knew of him, and particularly that he found this stranger was loath to be known.

"No," said Kalander, speaking aloud, "I am no herald to enquire of men's pedigrees; it sufficeth me if I know their virtues; which, if this young man's face be not a false witness, do better apparel his mind then you have done his body."

While he was speaking, there came a boy, in shew like a merchant's prentice, who, taking Strephon by the sleeve, delivered him a letter, written jointly both to him and Claius from Urania; which they no sooner had read but that with short leave-taking of Kalander, who quickly guess'd and smiled at the matter, and once again, though hastily, recommending the young man unto him, they went away, leaving Musidorus even loath to part with them, for the good conversation he had of them and obligation he accounted himself tied in unto them; and therefore, they delivering his chest unto him, he opened it, and would have presented them with two very rich jewels, but they absolutely refused them, telling him they were more then enough rewarded in the knowing of him, and without harkening unto a reply, like men whose hearts disdained all desires but one, gate speedily away, as if the letter had brought wings to make them fly. But by that sight Kalander soon judged that his guest was of no mean calling; and therefore the more respectfully entertaining him, Musidorus found his sickness, which the fight, the sea, and late travel had laid upon him, grow greatly; so that fearing some suddain accident, he delivered the chest to Kalander, which was full of most precious stones, gorgeously and cunningly set in diverse manners, desiring him he would keep those trifles, and, if he died, he would bestow so much of it as was needful to find out and redeem a young man naming himself Daiphantus, as then in the hands of Laconia pirates.

But Kalander, seeing him faint more and more, with careful speed conveyed him to the most commodious lodging in his house; where, being possess'd with an extreme burning fever, he continued some while with no great hope of life; but youth at length got the victory of sickness, so that in six weeks the excellency of his returned beauty was a credible embassador of his health; to the great joy of Kalander, who, as in this time he had by certain friends of his that dwelt near the sea in Messenia set forth a ship and a galley to seek and succor Daiphantus, so at home did he omit nothing which he thought might either profit or gratify Palladius.

For, having found in him (besides his bodily gifts, beyond the degree of admiration) by daily discourses, which he delighted himself to have with him, a mind of most excellent composition (a piercing wit, quite void of ostentation, high-erected thoughts seated in a heart of courtesy, an eloquence as sweet in the uttering as slow to come to the uttering, a behavior so noble as gave a majesty to adversity, and all in a man whose age could not be above one-and-twenty years), the good old man was even enamored with a fatherly love towards him; or rather became his servant by the bonds such virtue laid upon him; once he acknowledged himself so to be, by the badge of diligent attendance.

CHAPTER III

The pictures of Kalander's dainty garden-house. His narration of the Arcadian estate, the king, the queen, their two daughters, and their guardians, with their qualities, which is the ground of all this story.

But Palladius having gotten his health, and only staying there to be in place where he might hear answer of the ships set forth, Kalander one afternoon led him abroad to a well-arrayed ground he had behind his house, which he thought to shew him before his going, as the place himself more then in any other delighted. The backside of the house was neither field, garden, nor orchard; or rather it was both field, garden, and orchard: for as soon as the descending of the stairs had delivered them down, they came into a place cunningly set with trees of the most taste-pleasing fruits; but scarcely they had taken that into their consideration but that they were suddenly stepp'd into a delicate green; of each side of the green a thicket bend, behind the thickets again new beds of flowers, which being under the trees, the trees were to them a pavilion, and they to the trees a mosaical floor; so that it seemed that Art therein would needs be delightful by counterfaiting his enemy Error and making order in confusion.

In the middest of all the place was a fair pond, whose shaking crystal was a perfect mirror to all the other beauties, so that it bare shew of two gardens— one in deed, the other in shadows; and in one of the thickets was a fine fountain, made thus: a naked Venus, of white marble, wherein the graver had used such cunning that the natural blue veins of the marble were framed in fit places to set forth the beautiful veins of her body; at her breast she had her babe Aeneas, who seemed, having begun to suck, to leave that to look upon her fair eyes, which smiled at the babe's folly, the meanwhile the breast running. Hard by was a house of pleasure, built for a sommer retiring-place, whether Kalander leading him, he found a square room, full of delightful pictures, made by the most excellent workman of Greece. There was Diana when Acteon saw her bathing, in whose cheeks the painter had set such a color as was mix'd between shame and disdain; and one of her foolish nymphs, who weeping, and withal low'ring, one might see the workman meant to set forth tears of anger. In another table was Atalanta, the posture of whose limbs was so lively expressed that if the eyes were the only judges, as they be the only seers, one would have sworn the very picture had run. Besides many mo, as of Helena, Omphale, Iole; but in none of them all beauty seemed to speak so much as in a large table, which contained a comely old man, with a lady of middle age, but of excellent beauty; and more excellent would have been deemed, but that there stood between them a young maid, whose wonderfulness took away all beauty from her but that which it might seem she gave her back again by her very shadow. And such difference, being known that it did indeed counterfeit a person living, was there between her and all the other, though goddesses, that it seem'd the skill of the painter bestowed on the other new beauty, but that the beauty of her bestowed new skill of the painter.

Though he thought inquisitiveness an uncomely guest, he could not choose but ask who she was, that, bearing shew of one being indeed, could with natural gifts go beyond the reach of invention. Kalander answered that it was made by Philoclea, the younger daughter of his prince, who also with his wife were contained in that table; the painter meaning to represent the present condition of the young lady, who stood watched by an overcurious eye of her parents; and that he would also have drawn her eldest sister, esteemed her match for beauty, in her shepherdish attire, but that the rude clown her guardian would not suffer it; neither durst he ask leave of the prince for fear of suspicion. Palladius perceived that the matter was wrapp'd up in some secrecy, and therefore would for modesty demand no further; but yet his countenance could not but with dumb eloquence desire it; which Kalander perceiving, "Well," said he, "my dear guest, I know your mind, and I will satisfy it; neither will I do it like a niggardly answerer, going no further then the bounds of the question, but I will discover unto you as well that wherein my knowledge is common with others as that which by extraordinary means is delivered unto me, know-

ing so much in you, though not long acquainted, that I shall find your ears faithful treasurers."

So then sitting down in two chairs; and sometimes casting his eye to the picture, he thus spake: "This country Arcadia, among all the provinces of Greece, hath ever been had in singular reputation, partly for the sweetness of the air and other natural benefits, but principally for the well-tempered minds of the people, who (finding that the shining title of glory, so much affected by other nations, doth indeed help little to the happiness of life) are the only people which, as by their justice and providence geve neither cause nor hope to their neighbors to annoy them, so are they not stirred with false praise to trouble others' quiet, thinking it a small reward for the wasting of their own lives in ravening that their posterity should long after say they had done so. Even the muses seem to approve their good determination by choosing this country for their chief repairing-place, and by bestowing their perfections so largely here that the very shepherds have their fancies lifted to so high conceits as the learned of other nations are content both to borrow their names and imitate their cunning.

"Here dwelleth and reigneth this prince whose picture you see, by name Basilius, a prince of sufficient skill to govern so quiet a country, where the good minds of the former princes had set down good laws, and the well bringing-up of the people doth serve as a most sure bond to hold them. But to be plain with you, he excels in nothing so much as in the zealous love of his people, wherein he doth not only pass all his own foregoers but, as I think, all the princes living. Whereof the cause is, that though he exceed not in the virtues which get admiration, as depth of wisdom, height of courage, and largeness of magnificence, yet is he notable in those which stir affection, as truth of word, meekness, courtesy, mercifulness, and liberality.

"He, being already well stricken in years, married a young princess, named Gynecia, daughter to the king of Cyprus, of notable beauty, as by her picture you see; a woman of great wit, and in truth of more princely virtues then her husband; of most unspotted chastity, but of so working a mind, and so vehement spirits, as a man may say it was happy she took a good course, for otherwise it would have been terrible.

"Of these two are brought to the world two daughters, so beyond measure excellent in all the gifts allotted to reasonable creatures that we may think they were born to shew that Nature is no stepmother to that sex, how much soever some men, sharp-witted only in evil speaking, have sought to disgrace them. The elder is named Pamela, by many men not deemed inferior to her sister. For my part, when I marked them both, methought there was (if at least such perfections may receive the word of 'more') more sweetness in Philoclea, but more majesty in Pamela; methought love play'd in Philoclea's eyes and threat'ned in Pamela's; methought Philoclea's beauty only persuaded, but so persuaded as all hearts must yield; Pamela's beauty used violence, and such violence as no heart could resist. And it seems that such proportion is between their minds: Philoclea so bashful as though her excellencies had stol'n into her before she was aware, so humble that she will put all pride out of countenance—in sum, such proceeding as will stir hope, but teach hope good manners; Pamela of high thoughts, who avoids not pride with not knowing her excellencies, but by making that one of her excellencies to be void of pride—her mother's wisdom, greatness, nobility, but (if I can guess aright) knit with a more constant temper.

"Now, then, our Basilius being so publicly happy as to be a prince, and so happy in that happiness as to be a beloved prince, and so in his private blessed as to have so excellent a wife and so overexcellent children, hath of late taken a course which yet makes him more spoken of then all these blessings. For, having made a journey to Delphos and safely returned, within short space he brake up his court and retired himself, his wife, and children into a certain forest hereby, which he calleth his desert; wherein (besides a house appointed for stables, and lodgings for certain persons of mean calling, who do all household services) he hath builded two fine lodges. In the one of them himself remains with his younger daughter Philoclea (which was the cause they three were matched together in this picture), without having any other creature living in that lodge with him. Which, though it be strange, yet not so strange as the course he hath taken with the Princess Pamela, whom he hath placed in the other lodge; but how think you accompanied? Truly with none other but one Dametas, the most arrant, doltish clown that I think ever was without the privilege of a bable, with his wife Miso and daughter Mopsa, in whom no wit can devise anything wherein they may pleasure her, but to exercise her patience and to serve for a foil of her perfections. This loutish clown is such that you never saw so ill-favored a visar; his behavior such that he is beyond the degree of ridiculous; and for his apparel, even as I would wish him; Miso his wife, so handsome a beldame that only her face and her splay-foot have made her accused for a witch; only one good point she hath, that she observes decorum, having a froward mind in a wretched body. Between these two personages (who never agreed in any humor but in disagreeing) is issued forth Mistress Mopsa, a fit woman to participate of both

their perfections; but because a pleasant fellow of my acquaintance set forth her praises in verse, I will only repeat them, and spare mine own tongue, since she goes for a woman. These verses are these, which I have so often caused to be song that I have them without book.

"What length of verse can serve brave Mopsa's good to show,
Whose virtues strange and beauties such as no man them may know?
Thus shrewdly burd'ned then, how can my muse escape?
The gods must help, and precious things must serve to shew her shape.
Like great god Saturn fair and like fair Venus chaste;
As smooth as Pan, as Juno mild, like goddess Iris fac'd.
With Cupid she foresees, and goes god Vulcan's pace;
And for a taste of all these gifts she steals god Momus' grace.
Her forehead jacinth-like, her cheeks of opal hue,
Her twinkling eyes bedeck'd with pearl, her lips as sapphire blew;
Her hair like crapal-stone; her mouth, O heavenly wide;
Her skin like burnish'd gold, her hands like silver ure untried.
As for her parts unknown, which hidden sure are best,
Happy be they which well believe and never seek the rest.

"Now truly having made these descriptions unto you, methinks you should imagine that I rather feign some pleasant device then recount a truth, that a prince (not banished from his own wits) could possibly make so unworthy a choice. But truly, dear guest, so it is, that princes (whose doings have been often soothed with good success) think nothing so absurd which they cannot make honorable. The beginning of his credit was by the prince's straying out of the way, one time he hunted, where meeting this fellow, and asking him the way, and so falling into other questions, he found some of his answers (as a dog, sure, if he could speak had wit enough to describe his kennel) not unsensible, and all uttered with such rudeness, which he enterpreted plainness (though there be great difference between them), that Basilius, conceiving a sodain delight, took him to his court, with apparant shew of his good opinion; where the flattering courtier had no sooner taken the prince's mind but that there were straight reasons to confirm the prince's doing, and shadows of virtues found for Dametas. His silence grew wit, his bluntness integrity, his beastly ignorance virtuous simplicity; and the prince (according to the nature of great persons, in love with that he had done himself) fancied that his weakness with his presence would much be mended. And so, like a creature of his own making, he liked him more and more, and thus having first given him the office of principal herd-man, lastly, since he took this strange determination, he hath in a manner put the life of himself and his children into his hands. Which authority (like too great a sail for so small a boat) doth so oversway poor Dametas that if before he were a good fool in a chamber, he might be allowed it now in a comedy; so as I doubt me (I fear me indeed) my master will in the end (with his cost) find that his office is not to make men, but to use men as men are; no more then a horse will be taught to hunt or an ass to manage. But in sooth I am afraid I have geven your ears too great a surfet with the gross discourses of that heavy piece of flesh. But the zealous grief I conceive to see so great an error in my lord hath made me bestow more w r ls then I confess so base a subject de-serveth."

CHAPTER V

The sorrow of Kalander for his son Clitophon. The story of Argalus and Parthenia, their perfections, their love, their troubles, her impoisoning, his rare constancy, her strange refusal, their pathologies, her flight, his revenge on his rival, the mischief-worker Demagoras, then captain of the rebel Helots, who take him and Clitophon that sought to help him; but both are kept alive by their new captain.

But being come to the supping-place, one of Kalander's servants rounded in his ear; at which (his color changing) he retired himself into his chamber, commanding his men diligently to wait and attend upon Palladius and to excuse his absence with some necessary business he had presently to dispatch. Which they accordingly did, for some few days forcing themselves to let no change appear; but though they framed their countenances never so cunningly, Palladius perceived there was some ill-pleasing accident fallen out. Whereupon, being again set alone at supper, he called to the steward and desired him to tell him the matter of his suddain alteration; who, after some trifling excuses, in the end confessed unto him that his maister had received news that his son before the day of his near marriage chanc'd to be at a battail which was to be fought between the gentlemen of Lacedaemon and the Hel-ots; who winning the victory, he was there made prisoner going to deliver a friend of his taken prisoner by the Helots; that the poor young gentleman had offered great ransom for his life, but that the hate those paisants conceived against all gentlemen was such that every hour he was to look for nothing but some cruel death, which hetherunto had only been delayed by the captain's vehement dealing for him, who seemed to have a heart of more manly pity then

the rest. Which loss had stricken the old gentleman with such sorrow, as if aboundance of tears did not seem sufficiently to witness it, he was alone retired, tearing his beard and hair and cursing his old age that had not made his grave to stop his ears from such advertisements; but that his faithful servants had written in his name to all his friends, followers, and tenants (Philanax, the governor, refusing to deal in it as a private cause, but yet giving leave to seek their best redress so as they wronged not the state of Lacedaemon), of whom there were now gathered upon the frontiers good forces that he was sure would spend their lives by any way to redeem or revenge Clitophon. "Now, sir," said he, "this is my maister's nature, though his grief be such as to live is a grief unto him and that even his reason is darkened with sorrow, yet the laws of hospitality (long and holily observed by him) give still such a sway to his proceeding that he will no way suffer the stranger lodged under his roof to receive, as it were, any infection of his anguish, especially you, toward whom I know not whether his love or admiration be greater." But Palladius could scarce hear out his tale with patience, so was his heart torn in pieces with compassion of the case, liking of Kalander's noble behavior, kindness for his respect to himward, and desire to find some remedy, besides the image of his dearest friend Daiphantus, whom he judged to suffer either a like or a worse fortune; therefore, rising from the boord, he desired the steward to tell him particu-larly the ground and event of this accident, because by knowledge of many circumstances there might perhaps some way of help be opened. Whereunto the steward easily in this sort condiscended:

"My lord," said he, "when our good King Basilius, with better success then expectation, took to wife (even in his more then decaying years) the fair young princess Gynecia, there came with her a young lord, cousin-german to herself, named Argalus, led hether partly with the love and honor of his noble kins-woman, partly with the humor of youth, which ever thinks that good whose goodness he sees not; and in this court he received so good encrease of knowledge that, after some years spent, he so manifested a most virtuous mind in all his actions that Arcadia gloried such a plant was transported unto them, being a gentleman indeed most rarely accomplished, ex-cellently learned, but without all vainglory: friendly without factiousness; valiant, so as, for my part, I think the earth hath no man that hath done more heroical acts then he; howsoever now of late the fame flies of the two princes of Thessalia and Mace-don, and hath long done of our noble Prince Amphialus, who indeed, in our parts, is only ac-counted likely to match him; but I say for my part

I think no man for valor of mind and hability of body to be preferred, if equaled, to Argalus; and yet so valiant as he never durst do anybody injury; in behavior some will say ever sad, surely sober, and somewhat given to musing, but never uncourteous; his word ever led by his thought and followed by his deed, rather liberal then magnificent, though the one wanted not and the other had ever good choice of the receiver; in sum (for I perceive I shall easily take a great draught of his praises whom both I and all this country love so well), such a man was (and I hope is) Argalus as hardly the nicest eye can find a spot in, if the overvehement constancy of yet spotless affection may not in hard-wrested constructions be counted a spot; which in this manner began that work in him which hath made both him and itself in him over all this country famous. My maister's son Clitophon (whose loss gives the cause to this discourse, and yet gives me cause to begin with Argalus, since his loss proceeds from Argalus'), being a young gentleman as of great birth (being our king's sister's son), so truly of good nature, and one that can see good and love it, haunted more the company of this worthy Argalus then of any other, so as if there were not a friendship (which is so rare as it is to be doubted whether it be a thing indeed or but a word) at least there was such a liking and friendliness as hath brought forth the effects which you shall hear. About two years since it so fell out that he brought him to a great lady's house, sister to my maister, who had with her her only daughter, the fair Parthenia, fair indeed (fame, I think, itself daring not to call any fairer if it be not Helena, queen of Corinth, and the two incomparable sisters of Arcadia); and that which made her fairness much the fairer was that it was but a fair embassador of a most fair mind, full of wit, and a wit which delighted more to judge itself then to show itself; her speech being as rare as precious, her silence without sullenness, her modesty without affectation, her shamefastness without ignorance; in sum, one that to praise well one must first set down with himself what it is to be excellent, for so she is.

"I think you think that these perfections meeting could not choose but find one another and delight in that they found, for likeness of manners is likely in reason to draw liking with affection. Men's actions do not always cross with reason; to be short, it did so indeed. They loved, although for a while the fire thereof (Hope's wings being cut off) were blown by the bellows of dispair upon this occasion.

"There had been, a good while before, and so continued, a suitor to this same lady, a great nobleman, though of Laconia, yet near neighbor to Parthenia's mother, named Demagoras, a man mighty in riches and power, and proud thereof, stubbornly stout, loving nobody but himself and for his own delight's sake Parthenia, and pursuing vehemently his desire; his riches had so gilded over all his other imperfections that the old lady (though contrary to my lord her brother's mind) had given her consent, and, using a mother's authority upon her fair daughter, had made her yield thereunto, not because she liked her choice but because her obedient mind had not yet taken upon it to make choice; and the day of their assurance drew near when my young Lord Clitophon brought this noble Argalus, perchance principally to see so rare a sight as Parthenia by all well-judging eyes was judged.

"But though few days were before the time of assurance appointed, yet Love, that saw he had a great journey to make in short time, hasted so himself that, before her word could tie her to Demagoras, her heart hath vowed her to Argalus with so grateful a receipt in mutual affection that if she desired above all things to have Argalus, Argalus feared nothing but to miss Parthenia. And now Parthenia had learned both liking and misliking, loving and lothing, and out of passion began to take the authority of judgment, insomuch that when the time came that Demagoras (full of proud joy) thought to receive the gift of herself, she, with words of resolute refusal (though with tears shewing she was sorry she must refuse), assured her mother she would first be bedded in her grave then wedded to Demagoras. The change was no more strange then unpleasant to the mother, who, being determinately (lest I should say of a great lady 'wilfully') bent to marry her to Demagoras, tried all ways which a witty and hard-hearted mother could use upon so humble a daughter, in whom the only resisting power was love. But the more she assaulted, the more she taught Parthenia to defend; and the more Parthenia defended, the more she made her mother obstinate in the assault; who, at length finding that Argalus standing between them was it that most eclipsed her affection from shining upon Demagoras, she sought all means how to remove him, so much the more as he manifested himself an unremovable suitor to her daughter. First, by imploying him in as many dangerous enterprises as ever the evil stepmother Juno recommended to the famous Hercules; but the more his virtue was tried, the more pure it grew, while all the things she did to overthrow him did set him up upon the height of honor; inough to have moved her heart, especially to a man every way so worthy as Argalus, but she struggling against all reason because she would have her will and shew her authority in matching her with Demagoras, the more virtuous Argalus was, the more she hated him, thinking herself conquered in his conquests and therefore still imploying him in more and more dangerous attempts; meanwhile she used all extremities possible upon her fair daughter to make her geve over herself to her direction. But it was hard to judge whether he in doing or she in suffering shewed greater constancy of affection, for as to Argalus the world sooner wanted occasions then he valor to go thorow them, so to Parthenia malice sooner ceased then her unchanged patience. Lastly, by treasons Demagoras and she would have made away Argalus, but he, with providence and courage, so pass'd over all that the mother took such a spiteful grief at it that her heart brake withal, and she died.

"But then Demagoras, assuring himself that now Parthenia was her own she would never be his, and receiving as much by her own determinate answer, not more desiring his own happiness then envying Argalus' whom he saw with narrow eyes, even ready to enjoy the perfection of his desires, strength'ning his conceit with all the mischievous counsels which disdained love and envious pride could geve unto him, the wicked wretch (taking a time that Argalus was gone to his country to fetch some of his principal friends to honor the marriage which Parthenia had most joyfully consented unto), the wicked Demagoras, I say, desiring to speak with her, with unmerciful force (her weak arms in vain resisting) rubb'd all over her face a most horrible poison, the effect whereof was such that never leper look'd more ugly then she did; which done, having his men and horses ready, departed away in spite of her servants as ready to revenge as they could be in such an unexpected mischief. But the abhominableness of this fact being come to my Lord Kalander, he made such means, both by our king's intercession and his own, that by the king and senate of Lacedaemon Demagoras was upon pain of death banished the country; who, hating the punishment where he should have hated the fault, join'd himself with all the powers he could make unto the Helots, lately in rebellion against that state; and they, glad to have a man of such authority among them, made him their general, and under him have committed divers the most outragious villanies that a base multitude full of desperate revenge can imagine.

"But within a while after this pitiful fact committed upon Parthenia, Argalus returned (poor gentleman), having her fair image in his heart and already promising his eyes the uttermost of his felicity, when they (nobody else daring to tell it him) were the first messengers to themselves of their own misfortune. I mean not to move passions with telling you the grief of both when he knew her, for at first he did not, nor at first knowledge could possibly have virtue's aid so ready as not even weakly to lament the loss of such a jewel—so much the more as that skilful men in that art assured it was unrecoverable. But within a while, trueth of love (which still held the first face in his memory), a virtuous constancy, and even a delight to be constant, faith geven, and inward worthiness shining through the foulest mists took so full hold of the noble Argalus that not only in such comfort which witty arguments may bestow upon adversity, but even with the most aboundant kindness that an eye-ravished lover can express, he labored both to drive the extremity of sorrow from her and to hasten the celebration of their marriage; whereunto he unfeignedly shewed himself no less cheerfully earnest then if she had never been disinherited of that goodly portion which nature had so liberally bequeathed unto her; and for that cause deferred his intended revenge upon Demagoras because he might continually be in her presence, shewing more humble serviceableness and joy to content her then ever before.

"But as he gave this rare ensample (not to be hoped for of any other but of another Argalus), so of the other side she took as strange a course in affection; for where she desired to enjoy him more then to live, yet did she overthrow both her own desire and his, and in no sort would yield to marry him, with a strange encounter of love's affects and effects that he, by an affection sprong from excessive beauty, should delight in horrible foulness, and she, of a vehement desire to have him, should kindly build a resolution never to have him; for truth is that so in heart she loved him as she could not find in her heart he should be tied to what was unworthy of his presence.

"Truly, sir, a very good orator might have a fair field to use eloquence in if he did but only repeat the lamentable and truly affectionated speeches while he conjured her, by remembrance of her affection and true oaths of his own affection, not to make him so unhappy as to think he had not only lost her face but her heart; that her face, when it was fairest, had been but as a marshal to lodge the love of her in his mind, which now was so well placed as it needed no further help of any outward harbinger, beseeching her, even with tears, to know that his love was not so superficial as to go no further then the skin, which yet now to him was most fair since it was hers; how could he be so ungrateful as to love her the less for that which she had only received for his sake? That he never beheld it but therein he saw the loveliness of her love toward him, protesting unto her that he would never take joy of his life if he might not enjoy her for whom principally he was glad he had life. But (as I heard by one that overheard them) she, wringing him by the hand, made no other answer but this: 'My lord,' said she, 'God knows I love you; if I were princess of the whole world and had withal all the blessings that ever the world brought forth, I should not make delay to lay myself and them under your feet; or if I had continued but as I was (though, I must confess, far unworthy of you), yet would I (with too great joy for my heart to think of) have accepted your vouchsafing me to be yours, and with faith and obedience would have supplied all other defects. But first let me be much more miserable then I am ere I match Argalus to such a Parthenia. Live happy, dear Argalus! I geve you full liberty, and I beseech you take it; and I assure you I shall rejoice (whatsoever become of me) to see you so coupled as may be fit both for your honor and satisfaction.' With that, she burst out in crying and weeping, not able longer to contain herself from blaming her fortune, and wishing her own death.

"But Argalus with a most heavy heart still pursuing his desire, she fix'd of mind to avoid further intreaty and to fly all company, which, even of him, grew unpleasant unto her, one night she stole away, but whether, as yet is unknown, or indeed what is become of her.

"Argalus sought her long and in many places. At length, despairing to find her, and the more he despaired the more enraged, weary of his life but first determining to be revenged of Demagoras, he went alone disguised into the chief town held by the Helots; where, coming into his presence, guarded about by many of his soldiers, he could delay his fury no longer for a fitter time, but setting upon him, in despight of a great many that helped him, gave him divers mortal wounds, and himself (no question) had been there presently murthered but that Demagoras himself desired he might be kept alive, perchance with intention to feed his own eyes with some cruel execution to be laid upon him, but death came sooner then he look'd for; yet having had leisure to appoint his successor, a young man not long before delivered out of the prison of the king of Lacedaemon, where he should have suffered death for having slain the king's nephew, but him he named, who at that time was absent, making roads upon the Lacedaemonians, but being returned, the rest of the Helots, for the great liking they conceived of that young man (especially because they had none among themselves to whom the others would yield), were content to follow Demagoras' appointment. And well hath it succeeded with them, he having since done things beyond the hope of the youngest heads, of whom I speak the rather because he hath hetherto preserved Argalus alive under pretence to have him publiquely and with exquisite torments executed after the end of these wars, of which they hope for a soon and prosperous issue.

"And he hath likewise hetherto kept my young Lord Clitophon alive, who (to redeem his friend)

went with certain other noblemen of Laconia and forces gathered by them to besiege this young and new successor; but he, issuing out, to the wonder of all men, defeated the Laconians, slew many of the noblemen, and took Clitophon prisoner, whom with much ado he keepeth alive, the Helots being villanously cruel, but he tempereth them so, sometimes by following their humor, sometimes by striving with it, that hetherto he hath saved both their lives, but in different estates, Argalus being kept in a close and hard prison, Clitophon at some liberty. And now, sir, though, to say the truth, we can promise ourselves little of their safeties while they are in the Helots' hands, I have delivered all I understand touching the loss of my lord's son and the cause thereof, which, though it was not necessary to Clitophon's case to be so particularly told, yet the strangeness of it made me think it would not be unpleasant unto you."

CHAPTER VII

The articles of peace between the Lacedaemonians and Helots; Daiphantus his departure from the Helots with Argalus to Kalander's house; the offer of a strange lady to Argalus, his refusal, and who she was.

[When Kalander leads an expedition against the Helots to rescue Clitophon, Palladius gives him invaluable assistance. Not only is an honorable peace concluded, but also Palladius discovers his lost friend Daiphantus (that is, Pyrocles). Palladius, Kalander, and Clitophon return to Arcadia, whither Daiphantus follows them as soon as he has satisfactorily arranged the affairs of the Helots.]

. . . After a few days, settling them in perfect order, he took his leave of them, whose eyes bad him farewell with tears and mouths with kissing the places where he slept; and after making temples unto him as to a demigod, thinking it beyond the degree of humanity to have a wit so far overgoing his age and such dreadful terror proceed from so excellent beauty. But he for his sake obtained free pardon for Argalus, whom also (upon oath never to bear arms against the Helots) he delivered; and taking only with him certain principal jewels of his own, he would have parted alone with Argalus (whose countenance well shewed, while Parthenia was lost, he counted not himself delivered), but that the whole multitude would needs guard him into Arcadia. Where, again leaving them all to lament his departure, he by enquiry got to the well-known house of Kalander. There was he received with loving joy of Kalander, with joyful love of Palladius, with humble (though doulful) demeanor of Argalus (whom specially both he and Palladius regarded), with grateful serviceableness of Clitophon, and honorable admiration of all. For being now well viewed to have no hair of his face to witness him a man who had done acts beyond the degree of a man, and to look with a certain almost bashful kind of modesty, as if he feared the eyes of men who was unmoved with sight of the most horrible countenances of death, and as if Nature had mistaken her work to have a Mars's heart in a Cupid's body. All that beheld him (and all that might behold him did behold him) made their eyes quick messengers to their minds that there they had seen the uttermost that in mankind might be seen. The like wonder Palladius had before stirred, but that Daiphantus, as younger and newer come, had gotten now the advantage in the moist and fickle impression of eyesight. But while all men (saving poor Argalus) made the joy of their eyes speak for their hearts towards Daiphantus, Fortune (that belike was bid to that banket and meant then to play the good fellow) brought a pleasant adventure among them.

It was that as they had newly dined there came in to Kalander a messenger that brought him word a young noble lady, near kinswoman to the fair Helen, queen of Corinth, was come thether and desired to be lodged in his house. Kalander, most glad of such an occasion, went out and all his other worthy guests with him, saving only Argalus, who remained in his chamber, desirous that this company were once broken up that he might go in his solitary quest after Parthenia. But when they met this lady, Kalander streight thought he saw his niece Parthenia, and was about in such familiar sort to have spoken unto her; but she in grave and honorable manner giving him to understand that he was mistaken, he, half ashamed, excused himself with the exceeding likeness was between them, though indeed it seemed that [this] lady was of the more pure and dainty complexion. She said it might very well be, having been many times taken one for another. But as soon as she was brought into the house, before she would rest her, she desired to speak with Argalus publicly, who she heard was in the house. Argalus came in hastely and as hastely thought as Kalander had done, with sodain changes of joy into sorrow. But she, when she had stay'd their thoughts with telling them her name and quality, in this sort spake unto him: "My Lord Argalus," said she, "being of late left in the court of Queen Helen of Corinth as chief in her absence (she being upon some occasion gone thence) there came unto me the Lady Parthenia so disguised as I think Greece hath nothing so ougly to behold. For my part, it was many days before, with vehement oaths and some good proofs, she could make me think that she was Parthenia. Yet at last finding certenly

it was she, and greatly pitying her misfortune, so much the more as that all men had ever told me (as now you do) of the great likeness between us, I took the best care I could of her, and of her understood the whole tragical history of her undeserved adventure and therewithal of that most noble constancy in you, my Lord Argalus, which whosoever loves not shews himself to be a hater of virtue and unworthy to live in the society of mankind. But no outward cherishing could salve the inward sore of her mind, but a few days since she died, before her death earnestly desiring and persuading me to think of no husband but of you, as of the only man in the world worthy to be loved; withal she gave me this ring to deliver you, desiring you and by the authority of love commanding you that the affection you bare her you should turn to me, assuring you that nothing can please her soul more then to see you and me matched together. Now, my lord, though this office be not (perchance) suitable to my estate nor sex, who should rather look to be desired, yet an extraordinary desert requires an extraordinary proceeding, and therefore I am come (with faithful love built upon your worthiness) to offer myself and to beseech you to accept the offer; and if these noble gentlemen present will say it is great folly, let them withal say it is great love." And then she stay'd, earnestly attending Argalus his answer, who (first making most hearty sighs to do such obsequies as he could to Parthenia) thus answered her:

"Madame," said he, "infinitely bound am I unto you for this no more rare then noble courtesy, but most bound for the goodness I perceive you shewed to the Lady Parthenia"—with that the tears ran down his eyes, but he followed on—"and as much as so unfortunate a man, fit to be the spectacle of misery, can do you service, determine you have made a purchase of a slave (while I live) never to fail you. But this great matter you propose unto me, wherein I am not so blind as not to see what happiness it should be unto me, excellent lady, know that if my heart were mine to give, you before all other should have it; but Parthenia's it is, though dead. There I began, there I end all matter of affection. I hope I shall not long tarry after her, with whose beauty if I had only been in love I should be so with you who have the same beauty, but it was Parthenia's self I loved and love, which no likeness can make one, no commandment dissolve, no foulness defile, nor no death finish." "And shall I receive," said she, "such disgrace as to be refused?" "Noble lady," said he, "let not that hard word be used, who know your exceeding worthiness far beyond my desert, but it is only happiness I refuse, since of the only happiness I could and can desire I am refused."

He had scarce spoken those words when she ran to him, and, imbracing him, "Why then, Argalus," said she, "take thy Parthenia!" And Parthenia it was indeed. But because sorrow forbad him too soon to believe, she told him the truth with all circumstances: how being parted alone, meaning to die in some solitary place, as she happ'ned to make her complaint the Queen Helen of Corinth (who likewise felt her part of miseries), being then walking also alone in that lovely place, heard her, and never left till she had known the whole discourse. Which the noble queen greatly pitying, she sent her to a physician of hers, the most excellent man in the world, in hope he could help her, which in such sort as they saw performed; and she, taking with her of the queen's servants, thought yet to make this trial, whether he would quickly forget his true Parthenia or no. Her speech was confirmed by the Corinthian gentlemen who before had kept her counsel, and Argalus easily persuaded to what more then ten thousand years of life he desired, and Kalander would needs have the marriage celebrated in his house, principally the longer to hold his dear guests, towards whom he was now (besides his own habit of hospitality) carried with love and duty, and therefore omitted no service that his wit could invent and his power minister.

ROBERT GREENE

MENAPHON

When, sick and soul-weary toward the end of his dissolute life, Greene sneered at the "love pamphlets" which had made him "famous," he was something less than just to his own work. He was not a great writer—indeed, he was often a very bad one—but he had a fair education, a gift of copious language, and a professional knowledge of what the public wanted; and therefore his plays, romances, and pamphlets are useful specimens of popular literature in the eighties. Fresh from Cambridge and from his travels on the Continent, he began his career in imitation of Lyly. The genealogy of *Mamillia* (two parts, 1580, ?1583) is sufficiently explained by the subtitle, "a mirror or looking-glass for the ladies of England"; and, in the stream of romances that followed, Greene never dared to venture far beyond the stylistic and thematic boundaries of *Euphues* and *Arcadia*. In the nature of things, the twenty or so romances that he produced within the next few years could hardly reach the limits of art, but they all reveal his fertility and facility, and at least some of them have real charm. For example, *The Mirror of Modesty* (1584) is a fairly straightforward version of Susanna and the elders; *Gwydonius, the Card of Fancy* (1584) is a frothy and modishly complicated fiction; *Morando, the Tritameron of Love* (two parts, 1584, 1587) seeks to revive the philosophical debate which Lyly had imitated from Castiglione. But on these and the other romances of Greene's early period lies the heavy hand of euphuism, and if they had all perished our grief would not be inconsolable. However, toward the end of the eighties significant changes are discernible in Greene's work: the style becomes less precious, the pretentious philosophical digressions less heavy, the plots fuller and tighter and swifter; in short, Lyly's influence diminished as Sidney's increased. Just before Greene abandoned romance for rogue-pamphlets and autobiographical narrative, he produced a batch of novels that, though derivative like all his other fiction, have a freshness of style and a charm of plot that still keep them alive. *Pandosto, the Triumph of Time* (1588)—or *Dorastus and Fawnia*, as it was often called—is famous not only because it provided Shakespeare the plot of *A Winter's Tale* but also because for generations of readers (and through countless editions) it proved to be one of the best-loved legacies of Elizabethan fiction. *Perimedes the Blacksmith* (1588) is a vigorous retelling of a tale from Boccaccio's *Decamerone;* its preface, incidentally, contains a testy attack on Marlowe, whose success Greene, himself never a very popular dramatist, obviously resented just as he later resented Shakespeare's. One distinction of *Menaphon* (1589) is the breezy preface in which young Thomas Nashe flays alive a good many contemporary writers (see pp. 637-39); another is its plot (perhaps derived from the tale of Curan and Argentile in Warner's *Albion's England*), which immediately suggests *Arcadia* and *Pandosto* with its riddling oracle, disguised royalty, estranged and then united lovers, and dynastic involvements; a third is the lovely songs—some of them gems of Elizabethan lyricism—for which Sidney, and not Lyly, had provided the model. Entered in the Stationers' Register on August 23, 1589, the romance was published in the same year. Our text is based upon *Menaphon Camillas alarum to slumbering Euphues,* 1589 (STC 12272).

FROM MENAPHON: CAMILLA'S ALARUM TO SLUMBERING EUPHUES IN HIS MELANCHOLY CELL AT SILEXEDRA (1589)

To the Right Worshipful and Virtuous Lady, the Lady [Margaret] Hales, Wife to the Late Deceased Sir James Hales, Robert Greene Wisheth Increase of Worship and Virtue

When Alexander, right worshipful, was troubled with hottest fevers, Philip the physician brought him the coldest potions; extremes have their antidotes, and the driest melancholy hath a moistest sanguine; wise Hortenzia, midst her greatest dumps, either play'd with her children or read some pleasant verses; such as sorrow hath pinched, mirth must cure. This considered, hearing, madam, of the passions your ladyship hath uttered alate for the loss of your husband, a knight in life worshipful, virtuous, and full of honorable thoughts, discovering by such passionate sorrows the pattern of a loving and virtuous wife, whose joys lived in her husband's weal and ended with his life, I thought it my duty to write this pastoral history, containing the manifold injuries of fortune, that both your ladyship might see her inconstant follies and bear her frowns with more patience; and when your dumps were most deep, then to look on this little treatise for recreation. Wherein there be as well humors to delight as discourses to advise. Which if your ladyship shall vouch to accept, covering my presumption and faults with your wonted courtesy, I have the wished end of my labors. In which hope resting, I commit your ladyship to the Almighty.

Yours in all humble service,
Robert Greene

ARCADIA. THE REPORTS OF THE SHEPHERDS.

After that the wrath of mighty Jove had wrapp'd Arcadia with noisome pestilence, insomuch that the air, yielding prejudicial savors, seem'd to be peremptory in some fatal resolution, Democles, sovereign and king of that famous continent, pitying the sinister accidents of his people, being a man as just in his censures as royal in his possessions, as careful for the weal of his country as the continuance of his diadem, thinking that unpeopled cities were corasives to princes' consciences, that the strength of his subjects was the sinews of his dominions, and that every crown must contain a care, not only to win honor by foreign conquests but in maintaining dignity with civil and domestical insights—Democles, grounding his arguments upon these premises, coveting to be counted *pater patriae,* calling a parliament together, whether all his nobility, incited by summons, made their repair, elected two of his chief lords to pass unto

Delphos, at Apollo's oracle, to hear the fatal sentence either of their future misery or present remedy.

They, having their charge, posting from Arcadia to the tripos where Pythia sat, the sacred nymph that delivered out Apollo's dylonimas, offering, as their manner is, their orisons and presents, as well to intreat by devotion as to persuade by bounty, they had returned from Apollo this doom:

When Neptune, riding on the southern seas,
Shall from the bosom of his leman yield
Th' Arcadian wonder, men and gods to please,
Plenty in pride shall march amidst the field,
   Dead men shall war, and unborn babes shall frown,
   And with their fawchons hew their foemen down.

When lambs have lions for their surest guide,
And planets rest upon th' Arcadian hills,
When swelling seas have neither ebb nor tide,
When equal banks the ocean margin fills,
   Then look, Arcadians, for a happy time,
   And sweet content within your troubled clime.

No sooner had Pythia delivered this scroll to the lords of Arcady but they departed and brought it to Democles, who, causing the oracle to be read amongst his distressed commons, found the Delphian censure more full of doubts to amaze than fraught with hope to comfort; thinking rather that the angry god sent a peremptory presage of ruin than a probable ambiguity to applaud any hope of remedy, yet loath to have his careful subjects fall into the baleful labyrinth of despair, Democles began to discourse unto them that the interpreters of Apollo's secrets were not the conceipts of human reason but the success of long-expected events, that comets did portend at the first blaze but took effect in the dated bosom of the Destinies, that oracles were foretold at the Delphian cave but were shap'd out and finished in the council house.

With such persuasive arguments Democles appeased the distressed thoughts of his doubtful countrymen, and commanded by proclamation that no man should pry into the quiddities of Apollo's answer lest sundry censures of his divine secrecy should trouble Arcadia with some sudden mutiny. The king, thus smoothing the heat of his cares, rested a melancholy man in his courts, hiding under his head the double-faced figure of Janus, as well to clear the skies of other men's conceipts with smiles as to furnish out his own dumps with thoughts. . . .

Whiles thus Arcadia rested in a silent quiet, Menaphon, the king's shepherd, a man of high account among the swains of Arcady, loved of the nymphs as the paragon of all their country young-sters, walking solitary down to the shore to see if any of his ewes and lambs were straggled down to the strond to browse on sea ivy (wherefore they take special delight to feed), he found his flocks grazing upon the promontory mountains hardly; whereon resting himself on a hill that overpeered the great Mediterranean, noting how Phoebus fetched his lavoltas on the purple plains of Neptunus, as if he had meant to have courted Thetis in the royalty of his robes; the dolphins (the sweet conceipters of music) fetch'd their careers on the calmed waves, as if Arion had touched the strings of his silver-sounding instrument; the mermaids, thrusting their heads from the bosom of Amphitrite, sat on the mounting banks of Neptune drying their watery tresses in the sun-beams; Aeolus forbare to throw abroad his gusts on the slumbering brows of the sea-god, as giving Triton leave to pleasure his queen with desired melody and Proteus liberty to follow his flocks without disquiet.

Menaphon, looking over the champion of Arcady to see if the continent were as full of smiles as the seas were of favors, saw the shrubs as in a dream with delightful harmony and the birds that chanted on their branches not disturbed with the least breath of a favorable zephyrus. Seeing thus the accord of the land and sea, casting a fresh gaze on the water nymphs, he began to consider how Venus was feigned by the poets to spring of the froth of the seas, which drave him straight into a deep conjecture of the inconstancy of love, that, as if Luna were his lodestar, had every minute ebbs and tides, sometime overflowing the banks of fortune with a gracious look lightened from the eyes of a favorable lover, other-whiles ebbing to the dangerous shelf of despair with the piercing frown of a froward mistress. Menaphon in this brown study, calling to mind certain aphorisms that Anacreon had penn'd down as principles of love's follies, being as deep an enemy to fancy as Narcissus was to affection, began thus to scoff at Venus' deity:

"Menaphon, thy mind's favors are greater than thy wealth's fortunes, thy thoughts higher than thy birth, and thy private conceipt better than thy public esteem. Thou art a shepherd, Menaphon, who in feeding of thy flocks findest out nature's secrecy, and in preventing thy lambs' prejudice conceiptest the astronomical motions of the heavens, holding thy sheep-walks to yield as great philosophy as the ancients' discourse in their learned academies. . . . Love, Menaphon! Why, of all follies that ever poets feigned, or men ever faulted with, this foolish imagi-nation of love is the greatest. Venus, forsooth, for her wanton escapes must be a goddess, and her bastard a deity; Cupid must be young and ever a boy to prove that love is fond and witless; wings to make him

inconstant and arrows whereby to shew him fearful; blind (or all were not worth a pin) to prove that Cupid's level is both without aim and reason; thus is the god, and such are his votaries. As soon as our shepherds of Arcady settle themselves to fancy, and wear the characters of Venus stamp'd in their fore-heads, straight their attire must be quaint, their looks full of amours as their god's quiver is full of arrows; their eyes holding smiles and tears to leap out at their mistress' favors or her frowns; sighs must fly as figures of their thoughts, and every wrinkle must be temp'red with a passion; thus suited in outward proportion, and made excellent in inward consti-tution, they straight repair to take view of their mis-tress' beauty. . . ." And in this satirical humor, smiling at his own conceipts, he took his pipe in his hand, and between every report of his instrument sung a stanzo to this effect:

MENAPHON'S SONG

Some say Love,
Foolish Love,
Doth rule and govern all the gods.
I say Love,
Inconstant Love,
Sets men's senses far at odds.
Some swear Love,
Smooth'd-face Love,
Is sweetest sweet that men can have.
I say Love,
Sour Love,
Makes virtue yield as beauty's slave.
A bitter sweet, a folly worst of all,
That forceth wisdom to be folly's thrall.

Love is sweet.
Wherein sweet?
In fading pleasures that do pain.
Beauty sweet.
Is that sweet
That yieldeth sorrow for a gain?
If Love's sweet,
Herein sweet,
That minutes' joys are monthly woes.
'Tis not sweet
That is sweet
Nowhere but where repentance grows.
Then love who list if beauty be so sour.
Labor for me! Love, rest in prince's bower.

Menaphon, having ended his roundelay, rising up, thinking to pass from the mountain down to the valley, casting his eye to the seaside, espied certain fragments of a broken ship floating upon the waves, and sundry persons driven upon the shore with a calm walking all wet and weary upon the sands; wond'ring at this strange sight he stood amazed; yet desirous to see the event of this accident, he shrouded himself to rest unespied till he might perceive what would happen. At last he might descry it was a woman, holding a child in her arms, and an old man directing her, as it were her guide. These three (as distressed wracks), preserved by some further forepointing fate, coveted to climb the mountain, the better to use the favor of the sun to dry their drenched apparel; at last crawled up where poor Menaphon lay close, and, resting them under a bush, the old man did nothing but send out sighs, and the woman ceased not from streaming forth rivolets of tears that hung on her cheeks like the drops of pearled dew upon the riches of Flora. The poor babe was the touchstone of his mother's passions, for, when he smiled and lay laughing in her lap, were her heart never so deeply overcharged with her present sorrows, yet, kissing the pretty infant, she lightened out smiles from those cheeks that were furrowed with continual sources of tears; but if he cried, then sighs as smokes and sobs as thundercracks foreran those showers that with redoubled distress distilled from her eyes. Thus with pretty, inconstant passions trimming up her baby, and at last to lull him asleep, she warbled out of her woful breast this ditty:

SEPHESTIA'S SONG TO HER CHILD

Weep not, my wanton, smile upon my knee.
When thou art old there's grief enough for thee.
    Mother's wag, pretty boy,
    Father's sorrow, father's joy.
    When thy father first did see
    Such a boy by him and me
    He was glad, I was wo.
    Fortune chang'd made him so,
    When he left his pretty boy,
    Last his sorrow, first his joy.

Weep not, my wanton, smile upon my knee.
When thou art old there's grief enough for thee.
    Streaming tears that never stint,
    Like pearl drops from a flint,
    Fell by course from his eyes
    That one another's place supplies.
    Thus he griev'd in every part,
    Tears of blood fell from his heart,
    When he left his pretty boy,
    Father's sorrow, father's joy.

Weep not, my wanton, smile upon my knee.
When thou art old there's grief enough for thee.
    The wanton smil'd, father wept,
    Mother cried, baby lept;

    More he crow'd, more we cried,
    Nature could not sorrow hide.
    He must go, he must kiss
    Child and mother, baby bliss.
    For he left his pretty boy,
    Father's sorrow, father's joy.

Weep not, my wanton, smile upon my knee.
When thou art old there's grief enough for thee.

With this lullaby the baby fell asleep, and Sephestia, laying it upon the green grass, covered it with a mantle, and then, leaning her head on her hand and her elbow on her lap, she fell afresh to pour forth abundance of plaints, which Lamedon, the old man, espying, although in his face appeared the map of discontent and in every wrinkle was a catalogue of woes, yet to cheer up Sephestia, shrouding his inward sorrow with an outward smile, he began to comfort her in this manner. . . .

[Lamedon urges Sephestia, exiled by her royal father and parted from her husband Maximus ("who for thee hath suffered so many disfavors"), to possess her soul in patience and hope for the event of her misfortunes: "Fear not, for if the mother live in misery, yet hath she a scepter for the son; let the unkindness of thy father be buried in the cinders of obedience, and the want of Maximus be supplied with the presence of his pretty babe." Sephestia euphuistically agrees to follow such good advice.]

All this while Menaphon sat amongst the shrubs, fixing his eyes on the glorious object of her face; he noted her tresses, which he compared to the colored hyacinth of Arcadia, her brows to the mountain snows that lie on the hills, her eyes to the gray glister of Titan's gorgeous mantle, her alabaster neck to the whiteness of his flocks, her tears to pearl, her face to borders of lilies interseamed with roses. . . . As thus he mused in his new passions, Lamedon and Sephestia rose up and resolved to take their course which way the wind blew, passing so down the mountain to go seek out some town. At last, they pacing softly on, Lamedon espied Menaphon; desirous therefore to know the course of the country, he saluted him thus:

"Shepherd, for so far thy attire warrants me; courteous, for so much thy countenance imports; if distressed persons whom Fortune hath wronged and the seas have favored (if we may count it favor to live and want) may without offence crave so far aid as to know some place where to rest our weary and weather-beaten bones, our charges shall be paid, and you have for recompense such thanks as Fortune's outlaws may yield to their favorers." Menaphon, hearing him speak so gravely but not fitting his ear to his eye, stood staring still on Sephestia's face, which she perceiving flashed out such a blush from her alabaster cheeks that they look'd like the ruddy gates of the morning. This sweet bashfulness amazing Menaphon, at last he began thus to answer:

"Strangers, your degree I know not; therefore pardon if I give less title than your estates merit. Fortune's frowns are princes' fortunes, and kings are subject to chance and destiny. Mishap is to be salved with pity, not scorn; and we that are Fortune's darlings are bound to relieve them that are distress'd. Therefore follow me, and you shall have such succor as a shepherd may afford. . . ."

[As Menaphon leads the strangers to his house Sephestia contrives a fiction for his questions: "My name is Samela, my country Cyprus, my parentage mean, the wife of a poor gentleman now deceased. How we arrived here by shipwreck, gentle shepherd, inquire not, lest it be tedious for thee to hear it, and a double grief for me to rehearse it." When his guests retire, Menaphon, obviously wracked with the torments of love, refuses his sister Carmela's customary kindnesses so that she "blubbered," and he sighed, and "his men that came in and saw their master with a kercher on his head mourn'd." When at last he goes to bed, it is only to toss and turn in his passion; but at last he finds peace: "Samela is shipwrack'd, Menaphon relieves her; she wants, he supplies with wealth; he sues for love, either must she grant, or buy denial with perpetual repentance.' In this hope rested the poor shepherd, and with that Menaphon laid [his] head down on the pillow and took a sound nap, sleeping out fancy with a good slumber." The next morning he greeted her "with a firm lover's look; Samela, knowing the fowl by the feather, was able to cast his disease without his water, perceived that Cupid had caught the poor shepherd in his net, and unless he sought quickly to break out of the snare would make him a tame fool." As he shows her over his fields he insists on talking of love in spite of her efforts to dissuade him. At last she seems to give him some cause to hope.]

"Give me leave then, Menaphon, first to sorrow for my fortunes, then to call to mind my husband's late funerals, then if the Fates have assigned I shall fancy, I will account of thee before any shepherd in Arcady." This conclusion of Samela drave Menaphon into such an ecstasy for joy that he stood as a man metamorphosed; at last calling his senses together, he told her he rested satisfied with her answer, and thereupon lent her a kiss, such as blushing Thetis receives from her choicest leman. At this, Lamedon awak'd; otherwise Menaphon no doubt had replied, but, breaking off their talk, they went to view their pastures, and so, passing down to the place where the sheep grazed, they searched the shepherds' bags, and so emptied their bottles as Samela mervailed at such

an uncouth banquet. At last they returned home, Menaphon glorying in the hope of his success, intertaining Samela still with such courtesy that she, finding such content in the cottage, began to despise the honors of the court. Resting thus in house with the shepherd, to avoid tedious conceipts she framed herself so to country labors that she ofttimes would lead the flocks to the fields herself, and, being dress'd in homely attire, she seem'd like Oenone that was amorous of Paris. As she thus often traced alongst the plains she was noted, amongst the shepherds, of one Doron, next neighbor to Menaphon, who entered into the consideration of her beauty and made report of it to all his fellow swains, so that they chatted nought in the fields but of the new shepherdess. One day amongst the rest it chanced that Doron, sitting in parley with another country companion of his, amidst other tattle they prattled of the beauty of Samela. "Hast thou seen her?" quoth Melicertus (for so was his friend called). "Ay," quoth Doron, "and sigh'd to see her, not that I was in love, but that I grieved she should be in love with such a one as Menaphon." "What manner of woman is she?" quoth Melicertus. "As well as I can," answered Doron, "I will make description of her."

DORON'S DESCRIPTION OF SAMELA

Like to Diana in her summer weed,
  Girt with a crimson robe of brightest dye,
    goes fair Samela.
Whiter than be the flocks that straggling feed
  When wash'd by Arethusa faint they lie
    is fair Samela.

As fair Aurora in her morning gray,
  Deck'd with the ruddy glister of her love,
    is fair Samela.
Like lovely Thetis on a calmed day,
  Whenas her brightness Neptune's fancy move,
    shines fair Samela.

Her tresses gold, her eyes like glassy streams,
  Her teeth are pearl, the breasts are ivory
    of fair Samela.
Her cheeks like rose and lily yield forth gleams,
  Her brows bright arches fram'd of ebony.
    Thus fair Samela

Passeth fair Venus in her bravest hew,
  And Juno in the shew of majesty,
    for she is Samela;
Pallas in wit. All three, if you well view,
  For beauty, wit, and matchless dignity
    yield to Samela.

"Thou hast," quoth Melicertus, "made such a description as if Priamus' young boy should paint out the perfection of his Greekish paramour. Methinks the idea of her person represents itself an object to my fantasy, and that I see in the discovery of her excellence the rare beauties of ——." And with that he broke off abruptly with such a deep sigh as it seemed his heart should have broken, sitting as the Lapithes when they gazed on Medusa. . . . [When Doron asks the cause of his sorrow, Melicertus tells him of a former love of his whom, having with difficulty won her, he lost in death.] "Ah, Doron, there ends my joys, for no sooner had I triumph'd in my favors but the trophies of my fortunes fell like the herbs in Syria, that flourish in the morn and fade before night; or like unto the fly tyryma, that taketh life and leaveth it all in one day. So, my Doron, did it fare with me, for I had no sooner enjoyed my love but the heavens, envious a shepherd should have the fruition of such a heavenly paragon, sent unrevocable Fates to deprive me of her life, and she is dead—dead, Doron, to her, to myself, to all, but not to my memory, for so deep were the characters stamped in my inward senses that oblivion can never raze out the form of her excellence. . . ."

[Meanwhile, Menaphon continues his pursuit of Samela. At a gathering of the local rustics she succeeds in arousing the jealousy of Pesana ("a herdsman's daughter of the same parish that long had loved Menaphon") and the love of Melicertus, for beneath the rippling wit of the conversation deep passions are engaged.] Everyone departed to their own home, where they talked of the exquisite perfection of Samela, especially Melicertus, who, gotten to his own cottage and lien down in his couch by himself, began to ruminate on Samela's shape.

"Ah, Melicertus, what an object Fortune this day brought to thy eyes, presenting a strange idea to thy sight, as appeared to Achilles of his dead friend Patroclus. Tresses of gold like the trammels of Sephestia's locks, a face fairer than Venus'—such was Sephestia. Her eye paints her out Sephestia, her voice sounds her out Sephestia, she seemeth none but Sephestia; but seeing she is dead and there liveth not such another Sephestia, sue to her and love her, for that it is either a self-same or another Sephestia." In this hope Melicertus fell to his slumber; but Samela was not so content, for she began thus to muse with herself: "May this Melicertus be a shepherd, or can a country cottage afford such perfection? Doth this coast bring forth such excellence? Then happy are the virgins shall have such suitors, and the wives such pleasing husbands. But his face is not inchas'd with any rustic proportion, his brows contain the characters of nobility, and his looks in shepherd's weeds are lordly, his voice pleasing, his wit full of gentry. Weigh all these equally and consider, Samela, is it

not thy Maximus? Fond fool, away with these suppositions! Could the dreaming of Andromache call Hector from his grave? Or can the vision of my husband raise him from the seas? Tush, stoop not to such vanities; he is dead, and therefore grieve not thy memory with the imagination of his new revive, for there hath been but one Hippolytus found to be *virbius,* twice a man. To salve Samela, than, this suppose. If [he] court thee with hyacinth, intertain [him] with roses; if he send thee a lamb, present him an ewe; if he woo, be wooed; and for no other reason but he is like Maximus." Thus she rested, and thus she slept, all parties being equally content and satisfied with hope except Pesana, who, fett'red with the feature of her best-beloved Menaphon, sat cursing Cupid as a partial deity that would make more daylight in the firmament than one sun, more rainbows in the heaven than one Iris, and more loves in one heart than one settled passion. Many prayers she made to Venus for revenge, many vows to Cupid, many orisons to Hymaeneus, if she might possess the type of her desires. Well, poor soul, howsoever she was paid, she smothered all with patience, and thought to brave love with seeming not to love; and thus she daily drove out the time with labor and looking to her herd, hearing every day by Doron, who was her kinsman, what success Menaphon had in his loves. Thus Fates and Fortune dallying a doleful catastrophe to make a more pleasing *epitasis,* it fell out amongst them thus. Melicertus, going to the fields as he was wont to do with his flocks, drove to graze as near the swains of Menaphon as he might to have a view of his new-entertained mistress, who, according to his expectation, came thether every day. Melicertus, esteeming her to be some farmer's daughter at the most, could not tell how to court her; yet at length calling to remembrance her rare wit discovered in her last discourses, finding opportunity to give her both ball and racket, seeing the coast was clear and that none but Samela and he were in the field, he left his flock in the valley and stepp'd unto her, and saluted her thus:

"Mistress of all eyes that glance but at the excellence of your perfection, sovereign of all such as Venus hath allowed for lovers, Oenone's overmatch, Arcady's comet, beauty's second comfort, all hail! Seeing you sit like Juno when she first watch'd her white heifer on the Lincen downs, as bright as silver Phoebe mounted on the high top of the ruddy element, I was by a strange, attractive force drawn, as the adamant draweth the iron, or the jet the straw, to visit your sweet self in the shade and afford you such company as a poor swain may yield without offence; which if you shall vouch to deign of, I shall be as glad of such accepted service as Paris first was of his best-beloved paramour." Samela, looking on the shepherd's face and seeing his utterance full of broken sighs, thought to be pleasant with her shepherd thus: "Arcady's Apollo, whose brightness draws every eye to turn as the *heliotropion* doth after her lode, fairest of the shepherds, the nymphs' sweetest object, women's wrong in wronging many with one's due, welcome! And so welcome as we vouchsafe of your service, admit of your company, as of him that is the grace of all companies, and if we durst upon any light pardon would venter to request you shew us a cast of your cunning."

Samela made this reply because she heard him so superfine, as if Ephoebus had learn'd him to refine his mother tongue, wherefore thought he had done it of an inkhorn desire to be eloquent; and Melicertus, thinking that Samela had learn'd with Lucilla in Athens to anatomize wit and speak none but similes, imagined she smoothed her talk to be thought like Sapho, Phao's paramour.

Thus deceived either in other's suppositions, Samela followed her suit thus: "I know that Priamus' wanton [i.e. Paris] could not be without flocks of nymphs to follow him in the Vale of Ida, beauty hath legions to attend her excellence if the shepherd be true; if, like Narcissus, you wrap not your face in the cloud of disdain you cannot but have some rare paragon to your mistress, whom I would have you, in some sonnet, describe—Jove's last love if Jove could get from Juno." "My pipe shall presume and I adventure with my voice to set out my mistress' favor for your excellence to censure of, and therefore thus." Yet Melicertus, for that he had a farther reach, would not make any clownish description, chanted it thus cunningly:

MELICERTUS' DESCRIPTION OF HIS MISTRESS

Tune on my pipe the praises of my love,
And midst thy oaten harmony recount
How fair she is that makes thy music mount
And every string of thy heart's harp to move.

Shall I compare her form unto the sphere
Whence sun-bright Venus vaunts her silver shine?
Ah, more than that by just compare is thine,
Whose crystal looks the cloudy heavens do clear.

How oft have I descending Titan seen
His burning locks couch in the sea-queen's lap,
And beauteous Thetis his red body wrap
In wat'ry robes, as he her lord had been,

Whenas my nymph, impatient of the night,
Bad bright Atraeus with his train give place
Whiles she led forth the day with her fair face
And lent each star a more than Delian light.

Not Jove or Nature, should they both agree
To make a woman of the firmament,
Of his mix'd purity could not invent
A sky-born form so beautiful as she.

[When Samela demands the name of such a paragon, Melicertus ardently tells her it is she whom he loves. Without surrendering, she encourages him; and so they pass the hours with amorous talk and amorous verse until, at the approach of Lamedon and Menaphon, they leave each other, "kissing in conceit and parting with interchanged glances." And thus matters stand in a state of presumably arrested development as five years pass and Pleusidippus, Sephestia's son, grows to be a handsome and imperious boy: sprung from a line of kings, he assumes naturally the habit of authority even in the rustic wilds of Arcadia.]

In this sort did Pleusidippus draw forth his infancy till on a time, walking to the shore where he with his mother were wrack'd to gather cockles and pebble stones, as children are wont, there arrived on the strond a Thessalian pirate named Eurilochus; who, after he had foraged in the Arcadian confines, driving before him a large booty of beasts to his ships, espied this pretty infant. When, gazing on his face as wanton Jove gazed on Phrygian Ganymede in the fields of Ida, he exhaled into his eyes such deep impression of his perfection as that his thought never thirsted so much after any prey as this pretty Pleusidippus' possession; but, determining first to assay him by curtesy before he assailed him with rigor, he began to try his wit after this manner: "My little child, whence art thou? Where wert thou born? What's thy name? And wherefore wand'rest thou thus all alone on the shore?" "I pray ye, what are you, sir," quoth Pleusidippus, "that deal thus with me by interrogatories as if I were some runaway?" "Wilt thou not tell me, then, who was thy father?"

Said he, "Good sir, if ye will needs know, go ask that of my mother." "Hath said well, my lord," quoth Romanio, who was one of his especial associates; "for wise are the children in these days that know their own fathers, especially if they be begotten in dog-days, when their mothers are frantic with love and young men furious for lust. Besides, who knows not that these Arcadians are given to take the benefit of every Hodge when they will sacrifice their virginity to Venus, though they have but a bush of nettles for their bed? And sure this boy is but some shepherd's bastard at the most, howsoever his wanton face importeth more than appearance." Pleusidippus' eyes at this speech resolved into fire and his face into purple, with a more than common courage in children of his years and stature gave him the lie roundly in this reply: "Peasant, the bastard in thy face, for I am a gentleman. Wert thou a man in courage, as thou art a cow in proportion, thou wouldst never have so much empaired thy honesty as to derogate from my honor. Look not in my face, but level at my heart by this that thou seest"; and therewith let drive at him with such pebble stones as he had in his hat, insomuch that Romanio was driven to his heels to shun this sudden hailshot, and Eurilochus resolved into a laughter, and in terms of admiration most highly extolled so exceeding magnanimity in so little a body, which how available it proved to the confirmation of his fancy, that was before inflamed with his features, let them imagine that have noted the imbecility of that age and the unresisted fury of men at arms. Sufficeth at this instant to unfold (all other circumstance of praise laid apart) that Eurilochus, being far in love with his extraordinary lineaments, awaited no farther parley, but willed his men perforce to hoise him a-shipboard, intending as soon as ever he arrived in Thessaly, by sending him to the court as a present, to make his peace with his lord and master Agenor, who not long before had proclaimed him as a notorious pirate throughout all his dominions. Neither swarved he one whit from his purpose, for no sooner had he cast anchor in the port of Hadrionopolis but he arrayed him in choice silks and Tyrian purple, and so sent him as a prize to the king of that country; who, walking as then in his summer garden with his queen, the beauteous Eriphila, fell to discourse (as one well seen in philosophy) of herbs and flowers, as the savor or color did occasion; and, having spent some time in disputing their medicinable properties, his lady reaching him a marigold, he began to moralize of it thus merely: "I marvel the poets that were so prodigal in painting the amorous affection of the sun to his hyacinth did never observe the relation of love twixt him and the marigold. It should either seem they were loath to incur the displeasure of women by propounding it in the way of comparison any servile imitation for headstrong wives, that love no precepts less than those pertaining unto duty, or that that flower (not so usual in their gardens as ours) in her unacquainted name did obscure the honor of her amours to Apollo; to whose motions reducing the method of her springing, she waketh and sleepeth, openeth and shutteth her golden leaves, as he riseth and setteth." "Well did you forestall my exception," quoth Eriphila, "in terming it a servile imitation; for were the condition of a wife so slavish as your similitude would infer, I had as leave be your page as your spouse, your dog as your darling." "Not so, sweet wife," answered Agenor, "but the comparison holdeth in this, that as the marigold resembleth the sun both in color and form, so each man's wife ought every way to be the image of her husband, framing her countenance to smile when she sees him disposed to mirth, and contrariwise her eyes to tears, he being surcharged with melancholy. And as the marigold displayeth the orient ornaments of her beauty to the resplendant view of none but her lover Hyperion, so ought not a woman of modesty lay open the allurements of her face to any but her espoused fere, in whose absence, like the marigold in the absence of the sun, she ought to shut up her doors and solemnize continual night till her husband, her sun, making a happy return, unsealeth her silence with the joy of his sight. . . ."

[This witty colloquy is interrupted by the entrance of Romanio with Pleusidippus. The boy's beauty and charm work so powerfully on both the king and the queen that the pirates are pardoned on the spot and Pleusidippus is received almost as a demigod. "Whereupon Agenor, commanding him to be had in and used in every respect as the child of a prince, began in his solitary walk by his countenance to calculate his nativity and measure his birth by his beauty, contracting him in thought heir to his kingdom of Thessaly and husband to his daughter, before he knew whence the child descended or who was his father."]

But leaving young Pleusidippus thus spending his youth in the Thessalian court, protected with the tender affection of such a courteous foster-father as Agenor, return we where we left, back unto Arcady, and meet his mother, the fair Samela, returning from the folds; who, having discoursed by the way, as she came home, to Lamedon and Menaphon, what she late saw and observed in her son, they both conjoined their judgments to this conclusion: that he was doubtless born to some greater fortunes than the sheepcotes could contain, and therefore it behooved her to further his destinies with some good and liberal education, and not to detain him any longer in that trade of life which his fortune withstood, but by the way to rebuke him for tyrannizing so lordly over the boys, lest the neighbor shepherds might happily intrude the name of injury on them, being strangers, for his insulting over their children. With this determination came she home, and calling for Pleusidippus according to their former counsel, he would in no wise be found. Thereupon enquiry was made amongst all the shepherds, diligent search in every village, but still the most carefullest post returned with *non est inventus*. Which Samela hearing, thinking she had utterly lost him whom Fortune had saved, began in this manner to act her unrest: "Dissembling heavens, where is your happiness? Unconstant times, what are your triumphs? Have you therefore hetherto fed me with honey that you might at last poison me with gall? Have you fatted me so long with Sardenian smiles that, like the wrack of the sirens, I might perish in your wiles? Curst that I was to affy in your curtesy, curst that [I] am to taste of your cruelty! O Pleusidippus, livest thou, or art thou dead? No, thou art dead, dead to the world, dead to thy kinsfolks, dead to Cyprus, dead to Arcady, dead to thy mother Samela; and with thee dies the world's wonder, thy kinsfolks' comfort, Cyprus' soul, Arcady's hopes, thy mother's honors. . . ." [And so on. When Menaphon, seeking to comfort her, promises her more fair children if she will only yield to his long suit, she enrages him by her tart refusal. At last the worm turns.]

Therewith he scratch'd his head where it itch'd not, and, setting his cap he could not tell which way in a hot fustian fume, he utter'd these words of fury: "Strumpet of Greece, repayest thou my love with this lavish ingratitude? Have I therefore with my plenty supplied thy wants that thou with thy pride shouldst procure my wo? Did I relieve thee in distress to wound me in thy welfare with disdain? Deceitful woman"—and therewith he swore a holiday oath by Pan, the god of the shepherds—"either return love for love, or I will turn thee forth of doors to scrape up thy crumbs where thou canst, and make thee pitied for thy poverty that erstwhile wert honored in every man's eye through the supportance of thy beauty." "Belike then," quoth Samela, "when you intertained me into your house you did it not in regard of the laws of hospitality, but only with this policy to quench the flames of your fancy. Then, sir, have I mistook your honesty, and am less indebted to your courtesy." "Nay, I thought no less," said Menaphon, "when your straggling eye at our last meeting would be gadding throughout every corner of our company, that you would prove such a kind kistrel; but if you will needs be starting, I'll serve ye thereafter, I warrant you. Then see which of our beardless youngsters will take ye in when I have cast you forth. . . ." [And so they angrily part. Lamedon, "with certain remainder of money he had," bought the house of a deceased shepherd and there installed Samela. Meanwhile, Menaphon, sick with remorse and unrequited love, "spent whole eclogues in anguish." But Pesana, rejected for so many years, saw and seized the opportunity, so that Menaphon ("with good diet and warm broths, and especially by her careful attendance") gradually "began to gather up his crumbs, and listen by little and little to the love he late scorned."]

Leave we them to their equal desires as surfeiting either of other's society, and let us look back to Thessaly, where Samela's stripling (now grown up to the age of sixteen years) flourish'd in honor and feats of arms above all the knights of the court, insomuch that the echo of his fame was the only news talk'd on throughout every town in Greece. But Olympia, the mistress of his prowess (for so was the king's daughter named), was she that most of all exalted in the far-renowmed reports of his martial perfections, to whose praise he did consecrate all his endeavors, to whose exquisite form he did dedicate all his adventures. But hell-born Fame, the eldest daughter of Erinyes, envying the felicity of these two famous lovers, dismounted eftsoons from her brass-sounding buildings and unburdened herself of her secrets in the presence of young Pleusidippus, among whose catalogue she had not forgot to discover the incomparable beauty of the Arcadian shepherdess; whereof the young prince no sooner had received an inkling but he stood upon thorns till he had satisfied his desire with her sight. Therefore on a time sitting with his mistress at supper, when for table talk it was debated amongst them what country bred the most accomplish'd dames for all things, after strangers and others had delivered up their opinions without partiality, one amongst them all, who had been in Arcady, gave up his verdit thus freely:

"Gentlewomen," quoth he, "be it no disgrace for the moon to stoop to the sun, for the stars to give place when Titan appears, then I hope neither the Thessalians will be moved, nor the Grecians agrieved, if I make Apollo's Arcady beauty's meridian. . . . Our Arcadian nymphs are fair and beautiful, though not begotten of the sun's bright rays, whose eyes vaunt love's armory to the view, whose angelical faces are to the obscure earth instead of a firmament. View but this counterfeit"—and therewithal he shewed the picture of Samela—"and see if it be not of force to draw the sun from his sphere, or the moon from her circle, to gaze as the one did on the beauty of Daphne, or all night contemplate as the other on the form of Endymion." Pleusidippus, who all this while heard his tale with attentive patience, no sooner beheld the radiant glory of this resplendant face but as a man already installed in eternity he exclaimed thus abruptly, "O Arcady, Arcady, storehouse of nymphs and nursery of beauty!" At which words, Olympia starting up suddenly, as if she, a second Juno, had taken her Jove in bed with Alcmena, and overcasting the chamber with a frown that was able to mantle the world with an eternal night, she made passage to her choler in these terms of contempt: "Beardless upstart of I know not whence, have the favors of my bounty (not thy desert) ent'red thee so deeply in overweening presumption that thou shouldst be the foremost in derogation of our dignity and blaspheming of my beauty? I tell thee, recreant, I scorn thy clownish Arcady with his inferior comparisons as one that prizeth her perfection above any created constitution. . . ."

[Angrily replying to Olympia's slurs on his birth, Pleusidippus throws to her the glove she had given him for a lover's token and declares his intention of going to Arcadia immediately in search of true beauty. Although Agenor effects a precarious reconciliation between the haughty youth and the repentant girl ("her eyes red, and her cheeks all to-beblubbered with her jealous tears"), Pleusidippus is resolved to carry out his plan. Declining all entreaties to stay in Thessaly, he takes a ship bound for Arcadia, "so that in a day and night's sailing he arrived on the shore adjoining to the promontory where he, his mother, and his uncle Lamedon were first wrack'd."]

Leave we him wand'ring with some few of his train that came with him alongst the seaside to seek out some town or village where to refresh themselves, and let us awhile to the court of Democles, where our history began; who, having committed his daughter with her tender babe, her husband Maximus, and Lamedon (his uncle), without oar or mariner, to the fury of the merciless waves, determined to leave the succession of his kingdom to uncertain chance; for his queen with Sephestia's loss (whom she deemed to be dead) took such thought that within short time after she died. Democles, as careless of all weathers, spent his time epicure-like in all kind of pleasures that either art or expense might afford; so that for his dissolute life he seemed another Heliogabalus, deriving his security from that grounded tranquillity which made it proverbial to the world: "No heaven but Arcady." Having spent many years in this variety of vanity, Fame, determining to apply herself to his fancy, sounded in his ears the singular beauty of his daughter Samela. He, although he were an old colt, yet had not cast all his wanton teeth, which made him under the bruit of being sick of a grievous apoplexy steal from his court secretly in the disguise of a shepherd to come and seek out Samela; who, not a little proud of her new flock, liv'd more contented than if she had been queen of Arcady; and Melicertus, joying not a little that she was parted from Menaphon, used every day to visit her without dread and court her in such shepherd's terms as he had; which how they pleased her I leave to you to imagine, whenas not long after she vowed marriage to him solemnly in presence of all the shepherds, but not to be solemnized till the prophecy was fulfilled, mentioned in the beginning of this history. Although this penance exceeded the limits of his patience, yet hoping that the oracle was not uttered in vain, and might as well (albeit he knew not which way) be

accomplished in him as in any other, he was contented to make a virtue of necessity and await the utmost of his destiny. But Pleusidippus, who by this time had perfected his policies, exchanging his garments with one of the herdgrooms of Menaphon, tracing over the plains in the habit of a shepherd, chanced to meet with Democles as he was new come into those quarters; whom mistaking for an old shepherd, he began many impertinent questions belonging to the sheepcotes. At last he ask'd him if he knew Samela's sheepfold; who, answering doubtfully unto all alike, made him half angry; and had not Samela passed by at that instant to fill her bottle at a spring near the foot of the promontory he should like enough have had first handsel of our new shepherd's sheephook. But the wonder of her beauty so wrought with his wounded fancy that he thought report a partial spreader of her praises, and fame too base to talk of such forms. Samela, espying this fair shepherd so far overgone in his gazing, stepp'd to him and ask'd him if he knew her that he so overlook'd her.

"Pardon me, fair shepherdess," quoth Pleusidippus, "if it be a fault, for I cannot choose, being eagle-sighted, but gaze on the sun the first time I see it." "And truly I cannot choose but compare you to one of Aesop's apes, that, finding a glowworm in the night, took it for fire; and you, seeing a face full of deformities, mistake it for the sun."

"Indeed, it may be. Mine eyes made opposite to such an object may fail in their office, having their lights rebated by such brightness." "Nay, not unlike," quoth Samela, "for else out of doubt you would see your way better." "Why," quoth Pleusidippus, "I cannot go out of the way when I meet such glistering goddesses in my way." "How now, Sir Paris, are you out of your arithmetic? I think you have lost your wits with your eyes, that mistake Arcady for Ida and a shepherdess for a goddess." "However it please you," quoth Pleusidippus, "to derogate from my prowess by the title of Paris, know that I am not so far out of my arithmetic but that by multiplication I can make two of one in an hour's warning, or be as good as a cypher to fill up a place at the worst hand. . . ." Much other circumstance of prattle passed between them which the Arcadian records do not shew, nor I remember; sufficeth he pleaded love, and was repuls'd, which drove him into such a choler that, meeting his supposed shepherd (who, lying under a bush, had all this while overheard them), he ent'red into such terms of indignation as Jove shaking his earthquaking hair when he sat in consultation of Lycaon. Wherefore Democles, perceiving Pleusidippus repuls'd, who was every way grac'd with the ornaments of nature, began to cast his bad pennyworth's, in whose face age had furrowed her wrinkles, except he should lay his crown at her feet and tell her he was king of Arcadia; which in commonwealth's respects seeming not commodious, he thought to turn a new leaf and make this young shepherd the means to perfect his purpose. He had not far from that place a strong castle which was inhabited as then by none but tillsmen and herdgrooms; thether did he persuade Pleusidippus to carry her perforce, and effect that by constraint that he could not atchieve by intreaty; who, list'ning not a little to this counsel that was never platted for his advantage, presently put in practise what he of late gave in precepts, and, waiting till the evening that Samela should fold her sheep, having given his men the watchword, maugre all the shepherds adjoining, he mounted her behind him; and, being by Democles directed to the castle, he made such havoc among the stubborn herdsmen that will they, nill they, he was lord of the castle. Yet might not all this prevail with Samela, who, constant to her old shepherd, would not intertain any new love; which made Pleusidippus think all his harvest lost in the reaping, and blemish'd all his delights with a mournful drooping. But Democles, that look'd for a mountain of gold in a mole-hill, finding her all alone, began to discourse his love in more ample manner than ever Pleusidippus, telling her how he was a king, what his revenues were, what power he had to advance her, with many other proud vaunts of his wealth and prodigal terms of his treasure. Samela, hearing the name of a king and perceiving him to be her father, stood amazed like Medusa's metamorphosis, and, blushing oft with intermingled sighs, began to think how injurious fortune was to her shown in such an incestuous father. But he, hotspurred in his purpose, gave her no time to deliberate, but required either a quick consent or a present denial. She told him that the shepherd Melicertus was already intitled in the interest of her beauty, wherefore it was in vain what he or any other could plead in the way of persuasion. . . .

[The already thick plot now grows thicker. After Samela has "flung away to her withdrawing chamber in a dissembled rage," her father Democles resolves "either to obtain his love or satisfy his hate." Dressing again as a shepherd he goes "down to the plains, where he found all the swains in a mutiny about the recovery of their beautiful paragon." He tells them that a Thessalian "knight" holds Samela captive in the castle and intends to carry her away to Thessaly. At this news, both Melicertus and Menaphon declare their love for the distressed lady; each presses his claims so hard that they resolve to settle the matter by matching eclogues against each other, Democles to

be the judge. Melicertus, having "most curiously portrayed out his mistress' excellence," is awarded the guerdon "to bear sole rule and supremacy." He immediately assembles a force of some two hundred "stout, headstrong clowns," arrays himself in armor, and sets out for the castle, accompanied by Democles and his troop. Arriving there, he besieges Pleusidippus and Samela in their retreat. In an angry parley he challenges the youth to single combat, but the wily Democles persuades them to wait for three days. During the truce he sends to his own court for ten thousand soldiers, and when they arrive "secretly" he places them "in ambush" around the castle. When the day of combat comes Samela stands on the turret as the two champions prepare to fight, "grieving that for her cause such a stratagem should arise in Arcady, her countenance full of sorrow, and floods of tears falling from her eyes." The encounter between Pleusidippus and Melicertus is fearful, but they are so evenly matched and so valorous that neither can overcome. This is the chance Democles has been waiting for: he, "seeing his time, that both of them were sore weakened, gave the watchword, and the ambush leap'd out, slaughtered many of the shepherds, put the rest to flight, took the two champions prisoners, and, sacking the castle, carried them and the fair Samela to his court, letting the shepherdess have her liberty but putting Melicertus and Pleusidippus into a deep and dark dungeon." Meanwhile, Doron plights his troth to Carmela in a "merry eclogue."]

Again to Democles, who, seeing no intreaties would serve to persuade Samela to love, neither the hope of the Arcadian crown nor the title of a queen, lastly assayed with frowns and threats, but all in vain; for Samela, first restrained by nature, in that he was her father, and secondly by love, in that Melicertus lay imprisoned only for her sake, stood still so stiff to her tackling that Democles, changing love into hate, resolved to revenge that with death which no means else might satisfy. So that to color his frauds withal he gave Samela free license to visit Melicertus, which she had not long done but that by the instigation of the old king the jailer, confederate to his treachery, accuseth her of adultery, whereupon without further witness they both were condemned to die. These two lovers, knowing themselves guiltless in this surmised faction, were joyful to end their loves with their lives, and so to conclude all in a fatal and final content of minds and passions. But Democles set free Pleusidippus, as afraid the king of Thessaly would revenge the wrong of his knight, intertaining him with sumptuous banquets as befitted so brave and worthy a gentleman. The day came prefixed, wherein these parties should die. Samela was so

desirous to end her life with her friend that she would
not reveal either unto Democles or Melicertus what
she was; and Melicertus rather chose to die with his
Samela then once to name himself Maximus. Both
thus resolved were brought to the place of execution.
Pleusidippus, sitting on a scaffold with Democles,
seeing Samela come forth like the blush of the
morning, felt an uncouth passion in his mind, and
nature began to enter combat with his thoughts: not
love but reverence, not fancy but fear, began to
assail him, that he turn'd to the king and said: "Is
it not pity, Democles, such divine beauty should be
wrapp'd in cinders?" "No," quoth Democles,
"where the anger of a king must be satisfied." At
this answer Pleusidippus wrapp'd his face in his
cloak and wept, and all the assistants grieved to see
so fair a creature subject to the violent rage of
Fortune. Well, Democles commanded the deathsman to do his devoir, who, kneeling down and
craving pardon, ready to give Melicertus the fatal
stroke, there stepp'd out an old woman attired like
a prophetess, who cried out, "Villain, hold thy hand!
Thou wrongest the daughter of a king!" Democles,
hearing the outcry and seeing that at that word the
people began to mutiny and murmur, demanded
the old woman what she meant. "Now," quoth she,
"Democles, is the Delphian oracle performed. Neptune hath yielded up the world's wonder, and that is
young Pleusidippus, nephew to thee and son to fair
Sephestia, who here standeth under the name of
Samela, cast upon the promontory of Arcady with
her young son where she, as a shepherdess, hath
liv'd in labors temp'red with loves; her son, playing
on the shore, was conveyed by certain pirates into
Thessaly where (whenas he was supposed every way
to be dead) doing deeds of chivalry, he fulfilled the
prophecy; your Highness, giving the lion, were
guide unto the lambs in dissembling yourself a
shepherd; planets resting upon the hills was the picture of Venus upon their crests; and the seas that had
neither ebb nor tide was the combat twixt the father
and the son, that gave the waves of the seas in their
shields, not able to vanquish one another, but parting
with equal victory. For know, Democles, this
Melicertus is Maximus, twice betrothed to Sephestia
and father to young Pleusidippus. Now, therefore,
the oracle fulfilled, is the happy time wherein

Arcady shall rest in peace." At this the people gave a
great shout, and the old woman vanish'd. Democles,
as a man ravish'd with an ecstasy of sudden joy, sat
still and stared on the face of Sephestia. Pleusidippus
in all duty leap'd from his seat and went and covered
his mother with his robe, craving pardon for the
fondness of his incestuous affection, and kneeling at
his father's feet submiss, in that he had drawn his
sword and sought his life that first in this world gave
him life. Maximus first looked on his wife, and seeing by the lineaments of her face that it was Sephestia,
fell about her neck, and both of them, weeping in
the bosom of their son, shed tears for joy to see him
so brave a gentleman. Democles all this while sitting
in a trance, at last calling his senses together, seeing
his daughter revived whom so cruelly for the love
of Maximus he had banish'd out of his confines,
Maximus in safety, and the child a matchless paragon
of approved chivalry, he leap'd from his seat and
imbraced them all with tears, craving pardon of
Maximus and Sephestia; and to shew that the outward object of his wat'ry eyes had a sympathy with
the inward passion of his heart he impal'd the head
of his young nevew Pleusidippus with the crown
and diadem of Arcady; and for that his brother
Lamedon had in all distress not left his daughter
Sephestia, he took the matter so kindly that he
reconciled himself unto him and made him duke in
Arcady.

The success of this forerehearsed catastrophe growing so comical, they all concluded after the festival
solemnizing of the coronation (which was made
famous with the excellent deeds of many worthy
cavaliers) to pass into Thessaly to contract the
marriage twixt Pleusidippus and the daughter of the
Thessalian king. Which news spread through Arcady
as a wonder, that at last it came to Menaphon's ears,
who, hearing the high parentage of his supposed
Samela, seeing his passions were too aspiring and that
(with the Syrian wolves) he bark'd against the moon,
he left such lettice as were too fine for his lips and
courted his old love Pesana, to whom shortly after
he was married. And lest there should be left anything unperfect in this pastoral accident, Doron
smudg'd himself up and jump'd a marriage with his
old friend Carmela.

THOMAS LODGE

ROSALYNDE

Lodge had already experimented with prose fiction in *Forbonius and Prisceria* (1584), a grim little tale of frustrated love, before he joined Captain Clark's voyage to the Canaries in 1588. It was on that trip, as he remarks in the dedication to Lord Hunsdon, that he wrote another romance "to beguile the time with labor," and the result, published just after *Scylla's Metamorphosis* (1589) and just before he set forth on a second voyage in 1591, was *Rosalynde* (1590), one of the most durable monuments of Elizabethan fiction. Based upon the fourteenth-century *Tale of Gamelyn* (which was long attributed to Chaucer), Lodge's book provided Shakespeare the plot for *As You Like It* and attracted so many readers that it went through ten further editions by 1634—and no wonder, for it is a work of real charm and beauty. For the lusty plot of a wronged younger brother we may thank *The Tale of Gamelyn;* for the moralizing soliloquies, Lyly; for the pastoral setting and chivalric trappings, Sidney; but for the fluent progress of the story, the gracefully drawn pairs of lovers, and the lively interpolated lyrics we must thank Lodge himself. Written when Lyly's influence was waning and just before the advent of the brawling, journalistic narratives of Greene, Nashe, Deloney, and others, *Rosalynde* remains a charming memorial to a style that would presently be no more. Though without the heroic scope or dignity of Sidney's great novel, it is in many respects the Arcadian romance *par excellence* in English. Our text is based upon *Rosalynde. Euphues golden legacie: found after his death in his Cell at Silexedra,* 1590 (STC 16664).

FROM ROSALYNDE: EUPHUES' GOLDEN LEGACY (1590)

To the Right Honorable and His Most Esteemed Lord the Lord of Hunsdon, Lord Chamberlain of Her Majesty's Household and Governor of Her Town of Barwick, T[homas] L[odge], G[entleman], Wisheth Increase of All Honorable Virtues

Such Romans, right honorable, as delighted in martial exploits attempted their actions in the honor of Augustus because he was a patron of soldiers; and Virgil dignified him with his poems as a Moecenas of schollers—both jointly advancing his royalty as a prince warlike and learned. Such as sacrifice to Pallas present her with bays as she is wise and with armor as she is valiant, observing herein that excellent τὸ πρέπον which dedicateth honors according to the perfection of the person. When I ent'red, right honorable, with a deep insight into the consideration of these premises, seeing your lordship to be a patron of all martial men and a Moecenas of such as apply themselves to study, wearing with Pallas both the lance and the bay, and aiming with Augustus at the favor of all by the honorable virtues of your mind, being myself first a student and after falling from books to arms, even vowed in all my thoughts dutifully to affect your lordship. Having with Captain [John] Clarke made a voyage to the Ilands of Terceras and the Canaries, to beguile the time with labor I writ this book; rough, as hatch'd in the storms of the ocean and feathered in the surges of many perilous seas. But as it is the work of a soldier and a scholler, I presumed to shrowd it under your Honor's patronage, as one that is the fautor and favorer of all virtuous actions; and whose honorable loves, grown from the general applause of the whole commonwealth for your higher deserts, may keep it from the malice of every bitter tongue. Other reasons more particular, right honorable, challenge in me a special affection to your lordship, as being a scholler with your two noble sons, Master Edmond Carew and Master Robert Carew, two siens worthy of so honorable a tree, and a tree glorious in such honorable fruit, as also being scholler in the university under that learned and virtuous knight, Sir Edward Hoby, when he was Bachelor in Arts, a man as well lettered as well born, and, after the etymology of his name, soaring as high as the wings of knowledge can mount him, happy every way, and the more fortunate as blessed in the honor of so virtuous a lady. Thus, right honorable, the duty that I owe to the sons chargeth me that all my affection be placed on the father, for where the branches are so precious, the tree of force must be most excellent. Commanded and emboldened thus with the consideration of these forepassed reasons to present my book to your lordship, I humbly intreat your Honor will vouch of my labors and favor a soldier's and a scholler's pen with your gracious acceptance, who answers in affection what he wants in eloquence; so devoted to your Honor as his only desire is to end his life under the favor of so martial and learned a patron.

Resting thus in hope of your lordship's courtesy in deigning the patronage of my work, I cease, wishing you as many honorable fortunes as your lordship can desire or I imagine.

Your Honor's soldier,
Humbly affectionate
Thomas Lodge

To the Gentlemen Readers

Gentleman, look not here to find any sprigs of Pallas' bay tree, nor to hear the humor of any amorous laureate, nor the pleasing vein of any eloquent orator. *Nolo altum sapere,* they be matters above my capacity; the cobbler's check shall never light on my head, *ne sutor ultra crepidam;* I will go no further than the latchet, and then all is well. Here you may perhaps find some leaves of Venus' myrtle, but hewn down by a soldier with his curtle-ax, not bought with the allurement of a filed tongue. To be brief, gentlemen, room for a soldier and a sailor, that gives you the fruits of his labors that he wrought in the ocean, when every line was wet with a surge, and every humorous passion countercheck'd with a storm. If you like it, so; and yet I will be yours in duty if you be mine in favor. But if Momus or any squint-eyed ass that hath mighty ears to conceive with Midas and yet little reason to judge, if he come aboord our bark to find fault with the tackling, when he knows not the shrouds, I'll down into the hold and fetch out a rusty pollax that saw no sun this seven year, and either well bebaste him or heave the cockscomb overboord to feed cods. But courteous gentlemen that favor most, backbite none, and pardon what is overslipp'd, let such come and welcome; I'll into the steward's room and fetch them a can of our best bev'radge. Well, gentlemen, you have *Euphues' Legacy.* I fetch'd it as far as the Ilands of Terceras, and therefore read it, censure with favor, and farewell.

Yours,
T[homas] L[odge]

There dwelled adjoining to the city of Bordeaux a knight of most honorable parentage, whom Fortune had graced with many favors, and Nature honored with sundry exquisite qualities, so beautified with the excellence of both, as it was a question whether Fortune or Nature were more prodigal in deciphering the riches of their bounties. Wise he was, as holding in his head a supreme conceipt of policy, reaching with Nestor into the depth of all civil government; and to make his wisdom more gracious, he had that *salem ingenii* and pleasant eloquence that was so highly commended in Ulysses; his valor was no less than his wit, nor the stroke of his lance no less forcible than the sweetness of his tongue was persuasive; for he was for his courage chosen the principal of all the Knights of Malta. This hardy knight, thus enrich'd with virtue and honor, surnamed Sir John of Bordeaux, having passed the prime of his youth in sundry battails against the Turks, at last, as the date of time hath his course, grew aged. His hairs were silver-hued, and the map of age was figured on his forehead: honor sat in the furrows of his face, and many years were pourtrayed in his wrinkled liniaments, that all men might perceive his glass was run, and that Nature of necessity challenged her due. Sir John, that with the phoenix knew the term of his life was now expired, and could, with the swan, discover his end by her songs, having three sons by his wife Lynida, the very pride of all his forepassed years, thought now, seeing death by constraint would compel him to leave them, to bestow upon them such a legacy as might bewray his love and increase their ensuing amity. Calling, therefore, these young gentlemen before him, in the presence of all his fellow Knights of Malta, he resolved to leave them a memorial of his fatherly care in setting down a method of their brotherly duties. Having, therefore, death in his looks to move them to pity, and tears in his eyes to paint out the depth of his passions, taking his eldest son by the hand, he began thus:

SIR JOHN OF BORDEAUX' LEGACY HE GAVE TO HIS SONS

"O my sons, you see that fate hath set a period of my years, and Destinies have determined the final end of my days. The palm tree waxeth away-ward, for he stoopeth in his height, and my plumes are full of sick feathers touched with age. I must to my grave that dischargeth all cares, and leave you to the world that encreaseth many sorrows; my silver hairs containeth great experience, and in the number of my years are penn'd down the subtilties of Fortune. Therefore, as I leave you some fading pelf to countercheck poverty, so I will bequeath you infallible precepts that shall lead you unto virtue. First, therefore, unto thee, Saladyne, the eldest, and therefore the chiefest pillar of my house, wherein should be ingraven as well the excellence of thy father's qualities as the essential form of his proportion, to thee I give fourteen plowlands, with all my manor houses and richest plate. Next, unto Fernandyne I bequeath twelve plowlands. But unto Rosader, the youngest, I give my horse, my armor, and my lance, with sixteen plowlands; for if the inward thoughts be discovered by outward shadows, Rosader will exceed you all in bounty and honor. . . .

"O, man's life is like lightning that is but a flash, and the longest date of his years but as a bavin's blaze. Seeing, then, man is so mortal, be careful that thy life be virtuous, that thy death may be full of admirable honors; so shalt thou challenge fame to be thy fautor and put oblivion to exile with thine honorable actions. But, my sons, lest you should forget your father's axioms, take this scroul, wherein read what your father dying wills you to execute living." At this he shrunk down in his bed and gave up the ghost.

John of Bordeaux being thus dead was greatly lamented of his sons and bewailed of his friends, especially of his fellow Knights of Malta, who attended on his funerals, which were performed with great solemnity. His obsequies done, Saladyne caused, next his epitaph, the contents of the scroul to be pourtrayed out, which were to this effect:

THE CONTENTS OF THE SCEDULE WHICH SIR JOHN OF BORDEAUX GAVE TO HIS SONS

My sons, behold what portion I do give:
I leave you goods, but they are quickly lost;
I leave advice to school you how to live;
I leave you wit, but won with little cost;
But keep it well, for counsail still is one
When father, friends, and worldly goods are gone. . . .

Learn of the ant in summer to provide,
Drive with the bee the drone from out thy hive,
Build like the swallow in the summertide,
Spare not too much, my son, but sparing thrive.
Be poor in folly, rich in all but sin,
So by thy death thy glory shall begin.

Saladyne having thus set up the scedule, and hang'd about his father's hearse many passionate poems, that France might suppose him to be passing sorrowful, he clad himself and his brothers all in black, and in such sable suits discoursed his grief; but as the hyena when she mourns is then most guileful, so Saladyne under this shew of grief shadowed a heart full of contented thoughts. The tiger, though he hide his claws, will at last discover his rapine; the lion's looks are not the maps of his meaning, nor a man's phisnomy is not the display of his secrets. Fire cannot be hid in the straw, nor the nature of man so concealed but at last it will have his course; nourture and art may do much, but that *natura naturans,* which by propagation is ingrafted in the heart, will be at last perforce predominant according to the old verse: *Naturam expellas furca licet, tamen usque recurret.*

So fared it with Saladyne, for after a month's mourning was past he fell to consideration of his father's testament; how he had bequeathed more to his younger brothers than himself, that Rosader was his father's darling, but now under his tuition, that as yet they were not come to years, and he, being their gardin, might, if not defraud them of their due, yet make such havoc of their legacies and lands as they should be a great deal the lighter; whereupon he began thus to meditate with himself:

SALADYNE'S MEDITATION WITH HIMSELF

"Saladyne, how art thou disquieted in thy thoughts, and perplexed with a world of restless passions, having thy mind troubled with the tenor of thy father's testament, and thy heart fired with the hope of present preferment! By the one thou art counsail'd to content thee with thy fortunes, by the other persuaded to aspire to higher wealth. Riches, Saladyne, is a great royalty, and there is no sweeter physic than store. Avicen, like a fool, forgot in his *Aphorisms* to say that gold was the most precious restorative, and that treasure was the most excellent medicine of the mind. O Saladyne, what, were thy father's precepts breathed into the wind? Hast thou so soon forgotten his principles? Did he not warn thee from coveting without honor and climbing without virtue? Did he not forbid thee to aim at any action that should not be honorable? And what will be more prejudicial to thy credit than the careless ruin of thy brothers' welfare? . . . Tush, what words are these, base fool, far unfit (if thou be wise) for thy humor? What though thy father at his death talked of many frivolous matters, as one that doated for age and raved in his sickness? Shall his words be axioms, and his talk be so authentical that thou wilt, to observe them, prejudice thyself? No, no, Saladyne, sick men's wills that are parol and have neither hand nor seal are like the laws of a city written in dust, which are broken with the blast of every wind. What, man, thy father is dead, and he can neither help thy fortunes nor measure thy actions; therefore bury his words with his carcass, and be wise for thyself. What, 'tis not so old as true, *Non sapit, qui sibi non sapit.* Thy brother is young; keep him now in awe; make him not checkmate with thyself, for *Nimia familiaritas contemptum parit.* Let him know little, so shall he not be able to execute much; suppress his wits with a base estate, and though he be a gentleman by nature, yet form him anew and make him a peasant by nourture; so shalt thou keep him as a slave, and reign thyself sole lord over all thy father's possessions. As for Fernandyne, thy middle brother, he is a scholler and hath no mind but on Aristotle. Let him read on Galen while thou riflest with gold, and pore on his book till thou dost purchase lands; wit is great wealth; if he have learning it is enough. And so let all rest."

In this humor was Saladyne, making his brother Rosader his footboy for the space of two or three years, keeping him in such servile subjection as if he had been the son of any country vassal. The young gentleman bare all with patience, till on a day, walking in the garden by himself, he began to consider how he was the son of John of Bordeaux, a knight renowmed for many victories and a gentleman famouzed for his virtues; how, contrary to the testament of his father, he was not only kept from his land and intreated as a servant, but smothered in such secret slavery as he might not attain to any honorable actions.

"Ah," quoth he to himself, nature working these effectual passions, "why should I, that am a gentleman born, pass my time in such unnatural drudgery? Were it not better either in Paris to become a scholler, or in the court a courtier, or in the field a soldier, than to live a footboy to my own brother? Nature hath lent me wit to conceive, but my brother denied me art to contemplate; I have strength to perform any honorable exploit, but no liberty to accomplish my virtuous endeavors; those good parts that God hath bestowed upon me, the envy of my brother doth smother in obscurity; the harder is my fortune, and the more his frowardness."

With that, casting up his hand, he felt hair on his face, and perceiving his beard to bud, for choler he began to blush, and swore to himself he would be no more subject to such slavery. As thus he was ruminating of his melancholy passions, in came Saladyne with his men, and seeing his brother in a brown study, and to forget his wonted reverence, thought to shake him out of his dumps thus:

"Sirrah," quoth he, "what, is your heart on your halfpenny, or are you saying a dirge for your father's soul? What, is my dinner ready?"

At this question Rosader, turning his head askance, and bending his brows as if anger there had plowed the furrows of her wrath, with his eyes full of fire, he made this reply:

"Dost thou ask me, Saladyne, for thy cates? Ask some of thy churls who are fit for such an office; I am thine equal by nature, though not by birth, and though thou hast more cards in the bunch, I have as many trumps in my hands as thyself. Let me question with thee, why thou hast fell'd my woods, spoiled my manor houses, and made havoc of such utensals as my father bequeathed unto me? I tell thee, Saladyne, either answer me as a brother, or I will trouble thee as an enemy."

At this reply of Rosader's Saladyne smiled, as laughing at his presumption, and frowned, as checking his folly; he therefore took him up thus shortly:

"What, sirrah! Well, I see early pricks the tree that will prove a thorn; hath my familiar conversing with you made you coy, or my good looks drawn you to be thus contemptuous? I can quickly remedy such a fault, and I will bend the tree while it is a wand. In faith, sir boy, I have a snaffle for such a headstrong colt. You, sirs, lay hold on him and bind him, and then I will give him a cooling-card for his choler."

This made Rosader half mad, that, stepping to a great rake that stood in the garden, he laid such load upon his brother's men that he hurt some of them and made the rest of them run away. Saladyne, seeing Rosader so resolute and with his resolution so valiant, thought his heels his best safety, and took him to a loaft adjoining to the garden, whether Rosader pursued him hotly. Saladyne, afraid of his brother's fury, cried out to him thus:

"Rosader, be not so rash. I am thy brother and thine elder, and if I have done thee wrong I'll make thee amends. Revenge not anger in blood, for so shalt thou stain the virtue of old Sir John of Bordeaux. Say wherein thou art discontent, and thou shalt be satisfied. Brothers' frowns ought not to be periods of wrath; what, man, look not so sourly; I know we shall be friends, and better friends than we have been, for *Amantium irae amoris redintegratio est*."

These words appeased the choler of Rosader, for he was of a mild and courteous nature, so that he laid down his weapons, and upon the faith of a gentleman assured his brother he would offer him no prejudice; whereupon Saladyne came down, and after a little parley they imbraced each other and became friends, and Saladyne promising Rosader the restitution of all his lands, "and what favor else," quoth he, "any ways my ability or the nature of a brother may perform." Upon these sug'red reconciliations they went into the house arm in arm together, to the great content of all the old servants of Sir John of Bordeaux.

Thus continued the pad hidden in the straw, till it chanced that Torismond, king of France, had appointed for his pleasure a day of wrestling and of tournament to busy his commons' heads, lest, being idle, their thoughts should run upon more serious matters, and call to remembrance their old banished king. A champion there was to stand against all comers, a Norman, a man of tall stature and of great strength; so valiant that in many such conflicts he always bare away the victory, not only overthrowing them which he incount'red, but often with the weight of his body killing them outright. Saladyne, hearing of this, thinking now not to let the ball fall to the ground, but to take opportunity by the forehead, first by secret means convented with the Norman and procured him with rich rewards to swear that if Rosader came within his claws he should never more return to quarrel with Saladyne for his possessions. The Norman, desirous of pelf —as *Quis nisi mentis inops oblatum respuit aurum?*—taking great gifts for little gods, took the crowns of Saladyne to perform the stratagem.

Having thus the champion tied to his villanous determination by oath, he prosecuted the intent of his purpose thus. He went to young Rosader, who in all his thoughts reach'd at honor and gazed no lower than virtue commanded him, and began to tell him of this tournament and wrastling, how the king should be there, and all the chief peers of France, with all the beautiful damosels of the country.

"Now, brother," quoth he, "for the honor of Sir John of Bordeaux, our renowmed father, to famous that house that never hath been found without men approved in chevalry, shew thy resolution to be peremptory. For myself thou knowest, though I am eldest by birth, yet never having attempted any deeds of arms, I am youngest to perform any martial exploits, knowing better how to survey my lands than to charge my lance; my brother Fernandyne he is at Paris poring on a few papers, having more insight into sophistry and principles of philosophy than any warlike indeavors; but thou, Rosader, the youngest in years but the eldest in valor, art a man of strength, and darest do what honor allows thee. Take thou my father's lance, his sword, and his horse, and hie thee to the tournament, and either there valiantly crack a spear, or try with the Norman for the palm of activity."

The words of Saladyne were but spurs to a free horse, for he had scarce uttered them ere Rosader took him in his arms, taking his proffer so kindly that he promised, in what he might, to requite his courtesy. The next morrow was the day of the tournament, and Rosader was so desirous to shew his heroical thoughts that he pass'd the night with little sleep; but as soon as Phoebus had vailed the curtain of the night, and made Aurora blush with giving her the *bezo les labres* in her silver couch, he gat him up, and taking his leave of his brother, mounted himself towards the place appointed, thinking every mile ten leagues till he came there.

But leaving him so desirous of the journey, to Torismond, the king of France, who having by force banished Gerismond, their lawful king, that lived as an outlaw in the forest of Arden, sought now by all means to keep the French busied with all sports that might breed their content. Amongst the rest he had appointed this solemn tournament, whereunto he in most solemn manner resorted, accompanied with the twelve peers of France, who, rather for fear than love, graced him with the shew of their dutiful favors. To feed their eyes, and to make the beholders pleased with the sight of most rare and glist'ring objects, he had appointed his own daughter Alinda to be there, and the fair Rosalynde, daughter unto Gerismond, with all the beautiful damosels that were famous for their features in all France. Thus in that place did love and war triumph in a sympathy; for such as were martial might use their lance to be renowmed for the excellence of their chevalry, and such as were amorous might glut themselves with gazing on the beauties of most heavenly creatures. As every man's

eye had his several survey, and fancy was partial in their looks, yet all in general applauded the admirable riches that Nature bestowed on the face of Rosalynde; for upon her cheeks there seemed a battail between the Graces who should bestow most favors to make her excellent. The blush that gloried Luna when she kiss'd the shepherd on the hills of Latmos was not tainted with such a pleasant dye as the vermillion flourish'd on the silver hue of Rosalynde's countenance; her eyes were like those lamps that make the wealthy covert of the heavens more gorgeous, sparkling favor and disdain, courteous and yet coy, as if in them Venus had placed all her amorets, and Diana all her chastity. The trammels of her hair, folded in a caul of gold, so far surpass'd the burnish'd glister of the metal as the sun doth the meanest star in brightness; the tresses that folds in the brows of Apollo were not half so rich to the sight, for in her hairs it seemed Love had laid herself in ambush, to intrap the proudest eye that durst gaze upon their excellence. What should I need to decipher her particular beauties, when by the censure of all she was the paragon of all earthly perfection? This Rosalynde sat, I say, with Alinda as a beholder of these sports, and made the cavaliers crack their lances with more courage; many deeds of knighthood that day were perfourmed, and many prizes were given according to their several deserts.

At last, when the tournament ceased, the wrastling began, and the Norman presented himself as a challenger against all comers, but he looked like Hercules when he advanc'd himself against Achelous, so that the fury of his countenance amazed all that durst attempt to incounter with him in any deed of activity; till at last a lusty franklin of the country came with two tall men that were his sons, of good liniaments and comely personage. The eldest of these, doing his obeisance to the king, entered the list, and presented himself to the Norman, who straight cop'd with him, and as a man that would triumph in the glory of his strength, roused himself with such fury that not only he gave him the fall, but killed him with the weight of his corpulent personage; which the younger brother seeing, lept presently into the place, and, thirsty after the revenge, assailed the Norman with such valor that at the first incounter he brought him to his knees; which repuls'd so the Norman that, recovering himself, fear of disgrace doubling his strength, he stepp'd so sternly to the young franklin that, taking him up in his arms, he threw him against the ground so violently that he broke his neck, and so ended his days with his brother. At this unlook'd for massacre the people murmured, and were all in a deep passion of pity; but the franklin, father unto these, never changed his countenance, but as a man of a couragious resolution took up the bodies of his sons without any shew of outward discontent.

All this while stood Rosader and saw this tragedy; who, noting the undoubted virtue of the franklin's mind, alighted off from his horse, and presently sat down on the grass and commanded his boy to pull off his boots, making him ready to try the strength of this champion. Being furnished as he would, he clapp'd the franklin on the shoulder and said thus:

"Bold yeoman, whose sons have ended the term of their years with honor, for that I see thou scornest Fortune with patience and twhartest the injury of Fate with content in brooking the death of thy sons, stand a while, and either see me make a third in their tragedy or else revenge their fall with an honorable triumph."

The franklin, seeing so goodly a gentleman to give him such courteous comfort, gave him hearty thanks, with promise to pray for his happy success. With that Rosader vailed bonnet to the king, and lightly lept within the lists, where noting more the company than the combatant, he cast his eye upon the troup of ladies that glistered there like the stars of heaven; but at last, Love, willing to make him as amorous as he was valiant, presented him with the sight of Rosalynde, whose admirable beauty so inveigled the eye of Rosader that, forgetting himself, he stood and fed his looks on the favor of Rosalynde's face; which she perceiving blush'd, which was such a doubling of her beauteous excellence that the bashful red of Aurora at the sight of unacquainted Phaeton was not half so glorious.

The Norman, seeing this young gentleman fettered in the looks of the ladies, drave him out of his memento with a shake by the shoulder. Rosader, looking back with an angry frown as if he had been wakened from some pleasant dream, discovered to all by the fury of his countenance that he was a man of some high thoughts; but when they all noted his youth and the sweetness of his visage, with a general applause of favors, they grieved that so goodly a young man should venture in so base an action; but seeing it were to his dishonor to hinder him from his enterprise, they wish'd him to be graced with the palm of victory. After Rosader was thus called out of his memento by the Norman, he roughly clapp'd to him with so fierce an incounter that they both fell to the ground, and with the violence of the fall were forced to breathe; in which space the Norman called to mind by all tokens that this was he whom Saladyne had appointed him to kill; which conjecture made him stretch every limb, and try every sinew, that, working his death, he might recover the gold which so bountifully was promised him. On the contrary part, Rosader while he breathed

was not idle, but still cast his eye upon Rosalynde, who, to incourage him with a favor, lent him such an amorous look as might have made the most coward desperate; which glance of Rosalynde so fired the passionate desires of Rosader that, turning to the Norman, he ran upon him and braved him with a strong encounter. The Norman received him as valiantly, that there was a sore combat, hard to judge on whose side Fortune would be prodigal. At last, Rosader, calling to mind the beauty of his new mistress, the fame of his father's honors, and the disgrace that should fall to his house by his misfortune, roused himself and threw the Norman against the ground, falling upon his chest with so willing a weight that the Norman yielded Nature her due and Rosader the victory.

The death of this champion, as it highly contented the franklin as a man satisfied with revenge, so it drew the king and all the peers into a great admiration that so young years and so beautiful a personage should contain such martial excellence; but when they knew him to be the youngest son of Sir John of Bordeaux, the king rose from his seat and imbraced him, and the peers intreated him with all favorable courtesy, commending both his valor and his virtues, wishing him to go forward in such haughty deeds that he might attain to the glory of his father's honorable fortunes.

As the king and lords graced him with embracing, so the ladies favored him with their looks, especially Rosalynde, whom the beauty and valor of Rosader had already touched; but she accounted love a toy, and fancy a momentary passion, that, as it was taken in with a gaze, might be shaken off with a wink, and therefore feared not to dally in the flame; and to make Rosader know she affected him, took from her neck a jewel, and sent it by a page to the young gentleman. The prize that Venus gave to Paris was not half so pleasing to the Troyan as this gem was to Rosader; for if Fortune had sworn to make him sole monarch of the world, he would rather have refused such dignity than have lost the jewel sent him by Rosalynde. To retourn her with the like he was unfurnished, and yet that he might more than in his looks discover his affection, he stepp'd into a tent and, taking pen and paper, writ this fancy:

Two suns at once from one fair heaven there shin'd,
Ten branches from two boughs, tipp'd all with roses,
Pure locks more golden than is gold refin'd,
Two pearled rows that nature's pride incloses;
Two mounts fair marble-white, down-soft and dainty,
A snow-dy'd orb, where love increas'd by pleasure
Full woful makes my heart, and body fainty:
Her fair, my wo, exceeds all thought and measure.
In lines confus'd my luckless harm appeareth,
Whom sorrow clouds, whom pleasant smiling cleareth.

This sonnet he sent to Rosalynde, which when she read she blush'd, but with a sweet content in that she perceived love had allotted her so amorous a servant.

Leaving her to her new-intertained fancies, again to Rosader, who, triumphing in the glory of this conquest, accompanied with a troup of young gentlemen that were desirous to be his familiars, went home to his brother Saladyne's, who was walking before the gates to hear what success his brother Rosader should have, assuring himself of his death, and devising how with dissimuled sorrow to celebrate his funerals. As he was in this thought, he cast up his eye and saw where Rosader returned with the garland on his head, as having won the prize, accompanied with a crew of boon companions. Grieved at this, he stepped in and shut the gate. Rosader seeing this, and not looking for such unkind intertainment, blush'd at the disgrace, and yet, smothering his grief with a smile, he turned to the gentlemen and desired them to hold his brother excused, for he did not this upon any malicious intent or niggardize, but being brought up in the country he absented himself as not finding his nature fit for such youthful company. Thus he sought to shadow abuses proff'red him by his brother, but in vain, for he could by no means be suffered to enter; whereupon he ran his foot against the door and brake it open, drawing his sword and ent'ring boldly into the hall, where he found none, for all were fled but one Adam Spencer, an Englishman who had been an old and trusty servant to Sir John of Bordeaux. He, for the love he bare to his deceased maister, favored the part of Rosader, and gave him and his such intertainment as he could. Rosader gave him thanks, and, looking about, seeing the hall empty, said: "Gentlemen, you are welcome. Frolic and be merry; you shall be sure to have wine enough, whatsoever your fare be. I tell you, cavaliers, my brother hath in his house five tun of wine, and as long as that lasteth, I beshrew him that spares his liquor."

With that he burst open the buttery door, and with the help of Adam Spencer covered the tables and set down whatsoever he could find in the house; but what they wanted in meat, Rosader supplied with drink, yet had they royal cheer, and withal such a hearty welcome as would have made the coarsest meats seem delicates. After they had feasted and frolick'd it twice or thrice with an upsee freeze, they all took their leaves of Rosader and departed. As soon as they were gone Rosader, growing impatient of the abuse, drew his sword and swore to be revenged on the discurteous Saladyne; yet by the means of Adam Spencer, who sought to continue friendship and amity betwixt the brethren, and through the flattering submission of Saladyne, they were once again reconciled and put up all forepassed injuries with a peaceable agreement, living together for a good space in such brotherly love as did not only rejoice the servants but made all the gentlemen and bord'ring neighbors glad of such friendly concord. Saladyne, hiding fire in the straw and concealing a poisoned hate in a peaceable countenance, yet deferring the intent of his wrath till fitter opportunity, he shewed himself a great favorer of his brother's virtuous endeavors; where, leaving them in this happy league, let us return to Rosalynde.

Rosalynde returning home from the triumph, after she waxed solitary, love presented her with the idea of Rosader's perfection, and taking her at discovert strook her so deep as she felt herself grow passing passionate. She began to call to mind the comeliness of his person, the honor of his parents, and the virtues that, excelling both, made him so gracious in the eyes of everyone. Sucking in thus the honey of love by imprinting in her thoughts his rare qualities, she began to surfit with the contemplation of his virtuous conditions; but when she call'd to remembrance her present estate and the hardness of her fortunes, desire began to shrink, and fancy to vail bonnet, that between a chaos of confused thoughts she began to debate with herself in this manner:

ROSALYNDE'S PASSION

"Infortunate Rosalynde, whose misfortunes are more than thy years, and whose passions are greater than thy patience! The blossoms of thy youth are mix'd with the frosts of envy, and the hope of thy ensuing fruits perish in the bud. Thy father is by Torismond banish'd from the crown, and thou, the unhappy daughter of a king, detained captive, living as disquieted in thy thoughts as thy father discontented in his exile. Ah, Rosalynde, what cares wait upon a crown! what griefs are incident to dignity! what sorrows haunt royal palaces! The greatest seas have the sorest storms, the highest birth subject to the most bale, and of all trees the cedars soonest shake with the wind; small currents are ever calm, low valleys not scorch'd in any lightnings, nor base men tied to any baleful prejudice. Fortune flies, and if she touch poverty it is with her heel, rather disdaining their want with a frown than envying their wealth with disparagement. O Rosalynde, hadst thou been born low, thou hadst not fallen so high, and yet being great of blood thine honor is more if thou brookest misfortune with patience. Suppose I contrary Fortune with content, yet Fates, unwilling to have me anyway happy, have forced love to set my thoughts on fire with fancy. Love, Rosalynde! Becometh it women in distress to think of love? Tush, desire hath no respect of persons: Cupid is blind and shooteth at randon, as soon hitting a rag as a robe, and piercing as soon the bosom of a captive as the breast of a libertine. Thou speakest it, poor Rosalynde, by experience; for being every way distress'd, surcharged with cares and overgrown with sorrows, yet amidst the heap of all these mishaps, love hath lodged in thy heart the perfection of young Rosader, a man every way absolute as well for his inward life as for his outward liniments, able to content the eye with beauty and the ear with the report of his virtue. But consider, Rosalynde, his fortunes and thy present estate: thou art poor and without patrimony, and 10 yet the daughter of a prince; he a younger brother, and void of such possessions as either might maintain thy dignities or revenge thy father's injuries. And hast thou not learned this of other ladies, that lovers cannot live by looks, that women's ears are sooner content with a dram of *give me* than a pound of *hear me,* that gold is sweeter than eloquence, that love is a fire and wealth is the fuel, that Venus' coffers should be ever full? Then, Rosalynde, seeing Rosader is poor, think him less beautiful because he is in want, and 20 account his virtues but qualities of course for that he is not indued with wealth. Doth not Horace tell thee what method is to be used in love, *Quaerenda pecunia primum, post nummos virtus?* Tush, Rosalynde, be not overrash; leap not before thou look; either love such a one as may with his lands purchase thy liberty, or else love not at all. Choose not a fair face with an empty purse, but say as most women use to say, *Si nihil attuleris, ibis Homere foras.* Why, Rosalynde! Can such base thoughts harbor in such high beauties? 30 Can the degree of a princess, the daughter of Gerismond, harbor such servile conceits as to prize gold more than honor, or to measure a gentleman by his wealth, not by his virtues? No, Rosalynde, blush at thy base resolution, and say, if thou lovest, either Rosader or none. And why? because Rosader is both beautiful and virtuous."

Smiling to herself to think of her new-entertained passions, taking up her lute that lay by her, she warbled out this ditty:

ROSALYNDE'S MADRIGAL

Love in my bosom like a bee
　Doth suck his sweet:
Now with his wings he plays with me,
　Now with his feet.
Within mine eyes he makes his nest,
His bed amidst my tender breast;
My kisses are his daily feast,
And yet he robs me of my rest.
　Ah, wanton, will ye?

And if I sleep, then percheth he
　With pretty flight,
And makes his pillow of my knee
　The livelong night.

Strike I my lute, he tunes the string,
　He music plays if so I sing,
He lends me every lovely thing,
　Yet cruel he my heart doth sting.
　　Whist, wanton, still ye!

Else I with roses every day
　Will whip you hence,
And bind you, when you long to play,
　For your offense;
I'll shut mine eyes to keep you in,
I'll make you fast it for your sin,
I'll count your power not worth a pin.
　Alas, what hereby shall I win,
　　If he gainsay me?

What if I beat the wanton boy
　With many a rod?
He will repay me with annoy,
　Because a god.
Then sit thou safely on my knee,
And let thy bow'r my bosom be;
Lurk in mine eyes, I like of thee.
　O Cupid, so thou pity me,
　　Spare not but play thee.

Scarce had Rosalynde ended her madrigal before Torismond came in with his daughter Alinda and many of the peers of France, who were enamored of her beauty; which Torismond perceiving, fearing 30 lest her perfection might be the beginning of his prejudice, and the hope of his fruit end in the beginning of her blossoms, he thought to banish her from the court; "for," quoth he to himself, "her face is so full of favor that it pleads pity in the eye of every man; her beauty is so heavenly and devine that she will prove to me as Helen did to Priam; some one of the peers will aim at her love, end the marriage, and then in his wive's right attempt the kingdom. 40 To prevent therefore *had I wist* in all these actions, she tarries not about the court, but shall, as an exile, either wander to her father or else seek other fortunes." In this humor, with a stern countenance full of wrath, he breathed out this censure unto her before the peers, that charged her that that night she were not seen about the court; "for," quoth he, "I have heard of thy aspiring speeches and intended treasons." This doom was strange unto Rosalynde, and presently, covered with the shield of her in-50 nocence, she boldly brake out in reverend terms to have cleared herself; but Torismond would admit of no reason, nor durst his lords plead for Rosalynde, although her beauty had made some of them passionate, seeing the figure of wrath portrayed in his brow. Standing thus all mute, and Rosalynde amazed, Alinda, who loved her more than herself, with grief in her heart and tears in her eyes, falling down on her knees, began to intreat her father thus:

ALINDA'S ORATION TO HER FATHER IN DEFENSE OF FAIR ROSALYNDE

"If, mighty Torismond, I offend in pleading for my friend, let the law of amity crave pardon for my boldness; for where there is depth of affection, there friendship alloweth a priviledge. Rosalynde and I have been fostered up from our infancies, and nursed under the harbor of our conversing together with such private familiarities that custom had wrought an union of our nature, and the sympathy of our affections such a secret love that we have two bodies and one soul. Then mervail not, great Torismond, if, seeing my friend distress'd, I find myself perplexed with a thousand sorrows; for her virtuous and honorable thoughts, which are the glories that maketh women excellent, they be such as may challenge love, and race out suspicion. Her obedience to your Majesty I refer to the censure of your own eye, that since her father's exile hath smothered all griefs with patience, and in the absence of nature hath honored you with all duty, as her own father by nouriture, not in word uttering any discontent, nor in thought, as far as conjecture may reach, hammering on revenge; only in all her actions seeking to please you and to win my favor. Her wisdom, silence, chastity, and other such rich qualities I need not decipher; only it rests for me to conclude in one word, that she is innocent. If, then, Fortune, who triumphs in variety of miseries, hath presented some envious person as minister of her intended stratagem to taint Rosalynde with any surmise of treason, let him be brought to her face, and confirm his accusation by witnesses; which proved, let her die, and Alinda will execute the massacre. If none can avouch any confirmed relation of her intent, use justice, my lord (it is the glory of a king), and let her live in your wonted favor; for if you banish her, myself, as co-partner of her hard fortunes, will participate in exile some part of her extremities."

Torismond, at this speech of Alinda, covered his face with such a frown as tyranny seemed to sit triumphant in his forehead, and check'd her up with such taunts as made the lords, that only were hearers, to tremble.

"Proud girl," quoth he, "hath my looks made thee so light of tongue, or my favors incouraged thee to be so forward, that thou darest presume to preach after thy father? Hath not my years more experience than thy youth, and the winter of mine age deeper insight into civil policy than the prime of thy florishing days? The old lion avoids the toils, where the young one leaps into the net; the care of age is provident and foresees much; suspicion is a virtue where a man holds his enemy in his bosom. Thou, fond girl, measurest all by present affection, and as thy heart loves, thy thoughts censure; but if thou knewest that in liking Rosalynde thou hatchest up a bird to peck out thine own eyes, thou wouldst intreat as much for her absence as now thou delightest in her presence. But why do I alledge policy to thee? Sit you down, huswife, and fall to your needle; if idleness make you so wanton, or liberty so malipert, I can quickly tie you to a sharper task. And you, maid, this night be packing, either into Arden to your father, or whether best it shall content your humor, but in the court you shall not abide."

This rigorous reply of Torismond nothing amazed Alinda, for still she prosecuted her plea in the defense of Rosalynde, wishing her father, if his censure might not be revers'd, that he would appoint her partner of her exile; which if he refused to do, either she would by some secret means steal out and follow her, or else end her days with some desperate kind of death. When Torismond heard his daughter so resolute, his heart was so hard'ned against her that he set down a definitive and peremptory sentence that they should both be banished, which presently was done, the tyrant rather choosing to hazard the loss of his only child than anyways to put in question the state of his kingdom; so suspicious and fearful is the conscience of an usurper. Well, although his lords persuaded him to retain his own daughter, yet his resolution might not be revers'd, but both of them must away from the court without either more company or delay. In he went with great melancholy, and left these two ladies alone. Rosalynde waxed very sad, and sat down and wept. Alinda she smiled, and sitting by her friend began thus to comfort her. . . .

[Rosalynde] gave her hearty thanks, and then they sat them down to consult how they should travel. Alinda grieved at nothing but that they might have no man in their company, saying it would be their greatest prejudice in that two women went wand'ring without either guide or attendant.

"Tush," quoth Rosalynde, "art thou a woman, and hast not a sodain shift to prevent a misfortune? I, thou seest, am of a tall stature, and would very well become the person and apparel of a page; thou shalt be my mistress, and I will play the man so properly that, trust me, in what company soever I come I will not be discovered. I will buy me a suit, and have my rapier very handsomely at my side, and if any knave offer wrong, your page will shew him the point of his weapon."

At this Alinda smiled, and upon this they agreed, and presently gathered up all their jewels, which they trussed up in a casket, and Rosalynde in all haste provided her of robes, and Alinda, from her royal weeds, put herself in more homely attire. Thus fitted to the purpose, away go these two friends, having now changed their names, Alinda being called Aliena, and Rosalynde, Ganymede. They traveled along the vineyards, and by many byways at last got to the forest side, where they traveled by the space of two or three days without seeing any creature, being often in danger of wild beasts, and pained with many passionate sorrows. Now the black ox began to tread on their feet, and Alinda thought of her wonted royalty; but when she cast her eyes on her Rosalynde, she thought every danger a step to honor. Passing thus on along, about midday they came to a fountain, compass'd with a grove of cypress trees so cunningly and curiously planted as if some goddess had intreated nature in that place to make her an arbor. By this fountain sat Aliena and her Ganymede, and forth they pulled such victuals as they had, and fed as merrily as if they had been in Paris with all the king's delicates, Aliena only grieving that they could not so much as meet with a shepherd to discourse them the way to some place where they might make their abode. At last Ganymede, casting up his eye, espied where on a tree was ingraven certain verses; which as soon as he espied, he cried out:

"Be of good cheer, mistress, I spy the figures of men; for here in these trees be ingraven certain verses of shepherds, or some other swains that inhabit hereabout." . . .

[The men are old Corydon and young Montanus, and the latter has inscribed in the bark of a pine tree a poem expressing his hopeless passion for Phoebe. Presently the princesses wander on "into a fair valley" where they see two flocks of grazing sheep.] Then, looking about, they might perceive where an old shepherd sat, and with him a young swain, under a covert most pleasantly situated. The ground where they sat was diap'red with Flora's riches, as if she meant to wrap Tellus in the glory of her vestments; round about in the form of an amphitheater were most curiously planted pine trees, interseamed with limons and citrons, which with the thickness of their boughs so shadowed the place that Phoebus could not pry into the secret of that arbor; so united were the tops with so thick a closure that Venus might there in her jollity have dallied unseen with her dearest paramour. Fast by, to make the place more gorgeous, was there a fount so crystalline and clear that it seemed Diana with her dryades and hamadryades had that spring as the secret of all their bathings. In this glorious arbor sat these two shepherds, seeing their sheep feed, playing on their pipes many pleasant tunes, and from music and melody falling into much amorous chat. . . . [Drawing closer, the two girls overhear "A Pleasant Eglog between Montanus and

Corydon," a pastoral flyting on the pangs of unrequited love. Approaching the shepherds, the girls talk to them of love and of the delights of country life, the upshot being that Aliena agrees to buy a farm and settle there with her page.] Aliena resolved there to set up her rest, and by the help of Corydon swapt a bargain with his landlord and so became mistress of the farm and the flock, herself putting on the attire of a shepherdess and Ganymede of a young swain; every day leading forth her flocks with such delight that she held her exile happy, and thought no content to the bliss of a country cottage. Leaving her thus famous amongst the shepherds of Arden, again to Saladyne.

When Saladyne had a long while concealed a secret resolution of revenge, and could no longer hide fire in the flax, nor oil in the flame, for envy is like lightning, that will appear in the darkest fog, it chanced on a morning very early he call'd up certain of his servants, and went with them to the chamber of Rosader, which being open he ent'red with his crew, and surprised his brother being asleep, and bound him in fetters, and in the midst of his hall chained him to a post. Rosader, amazed at this strange chance, began to reason with his brother about the cause of this sodain extremity, wherein he had wrong'd, and what fault he had committed worthy so sharp a penance. Saladyne answered him only with a look of disdain, and went his way, leaving poor Rosader in a deep perplexity; who, thus abused, fell into sundry passions, but no means of relief could be had; whereupon for anger he grew into a discontented melancholy. In which humor he continued two or three days without meat, insomuch that, seeing his brother would give him no food, he fell into despair of his life. Which Adam Spencer, the old servant of Sir John of Bordeaux, seeing, touched with the duty and love he ought to his old master, felt a remorse in his conscience of his son's mishap; and therefore, although Saladyne had given a general charge to his servants that none of them upon pain of death should give either meat or drink to Rosader, yet Adam Spencer in the night arose secretly, and brought him such victuals as he could provide, and unlock'd him, and set him at liberty. After Rosader had well feasted himself, and felt he was loose, straight his thoughts aimed at revenge, and now, all being asleep, he would have quit Saladyne with the method of his own mischief. But Adam Spencer persuaded him to the contrary with these reasons:

"Sir," quoth he, "be content; for this night go again into your old fetters; so shall you try the faith of friends, and save the life of an old servant. Tomorrow hath your brother invited all your kindred and allies to a solemn breakfast only to see you, telling them all that you are mad and fain to be tied to a post. As soon as they come, make complaint to them of the abuse proffered you by Saladyne. If they redress you, why, so; but if they pass over your plaints *sicco pede,* and hold with the violence of your brother before your innocence, then thus: I will leave you unlock'd that you may break out at your pleasure, and at the end of the hall shall you see stand a couple of good pollaxes, one for you and another for me. When I give you a wink, shake off your chains, and let us play the men and make havoc amongst them, drive them out of the house and maintain possession by force of arms till the king hath made a redress of your abuses."

These words of Adam Spencer so persuaded Rosader that he went to the place of his punishment, and stood therewhile the next morning. About the time appointed, came all the guests bidden by Saladyne, whom he intreated with courteous and curious entertainment, as they all perceived their welcome to be great. The tables in the hall where Rosader was tied were covered, and Saladyne, bringing in his guests together, shewed them where his brother was bound and was inchain'd as a man lunatic. Rosader made reply, and with some invectives made complaints of the wrongs proffered him by Saladyne, desiring they would in pity seek some means for his relief. But in vain; they had stopp'd their ears with Ulysses, that were his words never so forcible, he breathed only his passions into the wind. They, careless, sat down with Saladyne to dinner, being very frolic and pleasant, washing their heads well with wine. At last, when the fume of the grape had ent'red peal-meal into their brains, they began in satirical speeches to rail against Rosader; which Adam Spencer no longer brooking, gave the sign, and Rosader, shaking off his chains, got a pollax in his hand and flew amongst them with such violence and fury that he hurt many, slew some, and drave his brother and all the rest quite out of the house. Seeing the coast clear, he shut the doors, and being sore anhung'red, and seeing such good victuals, he sate him down with Adam Spencer and such good fellows as he knew were honest men, and there feasted themselves with such provision as Saladyne had prepared for his friends. After they had taken their repast, Rosader rampier'd up the house, lest upon a sodain his brother should raise some crew of his tenants and surprise them unawares. But Saladyne took a contrary course, and went to the sheriff of the shire and made complaint of Rosader, who, giving credit to Saladyne, in a determined resolution to revenge the gentleman's wrongs, took with him five-and-twenty tall men, and made a vow either to break into the house and take Rosader, or else to coop him in till he made him yield by famine. In this determination, gathering a crew together, he went forward to set Saladyne in his former estate. News of this was brought unto Rosader, who, smiling at the cowardice of his brother, brook'd all the injuries of fortune with patience, expecting the coming of the sheriff. As he walk'd upon the battlements of the house, he descried where Saladyne and he drew near, with a troup of lusty gallants. At this he smil'd, and call'd up Adam Spencer, and shewed him the envious treachery of his brother and the folly of the sheriff to be so credulous.

"Now, Adam," quoth he, "what shall I do? It rests for me either to yield up the house to my brother and seek a reconcilement, or else issue out and break through the company with courage, for coop'd in like a coward I will not be. If I submit, ah, Adam, I dishonor myself, and that is worse than death, for by such open disgraces the fame of men grows odious. If I issue out amongst them, Fortune may favor me and I may escape with life. But suppose the worst; if I be slain, then my death shall be honorable to me and so inequal a revenge infamous to Saladyne."

"Why then, master, forward and fear not! Out amongst them; they be but faint-hearted lozels, and for Adam Spencer, if he die not at your foot, say he is a dastard."

These words cheered up so the heart of young Rosader that he thought himself sufficient for them all, and therefore prepared weapons for him and Adam Spencer, and were ready to intertain the sheriff; for no sooner came Saladyne and he to the gates but Rosader, unlook'd for, leap'd out and assailed them, wounded many of them, and caused the rest to give back, so that Adam and he broke through the prease in despite of them all, and took their way towards the forest of Arden. This repulse so set the sheriff's heart on fire to revenge that he straight raised all the country, and made hue and cry after them. But Rosader and Adam, knowing full well the secret ways that led through the vineyards, stole away privily through the province of Bordeaux, and escaped safe to the forest of Arden. Being come thether, they were glad they had so good a harbor; but Fortune, who is like the camelion, variable with every object and constant in nothing but inconstancy, thought to make them mirrors of her mutability, and therefore still cross'd them thus contrarily. Thinking still to pass on by the byways to get to Lyons, they chanced on a path that led into the thick of the forest, where they wand'red five or six days without meat, that they were almost famished, finding neither shepherd nor cottage to relieve them; and, hunger growing on so extreme, Adam Spencer, being old, began first to faint, and, sitting him down on a hill and looking about him, espied where Rosader lay as feeble and as ill perplexed, which sight made him shed tears and to fall into these bitter terms:

ADAM SPENCER'S SPEECH

"O, how the life of man may well be compared to the state of the ocean seas, that for every calm hath a thousand storms, resembling the rose tree, that for a few fair flowers hath a multitude of sharp prickles! All our pleasures end in pain, and our highest delights are crossed with deepest discontents. The joys of man, as they are few, so are they momentary, scarce ripe before they are rotten, and withering in the blossom, either parched with the heat of envy or Fortune. Fortune, O inconstant friend, that in all thy deeds art froward and fickle, delighting in the poverty of the lowest and the overthrow of the highest to decipher thy inconstancy, thou stand'st upon a globe, and thy wings are plumed with Time's feathers, that thou may'st ever be restless; thou art double-faced like Janus, carrying frowns in the one to threaten and smiles in the other to betray; thou profferest an eel and perfourmest a scorpion, and where thy greatest favors be, there is the fear of the extremest misfortunes, so variable are all thy actions. But why, Adam, dost thou exclaim against Fortune? She laughs at the plaints of the distressed, and there is nothing more pleasing unto her than to hear fools boast in her fading allurements, or sorrowful men to discover the sour of their passions. Glut her not, Adam, then with content, but thwart her with brooking all mishaps with patience. For there is no greater check to the pride of Fortune than with a resolute courage to pass over her crosses without care. Thou art old, Adam, and thy hairs wax white; the palm tree is already full of blooms, and in the furrows of thy face appears the calendars of death. Wert thou blessed by Fortune thy years could not be many, nor the date of thy life long; then, sith Nature must have her due, what is it for thee to resign her debt a little before the day? Ah, it is not this which grieveth me, nor do I care what mishaps Fortune can wage against me, but the sight of Rosader that galleth unto the quick. When I remember the worships of his house, the honor of his fathers, and the virtues of himself, then do I say that Fortune and the Fates are most injurious to censure so hard extremes against a youth of so great hope. O Rosader, thou art in the flower of thine age and in the pride of thy years, buxom and full of May. Nature hath prodigally inrich'd thee with her favors, and Virtue made thee the mirror of her excellence, and now, through the decree of the unjust stars, to have all these good parts nipped in the blade, and

blemish'd by the inconstancy of Fortune! Ah, Rosader, could I help thee, my grief were the less, and happy should my death be, if it might be the beginning of thy relief; but seeing we perish both in one extreme, it is a double sorrow. What shall I do? prevent the sight of his further misfortune with a present dispatch of mine own life? Ah, despair is a merciless sin!"

As he was ready to go forward in his passion, he looked earnestly on Rosader, and, seeing him change color, he rise up and went to him and, holding his temples, said:

"What cheer, master? Though all fail, let not the heart faint; the courage of a man is shewed in the resolution of his death."

At these words Rosader lifted up his eye and, looking on Adam Spencer, began to weep.

"Ah, Adam," quoth he, "I sorrow not to die, but I grieve at the manner of my death. Might I with my lance encounter the enemy, and so die in the field, it were honor and content; might I, Adam, combat with some wild beast and perish as his prey, I were satisfied; but to die with hunger, O Adam, it is the extremest of all extremes!"

"Master," quoth he, "you see we are both in one predicament, and long I cannot live without meat; seeing therefore we can find no food, let the death of the one preserve the life of the other. I am old, and overworn with age; you are young, and are the hope of many honors. Let me then die; I will presently cut my veins, and, master, with the warm blood relieve your fainting spirits; suck on that till I end, and you be comforted."

With that Adam Spencer was ready to pull out his knife, when Rosader, full of courage though very faint, rose up, and wish'd Adam Spencer to sit there till his retourn; "for my mind gives me," quoth he, "I shall bring thee meat." With that, like a madman, he rose up and ranged up and down the woods, seeking to encounter some wild beast with his rapier, that either he might carry his friend Adam food or else pledge his life in pawn of his loyalty.

It chanced that day that Gerismond, the lawful king of France banished by Torismond, who with a lusty crew of outlaws lived in that forest, that day in honor of his birth made a feast to all his bold yeomen, and frolick'd it with store of wine and venison, sitting all at a long table under the shadow of limon trees. To that place by chance Fortune conducted Rosader, who, seeing such a crew of brave men, having store of that for want of which he and Adam perished, he stepp'd boldly to the boord's end, and saluted the company thus:

"Whatsoever thou be that art master of these lusty squires, I salute thee as graciously as a man in extreme distress may; know that I and a fellow friend of mine are here famished in the forest for want of food; perish we must unless relieved by thy favors. Therefore, if thou be a gentleman, give meat to men, and to such men as are every way worthy of life. Let the proudest squire that sits at thy table rise and incounter with me in any honorable point of activity whatsoever, and if he and thou prove me not a man, send me away comfortless. If thou refuse this, as a niggard of thy cates, I will have amongst you with my sword; for rather will I die valiantly than perish with so cowardly an extreme."

Gerismond, looking him earnestly in the face, and seeing so proper a gentleman in so bitter a passion, was moved with so great pity that, rising from the table, he took him by the hand and bad him welcome, willing him to sit down in his place, and in his room not only to eat his fill but be lord of the feast.

"Gramercy, sir," quoth Rosader, "but I have a feeble friend that lies hereby famished almost for food, aged and therefore less able to abide the extremity of hunger than myself, and dishonor it were for me to taste one crumb before I made him partner of my fortunes; therefore I will run and fetch him, and then I will gratefully accept of your proffer."

Away hies Rosader to Adam Spencer, and tells him the news, who was glad of so happy fortune, but so feeble he was that he could not go; whereupon Rosader got him up on his back, and brought him to the place. Which when Gerismond and his men saw, they greatly applauded their league of friendship; and Rosader, having Gerismond's place assigned him, would not sit there himself, but set down Adam Spencer. Well, to be short, those hungry squires fell to their victuals, and feasted themselves with good delicates and great store of wine. As soon as they had taken their repast, Gerismond, desirous to hear what hard fortune drave them into those bitter extremes, requested Rosader to discourse, if it were not any way prejudicial unto him, the cause of his travel. Rosader, desirous any way to satisfy the courtesy of his favorable host, first beginning his exordium with a volley of sighs and a few lukewarm tears, prosecuted his discourse, and told him from point to point all his fortunes: how he was the youngest son of Sir John of Bordeaux, his name Rosader, how his brother sundry times had wronged him, and lastly how, for beating the sheriff and hurting his men, he fled.

"And this old man," quoth he, "whom I so much love and honor, is surnamed Adam Spencer, an old servant of my father's, and one that for his love never failed me in all my misfortunes."

When Gerismond heard this, he fell on the neck of Rosader, and next discoursing unto him how he was Gerismond, their lawful king exiled by Torismond, what familiarity had ever been betwixt his father, Sir John of Bordeaux, and him, how faithful a subject he lived, and how honorably he died, promising, for his sake, to give both him and his friend such courteous intertainment as his present estate could minister, and upon this made him one of his foresters. Rosader, seeing it was the king, crav'd pardon for his boldness, in that he did not do him due reverence, and humbly gave him thanks for his favorable courtesy. Gerismond, not satisfied yet with news, began to enquire if he had been lately in the court of Torismond, and whether he had seen his daughter Rosalynde or no. At this Rosader fetch'd a deep sigh and, shedding many tears, could not answer; yet at last, gathering his spirits together, he revealed unto the king how Rosalynde was banished, and how there was such a sympathy of affections between Alinda and her that she chose rather to be partaker of her exile than to part fellowship; whereupon the unnatural king banished them both; "and now they are wand'red none knows whether, neither could any learn since their departure the place of their abode." This news drive the king into a great melancholy, that presently he arose from all the company and went into his privy chamber, so secret as the harbor of the woods would allow him. The company was all dash'd at these tidings, and Rosader and Adam Spencer, having such opportunity, went to take their rest. Where we leave them, and return again to Torismond.

The flight of Rosader came to the ears of Torismond, who, hearing that Saladyne was sole heir of the lands of Sir John of Bordeaux, desirous to possess such fair revenues, found just occasion to quarrel with Saladyne about the wrongs he proff'red to his brother; and therefore, dispatching a herehault, he sent for Saladyne in all post-haste. Who, mervailing what the matter should be, began to examine his own conscience wherein he had offended his Highness; but imboldened with his innocence, he boldly went with the herehault unto the court; where, as soon as he came, he was not admitted into the presence of the king, but presently sent to prison. This greatly amazed Saladyne, chiefly in that the jailer had a straight charge over him to see that he should be close prisoner. Many passionate thoughts came in his head, till at last he began to fall into consideration of his former follies and to meditate with himself. . . . [The upshot is that Torismond, pretending to be enraged at Saladyne's treatment of Rosader, banishes him forever. The penitent villain bears his disgrace with humility, and determines to expiate his "former follies" by traveling "abroad in every coast till he had found out his brother Rosader."]

Rosader, being thus preferred to the place of a forester by Gerismond, rooted out the remembrance of his brother's unkindness by continual exercise, traversing the groves and wild forests, partly to hear the melody of the sweet birds which recorded, and partly to shew his diligent indeavor in his master's behalf. Yet whatsoever he did, or howsoever he walked, the lively image of Rosalynde remained in memory; on her sweet perfections he fed his thoughts, proving himself like the eagle a true-born bird, since as the one is known by beholding the sun, so was he by regarding excellent beauty. One day among the rest, finding a fit opportunity and place convenient, desirous to discover his woes to the woods, he engraved with his knife on the bark of a myrtle tree this pretty estimate of his mistress' perfection:

SONETTO

Of all chaste birds the phoenix doth excel,
Of all strong beasts the lion bears the bell,
Of all sweet flowers the rose doth sweetest smell,
Of all fair maids my Rosalynde is fairest.

Of all pure metals gold is only purest,
Of all high trees the pine hath highest crest,
Of all soft sweets I like my mistress' breast,
Of all chaste thoughts my mistress' thoughts are rarest.

Of all proud birds the eagle pleaseth Jove,
Of pretty fowls kind Venus likes the dove,
Of trees Minerva doth the olive love,
Of all sweet nymphs I honor Rosalynde.

Of all her gifts her wisdom pleaseth most,
Of all her graces virtue she doth boast.
For all these gifts my life and joy is lost
If Rosalynde prove cruel and unkind.

In these and such like passions Rosader did every day eternize the name of his Rosalynde; and this day especially when Aliena and Ganymede, inforced by the heat of the sun to seek for shelter, by good fortune arrived in that place where this amorous forester regist'red his melancholy passions. They saw the sodain change of his looks, his folded arms, his passionate sighs; they heard him often abruptly call on Rosalynde, who, poor soul, was as hotly burned as himself, but that she shrouded her pains in the cinders of honorable modesty. Whereupon, guessing him to be in love, and according to the nature of their sex being pitiful in that behalf, they sodainly brake off his melancholy by their approach,

and Ganymede shook him out of his dumps thus:

"What news, forester? hast thou wounded some deer and lost him in the fall? Care not, man, for so small a loss; thy fees was but the skin, the shoulder, and the horns; 'tis hunter's luck to aim fair and miss, and a woodman's fortune to strike and yet go without the game."

"Thou art beyond the mark, Ganymede," quoth Aliena; "his passions are greater, and his sighs discovers more loss; perhaps in traversing these thickets he hath seen some beautiful nymph, and is grown amorous."

"It may be so," quoth Ganymede, "for here he hath newly ingraven some sonnet; come, and see the discourse of the forester's poems."

Reading the sonnet over, and hearing him name Rosalynde, Aliena look'd on Ganymede and laugh'd, and Ganymede, looking back on the forester and seeing it was Rosader, blush'd; yet, thinking to shroud all under her page's apparel, she boldly returned to Rosader, and began thus:

"I pray thee tell me, forester, what is this Rosalynde for whom thou pinest away in such passions? Is she some nymph that waits upon Diana's train whose chastity thou hast deciph'red in such epethits? Or is she some shepherdess that haunts these plains whose beauty hath so bewitched thy fancy, whose name thou shadowest in covert under the figure of Rosalynde, as Ovid did Julia under the name of Corinna? Or say me forsooth, is it that Rosalynde of whom we shepherds have heard talk, she, forester, that is the daughter of Gerismond, that once was king, and now an outlaw in this forest of Arden?"

At this Rosader fetch'd a deep sigh, and said:

"It is she, O gentle swain, it is she; that saint it is whom I serve, that goddess at whose shrine I do bend all my devotions; the most fairest of all fairs, the phoenix of all that sex, and the purity of all earthly perfection."

"And why, gentle forester, if she be so beautiful, and thou so amorous, is there such a disagreement in thy thoughts? Happely she resembleth the rose that is sweet but full of prickles? or the serpent regius that hath scales as glorious as the sun and a breath as infectious as the aconitum is deadly? So thy Rosalynde may be most amiable and yet unkind; full of favor and yet froward, coy without wit, and disdainful without reason."

"O shepherd," quoth Rosader, "knewest thou her personage, graced with the excellence of all perfection, being a harbor wherein the Graces shroud their virtues, thou wouldst not breathe out such blasphemy against the beauteous Rosalynde. She is a diamond bright but not hard, yet of most chaste operation; a pearl so orient that it can be stained with no blemish; a rose without prickles; and a princess absolute as well in beauty as in virtue. But I, unhappy I, have let mine eye soar with the eagle against so bright a sun that I am quite blind; I have with Apollo enamored myself of a Daphne, not, as she, disdainful, but far more chaste than Daphne; I have with Ixion laid my love on Juno, and shall, I fear, embrace naught but a cloud. Ah, shepherd, I have reach'd at a star; my desires have mounted above my degree and my thoughts above my fortunes; I, being a peasant, having vent'red to gaze on a princess, whose honors are too high to vouchsafe such base loves."

"Why, forester," quoth Ganymede, "comfort thyself; be blithe and frolic, man. Love sowseth as low as she soareth high; Cupid shoots at a rag as soon as at a robe; and Venus' eye, that was so curious, sparkled favor on pole-footed Vulcan. Fear not, man; women's looks are not tied to dignity's feathers, nor make they curious esteem where the stone is found but what is the virtue. Fear not, forester; faint heart never won fair lady. But where lives Rosalynde now? at the court?"

"O no," quoth Rosader, "she lives I know not where, and that is my sorrow; banish'd by Torismond, and that is my hell; for might I but find her sacred personage, and plead before the bar of her pity the plaint of my passions, hope tells me she would grace me with some favor, and that would suffice as a recompense of all my former miseries."

"Much have I heard of thy mistress' excellence, and I know, forester, thou canst describe her at the full, as one that hast survey'd all her parts with a curious eye; then do me that favor to tell me what her perfections be."

"That I will," quoth Rosader, "for I glory to make all ears wonder at my mistress' excellence. . . ."

[Rosader then describes Rosalynde's merits and charms in a poem, and leaves the girls "to their prittle-prattle" with a promise to read them more of his passionate lyrics the next day. When they meet, as they had planned, Rosader, "fetching a deep sigh," bewails his sad lot in a "sonnet."]

ROSADER'S SONNET

In sorrow's cell I laid me down to sleep,
But waking woes were jealous of mine eyes;
They made them watch and bend themselves to weep,
But weeping tears their want could not suffice.
　　Yet since for her they wept who guides my heart,
　　They weeping smile, and triumph in their smart.

Of these my tears a fountain fiercely springs,
Where Venus bains herself incens'd with love,
Where Cupid bowseth his fair feath'red wings,
But I behold what pains I must approve.
　　Care drinks it dry, but when on her I think
　　Love makes me weep it full unto the brink.

Meanwhile my sighs yield truce unto my tears;
By them the winds increas'd and fiercely blow;
Yet when I sigh, the flame more plain appears,
And by their force with greater power doth glow.
　　Amids these pains, all phoenix-like I thrive,
　　Since love, that yields me death, may life revive.
　　　　Rosader en esperance

"Now, surely, forester," quoth Aliena, "when thou madest this sonnet thou wert in some amorous quandary, neither too fearful as despairing of thy mistress' favors, nor too gleesome as hoping in thy fortunes."

"I can smile," quoth Ganymede, "at the sonettos, canzons, madrigals, rounds, and roundelays that these pensive patients pour out when their eyes are more full of wantonness than their hearts of passions. Then, as the fishers put the sweetest bait to the fairest fish, so these Ovidians, holding *amo* in their tongues when their thoughts come at haphazard, write that they be wrapp'd in an endless laborinth of sorrow, when walking in the large leas of liberty they only have their humors in their inkpot. If they find women so fond that they will with such painted lures come to their lust, then they triumph till they be fullgorg'd with pleasures; and then fly they away, like ramage kites, to their own content, leaving the tame fool, their mistress, full of fancy, yet without ever a feather. If they miss, as dealing with some wary wanton that wants not such a one as themselves, but spies their subtilty, they end their amours with a few feigned sighs; and so their excuse is their mistress is cruel, and they smother passions with patience. Such, gentle forester, we may deem you to be, that rather pass away the time here in these woods with writing amorets than to be deeply enamored (as you say) of your Rosalynde." . . . [But Rosader, mournfully denying Ganymede's cynical taunts, insists on the sincerity of his passion in two more "sonnets," after which they all eat dinner.]

As soon as they had taken their repast, Rosader, giving them thanks for his good cheer, would have been gone, but Ganymede, that was loath to let him pass out of her presence, began thus: "Nay, forester," quoth he, "if thy business be not the greater, seeing thou sayst thou art so deeply in love, let me see how thou canst woo; I will represent Rosalynde, and thou shalt be as thou art, Rosader. See in some amorous eglogue, how if Rosalynde were present, how thou couldst court her; and while we sing of love, Aliena shall tune her pipe and play us melody." . . . [Thus they embark on a long "wooing eglogue" and so sing and pipe away the afternoon.]

All this while did poor Saladyne, banished from Bordeaux and the court of France by Torismond, wander up and down in the forest of Arden, thinking to get to Lyons, and so travel through Germany into Italy; but the forest being full of bypaths, and he unskilful of the country coast, slipp'd out of the way, and chanced up into the desart, not far from the place where Gerismond was, and his brother Rosader. Saladyne, weary with wand'ring up and down and hungry with long fasting, finding a little cave by the side of a thicket, eating such fruit as the forest did afford and contenting himself with such drink as nature had provided and thirst made delicate, after his repast he fell in a dead sleep. As thus he lay, a hungry lion came hunting down the edge of the grove for prey and, espying Saladyne, began to seize upon him; but seeing he lay still without any motion, he left to touch him, for that lions hate to prey on dead carcasses; and yet desirous to have some food, the lion lay down and watch'd to see if he would stir. While thus Saladyne slept secure, Fortune that was careful over her champion began to smile, and brought it so to pass that Rosader, having stricken a deer that, but lightly hurt, fled through the thicket, came pacing down by the grove with a boar-spear in his hand, in great haste. He spied where a man lay asleep, and a lion fast by him; amazed at this sight, as he stood gazing, his nose on the sodain bled, which made him conjecture it was some friend of his. Whereupon drawing more nigh, he might easely discern his visage, and perceived by his phisnomy that it was his brother Saladyne, which drave Rosader into a deep passion, as a man perplexed at the sight of so unexpected a chance, marveling what should drive his brother to traverse those secret desarts, without any company, in such distress and forlorn sort. But the present time craved no such doubting ambages, for either he must resolve to hazard his life for his relief, or else steal away and leave him to the cruelty of the lion. In which doubt he thus briefly debated with himself.

ROSADER'S MEDITATION

"Now, Rosader, Fortune that long hath whipp'd thee with nettles means to salve thee with roses, and, having cross'd thee with many frowns, now she presents thee with the brightness of her favors. Thou that didst count thyself the most distressed of all men mayst accompt thyself now the most fortunate amongst men, if Fortune can make men happy, or sweet revenge be wrapp'd in a pleasing content. Thou seest Saladyne thine enemy, the worker of thy misfortunes, and the efficient cause of thine exile, subject to the cruelty of a merciless lion, brought into this

misery by the gods, that they might seem just in revenging his rigor and thy injuries. Seest thou not how the stars are in a favorable aspect, the planets in some pleasing conjunction, the Fates agreeable to thy thoughts, and the Destinies perfourmers of thy desires, in that Saladyne shall die and thou free of his blood; he receive meed for his amiss and thou erect his tomb with innocent hands? Now, Rosader, shalt thou return to Bordeaux and enjoy thy possessions by birth and his revenues by inheritance; now mayst thou triumph in love and hang Fortune's altars with garlands. For when Rosalynde hears of thy wealth, it will make her love thee the more willingly; for women's eyes are made of chrisecoll, that is ever unperfect unless temp'red with gold, and Jupiter soonest enjoyed Danae because he came to her in so rich a shower. Thus shall this lion, Rosader, end the life of a miserable man, and from distress raise thee to be most fortunate." And with that, casting his boar-spear on his neck, away he began to trudge.

But he had not stepp'd back two or three paces, but a new motion stroke him to the very heart, that, resting his boar-spear against his breast, he fell into this passionate humor:

"Ah, Rosader, wert thou the son of Sir John of Bordeaux, whose virtues exceeded his valor, and yet the most hardiest knight in all Europe? Should the honor of the father shine in the actions of the son, and wilt thou dishonor thy parentage in forgetting the nature of a gentleman? Did not thy father at his last gasp breathe out this golden principle: Brothers' amity is like the drops of balsamum that salveth the most dangerous sores? Did he make a large exhort unto concord, and wilt thou shew thyself careless? O Rosader, what though Saladyne hath wronged thee, and made thee live an exile in the forest, shall thy nature be so cruel, or thy nurture so crooked, or thy thoughts so savage as to suffer so dismal a revenge? What, to let him be devoured by wild beasts! *Non sapit qui non sibi sapit* is fondly spoken in such bitter extremes. Loose not his life, Rosader, to win a world of treasure; for in having him thou hast a brother, and by hazarding for his life thou gettest a friend and reconcilest an enemy; and more honor shalt thou purchase by pleasuring a foe than revenging a thousand injuries."

With that his brother began to stir and the lion to rouse himself, whereupon Rosader sodainly charged him with the boar-spear, and wounded the lion very sore at the first stroke. The beast, feeling himself to have a mortal hurt, leap'd at Rosader, and with his paws gave him a sore pinch on the breast, that he had almost fall'n; yet as a man most valiant, in whom the sparks of Sir John of Bordeaux remained, he recovered himself, and in short combat slew the lion, who at his death roared so loud that

Saladyne awaked, and, starting up, was amazed at the sodain sight of so monstrous a beast lie slain by him, and so sweet a gentleman wounded. He presently, as he was of a ripe conceit, began to conjecture that the gentleman had slain him in his defense. Whereupon, as a man in a trance, he stood staring on them both a good while, not knowing his brother, being in that disguise. At last he burst into these terms:

"Sir, whatsoever thou be, as full of honor thou must needs be by the view of thy present valure, I perceive thou hast redress'd my fortunes by thy courage, and saved my life with thine own loss, which ties me to be thine in all humble service. Thanks thou shalt have as thy due, and more thou canst not have, for my ability denies me to perfourm a deeper debt. But if anyways it please thee to command me, use me as far as the power of a poor gentleman may stretch."

Rosader, seeing he was unknown to his brother, wond'red to hear such courteous words come from his crabbed nature; but, glad of such reformed nourture, he made this answer:

"I am, sir, whatsoever thou art, a forester and ranger of these walks, who, following my deer to the fall, was conducted hether by some assenting fate that I might save thee, and disparage myself. For, coming into this place, I saw thee asleep, and the lion watching thy awake, that at thy rising he might prey upon thy carcass. At the first sight I conjectured thee a gentleman, for all men's thoughts ought to be favorable in imagination, and I counted it the part of a resolute man to purchase a stranger's relief, though with the loss of his own blood; which I have perfourmed, thou seest, to mine own prejudice. If, therefore, thou be a man of such worth as I value thee by thy exterior liniaments, make discourse unto me what is the cause of thy present fortunes. For by the furrows in thy face thou seemest to be cross'd with her frowns; but whatsoever, or howsoever, let me crave that favor, to hear the tragic cause of thy estate."

Saladyne sitting down, and fetching a deep sigh, began thus:

SALADYNE'S DISCOURSE TO ROSADER UNKNOWN

"Although the discourse of my fortunes be the renewing of my sorrows, and the rubbing of the scar will open a fresh wound, yet that I may not prove ingrateful to so courteous a gentleman, I will rather sit down and sigh out my estate than give any offense by smothering my grief with silence. Know therefore, sir, that I am of Bordeaux, and the son and heir of Sir John of Bordeaux, a man for his virtues and valor so famous that I cannot think but the fame of his honors hath reach'd farther than the knowledge of his personage. The infortunate son of so fortunate

a knight am I; my name, Saladyne; who succeeding my father in possessions, but not in qualities, having two brethren committed by my father at his death to my charge, with such golden principles of brotherly concord as might have pierc'd like the sirens' melody into any human ear. But I, with Ulysses, became deaf against his philosophical harmony, and made more value of profit than of virtue, esteeming gold sufficient honor and wealth the fittest title for a gentleman's dignity. I set my middle brother to the university to be a scholler, counting it enough if he might pore on a book while I fed upon his revenues; and for the youngest, which was my father's joy, young Rosader"—and with that, naming of Rosader, Saladyne sate him down and wept. . . .

[At the sight of his brother's remorse Rosader reveals his identity. "Much ado there was between these two brethren, Saladyne in craving pardon and Rosader in forgiving and forgetting all former injuries; the one submiss, the other curteous, Saladyne penitent and passionate, Rosader kind and loving. . . ." When Rosader leads Saladyne to Gerismond, who welcomes him cordially, their reconciliation is complete, and so they sit down to a hearty meal of "red deer" provided by Adam Spencer.]

As soon as they had taken their repast and had well dined, Rosader took his brother Saladyne by the hand, and shewed him the pleasures of the forest, and what content they enjoyed in that mean estate. Thus for two or three days he walked up and down with his brother to shew him all the commodities that belonged to his walk.

In which time he was miss'd of his Ganymede, who mused greatly, with Aliena, what should become of their forester. Somewhile they thought he had taken some word unkindly, and had taken the pet; then they imagined some new love had withdrawn his fancy, or happely that he was sick, or detained by some great business of Gerismond's, or that he had made a reconcilement with his brother and so returned to Bordeaux.

These conjectures did they cast in their heads, but especially Ganymede, who, having love in her heart, proved restless and half without patience that Rosader wronged her with so long absence; for love measures every minute, and thinks hours to be days and days to be months, till they feed their eyes with the sight of their desired object. Thus perplexed lived poor Ganymede, while on a day, sitting with Aliena in a great dump, she cast up her eye, and saw where Rosader came pacing towards them with his forest bill on his neck. At that sight her color chang'd, and she said to Aliena:

"See, mistress, where our jolly forester comes."

"And you are not a little glad thereof," quoth Aliena; "your nose bewrays what porredge you love;

the wind cannot be tied within his quarter, the sun shadowed with a veil, oil hidden in water, nor love kept out of a woman's looks; but no more of that, *lupus est in fabula*."

As soon as Rosader was come within the reach of her tongue's end, Aliena began thus:

"Why, how now, gentle forester, what wind hath kept you from hence? that, being so newly married, you have no more care of your Rosalynde but to absent yourself so many days? Are these the passions you painted out so in your sonnets and roundelays? I see well hot love is soon cold, and that the fancy of men is like to a loose feather that wand'reth in the air with the blast of every wind."

"You are deceived, mistress," quoth Rosader; "'twas a copy of unkindness that kept me hence, in that, I being married, you carried away the bride; but if I have given any occasion of offense by absenting myself these three days, I humbly sue for pardon, which you must grant of course, in that the fault is so friendly confess'd with penance. But to tell you the truth, fair mistress and my good Rosalynde, my eldest brother by the injury of Torismond is banished from Bordeaux, and by chance he and I met in the forest."

And here Rosader discours'd unto them what had happ'ned betwixt them, which reconcilement made them glad, especially Ganymede. But Aliena, hearing of the tyranny of her father, grieved inwardly, and yet smoth'red all things with such secrecy that the concealing was more sorrow than the conceipt; yet that her estate might be hid still, she made fair weather of it, and so let all pass.

Fortune, that saw how these parties valued not her deity but held her power in scorn, thought to have a bout with them, and brought the matter to pass thus. Certain rascals that lived by prowling in the forest, who for fear of the provost marshal had caves in the groves and thickets to shrowd themselves from his trains, hearing of the beauty of this fair shepherdess Aliena, thought to steal her away, and to give her to the king for a present; hoping, because the king was a great lecher, by such a gift to purchase all their pardons, and therefore came to take her and her page away. Thus resolved, while Aliena and Ganymede were in this sad talk, they came rushing in, and laid violent hands upon Aliena and her page, which made them cry out to Rosader; who, having the valor of his father stamped in his heart, thought rather to die in defense of his friends than any way be touch'd with the least blemish of dishonor, and therefore dealt such blows amongst them with his weapon as he did witness well upon their carcasses that he was no coward. But as *ne Hercules quidem contra duos,* so Rosader could not resist a multitude, having none to back him; so that

he was not only rebated but sore wounded, and Aliena and Ganymede had been quite carried away by these rascals had not Fortune, that meant to turn her frown into a favor, brought Saladyne that way by chance, who, wand'ring to find out his brother's walk, encount'red this crew; and, seeing not only a shepherdess and her boy forced but his brother wounded, he heaved up a forest bill he had on his neck, and the first he stroke had never after more need of the phisition, redoubling his blows with such courage that the slaves were amazed at his valor. Rosader, espying his brother so fortunately arrived, and seeing how valiantly he behaved himself, though sore wounded rushed amongst them, and laid on such load that some of the crew were slain and the rest fled, leaving Aliena and Ganymede in the possession of Rosader and Saladyne.

Aliena, after she had breathed awhile and was come to herself from this fear, look'd about her, and saw where Ganymede was busy dressing up the wounds of the forester; but she cast her eye upon this courteous champion that had made so hot a rescue, and that with such affection that she began to measure every part of him with favor, and in herself to commend his personage and his virtue, holding him for a resolute man that durst assail such a troop of unbridled villains. At last, gathering her spirits together, she returned him these thanks:

"Gentle sir, whatsoever you be that have adventured your flesh to relieve our fortunes, as we hold you valiant so we esteem you courteous and to have as many hidden virtues as you have manifest resolutions. We poor shepherds have no wealth but our flocks, and therefore can we not make requital with any great treasures; but our recompense is thanks, and our rewards to our friends without feigning. For ransom, therefore, of this our rescue, you must content yourself to take such a kind gramercy as a poor shepherdess and her page may give, with promise, in what we may, never to prove ingrateful. For this gentleman that is hurt, young Rosader, he is our good neighbor and familiar acquaintance; we'll pay him with smiles and feed him with love-looks, and though he be never the fatter at the year's end, yet we'll so hamper him that he shall hold himself satisfied."

Saladyne, hearing this shepherdess speak so wisely, began more narrowly to pry into her perfection and to survey all her liniaments with a curious insight, so long dallying in the flame of her beauty that to his cost he found her to be most excellent. For Love that lurked in all these broils to have a blow or two, seeing the parties at the gaze, encount'red them both with such a veny that the stroke pierc'd to the heart so deep as it could never after be raced out. . . .

[But the three pairs of lovers—Rosader and Rosalynde, Saladyne and Alinda, Montanus and Phoebe—are, through one reason or another, frustrated in their desires. As Aliena and Ganymede ("both of them amorous, and yet diversely affected") sit pensively under an olive tree, old Corydon comes to fetch them that they may overhear, from the concealment of a thicket, Montanus' passionate wooing of the disdainful Phoebe. Montanus plies her with both English and French poems, but to no avail. Finally, Ganymede becomes so incensed at her coy and scornful behavior that she breaks in upon the startled pair.]

Ganymede, overhearing all these passions of Montanus, could not brook the cruelty of Phoebe, but starting from behind the bush said:

"And if, damsel, you fled from me, I would transform you as Daphne to a bay, and then in contempt trample your branches under my feet."

Phoebe at this sodain reply was amazed, especially when she saw so fair a swain as Ganymede; blushing therefore, she would have been gone, but that he held her by the hand, and prosecuted his reply thus:

"What, shepherdess, so fair and so cruel? Disdain beseems not cottages, nor coyness maids; for either they be condempned to be too proud or too froward. Take heed, fair nymph, that in despising love you be not overreach'd with love, and in shaking off all, shape yourself to your own shadow, and so with Narcissus prove passionate and yet unpitied. Oft have I heard, and sometimes have I seen, high disdain turn'd to hot desires. Because thou art beautiful be not so coy; as there is nothing more fair, so there is nothing more fading—as momentary as the shadows which grows from a cloudy sun. Such, my fair shepherdess, as disdain in youth desire in age, and then are they hated in the winter that might have been loved in the prime. A wrinkled maid is like to a parched rose, that is cast up in coffers to please the smell, not worn in the hand to content the eye. There is no folly in love to *had I wist,* and therefore be rul'd by me. Love while thou art young, lest thou be disdained when thou art old. Beauty nor time cannot be recall'd, and if thou love, like of Montanus; for as his desires are many, so his deserts are great."

Phoebe all this while gazed on the perfection of Ganymede, as deeply enamored on his perfection as Montanus inveigled with hers; for her eye made survey of his excellent feature, which she found so rare that she thought the ghost of Adonis had been leap'd from Elysium in the shape of a swain. When she blush'd at her own folly to look so long on a stranger, she mildly made answer to Ganymede thus:

"I cannot deny, sir, but I have heard of Love, though I never felt love; and have read of such a goddess as Venus, though I never saw any but her picture; and, perhaps"—and with that she wex'd red and bashful and withal silent; which Ganymede perceiving, commended in herself the bashfulness of the maid, and desired her to go forward.

"And perhaps, sir," quoth she, "mine eye hath been more prodigal today than ever before"—and with that she stay'd again, as one greatly passionate and perplexed.

Aliena, seeing the hare through the maze, bade her forward with her prattle, but in vain; for at this abrupt period she broke off, and with her eyes full of tears, and her face covered with a vermillion dye, she sate down and sighth. Whereupon Aliena and Ganymede, seeing the shepherdess in such a strange plight, left Phoebe with her Montanus, wishing her friendly that she would be more pliant to Love, lest in penance Venus joined her to some sharp repentance. Phoebe made no reply, but fetch'd such a sigh that Echo made relation of her plaint, giving Ganymede such an adieu with a piercing glance that the amorous girl-boy perceived Phoebe was pinch'd by the heel. . . .

[Meanwhile, Saladyne continues his suit to Aliena, who, though powerfully attracted to him, cannot overcome her doubts of all men's constancy.]

Saladyne, hearing how Aliena harp'd still upon one string, which was the doubt of men's constancy, he broke off her sharp invective thus: "I grant, Aliena," quoth he, "many men have done amiss in proving soon ripe and soon rotten; but particular instances infer no general conclusions, and therefore I hope what others have faulted in shall not prejudice my favors. I will not use sophistry to confirm my love, for that is subtilty; nor long discourses lest my words might be thought more than my faith; but if this will suffice, that by the honor of a gentleman I love Aliena, and woo Aliena, not to crop the blossoms and reject the tree, but to consummate my faithful desires in the honorable end of marriage."

At this word "marriage" Aliena stood in a maze what to answer, fearing that if she were too coy, to drive him away with her disdain, and if she were too courteous, to discover the heat of her desires. In a dilemma thus what to do, at last this she said: "Saladyne, ever since I saw thee I favored thee; I cannot dissemble my desires because I see thou dost faithfully manifest thy thoughts, and in liking thee I love thee so far as mine honor holds fancy still in suspense; but if I knew thee as virtuous as thy father or as well qualified as thy brother Rosader, the doubt should be quickly decided; but for this time to give thee an answer, assure thyself this, I will either marry with Saladyne or still live a virgin."

And with this they strained one another's hand; which Ganymede espying, thinking he had had his mistress long enough at shrift, said, "What, a match or no?"

"A match," quoth Aliena, "or else it were an ill market."

"I am glad," quoth Ganymede. "I would Rosader were well here to make up a mess."

"Well rememb'red," quoth Saladyne. "I forgot I left my brother Rosader alone, and therefore lest being solitary he should increase his sorrows, I will haste me to him. May it please you, then, to command me any service to him, I am ready to be a dutiful messenger."

"Only at this time commend me to him," quoth Aliena, "and tell him though we cannot pleasure him we pray for him."

"And forget not," quoth Ganymede, "my commendations; but say to him that Rosalynde sheds as many tears from her heart as he drops of blood from his wounds, for the sorrow of his misfortunes, feathering all her thoughts with disquiet till his welfare procure her content. Say thus, good Saladyne, and so farewell."

He, having his message, gave a courteous adieu to them both, especially to Aliena, and so, playing "Loath to depart," went to his brother. But Aliena, she perplexed and yet joyful, pass'd away the day pleasantly, still praising the perfection of Saladyne, not ceasing to chat of her new love till evening drew on; and then they, folding their sheep, went home to bed. Where we leave them and return to Phoebe. . . .

[Phoebe is in a truly sad plight: infatuated with Ganymede and despairing of his love, she loses her appetite, becomes ill, takes to her bed, and resorts to literary composition in the form of amorous epistles and poems. She commissions the luckless and faithful Montanus to deliver them to Ganymede. When he does so, Ganymede resolves to disabuse him.]

"I tell thee, Montanus, in courting Phoebe thou barkest with the wolves of Syria against the moon, and rovest at such a mark with thy thoughts as is beyond the pitch of thy bow, praying to Love when Love is pitiless and thy malady remediless. For proof, Montanus, read these letters, wherein thou shalt see thy great follies and little hope."

With that Montanus took them and perused them, but with such sorrow in his looks as they bewrayed a source of confused passions in his heart; at every line his color changed, and every sentence was ended with a period of sighs.

At last, noting Phoebe's extreme desire toward Ganymede and her disdain towards him, giving Ganymede the letter, the shepherd stood as though he had neither won nor lost. Which Ganymede perceiving wakened him out of his dream thus:

"Now, Montanus, dost thou see thou vowest great service and obtainest but little reward? But in lieu of thy loyalty, she maketh thee, as Bellerophon, carry thine own bane. Then drink not willingly of that potion wherein thou knowest is poison; creep not to her that cares not for thee. What, Montanus, there are many as fair as Phoebe, but most of all more courteous than Phoebe. I tell thee, shepherd, favor is love's fuel; then since thou canst not get that, let the flame vanish into smoke, and rather sorrow for a while than repent thee forever."

"I tell thee, Ganymede," quoth Montanus, "as they which are stung with the scorpion cannot be recovered but by the scorpion, nor he that was wounded with Achilles' lance be cured but with the same trunchion, so Apollo was fain to cry out that love was only eased with love and fancy healed by no medicine but favor. Phoebus had herbs to heal all hurts but this passion; Circes had charms for all chances but for affection, and Mercury subtil reasons to refell all griefs but love. Persuasions are bootless, reason lends no remedy, counsail no comfort, to such whom fancy hath made resolute; and therefore though Phoebe loves Ganymede, yet Montanus must honor none but Phoebe."

"Then," quoth Ganymede, "may I rightly term thee a despairing lover, that livest without joy and lovest without hope. But what shall I do, Montanus, to pleasure thee? Shall I despise Phoebe, as she disdains thee?"

"O," quoth Montanus, "that were to renew my griefs and double my sorrows; for the sight of her discontent were the censure of my death. Alas, Ganymede! though I perish in my thoughts, let not her die in her desires. Of all passions, love is most impatient; then let not so fair a creature as Phoebe sink under the burden of so deep a distress. Being lovesick, she is proved heartsick, and all for the beauty of Ganymede. Thy proportion hath entangled her affection, and she is snared in the beauty of thy excellence. Then, sith she loves thee so dear, mislike not her deadly. Be thou paramour to such a paragon; she hath beauty to content thine eye and flocks to enrich thy store. Thou canst not wish for more than thou shalt win by her; for she is beautiful, virtuous, and wealthy, three deep persuasions to make love frolic."

Aliena, seeing Montanus cut it against the hair and plead that Ganymede ought to love Phoebe, when his only life was the love of Phoebe, answered him thus:

"Why, Montanus, dost thou further this motion, seeing if Ganymede marry Phoebe thy market is clean marr'd?"

"Ah, mistress," quoth he, "so hath love taught me to honor Phoebe that I would prejudice my life to pleasure her, and die in despair rather than she should perish for want. It shall suffice me to see [her] contented, and to feed mine eye on her favor. If she marry, though it be my martyrdom, yet if she be pleased I will brook it with patience, and triumph in mine own stars to see her desires satisfied. Therefore, if Ganymede be as courteous as he is beautiful, let him shew his virtues in redressing Phoebe's miseries." And this Montanus pronounc'd with such an assured countenance that it amazed both Aliena and Ganymede to see the resolution of his loves; so that they pitied his passions and commended his patience, devising how they might by any subtilty get Montanus the favor of Phoebe. Straight, as women's heads are full of wiles, Ganymede had a fetch to force Phoebe to fancy the shepherd, *malgrado* the resolution of her mind; he prosecuted his policy thus:

"Montanus," quoth he, "seeing Phoebe is so forlorn, lest I might be counted unkind in not salving so fair a creature, I will go with thee to Phoebe, and there hear herself in word utter that which she hath discours'd with her pen; and then, as love wills me, I will set down my censure. I will home by our house, and send Corydon to accompany Aliena."

Montanus seemed glad of this determination and away they go towards the house of Phoebe. When they drew nigh to the cottage, Montanus ran afore, and went in and told Phoebe that Ganymede was at the door. This word "Ganymede," sounding in the ears of Phoebe, drave her into such an ecstasy for joy that, rising up in her bed, she was half revived, and her wan color began to wax red; and with that came Ganymede in, who saluted Phoebe with such a curteous look that it was half a salve to her sorrows. Sitting him down by her bedside, he questioned about her disease, and where the pain chiefly held her. Phoebe, looking as lovely as Venus in her night-gear, tainting her face with as ruddy a blush as Clytia did when she bewrayed her loves to Phoebus, taking Ganymede by the hand, began thus:

"Fair shepherd, if Love were not more strong then Nature, or fancy the sharpest extreme, my immodesty were the more and my virtues the less; for Nature hath framed women's eyes bashful, their hearts full of fear, and their tongues full of silence; but Love, that imperious Love, where his power is predominant, then he perverts all and wresteth the wealth of Nature to his own will: an instance in myself, fair Ganymede, for such a fire hath he kindled in my thoughts that to find ease for the flame, I was forced to pass the bounds of modesty, and seek a salve at thy hands for my secret harms. Blame me not if I be overbold, for it is thy beauty; and if I be too forward, it is fancy and the deep insight into thy virtues that makes me thus fond; for let me say in a word what may be contained in a volume: Phoebe loves Ganymede."

At this she held down her head and wept, and

Ganymede rose as one that would suffer no fish to hang on his fingers, made this reply:

"Water not thy plants, Phoebe, for I do pity thy plaints, nor seek not to discover thy loves in tears, for I conjecture thy trueth by thy passions; sorrow is no salve for loves, nor sighs no remedy for affection. Therefore frolic, Phoebe; for if Ganymede can cure thee, doubt not of recovery. Yet this let me say without offense, that it grieves me to thwart Montanus in his fancies, seeing his desires have been so resolute and his thoughts so loyal. But thou alledgest that thou art forc'd from him by fate; so I tell thee, Phoebe, either some star or else some destiny fits my mind rather with Adonis to die in chase than be counted a wanton in Venus' knee. Although I pity thy martyrdom, yet I can grant no marriage; for though I held thee fair, yet mine eye is not fettered. Love grows not, like the herb spattana, to his perfection in one night, but creeps with the snail, and yet at last attains to the top. *Festina lente,* especially in love, for momentary fancies are ofttimes the fruits of follies. If, Phoebe, I should like thee as the Hyperborei do their dates, which banquet with them in the morning and throw them away at night, my folly should be great, and thy repentance more. Therefore I will have time to turn my thoughts, and my loves shall grow up as the watercresses, slowly, but with a deep root. Thus, Phoebe, thou mayst see I disdain not, though I desire not; remaining indifferent till time and love makes me resolute. Therefore, Phoebe, seek not to suppress affection, and with the love of Montanus quench the remembrance of Ganymede; strive thou to hate me as I seek to like of thee, and ever have the duties of Montanus in thy mind, for I promise thee thou mayst have one more wealthy, but not more loyal." These words were corasives to the perplexed Phoebe, that sobbing out sighs, and straining out tears, she blubbered out these words:

"And shall I then have no salve of Ganymede but suspense, no hope but a doubtful hazard, no comfort, but be posted off to the will of time? Justly have the gods balanc'd my fortunes, who, being cruel to Montanus, found Ganymede as unkind to myself; so in forcing him perish for love, I shall die myself with overmuch love."

"I am glad," quoth Ganymede, "you look into your own faults, and see where your shoe wrings you, measuring now the pains of Montanus by your own passions."

"Truth," quoth Phoebe, "and so deeply I repent me of my frowardness toward the shepherd that, could I cease to love Ganymede, I would resolve to like Montanus."

"What, if I can with reason persuade Phoebe to

mislike of Ganymede, will she then favor Montanus?"

"When reason," quoth she, "doth quench that love that I owe to thee, then will I fancy him; conditionally, that if my love can be suppress'd with no reason, as being without reason, Ganymede will only wed himself to Phoebe."

"I grant it, fair shepherdess," quoth he; "and to feed thee with the sweetness of hope, this resolve on: I will never marry myself to woman but unto thyself."

And with that Ganymede gave Phoebe a fruitless kiss and such words of comfort that before Ganymede departed she arose out of her bed and made him and Montanus such cheer as could be found in such a country cottage; Ganymede in the midst of their banquet rehearsing the promises of either in Montanus' favor, which highly pleased the shepherd. Thus, all three content and soothed up in hope, Ganymede took his leave of his Phoebe and departed, leaving her a contented woman, and Montanus highly pleased. But poor Ganymede, who had her thoughts on her Rosader, when she call'd to remembrance his wounds, fill'd her eyes full of tears and her heart full of sorrows, plodded to find Aliena at the folds, thinking with her presence to drive away her passions. As she came on the plains she might espy where Rosader and Saladyne sate with Aliena under the shade; which sight was a salve to her grief, and such a cordial unto her heart that she tripp'd alongst the lawns full of joy.

At last Corydon, who was with them, spied Ganymede, and with that the clown rose, and, running to meet him, cried:

"O sirrah, a match, a match! our mistress shall be married on Sunday."

Thus the poor peasant frolick'd it before Ganymede, who coming to the crew saluted them all, and especially Rosader, saying that he was glad to see him so well recovered of his wounds.

"I had not gone abroad so soon," quoth Rosader, "but that I am bidden to a marriage, which, on Sunday next, must be solempnized between my brother and Aliena. I see well where love leads delay is loathsome, and that small wooing serves where both the parties are willing."

"Truth," quoth Ganymede; "but a happy day should it be if Rosader that day might be married to Rosalynde."

"Ah, good Ganymede," quoth he, "by naming Rosalynde, renew not my sorrows; for the thought of her perfections is the thrall of my miseries."

"Tush, be of good cheer, man," quoth Ganymede; "I have a friend that is deeply experienc'd in negromancy and magic; what art can do shall be acted for thine advantage. I will cause him to bring in Rosalynde, if either France or any bordering nation harbor her; and upon that take the faith of a young shepherd."

Aliena smil'd to see how Rosader frown'd, thinking that Ganymede had jested with him. But, breaking off from those matters, the page, somewhat pleasant, began to discourse unto them what had pass'd between him and Phoebe; which, as they laugh'd, so they wond'red at, all confessing that there is none so chaste but love will change. Thus they pass'd away the day in chat, and when the sun began to set they took their leaves and departed; Aliena providing for their marriage day such solempn cheer and handsome robes as fitted their country estate, and yet somewhat the better, in that Rosader had promised to bring Gerismond thether as a guest. Ganymede, who then meant to discover herself before her father, had made her a gown of green and a kirtle of the finest sendal, in such sort that she seemed some heavenly nymph harbored in country attire.

Saladyne was not behind in care to set out the nuptials, nor Rosader unmindful to bid guests, who invited Gerismond and all his followers to the feast, who willingly granted, so that there was nothing but the day wanting to this marriage.

In the meanwhile, Phoebe being a bidden guest made herself as gorgeous as might be to please the eye of Ganymede; and Montanus suited himself with the cost of many of his flocks to be gallant against that day, for then was Ganymede to give Phoebe an answer of her loves, and Montanus either to hear the doom of his misery or the censure of his happiness. But while this gear was a-brewing, Phoebe pass'd not one day without visiting her Ganymede, so far was she wrapp'd in the beauties of this lovely swain. Much prattle they had and the discourse of many passions, Phoebe wishing for the day, as she thought, of her welfare, and Ganymede smiling to think what unexpected events would fall out at the wedding. In these humors the week went away, that at last Sunday came.

No sooner did Phoebus' henchman appear in the sky, to give warning that his master's horses should be trapp'd in his glorious coach, but Corydon, in his holiday suit, mervailous seemly, in a russet jacket, welted with the same and faced with red worsted, having a pair of blue chamlet sleeves, bound at the wrests with four yellow laces, closed afore very richly with a dozen of pewter buttons; his hose was of gray karsie, with a large slop barr'd overthwart the pocketholes with three fair guards, stitch'd of either side with red thread; his stock was of the own, sewed close to his breech, and for to beautify his hose he had truss'd himself round with a dozen of newthreaden points of medley color; his bonnet was green, whereon stood a copper brooch with the picture of Saint Denis; and to want nothing that might make him amorous in his old days, he had a fair shirt-band of fine lockram, whipp'd over with Coventry blue of no small cost. Thus attired, Corydon bestirr'd himself as chief stickler in these actions, and had strowed all the house with flowers, that it seemed rather some of Flora's choice bowers than any country cottage.

Thether repaired Phoebe with all the maids of the forest, to set out the bride in the most seemliest sort that might be; but howsoever she help'd to prank out Aliena, yet her eye was still on Ganymede, who was so neat in a suit of gray that he seemed Endymion when he won Luna with his looks, or Paris when he play'd the swain to get the beauty of the nymph Oenone. Ganymede, like a pretty page, waited on his mistress Aliena, and overlook'd that all was in a readiness against the bridegroom should come; who, attired in a forester's suit, came accompanied with Gerismond and his brother Rosader early in the morning; where arrived, they were solempnly entertaine d by Aliena and the rest of the country swains, Gerismond very highly commending the fortunate choice of Saladyne, in that he had chosen a shepherdess whose virtues appeared in her outward beauties, being no less fair than seeming modest.

Ganymede, coming in and seeing her father, began to blush, Nature working affects by her secret effects. Scarce could she abstain from tears to see her father in so low fortunes—he that was wont to sit in his royal palaice, attended on by twelve noble peers, now to be contented with a simple cottage and a troup of reveling woodmen for his train. The consideration of his fall made Ganymede full of sorrows; yet, that she might triumph over Fortune with patience and not any way dash that merry day with her dumps, she smothered her melancholy with a shadow of mirth, and very reverently welcomed the king, not according to his former degree but to his present estate, with such diligence as Gerismond began to commend the page for his exquisite person and excellent qualities.

As thus the king with his foresters frolick'd it among the shepherds, Corydon came in with a fair mazer full of cider and presented it to Gerismond with such a clownish salute that he began to smile, and took it of the old shepherd very kindly, drinking to Aliena and the rest of her fair maids, amongst whom Phoebe was the foremost. Aliena pledged the king and drunk to Rosader; so the carowse went round from him to Phoebe, etc. As they were thus drinking and ready to go to church, came in Montanus, appareled all in tawny, to signify that he was forsaken; on his head he wore a garland of willow, his bottle hanged by his side, whereon was painted despair, and on his sheep-hook hung two sonnets, as labels of his loves and fortunes. . . .

[When Gerismond learns of Montanus' hopeless passion and reads his poetry he commands that Phoebe be brought before him. When he taxes her with cruelty to her faithful lover she replies that her case is as hopeless as Montanus'. "I am in love with a shepherd's swain, as coy to me as I am cruel to Montanus, as peremptory in disdain as I was perverse in desire. And that is . . . Aliena's page, young Ganymede."]

Gerismond, desirous to prosecute the end of these passions, called in Ganymede, who, knowing the case, came in graced with such a blush as beautified the crystal of his face with a ruddy brightness. The king, noting well the phisnomy of Ganymede, began by his favors to call to mind the face of his Rosalynde, and with that fetch'd a deep sigh. Rosader, that was passing familiar with Gerismond, demanded of him why he sighth so sore.

"Because, Rosader," quoth he, "the favor of Ganymede puts me in mind of Rosalynde."

At this word Rosader sight so deeply as though his heart would have burst.

"And what's the matter," quoth Gerismond, "that you quite me with such a sigh?"

"Pardon me, sir," quoth Rosader, "because I love none but Rosalynde."

"And upon that condition," quoth Gerismond, "that Rosalynde were here, I would this day make up a marriage betwixt her and thee."

At this Aliena turn'd her head and smil'd upon Ganymede, and she could scarce keep countenance. Yet she salved all with secrecy; and Gerismond, to drive away such dumps, questioned with Ganymede what the reason was he regarded not Phoebe's love, seeing she was as fair as the wanton that brought Troy to ruin. Ganymede mildly answered:

"If I should affect the fair Phoebe, I should offer poor Montanus great wrong to win that from him in a moment that he hath labored for so many months. Yet have I promised to the beautiful shepherdess to wed myself never to woman except unto her; but with this promise, that if I can by reason suppress Phoebe's love towards me, she shall like of none but of Montanus."

"To that," quoth Phoebe, "I stand; for my love is so far beyond reason as will admit no persuasion of reason."

"For justice," quoth he, "I appeal to Gerismond."

"And to his censure will I stand," quoth Phoebe.

"And in your victory," quoth Montanus, "stands the hazard of my fortunes; for if Ganymede go away with conquest, Montanus is in conceipt love's monarch; if Phoebe win, then am I in effect most miserable."

"We will see this controversy," quoth Gerismond, "and then we will to church. Therefore, Ganymede, let us hear your argument."

"Nay, pardon my absence awhile," quoth she, "and you shall see one in store."

In went Ganymede and dress'd herself in woman's attire, having on a gown of green, with kirtle of rich sandal, so quaint that she seemed Diana triumphing in the forest; upon her head she wore a chaplet of roses, which gave her such a grace that she looked like Flora perk'd in the pride of all her flowers. Thus attired came Rosalynde in, and presented herself at her father's feet, with her eyes full of tears, craving his blessing, and discoursing unto him all her fortunes, how she was banished by Torismond, and how ever since she lived in that country disguised.

Gerismond, seeing his daughter, rose from his seat and fell upon her neck, utt'ring the passions of his joy in wat'ry plaints, driven into such an ecstasy of content that he could not utter one word. At this sight if Rosader was both amazed and joyful, I refer myself to the judgment of such as have experience in love, seeing his Rosalynde before his face whom so long and deeply he had affected. At last Gerismond recovered his spirits, and in most fatherly terms entertained his daughter Rosalynde, after many questions demanding of her what had pass'd between her and Rosader.

"So much, sir," quoth she, "as there wants nothing but your grace to make up the marriage."

"Why, then," quoth Gerismond, "Rosader, take her: she is thine, and let this day solemnize both thy brother's and thy nuptials." Rosader, beyond measure content, humbly thanked the king, and imbraced his Rosalynde, who, turning towards Phoebe, demanded if she had shewn sufficient reason to suppress the force of her loves.

"Yea," quoth Phoebe, "and so great a persuasive that, please it you, madame, and Aliena to give us leave, Montanus and I will make this day the third couple in marriage."

She had no sooner spake this word but Montanus threw away his garland of willow, his bottle, where was painted dispair, and cast his sonnets in the fire, shewing himself as frolic as Paris when he hanseled his love with Helena. At this Gerismond and the rest smiled, and concluded that Montanus and Phoebe should keep their wedding with the two brethren. Aliena, seeing Saladyne stand in a dump, to wake him from his dream began thus:

"Why how now, my Saladyne, all amort? What, melancholy, man, at the day of marriage? Perchance thou art sorrowful to think on thy brother's high fortunes, and thine own base desires to choose so mean a shepherdess. Cheer up thy heart, man; for this day thou shalt be married to the daughter of a king; for know, Saladyne, I am not Aliena, but Alinda, the daughter of thy mortal enemy Torismond."

At this all the company was amazed, especially Gerismond, who, rising up, took Alinda in his arms, and said to Rosalynde:

"Is this that fair Alinda famous for so many virtues, that forsook her father's court to live with thee exil'd in the country?"

"The same," quoth Rosalynde.

"Then," quoth Gerismond, turning to Saladyne, "jolly forester, be frolic, for thy fortunes are great, and thy desires excellent; thou hast got a princess as famous for her perfection as exceeding in proportion."

"And she hath with her beauty won," quoth Saladyne, "an humble servant as full of faith as she of amiable favor."

While everyone was amazed with these comical events, Corydon came skipping in and told them that the priest was at church and tarried for their coming. With that Gerismond led the way, and the rest followed; where to the admiration of all the country swains in Arden their marriages were solemnly solemnized. As soon as the priest had finished, home they went with Alinda, where Corydon had made all things in readiness. Dinner was provided, and the tables being spread and the brides set down by Gerismond, Rosader, Saladyne, and Montanus that day were servitors; homely cheer they had, such as their country could afford, but to mend their fare they had mickle good chat, and many discourses of their loves and fortunes. About mid-dinner, to make them merry, Corydon came in with an old crowd, and play'd them a fit of mirth, to which he sung this pleasant song:

CORYDON'S SONG

A blithe and bonny country lass
   (Heigh ho, the bonny lass!)
Sat sighing on the tender grass
   And weeping said, "Will none come woo me?"
A smicker boy, a lither swain
   (Heigh ho, a smicker swain!),
That in his love was wanton fain,
   With smiling looks straight came unto her.

Whenas the wanton wench espy'd
   (Heigh ho, when she espy'd!)
The means to make herself a bride
   She simp'red smooth like bonnibell;
The swain, that saw her squint-eyed kind
   (Heigh ho, so squint-eyed kind!),
His arms about her body twin'd,
   And said, "Fair lass, how fare ye, well?"

The country kit said, "Well, forsooth
   (Heigh ho, well forsooth!),
But that I have a longing tooth,
   A longing tooth that makes me cry."
"Alas," said he, "what gars thy grief?
   (Heigh ho, what gars thy grief?)"
"A wound," quoth she, "without relief,
   I fear a maid that I shall die."

"If that be all," the shepherd said
   (Heigh ho, the shepherd said!),
"I'll make thee wive it, gentle maid,
   And so recure thy malady."
Hereon they kiss'd with many a oath
   (Heigh ho, with many a oath!),
And fore God Pan did plight their troath,
   And to the church they hied them fast.

   And God send every pretty peat
     (Heigh ho, the pretty peat!)
   That fears to die of this conceit
   So kind a friend to help at last.

Corydon having thus made them merry, as they were in the midst of their jollity, word was brought in to Saladyne and Rosader that a brother of theirs, one Fernandyne, was arrived, and desired to speak with them. Gerismond, overhearing this news, demanded who it was.

"It is, sir," quoth Rosader, "our middle brother, that lives a scholler in Paris; but what fortune hath driven him to seek us out I know not."

With that Saladyne went and met his brother, whom he welcomed with all curtesy, and Rosader gave him no less friendly entertainment; brought he was by his two brothers into the parlor where they all sate at dinner. Fernandyne, as one that knew as many manners as he could points of sophistry, and was as well brought up as well lettered, saluted them all. But when he espied Gerismond, kneeling on his knee he did him what reverence belonged to his estate, and with that burst forth into these speeches:

"Although, right mighty prince, this day of my brothers' marriage be a day of mirth, yet time craves another course; and therefore from dainty cates rise to sharp weapons. And you, the sons of Sir John of Bordeaux, leave off your amours and fall to arms; change your loves into lances, and now this day shew yourselves as valiant as hetherto you have been passionate. For know, Gerismond, that hard by, at the edge of this forest, the twelve peers of France are up in arms to recover thy right; and Torismond, troup'd with a crew of desperate runagates, is ready to bid them battail. The armies are ready to join; therefore shew thyself in the field to encourage thy subjects. And you, Saladyne and Rosader, mount you, and shew yourselves as hardy soldiers as you have been hearty lovers; so shall you, for the benefit of your country, discover the idea of your father's virtues to be stamped in your thoughts, and prove children worthy of so honorable a parent."

At this alarm given by Fernandyne, Gerismond leap'd from the boord, and Saladyne and Rosader betook themselves to their weapons.

"Nay," quoth Gerismond, "go with me; I have horse and armor for us all, and then, being well mounted, let us shew that we carry revenge and honor at our fawchions' points."

Thus they leave the brides full of sorrow, especially Alinda, who desired Gerismond to be good to her father. He, not returning a word because his haste was great, hied him home to his lodge, where he delivered Saladyne and Rosader horse and armor, and himself, armed royally, led the way; not having ridden two leagues before they discovered where in a valley both the battails were joined. Gerismond, seeing the wing wherein the peers fought, thrust in there, and cried "Saint Denis!" Gerismond laying on such load upon his enemies that he shewed how highly he did estimate of a crown. When the peers perceived that their lawful king was there, they grew more eager; and Saladyne and Rosader so behaved themselves that none durst stand in their way nor abide the fury of their weapons. To be short, the peers were conquerors, Torismond's army put to flight, and himself slain in battail. The peers then gathered themselves together, and saluting their king, conducted him royally into Paris, where he was received with great joy of all the citizens. As soon as all was quiet and he had received again the crown, he sent for Alinda and Rosalynde to the court, Alinda being very passionate for the death of her father, yet brooking it with the more patience in that she was contented with the welfare of her Saladyne.

Well, as soon as they were come to Paris, Gerismond made a royal feast for the peers and lords of his land, which continued thirty days, in which time summoning a parliament, by the consent of his nobles he created Rosader heir apparent to the kingdom; he restored Saladyne to all his father's land and gave him the dukedom of Nameurs; he made Fernandyne principal secretary to himself; and that fortune might every way seem frolic, he made Montanus lord over all the forest of Arden, Adam Spencer captain of the king's guard, and Corydon master of Alinda's flocks.

Here, gentleman, you may see in *Euphues' Golden Legacy* that such as neglect their fathers' precepts incur much prejudice; that division in nature, as it is a blemish in nurture, so 'tis a breach of good fortunes; that virtue is not measured by birth but by action; that younger brethren, though inferior in years, yet may be superior to honors; that concord is the sweetest conclusion, and amity betwixt brothers more forcible than fortune. If you gather any fruits by this *Legacy*, speak well of Euphues for writing it, and me for fetching it. If you grace me with that favor, you encourage me to be more forward; and as soon as I have overlook'd my labors, expect *The Sailor's Calendar*.

T[homas] Lodge

THOMAS NASHE

THE UNFORTUNATE TRAVELER

Although in his yeasty fertility Nashe tossed off *The Unfortunate Traveler* (1594) with the same careless ease with which he slapped together *Pierce Penniless* (1592) or *Have with You to Saffron Walden* (1596), this first realistic novel in English is his masterpiece. The same stabbing satire, the same indifference to form, the same joyous gift of language appear in all these major books; but *The Unfortunate Traveler* is set apart from his other work, and from the work of other men, in that it launches a new type of prose fiction in our language. Perhaps Nashe knew the English translation (1586) of the Spanish picaresque novel *Lazarillo de Tormes*, and he surely knew the coarse little anecdotes collected as the "jests" of Skelton and Scoggin (see p. 669); moreover, in the later work of Greene (for example, *A Groatsworth of Wit*) he had a model for earthy autobiographical narrative. But no English writer before Nashe had created a picaresque hero whose exploits and experiences were molded into a long realistic novel of contemporary life. Painter and his imitators had transcribed the sensational and romantic *novelle* of Bandello and other Italians; Lyly and his imitators had embroidered their fantastic excesses of style on the thinnest of narrative frames; Sidney and his imitators had revived the ancient formulas of Greek romance; but Nashe had no clear precedent for what he did, and therefore *The Unfortunate Traveler*, despite its ungainly faults of structure and its jagged narrative line, is a new departure. In a sense, the very faults become virtues by permitting the free play of Nashe's satire and the exercise of his piercing, restless power of observation. But it is in terms of character that this novel, like any other good novel, justifies itself. As we live with Jack Wilton through his harum-scarum soldiering, the sweating-sickness in England, the Anabaptist rising at Münster, the exploits with the Earl of Surrey and his fictitious Geraldine, and the lustful violence of Italy, he acquires a rounded, plastic quality possessed by no other fictional character of the age. Entered in the Stationers' Register on September 17, 1593, *The Unfortunate Traveler* went through two editions in 1594, the year of its publication. Our text is based upon *The Unfortunate Traveller. Or, The life of Jacke Wilton*, 1594 (STC 18380).

FROM THE UNFORTUNATE TRAVELER: OR, THE LIFE OF JACK WILTON (1594)

The Induction to the Dapper Monsieur Pages of the Court

Gallant squires, have amongst you! At mumchance I mean not, for so I might chance come to short commons, but at *novus, nova, novum*, which is in English, "news of the maker." A proper fellow-page of yours called Jack Wilton by me commends him unto you, and hath bequeathed for wastepaper here amongst you certain pages of his misfortunes. In any case, keep them preciously as a privy token of his good will towards you. If there be some better than other, he craves you would honor them in their death so much as to dry and kindle tobacco with them; for a need he permits you to wrap velvet pantofles in them also, so they be not wobegone at the heels, or weather-beaten like a black head with gray hairs, or mangy at the toes like an ape about the mouth. But as you love good fellowship and ames ace, rather turn them to stop mustard-pots than the grocers should have one patch of them to wrap mace in; a strong, hot, costly spice it is, which above all things he hates. To any use about meat and drink put them to and spare not, for they cannot do their country better service. Printers are mad whoresons; allow them some of them for napkins. Just a little nearer to the matter and the purpose: *Memorandum*, every one of you, after the perusing of this pamphlet, is to provide him a case of poniards, that, if you come in company with any man which shall dispraise it or speak against it, you may straight cry *Sic respondeo* and give him the stockado. It stands not with your honors, I assure ye, to have a gentleman and a page abus'd in his absence. Secondly, whereas you were wont to swear men on a pantofle to be true to your puissant order, you shall swear them on nothing but this chronicle of the king of pages henceforward. Thirdly, it shall be lawful for any whatsoever to play with false dice in a corner on the cover of this foresaid *Acts and Monuments*. None of the fraternity of the Minorites shall refuse it for a pawn in the times of famine and necessity. Every stationer's stall they pass by, whether by day or by night, they shall put off their hats to, and make a low leg, in regard their grand printed capitano is there entomb'd. It shall be flat treason for any of this forementioned catalogue of the point-trussers once to name him within forty foot of an alehouse; marry, the tavern is honorable. Many special grave articles more had I to give you in charge, which your Wisdoms, waiting together at the bottom of the great-chamber stairs or sitting in a porch (your parliament house), may better consider of than I can deliver; only let this suffice for a taste to the text and a bit to pull on a good wit with, as a rasher on the coals is to pull on a cup of wine. Heigh pass, come aloft! Every man of you take your places, and hear Jack Wilton tell his own tale.

About that time [1513] that the terror of the world and fever quartan of the French, Henry the Eight (the only true subject of chronicles), advanced his standard against the two hundred and fifty towers of Tournay and Turwin, and had the emperor and all the nobility of Flanders, Holland, and Brabant as mercenary attendants on his full-sail'd fortune, I, Jack Wilton (a gentleman at least), was a certain kind of an appendix or page, belonging or appertaining in or unto the confines of the English court, where what my credit was a number of my creditors that I cos'ned can testify. *Caelum petimus stultitia,* which of us all is not a sinner? Be it known to as many as will pay money inough to peruse my story that I followed the court or the camp, or the camp and the court, when Turwin lost her maidenhead and opened her gates to more than Jane Tross did. There did I (soft! let me drink before I go any further) reign sole king of the cans and black-jacks, prince of the pygmies, county palatine of clean straw and provant, and, to conclude, lord high regent of rashers of the coals and red herring cobs. *Paulo majora canamus.* Well, to the purpose. What stratagemical acts and monuments do you think an ingenious infant of my years might enact? You will say, it were sufficient if he slur a die, pawn his master to the utmost penny,

and minister the oath of the pantofle artificially. These are signs of good education, I must confess, and arguments of "In grace and virtue to proceed." O, but *aliquid latet quod non patet,* there's a further path I must trace; examples confirm; list, lordings, to my proceedings. Whosoever is acquainted with the state of a camp understands that in it be many quarters, and yet not so many as on London Bridge. In those quarters are many companies. Much company, much knavery, as true as that old adage, "Much curtesy, much subtilty." Those companies, like a great deal of corn, do yield some chaff; the corn are cormorants, the chaff are good fellows, which are quickly blown to nothing with bearing a light heart in a light purse. Amongst this chaff was I winnowing my wits to live merrily, and by my troth so I did; the prince could but command men spend their blood in his service, I could make them spend all the money they had for my pleasure. But poverty in the end parts friends; though I was prince of their purses, and exacted of my unthrift subjects as much liquid allegeance as any kaiser in the world could do, yet where it is not to be had the king must loose his right; want cannot be withstood, men can do no more than they can do. What remained, then, but the fox's case must help, when the lion's skin is out at the elbows?

There was a lord in the camp, let him be a Lord of Misrule if you will, for he kept a plain alehouse without welt or guard of any ivy bush, and sold cider and cheese by pint and by pound to all that came (at the very name of cider I can but sigh, there is so much of it in Rhenish wine nowadays). Well, *tendit ad sidera virtus,* there's great virtue belongs (I can tell you) to a cup of cider, and very good men have sold it, and at sea it is *aqua caelestis;* but that's neither here nor there; if it had no other patron but this peer of quart pots to authorize it, it were sufficient. This great lord, this worthy lord, this noble lord, thought no scorn (Lord, have mercy upon us!) to have his great velvet breeches larded with the droppings of this dainty liquor, and yet he was an old servitor, a cavalier of an ancient house, as might appear by the arms of his ancestors, drawn very amiably in chalk on the inside of his tent door.

He and no other was the man I chose out to damn with a lewd moneyless device; for coming to him on a day, as he was counting his barrels and setting the price in chalk on the head of them, I did my duty very devoutly, and told his Ale-y Honor I had matters of some secrecy to impart unto him, if it pleased him to grant me private audience. "With me, young Wilton?" quod he. "Marry, and shalt! Bring us a pint of cider of a fresh tap into the Three Cups here; wash the pot." So into a back room he led me, where after he had spit on his finger, and pick'd off two or three motes of his old moth-eaten velvet cap, and spunged and wrung all the rheumatic drivel from his ill-favored goat's beard, he bade me declare my mind, and thereupon he drank to me on the same.

I up with a long circumstance, alias a cunning shift of the seventeens, and discours'd unto him what entire affection I had borne him time out of mind, partly for the high descent and linage from whence he sprung, and partly for the tender care and provident respect he had of poor soldiers, that, whereas the vastity of that place (which afforded them no indifferent supply of drink or of victuals) might humble them to some extremity, and so weaken their hands, he vouchsafed in his own person to be a victualer to the camp (a rare example of magnificence and honorable curtesy), and diligently provided that without far travel every man might for his money have cider and cheese his bellyful; nor did he sell his cheese by the way only, or his cider by the great, but abas'd himself with his own hands to take a shoemaker's knife (a homely instrument for such a high personage to touch) and cut it out equally, like a true justiciary, in little pennyworths that it would do a man good for to look upon. So likewise of his cider, the poor man might have his moderate draught of it (as there is a moderation in all things) as well for his doit or his dandiprat as the rich man for his half sous or his denier. "Not so much," quoth I, "but this tapster's linen apron which you wear to protect your apparel from the imperfections of the spigot most amply bewrays your lowly mind. I speak it with tears, too few such noble men have we that will draw drink in linen aprons. Why, you are every child's fellow; any man that comes under the name of a soldier and a good fellow, you will sit and bear company to the last pot, yea, and you take in as good part the homely phrase of 'Mine host, here's to you,' as if one saluted you by all the titles of your barony. These considerations, I say, which the world suffers to slip by in the channel of forgetfulness, have moved me, in ardent zeal of your welfare, to forewarn you of some dangers that have beset you and your barrels."

At the name of dangers he start up, and bounc'd with his fist on the board so hard that his tapster, overhearing him, cried, "Anon, anon, sir! By and by!" and came and made a low leg and ask'd him what he lack'd. He was ready to have stricken his tapster for interrupting him in attention of this his so much desired relation, but for fear of displeasing me he moderated his fury, and only sending for the other fresh pint, will'd him look to the bar, and come when he is call'd, with a devil's name.

Well, at his earnest importunity, after I had moist'ned my lips to make my lie run glib to his journey's end, forward I went as followeth: "It chanced me the other night, amongst other pages, to attend where the king, with his lords and many chief leaders, sate in counsel; there, amongst sundry serious matters that were debated, and intelligences from the enemy given up, it was privily informed (no villains to these privy informers!) that you, even you that I now speak to, had—O would I had no tongue to tell the rest; by this drink, it grieves me so I am not able to repeat it!"

Now was my drunken lord ready to hang himself for the end of the full point, and over my neck he throws himself very lubberly, and intreated me, as I was a proper young gentleman and ever look'd for pleasure at his hands, soon to rid him out of this hell of suspense, and resolve him of the rest; then fell he on his knees, wrung his hands, and I think on my conscience wept out all the cider that he had drunk in a week before; to move me to have pity on him, he rose and put his rusty ring on my finger, gave me his greasy purse with that single money that was in it, promised to make me his heir, and a thousand more favors, if I would expire the misery of his unspeakable, tormenting uncertainty. I, being by nature inclined to Mercy (for indeed I knew two or three good wenches of that name), bad him harden his ears, and not make his eyes abortive before their time, and he should have the inside of my breast turn'd outward, hear such a tale as would tempt the utmost strength of life to attend it and not die in the midst of it. "Why," quoth I, "myself that am but a poor childish well-willer of yours, with the very thought that a man of your desert and state by a number of peasants and varlets should be so injuriously abused in hugger mugger, have wept all my urine upward. The wheel under our city bridge carries not so much water over the city as my brain hath welled forth gushing streams of sorrow; I have wept so immoderately and lavishly that I thought verily my palate had been turned to Pissing Conduit in London. My eyes have been drunk, outrageously drunk, with giving but ordinary entercourse through their sea-circled ilands to my distilling dreriment. What shall I say? That which malice hath said is the mere overthrow and murther of your days. Change not your color, none can slander a clear conscience to itself; receive all your fraught of misfortune in at once.

"It is buzzed in the king's head that you are a secret friend to the enemy, and under pretence of getting a license to furnish the camp with cider and such-like provant, you have furnish'd the enemy, and in empty barrels sent letters of discovery and corn innumerable."

I might well have left here, for by this time his white liver had mix'd itself with the white of his eye, and both were turned upwards, as if they had offered themselves a fair white for death to shoot at. The troth was, I was very loath mine host and I should part with dry lips; wherefore the best means that I could imagine to wake him out of his trance was to cry loud in his ear, "Ho, host, what's to pay? Will no man look to the reckoning here?" And in plain verity it took expected effect, for with the noise he started and bustled, like a man that had been scar'd with fire out of his sleep, and ran hastily to his tapster, and all to-belabored him about the ears for letting gentlemen call so long and not look in to them. Presently he rememb'red himself, and had like to fall into his memento again, but that I met him half ways and ask'd his lordship what he meant to slip his neck out of the collar so sodainly, and, being revived, strike his tapster so hastily.

"O," quoth he, "I am bought and sold for doing my country such good service as I have done. They are afraid of me, because my good deeds have brought me into such estimation with the comminalty. I see, I see, it is not for the lamb to live with the wolf."

"The world is well amended," thought I, "with your cidership; such another forty years' nap together as Epeminedes had would make you a perfect wise man." "Answer me," quoth he, "my wise young Wilton, is it true that I am thus underhand dead and buried by these bad tongues?"

"Nay," quoth I, "you shall pardon me, for I have spoken too much already; no definitive sentence of death shall march out of my well-meaning lips; they have but lately suck'd milk, and shall they so sodainly change their food and seek after blood?"

"O, but," quoth he, "a man's friend is his friend; fill the other pint, tapster. What said the king? Did he believe it when he heard it? I pray thee say; I swear by my nobility, none in the world shall ever be made privy that I received any light of this matter by thee."

"That firm affiance," quoth I, "had I in you before, or else I would never have gone so far over the shoes to pluck you out of the mire. Not to make many words (since you will needs know), the king says flatly you are a miser and a snudge, and he never hoped better of you."

"Nay, then," quoth he, "questionless some planet that loves not cider hath conspired against me."

"Moreover, which is worse, the king hath vowed to give Turwin one hot breakfast only with the bungs that he will pluck out of your barrels. I cannot stay at this time to report each circumstance that passed, but the only counsel that my long-cherished kind inclination can possibly contrive is now in your old days to be liberal; such victuals or provision as you

have, presently distribute it frankly amongst poor soldiers; I would let them burst their bellies with cider and bathe in it, before I would run into my prince's ill opinion for a whole sea of it. The hunter pursuing the beaver for his stones, he bites them off and leaves them behind for him to gather up, whereby he lives quiet. If greedy hunters and hungry tale-tellers pursue you, it is for a little pelf that you have; cast it behind you, neglect it, let them have it, lest it breed a farther inconvenience. Credit my advice, you shall find it prophetical; and thus have I discharged the part of a poor friend." With some few like phrases of ceremony, "Your Honor's poor suppliant," and so forth, and "Farewell my good youth, I thank thee and will remember thee," we parted.

But the next day I think we had a dole of cider, cider in bowls, in scuppets, in helmets; and to conclude, if a man would have fill'd his boots full there he might have had it; provant thrust itself into poor soldiers' pockets whether they would or no. We made five peals of shot into the town together of nothing but spigots and faucets of discarded empty barrels; every underfoot soldier had a distenanted tun, as Diogenes had his tub to sleep in. I myself got as many confiscated tapsters' aprons as made me a tent as big as any ordinary commander's in the field. But in conclusion, my well-beloved baron of double beer got him humbly on his marrybones to the king, and complained he was old and stricken in years, and had never an heir to cast at a dog, wherefore if it might please his Majesty to take his lands into his hands, and allow him some reasonable pension to live, he should be mervailously well pleased; as for wars, he was weary of them; yet as long as his Highness vent'red his own person, he would not flinch a foot, but make his withered body a buckler to bear off any blow advanced against him.

The king, mervailing at this alteration of his cider-merchant (for so he often pleasantly term'd him), with a little farther talk bolted out the whole complotment. Then was I pitifully whipp'd for my holiday lie, though they made themselves merry with it many a winter's evening after.

For all this, his good Ass-Headed Honor, mine host, persevered in his former request to the king to accept his lands and allow him a beadsmanry or out-brotherhood of brachet, which, through his vehement instancy, took effect; and the king jestingly said since he would needs have it so, he would distrain on part of his land for impost of cider, which he was behind with.

This was one of my famous atchievements, insomuch as I never light upon the like famous fool; but I have done a thousand better jests, if they had been book'd in order as they were begotten. It is pity posterity should be deprived of such precious records, and yet there is no remedy; and yet there is, too, for when all fails, well fare a good memory. Gentle readers—look you be gentle now, since I have call'd you so—as freely as my knavery was mine own it shall be yours to use in the way of honesty. . . . [Jack then relates further "jests" of his at the expense of a braggart captain and other butts. After the capture of Tournay and Térouanne he returns to England.]

I must not place a volume in the precincts of a pamphlet; sleep an hour or two and dream that Turney and Turwin is won, that the king is shipp'd again into England, and that I am close at hard-meat at Windsor or at Hampton Court. What, will you in your indifferent opinions allow me for my travail no more signory over the pages than I had before? Yes, whether you will part with so much probable friendly suppose or no, I'll have it in spite of your hearts. For your instruction and godly consolation, be informed that at that time I was no common squire, no undertrodden torch-bearer. I had my feather in my cap as big as a flag in the foretop, my French doublet gelt in the belly as though (like a pig ready to be spitted) all my guts had been pluck'd out, a pair of side-paned hose that hung down like two scales filled with Holland cheeses, my long stock that sate close to my dock and smothered not a scab or a lecherous hairy sinew on the calf of the leg, my rapier pendant like a round stick fast'ned in the tacklings for skippers the better to climb by, my cape-cloak of black cloth overspreading my back like a thornback or an elephant's ear (that hangs on his shoulders like a country huswife's banskin, which she thirls her spindle on), and, in consummation of my curiosity, my hands without gloves, all a more French, and a black budge edging of a beard on the upper lip, and the like sable auglet of excrements in the rising of the ankle of my chin. I was the first that brought in the order of passing into the court, which I derived from the common word *qui passa* and the herald's phrase of *arms passant,* thinking in sincerity he was not a gentleman, nor his arms currant, who was not first pass'd by the pages. If any prentice or other came into the court that was not a gentleman I thought it was an indignity to the preheminence of the court to include such a one, and could not be salv'd except we gave him *arms passant* to make him a gentleman.

Besides, in Spain none pass any far way but he must be examined what he is, and give threepence for his pass.

In which regard it was considered of by the common table of the cupbearers what a perilsome thing it was to let any stranger or outdweller approach so near the precincts of the prince as the great chamber without examining what he was and giving him his pass; whereupon we established the like order, but took no money of them as they did, only for a sign that he had not pass'd our hands unexamined we set a red mark on their ears, and so let them walk as authentical.

I must not discover what ungodly dealing we had with the black-jacks, or how oft I was crowned king of the drunkards with a court-cup. Let me quietly descend to the waning of my youthful days and tell a little of the sweating sickness that made me, in a cold sweat, take my heels and run out of England.

This sweating sickness [of which there were epidemics in 1485, 1508, 1517, 1528, 1551] was a disease that a man then might catch and never go to a hothouse. Many masters desire to have such servants as would work till they sweat again, but in those days he that sweat never wrought again. That Scripture then was not thought so necessary which says, "Earn thy living with the sweat of thy brows," for then they earn'd their dying with the sweat of their brows. It was inough if a fat man did but truss his points, to turn him over the perch. Mother Cornelius' tub? why, it was like hell; he that came into it never came out of it. Cooks that stand continually basting their faces before the fire were now all cashier'd with this sweat into kitchen stuff; their hall fell into the king's hands for want of one of the trade to uphold it. Felt-makers and furriers, what the one with the hot steam of their wool new taken out of the pan and the other with the contagious heat of their slaughter-budge and cony skins, died more thick than of the pestilence. I have seen an old woman at that season having three chins wipe them all away one after another, as they melted to water, and left herself nothing of a mouth but an upper chap. Look how in May or the heat of summer we lay butter in water for fear it should melt away, so then were men fain to wet their clothes in water as dyers do, and hide themselves in wells from the heat of the sun.

Then happy was he that was an ass, for nothing will kill an ass but cold, and none died but with extreme heat. The fishes called sea-stars, that burn one another by excessive heat, were not so contagious as one man that had the sweat was to another. Masons paid nothing for hair to mix their lime, nor glovers to stuff their balls with, for then they had it for nothing; it dropped off men's heads and beards faster than any barber could shave it. O, if hair breeches had then been in fashion, what a fine world had it been for tailors; and so it was a fine world for tailors nevertheless, for he that could make a garment slightest and thinnest carried it away. Cutters, I can tell you, then stood upon it to have their trade one of the twelve companies, for who was it then that would not have his doublet cut to the skin and his shirt cut into it, too, to make it more cold? It was as much as a man's life was worth, once to name a freeze jerkin; it was high treason for a fat gross man to come within five miles of the court. I heard where they died up all in one family, and not a mother's child escap'd, insomuch as they had but an Irish rug lock'd up in a press, and not laid upon any bed, neither. If those that were sick of this malady slept of it, they never wak'd more. Phisitions with their simples in this case wext simple fellows and knew not which way to bestir them.

Galen might go shoe the gander for any good he could do; his secretaries had so long called him divine that now he had lost all his virtue upon earth. Hippocrates might well help almanac-makers, but here he had not a word to say; a man might sooner catch the sweat with plodding over him to no end, than cure the sweat with any of his impotent principles. Paracelsus with his spirit of the buttery and his spirits of minerals could not so much as say "God amend him" to the matter. *Plus erat in artifice quam arte:* "there was more infection in the phisition himself than his art could cure." This mortality first began amongst old men, for they, taking a pride to have their breasts loose basted with tedious beards, kept their houses so hot with their hairy excrements that not so much but their very walls sweat out salt-peter, with the smothering perplexity; nay, a number of them had mervailous hot breaths, which, sticking in the briers of their bushy beards, could not choose but (as close air long imprisoned) ingender corruption.

Wiser was our Brother Banks of these latter days, who made his juggling horse a cut, for fear if at any time he should foist, the stink sticking in his thick bushy tail might be noisome to his auditors. Should I tell you how many pursevants with red noses and sergeants with precious faces shrunk away in this sweat, you would not believe me. Even as the salamander with his very sight blasteth apples on the trees, so a pursevant or a sergeant at this present, with the very reflex of his *fiery facies,* was able to spoil a man afar off. In some places of the world there is no shadow of the sun; *diebus illis* if it had been so in England, the generation of Brut had died all and some. To knit up this description in a pursenet: so fervent and scorching was the burning air which inclosed them that the most blessed man then alive would have thought that God had done fairly by him if he had turn'd him to a goat, for goats take breath not at the mouth or nose only, but at the ears also. . . . [Leaving England, Wilton returns to the Continent.

There he witnesses the battle of Marignano (1515) and the ruthless suppression of the Anabaptists at Münster (1534). Finally, at Middelburg, he meets Henry Howard, Earl of Surrey.]

What with wagons and bare ten toes having attained to Middleborough (good Lord, see the changing chances of us knights-arrant infants), I met with the right honorable Lord Henry Howard, Earl of Surrey, my late master. Jesu, I was persuaded I should not be more glad to see heaven than I was to see him. O, it was a right noble lord, liberality itself (if in this iron age there were any such creature as liberality left on the earth), a prince in content because a poet without peer.

Destiny never defames herself but when she lets an excellent poet die; if there be any spark of Adam's paradised perfection yet ember'd up in the breasts of mortal men, certainly God hath bestowed that his perfectest image on poets. None come so near to God in wit, none more contemn the world; *Vatis avarus non temere est animus,* saith Horace, *versus amat, hoc studet unum:* "Seldom have you seen any poet possessed with avarice, only verses he loves, nothing else he delights in"; and as they contemn the world, so contrarily of the mechanical world are none more contemned. Despised they are of the world, because they are not of the world; their thoughts are exalted above the world of ignorance and all earthly conceits.

As sweet angelical queristers they are continually conversant in the heaven of arts; heaven itself is but the highest height of knowledge; he that knows himself and all things else, knows the means to be happy; happy, thrice happy, are they whom God hath doubled his spirit upon, and given a double soul unto to be poets.

My heroical master exceeded in this supernatural kind of wit; he entertained no gross earthly spirit of avarice, nor weak womanly spirit of pusillanimity and fear that are feigned to be of the water, but admirable airy and fiery spirits, full of freedom, magnanimity, and bountihood. Let me not speak any more of his accomplishments, for fear I spend all my spirits in praising him, and leave myself no vigor of wit or effects of a soul to go forward with my history.

Having thus met him I so much adored, no interpleading was there of opposite occasions, but back I must return and bear half stakes with him in the lottery of travel. I was not altogether unwilling to walk along with such a good purse-bearer, yet musing what changeable humor had so sodainly seduced him from his native soil to seek out needless perils in those parts beyond sea, one night very boldly I demanded of him the reason that moved him thereto.

"Ah," quoth he, "my little page, full little canst

thou perceive how far metamorphosed I am from myself since I last saw thee. There is a little god called Love that will not be worship'd of any leaden brains; one that proclaims himself sole king and emperor of piercing eyes, and chief sovereign of soft hearts; he it is that, exercising his empire in my eyes, hath exorcised and clean conjured me from my content.

"Thou know'st stately Geraldine, too stately I fear for me to do homage to her statue or shrine; she it is that is come out of Italy to bewitch all the wise men of England; upon Queen Katherine Dowager she waits, that hath a dowry of beauty sufficient to make her wooed of the greatest kings in Christendom. Her high exalted sunbeams have set the phoenix nest of my breast on fire, and I myself have brought Arabian spiceries of sweet passions and praises to furnish out the funeral flame of my folly. Those who were condemned to be smothered to death by sinking down into the soft bottom of an high-built bed of roses never died so sweet a death as I should die if her rose-colored disdain were my deathsman.

"O thrice emperial Hampton Court, Cupid's inchanted castle, the place where I first saw the perfect omnipotence of the Almighty expressed in mortality, 'tis thou alone that, tithing all other men solace in thy pleasant scituation, affordest me nothing but an excellent begotten sorrow out of the chief treasury of all thy recreations.

"Dear Wilton, understand that there it was where I first set eye on my more than celestial Geraldine. Seeing her, I admired her; all the whole receptacle of my sight was unhabited with her rare worth. Long suit and uncessant protestations got me the grace to be entertained. Did never unloving servant so prentice-like obey his never pleased mistress as I did her. My life, my wealth, my friends had all their destiny depending on her command.

"Upon a time I was determined to travel; the fame of Italy, and an especial affection I had unto poetry, my second mistress, for which Italy was so famous, had wholly ravish'd me unto it. There was no dehortment from it, but needs thether I would; wherefore, coming to my mistress as she was then walking with other ladies of estate in paradise at Hampton Court, I most humbly besought her of favor that she would give me so much gracious leave to absent myself from her service as to travel a year or two into Italy. She very discreetly answered me that if my love were so hot as I had often avouched, I did very well to apply the plaister of absence unto it, for absence, as they say, causeth forgetfulness. 'Yet nevertheless since it is Italy, my native country, you are so desirous to see, I am the more willing to make my will yours. Aye, *pete Italiam,* "go and seek Italy," with Aeneas; but be more true than Aeneas; I hope that kind wit-

cherishing climate will work no change in so witty a breast. No country of mine shall it be more, if it conspire with thee in any new love against me. One charge I will give thee, and let it be rather a request than a charge: when thou comest to Florence (the fair city from whence I fetch'd the pride of my birth), by an open challenge defend my beauty against all comers.

" 'Thou hast that honorable carriage in arms that it shall be no discredit for me to bequeath all the glory of my beauty to thy well-governed arm. Fain would I be known where I was born, fain would I have thee known where Fame sits in her chiefest theater. Farewell, forget me not; continued deserts will eternize me unto thee, thy wishes shall be expired when thy travel shall be once ended.'

"Here did tears step out before words, and intercepted the course of my kind-conceived speech, even as wind is allayed with rain; with heart-scalding sighs I confirmed her parting request, and vowed myself hers while living heat allowed me to be mine own; *hinc illae lachrimae,* herehence proceedeth the whole cause of my peregrination."

Not a little was I delighted with this unexpected love story, especially from a mouth out of which was nought wont to march but stern precepts of gravity and modesty. I swear unto you I thought his company the better by a thousand crowns because he had discarded those nice terms of chastity and continency. Now I beseech God love me so well as I love a plain-dealing man; earth is earth, flesh is flesh, earth will to earth, and flesh unto flesh; frail earth, frail flesh, who can keep you from the work of your creation?

Dismissing this fruitless annotation *pro et contra;* towards Venice we progress'd, and took Rotterdam in our way, that was clean out of our way; there we met with aged learning's chief ornament, that abundant and superingenious clark, Erasmus, as also with merry Sir Thomas More, our countryman, who was come purposely over, a little before us, to visit the said grave father Erasmus; what talk, what conference we had then, it were here superfluous to rehearse, but this I can assure you, Erasmus in all his speeches seemed so much to mislike the indiscretion of princes in preferring of parasites and fools that he decreed with himself to swim with the stream, and write a book forthwith in commendation of folly. Quick-witted Sir Thomas More travel'd in a clean contrary province, for he seeing most commonwealths corrupted by ill custom, and that principalities were nothing but great piracies, which, gotten by violence and murther, were maintained by private undermining and bloodshed, that in the chiefest flourishing kingdoms there was no equal or well-divided weal

intended for popular consumption

one with another, but a manifest conspiracy of rich men against poor men, procuring their own unlawful commodities under the name and interest of the commonwealth; he concluded with himself to lay down a perfect plot of a commonwealth or government, which he would intitle his *Utopia*.

So left we them to prosecute their discontented studies, and made our next journey to Wittenberg.

At the very point of our enterance into Wittenberg, we were spectators of a very solemn scholastical 10 entertainment of the Duke of Saxony thether. Whom, because he was the chief patron of their university, and had took Luther's part in banishing the mass and all like papal jurisdiction out of their town, they crouch'd unto extremely. The chief ceremonies of their intertainment were these: first, the heads of their university (they were great heads, of certainty) met him in their hooded hypocrisy and doctorly accoustrements, *secundum formam statuti;* where by the orator of the university, whose picker- 20 devant was very plentifully besprinkled with rose-water, a very learned or rather ruthful oration was delivered (for it rain'd all the while) signifying thus much, that it was all by patch and by piecemeal stol'n out of Tully, and he must pardon them though in emptying their phrase books the world emptied his intrails, for they did it not in any ostentation of wit (which God knows they had not) but to shew the extraordinary good will they bare the duke (to have him stand in the rain till he was through wet); a 30 thousand *quemadmodums* and *quapropters* he came over him with; every sentence he concluded with *Esse posse videatur;* through all the nine worthies he ran with praising and comparing him; Nestor's years he assured him of under the broad seal of their supplications, and with that crow-trodden verse in Virgil, *Dum iuga montis aper.* he pack'd up his pipes and cried, "*Dixi.*"

That pageant overpast, there rush'd upon him a miserable rabblement of junior graduates, that all 40 cried upon him mightily in their gibrige, like a company of beggars, "God save your Grace, God save your Grace! Jesus preserve your Highness, though it be but for an hour!"

Some three half-pennyworth of Latin here also had he thrown at his face, but it was choice stuff, I can tell you, as there is a choice even amongst rags gathered up from the dunghill. At the town's end met him the burghers and dunstical incorporationers of Wittenberg in their distinguished liveries, their 50 distinguished livery faces, I mean, for they were most of them hot-livered drunkards, and had all the coat colors of sanguine, purple, crimson, copper, carnation that were to be had in their countenances. Filthy knaves, no cost had they bestowed on the

town for his welcome, saving new painted their houghs and bousing-houses, which commonly are fairer than their churches, and over their gates set the town arms carousing a whole health to the duke's arms, which sounded gulping after this sort, "Vanhotten, slotten, irk bloshen glotten gelderslike!" Whatever the word were, the sense was this, "Good drink is a medicine for all diseases."

A bursten-belly inkhorn orator called Vanderhulke they pick'd out to present him with an oration, one that had a sulpherous, big, swoll'n, large face, like a Saracen, eyes like two Kentish oysters, a mouth that opened as wide every time he spake as one of those old knit trap-doors, a beard as though it had been made of a bird's nest pluck'd in pieces, which consisteth of straw, hair, and dirt mix'd together. He was appareled in black leather new liquor'd, and a short gown without any gathering in the back, faced before and behind with a boist'rous bearskin, and a red nightcap on his head. To this purport and effect was this broccing double-beer oration:

"Right noble duke (*ideo nobilis quasi no bilis,* for you have no bile or choler in you), know that our present incorporation of Wittenberg, by me the tongueman of their thankfulness, a townsman by birth, a free German by nature, an orator by art, and a scrivener by education, in all obedience and chastity, most bountifully bid you welcome to Wittenberg. Welcome, said I? O orificial rhetoric, wipe thy everlasting mouth, and afford me a more Indian metaphor than that for the brave princely blood of a Saxon! Oratory, uncask the barr'd hutch of thy complements, and with the triumphantest trope in thy treasury do truage unto him! What impotent speech with his eight parts may not specify, this unestimable gift, holding his peace, shall as it were (with tears I speak it) do whereby as it may seem or appear to manifest or declare, and yet it is, and yet it is not, and yet it may be a diminutive oblation meritorious to your high pusillanimity and indignity. Why should I go gadding and fisgigging after firking flantado amfibologies? Wit is wit, and good will is good will. With all the wit I have, I here, according to the premises, offer up unto you the city's general good will, which is a gilded can, in manner and form following, for you and the heirs of your body lawfully begotten to drink healths in. The scholastical squitterbooks clout you up canopies and footclothes of verses. We that are good fellows, and live as merry as cup and can, will not verse upon you as they do, but must do as we can, and entertain you if it be but with a plain empty can. He hath learning inough that hath learn'd to drink to his first man.

"Gentle duke, without paradox be it spoken, thy horses at our own proper costs and charges shall knead up to the knees all the while thou art here in spruce beer and Lubeck liquor. Not a dog thou bringest with thee but shall be banketed with Rhenish wine and sturgion. On our shoulders we wear no lambskin or miniver like these academics, yet we can drink to the confusion of thy enemies! Good lambswool have we for their lambskins, and for their miniver, large minerals in our coffers. Mechanical men they call us, and not amiss, for most of us being *maechi,* that is, cuckolds and whoremasters, fetch our antiquity from the temple of Mecca, where Mahomet was hung up. Three parts of the world, America, Afric, and Asia, are of this our mechanic religion. Nero, when he cried, *"O quantus artifex pereo,"* profess'd himself of our freedom, insomuch as *artifex* is a citizen or craftsman, as well as *carnifex* a scholar or hangman. Pass on by leave into the precincts of our abhomination. Bonny duke, frolic in our bower, and persuade thyself that even as garlic hath three properties, to make a man wink, drink, and stink, so we will wink on thy imperfections, drink to thy favorites, and all thy foes shall stink before us. So be it. Farewell!"

The duke laugh'd not a little at this ridiculous oration, but that very night as great an ironical occasion was minist'red, for he was bidden to one of the chief schools to a comedy handled by scholars. *Acolastus, the Prodigal Child,* was the name of it, which was so filthily acted, so leathernly set forth, as would have moved laughter in Heraclitus. One, as if he had been planing a clay floor, stampingly trod the stage so hard with his feet that I thought verily he had resolved to do the carpenter that set it up some utter shame. Another flung his arms like cudgels at a pear tree, insomuch as it was mightily dreaded that he would strike the candles that hung above their heads out of their sockets, and leave them all dark. Another did nothing but wink and make faces. There was a parasite, and he with clapping his hands and thripping his fingers seemed to dance an antic to and fro. The only thing they did well was the prodigal child's hunger, most of their scholars being hungerly kept; and surely you would have said they had been brought up in hog's academy to learn to eat acorns, if you had seen how sedulously they fell to them. Not a jest had they to keep their auditors from sleeping but of swill and draff; yes, now and then the servant put his hand into the dish before his master, and almost chok'd himself, eating slovenly and ravenously to cause sport.

The next day they had solempn disputations, where Luther and Carolostadius scolded level coil. A mass of words I wot well they heap'd up against the mass and the pope, but farther particulars of their disputations I remember not. I thought verily they would have worried one another with words, they were so earnest and vehement. Luther had the louder voice, Carolostadius went beyond him in beating and bouncing with his fists. *Quae supra nos, nihil ad nos;* they uttered nothing to make a man laugh, therefore I will leave them. Marry, their outward gestures would now and then afford a man a morsel of mirth; of those two I mean not so much as of all the other train of opponents and respondents. One peck'd with his forefinger at every half syllable he brought forth, and nodded with his nose like an old singing man teaching a young querister to keep time. Another would be sure to wipe his mouth with his handkercher at the end of every full point, and ever when he thought he had cast a figure so curiously as he dived over head and ears into his auditors' admiration, he would take occasion to stroke up his hair, and twine up his mustachios twice or thrice over, while they might have leisure to applaud him. A third waver'd and waggl'd his head, like a proud horse playing with his bridle, or as I have seen some fantastical swimmer, at every stroke, train his chin sidelong over his left shoulder. A fourth sweat and foamed at the mouth for very anger his adversary had denied that part of the syllogism which he was not prepared to answer. A fifth spread his arms like an usher that goes before to make room, and thripp'd with his finger and his thumb when he thought he had tickled it with a conclusion. A sixt hung down his countenance like a sheep, and stutted and slavered very pitifully when his invention was stepp'd aside out of the way. A seventh gasp'd for wind, and groaned in his pronunciation as if he were hard bound with some bad argument. Gross plodders they were all, that had some learning and reading, but no wit to make use of it. They imagined the duke took the greatest pleasure and contentment under heaven to hear them speak Latin, and as long as they talk'd nothing but Tully he was bound to attend them. A most vain thing it is in many universities at this day that they count him excellent eloquent who stealeth not whole phrases but whole pages out of Tully. If of a number of shreds of his sentences he can shape an oration, from all the world he carries it away, although in truth it be no more than a fool's coat of many colors. No invention or matter have they of their own, but tack up a style of his stale gallimafries. The leaden-headed Germans first began this, and we Englishmen have surfeted of their absurd imitation. I pity Nizolius, that had nothing to do but pick thrids' ends out of an old overworn garment.

This is but by the way; we must look back to our disputants. One amongst the rest, thinking to be more conceited than his fellows, seeing the duke have a dog he loved well which sate by him on the tarras, converted all his oration to him, and not a hair of his tail but he kemb'd out with comparisons;

so to have courted him if he were a bitch had been very suspicious. Another commented and descanted on the duke's staff, new tipping it with many quaint epithits. Some cast his nativity, and promised him he should not die until the Day of Judgment. Omitting further superfluities of this stamp, in this general assembly we found intermixed that abundant scholar, Cornelius Agrippa. At that time he bare the fame to be the greatest conjurer in Christendom. Scoto, that did the juggling tricks before the queen, never came near him one quarter in magic reputation. The doctors of Wittenberg, doting on the rumor that went of him, desired him before the duke and them to do something extraordinary memorable.

One requested to see pleasant Plautus, and that he would shew them in what habit he went and with what countenance he look'd when he ground corn in the mill. Another had half a month's mind to Ovid and his hook nose. Erasmus, who was not wanting in that honorable meeting, requested to see Tully in that same grace and majesty he pleaded his oration *Pro Roscio Amerino,* affirming that till in person he beheld his importunity of pleading, he would in no wise be persuaded that any man could carry away a manifest case with rhetoric so strangely. To Erasmus' petition he easily condescended, and willing the doctors at such an hour to hold their convocation and every one to keep him in his place without moving, at the time prefixed in entered Tully, ascended his pleading place, and declaimed verbatim the forenamed oration, but with such astonishing amazement, with such fervent exaltation of spirit, with such soul-stirring gestures, that all his auditors were ready to install his guilty client for a god.

Great was the concourse of glory Agrippa drew to him with this one feat. And indeed he was so cloyed with men which came to behold him that he was fain, sooner than he would, to return to the emperor's court from whence he came and leave Wittenberg before he would. With him we traveled along. . . .

[Having accompanied Agrippa to the emperor's court, Surrey and Wilton next go to Venice, where they are imprisoned. Released through the good offices of Pietro Aretino, Wilton leaves Surrey to go to Florence with Diamante, a courtezan. Surrey rejoins them there to enter a tournament in honor of Geraldine and her birthplace; then he returns to England while Wilton proceeds to Rome, where again he suffers imprisonment (on a trumped-up charge of murder) and is aided by another courtezan, this time Juliana. In the company of Diamante he escapes to Bologna, where he witnesses the execution of the notorious Cutwolfe, a murderer.]

To Bolognia with a merry gale we posted, where we lodged ourselves in a blind street out of the way

and kept secret many days; but when we perceived we sail'd in the haven, that the wind was laid, and no alarum made after us, we boldly came abroad, and one day, hearing of a more desperate murtherer than Cain that was to be executed, we followed the multitude and grutch'd not to lend him our eyes at his last parting. Who should it be but one Cutwolfe, a wearish, dwarfish, writhen-fac'd cobbler, brother to Bartol the Italian that was confederate with Esdras of Granado, and at that time stole away my curtizan when he ravish'd Heraclide [in an earlier episode of the novel]. It is not so natural for me to epitomize his impiety as to hear him in his own person speak upon the wheel where he was to suffer.

Prepare your ears and your tears, for never till this thrust I any tragical matter upon you. Strange and wonderful are God's judgments; here shine they in their glory. Chaste Heraclide, thy blood is laid up in heaven's treasury; not one drop of it was lost, but lent out to usury. Water poured forth sinks down quietly into the earth, but blood spilt on the ground sprinkles up to the firmament. Murder is widemouth'd and will not let God rest till he grant revenge. Not only the blood of the slaught'red innocent but the soul ascendeth to His throne and there cries out and exclaims for justice and recompense. Guiltless souls that live every hour subject to violence, and with your dispairing fears do much empair God's providence, fasten your eyes on this spectacle that will add to your faith. Refer all your oppressions, afflictions, and injuries to the even-balanced eye of the Almighty; he it is that, when your patience sleepeth, will be most exceeding mindful of you.

This is but a glose upon the text. Thus Cutwolfe begins his insulting oration:

"Men and people that have made holiday to behold my pained flesh toil on the wheel, expect not of me a whining penitent slave that shall do nothing but cry and say his prayers and so be crush'd in pieces. My body is little, but my mind is as great as a giant's. The soul which is in me is the very soul of Julius Caesar by reversion. My name is Cutwolfe, neither better nor worse by occupation than a poor cobbler of Verona. Cobblers are men, and kings are no more. The occasion of my coming hether at this present is to have a few of my bones broken (as we are all born to die) for being the death of the emperor of homicides, Esdras of Granado.

"About two years since, in the streets of Rome, he slew the only and eldest brother I had, named Bartol, in quarreling about a curtizan. The news brought to me as I was sitting in my shop under a stall, knocking in of tacks, I think I rais'd up my bristles, sold pritchawl, spunge, blacking-tub, and punching-iron, bought me rapier and pistol, and to go I went. Twenty months together I pursued him, from Rome to

Naples, from Naples to Caiete passing over the river, from Caiete to Siena, from Siena to Florence, from Florence to Parma, from Parma to Pavia, from Pavia to Sion, from Sion to Geneva, from Geneva back again towards Rome, where in the way it was my chance to meet him in the nick, here at Bolognia, as I will tell you how. I saw a great fray in the streets as I pass'd along, and many swords walking, whereupon, drawing nearer, and enquiring who they were, answer was returned me that it was that notable bandetto Esdras of Granado. O, so I was tickled in the spleen with that word my heart hopp'd and danc'd, my elbows itch'd, my fingers frisk'd; I wist not what should become of my feet nor knew what I did, for joy. The fray parted, I thought it not convenient to single him out, being a sturdy knave, in the street, but to stay till I had got him at more advantage. To his lodging I dogg'd him, lay at the door all night where he ent'red for fear he should give me the slip any way. Betimes in the morning I rung the bell and craved to speak with him. Now to his chamber door I was brought, where knocking, he rose in his shirt and let me in, and when I was ent'red, bade me lock the door and declare my arrant, and so he slipp'd to bed again.

"'Marry, this,' quoth I, 'is my arrant. Thy name is Esdras of Granado, is it not? Most treacherously thou slew'st my brother Bartol about two years ago in the streets of Rome; his death am I come to revenge. In quest of thee ever since, above three thousand miles have I travel'd. I have begg'd, to maintain me, the better part of the way, only because I would intermit no time from my pursuit in going back for money. Now have I got thee naked in my power; die thou shalt, though my mother and my grandmother dying did intreat for thee. I have promis'd the Divel thy soul within this hour; break my word I will not; in thy breast I intend to bury a bullet. Stir not, quinch not, make no noise, for if thou dost it will be worse for thee.'

"Quoth Esdras: 'Whatever thou beest at whose mercy I lie, spare me and I will give thee as much gold as thou wilt ask. Put me to any pains, my life reserved, and I willingly will sustain them; cut off my arms and legs and leave me as a lazar to some loathsome spittle, where I may but live a year to pray and repent me. For thy brother's death the despair of mind that hath ever since haunted me, the guilty gnawing worm of conscience I feel, may be sufficient penance. Thou canst not send me to such a hell as already there is in my heart. To dispatch me presently is no revenge; it will soon be forgotten. Let me die a ling'ring death—it will be rememb'red a great deal longer. A ling'ring death may avail my soul, but it is the illest of ills that can befortune my

body. For my soul's health I beg my body's torment; be not thou a divel to torment my soul and send me to eternal damnation. Thy overhanging sword hides heaven from my sight; I dare not look up, lest I embrace my death's-wound unawares. I cannot pray to God and plead to thee both at once. Ay me! Already I see my life buried in the wrinkles of thy brows; say but I shall live, though thou meanest to kill me. Nothing confounds like to sudden terror; it thrusts every sense out of office. Poison wrapp'd up in sug'red pills is but half a poison; the fear of Death's looks are more terrible than his stroke. . . . Defer awhile thy resolution; I am not at peace with the world, for even but yesterday I fought, and in my fury threat'ned further vengeance; had I a face to ask forgiveness, I should think half my sins were forgiven. A hundred devils haunt me daily for my horrible murthers. The devils when I die will be loath to go to hell with me, for they desired of Christ he would not send them to hell before their time; if they go not to hell, into thee they will go and hideously vex thee for turning them out of their habitation. Wounds I contemn; life I prize light; it is another world's tranquillity which makes me so timerous. Everlasting damnation! Everlasting howling and lamentation! It is not from death I request thee to deliver me, but from this terror of torment's eternity. Thy brother's body only I pierc'd unadvisedly; his soul meant I no harm to at all. My body and soul both shalt thou cast away quite, if thou dost at this instant what thou mayst. Spare me, spare me, I beseech thee! By thy own soul's salvation, I desire thee, seek not my soul's utter perdition. In destroying me, thou destroyest thyself and me.'

"Eagerly I replied after this long suppliant oration: 'Though I knew God would never have mercy upon me except I had mercy on thee, yet of thee no mercy would I have. Revenge in our tragedies is continually raised from hell; of hell do I esteem better than heaven if it afford me revenge. There is no heaven but revenge. I tell thee, I would not have undertook so much toil to gain heaven as I have done in pursuing thee for revenge. Divine revenge, of which, as of the joys above, there is no fullness or satiety. Look how my feet are blistered with following thee from place to place! I have riven my throat with overstraining it to curse thee. I have ground my teeth to powder with grating and grinding them together for anger when any hath nam'd thee. My tongue with vain threats is boll'n and waxen too big for my mouth; my eyes have broken their strings with staring and looking ghastly as I stood devising how to frame or set my countenance when I met thee. I have near spent my strength in imaginary acting on stone walls what I determined to execute on thee.

Intreat not, a miracle may not reprieve thee! Villain, thus march I with my blade into thy bowels!'

" 'Stay, stay!' exclaimed Esdras, 'and hear me but one word further. Though neither for God nor man thou carest, but placest thy whole felicity in murther, yet of thy felicity learn how to make a greater felicity. Respite me a little from thy sword's point and set me about some execrable enterprise that may subvert the whole state of Christendom and make all men's ears tingle that hear of it. Command me to cut all my kindred's throats, to burn men, women, and children in their beds in millions by firing their cities at midnight; be it pope, emperor, or Turk that displeaseth thee, he shall not breathe on the earth. For thy sake will I swear and forswear, renounce my baptism and all the interest I have in any other sacrament. Only let me live, how miserable soever, be it in a dungeon amongst toads, serpents, and adders, or set up to the neck in dung. No pains I will refuse, however prorogued, to have a little respite to purify my spirit. O hear me, hear me! and thou canst not be hard'ned against me.'

"At this his importunity I paused a little, not as retiring from my wreakful resolution, but going back to gather more forces of vengeance. With myself I devised how to plague him double for his base mind. My thoughts travel'd in quest of some notable new Italianism whose murderous platform might not only extend on his body, but his soul also. The groundwork of it was this: that whereas he had promised for my sake to swear and forswear, and commit Julian-like violence on the highest seals of religion, if he would but this far satisfy me, he should be dismiss'd from my fury: First and foremost, he should renounce God and his laws and utterly disclaim the whole title or interest he had in any covenant of salvation. Next, he should curse Him to his face, as Job was willed by his wife, and write an absolute firm obligation of his soul to the Devil without condition or exception. Thirdly and lastly, having done this, he should pray to God fervently, never to have mercy upon him or pardon him.

"Scarce had I propounded these articles unto him but he was beginning his blasphemous abjurations. I wonder the earth opened not and swallowed us both, hearing the bold terms he blasted forth in contempt of Christianity; heaven hath thundered when half less contumelies against it have been uttered. Able they were to raise saints and martyrs from their graves and pluck Christ himself from the right hand of his Father. My joints trembled and quak'd with attending them; my hair stood upright, and my heart was turned wholly to fire. So affectionately and zealously did he give himself over to infidelity as if Sathan had got the upper hand of our

High Maker. The vein in his left hand that is derived from the heart with no faint blow he pierc'd, and with the full blood that flowed from it writ a full obligation of his soul to the Devil; yea, he more earnestly pray'd unto God never to forgive his soul than many Christians do to save their souls. These fearful ceremonies brought to an end, I bade him ope his mouth and gape wide. He did so (as what will not slaves do for fear?); therewith made I no more ado, but shot him full into the throat with my pistol. No more spake he after, so did I shoot him that he might never speak after or repent him. His body being dead look'd as black as a toad: the Devil presently branded it for his own.

"This is the fault that hath called me hether. No true Italian but will honor me for it. Revenge is the glory of arms and the highest performance of valure. Revenge is whatsoever we call law or justice. The farther we wade in revenge the nearer come we to the throne of the Almighty. To his scepter it is properly ascribed; his scepter he lends unto man when he lets one man scourge another. All true Italians imitate me in revenging constantly and dying valiantly. Hangman, to thy task, for I am ready for the utmost of thy rigor."

Herewith, all the people, outragiously incensed, with one conjoined outcry, yelled mainly: "Away with him, away with him! Executioner, torture him! Tear him, or we will tear thee in pieces if thou spare him!"

The executioner needed no exhortation hereunto, for of his own nature was he hackster good inough; old-excellent he was at a bone-ache. At the first chop with his wood-knife would he fish for a man's heart, and fetch it out as easily as a plum from the bottom of a porredge-pot. He would crack necks as fast as a cook cracks eggs; a fiddler cannot turn his pin so soon as he would turn a man off the ladder. Bravely did he drum on this Cutwolfe's bones, not breaking them outright, but, like a saddler knocking in of tacks, jarring on them quaveringly with his hammer a great while together. No joint about him but with a hatchet he had for the nones he disjointed half, and then with boiling lead souldered up the wounds from bleeding; his tongue he pull'd out, lest he should blaspheme in his torment; venimous stinging worms he thrust into his ears to keep his head ravingly occupied; with cankers scruzed to pieces he rubb'd his mouth and his gums; no limb of his but was lingeringly splinter'd in shivers. In this horror left they him on the wheel as in hell, where, yet living, he might behold his flesh legacied amongst the fowls of the air. Unsearchable is the book of our destinies. One murder begetteth another; was never yet bloodshed barren from the beginning of the world to this day. Mortifiedly abjected and daunted was I with this truculent tragedy of Cutwolfe and Esdras. To such straight life did it thenceforward incite me that ere I went out of Bolognia I married my curtizan, performed many almsdeeds, and hasted so fast out of the Sodom of Italy that within forty days I arrived at the king of England's camp twixt Ardes and Guines in France, where he with great triumphs met and entertained the emperor and the French king, and feasted many days. And so, as my story began with the king at Turnay and Turwin, I think meet here to end it with the king at Ardes and Guines. All the conclusive epilogue I will make is this: that if herein I have pleased any, it shall animate me to more pains in this kind. Otherwise I will swear upon an English chronicle never to be outlandish chronicler more while I live. Farewell as many as wish me well.

THOMAS DELONEY

JACK OF NEWBURY and THOMAS OF READING

Whether they are novels or not, Deloney's swift and artless tales mark a significant departure in the writing of English fiction. Himself a weaver and a well-known writer of ballads, he took as his main subject the bourgeois industrial life that he knew intimately, and the four "novels" which he produced at the very end of his career are the first successful effort in English to work the data of contemporary middle-class culture into popular prose fiction. The extent of his success is indicated by the fact that his books were literally read to pieces: although published between 1597 and 1600, they survive only as reprints dating from twelve to forty years after their first editions. Deloney can hardly be called a realist, whatever that vague label means. His materials are generally homely, and are treated in a homely style; but he also knew, and occasionally imitated with calamitous results, the euphuistic romances of the seventies and eighties. And even though as both a man and a writer he must have recoiled from the aristocratic and stylistic mannerisms of Fenton's and Lyly's drawing-room romances, he was not above cribbing from (and misusing) euphuistic works when, as he naïvely thought, he needed to heighten his style and vary his subjects. None the less, if, as has been suggested, Elizabethan fiction derives from the two broad streams of medieval romance and the anecdotal jestbooks, Deloney's work certainly climaxes the popular as opposed to the literary tradition. He occasionally seeks to imitate the presumed elegance of Pettie or Lyly or Sidney; but his spiritual brethren are the anonymous generations of storytellers who contrived the racy, unpretentious jestbooks (see p. 669), Greene of the cony-catching pamphlets, and Nashe of *The Unfortunate Traveler*. The romantic adventures of Robert, Duke of Normandy, and his Fair Margaret (in *Thomas of Reading*) and the story of St. Hugh and Princess Winifred (in the first part of *The Gentle Craft*) are, as it were, painful coloratura arias amid brash and vigorously told yarns of enterprising merchants and ambitious apprentices; on the other hand, in the splendid career of Simon Eyre (*The Gentle Craft*, Part I) and the terrifying death of Old Cole (*Thomas of Reading*)—which Shakespeare may possibly have remembered when he came to write *Macbeth*—we see Deloney at his best, a minor master of swift prose narrative. *Jack of Newbury* (entered in the Stationers' Register on March 7, 1597) is a group of eleven anecdotes strung together, after a fashion, on the career of the exemplary John Winchcomb, an apprentice of Newbury who married his master's widow and came to be a power in the realm. *The Gentle Craft* (of which the first part was entered in the Stationers' Register on October 19, 1597, and the second was probably printed in 1598) is a similar batch of tales, but about shoemakers instead of clothworkers. *Thomas of Reading* (which probably followed *The Gentle Craft* within a year or so) contains fifteen stories about weavers and merchant-princes in the reign of Henry I. Our texts are based upon the earliest extant editions: *The Pleasant History of John Winchcomb, in his younger yeares called Jack of Newberie. . . . Now the eight time Imprinted*, 1619 (STC 6559); *Thomas of Reading. Or, The sixe worthy yeomen of the West. Now the fourth time corrected and enlarged*, 1612 (STC 6569).

FROM THE PLEASANT HISTORY OF JOHN WINCHCOMB, IN HIS YOUNGER YEARS CALLED JACK OF NEWBURY (1619)

To All Famous Cloth-Workers in England I Wish All Happiness of Life, Prosperity, and Brotherly Affection

Among all manual arts used in this land none is more famous for desert or more beneficial to the commonwealth than is the most necessary art of clothing. And therefore as the benefit thereof is great, so are the professors of the same to be both loved and maintained. Many wise men therefore, having deeply considered the same, most bountifully have bestowed their gifts for upholding of so excellent a commodity, which hath been and yet is the nourishing of many thousands of poor people. Wherefore to you, most worthy clothiers, do I dedicate this my rude work which hath raised out of the dust of forgetfulness a most famous and worthy man whose name was John Winchcomb, *alias* Jack of Newbury, of whose life and love I have briefly written, and in a plain and humble manner that it may be the better understood of those for whose sake I take pains to compile it, that is, for the well-minded clothiers, that herein they may behold the great worship and credit which men of this trade have in former time come unto. If, therefore, it be of you kindly accepted, I have the end of my desire, and think my pains well recompensed; and, finding your gentleness answering my hope, it shall move me shortly to set to your sight the long-hidden history of Thomas of Reading, George of Gloucester, Richard of Worcester, and William of Salisbury with divers others who were all most notable members in the commonwealth of this land and men of great fame and dignity. In the mean space I commend you all to the most high God, who ever increase, in all perfection and prosperous estate, the long-honored trade of English clothiers.

Yours in all humble service,

T[homas] D[eloney]

CHAPTER I

In the days of King Henery the Eight, that most noble and victorious prince, in the beginning of his reign John Winchcomb, a broadcloth weaver, dwelt in Newbury, a town in Berkshire, who, for that he was a man of a merry disposition and honest conversation, was wondrous well beloved of rich and poor, especially because in every place where he came he would spend his money with the best, and was not at any time found a churl of his purse. Wherefore, being so good a companion, he was called of old and young Jack of Newbury, a man so generally well-known in all his country for his good fellowship that he could go in no place but he found acquaintance, by means whereof Jack could no sooner get a crown but straight he found means to spend it; yet had he ever this care, that he would always keep himself in comely and decent apparel, neither at any time would he be overcome in drink, but so discreetly behave himself with honest mirth and pleasant conceits that he was every gentleman's companion.

After that Jack had long led this pleasant life, being (though he were but poor) in good estimation, it was his master's chance to die and his dame to be a widow, who was a very comely, ancient woman, and of reasonable wealth. Wherefore she, having a good opinion of her man John, committed unto his government the guiding of all her workfolks for the space of three years together; in which time she found him so careful and diligent that all things came forward and prospered wondrous well. No man could intice him from his business all the week by all the intreaty they could use, insomuch that in the end some of the wild youths of the town began to deride and scoff at him.

"Doubtless," quoth one, "I doubt some female spirit hath inchanted Jack to his treadles and conjured him within the compass of his loom that he can stir no further." "You say true," quoth Jack, "and if you have the leisure to stay till the charm be done, the space of six days and five nights, you shall find me ready to put on my holiday apparel, and on Sunday morning for your pains I will give you a pot of ale over against the maypole." "Nay," quoth another, "I'll lay my life that as the salamander cannot live without the fire so Jack cannot live without the smell of his dame's smock." "And I marvel," quoth Jack, "that you, being of the nature of the herring (which so soon as he is taken out of the sea straight dies) can live so long with your nose out of the pot." "Nay, Jack, leave thy jesting," quoth another, "and go along with us. Thou shalt not stay a jot." "And because I will not stay, nor make you a liar," quoth Jack, "I'll keep me here still, and so farewell!"

Thus then they departed, and after they had for half a score times tried him to this intent and saw he would not be led by their lure they left him to his own will. Nevertheless, every Sunday in the afternoon, and every holiday, Jack would keep them company and be as merry as a pie, and having still good store of money in his purse one or other would ever be borrowing of him, but never could he get penny of it again, which when Jack perceived, he would never after carry above twelvepence at once in his purse, and that being spent he would straight

return home merrily, taking his leave of the company
in this sort:

My masters, I thank you, it's time to pack home,
For he that wants money is counted a mome,
And twelvepence a Sunday being spent in good cheer
To fifty-two shillings amounts in the year.
Enough for a craftsman that lives by his hands,
And he that exceeds it shall purchase no lands.
For that I spend this day I'll work hard tomorrow,
For wo is that party that seeketh to borrow.   10
My money doth make me full merry to be,
And without my money none careth for me.
Therefore, wanting money, what should I do here?
But haste home, and thank you for all my good cheer.

Thus was Jack's good government and discretion
noted of the best and substantialest men of the town,
so that it wrought his great commendations, and his
dame thought herself not a little blest to have such a   20
servant, that was so obedient unto her and so careful
for her profit. For she had never a prentice that
yielded her more obedience then he did or was more
dutiful, so that by his good example he did as much
good as by his diligent labor and travail, which his
singular virtue being noted by the widow, she began
to cast very good countenance to her man John, and
to use very much talk with him in private; and first,
by way of communication, she would tell unto him
what suitors she had, and the great offers they made   30
her, what gifts they sent her, and the great affection
they bare her, craving his opinion in the matter.

When Jack found the favor to be his dame's
secretary he thought it an extraordinary kindness,
and, ghessing by the yarn it would prove a good web,
began to question with his dame in this sort: "Although it becometh not me, your servant, to pry
into your secrets nor to be busy about matters of
your love, yet for so much as it hath pleased you to
use conference with me in those causes, I pray you,   40
let me intreat you to know their names that be your
suitors, and of what profession they be."

"Marry, John," saith she, "that you shall, and,
I pray thee, take a cushion and sit down by me."
"Dame," quoth he, "I thank you, but there is no
reason I should sit on a cushion till I have deserved
it." "If thou hast not, thou mightest have done,"
said she, "but faint soldiers never find favor." John
replied, "That makes me indeed to want favor, for I
durst not try maidens because they seem coy, nor   50
wives for fear of their husbands, nor widows, doubting their disdainfulness." "Tush, John," quoth she,
"he that fears and doubts womenkind cannot be
counted mankind; and take this for a principle, all
things are not as they seem. But let us leave this and

proceed to our former matter. My first suitor dwells
at Wallingford, by trade a tanner, a man of good
wealth, and his name is Crafts, of comely personage
and very good behavior, a widower, well thought of
amongst his neighbors; he hath proper land, a fair
house and well-furnished, and never a child in the
world, and he loves me passing well." "Why then,
dame," quoth John, "you were best to have him."
"Is that your opinion?" quoth she; "now trust me,
so it is not mine. For I find two special reasons to the
contrary: the one is that he, being overworn in
years, makes me overloth to love him; and the other
that I know one nearer hand."

"Believe me, dame," quoth Jack, "I perceive store
is no sore, and proffered ware is worse by ten in the
hundred than that which is sought; but, I pray ye,
who is your second suitor?" "John," quoth she, "it
may seem immodesty in me to bewray my love's
secrets; yet, seeing thy discretion and being persuaded
of thy secrecy, I will shew thee. The other is a man of
middle years but yet a bachelor, by occupation a
tailor dwelling at Hungerford, by report a very good
husband, such a one as hath crowns good store, and
to me he professes much good will; for his person,
he may please any woman." "Ay, dame," quoth
John, "because he pleaseth you." "Not so," said she,
"for my eyes are unpartial judges in that case; and
albeit my opinion may be contrary to others', if his
art deceive not my eyesight he is worthy of a good
wife, both for his person and conditions." "Then
trust me, dame," quoth John, "forsomuch as you are
without doubt of yourself that you will prove a good
wife and so well-persuaded of him, I should think
you could make no better a choice." "Truly, John,"
quoth she, "there be also two reasons that move me
not to like of him: the one, that being so long a
ranger he would at home be a stranger, and the other,
that I like better of one nearer hand." "Who is that?"
quoth Jack. Saith she, "The third suitor is the parson
of Spinhomeland, who hath a proper living; he
is of holy conversation and good estimation, whose
affection to me is great." "No doubt, dame,"
quoth John, "you may do wondrous well with him,
where you shall have no care but to serve God and
to make ready his meat." "O John," quoth she, "the
flesh and the spirit agrees not, for he will be so bent
to his book that he will have little mind of his bed;
for one moneth's studying for a sermon will make
him forget his wife a whole year." "Truly, dame,"
quoth John, "I must needs speak in his behalf, and
the rather for that he is a man of the church and your
near neighbor, to whom (as I guess) you bear the
best affection. I do not think that he will be so much
bound to his book or subject to the spirit but that
he will remember a woman at home or abroad."

"Well, John," quoth she, "iwis my mind is not that way, for I like better of one nearer hand." "No marvel," quoth Jack, "you are so peremptory, seeing you have so much choice, but I pray ye, dame," quoth he, "let me know this fortunate man that is so highly placed in your favor." "John," quoth she, "they are worthy to know nothing that cannot keep something. That man, I tell thee, must go nameless, for he is lord of my love and king of my desires. There is neither tanner, tailor, nor parson may compare with him; his presence is a preservative to my health, his sweet smiles my heart's solace, and his words heavenly music to my ears." "Why then, dame," quoth John, "for your body's health, your heart's joy, and your ears' delight delay not the time, but entertain him with a kiss, make his bed next yours, and chop up the match in the morning." "Well," quoth she, "I perceive thy consent is quickly got to any, having no care how I am match'd so I be match'd. Iwis, iwis, I could not let thee go so lightly, being loth that any one should have thee except I could love her as well as myself." "I thank you for your kindness and good will, good dame," quoth he, "but it is not wisdom for a young man that can scantly keep himself to take a wife; therefore I hold it the best way to lead a single life, for I have heard say that many sorrows follow marriage, especially where want remains; and beside, it is a hard matter to find a constant woman, for as young maids are fickle, so are old women jealous, the one a grief too common, the other a torment intolerable." "What, John," quoth she, "consider that maidens' fickleness proceeds of vain fancies, but old women's jealousy of superabounding love, and therefore the more to be borne withal." "But, dame," quoth he, "many are jealous without cause, for is it sufficient for their mistrusting natures to take exceptions at a shadow, at a word, at a look, at a smile, nay, at the twinkle of an eye, which neither man nor woman is able to expel. I knew a woman that was ready to hang herself for seeing but her husband's shirt hang on a hedge with her maid's smock." "I grant that this fury may haunt some," quoth she, "yet there be many other that complain not without great cause." "Why, is there any cause that should move jealousy?" quoth John. "Ay, by St. Mary is there," quoth she, "for would it not grieve a woman (being one every way able to delight her husband) to see him forsake her, despise and contemn her, being never so merry as when he is in other company, sporting abroad from morning till noon, from noon till night, and when he comes to bed, if he turn to his wife it is in such solemnness and wearisome, drowsy lameness that it brings rather lothsomeness than any delight. Can you then blame a woman in this case to be angry and

displeased? I'll tell you what, among brute beasts it is a grief intolerable; for I heard my granddame tell that the bell-wether of her flock, fancying one of the ewes above the rest and seeing Gratis the shepherd abusing her in abhominable sort (subverting the law of nature), could by no means bear that abuse, but, watching opportunity for revenge, on a time found the said shepherd sleeping in the field and suddenly ran against him in such violent sort that by the force of his wreathen horns he beat the brains out of the shepherd's head and slew him. If, then, a sheep could not endure that injury, think not that women are so sheepish to suffer it." "Believe me," quoth John, "if every horn-maker should be so plagued by a horned beast there should be less horns made in Newbury by many in a year. But dame," quoth he, "to make an end of this prattle, because it is an argument too deep to be discussed between you and I, you shall hear me sing an old song, and so we will depart to supper.

> "A maiden fair I dare not wed,
> For fear to have Actaeon's head;
> A maiden black is often proud,
> A maiden little will be loud;
> A maiden that is high of growth,
> They say, is subject unto sloth;
> Thus fair or foul, little or tall,
> Some faults remain among them all,
> But of all the faults that be,
> None is so bad as jealousy.
> For jealousy is fierce and fell,
> And burns as hot as fire in hell.
> It breeds suspicion without cause
> And breaks the bonds of Reason's laws.
> To none it is a greater foe
> Than unto those where it doth grow.
> And God keep me both day and night
> From that fell, fond, and ugly spright!
> For why of all the plagues that be,
> The secret plague is jealousy.
> Therefore I wish all womenkind
> Never to bear a jealous mind."

"Well said, John!" quoth she. "Thy song is not so sure, but thy voice is as sweet. But seeing the time agrees with our stomachs, though loth, yet will we give over for this time and betake ourselves to our suppers." Then calling the rest of her servants, they fell to their meat merrily. . . .

[Jack, cannily analyzing his prospects, "perceived that his dame's affection was great toward him," yet he weighed the advantages of money and position against the disadvantages of an aging and probably jealous wife, and "therefore resolved to be silent rather than to proceed further." Thus things rocked along for a month, the widow's desire to marry her servant growing daily more urgent but his reservations remaining unchanged. At last, resolving to take decisive action, she invited the tailor, the tanner, and the parson to her house on the following Thursday, permitting each one to understand that his prospects for matrimony were by no means dim. When they had all arrived (preceded by their love-offerings of pigs, geese, capons, mutton, and sack, wherewith the festive board groaned), the situation was delicate, for each suitor was surprised and resentful at the presence of the others. When dinner-time came, the widow and her three suitors, together with a neighbor ("an old woman with scant ever a good tooth in her head"), made the party, Jack "being chief servitor."]

After they had sitten a while and well refreshed themselves, the widow, taking a crystal glass fill'd with claret wine, drunk unto the whole company and bade them welcome. The parson pledged her, and so did all the rest in due order, but still in their company the cup pass'd over the poor old woman's nose, insomuch that at length the old woman (in a merry vein) spake thus unto the company: "I have had much good meat among you, but as for the drink I can nothing commend it." "Alas, good gossip," quoth the widow, "I perceive no man hath drunk to thee yet." "No, truly," quoth the old woman, "for churchmen have so much mind of young rabbits, old men such joy in young chickens, and bachelors in pigs' flesh take such delight that an old sow, a tough hen, or a gray cony are not accepted; and so it is seen by me, else I should have been better rememb'red." "Well, old woman," quoth the parson, "take here the leg of a capon to stop thy mouth." "Now by St. Anne, I dare not," quoth she. "No? Wherefore?" said the parson. "Marry, for fear lest you should go home with a crutch," quoth she. The tailor said, "Then taste here a piece of goose." "Now God forbid," said the old woman. "Let goose go to his kind; you have a young stomach; eat it yourself, and much good may it do your heart, sweet young man." "The old woman lacks most of her teeth," quoth the tanner, "and therefore a piece of tender chick is fittest for her." "If I did lack as many of my teeth," quoth the old woman, "as you lack points of good husbandry I doubt I should starve before it were long." At this the widow laugh'd heartily, and the men were stricken into such a dump that they had not a word to say. Dinner being ended, the widow with the rest rose from the table, and, after they had sitten a pretty while merrily talking, the widow called her man John to bring her a bowl of fresh ale, which he did. Then said the widow:

"My masters, now for your curtesy and cost I heartily thank you all, and in requital of all your favor, love, and good will I drink to you, giving you free liberty when you please to depart." At these words her suitors looked so sourly one upon another as if they had been newly champing of crabs. Which when the tailor heard, shaking up himself in his new russet jerkin and setting his hat on one side, he began to speak thus: "I trust, sweet widow," quoth he, "you remember to what end my coming was hither today. I have long time been a suitor unto you, and this day you promised to give me a direct answer." " 'Tis true," quoth she, "and so I have. For your love I give you thanks, and when you please you may depart." "Shall I not have you?" said the tailor. "Alas," quoth the widow, "you come too late." "Good friend," quoth the tanner, "it is manners for young men to let their elders be served before them. To what end should I be here if the widow should have thee? A flat denial is meet for a saucy suitor, but what sayst thou to me, fair widow?" quoth the tanner. "Sir," said she, "because you are so sharp set I would wish you as soon as you can to wed." "Appoint the time yourself," quoth the tanner. "Even as soon," quoth she, "as you can get a wife, and hope not after me, for I am already promised." "Now, tanner, you may take your place with the tailor," quoth the parson, "for indeed the widow is for no man but myself." "Master Parson," quoth she, "many have run near the goal and yet lost the game, and I cannot help it though your hope be in vain; besides, parsons are but newly suffered to have wives, and for my part I will have none of the first head." "What!" quoth the tailor, "is our merriment grown to this reckoning? I never spent a pig and a goose to so bad purpose before. I promise you, when I came in I verily thought that you were invited by the widow to make her and me sure together, and that the jolly tanner was brought to be a witness to the contract, and the old woman fetch'd in for the same purpose; else I would never have put up so many dry-bobs at her hands." "And surely," quoth the tanner, "I, knowing thee to be a tailor, did assuredly think that thou wast appointed to come and take measure for our wedding apparel." "But now we are all deceived," quoth the parson, "and therefore, as we came fools, so we may depart hence like asses." "That is as you interpret the matter," said the widow; "for I, ever doubting that a concluding answer would breed a jar in the end among you every one, I thought it better to be done at one instant, and in mine own house, than at sundry times and in common taverns. And as for the meat you sent, as it was unrequested of me, so had you your part thereof, and if you think good to take home the remainder prepare your wallets and you shall have it." "Nay, widow," quoth they, "although we have lost our labors, we have not altogether lost our manners. That which you have, keep; and God send to us better luck and to you your heart's desire." And with that they departed.

The widow, being glad she was thus rid of her guests, when her man John with all the rest sate at supper, she sitting in a chair by, spake thus unto them: "Well, my masters, you saw that this day your poor dame had her choice of husbands, if she had listed to marry, and such as would have loved and maintained her like a woman." "'Tis true," quoth John, "and I pray God you have not withstood your best fortune." "Trust me," quoth she, "I know not, but if I have I may thank mine own foolish fancy."

Thus it pass'd on from Bartholomewtide till it was near Christmas, at what time the weather was so wonderful cold that all the running rivers round about the town were frozen very thick. The widow, being very loth any longer to lie without company, in a cold winter's night made a great fire and sent for her man John; having also prepared a chair and a cushion, she made him sit down therein, and, sending for a pint of good sack, they both went to supper.

In the end, bedtime coming on, she caused her maid in a merriment to pluck off his hose and shoes, and caused him to be laid in his master's best bed, standing in the best chamber, hung round about with very fair curtains. John, being thus preferred, thought himself a gentleman, and lying soft after his hard labor and a good supper quickly fell asleep.

About midnight the widow, being cold on her feet, crept into her man's bed to warm them. John, feeling one lift up the clothes, asked who was there. "O, good John, it is I," quoth the widow; "the night is so extreme cold and my chamber walls so thin that I am like to be starved in my bed; wherefore, rather then I would any way hazard my health, I thought it much better to come hither and try your curtesy to have a little room beside you."

John, being a kind young man, would not say her nay, and so they spent the rest of the night both together in one bed. In the morning betime she rose up and made herself ready, and willed her man John to run and fetch her a link with all speed. "For," quoth she, "I have earnest business to do this morning." Her man did so. Which done, she made him to carry the link before her until she came to Saint Bartholomew's Chapel, where Sir John, the priest, with his clerk and sexton stood waiting for her. "John," quoth she, "turn into the chapel, for before I go further I will make my prayers to St. Bartholomew; so shall I speed the better in my business." When they were come in, the priest, according to

his order, came to her and asked where the bridegroom was. Quoth she, "I thought he had been here before me. Sir," quoth she, "I will sit down and say over my beads, and by that time he will come." John mused at this matter, to see that his dame should so sodainly be married and he hearing nothing thereof before. The widow rising from her prayers, the priest told her that the bridegroom was not yet come. "Is it true?" quoth the widow. "I promise you I will stay no longer for him if he were as good as George-a-Green, and therefore dispatch," quoth she, "and marry me to my man John." "Why, dame," quoth he, "you do but jest, I trow." "John," quoth she, "I jest not, for so I mean it shall be, and stand not strangely but remember that you did promise me on your faith not to hinder me when I came to the church to be married, but rather to set it forward. Therefore, set your link aside and give me your hand, for none but you shall be my husband." John, seeing no remedy, consented, because he saw the matter could not otherwise be amended, and married they were presently. When they were come home, John entertained his dame with a kiss, which the other servants seeing thought him something saucy. The widow caused the best cheer in the house to be set on the table, and to breakfast they went, causing her new husband to be set in a chair at the table's end with a fair napkin laid on his trencher. Then she called out the rest of her servants, willing them to sit down and take part of their good cheer. They, wond'ring to see their fellow John set at the table's end in their old master's chair, began heartily to smile and openly to laugh at the matter, especially because their dame so kindly sate by his side; which she, perceiving, asked if that were all the manners they could shew before their master. "I tell you," quoth she, "he is my husband, for this morning we were married, and therefore henceforward look you acknowledge your duty towards him." The folks looked one upon another, marveling at this strange news. Which when John perceived, he said: "My masters, muse not at all, for although by God's providence and your dame's favor I am preferred from being your fellow to be your master, I am not thereby so much puff'd up in pride that any way I will forget my former estate. Notwithstanding, seeing I am now to hold the place of a master, it shall be wisdom in you to forget what I was and to take me as I am, and in doing your diligence you shall have no cause to repent that God made me your master." The servants, hearing this, as also knowing his good government beforetime, pass'd their years with him in dutiful manner.

The next day the report was over all the town that Jack of Newbury had married his dame, so that when the woman walked abroad everyone bad God give her joy. Some said that she was match'd to her sorrow, saying that so lusty a young man as he would never love her, being so ancient. Whereupon the woman made answer that she would take him down in his wedding shoes and would try his patience in the prime of his lustiness, whereunto many of her gossips did likewise encourage her. Every day, therefore, for the space of a moneth after she was married it was her ordinary custom to go forth in the morning among her gossips and acquaintance to make merry and not to return home till night, without any regard of her household. Of which, at her coming home, her husband did very oftentimes admonish her in very gentle sort, shewing what great inconvenience would grow thereby, the which sometime she would take in gentle part and sometime in disdain, saying: "I am now in very good case, that he which was my servant but the other day will now be my master. This it is for a woman to make her foot her head. The day hath been when I might have gone forth when I would and come in again when it had pleased me without controlment; and now I must be subject to every Jack's check. I am sure," quoth she, "that by my gadding abroad and careless spending I waste no goods of thine. I, pitying thy poverty, made thee a man, and maister of the house, but not to the end I would become thy slave. I scorn, I tell thee true, that such a youngling as thyself should correct my conceit and give me instructions, as if I were not able to guide myself. But i'faith, i'faith, you shall not use me like a babe nor bridle me like an ass, and seeing my going abroad grieves thee, where I have gone forth one day I will go abroad three, and for one hour I will stay five." "Well," quoth her husband, "I trust you will be better advised." And with that he went from her about his business, leaving her sweating in her fustian furies.

Thus the time pass'd on till, on a certain day, she had been abroad in her wonted manner, and, staying forth very late, he shut the doors and went to bed. About midnight she comes to the door and knocks to come in, to whom he, looking out of the window, answered in this sort: "What, is it you that keeps such a knocking? I pray you get hence and request the constable to provide you a bed for this night; you shall have no lodging here." "I hope," quoth she, "you will not shut me out of doors like a dog or let me lie in the streets like a strumpet." "Whether like a dog or drab," quoth he, "all is one to me, knowing no reason but that as you have stayed out all day for your delight, so you may lie forth all night for my pleasure. Both birds and beasts, at the night's approach, prepare to their rest and observe a convenient time to return to their habitation. Look but upon the poor spider, the frog, the fly, and every other silly worm, and you shall see all these observe time to return to their home; and if you, being a woman, will not do the like, content yourself to bear the brunt of your own folly, and so farewell."

The woman, hearing this, made piteous moan and in very humble sort intreated him to let her in and to pardon this offense, and while she lived vowed never to do the like. Her husband, at length being moved with pity towards her, slipp'd on his shoes and came down in his shirt; the door being opened, in she went quaking, and as he was about to lock it again, in very sorrowful manner she said: "Alack, husband, what hap have I! My wedding ring was even now in my hand and I have let it fall about the door. Good, sweet John, come forth with the candle and help me to seek it." The man incontinent did so, and while he sought for that which was not there to be found she whipp'd into the house and, quickly clapping to the door, she lock'd her husband out. He stood calling with the candle in his hand to come in, but she made as if she heard not. Anon she went up into her chamber and carried the key with her, but when he saw she would not answer he presently began to knock as loud as he could at the door. At last she thrust her head out at the window, saying, "Who is there?" "'Tis I," quoth John. "What mean you by this? I pray you come down and open the door that I may come in."

"What, sir," quoth she, "is it you? Have you nothing to do but dance about the streets at this time of night and, like a spirit of the buttery, hunt after crickets? Are you so hot that the house cannot hold you?" "Nay, I pray thee, sweetheart," quoth he, "do not gibe any longer, but let me in." "O sir, remember," quoth she, "how you stood even now at the window like a judge on the bench and in taunting sort kept me out of my own house. How now, Jack, am I even with you? What, John my man, were you so lusty to lock your dame out of doors? Sirrah, remember you bad me go to the constable to get lodging; now you have leisure to try if his wife will prefer you to a bed. You, sir sauce, that made me stand in the cold till my feet did freeze and my teeth chatter, while you stood preaching of birds and beasts, telling me a tale of spiders, flies, and frogs, go try now if any of them will be so friendly to let thee have lodging. Why go you not, man? Fear not to speak with them, for I am sure you shall find them at home. Think not they are such ill husbands as you, to be abroad at this time of night."

With this, John's patience was greatly moved, insomuch that he deeply swore that if she would not let him in he would break down the door. "Why, John," quoth she, "you need not be so hot. Your clothing is not so warm; and because I think this will be a warning unto ye against another time how you shut me out of my house, catch, there is the key. Come in at thy pleasure, and look you go to bed to your fellows, for with me thou shalt not lie tonight." With that she clapp'd to the casement and got her to bed, locking the chamber door fast. Her husband, that knew it was in vain to seek to come into her chamber, and being no longer able to endure the cold, got him a place among his prentices and there slept soundly. In the morning his wife rose betime and merrily made him a caudle, and bringing it up to his bed asked him how he did.

Quoth John, "Troubled with a shrew who the longer she lives the worse she is. And as the people of Illyris kill men with their looks, so she kills her husband's heart with untoward conditions. But trust me, wife," quoth he, "seeing I find you of such crooked qualities that, like the spider, ye turn the sweet flowers of good counsel into venemous poison, from henceforth I will leave you to your own wilfulness, and neither vex my mind nor trouble myself to restrain you, the which if I had wisely done last night I had kept the house in quiet and myself from cold." "Husband," quoth she, "think that women are like starlings that will burst their gall before they will yield to the fowler, or like the fish scolopendra, that cannot be touched without danger. Notwithstanding, as the hard steel doth yield to the hammer's stroke, being used to his kind, so will women to their husbands where they are not too much cross'd. And seeing ye have sworn to give me my will, I vow likewise that my wilfulness shall not offend you. I tell you, husband, the noble nature of a woman is such that for their loving friends they will not stick (like the pelican) to pierce their own hearts to do them good. And therefore, forgiving each other all injuries pass'd, having also tried one another's patience, let us quench these burning coals of contention with the sweet juice of a faithful kiss, and, shaking hands, bequeath all our anger to the eating-up of this caudle." Her husband curteously consented. And after this time they lived long together in most godly, loving, and kind sort till, in the end, she died, leaving her husband wondrous wealthy.

FROM THOMAS OF READING, OR THE SIX WORTHY YEOMEN OF THE WEST (1612)

In the days of King Henry the First, who was the first king that instituted the High Court of Parliament, there lived nine men which for the trade of clothing were famous throughout all England. Which art in those days was held in high reputation, both in respect of the great riches that thereby was gotten as also of the benefit it brought to the whole commonwealth. The younger sons of knights and gentlemen, to whom their fathers would leave no lands, were most commonly preferred to learn this trade to the end that thereby they might live in good estate and drive forth their days in prosperity.

Among all crafts this was the only chief for that it was the greatest marchandize by the which our country became famous through all nations. And it was verily thought that the one half of the people in the land lived in those days thereby, and in such good sort that in the commonwealth there was few or no beggars at all. Poor people, whom God lightly blesseth with most children, did, by means of this occupation, so order them that by the time that they were come to be six or seven years of age they were able to get their own bread. Idleness was then banished our coast, so that it was a rare thing to hear of a thief in those days. Therefore it was not without cause that clothiers were then both honored and loved, among whom these nine persons in this king's days were of great credit, viz., Thomas Cole of Reading, Gray of Gloucester, Sutton of Salisbury, Fitzallen of Worcester (commonly called William of Worcester), Tom Dove of Exeter, and Simon of Southampton, alias Sup-Broth, who were by the king called the six worthy husbands of the West. Then were there three living in the North, that is to say, Cutbert of Kendal, Hodgekins of Halifax, and Martin Byram of Manchester. Every one of these kept a great number of servants at work—spinners, carders, weavers, fullers, dyers, shearmen, and rowers —to the great admiration of all those that came into their houses to behold them.

Now you shall understand these gallant clothiers, by reason of their dwelling-places, separated themselves in three several companies: Gray of Gloucester, William of Worcester, and Thomas of Reading, because their jorney to London was all one way, they conversed commonly together. And Dove of Exeter, Sutton of Salisbury, and Simon of Southampton, they in like sort kept company the one with the other, meeting ever altogether at Basingstoke; and the three northern clothiers did the like, who commonly did not meet till they came to Bosom's Inn in London.

Moreover, for the love and delight that these western men had each in other's company, they did so provide that their wains and themselves would ever meet upon one day in London at Jarrat's Hall, surnamed the Giant, for that he surpassed all other men of that age both in stature and strength, whose merriments and memorable deeds I will set down unto you in this following discourse.

CHAP. I. How King Henry Sought the Favor of All His Subjects, Especially of the Clothiers

This King Henry, who for his great learning and wisdom was called Beauclerk, being the third son to the renowned Conqueror, after the death of his brother William Rufus, took upon him the government of this land in the absence of his second brother, Robert, Duke of Normandy, who at this time was at wars against the infidels and was chosen king of Jerusalem, the which he, for the love he bare to his own country, refused and with great honor returned from the Holy Land, of whose coming when King Henry understood, knowing he would make claim to the crown, sought by all means possible to win the good will of his nobility and to get the favor of the commons by curtesy, for the obtaining whereof he did them many favors, thereby the better to strengthen himself against his brother.

It chanced on a time as he, with one of his sons and divers of his nobility, rode from London towards Wales to appease the fury of the Welshmen, which then began to raise themselves in arms against his authority, that he met with a great number of wains loaden with cloth coming to London; and seeing them still drive on, one after another so many together, demanded whose they were. The wainmen answered in this sort: "Cole's of Reading," quoth they. Then by and by the king asked another, saying, "Whose cloth is all this?" "Old Cole's," quoth he, and again anon, after he asked the same question to other, and still they answered, "Old Cole's." And it is to be rememb'red that the king met them in such a place, so narrow and streight, that he, with all the rest of his train, were fain to stand up close to the hedge whilest the carts passed by, the which, at that time being in number above two hundred, was near hand an hour ere the king could get room to be gone; so that by his long stay he began to be displeased, although the admiration of that sight did much qualify his fury, but breaking out in discontent by reason of his stay, he said he thought Old Cole had got a commission for all the carts in the country to carry his cloth. "And how if he have," quoth one of the wainmen, "doth that grieve you, good sir?" "Yea, good sir," said our king, "what say you to that?" The fellow, seeing the king, in asking that question, to bend his brows, though he knew not what he was, yet being abash'd, he answered thus:

"Why, sir, if you be angry nobody can hinder you, for possibly, sir, you have anger at commandment." The king, seeing him in uttering of his words to quiver and quake, laughed heartily at him, as well in respect of his simple answer as at his fear, and so, soon after, the last wain went by, which gave present passage unto him and his nobles, and thereupon ent'ring into communication of the commodity of clothing, the king gave order at his home return to have Old Cole brought before his Majesty to the intent he might have conference with him, noting him to be a subject of great ability. But by that time he came within a mile of Staines, he met another company of wains, in like sort laden with cloth, whereby the king was driven into a further admiration, and demanding whose they were, answer was made in this sort: "They be Goodman Sutton's of Salisbury, good sir." And by that time a score of them were pass'd he asked again, saying, "Whose are these?" "Sutton's of Salisbury," quoth they. And so still, as often as the king asked that question, they answer'd, "Sutton's of Salisbury." "God send me many such Suttons," said the king. And thus the farther he traveled westward, more wains and more he met continually, upon which occasion he said to his nobles that it would never grieve a king to die for the defense of a fertile country and faithful subjects. "I always thought," quoth he, "that England's valor was more than her wealth, yet now I see her wealth sufficient to maintain her valor, which I will seek to cherish in all I may, and with my sword keep myself in possession of that I have. Kings and lovers can brook no partners, and therefore let my brother Robert think that although he was heir to England by birth, yet I am king by possession. All his favorers I must account my foes, and will serve them as I did the ungrateful Earl of Shrewsbury, whose lands I have seized and banish'd his body." But now we will leave the king to his journey into Wales and, waiting his home return, in the meantime tell you of the meeting of these jolly clothiers at London. . . .

CHAP. IX. How the Bailiffs of London Could Get No Man to Be a Catchpole, and How Certain Flemings Took That Office upon Them, Whereof Many of Them Were Fled into This Realm by Reason of Certain Waters That Had Drowned a Great Part of Their Country

The city of London being at this time governed by bailiffs, it came to pass that in a certain fray two of their catchpoles were killed, for at that time they had not the name of sergeants, and you shall understand that their office was then so much hated and detested of Englishmen that none of them would take it upon him, so that the bailiffs were glad to get any man whatsoever and to give him certain wages to perform that office.

It came to pass, as I said before, that two of their officers, by arresting of a man, were at one instant slain, by means whereof the bailiffs were inforced to seek others to put in their rooms, but by no means could they get any, wherefore, according to their wonted manner, they made proclamation that, if there were any man that would present himself before them, he should not only be settled in that office during their lives but also should have such maintenance and allowance as for such men was by the city provided; and notwithstanding that it was an office most necessary in the commonwealth, yet did the poorest wretch despise it that lived in any estimation among his neighbors.

At last a couple of Flemings, which were fled into this land by reason that their country was drowned with the sea, hearing the proclamation, offered themselves unto the bailiffs to serve in this place, who were presently received and accepted, and according to order had garments given them which were of two colors, blue and red, their coats, breeches, and stockings, whereby they were known and discerned from other men.

Within half a year after, it came to pass that Thomas Dove of Exeter came up to London, who, having by his jollity and good fellowship brought himself greatly behindhand, was in danger to diverse men of the city; among the rest, one of his creditors fixed an officer to arrest him. The Dutchman, that had not been long experienced in such matters, and hearing how many of his fellows had been killed for attempting to arrest men, stood quivering and quaking in a corner of the street to watch for Tom Dove, and, having long waited, at length he spied him; whereupon he prepared his mace ready, and with a pale countenance proceeded to do his office, at what time, coming behind the man, sodainly with his mace he knock'd him on the pate, saying, "I arrest you!" giving him such a blow that he fell'd him to the ground.

The catchpole, thinking he had killed the man, he left his mace behind him and ran away; the creditor he ran after him, calling and crying that he should turn again; but the Fleming would not by any means come back, but got him quite out of the city and took sanctuary at Westminster.

Dove, being come to himself, arose and went to his inn, no man hind'ring his passage, being not a little glad he so escaped the danger. Yet, nevertheless, at his next coming to London another catchpole met with him and arrested him in the king's name.

Dove, being dismay'd at this mischievous chance, knew not what to do; at last he requested the catchpole that he would not violently cast him in prison, but stay till such time as he could send for a friend to be his surety; and although kindness in a catchpole be rare, yet was he won with fair words to do him this favor, whereupon Dove desired one to go to his host Jarrat, who immediately came unto him and off'red himself to be Dove's surety.

The officer, who never saw this man before, was much amazed at his sight, for Jarrat was a great and a mighty man of body, of countenance grim, and exceeding high of stature, so that the catchpole was wonderfully afraid, asking if he could find never a surety but the Divel, most fearfully intreating him to conjure him away and he would do Dove any favor. "What, will you not take my word?" quod Jarrat. "Sir," quod the catchpole, "if 'twere for any matter in hell I would take your word as soon as any divel's in that place, but seeing it is for a matter on earth, I would gladly have a surety."

"Why, thou whoreson cricket," quoth Jarrat, "thou magget a pie, thou spinner, thou paltry spider, dost thou take me for a divel, sirrah? Take my word, I charge thee, for this man, or else, Goodman Butterfly, I'll make thee repent it." The officer, while he was in the house, said he was content, but so soon as he came into the street he cried, saying, "Help, help, good neighbors, or else the Divel will carry away my prisoner." Notwithstanding, there was not one man would stir to be the catchpole's aid, which when he saw he took fast hold on Thomas Dove and would not by any means let him go.

Jarrat, seeing this, made no more to do, but coming to the officer gave him such a fillip on the forehead with his finger that he fell'd the poor Fleming to the ground; and while he lay in the street stretching his heels, Jarrat took Dove under his arm and carried him home, where he thought himself as safe as King Charlemagne in Mount Alban.

The next morning Jarrat conveyed Dove out of town, who afterward kept him in the country and came no more in the catchpole's claws. . . .

CHAP. XI. How Thomas of Reading Was Murd'red at His Host's House of Colebrooke Who Also Had Murd'red Many before Him; How Their Wickedness Was at Length Revealed

Thomas of Reading having many occasions to come to London, as well about his own affairs as also the king's business, being in a great office under his Majesty, it chanced on a time that his host and hostess of Colebrook, who through covetousness had murd'red many of their ghests and having every time he came thither great store of his money to lay up, appointed him to be the next fat pig that should be killed. For it is to be understood that, when they plotted the murther of any man, this was always their term, the man to his wife and the woman to her husband: "Wife, there is now a fat pig to be had if you want one." Whereupon she would answer thus, "I pray you put him in the hog-sty till tomorrow." This was when any man came thither alone without others in his company, and they saw he had great store of money.

This man should be then laid in the chamber right over the kitchen, which was a fair chamber and better set out then any other in the house; the best bedstead therein, though it were little and low, yet was it most cunningly carved and fair to the eye, the feet whereof were fast nail'd to the chamber floor in such sort that it could not in any wise fall; the bed that lay therein was fast sewed to the sides of the bedstead. Moreover, that part of the chamber whereupon this bed and bedstead stood was made in such sort that, by the pulling out of two iron pins below in the kitchen, it was to be let down and taken up by a drawbridge, or in manner of a trap-door. Moreover, in the kitchen, directly under the place where this should fall, was a mighty great caldron wherein they used to seethe their liquor when they went to brewing. Now the men appointed for the slaughter were laid into this bed, and in the dead time of the night, when they were found asleep, by plucking out the foresaid iron pins down would the man fall out of his bed into the boiling caldron and all the clothes that were upon him, where, being suddenly scalded and drowned, he was never able to cry or speak one word.

Then had they a little ladder ever standing ready in the kitchen by the which they presently mounted into the said chamber and there closely took away the man's apparel, as also his money in his male or cap-case, and then, lifting up the said falling floor, which hung by hinges, they made it fast as before.

The dead body would they take presently out of the caldron and throw it down the river, which ran near unto their house, whereby they escaped all danger.

Now if in the morning any of the rest of the ghests that had talk'd with the murthered man over eve chanc'd to ask for him, as having occasion to ride the same way that he should have done, the goodman would answer that he took horse a good while before day and that he himself did set him forward. The horse the goodman would also take out of the stable and convey him to a haybarn of his that stood from his house a mile or two, whereof himself did always keep the keys full charily, and when any hay was to be brought from thence, with his own hands he would deliver it; then, before the horse should go from thence he would dismark him, as if he ware a long tail he would make him curtal,

or else crop his ears, or cut his mane, or put out one of his eyes; and by this means he kept himself a long time unknown.

Now Thomas of Reading, as I said before, being mark'd and kept for a fat pig, he was laid in the same chamber of death, but by reason Gray of Gloucester chanc'd also to come that night he escaped scalding.

The next time he came he was laid there again, but before he fell asleep or was warm in his bed one came riding through the town and cried piteously that London was all on afire and that it had burned down Thomas Becket's house in Westcheap, and a great number more in the same street. "And yet," quoth he, "the fire is not quench'd."

Which tidings when Thomas of Reading heard, he was very sorrowful, for of the same Becket that day had he received a great piece of money and had left in his house many of his writings and some that appertained to the king also; therefore there was no nay but he would ride back again to London presently to see how the matter stood; thereupon, making himself ready, departed. This cross fortune caused his host to frown. "Nevertheless, the next time," quoth he, "will pay for all."

Notwithstanding, God so wrought that they were prevented then likewise by reason of a great fray that happ'ned in the house betwixt a couple that fell out at dice, insomuch as the murderers themselves were inforced to call him up, being a man in great authority, that he might set the house in quietness, out of the which, by means of this quarrel, they doubted to lose many things.

Another time, when he should have been laid in the same place, he fell so sick that he requested to have somebody to watch with him, whereby also they could not bring their vile purpose to pass. But hard it is to escape the ill fortunes whereunto a man is allotted, for albeit that the next time that he came to London his horse stumbled and broke one of his legs, as he should ride homeward, yet hired he another to hasten his own death; for there was no remedy but he should go to Colebrook that night; but by the way he was so heavy asleep that he could scant keep himself in the saddle, and when he came near unto the town his nose burst out suddenly a-bleeding.

Well, to his inn he came, and so heavy was his heart that he could eat no meat; his host and hostess, hearing he was so melancholy, came up to cheer him, saying, "Jesus, Master Cole, what ails you tonight? Never did we see you thus sad before. Will it please you to have a quart of burn'd sack?" "With a good will," quoth he, "and would to God Thomas Dove were here! He would surely make me merry, and we should lack no music. But I am sorry for the man with all my heart that he is come so far behindhand. But alas, so much can every man say, but what good doth it him? No, no, it is not words can help a man in this case; the man had need of other relief then so. Let me see: I have but one child in the world, and that is my daughter; and half that I have is hers, the other half my wife's. What then? Shall I be good to nobody but them? In conscience, my wealth is too much for a couple to possess, and what is our religion without charity? And to whom is charity more to be shewn then to decayed householders?

"Good my host, lend me a pen and ink and some paper, for I will write a letter unto the poor man straight, and something I will give him. That alms which a man bestows with his own hands he shall be sure to have delivered, and God knows how long I shall live!"

With that, his hostess dissemblingly answered, saying, "Doubt not, Master Cole, you are like enough by the course of nature to live many years." "God knows," quoth he, "I never found my heart so heavy before." By this time pen, ink, and paper was brought, setting himself to writing as followeth: "In the name of God, amen. I bequeath my soul to God and my body to the ground, my goods equally between my wife Elenor and Isabel, my daughter. Item, I give to Thomas Dove of Exeter one hundred pounds. Nay, that is too little. I give to Thomas Dove two hundred pounds, in money, to be paid unto him presently upon his demand thereof by my said wife and daughter."

"Ha, how say you, my host?" quod he. "Is not this well? I pray you read it." His host, looking thereon, said, "Why, Maister Cole, what have you written here? You said you would write a letter, but methinks you have made a will. What need have you to do thus? Thanks be to God, you may live many fair years." " 'Tis true," quoth Cole, "if it please God, and I trust this writing cannot shorten my days. But let me see, have I made a will? Now, I promise you, I did verily purpose to write a letter. Notwithstanding, I have written that that God put into my mind. But look once again, my host; is it not written there that Dove shall have two hundred pounds, to be paid when he comes to demand it?" "Yes indeed," said his host." "Well, then, all is well," said Cole, "and it shall go as it is for me. I will not bestow the new writing thereof any more."

Then folding it up, he sealed it, desiring that his host would send it to Exeter. He promised that he would; notwithstanding Cole was not so satisfied, but after some pause he would needs hire one to carry it. And so, sitting down sadly in his chair again, upon a sudden he burst forth a-weeping. They demanding the cause thereof, he spake as followeth:

"No cause of these tears I know, but it comes now into my mind," said Cole, "when I set toward this, my last journey to London, how my daughter took on, what a coil she kept to have me stay; and I could not be rid of the little baggage a long time, she did so hang about me. When her mother by violence took her away she cried out most mainly, 'O my father, my father, I shall never see him again!' "

"Alas, pretty soul," said his hostess, "this was but mere kindness in the girl, and it seemeth she is very fond of you. But alas, why should you grieve at this? You must consider that it was but childishness." "Ay, it is indeed," said Cole, and with that he began to nod. Then they asked him if he would go to bed. "No," said he; "although I am heavy, I have no mind to go to bed at all." With that, certain musicians of the town came to the chamber and, knowing Master Cole was there, drew out their instruments and very solemnly began to play.

"This music comes very well," said Cole. And when he had list'ned a while thereunto he said, "Methinks these instruments sound like the ring of St. Mary Overy's bells. But the bass drowns all the rest, and in my ear it goes like a bell that rings a forenoon's knell. For God's sake let them leave off, and bear them this simple reward." The musicians being gone, his host asked if now it would please him to go to bed. "For," quoth he, "it is well-near eleven of the clock."

With that, Cole, beholding his host and hostess earnestly, began to start back, saying, "What ail you to look so like pale death? Good Lord, what have you done that your hands are thus bloody?" "What, my hands?" said his host. "Why, you may see they are neither bloody nor foul. Either your eyes do greatly dazzle or else fancies of a troubled mind do delude you."

"Alas, my host, you may see," said he, "how weak my wits are. I never had my head so idle before. Come, let me drink once more, and then I will to bed and trouble you no longer." With that, he made himself unready, and his hostess was very diligent to warm a kerchef, and put it about his head. "Good Lord!" said he, "I am not sick, I praise God, but such an alteration I find in myself as I never did before."

With that the scritch-owl cried piteously, and anon after the night raven sate croaking hard by his window. "Jesu, have mercy upon me," quoth he. "What an ill-favored cry do yonder carrion birds make!" And therewithal he laid him down in his bed from whence he never rose again.

His host and hostess, that all this while noted his troubled mind, began to commune betwixt themselves thereof. And the man said he knew not what were best to be done. "By my content," quoth he, "the matter should pass, for I think it is not best to meddle on him." "What, man!" quoth she, "faint you now? Have you done so many, and do you shrink at this?" Then, shewing him a great deal of gold which Cole had left with her, she said, "Would it not grieve a body's heart to loose this? Hang the old churl! What should he do living any longer? He hath too much, and we have too little. Tut, husband, let the thing be done, and then this is our own."

Her wicked counsel was followed, and when they had list'ned at his chamber door they heard the man sound asleep. "All is safe," quoth they, and down into the kitchen they go, their servants being all in bed; and, pulling out the iron pins, down fell the bed and the man dropp'd out into the boiling caldron. He being dead, they betwixt them cast his body into the river, his clothes they hid away, and made all things as it should be. But when he came to the stable to convey thence Cole's horse, the stable door being open, the horse had got loose, and with a part of the halter about his neck and straw trussed under his belly, as the ostlers had dressed him o'er eve, he was gone out at the back side which led into a great field adjoining to the house, and so, leaping divers hedges, being a lusty ston'd horse, had got into a ground where a mare was grazing, with whom he kept such a coil that they got into the highway where one of the town, meeting them, knew the mare and brought her and the horse to the man that ow'd her.

In the mean space the musicians had been at the inn, and in requital of their evening's gift they intended to give Cole some music in the morning. The goodman told them he took horse before day; likewise there was a guest in the house that would have borne him company to Reading, unto whom the host also answered that he himself set him upon horseback, and that he went long ago. Anon comes the man that owed the mare, inquiring up and down to know and if none of them missed a horse, who said no. At last he came to the Sign of the Crane where Cole lay, and calling the hostlers, he demanded of them if they lack'd none. They said no. "Why then," said the man, "I perceive my mare is good for something, for if I send her to field single she will come home double." Thus it passed on all that day and the night following. But the next day after, Cole's wife, musing that her husband came not home, sent one of her men on horseback to see if he could meet him. "And if," quoth she, "you meet him not betwixt this and Cole-

brook, ask for him at the Crane; but if you find him not there, then ride to London, for I doubt he is either sick or else some mischance hath fallen unto him."

The fellow did so, and, asking for him at Colebrook, they answered he went homeward from thence such a day. The servant, musing what should be become of his master and making much inquiry in the town for him, at length one told him of a horse that was found on the highway, and no man knew whence he came. He, going to see the horse, knew him presently, and to the Crane he goes with him. The host of the house, perceiving this, was blank, and that night fled secretly away. The fellow, going unto the justice, desired his help. Presently after, word was brought that Jarman of the Crane was gone; then all men said he had surely made Cole away, and the musicians told what Jarman said to them when they would have given Cole music. Then the woman, being apprehended and examined, confessed the truth. Jarman soon after was taken in Windsor Forest. He and his wife were both hang'd after they had laid open all these things before expressed. Also he confessed that he, being a carpenter, made that false falling floor, and how his wife devised it. And how they had murd'red by that means sixty persons. And yet, notwithstanding all the money which they had gotten thereby, they prospered not, but at their death were found very far in debt.

When the king heard of this murder he was, for the space of seven days, so sorrowful and heavy as he would not hear any suit, giving also commandment that the house should quite be consumed with fire wherein Cole was murd'red, and that no man should ever build upon that cursed ground.

Cole's substance at his death was exceeding great. He had daily in his house an hundred men servants and forty maids; he maintain'd beside above two or three hundred people, spinners and carders and a great many other householders. His wife after never married, and at her death she bestowed a mighty sum of money toward the maintaining of the new-builded monastery. Her daughter was most richly married to a gentleman of great worship by whom she had many children. And some say that the river whereunto Cole was cast did ever since carry the name of Cole, being called the river of Cole and the town of Colebrook.

Part X MISCELLANEOUS PROSE

ROGER ASCHAM

TOXOPHILUS and THE SCHOOLMASTER

Ascham's own charming account, in "A Preface to the Reader," of the genesis of *The Schoolmaster* sufficiently explains his title and his intentions in expounding the pedagogical principles and practises which he had gathered from a lifelong cultivation of *bonae literae*. His posthumously published book is in a sense his testament, as well as a memorial to that stanch northern humanism which built not only an educational but also a political and a moral code upon the study of Christ and Cicero, religion and classical literature. The eminent group of men who shaped his education during his years at St. John's College, Cambridge—a group including Sir John Cheke, Robert Pember, John Redman, Edmund Grindal, Walter Haddon, and Thomas Wilson—comprised the second generation of Tudor humanists; and, if we may believe Ascham's warm tribute, they were worthy successors to such learned and pious teachers as Erasmus, Colet, More, and Lily. At any rate, the memory of his masters and the friendship of his contemporaries (especially of Cheke) sustained Ascham through all the changes and chances of his turbulent career both at home and abroad in exile, and when in 1563, toward the end of his life, he began the composition of a systematic treatise on education he inevitably based his work on the principles and the values he had acquired in the golden years at St. John's. Ascham labored at his treatise for five years, and in 1568, in his last letter to his old friend John Sturm, rector of the gymnasium at Strassburg, he sketched the plan that he had followed—a plan not very systematic, but one that allowed copiously for those autobiographical digressions that give *The Schoolmaster* much of its warmth and intimacy. The first book sets forth the inducements to learning, an argument against coercion and compulsion in the education of youth, and a famous attack on foreign travel (and on Italy); the less attractive second book expounds Ascham's technique of double translation, lists and discusses the authors (graded as to difficulty) proper for the acquisition of sound classical training, analyzes Latin prosody, and examines the style and merits of many Latin authors. When, at the age of fifty-four, Ascham died in 1568, he left *The Schoolmaster* not quite finished, but his impoverished widow published it two years later with a graceful dedication to Sir William Cecil, recently elected chancellor of Cambridge. Three other editions followed in 1571, and a fifth in 1589. Our text is based upon *The Scholemaster, Or plaine and perfite way of teachyng children . . . the Latin tong*, 1570 (STC 832).

Earlier than Ascham's *magnum opus* is *Toxophilus*, a treatise on archery, written in 1543–44 in an effort to secure the favor of Henry VIII and to demonstrate both the patriotism and the erudition of its author. Although balked by Henry's departure for the siege of Boulogne (July, 1544) from presenting the book to him, Ascham had the printed volume ready for a formal presentation on Henry's return the next year, and it was well received by the ill and aging monarch, who pensioned its author. The body of the work, on the uses of archery for both recreation and war and on the proper method of acquiring the skill, has only an antiquarian interest, but the dedication, justifying Ascham's use of the vernacular, and the purity and vigor of the prose make *Toxophilus* a landmark in the history of Tudor literature. After the first edition of 1545—*Toxophilus, The schoole of shootinge conteyned in two bookes* (STC 837)—on which our text is based, the work was not reprinted in Ascham's lifetime, but other editions followed in 1571 and 1589, no doubt stimulated by the success of *The Schoolmaster*.

FROM TOXOPHILUS (1545)

To All Gentlemen and Yeomen of England

Bias the wise man came to Croesus the rich king, on a time when he was making new ships, purposing to have subdued by water the out-isles lying betwixt Greece and Asia Minor. "What news now in Greece?" saith the king to Bias. "None other news but these," saith Bias, "that the isles of Greece have prepared a wonderful company of horsemen to overrun Lydia withal." "There is nothing under heaven," saith the king, "that I would so soon wish as that they durst be so bold to meet us on the land with horse." "And think you," saith Bias, "that there is anything which they would sooner wish then that you should be so fond to meet them on the water with ships?" And so Croesus, hearing not the true news, but perceiving the wise man's mind and counsel, both gave then over making of his ships, and left also behind him a wonderful example for all communewealths to follow: that is, evermore to regard and set most by that thing whereunto nature hath made them most apt, and use hath made them most fit.

By this matter I mean the shooting in the long

815

bow for Englishmen; which thing with all my heart I do wish, and if I were of authority, I would counsel all the gentlemen and yeomen of England not to change it with any other thing, how good soever it seem to be; but that still, according to the old wont of England, youth should use it for the most honest pastime in peace, that men might handle it as a most sure weapon in war. Other strong weapons, which both experience doth prove to be good, and the wisdom of the king's Majesty and his counsel provides to be had, are not ordained to take away shooting; but that both, not compared togither whether should be better then the other, but so joined togither that the one should be always an aid and help for the other, might so strengthen the realm on all sides that no kind of enemy, in any kind of weapon, might pass and go beyond us.

For this purpose I, partly provoked by the counsel of some gentlemen, partly moved by the love which I have always borne toward shooting, have written this little treatise; wherein if I have not satisfied any man, I trust he will the rather be content with my doing, bycause I am (I suppose) the first which hath said anything in this matter (and few beginnings be perfect, saith wise men); and also bycause, if I have said amiss, I am content that any man amend it: or, if I have said too little, any man that will to add what him pleaseth to it.

My mind is, in profiting and pleasing every man, to hurt or displease no man, intending none other purpose but that youth might be stirred to labor, honest pastime, and virtue, and, as much as lay in me, plucked from idleness, unthrifty games, and vice; which thing I have labored only in this book, shewing how fit shooting is for all kinds of men; how honest a pastime for the mind; how wholesome an excercise for the body; not vile for great men to use, not costly for poor men to sustain, not lurking in holes and corners for ill men at their pleasure to misuse it, but abiding in the open sight and face of the world, for good men, if it fault, by their wisdom to correct it.

And here I would desire all gentlemen and yeomen to use this pastime in such a mean that the outragiousness of great gaming should not hurt the honesty of shooting, which of his own nature is always joined with honesty; yet for men's faults oftentimes blamed unworthily, as all good things have been, and evermore shall be.

If any man would blame me, either for taking such a matter in hand, or else for writing it in the English tongue, this answer I may make him, that whan the best of the realm think it honest for them to use, I, one of the meanest sort, ought not to suppose it vile for me to write; and though to have written it in another tongue had been both more profitable for my study, and also more honest for my name, yet I can think my labor well bestowed, if with a little hinderance of my profit and name may come any furtherance to the pleasure or commodity of the gentlemen and yeomen of England, for whose sake I took this matter in hand. And as for the Latin or Greek tongue, everything is so excellently done in them that none can do better; in the English tongue, contrary, everything in a manner so meanly both for the matter and handeling that no man can do worse. For therein the least learned, for the most part, have been always most ready to write. And they which had least hope in Latin have been most bold in English; when surely every man that is most ready to talk is not most able to write. He that will write well in any tongue must follow this counsel of Aristotle, to speak as the common people do, to think as wise men do; and so should every man understand him, and the judgment of wise men allow him. Many English writers have not done so, but using strange words, as Latin, French, and Italian, do make all things dark and hard. Once I communed with a man which reasoned the English tongue to be enriched and increased thereby, saying, "Who will not praise that feast where a man shall drink at a dinner both wine, ale, and beer?" "Truly," quod I, "they be all good, every one taken by himself alone, but if you put malmsey and sack, red wine and white, ale and beer, and all in one pot, you shall make a drink neither easy to be known nor yet wholesome for the body." Cicero, in following Isocrates, Plato, and Demosthenes, increased the Latin tongue after another sort. This way bycause divers men that write do not know, they can neither follow it, bycause of their ignorancy, nor yet will praise it, for very arrogancy, two faults seldom the one out of the other's company.

English writers by diversity of time have taken diverse matters in hand. In our fathers' time nothing was read but books of feigned chevalry, wherein a man by reading should be led to none other end but only to manslaughter and bawdry. If any man suppose they were good inough to pass the time withal, he is deceived. For surely vain words do work no small thing in vain, ignorant, and young minds, specially if they be given anything thereunto of their own nature. These books (as I have heard say) were made the most part in abbeys and monasteries—a very likely and fit fruit of such an idle and blind kind of living.

In our time now, whan every man is given to know much rather than to live well, very many do write, but after such a fashion as very many do shoot. Some shooters take in hand stronger bows than they be able to maintain. This thing maketh them sometime to outshoot the mark, sometime to shoot far wide, and perchance hurt some that look on. Other that never learned to shoot, nor yet knoweth good shaft nor bow, will be as busy as the best, but such one commonly plucketh down a side, and crafty archers which be against him will be both glad of him, and also ever ready to lay and bet with him; it were better for such one to sit down than shoot. Other there be, which have very good bow and shafts, and good knowledge in shooting, but they have been brought up in such evil-favoured shooting [10] that they can neither shoot fair nor yet near. If any man will apply these things togither, [he] shall not see the one far differ from the other.

And I also, amonges all other, in writing this little treatise have followed some young shooters, which both will begin to shoot for a little money, and also will use to shoot once or twice about the mark for nought, afore they begin a-good. And therefore did I take this little matter in hand, to assay myself, and hereafter, by the grace of God, if the judgment of [20] wise men, that look on, think that I can do any good, I may perchance cast my shaft among other, for better game.

Yet in writing this book, some man will marvail, perchance, why that I, being an unperfect shooter, should take in hand to write of making a perfect archer; the same man, peradventure, will marvail how a whetstone, which is blunt, can make the edge of a knife sharp. I would the same man should consider also that in going about any matter there be [30] four things to be considered: doing, saying, thinking, and perfectness. First, there is no man that doth so well but he can say better, or else some men, which be now stark nought, should be too good; again, no man can utter with his tongue so well as he is able to imagine with his mind, and yet perfectness itself is far above all thinking; than, seeing that saying is one step nearer perfectness than doing, let every man leave marvailing why my word shall rather express, than my deed shall perform, perfect shooting. [40]

I trust no man will be offended with this little book, except it be some fletchers and bowyers,

thinking hereby that many that love shooting shall be taught to refuse such naughty wares as they would utter. Honest fletchers and bowyers do not so, and they that be unhonest ought rather to amend themselves for doing ill than be angry with me for saying well. A fletcher hath even as good a quarrel to be angry with an archer that refuseth an ill shaft as a bladesmith hath to a fletcher that forsaketh to buy of him a naughty knife; for as an archer must be content that a fletcher know a good shaft in every point for the perfecter making of it, so an honest fletcher will also be content that a shooter know a good shaft in every point for the perfiter using of it; bicause the one knoweth like a fletcher how to make it, the other knoweth like an archer how to use it. And seeing the knowledge is one in them both, yet the end diverse, surely that fletcher is an enemy to archers and artillery which cannot be content that an archer know a shaft as well for his use in shooting as he himself should know a shaft for his advantage in selling. And the rather, bycause shafts be not made so much to be sold, but chiefly to be used. And seeing that use and occupying is the end why a shaft is made, the making, as it were, a mean for occupying, surely the knowledge in every point of a good shaft is more to be required in a shooter than a fletcher.

Yet, as I said before, no honest fletcher will be angry with me, seeing I do not teach how to make a shaft, which belongeth only to a good fletcher, but to know and handle a shaft, which belongeth to an archer. And this little book, I trust, shall please and profit both parts; for good bows and shafts shall be better known to the commodity of all shooters, and good shooting may, perchance, be the more occupied to the profit of all bowyers and fletchers. And thus I pray God that all fletchers getting their living truly, and all archers using shooting honestly, and all manner of men that favor artillery, may live continually in health and merriness, obeying their prince as they should, and loving God as they ought; to whom, for all things, be all honor and glory for ever. Amen.

from THE SCHOOLMASTER (1570)

To the Honorable Sir William Cecil, Knight,
Principal Secretary to the Queen's
Most Excellent Majesty

Sundry and reasonable be the causes why learned men have used to offer and dedicate such works as they put abroad to some such personage as they think fittest, either in respect of ability of defense, or skill for judgment, or private regard of kindness and duty.

Every one of those considerations, sir, move me of right to offer this my late husband's, Master Ascham's, work unto you. For well rememb'ring how much all good learning oweth unto you for defense thereof, as the University of Cambridge, of which my said late husband was a member, have in choosing you their worthy chancellor acknowledged; and how happily you have spent your time in such studies and carried the use thereof to the right end, to the good service of the queen's Majesty and your country to all our benefits; thirdly, how much my said husband was many ways bound unto you, and how gladly and comfortably he used in his life to recognize and report your goodness toward him, leaving with me then, his poor widow, and a great sort of orphans a good comfort in the hope of your good continuance, which I have truly found to me and mine, and therefore do duly and daily pray for you and yours; I could not find any man for whose name this book was more agreeable for hope [of] protection, more meet for submission to judgment, nor more due for respect of worthiness of your part and thankfulness of my husband's and mine. Good I trust it shall do, as I am put in great hope by many very well-learned that can well judge thereof. Meet, therefore, I compt it that such good as my husband was able to do and leave to the common weal, it should be received under your name, and that the world should owe thank thereof to you, to whom my husband, the author of it, was for good received of you most dutifully bounden. And so beseeching you to take on you the defense of this book, to avaunce the good that may come of it by your allowance and further-ance to public use and benefit, and to accept the thankful recognition of me and my poor children, trusting of the continuance of your good memory of Master Ascham and his, and daily commending the prosperous estate of you and yours to God whom you serve and whose you are, I rest to trouble you.

Your humble Margaret Ascham

A PREFACE TO THE READER

When the great plage was at London, the year 1563, the queen's Majesty, Queen Elizabeth, lay at her castle of Windsor; where, upon the tenth day of December, it fortuned that in Sir William Cecil's chamber, her Highness' principal secretary, there dined together these personages: Master Secretary himself, Sir William Petre, Sir J. Mason, D[ean Nicholas] Wotton, Sir Richard Sackville, treasurer of the exchequer, Sir Walter Mildmay, chancellor of the exchequer, Master [Walter] Haddon, master of requests, Master John Astley, master of the jewel house, Master Bernard Hampton, Master Nicasius, and I. Of which number the most part were of her Majesty's most honorable privy council, and the rest serving her in very good place. I was glad than, and do rejoice yet to remember, that my chance was so happy to be there that day in the company of so many wise and good men togither as hardly than could have been picked out again out of all England beside.

Master Secretary hath this accustomed manner: though his head be never so full of most weighty affairs of the realm, yet at dinner-time he doth seem to lay them always aside; and findeth ever fit occasion to talk pleasantly of other matters, but most gladly of some matter of learning, wherein he will curtesly hear the mind of the meanest at his table.

Not long after our sitting down, "I have strange news brought me," saith Master Secretary, "this morning, that diverse scholars of Eton be run away from the school for fear of beating." Whereupon, Master Secretary took occasion to wish that some more discretion were in many schoolmasters in using correction than commonly there is, who many times punish rather the weakness of nature than the fault of the scholar; whereby many scholars, that might else prove well, be driven to hate learning before they know what learning meaneth, and so are made willing to forsake their book, and be glad to be put to any other kind of living.

Master Petre, as one somewhat severe of nature, said plainly that the rod only was the sword that must keep the school in obedience and the scholar in good order. Master Wotton, a man mild of nature, with soft voice and few words, inclined to Master Secre-tary's judgment, and said, "In mine opinion, the schoolhouse should be indeed, as it is called by name, the house of play and pleasure and not of fear and bondage; and, as I do remember, so saith Socrates in one place of Plato. And therefore, if a rod carry the fear of a sword, it is no marvel if those that be fearful of nature choose rather to forsake the play than to stand always within the fear of a sword in a fond man's handling."

Master Mason, after his manner, was very merry with both parties, pleasantly playing both with the shrewd touches of many cours'd boys and with the small discretion of many lewd schoolmasters. Master Haddon was fully of Master Petre's opinion, and said that the best schoolmaster of our time [Nicholas Udall] was the greatest beater, and named the person. "Though," quoth I, "it was his good fortune to send from his school unto the university one of the best scholars indeed of all our time, yet wise men do think that that came so to pass rather by the great toward-ness of the scholar than by the great beating of the master; and whether this be true or no, you yourself are best witness." I said somewhat farder in the matter, how and why young children were sooner allured by love than driven by beating to attain good learning; wherein I was the bolder to say my mind because Master Secretary curtesly provoked me thereunto; or else in such a company, and namely in his presence, my wont is to be more willing to use mine ears than to occupy my tongue.

Sir Walter Mildmay, Master Astley, and the rest said very little; only Sir Richard Sackville said nothing at all. After dinner I went up to read with the queen's Majesty. We read than togither in the Greek tongue, as I well remember, that noble oration of Demosthenes against Aeschines, for his false dealing in his ambassage to King Philip of Macedony. Sir Richard Sackville came up soon after, and, finding me in her Majesty's privy chamber, he took me by the hand and carrying me to a window said: "Master Ascham, I would not for a good deal of money have been this day absent from dinner. Where, though I said nothing, yet I gave as good ear, and do consider as well the talk that passed, as any one did there. Master Secretary said very wisely, and most truly, that many young wits be driven to hate learning before they know what learning is. I can be good witness to this myself; for a fond schoolmaster, before I was fully fourteen years old, drave me so with fear of beating from all love of learning as now, when I know what difference it is to have learning and to have little or none at all, I feel it my greatest grief and find it my greatest hurt that ever came to me that it was my so ill chance to light upon so lewd a schoolmaster. But seeing it is but in vain to lament things past, and also wisdom to look to things to come, surely, God willing, if God lend me life, I will make this my mishap some occasion of good hap to little Robert Sackville, my son's son. For whose bringing-up I would gladly, if it so please you, use specially your good advice. I hear say you have a son much of his age; we will deal thus togither: point you out a schoolmaster who by your order shall teach my son and yours, and for all the rest I will provide, yea though they three do cost me a couple of hundred pounds by year; and beside, you shall find me as fast a friend to you and yours as perchance any you have." Which promise the worthy gentleman surely kept with me until his dying day.

We had than farther talk togither of bringing-up of children, of the nature of quick and hard wits, of the right choice of a good wit, of fear and love in teaching children. We passed from children and came to young men, namely gentlemen; we talked of their too much liberty to live as they lust; of their letting loose too soon to overmuch experience of ill, contrary to the good order of many good old commonwealths of the Persians and Greeks; of wit gathered and good fortune gotten by some, only by experience without learning. And, lastly, he required of me very earnestly to shew what I thought of the common going of Englishmen into Italy. "But," saith he, "bicause this place and this time will not suffer so long talk as these good matters require, therefore I pray you, at my request and at your leisure, put in some order of writing the chief points of this our talk, concerning the right order of teaching and honesty of living, for the good bringing-up of children and young men; and surely, beside contenting me, you shall both please and profit very many others." I made some excuse by lack of hability and weakness of body. "Well," saith he, "I am not now to learn what you can do. Our dear friend, good Master [Thomas] Goodricke, whose judgment I could well believe, did once for all satisfy me fully therein. Again, I heard you say, not long ago, that you may thank Sir John Cheke for all the learning you have; and I know very well myself that you did teach the queen. And therefore, seeing God did so bless you to make you the scholar of the best master, and also the schoolmaster of the best scholar, that ever were in our time, surely you should please God, benefit your country, and honest your own name, if you would take the pains to impart to others what you learned of such a master and how ye taught such a scholar. And in uttering the stuff ye received of the one, in declaring the order ye took with the other, ye shall never lack neither matter nor manner, what to write nor how to write, in this kind of argument."

I beginning some farther excuse sodeinly was called to come to the queen. The night following I slept little, my head was so full of this our former talk, and I so mindful somewhat to satisfy the honest request of so dear a friend. I thought to prepare some little treatise for a New Year's gift that Christmas. But, as it chanceth to busy builders, so, in building this my poor schoolhouse (the rather bicause the form of it is somewhat new and differing from others), the work rose daily higher and wider than I thought it would at the beginning.

And though it appear now, and be in very deed, but a small cottage, poor for the stuff and rude for the workmanship, yet in going forward I found the site so good as I was loth to give it over, but the making so costly, outreaching my hability, as many times I wished that some one of those three, my dear friends with full purses, Sir Thomas Smith, Master Haddon, or Master [Thomas] Watson, had had the doing of it. Yet, nevertheless, I myself spending gladly that little that I gat at home by good Sir John Cheke, and that that I borrowed abroad of my friend Sturmius, beside somewhat that was left me in reversion by my old masters, Plato, Aristotle, and Cicero, I have at last patched it up as I could and as you see. If the matter be mean and meanly handled, I pray you bear both with me and it; for never work went up in worse weather, with mo lets and stops, than this poor schoolhouse of mine. Westminster Hall can bear some witness, beside much weakness of body, but more trouble of mind, by some such sores as grieve me to touch them myself, and therefore I purpose not to open them to others. And in middes of outward injuries and inward cares, to encrease them withal, good Sir Richard Sackville dieth, that worthy gentleman; that earnest favorer and furtherer of God's true religion; that faithful servitor to his prince and country; a lover of learning and all learned men; wise in all doings; curtess to all persons, shewing spite to none, doing good to many; and, as I well found, to me so fast a friend as I never lost the like before. Whan he was gone, my heart was dead. There was not one that wore a black gown for him who carried a heavier heart for him than I. Whan he was gone, I cast this book away; I could not look upon it but with weeping eyes, in rememb'ring him who was the only setter-on to do it, and would have been not only a glad commender of it, but also a sure and certain comfort to me and mine for it.

Almost two years togither this book lay scattered and neglected, and had been quite given over of me, if the goodness of one [?Cecil] had not given me some life and spirit again. God, the mover of goodness, prosper always him and his, as he hath many times comforted me and mine, and, I trust to God, shall comfort more and more. Of whom most justly I may say, and very oft and always gladly I am wont to say, that sweet verse of Sophocles, spoken by Oedipus to worthy Theseus: ἔχω [γὰρ] ἄχω διὰ σὲ, κoὐκ ἄλλον βροτῶν. This hope hath helped me to end this book; which, if he allow, I shall think my labors well imployed, and shall not much esteem the misliking of any others. And I trust he shall think the better of it, bicause he shall find the best part thereof to come out of his school [i.e. Plato's] whom he of all men loved and liked best.

Yet some men, friendly enough of nature but of small judgment in learning, do think I take too much pains and spend too much time in setting forth these children's affairs. But those good men were never brought up in Socrates' school, who saith plainly that no man goeth about a more godly purpose than he that is mindful of the good bringing-up both of his own and other men's children.

Therefore, I trust, good and wise men will think well of this my doing. And of other, that think otherwise, I will think myself they are but men to be pardoned for their folly and pitied for their ignorance.

In writing this book, I have had earnest respect to three special points: troth of religion, honesty in living, right order in learning. In which three ways I pray God my poor children may diligently walk; for whose sake, as nature moved and reason required and necessity also somewhat compelled, I was the willinger to take these pains.

For, seeing at my death I am not like to leave them any great store of living, therefore in my lifetime I thought good to bequeath unto them in this little book, as in my will and testament, the right way to good learning; which if they follow, with the fear of God, they shall very well come to sufficiency of living.

I wish also, with all my heart, that young Master Robert Sackville may take that fruct of this labor that his worthy grantfather purposed he should have done. And if any other do take either profet or pleasure hereby, they have cause to thank Master Robert Sackville, for whom specially this my *Schoolmaster* was provided.

And one thing I would have the reader consider in reading this book, that, bicause no schoolmaster hath charge of any child before he enter into his school, therefore I, leaving all former care of their good bringing-up to wise and good parents, as a matter not belonging to the schoolmaster, I do appoint this my *Schoolmaster* than and there to begin where his office and charge beginneth. Which charge lasteth not long, but until the scholar be made hable to go to the university to proceed in logic, rhetoric, and other kinds of learning.

Yet if my Schoolmaster, for love he beareth to his scholar, shall teach him somewhat for his furtherance and better judgment in learning that may serve him seven year after in the university, he doth his scholar no more wrong, nor deserveth no worse name thereby, than he doth in London who, selling silk or cloth unto his friend, doth give him better measure than either his promise or bargain was.

Farewell in Christ.

The First Book for the Youth

After the child hath learned perfitly the eight parts of speech, let him then learn the right joining togither of substantives with adjectives, the noun with the verb, the relative with the antecedent. And in learning farther his syntaxis, by mine advice, he shall not use the common order in common schools for making of Latins: whereby the child commonly learneth, first, an evil choice of words (and right choice of words, saith Caesar, is the foundation of eloquence); than, a wrong placing of words; and, lastly, an ill framing of the sentence, with a perverse judgment, both of words and sentences. These faults, taking once root in yougth, be never or hardly pluck'd away in age. Moreover, there is no one thing that hath more either dulled the wits or taken away the will of children from learning then the care they have to satisfy their masters in making of Latins.

For the scholar is commonly beat for the making, when the master were more worthy to be beat for the mending, or rather marring, of the same; the master many times being as ignorant as the child what to say properly and fitly to the matter.

Two schoolmasters have set forth in print, either of them, a book of such kind of Latins, Horman and Whittington. A child shall learn of the better of them that which another day, if he be wise and come to judgment, he must be fain to unlearn again.

There is a way, touched in the first book of Cicero *De oratore,* which, wisely brought into schools, truly taught, and constantly used, would not only take wholly away this butcherly fear in making of Latins, but would also with ease and pleasure, and in short time, as I know by good experience, work a true choice and placing of words, a right ordering of sentences, an easy understanding of the tongue, a readiness to speak, a facility to write, a true judgment both of his own and other men's doings, what tongue soever he doth use.

The way is this. After the three concordances learned, as I touched before, let the master read unto him the epistles of Cicero, gathered togither and chosen out by Sturmius, for the capacity of children. First let him teach the child cheerfully and plainly the cause and matter of the letter; then let him construe it into English so oft as the child may easily carry away the understanding of it; lastly, parse it over perfitly. This done thus, let the child, by and by, both construe and parse it over again; so that it may appear that the child doubteth in nothing that his master taught him before. After this, the child must take a paper book, and, sitting in some place where no man shall prompt him, by himself let him translate into English his former lesson. Then shewing it to his master, let the master take from him his Latin book, and, pausing an hour at the least, than let the child translate his own English into Latin again in another paper book. When the child bringeth it turned into Latin, the master must compare it with Tully's book, and lay them both togither; and where the child doth well, either in choosing or true placing of Tully's words, let the master praise him, and say, "Here ye do well." For I assure you, there is no such whetstone to sharpen a good wit and encourage a will to learning as is praise.

But if the child miss, either in forgetting a word, or in changing a good with a worse, or misordering the sentence, I would not have the master either frown or chide with him, if the child have done his diligence and used no trewandship therein. For I know by good experience that a child shall take more profit of two fauts gently warned of then of four things rightly hit; for than the master shall have good occasion to say unto him, "N., Tully would have used such a word, not this; Tully would have placed this word here, not there; would have used this case, this number,

this person, this degree, this gender; he would have used this mood, this tense, this simple rather than this compound; this adverb here, not there; he would have ended the sentence with this verb, not with that noun or participle," etc.

In these few lines I have wrapped up the most tedious part of grammar, and also the ground of almost all the rules that are so busily taught by the master, and so hardly learned by the scholar, in all common schools; which, after this sort, the master shall teach without all error, and the scholar shall learn without great pain; the master being led by so sure a guide, and the scholar being brought into so plain and easy a way. And therefore we do not contemn rules, but we gladly teach rules; and teach them more plainly, sensibly, and orderly than they be commonly taught in common schools. For whan the master shall compare Tully's book with his scholar's translation, let the master, at the first, lead and teach his scholar to join the rules of his grammar book with the examples of his present lesson, until the scholar by himself be hable to fetch out of his grammar every rule for every example; so as the grammar book be ever in the scholar's hand, and also used of him as a dictionary for every present use. This is a lively and perfit way of teaching of rules; where the common way used in common schools, to read the grammar alone by itself, is tedious for the master, hard for the scholar, cold and uncomfortable for them both.

Let your scholar be never afraid to ask you any doubt, but use discreetly the best allurements ye can to encourage him to the same, lest his ever much fearing of you drive him to seek some misorderly shift; as to seek to be helped by some other book or to be prompted by some other scholar; and so go about to beguile you much and himself more.

With this way of good understanding the matter, plain construing, diligent parsing, daily translating, cheerful admonishing, and heedful amending of faults, never leaving behind just praise for well doing, I would have the scholar brought up withal till he had read and translated over the first book of epistles chosen out by Sturmius, with a good piece of a comedy of Terence also.

All this while, by mine advice, the child shall use to speak no Latin; for as Cicero saith in like matter, with like words, *Loquendo, male loqui discunt;* and that excellent learned man G. Budaeus, in his Greek commentaries, sore complaineth that whan he began to learn the Latin tongue, use of speaking Latin at the table and elsewhere unadvisedly did bring him to such an evil choice of words, to such a crooked framing of sentences, that no one thing did hurt or hinder him more all the days of his life afterward, both for readiness in speaking and also good judgment in writing.

In very deed, if children were brought up in such a house, or such a school, where the Latin tongue were properly and perfitly spoken, as Tiberius and Caius Gracchi were brought up in their mother Cornelia's house, surely than the daily use of speaking were the best and readiest way to learn the Latin tongue. But now commonly in the best schools in England, for words right choice is smally regarded, true propriety wholly neglected, confusion is brought in, barbariousness is bred up so in young wits as afterward they be not only marr'd for speaking but also corrupted in judgment, as with much ado, or never at all, they be brought to the right frame again.

Yet all men covet to have their children speak Latin, and so do I very earnestly too. We both have one purpose; we agree in desire, we wish one end; but we differ somewhat in order and way that leadeth rightly to that end. Other would have them speak at all adventures; and, so they be speaking, to speak the master careth not, the scholar knoweth not, what. This is to seem, and not to be; except it be, to be bold without shame, rash without skill, full of words without wit. I wish to have them speak so as it may well appear that the brain doth govern the tongue, and that reason leadeth forth the talk. Socrates' doctrine is true in Plato, and well marked and truly uttered by Horace in *Arte poetica,* that, wheresoever knowledge doth accompany the wit, there best utterance doth always await upon the tongue. For good understanding must first be bred in the child, which being nourished with skill and use of writing (as I will teach more largely hereafter) is the only way to bring him to judgment and readiness in speaking; and that in far shorter time (if he follow constantly the trade of this little lesson) than he shall do by common teaching of the common schools in England.

But to go forward. As you perceive your scholar to go better and better on away, first, with understanding his lesson more quickly, with parsing more readily, with translating more speedily and perfitly then he was wont, after give him longer lessons to translate; and, withal, begin to teach him both in nouns and verbs what is *Proprium* and what is *Translatum;* what *Synonymum,* what *Diversum;* which be *Contraria,* and which be most notable *Phrases,* in all his lecture. As:

Proprium	{ *Rex sepultus est magnifice*
Translatum	{ *Cum illo principe, sepulta est et gloria et salus reipublicae*

Synonyma	{ *Ensis, gladius; Laudare, praedicare*
Diversa	{ *Diligere, amare; Calere, exardescere; Inimicus, hostis*
Contraria	{ *Acerbum et luctuosum bellum; Dulcis et laeta pax*
Phrases	{ *Dare verba; Abjicere obedientiam*

Your scholar then must have the third paper book, in the which, after he hath done his double translation, let him write, after this sort, four of these forenamed six, diligently marked out of every lesson.

Quatuor	{ *Propria* *Translata* *Synonyma* *Diversa* *Contraria* *Phrases*

Or else three, or two, if there be no mo; and if there be none of these at all in some lecture, yet not omit the order, but write these:

> *Diversa nulla,*
> *Contraria nulla, etc.*

This diligent translating, joined with this heedful marking in the foresaid epistles, and afterward in some plain oration of Tully, as *Pro lege Manilia, Pro Archia poeta,* or in those three *Ad C. Caesarem,* shall work such a right choice of words, so straight a framing of sentences, such a true judgment both to write skilfully and speak wittily, as wise men shall both praise and marvel at.

If your scholar do miss sometimes in marking rightly these foresaid six things, chide not hastely, for that shall both dull his wit and discorage his diligence; but monish him gently, which shall make him both willing to amend and glad to go forward in love and hope of learning.

I have now wished twice or thrice this gentle nature to be in a schoolmaster. And that I have done so neither by chance nor without some reason, I will now declare at large why in mine opinion love is fitter then fear, gentleness better than beating, to bring up a child rightly in learning.

With the common use of teaching and beating in common schools of England I will not greatly contend; which, if I did, it were but a small grammatical controversy, neither belonging to heresy nor treason, nor greatly touching God nor the prince; although in very deed, in the end, the good or ill bringing-up of children doth as much serve to the good or ill service of God, our prince, and our whole country as any one thing doth beside.

I do gladly agree with all good schoolmasters in these points: to have children brought to good perfitness in learning, to all honesty in manners, to have all fauts rightly amended, to have every vice severely corrected; but for the order and way that leadeth rightly to these points we somewhat differ. For commonly many schoolmasters, some as I have seen, mo as I have heard tell, be of so crooked a nature as, when they meet with a hard-witted scholar, they rather break him than bow him, rather mar him than mend him. For whan the schoolmaster is angry with some other matter, then will he soonest fall to beat his scholar; and though he himself should be punished for his folly, yet must he beat some scholar for his pleasure, though there be no cause for him to do so, nor yet fault in the scholar to deserve so. These ye will say be fond schoolmasters, and few they be that be found to be such. They be fond indeed, but surely overmany such be found everywhere. But this will I say, that even the wisest of your great beaters do as oft punish nature as they do correct faults. Yea, many times the better nature is sorer punished. For, if one by quickness of wit take his lesson readily, another by hardness of wit taketh it not so speedily, the first is always commended, the other is commonly punished: whan a wise schoolmaster should rather discreetly consider the right disposition of both their natures, and not so much weigh what either of them is able to do now, as what either of them is likely to do hereafter. For this I know, not only by reading of books in my study, but also by experience of life abroad in the world, that those which be commonly the wisest, the best learned, and best men also when they be old, were never commonly the quickest of wit when they were young. The causes why, amongest other which be many, that move me thus to think be these few which I will reckon.

Quick wits commonly be apt to take, unapt to keep; soon hot, and desirous of this and that; as cold, and soon weary of the same again; more quick to enter speedily than hable to pierce far; even like oversharp tools, whose edges be very soon turned. Such wits delight themselves in easy and pleasant studies, and never pass far forward in high and hard sciences. And therefore the quickest wits commonly may prove the best poets, but not the wisest orators; ready of tongue to speak boldly, not deep of judgment either for good counsel or wise writing. Also for manners and life quick wits commonly be, in desire, newfangle; in purpose, unconstant; light to promise anything, ready to forget everything, both benefit and injury, and thereby neither fast to friend nor fearful to foe; inquisitive of every trifle, not secret in greatest affairs; bold with any person; busy in every matter; soothing such as be present, nipping any that is absent; of nature, also, always flattering their betters, envying their equals, despising their inferiors; and, by quickness of wit, very quick and ready to like none so well as themselves.

Moreover, commonly, men very quick of wit be also very light of conditions; and thereby very ready of disposition to be carried overquickly, by any light company, to any riot and unthriftiness when they be young, and therefore seldom either honest of life or rich in living when they be old. For quick in wit and light in manners be either seldom troubled or very soon weary in carrying a very heavy purse. Quick wits also be, in most part of all their doings, overquick, hasty, rash, heady, and brainsick. These two last words, "heady" and "brainsick," be fit and proper words, rising naturally of the matter, and termed aptly by the condition of overmuch quickness of wit. In yougth also they be ready scoffers, privy mockers, and ever overlight and merry; in age, soon testy, very waspish, and always overmiserable. And yet few of them come to any great age, by reason of their misordered life when they were young; but a great deal fewer of them come to shew any great countenance, or bear any great authority abroad in the world, but either live obscurely, men know not how, or die obscurely, men mark not whan. They be like trees that shew forth fair blossoms and broad leaves in springtime, but bring out small and not long-lasting fruit in harvest-time; and that only such as fall and rot before they be ripe, and so never, or seldom, come to any good at all. For this ye shall find most true by experience, that amongest a number of quick wits in youth few be found in the end either very fortunate for themselves or very profitable to serve the commonwealth, but decay and vanish, men know not which way; except a very few, to whom peradventure blood and happy parentage may perchance purchase a long standing upon the stage. The which felicity, because it cometh by others' procuring, not by their own deserving, and stand by other men's feet, and not by their own, what outward brag soever is borne by them is indeed of itself, and in wise men's eyes, of no great estimation.

Some wits, moderate enough by nature, be many times marr'd by overmuch study and use of some sciences, namely music, arithmetic, and geometry. These sciences, as they sharpen men's wits overmuch, so they change men's manners oversore, if they be not moderately mingled and wisely applied to some good use of life. Mark all mathematical heads which be only and wholly bent to those sciences, how solitary they be themselves, how unfit to live with others, and how unapt to serve in the world. This is not only known now by common experience, but uttered long before by wise men's judgment and sentence. Galen saith, "Much music marreth men's manners"; and Plato hath a notable place of the same thing in his books *De republica*, well marked also and excellently translated by Tully himself. Of this matter I wrote once more at large, twenty year ago, in my book of shooting [i.e. *Toxophilus*, 1545]. Now I thought but to touch it to prove that overmuch quickness of wit, either given by nature or sharpened by study, doth not commonly bring forth either greatest learning, best manners, or happiest life in the end.

Contrariwise, a wit in youth that is not overdull, heavy, knotty, and lumpish, but hard, rough, and though somewhat staffish, as Tully wisheth, *otium quietum non languidum,* and *negotium cum labore, non cum periculo,* such a wit, I say, if it be at the first well handled by the mother, and rightly smoothed and wrought as it should, not overwhartly and against the wood, by the schoolmaster, both for learning and whole course of living proveth always the best. In wood and stone not the softest, but hardest, be always aptest for portraiture, both fairest for pleasure and most durable for profit. Hard wits be hard to receive, but sure to keep; painful without weariness, heedful without wavering, constant without newfangleness; bearing heavy things, though not lightly, yet willingly; ent'ring hard things, though not easely, yet deeply; and so come to that perfitness of learning in the end that quick wits seem in hope, but do not indeed, or else very seldom, ever attain unto. Also for manners and life, hard wits commonly are hardly carried either to desire every new thing or else to mervel at every strange thing; and therefore they be careful and diligent in their own matters, not curious and busy in other men's affairs; and so they become wise themselves, and also are counted honest by others. They be grave, steadfast, silent of tongue, secret of heart; not hasty in making, but constant in keeping any promise; not rash in uttering, but ware in considering every matter; and thereby not quick in speaking, but deep of judgment, whether they write or give counsel, in all weighty affairs. And these be the men that become in the end both most happy for themselves, and always best esteemed abroad in the world.

I have been longer in describing the nature, the good or ill success, of the quick and hard wits than perchance some will think this place and matter doth require. But my purpose was hereby plainly to utter what injury is offered to all learning, and to the commonwealth also, first by the fond father in choosing, but chiefly by the lewd schoolmaster in beating, and driving away the best natures from learning. A child that is still, silent, constant, and somewhat hard of wit is either never chosen by the father to be made a scholar, or else when he cometh to the school he is smally regarded, little looked unto; he lacketh teaching, he lacketh coraging, he lacketh all things, only he never lacketh beating, nor any word that may move him to hate learning, nor any deed that may drive him from learning to any other kind of living.

And when this sad-natured and hard-witted child is bet from his book, and becometh after either student of the common law, or page in the court, or servingman, or bound prentice to a merchant or to some handicraft, he proveth in the end wiser, happier, and many times honester, too, than many of these quick wits do by their learning.

Learning is both hind'red and injured, too, by the ill choice of them that send young scholars to the universities, of whom must needs come all our divines, lawyers, and physicians.

These young scholars be chosen commonly as young apples be chosen by children in a fair garden about St. James' tide. A child will choose a sweeting because it is presently fair and pleasant, and refuse a runnet bycause it is than green, hard, and sour; whan the one, if it be eaten, doth breed both worms and ill humors; the other, if it stand his time, be ordered and kept as it should, is wholesome of itself, and helpeth to the good digestion of other meats. Sweetings will receive worms, rot, and die on the tree, and never or seldom come to the gathering for good and lasting store.

For very grief of heart I will not apply the similitude; but hereby is plainly seen how learning is robbed of her best wits, first, by the great beating and, after, by the ill choosing of scholars to go to the universities; whereof cometh partly that lewd and spiteful proverb, sounding to the great hurt of learning and shame of learned men, that "the greatest clerks be not the wisest men."

And though I, in all this discourse, seem plainly to prefer hard and rough wits before quick and light wits, both for learning and manners, yet am I not ignorant that some quickness of wit is a singular gift of God, and so most rare emonges men; and, namely, such a wit as is quick without lightness, sharp without brittleness, desirous of good things without newfangleness, diligent in painful things without wearisomeness, and constant in good will to do all things well; as I know was in Sir John Cheke, and is in some that yet live, in whom all these fair qualities of wit are fully met togither.

But it is notable and true, that Socrates saith in Plato to his friend Crito, that that number of men is fewest which far exceed, either in good or ill, in wisdom or folly; but the mean betwixt both be the greatest number. Which he proveth true in diverse other things; as in greyhounds, emonges which few are found exceeding great or exceeding little, exceeding swift or exceeding slow. And therefore I speaking of quick and hard wits, I meant the common number of quick and hard wits; emonges the which, for the most part, the hard wit proveth many times the better learned, wiser, and honester man. And therefore do I the more lament that such wits commonly be either kept from learning by fond fathers, or beat from learning by lewd schoolmasters.

And speaking thus much of the wits of children for learning, the opportunity of the place and goodness of the matter might require to have here declared the most special notes of a good wit for learning in a child; after the manner and custom of a good horseman, who is skilful to know, and hable to tell others, how by certain sure signs a man may choise a colt that is like to prove another day excellent for the saddle. And it is pity that commonly more care is had, yea, and that emonges very wise men, to find out rather a cunning man for their horse than a cunning man for their children. They say nay in word, but they do so in deed; for to the one they will gladly give a stipend of two hundred crowns by year, and loth to offer to the other two hundred shillings. God that sitteth in heaven laugheth their choice to scorn, and rewardeth their liberality as it should; for he suffereth them to have tame and well-ordered horse, but wild and unfortunate children; and therefore in the end they find more pleasure in their horse than comfort in their children.

But concerning the true notes of the best wits for learning in a child, I will report not mine own opinion but the very judgment of him that was counted the best teacher and wisest man that learning maketh mention of; and that is Socrates in Plato, who expresseth orderly these seven plain notes, to choise a good wit in a child for learning:

1. Εὐφυής   5. φιλήκοος
2. Μνήμων   6. Ζητητικός
3. φιλομαθής   7. φιλέπαινος
4. φιλόπονος

And bicause I write English and to Englishmen, I will plainly declare in English both what these words of Plato mean, and how aptly they be linked, and how orderly they follow one another.

1. Εὐφυής

Is he that is apt by goodness of wit, and appliable by readiness of will, to learning, having all other qualities of the mind and parts of the body that must another day serve learning; not troubled, mangled, and halfed, but sound, whole, full, and hable to do their office; as, a tongue not stammering or over-hardly drawing forth words, but plain and ready to deliver the meaning of the mind; a voice not soft, weak, piping, womanish, but audible, strong, and manlike; a countenance not wearish and crabbed, but fair and comely; a personage not wretched and deformed, but tall and goodly; for surely a comely countenance with a goodly stature geveth credit to learning and authority to the person; otherwise, commonly, either open contempt or privy disfavor doth hurt or hinder both person and learning. And even as a fair stone requireth to be set in the finest gold, with the best workmanship, or else it leseth much of the grace and price; even so excellency in learning and namely divinity, joined with a comely personage, is a marvelous jewel in the world. And how can a comely body be better employed than to serve the fairest exercise of God's greatest gift? And that is learning. But commonly the fairest bodies are bestowed on the foulest purposes. I would it were not so; and with examples herein I will not meddle; yet I wish that those should both mind it and meddle with it which have most occasion to look to it, as good and wise fathers should do; and greatest authority to amend it, as good and wise magistrates ought to do. And yet I will not let openly to lament the unfortunate case of learning herein.

For if a father have four sons, three fair and well formed both in mind and body, the fourth wretched, lame, and deformed, his choice shall be to put the worst to learning, as one good enough to become a scholar. I have spent the most part of my life in the University, and therefore I can bear good witness that many fathers commonly do thus; whereof I have hard many wise, learned, and as good men as ever I knew make great and oft complaint. A good horseman will choise no such colt, neither for his own nor yet for his master's saddle. And thus much of the first note. . . .

[Ascham proceeds to discuss each of the other characteristics of a proper scholar: his good memory, his love of learning, his willingness to work, his desire to learn of others, his ability to ask questions, his delight in praise. Then, recurring to his earlier point that "love is fitter then fear, gentleness better than beating, to bring up a child rightly in learning," he urges schoolmasters to foster these seven qualities by mild and gentle treatment of their pupils. To refute those who argue that children naturally "mislike learning" and must be beaten to their books he sketches a charming and famous vignette of Lady Jane Grey.]

And one example whether love or fear doth work more in a child for virtue and learning I will gladly report; which may be hard with some pleasure and followed with more profit. Before I went into

Germany, I came to Broadgate in Leicestershire to take my leave of that noble Lady Jane Grey, to whom I was exceeding much beholding. Her parents, the duke and duchess, with all the household, gentlemen and gentlewomen, were hunting in the park. I found her in her chamber, reading *Phaedon Platonis* in Greek, and that with as much delight as some gentleman would read a merry tale in Boccace. After salutation and duty done, with some other talk, I asked her why she would leese such pastime in the park. Smiling, she answered me, "Iwis, all their sport in the park is but a shadow to that pleasure that I find in Plato. Alas! good folk, they never felt what true pleasure meant." "And how came you, madam," quoth I, "to this deep knowledge of pleasure, and what did chiefly allure you unto it, seeing not many women, but very few men, have attained thereunto?" "I will tell you," quoth she, "and tell you a troth which perchance ye will mervel at. One of the greatest benefits that ever God gave me is that he sent me so sharp and severe parents and so gentle a schoolmaster. For when I am in presence either of father or mother, whether I speak, keep silence, sit, stand, or go, eat, drink, be merry or sad, be sewing, playing, dancing, or doing anything else, I must do it, as it were, in such weight, measure, and number, even so perfitly, as God made the world; or else I am so sharply taunted, so cruelly threatened, yea presently sometimes with pinches, nips, and bobs, and other ways, which I will not name for the honor I bear them, so without measure misordered, that I think myself in hell till time come that I must go to Master Elmer; who teacheth me so gently, so pleasantly, with such fair allurements to learning, that I think all the time nothing whiles I am with him. And when I am called from him I fall on weeping, because whatsoever I do else but learning is full of grief, trouble, fear, and whole misliking unto me. And thus my book hath been so much my pleasure, and bringeth daily to me more pleasure and more, that in respect of it all other pleasures, in very deed, be but trifles and troubles unto me." I remember this talk gladly, both bicause it is so worthy of memory and bicause also it was the last talk that ever I had and the last time that ever I saw that noble and worthy lady. . . .

[Ascham then turns from his urging of greater gentleness in the classroom to a plea for "some more severe discipline" outside it, to produce that "good order of living" which has always characterized the most memorable commonwealths but which he finds sadly lacking in the England of his own day. He paints a gloomy picture of the lax conduct of English youth, particularly of noblemen's sons, who from seventeen to twenty-seven ("the most dangerous time of all a man's life, and most slippery to stay well in") are commonly allowed to run wild at court, where they follow the worst examples. The remedy lies chiefly "in observing private discipline every man carefully in his own house, and namely if special regard be had to youth, and that not so much in teaching them what is good as in keeping them from that that is ill."]

Athens, by this discipline and good ordering of yougth, did breed up, within the circuit of that one city, within the compass of one hundred year, within the memory of one man's life, so many notable capitains in war for worthiness, wisdom, and learning as be scarce matchable, no, not in the state of Rome in the compass of those seven hundred years whan it florished most.

And bicause I will not only say it, but also prove it, the names of them be these: Miltiades, Themistocles, Xantippus, Pericles, Cimon, Alcibiades, Thrasybulus, Conon, Iphicrates, Xenophon, Timotheus, Theopompus, Demetrius, and divers other mo; of which every one may justly be spoken that worthy praise which was geven to Scipio Africanus, who Cicero doubteth whether he were more noble capitain in war or more eloquent and wise counselor in peace. And if ye believe not me, read diligently Aemilius Probus in Latin and Plutarch in Greek; which two had no cause either to flatter or lie upon any of those which I have recited.

And beside nobility in war, for excellent and matchless masters in all manner of learning, in that one city in memory of one age were mo learned men, and that in a manner altogether, than all time doth remember, than all place doth afford, than all other tongues do contain. And I do not mean of those authors which by injury of time, by negligence of men, by cruelty of fire and sword, be lost; but even of those which by God's grace are left yet unto us; of which, I thank God, even my poor study lacketh not one. As, in philosophy, Plato, Aristotle, Xenophon, Euclid, and Theophrast; in eloquence and civil law, Demosthenes, Aeschines, Lycurgus, Dinarchus, Demades, Isocrates, Isaeus, Lysias, Antisthenes, Andocides; in histories, Herodotus, Thucydides, Xenophon, and, which we lack to our great loss, Theopompus and Ephorus; in poetry, Aeschylus, Sophocles, Euripides, Aristophanes, and somewhat of Menander, Demosthenes' sister son.

Now let Italian, and Latin itself, Spanish, French, Dutch, and English bring forth their learning and recite their authors; Cicero only excepted, and one or two mo in Latin, they be all patched clouts and rags, in comparison of fair woven broadcloths; and truly if there be any good in them, it is either learned, borrowed, or stol'n from some one of those worthy wits of Athens.

The remembrance of such a commonwealth, using

such discipline and order for yougth, and thereby bringing forth to their praise, and leaving to us for our example, such capitains for war, such counselors for peace, and matchless masters for all kind of learning, is pleasant for me to recite, and not irksome, I trust, for other to hear, except it be such as make neither count of virtue nor learning.

And whether there be any such or no, I cannot well tell; yet I hear say some young gentlemen of ours count it their shame to be counted learned; and perchance they count it their shame to be counted honest also; for I hear say they meddle as little with the one as with the other. A mervelous case, that gentlemen should so be ashamed of good learning and never a whit ashamed of ill manners! Such do lay for them that the gentlemen of France do so; which is a lie, as God will have it. Langaeus and Bellaeus, that be dead, and the noble Vidam of Chartres, that is alive, and infinite mo in France which I hear tell of prove this to be most false. And though some in France which will needs be gentlemen, whether men will or no, and have more gentleship in their hat than in their head, be at deadly feud with both learning and honesty; yet I believe if that noble prince, King Francis the First, were alive they should have neither place in his court nor pension in his wars, if he had knowledge of them. This opinion is not French, but plain Turkish, from whence some French fetch mo faults than this; which I pray God keep out of England, and send also those of ours better minds, which bend themselves against virtue and learning, to the contempt of God, dishonor of their country, to the hurt of many others, and at length to the greatest harm and utter destruction of themselves.

Some other, having better nature but less wit (for ill commonly have overmuch wit), do not utterly dispraise learning, but they say that, without learning, common experience, knowledge of all fashions, and haunting all companies shall work in yougth both wisdom and hability to execute any weighty affair. Surely long experience doth profet much, but most, and almost only, to him (if we mean honest affairs) that is diligently before instructed with precepts of well-doing. For good precepts of learning be the eyes of the mind to look wisely before a man, which way to go right and which not.

Learning teacheth more in one year than experience in twenty; and learning teacheth safely, when experience maketh mo miserable then wise. He hasardeth sore that waxeth wise by experience. An unhappy master he is that is made cunning by many shipwracks; a miserable merchant, that is neither rich nor wise but after some bankrouts. It is costly wisdom that is bought by experience. We know by experience itself that it is a mervelous pain to find out but a short way by long wandering. And, surely, he that would prove wise by experience, he may be witty indeed, but even like a swift runner that runneth fast out of his way, and upon the night, he knoweth not whither. And verily they be fewest of number that be happy or wise by unlearned experience. And look well upon the former life of those few, whether your example be old or young, who without learning have gathered by long experience a little wisdom and some happiness; and whan you do consider what mischief they have committed, what dangers they have escaped (and yet twenty for one do perish in the adventure), than think well with yourself whether ye would that your own son should come to wisdom and happiness by the way of such experience or no.

It is a notable tale that old Sir Roger Chamloe, sometime chief justice, would tell of himself. Whan he was ancient in inn of court, certain young gentlemen were brought before him to be corrected for certain misorders; and one of the lustiest said, "Sir, we be young gentlemen; and wise men before us have proved all fashions, and yet those have done full well." This they said because it was well known that Sir Roger had been a good fellow in his yougth. But he answered them very wisely: "Indeed," saith he, "in yougth I was as you are now; and I had twelve fellows like unto myself, but not one of them came to a good end. And therefore follow not my example in yougth, but follow my counsel in age, if ever ye think to come to this place or to these years that I am come unto, less ye meet either with poverty or Tyburn in the way."

Thus experience of all fashions in yougth, being in proof always dangerous, in issue seldom lucky, is a way indeed to overmuch knowledge, yet used commonly of such men which be either carried by some curious affection of mind, or driven by some hard necessity of life, to hasard the trial of overmany perilous adventures.

Erasmus, the honor of learning of all our time, said wisely that experience is the common schoolhouse of fools and ill men. Men of wit and honesty be otherwise instructed. For there be that keep them out of fire, and yet was never burned; that beware of water, and yet was never nigh drowning; that hate harlots, and was never at the stews; that abhor falsehood, and never brake promise themselves.

But will ye see a fit similitude of this adventured experience? A father that doth let loose his son to all experiences is most like a fond hunter that letteth slip a whelp to the whole herd; twenty to one he shall fall upon a rascal, and let go the fair game. Men that hunt so be either ignorant persons, prevy stealers, or nightwalkers.

Learning, therefore, ye wise fathers, and good bringing-up, and not blind and dangerous experience, is the next and readiest way that must lead your children, first to wisdom, and than to worthiness, if ever ye purpose they shall come there.

And to say all in short, though I lack authority to give counsel, yet I lack not good will to wish that the yougth in England, specially gentlemen, and namely nobility, should be by good bringing-up so grounded in judgment of learning, so founded in love of honesty, as, when they should be called forth to the execution of great affairs in service of their prince and country, they might be hable to use and to order all experiences, were they good, were they bad, and that according to the square, rule, and line of wisdom, learning, and virtue.

And I do not mean, by all this my talk, that young gentlemen should always be poring on a book, and by using good studies should leese honest pleasure and haunt no good pastime; I mean nothing less. For it is well known that I both like and love, and have always, and do yet still use, all exercises and pastimes that be fit for my nature and hability; and beside natural disposition, in judgment also I was never either Stoic in doctrine or Anabaptist in religion to mislike a merry, pleasant, and playful nature, if no outrage be committed against law, measure, and good order.

Therefore I would wish that, beside some good time fitly appointed and constantly kept to encrease by reading the knowledge of the tongues and learning, young gentlemen should use and delight in all courtly exercises and gentlemanlike pastimes. And good cause why; for the selfsame noble city of Athens, justly commended of me before, did wisely, and upon great consideration, appoint the muses, Apollo, and Pallas to be patrons of learning to their yougth. For the muses, besides learning, were also ladies of dancing, mirth, and minstrelsy; Apollo was god of shooting and author of cunning playing upon instruments; Pallas also was lady mistress in wars. Whereby was nothing else meant but that learning should be always mingled with honest mirth and comely exercises; and that war also should be governed by learning and moderated by wisdom; as did well appear in those capitans of Athens named by me before, and also in Scipio and Caesar, the two diamonds of Rome. And Pallas was no mo feared in wearing *aegida* than she was praised for choosing *oliva;* whereby shineth the glory of learning, which thus was governor and mistress in the noble city of Athens, both of war and peace.

Therefore to ride comely, to run fair at the tilt or ring, to play at all weapons, to shoot fair in bow or surely in gun, to vaut lustily, to run, to leap, to wrestle, to swim, to dance comely, to sing and play of instruments cunningly, to hawk, to hunt, to play at tennis and all pastimes generally which be joined with labor, used in open place and on the daylight, containing either some fit exercise for war, or some pleasant pastime for peace, be not only comely and decent, but also very necessary, for a courtly gentleman to use.

But of all kind of pastimes fit for a gentleman, I will, God willing, in fitter place more at large declare fully, in my book of the cockpit; which I do write to satisfy some, I trust with some reason, that be more curious in marking other men's doings than careful in mending their own faults. And some also will needs busy themselves in merveling, and adding thereunto unfriendly talk, why I, a man of good years and of no ill place, I thank God and my prince, do make choice to spend such time in writing of trifles, as the School of Shooting, the Cockpit, and this book of the First Principles of Grammar, rather than to take some weighty matter in hand, either of religion or civil discipline.

Wise men, I know, will well allow of my choice herein; and as for such who have not wit of themselves but must learn of others to judge right of men's doings, let them read that wise poet Horace in his *Arte poetica,* who willeth wise men to beware of his high and lofty titles. For great ships require costly tackling, and also afterward dangerous government: small boats be neither very chargeable in making, nor very oft in great jeopardy; and yet they carry many times as good and costly ware as greater vessels do. A mean argument may easely bear the light burden of a small faut, and have always at hand a ready excuse for ill handling; and some praise it is if it so chance to be better indeed than a man dare venture to seem. A high title doth charge a man with the heavy burden of too great a promise; and therefore saith Horace, very wittily, that that poet was a very fool that began his book with a goodly verse indeed but overproud a promise: *Fortunam Priami cantabo et nobile bellum.* And after as wisely: *Quanto rectius hic, qui nil molitur inepte,* etc.; meaning Homer, who, within the compass of a small argument of one harlot and of one good wife, did utter so much learning in all kind of sciences as, by the judgment of Quintilian, he deserveth so high a praise that no man yet deserved to sit in the second degree beneath him. And thus much out of my way, concerning my purpose in spending pen and paper and time upon trifles; and namely, to answer some that have neither wit nor learning to do anything themselves, neither will nor honesty to say well of other.

To join learning with comely exercises, Conto Baldesar Castiglione, in his book *Cortegiano,* doth trimly teach; which book advisedly read and diligently followed but one year at home in England would do a young gentleman more good, iwis, then three years' travel abroad spent in Italy. And I mervel this book is no more read in the court than it is, seeing it is so well translated into English by a worthy gentleman, Sir Thomas Hoby, who was many ways furnished with learning and very expert in knowledge of divers tongues.

And beside good precepts in books, in all kind of tongues, this court also never lacked many fair examples for young gentlemen to follow; and surely one example is more valiable, both to good and ill, than twenty precepts written in books; and so Plato, not in one or two, but diverse places, doth plainly teach.

If King Edward [VI] had lived a little longer, his only example had bred such a race of worthy learned gentlemen as this realm never yet did afford. And in the second degree two noble primroses of nobility, the young Duke of Suffolk [?Charles Brandon] and Lord H[enry] Ma[l]trevers, were such two examples to the court for learning as our time may rather wish than look for again. At Cambridge, also, in St. John's College, in my time, I do know that not so much the good statutes as two gentlemen of worthy memory, Sir John Cheke and Dr. Redman, by their only example of excellency in learning, of godliness in living, of diligency in studying, of counsel in exhorting, of good order in all thing, did breed up so many learned men in that one college of St. John's at one time as I believe the whole University of Louvain in many years was never able to afford.

Present examples of this present time I list not to touch; yet there is one example for all the gentlemen of this court to follow that may well satisfy them, or nothing will serve them, nor no example move them to goodness and learning.

It is your shame (I speak to you all, you young gentlemen of England) that one maid should go beyond you all in excellency of learning and knowledge of divers tongues. Point forth six of the best-given gentlemen of this court, and all they together shew not so much good will, spend not so much time, bestow not so many hours daily, orderly, and constantly, for the increase of learning and knowledge as doth the queen's Majesty herself. Yea, I believe that beside her perfit readiness in Latin, Italian, French, and Spanish, she readeth here now at Windsor more Greek every day than some prebendary of this church doth read Latin in a whole week. And that which is most praiseworthy of all, within the walls of her privy chamber she hath obtained that excellency of learning to understand, speak, and write both wittily with head and fair with hand as scarce one or two rare wits in both the universities have in many years reached unto. Amongst all the benefits that God hath blessed me withal, next the knowledge of Christ's true religion, I count this the greatest, that it pleased God to call me to be one poor minister in setting forward these excellent gifts of learning in this most excellent prince; whose only example if the rest of our nobility would follow, than might England be for learning and wisdom in nobility a spectacle to all the world beside. But see the mishap of men: the best examples have never such force to move to any goodness, as the bad, vain, light, and fond have to all illness.

And one example, though out of the compass of learning, yet not out of the order of good manners, was notable in this court not fully twenty-four years ago, when all the acts of Parlament, many good proclamations, diverse strait commandements, sore punishment openly, special regard privately, could not do so much to take away one misorder as the example of one big one of this court did, still to keep up the same; the memory whereof doth yet remain in a common proverb of Birching Lane.

Take heed, therefore, ye great ones in the court, yea, though ye be the greatest of all, take heed what ye do; take heed how ye live; for as you great ones use to do, so all mean men love to do. You be indeed makers or marrers of all men's manners within the realm. For though God hath placed you to be chief in making of laws, to bear greatest authority, to command all others; yet God doth order that all your laws, all your authority, all your commandements do not half so much with mean men as doth your example and manner of living. And, for example, even in the greatest matter, if you yourselves do serve God gladly and orderly for conscience sake, not coldly and sometime for manner sake, you carry all the court with you and the whole realm beside, earnestly and orderly to do the same. If you do otherwise, you be the only authors of all misorders in religion, not only to the court, but to all England beside. Infinite shall be made cold in religion by your example that never were hurt by reading of books.

And in meaner matters, if three or four great ones in court will needs outrage in apparel, in huge hose, in monstrous hats, in garish colors, let the prince proclaim, make laws, order, punish, command every gate in London daily to be watched, let all good men beside do everywhere what they can, surely the misorder of apparel in mean men abroad shall never be amended, except the greatest in court will order and mend themselves first. I know some great and good ones in court were authors that honest citizens of London should watch at every gate to take misordered persons in apparel; I know that honest Londoners did so; and I saw, which I saw than and report now with some grief, that some courtly men were offended with these good men of London. And that which grieved me most of all I saw the very same time, for all these good orders commanded from the court and executed in London—I saw, I say, come out of London even unto the presence of the prince a great rabble of mean and light persons in apparel, for matter against law, for making against order, for fashion, namely hose, so without all order as he thought himself most brave that durst do most in breaking order, and was most monsterous in misorder. And for all the great commandements that came out of the court, yet this bold misorder was winked at and borne withal in the court. I thought it was not well that some great ones of the court durst declare themselves offended with good men of London for doing their duty, and the good ones of the court would not shew themselves offended with ill men of London for breaking good order. I found thereby a saying of Socrates to be most true, that ill men be more hasty than good men be forward to prosecute their purposes, even as Christ himself saith of the children of light and darkness.

Beside apparel, in all other things too, not so much good laws and strait commandements as the example and manner of living of great men doth carry all mean men everywhere to like and love and do as they do. For if but two or three noblemen in the court would but begin to shoot, all young gentlemen, the whole court, all London, the whole realm, would straightway exercise shooting.

What praise should they win to themselves, what commodity should they bring to their country, that would thus deserve to be pointed at, "Behold, there goeth the author of good order, the guide of good men"! I could say more, and yet not overmuch. But perchance some will say I have stepp'd too far out of my school into the commonwealth, from teaching a young scholar to monish great and noble men; yet I trust good and wise men will think and judge of me that my mind was not so much to be busy and bold with them that be great now as to give true advice to them that may be great hereafter; who, if they do as I wish them to do, how great soever they be now by blood and other men's means, they shall become a great deal greater hereafter by learning, virtue, and their own deserts—which is true praise, right worthiness, and very nobility indeed. Yet, if some will needs press me that I am too bold with great men and stray too far from my matter, I will answer them with St. Paul, *Sive per contentionem, sive quocunque modo, modo Christus praedicetur*, etc. Even so whether in place or out of place, with my matter or beside my matter, if I can hereby either provoke the good or stay the ill I shall think my writing herein well imployed.

But to come down from great men and higher matters to my little children and poor schoolhouse again, I will, God willing, go forward orderly, as I purposed, to instruct children and young men both for learning and manners.

Hitherto I have shewed what harm overmuch fear bringeth to children and what hurt ill company and overmuch liberty breedeth in yougth; meaning thereby that from seven year old to seventeen love is the best allurement to learning; from seventeen to seven-and-twenty, that wise men should carefully see the steps of yougth surely stay'd by good order in that most slippery time, and specially in the court, a place most dangerous for yougth to live in without great grace, good regard, and diligent looking to.

Sir Richard Sackville, that worthy gentlemen of worthy memory, as I said in the beginning, in the queen's privy chamber at Windsor, after he had talked with me for the right choice of a good wit in a child for learning, and of the true difference betwixt quick and hard wits, of alluring young children by gentleness to love learning, and of the special care that was to be had to keep young men from licentious living, he was most earnest with me to have me say my mind also what I thought concerning the fancy that many young gentlemen of England have to travel abroad, and namely to lead a long life in Italy. His request, both for his authority and good will toward me, was a sufficient commandement unto me to satisfy his pleasure with uttering plainly my opinion in that matter. "Sir," quoth I, "I take going thither, and living there, for a young gentleman that doth not go under the keep and guard of such a man as both by wisdom can and authority dare rule him, to be mervelous dangerous." And why I said so than I will declare at large now, which I said than privately and write now openly; not bicause I do contemn either the knowledge of strange and diverse tongues, and namely the Italian tongue, which, next the Greek and Latin tongue, I like and love above all other, or else bicause I do despise the learning that is gotten or the experience that is gathered in strange countries; or for any private malice that I bear to Italy, which country, and in it namely Rome, I have always specially honored, because time was whan Italy and Rome have been to the great good of us that now live the best breeders and bringers-up of the worthiest men, not only for wise speaking but also for well doing in all civil affairs, that ever was in the world. But now that time is gone; and though the place remain, yet the old and present manners do differ as far as black and white, as virtue and vice. Virtue once made that country mistress over all the world; vice now maketh that country slave to them that before were glad to serve it. All men seeth it; they themselves confess it, namely such as be best and wisest amongest them. For sin, by lust and vanity, hath and doth breed up everywhere common contempt of God's word, private contention in many families, open factions in every city; and so, making themselves bond to vanity and vice at home, they are content to bear the yoke of serving strangers abroad. Italy now is not that Italy that it was wont to be; and therefore now not so fit a place as some do count it for young men to fetch either wisdom or honesty from thence. For surely they will make other but bad scholars that be so ill masters to themselves. Yet, if a gentleman will needs travel into Italy, he shall do well to look on the life of the wisest traveler that ever traveled thether, set out by the wisest writer that ever spake with tongue, God's doctrine only excepted; and that is Ulysses in Homer. Ulysses and his travel I wish our travelers to look upon, not so much to fear them with the great dangers that he many times suffered, as to instruct them with his excellent wisdom, which he always and everywhere used. Yea, even those that be learned and witty travelers, when they be disposed to praise traveling, as a great commendation and the best scripture they have for it, they gladly recite the third verse of Homer, in his first book of *Odyssea,* containing a great praise of Ulysses for the wit he gathered and wisdom he used in his traveling.

Which verse, bicause in mine opinion it was not made at the first more naturally in Greek by Homer, nor after turned more aptly into Latin by Horace, than it was a good while ago in Cambridge translated into English, both plainly for the sense and roundly for the verse, by one of the best scholars that ever St. John's College bred, Master Watson, mine old friend, sometime Bishop of Lincoln; therefore for their sake that have lust to see how our English tongue in avoiding barbarous riming may as well receive right quantity of syllables and true order of versifying (of which matter more at large hereafter) as either Greek or Latin, if a cunning man have it in handling, I will set forth that one verse in all three tongues for an example to good wits that shall delight in like learned exercise.

Homerus.—πολλῶν δ' ἀνθρώπων ἴδεν ἄστεα καὶ νόον ἔγνω.

Horatius.—*Qui mores hominum multorum vidit, et urbes.*

Master Watson:
All travelers do gladly report great praise of
Ulysses,
For that he knew many men's manners, and saw
many cities.

And yet is not Ulysses commended so much nor so oft in Homer bicause he was πολύτροπος, that

is, skilful in many men's manners and fashions, as bicause he was πολύμητις, that is, wise in all purposes and ware in all places; which wisdom and wareness will not serve neither a traveler except Pallas be always at his elbow, that is, God's special grace from heaven, to keep him in God's fear in all his doings, in all his journey. For he shall not always, in his absence out of England, light upon a gentle Alcinous and walk in his fair gardens full of all harmless pleasures; but he shall sometimes fall either into the hands of some cruel Cyclops or into the lap of some wanton and dallying Dame Calypso, and so suffer the danger of many a deadly den, not so full of perils to distroy the body as full of vain pleasures to poison the mind. Some siren shall sing him a song, sweet in tune, but sownding in the end to his utter destruction. If Scylla drown him not, Charybdis may fortune to swallow him. Some Circes shall make him of a plain Englishman a right Italian. And at length to hell, or to some hellish place, is he likely to go, from whence is hard returning, although one Ulysses, and that by Pallas' aid and good counsel of Tiresias, once escaped that horrible den of deadly darkness.

Therefore, if wise men will needs send their sons into Italy, let them do it wisely, under the keep and guard of him who, by his wisdom and honesty, by his example and authority, may be hable to keep them safe and sound in the fear of God, in Christ's true religion, in good order and honesty of living, except they will have them run headling into overmany jeopardies, as Ulysses had done many times if Pallas had not always governed him, if he had not used to stop his ears with wax, to bind himself to the mast of his ship, to feed daily upon that sweet herb moly, with the black root and white flow'r, given unto him by Mercury to avoid all the inchantments of Circes. Whereby the divine poet Homer meant covertly (as wise and godly men do judge) that love of honesty and hatred of ill which David more plainly doth call the fear of God, the only remedy against all inchantments of sin.

I know diverse noble personages, and many worthy gentlemen of England, whom all the siren songs of Italy could never untwine from the mast of God's Word, nor no inchantment of vanity overturn them from the fear of God and love of honesty.

But I know as many, or mo, and some sometime my dear friends, for whose sake I hate going into that country the more, who parting out of England fervent in the love of Christ's doctrine and well furnished with the fear of God, returned out of Italy worse transformed than ever was any in Circes' court. I know diverse that went out of England men of innocent life, men of excellent learning, who returned out of Italy not only with worse manners but also with less learning; neither so willing to live orderly, nor yet so hable to speak learnedly, as they were at home before they went abroad. And why? Plato, that wise writer and worthy traveler himself, telleth the cause why. He went into Sicilia, a country no nigher Italy by site of place than Italy that is now is like Sicilia that was then in all corrupt manners and licentiousness of life. Plato found in Sicilia every city full of vanity, full of factions, even as Italy is now. And as Homer, like a learned poet, doth feign that Circes by pleasant inchantments did turn men into beasts, some into swine, some into asses, some into foxes, some into wolves, etc., even so Plato, like a wise philosopher, doth plainly declare that pleasure by licentious vanity, that sweet and perilous poison of all youth, doth ingender in all those that yield up them elves to her four notorious properties,

1. λήθην
2. δυσμαθίαν
3. ἀφροσύνην
4. ὕβριν

The first, forgetfulness of all good things learned before; the second, dulness to receive either learning or honesty ever after; the third, a mind embracing lightly the worse opinion, and barren of discretion to make true difference betwixt good and ill, betwixt troth and vanity; the fourth, a proud disdainfulness of other good men in all honest matters. Homer and Plato have both one meaning, look both to one end. For if a man inglut himself with vanity, or walter in filthiness like a swine, all learning, all goodness, is soon forgotten. Than quickly shall he become a dull ass to understand either learning or honesty, and yet shall he be as subtle as a fox in breeding of mischief, in bringing in misorder, with a busy head, a discoursing tongue, and a factious heart in every private affair, in all matters of state, with this pretty property—always glad to commend the worse party, and ever ready to defend the falser opinion. And why? For where will is given from goodness to vanity, the mind is soon carried from right judgment to any fond opinion in religion, in philosophy, or any other kind of learning. The fourth fruit of vain pleasure, by Homer and Plato's judgment, is pride in themselves, contempt of others, the very badge of all those that serve in Circes' court. The true meaning of both Homer and Plato is plainly declared in one short sentence of the holy prophet of God, Hieremy, crying out of the vain and vicious life of the Israelites: "This people," saith he, "be fools and dull-heads to all goodness, but subtle, cunning, and bold in any mischief," etc.

The true medicine against the inchantments of Circes, the vanity of licentious pleasure, the intice-ments of all sin, is in Homer the herb moly, with the black root and white flower, sour at the first, but sweet in the end; which Hesiodus termeth the study of virtue, hard and irksome in the beginning, but in the end easy and pleasant. And that which is most to be marveled at, the divine poet Homer saith plainly that this medicine against sin and vanity is not found out by man, but given and taught by God. And for someone sake that will have delight to read that sweet and godly verse, I will recite the very words of Homer, and also turn them into rude English meter:

χαλεπὸν δέ τ᾽ ὀρύσσειν
ἀνδράσι γε θνητοῖσι θεοὶ δέ τε πάντα δύνανται.

In English thus:

No mortal man, with sweat of brow or toil of mind,
But only God, who can do all, that herb doth find.

Plato also, that divine philosopher, hath many godly medicines against the poison of vain pleasure, in many places, but specially in his epistles to Dionysius, the tyrant of Sicily. Yet against those that will needs become beasts with serving of Circes, the prophet David crieth most loud: *Nolite fieri sicut equus et mulus;* and by and by giveth the right medicine, the true herb moly, *In camo et freno maxillas eorum constringe;* that is to say, let God's grace be the bit, let God's fear be the bridle, to stay them from running headlong into vice, and to turn them into the right way again. David, in the second psalm after, giveth the same medicine, but in these plainer words, *Diverte a malo, et fac bonum.* But I am afraid that overmany of our travelers into Italy do not exchew the way to Circes' court, but go, and ride, and run, and fly thether; they make great haste to come to her; they make great suit to serve her; yea, I could point out some with my finger that never had gone out of England but only to serve Circes in Italy. Vanity and vice and any license to ill living in England was counted stale and rude unto them. And so, being mules and horses before they went, returned very swine and asses home again; yet everywhere very foxes with subtle and busy heads; and, where they may, very wolves with cruel malicious hearts. A mervelous monster, which for filthiness of living, for dulness to learning himself, for wiliness in dealing with others, for malice in hurting without cause, should carry at once in one body the belly of a swine, the head of an ass, the brain of a fox, the womb of a wolf. If you think we judge amiss, and write too sore against you, hear what the Italian saith of the Englishman, what the master reporteth of the scholar, who uttereth plainly what is taught by him and what is learned by you, saying, *Inglese Italianato è un diabolo incarnato;* that is to say, "You remain men in shape and fashion, but become devils in life and condition." This is not the opinion of one for some private spite, but the judgment of all in a common proverb which riseth of that learning and those manners which you gather in Italy. A good school-house of wholesome doctrine, and worthy masters of commendable scholars, where the master had rather difame himself for his teaching than not shame his scholar for his learning! A good nature of the maister, and fair conditions of the scholars! And now choose you, you Italian Englishmen, whether you will be angry with us for calling you monsters, or with the Italians for calling you devils, or else with your own selves that take so much pains, and go so far, to make yourselves both. If some yet do not well understand what is an Englishman Italianated, I will plainly tell him: he that by living and traveling in Italy bringeth home into England out of Italy the religion, the learning, the policy, the experience, the manners of Italy. That is to say, for religion, papistry or worse; for learning, less commonly than they carried out with them; for policy, a factious heart, a discoursing head, a mind to meddle in all men's matters; for experience, plenty of new mischieves never known in England before; for manners, variety of vanities and change of filthy living. These be the inchantments of Circes, brought out of Italy, to mar men's manners in England; much by example of ill life, but more by precepts of fond books, of late translated out of Italian into English, sold in every shop in London; commended by honest titles, the sooner to corrupt honest manners; dedicated over-boldly to virtuous and honorable personages, the easilier to beguile simple and innocent wits. It is pity that those which have authority and charge to allow and disallow books to be printed be no more circumspect herein than they are. Ten sermons at Paul's Cross do not so much good for moving men to true doctrine as one of those books do harm with inticing men to ill living. Yea, I say farder, those books tend not so much to corrupt honest living as they do to subvert true religion. Mo papists be made by your merry books of Italy than by your earnest books of Louvain. And bicause our great physicians do wink at the matter, and make no count of this sore, I, though not admitted one of their fellowship, yet having been many years a prentice to God's true religion and trust to continue a poor journeyman therein all days of my life, for the duty I owe and love I bear both to true doctrine and honest living, though I have no authority to amend the sore my-self, yet I will declare my good will to discover the sore to others.

St. Paul saith that sects and ill opinions be the works of the flesh and fruits of sin. This is spoken no more truly for the doctrine than sensibly for the reason.

And why? For ill doings breed ill thinkings; and of corrupted manners spring perverted judgments. And how? There be in man two special things: man's will, man's mind. Where will inclineth to goodness, the mind is bent to troth. Where will is carried from goodness to vanity, the mind is soon drawn from troth to false opinion. And so the readiest way to entangle the mind with false doctrine is first to intice the will to wanton living. Therefore, when the busy and open papists abroad could not by their contentious books turn men in England fast enough from troth and right judgment in doctrine, than the subtle and secret papists at home procured bawdy books to be translated out of the Italian tongue, whereby overmany young wills and wits allured to wantonness do now boldly contemn all severe books that sound to honesty and godliness. In our forefathers' time, whan papistry, as a standing pool, covered and overflowed all England, few books were read in our tongue, saving certain books of chevalry, as they said for pastime and pleasure; which, as some say, were made in monasteries by idle monks or wanton chanons. As one for example, *Morte Arthur;* the whole pleasure of which book standeth in two special points, in open manslaughter and bold bawdry. In which book those be counted the noblest knights that do kill most men without any quarrel and commit foulest advoulteries by subtlest shifts; as Sir Lancelot with the wife of King Arthur, his master; Sir Tristram with the wife of King Mark, his uncle; Sir Lamerock with the wife of King Lote, that was his own aunt. This is good stuff for wise men to laugh at or honest men to take pleasure at! Yet I know when God's Bible was banished the court and *Morte Arthur* received into the prince's chamber.

What toys the daily reading of such a book may work in the will of a young gentleman or a young maid that liveth wealthily and idlely, wise men can judge and honest men do pity. And yet ten *Morte Arthurs* do not the tenth part so much harm as one of these books made in Italy and translated in England. They open, not fond and common ways to vice, but such subtle, cunning, new, and diverse shifts to carry young wills to vanity and young wits to mischief, to teach old bawds new school-points, as the simple head of an Englishman is not hable to invent, nor never was hard of in England before, yea, when papistry overflowed all. Suffer these books to be read, and they shall soon displace all books of godly learning. For they, carrying the will to vanity, and marring good manners, shall easily corrupt the mind with ill opinions and false judgment in doctrine; first, to think ill of all true religion, and at last to think nothing of God himself, one special point that is to be learned in Italy and Italian books. And that which is most to be lamented, and therefore more needful to be looked to, there be mo of these ungracious books set out in print within these few moneths than have been seen in England many score year before. And bicause our Englishmen made Italians cannot hurt but certain persons, and in certain places, therefore these Italian books are made English to bring mischief enough openly and boldly to all states, great and mean, young and old, everywhere.

And thus you see how will inticed to wantonness doth easely allure the mind to false opinions; and how corrupt manners in living breed false judgment in doctrine; how sin and fleshliness bring forth sects and heresies; and therefore suffer not vain books to breed vanity in men's wills, if you would have God's troth take root in men's minds.

That Italian that first invented the Italian proverb against our Englishmen Italianated meant no more their vanity in living than their lewd opinion in religion. For in calling them devils he carrieth them clean from God; and yet he carrieth them no farder than they willingly go themselves; that is, where they may freely say their minds to the open contempt of God and all godliness, both in living and doctrine.

And how? I will express how, not by a fable of Homer, nor by the philosophy of Plato, but by a plain troth of God's word, sensibly uttered by David thus: these men, *abominabiles facti in studiis suis,* think verily and sing gladly the verse before, *Dixit insipiens in corde suo, non est Deus:* that is to say, they geving themselves up to vanity, shaking off the motions of grace, driving from them the fear of God, and running headlong into all sin, first lustily contemn God, than scornfully mock his Word, and also spitefully hate and hurt all well-willers thereof. Than they have in more reverence the *Triumphs* of Petrarch than the Genesis of Moses; they make more account of Tully's *Offices* than St. Paul's epistles; of a tale in Boccace than a story of the Bible. Than they count as fables the holy mysteries of Christian religion. They make Christ and his Gospel only serve civil policy. Than neither religion cometh amiss to them; in time they be promoters of both openly, in place again mockers of both privily, as I wrote once in a rude rime:

Now new, now old, now both, now neither;
To serve the world's course, they care not with whether.

For where they dare, in company where they like, they boldly laugh to scorn both protestant and papist. They care for no Scripture; they make no count of general councils; they contemn the consent of the church; they pass for no doctors; they mock the pope, they rail on Luther; they allow neither side; they like none but only themselves. The mark they shoot at,

the end they look for, the heaven they desire, is only their own present pleasure and private profit; whereby they plainly declare of whose school, of what religion, they be, that is, Epicures in living, and ἄθεοι in doctrine. This last word is no more unknown now to plain Englishmen than the person was unknown sometime in England, until some Englishman took pains to fetch that devilish opinion out of Italy. These men thus Italianated abroad cannot abide our godly Italian church at home; they be not of that parish; they be not of that fellowship; they like not the preacher; they hear not his sermons, except sometimes for company they come thither to hear the Italian tongue naturally spoken, not to hear God's doctrine truly preached.

And yet these men in matters of divinity openly pretend a great knowledge, and have privately to themselves a very compendious understanding of all, which nevertheless they will utter when and where they list. And that is this: all the mysteries of Moses, the whole law and ceremonies, the Psalms and prophets, Christ and his Gospel, God and the Devil, heaven and hell, faith, conscience, sin, death, and all, they shortly wrap up, they quickly expound with this one-half verse of Horace, *Credat Judaeus Apella.*

Yet though in Italy they may freely be of no religion, as they are in England in very deed too, nevertheless, returning home into England, they must countenance the profession of the one or the other, howsoever inwardly they laugh to scorn both. And though for their private matters they can follow, fawn, and flatter noble personages contrary to them in all respects, yet commonly they ally themselves with the worst papists, to whom they be wedded, and do well agree togither in three proper opinions: in open contempt of God's Word, in a secret security of sin, and in a bloody desire to have all taken away by sword or burning that be not of their faction. They that do read with indifferent judgment Pighius and Machiavel, two indifferent patriarchs of these two religions, do know full well that I say true.

Ye see what manners and doctrine our Englishmen fetch out of Italy; for finding no other there, they can bring no other hither. And therefore many godly and excellent learned Englishmen, not many years ago, did make a better choice, whan open cruelty drave them out of this country, to place themselves there [i.e. in Germany] where Christ's doctrine, the fear of God, punishment of sin, and discipline of honesty were had in special regard.

I was once in Italy myself, but I thank God my abode there was but nine days; and yet I saw in that little time, in one city [i.e. Venice], more liberty to sin than ever I hard tell of in our noble city of London in nine year. I saw it was there as free to sin, not only without all punishment, but also without any man's marking, as it is free in the city of London to choose without all blame whether a man lust to wear shoe or pantocle. And good cause why; for being unlike in troth of religion, they must needs be unlike in honesty of living. For, blessed be Christ, in our city of London commonly the commandements of God be more diligently taught and the service of God more reverently used, and that daily in many private men's houses, than they be in Italy once a week in their common churches; where masking ceremonies to delight the eye and vain sounds to please the ear do quite thrust out of the churches all service of God in spirit and troth. Yea, the lord mayor of London, being but a civil officer, is commonly for his time more diligent in punishing sin, the bent enemy against God and good order, than all the bloody inquisitors in Italy be in seven year. For their care and charge is, not to punish sin, not to amend manners, not to purge doctrine, but only to watch and oversee that Christ's true religion set no sure footing where the pope hath any jurisdiction. I learned when I was at Venice that there it is counted good policy when there be four or five brethren of one family, one only to marry, and all the rest to walter with as little shame in open lechery as swine do here in the common mire. Yea, there be as fair houses of religion, as great provision, as diligent officers to keep up this misorder, as Bridewell is, and all the masters there, to keep down misorder. And therefore, if the pope himself do not only grant pardons to furder these wicked purposes abroad in Italy, but also (although this present pope [?Pius V] in the beginning made some shew of misliking thereof) assign both meed and merit to the maintenance of stews and brothel-houses at home in Rome, than let wise men think Italy a safe place for wholesome doctrine and godly manners, and a fit school for young gentlemen of England to be brought up in.

Our Italians bring home with them other faults from Italy, though not so great as this of religion, yet a great deal greater than many good men can well bear. For commonly they come home common contemners of marriage and ready persuaders of all other to the same; not because they love virginity, nor yet because they hate pretty young virgins, but, being free in Italy to go whithersoever lust will carry them, they do not like that law and honesty should be such a bar to their like liberty at home in England. And yet they be the greatest makers of love, the daily dalliers with such pleasant words, with such smiling and secret countenances, with such signs, tokens, wagers purposed to be lost before they were purposed to be made, with bargains of wearing colors, flow'rs, and herbs, to breed occasion of ofter meeting of him

and her, and bolder talking of this and that, etc. And although I have seen some innocent of all ill, and stay'd in all honesty, that have used these things without all harm, without all suspicion of harm, yet these knacks were brought first into England by them that learned them before in Italy in Circes' court; and how courtly curtesses soever they be counted now, yet if the meaning and manners of some that do use them were somewhat amended, it were no great hurt neither to themselves nor to others.

Another property of this our English Italians is to be mervelous singular in all their matters: singular in knowledge, ignorant of nothing; so singular in wisdom (in their own opinion) as scarce they count the best counselor the prince hath comparable with them; common discoursers of all matters; busy searchers of most secret affairs; open flatterers of great men; privy mislikers of good men; fair speakers with smiling countenances and much curtesy openly to all men; ready backbiters, sore nippers, and spiteful reporters privily of good men. And being brought up in Italy, in some free city, as all cities be there, where a man may freely discourse against what he will, against whom he lust, against any prince, against any government, yea, against God himself and his whole religion; where he must be either Guelph or Ghibelline, either French or Spanish, and always compelled to be of some party, of some faction, he shall never be compelled to be of any religion; and if he meddle not overmuch with Christ's true religion, he shall have free liberty to embrace all religions, and become if he lust, at once, without any let or punishment, Jewish, Turkish, papish, and devilish.

A young gentleman, thus bred up in this goodly school to learn the next and ready way to sin, to have a busy head, a factious heart, a talkative tongue, fed with discoursing of factions, led to contemn God and his religion, shall come home into England but very ill taught, either to be an honest man himself, a quiet subject to his prince, or willing to serve God under the obedience of true doctrine or within the order of honest living.

I know none will be offended with this my general writing but only such as find themselves guilty privately therein; who shall have good leave to be offended with me until they begin to amend themselves. I touch not them that be good, and I say too little of them that be nought. And so, though not enough for their deserving, yet sufficiently for this time, and more elsewhen, if occasion so require.

And thus far have I wand'red from my first purpose of teaching a child, yet not altogether out of the way, bicause this whole talk hath tended to the only advancement of troth in religion an honesty of living;

and hath been wholly within the compass of learning and good manners, the special points belonging in the right bringing-up of youth.

But to my matter: as I began plainly and simply with my young scholar, so will I not leave him, God willing, until I have brought him a perfit scholar out of the school, and placed him in the university to become a fit student for logic and rhetoric; and so after to physic, law, or divinity, as aptness of nature, advice of friends, and God's disposition shall lead him.

The end of the first book

THE SECOND BOOK

After that your scholar, as I said before, shall come indeed first to a ready perfitness in translating, than to a ripe and skilful choice in marking out his six points, as

1. *Proprium*
2. *Translatum*
3. *Synonymum*
4. *Contrarium*
5. *Diversum*
6. *Phrases*

than take this order with him: read daily unto him some book of Tully, as the third book of epistles chosen out by Sturmius, *De amicitia, De senectute,* or that excellent epistle containing almost the whole first book *Ad Quintum fratrem;* some comedy of Terence or Plautus (but in Plautus skilful choice must be used by the master to train his scholar to a judgment in cutting out perfitly overold and unproper words); Caesar's *Commentaries* are to be read with all curiosity in specially, without all exception to be made either by friend or foe, [where] is seen the unspotted propriety of the Latin tongue, even whan it was, as the Grecians say, in ἀχμῇ, that is, at the highest pitch of all perfitness; or some orations of Titus Livius, such as be both longest and plainest.

These books I would have him read now, a good deal at every lecture; for he shall not now use daily translation, but only construe again, and parse, where ye suspect is any need; yet let him not omit in these books his former exercise in marking diligently and writing orderly out his six points. And for translating, use you yourself, every second or third day, to chose out some epistle *Ad Atticum,* some notable commonplace out of his orations, or some other part of Tully, by your discretion, which your scholar may not know where to find; and translate it you yourself into plain, natural English, and than give it him to translate into Latin again, allowing him good space and time to do it, both with diligent heed and good advisement. Here his wit shall be new set on

work; his judgment, for right choice, truly tried; his memory, for sure retaining, better exercised than by learning anything without the book; and here how much he hath profited shall plainly appear. Whan he bringeth it translated unto you, bring you forth the place of Tully; lay them together; compare the one with the other; commend his good choice and right placing of words; shew his faults gently, but blame them not oversharply; for of such missings, gently admonished of, proceedeth glad and good heed-taking; of good heed-taking springeth chiefly knowledge, which after groweth to perfitness if this order be diligently used by the scholar and gently handled by the master; for here shall all the hard points of grammar both easely and surely be learned up, which scholars in common schools, by making of Latins, be groping at with care and fear, and yet in many years they scarce can reach unto them. I remember whan I was young, in the North they went to the grammar school little children; they came from thence great lubbers, always learning and little profiting; learning without book everything, understanding within the book little or nothing. Their whole knowledge, by learning without the book, was tied only to their tongue and lips, and never ascended up to the brain and head, and therefore was soon spit out of the mouth again. They were as men always going but ever out of the way. And why? For their whole labor, or rather great toil without order, was even vain idleness without profit. Indeed, they took great pains about learning, but employed small labor in learning, whan by this way prescribed in this book, being straight, plain, and easy, the scholar is always laboring with pleasure and ever going right on forward with profit. . . .

In this place, or I proceed farder, I will now declare by whose authority I am led, and by what reason I am moved, to think that this way of double translation out of one tongue into another is either only, or at least chiefly, to be exercised, specially of youth, for the ready and sure obtaining of any tongue.

There be six ways appointed by the best-learned men for the learning of tongues and encrease of eloquence, as

1. *Translatio linguarum*
2. *Paraphrasis*
3. *Metaphrasis*
4. *Epitome*
5. *Imitatio*
6. *Declamatio*

All these be used and commended, but in order and for respects as person, hability, place, and time shall require. The five last be fitter for the master than the scholar, for men than for children, for the universities rather than for grammar schools; yet, nevertheless, which is fittest, in mine opinion, for our school, and which is either wholly to be refused or partly to be used for our purpose, I will, by good authority and some reason, I trust, perticularly of every one and largely enough of them all, declare orderly unto you. . . .

[Ascham then discusses, copiously and with many examples and digressions, the faults and merits of these six various techniques for learning a foreign language. He admires the first very much as the "most common and most commendable of all other exercises for youth." *Paraphrasis*—which "is not only to express at large with mo words, but to strive and contend (as Quintilian saith) to translate the best Latin authors into other Latin words"—admittedly "hath good place in learning," yet it is not for everyone: it is "an exercise not fit for a scholar, but for a perfit master, who in plenty hath good choice, in copy hath right judgment and grounded skill." *Metaphrasis* is like *paraphrasis* "save it is out of verse either into prose, or into some other kind of meter; or else out of prose into verse." *Epitome* may perhaps be profitable for him who practises it, but for others it is "a silly, poor kind of study, not unlike to the doing of those poor folk which neither till nor sow nor reap themselves, but glean by stealth upon other men's grounds." It is the solace of the lazy and the half-educated. "To dwell in epitomes and books of commonplaces, and not to bind himself daily by orderly study to read with all diligence principally the holiest Scripture and withal the best doctors, and so to learn to make true difference betwixt the authority of the one and the counsel of the other, maketh so many seeming and sunburnt ministers as we have, whose learning is gotten in a summer heat and washed away with a Christmas snow again, who nevertheless are less to be blamed than those blind bussards who in late years, of wilful maliciousness, would neither learn themselves nor could teach others anything at all." *Imitatio*, however, appeals to Ascham so much that to it he devotes the rest, and the greater part, of his second book.]

Imitation is a faculty to express lively and perfitly that example which ye go about to follow. And of itself it is large and wide, for all the works of nature in a manner be examples for art to follow.

But to our purpose: all languages, both learned and mother tongues, be gotten and gotten only by imitation. For as ye use to hear, so ye learn to speak; if ye hear no other, ye speak not yourself, and whom ye only hear, of them ye only learn. . . .

In the Greek and Latin tongue, the two only learned tongues, which be kept not in common talk but in private books, we find always wisdom and eloquence, good matter and good utterance, never or seldom asunder. For all such authors as be fullest of good matter and right judgment in doctrine be likewise always most proper in words, most apt in sentence, most plain and pure in uttering the same. And contrariwise in those two tongues all writers, either in religion or any sect of philosophy, whosoever be found fond in judgment of matter be commonly found as rude in uttering their mind. For Stoics, Anabaptists, and friars, with Epicures, libertines, and monks, being most like in learning and life, are no fonder and pernicious in their opinions than they be rude and barbarous in their writings. They be not wise, therefore, that say, "What care I for a man's words and utterance if his matter and reasons be good?" . . .

Ye know not what hurt ye do to learning that care not for words but for matter, and so make a divorce betwixt the tongue and the heart. For mark all ages, look upon the whole course of both the Greek and Latin tongue, and ye shall surely find that whan apt and good words began to be neglected, and properties of those two tongues to be confounded, than also began ill deeds to spring, strange manners to oppress good orders, new and fond opinions to strive with old and true doctrine, first in philosophy and after in religion, right judgment of all things to be perverted, and so virtue with learning is contemned and study left off; of ill thoughts cometh perverse judgment, of ill deeds springeth lewd talk. Which sour misorders, as they mar man's life, so destroy they good learning withal.

But behold the goodness of God's providence for learning: all old authors and sects of philosophy which were fondest in opinion and rudest in utterance, as Stoics and Epicures, first contemned of wise men and after forgotten of all men, be so consumed by times as they be now not only out of use but also out of memory of man, which thing, I surely think, will shortly chance to the whole doctrine and all the books of phantastical Anabaptists and friars and of the beastly libertines and monks.

Again behold, on the other side, how God's wisdom hath wrought that of *Academici* and *Peripatetici*, those that were wisest in judgment of matters and purest in uttering their minds, the first and chiefest that wrote most and best in either tongue, as Plato and Aristotle in Greek, Tully in Latin, be so either wholly or sufficiently left unto us as I never knew yet scholar that gave himself to like and love and follow chiefly those three authors but he proved both learned, wise, and also an honest man if he joined with all the true doctrine of God's Holy Bible, without the which the other three be but fine-edge tools in a fool or madman's hand.

But to return to imitation again: there be three kinds of it in matters of learning.

The whole doctrine of comedies and tragedies is a perfit imitation, or fair, lively painted picture of the life of every degree of man. Of this imitation writeth Plato at large in III *De republica*, but it doth not much belong at this time to our purpose.

The second kind of imitation is to follow for learning of tongues and sciences the best authors. Here riseth, emonges proud and envious wits, a great controversy whether one or many are to be followed, and, if one, who is that one—Seneca or Cicero, Sallust or Caesar, and so forth in Greek and Latin.

The third kind of imitation belongeth to the second, as when you be determined whether ye will follow one or mo, to know perfitly and which way to follow that one, in what place, by what mean and order, by what tools and instruments ye shall do it, by what skill and judgment ye shall truly discern whether ye follow rightly or no. . . .

If a man would take this pain also, whan he hath laid two places of Homer and Virgil, or of Demosthenes and Tully, togither, to teach plainly withal after this sort:

1. Tully retaineth thus much of the matter, these sentences, these words.
2. This and that he leaveth out, which he doth wittily to this end and purpose.
3. This he addeth here.
4. This he diminisheth there.
5. This he ordereth thus, with placing that here, not there.
6. This he altereth and changeth, either in property of words, in form of sentence, in substance of the matter, or in one or other convenient circumstance of the author's present purpose.

In these few rude English words are wrapp'd up all the necessary tools and instruments wherewith true imitation is rightly wrought withal in any tongue. Which tools, I openly confess, be not of mine own forging, but partly left unto me by the cunningest master, and one of the worthiest gentlemen that ever England bred, Sir John Cheke, partly borrowed by me out of the shop of the dearest friend I have out of England, Jo[hannes] St[urmius]. And therefore I am the bolder to borrow of him, and here to leave them to other, and namely to my children; which tools if it please God that another day they may be able to use rightly, as I do wish and daily pray they may do, I shall be more glad than if I were able to leave them a great quantity of land.

This aforesaid order and doctrine of imitation would bring forth more learning and breed up truer judgment than any other exercise that can be used, but not for young beginners, bicause they shall not be able to consider duly thereof. And truly, it may be a shame to good students who, having so fair examples to follow as Plato and Tully, do not use so wise ways in following them for the obtaining of wisdom and learning as rude ignorant artificers do for gaining a small commodity. For surely the meanest painter useth more wit, better art, greater diligence in his shop in following the picture of any mean man's face than commonly the best students do, even in the university, for the attaining of learning itself.

Some ignorant, unlearned, and idle student, or some busy looker upon this little poor book that hath neither will to do good himself nor skill to judge right of others, but can lustily contemn, by pride and ignorance, all painful diligence and right order in study, will perchance say that I am too precise, too curious, in marking and pitteling thus about the imitation of others; and that the old worthy authors did never busy their heads and wits in following so precisely either the matter what other men wrote or else the manner how other men wrote. They will say it were a plain slavery and injury too to shackle and tie a good wit and hinder the course of a man's good nature with such bonds of servitude in following other.

Except such men think themselves wiser then Cicero for teaching of eloquence, they must be content to turn a new leaf. . . . [And here Ascham buttresses his praise of imitation with citations from Cicero, Dionysius of Halicarnassus, Quintilian, Erasmus, Budaeus, Melanchthon, Sturmius, and many others.]

I have been a looker-on in the cockpit of learning these many years, and one cock only have I known which with one wing, even at this day, doth pass all other, in mine opinion, that ever I saw in any pit in England, though they had two wings. Yet nevertheless, to fly well with one wing, to run fast with one leg, be rather rare maistries much to be merveled at than sure examples safely to be followed. A bushop that now liveth, a good man whose judgment in religion I better like than his opinion in perfitness in other learning, said once unto me: "We have no need now of the Greek tongue, when all things be translated into Latin." But the good man understood not that even the best translation is, for mere necessity, but an evil-imped wing to fly withal or a heavy stump-leg of wood to go withal; such, the higher they fly, the sooner they falter and fail; the faster they run, the ofter they stumble and sorer they fail. Such as will needs so fly may fly at a pie and catch a daw. And such runners, as commonly they shove and shoulder to stand foremost, yet in the end they come behind others and deserve but the hopshackles, if the masters of the game be right judgers. . . .

If a good student would bend himself to read diligently over Tully, and with him also at the same time as diligently Plato and Xenophon with his books of philosophy, Isocrates and Demosthenes with his orations, and Aristotle with his rhetorics (which five, of all other, be those whom Tully best loved and specially followed), and would mark diligently in Tully where he doth *exprimere* or *effingere* . . . , and not only write out the places diligently, and lay them together orderly, but also to confer them with skilful judgment by those few rules which I have expressed now twice before—if that diligence were taken, if that order were used, what perfit knowledge of both the tongues, what ready and pithy utterance in all matters, what right and deep judgment in all kind of learning would follow is scarce credible to be believed.

These books be not many, nor long, nor rude in speech, nor mean in matter, but next the majesty of God's Holy Word most worthy for a man, the lover of learning and honesty, to spend his life in. Yea, I have heard worthy Master Cheke many times say, "I would have a good student pass and journey through all authors, both Greek and Latin, but he that will dwell in these few books only, first in God's Holy Bible, and than join with it Tully in Latin, Plato, Aristotle, Xenophon, Isocrates, and Demosthenes in Greek, must needs prove an excellent man." . . .

[Ascham urges that in accordance with his precepts of imitation the "hard, dry, and cold" precepts of Aristotle could be delightfully enriched with the "examples" of Plato.]

Cambridge, at my first coming thither but not at my going away, committed this fault in reading the precepts of Aristotle without the examples of other authors; but herein, in my time, these men of worthy memory, Master Redman, Master Cheke, Master Smith, Master Haddon, Master Watson, put so to their helping hands as that university, and all students there, as long as learning shall last shall be bound unto them, if that trade in study be truly followed which those men left behind them there.

By this small mention of Cambridge I am carried into three imaginations: first into a sweet remembrance of my time spent there, than into some careful thoughts for the grievous alteration that followed soon after, lastly into much joy to hear tell of the good recovery and earnest forwardness in all good learning there again.

To utter these my thoughts somewhat more largely were somewhat beside my matter, yet not very far out of the way, bycause it shall wholly tend to the good encoragement and right consideration of learning, which is my full purpose in writing this little

book, whereby also shall well appear this sentence to be most true, that only good men, by their government and example, make happy times in every degree and state. . . . [Ascham then digresses into an account of Nicholas Medcalfe (?1475–1539), the Master of St. John's College, Cambridge, in his student days, and into a vivid relation of Cambridge's misfortunes during the religious turmoils that "at length, by God's providence, had their end 16 November 1558" with the accession of Elizabeth. In its former glory under Cheke and Smith and Redman and Medcalfe, Cambridge had "four pillars of learning" and gave place "to no university, neither in France, Spain, Germany, nor Italy." But with the golden day promised by the new queen even greater glories lie ahead. Then returning to his discourse of imitation, Ascham surveys the *corpus* of classical literature under typical Renaissance categories or "kinds." Thus all writing takes the form of poetry or history or philosophy or oratory; and all poetry, in turn, may be described as comic or tragic or epic or lyric. This analysis leads to a discussion of classical metrics.]

This matter maketh me gladly remember my sweet time spent at Cambridge and the pleasant talk which I had oft with Master Cheke and Master Watson of this fault [that is, the "very mean" meters of Plautus and Terence], not only in the old Latin poets but also in our new English rimers at this day. They wished, as Virgil and Horace were not wedded to follow the faults of former fathers (a shrewd marriage in greater matters) but by right imitation of the perfit Grecians had brought poetry to perfitness also in the Latin tongue, that we Englishmen likewise would acknowledge and understand rightfully our rude, beggarly riming, brought first into Italy by Goths and Huns whan all good verses and all good learning, too, were destroy'd by them, and after carried into France and Germany, and at last received into England by men of excellent wit, indeed, but of small learning and less judgment in that behalf.

But now, when men know the difference and have the examples both of the best and of the worst, surely to follow rather the Goths in riming than the Greeks in true versifying were even to eat ackorns with swine when we may freely eat wheat bread emonges men. Indeed, Chaucer, Thomas Norton of Bristow, my Lord of Surrey, Master Wyatt, Thomas Phaer, and other gentlemen, in translating Ovid, Palingenius, and Seneca, have gone as far to their great praise as the copy they followed could carry them; but if such good wits and forward diligence had been directed to follow the best examples, and not have been carried by time and custom to content themselves with that barbarous and rude riming, emonges their other worthy praises which they have justly deserved, this had not been the least, to be counted emonges men of learning and skill more like unto the Grecians than unto the Gothians in handling of their verse. . . . [And thus Ascham sets off in pursuit of that will-o'-the-wisp, quantitative verse in English. To substitute it for syllabic verse would mean that "rash, ignorant heads, which now can easely reckon up fourteen syllables and easely stumble on every rime, either durst not, for lack of such learning, or else would not, in avoiding such labor, be so busy as everywhere they be, and shops in London should not be so full of lewd and rude rimes as commonly they are."]

You that be able to understand no more then ye find in the Italian tongue and never went farder than the school of Petrarch and Ariostus abroad or else of Chaucer at home, though you have pleasure to wander blindly still in your foul wrong way, envy not others that seek, as wise men have done before them, the fairest and rightest way; or else, beside the just reproach of malice, wise men shall truly judge that you do so, as I have said and say yet again unto you, bicause either for idleness ye will not or for ignorance ye cannot come by no better yourself.

And therefore even as Virgil and Horace deserve most worthy praise that they, spying the unperfitness in Ennius and Plautus, by true imitation of Homer and Euripides brought poetry to the same perfitness in Latin as it was in Greek, even so those that by the same way would benefit their tongue and country deserve rather thanks than dispraise in that behalf. . . .

[*The Schoolmaster* closes with a discussion of four writers—Cicero, Varro, Sallust, and Caesar—whom Ascham very much admires as objects of imitation. His treatment of Sallust is, he admits, a restatement of the teaching of "my dearest friend and best master that ever I had or heard in learning, Sir John Cheke." As such it is a notable example of the lasting influence

of a great teacher—one whose talents and energies went into the spoken rather than the written word. The last section of the book consists of a perfunctory analysis of Caesar.]

Caesar, for that little of him that is left unto us, is like the half face of a Venus, the other part of the head being hidden, the body and the rest of the members unbegun, yet so excellently done by Apelles as all men may stand still to maze and muse upon it, and no man step forth with any hope to perform the like.

His seven books *De bello Gallico* and three *De bello civili* be written so wisely for the matter, so eloquently for the tongue, that neither his greatest enemies could ever find the least note of partiality in him (a mervelous wisdom of a man, namely writing of his own doings), nor yet the best judgers of the Latin tongue nor the most envious lookers upon other men's writings can say any other but all things be most perfitly done by him.

Brutus, Calvus, and Calidius, who found fault with Tully's fulness in words and matter, and that rightly, for Tully did both confess it and mend it, yet in Caesar they neither did nor could find the like or any other fault.

And therefore thus justly I may conclude of Caesar that, where in all other the best that ever wrote in any time or in any tongue in Greek and Latin (I except neither Plato, Demosthenes, nor Tully) some fault is justly noted, in Caesar only could never yet fault be found.

Yet nevertheless, for all this perfit excellency in him, yet it is but in one member of eloquence, and that but of one side neither, whan we must look for that example to follow which hath a perfit head, a whole body, forward and backward, arms and legs and all.

RICHARD MULCASTER

THE ELEMENTARY

Though by no means a master of English prose himself, Richard Mulcaster was convinced, as he wrote to Leicester, that the "right writing of our English tongue" is a necessary component of sound education. As a great Elizabethan pedagogue—he was successively headmaster of the Merchant Taylors' School and highmaster of St. Paul's—he was in a position to implement his curricular reforms in a way denied to Ascham (whose *Schoolmaster* he revered). In his two major pronouncements, the *Positions* (1581) and *The Elementary* (1582), he maintains

the humanistic veneration for Latin, and he perpetuates (after his dry, pedantic fashion) the tradition of Renaissance courtesy books in prescribing "for the training-up of children either for skill in their book or health in their body"; but, unlike Elyot and Ascham, he is less concerned with the sons of "magistrates" and landed gentry than with the sons of small merchants and common citizens. Thus, though he does not share the aristocratic presuppositions of earlier humanists, he finds a compensation in democratizing (some would say vulgarizing) the tradi-

tion of Tudor education; and his earthy, realistic awareness of the everyday needs of that urban middle class
whose sons he had taught for some twenty years gives a
peculiar relevance to the creed which he announced to
his queen: "I love Latin, but worship English." Our text
is based upon *The First Part of the Elementarie Which
Entreateth Chefelie of the right writing of our English tung,*
1582 (STC 18250). So far as is known, its promised successor (a presumed "second part") never appeared.

FROM THE FIRST PART OF THE ELEMENTARY, WHICH ENTREATETH CHIEFLY OF THE RIGHT WRITING OF OUR ENGLISH TONGUE (1582)

To the Right Honorable My Very Good Lord, the
Lord Robert Dudley, Earl of Leicester . . .

Right honorable and my very good lord, as the
considerations which enforced me to offer her Majesty the first fruits of my public writing were exceeding great, so those reasons which induce me now to
present to your Honor this my second labor be not
very small. Her Majesty representeth the personage
of the whole land, and therefore claimeth a prerogative in duty both for the excellency of her place
wherewith she is honored as our prince and for the
greatness of her care wherewith she is charged as our
parent. . . . Now, my duty in that behalf towards
her Majesty being so discharged, whom the presenting of my book makes privy to my purpose, doth not
the very stream of duty and the force of desert carry
me straight from her Highness unto your Honor,
whether I have in eye your general goodness towards
all them which be learned themselves or your
particular favor towards my travail which teach
others to learn? . . . And though I begin the shew of
my devotion with a very mean sacrifice for so great
a saint (as what a simple present is a part of an
Elementary or an English ortography, to so great a
person and so good a patron?), yet am I in very good
hope that your Honor will accept it and measure my
good will not by the value of the present but by the
wont of your goodness. . . . And as the difference of
state between her Majesty and your Honor made me,
of mere force, to begin with her and to discend to
you, so the matter of that book which I presented
unto her is the occasion of this which I offer unto
you. In that book, among other things which the
discourse enforced as it enforced many (bycause it
doth meddle with all the needful accidents which
belong to teaching), I did promise an Elementary,
that is, the whole matter which childern are to learn,
and the whole manner how masters are to teach them,
from their first beginning to go to any school until
they pass to grammer, in both the best if my opinion
prove best. This point is of great moment, in my
judgment, both for young learners to be ent'red
with the best and for the old learned to be sound
from the first. This Elementary am I now to perform. Whose particular branches being many in
number and the book thereby growing to some
bulk, I thought it good to devide it into parts upon
sundry causes, but chiefly for the printer, whose sale
will be quick if the book be not big. Of those several
parts this is the first, wherein I entreat (though that
be but little) of certain general considerations which
concern the whole Elementary, but I handle specially
in it the right writing of our English tongue, a very
necessary point and of force to be handled ere the
child be taught to read, which reading is the first
principle of the whole Elementary. For can reading
be right before writing be righted, seeing we read
nothing else but what we see written? Or can writing
seem right, being challenged for wrong, before it be
cleared? . . . I have traveled in this point of our English writing somewhat more then ordinary. Wherein
what my judgment is your Honor may perceive even
by this my thus writing, which is as the common,
though more certain then the common, as my precepts will shew, bycause I write nothing without
cause why and most certain ground. For I have
sounded the thing by the depth of our tongue and
planted my rules upon our ordinary custom, the more
my friend bycause it is followed, nowhere my foe
bycause nowhere forced. Whereby I do perceive
why we ought to write thus as the common currant
is without the alteration of either custom or charact,
though with some correction of certain wants and
general direction for the whole pen. I begin to teach
this low bycause I would not leap, but rise by
degrees, entending to mount higher as my argument
grows higher. . . .

The most mighty and most merciful God preserve
her most excellent Majesty with long and happy life
to work this and many such effects to his honor, her
own renoun, and her people's good; and the same
good God preserve your Honor as a counseler of
most trust to a prince of most wisdom to beautify
nobility, to avance knowledge, to assist your country
in both true religion and politic rule; and amongst
other things not of least honor to further our schools
that even the young infant thorough this whole
realm may learn to know how much he is bound to

your honorable furtherance for his good bringing-up in the elementary principles of all learning before he do remove to any university, as all those students which are of the universities do both praise and pray for your honorable prosperity for that great encouragement which they receive by you both while they study there and when they serve abroad in public functions of the commonweal.

Your Honor's most bound in all dutifulness,
Richard Mulcaster   10

CHAPTER XI

The General Platform and Method of the Whole Elementary

I will set down the purtrat of the whole Elementary, and how I purpose to deal therein, before I meddle with any particular principle, that my reader, seeing my whole plat in so small a form, and no parcel thereof but within his compass, may the sooner perceive the drift of my labor and accordingly frame his hope of the thing and the good like to come by it, and stay his memory the better by the method and order which I promise to keep in it. I devide the consideration of the whole Elementary into two parts, whereof the first concerneth the matter and substance thereof and how I entend to deal therein; the second concerneth the manner and form of teaching it and how I wish that every circumstance were handled that both the teacher may deliver plainly with order and the learner receive quickly with profit. Wherefore the first part of this my general plat shall shew the matter of the Elementary and the handling thereof; the second shall shew the manner of teaching and the circumstances therein.

The matter of the whole Elementary consisting in five points—reading, writing, drawing, singing, and playing—I will so handle them in rew as I marshal them in order, and begin first at reading.

But bycause I take upon me in this Elementary, besides some friendship to secretaries for the pen and to correctors for the print, to direct such people as teach childern to read and write English, and the reading must needs be such as the writing leads unto, therefore, before I meddle with any particular precept to direct the reader, I will thoroughly rip up the whole certainty of our English writing so farfurth and with such assurance as probability can make me, bycause it is a thing both proper to my argument and profitable to my country. For our natural tongue being as beneficial unto us for our needful delivery as any other is to the people which use it, and having as pretty and as fair observations in it as any other hath, and being as ready to yield to any rule of art as any other is, why should I not take some pains to find out the right writing of ours, as other country-

men have done to find the like in theirs? And so much the rather bycause it is pretended that the writing thereof is mervelous uncertain and scant to be recovered from extreme confusion without some change of as great extremity. I mean, therefore, so to deal in it as I may wipe away that opinion of either uncertainty for confusion or impossibility for direction, that both the natural English may have wherein to rest and the desirous stranger may have whereby to learn. For the performance whereof and mine own better direction I will first examine those means whereby other tongues of most sacred antiquity have been brought to art and form of discipline for their right writing, to the end that by following their way I may hit upon their right, and at the least by their president devise the like to theirs where the use of our tongue and the property of our dialect will not yield flat to theirs. That done, I will set all the variety of our now writing and the uncertain force of all our letters in as much certainty as any writing can be by these seven precepts: general rule, which concerneth the property and use of each letter; proportion, which reduceth all words of one sound to the same writing; composition, which teacheth how to write one word made of mo; derivation, which examineth the offspring of every original; distinction, which bewrayeth the difference of sound and force in letters by some written figure or accent; enfranchisement, which directeth the right writing of all incorporate foren words; prerogative, which declareth a reservation, wherein common use will continue her precedence in our English writing as she hath done everywhere else, both for the form of the letter in some places which likes the pen better and for the difference in writing where some particular caveat will check a common rule. . . .

In reading I will keep this order: bycause the treatise of right writing doth pretend some help to the right in reading, I will first give certain rules to be observed in reading and spelling, according to those precepts which I gave in writing. And forsomuch as the goodness and virtue of matter is most fit for the young child in the first seasoning of his tender mind, and the matter itself is spread into two branches consonant unto the main distinction of the Ten Commandements, either for religion towards God and right opinion in faith or for civility towards men and right judgment in behavior, I will therefore cast the matter of reading so as it shall answer at full both to religion in faith and to civility in friendship. . . .

For his memory I will foresee that as he must practise it even from the first, so he may also practise it even upon the best, both for pleasure in learning and for profit after learning.

For his delight, which is no mean allurement to his

learning well, I will be as careful that the matter which he shall read may be so fit for his years and so plain to his wit as when he is at school he may desire to go forward in so comfortable an argument, and when he cometh home he may take great pleasure to be telling of his parents what pretty, petty things he doth find in his book, and that the parents also may have no less delight to hear their little one speak. . . .

For his capacity, I will so provide that the matter which he shall learn may be so easy to understand and the phrase which I will use so evident to perceive as both the one and the other shall cause nothing but courage.

For his forwarding, I mean to be somewhat curious that there be such consideration and choice for syllabs, words, and sentences, and for all their accidentary notes, as there shall want nothing which may seem worth the wishing for the full help of either spelling true or reading sure, that what child soever can read them well may read anything else well if the reading-master will keep that order in his teaching which I entend to give him in my precept, and do his infant no harm by hasting him on too fast and by measuring his forwardness not by his own knowledge but by fant'sy of his friends. If opportunity serve me and cause require that labor, I will pen the same things in the Latin tongue also to satisfy some people which will be best pleased so. . . .

The treatise of reading being thus ended, then will I on to the principle of writing, wherein I shall need neither to be curious ne yet long bycause the whole ortography which concerneth the right writing of our tongue will both help the writing-master and ease my labor in that behalf. . . .

This done, I must teach how to draw. Which drawing, bycause it is not so evidently profitable nor so generally received as writing and reading be, I will therefore prove in a pretty short discourse both how profitable it is and how it deserveth the learning even for profit sake, besides many petty pleasures. Then bycause drawing useth both number and figure wherewithal to work, I will cull out so much numb'ring from out of arithmetic, the mistress of numbers, and so much figuring out of geometry, the lady of figures, as shall serve fit for an elementary principle to the child's drawing without either hardness to fray him or length to tire him. . . . Last of all, forsomuch as drawing is a thing whose thorough help many good workmen do use which live honestly thereby and in good degree of estimation and wealth —as architecture, picture, embrodery, engraving, statuary, all modeling, all platforming, and many the like, besides the learned use thereof for astronomy, geometry, chorography, topography, and some other such—I will therefore pick out some certain figures proper to so many of the foresaid faculties as shall seem most fit to teach a child to draw, and withal I will shew how they be to be dealt with even from their first point to their last perfection. . . .

As for music, which I have devided into voice and instrument, I will keep this currant: the training-up in music, as in all other faculties, hath a special eye to these three points: the child himself that is to learn, the matter itself which he is to learn, and the instrument itself whereon he is to learn. Wherein I will deal so for the first and last, that is, for the child and the instrument, as neither of them shall lack whatsoever is needful either for framing of the child's voice, or for the righting of his finger, or for the pricking of his lessons, or for the tuning of his instrument. . . .

CHAPTER XIII

That the English Tongue Hath in Itself Sufficient Matter to Work Her Own Artificial Direction for the Right Writing Thereof

It must needs be that our English tongue hath matter enough in her own writing which may direct her own right if it be reduced to certain precept and rule of art, though it have not as yet been thoroughly perceived.

The causes why it hath not as yet been thoroughly perceived are the hope and despair of such as have either thought upon it and not dealt in it, or that have dealt in it but not rightly thought upon it. . . .

Yet notwithstanding all this, it is very manifest that the tongue itself hath matter enough in itself to furnish out an art, and that the same mean which hath been used in the reducing of other tongues to their right will serve this of ours, both for generality of precept and certainty of ground, as may be easily proved by these four arguments: the antiquity of our tongue, the people's wit, their learning, and their experience. For how can it be but that a tongue which hath continued many hundred years not only a tongue but one of good account both in speech and pen hath grown in all that time to some finesse and assurance of itself by so long and so general an use, though it be not as yet sounded, the people that have used it being none of the dullest, and traveling continually in all exercises that concern learning, in all practises that procure experience either in peace or war, either in public or private, either at home or abroad?

As for the antiquity of our speech, whether it be measured by the ancient Almane whence it cometh originally, or even but by the latest terms which it borroweth daily from forren tongues, either of pure necessity in new matters or of mere bravery to garnish itself withal, it cannot be young. . . .

For the account of our tongue, both in pen and

speech, no man will doubt thereof who is able to judge what those things be which make any tongue to be of account; which things I take to be three: the autority of the people which speak it, the matter and argument wherein the speech dealeth, the manifold use for which the speech serveth. For all which three our tongue needeth not to give place to any of her peers.

First to say somewhat for the people that use the tongue, the English nation hath alway been of good credit and great estimation ever since credit and estimation by history came on this side the Alps; which appeareth to be true even by foren chronicles (not to use our own in a case of our own), which would never have said so much of the people if it had been obscure and not for an history, or not but well worthy of a perpetual history.

Next for the argument wherein it dealeth, whether private or public, it may compare with some other that think very well of their own selves. For not to touch ordinary affairs in common life, will matters of learning in any kind of argument make a tongue of account? Our nation, then, I think, will hardly be proved to have been unlearned at any time in any kind of learning, not to use any bigger speech. Wherefore, having learning by confession of all men and uttering that learning in their own tongue for their own use, of very pure necessity (bycause we learn to use and the use is in our own) they could not but enrich the tongue and purchase it account.

Will matters of war, whether civil or foren, make a tongue of account? Our neighbor nations will not deny our people to be very warrious, and our own country will confess it, though loth to feel it, both by rememb'ring the smart and comparing with some other—neither to vaunt ourselves nor to gall our friends with any mo words. . . .

Will all kinds of trade and all sorts of traffic make a tongue of account? If the spreading sea and the spacious land could use any speech, they would both shew you where and in how many strange places they have seen our people, and also give you to wit that they deal in as much and as great variety of matters as any other people do, whether at home or abroad. . . .

All which reasons concerning but the tongue and the account thereof being put together, as of themselves they prove the nation's exercise in learning and their practise in other dealings, so they seem to infer no base-witted people, not to amplify it with more, bycause it is not for fools to be so well learned, to be so warrious, to be so well practised. I shall not need to prove any of these my positions either by foren or home history, seeing my reader stranger will not strive with me for them, and mine own nation will not gainsay me in them, I think, which knoweth them to be true and may use them for their honor.

Wherefore I may well conclude my first position: that if use and custom, having the help of so long time and continuance wherein to fine our tongue, of so great learning and experience which furnish matter for the fining, of so good wits and judgments which can tell how to fine, have griped at nothing in all that time, with all that cunning, by all those wits which they will not let go but hold for most certain in the right of our writing, that then our tongue hath no certainty to trust to, but writeth all at randon. But the antecedent, in my opinion, is altogether unpossible, wherefore the consequent is a great deal more then probable, which is that our tongue hath in her own possession and writing very good evidence to prove her own right writing; which, though no man as yet by any public writing of his seemeth to have seen, yet the tongue itself is ready to shew them to any whosoever which is able to read them and withal to judge what evidence is right in the right of writing. . . .

THOMAS LODGE

AN ALARUM AGAINST USURERS

Immature and ragged as it is, *An Alarum against Usurers* (1584) has several points of special interest. For one thing, it gets in a final lick at Stephen Gosson, whose *Plays Confuted in Five Actions* (1582) had viciously attacked Lodge for his reply (1579–80) to *The School of Abuse* (see pp. 599–600). Lodge's chesty little tract had apparently been suppressed as soon as it appeared, but he carried on his campaign against Gosson's obscurantism by dedicating the *Alarum* (the "primordia of my studies") to Sir Philip Sidney, an acknowledged champion of poetry, and by complaining in his preface of the ill treatment accorded him by Gosson and his fellows. The *Alarum* itself interestingly anticipates the development, in the nineties, of the autobiographical rogue-pamphlets of Greene and his imitators. Obviously written out of personal experience, the tract was devised, as Lodge tells Sidney, to paint "the image of a licentious usurer and the collusions of divelish incroachers." In spite of its vivid personal element, as a treatise designed for the education of well-bred young men its debt to Lyly's *Euphues* is obvious. Its sporadic plot (later used repeatedly by Greene in his own confessional pamphlets) concerns an engaging but foolish young man who, falling into the hands of moneylenders, comes to more grief than any engaging young man deserves. A medley of inadequately fused elements, it juxtaposes an ostensibly fictional narrative with realistic pictures of contemporary London, homely dialogue with passages of cloying euphuism, scenes of vivid drama with tedious and stilted moralizing. None the less, during the

years when *Euphues* and *Arcadia* were the admired of all admirers Lodge's jejune caveat anticipated a new kind of prose fiction. Registered on November 4, 1583, it was published together with Lodge's first prose romance, *The Delectable History of Forbonius and Prisceria*, and a verse satire, perhaps inspired by Gascoigne's *Steel Glass*, called *Truth's Complaint over England*. Barnabe Rich (whose *Strange and Wonderful Adventures of Don Simonides* Lodge had helped revise in 1581) and one John Jones contributed commendatory verses. Our text is based upon *An Alarum against Usurers. Containing Tryed experiences against worldly abuses*, 1584 (STC 16653).

FROM AN ALARUM AGAINST USURERS (1584)

To the Right Worshipful My Curteous Friends, the Gentlemen of the Inns of Court, Thomas Lodge of Lincoln's Inn, Gentleman, Wisheth Prosperous Success in Their Studies and Happy Event in Their Travails

Curteous gentlemen, let it not seem strange unto you that he which hath long time slept in silence now beginneth publicly to salute you, since, no doubt, my reasons that induce me hereunto be such as both you may allow of them (since they be well meant) and account of them (since they tend to your profit). I have published here, of set purpose, a tried experience of worldly abuses, describing herein not only those monsters which were banished Athens—I mean usurers—but also such devouring caterpillars who not only have fatted their fingers with many rich forfeitures but also spread their venim among some private gentlemen of your profession; which considered, I thought good, in opening the wound, to prevent an ulcer, and, by counseling before escape, forewarn before the mischief. Led, then, by these persuasions, I doubt not but as I have always found you favorable, so now you will not cease to be friendly, both in protecting of this just cause from unjust slander and my person from that reproach which, about two years since, an injurious caviler objected against me. You that know me, gentlemen, can testify that neither my life hath been so lewd as that my company was odious, nor my behavior so light as that it should pass the limits of modesty. This notwithstanding, a licentious Hipponax, neither regarding the asperity of the laws touching slanderous libelers nor the offspring from whence I came (which is not contemptible), attempted not only in public and reproachful terms to condemn me in his writings but also so to slander me as neither justice

should wink at so hainous an offense nor I pretermit a commodious reply. About three years ago one Stephen Gosson published a book intituled *The School of Abuse,* in which having escaped in many and sundry conclusions, I, as the occasion then fitted me, shap'd him such an answer as beseemed his discourse; which, by reason of the slenderness of the subject (because it was in defense of plays and playmakers), the godly and reverent that had to deal in the cause, misliking it, forbad the publishing, notwithstanding he, coming by a private, unperfect copy about two years since, made a reply, dividing it into five sections; and in his epistle dedicatory to the right honorable Sir Francis Walsingham he impugneth me with these reproaches: that I am become a vagrant person, visited by the heavy hand of God, lighter than liberty, and looser then vanity. . . . [The rest of Lodge's preface consists of his unfortunately delayed answer to Gosson's libels.] Good Stephen, . . . will I deal with thee as Philip of Macedon with Nicanor, who, not respecting the majesty of the king but giving himself over to the petulancy of his tongue, vainly inveighed against him; whom, notwithstanding, Philip so cunningly handeled that not only he ceased the rumor of his report but also made him as lavish in commending as once he was profuse in discommending. His attempt was thus performed: he, seeing Nicanor sorely pressed with poverty, relieved him to his content. Whereupon, altering his copy and breaking out into singular commendation of Philip, the king concluded thus: "Lo, curtesy can make of bad good, and of Nicanor an enemy Nicanor a friend." Whose actions, my reprover, I will now fit to thee, who having slandered me without cause, I will no otherwise revenge it but by this means: that now in public

I confess thou hast a good pen, and if thou keep thy method in discourse and leave thy slandering without cause, there is no doubt but thou shalt be commended for thy copy and praised for thy style. And thus, desiring thee to measure thy reports with justice, and you, good gentlemen, to answer in my behalf if you hear me reproached, I leave you to your pleasures, and for myself I will study your profit.

Your loving friend,
Thomas Lodge

Barnabe Rich, Gentleman Soldier, in Praise of the Author

If that which warns the young beware of vice
  And schools the old to shun unlawful gain,
If pleasant style and method may suffice,
  I think thy travail merits thanks for pain.
  My simple doom is thus in terms as plain:
That both the subject and thy style is good,
Thou needs not fear the scoffs of Momus' brood.

If thus it be, good Lodge, continue still.
  Thou need'st not fear goose-son or gander's hiss,
Whose rude reports, pass'd from a sland'rous quill,
  Will be determin'd but in reading this,
  Of whom the wiser sort will think amiss
To slander him whose birth and life is such
As false report his fame can never touch.

AN ALARUM AGAINST USURERS

No marvel though the wise man accompted all things under the sun vain, since the chiefest creatures be mortal; and no wonder though the world run at randon, since iniquity in these later days hath the upper hand. The alteration of states, if they be look'd into, and the overthrow of houses, if they be but easely laid in open view, what eye would not shed tears to see things so transitory? And what wisdom would not indeavor to dissolve the inconvenience? There is a state within this our commonwealth which, though it necessarily stand as a pillar of defense in this royal realm, yet such are the abuses that are grown in it that not only the name is become odious by some's error but also, if the thing be not narrowly look'd into, the whole land by that means will grow into great inconvenience. I mean the state of merchants who, though to public commodity they bring in store of wealth from forrein nations, yet such are their domestical practises that not only they inrich themselves mightily by others' misfortunes but also eat our English gentry out of house and home. The general faculty in itself is both ancient and laudable, the professors honest and virtuous, their actions full of danger and therefore worthy gain; and so necessary this sort of men be as no well-governed state may be without them.

But as among a tree of fruit there be some withered fallings, and as among wholesome herbs there grows some bitter coloquintida, so it cannot be but among such a number of marchants there should be some that degenerate from the true name and nature of marchants. Of these men I write and of none other; my invective is private; I will not write general. And were it not I respected the public commodity more then my private praise, this matter should have slept in hugger-mugger. Of these ungracious men I write who, having nothing of themselves, yet greedily grasp all things into their own hands.

These be they that find out collusions of statutes and compass land with commodity; these be the bolsterers of ungracious, petty brokers; and by these men (the more is the pity) the prisons are replenished with young gentlemen. These be they that make the father careful, the mother sorrowful, the son desperate. These be they that make crooked straight and straight crooked, that can close with a young youth while they cousen him, and feed his humors till they free him of his farms. In brief, such they be that glose most fair then when they imagine the worst, and unless they be quickly known they easely will make bare some of the best of our young heirs that are not yet stayed; whom zealously I beseech to overlook this my writing, for what is set down here, either as an eye-witness I will avow or, informed even by those gentlemen who have swallowed the gudgen and have been intangeled in the hook, I have approvedly set down.

Such be those sort of men that their beginning is of naught, set by the devotion of some honest marchants; of whom taking up their refuse commodity, they imploy it to this ungodly and unhonest purpose.

They find out, according to their own vein, some old, soaking, undermining solicitor whom they both furnish with money and expense to set him forth and get him more credit. This good fellow must haunt ordinaries, canvass up and down Powles, and, as the cat watcheth the prey of the mouse, so diligently intends he to the compassing of some young novice whom, by fortune, either he findeth in melancholic passions at the ordinary or at penniless devotion in Powles, or perhaps is brought acquainted with him by some of his own brotherhood. Him he handeleth in these or such-like terms, both noting place and circumstance:

"Gentleman, why be you so melancholy? How falleth it out that you are not more lightsome? Your young years, methinks, should loathe such sollom aspects; I may not any way imagine a cause why you should be pensive. You have good parents; you want no friends; and, more, you have livelihoods; which considered, truly you commit mere folly to be so mervailously sad and wonderfully sorrowful where you have no occasion.

"If you want money you have credit (a gift which whosoever injoyeth nowadays he is able to compass anything), and for that I see so good a nature in you (if proffered service stink not) I will very willingly (if so be you will open your estate to me) further you in what I may, and perhaps you shall find yourself fortunate in falling into my company."

The young gentleman, unacquainted with such-like discourses, counting all gold that glisters and him a faithful friend that hath a flattering tongue, opens all his mind to this subtile underminer, who so wringeth him at last that there is no secret corner in the poor gentleman's heart but he knoweth it; after that, framing his behavior to the nature of the youth —if he be sad, sober, if youthly, riotous, if lascivious, wanton—he laboreth so much that at last the bird is caught in the pitfall; and, perceiving the vein of the youth, he promiseth him some relief by his means. The gentleman, thinking he hath God Almighty by the heel, holds the Divel by the toe, and by this means is brought to utter wrack and ruin. The broker, furnished of his purpose, having learned the gentleman's name, lodging, want, and wealth, and finding all things correspondent to his purpose, hies him to his setter-up, who rejoiceth greatly at his good hap and rewards this wicked seducer with a piece of gold. To be brief, at first issue on the gentleman's bond this broking knave receives forty or fifty pounds of coarse commodity, making him believe that by other means money may not be had and swearing to him that there will be great loss and that he could wish the gentleman would rather refuse then take. But the youth, not esteeming the loss so he supply his lack, sets him forward and gives the willing jade the spur, who, finding all things meat in the mouth, makes sale of this marchandise to some one of his greatest fraternity; and if it be forty, the youth hath a good pennyworth if in ready money he receive twenty pound, and yet the money repayable at three moneths' end. The broker in this matter getteth double fee of the gentleman, treble gain in the sale of the commodity, and, more, a thousand thanks of this divelish usurer. Truly, gentlemen, it is wonderful to conceive (yet are there some of you can tell if I lie) how this sycophant that help'd our youth to get now learneth him to spend. What saith he?

"My young master, what make you with this old satten doublet? It is soil'd; it is unfit for a gentleman's wearing. Apparel yourself as you should be, and, ere few days pass, I will acquaint you with as brave a dame (a friend of mine) as ever you knew. O, how sweet a face hath she!" And thus dilating it with rethorical praises to make the gentleman more passionate, it falleth out that the mann'd falcon stoops to lure, and all things are fulfilled according to his broker's direction. Promises are kept on both parts, and my youth is brought acquainted with Mistress Minx. This harlot is an old, beaten dog and a maintainer of the brothel-house brotherhood, a stale for young novices and a limb of Sathan himself, whose behaviors and gestures are such as the world cannot imagine better. If the gentleman weep, she will wail; if he sorrow, she will sigh; if he be merry, she will not be modest. To conclude, her lesson is so taught her as she can reckon without book. Lord, what riotousness passeth in apparel, what lavishness in banketing, what looseness in living! And in very short space our youth, which was fligge, is now at leak, his purse is empty, and his mistress begins to low'r; which he perceiving and earnestly bent to continue his credit with his curtisan, comes to his ungracious broker, whom with fair terms he desireth and with humble suits more earnestly beseecheth to further his credit in what he may. Who, seeing which way the hare windeth, begins to blame him of his liberality (and yet only is the cause of his spending) and, after a few privy nips, bearing shew of good meaning but yet indeed his way is to try conclusions, he hasteth to the principal, his good master merchant, whom he findeth altogether prompt and ready at a beck to send abroad his refuse commodity for crack'd angels. What conclusion is between them both may easily be imagined, but the end is this: the broker returns to my solitary youth and recounts unto him first, to make him fearful, how many places he hath been at when he hath not visited one, how many he hath desired yet how few are ready to pleasure; at last he breaketh out and telleth him the whole, assuring him that he is to think well of his Master Scrape-Penny, the usurer, who is willing in hope of his well-doing to let him have once more of his incommodious commodity upon reasonable assurance. To be brief, the bargain is quickly beaten on, the broker layeth the loss, the gentleman esteemeth not so his need be served, the merchant laughs at his folly in his sleeve; and, to conclude, the bonds are delivered, the cursed commodity received, and at this second mart how speeds our yonker, think you? Perhaps of fifty pounds in ware he receiveth thirty pounds in ready money, and yet the money repayable at three months' end. O incredible and injurious dealings! O more then Judaical cousonage! Truly, gentlemen, this that I write is true. I myself know the paymaster. Nay, more, I myself know certainly that by name I can reckon among you some that have been bitten, who, left good portions by their parents and fair lands by their ancestors, are desolate now, not having friends to relieve them or money to affray their charges. . . .

[Lodge continues with the melancholy mishaps of the young "gentleman," tracing his deterioration until, after a prison term, he himself is forced to become a usurer's lure for the ruin of other unsuspecting youths. The *exemplum* is used to point the moral of legislative reform: "If we had as severe laws in England as once in Athens Solon set down, we should then cast a rein over the headstrong unruliness of these caterpillars." The peroration reaches a climax of sentimental indignation at the unjust treatment accorded such prodigal sons by the merchants who prey upon them:]

In these extremities that they are driven into, which of you either relieveth them or comforteth them in their sorrows? So far are you, you worldlings, from lessening their miseries as that, Perilluslike, you invent new tortures to drive them from your doors, calling them vacabonds and Bridewell birds who, in very truth, were your best masters and setters-up. But yourselves, with Perillus, shall taste of the engines you have provided for others, and the Lord shall pity the fatherless and comfort the afflicted when that dreadful day shall come in which the heavens shall be opened and the Son of Man shall come to judgment. How will the case then stand with you? Shall your wealth then acquite you? No, no! The Judge is not partial; he is just in all his doings and true in all his sayings. In that day the horror of your conscience shall condemn you; Sathan, whom you have served, shall accuse you; the poor, afflicted members of Christ shall bear witness against you, so that in this horror and confusion you shall desire the mountains to fall upon you and the hills to cover you from the fearful indignation of the Lord of Hosts

and the dreadful condemnation of the Lamb Jesus. When it shall be found out that you were rich, yet relieved none; that you were of wealth, yet comforted none; that you rather replenished the prisons then released the prisoner; that your life be found sauced with cruelty and no one action savoring of mercy, the Lord shall place you among the goats and pronounce his *ve* against you. He shall thunder out this sentence: "Go, you cursed, into everlasting fire prepared for the Divel and his angels." This is the reward of wickedness, this is the punishment of cruelty. Look upon this, therefore, you worldlyminded men, and consider of these sayings. Harden not your hearts, but be you converted. Relieve the poor, be harborsome, restore to the owner that you have wrested from him, and turn, turn, turn unto the Lord, I beseech you, lest you perish in your own abhominations. And to conclude, accompt of me as your well-wisher who for public commodity have opened your inconveniences and for brotherly amity counsailed you to call yourselves home. And I beseech you, as speedily reclaim you from your errors as I do brotherly admonish you of your escapes. How happy were I that, having less cause, might have less matter to write on. And hapless are you if, not won with these warnings, you give more occasion to be written on. Now stay you where you are and alter your natures, and where you were accustomed to do ill, now acquaint yourselves to follow goodness, and then it will thus fall out that I which exclaimed upon you for your vices will then honor you for your virtues; and where in common assemblies your name grows odious, in public audience you may be praised for your good life. The Lord send our gentlemen more wit, our usurers more conscience, and ungodliness a fall, so nobility shall not decay, but the sinner shall be reclaimed and wickedness confounded.

ROBERT GREENE

PAMPHLETS

Greene's abandoning euphuistic romance for grubby and ostensibly realistic disclosures of his and others' wicked ways is an event of considerable importance in late Elizabethan literature. It signalizes the slow death of Lyly's influence on writers of prose fiction, it establishes new subjects and new techniques for both Greene and his imitators, and it throws a bright glare of publicity on the private lives and relationships of Greene and his friends and enemies. Greene made his first tentative approaches toward realism and autobiography with his *Mourning Garment* (1590), *Never Too Late* (1590), and

Farewell to Folly (1591). In the first, the hero being an engaging young wastrel named Philador who penitently returns to his father after a career of frisky dissipation, Greene makes his formal farewell to amorous tales and announces his new interest in serious moral and social problems; the second, of which the second part is *Francesco's Fortunes*, concerns another misguided roué who deserts his wife, becomes a rascally but successful playwright, and at last is redeemed to conjugal felicity; the third is a string of monitory dialogues (in a lush and charming Italian setting) on lewdness, pride, and drunkenness. With these painfully edifying works Greene was fairly launched on the last stage of his career, and thereafter he poured forth a stream of pamphlets which in both style and subject marked a startling change from his earlier euphuistic romances.

In 1591 appeared *A Notable Discovery of Cozenage*, the first of his famed exposés of the London underworld and a work (the preface claims) held so subversive by card-sharpers and confidence-men that they had threatened the author with physical violence. In spite of the danger— and in spite of a brisk rejoinder (in which Greene almost surely had a hand) called *A Defense of Cony-Catching*— he plunged ahead valiantly, no doubt stirred more by his financial success than by his alleged moral indignation at urban vice. He continued to mine the new lode in a *Second Part of Cony-Catching* (1591), a sensational exposé of five kinds of rascality, each illustrated with a case-history; next followed a *Third and Last Part* (1592), a group of picaresque tales allegedly based upon the experiences of a justice of the peace, and *A Disputation between a He Cony-Catcher and a She Cony-Catcher* (1592), an energetic and informative flyting between two rogues hardened in iniquity. Perhaps the most interesting and ambitious of these hasty potboilers in social criticism is *A Quip for an Upstart Courtier* (1592). A curious resuscitation of the dream-allegory, it tells of the encounter between Velvet Breeches and Cloth Breeches (that is, urban sophistication and rustic simplicity), who, assembling a jury of twenty-four to adjudicate their claims of sovereignty, examine a large number of type-characters contrived to represent various foibles and vices. This work is notable, among other things, for the scurrilous and quickly suppressed passage on the Harvey family which brought Gabriel Harvey charging down to London hot for legal redress; the upshot, when he found that Greene had already died, was his furious *Four Letters* which sparked the subsequent controversy with Thomas Nashe (see pp. 859–60). To represent the batch of rogue-pamphlets of Greene's last period we give excerpts from

The Black Book's Messenger (1592), a sort of sob-sister account of a criminal named Ned Browne and a work-in-progress report of a projected but never completed *Who's Who* of the London underworld.

In the last year of his life Greene wrote with desperate haste about the sins of city slickers and about his own offenses against God and man. Relinquishing at last the cony-catching series, he returned in his final months to the autobiographical narrative already launched with the *Mourning Garment* and *Never Too Late*. *Greene's Groatsworth of Wit* (like the *Repentance* published posthumously late in 1592) recalls the earlier works by beginning with a thinly disguised fiction about one Roberto, a disinherited younger son who falls into evil ways; but the disguise is presently abandoned for a frank first-person confession of Greene's own misspent life. The famous concluding letter to his younger contemporaries contains the attack on the "upstart crow" Shakespeare for which Henry Chettle (who had edited the papers found after Greene's death) quickly apologized in his *Kind-Heart's Dream* of the following year (see p. 871). Chettle there explains that he had taken the liberty of toning down some of Greene's acerb comments (probably on Marlowe), but he disclaims credit for the offending passage that remained. The *Groatsworth* closes with a poignant— and probably genuine—letter from Greene to his long-suffering wife. *The Repentance of Robert Greene* (1592) also was apparently edited from fugitive confessional tracts, and its account of Greene's last wretched days corresponds in all essentials with Gabriel Harvey's angry report in the *Four Letters*.

Our texts are based upon *The Blacke Bookes Messenger. Laying open the Life and Death of Ned Browne*, 1592 (STC 12223); *Greenes, Groats-worth of witte, bought with a million of Repentance . . . Written before his death and published at his dyeing request*, 1592 (STC 12245); *The Repentance of Robert Greene Maister of Artes. Wherein by himselfe is laid open his loose life, with the manner of his death*, 1592 (STC 12306).

---

from THE BLACK BOOK'S MESSENGER (1592)

To the Curteous Reader, Health

Gentleman, I know you have long expected the coming-forth of my *Black Book*, which I long have promised, and which I had many days since finished had not sickness hindered my intent; nevertheless, be assured it is the first thing I mean to publish after I am recovered. This messenger to my *Black Book* I commit to your curteous censures, being written before I fell sick, which I thought good in the mean-time to send you as a fairing, discoursing Ned

Browne's villanies, which are too many to be described in my *Black Book*.

I had thought to have joined with this treatise a pithy discourse of the repentance of a cony-catcher lately executed out of Newgate, yet forasmuch as the method of the one is so far differing from the other I altered my opinion, and the rather for that the one died resolute and desperate, the other penitent and passionate. For the cony-catcher's repentance, which shall shortly be published, it contains a passion of great importance. First, how he was given over from all grace and godliness and seemed to have no spark of the fear of God in him, yet, nevertheless, through the wonderful working of God's spirit, even in the dungeon at Newgate the night before he died, he so repented him from the bottom of his heart that it may well beseem parents to have it for their children, masters for their servants, and to be perused of every honest person with great regard.

And for Ned Browne, of whom my Messenger 10 makes report, he was a man infamous for his bad course of life and well known about London. He was in outward shew a gentlemanlike companion, attired very brave, and to shadow his villany the more would nominate himself to be a marshal-man, who, when he had nipp'd a bung or cut a good purse, he would steal over into the Low Countries, there to taste three or four stoaps of Rhenish wine and then come over, forsooth, a brave soldier. But at last he leapt at a daisy for his loose kind of life, and therefore 20 imagine you now see him in his own person, standing in a great bay window with a halter about his neck, ready to be hanged, desperately pronouncing this, his whole course of life, and confesseth as followeth.

Yours in all curtesy,

R[obert] G[reene]

THE LIFE AND DEATH OF NED BROWNE, A NOTABLE CUTPURSE AND CONY-CATCHER

"If you think, gentlemen, to hear a repentant man speak or to tell a large tale of his penitent sorrows, 30 ye are deceived, for as I have ever lived lewdly, so I mean to end my life as resolutely, and not by a cowardly confession to attempt the hope of a pardon. Yet in that I was famous in my life for my villainies, I will at my death profess myself as notable by discoursing to you all merrily the manner and method of my knaveries, which if you hear without laughing, then after my death call me base knave and never have me in remembrance.

"Know therefore, gentlemen, that my parents 40 were honest, of good report and no little esteem amongst their neighbors, and sought (if good nurture and education would have served) to have made me an honest man; but as one selfsame ground brings forth flowers and thistles, so of a sound stock proved an untoward sien, and of a virtuous father a most vicious son. It boots little to rehearse the petty sins of my nonage, as disobedience to my parents, contempt of good counsail, despising of mine elders, filching, pettilashery, and such trifling toys; but with 50 these follies I inur'd myself till, waxing in years, I grew into greater villanies. For when I came to eighteen years old, what sin was it that I would not commit with greediness, what attempt so bad that I

would not endeavor to execute: cutting of purses, stealing of horses, lifting, picking of locks, and all other notable cosenages. . . .

"Thus animated to do wickedness, I fell to take delight in the company of harlots, amongst whom, as I spent what I got, so I suffered not them I was acquainted withal to feather their nests, but would at my pleasure strip them of all that they had. What bad woman was there about London whose champion I would not be for a few crowns to fight, swear, and stare in her behalf to the abuse of any that should do justice upon her? I still had one or two in store to crossbite withal, which I used as snares to trap simple men in; for if I took but one suspiciously in her company, straight I vers'd upon him and crossbit him for all the money in his purse. . . ."

[Ned Browne then proceeds to tell, in a series of biographical anecdotes, the nature of his villainies.]

A Pleasant Tale How Ned Browne Kiss'd a Gentlewoman and Cut Her Purse

". . . I saw a brave country gentlewoman coming along from Saint Bartlemew's in a satten gown and four men attending upon her; by her side she had hanging a marvelous rich purse embroid'red and not so fair without but it seemed to be as well-lined within. At this my teeth watered, and as the prey makes the thief, so necessity and the sight of such a fair purse began to muster a thousand inventions in my head how to come by it. To go by her and nip it I could not because she had so many men attending on her; to watch her into a press, that was in vain, for going towards St. John's Street I guess'd her about to take horse to ride home, because all her men were booted. Thus perplexed for this purse and yet not so much for the bung as the shells, I at last resolutely vowed in myself to have it though I stretch'd a halter for it; and so, casting in my head how to bring my fine mistress to the blow, at last I performed it thus. She standing and talking a while with a gentleman, I stepp'd before her and leaned at the bar till I saw her leave him, and then, stalking towards her very stoutly as if I had been some young cavalier or captain, I met her and curteously saluted her, and not only greeted her, but as if I had been acquainted with her I gave her a kiss, and so, in taking acquaintance closing very familiarly to her, I cut her purse. The gentlewoman, seeing me so brave, used me kindly, and blushing said she knew me not. 'Are you not, mistress,' quoth I, 'such a gentlewoman and such a man's wife?' 'No, truly, sir, quoth she, 'you mistake me.' 'Then I cry you mercy,' quoth I, 'and am sorry that I was so saucily bold.' 'There is no harm done, sir,' said she, 'because there is no offense taken.' And so we parted, I with a good bung and my gentlewoman with a kiss, which, I dare safely swear, she bought as dear as ever she did thing in her life; for what I found in the purse, that I keep to myself. Thus did I plot devices in my head how to profit myself, though it were to the utter undoing of anyone. . . .

"This, gentlemen, was my course of life, and thus I got much by villany and spent it amongst whores as carelessly. I sildom or never listened to the admonition of my friends, neither did the fall of other men learn me to beware, and therefore am I brought now to this end. Yet little did I think to have laid my bones in France; I thought, indeed, that Tyburn would at last have shak'd me by the neck, but having done villany in England, this was always my course: to slip over into the Low Countries, and there for a while play the soldier, and partly that was the cause of my coming hither, for growing odious in and about London for my filching, lifting, nipping, foisting, and crossbiting, that every one held me in contempt and almost disdained my company, I resolved to come over into France, by bearing arms to win some credit, determining with myself to become a true man. But as men, though they change countries, alter not their minds, so, given over by God into a reprobate sense, I had no feeling of goodness, but with the dog fell to my old vomit, and here most wickedly I have committed sacrilege, robb'd a church, and done other mischievous pranks for which justly I am condemned and must suffer death; whereby I learn that revenge deferr'd is not quittanc'd, that though God suffer the wicked for a time, yet he pays home at length. For while I lasciviously led a careless life, if my friends warned me of it, I scoff'd at them, and if they told me of the gallows I would swear it was my destiny; and now I have proved myself no liar, yet must I die more basely and be hang'd out at a window.

"O countrymen and gentlemen, I have held you long, as good at the first as at the last; take, then, this for a farewell: trust not in your own wits, for they will become too wilful oft and so deceive you. Boast not in strength nor stand not on your manhood so to maintain quarrels, for the end of brawling is confusion; but use your courage in defense of your country and then fear not to die, for the bullet is an honorable death. Beware of whores, for they be the sirens that draw men on to destruction; their sweet words are inchantments, their eyes allure, and their beauties bewitch. O take heed of their persuasions, for they be crocodiles that, when they weep, destroy. Truth is honorable, and better is it to be a poor, honest man than a rich and wealthy thief, for the fairest end is the gallows, and what a shame is it to a man's friends when he dies so basely. Scorn not labor, gentlemen, nor hold not any course of life bad or servile that is profitable and honest, lest in giving yourselves over to idleness and having no yearly maintenance you fall into many prejudicial mischiefs. Contemn not the virtuous counsail of a friend, despise not the hearing of God's ministers, scoff not at the magistrates; but fear God, honor your prince, and love your country. Then God will bless you as I hope he will do me for all my manifold offenses, and so, Lord, into thy hands I commit my spirit." And with that he himself sprung out at the window and died.

Here, by the way, you shall understand that going over into France he near unto Arx robb'd a church and was therefore condemned, and, having no gallows by, they hang'd him out at a window, fast'ning the rope about the bar; and thus this Ned Browne died miserably that all his lifetime had been full of mischief and villany, slightly at his death regarding the state of his soul. But note a wonderful judgment of God shewed upon him after his death: his body being taken down and buried without the town, it is verified that in the night-time there came a company of wolves and tore him out of his grave and eat him up, whereas there lay many soldiers buried and many dead carcasses that they might have prey'd on to have filled their hungry paunches. But the judgments of God as they are just so they are inscrutable, yet thus much we may conjecture, that as he was one that delighted in rapine and stealth in his life, so at his death the ravenous wolves devoured him and pluck'd him out of his grave as a man not worthy to be admitted to the honor of any burial. Thus have I set down the life and death of Ned Browne, a famous cutpurse and cony-catcher, by whose example if any be profited, I have the desired end of my labor.

FROM GREENE'S GROATSWORTH OF WIT BOUGHT WITH A MILLION OF REPENTANCE (1592)

The Printer to the Gentle Readers

I have published here, gentlemen, for your mirth and benefit Greene's *Groatsworth of Wit*. With sundry of his pleasant discourses ye have been before delighted, but now hath death given a period to his pen. Only this happened into my hands, which I have published for your pleasures. Accept it favorably because it was his last birth and not least worth, in my poor opinion. But I will cease to praise that which is above my conceit, and leave itself to speak for itself, and so abide your learned censuring.

Yours,

W[illiam] W[right]

To the Gentlemen Readers

Gentlemen, the swan sings melodiously before death that in all his lifetime useth but a jarring sound. Greene, though able inough to write, yet deeplier searched with sickness than ever heretofore, sends you his swan-like song for that he fears he shall never again carol to you wonted love-lays, never again discover to you youth's pleasures. However yet sickness, riot, incontinence have at once shown their extremity, yet if I recover you shall all see more fresh sprigs then ever sprang from me, directing you how to live yet not dissuading ye from love. This is the last I have writ, and I fear me the last I shall write. And however I have been censured for some of my former books, yet, gentlemen, I protest they were as I had special information. But passing them, I commend this to your favorable censures, that, like an embryon without shape, I fear me will be thrust into the world. If I live to end it, it shall be otherwise; if not, yet will I commend it to your courtesies that you may as well be acquainted with my repentant death as you have lamented my careless course of life. But as *nemo ante obitum felix,* so *acta exitus probat.* Beseeching, therefore, so to be deemed hereof as I deserve, I leave the work to your likings and leave you to your delights.

GREENE'S GROATSWORTH OF WIT

In an iland bounded with the ocean there was sometime a city situated, made rich by marchandize and populous by long peace; the name is not mentioned in the antiquary, or else worn out by time's antiquity. What it was, it greatly skills not, but therein thus it happened. An old new-made gentleman herein dwelt, of no small credit, exceeding wealth, and large conscience. He had gathered from many to bestow upon one, for, though he had two sons, he esteemed but one, that, being as himself brought up to be gold's bondman, was therefore held heir-apparant of his ill-gathered goods.

The other was a scholler and married to a proper gentlewoman and therefore least regarded, for 'tis an old-said saw, "To learning and law there's no greater foe than they that nothing know." Yet was not the father altogether unlettered, for he had good experience in a noverint, and by the universal terms therein contained had driven many a young gentleman to seek unknown countries. Wise he was, for

he bore office in his parish and sat as formally in his fox-furr'd gown as if he had been a very upright-dealing burgess. He was religious, too, never without a book at his belt and a bolt in his mouth, ready to shoot through his sinful neighbor.

And Latin he had somewhere learned, which, though it were but little, yet was it profitable, for he had this philosophy written in a ring, *Tu tibi cura,* which precept he curiously observed, being in self-love so religious as he held it no point of charity to part with anything of which he, living, might make use.

But as all mortal things are momentary, and no certainty can be found in this uncertain world, so Gorinius (for that shall be this usurer's name), after many a gouty pang that had pinch'd his exterior parts, many a curse of the people that mounted into heaven's presence, was at last with his last summons by a deadly disease arrested, whereagainst when he had long contended and was by phisitions given over, he call'd his two sons before him, and, willing to perform the old proverb, *Qualis vita finis ita,* he thus prepar'd himself and admonished them: "My sons (for so your mother said ye were, and so I assure myself one of you is, and of the other I will make no doubt), you see the time is come which I thought would never have approached, and we must now be seperated, I fear never to meet again. This sixteen years daily have I liv'd vexed with disease, and might I live sixteen more, however miserably, I should think it happy. But Death is relentless and will not be intreated, witless and knows not what good my gold might do him, senseless and hath no pleasure in the delightful places I would offer him. In brief, I think he hath with this fool, my eldest son, been brought up in the university and therefore accounts that in riches is no virtue. But thou, my son," laying then his hand on the younger's head, "have thou another spirit; for without wealth life is a death. What is gentry if wealth be wanting but base servile beggery? Some comfort yet it is unto me to think how many gallants sprung of noble parents have crouch'd to Gorinius to have sight of his gold—O gold, desired gold, admired gold—and have lost their patrimonies to Gorinius because they have not returned by their day that adored creature. How many schollers have written rimes in Gorinius' praise and received, after long capping and reverence, a sixpenny reward in sign of my superficial liberality? Briefly, my young Lucanio, how I have been reverenc'd thou seest when honester men, I confess, have been set far off; for to be rich is to be anything—wise, honest, worshipful, or what not. I tell thee, my son, when I came first to this city my whole wardrop was only a suit of white sheepskins, my wealth an old groat, my woning the wide world. At this instant—O grief to part with it—I have in ready coin threescore thousand pound, in plate and jewels fifteen thousand, in bonds and specialities as much, in land nine hundred pound by the year—all which, Lucanio, I bequeath to thee, only I reserve for Roberto, thy well-read brother, an old groat (being the stock I first began with), wherewith I wish him to buy a groatsworth of wit, for he in my life hath reprov'd my manner of life, and therefore at my death shall not be contaminated with corrupt gain. . . .

"Ah, Lucanio, my only comfort, because I hope thou wilt as thy father be a gatherer let me bless thee before I die. Multiply in wealth, my son, by any means thou mayst; only fly alchemy, for therein are more deceits than her beggarly artists have words, and yet are the wretches more talkative than women. But my meaning is thou shouldest not stand on conscience in causes of profit, but heap treasure upon treasure for the time of need; yet seem to be devout, else shalt thou be held vile; frequent holy excercises, grave company, and above all use the conversation of young gentlemen who are so wedded to prodigality that once in a quarter necessity knocks at their chamber doors; proffer them kindness to relieve their wants, but be sure of good assurance; give fair words till days of payment come, and then use my course, spare none. What though they tell of conscience (as a number will talk), look but into the dealings of the world, and thou shalt see it is but idle words. Seest thou not many perish in the streets and fall to theft for need whom small succor would relieve? Then where is conscience, and why art thou bound to use it more than other men? Seest thou not daily forgeries, perjuries, oppressions, rackings of the poor, raisings of rents, inhancing of duties, even by them that should be all conscience if they meant as they speak? But, Lucanio, if thou read well this book"—and with that he reach'd him Machiavel's works at large—"thou shalt see what 'tis to be so fool-holy as to make scruple of conscience where profit presents itself.

"Besides, thou hast an instance by the threadbare brother here, who, willing to do no wrong, hath lost his child's right; for who would wish anything to him that knows not how to use it? . . ."

[Following Gorinius' death, Roberto is so vexed at his unjust treatment that he seeks revenge upon the favored Lucanio. With the aid of Lamilia, a courtesan, he dupes the innocent and gullible younger brother into a career of dissipation and extravagance. Meanwhile, Roberto himself, "now famoused for an arch-playmaking poet," lives a most irregular life.] His purse, like the sea, sometime swell'd, anon, like the same sea, fell to a low ebb, yet seldom he wanted, his labors were so well esteemed. Marry,

this rule he kept: whatever he finger'd aforehand was the certain means to unbind a bargain, and, being ask'd why he so slightly dealt with them that did him good, "It becomes me," saith he, "to be contrary to the world, for commonly when vulgar men receive earnest they do perform; when I am paid anything aforehand I break my promise." He had shift of lodgings, where in every place his hostess writ up the woful remembrance of him, his laundress, and his boy; for they were ever his in household, beside retainers in sundry other places. His company were lightly the lewdest persons in the land, apt for pilfery, perjury, forgery, or any villainy. Of these he knew the casts to cog at cards, coossen at dice; by these he learn'd the legerdemains of nips, foists, cony-catchers, crossbiters, lifts, high-lawyers, and all the rabble of that unclean generation of vipers; and pithily could he paint out their whole courses of craft. So cunning he was in all crafts as nothing rested in him almost but craftiness. How often the gentlewoman his wife labored vainly to recall him is lamentable to note; but as one given over to all lewdness, he communicated her sorrowful lines among his loose trulls, that jested at her bootless laments. If he could any way get credit on scores, he would then brag his creditors carried stones, comparing every round circle to a groaning O, procured by a painful burden. The shameful end of sundry his consorts, deservedly punished for their amiss, wrought no compunction in his heart, of which one, brother to a brothel he kept, was truss'd under a tree as round as a ball. . . . [Relating Roberto's wicked life, Greene drops his mask to confess that he is himself Roberto: "Hereafter suppose me the said Roberto, and I will go on with that he promised. Greene will send you now his groatsworth of wit that never shewed a mitesworth in his life, and though no man now be by to do me good, yet ere I die I will by my repentance indeavor to do all men good." Thus he closes with the famous advice to his fellow-writers.]

O horrenda fames, how terrible are thy assaults! But vermis conscientiae, more wounding are thy stings. Ah, gentlemen that live to read my broken and confused lines, look not I should, as I was wont, delight you with vain fantasies; but gather my follies altogether, and, as ye would deal with so many parricides, cast them into the fire. Call them Telegones, for now they kill their father, and every lewd line in them written is a deep piercing wound to my heart; every idle hour spent by any in reading them brings a million of sorrows to my soul. O that the tears of a miserable man—for never any man was yet more miserable—might wash their memory out with my death, and that those works with me together might be interr'd! But sith they cannot, let this my last work witness against them with me, how I detest them. Black is the remembrance of my black works, blacker than night, blacker than death, blacker than hell.

Learn wit by my repentance, gentlemen, and let these few rules following be regarded in your lives:

1. First, in all your actions, set God before your eyes, for the fear of the Lord is the beginning of wisdom. Let his word be a lantern to your feet and a light unto your paths; then shall you stand as firm rocks and not be mocked.

2. Beware of looking back, for God will not be mocked; and of him that hath received much, much shall be demanded.

3. If thou be single, and canst abstain, turn thy eyes from vanity; for there is a kind of women bearing the faces of angels but the hearts of devils, able to intrap the elect if it were possible.

4. If thou be married, forsake not the wife of thy youth to follow strange flesh, for whoremongers and adulterers the Lord will judge. The door of a harlot leadeth down to death, and in her lips there dwells destruction; her face is decked with odors, but she bringeth a man to a morsel of bread and nakedness, of which myself am instance.

5. If thou be left rich, remember those that want, and so deal that by thy wilfulness thyself want not. Let not taverners and victualers be thy executors, for they will bring thee to a dishonorable grave.

6. Oppress no man, for the cry of the wronged ascendeth to the ears of the Lord; neither delight to increase by usury, lest thou loose thy habitation in the everlasting tabernacle.

7. Beware of building thy house to thy neighbor's hurt, for the stones will cry to the timber, "We were laid together in blood"; and those that so erect houses, calling them by their names, shall lie in the grave like sheep, and death shall gnaw upon their souls.

8. If thou be poor, be also patient, and strive not to grow rich by indirect means, for goods so gotten shall vanish like smoke.

9. If thou be a father, maister, or teacher, join good example with good counsail, else little avail precepts where life is different.

10. If thou be a son or servant, despise not reproof; for though correction be bitter at the first, it bringeth pleasure in the end.

Had I regarded the first of these rules, or been obedient to the last, I had not now at my last end been left thus desolate. But now though to myself I give *consilium post facta,* yet to others they may serve for timely precepts. And therefore, while life gives leave, I will send warning to my old consorts, which have lived as loosely as myself; albeit weakness will scarce

suffer me to write, yet to my fellow schollers about this city will I direct these few insuing lines:

To those gentlemen, his quondam acquaintance, that spend their wits in making plays, R[obert] G[reene] wisheth a better exercise, and wisdom to prevent his extremities

If woful experience may move you, gentlemen, to beware, or unheard-of wretchedness intreat you to take heed, I doubt not but you will look back with sorrow on your time past, and indeavor with repentance to spend that which is to come. Wonder not (for with thee will I first begin), thou famous gracer of tragedians [Marlowe], that Greene, who hath said with thee, like the fool in his heart, "There is no God," should now give glory unto His greatness; for penetrating is his power, his hand lies heavy upon me, he hath spoken unto me with a voice of thunder, and I have felt he is a God that can punish enemies. Why should thy excellent wit, his gift, be so blinded that thou shouldst give no glory to the giver? Is it pestilent Machiavellian policy that thou hast studied? O, peevish folly! What are his rules but mere confused mockeries, able to extirpate in small time the generation of mankind? For if *Sic volo, sic iubeo* hold in those that are able to command, and if it be lawful *fas et nefas* to do anything that is beneficial, only tyrants should possess the earth, and they striving to exceed in tyranny should each to other be a slaughter-man; till the mightiest outliving all, one stroke were left for Death, that in one age man's life should end. The broacher of this diabolical atheism is dead, and in his life had never the felicity he aimed at; but as he began in craft, lived in fear and ended in despair. *Quam inscrutabilia sunt Dei judicia!* This murderer of many brethren had his conscience seared like Cain; this betrayer of Him that gave his life for him inherited the portion of Judas; this apostata perished as ill as Julian; and wilt thou, my friend, be his disciple? Look but to me, by him persuaded to that liberty, and thou shalt find it an infernal bondage. I know the least of my demerits merit this miserable death, but wilful striving against known truth exceedeth all the terrors of my soul. Defer not, with me, till this last point of extremity; for little know'st thou how in the end thou shalt be visited.

With thee I join young Juvenal [probably Nashe], that biting satirist, that lastly with me together writ a comedy. Sweet boy, might I advise thee, be advis'd, and get not many enemies by bitter words; inveigh against vain men, for thou canst do it, no man better, no man so well; thou hast a liberty to reprove all and name none; for, one being spoken to, all are offended; none being blamed, no man is injured. Stop shallow water still running, it will rage, or tread on a worm and it will turn; then blame not schollers vexed with sharp lines, if they reprove thy too much liberty of reproof.

And thou [Peele] no less deserving than the other two, in some things rarer, in nothing inferior, driven, as myself, to extreme shifts, a little have I to say to thee; and were it not an idolatrous oath, I would swear by sweet St. George, thou art unworthy better hap, sith thou dependest on so mean a stay. Base-minded men all three of you, if by my misery you be not warn'd; for unto none of you, like me, sought those burrs to cleave; those puppets, I mean, that spake from our mouths, those antics garnish'd in our colors. Is it not strange that I, to whom they all have been beholding, is it not like that you, to whom they all have been beholding, shall, were ye in that case as I am now, be both at once of them forsaken? Yes, trust them not; for there is an upstart crow [Shake-speare], beautified with our feathers, that with his *tiger's heart wrapp'd in a player's hide* supposes he is as well able to bombast out a blank verse as the best of you; and being an absolute *Johannes fac totum,* is in his own conceit the only Shake-scene in a country. O that I might intreat your rare wits to be imployed in more profitable courses; and let those apes imitate your past excellence, and never more acquaint them with your admired inventions. I know the best husband of you all will never prove an usurer, and the kindest of them all will never prove a kind nurse; yet whilest you may, seek you better maisters; for it is pity men of such rare wits should be subject to the pleasure of such rude grooms.

In this I might insert two more that both have writ against these buckram gentlemen; but let their own works serve to witness against their own wickedness, if they persevere to maintain any more such peasants. For other newcomers, I leave them to the mercy of these painted monsters, who, I doubt not, will drive the best-minded to despise them; for the rest, it skills not though they make a jest at them.

But now return I again to you three, knowing my misery is to you no news; and let me heartily intreat you to be warned by my harms. Delight not, as I have done, in irreligious oaths; for from the blas-phemer's house a curse shall not depart. Despise drunkenness, which wasteth the wit and maketh men all equal unto beasts. Fly lust, as the deathsman of the soul, and defile not the temple of the Holy Ghost. Abhor those Epicures whose loose life hath made religion lothsome to your ears; and when they soothe you with terms of maistership, remember Robert Greene, whom they have so often flattered, perishes now for want of comfort. Remember, gentlemen, your lives are like so many lighted tapers that are with care delivered to all of you to maintain; these

with wind-puff'd wrath may be extinguish'd, which drunkenness put out, which negligence let fall; for man's time is not of itself so short but it is more short'ned by sin. The fire of my light is now at the last snuff, and for want of wherewith to sustain it, there is no substance left for life to feed on. Trust not then, I beseech ye, to such weak stays; for they are as changeable in mind as in many attires. Well, my hand is tir'd, and I am forc'd to leave where I would begin; for a whole book cannot contain their wrongs which I am forc'd to knit up in some few lines of words.

> Desirous that you should live,
> though himself be dying,
> Robert Greene . . .

A Letter Written to His Wife, Found with This Book after His Death

The remembrance of the many wrongs off'red thee and thy unreproved virtues add greater sorrow to my miserable state than I can utter or thou conceive. Neither is it lessened by consideration of thy absence (though shame would hardly let me behold thy face), but exceedingly aggravated, for that I cannot, as I ought, to thy own self reconcile myself, that thou might'st witness my inward wo at this instant that have made thee a woful wife for so long a time. But equal heaven hath denied that comfort, giving at my last need like succor as I have sought all my life, being in this extremity as void of help as thou hast been of hope. Reason would that after so long waste I should not send thee a child to bring thee greater charge, but consider he is the fruit of thy womb, in whose face regard not the father's faults so much as thy own perfections. He is yet Greene, and may grow straight if he be carefully tended; otherwise, apt enough (I fear me) to follow his father's folly. That I have offended thee highly I know, that you canst forget my injuries I hardly believe; yet persuade I myself, if thou saw my wretched estate thou couldst not but lament it, nay, certainly I know thou wouldst. All my wrongs muster themselves before me, every evil at once plagues me. For my contempt of God I am contemned of men; for my swearing and forswearing no man will believe me; for my gluttony I suffer hunger; for my drunkenness, thirst; for my adultery, ulcerous sores. Thus God hath cast me down that I might be humbled, and punished me for example of other sinners; and although he strangely suffers me in this world to perish without succor, yet trust I in the world to come to find mercy by the merits of my Savior, to whom I commend thee and commit my soul.

Thy repentant husband for his disloyalty,
Robert Greene

from THE REPENTANCE OF ROBERT GREENE, MAISTER OF ARTS (1592)

The Printer to the Gentlemen Readers

Gentlemen, I know you are not unacquainted with the death of Robert Greene, whose pen in his lifetime pleased you as well on the stage as in the stationers' shops; and to speak truth, although his loose life was odious to God and offensive to men, yet, forasmuch as at his last end he found it most grievous to himself (as appeareth by this, his repentant discourse), I doubt not but he shall for the same deserve favor both of God and men. And considering, gentlemen, that Venus hath her charms to inchant, that Fancy is a sorceress bewitching the senses and Folly the only enemy to all virtuous actions, and forasmuch as the purest glass is the most brickle, the finest lawn the soonest stain'd, the highest oak most subject to the wind, and the quickest wit the more easily won to folly, I doubt not but you will with regard forget his follies and, like to the bee, gather honey out of the good counsels of him who was wise, learned, and politic had not his lascivious life withdrawn him from those studies which had been far more profitable to him.

For herein appeareth that he was a man given over to the lust of his own heart, forsaking all godliness, and one that daily delighted in all manner of wickedness. Since other, therefore, have forerun him in the like faults and have been forgiven both of God and men, I trust he shall be the better accepted, that by the working of God's Holy Spirit returns with such a resolved repentance, being a thing acceptable both to God and men.

To conclude: forasmuch as I found this discourse very passionate and of wonderful effect to withdraw the wicked from their ungodly ways, I thought good to publish the same, and the rather for that by his repentance they may as in a glass see their own folly and thereby in time resolve that it is better to die repentant than to live dishonest.

Yours,

C[uthbert] B[urby]

The Life and Death of Robert Greene, Maister of Arts

I need not make long discourse of my parents, who for their gravity and honest life is well known and esteemed amongst their neighbors; namely, in the city of Norwich, where I was bred and born. But as out of one selfsame clod of clay there sprouts both stinking weeds and delightful flowers, so from honest parents often grow most dishonest children; for my father had care to have me in my nonage brought up at school, that I might through the study of good letters grow to be a friend to myself, a profitable member to the commonwealth, and a comfort to him in his age. But as early pricks the tree that will prove a thorn, so even in my first years I began to follow the filthiness of mine own desires, and neither to listen to the wholesome advertisements of my parents, nor be rul'd by the careful correction of my maister. For being at the University of Cambridge, I light amongst wags as lewd as myself, with whom I consumed the flower of my youth, who drew me to travel into Italy and Spain, in which places I saw and practis'd such villainy as is abhominable to declare. Thus by their counsail I sought to furnish myself with coin, which I procured by cunning sleights from my father and my friends, and my mother pampered me so long and secretly helped me to the oil of angels, that I grew thereby prone to all mischief; so that being then conversant with notable braggarts, boon companions, and ordinary spendthrifts, that practised sundry superficial studies, I became as a sien grafted into the same stock, whereby I did absolutely participate of their nature and qualities.

At my return into England I ruffeled out in my silks, in the habit of malcontent, and seemed so discontent that no place would please me to abide in, nor no vocation cause me to stay myself in; but after I had by degrees proceeded Maister of Arts, I left the University and away to London, where (after I had continued some short time and driven myself out of credit with sundry of my friends) I became an author of plays and a penner of love pamphlets, so that I soon grew famous in that quality, that who for that trade grown so ordinary about London as Robin Greene? Young yet in years, though old in wickedness, I began to resolve that there was nothing bad that was profitable; whereupon I grew so rooted in all mischief that I had as great a delight in wickedness as sundry hath in godliness; and as much felicity I took in villainy as others had in honesty.

Thus was the liberty I got in my youth the cause of my licentious living in my age, and being the first step to hell, I find it now the first let from heaven.

But I would wish all my native countrymen that read this my repentance, first, to fear God in their whole life, which I never did, secondly, to obey their parents and to listen unto the wholesome counsail of their elders; so shall their days be multiplied upon them here on earth, and inherit the crown of glory in the kingdom of heaven. I exhort them also to leave the company of lewd and ill livers; for conversing with such copesmates draws them into sundry dangerous inconveniences; nor let them haunt the company of harlots, whose throats are as smooth as oil, but their feet lead the steps unto death and destruction; for they like sirens with their sweet inchanting notes soothed me up in all kind of ungodliness.

O, take heed of harlots (I wish you, the unbridled youth of England), for they are the basilisks that kill with their eyes, they are the sirens that allure with their sweet looks; and they lead their favorers unto their destruction as a sheep is led unto the slaughter.

From whoredom I grew to drunkenness, from drunkenness to swearing and blaspheming the name of God; hereof grew quarrels, frays, and continual controversies which are now as worms in my conscience gnawing incessantly. And did I not through hearty repentance take hold of God's mercies, even these detestable sins would drench me down into the damnable pit of destruction; for *Stipendium peccati mors.*

O know, good countrymen, that the horrible sins and intolerable blasphemy I have used against the majesty of God is a block in my conscience, and that so heavy that there were no way with me but desperation, if the hope of Christ's death and passion did not help to ease me of so intolerable and heavy a burthen.

I have long with the deaf adder stopp'd mine ears against the voice of God's ministers; yea, my heart was hardened with Pharaoh against all the motions that the spirit of God did at any time work in my mind to turn me from my detestable kind of living.

Yet let me confess a trueth, that even once, and yet but once, I felt a fear and horror in my conscience, and then the terror of God's judgments did manifestly teach me that my life was bad, that by sin I deserved damnation, and that such was the greatness of my sin that I deserved no redemption. And this inward motion I received in Saint Andrew's church in the city of Norwich, at a lecture or sermon then preached by a godly learned man, whose doctrine, and the manner of whose teaching, I liked wonderful well; yea (in my conscience) such was his singleness of heart and zeal in his doctrine that he might have converted the most monster of the world.

Well, at that time, whosoever was worst, I knew myself as bad as he; for being new come from Italy (where I learned all the villanies under the heavens), I was drown'd in pride, whoredom was my daily exercise, and gluttony with drunkenness was my only delight.

At this sermon the terror of God's judgments did manifestly teach me that my exercises were damnable, and that I should be wip'd out of the book of life if I did not speedily repent my looseness of life and reform my misdemeanors.

At this sermon the said learned man (who doubtless was the child of God) did beat down sin in such pithy and persuasive manner that I began to call unto mind the danger of my soul, and the prejudice that at length would befall me for those gross sins which with greediness I daily committed; insomuch as sighing I said in myself, "Lord, have mercy upon me, and send me grace to amend and become a new man."

But this good motion lasted not long in me; for no sooner had I met with my copesmates but, seeing me in such a solemn humor, they demanded the cause of my sadness; to whom when I had discovered that I sorrowed for my wickedness of life, and that the preacher's words had taken a deep impression in my conscience, they fell upon me in jesting manner, calling me puritan and precisian, and wished I might have a pulpit, with such other scoffing terms that by their foolish persuasion the good and wholesome lesson I had learned went quite out of my remembrance; so that I fell again with the dog to my old vomit, and put my wicked life in practise, and that so throughly as ever I did before.

Thus although God sent his Holy Spirit to call me, and though I heard him, yet I regarded it no longer than the present time, when, sodainly forsaking it, I went forward obstinately in my miss. Nevertheless, soon after, I married a gentleman's daughter of good account, with whom I lived for a while; but forasmuch as she would persuade me from my wilful wickedness, after I had a child by her I cast her off, having spent up the marriage money which I obtained by her.

Then left I her at six or seven, who went into Lincolnshire and I to London, where in short space I fell into favor with such as were of honorable and good calling. But here note that though I knew how to get a friend, yet I had not the gift or reason how to keep a friend; for he that was my dearest friend, I would be sure so to behave myself towards him that he should ever after profess to be my utter enemy, or else vow never after to come in my company.

Thus my misdemeanors (too many to be recited) caused the most part of those so much to despise me that in the end I became friendless, except it were in a few alehouses, who commonly for my inordinate expenses would make much of me, until I were on the score far more than ever I meant to pay by twenty nobles thick. After I had wholly betaken me to the penning of plays (which was my continual exercise) I was so far from calling upon God that I sildom thought on God, but took such delight in swearing and blaspheming the name of God that none could think otherwise of me than that I was the child of perdition.

These vanities and other trifling pamphlets I penned of love and vain fantasies was my chiefest stay of living, and for those my vain discourses I was beloved of the more vainer sort of people, who, being my continual companions, came still to my lodging, and there would continue quaffing, carowsing, and surfeting with me all the day long.

But I thank God that he put it in my head to lay open the most horrible coosenages of the common cony-catchers, cooseners, and crossbiters, which I have indifferently handled in those my several discourses already imprinted. And my trust is that those discourses will do great good, and be very beneficial to the commonwealth of England.

But O, my dear wife, whose company and sight I have refrained these six years, I ask God and thee forgiveness for so greatly wronging thee, of whom I seldom or never thought until now. Pardon me, I pray thee, wheresoever thou art, and God forgive me all my offenses.

And now to you all that live and revel in such wickedness as I have done, to you I write, and in God's name wish you to look to yourselves and to reform yourselves for the safeguard of your own souls; dissemble not with God, but seek grace at his hands; he hath promis'd it, and he will perform it.

God doth sundry times defer his punishment unto those that run a wicked race; but *Quod defertur non aufertur* ("that which is deferr'd is not quittanc'd"), a day of reckoning will come, when the Lord will say, "Come, give account of thy stewardship." What God determineth, man cannot prevent; he that binds two sins together cannot go unpunish'd in the one; so long the pot goeth to the pit that at last it comes broken home.

Therefore, all my good friends, hope not in money, nor in friends, in favors, in kindred; they are all uncertain, and they are furthest off when men think them most nigh. O were I now to begin the flower of my youth, were I now in the prime of my years, how far would I be from my former follies! What a reformed course of life would I take! But it is too late; only now the comfortable mercies of the Lord is left me to hope in.

It is bootless for me to make any long discourse to such as are graceless as I have been. All wholesome warnings are odious unto them, for they with the spider suck poison out of the most precious flowers, and to such as God hath in his secret counsel elected, few words will suffice. But howsoever my life hath been, let my repentant end be a general example to all the youth in England to obey their parents, to fly whoredom, drunkenness, swearing, blaspheming, contempt of the Word, and such grievous and gross sins, lest they bring their parents' heads with sorrow to their graves, and lest (with me) they be a blemish to their kindred and to their posterity forever.

Thus may you see how God hath secret to himself the times of calling; and when he will have them into his vineyard, some he calls in the morning, some at noon, and some in the evening, and yet hath the last his wages as well as the first. For as his judgments are inscrutable, so are his mercies incomprehensible. And therefore let all men learn these two lessons: not to despair, because God may work in them through his Spirit at the last hour; nor to presume, lest God give them over for their presumption, and deny them repentance, and so they die impenitent; which *finalis impenitentia* is a manifest sin against the Holy Ghost.

To this doth that golden sentence of St. Augustine allude, which he speaketh of the thief hanging on the cross. "There was," saith he, "one thief saved and no more; therefore presume not; and there was one saved, and therefore despair not." . . .

The Manner of the Death and Last End of Robert Greene, Maister of Arts

After that he had penn'd the former discourse, then lying sore sick of a surfet which he had taken with drinking, he continued most patient and penitent; yea, he did with tears forsake the world, renounced swearing, and desired forgiveness of God and the world for all his offenses; so that during all the time of his sickness, which was about a moneth's space, he was never heard to swear, rave, or blaspheme the name of God, as he was accustomed to do before that time—which greatly comforted his well-willers to see how mightily the grace of God did work in him.

He confessed himself that he was never heartsick, but said that all his pain was in his belly. And, although he continually scoured, yet still his belly swell'd; and never left swelling upward until it swell'd him at the heart and in his face.

During the whole time of his sickness, he continually called upon God and recited these sentences following: "O Lord, forgive me my manifold offenses. O Lord, have mercy upon me. O Lord, forgive me my secret sins, and in thy mercy, Lord, pardon them all. Thy mercy, O Lord, is above thy works." And with such-like godly sentences he passed the time, even till he gave up the ghost.

And this is to be noted, that his sickness did not so greatly weaken him but that he walked to his chair and back again the night before he departed; and then, being feeble, laying him down on his bed about nine of the clock at night, a friend of his told him that his wife had sent him commendations, and that she was in good health; whereat he greatly rejoiced, confessed that he had mightily wronged her, and wished that he might see her before he departed; whereupon, feeling his time was but short, he took pen and ink and wrote her a letter to this effect:

Sweet wife, as ever there was any good will or friendship between thee and me, see this bearer (my host) satisfied of his debt; I owe him ten pound, and but for him I had perished in the streets. Forget and forgive my wrongs done unto thee, and Almighty God have mercy on my soul. Farewell till we meet in heaven, for on earth thou shalt never see me more. This 2 of September, 1592.

Written by thy dying husband,

Robert Greene

GREENE'S PRAYER IN THE TIME OF HIS SICKNESS

O Lord Jesus Christ, my Savior and Redeemer, I humbly beseech thee to look down from heaven upon me, thy servant that am grieved with thy Spirit, that I may patiently endure to the end thy rod of chastisement; and forasmuch as thou art lord of life and death, as also of strength, health, age, weakness, and sickness, I do therefore wholly submit myself unto thee to be dealt withal according to thy holy will and pleasure. And seeing, O merciful Jesu, that my sins are innumerable like unto the sands of the sea and that I have so often offended thee that I have worthily deserved death and utter damnation, I humbly pray thee to deal with me according to thy gracious mercy and not agreeable to my wicked deserts. And grant that I may, O Lord, through thy Spirit, with patience suffer and bear this cross which thou hast worthily laid upon me, notwithstanding how grievous soever the burthen thereof be, that my faith may be found laudable and glorious in thy sight to the increase of thy glory and my everlasting felicity. For even thou, O Lord, most sweet Savior, didst first suffer pain before thou wert crucified; since, therefore, O meek Lamb of God, that my way to eternal joy is to suffer with thee worldly grievances, grant that I may be made like unto thee by suffering patiently adversity, trouble, and sickness. And lastly, forasmuch as the multitude of thy mercies doth put away the sins of those which truly repent, so as thou rememb'rest them no more, open the eye of thy mercy and behold me a most miserable and wretched sinner, who for the same doth most earnestly desire pardon and forgiveness. Renew, O Lord, in me whatsoever hath been decayed by the fraudulent malice of Sathan or my own carnal wilfulness; receive me, O Lord, into thy favor; consider of my contrition and gather up my tears into thy heavenly habitation; and seeing, O Lord, my whole trust and confidence is only in thy mercy, blot out my offenses and tread them under feet so as they may not be a witness against me at the day of wrath. Grant this, O Lord, I humbly beseech thee, for thy mercy's sake. Amen.

THE GREENE-NASHE-HARVEY CONTROVERSY

The angry, scurrilous, and tedious controversy between Greene, Nashe, and Gabriel Harvey is one of the most celebrated (and bibliographically complicated) events of Tudor literary history. Greene and his disciple Nashe, university men whose brief but turbulent careers as professional writers of popular literature marked a new movement in English letters, found profit and delight in hurling their invective on Harvey and the academic tradition which he tried to defend. As professionals who can be fairly called hack-writers, they turned out with astonishing ease and speed euphuistic romances, plays, journalistic pamphlets ostensibly exposing the evils of low life, and merciless lampoons; as a scholar, a gentleman (as he, at least, believed), *laudator temporis acti,* and (as his letters to young Spenser show) something of a pompous fool, Harvey regarded himself as a champion of those traditional literary and moral values which the dissolute professionals so obscenely flouted. It is not surprising that Greene and Nashe should have detested Harvey, or that Harvey should have held them in fierce contempt; but it is surprising that their antagonisms should have swirled and eddied for some ten years through a bewildering mass of books and pamphlets. From this literature (if that term is not too pretentious) we not only learn a great deal about the personalities involved; we also get an intimate glimpse of an important stage of English literary history —that stage in which, for the first time, the tradition of learned or courtly amateurs (the tradition embracing Chaucer, Lydgate, More, Elyot, Wyatt, Sackville, Sidney, and many others) was yielding to a new race of professionals. When we remember that Shakespeare was finding his stride as a professional dramatist about the time that Sidney's well-bred attack on popular drama appeared, we can sense some of the larger implications of Nashe's and Harvey's noisy brawls.

Thanks to the researches of R. B. McKerrow we can now retrace at least the main stages of the controversy. Greene had apparently been hired by the Anglican bishops, toward the end of the eighties, to write against the audacious puritan attacks of "Martin Marprelate," and when Richard Harvey (Gabriel's younger brother) consequently attacked him in *Plain Perceval the Peace-maker of England* (1590) and at the same time found occasion, in *The Lamb of God,* to denounce young Nashe for his presumptuous preface to Greene's *Menaphon,* the fat was in the fire. In his *Quip for an Upstart Courtier* (1592) Greene replied with a vitriolic attack (perhaps written by Nashe and later canceled) on the elder Harvey, a rope-maker of

Saffron Walden, and on his sons Gabriel, Richard, and John; but when Gabriel, breathing fire and brimstone, came down to London to take legal action against Greene he learned that his enemy, young in years but old in sin, had just died of a surfeit of Rhine wine and pickled herring. Implacable in vengeance, he gathered such information as he could about Greene's dissolute life and sorry end and then began to write his *Four Letters* (1592) to justify his family's honor. Meanwhile, Nashe had published *Pierce Penniless* (1592), which contained, among other things, some very funny and very unflattering remarks about Richard Harvey's *Lamb of God;* as a result, in his third letter the enraged Gabriel abandoned the dead Greene for the living Nashe. Since Greene was necessarily *hors de combat,* Nashe gleefully assumed the responsibility for answering the *Four Letters* with *Strange News of the Intercepting Certain Letters* (1592), whereupon Harvey replied with *Pierce's Supererogation* (1593), an intolerably long and angry denunciation not only of Nashe but also of Greene, Dr. Andrew Perne (a Cambridge dignitary), and John Lyly (whose *Pap with an Hatchet,* an anti-Martinist tract of 1589, came in for furious if belated rebuttal). Although Nashe, peerless in invective, thrived on name-calling, he was then willing to call a halt, and in the preface to *Christ's Tears over Jerusalem* (1593) he handsomely offered a truce. Perhaps ignorant of Nashe's yielding mood, Harvey meanwhile carried on the fray with *A New Letter of Notable Contents* (1593), and Nashe, stung that his offer was rejected, retracted his kind words in a new preface to the second (?1594) issue of *Christ's Tears.* In 1596 he pushed his advantage brilliantly with *Have with You to Saffron Walden,* a masterpiece of invective that ruthlessly dissected Harvey and all his works. But Harvey, nothing if not persistent, had the last word in *The Trimming of T. Nashe* (1597), purportedly written by Richard Lichfield, the Cambridge barber to whom Nashe had ironically dedicated *Have with You.* There the matter seems to have rested until June 1, 1599, when the ecclesiastical authorities ordered the confiscation of all Nashe's and Harvey's books and prohibited their reprinting, and so the battle of the frogs and the mice came to an end. Two years later Nashe, still in his early thirties, was dead; and although Harvey lived on for three more decades he was at last content to let the dead lie in peace. Our texts are based upon *Foure Letters, and certaine Sonnets: Especially touching Robert Greene, and other parties, by him abused,* 1592 (STC 12900); *Strange Newes, Of the intercepting certaine Letters, and a Convoy of Verses,* 1592 (STC 18377) in *The Works of Thomas Nashe,* ed. Ronald B. McKerrow, volume I; *Kind-Harts Dreame, Conteining five Apparitions, with their Invectives against abuses raigning,* [1592] (STC 5123). (On Chettle see p. 849.)

GABRIEL HARVEY

from FOUR LETTERS AND CERTAIN SONNETS, ESPECIALLY TOUCHING ROBERT GREENE AND OTHER PARTIES BY HIM ABUSED (1592)

To All Courteous Minds That Will Voutchsafe the Reading

May I crave pardon at this instant as well for enditing that is unworthy to be published as for publishing that was unworthy to be endited? I will hereafter take precise order either never to importune you more or to solicit you for more especial cause. I was first exceeding loath to pen that is written, albeit in mine own enforced defense (for I make no difference between my dearest friends and myself), and am now much loather to divulge that is imprinted, albeit against those whose own pamflets are readier to condemn them then my *Letters* forward to accuse them. Vile acts would in some respects rather be concealed then recorded, as the darkness of the night better fitteth the nature of some unlucky birds then the brightness of the day. . . . But Greene (although pitifully blasted and how wofully faded) still flourisheth in the memory of some green wits, wedded to the wantonness of their own fancy and inamored upon every newfangled toy; and Pierce Penniless (although the Divel's orator by profession and his dam's poet by practise) in such a flush of notable good fellows cannot possibly want many to read him, enough to excuse him, a few to commend him, some to believe him or to credit any that tickeleth the right vein and feedeth the riotous humor of their licentious vanity. To stop the beginning is no bad purpose where the end may prove pernitious or perilous. Venom is venom, and will infect; when the dragon's head spitteth poison, what mischief may lurk in the dragon's tail? . . . That is done cannot *de facto* be undone; but I appeal to wisdom, how discreetly, and to justice, how deservedly it is done, and request the one to do us reason in shame of impudency and beseech the other to do us right in reproach of calumny. It was my intention so to demean myself in the whole and so to temper my style in every part that I might neither seem blinded with affection nor enraged with passion, nor partial to friend nor prejudicial to enemy, nor injurious to the worst nor offensive to any, but mildly and calmly shew how discredit reboundeth upon the autors as dust flyeth back into the wag's eyes that will needs be puffing it up. Which if I have altogether attained without the least oversight of distempered phrase, I am the gladder; if failed in some few incident terms (what tounge or pen may not slip in heat of discourse?), I hope a little will not greatly break the square either of my good meaning with humanity or of your good acceptation with indifferency. . . . London, this 16 of September.

Your thankful dettour,
G[abriel] H[arvey]

THE FIRST LETTER

To the Worshipful My Very Good Friend Master Emmanuel Demetrius, at His House by the Church in Lime Street in London

Master Demetrius, I earnestly commend this bearer, M[aster] Doctor Harvey, my good friend, unto you, being a very excellent general scholler who is desirous of your acquaintance and friendship, especially for the sight of some of your antiquities and monuments and also for some conference touching the state of forrain countries as your leisure may conveniently serve. You shall assuredly find the gentleman very honest and thankful, and me ready to reacquite your courtesy and favor to him so shewn in that I possibly may. And so, with the remembrance of my hearty recommendations, with like thanks for your two letters of forrein news received the last week, I commit you to the protection of the Almighty. Walden, this 29 of August, 1592.

Your loving friend,
Christopher Bird

Instead of other novels I send you my opinion in a plain but true sonnet upon the famous new work intituled *A Quip for an Upstart Courtier,* or, forsooth, *A Quaint Dispute between Velvet Breeches and Cloth Breeches,* as fantastical and fond a dialogue as I have seen, and, for some particulars, one of the most licentious and intolerable invectives that ever I read. Wherein the lewd fellow and impudent railer, in an odious and desperate mood, without any other cause or reason, amongst sundry other persons notoriously defamed, most spitefully and villanously abuseth an ancient neighbor of mine, one Master Harvey, a right honest man of good reckoning and one that above twenty years since bare the chiefest office in Walden with good credit, and hath maintained four sons in Cambridge and elsewhere with great charges, all sufficiently able to answer for themselves, and

three (in spite of some few Greenes) universally well reputed in both universities and through the whole realm. Whereof one returning sick from Norwich to Lynn in July last was past sense of any such malicious injury before the publication of that vile pamphlet. *Livor post fata quiescit, et bene a singulis audiant qui omnibus volunt bene.*

A Due Commendation of the Quipping Autor

Greene the Cony-catcher, of this dream the autor,
For his dainty devise deserveth the hauter:
A rakehell, a makeshift, a scribbling fool,
A famous bayard in city and school,
Now sick as a dog and ever brainsick,
Where such a raving and desperate Dick?
Sir-reverence, a scurvy Master of Art
Answered inough with a doctor's fart.
He scorns other answer, and Envy salutes
With shortest vowels and with longest mutes.   10
For farther trial himself he refers
To proof and sound judgment, that seldom errs.
    Now good Robin Goodfellow and gentle Greenesleeves,
    Give him leave to be quiet that none aggrieves.
        Miserrima fortuna quae caret inimico.

THE SECOND LETTER

To My Loving Friend Maister Christopher Bird of Walden

Maister Bird, in the absence of M[aster] Demetrius I delivered your letter unto his wife, whom I found very courteous. My next business was to enquire after the famous author, who was reported to lie dangerously sick in a shoemaker's house near Dowgate, not of the plague or the pocks, as a gentleman said, but of a surfet of pickle herring and Rhenish wine, or, as some suppose, of an exceeding fear. For in his extremest want he offered ten or, rather then fail, twenty shillings to the printer (a huge sum with him at that instant) to leave out the matter of the three brothers, with confession of his great fear to be called *coram* for those forged imputations. A conscious mind and undaunted heart seldom dwell together; he was not the first that bewrayed and punished his own guiltiness with blushing for shame, or trembling for dread, or drooping for wo. Many can heap misery inough upon their own heads, and need no more penalty but their own contrition and the censure of other. I would not wish a sworn enemy to be more basely valued or more vilely reputed then the common voice of the city esteemeth him that sought fame by diffamation of other but hath utterly discredited himself and is notoriously grown a very proverb of infamy and contempt. I little delight in the rehearsal of such paltry; but who like

Elderton for ballating, Greene for pamphleting, both for good fellowship and bad conditions? Railing was the ippocras of the drunken rimester and quipping the marchpane of the mad libeler. They scape fair that go scot-free in such saucy reckonings. I have known some, read of many, and heard of more, that wantonly quipped other and soundly nipped themselves. The hottest blood of choler may be cooled; and, as the fiercest fury of wildfire, so the fiercest wildfire of fury consumeth itself. Howbeit a common mischief would be prevented; and it generally concerneth all, and particularly behooveth everyone to look about him when he heareth the bells ringing backward and seeth the fire running forward and beholdeth even Death in person shooting his peremptory bolts. You understand me without a gloss, and here is matter inough for a new civil war, or shall I say for a new Trojan siedge, if this poor letter should fortune to come in print. I deal directly and will plainly tell you my fancy, if Titius continue to upbraid Caius with everything and nothing. I neither name Martin Marprelate nor shame Pap-with-a-Hatchet nor mention any other but Elderton and Greene, two notorious mates and the very ringleaders of the riming and scribbling crew. But Titius, or rather Zoilus in his spiteful vein, will so long flurt at Homer, and Thersites in his peevish mood so long fling at Agamemnon, that they will become extremely odious and intolerable to all good learning and civil government; and in attempting to pull down or disgrace other without order, must needs finally overthrow themselves without relief. Orators have challenged a special liberty and poets claimed an absolute license; but no liberty without bounds, nor any license without limitation. Invectives by favor have been too bold, and satires by usurpation too presumptuous; I overpass Archilochus, Aristophanes, Lucian, Julian, Aretine, and that whole venemous and viperous brood of old and new railers, even Tully and Horace otherwhiles overreached; and I must needs say, Mother Hubbard, in heat of choler, forgetting the pure sanguine of her sweet *Faerie Queene,* wilfully overshot her malcontented self, as elsewhere I have specified at large, with the good leave of unspotted friendship. Examples in some ages do exceeding much hurt. Sallust and Clodius learned of Tully to frame artificial declamations and pathetical invectives against Tully himself and other worthy members of that most florishing state. If Mother Hubbard in the vein of Chaucer happen to tell one canicular tale, father Elderton and his son Greene, in the vein of Skelton or Scoggin, will counterfeit an hundred dogged fables, libels, calumnies, slanders, lies for the whetstone, what not, and most currishly snarl and bite where they should most kindly fawn and lick. Every private excess is dangerous, but such

public enormities, incredibly pernitious and insupportable. And who can tell what huge outrages might amount of such quarrelous and tumultuous causes? Honor is precious, worship of value, fame invaluable. They perilously threaten the commonwealth that go about to violate the inviolable parts thereof. Many will sooner loose their lives then the least jot of their reputation. Lord, what mortal feuds, what furious combats, what cruel bloodshed, what horrible slaughterdom have been committed for the point of honor and some few courtly ceremonies! Though meaner persons do not so highly overprice their credit, yet who taketh not discourtesy unkindly, or slander displeasingly? For mine own part, I am to make an use of my adversary's abuse and will endeavor to reform any default whereof I may justly or probably be empeached. Some emulation hath already done me good, both for supply of great imperfections and for encrease of small perfections. I have (and who hath not?) found it better to be tickled and stinged of a busy enemy then to be coyed and lulled of an idle friend. Plutarch is gravely wise, and Machiavel subtilly politic; but in either of them, what sounder or finer piece of cunning then to reap commodity by him that seeketh my displeasure, and to play upon the advantage of his detection of my infirmities? Other caviling or mote-spying malice confoundeth itself, and I continue my accustomed simplicity to answer vanity with silence, though peradventure not without danger of inviting a new injury by intertaining an old. Patience hath trained me to pocket up more hainous indignities and even to digest an age of iron. They that can do little must be contented to suffer much. My betters need not take it grievously to be taunted or reproached in that book where St. Peter and Christ himself are Lucianically and scoffingly alledged, the one for begging, the other for granting a foolish boon, pretended ever since the fatal destiny of the gentle craft. Some men will have their swing and their bug's-words, though it be against all Gods-forbid; and what Caesar's might or Cato's integrity or what saint's devotion can stop such mouths? Yet neither themselves the better nor other the worse, that depend not on their allowance, but rely on their own justification and desire to confute their impudency not with words but with deeds. Howbeit I am not to prejudice my brother alive or to smother the wrong offered to my brother deceased, or to tolerate the least diffamation of my good father, whom no ill-willer could ever touch with any dishonesty or discredit in any sort. Nothing more dear or inestimable then a man's good name; and albeit I contemn such pelting injuries vainly devised against myself, yet am I not to neglect so intolerable a wrong so notoriously published against them. There is law for desperatest outlaws and order for most disorderly fellows. They that cannot govern themselves must be ruled by other, and pay for their folly. Whiles I was thus, or to like effect, resolving with myself and discoursing with some special friends, not only writing unto you, I was suddainly certified that the king of the paper stage, so the gentleman termed Greene, had played his last part, and was gone to Tarlton; whereof I protest I was nothing glad, as was expected, but unfeignedly sorry, as well because I could have wished he had taken his leave with a more charitable farewell, as also because I was now deprived of that remedy in law that I entended against him in the behalf of my father, whose honest reputation I was in many duties to tender. Yet to some conceited wit that could take delight to discover knaveries or were a fit person to augment the history of cony-catchers, O Lord, what a pregnant occasion were here presented to display lewd vanity in his lively colors and to decipher the very mysteries of that base art! Petty cooseners are not worth the naming; he, they say, was the monarch of crossbiters and the very emperor of shifters. I was altogether unacquainted with the man and never once saluted him by name; but who in London hath not heard of his dissolute and licentious living, his fond disguising of a Maister of Art with ruffianly hair, unseemly apparel, and more unseemly company; his vainglorious and thrasonical braving; his piperly extemporizing and Tarltonizing; his apish counterfeiting of every ridiculous and absurd toy; his fine coosening of jugglers and finer juggling with cooseners; his villanous cogging and foisting; his monstrous swearing and horrible forswearing; his impious profaning of sacred texts; his other scandalous and blasphemous raving; his riotous and outragious surfeiting; his continual shifting of lodgings; his plausible mustering and banqueting of roisterly acquaintance at his first coming; his beggarly departing in every hostess's debt; his infamous resorting to the Bankside, Shoreditch, Southwark, and other filthy haunts; his obscure lurking in basest corners; his pawning of his sword, cloak, and what not when money came short; his impudent pamphleting, phantastical interluding, and desperate libeling when other coosening shifts failed; his imploying of Ball (surnamed "Cutting" Ball) till he was intercepted at Tyburn, to levy a crew of his trustiest companions to guard him, in danger of arrests; his keeping of the foresaid Ball's sister, a sorry ragged quean, of whom he had his base son, Infortunatus Greene; his forsaking of his own wife, too honest for such a husband—particulars are infinite—his contemning of superiors, deriding of other, and defying of all good order?

Compare base fellows and noble men together, and what, in a manner, wanted he of the ruffianly and variable nature of Catiline or Antony but the honorable fortunes of Catiline and Antony? They that have seen much more then I have heard (for so I am credibly infourmed) can relate strange and almost incredible comedies of his monstrous disposition, wherewith I am not to infect the air or defile this paper. There be inough, and inough such histories, both dead and living, though youth be not corrupted or age accloyed with his legendary. Truly I have been ashamed to hear some ascertained reports of his most woful and rascal estate: how the wretched fellow (or shall I say the prince of beggars?) laid all to gage for some few shillings, and was attended by lice, and would pitifully beg a penny pot of malmsey, and could not get any of his old acquaintance to comfort or visit him in his extremity but Mistress Appleby and the mother of Infortunatus. Alas, even his fellow writer [i.e. Nashe], a proper young man if advised in time, that was a principal guest at that fatal banquet of pickle herring (I spare his name, and in some respects wish him well), came never more at him, but either would not or happily could not perform the duty of an affectionate and faithful friend. The poor cordwainer's wife was his only nurse, and the mother of Infortunatus his sole companion, but when Mistress Appleby came as much to expostulate injuries with her as to visit him. God help good fellows when they cannot help themselves! Slender relief in the predicament of privations and feigned habits. Miserable man that must perish or be succored by counterfeit or impotent supplies! I once bemoaned the decayed and blasted estate of M[aster] Gascoigne, who wanted not some commendable parts of conceit and endeavor; but unhappy M[aster] Gascoigne, how lordly happy in comparison of most unhappy M[aster] Greene! He never envied me so much as I pitied him from my heart; especially when his hostess Isam, with tears in her eyes and sighs from a deeper fountain (for she loved him dearly), told me of his lamentable begging of a penny pot of malmsey; and, sir-reverence, how lousy he and the mother of Infortunatus were (I would her surgeon found her no worse then lousy); and how he was fain, poor soul, to borrow her husband's shirt whiles his own was a-washing; and how his doublet and hose and sword were sold for three shillings; and beside, the charges of his winding sheet, which was four shillings; and the charges of his burial yesterday in the new churchyard near Bedlam, which was six shillings and fourpence; how deeply he was indebted to her poor husband, as appeared by his own bond of ten pounds which the good woman kindly shewed me and beseeched me to read the writing beneath, which was a letter to his abandoned wife in the behalf of his gentle host—not so short as persuasible in the beginning, and pitiful in the ending:

Doll, I charge thee, by the love of our youth and by my soul's rest, that thou wilt see this man paid; for if he and his wife had not succored me I had died in the streets.

Robert Greene

O what notable matter were here for a green head or Lucianical conceit that would take pleasure in the pain of such sorry, distressed creatures! Whose afflicted case, to every charitable or compassionate mind cannot but seem most commiserable, if not for their own cause, yet for God's sake, who deserveth infinitely of them whom he acquitteth, not according to judgment but according to mercy. I rather hope of the dead as I wish to the living, that grace might finally abound where wickedness did overflow, and that Christ in his divine goodness should miraculously forgive the man that in his divilish badness blasphemously reviled God. The dead bite not, and I am none of those that bite the dead. When I begin to conflict with ghosts, then look for my confutation of his fine *Quip* or quaint *Dispute*—whom his sweet hostess, for a tender farewell, crowned with a garland of bays, to shew that a tenth muse honored him more being dead then all the nine honored him alive. I know not whether Skelton, Elderton, or some likeflourishing poet were so enterred; it was his own request, and his nurse's devotion; and happily some of his favorites may imitate the example. One that wished him a better lodging then in a poor journeyman's house and a better grave then in that churchyard in Bedlam hath perfourmed a little piece of a greater duty to a laureate poet:

> Here lies the man whom Mistress Isam crown'd
>   with bays—
> She, she that joy'd to hear her Nightingale's
>   sweet lays.

Which another no sooner read but he immediately subscribed, as speaking to the ignorant passenger:

> Here Bedlam is, and here a poet garish,
> Gaily bedeck'd like forehorse of the parish.

Other epitaphs and funeral devotions I am promised by some that deeply affect inspired bards and the adopted sons of the muses, but you may imagine I have small superfluity of leisure to entend such business, and yet nothing of friend or foe can be unwelcome unto me that savoreth of wit or relisheth of humanity or tasteth of any good. In the mean, as ever before for a general defense, so still for a special apology, I refer myself to every indifferent judgment, and presume they will conceive well that perceive no ill. . . . I return to my private business. Good Maister Bird, commend me to my good friends and fare you heartily well. London, this 5 of September.

Your ever assured
Gabriel Harvey

THE THIRD LETTER

To Every Reader, Favorably or Indifferently Affected

Albeit for these twelve or thirteen years no man hath been more loth or more scrupulous then myself to underlie the censure of every curious conceit or rigorous judgment that pretendeth a deep insight in the perfections of wits and styles, insomuch that even actions of silence and patience have been commenced against me, and although I still dwell in the same opinion that nothing would be committed to a public view that is not exactly labored both for matter and manner and that importeth not some notable use to one or other effectual purpose, yet partly the vehement importunity of some affectionate friends and partly mine own tender regard of my father's and my brothers' good reputation have so forcibly overruled me that I have finally condescended to their passionate motion, and in an extraordinary case have respectively yielded my consent to an extraordinary course. Which I would unpartially commend to the reasonable allowance of every indifferent peruser that carrieth courtesy in his tongue or honesty in his heart. For mine own injury, the more I consider the less I estimate the same, as one born to suffer and made to contemn injuries. He that in his youth flattered not himself with the exceeding commendations of some greatest schollers in the world cannot at these years either be discouraged with misreport or daunted with misfortune. A premeditate and resolute mind lightly shaketh off the heaviest crosses of malice and easely passeth over a thousand grievances with a smile. . . .

A mad world where such shameful stuff [as Greene's libels] is bought and sold, and where such roisterly varlets may be suffered to play upon whom they lust and how they lust. Is this Greene, with the running head and the scribbling hand, that never lins putting forth new, newer, and newest books of the maker? If his other books be as wholesome gear as this, no marvel though the gay man conceive trimly of himself and stately scorn all beside. Greene, vile Greene, would thou werest half so honest as the worst of the four whom thou upbraidest, or half so learned as the unlearned'st of the three! Thank other for thy borrowed and filched plumes of some little Italianated bravery, and what remaineth but flat impudency and gross detraction, the proper ornaments of thy sweet utterance? . . .

That best and his only phisition knoweth what spiritual physic I commended unto him when I beheld in his meager and ghastly countenance that I cannot rehearse without some fit of compassion. We must in order follow him, that should in nature have gone before him, and I know not by what destiny he followed him first that fooled him last. How he departed, his ghostly mother Isam can truliest and will favorabliest report; how he lived, London rememb'reth. O, what a lively picture of vanity! But O, what a deadly image of misery! And O, what a terrible caveat for such and such! I am not to extenuate or prejudice his wit, which could not any way be great, though some way not the least of our vulgar writers, and many ways very ungracious; but who ever esteemed him either wise, or learned, or honest, or any way credible? How many gentlemen and other say of him, "Let the paltry fellow go. Lord, what a lewd companion was he! What an egregious makeshift!" Where should cony-catchers have gotten such a secretary? How shall coosenage do for a new register, or phantasticality for a new autor? They wrong him much in their epitaphs and other solemn devices that entitle him not at the least "The Second Toy of London, the Stale of Paul's, the Ape of Euphues, the Vice of the Stage, the Mocker of the Simple World, the Flouter of His Friends, the Foe of Himself," and so forth. What durst not he utter with his tongue, or divulge with his pen, or countenance with his face? Or whom cared he for but a careless crew of his own associates? Peruse his famous books, and instead of *Omne tulit punctum qui miscuit utile dulci* (that forsooth was his professed poesy), lo, a wild head full of mad brain and a thousand crotchets, a scholler, a discourser, a courtier, a ruffian, a gamester, a lover, a soldier, a traveler, a merchant, a broker, an artificer, a botcher, a pettifogger, a player, a coosener, a railer, a beggar, an omnigatherum, a gay nothing; a storehouse of bald and baggage stuff, unworth the answering or reading; a trivial and triobular autor for knaves and fools, an image of idleness, an epitome of fantasticality, a mirror of vanity, *vanitas vanitatum et omnia vanitas*. Alas, that any should say, as I have heard divers affirm, "His wit was nothing but a mint of knavery, himself a deviser of juggling feats, a forger of covenous practises, an inventor of monstruous oaths, a derider of all religions, a contemner of God and man, a desperate Lucianist, an abhominable Aretinist, an arch-atheist, and he arch-deserved to be well hanged seven years ago." Twenty and twenty such familiar speeches I overpass and bury the whole legendary of his life and death in the sepulcher of eternal silence. I will not condemn or censure his works, which I never did so much as superficially overrun, but as some few of them occursively presented themselves in stationers' shops and some other houses of my acquaintance. But I pray God they have not done more harm by corruption of manners then good by quickening of wit, and I would some buyers had either more reason to discern or less appetite to

desire such novels. The world is full inough of fooleries though the humor be not feasted with such luxurious and riotous pamphlets. . . .

Flourishing M[aster] Greene is most wofully faded, and whilest I am bemoaning his overpiteous decay and discoursing the usual success of such rank wits, lo, all on the suddain, his sworn brother, M[aster] Pierce Penniless (still more paltery, but what remedy? We are already over shoes and must now go through), lo, his inwardest companion, that tasted of the fatal herring, cruelly pinched with want, vexed with discredit, tormented with other men's felicity and overwhelmed with his own misery, in a raving and frantic mood most desperately exhibiteth his *Supplication to the Devil.* A strange title, an odd wit, and a mad whoreson, I warrant him. Doubtless it will prove some dainty device, queintly contrived, by way of humble supplication to the high and mighty prince of darkness; not dunsically botched up, but right formally conveyed according to the style and tenor of Tarlton's president, his famous play of the *Seven Deadly Sins,* which most deadly but most lively play I might have seen in London, and was very gently invited thereunto at Oxford by Tarlton himself, of whom I merrily demanding which of the seven was his own deadly sin he bluntly answered after this manner, "By God, the sin of other gentlemen—Lechery!" . . .

Good, sweet orator, be a devine poet indeed and use heavenly eloquence indeed, and employ thy golden talent with amounting usance indeed, and with heroical cantos honor right virtue and brave valor indeed, as noble Sir Philip Sidney and gentle Maister Spenser have done with immortal fame, and I will bestow more complements of rare amplifications upon thee then ever any bestowed upon them, or this tongue ever afforded, or any Aretinish mountain of huge exaggerations can bring forth. Right artificiality (whereat I once aimed to the uttermost power of my slender capacity) is not mad-brained or ridiculous or absurd or blasphemous or monstrous, but deep-conceited, but pleasurable, but delicate, but exquisite, but gratious, but admirable, not according to the fantastical mold of Aretine or Rabelais but according to the fine model of Orpheus, Homer, Pindarus, and the excellentest wits of Greece and of the land that flowed with milk and honey. For what festival hymns so divinely dainty as the sweet psalms of King David, royally translated by Buchanan? Or what sage gnomes so profoundly pithy as the wise proverbs of King Salomon, notably also translated? But how few Buchanans! Such lively springs of streaming eloquence and such right Olympical hills of amounting wit I cordially recommend to the dear lovers of the muses, and namely to the professed sons of the same, Edmund Spenser, Richard Stanyhurst, Abraham Fraunce, Thomas Watson, Samuel Daniel, Thomas Nashe, and the rest whom I affectionately thank for their studious endeavors, commendably employed in enriching and polishing their native tongue, never so furnished or embellished as of late. . . .

It is my earnest desire to begin and end such frivolous altercations at once, and were it not more for other then for myself, assuredly I would be the first that should cancel this impertinent pamflet and throw the other two letters with the sonnets annexed into the fire. Let them have their swing, that affect to be terribly singular. I desire not to be a black swan or to leave behind me any period in the style of the Divel's orator or any verse in the vein of his damn's poet, but rather covet to be nothing in print then anything in the stamp of needless or fruitless contention. As I am overruled at this present and as it standeth now, I am not to be mine own judge or advocate, but am content to be sentenced by every courteous or indifferent peruser that regardeth honesty in persons or truth in testimonies or reason in causes. Or, seeing some matters of fame are called in question, I am not only willing but desirous to underlie the verdict even of Fame herself, and to submit our whole credits to the voice of the people as to the voice of equity and the oracle of God, to whose gratious favors he recommendeth your courtesy, that neither flattereth the best nor slandereth the worst nor wilfully wrongeth any, but professeth duty to his superiors, humanity to his equals, favor to his inferiors, reason to all. And by the same rule oweth you amends for the premises, not speedily dispatched but hastily bungled up, as you see. London, this 8 and 9 of September.

The friend of his friends, and foe of none

GREENE'S MEMORIAL, OR CERTAIN FUNERAL SONNETS

To the Foresaid Maister Emmanuel Demetrius, Maister Christopher Bird, and All Gentle Wits That Will Voutsafe the Reading

SONNET 3
His Admonition to Greene's Companions

The flourishing and gaily-springing wight
That vainly me provok'd with vile reproach
Hath done his worst, and hath no more to broach.
Mauger the Divel of villanous despight

I cannot rail, whatever cause to rail;
For charity I lovingly imbrace
That me for envy odiously deface
But in their highest rage extremely fail.
I can do him no harm that is in heaven;
I can do him no good that is in hell;
I wish the best to his survivors fell,
Deeply acquainted with his six and seven.
O be not like to Death, that spareth none!
Your greenest flower and peacock's tail is gone.

SONNET 20
His Apology of His Good Father

Ah, my dear father and my parent sweet,
Whose honesty no neighbor can empeach,
That any ruffian should in terms unmeet
To your discredit shamefully outreach!
O rakehell hand that scribbled him a knave,
Whom never enemy did so appeach,
Repent thy wicked self that so didst rave
And cancel that which Slander's mouth did teach!
Nor every man nor every trade is brave;
Malt, hairs, and hemp, and sackcloth must be had;
Truth him from odious imputations save
And many a gallant gentleman more bad.
Four sons him cost a thousand pounds at lest.
Well may he fare and thou enjoy thy rest!

TO THE RIGHT WORSHIPFUL, MY SINGULAR GOOD FRIEND, M[ASTER] GABRIEL HARVEY, DOCTOR OF THE LAWS

Harvey, the happy above happiest men
I read, that, sitting like a looker-on
Of this world's stage, doest note with critique en
The sharp dislikes of each condition,
And as one careless of suspicion
Ne fawnest for the favor of the great,
Ne fearest foolish reprehension
Of faulty men which danger to thee threat;
But freely doest of what thee list entreat
Like a great lord of peerless liberty,
Lifting the good up to high honor's seat
And the evil damning evermore to die.
For life and death is in thy doomful writing,
So thy renowm lives ever by endighting.

Dublin, this eighteenth of July, 1586.
Your devoted friend during life,
Edmund Spenser

FROM STRANGE NEWS OF THE INTERCEPTING CERTAIN LETTERS AND A CONVOY OF VERSES AS THEY WERE GOING PRIVILY TO VICTUAL THE LOW COUNTRIES (1592)

To the Gentlemen Readers

Gentlemen, the strong faith you have conceiv'd that I would do works of supererogation in answering the doctor [Gabriel Harvey] hath made me break my day with other important business I had, and stand darting off quills a while like the porpentine.

I know there want not well-willers to my disgrace who say my only muse is Contention, and other that, with Tiberius Caesar pretending to see in the dark, talk of strange objects by them discovered in the night when in truth they are nothing else but the glimmering of their eyes.

I will not hold the candle to the Devil, unmask my holiday muse to envy; but if any such deep, insighted detracter will challenge me to whatsoever quiet adventure of art wherein he thinks me least conversant, he shall find that I am *tam Mercurio quam Marti,* a scholler in something else but contention.

If idle wits will needs tie knots on smooth bulrushes with their tongues, faith, the world might think I had little to attend if I should go about to unloose them with my pen.

I cannot tell how it comes to pass, but in these ill-ey'd days of ours every man delights with Ixion to beget children of clouds, dig for pearls in dunghills, and wrest oil out of iron.

Poor *Pierce Penniless* have they turn'd to a conjuring book, for there is not that line in it with which they do not seek to raise up a ghost, and, like the hog that converts the sixth part of his meat into bristles, so have they converted six parts of my book into bitterness.

Aretine, in a comedy of his, wittily complaineth that upstart commenters, with their annotations and gloses, had extorted that sense and moral out of Petrarch which, if Petrarch were alive, a hundred strappadoes might not make him confess or subscribe to; so may I complain that rash heads, upstart interpreters, have extorted and rak'd that unreverent meaning out of my lines which a thousand deaths cannot make me e'er grant that I dream'd of. . . .

From the admonition of these uncurteous misconsterers I come to the kill-cow champion of the three brethren. He, forsooth, will be the first that shall give *Pierce Penniless* a *non placet.*

It is not inough that he bepiss'd his credit about twelve years ago [i.e. 1580] with *Three Proper and Witty Familiar Letters,* but still he must be running on the letter and abusing the queen's English without pity or mercy.

Be it known unto you, Christian readers, this man is a forestaller of the market of fame, an ingrosser of glory, a mountebank of strange words, a mere marchant of babies and cony-skins.

Hold up thy hand, G[abriel] H[arvey]! Thou art here indited for an incrocher upon the fee simple of the Latin, an enemy to carriers as one that takes their occupation out of their hands and dost nothing but transport letters up and down in thy own commendation, a conspirator and practiser to make printers rich by making thyself ridiculous, a manifest briber of booksellers and stationers to help thee to sell away thy books (whose impression thou paid'st for) that thou mayst have money to go home to Trinity Hall to discharge thy commons.

I say no more but Lord have mercy upon thee, for thou art fall'n into his hands that will plague thee.

Gentlemen, will you be instructed in the quarrel that hath caus'd him lay about him with his pen and inkhorn so couragiously? About two years since (a fatal time to familiar epistles) a certain theological gimpanado, a demi-divine no higher than a tailor's pressing-iron, brother to this huge book-bear that writes himself "One of the Emperor Justinian's courtiers [i.e. a student of civil law]," took upon him to set his foot to mine and overcrow me with comparative terms. I protest I never turn'd up any cowsheard to look for this scarab fly. I had no conceit as then of discovering a breed of fools in the three brothers' books; marry, when I beheld ordinance planted on edge of the pulpit against me and that there was no remedy but the blind vicar would needs let fly at me with his church-door keys and curse me with bell, book, and candle because in my alphabet of idiots I had overskipp'd the H's, what could I do but draw upon him with my pen and defend myself with it and a paper buckler as well as I might?

Say I am as very a Turk as he that three years ago ran upon ropes if ever I spell'd either his or any of his kindred's name in reproach before he bark'd against me as one of the enemies of the Lamb of God and fetch'd allusions out of the buttery to debase me.

Here beginneth the fray. I upbraid godly predication with his wicked conversation; I squirt ink into his decayed eyes with iniquity to mend their diseased sight that they may a little better descend into my scholarship and learning. . . .

Sweet gentlemen, be but indifferent and you shall see me desperate. Here lies my hat and there my cloak, to which I resemble my two epistles, being the upper garments of my book as the other of my body. Saint Fame for me, and thus I run upon him.

Thomas Nashe

HERE BEGINNETH THE FIRST EPISTLE . . .

There was a learned doctor of physic (to whom Greene in his sickness sent for counsail) that, having read over the book of *Velvet Breeches and Cloth Breeches* and laughing merrily at the three brothers' legend, will'd Greene in any case either to mitigate it or leave it out, not for any extraordinary account he made of the fraternity of fools but for one of them was proceeded in the same faculty of physic he profess'd, and willingly he would have none of that excellent calling ill spoken of.

This was the cause of the alt'ring it, the fear of his phisition's displeasure, not any fear else.

I keep your "conscious mind," with all other odd ends of your half-fac'd English, till the full conclusion of my book, where, in an honorable index, they shall be placed according to their degree and segniority.

We are to vex you mightily for plucking Elderton out of the ashes of his ale and not letting him injoy his nappy muse of ballad-making to himself, but now, when he is as dead as dead beer, you must be finding fault with the brewing of his meters.

Hough, Thomas Deloney, Philip Stubbes, Robert Armin, etc.! Your father Elderton is abus'd. Revenge, revenge on coarse paper and want of matter that hath most sacriligiously contaminated the divine spirit and quintessence of a penny a quart.

Helter-skelter, fear no colors, course him, trounce him! One cup of perfect bonaventure licuor will inspire you with more wit and scholarship than he hath thrust into his whole packet of letters. . . .

As touching the liberty of orators and poets, I will confer with thee somewhat gravely, although thou beest a goosecap and hast no judgment. A liberty they have, thou sayest, "but no liberty without bounds, no license without limitation." Jesu, what mister wonders dost thou tell us! Everything hath an end, and a pudding hath two. "That liberty, poets of late in their invectives have exceeded"; they have borne their sword up where it is not lawful for a poynado, that is but the page of prowess, to intermeddle.

Thou bring'st in *Mother Hubbard* for an instance. Go no further, but here confess thyself a flat nodgcomb before all this congregation, for thou hast dealt by thy friend as homely as thou didst by thy father. Who publicly accus'd or of late brought *Mother Hubbard* into question, that thou shouldst by rehearsal rekindle against him the sparks of displeasure that were quenched? Forgot he "the pure sanguine of his *Faerie Queene*," say'st thou? A pure sanguine

sot art thou, that in vainglory to have Spenser known for thy friend, and that thou hast some interest in him, censerest him worse than his deadliest enemy would do. If any man were undeservedly touch'd in it, thou hast revived his disgrace that was so touch'd in it by renaming it when it was worn out of all men's mouths and minds. Besides, whereas before I thought it a made matter of some malitious moralizers against him, and no substance of slander in truth, now, when thou, that proclaimest thyself the only familiar of his bosom and therefore shouldst know his secrets, gives it out in print that he overshot himself therein, it cannot chuse but be suspected to be so indeed.

Immortal Spenser, no frailty hath thy fame but the imputation of this idiot's friendship! Upon an unspotted Pegasus should thy gorgeous-attired *Faerie Queene* ride triumphant through all Report's dominions, but that this mud-born bubble, this bile on the brow of the University, this bladder of pride new blown challengeth some interest in her prosperity. Of pitch who hath any use at all, shall be abus'd by it in the end.

High grass that florisheth for a season on the house-top, fadeth before the harvest calls for it, and may well make a fair shew, but hath no sweetness in it. Such is this ass *in presenti,* this gross painted image of pride, who would fain counterfeit a good wit, but scornful pity, his best patron, knows it becomes him as ill as an unweldy elephant to imitate a whelp in his wantonness. . . .

Gaffer Jobbernoll, once more well overtaken, how dost thou? How dost thou? Hold up thy head, man, take no care! Though Greene be dead, yet I may live to do thee good.

But "by the means of his death thou art deprived of the remedy in law which thou intended'st to have had against him for calling thy father rope-maker." Mas, that's true. What action will it bear? *Nihil pro nihilo,* none in law. What it will do upon the stage I cannot tell, for there a man may make action besides his part when he hath nothing at all to say; and if there, it is but a clownish action that it will bear, for what can be made of a rope-maker more than a clown? Will Kemp, I mistrust it will fall to thy lot for a merriment one of these days.

In short terms, thus I demur upon thy long Kentish-tail'd declaration against Greene.

He inherited more virtues than vices: a jolly, long, red peak like the spire of a steeple, he cherish'd continually without cutting, whereat a man might hang a jewel, it was so sharp and pendant.

Why should art answer for the infirmities of manners? He had his faults, and thou thy follies.

Debt and deadly sin who is not subject to? With

any notorious crime I never knew him tainted (and yet tainting is no infamous surgery for him that hath been in so many hot skirmishes).

A good fellow he was, and would have drunk with thee for more angels then the lord thou libel'd'st on "gave thee in Christ's College"; and in one year he piss'd as much against the walls as thou and thy two brothers spent in three.

In a night and a day would he have yark'd up a pamphlet as well as in seven year, and glad was that printer that might be so blest to pay him dear for the very dregs of his wit.

He made no account of winning credit by his works, as thou dost, that dost no good works but thinks to be famosed by a strong faith of thy own worthiness. His only care was to have a spell in his purse to conjure up a good cup of wine with at all times.

For the lousy circumstance of his poverty before his death, and sending that miserable writ to his wife, it cannot be but thou liest, learned Gabriel.

I and one of my fellows, Will Monox—hast thou never heard of him and his great dagger?—were in company with him a month before he died at that fatal banquet of Rhenish wine and pickled hearing (if thou wilt needs have it so), and then the inventory of his apparel came to more than three shillings (though thou say'st the contrary). I know a broker in a spruce leather jerkin with a great number of gold rings on his fingers and a bunch of keys at his girdle shall give you thirty shillings for the doublet alone if you can help him to it. Hark in your ear, he had a very fair cloak with sleeves of a grave, goose-turd green; it would serve you as fine as may be. No more words. If you be wise, play the good husband and listen after it; you may buy it ten shillings better cheap than it cost him. . . .

THE ARRAIGNMENT AND EXECUTION OF THE THIRD LETTER . . .

. . . The hexamiter verse I grant to be a gentleman of an ancient house (so is many an English begger), yet this clime of ours he cannot thrive in; our speech is too craggy for him to set his plow in; he goes twitching and hopping in our language like a man running upon quagmires, up the hill in one syllable and down the dale in another, retaining no part of that stately, smooth gait which he vaunts himself with amongst the Greeks and Latins.

Homer and Virgil, two valorous authors, yet were they never knighted; they wrote in hexameter verses; ergo, Chaucer and Spenser, the Homer and Virgil of England, were far overseen that they wrote not all their poems in hexamiter verses also.

In many countries velvet and satten is a commoner wear than cloth amongst us; ergo, we must leave wearing of cloth and go every one in velvet and satten because other countries use so. . . .

Master Stanyhurst (though otherwise learned) trod a foul, lumb'ring, boist'rous, wallowing measure in his translation of Virgil. He had never been prais'd by Gabriel for his labor if therein he had not been so famously absurd.

Greene, for dispraising his practise in that kind, "is the Greene maister of the black art, the founder of ugly oaths, the father of misbegotten Infortunatus, the scrivener of crossbiters, the patriarch of shifters," etc.

"The monarch of crossbiters, the wretched fellow-prince of beggars, emperor of shifters" he had call'd him before, but like a drunken man that remembers not in the morning what he speaks overnight, still he fetcheth metaphors from cony-catchers and doth nothing but torment us with tautologies.

Why, thou arrant butter-whore, thou cotquean and scrattop of scolds, wilt thou never leave afflicting a dead carcass, continually read the rethorick-lecture of Ram Alley? A wisp, a wisp, a wisp, rip, rip, you kitchin-stuff wrangler. . . .

The flours of your Four Letters it may be I have overlook'd more narrowly and done my best devoir to assemble them together into pathetical posy, which I will here present to Maister Orator Edge for a New Year's gift, leaving them to his wordy discretion to be censured whether they be currant in inkhornism or no:

"Conscious mind; canicular tales; egregious an argument (whenas 'egregious' is never used in English but in the extreme ill part); ingenuity; jovial mind; valarous authors; inkhorn adventures; inkhorn pads; putative opinions; putative artists; energetical persuasions; rascality; materiality; artificiality; fantasticality; divine entelechy; loud mentery; deceitful perfidy; addicted to theory; the world's great incendiary; sirenized furies; soveraignty immense; abundant cautels; cautelous and advent'rous; cordial liquor; Catilinaries and Philippics; perfunctory discourses; David's sweetness Olympic; the Idee high and deep abyss of excellence; the only unicorn of the muses; the Aretinish mountain of huge exaggerations; the gratious law of amnesty; amicable terms; amicable end; effectuate; addoulce his melody; Magi; poly-mechany; extensively employ'd; precious trainment; novelets; notoriety; negotiation; mechanician."

Nor are these all, for every third line hath some of this overrack'd absonism. Nor do I altogether scum off all these as the new-ingend'red foam of the English, but allow some of them for a need to fill up a verse—as "trainment," and one or two words more which the liberty of prose might well have spar'd.

In a verse, when a word of three syllables cannot thrust in but sidelings, to joint him even we are oftentimes fain to borrow some lesser quarry of elocution from the Latin, always retaining this for a principle: that a leak of indesinence, as a leak in a ship, must needly be stopp'd with what matter soever.

Chaucer's authority, I am certain, shall be alledg'd against me for a many of these balductums. Had Chaucer liv'd to this age, I am verily persuaded he would have discarded the ton half of the harsher sort of them. They were the oouse which overflowing barbarism, withdrawn to her Scottish northern channel, had left behind her. Art, like young grass in the spring of Chaucer's florishing, was glad to peep up through any slime of corruption, to be beholding to she car'd not whom for apparail, traveling in those cold countries. There is no reason that she, a banish'd queen into this barrain soil, having monarchiz'd it so long amongst the Greeks and Romans, should, although war's fury had humbled her to some extremity, still be constrained, when she hath recover'd her state, to wear the robes of adversity, jet it in her old rags, when she is wedded to new prosperity. *Utere moribus praeteritis,* saith Caius Caesar in Aulus Gellius, *loquere verbis praesentibus.*

Thou art mine enemy, Gabriel, and that which is more, a contemptible underfoot enemy, or else I would teach thy old Trewantship the true use of words, as also how more inclinable verse is than prose to dance after the horrizonant pipe of inveterate antiquity. It is no matter, since thou hast brought godly instruction out of love with thee; use thy own destruction, reign sole emperor of inkhornism! I wish unto thee all superabundant increase of the singular gifts of absurdity and vainglory; from this time forth for ever, ever, ever, evermore may'st thou be canonized as the nonpareil of impious epistlers, the short shredder-out of sandy sentences without lime, as Quintilian termed Seneca all lime and no sand, all matter and no circumstance; the factor for the fairies and night-urchins in supplanting and setting aside the true children of the English, and suborning inkhorn changelings in their stead; the galimafrier of all styles in one standish, as imitating everyone and having no seperate form of writing of thy own; and, to conclude, the only feather-driver of phrases and putter-of-a-good-word-to-it-when-thou-hast-once-got-it that is betwixt this and the Alps. So be it, world without end. Chroniclers, hear my prayers; good Master Stowe, be not unmindful of him. . . .

But something even now, Gabriel, thou wert girding against my "prefaces and rimes, and the tympany of my Tarltonizing wit." Well, these be your words, "prefaces and rimes." Let me study a little—"prefaces and rimes"—*minime vero, si ais nego.* I never printed rime in my life, but those verses in the beginning of *Pierce Penniless,* though you have set forth

> The stories quaint of many a doughty fly,
> That read a lecture to the vent'rous elf.

And so forth, as followeth in chambling row. Prefaces two, or a pair of epistles, I will receive into the protection of my parentage, out of both which, suck out one solecism or misshapen English word if thou canst for thy guts.

Wherein have I borrowed from Greene or Tarlton, that I should thank them for all I have? Is my style like Greene's or my jests like Tarlton's? Do I talk of any counterfeit birds, or herbs, or stones, or rake up any newfound poetry from under the walls of Troy? If I do, trip me with it; but I do not; therefore I'll be so saucy as trip you with the grand lie. Ware stumbling of whetstones in the dark there, my maisters!

This will I proudly boast (yet am I nothing akindred to the three brothers), that the vein which I have, be it a median vein or a madman, is of my own begetting, and calls no man father in England but myself, neither Euphues, nor Tarlton, nor Greene.

Not Tarlton nor Greene but have been contented to let my simple judgment overrule them in some matters of wit. *Euphues* I read when I was a little ape in Cambridge, and then I thought it was *ipse ille;* it may be excellent good still, for ought I know, for I look'd not on it this ten year; but to imitate it I abhor, otherwise than it imitates Plutarch, Ovid, and the choicest Latin authors.

If you be advis'd, I took "shortest vowels and longest mutes" in the beginning of my book, as suspitious of being accessary to the making of a sonnet whereto Maister Christopher Bird's name is set; there I said that you mute forth many such phrases in the course of your book, which I would point at as I pass'd by. Here I am as good as my word, for I note that thou, being afraid of beraying thyself with writing, wouldest fain be a mute, when it is too late to repent. Again thou reviest on us and say'st that mutes are coursed and vowels haunted. Thou art no mute, yet shalt thou be haunted and coursed to the full. I will never leave thee as long as I am able to lift a pen.

Whether I seek to be counted a terrible bull-begger or no, I'll bait thee worse than a bull, so that thou shalt desire somebody on thy knees to help thee with letters of commendation to Bull the hangman, that he may dispatch thee out of the way before more affliction come upon thee. All the invective and satirical spirits shall then be thy familiars, as the furies in hell are the familiars of sinful ghosts, to follow them and torment them without intermission; thou shalt be double-girt with girds, and scoff'd at till those that stand by do nothing but cough with laughing.

Thou sayest I profess the art of railing; thou shalt not say so in vain, for, if there be any art or depth in it more than Aretine or Agrippa have discovered or div'd into, look that I will sound it and search it to the uttermost, but ere I have done with thee I'll leave thee the miserablest creature that the sun ever saw.

There is no kind of peaceable pleasure in poetry, but I can draw equally in the same yoke with the haughtiest of those foul-mouth'd backbiters that say I can do nothing but rail. I have written in all sorts of humors privately, I am persuaded, more than any yoong man of my age in England. . . .

HENRY CHETTLE

FROM KIND-HEART'S DREAM CONTAINING FIVE APPARITIONS WITH THEIR INVECTIVES AGAINST ABUSES REIGNING (1592)

To the Gentlemen Readers

It hath been a custom, gentlemen, in my mind commendable, among former authors (whose works are no less beautified with eloquent phrase than garnished with excellent example) to begin an exordium to the readers of their time. Much more convenient, I take it, should the writers in these days (wherein that gravity of enditing by the elder excercised is not observ'd, nor that modest decorum kept which they continued) submit their labors to the favorable censures of their learned overseers. For, seeing nothing can be said that hath not been before said, the singularity of some men's conceits (otherways excellent well deserving) are no more to be soothed than the peremptory posies of two very sufficient translators commended. To come in print is not to seek praise, but to crave pardon; I am urg'd to the one and bold to beg the other; he that offends, being forc'd, is more excusable than the wilful faulty; though both be guilty, there is difference in the guilt. To observe custom and avoid as I may cavil, opposing your favors against my fear, I'll shew reason for my present writing and after proceed to sue for pardon. About three moneths since died M[aster] Robert Greene, leaving many papers in sundry booksellers' hands, among other his *Groatsworth of Wit,* in which a letter written to divers playmakers is offensively by one or two of them taken; and, because on the dead they cannot be avenged, they wilfully forge in their conceits a living author; and after tossing it to and fro, no remedy but it must light on me. How I have all the time of my conversing in printing hind'red the bitter inveighing against schollers it hath been very well known, and how in that I dealt I can sufficiently prove. With neither of them that take offense was I acquainted, and with one of them [?Marlowe] I care not if I never be. The other [Shakespeare], whom at that time I did not so much

spare as since I wish I had, for that as I have moderated the heat of living writers and might have us'd my own discretion (especially in such a case, the author being dead), that I did not I am as sorry as if the original fault had been my fault, because myself have seen his demeanor no less civil than he exellent in the quality he professes. Besides, divers of worship have reported his uprightness of dealing which argues his honesty, and his facetious grace in writing that approves his art. For the first, whose learning I reverence, and at the perusing of Greene's book stroke out what then in conscience I thought he in some displeasure writ, or, had it been true, yet to publish it was intolerable—him I would wish to use me no worse than I deserve. I had only in the copy this share: it was ill written, as sometime Greene's hand was none of the best; licens'd it must be ere it could be printed, which could never be if it might not be read. To be brief, I writ it over, and, as near as I could, followed the copy; only in that letter I put something out, but in the whole book not a word in, for I protest it was all Greene's, not mine nor Maister Nashe's, as some unjustly have affirmed. Neither was he the writer of an epistle to the second part of *Gerileon,* though by the workman's error "T. N." were set to the end. That I confess to be mine, and repent it not.

Thus, gentlemen, having noted the private causes that made me nominate myself in print, being as well to purge Master Nashe of that he did not as to justify what I did, and withal to confirm what M[aster] Greene did, I beseech ye accept the public cause, which is both the desire of your delight and common benefit. For though the toy be shadowed under the title of *Kind-Heart's Dream* it discovers the false hearts of divers that wake to commit mischief. Had not the former reasons been, it had come forth without a father, and then should I have had no cause to fear offending or reason to sue for favor. Now am I in doubt of the one, though I hope of the other, which if I obtain, you shall bind me hereafter to be silent till I can present ye with something more acceptable.

Henry Chettle

Kind-Heart's Dedication of His Dream to All the Pleasant Conceited Wheresoever

Gentlemen and good fellows (whose kindness, having christened me with the name of Kind-Heart, binds me in all kind course I can to deserve the continuance of your love), let it not seem strange, I beseech ye, that he that all days of his life hath been famous for drawing teeth should now, in drooping age, hazard contemptible infamy by drawing himself into print. For such is the folly of this age, so witless, so audacious, that there are scarce so many peddlers brag themselves to be printers because they have a bundle of ballads in their pack as there be idiots that think themselves artists because they can English an obligation or write a true staff to the tune of "Fortune." This folly, raging universally, hath infired me to write the remembrance of sundry of my deceased friends, personages not altogether obscure, for then were my subject base, nor yet of any honorable carriage, for my style is rude and bad; and to such as I it belongs not to jest with gods. Kind-Heart would have his companions esteem of estates as stars on whom mean men may look but not overlook. I have heard of an eloquent orator that, trimly furnished with war's abiliments, had on his shield this motto, *Bona fortuna;* yet at the first meeting of the enemy fled without fight. For which being reproved he replied, "If I have saved myself in this battle by flight, I shall live to chase the enemy in the next." So, gentlemen, fares it with me if envious misconsterers arm themselves against my simple meaning and wrest every jest to a wrong sense. I think it policy to fly at the first fight till I gather fresh forces to repress their folly. Neither can they, whatever they be, deal hardly with Kind-Heart, for he only delivers his dream with every apparition simply as it was uttered. It's fond for them to fight against ghosts; it's fearful for me to hide an apparition; by concealing it I might do myself harm and them no good; by revealing it, ease my heart and do no honest men hurt. For the rest, although I would not willingly move the meanest, they must bear as I do or mend it as they may. Well, lest ye deem all my dream but an epistle I will proceed to that without any further circumstance.

THE DREAM

Sitting alone not long since, not far from Finsbury, in a taphouse of antiquity, attending the coming of such companions as might wash care away with carowsing, Sleep, the attendant upon distemp'red bodies, bereft the sun's light by covering mine eyes with her sable mantle and left me in night's shade though the day's eye shin'd. So powerful was my received potion, so heavy my passion, whence (by my hostess' care) being removed to a pleasant parlor, the windows opening to the east, I was laid softly on a down bed and covered with equal furniture, where how long I slept quietly I am not well assured, but in the time I intended to rest I was thus by visible apparitions disturb'd.

First, after a harsh and confused sound, it seemed there entered at once five personages severally attired and diversly qualified; three bearing instruments, their favors pleasant; two appearing to be artists, their countenances reverend.

The first of the first three was an odd old fellow, low of stature; his head was covered with a round cap, his body with a side-skirted tawny coat, his legs and feet truss'd up in leather buskins; his gray hairs and furrowed face witnessed his age; his treble viol in his hand assured me of his profession. On which (by his continual sawing, having left but one string) after his best manner he gave me a hunt's-up. Whom, after a little musing, I assuredly rememb'red to be no other but old Anthony Now-Now.

The next, by his suit of russet, his button'd cap, his tabor, his standing on the toe, and other tricks, I knew to be either the body or resemblance of Tarlton, who, living, for his pleasant conceits was of all men liked, and, dying, for mirth left not his like.

The third, as the first, was an old fellow, his beard milk-white, his head covered with a round, low-crown'd rent silk hat on which was a band knit in many knots wherein stuck two round sticks after the juggler's manner. His jerkin was of leather cut, his cloak of three colors, his hose pan'd with yellow drawn out with blue, his instrument was a bagpipe, and him I knew to be William Cuckoo, better known than lov'd, and yet some think as well lov'd as he was worthy.

The other two had in their countenances a reverent grace; the one which was the elder, seeming more severe, was in habit like a doctor. In his right hand he held a compendium of all the famous physicians' and surgeons' works belonging to theoric, in his left hand a table of all instruments for man's health appertaining to practise.

At the sight of this doctor you may think, gentlemen, Kind-Heart was in a piteous case; for I verily believed he had been some rare artist that, taking me for a dead man, had come to anatomize me, but taking comfort that my thrumm'd hat had hanging at it the ensigns of my occupation, like a tall fellow (as to me it seemed) I look'd him in the face and beheld him to be Maister Doctor Burcot, though a stranger, yet in England for physic famous.

With him was the fifth, a man of indifferent years, of face amiable, of body well-proportioned, his attire after the habit of a scholler-like gentleman (only his hair was somewhat long), whom I supposed to be Robert Greene, Maister of Arts, of whom, however some suppose themselves injured, I have learned to speak, considering he is dead, *nil nisi necessarium*. He was of singular pleasance the very supporter and—to no man's disgrace be this intended—the only comedian of a vulgar writer in this country.

Well, thus these five appeared, and by them in post pass'd a knight of the post, whom in times past I have seen as highly promoted as the pillory; but I have heard since he was a divel that play'd the carrier of [Nashe's] Pierce Penniless' packet to Lucifer and was now returning to contaminate the air with his pestilent perjuries and abhominable false-witness-bearing.

How Pierce his supplication pleased his patron I know not, but sure I take it this friend had a foul check for meddling in the matter; for when all these five before-named had made proffer of several bills invective against abuses reigning, this divelish messenger repulsed them wrathfully and bad them get some other to be their packet-bearer if they list, for he had almost hazarded his credit in hell by being a broker between Pierce Penniless and his lord; and so, without hearing their reply, flew from them like a whirlwind. With that, after a small pause, in a round ring they compassed my bed, and, thrusting into my hand all their papers, they at once charged me to awake and publish them to the world.

This charge seemed to me most dreadful of all the dream because in that the distinguishing of their several voices was heard far from the frequent manner of men's speech. In fine, Cuckoo with his pipes and Antony with his crowd, keeping equal equipage, first left my sight; Tarlton with his tabor, fetching two or three leaden frisks, shortly followed; and the doctor and Maister Greene immediately vanished.

With this not a little amazed, as one from a trance revived I rous'd up myself, when sodainly out of my hand fell the five papers, which confirmed my dream to be no fantasy. Yet (for that I knew the times are dangerous) I thought good advisedly to read them before I presumed to make them public. . . . [There follow the five epistles of the five "apparitions," the third being Greene's.]

Robert Greene to Pierce Penniless

Pierce, if thy carrier had been as kind to me as I expected I could have dispatched long since my letters to thee, but it is here as in the world, *donum a dando derivatur,* where there is nothing to give, there is nothing to be got. But having now found means to send to thee, I will certify thee a little of my disquiet after death, of which I think thou either hast not heard or wilt not conceive.

Having with humble penitence besought pardon for my infinite sins and paid the due to death, even in my grave was I scarce laid when Envy (no fit companion for Art) spit out her poison to disturb my rest. *Adversus mortuos bellum suscipere, inhumanum est.* There is no glory gained by breaking a dead man's skull. *Pascitur in vivis livor, post fata quiescit.* Yet it appears contrary in some that, inveighing against my works, my poverty, my life, my death, my burial, have omitted nothing that may seem malicious. For my books, of what kind soever, I refer their commendation or dispraise to those that have read them. Only for my last labors affirming, my intent was to reprove vice and lay open such villanies as had been very necessary to be made known, whereof my *Black Book,* if ever it see light, can sufficiently witness.

But for my poverty, methinks wisdom would have brideled that invective, for *cuius potest accidere, quod cuiquam potest.* The beginning of my dispraisers is known; of their end they are not sure. For my life, it was to none of them at any time hurtful; for my death, it was repentant, my burial like a Christian's.

> Alas, that men so hastily should run
> To write their own dispraise as they have done.

For my revenge, it suffices that every half-ey'd humanitian may account it *instar belluarum immanissimarum saevire in cadaver.* For the injury off'red thee, I know I need not bring oil to thy fire. And albeit I would dissuade thee from more invectives against such thy adversaries (for peace is now all my plea), yet I know thou wilt return answer that since thou receivedst the first wrong, thou wilt not endure the last.

My quiet ghost, unquietly disturbed, had once intended thus to have exclaim'd:

"Pierce, more witless than penniless, more idle than thine adversaries ill-imploy'd, what foolish innocence hath made thee (infant-like) resistless to bear whatever injury Envy can impose?

"Once thou commendedst immediate conceit and gavest no great praise to excellent works of twelve years' labor; now, in the blooming of thy hopes, thou sufferest slander to nip them ere they can bud, thereby approving thyself to be of all other most slack, being in thine own cause so remiss.

"Color can there be none found to shadow thy fainting, but the longer thou defer'st, the more grief thou bring'st to thy friends, and givest the greater head to thy enemies,

"What canst thou tell if, as myself, thou shalt be with death prevented? And then how can it be but thou diest disgrac'd, seeing thou hast made no reply to their twofold edition of invectives?

"It may be thou think'st they will deal well with thee in death, and so thy shame in tolerating them will be short; forge not to thyself one such conceit, but make me thy president and remember this old adage: *Leonem mortuum mordent catuli.*

"Awake, secure boy, revenge thy wrongs, remember mine. Thy adversaries began the abuse; they continue it; if thou suffer it, let thy life be short in silence and obscurity, and thy death hasty, hated, and miserable."

All this had I intended to write, but now I will not give way to wrath, but return it unto the earth from whence I took it, for with happy souls it hath no harbor.

Robert Greene

THOMAS NASHE

PIERCE PENNILESS and CHRIST'S TEARS OVER JERUSALEM

Although Nashe's prose is often hasty and slovenly, it is rarely dull, and from the very beginning of his short career he exhibits the verve, intellectual vigor (if not profundity), and verbal audacity that are so fully exemplified in *Pierce Penniless His Supplication to the Devil.* That work, his first major success, is a satire of contemporary foibles and vices articulated by the thinnest of narrative devices. In the proem the author, disgusted at the poor reception accorded men of training and talent, resolves to petition the Devil for aid, and, after considerable jockeying about, he finds a knight of the post to deliver his supplication for money and fame to the Prince of Darkness. Thereafter the work turns into an immensely zestful survey of contemporary abuses—but abuses fleshed out and made dramatically urgent as various personified sins. Nashe pours his wrath or contempt on Avarice, Pride, the pedantry of antiquaries, Richard Harvey's *Lamb of God* (see p. 859), Gluttony, puritan antagonists of popular drama, and other objectionable things; then follow a quasi-serious discussion of hell and devils, a presumably allegorical beast-fable, a closing address to the reader, and a eulogistic epilogue about a certain Amyntas who is perhaps Ferdinando Stanley, Earl of Derby. Entered in the Stationers' Register on August 8, 1592, *Pierce Penniless* was probably published early in September—or at any rate in time for Gabriel Harvey to acknowledge the attack on his brother Richard by denouncing Nashe in the third of his *Four Letters* (dated September 8–9, 1592). Nashe's sprawling pamphlet was such an immediate success that three more editions were required before the following spring, and a fourth in 1595. Our text is based upon *Pierce Penilesse his Supplication to the Divell,* 1592 (STC 18371).

Christ's Tears over Jerusalem (1593) must have been something of a surprise to both Nashe and his readers, so different is it from the savage satire and wry humor of his earlier and later work. The unexpected peace offer to

Gabriel Harvey in the preface—an offer quickly and characteristically rescinded in the second (1594) issue—may indicate that Nashe, the *enfant terrible* of the university wits, had at least temporarily assumed the Christian virtues of charity and humility; and the work itself seems to derive from a genuine sense of public and private sin. However, it is much more plausible to regard *Christ's Tears* as a skilful occasional piece than as an honest *mea culpa.* The occasion was the plague that in 1592–93 had desolated London, closed the theaters, and sent the well-to-do scurrying to safety in the country; Nashe rises to the occasion with his customary skill and vigor. The long first section (omitted in our excerpts) is a deft reworking of Peter Morvyn's translation (1558) of Joseph Ben Gorion's *History of the Latter Times of the Jews' Commonweal,* a ninth- or tenth-century account of the Jews' offenses against God and their subsequent afflictions climaxed by the destruction of Jerusalem. The second part, on the sins of London, affords Nashe a splendid opportunity for the kind of acidulous social commentary in which he excelled; he underscores the obvious inference that as God dealt with the Jews so He may deal with the unrepentant English. In this part, as in *Pierce Penniless,* Nashe employs the ancient device of personified sins, and his vivid account of London's iniquities is built around a procession of the "sons" (Ambition, Atheism, Vainglory, *et al.*) and "daughters" (Disdain, Gorgeous Attire, and Delicacy) of Pride. A prayer against the plague provides an appropriate coda. Entered in the Stationers' Register on September 8, 1593, the work was probably published immediately, for Harvey's *New Letter* (entered on September 16) contains several references to it. Our text is based upon *Christs Teares Over Jerusalem. Wherunto is annexed, a comparative admonition to London,* 1593 (STC 18366) in *The Works of Thomas Nashe,* ed. Ronald B. McKerrow, volume II.

FROM PIERCE PENNILESS HIS SUPPLICATION TO THE DEVIL (1592)

Having spent many years in studying how to live (and liv'd a long time without money), having tired my youth with folly and surfetted my mind with vanity, I began at length to look back to repentance and address my endeavors to prosperity; but all in vain I sate up late and rose early, contended with the cold and conversed with scarcity; for all my labors turned to loss, my vulgar muse was despised and neglected, my pains not regarded or slightly rewarded, and I myself (in prime of my best wit) laid open to poverty. Whereupon, in a malecontent humor, I accused my fortune, rail'd on my patrons, bit my pen, rent my papers, and rag'd in all points like a mad man. In which agony tormenting myself a long time, I grew by degrees to a milder discontent; and, pausing a while over my standish, I resolved in verse to paint forth my passion, which, best agreeing with the vein of my unrest, I began to complain in this sort:

Why is't damnation to dispair and die
When life is my true happiness' disease?
My soul, my soul, thy safety makes me fly
The faulty means that might my pain appease.
　　Divines and dying men may talk of hell,
　　But in my heart her several torments dwell. . . .

Without redress complains my careless verse,
And Midas-ears relent not at my moan;
In some far land will I my griefs rehearse
Mongst them that will be mov'd when I shall groan.
　　England, adieu, the soil that brought me forth,
　　Adieu, unkind, where skill is nothing worth.

These rimes thus abruptly set down, I toss'd my imaginations a thousand ways to see if I could find any means to relieve my estate; but all my thoughts consorted to this conclusion: that the world was uncharitable, and I ordain'd to be miserable. Thereby I grew to consider how many base men, that wanted those parts which I had, enjoyed content at will and had wealth at command. I call'd to mind a cobbler that was worth five hundred pound, an hostler that had built a goodly inn and might dispend forty pound yearly by his land, a carman in a leather pilch that had whipp'd out a thousand pound out of his horse' tail. And have I more wit than all these? thought I to myself. Am I better born? Am I better brought up? Yea, and better favored? And yet am I a begger? What is the cause? How am I cross'd? Or whence is this curse? . . .

Gentle Sir Philip Sidney, thou knew'st what belong'd to a scholler; thou knew'st what pains, what toil, what travail conduct to perfection. Well couldst thou give every virtue his encouragement, every art his due, every writer his desert—cause none more virtuous, witty, or learned than thyself.

But thou art dead in thy grave and hast left too few successors of thy glory, too few to cherish the sons of the muses, or water those budding hopes with their plenty which thy bounty erst planted.

Believe me, gentlemen, for some cross mishaps have taught me experience. There is not that strict observation of honor which hath been heretofore. Men of great calling take it of merit to have their names eterniz'd by poets, and whatsoever pamphlet or dedication encounters them, they put it up in their sleeves and scarce give him thanks that presents it. . . .

For whereas those that stand most on their honor have shut up their purses and shift us off with court holy-bread, and, on the other side, a number of hypocritical hotspurs, that have God always in their mouths, will give nothing for God's sake, I have clapp'd up a handsome supplication to the Divel and sent it by a good fellow that I know will deliver it.

And because you may believe me the better, I care not if I acquaint you with the circumstance.

I was inform'd of late days that a certain blind retailer called the Divel used to lend money upon pawns or anything, and would let one for a need have a thousand pounds upon a statute-merchant of his soul; or, if a man ply'd him thoroughly, would trust him upon a bill of his hand without any more circumstance. . . .

These manifest conjectures of plenty assembled in one common place of ability, I determined to claw Avarice by the elbow till his full belly gave me a full hand, and let him blood with my pen (if it might be) in the vein of liberality; and so, in short time, was this paper monster, *Pierce Penniless,* begotten.

But written and all, here lies the question: where shall I find this old ass, that I may deliver it? . . .

[Having unsuccessfully searched for the Devil in Westminster Hall, Nashe, hungry and despondent, went to St. Paul's.] Two hungry turns had I scarce fetch'd in this waste gallery when I was encount'red by a neat, pedantical fellow in form of a citizen, who, thrusting himself abruptly into my company like an intelligencer, began very earnestly to question with me about the cause of my discontent, or what made me so sad, that seemed too young to be acquainted with sorrow. I, nothing nice to unfold my estate to any whatsoever, discours'd to him the whole circumstance of my care, and what toil and pains I had took in searching for him that would not be heard of. "Why, sir," quoth he, "had I been privy to your purpose before, I could have eas'd you of this travail, for if it be the Divel you seek for, know

I am his man." "I pray, sir, how might I call you?" "A knight of the post," quoth he, "for so I am termed; a fellow that will swear you anything for twelvepence, but, indeed, I am a spirit in nature and essence that take upon me this humain shape only to set men together by the ears and send souls by millions to hell."

"Now trust me, a substantial trade. But when do you think you could send next to your maister?" "Why, every day, for there is not a cormorant that dies, or cutpurse that is hanged, but I dispatch letters by his soul to him and to all my friends in the low countries; wherefore, if you have anything that you would have transported, give it me, and I will see it delivered."

"Yes, marry, have I," quoth I, "a certain supplication here unto your maister, which you may peruse if it please you." With that he opened it and read as followeth:

To the High and Mighty Prince of Darkness, Donsell dell Lucifer, King of Acheron, Styx, and Phlegeton, Duke of Tartary, Marquess of Cocytus, and Lord High Regent of Limbo, his distressed orator, Pierce Penniless, wisheth encrease of damnation and malediction eternal, *per Iesum Christum Dominum nostrum.* . . .

[Nashe then proceeds, in his supplication, to invoke, with copious descriptions and examples, the Seven Deadly Sins that attend the Devil; thus Envy appears, following Pride:] Out upon it, how long is Pride a-dressing herself! Envy, awake, for thou must appear before Nicalao Malevolo, great muster-maister of hell. Mark you this sly mate, how smoothly he looks. The poets were ill-advised that feigned him to be a lean, gag-tooth'd beldam with hollow eyes, pale cheeks, and snaky hair; for he is not only a man, but a jolly, lusty old gentleman that will wink, and laugh, and jest drily as if he were the honestest of a thousand; and I warrant you shall not hear a foul word come from him in a year. I will not contradict it, but the dog may worry a sheep in the dark and thrust his neck into the collar of clemency and pity when he hath done; as who should say, "God forgive him! He was asleep in the shambles when the innocent was done to death." But openly, Envy sets a civil, fatherly countenance upon it, and hath not so much as a drop of blood in his face to attaint him of murther. I thought it expedient, in this my supplication, to place it next to Pride, for it is his adopted son. And hence comes it that proud men repine at others' prosperity, and grieve that any should be great but themselves. *Mens cuiusque, is est quisque;* it is a proverb that is as hoary as Dutch butter. If a man will go to the Divel, he may go to the Divel; there

are a thousand juggling tricks to be used at "Hey pass, come aloft," and the world hath cords enough to truss up a calf that stands in one's way. Envy is a crocodile that weeps when he kills, and fights with none but he feeds on. This is the nature of this quick-sighted monster: he will endure any pains to endamage another, waste his body with undertaking exploits that would require ten men's strengths rather than any should get a penny but himself, blear his eyes to stand in his neighbor's light, and (to conclude) like Atlas underprop heaven alone rather than any should be in heaven that he lik'd not of, or come unto heaven by any other means but by him.

You goodman wand'rer about the world, how do ye spend your time that you do not rid us of these pestilent members? You are unworthy to have an office if you can execute it no better. Behold another enemy of mankind besides thyself, exalted in the south, Philip [II] of Spain: who [is] not content to be the god of gold and chiefest commander of content that Europe affords, but now he doth nothing but thirst after human blood when his foot is on the threshold of the grave; and as a wolf, being about to devour a horse, doth balist his belly with earth that he may hang the heavier upon him, and then forcibly flies in his face, never leaving his hold till he hath eaten him up, so this wolvish, unnatural usurper, being about to devour all Christendom by invasion, doth cram his treasures with Indian earth to make his malice more forcible, and then flies in the bosom of France and Belgia, never withdrawing his forces (as the wolf his fast'ning) till he hath devoured their welfare and made the war-wasted carcasses of both kingdoms a prey for his tyranny. Only poor England gives him bread for his cake, and holds him out at the arms' end. His armados (that, like a high wood, overshadowed the shrubs of our low ships) fled from the breath of our cannons as vapors before the sun, or as the elephant flies from the ram, or the sea-whale from the noise of parched bones. The winds, envying that the air should be dimmed with such a chaos of wooden clouds, raised up high bulwarks of bellowing waves whence death shot at their disord'red navy; and the rocks with their overhanging jaws eat up all the fragments of oak that they left. So perish'd our foes; so the heavens did fight for us. *Praeterit Hippomenes, resonant spectacula plausu.*

I do not doubt, Doctor Divel, but you were present in this action, or passion rather, and help'd to bore holes in ships to make them sink faster, and rence out galley-foists with salt water, that stunk like fusty barrels with their maisters' fear. It will be a good while ere you do as much for the king as you did for his subjects. I would have ye persuade an army of gouty usurers to go to sea upon a boon voyage; try if you can tempt Envy to embark himself in the maladventure and leave troubling the stream, that poets and good fellows may drink and soldiers may sing *placebo* that have murmured so long at the waters of strife.

But that will never be; for so long as Pride, Riot, and Whoredom are the companions of young courtiers they will always be hungry, and ready to bite at every dog that hath a bone given him beside themselves. Jesu, what secret grudge and rancor reigns amongst them, one being ready to dispair of himself if he see the prince but give his fellow a fair look, or to die for grief if he be put down in bravery never so little. Yet this custom have our false hearts fetch'd from other countries, that they will swear and protest love where they hate deadly, and smile on him most kindly whose subversion in soul they have vowed. *Fraus sublimi regnat in aula.* 'Tis rare to find a true friend in kings' palaces. Either thou must be so miserable that thou fall into the hands of scornful pity, or thou canst not escape the sting of Envy. In one thought assemble the famous men of all ages, and tell me which of them all sate in the sunshine of his sovereign's grace, or wex'd great of low beginnings, but he was spite-blasted, heaved at, and ill spoken of—and that of those that bare them most countenance. But were Envy nought but words it might seem to be only women's sin; but it hath a lewd mate hanging on his sleeve called Murther, a stern fellow that, like a Spaniard in fight, aimeth all at the heart; he hath more shapes than Proteus, and will shift himself upon any occasion of revengement into a man's dish, his drink, his apparel, his rings, his stirrups, his nosegay.

O Italy, the academy of manslaughter, the sporting-place of murther, the apothecary shop of poison for all nations! How many kind of weapons hast thou invented for malice? Suppose I love a man's wife whose husband yet lives, and cannot enjoy her for his jealous overlooking; physic, or rather the art of murther (as it may be used), will lend one a medicine which shall make him away in the nature of that disease he is most subject to, whether in the space of a year, a month, half a year, or what tract of time you will, more or less.

In Rome the papal chair is wash'd every five year at the furthest with this oil of aconitum. I pray God the king of Spain feasted not our Holy Father Sextus [V] that was last with such conserve of henbane, for it was credibly reported he loved him not, and this [Clement VIII] that is now is a God made with his own hands, as it may appear by the pasquil that was set up of him, in manner of a note, presently after his election: *Sol, Re, Me, Fa,* that is to say, *Solus rex me facit* ("only the king of Spain made me pope"). I

am no chronicler from our own country, but if probable suspicion might be heard upon his oath, I think some men's souls would be canonized for martyrs that on the earth did sway it as monarchs.

Is it your will and pleasure, noble lantsgrave of Limbo, to let us have less carousing to your health in poison, fewer underhand conspirings, or open quarrels executed only in words, as they are in the world nowadays; and if men will needs carouse, conspire, and quarrel, that they may make Ruffians Hall of hell, and there bandy balls of brimstone at one another's head and not trouble our peaceable paradise with their private hurlyburlies about strumpets, where no weapon, as in Adam's paradise, should be named, but only the angel of providence stand with a fiery sword at the gate to keep out our enemies?

A perturbation of mind like unto Envy is Wrath, which looketh far lower than the former; for, whereas Envy cannot be said to be but in respect of our superiors, Wrath respecteth no degrees nor persons, but is equally armed against all that offend him. A harebrain'd little dwarf it is with a swarth visage, that hath his heart at his tongue's end if he be contrari'd, and will be sure to do no right nor take no wrong. If he be a judge or a justice (as sometimes the lion comes to give sentence against the lamb), then he swears by nothing but by Saint Tyburn, and makes Newgate a noun substantive whereto all his other words are but adjectives. Lightly, he is an old man (for those years are most wayward and teatish), yet be he never so old or so froward, since Avarice likewise is a fellow-vice of those frail years, we must set one extreme to strive with another and allay the anger of oppression by the sweet incense of a new purse of angels; or the doting planet may have such predominance in these wicked elders of Israel that, if you send your wife or some other female to plead for you, she may get your pardon upon promise of better acquaintance. But whist! These are the works of darkness, and may not be talk'd of in the daytime. Fury is a heat or fire, and must be quench'd with maids' water. . . .

I heard a tale of a butcher who, driving two calves over a common that were coupled together by the necks with an oaken with, in the way where they should pass there lay a poor, lean mare with a gall'd back; to whom they coming (as chance fell out), one of one side and the other of the other, smelling on her as their manner is, the midst of the with that was betwixt their necks rubb'd her and grated her on the sore back, that she started and rose up, and hung them both on her back as a beam; which being but a rough plaister to her raw ulcer, she ran away with them (as she were frantic) into the fens, where the butcher could not follow them, and drown'd both herself and them in a quagmire. Now the owner of the mare is in law with the butcher for the loss of his mare, and the butcher enterchangeably endites him for his calves. I pray ye, Timothy Tempter, be an arbitrator betwixt them, and couple them both by the necks as the calves were, and carry them to hell on your back; and then, I hope, they will be quiet. . . .

With the enemies of poetry I care not if I have a bout, and those are they that term our best writers but babbling ballad-makers, holding them fantastical fools that have wit but cannot tell how to use it. I myself have been so censured among some dull-headed divines, who deem it no more cunning to write an exquisite poem than to preach pure Calvin or distil the juice of a commentary in a quarter-sermon. Prove it when you will, you slow-spirited Saturnists, that have nothing but the pilfries of your pen to polish an exhortation withal; no eloquence but tautologies to tie the ears of your auditory unto you; no invention but "here is to be noted, I stole this note out of Beza or Marlorat"; no wit to move, no passion to urge, but only an ordinary form of preaching, blown up by use of often hearing and speaking; and you shall find there goes more exquisite pains and purity of wit to the writing of one such rare poem as Rosamond than to a hundred of your dunstical sermons.

Should we (as you) borrow all out of others, and gather nothing of ourselves, our names should be bafful'd on every bookseller's stall, and not a chandler's mustard-pot but would wipe his mouth with our waste paper. "New herrings, new!" we must cry, every time we make ourselves publique, or else we shall be christened with a hundred new titles of idiotism. Nor is poetry an art whereof there is no use in a man's whole life but to describe discontented thoughts and youthful desires; for there is no study but it doth illustrate and beautify. How admirably shine those divines above the common mediocrity that have tasted the sweet springs of Pernassus!

Silver-tongu'd [Henry] Smith, whose well-tun'd style hath made thy death the general tears of the muses, quaintly couldst thou devise heavenly ditties to Apollo's lute, and teach stately verse to trip it as smoothly as if Ovid and thou had but one soul. Hence alone did it proceed that thou wert such a plausible pulpit man, that before thou ent'redst into the rough ways of theology thou refinedst, preparedst, and purifiedest thy mind with sweet poetry. If a simple man's censure may be admitted to speak in such an open theater of opinions, I never saw abundant reading better mix'd with delight, or sentences which no man can challenge of prophane affectation sounding more melodious to the ear or piercing more deep to the heart.

To them that demand what fruits the poets of our time bring forth, or wherein they are able to prove themselves necessary to the state, thus I answer: first and foremost, they have cleansed our language from barbarism and made the vulgar sort here in London (which is the fountain whose rivers flow round about England) to aspire to a richer purity of speech than is communicated with the comminalty of any nation under heaven. The virtuous by their praises they encourage to be more virtuous; to vicious men they are as infernal hags to haunt their ghosts with eternal infamy after death. The soldier, in hope to have his high deeds celebrated by their pens, despiseth a whole army of perils, and acteth wonders exceeding all human conjecture. Those that care neither for God nor the Devil, by their quills are kept in awe. *Multi famam,* saith one, *pauci conscientiam verentur.*

Let God see what he will, they would be loath to have the shame of the world. What age will not praise immortal Sir Philip Sidney, whom noble Salustius (that thrice singular French poet) hath famoused; together with Sir Nicholas Bacon, lord keeper, and merry Sir Thomas More, for the chief pillars of our English speech. Not so much but Chaucer's host, [Harry] Bailly in Southwark, and his wife of Bath he keeps such a stir with, in his *Canterbury Tales,* shall be talk'd of whilst the Bath is us'd or there be ever a bad house in Southwark. Gentles, it is not your lay chronographers, that write of nothing but of mayors and sheriffs and the dear year and the great frost, that can endow your names with never-dated glory; for they want the wings of choice words to fly to heaven, which we have; they cannot sweeten a discourse, or wrest admiration from men reading, as we can, reporting the meanest accident. Poetry is the honey of all flowers, the quintessence of all sciences, the marrow of wit, and the very phrase of angels. How much better is it, then, to have an elegant lawyer to plead one's cause than a stutting townsman that loseth himself in his tale and doth nothing but make legs; so much it is better for a nobleman or gentleman to have his honor's story related, and his deeds emblazon'd, by a poet than a citizen.

Alas, poor Latinless authors, they are so simple they know not what they do; they no sooner spy a new ballad, and his name to it that compil'd it, but they put him in for one of the learned men of our time. I marvel how the masterless men, that set up their bills in Paul's for services, and such as paste up their papers on every post, for arithmetique and writing schools, scape eternity amongst them. I believe both they and the knight marshal's men, that nail up mandates at the court gate for annoying the palace with filth or making water, if they set their names to the writing, will shortly make up the number of the learned men of our time, and be as famous as the rest. For my part, I do challenge no praise of learning to myself, yet have I worn a gown in the University, and so hath *caret tempus non habet moribus;* but this I dare presume, that if any Maecenas bind me to him by his bounty or extend some round liberality to me worth the speaking of, I will do him as much honor as any poet of my beardless years shall in England. Not that I am so confident what I can do, but that I attribute so much to my thankful mind above others, which I am persuaded would enable me to work miracles.

On the contrary side, if I be evil intreated, or sent away with a flea in mine ear, let him look that I will rail on him soundly; not for an hour or a day, whiles the injury is fresh in my memory, but in some elaborate polished poem, which I will leave to the world when I am dead, to be a living image to all ages of his beggerly parsimony and ignoble illiberality; and let him not (whatsoever he be) measure the weight of my words by this book, where I write *quicquid in buccam venerit,* as fast as my hand can trot; but I have terms (if I be vex'd) laid in steep in aqua fortis and gunpowder that shall rattle through the skies and make an earthquake in a peasant's ears. Put case (since I am not yet out of the theme of wrath) that some tired jade [i.e. Richard Harvey in *The Lamb of God*] belonging to the press, whom I never wronged in my life, hath named me expressly in print (as I will not do him) and accused me of want of learning, upbraiding me for reviving in an epistle of mine the reverent memory of Sir Thomas More, Sir John Cheke, Doctor Watson, Doctor Haddon, Doctor Carr, Maister Ascham, as if they were no meat but for his Maistership's mouth, or none but some such as the son of a rope-maker were worthy to mention them. To shew how I can rail, thus would I begin to rail on him, "Thou that hadst thy hood turn'd over thy ears when thou wert a bachelor, for abusing of Aristotle and setting him upon the school gates painted with ass's ears on his head, is it any discredit for me, thou great babound, thou pigmy braggart, thou pamphleter of nothing but paeans, to be censured by thee, that hast scorned the prince of philosophers? Thou that in thy dialogues sold'st honey for a halpenny, and the choicest writers extant for cues apiece, that camest to the logic schools when thou wert a freshman and writ'st phrases, off with thy gown and untruss, for I mean to lash thee mightily. Thou hast a brother [i.e. John Harvey, the writer of almanacs], hast thou not, student in almanacs (go to, I'll stand to it), he father'd one of thy bastards (a book, I mean) which being of thy begetting was set forth under his name?" . . .

The nurse of this enormity [Drunkenness] . . . is Idleness or Sloth, which, having no painful providence to set himself awork, runs headlong, with the reins in his own hand, into all lasciviousness and sensuality that may be. Men, when they are idle and know not what to do, saith one, "Let us go to the Stilyard and drink Rhenish wine." "Nay, if a man knew where a good whorehouse were," saith another, "it were somewhat like." "Nay," saith the third, "let us go to a dicing house or a bowling alley, and there we shall have some sport for our money." To one of these three—"At hand," quoth Pick-Purse—your Evil Angelship, Maister Many-Headed Beast, conducts them, *ubi quid agitur* betwixt you and their souls be it, for I am no drawer, box-keeper, or pander to be privy to their sports. If I were to paint Sloth (as I am not seen in the sweetening), by Saint John the Evangelist I swear I would draw it like a stationer that I know, with his thumb under his girdle, who, if a man come to his stall and ask him for a book, never stirs his head or looks upon him, but stands stone still and speaks not a word, only with his little finger points backwards to his boy, who must be his interpreter; and so all the day, gaping like a dumb image, he sits without motion, except at such times as he goes to dinner or supper, for then he is as quick as other three, eating six times every day. If I would range abroad and look in at sluggards' keyholes, I should find a number lying abed to save charges of ordinaries, and in winter, when they want firing, losing half a week's commons together to keep them warm in the linen. And hold you content, this summer an undermeal of an afternoon long doth not amiss to exercise the eyes withal. Fat men and farmers' sons, that sweat much with eating hard cheese and drinking old wine, must have some more ease than young boys that take their pleasure all day running up and down.

Setting jesting aside, I hold it a great disputable question which is a more evil man, of him that is an idle glutton at home or a retchless unthrift abroad. The glutton at home doth nothing but engender diseases, pamper his flesh unto lust, and is good for none but his own gut; the unthrift abroad exerciseth his body at dancing school, fence school, tennis, and all such recreations; the vintners, the victualers, the dicing houses, and who not get by him. Suppose he lose a little now and then at play; it teacheth him wit. And how should a man know to eschew vices, if his own experience did not acquaint him with their inconveniences? *Omne ignotum pro magnifico est:* "that villainy we have made no assays in, we admire." Besides, my vagrant reveler haunts plays and sharpens his wits with frequenting the company of poets; he emboldens his blushing face by courting fair women on the sodain, and looks into all estates by conversing with them in public places. Now tell me whether of these two, the heavy-headed gluttonous house-dove, or this lively wanton young gallant, is like to prove the wiser man and better member in the commonwealth. If my youth might not be thought partial, the fine qualified gentleman, although unstay'd, should carry it clean away from the lazy clownish drone.

Sloth in nobility, courtiers, schollers, or any men is the chiefest cause that brings them in contempt. For as industry and unfatigable toil raiseth mean persons from obscure houses to high thrones of authority, so sloth and sluggish security causeth proud lords to tumble from the towers of their starry discents and be trod underfoot of every inferior besonian. Is it the lofty treading of a galliard or fine grace in telling of a love tale amongst ladies can make a man reverenc'd of the multitude? No; they care not for the false glistering of gay garments or insinuating courtesy of a carpet peer; but they delight to see him shine in armor and oppose himself to honorable danger, to participate a voluntary penury with his soldiers and relieve part of their wants out of his own purse. That is the course he that will be popular must take, which if he neglect and sit dallying at home, nor will be awak'd by any indignities out of his love dream, but suffer every upstart groom to defy him, set him at naught and shake him by the beard unreveng'd, let him straight take orders and be a churchman, and then his patience may pass for a virtue; but otherwise he shall be suspected of cowardice and not car'd for of any. The only enemy to Sloth is contention and emulation, as to propose one man to myself that is the only mirror of our age and strive to outgo him in virtue. But this strife must be so tempered that we fall not from the eagerness of praise to the envying of their persons, for then we leave running to the goal of glory to spurn at a stone that lies in our way; and so did Atlante in the middest of her course stoop to take up the golden apple that her enemy scattered in her way, and was outrun by Hippomenes. The contrary to this contention and emulation is security, peace, quiet, tranquillity—when we have no adversary to pry into our actions, no malicious eye whose pursuing our private behavior might make us more vigilant over our imperfections than otherwise we would be.

That state or kingdom that is in league with all the world, and hath no forrain sword to vex it, is not half so strong or confirmed to endure as that which lives every hour in fear of invasion. There is a certain waste of the people for whom there is no use but war; and these men must have some employment still to cut them off. *Nam si foras hostem non habent, domi*

invenient: "if they have no service abroad, they will make mutinies at home." Or if the affairs of the state be such as cannot exhale all these corrupt excrements, it is very expedient they have some light toys to busy their heads withal, cast before them as bones to gnaw upon, which may keep them from having leisure to intermeddle with higher matters.

To this effect, the policy of plays is very necessary, howsoever some shallow-brain'd censurers (not the deepest searchers into the secrets of government) mightily oppugn them. For whereas the afternoon being the idlest time of the day, wherein men that are their own masters (as gentlemen of the court, the Inns of the Court, and the number of captains and soldiers about London) do wholly bestow themselves upon pleasure, and that pleasure they devide (how virtuously, it skills not) either into gaming, following of harlots, drinking, or seeing a play; is it not then better (since of four extremes all the world cannot keep them but they will choose one) that they should betake them to the least, which is plays? Nay, what if I prove plays to be no extreme, but a rare exercise of virtue? First, for the subject of them, for the most part it is borrowed out of our English chronicles, wherein our forefathers' valiant acts (that have line long buried in rusty brass and worm-eaten books) are revived, and they themselves raised from the grave of oblivion, and brought to plead their aged honors in open presence; than which, what can be a sharper reproof to these degenerate effeminate days of ours?

How would it have joyed brave Talbot, the terror of the French, to think that after he had line two hundred years in his tomb he should triumph again on the stage, and have his bones new embalmed with the tears of ten thousand spectators at least (at several times) who in the tragedian that represents his person imagine they behold him fresh bleeding.

I will defend it against any collian or clubfisted usurer of them all, there is no immortality can be given a man on earth like unto plays. What talk I to them of immortality that are the only underminers of honor, and do envy any man that is not sprung up by base brokery like themselves? They care not if all the ancient houses were rooted out, so that like the burgomasters of the Low Countries they might share the government amongst them as states, and be quartermaisters of our monarchy. All arts to them are vanity; and if you tell them what a glorious thing it is to have Henry the Fifth represented on the stage leading the French king prisoner, and forcing both him and the dolphin to swear fealty, "I, but," will they say, "what do we get by it?" Respecting neither the right of fame that is due to true nobility deceased, nor what hopes of eternity are to be proposed to advent'rous mind to encourage them forward, but only their execrable lucre and filthy unquenchable avarice.

They know when they are dead they shall not be brought upon the stage for any goodness, but in a merriment of the usurer and the Divel, or buying arms of the herald, who gives them the lion without tongue, tail, or tallents, because his maister whom he must serve is a townsman and a man of peace, and must not keep any quarreling beasts to annoy his honest neighbors.

In plays, all coosonages, all cunning drifts overgilded with outward holiness, all stratagems of war, all the cankerworms that breed on the rust of peace, are most lively anatomiz'd; they shew the ill success of treason, the fall of hasty climbers, the wretched end of usurpers, the misery of civil dissension, and how just God is evermore in punishing of murther. And to prove every one of these allegations could I propound the circumstances of this play and that play, if I meant to handle this theme otherwise than *obiter*. What should I say more? They are sour pills of reprehension wrapp'd up in sweet words. Whereas some petitioners of the counsail against them object they corrupt the youth of the city and withdraw prentices from their work, they heartily wish they might be troubled with none of their youth nor their prentices; for some of them (I mean the ruder handicrafts' servants) never come abroad but they are in danger of undoing; and as for corrupting them when they come, that's false; for no play they have encourageth any man to tumults or rebellion, but lays before such the halter and the gallows; or praiseth or approveth pride, lust, whoredom, prodigality, or drunkenness, but beats them down utterly. As for the hindrance of trades and traders of the city by them, that is an article foisted in by the vintners, alewives, and victualers, who surmise if there were no plays they should have all the company that resort to them lie bowzing and beer-bathing in their houses every afternoon. Nor so, nor so, good brother bottle-ale, for there are other places besides where money can bestow itself; the sign of the smock will wipe your mouth clean; and yet I have heard ye have made her a tenant to your taphouses. But what shall he do that hath spent himself? Where shall he haunt? Faith, when dice, lust, and drunkenness, and all, have dealt upon him, if there be never a play for him to go to for his penny, he sits melancholy in his chamber, devising upon felony or treason and how he may best exalt himself by mischief.

In Augustus' time (who was the patron of all witty sports) there happened a great fray in Rome about a player, insomuch as all the city was in an uproar; whereupon, the emperor (after the broil was somewhat overblown) call'd the player before him, and ask'd what was the reason that a man of his quality durst presume to make such a brawl about nothing. He smilingly replied, "It is good for thee, O Caesar, that the people's heads are troubled with brawls and quarrels about us and our light matters; for otherwise they would look into thee and thy matters." Read Lipsius or any prophane or Christian politician, and you shall find him of this opinion. Our players are not as the players beyond sea, a sort of squirting bawdy comedians that have whores and common curtizans to play women's parts, and forbear no immodest speech or unchaste action that may procure laughter; but our scene is more stately furnish'd than ever it was in the time of Roscius, our representations honorable and full of gallant resolution, not consisting like theirs of a pantaloon, a whore, and a zany, but of emperors, kings, and princes; whose true tragedies (*Sophocleo cothurno*) they do vaunt.

Not Roscius nor Aesop, those admired tragedians that have lived ever since before Christ was born, could ever perform more in action than famous Ned Allen. I must accuse our poets of sloth and partiality that they will not boast in large impressions what worthy men (above all nations) England affords. Other countries cannot have a fiddler break a string but they will put it in print, and the old Romans in the writings they published thought scorn to use any but domestical examples of their own home-bred actors, schollers, and champions, and them they would extol to the third and fourth generation; cobblers, tinkers, fencers, none escap'd them, but they mingled them all in one gallimafrey of glory.

Here I have used a like method, not of tying myself to mine own country, but by insisting in the experience of our time; and if I ever write anything in Latin (as I hope one day I shall), not a man of any desert here amongst us but I will have up. Tarlton, Ned Allen, Knell, Bentley, shall be made known to France, Spain, and Italy; and not a part that they surmounted in, more than other, but I will there note and set down, with the manner of their habits and attire.

FROM CHRIST'S TEARS OVER JERUSALEM (1593)

To the Reader

Nil nisi flere libet. Gentles, here is no joyful subject towards; if you will weep, so it is. I have nothing to spend on you but passion. A hundred unfortunate farewells to fantastical satirism. In those veins heretofore have I misspent my spirit and prodigally conspir'd against good hours. Nothing is there now so much in my vows as to be at peace with all men, and make submissive amends where I have most displeased. Not basely fear-blasted or constraintively overruled, but purely pacificatory suppliant, for reconciliation and pardon do I sue to the principalest of them gainst whom I profess'd utter enmity. Even of Maister Doctor Harvey I heartily desire the like, whose fame and reputation (though through some precedent injurious provocations and fervent incitements of young heads) I rashly assailed; yet now better advised, and of his perfections more confirmedly persuaded, unfeignedly I entreat of the whole world from my pen his worths may receive no impeachment. All acknowledgments of aboundant scholarship, courteous, well-governed behavior, and ripe, experienc'd judgment do I attribute unto him. Only with his mild, gentle moderation hereunto hath he won me.

Take my invective against him in that abject nature that you would do the railing of a sophister in the schools, or a scolding lawyer at the bar, which none but fools will wrest to defame. As the title of this book is *Christ's Tears,* so be this epistle the tears of my pen. Many things have I vainly set forth whereof now it repenteth me. St. Augustine writ a whole book of his *Retractations.* Nothing so much do I retract as that wherein soever I have scandaliz'd the meanest. Into some spleenative veins of wantonness heretofore have I foolishly relapsed, to supply my private wants; of them no less do I desire to be absolved then the rest, and to God and man do I promise an unfeigned conversion.

Two or three trivial volumes [?*The Terrors of the Night* and *The Unfortunate Traveler*] of mine at this instant are under the printers' hands, ready to be published; which, being long bungled up before this, I must crave to be included in the catalogue of mine excuse. To a little more wit have my encreasing years reclaimed me then I had before. Those that have been perverted by any of my works, let them read this, and it shall thrice more benefit them. The autumn I imitate in shedding my leaves with the trees, and so doth the peacock shed his tail. Buy who list, contemn who list; I leave every reader his free liberty. If the best sort of men I content, I am satisfiedly successful.

Farewell, all those that wish me well; others wish I more wit to.

Thomas Nashe . . .

Since these be the days of dolor and heaviness [owing to the plague of 1592–93], wherein, as holy David saith, the Lord is known by executing judgment and the ax of his anger is put to the root of the tree, and his fan is in his hand to purge his floor, I suppose it shall not be amiss to write something of mourning, for London to harken counsail of her great-grandmother Jerusalem.

Omnipotent Savior, it is thy tears I intend to write of, those affectionate tears which in the twenty-third and twenty-fourth of Matthew thou wepst over Jerusalem and her temple. Be present with me, I beseech thee, personating the passion of thy love. O dew thy spirit plentifully into my ink, and let some part of thy divine dreariment live again in mine eyes. Teach me how to weep as thou wepst, and rent my heart in twain with the extremity of ruth. I hate in thy name to speak coldly to a quick-witted generation. Rather let my brains melt all to ink, and the floods of affliction drive out mine eyes before them, then I should be dull and leaden in describing the dolor of thy love. Far be from me any ambitious hope of the vain merit of art; may that living vehemence I use in lament only proceed from a heaven-bred hatred of uncleanness and corruption. Mine own wit I clean disinherit; thy fiery, cloven-tongued inspiration be my muse. Lend my words the forcible wings of the lightnings, that they may pierce unawares into the marrow and reins of my readers. New mint my mind to the likeness of thy lowliness; file away the superfluous affectation of my prophane, puff'd-up phrase that I may be thy pure, simple orator. I am a child, as thy holy Jeremy said, and know not how to speak, yet *omnia possum in eo qui me confortat:* "I can do all things through the help of Him that strengtheneth me." The tongues of infants it is thou that makest eloquent, and teachest the heart understanding. Grant me, that am a babe and an infant in the mysteries of divinity, the gracious favor to suck at the breasts of thy sacred revelation, to utter something that may move secure England to true sorrow and contrition. All the pores of my soul, assembled in their perfectest array, shall stand waiting on thy incomprehensible wisdom for arguments, as poor young birds stand attending on their dam's bill for sustenance. Now help, now direct; for now I transform myself from myself to be thy unworthy speaker to the world. . . .

[After a long and fervent account of the sinful

history of Jerusalem, Nashe calls London to repentance lest it also suffer the righteous anger of
God.] Hetherto stretcheth the prosecution of thy
[i.e. Jerusalem's] desolation. Now to London must I
turn me, London that turneth from none of thy left-
hand impieties. As great a desolation as Jerusalem
hath London deserved. Whatsoever of Jerusalem I
have written was but to lend her a looking-glass.
Now enter I into my true tears, my tears for London,
wherein I crave pardon though I deal more search-
ingly then common soul-surgeons accustom, for in
this book wholly have I bequeathed my pen and my
spirit to the prosternating and enforrowing the
frontiers of sin. So let it be acceptable to God and his
church what I write, as no man in this treatise I will
particularly touch, none I will semovedly allude to,
but only attaint vice in general.

Pride shall be my principal aim, which in London
hath platformed another sky-undersetting tower of
Babel. Jonathan shot five arrows beyond the mark; I
fear I shall shoot fifteen arrows behind the mark in
describing this high-tow'ring sin.

O Pride, of all heaven-relapsing premunires the
most fearful! Thou that ere this hast disparadis'd our
first parent Adam, and unrighteous'd the very angels,
how shall I arm mine elocution to break through the
ranks of thy hilly stumbling-blocks? After the
destruction of Antwerp [by the Duke of Parma in
1585], thou (being thrust out of house and home,
and not knowing whither to betake thee) at haphazard embarkedst for England. Where, hearing
rich London was the full-streamed well-head, unto it
thou hastedst, and there hast dwelt many years,
begetting sons and daughters. Thy sons' names are
these: Ambition, Vainglory, Atheism, Discontent,
Contention; thy daughters', Disdain, Gorgeous Attire, and Delicacy. O had Antwerp still florished that
thou hadst ne'er come hether to misfashion us, or
that there were any city would take thy children to
halfs with us! . . .

Riches have hurt a great number in England who,
if their riches had not been, had still been men and
not Timonists. Riches as they have renowned, so
they have reproached, London. It is now grown a
proverb that "there is no merchandise but usury."
I dare not affirm it, but, questionless, Usury crieth to
the children of Prodigality in the streets: "All you
that will take up money or commodities on your
land or possibilities to banquet, riot, and be drunk,
come unto us and you shall be furnished; for gain
we will help to damn both your souls and our own."
God in his mercy never call them to their audit!
God in his mercy rid them all out of London, and
then it were to be hoped the plague would cease,
else never.

Jeremy saith, "Woe be to him that buildeth his
house with unrighteousness, and his chambers without equity; whose eyes and whose heart are only for
covetousness and to shed innocent blood." The eyes
and the heart of usurers are only for covetousness
and to shed innocent blood. Mo gentlemen by their
entanglement and exactions have they driven to
desperate courses, and so consequently made away
and murdered, then either France, the Low Countries, or any foreign siege or sea voyage this forty
years. Tell me, almost what gentleman hath been
cast away at sea, or disasterly soldieriz'd it by land,
but they have enforc'd him thereunto by their fleec-
ing? What is left for a man to do, being consumed
to the bare bones by these greedy horse-leeches and
not having so much reserved as would buy him
bread, but either to hang at Tyburn or pillage and
reprisal where he may? Huge numbers in their stinking prisons they have starved, and made dice of their
bones for the Devil to throw at dice for their own
souls.

This is the course nowadays everyone taketh to be
rich: being a young trader, and having of old
Mumpsimus (his avaricious maister) learn'd to be his
crafts-maister, for a year or two he is very thrifty,
and husbandly he pays and takes as duly as the clock
strikes; he seemeth very sober and precise, and
bringeth all men in love with him. When he thinketh
he hath thorowly wrung himself into the world's
good opinion, and that his credit is as much as he will
demand, he goes and tries it, and on the tenter-hooks
stretches it. No man he knoweth but he will scrape a
little book-curtesy of; two or three thousand pound,
perhaps, makes up his mouth. When he hath it all in
his hands, for a month or two he revels it, and cuts
it out in the whole cloth.

He falls acquainted with gentlemen, frequents
ordinaries and dicing-houses daily, where, when some
of them in play have lost all their money, he is very
diligent at hand, on their chains, or bracelets, or
jewels to lend them half the value. Now this is the
nature of young gentlemen, that where they have
broke the ice and borrow'd once they will come again
the second time; and that these young foxes know
as well as the beggar knows his dish. But at the second
time of their coming it is doubtful to say whether
they shall have money or no. The world grows hard,
and we all are mortal. Let them make him any assurance before a judge, and they shall have some
hundred pounds *per consequens* in silks and velvets.
The third time if they come, they shall have baser
commodities; the fourth time, lute strings and gray
paper. And then, "I pray pardon me, I am not for
you. Pay me that you owe me and you shall have
anything."

When thus this young usurer hath thrust all his pedlary into the hands of novice heirs and that he hath made of his three thousand nine thousand in bonds and recognisances, besides the strong faith of the forfeitures, he breaks and cries out amongst his neighbors that he is undone by trusting gentlemen. His kind heart hath made him a beggar; and warns all men, by his example, to beware how they have any dealings with them. For a quarter of a year or thereabouts he slips his neck out of the collar and sets some grave man of his kindred (as his father-in-law or such-like) to go and report his lamentable mischance to his creditors, and what his honest care is to pay every man his own as far as he is able. His creditors, thinking all is gospel he speaks, and that his state is lower ebbed then it is, are glad to take anything for their own, so that whereas three thousand pound is due, in his absence all is satisfied for eight hundred (his father-in-law making them believe he lays it out of his own purse).

All matters thus under hand discharged, my young merchant returns and sets up fresher then ever he did. Those bonds and statutes he hath he puts in suit amain. For a hundred-pound commodity (which is not forty pound money) he recovers by relapse some hundred pound a year. In three terms, of a bankrout he wexeth a great landed man, and may compare with the best of his company. O intolerable usury! Not the Jews, whose peculiar sin it is, have ever committed the like. . . .

The third son of Pride [after Ambition and Vainglory] is Atheism, which is when a man is so tympaniz'd with prosperity, and entranced from himself with Wealth, Ambition, and Vainglory, that he forgets he had a Maker, or that there is a heaven above him which controls him. Too much joy of this world hath made him drunk. I have read of many whom extreme joy and extreme grief hath forced to run mad; so with extreme joy runs he mad, he waxeth a fool and an idiot, and then he says in his heart, "There is no God." Others there be of these soul-benumbed atheists who (having so far ent'red in bold blasphemies and Scripture-scorning ironies against God that they think if God be a God of any justice and omnipotence it cannot stand with that his justice and omnipotence to suffer such despite unpunished) for their only refuge persuade themselves there is no God, and with their prophane wits invent reasons why there should be no God. . . .

Of atheists this age affordeth two sorts, the inward and the outward. The inward atheist is he that devours widows' houses under pretense of long prayers, that (like the panther) hideth his face in a hood of religion when he goeth about his prey. He would profess himself an atheist openly but that, like the

Pharisees, he feareth the multitude. Because the multitude favors religion, he runs with the stream, and favors religion—only for he would be captain of a multitude. To be the god of gold, he cares not how many gods he entertains. Church-rights he supposeth not amiss to busy the common people's heads with, that they should not fall aboard princes' matters. And as Numa Pompilius in Rome, and Minos in Athens, kept the people in awe, and thrust what tyrannous laws they list upon them (the one under pretense he did nothing without conference of the nymph Egeria, the other under color he was inspired in a certain hollow cave by Jupiter), so he makes conscience and the spirit of God a long sidecloak for all his oppressions and policies. A holy look he will put on when he meaneth to do mischief, and have Scripture in his mouth even whiles he is in cutting his neighbor's throat. . . .

The outward atheist, contrariwise, with those things that proceed from his mouth defileth his heart. He establisheth reason as his God, and will not be persuaded that God—the true God—is, except He make him privy to all the secrecies of His beginning and government. Straitly he will examine Him where He was, what He did, before He created heaven and earth; how it is possible He should have His being from before all beginnings. Every circumstance of His providence he will run thorough, and question why He did not this thing, and that thing, and the other thing according to their humors.

Being earthly bodies, unapt to ascend, in their ambitious cogitation they will break ope and ransack His closet; and if, conveniently, they may not come to it, then they will derogate and deprave him all they can. Little do they consider that as the light which shined before Paul made him blind, so the light of God's invisible mysteries, if ever it shine in our hearts, will confound and blind our carnal reason.

Philosophy's chief fulness, wisdom's adopted father next unto Salomon, unsatiable art-searching Aristotle, that in the round compendiate bladder of thy brain conglobedst these three great bodies (heaven, earth, and the wide world of waters), thine Icarian-soaring comprehension, tossed and turmoiled but about the bounds and beginning of Nilus, in Nilus drown'd itself, being too sely and feeble to plunge thorow it.

If knowledge's second Salomon had not knowledge enough to engrasp one river, and alledge probability of his beginning and bounding, who shall engrasp or bound the heaven's body? Nay, what soul is so metaphysical subtile that can humorously sirenize heaven's soul, Jehovah, out of the concealments of his Godhead? He that is familiar with all earthly states must not think to be familiar with the state of heaven. The very angels know not the day nor hour of the Last Judgment; if they know not the day nor hour of the Judgment (which is such a general thing), more private circumstances of the Godhead, determinately, they are not acquainted with. And if not angels, his sanctified attendants, much less are they revealed to sinners. Idle-headed atheist, ill wouldst thou, as the Romans, acknowledge and offer sacrifice to many gods, that wilt not grant one God. From thy birth to this moment of thine unbelief, revolve the diary of thy memory and try if thou hast ne'er pray'd and been heard; if thou hast been heard and thy prayer accomplish'd, who hath heard thee, who hath accomplish'd it? Wilt thou ratifiedly affirm that God is no God because, like a noun substantive, thou canst not essentially see him, feel him, or hear him? . . .

I cannot be persuaded any poor man, or man in misery (be he not altogether desperate of his estate), is an atheist. Misery, mauger their hearts, will make them confess God. Who heareth the thunder, that thinks not of God? I would know who is more fearful to die, or dies with more terror and affrightment, then an atheist. Discourse over the ends of all atheists, and their deaths, for the most part, have been drunken, violent, and secluded from repentance. The black, swutty visage of the night, and the shady fancies thereof, ascertains every guilty soul there is a sin-hating God.

How can bellows blow except there be one that binds and first imprisons wind in them? How can fire burn if none first kindle it? How can man breathe except God puts first the breath of life into him? Who leadeth the sun out of his chamber, or the moon forth her cloudy pavilion, but God? Why doth not the sea swallow up the earth, whenas it overpeers it and is greater then it, but that there is a God that snaffles and curbs it? . . . .

University men that are called to preach at the Cross and the court, arm yourselves against nothing but atheism; meddle not so much with sects and foreign opinions, but let atheism be the only string you beat on; for there is no sect now in England so scattered as atheism. In vain do you preach, in vain do you teach, if the root that nourisheth all the branches of security be not thorowly digg'd up from the bottom. You are not half so well acquainted as them that live continually about the court and city how many followers this damnable paradox hath, how many high wits it hath bewitch'd. Where are they that count a little smatt'ring in liberal arts and the reading over the Bible with a late comment sufficient to make a father of divines? What will their disallowed Bible or late comments help them if they have no other reading to resist atheists? Atheists, if ever they be confuted, with their own prophane authors they must be confuted. . . .

Comfort us, Lord. We mourn; our bread is mingled with ashes, and our drink with tears. With so many funerals are we oppressed that we have no leisure to weep for our sins for howling for our sons and daughters. O hear the voice of our howling, withdraw thy hand from us, and we will draw near unto thee.

Come, Lord Jesu, come, for as thou art Jesus, thou art pitiful. Challenge some part of our sin-procured scourge to thy cross. Let it not be said that thou but half satisfiedst for sin. We believe thee to be an absolute satisfier for sin. As we believe, so for thy merit's sake we beseech thee let it happen unto us.

Thus ought every Christian in London, from the highest to the lowest, to pray. From God's justice we must appeal to his mercy. As the French king, Francis the First, a woman kneeling to him for justice, said unto her, "Stand up, woman, for justice I owe thee; if thou begst anything, beg for mercy." So if we beg of God for anything, let us beg for mercy, for justice he owes us. Mercy, mercy, O grant us, heavenly Father, for thy mercy!

RICHARD HAKLUYT

DIVERS VOYAGES and THE PRINCIPAL NAVIGATIONS

Although not the first, Richard Hakluyt is by far the most famed compiler of voyages and travel narratives in the English language. Just as Continental navigators, first venturing into uncharted seas, provided the Tudors an example they were slow to follow, so Continental historians and cosmographers set a precedent for Hakluyt's great compilations. In 1504 the Spaniard Petrus Martyr published the first *Decade* of his *De orbe novo,* and when his work was at last finished in 1532 it was quickly imported or adapted for Italian, French, and German consumption. Also during the early sixteenth century the similar cosmographical works of Giovanni Battista Ramusio, Gonzalo Fernández de Oviedo y Valdés, and Francisco López de Gómara served both to describe past expeditions and stimulate new ones.

Although there were sporadic accounts of voyages during the reigns of the early Tudors, Hakluyt's only important English predecessor was Richard Eden, who, in 1553, translated from Sebastian Münster's Latin the *Universal Cosmography*, a compendious record of Portuguese and Spanish explorations. This he followed in 1555 with a compilation from Petrus Martyr and other cosmographers, the *Decades of the New World*, and in 1561 with *The Art of Navigation*, translated from a well-known treatise by Martin Cortes. Eden himself had been subsidized by the newly formed Muscovy Company, and in the early years of Elizabeth's reign English navigators, generally in the employment of trading companies, unfurled their queen's standard in quarters of the globe which their grandfathers had known only remotely if at all. Sir Hugh Willoughby and Richard Chancellor's expedition to Russia, the first exploits of Hawkins and Drake against the prodigious power of Catholic Spain, Sir Humphrey Gilbert's search for a northwest passage to Cathay, and Sir Martin Frobisher's futile but valiant efforts to circumnavigate Canada—all of which were duly celebrated in print—were the most famed of the early Elizabethans' colonial adventures; but there were others too, and only three years after Richard Willes published an enlarged edition of Eden's *Decades of the New World* (1577) Drake returned in triumph from his voyage of circumnavigation. Thereafter the English stood poised for their vigorous if belated effort to win money, power, and Protestant converts across the seas.

It was to encouraging this effort that Richard Hakluyt dedicated his life. In 1582, addressing to Sir Philip Sidney his first work, *Divers Voyages Touching the Discovery of America*, he wrote in the fervent hope of stimulating, for both religious and commercial reasons, systematic colonization of "such fertile and temperate places as are left as yet unpossessed" by the Spaniards and Portuguese. Gaining the patronage of Lord Howard of Effingham, in 1583 he was appointed chaplain to Lord Howard's brother-in-law, Sir Edward Stafford, the English ambassador in Paris. There he could devote himself to the work that he was born to do, and during the next five years he pursued the researches that resulted in his translation of Laudonnière's *Notable History Containing Four Voyages Made by Certain French Captains unto Florida* (1587), an elaborate edition (in Latin) of Petrus Martyr's *De orbe novo* (1587) which he dedicated to Sir Walter Raleigh, and finally (after his return to England) the first instalment of his *magnum opus*, *The Principal Navigations, Voyages, and Discoveries of the English Nation Made by Sea or over Land to the Most Remote and Farthest Distant Quarters of the Earth at Any Time within the Compass of These 1500 Years* (1589). A decade later this work was expanded into three stately folios (1598, 1599, 1600) to become, in Froude's proud words, the prose epic of the modern English nation.

As Hakluyt explains to "the Favorable Reader" in the second edition of his work, he had tried to marshal his immense erudition and his sprawling materials into some sort of order, dealing first with all English voyages "to the south and southeast parts of the world," then with those to "the north and northeastern" parts, and finally, "in the third and last room," with "the western navigations and travails" of English mariners. Within this copious framework the *Principal Navigations* is almost as trackless and as various as the seas which haunted Hakluyt's imagination. There one may find almost everything: the legendary voyages of King Arthur and the early Britons, the sea-journeys of Ohthere and Wulfstan, letters and charters of Edward I and many other monarchs, commercial treaties between English and Baltic merchants of the Middle Ages, Anthony Jenkinson's fabulous trips through Russia to Persia, documents of the Muscovy Company (including the exploits of Willoughby and Chancellor), Drake's foray on Cadiz, Hawkins' glorious and inglorious feats of piracy and seamanship, Sir Walter Raleigh's Guiana expeditions, and many, many more. After Hakluyt, then Archdeacon of Westminster, died in 1616, part of his huge manuscript collections came into the possession of Samuel Purchas, who carried on his predecessors' labors in *Purchas His Pilgrims*, a compilation that by its last edition of 1625 had grown to gigantic proportions.

Our texts are based upon *Divers voyages touching the discoverie of America, and the Ilands adjacent unto the same*, 1582 (STC 12624); *The Principall Navigations, Voiages and Discoveries of the English nation . . . By Richard Hakluyt Master of Artes, and Student sometime of Christ-church in Oxford*, 1589 (STC 12625); *The Principal Navigations . . . Divided into three severall Volumes*, 1598–[1600] (STC 12626).

FROM DIVERS VOYAGES TOUCHING THE DISCOVERY OF AMERICA (1582)

A Very Late and Great Probability of a Passage by the Northwest Part of America in 58 Degrees of Northerly Latitude

An excellent learned man of Portingale, of singular gravity, authority, and experience, told me very lately that one Anus Cortereal, captain of the Ile of Tercera, about the year 1574 (which is not above eight years past) sent a ship to discover the Northwest Passage of America, and that the same ship, arriving on the coast of the said America in fifty-eight degrees of latitude, found a great entrance exceeding deep and broad, without all impediment of ice, into which they passed above twenty leagues and found it always to trend toward the south, the land lying low and plain on either side; and that they persuaded themselves verily that there was a way open into the South Sea. But their victails failing them, and being but one ship, they returned back again with joy. This place seemeth to lie in equal degrees of latitude with the first entrance of the Sound of Denmark between Norway and the headland called in Latin *Cimbrorum promontorium,* and therefore like to be open and navigable a great part of the year. And this report may be well annexed unto the other eight reasons mentioned in my epistle dedicatory for proof of the likelihood of this passage by the northwest.

To The Right Worshipful and Most Virtuous Gentleman, Master Philip Sidney, Esquire

I marvel not a little, right worshipful, that since the first discovery of America (which is now full four-score and ten years), after so great conquests and plantings of the Spaniards and Portingales there, that we of England could never have the grace to set fast footing in such fertile and temperate places as are left as yet unpossessed of them. But again, when I consider that there is a time for all men, and see the Portingales' time to be out of date and that the nakedness of the Spaniards and their long-hidden secrets are now at length espied, whereby they went about to delude the world, I conceive great hope that the time approacheth and now is that we of England may share and part stakes (if we will ourselves) both with the Spaniard and the Portingale in part of America and other regions as yet undiscovered. And surely if there were in us that desire to advance the honor of our country which ought to be in every good man we would not all this while have foreslown the possessing of those lands which of equity and right appertain unto us, as by the discourses that follow shall appear most plainly. Yea, if we would behold with the eye of pity how all our prisons are pestered and filled with able men to serve their country, which for small robberies are daily hanged up in great numbers, even twenty at a clap out of one jail (as was seen at the last assizes at Rochester), we would hasten and further every man to his power the deducting of some colonies of our superfluous people into those temperate and fertile parts of America, which, being within six weeks' sailing of England, are yet unpossessed by any Christians, and seem to offer themselves unto us, stretching nearer unto her Majesty's dominions then to any other part of Europe. We read that the bees, when they grow to be too many in their own hives at home, are wont to be led out by their captains to swarm abroad, and seek themselves a new dwelling-place. If the examples of the Grecians and Carthaginians of old time and the practise of our age may not move us, yet let us learn wisdom of these small, weak, and unreasonable creatures. It chanced very lately that upon occasion I had great conference in matters of cosmography with an excellent learned man of Portingale, most privy to all the discoveries of his nation, who wondered that those blessed countries from the point of Florida northward were all this while unplanted by Christians, protesting with great affection and zeal that if he were now as young as I (for at this present he is three-score years of age) he would sell all he had, being a man of no small wealth and honor, to furnish a convenient number of ships to sea for the inhabiting of those countries and reducing those gentile people to Christianity. Moreover, he added that John Barros, their chief cosmographer, being moved with the like desire, was the cause that Bresilia was first inhabited by the Portingales, where they have nine baronies or lordships and thirty engines or sugar mills, two or three hundred slaves belonging to each mill, with a judge and other offices and a church, so that every mill is, as it were, a little commonwealth; and that the country was first planted by such men as for small offenses were saved from the rope. This he spake not only unto me and in my hearing, but also in the presence of a friend of mine, a man of great skill in the mathematics. If this man's desire might be executed, we might not only for the present time take possession of that good land, but also in short space by God's grace find out that short and easy passage by the northwest which we have hetherto so long desired and whereof we have many good and more then probable conjectures, a few whereof I think it not amiss here to set down, although your Worship know them as well as myself. First, therefore, it is not to be forgotten that Sebastian Gabot wrote to Master Baptista Ramusius that he verily believed that all the north part of America is divided into ilands. Secondly, that Master John Verarzanus, which had been thrice on that coast, in an old, excellent map which he gave to King Henry the Eight and is yet in the custody of Master [Michael] Locke doth so lay it out as it is to be seen in the map annexed to the end of this book, being made according to Verarzanus' plat. Thirdly, the story of Gil Gonsalva recorded by Franciscus Lopes de Gomara, which is said to have sought a passage by the northwest, seemeth to argue and prove the same. . . . Seventhly, the experience of Captain Frobisher on the hither side and Sir Francis Drake on the back side of America, with the testimony of Nicolaus and Anthonius Zeni, that Estotilanda is an iland doth yield no small hope thereof. Lastly, the judgment of the excellent geographer Gerardus Mercator, which his son Rumold Mercator, my friend, shewed me in his letters and drew out for me in writing, is not of wise men lightly to be regarded. . . . "You write," saith he to his son, "great matters, though very briefly of the new discovery of Frobisher, which I wonder was never these many years heretofore attempted. For there is no doubt but that there is a straight and short way open into the west, even unto Cathay, into which kingdom if they take their course aright, they shall gather the most noble merchandise of all the world and shall make the name of Christ to be known unto many idolatrous and heathen people." And here to conclude and shut up this matter, I have heard myself of merchants of credit that have lived long in Spain that King Philip [II] hath made a law of late that none of his subjects shall discover to the northwards of five and forty degrees of America, which may be thought to proceed chiefly of two causes: the one, least passing farther to the north they should discover the open passage from the South Sea to our North Sea; the other, because they have not people enough to possess and keep that passage, but rather thereby should open a gap for other nations to pass that way. Certes if hetherto in our own discoveries we had not been led with a preposterous desire of seeking rather gain then God's glory, I assure myself that our labors had taken far better effect. But we forgot that godliness is great riches and that if we first seek the kingdom of God all other things will be given unto us, and that as the light accompanieth the sun and the heat the fire, so lasting riches do wait upon them that are zealous for the advancement of the kingdom of Christ and the enlargement of his glorious Gospel; as it is said, "I will honor them that honor me." I trust that now, being taught by their manifold losses, our men will take a more godly course and use some part of their goods to his glory; if not, he will turn even their covetousness to serve him as he hath done the pride and avarice of the Spaniards and Portingales, who, pretending in glorious words that they made their discoveries chiefly to convert infidels to our most holy faith (as they say), in deed and truth sought not them, but their goods and riches. Which thing that our nation may more speedily and happily perform, there is no better mean in my simple judgment then the increase of knowledge in the art of navigation and breeding of skilfulness in the seamen; which Charles [V] the emperor and the king of Spain that now is, wisely considering, have in their contractation-house in Sivill appointed a learned reader of the said art of navigation and joined with him certain examiners, and have distinguished the orders among the seamen, as the groomet (which is the basest degree), the mariner (which is the second), the master

(the third), and the pilot (the fourth), unto the which two last degrees none is admitted without he have heard the reader for a certain space (which is commonly an excellent mathematician, of which number were Pedro di Medina, which writ learnedly of the art of navigation, and Alonso di Chavez and Hieronimus di Chavez, whose works likewise I have seen), and being found fit by him and his assistants, which are to examine matters touching experience, they are admitted with as great solemnity and giving of presents to the ancient masters and pilots and the reader and examiners as the great doctors in the universities, or our great sergeants at the law when they proceed, and so are admitted to take charge for the Indies. And that your Worship may know that this is true, Master Steven Borrows, now one of the four masters of the queen's navy, told me that newly after his return from the discovery of Moscovy by the north, in Queen Marie's days, the Spaniards, having intelligence that he was master in that discovery, took him into their contractation-house at their making and admitting of masters and pilots, giving him great honor, and presented him with a pair of perfumed gloves worth five or six ducats. I speak all this to this end, that the like order of erecting such a lecture here in London or about Ratcliffe in some convenient place were a matter of great consequence and importance for the saving of many men's lives and goods, which now, through gross ignorance, are daily in great hazard to the no small detriment of the whole realm. For which cause I have dealt with the right worshipful Sir Francis Drake, that seeing God hath blessed him so wonderfully he would do this honor to himself and benefit to his country, to be at the cost to erect such a lecture; whereunto in most bountiful manner at the very first he answered that he liked so well of the motion that he would give twenty pounds by the year standing and twenty pounds more beforehand to a learned man, to furnish him with instruments and maps, that would take this thing upon him; yea, so ready he was that he earnestly requested me to help him to the notice of a fit man for that purpose, which I, for the zeal I bare to this good action, did presently, and brought him one who came unto him and conferred with him thereupon, but in fine he would not undertake the lecture unless he might have forty pound a year standing, and so the matter ceased for that time; howbeit, the worthy and good knight remaineth still constant, and will be, as he told me very lately, as good as his word. Now if God should put into the head of any noble man to contribute other twenty pound to make this lecture a competent living for a learned man, the whole realm no doubt might reap no small benefit thereby.

To leave this matter and to draw to an end, I have here, right worshipful, in this hasty work first put down the title which we have to that part of America which is from Florida to 67 degrees northward by the letters-patents granted to John Gabot and his three sons Lewis, Sebastian, and Santius, with Sebastian's own certificate to Baptista Ramusius of his discovery of America and the testimony of [Robert] Fabian, our own chronicler. Next, I have caused to be added the letters of M[aster] Robert Thorne to King Henry the Eight and his discourse to his ambassador, Doctor [Edward] Ley, in Spain of the like argument, with the king's setting-out of two ships for discovery in the 19 year of his reign. Then I have translated the voyage of John Verarzanus from thirty degrees to Cape Briton (and the last year at my charges and other of my friends by my exhortation I caused Jacques Cartier's two voyages of discovering the Grand Bay and Canada, Saguinay, and Hochelaga to be translated out of my volumes, which are to be annexed to this present translation).

Moreover, following the order of the map and not the course of time, I have put down the discourse of Nicholaus and Antonius Zeni. The last treatise of John Ribault is a thing that hath been already printed, but not now to be had unless I had caused it to be printed again. The map is Master Michael Locke's, a man for his knowledge in divers languages and especially in cosmography able to do his country good, and worthy, in my judgment, for the manifold good parts in him of good reputation and better fortune. This cursory pamphlet I am overbold to present unto your Worship, but I had rather want a little discretion then to be found unthankful to him which hath been always so ready to pleasure me and all my name.

Here I cease, craving pardon for my overboldness, trusting also that your Worship will continue and increase your accustomed favor toward these godly and honorable discoveries.

Your Worship's humble always to command,

R[ichard] H[akluyt]

FROM THE PRINCIPAL NAVIGATIONS . . . OF THE ENGLISH NATION (1589)

To the Right Honorable Sir Francis Walsingham . . .

Right honorable, I do remember that being a youth and one of her Majesty's scholars at Westminster, that fruitful nursery, it was my hap to visit the chamber of M[aster] Richard Hakluyt, my cousin, a gentleman of the Middle Temple, well known unto you, at a time when I found lying open upon his boord certain books of cosmography, with an universal map. He, seeing me somewhat curious in the view thereof, began to instruct my ignorance by shewing me the division of the earth into three parts after the old account, and then, according to the latter and better distribution, into more; he pointed with his wand to all the known seas, gulfs, bays, straights, capes, rivers, empires, kingdoms, dukedoms, and territories of each part, with declaration also of their special commodities and particular wants, which by the benefit of traffic and entercourse of merchants are plentifully supplied. From the map he brought me to the Bible, and, turning to the 107 Psalm, directed me to the twenty-third and twenty-fourth verses, where I read that they which go down to the sea in ships and occupy by the great waters, they see the works of the Lord and his wonders in the deep, etc. Which words of the prophet, together with my cousin's discourse (things of high and rare delight to my young nature), took in me so deep an impression that I constantly resolved if ever I were preferred to the university where better time and more convenient place might be minist'red for these studies I would by God's assistance prosecute that knowledge and kind of literature, the doors whereof (after a sort) were so happily opened before me.

According to which my resolution, when, not long after, I was removed to Christ Church in Oxford, my exercises of duty first performed, I fell to my intended course, and by degrees read over whatsoever printed or written discoveries and voyages I found extant either in the Greek, Latin, Italian, Spanish, Portugal, French, or English languages, and in my public lectures was the first that produced and shewed both the old imperfectly composed and the new lately reformed maps, globes, spheres, and other instruments of this art for demonstration in the common schools, to the singular pleasure and general contentment of my auditory. In continuance of time, and by reason principally of my insight in this study, I grew familiarly acquainted with the chiefest captains at sea, the greatest merchants, and the best mariners of our nation; by which means having gotten somewhat more then common knowledge, I passed at length the narrow seas into France with Sir Edward Stafford, her Majesty's careful and discreet ligier, where, during my five years' abode with him in his dangerous and chargeable residency in her Highness' service, I both heard in speech and read in books other nations miraculously extolled for their discoveries and notable enterprises by sea, but the English of all others for their sluggish security and continual neglect of the like attempts, especially in so long and happy a time of peace, either ignominiously reported or exceedingly condemned; which singular opportunity if some other people our neighbors had been blessed with, their protestations are often and vehement, they would far otherwise have used. . . . Thus both hearing and reading the obloquy of our nation, and finding few or none of our own men able to reply herein, and further, not seeing any man to have care to recommend to the world the industrious labors and painful travels of our countrymen; for stopping the mouths of the reproachers, myself being the last winter returned from France with the honorable the Lady Sheffield, for her passing good behavior highly esteemed in all the French court, determined notwithstanding all difficulties to undertake the burden of that work wherein all others pretended either ignorance or lack of leisure or want of sufficient argument, whereas (to speak truly) the huge toil and the small profit to insue were the chief causes of the refusal. I call the work a burden in consideration that these voyages lay so dispersed, scattered, and hidden in several hucksters' hands that I now wonder at myself to see how I was able to endure the delays, curiosity, and backwardness of many from whom I was to receive my originals. . . .

To harp no longer upon this string, and to speak a word of that just commendation which our nation do indeed deserve, it cannot be denied but as in all former ages they have been men full of activity, stirrers abroad, and searchers of the remote parts of the world, so in this most famous and peerless government of her most excellent Majesty, her subjects through the special assistance and blessing of God in searching the most opposite corners and quarters of the world, and, to speak plainly, in compassing the vast globe of the earth more then once, have excelled all the nations and people of the earth. For which of the kings of this land before her Majesty had their banners ever seen in the Caspian Sea? Which of them hath ever dealt with the emperor of Persia, as her Majesty hath done and obtained for her merchants large and loving privileges? Who ever saw, before this regiment, an English ligier in the stately porch of the grand signor at Constantinople? Who ever found English consuls and agents at Tripolis in Syria, at Aleppo, at Babylon, at Balsara, and, which is more, who ever heard of Englishman at Goa before now? What English ships did heretofore ever anker in the mighty River of Plate, pass and repass the unpassable (in former opinion)

Straight of Magellan, range along the coast of Chili, Peru, and all the back side of Nova Hispania further then any Christian ever passed, traverse the mighty breadth of the South Sea, land upon the Luzones in despight of the enemy, enter into alliance, amity, and traffic with the princes of the Moluccaes and the Isle of Java, double the famous Cape of Bona Speranza, arrive at the Isle of Santa Helena, and last of all return home most richly laden with the commodities of China, as the subjects of this now florishing monarchy have done? . . .

Now whereas I have always noted your wisdom to have had a special care of the honor of her Majesty, the good reputation of our country, and the advancing of navigation, the very walls of this our island, as the oracle is reported to have spoken of the sea forces of Athens; and whereas I acknowledge in all dutiful sort how honorably both by your letter and speech I have been animated in this and other my travels, I see myself bound to make presentment of this work to yourself, as the fruits of your own incouragements and the manifestation both of my unfeigned service to my prince and country and of my particular duty to your Honor; which I have done with the less suspicion either of not satisfying the world or of not answering your own expectation, in that according to your order it hath passed the sight and partly also the censure of the learned physician M[aster] Doctor James, a man many ways very notably qualified.

And thus beseeching God, the giver of all true honor and wisdom, to increase both these blessings in you with continuance of health, strength, happiness, and whatsoever good thing else yourself can wish, I humbly take my leave. London, the seventeenth of November.

Your Honor's most humble
always to be commanded,
Richard Hakluyt

Richard Hakluyt to the Favorable Reader

I have thought it very requisite for thy further instruction and direction in this history, good reader, to acquaint thee briefly with the method and order which I have used in the whole course thereof; and by the way also to let thee understand by whose friendly aid in this my travel I have been furthered, acknowledging that ancient speech to be no less true then ingenious, that the offense is great *non agnoscere per quos perfeceris,* "not to speak of them by whom a man in his indeavours is assisted."

Concerning my proceeding therefore in this present work, it hath been this. Whatsoever testimony I have found in any author of authority appertaining to my argument, either stranger or natural, I have recorded the same word for word, with his particular name and page of book where it is extant. If the same were not reduced into our common language I have first expressed it in the same terms wherein it is originally written, whether it were a Latin, Italian, Spanish, or Portingal discourse, or whatsoever else, and thereunto in the next room have annexed the signification and translation of the words in English. . . .

Moreover, I meddle in this work with the navigations only of our own nation; and albeit I allege in a few places (as the matter and occasion required) some strangers as witnesses of the things done, yet are they none but such as either faithfully remember or sufficiently confirm the travels of our own people, of whom (to speak truth) I have received more light in some respects then all our own historians could afford me in this case, Bale, Foxe, and Eden only excepted.

And it is a thing withal principally to be considered that I stand not upon any action performed near home, nor in any part of Europe commonly frequented by our shipping, as for example not upon that victorious exploit not long since atchieved in our narrow seas against that monstrous Spanish army under the valiant and provident conduct of the right honorable the Lord Charles Howard, high admiral of England; not upon the good services of our two worthy generals in their late Portugal expedition; not upon the two most fortunate attempts of our famous chieftain Sir Francis Drake, the one in the Bay of Cales upon a great part of the enemy's chiefest ships, the other near the islands upon the great carrack of the East India . . . ; these (albeit singular and happy voyages of our renowmed countrymen) I omit as things distinct and without the compass of my prescribed limits, being neither of remote length and spaciousness, neither of search and discovery of strange coasts, the chief subject of this my labor.

Thus much in brevity shall serve thee for the general order. Particularly I have disposed and digested the whole work into three parts or, as it were, classes, not without my reasons. In the first I have martialed all our voyages of any moment that have been performed to the south and southeast parts of the world, by which I chiefly mean that part of Asia which is nearest and of the rest hithermost towards us; for I find that the oldest travels as well of the ancient Britains as of the English were ordinary to Judea, which is in Asia, termed by them the Holy Land, principally for devotion's sake according to the time, although I read in Joseph Ben Gorion, a very authentical Hebrew author, a testimony of the passing of twenty thousand Britains, valiant soldiers, to

the siege and fearful sacking of Jerusalem under the conduct of Vespasian and Titus, the Roman emperor, a thing indeed of all the rest most ancient. But of latter days I see our men have pierced further into the East, have passed down the mighty River Euphrates, have sailed from Balsara through the Persian Gulf to the city of Ormuz and from thence to Chaul and Goa in the East India, which passages, written by the parties themselves, are herein to be read. To these I have added the navigations of the English made for the parts of Africa, and either within or without the Straights of Gibraltar: within, to Constantinople in Romania, to Alexandria and Cairo in Egypt, to Tunez, to Goletta, to Malta, to Algier, and to Tripolis in Barbary; without, to Santa Cruz, to Asafi, to the city of Marocco, to the River of Senega, to the Isles of Cape Verde, to Guinea, to Benyn, and round about the dreadful Cape of Bona Speranza as far as Goa.

The north and northeastern voyages of our nation I have produced in the second place because our access to those quarters of the world is later and not so ancient as the former; and yet some of our travails that way be of more antiquity by many hundred years then those that have been made to the western coasts of America. Under this title thou shalt first find the old northern navigations of our British kings, as of Arthur, of Malgo, of Edgar Pacificus, the Saxon monarch, with that also of Nicholaus de Linna under the North Pole; next to them in consequence the discoveries of the Bay of Saint Nicholas, of Colgoieve, of Pechora, of the Isles of Vaigats, of Nova Zembla, and of the sea eastwards towards the River of Ob; after this, the opening by sea of the great dukedom and empire of Russia, with the notable and strange journey of Master Jenkinson to Boghar in Bactria. . . .

Touching the western navigations and travails of ours, they succeed naturally in the third and last room, forasmuch as in order and course those coasts and quarters came last of all to our knowledge and experience. Herein thou shalt read the attempt by sea of the son of one of the princes of North Wales in sailing and searching towards the west more then four hundred years since, the offer made by Christopher Columbus, that renowned Genovese, to the most sage prince of noble memory, King Henry the Seventh, with his prompt and cheerful acceptation thereof and the occasion whereupon it became fruitless and at that time of no great effect to this kingdom; then follow the letters-patents of the foresaid noble prince given to John Cabot, a Venetian, and his three sons to discover and conquer in his name and under his banners unknown regions, who with that royal incouragement and contribution of the king himself, and some assistance in charges of

English marchants, departed with five sails from the port of Bristol accompanied with three hundred Englishmen, and first of any Christians found out that mighty and large tract of land and sea from the Circle Arctic as far as Florida, as appeareth in the discourse thereof. The triumphant reign of King Henry the Eighth yielded some prosecution of this discovery, for the three voyages performed and the four intended for all Asia by his Majesty's self do approve and confirm the same. Then in process of years ariseth the first English trade to Brasil, the first passing of some of our nation in the ordinary Spanish fleets to the West Indies and the huge City of Mexico in Nova Hispania. Then immediately ensue three voyages made by M[aster] John Hawkins, now knight, then esquire, to Hispaniola and the Gulf of Mexico, upon which depend six very excellent discourses of our men, whereof some for fifteen or sixteen whole years inhabited in New Spain and ranged the whole country, wherein are disclosed the chiefest secrets of the West India, which may in time turn to our no small advantage. The next leaves thou turnest do yield thee the first valiant enterprise of Sir Francis Drake upon Nombre de Dios, the mules laden with treasure which he surprised, and the house called the Cruzes which his fire consumed; and therewith is joined an action more venterous then happy of John Oxnam of Plymouth (written and confessed by a Spaniard), which with his company passed over the straight Istme of Darien and, building certain pinnesses on the west shore, was the first Englishman that entered the South Sea. To pass over Master Frobisher and his actions, which I have also newly though briefly printed, and as it were revived, whatsoever Master John Davys hath performed in continuing that discovery which Master Frobisher began for the Northwest Passage I have faithfully at large communicated it with thee that so the great good hope and singular probabilities and almost certainty thereof which by his industry have risen may be known generally of all men, that some may yet still prosecute so noble an action. Sir Humphrey Gilbert, that couragious knight, and very expert in the mysteries of navigation, amongst the rest is not forgotten; his learned reasons and arguments for the proof of the passage before named, together with his last more commendable resolution then fortunate success, are here both to be read. The continuance of the history produceth the beginnings and proceedings of the two English colonies planted in Virginia at the charges of Sir Walter Raleigh, whose entrance upon those new inhabitations had been happy if it had been as seriously followed as it was cheerfully undertaken. . . .

For the conclusion of all, the memorable voyage of Master Thomas Candish into the South Sea and from thence about the globe of the earth doth satisfy me, and I doubt not but will fully content thee; which as in time it is later then that of Sir Francis Drake, so in relation of the Philippinas, Japan, China, and the Isle of Saint Helena it is more particular and exact, and therefore the want of the first made by Sir Francis Drake will be the less; wherein I must confess to have taken more then ordinary pains, meaning to have inserted it in this work, but being of late (contrary to my expectation) seriously dealt withal not to anticipate or prevent another man's pains and charge in drawing all the services of that worthy knight into one volume, I have yielded unto those my friends which pressed me in the matter, referring the further knowledge of his proceedings to those intended discourses. . . .

Now because peradventure it would be expected as necessary that the descriptions of so many parts of the world would far more easily be conceived of the readers by adding geographical and hydrographical tables thereunto, thou art by the way to be admonished that I have contented myself with inserting into the work one of the best general maps of the world only until the coming-out of a very large and most exact terrestrial globe, collected and reformed according to the newest, secretest, and latest discoveries, both Spanish, Portugal, and English, composed by M[aster] Emery Mollineux of Lambeth, a rare gentleman in his profession, being therein for divers years greatly supported by the purse and liberality of the worshipful marchant M[aster] William Sanderson.

This being the sum of those things which I thought good to admonish thee of, good reader, it remaineth that thou take the profit and pleasure of the work, which I wish to be as great to thee as my pains and labor have been in bringing these raw fruits unto this ripeness, and in reducing these loose papers into this order. Farewell.

FROM THE PRINCIPAL NAVIGATIONS (1598-1600)

The course which Sir Francis Drake held from the haven of Guatulco in the South Sea on the back side of Nueva Espanna to the northwest of California as far as forty-three degrees, and his return back along the said coast to thirty-eight degrees, where finding a fair and goodly haven he landed; and staying there many weeks, and discovering many excellent things in the country and great shew of rich mineral matter, and being offered the dominion of the country by the lord of the same, he took possession thereof in the behalf of her Majesty, and named it Nova Albion.

We kept our course from the Isle of Cano, which lieth in eight degrees of northerly latitude, and within two leagues of the main of Nicaragua, where we calked and trimmed our ship, along the coast of Nueva Espanna, until we came to the haven and town of Guatulco, which, as we were informed, had but seventeen Spaniards dwelling in it, and we found it to stand in fifteen degrees and fifty minutes.

As soon as we were ent'red this haven we landed, and went presently to the town and to the town-house, where we found a judge sitting in judgment, he being associate with three other officers, upon three Negroes that had conspired the burning of the town, both which judges and prisoners we took, and brought them a-shipboard and caused the chief judge to write his letter to the town, to command all the townsmen to avoid, that we might safely water there. Which being done, and they departed, we ransacked the town and in one house we found a pot of the quantity of a bushel full of royals of plate, which we brought to our ship.

And here one Thomas Moone, one of our company, took a Spanish gentleman as he was flying out of the town, and, searching him, he found a chain of gold about him and other jewels, which we took and so let him go.

At this place our general, among other Spaniards, set ashore his Portugal pilot, which he took at the Island of Cape Verde out of a ship of Saint Marie, port of Portugal, and, having set them ashore, we departed thence.

Our general at this place and time thinking himself, both in respect of his private injuries received from the Spaniards as also of their contempts and indignities offered to our country and prince in general, sufficiently satisfied and revenged, and supposing that her Majesty at his return would rest contented with this service, purposed to continue no longer upon the Spanish coasts, but began to consider and to consult of the best way for his country.

He thought it not good to return by the straits, for two special causes: the one, lest the Spaniards should there wait and attend for him in great number and strength, whose hands he, being left but one ship, could not possibly escape. The other cause was the dangerous situation of the mouth of the straits of the south side, with continual storms raining and blust'ring, as he found by experience, besides the shoals and sands upon the coast. Wherefore he thought it not a good course to adventure that way. He resolved, therefore, to avoid these hazards, to go

forward to the Islands of the Malucos, and therehence to sail the course of the Portugals by the Cape of Bona Sperança.

Upon this resolution, he began to think of his best way for the Malucos, and finding himself, where he now was, becalmed, he saw that of necessity he must be enforced to take a Spanish course, namely to sail somewhat northerly to get a wind. We therefore set sail and sailed 800 leagues at the least for a good wind, and thus much we sailed from the 16 of April (after our old style) till the third of June.

The fift day of June, being in forty-three degrees towards the pole Arctic, being speedily come out of the extreme heat, we found the air so cold that our men, being pinched with the same, complained of the extremity thereof, and the further we went, the more the cold increased upon us, whereupon we thought it best for that time to seek land, and did so, finding it not mountainous, but low plainland, and we drew back again without landing, till we came within thirty-eight degrees towards the line. In which height it pleased God to send us into a fair and good bay, with a good wind to enter the same.

In this bay we ankered the seventeenth of June, and the people of the country, having their houses close by the water's side, shewed themselves unto us, and sent a present to our general.

When they came unto us, they greatly wond'red at the things which we brought, but our general, according to his natural and accustomed humanity, curteously intreated them, and liberally bestowed on them necessary things to cover their nakedness, whereupon they supposed us to be gods, and would not be persuaded to the contrary. The presents which they sent unto our general were feathers and cawls of network.

Their houses are digged round about with earth, and have from the uttermost brims of the circle clifts of wood set upon them, joining close together at the top like a spire steeple, which by reason of that closeness are very warm.

Their bed is the ground with rushes strawed on it, and, lying about the house, they have the fire in the middest. The men go naked, the women take bulrushes and kemb them after the manner of hemp, and thereof make their loose garments, which being knit about their middles hang down about their hips, having also about their shoulders a skin of deer, with the hair upon it. These women are very obedient and serviceable to their husbands.

After they were departed from us, they came and visited us the second time, and brought with them feathers and bags of tabacco for presents. And when they came to the top of the hill, at the bottom whereof we had pitched our tents, they stayed themselves, where one appointed for speaker wearied himself with making a long oration, which done, they left their bows upon the hill and came down with their presents.

In the meantime the women remaining on the hill tormented themselves lamentably, tearing their flesh from their cheeks, whereby we perceived that they were about a sacrifice. In the meantime our general, with his company, went to prayer and to reading of the Scriptures, at which exercise they were attentive and seemed greatly to be affected with it. But when they were come unto us they restored again unto us those things which before we had bestowed upon them.

The news of our being there being spread through the country, the people that inhabited round about came down, and amongst them the king himself, a man of a goodly stature and comely personage, with many other tall and warlike men, before whose coming were sent two ambassadors to our general to signify that their king was coming, in doing of which message their speech was continued about half an hour. This ended, they by signs requested our general to send something by their hand to their king, as a token that his coming might be in peace. Wherein our general having satisfied them, they returned with glad tidings to their king, who marched to us with a princely majesty, the people crying continually after their manner, and, as they drew near unto us, so did they strive to behave themselves in their actions with comeliness.

In the forefront was a man of a goodly personage, who bare the scepter or mace before the king, whereupon hanged two crowns, a less and a bigger, with three chains of a merveilous length. The crowns were made of knitwork wrought artificially with feathers of divers colors. The chains were made of a bony substance, and few be the persons among them that are admitted to wear them, and of that number also the persons are stinted, as some ten, some twelve, etc. Next unto him which bare the scepter was the king himself, with his guard about his person, clad with cony skins and other skins. After them followed the naked common sort of people, every one having his face painted, some with white, some with black, and other colors, and having in their hands one thing or other for a present, not so much as their children but they also brought their presents.

In the meantime, our general gathered his men together, and marched within his fenced place, making against their approaching a very warlike shew. They being trooped together in their order, and a general salutation being made, there was presently a general silence. Then he that bare the scepter before the king, being informed by another whom they assigned to that office, with a manly and lofty voice proclaimed that which the other spake to him in secret, continuing half an hour, which ended and a general amen, as it were, given, the king, with the whole number of men and women (the children excepted), came down without any weapon, who descending to the foot of the hill set themselves in order.

In coming towards our bulwarks and tents, the scepter-bearer began a song, observing his measures in a dance, and that with a stately countenance, whom the king with his guard, and every degree of persons following, did in like manner sing and dance, saving only the women, which danced and kept silence. The general permitted them to enter within our bulwark, where they continued their song and dance a reasonable time. When they had satisfied themselves, they made signs to our general to sit down, to whom the king and divers others made several orations, or rather supplication, that he would take their province and kingdom into his hand and become their king, making signs that they would resign unto him their right and title of the whole land and become his subjects. In which to persuade us the better, the king and the rest with one consent and with great reverence, joyfully singing a song, did set the crown upon his head, inriched his neck with all their chains, and offered unto him many other things, honoring him by the name of *Hioh*, adding thereunto, as it seemed, a sign of triumph, which thing our general thought not meet to reject, because he knew not what honor and profit it might be to our country. Wherefore in the name and to the use of her Majesty he took the scepter, crown, and dignity of the said country in his hands, wishing that the riches and treasure thereof might so conveniently be transported to the inriching of her kingdom at home as it aboundeth in the same.

The common sort of the people, leaving the king and his guard with our general, scattered themselves together with their sacrifices among our people, taking a diligent view of every person; and such as pleased their fancy (which were the youngest) they, inclosing them about, off'red their sacrifices unto them with lamentable weeping, scratching, and tearing the flesh from their faces with their nails, whereof issued abundance of blood. But we used signs to them of disliking this, and stayed their hands from force, and directed them upwards to the living God, whom only they ought to worship. They shewed unto us their wounds, and craved help of them at our hands, whereupon we gave them lotions, plaisters, and ointments agreeing to the state of their griefs, beseeching God to cure their diseases. Every third day they brought their sacrifices unto us, until they understood our meaning, that we had no pleasure in them. Yet they could not be long absent from us, but daily frequented our company to the hour of our departure, which departure seemed so grievous unto them that their joy was turned into sorrow. They intreated us that being absent we would remember them, and by stealth provided a sacrifice, which we misliked.

Our necessary business being ended, our general with his company traveled up into the country to their villages, where we found herds of deer by a 10 thousand in a company, being most large and fat of body.

We found the whole country to be a warren of a strange kind of conies, their bodies in bigness as be the Barbary conies, their heads as the heads of ours, the feet of a want, and the tail of a rat, being of great length; under her chin on either side a bag into the which she gathereth her meat when she hath filled her belly abroad. The people eat their bodies and make great account of their skins, for their king's 20 coat was made of them.

Our general called this country Nova Albion,

and that for two causes: the one in respect of the white banks and cliffs which lie towards the sea, and the other because it might have some affinity with our country in name, which sometime was so called.

There is no part of earth here to be taken up wherein there is not some special likelihood of gold or silver.

At our departure hence our general set up a monument of our being there, as also of her Majesty's right and title to the same, namely, a plate nailed upon a fair great post, whereupon was ingraven her Majesty's name, the day and year of our arrival there, with the free giving-up of the province and people into her Majesty's hands, together with her Highness' picture and arms, in a piece of sixpence of current English money under the plate, whereunder was also written the name of our general.

It seemeth that the Spaniards hitherto had never been in this part of the country, neither did ever discover the land by many degrees to the southwards of this place.

SIR WALTER RALEIGH

THE LAST FIGHT OF THE *REVENGE* AT SEA

Raleigh's romantic, zestful account of his cousin Sir Richard Grenville's fatal encounter with the Spaniards off the Azores—an account that tells us a great deal about the nationalistic and religious currents sweeping England in Elizabeth's reign—was published anonymously in 1591. Hakluyt inevitably appropriated it for the second edition

of the *Principal Navigations,* and his attribution of the authorship to Raleigh has been accepted ever since. Our text is based upon *A Report of the Truth of the fight about the Iles of Açores, this last Sommer. Betwixt the Revenge, one of her Maiesties Shippes, And an Armada of the King of Spaine,* 1591 (STC 20651).

A REPORT OF THE TRUTH OF THE FIGHT ABOUT THE ILES OF AÇORES THIS LAST SUMMER BETWIXT THE *REVENGE,* ONE OF HER MAJESTY'S SHIPS, AND AN ARMADA OF THE KING OF SPAIN (1591)

Because the rumors are diversely spread, as well in England as in the Low Countries and elsewhere, of this late encounter between her Majesty's ships and the Armada of Spain; and that the Spaniards according to their usual manner fill the world with their vainglorious vaunts, making great apparance of victories, when on the contrary themselves are most commonly and shamefully beaten and dishonored; thereby hoping to possess the ignorant multitude by anticipating and forerunning false reports; it is agree- 10 able with all good reason, for manifestation of the truth, to overcome falsehood and untruth, that the

beginning, continuance, and success of this late honorable encounter of Sir Richard Grinvile and other her Majesty's captains with the Armada of Spain should be truly set down and published without partiality or false imaginations. And it is no marvel that the Spaniard should seek by false and sland'rous pamphlets, advisoes, and letters to cover their own loss and to derogate from others their due honors, especially in this fight being performed far off; seeing they were not ashamed in the year 1588, when they purposed the invasion of this land, to publish in sundry languages, in print, great victories in words, which they pleaded to have obtained against this realm; and spread the same in a most false sort over all parts of France, Italy, and elsewhere. When shortly after it was happily manifested in very deed to all nations how their navy, which they termed invincible, consisting of 240 sail of ships, not only of their own kingdom but strengthened with the greatest argosies, Portugal carracks, Florentines, and huge hulks of other countries, were by thirty of her Majesty's own ships of war, and a few of our own marchants, by the wise, valiant, and most advantagious conduction of the Lord Charles Howard, high admiral of England, beaten and shuffeled togither; even from the Lizard in Cornwall, first to Portland, where they shamefully left Don Pedro de Valdes with his mighty ship; from Portland to Cales, where they lost Hugo de Moncado, with the gallias of which he was captain; and from Cales driven with squibs from their anchors, were chased out of the sight of England, round about Scotland and Ireland. Where for the sympathy of their barbarous religion hoping to find succor and assistance, a great part of them were crush'd against the rocks, and those other that landed, being very many in number, were notwithstanding broken, slain, and taken, and so sent from village to village, coupled in halters, to be shipped into England. Where her Majesty of her princely and invincible disposition disdaining to put them to death, and scorning either to retain or entertain them, were all sent back again to their countries, to witness and recount the worthy achievements of their invincible and dreadful navy. Of which the number of soldiers, the fearful burthen of their ships,· the commanders' names of every squadron, with all other their magazines of provisions, were put in print as an army and navy unresistible and disdaining prevention. With all which so great and terrible an ostentation they did not in all their sailing round about England so much as sink or take one ship, bark, pinnes, or cockboat of ours, or ever burn'd so much as one sheepcote of this land. Whenas on the contrary Sir Francis Drake, with only eight hundred soldiers, not long before landed in their Indies and forced Santiago, Santo Domingo, Cartagena, and the forts of Florida. And after that Sir John Norris marched from Peniche in Portugal, with a handful of soldiers, to the gates of Lisbon, being above forty English miles. Where the Earl of Essex himself and other valiant gentlemen braved the city of Lisbon, encamped at the very gates; from whence after many days' abode, finding neither promised party nor provision to batter, made retrait by land in despight of all their garrisons both of horse and foot.

In this sort I have a little digressed from my first purpose, only by the necessary comparison of theirs and our actions; the one covetous of honor without vaunt or ostentation; the other so greedy to purchase the opinion of their own affairs and by false rumors to resist the blasts of their own dishonors as they will not only not blush to spread all manner of untruths, but even for the least advantage, be it but for the taking of one poor adventurer of the English, will celebrate the victory with bonfires in every town, always spending more in faggots then the purchase was worth they obtained. Whenas we never yet thought it worth the consumption of two billets when we have taken eight or ten of their Indian ships at one time and twenty of the Brasill fleet. Such is the difference between true valure and ostentation, and between honorable actions and frivolous vainglorious vaunts. But now to return to my first purpose.

The Lord Thomas Howard, with six of her Majesty's ships, six victualers of London, the bark *Ralegh,* and two or three pinnaces, riding at anchor near unto Flores, one of the westerly ilands of the Azores, the last of August in the afternoon, had intelligence by one Captain Middleton of the approach of the Spanish Armada. Which Middleton being in a very good sailer had kept them company three days before, of good purpose, both to discover their forces the more, as also to give advice to my Lord Thomas of their approach. He had no sooner delivered the news but the fleet was in sight.

Many of our ships' companies were on shore in the iland, some providing ballast for their ships, others filling of water and refreshing themselves from the land with such things as they could either for money or by force recover. By reason whereof our ships being all pestered and roomaging, everything out of order, very light for want of ballast. And that which was most to our disadvantage, the one-half part of the men of every ship sick and utterly unserviceable. For in the *Revenge* there were ninety diseased; in the *Bonaventure* not so many in health as could handle her mainsail. For had not twenty men been taken out of a bark of Sir George Cary's, his being commanded to be sunk, and those appointed to her, she had hardly ever recovered England. The rest for the most part were in little better state. The names of her Majesty's ships were these as followeth: the *Defiance,* which was admiral, the *Revenge,* vice-admiral, the *Bonaventure* commanded by Captain Cross, the *Lion* by George Fenner, the *Foresight* by M[aster] Thomas Vavasour, and the *Crane* by Duffield. The *Foresight* and the *Crane* being but small ships; only the other were of the middle size; the rest, besides the bark *Ralegh* commanded by Captain Thin, were victualers and of small force or none.

The Spanish fleet having shrouded their approach

by reason of the iland, were now so soon at hand as our ships had scarce time to weigh their anchors, but some of them were driven to let slip their cables and set sail. Sir Richard Grinvile was the last weighed, to recover the men that were upon the iland, which otherwise had been lost. The Lord Thomas with the rest very hardly recovered the wind, which Sir Richard Grinvile not being able to do was persuaded by the maister and others to cut his mainsail and cast about, and to trust to the sailing of the ship; for the squadron of Sivil were on his weather bow. But Sir Richard utterly refused to turn from the enemy, alledging that he would rather choose to die then to dishonor himself, his country, and her Majesty's ship, persuading his company that he would pass through the two squadrons in despight of them, and enforce those of Sivil to give him way. Which he performed upon divers of the foremost, who, as the mariners term it, sprang their luff, and fell under the lee of the *Revenge*. But the other course had been the better, and might right well have been answered in so great an impossibility of prevailing. Notwithstanding, out of the greatness of his mind he could not be persuaded.

In the meanwhile as he attended those which were nearest him, the great *San Philip*, being in the wind of him and coming towards him, becalmed his sails in such sort as the ship could neither make way nor feel the helm, so huge and high carged was the Spanish ship, being of a thousand and five hundreth tons. Who after laid the *Revenge* aboard. When he was thus bereft of his sails, the ships that were under his lee, luffing up, also laid him aboard; of which the next was the admiral of the Biscaines, a very mighty and puissant ship commanded by Brittandona. The said *Philip* carried three tire of ordinance on a side, and eleven pieces in every tire. She shot eight forthright out of her chase, besides those of her stern ports.

After the *Revenge* was intangled with this *Philip*, four other boarded her, two on her larboard and two on her starboard. The fight thus beginning at three of the clock in the afternoon continued very terrible all that evening. But the great *San Philip* having received the lower tire of the *Revenge*, discharged with crossbar-shot, shifted herself with all diligence from her sides, utterly misliking her first entertainment. Some say that the ship found'red, but we cannot report it for truth unless we were assured.

The Spanish ships were filled with companies of soldiers, in some two hundred besides the mariners, in some five, in others eight hundreth. In ours there were none at all, beside the mariners, but the servants of the commanders and some few voluntary gentlemen only. After many enterchanged volleys of great ordinance and small shot, the Spaniards deliberated to enter the *Revenge*, and made divers attempts, hoping to force her by the multitudes of their armed soldiers and musketeers, but were still repulsed again and again, and at all times beaten back into their own ships or into the seas.

In the beginning of the fight the *George Noble* of London, having received some shot thorow her by the armados, fell under the lee of the *Revenge* and asked Sir Richard what he would command him, being but one of the victualers and of small force. Sir Richard bid him save himself and leave him to his fortune.

After the fight had thus without intermission continued while the day lasted and some hours of the night, many of our men were slain and hurt, and one of the great gallions of the armada and the admiral of the hulks both sunk, and in many other of the Spanish ships great slaughter was made. Some write that Sir Richard was very dangerously hurt almost in the beginning of the fight and lay speechless for a time ere he recovered. But two of the *Revenge*'s own company, brought home in a ship of line from the ilands, examined by some of the lords and others, affirmed that he was never so wounded as that he forsook the upper deck till an hour before midnight; and then being shot into the body with a musket, as he was a-dressing was again shot into the head, and withal his chirurgeon wounded to death. This agreeth also with an examination taken by Sir Francis Godolphin of four other mariners of the same ship being returned, which examination the said Sir Francis sent unto Maister William Killigrew of her Majesty's privy chamber.

But to return to the fight, the Spanish ships which attempted to board the *Revenge,* as they were wounded and beaten off, so always others came in their places, she having never less then two mighty gallions by her sides and aboard her. So that ere the morning, from three of the clock the day before, there had fifteen several armados assailed her; and all so ill approved their entertainment as they were by the break of day far more willing to harken to a composition then hastily to make any more assaults or entries. But as the day encreased, so our men decreased; and as the light grew more and more, by so much more grew our discomforts. For none appeared in sight but enemies, saving one small ship called the *Pilgrim,* commanded by Jacob Whiddon, who hovered all night to see the success, but in the morning bearing with the *Revenge* was hunted like a hare amongst many ravenous hounds, but escaped.

All the powder of the *Revenge* to the last barrel was now spent, all her pikes broken, forty of her best men slain, and the most part of the rest hurt. In the beginning of the fight she had but one hundreth free from sickness, and fourscore and ten sick, laid in hold upon the ballast. A small troop to man such a

ship, and a weak garrison to resist so mighty an
army. By those hundred all was sustained, the volleys,
boardings, and ent'rings of fifteen ships of war,
besides those which beat her at large. On the contrary,
the Spanish were always supplied with soldiers
brought from every squadron; all manner of arms
and powder at will. Unto ours there remained no
comfort at all, no hope, no supply either of ships,
men, or weapons; the masts all beaten overboard,
all her tackle cut asunder, her upper work altogither   10
rased, and in effect evened she was with the water,
but the very foundation or bottom of a ship, nothing
being left overhead either for flight or defense.

Sir Richard, finding himself in this distress and
unable any longer to make resistance, having endured
in this fifteen hours' fight the assault of fifteen several
armados all by turns aboard him, and by estimation
eight hundred shot of great artillery, besides many
assaults and entries; and that himself and the ship
must needs be possessed by the enemy, who were   20
now all cast in a ring round about him, the *Revenge*
not able to move one way or other but as she was
moved with the waves and billow of the sea; commanded the maister gunner, whom he knew to be a
most resolute man, to split and sink the ship; that
thereby nothing might remain of glory or victory
to the Spaniards, seeing in so many hours' fight and
with so great a navy they were not able to take her,
having had fifteen hours' time, fifteen thousand men,
and fifty-and-three sail of men-of-war to perform it   30
withal; and persuaded the company, or as many as
he could induce, to yield themselves unto God and to
the mercy of none else, but as they had like valiant
resolute men repulsed so many enemies they should
not now shorten the honor of their nation by prolonging their own lives for a few hours or a few days.

The maister gunner readily condescended, and
divers others; but the captain and the maister were of
another opinion, and besought Sir Richard to have
care of them; alleging that the Spaniard would be as   40
ready to entertain a composition as they were willing
to offer the same; and that there being diverse
sufficient and valiant men yet living, and whose
wounds were not mortal, they might do their country and prince acceptable service hereafter. And that
where Sir Richard had alleged that the Spaniards
should never glory to have taken one ship of her
Majesty, seeing they had so long and so notably
defended themselves, they answered that the ship
had six foot water in hold, three shot under water   50
which were so weakly stopped as with the first
working of the sea she must needs sink, and was
besides so crush'd and bruised as she could never be
removed out of the place.

And as the matter was thus in dispute, and Sir

Richard refusing to harken to any of those reasons,
the maister of the *Revenge* (while the captain wan
unto him the greater party) was convoy'd aboard
the general, Don Alfonso Bassan. Who finding none
overhasty to enter the *Revenge* again, doubting lest
Sir Richard would have blown them up and himself,
and perceiving by the report of the maister of the
Revenge his dangerous disposition, yielded that all
their lives should be saved, the company sent for
England, and the better sort to pay such reasonable
ransom as their estate would bear, and in the mean
season to be free from galley or imprisonment. To
this he so much the rather condescended as well, as
I have said, for fear of further loss and mischief to
themselves, as also for the desire he had to recover
Sir Richard Grinvile, whom for his notable valure
he seemed greatly to honor and admire.

When this answer was returned, and that safety
of life was promised, the common sort being now
at the end of their peril, the most drew back from
Sir Richard and the maister gunner, being no hard
matter to dissuade men from death to life. The
maister gunner, finding himself and Sir Richard
thus prevented and maistered by the greater number,
would have slain himself with a sword, had he not
been by force withheld and locked into his cabin.
Then the general sent many boats aboard the *Revenge,*
and diverse of our men, fearing Sir Richard's disposition, stole away aboard the general and other ships.
Sir Richard, thus overmatched, was sent unto by
Alfonso Bassan to remove out of the *Revenge,* the
ship being marvelous unsavory, filled with blood and
bodies of dead and wounded men like a slaughterhouse. Sir Richard answered that he might do with
his body what he list, for he esteemed it not, and as
he was carried out of the ship he swounded, and
reviving again desired the company to pray for him.
The general used Sir Richard with all humanity, and
left nothing unattempted that tended to his recovery, highly commending his valor and worthiness, and greatly bewailed the danger wherein he
was, being unto them a rare spectacle and a resolution sildom approved, to see one ship turn toward
so many enemies, to endure the charge and boarding
of so many huge armados, and to resist and repel the
assaults and entries of so many soldiers. All which and
more is confirmed by a Spanish captain of the same
armada, and a present actor in the fight, who being
severed from the rest in a storm was by the *Lion* of
London, a small ship, taken, and is now prisoner in
London.

The general commander of the armada was Don
Alfonso Bassan, brother to the Marquess of Santa
Cruz. The admiral of the Biscaine squadron was
Brittandona. Of the squadron of Sivil, the Marquess

of Arumburch. The hulks and flyboats were commanded by Luis Coutinho. There were slain and drowned in this fight well near two thousand of the enemies, and two especial commanders, Don Luis de Sant John and Don George de Prunaria de Malaga, as the Spanish captain confesseth, besides divers others of special account whereof as yet report is not made.

The admiral of the hulks and the *Ascension* of Sivil were both sunk by the side of the *Revenge;* one other recovered the road of St. Michael's and sunk also there; a fourth ran herself with the shore to save her men. Sir Richard died, as it is said, the second or third day aboard the general, and was by them greatly bewailed. What became of his body, whether it were buried in the sea or on the land, we know not; the comfort that remaineth to his friends is that he hath ended his life honorably in respect of the reputation won to his nation and country, and of the same to his posterity, and that being dead he hath not outlived his own honor.

For the rest of her Majesty's ships that ent'red not so far into the fight as the *Revenge,* the reasons and causes were these. There were of them but six in all, whereof two but small ships; the *Revenge* ingaged past recovery; the Iland of Flores was on the one side, fifty-three sail of the Spanish, divided into squadrons, on the other, all as full filled with soldiers as they could contain; almost the one-half of our men sick and not able to serve; the ships grown foul, unroomaged, and scarcely able to bear any sail for want of ballast, having been six months at the sea before. If all the rest had ent'red, all had been lost. For the very hugeness of the Spanish fleet, if no other violence had been off'red, would have crush'd them between them into shivers. Of which the dishonor and loss to the queen had been far greater then the spoil or harm that the enemy could any way have received. Notwithstanding, it is very true that the Lord Thomas would have ent'red between the squadrons, but the rest would not condescend; and the maister of his own ship off'red to leap into the sea rather then to conduct that her Majesty's ship and the rest to be a prey to the enemy, where there was no hope nor possibility either of defense or victory. Which also in my opinion had ill sorted or answered the discretion and trust of a general, to commit himself and his charge to an assured destruction, without hope or any likelihood of prevailing; thereby to diminish the strength of her Majesty's navy and to enrich the pride and glory of the enemy. The *Foresight* of the queen's, commanded by M[aster] Thomas Vavasour, performed a very great fight, and stay'd two hours as near the *Revenge* as the weather would permit him, not forsaking the fight

till he was like to be encompassed by the squadrons and with great difficulty cleared himself. The rest gave divers volleys of shot and ent'red as far as the place permitted, and their own necessities to keep the weather gage of the enemy, until they were parted by night.

A few days after the fight was ended and the English prisoners dispersed into the Spanish and Indy ships there arose so great a storm from the west and northwest that all the fleet was dispersed, as well the Indian fleet which were then come unto them as the rest of the armada that attended their arrival, of which fourteen sail, togither with the *Revenge,* and in her two hundred Spaniards, were cast away upon the Isle of St. Michael's. So it pleased them to honor the burial of that renowned ship the *Revenge,* not suff'ring her to perish alone, for the great honor she achieved in her lifetime. On the rest of the ilands there were cast away in this storm fifteen or sixteen more of the ships of war; and of a hundred and odd sail of the Indy fleet, expected this year in Spain, what in this tempest, and what before in the Bay of Mexico and about the Bermudas, there were seventy and odd consumed and lost, with those taken by our ships of London, besides one very rich Indian ship which set herself on fire, being boarded by the *Pilgrim,* and five other taken by Maister Watts his ships of London, between the Havana and Cape St. Antonio. The fourth of this month of November we received letters from the Tercera affirming that there are three thousand bodies of men remaining in that iland, saved out of the perished ships; and that by the Spaniards' own confession there are ten thousand cast away in this storm, besides those that are perished between the ilands and the main. Thus it hath pleased God to fight for us and to defend the justice of our cause against the ambitious and bloody pretenses of the Spaniard, who seeking to devour all nations are themselves devoured. A manifest testimony how injust and displeasing their attempts are in the sight of God, who hath pleased to witness by the success of their affairs his mislike of their bloody and injurious designs purposed and practised against all Christian princes, over whom they seek unlawful and ungodly rule and empery.

One day or two before this wrack happ'ned to the Spanish fleet, whenas some of our prisoners desired to be set on shore upon the ilands, hoping to be from thence transported into England, which liberty was formerly by the general promised, one Morice Fitz-John, son of old John of Desmond, a notable traitor, cousin-german to the late Earl of Desmond, was sent to the English from ship to ship to persuade them to serve the king of Spain. The arguments he used to induce them were these: the increase of pay, which he promised to be trebled; advancement to the better sort; and the exercise of the true Catholic religion and safety of their souls to all. For the first, even the beggarly and unnatural behavior of those English and Irish rebels that served the king in that present action was sufficient to answer that first argument of rich pay. For so poor and beggarly they were as for want of apparel they stripped their poor countrymen prisoners out of their ragged garments worn to nothing by six months' service, and spared not to despoil them even of their bloody shirts from their wounded bodies, and the very shoes from their feet; a notable testimony of their rich entertainment and great wages. The second reason was hope of advancement if they served well and would continue faithful to the king. But what man can be so blockishly ignorant ever to expect place or honor from a forrain king, having no other argument or persuasion then his own disloyalty; to be unnatural to his own country that bred him, to his parents that begat him, and rebellious to his true prince to whose obedience he is bound by oath, by nature, and by religion? No, they are only assured to be imployed in all desperate enterprises, to be held in scorn and disdain ever among those whom they serve. And that ever traitor was either trusted or advanced I could never yet read, neither can I at this time remember any example. And no man could have less becomed the place of an orator for such a purpose then this Morice of Desmond. For the earl his cosen, being one of the greatest subjects in that kingdom of Ireland, having almost whole countries in his possession, so many goodly manors, castles, and lordships, the count palatine of Kerry, five hundred gentlemen of his own name and family to follow him, besides others—all which he possessed in peace for three or four hundred years—was in less then three years after his adhering to the Spaniards and rebellion beaten from all his holds, not so many as ten gentlemen of his name left living, himself taken and beheaded by a soldier of his own nation, and his land given by a Parliament to her Majesty and possessed by the English; his other cosen, Sir John of Desmond, taken by M[aster] John Zouch and his body hanged over the gates of his native city to be devoured by ravens; the third brother, Sir James, hanged, drawn, and quartered in the same place. If he had withal vaunted of this success of his own house, no doubt the argument would have moved much and wrought great effect; which because he for that present forgot, I thought it good to remember in his behalf. For matter of religion, it would require a particular volume if I should set down how irreligiously they cover their greedy and ambitious pretenses with that veil of piety. But sure I am that there is no kingdom or commonwealth in all Europe but, if they be reformed, they then invade it for religion sake; if it be, as they term, Catholic, they pretend title, as if the kings of Castile were the natural heirs of all the world; and so between both no kingdom is unsought. Where they dare not with their own forces to invade, they basely entertain the traitors and vacabonds of all nations, seeking by those and by their runnagate Jesuits to win parts, and have by that mean ruined many noble houses and others in this land, and have extinguished both their lives and families. What good, honor, or fortune ever man yet by them achieved is yet unheard of or unwritten. And if our English papists do but look into Portugal, against whom they have no pretense of religion, how the nobility are put to death, imprisoned, their rich men made a prey, and all sorts of people captived, they shall find that the obedience even of the Turk is easy and a liberty in respect of the slavery and tyranny of Spain. What they have done in Sicil, in Naples, Milan, and in the Low Countries; who hath there been spared for religion at all? And it cometh to my remembrance of a certain burgher of Antwerp, whose house being ent'red by a company of Spanish soldiers, when they first sacked the city, he besought them to spare him and his goods, being a good Catholic, and one of their own party and faction. The Spaniards answered that they knew him to be of a good conscience for himself, but his money, plate, jewels, and goods were all heretical and therefore good prize. So they abused and tormented the foolish Fleming, who hoped that an *Agnus Dei* had been a sufficient target against all force of that holy and charitable nation. Neither have they at any time, as they protest, invaded the kingdoms of the Indies and Peru and elsewhere but only led thereunto rather to reduce the people to Christianity then for either gold or empery. Whenas in one only iland, called Hispaniola, they have wasted thirty hundred thousand of the natural people, besides many millions else in other places of the Indies; a poor and harmless people, created of God, and might have been won to his knowledge, as many of them were, and almost as many as ever were persuaded thereunto. The story whereof is at large written by a bishop of their own nation called Bartholomew de las Casas, and translated into English and many other languages, intituled *The Spanish Cruelties*. Who would therefore repose trust in such a nation of ravinous strangers, and especially in those Spaniards, which more greedily thirst after English blood then after the lives of any other people of Europe, for the many overthrows and dishonors they have received at our hands, whose weakness we have discovered to the world, and whose forces at home, abroad, in Europe, in India, by sea and land, we have even with handfuls of men and ships overthrown and dishonored? Let not therefore any Englishman, of what religion soever, have other opinion of the Spaniards but that those whom he seeketh to win of our nation he esteemeth base and traitorous, unworthy persons, or unconstant fools; and that he useth his pretense of religion for no other purpose but to bewitch us from the obedience of our natural prince, thereby hoping in time to bring us to slavery and subjection, and then none shall be unto them so odious and disdained as the traitors themselves, who have sold their country to a stranger, and forsaken their faith and obedience, contrary to nature or religion, and contrary to that humane and general honor, not only of Christians, but of heathen and irreligious nations, who have always sustained what labor soever, and embraced even death itself, for their country, prince, or commonwealth.

To conclude, it hath ever to this day pleased God to prosper and defend her Majesty, to break the purposes of malicious enemies, of forsworn traitors, and of unjust practises and invasions. She hath ever been honored of the worthiest kings, served by faithful subjects, and shall by the favor of God resist, repel, and confound all whatsoever attempts against her sacred person or kingdom. In the meantime let the Spaniard and traitor vaunt of their success; and we her true and obedient vassals guided by the shining light of her virtues shall always love her, serve her, and obey her to the end of our lives.

FRANCIS BACON

ESSAYS and THE ADVANCEMENT OF LEARNING

The *Essays,* Bacon's first and most lasting literary success, poses almost insuperable bibliographical problems. Unquestionably inspired by Montaigne, but with none of Montaigne's fascinating egotism and winsome charm, Bacon first set down his stylistically terse and morally callous advice to ambitious men of his own class when he himself was pushing hard for that high position which he gained so slowly and lost so easily. Entered in the Stationers' Register on February 5, 1597, ten of the essays, with a dedication to Bacon's brother Anthony, were published by John Windet in 1597 in *Essays, Religious Meditations, Places of Persuasion and Dissuasion.* Clearly indicative of the author's hard, ambitious cast of mind, these original essays (on study, discourse, ceremonies and respects, followers and friends, suitors, expense, regiment of health, honor and reputation, faction, and negotiating) were combined in a thin octavo with "Meditationes sacrae," a set of religious meditations in Latin, and "The Colors of Good and Evil" (or "places of persuasion and dissuasion," as the titlepage had it). The popularity and the bibliographical problems followed apace. A second edition (with the "Meditations" in English) appeared in 1598, and presumably pirated editions (without "The Colors of Good and Evil") from the shop of John Jaggard were issued in 1606 and 1612, as well as an apparently authorized edition by John Beale in 1612. Finally, in 1613 Bacon himself revised and enlarged the 1598 edition by expanding all the original essays (except "Of Honor and Reputation") and adding to them twenty-nine new pieces for *The Essays of Francis Bacon, Knight, the King's Attorney-General*—a collection that Jaggard issued at least three times in the course of the year and that his widow Elizabeth reprinted in 1624. The third and last edition which Bacon supervised appeared in 1625, a year before his death. Containing fifty-eight essays (twenty of them new and the others altered or enlarged from the 1613 edition), it embodies Bacon's maturest revisions and is the last edition with any textual authority. But the popularity of the *Essays* continued strong throughout the early seventeenth century. Bacon himself presumably authorized an Italian translation of the 1613 edition which appeared in three issues in 1617 and 1618, Sir Arthur Gorges published his French version in 1619, and later English editions were published posthumously in 1629, 1632, and 1639. A Latin translation, which Bacon probably planned, and in which Thomas Hobbes may have had a hand, was published by Dr. William Rawley, Bacon's "learned chaplain" and literary executor, as *Sermones fideles sive interiora rerum* in 1638. Our text is based upon *The Essayes or Counsels, Civill and Morall, of Francis Lo. Verulam, Viscount St. Alban. Newly enlarged,* 1625 (STC 1147).

If the essays are flinty nuggets of worldly wisdom by a worldly and ambitious man, Bacon's *Two Books . . . of the Proficience and Advancement of Learning* is a noble projection of the ideas and ideals to which he, as a philosopher, clung through all the sinuous turns of his busy life. Addressed to the new king shortly after his coronation, and written in a rolling, sonorous prose which readers of the *Essays* would hardly recognize as Baconian, *The Advancement of Learning* is at once a defense of human knowledge, a sharp-eyed scrutiny of its defects, and an ambitious project for its improvement and progress. Book I refutes the libels of fools and zealots against the dignity of the human mind; Book II, an essay in epistemology, sketches that "great instauration," or reconstruction, of the aims and methods of human learning which Bacon envisaged as the major work of his age. Thus the book both evaluates the rich accretions of Renaissance culture and sketches a methodology for refining and extending the gains of the modern intellect. Much later, in the "*Distributio operis, or plan of the work*" prefixed to the *Novum organum* (1620), Bacon locates *The Advancement of Learning* within the gigantic scheme which he compendiously called *The Great Instauration*. As he projected a truly modern philosophy, he planned, first, "a summary or general description of the knowledge which the human race at present possess" (*The Advancement of Learning,* perhaps); second, a systematic treatise on methodology (the *Novum organum,* which survives in a fragment of two books); third, a "natural and experimental history for the construction of

philosophy"; fourth, a "ladder of the intellect"; fifth, "the forerunners or anticipations of the new philosophy"; and, sixth, a crowning work on "active science." Neither Bacon nor any other man could hope to achieve such an elaborate scheme, and the various fragments and prefaces that have survived (*Historia vitae et mortis, Valerius terminus, Sylva sylvarum, Historia densi et rari,* and so on) can only conjecturally be located within the vast project. As it is, however, *The Advancement of Learning* (and its greatly expanded Latin version called *De augmentis scientiarum,* 1623) and the *Novum organum* are sufficiently perfected to indicate the magnitude of Bacon's dream. Our text is based upon *The Twoo Bookes of Francis Bacon. Of the proficience and advancement of Learning, divine and humane. To the King,* 1605 (STC 1164).

FROM ESSAYS OR COUNSELS CIVIL AND MORAL (1625)

1. Of Truth

"What is truth?" said jesting Pilate; and would not stay for an answer. Certainly there be that delight in giddiness, and count it a bondage to fix a belief; affecting free will in thinking as well as in acting. And though the sects of philosophers of that kind be gone, yet there remain certain discoursing wits which are of the same veins, though there be not so much blood in them as was in those of the ancients. But it is not only the difficulty and labor which men take in finding out of truth, nor again that when it is found it imposeth upon men's thoughts, that doth bring lies in favor, but a natural though corrupt love of the lie itself. One of the later school of the Grecians examineth the matter, and is at a stand to think what should be in it, that men should love lies where neither they make for pleasure, as with poets, nor for advantage, as with the merchant, but for the lie's sake. But I cannot tell; this same truth is a naked and open daylight, that doth not shew the masques and mummeries and triumphs of the world half so stately and daintily as candle-lights. Truth may perhaps come to the price of a pearl, that sheweth best by day; but it will not rise to the price of a diamond or carbuncle, that sheweth best in varied lights. A mixture of a lie doth ever add pleasure. Doth any man doubt that if there were taken out of men's minds vain opinions, flattering hopes, false valuations, imaginations as one would, and the like, but it would leave the minds of a number of men poor shrunken things, full of melancholy and indisposition and unpleasing to themselves? One of the fathers, in great severity, called poesy *vinum*

daemonum because it filleth the imagination and yet it is but with the shadow of a lie. But it is not the lie that passeth through the mind, but the lie that sinketh in and settleth in it, that doth the hurt; such as we spake of before. But howsoever these things are thus in men's depraved judgments and affections, yet truth, which only doth judge itself, teacheth that the inquiry of truth, which is the love-making or wooing of it, the knowledge of truth, which is the presence of it, and the belief of truth, which is the enjoying of it, is the sovereign good of human nature. The first creature of God, in the works of the days, was the light of the sense; the last was the light of reason; and his sabbath work ever since is the illumination of his Spirit. First he breathed light upon the face of the matter or chaos; then he breathed light into the face of man; and still he breatheth and inspireth light into the face of his chosen. The poet [Lucretius] that beautified the sect [the Epicureans] that was otherwise inferior to the rest saith yet excellently well: "It is a pleasure to stand upon the shore and to see ships toss'd upon the sea; a pleasure to stand in the window of a castle and to see a battail and the adventures thereof below; but no pleasure is comparable to the standing upon the vantage ground of Truth"— a hill not to be commanded, and where the air is always clear and serene—"and to see the errors, and wand'rings, and mists, and tempests in the vale below"; so always that this prospect be with pity, and not with swelling or pride. Certainly it is heaven upon earth to have a man's mind move in charity, rest in providence, and turn upon the poles of truth.

To pass from theological and philosophical truth

to the truth of civil business, it will be acknowledged even by those that practise it not that clear and round dealing is the honor of man's nature; and that mixture of falsehood is like allay in coin of gold and silver, which may make the metal work the better, but it embaseth it. For these winding and crooked courses are the goings of the serpent, which goeth basely upon the belly and not upon the feet. There is no vice that doth so cover a man with shame as to be found false and perfidious. And therefore Mountaigny saith prettily, when he enquired the reason why the word of the lie should be such a disgrace and such an odious charge—saith he, "If it be well weighed, to say that a man lieth is as much to say as that he is brave towards God and a coward towards men." For a lie faces God and shrinks from man. Surely the wickedness of falsehood and breach of faith cannot possibly be so highly expressed as in that it shall be the last peal to call the judgments of God upon the generations of men; it being foretold that when Christ cometh, "he shall not find faith upon the earth."

2. Of Death

Men fear death, as children fear to go in the dark; and as that natural fear in children is increased with tales, so is the other. Certainly the contemplation of death as the wages of sin and passage to another world is holy and religious; but the fear of it as a tribute due unto nature is weak. Yet in religious meditations there is sometimes mixture of vanity and of superstition. You shall read in some of the friars' books of mortification that a man should think with himself what the pain is if he have but his finger's end pressed or tortured, and thereby imagine what the pains of death are when the whole body is corrupted and dissolved; when many times death passeth with less pain then the torture of a limb; for the most vital parts are not the quickest of sense. And by him that spake only as a philosopher and natural man, it was well said, *Pompa mortis magis terret, quam mors ipsa.* Groans and convulsions, and a discolored face, and friends weeping, and blacks, and obsequies, and the like, shew death terrible. It is worthy the observing that there is no passion in the mind of man so weak but it mates and masters the fear of death; and therefore death is no such terrible enemy when a man hath so many attendants about him that can win the combat of him. Revenge triumphs over death; love slights it; honor aspireth to it; grief flieth to it; fear preoccupateth it; nay, we read, after Otho the emperor had slain himself, pity (which is the tenderest of affections) provoked many to die, out of mere compassion to their sovereign and as the truest sort of followers. Nay, Seneca adds niceness and society:

Cogita quamdiu eadem feceris; mori velle, non tantum fortis, aut miser, sed etiam fastidiosus potest. A man would die, though he were neither valiant nor miserable, only upon a weariness to do the same thing so oft over and over. It is no less worthy to observe how little alteration in good spirits the approaches of death make; for they appear to be the same men till the last instant. Augustus Caesar died in a complement: *"Livia, conjugii nostri memor, vive et vale."* Tiberius in dissimulation; as Tacitus saith of him, *Jam Tiberium vires et corpus, non dissimulatio, deserebant.* Vespasian in a jest, sitting upon the stool, *"Ut puto Deus fio."* Galba with a sentence, *"Feri, si ex re sit populi Romani,"* holding forth his neck. Septimius Severus in dispatch: *"Adeste si quid mihi restat agendum."* And the like. Certainly the Stoics bestowed too much cost upon death, and by their great preparations made it appear more fearful. Better saith he *qui finem vitae extremum inter munera ponat naturae.* It is as natural to die as to be born; and to a little infant, perhaps, the one is as painful as the other. He that dies in an earnest pursuit is like one that is wounded in hot blood; who, for the time, scarce feels the hurt; and therefore a mind fix'd and bent upon somewhat that is good doth avert the dolors of death. But above all, believe it, the sweetest canticle is *Nunc dimittis,* when a man hath obtained worthy ends and expectations. Death hath this also, that it openeth the gate to good fame, and extinguisheth envy. *Extinctus amabitur idem.*

6. Of Simulation and Dissimulation

Dissimulation is but a faint kind of policy or wisdom, for it asketh a strong wit and a strong heart to know when to tell truth and to do it. Therefore it is the weaker sort of politics that are the great dissemblers.

Tacitus saith, "Livia sorted well with the arts of her husband and dissimulation of her son," attributing arts or policy to Augustus and dissimulation to Tiberius. And again, when Mucianus encourageth Vespasian to take arms against Vitellius, he saith, "We rise not against the piercing judgment of Augustus, nor the extreme caution or closeness of Tiberius." These properties, of arts or policy and dissimulation or closeness, are indeed habits and faculties several and to be distinguished. For if a man have that penetration of judgment as he can discern what things are to be laid open, and what to be secreted, and what to be shewed at half lights, and to whom and when (which indeed are arts of state and arts of life, as Tacitus well calleth them), to him a habit of dissimulation is a hinderance and a poorness. But if a man cannot obtain to that judgment, then it is left to him generally to be close and a dissembler. For where a man cannot choose or vary in particulars, there it is good to take the safest and wariest way in general; like the going softly by one that cannot well see. Certainly the ablest men that ever were have had all an openness and frankness of dealing and a name of certainty and veracity; but then they were like horses well managed, for they could tell passing well when to stop or turn; and at such times when they thought the case indeed required dissimulation, if then they used it, it came to pass that the former opinion spread abroad of their good faith and clearness of dealing made them almost invisible.

There be three degrees of this hiding and veiling of a man's self. The first, closeness, reservation, and secrecy—when a man leaveth himself without observation, or without hold to be taken what he is. The second, dissimulation, in the negative—when a man lets fall signs and arguments that he is not that he is. And the third, simulation, in the affirmative—when a man industriously and expressly feigns and pretends to be that he is not.

For the first of these, secrecy: it is indeed the virtue of a confessor. And assuredly the secret man heareth many confessions. For who will open himself to a blab or babbler? But if a man be thought secret, it inviteth discovery, as the more close air sucketh in the more open; and as in confession the revealing is not for worldly use, but for the ease of a man's heart, so secret men come to the knowledge of many things in that kind, while men rather discharge their minds then impart their minds. In few words, mysteries are due to secrecy. Besides (to say truth) nakedness is uncomely, as well in mind as body; and it addeth no small reverence to men's manners and actions if they be not altogether open. As for talkers and futile persons, they are commonly vain and credulous withal. For he that talketh what he knoweth will also talk what he knoweth not. Therefore set it down *that an habit of secrecy is both politic and moral*. And in this part it is good that a man's face give his tongue leave to speak. For the discovery of a man's self by the tracts of his countenance is a great weakness and betraying, by how much it is many times more marked and believed then a man's words.

For the second, which is dissimulation: it followeth many times upon secrecy by a necessity; so that he that will be secret must be a dissembler in some degree. For men are too cunning to suffer a man to keep an indifferent carriage between both, and to be secret, without swaying the balance on either side. They will so beset a man with questions, and draw him on, and pick it out of him, that, without an absurd silence, he must shew an inclination one way; or if he do not, they will gather as much by his silence as by his speech. As for equivocations or oraculous speeches, they cannot hold out long. So that no man can be secret, except he give himself a little scope of dissimulation; which is, as it were, but the skirts or train of secrecy.

But for the third degree, which is simulation and false profession: that I hold more culpable and less politic, except it be in great and rare matters. And therefore a general custom of simulation (which is this last degree) is a vice, rising either of a natural falseness or fearfulness, or of a mind that hath some main faults, which because a man must needs disguise it maketh him practise simulation in other things, lest his hand should be out of ure.

The great advantages of simulation and dissimulation are three. First, to lay asleep opposition and to surprise. For where a man's intentions are published, it is an alarum to call up all that are against them. The second is to reserve to a man's self a fair retreat. For if a man engage himself by a manifest declaration, he must go through or take a fall. The third is the better to discover the mind of another. For to him that opens himself men will hardly shew themselves adverse; but will fair let him go on, and turn their freedom of speech to freedom of thought. And therefore it is a good shrewd proverb of the Spaniard, "Tell a lie and find a troth." As if there were no way of discovery but by simulation. There be also three disadvantages, to set it even. The first, that simulation and dissimulation commonly carry with them a shew of fearfulness, which in any business doth spoil the feathers of round flying up to the mark. The second, that it puzzleth and perplexeth the conceits of many that perhaps would otherwise cooperate with him; and makes a man walk almost alone to his own ends. The third and greatest is that it depriveth a man of one of the most principal instruments for action, which is trust and belief. The best composition and temperature is to have openness in fame and opinion; secrecy in habit; dissimulation in seasonable use; and a power to feign, if there be no remedy.

8. Of Marriage and Single Life

He that hath wife and children hath given hostages to fortune; for they are impediments to great enterprises either of virtue or mischief. Certainly the best works and of greatest merit for the public have proceeded from the unmarried or childless men, which both in affection and means have married and endowed the public. Yet it were great reason that those that have children should have greatest care of future times; unto which they know they must transmit their dearest pledges. Some there are who, though they lead a single life, yet their thoughts do end with themselves, and account future times impertinences. Nay, there are some other that account wife and children but as bills of charges. Nay more, there are some foolish rich, covetous men that take a pride in having no children because they may be thought so much the richer. For perhaps they have heard some talk, "Such an one is a great rich man," and another except to it, "Yea, but he hath a great charge of children"; as if it were an abatement to his riches. But the most ordinary cause of a single life is liberty, especially in certain self-pleasing and humorous minds which are so sensible of every restraint as they will go near to think their girdles and garters to be bonds and shackles. Unmarried men are best friends, best masters, best servants; but not always best subjects; for they are light to run away, and almost all fugitives are of that condition. A single life doth well with churchmen; for charity will hardly water the ground where it must first fill a pool. It is indifferent for judges and magistrates; for if they be facile and corrupt, you shall have a servant five times worse than a wife. For soldiers, I find the generals commonly in their hortatives put men in mind of their wives and children; and I think the despising of marriage amongst the Turks maketh the vulgar soldier more base. Certainly wife and children are a kind of discipline of humanity; and single men, though they be many times more charitable, because their means are less exhaust, yet, on the other side, they are more cruel and hardhearted (good to make severe inquisitors), because their tenderness is not so oft called upon. Grave natures, led by custom and therefore constant, are commonly loving husbands; as was said of Ulysses, *Vetulam suam praetulit immortalitati.* Chaste women are often proud and froward, as presuming upon the merit of their chastity. It is one of the best bonds both of chastity and obedience in the wife if she think her husband wise; which she will never do if she find him jealous. Wives are young men's mistresses, companions for middle age, and old men's nurses. So as a man may have a quarrel to marry when he will. But yet he was reputed one of the wise men that made answer to the question when a man should marry, "A young man not yet, an elder man not at all." It is often seen that bad husbands have very good wives; whether it be that it raiseth the price of their husband's kindness when it comes, or that the wives take a pride in their patience. But this never fails if the bad husbands were of their own choosing, against their friends' consent; for then they will be sure to make good their own folly.

16. OF ATHEISM

I had rather believe all the fables in the *Legend* and the Talmud and the Alcoran then that this universal frame is without a mind. And therefore God never wrought miracle to convince atheism, because his ordinary works convince it. It is true that a little philosophy inclineth man's mind to atheism; but depth in philosophy bringeth men's minds about to religion. For while the mind of man looketh upon second causes scattered, it may sometimes rest in them, and go no further; but when it beholdeth the chain of them, confederate and linked together, it must needs fly to Providence and Deity. Nay, even that school which is most accused of atheism doth most demonstrate religion; that is, the school of Leucippus and Democritus and Epicurus. For it is a thousand times more credible that four mutable elements and one immutable fift essence, duly and eternally placed, need no God, then that an army of infinite small portions or seeds unplaced should have produced this order and beauty without a divine marshal. The Scripture saith, "The fool hath said in his heart, there is no God"; it is not said, "The fool hath thought in his heart"; so as he rather saith it by rote to himself, as that he would have, then that he can throughly believe it or be persuaded of it. For none deny there is a God but those for whom it maketh that there were no God. It appeareth in nothing more that atheism is rather in the lip then in the heart of man then by this: that atheists will ever be talking of that their opinion, as if they fainted in it within themselves, and would be glad to be strength'ned by the consent of others. Nay more, you shall have atheists strive to get disciples, as it fareth with other sects. And, which is most of all, you shall have of them that will suffer for atheism, and not recant; whereas if they did truly think that there were no such thing as God, why should they trouble themselves? Epicurus is charged that he did but dissemble for his credit's sake when he affirmed there were blessed natures, but such as enjoyed themselves without having respect to the government of the world. Wherein they say he did temporize, though in secret he thought there was no God. But certainly he is traduced, for his words are noble and divine: *Non deos vulgi negare profanum, sed vulgi opiniones diis applicare profanum.* Plato could have said no more. And although he had the confidence to deny the administration, he had not the power to deny the nature. The Indians of the west have names for their particular gods, though they have no name for God; as if the heathens should have had the names "Jupiter," "Apollo," "Mars," etc., but not the word *deus;* which shews that even those barbarous people have the notion, though they have not the latitude and extent of it. So that against atheists the very savages take part with the very subtilest philosophers. The contemplative atheist is rare: a

Diagoras, a Bion, a Lucian perhaps, and some others; and yet they seem to be more then they are, for that all that impugn a received religion or superstition are by the adverse part branded with the name of atheists. But the great atheists indeed are hypocrites, which are ever handling holy things, but without feeling; so as they must needs be cauterized in the end. The causes of atheism are: divisions in religion, if they be many; for any one main division addeth zeal to both sides, but many divisions introduce atheism. Another is, scandal of priests; when it is come to that which St. Bernard saith, *Non est jam dicere, ut populus sic sacerdos; quia nec sic populus ut sacerdos.* A third is, custom of profane scoffing in holy matters, which doth by little and little deface the reverence of religion. And lastly, learned times, specially with peace and prosperity, for troubles and adversities do more bow men's minds to religion. They that deny a God destroy man's nobility, for certainly man is of kin to the beasts by his body; and if he be not of kin to God by his spirit, he is a base and ignoble creature. It destroys likewise magnanimity and the raising of human nature; for take an example of a dog, and mark what a generosity and courage he will put on when he finds himself maintained by a man, who to him is instead of a God, or *melior natura*—which courage is manifestly such as that creature, without that confidence of a better nature then his own, could never attain. So man, when he resteth and assureth himself upon divine protection and favor, gathereth a force and faith which human nature in itself could not obtain. Therefore, as atheism is in all respects hateful, so in this, that it depriveth human nature of the means to exalt itself above human frailty. As it is in particular persons, so it is in nations. Never was there such a state for magnanimity as Rome. Of this state hear what Cicero saith: *Quam volumus licet, patres conscripti, nos amemus, tamen nec numero Hispanos, nec robore Gallos, nec calliditate Paenos, nec artibus Graecos, nec denique hoc ipso hujus gentis et terrae domestico nativoque sensu Italos ipsos et Latinos; sed pietate ac religione, atque hac una sapientia, quod deorum immortalium numine omnia regi gubernarique perspeximus, omnes gentes nationesque superavimus.*

50. OF STUDIES

Studies serve for delight, for ornament, and for ability. Their chief use for delight is in privateness and retiring; for ornament, is in discourse; and for ability, is in the judgment and disposition of business.

For expert men can execute and perhaps judge of particulars, one by one; but the general counsels, and the plots and marshaling of affairs, come best from those that are learned. To spend too much time in studies is sloth; to use them too much for ornament is affectation; to make judgment wholly by their rules is the humor of a scholler. They perfect nature, and are perfected by experience; for natural abilities are like natural plants, that need proyning by study; and studies themselves do give forth directions too much at large, except they be bounded in by experience. Crafty men contemn studies, simple men admire them, and wise men use them; for they teach not their own use, but that is a wisdom without them, and above them, won by observation. Read not to contradict and confute, nor to believe and take for granted, nor to find talk and discourse, but to weigh and consider. Some books are to be tasted, others to be swallowed, and some few to be chewed and digested; that is, some books are to be read only in parts; others to be read, but not curiously; and some few to be read wholly, and with diligence and attention. Some books also may be read by deputy, and extracts made of them by others; but that would be only in the less important arguments, and the meaner sort of books; else distilled books are like common distilled waters, flashy things. Reading maketh a full man; conference a ready man; and writing an exact man. And therefore, if a man write little, he had need have a great memory; if he confer little, he had need have a present wit: and if he read little, he had need have much cunning, to seem to know that he doth not. Histories make men wise; poets witty; the mathematics subtile; natural philosophy deep; moral grave; logic and rhetoric able to contend. *Abeunt studia in mores.* Nay, there is no stond or impediment in the wit but may be wrought out by fit studies; like as diseases of the body may have appropriate exercises. Bowling is good for the stone and reins; shooting for the lungs and breast; gentle walking for the stomach; riding for the head; and the like. So if a man's wit be wand'ring, let him study the mathematics; for in demonstrations, if his wit be called away never so little, he must begin again. If his wit be not apt to distinguish or find difference, let him study the schoolmen; for they are *cymini sectores.* If he be not apt to beat over matters, and to call up one thing to prove and illustrate another, let him study the lawyers' cases. So every defect of the mind may have a special receit.

Knowledge is like a pyramid— each layer suggest another
at Top—science by which God created th—
world—

FRANCIS BACON 907

FROM THE TWO BOOKS . . . OF THE PROFICIENCE AND ADVANCEMENT OF LEARNING, DIVINE AND HUMAN (1605)

THE FIRST BOOK

To the King

There were under the law, excellent king, both daily sacrifices and free-will offerings; the one proceeding upon ordinary observance, the other upon a devout cheerfulness. In like manner there belongeth to kings from their servants both tribute of duty and presents of affection. In the former of these I hope I shall not live to be wanting, according to my most humble duty and the good pleasure of your Majesty's employments; for the latter, I thought it more respective to make choice of some oblation which might rather refer to the propriety and excellency of your individual person than to the business of your crown and state.

Wherefore representing your Majesty many times unto my mind, and beholding you not with the inquisitive eye of presumption to discover that which the Scripture telleth me is inscrutable, but with the observant eye of duty and admiration; leaving aside the other parts of your virtue and fortune, I have been touched, yea, and possessed, with an extreme wonder at those your virtues and faculties which the philosophers call intellectual: the largeness of your capacity, the faithfulness of your memory, the swiftness of your apprehension, the penetration of your judgment, and the facility and order of your elocution; and I have often thought that, of all the persons living that I have known, your Majesty were the best instance to make a man of Plato's opinion, that all knowledge is but remembrance, and that the mind of man by nature knoweth all things, and hath but her own native and original motions (which by the strangeness and darkness of this tabernacle of the body are sequest'red) again revived and restored; such a light of nature I have observed in your Majesty, and such a readiness to take flame and blaze from the least occasion presented, or the least spark of another's knowledge delivered. And as the Scripture saith of the wisest king, that "His heart was as the sands of the sea," which though it be one of the largest bodies yet it consisteth of the smallest and finest portions; so hath God given your Majesty a composition of understanding admirable, being able to compass and comprehend the greatest matters, and nevertheless to touch and apprehend the least; whereas it should seem an impossibility in nature for the same instrument to make itself fit for great and small works. And for your gift of speech, I call to mind what Cornelius Tacitus saith of Augustus Caesar: *Augusto profluens, et quae principem deceret, eloquentia fuit;* for if we note it well, speech that is uttered with labor and difficulty, or speech that savoreth of the affectation of art and precepts, or speech that is framed after the imitation of some pattern of eloquence, though never so excellent—all this hath somewhat servile, and holding of the subject. But your Majesty's manner of speech is indeed prince-like, flowing as from a fountain, and yet streaming and branching itself into nature's order, full of facility and felicity, imitating none, and inimitable by any. And as in your civil estate there appeareth to be an emulation and contention of your Majesty's virtue with your fortune: a virtuous disposition with a fortunate regiment; a virtuous expectation (when time was) of your greater fortune with a prosperous possession thereof in the due time; a virtuous observation of the laws of marriage with most blessed and happy fruit of marriage; a virtuous and most Christian desire of peace with a fortunate inclination in your neighbor princes thereunto; so likewise in these intellectual matters there seemeth to be no less contention between the excellency of your Majesty's gifts of nature and the universality and profection of your learning. For I am well assured that this which I shall say is no amplification at all, but a positive and measured truth; which is, that there hath not been since Christ's time any king or temporal monarch which hath been so learned in all literature and erudition, divine and human. For let a man seriously and diligently revolve and peruse the succession of the emperors of Rome, of which Caesar the dictator, who lived some years before Christ, and Marcus Antoninus were the best learned; and so descend to the emperors of Grecia, or of the West, and then to the lines of France, Spain, England, Scotland, and the rest, and he shall find this judgment is truly made. For it seemeth much in a king if by the compendious extractions of other men's wits and labors he can take hold of any superficial ornaments and shews of learning, or if he countenance and prefer learning and learned men; but to drink indeed of the true fountains of learning, nay, to have such a fountain of learning in himself, in a king, and in a king born, is almost a miracle. And the more, because there is met in your Majesty a rare conjunction as well of divine and sacred literature as of prophane and human; so as your Majesty standeth invested of that triplicity which in great veneration was ascribed to the ancient Hermes: the power and fortune of a king, the knowledge and illumination of a priest, and the learning and universality of a philosopher. This propriety inherent and individual attribute in your Majesty deserveth to be expressed not only in the fame and admiration of the present time, nor in the history or tradition of the ages succeeding, but also in some solid work, fixed memorial, and immortal monument bearing a character or signature both of the power of a king and the difference and perfection of such a king.

Therefore I did conclude with myself that I could not make unto your Majesty a better oblation then of some treatise tending to that end; whereof the sum will consist of these two parts: the former concerning the excellency of learning and knowledge, and the excellency of the merit and true glory in the augmentation and propagation thereof; the latter, what the particular acts and works are which have been imbraced and undertaken for the advancement of learning, and again what defects and undervalues I find in such particular acts; to the end that though I cannot positively or affirmatively advise your Majesty, or propound unto you framed particulars, yet I may excite your princely cogitations to visit the excellent treasure of your own mind, and thence to extract particulars for this purpose agreeable to your magnanimity and wisdom.

In the entrance to the former of these—to clear the way, and as it were to make silence to have the true testimonies concerning the dignity of learning to be better heard without the interruption of tacit objections—I think good to deliver it from the discredits and disgraces which it hath received, all from ignorance, but ignorance severally disguised; appearing sometimes in the zeal and jealousy of divines, sometimes in the severity and arrogancy of politiques, and sometimes in the errors and imperfections of learned men themselves.

I hear the former sort say that knowledge is of those things which are to be accepted of with great limitation and caution; that th' aspiring to overmuch knowledge was the original temptation and sin, whereupon ensued the fall of man; that knowledge hath in it somewhat of the serpent, and therefore where it ent'reth into a man it makes him swell—*Scientia inflat;* that Salomon gives a censure that "There is no end of making books," and that "Much reading is weariness of the flesh"; and again in another place, that "In spacious knowledge there is much contristation," and that "He that encreaseth knowledge encreaseth anxiety"; that Saint Paul gives a caveat that we be not spoiled through vain philosophy; that experience demonstrates how learned men have been arch-heretiques, how learned times have been enclined to atheism, and how the comtemplation of second causes doth derogate from our dependence upon God, who is the first cause.

To discover then the ignorance and error of this opinion and the misunderstanding in the grounds thereof, it may well appear these men do not observe or consider that it was not the pure knowledge of nature and universality, a knowledge by the light whereof man did give names unto other creatures in Paradise, as they were brought before him, according unto their properties, which gave the occasion to the fall; but it was the proud knowledge of good and evil, with an intent in man to give law unto himself and to depend no more upon God's commandements, which was the fourm of the temptation. Neither is it any quantity of knowledge how great soever that can make the mind of man to swell; for nothing can fill, much less extend, the soul of man but God and the contemplation of God. And therefore Salomon, speaking of the two principal senses of inquisition, the eye and the ear, affirmeth that the eye is never satisfied with seeing, nor the ear with hearing; and if there be no fulness, then is the continent greater than the content; so of knowledge itself and the mind of man, whereto the senses are but reporters, he defineth likewise in these words, placed after that calendar or ephemerides which he maketh of the diversities of times and seasons for all actions and purposes, and concludeth thus: "God hath made all things beautiful or decent in the true return of their seasons; also he hath placed the world in man's heart, yet cannot man find out the work which God worketh from the beginning to the end"; declaring not obscurely that God hath framed the mind of man as a mirror or glass capable of the image of the universal world, and joyful to receive the impression thereof, as the eye joyeth to receive light; and not only delighted in beholding the variety of things and vicissitude of times, but raised also to find out and discern the ordinances and decrees which throughout all those changes are infallibly observed. And although he doth insinuate that the supreme or summary law of nature, which he calleth "the work which God worketh from the beginning to the end," is not possible to be found out by man; yet that doth not derogate from the capacity of the mind, but may be referred to the impediments, as of shortness of life, ill conjunction of labors, ill tradition of knowledge over from hand to hand, and many other inconveniences whereunto the condition of man is subject. For that nothing parcel of the world is denied to man's enquiry and invention he doth in another place rule over, when he saith, "The spirit of man is as the lamp of God, wherewith he searcheth the inwardness of all secrets." If then such be the capacity and receit of the mind of man, it is manifest that there is no danger at all in the proportion or quantity of knowledge, how large soever, lest it should make it swell or outcompass itself; no, but it is merely the quality of knowledge, which be it in quantity more or less, if it be taken without the true corrective thereof, hath in it some nature of venom or malignity, and some effects of that venom, which is ventosity or swelling. This corrective spice, the mixture whereof maketh knowledge so sovereign, is charity, which the apostle immediately addeth to the former clause; for so he saith, "Knowledge bloweth up, but charity buildeth up"; not unlike unto that which he delivereth in another place: "If I spake," saith he, "with the tongues of men and angels, and had not charity, it were but as a tinkling cymbal." Not but that it is an excellent thing to speak with the tongues of men and angels, but because if it be severed from charity, and not referred to the good of men and mankind, it hath rather a sounding and unworthy glory than a meriting and substantial virtue. And as for that censure of Salomon concerning the excess of writing and reading books, and the anxiety of spirit which redoundeth from knowledge, and that admonition of Saint Paul that we be not seduced by vain philosophy; let those places be rightly understood, and they do indeed excellently set forth the true bounds and limitations whereby human knowledge is confined and circumscribed; and yet without any such contracting or coarctation but that it may comprehend all the universal nature of things. For these limitations are three. The first, that we do not so place our felicity in knowledge as we forget our mortality. The second, that we make application of our knowledge to give ourselves repose and contentment, and not distaste or repining. The third, that we do not presume by the contemplation of nature to attain to the mysteries of God. . . .

Now I proceed to those errors and vanities which have interveined amongst the studies themselves of the learned; which is that which is principal and proper to the present argument, wherein my purpose is not to make a justification of the errors, but, by a censure and separation of the errors, to make a justification of that which is good and sound, and to deliver that from the aspersion of the other. For we see that it is the manner of men to scandalize and deprave that which retaineth the state and virtue, by taking advantage upon that which is corrupt and degenerate; as the heathens in the primitive church used to blemish and taint the Christians with the faults and corruptions of heretiques. But nevertheless I have no meaning at this time to make any exact animadversion of the errors and impediments in matters of learning which are more secret and remote from vulgar opinion; but only to speak unto such as do fall under, or near unto, a popular observation.

There be therefore chiefly three vanities in studies, whereby learning hath been most traduced. For those things we do esteem vain which are either false or frivolous, those which either have no truth or no use; and those persons we esteem vain which are either credulous or curious; and curiosity is either in matter or words; so that in reason as well as in experience there fall out to be these three distempers (as I may term them) of learning: the first, fantastical learning; the second, contentious learning; and the last, delicate learning; vain imaginations, vain altercations, and vain affectations; and with the last I will begin.

Martin Luther, conducted no doubt by an higher Providence, but in discourse of reason, finding what a province he had undertaken against the bishop of Rome and the degenerate traditions of the church, and finding his own solitude being no ways aided by the opinions of his own time, was enforced to awake all antiquity, and to call former times to his succors to make a party against the present time; so that the ancient authors, both in divinity and in humanity, which had long time slept in libraries, began generally to be read and revolved. This by consequence did draw on a necessity of a more exquisite travail in the languages original wherein those authors did write, for the better understanding of those authors and the better advantage of pressing and applying their words. And thereof grew again a delight in their manner of style and phrase, and an admiration of that kind of writing; which was much furthered and precipitated by the enmity and opposition that the propounders of those primitive, but seeming new, opinions had against the schoolmen, who were generally of the contrary part, and whose writings were altogether in a differing style and fourm; taking liberty to coin and frame new terms of art to express their own sense and to avoid circuit of speech, without regard to the pureness, pleasantness, and (as I may call it) lawfulness of the phrase or word. And again, because the great labor that then was with the people (of whom the Pharisees were wont to say, *Execrabilis ista turba, quae non novit legem*), for the winning and persuading of them, there grew of necessity in chief price and request eloquence and variety of discourse, as the fittest and forciblest access into the capacity of the vulgar sort. So that these four causes concurring, the admiration of ancient authors, the hate of the schoolmen, the exact study of languages, and the efficacy of preaching, did bring in an affectionate study of eloquence and copy of speech, which then began to flourish. This grew speedily to an excess; for men began to hunt more after words than matter, and more after the choiceness of the phrase, and the round and clean composition of the sentence, and the sweet falling of the clauses, and the varying and illustration of their works with tropes and figures, then after the weight of matter, worth of subject, soundness of argument, life of invention, or depth of judgment. Then grew the flowing and watery vein of Osorius, the Portugal bishop, to be in price. Then did Sturmius spend such infinite and curious pains upon Cicero the orator and Hermogenes the rhetorician, besides his own books of periods and imitation and the like. Then did Carr of Cambridge and Ascham, with their lectures and writings, almost deify Cicero and Demosthenes, and allure all young men that were studious unto that delicate and polished kind of learning. Then did Erasmus take occasion to make the scoffing echo: *Decem annos consumpsi in legendo Cicerone,* and the echo answered in Greek: "Ονε, *Asine.* Then grew the learning of the schoolmen to be utterly despised as barbarous. In sum, the whole inclination and bent of those times was rather towards copy than weight.

Here, therefore, the first distemper of learning, when men study words and not matter; whereof though I have represented an example of late times, yet it hath been and will be *secundum majus et minus* in all time. And how is it possible but this should have an operation to discredit learning, even with vulgar capacities, when they see learned men's works like the first letter of a patent or limmed book, which though it hath large flourishes, yet it is but a letter? It seems to me that Pygmalion's frenzy is a good emblem or portraiture of this vanity; for words are but the images of matter; and except they have life of reason and invention, to fall in love with them is all one as to fall in love with a picture.

But yet notwithstanding it is a thing not hastily to be condemned, to clothe and adorn the obscurity even of philosophy itself with sensible and plausible elocution. For hereof we have great examples in Xenophon, Cicero, Seneca, Plutarch, and of Plato also in some degree; and hereof likewise there is great use; for surely to the severe inquisition of truth, and the deep progress into philosophy, it is some hindrance; because it is too early satisfactory to the mind of man, and quencheth the desire of further search, before we come to a just period; but then if a man be to have any use of such knowledge in civil occasions, of conference, counsel, persuasion, discourse, or the like, then shall he find it prepared to his hands in those authors which write in that manner. But the excess of this is so justly contemptible that as Hercules, when he saw the image of Adonis, Venus' mignion, in a temple, said in disdain, *Nil sacri es;* so there is none of Hercules' followers in learning, that is, the more severe and laborious sort of enquirers into truth, but will despise those delicacies and affectations as indeed capable of no divineness. And thus much of the first disease or distemper of learning.

The second, which followeth, is in nature worse then than the former; for as substance of matter is better than beauty of words, so contrariwise vain matter is worse than vain words; wherein it seemeth the reprehension of Saint Paul was not only proper for those times, but prophetical for the times following, and not only respective to divinity, but extensive to all knowledge: *Devita prophanas vocum novitates, et oppositiones falsi nominis scientiae.* For he assigneth two marks and badges of suspected and falsified science: the one, the novelty and strangeness of terms; the other, the strictness of positions, which of necessity doth induce oppositions, and so questions and altercations. Surely, like as many substances in nature which are solid do putrefy and corrupt into worms, so it is the property of good and sound knowledge to putrefy and dissolve into a number of subtile, idle, unwholesome, and (as I may term them) vermiculate questions, which have indeed a kind of quickness and life of spirit, but no soundness of matter or goodness of quality. This kind of degenerate learning did chiefly reign amongst the schoolmen, who—having sharp and strong wits, and aboundance of leisure, and small variety of reading, but their wits being shut up in the cells of a few authors (chiefly Aristotle, their dictator) as their persons were shut up in the cells of monasteries and colledges, and knowing little history, either of nature or time—did out of no great quantity of matter, and infinite agitation of wit, spin out unto us those laborious webs of learning which are extant in their books. For the wit and mind of man, if it work upon matter, which is the contemplation of the creatures of God, worketh according to the stuff, and is limited thereby; but if it work upon itself, as the spider worketh his web, then it is endless, and brings forth indeed copwebs of learning, admirable for the fineness of thread and work, but of no substance or profit. . . .

For the third vice or disease of learning, which concerneth deceit or untruth, it is of all the rest the foulest, as that which doth destroy the essential fourm of knowledge, which is nothing but a representation of truth; for the truth of being and the truth of knowing are one, differing no more than the direct beam and the beam reflected. This vice therefore brancheth itself into two sorts: delight in deceiving, and aptness to be deceived—imposture and credulity; which, although they appear to be of a divers nature, the one seeming to proceed of cunning and the other of simplicity, yet certainly they do for the most part concur; for as the verse noteth, *Percontatorem fugito, nam garrulus idem est,* an inquisitive man is a prattler; so upon the like reason a credulous man is a deceiver. As we see it in fame, that he that will easily believe rumors will as easily augment rumors and add somewhat to them of his own; which Tacitus wisely noteth when he saith, *Fingunt simul creduntque;* so great an affinity hath fiction and belief.

This facility of credit, and accepting or admitting things weakly authorized or warranted, is of two kinds, according to the subject; for it is either a belief of history (as the lawyers speak, matter of fact), or else of matter of art and opinion. As to the former, we see the experience and inconvenience of this error in ecclesiastical history, which hath too easily received and regist'red reports and narrations of miracles wrought by martyrs, hermits, or monks of the desert, and other holy men, and their reliques, shrines, chapels, and images; which though they had a passage for time, by the ignorance of the people, the superstitious simplicity of some, and the politique toleration of others, holding them but as divine poesies; yet after a period of time, when the mist began to clear up, they grew to be esteemed but as old wives' fables, impostures of the clergy, illusions of spirits, and badges of Antichrist, to the great scandal and detriment of religion.

So in natural history, we see there hath not been that choice and judgment used as ought to have been; as may appear in the writings of Plinius, Cardanus, Albertus, and divers of the Arabians, being fraught with much fabulous matter, a great part not only untried but notoriously untrue, to the great derogation of the credit of natural philosophy with the grave and sober kind of wits. Wherein the wisdom and integrity of Aristotle is worthy to be observed, that, having made so diligent and exquisite a history of living creatures, hath mingled it sparingly with any vain or feigned matter; and yet on thother [side] hath cast all prodigious narrations which he thought worthy the recording into one book; excellently discerning that matter of manifest truth, such whereupon observation and rule was to be built, was not to be mingled or weakened with matter of doubtful credit; and yet again, that rarities and reports that seem uncredible are not to be suppressed or denied to the memory of men.

And as for the facility of credit which is yielded to arts and opinions, it is likewise of two kinds: either when too much belief is attributed to the arts themselves, or to certain authors in any art. The sciences themselves which have had better intelligence and confederacy with the imagination of man than with his reason are three in number: astrology, natural magic, and alcumy; of which sciences nevertheless the ends or pretenses are noble. For astrology pretendeth to discover that correspondence or concatenation which is between the superior globe and the inferior; natural magic pretendeth to call and reduce natural philosophy from variety of speculations to the magnitude of works; and alcumy pretendeth to make separation of all the unlike parts of bodies which in mixtures of nature are incorporate. But the derivations and prosecutions to these ends, both in the theories and in the practises, are full of error and vanity, which the great professors themselves have sought to veil over and conceal by enigmatical writings, and referring themselves to auricular traditions, and such other devices to save the credit of impostures. And yet surely to alcumy this right is due, that it may be compared to the husbandman whereof Aesop makes the fable, that when he died told his sons that he had left unto them gold buried underground in his vineyard; and they digged over all the ground, and gold they found none, but by reason of their stirring and digging the mold about the roots of their vines, they had a great vintage the year following; so assuredly the search and stir to make gold hath brought to light a great number of good and fruitful inventions and experiments, as well for the disclosing of nature as for the use of man's life.

And as for the overmuch credit that hath been given unto authors in sciences, in making them dictators, that their words should stand, and not counsels to give advice; the damage is infinite that sciences have received thereby, as the principal cause that hath kept them low, at a stay without growth or advancement. For hence it hath comen that in arts mechanical the first deviser comes shortest, and time addeth and perfecteth, but in sciences the first author goeth furthest, and time leeseth and corrupteth. So, we see, artillery, sailing, printing, and the like were grossly managed at the first, and by time accommodated and refined; but contrariwise the philosophies and sciences of Aristotle, Plato, Democritus, Hippocrates, Euclides, Archimedes, of most vigor at the first, and by time degenerate and imbased; whereof the reason is no other but that in the former many wits and industries have contributed in one, and in the latter many wits and industries have been spent about the wit of some one, whom many times they have rather depraved than illustrated. For as water will not ascend higher than the level of the first spring-head from whence it descendeth, so knowledge derived from Aristotle, and exempted from liberty of examination, will not rise again higher than the knowledge of Aristotle. And therefore, although the position be good, *Oportet discentem credere,* yet it must be coupled with this, *Oportet edoctum judicare;* for disciples do owe unto maisters only a temporary belief and a suspension of their own judgment till they be fully instructed, and not an absolute resignation or perpetual captivity; and therefore to conclude this point, I will say no more but, so let great authors have their due as time, which is the author of authors, be not deprived of his due, which is furder and furder to discover truth. Thus have I gone over these three diseases of learning; besides the which there are some other rather peccant humors then fourmed diseases, which nevertheless are not so secret and intrinsic but that they fall under a popular observation and traducement, and therefore are not to be passed over.

The first of these is the extreme affecting of two extremities, the one antiquity, the other novelty; wherein it seemeth the children of Time do take after the nature and malice of the father. For as he devoureth his children, so one of them seeketh to devour and suppress the other; while antiquity envieth there should be new additions, and novelty cannot be content to add, but it must deface. Surely the advice of the prophet is the true direction in this matter, *State super vias antiquas, et videte quaenam sit via recta et bona, et ambulate in ea.* Antiquity deserveth that reverence that men should make a stand thereupon, and discover what is the best way; but when the discovery is well taken, then to make progression. And to speak truly, *antiquitas saeculi juventus mundi.* These times are the ancient times, when the world is ancient, and not those which we account ancient *ordine retrogrado,* by a computation backward from ourselves.

Another error, induced by the former, is a distrust that anything should be now to be found out which the world should have missed and passed over so long time; as if the same objection were to be made to time that Lucian maketh to Jupiter and other the heathen gods, of which he wond'reth that they begot so many children in old time and begot none in his time, and asketh whether they were become septuagenary, or whether the law *pappia,* made against old men's marriages, had restrained them. So it seemeth men doubt lest time is become past children and generation; wherein contrariwise we see commonly the levity and unconstancy of men's judgments, which, till a matter be done, wonder that it can be done; and as soon as it is done, wonder again that it was no sooner done; as we see in the expedition of Alexander into Asia, which at first was prejudged as a vast and impossible enterprise; and yet afterwards it pleaseth Livy to make no more of it than this, *nil aliud quam bene ausus vana contemnere.* And the same happened to Columbus in the western navigation. But in intellectual matters it is much more common; as may be seen in most of the propositions of Euclid, which till they be demonstrate, they seem strange to our assent; but being demonstrate, our mind accepteth of them by a kind of relation (as the lawyers speak) as if we had known them before.

Another error, that hath also some affinity with the former, is a conceit that of former opinions or sects, after variety and examination, the best hath still prevailed and suppressed the rest; so as if a man should begin the labor of a new search, he were but like to light upon somewhat formerly rejected, and by rejection brought into oblivion; as if the multitude, or the wisest for the multitude's sake, were not ready to give passage rather to that which is popular and superficial than to that which is substantial and profound; for the truth is that time seemeth to be of the nature of a river or stream, which carrieth down to us that which is light and blown up, and sinketh and drowneth that which is weighty and solid. . . .

Another error is an impatience of doubt, and haste to assertion without due and mature suspension of judgment. For the two ways of contemplation are not unlike the two ways of action commonly spoken of by the ancients; the one plain and smooth in the beginning, and in the end impassable; the other rough and troublesome in the entrance, but after a while fair and even. So it is in contemplation; if a man will begin with certainties, he shall end in doubts; but if he will be content to begin in doubts, he shall end in certainties.

Another error is in the manner of the tradition and delivery of knowledge, which is for the most part magistral and peremptory, and not ingenuous and faithful; in a sort as may be soonest believed, and not easiliest examined. It is true that in compendious treatises for practise that fourm is not to be disallowed. But in the true handling of knowledge, men ought not to fall either on the one side into the vein of Velleius the Epicurean, *nil tam metuens, quam ne dubitare aliqua de re videretur,* nor on the other side into Socrates his ironical doubting of all things, but to propound things sincerely, with more or less asseveration, as they stand in a man's own judgment proved more or less.

Other errors there are in the scope that men propound to themselves, whereunto they bend their endeavors; for whereas the more constant and devote kind of professors of any science ought to propound to themselves to make some additions to their science, they convert their labors to aspire to certain second prizes; as to be a profound interpreter or commenter, to be a sharp champion or defender, to be a methodical compounder or abridger; and so the patrimony of knowledge cometh to be sometimes improved, but seldom augmented.

But the greatest error of all the rest is the mistaking or misplacing of the last or furthest end of knowledge. For men have ent'red into a desire of learning and knowledge, sometimes upon a natural curiosity and inquisitive appetite; sometimes to entertain their minds with variety and delight; sometimes for ornament and reputation; and sometimes to inable them to victory of wit and contradiction; and most times for lucre and profession; and seldom sincerely to give a true account of their gift of reason, to the benefit and use of men; as if there were sought in knowledge a couch, whereupon to rest a searching and restless spirit; or a tarrasse, for a wand'ring and variable mind to walk up and down with a fair prospect; or a tower of state, for a proud mind to raise itself upon; or a fort or commanding ground, for strife and contention; or a shop, for profit or sale; and not a rich storehouse, for the glory of the Creator and the relief of man's estate. But this is that which will indeed dignify and exalt knowledge, if contemplation and action may be more nearly and straightly conjoined and united together than they have been; a conjunction like unto that of the two highest planets, Saturn, the planet of rest and contemplation, and Jupiter, the planet of civil society and action. Howbeit, I do not mean, when I speak of use and action, that

end before-mentioned of the applying of knowledge to lucre and profession; for I am not ignorant how much that diverteth and interrupteth the prosecution and advancement of knowledge; like unto the golden ball thrown before Atalanta, which while she goeth aside and stoopeth to take up, the race is hind'red, *declinat cursus, aurumque volubile tollit.* Neither is my meaning, as was spoken of Socrates, to call philosophy down from heaven to converse upon the earth; that is, to leave natural philosophy aside, and to apply knowledge only to manners and policy. But as both heaven and earth do conspire and contribute to the use and benefit of man, so the end ought to be, from both philosophies to separate and reject vain speculations and whatsoever is empty and void, and to preserve and augment whatsoever is solid and fruitful; that knowledge may not be as a curtezan, for pleasure and vanity only, or as a bond-woman, to acquire and gain to her master's use, but as a spouse, for generation, fruit, and comfort.

The following items, arranged to correspond with the principal sections of the anthology, are not formal bibliographies but rather suggestions for the use of students who may wish to study further the authors treated in this book.

ABBREVIATIONS

CBEL	Cambridge Bibliography of English Literature
CHEL	Cambridge History of English Literature
ELH	Journal of English Literary History
ES	English Studies
HLB	Huntington Library Bulletin
HLQ	Huntington Library Quarterly
JEGP	Journal of English and Germanic Philology
MLN	Modern Language Notes
MLQ	Modern Language Quarterly
MLR	Modern Language Review
MLS	Modern Language Studies
MP	Modern Philology
PMLA	Publications of the Modern Language Association of America
PQ	Philological Quarterly
RES	Review of English Studies
SP	Studies in Philology
TLS	(London) Times Literary Supplement

General Works

The sixteenth century has long exerted a strong attraction for historians. Two great monuments of a great age of historical research are the massive studies of James Anthony Froude and John Lingard, one a disenchanted Anglo-Catholic and the other a devout Romanist. To celebrate the triumph of English Protestantism Froude's brilliant but not always reliable narrative (12 vols., 1856–70) covers the course and consequences of the Reformation from the fall of Wolsey to the defeat of the Armada; Lingard's work (8 vols., 1819–30; rev. ed., 10 vols., 1849–51) is, in its quieter way, equally impressive. Shorter and more recent studies are G. M. Trevelyan's History of England (1926), bk. III; The Cambridge Modern History, vols. I–IV (1902–6); E. P. Cheyney's standard History of England from the Defeat of the Armada to the Death of Elizabeth (2 vols., 1914–26); H. A. L. Fisher's and A. F. Pollard's contributions to the great Political History of England (vol. V, 1906; vol. VI, 1910); J. B. Black's Reign of Elizabeth (1936); and J. E. Neale's spirited biography of Queen Elizabeth (1934).

A pioneer work in Renaissance intellectual history is H. O. Taylor's Thought and Expression in the Sixteenth Century (2 vols., 1920); on a more modest scale Hardin Craig's Enchanted Glass (1936) and E. M. W. Tillyard's Elizabethan World Picture (1943) are both stimulating. Shakespeare's England (rev. ed., 2 vols., 1926) contains authoritative essays by various scholars on many aspects of Elizabethan culture, and L. B. Wright's Middle-Class Culture in Elizabethan England (1935) is a useful complement to more formal histories of the period.

For general literary history, the standard CHEL, vols. III (1908) and IV (1909), and W. J. Courthope's History of English Poetry, vols. II (1897) and III (1904), are, though somewhat dated, full of good things. Other, and shorter, studies are the literary histories of the period by George Saintsbury (1887), F. E. Schelling (rev. ed., 1927), Esther Dunn (1936), Tucker Brooke (in A Literary History of England, ed. A. C. Baugh, 1948), and Vivian de Sola Pinto (rev. ed., 1950), the last with copious bibliographies. Douglas Bush's Mythology and the Renaissance Tradition (1932) analyzes classical influences in Elizabethan poetry, and Hallett Smith's Elizabethan Poetry (1952) is a study of the principal genres (pastoral, satirical, heroic, etc.) of the period.

Three works indispensable for the advanced study of Elizabethan literature are Edward Arber's Transcript of the registers of the Stationers' Company (5 vols., 1875–94), A. W. Pollard and G. R. Redgrave's Short-Title Catalogue of Books Printed in England, Scotland, and Ireland, and of English Books Printed Abroad, 1475–1640 (1926), and CBEL (4 vols., 1941). Recent Renaissance scholarship is summarized annually in the spring issue of SP.

I. The Historical Setting

MICHAEL DRAYTON: See section VI, below.

WILLIAM WARNER: His modern reputation may be gauged by the fact that the last edition of Albion's England was that in Chalmers' English Poets, vol. IV (1810). Pan His Syrinx (1584), Warner's collection of prose tales, has been edited by Wallace Bacon (1950).

SAMUEL DANIEL: See section VI, below.

RICHARD GRAFTON: A Chronicle at Large was reprinted by Sir Henry Ellis (2 vols., 1809) in a series with other Elizabethan histories, the texts of which are generally unreliable. Grafton is the subject of two biographical studies (1895, 1901) by J. A. Kingdon.

RAPHAEL HOLINSHED: Owing to its relevance to Shakespeare, the Chronicles has been edited several times. Sir Henry Ellis reprinted the whole work (6 vols., 1807–8), and the parts used by Shakespeare have been edited by W. G. Boswell-Stone (1896), as well as by R. S. Wallace and Alma Hansen (1917) and by Allardyce and Josephine Nicoll for Everyman's Library (1927). Boswell-Stone has also explored the relation between Holinshed and Shakespeare (1896), and there are other studies by Christabel Fiske (1910) and Wilhelm Mutz (1936). F. J. Furnivall has edited separately (3 vols., 1877–81) parts of WILLIAM HARRISON's Description of England.

EDWARD HALL: The complete Union was reprinted by Sir Henry Ellis (1809), and the part dealing with

Henry VIII by Charles Whibley (1904). Its interesting bibliographical problems have prompted articles by R. M. Smith (*JEGP*, XVII, 1918), A. F. Pollard (*Bulletin* of the Institute of Historical Research, IX, 1931–32), and Graham Pollard (the same, X, 1932–33). Hall's influence on Shakespeare has been explored by W. G. Zeeveld (*ELH*, III, 1936).

JOHN STOW: *A Survey of London* has been edited by W. J. Thoms (1842, 1876), Henry Morley (1890), and (most usefully) C. L. Kingsford (2 vols., 1908). There is also a reprint in Everyman's Library (1912).

SIR THOMAS MORE: There is a whole library of books about this great man. The 1557 compilation of his English works is being sumptuously edited (with facsimile texts) by W. E. Campbell and A. W. Reed (2 vols. to date, 1931, 1937), while the *Utopia* has gone through many modern editions, the best being those of J. H. Lupton (with both English and Latin texts, 1895), J. C. Collins (1904), and J. R. Lumby (1935). Elizabeth Rogers has edited More's *Correspondence* (1947). Of the many works of biography and commentary, first mention should be given to R. W. Chambers' *Sir Thomas More* (1935). A small classic in its own right is Frederic Seebohm's *Oxford Reformers of 1498: Colet, More, Erasmus* (3d ed., 1887), which may be supplemented by Enid Routh's *Sir Thomas More and His Friends* (1934). E. L. Surtz has written a series of articles on More's religious and political thought (*ELH*, XVI, 1949; *PMLA*, LXIV, 1949; *SP*, XLVI, 1949; *PQ*, XXIX, 1950, and XXXII, 1953). *Utopia* has received several extended treatments: for example, Karl Kautsky's *Thomas More und seine Utopia* (1888; English trans. by H. J. Stenning, 1927), W. E. Campbell's *More's Utopia and His Social Teaching* (1930) and *Erasmus, Tyndale, and More* (1949), and J. O. Hertzler's *History of Utopian Thought* (1923), as well as recent studies by Russell Ames (1949) and J. H. Hexter (1952). The Tudor lives of More (with the exception of Nicholas Harpsfield's, which was not printed until 1932) are discussed by R. W. Chambers in a British Academy lecture of 1927. There are suggestive studies of *The History of King Richard the Third* by W. G. Zeefeld (*PMLA*, LV, 1940) and L. F. Dean (the same, LVIII, 1943).

WILLIAM ROPER: All the available material, textual and biographical, is brought together by Elsie V. Hitchcock in the edition (1934) prepared for the Early English Text Society.

GEORGE CAVENDISH: This shadowy man is treated in most modern biographies of Wolsey, of which A. F. Pollard's (1929) is the best. P. L. Wiley has studied Cavendish's influence in the later Renaissance (*SP*, XLIII, 1946).

II. Early Tudor Literature

STEPHEN HAWES: W. E. Mead has edited the *Pastime* for the Early English Text Society (1928), while certain questions of sources and influence are treated in articles in *RES* by C. W. Lemmi (V, 1929), Whitney Wells (VI, 1930), and C. F. Bühler (X, 1934).

JOHN SKELTON: Though imperfect, Alexander Dyce's edition of *The Poetical Works* (3 vols., 1855) is still the best, and certainly preferable to the modernized version by Philip Henderson (1931). Useful selections have been edited by W. H. Williams (1902), Richard Hughes (1924), and Vivian de Sola Pinto (1950). In addition to a long discussion of Skelton in John Berdan's *Early Tudor Poetry* (1920) there are biographical and critical studies by L. J. Lloyd (1938), William Nelson (1939), I. A. Gordon (1943), and H. L. R. Edwards (1949). W. H. Auden has contributed a provocative essay on Skelton to *The Great Tudors* (ed. Katharine Garvin, 1935), and some of the vexed questions of dating the poems are discussed by Helen Sale (*MLN*, LII, 1937) and William Nelson (*PMLA*, LIII, 1938). There is a recent article by Alan Swallow (*PQ*, XXXII, 1953).

ALEXANDER BARCLAY: The *Eclogues* has been well edited by Beatrice White for the Early English Text Society (1928); her introduction may be supplemented by the discussions of C. H. Herford, *Studies in the Literary Relations of England and Germany* (1886), and John Berdan, *Early Tudor Poetry* (1920). J. R. Schultz has published two articles on the *Eclogues* (*MLN*, XXXV, 1920; *JEGP*, XXXII, 1933), and Fitzroy Pyle has discussed Barclay's metrics (*MLR*, XXXII, 1937).

SIR THOMAS MORE: See section I, above.

SIR THOMAS CHALONER: Although Chaloner's translation of *The Praise of Folly* has apparently never been reprinted, Erasmus himself has provided the stimulus for dozens of books. In addition to several works listed under Sir Thomas More in section I, above, one may consult Douglas Bush's admirable short discussion in *The Renaissance and English Humanism* (1939), L. E. Elliott-Binn's *England and the New Learning* (1937), and two solid studies by Preserved Smith, *The Age of the Reformation* (1920) and *Erasmus* (1923). H. H. Hudson has published an excellent modern translation with commentary (1941) of *The Praise of Folly*.

SIR THOMAS ELYOT: *The Book Named the Governor* has been well edited by H. H. S. Croft (2 vols., 1880), and has also been reprinted in Everyman's Library (1907). There is a modern edition of *Of the Knowledge Which Maketh a Wise Man* by E. J. Howard (1946); and a facsimile reproduction of the 1541 *Castle of Health* is included in the Scholars' Facsimiles & Reprints series (1936). Elyot's place in the history of Renaissance thought is treated by S. S. Laurie, *Studies in the History of Educational Opinion from the Renaissance* (1903), and by L. K. Born in the introduction to his translation (1936) of Erasmus' *Education of a Christian Prince*. Elyot's influence on Shakespeare has been investigated by D. T. Starnes (University of Texas *Studies in English*, VII, 1927) and Douglas Bush (*MLN*, LII, 1937), and his methods as a translator by James Wortham (*HLQ*, XI, 1948).

JOHN HEYWOOD: Discussions of Heywood's importance both as a poet and as a dramatist may be found in John Berdan's *Early Tudor Poetry* (1920), Rupert de la Bère's *John Heywood: Entertainer* (1937), and R. G. W. Bolwell's *Life and Works of John Heywood* (1921). *The Spider and the Fly* was edited (1894) for the Spenser Society by Sir A. W. Ward, some of whose opinions about its date are challenged in a study by Jakob Haber (1900). The 1562 *Works*, containing Heywood's epigrams, has been issued by the Spenser Society (1867) and edited by J. S. Farmer (1908), and there are articles in *MP* on his biography and influence by T. S. Graves (X, 1913; XXI, 1923) and H. N. Hillebrand (XIII, 1916).

III. The Reformation in England

TRANSLATIONS OF THE BIBLE: Although the bibliography of the various English versions of the Bible is huge, the following selected titles may be of use. B. F. Westcott's *General View of the History of the English Bible* (rev. by W. A. Wright, 1905) is a standard work, and there are others by George Milligan (*The English Bible, a Sketch of Its History*, 1895; *The New Testament and Its Transmission*, 1932), H. W. Hoare (*The Evolution of the English Bible*, 1901), and W. J. Heaton (*Our Own English Bible: Its Translators and Their Work*, 3 vols., 1913). A. W. Pollard's *Records of the English Bible . . . 1525–1611* (1911) is especially valuable. For the literary influence of the Bible the well-known studies by A. S. Cook (1892) and R. G. Moulton (1895) are useful; they may be supplemented with more recent works by Kathleen Innes (1930), C. A. Dinsmore (1931), C. C. Butterworth (1941), and David Daiches (1941), the last two on the King James Version.

SIR THOMAS MORE: See section I, above.

JOHN COLET: Between 1867 and 1876 J. H. Lupton edited most of Colet's extant Latin and English works, a number of them from manuscripts; and he printed some of them (including the sixteenth-century English translation of the Convocation Sermon and *A Right Fruitful Monition*) in the standard *Life* (1887). A more recent biography is that by Sir John Marriott (1933), and there is an extended discussion of Colet's role as a humanist in Frederic Seebohm's *Oxford Reformers* (3d ed., 1887). Friedrich Dannenberg's *Das Erbe Platons in England* (1932) has several chapters on the Platonic elements in Colet's thought.

HUGH LATIMER: G. E. Corrie edited for the Parker Society Latimer's sermons and literary remains (2 vols., 1844–45), and there are reprints of some of the sermons in Edward Arber's *English Reprints* (1868) and in Everyman's Library (1906). The biography by R. M. and A. J. Carlyle (1899) is still useful, and there is a sensitive "essay in interpretation" by C. M. Gray (1950).

THOMAS STERNHOLD and JOHN HOPKINS: A convenient summary of the immense bibliography of Tudor hymnology is available in *CBEL*, I, 677–79, which may be supplemented by John Julian's standard *Dictionary of Hymnology* (rev. ed., 1915).

THE BOOK OF COMMON PRAYER: The 1549 version has been edited by H. B. Walton and P. G. Medd (1869); there is also a reprint in Everyman's Library (1910). CRANMER's important part in its compilation is treated in A. F. Pollard's biography (1904), and the complicated history of the various revisions is traced in Francis Proctor and W. H. Frere's *New History of the Book of Common Prayer* (rev. ed., 1914) and more briefly in Edward Bright and K. D. Mackenzie's contribution to *Liturgy and Worship* (ed. W. K. L. Clarke, 1932). There are other studies by John Dowden (1899) and J. H. Benton (1910), and E. C. Ratcliff has published (1949) an anthology of excerpts from various versions of the Prayer Book between 1549 and 1661.

JOHN JEWEL: The complete works have been edited by John Ayer for the Parker Society (4 vols., 1845–50) and by R. W. Jelf (8 vols., 1848).

JOHN FOXE: Among the almost numberless reprints and expansions of *Acts and Monuments*, Josiah Pratt's edition (8 vols., 1877) is especially useful. J. F. Mozley has discussed the work at length in *John Foxe and His Book* (1940).

RICHARD HOOKER: John Keble's edition (1836) of the *Works* has been revised and expanded by R. W. Church and Francis Paget (3 vols., 1888), and there are separate editions of bk. I by R. W. Church (1868), bk. V by Ronald Bayne (1902), and the controversial bk. VIII by R. A. Houk (1931); in addition bks. I–V are available in Everyman's Library (2 vols., 1907). One of the classic biographies in the language is Izaak Walton's life of Hooker, which has been prefixed to most editions of the *Laws* since that of 1666. C. J. Sisson's *Judicious Marriage of Mr. Hooker* (1940) is valuable, and D. C. Boughner has studied Hooker's style (*RES*, XV, 1939). Two recent efforts to locate Hooker within the framework of Renaissance theological and political thought are those by E. T. Davies (1946) and F. J. Shirley (1949).

IV. Poetical Miscellanies, Ballads, and Song Books

THE COURT OF VENUS and *A BOOK OF BALLETS:* Following the descriptions of these early miscellanies by Agnes Foxwell (*The Poems of Sir Thomas Wiat*, 2 vols., 1913) and Charlotte Stopes (*Shakespeare's Industry*, 1916), further information about the three extant fragments was revealed by R. H. Griffith and R. A. Law in two articles (*TLS*, 5 July 1928; University of Texas *Studies in English*, X, 1930). Sir E. K. Chambers has a short discussion in *Sir Thomas Wyatt and Some Collected Studies* (1933), and an edition of all the fragments has been made by Russell Fraser (1955).

SONGS AND SONNETS (TOTTEL'S *MISCELLANY*): This famous book has been edited by Hyder

Rollins (2 vols., 1928–29), who gives some additional notes on it in an article in *Joseph Quincy Adams Memorial Studies* (1948). Its principal contributors have received treatment by various scholars. SURREY's poetry is interestingly discussed by W. J. Courthope (*A History of English Poetry*, vol. III, 1904) and John Berdan (*Early Tudor Poetry*, 1920); F. M. Padelford examined some of the manuscript poems in *Anglia* (XXIX, 1906) and much later (1920) edited the poetical remains (rev. ed., 1928); there is a monograph on Surrey by Edwin Casady (1938). For WYATT, Agnes Foxwell has written a *Study* (1911) and edited the *Poems* (2 vols., 1913); more recent are E. M. W. Tillyard's selection with perceptive critical discussion (1929), Kenneth Muir's edition of the *Collected Poems* (1949), and Alan Swallow's volume of excerpts (1949). Sir E. K. Chambers' discussion in *Sir Thomas Wyatt and Some Collected Studies* (1933) is also useful. GRIMALD's extant work in English and Latin has been edited by L. R. Merrill (1925), and there are articles on his translations (H. H. Hudson, *MLN*, XXXIX, 1924) and his metrics (G. P. Shannon, *PMLA*, XLV, 1930). Ruth Hughey has cleared up several misconceptions about his possible role as the first editor of Tottel's *Miscellany* (*Library*, XV, 1935).

JOHN HALL: Hyder Rollins has studied the relationship between *The Court of Virtue* and Tottel's *Miscellany* (*TLS*, 14 January 1932). There is no modern edition.

THE PARADISE OF DAINTY DEVICES: There is a modern edition by Hyder Rollins (1927) and a study of the sources of some of the poems by D. T. Starnes (*PQ*, VI, 1927).

A GORGEOUS GALLERY OF GALLANT INVENTIONS: There is a modern edition by Hyder Rollins (1926).

A HANDFUL OF PLEASANT DELIGHTS: Hyder Rollins has discussed questions of date and authorship in three articles (*JEGP*, XVIII, 1919; *MLN*, XLI, 1926; *Joseph Quincy Adams Memorial Studies*, 1948), and has also published a modern edition (1924).

BRETON'S BOWER OF DELIGHTS: There is a modern edition by Hyder Rollins (1933).

THE PHOENIX NEST: There is a modern edition by Hyder Rollins (1931).

ENGLAND'S HELICON: This splendid miscellany has received a good deal of attention. There are modern editions by A. H. Bullen (1887, 1899), Hugh Macdonald (1925), and Hyder Rollins (2 vols., 1935), as well as discussions by Hugh Macdonald (*TLS*, 23 and 30 April and 7, 14, and 21 May 1925), J. W. Hebel (*Library*, V, 1924–25), and Hyder Rollins (*TLS*, 1 October 1931).

A POETICAL RHAPSODY: There are modern editions by A. H. Bullen (2 vols., 1890–91) and Hyder Rollins (2 vols., 1931–32), as well as shorter studies by G. C. Moore Smith (*RES*, I, 1925) and Hyder Rollins (*SP*, XXIX, 1932).

BROADSIDE BALLADS: There are several good collections of sixteenth- and seventeenth-century broadside ballads. *The Roxburghe Ballads* (9 vols., 1871–99), *The Shirburn Ballads* (ed. Andrew Clark, 1907), and *Ballads & Broadsides Chiefly of the Elizabethan Period* (ed. H. L. Collmann, 1912) bring together a wealth of material. Hyder Rollins has edited several collections, including *Old English Ballads, 1553–1625* (1920), *A Pepysian Garland . . . 1595–1639* (1922), *The Pack of Autolycus* (1927), and *The Pepys Ballads* (8 vols., 1929–32). Sir Charles Firth wrote a series of excellent articles for the *Transactions* of the Royal Historical Society (III, 1909; V, 1911; VI, 1912) and contributed a general discussion of the subject to *Shakespeare's England* (rev. ed., 1926). See also Rollins' article in *PMLA* (XXXIV, 1919) and his *Analytical Index to the Ballad-Entries (1557–1709) in the Registers of the Company of Stationers of London* (1924).

SONG BOOKS: E. H. Fellowes has published copiously on Elizabethan madrigals (*English Madrigal Verse, 1588–1632*, 1920; *The English Madrigal Composers*, 1921; *The English Madrigal*, 1925), and has printed a study of Byrd (2d ed., 1948) as well as editions of Dowland, Morley, and others in *The English Madrigal School* (36 vols., 1913–24). Useful also are his editions for *The English School of Lutenist Song Writers* (series I, 16 vols., 1920–32; series II, 16 vols., 1925–27). There are many smaller collections of Elizabethan songs by A. H. Bullen (*Lyrics from the Song-Books of the Elizabethan Age*, 1887; *More Lyrics*, 1888), "Peter Warlock" (i.e. Philip Heseltine, 1927), and others. Of the many commentaries and studies on the subject those by R. R. Steele (*The Earliest English Music Printing*, 1903), W. H. G. Flood (*Early Tudor Composers*, 1925), J. M. Gibbon (*Melody and the Lyric from Chaucer to the Cavaliers*, 1930), H. E. Wooldridge (*The Polyphonic Period, Part II* [in *The Oxford History of Music*, 1932]), and Germaine Bontoux (*La chanson en Angleterre au temps d'Élizabeth*, 1936) are recommended. An excellent general study is Bruce Pattison's *Music and Poetry of the English Renaissance* (1948), and a convenient short discussion is in Hallett Smith's *Elizabethan Poetry* (1952). William Chappell's *Popular Music of the Olden Time* (2 vols., 1855–59) is an old but indispensable treatment of "ayres" and ballad tunes. CAMPION has received a good deal of special attention, there being selections or ostensibly complete editions by A. H. Bullen (1889) and Ernest Rhys (1896); the standard modern edition of his *Works* is that of Percival Vivian (1909), who also contributed a discussion to *CHEL* (vol. IV, 1909). On a larger scale are Thomas MacDonagh's *Thomas Campion and the Art of English Poetry* (1913) and M. M. Kastendieck's *England's Musical Poet, Thomas Campion* (1938).

V. Early Elizabethan Poetry

A MIRROR FOR MAGISTRATES: Lily B. Campbell has edited (1938) the 1559 *Mirror* with the additions of 1563, 1578, and 1587, and in a second volume (1946) the Higgins-Blenerhasset versions with subsequent additions. W. F. Trench made a study (1898) of the sources and influence of the *Mirror* and also wrote an article on WILLIAM BALDWIN, its first editor (*MLQ*, I, 1899). J. W. Cunliffe contributed a useful short account to *CHEL* (vol. III, 1908); Douglas Bush has studied the "classical lives" in the *Mirror* (*SP*, XXII, 1925); and Eveline I. Feasey has added to our knowledge of Baldwin's career (*MLR*, XX, 1925). There is a series of articles by Willard Farnham (*MP*, XXIII, 1926, XXIX, 1932; *JEGP*, XXV, 1926). Miss Campbell has studied some special bibliographical problems in *HLB*, no. 6, 1934. Certain of her conclusions have been challenged by Fitzroy Pyle (*TLS*, 28 December 1935), who has also written on SACKVILLE's relation to the *Mirror* (*RES*, XIV, 1938). The relationship between medieval and Tudor notions of history and the Elizabethan chronicle play has prompted a good deal of work: in addition to an article in *HLQ* (I, 1938) Miss Campbell has written *Shakespeare's "Histories": Mirrors of Elizabethan Policy* (1947), a subject explored earlier by Willard Farnham (*The Medieval Heritage of Elizabethan Tragedy*, 1936) and E. M. W. Tillyard (*Shakespeare's History Plays*, 1944).

THOMAS TUSSER: *Five Hundreth Points* has been edited by W. Payne and S. J. Herrtage for the English Dialect Society (1878), and by Dorothy Hartley (1931) with a facsimile reproduction of the 1557 edition.

BARNABE GOOGE: Edward Arber (whose texts are untrustworthy) edited the 1563 *Eglogues, Epitaphs, and Sonnets* (1871). T. P. Harrison has studied the relationship between Googe's eclogues and Montemayor's *Diana* (University of Texas *Studies in English*, V, 1925), and H. H. Hudson has written on Googe's sonnets (*PMLA*, XLVIII, 1933).

THOMAS HOWELL: A. B. Grosart has edited all of Howell's extant poetry (1879) and Sir Walter Raleigh the 1581 *Devices*, with a useful introduction (1906).

GEORGE TURBERVILE: There is no modern edition of the *Eglogues*, but Douglas Bush has published a facsimile reproduction with an introduction (1937); James Maidment long ago (1837) reprinted the *Tragical Tales*; J. P. Collier reprinted (1867) the *Epitaphs, Epigrams, Songs, and Sonnets*; and F. S. Boas has edited (1928) Turbervile's translation of Ovid. Hyder Rollins has turned up some new facts about Turbervile's life (*MP*, XV, 1918), and René Pruvost has studied the sources of some of his *Tragical Tales* (*RES*, X, 1934).

GEORGE GASCOIGNE: W. C. Hazlitt edited *The Complete Poems* (2 vols., 1869-70), but his work has been superseded by the edition of J. W. Cunliffe (2 vols., 1907-10). B. M. Ward has published a partial (1926) and C. T. Prouty a complete edition (1942) of *A Hundreth Sundry Flowers*. Ward has also written a series of articles on biographical and bibliographical problems (*RES*,

II, 1926; III, 1927; III, 1928), and Leicester Bradner has discussed *The Adventures Passed by Master F. J.* (*PMLA*, XLV, 1930). F. E. Schelling's *Life and Writings* (1893) and J. W. Cunliffe's chapter in *CHEL* (vol. III, 1908) have been superseded by C. T. Prouty's *George Gascoigne, Elizabethan Courtier, Soldier, and Poet* (1942). S. A. Tannenbaum's *Concise Bibliography* (1942) is a handy guide, especially to the long series of articles on Gascoigne's life and work in *RES* between 1926 and 1938.

GEORGE WHETSTONE: *The Rock of Regard* has been reprinted by J. P. Collier (1867), and Thomas Izard has published (1942) a biographical and critical study.

VI. Later Elizabethan Poetry

THOMAS WATSON: His so-called sonnets have been reprinted by the Spenser Society (1869) and his *Poems* by Edward Arber (1870). F. I. Carpenter (*JEGP*, II, 1899) and Janet [Espiner-]Scott (*MLR*, XXI, 1926) have investigated some of his sources, and Mark Eccles has interestingly treated his biography in *Christopher Marlowe in London* (1934).

SIR WALTER RALEIGH: The standard edition is still that published at Oxford in 1829 (8 vols.), but selections from the prose have been edited by G. E. Hadow (1917) and from both the prose and poetry by F. C. Hersey (1931). John Hannah's edition of the poetry (last revised in 1910) has been superseded by that of Agnes Latham (1951). In addition to the memoirs by William Oldys and Thomas Birch included in the Oxford edition, there are biographical studies by Edward Edwards (2 vols., 1868), Hugh de Sélincourt (1908), John Buchan (1911), and Eric Ecclestone (1941)—to mention only a few. Raleigh's intellectual and philosophical position has been studied by Irving Anthony (1934), Muriel Bradbrook (*The School of Night*, 1936), and E. A. Strathmann (*Sir Walter Raleigh: a Study in Elizabethan Skepticism*, 1951).

SIR PHILIP SIDNEY: The standard modern edition is that by Albert Feuillerat (4 vols., 1912-26), and there are also several useful reprints of separate works: the *Arcadia* in a facsimile reproduction of the 1590 version by H. Oskar Sommer (1891) and in a modernized version by E. A. Baker (1907); *Astrophel and Stella* in editions by Edward Arber (1877), A. W. Pollard (1888), Sir Sidney Lee (in *Elizabethan Sonnets*, 2 vols., 1904), and Mona Wilson (1931); *The Defense of Poesy* in editions by Edward Arber (1868), A. S. Cook (1890), Evelyn Shuckburgh (1891), and J. C. Collins (1907). There are biographies by M. W. Wallace (1915), Mona Wilson (1931), C. H. Warren (1936), and A. H. Bill (1937); and K. O. Myrick's *Sir Philip Sidney as a Literary Craftsman* (1935) is a valuable critical study. Of the numerous other critical and biographical works (conveniently listed in S. A. Tannenbaum's *Concise Bibliography*, 1941), a few deserve special mention: there are two substantial studies of the *Arcadia* and its revisions by R. W. Zandvoort (1929) and M. S. Goldman (1934), as well as articles by A. G. D. Wiles (*SP*, XXXIX, 1942), W. D. Briggs (*SP*, XXVIII, 1931), and E. A. Greenlaw (in *Anniversary Papers by Colleagues and Pupils of George Lyman Kittredge*, 1913). Theodore Spencer has discussed Sidney's merits as a poet (*ELH*, XII, 1945), and there are many biographical studies concerning his relations with Penelope Devereux, for example those by H. H. Hudson (*HLB*, no. 7, 1935), T. H. Banks (*PMLA*, L, 1935), W. G. Friedrich (*ELH*, III, 1936), and D. E. Gaughan (*MLR*, XXXIII, 1938).

EDMUND SPENSER: The indefatigable Spenserians have been so prolific that one can hardly do better than have immediate recourse to F. I. Carpenter's *Reference Guide to Edmund Spenser* (1923, supplement by D. F. Atkinson, 1937). The excellent Variorum Edition (9 vols. in 10, 1933–49) supersedes the many earlier editions of separate works. The best biography is that by A. C. Judson (1945), and H. S. V. Jones's *Spenser Handbook* (1930) is helpful. Of the numberless critical and biographical studies, three are especially useful: W. L. Renwick's *Edmund Spenser, an Essay on Renaissance Poetry* (1925), B. E. C. Davis' *Edmund Spenser, a Critical Study* (1933), and C. S. Lewis' *Allegory of Love* (1936). On a smaller scale Hallett Smith's discussions in *Elizabethan Poetry* (1952) are stimulating.

ROBERT GREENE: A. B. Grosart's *Life and Complete Works in Prose and Verse* (15 vols., 1881–86) may be supplemented by J. C. Collins' *Plays and Poems* (2 vols., 1905), although neither is satisfactory. Most of the numerous studies listed in S. A. Tannenbaum's *Concise Bibliography* (1939) are concerned with the plays and novels (see under Greene in Section IX, below), but there is an interesting discussion of the songs by Alice Meynell in *The Second Person Singular* (1921).

THOMAS LODGE: *The Complete Works* (with the exception of the translations) was published by the Hunterian Club with a "Memoir" by Sir Edmund Gosse (4 vols., 1883). There are full-length studies by N. B. Paradise (1931) and E. A. Tenney (1935), and new biographical information is given in *Thomas Lodge and Other Elizabethans* (ed. C. J. Sisson, 1933). S. A. Tannenbaum issued a bibliography in 1940.

CHRISTOPHER MARLOWE: *The Works and Life* prepared under the general direction of R. H. Case (6 vols., 1930–33) supersedes the earlier editions of Alexander Dyce (3 vols., 1850), Francis Cunningham (1870), and A. H. Bullen (3 vols., 1885), but Tucker Brooke's one-volume *Works* (1910) is excellent. Although most of the many critical studies have centered on the plays, there are discussions of the poetry in the studies of Una Ellis-Fermor (1927), John Bakeless (1942), and Harry Levin (1952). The investigation of Marlowe's life has prompted some fascinating modern studies: J. L. Hotson's *Death of Christopher Marlowe* (1925), F. S. Boas' *Marlowe and His*

Circle (1929) and *Christopher Marlowe* (1940), and Mark Eccles' *Christopher Marlowe in London* (1934). There is an important discussion of Marlowe's canon by Tucker Brooke (*PMLA*, XXXVII, 1922). Douglas Bush has a long discussion of *Hero and Leander* in *Mythology and the Renaissance Tradition* (1932), as well as two earlier studies (*MLN*, XLII, 1927; *PMLA*, XLIV, 1929).

RICHARD BARNFIELD: The poems have been edited by A. B. Grosart (1876), Edward Arber (1882), and A. H. Bullen (in *Some Longer Elizabethan Poems*, 1903).

SAMUEL DANIEL: The *Complete Works* is available in the edition of A. B. Grosart (5 vols., 1885–96), but a good modern edition is lacking. A. C. Sprague has edited a selection of the major works (1930), however, and Harry Sellers has discussed the bibliographical problems of Daniel's poetry (*Proceedings & Papers* of the Oxford Bibliographical Society, II, 1928–30). Also useful are G. K. Brady's critical study (1926), S. A. Tannenbaum's bibliography (1942), and F. W. Moorman's discussion of the relations between *The Civil Wars* and Shakespeare's history plays (*Jahrbuch der deutschen Shakespeare-Gesellschaft*, XL, 1904). There is a recent study of the manuscript of *The Civil Wars* by Cecil Seronsy (*JEGP*, LII, 1953).

MICHAEL DRAYTON: The *Complete Works* has been authoritatively edited by J. W. Hebel, Kathleen Tillotson, and B. H. Newdigate (5 vols., 1931–41). Although this edition supersedes all previous work on the subject, Sir Oliver Elton's *Michael Drayton, a Critical Study* (1905) is still useful. More recently, Russell Noyes has studied Drayton's reputation since 1631 (1935), B. H. Newdigate his contemporary reputation (1941); and S. A. Tannenbaum has published a bibliography (1941). There are shorter essays by A. H. Bullen (in *Elizabethans*, 1924) and F. L. Lucas (in *Authors Living and Dead*, 1926). Cyril Brett has edited the *Minor Poems* (1907) with a good introduction.

GEORGE CHAPMAN: The poems and plays have been edited by T. M. Parrott (2 vols., 1910–14), the poems alone by Phyllis Bartlett (1941). There are reprints of the 1611 *Iliad* by Richard Hooper (2d ed., 2 vols., 1865) and Henry Morley (2d ed., 1886), of the *Odyssey* by Richard Hooper (2d ed., 2 vols., 1874), and of *The Whole Works of Homer* (5 vols., 1930–31). Swinburne's famous essay is included in the third volume of *The Works* (ed. R. H. Shepherd, 3 vols., 1874–75). Although most Chapman scholarship is concerned with the plays, there are some interesting modern studies of the poetry: F. L. Schoell has investigated some of the sources in two articles (*MP*, XIII, 1916, and *Revue de littérature comparée*, III, 1923) and in *Études sur l'humanisme continental en Angleterre à la fin de la renaissance* (1926). There is a critical essay in A. H. Bullen's *Elizabethans* (1924) and a "revaluation" by James Smith (*Scrutiny*, IV, 1935–36), which should be compared with the tercentenary article in *TLS* (10 May 1934). R. W. Battenhouse has published an interesting interpretation of *The Shadow of Night* (*SP*, XXXVIII, 1941), and Muriel Bradbrook has explored certain aspects of Chapman's biography and intellectual interests in *The School of Night* (1936). Of special importance are Phyllis Bartlett's articles on the translations (*ELH*, II, 1935; *PMLA*, XVII, 1942).

ROBERT SOUTHWELL: His poems were issued by W. B. Turnbull (1856) and A. B. Grosart (1872), and in addition there are selections by Christobel M. Hood (1926). Some of the biographies are hagiographic, but there is a good modern study by Pierre Janelle (1935) and a *Bibliographical Study* by J. H. McDonald (1937).

JOSEPH HALL: The standard edition is that of Philip Wynter (10 vols., 1863), but A. B. Grosart has issued *The Complete Poems* (1879) and Arnold Davenport the *Collected Poems* (1949). The *Life* by George Lewis (1886) is now dated, but there are two valuable articles by S. M. Salyer (*PQ*, VI, 1927; *SP*, XXV, 1928). An old but still useful book is R. M. Alden's *Rise of Formal Satire in England* (1899), and relevant to Hall and other Elizabethan satirists are two studies of the epigram by T. K. Whipple (1925) and H. H. Hudson (1947).

JOHN MARSTON: The works were edited by J. O. Halliwell [-Phillipps] (3 vols., 1856) and A. H. Bullen (3 vols., 1887), and the poems by A. B. Grosart (1879); *The Scourge of Villany* has been reprinted separately by G. B. Harrison (1925). Theodore Spencer has written a critical essay (*Criterion*, XIII, 1934), and M. S. Allen a full-length study (1920).

EVERARD GUILPIN: *Skialetheia* was edited by J. P. Collier (1870), and there is a facsimile reprint published for the Shakespeare Association (1931). R. E. Bennett has written an article on Guilpin and Donne (*RES*, XV, 1939).

JOHN WEEVER: There is an edition of the *Epigrams* by R. B. McKerrow (1911).

SIR JOHN DAVIES: A. B. Grosart edited the complete works (3 vols., 1869–76), the poems alone (2 vols.) in 1876. There is an edition of the epigrams by Hugh Macdonald (1925), and *Nosce Teipsum* and *Orchestra* were both included in A. H. Bullen's *Some Longer Elizabethan Poems* (1903); *Orchestra* has been edited by E. M. W. Tillyard (1945). Clare Howard has issued (1941) facsimile texts of all the major poems, together with the "Gulling Sonnets" transcribed from manuscript. There are articles on *Nosce Teipsum* by L. I. Bredvold (*PMLA*, XXXVIII, 1923), G. T. Buckley (*MP*, XXV, 1927), and M. P. Tilley (*MLN*, XLIV, 1929), as well as fuller studies of Davies as a philosophical poet by E. H. Sneath (1903) and Mabel Holmes (1921).

JOHN DONNE: Since the publication of Sir Herbert Grierson's fine edition of the poems (2 vols., 1912; the text alone, 1929) there has been written a whole library of books on Donne and his fellows. John Hayward's edition of *The Complete Poetry and Select Prose* (1929) is useful, and R. E. Bennett's of *The Complete Poems* (1942) contains new material; there is a selection from the prose and poetry by W. S. Scott (1946). F. W. Payne's brief critical study (1926) and *A Garland for John Donne* (ed. Theodore Spencer, 1931) are both stimulating, as are George Williamson's *Donne Tradition* (1930) and C. M. Coffin's *John Donne and the New Philosophy* (1937). On a broader scale there are studies of metaphysical poetry by Joan Bennett (1934), J. B. Leishman (1934), and Helen C. White (1936). Izaak Walton wrote a famous life of Donne for the 1640 edition of the sermons, and Sir Edmund Gosse's *Life and Letters* (2 vols., 1899) is still of use. J. B. Leishman's recent *Monarch of Wit* (1951) is splendid. The extensive periodical literature on Donne between 1900 and 1942 is itemized in William White's bibliography (1942).

BEN JONSON: The great edition by C. H. Herford and Percy and Evelyn Simpson (11 vols., 1925–52) is now complete, and on questions of text, biography, and interpretation it supersedes all previous work. There is an edition of *Epigrams*, *The Forest*, and *Underwoods* prepared by H. H. Hudson for the Facsimile Text Society (1936), and *Timber or Discoveries* has been edited by F. E. Schelling (1892), Maurice Castelain (1906), and G. B. Harrison (1923). Although the best account of Jonson's life and works is that in the first two volumes of Herford and Simpson's edition, the biographies by Maurice Castelain (1907) and G. Gregory Smith (1919) may profitably be consulted.

SONNET SEQUENCES: Sir Sidney Lee's *Elizabethan Sonnets* (2 vols., 1904) reprints—with extremely bad texts—most of the important sequences, together with a long historical introduction; Martha Crow's *Elizabethan Sonnet-Cycles* (4 vols., 1896–98) is even more inclusive. There are good general treatments by Janet [Espiner-] Scott (*Les sonnets élisabethains*, 1929), Lu Emily Pearson (*Elizabethan Love Conventions*, 1933), and Lisle C. John (1938). Hallett Smith's chapter on the sonnet sequences in *Elizabethan Poetry* (1952) is stimulating, especially on the major sonneteers. The standard modern edition of FULKE GREVILLE (*Caelica*) is that of Geoffrey Bullough (2 vols., 1938). GILES FLETCHER's *Licia* has been edited by A. B. Grosart (1870) and Edward Arber (1896) and reprinted by Lee and Crow. HENRY CONSTABLE's *Diana* has been edited by Arber (1879) and reprinted by Lee and Crow. WILLIAM PERCY's *Coelia* has been edited by Grosart (1877) and Arber (1883) and reprinted by Lee. ZEPHERIA is reprinted by Lee. BARTHOLOMEW GRIFFIN's *Fidessa* has been edited by Grosart (1876) and Arber (1882) and reprinted by Lee and Crow. ROBERT TOFTE's *Laura* has been edited by Arber (1896) and reprinted by Lee. Most of the mountainous material on SHAKESPEARE'S *Sonnets* has been digested by Hyder Rollins for the New Variorum Edition (2 vols., 1944); among the many modern editions those by T. G. Tucker (1924) and Tucker Brooke (1936) are particularly useful, and Edward Hubler has written a short but sensitive critical study (1952).

VII. Translations

On the general subject of Tudor translations F. O. Matthiessen's *Translation, an Elizabethan Art* (1931) and A. F. Clements' *Tudor Translations, an Anthology* (1940) are both good. They may be supplemented by C. H. Conley's *First English Translators of the Classics* (1927) and H. B. Lathrop's *Translations from the Classics into English from Caxton to Chapman 1477–1620* (1933). Many notable translations of the period are reprinted in the two series of Tudor Translations (32 vols., 1892–1903; 12 vols., 1924–27), and Charles Whibley, the general editor of the second series, contributed a discussion to *CHEL* (vol. III, 1908). Henrietta Palmer's *List of English Editions and Translations of Greek and Latin Classics Printed before 1641* (1911) is a standard bibliographical guide.

HENRY HOWARD, EARL OF SURREY: All the available information about the three sixteenth-century versions of his translation of Virgil is brought together in Herbert Hartman's edition (1933) of the *Fourth Book* published by John Day in 1554, the dating of which Gladys Willcock has studied separately (*MLR*, XIV, 1919). On the unprinted manuscript version (British Museum MS. Hargrave 205) F. M. Padelford's edition of Surrey's *Poems* (rev. ed., 1928) is informative.

THOMAS PHAER: His translation of Virgil has apparently not been reprinted since the early seventeenth century.

SIR THOMAS HOBY: His translation of *The Courtier* has been edited by Sir Walter Raleigh for the Tudor Translations (1900), and there is a reprint in Everyman's Library (1928). Hoby's own interesting *Travels and Life*, treating his experiences on the Continent between 1547 and 1555, has been edited from manuscript by Edgar Powell (1902). Julia Ady has written a long study of Castiglione (2 vols., 1908), and Walter Schrinner has more recently investigated his importance in *Castiglione und die englische Renaissance* (1939).

ARTHUR GOLDING: His translation of Ovid's *Metamorphoses* has been edited by W. H. D. Rouse (1904), and his varied career has been studied by L. T. Golding in *An Elizabethan Puritan* (1937).

SIR THOMAS NORTH: His great translation of Plutarch has been reprinted several times in whole or in part, among others by W. W. Skeat (1875), George Wyndham (for the Tudor Translations, 6 vols., 1895–96), and Tucker Brooke (2 vols., 1909). Thomas M. Cranfill has turned up some new biographical facts (*HLQ*, XIII, 1949).

RICHARD STANYHURST: His translation of Virgil

was reprinted by Edward Arber (1880), and there is a modern edition by Dirk van der Haar (1933).

CHRISTOPHER MARLOWE: See section VI, above.

SIR JOHN HARINGTON: His version of Ariosto has not been reprinted since the early seventeenth century, but Townsend Rich has written an able study of the work (1940).

PHILEMON HOLLAND: His version of Plutarch's *Moralia* has been edited by Joseph Jacobs (1888) and F. B. Jevons (1892), and there is a partial reprint in Everyman's Library (1911).

JOHN FLORIO: His translation of Montaigne has been edited by George Saintsbury for the Tudor Translations (3 vols., 1892–93), A. R. Waller (6 vols., 1897), Desmond MacCarthy (3 vols., 1928), and J. I. M. Stewart (2 vols., 1931). There is also a reprint in Everyman's Library (3 vols., 1910). Clara de Chambrun's *Giovanni Florio, un apôtre de la renaissance en Angleterre* (1921) may be supplemented by Frances Yates's *John Florio, the Life of an Italian in Shakespeare's England* (1934).

GEORGE CHAPMAN: See section VI, above.

VIII. Critical Theory

Most of the important critical documents are brought together in *Elizabethan Critical Essays* (ed. G. Gregory Smith, 2 vols., 1904). The subject is treated historically and critically in J. E. Spingarn's *History of Literary Criticism in the Renaissance* (6th impression, 1930), George Saintsbury's *History of English Criticism* (1911), C. S. Baldwin's *Renaissance Literary Theory and Practice* (ed. D. L. Clark, 1939), Elizabeth Sweeting's *Early Tudor Criticism* (1940), and J. W. H. Atkins' *English Literary Criticism: the Renaissance* (2d ed., 1951).

SIR THOMAS ELYOT: See section II, above.

THOMAS WILSON: *The Art of Rhetorique* has been edited by G. H. Mair (1909). There is a discussion in W. G. Crane's *Wit and Rhetoric in the Renaissance* (1937), and R. H. Wagner has written several studies, for example a contribution to *Papers in Rhetoric* (ed. D. C. Bryant, 1940) and an article on bibliographical problems (*MLN*, XLIV, 1929).

GEORGE GASCOIGNE: *Certain Notes* has been reprinted by G. Gregory Smith and by George Saintsbury in *Loci Critici* (1903). See also section V, above.

STEPHEN GOSSON: *The School of Abuse* has been reprinted by J. P. Collier (1841) and Edward Arber (1868), and there is a monograph on Gosson by William Ringler (1942).

THOMAS LODGE: His attack on Gosson is reprinted (in part) by G. Gregory Smith, and there are articles on its "missing title" and its source by J. Dover Wilson (*MLR*, III, 1908) and William Ringler (*RES*, XV, 1939).

SIR PHILIP SIDNEY: See section VI, above.

GABRIEL HARVEY and EDMUND SPENSER: Their correspondence is reprinted in some editions of

Spenser and is discussed by J. R. Caldwell (*PMLA*, XLI, 1926) and Josephine Bennett (*MP*, XXIX, 1931). William Ringler has written on "Master Drant's Rules" (*PQ*, XXIX, 1950), and Gladys Willcock has investigated the vogue of classical meters (*MLR*, XXIX, 1934).

WILLIAM WEBBE: His *Discourse* has been edited by Edward Arber (1870) and reprinted by G. Gregory Smith.

ABRAHAM FRAUNCE: *The Arcadian Rhetoric* is partially summarized by G. Gregory Smith, and Ethel Seaton has published an excellent edition for the Luttrell Society (1950).

THOMAS NASHE: R. B. McKerrow's edition of the *Works* (5 vols., 1904–10) is one of the most notable achievements of Renaissance scholarship. There are extracts from Nashe's critical tracts in G. Gregory Smith, and S. A. Tannenbaum has published a bibliography (1941).

GEORGE PUTTENHAM: *The Art of English Poesy* has been edited by Gladys Willcock and Alice Walker (1936), and B. M. Ward has studied the authorship of the treatise (*RES*, I, 1925).

SIR JOHN HARINGTON: The *Apology* has been reprinted by G. Gregory Smith. See also section VII, above.

FRANCIS MERES: D. C. Allen has edited (1933) the section on "Poetrie" from *Palladis Tamia* and has contributed an introduction to the whole book as issued by Scholars' Facsimiles & Reprints (1938).

THOMAS CAMPION: The *Observations* has been reprinted by G. Gregory Smith and (with Daniel's *Defense*) by G. B. Harrison (1925). See also section IV, above.

SAMUEL DANIEL: The *Defense* has been reprinted by G. Gregory Smith and (with Campion's *Observations*) by G. B. Harrison (1925). See also section VI, above.

BEN JONSON: See section VI, above.

IX. Prose Fiction

An adequate study of the Elizabethan novel is yet to be written, but there are general discussions in Sir Walter Raleigh's *English Novel* (1894, rev. ed. 1935), W. L. Cross's *Development of the English Novel* (1899), and George Saintsbury's *English Novel* (1913). J. J. Jusserand's *Roman anglais* (1886; Eng. trans. by Elizabeth Lee, 1890, rev. ed. 1899) is, though somewhat dated, still valuable, and E. A. Baker's *History of the English Novel*, vol. II (*The Elizabethan Age and After*, 1929), is a standard work. Special influences are treated in S. L. Wolff's *Greek Romances in Elizabethan Prose Fiction* (1912), J. G. Underhill's *Spanish Literature in the England of the Tudors* (1899), and Mary Augusta Scott's *Elizabethan Translations from the Italian* (1916). The literature of roguery is discussed in two studies by F. W. Chandler (*Romances of Roguery*, 1899; *The Literature of Roguery*, 1907) and in Frank Aydelotte's *Elizabethan Rogues and Vagabonds* (1913).

Arundell Esdaile's *List of English Tales and Prose Romances Printed before 1740* (1912) is a useful bibliography. There are reprints of Elizabethan tales and novels in J. P. Collier's *Shakespeare's Library* (rev. by W. C. Hazlitt, 6 vols., 1875), *Shorter Novels: Elizabethan and Jacobean* (Everyman's Library, 1929), and *Elizabethan Tales* (ed. E. J. O'Brien, 1936).

JESTBOOKS: The standard collection is *Shakespeare's Jest-Books* (ed. W. C. Hazlitt, 3 vols., 1864). Ernst Schulz's *Englischen Schwankbücher* (1912) may be supplemented by F. P. Wilson's useful discussion in *HLQ* (II, 1938–39).

WILLIAM PAINTER: *The Palace of Pleasure* has been reprinted by Joseph Jacobs (3 vols., 1890) and Hamish Miles (4 vols., 1929), and ten tales are included in Peter Haworth's *Elizabethan Story-Book* (1928). Douglas Bush has studied some of Painter's classical tales in *JEGP* (XXIII, 1924).

SIR GEOFFREY FENTON: *Certain Tragical Discourses* has been reprinted by R. L. Douglas (2 vols., 1898), and a selection from Belleforest's *Histoires tragiques* has been published with a useful introduction by R. S. Hook (1948).

GEORGE PETTIE: *A Petite Palace* has been edited by Sir Israel Gollancz (2 vols., 1908) and Herbert Hartman (1938). There are articles by Douglas Bush (*PQ*, V, 1926; *JEGP*, XXIII, 1924, XXVII, 1928) and D. T. Starnes (*SP*, XXXVII, 1940) on Pettie's sources, and studies of his influences (as on Lyly) in a monograph by M. P. Tilley (1926) and in articles by C. J. Vincent (*MLN*, LIV, 1939) and J. Swart (*ES*, XXIII, 1941).

BARNABE RICH: The *Farewell* has been reprinted by J. P. Collier (in *Eight Novels Employed by English Dramatic Poets*, 1846), and there are studies by D. T. Starnes (*SP*, XXX, 1933), H. J. Webb (*JEGP*, XLII, 1943), and Thomas M. Cranfill (*ELH*, XVI, 1949; *SP*, XLVI, 1949), in addition to a biography by Cranfill and Dorothy H. Bruce (1953).

THOMAS UNDERDOWN: *An Ethiopian History* has been reprinted by Charles Whibley (1895; rev. by F. A. Wright, 1923) and George Saintsbury (1924). The standard study of Greek romances in English is that of S. L. Wolff (1912), but Zoë Glava has written on Heliodorus (1937) and Charles Whibley has an essay on him in *Studies in Frankness* (1910). Elizabeth H. Haight has published two useful studies (1943, 1945) on Greek romances.

GEORGE GASCOIGNE: See section V, above.

JOHN LYLY: The standard edition of the *Complete Works* is that of R. W. Bond (3 vols., 1902); *Euphues* has been separately edited by M. W. Croll and Harry Clemens (1916). There are full-length studies by J. Dover Wilson (1905), Albert Feuillerat (1910), and Violet Jeffrey (1928); and Lyly's style and influence have been studied by many scholars, among others C. G. Child (1894), M. P. Tilley (*Elizabethan Proverb Lore*, 1926), William Ringler (*PMLA*, LIII, 1938), and G. W. Knight (*RES*, XV, 1939). S. A. Tannenbaum has published *A Concise Bibliography* (1940).

SIR PHILIP SIDNEY: See section VI, above.

ROBERT GREENE: *Menaphon* has been reprinted (with Lodge's *Margarite of America*) by G. B. Harrison (1927), and René Pruvost's *Robert Greene et ses romans* (1938) discusses all the novels. See also section VI, above.

THOMAS LODGE: See section VI, above.

THOMAS NASHE: *The Unfortunate Traveler* has been reprinted by Sir Edmund Gosse (1892), S. C. Chew (1926), H. F. B. Brett-Smith (1927), and Haydn Mackey (1930). See also section VIII, above.

THOMAS DELONEY: The best available edition is that of F. O. Mann (1912). Both *Jack of Newbury* and *Thomas of Reading* have been reprinted by W. H. D. Rouse (1920) and are included in *Shorter Novels* (Everyman's Library, 1929). Earlier, *Jack of Newbury* was reprinted by J. O. Halliwell[-Phillipps] (1859) and *Thomas of Reading* by W. J. Thoms (in *Early English Prose Romances*, rev. ed., 3 vols., 1858). There are several articles by Hyder Rollins (*PMLA*, L, 1935, LI, 1936; *Harvard Studies and Notes in Philology and Literature*, XIX, 1937) and a monograph by Abel Chevalley (1926).

X. Miscellaneous Prose

ROGER ASCHAM: The only collected edition is the *Whole Works* edited by J. A. Giles (3 vols. in 4, 1864–65), but there is a useful reprint of the *English Works* (ed. W. A. Wright, 1904). *The Schoolmaster* has been edited separately by J. E. B. Mayor (1863) and Edward Arber (1870). Apart from Giles's introduction, the most useful biography is a German monograph by Alfred Katterfeld (1879), and there are articles by L. B. Radford (*Quarterly Review*, CCLVI, 1931) and G. B. Parks (*HLQ*, I, 1937–38). S. A. Tannenbaum has published a bibliography (1946).

RICHARD MULCASTER: *The First Part of the Elementary* has been edited by E. T. Campagnac (1925), the *Positions* by R. H. Quick (1888). Mulcaster's theories of language are discussed by A. C. Baugh in *A History of the English Language* (1935), and R. F. Jones has written an article on the subject (Washington University *Studies*, XIII, 1926).

THOMAS LODGE: *An Alarum against Usurers* was edited for the Shakespeare Society by David Laing (1853). See also section VI, above.

ROBERT GREENE: G. B. Harrison has reprinted most of Greene's rogue pamphlets for the Bodley Head Quartos, *The Black Book's Messenger* in 1924, *A Groatsworth of Wit* in 1923, and *The Repentance* in 1923. The cony-catching pamphlets are reprinted by A. V. Judges

in *The Elizabethan Underworld* (1930). Frank Aydelotte's general discussion in *Elizabethan Rogues and Vagabonds* (1913) is useful, and Harold Jenkins has studied the authenticity of *A Groatsworth* and *The Repentance* (*RES*, XI, 1935). See also section VI, above.

THE GREENE–NASHE–HARVEY CONTROVERSY: For modern editions of Greene's and Nashe's works see sections VI and VIII, respectively. The controversy is learnedly surveyed by R. B. McKerrow in his edition of Nashe; there are also monographs on the subject by E. G. Harman (1923) and Chauncey Saunders (1931). A. B. Grosart has edited Harvey's *Works* (3 vols., 1884–85), and G. B. Harrison has reprinted (1922) *Four Letters*, the bibliographical problems of which have been studied by F. R. Johnson (*Library*, XV, 1934–35); see also section VIII, above.

THOMAS NASHE: See section VIII, above.

RICHARD HAKLUYT: The standard reprints of Elizabethan travel narratives are those in the sumptuously edited publications of the Hakluyt Society. *Divers Voyages* was reprinted by the Society in 1850, *The Principal Navigations* (in 12 vols.) in 1903–5, and there is also a partial edition of the *Navigations* in Everyman's Library (8 vols., 1907). Froude's famous essay ("England's Forgotten Worthies") is included in the first series of *Short Studies of Great Subjects* (1867–68). For longer studies there are E. J. Payne's *Voyages of the Elizabethan Seamen* (2d ed., 2 vols., 1893–1900), Sir Walter Raleigh's introduction for the Hakluyt Society's edition of *The Principal Navigations* published separately as *The English Voyages of the Sixteenth Century* (1910), and G. B. Parks's *Richard Hakluyt and the English Voyages* (1928).

SIR WALTER RALEIGH: Apart from its inclusion in the 1598 edition of Hakluyt's *Principal Navigations*, *A Report* has been reprinted in later editions of that work and separately by Edward Arber (?1895). See also section VI, above.

FRANCIS BACON: The standard edition of the works is that by James Spedding, R. L. Ellis, and D. D. Heath (14 vols., 1857–74), but there are many reprints of the *Essays* and the *Advancement*, the former by W. A. Wright (1868), Edward Arber (*A Harmony of the Essays*, 1871), and E. A. Abbott (5th ed., 2 vols., 1882), the latter by W. A. Wright (1869, 1900), J. E. Creighton (rev. ed., 1899), and Thomas Case (190–). Among the many biographies, that by James Spedding (7 vols., 1861–74; abridged ed., 2 vols., 1878) remains standard, but there are useful shorter works by E. A. Abbott (1885), R. W. Church (1884), Mary Sturt (1932), and Charles Williams (1933). E. N. S. Thompson has written a study of the seventeenth-century essay (1926), and there are articles on Bacon's *Essays* by R. S. Crane (in the *Schelling Anniversary Papers*, 1923) and Jacob Zeitlin (*JEGP*, XXVII, 1928). M. W. Croll's important analysis of Bacon's style was contributed to the *Schelling Anniversary Papers* (1923), and K. R. Wallace has treated the subject more fully in *Francis Bacon on Communication and Rhetoric* (1943). Two recent studies of seventeenth-century prose which pay considerable attention to Bacon are George Williamson's *Senecan Amble* (1951) and R. J. Jones's *Triumph of the English Language* (1953). Of the many works on Bacon's

philosophical position that of C. D. Broad (1926) is especially useful, as is the short discussion in Basil Willey's *Seventeenth Century Background* (1934). There are shorter essays by Geoffrey Bullough and Rudolf Metz in *Seventeenth Century Studies Presented to Sir Herbert Grierson* (1938).

Glossary of English Words and Phrases
Including a List of Archaic Spellings[1]

a, *adj.*, one; *prep.*, in; of; *pron.*, he
abashment, confusion from surprise
abator, abater
abcedarian, abecedarian, one engaged in learning the alphabet
abeston, asbestos
abhominable(ness), abominable(ness)
abhomination, abomination
abhor from the sense, shrink with dislike from (others') sense
abidden, *adj.*, enduring, lasting; *v.*, endured; resist; submit to
abide the sale, wait for a buyer
abiden, abode, lived
abiders, strong, men with great power of endurance
abiding, dwelling place
abiliments, habiliments
abject, *n.*, degraded person; *v.*, **abjected his rigor**, i.e. cast off
aboard, laid, came alongside for fighting
abod, abode
abominable house, i.e. large house or college
aboord, aboard
aboundance, abundance
aboundant(ly), abundant(ly)
abroach, set, published, diffused
absent, *n.*, absence; *v.*, **absented his eyes**, i.e. kept them away (from); **absented lover**, i.e. absent
absolute, finished; entire; perfect
absolutely performed, i.e. perfectly
absonism, solecism
absteigned, abstained
aburn, auburn
abuse, deceive; violate, defile
abusion, abuse
abusively call, i.e. incorrectly
aby(e), pay the penalty for; make amends for
acception of persons, i.e. corrupt favoritism, due to a person's rank or influence
accersited, summoned
accessary, accessory
accident, happening; misfortune; **accidents in teaching**, i.e. accidence
accidentary, grammatical, inflexional
accloyed, nauseated
accommodate, *pa. part.*, accommodated
accompable, sociable
accompt, accoumpt, accounpt, *n.*, account; *v.*, tell; esteem (of), value
accouster, accouter
accoustrements, accouterments, clothes
accrew, come as an addition (to)
accursed, *v.*, cursed, swore
accurtation, shortening
accustomable, customary
accustomably, customarily
accustomed poets, i.e. habitual
acer, maple tree
ackorns, acorns

aconitum, aconite, wolfsbane
acquaint, *pa. part.*, acquainted
acquentance, acquaintance
acquite, acquit, release
across, arms, i.e. embracing or folded
actife, active
adamant, (fancy's) magnet
adayes, daily
adder, deaf: *see* Psalms lviii.4 f.
addict thyself, devote thyself (to)
addoulce, ?make fragrant
adepted superiority, i.e. gained, acquired
adew, adieu
adjorn, adjourn; **being adjorned**, i.e. adjourned, remanded for justice to another day
adjuvate, assist, aid
administrations, all common, i.e. actions of serving in offices
admiral, flagship
admiration, wonder, astonishment
admire, wonder
admit (of), approve; **admitted to wear**, i.e. permitted
adni(c)hilate, annihilate(d)
adoptive, (daughters) by adoption
a-dressing, having wounds dressed
adultry, adultery
adust, atrabilious, sallow
adustion, hotness and dryness of the body's humors
adventure, venture, dare; **adventured experience**, i.e. gained at a risk; **at adventure**, at random, recklessly; **at all adventures**, in any case
adverse, *n.*, adversary
advertise, advertize, inform, tell, notify
advertisement, information; tidings; instruction, counsel; warning, precept
advise her visage, look at her face; **advised with**, thought of in connection with; **advised with judgment**, i.e. pondered
advisoes, official dispatches
advouch, avouch
advoultery, advoutry, adultery
aegida, Jupiter's shield
aeglogue, eclogue
aemule, emulate
afear(e)d, afraid
afer, afar
affair, action, performance
affect, *n.*, passion, love; **working affect**, producing an effect; *v.*, love; prefer, like
affectation, natural, i.e. inclination, bent
affected, *adj.*, cherished; loving (friend); *v.*, loved; used
affection, affectation (of words); feeling; partiality; passion, lust; animosity; **affections of words**, i.e. properties, qualities
affectionate to his own mind, i.e. prejudiced, partial
affectionated speeches, i.e. affectionate
affiance, faith, confidence
affied, affianced
affinity, association, argument

affray, afray, *n.*, fray, assault; *v.*, frighten; **afrayed**, afraid; **affray charges**, i.e. defray
affy, trust, confide
aforce, afforce, attempt
afore, before
afray, afrayed: *see* affray
afront, *prep.*, before
after-claps, unexpected blows or misfortunes
after-loss, future grief, later loss
after-wit, knowledge after the event
again, *prep.*, against; in anticipation of; drawing towards (Christmas)
against, sit, i.e. opposite
agen, again
aglets, the tags of a woman's garters
a-good, heartily, thoroughly
agreeable to the Latin, i.e. close, literal
agrieve, aggrieve; grieved
agrise, quake, be full of horror
air, part-song; beat the air, i.e. couldn't find me in the lists or tournament
ajoining, adjoining
aknow, recognize
acknowledge, acknowledge
a-land, ashore
alarm, fresh, further incitement
alate, of late, recently
alay, dilution
albe, although
alchimy, alchemy
alcumists, alchemists
alcumy, alchemy
alegge, alleviate
ale-joust, ale-just, a pot with handles
alienate, *pa. part.*, withdrawn
alight'ned, illumined
all a more, ?à la mode
all amort, dull, dead
all and some, entirely, the sum x al
all had it, even if it had
all one, quite the same
all they, they all
all to- (*plus a verb*), wholly, utterly
all were, even though it (there) were
allay, *n.*, alloy; *v.*, qualify, mix
alledge, allege; cite
allegeance, alleviation, relief
allegoria, a sort of envoy pointing the moral of the poem that precedes
allow (of), approve, praise
allowance, approval
allude, hint, suggest (an effect)
all-where, everywhere
almery, ambry, storehouse
almoner, functionary in the household of a bishop
almonry, place where alms were distributed
alonely, only; solitarily
alongst, down the length of
als, also
alsoone, as soon
altitude, height
altogither, altogether
alway, always
am to, I, I must

---

amain, at once

amaranth, imaginary fadeless flower

amarous, amorous

amate, dismay

amazed, Rome, i.e. was amazed

amazement, astonishing, ?i.e. impressiveness

ambages, beating about the bush

ambassade, ambassador and his suite; business entrusted to, or message borne by, an ambassador

ambassadge, ambassage, the business of ambassadors; mission

ambry, repository

amearst, amerced, punished

amel'd, enameled

amenaunce, bearing, conduct

amended Dover, i.e. rebuilt

amendement, amendment

ames ace, ambs-ace, two aces, the smallest throw at dice

amfibologies, ambiguous discourses

amiable picture, i.e. lovely

amiably drawn, i.e. admirably

amiddes, amids, amidmong, amidst

amiss, crime

amisse, amice, white-lined square worn by celebrant priests

among, *adv.*, all the while (merry)

amonges(t), amongs, amongst

amorets, love glances; love songs

amounting, *adj.*, mounting, increasing

amusing to pray, engaging himself to pray

an, *conj.*, and; if

anapestiques, anapests

anatomy, detailed examination

ancient, senior member, one of the governing body; standard, flag; insignia; ancientest, oldest race of men

and, *often* = if; and if, if

angels, gold coins worth about ten shillings; oil of angels, money (slang)

angle, *n.*, fishing-hook

Angle-, Anglo-

anhungered, overcome with hunger

anker, anchor

ankle of my chin, ?i.e. angle

annotation, digression

annoy, *n.*, trouble, pain

anone, anon

another, other, additional

answered, been, been justified

antic, antick, *n.*, clown; dance an antic, dance grotesquely; mad anticks or antiques, i.e. tricks; *v.*, antick it, perform antics

antiquary, antiquity

antiques, mad: *see* antic

any of them (both), i.e. either

apall, appal

apart, *v.*, put away, remove (grief)

apay, satisfy

apear, appear

apease, pacify (a fight); apeased (appeased) through the deep flood, through the tranquil seas (*tranquilla per alta*)

aperns, aprons

apes (in hell), lead, the (proverbial) punishment for spinsters

apoint, appoint

apologize translation, i.e. apologize for

apon, upon

apostata, apostate

appair, deteriorate, impair; once appair, sometime deteriorate

appale, make pale with fear

apparail, apparel

apparance, appearance

apparant(ly), apparent(ly), clear(ly)

appareil, apparel

apparence, appearance

apparition, semblance

appeach, accuse

appendix, attendant, page

appertenent, appertinent, appertaining (to)

appetence, desire, appetite

apply, work assiduously (for); applied with lessons, i.e. instructed

apposed, opposed

apprentissage, apprenticeship

approper, assign to

approvaunce, approval

approve, find out by testing; prove

approvedly, written, i.e. in an approved manner

aproach, approach

aqua fortis, nitric acid

araxa, a fabulous herb noisome to virginity

arbiterment, arbitrament

archigrammatian, ?chief grammarian

architecture, architector, architect

aread: *see* areed

areared, erected

areed, aread, make known, tell

argument, subject; summary of the subject; arguments of age, i.e. signs, tokens

armado, armada, fleet; ship of war

armary, armory

armony, harmony

arms across, folded or embracing arms

arr, err

arrant, errand

arras, tapestry (quilts)

array, *n.*, plight, situation

arrive, *n.*, arrival

art should win her, i.e. artifice, trickery

artificer, one who practises any art; trickster

artificial, displaying special art or skill

artificiality, artfulness, skill

artificially, with art

artillery, the practise of using artillery or archery

art-masters, those skilled in arts; professed rhetoricians

as, *conj.*, as if; so that; such as; that; as what is hid, for, indeed, what is hidden

ascendent, fortunate, favorable ascendant, a lucky degree of the zodiac

ascent, staircase

ascertains God, night, i.e. assures one of His existence

ascited, summoned

assembly, assembly

asken, ask

askes, ashes

aslake, grow less, cease

asonder, asunder

aspire, blow; breathe into; fly upward

assawt, assault

assay, *n.*, effort, attempt; tasting food and drink before giving it to the king; trial; made assay, made trial of; *v.*, essay, try; a fellowship assay, in good fellowship try (to sing)

assemble, *n.*, assembly

assend, ascend

assentation, assenting to others' opinions

assott, befooled

assoyle, acquit oneself

assuage, asswage, diminish, lessen

assubtiling, subtilizing

assurance, assuring, betrothal

asswage: *see* assuage

astart, astert, escape

astate, estate; of exalted rank

astert: *see* astart

astoined, astonied, astonned, astoned, stunned, astonished

astrology, a fair, ?*misprint for* astrolabye, an astrolabe

astronomer, astrologer

astronomy, astrology

atach, attach

atchieve(ment), achieve(ment)

a-thrust, a-thurst, athirst, thirsty

athwart, (speak) in opposition to

atomus, atomy, atom

atones, at once

attached, arrested; attacked (with drouth); attached of, imprisoned by

attaint, *n.*, sin; *v.*, affect, seize upon; attainted at his hands, i.e. attained, got

attempred, attuned

attemptate, attempt

attend, hear, listen; wait for; attend blissfulness, i.e. expect

attent, *n.*, attention

attone, *n.*, agreement

attones, at once

atturney, attorney

atween, between

aucthor, auctor, author

aucthority, auctority, authority

aught, *adv.*, at all

auglet, aglet, fringe

augur, seer, prophet

auncetors, ancestors

auricular, hearsay; oral

autentique, *adj.*, authentic; *v.*, authenticate

auter, altar

author, autor, prompter, mover

authorize, give authority to

autor(ity), author(ity). *See* author

autumpn, autumn

avail, *n.*, advantage; *v.*, bring down; set, disappear

avale, go down, get down; lower, debase; slacken

avance, avaunce, advance, further

avena, pastoral pipe (Italian)

aventure, adventure (*q.v.*); at all aventures, all by chance

avise, advise

avize him, bethink himself

avoid, go away, leave; go (into exile); avoid from, escape; water might avoid, i.e. run off

avoord, afford, supply

avow, *n.*, solemn promise; *v.*, avow the saying, i.e. approve it

await, laid, ambushed, surrounded

awake, *n.*, awakening

away-ward, not straight

aweight, *pa. part.*, weighed down, oppressed

awful eyes, i.e. full of awe

awhape, dismay

awn, own

awnswered, answered

awork, to work, on work

awry-transformed, corrupted (by travel)

ax(e), *v.*, ask

axiomaes, axioms, maxims

axtree, trunk of an ash tree

ay(e), ever; ay(e) me, alas

ayre, air

azures, stones of lapis lazuli

babes, boys, students

bable, bauble

babound, baboon

baby, doll, toy; **look babies in his eyes,** make small images of oneself reflected in his eyes

bad, *v.*, bade, ordered

badged coach, i.e. with armorial bearings

bafful'd, treated with scorn

baggage, despicable (stuff); refuse, dirt (in beer)

bain, *n.*, bath; *v.*, wash, bathe

baiting-place, i.e. that which refreshes one's wit

bald rimers, trivial, paltry poets

balductum, *adj.*, trashy; *n.*, trash

bale, destruction, misery

balien (Old French *baleine*, Latin *balaena*), whale

balist, ballast

balk, *n.*, dividing ridge; post, board; *v.*, **from his liking balk,** to lie out of the way of his liking

ballade, poetry of the ballade form

ballat, ballet, ballatry, ballad(s)

ballating, ballad-writing

balliards, billiards

balls, stuff their, stuff tennis balls with hair

balsamum, balm

ban, *v.*, curse

band, agreement; bond; bondage; *pa. part.*, bound

bandetto, bandit

banes, banns (of marriage)

banket(ing), banquet(ing)

bankrot, bankrout, bankrupt; bankruptcy

banquests minds, i.e. banqueteth

banskin, barmskin, leather apron

barbariousness, barbarousness

barbill, barbel, freshwater fish of the carp tribe

barded, covered with armor

bare of his palm, i.e. the bare skin of

barley-break, a country game like prisoner's bars

barleyhood, fit of drunkenness

barm, froth on ale; yeast, leaven

barmy, yeasty

barn, bairn; man

barnacle, i.e. the fabulous barnacle-goose

barrain, barren

barreled beef, i.e. packed in barrels

barriers, fighting at, i.e. in the lists, divided in the center by a low fence

base, bidding, game of prisoner's base; **run a base,** play prisoner's base

base-court, outer courtyard occupied by servants

basest clouds, i.e. the darkest

bash at it, i.e. be abashed by

basilisks, fabulous reptiles

bason, basin

bass, kiss

bastinado, a blow with a stick or cudgel

bastion, ball

bastle, bastille, tower

bat, a quarterstaff

batchelor, bachelor; batchelor knight, i.e. young, a novice in arms

bate, *n.*, debate, strife; *v.*, lessen in force or intensity; bating, abating, subtracting

battail, battle; troops in battle array

batter, provision to, i.e. to seize upon

battle, body of troops in battle array

battled walls, walls fortified with battlements

baud, *v.*, foul, dirty

bauldrick, belt, girdle

bavin, brushwood

bawdery, bawdry

bawds, preachers are, i.e. pander to evil designs

bay, embankment, dam; at that bay, in such close quarters

bayard, blind, bay horse, a type of recklessness; bayard in school, self-confident in ignorance

be, are; been; be to have, have occasion to

bead-roll, list of souls to be prayed for

beads, bid one's, tell one's beads, pray

beadsmanry, the place of a beadsman in an almshouse

bear, Warwick's, "the ancient [heraldic] coat of that earldom"

bear in hand, i.e. assert, maintain; cajole, delude with promises; bear it out, survive

beat his brain, labored

beating, in, being beaten

beautreux, ?protection

beavers, visors of helmets

bebaste, beat with a cudgel

beblister, blister badly

because, *often* = in order that; why

beck, beak; gesture; nod

becomed, less, less suited

becoming of, gracing

bed, hunted for the, i.e. for its skin for bed-covers

bedfellaw, bedfellow

bedight, dressed

bedrent, soaked

bedward, to, towards bed

been, bene, are; be

beforetime(s), previously

beforn, before

befortune, happen to

began, *pa. part.*, begun

begate, begot

begged for fools, set down for fools

begger(ly), beggery, beggar(ly), beggary

begon, begun

begsters, beggars

behalfs, behalves

behavor, behavior

behight, decide, ordain; ladies behight, called or named ladies

behild, beheld

behindhand, insolvent

beholding, beholden, indebted

behooveful, expedient, useful

behove, *n.*, behoof; *v.*, behoove

beldam, loathsome male

beldame, aged woman

belike, apparently

belimmed, disfigured

bell, bear the, surpass, succeed

bellibone, fair maid

beloved with, beloved by

bemist, becloud, dim

bemole, i.e. in B mollis, "softened B"

bend argent, a white ordinary formed by two parallel lines on a shield (in heraldry)

bended moon, i.e. crescent

bene, been; are; be

benefit of clergy, exemption from criminal process before a secular judge to laymen who could read their "neck-verse" (*q.v.*)

benight, bring darkness to

bent enemy, i.e. resolute; bent of the brow, i.e. bending

benum, benumb

berain, wet (with tears)

beraying, befouling

bereafing, bereaving

bereave, deprive of

beryl glass, a mirror the color of beryl (pale sea-green)

beseek, beseech

beseen, well, beautiful

beshrew, curse (one)

besides, *prep.*, beside

besiedge, besiege

besiness, business

besonian, bezonian, beggar, scoundrel

besprent, sprinkled

bested, hard, hard pressed; ill bested, in unhappy plight

bestness, the quality of being best

bestoul, bestoled, moved stealthily on

bestraught, distraught, distracted

besy, busy

besyty, busyty, fussiness, officiousness

bet, beat, beaten

betake you, hath, i.e. given to

betide, *n.*, fortune

betied, tied fast

betil, beetle

bett, better (off)

better part, i.e. the larger

betwext, betwixt

bev'radge, beverage

bewrap, cover, envelop

bewray, reveal, make known; betray

bias, against the, i.e. the weight in the side of a bowl that makes it run against the slope of a bowling green

bibble, tipple, drink

bicause, because

bid beads, tell (count) rosary beads, pray

bidding base: *see* base

bilboes, swords (from Bilboa, Spain)

bile, *n.*, boil

bill, bill of complaint; halberd; scythe

billets, written documents

billmen, halberdiers

bin, been

binden, bind

birle them, pour drink for them

bisket, biscuit

bit, *n.*, (bloody) bite

bitter, *n.*, bittern; *adj.*, bitter to enemies, i.e. cruel

black bowl, drinking bowl

black-jack, jack, leather beer-jug

blacks, mourning garments

blacksmith with a polt-foot, Vulcan

blake, black

blank, to be, i.e. utterly disconcerted; put their blanks, a pun on the French copper coin so called and blank verse

blanket hose, hose of undyed woolen stuff

blast, storm

blaze, *v.*, portray, set forth; *n.*, **blaze of her beauty**, i.e. blazing star

blazon, record of excellences

ble, color, complexion

blear his eyes, dim his vision, hoodwink

blen, blend

blenches, faults

blend, defile, obscure (beauty); **blent**, polluted

bless, *n.*, bliss

blew, blue

blind master, Cupid

bliss, *v.*, bless; **blist**, blest

blo, blackish blue

block and stork, a reference to a fable of Aesop

blommer, ?uproar

blood, children, heirs; **burn in her blood**, i.e. burn alive; **gentle bloods**, aristocrats

bloosmes, blossoms

blow, **bring one to the**, i.e. to the desired end

blunting, for, for fear of blunting

boad, **bootless**, dwelt unprofitably

board, table

boatis, boats

bob, *n.*, a rap on the knuckles or on the head; a taunt, gibe; *v.*, **bobbed lips**, ?lips swollen with blows; **bobbing**, beating

bode, dwelt; endured, suffered

bodkin, dagger

bodrags, raids

boil meat, i.e. boiled

boisterous bearskin, i.e. of stiff texture

boistrous, boisterous

boll'n, swollen

bolted out, sifted

bonaventure liquor (unexplained term)

bonden, bound; **bonden men**, bondmen, serfs

bonnibel, fair maid

book-bear, *nonce word formed on* bugbear

book-bearer, prompter in a theater

bookcurtesy, credit

boon, entreaty; **boon voyage**, i.e. prosperous

boor, unlearned man

boord, **bord**, board, table; **over the bord**, off the ship. *See* bourd

borderers, people living in adjoining countries

borne outward, i.e. carried out for burial

borrell, rustic, rude

borrow, *n.*, burrow; **borrow base**, base borrowing

bosom-hung, hanging down upon the bosom

bot, *v.*, bit

botcher, patcher, bungler

bote, *v.*, bit

bottom, clew on which to wind thread

boullion, bullion

bound, *n.*, boundary; *v.*, **as she bounds**, i.e. marks out or describes the bounds of

bounden, bound, forced; indebted

bounders, boundary markers

bourd, **boord**, *n.*, board, table; jest; *v.*, make game of, jest

boure, bower, chamber

bourn, burn

bousing-houses, low alehouses

bove, above

bow, **made unto the**, i.e. subject to his will; **bring to the bows**, i.e. into one's control

bowge (**bouge**) **of court**, allowance of victuals granted to a king's household

bowl is rammed, i.e. the ball, bullet

bown, bound

bowse, bathe; dip

bowsy, bloated by drink

bowzing, drinking

box, wood of the box tree; **in a wrong box**, in error

box-keeper, keeper of the dice and box at a gaming table

brabbling, noisy cries

brack, flaw

bracket, **out-brothership of** (unexplained phrase)

braid (**brayd**), **at a**, suddenly

brake, *n.*, bridle; thicket; **take in a brake**, i.e. in a trap; *v.*, broke

brall, brawl

branch'd with coral, adorned with a branch-like pattern in coral

branch-imbosted, embossed with branches

brand, marriage torch

brandered, embroidered

brass-bold, bold as brass

brast, burst

braught, brought

braunce, branch

brave, *adj.*, fine, noble; finely dressed; gallant; handsome, beautiful; *v.*, flaunt

bravely, beautifully

bravery, boasting, bragging; daring, courage; extravagant dress; ornamentation, beauty; ostentation

brawl, French dance resembling a cotillion; **brake the brawl**, quit the dance

brawn-fallen, shrunken in flesh

bray, *n.*, scream, yell

brayd, **at a**, suddenly

bread for cake, give, i.e. be a match for

break, go bankrupt; **break with one**, make known to one

breast, power of singing; musical voice

breath, *v.*, breathe

breathe, catch one's breath

breed, *n.*, offspring

breek, breech-cloth

breem, raging, stormy

breers, briers

bren(**ning**), burn(ing); **brent**, burnt

breres, briers

bretheren, brethren

bretherhed, brotherhood

brethern, brethren

brevia, short (syllables)

breviation, **in**, in miniature

brickle, brittle

bricky towers, i.e. of the Temple, London

bride it, play or act the bride

brideled, bridled

bright, *adj.* beautiful; *n.*, beauty

brightsome fairs, glowing beauties

briginders, briganders, body armor for foot soldiers

brin(**ning**), burn(ing)

broach, (Momus') spear

broacher, introducer

brocage, pandering

broccing, ?broking (a term of abuse)

broker, pander; pawnbroker; secondhand-clothes dealer

brokery, base dealing

brood, *n.*, offspring

brook, *v.*, endure, tolerate

brothel, bagnio; a prostitute

brothel-house, brothel

brothelry, lewdness

brothren's, brethren's

bruit, report; reputation

brunt, **at a sudden**, i.e. a pull when there is no momentum on the load to make it easier

brust, burst

brute, **so noble a**, i.e. hero (like Brut)

bruze, bruise

bubs, bubbles

buckeler, buckler

budge, fur

budget, bag, wallet

bug's-words, words meant to terrify

bull, **heavenly**, the constellation Taurus

bull-begger, bugbear

bullifant, bull (*pun on* elephant)

bulrushes, **tie knots on smooth**, i.e. unreasonably find fault with

bumbast, *n.*, bombast, wool; *v.*, stuff, pad

bump, the cry of the bittern

bung, purse

burd, board, approach

burdened, accused

burn'd sack, heated Spanish white wine

burneux, sauce made of butter, salt, etc.

bursten, burst

burthen, *n.*, burden; chorus; *v.*, burden

bushop, bishop

busk, corset

buskins, high shoes

busk-point, corset-lace

bussards, buzzards

busy biting, sharp, corroding desire

but if, unless

but only, only

butcherous, butcherly, murderous

butt, **to level at a**, aim at a mark

butter-whore, butter-woman

buttery, room where provisions are stored; **spirit of the buttery**, spirit of wine, drunkenness; the spirit Paracelsus kept in the pommel of his sword

buxom, vigorous, jolly

by, against (poetry, etc.); **on the by**, in passing

by and by, immediately

by cause, **bycause**, because

byfore, before

byle, boil

byleve, believe

bylief, belief

bylive, belive, at once; quickly

bynempt, named

by-pleasures, pleasures on the side

byside, beside

bytween, between

byword, proverb

cabin, poor dwelling

caddis, coarse cheap serge

cadence, fall of the voice; rhythm; rime

caduceus, Mercury's staff

caffa, rich silk cloth

calendars, outward signs (of death)

calender, calendar

calenture, tropical delirium

callet, a drab

calms, **wooden**, enclosing frames

calmy, calm(ing)

came of, **what**, i.e. became of; **came over him with**, bore him down, insisted camelion, chameleon

cameric, cambric

cammassado, camisado, night attack

cammock, shepherd's crook

camously, concavely (i.e. pug-nosed)

camphire, camphor

can say, did say; **can better good**, knows better what good actions are; **that nought can**, who knows nothing; **canned**, known, understood

canapy, canopy

cancred, malignant

candle-stuff, work done by candlelight

canicular, pertaining to a dog

canker, wild dog-rose

cannapy, canopy

cannat, cannot

canned: see can

cantharides, medical preparation

cantion, song

cantle, slice

canton point, square division on a shield (in heraldry)

canzon, a song

canzonet, a little or short song

cap and knee, bareheaded and kneeling

cap-a-pie, (armed) from head to foot

capcase, wallet

cape-cloak, cloak

capering coat, ?dancing coat

capitain, captain

capitano, headman, chief

capping, removing their caps in reverence

captive, one bound (true) in love

caract, a mark of accent

carcass, human body

card, *n.*, chart, map; **card of ten**, the ten of trumps; *v.*, play at cards

career, gallop; **fetch their careers**, make sudden, nimble turns

careful(ly), sorrowful(ly)

careless, carefree; **careless hair**, i.e. untended

caren, care

carged, charged, loaded

cark, *n.*, anxious solicitude; trouble, care; *v.*, toil and moil; **cark and care**, be anxious

carl, churl

carman, carter, carrier

carnosity, fleshiness

carouse, carowse, *n.*, health-drinking; *v.*, drink up

carp, find fault with; sing or recite; **carp deore**, ?gilded (*doré*) carp

carpet peer, unworthy courtier; **garnish with carpets**, i.e. table covers

carrack, large warship, galleon

carren, carrion

carrion, carrion crow

carterly, churlish

carver, be one's own, choose for oneself at one's own discretion

case, *n.*, skin; **in case to**, in a condition to

casket, money-box

cast, *n.*, (foolish) manner; **gay, goodly cast**, fine piece of ingenious action; *v.*, add; be condemned; calculate astrologically; consider, plan; diagnose; scheme; **cast away**, ruined; **cast robes**, discarded garments

casual, subject to chance or accident

casually, by chance

casualty(e), hapzardness

cate, viand

cater, caterer

cattle, property, livestock; wretched men

causd', causde (caused)

cause, *conj.*, because

cautel, caution, proviso

cautelous, crafty

cave, *v.*, be careful, beware (Latin)

cavilations, quibbles, trickery

cawl, cap, headdress

cawry mawry, ?a kind of coarse, rough material

cease one's fame, i.e. put an end to

ceasures, cesuras

ceaze, seize

celestine, celestial

celler, cellar

censere, censure

censing, the burning of incense

censure, *n.*, judgment; *v.*, appraise, judge

centon, cento, patchwork

ceremonies, images and other sacred objects

certain, *n.*, some persons

certenly, certainly

certes, certainly

cesterns, cisterns

cha, I have (*dialectic*)

chafe, anger

chaffar, chaffer, *n.*, buying and selling; merchandise; *v.*, buy and sell

chain-shot, bullets fastened together (i.e. a violent attack)

chair, the soul's, i.e. dwelling place

challenge me, lay claim to me

cham, I am (*dialectic*)

chamber of presence, audience room

chamberers, valets

chamberlin, chamberlain

chambling, ?shambling (verse)

chamboring, chambering, sexual indulgence

chamlet, camlet, rich cloth of silk and wool

champain, champion, champian, a plain

chance, stand to the main, keep to the chief issue

chanceable, fortuitous

chancelor, secretary

chandlery, chandry, a place where candles, etc., were kept

channel, gutter

chanons, canons

chaped staff, i.e. furnished with a chape or ornamental metal mounting

chapeleyne, chaplain

chapiter, chapter

char, chair

charact, letter

chardge, charge (*q. v.*)

charet, cart, chariot

charge, load; **charged necks**, i.e. loaded down; **charged with forgetfulness**, i.e. laden

chargeable, chargeful, expensive

charm, play (a pipe)

charter, privilege, freedom of action

chase, unenclosed park land; a ship's bow; **out of her chase**, i.e. her chase-guns in the bow

Chatholike, Catholic

chave, I have (*dialectic*)

chaw, chew

cheap, good, low-priced

cheapen, bargain for

check, rebuke, revile; **check the ground**, strike or stamp with the hoof

chee vore thee, I warn you (*dialectic*)

cheer, countenance; entertainment; joy, gladness

cheese, choose

cheezel, chisel

cherely, cheerily

cherissing, cherishing

cherm, chirm, noise

cherry-fair, boisterous fair held in cherry orchards for the sale of fruit

cherubines, cherubyns, cherubim

cherup, chirrup

chese, choose

chest, coffin

chests, chess

chevalry, chevalree, chivalry

cheven, chevin, the chub fish

cheving, evil, bad success

chevisance, dealing for profit

chevisaunce, an unidentified flower, possibly the wallflower

chewse, choose

child of light, Lucifer

childer(n), children

chill, I will (*dialectic*)

chill shivering, shivering with cold

chipped by winter, i.e. chapped

chippes, bread-crust parings

choise, *v.*, choose

chop, dart to (the window); **chop and change**, change, alter; **chop up**, conclude

choploge, contentious arguer

chorl: see churl

chorlish(ly), churlish(ly)

chosen but, cannot be, i.e. it cannot be otherwise than that

chrisecoll, chrysocoll, gold solder

Christen, Christian

Christendom, ill, poor Christianity

Christenly, in a Christian manner

Christes, Christ's

church, one poor, i.e. Romulus' sanctuary for criminals

churchward, to the, towards the church

churl, chorl, fellow, man

chuse, choose

chwot, I know (*dialectic*)

cimented, cemented

cind'ring, burning to cinders

circle, magic circle to which a ghost is to be summoned

circlet of a turtle, the iridescent band around a dove's neck

circuled, circled

citezins, citizens

citheron, cithern

citrine, lemon-colored

civil, civilized

clad, clothe, dress

clam, climbed

clap, *n.*, applause; mishap, a blow from Fortune; *v.*, a door clapped, i.e. slammed; **clapped to**, struck

clare, clear

clark, clarkly: see clerk, clerkly

cleanly, dexterous (knavery)

cleeves, cliffs

clepe, call; clip, embrace; **cleped**, is called

clergy, ability to read (a neck-verse, *q.v.*)

clerk, clark, scholar; cleric

clerkly, clarkly, learned; **clerkly opened**, learnedly set forth or explained

clifs, clefs

clift, cliff; cleft, a split of wood; opening (of a window)

clim, clime, climb

clinged her, clung to, embraced

clip, surround closely, embrace

clives, cliffs

clock, what is (it) of the, what time is it

clocking, clucking

clog at my heel, a reference to Wyatt's being on parole to his father during his "exile"

cloins, clowns, rustics

clong, clung

clook, cloak

close, *n.*, farmyard; *adj.*, close nuns, i.e. strictly secluded

clot land, i.e. free it from clods

cloth, clothes; cut it out in the whole cloth, live extravagantly

clout, *n.*, cloth, clothes; *v.*, mend (a shoe); clouted, bandaged (leg)

clown, ill-bred man; rustic

clung with cold, i.e. shriveled

clush-clash, clashing

co, jackdaw

coarctation, restriction

coarcted, restrained, repressed

coast, *v.*, approach

coat, of his, of his class, like himself

cob, head of (red) herrings

cocker, *n.*, kind of boot; *v.*, pet

cocket, sealed permit

cockle, a weed

cockney, spoiled child

cock's blood, i.e. God's

cockscomb, coxcomb; fool's cap

cockwats, ?cockwards, cuckolds

codling, young codfish

cofferer, treasurer

cog(ger), deceive(r), cheat(er)

cogging, cheating at dice, deceitfulness

coil, kept a, made a fuss

coistrel, base fellow

coits, quoits

cold, *v.*, could

collace, cullis, strong clear meat broth

collaud, praise highly

collectors, compilers

colledge, college

collet, collet(t)e, collect, form of prayer; acolyte

collian, wretch

colliquintida: *see* coloquintida

colonies, settlers

coloquintida, colliquintida, bitter herb or apple

color, *n.*, pretence, pretext; color of rhetoric, ornament of style or diction; fear no color, fear no foe; set some color upon, give a specious excuse for; *v.*, disguise, cloak

colorable, colored, specious, plausible

colosse, the Colossus; colosses, colossuses

combat, by, trial by combat

comberous, combrous, cumbrous, clumsy

come, where to be, i.e. to go; comed, having come; comen, come; been comen, are (have) come; comen of, come from

comedients, comedians

comelily, in a comely manner

comen, *adj.*, common; *v.*, come (*q.v.*)

comerous crab's, cumbrous crab is

comey, come

commandement, commandment

commaund with you, *v.*, ?communed, talked

commen(ly), common(ly)

commenweal, commonwealth

comminalty: *see* commonalty

comminers, commoners

commiserable, pitiable

commissaries, representatives of bishops

commodious, convenient; helpful, beneficial

commodity, advantage, benefit

common, in, in the abstract; go in common, be a common (lewd) woman; common words, syllables optionally short or long

commonalty, comminalty, communalty, the people of the nation

commoning: *see* commune

commonplaces, stock examples or tales illustrating general truths; parables

commons, come to short, i.e. to insufficient food; discharge commons, pay for one's food

communalty: *see* commonalty

commune, talk; communing (commoning) of the matter, i.e. discussing it

commune(ly), common(ly)

communer, cummener, commoner

communewealth, commonwealth; general good

communication, conversation

community of women, i.e. sharing in common; the same community, i.e. common ownership

compace, compass, surround

compact, *pa. part.*, composed of

company with, *v.*, associate with

companies, the twelve, the London Guilds

compare, comparison; well compare, find an equal to

compass, *n.*, artifice; calculation; fetch a compass about, make a circuit or detour; *v.*, achieve, bring about; circumvent; contrive (a bad purpose); seize, lay hold of (land)

compast course, i.e. circular

compendiate, contracted, diminutive

compendious living, i.e. economical

compfort, comfort

complement, compliment; complimentary language

complemento, compliment

complexion, humor of the body

complot(ment), plot

complynes, complins, the last (Catholic) service of the day

composition, entertain or harken to a, i.e. to terms of surrender; be at composition with, make a treaty or agreement

compost, compote, fruit preserved in wine, etc.

compound, for to, make terms, settle; compounds strange, unfamiliar compound words

compt, count

comptrol, control

con, know; learn by heart

concei(p)t: *see* concept

concei(p)ted, clever, amusing, witty

conceipters, those fond (of)

concend, kindle, inflame

concept, concei(p)t, concet, consait, concept, notion, idea, thought; fancy article; fancy trifle to eat; imagination; fancy; jest; judgment, estimation, opinion; witty ex-

pression; inward conceit, perception, understanding; out of conceit, displeased, dissatisfied; taken in conceit, taken into Fortune's favor

concileth, counseleth

conclusion, final arranging (of a treaty)

concordances, three, grammatical agreements in gender, person, and number

concupiscible, the concupiscible faculty of the soul

condempn, condemn

condescend, agree

condign merits, i.e. deserving, worthy

condiscended, condescended, consented

condisciples, fellow-disciples, fellow-students

condit, conduit

conduction, leadership

conference of books, collation or comparison of texts

conferring, comparing

confettered, confederated, allied

confort, comfort

confound, shall I be, i.e. confounded

confuse mixture, i.e. confused

congé, congee, farewell

conger, eel

conglobe, form into a rounded compact mass

conject, *v.*, conjecture

conne, can; know

conning, reading; cunning (*q.v.*)

consait: *see* concept

conscience, thought it no, made no conscience or "bones" about it

conscious mind, i.e. conscientious

consecrate, *pa. part.*, consecrated

consent, music's, i.e. harmony, accord

conserve, *n.*, confection, preserves; *v.*, preserve

considerance to, consideration of

consither, consider

consolidate, *pa. part.*, solidified

consort, friend; musical accord of instruments and voice

conspire with, agree with (Plato)

conster, construe

constitucion, constitution

constitute, *pa. part.*, constituted

constraintively, constrainingly

construpate, rape

consture, construe

consuetude, custom

consume, expire, end

contempn, contemn

contentation, acceptance of a situation; satisfaction, contentment

contention, to my, i.e. contentment, pleasure

contestation, contention, dispute

contiguate, contiguous to

continens, a stone "named for the contrary" which faithless lovers wear

continent, container; the earth

continuance, course of time; in continuance, eventually

continued poems, i.e. long

contractation-house, Seville exchange or treasury where West Indian trade contracts were made

contrary, *v.*, contradict, argue against; strive against

contraversy, controversy

contrectation, handling, fingering

contribute France, i.e. levy tribute upon

contributories, contributors

contristation, the state of being saddened

control a piece, i.e. find fault with, rebuke

convart, convert, turn

conveigh, *n.*, convey, conduct of life; ?path; *v.*, convey; escort

conveighance, conveyance, conduct

convenable, suitable

conveniency, suitability

convent, body of monks

convented, met

conversant among men, i.e. associating with

conversation of the citizens, i.e. the behavior of; priests' conversation, i.e. intercourse, society

converse, associate familiarly

conversion, translation

converted, would have, i.e. turned from sinful life

conveyance, style; close conveyance, thievery

convict, *pa. part.*, convicted

convince, convict; refute

convoy, happy, i.e. a thing that conducts

cony-catchers, cheats, confidence-men

cookemate, partner, mate

cooling-card, something that cools one's passion

coople, couple

coosen, coosin, cos(s)en, cousen, couson, cozen

coosenage, coosinage, coosonage, cosenage, cosonage, cousonage, cozenage

coosener, cosener, cozener

coote, coat

cope, canopy (of the heavens); a cleric's cloak

copesmate, companion, confederate

cople, couple

copps, copse

copweb, cobweb

copy, copious quantity; copiousness (of language); alter or change copy, change one's tone or course of action

corage, courage

coraging, encouragement

coram, be called, called publicly to account

corasives, corrosives

cordwainer, shoemaker (in cordovan leather)

cormarant, cormorant, miser

corn, grain, wheat; ale in corns, ?ale as drawn off the malt

corn-fed, well-fed

coronall, garland

coronation, carnation

corp, corps, corse, (living) body; corpse

corrage, courage

correctors, critics

corriers, curriers

corrival, rival suitor

corsay, corsie, cause of grief

corse: see corp

cortesie, cortesy, courtesy

cosen, *n.*, cousin, relative; *v.*, cozen

cosenage, cosonage, cozenage

cosener, cozener

cos(s)en, cozen

cost, coast, way; pomp, ornament

costifeness, constipation

cote, sheepfold; house; coat armor

cotquean, man who acts the housewife

couch unto, submit, stoop to

could his good, knew his own welfare; could skill of, had skill in; could sophistry, i.e. knew

coumpinable, companionable, sociable

coumpt, count

councel: see counsel

counsail, council; counsel

counsailor, counselor

counsel, councel, council, group; counselor; the Sanhedrin

counseler, counselor

count, make no, do not esteem; count the clock, i.e. count its strokes

countenance, courtly, social appearance

counterfait, counterfect, counterfeict, counterfet, *n.*, counterfeit; a picture; written in counterfeit, i.e. in a disguised hand; *v.*, disguise, imitate

counterfaitor, counterfeiter, imitator

countering, singing an accompaniment to a melody or plain-song

counterpanes, copies, duplicates

counterpoint, artifice; counterpane

counterpoise, counterweigh

countervail, be equivalent in value to

country, *adj.*, native

coupe, coop; prison

coupled, married

couplement, union

couples, riming couplets; couples soly, seem individually a couple; without couples, without coupling or union

courage, lustiness

couragious, courageous

cours'd boys, i.e. flogged

course accompt, (treat as) a matter of course or unimportant; by course, in turn, alternately; in course, not in kind, i.e. one hundred suns, or days, not one hundred sons

coursing of a letter, using alliteration, "running in rattling rows"

court it, play the courtier

court-cup, ?cup made of ash

courtein, curtain, quilt

courtesy, pinch, stand on ceremony; strain courtesy, act with less than due courtesy

court-holy-bread, i.e. fair words

courting, attendance at court

courtisan(e), courtezan

courtling, courtier

courtnoles, *contemptuous for* courtiers

cousen, cozen

cousin-german, first cousin

couson(age), cozen(age)

couth, knew how to; could

covart, in, in covert or hiding

covenable, suitable, convenient

covenous, covinous, deceitful

coverture, a covering

covetise, covetousness

covin, fraud

cowardry, cowardice

cowsh(e)ard, cow-dung

cowslops, cowslips

coy, coax, blandish; coy her, act coyly

crab, apple

crabby, crabbed, rough

crack a word, i.e. utter briskly

cracknelles, crisp kind of biscuit

craesie, cracked

craftely, craftily

craggy, difficult

crake of, boast of

crambe, distasteful repetition

crampfish, ray

crapal-stone, crapaud-stone (supposedly produced in a toad's head)

crased, cracked; broken down

cratch, manger

crazed, cracked

creacion, creation

credence, message

cremosin, crimson

cretick, critic

crevis, crayfish

cricking chaps, jaws making a sharp abrupt sound

crisped, curled

Crist(en), Christ(ian)

crook, winding (as of a maze)

crooked eclipses, i.e. malignant

croppy, crop, stomach

cross-bar, misfortune

crossbar-shot, cannon ball with projecting bars

crossbite(r), swindle(r)

crouch'd unto, bowed (deferred) humbly to

croud, crowd, fiddle

crowder, fiddler

crowns, silver coins (five shillings)

crow-trodden, abused

crud, curd

cruddy, curd-like in appearance

crudities, undigested food

crum, crumb

crumpled knot, i.e. curled

crystal temple, crystalline sphere

crystalline, *n.*, crystal

cucking-stool, stool for ducking people in water

cuckove, cuckoo

cue, half a farthing

cuffing, vanquishing

cullisses, strong clear meat broths

culter, coulter, blade of a plowshare

culver, dove

cumber, perplex, trouble

cumberments, encumbrances

cummuner, commoner

cun, can

cunnigare, cunninger, more skilful (*dialectic*)

cunning, conning, *adj.*, skilful, learned; *n.*, learning, study; knowledge; skill

curats, cuirasses

cure, care, attention; cure of soul(s), office of a curate; cured, taken care of

curiosity, affectation; elaborateness; fantasticality; nice ceremony; whims, fastidiousness

curious, beautifully wrought; difficult to please, fastidious; elaborate; curious of, solicitous about

curiously, elaborately; read curiously, i.e. attentively

curral, coral

currant, *adj.*, fluent; genuine, sterling; *n.*, current, custom, order

currantness, currentness, fluidity

curst, ill-tempered; vicious

curtal, horse with its tail docked; cutting off. *See* curtol(l)

curteous, curtess, curties, courteous

curtesly, courteously

curtesses, courtesies

curtesy, curtsy, courtesy

curtezan, curtizan, curtisan, courtezan

curties: see curteous

curtle-ax, curtal-ax, cutlass

curtol(l), *n.*, curtail, word with a syllable cropped off; *v.*, curtail, shorten. *See* curtal

curtsy: *see* curtesy

cushion, missed the, made a mistake

custom in swearing, i.e. the practise or use of

customably, usually

cut, curtail (horse); **keep his cut**, be coy or reserved, keep his distance; **kept cut at home**, returned and stayed at home

cylindrus, fabulous stone that makes a thunderclap as it rolls

daded, (children) supported as they learn to walk

dag, heavy pistol

dagged, bemired

dagswain, coarse coverlet of rough shaggy material

dainously, disdainfully

daintily, fastidiously

dainty, rare, scarce; **have dainty**, have pleasure or delight

daisy, leap at a, to be hanged

dalliance of children, i.e. their playing

dallop, clump of grass or weeds

dam, mother

damask rose, rose of mingled red and white

damasked, variegated, streaked

dame, mother; sweetheart

damn's, dam's, mother's

dampnable, damnable

dampnation, damnation

dampned, damned

damsines, plums

dan, master, sir

dancing him, i.e. dandling

dandiprat, English coin worth threepence

danged, dashed down

danger, harm, damage; grudging; power, domination; **coming within danger**, in range to inflict physical injury; **in danger to**, indebted to

dankish, humid

dant, *n.*, loose woman; *v.*, daunt

dapper, trim and lovely (ditties)

dark, *v.*, darken

darkth, darkness

darnel, deleterious grain which grows as a weed among wheat

dart-thirling, dart-piercing

dataries, officers who date and register papal documents

date, end (of life); age, period of time; **dateth me**, puts an end to me

date-exceeding, superior to one's time

daw, *n.*, jackdaw; *v.*, dawn

dawcock, silly bird

daylight, on the, in daylight

dazzle, dim with excess of brightness

dead, *v.*, deaden

deafed, deafened

deal, every, every bit or part

deambulations, taking walks

dearling, darling

dearworth, beloved

deathsman, executioner

debate, (friendly) contest; quarrel

decasyllabon, ten-syllable verse

deceipt(ful), deceit(ful)

deceivable, deceitful

decern, discern

decerped, decerpt, excerpted; extracted, plucked out

decipher, write down; recount; **decipher inconstancy**, i.e. make it known

decline, depreciate (verse); **decline from them**, i.e. avoid, shun

decoct, digest; digested

decoction, digestion

decrepity, decrepitude

dedicate, *pa. part.*, dedicated

deduce the course, i.e. trace, deal with; **deduced to chambers**, i.e. diverted

deducted spirit, i.e. weakened; **deducting**, leading out

deedly, deadly

deemer, a judge

deep in, busy oneself in; **deep oaths**, i.e. solemn

defalk'd, diminished

defame, *n.*, slander; bad reputation

default, defaut, fault; **never in default**, never failing in his duty; **made defaut**, defaulted, failed to appear

defeature, ruin

defectious, defectuous, defective

defence, prohibition

defend away, fend off, avert

defensed, defended

deffly, deftly

deflour, deflower

defluxion, flowing (of blood)

defoiled, defiled

defray, pay; settle

defus'd, diffused

degendering, degenerating

degenerate, *pa. part.*, degenerated

degree, step (of a staircase); **dearest in degree**, as dearly as possible; **high degree**, top rung or step

dehortation, dehorting, dehortment, earnest dissuasion

deject, *v.*, cast down

delapidation, the action of impairing ecclesiastical property belonging to an incumbency

delated, dilated, deferred; **delated sufficiently**, i.e. related, reported

delicate, *n.*, delicacy, choice viand

deligence, diligence

delighted, odors most, i.e. delightful

delightsome, delightful

dell, pit

delt, dealt

delve, dig

demean, conduct oneself, behave; conduct (the choir); **demean covertly**, ?secretly conduct or manage; **demean well**, treat (me) well

demeanor, demeanure, behavior

demen, *v.*, judge

deminish, diminish

demisse, submissive

dempt and dread, deemed and dreaded

denay, *n.*, denial; *v.*, deny

denier, coin of small value

denisoned, denizened, (foreign wit or words) naturalized (in English)

denizon, denizen, citizen

denotated, denoted

dent, stroke (of swords)

dented cheeks, i.e. hollow, sunken

deore, ?*doré* (French), gilded

depaint, depeinct, adorn (with flowers); depict, paint

depart, *n.*, departure; separation; *v.*, die;

divide; **depart from**, give up, divide; **departed**, dead, separated from the body; **departed us**, i.e. separated

depeinct: *see* depaint

depend, hang down; result from

deprave, decry, "run down"; misconstrue

deprehend, detect, perceive; discover

deprived, divested of office

depured, clear

deputed thee, i.e. made a deputy

derived upon, directed at

derkness, darkness

derring-do, daring deeds

desart, desert

desarve, deserve

desastrous, disastrous

descant, harmony, melody sung above the plain-song of the tenor

desceit, deceit

descent, are the high, i.e. descendants

descern, discern

descride, perceived

descrive, describe

dese, go to the, go to the dais, take the best place

desembled, dissembled

deserned, discerned

desevered, separated

desinence, termination

desire, kindly wise, natural desire for wisdom

desolve, dissolve

despight, despite

despiteous, pitiless

despoiled, disrobed (of clothes or leaves)

desseign, design

desteny, destiny

destress, distress

detecting his sex, i.e. accusing

determinate, conclusive; final (answer); ended, out of date

determinately, determinedly

determination, authoritative decision

determine, end, conclude; officially decide

detracter, detractor

detray, subtract

dettour, debtor

devesting, divesting

device, talk (of pastimes)

devide, divide

devine, *adj.*, divine; *n.*, preacher; *v.*, foretell

devinity, divinity

devise, discern; plan; **devise me**, lay plans to do me evil

devision, division

devoir, duty

divorce(ment), divorce(ment)

devote, *adj.*, devoted (kind)

devotion, take the, i.e. an offering made in church as an act of devotion

dew, *adj.*, due

dewle, dole, grief

dial, clock, timepiece

diamant, diamond

diapered, variegated (with flowers)

dich, ditch

dictanum, fabulous herb

did to, caused to. *See* do

die, copulate; **died up all**, all utterly perished; **slur a die**, method of cheating at dice

diets, Dutch, i.e. parliaments, conventions

dif(f)amation, defamation

dif(f)ame, defame

different flowers in odor, flowers different in odor

diffuse problem or question, i.e. obscure, difficult; diffuse to find, i.e. difficult

digest, bear, endure

dight, dress(ed); made, written; repaired; dight him, make (made) himself ready

digladiations, wranglings

dilectation, delectation

dimensive, (the soul's) dimensions

dimiss, dismiss, divorce

ding, strike

dint, indentation; stroke of lightning

diot, diet

directly a poet, i.e. properly; directly tell, i.e. precisely

directory, book of rules; guide

dirige, dirge

dirivied, derived

disable oneself, i.e. disparage

disadventrous, disastrous

disallow, disapprove; reject

discease, decease

disceatful, deceitful

disceipt, disceit, deceit

discend, descend

discent, descent; step down

discern, n., discernment

discharge, to their, to their relief from obligation

discipher, decipher; disclose

discolored stone, i.e. variously colored

discorage, discourage

discourage, n., discouragement

discourse them, i.e. tell

discovert, at, off guard

discrepance, difference

discrete, discreet

discribe, describe; discribed, apportioned

discrive, describe; descry

discry, descry, see

discure, discover, reveal

discurteously, discourteously

discuss, n., decision; v., discuss laws, try (as a judge) by law

disdeign, disdain

disease, n., trouble, sorrow; v., trouble

diserdes, dizzards, blockheads

disfurnishing, depriving

disgest(ion), digest(ion)

disherit, disinherit

dishonest, unchaste, unvirtuous

disjoin, cut, kill

dislodging, n., death

dismark a horse, i.e. remove its distinguishing marks

dismounted hills, i.e. leveled

disordinately, excessively

dispair, despair

disparadiz'd, cast out of Paradise

disparage, damage (myself)

disparent ground, ?bank (of the fountain) with divers flowers; disparent lawn, ?i.e. transparent

dispatched by, disposed of (their business being settled)

dispearing, despairing

dispend, spend

dispense, expenditure

dispersedly, (write) in a scattered manner

dispicions, discussions

dispise, despise

---

dispiteful, despiteful

dispitious, dispiteous, merciless

display, spread out; displayed alike, (eagles) matched in combat

displeasant, displeasing

displow, plow up

dispose head, set the head against (the body); disposd', disposde (disposed)

disprove, disapprove of

disputative, theoretical

disputing, discoursing about

disray'd, deprived, stripped

disseised, deprived

dissemblable, dissimilar

dissimule(r), dissemble(r), pretend(er)

dissiphered, deciphered

distemperature, disorder

distenanted tun, empty cask

distrain, distrein, squeeze; distrain on, levy a distress or sale on land; distrained, afflicted, oppressed

distroy, destroy

distruction, destruction

disuse himself, abandon (mirth); disuse my ear, i.e. disaccustom

ditched, surrounded with a ditch

ditches, holes, pits

divel, devil

divendop, dabchick, didapper

divers, diverse

diverse, divers, different; many people

diversly, variously

divil, devil

divine, n., divine (church) service; v., divine upon, make conjectures about; divining eyes, i.e. guessing

divulged, books, i.e. published

dizains, ten-line stanzas

do, often = cause (to), make, as do bleed, cause to bleed, do him die, cause him to die; do on, put on; do way, do away with

doat, dote

dock, buttocks

doctors, very learned men

doctrinable, instructive

doctrinal, n., textbook

documents martial, i.e. warnings, instructions

dog-days, hot days influenced by the dog-star, Sirius

doings, actions; verses, poems; works

doit, Dutch coin about equal to a farthing

dole, grief. See dool(e)

dollar, Philip's, the peso, or piece of eight, current in Spain

dollop, clump of grass or weeds

dolphin, dauphin

dolphinet, female dolphin

domb, dumb

dome, house; judgment, opinion; Judgment Day

domesday, Day of Doom, Judgment Day

domestical, domestic

domify, be in the ascendant

dominical, lordly

domp, dump, melancholy fit

don, dan, sir

done, as fellows, i.e. do

dongeon, dungeon

donny, dunny, dusky brown

dooble, double

dooen, done

dool(e), n., grief, sorrow; v., lament, grieve

---

doom, judgment, verdict

doomful, fateful

dormants, sleepers, horizontal beams

dorres, drone bees

doth, occasionally = the plural do

dotterel, plover

double-mailed, doubly clad or covered

doubleness, duplicity

doublings, sudden turnings

doubt, n., doubtful question; doubt of, the fear of; v., fear, dread; hesitate, scruple; suspect; doubted, (it was) doubtful; suspected; doubted knights, i.e. redoubted, feared

doubtance, hesitation

doubtful, fearful

dought, doubt

doughter, daughter

doulful, doleful

doutless, doubtless

dowdy, n., ?harlot, or ?some notorious real woman

drad, dread(ed)

draff, refuse, dregs

drane, drone

draught, draft, outline

drave, drove

draw the deer, i.e. hunt out

drawen, drawn

drawer, tapster

drawn with stars, i.e. ornamented

drawningly, drawlingly

drawttis, draughts

dread, v., dreaded (as in Skelton)

dreadfully to set hands, i.e. with awe or fear

drear, n., sadness

dreariment, dreary or dismal condition

dred(e), dreed, dread

dreful, dreadful

drench, drown; soak; drench down, plunge down (to hell)

drere, grief, sorrow

dreriment, gloom, sorrow

drery, dreary; cruel (Mars)

dress oneself, address, apply, oneself; dress to war, i.e. prepare for

dresser, one who prepares food for cooking

dreve it off, prolong it

drevel, drivel, dirty person

dreven, drevin, driven

dribbed shot, arrows shot so that they fall short of the mark

drifts, plans, schemes

drit, dirt

drive the king, this news, i.e. drove

droncken, drunken (person)

drone, wind instrument or bagpipe

dronkard, drunkard

dronk(en), drunk(en), intoxicated

dronkenness, drunkenness

dronny, v., drone

dropping, n., drop

droppy, drop

drougth, drought

drowned, boat, i.e. submerged, sunken

drowsy, (complexion) characterized by sleepiness

droyle, drudge

dry-bobs, bitter gibes

dryth, dryness

dub, beat or sound of a drum

dum, dumb

dump, melancholy fit

dumped, (being) in the dumps or sad

dungy, vile, defiling

dunsically, duncically, stupidly

dunstical, stupid

dure, endure, last

dureless, not lasting

dusked, darkened, sullied

duskish, blackish

dyld ye, God, God 'ield (yield, i.e. reward) you

dylonimas, ?oracles

dyne, dun, dark

dyscrasy, disordered condition of the body, distemper

eachwhere, everywhere

eager, biting (poems or subjects)

ear, give ear to; plow; **fall together by the ears**, i.e. fight

ear-giving, listening

ear-marked beasts abroad, branded, stray cattle

earn, yearn

earnest, *n.*, pledge or partial payment

earth, my sinful, my body

easely, easily

easement, defecation

easilier, more easily

eat (up), ate (up); eaten

eath, easy; easily

economic art, i.e. pertaining to the management of private affairs

economy of poems, i.e. structure, arrangement

edders, adders

edified, Troy was, i.e. built

eeke, increase

effect, *n.*, (secret) affection; **effect of soul**, ?power of soul

effectuously, effectually, urgently

efficient cause, cause that makes effects what they are

eft, again, afterward

eftsoon(s), a second time, again; soon afterward

egal(l), equal

eglog, egloge, eglogue, eclogue

eight, *ord.*, eighth

either . . . either, either . . . or; **either other**, each other

eke, also

ela, highest note of the scale

eld, old age

elder, the, writers of old

elect, *n.*, soul "elected" for salvation; *pa. part.*, selected

elemented, composed

elevate, *pa. part.*, elevated; lengthened

eleventh article, a reference to Andreas Capellanus' code of love

elf, child, creature

elixar, elixir

els, else

elsewhen, at other times

elucubrators, historians

elumine, illumine

embase, imbase, lower; lower in value

embassador, ambassador

embattailed, drawn up in battle array

embayed, enveloped, surrounded

embrewed, bloodstained

embro(a)dered, embroidered, ornamented

embrodery, embroidery

embryon, embryo

embuskined, wearing buskins or high boots (i.e. writing tragedy)

emispery, hemisphere

emmarble, convert into marble

emong, emonges(t), emongst, among, amongst

empair, *n.*, impairment; *v.*, impair, discredit; insult, harm

empaled, impaled, encircled

empeach, impeach

emperess, empress

emperial, imperial

empery, empire, rule; territory of a ruler; power

empierce, penetrate

emported, imported, made known

empressed, oppressed

emprisonment, imprisonment

enamel, *n.*, beauty, ornament; *v.*, beautify with various colors

enbold, embolden

enbrace, embrace

encense, breathe out; diffuse

enchase, engrave; **enchasing**, surrounding

encheer, cheer

enclinable, inclinable

encline, incline

enclude, include

encomber, encumber

encomions, encomiums

encorage, encourage

encrease, encresse, increase

endamage, damage

endebted, indebted

endewed, endued, endowed

endewors, endeavors

endight, endite, compose

endite, indict, bring charges against; **write verses**

endosse, inscribe

enduced, induced

enduction, induction, inducement

endued, endowed

enflame, inflame

enform, inform; shape or mold

enforrowing, enfurrowing, plowing up

enfranchised, freed, released

enfuse, infuse, impart by divine influence; pour in

enfyre, harden by fire

engine, contrivance; instrument; snare, plot

English, *v.*, translate into English; write in English

engrained, dyed

engrasp, take in one's grasp

engrave, ingrave, bury (themselves)

engross, monopolize; write in large letters

enhanced, lifted

enherit(ance), inherit(ance)

enimity, enmity

enlarge, fearing to, i.e. to release

enlumine, illuminate

enneude, restored, made new

enow, enough

enprison(ment), imprison(ment)

enprowed, improved

enquisitive, inquisitive

enragement, rapture

enranged, arranged, placed in a row

enritch, enrich

enrol'd, recorded with honor

ens, being; the existent

ensample, example

ensearch, search for, examine

enseignment, ensignment, teaching

ensence, incense

ensensed, burned out, diffused

ensign, leader (bell-wether); sign, token

ensignuate, insinuate

enstall'd, installed

enstruct, instruct

ensucket, sweetened

ensure, assure

entelechy, ?(divine) spirit in man

entend, attend (to); be in accord with; intend; **entended to observe**, i.e. exerted their minds to

entendment, intendment, the faculty of understanding

entent, intent

enter, inter

enterance, entrance

enterchangeably, interchangeably, alternately

entercourse, intercourse

enterdeal, mutual dealing

entergraft, intergraft, join

enterlace, interlace

enterline, interline

enterludes, interludes, plays

entermeddling, intermingling

entermingle, mix together

entermit, entermete, concern oneself with

enterpretation, interpretation

enterpret(er), interpret(er)

enterprise, design in an undertaking

enterserted, interpolated

enterview, interview

enthrilling, piercing

entire friend, i.e. wholly devoted

entituling, dedicating

entrayled, interlaced

entreat (upon), treat of, deal with

entry, for his, as his introduction

envies her vows, i.e. censures, inveighs against them

environing one, i.e. surrounding

epanorthosis, a figure in which the word is recalled in order to substitute a correcter term

epethit, epithit, epithet

Epicure, Epicurean

epiphonematicos, related to the rhetorical device of closing a passage with an exclamatory sentence or a striking reflection

episteler, cleric who reads the Epistle in the Mass

epitasis, (second) part of a play where the plot thickens

epithit, epithet

equal, people of the same (age); **equal doom**, fair judgment; **equal heaven**, i.e. just; **equal visage**, tranquil face

ere, ever

err, run, wander

erudition, education, instruction

escaped in conclusions, i.e. eluded notice

escapes, venial errors

escuir, esquire

especial, *adv.*, especially

esperance, hope

essay, trial specimen; **worse essays**, trials of worse (friendships)

essence to the eye, i.e. substance or entity

estate, class of people; form of government; person of high rank; **of estate**, of high rank

esteemid, esteemed
estimate, thy, i.e. value
estraunged, furre. absent far abroad
estridge, ostrich
eternizement, immortal fame
ethe, easy
ethnic, pagan
eughen, yewen, made of yew
eve, over, in the (preceding) evening
event, v., bring to pass; ?expose
ever-during, everlasting
every, everybody, everyone; each
everychone, everyone
everydel(l), every bit or part
evidences of hers, her title deeds
evidently prove or declare, i.e. distinctly
evil captain, poor commander
evil-imped, badly engrafted (of falcons' feathers)
ewer, ewerer, servant who passes water for guests at the table to wash their hands
ewery, room in which water ewers, towels, etc., were kept
ewgh, yew
exactly to be eschewed, to be completely avoided
except, *often* = unless
excepted, must be, i.e. accepted
excercise, exercise
exchew, eschew
excogitated, devised
excommunicate, *pa. part.*, excommunicated
excrements, outgrowths (of hair)
excusation, apology
exel(l)ent, excellent
exequies, funeral rites
exhaled, drew up, raised
exhaust, *pa. part.*, exhausted
exhibition, scholarship (at a college)
exhort, n., exhortation
existimation, estimation, repute
exordium, introduction
exornation, adornment
expansure, expansion
experiency, experience
experimented secrecy, i.e. proved by experience
expire, bring to an end; fulfil
expoun, expown, expound; is expound, is expounded
express her limbs, i.e. press, squeeze
exquisite censure, careful criticism; exquisite study to the learner, i.e. abstruse, overlabored
exsamples, examples
exspected, expected
exspire, expire, breathe out
extasy, ecstasy
extensive to knowledge, i.e. applicable
extirp, exterminate, extirpate
extrude, thrust out
exul, exile
eyas, newly fledged hawk
eye of pheasants, i.e. a brood
eyen, eyne, eyes

fabble, talking, jabbering
fable, n., plot, subject; v., lie
faburden, droning accompaniment
face, with forced, with faces in forced calm
facetious grace, polished style
facies, fiery, *a pun on the writ called* fieri facias *and* frery faces

facinorous, infamous
facion, fashion
fact, deed; crime
factor, agent
faculty, profession; branch of knowledge
facundity, eloquence
fade, be so, i.e. faded
faery's want, fairyland's deprivation
fain, glad; obliged
fainted limbs, i.e. exhausted
faintful knees, knees weak, ready to fail
fainty, faint
fair, adj., beautiful; adv., complacently; n., beauty
fairing, present brought from a fair
fall, in the, in death
falling, (fruit) dropping off
falling band, collar falling flat around the neck
falling evil or sickness, epilepsy
fals(e)hed, falsehood
falyre, ?fellow
fame, common talk; public report
familiar, demon supposed to come at a call; friend
famosest, most famous
famo(u)s, famo(u)ze, v., make famous
fan, v., winnow away chaff; n., God's fan, ?wing or broom
fancy, love, passion
fantasy, fant'sy, phantasy, n., fancy; desire; the faculty of perception; v., be favorably inclined to; love; picture to oneself, call to mind
fardel, fardle, pack, parcel
farder, farther, more
fardest, farthest, remotest
fardle: *see* fardel
far-fatcher, far-fetcher
farfet, farfetched
farforth, farfurth, far, in so far as
far-published, widely known
farthermore, furthermore
fashion, (human) figure or build; mode of action
fat brains, i.e. slow-witted; fat fume, full-bodied fragrance; swept the fat from my beard, i.e. forestalled the results of my enterprise
fatal thread, thread of life (spun by the Fates)
father, without a, anonymously
father-sexton, Time
fatigate, tire; *pa. part.*, fatigued
fatted, covered thickly
faut, fawt, faut
fautless, faultless
fautor, adherent, partisan
fauty, faulty
favel, flattery
favor, look, countenance; full of favor, i.e. beauty
fawchion, fawchon, falchion, sword
fawned into, enticed
fawt: *see* faut
fawth, ?faugh (*expression of disgust*)
feader, feather
fear, *trans. v.*, deter; frighten
fearce, fierce
fearfulest, most apprehensive
feat, apt; feat and use, the art of steering (by the loadstone)
feateously, dexterously

feature, formal, regular form
featured, well formed or fashioned
feder, feather; fed'red, feathered
fee, money; property; wealth; in fee, in (her) service; lie but for fee, remain in jail for a fee due to the jailer; fee simple, absolute possession
feint, feign; faint
fell, n., skin
fellow, sweetheart (female); fellows, equals
felly, cruelly
fenced, shielded
fer, far
ferdillant, ?flashing
fere, phere, mate, fellow, equal
ferm, farm; rent
ferret silk, floss silk
ferther, farther
fervent, burning, hot; intense (cold)
fest, feast
fet, n., feat; ?handsome person; v., fetch, draw; reach
fetch, n., scheme, trick, stratagem; v., fetched, reached
fetch-water, water carrier
fever, French, venereal disease
few, in, in short
fewel, fuel
fiaunt, warrant
field, lodged with his, i.e. in the field, ready for battle
fieldfare, species of thrush
fieldish, rural
fiest, fart
fift, ord., fifth
fifteen, tax of one-fifteenth imposed on personal property
fig, v., pick pockets
figure, executed by, i.e. in effigy
file, polish, elaborate to perfection; curious file, filed quill, "polished" pen; file their hands, i.e. defile
fine, n., end; v., refine
fine-filed, finely turned, well-wrought
finesse, fineness
fingar, finger
firing, n., fuel
firking flantado, i.e. high-flown, bombastic
fisgig, n., gadding wench; v., gad around
fistis, fists
fit, song or poem; strain of music
fitches, heraldic term from the French *fiché*, fixed
fitted, been, i.e. forced out by fits
fitten, untruth, invention
fittes, is fitting
fix an officer, i.e. appoint definitely
flake, flash (of flame)
flamb, flame
flame, sweetheart; fragrant flame, i.e. of love
flame-god, Apollo
flamid, flamed
flampeyn, flampoint, a pie or tart
flang, flung
flaring, shining brightly
flashy, insipid
flasket, long shallow basket
flasks of the sun, i.e. flashes
flaws, squalls (of wind)
flea in my ear, have or send away with a, i.e. a stinging reproof
flee, fly

fleet, flit, hasten; flow swiftly; **fleet hence,** die; **thou fleets,** i.e. fleetest

fleeting, *n.,* inconstancy; *adj.,* **fleeting audience,** i.e. fickle

flegm, phlegm

fleshed, initiated; inured to bloodshed; **fleshed to the press,** habituated in publishing

fleum(atic), phlegm(atic)

flick, flitch (of bacon)

flickerings, dallyings, fondlings

fledge, fligge, fledged

flip flap, part of the clothes that flaps

flitter, flutter

flockbed, mattress with wool stuffing

flocket, garment with large sleeves

flong, flung

florish, flourish

floud, flood

flounce, a flopping movement

flour, *often* = flower

flour-de-luces, fleurs-de-lis

floured, flowered, flourished

flourished, garnished, ornamented

flowre delice (or de luce), iris

flurt, flirt, mock

flush birds, i.e. ready to fly

fly at, let, attacked with fury

fode forth, fob off with excuses

foggy fat, bloated with fat

foil, *n.,* the backing on a glass to produce a reflection; setting for a jewel; *v.,* set (as a jewel)

foist, *n.,* pickpocket; *v.,* break wind; cheat

fold, put sheep in a fold; **hand she fold, i.e.** folded

fon, foolish fellow

fond, foolish, bungling

fondly, foolishly

fondness, foolishness

fone, foes

fonny, foolishly amorous

foolis filly, foolish young jade

foot it, dance

foot-saunt, cent-foot, game at cards

for, *various meanings like* against, because (of), despite, instead of, for fear of, notwithstanding

for that, for why, because; in order that

forain, foreign

forasmych, forasmuch

forbare her, i.e. kept away from

forbathed, bathed, submerged

forbecause, because

forbed(e), forbid

forbod(en), forbid(den)

forborne, being, being omitted

force, care for; strive; **force not,** be of no consequence; **force on,** care about; **force to tell,** i.e. hesitate; **of force,** (hunt) in the open with the hounds in full cry; necessarily; **forced face,** faces hiding their tears in forced calm

forcy Gauls, i.e. powerful Frenchmen

ford, go ahead; **fair ford,** Oxford University; **fleeting ford,** the sea

forder, further

fordge, forge

fordinning, filling with noise

fordon(n)e, undone, ruined

fore, *prep.,* before

fore-backwardly, in an unnatural order

fore-bemoaned, already bemoaned

foreconceit, preconception

foredone, undone, ruined

foredoom, judgment pronounced in advance

forefauts, sins committed before

forefront, foremost part

forego, precede

for(e)gone, gone earlier; entirely gone

foreheads of the trees, i.e. tops

forehorse, foremost horse in a team

foreland, promontory

foren(n)e, foreign

forepassed, forepast, passed, gone; **forepassed reasons,** i.e. already given

forepenned, written in advance

forepointing, pointing out beforehand

foreran, preceded

forereading, foreseeing

forerehearsed, told before

forerun, preceded

foresaid, excluded

foreset, prefixed

foresettled, settled in advance

foreslown, forslown, lost by sloth or neglect

forestall, buy up beforehand (for speculation)

forestore, *n.,* supply laid up in advance

forethought, thought of in advance

foretime, past ages

foreward, vanguard

forewent, went before; already gone

foreworn, forworn, decayed (house)

forfaint, very faint

forfait, forfeit

forfeit most concerned, such a, such a crime or offense

forgat(e), forgot

forge, invent; **forge in their conceits,** invent out of their imagination

forgedly, deceitfully

forgery, dishonest act; false artifice, deceit

forgeve, forgive

forgo, forsake

forgone, lost, completely gone

forhe(a)d, forehead

forhewed, cut to pieces

forlore, forlorn, lost; gone; abandoned

form, kneeling at a, i.e. a bench; **lowest form,** most elementary class

formal priest, i.e. regularly ordained; **formal tales,** i.e. in outward form

formally compact, handsomely formed

former ages, i.e. the first, primeval; **former part,** i.e. the first, initial

formest, foremost, first

fornace, furnace

fornish, furnish

forow, furrow

forpast, passed before or by

forrai(g)n, forre(i)n, foren(ne), foreign

forsaking, declining to accept (money)

forsomuch, forasmuch

forspent, exhausted

forstall, forestall, buy goods to increase their price

forsunk, sunk down

forswatt, covered with sweat

forswonck, worn out with labor

forteress, fortress

forth farder, so, so farther forth

forthy, therefore

fortitude, maximum strength

fortuneless, unfortunate

forwaste, worn out; gone forever

forweary, tired out

forwithered, dried up

forworn, worn out

foster, forester

foughten fields, battlefields

foul, dirty; ugly

foulness, ugliness

founden, found

fourm, form

fournitours, fournitures, furnishings

fourtenight, fortnight

fraight, freight

frame, *n.,* form; **in such frame,** in such a (wretched) condition; **out of frame,** out of order, confused; **witty frame,** i.e. form or shape; *v.,* be fit for; make; prosper, succeed; **frame a form,** make a model; **frame themselves,** i.e. contrive, prepare; **framed in the front,** ?i.e. drawn up, stationed

frank of, liberal with

frankencense, frankincense

franklin, freeholder

frankposts, ?angle-posts in a frame house

franzy, frenzy

fraught, freight, load; supplied, filled

fraunchis, franchise

fray, *n.,* brawl; fright; *v.,* frighten; **fray with,** fight

freak, whim, vagary

fream, roar

freat, frete, gnaw. *See* fret

free, generous, liberal

freedom, of our, holding membership in our trade or guild

freer, friar

freeseled, frizzled

freeze (frieze) jerkin, sleeveless jacket (*with a pun on* frieze, *coarse woolen cloth, and* freeze)

freight with learning, i.e. laden

freke, fellow; freak (*q.v.*)

frenne, stranger

frere, friar

freshman, novice

fret, frete, *n.,* ?flaw; *v.,* eat away; rub, wear. *See* freat

friend, lover; mistress; **friended,** having friends

frier, friar

fright, *pa. part.,* freighted, fraught

frightful herds, i.e. full of fear

frind, friend

frippery, (looking like an) old-clothes shop

friscoles vet, fetch (cut) friscals or capers (*dialectic*)

frise frock, i.e. made of frieze, coarse woolen cloth

frisk, move briskly or sportively; **fetching a frisk,** leaping and dancing

frolic, be, be merry; **frolic(k) it,** make merry

fromward, turned away from

front, *n.,* forehead; *v.,* confront

frontless, shameless

froslings, naughty, (goslings) injured by frost, hence worthless

frost, farewell, *a proverb*

frost-dead, killed by frost

frotting, rubbing

frought, fraught

froward, *adj.,* evilly disposed; *n.,* forward things

frowie, stale, musty

fruct, fruit

fruits, increase, profits

frument, wheat

frump, *n.*, mocking speech; *v.*, mock

fry, crowd of insignificant poets; young men or people

fulfil the mind, i.e. fill up

fume, exhalation; fit of anger; smoke from fire; vapor from the stomach

fumigation, odorous smoke generated by incense

funerals, *plural with singular sense*

furder, further

furmenty, frumenty, a dish of wheat boiled in milk

furniture, the action of furnishing; (down) bedding; equipment; occupants; **equal furniture,** the same kind of bedding; **for her furniture,** i.e. equipped (with an escort)

furor, madness

furous, furious

furre, far; **furre estraunged,** absent far abroad

furrows, wrinkles

furth, forth

furthwith, forthwith

fury, poetic inspiration

fustian, great display (of)

futile, talkative (persons)

gaale, gale, favorable winds

gables, slept on, i.e. on or beside the stern cables

gader, gather

gage, to, in pawn

gaggling, cackling

gag-tooth'd, having prominent teeth

gainsend, send again

gainstood, opposed

gainward, facing, towards

galding, galling

galimafrier, gallimaufryer, one who writes in a hodgepodge style

gall, no broken, i.e. cuckold

galland, gallant; gallon

galley-foists, barges

galliard, quick, lively dance

gallias, galleys

gallimafr(e)y, gallimaufry, hodgepodge

gallions, galleons

gallowp, gallop

gallow-tree, gallows

gambone, gammon, flitch of bacon

game, delight, sport

gan, began; did

gander, shoe the, i.e. undertake a useless task

gang, go

gant, gannet

gape on, long for

gar, garre, cause

garboils, tumults

garded, trimmed with gards or facings

gardein, garden

gardin, guardian

gare, ready, eager

garner, storehouse

garre: *see* gar

gasping net, i.e. widespread

gaspy, gasp

gat(e), *n.*, goat; *v.*, got

gaud, gewgaw

gauge, gage, pledge

gave him his mind, i.e. suggested to him

gawdy, gaudy, gaily dressed

gaze, at the, in bewilderment; **gaze her,** stare at herself; **taken the gaze,** seen

gear, affair; dress; **all this gear,** all these things

geason, rare

geast, guest

geets, clothes

gelliflowers, gillyflowers

gelousy, jealousy

gelt, *n.*, money; *v.*, cut

genealogy, offspring

general, the, the admiral; **aboord the general,** aboard the admiral's ship

generally, all, as a whole

genial, generative; **genial brands,** *error for* genial (nuptial) bands (bonds)

gentil, gentle

gentile, heathen

genus and difference, the class and distinguishing attribute

gerfalcon, large falcon

gess, guess

gest, action; story

get, beget (a child); got

gether, gather

geve, give

ghess, guess

ghest, guest

Ghospel, Gospel

ghost, senseless, dead body

ghostly, spiritual(ly); **ghostly enemy,** spiritual enemy (Satan)

gibbrish, gibrige, gibberish

gill, girl, woman

gilly, gillie, a mare (i.e. a giddy young woman)

gilt, *n.*, gold, money

gimpanado (word of unknown meaning)

gin, *n.*, snare, trap; *v.*, begin

gipsen, gipsy

gird, *n.*, gibe

girlond, gyrlond, garland

giust, joust

give, *sometimes* = misgive, *as* my mind gives me, i.e. has a foreboding; **giving the lion,** i.e. representing, portraying; **given best,** most gifted

gladded, pleased, full of joy

glair, **gummy,** slimy matter

glaive, sword

glassy bed, the ocean

glazeworm, glowworm

glazing glass, i.e. polished

gleak, glyeke, *n.*, gleak, jibe; *v.*, **gave the gleak,** made sport of

gleaves, glaives, swords

glebe, cultivated land; clods containing ore

glebeland, a portion of land assigned to a clergyman as part of his benefice

glede: *see* gleed

glee of meadows, i.e. beauty

gleed, glede, fire; ember

gleesome, gleeful

glide, *n.*, the gliding portion of a stream or river

glim, gleam, shine

glimse, glimpse; glitter

glitterand, glittering

glode, glided

glom(e), *n.*, a glum or sullen look; *v.*, look glum

glomy, gloomy

gloome, become dusk

gloot, glut

gloried, glorified

glose, gloze, *n.*, false show; gloss; panegyric; *v.*, cajole; deceive; talk flatteringly

glotony, gluttony

gloze: *see* glose

glyeke: *see* gleak

gnibbling, nibbling

gnomes, maxims

gnosis, knowledge

go, walk; **go bet,** go faster; **is go,** is gone

goar-blood, gore-blood, clotted blood

Godbewyes, God-be-with-you's, farewells

godded him, deified him

goddes, god's

Goddilge (dyld) ye, God yield (reward) you

goddish, divine

Godsake, God's sake

Godward, to, towards God

goith, goeth

gojon, gudgeon

golden thumb, an allusion to the proverbial dishonesty of millers

golf, goaf, grain stacked in one bay of a barn

good worth, goods, wealth

goodman, prefix to a designation of occupation

goolds, marigolds

goosecap, booby

goose-son, *pun on the name* Gosson

gorgious, gorgeous

gose, goose

goshawk, large short-winged hawk

goship, gossip, friend

gospeler, priest who reads the Gospel in the Mass

gossop, gossip

got(ten), begot(ten)

goverment, government, conduct

governals, rules of conduct

governance, control, influence; discipline, rule of practise; good behavior; governing

government, conduct; working, propelling

gowndy, i.e. sore, running (eyes)

gowned beast, horse decorated with drapery

graff, implant; **graffed,** grafted

grafts, shoots, branches

grail, sung the, i.e. the gradual, an antiphon sung between the Epistle and the Gospel in the Mass

grain, (dyed in) fast color; **grains,** the fork of the body

grame, anger

gramercy, thanks

grammarians, deep-read, men who have not got beyond grammar

grammer, grammar

granade, grenado, pomegranate

grantfather, grandfather

graple, grapple

grass, take heart at, i.e. take heart of grace, pluck up your spirits

grasshopper, newsful, the Royal Exchange, London

grating, for, for fear of grating; **grating his heart,** i.e. consuming, fretting

gratious, gracious

grave, make sculpture; write down; **graved,** buried; chiseled, cut

graver, *n.*, sculptor

gravety, gravity

great, sell by the, i.e. at wholesale

greaves, thickets

gree, agree; great in gree, i.e. in rank or station

greement, agreement

green, *n.*, greenery; *adj.*, green wine, i.e. not mellowed in keeping

greenesse, greenness

greenyard, enclosure covered with grass

greet, weep, mourn

gressop, grasshopper

grief, gown of, i.e. of gries (French *gris*), gray

griesly, grisly, horrible

grill, *adj.*, fierce, cruel

grinckcome's grease, ointment used for the treatment of grincome, or syphilis

grip of pain, i.e. gripe

gripe, *n.*, vulture; *v.*, squeeze

gripple, greedy

grisled, grisly, horrible

grissells, gristles

grizzled, gray (moss)

groaping, groping, handling, grasping

groat, grote, fourpenny coin

groom, shepherd; young man

groomet, grummet, cabin boy

groping flowers, i.e. reaching for or plucking them

grossy, *dialectic for* thickish, luxuriant (*or perhaps a misprint for* grassy)

grote: *see* groat

ground, warble the, i.e. the melody or plain-song

groundplat, groundplot, outline

groundsel, timber in foundations of houses

grutch, *n.*, grumbling; *v.*, grudge

guard, ornament, trimming; guarded, ornamented with lace, etc.; tricked out

gudgen, gudgeon (a fish)

guerdon, reward

guerison, cure, healing

guestwise, as a guest

gules, red

gulfy, full of eddies

gultching, gulching, swallowing

gup, ?go up (cry of anger to a horse)

gurnard, kind of fish

guzzle, gutter, drain; guzzle dogs, dogs from the gutter

gylden, gilded

gyrlond, garland

habandon, abandon

haberdasher, seller or peddler of small wares

hability, ability

habit, amorous, lover's dress

hable, able

habominable, abominable

haboundance, abundance

had I wist, if I had known

haft, cheat, trick

hagbussers, harquebusers, early type of portable guns

haggard, wild female hawk

haggardness, wildness

hagger, wild

hail, ill, bad luck

hails, hales, tents, huts

hailsed, saluted

hain, mean wretch

hainous, heinous

hair, cut against the, i.e. against the "grain"

hakes, short fire-arms

hale, drag, pull; tear on the rack

half, God's, i.e. behalf, sake

half-faced, imperfect

halfpenny (halpenny), have one's heart on a, to have a particular object in view

halfs, to, in equal shares

half-sous, half a sou, worth about a penny and a quarter

hallow, loud shout; all hallow, all saints

halpenny: *see* halfpenny

halt, limp

hamper, entangle

han, have

handel, handle

handgoons, handguns, small arms

handkercher, handkerchief

hands, shake, i.e. say farewell, part

handsel, first use; reward; han(d)seled, first proved or tested

handsomely removing him, i.e. dexterously

handy strokes, hand-to-hand blows

handycraftmen, handicraftsmen

hap, event, fortune; have hap, have the fortune (to)

happ(e)ly, happily, haply

harald, herald

harbenger, harbinger

harber, harbor

harborsome, hospitable

hard, dull; if husband be hard, i.e. stingy; hard together, nearby, close to; *v.*, heard

hardely, hardly, hardily, assuredly, certainly; courageously; with difficulty

hardle, hurdle, sledge on which criminals were drawn to execution

hardly: *see* hardely

hard-meat, at, in retirement

hardwitted, dull at learning

hardyhedde, boldness

harkening, harking, *n.*, listening, attention

harlotry, ribaldry

harm, (Richard III's withered) arm

harness, armor; harnessed, appareled; dressed in armor

harold, herald

harried, drawn (dead on a horse)

hartless, timid

hasard, hazard

haskardy, baseness

haste, hasten

hastely, hastly, hastily

hate-man, misanthropic

hatered, hatred

haughty hill, i.e. high; haughty thoughts, ?liberties taken in translating Virgil

hault, haut, haughty, high

haultie, haulty, hauty, haughty, exalted

haunt, *n.*, frequent visits; *v.*, visit; frequent; haunted path, frequented walk

haut: *see* hault

hauter, halter

hauty: *see* haultie

have after, I'll come along

haveour, havor, bearing; deportment moral and physical

having, you should be, i.e. greedy, grasping

havor: *see* haveour

hawbart, halberd

haws, hawthorn fruit

hay, country dance on the order of a reel; net for trapping rabbits

hay-de-guise, a kind of serpentine dance

he, *n.*, man; *as pron. often* = it

head, great, large deer antlers, i.e. a cuckold; have Actaeon's head, be a cuckold; hung his old head, shed his antlers

headling, headlong

headlonds, strips of land in a field left unplowed for turning a plow at the end of a furrow

heady, passionate

heaped, feast hath, i.e. added

hear, *n.*, hair

hearing, herring

hear-lace, hair-lace

hearse, coffin; funeral-pall; tomb, grave

heartely, heartily

heast: *see* hest

heaviness, sorrow

heavy Cicero or Saturn, i.e. melancholy, sad

hebon, ebon, black ink

hecatombs, great public sacrifices among the Greeks; large number

hecco, woodpecker

heckle, instrument for combing flax

heed, *n.*, head

heedily, heedfully

heedling, headlong

heedy, heedful people

heels, set by the, put in the stocks

heer, hair

heighnous, heinous

height, altitude (of a star) in navigation

helas, alas

heliotropion, heliotropium, marigold

helitropium, heliotropian, purple

hell-danting, hell-daunting

helms of knights, knights in full armor

helpless harms, i.e. inevitable, for which help is impossible

hem, *pron.*, them

hempen tragedy, i.e. execution by hanging

hencefurth, henceforth

hent, arrived at; laid hold of

her, *often the sign of the genitive, as* daughter her name

herault, herald

herbage, pike in, ?i.e. in a bed or garnish of herbs

herbarists, writers on plants

herber, arbor; harbor

herd, fitting a, suitable for a herdsman

herehault, herald

herehence, from this

herk(en), hark(en)

herod, herald

herring-bones, kind of stitches

hert, heart

heryed, heried, praised

hest, heast, command, bidding

hesting, design

het, heated

hether, hither

hetherto, hetherunto, hitherto

hetherwards, hitherward

hew, hue; face; beauty

hexamiter, hexameter

hey pass, etc., a juggler's phrase

heywards, haywards, herdsmen of cattle feeding on a common

hiachinth, hiacynth, hyacinth; sapphire

hidder, hither

hidious, hideous

hierd, herd

high-carged, high-charged
high-lawyers, highwaymen
hight, *n.*, height; *v.*, is called or named
high-welked, ?high in the welkin
hild, held
hilts, handle of a sword (*plural for singular*)
him, *often* = it
himward, to, towards him
hind, rustic, farmer
hinderance, hindrance
hing, hung
hippocentaurs, fabulous creatures combining
  forms of a man and a horse
hips, fruit of roses
hire, reward; payment
his, *often* = its; *sign of the genitive, as* gentleman his name, the reader his view, *etc.*
historial, historical
historify, narrate
history, *often* = story (fiction)
hit, *pron.,* it
hither-deduced, thence descended from
hitself, itself
hobby, small species of falcon
hoddypeak, hoddypeck, blockhead, simpleton
hofes, hoofs
hoise, hoist, raise; cry out
hold, *n.,* fortified place
holden, hold; held
holding of, pertaining to (the subject)
holiday oath, oath fit for a holiday (not
  serious)
holland, linen
hollow eyes, i.e. sunken
holm, holly tree
holp(en), helped
holt, wooded hill
holy day, holiday
home, *interj.,* hum!
homeliness, kindliness
homely, rude; rudely; unpretentiously
hond, hand
honest, *adj.,* chaste; honest for my name,
  i.e. honorable to; honest to use, i.e. befitting; *v.,* honest your name, i.e. honor
honestly, virtuously
honesty, chastity, virtue; never have honesty
  of, i.e. honor, respect, from
honger, hunger
honorous, honorable
hoong, hung
hoop, encircle, gird
hoop(e), hope
hooved, lingered, waited
hopelost, desperate
hopharlots, coarse coverlets
hoppy, hop
hopshackles, hobbles
horizon twixt, boundary between
horn-maker, maker of cuckolds
horns, grafting, cuckolding
horologe, horology, timepiece
horrizonant, inharmonious
horse, *often the plural*
horse-co(u)rsers, dealers in horses
horse-nest, mare's nest
horshowe, horseshoe
host, army
hote, mentioned
hothouse, brothel
hotspurs, rash persons
hough, *interj.,* ho!; *n.,* ?tavern

house, bad, brothel
hous(e)band, husband
housekeeping, hospitality
housel, the Mass or Eucharist
hove, linger
huckles, hips
huddes, huds, hoods
huddle, *n.,* stooped old man
huddled up, compiled hastily and carelessly
hudge(ness), huge(ness)
hudwinked, hoodwinked
hue, beauty; complexion; face
huff-snuff, braggart
hugger-mugger, in, secretly
hugy, huge
huke, loose garment
hulks, admiral of the, i.e. the chief supply
  ship
hulling, a ship, i.e. drifting to the wind
humain, humane, human
humanitian, scholar
humect, moisten
humerly, *interj.*
humiliatedo, abjection, insignificance
humor, fluid of the body; temperament;
  vapor; whimsical action, caprice
humorous, humid; ill humored; humorous
  minds, minds governed by their own
  fancies or inclinations; humorous times,
  i.e. capricious, fanciful
humorously lure, ?i.e. fantastically
hundreth, hundred
hungerly, in a half-famished condition
hunger-starved, starved
hunt the letter, use alliteration
hunt's-up, a tune played to rouse one from
  sleep
hurd, hoarding
husband, *n.,* businessman; tiller, farmer; *v.,*
  manage prudently
husbandly, in a businesslike manner
hushing, quiet (woods)
huswife, housewife
huswif(e)ry, housekeeping
hutch, coffer
hydrographical, referring to rivers, lakes,
  etc.
hydroptique, having an insatiable thirst
hypocrasy, hypocrisy
hyre, *adv.,* higher

I, *often* = aye
iambicques, iambics
ich, I (*dialectic*); icham, I am
idea, the Platonic archetype of any class of
  things
idee, idea, image
idilion, idyl
idiot, holy, i.e. a person without learning
idlely, idly
ignorant to, having no knowledge of; ignorants, ignorant people
iland, island
ile, isle
ile-ward, towards the isle
illecebrous, alluring
ill-faring, in bad condition
illudes, evades
illuminate, *pa. part.,* illuminated
illustrate, *adj.,* illustrious
imaginarily, in imagination
imaginary lines, i.e. imaginative
imbark, embark

imbase, lower; lower in value; imbased
  minds, i.e. debased
imbattle, fight; imbattle his host, i.e. form
  it in battle array
imber, ember; one of the quarterly periods
  of fasting and prayer
imboss, emboss
imbrace, embrace
imbrauder, imbroider, embroider
imbroil, embroil
imp, *n.,* child; fellow, man; *v.,* engraft
  (wings)
impaled, encircled
impart my pain, i.e. share in, partake of
impassible, incapable of suffering injury
impeach, *n.,* impeachment, accusation
imperial, *n.,* kingdom
impertinences, things of little importance
impery, empery, empire
impetrate, procure
imploy, employ
impoisoning, being poisoned
impolished, unpolished
import, impart (to me)
importable, insupportable
impose on men's thoughts, i.e. place restrictions on; imposed names, names assigned
  to individuals
impression, printing; English impressions,
  i.e. translations, versions
imprinter, printer
in, *sometimes* = on
"In speech," grammar (from the opening
  words of William Lily's *Grammar*, 1577)
inable, enable
inamel, enamel (*q.v.*)
inamour, enamor
inartificially, clumsily, unskilfully
inaspiring, unambitious
inaugured, invested (with), consecrated
incaged, encaged
incamp, encamp
incantivanty, ?incontinently, at once
incense, inflame (with passion); kindle, excite
incesteous, incestious, incestuous
inchant(ment), enchant(ment)
inchase, enchase, engrave
incident terms, i.e. incidental
inclose, enclose
included, enclosed
incommodious, unprofitable
incommodity, discomfort, injury
incompass, encompass
incomperable, incomparable
incontinency, unrestraint (of the tongue)
incontinent(ly), at once
inconveniencies, unseemly acts, offences
inconveniently, expel, i.e. improperly, un-
  suitably
incoragement, encouragement
incorporationers, members of the city
  corporation
incounter, encounter
incourage, encourage
incroach, encroach; gradually extend
incrocher, encroacher
incrouching, fawning (eloquence)
incumber, encumber
incumb(e)rancies, encumbrances
indagations, investigations
indeavor, endeavor
indenize, endenize, naturalize

indepressed, not dejected

indesinence, want of proper ending

indifference, indifferency, impartiality

indifferent, impartial, unprejudiced; not different in length or accent; **indifferent years**, moderate age

indigest, undigested, formless

inditched, buried

indite, indict

individuum, indivisible entity

indow, endow

indubitate, undoubted

induce, introduce

induction, initiation

indue, endue, endow

indurate, morally hardened

indure, endure

inequal, unequal

infame, infamous

infant, young man

infarced, enfarced, stuffed

infect, *pa. part.*, infected

infired, enflamed; inspired

infold, enfold

inforce, enforce, force

inform the womb, i.e. shape, mold

infortunate, unfortunate

infortune, misfortune

infourm, inform

infuse, *n.*, infusion

ingage, engage

ingarlanded, engarlanded

ingender, engender

ingent, very great

ingeny, intellect

inglut, englut

ingrained, (satin) dyed in the fiber

ingrateful, ungrateful

ingrave, engrave; **ingraven**, engraved, written

ingross, engross, buy up wholesale for a monopoly; include in a list

ingurgitations, guzzling

inhanced, enhanced

inhearse, enclose as in a coffin

injoin, enjoin

injoy, enjoy

injuried, injured

injurious reader, i.e. wilfully offensive

injust, unjust

inkhorn, *adj.*, pedantic; *n.*, **smell of the inkhorn**, be pedantic

inkhornism, pedantic word or expression

inkpot, *adj*. pedantic

inlarge, enlarge

inless, diminish

inlightened, enlightened

inly, heartily

inough, inow, enough

inpalpable, impalpable, imperceptible to the touch

inprinted, printed

inquisition, senses of, i.e. for finding out facts

inrage, enrage

inrich, enrich

inscience, ignorance

inshrine, enshrine

insighted detractor, i.e. having insight

insinuation of testaments, ?deliveries of wills for probate

insolence, (furious) exultation

insolent, swelling, exulting

instance, required with, asked with urgency of speech

instant entreaty, i.e. urgent; **be instant upon**, be urgent with

instantly craved, or laid at, i.e. persistently urged or sued

instep, high in the, i.e. full of pride

instinction, celestial, i.e. inspiration

instruct, *pa. part.*, instructed

instyle, call by the name of

insue, ensue

insult, triumph; **insult in**, boast of; **insulting**, boasting

intangeled, intangled, entangled

intellectife, intellective, intellectual

intellectual, intelligence, mind; (will) apprehensible only by the mind

intelligence, mental intercourse; news

intelligencer, bringer of news; informer, spy

intend thereto, pay attention to it; **intend wars**, i.e. fix the mind or attention on

intendment, intention

intent, a smith's, i.e. use

intentions, second, secondary conceptions of things (logic term)

intercepted at Tyburn, i.e. hanged

interessed, interested

interinanimates, animates mutually

interluding, playwriting

intermeddle, concern onself; intermingle

interprise, undertaking

interseamed, interspersed

intertain, entertain

interveined, intersected as with veins

intestine broils, domestic or civil quarrels

inthrall, enthrall

intice(r), entice(r)

intire(ly), entire(ly)

intitle, intitule, entitle; **intituled to**, dedicated to

intrails, intrals, entrails

intrap, entrap

intreat, entreat, beg; treat, behave to; treat of, discuss

intreatance, entreaty

intrinsicate, entangled

introit, antiphon or psalm at the beginning of a communion or other service

invegled, inveigled

invehing, inveighing

inveloped, enveloped

invent, find

inventer, inventor

inventife, inventive

invention, literary composition; **daily inventions**, i.e. fashions

invigilate, watch carefully

invile, render vile, debase

inviron, environ

involved in earth, i.e. wrapped, interred

invulgared, divulged to the common people

inwrap, enwrap

ippocras, hippocras, spiced wine

irksome cave, i.e. loathsome

ironies against God, i.e. contemptuous remarks

irregular idiot, i.e. disorderly, lawless

isop, hyssop

istme, isthmus

it, *sometimes* = its

itch, shift one's position a little (to)

ivy bush, the sign of an alehouse

iwis, certainly, truly

jacincts, jacinths, sapphires

jack, (foulmouthed) knave; *misused for* the key of a virginal. *See* black-jack

jalous, jealous

janglery, idle talk

jape, jest; **make a jape**, make light of

jar, *n.*, blow, fight; *v.*, quarrel, dispute

jarging, creaking

jast you, ?chase you!

javel, low or worthless fellow

jealious, jealous

jeliflowers, gillyflowers

jeoberdy, jeoberty, jeopardy

jeopardous, hazardous

jerks, gibes; lashes

jet (it), strut, swagger

jetty, projecting part of a building

jobbernoll, blockhead

joined beds, beds made by joiners

jointed, (her neck) disjointed

jolly, gallant, fine; showy, splendid

jorney, journey

journey, that day's, i.e. fight, battle

joy, *v.*, enjoy

joyly, jolly

jubilee, a monk's, i.e. a year of plenary indulgence for doing certain pious works

jump a marriage, i.e. make up hastily; **jump with**, *adv. phr.*, exactly with, *v.*, agree completely with

juncat, junket, delicacy to eat; sweet confection

just, joust; **justs**, joust (*plural used for singular*)

justicer, administrator of justice

justiciary, administrator of justice

kaiser, kesar, king, emperor

karn, kern, rascal

karsie, kersey, coarse narrow cloth

kaw me and I'll kaw thee, flatter me and I'll flatter you; do me a good turn and I'll do you another

kay, key

keel, *v.*, become cold

keep, *n.*, what is left, a charge; **take keep**, give heed; *v.*, **keep him**, kept himself; **none may keep in**, i.e. live, dwell

keke, kick

kemb, comb

ken, know

kendle, kindle

kenning, in, in sight or view (of)

kerchef, kercher, kerchief

kerke, kirk, church

kernes, peasants, rascals

kesar: see kaiser

kest, cast

kestrel, small hawk

kibe, chilblain

kill-cow, *adj.*, bullying; *n.*, braggart

kim kam, crooked

kind, *adj.*, natural; well-bred (spaniel); *n.*, each sex; nature; Nature; *often the plural* kinds; **frames to its kind**, makes it natural; **not in kind**, of a different nature; **of kind**, from or by nature, natural(ly)

kindly, *adj.*, natural; *adv.*, according to its nature; properly, fittingly

kindness, love

kine, cattle. *See* kye

kinred, kindred

kinsfolks, relatives

kirtle, gown

kistrel(l), coistrel, knave; kestrel, small hawk

kit, kitten, girl

knacks, tricks of rhetoric

knave, boy's servant

knaw, gnaw; knawn, gnawn, gnawed

knead up to the knees, ?tread up and down

knedded, kneaded, shaped, formed

knight of the post, perjured witness

knight-arrant, knight-errant

knit trap-doors, i.e. fastened

knot, bird of the snipe family; design of crossing lines; flower bed; motto, saying; curious knots, fancifully patterned flower-beds

knotty youth, i.e. rough and hard in character

knowen, known

knowledge, v., admit, acknowledge

kough, ?chough or co, jackdaw

kuss, kiss

kusshins, cushions

kye, cows. See kine

kyst, cast (dice)

laberinth, laborinth, labyrinth

laborsome, laborious

lack, a bull that was a, i.e. that was lost

lad, v., led

ladies nine, the muses

laid at, assailed, sued; laid bellies, i.e. that have been delivered of births; laid to, charged against; laid upon me, quoted against me; ligge so laid, lie so prostrated

Lammas, latter: see latter

lamp, the eye; planet, star; the sun and the moon

lampatram, ?a drab

lamping eyes, i.e. resplendent, flashing

lanch, launch

lanners, species of falcons

lanthern, lanthorn, lantern

lantsgrave, lantzgrave, landgrave, German count

lap up (in), bind together; wrap in

larded, ornamented; soiled

lardge, large

large, a, and a long, musical characters; a large contained two or three longs, one long two or three breves; at large, or in letters, i.e. with one's full name or initials

largely, at length, in detail

lass, adj., less

latch, catch

lated in the night, i.e. belated

Latins, translations into Latin

latter breath, last breath; latter day, the last day (Doomsday); at latter Lammas, at a (Lammas) day that will never come

lauds, n., praises; a religious service or office

laughs the songs, i.e. derides them

launch, lance

laund: see lawn

laundery, laundry room

laureate, poet

lauriat, laureate

lavasse, lavish

lavoltas, fetch, do lively dances (for two persons)

lawn, piece or garment of lawn; lawn or laund, untilled ground

laws, either of the, i.e. civil and canon laws

laxative letters, i.e. relaxing, bringing relief

lay, n., layman; v., save (for old age). See laid

laystall, dumping ground

lazar, leper

lea, pasture (Neptune's waters)

leach, leech, doctor; leach damask, leach lumbard, dishes of sliced meat, eggs, fruit, and spices in jelly

leads, n., lead-covered balustrades or roofs; v., leads in dales, i.e. dwells in

leak, at, passing away

leam, ray, gleam

lean them, i.e. lend, furnish

leaning, n., inclination

leap with him, coincide with his convenience

learn me, teach me

learnless, devoid of learning

lease, n., allotted time; v., leese, lose

leasing, leesing, lie, lying; fictions; whetstone leasings, lies qualifying one for having a whetstone round his neck, the sign of a great liar

leasor, leisure

leastwise, at the, at least

leaveless, leafless

leavy, leafy

lecture, course of lectures; reading (of texts)

ledder, leather

lee, river

lee shores, shores that the wind blows upon

leech, doctor

leechcraft, art of healing

leefe, lief, agreeable

leeful, leful, lawful

leeks, likes, loves

leer, lear, tape binding the edges of fabric

leese, lese, impair; lose

leesing: see leasing

left to, refrained from

leftenants, lieutenants, representatives

leful: see leeful

leg, make a, bow

lege de moy, the name of some dance

legendary, his, stories about him

legier, nimble

leir, lair

leman, lemmon, mistress

lene, lend

lenger, longer

length, v., prolong

lep(t), leap(ed)

lere, lore; skin, complexion

lese: see leese

less, conj., lest; I would no less, i.e. I was pleased to be addressed by Cupid

lest, at, at least

let, n., hindrance, obstacle; v., cease, stop; hinder, restrain; let to, refrain from; letted, prevented

letany, litany

letcher, lecherous man

letchery, lechery

letten, let

letter, leave this, i.e. this text, subject; running on the letter, alliterating

letter'd, educated

letter-graven, inscribed (with memorial lines)

lettice, lettuce

leuse, loose

levation, elevation of the Host in the Mass

level, n., goal; v., aim; level coil, *lève-cul*, a rough, noisy game

lever, liefer, dearer

levin, lightning

lewd, ignorant; wicked

lewsed, loosed, let go

lewterer, loiterer

liberality, liberal bounty; extravagance

libertine, one who follows his own inclinations

liberty, licentious living

licentiate, freed from rules

licuor, liquor

lied, a village, i.e. lay, was situated

lief, dear, pleasant

liefe, (my) beloved

liegeland, ?a condition of fawning servitude

lien, lain

lift, n., thief; at a dead lift, the pull of oxen at a dead weight beyond their power to move; v., sometimes = steal; pa. part., lifted

lifull, lifeful (heat)

ligge(n), lie; ligge so laid, lie so prostrated; liggen in lead, lie in a leaden shroud

light, adj., loose, wanton; swift, quick; unencumbered; adv., quickly; n., lung; window; v., lighten; light(ed) upon, settle(d); lighted, fell and settled; gave light

lightening, lightning

lightly, easily; commonly, often; probably; readily

light'ned, made luminous

lightsome, cheerful

lightsomeness, brightness

ligier, ledger, ambassador

ligne, line

like, be pleasing to; like of, like, love; like well, pleases (you); of a like, probably, belike; it is like, i.e. likely

lim, n., limb; v., limn, draw; limmed book, i.e. illuminated

limbec(k), alembic

lime-finger, thief

limiter, lymiter, friar licensed to beg in certain limits

limon, lemon

lin, cease, stop

li'n, lien, lain

linage, lineage

lind, light as, i.e. as a linden tree

line, n., the equator; pa. part., lain

linger out, protract; lingered the time, i.e. prolonged

liniaments, lineaments; outlines, figure

link, one of the divisions of black puddings; torch

lip-labor, vain repetition of words

lippes, lips

lip-threats, spoken threats

liqueress, licorice

liquor'd, polished

list, wish; list of green, green border

listful, attentive

literature, humane learning

lither, nimble

little and little, by, gradually

live, on, alive

liveless, lifeless

livelihood, inheritance; liveliness

livelike, like life

livelod(e), livelihood

lively, adj., adv., in a lifelike way; lifelike,

natural; living; quick; vigorously; warm and vigorous; **lively death,** i.e. quick and easy; **lively food,** i.e. necessary for life; *n.,* lifelikeness

livery faces, ?faces showing diseased livers

live's, life's

livory, livery

lizard, dragon

load, had, had been freighted with

loaded, laden

loaf, sugar-loaf

loaft, loft

lockram, linen

loden, laden

loding, loading

loft, *adj.,* raised aloft

lond, land

long, *v.,* belong

longitude of days, a long time

loof, luff, lie close to the wind

look how, just as; **look it,** seek it; **look what,** whatever

loord, lout

loose, *often* = lose; **make our loose,** i.e. loosing, letting go

lope, leaped

lord it, flaunt like a lord

lording, sir, gentleman

lore, learning

lorell, lorrell, lorel, blackguard

lorn, lost

lose, *v., often* = loose

losel, scoundrel

lot, condition of life

lothful eyes, i.e. reluctant

lothly, unwilling

lourdayn, lourden, lurdan(e), loafer, rascal

lovely live, i.e. lovingly

low countries, the, hell

lower, *n.,* lour, gloomy look; *v.,* frown

lowted, bowed, reverenced

lozel, losel, scoundrel

lubber, stupid fellow

lubberlike, loutish

lubberly, clumsily

luff, spring their, head too far into the wind

lumbard: *see* leach

lumining, illumining

lunary, a garden plant called "honesty"

lupa, wolf or prostitute

lurdan(e): *see* lourdayn

lurk, keep hidden

lusking, lying idly

lust, *n.,* pleasure; wish, desire; *v.,* list, wish; desire sinfully

lustful, lusty, vigorous

lustless, lacking vigor

lusty, beautiful (words); delightful; vigorous, lively

lustyhed, lustihead, pleasure, enjoyment

lyeke, like

lyen, lain

lymiter: *see* limiter

maden, made

magget a pie, maggot in a pie

magistracy, office (position) of a magistrate

magistral, dogmatic

magnifical, magnificent

maiden knight, one inexperienced in fighting

maidenhear, maidenhair

maim, *n.,* bodily injury; calamity

mainge, maingy, mange, mangy

mainly, cry, i.e. loudly

maister, master; **blind maister,** Cupid

maistress, mistress

maistries, masteries, feats

make, *n.,* mate; *v.,* **make so excellent,** write verses so well; **for whom it maketh,** i.e. to whom it would be advantageous

maker, poet

making, *n.,* poetry

malapert, malipert, presumptuous, saucy

male, mail, bag

malecontent, malcontent

malefices, evil deeds

malgrado, in spite of

malice, seek to injure

malign at, speak evil of

malingn, malign

malipert: *see* malapert

malist, envied

malitious, malicious

malmesey, malmsey, a wine

malt, maul, wooden club

manage, manege, handle or train a horse; put through (or perform) the exercises of the manège

mane, crest

manege: *see* manage

mangeled, mangled

manicled, manacled

manless, unmanly

manlike, manly

manner, kind or sort of; = manner's or manners' (*uninflected genitive*)

mannerly in reproving, i.e. becomingly

manning, escorting

mansleers, manslayers

manticor, fabulous deadly beast

manurage, cultivation (of land)

many, *n.,* meinie, crowd

many-formed, various

map, the very image of, picture

marchandise, marchandize, merchandise

marchant, merchant; merchant ship

marches, *n.,* frontier borderlands

mare, specter, hag (Medusa); **away the mare,** away with melancholy

marees: *see* marish

margarites, pearls

margent, margin

marigold, the, i.e. Clytie

marinar, mariner

marish, marees, marsh

mark, money, two-thirds of a pound (*sometimes the plural*)

marlions, merlins, hawks

marry, *interj.,* why, to be sure

marrybones, marrowbones

martial, marshal, arrange

marshal-man, martial-man

martin(et), a bird

martyr, constant sufferer in love

marvail(ous), marveil(ous), marvel(ous)

mas, master

mash-fat, mashing-vat

maship, mastership

mask, *n.,* masque; *v.,* hide; enmesh

masker(y), masquer(ade)

massy, massive

mast, fruit of forest trees

masterless men, i.e. unemployed

mast'ring vein, master-vein, a great artery

mate, checkmate, foil; **mated,** amazed; checkmated

mathematics, sciences

matteres, mattress

mauger, in spite of

mavis, song-thrush

maw, stomach

maze, on, in amazement; **seeing the hare through the maze,** i.e. seeing what was going on beneath the surface

mazed face, i.e. bewildered, terrified

mazer, wooden cup

me, *dative of interest (ethical dative), as in* seat me him, placed me him, talk me, etc.

me likes, it likes (pleases) me

me seems, it seems to me

meal-mouthed, not outspoken

mean, intercessor; means; medium; method; middle; middle course; poor (estate); tenor or alto; **in a mean,** with moderation; **without mean,** immoderately; **mean season,** meantime

meany: *see* meinie

mears, landmarks

measurable, metrical, quantitative

measurableness, moderation

measure, dance; poetical rhythm; **measured,** metrical or quantitative (verse)

meat, food in general

mechanic(al), mean, vulgar

meddle, concern oneself (with); mix

meddling, association, dealing

median, vein, vein in the arm

medicynd, cured

medley color, i.e. mixed

meed, *n., v.,* reward

meetly, suitably

meinie, meany, meny, army; multitude (of persons); drove (of asses)

mell, meddle

memento, musing

memories, memorial services for the dead

memorize my birth, i.e. memorialize

menaging, managing, controlling

mennes, minnows

mentery, lying

meny: *see* meinie

merchant, fellow, chap

mere liberality, i.e. pure

merely, merrily; not only

meremaids, mermaids

merit, reward

merle, blackbird

merlin, small falcon

mervail, merveil, mervel, mervoil, marvel

meseems, it seems to me

meself, myself

mess, make up a, i.e. a group of four persons (at a banquet)

messager, messenger

met, good, good measure

metely, meetly, fitly

meten, meted, given

meth, mead

methink(s), it seems to me

mettles, metals

meve, move

mew, *n.,* place of concealment; **in mew,** cooped up; *v.,* shut up; molt, shed

meward, to, towards me

meynt, menged, mingled

mich, much

miche, skulk

mickle, great; much

middest, midst, middle

middleward, middle body of an army

midland sea, the Mediterranean

mids, middes, midst

mignion, minion

mile, *often the plural*

millons, melons

minacing, menacing

mind, to her, to her liking

mine, Indias of, i.e. with mines (of precious stones)

ming, meng, produce (honey) by mixing

minish, lessen

ministers, agents, attendants

ministery, ministry

minorites, fraternity of the, ?class of persons of minor rank

minstreil, minstrel

mirrhor, mirrold, mirror

mischieves, mischiefs

misconster, misinterpret

misconsterer, one who misconstrues

misdempt, misdeemed, judged wrongly

miser, wretch

misfashion, make out of shape

misgone, gone astray

misguide, trespass

mislike, displease; **mislike with him**, disapprove of him

mismetering, spoiling the meter of

misorder, bad order, disorder; error; **misordered life**, i.e. ill-conducted

misorderly, irregular

misprision, growing upon, being based upon a mistake

misproud, arrogant

misruly, disorderly

miss, absence, death; injury, lack, deficiency, privation; mistake; sinning; **missing**, *n.*, error; *adj.*, that misses its aim

misseek, seek wrongly

mistaste thy chaps, i.e. be distasteful to

mister, kind of

mistriss, mistress

miswend, go astray

miter, meter; crown

mithridate, antidote against poison

miting, a diminutive creature

mixed hands, i.e. joined

mo, moe, more

mockado, kind of cloth

mocking-stock, laughing-stock

mode, furious, i.e. mood

module, sing

moe: *see* mo

moiling, toiling

moist, *n.*, wetness; *adj.*, **moist brain**, i.e. watery, weak

moisted, moistened, soaked

mold, earth; earth = human body; **mold celestial**, celestial form or earth

moldwarp(e), mole

mole, iron, i.e. mold

mollify, soften

molt, *pa. part.*, melted

moly, fabulous herb (in Homer)

mome, blockhead

monarch, absolute ruler

moneth, month

mong, mongst, among

moniment, monument

monish, admonish

monith, month

monition, admonition

monkery, body of monks

monsterous, monstruous, monstrous

montaigne, mountain

month's mind, strong desire

monticors, manticoras, fabulous wild beasts

monuments, documents, records

mood, mode (in music)

moon, cast beyond the, go to extravagant lengths

mooting, debating

moralizing Death, i.e. exemplifying

morder(er), murder(er)

more, all a, ?à la mode

morgage, mortgage

morn, *v.*, mourn

morphew, leprous eruption

morreyn, murrain

mortal rage, fury of death

morter, mortar

mortify oneself, be an ascetic; **mortify the blood**, i.e. destroy its vigor; **mortified**, numbed, insensible

mortuaries, gifts claimed by a vicar from the estate of a deceased parishioner

most monster, i.e. the greatest

mostwhat, for the most part

mote, may; might

motion, proposal; **motioned**, presented, set forth; **motioned in season**, proposed at the right moment

mott, measured

mottle cream, i.e. mottled

mough, mo, more

mought, might; could

mout, moult

mouth, makes up his, finishes a meal with something delicious, i.e. satisfies

move, *v.*, anger; **in moving**, in power of affecting the mind

moyle, defile

much deal, a, a great part; **much pleasant**, very pleasant

muchwhat, almost, pretty much

muckhill, manure-heap

muckworm, money-grubber

mue, in, in mew, cooped up

mulling, term of endearment

mumchance, card game

mumpsimus, bigoted opponent of reform

murr, severe form of catarrh

murther(er), murder(er)

muscul, mussel

muse, *n.*, *often* = poet; profound meditation; **in her muses**, in a state of abstraction; *v.*, ponder over, wonder at

muse-foe, poetry-hating

mushromp, mushroom

musket, sparrowhawk

muss, muzzle, mouth

mute forth, void excrement

mych, much

myriad, ten thousand (Egyptian) coins of some understood value

mystery, profession, art

N., *nomen*, name

nacion, nation

naked bed, to my, naked to my bed

namecouth, famous

named me, called me by name

namely, particularly, especially

napkin(g), handkerchief; ?tympan-sheet

nappy, drunken (muse); heady, strong (ale)

narre, nearer

narrow, went, walked carefully

nat, not

natheless, nevertheless

nathemore, never the more

nativity, the moment of birth; infancy

natural, *n.*, natural character; native citizen; *adj.*, **natural author** or **people**, i.e. native

naturate, created

naturing, creating and giving to each thing its specific nature

natwithstanding, notwithstanding

naught, *adj.*, bad, wicked; worthless

naughtiness, wickedness

naughty, inferior (wares); wicked; worthless

ne, *neg.*, not

near, nearer; never the near, no closer to one's purpose or end

neare, *adv.*, ne'er

neat, unwatered (wine)

neathermost, lowest

neck-verse, the beginning of the 51st Psalm in Latin, read by a criminal who claimed benefit of clergy (*q.v.*)

necligent, negligent

needly, necessarily

needments, necessaries

negromancy, necromancy

neighbrod, neighborhood

neither, not any one; **neither of both**, neither one; **neither . . . neither**, neither . . . nor

nembleness, nimbleness

nepenthe(s), a drink of herb of forgetfulness

nephews, descendants

nethelesse, nevertheless

neven, name

never-singling, who never makes single (unmarried)

nevew, nephew

new, *adv.*, anew, again

newelties, novelties

newfangle, *adj.*, new; carried away with what is new; *n.*, new thing or fashion; **newfangled**, fashionably dressed; inconstant; **newfangleness**, inconstancy

news-stir, fuss or excitement

new-threaden, newly threaded

next, nearest

nice, careful, precise; inclined to foolish tricks; scrupulous

nick, precise moment

niggardize, *n.*, niggardliness

niggish, stingy

nightes, night's

nightwalkers, bullies, thieves

nill, *neg. v.*, will not

nip, cutpurse; **give the nip**, utter a reproof; **nip a bung**, lift or cut a purse

nipper, slanderer

nis, *neg. v.*, is not

nobles, thick by, by a margin of coins worth ten shillings

noblesse, nobility

nobs, a term of endearment

nocent, guilty

nocturn, one of the divisions of the office of matins

nocturnal, verse night-piece

noddle, head

nodgcomb, simpleton

noise, (music of a) trumpet; melodious sound (of music)

noll, head

nomber, number

none, *adj.*, no

nones, for the, for the nonce or special purpose

noonstead, position of the sun at noon

nope, bullfinch

noppy, heady, strong (ale)

nor . . . nor, neither . . . nor

norise, nurse

norish, nourish

nosethrills, nosthrils, nostrils

not, *neg. v.*, know not

nother, neither; nother . . . neither, neither . . . nor

nothing, *adv.*, not at all; nothing parcel, no part

noughtiness, worthlessness

nought of her body, i.e. adulterous

noughts, at, of no value, a mere nothing

nource, nourcies, nurse(s)

nouriture, nourture, nurture

nourse, nurse

nousel, train, educate

novelets, little new books

novels, news, novelties

noverint, a writ; noverint trade, the trade of a scrivener

noy, *n.*, annoyance, pain; *v.*, annoy; injure

noyer, injurer, enemy

noyful, injurious

number, rhythm; verse; quantitative verse; metrical feet

numbered laughter, ?i.e. rhythmical

numb'ring men, mathematicians

numbrous, metrical

numerosity, rhythmic quality

numerous poetry, quantitative verse

numming, numbing

nun, Venus', i.e. priestess

nuntius, messenger

nutrify, nourish

nymphist brood, children resembling the nymphs (i.e. characters of fiction)

obedience, under one's, i.e. rule, control

obiter, by the way

oblivious ground, i.e. attended by oblivion (the grave)

obraid, upbraid

observancy, observation

obtestate, beseech

occion, ocean

occupier of farming, i.e. practitioner

occupy, do business; make use of

occurred upon, happened upon

occursively, by the way

odd rimes, i.e. uneven, discrepant

odible, odious

odored, perfumed

of, *used in various senses as* by, for, from, in, off, on, with

offend at, take offense at; offend herself, i.e. harm, hurt

offensively taken, i.e. with resentment

offspring, origin, birth; family, race

ofter, oftner, oftener

oftscome, offscum, scum, refuse

ointed, anointed

old excellent, very excellent; my old excuse, my excuse when I am old

oliphant, elephant

oliva, olive branch

omely, homily

omnigatherum, catchall

on live, alive; on the daylight, i.e. in

once, at, at one time

ones, *adv.*, once

onles(s), unless

only, alone; not only the cause, i.e. not the only

onto, unto

ony, any

oouse, ooze

opbraid, upbraid

open and plain, freely and plainly

open-breasted, with the breast exposed

opened, clerkly, learnedly set forth or explained

oppugn, call into question

optain, obtain

or, *adj., n.*, gold; *adv., conj.*, ere, before; or ever, before; or . . . or, either . . . or

oraculous, oracular

oraisons, orisons

oration, language

orator, one who prays for another

order, arrange; prepare; ordered people, i.e. governed; ordering of poetry, i.e. the treatment

orderless, in a disorderly way

orderly, *adv.*, in a well-behaved manner; regularly, methodically

ordinal, ritual

ordinance, ordinaunce, device, plan; ordnance, artillery

ordinary, church official who has immediate jurisdiction in church affairs; eating-house or tavern; a meal provided in an eating-house; of ordinary, ordinarily

ordinate, govern

ordinately, in due order

organons, organs

orient, glowing (cheeks); precious (pearl)

orificial, ?bombastic

origanum, one of the labiate herbs like marjoram

oringes, oranges

orizon, horizon

ortography, orthography

ost, host

ostentate, make a show of

ostess, hostess

ostler, hostler

other, *conj.*, either; otherwise; *plural pron.*, others; other some, some others

otherways, otherwise

otherwhile(s), sometimes; at other times; otherwhile vacations, occasional recreations

ought, *n.*, aught, any part; *v.*, owed

ougly, ugly

ourself(s), ourselves

out alas, alas

outbrast, burst forth

outbrayed, uttered, yelled

out-brothership, non-resident membership in a fraternity

outduring, outlasting

outlandish, foreign

outrage in apparel, i.e. run riot

outragious, outrageous

outray, vanquish

outward, borne, i.e. as corpses are carried out feet first

outwent, surpassed

outwroong, wrung out

ouzell, blackbird

over end, upper part

overcrow me, exult or triumph over me

overcurious, too fastidious

overflown, submerged

overgo, surpass; overgone in love, i.e. overpowered

overhail, draw over

overhaled, overtook

overlaid with a plume, i.e. surmounted

overlash, be extravagant; overlashing, *adj.*, excessive; *n.*, extravagance

overlay, overwhelm

overlive, live too long

overlook, examine, scrutinize; see to it

overmatch, Oenone's, i.e. superior

overpass, pass

overrun, glance at

overseen, deceived; ill-advised

overseer, critical reader; overseer of the print, editor of the book

overshot, carried to excess

overstraight, overstrait, too strict

overthrow, defeat; *pa. part.*, overthrown; overthrew, *intrans. v.*, fell over

overthwart, across, adverse; contradictory; hostile

overthwartly, contrariwise

overthwartness, perversity

overture, a plain, i.e. an exposed place

overweening, overestimation

overwhart, overthwart, across

overwhartly, perversely, "crossly"

overworn, worn out

owches, ouches, bracelets

owe, own; the own, its own (i.e. part of the slop or breeches)

ox, black, (proverbial for) misfortune

pad (toad) in the straw, a hidden danger

paeans, a reference to Harvey's *Ephemeron, sive Paean* (1583)

paederastice, pederasty

pageants, tricks

pageyond, pageant

painful, diligent, laborious (poet, warrior, etc.)

painim, paynim

paint out, depict in words

painted, beautified with their presence; variegated and adorned; painted cloth, picture

painty, paint, feign

paisant, peasant

paised, peised, weighed

paladines, paladins, legendary heroes

palaice, palace

palatine tower, i.e. of a royal palace

pale, hang his head on a, shed his antlers on the rail fence

paled, fenced

palettes, pates, heads

palice, palace

pall, robe, vestment

palmastrers, palmisters

palm-play, a game resembling tennis played with the palms of the hands

paltery, paltry

pamflet, pamphlet, book; little book of poems

pane, holy-crossed, garment with criss-crossed strips cut out for ornamental purposes

paned, (satin) with other material inserted between its stripes

panion, companion, fellow

pantaloon, foolish old man (in Italian drama)

panter, household officer in charge of the pantry

panticle, pantocle, pantofle, a slipper; stand on one's pantuffles, show pride

paper-clothed post, post on which publishers' advertisements were pasted

paradventure, peradventure, perhaps

paragon, equal; mate; by paragon, by comparison

paramour, sweetheart

paravant, preeminently

paraventure: peradventure, perhaps

parceived, perceived

parcel, small piece (of verse); nothing parcel, no part

parchmenteers, sellers of parchment

parde(e), pardie, pardy, by God!, verily

parel, peril

parfectly, perfectly

parfit, perfect

parget, plaster spread on a wall

parhaps, perhaps

parings, scrapings, refuse (of language)

Parlament, Parliament

parle, talk

parley, speech

parol(e), word of mouth; parol wills, i.e. oral, not written

paronomasia, word-play

parsever, persevere

parsneps, parsnips

parson, his own, i.e. person; pinched him on the parson's side, ?prevented him from having his wedding

parsonage, personage

part, melody (of a song); party, side; region of a country; for the most part, sometimes (Latin *nonnunquam*); set in parts, compose part songs

parted alone, i.e. departed; parted out of, left; the fray parted, i.e. being broken up

parten, share

parteners, partners

particular, for my own, for my own part; it is my own particular, i.e. my concern or business

partizans, long-handled spears

partlet strips, a sort of collar or ruff

partrich, partridge

party, part, side; region

pasquil, lampoon

pass, surpass; pass all, excel; pass for, care, have regard for; pass in, excel; pass little, care little; pass not, care not; make no attempt to judge; pass upon, care for; pass well, be well received

passage, passadge, exchange of blows; movings or turnings (in a dance); passages to be kept, i.e. crossings to be guarded

passen, surpass

passenger, passinger, passerby; vessel carrying passengers; walker

passing hap, ?excessive prosperity

passinger: see passenger

passion, love poem; impassioned speech; painful disorder (of drunkenness)

passionate, v., mourn; adj., passionate kindness, lover's affection

passport, voucher; permit (for paupers to proceed to a certain place)

passportless, unprovided with a permit to travel

pastery, place where pastry is made

pastor, shepherd

patch, ill, ?poor piece of ground

path in heaven, the Milky Way

pathetical, pathetic

pathologies, ?diseases, love-sicknesses

paunched, stabbed in the paunch

paunchis, paunches

pautner, wallet

pavilion, tent

pavine, pavan, a dance

pawnce, pansy

pay them home, give them their deserts; to my pay, to my satisfaction

paylet, pallet, straw-stuffed bed

peak, pointed beard

peal-meal, pell-mell

pearl of Greece, Alexander the Great

pease, n., pea; v., become still; peasing, peizing, weighing

pease-porredge ordinary, a cheap pea-soup meal

peason, peas

peat, girl

peccant, unhealthy

peck, foolish, ?foolish contemptible creature

peculiar, adj., one's own; n., peculiarity; one's own property

pedanteria, pedantic knowledge

pedegree, pedigree

pedlary, peddlers' wares

peebles, pebbles

peeced pineons, i.e. patched feathers

peevish, pievish, foolish, silly

peevishness, folly

peinct(ing), paint(ing)

peize, press downwards by its weight

pelf, property, goods; wealth, well-being

pelts, garments made of skins

penates, household gods of Rome

pencil, artist's paint brush

penny chick, ?worthless little chicken

penny-fathers, misers

penny-knaves, low readers who buy only the cheapest publications

pennyrial, pennyroyal

pensife, pensiful, pensive

people, gliding, i.e. fish

percase, perchance

percel, parcel; part

perceley, parsley

perch, turn him over the, "do for him"

percial, pershal, partial, prejudiced

perdee, perdie, perdy, by God!, verily

perdurable, lasting

perfet, perfit, adj., v., perfect

perfitness, perfectness

perforce, forcibly; in spite of

perfourm, perform

periods, sentences

peripatetical path, in the nature of a formal or strutting walk

perk'd, decked

perled, pearled, dew-besprinkled

perler, parlor

perling, forming pearl-like drops

pernitious, pernicious

perplexity, smothering, i.e. oppression

perse, pierce

persever, persevere

pershal, partial

personage, (child's) body; parsonage

persuaded with him, i.e. pleaded

persue, pursue

persward, persuade

pertaker, partaker

perticipate, participate

perticular, perticuler, particular

pertinacy, pertinacity

pertition, partition, division

pervial, easily seen through

pery, gust of wind

pestered, ships being, i.e. busied in various tasks

pet, take the, be offended

petegree, petigree, pedigree

pettifogger, rascal, pretender

pettilashery, petty larceny

petty, little schoolboy

pewled, puled, whined

phancy, fancy

phane, fane

phantastical(ly), fantastical(ly)

phantasy: see fantasy

phere, mate, fellow, equal

phillop, fillip, smart blow

phisicion, phisition, physician

phisnamy, phisnomy, physnamy, physnomy, physiognomy; general appearance

phrases, idioms

phrenzy, frenzy

phylarch, head-bailiff

physitians, physicians; men who cure moral or political ills

physnamy, physnomy: see phisnamy

pick out, trick out, adorn

picked, adj., ornate; picked staff, i.e. having a sharp point

picker-devant, picke-devant, short pointed beard

picking, keep him from, i.e. from stealing

pickthank, flatterer, sycophant

picture of marble, sculptured figure

pie, collection of rules made in the pre-Reformation church; magpie

piece, such a, i.e. woman; wine in the piece, i.e., in the cask

pievish, peevish

pight, pitched, placed

pike, n., rock; v., pick

pilch, outer garment of skin dressed with the hair

pile, metal arrowhead

pilements, piled heaps (of stone)

pilfries, pilferies, plagiarisms

pill, pillage, plunder

pillar-bearers, bearers of portable pillars as ensigns of dignity or office

pill'd, bald; miserable (luck); threadbare

piller, pillar

pillion, cap or hat

pinch you of, stint you of; pinched by the heel, caught

pine, n., suffering, punishment; v., die; pined ghost, tormented spirit

pineon, pinion

pinnes(s), pinnace

pipes of men, i.e. voices

piracies, ?despoilers

pirrie, squall, blast of wind

pismere, pismire, ant

pistle, epistle

pistrinum, a mill used as a place in which to punish slaves

piteous law, i.e. merciful

pitious(ly), piteous(ly)

pitteling, piddling, trifling

pituously, piteously

place, *sometimes* = house, palace; **come in place**, i.e. into the royal presence; **places of Homer**, i.e. passages in his book; **places of logic**, i.e. topics or subjects (Latin *loci*)

placebo, *sing*, act the sycophant

plagards, placards, licenses

plage, plague

plaice, a fish

plaice-mouthed, having a small, puckered mouth

plain, complain; **my goddess plain**, i.e. absolutely

plain-song, simple melody or theme

plaister, plaster

planchers, wooden planks

plane, footed like a, i.e. like a plane tree

planet-like, (music) of the spheres

plangors, piercing lamentations

plashed, splashed

plat, *n.*, locality; *n., v.*, outline, plan; plot

platform, plot, device; **platforming**, outlining, sketching

play, sexual intercourse; **play in the veins**, ?misprint for plag(u)e

playferes, playmates, companions

plea, action at law

plead, *n.*, plea, discussion

pleaders, advocates in a law-court

pleasa(u)nce, pleasor, delight, pleasure

plenarly, fully

plight, pleat; **in plight**, in a condition to

pluck, pull (the pot); **pluck down**, bring down, ruin; **pluck down a side**, pull down the score on one side; **hold plucking on**, endure the strain of pulling (a shoe) on

plumps, bands, companies

pluralities, (holding) more than one church benefice at a time

pocks, pox, syphilis

poesie, poesy, poem; motto; posy, flower

poet laureate, eminent poet; a title conferred by certain universities

point, poinct, *n.*, lace attaching the hose to the doublet; *v.*, appoint

pointel, stylus, pencil

point-trussers, pages who tied their masters' points or laces

poise of his body, i.e. weight; **poise of lead**, heavy substance, weight; **poised**, weighed

poke full, bag full

pole, mounting, support for climbing plants

pole-foot, *error for* polt-foot (*q.v.*)

pole-head, tadpole (*fig.*)

policy, device; statecraft

politic, politique, *n.*, politician

poll, clip, plunder

pollax, pole-ax

polt-foot, poult-foot, clubfoot; **blacksmith with a polt-foot**, Vulcan

polymechany, multifarious contrivance or invention

polypus, fabulous fish that changes colors

pommice, pumice

ponderous, weighty, important

pooffed, puffed

poor surety, security in poverty

popilous, populace

popinjay, parrot

porch of the signors, i.e. hall of justice

porpentine, porcupine

porperous, porpoise

porphirius, fabulous serpent with poison but no teeth

porredge, porridge

port, deportment; gate; style of living

portch, porch

portliness, stateliness

portly pace, dignified walk

portrait, portraict, *v.*, portray

port-sale, public sale to the highest bidder

pose, *n.*, posy (*q.v.*); **had the pose**, i.e. catarrh

positions, dogmas

possible, *adv.*, possibly

post, courier with messages; **(in) post**, in haste; **paper-clothed posts**, advertising posts bearing printed titlepages or broadsides

posy, ?flower of rhetoric; motto in verse; motto or proverb

potgoons, potguns, mortars

pottle, liquid measure equal to two quarts

pottle-pitcher, pitcher holding about two quarts

poult-foot: *see* polt-foot

pounced, all, perforated for ornament

pound, place of confinement; **pounded**, put in the pound for strayed cattle

pourpose, purpose

pourtray, portray

pover, poor

powers, the olive, i.e. pours, emits oil

poynado, poniard

practic, deception, trick

practique, practic, a practical man

practisie, practise, action

pranis, prawns

prank (out), dress up; **prank up**, make ostentatious show

praty, pretty

praxis, action

preace, *v.*, praise; press; *n.*, **be evermore in preace**, i.e. in praise; **in preace**, (put) to exercise or in practise; **put in preace**, set forth for competition

preach at Tyburn Cross, make a speech of repentance before being hanged

prease, prece, prese, *n., v.*, press, throng; **in prece**, in a press or throng

precedent, matter, i.e. preceding

precious faces, i.e. showing effects of drinking

precisian, puritan; purist

predication, preaching

preeving, proving

prefar, prefer

prefixed, fixed (star); set in advance

pregnance, abundance; imaginative power

preheminence, preeminence

preife, trial

prejudice, *n.*, injury, harm; *v.*, **prejudice my life**, i.e. endanger it

premeditate mind, i.e. a deliberate

preminence, preeminence, merit

premunires, serious crimes

preoccupate, anticipate

preparement, preparation

prepense, consider beforehand

prepose, prefix

prepotent, preeminently powerful

prerogatife, prerogative

prescript, *n.*, decree, order; *ppl. adj.*, prescribed

prese: *see* prease

presently, now, at once; personally, on the spot

president, precedent, guide

preson, prison

prest, alert, brisk; ready, eager

presumptious, presumptuous

pretely, prettily

pretence, claim to authority

pretend to commend, i.e. attempt to; **pretended mischief**, i.e. intended

pretermit, omit, fail to make

prethee, prithee, (I) pray thee

pretious, precious

pretty space or while, moderate length of time; **pretty way off**, at a considerable distance

prevent, *often* = forestall, anticipate

previly, privily

preving ill, ill proving, a bad end

prevy, privy, secret

prey a daw, ?catch a silly bird (*or perhaps* prove, make trial of)

price, esteem, estimation; value; **at a higher price**, of greater worth or value; **in price**, be esteemed

pricisianists, hidebound purists

prick, *n.*, hairpin; object, end; **prick and price**, success and its acknowledgment; *v.*, spur; write music with pricks, dots, etc.

prick-me-dainty, woman dressed in a finical manner

prickposts, posts placed between the principal corner-posts

pride, *v.*, make proud; *n.*, **foul pride**, sexual desire, "heat"

prime, primetide, the spring

princes, many, i.e. princesses

principal for a princess, i.e. are princely for; **principals**, rafters, posts; the two principal feathers in each wing

princox, saucy boy

prison the water, i.e. grasp it (French *empoigner*)

prison-base, a country game

pritch-awl, shoemaker's awl

prithee, (I) pray thee

private, in his, i.e. private affairs

privateness, referring to attacks on private individuals

priviledge, privilege

privity, my, my participation in the knowledge of

privy, sweet, i.e. privet

prize, playing a, engaging in a fencing match

proaching, approaching

proceed, get a degree

procurator, official agent; procurator general, agent-general

procurer, pander

product, *v.*, bring forward, produce; prolong (your days)

profe, proof

profection, proficiency

proferred with foot, i.e. put forth, advanced

professor, one who makes a profession of a craft or trade

profet, profit

proficience, advance, improvement

progeny, ancestors; **issue of a high progeny,** the descendant of noble ancestors

prollers, prowlers, cheaters

prolocutor, spokesman

promess, promise

pronostication, prognostication

proof, comforted by his, i.e. his experience

proparty, property

proper, admirable; fine; lusty; one's own: pretty, handsome

property, **be of the,** i.e. of the nature; **property of a patron,** i.e. his characteristics

prophane, profane

propise, propitious, advantageous

proportion, *n.,* metrical rhythm or harmony; *v.,* **proportion thee,** compare thee proportionately

proportionable, corresponding

propounded, *intrans. v.,* made a proposal

propriety, peculiarity (of your person); property, characteristics

prorogued, prolonged

prosecution, some, i.e. development

prosopopeia, personification

prospective, point of view

prosternating, prostrating

proud-pied, splendidly variegated

provant, provisions for troops

prove, *n.,* proof, outcome; *v.,* make trial of; put to the test

provenzal, ?provincial

provest, provost, head of a religious chapter

provoked London, i.e. incited, caused

provulgation, publication

prowess, character

proyning, pruning

public weal, commonwealth

publish, bring into public notice; show (their faces)

puddled, miry, foul (pit)

pui'nee, puisne, underling

puissance, armed forces; strength

pulcritude, beauty

pull on, induce

pullen, poultry

pullet, tyro, beginner (*fig.*)

pultesses, poultices

puny, novice

punyete, pungent

puppet, person whose acts are controlled by another

puppetry, a dress as of a puppet

purchase, *n.,* booty, plunder; *v.,* acquire wealth; procure

pure, *n.,* purity

purl'd, embroidered, edged

purpensed, premeditated

purpose, *n.,* conversation; **as to purpose,** i.e. as in talking

pursenet, bag-shaped net

pursevants, pursuivants, state messengers

pursy, fat

purtraiture, portraiture

purtrat, portrait, picture

purveyor, steward, manager

puscul, pustule, pimple

put him by it, refuse it to him

put-pin, game of push-pin

puttock, kite

puwyt, pewit, lapwing

pyramis, pyramid

pyx, vessel in which the Host of the Sacrament is kept

qu, set a, i.e. a cue, a half-farthing (= slightly esteem)

quadrant pavilion, pavilion of a square form

quail, destroy, kill; fade away; quell

quaint gown, i.e. beautiful

quake, *n.,* quack

qualified, accomplished, perfect

qualifier of kings, i.e. controller, injurious affecter

quality, accomplishment; character; profession, trade; profession of acting

quantity, size or weight; length or shortness of syllables

quarl, quarrel, crossbow arrow; provocation; reason (for marrying)

quarrel, *n.,* cause, reason, pretext

quarrelous, querulous

quartan, recurrent (every fourth day)

quartermaister, assistant ruler

quarter-sermon, quarterly sermon

quarterzains, quatorzains, sonnets

quat, surfeit

quaving, quivering

quean, whore

queasy, nauseating

queatch, quetch, (dare not) utter a sound, i.e. show complete submission to

queate, quiet

queere, choir

queimishly, squeamishly

queint, strange (Bellona)

queintly, quaintly

quell, kill

quere, choir

querestrer, querister, chorister

quest, inquest, inquiry

quick, alive; the living; **some quick,** some living thing

quickness of sentence, freshness of thought

quickset, screened, fenced

quid, quiddity, quibble

quidams, somebodies, certain persons

quiddity, subtlety, quibble

quiere, quire, choir

quietus, receipt

quight, quite

quillities, quillets, quibbles

quinch, flinch

quip pride, i.e. use sarcastic remarks about

quire, choir

quirister, chorister

quit, *v.,* acquit; repay; requite

quite, *v.,* quit, release; requite

quittanced, paid, remitted

quod, quoth

quoke, quaked, shook

quotidian, of daily recurrence

rabbet, rabbit; woman

rabbins, rabbis

rabet, slot or groove

raca, racha, vain fellow (Biblical)

race, *v.,* raze; **race out,** obliterate; *n.,* feed **his race,** i.e. his family

racha: see raca

rack, *n.,* floating vapor; cloud; *v.,* **rack the Scriptures,** i.e. give a forced interpreta-

tion to; **rack rents,** raise rent inordinately; **rack treasure,** i.e. extort; **racking,** *adj.,* extortionate (steward); *n.,* extortion

rac't, rooted out. *See* race

rad, read

radel, raddle, slender post

rage, poetic inspiration

raght, raught, reached

raine, *n.,* reign; rule, dominion

raint, ?be rent or torn out

raisins, rasens, rasing-pieces (of a house)

raison(ably), reason(ably)

rakehell, *adj.,* dissolute; *n.,* scoundrel

ramage, untamed

ramp, bold, vulgar girl; **ramping girls,** girls who act loosely

rampier, ramper, rampart; **rampiered,** barricaded

ranck riches, i.e. abundant

randon, random

ranger, rake, libertine

rank, (rife and) numerous

rankled, fretted (in anger)

ransick, ransack

rap'd, fury, i.e. overpowered

rape, Greekish, i.e. Helen of Troy

rapting, enrapturing (tunes)

rascal, young deer

rase, erase; raze

rasens: *see* raisins

rash view, rapid glance

rasher, thin slice

rashly, hastily; rapidly

rated, scolded

rathe, *adj.,* early; *adv.,* swiftly; **the rather,** all the sooner

raught, reached; snatched; **raught to him,** taken in hand

ravin, voracity, gluttony

ravine, ravin, rapine

ravinous, ravenous

ray, (battle) array

raze, erase, destroy

reach a sigh, i.e. heave

reacquite, requite

read, declare, tell; see, discover; deem

reader, lecturer; lecturer on law; reader in court; **reader stranger,** foreign reader

ready, make oneself, dress

reaport, reapport, report

reapose, reappose, repose, place

rear, *adj.,* underdone (eggs); *v.,* raise or start a war; **teared ridge,** high coping of a roof

rearward, rearguard

reason, *n.,* discourse, speech; *v.,* debate, argue; talk, discourse

reasonings, discussions, talks

reasty, rancid

reave, deprive, take away

reaver, robber

rebated, abated; driven back

rebato, stiff collar

rebel, for my, i.e. rebellion

rebending, bending, hanging

reboke, belch

receit, receipt, the act of receiving; recipe; comprehensiveness; remedy

rechate, recheat, blow a series of notes on a horn to call the hounds together

rechless, heedless

reck, care; reckon, add

recken(ing), reckon(ing)

reckon, count

recoil, retire (to rest)

recomfort, comfort

recompt, recount

recongnies, recognize

record, *often* = sing

recorders, birds' throats

recovered her lodging, or the isle, i.e. reached

recueled, recueiled, gathered together

recuperable, recoverable

recure, cure; recover

red, *v.*, read, perceive; *adj.*, red ones, gold coins

redargution, reproof

rede, *n.*, advice; *v.*, consider

redges, ridges

redoubted, dreaded, feared; redoubted mistress, i.e. respected

redouned, reechoed

redress, relieve

reduce, bring (back); expressed (in English); lead, direct; take back; reduce from error, i.e. lead away from

reed, reede, precept; this reede is ryfe, this precept is common

reek, be exhaled; reeking, vaporous

refection, water of, "baptism of regeneration"

refel, refell, refute

reflayre, reflair, odor

reflex, reflection

reformed kingdom, i.e. Protestant; reformed versifying, writing in quantitative verse

refreshing, *n.*, refreshment

reft, bereft; deprived of

regal, *n.*, (a block of wood in a) slot, groove

regality, sovereign rule

regardful, worthy of regard

regiment, control; education; government

region cloud, cloud of the upper air

register, record; in register, on record

regius, fabulous snake

regreet, return of the greeting (in the line preceding)

rehearsal, recital

rehearse, declare, repeat; read aloud; utter, tell

reign, empire

rein, kidney

reined, guided

reise, raise

reject, *pa. part.*, rejected

rejoice, *n.*, rejoicing, joy

reke, ne, (I) reck not

relapse, recovers by, i.e. by failure to meet a claim on time

relent, abate; relinquish, give up; show pity

religious, *n.*, person(s) bound by monastic vows

remain of Troy, the, i.e. remnant

remainder, *adj.*, remaining; *n.*, the right to succeed to the title

remembered before, mentioned earlier

remeve, remove

reminant, remnant

remorse, *n.*, pity, mercy; *v.*, show pity

ren, renne, run

rence, rinse

render, surrender (thee)

reneging, renouncing

renne: *see* ren

renome, renoum, renowm, renoun, renown

rent, *n.*, tribute, tax; *v.*, pay the tribute or price; rend; mangle

renying, renaying, abjuring

repairs a crown, i.e. ornaments it

repast, *v.*, refresh with food

repaste, repast

repeater, trainer (of a choir)

repent, fond, foolish repentance

report, fame

reprisal, *v.*, make reprisal, loot

reproachfully condemn, i.e. in a shameful way

reputacion, reputation

require, request, ask; require you no word, beg you not to mention a word

reredos, plate at the back of a fireplace

res'due: *see* residue

resemblant, similar

reserved, preserved; with the exception of

residence, sediment (in blood)

residency in service, i.e. continuance

residue, res'due, the remainder; the common herd

resine, resign

resistence, resistance

resolute, absolute, final; constant

resolve, consider; dissolve into; explain

resorted, his house was, i.e. frequented

respect, heed not (faults); take into account

respective, respectful

respiring, taking a rest from

resplendant, resplendishant, resplendent

rest, desist, cease; rest upon her, rest herself upon; to set this rest, to be determined on

restore, *n.*, restoration

resumed, *pa. part.*, taken back

retailer, small dealer or trader

retch, reach

retchless, reckless

rethorical, rhetorical

rethorician, rhetorician

rethorick, rhetoric

rethrogard, retrograde

retire, *n.*, retirement

retorn, return

retorting snakes, i.e. twisting, writhing

retourn, return

retractation, retraction

retrait, retreat

returnable, deceit is, i.e. capable of being returned

reverend, *n.*, reverence

reverent, reverend

reverture, return

revested, reclothed

revie, on, outgo

revive, *n.*, revival, resurrection

revoke, recall; revoked home, called back home

revoluting, revolving

revolved, authors, i.e. (read and) studied

rew, rue; row; in rew, successively

rewalting, throwing down

rhabarbarum, rhubarb root

rhetoric, skill in using persuasive language

rhythm, rime; rhythm royal, rime royal (stanza)

rhythmers, rimers

rhythming, riming

rial, royal

ribaud, ribald; foul ribaud, wicked ribald man

ribaudry, ribawdry, ribaldry

ribbind, riband, ribbon

ribibe, abusive term for an old woman

ribskin, leather apron worn while ribbing flax

riches, *occasionally a singular noun*

rid them, kill them

riding rime, heroic couplet

rife, abundant; common; most rifest, most readily

riflest with gold, gamble, play at dice

right, justly entitled to the name of (comedy, poet, etc.)

rightuous, righteous

rightwesnes, righteousness

rime, *often* = rhythm

rine, rind

ring, run at, a sport in which a rider tries to carry off suspended rings on the point of his lance

ringled, ringed (bit)

riotize, *n.*, riotous living

ripe, marriageable (daughters)

rise up, he, i.e. rose

rising, next a body's, i.e. immediately after getting out of bed

rive, split

rivel'd, shriveled

riverets, small rivers or streams; the veins

rivolets, rivulets

roach, roch, fish of the carp family

road, foray, raid; roadstead (for ships)

roamed in bed, i.e. tossed, turned

roast, rule the, have full authority

robble hobble: *see* rounce

roch: *see* roach

rochet, red gurnand (a kind of fish)

rochette, rochet, bishop's vestment

rock, distaff

rockat, a fabulous weed that breeds inconstancy

rocket, the fish rochet; a sort of garment

roiling, rolling

roisters, roisterers, bullies

roisting, roistering, boisterous

rondlet, rondelet, short rondeau

rood, cross

room, place, office

roomaging, rummaging, arranging goods in the hold of a ship

rope in, seize

roset gray, russet gray

rote, *v.*, rot

rough-heawen, rough-hewn

rounce robble hobble, words attempting to represent the sound of thunder

round, *adj.*, direct (flying); *n.*, dance; this round, the earth; *v.*, round in, whisper in (the ear). *See* rowned

roundelays, short songs with refrains

roused water, i.e. disturbed, stirred up

rousted, roosted

rout, *n.*, band, crowd; species of wild goose; *v.*, snore

row, in (on), in turn or order

rowen, second crop of hay

rowers, workmen who put a nap on cloth

rowme, room

rowned, whispered. *See* round

royals, gold coins

ruc, roc, a fabulous bird

ruck, *v.*, crouch, huddle together

rud, red, ruddiness

rudded, made ruddy

ruddock, the redbreast; gold coin

rude, brutal; rough; inexperienced

rue from prosperity, i.e. fall, decline

ruff, rough

ruffeled: *see* ruffle

ruffinous, ruffianly

ruffle, ruffel, *n.*, riotous disturbance; *v.*, swagger; ruffling, ruffeling, bearing themselves arrogantly; forming ruffles; ruffeled out, swaggered

ruggy, wild, stormy

rule over, decide

runagate, runnagate, vagabond; apostate

runnet, rennet, kind of French dessert apple

running copy, rapidly made copy

rusten, rust

ruth, pity; lamentation

rutter, cavalry soldier

rutty, full of ruts

ryfe, rife, abundant, common

rym ram ruff, nonsense-words from Chaucer's Parson, indicating the craze for alliteration

rythme, rhythm

rythming, riming

Sabaoth, Sabboth, Sabbath

saciety, satiety

sacraligious, sacrilegious

sacriledge, sacrilege

sacriligiously, sacrilegiously

sad, serious; sober, grave

safeguard, protector, covering; safety

saffron bag, bag in which saffron is kept

sailer, sailor; good sailer, i.e. sailing vessel

sain, say; said

sainct, saint, *often* = lover, sweetheart, mistress

saintish, saintlike

sainty, saint

saker, cannon; large lanner falcon

salf, safe

sallet, salad

sallows, willow-like shrubs

salt, saltcellar; sit above the salt, i.e. at the upper part of the table among the honored guests

saluted, sorrow to be, i.e. salved, healed

salvage, *adj.*, savage

salve, *v.*, atone for; save

samples, by, by examples

sandal, sendal, thin silken material

sanguine, ?sanguine "complexion"; moistest sanguine, i.e. temperament or "complexion"

sans, without (French)

sapphic verse, meter used by and named after Sappho

sarcasmus, sarcastic

sardenian, sardonian, sardonic

sate, sat

satiricques, satirists

satirism, satire

satten, satin

sauce, have eaten, be abusive

saucing bell, saunce or sanctus bell, rung at the Sanctus in the Mass

savecundites, safe-conducts

savely, safely

saverly, savorly, effectively

savety, safety

sav'riness, savoriness, having savor

saw, *n.*, line, saying; (powerful) command

sayne, say; said

scalp, skull

scan verse, i.e. criticize, estimate the value of

scandalize thee, bring shame or discredit on thee

scantly, centered, i.e. barely, scarcely

scape, *n.*, error; *n.*, *v.*, escape

scasely, scarcely

scath, scathe, damage

scedule, letter; schedule; document; scroll containing writing

schema, scheme, figure

scheme, rhetorical device of deviating from the ordinary use and arrangement of words for effectiveness or beauty

schol(l)er, scholar, pupil

school, after my, i.e. my instruction

schooler, scholar, pupil

schoolery, education

schoolmen, medieval philosophers

science, knowledge in general; trade or profession

scilence, silence

scituate, situated

scituation, situation

sclander, slander

sclender, slender

scol(l)er, scholar, pupil

scolopidus, fabulous fish whose color changes with the moon

sconce, head

score, on, on the scores, (debt) recorded by tally or marks; run on the score, incur debts

scorns, wrought with, i.e. with insults

scorser, jobber dealing in horses

scortch, scorched, parched by the sun

scot, payment for entertainment

scout her, mock at her

scratting, scratching

scrattop, *term of abuse*

scrawling, spreading the limbs abroad in a sprawling manner

scriech'd, screeched

scrip, small bag or satchel

scripture, writing (in diamond letters)

scritch-owl, screech-owl

scroul, scroll

scrupule, scruple

scruzed, squeezed

scuppets, shovels

scurrile, scurrilous

scuse, excuse

sdeign(ful), disdain(ful)

sea-agget, sea-agate, an agate with green wave-like markings (?)

sea-beat, tossed about by the waves

sea-gaols, sea-jails

seals of religion, marks of Christianity like baptism and the sign of the cross

seamew, gull

search of nature, ?searching effect of

sea-room, space at sea in which a ship can be maneuvered

season, time, period; season the world, i.e. seisen, seize upon; seasoned deer, deer habituated to a place

seat, her ancient, their native place

second intentions, the *intentio secunda* of logic

secretary, confidant; disciple

sect, class or kind of persons; division, group

secular, layman

secure of, free from apprehension of

sedean, subdean

seducer, one who tempts another to desert his allegiance

seek, all to, without the skill (of); be to seek, be lacking, deficient; to seek of, without, lacking

seely, sely, siely, hapless, innocent. *See* silly

seem'd her, beseemed her

seeming, *adj.*, seemly; *n.*, judgment

seen, see; seen in, experienced in; be seen unto thee, seem good or proper to you

seethe, boil

segn(i)ority, seniority; rank

seized of the throne, i.e. in possession of

seld, seldom

self, *adj.*, same

sely: *see* seely

semblable, similar

semblably, similarly

semblant, made, pretended

sem'briefs, notes of music

sembstantial, substantial

semovedly, ?separately, individually

senary, senarius, iambic trimeter

sence, *conj.*, since; *v.*, cense, offer incense to

sendal, sandal, thin silken material

sennet, sennight, a week

senows, sinews

sens, since

sensative, sensitive

sense, creatures wanting, inanimate things

sensible, perceptible by the senses

sensitife, sensitive

sensuality, the lower nature as opposed to reason

sented, well, having keen perception

sentence, aphorism, saying; thought, meaning

sentuary, sanctuary

separate, *pa. part.*, separated

seperate, separate

sepulture, sepulcher

sequel, subsequent events (in life and work)

sequence, lose his, i.e. letters, prose epistles

sequent, successive

sequestration, diversion of the income of a benefice to the advantage of the creditors of the incumbent

sergeant, police officer

servant, lover

set, *n.*, setting, end; *v.*, set by, esteem

settel, settle

setter-on, inciter, instigator

setter-up, backer, employer

seventeen, a shift of (unexplained phrase)

several, *adj.*, separate, distinct; each in its (or her) place; *n.*, private plot of land

severally, separately; variously

severe books, i.e. serious

sew, act as a sewer or waiter; sue, follow (the chase)

sewers, attendants supervising the arrangement of the table, etc.

sextile month, the old sixth month, August

shackeled, shackled

shader, shadier

shadow, *n.*, reflection; portrait, picture; symbol, image; shadow . . . shadow, intimate friend . . . pretext; *v.*, hide; shadowed works, i.e. heretical books

shagged, jagged

shaked, shook

shalm: *see* shawm

shamefast(ness), bashful(ness), modest(y)

shap, shape, pudendum

sharp life, i.e. rough, hard

shave to the quick, strip, plunder

shawm, shalm, hautboy or "waits"

she, *n.*, girl, woman

sheapherd, shepherd

shear, *n.*, a pair of shears

shed, be shed, dispersed; **sheddeth in the sky**, i.e. pours out

sheeding, shedding

sheene, bright, beautiful

sheepherd, shepherd

sheer shaking nought, sheer worthless

shelf, submerged ledge of rocks

shells, money (*slang*)

shend, *n.*, disgrace; *v.*, destroy; surpass; **shent**, harmed

shepheard, shephierd, shepherd

shevered, shivered, broken

shew, show; theatrical performance; **bearing shew**, having the appearance

shewers, sewers (*q.v.*)

shidered, splintered

shield, God, God forbid

shift, *v.*, live by fraud; shed (skins); **shift oneself**, change clothes

shifters, tricksters

shild, shield

shiller, more resonant

shilt'reth, sheltereth

shipboard, side of the ship

shipwrack, shipwreck, ruin; **shipwrack treasure**, treasure from wrecked ships

shiriff, sheriff

shit, shut

shivered out, split into

shoe-clout, shoe-cloth

shold, should

shone, shoon, shoes

shoot, levels his, i.e. aims his shot

shortly shrank, i.e. quickly, speedily

shoveler, shovelard, spoonbill

shower, that sharp, i.e. the pangs or throes (of death)

shrew, wicked man

shrewd array, evil situation

shrewdly bruised, i.e. severely

shriching, shritching, shrieking

shricked, shrieked

schriech, screech (owl)

shrift, confession

shright, shrieked

shrike, shriek

shrined up, enclosed

shrives, sheriffs

shronk, shrunk

shrood, shroud, shrowd, cover; enclose; hide; shelter; **shrowds, shrouds**, a ship's ropes; **golden shrouds**, i.e. hair, tresses

shrugging, ?chilling (air)

shuffeled, shuffled, jumbled together

sib, akin, related

sich, such

sicker, assured; certain; surely

side, his hood was, i.e. long

side-cloak, wide cloak

sidelings, edgeways

side-paned, striped with colored cloth

sidings, instances of taking sides

siedge, siege

siege, abundant, big bowel movement

siely: *see* seely

sien, scion

sigh, lament with sighing, sigh for

sight, sighth, sithed, sighed

sign, under or through the, i.e. of the zodiac

sike, *adj.*, such; *n.*, sigh

siker, free from danger; surely

sildom, seldom

silly, hapless, innocent, simple

similitude, likeness, appearance; **by any similitude**, in all probability

simper-the-cocket, a simpering coquette

simple, *n.*, word without a prefix

simples, herbs, medicines

simplesse, simplicity

simulation, the feigning to be what one is not

sine, sign

single money, small change

singled, drawn aside or apart; **singled the deer**, i.e. separated it from the herd

singly, without more than

singular, single detail; **singular friend**, particular friend; **singular persons**, individuals

singuler(ly), singular(ly)

singults, sobs

sink, faint

sin-leapered, sin-lepered or foully infected

sinow(y), sinew(y)

sippet, a little sip

sirenize, lure down

sir-reverence (= save your reverence), with all respect for you (*used by way of apology before an unseemly expression*)

sirrop, syrup

sister son, i.e. sister's son; **youngest sister**, Atropos, the Fate; **three sisters**, the Fates

sit, behoove; *often* = sat; **sit near me**, concern me deeply; **sit with you**, befit you

sith, since

sithe, sigh; time

sithen, sithence, since

sithens, afterwards; since; since that time

sitten, sat

six and seven, carelessness about the consequences of one's actions; **at six and seven**, at loose ends

sixain, six-line stanza

sixt, *ord.*, sixth

sized, had "sizes" (scores) entered against oneself

skewed, skewbald, irregularly colored

skill, *n.*, knowledge, art; **could skill of**, had knowledge of; **without my skill**, not in my knowledge; *v.*, understand; **it skills not**, i.e. doesn't matter

skinker, tapster

skirr, fly rapidly

skom, skim

skommer, scummer, ladle for removing scum

skull, helmet

slack, *n.*, feeble verse

slacking, loosening, raising

slade, dell, valley

slake, cease; **slakid**, slaked

slaty or slider, miry or slippery

slaughter-budge, cheap lambskin fur from the slaughterhouse

slaughterdom, slaughter, massacre

slea, slee, slay

sleekstone, smooth stone used for polishing

sleeps thy death, i.e. disregards it

sleight, trick, contrivance

slice, cooking utensil

slightly, dealt, i.e. slightingly

slipper, slippery, variable; **slipper hap**, unstable fortune

slo, slay

slomber, slumber

slop, loose breeches

slot, by, by the track (of a deer)

slough, ditch, drain; skin (of a serpent)

sloughishness, sluggishness

slought, sloth, slough

slouth(ful), sloth(ful)

sluces, sluices, channels

slug, lie lazily

slup, swallow

smack, taste, tasting; **loving smack**, taste of love

smally, little

smaradges, emeralds

smart, sorrow, pain

smicker, smart

smock, sign of the, i.e. a harlot

smock-sworn, (a page) of loose conduct with women

smogue, smug, smart

smoky or smoking sighs, i.e. steaming

smoothing age, i.e. flattering

smored, smothered

smother, make straw to, i.e. smolder

smudged up, smartly dressed

snaky rod, Mercury's caduceus

snaphaunce, ready answer or argument

snapped, captured suddenly (by Ulysses)

sneveling, sniveling

snib, chide, snub

snite, snipe

snottery, filthiness

snout-fair, fair-faced, comely

snudge, skinflint

so as, so that

soak a purse, i.e. drain it dry; **soaken**, soaked dry or up; **soaking lawyer**, one who drains or exhausts his client's money

soch, such

sod, seethed, boiled

sod(d)ain, sod(d)eyn, soden, sodein, sud(d)ain, suddein, sudden

soder, solder

sol fa, solf(e), singing notes to the sol-fa syllables

solace, make, have sport

solacious, full of solace

soldierized it, served as a soldier

solemply, solemnly

solempn, solemn

solempnity, occasion of ceremony

solf(e): *see* sol fa

solicet, solicit

solicitor, agent, deputy

sollom, solemn

soly, alone

somd, pledged; (with wings) full fledged

some, one (*impersonal, often in Skelton*); **some's**, someone's

somedeal, somedele, somewhat

sommance, sommonce, summons

sommer, summer

Sonday, Sunday

sondry, sundry

sonetto, sonnet, song

song, *v.*, sung

sonned, exposed to the sun

sonnet, song, short lyric

sooly, solely

soope, sup

soot(e), fragrant, sweet; sweetly

sooth, truth

soothe his person, i.e. flatter immoderately

soothly, truly

soothsay, v., prophesy

sopheme, sophism

sophister, Sophist; specious reasoner; student of philosophy

soppy, sop

sops in wine, mottled red and white carnations

sorceries, sins, crimes

sort, n., company, set; class of people; considerable number; manner; *sometimes the plural* kinds; in sort, in a group; in such sort, in such a manner or way; v., consort, associate, with; it sorteth in suit, it happens in the end; sorted to effect, came to effect, was successful

sortable, fitting, suitable

souldered, soldered

souldiour, souldior, soldier

souls sensative, partaking of the second of the three levels of "soul" described by Aristotle

soun, sound

sound, n., swoon; v., have a tendency to; probe, examine; sing of; signify, imply; understand; swoon; sound to, have a connection with

sourded, arisen

southern, n., southern English

southest, southeast

soverai(g)n(ty), sovereign(ty)

sown, n., sound; v., swoon

sownding, sink in, penetrate as far as destruction

sowning, sounding, investigating

sowse, drench; souse, fall; swoop (like a hawk)

spair, spare, opening or slit in a woman's dress

spangs, spangles

spare: *see* spair

spatious, spacious

spattana, mythical herb

spattle, spatula

speces, spices

species, supposed emanation from outward things forming the direct object of sensual cognition

sped, am, am versed in

"speech, In": *see* In speech

speed, n., success (in love); v., succeed, prosper

speedely, speedily

spell, read; spelled his name, i.e. uttered; spelled in reproach, i.e. wrote out; need no spell, i.e. no verse used as a charm

spence, room in which liquor is stored

spercled, disheveled (hair)

spere, sphere; (Cynthia's) orbit

spertling, spirtling, being spattered

spettle, spittle

spicery, room for the keeping of spices

spick, fat meat

spight(ful), spite(ful)

spill, go to ruin; harm, ruin

spink, chaffinch

spinner's web, i.e. spider's

spire, top of a tree

spirit of the buttery, spirit of wine, drunkenness; the spirit Paracelsus kept in the pommel of his sword; spirit of minerals, mineral medicine

spiritual(i)ty, the clergy

spittle, hospital

spleenative, spleenful, of hot temper

splendant, splendent, splendidious, splendid, grand

spoil, n., destruction; v., plunder; spoil himself, commit suicide; peril of spoiling, i.e. of robbery

sprete, spright, spirit

spring, grow, bud

sprinkeling wine, i.e. sprinkling, sparkling

sprinkles up, flies up in fine drops

sprit(e), spirit

spriteless, dispirited

sprong(en), sprung

spruce beer, beer made from the leaves and small branches of the spruce fir

spunge, sponge

spurn at, scorn

squib, exploding missile; flashy fellow

squint-eyed, indirect

squire, aim with a, i.e. a square, a guiding principle

squirting actors, i.e. contemptible

squitter-books, scribblers

stablish, establish

stack, stake, funeral pyre; stack, v., stuck

staff, stanza (*plural* staves)

staffish, stubborn

staid, stayed, supported

stain, disgrace, injure; grow dim; impair the beauty of, surpass

stake: *see* stack

stale, n., decoy, lure; decoy bird; pretext; v., stole

stalk, pursue game; walk

stamp's sake, (for) the sake of the coinage

stanched, staunched

stanchless, staunchless

stand, at a, at a loss; take stand, take (like a hawk) a position of rest from flight; have stand in the way or upon, i.e. stood; stand me upon, behoove me; stand of their feet, i.e. on them; stood upon, was concerned with

standing by the year, i.e. a fixed salary

standish, inkstand

stang, pole

stanzo, stanza

star, wat'ry, i.e. the moon

staring hair, i.e. standing on end

start, n., (great) distance; v., escape; started, sprang in (or out); is start, has broken away; start up, started up

starter, one given to wandering; runaway

starve, sterve, die; kill

state, estate; individual condition; state . . . state, condition . . . greatness. *See* states

stately place, i.e. Leicester House, afterwards Essex House

states, all classes of society; estates, people of high rank; rulers. *See* state

statute merchant, a bond upon which, if unpaid, an execution could be awarded against the body or goods of the signer

staves, stanzas (*singular* staff)

stay, n., support; at a stay, at a standstill; come upon the stays, turn a ship to the

windward for tacking; in secret stay, from safe ambush; v., arrest, imprison; restrain, hold back; support

stayless, unsupported

stead, steed, n., place; use, help; in steed, (be) of help; v., profit, be of use; serve the needs of, help; nothing steed, be of no stead or avail

steal to see, come insensibly to see; stealing, (fables) acting secretly

steaming, flaming, glowing (eyes); ?rising, ascending (mountain)

steed: *see* stead

'steem, esteem

steep, laid in, put to soak; steep his face, i.e. plunge it into water

stench, steinch, staunch

stent, n., stint, stop, pause; v., cease

ster, star

stercory, excrement

sterry, starry

stert, started

sterve: *see* starve

stews, brothels

sticked, stuck, stabbed

stickled, quelled

stickler, manager; umpire

stiff sound, i.e. loud

stiffly, behave, i.e. stubbornly

still, adv., always, continually; n., distilling glass; down still, v., distil or trickle down

stilly, still

stilts, corked, high shoes, boots

stinged, stung

stint, cease

stir, n., fuss, commotion; v., impel

stith, anvil

stoaps, stoups

stock, hose, stocking; stock and stock, posts

stockado, a thrust

stocked, punished in the stocks

stock-father, progenitor of a race

stode, stood

stoin, amazed, astonished

stomach, stomack, courage, pride; in, of stomach, in pride

stond, n., impediment; v., stand

stone, testicle; the stone, i.e. in the kidneys; ston'd horse, stallion

stong, stung

stood upon, was concerned with

stoop me, humiliate or subdue me; stoop her veil, i.e. lower it

stopple, stopper, cap

store, abundance; breeding animals, livestock; provision, food; sufficient quantity

story, history

stound, loud noise; moment, time; time of trial and fear

stoung, stung

stour, stowre, affliction; cloud of spray; combat, battle; moment, occasion

stout, adv., stubbornly

stowre: *see* stour

strack, struck

straggeler, straggler, vagabond; strumpet (Helen of Troy)

straight, adj., *often* = strait, narrow; strict; n., strait, narrow passage of water

strain, n., sort, kind; v., restrain, confine; constrain; strained ghost, constrained spirit

strait, adj., adv., straight; narrow(ly),

crowded; *n.*, narrow, confined place (in a forest); ravine, gorge

straitly, narrowly, closely

strake, struck

strange, foreign (princes); **make it strange**, hold it (love) at a distance

stranger, foreigner

strangy, strange

strappado, a form of punishment or torture

stratagemical, strategical

strave, strove

straw, strew

strawry, ?as if newly come from straw

streict, streight, straight; strait

streightways, straightway

streken, stricken

strenght, strength

stricken, advanced (in age)

strict embraces, i.e. tight, close

striked out, stretched out

striken, struck, stricken

stripe, beat, whip

strok, stroke, stroken, struck; furled; **bear a stroke**, play a part

strompet, strumpet

strond, strand; **Latin stronds**, a reference to the strands of Gaeta in Latium

stroock, strook(en), struck; stricken

strow, strew; **strowed**, strown, strewn

stroyed, destroyed

struggeling, struggling

stub, stump of a tree

stubbed, short and thick

stubbernness, stubbornness

stud, stock, stem

studient, student

stuff, (misshapen) persons; subject-matter

stungen, stung

stur, *n.*, stir, commotion; *v.*, stir

sturgion, sturgeon

stut, stutter

style, princely, royal title

'suage, assuage, lessen

subjective duty, i.e. submissive

submiss, submissive; low (voice)

subscribe to me, i.e. submit

substance of the people, i.e. the majority

subtil, subtle

subtil(i)ty, subtlety; ingenious contrivance

subtilly, subtly, cleverly

subtle sand, i.e. finely powdered; **subtle water**, i.e. rarefied

subvert the towns, i.e. raze them to the ground

success, result; sequel

sucklings, youthful sons

sud(d)ain, suddein, sudden

sue, follow

sufferance, forbearance

suffrages, prayers

suffraine, sovereign

sugared meats, delicious food

suggest me, tempt me

suit, puts in, takes legal action against; **of all suits**, of all sorts

suited, dressed (himself)

sulking, plowing (the sea)

sullain, sullein, sullen; gloomy (earth); solemn (gravity)

sulphur, chapel of, i.e. Mantuan's *sulphuris arcem* = Solferino, a village in northern Italy

sum, reckon, count, add; summarize; **sum**

my count, balance my account (with Nature)

summer, the spring; **summer** or **dormant**, horizontal bearing beam in a house; **summer's story**, gay fiction

sumpteous, sumptious, sumptuous

sumpterman, driver of a packhorse

sunny tract, the course or path of the sun

sun-staining, surpassing the glory of the sun

superficies, surface

superfine, overrefined

superfinesse, excessive refinement

superflue, superfluous

supersticion, superstition

superstitious in their praises, i.e. extravagantly devoted in

superstitiously accompt, scrupulously account

supple, soft, yielding

supple-hearted, soft-hearted

suppliant, purely, i.e. supplicating

supportance, assistance

suppose, *n.*, supposition; *v.*, **pretend a title to suppose**, pretend a right to judge

supprise, surprise; **supprised**, appearing suddenly

surcease, stop, cease

surcingled, fastened with a girth

sure together, engaged to marry

sure-keeping, imprisonment

surely set, i.e. securely, firmly fixed

surfet, surfit, surfeit

surmised law, i.e. falsely devised

surmount, excel; overcome; swell; **surmount the Parliament**, ?i.e. summon

surphuled, surfled, painted with cosmetics

surquedry, arrogance; excess; surfeit

surrounded with tears, i.e. overflowed

surveyor, one who supervises the cooking and serving of food

suspect, *n.*, suspicion; *pa. part.*, suspected

suspition, suspicion

sustenation, sustinance, sustenance

suttelties, subtleties, symbolical devices

suttle, subtle

swage, assuage, lessen

swallow, singing, i.e. Davies' friend Richard Martin (since a martin is a species of swallow)

swap, cut; strike

sware, swore

swarth, swarthy

swartrutter, irregular troops in black and with blackened faces

swarve, swerve

swashly, with a dashing or splashing sound

swath, strip, broad track; **swathing**, swaddling (clothes)

sway, bear, exert power; manage

sweard, sword

sweared, swore

sweat, plaguy, the sweating sickness

sweetening, seen in the, skilled in flattery

sweeting, sweet-flavored kind of apple

sweet-scenting, sweet-smelling

swelling, pregnancy

swelth, foul water

swerd, sword

swete, sweat

swinge, burn; drink up; **bear the swinge**, have power

swink(er), labor(er)

swole, swelled, puffed out

swom, swam, swum

swounded, fainted

swutty, sooty

syllab, syllable

sylvan, *n.*, rustic; **feathered sylvan**, bird

sympathia, common liability to

symphony, harmony of speech-sounds in verse

synderesis, the function of conscience that guides conduct; the habitual knowledge of the primary principles of moral action

synodals, prayers to be used for festivals observed by a diocesan synod

syntaxis, syntax

syphogranty, city ward

syrly(e), surly

syrop, syrup

sythe, time

tabacco, tobacco

taber, tabor, small drum

table, alehouse sign; board on which a picture is painted; picture; **tables**, backgammon; astronomical charts

tablets, flat pieces of jewelry

tableture, tablature, musical notation

tabret, small tabor

tackling, stick to his, hold his position

ta'en, taken

taffeta fools, i.e. overdressed, fastidious

taint, prohibit; **tainted wound**, i.e. tented, kept open; **tainting her face**, i.e. coloring

take, *pa. part.*, taken

takings, wages, charges

talants: *see* talents

tale, on the, i.e. the tally

talents, tal(l)ants, tallents, talons

tall, brave; great (damage)

tal(l)ants, tallents: *see* talents

tapets, carpets of grass

tapist(e)ry, tapestry

tare, tore

targe(t), shield

targeteer, foot soldier armed with a target

tarras(se), terrace

tarsel, tercel, male hawk

taurus, fabulous bird that bellows like a bull

tawdry lace, lace band bought at St. Awdrey's fair

tawed, whitened (like leather)

tawny, *adj.*, yellowish-brown color; *n.*, cloth of a tawny color

taxing, private, censuring individuals

tead, torch

teatish, tettish, irritable

tedious beards, i.e. long; **tedious impression**, i.e. annoying, disagreeable

tediousness, weariness

teen, grief

teenest, ?keenest

teg, contemptuous term ("hog") for a woman

tell(o'er), count; **telled**, told

temper Tartarus, i.e. control

temperance, properly proportioned state; temperament

temperature, (goodly) combination; moderation; temperate climate

tempestious, tempestuous

temporal(i)ty, the laity

ten, card of, the ten of trumps; **ten toes**, nags

tench, a fish

tendance, long, long waiting in expectation

tender-eared, sensitive to criticism

tenor, in lovely, in beautiful agreement

tentive, attentive

tenure, tenor, purport

term, period of life; session of a law court; terms divine, ages of immortality

terminant, *adj.*, final; *n.*, ending

terminate heaven's movings, i.e. express them in words

termless, boundless

tessew, tissue

testars, testers, bed canopies

th', *sometimes* = they

than, *adv.*, then (*q.v.*)

thank, *n.*, gratitude

thankful studies, i.e. deserving thanks; thankful trees, i.e. agreeable, pleasant

thanksgeving, thanksgiving; Holy Communion

that, *often* = him who, so that, *the plural* those *or* those who, what, that which, what, when; that one, that other, the one, the other

theatch, thatch

theeself, thyself

theim(selves), them(selves)

theirselfes, themselves

theis, these

thelf, the elf, creature

them seemed, it seemed to them

themself, themself(e)s, themselves

then, *conj.*, than (*in Pettie's letter* then than = than then)

theoric, theory

there, *conj.*, to the place where

therefore, *sometimes* = therefor

therewhile, meanwhile; until

thetch, thatch

thether, thither; there

thetherward, thitherward, thither

thick, *n.*, thicket

thick-farcing, stuffing full

thider, thither

thilk(e), that (same), this (same)

thing, *often the plural*; thing self, thing itself

thirl, pierce; spin; thrill

this another, i.e. this is another reason; this make I, thus I make; this marks, i.e. these marks

tho, *adv.*, then; though

thomb, thumb

thone, the one

thornback, thorny ray, a kind of fish

thorough, thorow, through

thorough-seeing, seeing through

thorowly, thoroughly

thother, the other

thought, mind; melancholy; took such thought, was so grieved

thous, thou art

thralling, enslaved

thrasonical, vainglorious

thraves, bundles

thread, fatal or vital, thread of life

threasure, treasure

threaten, anticipate, foretell

threde, threed, thread

threstil, throstle, thrush

thret, threat

thrid, thread

thriftless, unprofitable (praise)

thrill the thickets, i.e. penetrate, pierce

thrip, snap

thristy, thirsty

thriving, causing to thrive

throng, (lie) crowded; squeeze, crush; they throng in, i.e. thronged in

through, thorough; thoroughly

throughly, thoroughly

thrumm'd, fringed (hat)

thrust, *n.*, thirst; *v.*, thrust her through both hands, pushed against her with both hands

thry-fallow, trifallow, plow fallow land a third time

thunder-scorning, (the laurel tree, or Daphne, supposedly) unhurt by lightning

thurification, the burning of incense

tickel, tickle

ticking, touching wantonly

tickle, *adj.*, fickle, capricious

tide, *n.*, time; fixed tide, appointed time; *v.*, happen

tierse, terse, neat

tillsmen, farmers

tilth, arable land

time, by, betimes; time in hope, future time; time removed, time of (my) absence; with the time, following the fashion

timeless, untimely

timely hermit, one who early became a hermit

timerous, timorous

tincted, tinctured, colored

tincture, color

tine, perish

tinkerly, bungling, clumsy

tippet, hood

tire, *n.*, attire, garment; tier, row of guns in a warship; *v.*, dress; pull; tire upon, devour; tiring meat, meat for a hawk to tire or tear

tissue, rich cloth interwoven with gold or silver

tissue-slop, (man dressed in) wide baggy breeches or hose made of tissue (*q.v.*)

tithing, giving a share of

titlers, those who claim a legal title

titters, clothes in, i.e. tatters

tittle-tattle, petty gossip

to, *often* = against, as, for ("to husband," "to wife," "to your mistress," etc.), equal to

to weet, to wete, to wit

toesed, toyed, pulled (ears)

tofore, heretofore

togethers, together

togged, tugged

togither, together

to-jagged, torn to rags

token, pudendum

told, is, is counted, esteemed

ton(e), the one

tong, tongue

tongueman, orator, speaker

tongues, diversity of, various dialects

tonnel, cask for beer

tonnish gib, beer-brewing old cat

too too, very, excessively

tooken, taken, won over

toong, tongue

toot, look inquisitively about

to-piteously, very pitifully

topping, having supremacy over

to-ragged, badly rent and torn

torch-bearer, Apollo, the sun

tord, turd

to-rent, rend to pieces; utterly ragged

torn, tourn, *v.*, turn

torteyse, tortoise

torves, turves, turfs

toss my books, i.e. turn over their leaves, read

tother, the other

tottered, tattered

tottering truth, i.e. wavering

touch, *n.*, black marble; inward touch, mental or moral perception; *v.*, touch me, speak to me of; in touching, to the touch

toung(u)e, tongue

tour, tower

tourn, turn

toward, towards, *adv.*, at hand, imminent

towardliness, promise

towards: *see* toward

townish, living in a town

towre, soar (like a falcon) far up in circles; (deer) stand high

toy, *n.*, amorous sporting; fantastic notion; fantastic speech; tricky action; trifle; trifling work or action; *v.*, trifle, sport

trace, walk

tract, course; expanse, length; trait; feature; sunny tract, the course or path of the sun

trade, follow the, i.e. the path, course; traded in languages, i.e. practised

tradition, communication (of knowledge)

tragedians, vainglorious, i.e. writers of tragedy

train, *n.*, follower(s), attendant(s); treachery, trickery; (peacock's) tail; snare; *v.*, be attracted (to); entice; train the time, i.e. drag it out wearily; trained, attended by; allured (wills or desires)

trainment, process of training

traison, treason

traiterous, traitorous

tralucent, translucent

trammels, tresses of hair

transcend, cross, go over

transcription, pass by, circulate in manuscript copies

transfix, pierce through, destroy

translate, change; translate a tree, i.e. move, transplant

translation of words, words used metaphorically

transparant, transparent

transperse, transpierce, pierce through

transumption, metaphor

travail, traveil, suffering; travel; work; in traveil of, in labor pains

trave, curtain or screen

travel, travail, labor; traveled pen, i.e. travailed, wearied

travers, screened-off apartment

traverse, in, in dispute, controversy; many traverses, i.e. troubles

treachor, traitor

treacle, medicinal compound

tread, copulate with; tread it, dance

treasor(e), treasure

treen, *adj.*, wooden; *n.*, trees

trencher-chaplain, domestic chaplain

trentals, series of thirty requiem masses

trepidation of the spheres, the precession of the equinoxes

tressure, narrow band on a shield

trewand(ship), trewant(ship), truant(ship)

trial by battle or combat, i.e. by a personal encounter between disputing parties

tribracques, tribrachs

tricksy, smartly

tried gold, i.e. refined

trilling, trickling

trim, ornamental dress; **trim up**, ?rebuke

trimetra, iambic trimeters

trimly, effectively, finely

trim-tram, neat ornament; piece of nonsense

trinall, threefold

triobolar, triobular, paltry

tripes, guts

triplicities, triads

tripos, tripod

tripping in, bringing in

triumvirate, my heart's, i.e. three joint rulers

troad: *see* trode

troan, throne

troath, troth

trochaicques, trochaic verses

trochilus, a fabulous bird which lives in a crocodile's mouth

trode, troad, *n.*, path, track; *v.*, trod

trompet, trumpet

trone, throne

troop'd, followed

trophies, memorials

troth, truth. *See* trouth

troubleous, troublous

troublous, turbid (wine)

troup, troop, band

trouth, *n.*, truth; *n., v.*, pledge

trow, believe, think; trust

truage, allegiance; tribute

truckle-bed, trundle-bed

truculent tragedy, i.e. barbarous

true, *n.*, truth; *adj.*, **true man**, i.e. honest

trueth, truth

trull, lass, girl

trunchion, truncheon; lance

truss, close-fitting body garment; pack, bag; **truss his points**, tie the laces holding up his hose

trustely, with confidence

tub, tale of a, a trifling cock-and-bull story

tuch, touch

tun, *n.*, cask; *sometimes the plural* casks; *v.*, **tuns dung**, ?i.e. tumbles in it

tune, *often* = tone

tunning, brewing

turbot, a fish

turk, die upon a, i.e. on a scimitar

turken, change, modify

Turkey work, Turkish tapestry work

turment, torment

turmoil themself, worry or trouble themselves

turning of books, i.e. translating

turtles' blood, i.e. doves'

twattle, tell idly

tway, two

tween, between

twhartest, thwartest

twish, exclamation of contempt

twist, thread, cord; thread of life

Tyburn, purchase a, win a certain death; **Tyburn play**, hanging

tydie, a small bird of an unknown kind

tympanized, puffed up

tympany, swelling

tyran, tyranne, tyrant

uglesome, ugglesome, horrible

ultra-equinoctials, those living beyond the equinox

umbratical, remaining in seclusion

unacquainted name, i.e. unfamiliar

unactit, unacted, undone

unapt, unusable (words)

unaware(s), at, unexpectedly

unbelieved, unbelievable

unbrace your hearts, free yourself from restraint; **unbraced**, with clothing unfastened

uncase, strip off one's garments

uncessant(ly), incessant(ly)

unclip, unclasp

uncoined, deprived of one's coin or wealth

uncompound, *pa. part.*, uncompounded

unconsuming lines, i.e. immortal verses

unconvenient, inconvenient

uncouth, strange; unfamiliar, unknown

uncredible, incredible

uncrudded, uncurdled

uncumber, *v.*, disencumber, reveal; *adj.*, not encumbered

undecent, indecent

underfoot, abject, downtrodden, inferior

under-kingdoms, inferior kingdoms

underlaid shoes, i.e. with additional soles

undermeal, afternoon nap

underminer, subverter, a cheat

under-room, low estimation

undersong, refrain

understand, understanded, understanden, *pa. part.*, understood

undertaker, challenger; one engaged in the serious study of a subject

undervalues, insufficiencies in worth

undiscreet, indiscreet

undiscrete, indiscrete, not divided into distinct parts

undoubted, undoughtedly, undoubtedly

undowed, without dowry

uneasiness, difficulty

uneath, uneth, not easily

unexercised, untrained

unfatigable, indefatigable

unfended, unprotected

unfiled rimes, i.e. unpolished

unfurnished, left, i.e. unprepared, not provided

ungrateful, unpleasant (love)

ungratefully, unkindly

unhabited, sight, i.e. incapable of any other sight

unhable, unable

unhansome, not handsome

unhaply, unhappily

unhappy, ill-fated

upholsters, upholsterers

unhonest, indecent, lewd

unhospital, made nature, i.e. inhospitable

univarsally, universally

unkempt, uncombed

unkenned, unkent, unknown

unkind(ly), unnatural(ly)

unlightsome, without light

unlust, repulsiveness

unmangeled, unmangled

unmann'd, untrained

unmeasurable, immense

unmustered, not put on the muster-roll

unneth, unnethes, uneath (*q.v.*), with difficulty

unnurtured, ill-bred

unparfited, unperfected

unpartial(ly), impartial(ly)

unperfight, imperfect

unperfitness, imperfection

unpossible, impossible

unproper, improper

unready, made, undressed

unreave, take to pieces

unrespected, unlooked on, neglected

unresistible, irresistible

unreverent, irreverent

unrevocable, irrevocable

unrighteous'd, corrupted

unroomaged, not rummaged or arranged in the ships' holds

unsatiable, insatiable

unseasoned one's ears, i.e. deprived of relish or enjoyment

unseperable, inseparable

unset leeks, i.e. young, untransplanted

unshadow my conceit, throw light on my purpose

unshamefastness, immodesty

unshameful, shameless

unsitting, unfitting

unsound, not mentally normal

unsowndy, unsound (eyes)

unstayed, fickle (youth); unstable

unstored of, unprovided with

unsufficient, insufficient

unsure, not fixed (as to time)

unswept stone, i.e. in unswept stone

untainted, uninjured, untouched

unthrift subjects, i.e. spendthrift

until, prep., *often* = unto

untimely words, i.e. obsolete, archaic

unto name, for a name, is called

untolerable, intolerable

untruss, take down one's breeches

untrust, distrust

unwares, at, unaware

unweeting, unwittingly

unweldy, unwieldy

unwist, unknown

unwroken, unrevenged

upbraid, reproach, blame

uplandish, high (ground); rustic

uprender, give up, surrender

upright, right, well-balanced

uprist, risen out of

upsee freeze, carouse, toast

upsteaming, rising up

upsupped, drunk

uptill, against

upweigh, lift up

urdge, urge

ure, ounce of unrefined silver; use, practise

usance, interest (as on money)

usd', usde (used)

use, custom; lending out at interest; order of church service and ritual; **to his use**, for his advantage

utas, octave, eighth day following a church festival

utensal, utensil, useful article

utter, *adj.*, fully qualified (barrister); *adv.*, **stand utter**, stand back; *v.*, publish; put forth; sell

utterance, good, i.e. sale or circulation (of music books)

utterly, absolutely (refused); verily (among you)

utterside, exterior

vacabonds, vagabonds

vacations, public, i.e. occupations, business

vade, vanish

vagarant, vagrant

vagary, devious journey

vail, *n.*, veil; *v.*, avail; take off (a cap);

vailed the curtain, i.e. lowered; **vail'd to the ground,** i.e. bowed in reverence

valarous, valerous, valorous

valew, value; **pay valews,** i.e. an adequate or equivalent return

valiable, of advantage

valianst, most valiant

vallew, value; valor

valor, like, i.e. value

valure, valor; value

vance, advance, improve; raise

vanishing her tire, putting off her robe

vapored eyes, i.e. tearful; **vapored tears,** i.e. formed from vapor

vaporing out, breathing out in the form of vapor

vare, fare (*dialectic*)

variable flowers, i.e. various

variance, at, in enmity with one another

varlets, attendants on warriors

varrow, farrow (*dialectic*)

vary, made them, gave a different account of them

vastity, desolation

vather, father (*dialectic*)

vaunt their meters or **pens,** i.e. display them in a stately manner

vauntguard, vantguard, vanguard

vaut, *n.,* vault; the inside of the Trojan horse; *v.,* vault, leap; **vauted skies,** i.e. arched

vaward, vanguard

ve, we (*used for I*)

veatch, fetch, get (*dialectic*)

vechy, heavy, bulky

vegetatife, vegetative, having the faculty of growth

venemous(ly), venomous(ly)

venim(ous), venom(ous)

venter, venture

venterous, vent'rous, venturous

ventosity, puffiness

ventures, *n.,* adventures

veny, assault

veow, few (*dialectic*)

ver, the spring

verdingale, verdingall, vardingale, farthingale, hoops for women's skirts

verdit, verdict

verdure, a bowl's, i.e. odor

verefy, verify

verely, verily

verjuice, sour-looking

verlay, virelay, song or brief lyric

vermeil, vermillion

vermiculate, worm-eaten

vermill, vermillion

verse (upon), cozen, cheat

versicles, verses and responses

versifying, *sometimes* = writing quantitative verse

versing-box, *perhaps connected with* verse (*q.v.*)

very, *adj.,* true

vet, friscoles, fetch friscals, cut capers (*dialectic*)

vetcht May, fetched (welcomed in) May (*dialectic*)

vicaries, vicars

vicissitudes of times, changes of season

vicker, vicar

victail, vitail, vittle, victual, food or (*plural*) provisions

victualer, ship carrying provisions

vifteen, fifteen (*dialectic*)

vild(ly), vile(ly)

villan, villein, occupier of land in a feudal vill

vinaigar, vineger, vinegar

vintener, vintiner, vintner

viol, vial

virelayes, short lyrics written in an old French measure

virtue of her eyes, i.e. the magnet

visar, viser, visor, face

visard, mask

viser: see visar

visitors, ecclesiastics appointed to inspect churches

visnomy, physiognomy

vitail: see victail

vitiate, *pa. part.,* vitiated, infected

vittle: see victail

vix good, scarcely or hardly good

vizar-faced, visor-faced

vocal, *n.,* vowel

void hours, i.e. idle; **let all sweet void,** i.e. go away; **the stars voided,** i.e. disappeared

volk, folk (*dialectic*)

volubility, revolving, rotating (of stars)

voluntary gentlemen, gentlemen volunteers

vor, for (*dialectic*)

vouch of, deign to accept

vouchsave, voutchsafe, voutsafe, vouchsafe; **vouchsafing my cloak,** i.e. graciously accepting

vound, found (*dialectic*)

vulgar, *adj.,* in the vernacular; popular; ordinary; *n.,* native language

wad of hay, i.e. bundle

wade, go, act; proceed

wadge, wage, fight

wafery, room in which wafers or cakes are made

waft with his hand, i.e. wave as a signal; **waft to and fro,** i.e. sail

wag, mischievous baby or boy

wagains, wagons

waged, meanly, poorly paid

wailful(ly), woful(ly)

wain(e), chariot

wainmen, cart drivers

wait, laid, lurked or plotted in concealment

walking head, ?i.e. wandering or throbbing; **swords walking,** i.e. in play or use; **walking with his words,** i.e. accompanying them; **plows not walking,** i.e. not in motion and use

wallowish, insipid, nauseous

walter, lie sprawling

wambling, nauseated

wan, won

wane, *n.,* decreasing

wanhope, despair

want, *n.,* a mole

wanton, *adj.,* playful, sportive; gay; *n.,* lewd son (Paris); playful babe; sportive girl

wanton it, sport amorously

wantonize, act wantonly

wantonness, caprice, playfulness

warbeling, warbling

ward, *n.,* guard; private chamber; *v.,* guard

warder, truncheon, staff

wardrop, wardrobe; dressing-room

ware, *adj.,* aware; careful, wary; *n.,* watchful care; *v.,* beware; wore; **ware red,** *error for* waxed red

warely, warily, carefully

wark, work

warly, warlike

warm, *n.,* warmth

warranti(s)e, warrant, sanction

warreid, assailed

warrious, warlike

warst, worst

wart, wert

waspy, wasp

wasted time, past ages

watching, (overnight's) debauch; sleeplessness

water-forow, water-furrow, make a furrow to let water run off

water-rimer, John Taylor, the so-called Water-Poet

water-work, machinery (erected in 1594–95) for distributing water from the Thames

wavering starter, a deserter from a cause

wax, *n.,* increasing; *v.,* grow, increase; **waxing brain,** i.e. aging

way, sell by the, i.e. by the wey, a unit of weight; **in his way,** on his journey

weal public (publique), commonwealth

wealked, welked, withered

wealth, well-being

wealthily, well

weapon, *sometimes the plural*

wear her, possess or enjoy her; **for wearing,** for fear of impairing

weare, were

wearish, sickly; wizened

weasant, gullet

weather, withers (of a horse); **keep the weather gage,** be to the windward

weathering, the state of being pulverized and made plowable by the elements

weed, garment, clothes; **noted weed,** well-known style

ween, think, suppose

weet, know; **to weet,** to wit

weeting, knowledge (of)

weetless, ignorant

weigh, regard or esteem; **weigh without,** estimate from the outside or by other people; **weighing that,** considering

weld, wield; wear (a crown)

welk, whelk; welked Phoebus, fading sun; **welked tower,** i.e. dried up, dulled in luster

well, worldly, i.e. welfare

well-apay'd, well-satisfied

well-beseen, good looking, beautiful

well fare good memory, i.e. good memory is a useful thing

well-favoredly, lavishly

well-publique, commonwealth

well-sorted, in harmony, well-agreed

well-tewed, fatigued, worked hard

well-whittled, very drunk, intoxicated

well-willer, one friendly to

welt and guard, in, in ornamental dress; **welt or guard, without,** i.e. unadorned

welted, edged

welter, weltre, wallow, roll

welt'ring, political agitation

wemen, women

wench, girl, woman; sweetheart

wend, change or turn; go; thought

wening, weening, thinking

went, had, i.e. weened, thought

wepst, weptst

were(n), wear
werk, work, deed
western isle, i.e. Ireland
wete, to, to wit
wex, *n.*, wax; *v.*, grow, increase
whan(as), when(as)
whare, where
wharrow, grooved pulley in a spinning-wheel
what, *often* = why; **most what**, for the most part; **what is he for a lad**, what sort of boy is he
wheat dough, i.e. the Sacrament
whelm, overwhelm (cut down with swords)
whenas, when
where, whence; whereas; whether
whereagainst, against which
whereas, wherein, where
whereso, wherever
wherewithal, pecuniary means
wherling, whirling
whether, which of the two; whither, where
whetstones, **stumbling of,** ?telling lies for the proverbial whetstone (*see* leasing)
whey-wormed, (pimples) with a whey-like discharge
which, *often* = who, what
which-like, of which kind
while, we had, i.e. opportunity
whileas, while
whilere, erewhile
whiles, while, when
whilest, whilst
whilom, once, formerly
whim wham, fantastic trinket
whirries, wherries
whissing, whizzing, hissing
whist, hushed, quiet
whistered, whispered
whistlen, whistle
white, *adj.*, gracious, favorable; *n.*, the mark at which an arrow is aimed; **hit the white,** succeed
whited, made white
whitflaw, whitlow, inflammatory sore in the finger
whither, whether, which
whiting, a term of endearment
whittle, *n.*, knife
who, *often* = the neuter which
whom, *excl.*, hum!
whop'd, whooped
whot(ly), hot(ly)
widered, withered
wife, on a, at a woman; **wifes,** wives
wiflers, whifflers, armed attendants to clear the way for a procession
wight, *adj.*, active; *n.*, creature, person
wig-wag, writhing motion
will, lawless, carnal desire
willow garland, emblem of ill luck in love
wimble, gimlet; wimple, veil
windlass, decoy, ensnare
windows, openings in shoes
wink, close the eyes; nod (in sleep)
winter-love, cold or conventional love
winter-starved, killed by winter (or age)
winter-withered, (face) wrinkled by age
wisards, wise men
wise, **in a wonder,** in a wonderful manner; **by wise of,** by means of
wisper, whisper
wist, knew, known; **had I wist,** if I had known

wistly, intently
wit, *n.*, wisdom; *v.*, **know**
witen, *v.*, blame
with, *n.*, halter, yoke
withouten, without
wittily, wisely
wittol(d), cuckold
witty, wise
wive it, act the part of a wife
wive's, wife's
wo worth, wo be to
wold, would
womanhead, womanhood, womankind
womb, stomach
won, *n.*, dwelling; *v.*, dwell, live
wonder (wise), in a, wondrously
wonderly beseen, of strange appearance
wonderous, wonderfully; wondrous
wonders, wondersly, wondrously
woning, dwelling
wood, *adj.*, vehement, crazy
wooden clouds or rimers, i.e. stiff and lifeless
woodhack, woodpecker
woodoses, woodwoses, savage wild men of the woods
woosel(l), ouzel, blackbird
wordish, consisting of words
wordle, world
wordly, worldly (matters)
wore, *pa. part.*, worn out
world, it is a, i.e. a wonderful thing
worm, (stinging) insect
worn, experienced in; past
worrowed, worried, (a cat) shook and bit
worth, take in, take at its proper value
worthely, worthily
wot(e), know, knows
woundless, unwounded
wounds, the five, i.e. of the crucified Christ
woxen, grew, grown, increased
wrack, wreck, disaster
wrackful tempests, i.e. causing shipwrecks
wrang, wrung
wrastle(r), wrestle(r)
wrate, wrote
wraught, wrought
wray, reveal
wreak, *n.*, injury, damage; *v.*, reck; revenge
wreakful, vengeful
wreathen, curved (horns)
wreck my wrong, i.e. wreak, avenge
wrests, wrists
wrete, written
wrethocks, puny fowls
wright, write; build, construct
wrigs, wriggles
writhed, twisted
writhen-faced, with a contorted face
wroken, wreaked, avenged
wrong(en), wroong, wrung; pinched, twisted
wull, will
wyten, *v.*, blame

yallow, yellow
yane, yawn
yarked up, put together hastily
ybared, made bare
ybent, bent
yblent, blinded
yblist, blessed
yborn, born
ybound, bound
ybreathed, exercised, put into breath

ycharged, loaded
yclad, clothed
yclepe, ycleepe, call, name
yclipped, yclept, named
ycompassed, ycompast, encircled
ycouched, bedded
ycounted, counted; esteemed
ycoupled, mated
ydone, done
ye, *adv.*, yea
year, *often the plural*; **by year,** a year, each year
yearth(ly), earth(ly)
yede, go; yeed, went
yeld, great, great eld or age
yelks, yolks of eggs
yelky, resembling an egg yolk
yenough, enough
yer, *adv., conj.*, ere, before
yerking, lashing, flogging
yeven, given
Yew, an, a Jew
yfere, together
yfiled, filed
yfound, found
yfraught, loaded, filled
ygirt, girded
ygoe, ago
ygotten, gotten
yit, yet
ylain, laid, placed
ylike, alike
ymade, made
ymay, may
ymounted, mounted
yode, went
yonker(ly): *see* younker
yoong, young
you, *dative of interest (ethical dative)* **as in** would he allege you examples, bring you Ajax, etc.
yought, yougth, youth
youngers, my, people younger than I
youngth, youth
younker, yonker, fashionable young man; youngster; **yonkerly,** befitting a young gentleman
yourself(e)s, yourselves
youthly, youthful
ypent, penned up
ypocrisy, hypocrisy
ypocrite, hypocrite
yrapt, rapt
yrun, run, gone
yseen, seen
yshrilled, sounded shrill
yspread, spread
ytanned, tanned
ytorn, torn, devoured
ytossed, tossed
yvanished, disappeared
ywist, had I, had I known
ywroken, avenged
ywrought, wrought, created

zaw, saw (*dialectic*)
zay, say (*dialectic*)
zed, said (*dialectic*)
zephires, zephyrs
zo, so (*dialectic*)
zow, sow (*dialectic*)
zun, sun (*dialectic*)
zure, sure (*dialectic*)
zweet, sweet (*dialectic*)

Glossary of Names and Foreign Words and Phrases

The following list does not include every proper noun that appears in the text. Two classes of words have as a rule been omitted: (1) names for which the context supplies adequate identification, like the genealogical and military catalogues in Warner and Holinshed; (2) extremely familiar personal and place names, like Abraham, Adam, Paris, Rome. But all unusual spellings have been entered,[1] even those whose modern equivalents fall into the second class above. Foreign phrases which are translated or explained in the text are not repeated below.

A loco . . . juxta B, "in place A . . . near B"

a porta inferi, "from the gate of hell"

Aaron, first high priest of the Israelites, brother of Moses

ab extrema pueritia, "from earliest youth"

ab ovo, "from the egg," i.e. from the beginning

abeunt studia in mores, "studies pass into morals" (Ovid, *Heroides* XV.83)

Abiron, Abiram, member of Korah's conspiracy against Moses and Aaron (see Numbers xvi.1–46)

abominabiles facti . . ., "they have done abominable works" (Vulgate Psalms xiii.1)

Abradates, Sidney's error for Araspes, of whom Xenophon's *Cyropaedia* relates the tale mentioned by Sidney

Absolon, Absalom, rebellious son of David, king of Israel (see II Samuel xiii–xix)

Abstemio, Lorenzo, Laurentius Abstemius, Italian writer and ducal librarian at the court of Urbino (*q.v.*), famed for his *Hecato-mythium* (1499)

Abydos, town on the Hellespont, in Asia Minor, legendary home of Leander (*q.v.*) and site of Xerxes' bridge

Academici, Academics, members of the philosophic school that Plato conducted at the Academy, a public pleasure-ground in the suburbs of Athens; Platonists

Acca Larentia, wife of the shepherd Faustulus, called Lupa ("she-wolf") because she nursed Romulus and Remus after they were taken from the wolf who had suckled them

Achaeus Erithriaeus (b. 484 B.C.), Greek poet who contended with Sophocles and Euripides. Although he wrote some forty plays he won the dramatic prize only once.

Achelous (Acheloy), river-god whom Hercules fought for the love of Dejanira. According to Ovid, the horn which Hercules took from Achelous was transformed by the Naiads into the horn of plenty.

Achelow, Thomas: see Achlow

Acheron(te), a river in Hades

Achillas, one of the guardians of young King Ptolemy who joined the conspiracy of Pothinus (*q.v.*) against Julius Caesar and for a short time controlled most of Alexandria. He was executed at the command of Arsinoë, Ptolemy's youngest sister, in 47 B.C.

Achil(les), Greek champion in the Trojan War

Achlow (Achelow, Atchelow), Thomas, Elizabethan poet of whom little is known except that *England's Parnassus* (1600) includes several extracts from his work

Acidalian, referring to Acidalia, a surname of Venus, from the well Acidalius near Orchomenos, where she bathed with the Graces

Acolastus, the Prodigal Child, Latin comedy (written 1529) by William Fullonius (Gulielmus Gnapheus), translated in 1540 by John Palsgrave

Açores, Isles of, the Azores

acta exitus probat, "the outcome is the test of the action"

Act(a)eon, hunter who was turned into a stag by Diana (Artemis)

because he watched her bathing; he was destroyed by his own dogs.

Acts and Monuments, Protestant martyrology compiled by John Foxe and popularly known as "The Book of Martyrs" (see pp. 173–74)

Ad Atticum, series of nearly four hundred epistles from Cicero to his friend Titus Pomponius Atticus

Ad C. Caesarem, letters to Julius Caesar in Cicero's *Epistolae ad familiares*

ad Dominum cum tribularer clamavi, "in my distress I cried unto the Lord" (Vulgate Psalms cxix.1)

ad lectorem, "to the reader"

ad Musam, "to the muse"

ad ornatissimum virum, "to the most illustrious man"

Ad Quintum fratrem, series of twenty-nine epistles from Cicero to his brother Quintus

adesti si quid mihi restat agendum, "come, if anything remains for me to do"

Admetus: see Alcest(is)

Adon(is), beautiful youth, beloved of Venus (Aphrodite), who died from the wound of a boar's tusk

Adrian: see Hadrian(us)

Advent, ecclesiastical period including the four Sundays before the celebration of Christ's nativity

adversus mortuos bellum . . ., "it is barbarous to attack the dead"

Aeaea, island in the straits between Italy and Sicily. The term is sometimes used as a surname for Circe and Calypso.

Aegeria: see Egeria

Aegipt(ian), Egypt(ian)

Aeglogues, the *Eclogues* of Virgil: see *Bucolics*

Aelianus, Claudius (fl. 250), Italian who wrote, in Greek, a miscellaneous history of anecdote and biography (*Varia historia*) and a study of the peculiarities of animals (*De animalium natura*)

Aemilius Probus: see Nepos

Aeneas, the hero of Virgil's *Aeneid*

Aeneas Sylvius, Enea Silvio Piccolomini (1405–64), later Pope Pius II, Italian humanist whose erotic novel *Euryalus and Lucretia* was much admired in the Renaissance

Aeneidos, Aeneis, Aeney, the *Aeneid* of Virgil

Aeolus (Aeole, Eolus), god of the winds

Aeschines (389–314 B.C.), Athenian orator, antagonist of Demosthenes (*q.v.*)

Aeson, father of Jason, restored to life by Medea after his suicide

Aesop (Esop), reputed sixth-century writer of fables, said to have been born a slave

Aesop(e), Clodius, Roman tragedian and friend of Cicero

Aetion, Eëtion, father of Andromache (*q.v.*)

Aetna: see Etna

Afric(k), Afrique, Africa(n); **Council of Africk**, the Council of Africa, an important synod convened to deal with the controversy agitated by the Donatists (*q.v.*) following the death of Menurius, bishop of Carthage, in 311

Agag, Amalekite king who, spared by Saul contrary to his vow, was killed by order of Samuel (see I Samuel xv)

Agamemnon, son of Atreus, brother of Menelaus, husband of Clytemnestra, leader of the Greeks in the Trojan War

Aganippe (Aganippa), a fountain on Helicon (*q.v.*) sacred to the muses

agendo nihil agere, "be busy doing nothing"

Agesilaus, king of Sparta (399–361 B.C.) and ally of the Asiatic Greeks against the Persians

Agincourt, French village near St. Pol, scene of Henry V's famous victory over the French on October 25, 1415

agitante calescimus illo, "[there is a god within us;] stirring, he warms our bosom" (Ovid, *Fasti* VI.5)

Agnus Dei, "Lamb of God," a disk bearing the figure of a lamb as a symbol of Christ, much used by Roman Catholics

---

[1] Except that the purely typographical *i/j* and *u/v* alternations in Spenser have been modernized.

Agricola, Rodolphus (1443–85), Dutch scholar, painter, and musician whose *De inventione dialectica* enjoyed wide popularity

Agrippa, Marcus Vipsanius (63–12 B.C.), Roman general and protégé of Augustus, whose daughter Julia was his third wife

Agrippa von Nettesheim, Cornelius Heinrich (1486–1535), German physician and occultist notorious for his *De occulta philosophia* and *De incertitudine et vanitate scientiarum*

Ajaces, (the two) Ajaxes: *see* Ajax

Ajax, (1) Greek warrior, son of Telamon, famous for his size and strength. At Troy, Agamemnon's decision to award Achilles' arms to Odysseus drove him to madness and suicide. (2) The so-called Lesser Ajax, son of Oileus, king of the Locrians, who fought with the Greeks at Troy and was drowned on the return voyage

al Portugese, "in the Portuguese manner"

Alanson: *see* Alençon

Albanact, one of the sons of Brut (*q.v.*)

Albertus Magnus (?1193–1280), scholastic philosopher and teacher of Aquinas, for his erudition called *Doctor Universalis*

Albinus, Clodius, Roman governor of Gaul and then of Britain (192–197)

Albion, ancient name for Britain

Albion, i.e. William Warner's *Albion's England* (see p. 9)

Albumazar, Albumazer (?805–885), Arabian astronomer

Alc(a)eus (611–580 B.C.), lyric poet of Mytilene in Lesbos

Alcest(is), wife of Admetus, a Thessalian king, in whose place she agreed to die after he had offended Artemis; Hercules brought her back from Hades and restored her to her husband.

Alcibiades, Alcybiades (450–404 B.C.), Athenian general and politician, pupil of Socrates. He shifted allegiance from Athens to Sparta to Persia and then again to Athens, and was finally murdered when he deserted Athens for the second time.

Alcides, a patronymic of Hercules, who was a descendant of Alcaeus, son of Perseus and Andromeda

Alcinous, in the *Odyssey*, the king of the Phaeacians who hospitably entertained Odysseus on his return from Troy

Alcmena, Alcumena, Alcmene: *see* Amphitruo

Alcybiades: *see* Alcibiades

Aldersgate Street, thoroughfare leading from Aldersgate, in the old wall of London

Alecto: *see* Furies

Alençon (Alanson), former courtship and duchy of France whose counts and dukes were prominent for their military and diplomatic services from the fourteenth to the sixteenth century

Aleppo, ancient Syrian city of Beroea

Alexander III of Macedon (the Great, 356–323 B.C.), pupil of Aristotle, conqueror of Greece, Syria, Egypt, and Persia

Alexander VI (1431–1503), Rodrigo Borgia, worldly pope whose policy was to curb secular inroads on the feudal holdings of the Papal States

Alexander, Alexandros, name given to Paris (*q.v.*) for his valor; it means "defender of men."

Alexander Aetolus or **the Aetolian** (fl. 260 B.C.), Greek tragic poet

Alexander Phereus, tyrant of Pherae in Thessaly (369–367 B.C.) who was murdered by his wife Thebe

Alexandros: *see* Alexander

Algier, Algeria, country in northern Africa, in antiquity called Numidia

aliquid latet quod non patet, "something is concealed which is not evident"

aliquid salis, "something salty," i.e. something of value

All Saints' (Day), November 1

Allen (Alleyn), Edward (1566–1626), Elizabethan tragedian, the creator of Marlowe's tragic heroes

alli veri figlioli delle Muse, "to the true sons of the muses"

Almain(e), Almane, Germany; German

Alphonsus of Aragon (Alphonsus a Sancta Maria, 1396–1456), bishop of Burgos and diplomat, whose history of Spain was printed in 1545

Alphonsus of Naples (i.e. Alphonso, or Alfonso, II, 1448–95), king of Naples (1494–95) who abdicated in favor of his son

Ferdinand II (1469–96) when Charles VIII of France threatened his capital

Amadis de Gaule, Spanish or Portuguese romance of chivalry which in the fifteenth-century Spanish version of Garcia de Montalvo achieved great popularity. It concerns the adventures of Amadis, illegitimate son of Perion, king of Gaul, who, abandoned as an infant, was raised at the Scottish court, won the hand of Oriana, princess of England, and returned to Gaul in triumph.

Amalech, Amalek, grandson of Esau, founder of a nomadic tribe traditionally hostile to the Israelites

amantium irae amoris redintegratio est, "the quarrels of lovers are the renewing of love" (adapted from Terence, *Andria* 555)

Ambri, ?the modern Amesbury, a village on Salisbury Plain near Stonehenge

Ambrose, St. (ca. 340–397), celebrated theologian and bishop of Milan, a father of the Latin church

Aminta's friend, i.e. Thomas Watson (*q.v.*), whose Latin version of Tasso's *Aminta* appeared in 1585

amo, "I love"

Amon: *see* Aymon

Amphestus, a man, says Lodge (*A Fig for Momus*), who "burnt his face because his beard was long." Anthony Nixon makes the same allusion but spells the name *Amplestus* in *The Scourge of Corruption* (1615), sig. C1.

Amphion, in Greek legend, a musician, the sweetness of whose lyre caused the stones of demolished Thebes to leap back into place

Amphitrio: see *Amphitruo*

Amphitrite, sea-goddess, daughter of Nereus, wife of Poseidon, and mother of Triton

Amphitruo, son of Alcaeus who won Alcmene after great trials and perils, only to have her seduced by Zeus posing as the real Amphitruo

Amphitruo, Amphitrio, Amphitryon, Plautine comedy involving magic and mythology. Sidney regarded it as a tragi-comedy probably because of the introduction of such serious characters as gods and heroes.

Ampthill, English town west of Bedford

Amyntas, a paraphrase in Latin hexameters of Tasso's *Aminta* by Thomas Watson (see p. 317)

Amyot, Jacques (1513–93), French humanist whose translations of *Theagenes and Chariclea* (1547), Diodorus Siculus (1554), *Daphnis and Chloe* (1559), and Plutarch (1559, 1572) were widely popular. Both North and Holland drew on him for their versions of Plutarch's *Lives* and *Morals* (see pp. 546, 565).

Anabaptists, sixteenth-century sect seeking religious and social reforms

Anacreon (ca. 563–478 B.C.), Greek lyric poet whose extant work mainly concerns the pleasures of love and wine

Anatomy of Absurdities (Absurdity), The, satirical tract (1589) by Thomas Nashe (*q.v.*)

Anaxagoras (ca. 500–428 B.C.), Greek philosopher who lived in Athens

Anchises (Anchisis), prince of Troy and father (by Aphrodite) of Aeneas

Ancor: *see* Anker

Andalo, ?Andalò di Negro (or Andalone de Negri), Boccaccio's teacher in astronomy

Andocides (ca. 467–391 B.C.), Athenian orator and philosopher exiled for an alleged desecration of the images of Hermes

Andromache (Andromaca), wife of Hector and mother of Scamandrius (or Astyanax)

Andromeda: *see* Perseus

Andronicus, Livius (fl. 240 B.C.), earliest Roman poet, a freed Greek slave who learned Latin at Rome and adapted many Greek tragedies and comedies

Andwarp, Antwerp (*q.v.*)

Angelica, heroine of the Italian romances about Orlando (i.e. Roland). In Boiardo's *Orlando Innamorato* and Ariosto's *Orlando Furioso* the hero goes mad for her love.

Angelus Politianus: *see* Politian(us)

Angleso Italiana, "English Italianated"

Angus, Earl of: *see* Douglas (George)

Anjou, ancient province in central France

Anker (Ancor), river in Warwickshire, a tributary of the Tame

Anna, Anne, (1) in Virgil's *Aeneid*, the sister of Dido, queen of Carthage; (2) ?Anne Boleyn, second wife of Henry VIII and mother of Queen Elizabeth

Ann(e), St., mother of the Virgin Mary; her feast day in the Roman church is July 26.

Annes, Agnes, Nicholas Grimald's mother

anno millimo . . . , a nonsensical date ("in the year one thousand million trillion")

Anomos, anonymous or unknown writer

Antenor, Trojan statesman spared by the Greeks at the sack of Troy because of his earlier efforts at conciliation

Anthony Now-Now, traditional name for an itinerant fiddler

Antigone, daughter of Oedipus and Jocasta who incurred the anger of Creon, tyrant of Thebes, by burying her brother Polynices (*q.v.*) after he was killed by his brother Eteocles. Creon caused her to be buried alive, whereupon his son Haemon killed himself. Her story was treated dramatically by Sophocles in his *Antigone*, a tragedy translated (1581) by Thomas Watson (*q.v.*) into Latin.

Antinous, one of the suitors of Penelope slain by Odysseus

antiquitas sacculi juventus mundi, "the antiquity of time is the youth of the world"

Antisthenes (ca. 444–371 B.C.), pupil of Socrates who founded the Cynic school of philosophy

Antonius, Marcus (ca. 83–30 B.C.), celebrated Roman triumvir and general. Attaching himself to Caesar's rising star in 50, he served brilliantly in the civil wars and at Pharsalia, becoming consul in 44. Bitterly denounced by Cicero after Caesar's assassination, he fled from Rome to form the second triumvirate with Octavianus and Lepidus (43), the next year defeated Brutus and Cassius at Philippi, and then, passing over to Egypt, began his notorious association with Cleopatra. The triumvirate was patched up again in 40 and 37, but Antony could not tear himself away from Alexandria for long at a time. When he divorced Octavia, Octavianus' sister, war broke out, and Antony and Cleopatra were defeated at the great sea-battle of Actium in 31. The next year the two lovers committed suicide in Egypt.

Antwerp (Antwarp, Andwarp), capital of the province of Antwerp on the Schelde sixty miles from the North Sea

Apelles (fl. early fourth century B.C.), Greek painter whose portrait of Aphrodite Anadyomene was carried to Rome by Augustus

Apennine(s), mountain-range running the length of the Italian peninsula

Aphrodite, goddess of love and wedlock (Venus), usually regarded as having risen from the sea at Cyprus (hence her epithet *Cyprian*); wife of Hephaestus (Vulcan) and mother of Eros (Amor or Cupid)

Apicius, Marcus Gabius, notorious Roman epicure in the reigns of Augustus and Tiberius

Apocalypse, the Book of Revelation

Apocrypha, fourteen non-canonical books (mainly on Jewish history) included in the Vulgate but ordinarily excluded from Protestant versions of the Old Testament and classed as *pseudepigrapha*, or works not authoritative in matters of doctrine

Apollo, god of light, reason, and art; often identified with Helios, the sun-god

Apollodorus Tarsensis, according to Ravisius Textor, a tragic dramatist contemporary with Menander (342–?291 B.C.)

Appleby, Mistress, Robert Greene's landlady in his last illness

Apuleius, Lucius (b. ca. 125), Numidian who became a famed Platonist and rhetorician at Rome; author of *The Metamorphoses* (or *The Golden Ass*), a romance satirizing religious credulity and decayed public morals

aqua caelestis, a powerful restorative drug

Aquinas, St. Thomas (?1225–74), *Doctor Angelicus*, greatest of scholastic philosophers, and vastly influential theologian. His many works—notably the *Summa theologiae* and *Summa contra Gentiles*—represent the systematic fusion of Christian dogma and pagan (especially Aristotelian) philosophy.

Aquitaine, i.e. France. Aquitania was one of the four divisions of Roman Gaul.

Arachne, Lydian maiden who challenged Minerva to a contest in weaving and was changed by her into a spider

Arar(is), a river in Gaul (the modern Saône)

Aratus, Greek astronomer (fl. 270 B.C.) whose astronomical poem *Phenomena* was translated by Cicero and Caesar Germanicus and was known to the Renaissance in the *Metaphrasis Arati* of Avicenna. St. Paul quotes from Aratus in Acts xvii.28.

arbor vittorioso triomphale . . . , "victorious and triumphant tree, guerdon of emperors and poets"

Arcadia (Arcadie, Arcady), region in the Peloponnesus famous for the virtue and simplicity of its rural life. It became a symbol of pastoral perfection when Sannazaro made it the scene of his influential novel at the end of the fifteenth century.

archa f[o]ederis, "the ark of the covenant" (Vulgate Deut. x.8)

Archelaus, Archelaos of Athens (fl. fifth century B.C.), reputedly the teacher of Socrates

Archesilaus Pyrtanaeus, a man mentioned by Ravisius Textor as having drunk himself to death at an orgy

Archilochus (d. ca. 676 B.C.), Ionian satirist

Archimedes (ca. 287–212 B.C.), celebrated geometer of Syracuse famous for his application of pure geometry to mechanics

Arden, famous ancient forest that once covered perhaps all the midland and eastern counties of England

Ard(es), town near Puy-de-Dome, France, south of Clermont-Ferrand

῎Αρειος πάγος, Areopagus, the so-called Hill of Mars in Athens, site of the highest court and a favorite place for public speeches. In his letters to Harvey, Spenser gives the name to the literary group around Sidney at Leicester House (*q.v.*).

Arete, in the *Odyssey*, wife of Alcinous, king of the Phaeacians

Arethusa, a nymph of Ortygia transformed into a fountain

Aretine, Pietro Aretino (1492–1556), Italian satirist and dramatist notorious for his profligate ways; hence **Aretinish, Aretinist**. E. K., in his gloss to "January" in Spenser's *Shepherd's Calendar*, mistakenly calls him Unico Aretino.

areytos, aréitos, West Indies dance-songs

Arge, Argos (*q.v.*). Grimald's reference is to Biton and Cleobis, sons of a priestess in Argos whose chariot they dragged for forty-five furlongs during a festival.

Argive, pertaining to Argos (i.e. Grecian)

Argonauts, heroes who, led by Jason, sailed in the Argo to Colchis to capture the Golden Fleece

Argos, Agamemnon's kingdom, of which Mycenae was the capital

ἀργυρέον μέλος, "silver song"

Argus, the guardian with a hundred eyes who was killed by Hermes while protecting Io (*q.v.*)

Ariadne, daughter of Minos of Crete (*q.v.*), who gave to Theseus (*q.v.*) the clue for escaping from her father's labyrinth and then fled with him to Naxos, where he abandoned her

Arion (fl. ca. 700 B.C.), Greek poet, native of Lesbos, who won fame at the court of Periander, tyrant of Corinth, for his skill on the cithara. Thrown overboard on a voyage from Sicily, he so charmed the dolphins with his lyre that they carried him to shore.

Ariosto, Alphonsus (Alfonso, d. 1526), brother of Ludovico and friend of Bembo and Castiglione. *The Courtier* is said to have been written at his suggestion.

Ariosto (Ariostus), Ludovico (1474–1533), great Italian epic poet, author of the Plautine comedies *Cassaria* and *Suppositi*, retainer of Alfonso d'Este, Duke of Ferrara. He completed *Orlando Furioso* in 1532 (see p. 561).

Aristippus (fl. 380 B.C.), pupil of Socrates who founded the Cyrenaic school of philosophical hedonism at Cyrene in Africa

Aristophanes (ca. 450–380 B.C.), greatest of Greek comic dramatists, author of *The Knights*, *The Clouds*, *The Birds*, *The Frogs*, *Lysistrata*, etc.

Arius (?256–336), presbyter of Alexandria, founder of the Arian heresy which, denying the Trinitarian dogma and the divinity of Christ, was condemned at the Council of Nicaea in 325

arma amens capio . . . , "distracted, I take up arms, though arms are foolish" (Virgil, *Aeneid* II.314)

Armenia the Less, i.e. Armenia Minor, the part of Armenia west of the Euphrates

Armin, Robert (fl. 1610), comic actor and dramatist

Armony, Skelton's rendering of *Armenia*

Armoric, Breton (from *Armorica*, the Roman name for Brittany)

arms passant, a heraldic device (*passant* means "walking" or "passing")

Arno, Arnus, river in Tuscany on which Florence and Pisa are situated

Arraignment of Paris, The, pastoral drama in verse by George Peele, played before Queen Elizabeth and published in 1584

Art of English Poetry, The, i.e. *The Art of English Poesy* (1589) by George Puttenham (see pp. 639–40)

Arte poetica, i.e. *Ars poetica*, a verse-epistle to the Pisos by Horace (*q.v.*)

artem qui tractant musicam, "they practise the musical art"

Artemis (Diana), twin sister of Apollo, goddess of the moon and patroness of the female sex, from her birthplace on the island of Delos sometimes called Delia

Arthur(e), King, perhaps a British chieftain of the sixth century who, in the later Middle Ages, became celebrated as the first great king of Britain

artifex, "artist"

Arundel, Thomas (1353–1414), chancellor during Richard II's regency (1386–89) and archbishop of Canterbury (1396), who was banished but returned to power with Henry IV's accession. He was notorious for his persecution of the Lollards.

Aruntius Stella (fl. 100), Roman statesman and friend of Statius and Martial. Statius celebrated his marriage in an *Epithalamion*.

Arx, ?Aix, an ancient French town north of Marseilles

Asafi, i.e. Safi or Asfi, Moroccan seaport on the Atlantic

Ascanius, son of Aeneas

Ascension Day, the day commemorating Christ's ascension to heaven, the fortieth day after Easter

Ascham, Margaret, *née* Howe, wife of Roger Ascham (*q.v.*), whom she married in 1554

Ascham, Roger (1515–68), teacher and humanist, educated at St. John's College, Cambridge (B.A. and fellow 1534, M.A. 1537); tutor of Elizabeth both before and after her accession (1548, 1558); secretary to Sir Richard Morysin, English ambassador to Charles V (1550–53); prebendary of York (1559): see p. 815

Ascraeus: *see* Hesiod(us)

Ashore, Ashour, a copse at Penshurst (*q.v.*)

Assuerus, Asur (or Assur), ancient national deity of Assyria

Astley, John (d. 1595), trusted confidential servant in Princess Elizabeth's household, and master of the jewel house after her accession in 1558. His *Art of Riding* was published in 1584.

Aston, Sir Walter, Baron Aston of Forfar (1584–1639), Stuart diplomat and generous patron of Michael Drayton

Astr(a)ea, goddess of justice who, after living among men, fled the earth in the Age of Brass and was stellified as the constellation Virgo

Astrophel (Astrophil), Sir Philip Sidney

Astyanax, Trojan name for Scamandrius, son of Hector and Andromache, who was slaughtered by the Greeks at the fall of Troy

Astydamas Atheniensis (fl. 390 B.C.), Greek tragic poet, nephew of Aeschylus, who wrote two hundred forty tragedies and won the dramatic prize fifteen times

Atalanta (Atalante, Atlante), maiden famed as a huntress, who received the prize from Meleager for her part in the Calydonian boar-hunt (*q.v.*). It is perhaps a different Atalanta who (in a Boeotian myth) was won by Hippomenes when, in a foot-race, he diverted her by rolling three golden apples in her path.

Atchelow, Thomas: *see* Achlow

Ate, daughter of Zeus, personification of infatuation or reckless crime; later she, like Dice or Nemesis, was regarded as an avenger of unrighteousness.

Atheniensis, citizen of Athens

ἄθεοι, "atheists"

Athon, according to Lyly, a region famous for its hares

Athos, holy mountain on the peninsula of Chalcidice in Macedonia

Atilius: *see* At(t)ilius

Atlante: *see* Atalanta

Atlantic Iland, i.e. Atlantis, a mythical island in the Atlantic thought by the ancients to have sunk into the sea

Atlanticum, Sea, the Atlantic Ocean

Atlas, a Titan, brother of Prometheus, whom Zeus condemned to support the heavens with his hands and shoulders

Atraeus, Arcturus, bright star in the northern hemisphere

Atreus, king of Mycenae, son of Pelops, and father of Agamemnon, who slew the sons of his brother Thyestes and was himself slain by his nephew Aegisthus

Atrides, a patronymic, "son(s) of Atreus," i.e. Agamemnon or Menelaus or both

Atropos, the Fate who cuts the thread of life: *see* Parcae

Attalus (d. 197 B.C.), king of Pergamon, famed for his victory (as an ally of Rome) over the Gauls

At(t)ilius, Marcus, one of the earliest Latin poets, a prolific writer of both comedies and tragedies

audivi vocem, "I heard a voice"

Augustine (Austin), Bishop of Hippo, the golden Augustine, Aurelius Augustinus (354–430), one of the four great fathers of the Roman church. A powerful antagonist of the Donatist, Pelagian, and Manichean heresies, he influenced the whole body of medieval dogma, and his *Confessions* and *The City of God* have remained literary classics of Christianity.

Augustine, one of an order of friars (sometimes called Austin friars) established in 1256 by Pope Alexander IV

Augusto profluens . . ., "Augustus' eloquence was flowing, as was proper for a prince"

Augustus Caesar, Caius Octavianus (63 B.C.–A.D. 14), first Roman emperor, nephew of Julius Caesar, who became the popular champion against Antony after Caesar's assassination; in 43 he joined forces with Antony and Lepidus to form the second triumvirate and with them won a decisive victory over Brutus and Cassius at Philippi in 42; he defeated Antony and Cleopatra at Actium (31) and thus inaugurated the Augustan age of peace and Roman power after the civil wars had almost destroyed the republic.

Aurelius, Marcus Aurelius Antoninus (121–180), Roman emperor (with Commodus) who spent most of his reign (161–180) administering affairs of the northern provinces. He is best remembered for his Greek *Meditations*, a Stoic commonplace-book that is one of the most attractive philosophical works of antiquity. Gascoigne's references to his success with "Boemia" and to "Faustine" (Aurelius' notoriously profligate wife) suggest that he was following Lord Berners' translation (1534) of Antonio de Guevara's *Libro aureo de Marco Aurelio*, a set of elegantly fictitious letters of which No. 15 bears the heading, "A Letter Sent by Mark the Emperor to Boemia, Lover of His, That Would Have Gone with Him to the Wars."

Aurora, goddess of the dawn

Ausonius, Decius [Meres's error for **Decimus**] **Magnus** (ca. 310–ca. 394), poet and rhetorician, a native of Bordeaux (hence called "Gallus"), tutor to the future Emperor Gratian, at whose hands he later enjoyed many official appointments

Austin: *see* Augustine

aut si carminibus: in attributing this tag to Ovid, E. K. (in the gloss to "October" of *The Shepherd's Calendar*) may have been thinking of *Amores* III.vii.27–30; actually he seems to be misquoting Virgil, *Aeneid* IV.487 (*haec se carminibus*, etc.): "with her spells she promises to free the hearts of whom she wills."

Avern(us), the underworld, so called from *Avernus Lacus*, a deep volcanic lake close to the promontory near Cumae, Italy, which the ancients regarded as the entrance to the underworld. "To lead apes in Avernus" was proverbially a spinster's destiny.

Avicen(na), Ibn Sina (980–1037), Arabian physician and philosopher, influential commentator on Aristotle and Galen, and author of more than a hundred works, many of them on medicine

Awen (or Owen), William, publisher of the 1554 Surrey partial translation of Virgil. Perhaps he is the Owen (or Awen) who was a bookseller at the Little Shop at the North Door of St. Paul's in 1562–63, and who had earlier (ca. 1548) dwelt in Paternoster Row at the Sign of the Cock.

Axe, river in Devon

Aylmer (Elmer), John (1521–94), tutor of Lady Jane Grey, bishop of London (1577), perhaps the model for Spenser's Morrell (a type of "proude and ambitious pastours") in "July" of *The Shepherd's Calendar*

Aymon (Amon), in medieval French romance (notably *The Four*

Sons of Aymon) the father of Rinaldo, Guiscard, Alard, and Richard, all of them champions of Charlemagne

Azarian Mountains, Drayton's rendering of Geoffrey of Monmouth's *montes Azare* or *Zarec* (II.xi), which is perhaps related to the town of Azamor, a Moroccan seaport

Babel, according to Genesis xi.4–9, an ancient city whose people fell into a confusion of tongues when they tried to build a tower to reach to heaven

Babylon, capital of ancient Babylonia on the Euphrates; Babel (*q.v.*)

Bacchus, a name for Dionysus, god of wine and revelry

Bacon, Francis, first Baron Verulam and Viscount St. Albans (1561–1626), philosopher and politician. After serving as solicitor-general (1607), attorney-general (1613), privy councilor (1616), and lord chancellor (1618), he fell from power on a charge of bribery in 1621. See pp. 901–2.

Bacon, Sir Nicholas (1509–79), Tudor statesman, lord-keeper of the great seal (1558), father of Francis Bacon

Bactria, in antiquity a central Asiatic country and province of the Persian Empire on the River Oxus

Baeotia: *see* Boeotia

Bailly, Harry, innkeeper of the Tabard in Southwark and a prominent character in Chaucer's *Canterbury Tales*

Baily College, Balliol College, Oxford

Bajazet (1347–1403), Turkish sultan whose conquests and cruelties were finally checked by Timur (Marlowe's Tamburlaine) at Angora in 1402. According to the legend which Marlowe employed, his last days were spent in an iron cage, against the bars of which he dashed out his brains.

Baldwin, William (fl. 1547), author, clergyman, and schoolmaster who superintended the compilation of *A Mirror for Magistrates* and contributed to its early editions (1559 ff.): see p. 269

Bale, John (1495–1563), author and bishop of Ossory (1553) whose fiery Protestantism made for a tempestuous life. In addition to martyrologies he wrote a valuable history of English literature (*Illustrium majoris Britanniae scriptorum summarium,* 1548) and some fiercely polemic plays, of which the most notable is *King John*.

Ball, "Cutting," presumably a rascally friend of Robert Greene's who was hanged at Tyburn

Balsar(a), Bulsaur, a city in Bombay, India

Bandel(lo), Matteo (ca. 1480–1562), Italian prelate and bishop of Agen, France (1550), whose *novelle* (1554, 1573) became very popular in England through adaptations and translations (see pp. 671–72)

Banks, ——, (fl. 1588–1637), famous showman whose trained horse Morocco was one of the most popular attractions of the day

Bankside, district in London lying on the south bank of the Thames in Southwark, notorious for its theaters and disreputable houses of amusement

Banktree, ?river in Essex

Bannockburn, village in Stirlingshire, Scotland, where Edward II suffered a great defeat from the Scots under Robert Bruce on June 24, 1314

Baptista, Leo, ?Italian architect

Barbarus, Hermol(a)us, Ermolao Barbaro (1454–95), Italian diplomat and humanist, patriarch of Aquileia, author of various translations and of a critical commentary on Pliny's *Historia naturalis*

Barbary, general name for the coastal countries of North Africa west of Egypt

Barclay, Alexander (?1475–1552), poet and clergyman. He translated Brant's *Narrenschiff* as *The Ship of Fools* (1508), wrote his *Eclogues* while a Benedictine monk at Ely, and later became a Franciscan at Canterbury. See p. 81.

Barnaby, St. Barnabas, on whose feast day (June 11) the wedding celebrated in Spenser's *Epithalamion* took place

Barnes, Robert (Friar Barons) (1495–1540), Protestant martyr who, driven into exile by Wolsey, returned to England after Wolsey's fall and achieved a measure of power on diplomatic missions to Lutheran divines in Germany until he relapsed into his old heresies, fell foul of Bishop Gardiner, and was subsequently burned at the stake

Barnfield, Richard (1574–1627), poet: see p. 396

Barons, Friar: *see* Barnes

Barros, John, João de Barros (1496–1570), Portuguese historian whose chief works are *O Imperador Clarimundo,* a romance of chivalry, and *Asia* (1552–1615), a history of Portuguese expansion in the Orient

Bartas, Guillaume de Salluste du (1544–90), French poet whose active diplomatic and military career was linked with the fortunes of Henri of Navarre. His most popular work was *La première semaine,* a long didactic and religious poem which gained great popularity in England through the translation completed by Joshua Sylvester in 1606.

Bartholomew, one of the twelve apostles, probably to be identified with Nathaniel. According to legend he was flayed alive and then crucified head downward in Armenia.

Bartholomewtide, August 24

Barton, Elizabeth (?1506–34), nun (or holy maid) of Kent, a serving-girl whose religious mania and trances led her to feign divine inspiration. Directed by certain Catholic monks of Canterbury, she vehemently denounced Henry VIII's divorce and break with Rome, with the result that she and her accomplices were executed for treason.

Barwick: *see* Berwick

Basil (329–379), a father of the Greek church, unrelenting foe of the Arian heresy, and author of many works of homiletics, commentary, and doctrinal controversy

Basingstoke, town in Hampshire, England

Bathsheba (Bersabe), mother of Solomon by David, who contrived to have her husband Uriah killed in battle so that he might have her (see II Samuel xi)

Baucis, wife of Philemon (*q.v.*)

Bavier, Bavaria

Bayard, magical horse in medieval chivalric romances; hence a mock-heroic name for any horse

Bear, ?the Great Bear (*Ursa Major*), a constellation in the northern hemisphere

Beatrice (Beatrix): *see* Portinari

Beaufort, Edmund, second Duke of Somerset (d. 1455), commander active in the Hundred Years' War whose power declined as the Yorkists rose to strength under Henry VI. Imprisoned in the Tower when the Duke of York became protector, he was later killed in the first battle of St. Albans.

Beaufort, Sir Thomas, Duke of Exeter (d. 1427), illegitimate son of John of Gaunt by Catherine Swynford, a vexation to all anti-Lancastrians, and admiral of the fleet as well as chancellor (1410–12). A negotiator of the Treaty of Troyes following Agincourt, he became a member of the council under Gloucester's protectorate.

Beaulan, Samuel, according to Selden the author of a gloss of Nennius' *Historia Britonum*

Bede (673–735), abbot of Jarrow whose nearly forty works include the *Historia ecclesiastica,* an invaluable account of early Britain

Bedelem: *see* Bedlam

Bedford, Countess of: *see* Russell

Bedford, Duke of: *see* John of Lancaster

Bedlam, Bedelem (a corruption of *Bethlehem*), the hospital of St. Mary of Bethlehem in London, originally a priory dating from about 1247, but long used as a lunatic asylum

Be(e)lzebub, originally a Philistine god worshiped as the destroyer of flies; in Christian demonology one of Satan's lieutenants in the infernal regions

Belgia, Belgium, in the sixteenth century one of the Spanish provinces that united in revolt against Spain; **Belgic,** Belgian

Bellaeus, Remy Belleau (ca. 1327–77), French poet and humanist

Belleforest, François de (1530–83), French writer and historiographer in the court of Margaret of Navarre. His translation of Bandello continued that of Pierre Boaistuau (called Launay), to whose six tales Belleforest added six more, publishing all twelve in 1559; in 1564 the first of a series of successive expansions appeared, others following in 1565, 1567, 1571 (2), 1579, 1580, 1582.

Bellerophon, Corinthian hero who, on the winged horse Pegasus, killed the monster Chimera. When, in his excessive pride, he tried to mount to heaven on Pegasus, Zeus maddened the steed with a gadfly so that Bellerophon fell and perished.

Bellona, sister of Mars and the goddess of war

Belzebub: *see* Be(e)lzebub

Bembo (Bembus), Pietro (1470–1547), Italian humanist, cardinal, lover of Lucretia Borgia, author of many poems and epistles as well as *Gli Asolani* (dialogues on the nature of love)

Benacus, i.e. Lake Garda in northern Italy, from which the Mincius (*q.v.*) flows

Benedic(t) Biscop (?628–690), Northumbrian monk who built the monastery of St. Peter at the mouth of the River Wear and of St. Paul at Jarrow, collector of manuscripts, and guardian of Bede. Traditionally he was the pioneer in England in the construction of stone buildings and the making of glass.

Benedictine, follower of the rule of St. Benedict of Nursia (ca. 480–543), founder of the famous monastery of Monte Cassino

Bennet, St., ?St. Benedict: *see* Benedictine

Bentley, an actor mentioned in Thomas Heywood's *Apology for Actors* (1612) as having been the favorite of an earlier generation

Benyn, Benin, formerly a name for the eastern part of Upper Guinea

Berkeley Castle, Norman castle between Bristol and Gloucester, the site of Edward II's murder

Bernard, St. (of Clairvaux, 1090–1153), French clergyman famed for his reform of the Cistercian order and for his wide influence in doctrinal matters, engineer of Abelard's condemnation at the Council of Sens (1140), powerful preacher of the Second Crusade in 1146

Bernardine, member of the branch of the Cistercian order founded by St. Bernard (*q.v.*)

Bersabe: *see* Bathsheba

Berwick (Barwick), Northumbrian seaport at the mouth of the Tweed

Bess, Lady, i.e. Elizabeth Woodville (*q.v.*), queen of Edward IV

Bethphage, in Scriptural geography, a Palestinian village situated on the Mount of Olives

Bewe, Master, unidentified contributor of at least two poems to *The Paradise of Dainty Devices* (see p. 212). It has been somewhat implausibly suggested that *Bewe* is an anagram for (William) *Webbe,* author of *A Discourse of English Poetry* (1586: see p. 628).

Beza, Theodore, Théodore de Bèze (1519–1605), Calvin's colleague and successor in Geneva, in the later sixteenth century the most influential Protestant leader on the Continent, prolific writer on theological subjects

bezo las manos, "kiss on the hands"; *bezo les labres,* "kiss on the lips"

Bias (fl. 550 B.C.), one of the Seven Sages of Greece, noted for his apothegms

Bib(b)iena, Bernardo Dovizio (1470–1520), Italian poet and friend of Raphael, secretary of Giovanni Cardinal de' Medici and later himself a cardinal, author of the comedy *Calandria* (1521)

Biblis, a woman of Miletus who was changed into a fountain because of her passion for her brother Caunus

Bion (fl. ca. 250 B.C.), a slave of Borysthenes, near the mouth of the Dnieper, who, when freed by his master, became a Cynic philosopher at Athens

Birchin(g) Lane, London street famed for its drapers' shops; "to send to Birching Lane" means to administer a whipping.

Bird, Christopher, a fellow-townsman of the Harveys at Saffron Walden, represented as the writer of the first epistle in Gabriel Harvey's *Four Letters*

Bithynia, ancient country in Asia Minor

Blackheath Field, an open common in Kent, the scene of Wat Tyler's rebellion in 1381, of Jack Cade's in 1450, and of the Cornish rebels' defeat on June 22, 1497

Blackleech, Nicholas, a friend of Richard Barnfield

Blount, Charles, Earl of Devonshire and eighth Baron Mountjoy (1563–1606), prominent Elizabethan courtier and soldier, patron of Samuel Daniel, and lover (later, in 1605, husband) of Penelope Rich, Sidney's "Stella" (*q.v.*)

Blount (Blunt), Edward (fl. 1588–1632), publisher and freeman of the Stationers' Company who printed many famous books,

among them Florio's translation of Montaigne (1603), Marlowe's *Hero and Leander* (1598), and the First Folio of Shakespeare (1623)

Blount (Blunt), Sir Walter (d. 1403), Lancastrian stalwart, friend and executor of John of Gaunt

Bocardo, ancient gate near the Church of St. Michael, Oxford. Before its destruction (1771) the room over the gate was used as a prison.

Boccaccio (Boccace, Bochas), Giovan(ni) (1313–75), a literary leader of the Italian Renaissance, author of the *Decamerone* (a frame-story of one hundred vernacular tales, 1353), *Il Filocolo, Il Teseide, Amorosa Fiammetta, Il Filostrato,* as well as such later Latin works as *De genealogia deorum, De casibus virorum et feminarum illustrium,* and *De claris mulieribus*

Boemia: *see* Aurelius

Boeotia (Baeotia), district in ancient Greece whose inhabitants were notorious for their stupidity

Boethius, Anicius Manlius Severinus (ca. 475-ca. 524), late Roman philosopher and politician (at the court of Theodoric, king of the Ostrogoths), author of the vastly influential *De consolatione philosophiae* (which he wrote in prison while awaiting his execution) and of an elaborate commentary on the *Topica* of Cicero as well as commentaries and translations of other philosophers

Boghar, Bokhara, a city in central Asia

Bohun, Mary de, first wife (m. 1380) of Henry Bolingbroke (later Henry IV), and mother of Henry V

Bois Saint Vincent, i.e. Bois de Vincennes, formerly the site of a castle and royal residence just east of Paris

Boleyn (Bulleine), Anne (1507–36), first the mistress (ca. 1527) and then the second wife (m. 1533) of Henry VIII, and mother of Queen Elizabeth. She was executed on a charge of adultery and incest after her marriage had been declared invalid.

Boleyn, George, Viscount Rochford (d. 1536), brother of Anne Boleyn (*q.v.*), whose fortunes rose with his sister's until he was charged with incest and high treason, convicted, and executed

Boleyn (Bulleine), Sir Thomas, Earl of Wiltshire (1477–1539), energetic Tudor politician who rose rapidly after his daughter Anne began her liaison with Henry VIII. Created Earl of Wiltshire and Ormonde in 1529 and lord privy seal the next year, he not unnaturally took an active part in the divorce proceedings against Queen Catherine.

Bolingbroke, Bullingbrook: *see* Henry IV

Bolognia, Bologna, Italian city at the foot of the Apennines

bona fide, "in good faith"

bona fortuna, "good fortune"

Bona Sperança (Speranza), Cape of, the Cape of Good Hope, a promontory at the southwest extremity of Africa, discovered by Vasco da Gama in 1497

Boniface, Count, St. Boniface, bishop of Rome (418–422)

Bordeaux, ancient capital city of the Gironde, France, on the Garonne

Boreas, the north wind, brother of Zephyrus, Eurus, and Notus, who lived in a cave on Mt. Haemus in Thrace

Borough: *see* Borrows

Borough(bridge), village in Yorkshire where Edward II defeated the barons under Thomas, Earl of Lancaster, in 1322

Borrows (Borough), Stephen (Steven) (1525–84), navigator, master of the first ship to reach Russia from England (1553), and prominent explorer of the Baltic

Bosom's Inn, i.e. Blossom's Inn in Cheapside, London

Boulogne (Bulloigne), French seaport on the English Channel. Captured by Henry VIII in 1544, it was restored to France in 1550.

Bourges, ancient French city noted for its cathedral and university

Bourman, Nicholas, ballad-writer in whose name three broadsides were licensed in the Stationers' Register between 1571 and 1602

Brabant (Braband), province of modern Belgium (formerly a duchy), the capital city of which is Brussels

Bramston(e), village near Flodden Field (*q.v.*)

Brandon, Charles, ?third Duke of Suffolk (?1537–51), educated by Thomas Wilson, from whom he went to St. John's College, Cambridge, where he died of the sweating sickness; or perhaps the illegitimate son (1544-51) of Charles Brandon, first Duke of Suffolk

Brasill, Bresil, Bresil(l)ia, Brazil

Breton (Britton), Nicholas (?1553-?1626), poet, stepson of George Gascoigne, probably a student of Oriel College, Oxford, author of satires, romances, and pastorals including *A Florish upon Fancy* (1577), *The Pilgrimage to Paradise* (1592), *The Will of Wit* (1597), *Pasquil's Madcap* (1600), *A Mad World, My Masters* (?1603), *Divine Considerations of the Soul* (1608): see p. 228

Bridewell, favorite palace of Henry VIII at the mouth of a tidal stream, the Fleet, between Whitefriars and Blackfriars, later a workhouse, and then a prison, most of which was demolished in 1863

Briget, Bridget; **Brigets bowre,** perhaps Spenser's confusion of the well and chapel of St. Blaze, located in the park of the bishop of Rochester at Bromley, Kent

Bristow, Bristol, important seaport at the mouth of the Avon on the Severn estuary

Britan, Briton

Britannia, England

Briton, Cape, Cape Breton, island off the east coast of Canada

Britton: *see* Breton

Broadgate, Bradgate, Leicestershire, birthplace of Lady Jane Grey

Brooke, Christopher (d. 1628), poet friendly with such writers and scholars as Selden, Jonson, and Drayton; roommate of Donne at Lincoln's Inn

Browne, William (1591-?1643), poet and retainer of the Herbert family

Brownshold, ?Leighton-Bromswold, Huntingdonshire

Bruges, capital of the province of West Flanders

Bruno, Giordano (1548-1600), Italian philosopher born at Nola (hence his sobriquet "Nolano"), who, though a Dominican, incurred the hatred and suspicion of the Roman church for his heterodox works. After a life of teaching and writing in Switzerland, France, England, and Germany he returned to Italy in 1592, was seized by the Inquisition, and after long imprisonment was burned as a heretic in Rome.

Brut, Brute, Brutus, legendary great-grandson (or, according to some accounts, grandson) of Aeneas, who, after many wanderings, became the first king of Britain (see p. 3)

Brutain, Britain

Brute: *see* Brut

Bruton, William a, i.e. William Brereton (d. 1536), courtier executed on a charge of high treason for complicity in Anne Boleyn's alleged misdeeds

Brutus: *see* Brut

Brutus Albinus, Decimus Junius, Roman general who was one of Caesar's assassins. He was betrayed by Camillus, of Gaul, to Antony and was executed in 43 B.C.

Brutus, Lucius Junius, hero of the Roman republic who, as consul in 509 B.C., led the popular revolt against the Tarquins after the rape of Lucretia (*q.v.*). One of his acts as consul was to condemn his own sons to death for plotting the return of the Tarquins.

Brutus, Marcus Junius (85-42 B.C.), Roman politician who abandoned Pompey's dying cause to join Caesar after the battle of Pharsalia (48), conspired with Cassius in the assassination of Caesar (44), and committed suicide after his defeat by Octavius and Antony at Philippi (42)

Bruxelle(s), Brussels, capital of the province of Brabant and of Belgium

Bryan, Sir Francis (d. 1550), courtier and diplomat under Henry VIII and Edward VI, friend of Wyatt, contributor to Tottel's *Miscellany* (although none of his work can now be identified)

Bryskett, Lodowick (or **Lewis,** fl. 1571-1611), poet, translator, and friend of Sidney and Spenser who owned land and held various government posts in Ireland between 1577 and 1600

Bubonax, perhaps Sidney's confusion of Hipponax and Bupalus. Hipponax (*q.v.*) so roughly criticized Bupalus' statuary that the artist hanged himself.

Buchanan, George (1506-82), Scottish humanist, tutor of James VI, author of *De jure regni apud Scotos* (1579), a history of Scot-

land, dramas (*Baptistes, Jephthes*), and translations of *Medea* and *Alcestis*

Buckhurst, Lord: *see* Sackville (Thomas)

Buckingham, Duke of: *see* Stafford (Henry)

Buckston, i.e. Buxton, a town in Derbyshire famous for its saline waters in both hot and cold springs

Bucolics (Bucoliques), Virgil's *Eclogues*, ten short poems which are probably his earliest work (ca. 41-37 B.C.)

Budaeus or Budé, Guillaume (1467-1540), French humanist and scholar, friend of Erasmus, royal librarian to François I, author of *De asse,* a famed work on ancient coinage

Bull, (1) the public hangman who was succeeded by the infamous Derrick, notorious in the early seventeenth century for his cruelty and rapacity; (2) the zodiacal sign Taurus

Bulleine: *see* Boleyn

Bullingbrook, i.e. Bolingbroke: *see* Henry IV

Bulloigne: *see* Boulogne

Bunel, Peter (or **Pierre,** 1499-1546), French humanist and author of a set of *Epistolae* modeled upon Cicero

Burby, Cuthbert, London bookseller (1592-1607) among whose products were Greene's *Repentance* and Harvey's *Trimming of Thomas Nashe*

Burcot, Master Doctor, unidentified person mentioned in Chettle's *Kind-Heart's Dream*

Burghley, Baron: *see* Cecil

Burgoyne (Burgognie), Duke of: *see* Philip, Duke of Burgundy

Burton, battle of, encounter in 1322 between Edward II and forces under Thomas, Earl of Lancaster, at Burton-on-Trent, a town in Staffordshire

Byrd, William (?1538-1623), composer and musician, gentleman of the Chapel Royal who shared with Thomas Tallis the honorary post of organist of the Chapel Royal and the monopoly (1575) for selling printed music and ruled music paper; prolific composer of vocal and instrumental works, many of which are preserved in the so-called *Queen Elizabeth's Virginal Book* in the Fitzwilliam Museum, Cambridge

Byrt, John (fl. 1525), a troublesome Protestant mentioned with asperity in More's *Apology*

Cabala, Kabbala, set of Jewish mystical commentaries on the Scripture, written between the ninth and thirteenth centuries

Cabelimus: G. Gregory Smith (*Elizabethan Critical Essays,* I, 71) emends Lodge's perplexing "which Cabelimus calleth Porum" to "which Persius calleth Caballinus." The reference is to the first line of the prologue of Persius' satires: *Nec fonte labra prolui caballino,* "I never wet my lips in the Nag's Spring," that is, in the Spring Hippocrene, struck out by the hoof of Pegasus on the top of Mt. Helicon.

Cabot, John, Giovanni Caboto (fl. 1495), Italian navigator in English service who, sailing from Bristol in 1497 in search of the Northwest Passage under letters patent from Henry VII, discovered Nova Scotia. He presumably died on a second voyage in 1498.

Cabot (Gabot), Sebastian (1474-1557), second son of John Cabot (*q.v.*), who accompanied his father on the 1497 voyage, entered the service of Charles V, and in the fifties explored the Baltic for the Company of Merchant Adventurers of London, of which he was the first governor

Cadmus (Cadinus), son of Agenor, king of Phoenicia, who, sent by his father in search of his sister Europa (or Io, *q.v.*), settled in Boeotia and founded the city of Thebes. Later he killed a dragon and sowed its teeth, from which soldiers sprang up.

caecus amor sui, "self-love is blind" (Horace, *Odes* I.xviii.14)

caelum petimus stultitia, "in our folly we try to scale the heavens" (adapted from Horace, *Odes* I.iii.38)

Caenis, ?Caeneus, one of the Lapithae (*q.v.*), originally a girl (Caenis) beloved of Poseidon, who changed her into a man and then made him invulnerable. He participated in the voyage of the Argonauts and in the Calydonian boar-hunt (*q.v.*), was buried beneath a tree by the Centaurs at the marriage of Pirithous, and in Hades became a woman again.

Caesar, Caius Julius (100-44 B.C.), Roman general and politician, dictator (49-44), and writer on military subjects. The *Com-*

mentarii, the only one of his original works extant, treats the first seven years of the Gallic wars in seven books (*De bello Gallico*) and the history of part of the civil war in three books (*De bello civili*).

Caiet(a), nurse in the family of Aeneas for whom the promontory of Gaeta, in Latium, was allegedly named

Caiete, Gaeta, seaport in the province of Caserta, Italy

Caius Gracchus: *see* Gracchi

Caius Octavianus Augustus Caesar: *see* Augustus Caesar

Calais (Calis), seaport in Pas-de-Calais, France, on the narrowest part of the Strait of Dover. It was held by England from 1347 to 1558.

Calcedon, Chalcedon, ancient city in Asia Minor, the site of the fourth Ecumenical Council in 451

Calchas, Greek soothsayer in the Trojan War: *see* Thestorides

Cales, Cadiz, ancient port in southeast Spain, in the sixteenth century an important base for Spanish shipping and exploration. In 1587 Sir Francis Drake (*q.v.*) destroyed an armament in the harbor, and in 1596 an English force under the command of Robert Devereux, Earl of Essex (*q.v.*), sacked the city.

Calicut (Caliquit), seaport in the Malabar district of Madras, India

Calidius, Marcus (d. 48 B.C.), Roman politician who followed Caesar in the civil war and was rewarded with the governorship of Gallia Togata

Caligula (Caius Caesar, 12–41), third emperor of the Roman Empire who succeeded his uncle Tiberius in 37 and became notorious for his cruelties and dissipations

Caliquit: *see* Calicut

Calis: *see* Calais

Callias (fl. 380 B.C.), scion of a noble Athenian family who notoriously dissipated his ancestral wealth. The scene of Xenophon's *Banquet* and Plato's *Symposium* is laid at his house.

Callimachus (d. ca. 240 B.C.), Greek critic, poet, and grammarian, reputedly chief librarian of the great Alexandrian library

Calliope, muse of epic poetry

Callisthenes (d. ca. 328 B.C.), philosopher and cousin and student of Aristotle who accompanied Alexander the Great to Asia and was executed for offending his master

Callisto, Arcadian huntress, attendant of Artemis, whom Zeus loved and transformed into a she-bear, whereupon she was killed by Artemis

Calpurnia, last wife of Julius Caesar (m. 59 B.C.)

Calvin (Cauvin), John (1509–64), Protestant reformer and theologian whose *Institutes* (1536 ff.) was the most influential document of reformed theology in England

Calvus, Caius Licinius Macer (82–47 B.C.), Roman poet and orator whose speeches and poems were much admired by Catullus and Ovid

Calydonian boar-hunt, the chase of a ferocious boar sent by Artemis to ravage the country of Oeneus, king of Calydon, as punishment for a neglected sacrifice. Meleager and his companions (including in some accounts his paramour Atalanta) slew the boar.

Calypso, nymph who entertained Odysseus for seven years on her island of Ogygia

Cam, Skelton's mistake for Ham, one of the sons of Noah

Camber, traditionally one of Brut's sons who was supposed to have given his name to Cambria (Wales)

Cambro-Briton (Cambro-Britan), Welshman

Camden, William (1551–1623), antiquarian and historian, headmaster of Westminster School, whose erudition became legendary: see p. 21

Camenes, the Camenae, prophetic nymphs of Italy, sometimes identified with the muses

Campion, Thomas (d. 1620), poet, musician, and physician whose lyrics are among the most flawless in English: see pp. 255, 653–54

Canaan, Palestine

Canaries, the Canary Islands, a group lying about sixty miles off the west coast of Africa

Candaules: *see* Gyges

Candish, Thomas: *see* Cavendish (Thomas)

Canidia, Neapolitan courtezan with whom Horace was infatuated and whom he denounced as a sorceress when she deserted him

Canna(e), town near Apulia, Italy, where Hannibal won his most decisive victory over Rome in 216 B.C.

Cano, Isle of, Caño Island, off the west coast of Costa Rica

Canossa, Lodovico (Count Lewis of Canossa, 1476–1532), close friend of Castiglione who joined the court of Urbino in 1498 and was named bishop of Bayeux in 1516

Cantabridge, Cambridge

Cantacuzene (Cantacuzenus), Joannes (ca. 1300–1383), Byzantine emperor who wrote a history of the mid-fourteenth century

Cantica canticorum, the Song of Solomon or Canticles, probably composed as a marriage ode for Solomon's wedding with the daughter of Pharaoh, although it has commonly been allegorized as the union of Christ and his spouse the Church

Cape Verd(e), Isles of, group of islands in the Atlantic west of Cape Verd, Africa

cap(itum), "chapter"

Cappadocia, ancient country (later a Roman province) in Asia Minor

Capra, zodiacal sign of the Goat; originally the nymph or goat who nursed the infant Zeus in Crete

Capys, (1) son of Assaracus and father of Anchises; (2) a companion of Aeneas

Carbo, probably either Caius Papirius Carbo or his son of the same name, both prominent statesmen at the turn of the first century B.C.

Cardan(us), Girolamo Cardano (1501–76), Italian physician, mathematician, astrologer, and philosopher

caret tempus non habet moribus, Nashe's bad Latin which, says McKerrow (*Nashe*, IV, 120), defies translation. Perhaps the implication is that even dunces have studied at universities.

Carew (Carey), Edmund and **Robert**, two of the seven sons of Henry Carey, first Lord Hunsdon (?1524–96), and brothers of George Carey, second Baron Hunsdon (*q.v.*), whom Lodge, in the dedication to *Rosalynde*, incorrectly calls their father. Edmund, the sixth son, was knighted by Leicester in the Netherlands in 1587; Robert, the youngest, was created first Earl of Monmouth in 1626.

Carey, George, second Baron Hunsdon (1547–1603), prominent statesman and diplomat under Elizabeth, who named him lord chamberlain of her household in 1597

Caria, a part of Asia Minor lying between Lydia and Phrygia and the Aegean Sea

Cariclea, Caricles: *see* Theagenes

Carlisle, Bishop of: *see* Merke

Carmelite, a friar of the Order of Our Lady of Mount Carmel, established in Syria in the twelfth century; a White Friar

carmina, "songs"

Carmina proverbialia, a popular collection of riming Latin proverbs (1577)

Carnarvon, i.e. Edward II, so called from his birth at the castle of Carnarvon, Wales (April 25, 1284)

carnifex, "executioner, murderer"

Carolostadius Andreas Karlstadt or Bodenstein (?1480–1541), German reformer and antagonist of Luther

Carr, Nicholas (1524–68), Greek scholar and regius professor of Greek at Cambridge, who published Latin versions of Eusebius and Demosthenes

Carra, Carrae (or Carrhae), Mesopotamian city where Crassus (*q.v.*) was murdered after his defeat by the Parthians in 53 B.C.

Carrow, village east of Norwich, formerly the site of a Benedictine nunnery

Cartagena, seaport of Colombia, situated on an island between the Caribbean Sea and the Bay of Cartagena

Carthage, Carthago, ancient city and state in North Africa a few miles northeast of modern Tunis. In the three Punic wars with Rome (264–241, 218–201, 149–146 B.C.) its great commercial power was broken; it later became an important center of Latin Christianity, and was finally destroyed by the Saracens about 697.

Cartier, Jacques (1491–1557), French explorer who made three voyages to Canada between 1534 and 1542, the last an unsuccessful attempt at colonization

Casas, Bartholomew (i.e. **Bartolomé**) **de las** (1474-1566), Spanish missionary to the Indians and vigorous critic of the oppressive colonial policy of Spain. In citing *The Spanish Cruelties* Raleigh apparently meant *The Spanish Colony,* an excoriation of colonial policy published in English translation in 1583. Las Casas' *Brief Narration of the Destruction of the Indies by the Spaniards* was included in *Purchas His Pilgrims* (1625).

Casca, Publius Servilius Casca, tribune of the plebs (44 B.C.) who struck the first blow at Caesar's assassination

Caspian Sea, salt inland sea between Europe and Asia, bounded by Russia on the north and Persia on the south

Cassandra, daughter of Priam and Hecuba who foretold the fall of Troy. She had repulsed Apollo, who gave her the gift of prophecy with the stipulation that her prophecies would never be believed.

Cassel(s), Kassel, town in the Departement du Nord, France, twenty miles south of Dunkirk

Cassius, Caius, fellow-conspirator of Brutus in the assassination of Caesar, and eventually a suicide at Philippi (42 B.C.)

Castalia (Castalius), fountain on the slopes of Mt. Parnassus, sacred to Apollo and the muses

Castell, Castile, old kingdom in the northern and central parts of Spain, united (1479) with Aragon after the marriage of Isabella of Aragon and Ferdinand of Castile

Castiglione, Baldassare (1478-1529), Italian diplomat and writer in the service first of the House of Sforza at Milan and then of the House of Malatesta at Urbino; author of *Il Cortegiano* (see p. 522)

Castilian, i.e. Spaniard

Catadupi, Catadupa, ancient name for the cataracts of the Nile and the adjacent parts of Ethiopia

Cathay, northern China

Catherine, Lady, Catherine of Valois (q.v.)

Catherine, Queen, Catherine of Aragon (q.v.)

Catherine of Aragon (1485-1536), daughter of Ferdinand and Isabella, fiancée of Arthur, Prince of Wales (d. 1502), wife of Henry VIII (m. 1509), mother of Mary Tudor, who became queen in 1553. Henry's efforts to secure an annulment of his marriage with Catherine were largely responsible for the English break with Rome.

Catherine of Valois (1401-37), daughter of Charles VI of France, wife of Henry V of England (m. 1420), mother of Henry VI. After her husband's death she plotted with (and perhaps secretly married) Owen Tudor, by whom she bore Edmund, Earl of Richmond and father of Henry VII, founder of the Tudor dynasty.

Catilinaries, referring to Catiline, Roman conspirator (q.v.)

Catiline, Lucius Sergius Catilina (ca. 108-62 B.C.), dissolute and unscrupulous Roman politician whose conspiracy against the republic (63) was exposed and demolished by Cicero in four brilliant orations leading to his capture and execution

Cato the Censor, Marcus Porcius Cato (234-149 B.C.), Roman statesman and writer (*De re rustica* and *Origines*) famed for his unyielding opposition to Carthage in the third Punic War and for his efforts to revive the old ideals of Roman virtue and integrity

Cato the Younger, Marcus Porcius Cato (surnamed Uticensis, 95-46 B.C.), great-grandson of Cato the Censor, ally of Cicero against Catiline and of Pompey against Caesar. Famed as a conservative and a custodian of all antique Roman virtues, he committed suicide after the death of Pompey rather than live under a new and, as he thought, wicked dispensation.

Catri, Mt., Monte Catria, a peak in the Apennines near Urbino (q.v.)

Caux (Pays de Caux or **Kaux),** small district in Normandy on the estuary of the Seine

cave, "beware"

Cavendish, George (1500-?1561), retainer and biographer of Cardinal Wolsey: see p. 53

Cavendish (Candish), Thomas (1560-92), navigator who in 1585 commanded a ship under Sir Richard Grenville on Raleigh's Virginia expedition, in 1586 began the voyage of circum-

navigation which ended in 1588, died at sea while returning from a second attempt at circumnavigation

c'e est la signe . . . , "this is the sign of the king to maintain joy, and to all his people it indicates his will"

Cecil, William, Baron Burghley (1520-98), Elizabeth's most trusted counselor, secretary of state (1550), lord high treasurer (1572), chief minister for nearly forty years

Celenes, Celaeno, chief of the Harpies (q.v.)

Celiano, Livio, author of a volume of *Rime* published in 1587

Centaurs, the Centauri ("bull-killers"), an ancient race who inhabited Mt. Pelion in Thessaly, so fierce that they came to be represented as creatures half horse, half man

Cerberus, watch-dog at the entrance of hell, usually represented as having three heads, a serpent's tail, and a mane of serpents' heads

Ceres, goddess of grain and harvest, later associated by the Romans with the Greek Demeter

Cethro, Mount, the island of Cythera

Chabrias, Athenian general who won brilliant victories against the Persians and the Spartans before his death at the siege of Chios in 357 B.C.

Chabris (Chabry), town in France north of Châteauroux

Chaldees, Chaldeans, in antiquity inhabitants of the area between Babylon and the Persian Gulf, a people famous for their knowledge of astronomy and astrology

Chaloner, Sir Thomas (1521-65), diplomat and author who served on a mission to Charles V, became a follower of Somerset, and was employed on diplomatic missions by both Mary and Elizabeth. A writer by avocation, he was a friend of Cheke and Haddon, translator of Chrysostom and Erasmus, author of various Latin epigrams and epitaphs, and contributor to the first extant edition of *A Mirror for Magistrates.*

Chamloe (Chomley), Sir Roger (d. 1565), named lord chief justice on March 21, 1552

Chanticleer, common name for a rooster (from Chaucer's "Nun's Priest's Tale")

Chaos, the infinite, vacant space out of which gods, men, and all things arose

Chapman, George (?1559-1634), poet, translator, and playwright: see pp. 445-46, 577

Chariclea, Charicles: *see* Theagenes

Charlemagne, Charles the Great (742-814), king of the Franks and emperor of the west, the great French leader whose deeds provided the subject for a vast body of medieval romance and Renaissance epic. The principal source of the Carolingian legend was the chronicle attributed to Turpin, archbishop of Rheims, but actually composed in the eleventh or twelfth century; later versions were the *Chanson de Roland* and the epics of Boiardo and Ariosto.

Charles V (1500-1558), emperor of the Holy Roman Empire (1519-55), father of Philip II of Spain. As head of the House of Hapsburg and nephew of Catherine of Aragon, first wife of Henry VIII, he was the Continental monarch whom Henry most feared and hated.

Charles VI (1368-1422), king of France (1380-1422) whose reign (during much of which he was insane) was agitated by a fierce struggle for power between the dukes of Burgundy and Orléans and by civil war following the murder of Orléans in 1407. In collusion with the Burgundians his wife Isabella acknowledged Henry V's right to the French crown at Charles's death, but her son Charles VII redeemed the honor and possessions of the House of Valois.

Charles VII (1403-61), king of France (1422-61) who, though disinherited by his mother Isabella (or Isabeau) at the Treaty of Troyes and challenged after his accession by Henry VI's claims to the French crown, earned his sobriquet "Victorious" by uniting all French factions, and regaining from the English all French soil except Calais. He was crowned at Rheims (1429) by Joan of Arc.

Charles the Great: *see* Charlemagne

Charon, the ferryman who transported the souls of the properly buried dead across the rivers of the underworld. For his fee, an obolus was placed in the mouth of the corpse before burial.

Charterhouse, Carthusian monastery near Aldersgate Street in London, founded in 1371 and dissolved by Henry VIII. The buildings were later used for an almshouse and a famous school for boys.

Charybdis: *see* Scylla and Charybdis

Chaucer, Geoffrey (ca. 1340–1400), greatest English poet before the sixteenth century, widely read by the Elizabethans despite their limited knowledge of his language and prosody

Chaul, Hindustani seaport south of Bombay

Chavez, Alonso di, sixteenth-century Spanish cosmographer and examiner of pilots

Chavez, Hieronimus di, Geronimo Chavez, sixteenth-century Spanish cosmographer

Cheap(side), thoroughfare in the City of London

Cheke, Sir John (1514–57), humanist and teacher, tutor to Edward VI, provost of King's College, Cambridge, secretary of state (1553), Marian exile at Strassburg, editor of Greek texts and author of works of Protestant theology

Chelsea, district of London three miles southwest of St. Paul's, in the sixteenth century a country village beyond Westminster

Chettle, Henry (d. ?1607), dramatist and printer, Robert Greene's literary executor: see p. 849

Cheviot (Hills), range of hills in Northumberland and Roxburghshire

Chichele (Chicheley), Henry (?1362–1443), archbishop of Canterbury, supporter of Henry V's persecution of Lollards and of his French wars, founder of All Souls' College, Oxford

Chloris, goddess of flowers, wife of Zephyrus

Chomley: *see* Chamloe

Christ Church, Oxford, college founded by Cardinal Wolsey in 1525 as Cardinal College, refounded as King Henry VIII's College in 1532, and again as Christ Church in 1546

Chrysa, city on the coast of the Troad, noted for its shrine dedicated to Apollo Smintheus

Chryses, in Homer, a priest of Apollo whose daughter Chryseis was the cause of a serious quarrel between Agamemnon and Achilles

Chrysostom(us), St. John (ca. 347–407), a father of the Greek church, famous preacher at Antioch (his name means "golden-mouthed"), patriarch of Constantinople (398–404)

Churchyard, Thomas (?1520–1604), long-lived miscellaneous writer of many ballads and poems, contributor to *A Mirror for Magistrates, The Paradise of Dainty Devices,* and *A Gorgeous Gallery,* author of *The First Part of Churchyard's Chips* (1575), *Churchyard's Challenge* (1593), etc.

Cicero, Marcus Tullius (Tully, 106–43 B.C.), Roman politician, orator, and moralist whose works were universally admired and imitated in the early Renaissance. After much shifting he joined Pompey's faction in 49, was proscribed by the second triumvirate, and was executed. A large number of his works are extant: fifty-seven orations, four bodies of correspondence, and many treatises on philosophy, oratory, politics, and morality (*De oratore, De republica, De legibus, De officiis, Tusculanae disputationes,* etc.).

Cilicia, district in southeastern Asia Minor

Cilla, small town in the Troad famed for its temple to Apollo

Cimber, Lucius Tillius, partisan of Caesar, who rewarded him with the province of Bithynia. Later Cimber took a vital part in Caesar's assassination and raised a fleet for the service of Brutus and Cassius.

Cimbrorum promontorium, the Skaw, a cape at the northeastern extremity of Jutland, Denmark

Cimmerian, pertaining to Cimmeria, a region north of the Black Sea thought by the ancients to lie in perpetual darkness

Cimon (d. 449 B.C.), Athenian general who defeated the Persians in 466

Cinthia: *see* Cynthia

Circe(s), a sorceress, daughter of Helios, who lived on the island of Aeaea, where she entertained Odysseus and turned some of his companions into swine

circum praecordia ludit, "he plays about the most intimate things" (Persius, *Satires* I.117)

Cithera: *see* Cythera

City of the Trinity, perhaps Nicaea, in Bithynia, where the Nicene Creed (325), establishing Trinitarian dogma, was promulgated

Clarence, Duke of: *see* Thomas, Duke of Clarence

Clarenceaulx, Clarenceux, the second king-of-arms in the Heralds' College, whose office is to supervise funerals of all baronets, knights, and esquires south of the Trent

Clark(e), John, perhaps the John Clark who was one of the commanders with Sir Richard Grenville in the Virginian expedition of 1585

Claudianus, Claudius (ca. 365–ca. 408), Latin poet whose voluminous works include panegyrics, epigrams, versified history, and the *Raptus Proserpinae* (a fragmentary epic)

Clauser(us), Conrad (?1520–1611), German humanist whose edition of Cornutus' *De natura deorum gentilium commentarius* was published at Basle in 1543

Clement VII (ca. 1342–94), antipope elected in 1378 to challenge the claims of Urban VI

Clement(s), John (d. 1572), physician educated at St. Paul's School under Colet, tutor in Sir Thomas More's household at Chelsea, and lecturer in rhetoric and reader in Greek at Oxford before his unyielding Catholicism drove him into exile at Elizabeth's accession

Cleopatra (69–30 B.C.), daughter of Ptolemy Auletes of Egypt, his successor (jointly with her brother) in 51, Julius Caesar's mistress in Rome (46–44), Antony's after he was named ruler of the East by the second triumvirate, with him a suicide after their defeat by Octavius at Actium in 31

Cleopatra, a tragedy by Samuel Daniel, published in 1594

Clerk, John (d. 1541), early Tudor ecclesiastic who, though raised to eminence by Wolsey (for whom he tried to obtain the papacy in 1523), assented to Henry VIII's divorce and continued in high favor with the king. He was named bishop of Bath and Wells in 1523.

Clifford, Margaret, Countess of Cumberland (?1560–1616), with her sister Lady Anne (not Lady Marie, as Spenser mistakenly calls her) the recipient of the dedication of *Four Hymns.* They were daughters of Francis Russell, second Earl of Bedford.

Clifford, Rosamond (d. ca. 1176), daughter of Walter de Clifford and mistress of Henry II, who publicly announced their relationship and built for her a handsome tomb at Godstow Nunnery. The legendary (but baseless) account of her death through the machinations of the jealous Queen Eleanor long survived in popular mythology and formed the plot of one of the most popular poems of the late sixteenth century, Samuel Daniel's *Complaint of Rosamond* (1592): see pp. 405–10.

Clodius, Publius Clodius Pulcher, notorious profligate whom Cicero brilliantly prosecuted for his defamation of the mysteries of the Bona Dea, and who in retaliation played an important part in Cicero's exile in 57 B.C.

Clotho: *see* Parcae

Clytia, Clytie, an Oceanid infatuated with Apollo

Cobham, Lord: *see* Oldcastle

Cocytus, tributary of Acheron, a river in Hades

Codrus, a perhaps fictitious poetaster attacked by Virgil and Juvenal

cogita quamdiu . . . , "think how often you have done the same thing. One may wish to die not so much because he is brave or miserable as because he is disgusted with life."

Colch(is), Colchos, Asiatic country between the Caucasus and the Black Sea, allegedly the home of Medea and of the Golden Fleece sought by Jason and his Argonauts

Colebrook, Colnbrook, a village in Buckinghamshire

Colet, John (?1467–1519), dean of St. Paul's and founder of St. Paul's School, humanist, friend of Erasmus and More: see p. 150

Colgoieve, ?Arctic port

Colin Clout, name adopted by Edmund Spenser in *The Shepherd's Calendar* and *Colin Clout's Come Home Again,* derived from Skelton's *Colin Clout* (ca. 1519), a satire of ecclesiastical abuses

Collatia, Sabine town in Latium on the River Anio

Collatinus, Tarquinius: *see* Lucretia

colonia deducta, "a colony broken off"

Columbus, Christopher (?1446–1506), Genoese navigator, the discoverer of America

Columella, Lucius Junius Moderatus, Spanish writer of Gades (Cadiz), contemporary with Seneca. His *De re rustica,* a treatise on agriculture and domestic animals, was long popular; bk. X, in dactylic hexameters, forms a kind of supplement to Virgil's *Georgics.*

Colwell, Thomas, London printer from 1561 to 1575

Commines, Philippe de (?1445–?1511), French politician and statesman who participated in and wrote a history of the long struggle between Charles the Bold and Louis XI

confitebor tibi, Domine, in toto corde meo, "I will confess to thee, Lord, with my whole heart" (Vulgate Psalms ix.2)

Conon (d. ?392 B.C.), Athenian general who defeated the Spartan fleet in 394

consilium post facta, "good advice too late"

Conspiracy of Catiline, The, Sallust's *Catilina* or *Bellum Catilinarium,* a valuable eye-witness account of Catiline's conspiracy in 63 B.C.

Constable, Henry (1562–1613), sonneteer: see p. 496

Constantine, George (?1501–59), Protestant reformer who worked with Tyndale in Antwerp, came to England to sell banned heretical books, was arrested, and saved himself by turning king's evidence in 1530

contrarium (plural *contraria*), "contrary, antonym"

Cook(e), Anthony (1555–1604), owner of the manor of Hartshill who was knighted by Essex at Cadiz in 1596

coram, "openly, publicly"

Corduba, Cordova, capital of the province of Cordova in Spain, birthplace of Seneca and Lucan

Corin(eus), a companion of Brut (*q.v.*): see Gogmagog

Corinna: *see* Ovid(ius)

Corinth, city of Greece near the Gulf of Corinth, one of the chief centers of literature and commerce in antiquity. Defeated by Sparta in 394 B.C., it was sacked and burned by the Romans in 146 B.C. and rebuilt by Julius Caesar in 46 B.C.

Coriolanus, Caius (or Cnaeus) Marcius, Roman legendary hero of the fifth century B.C. A champion of the patricians, he deserted Rome in anger at the plebeians to join the Volscians and was then won back by his mother Veturia (in Shakespeare's play, Volumnia).

Cornelia, (1) mother of the Gracchi (*q.v.*); (2) according to Lyly, a woman who married beneath her station (apparently a reference to an unidentified Italian *novella*)

Cornelius' tub, Mother, sweating tub used in the treatment of venereal disease

Cornutus, Lucius Annaeus, Stoic philosopher who lived in Rome until Nero banished him in 68 for too freely criticizing the emperor's poetry. The most important of Cornutus' works, virtually all of which are lost, was a commentary on Aristotle.

Cornwell, Cornwall

corrigat qui potest, "let him correct who can"

Cortegiano, Il, *The Courtier,* by Baldassare Castiglione (see p. 522)

Cortereal, Anus, perhaps a relation of the well-known Gaspar Cortereal (b. ca. 1450), Portuguese navigator who explored Labrador about 1500 and died a year later during a second voyage to the same region

Corynna, Corinna, the mistress of Ovid (*q.v.*)

Counter, ancient name given to three London prisons, one in the Poultry, one in Wood Street, and one in Southwark

Court of Wards, a court established by Henry VIII for the trial of causes relating to wardships. Later called Court of Wards and Liveries, it was abolished in 1660.

Coventry blue, a kind of blue thread used for embroidery, made at Coventry in Warwickshire

Coytus, ?Italian stream

Crab, zodiacal sign of Cancer, which the sun enters in late June

Craft of Love, i.e. the *Ars amatoria* of Ovid (*q.v.*)

crambe bis positum mors est, "cabbage twice cooked [i.e. a tale twice told] is deadly"

Cranmer, Thomas (1489–1556), Tudor ecclesiastic whose rise began when he supported Henry VIII's divorce. Following his elevation to the archbishopric of Canterbury (1533) he vigorously supported Henry's ecclesiastical policy and furthered his matrimonial ventures. After the accession of Edward VI he supervised the production of the first Book of Common Prayer and promulgated the Forty-two Articles of 1552. With Mary's accession in 1553 his position became very grave. Condemned for heresy by Cardinal Pole, he recanted all his alleged errors, but he repudiated his recantation before he was burned at the stake.

cras, "tomorrow"

Crassus, Marcus Licinius Crassus Dives (ca. 114–53 B.C.), Roman general and politician, member of the first triumvirate with Caesar and Pompey, treacherously slain following his disastrous defeat by the Parthians while he was governor of Syria: hence Lucan's allusion, "slaughter'd Crassus' ghost walks unreveng'd"

Crates, Cynic philosopher who flourished about 320 B.C.

Crécy, Cressy, village in northern France where, on August 26, 1346, Edward III won a famous victory against the French under Philip VI

credat Judaeus Apella, Ascham quotes only part of the line, omitting *non ego:* "Apella, the Jew, may believe—not I" (Horace, *Satires* I.v.100).

credo videre bona Domini, "I believe to see the goodness of the Lord" (Vulgate Psalms xxvi.13)

Cressid(a): *see* Troilus

Cressus: *see* Croesus

Cressy: *see* Crécy

crevisse de eau douce, freshwater crayfish

Crispin and Crispinian, noble Roman brothers who fled from persecution to Soissons and became shoemakers. St. Crispin, the patron saint of shoemakers, was executed in 287; his feast day is October 25.

Crito(n), a friend of Socrates and of Plato, who named a dialogue after him

Croesus (Cressus), king of Lydia who, succeeding his father in 560 B.C., extended his realm immensely and became fabulously wealthy. Herodotus (I.xxix) tells the famous story of his visit from Solon.

Cromwell, Thomas, Earl of Essex (?1485–1540), early Tudor politician who, beginning his rise to power under Wolsey, continued to advance after his master's fall; he held increasingly important posts during the thirties, taking an active part in the dissolution of the smaller monasteries and finally becoming lord great chamberlain in 1539. Henry VIII, dissatisfied with Cromwell's negotiation of his marriage with Anne of Cleves, permitted his execution on a charge of treason.

Cross: *see* Paul's Cross

Crossed (Friar), i.e. Crutched Friar, one of a Catholic religious order in England whose members wore the sign of the cross on their staves and habits

cuius potest accidere . . . , "whatever can happen to someone can happen to whom you please"

Cumberland, Lady Margaret, Countess of: *see* Clifford (Margaret)

Cupid(e), Cupido, the god of love, son of Hermes (Mercury) and Aphrodite (Venus), represented as a handsome winged boy—sometimes blind or blindfolded—armed with arrows, the wound of which induced passion

Cureti, the Curetes, attendants of Zeus

Curtius Rufus, Quintus, Roman author of a history of Alexander the Great, written perhaps during the reign of Vespasian (70–79)

Cyclopian, pertaining to the Cyclops (*q.v.*)

Cyclops, one of a race of one-eyed giants who forged Zeus's thunderbolts and served as helpers in the forge of Hephaestus (Vulcan). In the *Odyssey,* Polyphemus, the chief Cyclops, held Odysseus prisoner in his cave until Odysseus made him drunk and blinded him.

Cyllar(us), a Centaur killed at the wedding-feast of Pirithous

cymini sectores, "hair-splitters"

Cynics, philosophical sect founded by Antisthenes of Athens, a student of Socrates, whose central doctrine was that virtue is the result of rational self-control. Diogenes of Sinope, a pupil of Antisthenes, became notorious for his excessive asceticism.

Cynthia (Cynthea, Cinthia), a name for Diana (or Artemis), the moon-goddess, from Mt. Cynthus, her birthplace in Delos

Cynthian, pertaining to Cynthia (Diana)

Cypres: *see* Cyprus

Cyprian queen, i.e. Aphrodite, from her birthplace on Cyprus

Cyprus (Cypres), large island in the eastern Mediterranean, famous in antiquity as the birthplace of Aphrodite

Cypselus, Corinthian tyrant of the seventh century B.C.

Cyrrhus, the sun; a Syrian city

Cyrus (d. 529 B.C.), founder of the Persian empire, who consolidated his conquest of Ecbatana, Media, and Babylonia into a power that presaged the later Macedonian and Roman empires. It was Cyrus who permitted the exiled Jews to return to Jerusalem from Babylon. *See* Xenophon's *Cyrus*.

Cythera (Cithera), mountainous island off the southeast point of Laconia, famous for its worship of Aphrodite, who was in consequence often called Cytherea or Cythereis

D., M., ?"Master [afterward Sir Edward] Dyer" (*q.v.*)

Daedalus, an Athenian who personified skill in arts and crafts. Having constructed a labyrinth in Crete (*see* Minos of Crete), he was imprisoned in it with his son Icarus because he gave the clue to Ariadne; they escaped with waxen wings of Daedalus' contrivance, but when Icarus flew too near the sun the wax melted and he plummeted into the (Icarian) sea.

Damascus, ancient capital of Syria

Dametas, used as a herdsman's name by both Theocritus and Virgil; in Renaissance pastorals (e.g. those of Googe and Sidney) the name became almost a generic title for a (usually foolish) rustic.

Damocles, Syracusan courtier who, according to Cicero, flattered the tyrant Dionysius on his felicity, which he was thereupon invited to share. But when, at a spendid royal banquet, he happened to look up, he saw just above his head a sword suspended by a single horse-hair.

Damon (fl. first half of the fourth century B.C.), a Pythagorean of Syracuse famed for his friendship with Pythias (or Phintias), a member of the same brotherhood. When Pythias was condemned to die for conspiring against the tyrant Dionysius, Damon acted as hostage while the culprit was winding up his affairs, and was saved from execution only at the last moment by Pythias' reappearance. Dionysius thereupon freed them both and joined their brotherhood.

Dan, one of the twelve Hebrew tribes (see Joshua xix:40)

Danaë, mother of Perseus by Zeus, who visited her in a shower of gold while she was imprisoned by her father in a brazen tower

Danaus, founder of Argos and ancestor of the Greeks (the Danai)

Daniel, Old Testament prophet who lived for many years in Babylon

Daniel, Samuel (1562–1619), poet and humanist: see pp. 12, 402, 653–54

Daphne, nymph whose lover Leucippus pursued her in woman's clothing and was in consequence killed at Apollo's command. Apollo himself then sought her love but at her request transformed her into a bay tree.

Darby: *see* Derby

Dardanus, traditional ancestor of the Trojans; hence **Dardan**, Trojan

Dares Phrygius, Trojan priest mentioned by Homer (*Iliad* V.9) to whom was long attributed a now lost epic on the Trojan War that was thought to be older than the Homeric poems. *De excidio Trojae historia*, a Latin translation attributed to Cornelius Nepos (*q.v.*), was popular in the Middle Ages, and it, together with a spurious diary allegedly by one Dictys Cretensis (a Cretan soldier), is the chief source of the medieval Trojan legends (e.g. of Troilus and Cressida)

Darien, Isme of, the Isthmus of Darien, or Panama

Darius, mighty Persian king who, succeeding Cambyses in 521 B.C., restored order to his huge empire and then began a westward expansion which threatened to engulf all Greece. He was finally checked at Marathon in 490 B.C.

Dart (Dert), river in Devon that empties into the harbor of Dartmouth

Dathan, member of Korah's conspiracy against Moses and Aaron (see Numbers xvi.1–46)

David, second king of Israel, father of Solomon

Davie Diker: *see* Davy Dicar

Davies, Sir John (1569–1626), statesman and poet: see pp. 467–68

Davison, Francis (?1575–?1619), poet and editor of *A Poetical Rhapsody*: see pp. 242–43

Davison, Walter (1581–ca. 1608), younger brother and collaborator of Francis Davison (*q.v.*)

Davus, cunning slave in Terence's *Andria;* stock-name for a knave

Davy Dicar (Davie Diker), proverbial name for a plowman

Davys, John (?1550–1605), navigator who while searching for the Northwest Passage discovered Davys Strait and explored Baffin's Bay (1587)

De amicitia, On Friendship, a treatise by Cicero addressed to Atticus

De civitate Dei, The City of God, the chief work (426) of Augustine (*q.v.*), a monumental survey of sacred and profane history seeking to justify the ways of God to man and specifically to explain the sack of Rome by Alaric in 410

de ente et non ente, "of being and non-being"

de facto, "in fact"

De fastis (Fasti), a long poem by Ovid (only six of the twelve books being extant) in which the various festivals and celebrations of the Roman year are given their historic and mythological backgrounds

de ignoto, "concerning a nameless one"

De legibus, The Laws, Plato's last dialogue

De officiis: see *Offices*

De oratore, systematic treatise on oratory, in three books, which Cicero wrote in 55 B.C. at the request of his brother Quintus

de profundis clamavi, "out of the depths have I cried [unto thee, O Lord]" (Vulgate Psalms cxxix.1)

de quibus in superioribus . . . , "concerning which [you have written] in that former very sweet, long letter of yours"

De republica, The Republic, Plato's famous dialogue on the ideal commonwealth

De senectute, On Old Age, a treatise written by Cicero to Atticus

Debora(h), Hebrew prophetess and judge who sang a song of victory when Barak overcame the tyrant Jabin (see Judges v)

decem annos consumpsi . . . , "I have spent ten years in reading Cicero." To this statement of the ass (Latin *asine*) of a pedant, echo appropriately returns the last two syllables, *-one* (Greek *ŏve,* "ass").

decidunt celsa graviore lapsu, attributed by E. K. to Seneca in his gloss to Spenser's "July" but apparently adapted from Horace (*Odes* II.x.10–11): *celsae graviore casu Decidunt turres* ("high towers topple with a heavier ruin")

Decius Brutus: see Brutus Albinus

declinat cursus . . . , "she turns from the race and lifts up the rolling gold [ball]" (Ovid, *Metamorphoses* X.667)

Deiopey, i.e. Deiopea, in Virgil (*Aeneid* I.73) a lovely nymph who attends Juno

Delf(t), town in the western Netherlands

Delia, surname for Artemis (*q.v.*), from the island of Delos, her birthplace; hence **Delian**

Delia's servant, i.e. Samuel Daniel (*q.v.*)

Delilah, paramour of Samson (*q.v.*)

della Mirandola: see Pico della Mirandola

Deloney, Thomas (?1543–?1600), ballad-writer, novelist, and silk-weaver: see p. 800

Delos, smallest island of the Cyclades, legendary birthplace of Apollo and Artemis and in antiquity the site of a famous shrine dedicated to Apollo

Delphi, Delphos, town in Phocis, Greece, at the foot of Mt. Parnassus, the site of a famous oracle of Pythian Apollo

Delphrigus, ?hero of a lost Elizabethan play (see McKerrow, *Nashe,* IV, 458)

Demades (d. 318 B.C.), brilliant Athenian orator who, because he supported the Macedonian party, was the inveterate enemy of Demosthenes

Demea, stock-character of the harsh father in Terence's comedies

Demeter, goddess of vegetation, patroness of social order and of marriage, mother of Persephone

Demetrius (ca. 338–283 B.C.), Macedonian king who captured Athens and Megara in 307

Demetrius, Emmanuel, recipient of the dedication of the first of Gabriel Harvey's *Four Letters;* perhaps, says McKerrow (*Nashe,* IV, 161), a distinguished foreign merchant

Demetrius Phalereus (b. ca. 345 B.C.), Athenian orator, statesman, and poet who governed Athens for ten years with such success that more than three hundred statues were erected in his honor. Later, as a retainer of Ptolemy Lagi, he lived at Alexandria and probably had much to do with the establishment of his master's great library.

Democritus (ca. 460–ca. 357 B.C.), the "laughing philosopher," born in Abdera, Thrace, who developed the atomistic materialism of Leucippus in a series of works which survive only as fragments

Demopho(o)n, member of the Grecian host before Troy who freed his grandmother Aethra from her slavery with Helen. Returning from Troy he won the love of Phyllis, a Thracian princess, but when, delayed in Africa, he failed to return for his wedding she committed suicide and was transformed into a tree.

Demosthenes (ca. 384–322 B.C.), Athenian orator and statesman who made his reputation with a series of orations on the Macedonian threat to Athens. As leader of the so-called patriotic party (in opposition to Aeschines' temporizing policies) he organized the allies against Philip of Macedon and continued to resist the northern invaders until the battle of Chaeronea (338) marked the end of Athenian independence. He died a suicide in exile.

Denis (Denys), St., apostle to the Gauls and patron saint of France who, according to legend, was beheaded at Paris in 272

Deo gratias, "thanks be to God"

Deo opt[imo] max[imo] gloria, "glory to God most good, most great"

Derby (Darby) or **Derbyshire**, county in England between Yorkshire and Leicestershire, famous for its rugged and picturesque scenery

Derby, Earl of: *see* Stanley (Edward)

Dert: *see* Dart

Dertford, i.e. Dartford, a town in Kent, England

Desmond, Earl of: *see* Fitzgerald

Despenser, Hugh le (1262–1326), with his son **Hugh** (d. 1326) a favorite of Edward II in his quarrels with the barons over Piers Gaveston (*q.v.*). Both suffered exile for their friendship with the king, and when they fell into the hands of his estranged queen Isabella they were summarily executed. The family was often referred to as "the Spencers."

Desportes, Philippe (1546–1606), French poet, ecclesiastic, and statesman, as an imitator of Petrarch, Ariosto, and Sannazaro very influential in adapting Italian lyric forms (especially the sonnet) in such works as *Diane, Les amours d'Hippolyte, Élégies*, etc.

Destinies, the Fates or Parcae (*q.v.*)

desunt nonnulla, "something is lacking"

Deucalidon: *see* Ducalidon

Deucalion, king of Phthia in Thessaly who with his wife Pyrrha was saved from a deluge sent by Zeus. To repopulate the earth they cast stones on the ground, and the stones became men and women.

Devereux, Penelope: *see* Rich (Penelope)

Devereux, Robert, second Earl of Essex (1566–1601), favorite and most powerful courtier of Elizabeth's later reign, privy councilor (1593), commander of the Cadiz expedition (1596), earl-marshal (1597), lord-lieutenant of Ireland (1599). His unsatisfactory conduct in Ireland led to a rupture with the queen, an abortive rebellion, and his execution.

Deviere, Edward: *see* Vere

devita prophanas . . . , "avoid profane and vain babblings, and oppositions of science falsely so called" (adapted from Vulgate I Timothy vi.20)

Diagoras (fl. 425 B.C.), Greek philosopher (surnamed "the Atheist") who was forced to flee Athens because of his blasphemies about the Eleusinian mysteries and popular religion

Dian(a), goddess of the moon and patroness of the female sex

Dictys Cretensis, reputed author of a Trojan epic entitled *Ephemeris belli Trojani*: *see* Dares Phrygius

Dido, in Virgil's *Aeneid* a queen of Carthage who fell in love with Aeneas when he was shipwrecked after the fall of Troy. When, by command of the gods, he forsook her, she killed herself.

diebus illis, "in those days"

Dieu te garde, "God protect you"

difficile est satyram non scribere, "it is difficult not to write satire" (Juvenal, *Satires* I.30)

Digby, Sir Everard (1578–1606), noted Catholic convert who, knighted by James I in 1603, took part in the Gunpowder Plot and was executed for treason

Dinarchus (b. ca. 361 B.C.), orator who was born in Corinth but lived mainly in Athens, where he supported the Macedonian party

Diogenes (ca. 412–323 B.C.), Greek Cynic philosopher and eccentric, notorious for his blunt honesty and his contempt of foolish convention

Diogenes Laertius (fl. ca. 200), author of a gossipy set of philosophers' lives in ten books, a rambling but valuable work

Diomed(es), in Homer, king of Argos and one of the bravest of the Greeks before Troy; in post-Homeric legend he became a lover of Cressida and a rival of Troilus.

Dion Cassius (ca. 155–ca. 230), Roman historian and politician whose great work was a history of Rome in eighty books written in Greek, only part of which survives

Dione, Titaness who was the mother of Aphrodite by Zeus

Dionisius Areopagita (Dionyse), Dionysius the Areopagite, an Athenian converted by St. Paul about 50 (see Acts xvii.34), long revered as the supposed author of several mystical treatises which are now commonly regarded as forgeries of the fifth or sixth centuries

Dionysius (ca. 430–367 B.C.), tyrant of Syracuse in Sicily who waged successful war against Carthage and attained great power among the Italian Greeks. A patron of letters, he entertained Plato at his court.

Dionysius of Halicarnassus, Greek writer of the first century B.C. who gained a great reputation in Rome, where he lived and taught. Of his many works there survives part of his *Antiquities of Rome*, as well as various rhetorical and critical treatises (*On Imitation, Remarks on the Early Orators, On Thucydides*, etc.).

Dionysus: *see* Bacchus

Διὸς δ᾽ ἐτελείετο βουλή, "the will of Zeus was being fulfilled" (*Iliad* I.5)

Diotima, in Plato's *Symposium*, a woman who expounds mystical doctrines of love to Socrates

dirige, "direct [my steps]"

Dis (pater), a name for Pluto, god of wealth and of the underworld

discreta quantitas, "quantity pure and simple"

dispositio, "arrangement"

Diss, town in Norfolk south of Norwich

diversa, words of closely similar meaning but not synonyms

diverte a malo et fac bonum, "turn away from evil and do good" (Vulgate Psalms xxxiii.15)

Dives and Lazarus, the rich man and the beggar in Jesus' parable recorded in Luke xvi.19–31

dixi, "I have spoken"

dixit insipiens in corde suo . . . , "the fool hath said in his heart, There is no God. They are corrupt, they have done abominable works, there is none that doeth good" (Vulgate Psalms xiii.1)

Dolabella, Publius Cornelius (ca. 70–43 B.C.), Cicero's son-in-law who sought to recoup his dissipated fortune by throwing in his lot with Caesar; later shifting to Antony's party, he was named governor of Syria and was killed in battle by Cassius at Laodicea.

Dolopes, Dolopans, warlike people of Dolopia, Thessaly, whom Homer mentions as fighting before Troy; hence **Dolopian**, pertaining to the Dolopes

domine, "master"

Domine, exaudi orationem meam, "Lord, hear my prayer" (adapted from Vulgate Psalms cxxix.2)

Dominus vobiscum, "the Lord be with you"

Donate: *see* Donatus

Donati, Eduardo, a presumably fictitious friend to whom Gascoigne dedicated his *Certain Notes of Instruction*

Donatists, heretical Christian sect of the fourth century headed by Donatus, bishop of Carthage. They believed that the validity of the sacraments depended on the spiritual purity of the minister and that personal sanctity was essential for membership in the church.

Donatus (Donate), Aelius (fl. 350), Roman grammarian and rhetorician, teacher of St. Jerome, author of an *Ars grammatica* that in its abridged form (*Donatus pro puerilis*) was immensely popular for centuries

Donne, John (1572–1631), poet and divine: see p. 482

Doric, pertaining to Doris, a district in Asia Minor on the coast of Caria. In music the Doric was an ancient Greek mode prevailingly solemn and simple.

Dorset, Lord Marquess: *see* Grey (Thomas)

Douglas, Archibald, fourth Earl of Douglas and first Duke of Touraine (?1369–1424), first an enemy and then an ally of Hotspur, captured by the English at Shrewsbury, a supporter of Henry V in his French wars

Douglas, George, first Earl of Angus (?1380–1403), Scottish nobleman who, taken prisoner at Homildon, died of the plague in England

Dover, seaport in Kent, on the Strait of Dover

Dowgate, the original water-gate of the city of London, situated at the junction of the Wallbrook and the Thames

Dowland, John (?1563–?1626), lutenist and composer: see p. 255

Drake, Sir Francis (?1540–96), most celebrated of Elizabethan sea-dogs, commander of three voyages to the West Indies in the early seventies. In 1577 he began the voyage of circumnavigation for which Elizabeth knighted him in 1581.

Drant, Thomas (d. ?1578), member of St. John's College, Cambridge, chaplain to Archbishop Grindal (*q.v.*), archdeacon of Lewes (1570), advocate of classical meters in English poetry, translator of Horace's *Epistles, Satires,* and *Art of Poetry*

Drayton, Michael (1563–1631), poet: see pp. 3, 421–23

Drury, Sir William (1527–79), courtier and soldier, lord-justice to the council in Ireland. His most spectacular military feat was the capture of Edinburgh Castle in 1573.

Dryad(e)s: *see* Nymphae

Ducalidon, Deucalidon, sea to the north of Scotland

ducunt volentes fata . . . , "Fate leads the willing, drags the unwilling" (adapted from Seneca, *Epistles* cvii)

Dudley, Ambrose, Earl of Warwick (?1528–90), Tudor politician who, though convicted of treason for supporting his sister-in-law Lady Jane Grey, was pardoned and succeeded his father to the earldom in 1561. Thereafter he was named lieutenant of the Order of the Garter in 1575 and defended Mary Queen of Scots in 1586.

Dudley, Anne, daughter of Francis Russell, second Earl of Bedford, and third wife of Ambrose Dudley, Earl of Warwick. In dedicating his *Four Hymns* to her and her sister, Spenser mistakenly calls her Marie.

Dudley, Lady Jane (1537–54), daughter of Henry Grey, Duke of Suffolk, and wife of Guildford Dudley. Her husband's family conspired to transfer the succession from the Tudor to the Dudley family, and as a result the unfortunate girl, a highly cultivated and charming victim of her relatives' dynastic ambitions, was proclaimed queen in 1553 on the death of Edward VI. When her father-in-law's troops were routed by Mary's forces she was captured and executed.

Dudley, Robert, Earl of Leicester (?1532–88), in Elizabeth's early reign her favorite and most powerful courtier, thought by some to have been her lover and to have murdered his wife Amye Robsart in order to be free to marry the queen. His pretensions to the throne were persistently blocked by Cecil and the old nobility, and his two subsequent marriages lost him the queen's favor, even though he continued to hold high posts (e.g. governor of the United Provinces) until his death.

dulce bellum inexpertis, "war is delightful to those who have never tried it"

dum iuga montis aper, "while the boar loves the mountain" (Virgil, *Eclogues* V.76)

dum sibi quisque placet . . . , "while each of us flatters himself, we are a credulous mob" (Ovid, *Remedia amoris* 686)

Duns Scotus, Joannes (?1265–?1308), *Doctor Subtilis,* English Franciscan whose writings on metaphysics, logic, and theology generally opposed Thomistic rationalism

Dunsany, Lord Baron of, ?Patrick Plunkett, seventh Baron Dunsany (d. 1602)

Dunstable, town in Bedfordshire, England

Dyer, Sir Edward (d. 1607), protégé of the Earl of Leicester and a gifted "courtly maker" who became the friend of Sidney and Spenser as well as a contributor to various poetical miscellanies

e naturali et sponte . . . , "produced by natural and spontaneous composition"

Echo, mountain-nymph who pined away for love of Narcissus (*q.v.*) until only her voice was left

Edes, Richard (1555–1604), dean of Worcester and noted preacher, allegedly the author of a tragedy called *Julius Caesar* acted at Christ Church in 1582 and of various poems in Latin and English

Edgar Pacificus (944–975), king of the English who organized an efficient naval defense against the northern pirates

Edge, Master Orator, ?Giles Edge, a B.A. of Cambridge

Edmund of Had(d)enham, Edmundus de Hadenham (fl. 1307), ecclesiastical chronicler of Rochester

Edward II (1284–1327), king of England (1307–27) whose favorite Piers Gaveston (*q.v.*) so angered the powerful barons that they eventually broke into open rebellion. After increasing difficulties with his French wife Isabella, defeat by the Scots under Robert Bruce at Bannockburn (1314), and further troubles with the barons, the king was deposed by Parliament and murdered at Berkeley Castle.

Edward III (1312–77), king of England (1327–77), one of the most powerful political figures of the fourteenth century, famous for his victories in France, father of the Black Prince and John of Gaunt, grandfather of Richard II and Henry IV

Edward IV (1442–83), king of England (1461–83), son of Richard, Duke of York, and brother of Richard, Duke of Gloucester (later Richard III). By his marriage (1464) to Elizabeth Woodville (*q.v.*) alienating the powerful Earl of Warwick, Edward so declined in prestige and power that he had to flee abroad (1470–71) when Warwick (the so-called "king-maker") released Henry VI from the Tower and restored him, though an imbecile, to the throne. Although Edward regained control of England at the battles of Barnet and Tewkesbury (1471), his last years were disturbed by the machinations of his traitorous brothers, the dukes of Clarence and Gloucester.

Edward V (1470–83), king of England (April–June, 1483), boy-king under the regency of his unscrupulous uncle Richard, Duke of Gloucester, who presumably had him and his brother secretly murdered in the Tower so that he might succeed as Richard III

Edward, Duke of York: *see* Plantagenet (Edward)

Edwards, Richard (?1523–66), master of the children of the Chapel Royal (1561), for whom he composed the comedy *Damon and Pythias,* his only extant play. Ten years after his death his commonplace-book was pieced out with other lyrics to form *The Paradise of Dainty Devices* (see p. 212).

effingere, "to fashion"

Egeria, Aegeria, one of the Camenae (*see* Camenes) who instructed Numa Pompilius (*q.v.*) in matters of ceremony and worship

Egyptian, gipsy

Elagabalus: *see* Heliogabalus

Elderton, William (d. ?1592), ballad-writer and master of a company of comedians

elegiae, "elegies"

Elephant, a London tavern

Elias (Helias), Elijah, a Hebrew prophet of the ninth century B.C.

Elice: *see* Elis

Elicon: *see* Helicon

Eliphantina, Elephantine (or Elephantis), island and city in the Nile below the Little Cataract and on the Ethiopian frontier

Elis (Elice), fertile country on the west coast of the Peloponnesus, site of a famous sanctuary and festival of Zeus

Elisa(e), Eliza, Elizabeth I (*q.v.*)

Elizabeth, queen of Edward IV: *see* Woodville (Elizabeth)

Elizabeth, queen of Henry VII (1465–1503), daughter of Edward IV and Elizabeth Woodville, and mother of Henry VIII

Elizabeth I (1533–1603), queen of England (1558–1603), daughter of Henry VIII and Anne Boleyn

Elmer: *see* Aylmer

Elpenor, companion of Ulysses (Odysseus) during his long stay with Circe. While drunk, he died in a fall from the roof of her house. His shade met Ulysses in the underworld to beg that his body might be burned, and on his return to the earth Ulysses performed this last act of friendship.

Eltham, town in Kent, formerly the site of a royal residence

Elyot, Sir Thomas (?1490–1546), statesman, humanist, and translator: see pp. 105–6

Elysium, abode of the good souls and of the heroes exempt from death

Emesos, Emesa (or Emissa), Syrian city once the capital of Phoenice Libanesia

Empedocles (ca. 490–430 B.C.), Greek philosopher and poet of Agrigentum, Sicily. A follower of Pythagoras and Parmenides, he was thought to have had magical powers of divination and healing, and to have thrown himself into the crater of Mt. Etna.

Empson, Sir Richard (d. 1510), with Edmund Dudley the notorious and cordially detested tax-collector for Henry VII. Both men were executed on an insubstantial charge of treason by Henry VIII.

en esperance, "in hope"

Endymion, a lovely shepherd-boy who, sleeping in a cave on Mt. Latmus, attracted the love of Selene, the moon-goddess

Ene, Aeneas

Ennius, Quintus (239–169 B.C.), early Roman epic poet, one of the founders of Latin literature. Only fragments survive of his *Annals,* an epic in eighteen books on the history of Rome.

ens, quiddity of, scholastic jargon for "the essence of being"

Eolia, in Virgil, one of the *Aeoliae Insulae* (i.e. Lipari Islands) north of Sicily, home of Aeolus, god of the winds

Eolus: *see* Aeolus

Epaminondas (ca. 418–362 B.C.), Theban general who defeated the Spartans at Leuctra in 371

Epeminedes, Epimenides, Cretan poet of the seventh century B.C. who was alleged to have slept for fifty-seven years

Ephoebus, one of the speakers in "Euphues and His Ephoebus," a dialogue (based upon Plutarch's tract concerning the education of children) appended to Lyly's *Euphues: The Anatomy of Wit*

Ephorus (ca. 400–ca. 330 B.C.), Greek author of a history of Greece and its neighbors down to 340 B.C., which survives only in fragments

Epicure, Epicurean

Epicurus (342–270 B.C.), founder of the Epicurean school (which he opened in Athens in 306), author of some three hundred works (most of them now lost) developing the atomistic materialism of Democritus and the ethical principle that pleasure is the end of rational conduct

epigrammata, "epigrams"

epilogus, "epilogue"

Epistles, Drayton's *England's Heroical Epistles* (see p. 423) or Daniel's *Poetical Epistles* (see p. 402)

Epistolae obscurorum virorum, "Letters of Obscure Men," a collection of forty-one anonymous letters published in 1515 sharply satirizing the ignorance and depravity of Roman Catholic monastics

Epius Stolo, Stilo (*q.v.*)

Erasmus, Desiderius (ca. 1465–1536), most celebrated and influential of northern humanists, several times a visitor in England, friend of More and Colet, copious writer whose works include an edition and Latin translation of the New Testament (1516), a series of *Colloquies, Encomium Moriae* (1512), *Adagia* (1500 ff.), *Enchiridion militis Christiani* (1503), and thousands of epistles: see p. 103

Erato, muse of erotic poetry and of the lyre

Erebus, deity of the underworld; hence, the underworld itself

ergo, "therefore"

Erictheus, Erechtheus, legendary king of Athens

Eriny(e)s: *see* Furies

Eris, goddess of discord, sister of Ares, the god of war

Erpingham, Sir Thomas (1357–1428), long-time retainer of John of Gaunt who continued to serve his son Henry IV and his grandson Henry V. Following the victory at Agincourt he was entrusted with various diplomatic missions to France.

Erycine, Erycina, surname for Aphrodite (Venus), from Mt. Eryx in Sicily

Erythius, island of Erythia, one of the "fortunate islands" or Islands of the Blest (the modern Canary Islands) which the Greeks regarded as the place in the far west where the souls of the good were made happy

Esaia(s), Esaie, Esay, Isaiah, Hebrew prophet of the eighth century B.C.

Esop: *see* Aesop

Esoras, Ezra, Hebrew prophet and religious reformer of the fifth century B.C.

Esperides: *see* Hesperides

esprit, "spirit"

esse posse videatur, "it is apparent that it may be"

Essex, county in eastern England

Essex, Earl of: *see* Devereux (Robert)

est mihi namque domi . . . , "at home I have a stern father and stepmother" (Virgil, *Eclogues* III.33–4)

est Ulubris . . . , "[what you seek] is at Ulubrae, if a well-tempered mind does not fail you" (Horace, *Epistles* I.xi.30)

Estotiland(a), mythical region once thought to be in the northern part of North America near the Arctic Circle

et Catilinam quocunque in populo . . . , "you may see a Catiline among any people under the sky" (Juvenal, *Satires* XIV.41–2)

et ecce, nunc in pulvere dormio, "and behold, now I sleep in dust"

et sic de similibus, "and likewise in similar cases"

Eteocles: *see* Polynices

Ethicae, Ethics, general title for Aristotle's three treatises on ethics, politics, and economics. The chief of the ethical treatises, the so-called *Nicomachean Ethics* in ten books, discusses virtue as the mean between two extremes.

Etna (Aetna, Ethna), highest volcano in Europe and the largest mountain in Sicily, situated on the east of the island north of Catania

Eton, village on the Thames opposite Windsor, the site of Eton College, a famous boys' school founded in 1440 by Henry VI

Etruria, a kingdom of Italy along the Mediterranean, corresponding to modern Tuscany. The Etruscans, developing a formidable naval power, ruled in Rome until about 500 B.C.

Euander: *see* Evander

Euboea, largest of the Aegean islands that belonged to Greece. According to Hesiod, Io gave birth to Epaphus on Euboea.

Euclid(es), (fl. 300 B.C.), famous Alexandrian geometer whose *Elements,* in thirteen books, established the basis of classical geometry

Eudemonidas: Montaigne perhaps means Eudemus, a Peripatetic philosopher of Cyprus to whom Aristotle dedicated one of his lost dialogues (*Eudemos*)

Eumenides, the Furies (*q.v.*)

Eunuch(us), a comedy by Terence, modeled on Menander, that was performed in 162 B.C.

Euphorbus, Trojan warrior killed by Menelaus, whose soul Pythagoras claimed to have inherited through transmigration

Euphrates, Mesopotamian river mentioned in Genesis ii.14 as one of the four rivers of Paradise

Euphues, a novel in two parts (1578, 1580) by John Lyly: see p. 710

Eupolis (449–ca. 411 B.C.), with Aristophanes and Cratinus one of the masters of the old comedy in Athens

Europa, a name for Io (*q.v.*)

Euryalus, friend of Nisus (*q.v.*)

Eurydice, lover of Orpheus (*q.v.*)

Eusebius of Caesarea (ca. 264–ca. 340), celebrated theologian and historian

Eustathius (d. ?1194), Greek scholar, archbishop of Thessalonica, famed for his commentary on Homer

Euxine Sea, the Black Sea

Evander (Euander), son of Hermes and the nymph Themis, leader of a Greek colony in Latium before the Trojan War

Evippe's daughters, nine sisters who challenged the muses in song and were punished by being changed into magpies

ex consequenti, "in consequence"

ex uno puncto impudentiae, "from one point of impudence"

Excester, Exeter (*q.v.*)

execrabilis ista turba . . . , "the people who know not the law are cursed" (perhaps a paraphrase of Vulgate St. John vi.49)

Exeter (Excester), capital of Devonshire, an ancient cathedral city and seaport

Exeter, Duke of: *see* Beaufort

Exmew(e), William (?1507–35), steward of the London Charterhouse who was executed for denying Henry VIII's supremacy

Exmoor, district in the west of Somerset and the north of Devon, composed mainly of hills and marshes

ἔχω γὰρ ἄχω . . . , "everything I have I owe to you alone" (Sophocles, *Oedipus at Colonus* 1129)

exordium ad preparandos animos, "an opening to prepare the spirit"

explicit Convivium, "the Banquet ends"

explicit Hymnus, "the Hymn ends"

exprimere, "to press, squeeze out"

extinctus amabitur idem, "when he is dead he will be beloved too" (Horace, *Epistles* II.i.14)

Exton, Sir Piers of: *see* Piers of Exton

extra iocum, "joking aside"

Fabian, pertaining to the Fabia Gens (*Fabii*), an ancient patrician family of Rome

Fabian (Fabyan), Robert (d. 1513), chronicler who expanded his diary into *The Concordance of Histories,* a compilation covering English history from the arrival of Brut to the death of Henry VII

facundi calices quem . . . , "whom has the flowing bowl not made eloquent?" (Horace, *Epistles* I.v.19)

Fall of Princes, The, John Lydgate's longest work, some 26,000 lines based on the French prose of Laurent de Premierfait's *De cas des nobles hommes et femmes,* itself an expanded redaction of Boccaccio's *De casibus virorum . . . illustrium.* Written between 1430 and 1438, its subject is the fall of great personages, both historical and mythological, and its theme the fatal consequences of pride and ambition.

Familiar Letters, i.e. Spenser and Harvey's *Three Proper and Witty Familiar Letters* (1580): see pp. 624–25

fas et nefas, "good and bad"

Fasti: *see De fastis*

Fates: *see* Parcae

Father-Sexton, Father Time

Faunus, a rural deity, son of Picus (*q.v.*)

Faustina (Faustine), Annia (d. 175), daughter of the Emperor Antoninus Pius and profligate wife of Marcus Aurelius

Favorinus, Phavorinus (ca. 80–150), a rhetorician born in Gaul who became a pupil of Dio Chrysostom and later a favorite of the Emperor Hadrian

Feast of the Trinity: *see* Trinity

Fenton, Sir Geoffrey (?1539–1608), translator and statesman. His translation of Belleforest (1567: see p. 671) was followed by *Monophylo, a Philosophical Discourse and Division of Love* (1572) and by a translation of Guicciardini's *Wars of Italy* (1579), after which he spent the rest of his life administering the English occupation of Ireland.

Ferdinand of Naples, i.e. Ferdinand II (1469–96), king of Naples (1495–96)

Ferdinando: *see* Stanley (Ferdinando)

ferendo natura, adapted from Virgil, *Aeneid* V.710: *superanda omnis fortuna ferendo est,* "all fortune is to be overcome by bearing it"

feri, si ex re sit populi Romani, "strike, if it be for the good of the Roman people"

feriuntque summos fulmina montes, "lightning strikes the summits of the mountains" (adapted from Horace, *Odes* II.x.11)

Ferrau, Ferraw, in Ariosto's *Orlando Furioso* a Saracen who, dropping his helmet in a stream, vowed never to wear another unless he had won it from Orlando. But Orlando killed him with a wound in the navel, his only vulnerable spot.

Ferrers, George ("Edward Ferris" or Ferrys, ?1500–1579), politician and writer, master of the king's pastimes (1551), collaborator of William Baldwin in preparing *A Mirror for Magistrates,* to which he contributed the histories of Robert Tresilian, Thomas of Woodstock, and Richard II in the first

extant edition (1559) and that of Edmund, Duke of Somerset in the second (1563)

Ferris, Ferrys: *see* Ferrers

festina lente, "make haste slowly"

fiat, "let it be done"; hence, an authoritative decree

figura verbi, "figure of speech"

finalis impenitentia, "impenitence to the end"

Finsbury (Field), district of London lying north of the Thames and west of Shoreditch, in the sixteenth century frequented by the lower classes for recreation and shooting

Fiorentino, Ser Giovanni, Italian writer of the late fourteenth century whose *Il Pecorone* ("the Great Stupid One"), begun about 1378, is a loose collection of tales and anecdotes ostensibly related by a friar and a nun to console themselves for their unconsummated passion

Fi(o)renzuola, Agnolo (1493–?1545), Italian humanist and writer whose satires, sonnets, novels, and dramas enjoyed wide popularity

fiorir faceva . . . , "it made my feeble wit to flourish in its shade and grow amid sorrows" (Petrarch, *Rime* 60)

Fish Street (Hill), thoroughfare running from Eastcheap to Lower Thames Street, and so a principal approach to old London Bridge

Fisher, John (1459–1535), bishop of Rochester and uncompromising opponent of the English reformation who, like More, was executed for refusing to acknowledge Henry VIII as head of the church

Fitzalan, Henry, Lord Mautravers (Maltravers, 1538–56), son of the twenty-fourth Earl of Arundel who died, aged eighteen, at Brussels while on an embassy to the king of Bohemia

Fitzgerald, Gerald, fifteenth Earl of Desmond (d. 1583), one of the most persistent and troublesome of the Irish rebels in Elizabeth's reign

Fitzstephen(s), William (d. ?1190), friend and biographer of Thomas à Becket, and a horrified eye-witness of his assassination. Stow drew heavily on his *Vita Sancti Thomae* for information about London in the Middle Ages.

Flamininus, Titus Quintius (ca. 230–174 B.C.), Roman general who defeated Philip V of Macedonia and proclaimed the liberation of all Greece in 196

Flanders, ancient country along the North Sea from the Strait of Dover to the mouth of the Schelde. **Flanders cheer**, excessive eating and drinking

Flavius, Lucius Caesetius, a tribune of the plebs (44 B.C.) whom Julius Caesar deposed because he and Caius Epidius Marullus (also a tribune) had removed crowns from the statues of the dictator

Fleet Street, a street running from Ludgate Circus to the Strand in London

Fleming, Abraham (?1552–1607), antiquarian and poet whose works include translations of Virgil's *Eclogues* and *Bucolics* (1575) and Musaeus' *Hero and Leander* (ca. 1577)

Fletcher, Giles (?1549–1611), ambassador and poet: see p. 496

Flodden (Field), site of a battle in Northumberland on September 9, 1513, in which the English under the Earl of Surrey decisively defeated the Scots under James IV

Flora, goddess of flowers and springtime

Florence, Italian city on the Arno, a center of art and learning in the Renaissance, home of Dante, Boccaccio, Poggio, Giotto, Donatello, Leonardo da Vinci, Raphael, Michelangelo, and many other famous men

Florentine, a kind of ship

Florio, John (?1553–1625), teacher of languages, translator of Montaigne (1603: see p. 568), author of an Italian-English dictionary (1598)

flos volucrum formose . . . , "farewell, sweet bird! Philip, you lie beneath this marble, you who were ever dear to me. As long as the stars shine in the sky your image will be engraved on my heart."

Flower, Francis, mentioned in Thomas Howell's *Garden of Amity,* perhaps the same Francis Flower who was elected demy of Magdalen College, Oxford, in 1560 and fellow in 1565, and to whom Thomas Newman dedicated his surreptitious edition of Sidney's *Astrophel and Stella* in 1591 (see pp. 323–24)

Flushing, seaport in the province of Zealand, in the Low Countries, famed in the sixteenth century for the part its citizens took in the revolt from Spain

formidine poenae, "through fear of punishment"

fortunam Priami cantabo et nobile bellum, "of Priam's fate and famous wars I'll sing" (Horace, *Ars poetica* 137)

Fortune (*My Foe*), a popular street ballad (sometimes called "The Hanging Ballad")

Foxe, John (1516–87), martyrologist: see pp. 173–74

Fracastorius, Girolamo Fracastoro (1483–1553), Italian physician and poet whose many works included the Latin poem *Syphilis* (1530)

Francis of Assisi, St. (?1181–1226), noted mystic, founder of the Franciscan Order

Fraunce, Abraham (fl. 1587–1633), retainer of Mary Herbert, Countess of Pembroke, and author of various poems, rhetorical treatises, and translations: see pp. 633–34

fraus sublimi regnat in aula, "crime sits exalted in the lofty palace" (Seneca, *Hippolytus* 982)

Frederick of Urbino: see Urbino

Friar Barons, i.e. Robert Barnes (*q.v.*)

Frith, John (1503–33), Protestant martyr, collaborator of Tyndale, and author of various controversial works against More and Fisher

Frobisher, Sir Martin (?1535–94), navigator who made his first voyage to Guinea in 1554 and several others in search of the Northwest Passage in the seventies, vice-admiral in Drake's West Indian expedition in 1586, a squadron-leader against the Armada in 1588

fugientem haec terra . . . , "shall this land see [Turnus] fleeing? Is it so hard to die?" (*Aeneid* XII.645–46)

Fulvia (d. 40 B.C.), with Mark Antony (her third husband) a political power in the disorders following the assassination of Julius Caesar. When she failed to check the rising power of Octavianus (later Augustus Caesar) she fled to Greece, where she died.

Furies, the Latin Furiae (or Dirae), the Greek Erinyes (or Eumenides), female avengers usually thought of as Alecto (the unresting), Megaera (the jealous), and Tisiphone (the avenger)

Furnival's Inn, one of the Inns of Court (*q.v.*), established about 1406 and purchased by Lincoln's Inn in 1547. It ceased to exist as a legal community in 1817.

Gaba (named by Elyot as the city from which David fetched the Ark of the Covenant), apparently an error for Gibeah (see II Samuel vi.3)

Gabot, Sebastian: see Cabot (Sebastian)

Gades, ancient Phoenician outpost in the farthest west, on the site of modern Cadiz, Spain

Galen, Greek physician, born at Pergamum about 130, whose writings made him the supreme medical authority until almost the end of the Renaissance. Of the some five hundred treatises he is supposed to have written, about eighty-three are extant, several of which were translated by Thomas Linacre (*q.v.*) in the early sixteenth century.

Gales, Galicia

Gallia, France

Gallus, Caius Cornelius (?69–26 B.C.), Roman poet, orator, and politician who supported Octavius in his struggle against Antony

Gamage, i.e. Barbara Gamage (d. 1621), first wife of Robert Sidney, Viscount Lisle and first Earl of Leicester

Ganymed(e), lovely youth who served as cup-bearer to Zeus, thus supplanting Hebe. According to one legend, Zeus's eagle brought him to Olympus from his native Troy.

gardez le fortune . . . , "watch out for both good and bad fortune"

Gardiner, Stephen (?1483–1555), prominent Tudor clergyman who supported Henry VIII's break with Rome and rose to great power after the fall of Thomas Cromwell. He suffered a loss of favor in Edward VI's reign but lived to become Mary's lord chancellor.

Gascoigne, Gascony, ancient duchy of France

Gascoigne (Gascon), George (1542–77), poet, translator, and soldier: see pp. 298–99

Gascoigne, Sir William (?1350–1419), chief justice who relinquished his office after Henry V's accession. The apparently baseless legend that he was forced to do so because of his stern attitude toward the king's early escapades first appeared in Elyot's *Book Named the Governor*, whence it passed to Hall's chronicle and so on to Shakespeare.

Gascon, [George]: see Gascoigne (George)

Gaveston, Piers, Earl of Cornwall (d. 1312), first the playmate and then the confidant of Edward II, over whom he exerted the most baleful influence. When the king recalled him from the exile into which the angry barons had forced him, he was captured and summarily executed.

Gellius, Aulus (b. ca. 130), Roman grammarian whose *Noctes Atticae*, in twenty books, is a useful compendium of history, philosophy, literary gossip, and natural science

Gemine, Gemini, the Twins, a constellation, representing Castor and Pollux, that gives its name to a sign of the zodiac

Geneva, capital of the canton of Geneva, Switzerland, in the sixteenth century the center of Continental Calvinism from the fact that Calvin established there his theocracy

Gentile, heathen, pagan

Geoffery, i.e. Geoffrey Chaucer (*q.v.*)

George, Duke of Clarence (1449–78), brother of Edward IV who allied himself with Richard Neville, Earl of Warwick, to force the king into exile. Alleged to have used necromancy to kill Edward, he was committed to the Tower, attainted by Parliament, and sentenced to death; his execution was secret, but he was long thought to have been drowned in a butt of malmsey (as in Shakespeare's *Richard III*, I.iv).

George, St., patron saint of England. According to legend he was a native of Cappadocia who became a powerful commander under the Emperor Diocletian and died a Christian martyr in 303. By accretion the legend grew to include his fight with a dragon (the Devil), and from the reign of Edward III he was regarded as the patron saint of the Order of the Garter and of the English. His feast day is April 23, which is also celebrated as Shakespeare's birthday.

George-a-Green, pinner (or pound-keeper) of Wakefield celebrated in legend for his patriotism and his physical prowess, the subject of a play (?1595) probably by Robert Greene

George-nobles, gold coins worth 6*s.* 8*d.*

Georgics, poem by Virgil, in four books, on agriculture, tree cultivation, bee-keeping, and domestic animals

Geraldine, i.e. Geraldine (or Elizabeth) Fitzgerald (ca. 1528–89), youngest daughter of the ninth Earl of Kildare. She went from the household of Princess Mary to that of Queen Catherine Howard, marrying Sir Anthony Browne (1543) and after his death Sir Edward Clinton, first Earl of Lincoln (1548). Surrey probably knew her—as a child of nine—when she was in Princess Mary's household, but his sonnet to her can hardly be taken as evidence of a *grande passion*, and the sixteenth-century development of their affair was a romantic fabrication.

Gerileon (*of England*), Anthony Munday's translation (1592) from the French of Estienne de Maisonneufve

Germain, German

Ghibelline: see Guelf

Gilbert, Sir Humphrey (?1539–83), navigator who, after long agitation for a "new passage" to Cathay, made two voyages to America, on the second of which he established the first English colony in the New World and lost his life during the voyage home

Gildas (?516–?570), British historian whose *De excidio Britanniae* does not mention King Arthur although it treats the victory of Mt. Badon (?520) which was later included in lists of his military triumphs

gile che mirrour . . . , "the power of this mirror made me turn away"

Giles, Peter (Petrus Aegidius, ca. 1486–1533), pupil and later a close friend of Erasmus, and after 1510 town-clerk of Antwerp

Girald, Giraldus de Barri, called **Cambrensis** (?1146–?1220), Welsh historian and topographer, archdeacon of Brecknock, and energetic ecclesiastical politician, whose works include *Topographia Hibernica* and *Itinerarium Cambriae*

giunto Alexandro . . . , "when Alexander came to the great tomb of fierce Achilles he said, with a sigh, 'O happy one who found such clarion-room [and one who related so splendidly what you dared to do]' " (Petrarch, *Rime* 187)

Glendower, Owen (?1359–?1416), Owain ab Gruffydd, Welsh politician who served with Richard II against the Scots but rebelled against Henry IV and claimed the title Prince of Wales. Although he failed to join the Percys at Shrewsbury, he ravaged the English border and lost his wife and sons to the English; he was finally (1415) pardoned by the king. Nothing is known of his death.

Gloucester (Gloster), Duke of, i.e. Thomas of Woodstock (*q.v.*)

Gnatho, stock-character of a parasite from Terence's *Eunuch* γνῶσις, "knowledge"

Goa, capital of Portuguese India and thus a vital colonial outpost in the sixteenth century

Goad, Roger (1538–1610), provost of King's College, Cambridge, from 1570 and vice-chancellor of the university in 1576, 1595, and 1607

Goat, Capricornus, the zodiacal sign that the sun enters toward the end of December

Godstow (Nunnery), burial-place of Rosamond Clifford (*q.v.*) near Oxford

Gogmagog, according to Geoffrey of Monmouth, a giant who ruled the west of England before Brut landed at Totnes; he was thrown into the sea by Corineus, Brut's companion.

Golden Fleece, prize sought by the Argonauts (*q.v.*)

Golden Legend, the *Legenda aurea,* a collection of saints' lives compiled by James of Voragine in the thirteenth century and printed by Caxton in 1483

Goldey, i.e. Thomas Lodge (*q.v.*)

Golding, Arthur (?1536–?1605), translator: see p. 539

Goletta, seaport of Tunis, about eleven miles north of that city

Gómara, Francisco López (or Lopes) de (1510–ca. 1560), Spanish priest and historian who in 1540 became secretary and chaplain to Hernando Cortés, although he was probably never in America. His *Historia general de las Indias* (1552–53) was very popular and widely translated.

Gomor, Gomorrah: *see* Sodom

Gonsalva, Gil, i.e. Gil González Dávila (ca. 1460–ca. 1528), Spanish discoverer who, in spite of the jealousy and antagonism of the colonial governors, explored much of what is now Nicaragua and Honduras

Gonzaga, Cesar(e) (ca. 1475–1512), cousin of Baldassare Castiglione and trusted retainer of Duke Guidobaldo of Urbino

Gonzaga, Elizabeth (or Elisabetta), Duchess of Urbino (1471–1526), daughter of Federico Gonzaga, Marquess of Mantua, who married Duke Guidobaldo of Urbino in 1489 and became an intimate of his famous sister-in-law Isabella d'Este

Goodricke (Goodrich), Thomas (d. 1544), bishop of Ely and lord chancellor in 1552–53, one of the compilers of the Book of Common Prayer

Googe, Barnabe (1540–94), poet and translator: see p. 286

Gorboduc, five-act Senecan tragedy in blank verse (published in 1565) by Thomas Sackville and Thomas Norton

Gordian, pertaining to Gordius, an ancient king of Lydia who, in response to an oracle's prophecy, sought to perpetuate his reign by yoking oxen to his car with a knot that no one could untie. Alexander the Great cut the knot with his sword.

Gorgonean, Gorgonical, pertaining to the Gorgons (*q.v.*)

Gorgons, three daughters of Phorcys and Ceto (Stheno, Euryale, and Medusa [*q.v.*]) who, girded with serpents and armed with brazen claws, lived in the Western Ocean near Night and the Hesperides

Gosson, Stephen (1554–1624), disgruntled playwright and antagonist of the popular stage, later a clergyman at Great Wigborough and St. Botolph's, Bishopsgate, London: see p. 599

Gothian, Goth

Gower, John (ca. 1325–1408), poet, contemporary and friend of Chaucer, whose three major works (in as many languages) are *Speculum meditantis* (French), *Vox clamantis* (Latin), and *Confessio amantis* (English)

Gracchi, two famous Roman statesmen (Caius Sempronius Gracchus and Tiberius Sempronius Gracchus) whose mother was Cornelia, daughter of Scipio Africanus Major. Both were killed—Tiberius in 133 and Caius in 121 B.C.—as a result of their proposed agrarian reforms. Their mother, who carefully supervised their education, became so famed for her maternal virtues that the Romans erected to her a statue with the inscription "Cornelia, Mother of the Gracchi."

Graea(e), three gray-haired guardians of the Gorgons, who had only one eye and one tooth among them

Graeca cum Latinis, "Greek with Latin"

Grafton, Richard (d. ca. 1572), chronicler and printer: see p. 20

Granado, Granada, city (formerly a kingdom) on the Mediterranean coast of Spain, the last stronghold of the Moors on the peninsula

Grand Bay, the St. Lawrence estuary in Canada

Granta, the River Cam; in Grimald, Cambridge University

Grasshopper, i.e. the Royal Exchange in London, the steeple of which displayed a grasshopper, the crest of Sir Thomas Gresham, its founder (1565)

Grays, Grimald's rendering of *Graiae* ("Greek") in his translation from Beza's *Mors Ciceronis*

Grecia, Greece

Grecian maid, a, and eagle fierce, a reference to a wonderful grateful eagle of Sestos told of by Pliny, *Natural History* X.5

Greene, Infortunatus, according to Gabriel Harvey, Greene's son by the sister of "Cutting" Ball. Actually the name seems to have been Fortunatus.

Greene, Robert (?1560–92), pamphleteer, novelist, poet, and playwright: see pp. 379, 751, 848–49, 859–60

Greensleeves, proverbial name for an inconstant woman, the subject of one of the most popular of Elizabethan ballads. The reference to Robert Greene as Greensleeves in Harvey's *Four Letters* puns on the ballad title.

Greenwich, suburb southeast of London on the Thames

Gregory, probably Pope Gregory XIII, pope from 1572 to 1585, and therefore an important opponent of Elizabethan Calvinism

Grenville (Grinvile), Sir Richard (?1541–91), naval commander who commanded for Sir Walter Raleigh, his cousin, the expedition for the colonization of Virginia in 1585. Later he preyed upon Spanish shipping, organized the naval defenses of western England before the Armada, and served as second in command of the Azores fleet. The loss of his ship *The Revenge* and Grenville's death were stirringly told by Raleigh: see pp. 895–901.

Greville, Sir Fulke, first Baron Brooke (1554–1628), intimate friend of Sidney at Shrewsbury and Cambridge, secretary for the principality of Wales (1583–1628), and chancellor of the exchequer (1614–21); author of a biography of Sidney, plays, and sonnets

Grey, Arthur, fourteenth Baron Grey de Wilton (1536–93), a prominent Elizabethan statesman, Spenser's chief as lord-deputy of Ireland (1580–82), commissioner at the trials of the Duke of Norfolk (1574) and Mary Queen of Scots (1586)

Grey, Lady Jane: *see* Dudley (Lady Jane)

Grey, Lord Richard (d. 1483), with his brother Thomas (*q.v.*) a loyal supporter of Edward IV, accused by the Duke of Gloucester (later Richard III) of estranging the king from his family. After Gloucester had contrived the murder of Richard, Thomas actively supported the pretender Richmond (later Henry VII).

Grey, Thomas, first Marquis of Dorset (1451–1501), a supporter of Richmond (later Henry VII) before Bosworth Field. Following the death of Edward IV he took Jane Shore (*q.v.*) as his mistress and lived to become an early patron of Thomas Wolsey (*q.v.*).

Grey of Heaton, Sir Thomas (d. 1415), executed traitor to Henry V

Grey of Wilton, Lord: *see* Grey (Arthur)

Grey Friars, i.e. *Fratri Minores* (or Minorites), in the Roman Catholic Church a mendicant order founded by St. Francis of Assisi; also called Franciscans. The other mendicant orders are Dominicans (Friars Major), Carmelites (White Friars), and Augustinians (Austin Friars).

Griffin, Bartholomew (fl. 1596), sonneteer: see p. 496

Grimald, Nicholas (1519–62), chaplain of Bishop Ridley, poet, and translator. Imprisoned for his faith during Mary's reign, he saved himself by recanting and shortly thereafter contributed forty poems to the first (1557) edition of Tottel's *Miscellany*, most of them translations from classical and Renaissance Latin. He also translated Cicero's *De officiis* (1553). His two Latin dramas, *Archi-propheta* (1548) and *Christus redivivus* (1543), were probably products of his university days at Cambridge and Oxford.

Grindal, Edmund (?1519–83), archbishop of Canterbury (1576) whose unyielding Protestantism lost him the favor of Elizabeth even though it won for him the powerful protection of Cecil. Spenser eulogizes Grindal as "Algrind" in *The Shepherd's Calendar*.

Grindal, William (d. 1548), tutor of Queen Elizabeth and a favorite pupil of Roger Ascham (*q.v.*)

Grenvile, Sir Richard: *see* Grenville

Grocyn, William (?1446–1519), ecclesiastic and scholar who, after a visit to Italy (1488–90), returned with a knowledge of Greek to lecture at Oxford. Although he wrote virtually nothing he was a powerful teacher and a strong influence on such humanists as More, Linacre, and Erasmus.

Guatulco, Acapulco, a port on the west coast of Mexico

Guelf (or Guelph) and Ghibelline, leading political factions of medieval Italy, supporting respectively papal and popular as opposed to imperial and aristocratic interests

Guicciardin(i), Francesco (1483–1540), Florentine statesman whose *Storia d'Italia* is one of the first great works of modern history

Guidobaldo, Duke of Urbino: *see* Urbino

Guilhemites, Guillemins, hermits of the order of friars founded in the twelfth century by disciples of St. William

Guinea, region along the western coast of Africa between Cape Roxo and Cape Negro

Guines, French village in Pas-de-Calais

Gulike, in the country of, Robinson's mistranslation of More's *in castello* (in the fort). A capital C in the printed text caused Robinson to translate the phrase as "in Castellum." *Castellum* was the Latin name of Jülich, a town near Cologne.

Gundulf (?1024–1108), bishop of Rochester, allegedly the builder of the Tower of London, St. Leonard's Tower, and other Norman monuments

Guy of Warwick, legendary hero of English romance whose earliest exploits seem to date from the twelfth century. In addition to a popular verse romance from the early fourteenth century, there are many ballads about him, and especially about his victory over Colbrand, a Danish champion.

Gyges and Candaules, a story in Plato's *Republic* about a Lydian shepherd who found, in a chasm, a ring that could make him invisible. When sent on an embassy to King Candaules he used the ring in seducing his queen and then, with her assistance, in assassinating Candaules and securing the throne for himself.

H., Lady Elizabeth, perhaps Lady Hatton, one of the four daughters of Sir William Hatton, who died in March, 1597. But the allusion in Jonson's epitaph is intentionally obscure.

Haddon, Walter (1516–72), vice-chancellor (1549–50) and regius professor of civil law (1551) at Cambridge; master of Trinity (1552) and president of Magdalen College, Oxford (1552–53); under Elizabeth, master of requests, ecclesiastical commissioner, and judge of the prerogative court. His main literary work, written in collaboration with Sir John Cheke (*q.v.*), was *Reformatio legum ecclesiasticarum* (1571).

Hades, Pluto, god of the underworld; hence the underworld itself

Hadrianopolis (Hadrionopolis), Thracian city found by Hadrian (*q.v.*)

Hadrian(us) (Adrian), Publius Aelius (76–138), Roman emperor (117–138) in succession to Trajan, his uncle

haec memini . . . , "these things I remember, how the vanquished Thyrsis vainly struggled. Since then it has been Corydon, only Corydon, with us." (Virgil, *Eclogues* VII.69–70)

Hakluyt, Richard (?1552–1616), geographer and archdeacon of Westminster: see pp. 885–86

Halcyon, a bird (probably the kingfisher) which the ancients thought to breed in a floating nest and with its singing to calm the waves and winds

Hales, Lady Margaret, daughter of Thomas Hales of Henley-on-Thames, and mother, by Sir James Hales, of Humphrey, Edward,

and Mildred. Her husband, who had played a prominent part in the maneuvers concerning the succession of Edward VI, went mad and committed suicide in 1554.

Halifax, town in the West Riding of Yorkshire west of Leeds, long an important manufacturing center for woolens and cottons

Hall (Halle), Edward (d. 1547), English chronicler: see pp. 19–20

Hall, John (?1529–?1566), poet and physician, author of *The Court of Virtue:* see p. 209

Hall, Joseph (1574–1656), satirist, Anglican controversialist, bishop of Exeter and of Norwich: see p. 455

Haly, probably Ali-Ibn-Yoonas (d. 1008), eminent Arabic astronomer

Hamadryades, a class of nymphs or Nymphae (*q.v.*)

Haman, in the Book of Esther (chaps. iii–vii) a Persian courtier whose scheme to destroy the Jews was frustrated by Esther and Mordecai, and who was hanged on the gallows he had built for Mordecai

Hampton, Bernard (or Barnard), made one of the clerks of the Privy Council on September 23, 1551

Hampton (Court), royal residence built by Cardinal Wolsey some ten miles southwest of London on the Thames

Hannibal, (1) Carthaginian general (247–ca. 183 B.C.) of the second Punic War. The son of Hamilcar Barca, he succeeded Hasdrubal as general in Spain in 221, conquered that country, crossed the Alps in 218, ravaged Italy in a series of stunning victories over the Romans, and was finally defeated by Scipio Africanus Major at Zama in 202. He spent his last years in exile and committed suicide in Bithynia. (2) Count Hannibal Gonzaga, a Spanish cavalry officer killed at Zutphen

Harburn, tributary of the River Dart which rises in Dartmoor

Harding, Thomas (1516–72), divine who, named warden of New College, Oxford, by Edward VI, abandoned Protestantism at Mary's accession and later (1564–68) carried on a long controversy with John Jewel, bishop of Salisbury

Hardyng, John (1378–?1465), chronicler who, in the service of Hotspur and then of Henry V, saw action at Homildon and Agincourt. His chronicle in its original Lancastrian version ended with the year 1436, but a Yorkist version came down to 1461. Grafton published a mutilated redaction in 1543.

Harfleur, French seaport in Seine-Inférieure at the mouth of the Seine

Harington, Sir John (1561–1612), godson of Queen Elizabeth who translated *Orlando Furioso* at her command, accompanied Essex to Ireland, and gained a great reputation as a wit: see p. 561

Harpalus, Macedonian general under Alexander the Great, notorious for his excesses while satrap of Babylon and for his disloyalty to his master

Harpies, ravenous winged monsters with the faces of women and the bodies of birds of prey, fearful ministers of divine vengeance who polluted everything they touched

Harrison, William (1534–93), topographer and chronicler, canon of Windsor (1586), collaborator of Holinshed, and author of *The Description of England:* see p. 20

Harry, i.e. Henry VIII of England (*q.v.*)

Harvey, Gabriel (?1545–1630), fellow of Pembroke Hall and then of Trinity Hall, Cambridge, friend of Spenser, lecturer and writer on rhetoric, and party to a vicious quarrel with Greene and Nashe: see pp. 624–25, 859–60

Harvey, John (?1563–92), brother of Gabriel, writer on astrology, and physician at King's Lynn

Harvey, Richard (d. ?1623), brother of Gabriel, astrologer, and divine, whose *Plain Percival* (contributed to the Martin Marprelate controversy) and *Theological Discourse of the Lamb of God* (1590) provoked Greene to attack the Harvey family in *A Quip for an Upstart Courtier:* see pp. 859–60

Harwich(port), seaport in Essex, England

Hastings, Lord Henry, third Earl of Huntingdon (1535–95), heir-presumptive to the throne through his mother; a statesman active in Scottish affairs and president of the north in 1572

Hastings, William, Baron Hastings (?1430–83), ardent Yorkist whom Edward IV created a peer and made lord chamberlain in 1461. After Edward's death he refused to follow Gloucester and was consequently executed.

Haterius, Quintus (d. 26), senator and rhetorician in the time of Augustus and Tiberius

Hatton, Sir Christopher (1540–91), prominent member of Elizabeth's court (accused by Mary Queen of Scots of being Elizabeth's lover) and a generous patron of writers, notably Churchyard and Spenser. As a young man in the Inner Temple he wrote the fourth act of *Tancred and Gismund,* a play acted in 1568.

haud ictus sapio, "although beaten down, I have not learned wisdom"

Haward, Henry: *see* Howard (Henry)

Haward, Lord [Thomas]: *see* Howard (Thomas)

Hawes, Stephen (d. ?1523), groom of the chamber to Henry VII, author of *The Pastime of Pleasure* and shorter poems: see p. 61

Hawkins, Sir John (1532–95), naval commander who began his career as a slave-trader in the Caribbean and became a great vexation to the Spaniards. As comptroller and treasurer of the navy he did much to build up Elizabethan sea-power. He took a prominent part against the Armada in 1588 and died on a voyage to the West Indies with Drake.

Heath, John (fl. 1615), epigrammatist whose *Two Centuries of Epigrams* (1610) treats many of his famous contemporaries

Heautontimoroumenos, "The Self-Tormenter," a comedy by Terence first performed in 163 B.C.

Heavy Hill, ascent to Tyburn or the gallows

Hebe, goddess of spring and youth, and, until supplanted by Ganymede (*q.v.*), cup-bearer of Zeus. The daughter of Zeus and Hera, she became the wife of Hercules after his deification.

Hebrician, Hebraist

Hecuba, wife of Priam (*q.v.*)

Hekatompathia ('Εκατομπαθία), "a hundred passions or sonnets" by Thomas Watson: see p. 317

Helen(a), fabulously beautiful daughter of Zeus and Leda and wife of Menelaus whose abduction by Paris, son of Priam, caused the Trojan War

Helias: *see* Elias

Helice, the Great Bear (*Ursa Major*), a constellation in the northern hemisphere

Helicon, mountain in Boeotia celebrated as the home of the muses; it contained the sacred fountains of Aganippe and Hippocrene.

Heliodorus, Syrian bishop of Tricca, Thessaly, at the end of the fourth century who wrote, in Greek, *The Ethiopian History* (*Aethiopica*), one of the most popular "novels" of the Renaissance (see pp. 696–97)

Heliogabulus (Elagabalus), Varius Avitus Bassianus (205–222), Roman emperor notorious for his debauchery and irresponsibility who was put to death by his own pretorian guard

Helle, mythical Theban princess who, riding on a golden ram with her brother Phrixus, fell into the sea and thus gave her name to the Hellespont

Hellespont, the Dardanelles, a strait connecting the Aegean and the Sea of Marmora

Helots, class of serfs among the ancient Spartans. Owned by the state and bound to the soil, they served as light-armed troops in time of war and were often systematically massacred to keep down their numbers and thus reduce the danger of revolution. Sidney uses the word for the peasants of Laconia who form a lawless and rebellious mob.

Hengist, with Horsa the traditional leader of the Jutes who invaded Britain about 449 and were given the Isle of Thanet for a dwelling-place by King Vortigern

Henri III (1551–89), king of France (1574–89), last of the Valois, whose reign was agitated by almost incessant civil and religious wars

Henry I, surnamed Beauclerc (1068–1135), fourth son of William the Conqueror, king of England (1100–1135) in succession to William II

Henry II (1133–89), king of England (1154–89), lover of Rosamond Clifford (*q.v.*)

Henry IV (1367–1413), Henry of Bolingbroke, king of England (1399–1413), son of John of Gaunt and grandson of Edward III. In deposing and succeeding his cousin Richard II he inaugurated the Lancastrian dynasty.

Henry V (1387–1422), king of England (1413–22), famous warriorking, son of Henry IV and father of Henry VI

Henry VI (1421–71), king of England (1422–61, 1470–71), weakest of the Lancastrian dynasty. He succeeded his father Henry V when only nine months old, his uncle Humphrey of Gloucester acting as protector. Incapacitated by sporadic fits of insanity, he was constantly harassed by Yorkist claims to the succession until Edward, Duke of York, defeated him at Towton and became Edward IV. Briefly restored to the throne by the Earl of Warwick in 1470, he was again deposed by Edward and murdered in the Tower, perhaps by Richard, Duke of Gloucester (later Richard III).

Henry VII (1457–1509), king of England (1485–1509), first Tudor monarch, who established his dynasty after defeating Richard III, last of the Yorkists, at Bosworth in 1485. He was the father of Henry VIII, and so the grandfather of Edward VI, Mary, and Elizabeth.

Henry VIII (1491–1547), king of England (1509–47), son of Henry VII, father of Edward VI, Mary, and Elizabeth

Henry, Duke of Buckingham: *see* Stafford (Henry)

Henry, Earl of Northumberland: *see* Percy (Henry)

Henry of Huntingdon (?1084–1155), archdeacon of Huntingdon and author of *Historia Anglorum*

Henry, Prince of Wales (1594–1612), Henry Frederick, eldest son of James I, in spite of his youth a generous patron of writers, whose untimely death of typhoid fever was the subject of many elegies, some of them by very eminent men of letters

Heraclitus (ca. 535–ca. 475 B.C.), Greek philosopher whose main work, *On Nature,* develops in a very cryptic and obscure style the thesis that everything but fire, the primordial element, changes and passes away

Herbert, Mary, Countess of Pembroke (1561–1621), Sir Philip Sidney's sister, wife of Henry Herbert, second Earl of Pembroke, famous patroness of literature who inspired her brother's *Arcadia* and was praised by Spenser, Daniel, Breton, Jonson, and many others. Like her brother a zealous Protestant, she collaborated with him in a metrical version of the Psalms and in translating Plessis du Mornay's *Discourse of Life and Death* (1593). Her elegy on Sidney was appended to Spenser's *Astrophel.*

Herbert, William, third Earl of Pembroke of the second creation (1580–1630), pupil of Samuel Daniel, lover of Mary Fitton (one of Elizabeth's women-in-waiting whose name has been implausibly linked with Shakespeare's), trusted courtier of James I (becoming lord chamberlain in 1615), and patron of eminent writers. It was to him, as lord chamberlain, and his brother Philip that the First Folio of Shakespeare was dedicated in 1623, and he has been identified by some as the "Mr. W. H." to whom Shakespeare's *Sonnets* was dedicated by Thomas Thorpe.

Herculea proles, "a descendant of Hercules"

Hercules, son of Zeus and Alcmene, the powerful hero who came to be worshiped as the god of strength and courage. Juno set him to twelve labors—strangling the Nemean lion, killing the Lernean hydra, cleansing the Augean stables, capturing the Cretan bull, etc.—which earned him immortality. *See* Nessus.

Hereford (Herford), Earl of, title borne by two kings of England, Edward II and Henry IV (*qq.v.*)

Herennius, centurion in command of the troops who murdered Cicero near Formiae on December 7, 43 B.C.

Herford: *see* Hereford

Hermes, herald and messenger of the gods. Born on Mt. Cyllene in Arcadia, the son of Zeus and Maia, he became the protector of herdsmen, science, commerce, and invention, and the patron of rogues and travelers.

Hermes (or Mercurius) Trismegistus, reputed author of a body of syncretistic works on philosophy and religion of about the fourth century. The so-called Hermetic writings, combining elements of Neo-Platonic, Judaic, and cabalistic theosophy, were presumably contrived to check the ascendancy of Christianity.

Hermippus (fl. 200 B.C.), philosopher of Smyrna whose now lost biographical study was greatly admired in antiquity

Hermogenes (fl. 175), Greek rhetorician and protégé of Marcus Aurelius whose five treatises on rhetoric were long used as school manuals

Hero, beautiful priestess of Aphrodite at Sestos on the Hellespont, beloved of Leander, a youth of Abydos on the opposite shore, who nightly swam across to her. When he was drowned one stormy night, she flung herself into the sea.

Herodotus (ca. 484–ca. 424 B.C.), first of the great Greek historians, whose nine-book treatment of the Persian invasions has earned for him the title "Father of History"

Hesiod(us) or **Ascraeus** (fl. 735 B.C.), Greek poet of Boeotia whose *Works and Days* and *Theogony* deal respectively with rural economy and the gods of Greece

Hesperian land, the western land, i.e. Spain

Hesperides (Esperides), maidens in the far west who guarded the golden apples which Gaea (Earth) designed as a wedding-gift for Hera

Hesper(us), the evening star, son of Astraeus and Eos, recognized as identical with Phosphorus, the morning star

Hesse(n), principality in western Germany

Hetrurian, pertaining to Etruria (*q.v.*)

heu, heu, me, "wo, wo is me"

Heywood, Jasper (1535–98), son of John Heywood the epigrammatist. He served as page to Princess Elizabeth, attended Oxford, left England because of his Catholicism, and served for seventeen years as professor of moral theology in the Jesuit college at Dillingen, Bavaria. Returning to England on a Jesuit mission in 1581, he was arrested and exiled, and at last died in Naples, where he had been sent by his order. Heywood translated three plays of Seneca (*Troas,* 1559, *Thyestes,* 1560, *Hercules furens,* 1561) which were included in Thomas Newton's *Seneca His Ten Tragedies* (1581), and eight of his poems found their way into *The Paradise of Dainty Devices* (1576).

Heywood, John (?1497–?1580), epigrammatist, dramatist, and poet who long served the early Tudor family as a singer and musician: see pp. 120–21

Hibernic, Irish

Hieremias, Hieremy, Jeremiah

Hiero (d. 467 B.C.), tyrant of Syracuse, in Sicily, who was famed as a patron of writers

Hierom(e), Jerome (*q.v.*)

Hierusalem, Jerusalem

High Court of Parliament, old title for the English Parliament suggestive of its function as a judicial body

Hille, ——, possibly (see G. Gregory Smith, *Elizabethan Critical Essays,* I, 411) the R. Hill who contributed to *The Paradise of Dainty Devices* (1576)

Hilliard, Nicholas (1537–1619), miniature-painter and goldsmith to Queen Elizabeth whose fame was so great that James I in 1617 gave him the sole right to execute royal portraits

Hilton, John (d. 1657), composer and organist of St. Margaret's, Westminster, contributor to *The Triumphs of Oriana* (1601)

hinc illae lacrimae, "hence these tears" (Horace, *Epistles* I.xix.41)

Hippocrates (ca. 460–ca. 377 B.C.), Greek physician, the "Father of Medicine." The eighty-odd extant treatises attributed to him probably contain a good deal of work by his pupils and followers.

Hippocrene, fountain on Helicon (*q.v.*) sacred to the muses, said to have been struck out by the hoof of Pegasus

Hippolytus, son of Theseus and Hippolyta, pursued by his stepmother Phaedra (*q.v.*), who, when her incestuous advances were repulsed, contrived his destruction. The story forms the plot of Euripides' *Hippolytus* and Seneca's *Phaedra.*

Hippomenes, suitor of Atalanta (*q.v.*)

Hipponax, (fl. 546–520 B.C.), Greek poet of Ephesus, noted for the bitterness of his satires

Hippoplace, Chapman's rendering of Homer's Ὑποπλακίη, "under Placus" (*Iliad* VI.397): see Plac(i)us

Hispaniola, Española, the name given by Columbus to the Island of Haiti

Hoby, Sir Edward (1560–1617), courtier and literary patron. A son of Sir Thomas Hoby, he was educated at Eton and at Trinity College, Oxford, received his knighthood from Elizabeth (1582), joined the Cadiz expedition (1596), and became a great favorite of James I.

Hoby, Sir Thomas (1530–66), minor diplomat and translator of Castiglione: see p. 522

hoc opus, hic labor est, "this is the task, this the labor" (Virgil, *Aeneid* VI.129)

Hochelaga, Indian village on the site of Montreal when it was discovered by Cartier in 1535

Hodge (Plowman), type-name for a rustic or plowman

Hoe, hill and promontory overlooking Plymouth Harbor on the south coast of England

Holborn, district of London, formerly the site of Ely Place, the splendid palace of the bishops of Ely, and of various Inns of Court (*q.v.*)

Holdenby, Holmby House, Sir Christopher Hatton's country place near Northampton

Holinshed, Raphael (d. ?1580), chronicler, translator, and printer's assistant: see p. 20

Holland (cloth), linen fabric originally made in the province of Holland in the Netherlands

Holland, Philemon (1552–1637), translator and schoolmaster: see p. 565

Holofernes, general of Nebuchadnezzar killed by Judith (*q.v.*)

Homildon, Humbleton, height north of Wooler in Northumberland

Honterus, Joannes, author of *Rudimenta cogmographica* (1548), a three-book cosmography in Latin verse

Hooker, Richard (?1554–1600), divine and Anglican apologist: see pp. 179–80

Hopkins, John (d. 1570), schoolmaster who published (and expanded) the second edition of Sternhold's metrical versions of the Psalms in 1549: see pp. 160–61

Horace, Quintus Horatius Flaccus (65–8 B.C.), Roman poet who achieved immense popularity in the classical revival of the Renaissance. His two books of *Satires,* thirty *Epodes,* four books of *Odes,* and two books of *Epistles*—all the work of a graceful society poet—were admired, imitated, and translated throughout Europe.

Horman, William (d. 1535), master (1485) and fellow (1502) of Eton who attacked the grammatical works of Robert Whittington in his *Antibossicon* (1521) and printed a set of Latin aphorisms called *Vulgaria* (1519)

Hortenzia, according to Greene, a widow who consoled herself with her children

Hospital of France: *see* L'Hospital

Hotspur: *see* Percy (Sir Henry, 1364–1403)

Houghton, Master, a friend of Giles Fletcher

Howard, Lady Catherine (or Katherine), fifth queen of Henry VIII, executed on February 13, 1542, for alleged improper premarital conduct. She was a cousin of the poet Surrey.

Howard, Charles, second Baron Howard of Effingham, first Earl of Nottingham (1536–1624), naval commander and statesman, lord chamberlain (1574–85), lord high admiral (1585), chief commander against the Spanish Armada (1588)

Howard, Sir Edward (?1477–1513), member of one of the greatest families of Tudor England, whose distinguished naval career led to his appointment as lord high admiral in 1513, the year in which he lost his life in action against the French

Howard (Haward), Henry, Earl of Surrey (by courtesy) (?1517–47), son of Thomas Howard, afterward third Duke of Norfolk (*q.v.*), distinguished courtier who was condemned and executed on a foolish charge of quartering royal arms and advising his sister to become Henry VIII's mistress; a voluminous contributor to Tottel's *Miscellany:* see pp. 194–95, 517

Howard, Thomas, Earl of Surrey and third Duke of Norfolk of the Howard house (1473–1554), hero of Flodden Field and an inveterate enemy of Cardinal Wolsey (and later of Thomas Cromwell). He followed Henry VIII with unswerving loyalty even in the execution of his niece Anne Boleyn, was himself saved from the headsman's ax only by the death of his master, and lived to play an active part against Northumberland and Wyatt in their insurrections against Queen Mary.

Howard, Thomas, fourth Duke of Norfolk of the Howard house (1536–72), son of Henry Howard, the poet. Named by Elizabeth to her privy council, he promptly incurred the powerful enmity of the Earl of Leicester, became involved in Ridolfi's plot to assist a Spanish invasion and to marry Howard himself to Mary

Queen of Scots in order to establish a Catholic dynasty in England, and was executed for treason.

Howell, Thomas (fl. 1568), minor "courtly maker" of Elizabeth's early reign: see pp. 289–90

Hubbard, Mother, referring to Spenser's satire, *Mother Hubberd's Tale* (see p. 332)

humanus deus, "a god in human form"

Humber, estuary formed by the junction of the Trent and the Ouse between Yorkshire and Lincolnshire. Geoffrey of Monmouth identifies Humber as a king of the Huns who, invading England during Locrine's reign, was driven into the river that bears his name.

humiliatedo, abjection, insignificance

Humphrey, Duke of Gloucester ("Good Duke Humphrey," 1391–1447), youngest son of Henry IV. Though a man of some cultivation and the patron of Lydgate, Capgrave, and other writers, he was as bloody and self-seeking as the other Plantagenets. His unsuccessful regency led to the troubles of Henry VI's reign, and he died a prisoner of his nephew, the king.

Hungerford, town in Wiltshire west of Reading

Hunnis, William (d. 1597), musician, poet, and gentleman of the Chapel under Edward VI, master of the Chapel under Elizabeth (1566), and author of a metrical version of the Psalms as well as an original work called *A Hive Full of Honey* (1578)

Hunsdon, parish and village in Hertfordshire, the site of Hunsdon House

Hunsdon, Lord: *see* Carey (George)

Hyacinth(us), son of Amyclas, king of Sparta, who, preferring Apollo's love to Zephyrus', was killed by a quoit blown by the latter from Apollo's hand, whereupon Apollo changed his blood into the flower that bears his name

Hyades, the seven daughters of Hyas (a mystic surname for Dionysus) whom Zeus placed in the constellation of Taurus (the Bull) to assuage their grief at their father's death. Grimald twists the legend to make Lyai (Lyaeus or Bacchus) responsible for their stellification in reward for their care of him as an infant.

Hybla, Hybla Minor or Megara Hyblaea, in antiquity a city of Sicily famous for its honey. It is often confused with Hybla Major, a city on the slopes of Mt. Etna northwest of Catania.

Hylonomo (Hylonome), female Centaur beloved of Cyllarus

Hymen (Hymaeneus), originally a marriage-song with the Greeks; later, by personification, the god of marriage, a tall and comely youth bearing a nuptial torch

Hymnus in Noctem, "Hymn to Night"

Hyperborei, in Greek legend, a fabulous people living in the far north in a state of perpetual bliss

Hyperia, a spring in Thessaly

Hyperion, a Titan, son of Uranus and Gaea, and father (by his sister Theia) of Helios, Selene, and Eos

I Loathe That I Did Love, a ballad-tune (named from the first line of Lord Vaux's "The Aged Lover Renounceth Love" in Tottel's *Miscellany*); the poem and tune were registered for publication as a broadside in 1563–64.

iambicum trimetrum, "iambic trimeter," a verse of six iambics (feet consisting of a short and a long syllable), the first, third, and fifth of which may be variously altered. Corresponding roughly to the modern Alexandrine, it was the principal meter of Greek drama.

Iberus' lord, i.e. Philip II of Spain (*q.v.*)

Icarian, soaring, flying high like Icarus, son of Daedalus (*q.v.*)

Ida (Ide), mountain-range in Mysia, Asia Minor, the scene of the rape of Ganymede (*q.v.*) and the judgment of Paris. Homer has his deities watch the war on the Trojan plain from the summit of Mt. Ida. Hence Idalian.

ideo nobilis quasi no bilis, "therefore noble in having no bile," Nashe's bilingual pun on "noble" and "no bile"

idioma, "idiom"

Idomen(eus), a king of Crete who, as a former suitor of Helen, fought with the Greeks before Troy

Idyllia, some thirty bucolic poems attributed to Theocritus (*q.v.*)

ignes fatui, "will-o'-the-wisps"

Ignoto, unknown or anonymous author

il est escrit, pur voir & eit [an error for *dit*] . . . , "it is written, as true and accomplished, by marriage pure, that this war will not last"

Iliados, Iliads, Ilias, the *Iliad* of Homer

Ilion, Ilium, Troy, in antiquity a city in Mysia, Asia Minor, identified with the legendary Troy described by Homer

Illyris, Illyria, an ancient country on the east coast of the Adriatic

Immerito, "the undeserving one," Spenser's sobriquet in writing to Gabriel Harvey

in exitu Israel de Aegypto, "when Israel went out of Egypt" (Vulgate Psalms cxiii.1)

in manus tuas, Domine, "into thy hands, O Lord" (Vulgate Psalms xxx.6)

in nullius verba jurati, "sworn to no prescribed oath," i.e. not bound to follow any one formula or practise (perhaps adapted from Horace, *Epistles* I.i.14)

in obitum Ed. Spenser . . . , "on the death of Edmund Spenser, most eminent of poets"

in presenti, ass, a pun on a tag from the famous Latin grammar by William Lily (?1468–1522): *-as in presenti, perfectum format in -avi,* "forms ending in *-as* in the present tense end in *-avi* in the perfect tense"

inamorato Curio, "infatuated Curio"

Ind(ie), Indy, India, the Indies

indignatio principis mors est, "the wrath of a prince is death"

individuum, "an indivisible unity"

indulgere genio, "to indulge one's inclinations" (Persius, *Satires* V.151)

Indy: *see* Ind(ie)

Infortunatus: *see* Greene (Infortunatus)

Inns of Court, legal societies in London which both maintain instruction in the law and call candidates to the bar. They now comprise the Inner Temple, the Middle Temple, Lincoln's Inn, and Gray's Inn.

instar belluarum . . . , "the nature of the most savage beasts to do violence to a corpse"

instar cotis, "like flint"

Institution of a Christian Prince, The, Erasmus' *Institutio Christiani principis* (1516), a manual of statecraft written for the instruction of Charles V

intentio animi actio, "intention is the action of the mind"

intercalares, i.e. days inserted into the calendar

intonsi Catones, "unshorn Catos"

Io or Europa, daughter of Inachus, king of Argos, whom Hera jealously turned into a white heifer and put under the guard of Argus of the hundred eyes. When Argus was killed by Hermes (Mercury) at Zeus's command, Hera sent a gadfly to torment Io, until at last, in Africa, she regained her humanity and bore Epaphus to Zeus.

io paean, "shout huzza!"

Iole, captive princess beloved by Hercules: *see* Nessus

Ion, a dialogue of Plato's concerning the nature of poetic inspiration

Ionia, region on the western coast of Lydia and Caria, Asia Minor, and the adjacent islands of Chios and Samos

Ionique (harmony), the Ionian mode of Greek music

Iope, name of a lovely, dead woman which Campion imitated from Propertius (*Elegies* II.28): *vobiscum est Iope, vobiscum candida Tyro,* "with you [i.e. the dead] is Iope, with you is snowy Tyro"

Iphicrates, Athenian general who defeated the Spartans near Corinth in 392 B.C.

ipse ille, "the very thing"

Ipswich, seaport and chief city of Suffolk, a county in England

Iris, female messenger of the gods, sometimes regarded as the personification of the rainbow

Irishe, Master, Bishop Ridley's host the night before his execution. His wife is described in an old marginal gloss in Foxe's *Acts and Monuments* as "a great papist before."

Irus, a beggar of ancient Ithaca, famed for his size and his voracity. In the *Odyssey* he appears as the messenger of Penelope's suitors.

Isabeau or Isabella (of Bavaria, 1370–1435), wife of Charles VI of France, who, after her husband became insane (1392), lived a dissolute life, swinging politically between the Armagnacs and the Burgundians. The implacable enemy of her son, later Charles VII, she signed away his inheritance at the Treaty of Troyes (1420), and as a result of the same treaty her daughter Catherine married Henry V.

Isaeus, Attic orator of the fourth century B.C., eleven of whose orations survive

Isam, Mistress, presumably the wife of a shoemaker near Dowgate, Greene's landlady in his last illness

Isis, (1) prominent female deity of Egyptian mythology, the wife and sister of Osiris and mother of Horus. In the Hellenic period her worship was introduced into Greece, and later she became a popular mystery-deity at Rome. (2) A name sometimes given to the upper reaches of the Thames

Isocrates (436–338 B.C.), distinguished Athenian orator and teacher of eloquence, twenty-one of whose orations survive

Isthmus, the Isthmian sanctuary on the Isthmus of Corinth, in antiquity the site of the Isthmian games

Italia, Italy

Italianism, trickery

iubeo stultum . . . : see *jubeo stultum*

Ixion, king of the Lapithae, father of Pirithous and (by a cloud formed by Zeus into the shape of Hera) of the Centaurs. For boasting of his alleged conquest of Hera, Zeus fastened him to a perpetually turning wheel in Hades.

Jack Straw, leader of the insurgent Essex landsmen in the Peasants' Revolt of 1381

Jacobite, a Jacobin, or Dominican friar

Jacqueline (Jaquet) of Hainault, wife (m. 1422) of Humphrey, Duke of Gloucester. After the annulment of the marriage in 1428 he married his mistress Eleanor Cobham.

jam sed poteras tutior esse domi, "but now you could be safer at home"

jam Tiberium . . . , "now his strength and his body were failing Tiberius, but not his guile" (Tacitus, *Annals* VI.50)

James I (1394–1437), king of Scotland (1406–37), author of *The King's Quire*. During his nineteen-year imprisonment by the English he married Lady Jane Beaufort, granddaughter of John of Gaunt.

James V (1512–42), king of Scotland (1513–42), nephew of Henry VIII of England and father of Mary Stuart

James, Doctor, presumably a learned friend of Richard Hakluyt (*q.v.*)

James, St., the apostle James, son of Zebedee. His feast day is July 25.

Jane, Queen, Joan, regent of Brittany, second wife (m. 1402) of Henry IV

Janus, god of beginnings and endings after whom our first month is named. His temple (or "phane") was built in Rome by Duilius during the first Punic War, restored by Augustus, and dedicated by Tiberius. When Rome was at war its gates were ajar; when at peace, they were closed.

Japhet(h), third son of Noah

Jaquet: *see* Jacqueline

Jarrat's Hall, ancient building in Basing Lane, near Bread Street, London

Jason, leader of the Argonauts' expedition to Colchis to gain the Golden Fleece

Java, Isle of, one of the Sunda Islands between Sumatra and Borneo

Jaye, George: *see* Joye

Jean de Meun (John de Mehune), Jean Clopinel (ca. 1250–ca. 1305), French poet who completed, after a lapse of some forty years, *Le roman de la rose*, a dream-vision begun by Guillaume de Lorris about 1237

Jeffery, Geoffrey

Jenkinson, Anthony (d. 1611), merchant and traveler who wrote an account of his journey through Russia to Persia in 1558–60

Jeremy, Jeremiah

Jerome (Hierom), St., Eusebius Hieronymus (?340–420), one of the four great fathers of the Roman church; his Latin version of the Scriptures (the so-called Vulgate) is still the received text of that church.

Jerusalem Chamber, a room on the southwest side of Westminster Abbey, long the meeting-place for the Upper House of Convocation of the Province of Canterbury. The name probably derived from the subject-matter of the tapestries decorating the chamber.

Jewel, John (1522–71), bishop of Salisbury and Anglican apologist: see p. 168

Jeynes, ?town in France

joco (i.e. *gioco*) *de canne*, a courtly game involving the throwing of sticks

Jodelle, Étienne (1532–73), founder of French tragedy and member of the literary group called the Pléiade; his works include *Cléopâtre captive* (1552) and *Didon* (1553).

Johannes fac totum, "Jack of all trades"

Johannes (or John) Picus de Mirandula: *see* Pico della Mirandola

John, (1) the apostle John, reputed author of the Fourth Gospel, three epistles, and the Book of Revelation; (2) king of England (1199–1216) noted for his cruelty and corruption

John a Stile, John a Noakes, fictitious names in a legal action

John de Mehune: *see* Jean de Meun

John of Gaunt, Duke of Lancaster (1340–99), fourth son of Edward III, uncle of Richard II, father of Henry IV, one of the most energetic and powerful political figures of his time

John of Lancaster, Duke of Bedford (1389–1435), third son of Henry IV who, on the death of his brother Henry V, became regent of France. He is best remembered for buying Joan of Arc from the Burgundians and then burning her as a witch at Rouen (1431). In the same year he caused young Henry VI to be crowned king of France at Notre Dame.

Jonas, Jonah

Jonathan, Hebrew commander, son of Saul and friend of David

Jones, Richard (fl. 1564–1602), prolific but not entirely reputable printer whose products were generally of a popular sort—ballads, chapbooks, romances, etc.—although he also published such notable works as Marlowe's *Tamburlaine*, Nashe's *Pierce Penniless, Breton's Bower of Delights*

Jonson, Ben (?1573–1637), poet and playwright: see pp. 490–91

Joseph Ben Gorion, reputed author of a ninth- or tenth-century history of the Jews translated by Peter Morvyn (or Morwen) in 1558 as *A Compendious History of the Jews' Commonweal*

Josephus, Flavius (Jewish name Joseph Ben Matthias, 37–95), Jewish historian who attached himself to the Roman conquerors of his country and lived luxuriously at Rome under the protection of Vespasian and Titus. There he wrote his great works, *The Jewish War* (in seven books) and *Antiquities of the Jews* (in twenty books), dying, perhaps a Jewish martyr, in the reign of Domitian.

Jove: *see* Jupiter, Zeus

Joye (or Jaye), George (d. 1553), Protestant controversialist who, from his exile at Strassburg, issued defenses of his alleged heresies and translations of Isaiah, Jeremiah, and the Psalms, and also assisted William Tyndale (*q.v.*) in his controversy with More. Intransigent to the end, he died in England while involved in a bitter quarrel with Stephen Gardiner (*q.v.*).

jubeo stultum esse libenter, "I command him to be a fool freely"

Jubiter: *see* Jupiter

Judaical, Hebrew

Judas (Iscariot), the disciple who betrayed Jesus; hence a type-name for a traitor

Judas the Apostle (Jude), one of the twelve apostles, probably to be identified with Thaddeus and Lebbaeus (see Luke vi.16, Acts i.13)

Judicum, the Book of Judges

Judith, heroine of the Apocryphal Book of Judith, a historical romance, dating probably from the Maccabean period, which has survived in both Greek and Latin versions. Judith's city of Bethulia was besieged by Holofernes, an Assyrian general. She entered his camp, ostensibly to betray her people, and killed him in his drunken sleep.

Julia (39 B.C.–A.D. 14), daughter of Augustus Caesar and one of the most profligate women of the age. Thrice married (the third time to Tiberius Nero), she was at last banished by her father in punishment for her immorality.

Julian the Apostate, Flavius Claudius Julianus (331–363), Roman emperor who was reared a Christian but became a pagan on his accession in 361. At his death, in a battle against the Persians, he is alleged to have cried, "Thou hast conquered, O Galilean!" (*Vicisti, Galilaee!*). A prolific and accomplished writer, he left polished letters, orations, and satires (e.g. *The Caesars,* satirizing the Roman emperors, and *Misopogon,* an attack on the licentious citizens of Antioch).

Julian-like, resembling Julian the Apostate (*q.v.*)

Julians, ?Roman Catholics

Julie III, Pope Julius III (Gianmaria de' Medici), pope from 1550 to 1555

Julie, Caius: *see* Caesar

Julio (Julius), Duke of Brunswick (1528–89), German noble who succeeded his father Henry II as Duke of Brunswick-Wolfenbüttel in 1568

Julius II (1443–1513), Giuliano della Rovere, the warlike pope who, succeeding Alexander VI, became a famous patron of literature and art while waging incessant diplomatic warfare against the aggrandizements of Venice and France. He convened the fifth Lateran Council in 1512.

Junius, Franciscus (1545–1602), French Protestant who taught theology at Neustadt, Heidelberg, and Leyden. While at Heidelberg he assisted Emanuel Tremellius (whose daughter he married) in his Latin version of the Old Testament (1579).

Juno, queen of heaven, sister and wife of Jupiter, and protectress of marriage. She corresponded to and assimilated most of the characteristics of the Greek Hera.

Jupiter (Jubiter), Jove, supreme deity of Roman mythology (corresponding to the Greek Zeus), god of law, right, and national dignity. He was worshiped as Optimus Maximus in his temple on the Capitoline Hill in Rome.

jus, "law"

Justinian, Flavius Anicius Justinianus, surnamed "The Great" (483–565), Byzantine emperor from 527 until his death. His wife Theodora and his generals Belisarius and Narses were instrumental in making his reign memorable, both in civil and religious settlements and in military conquests. His codification of Roman law in the so-called Justinian Code (the *Corpus juris civilis*) is a landmark in the history of jurisprudence.

Justin(us), Roman historian of the fourth or fifth century whose *Historiae Philippicae* is an epitome of Trogus Pompeius' now lost work of the same name, ostensibly a history of Macedon but actually a universal history

Juvenal, Decimus Junius Juvenalis (ca. 60–140), Roman satirist whose extant work consists of sixteen satires (in five books), much admired and imitated in the late sixteenth century in England (see p. 455)

K., E.: *see* Kirke

Katherine, Catherine of Aragon (*q.v.*)

Katherine, Queen: *see* Howard (Lady Catherine)

Katherine, St., according to tradition, a martyr of the primitive church who was tortured and then beheaded by the emperor Maximian at Alexandria in 307. Her feast day is November 25.

Kaux: *see* Caux

Kemp, Will (fl. 1600), comic actor and dancer, a member of the company of players under the successive patronage of Leicester, Lord Strange, and Lord Hunsdon. He gained fame by dancing a morris-dance from London to Norwich, an exploit which he described in *Kemp's Nine Days' Wonder* (1600).

Kendal-green, a kind of green woolen cloth, named from Kendal in Westmorland, its place of manufacture

Kendall, Timothy (fl. 1577), epigrammatist and minor poet

Kenilworth (Killingworth), ancient town near Warwick, site of a castle now in ruins

Kent, county in southeast England

Kentish-tailed, i.e. long-tailed

Kilcolman, manor and castle in County Cork, Spenser's home in Ireland

Killingworth: *see* Kenilworth

Kimbalton, town and site of a castle in Huntington, England

Kindheart, name for an itinerant tooth-puller

King's College, Cambridge college founded by Henry VI in 1441 and patronized by Henry VII and Henry VIII. Its chapel,

built between 1446 and 1515, is one of the architectural glories of England.

King's Head, a tavern on Fish Street Hill (*q.v.*) famous for its wine

Kingston, Sir William (d. 1540), Tudor stalwart who fought at Flodden, accompanied Henry VIII to the Field of the Cloth of Gold, and served in various important posts as captain of the guard, constable of the Tower, and controller of the royal household

Kinwelmarsh, Francis (d. ?1580), minor poet, several of whose poems are included in *The Paradise of Dainty Devices.* A fellow-student at Gray's Inn with George Gascoigne (ca. 1557), with whom he collaborated on *Jocasta* (a blank-verse rendering of Euripides' *Phoenissae*) in 1566, he was elected to Parliament in 1572 and was remembered long enough to be mentioned favorably by William Webbe in *A Discourse of English Poetry* (1586).

Kirk, Mistress, ?Spenser's London landlady

Kirke, Edward (1553–1613), a friend of Spenser's at Pembroke Hall, Cambridge, and probably the E. K. who wrote the gloss to Spenser's *Shepherd's Calendar.* Efforts to prove that Spenser himself was the author of the gloss have been generally unsuccessful.

Kirkham, Henry, bookseller in London from 1570 to 1593 who dealt mainly in broadside ballads

Knell, [?Thomas], an actor who flourished in the 1580's

Knights of Malta, i.e. the Order of the Hospitalers of St. John of Jerusalem, an ancient quasi-monastic body that developed into a military organization during the Crusades. After the Knights' vain defense of Acre, which fell to the Moslems in 1291, they moved to Cyprus, then to Rhodes, and finally to Malta, which they controlled from the early sixteenth until it was seized by Napoleon in the late eighteenth century.

Kyd, Thomas (?1557–95), dramatist whose *Spanish Tragedy* (printed ?1592) was one of the most popular and influential plays of the period; he is also generally credited with *Solyman and Perseda* (printed 1599) and was perhaps the author of an early version of *Hamlet* that has not survived.

Kyrie eleison, "Lord, have mercy upon us" (a petition used in various religious offices)

La Lubber, ?a lost ballad

la royne ma file . . . , "the queen my daughter in this isle, for good reason, has renown"

Laberius, Decimus (ca. 105–43 B.C.), Roman *eques* who wrote farces, satires, and an epic on Caesar's Gallic wars of which only a few fragments survive

Lacedemon, Lacedaemonian, i.e. pertaining to ancient Sparta

Laconia, southeastern part of the Peloponnesus lying to the south of Arcadia; hence **Laconian**

Lacy, Alexander, London printer who was made free of the Stationers' Company in 1556, and from then until his retirement in 1571 dealt mainly in broadside ballads

Ladyes bowre, our, i.e. the famous shrine of the Virgin at Loretto in eastern Italy

Laelius, Caius (surnamed Sapiens, fl. ca. 140 B.C.), celebrated Roman orator and philosopher whom Cicero made the chief character of his *De amicitia*

Laestrygones, savage Sicilian tribe who destroyed eleven of Odysseus' twelve ships and devoured his companions (*Odyssey* X.82 ff.)

Lais, the name of two famous Greek courtezans: the elder (a native of Corinth) lived in the fifth century B.C., the younger (who was brought from Sicily to Corinth) in the fourth B.C.

Lambeth, district of London on the south bank of the Thames. Since 1197 Lambeth Palace has been the city residence of the archbishops of Canterbury.

Lamerock, King, i.e. Sir Lamorak de Galis, lover of King Lot's wife Morgause, the sister of King Arthur

Lammas, at latter, at a (Lammas) day that will never come. Lammas day (August 1) was originally celebrated as a harvest festival.

Lancaster, Duke of: *see* John of Gaunt

Lancaster, Earl of: *see* Thomas, Earl of Lancaster

Langaeus, ?a friend of Ascham

Langland, William (?1330–?1400), supposed author of *Piers Plowman* (q.v.)

Langley, Edmund (or Edmond) de, first Duke of York (1341–1402), fifth son of Edward III who, though a member of the council of regency for his nephew Richard II, supported the claims of Henry of Lancaster (afterwards Henry IV) and retired from active politics after the deposition of Richard

Laocoon, priest of Apollo at Troy whom the god destroyed (together with his two sons) for having warned the city against the Trojan horse

Lapithae (Lapithes), Thessalian people descended from Lapithes, a son of Apollo and brother of Centaurus. The Lapithae were ruled by Pirithous, at whose marriage with Hippodamia there occurred a fierce battle between the Lapithae and the Centaurs.

Las Casas, Bartholomew de: see Casas

Latimer, Hugh (?1485–1555), bishop of Worcester and prominent Protestant reformer and preacher who, with Bishop Ridley, died a victim of Mary's Catholic policy: see pp. 150, 176–78

Latins, translations into Latin

Latinus, king of Latium whose daughter Lavinia married Aeneas

Latmian shepherd, Endymion (q.v.)

Latmus, Latmos, mountain-range in Caria, the site of Endymion's cave

Latona(e), Roman name for the Greek goddess Leto, mother (by Jupiter) of Apollo and Diana

lauda, anima mea, Dominum, "praise the Lord, O my soul" (Vulgate Psalms cxlv.2)

Launay, surname of Pierre Boaistuau: see Belleforest

Laura, lady celebrated by Petrarch as his ideal love

Lavinia, daughter of Latinus (q.v.); hence **Lavine**, Italian

Lazarus: see Dives

Leander, lover of Hero (q.v.)

Lear: see Leir

Leda, a girl seduced by Zeus in the form of a swan and by him the mother of Helen, Castor, and Pollux; another daughter, by her husband Tyndareus, king of Sparta, was Clytemnestra.

Lederhead, town in Surrey near Epsom

Lee, ——, a friend of Giles Fletcher

Lee (Ley), Edward (?1482–1544), archbishop of York (1531) who was employed by Henry VIII on various embassies, including one to Spain

Lee, Sir Henry (1530–1610), nephew of Sir Thomas Wyatt who entered Henry VIII's service in 1545 and served the Tudors the rest of his life, rising at last (1590) to be Elizabeth's master of the ordnance. Foxe describes him as being present at the execution of Latimer and Ridley.

Legend: see *Golden Legend*

Legge, Thomas (1535–1607), master of Caius College, Cambridge (1573–1607), and author of a Latin tragedy on Richard III which was acted in 1579

Leicester, ancient British and Roman town, capital of Leicestershire, and a favorite seat of Richard III

Leicester, Earl of: see Dudley (Robert)

Leicester House, a famous mansion in the Strand, London. Originally the town-house of the bishop of Exeter, at the Reformation it passed into the hands of William Lord Paget; it was subsequently given by Elizabeth to Robert Dudley, Earl of Leicester, and then to Robert Devereux, Earl of Essex (from the latter taking the name Essex House at the end of the sixteenth century).

Leicestershire, English county in the north midlands

Leiden, Leyden, city in the province of South Holland on the Rhine, in the sixteenth century a center of the wool trade and after 1575 the site of a famous university

Leir, Llyr, Lear, worshiped as a sea-god by the ancient Britons, perhaps related to the Lir of Gaelic mythology. Geoffrey of Monmouth (II.11–15) makes him a descendant of Brut and a king of Britain, and thereafter the tale of him and his three daughters became very popular, appearing in the 1574 edition of *A Mirror for Magistrates*, Holinshed's *Chronicles*, Warner's *Albion's England*, Spenser's *Faerie Queene*, and a play called *The True Chronicle History of King Leir* (licensed 1594, printed 1605). In all pre-Shakespearean versions Leir dies peacefully after a reunion with his youngest daughter.

Leith, seaport and suburb of Edinburgh on the Firth of Forth

Leland, John (?1506–52), antiquarian who projected a huge history of England that was cut short by his madness and death (see p. 19)

Lemster, Leominster, a town in Herefordshire, England

Leo, "the Lion," zodiacal sign for July

leonem mortuum . . . , "puppies bite a dead lion"

Leonidas, Spartan king killed at Thermopylae in 480 B.C.

Lepidus, Marcus Aemilius, member of the second triumvirate with Octavian and Antony (43 B.C.); he was deposed in 36 and died in 13.

Lercegia, ?Mediterranean island

Lerna, marshy region south of Argos in Greece

Lesbian, pertaining to Lesbos (q.v.)

Lesbos, island in the Aegean Sea off Mysia, Asia Minor, in antiquity a famous center of literary culture

Letany: see Litany

Lethe(us), goddess of oblivion; also a river in Hades, the waters of which were thought to cause oblivion

Leuca(e), town in Ionia, Asia Minor

Leucippus (fl. 500 B.C.), early Greek philosophical materialist, founder of the so-called atomic school

levavi oculos . . . , "I have lifted up mine eyes unto the hills" (Vulgate Psalms cxx.1)

Lever (Leaver), Ralph (d. 1585), archdeacon of Northumberland, master of Sherburn Hospital, and author of *The Art of Reason* (1573), whose brother **Thomas** (1521–77) was a famous puritan preacher, canon of Durham, and master of Sherburn Hospital

Lewis of Canossa, Count: see Canossa

Lex Ecclesi(a)e, "church or canon law"

Ley, Edward, ?Edward Lee (q.v.)

Leyden: see Leiden

L'Hospital, Michel de (?1507–73), French statesman who became chancellor in 1560 and fell from power because of his liberal attitude toward the Protestants

Libany, Skelton's rendering of Libya

lib(er), "book"

libera me, "deliver me"

liberalissimo Signor Immerito, "most gentlemanly Signor Immerito"

libertino patre natus, "born of a freed-slave father"

libri primi finis, "the end of the first book"

Libyan (Liby, Lyban), pertaining to Libya, in antiquity a name loosely denoting Africa (or sometimes Africa exclusive of Egypt and Ethiopia)

Lician (Lycian) frog, unexplained allusion

Lidgate, John: see Lydgate

Limbo, supposed border-land of hell, home of those souls barred from heaven through no fault of their own (e.g. the souls of good men who died before the coming of Christ or the souls of unbaptized infants)

Lime Street, thoroughfare in London between Fenchurch Street and Houndsditch

Linacre, Thomas (ca. 1460–1524), physician and humanist, who returned to England (1492) from taking a medical degree at Padua to teach Greek, translated many of Galen's treatises into Latin, and composed a Latin grammar (*Rudimenta grammatices*) for the use of Princess Mary. He was one of the founders of the College of Physicians in London.

Lincen downs, unexplained allusion

Linche (Lynche), Richard (fl. 1596–1601), minor poet, supposed author of a volume of sonnets entitled *Diella* (1596)

Lincoln green, yellowish-green color

Lincoln's Inn, one of the Inns of Court (q.v.), named for the Earl of Lincoln who built his town-house on the site in the fourteenth century

Linus, common Greek exclamation of lamentation (*linos*) and distress, personified as a son of Apollo. In one legend he was brought up by shepherds and afterward torn to pieces by dogs; in another he was killed by Apollo for daring to challenge his musical skill.

Lion (Lyon), the chased, i.e. Leo, the zodiacal sign for July

Lipsius, Justus (1547–1606), Belgian scholar and philologist who published an important edition of Tacitus (1575) and wrote several influential treatises informed by Neo-Stoic moral philosophy

Litany (Letany), a form of liturgical prayer in which the petitions are spoken by the clergy and congregation alternately. The Latin Rite makes use of various litanies; the Book of Common Prayer has one, under the heading "The Litany and Suffrages."

literas nescivit, "he was ignorant of letters"

Littleton, Sir Thomas (1422–81), jurist and legal writer, author of *Tenures,* a famous work in law-French which, with Coke's commentaries, was long the authority on English real property law; hence **Littletonian,** law-student who knows only enough French to read the *Tenures*

Livia, conjugii nostri memor . . . , "Livia, remembering our marriage, live and farewell!"

Livie: see Livy

Livius Andronicus: *see* Andronicus

livor post fata quiescit, et bene a singulis audiant qui omnibus volunt bene, the first clause is apparently adapted from Ovid (*Amores* I.xv.39): *pascitur in vivis livor, post fata quiescit* ("envy feeds on the living; it ceases when they are dead"); the second clause is presumably Harvey's own: "and let those who are well disposed toward all be praised by everyone."

Livy (Livie), Titus Livius (59 B.C.–A.D. 17), greatest of Roman historians, author of a history of Rome in one hundred forty-two books, of which thirty-five are extant

Lizard, promontory in Cornwall, the southernmost point in England

Llyr: *see* Leir

Loath to Depart: see *Loth to Depart*

Loches, ancient town southeast of Tours, France. Its massive chateau was once a favorite seat of the counts of Anjou, the Plantagenets, and the French kings.

Locke, Michael: *see* Lok

Locrine, Logrin, according to Geoffrey of Monmouth, Brut's eldest son, who succeeded his father as king of Britain. Spenser gracefully retells his story (*The Faerie Queene,* II.x.13–20), and *The Lamentable History of Locrine* (1595), perhaps by George Peele, was included in the Third Folio (1664) of Shakespeare, although it has long since been rejected from the canon.

Lodge, Thomas (?1558–1625), versatile man of letters: see pp. 382, 599, 763, 844–45

Lodwick, i.e. Lodowick (or Lewis) Bryskett (*q.v.*)

Logicales, Parva logicales, the last section of Petrus Hispanus' *Summulae logicalia,* an influential thirteenth-century manual of logic

Lok (Locke), Michael (fl. 1615), famous traveler who served for many years in the Orient as governor of the Cathay Company and translated part of Peter Martyr's *History of the West Indies* (1613)

Lollards, English or Scottish followers of the teachings of John Wyclif (*q.v.*), in the fourteenth and fifteenth centuries the most notorious and savagely persecuted heretical sect in England

Longeous, Longi(n)us, according to legend a blind soldier who thrust his spear into Christ on the cross, regained his sight through the blood which spurted on his eyes, was promptly converted, and eventually suffered martyrdom after many travels and adventures. His story was often treated in medieval literary and pictorial art.

Longobards, Langobardi, Lombards, natives of Lombardy, a former kingdom of northern Italy with Milan as its capital

loquendo, male loqui discunt, "by speaking, they teach how to speak badly"

Lord Chancellor's tomb, Sir Christopher Hatton's monument in St. Paul's Cathedral

Lord of Lorn, a ballad (Child No. 271), "The Lord of Lorn and the False Steward," registered on October 6, 1580. *See also* Lorn

Lord of Misrule, person chosen to direct sports and revels at court

Lorn, lord of, head of a Scottish clan (who took the patronymic Macdonald) notorious for its resistance to the Scots monarchy. From the end of the fourteenth century its chiefs assumed the title "Lord of the Isles" (i.e. the Hebrides), John Macdonald (ca. 1386) being the first to bear that title

Lote, King, Lot, king of Orkney, father by his wife Morgause of Gawain, one of the most prominent knights of King Arthur's Round Table

Loth to Depart, common ballad-tune for a song sung on taking leave of friends

Louvain, formerly the capital city of the province of Brabant in the Low Countries

Love Labor's Won, a presumably lost or retitled play mentioned by Francis Meres (*q.v.*) as one of Shakespeare's early successes. It has been conjecturally identified with *All's Well That Ends Well* and *Troilus and Cressida.*

Lovelace, William, a friend of Barnabe Googe

Lubeck, Lübeck, Baltic port in northern Germany

Lucan(us), Marcus Annaeus (39–65), Roman poet. Taken to Rome from his native Corduba (i.e. Cordova, Spain), he won such acclaim that Nero jealously forbade him to recite in public. Lucan joined the conspiracy of Piso and then, promised pardon, ruthlessly betrayed all his accomplices, even his mother; but when he saw that his treachery would not save him from a traitor's death he committed suicide. Of his various poems there survives only the *Pharsalia,* an unfinished epic in ten books on the long struggle between Caesar and Pompey.

Lucian (ca. 120–ca. 200), Greek satirist and humorist whose dialogues ("Dialogues of the Gods," "Dialogues of the Dead," etc.) have gained him a lasting reputation for skepticism and impiety; hence **Lucianist, Lucianically**

Lucifer, "the Light-Bringer," the morning star, the planet Venus when it appears before sunrise (called Hesperus, the evening star, when it appears in the evening). Owing to a mistaken interpretation of Isaiah xiv.12 ("How art thou fallen from heaven, O Lucifer, son of the morning") the name has been applied in Christian myth to Satan, the rebel archangel who waged war on God and was hurled from heaven.

Lucilius, Caius (d. 103 B.C.), founder of Latin satire, whose *Saturae,* originally in thirty books, has survived only in fragments

Lucilla, heroine of Lyly's *Euphues: The Anatomy of Wit* (1578)

Lucrece, Lucrecia: *see* Lucretia

Lucrece (or *The Rape of Lucrece*), poem by Shakespeare published in 1594

Lucretia (Lucrece, Lucrecia), in Roman legend the wife of Tarquinius Collatinus. Her suicide, following her rape by Sextus Tarquinius, led to an insurrection headed by Lucius Brutus, the expulsion of Tarquin Superbus, and the founding of the Roman republic.

Lucretius, Titus Lucretius Carus (ca. 96–55 B.C.), author of *De rerum natura,* a didactic and philosophical poem in six books

Lucullus, Lucius Licinius (ca. 114–57 B.C.), Roman general and administrator who became proverbial for his luxurious and elegant tastes, and especially for the magnificence of his banquets; hence **Lucull(i)an.** He was a generous patron of scholars and writers

Lucy, St., virgin martyr of Alexandria (ca. 304). Her feast day is December 13.

Lud, according to Geoffrey of Monmouth, an ancient king of Britain who built the walls around Brut's capital. Perhaps his name survives in Ludgate, an ancient gate of London, part of which was eventually used as a debtors' prison.

Luna, goddess of the moon

Lupercalia, ancient Roman festival celebrated yearly in February. Originally a ritual purification with human sacrifices, it developed into a sportive event in which the celebrants ran around the Palatine walls striking everyone they met with thongs cut from the hides of slaughtered goats and dogs.

lupus est in fabula, "the wolf is in the story" (adapted from Terence, *Adelphi* 537), i.e. now the villain appears

Lusty Gallant, The, a broadside ballad to the tune of which were set pieces in both *A Gorgeous Gallery* and *A Handful of Pleasant Delights*

Luther, Martin (1483–1546), father of the German reformation, whose heretical influence in England was so strong in the 1520's that Henry VIII (vastly assisted by his bishops) wrote against him *Assertio septem sacramentorum* (1521), a treatise that won from the pope for him and his successors the title *Defensor fidei*

Luzones, the Philippine Islands

Lyai, Lyaeus, surname of Bacchus (*q.v.*)

Lyban: see Libyan

Lycaon, impious king of Arcadia whom Zeus, to punish for his sins, turned into a wolf. In other versions of the myth he is destroyed by lightning.

Lycophron (fl. 260 B.C.), poet of Alexandria who wrote a treatise on comedy, now lost. His *Cassandra,* a long iambic monologue full of erudition, earned for him the epithet "obscure." Ovid (*Ibis* 553) tells that he was killed by an arrow.

Lycoris, Cytheris, a famous courtezan, mistress of Antony and later of the poet Gallus (*q.v.*)

Lycurgus, Spartan lawgiver (probably of the ninth century B.C.) traditionally credited with initiating the rigors and discipline of Spartan life and laws

Lydgate (Lidgate), John (?1370–?1451), in spite of his present low reputation, one of the English poets most admired in the sixteenth century. Ordained a priest in 1397, he enjoyed the patronage and commissions of the corporation of London (for celebrating various civic functions), the Prince of Wales (for *The Troy Book,* which he finally completed in 1420), and Humphrey, Duke of Gloucester. His last years were passed in the monastery of Bury St. Edmunds. Among his many works some of the more important are *The Story of Thebes* (written ca. 1420), *The Fall of Princes* (*q.v.*), and *The Pilgrimage of Man* (translated from the French of Guillaume de Deguilleville).

Lydia, country on the western coast of Asia Minor bordering on the Aegean

Lydian (harmony), a mode of Greek music known for its soft and enervating quality

Lyly, John (?1554–1606), dramatist and novelist: see p. 710

Lynceus, one of the Argonauts famed for his keen vision

Lynn (Regis) or **King's Lynn**, seaport in Norfolk, England

Lyon: see Lion

Lyons, ancient French city at the confluence of the Rhone and Saône rivers

Lysander (d. 395 B.C.), Spartan general who seized Athens and destroyed its walls in 404

Lysias (d. ca. 380 B.C.), powerful and influential Athenian orator whose thirty-four extant orations reveal a new colloquial vigor and simplicity in Attic prose. A professional speech-maker, he composed many of his orations for clients.

Lysip(pus) (ca. 372–316 B.C.), Greek sculptor famous for his innovations in style and for his patronage from Alexander the Great

Macedo(n), a name for Alexander III of Macedon, or Alexander the Great (*q.v.*)

Macedon(y), Macedonia, an ancient country in the Balkan Peninsula

Machiavel(li), Niccolo (1469–1527), Italian diplomat and politician who, after his career was blocked by the Medici on their restoration in 1513, devoted the rest of his life to writing. In addition to *Mandragola* and other comedies, he wrote *Il principe* (notorious in the Renaissance for its cynical views on political morality), *Istorie fiorentine, Arte della guerra,* and a set of *Discorsi* on Livy.

Macrobius, Ambrosius Theodosius (fl. early fifth century), Roman grammarian, author of a famous commentary on the *Somnium Scipionis* from the sixth book of Cicero's *De republica*

Madame le Royne, "Madame the Queen"

Madonna Coelia, E. K.'s reference (in the gloss to "January" of *The Shepherd's Calendar*) is to *Lettre amorose de madonna Celia gentildonna Romana. Scritte al suo amante* (1562).

Maecenas (Mecaenas, Moecenas), Caius Cilnius (d. 8 B.C.), Roman statesman and patron of writers, among them Virgil and Horace

Magdalen College, college in Oxford founded by Bishop Waynflete in 1457

Magdalen(e): see Mary Magdalen(e)

Magellan, Straight of, the Strait of Magellan, a sea-passage separating the South American mainland from Tierra del Fuego, and connecting the Atlantic and Pacific oceans

Magnificat, in ecclesiastical services the song of the Virgin Mary (Luke i.46–55), usually sung at vespers or evensong

magnum loqui, nitique cothurno, adapted from Horace, *Ars poetica* 280: *et docuit magnumque loqui nitique cothurno,* "and taught a lofty speech as well as a stately gait on the buskin"

Maia, mother of Hermes by Zeus

Maide, the righteous, Astraea (*q.v.*)

Maiden Tower, Edinburgh Castle

Maine, former government in northern France

Malgo, according to Geoffrey of Monmouth (*q.v.*), an early king of England who recovered certain foreign holdings (Ireland, Denmark, Norway, etc.) which had been won by King Arthur and subsequently lost

malgrado, "in spite of"

Malmesbury, William of: see William of Malmesbury

Malta, chief of the Maltese Islands, a group in the central Mediterranean. See Knights of Malta

Maltrevers, Lord Henry: see Fitzalan

Malucas, Malucos: see Molucca(e)s

Mandeville, Sir John, allegedly the author of a famous fourteenth-century book of travels in Turkey, Armenia, Egypt, Ethiopia, and similarly remote places. Actually the work was compiled (as a guide to pilgrims to the Holy Land) from the writings of William of Boldensele and Friar Odoric of Pordenone, and the English version was put together by someone in the early fifteenth century.

Manilius, sometimes called Manlius or Mallius, a Roman poet, perhaps of the Augustan age, whose *Astronomica* is an astrological poem in five books

Mantua, man of, i.e. Virgil (*q.v.*)

Mantuan(us) or **Mantuano**, i.e. Baptista Spagnuoli (1448–1516), pastoral poet (see p. 81)

Manzolli, Pietro Angelo (b. ca. 1490), Italian astrologer whose *Zodiacus vitae* (1543) was widely popular throughout Europe, even though it was banned by the Inquisition for its alleged rationalistic tendencies. Barnabe Googe's English translation, *The Zodiac of Life,* appeared between 1560 and 1565.

Marathon, plain northeast of Athens where in 490 B.C. the Athenians won a decisive victory against the invading Persians

March: see Mortimer (Roger de)

Marchies, the Marches (i.e. borders) of Wales and England

Marcury: see Mercury

Marcus Antonius: see Antonius

Marcus Aurelius Antoninus: see Aurelius

Marcus, Consul, i.e. Marcus Tullius Cicero (*q.v.*)

Mardoche, i.e. Mordecai: see Haman

Margaret Tudor (1489–1541), daughter of Henry VII, wife of James IV of Scotland, and mother of James V. The last was the father of Mary Queen of Scots, whose son became James I of England and established the Stuart dynasty.

Marie, Queen: see Mary I

Maritius of Hesse, Maurice, landgrave of Hesse-Cassel (1592–1627), son of William IV, founder of the line

Marius, Caius (ca. 155–86 B.C.), famed general and consul, whose rivalry with Sulla led to civil war in 88; though driven from Rome, he returned with Cinna and captured the city in 87, a year before his death.

Mark, King, in medieval romance a king of Cornwall, husband of Iseult (Ysoude) and uncle of Tristram (*q.v.*)

Marlorat, Augustine (1506–63), prominent German reformer and theologian

Marlowe, Christopher (1564–93), poet and dramatist: see pp. 388, 557–58

Maro, family name of Virgil (*q.v.*)

Marocco, Morocco, a country in northwestern Africa

Marot, Clément (1497–1544), French Protestant poet whose adaptations of Italian verse-forms (and especially the sonnet) exerted considerable influence on sixteenth-century English poetry

Marprelate, Martin, pseudonym of a group of Elizabethan puritan controversialists whose pamphlets attacking the Anglican establishment and its bishops were a great vexation to the authorities at the end of the 1580's

Mars, god of war and protector of agriculture, corresponding to the Greek Ares

Marshalsea, ancient prison in Southwark, a London district on the south bank of the Thames

Marston, John (?1575–1634), poet, dramatist, and divine: see pp. 458–59

Martial(is), Marcus Valerius (43–ca. 104), Latin satirist who was born and died in Spain but spent most of his adult life in Rome, where he enjoyed the patronage of Titus and Domitian as well as great popularity with the reading public. His extant works consist of fourteen books of *Epigrammata,* poems rich in comment on the social life and personages of the first century of the Empire.

Martialists, devotees of Mars, the god of war

Martin, Martin Luther (*q.v.*)

Martin Marprelate: *see* Marprelate

Martius: *see* Coriolanus

Martyr, Peter (1455–1526), Italian courtier and historian who entered the service of Queen Isabella of Spain, held high diplomatic posts, and wrote a history of early American exploration in *De orbe novo: see* Spanish *Decades*

Marullus, Caius Epidius: *see* Flavius

Mary I (Queen Marie, 1516–58), queen of England (1553–58), only surviving child of Henry VIII and Catherine of Aragon, famed for her attempt to restore Catholicism during her reign. She married Philip of Spain (later Philip II) in 1554 but died without issue and was succeeded by her half-sister Elizabeth.

Mary Magdalen(e), a woman mentioned in the gospels as a demoniac who had been exorcised of seven devils by Jesus, and as a witness of the crucifixion, the empty tomb, and the risen Jesus. She is commonly confused with the "sinner" whose regeneration Luke describes (vii.37–50).

Mason, Sir John (1503–66), a favorite statesman of Henry VIII who was knighted (1547) by Edward VI and continued in high favor with Mary. Elizabeth employed him as a counselor in foreign policy.

Massic (wine), famous wine produced on Massicus Mons in the Roman Campagna. Falernian wine came from the eastern slope of this mountain.

Mauretania, Mauritania, ancient name for Barbary, i.e. North Africa

Mausolean, like the tomb of Mausolus, king of Caria, one of the wonders of the ancient world, erected at Halicarnassus in Asia Minor around 350 B.C.

Maximilian (1459–1519), emperor of the Holy Roman Empire (1493–1519) who in 1513 assisted Henry VIII against the French at the so-called Battle of the Spurs

Maximius (i.e. Maximus) Tyrius (fl. ca. 160), Tyrian rhetorician and Platonist—allegedly a tutor of Marcus Aurelius—from whose work have survived some forty treatises on theological and ethical subjects

me judice, "in my judgment"

Meander, (1) Menander (*q.v.*); (2) the Maeander, a river in western Asia Minor famed for its windings, the modern Mendere

Meaux, French town on the Marne about twenty-five miles northeast of Paris

Mecaenas: *see* Maecenas

Mecca, Arabian city, birthplace of Mohammed and spiritual center of Islam

Medcalfe, Nicholas: *see* Metcalfe

Medices, the Medici, a Florentine family, grown rich in banking, that ruled Florence and Tuscany in the late fifteenth and early sixteenth centuries and gained fame for their patronage of literature and art

Medina, Pedro de, cosmographer of Seville whose works include *L'arte del navegar* (1545) and *Regimento de navegación* (1563)

mediocribus esse poetis . . . , "neither gods nor men nor booksellers have admitted mediocrity in poets" (Horace, *Ars poetica* 372–73)

Medoro, in Ariosto's *Orlando Furioso,* a young Moor with whom Angelica returns to her native Cathay after her escape from Rogero

Medusa, one of the three Gorgons (*q.v.*), slain by Perseus (*q.v.*); her head, which turned to stone anyone who looked at it, was afterward borne on the shield of Athena.

Medway, river which joins the Thames at Sheerness to form a great estuary

Meg(a)era, one of the Furies (*q.v.*)

Mehune, John de: *see* Jean de Meun

Melanchates, hound belonging to Actaeon (*q.v.*)

Melanc(h)thon, Philipp (1497–1560), collaborator of Luther and a leader of the German reformation whose most important theological work is *Loci communes* (1521); a man of wide learning and humanistic interests, he also published translations of Euripides, Lucian, Pindar, and Plutarch.

Melchizedek, in ancient Hebrew history, a king of Salem and a priest who hospitably entertained Abraham and received tithes from him; hence, the model of a worthy cleric

Melibaeus (Meliboeus), common name for a shepherd in pastoral poetry

melior natura, "higher nature"

melius Chrysippo et Crantore, "better than Chrysippus and Crantor" (Horace, *Epistles* I.ii.4). Horace is saying that Homer tells us more about the Trojan War than eminent philosophical historians, that is, that poetry is superior to history.

Melpomene, muse of tragedy

Melun, French town on the Seine southeast of Paris

Memnon, solar hero, thought of as a youth of great beauty, who, as a warrior in the Trojan War, was slain by Achilles. The Greeks gave his name to a colossus at Thebes, in Egypt, which, when struck by the rays of the rising sun, gave forth a resounding chord of music.

memorandum, "something to be remembered"

Memory, Queen, Mnemosyne, mother of the muses

Memphis, ancient capital of Egypt, on the Nile south of Cairo

Menalus, mountain in Arcadia, Phoebe's home

Menander (Meander, 342–ca. 291 B.C.), Athenian comic playwright, chief writer of the so-called New Comedy, whose work survives only in fragments

Menelaus, in Homeric legend, son of Atreus, brother of Agamemnon, and husband of Helen, the famous beauty whose abduction by Paris precipitated the Trojan War

Menenius Agrippa, early Roman statesman who, as consul in 503 B.C., conquered the Sabines. He was famed as a peacemaker, and his fable of the belly and its members (which Shakespeare used in *Coriolanus*) is said to have resolved the differences between the patricians and plebeians in 493.

mens, "mind"

mens cuiusque, is est quisque, "the soul of each man is himself" (Cicero, *De republica* VI.xxiv.26)

Mercator, Gerardus, Gerhard Kremer (1512–94), Flemish geographer who received from Charles V a commission to manufacture a terrestrial and a celestial globe. He invented the Mercator system projection. His chief works are *Tabulae geographicae* (1578–84) and *Atlas* (1595). His son **Rumold (or Romoldus)** assisted his father in preparing the *Orbis terrarum compendiosa descriptio* (1587) and also completed and published a series of maps which the elder Mercator had begun.

Mercurius Trismegistus, i.e. Hermes Trismegistus (*q.v.*)

Mercury (Marcury), in Roman mythology the equivalent of the Greek Hermes, son of Jupiter and Maia, and his father's messenger

Meres, Francis (1565–1647), schoolmaster and divine: see pp. 650–51

Merke, Thomas (d. 1409), vigorous ecclesiastical politician and bishop of Carlisle who accompanied Richard II to Ireland and thereafter defended his interests against those of Henry Bolingbroke, later Henry IV. For his loyalty to Richard he was eventually deprived of his bishopric.

Merlin, in Arthurian romance a venerable magician. According to Geoffrey of Monmouth he brought the great stones of Stonehenge from Ireland to Salisbury Plain.

Meroe, ancient capital of Ethiopia

Messeides, fountain in Thessaly

Messenia, in antiquity a country in Peloponnesus adjacent to Laconia (*q.v.*)

Metamorphosi(o)s, the *Metamorphoses,* Ovid's longest and most elaborate poem, consisting of fifteen books treating legends and fables about deific and human transformations from the Creation to the stellification of Julius Caesar. Arthur Golding's influential English translation was completed in 1576 (see p. 539).

Metcalfe (Medcalfe), Nicholas (?1475–1539), archdeacon of Rochester (1515) and master of St. John's College, Cambridge (1516–37)

Metellian, pertaining to a famous plebeian family of ancient Rome

Metellus Cimber: *see* Cimber

Metrodorus (d. 277 B.C.), most brilliant of Epicurus' disciples who, if we may believe Cicero (for Metrodorus' own works are lost), debased his master's doctrines into the grossest sensualism

Meun, Jean de: *see* Jean de Meun

Mich(a)el, Mount, St. Michael's Mount, a lofty rock rising out of the sea near Penzance in Cornwall, once the seat of a religious foundation

Mich(a)elmas, feast of the archangel Michael, celebrated on September 29

Midas, famous king of Phrygia who, given his wish by Dionysus, turned everything he touched into gold. When he refused to award the prize to Apollo in a musical contest with Pan, his ears were turned into those of an ass. **Midasses,** pun on *Midas* and *asses*

Middle Temple, part of the Temple, a district between Fleet Street and the Thames, which in the Middle Ages was the London lodge of the Knights Templars. When the order was suppressed by Edward II, the Temple passed from one nobleman to another until it came into the possession of the Knights Hospitalers of St. John of Jerusalem, who in 1346 leased part of it to students of the common law. The Middle Temple and the Inner Temple have ever since been occupied by barristers. *See* Inns of Court

Middleborough, Middleburgh, Middelburg, capital of the province of Zealand in the Low Countries

Middlesex, county in southeast England

Mildmay, Sir Walter (?1520–89), chancellor of the exchequer and founder of Emmanuel College, Cambridge, a center of puritanism

Mileiades, Miltiades (*q.v.*)

Milo (fl. 510 B.C.), famous athlete who was six times victor in wrestling at both the Olympic and the Pythian games. He could carry a heifer because he had carried it every day as it grew from a calf.

Miltiades (Mileiades, d. ca. 489 B.C.), Athenian general who defeated the Persians at Marathon in 490 B.C.

Milton, John (?1563–1647), father of the poet, a prosperous scrivener of Cheapside who, as a gifted musical amateur, contributed both music and lyrics to various miscellanies

Mincius, the Mincio, a river in northern Italy that joins the Po near Mantua

Minerva (Minerve), one of the most important deities in the Roman pantheon. A virgin daughter of Jupiter, she, like her Greek equivalent Athena or Pallas, was the goddess of wisdom, of war, and of the liberal arts.

minime vero, si ais nego, "no, not at all; if you say it, I deny it"

Minors, i.e. Minorites: *see* Grey Friars

Minos of Athens (an error for Crete), legendary king of Crete, owner of the Minotaur or bull-man, for which he engaged Daedalus (*q.v.*) to construct a labyrinth

mirres vous y, "behold yourself therein"

Mirror of Magistrates, i.e. *A Mirror for Magistrates*: see p. 269

miseremini mei, "take pity on me"

miserrima fortuna quae caret inimico, "it is a most wretched fortune which has no enemy"

Mithridates (Mithradates) the Great (ca. 132–63 B.C.), king of Pontus who for much of his long reign (120–63) was one of the most aggressive and successful opponents of Roman power in the Near East. Checked by Sulla in 84, he rebelled again in 83 and 74; his power was finally broken by Pompey in 66.

Mnemosyne, goddess of memory, and mother (by Zeus) of the muses

Moab, the Moabites, a warlike Semitic tribe inhabiting the region around the southeastern end of the Dead Sea, for centuries the enemies of the Israelites

Moecenas: *see* Maecenas

Mole, Spenser's name for the Ballyhoura Hills and the Galtee Mountains north of Kilcolman, Ireland

Mollineux, Emery, globe-maker and friend of Richard Hakluyt

Mollineux, Sir Richard, friend of Giles Fletcher

Molucca(e)s (Malucas, Malucos), the Spice Islands, a group in the Malay Archipelago east of Celebes

Momus, god of mockery and censure; a carping critic

Monmouth, county (and city) formerly in Wales but after 1535 a part of England

Monox, Will, unidentified character mentioned by Nashe

Montaigne (Mountaigny), Michel Eyquem de (1533–92), French essayist (see p. 568); also the name of Montaigne's ancestral home near Bordeaux

monte potiri, "to get up the hill"

Montpellier, capital of the modern department of Hérault in southern France; its famous college of medicine dates from the twelfth century.

Mordack (Mordake, Murdoch), Lord, Earl of Fife, Scottish nobleman about whom Grafton, Holinshed, and Shakespeare (*1 Henry IV,* I.i.71) were all confused. The governor, or regent, of Scotland was Robert Stewart, first Duke of Albany (?1340–1420), and it was his eldest son who was Lord Mordack, Earl of Fife.

More, Alice, Sir Thomas More's second wife, whom he married (1511) less than a month after the death of Jane, his first wife. Alice was the widow of John Middleton, a prominent and wealthy merchant who died in 1509.

More, Sir John (?1453–1530), father of Sir Thomas More and judge of the king's bench in 1523

More, Sir Thomas (1478–1535), humanist, lord chancellor, Catholic controversialist, and martyr: see pp. 42, 86, 141–42

Morello, Sigismondo Morello da Ortona, about whom little is known other than that he was highly regarded as a musician in the court of Urbino. In Castiglione's *Courtier* he appears as the staid and elderly butt of many pranks.

Morley, Thomas (1557–?1604), a pupil of Byrd, organist of St. Paul's (1591), and gentleman of the Chapel Royal, who in 1598 was granted a monopoly for printing books of music and selling ruled paper. His own publications include madrigals and instrumental music, as well as *A Plain and Easy Introduction to Practical Music* (1597), the first good musical treatise published in England and a manual that retained its popularity for two centuries.

Morpheus, son of Sleep and god of dreams

mors omnibus communis, "death is common to all"

Morte (d')Arthur, Sir Thomas Malory's prose redaction of the Arthurian story, a work of twenty-one books covering both the fall of the Round Table and Lancelot's unsuccessful quest of the Holy Grail. It was published by Caxton in 1485.

Mortimer, Edmund de, fifth Earl of March and third Earl of Ulster (1391–1425), powerful baron who succeeded his father Roger (1374–98) as heir-presumptive to Richard II. Though used as a pawn by the Percys against Henry IV, he survived their disastrous rebellion and lived to become a supporter of Henry V.

Mortimer, Roger de, eighth Baron of Wigmore and first Earl of March (?1287–1330), head of one of the great baronial families of Plantagenet England. Early contesting the abuses of Edward II's reign, he and his father were both imprisoned in the Tower of London for their opposition to the Despensers (*q.v.*), but Roger escaped in 1324 to become the ally and lover of Edward's estranged queen Isabella. After the king's murder at Berkeley Castle Roger virtually ruled England in the early years of Edward III's reign through his influence over the queen-mother, but at last, checked by Henry IV and William de Montacute, he was condemned by Parliament for the murder of Edward II and for usurping royal power, and so died a felon's death at Tyburn.

Morton, John Cardinal (?1420–1500), canon lawyer who through his shrewd support of the House of Lancaster rose rapidly in the church. After the battle of Tewkesbury he continued to prosper (becoming bishop of Ely in 1479), and, although he was imprisoned during Richard III's reign of terror, he was elevated to the see of Canterbury by Henry VII in 1486, became lord chancellor a year later, and attained the cardinalate in 1493.

Morton may have been responsible for the Latin version of More's *History of King Richard the Third* (see p. 42), and it was on his recommendation that More was admitted to Canterbury Hall, Oxford, in 1492. Though an unscrupulous and self-seeking politician, he is depicted most sympathetically in More's *Utopia*.

Moschus (fl. 200 B.C.), Greek bucolic poet of Syracuse

Moscovy: *see* Muscovy

Moses, earliest lawgiver of the Israelites and founder of their nation; **five books of Moses,** the Pentateuch, the authorship of which is ascribed to Moses by Jewish tradition, if not by modern scholarship

Mount: *see* Mich(a)el (Mount)

Mountaigny: *see* Montaigne

Mountjoy, Lord: *see* Blount (Charles)

Mowbray, Thomas, twelfth Baron Mowbray and first Duke of Norfolk (?1366–99), a nobleman who sided with Gloucester and John of Gaunt (*qq.v.*) against Richard II but later became reconciled with the king and accompanied him to Ireland. Probably responsible for Gloucester's death in Calais, he was accused of treason by Henry Bolingbroke, was banished, and died in Venice.

Mucianus, Licinius, Roman statesman and orator, consul in 52, 70, and 75

Mulcaster, Richard (?1530–1611), first headmaster of Merchant Taylors' School (1561–86) and highmaster of St. Paul's School (1596–1608): see pp. 840–41

Mulla(e), Irish river which flowed by Kilcolman, Spenser's home

multi famam pauci . . . , "many respect fame, but only a few, conscience" (adapted from Pliny, *Epistles* III.20)

multos puto ad sapientiam . . . , "I think many could have attained wisdom if they had not thought that they had attained it"

multum ex illa . . . , "much of it remains for those who shall come hereafter"

Mumpsimus, a proverbial name for an old person (or, more specifically, for an old townsman or merchant)

Munda, a town in southern Spain where Caesar defeated the sons of Pompey in 45 B.C.

Munday, Anthony (1553–1633), poet and playwright, author of *The English Roman Life* (1582), many plays (most of which are lost), translations of popular romances (e.g. *Palladino of England*, 1588, and *Amadis de Gaule*, 1589–95), ballads, and city pageants

Mundy, John (d. 1630), English musician, for some forty years organist of St. George's Chapel, Windsor, and composer of many vocal and instrumental pieces

Murdoch: *see* Mordack

Muretus, Marc Antoine Muret (1526–85), French humanist who taught at Poitiers, Bordeaux, Paris, and elsewhere, a prolific letter-writer and editor of classical texts

Musa, mihi causas . . . , "O muse, recall to me the causes, what divinity was injured" (Virgil, *Aeneid* I.8)

Musaeus, (1) semi-mythological poet of Greece (the son of Orpheus) whose works were thought to be about the mysteries of Demeter at Eleusis; (2) Greek grammarian, of the fifth or sixth century, who wrote a celebrated poem on Hero and Leander (see p. 388)

Muscovite, Russian

Muscovy (Moscovy), Russia

Museus, i.e. Samuel Daniel (*q.v.*)

Mutin toils, a reference to the siege and battle of Mutina (a town in Gallia Cispadana) in which Decimus Brutus withstood Antony from December, 44, to April, 43 B.C.

Myron (ca. 500–440 B.C.), Greek sculptor, especially of athletes, whose most famous work is the Discobolus

Myrrha, mother of Adonis by an incestuous relationship with her father

Naiad(e)s, a class of water nymphs: *see* Nymphae

Nameurs, Nemours, a French town near Fontainebleau

Nanphant (Nanfan), Sir Richard (d. 1507), deputy of Calais and trusted diplomat in the service of Henry VII

Napolitans, Neapolitans

Narbonne, ancient district (the Latin Narbonensis in southern Gaul) around the city of Narbonne in Languedoc, united with the French crown in 1507–8

Narciss(us), beautiful son of Cephissus and the nymph Liriope who so much admired his own beauty that he rejected the love of Echo; thereafter he pined away for his own reflection in the water of a pool and was metamorphosed into a flower.

narratio, "narration," in rhetoric the part of an oration in which the facts of a situation are stated

Nashe, Thomas (1567–1601), pamphleteer and novelist: see pp. 788, 859–60, 874

Naso, i.e. Ovid (*q.v.*)

Nathan, Hebrew prophet in the time of David, Solomon's teacher (see II Samuel vii)

natura naturans, "Nature creating Nature"

natura naturata, "created Nature"

natura nihil fecit frustra, "Nature does nothing in vain"

naturam expellas furca . . . , "you may repel Nature with a pitchfork, but she still returns" (Horace, *Epistles* I.x.24)

ne evilescent, "they do not become vulgar"

ne Hercules quidem contra duos, "even Hercules is powerless against two opponents"

ne quando male cantando, "lest ever by singing badly"

ne quid nimis, "nothing too much"

ne sutor ultra crepidam, "let the cobbler not go above the sole," i.e. shoemaker, stick to your last

Nebo, in Biblical geography (Deuteronomy xxxii.49) a mountain in the land of Moab, site of Moses' death. Latimer speaks of it as a Moabite city notorious for its wickedness.

negotium cum labore . . . , "time filled with work but not with danger"

Nehemias, the Book of Nehemiah

nemo ante obitum felix, "no one may be accounted happy before his death" (perhaps adapted from Ovid, *Metamorphoses* III.136–37)

Nennius (fl. 746), traditional author of *Historia Britonum*, which mentions King Arthur as a *dux bellorum* leading the Britons against their Saxon oppressors. The *Historia* (which has survived in several versions) was one of the sources fancifully expanded by Geoffrey of Monmouth.

Neoptolemus (d. ca. 321 B.C.), Macedonian general, one of the trusted lieutenants of Alexander the Great

Nepos, Cornelius, Roman historian of the first century B.C., friend of Cicero, Atticus, and Catullus, author of many works now lost, including a universal history, a life of Cicero, and various epistles. The extant *Vitae excellentium imperatorum*, which contains biographies of famous military leaders, probably preserves some of his writing, although it is now regarded as largely the work of one Aemilius Probus, a fourth-century historian.

Neptune (Neptunus), god of the sea, corresponding to the Greek Poseidon

Nereis, daughter of Nereus and Doris; the plural form, **Nereides,** is used for all fifty daughters of the couple, and hence for a class of Nymphae (*q.v.*).

Nero Claudius Caesar Drusus Germanicus (37–68), infamous Roman emperor, last of the Julio-Claudian dynasty. He succeeded his stepfather Claudius (who had adopted him) when Claudius was poisoned by Agrippina, his wife and Nero's mother, in 54. Nero had Claudius' son Britannicus poisoned in 55 and Agrippina herself assassinated in 59; thereafter his reign was one of terror. He divorced and then murdered Octavia to marry Poppaea, who was eventually killed by a kick from her husband. He undertook a wholesale persecution of the Christians in order to divert attention from the burning of Rome (64), for which some had held him responsible; the following year he demanded the suicide of his former tutor Seneca and the poet Lucan (*qq.v.*). Three years later, when Galba raised a successful insurrection against his tyrannies, he himself committed suicide.

nescio quid magis nascitur Iliade, "something greater than the *Iliad* (i.e. the *Aeneid*) springs to birth" (Propertius, *Elegies* II.xxxiv.66). Meres apparently misinterpreted, "I know not what greater poem than the *Iliad* has come to birth."

Nessus, Centaur killed by Hercules when he tried to abduct Hercules' wife Dejanira. When Hercules later fell in love with Iole,

Dejanira gave him a shirt steeped in Nessus' blood (which she had been told would restore his love), and his skin was consumed by the poison of his own arrow. Dejanira thereupon killed herself, and Hercules was carried off to Olympus from a pyre which he himself had built and ignited.

Nestor, in Homeric legend, king of Pylus, the oldest of the Grecian leaders in the Trojan War

Neville, Ralph, first Earl of Westmorland (1364–1425), stalwart Lancastrian who opposed Richard II, assisted at Henry IV's coronation, powerfully concerned himself with Scottish affairs after the battle of Shrewsbury (1403), and lived to act as an executor of Henry V's will

New Inn, inn of the Middle Temple (*q.v.*), so called because it was formed by students previously attached to St. George's Inn. The buildings have long since disappeared.

Newbury, town in Berkshire, for centuries a center of the textile industry

Newgate, famous old London prison

Newhaven (New Haven), seaport in Sussex on the English Channel at the mouth of the Ouse

Newman, Thomas (fl. 1578–93), a somewhat disreputable London printer whose most notable venture was an unauthorized edition of Sidney's *Astrophel and Stella* (in two impressions) in 1591 (see pp. 323, 402)

Nicalao Malevolo, Nashe's euphemism for the Devil

Nicanor, son of Parmenion, a trusted officer in the service of Philip and Alexander of Macedon

Nicasius, ?a friend of Ascham

Nicholaus de Linna, Nicholas of Lynne (fl. 1386), Carmelite monk and lecturer at Oxford who is conjectured to have made an arctic voyage

Nicocles, king of Salamis in Cyprus who succeeded his father Evagoras in 374 B.C. For Isocrates' panegyric on his father's virtues he paid the magnificent fee of twenty talents.

Nicomachus Phrygius, Greek dramatist, according to Ravisius Textor the author of eleven tragedies

nihil pro nihilo, "nothing for nothing"

nil aliud quam bene ausus vana contemnere, "it was nothing else than that he dared well to despise vain fears" (Livy IX.7)

nil habet infelix . . ., "unhappy poverty has in it nothing worse than the fact that it makes men ridiculous" (Juvenal, *Satires* III.152–53)

nil nisi flere libet, "I care for nothing but weeping" (Ovid, *Tristia* III.ii.19)

nil nisi necessarium, "nothing except what is necessary"

nil sacri es, "you are no god"

nil tam metuens . . ., "fearing nothing so much as to seem to be in doubt about something"

Nilus, the River Nile

nimia familiaritas contemptus parit, "too much familiarity breeds contempt"

nimis curiosus in aliena republica, "excessively curious about foreign parts," i.e. too much concerned with matters that are none of my affair

Ninus, mythical Assyrian king and husband of Semiramis, who built for him a famous tomb in Babylon

Niobe, daughter of Tantalus and wife of Amphion, king of Thebes, whose many children were killed by Apollo and Artemis to punish her for boasting of them, whereupon grief-stricken Niobe was metamorphosed into a stone by Zeus

Nisus, follower of Aeneas on his voyage to Italy who died with his friend Euryalus in a night attack on the Rutulian camp. The two warriors have become symbols of unselfish friendship.

Nizolian paper-books, i.e. the collection of Ciceronian phrases published in 1535 by Marius Nizolius (?1498–1576), Italian humanist and lexicographer

nodum in scirpo quaerere, "to seek a knot in a bulrush," i.e. to find a difficulty where none exists (adapted from Terence, *Andria* 941)

Noe, Noah

Nolano, i.e. Giordano Bruno (*q.v.*), from his birthplace Nola, an Italian town near Naples

nolite fieri . . . constringere, "be yet not as the horse, or as the mule, which have no understanding, whose mouth must be held in with bit and bridle" (adapted from Vulgate Psalms xxxi.9)

nolo altum sapere, "I do not wish to know higher things" (adapted from Vulgate Romans xi.20)

Nombre de Dios, Spanish port on the Caribbean coast of the Isthmus of Panama

nomen, "name"

non convalescit planta . . ., "no plant grows strong which is too often moved"

non deos vulgi . . ., "it is not profane to denounce the gods of the vulgar, but it is profane to apply the opinions of the vulgar to the gods"

non domini nostri . . ., "they were not our commanders but our guides"

non equidem invideo . . ., "truly, I do not envy you, but rather marvel [at your good fortune]" (Virgil, *Eclogues* I.11)

non est inventus, "he has not been found"

non est jam dicere . . ., "it cannot now be said, 'Like priest, like people,' for the people are not like the priests"

non nobis, Domine . . ., "not to us, O Lord, not to us, but to thy name give the glory" (Vulgate Psalms cxiii.1)

non placet, "it is not pleasing"

non sapit, qui sibi non sapit, "he knows nothing who does not know himself"

Norfolk, Duke of: *see* Howard (Thomas, Earl of Surrey and third Duke of Norfolk of the Howard house)

Norman subtleties, i.e. legal jargon (derived from Norman French)

Norris, Henry (d. 1536), gentleman of the king's chamber to Henry VIII and a favorite of Anne Boleyn; though probably innocent, he was arrested on a charge of intimacy with Anne, convicted of high treason, and executed.

Norris, Sir John (?1547–97), military commander who had a distinguished career in Ireland and the Low Countries, and served with Drake on the Spanish expedition of 1589

North, Sir Thomas (?1535–?1601), translator of Plutarch and other moral philosophers: see pp. 545–46

North Sea, in the sixteenth century a common name for the Caribbean Sea, in contradistinction to the South Sea (i.e. the Pacific Ocean). Sometimes the term was applied to the whole Atlantic.

Northamptonshire, county in the south midlands of England

Northern Jig, popular ballad-tune called "Dainty, Come Thou to Me"

Norton, Thomas ("of Bristow"), mid-fifteenth-century member of Parliament and diplomatic agent for Edward IV who studied alchemy and wrote chemical treatises in verse (e.g. *The Ordinal of Alchemy*)

Norwich, capital city of Norfolk, England, famous for its cathedral

nostri Cato maxime saecli, "O greatest Cato of our age"

Nottingham, capital of Nottinghamshire, in north central England

Nova Hispania, New Spain, loosely used for all South and Central America

Nova Zembla, uninhabited double island in the Arctic Ocean

novus, nova, novum, i.e. the declension of the Latin adjective "new"

nox est perpetua . . ., "[we] must sleep one never-ending night" (Catullus, *Carmina* V.4)

Nueva España (Espanna), New Spain: *see* Nova Hispania

Numa Pompilius, according to legend the second king of Rome (715–672 B.C.), and the originator of many Roman institutions like the flamens, vestal virgins, and the worship of Terminus

Numantia, Numidia, ancient country in North Africa corresponding roughly to Algeria

nunc dimittis, "now let [thy servant] depart" (Vulgate Luke ii.29–32); used as a hymn or canticle in the public worship of many churches

Nuncius, messenger

Nuns Black, the Black Nuns or Benedictines, one of whose schools for young girls was at Carrow in Norfolk

Nymphae, various female divinities, some of them regarded as goddesses of nature, some as personifications of tribes, races, and states. In the first category were the Oceanides (daughters of Oceanus and nymphs of the ocean), Nereides (daughters of Nereus and nymphs of the Mediterranean), Oreades (nymphs of mountains), Potameides (nymphs of various streams), and Dryades or Hamadryades (nymphs of trees); in the second category were those nymphs whose names derived from the regions they protected (e.g. Lemniae).

O dea certe, "a goddess truly" (Virgil, *Aeneid* I.328)

O horrenda fames, "O dreadful poverty"

O quam te memorem virgo, "by what name should I call thee, maiden?" (Virgil, *Aeneid* I.327)

O quantus artifex pereo, "what an artist is lost in me"

Ob, the Obi, a Siberian river flowing into the Gulf of Obi in the Arctic Ocean

obiter, "by the way, incidentally"

Observant, member of a branch of the Franciscans devoted to the primitive ideals of their order, especially to the ideal of poverty

obsoleta et inusitata, "obsolete and unpractised"

occidendos esse, "that they must be destroyed"

Ocean(us), (1) in Greek mythology, god of the ocean and father of the Oceanides; (2) great body of water encircling the plain of the earth

Octavia (d. 11 B.C.), sister of Augustus Caesar who married Marcus Antonius in 40 in an effort to reconcile him and her brother, but was divorced by her husband after he had abandoned her for Cleopatra

Octavi(an)us: *see* Augustus Caesar

odi profanum vulgus et arceo, "I hate the uncultivated crowd and keep them at a distance" (Horace, *Odes* III.i.1)

ὁδῷ βαδίζειν . . . , "proceed methodically in the creation of the universe"

Odyssea, Odysses, the *Odyssey* of Homer

Odysseus (or Ulysses), son of Laertes, husband of Penelope, father of Telemachus, king of Ithaca, the Grecian leader who was one of the wisest and wiliest heroes of the Trojan War, famed for his practical wisdom and for his exploits on his long wanderings homeward from Troy

Oecolampadian, follower of Joannes Oecolampadius (1482–1531), a German reformer and theologian whose real name was Heussgen

Oedipus Coloneus, i.e. *Oedipus at Colonus,* the last play of Sophocles (*q.v.*)

Oenon(e), daughter of the river-god Cebren and wife of Paris when he was a shepherd on Mt. Ida. Deserted by him for Helen, she refused to cure him when he was brought to her with a fatal wound, repented too late, and took her own life.

Oeta, mountain in southern Thessaly

Offices, i.e. *De officiis,* a treatise on moral and political philosophy in three books which Cicero wrote in 44 B.C. for the edification of his son. It achieved immense prestige in the Renaissance.

Ohthere and Wulfstan, two ninth-century voyagers whose accounts of their travels were inserted into King Alfred's translation of Orosius' *Universal History*

Old Jewry, street in the City of London near Cheapside, probably occupied by the Jews before their expulsion from England in 1290

Old Sarum, ancient Celtic and then Roman fortress about two miles from Salisbury in Wiltshire, until about 1220 the site of the episcopal see now in Salisbury

Oldcastle, Sir John, called Lord Cobham (d. 1417), influential Lollard whom Henry V and Archbishop Arundel harried for years before he was at last condemned by Parliament to a traitor's death (see p. 175)

olere Atticum, "to savor of Attica," i.e. to be artistic

olim jam nec perit . . . , "for a long time I have neither gained nor lost anything; I have more provisions than I have a journey to go" (Seneca, *Epistles* lxxvii)

oliva, "olive branch"

Olivet, Mt., a ridge situated east of Jerusalem

Olympia, valley in the Peloponnesus, the site of a famous sanctuary of Zeus and of the Olympic games

Olympias, wife of Philip II of Macedon and mother of Alexander the Great

Olympus, (1) Olympia (*q.v.*); (2) a mountain on the borders of Macedonia and Thessaly regarded as the home of the gods; hence **Olympical**

omne tulit punctum . . . , "he has carried every point who has combined the useful and the pleasant" (Horace, *Ars poetica* 343)

omne vafer . . . , "he contrives to examine every fault while his friend laughs" (Persius, *Satires* I.116)

omnis spiritus laudet Dominum, "let everything that has breath praise the Lord" (Vulgate Psalms cli.6)

Omphale, Lydian princess who became Hercules' mistress when he agreed to work three years for wages in order, as he thought on an oracle's advice, to cure a lingering disease. He spun wool and wore a woman's garments while in her service.

ὄνε, *asine,* Greek and Latin, respectively, for *ass:* see *decem annos consumpsi . . .*

opera, "the works [of the Lord are great]" (Vulgate Psalms cx.2)

oportet discentem credere, "the student should believe"

oportet edoctum judicare, "the learned should judge"

Ops, wife of Saturn and goddess of plenty and fertility

Orange, House of, princely family of the Netherlands

Orange, Prince of: *see* William I

Orchady, Iles of, *Orcades Insulae,* Orkney and Shetland Isles, a group north of Scotland

Oreades, a class of Nymphae (*q.v.*)

oremus: Deus, cui proprium est miseri et parcere, "let us pray: O God, whose property it is to be merciful and to spare"

Orestes, son of Agamemnon and Clytemnestra and brother of Electra who, having avenged his father's murder by killing his mother and her lover Aegisthus, was pursued by the Erinyes

Organon, the logical treatises of Aristotle

Oriana, legendary English princess and mistress of Amadis of Gaul. The name was frequently applied to Queen Elizabeth by her encomiasts.

Origen (ca. 185–ca. 253), Alexandrian theologian, one of the fathers of the Greek church

Orion, mighty hunter who, after his death at the hands of Artemis, was changed into a constellation

Orlando, Roland, the most famous of Charlemagne's paladins, killed in battle with the Moors at Roncesvalles in 778. He is the hero of a chronicle attributed to Turpin (d. 794), archbishop of Rheims, but actually written in the twelfth century, of the *Chanson de Roland* (an eleventh-century *chanson de geste*), of Boiardo's *Orlando Innamorato,* and of Ariosto's *Orlando Furioso.*

Ormuz, Ormus (or Hormuz), ancient Persian city at the entrance of the Persian Gulf. About 1300 it was moved to an island in the Strait of Ormus and became legendary for its commerce and its wealth.

Orphean, pertaining to Orpheus (*q.v.*)

Orpheus, husband of Eurydice who could charm both living and inanimate objects with the irresistible music of his lyre. Going down to Hades to bring back his wife from the dead, he lost her when, against Pluto's command, he looked back as she followed him.

os rabidum, fera corda domans, "[so much the more he wearies] her foaming lips, quiets her savage heart, [and shapes her to his purpose]" (Virgil, *Aeneid* VI.79–80)

Osiris, a deity of the ancient Egyptians who, going abroad to spread the arts of civilization, left his kingdom in charge of his wife Isis (*q.v.*), only to be killed on his return by his brother Set (Typhon). Isis and her son Horus, however, lovingly assembled the scattered parts of his butchered body and erected statues to his divinity. Thus Osiris came to be regarded as the god of the dead, Horus as the god of renewed life.

Osorius, Jeronymo Osorio (1506–80), Portuguese historian and humanist ("the Cicero of Portugal"), bishop of Silves, whose chief work is a Latin history of the reign of Emanuel I (1571)

Otho, Marcus Salvius (32–69), friend of Nero who helped to overthrow Galba, Nero's successor, and himself became emperor for a few months in 69, only to die by his own hand when Vitellius raised a successful insurrection against him

otium quietum non languidum, "calm but not indolent leisure"

Ottoman, ruling dynasty of the Turkish empire from about 1300 to 1922

Our Lady's Church (in Antwerp), the Cathedral of Notre Dame, recently completed when More visited Antwerp in the early sixteenth century

Ovid(ius) (Ovide), Lucius Publius Ovidius Naso (43 B.C.–A.D. ?17), one of the literary ornaments of the Augustan age. Trained as a lawyer and an orator, he abandoned his political career for poetry. Though thrice married, his favorite mistress (whom he celebrated as Corinna) was perhaps Julia, daughter of Augustus, and he moved freely in the highest circles until, for reasons still not clear, he was banished (A.D. 9) to Tomi on the Black Sea, where he died in exile. His chief extant works are the early *Amores, Heroides* (a set of amatory epistles), *Ars amatoria, Metamorphoses* (*q.v.*), *Fasti* (a sort of poetical Roman calendar), *Tristia* (elegies written during his exile), and the poignant *Ex Ponte.* Of a tragedy called *Medea* only two lines are extant.

Owen, William: *see* Awen

Oxenford, Oxford

Oxford, Earl of: *see* Vere

Oza: *see* Uzza(h)

Ozee, Hosea, a Hebrew prophet of the eighth century B.C.

Pacolet's horse, a magic horse, the creation of the dwarf Pacolet, in *Valentine and Orson,* a French romance of the Charlemagne cycle first printed in 1495

paederastice, pederasty

Paget, William, first Baron Paget of Beaudesert (1505–63), trusted courtier and diplomat in the service of Henry VIII and a political power in the reigns of Edward VI and Mary; succeeded by his eldest son, **Henry, second Baron Paget of Beaudesert** (d. 1568)

Painter, William (?1540–94), translator and clerk of the ordnance for Elizabeth: see p. 671

Paladin of France, i.e. Orlando (*q.v.*) or Roland, celebrated French hero and follower of Charlemagne driven mad by his love for Angelica (*q.v.*)

Palamedes, Greek warrior in the Trojan War who was killed through the jealous machinations of Ulysses

Palemon, a sea-god

Palingenius, i.e. Pietro Angelo Manzolli (*q.v.*)

Palinurus (Palinure), helmsman of Aeneas who met his death off the coast of Sicily (see Virgil, *Aeneid* III.202, V.832 ff.)

Palladium, in Homer, a statue of the goddess Pallas Athena, on the preservation of which the safety of Troy was thought to depend; when Odysseus and Diomedes carried it off, Troy fell. Hence, anything thought to afford safety and protection.

Pallas, Minerva (*q.v.*)

Pallavicin, Lord Gaspar, Gasparo Pallavicino (1486–1511), Italian nobleman whom Castiglione depicts in *The Courtier* as a youthful misogynist

Pan, god of pastures and flocks, represented with the head and body of an old man and the hindquarters of a goat

Pandar(us) (Pandare), uncle of Cressida and the go-between in her affair with Troilus (*q.v.*); hence a type-name for a pander

Pandion, King, of Athens, father of Procne and Philomela (*q.v.*)

pantomimi, "pantomimists"

Paphian, pertaining to Paphos (*q.v.*)

Paphos, name of two cities in Cyprus, the older one, near the southwestern coast, famed for its worship of Astarte or Venus

Pap-with-a-Hatchet, i.e. John Lyly, whose *Pap with an Hatchet* (1589), an angry rebuttal to the Martin Marprelate tracts, contains an attack on Gabriel Harvey

Paralipomenon, Books of, i.e. I and II Chronicles

Parcae, the Fates or spinners of destiny. Clotho spun the thread of life, Lachesis fixed its length, and Atropos severed it.

Pargame, Pergamon, ancient Greek kingdom in Asia Minor

Paris (or Alexander), second son of King Priam of Troy. Because his mother Hecuba dreamed before his birth that she had brought forth a firebrand, she gave him as an infant to a shepherd who left him on Mt. Ida, where he was raised by a she-bear. When he awarded a prize for beauty to Aphrodite over Hera and Athena, she helped him to abduct Helen, wife of King Menelaus of Sparta, and thus precipitated the Trojan War. *See* Oenone

Parlament, Parlement, Parliament

Parmenides (fl. ca. 500 B.C.), Greek philosopher and chief of the Eleatic school of metaphysicians who held the permanence and unity of being and denied the possibility of change

Parnassus, Parnasse, Greek mountain-ridge near Delphi, famed as a haunt of Apollo, the muses, and the nymphs, and consequently sacred to poetry and art

Parthenius Nicaeus (i.e. of Nicaea), famous grammarian who taught Virgil Greek

Parthian, pertaining to Parthia, an ancient country in western Asia southeast of the Caspian Sea

Partition of Rhetoric, Cicero's *De partitione oratoria dialogus,* a catechism written in 46 B.C. for the instruction of his son Marcus

Partlet, Partlot, Pertelote, the hen in Chaucer's "Nun's Priest's Tale"

pascitur in vivis livor . . . , "envy feeds on the living; it ceases when they are dead" (Ovid, *Amores* I.xv.39)

Pater noster, "Our Father," the opening words of the Lord's Prayer; hence, the prayer itself

pater patriae, "father of his country" (Juvenal VIII.244)

Paterculus, Caius Velleius (?19 B.C.–A.D. ?30), Roman historian who held high military and administrative posts under Tiberius and wrote a brief epitome of Roman history that survives only in fragments

patet omnibus veritas . . . , "truth lies open to all; it is preempted by no one man; much of it is left too for those who shall come hereafter"

Patroclus, in the *Iliad,* bosom friend of Achilles, who, when Patroclus dies at Hector's hands, rouses himself from his lethargy, rejoins the war, and kills Hector

Paulet, Sir William, first Marquis of Winchester, first Earl of Wiltshire, and first Baron St. John (?1485–1572), prominent politician in the court of Henry VIII who assisted in overthrowing Somerset's protectorate, proclaimed Mary's succession in opposition to Lady Jane Grey, and continued in high posts under Elizabeth, the fourth Tudor sovereign he had served

Paulet(t) (Poulet), Sir Ames (Amyas, Amias, d. 1538), Tudor retainer who served in France during the reign of Henry VIII

paulo majora canamus, "let us sing of somewhat nobler things" (Virgil, *Eclogues* IV.1)

Paul's, St. Paul's (*q.v.*); dean of Paul's, John Colet (*q.v.*)

Paul's Cross, a cross in the northeast churchyard of old St. Paul's, a favorite place for sermons and public assemblies

Paulus, Lucius Aemilius, Roman consul who sought to avert the battle of Cannae (216 B.C.) and lost his life in it

Pavy, Salomon (d. 1602), child actor who performed in several of Jonson's plays as one of the children of Queen Elizabeth's Revels

Peak, hilly region in Derbyshire, England, famed for its picturesque scenery

Pechora, ?an Arctic port

pedanteria, "school learning"

Peele, George (?1558–?1597), poet and playwright educated at Oxford, cut off by his father for his dissipations and thus driven to make a living in the new commercial theaters of the metropolis. As a "university wit" who lived by his pen, he wrote much and in various forms: many lyrics, plays (e.g. *The Arraignment of Paris,* ca. 1581, and *The Battle of Alcazar,* printed 1594), pageants, and miscellaneous verse (e.g. *Polyhymnia,* 1590, and *The Honors of the Garter,* 1593).

Pegasus (Pegase), winged horse of the muses that sprang from the blood of Medusa when she was killed by Perseus; hence, poetic inspiration

Peloponnesus, southern peninsula of Greece

Pelops, son of Tantalus and father of Atreus and Thyestes. He had a shoulder of ivory.

Pembroke, Countess of: *see* Herbert (Mary)

Pembroke, Earl of: *see* Herbert (William)

Pembroke Hall or **College,** a college of Cambridge, founded by the Countess of Pembroke in 1347

Penelope, wife of Odysseus and mother of Telemachus who, while waiting for her husband's return from the Trojan War, stood off her suitors by weaving a web by day and unraveling it by night, all the while promising to marry when it was finished

Peneus, name of two rivers in Greece, one in Elis, the other in Thessaly

Penshurst (Place), seat of the Sidney family at the junction of the Eden and the Medway in Kent, famous as the birthplace of Sir Philip Sidney and the site of Lady Pembroke's literary coterie

per allegoriam, "by means of allegory"

per consequens, "in consequence"

per force sans resoun . . . , "by strength without reason I have captured this beast"

per Iesum Christum . . . , "through Jesus Christ our Lord"

per licentiam poeticam, "by poetic license"

per mare, per terras . . . , "by land, by sea, living and dead, thy Immerito" (adapted from Ovid, *Heroides* VII.88)

per postliminium, "by way of postliminium," that is, a return to one's threshold; figuratively, a return to one's former condition and privileges

per synecdochen, "by means of synecdoche"

percontatorem fugito . . . , "avoid an inquisitive person, for he is also gossipy" (Horace, *Epistles* I.xviii.69)

Percy and Douglas, the old song of, either "Chevy Chase" or "The Battle of Otterburn," both old border-ballads

Percy, Sir Henry, first Earl of Northumberland (1342–1408), in turn a Lancastrian, a supporter of Richard II, an ally of Henry Bolingbroke, and a rebel with his son Hotspur against Henry IV. He was pardoned after the disaster of Shrewsbury, but when he joined the conspiracy with Owen Glendower and Sir Edmund de Mortimer in 1405, he was declared a traitor and fled to the Scots. The revolt was crushed, but he survived to be killed in a border foray in 1408.

Percy, Sir Henry (1364–1403) the "Hotspur" of Shakespeare's *Henry IV,* eldest son of Sir Henry Percy, first Earl of Northumberland. An early supporter of Henry Bolingbroke against Richard II, he defeated the Scots at Homildon in 1402, then broke with Bolingbroke (by that time Henry IV), and in 1403 proclaimed Sir Edmund de Mortimer the rightful king. Making common cause with Archibald Douglas and Owen Glendower, he was killed and his cause was lost at Shrewsbury.

Percy, Sir Henry, ninth Earl of Northumberland (1564–1632), called the "Wizard Earl" from his interest in scientific experiments, notorious for his choleric temperament and his dissatisfaction with James I's treatment of the Roman Catholics

Percy, Sir Thomas, Earl of Worcester (?1344–1403), a follower of his brother Henry's shifting allegiances between the houses of York and Lancaster, captured and beheaded at Shrewsbury

Percy, William (1575–1648), sonneteer: see p. 496

Pereni, the Pyrenees (*q.v.*)

Pergame, Pergamus (or Pergamum), in the *Iliad* the citadel of Troy

Periander, Corinthian tyrant (625–585 B.C.) whose cruelty became proverbial

Pericles (ca. 495–429 B.C.), Athenian statesman and orator who, heading the democratic party, gained virtual control of his city around 444. He was conspicuous both as a patron of art and as a general in the early stages of the Peloponnesian War.

Perillus, inventor of the brazen bull in which the Sicilian tyrant Phalaris burned his victims alive—the first victim being Perillus himself

Perionius, Joachimus, i.e. Joachim Périon (?1499–1559), French humanist and scholar, editor of Aristotle, St. Basil, Justin Martyr, and various Latin writers

Peripatetici, Peripatetics, Aristotelian philosophers, so called because Aristotle lectured to his students as he walked through his school in the Lyceum at Athens

Periz, Consalvo, i.e. Gonçalo Perez, whose *La Ulyxea de Homero* appeared in 1553

Pernasse, Pernassus, Parnassus (*q.v.*); Cambridge (in Grimald)

Persephone, Greek deity corresponding to Proserpina (*q.v.*)

Perseus, heroic son of Zeus and Danaë who slew the Gorgon Medusa so that he could liberate and then marry Andromeda

Persius, (1) Aulus Persius Flaccus (34–62), Roman satirist whose six satires contain much comment on contemporary life judged by Stoic precepts; (2) Perseus (*q.v.*)

Perusian, pertaining to Perusia or Perugia, the ancient Italian town where Marcus Antonius' brother was besieged by Octavian in 41 and 40 B.C.

Peterborough, English city in Northamptonshire some seventy miles north of London

petere principium, "to beg the question"

Peter('s) pence, Peter-penny, before the Reformation an annual tax (paid to the papal see) of a penny from each householder owning land of a certain value

Petrarch (Petrark, Petrarque), Francesco Petrarca (1304–74), father of modern Italian literature and writer of international influence in the Renaissance. His platonic adoration of Laura (*q.v.*) is memorialized in two sets of sonnets which were widely imitated in late sixteenth-century England (see p. 495). In 1337 he retired to Vaucluse, near Avignon, in order to devote himself to writing; four years later he received a laurel crown on the ruins of the Capitol in Rome, and thereafter his life was filled with literature and diplomacy (principally in the service of the Visconti). In Latin, a language he cultivated with almost religious zeal, he wrote a series of quasi-Ciceronian essays, *Africa* (an epic on Scipio Africanus), and many letters and orations. In Italian, which he powerfully helped to make a literary language, he wrote the *Rime* or *Canzoniere* in honor of Laura and the long allegorical *Trionfi.*

Petre, Sir William (?1505–72), secretary of state from 1543 to 1566

Petrona, unidentified allusion

Pettie, George (1548–89), translator of Guazzo's *Civil Conversation* (1581) and author of *A Petite Palace of Pettie His Pleasure:* see pp. 671–72

Phaebus: *see* Phoebus

Phaedon Platonis, the *Phaedo* of Plato, a beautiful dialogue concerning the last days and death of Socrates

Phaedra, daughter of Minos and Pasiphaë, sister of Ariadne, and wife of Theseus. When her passion for her stepson Hippolytus was repulsed, she unjustly caused Theseus to have him killed and then committed suicide. The story has been treated by Euripides, Seneca, and Racine, and also by Sophocles in a tragedy no longer extant.

Phaedrus, a dialogue by Plato concerning the immortality of the soul

Phaer, Thomas (?1510–60), lawyer and physician who wrote medical and legal treatises and made a partial translation of Virgil's *Aeneid:* see p. 519

Phaet(h)on, surname of Helios, the sun-god; also the son of Helios, who, obtaining his father's permission to drive the chariot of the sun, set the earth afire, and was slain by Zeus with a thunderbolt

Phalaris, tyrant of Agrigentum in Sicily (ca. 570–550 B.C.) who became notorious for roasting his enemies in a brazen bull: *see* Perillus

Phao(n), Phaos, boatman of Mitylene in Lesbos upon whom Venus bestowed youth and beauty, whereupon Sappho, the poetess, fell in love with him, was repulsed, and committed suicide. The story is the subject of Lyly's play *Sapho and Phao.*

Phar, tower of, i.e. Pharos, an island off Alexandria, site of a famous lighthouse

Pharisees, ancient Jewish sect notable for its rigid adherence to Mosaic and tribal law

Pharnaces, king of Pontus and son of Mithridates the Great who revolted against the Roman power after his father's suicide in 63 B.C. and was finally subdued by Caesar at the battle of Zela in 47

Pharsalia, the site, in Thessaly, of the battle in which Caesar defeated Pompey in 48 B.C.

Phavorinus: *see* Favorinus

Phebe: *see* Ph(o)ebe

Phebus: *see* Pho(e)bus

Phemius, famous minstrel whose songs entertained Penelope's suitors in her palace at Ithaca

Phidias (ca. 500 B.C.–ca. 430 B.C.), celebrated sculptor who, under the patronage of Pericles, created some of the most memorable statues of antiquity

Philemon, an aged Phrygian who with his wife Baucis hospitably received Zeus and Hermes, disguised as ordinary travelers, after they had been spurned elsewhere. For reward, Zeus saved the kindly couple when he inundated the region; and when they died (at the same moment) he transformed them into trees.

Philip II (1527–98), king of Spain (1556–98). His policy of restoring and strengthening Catholic power in Europe and America led to his marriage with Mary I of England (*q.v.*), the revolt of the Netherlands (1567–79), his great victory over the Turks at Lepanto (1571), his program of vigorous colonial expansion, and his attempted invasion of England (1588).

Philip, Duke of Burgundy (or Burgoyne, 1396–1467), as regent of France a signer of the Treaty of Troyes with Henry V (1420) and an ally of England against Charles VII until 1435

Philip of Macedon (382–336 B.C.), a king whose reign was one of successful aggression culminating in a great victory over the Athenians and their allies at Chaeronea (338) and the subsequent conquest of the Peloponnesus; father of Alexander the Great

Philip, Sir, i.e. Sir Philip Sidney (*q.v.*)

Philip, a, or a Gregory, i.e. Philip II of Spain (*q.v.*) and Pope Gregory (probably XIII or XIV)

Philippes, Philippi, Macedonian city northeast of Saloniki, the site of two famous battles (42 B.C.) in which Octavius and Antony defeated the republican forces of Brutus and Cassius. St. Paul founded a church at Philippi and addressed one of his epistles to its members.

Philippinas, the Philippine Islands

Phillips, Henry (d. 1535), young Roman Catholic student at Louvain who, after insinuating himself into William Tyndale's confidence, betrayed him to the imperial officers (May, 1535) and thus opened the way to his execution

Phillis: *see* Demopho(o)n

Philomela, daughter of Pandion, sister of Procne, and sister-in-law of Tereus. According to Ovid's version of her story (*Metamorphoses* VI.565 ff.), Tereus ravished her and cut out her tongue, but she revealed his crime by depicting it in a piece of weaving, and in revenge Procne fed to Tereus their son Itys. Just as Tereus was about to overtake the fleeing sisters, Procne was changed into a swallow, Philomela into a nightingale, and Tereus into a hawk.

Philomene, Philomela (*q.v.*), the nightingale

φιλοφιλόσοφος, "a lover of philosophers"

Philopoemen (ca. 252–183 B.C.), one of the last great Greek patriots, general of the Achaean League, and persistent opponent of both Roman and Spartan aggression. He was finally captured and murdered by the Messenians.

Phlegethon, river of fire in the underworld, flowing into Acheron (*q.v.*)

Phocion (ca. 402–317 B.C.), Athenian general and statesman who, as head of the aristocratic party, urged compromise and peace with Philip of Macedon. He was subsequently executed by the democratic party for treason.

Phocylides (b. ca. 560 B.C.), Greek epic and elegiac poet of whose work only a few gnomic fragments remain

Ph(o)ebe, (1) a Titaness, daughter of Uranus and Gaea; (2) a surname of Diana (or Artemis) as goddess of the moon

Pho(e)bus (Phaebus), "the Shining One," an epithet for Apollo; the sun

Phoebus' son, Aesculapius, famed physician whom the Greeks honored as the god of medicine

Phosphorus, the morning star: *see* Hesperus

Phyllis: *see* Demopho(o)n

Pia, Lady Emilia (d. 1528), youngest daughter of Marco Pio and wife of Count Antonio de Montefeltro, a natural half-brother of Duke Guidobaldo. After her husband's death in 1500 she became a confidante of the Duchess Elizabeth at the court of Urbino.

Pico della Mirandola (Johannes Picus de Mirandola, 1463–94), Italian philosopher and theologian, pupil of Ficino, author of various works seeking to synthesize pagan, Christian, and Jewish thought

Picus, a deity of agriculture, son of Saturn and father of Faunus. The first king of Latium, he was transformed into a woodpecker (*picus*) because he remained faithful to Pomona and rejected the love of Circe. When Pettie refers to "Singer" he is apparently translating *Canens,* the name of another of Picus' would-be mistresses.

Pierce Penniless, i.e. Thomas Nashe, author of *Pierce Penniless His Supplication to the Devil* (1592): see p. 874

Pierce Plowman, i.e. *Piers Plowman* (*q.v.*)

Pieria, a district in Thessaly, the legendary birthplace of the muses (sometimes called the Pierides) and Orpheus

Pierias, (1) Pieria (*q.v.*); (2) ?Nicholas Pierius, author of *Dissertatio . . . de idea caloris humani vera,* of which a 1762 editon survives

Pierides, the muses: *see* Pieria

Piers of Exton, Sir, allegedly the murderer of Richard II, although Piers himself has never been identified nor have the details of Richard's death been established. Grafton's version has been given a long life by Shakespeare, but another legend, widely popular in the generation after Richard's death, was that the king escaped to Scotland; see C. Oman, *The History of England from the Accession of Richard II. to the Death of Richard III.* (1906), pp. 165–66.

Piers Plowman, *The Vision of Piers the Plowman,* supposedly by William Langland, a long allegorical poem in alliterative verse, on the social and moral problems of the fourteenth century. Its narrative concerns the quest of an innocent plowman for the shrine of Truth. Francis Meres evidently supposed that Piers Plowman was the author's name.

Pighius, Albertus (1490–1542), a Dutch Catholic whose writing included both controversial works against the Protestants and mathematical treatises

Pilate, Pontius (fl. 30), Roman procurator of Judea under whom Jesus of Nazareth was tried and executed

Pilkington, Leonard (?1527–99), with his brother **James** (?1520–76) a prominent Protestant reformer, Marian exile, and ecclesiastic in Elizabeth's reign

Pindar (ca. 522–443 B.C.), Greek lyric poet of Thebes famed for his *Epinicia,* four books of triumphal odes celebrating the Olympic games. Their elevation of style and metrical complexity have been often (and usually unsuccessfully) imitated by English poets.

Pindus, range of mountains in northern Greece

Pirithous (Pyrothus), king of the Lapithae (*q.v.*)

pistrinum, mill where slaves were compelled to toil as punishment

placebo, sing, act with servile complaisance; *placebo . . . dilexi,* "I shall please . . . I have loved," phrases from the Vespers for the Dead (Vulgate Psalms cxiv)

placet, "it pleases"; hence, approval

Plac(i)us, mountain of Mysia, near Thebes

Plain, Salisbury Plain (*q.v.*)

Plantagenet, Edward, actually Edward of Norwich, second Duke of York (?1373–1415). First a supporter of Richard II and then of Henry IV, his devotion to the Lancastrians was proved at Agincourt, where he fell in battle.

Plantin, Christophe (1514–89), French printer of Antwerp, famed for the beauty of his editions of the Bible in Hebrew, Latin, and Dutch and of Greek and Latin classics. His masterpiece was the *Biblia polyglotta* (1569–73), a project supported by Philip II of Spain.

Plate, River of, Rio de la Plata, La Plata, or Plate, the large estuary between Uruguay and Argentina

Plato (?429–347 B.C.), celebrated Greek philosophical idealist, pupil of Socrates and teacher of Aristotle, whose dialogues have had an incalculable influence on Western thought

Platonics, Platonists

plaudite, "applaud"; hence, applause

Plautus, Titus Maccius (ca. 254–184 B.C.), Roman comic dramatist who translated and adapted the new Attic comedy (especially that of Menander) into Latin. Twenty of his comedies are extant. **Plautus grinding corn in the mill,** an allusion to the tradition that Plautus worked in a flour-mill, writing plays in his spare time to earn additional money

Pliny (Plinius), Caius Plinius Secundus (23–79), Roman naturalist who also followed a high career in war and politics. His *Historia naturalis,* in thirty-seven books, is encyclopedic in its treatment of geography, medicine, and art. Although often wildly inaccurate in discussing geology and botany—hence the phrase, Pliny's unnatural natural history—for centuries it enjoyed great popularity.

Plotinus (?205–?270), Neoplatonic philosopher, author of the *Enneads*

Plutarch (ca. 46–ca. 120), Greek biographer and philosopher, born at Chaeronea in Boeotia, who, after a successful career as rhetorician in Rome, returned to his native village to write the famous *Parallel Lives* (see pp. 545–46). His more than sixty other works are usually lumped together as *Moralia*, most of them ethical treatises but some historical and anecdotal (see p. 565).

Pluto(n), god of the underworld

Po, largest river in Italy, rising in the French Alps and emptying into the Adriatic through several mouths

poeta nascitur, orator fit, "a poet is born, an orator is made" (perhaps adapted from *nascimur poetae, fimus oratores*, a remark attributed to Cicero)

poetica licentia, "poetic license"

Pogetto, ?town in France

Poins (Poyntz), John, member of an ancient Essex family and close friend of Sir Thomas Wyatt

Poitiers (Poiters), town in western France near which Edward the Black Prince defeated the French on September 19, 1356

Politian(us), Angelus, Angelo Poliziano (1454–94), one of the most brilliant humanists and scholars of the Italian Renaissance, protégé of Lorenzo the Magnificent, author of various Latin poems, a partial translation (in Latin) of the *Iliad*, and (in the vernacular) *La giostra, La favola di Orfeo*, and *Le stanze*

Polybius (ca. 204–ca. 122 B.C.), a Greek who, having spent several years in Rome as a prisoner, wrote a massive history of Rome in forty books, of which only the section on the Punic wars survives

Polycrates (d. 522 B.C.), tyrant of Samos. Herodotus relates that he threw a valuable ring into the sea in order to avert the possible jealousy of the gods at his extraordinary good fortune, but a few days later found the ring in the belly of a fish which had been given him.

Polydorus: *see* Polymnestor

Polymnestor, a king of the Thracian Chersonesus to whom Priam entrusted his youngest son Polydorus. When Troy fell, Polymnestor killed his ward for his treasure, and in retaliation Hecuba (*q.v.*) and other Trojan women killed Polymnestor's two children and put out his eyes. The legend forms the plot of Euripides' *Hecuba*.

Polynices, prince of Thebes who, when exiled by his brother Eteocles, attacked the city with six other heroes; in the ensuing battle both brothers were killed. The incident is treated by Aeschylus in *Seven against Thebes* and by Statius (*q.v.*) in the *Thebaid*. See Antigone

Pomfret: *see* Pontefract

pompa mortis . . . , "the pomp of death terrifies more than death itself"

Pompeia, daughter of Sulla (*q.v.*) who was divorced by Julius Caesar because of her alleged affair with Clodius (*q.v.*)

Pompey the Great, Cneius Pompeius Magnus (106–48 B.C.), with Caesar and Crassus a member of the first triumvirate (60 B.C.), whose developing conservatism led to a rupture and civil war in 49. A year later his forces were routed at Pharsalia, and he fled to Egypt, where he was murdered.

Pomponius Laetus, Julius, Guilio Pomponio Leto (?1425–93), Italian humanist whose *Opera varia* appeared in 1521

Pomponius Secundus, according to Ravisius Textor a writer of tragedies, favorite of the emperor Germanicus, and friend of Seneca

Pontanus, Joannes Jovianus, Giovanni Gioviano Pontano (1426–1503), founder of the Neapolitan Academy, whose best-known poem was *Urania*

Ponte, Pontus, ancient country in Asia Minor which rose to its greatest power under Mithridates the Great, was subdued by Pompey, and became a Roman province

Pontefract (Pomfret), ancient town in the West Riding of Yorkshire. Its famous castle—scene of the violent death of Richard II and (under Richard III) of Rivers, Grey, and Vaughan—has long been in ruins.

Ponticus Virunnius, Italian humanist whose *Historia Britannica* (1508) was an abridgment of Geoffrey of Monmouth's *Historia regum Britanniae*

Pope, Sir Thomas (?1507–59), Tudor statesman high in Henry

VIII's favor, who retired during Edward VI's reign and returned to public life to become a member of Mary's privy council and a trusted adviser of Elizabeth. In 1555 he founded Trinity College, Oxford.

Popillius, Gaius Popillius Laenas, a native of Picenum whom Cicero gratuitously and successfully defended in a legal action

Porphyry (233–ca. 304), Neoplatonist and adversary of Christianity

Port Esquiline, a privy

Portes, Philippe Desportes (*q.v.*)

Portinari, Beatrice or **Beatrix** (1266–90), wife of Simone de' Bardi, celebrated as the ideal woman by Dante in his *Vita nuova* and *Divina commedia*

Portingal(e), Portugal; Portuguese

Portland, the Isle of Portland, a peninsula in Dorset, England

Portugal, Portuguese

Porum: *see* Cabelimus

Poseidon, one of the chief Olympians, god of the sea. The brother of Zeus and husband of the Nereid Amphitrite, he was attended by a swarm of Nereids, Tritons, and sea-monsters.

Posidonius, celebrated Greek Stoic philosopher of the first century B.C. who, as a teacher at Rhodes, had among his students Cicero and Pompey. His many works survive only in fragments, but Cicero's *De officiis*—one of the most influential treatises of classical morality—reflects many of his doctrines.

Potameides, a class of Nymphae (*q.v.*)

Pothinus, the eunuch who, as young King Ptolemy's guardian, plotted against Julius Caesar after Pompey's assassination and was consequently put to death

Pouk(e): *see* Puck

Poules, Powel's, Powles: *see* St. Paul's; **dean of Powel's**, John Colet (*q.v.*)

Poyntz, John: *see* Poins

Praelia porcorum, alluding to the *Pugna porcorum per P. Porcium poetam* (1550) by Joannes Leo Placentius, a poetical burlesque in which every word begins with *p*

praeterit Hippomenes . . . , "Hippomenes passed her while the spectators roared with applause" (Ovid, *Metamorphoses* X.668)

πρᾶξις, "action, conduct"

Praxitel(es), Greek sculptor of the early fourth century B.C. whose Aphrodite of Cnidus was one of the most admired works of antiquity

Prester John, mythical Christian king of Ethiopia (or of the far Orient)

Preston, Thomas (1537–98), master of Trinity Hall, Cambridge (1584–98), vice-chancellor of the university, and amateur dramatist who wrote the notoriously bombastic *Cambyses, King of Persia* (1569)

Priam(us), last king of Troy, husband of Hecuba, and father of fifty sons, among them Hector and Paris

Priamus' boy, Priamus' wanton, i.e. Paris (*q.v.*)

prima facie, "at first appearance"

prima materia, the original substance of the universe

primus verborum artifex, "chief artist with words"

Priscian, Priscianus Caesariensis (fl. 500), author of the highly influential *Institutiones grammaticae*

Pro Archia poeta, Cicero's oration (61 B.C.) in defense of the poet Archias when he was charged with assuming Roman citizenship illegally. The defense rested mainly on Archias' merits as a writer.

pro et contra, "for and against"

pro forma, "as a matter of form"

Pro lege Manilia, Cicero's oration (66 B.C.) in support of a bill introduced by Caius Manilius to extend the military and administrative powers of Pompey

Pro Roscio Amerino, Cicero's oration (80 B.C.) successfully defending Sextus Roscius, a youth maliciously accused of murdering his father

probabile, i.e. the rudiments of logic

Procopius (ca. 490–ca. 565), Byzantine historian who accompanied Belisarius on his campaigns and wrote a history of the various wars of Justinian

Procrustes, legendary Attic bandit who tortured his victims on a bed: if too short to fit it they were stretched longer, if too long they lost their legs.

Proctor, Thomas (fl. 1578–84), editor of *A Gorgeous Gallery of Gallant Inventions* (see pp. 219–20)

proemium (*in librum primum*), "introduction (to the first book)"

Prometheus, son of Iapetus and brother of Atlas and Epimetheus, the "fire-bringer" and benefactor of mankind. When Zeus denied the use of fire to the human race, Prometheus stole it from the chariot of the sun and brought it to man in a hollow reed. In retaliation, Zeus had him chained on a peak in the Caucasus where his liver was daily devoured by an eagle, only to grow again at night. He was finally rescued by Hercules.

Propertius, Sextus (b. ca. 51 B.C.), Roman elegiac poet whose extant writings are mainly concerned with his illicit affair with a tantalizing woman whom he called Cynthia

proprium (plural *propria*), "literal statement"

Proserpina, Proserpine, in Roman mythology, the great goddess corresponding to the Greek Persephone, daughter of Ceres and wife of Pluto. Each year she spent six months on Olympus and six months in Hades, and as a personification of seasonal changes she was associated with the Eleusinian mysteries.

prosodia, "prosody"

prosopopeia, "personification"

Proteus, the "ancient one of the sea," noted for his power to assume different shapes

Provincia, Provençe, an ancient district in southern France

Ptolemy, Lucius Claudius Ptolemaeus (fl. 140), Alexandrian astronomer and geographer. His geocentric astronomy, as formulated in the *Syntaxis,* was first seriously challenged by Copernicus in the sixteenth century.

Ptolemy Lagi or **Soter** (d. 283 B.C.), founder (after a brilliant career in Alexander the Great's services) of the Greek dynasty in Egypt. Obtaining the government of Egypt as his legacy on Alexander's death, he assumed the title of king in 306 and abdicated in favor of his son Ptolemy II in 285.

Ptolemy V, king of Egypt (204–181 B.C.)

Puck, Pouk(e), mischievous and playful elf of folklore; Robin Goodfellow

Pugliano, John Pietro, equerry of Emperor Maximilian II, noted as an equestrian expert

Puttenham, George (d. 1590), supposed author of *The Art of English Poesy:* see pp. 639–40

Pygmalion, sculptor, king of Cyprus, who was so infatuated with a statue he had carved that Aphrodite turned it into a lovely woman, Galatea, and gave her to him for his wife

Pylades, friend of Orestes (*q.v.*) and husband of Electra

Pyren, pertaining to the Pyrenees (*q.v.*)

Pyrenees (Pereni), range of mountains on the borders of France and Spain

Pyrothus: *see* Pirithous

Pyrrho (ca. 360–270 B.C.), Greek philosopher who founded a school of philosophical skepticism; hence **Pyrrhonian,** a skeptic

Pyrrhus, (1) Neoptolemus, son of Achilles, who became a hero in the Trojan War. One of the Greeks concealed in the wooden horse, he slaughtered Priam himself and ultimately married Andromache, Hector's widow. (2) King of Epirus and renowned Greek general (ca. 318–272 B.C.) who, as an ally of Tarentum against Rome, won famous victories at Heraclea (280) and Asculum (279) but was defeated at Beneventum (275)

Pythagoras (ca. 582–ca. 500 B.C.), Greek philosopher and mathematician who founded a famous school at Crotona, Magna Graecia

Pythagorists, Pythagoreans or followers of Pythagoras (*q.v.*)

Pythia, Apollo's priestess at Delphi

Pythius, surname for Apollo, who killed the python at Delphi

qua authoritate . . . , "which authority certain barbarous and uncivilized persons would twist to mean that poets should be exiled from the state"

Quadrivium: *see* Trivium

quae supra nos . . . , "what is above us is nothing to us"

quaecumque scripta sunt . . . , "whatever things were written were written for our learning" (Romans xv.4)

quaerenda pecunia . . . , "seek money first, virtue after money" (Horace, *Epistles* I.i.53–54)

qualis vita finis ita, "as his life was, so his end was"

quam inscrutabilia . . . , "how inscrutable are God's judgments"

quam volumus licet . . . , "we may think as we like, conscript fathers, nevertheless we do not surpass the Spaniards in number, nor the Gauls in strength, nor the Carthaginians in craft, nor the Greeks in arts, nor finally the Italians and Latins themselves in the homely and native good sense of this people and land; but in piety and religion, and in this one wisdom, that we perceive all things to be ruled and governed by the power of the immortal gods, we excel all people and nations"

quamvis iam obsoleta, "however obsolete now"

quanto rectius hic . . . , "how much better is he who makes no foolish effort" (Horace, *Ars poetica* 140)

quarter-trey-deuce, "four-three-two" (dicing terms)

quatuor, "four"

queis meliore . . . , "whose hearts Titan has made of better clay" (adapted from Juvenal, *Satires* XIV.34–35)

quem penes arbitrium . . . , "which governs both the force and the form of speech" (adapted from Horace, *Ars poetica* 72)

quem toties honoris . . . , "whom I name so often for the sake of esteem and love"

quemadmodums and *quapropters,* "how's and wherefore's"

qui finem vitae . . . , "who regards the end of life as one of the rewards of nature"

qui monet . . . , "he who reminds you to do what you are doing already [by so doing praises your actions]" (Ovid, *Tristia* V.xiv. 45–46)

qui passa, "who goes there?"

qui quae desperat . . . , "who, despairing to be able to excel, leaves off"

qui sceptra saevus . . . , "he who rules with a harsh government fears the fearful; the fear returns upon its author" (adapted from Seneca, *Oedipus* 705)

quia ecce, nunc in pulvere dormio, "for behold, now I sleep in dust"

quia spicula . . . , "because small stings hurt less when they are foreseen"

quicquid conabar . . . , "whatever I tried to write became poetry"

quicquid in buccam venerit, "whatever occurs to me" (literally, "whatever comes to my mouth")

quid non, "what not"

quid placet ergo, "that which therefore pleases"

Quintilian(us), Marcus Fabius (ca. 35–ca. 95), Roman rhetorician, who won great fame in his own lifetime and a great reputation for centuries through his *De institutione oratoria,* a systematic treatise, in twelve books, on all branches of rhetoric. After Poggio's discovery of a perfect manuscript of the work in the monastery of St. Gall its popularity and influence in the Renaissance were immense.

Quip for an Upstart Courtier, A, or *a Quaint Dispute between Velvet Breeches and Cloth Breeches,* satirical pamphlet (1589) by Robert Greene of which one passage (canceled in later editions) gave great offense to Gabriel Harvey and his brothers and so sparked the controversy involving Greene, Nashe, and the Harveys (see pp. 859–60). The work is an attack on upstart urban fashions (symbolized by Velvet Breeches), which are contrasted unfavorably with solid, old-fashioned virtues (symbolized by Cloth Breeches).

quis nisi mentis . . . , "who in his senses refuses offered money?"

quod tamen condonabimus . . . , "which, however, I condone in such a poet and because of your very great authority in these matters"

quodlibet, "whatever you like"

quot caelum stellas . . . , "Rome has as many girls as the sky has stars" (Ovid, *Ars amatoria* I.59)

quot homines, tot sententiae, "so many men, so many opinions"

Rabelais, François (ca. 1495–1553), French satirist and humorist, trained as a monk and also a practising physician, who wrote *Pantagruel* (1533) and *Gargantua* (1535), vigorous satires of such popularity that a third part was published in 1545, a fourth in 1552, and a fifth posthumously in 1564

rac(h)a, "vain fellow"

Raleigh, Sir Walter (?1552–1618), one of the ornaments of Elizabeth's reign, military and naval commander, explorer, courtier, and writer of prose and verse: see pp. 320, 895

Ram Alley, low-class district between Fleet Street and the Temple in London

Ramus, Petrus, Pierre de la Ramée (1515–72), French educator and logician, whose anti-Aristotelian logic enjoyed great popularity in the late Renaissance. He died a Protestant martyr in the St. Bartholomew's Day massacre.

Ramusio (Ramusius), Giovanni Battista (or Baptista, 1485–1557), Venetian statesman and writer keenly interested in navigation. He corresponded widely with Oviedo, the Cabots, and other explorers, and finally summarized his knowledge in *Delle navigationi e viaggi* (1550–63), an important collection of travel-narratives.

raptim, "greedily, hastily"

Ratclif(fe), district in the east end of London near the Tower

Ratcliffe (Radcliffe), Margaret (d. 1599), daughter of Sir John Radcliffe and a maid of honor at Elizabeth's court. When her brother, Sir Alexander Radcliffe, was lost in the Irish wars she reputedly grieved herself to death. She was buried in Westminster Abbey at the queen's own command.

Red Horse, Vale of, valley south of Stratford-on-Avon in Warwickshire

redde rationem, "give your reason," i.e. cite your evidence

Redford, John (fl. 1535), musician, poet, and dramatist, who was probably organist and almoner at St. Paul's in London

Redman, John (1499–1551), Lady Margaret professor, Cambridge, and subsequently (1546–51) first master of Trinity College

Renaldo: *see* Rinaldo

Report, Fame

requiem eternam . . . , "grant them eternal rest, O Lord"

res temporibus . . . , "it is necessary to fit the thing to the time, not the time to the thing"

respice finem, "think of the end," i.e. of death

Retractations, St. Augustine's *Retractationes,* written in 428, in which he surveys his life's work and corrects certain erroneous opinions he had formerly held

Reuchlin, Johann (1455–1522), German humanist and Semitic scholar, whose defense of Jewish literature brought him into conflict with the Dominicans and various reactionaries (especially the converted Jew Pfefferkorn). In addition to various scholarly works on Greek and Latin literature he wrote an influential Hebrew grammar (*Rudimenta Hebraica,* 1506) and published the cabalistic works *De verbo mirifico* and *De arte cabbalistica.*

rex regum, "king of kings"

Rhadamant(hus), with Aeacus and his own brother Minos one of the judges of the underworld in Greek mythology

Rhamnusia, i.e. Nemesis, goddess of retributive justice, so named from her temple at Rhamnus in Attica

Rhe(i)ne, the River Rhine

Rhenish, Rhine (wine)

Rhone, river which rises in the Rhone glacier in Switzerland and flows through France into the Mediterranean

Ribau(l)t, John or **Jean** (1520–65), French navigator who established an unsuccessful colony of French Protestants in South Carolina. He was killed by the Spaniards on a subsequent expedition to Florida.

Rich, Barnabe: *see* Rich(e)

Rich, Penelope (?1562–1607), sister of Robert Devereux, second Earl of Essex (*q.v.*), and the beloved of Sir Philip Sidney, who addressed her as "Stella" in *Astrophel and Stella* (see p. 323). She married Robert Rich, third Baron Rich (afterward first Earl of Warwick) in 1581, and became the mistress of Charles Blount (*q.v.*), Lord Mountjoy, after Sidney's death in 1586. When her husband finally divorced her in 1605, she married Mountjoy, by then the Earl of Devonshire.

Rich, Robert, husband of Penelope Rich (*q.v.*)

Richard I (Richard Coeur-de-Lion, 1157–99), king of England (1189–99), famed for his part in the Third Crusade

Richard II (1367–1400), king of England (1377–99), grandson of Edward III, whom he succeeded when still a boy. Richard was deposed and probably murdered at the instigation of his cousin Henry Bolingbroke, later Henry IV.

Richard III (1452–85), king of England (1483–85), last of the Yorkist dynasty, whose defeat on Bosworth Field (1485) by the Earl of Richmond (later Henry VII) marked the beginning of the Tudor age

Richard, Earl of Cambridge (d. 1415), second son of Edmund de Langley, first Duke of York, who plotted to depose Henry V in favor of Edmund, Earl of March, and was therefore executed for treason

Richard, third Duke of York (1411–60), grandson of Edmund, fifth son of Edward III; long a claimant to the throne occupied by Henry VI, he died in battle a year before his son crowned the Yorkist hopes by defeating Henry at Towton and assuming the title of Edward IV (*q.v.*).

Rich(e), Barnabe (?1540–1617), soldier and miscellaneous writer: see p. 672

Ridley, Nicholas (?1500–55), prominent divine and reformer, master of Pembroke Hall, Cambridge (1540), and bishop of Rochester (1547) and London (1550). When Lady Jane Grey, whom he supported, was captured, he threw himself for mercy on Queen Mary but found none. Deprived of his bishopric and (with Latimer and Cranmer) declared a heretic, he was burned at the stake with Latimer (see pp. 176–78).

Rinaldo (Renaldo), one of the knights of Charlemagne and a favorite character in medieval romance. One of the four sons of Aymon (*q.v.*), he was Orlando's cousin, and in Ariosto's *Orlando Furioso* his unsuccessful rival for Angelica's love.

Rising in the North, a rebellion (1569) led by powerful northern noblemen for the purpose of replacing Elizabeth with Mary Queen of Scots and thus making England a Catholic country again. Although the rebels took Durham, they were easily (and ferociously) suppressed.

Rivenhall, village in Essex, England, Tusser's birthplace

Rivers, Earl: *see* Woodville (Anthony)

Robert, king of Sicily, Robert d'Anjou, king of Naples from 1309 to 1343, patron of both Petrarch and Boccaccio

Robin Goodfellow, Puck (*q.v.*)

Robin Hood, legendary English outlaw and champion of the poor. The many ballads about him describe him and his merry band— Friar Tuck, Maid Marian, Little John, Allen-a-Dale, and others— as living a carefree life in Sherwood Forest and in Barnsdale, Yorkshire, robbing the rich to succor the poor.

Rochester, ancient city and seaport in Kent, situated on the Medway

Rochford, Lord: *see* Boleyn (George)

Roland: *see* Orlando

Romain, Roman

Romaunt of the Rose, The, Middle English dream allegory of nearly eight thousand lines in couplets, a translation and expansion (in part by Chaucer) of the French *Roman de la Rose* by Guillaume de Lorris and Jean de Meun (*q.v.*)

Romea, Romeo

Romulus, legendary founder and first king (753–716 B.C.) of Rome, son of Mars and the vestal Rhea Silvia

Rone, i.e. Rouen, ancient French city on the River Seine

Roper, Margaret (1505–44), Sir Thomas More's eldest and favorite child, wife of his biographer, and a constant comfort during his last imprisonment. A well-established legend has it that she bought her father's head a month after his execution and preserved it in spices until her own death.

Roper, William (1498–1578), Sir Thomas More's son-in-law and first biographer: see p. 47

Rosamond or **Rosamund,** Rosamond Clifford (*q.v.*)

Roscius, Quintus (d. ca. 62 B.C.), famed Roman comic actor whom Cicero admired and studied with

Rotterdam(e), seaport in the province of South Holland at the junction of the Rotte and the New Meuse

Rovere, Giovanni della: *see* Urbino

Row Well, Ye Mariners, a ballad licensed in 1565–66, the tune of which became very popular

Rowland, i.e. Michael Drayton (*q.v.*)

Roydon, Matthew (fl. 1580–1622), a poet familiar with Sidney, Marlowe, Lodge, and Chapman, author of a well-known elegy on Sidney which was printed with Spenser's *Astrophel*, and an alleged member of the band of supposed atheists around Marlowe

Ruffians Hall, a name given to Smithfield, an open space outside the northwest walls of London

Russell, Lucy (d. 1627), daughter of John, first Baron Harington, and wife of Edward Russell, third Earl of Bedford, a noted friend and patroness of such writers as Jonson, Donne, Daniel, Drayton, and Chapman. Although Drayton dedicated *Mortimeriados* (1596) to her, his admiration apparently cooled: earlier, in the eighth eclogue of *Idea. The Shepherd's Garland* (1593), he had reproached her (Selena) with neglecting him (Rowland), and in the second version of *Mortimeriados* (i.e. *The Barons' Wars*, 1603) he deleted every reference to her.

Rutuli(an), pertaining to the Rutuli, an ancient Italian tribe inhabiting the coast of Latium south of the Tiber. Turnus (*q.v.*), their most famous king, was killed by Aeneas.

ρυθμός, "rhythm"

Saba, Sheba (see I Kings x.1–13)

Sabines, a people living in central Italy who were absorbed into the new Roman tribe when Romulus planned and executed a wholesale abduction of their women to provide wives for his young men

Sabrina, Sabrin(e), the River Severn (*q.v.*)

Sackville, Sir Richard (d. 1566), cousin of Anne Boleyn, member of Parliament under Henry VIII and of Mary's privy council in 1554

Sackville, Robert, second Earl of Dorset (1561–1609), pupil of Roger Ascham

Sackville, Thomas, first Earl of Dorset and Baron Buckhurst (1536–1608), contributor to *A Mirror for Magistrates,* co-author of *Gorboduc,* and prominent Elizabethan statesman

Sadolet(o), Jacopo (1477–1547), papal secretary and eventually cardinal (1536), noted for his learning. Two of his works—*De liberis recte instituendis* (1533) and *De laudibus philosophiae* (1538)—attained great popularity.

Saffron Walden, town in Essex, England, birthplace of Gabriel Harvey and his brothers

Sagittarius, "the Archer," a constellation and zodiacal sign

Saguinay, the Saguenay, a river in the province of Quebec, Canada

Sailor's Calendar, a work announced by Lodge at the end of *Rosalynde* which, so far as is known, was never published

Saint Albans, Abbey of, now the cathedral of Saint Albans (formerly Verulam) in Hertford, a town apparently built around an ancient Benedictine monastery

Saint Alban(s), Lord, Francis Bacon (*q.v.*)

Saint Andrew's, ancient church (originally a Dominican priory) in Norwich

Saint Angel, the castle of Sant' Angelo, the remodeled tomb of Emperor Hadrian in Rome, in the Middle Ages and the Renaissance used as a fortress by the popes

St. Anthony's, school on Threadneedle Street, London, which More attended

St. Bartlemew, St. Bartholomew the Great, an ancient London church founded in 1123

St. James's tide: i.e. the middle of summer, St. James's feast day being July 25

St. John's College, Cambridge, a college founded in 1511 by Lady Margaret Beaufort, a famous center of humanistic culture in the sixteenth century

St. John's Street, street in Clerkenwell, a shabby district just north of the City of London

St. Lawrence, church of, ancient church in Old Jewry (*q.v.*) which was rebuilt by Wren. A stained-glass window unveiled in 1900 commemorates Sir Thomas More.

St. Lucy's day, December 13

St. Mary Overy's, now Southwark Cathedral

St. Michael's, the largest of the Azores

St. Nicholas, Bay of, ?an Arctic estuary

St. Patrick's Purgatory, in the Middle Ages a famous place of pilgrimage (thought by some the entrance to an earthly purgatory) in a cave on an island in Lough Derg, Ireland

St. Paul's (Poules, Powel's, Powles), London cathedral destroyed in the fire of 1666. Nearly 600 feet long, and with a wooden spire 460 feet high, it was for generations not only the ecclesiastical center of London but also a focus of social and mercantile life.

St. Peter's day, June 29

Saint Quintine, St. Quentin, a French city on the Somme

salem ingenii, "salt of wit"

Salic Law, early (sixth century) Frankish or Salian collection of laws (*leges barbarorum*) that is mainly a penal code. Although it had no clause relevant to the succession of the French crown, the Plantagenets never tired of basing their preposterous French claims upon it.

Salisbury (Sarisbury), capital city of Wiltshire, England, to which an episcopal see was transferred from nearby Old Sarum about 1220

Salisbury Plain, undulating district in Wiltshire between Salisbury and Devizes

Sallust(ius), Caius Sallustius Crispus (86–34 B.C.), Roman historian who, having been exiled from his native city, followed Caesar on his African campaigns and became governor of Numidia. His chief works were the *Catilina* (on Catiline's conspiracy) and the *Jugurtha* (on the Jugurthine wars).

Salmacis, according to Ovid, a lovely nymph of a fountain in Caria who fell in love with Hermaphroditus when he bathed there. They were united into one person.

Salomon: *see* Solomon

Saluste, Salustius, i.e. Guillaume du Bartas (*q.v.*)

Samford, Hugh, a friend of Samuel Daniel

Samian, pertaining to Samos (*q.v.*); **Samian saws,** gnomic sayings like those of Pythagoras of Samos

Samos, Aegean island noted as a center of literary and philosophical culture

Samson (Sampson), legendary Jewish champion whose fabulous feats of strength against the Philistines ended when he was shorn of his hair—and his strength—by Delilah, his mistress, who betrayed him to his enemies. Though blinded and in captivity, he redeemed his honor by razing the Philistinian temple and thus destroying his captors along with himself. See Judges xiii–xvi.

Samson's post, a kind of mousetrap

Sanazarus: *see* Sannazar(o)

Sand, a poet mentioned by Webbe, probably the "D. S." and "D. Sand(e)" who contributed to *The Paradise of Dainty Devices*

Sannazar(o) (Sanazarus), Jacopo (1458–1530), Neapolitan poet whose *Arcadia* (1504), a prose pastoral in Italian, was one of the most popular books of the sixteenth century. He also wrote, in Latin, *De partu virginis* and other poems.

Santa Cruz de Teneriffe, seaport and capital of the Canary Islands

Santa Helena, Isle of, St. Helena, island in the South Atlantic about twelve hundred miles west of Africa

Santiago (de Cuba), a seaport and capital of the province of Oriente, Cuba

Santo Domingo, the island of Haiti in the Greater Antilles, next to Cuba the largest island in the West Indies

Sapho, in Lyly's play *Sapho and Phao* a princess of Syracuse and Phao's mistress

Sap(p)ho (fl. ca. 600 B.C.), celebrated Greek lyric poet, probably born in Lesbos, whose work is all lost except for an ode to Aphrodite and a few lovely lyrics. She was supposed to have thrown herself from the Leucadian promontory when Phaon, a handsome youth, rejected her love.

Sara(h), wife of Abraham and mother of Isaac, whom she bore when an old woman

Sarasin, Saracen

Sardenian, Sardinian, pertaining to Sardinia, a large island in the western Mediterranean

Sarisbury: *see* Salisbury

Sarum: *see* Old Sarum

Sathan, Satan

Saturn(e), Saturn(i)us, ancient Italian deity (corresponding to the Greek Cronus) whose reign was celebrated as the Golden Age because he brought civilization and order out of barbarism. He and his wife Ops were patrons of agriculture and vegetation.

Saturnist, morose or saturnine person

Saul, first king of Israel (see I Samuel ix)

Savoy, former duchy, now the departments of Savoie and Haute-Savoie, in southern France

Saxony, province (formerly a kingdom) of Germany, in the early sixteenth century a center of the Lutheran reformation

Scaliger, Julius Caesar (1484–1558), Italian humanist and doctor who wrote commentaries on Aristotle, Hippocrates, and Theophrastus, medical works, and a very influential *Poetices*. His son **Joseph Justus Scaliger** (1540–1609), also a scholar of international prestige, edited Catullus, Propertius, and Tibullus, but his main works were *De emendatione temporum* and *Thesaurus temporum*.

Scamandrius, i.e. Astyanax, son of Hector and Andromache

Scaurus, Mamercus, poet and orator who, as a senator, offended Tiberius on his accession in 14. He committed suicide in 34 when accused of *lèse-majesté*.

School of Abuse, The, an attack (1579) on plays and popular amusements by Stephen Gosson (see p. 599)

Schoolmen, scholastic philosophers and theologians

scientia inflat, "knowledge puffeth up" (I Corinthians viii.1)

Scipio, illustrious Roman family of the Cornelia *gens*

Scipio Africanus, Publius Cornelius Scipio Africanus Major (ca. 234–ca. 183 B.C.), Roman general who defeated Hasdrubal (209) and conquered Spain. When he invaded Africa and defeated Hannibal at Zama in 202 he brought the second Punic War to a close.

Scipio Nascia, Publius Cornelius, a young man declared by the senate in 204 B.C. to be the best citizen of the state. Later he followed a distinguished military and political career and became a noted jurist.

Scoggin (Scogan), John (fl. 1480), court-fool of Edward IV. The anonymous *Jests of Scoggin,* often associated with him, was published in 1565–66.

Scorpio, "the Scorpion," a constellation and zodiacal sign

Scoto, according to R. B. McKerrow (*Nashe,* V, 378) an Italian juggler popular in England during the 1580's

Scotus, Joannes Duns: *see* Duns Scotus

Scrope (Scroop), Henry le, third Baron Scrope of Masham (?1376–1415), executed traitor to Henry V

Sculler, the, John Taylor (*q.v.*)

Scylla and Charybdis, respectively a nymph beloved of Glaucus and a greedy woman who stole the oxen of Hercules. Scylla was turned into a monster by the jealous Circe, and in consternation flung herself into the sea. For her theft Charybdis was struck with a thunderbolt by Zeus and turned into a whirlpool. In ancient geography they thus represented a rock and a whirlpool in the Strait of Messina.

Scyrum, Scyros, an island in the Aegean, where, according to John Lyly, the natives pull up old fig trees when young ones begin to grow

Scythian, pertaining to Scythia, in ancient geography a region to the north and east of the Caspian Sea

se defendendo, "in self-defense"

Sebond(e) or **Sabunde, Raymond** (d. ca. 1432), Spanish physician and theologian whose *Theologia naturalis* (1496), a treatise of natural and rational theology, was translated by Montaigne at his father's request

secundum forman statuti, "according to the form of the statute" (a legal term)

secundum majus et minus, "to a greater or less degree"

sed te solum iam tum suspicabar . . . , "but already, at that time, I believed that you alone had taste, with Ascham; now I see that the court fosters excellent English poets"

sedes nulla datur . . . , "no place is given to a trochee except in the sixth foot"

Segar, Francis (fl. 1549–63), translator and poet who published metrical versions of the Psalms (1553) and contributed the history of Richard Plantagenet to the 1563 edition of *A Mirror for Magistrates*

Selden, John (1584–1654), jurist, Parliamentarian, and antiquarian, one of the most learned men of the age, who contributed the "Illustrations" (or historical commentary) to Drayton's *Poly-Olbion*. In addition to other works that groan with erudition

(*History of Tithes,* 1618; *De diis Syriis,* 1617; *Mare clausum,* 1635; *De jure naturali,* 1640) there survives his charming *Table Talk*.

Sem: *see* Shem

Semiramis, mythical Assyrian queen, wife of Ninus, and builder of Babylon

Seneca (the Elder), Marcus Annaeus Seneca (b. ca. 61 B.C.), father of Lucius Annaeus Seneca and grandfather of the poet Lucan; a rhetorician who, born in Cordoba, acquired his great fame in Rome. Only fragments of his works on rhetoric survive.

Senec(a) (the Younger), Lucius Annaeus Seneca (ca. 4 B.C.–A.D. 65), Roman Stoic philosopher and poet, tutor of Nero. For a time a successful politician, he was ordered to commit suicide when he fell from the emperor's favor. He wrote many philosophical essays (*De consolatione, De animi tranquillitate, De clementia,* etc.) as well as some ten closet dramas (*Medea, Oedipus,* etc.) which exerted a profound influence on Elizabethan playwrights.

Seneca, English, perhaps Nashe's contemptuous reference to the group of translations edited by Thomas Newton as *Seneca His Ten Tragedies* (1581), or perhaps a slurring allusion to some contemporary writer whose bombastic style he found offensive. One view identifies the writer in question as Thomas Kyd (*q.v.*) and finds in the passage evidence for his authorship of an early *Hamlet* (no longer extant) on which Shakespeare drew.

Senega, River of, the Senegal, a river in western Africa

Senlis, ancient French town about thirty miles northeast of Paris

sententias loquitur carnifex, "even a murderer can talk morality"

Septuagesima, period beginning with the third Sunday before Lent and ending with the Saturday before Easter; **Septuagesima Sunday** is the third before Lent and the ninth before Easter.

Serlio (Serlo), Sebastian (1473–1554), Italian painter, engraver, and architect, builder of part of Fontainebleau and author of *Regole generali d'architectura*

Sertorius, Quintus (d. 72 B.C.), Roman general whose devotion to his mother is mentioned by Plutarch

Servilian, pertaining to the Servilia *gens,* one of the most ancient Roman tribes

servum pecus, "a slavish herd"

Sestian, pertaining to Sestos (*q.v.*)

Sestos, Thracian town on the Hellespont, the legendary home of Hero (*q.v.*) and the point of debarkation for Xerxes in his invasions of Europe

Seven Deadly Sins, extemporary play arranged by the famous clown Richard Tarlton (*q.v.*). Only the "platt" or scenario of the second part is extant.

Seven Psalms, the so-called Penitential Psalms (nos. 6, 32, 38, 51, 102, 130, 143)

Severn, river (the Latin *Sabrina*) which rises in Wales and flows into the Bristol Channel

Severus (the Cruel), Lucius Septimius, Roman emperor (193–211) whose long and successful reign was marked by the ruthless suppression of his rivals, great victories over the Parthians and the Britons, and improvements in the administration of justice under the direction of the jurist Papinianus

Severus (the Excellent), Flavius Valerius, Roman emperor (306–307) who, unable to establish his title against Maxentius, surrendered and was compelled to commit suicide

Sextus V: *see* Sixtus V

Sextus Propertius: *see* Propertius

Sextus Tarquinius, the ravisher of Lucretia (*q.v.*)

Seymour, Edward, first Earl of Hertford and first Duke of Somerset (?1506–52), prominent Tudor politician who became protector on the accession of Edward VI (1547), lost his title and much of his power through the antagonism of John Dudley, Earl of Warwick (1550), and was finally executed for allegedly conspiring with Arundel Paget and Sir Thomas Palmer against **Warwick.** His wife, born **Lady (Anne) Stanhope,** was a woman famed for her beauty.

Seymour, Lady Jane (?1509–1537), third wife of Henry VIII (who married her immediately after Anne Boleyn's execution) and mother of Edward VI

Seymour, Thomas, Baron Seymour of Sudeley (?1508–49), brother of Edward and Jane, second husband of Catherine Parr (sixth wife and widow of Henry VIII). He was executed for treason as a result of opposing the authority of his brother as protector in the early reign of Edward VI.

Sforce, Lodowick, Lodovico Sforza (the Moor), powerful duke of Milan who came to his eminence, it was commonly alleged, by murdering Giovanni Sforza, his predecessor. Taken prisoner to France in 1500, he died at Loches about 1510.

Shakespeare, William (1564–1616), greatest of English poets and playwrights: see pp. 496–97

Shaw (Shaa), Ralph (or **John,** d. 1484), prebendary of London. His brother, Sir Edmund Shaw, was a prominent merchant who became sheriff, lord mayor, and privy councilor of Richard III.

Sheffield, Lady Douglas, sister of Charles Howard, second Baron Howard of Effingham (*q.v.*), chief commander against the Spanish Armada in 1588. Her celebrated brother was presumably a patron of Richard Hakluyt, and Lady Sheffield also befriended him. Wife of John, second Baron Sheffield of Butterwick, Lincolnshire (d. 1568), she was the mother of Edmund Sheffield, first Earl of Mulgrave.

Shem (Sem), one of the three sons of Noah

Shepherd's Calendar, The, set of twelve pastoral poems (1579) by Edmund Spenser: see p. 331

Shore, Jane (d. ?1527), famous royal concubine. Married to William Shore, a Lombard Street goldsmith, she became the mistress of Edward IV. After his death she engaged the attention of Thomas Grey, first Marquis of Dorset, and was at last (1483) accused by Richard III of sorcery and compelled to do public penance.

Shoreditch, district of London on the north bank of the Thames, according to legend named for Jane Shore (*q.v.*), who died there in a ditch

Shore's wife, i.e. Jane Shore (*q.v.*)

Shrewsbury, capital city of Shropshire and site of Henry IV's great victory over the Percys in 1403

Shrove Tuesday, the day before Ash Wednesday (the beginning of Lent), long celebrated as a day of merrymaking

si fortunatus inf(o)elix, "if one is fortunate he is unhappy"

si iniquitates, "if [thou shouldest mark] iniquities" (Vulgate Psalms cxxix.3)

si nihil attuleris . . . , "Homer, if you bring nothing, you will have to go away" (Ovid, *Ars amatoria* II.280)

si quid mea carmina possunt, "if my songs have any force" (Virgil, *Aeneid* IX.446)

Sibyl(la) (Sybella), the Cumaean sibyl, a prophetess whose cryptic utterances, in Greek hexameters, were cherished with great reverence by the Romans

sic malus egregium . . . , "thus the lowliest poet greets a poet transcendent; one who is new, a poet long known; one not unfriendly, a friend"

sic respondeo, "thus I reply"

sic volo, sic jubeo, "I command as I wish"

sicco pede, "with dry feet," i.e. without getting involved

Sicil(ia), Sicily; **Sicil(ian) brethren,** i.e. Amphinomus and Anapus, famed for carrying their parents to safety during an eruption of Mt. Etna

Sidney, Sir Philip (1554–86), famed Elizabethan courtier, soldier, and writer: see pp. 323, 599–600, 737

Siene, Syene, ancient Egyptian city on the Nile near modern Asswan

Sigeus, ?Sigeum, town in the Troad in Asia Minor at the entrance of the Hellespont

signat cuncta manu . . . , "Polymnia signals with her clasped hands and speaks"

Silius Italicus, Caius (b. ca. 25), Roman poet and statesman whose *Punica,* an epic in seventeen books on the second Punic War, is a limping imitation of the *Aeneid*

Silvanus, god who protected fields and herds. Ovid (*Metamorphoses* X.120 ff.) tells of his love of Cyparissus, a lovely boy who was changed into a cypress.

similiter cadenses or *similiter desinentia,* "ending similarly," rhetorical device of ending units of discourse with words of similar sounds, or of using rime in poetry

Simmes, Valentine, London printer from about 1585 to 1622,

publisher of some early quartos of Shakespeare's plays, and a man often in trouble for printing books offensive to the authorities or for appropriating the property of his competitors

Simois, small river near Troy

Simonides (fl. ca. 660 B.C.), Greek iambic poet, native of Samos, who wrote both gnomic and satiric verses

Simony, Sir, a dishonest priest. Simony is the act of selling ecclesiastical preferments or emoluments, so named from Simon Magus, who offered money to the apostles (see Acts viii.18–19).

sine linea, "without limit" (from the proverbial phrase *nulla dies sine linea,* "no day without an end")

Singer, Pettie's translation of the Latin *Canens:* see Picus

Sinon (Synon), Greek warrior who, after the Trojan horse was completed, let himself be captured by the Trojans and then persuaded them to haul the horse into the citadel, thus precipitating the fall of Troy

Sion: *see* Zion

Siren(e)s, sea-nymphs whose songs enchanted their listeners and drew them to destruction

Sisyphus, son of Aeolus, who, according to Homer, was the craftiest of men. In Hades he was condemned to roll a stone perpetually up a hill, from the top of which it always rolled back to the starting-place

sive bonum sive malum fama est, "be the outcome good or bad"

sive per contentionem . . . , "whether in contention or in any way whatever, Christ is proclaimed"

Sivil(l), Seville, Spanish port once famed as a base of colonial exploration

Sixtus (Sextus) V, pope (1585–90) who encouraged Spanish control of the Vatican

Skelton, John (?1460–1529), clergyman and poet: see pp. 65–66

Sme(a)ton, Mark (d. 1536), professional musician at the court of Henry VIII, charged with improper relations with Anne Boleyn, and hanged

Smintheus, surname of Apollo, probably derived from *sminthos* ("mouse") because the mouse was often regarded as a symbol of prophetic power

Smith, Dr., a preacher at the execution of Ridley and Latimer

Smith, Henry (?1550–91), puritan preacher who gained a great reputation for his sermons at St. Clement Danes in London

Smith (Smith), Sir Thomas (1513–77), Tudor lawyer and statesman, whose *De republica Anglorum,* an important treatise on English law, was published in English in 1583

Smith, William (fl. 1596), minor poet whose sonnet-cycle *Chloris* (1596) was dedicated to Spenser

Smithfield, district north of St. Paul's in London, a favorite place for sports, fairs, and (in the reign of Mary) executions

Smith, Sir Thomas: *see* Smith (Sir Thomas)

Sodom and Gomor(rah), cities in the Vale of Siddim that God destroyed for their wickedness (see Genesis xiv.8–24)

sola Sophocleo . . . , "your songs alone worthy of Sophocles' buskin" (Virgil, *Eclogues* VIII.10)

Solomon (Salomon), son of David and proverbially wise king of tenth-century Israel

Solon (ca. 638–559 B.C.), Athenian lawmaker, proverbial for his legal wisdom

Somerset, Duke of: *see* Beaufort (Edmund)

Sommer(s) (Summers), William (d. 1560), court-fool of Henry VIII

sonare, "to sound"

Sophocleo cothurno, "with Sophoclean dignity"

Sophocles (ca. 495–406 B.C.), one of the three great tragic poets of Greece, seven of whose plays survive

Sorbonist, one trained at the Sorbonne, the theological college of the University of Paris; hence, a follower of scholastic philosophy

sortes Virgilianae, the effort to prophesy future events by opening a volume of Virgil at random and interpreting the first passage lit upon. The same device is sometimes employed with Homer and the Bible.

Sotades Maronites (fl. ca. 280 B.C.), a native of Maronea in Thrace notorious for his lascivious iambics

Sothray, Surrey

Soto, Spanish friar who attended Cranmer (*q.v.*) during his imprisonment

South Sea, the Pacific Ocean, so named by its discoverer Balboa in 1513

Southwark, district on the south bank of the Thames around London Bridge

Southwell, Robert (?1561–95), Jesuit martyr and religious poet: see p. 452

Spanish *Decades*, travel-narratives of the Italian cosmographer Peter Martyr (*q.v.*), whose *Decades* of *De orbe novo* appeared between 1511 and 1532 and were translated into English by Richard Eden in 1555

Spencer(s): *see* Despenser

Spenser, Edmund (?1552–99), most important non-dramatic poet of the Elizabethan period: see pp. 330–32, 624–25

Spinhomeland, Speenhamland, a suburb of Newbury (*q.v.*)

Spondanus, Jean de Sponde (1557–95), French humanist whose Latin translation of Homer was published in 1583

Stafford, capital of Staffordshire, a midland county of England

Stafford, Sir Edward (?1552–1605), Elizabeth's ambassador at Paris from 1583 to 1590, during most of which time Richard Hakluyt was in his entourage

Stafford, Henry, first Baron Stafford (1501–63), Tudor politician whose zeal for the Reformation recommended him to Henry VIII and Edward VI; he was forced to recant in Mary's reign, but under Elizabeth he was lord-lieutenant of Staffordshire.

Stafford, Henry, second Duke of Buckingham (?1454–83), close associate of the future Richard III in his rise to power, but his enemy after Richard became king. He raised an insurrection and was captured and executed at Salisbury. His downfall is treated by Thomas Sackville (*q.v.*) in the 1563 edition of *A Mirror for Magistrates*.

Standley, Lord: *see* Stanley (Thomas)

Stanhope, Lady Anne: *see* Seymour (Edward)

Stanley, Edward, third Earl of Derby (1508–72), powerful politician under Henry VIII who served in the privy council of both Edward VI and Elizabeth

Stanley, Ferdinando, fifth Earl of Derby (?1559–94), friend and patron of writers, whom Spenser praises as "Amyntas" in *Colin Clout's Come Home Again*

Stanley (Standley), Thomas, first Earl of Derby (?1435–1504), Yorkist stalwart who survived Gloucester's displeasure in 1483 and was retained in office after the duke's accession as Richard III. With a wonderful flair for neutrality he did not take sides at Bosworth, and after the battle he hailed Richmond's victory. In reward Henry VII raised him to the peerage in 1485.

Stanneries, Stannaries, tin mines of Cornwall and Devon

Stanyhurst, Richard (1547–1618), translator of Virgil and historian: see pp. 20, 553

state super vias . . . , "stand in the old ways and see which is the right and good way, and walk in it" (Vulgate Jeremiah vi.16)

Statius, Publius Papinius (ca. 45–96), Roman poet, author of the *Thebaid* (a twelve-book epic on the Seven against Thebes) and of a collection of poems called *Silvae*

Steelyard (Stilyard), district of London on the north bank of the Thames just above London Bridge, long noted for its great warehouses, English headquarters of the Hanseatic League before its expulsion in 1597

Stella: *see* Rich (Penelope)

Stephan, St. Stephen (d. 1038), king and patron saint of Hungary

Sternhold, Thomas (d. 1549), musician and poet: see pp. 160–61

Stesichorus (ca. 630–550 B.C.), Greek lyric poet of Himera in Sicily

Still, John (?1543–1608), master of St. John's College, Cambridge (1574–77), and of Trinity (1577–1608), bishop of Bath and Wells (1593–1608), noted classical scholar who perhaps wrote *Gammer Gurton's Needle*, a comedy produced at Christ's College and published in 1575

Stillbon, a messenger (see Chaucer, "The Pardoner's Tale," l. 603)

Stilo, Aelius Praeconinus, Roman grammarian who taught Varro and Cicero

Stilyard: *see* Steelyard

Stilyard Tavern, inn above London Bridge

stipendium peccati mors, "the wages of sin is death" (Vulgate Romans vi.23)

Stoics, followers of the Greek philosopher Zeno, who founded a school at Athens about 308 B.C.

Stokesley, John (?1475–1539), Tudor ecclesiastic and statesman who served Henry VIII ably in divorce proceedings and was rewarded with the bishopric of London (1530–39)

Stony Stratford (or Stratford), town in Buckinghamshire, England, near Newport-Pagnell

Stow, John (?1525–1605), antiquarian and chronicler: see pp. 20–21

Strabo (ca. 63 B.C.–A.D. 24), Greek geographer whose description of Europe, Asia, Libya, and Egypt, in seventeen books, was one of the most exhaustive works of antiquity

Straparola (Straparole), i.e. Giovanni Francesco (d. ca. 1557), Italian novelist and poet whose collections of tales called *Tredeci piacevoli notti* were published at Venice in 1550 and 1554

Straw, Jack: *see* Jack Straw

Stubb(e)s, Philip (fl. 1583–91), puritan pamphleteer whose *Anatomy of Abuses* (1583), an attack upon the stage and popular entertainments that went through several editions, was answered by Nashe in the *Anatomy of Absurdity* (1589)

Sturm(ius), Johannes (1507–89), German humanist, after 1538 rector of the Strassburg gymnasium which was constituted a university in 1566, editor of Cicero, and correspondent of Roger Ascham

Stygian, pertaining to the Styx (*q.v.*) or to the underworld in general

Styx, a great river thought to flow through the underworld

sub dio, "under the sky," i.e. in the open

subire poenam capitis, "to undergo capital punishment"

subjectum circa quod, "a subject about which"

substantiam intellectu predictam, "a substance predicated in the intellect"

Suffenus, a poet ridiculed by Catullus

sufflaminandus erat, "he should have been clogged"

Suffolk, Duke of: *see* Brandon (Charles)

suis et ipsa Roma viribus ruit, "and Rome is tottering through her own strength" (Horace, *Epodes* XVI.2)

Sulla (Sylla), Lucius Cornelius (ca. 138–78 B.C.), Roman politician who, after a long struggle in the civil war with Marius, became dictator in 82

Sulpicia, Roman poetess of the reign of Domitian (81–96) whose only extant work (*De edicto Domitiani*) is a satire on the emperor's banishment of poets and writers

Summers, William: *see* Sommer(s)

suorum Christus humillimus, "Christ the most humble of all his creatures"; *suorum Deus altissimus*, "God the most exalted of all his creatures"

Supplication to the Devil, i.e. Nashe's *Pierce Penniless* (1592): see p. 874

Surrey, Earl of: *see* Howard (Henry)

Surrye, Surrey

Susanna, heroine of an Apocryphal book detached from the beginning of the Book of Daniel. The wife of Joachim, she is surprised by two lustful elders as she enters her bath. Accused of unchastity after she repulses them, she is proved innocent by the sagacious Daniel.

sustine pro nunc, "endure for the nonce"

Sybella: *see* Sibyl(la)

Sychaeus, in Virgil's *Aeneid*, the former husband of Dido, queen of Carthage

Sylla: *see* Sulla

Sylvan, deity of the woods

Sylvius, Aeneas: *see* Aeneas Sylvius

sympathia, "sympathy"

Symphlagades, the Symplegades, islands off the mouth of the Bosphorus, sometimes called the Cyanean Rocks and thought to crush boats trying to sail between them. Orpheus held them in place with the music of his lyre when the Argonauts sailed between them.

Symposium, a famous dialogue by Plato in which Socrates analyzes the nature of love

Synah, Mt., Sinai, the mountain from which the law was given to Moses (see Exodus xix)

Synon: see Sinon

synonymum (plural *synonyma*), "synonym"

Syracuse, capital of the province of Syracuse, on the island of Ortygia off the east coast of Sicily, a famous outpost of Greek culture

Syrian Dog, Sirius, the dog-star

Syrinx, a nymph changed by Pan into a reed

Syrtes, two dangerous gulfs off the north coast of Africa. Syrtis Major, opposite the mouth of the Adriatic, is mentioned in Acts xxvii.17; Syrtis Minor, near ancient Carthage, was notorious for its rocky reefs.

Tables (of Ptolemy), celebrated manual of geography in eight books by Lucius Claudius Ptolemaeus (see Ptolemy)

Tacitus, Cornelius (ca. 55–ca. 117), Roman historian whose works include the famous *Germania* (a valuable study of the primitive Teutons) as well as the fragmentary *Historiae* (Roman history from Galba to Domitian) and *Annales* (from the death of Augustus to the death of Nero). Tacitus' prose, unlike Cicero's, is conspicuous for its terse, incisive quality.

Tagus, longest river of the Iberian peninsula, emptying into the Bay of Lisbon

Talbot, Gilbert, seventh Earl of Shrewsbury (1553–1616), Elizabethan courtier notorious for wrangling with his family and his peasantry

Talbot, John, first Earl of Shrewsbury (d. 1453), dashing military commander whose distinguished career in the Hundred Years' War earned him the sobriquet "Terror of the French"

Tales of Canterbury, Chaucer's *Canterbury Tales*

Taliesin, Cymric bard of perhaps the sixth century, a contemporary and perhaps a friend of Gildas (*q.v.*), whose songs in celebration of his people's victories were very popular among the ancient Welsh

Talmud, the body of Jewish traditional and oral laws and commentaries on the Pentateuch

tam Marti quam Mercurio, "as much of Mars as of Mercury" (i.e. as much a soldier as a poet)

tam Mercurio quam Marti, "as much of Mercury as of Mars"

Tamar (Tamer), river between Cornwall and Devon

Tamburlain(e), Tamerlane (Tim[o]ur, ?1333–1405), Mongol conqueror of most of southern and western Asia; the hero of Marlowe's two-part play (1590)

Tamer: see Tamar

tandem aliquando, "finally, at length"

tanquam in oratione perpetua, "as if in ordinary speech"

tanquam per ignem, "even through fire"

Tantal(us), Tantale, son of Zeus, father of Pelops and Niobe, king of Mt. Sipylus in Lydia, who, because he revealed the secrets of the gods, was made to stand in Tartarus up to his chin in water under a fruit-tree; when he sought to eat or drink, both the water and the fruit retreated beyond his grasp.

Taprobam, a Greek corruption of the native name (Taprobane) for Ceylon. Thus More's Utopia would lie somewhere between India and South America.

Tarlton, Richard (d. 1588), comic actor who became widely popular for his improvised doggerels and jigs, and a subject of many jests and anecdotes, some of which were brought together in *Tarlton's Jests* (?1582–?1611); hence **Tarltonizing,** behaving like a clown

Tarquinius Superbus, in Roman legendary history, the seventh and last king of Rome (ca. 534–510 B.C.), whose downfall was caused by the outrage committed by his son Sextus on Lucretia (*q.v.*)

Tartar(us), an abyss that, according to Homer, is as far below Hades as Hades is below heaven; in general, the lower world

Taylor, John, the Sculler (1580–1653), London waterman on the Thames whose doggerel poems and well-publicized journeys made him a grotesque celebrity and earned him the title "Water-Poet." He published *All the Works of John Taylor, the Water-Poet* in 1630.

Te Deum, ancient Christian hymn of praise

Teian, name given to Anacreon (*q.v.*), from his birthplace in Teos, Asia Minor

Telegones, *Telegoni,* general name for Ovid's amatory poems (which presumably precipitated his exile), from Telegonus, the son of Odysseus and Circe who, according to one legend, unwittingly killed his father

Tellus, goddess personifying the earth

Tempe, proverbially a lovely valley in Thessaly where Apollo purified himself after slaying the python and where he pursued Daphne before her transformation into a laurel

temperatum dicendi genus, "middle style of writing"

Templar Knights, the Knights Templars, a military order founded at Jerusalem in the twelfth century by the Crusaders. The Knights of St. John occupied "those bricky towers" which were subsequently leased to the students of the common law and became the Inns of Court: *see* Middle Temple.

Temple Bar, formerly a famous gateway before the Temple in London, which divided Fleet Street and the Strand

tempus adest plausus . . . , "the time for applause is here; the golden procession comes" (Ovid, *Amores* III.ii.44)

tempus edax rerum, "time the devourer of things" (Ovid, *Metamorphoses* XV.234)

Temsice, George, Georgius a Tempseca, in the early sixteenth century provost of the town of Cassel(s) (*q.v.*) and a friend of More

tendit ad sidera virtus, "virtue tends toward the stars"

Tenedos, small island in the Aegean Sea off the Troad, Asia Minor

Tercera(s), Terceira, one of the Azores

Terence, Publius Terentius Afer (ca. 190–159 B.C.), Roman comic playwright who, born a slave in Carthage, was freed by his master and subsequently went to Greece, where he translated many of the comedies of Menander (*q.v.*); among his extant plays are *Andria, Eunuchus, Phormio,* and *Adelphi.*

Tereus, ravisher of Philomela (*q.v.*)

τερμίνθου τράγων . . . , "the goat that nibbles on the dangling terebinth" (Theocritus, *Epigrams* I.6)

Terpsichore, muse who was the patroness of the choral dance

Tertullian, Quintus Septimius Florens Tertullianus (?150–?230), Carthaginian convert to Christianity who became one of the fathers of the Latin church

testis temporum . . . , "witness of the times, light of truth, life of memory, mistress of life, messenger of antiquity"

Tetersall, Tattershall, town in Lincolnshire, formerly the site of an ancient castle

Tethys, sea-goddess, daughter of Uranus and Gaea, wife of Oceanus, and mother of the Oceanides

Teucrian, Trojan (from Teucer, son of the river-god Scamander, first king of Troy)

Thales (ca. 640–546 B.C.), philosopher of Miletus, Asia Minor, whose cosmology was based upon the premise that water is the primordial element of all things

Thamis(is), the River Thames

Thamyras (Thamyris), ancient Thracian bard who, presumptuously challenging the muses to a contest of singing, was blinded and deprived of his gift of song

Thanet, island off the east end of Kent, England

Theagenes, hero of the *Aethiopica* of Heliodorus (*q.v.*). The adventures of Theagenes, a Thessalian, and Chariclea (or Cariclea), daughter of an Ethiopian queen and foster-daughter of Charicles (or Caricles), a Delphian priest, furnished the model for many imitations in Renaissance romances after Thomas Underdown's translation (?1569) of *An Ethiopian History* (see pp. 696–97).

Theater, the first commercial London playhouse, a wooden structure built by James Burbage in 1576 in Shoreditch. When it was taken down in 1598 some of its materials were used in the construction of the Globe, Shakespeare's theater on the Bankside. The Curtain, built in 1577 in Shoreditch, remained open until the accession of Charles I.

Theater of God's Judgments, popular moral treatise (1597 ff.) by Thomas Beard, a puritan schoolmaster and divine (d. 1632)

Theban brothers, i.e. Polynices and Eteocles, legendary Grecian heroes: *see* Polynices

Thebes, ancient Greek city in Boeotia, long a rival of Athens; hence **Theban**

Themis, (1) Greek goddess personifying law, order, and abstract right; **Themis' daughters,** i.e. the Fates: see Parcae. (2) The River Thames

Themistocles (?527–?460 B.C.), Athenian statesman who, in spite of much opposition, built up the Greek fleet that defeated the Persians at Salamis in 480. Finally exiled by the ungrateful Athenians, he died in Persia as a pensioner of Artaxerxes.

Themmes, the River Thames

Theocrit(us) (fl. 270 B.C.), Greek poet born in Syracuse who celebrated the loves and rustic virtues of Sicilian shepherds in a series of pastoral idyls written in the Doric dialect. His extant work consists of epigrams and fragments and some thirty eclogues, some of doubtful authenticity.

Theodorus (the Atheist), probably Theodorus of Cyrene (fl. fourth century B.C.), Epicurean philosopher whose doctrines were so materialistic that he was banished from Athens

Theogony, poem on nature and the origin of the gods by Hesiod (q.v.)

Theophrast(us) (ca. 372–ca. 288 B.C.), Greek philosopher who inherited his master Aristotle's library and succeeded him as head of the Lyceum. Although parts of his many serious works on history and metaphysics survive, his most influential writings have been some thirty character-sketches ("The Grumbler," "The Braggart," etc.) which stimulated many imitations in the early seventeenth century.

Theopompus, Greek historian of the fourth century B.C. Fragments of his *Hellenics* and *Philippics* survive.

Theriomastix, i.e. "scourge of beasts"

Thersites, a crippled railer in Homer's *Iliad* and a cynical clown in Shakespeare's *Troilus and Cressida*

Theseus, son of Aegeus, king of Athens, who, brought up in Troezen at his maternal grandfather's court, came to Athens after many fabulous adventures. Later he slew the Minotaur with the help of Ariadne, daughter of Minos, whom he subsequently abandoned on the island of Naxos; he waged war on the Amazons with the aid of Pirithous, king of the Lapithae, who also went to Hades with him to rescue Proserpina; and he took part in the voyage of the Argonauts.

Thesperian, i.e. the Hesperian: see Hesperides

Thespian (bowl), pertaining to Thespiae, a Boeotian city famed for its worship of Eros and the muses

Thespis Atticus (fl. 550 B.C.), father of Greek tragedy, who introduced into the Dionysian chorus an actor taking various roles in different masks

Thessalian plains, i.e. the site of Philippi, scene of the two battles where Octavius and Antony defeated Brutus and Cassius

Thestorides, i.e. the son of Thestor, a common patronymic for Calchas, a priest of Apollo who foretold the length of the Trojan War and advised the Greeks to build the wooden horse

Thetis, chief of the Nereids, mother of Achilles

Thomas, Duke of Clarence (?1388–1421), second son of Henry IV and Mary de Bohun and brother of Henry V, whose trusted lieutenant he became. He was killed in a skirmish in France while seeking, it was thought, another victory as great as Agincourt.

Thomas, Duke of Norfolk: see Howard (Thomas, fourth Duke of Norfolk)

Thomas, Earl of Lancaster, Leicester, Derby, Lincoln, and Salisbury (?1277–1322), brother of Edward I who became leader of the opposition to Piers Gaveston in Edward II's reign. When he finally brought about Gaveston's execution, he turned his enmity to the Despensers, who had succeeded to Gaveston's place in the king's affections. After Edward's defeat at Bannockburn, Lancaster had him in his power, but vacillation led to his own capture and execution. Though hardly deserving the honor, he was subsequently regarded as a martyr for his vigilant opposition to Edward's misgovernment.

Thomas, Earl of Worcester: see Percy (Thomas, Earl of Worcester)

Thomas of Woodstock, Earl of Buckingham and Duke of Gloucester (1355–97), seventh and youngest son of Edward III and a political power during the early reign of his nephew Richard II. Finally checked (1389) and imprisoned at Calais (1397) by

the king, he was probably murdered—perhaps by Thomas Mowbray (q.v.)—at Richard's instigation.

Thopas, Sir, in Chaucer's unfinished "Rime of Sir Thopas" in *The Canterbury Tales,* a knight who burlesques the medieval metrical romances and the literary tradition of knight-errantry

Thorne, Robert (d. 1527), merchant and geographical writer who helped to finance Sebastian Cabot's voyage to North America in 1526 and wrote Henry VIII a letter (reprinted by Hakluyt) urging expeditions to the Indies by a northeast passage

Thorpe, Thomas (?1570–?1635), London publisher of dubious integrity who procured and published Marlowe's translation of Lucan (see p. 558), plays by Chapman and Jonson, and Shakespeare's *Sonnets* (see pp. 496–97)

Thoscane, Tuscan

Thrasimene, Trasimenus, a lake in the province of Perugia, Italy, where Hannibal gained a great victory over the Romans under Flaminius in 217 B.C.

Thraso, stock-character of the braggart in Terence's *Eunuch*

Thrasybulus (d. ca. 389 B.C.), Athenian general who overthrew the Thirty Tyrants in 403 B.C. and restored Athenian democracy

Three Proper and Witty Familiar Letters, Harvey' published correspondence with young Spenser: see pp. 624–25

Thucydides (ca. 471–ca. 401 B.C.), great Greek historian of the Peloponnesian War

Thule (Thulee, Thuly), the Romans' Ultima Thule, a name given by the geographer Pytheas of Marseilles to a region or an island north of Britain in or near the Arctic Circle; hence, any mythically remote northern region

θυμὸς δὴ μέγας ἐστὶ . . . , "the heart of kings is proud, and fostered by heaven; for their glory is from god, and Zeus, god of counsel, loves them" (Homer, *Iliad* II.196–97)

Thuscan, Tuscan

Tiber (Tybur), the river which flows through Rome

Tiberius Claudius Nero Caesar (42 B.C.–A.D. 37), Roman emperor, who, succeeding his stepfather Augustus in A.D. 14, left administrative affairs chiefly to the notorious Sejanus

Tiberius Gracchus: see Gracchi

Tibullus, Albius (ca. 54–18 B.C.), Roman elegiac poet who addressed many of his works to his mistress Delia

Tilbury, fort on the right bank of the Thames opposite Gravesend

Tillage, i.e. Virgil's *Georgics* (q.v.)

Time, the Greek Cronus, the original supreme god, who devoured his children as soon as they were born

Time-Ruins, i.e. Spenser's *Ruins of Time,* an elegiac poem included in *Complaints* (1591)

Timon, notorious Athenian misanthrope of the late fifth century B.C.

Timon Apolloniates, identified by Ravisius Textor as a writer of tragedies, comedies, satires, and other literary forms

Timonists, misanthropists (see Timon); perhaps (in Nashe's *Christ's Tears over Jerusalem*) misers

Timotheus, (1) Athenian naval commander (d. ca. 354 B.C.) who captured Samos from the Persians in 365; (2) Athenian musician (d. ca. 357 B.C.) famed for his dithyrambic poetry

Tiresias, a Theban whom Athena blinded when he saw her bathing. Relenting, she gave him the vision of a seer when she could not restore his sight.

Tirynthian groom, Hercules (q.v.), who was brought up at Tiryns in Argolis

Tisiphone: see Furies

Titan, Helios, the sun, with his sister Semele (the moon) a child of Hyperion and Thea, two of the twelve Titans who were the sons and daughters of Uranus (heaven) and Gaea (the earth)

Tithon(us), son (or brother) of Laomedon, who was beloved by Eos (Aurora). The gods gave him the gift of immortality, but not of eternal youth, and in his old age he was transformed into a grasshopper.

Titius, a poetaster in Horace's *Epistles* I.iii

Titus and Gysippus, two devoted friends whose story is told in Boccaccio's *Decamerone* X.viii

Titus Flavius Sabinus Vespasianus (?40–81), Roman general (later emperor, 79–81) who captured and sacked Jerusalem in 70

Titus Livius: *see* Livy

Tityre, tu patulae . . . , "thou, Tityrus, reclining beneath the beech's shade" (Virgil, *Eclogues* I.1)

Tityrus, (1) common name for a shepherd in classical and Renaissance pastoral poetry; (2) in Spenser's *Shepherd's Calendar*, Virgil or Chaucer

Tityrus, i.e. Virgil's *Eclogues*

Tityus, giant who was killed by Apollo (or, in some versions of the legend, Zeus) for assaulting Artemis at the instigation of Hera

Tmolus, mountain-range in Asia Minor running east and west through Lydia

τὸ πρέπον, "decorum, comeliness"

Tofte, Robert (d. 1620), sonneteer: *see* p. 496

Toletan, Toletum, modern Toledo, city in central Spain, the scene of some thirty synods and church councils between the fifth and sixteenth centuries

τὸν πάντα κόσμον . . . , "the creator made the whole universe, not with his hands but by reason"

topica, a treatise on forms of argument or a system of forms or commonplaces of argument or oratory (e.g. the *Topica* of Aristotle)

Torquatus, judicial, i.e. Ben Jonson, from Manlius Torquatus, a Roman dictator (353 B.C.) noted for his severity

Totnes, town in Devon on the River Dart, one of the most ancient settlements in England and the legendary site of Brut's landing

Toulouse, city in southern France on the Garonne River

Tournay, town in the province of Hainaut, Belgium

Tower of Babylon, the tower of Babel (*q.v.*)

Tower (of London), famous pile on the Thames at the southeast angle of the old walled City of London, an agglomeration of buildings dating from various periods but chiefly the work of William the Conqueror and his successors through Henry III

Trajan(us), Marcus Ulpius (ca. 53–117), Roman emperor who, after a brilliant career in the provinces, succeeded Nerva in 98 and thereafter annexed Dacia and part of Arabia to the Empire

translatum (plural *translata*), "figurative statement"

Trebey, Trebia, the site of one of Hannibal's victories over the Romans near the River Trebbia in northern Italy in 218 B.C.

Tremellius, Emanuel: *see* Junius (Franciscus)

Tresilian, Sir Robert (d. 1388), eminent jurist of the reign of Richard II who was charged with impugning the royal prerogative, fled for his life, and was captured and summarily executed

trimetra, "trimeters"; *see iambicum trimetrum*

Trinity, Feast of the, Trinity Sunday, the Sunday after Whitsunday, observed as a festival in celebration of the Trinity

Trinity (Hall), college of Cambridge University founded in 1350 and composed mainly of law-students

Tripoli(s), city of Syria, established by the ancient Phoenicians and long noted as a commercial center

tripos, the tripod from which the priestess of Apollo at Delphi delivered her pronouncements; hence, the Delphic oracle

Trismegistus: *see* Hermes Trismegistus

Tristram, in medieval romance a knight who loves Iseult (or Ysoude), wife of his uncle King Mark of Cornwall. The story of Tristram and Iseult, much older than the parallel story of Lancelot and Guinevere, appears in many versions, of which that in Malory's *Morte d'Arthur* (*q.v.*) is the most familiar.

trita et obvia, "commonplace and obvious"

Triton, son of Poseidon and Amphitrite and a powerful divinity of the ocean depths. In later myths Tritons were regarded as rather sportive subordinate sea-deities who consorted with the Nereids.

Triumphs, i.e. the *Trionfi* of Petrarch (*q.v.*), a set of allegorical poems in terza rima with prose commentaries

Trivia, (1) a title of Hecate as goddess of the crossroads (a Latin translation of the Greek *trioditis*); (2) a title of Diana

Trivium, in medieval schools the lower division of the seven liberal arts, comprising grammar, rhetoric, and logic; the upper division (the *Quadrivium*) comprised arithmetic, geometry, astronomy, and music.

Troiane, Trojan

Troilus (Troylus), son of Priam who, in post-Homeric legend,

became infatuated with Cressida, daughter of Calchas, only to lose her to Diomede, a Greek warrior. Their unhappy story has been treated by Benoit de Sainte-More, Boccaccio (in the *Filostrato*), Chaucer, Henryson, Shakespeare, Dryden, and many others.

Troilus and Cress(e)id, i.e. Chaucer's *Troilus and Criseyde*, a poem of more than eight thousand lines of rime royal based upon Boccaccio's *Filostrato* and probably written in the 1380's. *See* Troilus

Trojan knight, i.e. Aeneas (*q.v.*)

Trophonius' cave, site of an oracle in Boeotia sacred to Trophonius, a fabulous Greek architect (thought by some to be the son of Apollo himself) who built the temple of Apollo at Delphi

Tros, legendary king of Phrygia who gave his name to Troy

Tross, Jane, a London harlot

Troyan(e), Trojan

Troylus: *see* Troilus

Troynovant, "New Troy," name given to London, the supposed capital of Brut, in the early chronicles

tu nihil invita . . . , "do nothing and say nothing against the will of Minerva"

tu tibi cura, "look to yourself"

Tudor, Margaret: *see* Margaret Tudor

Tullia, daughter of Servius Tullius (*q.v.*) and second wife of Tarquinius Superbus (*q.v.*)

Tullie, Tully: *see* Cicero

Tullius, Servius, according to legend the sixth king of Rome, deposed by Tarquinius Superbus (*q.v.*)

Tunez, Tunis, seaport in northern Africa, near the site of ancient Carthage

Tunstall, Cuthbert (1474–1559), distinguished divine, statesman, and humanist (master of the rolls and bishop successively of London and Durham), who was a warm friend of More and appears in the *Utopia*. High in Henry VIII's favor, he lost power under Edward VI, and though restored to his offices by Mary was promptly deprived by Elizabeth for refusing to take the oath of supremacy.

Turbervile, George (?1540–?1610), poet and translator: *see* p. 291

Turnebus, Adrianus, Adrien Turnèbe (1512–65), French humanist whose international reputation was based largely on his knowledge of Greek. His *Adversaria* (three parts, 1564–73) restores the proper readings of many classical texts.

Turner, William (d. 1568), divine and botanist who, though in trouble under both Mary and Elizabeth for his intransigent Protestantism, inaugurated the scientific study of botany in England with his treatises on the subject

Turnus, Rutulian king who resisted Aeneas' conquest of Latium when King Latinus gave his daughter Lavinia to the invader instead of to him. Subsequently he died bravely in battle with Aeneas.

Turon, Tours, city in western France on the Loire

Turwin, Térouanne, town in northern France

Tuscan(y), formerly a duchy (corresponding to ancient Etruria) in central Italy, during the Renaissance an important center of art and literature. Its dialect became the literary language of Italy.

Tusculan Questions (or Disputations), Cicero's *Tusculanae disputationes*, a dialogue, in five books addressed to Marcus Brutus, on practical philosophy. The conversations comprising the various books were supposed to have been held at Cicero's estate at Tusculum.

Tusser, Thomas (?1524–80), poet and writer of versified almanacs: *see* p. 282

Tweed, river separating Berwickshire and Northumberland, and thus the traditional boundary of Scotland and England

Twick'nam (Twickenham), town on the Thames near London, where the Countess of Bedford had a house which Donne often visited

Twyne, Thomas (1543–1613), physician whose main literary work was the completion of Thomas Phaer's translation of Virgil's *Aneid* (see p. 519)

Tybur: *see* Tiber

Tyburn, former site of public executions in London, near what is now the Marble Arch

Tydeus, king of Calydon who, compelled to leave Calydon because of a murder, found refuge with Adrastus in Argos and married his daughter. When he was mortally wounded in a battle with the Thebans, Athena tried to restore him with a magic remedy that would immortalize him, but when she saw him eat the brain of Melanippus she left him to die.

Tymetes, Stanyhurst's rendering of *Thymoetes,* the name of a Trojan elder

Tyndale, William (d. 1536), translator of the Bible: see p. 131

Tyndar(eus), king of Sparta whose wife was Leda (*q.v.*)

Tyre (Tyrus), ancient Phoenician city which Alexander the Great reduced after a siege of nine months

Tyrell, Sir James (d. 1502), notorious Yorkist adventurer, master of the horse under Richard III, who got into difficulties with Henry VII, was compelled to admit his guilt for the murder of the princes in the Tower, and was beheaded

Tyrrhene, i.e. Tyrrhenian, that part of the Mediterranean Sea bounded by Sicily, Italy, Corsica, and Sardinia

Tyrtaeus (fl. ca. 650 B.C.), elegiac poet of Sparta, whose works were noted for their inspirational and patriotic effect on his countrymen

Tyrus: *see* Tyre

Tyryma (Tyryme) the fly, fabulous fly mentioned by Lyly and Greene

ubi quid agitur, "where what happens"

Udall, Nicholas (1505–56), schoolmaster and scholar, notorious as the "flogging master" of Eton (1534–41), author of *Ralph Roister Doister,* a comedy probably written for the boys of Eton and published in 1566

Ulster, the northern part of Ireland

Ulysses, Latin name for Odysseus (*q.v.*)

Underdown(e), Thomas (fl. 1566–87), translator of Heliodorus: see pp. 696–97

une sans plus, "one without others"

uno partu in rempublicam prodiere, "to proceed from single off-spring to the republic," i.e. to convey an impression of the whole by mentioning typical members

Urania (Uranie), muse of astronomy and arbitress of fate

Urbin(o), city in the province of Pesaro and Urbino, Italy, in the fifteenth and early sixteenth centuries a famous literary and artistic center under the patronage of the Montefeltro family. Its most notable member was Federico, lord of Urbino from 1444 to 1482 and an extremely able *condottieri* chief who increased his power by marrying Battista, a niece of Francesco Sforza. Their daughter married Giovanni della Rovere, the favorite nephew of Pope Sixtus IV, and their only son, Guidobaldo, married Elizabeth Gonzaga (of the ruling house of Mantua) in 1489. In 1497 Guidobaldo was expelled from Urbino by Cesare Borgia, but regained his dukedom after Borgia's death in 1507. Dying in 1508 as the last duke of his line, he bequeathed his coronet to Francesco Maria della Rovere, nephew of Pope Julius II. It was the court of Urbino in its golden age that Castiglione celebrated in *The Courtier.*

Ursinus Velius, Caspar, poet and humanist whose *Poematum libri quinque* was published by Froben at Basle in 1522

ut lateat virtus . . . , "that good may lie concealed near evil" (adapted from Ovid, *Ars amatoria* II.662)

ut puto deus fio, "I think I am becoming a god"

ut vales, "how are you?"

utere moribus praeteritis . . . , "follow ancient manners, but use modern language"

Utopia, Sir Thomas More's description of an ideal commonwealth (see p. 86)

Uzza(h) (Oza), Israelite who, named to drive the cart containing the Ark of the Covenant from Gibeah, put forth his hand to steady it and was smitten by God for his impiety (see I Chronicles xiii.9)

vacuum curis divina cerebrum poscit, line ascribed to Mantuan by E. K. in his gloss to "October" in Spenser's *Shepherd's Calendar,* but perhaps actually an adaptation of Ovid's *Heroides* XV.14: *vacuae carmina mentis opus,* "songs are the work of carefree minds"

Vaigats, Isle of, Vaigatch, an island in the Arctic Ocean southeast of Nova Zembla

vale, "farewell"

Valerian(us), Lucius Publius Aurelius Licinius, Roman emperor whose short reign (254–260) was one of disorder and confusion. He was captured by the Persians in 260 and executed about 269.

Valla, Lorenzo or **Laurentius** (ca. 1407–57), Italian humanist and celebrated Latinist, best known for his brilliant exposé of the papacy's forged "Donation of Constantine"

vanitas vanitatum . . . , "vanity of vanities and nothing but vanity" (adapted from the Vulgate Ecclesiastes i.2)

Varro, Marcus Terentius (116–ca. 27 B.C.), most learned of Roman scholars, of whose more than seventy works on almost every branch of knowledge only *De lingua Latina* and *De re rustica* survive

vaticinari, "to prophesy"

vaticinium, "prophecy, prediction"

Vaux, Sir Nicholas, first Baron Vaux of Harrowden (d. 1523), courtier and soldier

Vaux, Thomas, second Baron Vaux of Harrowden (1510–56), prominent courtier of Henry VIII and one of the best-known "courtly makers," author of various lyrics in Tottel's *Miscellany* (1557) and *The Paradise of Dainty Devices* (1576)

ve, "woe, curse"

Velius, Caspar Ursinus: *see* Ursinus Velius

Velleius Paterculus: *see* Paterculus

Velvet Breeches and Cloth Breeches, i.e. Greene's *Quip for an Upstart Courtier* (1589) (*q.v.*)

Venus, goddess of sensual love and beauty, corresponding to the Greek Aphrodite

Venus, Shakespeare's *Venus and Adonis* (1593)

Ver, spring

Verarzanus, John, Giovanni da Verrazano (ca. 1480–ca. 1527), Italian navigator who, in the service of France, explored the coast of North America from Carolina to Newfoundland in 1524

Vere, Edward de (Deviere), seventeenth Earl of Oxford (1550–1604), son-in-law of William Cecil and prominent member of Elizabeth's court, noted for his patronage of writers (Lyly, Spenser, Golding, Munday, Underdown, and others). Specimens of his own poetry were published in *The Paradise of Dainty Devices* (1576), *The Phoenix Nest* (1593), and *England's Helicon* (1600).

Vergivian seas, Drayton's rendering of Philemon Holland's *Oceanus Vergivius* in his translation of Camden's *Britannia.* The term appears to be synonymous with *Ducalidon* (*q.v.*), i.e. the sea to the north of Scotland.

vermis conscientiae, "worm of conscience"

Verona, city in northern Italy

verum ne quid durius, "but nothing is more difficult [than to procure patronage from a nobleman]"

veruntamen te solum . . . , "on the contrary, I shall follow only you (as I have often declared), yet never indeed equal you, as long as I live"

Vespasian(us), Titus Flavius Sabinus (9–79), Roman emperor (70–79) who rose from humble birth. In his reign his son Titus destroyed Jerusalem (70) and Agricola extended Roman control over Britain.

Vespuce, Amerike, Amerigo Vespucci (1452–1512), Italian navigator who, in the service of Spanish merchants, made and wrote accounts of four voyages to America between 1497 and 1503. America is named for him.

Vesta, important goddess of ancient Rome, corresponding to the Greek Hestia. The virgin deity of the hearth, she protected the family altar as well as the central altar of the tribe or race, and her undying sacred fire, which Aeneas carried from flaming Troy, was guarded by six vestal virgins.

vetulam suam . . . , "he preferred his aged wife to immortality"

Veysey, John (?1465–1554), prominent politician and civil servant under Henry VIII who lost favor with Edward VI and was restored to power by Mary

vicimus et domuum . . ., "victory is mine, and I tread my conquered love under foot"

Vidam of Chartres, i.e. the *vice-dominus* of Chartres, a friend of Ascham (*q.v.*)

videte quaeso . . ., "I ask that you observe and be favorable with your tongues and thoughts," i.e. be silent and attend (adapted from Ovid, *Amores* III.ii.43)

vim vi repellere, "to repel force with force"

vinum daemonum, "devils' wine"

Virgil(e), Publius Virgilius Maro (70–19 B.C.), greatest of Roman poets, author of the *Aeneid, Georgics, Eclogues* (or *Bucolics*), a writer of immense prestige in the Renaissance

Virgin(e), Virgo, "the Virgin," constellation and zodiacal sign

Virginia, in Latin legend, daughter of the plebeian Virginius, who killed her to save her from the decemvir Appius Claudius and thus precipitated the downfall of the decemvirate (449 B.C.)

Virgo: *see* Virgin(e)

virtutis amore, "through love of virtue"

Visitors, ecclesiastics appointed to inspect churches

Vitellius, Aulus (15–69), Roman emperor raised to power by the army in 69 but overthrown and shamefully executed by the forces of Vespasian in the same year

Vitruvius Pollio, Marcus, military engineer under Julius Caesar who in his extreme old age completed and dedicated to Augustus his *De architectura*, the only surviving Roman treatise on the subject and a powerful influence on Renaissance and neoclassical architects

vivit post funaera virtus, "virtue lives beyond the grave"

Vivit. Vivit? . . ., emended from Sidney's *vivit et vincit*, apparently a slip in his quoting Cicero's first oration against Catiline as an example of "the figure of repetition." The whole passage (*Oratio in Catilinam* I.2) follows: *O tempora, O mores! Senatus haec intelligit, consul videt; hic tamen vivit. Vivit? Immo vero etiam in senatum venit.* "What a time, what morals! The senate knows these things, the consul sees them—and still this man lives. Lives? He even walks into the senate itself."

vix, "scarcely"

Vlissing, Flushing, port in the Low Countries of which Sir Philip Sidney was governor at the time of his death in 1586

vox populi vox Dei est, "the voice of the people is the voice of God"

Vulcan(e), son of Jupiter and Juno and lame god of fire and of metals, corresponding to the Greek Hephaestus

Vylford, Vilvorde, castle that in the early sixteenth century served as the state prison of the Low Countries

Wakefield, city in the West Riding of Yorkshire south of Leeds

Walden: *see* Saffron Walden

Wallingford, town in Berkshire, England

Walsingham, town in Norfolk, site of a shrine of the Virgin much visited by medieval pilgrims

Walsingham, Sir Francis (?1530–90), prominent Elizabethan statesman, trusted lieutenant of Cecil (*q.v.*), and father-in-law of Sir Philip Sidney

Walter of Oxford, a perhaps fictitious writer cited by Geoffrey of Monmouth as his source for the legend of Brut

Walthamstow, town in Essex, now a suburb of London

Warbeck, Perkin (1474–99), Flemish-born pretender in the reign of Henry VII. Though accepted by the Yorkists, the Scots, and the French, who were eager to unseat Henry, his invasion of Cornwall in 1497 was a fiasco, and before his execution he confessed his imposture.

Warham, William (?1450–1532), prominent divine and civil servant, archbishop of Canterbury for twenty-eight years. He lived long enough to come into conflict with Wolsey and to delay Henry VIII's divorce from Catherine of Aragon.

Warner, William (?1558–1609), poet, translator, and lawyer: see p. 9

Warwick, Countess of: *see* Dudley (Anne)

Warwick, Earl of: *see* Dudley (Ambrose)

Waterford, maritime county of Munster, Ireland

Watson, Thomas (1513–84), Roman Catholic divine and humanist who became bishop of Lincoln under Mary, only to be removed and imprisoned by Elizabeth for twenty-five years before his death. Ascham professed to admire his now lost translation, in quantitative verse, of the *Odyssey*, bk. I.

Watson, Thomas (?1557–92), poet, scholar, and translator: see p. 317

Webbe, William (fl. 1586), author of *A Discourse of English Poetry* (1586): see p. 628

Weever, John (1576–1632), obscure epigrammatist: see p. 466

West India, West Indies

Westminster, formerly a city, now a borough of London, between Temple Bar and Kensington, the governmental center of England

Westminster Hall, building adjoining the Houses of Parliament on the west, originally part of the ancient palace of Westminster. Begun by William Rufus, the Hall was burned at the end of the thirteenth century and was restored by Edward II and Richard II.

Westminster School, famous preparatory school, established in Westminster Abbey by Henry VIII and reorganized by Elizabeth

Westmorland, Earl of: *see* Neville (Ralph)

Weston, Sir Francis (?1511–36), courtier and gentleman of the privy chamber for Henry VIII, executed on a charge of misconduct with Anne Boleyn

Whetstone(s), George (?1544–?1587), poet and translator: see p. 312

White Friars: *see* Grey Friars

White Rose and the Red, i.e. *The Civil Wars* by Samuel Daniel: see p. 12

Whitsunday, the seventh Sunday after Easter

Whittington, Robert (fl. 1519), translator (of Cicero and Seneca) and author of grammatical treatises

William the Conqueror, Duke of Normandy (1027–87), natural son of Robert, Duke of Normandy, who invaded England in 1066, defeated Harold at Hastings, and became the first Norman king of England

William Rufus, William II (d. 1100), third son of William the Conqueror, who succeeded to the throne in 1087

William I (Prince of Orange), William the Silent of Orange-Nassau (1533–84)

William, Lord Marquis of Winchester: *see* Paulet (Sir William)

William of Malmesbury (d. ?1143), English historian, author of *Gesta regum Anglorum* and *Historia novella*

William Cuckoo, perhaps an itinerant juggler

Williams, John, Baron Williams of Thame (?1500–1559), prominent Tudor politician whose role at the execution of Ridley and Latimer is described by John Foxe in his *Acts and Monuments*

Wilson, Thomas (?1525–81), statesman and scholar: see pp. 588–89

Wilton, town in Wiltshire, England, near Salisbury. Nearby Wilton House, founded by William Herbert, first Earl of Pembroke of the second creation, was a famous country house associated with Sir Philip Sidney, his sister, and their literary coterie.

Winchcomb(e), John (d. 1520), clothier who rose from apprentice to merchant-prince, the subject of many legends and chapbook stories. He allegedly equipped and led a troop of several hundred men at Flodden Field, an exploit described by Deloney in *Jack of Newbury* (Winchcomb's sobriquet).

Winchester, Lord Marquis of: *see* Paulet (Sir William)

Windsor, town on the Thames in Berkshire some twenty miles west of London, the site of Windsor Castle, a famous royal residence founded by William the Conqueror

Wisdom, Robert (d. 1568), ardent Protestant who went into exile during Queen Mary's reign but returned to become archdeacon of Ely in 1560. Some of his metrical versions of the Psalms were common objects of ridicule in the seventeenth century.

Wittenberg, town in Saxony, Prussia, an important center of the German reformation

Wolsey, Thomas (?1475–1530), powerful English prelate and statesman: see pp. 53–58

Woodville, Anthony, Baron Scales and second Earl Rivers (?1442–83), apostate Lancastrian who rose rapidly after he shifted his allegiance to Edward IV. As guardian of Prince Edward he earned the enmity of the Duke of Gloucester (later Richard III), who contrived his downfall and had him executed for treason. Several of his translations from the French (e.g. *The Dictes and*

Sayings of the Philosophers, 1477) were published by William Caxton.

Woodville, Elizabeth (?1437–92), queen of Edward IV, whose later life was spent in struggle with and flight from the dukes of Clarence and Gloucester. Her two sons were presumably murdered in the Tower at the instigation of their uncle Gloucester, later Richard III. Elizabeth refounded and endowed Queens' College, Cambridge.

Worde, Wynkyn de (d. ?1534), an Alsatian who migrated to London and there became William Caxton's apprentice and successor, printer of many of the most notable books of the early sixteenth century

Worthies, the Nine, Hector, Alexander the Great, Julius Caesar, Joshua, David, Judas Maccabaeus, Arthur, Charlemagne, and Godfrey of Bouillon

Wotton, Edward, first Baron Wotton (1548–1626), one of Elizabeth's most trusted diplomats, who continued his career under the Stuarts and became treasurer of the royal household in 1616

Wotton, Nicholas (?1497–1567), early Tudor diplomat and divine who served in high posts under Henry VIII, Edward VI, Mary, and Elizabeth

Wright, William, bookseller in London from 1591 to 1603 who dealt mainly in broadsides and ephemeral literature

Wulfstan: *see* Ohthere

Wyatt, Sir Thomas (?1503–42), diplomat and poet: see pp. 191, 194–95

Wyclif, John (d. 1384), religious reformer: see p. 131

Xant(h)ippus, Spartan commander who organized the Carthaginian forces in the first Punic War and defeated the Romans under Regulus in 255 B.C.

Xenocrates (396–314 B.C.), pupil of Plato and then of Aristotle who became president of Aristotle's Academy. Only the titles of his numerous works survive.

Xenophon (ca. 430–ca. 357 B.C.), Greek historian and essayist whose works include the *Anabasis* (the history of an expedition of

Cyrus the Younger in which he took part), the *Memorabilia* (a defense of his teacher Socrates), *Hellenica,* and *Cyropaedia*

Xenophon's Cyrus, the main character in Xenophon's *Cyropaedia,* a didactic work on the education and wisdom of Cyrus the Great

Xerxes (?519–465 B.C.), king of Persia whose projected invasion of Greece was turned back at Salamis (480 B.C.)

Y., S., perhaps the "M[aster] Yloop" (possibly an anagram for *Pooley*) who contributed verses to *The Paradise of Dainty Devices*

Yong, Bartholomew (fl. 1577–98), translator: see pp. 237–38

Yonge, Nicholas (d. 1619), musician and publisher: see p. 255

Zela (Ziela), ancient city in Pontus (modern Armenia)

Zeni(e), Nicolaus and **Anthonius,** i.e. Nicolo and Antonio Zeno, two navigators whose account of their alleged discoveries in northern waters were included in Hakluyt's *Divers Voyages* (1582)

Zeno (d. ca. 264 B.C.), Greek philosopher, a native of Cyprus, who founded the school of Stoic philosophy in Athens

Zenophontes, Skelton's rendering of *Xenophon* (q.v.)

Zephyr(us), Zepher(us), the personification of the west wind, mildest and gentlest of the sylvan deities

Zeus, supreme deity of Greek mythology. Son of Cronus and Rhea, he dethroned and succeeded his father to become the omnipotent and omnipresent god of law, reason, and cosmic justice. The chief centers of his worship were at Olympia in Elis and at Dodona in Epirus.

Zeuxis, Greek painter of the late fifth century B.C. who, in a contest with his rival Parrhasius, painted a bunch of grapes so realistically that birds flew at the picture to eat the fruit

Zion or **(Sion) Mt.,** hill on which was situated the old city of Jerusalem; symbolically, the whole of Jerusalem as a holy city, the Christian church, and heaven

Zoilus, rhetorician of the fourth century B.C. whose ruthless criticism of Homer made him the prototype of severe and carping critics

zuccado des labros, "kiss on the lips"

Zwin(g)lian, follower of Huldreich Zwingli (1484–1531), prominent Swiss theologian and reformer

INDEX OF AUTHORS, TITLES, AND FIRST LINES OF POEMS

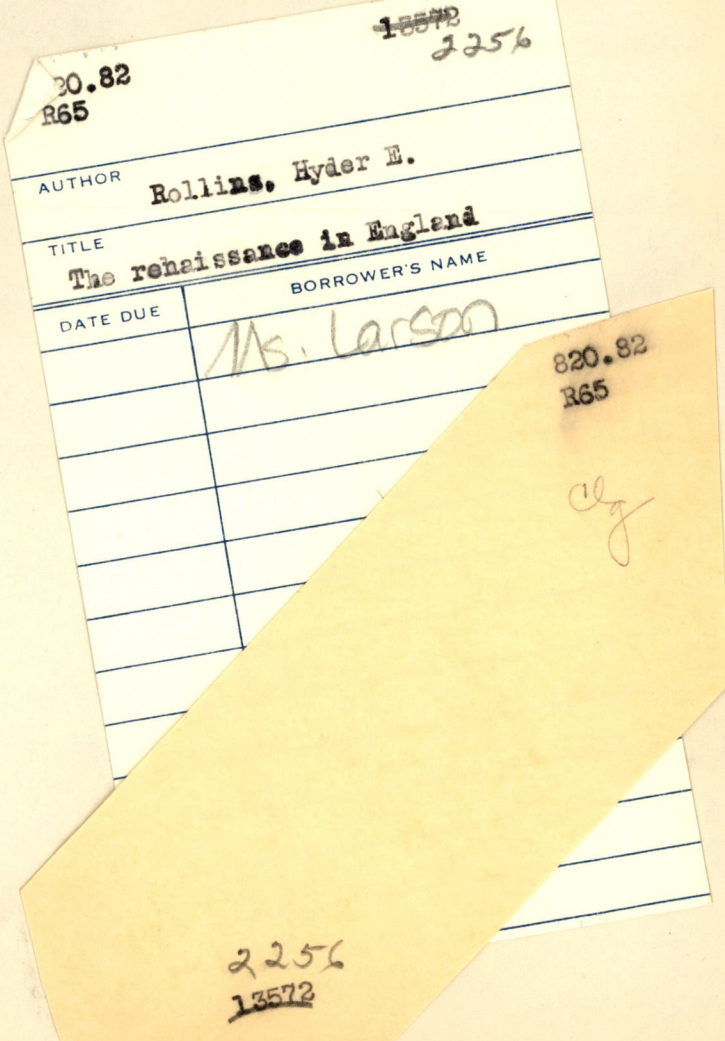